LOCAL GOVERNMENT LAW

Fourth Edition

Osborne M. Reynolds, Jr.
Professor of Law Emeritus
University of Oklahoma

HORNBOOK SERIES®

WEST ACADEMIC PUBLISHING

444 Cedar Street, Suite 700
St. Paul, MN 55101
1-877-888-1330

Printed in the United States of America

ISBN: 978-1-62810-121-8

Acknowledgments

This book—in both its original and its current edition—could best have been written by Prof. James E. Westbrook of the University of Missouri School of Law. He was originally scheduled to write the first edition, but had to forego the opportunity because of the press of administrative duties while he served at that time as Dean/Director of the University of Oklahoma Law Center. My thanks to him for recommending me to undertake the task.

Many of my colleagues, students and friends have provided valuable suggestions and help in my preparation of this book: Prof. Randall Coyne, Dr. Janet Crane, Prof. John Edwards, Prof. Laura Gasaway, Robert N. Gee, Prof. Jean Giles, Prof. Mark Gillett, Steven Graham, Prof. Katheleen Guzman, Paul D. Q. Haddock, Peggy Haddock, Brian Halloran, Prof. Anita Hill, Prof. Jim Hoover, Prof. Clifford Jones, Prof. Peter B Kutner, Prof. Judith Maute, Ann Millard, Marilyn Nicely, Prof. Jenni Parrish, Giselle Perryman, Ron Phelps, Steven Presson, Prof. Mike Roberts, Dustin Rowe, Prof. Alma Nickell Singleton, Prof. George Slusarz, Prof. Mickie Voges, and Prof. Maureen Weston.

Special thanks to Clara Walker, who was my high-school American Government teacher and first inspired my interest in the field of Local Government Law; to Sharon and Miles Pabst, and to Rick, Tim, Minh, and Sarah Weldon for friendship and support over many years; to Sandra Hathy and to the Bates and Postic families for their encouragement and loyalty; to my many students in Local Government Law, Land Use Control and Directed Research whose research papers provided me with insights and ideas; to Misti Box, Misty Lasater, Dawn Tomlins, Donna Wade, and the entire Faculty Support Staff (past and present) of the University of Oklahoma College of Law, who worked tirelessly, patiently and most competently in the preparation of this book; and to the administration (past and present) of the University of Oklahoma College of Law for summer research grants.

Summary of Contents

Table of Contents

LOCAL GOVERNMENT LAW

Fourth Edition

Chapter 1

THE STUDY OF LOCAL GOVERNMENT TODAY

Analysis

§ 1.1 The "Urban Crisis"

Two themes recurring throughout history—sometimes in conflict with one another—have been the search for individual freedom and happiness, and the need of individuals to unite with other persons for mutual security and well-being. Achieving a balance between the desired independence and the inevitable interdependence has generally required the establishment of local governments to serve the social and cultural needs of a community, while leaving the individual members of the community free from unreasonable restraints in their personal lives. Over the past several centuries, a prevalent trend has been the creation of, and transfer of powers to, strong central governments, controlling ever-wider areas. But it has always been recognized that many functions can best be provided at the community level, where the government is not a distant, dimly perceived entity, but is close to—and can be kept responsive to—its constituents. Thus, it is likely that—whatever the future of national governments and (perhaps eventually) world government—, the need for local governments will always be felt. The recent growth and sheer size of population have exerted pressure for larger units of government. But the demand of individuals that their voices be heard always exerts, at least in any democratic system, a counter-pressure for smaller units, in which each person's opinion and vote can have greater impact.

It is widely agreed that local governments, particularly those in urban areas, are beset in modern times by countless problems—crime, pollution of the air and of water supplies, financial crises. The popular press has at times been filled with articles on the "urban crisis." Many cities in the United States are considered to be in a "downward slide" from which recovery is extremely difficult.[1] The problems of cities in some other countries of the world are far worse: Calcutta, India, where thousands have no home but the open street, has been cited as an extreme example of "what happens when urban

1 See "Cities in Peril," U.S.News and World Rep., April 7, 1975, at 29. The various articles on the following pages of the magazine discuss in more detail many of the urban problems. On the problems of American cities in particular, see "The Economic Crisis of Urban America," Bus. Week, May 18, 1992, at 38, discussing the poverty, economic injustice, and racism prevalent in urban areas. See also Bissinger, A Prayer for the City (Random House 1997), reviewed Bus. Week, Jan. 19, 1998, describing the problems of Philadelphia. As to the concurrent movements toward "globalization" and "localism" that are mentioned in the text, see generally Hess, Localist Movements in a Global Economy—Sustainability, Justice, and Urban Development in the United States (MIT Press 2009).

population is allowed to run wild."[2] The congestion and pollution of Tokyo have shocked some visitors.[3] Indeed, in 1969 the Secretary-General of the United Nations reported that the city as an institution was, throughout most of the world, a failure.[4]

Sooner or later—particularly in the United States—, any discussion of the "urban crisis" is likely to turn to one subject: the need for more money. Cities find themselves barely able to maintain basic services, such as water delivery and garbage collection, and without the means to undertake new construction, or even substantial repairs to existing facilities.[5] When taxes are raised in order to supply more money, increasing numbers of residents and businesses often join the flight to the suburbs, so that the tax-increases become self-defeating and the city's central core deteriorates.[6] The people "left

---

[2] "If You Think America Has Slums—," U.S.News & World Rep., June 23, 1969, at 64. See "Jam-Packed Calcutta: Where Unrest Lurks," U.S.News & World Rep., June 27, 1977, at 36. See generally Chatterjee, Calcutta Region: Problems, Planning, and Development, Focus, Sept., 1976, at 9.

[3] See "Tokyo: The Problem City After the Shock," Bus. Week, Oct. 9, 1971, at 66, discussing Tokyo's problems and form of government. See also Koitabash & Matsuzaki, Seven Sins of Tokyo's Government, Atlas World Press Rev., April 1979, at 46. Mexico City is another urban center often cited for its myriad problems: There is heavy air pollution; much of the land is sinking; congested living conditions and traffic snarls are found in many areas; and there is social unrest. See Carruthers, Mexico Revisited, Essence, Oct., 1980, at 27; "Mexico City Sinking in Fossil Clay," Sci.Digest, Jan., 1977, at 24. See generally on the problems of Mexico City "A Proud Capital's Distress," Time, Aug. 6, 1984, at 26. On the world population explosion, particularly in "Third World" countries, see generally "People, People, People," *id.* at 24. See also "And If Mexico City Seems Bad . . . ," *id.* at 36, discussing the problems of Cairo, Calcutta, and Shanghai. On methods of dealing with population-explosion problems, see Lassonde, Coping with Population Challenges (Island Press 1997).

Traffic remains a key difficulty in Mexico City. But "Bangkok trumps Mexico City, Los Angeles and other megacities in its capacity to come to a standstill." Beech, Megacities—The Capital of Gridlock, Time, March 24, 2008, at 4, stating "Police don't consider traffic bad until a car is stationary for at least an hour. Really bad is two hours." *Id.* at 4.

[4] "The Cities—A Failure Everywhere," Time, Sept. 12, 1969, at 63, discussing Secretary-General U Thant's report to the Economic and Social Council of the United Nations. See generally Blank, The City and the World, 44 Colum. J. Transnat'l L. 875 (2006).

[5] See "Race Against Ruin in Budget-Strapped Cities," U.S.News & World Rep., May 18, 1981, at 84. On financial problems of U.S. cities, see generally Chapter 15 *infra*. On the effect on city planning—sometimes, perhaps, too great an effect—that has been exerted by proponents of the view that the financial plight of the central cities is the most serious problem facing urban America, see Comment, Urban Redevelopment and the Fiscal Crisis of the Central City, 21 St. Louis U.L.J. 820 (1978). On the repairs needed for various public works in America, see generally "To Rebuild America—$2.5 Trillion Job," U.S. News & World Rep., Sept. 27, 1982, at 57. See also Yardley, Building Costs Deal Heavy Blow to Local Budgets, N.Y. Times, Jan. 26, 2008, at A1, noting the aggravation of municipal problems due to climbing construction costs: "State and local governments in many parts of the country are struggling to pay for roads, bridges and other building projects because of rising construction costs, adding another burden to budgets already stressed by the troubled housing market." One state's experience is described in Juergensmeyer, Infrastructure and the Law: Florida's Past, Present, and Future, 23 J. Land Use & Envtl. L. 441 (2008). Excellent, detailed analysis of the infrastructure throughout the U.S. is found in Symposium, A 2020 View of Urban Infrastructure, 42/43 Urban Law. 1–423 (2010–11).

[6] See "The City: Problems of a Prototype," Time, March 21, 1969, at 21, discussing in particular the problems of Newark, New Jersey, but noting that similar difficulties were developing in most of the country's older cities. See generally Burchell & Listokin (eds.), Cities Under Stress (Center for Urban Policy Research 1981), containing essays on the causes and effects of, and possible solutions to, urban fiscal decline. Another city whose experiences are often cited as illustrating urban decline is Detroit. See Okrent, "Notown," Time magazine, Oct. 5, 2009, at 26. Detroit's population fall 25% over the decade from 2000 to 2010, a loss that was called "dramatic testimony to the crumbling industrial base of the U.S. Midwest, black flight to the suburbs and the tenuous future of what was once a thriving metropolis." Seelye, Detroit Census Affirms Urban Collapse, N.Y. Times, World News Section, March 24, 2011, at 3 (Global Edition). As to possible solutions to Detroit's problems, see Perman, Made in Detroit, Time magazine, March 31, 2014, at 46. As to the documentary film—"Detropia"—made about Detroit's downfall, see the review by Denby, The Current Cinema—Good Fights, The New Yorker, Sept. 10, 2012, at 108. Compare Williams, Letter From Michigan—Drop Dead, Detroit!, The New Yorker, Jan. 27, 2014, at 32, contrasting the decline of Detroit with the relative prosperity of neighboring suburban Oakland County. See also Hammer, The Fate of the Detroit Public Schools:

behind" in the city are those who cannot afford to flee—*i.e.*, those most in need of services from the city but least able to pay to support such services.[7] Large numbers of persons belonging to racial minorities are often among those left in the city centers; and they are particularly in need of help to move into the mainstream of society, but frequently unable to pay for such help.[8] Thus, a city may be caught in a vicious cycle of rising costs and shrinking tax-base.

Throughout most of the twentieth century, the large growth in this country occurred chiefly in the suburbs—and chiefly at the expense of central cities. This was the trend in 1970.[9] But some changes did begin to appear during the following decade. By 1976, metropolitan areas—not just central cities but such cities *and* their suburbs—began to lose population, with small communities and rural regions experiencing the greatest growth.[10] The general population-tilt away from the metropolitan areas and toward the rural sections of the country was called unprecedented in the modern history of the

---

Governance, Finance and Competition, 13 J.L. Soc'y 111 (2011); Kanner, Detroit and the Decline of Urban America, 2013 Mich. St. L. Rev. 1547. Eventually, a group of private donors banded together with community development agencies, private businesses, and the state of Michigan to make a settlement of Detroit's financial obligations. See Foroohar, Detroit's Turnup—An Unlikely Deal Lifts Motown Out of Bankruptcy, Time magazine, Nov. 24, 2014, at 24. See generally Ager, Taking Back Detroit, Natl. Geographic, May 2015, at 56. See also Section 15.14, note 165, *infra*. On the devastating effect that the economic downturn of the late 1980's and early 1990's had on many cities, see "Gloom and Boom Towns," U.S. News & World Rep., Oct. 19, 1990, at 80. By 2000, the percentage of Americans on welfare was considerably higher in the nation's 100 largest cities than in the rest of the country. See "Mean Streets," The Economist, July 22, 2000, at 31, citing Allen & Kirby, Unfinished Business: Why Cities Matter to Welfare Reform (Brookings Institution 2000) (welfare case-loads in the 89 counties containing the 100 largest cities rose from 48% of national total in 1994 to 58% in 1999).

[7] See "St. Louis Sings the Blues—The 'Gateway to the West' Tries to Stop Its Urban Exodus," Time, May 4, 1981, at 30, noting, "The people left in St. Louis proper are, to a large extent, the poor, the elderly, and the unemployed." See also Herbers, St. Louis Struggles to Cope With Federal Cutbacks, N.Y.Times, Oct. 20, 1981, at A22. As to possible solutions to the problems of St. Louis, see Note, From Cautionary Example to "City on a Hill": Revitalizing Saint Louis May Require an Innovative Regional Taxation Model, 91 Wash. U.L. Rev. 1035 (2014).

[8] See Shearer, Exodus (in "Parade's Special" column), Parade magazine, July 30, 1978, observing, "As whites continue to leave metropolitan areas, nonwhite and Hispanic people move in. These groups are generally poorer and less educated than the whites and reproduce at a more prolific rate." Cf. Herbers, Census Finds Blacks Gaining Majorities in Big Cities, N.Y.Times, April 16, 1981, at 1, col. 1. See generally Solomon, Building a Segregated City: How We All Worked Together, 16 St. Louis U. Pub. L. Rev. 265 (1997).

[9] See "Flight from the Cities—It's Growing," U.S.News & World Rep., Sept. 7, 1970, at 33, with accompanying table of figures, from the 1970 census, on metropolitan areas of more than 500,000 people. The article points out that between 1960 and 1970, suburban population in the United States increased by more than 25% while the population of central cities increased less than 10%. See generally Symposium, Suburban Seventies, 422 Annals 1–151 (Nov., 1975). On the beginnings of suburban America, see Binford, The First Suburbs: Residential Communities on the Boston Periphery, 1815–1860 (Univ. of Chicago Press 1985). See generally Stilgoe, Borderland: Origins of the American Suburb, 1820–1939 (Yale Univ. Press 1988), noting that the most important factors leading to the development of the suburbs were the Romanticism manifested in love for rural scenery and the industrialism that produced the necessary machinery for commuting. The "powerful hold on the American imagination" that has long been exerted by suburbs is well described in "Suburbia: The New American Plurality," Time, March 15, 1971, at 14.

[10] See "Drift Away from Big Cities Goes On," U.S.News and World Rep., Nov. 15, 1976, at 94, with accompanying table of figures on changes in the 70 most populous metropolitan areas between 1970 and 1975. Nonetheless, the 1980 census showed that for the first time, more Americans lived in suburbs than in either central cities or non-metropolitan areas. On the problems of some older suburbs that have been passed-by in more recent development, see Listokin & Beaton, Revitalizing the Older Suburb (Center for Urban Policy Research 1983). On suburban problems and ways to solve them, see generally Lucy & Phillips, Confronting Suburban Decline: Strategic Planning for Metropolitan Renewal (Island Press 2000); Adler, Bye-Bye, Suburban Dream, Newsweek, May 15, 1995, at 40. See also Cervero, Suburban Gridlock (Center for Urban Policy Research 1986); Jackson, Crabgrass Frontier: The Suburbanization of the United States (Oxford 1985).

United States,[11] and ultimately proved short-lived, with the 1980's and 1990's seeing a return to the strong growth of metropolitan areas, particularly the suburbs.[12]

Some older and decaying suburbs are joining the cities in the ranks of "problem children" of modern society, while the difficulties of the center-cities remain—often exacerbated by long-held prejudices of residents of less-populous areas, who may view cities as vice-ridden, wasteful, and unhealthy.[13] Labor problems, involving municipal

---

[11] "Slowdown for 'Strip Cities': Reversal of Century-Old Trend," U.S.News & World Rep., March 7, 1977, at 39, stating "In the 1970's, it's the non-metropolitan areas that show the faster growth rate—not the cities and suburbs." But many suburbs continued to grow rapidly; and in general, they definitely outpaced center-cities in growth during the 1970's. See "Tale of America's Shrinking Cities—Suburban Surge—What '80 Census Shows," U.S.News & World Rep., March 23, 1981, at 66.

[12] The 1990 Census showed that the nation's flirtation with a return to rural areas had been largely a phenomenon of the 1970's and had abruptly ended in the 1980's, when 90% of the population growth occurred in metropolitan areas of a million people or more. See Usdansky, Need for Little Places Disappeared, USA Today, Jan. 6, 1992, at 1, observing that today in the United States, just over one person in ten lives in a city with fewer than 10,000 residents. Rural communities that are located far from major metropolitan areas have often been particularly hard-hit by the movement toward urban areas. See "Small-Town Blues," Time, March 27, 1989, at 66, noting that during the 1980's rural areas developed jobs at only 40% of the rate in metropolitan centers and that deregulation in the transportation industry led to a decline in rail, truck, bus, and airline service to smaller communities, contributing to an economic downturn in those communities. See generally Graham, Where Have All the Small Towns Gone?, Parade magazine, Dec. 13, 1998, at 6.

The 2000 census showed that 50 metropolitan areas had a population of over a million, with a total population of 164 million people or 58.2% of the national total. New York Times Almanac for 2002, at 244. The total population of *all* metropolitan areas (including those with less than a million people) was 226 million—over 80% of all U.S. residents. Nearly 30% (84.1 million) lived in metropolitan areas of 5 million people or more. *Id.* at 264. See generally Lemann, Get Out of Town, The New Yorker, June 27, 2011, at 76, stating "During the first half of the twentieth century, vast numbers of Americans moved to the cities; during the second half, vast numbers moved to the suburbs. By 2000, the United States had become a majority-suburban nation." *Id.* Some turnover did occur, however, in 2010–11, when a trend first noticed in 2007 culminated in larger metropolitan area growth than suburban growth from April 1, 2010, to July 1, 2011. See Dockterman, Suburban Slowdown, Time magazine, July 16, 2012, at 16, attributing some of the turnaround to economic factors that have made the suburbs less affordable. See also Nelson, The Mass Market for Suburban Low-Density Development Is Over, 44 Urban Law. 811 (2012), noting that the development of the majority-suburban nation was made possible by inexpensive gasoline, rising incomes, broadly distributed wealth, and easy home-buying credit—all of which have changed. *Id.* at 812–14. But see Lewyn, Sprawl in Canada and the United States, 44 Urban Law. 85 (2012), concluding that suburban sprawl is less extensive in Canada than in the United States and thus should not be regarded as an inevitable result of affluence and the free market. *Id.* at 87, 133.

The 2010 census showed 52 metropolitan areas with over a million population, with only 5 of those areas (Detroit, Pittsburgh, Cleveland, New Orleans, and Buffalo) having lost population since 2000. World Almanac for 2012, at 612.

[13] See (J. V. Lindsay, The City Norton 1970), reviewed, Time, March 23, 1970, at 85. On the spread of urban problems to some suburbs, see Allman, Urban Crisis Leaves Town, Harper's, Dec., 1978, at 41. See also Podeschi, Reality of Our Suburban Myths, Intellect, Jan., 1975, at 234. Levittown, New York, has been called the first suburb in the United States. Soaring energy use, and accompanying soaring costs, have been a great problem in that Long Island community, as in many suburbs; but the Green Levittown program, launched by county officials in 2007, aims to solve those problems by persuading residents to upgrade their homes, improving energy efficiency and cutting fuel bills. See Walsh, A New Blueprint for Levittown, Time, Jan. 28, 2008, at 108. On suburban problems and the legal difficulties of solving them, see generally Stahl, The Suburb as a Legal Concept: The Problem of Organization and the Fate of Municipalities in American Law, 29 Cardozo L. Rev. 1193 (2008). On the particular problems of America's earliest suburbs, see R. Puentes & D. Warren, One-Fifth of America: A Comprehensive Guide to America's First Suburbs (Brookings Institution 2006), noting such situations in these oldest suburbs as concentrations of elderly and immigrant populations and of outmoded houses and commercial buildings. On changes in the nature of suburban growth, see also Dougherty, The End of White Flight, Wall St. J., July 19–20, 2008, at A1 (Weekend Edition), noting that the diminution of white population in center-cities because of "flight" to the suburbs has slowed and in some cases even been reversed. It has been noted that "the suburban dream of the big house with the big lawn is vanishing," and that some suburbs are being "remade" so as to correct the sprawl that had occurred, making the redeveloped

workers who are increasingly militant, increasingly organized, and often in search of higher pay, have also contributed to the "many-sided squeeze" on the cities.[14] Urban-renewal projects have resulted in impressive new buildings, and sometimes in a degree of rejuvenation for traditional "downtowns"—but the overall trend toward decline in population and per capita wealth of most older cities has nonetheless persisted.[15] It has even been suggested that many of the large cities of the northeastern United States have outlived their usefulness.[16]

Some of the "urban decline" may be attributed simply to shifts of population and industry away from northern sections of the country—a realignment that inevitably causes some temporarily depressed conditions in those sections but that results in healthy growth elsewhere.[17] Further, there are those who believe that the older cities are not beyond saving—that a "second industrial revolution," involving increased economic aid and tax benefits for such cities, can reverse the cycle of urban decay.[18]

---

suburbs "more sustainable—environmentally and economically." Walsh, Recycling the Suburbs, Time magazine, March 23, 2009, at 48.

[14] See "Cities—A Many-Sided Squeeze," Time, Dec. 16, 1974, at 30, discussing the 50th anniversary meeting of the National League of Cities. See generally Gonzalez, The American City, 16 Berkeley La Raza L.J. 195 (2005). On the financial strain placed on cities by the "war on terrorism," see "America's Cities Are Seeking Red Over Code Orange," Bus. Week, June 9, 2003, at 55 (in the Washington Outlook column, edited by Dunham). See generally El Nasser, Cities Struggle in Sept. 11's Wake, USA Today, Jan. 28, 2002, at 3A.

[15] Herbers, Study Says Old Cities Continue to Decline Despite Rejuvenation, N.Y.Times, July 7, 1980, at 1, col. 1, summarizing a report for which the research was co-directed by Richard P. Nathan of Princeton University (formerly a fellow at the Brookings Institution in Washington) and James W. Fossett of the University of Michigan. The *Times* article quotes from the authors' conclusions: "In spite of optimistic reports and the physical evidence of construction in Baltimore's Inner Harbor and Chicago's North Shore, a doubling of median office rents in Manhattan in the last five years, an impressive amount of housing rehabilitation in such areas as Adams-Morgan in Washington and Queen Village in Philadelphia, it is far from clear that many older cities have turned the corner or even bottomed out." *Id.* On efforts to rejuvenate central cities, see generally Halpern, Rebuilding the Inner City: A History of Neighborhood Initiatives to Address Poverty in the United States (Columbia Univ. Press 1995), reviewed 22 Rev. L. & Soc. Change 839 (1996–97). See also Macdonald, America's Cities: A Report on the Myth of Urban Renaissance (1984), reviewed Wash. Post, Aug. 19, 1984, Book Review Section, at 3.

[16] See "Burning Up the Snowbelt," Time, Jan. 12, 1981, at 19, describing proposals presented to Pres. Carter in Jan., 1981, by the President's Commission for a National Agenda for the Eighties. The report calls decline of many of the Northeastern cities inevitable; urges the government to assist the urban poor of such cities to migrate to the "Sunbelt," where more jobs are available; and concludes that cities in general are not permanent. See generally Beauregard, Atop the Urban Hierarchy (Rowman & Littlefield 1989), describing growth and decline in the five largest cities of the United States during the post-World War II years and noting the movement of people and industries from the Northeast and Midwest (including New York, Chicago, and Philadelphia) to the Sunbelt (including Los Angeles and Houston).

[17] See "U.S. Study Confirms Growth of Sun Belt," N.Y.Times, May 3, 1981, at 18, col. 6, discussing a Commerce Department study which showed that money flowed steadily from the Northeast to the South and West in the past decade, but that the Northeast continues to rank high in per capita income. See generally Alpern & Borger, Roughly 226,504,825 Noses, Newsweek, Jan. 12, 1981, at 30; "Where We Are," Time, Dec. 29, 1980, at 16. See also Abbott, The New Urban America: Growth and Politics in Sunbelt Cities (Univ. of North Carolina Press 1987). Throughout the 1980's and 1990's, the fastest growing states and metropolitan areas were in the West and South. See Holmes, United States Population—A Profile of America's Diversity—The View from the Census Bureau, 1998, in World Almanac and Book of Facts 373 (1999).

[18] See "Mr. Fixit for the Cities," Newsweek, May 4, 1981, at 26, describing the ideas and work of urban planner Felix Rohatyn, who, among many other activities, was head of New York's Municipal Assistance Corporation. Cf., discussing problems and progress in seven large American cities, "The Older America," *id.* at 30–35. As to the extent that aid and regulation aimed at the revival of cities should or should not come from the *federal* government, see generally Adelman & Engel, Adaptive Federalism: The Case Against Reallocating Environmental Regulatory Authority, 92 Minn. L. Rev. 1796 (2008). See also Zakaria, A Recovery With Many Fathers, Time magazine, June 10, 2013, at 32, attributing improvements in the economy partly to "good national government" as well as state and local government efforts.

There are "bright spots" in the urban picture that may justify such optimism: Some cities, such as Dallas, still operate efficiently most of the time;[19] and even some older cities, such as Baltimore, have been partially rejuvenated by urban-renewal projects.[20] Residents of a number of inner-city neighborhoods have exhibited remarkable energy and dedication in striving to reclaim those areas from decay.[21] Since the 1960's, racial tensions, civil disorders, attacks on the police and similar problems have lessened in many cities.[22]

Certainly the cities of the United States continue to provide many benefits to their residents; they remain impressive cultural and commercial centers, with museums housing invaluable collections, and shops offering for sale an endless array of goods.[23] The theory has even been put forth that the "urban crisis" has always been considerably exaggerated—that the problems of city life are merely the necessary, and not unduly high, price of living in a vital environment.[24] Undoubtedly, the lure of the "great city"

As to the role of *state* governments in this area, see Gluck, The States as Laboratories of Statutory Interpretation: Methodological Consensus and the New Modified Textualism, 119 Yale L. J. 1750 (2010). See generally Dinan, State Constitutional Politics, 45 Tulsa L. Rev. 747 (2010); Symposium, The Law of American State Constitutions, 45 New Eng. L. Rev. 797–912 (2011). See also Zackin, Looking for Rights in All the Wrong Places: Why State Constitutions Contain America's Positive Rights (Princeton Univ. Press 2013).

As to the desirability of handling some matters at the *local* (as opposed to state or federal) level, see Kalis & Hlafcsak, Healthcare Reform: Let's Act Locally, 50 Duq. L. Rev. 253 (2012).

[19] "A City that Still Works," Time, April 27, 1981, at 48.

[20] See Beck & Whitmore, Baltimore's Comeback, Newsweek, Jan. 15, 1979, at 34; Goldstein, A City with More, American Way, June, 1981, at 78; "What Is Reviving Baltimore," Bus. Week, Aug. 15, 1977, at 122. Cf. Chamberlain, No Fiscal Blues in Baltimore or Blackwell, Am.City & County, Jan., 1976, at 92. On Baltimore's success with urban-renewal and "homestead" projects, see also Chapter 20 *infra*. On the successful downtown-rejuvenation projects in several cities—Baltimore, Boston, and Philadelphia—of urban developer James Rouse, see "He Digs Downtown," Time, Aug. 24, 1981, at 42. The article noted that Rouse's credo—"The only legitimate purpose of a city is to provide for the life and growth of its people"—was similar to the belief expressed by Aristotle that "The goal of the city is to make man happy and safe." *Id.* at 44. A key part of Baltimore's harbor revitalization is the National Aquarium, owned by the city and built without federal funds. "Symphony on Pier 3," *id.* at 45. On continuing restoration and rejuvenation in downtown Baltimore, see Berke, Downtown Upturn—Baltimore Restoration on the Rise, Preservation News, Aug., 1984, at 1. On persisting problems in Baltimore, see Donnelly, Rounding Up the Usual Suspects, Time, Sept. 6, 1999, at 8. See generally Olson, Baltimore—The Building of an American City (Johns Hopkins Univ. Press Bicentennial ed. 1997). On San Francisco's efforts at inner city residential redevelopment, see Phillips, Residential Rehabilitation Financing, 15 Urban L.Ann. 53 (1978).

[21] See "Cities in the 1980's: A Dialogue," Historic Preservation May/June, 1981, at 48, presenting a discussion by three panelists on the merits of preservation and rejuvenation of old neighborhoods vs. the building of new projects and communities.

[22] See "City Woes: Easing a Bit, Mayors Say," U.S.News & World Rep., June 28, 1971, at 32, describing attitudes of civic leaders attending the 1971 U.S.Conference of Mayors.

[23] Koltun, The Unexpected City, American Way, May, 1971, at 31. See generally Geddes (ed.), Cities in Our Future (Island Press 1996), studying five North American cities, their development, their handling of problems, and their plans for the future. The growth of the telecommunications industry has proven a boon to some large American cities and resulted in a degree of revival. See "Brighter Lights for Big Cities," Bus. Week, May 4, 1998, at 88. In the 1990's crime and health problems were sometimes found to be receding faster in the larger cities than in the smaller ones. See Janofsky, As Larger Cities Gain Ground on Ills, Smaller Ones Lose, N.Y. Times, Dec. 5, 1995, at B-10. See also Katz, City Centered, Time magazine, Nov. 1, 2010, at 62, saying that the U.S. should invest more in its metropolitan areas and commenting that "We mytholize the benefits of small-town America, but it's the major metros that make the country thrive." *Id.*

[24] See E. Banfield, The Unheavenly City (1970), reviewed 6 J.Human Resources 251 (1971); Time, June 1, 1970, at 64; 19 U.C.L.A.L.Rev. 148 (1971). Some of Banfield's ideas proved highly controversial, such as his theory that many blacks remain mired in poverty not because of discrimination but because of a class outlook which they share with lower-class whites: they are rigidly present-minded and do not postpone immediate pleasure for future gain. Good discussions of the book include Freeman, Toward an Understanding of the Urban Crisis, 1 Pol.Sci.Reviewer 125 (1971); Friedmann, The Unheavenly City, J. American Inst. of Planners

continues to exert an irresistible pull on countless persons.[25] Many U.S. cities remain relatively comfortable, healthy places in which to live.[26] The continued importance of metropolitan areas is emphasized by two trends of recent times: (1) There has been a *long-run* tendency of large cities and their suburbs in some areas of the country—such as that between Boston and Washington, D.C.—to blend into one another, forming a single "super-city" or "megalopolis."[27] (2) There has been a sporadic trend in many cities toward movement back into the city-center, away from suburbs and rural areas—a process sometimes called "reverse flight" or "reverse exodus."[28] Of course, continued or renewed growth of cities is seldom an unmitigated blessing. There is little doubt that on a *world-wide* basis, most cities are continuing to grow—and that much of the urban growth is in "Third World" nations where cities are often ill-equipped to handle rapid or substantial growth.[29] Cities have been called one of the chief motivating factors in

---

122 (1971); Mundel, The Emperor's Time Horizon—A Naked Walk Through the Urban Crisis, 67 Nw.U.L.Rev. 303 (1972); Nisbet, The Urban Crisis Revisited, 7 Intercollegiate Rev. 1 (1970); Sennett, "Survival of the Fittest," N.Y.Rev. of Books, Aug. 13, 1970; Todd, A Theory of the Lower Class—Edward Banfield: The Maverick of Urbanology, The Atlantic, Sept., 1970, at 51. On the controversy caused by the book, see Marmor, Banfield's "Heresy," Commentary, July, 1972, at 86; McLaughlin, Is Banfield Really Diabolical?, 72 Pa.Gazette 25 (Nov., 1973). A new version, with some modifications and explanations of the original theories, was published in 1974—Banfield, The Heavenly City Revisited (1974).

[25] See "What Makes a City Great," Time, Nov. 14, 1969, at 47. The author of this essay quotes Henry James on London: "It is not a pleasant place; it is not agreeable, or cheerful, or easy, or exempt from reproach. It is only magnificent." And Lewis Mumford on Rome: "(W)hen the worst has been said about urban Rome, one further word must be added: to the end, men loved her."

[26] See "Ranking the Cities," Time, Sept. 29, 1975, at 83, reporting on the Midwest Research Institute's rating of American cities as to the "quality of life" they offer.

[27] See "Getting Bigger All the Time: U.S. Supercities," U.S.News & World Rep., June 11, 1973, at 39. See generally on the growth and management of "supercities," H. W. Eldredge, Taming Megalopolis (Anchor Books 1967).

[28] See "Downtown Is Looking Up," Time, July 5, 1976, at 54. See also, on increased activity and construction in downtown areas, "A Towering Rise in Downtown Construction," Business Week, March 5, 1979, at 91; "Comeback Starts for Big-City Downtowns," U.S.News & World Rep., Aug. 3, 1970, at 17. On the role that zoning law can play in revitalizing center-city areas, see Cook, Zoning for Downtown Urban Design (Lexington Books 1982). See generally Anderson, Streetwise: Race, Class, and Change in an Urban Community (Univ. of Chicago Press 1990), describing the effects of "reverse flight" from the suburbs to the center-cities—a process sometimes called "gentrification." Some older cities that are continuing to lose overall population are nonetheless enjoying benefits from some degree of reverse flight: smaller but more affluent households are being attracted to downtown areas, improving these downtowns' economic base. See "Smaller Is Better in New Urban Revival," U.S.A. Today, Aug. 16, 1999, at 1A, describing the experiences of such cities as Boston, Chicago, Cleveland, Louisville, Providence, and Washington, D.C. See also McGee, Seattle's Central District, 1990–2006: Integration or Displacement?, 39 Urban Law. 167 (2007), describing the "gentrification" of the center core of Seattle and the resulting dispersal of the Black population throughout the metropolitan area as white residents are increasingly attracted by "the proximity, the convenience, and the 'hip-ness' of living close to downtowns where they work and play." *Id.* at 170. Thus, for better or worse, the Central Area African-American community "continues to unravel as Euro Americans return to America's inner cities." *Id.* at 231. Another notable trend has been the increased tendency of young American workers to remain in the cities in which they find employment rather than attempting to flee the cities for the suburbs. See Shah, More Young Stay Put in the Biggest Cities, Wall St. J., Jan. 20, 2015, at A-3. But see Hudson, Many Millennials Yearn for Suburban Homes, Wall St. J., Jan. 22, 2015, at A-2, citing a survey of persons born since 1977 that showed most of them want to live in single-family homes outside urban centers, even if they currently reside in a city.

[29] "City Life," Parade, Nov. 30, 1980, at 25, noting as to forecasts for the 21st century: "If UN population projections prove correct, the new century will find 67 cities of 1 million or more in China alone. Mexico City will be the world's largest city, with 31 million inhabitants. And the most populous cities on earth will belong to the nations of the Third World." A global Gallup Poll taken in 1976 showed that most of the rural inhabitants of the developing nations of the world would like to move to the cities—while people living in the big cities of industrialized nations often responded by saying they would like to move to small towns or rural areas.

human progress, perhaps surpassed only by agriculture.[30] But the same authorities have recognized that cities, with their congestion, can at times suffer the most serious health and safety problems found anywhere.[31] While the United States has not endured the urban calamities occurring in some parts of the world, many cities continue to show signs of economic distress and physical decay; and a few impressive new buildings and developments should not be allowed to lull us into a sense of complacency about urban problems.[32]

Further, recent changes in society in the United States have brought difficulties not only to the large cities but also to the small towns. Small-town life has long figured prominently in the "American dream," but those who move from a city to such a town may find themselves confronted with depressingly familiar situations—decaying

---

[30] See 1 McQuillin, Municipal Corporations §1.01, at 3 (3d rev. ed. 1999), citing State ex rel. Audrain County v. City of Mexico, 355 Mo. 612, 197 S.W.2d 301 (1946). On the early history of cities in the world, see 1 McQuillin, *supra*, §§1.02–.05. On the world's earliest cities, see R. Whitehouse, The First Cities (E.P.Dutton 1977). On urban relocation in ancient times, see Demand, Urban Relocation in Archaic and Classical Greece: Flight and Consolidation (Univ. of Oklahoma Press 1990). On the way in which the human condition has been shaped in *recent* years by the modern urban environment, see S. Greer, The Urbane View—Life and Politics in Metropolitan America (Oxford Univ. Press 1972). As to the "tide of urbanization that has spread around the world," see Kungig, Cities Are the Solution, Natl. Geographic, Dec., 2011, at 124, 133, noting the growth of urban areas throughout much of the world and the increasingly accepted belief that cities may be the best hope of lifting people out of poverty and at the same time preserving the environment. See generally as to the effects throughout the world of urbanization, Brugmann, Welcome to the Urban Revolution—How Cities Are Changing the World (Bloomsbury Press 2009), stating (at ix) "We are organizing the planet itself into a City: into a single, complex, connected, and still very unstable urban system." See also P.D. Smith, City (Bloomsbury Press 2012), reviewed in The New Yorker, Aug. 6, 2012, at 73, noting that Smith's book is a "guidebook for the urban age that ranges from the Mesopotamian cities of Eridu and Ur to the unbuilt cities of the future." As to the effects of urban neighborhoods on people's lives, see Sampson, Great American City: Chicago and the Enduring Neighborhood Effect (2012), reviewed by Stahl, Mobility and Community in Urban Policy: An Essay on *Great American City* by Robert J. Sampson, 46 Urban Law. 625 (2014), advocating "place-based" policies that shape people's lives.

On the city as an important part of society's development, see generally L. Mumford, The City in History (Harcourt, Brace & World 1961). See also the symposium on the Mumford book in 1962 Wash.U.L.Q. 285 (including review by Mandelker at 299). As to cities as "incubators for innovative government strategies and techniques," and as having considerable power in our current political system, see Martin, Federalism and Municipal Innovation: Lessons From the Fight Against Vacant Properties, 46 Urban Law. 361 (2014).

[31] See 1 McQuillin, *supra* note 30, §1.07, at 8, describing problems of urban life over the centuries and progress in solving those problems. The author notes, regarding ancient and medieval times that "The conditions that prevailed in congested urban communities, especially in industrial cities and towns, are difficult to believe today." This author also observes that the differences between urban and rural life are not so great in the civilized world today as they were during the early years of the twentieth century. *Id.* On congestion in modern American cities, see "Crowds and More Crowds—No End to Urban Hassles," U.S. News & World Rep., April 5, 1982, at 47.

[32] See "America's 'False Sense of Complacency About Its Cities,'" U.S.News & World Rep., Dec. 8, 1980, at 72 (interview with Richard P. Nathan, Director of the Urban and Regional Research Center of Princeton). Mr. Nathan notes three approaches for helping troubled cities; aid to city governments of those cities most in need; grants directly to needy persons; and aid to businesses to encourage them to locate in distressed areas. On the use of the term "Los Angelization" to refer to the process, exemplified by the Southern California metropolis, by which rapid population growth, uncontrolled development, rampant crime, and environmental harm can combine to produce urban decay, see Bonfante, Everybody's Fall Guy, Time, June 10, 1991, at 22. On the future of the city, see generally Symposium Issue, The City in the 21st Century, 32 Urban Law. Issue No. 3 (2000). As to the importance of local governments in developing a sustainable environment, see Verchick, Why the Global Environment Needs Local Government: Lessons from the Johannesburg Summit, 35 Urban Law. 471 (2003), noting that the World Summit for Sustainable Development held in Johannesburg, South Africa, in the summer of 2002 produced a "Plan of Implementation" that emphasized the role of local government. *Id.* at 472.

downtowns, housing shortages, inadequate government revenues.[33] Some of these problems have long existed or been developing in smaller communities, but recent decades have seen great increases in such difficulties as hostility toward new residents, and criminal activity.[34] Also in recent decades, large population centers develop not only from once-small towns but from once-rural counties; these latter developments tend to grow in a sprawling fashion, lacking an organized pattern or any clear center, and experiencing special problems in serving their far-flung residents.[35]

In-between the colorful, if sometimes decaying, big cities and the comfortable, if sometimes idealized, small towns are America's "medium-size" cities. Frequently ignored—while writers, social scientists, and government planners concentrate on the two extremes—, these cities are also, in many cases, experiencing greater growth, importance, and difficulties.[36]

---

[33] "Small Town, U.S.A.: Growing and Groaning," Time, Sept. 1, 1980, at 73 (Time Essay). See generally, on the changes in America's small communities, R. Lingeman, Small Town America (1980). See also A. J. Vidich & J. Bensman, Small Town in Mass Society—Class, Power, and Religion in a Rural Community (Princeton University 1958) (also published by Anchor Books, 1960). Compare Symposium, Preventing the Ghost Town—What Rural Communities Need to Do to Survive in the Modern Economy, 23 Kan. J.L. & Pub. Pol'y, 345–436 (2014).

[34] "Population Surge Shakes Up Small Towns," U.S.News & World Rep., May 18, 1981, at 76. See Freilich, White-Wasson & Cofer, 1979–1980 Annual Review of Local Government Law: Municipal Liability and Other Certain Uncertainties, 12 Urban Lawyer 577, 599–606 (1980) ("Growth Policies"), stating that the goal of many Americans is a rural lifestyle with an urban income, but that often "The dream of the simple rural lifestyle has turned into a nightmare of endless fast-food chains, gas stations, and suburban office-industrial complexes burgeoning with employee parking lots." *Id.* at 599. Another wave of emigration from metropolitan areas, such as had occurred in the late 1970's, hit some small towns in the late 1990's, again bringing both benefits and problems. See Pooley, In Search of a Better Life, Time, Dec. 8, 1997, at 52. On small towns in America, see generally Vidich & Bensman, Small Town in Mass Society—Class, Power and Religion in a Rural Community (Princeton Univ. Press 1958). The more recent migrations to small communities and rural areas have often been to vacation or retirement areas or areas that have strong technology infrastructures. See "The Boonies are Booming," Bus. Week, Oct. 9, 1995, at 104. See generally "The Changing Heartland," Bus. Week, Sept. 9, 2002, at 80, noting that "rural towns that once looked askance at the ills of the big city are confronting a rise in everything from out-of-wedlock births to divorces." *Id.* at. 80.

[35] See Herbers, Small Towns Blazing a Trail to Metropolitan Status, N.Y.Times, Dec. 11, 1980, at A18, stating, "The new trend is toward urbanized counties without any clear center but with enough people, wealth, and development to make them vastly different from sparsely settled places." The urbanized counties described in this article—more urbanized than traditional suburbs, but still not quite like traditional cities—have been called "megacounties." See "The Boom Towns," Time, June 15, 1987, at 14, giving as examples Du Page County, Illinois; Gwinnett County, Georgia; Fairfax County, Virginia; Orange County, California; and Johnson County, Kansas. In many growing metropolitan areas, multiple centers of development are now appearing, sometimes spread out over hundreds of square miles. See Garreau, Edge City: Life on the New Frontier (Doubleday 1991), reviewed 24 Urban Law. 233 (1992); Heenan, The New Corporate Frontier: The Big Move to Small Town, U.S.A. (McGraw-Hill 1991), both reviewed Bus. Week, Sept. 30, 1991, at 10. On growth of far-flung "exurban" areas beyond the traditional center cities and suburbs, see "Moving Out to the City," Bus. Week, Sept. 25, 1989, at 148. See generally Symposium: Urban Sprawl, 29 Urban Law. 157–250 (1997). See also Daniels, When City and Country Collide: Managing Growth in the Metropolitan Fringe (Island Press 1998); Lacayo, The Brawl Over Sprawl, Time, March 22, 1999, at 44. Some suburbs are fighting the development of far-flung fringe areas by attempting to lure residents and businesses back. See "The Burbs Fight Back," Bus. Week, June 2, 1997, at 147, describing particularly the efforts of Euclid, Ohio. On efforts to combat urban sprawl, see generally Carey, New Neighborhoods Can Combat Urban Sprawl, Bus. Week, Aug. 30, 1999, at 110. See also Chapter 21 *infra*. As to the characteristics of rural vs. urban people and places, see Pruitt, Rural Rhetoric, 39 Conn. L. Rev. 159 (2006), discussing the legal relevance of rurality and urging judges to pay closer attention to the differences among the many places and people they label "rural."

[36] See Stuart, Mid-Sized American Cities Getting New Attention, N.Y.Times, March 16, 1981, at 1, col. 4. (The article defines a "medium-sized city" as between 50,000 and 250,000 population.) On the special problems of cities *under* 50,000 in population, see Banovetz (ed.), Small Cities and Counties: A Guide to Managing Services (International City Management Ass'n 1984), reviewed 18 Urban Law. 769 (1986). See

§ 1.2 Scope of Local Government Law

American municipalities of all sizes are thus encountering formidable challenges. While many parts of the country have become highly urbanized, in some states the bulk of the population remains concentrated in smaller communities.[37] But all the communities share certain characteristics, patterns, and problems; courses in Local Government Law concentrate on these common features. An attorney can, in a number of ways, be drawn into dealing with modern municipal problems; and the Local Government course may prove highly useful in at least four ways: (1) Some attorneys work within a local government themselves, as where they work in the city attorney's office, as attorney for a school district, etc. (2) Even the private practitioner who does not have any local government for a client may frequently encounter problems of Local Government Law—zoning matters, tort actions against a city, etc. Private citizens can seldom escape from some dealings with various units of local government, and many of these dealings require the help of an attorney. (3) Lawyers often become involved, quite aside from their law practice, in local politics and government—as officeholders or candidates for office, or simply as concerned citizens. The Local Government course should lead to greater understanding of such frequently encountered local problems as crime control, land-use planning, and financial inadequacies. (4) Lawyers, whether or not dealing at all with *local* government, can hardly avoid contact, as lawyers and as citizens, with *some* levels of government. The Local Government course gives a good overview of the inter-relationships of our various levels of government in this country, and thus of our whole political system. Since the "Jeffersonian revolution" brought about by the first edition of Jefferson Fordham's excellent case-book on Local Government Law in 1949, courses in this area have covered not merely cities and towns, but all units of government at the local level, plus the role of state and federal governments in urban areas.[38]

---

generally National League of Cities, The State of the Small City: A Survey of the Nation's Cities and Towns Under 50,000 (1987).

[37] See, *e.g.*, "Oklahoma 1970: The Dust Bowl of the '30's Revisited," Time, Jan. 26, 1970, at 16, noting that most of that state's population resides in rural communities.

[38] The original edition was Fordham, Local Government Law (1949) reviewed 3 Okl.L.Rev. 123 (1950); the latest edition is Fordham, Local Government Law (2d rev. ed. 1986). On the "Jeffersonian revolution" caused by the first edition, see Mandelker, Managing Our Urban Environment vii–viii (1966) (Preface to 1st ed.—found at xvii–xviii in 2d ed. 1971), noting also the new emphasis placed on environmental concerns by that book. Mandelker also observes that there is continuing debate over whether land-use controls (zoning, etc.) should be taught as part of property courses, within local government courses, or as the subject-matter of a separate course; all three methods have been, and continue to be, employed. Mandelker, *supra*, at viii (at xviii in 2d ed.). See also Redlich, The Scope of Urban Legal Studies, 8 Osgoode Hall L.J. 365 (1970) (part of a symposium on urban legal studies). On the importance of Jefferson Fordham and his casebook, see also "Call for Nominations: 11th Annual Jefferson B. Fordham Awards," 32 State & Local Law News, No. 2, Winter, 2008, at 3: "His 1949 case book on local government law revolutionized the teaching of state and local government law and addressed dynamic legal issues such as planning and finance, housing and blight, and transportation and congestion, in short, the entire range of urban problems whose solution required a larger concept of community." On the current condition of local government law, see "What Is Urban Law Today?": A Symposium on the Field's Past, Present, and Future in Honor of the Fordham Urban Law Journal's Fortieth Anniversary, 40 Fordham Urb. L. J. 1579–1973 (2013). See also Symposium, Super Aoki—A Tribute to Keith Aoki, 45 U.C. Davis L. Rev. 1585–1957 (2012), especially Barron, Keith and the Good City, *id.* at 1945, & Su, Locating Keith Aoko: Space, Geography, and Local Government Law, *id.* at 1637.

A good article on the trends in the relationship of the federal government to other governments within the United States is Freilich, Frye & Carpenter, The New Federalism—American Urban Policy in the 1980's: Trends and Directions in Urban, State and Local Government Law, 15 Urban Law. 159 (1983). See generally

The material in this book is presented in the following order: First, there is discussion of the various units of government below the state level, such as cities, towns, counties, etc. Then, attention is turned to the *forms* of government within such units (with particular attention to city and town government). Attention is next focused on the relationship of local government to the state and federal. Here we consider local home-rule, state and federal pre-emption, etc. After that, we concentrate on the local unit itself—first, its powers, and then the limitations on those powers. (Again, there is particular emphasis on the powers and limitations of cities and towns.) We look to the forms that local legislative action may take. After that, we are ready to concentrate on the three most important ingredients in local government—territory, people, and money. In looking to the territorial make-up of local units, we consider such matters as incorporation and annexation. In looking at the "people" aspect of local government, we concentrate on those who work for that government—the officers and employees—and their relationship to their constituents. In considering local finances, we discuss the manner in which localities may raise and spend money.

At that point, we have covered the basic make-up of local units and their relationship with other levels of government. But what does local government *do*? The next chapters concentrate on the activities of local units: First (since these activities overlap the immediately preceding subject of local finances), we look at efforts to encourage business and industry into the community, and at local government's involvement in the utility business. Local government is extremely active in the field of land-use control and planning, including (with aid from other levels of government) the rejuvenation of downtown areas and the building of new communities. Several chapters are devoted to this area. Two other important municipal activities are then discussed, each in its own chapter: regulating trades, businesses, and comparable (chiefly commercial) activities; and controlling crime and violence.

Finally, we look to the means for holding local governments liable and/or making them more responsive to their citizens. What are a local government's contractual obligations? What is such a government's potential liability in tort? What exceptional measures are available to bring about the passage or defeat of legislation, to give voters a chance to oust persons from local office, or to force action on the part of local government? These matters are considered in the final chapters.

An effort has been made to cover those topics most often dealt with in basic law-school courses in Local Government Law (or, to use the older name, "Municipal Corporations"). Since a "crash course" in Land Use Controls is often a part of Local Government, a considerable amount of land-use material is included herein—though courses devoted exclusively to that subject will probably go into more depth. Four topics relevant to Local Government Law have not, it should be noted, been included here in any detail, as they are so broad as to require entire volumes by themselves—or at least lengthy chapters that would have extended this work beyond reasonable limits: (1)

Symposium, Federalism: Issues Before the Supreme Court, 18 Urban Law. 483–705 (1986). See also Section 7.1 *infra* and cites therein. For differing views on the superior ability of local, as opposed to state and federal, governments to solve problems, compare Briffault, Our Localism, 90 Colum. L. Rev. 1, 346 (1990) (criticizing the frequently expressed idea that local power is superior), with Frug, Whose Localism Is "Our Localism"?, Ass'n of American Law Schools Section on Local Government Newsletter, Dec., 1990, at 4. See generally Lake (ed.), Readings in Urban Analysis (Center for Urban Policy Research 1983); Martinez & Libonati, State and Local Government Law—A Transactional Approach (Anderson Publ.2000).

Constitutional law as applied to local governments and their actions. This, obviously, is best covered in a separate law-school course; and a Constitutional Law course is a helpful basis for, though not an absolute prerequisite to, the study of Local Government.[39] (2) Civil rights in general—and in particular, the longstanding struggle over desegregation of the schools. These topics are well handled in special seminars. (3) Overlapping the prior topic—the law of schools and school districts. School districts are herein discussed as one kind of unit of local government. But their unique and myriad problems deserve their own book, and several excellent works exist on this subject.[40] (4) Local

---

[39] A constitutional-law problem of particular difficulty that is frequently encountered in the area of local government is that of "equal protection"; a most helpful discussion is found in Houle, Compelling State Interest vs. Mere Rational Classification: The Practitioner's Equal Protection Dilemma, 3 Urban Lawyer 375 (1971). See generally Tussman & ten Broeck, The Equal Protection of the Laws, 37 Calif.L.Rev. 341 (1949).

On constitutional theory and history, see C. J. Friedrich, Constitutional Government and Democracy—Theory and Practice in Europe and America (4th ed. 1968); A. E. Sutherland, Constitutionalism in America—Origin and Evolution of Its Fundamental Ideas (Blaisdell Publ.1965).

On the application of U.S. constitutional law to local governments, see Gelfand, Federal Constitutional Law and American Local Government (Michie 1984). See also Tushnet, Red, White and Blue: A Critical Analysis of Constitutional Law (Harvard Univ. Press 1988), reviewed 22 Urban Law. 171 (1990).

[40] See, *e.g.*, L. O. Garber & N. Edwards, The Law Relating to the Creation, Alteration, and Dissolution of School Districts (Interstate Publ.1962); S. Goldstein, Law and Public Education: Cases and Materials 9–12 (1974): J. L. McDaniel & E. C. Bolmeier, Law Governing Acquisition of School Property (W. H. Anderson 1966). See also L. O. Garber & N. Edwards, The Law Governing School Property and School-Building Construction (Interstate Publ.1964); L. O. Garber & N. Edwards, Tort and Contractual Liability of School Districts and School Boards (Interstate Publ.1963).

On school desegregation, see Dimond, Beyond Busing: Inside the Challenge to Urban Segregation (Univ. of Michigan Press 1985). On important U.S. Supreme Court cases regarding public education, see Swiger, Bittle & Gregory, The Supreme Court and Public Education: A View of the Past Year, 17 Urban Law. 911 (1985). On developments in American education, see generally Special Conferences Issues, Vol. 14, No. 3 (Summer, 1982) & Vol. 15, No. 1 (Winter, 1983) of The Urban Lawyer. An excellent work on the history of efforts to desegregate the public schools is Tushnet, The NAACP's Legal Strategy Against Segregated Education, 1925–1950 (Univ. of North Carolina Press 1987). See generally Morris, The Constitution and American Public Education (Carolina Academic Press 1989). On changing and differing views of the leading school desegregation case of Brown v. Board of Educ., 347 U.S. 483, 74 S.Ct. 686, 98 L.Ed. 873 (1954), see Garrow, Hopelessly Hollow History: Revisionist Devaluing of *Brown v. Board of Educ.*, 80 Va. L. Rev. 7 (1994); Klarman, *Brown*, Racial Change, and the Civil Rights Movement, 80 Va. L. Rev. 7 (1994); Rosenberg, *Brown* Is Dead! Long Live *Brown*!: The Endless Attempt to Canonize a Case, 80 Va. L. Rev. 161 (1994); Tushnet, The Significance of *Brown v. Board of Education*, 80 Va. L. Rev. 173 (1994); Symposiums, *Brown v. Board of Education*, 20 S. Ill. U.L.J. 1–115 (1995) & *Brown v. Board of Education*: Forty Years Later, 4 Temple Pol. & Civil Rights L. Rev. 211–99 (1995). See also Note, *Board of Education of Oklahoma City v. Dowell*: Protection of Local Authority or Disregard for the Purpose of *Brown v. Board of Education*?, 41 Catholic U.L. Rev. 779 (1992). On continuing problems and developments as to desegregation of American public schools, see Symposium, Separate but Unequal: The Status of America's Public Schools, 8 Mich. J. Race & L. 151 (2002). On the *Brown v. Board of Education* case in particular, see Ellis, *Brown v. Board of Education*: Right Result, Wrong Reasoning, 56 Mercer L. Rev. 715 (2005). See generally Symposium, Fifty Years of Reflection: *Brown v. Board of Education* and Its Universal Implications, 32 Fordham Urban L.J. vii–viii, 1–170 (2004). See also Note, The School Choice Provision of the No Child Left Behind Act and Its Conflict with Desegregation Orders, 13 Boston U. Pub. Interest L.J. 79 (2003). For thorough analysis of the legacy of the *Brown* case, see Minow, In *Brown*'s Wake—Legacies of America's Educational Landmark (2010). See generally Alger, From Desegregation to Diversity and Beyond: Our Evolving Legal Conversation on Race and Higher Education, 36 J. College & University L. 983 (2010). See also Schmidt, "Freedom Comes Only from the Law": The Debate over Law's Capacity and the Making of *Brown v. Board of Education*, 2008 Utah L. Rev. 1493. As to more recent cases on school integration, see Note, School Integration in the Wake of *Parents Involved* and *Meredith*, 40 Rutgers L. J. 535 (2009); Symposium, *Brown* Undone?: The Future of Integration in Seattle After *PICS v. Seattle School District No. 1*, 31 Seattle U.L. Rev. 863–936 (2008). A good summary of the long struggle for racial integration in the Little Rock, Arkansas, school district is found in Brown, The Little Rock School District's Quest for Unitary Status, 30 U. Ark. Little Rock L. Rev. 267 (2008). The 60th anniversary of the *Brown* case was observed with the Symposium, *Brown v. Board* at 60: Looking Back, Looking Forward, 53

administrative agencies and local courts.[41] These also are well covered in other works and present questions that are best handled in Administrative Law and Judicial Process courses.

A considerable variety of sources have been cited when dealing with such subjects as modern urban problems, forms of local government, etc. The citations are not limited to cases, statutes, and other "legal" authorities, but include newspaper and magazine articles, as these often give valuable information on, and insight into, the current urban situation. Laws on municipal matters can only be effectively studied and analyzed if considered in light of the real-life urban situations with which they deal. The laws are, after all, only *one* part of a multi-faceted attempt to deal with human problems.

§ 1.3 A Prevalent Distinction: Governmental v. Proprietary

One distinction in Local Government Law is so often encountered that, although it is also much criticized, it should be noted at the outset. That is the distinction between *governmental* (or public), and *proprietary* (or corporate, or business-like), functions of local units. A governmental function is supposedly one connected with the governing aspects of the locality's existence: the passing of legislation, the handing down of judicial decisions. Police and fire protection are usually included in this category, since they are activities typically performed by a government (though the same or similar activities are occasionally undertaken by private enterprise). If a function is uniquely capable of being performed by some level of government and/or is most often engaged-in by governments rather than by private persons, that function will likely be termed "governmental." Proprietary functions are, on the other hand, not uniquely suited to governmental rendition; they may equally well be conducted by private enterprise, and often are so performed. For instance, the providing of utility services (electric, gas, water, etc.) is nearly always classified as proprietary. The distinction has resulted in much hairsplitting, and is today less popular and less utilized than in past decades. It is definitely on the wane in the area where it once had its greatest degree of use—that of local governmental immunity in tort.[42] But cases relying on the distinction must still be

---

Washburn L.J. 439–544 (2014). See also Landsberg, Enforcing Desegregation: A Case Study of Federal District Court Power and Social Change in Macon County, Alabama, 48 Law & Soc'y Rev. 867 (2014).

[41] On local court systems, see B. W. Daynes, An Assessment of the Courts of Limited Jurisdiction (American Judicature Soc'y 1968); H. Jacob, Urban Justice—Law and Order in American Cities (Prentice-Hall 1973); K. M. Knab (ed.), Courts of Limited Jurisdiction: A National Survey (American Judicature Soc'y 1977). See generally Nelson, Cases and Materials on Judicial Administration and the Administration of Justice (1974).

[42] See Chapter 26 *infra*.

On the distinction, see generally Doddridge, Distinction Between Governmental and Proprietary Functions of Municipal Corporations, 23 Mich.L.Rev. 325 (1925); Note, Torts—Governmental Immunity—City Not Immune from Liability for Injuries Resulting from Malpractice in Municipal Hospital Because Operation of Hospital Is Not a Governmental Function, 57 U.Detroit J. Urban L. 165 (1979). On the history of the distinction, see Barnett, The Foundations of the Distinction Between Public and Private Functions in Respect to the Common Law Tort Liability of Municipal Corporations, 16 Or.L.Rev. 250 (1937). For criticism of the distinction, see Seasongood, Municipal Corporations: Objections to the Governmental or Proprietary Test, 22 Va.L.Rev. 910 (1936). Seasongood's classic article from 1936 was reprinted at 53 U. Cinc. L. Rev. 469 (1984). See also Comment, Postscript: Tracing the Governmental-Proprietary Test, 53 U. Cinc. L. Rev. 561 (1984). The governmental-proprietary distinction often retains significance in the area of intergovernmental tax immunity. See Flowing Wells Irrigation Dist. v. City of Tucson, 176 Ariz. 623, 863 P.2d 915 (Tax 1993), discussing the meanings of "governmental" and "proprietary," declaring that governmental activities are generally exempt from taxation by another government while proprietary activities are taxable, and holding that a municipality could tax an irrigation district's furnishing of water for residential uses since that is a proprietary function.

read at times for their other precedential value; many recent cases and statutes cannot be understood without an appreciation of their history, which often includes the governmental-proprietary distinction; and in some areas of Local Government Law, the distinction remains very much alive. Thus, the student should be aware, at the outset of a Local Government course, of the terminology; particular uses of the distinction, and cases thereon, appear throughout this work.

Chapter 2

UNITS OF LOCAL GOVERNMENT

Analysis

§ 2.1 English Background

The development of local government in America followed patterns earlier established in England. Even before the Norman Conquest of 1066, England was divided into shires or counties, and within these counties there were units of local government known as "townships." A township might be a free community or might be a colony of some great landowner.[1] Following the Conquest, the feudal system of tenure grew stronger; the powers of the landowning lords increased at the expense of the pre-existing units of local government. The king began to exercise direct control over these governments. For instance, the sheriff became the crown representative in each county, with control over such diverse matters as tax collection and administration of the jails.[2] Eventually, the rulers became afraid of the considerable power that had come to rest with the sheriffs; and by the 16th century, most of the powers of local government were transferred to new county-wide governing bodies whose members were called "justices

[1] See 1 Stubbs, Constitutional History of England 88–91 (6th ed. 1897, reprinted 1967); Taswell-Langmead, English Constitutional History 13 (6th ed. Ashworth 1905). See generally 1 Holdsworth, History of English Law 20–24 (4th ed. 1927).

[2] Fordham, Local Government Law 3 (2d rev. ed. 1986).

of the peace." These officials enjoyed powers that today would be regarded as legislative, in addition to their judicial duties.[3]

As governmental activities expanded, the justice-of-the-peace system proved ill-equipped to handle the ever-increasing tasks. Under the Tudor rulers, primacy in local government was assumed by another unit of local government, borrowed from church administration and known as the "parish". Soon the administration of taxes and the providing of many local services were being handled by the parishes.[4]

Meantime, some of the more populous centers had come to enjoy a separate status. Even before the Norman Conquest, some communities were more developed, more urban than others. Those that were military or marketing centers for their regions came to be called "boroughs." During the feudal period, many of these obtained, from the lord of the particular area, charters granting special privileges and freedoms. The boroughs, under these charters, enjoyed considerable power of self-government and developed their own judicial bodies. Often these were called "councils" and consisted of a presiding officer, known as a "mayor," and members, known as "aldermen." Again, such a body would usually function not only as a court, but also as a local legislature. When functioning legislatively, the mayor and aldermen would be joined by additional members, known as "common councilmen." In London and some of the other more populous boroughs, all these members were elected by the freemen of the community.[5]

For many years, the Crown struggled with the growing economic and political power of the boroughs, as well as with the increasing power of the national Parliament. After the Great Rebellion of 1688, however, attempts at central control of the local governments decreased. More and more responsibilities were given the local units by Parliament. In the eighteenth century, the judicial and administrative functions of officers were separated so that the same person or body would no longer exercise both. And "ad hoc" or "special function" units of government proliferated to handle such miscellaneous problems as poor relief and highway construction.[6]

Since English local government did not develop very systematically, weaknesses were apparent—and by the early 1800's were serious: the ad hoc agencies created a complex situation in which unified attack on a problem was difficult; there was too little central control, etc.[7] The Municipal Corporations Act of 1835[8] attempted to remedy these ills. It marked the beginning of regulation of local government by means of legislation and the end of the old idea of special privileges given by charters from lords or the Crown.

---

3 1 Stubbs, Constitutional History of England 647–52 (6th ed. 1897, reprinted 1967). On the role of the constable as an agent of the justices of the peace—and the strange survival of this office, in modified form, in a few American cities, see Note, The Philadelphia Constable, 104 U.Pa.L.Rev. 508 (1956).

4 Odgers, Local Government 39–50 (2d ed. Odgers & Naldrett 1907). See Webb & Webb, English Local Government from the Revolution to the Municipal Corporations Act: The Parish and the County (London 1906).

5 3 Stubbs, Constitutional History of England 577–611 (6th ed. 1897, reprinted 1967). Cf. 4 Holdsworth, History of English Law 136–37 (4th ed. 1927). See generally Maitland, Township and Borough (1898).

6 See Webb & Webb, Statutory Authorities for Special Purposes chs. 5 & 6 (1922).

7 10 Holdsworth, History of English Law 332–42 (4th ed. 1927). Cf. Odgers, Local Government 19 (2d ed. Odgers & Naldrett 1907). See generally, 1 Bryce, Modern Democracies 131 (1921).

8 5 & 6 Will. IV, c. 76. See Bebout, An Ancient Partnership—Local Government, Magna Carta, and the National Interest 31–33 (Univ. of Virginia Press 1966); Redlich & Hirst, The History of Local Government in England 526 (1958).

Many of its features of municipal organization were carried over to the counties by the Local Government Act of 1888.[9]

Under the legislation of the 1800's, two types of county were created in England: (1) The county borough existed in many of the more urban areas and had an elected borough council as its governing body. (2) The administrative counties existed in the rest of the country, except London. These latter were further subdivided into various districts, each of which had its own governing council, thus creating a two-tier system of government for the administrative counties.[10] Throughout the 20th century, there has been a general trend toward centralization of governmental power in Britain—a trend that accelerated during World War II.[11] Thus, while taxation of property remained a local power, the function of valuation of property for tax purposes was shifted to the national government.

London was long governed under a different system from the rest of the country, and powers were divided among many administrative authorities. Finally, a 1963 statute[12] established a 2-tier government for the London metropolitan area. The Greater London Council, made up of representatives from single-member districts throughout the area, has real power over matters of metropolitan import, while local councils retained control of matters of more limited concern.[13]

The entire British system of local government underwent another sweeping change in 1972 with passage of the Local Government Act of that year.[14] All the former counties and county boroughs were abolished and replaced by 6 metropolitan and 38 non-metropolitan counties, each subdivided into districts. (Some comparatively minor changes were also made in the governance of the London area.) A two-tier system was thus created for the whole country, and the local subdivisions are now left largely unrestrained as to their governmental set-up and functioning.

From the British experience Americans drew much terminology, some ideas on division of responsibility, and the important concept (drawn from the old borough charters) of charters granting powers and privileges to local governments.

§ 2.2 History of Local Government in the United States

Counties, modeled on those in England, were among the first important units of local government established in the English Colonies in North America. Thus, counties were created in Massachusetts in 1643—the first colony to form such units. Somewhat later, Connecticut delegated to an officer in each county the task of prosecuting criminal suspects—and the job of "county attorney" or "public prosecutor" was born. New York developed boards of freeholders elected to levy and administer taxes within each county.

---

[9] 51 & 62 Vict., c. 41.

[10] See Hart, Introduction to the Law of Local Government and Administration (8th ed. 1968).

[11] See Jennings, Principles of Local Government 187 (3d ed. 1948). On the importance of the central government in England throughout much of that country's earlier history, see Dicey, Introduction to the Study of the Law of the Constitution 175 (5th ed. 1897).

[12] The London Government Act of 1963, 12 & 13 Elizabeth 2, c. 33.

[13] See Williams, The London Government Act of 1963, 27 Mod.L.Rev. 447 (1964).

[14] The Local Government Act of 1972, noted 1973 Mod.L.Rev. 412. See Arnold-Baker, The Local Government Act of 1972, at 5–15 (Butterworth Co. 1973).

Commissioners elected at large administered the county under the Pennsylvania system—and similar bodies of "county commissioners" exist in many states today.

There were few important urban centers in colonial days, and thus municipal government was not widely developed. But the idea of a "charter" to a municipality was brought from England, with the governor, as representative of the Crown, generally issuing such documents. Taxing and other powers granted by such charters were normally quite limited. Governments for municipalities followed the pattern of the English boroughs.[15]

Reflecting the reaction against the power of the Crown and its representatives, state constitutions adopted after the American Revolution provided for weak governors and strong legislatures. Control over local government thus largely passed to the legislative branch, and legislative control over local government was considered to be unlimited except by specific constitutional provisions.[16] In establishing municipal governments, drafters of city charters often followed the federal and state examples, providing separate branches of government and a system of checks and balances. Often there was little concentration of authority. Weak city executives, spoils systems for filling municipal offices, undue meddling in city affairs by state legislatures—these were among the ills that beset American cities in the 19th century and into the early decades of the 20th.[17] Such abuses eventually brought the reforms of "home rule," prohibitions of special laws, etc. that are discussed in Chapters 5 and 6 *infra*. Of course, as old problems were solved (at least partially), new ones—financial difficulties, deterioration of city centers, etc.—have appeared.

§ 2.3 Distinction Between Public (or Municipal) Corporations and Public Quasi-Corporations

Units of local government—that is, government below the state level—in the United States are sometimes divided into two basic categories: public or municipal corporations, and public quasi-corporations.[18] Public or municipal corporations are legal entities with

---

[15] On local governments in the colonies, see Fairlie, Essays on Municipal Administration ch. 4 (1908); Fairlie & Kneier, County Government and Administration ch. 2 (1930); Reed, Municipal Government in the United States ch. 5 (rev. ed. 1934). Cf. McBain, The Legal Status of the American Colonial City, 40 Pol.Sci.Quart. 177 (1925).

[16] Fordham, Local Government Law 19 (rev. ed. 1975). See City of Covington v. Kentucky, 173 U.S. 231, 19 S.Ct. 383, 43 L.Ed. 679 (1899); Meriwether v. Garrett, 102 U.S. 472, 26 L.Ed. 197 (1880); Town of Mt. Pleasant v. Beckwith, 100 U.S. 514, 10 Otto 514, 25 L.Ed. 699 (1879); People ex rel. Drake v. Mahaney, 13 Mich. 481 (1865); State ex rel. Hawes v. Mason, 153 Mo. 23, 54 S.W. 524 (1899), all of which discuss and uphold the complete legislative power over municipal corporations. Cf. City of St. Louis v. Sheilds, 52 Mo. 351 (1873) (legislatures can alter or repeal at will all acts affecting municipal corporations).

[17] See Fairlie & Kneier, County Government and Administration ch. 3 (1930); Griffith, A History of American City Government 1870–1900 (1974). See generally Patton, The Battle for Municipal Reform (1941). See also 1 Bryce, American Commonwealth 608 (1st ed. 1888). On the continuing themes in American local government law of the lack of local power and the need for greater local autonomy, see Briffault, Our Localism, 90 Colum. L. Rev. 1, 346 (1990). See generally Monkkonen, America Becomes Urban: The Development of U.S. Cities and Towns 1780–1980 (Univ. of California Press 1988). On the "all black" racially segregated communities that at one time were formed in Kansas, Oklahoma and a few other states, see Johnson, Acres of Aspiration—The All-Black Town in Oklahoma (Eakin Press 2002), saying that the heyday of such towns was between 1890 and 1910, when American capitalism changed from agrarian to urban.

[18] 1 Dillon, Municipal Corporations 24, 65 (5th ed. 1911); 1 McQuillin, Municipal Corporations §§ 2.07–2.13, 2.23 (3d rev. ed. 1999); Stason & Kauper, Cases and Materials on the Law of Municipal Corporations 1 (1959). See Leviton v. Board of Education, 374 Ill. 594, 30 N.E.2d 497 (1940) (city or village is voluntary,

broad powers of local government. Typically, they have definite geographic boundaries within which resides a relatively compact population. Examples are the units of local government commonly called cities, towns, and villages. The term "borough" also often (but not invariably) indicates such a unit. Contrasted with these are the public quasi-corporations, which have traditionally been considered less organized and less powerful. They do not necessarily have a compact population and indeed may be quite rural in character. Typical examples include counties, townships, New England towns. Such ad hoc units as school districts, other special function districts, and public authorities are also often included in this category—though they may be listed merely as "miscellaneous units" of local government.

The distinction drawn between the two basic categories rests largely on two supposed differences. (1) The public quasi-corporations are historically mere arms of the state, created for purposes of convenience of administration. It was not practical in the early days of this country for a state to be governed entirely from the state capital. Geographic subdivisions were needed. Therefore, the quasi-corporations were created. Although (like municipal or public corporations) they generally have definite geographic limits, they serve *state* needs and interests, not local ones, within those limits. They act as administrative agents of state government. The municipal or public corporations, on the other hand, are not mere administrative arms of the state and never have been. They don't exist to serve the state but to serve a particular locality—that is, they exist to provide municipal services. Though their powers are limited by state law, they exercise the functions allowed them by that law for the good of their own populace and not for state-wide purposes. (2) Public quasi-corporations are often called "involuntary" because they were not created at the instance of their residents. At the time of statehood or some other time in their state's early history, they were established by the drafters of the state constitution or framers of the state government. Their boundaries, though they may follow geographical landmarks such as rivers or mountain ranges, are basically just lines drawn on a map—they don't indicate any particular unity of the people residing therein, merely some degree of geographic proximity. Municipal or public corporations, however, are often termed "voluntary." They are formed (at least under modern law) through the voluntary action of their residents. To form such a corporation, the residents normally follow a procedure prescribed by state law for "incorporation." This process usually

---

municipal corporation, not quasi-municipal corporation). Note that where this distinction is made, the terms "public corporation" and "municipal corporation" are used interchangeably to indicate one category, while the terms "public quasi-corporation," "quasi-public corporation," and "quasi-municipal corporation" are similarly used to indicate the other category. On the meaning of the term "political subdivision," which is often encountered in legislation dealing with units of local government, see Fowler v. Norman Municipal Hosp., 810 P.2d 822 (Okl.1991) (municipal hospital was not "political subdivision" within meaning of Government Tort Claims Act); Weston County Hosp. Joint Powers Bd. v. Westates Constr. Co., 841 P.2d 841 (Wyo.1992) (joint powers board created by two towns and a county was not a "political subdivision"). Compare Beaulieu v. Florquist, 2001 Wyo. 33, 20 P.3d 521 (2001) (municipality was a "political subdivision" within constitutional provisions relevant to claims for damages against city; counties, towns and school districts all said to be political subdivisions). Cf. Sanderson Lincoln Mercury, Inc. v. Ford Motor Co., 205 Ariz. 202, 63 P.3d 428 (App. 2003) (municipality is political subdivision of state, and the number, nature and duration of its powers rest in the absolute discretion of the state). See also Springfield Util. Bd. v. Emerald People's Util. Dist., 339 Or. 631, 125 P.3d 740 (2005) (terms "municipality" and "municipalities" have no fixed meanings; their meaning depends on context in which they are used).

requires either a vote or a petition by a designated portion of the populace. Thus, a voluntary exercise of will is required for such a unit of local government to be formed.[19]

As the natures and functions of many public quasi-corporations have become more similar to those of cities over recent decades, the distinction between public or municipal corporations on the one hand, and public quasi-corporations on the other, has become increasingly blurred.[20] And the terminology may be considered a throw-back to days when all "public" corporations and their relatives were considered similar, in the governmental sphere of activity, to "private" corporations in the business world. But the distinction is still sometimes of importance. Thus, public quasi-corporations, as arms of the state, normally enjoy the same degree of immunity from tort liability as enjoyed by the state, while municipal corporations have long been recognized as having a separate identity.[21] The latter are not necessarily governed by the same rules of immunity as the state, and traditionally have been immune in tort as to their governmental activities but not their proprietary.[22]

---

[19] See Curtis v. Eide, 19 A.D.2d 507, 244 N.Y.S.2d 330 (1963) (New York towns and counties involuntary; villages and cities voluntary); Mountain States Tel. & Tel. Co. v. Salt Lake County, 702 P.2d 113 (Utah 1985) (counties are subdivisions of the state, act only as arms of the state, and are imposed on state citizens, whereas city residents choose to be bound by city government). Cf. Mohave County v. City of Kingman, 160 Ariz. 502, 774 P.2d 806 (1989) (county not liable for cost of housing persons charged with violating a city ordinance but is liable for housing those charged with violating a state statute). See generally 1 Dillon, Municipal Corporations §§ 35–39 (5th ed. 1911), listing distinctions between public corporations and public quasi-corporations. Additional distinctions mentioned by that author are that the quasi-corporations are less complete forms of corporate entities and that public or municipal corporations have both a public and a private (corporate or business-like) character, while the quasi-corporations have only a public (governmental) character. See also Chapter 12 *infra*.

[20] See Schmidt v. Masters, 7 Or.App. 421, 490 P.2d 1029 (1971); City of West Allis v. County of Milwaukee, 39 Wis.2d 356, 159 N.W.2d 36 (1968), cert. denied 393 U.S. 1064, 89 S.Ct. 717, 21 L.Ed.2d 707; Glauberman, County Home Rule: An Urban Necessity, 1 Urban Lawyer 170 (1969), all discussing the municipal powers often given counties. Cf. Uricich v. Kolesar, 132 Ohio St. 115, 5 N.E.2d 335 (1936), holding that a county is a "body politic and corporate" within the meaning of a garnishment statute. See generally Note, The Urban County, A Study of New Approaches to Local Government in Metropolitan Areas, 73 Harv. L.Rev. 526 (1960). On the other hand, it can be contended that municipal corporations, such as cities, are similar to public quasi-corporations, such as counties, in that both categories consist of non-sovereign subdivisions of the state. See Reynolds v. Sims, 377 U.S. 533, 575, 84 S.Ct. 1362, 1388, 12 L.Ed.2d 506, reh. denied 379 U.S. 870, 85 S.Ct. 12, 13 L.Ed.2d 76 (1964). Cf. United Bldg. & Constr. Trades Council v. Mayor & Council of Camden, 465 U.S. 208, 104 S.Ct. 1020, 79 L.Ed.2d 249 (1984) (municipality said to be mere political subdivision of state); Matthews v. Wenatchee Heights Water Co., 92 Wash.App. 541, 963 P.2d 958 (1998) (in its broad sense, "municipal corporation" within meaning of state constitutional provision prohibiting such entities from owning stocks or bonds is limited to its strict and proper meaning, excluding quasi-public corporations); City of Seattle v. State, 103 Wash.2d 663, 694 P.2d 641 (1985) (municipalities are political subdivisions of state). For a critical view of the traditional idea that all units of local government have very limited powers, see Libonati, Do Local Governments Have Rights?, 10 Urban, State & Local L. Newsletter, No. 3, at 1, 13 (Summer, 1987). See generally Frug, The City as a Legal Concept, 93 Harv. L. Rev. 1059 (1980).

[21] See Champlin Petroleum Co. v. Board of County Commissioners, 526 P.2d 1142 (Okl.1974) (operation of landfill is governmental function, but in any case county, like state, enjoys immunity as to all activities). Cf. Hale v. Port of Portland, 308 Or. 508, 783 P.2d 506 (1989) (port district, as part of state government, is immune from tort suit to same extent as is state). But see Gooden v. County Comm'n of Webster County, 171 W.Va. 130, 298 S.E.2d 103 (1982) (county commissions not instrumentalities of state and not entitled to same immunity as state; should be treated the same as municipal governments). Cf. Kahale v. City & County of Honolulu, 104 Hawai'i 341, 90 P.3d 233 (2004) (tort claims against cities and towns are governed by same statute of limitations as is applicable to counties, not by statute applicable to state).

[22] See Bailey v. Mayor of City of New York, 3 Hill (N.Y.) 531 (1842); City of Memphis v. Bettis, 512 S.W.2d 270 (Tenn.1974); Borchard, Government Liability in Tort, 34 Yale L.J. 127, 132–36 (1924). Sometimes this distinction has been "carried over" and applied even to public quasi-corporations so that they too might be held liable for "proprietary" (*i.e.*, business-like) activities. See Annot., State's Immunity from Tort Liability as Dependent on Governmental or Proprietary Nature of Function, 40 A.L.R.2d 927 (1955). See generally Fuller

For purposes of description and analysis, many writers in recent times have preferred to classify units of government according to their structure, their functions (*e.g.*, units that perform general governmental functions vs. those that, like school districts or housing authorities, perform a limited, specialized range of services), their population, or their dependence on and independence from other governmental entities.[23]

Whatever classification is used, the same sub-categories must be considered: cities, towns, and villages (often lumped together as "municipalities"); counties; townships; New England towns; school districts and other special function districts; public authorities—and a few miscellaneous situations. The three basic categories of public quasi-corporations—counties, townships, and New England towns—may be looked upon as alternative arrangements; in any given jurisdiction, one of these forms will usually be of importance, and the other two will either be non-existent or of little importance as to local government.

§ 2.4 Municipalities: Cities, Towns, etc.

The terms "city," "town," and "village" have rather well-recognized meanings in everyday language, and, apart from statute, their legal meanings are the same as the everyday ones. "City" is used to indicate a major center of population, usually existing in relatively dense form. "Town" and "village" indicate smaller, often less organized communities. In some jurisdictions, a locality can change its designation from one of these terms to another merely by vote of the governing body,[24] without necessarily producing any effect except in language.[25] When a community is initially incorporating (*i.e.*, organizing under some form of municipal government), there are, however, often statutory requirements as to minimum population within the area proposed for the incorporation. These requirements may vary according to whether the proposed community is intended to be a "city" or "town," with a higher population required for the former.[26] Different statutes, on such matters as form of municipal government, will then

---

& Casner, Municipal Tort Liability in Operation, 54 Harv.L.Rev. 537 (1941); James, Tort Liability of Local Governmental Units and Their Officers, 22 U.Chi.L.Rev. 610 (1955); Smith, Municipal Tort Liability, 48 Mich.L.Rev. 41 (1949). Increasingly, the tort immunity of state and local governments is being abolished. See Hicks v. State, 88 N.M. 588, 544 P.2d 1153 (1975) (with appendix noting the status of this doctrine in the various states); Van Alstyne, Governmental Tort Liability: A Decade of Change, 1966 U.Ill.L.F. 919. See generally Chapter 26 *infra*.

[23] See Valente & McCarthy, Local Government Law 5 (4th ed. 1992). Cf. 1981 Municipal Yearbook 180 classifying units of local government according to their form of government.

[24] See Lusby v. Cozby, 402 S.W.2d 799 (Tex.Civ.App.1966) (municipality changed to different category by ordinance passed by city council).

[25] Thus, Art. 1153a of Vernon's Ann.Tex.Civil Code (1963) applied in the Lusby case, *supra* note 24, states the Texas law: Any town may, by ordinance of its governing body, change its designation from town to city, but this does not affect the corporate existence or powers of the municipality. On the differences within American states as to the meaning of terms such as "city" and "town," and the resulting differences as to powers and functions of the various entities, see Zeinemann, Overlooked Linkages Between Municipal Incorporations and Annexation Laws: An In-Depth Look at Wisconsin's Experience, 39 Urban Law. 257, at 257–58 (2007).

[26] See Mandelker, Standards for Municipal Incorporations on the Urban Fringe, 36 Tex.L.Rev. 271 (1958); Note, The Minnesota Municipal Commission—Statewide Administrative Review of Municipal Annexations and Incorporations, 50 Minn.L.Rev. 911 (1966); Note, Municipal Corporations: Formation: Judicial Review of Necessity for Urban Character, 3 Okl.L.Rev. 449 (1950). Compare Harvey v. Osborn, 55 Ind. 535, 542 (1877) (a city is a large, incorporated town), with Day v. Mayor of Morristown, 62 N.J.L. 571, 41 A. 964 (1898) ("cities" does not include incorporated towns). But cf. First National Bank v. Camp, 342 F.Supp. 871 (N.D.Ind.1971), aff'd 463 F.2d 595 (7th Cir.) ("city or town" in statute on branch banking can include even

sometimes apply to "cities" as opposed to "towns." In a few jurisdictions, the term "village" is used to indicate incorporations even less populous than towns—or is simply used interchangeably with "town."[27] Occasionally the word "borough" is employed to indicate small communities, or units within large communities.[28]

All of these terms refer to local units that have much in common so far as functions and officers are concerned; all the units may loosely be termed "municipal." The range of activities in which these municipalities engage has greatly expanded over the years. In the beginning, people banded together in communities at least partially for purposes of self-protection and defense. Thus, police protection is among the oldest of municipal services. Traffic control, trade regulation, and inevitably, tax-collecting are also among the local activities that go back to the earliest days of the United States. Some provision for lighting of public areas was, in addition, often an early service of municipal government. And a local court system sometimes soon developed under the aegis of a city or town. As the United States grew and developed through the 19th century, such essential public services as street paving and maintenance, garbage collection, fire protection, and the maintaining of parks came to be associated with municipal government. In some areas of the country, cities and towns have also played an important role in providing education for the community's children.[29] In this century,

---

an unincorporated community). In England, city status traditionally had nothing to do with population but indicated a place that was the seat of a bishop. State v. Green, 126 N.C. 1032, 35 S.E. 462 (1900). See generally Frug, The City as a Legal Concept, 93 Harv. L. Rev. 1059 (1980); Williams, The Constitutional Vulnerability of American Local Government: The Politics of City Status in American Law, 1986 Wis. L. Rev. 83. See also Crestview Water & Sanitation Dist. v. Board of Directors of Metropolitan Denver Sewage Disposal Dist., 640 P.2d 265 (Colo.App.1981) ("municipality" and "city," as those words used in statutes governing representation of board of directors of metropolitan sewage disposal district, distinguished from "district"). On the creation of cities, see generally Frug, City Making: Building Communities Without Building Walls (1999), reviewed by Ford, Bourgeois Communities, 56 Stan. L. Rev. 231 (2003).

27 See Town of Enfield v. Jordan, 119 U.S. 680, 7 S.Ct. 358, 30 L.Ed. 523 (1887) ("village" is small collection of houses in country, but in Delaware is synonymous with "town"); King v. Sweatt, 115 F.Supp. 215, 221 (W.D.Ark.1953) (village is small urban community); Truax v. Pool, 46 Iowa 256 (1877) (village is smaller than a town and is more occupied by agriculturists); State ex rel. Scott v. Lichte, 226 Mo. 273, 126 S.W. 466 (1910) (small town is a village); In re Eiss, 205 App.Div. 691, 199 N.Y.S. 544 (1923), dism'd 236 N.Y. 638, 142 N.E. 315 (village is small municipal corporation); State ex rel. Town of Holland v. Lammers, 113 Wis. 398, 89 N.W. 501 (1902) (village is assembly of houses less than a city). It is agreed that a village is a municipal corporation, not a public quasi-corporation. Village of Kenmore v. Erie County, 252 N.Y. 437, 169 N.E. 637 (1930); Sitte v. Paulson, 56 N.D. 146, 216 N.W. 344 (1927). See generally R. Critchfield, Villages (Anchor Press 1981).

28 See Crose v. City Council of Los Angeles, 175 Cal. 774, 167 P. 386 (1916) (borough is a unit composing a territorial fraction of a city); State ex rel. Railroad & Warehouse Commission v. Minneapolis & St. Louis Railway Co., 76 Minn. 469, 79 N.W. 510 (1899) (borough is an incorporated municipality); Dempster v. United Traction Co., 205 Pa. 70, 54 A. 501 (1903) (borough is a compact settlement—a town or village). Cf. In re Greenwald, 179 App.Div. 672, 167 N.Y.S. 154 (1917), aff'd 221 N.Y. 688, 117 N.E. 1068, on meaning of "borough office." On the current status of boroughs and borough offices in New York City, see Note, The Borough President: Community Leader or Excess Political Baggage, 42 N.Y.L. School L. Rev. 1197 (1998). But in Alaska, boroughs are public quasi-corporations, comparable to counties. See Walters v. Cease, 394 P.2d 670 (Alaska 1964).

29 On the functions of municipalities, and the growth of these functions, see Anderson & Weidner, American City Government 122–68 (rev. ed. 1950); Bromage, Introduction to Municipal Government and Administration 43–57, 399–567 (2d ed. 1957); H. G. James, Municipal Functions (1917); Reed, Municipal Government in the United States ch. 4 (1934). Cf. 2 E. S. Griffith, The Modern Development of City Government in the United Kingdom and the United States ch. 8 (1927). For criticism of the way in which city services are currently offered, see Frug, City Services, 73 N.Y.U.L. Rev. 23 (1998), proposing that such services as education and crime control be used as a mechanism for expanding the capacity of metropolitan residents to live in a diverse society, rather than as a means to separate and divide metropolitan population.

municipal government has become increasingly concerned with such matters as public transportation; utility services; the operation of hospitals and other health-care facilities; social welfare programs; and even the operation of ordinary businesses.[30] As city budgets have grown along with city functions, there has been increased need for new sources of tax money; and inducement of business into the community has thus become an accepted, necessary activity.[31]

The functions of local government vary, naturally, according to the size of the community. So do the numbers and titles of municipal officers. But again, there are many similarities in all municipalities. The legislative officers of municipalities in this country—that is, members of the city council or similar body—have long been popularly elected, though the number of people eligible to vote for them was at one time often limited by restrictions on the franchise. Such restrictions are now largely removed. And the party caucuses and primaries of the past are often replaced by non-partisan elections and/or nomination by petition. Such innovative devices as preferential ballots (where the voter indicates his 1st, 2nd, etc. preferences for an office), proportional representation, and popular recall have been tried in some communities, often before their use would possibly be considered by higher levels of government. Thus, municipalities have sometimes been laboratories for governmental experimentation.[32]

Into the early part of the 20th century, the tendency of localities was to have more and more of their administrative officials popularly elected. But this led to long ballots, voter apathy, and consequent corruption. Gradually, it was recognized that a system of appointment of lower-level officials was really preferable *if* the system were not the old "spoils" method of political appointment but was a civil service or "merit" system. Such methods of obtaining and retaining local government officers are now utilized in most large cities and many small ones. Increasingly, even such officers as the city clerk, city attorney, and members of the local judiciary are appointed rather than elected. Creation

---

[30] See People ex rel. Curren v. Wood, 391 Ill. 237, 62 N.E.2d 809 (1945) (municipal airport upheld); Duncan v. Smith, 262 S.W.2d 373 (Ky.1953) (public funds may be used for relief of indigent, including legal assistance); Albritton v. City of Winona, 181 Miss. 75, 178 So. 799 (1938) (city could own clothing manufacturing plant); Maney v. Oklahoma City, 150 Okl. 77, 300 P. 642 (1931) (in operating water plant, city is to be treated the same as a private business); Ruth v. Oklahoma City, 143 Okl. 62, 287 P. 406 (1930) (city may operate utilities, airports, and hospitals). Cf. Standard Oil Co. v. City of Lincoln, 114 Neb. 243, 207 N.W. 172, 208 N.W. 962 (1926), aff'd 275 U.S. 504, 48 S.Ct. 155, 72 L.Ed. 395 (municipal operation of gas station upheld).

[31] Hawkins v. City of Greenfield, 248 Ind. 593, 230 N.E.2d 396 (1967) (municipal industrial development legislation held constitutional); Port Authority v. Fisher, 275 Minn. 157, 145 N.W.2d 560 (1966) (judicial approval of city's industrial development project); Harrison v. Claybrook, 372 P.2d 602 (Okl.1962) (authority created by city to obtain local industrial development). But see Mitchell v. North Carolina Industrial Development Financing Authority, 273 N.C. 137, 159 S.E.2d 745 (1968) (no public purpose; good review of authorities). See generally Pinsky, State Constitutional Limitations on Public Industrial Financing, 111 U.Pa.L.Rev. 265 (1963).

[32] On proportional representation, see Reed, Municipal Government in the United States ch. 16 (1934). See generally Hallett, Proportional Representation (Nat'l Municipal League 1940). On initiative, referendum, and recall, see Bromage, Introduction to Municipal Government and Administration ch. 17 (1925). Cf. Bird & Ryan, The Recall of Public Officers (1930), discussing the development and operation of recall procedures in California. See generally the last chapter of this work *infra*. On municipal elections, see generally 3 McQuillin, Municipal Corporations §§ 12.02–.26 (3d rev. ed. 1990).

of municipal offices is generally a legislative function, but is often now delegated from the state to the legislative body of the city itself.[33]

Municipalities of all kinds and sizes share not only similar functions and governments; they also share many common problems. Larger centers of population have been confronted with mass migrations to the suburbs and to rural areas, leaving the core-city without the taxable wealth needed to provide cultural and other services that would benefit the whole metropolitan area. Suburban communities may struggle to provide facilities that previously were provided by the center-cities; but the suburban unit costs will generally be high because the service base is small. Special districts may then be established to broaden the service base. But there is then created a fragmented situation of numerous overlapping districts, sometimes overlapping in their functions as well as their areas, often confusing to the citizen wondering where to turn for a particular service.[34] It is hoped that plans currently being proposed and adopted—involving further decentralization in some instances, greater "regionalism" in others—may hold common solutions to many of these common problems.

§ 2.5 Counties

Counties are probably the most important of the public quasi-corporations. In one form or another, they are said to exist in every state, though they exist as "parishes" in Louisiana and—in a form roughly comparable to most counties—as "boroughs" in Alaska and in New York City. They have never actually functioned as governmental units in Rhode Island, Connecticut, or the District of Columbia. With those qualifications, counties are indeed found throughout the United States, but their greatest importance is in many of the Western and Southern states.[35] They vary considerably in size and number: Texas has the largest total, 254; California has the comparatively small number

---

[33] See Oklahoma City v. Century Indemnity Co., 178 Okl. 212, 62 P.2d 94 (1936) (municipal offices can be created either by state legislation or by city itself where power is delegated); Blinn v. Hassman, 162 Okl. 1, 18 P.2d 881 (1933); In re Templeton, 399 Pa. 10, 159 A.2d 725 (1960) (creation of borough police department is legislative function); State v. Berberian, 100 R.I. 413, 216 A.2d 507 (1966). See generally Bromage, Introduction to Municipal Government and Administration 335–58 (2d ed. 1957); Willoughby, Principles of Public Administration 211–380 (1927). On creation and scope of a civil-service system, see Munro, Municipal Administration ch. 3 (1934); Proctor, Principles of Public Personnel Administration (1921). Cf. Commonwealth ex rel. Truscott v. Di Lauro, 387 Pa. 506, 128 A.2d 348 (1957) (city council had delegated power to abolish office).

[34] Committee for Economic Development, Modernizing Local Government 28 (1966). For a critique of local government in the United States, and suggestions for possible improvement, see Liebmann, The New American Local Government, 34 Urban Law. 93 (2002).

[35] See Fordham, Local Government Law 27–29 (2d rev. ed. 1986); Valente & McCarthy, Local Government Law 7–8 (4th ed. 1992). See generally Bollens, American County Government (1969). For a long time, counties were not important units of government in Hawaii, but they now exist and can enjoy broad home-rule powers. See Hawaii Government Employees' Ass'n v. County of Maui, 59 Haw. 65, 576 P.2d 1029 (1978).

A few Eastern states, such as Maryland, also have relatively strong county governments. See Ann.Code of Maryland, Arts. 25 (powers of county commissioners), 25A (chartered counties), & 25B (home rule for counties). Where counties enjoy home rule, they become much stronger, more independent units of local government than they have traditionally been. See Chapter 6 *infra*. As to the power of Alaskan boroughs, which are comparable to counties, see Cutler v. Kodiak Island Borough, 290 P.3d 415 (Alaska 2012) (borough may only exercise powers specifically enumerated in Title 29 of Alaska Statutes and powers necessarily or fairly implied in or incident to the purposes of the powers and functions conferred in that title).

of 58. There are a total of 3,141 counties in the country.[36] Usually, the county includes any incorporated municipalities within its area, thus producing possible problems of division of responsibility; but in Virginia, county jurisdiction does not cover incorporated areas. In the financial crunch of the 1930's, county governments often were poorly financed and tended to lose power. But in recent decades, their power has increased. They have frequently adopted forms of government, and undertaken functions, traditionally associated with municipalities. And they have become increasingly involved in federal, as well as state, programs in such areas as rural housing.[37]

The functions of counties have long included such matters as administration of justice, custody and preservation of official documents, highway maintenance, and assessment of property for tax purposes. But in addition, they have now become much involved in fire protection, sanitation activities, and the operation of airports. In many states, the counties operate hospitals and health-related programs, and sometimes they, like the cities, are now engaged in industrial development. It is significant that from 1942 to 1962, the expenditures of all U.S. counties increased six-fold, to $9 billion; for that was an era of great expansion in county activity.[38]

But there is still some reluctance to grant too many powers to counties. In many jurisdictions, they are considered structurally archaic and lacking any real executive power. Many do not have a well-developed merit system for the selection of administrative personnel. The criticism is also made that counties are too numerous and too small in population, with over half having less than 25,000 residents.[39] If there truly are more counties than necessary, this probably is because many were established in "horse-and-buggy" days, when it was thought desirable that everyone be within an hour's ride or so, by horse-drawn vehicle, of the county seat. Modern means of transportation have put people within a few hours' drive of places that used to be considered distant. But it is difficult to eliminate or consolidate units of government once they are

---

[36] New York Times Almanac for 2002, at 259. Cf. United States Bureau of the Census, 1970 Census User's Guide, Part 1, at 79 (1971), listing a total at that time of 3,049 counties in the United States.

[37] Fordham, Local Government Law 28–29 (2d rev. ed. 1986). Cf. Town of Lockport v. Citizens for Community Action at the Local Level, Inc., 430 U.S. 259, 97 S.Ct. 1047, 51 L.Ed.2d 313 (1977), upholding New York laws requiring approval of a majority of voters within city limits and a majority of voters living outside city limits before a new county charter can be adopted. On the unusual nature of some local units in Virginia, see Bain, A Body Incorporating City-County Separation in Virginia 26 (1967) (Virginia cities are separate city-county units, performing functions usually performed by counties elsewhere). The traditional attitude regarding the limited powers of counties is well illustrated by Board of County Comm'rs v. Bainbridge, Inc., 929 P.2d 691 (Colo.1996) (counties could not impose school impact fees in addition to those provided by statute; as political subdivisions of state, counties have only the powers expressly granted them by state constitution or legislation). On the nature of counties, see generally Eigerman, California Counties: Second-rate Localities or Readymade Regional Governments?, 26 Hastings Const. L.W. 621 (1999).

[38] Committee for Economic Development, Modernizing Local Government 28–29 (1966). See Fordham, *supra* note 35, at 29; Salant, County Governments: An Overview, 17 Intergovernmental Respective (ACIR Winter, 1991). See generally Fairlie & Kneier, County Government Administration (1930); 1 McQuillin, Municipal Corporations §§ 1.23–.28.50 (3d rev. ed. 1999). See also Claunch, Toward a More Effective County Government, 35 Tex.L.Rev. 986 (1957).

[39] Committee for Economic Development, *supra* note 38, at 29. On possible reforms, see National Ass'n of Counties, From America's Counties Today (1973). Nonetheless, a new county occasionally comes into existence, as when the northern part of Yuma County, Arizona, broke away and became La Paz County as of January 1, 1983, despite having only one incorporated community. See "New County Begins Life Peacefully," Arizona (Tucson) Daily Star, Jan. 1, 1983, at 1.

established; their officers and employees obviously come to have a vested interest in their continued existence.

Under one-person one-vote decisions of the courts, the counties lost the automatic identification that they often had in the past with legislative districts. The legislative districts have necessarily been redesigned. Counties so far have remained active units of government in their own right. But since the legislative re-districting, it has been suggested by some observers that the counties eventually will have to be re-designed or risk losing their importance in the political structure.[40]

§ 2.6 Townships

There are over 16,000 townships functioning as units of local government now in the United States.[41] Historically, this unit has had its greatest importance in some Northern and Midwestern states. Today its greatest strength is in the North Central and Middle Atlantic regions and in the State of Washington. (The "towns" of New York State and Wisconsin are basically the same as townships.) In some other jurisdictions, townships exist as geographic designations, used in the defining of property boundaries, but not as units of local government.[42]

Traditionally, the township had an area of 36 square miles; and this is still often its size. Among its functions have been highway construction and maintenance, relief programs for poor persons, and, in many jurisdictions, education. Sometimes the township has assisted the state in tax administration and law enforcement. In many states, townships have declined in power, no longer play any role in providing education, and now function as governmental entities only in rural areas. For instance, the township is no longer of much importance in such traditional "township states" as Indiana and Iowa. But where the township has survived as a governmental unit—as in Michigan—it has often been granted broader powers, ceased to be purely an arm of the state, and become increasingly involved in such programs as police and fire protection, sanitation, and utility services. The growth of the suburbs has made many townships in such states as Michigan, New Jersey, and Wisconsin increasingly urban in character—thus producing a situation in which these units *must* either provide urban services or else cease to be of importance.[43]

§ 2.7 New England Towns

The "New England town" is roughly comparable to the "township" and distinguishable from the towns (*i.e.*, small municipalities) that exist in parts of the

---

40 Committee for Economic Development, *supra* note 38, at 29. Cf. Fordham, Some Questions and No Answers Anent Urban Regionalism, 1971 Utah L.Rev. 11.

41 New York Times Almanac for 2002, at 211; United States Bureau of the Census, 1987 Census of Governments vi (1987). Cf. Committee for Economic Development, *supra* note 38, at 30.

42 See Valente & McCarthy, Local Government Law 8–9 (4th ed. 1992), quoting from 1987 Census of Governments. See also Patrick Media Group, Inc. v. Department of Transp., 533 Pa. 188, 620 A.2d 1125 (1993), noted 32 Duquesne L. Rev. 377 (1994), holding that townships are not "incorporated municipalities" within the meaning of a state statute prohibiting construction of outdoor signs within 660 feet of the right-of-way of interstate highways but containing an exception for some areas of "incorporated municipalities."

43 See Committee for Economic Development, *supra* note 38, at 30. Cf. Perkins, Government of "Rurban" Areas, 37 Am.Pol.Sci.Rev. 306 (1943). See generally Rusch, *Douville v. Christensen*: An Answer to the Issue of Township Responsibility for the Improvement of Section Line Rights of Way, 48 S.D. L. Rev. 247 (2002–2003).

country other than New England. The six New England states contain over 1400 of these unusual "towns."[44] In states having this form of local government, the whole state is normally divided into "towns," much as many other jurisdictions are divided into counties. New England towns are extensively used by the state as units of administration in elections and for purposes of taxation and keeping of land records. But they have long been granted more extensive powers than most of the other public quasi-corporations and have always enjoyed a degree of independence that only in recent years has come to be enjoyed also by counties and, at least in some jurisdictions, by townships. Many of the functions of New England towns are those often associated elsewhere with municipalities: operation of utilities, sewage collection, park maintenance, police and fire protection, etc. By the 1960's, these units were spending well over $1 billion a year.[45]

Unincorporated and loose-knit, the New England town is a hybrid among units of local government. In addition to performing the above-mentioned municipal-type services, it often serves functions associated elsewhere with the county: road maintenance and welfare administration, for instance. And it remains important in providing education—a service performed by school districts in many states. The most renowned aspect of New England towns has probably been their method of functioning as direct democracies, through annual town meetings. But representative assemblies have now been substituted for such meetings by some towns. As with the counties and townships, the criticism is now often made that New England towns are too numerous and that each is unnecessarily small in size—about two-thirds of them have less than 10,000 people.[46]

§ 2.8 Special Function Districts

Of the approximately 83,000 units of local government in the United States, more than one-third—over 34,000—are classified as "special function units."[47] These are also called "special districts" or "ad hoc units," and they have steadily increased in number over recent years.[48] Like school districts (which are sometimes listed as a sub-category of special function districts), these units perform a single function or a limited range of functions; but unlike school districts, they do not necessarily exist throughout any given state—they are created to serve particular areas or provide facilities at particular locations. Thus, a "sewer district" may exist for one area of a state, while in other parts of the same state, comparable functions are handled by other local governments and

---

[44] United States Bureau of the Census, 1997 Census of Governments 2 (1997). See generally Bryce, American Commonwealth ch. 48 (1921); Local Government Law 28 (2d rev. ed. 1986). There is an interesting comparison of the "township" and the "New England town" in 1 McQuillin, Municipal Corporations § 1.–32 (3d rev. ed. 1999).

[45] Committee for Economic Development, *supra* note 38 at 29–30.

[46] *Id.* at 30.

[47] New York Times Almanac for 2002, at 211; United States Bureau of the Census, 1987 Census of Governments vi (1987); the total of "special districts" includes 1,374 *dependent* school districts, but does not include the separately listed 15,174 *independent* school districts. Cf. United States Bureau of the Census, 1970 Census User's Guide, Part 1, at 79 (1971), listing over 81,000 units of local government, including over 21,000 special districts. On the numbers of "special districts" of various kinds (fire protection districts, water districts, etc.), see United States Bureau of the Census, 1987 Census of Governments Table G (1987).

[48] Valente & McCarthy, Local Government Law 11 (4th ed. 1992), also noting distribution of special function districts within the various states.

there is no need for a special unit to handle sewer service.[49] These limited-purpose "special function units" invariably overlap the geographic boundaries of the other units of local government, contributing at times to a governmental maze.[50] Because of the number and variety of special districts on Long Island, overlapping as to territory but separated as to functions, it has been said that "To liken Long Island to the Balkans at the turn of the century would be a gross understatement."[51] The proliferation of special districts has continued into the twenty-first century, leading one commentator to conclude that "The number of special districts, public authorities, and other single or limited purpose government units is increasing at a rate that eclipses the growth of all other political subdivisions nationwide, having nearly tripled in number over the last fifty years."[52]

Until the 1930's, special districts were considered exceptional and outside the usual governmental structure; but since then, their growth has been dynamic.[53] They are often treated as public quasi-corporations or simply as miscellaneous agencies of the state, and this is probably accurate where they owe their life to state legislation. But some are created by municipalities, usually under enabling legislation passed by the state, and are then really agents of the creating city or town.[54] It has thus been said that this unit "eludes meaningful delineation and categorization" and is "the chameleon among local governments."[55] It has been suggested that such units if at first used to provide some limited services to a metropolitan area, might eventually evolve into general, all-purpose governments for such an area;[56] but in practice this has not occurred.

Special function districts may be said to have three common characteristics: (1) They differ from such general units of local government as municipalities and counties in that the special districts provide only one function or a few related functions.[57] (2) They enjoy a high degree of fiscal and administrative independence from all other governments, thus differentiating them from subordinate districts and from most "public

---

49 4 United States Bureau of the Census, 1977 Census of Governments (Finances of Special Districts) 1 (1977).

50 See United States Advisory Commission on Intergovernmental Relations, 14th Annual Report (Striking a Better Balance) 26 (1972).

51 Kaplan, The Balkanization of Suburbia, Harper's, Oct., 1971, at 72, 73. See generally Teaford, City and Suburb: The Political Fragmentation of Metropolitan America, 1850–1970 (Johns Hopkins Press 1979). Compare Rizzo, Protecting the Environment at the Local Level: New York City's Special District Approach, 13 Fordham Envtl. L.J. 225 (2002).

52 Laurie Reynolds, Local Governments and Regional Governance, 39 Urban Law. 483, 484–85 (2007).

53 See Bollens, Special District Government in the United States (1964); Pock, Independent Special Districts: A Solution to the Metropolitan Area Problems (1962); United States Advisory Commission on Intergovernmental Relations, Special District Government in the United States (1954).

54 See 1 McQuillin, Municipal Corporations §§ 2.28–2.29 & 2.30 (3d rev. ed. 1999). See generally State Farm Mut. Auto. Ins. Co. v. City of Lakewood, 788 P.2d 808 (Colo.1990) (due process did not require city council to provide landowners with notice or right to vote on decision to establish special district).

55 Pock, Independent Special Districts: A Solution to the Metropolitan Area Problems 19 (1962). See also Boardman v. Oklahoma City Housing Authority, 445 P.2d 412 (Okl.1968), where a housing authority is held not to be either an arm of the state or of the municipality in which it is located.

56 Fuchs, Regional Agencies for Metropolitan Areas, 22 Wash.U.L.Q. 64 (1936).

57 Bollens, Special District Governments in the United States 5 (1964), noting that in this regard, special districts resemble the townships of some Midwestern states.

authorities."[58] (3) Typically, they are not geographically coterminous with other units of government, but overlap municipal, county, and sometimes even state lines.[59]

Despite the complexity they create, these districts have enjoyed phenomenal growth. They have been said to outnumber cities in this country today and to be six times as numerous as counties.[60] They are of importance in every state except Alaska; but twelve states account for 61% of such units.[61] What functions do the districts perform, and what has contributed to their growth? Special districts might be created to perform any one or more of an endless list of services, but among the frequently encountered ones are fire protection, water supply and conservation, highway construction and/or maintenance, creation and maintenance of parks and recreational facilities, soil conservation, the provision of cultural facilities such as libraries, control of parking and/or providing additional parking areas, lighting of streets and other public areas, garbage collection, and providing and maintaining sewers. Some-times even police protection is furnished via a special district.[62] There is some trend toward special districts performing services, such as providing mass transit and controlling air pollution, for multi-county areas; but the bulk of such districts still perform in narrower confines.[63] Federal aid has stimulated the creation of some such districts, as in the areas of public housing and soil conservation. They have often been created to avoid debt limitations that in most states apply to municipalities. Even if these limitations are also made applicable to special districts, there is an obvious "solution": create additional districts with ever-narrower areas or functions.[64] Also, these districts have proliferated because they are considered democratic: they tax or assess the residents of the particular geographic area; they are governed by boards elected or appointed from among the residents of the area; and they provide services that are primarily beneficial to those residing in the area.[65]

---

[58] *Id.* See generally R. Smith, Public Authorities, Special Districts and Local Governments (1964).

[59] United States Advisory Commission on Intergovernmental Relations, Special Districts 12, 22–24 (1964). Cf. Committee for Economic Development, Modernizing Local Government 32 (1966).

[60] R. Smith, Public Authorities, Special Districts and Local Governments ix (1964). The figures given in this study lump "public authorities" together with "special districts."

[61] Valente & McCarthy, Local Government Law 11 (4th ed. 1992), quoting from 1987 Census of Governments. See Committee for Economic Development, *supra* note 38.

[62] On functions performed by special districts throughout the U.S., see Valente & McCarthy, *supra* note 60, at 10–11. Cf. United States Advisory Commission on Intergovernmental Relations, Special Districts ch. 3 (1964). See generally Hankerson, Special Governmental Districts, 35 Tex.L.Rev. 1004 (1957).

[63] United States Advisory Commission on Intergovernmental Relations, Urban America and the Federal System 76, 77 (1969), stating that of over 7000 special districts in metropolitan areas, only a little over 500 are multi-county districts dealing with area-wide services.

[64] See Bowmar, The Anachronism Called Debt Limitation, 52 Iowa L.Rev. 863, 868–73 (1967) (debt limitation is applied separately to each governmental unit). But cf. Cerajewski v. McVey, 225 Ind. 67, 72 N.E.2d 650 (1947), where it was held that a special district will not be treated as a separate governmental entity for debt-limitation purposes if the sole reason for its creation was evasion of that limitation. For further development of this rule in Indiana, see Datisman v. Gary Public Library, 241 Ind. 83, 170 N.E.2d 55 (1960); Rappaport v. Department of Public Health, 227 Ind. 508, 87 N.E.2d 77 (1949). See generally United States Advisory Commission on Inter-Governmental Relations, State Constitutional and Statutory Restrictions on Local Government Debt (1961). The Indiana attitude is unusual, and courts more often strive to find debt limitations inapplicable to special districts. See Berry v. Milliken, 234 S.C. 518, 109 S.E.2d 354 (1959). Cf. Morris, Evading Debt Limitations with Public Building Authorities: The Costly Subversion of State Constitutions, 68 Yale L.J. 234 (1958).

[65] See Fordham, Local Government Law 35 (2d rev. ed. 1986). But cf. Kendall v. Douglas, Grant, Lincoln & Okanogan Counties Pub. Hosp. Dist., 118 Wash.2d 1, 820 P.2d 497 (1991), stating that the formation of a

Many observers feel that this nation has gone overboard in the use of special districts. While originally they were often limited to relatively rural areas that had few other units of local government, they are now being employed in most metropolitan areas, the residents of which may live under 6 or more layers of special districts. The resulting fragmentation has rendered more difficult any attempts at coordinated government of a region, as well as making it difficult for residents to know who is responsible for any particular service to which they're entitled. Further, the governing boards of special districts often lack much legal power, and may not be politically responsive if, as is sometimes the case, the members are appointed or have ex officio membership. Thus, consolidating and restructuring of special function districts are often suggested, even if seldom achieved.[66]

§ 2.9 School Districts

School districts may be considered a subcategory of special function districts; they are special districts whose function is the providing of public education. But it is well to consider them separately for at least four reasons: (1) They are so numerous. There are about half as many of them in the United States as there are all other special districts combined.[67] (2) In some areas, particularly in the West, they existed before there were organized cities, towns, or other units of local government. And throughout much of the country, they have a history and administration separate from that of other governments because of local desire to "keep politics out of the schools."[68] (3) School districts are often

---

multicounty hospital district would violate equal protection if the boundary lines were intentionally drawn so as to discriminate against an identifiable political group and if there was actual discriminatory effect. But no such violation was here found. As to the powers of the boards that generally govern special function districts, see Bull Lake Fire Dist. v. Lincoln County, 313 P.3d 174 (Mont. 2013) (powers and duties regarding firefighting services were specifically granted by state law to district's board of trustees and fire chief; they, and not the county, could determine scope of district's emergency firefighting services).

[66] See United States Advisory Commission on Intergovernmental Relations, Government Structure, Organization and Planning in Metropolitan Areas 26–30 (1961), where it is suggested that the functions of many special districts might be transferred to general governmental units and that many other special districts could be consolidated into multi-functional districts with elected governing boards. On the large number of governments existing in some urban areas, see United States Advisory Commission on Intergovernmental Relations, Urban America and the Federal System 75 (1969), noting that metropolitan counties contain an average of 48 governments, including 12 school districts and 16 special districts. Proliferation of special function districts has been particularly prevalent in suburban areas and urbanized counties. See "The Boom Towns," Time, June 15, 1987, at 14, quoting (at 16) a Du Page County, Illinois, official as saying, "We're a city with 35 municipalities, nine townships and only the Lord knows how many special districts, fire districts, sanitary districts, school districts." See generally Comment, Merging and Dissolving Special Districts, 31 Yale J. on Regulation 493 (2014).

[67] See United States Bureau of the Census, 1997 Census of Governments vi (1997), listing 13,726 independent school districts and 34,683 "special districts". The approximately 1,500 "dependent" school districts are not counted as separate governments at all. Cf. United States Bureau of the Census, 1970 Census User's Guide, Part 1, at 79 (1971), listing 21,782 school districts and 21,264 other "special districts" as of 1967.

[68] Committee for Economic Development, *supra* note 38, at 31. There is precedent, however, for a state taking control of a school district if the district is in severe financial difficulty or if—as in one New Jersey situation—the district is totally failing to satisfy the educational needs of its students. See Hanley, New Jersey Seizes School District in Jersey City, Citing Total Failure, N.Y. Times, Oct. 5, 1989, at 1 (New Jersey seized control of the Jersey City public schools, finding the district was failing to meet students' constitutional right to a thorough and efficient education). See generally Note, Reform of New Jersey's Public Schools: Towards Regionalization, 62 Rutgers L. Rev. 1063 (2010). Statutes in some states now give city mayors considerable power to control public schools—a situation brought about by public dissatisfaction with the performances of the schools in many large cities. See Stodghill, Mayors Rule the Schools, Time, April 12, 1999, at 74, particularly describing the "takeover" of public schools by the mayors of Chicago and Detroit. In 2011, the worst performing schools in Detroit were removed from the city's school system and run by a new state

organized in every part of each state so that any given location within the state will be within some school district. Other special function districts exist on a "hit-or-miss" basis—thus, a given locality within a state may be within a sewer district, or may have its sewer service provided by some unit of government other than a special district, or may simply have no governmental authority responsible for sewer service at all.[69] (4) There are two further sub-categories of school districts—dependent and independent. And while independent school districts are fairly similar to other special function districts, dependent school districts are not really separate governmental entities at all.

Dependent school districts are geographically coterminous with some other unit of local government such as county, municipality, New England town, or township. They cannot levy taxes or issue bonds without approval of this other governmental unit. Often the members of the governing board are appointed by some officer or agency of the other unit, though occasionally they are elected by voters of the area. There are about 1500 dependent school systems in the United States. Five states and the District of Columbia have an entirely dependent school system. A substantial number of the public-school students in New Jersey, New York, Pennsylvania, and Wisconsin attend schools in dependent districts.[70]

Most public-school students—about 75%—are enrolled in independent districts, of which there are close to 14,000.[71] The boundaries of these districts are often not the same as the boundaries of any other governmental units. The members of the governing board are normally elected at large, often in separate, nonpartisan elections. And the districts levy taxes and issue bonds subject to state law but without approval being needed from some other governmental entity. These districts were often created very early in the history of a region's settlement, because education was considered a uniquely important governmental function that should be entrusted to a specially selected group of citizens, not to politicians elected to handle other services.[72]

Because many independent school districts were established so long ago, when transportation was far less developed than today, many districts were quite small—and often so remain even now. As late as 1962, of the 6000 independent school districts in metropolitan areas, 600 had less than 50 pupils—and a much larger number of such districts in rural areas had small enrollments.[73] This is one field, however, in which

---

authority charged with improving them over the next 5 years. See Dolan, State to Run Detroit's Worst Schools, Wall St. J., June 21, 2011, at A2. See generally Bowman, State Takeovers of School Districts and Related Litigation: Michigan as a Case Study, 45 Urban Law. 1 (2013). See also Oluwole & Green, State Takeovers of School Districts: Race and the Equal Protection Clause, 42 Ind. L. Rev. 343 (2009). On Detroit's problems, see also Section 1.1, note 6, *supra*.

[69] 4 United States Bureau of the Census, 1977 Census of Governments (Finances of Special Districts) 1 (1977).

[70] Committee for Economic Development, *supra* note 38, at 31.

[71] New York Times Almanac for 2002, at 211. Cf. United States Bureau of the Census, 1970 Census User's Guide, Part 1 (1971).

[72] Committee for Economic Development, *supra* note 38, at 30–31. Cf. Stein v. Highland Park Independent School District, 540 S.W.2d 551 (Tex.Civ.App.1976), ref'd n.r.e., appeal after remand 574 S.W.2d 807, error dism'd, a nuisance suit discussing the nature of school districts as "quasi-municipal corporations." *Id.* at 553. See also Winters v. Oklahoma City, 740 P.2d 724 (Okl.1987), where sanctions were imposed on an attorney for the "bad faith" exhibited by filing lawsuits against a city for alleged act of employees of an independent school district, since such acts were clearly not the city's responsibility.

[73] Committee for Economic Development, *supra* note 38, at 31–32.

considerable consolidation of local government has occurred. Between 1942 and the mid-60's, the number of independent districts was reduced by 75%[74] and the process of consolidation has been continuing.[75] Financial difficulties have given impetus to the movement toward at least some degree of unity among such districts[76] as have mandates from the state, and state school-aid formulas that encourage consolidation.[77] On the other hand, as some major centers of population have continued to grow, a single school district for an area has come to be considered inadequate by some critics, and splits have been proposed.[78]

There are, of course, numerous variations within the school-district patterns and means of financing public schools above described.[79] In most states, such as Texas, dependent districts exist in some areas, while other localities have independent

---

[74] *Id.* at 31.

[75] See Fordham, Local Government Law 37 (2d rev. ed. 1986).

[76] See *Id.* at 35, noting the situation in Pennsylvania, where financial difficulties led to numerous school "jointures," a form of school consolidation under which contiguous districts join in financing common facilities through creation of a public authority. The authority issues bonds payable out of revenue which comes through rentals paid by the school districts under a lease of the new facilities. Such financial cooperation is sometimes eventually followed by full-fledged governmental consolidation.

[77] Committee for Economic Development, *supra* note 38, at 31. Cf. Ruvoldt, Educational Financing in New Jersey: Robinson v. Cahill and Beyond, 5 Seton Hall L.Rev. 1 (1973), describing recent developments in the financing of public education and the importance in New Jersey of a specific state constitutional mandate to provide quality education. As to the size and boundaries of school districts, see generally Comment, When Bigger Is Not Always Better: Making "Cents" of Illinois School District Reform Proposals, 36 So. Ill. U.L. J. 571 (2012). See also Kiel, The Endangered School District: The Promise and Challenge of Redistributing Control of Public Education, 22 Boston Univ. Pub. Interest L.J. 403 (2013); Note, How Uncertainty in the Redrawing of School Districts Affects Housing Prices—A Case Study: Comparing Neighborhoods in Charlotte, North Carolina, and Columbia, Maryland, 2 U. Baltimore J. Land & Dev. 113 (2013).

[78] See Booty, Split Districts Proposed, Dallas Morning News, Jan. 11, 1977, noting proposals that the 210,000-student Houston school district and the 140,000-student Dallas district each be split into several independent districts. A statutory limit on the size of school districts in Texas was also suggested. See generally Saiger, The School District Boundary Problem, 42 Urban Law. 495 (2010). See also Kiel, The Enduring Power of Milliken's Fences, 45 Urban Law. 137 (2013), noting that the majority opinion in Milliken v. Bradley, 418 U.S. 717, 94 S.Ct. 3112 (1974), treated school district boundaries like fences surrounding sovereign entities that cannot be ignored even to remedy unconstitutional segregation; these "fences" assure local control of education. The Kiel article suggests that this ruling resulted ultimately in urban schools that serve a largely minority population and suburban schools that serve a largely white population. Kiel, *supra*, at 138.

[79] On the different sources that have been used in the financing of public education, see 49 NEA Research Bull. 53 (1971). See generally Fox & Hurd, Finances of Large-City School Systems: A Comparative Analysis (1971); 1 Levin, Muller, Scanlon & Cohen, Public School Finance: Present Disparities and Fiscal Alternatives (1972). See also 1 United States Bureau of the Census, 1967 Census of Governments 17, with a state-by-state tabulation of the number of school districts compared to the number of other local governmental units. There has been some trend toward school districts seeking donations from private and corporate donors. See Maeroff, Financially Pressed School Districts Are Trying to Obtain Private Funds, N.Y. Times, Nov. 9, 1982, at 17. On the search for new sources of financing for public schools, see generally Smolowe, Beyond Bake Sales—Parents and Principles Collide as Fund Raising Becomes a Way of Life in the Public Schools, Time, April 24, 1995, at 62; "A Crash Course in Creative Financing—Schools Are Broke, and the Search for Funds Is Breaking Fresh Ground," Bus. Week, Sept. 6, 1993, at 24. Across the U.S., a number of publicly funded schools are being operated by for-profit school-management companies. See "For-Profit Schools," Bus. Week, Feb. 7, 2000, at 64. On an experiment in Hartford, Connecticut, that involved turning operation of the public schools over to a private company, see "Schools for Profit," Time, Oct. 17, 1994, at 48. On problems with American public education, see generally Hirsch, The Schools We Need and Why We Don't Have Them (Doubleday 1996), reviewed 32 Urban Law. 165 (2000). On the degree of success achieved by experiments using private businesses to help city schools, see France, Can Business Save New York Schools?, Bus. Week, June 9, 2003, at 106 (recruiting business leaders to take full-time jobs in city government in order for them to apply business principles to the problems of public education); Winters, Grading the Philadelphia Experiment, Time, June 23, 2003 (for-profit firms used to reform city schools). See generally Section 16.2 *infra*.

districts.[80] Often, as in New York, independent school districts exist largely outside the major population centers, while the big cities have districts dependent on the municipalities.[81] In some jurisdictions, such as Massachusetts, districts that are nominally dependent on a municipality really enjoy a great deal of fiscal freedom.[82] Sometimes, there are separate districts for the providing of different levels of education—*e.g.*, separate elementary-school districts and high-school districts in a particular area. Undoubtedly, however, the trend is away from such an extreme amount of separation and decentralization.[83]

§ 2.10 Public Authorities

Public authorities are sometimes lumped together with special districts,[84] or are treated as a subcategory under some such general heading as "special function units."[85] But the term does sometimes connote a slightly different entity from "special function district." Public authorities as we know them today are usually said to have originated with the Port of New York Authority, created in 1921, to build and operate harbor, and related, facilities; but it has been noted that the term was at that time borrowed from

---

80 Vernon's Tex.Code Ann.Educ. Code chs. 19 & 22–24, providing for "common" (*i.e.*, dependent) school districts under the county, independent school districts governed by "boards of trustees," and previously established "municipal school districts" that under the present law are treated as independent districts. It is possible for an independent district to transfer control of the schools to an incorporated city or town therein. Vernon's Tex.Code Ann.Educ.Code § 19.162. "County-line districts" overlapping county boundaries can also be created; *Id.* § 19.101. And all types of districts can be consolidated with other districts. *Id.* § 19.231. Cf. the Oklahoma system of both dependent and independent districts as provided in 70 Okl.Stat.1981, § 4.

81 "Common" or "central" school districts in New York are fiscally independent special districts whose boundaries do not necessarily correspond with those of other local units—though sometimes such districts are coterminous with incorporated villages. Garber & Hageny, The Law and the Teacher in New York State 43–44 (1967). (Note that a "common" school district in New York is just the opposite of a "common" district in Texas, described *supra* note 80.) A number of the major cities in New York, however, including Albany, Buffalo, and Yonkers, have a local Board of Education whose members are appointed by elected city officials and whose budgets are dependent on city appropriations. Garber & Hageny, *supra* at 45. Thus, these systems are basically dependent. With a few variations, this is the type system that exists in New York City. See Mayor's Advisory Panel on Decentralization of the New York City Schools, Reconnection for Learning 7 (1967). Cf. Mayer, Frustration Is the Word for Ocean Hill, N.Y.Times Magazine 28, 59–62 (May 14, 1968), criticizing the amount of central control of the city's schools. Another variation exists in Syracuse and Rochester, where the cities have dependent school districts with popularly elected boards of education. See N.Y.Education Law § 2553–76. It has been noted that, through state aid or otherwise, some "dependent" systems really become rather independent of the general local government. See Sayre & Kaufman, Governing New York City 279–85 (1960). See generally Salisbury, Schools and Politics in the Big City, 37 Harv.Educ.Rev. 408 (1967).

82 As to the fiscal independence of Massachusetts school committees, which are popularly elected in all Massachusetts cities and towns, see Ring v. City of Woburn, 311 Mass. 679, 43 N.E.2d 8 (1942). A similar situation exists in New York State for cities under 125,000 population. N.Y.Education Law §§ 51 & 53. The Boston school system, however, does not operate solely under the general Massachusetts law as to fiscal support for schools—Mass.Gen.Laws Ann. c. 71, § 34—but also under other statutes—Act 1936, ch. 224, as amended by Acts 1963, ch. 786, § 3—giving somewhat more power to officials of the city.

83 See Fordham, Local Government Law 36–37 (2d rev. ed. 1986).

84 See R. Smith, Public Authorities, Special Districts, and Local Governments ix (1964). Authorities are sometimes held to be neither municipal nor quasi-public corporations but a separate form of entity altogether. Kennelly v. Kent County Water Authority, 79 R.I. 376, 89 A.2d 188 (1952). See 1 McQuillin, Municipal Corporations §§ 2.13 & 2.29a (3d rev. ed. 1999). Cf. Boardman v. Oklahoma City Housing Authority, 445 P.2d 412 (Okl.1968) (housing authority was not agency or instrumentality of city or county or a subdivision of state; thus not subject to debt limitations).

85 See Fordham, *supra* note 83, at 39–40.

the Port of London Authority.[86] And the designation has sometimes been used to describe similar ad hoc units that existed in England in the 18th and 19th century.[87]

The Port of New York Authority may well be considered the prototype of the modern "authority." This was created by an interstate compact made by the states of New York and New Jersey and approved by Congress. Parallel statutes enacted in both participating states establish the method of government. The Authority has twelve members, known as "commissioners," six appointed by the governor of each state to serve terms of 6 years each. The governors enjoy veto power over actions of the Authority commissioners, as well as power to remove a commissioner for cause. Additional parallel legislation has occasionally been enacted in New York and New Jersey authorizing the Authority to undertake specific projects. All of these have been planned to be self-liquidating from tolls, with the initial capital being raised through sale of Authority bonds. For instance, construction of Lincoln Tunnel under the Hudson River was undertaken in this manner in 1931.[88] When the Authority later commenced additional construction on the original tunnel without obtaining specific authorization from either state legislature, this was held to be an improper, *ultra vires* act.[89]

As with special districts, creation of public authorities, such as housing authorities, has been stimulated by federal aid. Use of the term "authority" has no doubt also been encouraged by creation of such federal agencies as the United States Housing Authority (now part of the Department of Housing and Urban Development) and the Tennessee Valley Authority. Authorities have been much used by municipalities in some states, such as Pennsylvania, to perform proprietary ("business-like") functions—and to do so in a way that will avoid budgetary limitations imposed on the cities and towns themselves.[90]

Many public authorities are little different from special function districts; both types of entity usually perform only a single function, or a few related functions. But five possible differences may be noted.[91] (1) Authorities are usually associated with the construction and operation of public facilities which are intended to produce revenue and which are initially financed by the issuance of bonds payable solely from these revenues, not from general tax money. The revenue is normally generated by tolls or user charges

---

[86] *Id.* at 39.

[87] See Webb & Webb, Statutory Authorities for Special Purposes (1922).

[88] On the history and activities of the Port of New York Authority, see Michelman & Sandalow, Materials on Governments in Urban Areas 715–18 (1970). See also Kolbert, Comment—Red Light, The New Yorker, Jan. 27, 2014, at 19, noting that the Port Authority now operates the George Washington Bridge, the three major airports in the New York metropolitan area, the Holland Tunnel, and several other transit facilities, in addition to the Lincoln Tunnel. *Id.* at 19–20. A case interpreting the bi-state compact creating the Port Authority is Port Authority Trans-Hudson Corp. v. Feeney, 495 U.S. 299, 110 S.Ct. 1868, 109 L.Ed.2d 264 (1990), holding that the consent-to-suit provision in the compact waived Eleventh Amendment immunity.

[89] Port of New York Authority v. Township of Weehawken, 14 N.J. 570, 103 A.2d 603 (1954).

[90] Sause, Municipal Authorities, The Pennsylvania Experience 1–10 (Commonwealth of Pennsylvania, Bureau of Municipal Affairs 1962). The author defends authorities as usually responsive to public opinion—at least in the Pennsylvania experience—even though not subject to close public control. *Id.* at 39–49. Cf. Hartman & Carr, Housing Authorities Reconsidered, 35 J.Am.Inst. Planners 10 (1969). The Pennsylvania statutes authorizing municipal authorities are found at 53 Pa.Stat. §§ 301–401 (1997). See generally Strickland, Inside the Trojan Horse (Logo Publ.1969). See also Sanders v. Washington Metropolitan Area Transit Auth., 819 F.2d 1151 (D.C.Cir.1987) (transit authority created by interstate compact held to have Eleventh Amendment immunity from suit on civil rights and constitutional claims).

[91] See Fordham, *supra* note 83, at 38.

collected from those who make use of the facility. Special function districts may occasionally be associated with the building and operation of such facilities also, but this is less often true of them—and any facilities that they construct are often paid for by taxes.[92] (2) Authorities may lack any definite geographic limits; special districts usually have definite boundaries. (3) Authorities may lack any definite body of inhabitants or constituents; special districts are usually created to serve a particular group of persons. (4) Authorities have little if any legislative power, and are more thoroughly under the control of their creating units of government than are special districts (with the exception of the even less powerful *dependent* school districts). (5) Authorities have from their inception been extremely "ad hoc" in nature—sometimes created by a single municipality, sometimes by several cities or towns; sometimes created by one state, sometimes by two or more. Such flexibility may be increasingly found among special districts also, but the word "authority" always puts us on guard that we are dealing with a kind of unit that lacks any firm pattern.[93]

Authorities, like special districts, have increased greatly in number in recent decades, but amid oft-raised contentions that the resulting fractionalization of government functions is excessive.[94] The argument is sometimes made that city

---

[92] In some states, however, neither districts nor authorities have taxing power. Thus, under art. X, § 9, of the Oklahoma Constitution, *ad valorem* taxing powers are limited to counties, cities, towns, and school districts. It has been held that other units of local government cannot raise money by *ad valorem* taxes—but can raise money through property assessments (which may be figured on an *ad valorem* basis) if the assessments reflect special benefits to the properties so burdened. Application of Erick Hospital District, 444 P.2d 216 (Okl.1968). Cf. Myles Salt Co. v. Board of Commissioners, 239 U.S. 478, 36 S.Ct. 204, 60 L.Ed. 392 (1916) (inclusion of land in drainage district, and assessment of such land therefor, amounted to confiscation where land would not be benefited by district's activities). But cf. Yribarne v. County of San Bernardino, 218 Cal.App.2d 369, 32 Cal.Rptr. 847 (1963), appeal dism'd 376 U.S. 783, 84 S.Ct. 1134, 12 L.Ed.2d 83; In re Orosi Public Utility District, 196 Cal. 43, 235 P. 1004 (1925) (property may, without notice and hearing, be included in special district and subjected to general tax therefor—though it may not be so included in assessment district drawn for purpose of assessing to pay for some local benefit); Ruberoid Co. v. North Pecos Water & Sanitation District, 158 Colo. 498, 408 P.2d 436 (1965) (land can be included in special district though not specifically benefited thereby where district does not depend on special assessment for revenue but can levy *ad valorem* taxes). The Pennsylvania authorities, discussed *supra* note 90, are largely limited to revenue financing. See Tranter v. Allegheny County Authority, 316 Pa. 65, 173 A. 289 (1934).

[93] See Greensboro-High Point Airport Authority v. Johnson, 226 N.C. 1, 36 S.E.2d 803 (1946), discussing the nature of authorities and dealing with one created to operate an airport for two municipalities and a county. Cf. James v. Board of Commissioners, 200 Colo. 28, 611 P.2d 976 (1980) (Denver Urban Renewal Authority not a "state agency or authority" within Open Meetings Law). See also L.G. Lefler, Inc. v. Tucson Airport Auth., Inc., 141 Ariz. 23, 684 P.2d 904 (App. 1984) (Tucson Airport Authority was actually the city of Tucson acting through an agency); City of Norwich v. Housing Auth. of Town of Norwich, 216 Conn. 112, 579 A.2d 50 (1990) (city could abolish two earlier-created housing authorities and create a replacement to which the predecessors' assets and functions would be transferred); Mount Spokane Skiing Corp. v. Spokane County, 86 Wash.App. 165, 936 P.2d 1148 (1997) (county could create authority to operate ski facilities in state-owned ski area). In Commesso v. Hingham Housing Auth., 399 Mass. 805, 507 N.E.2d 247 (1987), a housing authority was held not to be an independent body politic, but rather a "public employer" within the meaning of the Massachusetts Tort Claims Act, and thus entitled to due notice of a claim against it. Compare Karlin v. Massachusetts Turnpike Auth., 399 Mass. 765, 506 N.E.2d 1149 (1987) (Massachusetts Turnpike Authority not entitled to governmental immunity). On the general lack of power of authorities, see Olson v. City of Golden, 53 P.3d 747 (Colo. App. 2002) (city urban renewal authority had no power to levy taxes or assessments of any kind or to conduct any kind of elections). But cf. Housing Auth. of City of Pasco & Franklin County v. City of Pasco, 120 Wash.App. 839, 86 P.3d 1217 (2004) (housing authority is independent entity, not a department of city; city had no authority to dissolve one such authority and create another).

[94] See Valente & McCarthy, Local Government Law 16–17 (4th ed. 1992), listing "problems aggravated by fractionated local government." See generally United States Advisory Commission on Intergovernmental Relations, Urban America and the Federal System (1969). For a positive view of the role of authorities in the

governing bodies are delegating away, to the special boards and commissions that run such entities as public authorities, too much of the discretion and power that the members of the governing body are elected to exercise.[95] Because of its flexibility and its potential for avoiding fiscal restraints that are imposed on municipalities, the device is likely, however, to remain quite popular.

§ 2.11 Federal-Local Units

There is only one real "federal local unit" in the United States, and that is Washington, D.C.; but similar units are used in some other countries for the governing of the national capital.[96] Except for a brief period of self-government in the 1870's,[97] the District of Columbia was long under the control of the U.S. Congress, which legislated directly for the District. A few powers of government were delegated by Congress to three District "commissioners"—two resident civilians appointed by the President with the advice and consent of the Senate and one officer in the Army Corps of Engineers detailed by the President for this duty.

In 1953, the Supreme Court upheld the validity of legislation passed by District's assembly during the brief period of self-government, and clearly said that self-government could again at any time be delegated by Congress to the District.[98] But Congress was slow to act. In 1967, President Lyndon Johnson exercised his powers as Chief Executive to bring about a limited reorganization of the District's administrative and executive branches.[99] Under this, a single Commissioner and bi-partisan nine-member Council, both appointed by the President with the Senate's advice and consent, replaced the 3-commissioner system. In 1971, District residents were for the first time (except, again, for that brief time in the 1870's) allowed to elect a delegate—though only

---

development of urban areas, see Gilbert, Stevenson, Girardet & Stren, Making Cities Work—The Role of Local Authorities in the Urban Environment (Island Press 1996).

[95] See Stewart v. City of Cheyenne, 60 Wyo. 497, 154 P.2d 355 (1944), in which the court relied on a common type of constitutional provision against delegating municipal functions to special commissions, in order to strike down a statute allowing the city council to establish a board to supervise a municipal utility. It was said that no board could perform municipal functions unless under the direct control of the elected municipal officials. *Id.* at 528, 154 P.2d at 366. But cf. People ex rel. Stokes v. Newton, 106 Colo. 61, 101 P.2d 21 (1940), finding no improper devolution of authority to state-created housing authorities in metropolitan areas and indicating such authorities would not constitute an undue interference with municipal affairs. For a study of an authority that allegedly abused its power, see Osborn, New York's Urban Development Corporation: A Study on the Unchecked Power of a Public Authority, 43 Brooklyn L. Rev. 237 (1977).

[96] See Tokyo: The Problem City After the Shock, Business Week Oct. 9, 1971, at 66, 69, noting, "The federal administration governs Tokyo as Congress governs Washington, D.C.," and discussing the resulting problems. Similarly, the Federal District in Mexico is administered by the federal government, with a mayor appointed by the president. See Ward, Creating a Metropolitan Tier of Government in Federal Systems: Getting "There" from "Here" in Mexico City and in Other Latin American Megacities, 40 S. Tex. L. Rev. 603 (1999). And Canberra, Australia, is a capital territory, not a state. See Shaefer, Canberra, 30 Urban Law. 251 (1998).

[97] Self-government was accorded by an Act of February 21, 1871, 16 Stat. 419 (1871), but was repealed by an Act of June 20, 1874, 18 Stat. 116 (1874).

[98] District of Columbia v. John R. Thompson Co., 346 U.S. 100, 73 S.Ct. 1007, 97 L.Ed. 1480 (1953). On the form of government that existed in Washington, D.C., from the 1874 repeal of the home-rule statute until changes were initiated in the 1960's, see Schmeckebier, The District of Columbia: Its Government and Administration (The Brookings Institute 1929).

[99] Pres. Johnson acted under the Act of June 20, 1949, 63 Stat. 203, 5 U.S.C.A. § 901, which allowed the reorganization plan to take effect if neither house of Congress acted adversely within 60 days of the plan's submission. The plan went into operation August 11, 1967. See Library of Congress Legislative Reference Service, Congressional Action on District of Columbia Home Rule, 1947–73 (1974).

a non-voting delegate—to Congress. Finally, in 1973, Congress restored "home rule" to Washington, D.C.[100] The charter approved by the District electorate provided an elected mayor and thirteen-member council. The mayor has real executive duties, and the council has broad law-making power. But the control of Congress was by no means totally removed. Local legislative measures are subject to Congressional veto; District budgets and spending are subject to Presidential and Congressional control; and any amendments to the District's charter are effective only if approved by Congress.[101]

Two significant U.S. Supreme Court cases in 1973 discussed the nature of the District of Columbia. In one,[102] a defendant convicted of violating the District of Columbia Code argued his conviction was invalid because the judges of the court in which his conviction occurred—the Superior Court of the District—did not enjoy lifetime tenure, in alleged violation of Article III of the U.S. Constitution. The case came before the high Court on appeal, rather than by writ of certiorari, and the Court first determined that this was not proper. Appeal from a Court of Appeals lies where a U.S. statute is struck down or a state statute sustained. The statute here involved was sustained—but a District statute does not come within the term "*state* statutes." However, the Court treated the jurisdictional statement of defendant as a petition for

---

[100] Public Law 93–198, 87 Stat. 774 (Dec. 24, 1973).

[101] *Id.* See Fordham, Local Government Law 42 (2d rev. ed. 1986). Cf. Home Rule: The Politicizing Begins, Washington Star-News, Jan. 6, 1974, § D, at 1. On subsequent temporary modifications of the District of Columbia's home rule made necessary by the District's financial problems, see Comment, Tough Love in the District: Management Reform Under the District of Columbia Financial Responsibility and Management Assistance Act, 47 Am. U.L. Rev. 993 (1998), discussing the District of Columbia Financial Responsibility & Management Assistance Act of 1995, Public Law 104–8, 109 Stat. 97 (April 17, 1995). On subsequent lifting of the restraints imposed by that legislation, see Note, Democracy or Distrust? Restoring Home Rule for the District of Columbia in the Post-Control Board Era, 111 Harv. L. Rev. 2045 (1998) (urging eventual adoption by Congress of greater autonomy for the District); "District of Columbia Is Back on Path to Self-Government," N.Y. Times, Feb. 22, 1999, at A-13. See generally Palmer, Waiting for Democracy: Congress, Control Boards and the Pursuit of Self-Determination in the District of Columbia, 19 Hamline J. Pub. L. & Pol'y 339 (1997). See also Note, DCERA: A Solution for the District of Columbia's People Problem, 86 Geo. L.J. 181 (1997), advocating legislation that would help reverse migration out of the District. A proposed Constitutional amendment, approved by Congress and submitted to the states for ratification in 1978, would have accorded the District of Columbia actual voting representation in both houses of Congress; presently, the District has only a nonvoting delegate to the House of Representatives. See "Victory for D.C.," Time, Sept. 4, 1978, at 15. That amendment failed to obtain ratification by the states, but proposals continue to be made that would grant District residents the same rights to vote and be represented as are enjoyed by other U.S. citizens. See Raskin, Is This America? The District of Columbia and the Right to Vote, 34 Harv. Civ. Rights-Civ. Lib. L. Rev. 39 (1999); Symposium, Is There a Constitutional Right to Vote and Be Represented? The Case of the District of Columbia, 48 Am. U.L. Rev. 589–727 (1999). On the possibility of statehood for Washington, D.C., see Raven-Hansen, The Constitutionality of D.C. Statehood, 60 Geo. Wash. L. Rev. 169 (1991). See generally Barnes, Towards Equal Footing: Responding to the Perceived Constitutional, Legal and Practical Impediments to Statehood for the District of Columbia, 13 U. District of Columbia L. Rev. 1 (2010). On the question of the validity of Washington's current situation as to representation in Congress, see Turley, Two Clever by Half: The Unconstitutionality of Partial Representation of the District of Columbia in Congress, 76 Geo. Wash. L. Rev. 305 (2008).

A good historical account of the establishing of the District, and of Congressional control over it, is found in Bowling, The Creation of Washington, D.C.: The Idea and Location of the American Capital (George Mason Univ. Press 1991). On the subsequent development of Washington, D.C., see generally "A Place to Hate and Love," Time, Nov. 10, 1980, at 24.

[102] Palmore v. United States, 411 U.S. 389, 93 S.Ct. 1670, 36 L.Ed.2d 342 (1973). Cf. Whalen v. United States, 445 U.S. 684, 100 S.Ct. 1432, 63 L.Ed.2d 715 (1980) (Court need not defer to decisions of District of Columbia courts on local matters to same extent it defers to decisions of *state* courts on questions of state law); Key v. Doyle, 434 U.S. 59, 98 S.Ct. 280, 54 L.Ed.2d 238 (1977), reh. denied 434 U.S. 1025, 98 S.Ct. 753, 54 L.Ed.2d 773 (law applicable only in District of Columbia is not a "statute of the United States" within rule on Court's review of judgments of a State's highest court that hold invalid a U.S. statute).

writ of certiorari, granted the petition, and reached the merits of the case. The Justices then noted Congress's plenary power over the District under Art. I, § 8, cl. 17, of the U.S. Constitution. They also noted Congress's broad powers to establish inferior federal courts and held that not all federal questions need be decided by Art. III judges. Thus, they held that it was perfectly valid for Congress to create one set of Washington, D.C., courts with Art. III characteristics and with jurisdiction to hear matters of national concern, and to create a separate court system, without Art. III characteristics, to deal with local matters. Judges in this latter court system need not be granted lifetime tenure.

The other case was a civil action for damages against the District of Columbia and some of its agents due to an alleged beating inflicted by District police officers.[103] The Court considered the possible liability under the Federal Civil Rights Act, 42 U.S.C.A. § 1983, which at that time applied only to acts committed under color of law of a State or Territory. The Court said that whether the District of Columbia is a "state" or "territory" within the meaning of any statute must be determined according to the meaning and purpose of the particular legislation. It was noted that the statute immediately preceding the one here involved had been held applicable to the District.[104] But that statute dealt with the right of all citizens to inherit, purchase, lease, and convey property, and was enacted in fulfillment of the Thirteenth Amendment's total proscription of slavery in all parts of the United States. By contrast, 42 U.S.C.A. § 1983 was enacted in enforcement of the Fourteenth Amendment, whose commands are addressed only to the States and Territories and those acting under their authority. Thus, this civil rights statute did not apply to actions committed under authority of the District (though the statute was amended in 1979 to make it applicable to such actions). These cases show that the District of Columbia is another ad hoc unit, still unique among municipalities in its dependence on Congress; distinct from the States and Territories, and by no means always included in general legislation directed at the rest of the nation.

Indian reservations may be considered somewhat analogous to a federal local unit. They are under the ultimate and plenary control of Congress, but considerable power of tribal self-government is often now recognized.[105] States and local governments have

---

[103] District of Columbia v. Carter, 410 U.S. 959, 93 S.Ct. 1411, 35 L.Ed.2d 694 (1973).

[104] Hurd v. Hodge, 334 U.S. 24, 68 S.Ct. 847, 92 L.Ed. 1187 (1948), applying 42 U.S.C.A. § 1982. Cf. De Geofroy v. Riggs, 133 U.S. 258, 10 S.Ct. 295, 33 L.Ed. 642 (1890) (Washington, D.C., within words "states of the Union" in treaty with France allowing French citizens to inherit property in such states).

[105] See Cohen, Indian Rights and the Federal Courts, 24 Minn.L.Rev. 145, 179 (1940); Crosse, Criminal and Civil Jurisdiction in Indian Country, 4 Ariz.L.Rev. 57, 58–62 (1962); Emery, Tribal Government in North America: The Evolution of Tradition, 32 Urban Law. 315 (2000); Resnik, Multiple Sovereignties: Indian Tribes, States, and the Federal Government, 79 Judicature, No. 3, at 118 (Nov.-Dec., 1995); Comment, Tribal Self-Government and the Indian Reorganization Act of 1934, 70 Mich.L.Rev. 955 (1972). See also K. Johnson, Sovereignty, Citizenship, and the Indian, 15 Ariz. L.Rev. 973 (1973). On the status of Indian reservations, see generally Case Comment, An Express Reservation? An Analysis of Reservations Under the Equal Footing Doctrine, 32 Pub. Land & Resources L. Rev. 203 (2011). For an example of the shared control by the federal government and the Indian tribes, see Comment, Tribal Control in Federal Sentencing, 99 Cal. L. Rev. 1409 (2011).

The Economic Opportunity Act of 1964, 42 U.S.C.A. §§ 2701–981, creating various federally financed social service programs, uses the term "community" to include Indian reservations as well as cities, towns, and other political subdivisions. 42 U.S.C.A. § 2790(c). See Comment, Indian Legal Services Programs: The Key to Red Power, 12 Ariz.L.Rev. 594 (1970). See generally Note, The Indian: The Forgotten American, 81 Harv.L.Rev. 1818 (1968). On the housing problems often faced by Native Americans living on reservations, see Listokin, Confronting the Barriers to Native American Homeownership on Tribal Lands: The Case of the Navajo Partnership for Housing, 33 Urban Law. 433 (2001).

only such powers regarding the reservations as are allowed them by Congress, and grants of such power are subject to any conditions (for instance, consent of the tribe in some instances) that Congress may reasonably provide.[106]

Trust allotments to individual Indians, which need not be within a reservation, remain under the exclusive jurisdiction and control of Congress for all purposes relating to the guardianship and protection of Indians. See Oklahoma Tax Comm'n v. Sac & Fox Nation, 508 U.S. 114, 113 S.Ct. 1985, 124 L.Ed.2d 30 (1993) ("Indian Country" includes formal and informal reservations, dependent Indian Communities, and Indian allotments; if tribal member lives in "Indian Country," such member is outside state's taxing jurisdiction); Ahboah v. Housing Auth. of Kiowa Tribe, 660 P.2d 625 (Okl.1983) (state had no jurisdiction over forcible entry and detainer action brought against Indian lessees of trust allotments). Cf. State ex rel. May v. Seneca-Cayuga Tribe of Okla., 711 P.2d 77 (Okl.1985) (Indian allotment is "Indian Country" and state regulation of bingo games in such territory is permissible only if, and to the extent that, the activity affects non-Indians or Indians who are non-members of a self-governing unit). But see Arizona Dep't of Rev. v. Blaze Constr. Co., 526 U.S. 32, 119 S.Ct. 957, 143 L.Ed.2d 27 (1999) (performance of contract on Indian reservation does not except proceeds from taxation); Cass County v. Leech Lake Band of Chippewa Indians, 524 U.S. 103, 118 S.Ct. 1904, 141 L.Ed.2d 90 (1998) (when Congress makes Indian reservation land freely alienable, land becomes subject to state and local taxation even if repurchased by an Indian tribe); Oklahoma Tax Comm'n v. Citizen Band Potawatomi Indian Tribe, 498 U.S. 505, 111 S.Ct. 905, 112 L.Ed.2d 1112 (1991), on remand 932 F.2d 1355 (10th Cir.1991), appeal after remand 969 F.2d 943 (10th Cir.1992) (when transactions occur on Indian trust lands, state is free to collect taxes on sales to members); State ex rel. Oklahoma Tax Comm'n v. Bruner, 815 P.2d 667 (Okl.1991) (tribal immunity does not prevent state from requiring Indian retailers doing business on reservations to collect sales tax on sale of cigarettes to nontribal members). Cf. Oklahoma Tax Comm'n v. Chickasaw Nation, 515 U.S. 450, 115 S.Ct. 2214, 132 L.Ed.2d 400 (1995) (state could not apply motor fuels tax to fuels sold by Indian tribe in Indian Country but could tax income of all persons residing outside Indian Country); County of Yakima v. Confederated Tribes & Bands of Yakima Indian Nation, 502 U.S. 251, 112 S.Ct. 683, 116 L.Ed.2d 687 (1992), on remand 960 F.2d 793 (9th Cir.1992) (county could impose ad valorem tax on reservation land patented in fee but could not enforce its excise tax on sales of such land). On the taxation powers of states and of tribal authorities, see Wagnon v. Prairie Band Potawatomi Nation, 546 U.S. 95, 126 S.Ct. 676, 163 L.Ed.2d 429 (2005) (states are categorically barred from placing the legal incidence of excise tax on a tribe or on tribal members for sales made inside Indian country without Congressional authorization; but Kansas motor fuel tax imposed on *non-Indian* distributor for fuel supplied gas station operated by tribe on reservation property was valid and posed no affront to tribe's sovereignty). See generally EchoHawk, Balancing State and Tribal Power to Tax in Indian Country, 40 Idaho L. Rev. 623 (2004); Stone & Ross–Petherick,The "Who and Where" Means the State Takes All: State Taxation Crosses Into Indian Country, 30 Am. Indian L. Rev. 385 (2005–06); Tabor, Sovereignty in the Balance, Taxation by Tribal Governments, 15 U. Fla. J.L. & Pub. Pol'y 349 (2004); Note, Taxation of Indians: An Analysis and Comparison of New Mexico and Oklahoma State Tax Laws, 41 Tulsa L. Rev. 91 (2005). See also Fletcher (with commentaries by Carlson & Laverdure), In Pursuit of Tribal Economic Development as a Substitute for Reservation Tax Revenue, 80 N.D. L. Rev. 809 (2004); Koenig & Stein, Federalism and the State Recognition of Native American Tribes: A Survey of State-Recognized Tribes and State Recognition Processes Across the United States, 48 Santa Clara L. Rev. 79 (2008).

On the definition of "Indian country," over which the states generally lack jurisdiction, see State of New Mexico v. Quintana, 143 N.M. 535, 178 P.3d 820 (2008) (to be dependent Indian country, a community must have been set aside by the federal government for use of the Indians as Indian land and must be under federal superintendence; here, the land did not meet the first requirement, as there was no explicit congressional or executive action setting aside the land for use of the Indians as Indian land; thus the state did not lack jurisdiction). See generally Jensen, Taxation and Doing Business in Indian Country, 60 Me. L. Rev. 1 (2008).

[106] Perhaps the most famous example of legislation by which Congress allowed the states possible jurisdiction over Indian reservations is Public Law 280, passed in 1953. 18 U.S.C.A. § 1162 (criminal jurisdiction); 28 U.S.C.A. § 1360 (civil jurisdiction). See Goldberg, Public Law 280: The Limits of State Jurisdiction Over Reservation Indians, 22 U.C.L.A.L.Rev. 535 (1975). This law granted several states jurisdiction over persons and property within reservations, and gave all other states the option of asserting such jurisdiction. Amendments in 1968 rendered future assertions of state jurisdiction under the Act subject to consent of the affected Indians, and allowed the states to return to the federal government jurisdiction that they had once assumed. 25 U.S.C.A. §§ 1321–26. There has been debate over such matters as the extent to which Public Law 280 might allow municipalities the right to zone land on Indian reservations. See (in chronological order) Reynolds, Zoning the Reservation—Village of Euclid Meets Agua Caliente, 2 Am.Ind.L.Rev. 1 (No. 2 1974); Note, Zoning: A Rebuttal to "Village of Euclid Meets Agua Caliente," 4 Am.Ind.L.Rev. 141 (1976); Reynolds, Agua Caliente Revisited: Recent Developments as to Zoning of Indian Reservations, 4 Am.Ind.L.Rev. 249 (1976). See generally Note, Jurisdiction: Public Law 280—Local Regulation of Protected Indian Lands, 6 Am.Ind.L.Rev. 403 (1979). See also Kane, Jurisdiction Over Indians and Indian

Reservations, 6 Ariz.L.Rev. 237 (1965); Comment, The Indian Stronghold and the Spread of Urban America, 10 Ariz.L.Rev. 706 (1968). In California v. Cabazon Band of Mission Indians, 480 U.S. 202, 107 S.Ct. 1083, 94 L.Ed.2d 244 (1987), the Supreme Court held that while state criminal laws are, under Public Law 280, fully applicable to an Indian reservation, civil laws are applicable only when relevant to private civil litigation in state court. The Court expressed doubt that any laws of local (as opposed to state) governments are, under Public Law 280, applicable to reservations but found it unnecessary to decide that question since the county gambling ordinance here involved was regulatory, not criminal, in nature and thus definitely inapplicable. *Id.* at 212 n. 11, 107 S.Ct. at 1089–90 n. 11. See generally Conway, Inherently or Exclusively Federal: Constitutional Preemption and the Relationship Between Public Law 280 and Federalism, 15 U. Pa. J. Const. L. 1323 (2013); Dimitrova-Grajzl, Grajzl & Guse, Jurisdiction, Crime, and Development: The Impact of Public Law 280 in Indian Country, 48 Law & Soc'y Rev. 127 (2014); Goldberg-Ambrose, Public Law 280 and the Problem of Lawlessness in California Indian Country, 44 U.C.L.A.L.Rev. 1405 (1997). On the effect that Public Law 280 has on various areas of the law, see Washburn & Thompson, A Legacy of Public Law 280: Comparing and Contrasting Minnesota's New Rule for the Recognition of Tribal Court Judgments with the Recent Arizona Rule, 31 Wm. Mitchell L. Rev. 479 (2004); Note, Baffling Distinctions Between Criminal and Regulatory: How Public Law 280 Allows Vague Notions of State Policy to Trump Tribal Sovereignty, 8 J. Gender, Race & Just. 449 (2004).

Gambling on Indian reservations is now controlled by federal legislation—the Indian Gaming Regulatory Act of 1988, 25 U.S.C.A. §§ 2701–21. See generally Santoni, The Indian Gaming Regulatory Act: How Did We Get Here?, Where Are We Going?, 26 Creighton L. Rev. 387 (1993); Comment, The Indian Gaming Regulatory Act of 1988: Did Congress Forget About the *Other* Commerce Clause?, 10 Thomas M. Cooley L. Rev. 665 (1993); Comment, The Reservation Gaming Craze: Casino Gambling Under the Indian Gaming Regulatory Act of 1988, 15 Hamline L. Rev. 471 (1992); Note, The Indian Gaming Regulatory Act and the Constitution: The Eleventh Amendment's Impact on Indian Gaming and Entrepreneurship, 21 Thurgood Marshall L. Rev. 205 (1995). In Seminole Tribe of Florida v. Florida, 517 U.S. 44, 116 S.Ct. 1114, 134 L.Ed.2d 252 (1996), the Supreme Court held invalid the portion of the Indian Gaming Regulatory Act by which Congress attempted to abrogate the states' Eleventh Amendment immunity and to authorize Indian tribes to bring suits in federal court against states in order to compel those states to negotiate in good faith with the tribes in order to form compacts under the Regulatory Act. For criticism of the *Seminole* case, see Note, *Seminole Tribe v. Florida*: The Supreme Court's Botched Surgery of the Indian Gaming Regulatory Act, 24 J. Legis. 149 (1998). Cf. Michigan v. Bay Mills Indian Community, ___ U.S. ___, 134 S.Ct. 2024, 188 L.Ed.2d 1071 (2014) (abrogation of tribal immunity in Indian Gaming Regulatory Act applies to gaming on, but not off, Indian lands; good review of immunity cases). See generally Martin, The Supreme Court Erects a Fence Around Indian Gaming, 39 Okla. City U.L. Rev. 45 (2014). On suggestions for changes in the law governing gambling on Indian reservations, see Rand & Light, How Congress Can and Should "Fix" the Indian Gaming Regulatory Act: Recommendations for Law and Policy Reform, 13 Va. J. Soc. Pol'y & L. 396 (2006). See generally Note, Will States Continue to Provide Exclusivity in Tribal Gaming Compacts or Will Tribes Bust on the Hand of the State in Order to Expand Indian Gaming?, 29 Am. Ind. L. Rev. 319 (2004–05). See also Berman, Such Gaming Causes Trouble: Constitutional and Statutory Confusion With the Indian Gaming Regulatory Act, 23 Seton Hall J. Sports & Ent. L. 281 (2013); Rand, Caught in the Middle: How State Politics, State Law, and State Courts Constrain Tribal Influence Over Indian Gaming, 90 Marq. L. Rev. 971 (2007). See generally on jurisdictional issues under the Indian Gaming Act, Note, Jurisdictional Ambiguities Among Sovereigns: The Impact of the Indian Gaming Regulatory Act on Criminal Jurisdiction on Tribal Lands, 26 Ariz. J. Int'l & Comp. L. 229 (2009); Symposium, Indian Gaming Regulatory Act, 42 Ariz. St. L. J. 1–338 (2010). See also Braccio, How the Anti-Gaming Backlash Is Redefining Tribal Government Functions, 34 Am. Ind. L. Rev. 171 (2009); Jensen, Indian Gaming on Newly Acquired Lands, 47 Washburn L. J. 675 (2008).

As to Internet gambling and its regulation, see Comment, Internet Gambling: A Road to Strengthening Tribal Self-Government and Increasing Tribal Self-Sufficiency While Protecting American Consumers, 37 Am. Ind. L. Rev. 229 (2012–13).

On the power of Indian tribes to regulate land uses, see Brendale v. Confederated Tribes & Bands of Yakima, 492 U.S. 408, 109 S.Ct. 2994, 106 L.Ed.2d 343 (1989), reh. denied 492 U.S. 937, 110 S.Ct. 22, 106 L.Ed.2d 634 (1989) (tribe has authority to zone property in areas of its reservations that are closed to general public but not in "open" areas). On the nature of tribal housing authorities, see Eaves v. State, 795 P.2d 1060 (Okl. Crim. App. 1990), reh. denied 800 P.2d 251 (1990) (tribal housing authority not subject to jurisdiction of state courts). See generally Note, Modern Problems in HUD Indian Housing Authorities, 16 Okla. C.U.L. Rev. 441 (1991). For an interesting comparison of Indian tribal governments and typical city governments in the United States, see Worthen, Two Sides of the Same Coin: The Potential Normative Power of American Cities and Indian Tribes, 44 Vand. L. Rev. 1273 (1991). See generally, comparing how tribal governments and other local governments handle similar issues, Sutton, Divergent But Co-Existent: Local Governments and Tribal Governments Under the Same Constitution, 31 Urban Law. 47 (1999). On the ways in which the need for economic development of Indian lands has influenced land-use regulation, see Logsdon, Jurisdiction to

§ 2.12 Assessment Districts

One final creation must be distinguished from all the foregoing. This creation has many names: a local taxing or assessment area or district; an improvement district; a maintenance district, etc.—though "assessment district" is probably the most common. The term "district" seems to indicate the unit of local government known as the "special function district" (discussed *supra*). But the assessment district or area is not really a unit of government at all. Its principal function is merely to delimit the territory on which a special tax or assessment is imposed in order to pay the cost of a public improvement or service. Normally, the property chosen for the assessment is considered to be specially benefited by the improvement or service. Naturally, lines must be drawn to indicate the bounds of this specially benefited, and therefore specially assessed, property—and these lines can be said to delimit the "assessment district." Often the assessments are then divided according to the benefits thought to have been received by each parcel of land; thus, an assessment for installation of sidewalks may be distributed among property owners in proportion to their front footage along the walk.[107]

Assessment districts are often utilized when a street is widened, paved, or re-paved. All the property along, or within a certain distance of, the street may be specially assessed.

The distinction between the true special function district and the mere assessment area is often blurred; but five factors should be considered in determining which is which.[108] (1) The special function district generally has its own governing board, separate

---

Regulate Land Uses in Indian Country: Basic Concepts and Recent Developments, 33 Urban Law. 765 (2001). See as to state v. tribal authority on reservation land, Nevada v. Hicks, 533 U.S. 353, 121 S.Ct. 2304, 150 L.Ed.2d 398 (2001) (most conduct on a reservation, if it involves only Native Americans, falls outside state jurisdiction; but this is not true where state interests are implicated). See generally Symposium, State-Tribal Relations: Past, Present, and Future, 47 Tulsa L. Rev. 503–720 (2012). See also as to Indian sovereignty Fletcher, Tribal Membership and Indian Nationhood, 37 Am. Indian L. Rev. 1 (2012–13); Duthu, Shadow Nations: Tribal Sovereignty and the Limits of Legal Pluralism (Oxford Univ. Press 2013).

[107] Sato & Van Alstyne, State and Local Government Law 5–6 (2d ed. 1977). See generally Stevens v. City of Missoula, 205 Mont. 274, 667 P.2d 440 (1983) (boundaries of assessment district should be drawn so that improvement benefits the included properties in substantially more intense manner than it benefits properties outside the district, but fact that outside property derives some general benefit does not affect the special benefit to district properties). It has been held that a municipality cannot include land located outside its boundaries in an assessment district. Madden v. Governing Body of Lenexa, 239 Kan. 397, 721 P.2d 261 (1986). See also Section 15.6 *infra.*

[108] See Sato & Van Alstyne, *supra* note 107, at 8. Cf. Fordham, Local Government Law 38–39 (2d rev. ed. 1986). See also In re Orosi Public Utility District, 196 Cal. 43, 235 P. 1004 (1925), finding that notice and hearing are constitutionally required in California before a property owner's land can be included in an assessment district, but not before it can be included in a special function district, since the former involves an assessment based on local benefits while the latter supplies general needs and is supported by general taxes. Cf. California Portland Cement Co. v. Picture Rocks Fire Dist., 143 Ariz. 170, 692 P.2d 1019 (App.1984), noting that property cannot be included in an assessment district unless it is specially benefited by the service or facility for which it is assessed, but a true special function district—as, in this case, a fire district—can tax property within the district even if that specific property receives no special benefit.

Where a mere assessment district, rather than a special function district, is found to exist, one result is that any liability for "district" actions must rest with the creating unit of local government. Bauer v. County of Ventura, 45 Cal.2d 276, 289 P.2d 1 (1955) (county, not drain maintenance "district," liable for flooding); Mortimer v. Acquisition & Improvement District, 105 Cal.App.2d 298, 233 P.2d 113 (1951) (county liable for indebtedness on bond issue in name of non-independent improvement district).

Comparable to assessment districts are "administrative areas" or "administrative districts" created by some local government units for purposes of administrative convenience, but with the "districts" having no corporate powers or responsibilities of their own. Similarly, "zoning districts" have no independent existence;

from that of any other unit of government, and often independently selected. The assessment district or area usually has no governing board of its own. (2) Some statutory declaration of continuing or perpetual existence typically supports the special function district, while an assessment district lacks this—and, indeed, by its very nature is usually intended to last only until certain assessments are collected. (3) The special function district has power to engage in such corporate functions as acquiring, owning, and selling property in its own name; the assessment district lacks these powers. (4) Though limitations and controls may exist, the special function district also often has power to incur indebtedness in its own name. The assessment district does not. (5) By statute or otherwise, special function districts usually have power to sue and are themselves subject to suit. Assessment areas have no such power or liability. Judicially, they act, or are acted against, only through the creating government.

Sometimes it is necessary to look to enabling legislation or other relevant statutes to determine whether a true special function district exists, or only an assessment area. It should be noted that both do rest on a similar underlying principle: that those specially benefited by a facility or service should bear the cost burden.

§ 2.13 Movement Toward Decentralization

Two very different trends are apparent in the United States today in respect to the organization of local government. On the one hand, many suggestions are made, and some effort has been put forth, to "decentralize" the large centers of population by creating neighborhood units of government. On the other hand, there is considerable movement, especially in the field of land use planning, toward greater "centralization"—toward regional planning and government.

Proposals for decentralization are far from new. Leonardo da Vinci suggested that 16th century Milan be broken into ten cities of 30,000 people each. More recently, writer Lewis Mumford has suggested a population range of 30,000 to 300,000 as ideal for cities; a proposal has been made that New York City be divided into units of 100,000 people; and a Royal Commission has recommended organizing London into boroughs of 200,000 each.[109]

One plan occasionally implemented in recent years involves the creation of "community corporations" or "neighborhood corporations" to deal with problems of the inner city. Proposals usually call for a non-profit corporation to be formed under general state law. All voting-age residents of the geographical area defined as the corporation's

---

the term simply refers to areas set aside for certain allowed uses (and not for other uses) by a city or other zoning authority. And "districts" defining the constituency, for election purposes, of members of the city council or other governing bodies normally have no separate governmental existence. All these "districts" really amount to little more than lines drawn on the map by, and for the convenience of, some unit of local government. See Sato & Van Alstyne, *supra* note 107, at 6–7.

[109] These various proposals are summarized in "John Lindsay's Ten Plagues," Time, Nov. 1, 1968, at 20, 29. The idea that New York City might be divided into units of 100,000 people each is quoted from Jacobs, The Death and Life of Great American Cities (1951). Jacobs actually suggests that the size of such districts might vary from about 50,000 to 200,000 residents. *Id.* at 130–31, 425. It has been suggested that an area where decentralized government may be particularly needed is environmental law. See Nolon, In Praise of Parochialism: The Advent of Local Environmental Law, 26 Harv. Envtl. L. Rev. 365 (2002). On the other hand, "Subnational debt restructuring has emerged as one of decentralization's most difficult problems." Schwarcz, Global Decentralization and the Subnational Debt Problem, 51 Duke L.J. 1181 (2002), at 1181. See generally Schragger, Decentralization and Development, 96 Va. L. Rev. 1837 (2010).

jurisdiction are eligible for corporation membership. If stock is issued, members of this same group are eligible to buy the shares, generally at nominal prices. A board of directors is popularly elected, sometimes at large and sometimes from sub-districts within the area.[110] Foundation grants and/or gifts from individuals are normally needed to initiate such a corporation. Once the corporation's activities are started, federal grants or loans may be available to aid such projects as community planning and low-cost housing construction.[111] The corporation might eventually develop profit-making businesses of its own. In addition to serving (through planning, housing, and anti-poverty activities) toward revitalizing depressed neighborhoods, such corporations could help bring city government to local neighborhoods by establishing and operating "little city halls," "neighborhood school districts," etc.[112]

But quite aside from the use of private corporations and the need for improving inner-city neighborhoods, suggestions are made for decentralizing existing municipalities in order to encourage citizen participation and make government more

---

[110] See Miller, Community Capitalism and the Community Self-Determination Act, 6 Harv.J.Legis. 413 (1969); Note, Community Development Corporations: A New Approach to the Poverty Problem, 82 Harv.L.Rev. 644 (1969). Cf. Schmandt, Decentralization: A Structural Imperative, in Neighborhood Control in the 1970's, at 20, 24–77 (G. Frederickson ed. 1973). See generally Kotler, Two Essays on the Neighborhood Corporation, in United States Congress, Joint Economic Committee, Urban America: Goals and Problems 170 (1967). Community Development Corporations have had their greatest impact in the area of developing new housing. See Grogan & Proscio, Comeback Cities: A Blueprint for Urban Neighborhood Revival (Westview Press 2000), reviewed by McNatt, Bringing the City Back to Life, Bus. Week, Jan. 8, 2001.

[111] Thus, community corporations might be grantees under the "community action programs" of Title II of the Economic Opportunity Act, 78 Stat. 516 (1964), as amended, 42 U.S.C.A. §§ 2781–2837, or under the urban planning assistance provisions of section 701 of the Housing Act of 1954, 68 Stat. 640, as amended, 40 U.S.C.A. § 461. Such corporations might be given membership on metropolitan planning agencies, which can perform grant-clearance functions for a region under section 204 of the Demonstration Cities and Metropolitan Development Act of 1966, 80 Stat. 1262, 42 U.S.C.A. § 3334. See Michelman & Sandalow, Cases and Materials on Government in Urban Areas 138–39 (1970).

[112] Michelman & Sandalow, *supra* note 111, at 137–40. The authors list possible activities of community corporations. *Id.* at 137–38. See United States Advisory Commission on Intergovernmental Relations, New Proposals for 1969: Suggested Legislation on Neighborhood Sub-Units of Government (1969). See also Rohe & Gates, Planning with Neighborhoods (Univ. of North Carolina Press 1985), urging a neighborhood-based approach to planning in order to increase citizen interest and participation in community activities. On the rise in recent years of privately organized residential community associations—both in high-rise buildings and in other neighborhoods—, see Liebmann, Devolution of Power to Community and Block Associations, 25 Urban Law. 335 (1993). See generally Liebmann, Solving Problems Without Large Government (Praeger 2000); Liebmann, The Little Platoons: Sub-Local Governments in Modern History (Praeger 1995), reviewed 28 Urban Law. 560 (1996), comparing community-level governments within 7 countries, including residential community associations in the United States. See also Barton & Silverman, Common Interest Communities, Private Governments and the Public Interest (Univ. of Calif. Press 1994), reviewed 27 Urban Law. 631 (1995), discussing such common interest developments as condominiums, planned unit developments and housing cooperatives, and comparing them to traditional neighborhood associations; Briffault, The Rise of Sublocal Structures in Urban Governance, 82 Minn. L. Rev. 503 (1997); Note, Ticky Tacky Little Government? A More Faithful Approach to Community Associations Under the State Action Doctrine, 40 Fla. St. U.L. Rev. 201 (2012). Compare the "community redevelopment agencies," used for some urban renewal projects, discussed in California Redevelopment Assn. v. Matosantos, 53 Cal. 4th 231, 135 Cal. Rptr. 3d 683, 267 P.3d 580 (2011) (states have extraordinarily wide latitude in creating various political subdivisions within state and conferring authority on them; legislature has corollary power to dissolve these same entities when deemed necessary and proper). Compare also the increasing use of "community benefit agreements," where "A developer enters into a private contract, usually with a coalition of community, faith-based, or special interest groups in exchange for their support, cooperation, or forbearance regarding the proposed development." Musil, The Sleeping Giant: Community Development Agreements and Urban Development, 44 Urban Law. 827, 829 (2012). See also Siegel, Community Benefit Agreements in a Union City: How the Structure of CBAs May Result in Inefficient, Unfair Land Use Decisions, 46 Urban Law. 419 (2014).

accessible to the average resident.[113] These aims are considered particularly desirable where governance of the public schools is involved.[114] But in all phases of urban government, the need for citizen involvement and understanding is increasingly felt. One method to achieve this is through the use of "citizen advisory committees"—groups of community members who must at least be consulted before action is taken affecting their particular neighborhood.[115] Such boards, with the members appointed by borough presidents, have been utilized to some extent as to planning activities in New York City.[116]

Another method of lessening the alienation between citizens and local governments is to develop neighborhood city halls and sub-county courthouses. Again New York City, through funding by private foundations, has experimented with six little city halls—five in different city areas plus one mobile unit. These act as complaint and information centers, with complaints sent to an administrator in the office of the mayor, who then forwards the matter to an appropriate agency.[117] A variation on this is the "multiservice center." Such centers have been established in various sections of some cities and counties to provide information and to handle complaints but also to offer a variety of other services, sometimes including recreational programs, job training, and day-care for children.[118] A similar system is used in Dayton, Ohio, where five "priority boards"

---

[113] See Babcock & Bosselman, Citizen Participation: A Suburban Suggestion for the Central City, 32 Law & Contemp.Prob. 221 (1967). Cf. Kotler, Neighborhood Government ch. 1 (1969), noting the development of many big-city "neighborhoods" as independent settlements before they became part of a city. It has also been suggested that *county* governance might well be decentralized by turning over to municipalities within the county such functions as road maintenance and snow plowing. See Cerra, Cohalan Proposing Changes in Suffolk, N.Y.Times, Dec. 9, 1979, at 33, col. 6. See generally Frug, Decentering Decentralization, 60 U. Chi. L. Rev. 253 (1993), offering a non-traditional view of decentralization while recognizing (at 257) some of the traditional benefits: the freedom gained by the citizen from being able to participate in the basic societal decisions that affect one's life; the creativity resulting from the ability to experiment in solving public problems and tailoring solutions to local needs; and the energy derived from democratic forms of organization. See also Frug, Administrative Democracy, 40 U. Toronto L. J. 559 (1990). In modern times, the development of suburbs, often governed separately from the central city, has in itself resulted in a degree of decentralization. See Dilworth, The Urban Origins of Suburban Autonomy (Harvard Univ. Press 2005), reviewed in Garnett, Unsubsidizing Suburbia, 90 Minn. L. Rev. 459 (2005).

[114] See Mayor's Advisory Panel on Decentralization of the New York City Schools, Reconnection for Learning 22–40 (1967). On the decentralization plan for New York City eventually adopted by the New York legislature, see Michelman & Sandalow, *supra* note 111, at 487–90. On experiments with decentralization in the New York City public schools, see Rogers, Does Decentralization Work?, 14 Urban Law. 515 (1982). See also Goodlad, A Place Called School: Prospects for the Future (McGraw-Hill 1984), indicating that lasting improvements in education are likely to result only if specific needs can be identified at the school level, not the district level. On the extent to which politics have continued to dominate the governing of New York City schools even after some degree of decentralization, see Berger & Kolbert, New York Schools and Patronage: Experience Teaches Hard Lessons, N.Y. Times, Dec. 11, 1989, at A-1. See generally Faber, Is Local Control of the Schools Still a Viable Option?, 14 Harv. J.L. & Pub. Policy 447 (1991).

[115] See Schmandt, *supra* note 110, at 20, noting that such committees may be looked on by city administrators as merely devices for obtaining consent to bureaucratic actions. See generally Parlow, Civic Republicanism, Public Choice Theory, and Neighborhood Councils: A New Model for Civic Engagement, 79 U. Colo. L. Rev. 137 (2008). See also Parlow, Revolutions in Local Democracy? Neighborhood Councils and Broadening Inclusion in the Local Political Process, 16 Mich. J. Race & L. 81 (2010); Stahl, Neighborhood Empowerment and the Future of the City, 161 U. Pa. L. Rev. 939 (2013). Compare Chemerinsky & Kleiner, Federalism From the Neighborhood Up: Los Angeles's Neighborhood Councils, Minority Representation, and Democratic Legitimacy, 32 Yale L. & Pol'y Rev. 569 (2014).

[116] Yates, Neighborhood Democracy 39–43, 74–77 (1973).

[117] See Levitt & Feldbaum, State and Local Government and Politics 90–91 (1973). Cf. Yates, *supra* note 116, at 29.

[118] Stenberg, Decentralization and the Cities, in 1972 Municipal Yearbook 88, 91–92, 95.

have been established. These are composed of representatives elected by residents of their areas; they have sponsored job training and a variety of other service programs.[119] Some proposals for city decentralization go beyond any of the above-noted measures. Thus, it has been suggested that a large city might be restructured into 40 or 50 "service districts," each with its own police, sanitation, health, and other service units, with the units having considerable local autonomy in their field of service.[120]

Finally, an old idea that has gained new life under recent decentralization proposals is the use of public hearings and open meetings. Public hearings have been held in some communities in recent years, with a good deal of participation occurring, on such subjects as relations between the public and the police.[121] And some local government legislative bodies (city councils, etc.) have held open meetings in various neighborhoods within their locality, facilitating attendance by area residents.[122]

There has been more talk than action so far on decentralization. But the success of some experiments, plus increased community pressure to make local government less remote, may well lead to additional innovations. Most experimenting has so far occurred in densely populated centers; but decentralization, where money and personnel are available, might also be considered by units of government covering wide expanses of largely rural territory.

§ 2.14 Movement Toward Centralization

"Regionalism" in the local government field takes many forms. Intergovernmental contracts and agreements have been called "the most widely used formal method of accommodating governmental problems to geographic boundaries."[123] The two main types of such agreements are service contracts, under which one local government provides services to another, and joint enterprise contracts, under which two or more

---

[119] Cole, Citizen Participation and the Urban Policy Process 31–32 (1974).

[120] See N.Y.Times, Feb. 4, 1975, at 1, col. 1, discussing such a proposal for New York City, made by the State Charter Revision Commission. Cf. United States Advisory Commission on Intergovernmental Relations, ACIR State Legislative Program: New Proposals for 1969, at 803 (1968). See generally National Commission on Urban Problems, Building the American City 350–53 (House Doc.No. 91–34, 1st Cong., 1st Sess. 1968).

[121] Levitt & Feldbaum, State and Local Government and Politics 68–70 (1973). See also Gellhorn, Public Participation in Administrative Proceedings, 81 Yale L.J. 359 (1972).

[122] See Stenberg, *supra* note 118, at 88. Stenberg reported, however, that less than a fifth of cities and counties responding to his survey had held official meetings in neighborhood areas.

[123] United States Advisory Commission on Intergovernmental Relations, A Handbook for Interlocal Agreements and Contracts 18 (1967). Municipal annexations of ever-expanding territory may also be considered a common means of achieving regional government. See Sengstock, Annexation: A Solution to the Metropolitan Area Problem (Mich. Legal Publications 1985). See generally Sections 12.4–12.7 *infra*. On the need "to facilitate principled inter-city negotiations for the purpose of building more effective regional communities," see generally Lorenz, Good Fences Make Bad Neighbors, 33 Urban Law. 45, 46 (2001).

On regionalism in local government, see generally Griffith, Regional Government Reconsidered, 21 J.L. & Pol. 505 (2005); Note, Regionalism, the Supreme Court, and Governance: Healing Problems that Know No Bounds, 8 Howard Scroll 21 (2006). For a critique of the various methods used to implement some degree of regional government, particularly through the creation of regional special districts or public authorities, see Laurie Reynolds, Local Governments and Regional Governance, 39 Urban Law. 483 (2007). As to the general advantages of regionalism v. localism, see Saiger, Local Government Without Tiebout, 41 Urban Law. 93 (2009), discussing Tiebout, A Pure Theory of Local Expenditures, 64 J. Pol. Econ. 416 (1956), and observing that "Regionalization abandons the advantages of local governance with respect to whatever functions are regionalized, which, for most proponents, are most of the important ones." Saiger, *supra*, at 117. See generally Frug, Against Centralization, 48 Buffalo L. Rev. 31 (2000). Compare Gillett, Regionalization and Interlocal Bargains, 76 N.Y.U.L. Rev. 190 (2001).

local units jointly undertake some project for their common needs. In the past, such agreements sometimes ran into difficulty because of lack of power on the part of the participating units, as where a city was found to have no authority to provide services outside its territorial limits.[124] But now most states have enacted Interlocal Cooperation Acts. These vary as to the units of local government covered and the powers granted; but they all allow some agreements by which one unit of government may undertake to render services for another—such as a city for a county or vice versa.[125] In recent years, intergovernmental agreements for cooperation during times of emergency have become especially common.[126] But many obstacles may be encountered when one government attempts an agreement with another,[127] leading one commentator to conclude that voluntary cooperation among local governments "is the least satisfactory response to decentralization and has the fewest applications to growth-related problems."[128]

One of the most common types of intergovernmental contracts is the "Lakewood Plan," by which a county government, for a service charge, performs certain functions—often ones that are traditionally associated with municipal government, such as police and fire protection—for municipalities within the county. The name was derived from a 1954 agreement between the County of Los Angeles, California, and the city of Lakewood.[129] Such plans eliminate the artificial barriers otherwise imposed by jurisdictional lines, so that fire protection, for instance, can be offered by the county throughout its territory—not just in the unincorporated areas. Each municipality in the county, then, does not have to offer its own fire-protection service. This eliminates duplication of facilities and often results in cost savings and more efficient service.[130] Note that while the Lakewood Plan contemplates two-party agreements, the agreed-upon services are offered by only one of the parties—usually the more comprehensive unit, such as the county. This is sometimes referred to as a "vertical" system of

---

[124] See Port of Peninsula v. E. H. Bendiksen Co., 71 Wn.2d 530, 429 P.2d 859 (1967).

[125] See Handbook, *supra* note 123, at 23–29. Cf. United States Advisory Commission on Intergovernmental Relations, 14th Annual Report 51 (1973). See generally Merrill, Our Unrealized Resource—Intermunicipal Cooperation, 23 Okl.L.Rev. 349 (1970). In Utah County v. Ivie, 2006 Utah 33, 137 P.3d 797 (2006), it was held that the Interlocal Cooperation Act did not preclude a county and a city from exercising their general contracting powers to enter a condemnation agreement, since the Act was intended to expand, not limit, local governments' ability to cooperate.

In Lockheed Information Mgmt. Servs. Co. v. City of Inglewood, 17 Cal.4th 170, 70 Cal.Rptr.2d 152, 948 P.2d 943 (1998), the court dissolved an injunction against a municipal agency's furnishing computing and related services to other cities regarding parking tickets. But cf. Brittain v. Village of Liverpool, 172 Misc.2d 201, 657 N.Y.S.2d 298 (Sup. Ct. 1997) (merger of village and city police departments, while not an abuse of discretion, violated referendum and civil service laws).

[126] See Cohn, Mutual Aid: Intergovernmental Agreements for Emergency Preparedness and Response, 37 Urban Law. 1 (2005). See generally Abbott & Hetzel, A Checklist for State and Local Government Attorneys to Prepare for Possible Disasters, 37 Urban Law. 489 (2005).

[127] See Myers, Obstacles to Bargaining Between Local Governments: The Case of West Haven and Orange, Connecticut, 37 Urban Law. 853 (2005).

[128] A. Downs, New Visions for Metropolitan America 170–71 (1994). See generally Laurie Reynolds, Intergovernmental Cooperation, Metropolitan Equity, and the New Regionalism, 78 Wash. L. Rev. 93 (2003).

[129] Kuyper, Intergovernmental Cooperation: An Analysis of the Lakewood Plan, 58 Geo.L.J. 777 (1970).

[130] See Note, The Urban County: A Study of New Approaches to Local Government in Metropolitan Areas, 73 Harv.L.Rev. 526, 545, 558 (1960). On the general trend toward services being offered by counties, or other area-wide units of government, rather than by municipalities, see Herbers, City Services Assumed by Bigger Governments, N.Y. Times, Feb. 20, 1984, at 11.

contracting because it involves government bodies at various political levels.[131] Modified plans, of course, are possible under which any number of units agree to perform services for one another.

While intergovernmental contracts typically deal with a limited range of services and establish no new unit of government, the need is sometimes felt for representatives of various units of government to meet together in some organized fashion and discuss common problems. Thus, the move toward regionalism is also seen in the establishment of formal organizations of government officials within various geographic areas (usually large metropolitan centers). These organizations are often called "councils of governments," or "metropolitan regional councils," or "associations of governments.". A typical organization might include representatives of a center-city, the surrounding suburban municipalities, and the county or counties within which the urban area lies.[132] The typical such group is also voluntary, with any member entitled to withdraw at any time, and rather powerless, lacking the sovereign powers of government except as they may be exercised by the cooperation of the individual members.[133] But some state laws have designated councils of government as official planning-coordinating agencies for their region; and in any case, such groups provide valuable forums for discussion of regional planning, environmental problems, and transportation needs.[134]

Councils of government have been said to have five characteristics:[135] (1) They cut across the lines of several local jurisdictions, and occasionally encompass parts of several states. (2) They are often composed of the chief elected officials of the governments represented. (3) They are primarily forums for discussion and have no powers to compel membership, attendance, or compliance with their recommendations. (4) They are multi-purpose and deal with a variety of metropolitan problems. (5) They usually employ a full-time staff. Since the first such Council was organized in the Detroit area in 1954, there has been steady growth in the number of regional councils—a growth stimulated

---

[131] Kuyper, *supra* note 129, at 793. Where various governmental units contract to undertake a joint operation, there is authority that the agreement is valid only if each contracting unit has power to perform the contract. Kaufman v. Swift County, 225 Minn. 169, 30 N.W.2d 34 (1947) (all parties to contract for joint operation of hospital must have power to run hospital). But see Council of State Governments, Suggested State Legislation Program for 1957, at 94 (1956) (cooperation statutes are intended to authorize interlocal projects even if only one of the units would have power to act alone). See generally Comment, Interlocal Cooperation: The Missouri Approach, 33 Mo.L.Rev. 442 (1968).

State departments of community affairs, or other state agencies dealing with local governmental affairs, have encouraged interlocal cooperation and agreements in some states. See Grant, Urban Needs and State Response, in American Assembly, The States and the Urban Crisis 77–88 (1970).

[132] See United States Advisory Commission on Intergovernmental Relations, Metropolitan Councils of Government (1966).

[133] See Rollow v. West, 479 P.2d 962 (Okl.1971) (voluntary association of counties and municipalities did not have power of eminent domain). See generally Mogulof, Governing Metropolitan Areas—A Critical Review of Councils of Government and the Federal Role (Urban Institute 1971).

[134] See Zimmerman, Metropolitan Ecumenism: The Road to the Promised Land?, 44 U.Det.J.Urban L. 433 (1967). An example of transportation studies and discussions conducted under auspices of a Council of Governments is supplied by North Central Texas Council of Governments efforts in behalf of commuter rail service for the Dallas-Ft.Worth area. See Thompson, Rail Service Plan Lauded by Officials, Dallas Morning News, Jan. 19, 1977. The possibility that councils of government might develop into true regional governments has been mentioned, but this hasn't so far occurred. See Dixon, Rebuilding the Urban Political System: Some Heresies Concerning Citizen Participation, Community Action, Metros, and One Man-One Vote, 58 Geo.L.J. 955, 968 (1970).

[135] United States Advisory Commission on Intergovernmental Relations, 1968 State Legislative Program 388–89.

in part by some federal-aid programs being made dependent on the participation of such a group.[136]

For years, some special function districts have dealt with a particular problem—air pollution, for instance—throughout an entire region including a number of municipalities and other units of local government.[137] But what about a general function government for an entire metropolitan area? Recently, many proposals for such governments have been made, and a few have been adopted—usually by way of consolidation of city governments with the county government in an urban area.[138] The first complete consolidation of the 20th century occurred in 1963 when Nashville, Tennessee, consolidated with Davidson County. The move has been credited with helping end city-suburban clashes since the center city no longer has to worry about losing its tax base if businesses move out into the surrounding area.[139]

---

[136] *Id.* at 388–90, noting federal grants for regional planning that are available to regions having a representative organization of public officials from the various governments in the area.

Some advisory councils are composed of, or include, private citizens who are not the chief officials of the representative governments. See Note, Regional Citizen Advisory Councils: Their Role in Oil Spill Prevention, and Response, 24 Geo. Int'l Envtl. L. Rev. 169 (2012).

[137] For instance, the Bay Area Air Pollution Control Law, West's Ann.Cal. Health & Safety Code §§ 24345–74, creates the Bay Area Air Pollution Control District to deal with air pollution in the San Francisco Bay area. On possible constitutional issues, see Brooks, The Metropolis, Home Rule, and the Special District, II Hast.L.J. 110, 246 (1959–60). Cf. Municipality of Metropolitan Seattle v. City of Seattle, 57 Wn.2d 446, 357 P.2d 863 (1960). See generally Ziegler, The Case for Metropolitan Growth Management in the 21st Century: Regional Urban Planning and Sustainable Development in the United States, 41 Urban Law. 147 (2008).

[138] See Blair, American Local Government 254–56 (1964); Bollens & Schmandt, The Metropolis; Its People, Politics and Economic Life 173–75 (1965). On the effects of city-county consolidation, see Butler v. Local 2033, 186 Mont. 28, 606 P.2d 141 (1980), voiding promotions within the sheriff's department as not in accord with county-municipality charter. See generally Jones, Metropolitan Detente: Is It Politically and Constitutionally Possible?, 36 Geo. Wash.L.Rev. 141 (1968). Since 1875, St. Louis, Missouri, has been both a city and a county, exhibiting an early form of "consolidation." On the other hand, "city-county separation" has in the past occurred in a number of metropolitan areas—that is, the city has been detached from the county that formerly included it and has been made into a separate county or other form of governmental unit. This has occurred in the areas of Baltimore, Denver, and San Francisco. Bollens & Schmandt, *supra*, at 427 note 12. See United States Advisory Commission on Intergovernmental Relations, Alternative Approaches to Governmental Reorganization in Metropolitan Areas 68 (1962). Despite the city-county consolidation in St. Louis, mentioned *supra*, the metropolitan area is fragmented into a central city and many suburbs and has been suggested as a prime candidate for a regional government. See Note, A Regional Government for Fragmented St. Louis: Even the "Favored Quarter" Would Benefit, 83 Wash. U.L.Q. 361 (2005). See also Board of Trustees v. Butte-Silver Bowe County, 353 Mont. 326, 221 P.3d 1175 (2009), dealing with governance of a public library for a county that had consolidated with a city therein.

Consolidation of city-and-county was not entirely a 20th-century development. Besides the St. Louis situation mentioned *supra*, a partial consolidation of Boston and Suffolk County, as well as total consolidations in the New York and Philadelphia areas, occurred before 1900. See Bollens & Schmandt, *supra*, at 427–28. In the 20th century, Kentucky was among the first states to provide for city-county consolidation. See Lewis, Kostas & Carnes, Consolidation—Complete or Functional—of City and County Governments in Kentucky, 42 Ky.L.J. 295 (1953). For discussion of the effects of city-county consolidation on voting rights, see Clark, Voting Rights and City-County Consolidations, 43 Houston L. Rev. 621 (2006). See generally Frug, City Making: Building Communities Without Building Walls (1999), reviewed in Lees, Expanding Metropolitan Solutions Through Interdisciplinarity, 26 N.Y.U. Rev. L. & Soc. Change 347 (2000–01). See also note 26 *supra*, and accompanying text.

[139] "Nashville Thrives on a City-County Merger," Bus. Week, Sept. 25, 1971, at 133–38. The consolidation occurred under an enabling act passed by the Tennessee legislature in 1957; Public Acts 1957, c. 120, Tenn.Code Ann. ch. 6, amended by Public Acts 1961, c. 199. The 1961 amendment specified that a commission to write a charter for the consolidated government might be created either as provided in the earlier legislation or by a private act of the legislature. A charter commission was then named by private act—Private Acts 1961, c. 408. The subsequently adopted charter was upheld against constitutional attacks in Frazer v. Carr, 210 Tenn. 565, 360 S.W.2d 449 (1962). Cf. Metropolitan Government v. Poe, 215 Tenn. 53, 383

An even earlier consolidation had occurred in Baton Rouge-East Baton Rouge Parish, Louisiana; but this was less-thoroughgoing, with budgets of the various units kept separate.[140] Since the Nashville consolidation, similar reforms have occurred in Jacksonville, Florida, and Indianapolis, Indiana.[141] An interesting example of consolidation of a center city and its suburban municipalities has also occurred in Winnipeg, Canada, where the union has been accompanied by a degree of decentralization, supplied by provision for community committees and advisory groups in the different geographic sections.[142] But the creation of metropolitan-wide governments has sometimes met with failure due to the desire of suburban voters for local autonomy. A movement, frequently called "New Regionalism," accepts the futility

---

S.W.2d 265 (1964); Robinson v. Briley, 213 Tenn. 418, 374 S.W.2d 382 (1963); Glasgow v. Fox, 214 Tenn. 656, 383 S.W.2d 9 (1964); Winter v. Allen, 212 Tenn. 84, 367 S.W.2d 785 (1963), all dealing with the effect of the new charter on various county offices. On typical activities of Nashville's consolidated government, see Metro & State section, The (Nashville) Tennessean, Jan. 11, 1981. On the continued prosperity of Nashville, see Meacham, Red-Hot Town, Time magazine, March 17, 2014, at 28.

[140] See Bollens & Schmandt, *supra* note 138, at 431–32.

[141] The Jacksonville consolidation occurred under Fla.Laws 1967, ch. 1320, as authorized by West's Fla.S.A.Const.Art. 8, § 9 (1967—adopted in 1934). The Indianapolis consolidation with Marion County was legislated into effect by Indiana Acts 1969, c. 173, now found at Ind.Code 1976, 18–4–1–1 to 18–4–24–25. On the success of the unified government for the Indianapolis area, see " 'India-no-place' No More," Time, June 11, 1984, at 30. See generally Owen & Wilbern, Governing Metropolitan Indianapolis: The Politics of UNIGOV (Univ. of Calif. Press 1985). There was no popular vote taken in the Indianapolis situation, but the statute was upheld in Dortch v. Lugar, 255 Ind. 545, 266 N.E.2d 25 (1971). Other consolidations have usually involved a vote of electors throughout the consolidated area. See White, Differential Property Taxation in Consolidated City-Counties, 63 Nat.Civic Rev. 301, 302 (1974). On the Jacksonville consolidation, see De-Grove, The City of Jacksonville: Consolidation in Action, in 2 United States Advisory Commission on Intergovernmental Relations, Regional Governance—Case Studies 17–25 (1973). See generally Martin, Consolidation: Jacksonville-Duval County (1968). Other interesting examples of city-county consolidation are discussed in Hart v. City of Columbus, 125 Ga.App. 625, 188 S.E.2d 422 (1972) (consolidation of city of Columbus with Muscogee County); Holsclaw v. Stephens, 507 S.W.2d 462 (Ky.1973) (city of Lexington with Fayette County); Moore, The Lexington-Fayette Urban County Board of Adjustment: Fifty Years Later, 100 Ky. L. J. 435 (2011–12). Cf. Dusch v. Davis, 387 U.S. 112, 87 S.Ct. 1554, 18 L.Ed.2d 656 (1967) (consolidation of Virginia Beach, Virginia, with county; borough form of government adopted); Polk County Bd. of Supervisors v. Polk Commonwealth Charter Comm'n, 522 N.W.2d 783 (Iowa 1994) (proposed charter for consolidated city-county government was rightly ordered placed before the voters); State ex rel. Tomasic v. Unified Government of Wyandotte County/Kansas City, 264 Kan. 293, 955 P.2d 1136 (1998) (statute authorizing city-county consolidation upheld as constitutional). See also Harter, Municipal Consolidation: Notes for the Small-Town Practitioner, 24 Urban Law. 761 (1992), discussing efforts to consolidate the governments of Ohio County, Indiana, and that county's seat, Rising Sun. Movement of population from the central city to suburbs on the edge of the city has sometimes resulted in a "hollowing out" of the city's core. Consolidation of city and county has been seen as a step that may help avoid this hollowing of the downtown area. See Baker, Using Special Assessments as a Tool for Smart Growth: Louisville's New Metro Government as a Potential Example, 45 Brandeis L.J. 1 (2006), discussing the merger of Louisville, Kentucky, with its surrounding county: "With a more compact and centralized regional community as the goal, the challenge of Louisville's new metro government, or others like it, is how to shape the development at the edge and encourage it at the core." *Id.* at 4.

[142] Fuga, New Winny's Government Is Unique Experiment, 62 Nat.Civic Rev. 189 (1973). See Axworthy, Winnipeg University, in United States Advisory Comm'n on Intergovernmental Relations, A Look to the North: Canadian Regional Experience 83–108 (1974). But Winnipeg had problems with deterioration of its city core, and with scant representation of the downtown area on the regional governing committee. See "Wasteland . . . Canada: Our Own Urban Ghetto," Maclean's, Nov. 27, 1978, at 54. See generally Brownstone & Plunkett, Metropolitan Winnipeg—Politics and Reform of Local Government (Univ. of Calif. Press 1983). For another example of consolidation in Canada, see Note, The Effects of Quebec's Municipal Merger Law on Montreal: Mega-City or Mega-Blunder?, 11 Cardozo J. Int'l & Comp. L. 1127 (2004). See also the discussion of the Toronto area two-tier government at notes 146–147 and accompanying text, *infra* this section.

of seeking consolidated regional governments and aims instead for regional structures that do not supplant local governments.[143]

Inevitably, the question has arisen of whether there might not be some workable middle-ground between the extremes of the impotent councils of government and the total consolidation of municipalities with a higher level of government. In the Dade County-Miami area of Florida a two-tier "federated" metropolitan government has been established, with matters of county-wide concern being handled by a nine-member county commission composed of representatives elected from each of 8 districts and a county mayor elected at large. Matters of more limited, local concern can still be handled by the various municipalities; but the arrangement is quite flexible and provides the possibility of most city services being transferred to the county whenever city officials so decide.[144] A similar, and highly successful, arrangement has been adopted for the Twin Cities area of Minnesota, though here the members of the Metropolitan Council are appointed by the governor. This 15-member group oversees such area-wide activities as watershed development, sewers, transit, and operation of the airport. It can veto any major project conflicting with its plan for the region's future. Local matters, including police and fire protection, are left to the participating municipalities. A tax-pooling law allows 40% of the taxes from new industrial and commercial establishments to be shared by the entire region—thus lessening the danger of a "scramble" by the various municipalities, each trying to get new business for itself.[145]

Another two-tier arrangement is found in Toronto, Canada. In 1953, the province of Ontario—exercising powers rarely found in states in the United States—ordered a limited consolidation of Toronto and 13 formerly autonomous suburbs. (Later, the participating units were compressed into the center-city and five suburban boroughs.) The Metro Council for the whole region is made up of representatives of the various units and handles such area-wide services as sewers, highways, housing, and public transportation. Left to the city and boroughs are such matters as garbage collection and local zoning.[146] Although rapid population growth in the region and political problems have raised some obstacles to the Toronto metropolitan government's success, the

---

[143] See Cashion, Localism, Self-Interest, and the Tyranny of the Favored Quarter: Addressing the Barriers to New Regionalism, 88 Geo. L.J. 1985, 2027–48 (2000).

[144] Lotz, Metropolitan Dade County, in 2 United States Advisory Comm'n on Intergovernmental Relations, Regional Governance—Case Studies 6–16 (1973). See Note, The Urban County: A Study of New Approaches to Local Government in Metropolitan Areas, 73 Harv.L.Rev. 526, 529–33 (1960). West's Fla.S.A.Const. Art. 8, § 1, provides for home rule for "charter counties." On the interpretation of this "home rule amendment" and its application to the Miami consolidation, see Miami Shores Village v. Cowart, 108 So.2d 468 (Fla.1958). Cf. Carol City Utilities, Inc., v. Dade County, 183 So.2d 227 (Fla.App.1966); City of Coral Gables v. Burgin, 143 So.2d 859 (Fla.1962); Dade County v. Mercury Radio Service, Inc., 134 So.2d 791 (Fla.1961). See generally Sofen, The Miami Metropolitan Experiment (rev. ed. 1966). On early problems of Miami's Metro, see Comment, Metro and Its Judicial History, 15 Miami L.Rev. 283 (1961). See also Bucki, Regionalism Revisited: The Effort to Streamline Governance in Buffalo and Erie County, New York, 71 Albany L. Rev. 117 (2008).

[145] See Kolderie, Governance in the Twin Cities Area of Minnesota, in United States Advisory Comm'n on Intergovernmental Relations, Promise and Performance 111–38 (1973). Cf. Flatermayer, "Metro" Government, Twin-Cities Style, Life, Jan. 24, 1972, at 28; Haigh, The Metropolitan Council, 40 Wm. Mitchell L. Rev. 160 (2013). The statutory provisions on the Twin Cities' Metro government are found at Minn.Stat.Ann. ch. 473, noted 62 Nat'l Civic Rev. 189 (1973).

[146] See Kaplan, Urban Political Systems: A Functional Analysis of Metro Toronto (1967); Milner, The Metropolitan Toronto Plan, 106 U.Pa.L.Rev. 570 (1957). See generally Royal Commission on Metropolitan Toronto, Report (1965).

arrangement in general has been praised, and certainly credited with helping comprehensive, area-wide planning for new developments.[147]

The two-tier approaches to centralization in Miami, Minneapolis-St. Paul, and Toronto have numerous differences. The Toronto situation, prior to the Metro government, was not typical of many big-city situations in the United States (the central city was relatively prosperous, there were no serious racial problems, there was no great profusion of local governments, etc.); and thus any successes there may have limited significance. The Twin Cities plan is subject to criticism for being undemocratic and for creating a regional authority that governs mostly through veto. The Miami plan leaves much to *ad hoc* decisions by the participating municipalities, county governing body, and ultimately the courts. But all the plans recognize that there is a need for greater regional planning as to some matters of local governmental concern, and also a need for greater local autonomy as to other matters. "In some respects, modern society will require even more centralization than now exists; in some respects, to make it bearable as well as workable, it will require more decentralization. Achieving a balance between these two needs is perhaps the most important and difficult problem for the near future. . . ."[148] Thus we can expect continued moves in the direction of both regionalism and decentralization.

Regionalism, of course, need not stop at state lines any more than at city boundaries. General function units overlapping state lines have not yet appeared, but some special units—like the Port of New York Authority and school districts in New England states—have been created by interstate compact.[149] It has been suggested that similar compacts might be used to create general-function regional governments.[150] It may be argued that Congressional consent is not even needed unless the Federal-state political balance would be affected.[151]

---

147 "Toronto Learns to Live with Bigness," Bus. Week, Aug. 19, 1972, at 64–66. See Smallwood, Metro Toronto: A Decade Later (Toronto Bureau of Municipal Research 1963); Rose, A Decade of Metropolitan Government in Toronto, 13 Buffalo L.Rev. 539 (1964). Cf. Smallwood, Changes Suggested for Toronto, 54 Nat'l Civic Rev. 559 (1965), discussing the changes recommended in the Report of the Royal Commission, *supra* note 146. Some of these changes were subsequently enacted. See Michelman & Sandalow, Materials on Government in Urban Areas 944 (1970). On the problems encountered by Metro, see Baker, Metro Toronto's Prestige, Efficiency, Morale on Decline, The Globe & Mail, May 9, 1973, at 4. See generally Rose, Metropolitan Government in Toronto: 1953–1973, in United States Advisory Commission on Intergovernmental Relations, A Look to the North: Canadian Regional Experience 33 (1974).

148 "John Lindsay's Ten Plagues," Time, Nov. 1, 1968, at 20, 29. See generally 4 United States Advisory Commission on Intergovernmental Relations, Governmental Functions and Processes: Local and Areawide—Substate Regionalism and the Federal System (1974); Symposium, Restructuring Metropolitan Area Government, 58 Geo.L.J. 663 (1970). The "new federalism" of the Reagan administration illustrated another kind of restructuring of governmental responsibilities, shifting more tasks to state and local governments and away from the federal government.

149 See Fordham, Local Government Law 39–40 & 916–18 (2d rev. ed. 1986). Cf. People ex rel. Younger v. County of El Dorado, 5 Cal.3d 480, 96 Cal.Rptr. 553, 487 P.2d 1193 (1971), discussing the interstate compact establishing a regional planning body for the Lake Tahoe area of California and Nevada. See generally Zimmerman, Interstate Cooperation: Compacts and Administrative Agreements (State Univ. of N.Y. Press 2012). But see Litwak, State Border Towns and Resiliency: Barriers to Interstate Intergovernmental Cooperation, 50 Idaho L. Rev. 193 (2014).

150 Engdahl, Interstate Urban Areas and Interstate "Agreements" and "Compacts": Unclear Possibilities, 58 Geo.L.J. 799, 801 (1970).

151 Virginia v. Tennessee, 148 U.S. 503, 519, 13 S.Ct. 728, 734, 37 L.Ed. 537 (1893) (dictum). Cf. State of West Virginia ex rel. Dyer v. Sims, 341 U.S. 22, 71 S.Ct. 557, 95 L.Ed. 713 (1951), enforcing an interstate compact; the Court held that it was not bound by state law and could make its own determinations of validity.

Full-fledged consolidation does not have to be limited—logically, at least—to the local level either, and the suggestion of some of our *states* consolidating, leading to fewer state governments, has been made.[152] For political reasons, this, of course, is unlikely to occur. And again, there are countertrends: It has been suggested that some of our major urban areas—such as New York City—should be separate states.[153] And it may be argued that what we need is not so much a change in the number of states as more active participation by the states in finding solutions to the problems of urban America.[154]

[152] See "Boston, Plym., and Boise, Bitt.," Time, Dec. 17, 1973, at 10, discussing a proposal, made by a retired professor of geography at California State University at Los Angeles, that the Union be restructured into 38 states instead of the present 50. A similar, though less detailed, proposal was made in 1970 by the late columnist Peter Lisagor.

[153] See "Should New York City Be the 51st State?," Time, June 21, 1971, at 14–15, noting that the approval of New York City voters, the New York state legislature, and the U.S. Congress would be needed. The article also notes the importance of determining what issues are best left to be decided by neighborhoods, what by cities, etc. *Id.* at 15. There have also been proposals for the separation of the borough of Staten Island from New York City. See City of New York v. State of New York, 76 N.Y.2d 479, 561 N.Y.S.2d 154, 562 N.E.2d 118 (1990), noted 19 Fordham U.L.J. 147 (1991), 8 Touro L. Rev. 795 (1992) (sustaining legislation prescribing a procedure for determining borough inhabitants' interest in secession). See generally Briffault, Voting Rights, Home Rule, and Metropolitan Governance: The Secession of Staten Island as a Case Study in the Dilemmas of Local Self-Determination, 92 Colum. L. Rev. 775 (1992): Viteritti, Municipal Home Rule and the Conditions of Justifiable Secession, 23 Fordham U.L.J. 1 (1995). On the possible secession of portions of Los Angeles from that city, see Frug, Is Secession from the City of Los Angeles a Good Idea?, 49 U.C.L.A. L. Rev. 1783 (2002). See also, on a proposal to divide California into several states, Vella, The State of Silicon Valley, Time magazine, July 28, 2014, at 14.

[154] See United States Advisory Commission on Intergovernmental Relations, Urban America and the Federal System 101–05 (1969). On the need for a regional approach to social and economic problems, see generally Cashin, Localism, Self-Interest, and the Tyranny of the Favored Quarter: Addressing the Barriers to New Regionalism, 88 Geo.L.J. 1985 (2000). Foster-Bey, Bridging Communities: Making the Link Between Regional Economies and Local Community Development, 8 Stanford L. & Pol'y Rev. 25 (1997). See also Boudreaux, E Pluribus Unum Urbs: An Exploration of the Potential Benefits of Metropolitan Government on Efforts to Assist Poor Persons, 5 Va. J. Soc. Pol'y & L. 471 (1998). On the need for metropolitan governments, see generally Peirce (with Johnson and Hall), Citistates: How Urban America Can Prosper in a Competitive World (Seven Locks Press 1993); Rusk, Cities Without Suburbs (Woodrow Wilson Center Press 1993), both favoring such governments. Both these books are criticized in Zelinsky, Metropolitanism, Progressivism and Race, 98 Colum. L. Rev. 665 (1998). For a proposal that would replace the traditional legal concept of "cities" with an alternative based on "community building" and that would encourage localities within a metropolitan area to forge closer ties with one another, see Frug, City Making: Building Communities Without Building Walls (Princeton Univ. Press 1999), reviewed in Hills, Romancing the Town: Why We (Still) Need a Democratic Defense of City Power, 113 Harv. L. Rev. 2009 (2000). Some efforts toward interlocal cooperation or consolidation are limited to particular areas of municipal activity. See, *e.g.*, Parker, Juvenile Assessment Centers: A Study in Local Government Collaboration, 31 Stetson L. Rev. 203 (2002).

Chapter 3

FORMS OF GOVERNMENT WITHIN LOCAL UNITS

Analysis

§ 3.1 Forms of Municipal Government—In General

Modern American municipalities exercise the three basic kinds of governmental power—legislative, executive, and judicial. In the early years of our country, the legislative branch of city government—usually a city council—was normally supreme.[1] But in many cities, this is no longer true. There are today many variations in the distribution of power within city government. Three main types of city government can, however, be identified: the mayor-council form; the commission plan; and the city manager (or "council-manager") plan. Other terms—such as "aldermanic"—are sometimes encountered; but most plans will fit into one of the three main categories.

In many states, there are statutes setting forth the recognized types of government for municipalities within that state: the mayor-council form, etc. These statutes are often augmented by legislation setting forth in some detail how each of the recognized types of city government operates. But frequently it can be observed that some cities in the state will have a form of government not listed in the statutes—for instance, the commission form where the state statutes are silent on this type of arrangement. How is this possible? Of course, the answer might sometimes be that the state statutes are not always intended to set forth the *only* permissible forms of municipal government to the exclusion of all others. But even if the statutory forms *are* intended as exclusive, the form of government that a city chooses is, within constitutional limitations, considered a matter of purely local concern.[2] This means that, as further discussed in Chapter 6

---

1 Stason & Kauper, Cases and Materials on Municipal Corporations 4 (1959). See generally Zink, Government of Cities in the United States (rev. ed. 1948). The historical background of modern American city governments is well described in Griffith, A History of American City Government: The Colonial Period (1938; reissued by Da Capo Press 1972); Griffith & Adrian, A History of American City Government—The Formation of Traditions, 1885–1870 (University Press of America 1983).

2 See Hinz v. Hubbard, 95 Okl. 164, 216 P. 440 (1923) (whether powers are exercised by mayor and council, or by board of commissioners, is matter of purely local concern); Lackey v. State, 29 Okl. 255, 116 P.

infra, a "home-rule city" is free to adopt any constitutionally allowable governmental arrangement—the commission form, to return to the example, even though state statutes say nothing about this. It is, naturally, also true that if a "home-rule-city" does choose one of the forms of government set forth in state statutes, it does not have to follow the statutory pattern as to the details of that arrangement.[3] It could, for instance, adopt the city-manager plan in a state recognizing this form of government in the state statutes—but the "home-rule-city" could then proceed to confer on the city manager (and other officials) a greater or lesser degree of power than would be conferred under those state statutes. All these matters are of basically municipal concern, and thus the "home-rule-cities" are free to decide them for themselves, limited only by the state and federal constitutions.

Nonetheless, state statutes setting forth the details of the various forms of city government are of importance. Such statutes in non-home-rule cities take the place of, or serve as a kind of, city charter.[4] And even the home-rule cities often follow the statutory pattern.

§ 3.2 Mayor-Council Form of Government

The mayor-council form of city government is considered the "traditional" form of municipal government in the United States, and remains the second most common form. This form is especially popular among smaller municipalities, but some of the nation's largest cities, such as New York and Chicago, also have it.[5]

In the early days of this country, the council was clearly supreme under this form of government. Often it chose the mayor (usually from among its own members), and normally the mayor—however chosen—had very little power. (Occasionally, there was no mayor at all; and the government would have to be considered a pure "council form.") In time, the mayor in most cities came to be elected popularly by voters of the whole city, though the system of the council choosing the mayor from its own members has never entirely disappeared. Gradually, the mayor often came to enjoy greater powers—powers of veto over at least certain measures, power to approve or disapprove the city budget, power to appoint and remove certain city officials. Members of the council are elected, in

---

913 (1911) (city with home-rule charter could adopt commission form of government even though state statutes did not provide for such form); State ex rel. City of West Orange v. City of Orange, 300 S.W.2d 705 (Tex.Civ.App.1957) ref'd n. r. e. When Oklahoma City, the city involved in the *Lackey* case *supra*, subsequently changed from the commission to the city-manager form of government, this move was also held valid. Moore v. Oklahoma City, 122 Okl. 234, 254 P. 47 (1927). Cf. Mollner v. City of Omaha, 169 Neb. 44, 98 N.W.2d 33 (1959) (electors of city may be allowed to participate in legislative process); State ex rel. Canada v. Phillips, 168 Ohio St. 191, 151 N.E.2d 722 (1958) (appointment of local police officers not governed by state statute).

[3] See Broadway National Bank v. Parking Authority, 40 N.J. 227, 191 A.2d 169 (1963); Boatman v. Waddle, 264 P.2d 730 (Okl.1953) (home-rule city may amend form of government, retain certain departments and abolish others, etc.); City of Tulsa v. Langley, 196 Okl. 680, 168 P.2d 116 (1946) (home-rule city may create separate body to manage water department). Cf. Adams v. Bryant, 236 Ark. 859, 370 S.W.2d 432 (1963) (city may create light-and-water commission); State ex rel. Brown v. Dunnaway, 207 Okl. 144, 248 P.2d 232 (1952) (operation of library is of purely local concern).

[4] See 2A McQuillin, Municipal Corporations §§ 9.02, 9.03, 9.07, 9.22, 10.09, 10.10 (3d rev. ed. 1996). But cf. Morehead v. Dyer, 518 P.2d 1105 (Okl.1973) (city voters of non-home rule city cannot by initiative petition amend city charter since they have no such charter).

[5] See 1981 Municipal Yearbook 180, giving data on the forms of government in 4,157 cities of 2500 or more population. Cf. National Municipal League, Forms of Municipal Government, Chart A (1966), showing the mayor-council form was still the most frequently used type of city government as of 1966.

many cities, from various districts of the city, usually called "wards." But often at least one member of the council, in addition to the mayor, is elected at large.[6]

The mayor-council form is often sub-divided into two categories: the weak-mayor system and the strong-mayor system. Typically, the weak-mayor format includes a large city council, the members of which are mostly or entirely elected from wards—thus increasing their commitment to a particular area of the city. The mayor has little if any veto power over legislation passed by the council. He has limited administrative authority, with most heads of city departments being chosen by the council or elected by the voters.[7] Under the strong-mayor plan, there are more clear-cut lines of responsibility, and the system is more analogous to our federal government. While policy-making still rests with the council, the mayor is a true chief administrative officer of the city. He has power to appoint and remove the heads of most departments of city government. He has a veto power over most legislation. The budget requires his approval and/or he is active in its preparation for submission to the council.[8] Many attempts have been made to improve on this form; but almost all other forms and proposals use as a starting-point the mayor-council system—usually the *strong*-mayor council system.

---

[6] See Reed, Municipal Government in the United States chs. 11 & 12 (1934). See generally Munro, Municipal Government and Administration chs. 18 (on city councils) & 19 (on the office of mayor) (1925). For historical background on this form of government, see Bryce, The American Commonwealth chs. 50–52 (2d ed. 1891). On the veto power given the mayor in some municipalities, see Municipality of Anchorage v. Repasky, 34 P.3d 302 (Alaska 2001), where the mayor's veto power was held to extend even to a line-item veto over the school district's budget.

[7] Fordham, Local Government Law 33 (2d rev. ed. 1986). This form is contrary to the traditional American policy of giving more power to executive officers than to legislative bodies. See 2A McQuillin, Municipal Corporations § 9.10 (3d rev. ed. 1996). Cf. Patterson v. American Fork City, 2003 Utah 7, 67 P.3d 466 (2003) (mayor lacked power to bind the city council on a settlement agreement). On a mayor's powers, see generally Law, Who Gets to Interpret the Constitution? The Case of Mayors and Marriage Equality, 3 Stanford J. Civ. Rights and Civil Liberties 1 (2007). See also Schragger, Can Strong Mayors Empower Weak Cities? On the Power of Local Executives in a Federal System, 115 Yale L.J. 2542 (2006).

[8] Fordham, *supra* note 7. See generally 2A McQuillin, Municipal Corporations § 9.18 (3d rev. ed. 1996). On the duties of, and problems encountered by, mayors in large U.S. cities in modern times, see Pickert, Can He Write a New L.A. Story?, Time magazine, March 31, 2014, at 42 (profiling Mayor Garcetti of Los Angeles); "A Mayor for All Seasons," Time, June 15, 1981, at 22; "Copious Coping: How Other Mayors Fare," *id.* at 29. Compare the obituary for Kevin White, long-time mayor of Boston, in Time magazine, Feb. 13, 2012, at 19. See generally Sherman, Your Mayor, Your "Friend": Public Officials, Social Networking, and the Unmapped New Public Square, 31 Pace L. Rev. 95 (2011). For an amusing description of the position of mayor in Great Britain and the development of that office, see also Wright, The Lighter Side of Local Government, ch. 1 ("His Worship the Mayor") (George Allen & Unwin, Ltd. 1935). In 2005, a vigorous debate on the strong-mayor form of government occurred in Dallas, Texas, when an initiative submitted to the voters proposed such a government for that city, rather than the present city-manager form. See Levinthal, Miller Makes Pitch for Strong-Mayor System, Dallas Morning News, Feb. 11, 2005, at 5B; "Who Should Have the Reins at City Hall?," Dallas Morning News, Feb. 13, 2005, at 4H. At the May 7, 2005, election the voters rejected the strong-mayor initiative. See Ramshaw & Jeffers, Seizing the Poll Question, Dallas Morning News, May 9, 2005, at 1A; Ragland, Key Voting Blocs Didn't Want Strong Mayor, Dallas Morning News, May 9, 2005, at 1B (noting that opposition centered on the argument that the proposed strong-mayor government would allow the mayor to become a dictator).

On the probable effect of the ongoing digital revolution, such as the Internet, on the quality of service offered by mayors and other local government officials, see Ellickson, Monitoring the Mayor: Will the New Information Technologies Make Local Officials More Responsible?, 32 Urban Law. 391 (2000).

On the executive branch of local governments in general, see The Most Dangerous Branch? Mayors, Governors, Presidents, and the Rule of Law: A Symposium on Executive Power, 115 Yale L.J. 2215–2651 (2006).

§ 3.3 Commission Form of Government

The commission form of city government was first developed as the result of a hurricane. A devastating storm, and consequent flooding, struck Galveston, Texas, in 1900, leaving the city with many human casualties, much destroyed and abandoned property, and a mayor-council government that was unable to cope with the exigencies of the situation. Under an act passed by the Texas legislature in 1901, the city government was taken over by a five-member "commission," partly appointed by the governor and partly elected. In 1903, the plan was modified so that all members of the commission were thereafter elected at large. The key to the plan was the unity of the legislative and administrative branches of the government: The commission served, like a council, as the city's legislative body; but in addition, each member of the commission headed some city department, such as the police department, fire department, etc.[9]

The commission worked efficiently in handling the clean-up and reconstruction needed in Galveston. The favorable publicity concerning the Galveston system resulted in similar commissions being adopted in a number of other United States cities during the period up to about 1915. Under legislative authorization in Iowa, the city of Des Moines was among the leaders in adopting this form of government, and thus the plan is often called the "Des Moines plan." Over 500 cities—mostly smaller cities—adopted this system at one time or another, usually during the early years of the 20th century. Most commissions have five members, though a few have only 3 while a few have 7 or more. It is generally necessary that each commissioner work full-time at his job since he is serving as both legislator and administrator.[10]

Despite the system's relative efficiency, its popularity proved short-lived. Few cities have adopted this form of government in recent years, and many cities that once had it have switched to other systems. Five main reasons can be given for the plan's downfall.[11] (1) It violates the American concept of "separation of powers," under which one branch can serve as a check on the actions of the other branches (the "checks and balances" principle). This tends to arouse fears of too much power, with too little control, in the hands of a few individuals. (2) While the fairly small size of most commissions contributed to efficiency, this feature made commissions vulnerable to charges of not being fully representative of the diverse elements in many cities' population. Partly for this reason, the commission form never became popular in larger cities. (3) The

---

[9] See Brown v. Galveston, 97 Tex. 1, 75 S.W. 488 (1903), in which the Texas Supreme Court discussed and upheld the Galveston city charter providing the commission form of government. This decision disagreed with that of the Texas Court of Criminal Appeals in Ex parte Lewis, 45 Tex.Cr.R. 1, 73 S.W. 811 (1903), where the state legislation amending the Galveston charter so as to establish the commission government was declared invalid as violative of the right of local self-government. The Texas courts rendering these two decisions were equals in the judicial hierarchy, but Texas law today is in accord with the Supreme Court ruling that there is no inherent right of local self-government. See State ex rel. Burnet County v. Burnet County Hospital Authority, 495 S.W.2d 300 (Tex.Civ.App.1973), ref'd n. r. e. The present statutes concerning the commission form of government in Texas are found at Vernon's Ann.Tex.Civ.Code arts. 1154–64. The basic idea of a commission form of government has been called at least as old as the Roman Empire. Fassett, Handbook on Municipal Government 37 (1922).

[10] Stason & Kauper, Cases and Materials on the Law of Municipal Corporations 5–6 (1959). See Bromage, Introduction to Municipal Government and Administration 278–91 (2d ed. 1957); Munro, Municipal Government and Administration ch. 20 (1925). See generally Reed, Municipal Government in the United States ch. 13 (1934); C. R. Woodruff, City Government by Commission (D.Appleton 1911).

[11] See Stason & Kauper, *supra* note 10, at 6. Cf. Fordham, Local Government Law 34 (2d rev. ed. 1986), commenting "Little wonder the plan has lost much ground."

specialized personnel needed for the plan's success often could not be obtained. The plan requires full-time city officers trained and willing to specialize in the operation of their various individual departments. Many cities—especially the smaller ones to which the plan might otherwise be suited—simply could not afford to pay adequate salaries to procure and retain competent, full-time department heads. Since these department heads are subject to voter approval or disapproval at elections, there is considerable uncertainty of tenure, making the positions still less attractive. (4) The system tends, by making each commission member the head of a department, to foster a specialized, "departmentalized" outlook that is not conducive to the broad overview that the commission members need in their policy-making role as legislators. Similarly, the system leads to rather fixed, inflexible areas of administrative responsibility. (5) The commission plan's popularity simply could not survive the rapid growth of the council-manager plan, discussed in the following section. Thus Des Moines, the city most associated with the commission plan, adopted a council-manager form of government in 1968.[12]

Some faults often associated with the commission plan are capable of being eliminated. In some cities, the various commissionerships (police, fire, etc.) were divided up on the basis of seniority, the longest-serving commission member having first choice. This could result in some commissioners—particularly junior ones—heading a department in which they had no interest and which they knew little about. The system has probably worked best where each commissioner is elected to a specific job: Police Commissioner, Water Commissioner, and so on.[13]

The mayorship under the commission form tends to become a weak office. The mayor is often little more than a presiding officer and public-relations person. Frequently, the mayorship goes with a particular commissionership that entails other duties as well. The system probably works best if the mayor is specifically elected to the mayorship, is elected at large by the community, and has some real executive power as mayor, with few other ("non-mayorial") administrative responsibilities.[14]

Thus, though the commission plan was sometimes adopted as a reaction against the weak-mayor plan, it often proved even less workable than its predecessor. It did contribute to American city government the use of shorter ballots, a greater degree of particularization in administrative responsibility, and a system that proved efficient in

---

[12] 9 Encyclopedia Americana 15 ("Des Moines") (1979). The Des Moines commission government always included a number of features not generally found under such a plan: nonpartisan elections, career service for city workers, and provisions for direct legislation and for recall of city elective officers. The other city associated with the original development of the commission plan—Galveston, Texas—also now employs a city manager. 12 Encyclopedia Americana 257–58 ("Galveston") (1979) (council-manager plan adopted in 1961).

[13] For instance, the city of Tulsa, Oklahoma, long had a commission form of government, adopted by the electorate in 1908; the commissioners were the Mayor, Finance and Revenue Commissioner, Police and Fire Commissioner, Streets and Public Property Commissioner, and Waterworks and Sewerage Commissioner—each elected to the specific job. But Tulsa switched to a mayor-council form in 1990. See Tulsa World, April 4, 1990, at A-1, A-4.

[14] See Fordham, *supra* note 11. Cf. Sato & Van Alstyne, Local Government Law 220 (2d ed. 1977).

the *short*-term for meeting emergencies.[15] But its faults have outweighed these contributions, and less than 3% of American municipalities now use this plan.[16]

§ 3.4 City Manager Form of Government

The council-manager plan of city government is now the most popular form, at least among municipalities of any size. About half of American cities have this form.[17] Staunton, Virginia, was the first American municipality to experiment with this plan, back in 1908.[18] But the first major city to adopt the plan (variously called "council-manager plan," "city-manager plan," or simply "manager plan") was Dayton, Ohio, in 1914. (Thus, this is sometimes termed the "Dayton plan.") The Dayton charter adopted to implement this method of government shifted most administrative power to an official, appointed by the city legislative body, known as the city manager.[19] By 1958, over 1,500 local governments in this country—including towns, villages, counties, and townships—had employed a similar manager.[20]

The council-manager plan, unlike the commission form, does not violate the concept of separation of powers. Here, the members of the council perform their traditional policy-making and legislating functions; but they have no administrative responsibilities. The city manager is a kind of business executive for the city—the head administrative officer, with supervisory power over the heads of most or all city departments. Many—sometimes all—such department heads are appointed, and subject to removal, by the manager, with council consent occasionally required. The manager himself is appointed by the council, and subject to removal by that body. Due to the concentration of administrative power in the one person, this system has proved more efficient than the commission plan. And by placing the administrative control in the hands of a non-elective professional manager, this plan has the advantage over the mayor-council system of keeping politics relatively removed from the day-to-day governmental operations (at least in theory). Since the manager answers to the council and not the electorate, his tenure is considered somewhat more secure than that, for instance, of a mayor.[21]

---

15 See Sato & Van Alstyne, *supra* note 14. Cf. Rodee, Anderson, & Christol, Introduction to Political Science 203 (1957).

16 1981 Municipal Yearbook 180. Most cities having this form of government fell in the population range between 100,000 and 500,000. See 1972 Municipal Yearbook 16. Cf. National Municipal League, Forms of Municipal Government Chart A (1966).

17 Yearbook, *supra* note 16.

18 The New Columbia Encyclopedia 2613 ("Staunton") (1975); 25 Encyclopedia Americana 638 ("Staunton") (1979). The Staunton experiment attracted the attention of Richard S. Childs, secretary of the National Short Ballot Association; and that group soon switched from promoting the commission form of government to the manager plan. Sumter, South Carolina, was the next city after Staunton to adopt the manager plan—doing so in 1912. See 6 Encyclopedia Americana 755 ("city manager") (1979); 3 Encyclopedia Britannica 334 ("city manager") (1998). See generally 3 Encyclopedia Britannica 334 ("city government") (1998).

19 Stason & Kauper, *supra* note 10, at 6. See 2A McQuillin, Municipal Corporations § 9.21 (3d rev. ed. 1996). See generally Bromage, Urban Policy Making: The Council-Manager Partnership (1970).

20 "News in Review: Manager Localities Number 1550," 47 Nat'l Mun.Rev. 71 (1958). Cf. 5 Encyclopedia Britannica 812 ("City government") (1971), stating that by the middle of the 20th century, half of all cities in the U.S. with more than 25,000 population had the manager form of government.

21 See Stason & Kauper, *supra* note 10, at 6. See generally Bromage, Introduction to Municipal Government and Administration 292–312 (2d ed. 1957); Munro, Municipal Government and Administration ch. 21 (1925); Reed, Municipal Government in the United States ch. 14 (1934); Sato & Van Alstyne, *supra* note

Under the council-manager plan, the manager often is accorded considerable control over fiscal matters, including the preparing of the city budget and the submitting of it to the council for approval. Increasingly, many city managers are professionally trained for their work. Normally, a council, in choosing a manager, does not have to select from among local people but may hire a non-resident.[22] Frequently it may "hire away" the successful city manager of some other municipality.

The city-manager plan has been particularly popular among medium-size cities in the United States. Though generally hailed as a responsible, professionalized form of government, it has not met with the approval of all students of urban affairs. Three main criticisms have been leveled: (1) The mayor, though the chief elected officer of the city under this plan, tends, as under the commission form, to have a weak office. With so much administrative power given the manager, the mayor's job may inevitably become little more than that of a "ribboncutter" at city ceremonies and presiding officer at council meetings.[23] (2) Too much power, it is sometimes alleged, comes to rest with the manager. Though technically answerable to and removable by the council, the manager may actually become a dictator of city policy by virtue of being the only person who really knows what's going on in the various city departments on a day-to-day basis. So much power, it is sometimes contended, should not be given an official who is not directly responsible to the electorate.[24] (3) There is, it is sometimes said, a lack of political leadership and responsiveness in government under the manager plan. Especially if (as often) the particular plan provides for a rather small city council (sometimes elected at large), there may not be adequate representation of minorities and the divergent groups that make up the city population.[25]

But overall, the trend still seems toward general approval and increased adoption of the manager plan among American municipalities and other units of local government.

§ 3.5 Miscellaneous Forms of Municipal Government

There are numerous variations in the three basic types of municipal government above described. Just as the English boroughs varied from one another as they developed, so "cities," "towns," and other units of local government differ considerably within the United States, particularly from one region of the country to another.[26] And the forms of government vary also, so that, for instance, a council-manager plan in one

---

14. On the powers of a city manager, see Nottingham v. City of Yukon, 766 P.2d 973 (Okl.1988) (power to compromise claim against municipality is lodged with legislative branch of government and is beyond authority of city manager).

[22] Fordham, Local Government Law 34 (2d rev. ed. 1986). See 3 McQuillin, Municipal Corporations §§ 12.59 & 12.61 (3d rev. ed. 1990).

[23] See Schneier, Strong Mayor System, (Tucson) Arizona Daily Star, Dec. 31, 1972, § E, at 1, alleging that the public looks to the mayor for political leadership but that under the manager plan, the mayor has no more power than any other member of the city council. On qualifications for, and legal powers of, chief executive officers (*i.e.*, city managers and mayors) of municipalities, see generally Rhyne, Mayor: Chief Municipal Executive Law (Local Government Law Series 1985). On city managers in particular, see *id.* §§ 1.3 & 2.3. On the increasing activism of mayors in some cities, see Cohen, City Boosters, Time, Aug. 18, 1997, at 20; "Rich Daley's Kind of Town," Bus. Week, March 1, 1999.

[24] See Thompson & Tatum, Who Has the Power?, The Dallas Morning News, Jan. 30, 1977, § G, at 1.

[25] See Bollens & Schmandt, The Metropolis 116–17 (2d ed. 1970).

[26] See Valente & McCarthy, Local Government Law 4–7 (4th ed. 1992).

city may be quite different from the same plan implemented in another city. Variations are found, for instance, in the number of officers elected rather than appointed; in the size of the city legislative body; in whether members of the legislative body are elected at large or by wards, or some by each method; in the degree to which partisan political parties participate in the city's election process.[27] The student must be careful to look beyond labels—merely because a city's governing body is called a "commission," for instance, it is not safe to assume that the city actually has the commission form of government that was developed by Galveston and Des Moines.

The word "aldermanic" sometimes appears as a description of a city government. The aldermen, in this form of government, are members of the municipal legislative body; and occasionally they also exercise some local judicial powers, acting as something akin to justices of the peace. The "aldermanic" form may be considered a category within the mayor-council system. The aldermen most commonly are elected for two-year terms, from particular wards of the city. But the words "alderman" and "aldermanic" are used rather infrequently these days, and increasingly only in reference to the legislative bodies of small municipalities.[28]

Sometimes new forms of local government are developed that may be considered hybrids—combinations of the desirable features of two or more of the traditional types. For instance, there are often attempts to combine some of the elements of the strong mayor-council system with the city manager plan. Under such a hybrid system, the manager may be appointed by the mayor, or at least be directly responsible to him. The mayor thus retains considerable power, but the manager exercises day-to-day supervisory authority over some or all of the city departments.[29]

As illustrated by the regional authorities described in Chapter 2, some overall trend is apparent toward increased central power—toward taking power from the units that govern very limited areas and transferring it to those that govern wider territories and more constituents.[30] But the need for some amount of central-local sharing of power—for some degree of decentralization of control—continues to be felt also, leading to constant tension and shifting.[31]

§ 3.6 Forms of Government in Public Quasi-Corporations

In the governmental forms utilized by public quasi-corporations in the United States, there are even more variations than are found among the governments of municipalities. Counties—and their counterparts, such as townships—are sometimes established by constitution, sometimes by statute. Often they are governed by boards or commissions elected by voters, but occasionally the board members are appointed, or some serve on an ex-officio basis. Two common features of such governments have,

---

27 Sato & Van Alstyne, *supra* note 14, at 220.

28 See Black, Law Dictionary 70 ("Alderman") and related terms (6th ed. 1990); Cyclopedic Law Dictionary 49 ("Alderman") (1940); 1 Encyclopedia Britannica 231 ("Alderman") (1994). Sometimes under the aldermanic form of government, the mayor has considerable power to appoint other officials. See 11 Okl.St. Ann. 1991, §§ 9–101–106. See generally 2A McQuillin, Municipal Corporations § 9.17 (3d rev. ed. 1996). But often when the word "aldermanic" is now used, it connotes a rather old form of governmental structure under which the mayor is rather weak.

29 Fordham, Local Government Law 34 (2d rev. ed. 1986).

30 See Bollens & Schmandt, *supra* note 25, at 431.

31 See Reed, Municipal Government in the United States 31 (1934).

however, been noted: (1) There is a general governing body, usually called either a board of commissioner or board of supervisors, charged with both policy-making and administrative functions. (2) There are considerable numbers of other officers and boards, some elected, many appointed by the general governing body.[32]

Most often, the governing body of the county, or comparable unit, is entirely elected by the people—sometimes at large, but often by districts or through a combination of the two methods. The weakness of many of these governments has led to pressure for the appointment or election of a manager comparable to a city manager—a person with real supervisory power over other officers and with authority to prepare the governmental unit's budget.[33] But county officers sometimes resist the creation of such a supervisory post. A compromise often reached is establishment of the position of "county administrator" (or something similar), who is given supervisory functions over daily operation of the government but who has little if any power to appoint or remove others or to direct the preparation of the budget.[34]

A few jurisdictions still employ judicial-type governing bodies for their counties—sometimes called "county courts." These are obviously survivals from English local government of an early day, and have been said to be more suited to the Middle Ages than to modern times.[35] Urbanization of many counties, and the demand for city services even in rural areas, have caused increased pressure for the reform of outmoded patterns of county government. Increasingly, the need is recognized as urgent for (1) a true executive officer or body in each county and comparable unit, (2) a professional manager or administrator to coordinate routine administration and keep it separate from policy-making, and (3) in some instances, consolidation of county government with that of the major city (if any) within the county.[36] Change, however, sometimes comes slowly, not only because of inertia, but because the governmental pattern for counties, and other public quasi-corporations, is often established by state constitution and can thus be changed only by pursuing the time-consuming amendment process.

Special function districts (and comparable units, such as public authorities) are controlled by governing boards, the members of which are, more often than not, elected by voters within the district. But again, there are variations. As to some types of districts, such as school districts, there is an overwhelming tendency toward election of board members. But in other districts, such as for housing, appointment of board members is quite common. Sometimes—often in soil conservation districts, for instance—there is a combination of election and appointment. Where appointment occurs, this power generally rests with the governing body of the governmental unit that

---

[32] Snider, Local Government in Rural America 119 (1957). Cf. Fordham, Local Government Law 31 (2d rev. ed. 1986). Typical of the county offices often filled by popular election are those specified in California as to counties not having a home-rule charter (unless these offices are specifically made appointive by the voters): the treasurer, county clerk, auditor, sheriff, tax collector, district attorney, recorder, assessor, public administrator, and coroner. West's Ann.Cal.Gov.Code § 24009.

[33] Mitau, State and Local Government 382 (1966). Virginia has for many years provided for county managers. See Spicer, Ten Years of County Manager Government in Virginia (Univ. of Va.Ext.1945).

[34] Bollens & Schmandt, *supra* note 25, at 118. Cf. Fordham, *supra* note 7, at 29.

[35] Fordham, *supra* note 32, noting the former Tennessee system of county courts of quarter sessions made up of the justices of the peace of the counties. Tennessee now provides for elected county governing bodies. Tenn. Const. art. 7, § 1.

[36] See Fordham, *supra* note 32, noting From America's Counties Today 11 (Natl. Ass'n of Counties 1973).

created the district—or that at least received the petition seeking the district's establishment. Thus, the governing body of the county in which the district is situated often has this appointing power. Sometimes a court, or the presiding judge of a court, within whose jurisdiction the district lies is given the power by statute. Other statutes designate the governor to appoint the boards of some districts, particularly if, as with a port authority, the district's activities have state-wide effect. Similarly, mayors may have power, by statute, charter, or ordinance, to name the members of district boards where the district engages in only limited, local functions. Occasionally, but infrequently, state administrative officers or agencies, state legislatures, or city legislative bodies appoint the members of district boards. A legislative body will usually delegate most of this responsibility to a committee, or will simply accept the recommendation of members of the legislature from the geographic area affected.[37]

Over the past quarter century, there has been a trend toward having members of district boards appointed both *by* and *from among* the members of the governing bodies of the city and/or county within which the district lies. This is known as a "constituent-unit system" of appointment. Where, as is increasingly true, a district overlaps several counties and other local units, a designated number of representatives of each such unit may be chosen. Sometimes where a district overlaps several counties, each county will name two representatives to the district board—one chosen by the county governing body, and one chosen by a selection committee made up of a representative of each city in the county. The constituent-unit method of appointment is designed to prevent undue increase in the number of elected and appointed officials and to encourage coordination of the activities of the participating governments. But the method has been criticized as resulting in the selection of persons not directly accountable to the voters of the district and as leading to inadequate representation of minority groups.[38]

"New England towns," though comparable to counties, present something of a special case as to their form of government, since traditionally their officers have been elected and other important business handled at an annual town meeting, with special meetings called to deal with unusual situations. As population growth has made town meetings impossible in some communities, modified meetings, composed of representatives of the various precincts in the area, have been employed.[39] Some of these meetings are still quite large. But some New England towns have abandoned the meetings altogether and are electing representative assemblies.

Township meetings—though often with less participation and less power than the New England town meetings—have been regularly held in the townships of some North Central states—a fact attributed to population movements from New England into that area.[40] But otherwise, the government of townships is often quite similar to that of counties. There is usually a governing board of supervisors or trustees. There are often a large number of lesser officials, many of them elected, many rather powerless.[41] The

---

37 Bollens, Special District Governments in the United States 31–38 (Univ. of Calif.Press 1957).

38 Sato & Van Alstyne, *supra* note 14, at 222.

39 See Sly, Town Government in Massachusetts 164 (1930). Cf. Committee for Economic Development, Modernizing Local Government 29–30 (1966). See generally Bryce, American Commonwealth ch. 48 (1921).

40 Fairlie & Kneier, County Government and Administration 458 (1930).

41 See Fordham, Local Government Law 29–30 (2d rev. ed. 1986).

governments of townships have been criticized as extremely inefficient,[42] and it has been suggested that these governments should either be abolished and their functions assumed by counties or other units,[43] or they should be strengthened into governments of real authority, as by giving them home-rule powers. The latter alternative has been chosen in Pennsylvania.[44] In some other states, a step has at least been taken toward improving the efficiency of township government by creating a real chief executive office, in addition to having the policy-making township board.

§ 3.7 Effect of One-Person One-Vote Principle

An important influence on the composition of governing bodies in recent years has been the U.S. Supreme Court's adoption of the one person-one vote principle which requires equality in the population of legislative districts. This was applied to state legislatures in the early 1960's.[45] In 1964 the Court ruled that this principle must govern the election of members to the U.S. House of Representatives.[46] Almost mathematical

---

[42] In Bromage, Recommendations on Township Government—A Supplement, 23 Nat'l Mun.Rev. 139 (1934), it is suggested that township governments be eliminated because most such units are too small for adequate financing and for efficient operation, because the cost to the public of these governments is quite high on a per capita basis, because the use of such units for the selection of members on county governing bodies contributes to petty politics, provincialism, and county bodies of unwieldy size, and because the township is an artificial creation having no relation to trade or industrial areas.

[43] See Committee for Economic Development, *supra* note 39, at 42.

[44] Home rule is extended to townships as well as counties and municipalities by Pa.Const. Art. 9, §§ 2, 14.

[45] The leading cases are Reynolds v. Sims, 377 U.S. 533, 84 S.Ct. 1362, 12 L.Ed.2d 506 (1964), reh. denied 379 U.S. 870, 85 S.Ct. 12, 13 L.Ed.2d 76 (both houses of state legislature must be apportioned according to population); Baker v. Carr, 369 U.S. 186, 82 S.Ct. 691, 7 L.Ed.2d 663 (1962), on remand 206 F.Supp. 341 (M.D.Tenn.) (finding violation of equal protection where Tennessee General Assembly was not regularly reapportioned according to population). See McKay, Reapportionment: Success Story of the Warren Court, 67 Mich.L.Rev. 223 (1968). Cf. Kilgarlin v. Hill, 386 U.S. 120, 87 S.Ct. 820, 17 L.Ed.2d 771 (1967), reh. denied 386 U.S. 999, 87 S.Ct. 1300, 18 L.Ed.2d 352; WMCA, Inc. v. Lomenzo, 377 U.S. 633, 84 S.Ct. 1418, 12 L.Ed.2d 568 (1964) (invalidating system under which counties were used to establish legislative boundaries, with less populous rural counties receiving more representational strength than more populous counties). See also Gray v. Sanders, 372 U.S. 368, 83 S.Ct. 801, 9 L.Ed.2d 821 (1963), invalidating a "county unit vote" system used in primary elections for state offices. The legislative reapportionments required under these decisions have to some extent corrected the rural bias previously found in many state legislatures, but new coalitions between rural and suburban interests have often been formed, preventing the center-cities from enjoying very many great gains. See Bicker, The Effects of Malapportionment in the States—A Mistrial, in Reapportionment in the 1970's, at 151 (Polsky ed. 1971). On the question of using elector population or total population in legislative reapportionment, see Garza v. County of Los Angeles, 918 F.2d 763 (9th Cir.1990), cert. denied 498 U.S. 1028, 111 S.Ct. 681, 112 L.Ed.2d 673 (1991), noted 41 Case W. Res. L. Rev. 1013 (1991) (apportionment properly based on total population rather than number of voting age citizens). On the question of whether illegal aliens should be included in the population base, see Note, The Exclusion of Illegal Aliens from the Reapportionment Base: A Question of Representation, 41 Case W. Res. L. Rev. 969 (1991). As to whether the apportionment of Congressional districts should be based on voting-age population, as opposed to overall population, see Kalson v. Paterson, 542 F.3d 281 (2d Cir. 2008) (United States Constitution does not require apportionment on basis of voting-age population).

[46] Wesberry v. Sanders, 376 U.S. 1, 84 S.Ct. 526, 11 L.Ed.2d 481 (1964). See United States Dep't of Commerce v. Montana, 503 U.S. 442, 112 S.Ct. 1415, 118 L.Ed.2d 87 (1992), upholding a federal statute which provides that after each decennial census the number of representatives to which each state is entitled shall be determined by a method known as the "method of equal proportions." Cf. Wisconsin v. City of New York, 517 U.S. 1, 116 S.Ct. 1091, 134 L.Ed.2d 167 (1996) (Secretary of Commerce's decision not to adjust census results to rectify undercounting of minority groups upheld as within constitutional bounds of discretion). See generally "Cities Want Inclusive Tally to Be One That Counts," U.S.A. Today, Aug. 16, 1999, at 2A. On the possibility of United States *Senate* districting, see Smith, Rediscovering the Sovereignty of the People: The Case for Senate Districts, 75 N.C.L. Rev. 1 (1996). As to the possibility of increasing the size of the U.S. House

equality in Congressional districts came to be required by the Court,[47] and it seemed the same attitude would govern as to state legislative districts.[48] But in time, the Court took a more lenient view of minor inequalities at the *state* level. Thus, it has been held that minor deviations from equality do not make out a prima facie case of unconstitutionality,[49] and that deviations of even 16% from perfect equality may be

---

of Representatives, see Note, Apportionment or Size? Why the U.S. House Should Be Expanded, 62 Ala. L. Rev. 1069 (2011).

[47] See White v. Weiser, 412 U.S. 783, 790, 93 S.Ct. 2348, 37 L.Ed.2d 335 (1973) (districting system for congressional seats invalidated where there was a maximum deviation of 2.43% from the ideal); Kirkpatrick v. Preisler, 394 U.S. 526, 89 S.Ct. 1225, 22 L.Ed.2d 519 (1969), reh. denied 395 U.S. 917, 89 S.Ct. 1737, 23 L.Ed.2d 231. But see Tennant v. Jefferson County Comm'n, 567 U.S. ___, 133 S.Ct. 3, 183 L.Ed.2d 660 (2012) (West Virginia congressional redistricting plan did not violate constitutional "one person one vote" principle, although the plan resulted in a population variance of 0.79% between the largest and smallest districts, where it furthered legitimate state objectives of not splitting counties, avoiding contests between incumbents, and minimizing population shifts between districts). See generally Annot., Constitutionality of Congressional Apportionment—Supreme Court Cases, 77 L.Ed.2d 1474 (1985). Compare Fryman, National Reapportionment: Geographic Patterns and Implications for States, 58 State Gov't 90 (1985); Note, The Road to Better Redistricting: Empirical Analysis and State-Based Reforms to Counter Partisan Gerrymandering, 73 Ohio St. L. J. 839 (2012). See also Arizona State Legislature v. Arizona Independent Redistricting Comm'n, ___ U.S. ___, 135 S.Ct. 2652 (2015), upholding the state's use of an independent conressional redistricting commission created by ballot initiative.

On the use of Congressional redistricting so as to achieve greater minority representation in Congress, see Shaw v. Reno, 509 U.S. 630, 113 S.Ct. 2816, 125 L.Ed.2d 511 (1993), noted 17 Harv. J.L. & Pub. Pol. 283 (1994), 70 Ind. L.J. 255 (1994), 73 Neb. L. Rev. 383 (1994), 21 Okla. C.U.L. Rev. 577 (1996) (redistricting legislation that is so extremely irregular on its face that it can rationally be viewed only as an effort to segregate the races for purposes of voting, without regard for traditional districting principles and with no compelling justification, states a claim for possible equal-protection relief). Cf. Miller v. Johnson, 515 U.S. 900, 115 S.Ct. 2475, 132 L.Ed.2d 762 (1995), on remand 922 F.Supp. 1556 (S.D.Ga.1995), upholding a district court finding that Georgia's Congressional redistricting plan was, unless narrowly tailored to serve a compelling state interest, a violation of equal protection given the irregular shape of a Congressional district and the evidence showing that the Georgia Legislature was motivated by a predominant desire to create a majority-black district. See generally Griffith, Defense Strategies in Voting Rights Litigation After *Shaw* and *Miller*, 29 Urban Law. 757 (1997) & 28 Urban Law. 715 (1996); Guinn & Sewell, *Miller v. Johnson*: Redistricting and the Elusive Search for a Safe Harbor, 47 Baylor L. Rev. 895 (1995); Note, Constitutional Limits on Racial Redistricting: *Miller v. Johnson*, 19 Harv. J.L. & Pub. Pol. 188 (1995); Note, *Miller v. Johnson*: The Supreme Court "Remaps" *Shaw v. Reno*, 56 La. L. Rev. 981 (1996); Note, *Miller v. Johnson*: Drawing the Line on Racial Gerrymandering, 17 N. Ill. U.L. Rev. 155 (1996). See also Aguilar, Congressional Redistricting in Texas: Time for a Change, 27 Stetson L. Rev. 781 (1998). An excellent symposium on Voting Rights and Elections is found at 1995 U. Chi. L.F. 1–599; see particularly Briffault, Race and Representation After *Miller v. Johnson*, *id.* at 23. For subsequent developments regarding the issues raised in *Miller v. Johnson*, *supra*, see Abrams v. Johnson, 521 U.S. 74, 117 S.Ct. 1925, 138 L.Ed.2d 285 (1997), upholding the Congressional redistricting plan of the district court. For later developments in the *Shaw v. Reno* litigation *supra*, see Shaw v. Hunt, 517 U.S. 899, 116 S.Ct. 1894, 135 L.Ed.2d 207 (1996) (redistricting plan found not narrowly tailored to serve compelling state interest and thus violative of equal protection), followed by Hunt v. Cromartie, 526 U.S. 541, 119 S.Ct. 1545, 143 L.Ed.2d 731 (1999) (triable issues found as to whether new redistricting plan was drawn with impermissible racial motive). In the *Hunt v. Cromartie* litigation, the Supreme Court subsequently ruled that the district court's finding that race, not politics, was the predominant factor in the state legislature's Congressional redistricting plan was clearly erroneous. Easley v. Cromartie, 532 U.S. 234, 121 S.Ct. 1452, 149 L.Ed.2d 430 (2001) (those who claim that legislature has improperly used race as a criterion on drawing a district must at a minimum show that the legislature subordinated traditional race-neutral districting principles to racial considerations; race must not simply have been one motivation but the predominant motivating factor in the districting decision).

[48] See Swann v. Adams, 385 U.S. 440, 87 S.Ct. 569, 17 L.Ed.2d 501 (1967).

[49] Gaffney v. Cummings, 412 U.S. 735, 93 S.Ct. 2321, 37 L.Ed.2d 298 (1973). It has also been held that legislative apportionment may be based on voter registration figures, at least where the distribution of legislators does not differ sharply from what would result under a population basis. See Burns v. Richardson, 384 U.S. 73, 93, 86 S.Ct. 1286, 16 L.Ed.2d 376 (1966); Reynolds v. Gallion ex rel. Attorney General of Alabama, 308 F.Supp. 803 (M.D.Ala.1969). Cf. Ely v. Klahr, 403 U.S. 108, 91 S.Ct. 1803, 29 L.Ed.2d 352 (1971); Pate v. El Paso County, 337 F.Supp. 95 (W.D.Tex.1970), aff'd 400 U.S. 806, 91 S.Ct. 55, 27 L.Ed.2d 38.

justified by a state policy of making districts correspond to local governmental boundaries.[50]

Early one person-one vote decisions of the U.S. Supreme Court also indicated considerable flexibility in application of the principle to *local* units of government—and possible non-application of the rule to special function units.[51] But the Court then

---

In Davis v. Bandemer, 478 U.S. 109, 106 S.Ct. 2797, 92 L.Ed.2d 85 (1986), the Court, declaring that political gerrymandering cases are properly justiciable under the Equal Protection clause, ruled that unconstitutional discrimination in reapportionment of a state legislature occurs only when the electoral system is arranged so as to degrade consistently a voter's or group of voters' influence on the political process, not necessarily whenever it is made more difficult for a particular group to win elections. See generally Pac, Miller, Packman & Hill, *Davis v. Bandemer*—Political Gerrymandering Challenged on Equal Protection Grounds, 17 Urban Law. 945 (1985), noting that the U.S. Supreme Court had never ruled on the general constitutionality of political gerrymandering and stating that a finding that it is unconstitutional would raise troubling questions concerning judicial involvement in the political process. In Vieth v. Jubelirer, 541 U.S. 267, 124 S.Ct. 1769, 158 L.Ed.2d 546 (2004), the Supreme Court overruled Davis v. Bandemer, *supra*, and held that a pro-Republican redistricting plan passed by the Pennsylvania legislature was a nonjusticiable political question. See also Duncombe & Stewart, Idaho's Unique Approach to State Legislative Apportionment: Statewide Floterial District, 58 State Gov't 96 (1985). On the unusual situation in Nebraska, where the state constitution requires that election districts for the unicameral legislature follow county lines wherever practicable, see Day v. Nelson, 240 Neb. 997, 485 N.W.2d 583 (1992), noted 72 Neb. L. Rev. 888 (1993), giving a strict interpretation to the constitutional requirement. See generally Note, The Frequency of Redistricting in Nebraska and the Balance Between One Person, One Vote and Electoral Stability: How Often Is Too Often?, 82 Neb. L. Rev. 575 (2003), analyzing Chambers v. Lautenbaugh, 263 Neb. 920, 644 N.W.2d 540 (2002).

[50] See Mahan v. Howell, 410 U.S. 315, 93 S.Ct. 979, 35 L.Ed.2d 320 (1973), modified 411 U.S. 922, 93 S.Ct. 1475, 36 L.Ed.2d 316. Cf. Gaffney v. Cummings, *supra* note 49, at 745, declaring that minor deviations from equality among state legislative districts may be permissible and may not require justification by the state, though a stricter standard has been applied to U.S. Congressional districts. In Brown v. Thomson, 462 U.S. 835, 103 S.Ct. 2690, 77 L.Ed.2d 214 (1983), the Court, in upholding reapportionment of the Wyoming House of Representatives, said that an honest, good-faith effort to construct districts as nearly equal in population as practicable would suffice. Under the Voting Rights Act of 1965, a deviation from ideal district size exceeding 10% in the apportionment of state legislative districts establishes a prima facie case of improper discrimination, but such a deviation may be justified by a state policy of preserving the boundaries of political subdivisions. See Alabama Legislative Black Caucus v. Alabama, ___ U.S. ___, 135 S.Ct. 1257 (2015) (jurisdiction, even when covered by Voting Rights Act, is not required to maintain a particular numerical minority percentage); Voinovich v. Quilter, 507 U.S. 146, 113 S.Ct. 1149, 122 L.Ed.2d 500 (1993), on remand 157 F.R.D. 36 (N.D.Ohio 1994). Cf. Johnson v. De Grandy, 512 U.S. 997, 114 S.Ct. 2647, 129 L.Ed.2d 775 (1994) (no violation of Voting Rights Act found in legislative redistricting where minority voters formed effective voting majorities in a number of districts roughly proportional to the minority voters' respective shares in the voting age population, even though it might have been possible to create additional districts in which minority voters represented a majority); Pope v. County of Albany, 687 F.3d 565 (2d Cir. 2012) (no violation of Voting Rights Act where no evidence that white majority votes were sufficiently in a bloc to defeat minority's preferred candidate). On what constitute violations of the Voting Rights Act's voting-dilution provision, see League of United Latin American Citizens v. Perry, 548 U.S. 399, 126 S.Ct. 2594, 165 L.Ed.2d 609 (2006). See generally on the Voting Rights Act, Symposium, The Value of the Vote: The 1965 Voting Rights Act and Beyond, 49 Howard L.J. 669–842 (2006); Symposium 2012: The Voting Rights Act of 1964: Where Do We Go From Here?, 64 Rutgers L. Rev. 925–1064 (2012). See also Georgia v. Ashcroft, 539 U.S. 461, 123 S.Ct. 2498, 156 L.Ed.2d 428 (2003) (assessment of racially retrogressive effect under Act depends not only on ability of minority group to elect candidate of its choice but on all relevant circumstances, including extent of group's opportunity to participate in political process). In Shelby County, Alabama v. Holder, ___ U.S. ___, 133 S.Ct. 2612 (2013), noted 44 Cumb. L. Rev. 153 (2013–14), the "preclearance" provision of the Voting Rights Act—under which no change in voting procedures could take place in specified jurisdictions until approved by federal authorities in Washington, D.C.—was declared unconstitutional, as the disparate geographic coverage of the preclearance requirement was found no longer needed to remedy past racial discrimination. For a contrary argument, see Note, Blocking the Ballot: Why Florida's New Voting Restrictions Demonstrate a Need for Continued Enforcement of the Voting Rights Act Preclearance Requirement, 62 Cath. U.L. Rev. 541 (2013).

[51] See Dusch v. Davis, 387 U.S. 112, 87 S.Ct. 1554, 18 L.Ed.2d 656 (1967) (upholding city-county consolidation; eleven-member governing body was made up of 4 members elected at large without regard to residence, and 7 elected at large with one residing in each of 7 districts of widely varying population); Sailors v. Board of Education, 387 U.S. 105, 87 S.Ct. 1549, 18 L.Ed.2d 650 (1967) (upholding governing board for

wavered in its flexible attitude. In 1968, the one person-one vote doctrine was clearly made applicable to general function local units—a county in the particular case.[52] Then in 1970, the rule was extended to a special function unit (a college district), and applied strictly.[53] The rigidity was criticized as unnecessarily detrimental to the preservation of traditional political subdivisions, and it was suggested that greater use of appointment of governing boards, or the use of weighted voting, might be tried.[54] But resort to such measures proved unnecessary, as in 1971 the Court, in another case dealing with a county governing body, reaffirmed that local governments need flexibility in their legislative districts and that greater deviations from absolute equality may be allowed here than in the case of Congressional districts.[55]

Enunciation of the one-person one-vote principle has raised two new questions: (1) Is the use of at-large election of local governmental officers valid, or must members of local governing bodies be elected from wards or districts within the general area? (2) In special-function districts, may the right to vote for district officers be limited to those with a particular interest in the district's functions?

The Supreme Court has upheld at-large elections,[56] and has ruled that the use of multi-member districts (in which a number of members are elected to a governing body

---

county schools though board was not chosen by county voters). On the validity of "super-majority vote" requirements at the local level, see Section 4.2, notes 43–44 *infra*.

[52] Avery v. Midland County, 390 U.S. 474, 88 S.Ct. 1114, 20 L.Ed.2d 45 (1968), on remand 430 S.W.2d 487 (Tex.). See Kawamoto v. Okata, 75 Haw. 463, 868 P.2d 1183 (1994), applying the one-person one-vote principle to a city council. See generally Briffault, Who Rules at Home?: One Person/One Vote and Local Governments, 60 U. Chi. L. Rev. 339 (1993).

[53] Hadley v. Junior College District, 397 U.S. 50, 90 S.Ct. 791, 25 L.Ed.2d 45 (1970), on remand 460 S.W.2d 1 (Mo.) (built-in bias in favor of less populous sub-areas within district).

[54] See Fordham, Some Questions and No Answers Anent Urban Regionalism, 1971 Utah L.Rev. 11, 16–17. The use of a proportional representation method of voting for city council members was upheld in McSweeney v. City of Cambridge, 422 Mass. 648, 665 N.E.2d 11 (1996).

[55] Abate v. Mundt, 403 U.S. 182, 91 S.Ct. 1904, 29 L.Ed.2d 399 (1971) (total deviation of 11.9% from population equality). Cf. Reynolds v. Sims, 377 U.S. 533, 578, 84 S.Ct. 1362, 1390, 12 L.Ed.2d 506 (1964), reh. denied 379 U.S. 870, 85 S.Ct. 12, 13 L.Ed.2d 76 (greater percentage deviations may be tolerable for local government apportionment plans); Fairley v. City of Hattiesburg, 584 F.3d 660 (5th Cir. 2009) (redistricting of city wards did not violate one-person one-vote principle where population of the ward in question deviated only 4.8% from ideal population). A rule of thumb applied by some courts (based partly on U.S. Supreme Court cases dealing with state legislatures—see note 50 *supra*) is that deviations in local governmental districts of more than 10% are unlawful unless some special justification is shown, but deviations of 10% or less are generally valid. See Kentopp v. Anchorage, 652 P.2d 453 (Alaska 1982). In Board of Estimate of City of New York v. Morris, 489 U.S. 688, 109 S.Ct. 1433, 103 L.Ed.2d 717 (1989), the Court applied the one-person one-vote principle to a city board of estimate and ruled that (1) the fact that members elected citywide could outvote the members elected from individual boroughs did not preclude a finding that the principle was violated, and (2) no governmental interest was shown that justified a 78% deviation from equality. See Note, One Person, One Vote: Is It Time for a New Constitutional Principle?, 8 N.Y.L. School J. Hum. Rights 523 (1991). See also Kilbury v. Franklin County, 151 Wash.2d 552, 90 P.3d 1071 (2004) (voters who challenged approval, by county board of commissioners, of redistricting plan for county commissioner districts failed to show arbitrary or capricious conduct in considering requirement that districts be compact); Note, One Person, No Vote? A Participatory Analysis of Voting Rights in Special Purpose Districts, 27 T. Jefferson L. Rev. 57 (2004). The scope of the one-person one-vote principle is well discussed in Toplak, Equal Voting Weight of All: Finally "One Person, One Vote" From Hawaii to Maine?, 81 Temple L. Rev. 123 (2008). As to the principle's application to college campuses, see Note, One Student One Vote? Equal Protection and Campus Elections, 35 J. College & University L. 217 (2008).

[56] City of Mobile v. Bolden, 446 U.S. 55, 100 S.Ct. 1490, 64 L.Ed.2d 47 (1980), on remand 626 F.2d 1324 (5th Cir.) (no violation of Fifteenth Amendment); Dusch v. Davis, *supra* note 51; Burns v. Richardson, *supra* note 49. At-large elections have sometimes been considered a desirable solution to the corruption of "ward politics." See E. Banfield & J. Wilson, City Politics 151 (1963). See generally New York State Cities, Towns,

by an entire area, rather than single members being elected from sub-districts within the area) does not constitute invidious discrimination per se.[57] But the Court indicated, in some cases in the 1960's involving state bodies, that a multi-member system of representation might be found violative of equal protection if it could be shown to minimize or cancel out the voting strength of a minority group that, under a single-member system, would be able to assert its voting power.[58] In a 1973 case involving state legislative districts, the use of multi-member districts was ruled invalid where it was shown that the system had the effect of making the nomination and election process not equally open to participation by certain minority groups.[59] There is also authority that any at-large system is unconstitutional if adopted with the *intent* of furthering discrimination against a particular race or group.[60]

The general rule remains that at-large and multi-member districts, on the state or local level, are not necessarily invalid.[61] To establish the unconstitutionality of such a

---

Villages, and School Districts and the Challenge of Growing Population Diversity, 5 Alb. Gov't L. Rev. 733 (2012).

As to staggered elections, see Comment, One-Person, No-Vote: Staggered Elections, Redistricting, and Disenfranchisement, 121 Yale L. J. 2013 (2012).

[57] Whitcomb v. Chavis, 403 U.S. 124, 91 S.Ct. 1858, 29 L.Ed.2d 363 (1971), on remand 57 F.R.D. 32 (D.C.Ind.), noted 26 Ark. L. Rev. 75 (1972), 85 Harv. L. Rev. 135 (1971), 5 Ind. L.F. 167 (1971), 50 N.C.L. Rev. 104 (1971), 3 Seton Hall L. Rev. 178 (1971).

[58] Burns v. Richardson, *supra* note 49; Fortson v. Dorsey, 379 U.S. 433, 85 S.Ct. 498, 13 L.Ed.2d 401 (1965), noted 33 Geo. Wash. L. Rev. 1127 (1965), 1965 U. Ill. L. F. 596. See generally Stahl, The Artifice of Local Growth Politics: At-Large Elections, Ballot-Box Zoning, and Judicial Review, 94 Marq. L. Rev. 1 (2010).

[59] White v. Regester, 412 U.S. 755, 93 S.Ct. 2332, 37 L.Ed.2d 314 (1973), conformed to 378 F.Supp. 640 (W.D.Tex.) (multi-member Texas legislative districts invalidated), noted 23 De Paul L. Rev. 821 (1974), 41 U. Chi. L. Rev. 398 (1974), 13 Washburn L.J. 124 (1974). Cf. Wallace v. House, 377 F.Supp. 1192 (W.D.La.1974), aff'd in part, rev'd in part 521 F.2d 816 (5th Cir.), reh. denied 521 F.2d 816, vac'd 425 U.S. 947, 96 S.Ct. 1721, 48 L.Ed.2d 191, on remand 538 F.2d 1138, reh. denied 541 F.2d 282, cert. denied 431 U.S. 965, 97 S.Ct. 2921, 53 L.Ed.2d 1060 (at-large system of electing town aldermen found to discriminate against black citizens).

[60] Cherry v. County of New Hanover, 489 F.2d 273 (4th Cir.1973) (staggered-term voting system in North Carolina county upheld absent a showing that system was adopted in order to further racial discrimination). Cf. Gomillion v. Lightfoot, 364 U.S. 339, 81 S.Ct. 125, 5 L.Ed.2d 110 (1960); Howard v. Adams County Board of Supervisors, 453 F.2d 455 (5th Cir.1972), cert. denied 407 U.S. 925, 92 S.Ct. 2461, 32 L.Ed.2d 812; Sims v. Baggett, 247 F.Supp. 96 (M.D.Ala.1965). But cf. Zimmer v. McKeithen, 485 F.2d 1297, 1304, n. 16 (5th Cir.1973), aff'd 424 U.S. 636, 96 S.Ct. 1083, 47 L.Ed.2d 296, saying that a reapportionment plan cannot be invalidated merely because of the racial motivations of those who devised it. In Rogers v. Herman Lodge, 458 U.S. 613, 102 S.Ct. 3272, 73 L.Ed.2d 1012 (1982), reh. denied 459 U.S. 899, 103 S.Ct. 198, 74 L.Ed.2d 160 (1982), the Court invalidated an at-large voting system in a rural Georgia county in which no black had ever been elected to the county governing body. The Court found that the evidence supported the District Court's conclusion that the at-large system was being maintained for the invidious purpose of diluting the voting strength of the black population and thus violated equal protection. The U.S. Supreme Court has also invalidated a state law disenfranchising persons convicted of crimes involving "moral turpitude" where the law was found to have racially disproportionate impact *and* to have been passed with discriminatory intent. Hunter v. Underwood, 471 U.S. 222, 105 S.Ct. 1916, 85 L.Ed.2d 222 (1985). See generally "Census and Reapportionment" in Freilich, Marshall & Flick, Urban Problems Regenerated: A Twenty-Year View, 22 Urban Law. 537, 540–44 (1990).

[61] Mahan v. Howell, *supra* note 50, at 335, Whitcomb v. Chavis, *supra* note 57; Dusch v. Davis, *supra* note 51; Kilgarlin v. Hill, 386 U.S. 120, 87 S.Ct. 820, 17 L.Ed.2d 771 (1967), reh. denied 386 U.S. 999, 87 S.Ct. 1300, 18 L.Ed.2d 352; Lipscomb v. Jonsson, 459 F.2d 335, 337 (5th Cir.1972). See Washington v. Finlay, 664 F.2d 913 (4th Cir.1981), cert. denied 457 U.S. 1120, 102 S.Ct. 2933, 73 L.Ed.2d 1333 (1982) (finding that at-large system—adopted in 1910 due to abuses of ward system—was not racially motivated held not clearly erroneous). Cf. Ferrell v. State of Oklahoma ex rel. Hall, 339 F.Supp. 73 (W.D.Okl.1972), aff'd 406 U.S. 939, 92 S.Ct. 2045, 32 L.Ed.2d 328, petition for reh. denied 408 U.S. 932, 92 S.Ct. 2489, 33 L.Ed.2d 344; Gunderson v. Adams, 328 F.Supp. 584 (S.D.Fla.1970), aff'd 403 U.S. 913, 91 S.Ct. 2225, 29 L.Ed.2d 692. See generally Freilich, White-Wasson, & Cofer, 1979–1980 Annual Review of Local Government Law: Municipal Liability and Other Certain Uncertainties, 12 Urban Lawyer 577, 649–51 (1980).

system, a challenging group must show that its members are accorded less opportunity than other residents of the area to elect legislators or other officers of their choice.[62] The Supreme Court has indicated that single-member districts may be constitutionally preferable.[63] And this *can* be taken as showing that multi-member districts should be used only if they will afford minorities a *greater* opportunity to participate in the political

---

[62] White v. Regester, *supra* note 59, at 766; Zimmer v. McKeithen, 485 F.2d 1297 (5th Cir.1973), aff'd 424 U.S. 636, 96 S.Ct. 1083, 47 L.Ed.2d 296. See Whitcomb v. Chavis, *supra* note 57, at 149–50. On the evidence required to prove "voter dilution" such as violates Equal Protection, see Cardwell, Voter Dilution and the Standard of Proof, 14 Urban Law. 863 (1982). Cf. Engstrom & McDonald, Quantitative Evidence in Vote Dilution Litigation: Political Participation and Polarized Voting, 17 Urban Law. 369 (1985). See generally Ho, Minority Vote Dilution in the Age of Obama, 47 U. Rich L. Rev. 1041 (2013); Note, Tracking the Court Through a Political Thicket: At-Large Election Systems and Minority Vote Dilution, 23 Urban L. Ann. 227 (1982). Even if the discriminatory *intent* necessary to prove an Equal Protection violation is missing, discriminatory *effect* sufficient to violate the Voting Rights Act of 1965 may sometimes be shown. On the factors to be weighed in determining if the use of multimember districts for a state legislature amounts to a violation of that Act, see Thornburg v. Gingles, 478 U.S. 30, 106 S.Ct. 2752, 92 L.Ed.2d 25 (1986); the extent to which minority group members have been elected to office in the jurisdiction and the extent to which voting is racially polarized are said to be key factors. Compare Clarke v. City of Cincinnati, 40 F.3d 807 (6th Cir.1994), cert. denied 514 U.S. 1109, 115 S.Ct. 1960, 131 L.Ed.2d 851 (1995) (at-large election of council members upheld; insufficient indication of white bloc voting found under *Thornburg*). On the effects of the *Thornburg* case *supra*, see Wildgen, Adding *Thornburg* to the Thicket: The Ecological Fallacy and Parameter Control in Vote Dilution Cases, 20 Urban Law. 155 (1988). Compare Engstrom & McDonald, Definitions, Measurements, and Statistics: Weeding Wildgen's Thicket, 20 Urban Law. 175 (1988); Engstrom & McDonald, Quantitative Evidence in Vote Dilution Litigation, Part II: Minority Coalitions and Multivariate Analysis, 19 Urban Law. 65 (1987). Cf. Brown v. Board of Comm'rs of Chattanooga, 722 F.Supp. 380 (E.D.Tenn.1989) (at-large method of electing city commissioners violated Voting Rights Act). But cf. Baird v. Consolidated City of Indianapolis, 976 F.2d 357 (7th Cir.1992), cert. denied 508 U.S. 907, 113 S.Ct. 2334, 124 L.Ed.2d 246 (1993) (at-large district for election of members of city-county metropolitan council held not a violation of Voting Rights Act even though such districts could be redrawn so as to create another black majority district). See also Loewen & Grofman, Recent Developments in Methods Used in Vote Dilution Litigation, 21 Urban Law. 589 (1989). Valuable comments on vote dilution litigation appear in Volume 22 of The Urban Lawyer: Wildgen, Vote Dilution Litigation and Cold Fusion Technology, 22 Urban Law. 487 (1990); Engstrom: Getting the Numbers Right: A Response to Wildgen, 22 Urban Law. 405 (1990). See also Greene v. Marin County Flood Control & Water Conservation Dist., 49 Cal. 4th 277, 109 Cal. Rptr. 3d 620, 231 P.3d 350 (2010) (state constitutional provision prohibiting property qualification for electors, and the one-person, one-vote requirement rooted in the state and federal equal protection provisions, do not apply to fee and assessment elections conducted by limited purpose government agencies that disproportionally affect certain property owners).

[63] Connor v. Johnson, 402 U.S. 690, 692, 91 S.Ct. 1760, 1762, 29 L.Ed.2d 268 (1971), on remand 330 F.Supp. 521 (S.D.Miss.), reh. denied 403 U.S. 924, 91 S.Ct. 2220, 29 L.Ed.2d 702, vac'd in part and remanded 404 U.S. 549, 92 S.Ct. 656, 30 L.Ed.2d 704, saying, "We agree that when district courts are forced to fashion apportionment plans, single-member districts are preferable to multi-member districts as a general matter." See Wise v. Lipscomb, 437 U.S. 535, 98 S.Ct. 2493, 57 L.Ed.2d 411 (1978), on remand 583 F.2d 212 (5th Cir.), appeal after remand 643 F.2d 319 (court-drawn reapportionment plan should prefer single-member over multi-member districts unless there is strong justification for the contrary).

The Voting Rights Act Amendments of 1982, 42 U.S.C.A. § 1973, outlaw any standard or practice that results in denial or abridgement of a U.S. citizen's right to vote, where such denial occurs due to that person's race or color. Under this law, even single-member districts are not allowed unnecessarily to diminish the voting strength of racial minorities. See Blacksher, Drawing Single-Member Districts to Comply with the Voting Rights Amendments of 1982, 17 Urban Law. 347 (1985). Cf. Houston Lawyers' Ass'n v. Attorney General of Texas, 501 U.S. 419, 111 S.Ct. 2376, 115 L.Ed.2d 379 (1991) (vote dilution provision of Voting Rights Act applies to election of trial judges). See generally Wright, The Bench and the Ballot: Applying the Protections of the Voting Rights Act to Judicial Elections, 19 Fla. St. U.L. Rev. 669 (1992). Compare Holder v. Hall, 512 U.S. 874, 114 S.Ct. 2581, 129 L.Ed.2d 687 (1994), on remand 37 F.3d 1456 (11th Cir.1994) (size of governing body, such as use of single county commissioner rather than multi-member board, not subject to challenge under Voting Rights Act). See generally Ross, The Voting Rights Act: Interpretation of the Statutory Text, the Political Subtext, and the Constitutional Overlay, 26 Urban Law. 723 (1994), noting the trend against an expansive reading of the Voting Rights Act. See also Grofman, Handley & Niemi, Minority Representation and the Quest for Voting Equality (Cambridge Univ. Press 1992), discussing the issue of minority representation since passage of the Voting Rights Act.

process than would single-member districts, or if the multi-member districts would advance some other significant interests of the community.[64] But this may be making too much of the Court's "preference" for single-member districts. It would seem the Court is nonetheless going to uphold multi-member voting unless a resultant and significant denial of impact on the political process is shown.[65]

As to the second question—Normally, the right to vote cannot be limited so as to include only property owners, taxpayers, or other groups determined by wealth, race, sex, education, etc.[66] But an exception has been recognized where certain special function districts are concerned. If the activities of the district are limited in nature and have a disproportionately greater impact on some residents of an area than on others, the right to vote on matters of creation and governance of the district may be limited to those specially affected.[67] Thus, the right to vote for directors of an irrigation district may be

---

[64] Zimmer v. McKeithen, *supra* note 62. See Mahan v. Howell, *supra* note 50. The significant interests of the community that are advanced by the use of multi-member districts must not be rooted in racial discrimination. See Taylor v. McKeithen, 407 U.S. 191, 194, 92 S.Ct. 1980, 1982, 32 L.Ed.2d 648, conformed to 499 F.2d 893 (5th Cir.) (1972). See generally Parker, County Redistricting in Mississippi: Case Studies in Racial Gerrymandering, 44 Miss. L.J. 391 (1973).

[65] See Recent Cases, 87 Harv.L.Rev. 1851, 1859 (1974). Cf. Turner v. McKeithen, 490 F.2d 191 (5th Cir.1973) (proposal for reapportionment of school board and police jury unconstitutionally diluted the potential for political participation by black community). The Supreme Court has also upheld continued use of "super-majority" requirements in elections, at least if the required majority is not so large as to give a veto power to a small group. See City of Eastlake v. Forest City Enterprises, Inc., 426 U.S. 668, 96 S.Ct. 2358, 49 L.Ed.2d 132 (1976) (55% requirement for approval of change in land use); Gordon v. Lance, 403 U.S. 1, 91 S.Ct. 1889, 29 L.Ed.2d 273 (1971) (60% approval of bonded indebtedness or tax increase). See also Section 4.2 note 44 *infra* and accompanying text. In City of Port Arthur v. United States, 459 U.S. 159, 103 S.Ct. 530, 74 L.Ed.2d 334 (1982), the Court upheld a plan that included at-large election of some members of the city council but approved the District Court holding that the majority-vote requirement as to the at-large council seats must be eliminated as a reasonable hedge against the possibility that the plan contained a purposefully discriminatory element. On the validity of majority-, rather than plurality-, vote requirements and the use of runoff elections, see generally McDonald, Butler, Theodoulou, Stekler & Godwin, The Majority Vote Requirement and Runoff Elections, 17 Urban Law, 429 (1985). A good discussion of super-majority requirements is Symposium, *Guinn v. Legislature of Nevada*, 4 Nev. L.J. 491–572 (2004); see particularly Johnson, Supermajority Provisions, *Guinn v. Legislature* and a Flawed Constitutional Structure; *id.* at 491.

[66] City of Phoenix v. Kolodziejski, 399 U.S. 204, 90 S.Ct. 1990, 26 L.Ed.2d 523 (1970) (voting on municipal general-obligation bonds cannot be limited to taxpayers); Cipriano v. City of Houma, 395 U.S. 701, 89 S.Ct. 1897, 23 L.Ed.2d 647 (1969) (voting on revenue bonds cannot be limited to taxpayers); Burrey v. Embarcadero Municipal Improvement District, 5 Cal.3d 671, 97 Cal.Rptr. 203, 488 P.2d 395 (1971) (voting in "improvement district" that was really a general function unit could not be limited to landowners). In general, limitations on the right to vote that are based on age, residence or citizenship can be upheld if supported by a rational purpose; but other limitations require a compelling state interest. See Harper v. Virginia State Board of Elections, 383 U.S. 663, 86 S.Ct. 1079, 16 L.Ed.2d 169 (1966); Gray v. Sanders, 372 U.S. 368, 83 S.Ct. 801, 9 L.Ed.2d 821 (1963). Cf. City of Seattle v. State, 103 Wash.2d 663, 694 P.2d 641 (1985) (state did not have compelling interest in granting greater voting rights to property owners in annexation proceedings; statute invalidated). But cf. Snead v. City of Albuquerque, 663 F.Supp. 1084 (D.N.M.1987), judgment aff'd 841 F.2d 1131 (10th Cir.1987), cert. denied 485 U.S. 1009, 108 S.Ct. 1475, 99 L.Ed.2d 704 (1988), upholding a constitutional provision and statute giving nonresident property owners living within a county the right to vote on the creation of municipal indebtedness.

[67] Associated Enterprises, Inc. v. Toltec Watershed Improvement District, 410 U.S. 743, 93 S.Ct. 1237, 35 L.Ed.2d 675 (1973) (upholding Wyoming statute limiting the vote on creation of a watershed district to landowners and weighting the voting according to acreage owned). See Avery v. Midland County, *supra* note 52, at 483–84, noting the possibility that special function units (as opposed to general function ones) might accord more voting power to the citizens most affected by the organization's activities. In Petition of Lower Valley Water & Sanitation Dist., 96 N.M. 532, 632 P.2d 1170 (1981), the court found that a water and sanitation district, which had power to levy ad valorem taxes and to administer health services, was of general interest; therefore, restriction of voting rights on any basis other than age, residence or citizenship would be invalid if not supported by a compelling state interest. But here the restriction applied at the stage of petitioning to create a new district—25% of the taxpaying electors of a proposed sewage district must sign a

limited to landowners within the area.[68] The impact of this exception will only become clearer with further interpretation; but it is questionable whether the exception can be extended much beyond irrigation districts and units principally concerned with land and other natural resources.[69]

---

petition. Since the petition was a step removed from the actual voting process, the court concluded that a rational justification would suffice to sustain the "taxpaying electors" limitation, and such justification was here found. Cf. Southern Cal. Rapid Transit Dist. v. Bolen, 1 Cal.4th 654, 3 Cal.Rptr.2d 843, 822 P.2d 875 (1992), cert. denied 505 U.S. 1220, 112 S.Ct. 3031, 120 L.Ed.2d 901 (1992), where rapid transit special benefit assessment districts were ruled to be special-purpose units of government and a voting scheme by which only owners of commercial real property located in the proposed districts would be allowed to vote on district creation was upheld as reasonably related to legislative objectives.

[68] Salyer Land Co. v. Tulare Lake Basin Water Storage District, 410 U.S. 719, 93 S.Ct. 1224, 35 L.Ed.2d 659 (1973). See Ball v. James, 451 U.S. 355, 101 S.Ct. 1811, 68 L.Ed.2d 150 (1981) (voting in elections for directors of agricultural improvement and power district could be limited to landowners, with votes essentially apportioned according to acreage owned). Cf. Millis v. Board of County Commissioners, 626 P.2d 652 (Colo.1981) (excluding out-of-state property owners from voting on a water-district matter while granting that right to Colorado residents who own property within the district, but do not live therein, does not violate 14th Amendment). See generally Martin, "One Person, One Vote" and California's Water Districts, 8 Nat.Res.Law. 9 (1975).

[69] See Sato & Van Alstyne, Local Government Law 46 (2d ed. 1977), questioning whether, if the *Salyer* case, *supra* note 68, is limited to irrigation districts, there is adequate judicial recognition that the activities of such districts will also affect downstream, or other, users of the water supply. See generally The Supreme Court, 1972 Term, 87 Harv.L.Rev. 57, 94–105 (1973). So far, the one-person one-vote rule has not been extended to invalidating appointed, rather than elected, local boards and officers. See Sailors v. Board of Educ., *supra* note 51; Nahmod, Reflections on Appointive Local Government Bodies and a Right to an Election, 11 Duquesne L.Rev. 119 (1972). Cf. People ex rel. Younger v. County of El Dorado, 5 Cal.3d 480, 96 Cal.Rptr. 553, 487 P.2d 1193 (1971) (upholding statute providing for regional planning agency with governing body made up entirely of appointed members; one-person one-vote principle found inapplicable to appointed body even if it has legislative powers). See also Donahue v. Secretary of the Commonwealth, 403 Mass. 363, 530 N.E.2d 792 (1988) (one-person one-vote principle does not require election of a county court clerk by all the citizens of the state rather than just one county even though the clerk acts as clerk for the single justice of the state's Supreme Judicial Court when the single justice sits in Boston).

Chapter 4

LIMITS ON STATE CONTROL OF MUNICIPALITIES: INHERENT HOME RULE

Analysis

§ 4.1 History of Inherent Home Rule

In the late 19th century, and early years of the 20th, a few courts, mostly in the Midwest, endorsed "an extra-constitutional doctrine" known as inherent home rule.[1] This doctrine states that, quite apart from any constitutional or statutory provisions allowing home rule to cities that are granted their own charter, a city has a natural, "inherent" right to govern its own affairs where purely local matters are concerned. The doctrine requires a distinction to be made between matters of purely municipal or local import, and those of general, statewide concern. As to the former, the city is entitled to be free of state interference, and the city's laws will prevail over state law in cases of conflict. As to matters of statewide concern, however, the city is subordinate to the state, and in situations of conflict, state law will prevail over that of the municipality.[2]

---

[1] Mandelker, Managing Our Urban Environment 259 (2d ed. 1971).

[2] McBain, The Doctrine of an Inherent Right of Local Self-government, 16 Colum.L.Rev. 190, 299 (1916), noting that the doctrine has been generally rejected. See Eaton, The Right to Local Self-Government, 13 Harv.L.Rev. 441, 570, 638 (1900); 14 Harv.L.Rev. 20, 116 (1900). See generally Dillon, Municipal Corporations § 99 (5th ed. 1911); 2 McQuillin, Municipal Corporations § 4.82 (3d rev. ed. 1996). See also Schouler, Self-Rule in the Cities, 20 Yale L.J. 463 (1911).

This doctrine was endorsed in Michigan in 1871,[3] and was at one time or another clearly adopted by Indiana,[4] Iowa,[5] and Kentucky.[6] Montana has recognized the right of cities to inherent home rule where their proprietary affairs (*i.e.*, those of a corporate or business nature, as opposed to those of a governmental nature) are involved.[7] The Texas Court of Criminal Appeals once embraced the doctrine,[8] but in the same year the Texas Supreme Court rejected it.[9] There are old dicta in California,[10] Nebraska,[11] and North Carolina[12] that support inherent home rule. A series of three Oklahoma cases in the 1930's approved of the doctrine,[13] but the statements in the latter two were clearly dicta. And the first of the Oklahoma cases would really seem to stand for a right of majority rule, rather than inherent home rule, as the court there invalidated a law requiring a 60% affirmative vote to authorize the sale of a municipal light and power plant on the ground this was in conflict with a fundamental principle of governance by majority vote.[14]

The inherent home-rule principle may be based on the theory that a natural right of local self-government goes with legislative creation of a municipal corporation. It is sometimes also said that the right of local self-government is one of those retained by or reserved to the people under the 9th and 10th amendments to the U.S. Constitution.[15] In making the necessary distinction under this doctrine between matters of local concern and those of statewide import, courts may utilize the related distinction between

---

3 People ex rel. Le Roy v. Hurlbut, 24 Mich. 44 (1871). Cf. City of Detroit v. Detroit & Howell Plank-Road Co., 43 Mich. 140, 5 N.W. 275 (1880). But see McBain, *supra* note 2, at 192–96.

4 City of Logansport v. Public Service Commission, 202 Ind. 523, 177 N.E. 249 (1931); State ex rel. Jameson v. Denny, 118 Ind. 382, 21 N.E. 252 (1889). See State ex rel. Schroeder v. Morris, 199 Ind. 78, 155 N.E. 198 (1927), recognizing inherent home-rule but holding that this principle did not invalidate a state law on municipal fire-department employees, as this had to do with matters of statewide concern (health and safety).

5 State ex rel. White v. Barker, 116 Iowa 96, 89 N.W. 204 (1902); State ex rel. Howe v. Mayor of Des Moines, 103 Iowa 76, 72 N.W. 639 (1897) (statute struck down giving power to determine tax to local library board; legislature cannot delegate power of municipal taxation to a board not responsible to electorate of municipality). But cf. State ex rel. Witter v. Forkner, 94 Iowa 1, 62 N.W. 772 (1895) (liquor law not unconstitutional merely because it delegated to the people in certain cities the power to repeal or abrogate its provisions, as act did not depend on popular vote to give it validity but only to determine limits of its operation). Statutes (such as those involved in State ex rel. Howe, *supra*) giving local bodies taxing powers are also sometimes declared invalid on the ground they delegate unrestricted authority. See Wilson v. Philadelphia School District, 328 Pa. 225, 195 A. 90 (1937).

6 City of Lexington v. Thompson, 113 Ky. 540, 68 S.W. 477 (1902) (statute fixing pay of members of city fire department held invalid). Cf. Orr v. Bracken County, 81 Ky. 593 (1884) (turnpike company). But cf. Campbell v. Board of Trustees, 235 Ky. 383, 31 S.W.2d 620 (1930) (statute requiring city to levy tax to create firemen's pension fund violated state constitutional provision forbidding state from imposing tax for municipal purposes).

7 State of Montana ex rel. Kern v. Arnold, 100 Mont. 346, 49 P.2d 976 (1935). Cf. Helena Consolidated Water Co. v. Steele, 20 Mont. 1, 49 P. 382 (1897) (applying state constitutional provision forbidding state from imposing on a municipality any new liability with respect to past transactions or considerations).

8 Lewis, 45 Tex.Cr.R. 1, 73 S.W. 811 (1903).

9 Brown v. Galveston, 97 Tex. 1, 75 S.W. 488 (1903).

10 People v. Lynch, 51 Cal. 15 (1875).

11 State ex rel. Attorney General v. Moores, 55 Neb. 480, 76 N.W. 175 (1898).

12 Asbury v. Town of Albemarle, 162 N.C. 247, 78 S.E. 146 (1913).

13 Bartlesville Water Co. v. Brann, 166 Okl. 251, 27 P.2d 345 (1933); City of Ardmore v. Excise Board, 155 Okl. 126, 8 P.2d 2 (1932); Thomas v. Reid, 142 Okl. 38, 285 P. 92 (1930).

14 Thomas v. Reid, *supra* note 13. See Recent Cases, 44 Harv.L.Rev. 133 (1930).

15 See State ex rel. White v. Barker, *supra* note 5.

governmental activities and proprietary activities. Thus, as a rule of thumb, governmental matters may be considered of statewide concern, as they are matters in which the city acts as a kind of agency of the state. Proprietary matters, on the other hand, are those in which the city, by definition, is acting in much the same role as a private business, as, for instance, when the city operates a water utility. These proprietary matters may be considered as a general rule to be of purely local concern.[16]

In those relatively few cases actually applying inherent home rule, the situation presented was often that of the state legislature attempting to create and/or appoint boards or agencies to deal with local matters, such as operation of a city utility.[17] It is understandable that both local governments and state courts might rebel against this interference, but inherent home rule is not essential to overthrowing such actions. Today the interference could often be invalidated under state constitutional prohibitions of special legislation or of state commissions to deal with municipal property, such as are discussed in the following chapter. The need for a doctrine of inherent home rule has also been lessened by the adoption in most states of constitutional or statutory methods under which certain qualifying cities may obtain a home-rule charter. When such a charter is obtained, the effect is then much the same as if inherent home rule were applied: state law prevails as to statewide matters but city law prevails as to matters of purely municipal concern.[18]

§ 4.2 General Rejection of Concept; Its Continuing Significance

The doctrine of inherent home rule has now been clearly rejected in almost all U.S. jurisdictions and may thus be considered of little contemporary significance.[19] But it has been noted that it has a "persistence in the romantic literature of local government law"[20] that often requires contrary citations simply to establish the principle's current non-existence.

Even where a state legislature has attempted to establish a board of water commissioners for a city, or some other body to operate a city utility, the inherent home-rule doctrine has been generally rejected.[21] Many cases affirm the supremacy of the state

---

[16] Dillon, Municipal Corporations § 58 (5th ed. 1911). See Kansas City v. Marsh Oil Co., 140 Mo. 458, 41 S.W. 943 (1897). Cf. Proprietors of Mount Hope Cemetery v. City of Boston, 158 Mass. 509, 33 N.E. 695 (1893) (city could not be compelled by state to transfer, without compensation, cemetery which it owned to a new corporation); City of Newport v. Horton, 22 R.I. 196, 47 A. 312 (1900) (recognizing right of local self-government but finding that law authorizing state governor to appoint board of police commissioners—who in turn appointed police chief—did not infringe such right since police chief was state, not local, officer). See generally Doddridge, The Distinction Between Governmental and Proprietary Functions of Municipal Corporations, 23 Mich.L.Rev. 325 (1925).

[17] Mandelker, Managing Our Urban Environment 259 (2d ed. 1971). Examples include City of Logansport v. Public Service Commission, 202 Ind. 523, 177 N.E. 249 (1931) (appointment by the governor); State ex rel. Jameson v. Denny, *supra* note 4; State ex rel. White v. Barker, *supra* note 5.

[18] See 1 Antieau, Municipal Corporation Law §§ 3.14–.21 (1998); Bromage, Home Rule Puzzle, 46 Nat'l Mun.Rev. 118 (1957); Walker, Toward a New Theory of Municipal Home Rule, 50 Nw.U.L.Rev. 571 (1955). See generally Jones, "Municipal Affairs" in the California Constitution, 1 Cal.L.Rev. 132 (1912).

[19] See Rhyne, Municipal Law § 4.2, at 61–62 (1957), with list of relevant cases.

[20] Mandelker, *supra* note 17.

[21] Coyle v. Gray, 12 Del. 44, 30 A. 728 (1884) (board of water commissioners established for city of Wilmington). Cf. Datisman v. Gary Public Library, 241 Ind. 83, 170 N.E.2d 55 (1960) (act providing method of

legislature and its laws over the city government and its enactments.[22] Most states that once endorsed inherent home rule have repudiated it. In Michigan, where inherent home-rule originated, it would seem largely rejected by the holding that all municipalities are subject to the general laws of the state and the indication that the only recognized "home rule" is that accorded by the state constitution.[23] Similarly in Indiana, the doctrine would appear to have little remaining importance, since it has been held that the state legislature may prescribe the manner of selection for, and the duties of, municipal officers.[24] In Iowa, the doctrine has now been discarded.[25] In Texas, the theory was cast out by the state supreme court almost as soon as another court in that state had endorsed it.[26] Nebraska long ago rejected any early indication that it might adopt the doctrine.[27] Since the 1930's, Oklahoma cases have often asserted the supremacy of the state legislature and thus impliedly ruled against inherent home rule.[28] Modern California and North Carolina cases seem squarely opposed to the doctrine.[29] The Kentucky Court of Appeals has announced its rejection.[30] Montana,

---

appointing local library board). See also McQuillin, Limitations of Legislative Control of Municipal Corporations, 34 Am.L.Rev. 505, 510–15 (1900), favoring inherent home-rule in such situations.

22 Amyot v. Caron, 88 N.H. 394, 190 A. 134 (1937); Booth v. McGuinness, 78 N.J.L. 346, 75 A. 455 (1910); State ex rel. City of Minot v. Gronna, 79 N.D. 673, 59 N.W.2d 514 (1953); City of Providence v. Moulton, 52 R.I. 236, 160 A. 75 (1932); Madison Metropolitan Sewerage District v. Committee on Water Pollution, 260 Wis. 229, 50 N.W.2d 424 (1951). The power of the state legislature to force a municipality to pay a nonbinding demand, where an equitable obligation exists, has even been recognized. Forman v. Sewerage & Water Board, 135 La. 1031, 66 So. 351 (1914) (but legislature cannot compel payment where is no moral or equitable obligations); McBain, The Law and Practice of Home Rule 24–25 (1916). But it has been held in a few cases, and said in a number of others, that due process prevents a state from compelling a city to levy a tax or incur a debt for a purely local purpose. See McBain, Due Process of Law and the Power of the Legislature to Compel a Municipal Corporation to Levy a Tax or Incur a Debt for a Strictly Local Purpose, 14 Colum.L.Rev. 407 (1914). Cf. 1 Dillon, Municipal Corporations §§ 119–20 (5th ed. 1911). This doctrine may be considered an actual recognition of some degree of inherent home-rule. See Fordham, Local Government Law 57 (rev. ed. 1975). See generally Davison, Leaps and Bounds, 108 Mich. L. Rev. 957 (2010), reviewing Frug & Barron, City Bound: How States Stifle Urban Innovation (Cornell Univ. Press 2008).

23 City of Highland Park v. Fair Employment Practices Commission, 364 Mich. 508, 111 N.W.2d 797 (1961) (city held subject to state fair employment practices legislation).

24 Datisman v. Gary Public Library, *supra* note 21. Cf. City of South Bend v. Krovitch, 149 Ind.App. 438, 273 N.E.2d 288 (1971), rejecting inherent home rule and saying local autonomy theory is now practically nonexistent in Indiana.

25 See Maddy v. City Council, 226 Iowa 941, 285 N.W. 208 (1939) (powers of city derived solely from legislative grant).

26 Brown v. Galveston, 97 Tex. 1, 75 S.W. 488 (1903), rejecting Ex parte Lewis, 45 Tex.Cr.R. 1, 73 S.W. 811 (1903). See McBain, The Doctrine of an Inherent Right of Local Self-Government, 16 Colum.L.Rev. 190, 206 (1916). The Texas Court of Criminal Appeals, which applied the doctrine in the *Lewis* case, *supra*, and the Texas Supreme Court, which rejected the doctrine in the *Brown* case, *supra*, had equal authority in the state judicial system. *Id.* But the inherent home-rule doctrine seems clearly rejected in Texas today. See State ex rel. Burnet County v. Burnet County Hospital Authority, 495 S.W.2d 300 (Tex.Civ.App.1973), ref'd n. r. e.

27 Redell v. Moores, 63 Neb. 219, 88 N.W. 243 (1901).

28 See City of Claremore v. Oklahoma Tax Commission, 197 Okl. 223, 169 P.2d 299 (1946); City of McAlester v. Grand Union Tea Co., 186 Okl. 487, 98 P.2d 924 (1940). Cf. Ex parte Higgs, 97 Okl.Cr. 338, 263 P.2d 752 (1953) (statute authorizing municipalities to prohibit Sunday sale of beer for on-premises consumption did not authorize prohibition of such sales for *off*-premises consumption).

29 See Golden Gate Bridge & Highway District v. Felt, 214 Cal. 308, 5 P.2d 585 (1931); Town of Highlands v. Hickory, 202 N.C. 167, 162 S.E. 471 (1932).

30 Board of Trustees v. City of Paducah, 333 S.W.2d 515 (Ky.1960). See Warley v. Board of Park Commissioners, 233 Ky. 688, 26 S.W.2d 554 (1930); Board of Trustees v. Schupp, 223 Ky. 269, 3 S.W.2d 606 (1928), in both of which the Court of Appeals appeared to reject inherent home rule without the clear overruling of prior authority that is contained in the later *City of Paducah* case *supra*. Cf. Campbell v. Board of Trustees, 235 Ky. 383, 31 S.W.2d 620 (1930), where it is noted that the leading Kentucky case on inherent home-rule

which formerly applied the doctrine in proprietary matters, now appears to reject it.[31] All the above-mentioned states, now including even Kentucky and North Carolina,[32] have constitutional provisions or broad statutes allowing cities wide home-rule powers. Thus, the need for a principle of *inherent* home rule is greatly diminished. And such a doctrine may be considered inconsistent with the governmental framework in the United States, under which it is the states, not the municipalities, that have reserved areas of power under the federal Constitution.[33]

But the doctrine may be thought to have some continuing influence, particularly in states that once indicated approval of inherent home rule. In California, for instance, the distinction between municipal affairs and matters of statewide concern persists under a 1970 revision of the state constitution.[34] The distinction is, under modern law, simply applied if, and only if, a particular city has obtained a home-rule charter, rather than as a matter of *right* inherent in all municipalities. This local-v.-statewide distinction continues to be applied, under constitutional or statutory home rule, in many other states, and may occasionally persist partly because of early cases recognizing inherent

---

could have been based instead on a specific constitutional provision. The last important assertion of inherent home-rule in Kentucky occurred in a 1940 Court of Appeals case, Board of Aldermen v. Hunt, 284 Ky. 720, 145 S.W.2d 814 (1940).

[31] The older Montana view is illustrated by State of Montana ex rel. Kern v. Arnold, 100 Mont. 346, 49 P.2d 976 (1935) (inherent home rule applies to *proprietary* affairs, including some aspects of fire department operations). But Montana's Constitution now provides for municipal home rule (Mont. Const. Art. XI, §§ 5–6 (1972)), and its statutes provide the details of the form of government for municipalities with home-rule charters (Mont. Stat. Ann. §§ 7–3–701–09 (1997)). Apart from the home-rule powers granted under these state laws, there would appear to be no home rule now in Montana even in proprietary areas. See Leischner v. Knight, 135 Mont. 109, 337 P.2d 359 (1959) (as to operation of water system, cities have only the powers granted or implied by statute). But Montana does still broadly interpret the proprietary powers of cities that have, via state constitution and statutes, obtained home rule. See Lechner v. City of Billings, 244 Mont. 195, 797 P.2d 191 (1990) (although Montana statutes don't specifically provide for municipality to impose system development fees in order to fund expansion of water and sewer system, municipality's power to institute such system must be liberally construed, resolving all doubts in favor of finding the power).

[32] Kentucky cities may be classified by the Legislature under Ky.Const. § 156a and are divided into 6 classes by Ky.Rev.Stat. 81.010. Powers of cities of the first class are provided by Ky.Rev.Stat. 83.420, 83.430 & 83.440 (board of aldermen). Other classes of cities are dealt with in 82.081 & 82.082. See Commonwealth v. Beasy, 386 S.W.2d 444 (Ky.1965) (city of first class could enact penal anti-discrimination ordinance). Cf. Hyman v. Boldrick, 153 Ky. 77, 154 S.W. 369 (1913), (upholding city ordinance regulating hours of operation of pawnbrokers, secondhand dealers, and junk merchants). See generally Keiper v. City of Louisville, 152 Ky. 691, 154 S.W. 18 (1913).

Powers of North Carolina cities are provided by N.C.Gen.Stat. § 160A–1, 160A–4 (provisions of charters to be broadly construed), 160A–11 (corporate powers). As to older North Carolina law, see State v. Furio, 267 N.C. 353, 148 S.E.2d 275 (1966) (city is agency of state and has no governmental power except as granted by legislature); Starbuck v. Town of Havelock, 252 N.C. 176, 113 S.E.2d 278 (1960); Stephenson v. City of Raleigh, 232 N.C. 42, 59 S.E.2d 195 (1950) (municipal corporation is political subdivision of state); State v. Dannenberg, 150 N.C. 799, 63 S.E. 946 (1909) (doubt concerning municipal power is resolved against its existence). Cf. Conover v. Jolly, 277 N.C. 439, 177 S.E.2d 879 (1970) (no inherent police power in city); Gunter v. Sanford, 186 N.C. 452, 120 S.E. 41 (1923) (municipality controls matters of special municipal concern).

[33] See McBain, The Doctrine of an Inherent Right of Local Self-Government, 16 Colum.L.Rev. 190, 299 (1916). But see Eaton, The Origin of Municipal Incorporation in England and the United States, 25 Rep.Am.Bar Ass'n 292 (1902), supporting the doctrine. See generally McQuillin, Constitutional Right of Local Self-Government of Municipalities, and Principles Applicable to Central Control, 35 Am.L.Rev. 510 (1901).

[34] Cal.Const. Art. 11, § 5. This was done despite the criticism, by a justice of the state supreme court at an early date, that the words "municipal affairs" are "impossible." Ex parte Braun, 141 Cal. 204, 213, 74 P. 780, 784 (1903). See Jones, "Municipal Affairs" in the California Constitution, 1 Calif.L.Rev. 132 (1912). See generally Peppin, Municipal Home Rule in California III, 32 Calif.L.Rev. 341 (1944) & Municipal Home Rule in California IV, 34 Calif.L.Rev. 644 (1946).

home rule.[35] When applied, the distinction is generally drawn in order to determine whether state law or municipal law governs, in situations of conflict between the two, where the city has enacted some law pursuant to authorization in its charter. But some authority goes farther and holds that as to matters of purely local concern, a city with a home-rule charter is completely free of state control and may do anything not *forbidden* by its charter. Under this view, the charter is, as to matters of purely local concern, only a limitation on city power, not a grant of power, and the city may act despite charter silence.[36]

It has been observed[37] that, under inherent home rule, the further distinction between governmental and proprietary affairs has also sometimes been employed, with the former considered of statewide import and the latter of only municipal concern. There is no doubt that the governmental-proprietary dichotomy has continuing importance, though this would seem to be entirely independent of and unaffected by the distinction's use in inherent home rule. This distinction is often still employed, for instance, in the area of municipal tort liability, with the municipality being potentially liable under common law for its proprietary activities but not its governmental.[38]

The state, it is generally held, may use its power of eminent domain to condemn without compensation the property of a municipality within that state, if the property was held by the city in its governmental capacity. But if property held by the city in its proprietary capacity is condemned by the state, compensation must be awarded.[39]

---

35 See Vanlandingham, Municipal Home Rule in the United States, 10 Wm. & Mary L.Rev. 269 (1968). The distinction between municipal affairs and statewide ones has proven difficult and has not produced uniform results among the various states as to any given subject. See Sato, "Municipal Affairs" in California, 60 Cal.L.Rev. 1055, 1058 (1972); Westbrook, Municipal Home Rule: An Evaluation of the Missouri Experience, 33 Mo.L.Rev. 45, 76 (1968). See generally Mott, Strengthening Home Rule, 39 Nat'l Mun.Rev. 172 (1950). It has been observed that the term "municipal affairs" is really capable of no fixed meaning and inevitably fluctuates with changing conditions. Rhyne, Municipal Law 64 (1957). See also Sandalow, The Limits of Municipal Power under Home Rule: A Role for the Courts, 48 Minn. L.Rev. 643 (1964), urging a broad grant of home-rule power, though with the state legislature clearly remaining supreme.

36 See Wiley v. City of Berkeley, 136 Cal.App.2d 10, 288 P.2d 123 (Dist.Ct.1955); State ex rel. McClure v. Hagerman, 155 Ohio St. 320, 98 N.E.2d 835 (1951). See generally Owens, Comparative Powers of Charter and Non-Charter Municipalities Under Ohio Home Rule, 9 Ohio St.L.J. 121 (1948). But most courts treat the municipal charter as a *grant* of power and hold that the municipality's acts must be authorized by the home-rule charter or by general state laws. See 2 McQuillin, Municipal Corporations § 10.09 (3d ed. 1966 rev.). Indeed, the criticism has been made that many courts are too strict in their interpretation of charter powers. See Winter, Municipal Home Rule: A Progress Report?, 36 Neb.L.Rev. 447 (1957).

37 See note 16 *supra* and accompanying text. Cf. Green v. City of Amarillo, 244 S.W. 241 (Tex.Civ.App.1922), aff'd 267 S.W. 702 (Tex.Com.App.). See generally Ruud, Legislative Jurisdiction of Texas Home Rule Cities, 37 Tex.L.Rev. 682, 687 (1959). But see Oregon ex rel. Heinig v. City of Milwaukie, 231 Or. 473, 483 n. 16, 373 P.2d 680, 685–86 n. 16 (1962), rejecting the use of the governmental-v.-proprietary distinction in determining what matters are of local concern and what of statewide.

38 See Antieau, The Tort Liability of American Municipalities, 40 Ky.L.J. 131 (1951); Fuller & Casner, Municipal Tort Liability in Operation, 54 Harv.L.Rev. 437 (1971); Seasongood, Municipal Corporations: Objections to the Governmental or Proprietary Test, 22 Va.L.Rev. 910 (1936). See generally Barnett, The Foundations of the Distinction between Public and Private Functions in Respect to the Common-Law Tort Liability of Municipal Corporations, 16 Or.L.Rev. 250 (1937). See also Chapter 26 *infra*.

39 People ex rel. Department of Public Works v. City of Los Angeles, 220 Cal.App.2d 345, 33 Cal.Rptr. 797 (Dist.Ct.1963); Town of Winchester v. Cox, 129 Conn. 106, 26 A.2d 592 (1942); Parr, State Condemnation of Municipally-Owned Property: The Governmental-Proprietary Distinction, 11 Syracuse L.Rev. 27 (1959). See generally 11 McQuillin, Municipal Corporations § 32.72 (3d rev. ed. 1991); 26 Am.Jur.2d Eminent Domain §§ 178–79 (1966). Counties, on the other hand, are mere agencies of the state, and the state may take, damage, or transfer county property without compensation, regardless of the nature of the property's use. See Board of Education v. Martin, 92 Cal. 209, 28 P. 799 (1891); City of Edwardsville v. Madison County, 251 Ill. 265, 96

And property held by a city for public use in a governmental capacity, as for a park, cannot be disposed of by the city unless (1) there is specific legislative authorization, or (2) the public use has been abandoned, or (3) the property has become unsuitable or inadequate for the public use to which it had been put.[40] Where, however, the city owns property in its proprietary capacity, as in connection with the operation of a utility, no such limitations exist as to disposing of that property.[41]

In the above-mentioned areas, and numerous others, the governmental-proprietary distinction continues to be employed, despite its vagueness; and it will be encountered again and again.[42] But this distinction, of course, was only a "rule-of-thumb" guide sometimes employed under inherent home-rule, and the guide's continued significance gives no new life to the inherent home-rule doctrine itself. And while the municipal-v.-

---

N.E. 238 (1911); Heffner v. Cass & Morgan Counties, 193 Ill. 439, 62 N.E. 201 (1901). The same is true of special function districts. See Reclamation Dist. No. 1500 v. Superior Court, 171 Cal. 672, 154 P. 845 (1916). It has often been held in general terms that the state legislature may direct a transfer of public property from one public entity to another without compensation. Reclamation District No. 70 v. Birks, 159 Cal. 233, 113 P. 170 (1911) (transfer of land-district property to newly created reclamation district); Chester County Institution District v. Commonwealth, 341 Pa. 49, 17 A.2d 212 (1941) (compelled transfer of mental health institutions from county districts to state). This "change of management" or "change of trustees" theory has occasionally been used to justify an uncompensated transfer of even municipally owned property to another governmental entity without regard to the possible proprietary nature of the municipality's use of the property. See Monaghan v. Armatage, 218 Minn. 108, 15 N.W.2d 241 (1944), appeal dism'd 323 U.S. 681, 65 S.Ct. 436, 89 L.Ed. 552 (1945) (transfer of municipal airport to airport commission); Hickey v. Burke, 78 Ohio App. 351, 69 N.E.2d 33 (1946), appeal dism'd 147 Ohio St. 217, 70 N.E.2d 274 (transfer of city psychopathic hospital to state).

In Department of Transp. v. City of Atlanta, 255 Ga. 124, 337 S.E.2d 327 (1985), the court found that the state Department of Transportation lacked authority to condemn property owned by a city and dedicated to a public use, such as park land. The court emphasized that the state had the power of eminent domain over city property and *could* authorize the Department of Transportation to exercise that power, but the relevant statute gave the Department the power to condemn only private property, and that grant did not cover acquisition of city park lands. See also Jobe v. Weyerhaeuser Co., 37 Wash.App. 718, 684 P.2d 719 (1984) (state statute entitling private person's to condemn an easement under certain circumstances could not be used to justify a private person's condemning of state or city land).

[40] Opinion of the Justices to the Senate, 369 Mass. 979, 338 N.E.2d 806 (1975) (holding unconstitutional a statute authorizing city to construct public school on park land); State ex rel. Remy v. Agar, 559 P.2d 1235 (Okl.1977) (city could not sell land used for city dump where use had not been abandoned or become unsuitable); Board of County Commissioners v. Mullins, 202 Okl. 628, 217 P.2d 835 (1950). Sometimes this restriction is based on a conveyance of the property to the municipality for specified purposes, as in the *Opinion of the Justices, supra*, or on an actual dedication to public use, as in the *Mullins* case *supra*; but the rule has even been applied where there is no evidence of conveyance in trust or of a public dedication, as in the *Agar* case, *supra*. But cf. Fielding v. Board of Education, 76 N.J.Super. 50, 183 A.2d 767 (1962), aff'd 39 N.J. 85, 187 A.2d 599 (use of parkland for school held valid where city held park in fee and not under any trust). Even where the city clearly holds land in trust, or under a dedication to public use, exceptions are occasionally recognized to the restrictions on transfer. See City of Wilmington v. Lord, 340 A.2d 182 (Del.Super.1975) (city, acting through water department, could condemn part of city golf course for water tank); Paepcke v. Public Building Commission, 46 Ill.2d 330, 263 N.E.2d 11 (1970) (under statute, park land could be diverted to other recreational uses or school purposes if original public uses not greatly impaired); Sharp v. City of Guthrie, 49 Okl. 213, 152 P. 403 (1915) (legislature can relieve city from trust obligation and authorize sale). See generally Sax, The Public Trust Doctrine in Natural Resource Law: Effective Judicial Intervention, 68 Mich.L.Rev. 471 (1970). See also People v. Holladay, 93 Cal. 241, 29 P. 54 (1892), appeal dism'd 159 U.S. 415, 16 S.Ct. 53, 40 L.Ed. 202 (municipal lands dedicated to public use cannot be acquired by private persons through adverse possession).

[41] See City of Northglenn v. City of Thornton, 193 Colo. 536, 569 P.2d 319 (1977) (waterworks property not held in trust). On the governmental-v.-proprietary distinction as applied to sale and other disposition of municipal property, see also Chapter 19 *infra*.

[42] See Doddridge, The Distinction between Governmental and Proprietary Functions of Municipal Corporations, 23 Mich. L.Rev. 325 (1925).

statewide distinction also persists, this—whatever its origins might owe to inherent home rule—is now a creature of judicial interpretation of statutes and constitutions.

One of the cases approving of inherent home rule[43] actually applied a principle that might more accurately be called "majority rule," and struck down a statute that required a 60% affirmative vote for sale of municipal electric plants. Majority rule is, of course, a separate matter from inherent home-rule, and the majority-rule principle might still be applied under some state constitutions. However, the U.S. Supreme Court has held that the federal Constitution is not violated by state laws requiring a greater than majority vote for certain measures to be passed or steps taken.[44] So the majority-rule principle would, like inherent home-rule, now seem of very limited use in striking down state statutes.

Some limitations on state power over cities may be inferred from the very existence of cities and of our democratic form of government—but these limitations are rare. It has, for instance, been suggested that the state cannot direct a city to use property in ways inconsistent with the purposes for which it was acquired, or to take property without compensating those from whom it is taken, or to transfer public property to private persons or private uses.[45] Even these limitations would seem inferable not only from our governmental framework but also from constitutional provisions that exist in most states. Thus, "inherent" limitations on state control of municipalities are at best extremely few in number—and are such as to be of little use since they almost surely duplicate limitations that can be found more clearly spelled-out in written laws. The overwhelming majority view, then, is that any right of a municipality to control its own affairs is not an inherent right but is dependent on the legislative will or some specific constitutional provision.

---

[43] Thomas v. Reid, 142 Okl. 38, 285 P. 92 (1930). The statute involved in this case has been amended so as to require only a majority vote. 11 Okl. Stat.1981, § 35–201–02.

[44] Gordon v. Lance, 403 U.S. 1, 91 S.Ct. 1889, 29 L.Ed.2d 273 (1971) (60% approval of bonded indebtedness or tax increase). See City of Eastlake v. Forest City Enterprises, Inc., 426 U.S. 668, 96 S.Ct. 2358, 49 L.Ed.2d 132 (1976) (changes in land use had to be approved by 55% vote in referendum). Cf. Gray v. Town of Darien, 927 F.2d 69 (2d cir.1991), cert. denied 502 U.S. 856, 112 S.Ct. 170, 116 L.Ed.2d 133 (1991) (town charter required that those wishing to reverse an action of the Town Meeting must obtain not only a majority of votes cast in a referendum but must also obtain the vote of 25% of all enrolled municipal electors; held constitutional).

[45] Coyle v. Gray, 12 Del. 44, 30 A. 728 (1884). Occasionally, the due process clause of the Fourteenth Amendment to the United States Constitution has been found to prevent transfer of city property to private uses. See Proprietors of Mount Hope Cemetery v. City of Boston, 158 Mass. 509, 33 N.E. 695 (1893). But cf. Opinion of the Justices, 323 Mass. 759, 79 N.E.2d 889 (1948) (advisory opinion) (would not be taking without due process for legislature to force cities to quit selling cemetery monuments). The possible use of the contract clause of the U.S. Constitution to prevent legislative interference with city property is explored by McBain, The Rights of Municipal Corporations under the Contract Clause of the Federal Constitution, 3 Nat'l Mun. Rev. 284 (1914).

Chapter 5

LIMITS ON STATE CONTROL OF MUNICIPALITIES: SPECIFIC CONSTITUTIONAL LIMITATIONS

Analysis

§ 5.1 General Rule of Complete State Control

As the doctrine of inherent home rule, discussed in Chapter 4 *supra*, has been almost universally rejected, municipalities in the United States are subject to the complete control of the states in which they are located except as such control is limited by constitutional provisions.[1] State control of cities and towns has been described as "plenary."[2] And, although municipalities are sometimes distinguished from public quasi-corporations, such as counties—with the former said to exist for purposes of local self-government and the latter only for purposes of state administration—, the distinction becomes largely meaningless where the degree of state control is the issue: even municipalities are then considered mere political subdivisions of the state.[3] Thus, the state may take away the powers of municipalities,[4] may transfer their functions to other

[1] Barnes v. District of Columbia, 91 U.S. 540, 23 L.Ed. 440 (1876); Opinion of the Justices, 323 Mass. 759, 79 N.E.2d 889 (1948); Town of Lisbon v. Lisbon Village District, 104 N.H. 255, 183 A.2d 250 (1962); Elizabethton v. Carter County, 204 Tenn. 452, 321 S.W.2d 822 (1958). Cf. Northwestern School District v. Pittenger, 397 F.Supp. 975 (W.D.Pa.1975) (municipality has no rights under the U.S. Constitution which it may invoke against its creator state). On state control of municipalities and limits thereon, see generally Hill, State Laws Governing Local Government Structure and Administration (Univ. of Ga. 1978). See also Zimmerman, State-Local Relations—A Partnership Approach (Praeger Press 1983), also discussing the federal government's influence on state-local relations.

[2] State v. City of Boca Raton, 172 So.2d 230, 232 (Fla.1965). Cf. Pumphrey v. City of Baltimore, 47 Md. 145 (1877). See generally Libonati, Intergovernmental Relations in State Constitutional Law: A Historical Overview, 496 Annals 107 (1988).

[3] See Becker v. Adams, 37 N.J. 337, 181 A.2d 349 (1962) (state legislative control of cities is almost unlimited); Mountlake Terrace v. Wilson, 15 Wn.App. 392, 549 P.2d 497 (1976) (city is mere political subdivision of state and cannot challenge state retirement-system statute).

[4] Jefferson County v. City of Anchorage, 393 S.W.2d 608 (Ky.1965).

governmental units,[5] and may turn their property over to other governmental entities without making compensation.[6]

The Contract Clause of the United States Constitution has been held to accord a municipality no protection against repeal or amendment of its governing charter by the state.[7] Nor does the Privileges and Immunities Clause of that Constitution apply to state action affecting municipalities.[8] The same is true of the Equal Protection Clause so long as no rights of third persons are involved.[9] Even the Due Process Clause of the Federal Constitution has usually been found to have no application to actions taken against a municipality by its parent state.[10] The Due Process Clauses of *state* constitutions may

---

[5] Cobo v. O'Bryant, 116 So.2d 233 (Fla.1959).

[6] Higginson v. Treasurer, 212 Mass. 583, 99 N.E. 523 (1912); People v. Kerr, 27 N.Y. 188 (1863). See Robertson v. Zimmermann, 268 N.Y. 52, 196 N.E. 740 (1935) (city sewer system turned over to public authority). Cf. Enger v. Colorado Airport Authority, 181 Colo. 253, 508 P.2d 1245 (1973) (city and county property turned over to airport authority).

[7] See Hunter v. Pittsburgh, 207 U.S. 161, 28 S.Ct. 40, 52 L.Ed. 151 (1907); Covington v. Kentucky, 173 U.S. 231, 19 S.Ct. 383, 43 L.Ed. 679 (1899) (holding that statute conferring tax exemptions on city was not contract within Contract Clause); Meriwether v. Garrett, 102 U.S. 472, 26 L.Ed. 197 (1880). Cf. Pawhuska v. Pawhuska Oil & Gas Co., 250 U.S. 394, 39 S.Ct. 526, 63 L.Ed. 1054 (1919) (no violation of Contract Clause where state withdrew city's power to regulate utility rates); Williamson v. New Jersey, 130 U.S. 189, 9 S.Ct. 453, 32 L.Ed. 915 (1889) (grant of power of taxation to city can be withdrawn without violating Contract Clause); Safety Harbor v. Birchfield, 529 F.2d 1251 (5th Cir.1976) (state can authorize annexation even where such act would violate contract between cities involved).

The situation is different, however, where rights of third parties, not just the state and the municipality, are concerned. Thus, it has been held if the state has given a city the power of taxation in order to pay off its bonds and bonds are thereafter purchased by individuals in reliance on the city's power, the state cannot, without providing an adequate substitute, take away or interfere with this power of taxation of the city. Wolff v. New Orleans, 103 U.S. 358, 26 L.Ed. 395 (1880); Von Hoffman v. Quincy, 71 U.S. (4 Wall.) 535, 18 L.Ed. 403 (1886). Cf. State ex rel. Markel v. Columbus, 139 Ohio St. 351, 40 N.E.2d 144 (1942).

[8] Williams v. Mayor & City Council of Baltimore, 289 U.S. 36, 53 S.Ct. 431, 77 L.Ed. 1015 (1933); Marshfield v. Towns of Cameron, 24 Wis.2d 56, 127 N.W.2d 809 (1964). See generally Town of Chino Valley v. State Land Department, 119 Ariz. 243, 580 P.2d 704 (1978) (municipality cannot invoke personal rights of its citizens against the state).

[9] Newark v. New Jersey, 262 U.S. 192, 43 S.Ct. 539, 67 L.Ed. 943 (1923) (city sought to avoid payment of state water charge not applied to all cities in state); State ex rel. Zilisch v. Auer, 197 Wis. 284, 221 N.W. 860 (1928). Cf. State ex rel. Spink v. Kemp, 365 Mo. 368, 283 S.W.2d 502 (1955). But state exercises of control over municipalities might be attacked where rights of third persons under the Equal Protection Clause may have been violated. See Rimarcik v. Johansen, 310 F.Supp. 61 (D.Minn.1970), vac'd 403 U.S. 915, 91 S.Ct. 2222, 29 L.Ed.2d 691, appeal dism'd 403 U.S. 914, 91 S.Ct. 2222, 29 L.Ed.2d 691. Cf. Gomillion v. Lightfoot, 364 U.S. 339, 81 S.Ct. 125, 5 L.Ed.2d 110 (1960) (state action denying black citizens the right to vote). In Washington v. Seattle School Dist. No. 1, 458 U.S. 457, 102 S.Ct. 3187, 73 L.Ed.2d 896 (1982), a school board successfully invoked the Equal Protection Clause to invalidate a Washington State initiative measure that barred the use of mandatory busing for purposes of racial integration. The State of Washington continues, however, to adhere to the general rule that a local government has no rights against the State under the Equal Protection Clauses of the state and federal constitutions. See City of Seattle v. State, 103 Wash.2d 663, 694 P.2d 641 (1985) (city has no rights itself but has standing to raise equal protection claims of its potential residents challenging statute that allows property owners to block annexation of those potential residents). See generally Libonati, Do Local Governments Have Rights?, 10 Urban, State & Local L. Newsletter No. 3, at1, 12 (Summer, 1987); Kushner, Government Discrimination: Equal Protection Law and Litigation (Clark Boardman Co. 1988). See also Alaska Inter-Tribal Council v. State of Alaska, 110 P.3d 947 (Alaska 2005) (residents of "off-road," predominantly Alaska Native communities, who sued the state for allegedly violating their equal protection rights by adopting a discriminatory system of law enforcement, failed to establish a prima facie case of discrimination based on race, and thus the burden of persuasion was properly placed on the residents rather than the state). On suits by local units against the state, see Note, Subdivisions, Standing and the Supremacy Clause: Can a Political Subdivision Sue Its Parent State Under Federal Law?, 103 Mich. L. Rev. 1899 (2005).

[10] See City of Trenton v. New Jersey, 262 U.S. 182, 43 S.Ct. 534, 67 L.Ed. 937 (1923); Associated Hospital Service, Inc. v. City of Milwaukee, 13 Wis.2d 447, 109 N.W.2d 271 (1961). Cf. Board of Levee Comm'rs v. Huls, 852 F.2d 140 (5th Cir.1988) (agency of state—in this case, the levee board created by Louisiana to

occasionally be found to prevent the state's acquiring without compensation municipal property held in a private (or "proprietary") capacity,[11] but this result is often based at least partly on interpretations of the state constitutional provisions limiting exercises of the power of eminent domain.[12] Certainly, state constitutional Due Process Clauses give municipalities few if any rights against the parent state where anything other than private ownership of property by such municipalities is concerned.

Thus, such protection as a city or town may have against state action must usually be derived from the fairly specific restrictions, found in most state constitutions, that are squarely aimed at state control of municipalities. A considerable assortment of such restrictions can be found in the various state constitutions,[13] but most can be placed in one of six categories[14]—or a final category of Home Rule Provisions, to be discussed in Chapter 6 *infra*.

§ 5.2 Requirement of Local Consent to Street Franchise

The first type of restriction commonly encountered in state constitutions and relating to state power over municipalities is a requirement that no street franchise be granted without local consent. The term "franchise," as used in this sense, means the right of a public utility (such as gas, electric, water, or telephone companies) to use the public streets and ways for such purposes as the laying of pipes or stringing of wires[15]—some purpose other than that of travel, which is the primary intended use of such ways.[16] These provisions mean that the state legislature, or some other state body or official, cannot grant a utility a franchise as to local streets without obtaining the permission of the locality's government. Many of these constitutional restrictions apply only to the

---

protect New Orleans from flooding by Mississippi River—cannot sue the parent state under the Fifth and Fourteenth Amendments for an uncompensated taking of property in alleged violation of due process). But a city in one state can attack on due process grounds the ordinance of a city in another state, since that state is not the city's "parent." Township of River Vale v. Town of Orangetown, 403 F.2d 684 (2d Cir.1968), noted 83 Harv.L.Rev. 679 (1969).

[11] Shirk v. Lancaster City, 313 Pa. 158, 169 A. 557 (1933); Sossamon v. Greater Gaffney Metropolitan Utilities Area, 236 S.C. 173, 113 S.E.2d 534 (1960) (state legislature cannot, without compensation, appropriate city water system for use of other governmental units). See Proprietors of Mt. Hope Cemetery v. Boston, 158 Mass. 509, 33 N.E. 695 (1893) (legislature could not compel Boston to turn cemetery over to private corporation without compensation); People ex rel. Board of Detroit Park Commissioners v. Common Council, 28 Mich. 228 (1873). But see Commonwealth of Pennsylvania v. Westmoreland-Fayette Municipal Sewage Authority, 18 Pa.Cmwlth. 555, 336 A.2d 704 (1975).

[12] See Shirk v. Lancaster City, 313 Pa. 158, 169 A. 557 (1933). It was the traditional rule that property held by the city in its public or governmental capacity can be condemned and taken by the parent-state without compensation. See In re Condemnation of Land by Pennsylvania Turnpike Commission, 347 Pa. 643, 32 A.2d 910 (1943), overruled by Specter v. Com., 462 Pa. 474, 341 A.2d 481 (1975). Cf., questioning the traditional rule, State v. Cooper, 24 N.J. 261, 131 A.2d 756 (1957), cert. denied Cooper v. State of N.J., 355 U.S. 829, 78 S.Ct. 41, 2 L.,Ed.2d 42 (1957).

[13] See 2 McQuillin, Municipal Corporations ch. 4 (3d rev. ed. 1996); Fordham, Local Government Law 58–69 (2d rev. ed. 1986); Sturm, Thirty Years of State Constitution Making 107 (1970). See generally Columbia Univ., Constitutions of the United States—National and State (1962); Winters, State Constitutional Limitations (1961).

[14] See Stason & Kauper, Municipal Corporations 25–30 (3d ed. 1959).

[15] Oklahoma Gas & Electric Co. v. Total Energy, Inc., 499 P.2d 917 (Okl.1972) (no franchise from municipality needed where utility was not using public streets in its distribution and sale of electricity).

[16] See Nelson v. Duquesne Light Co., 338 Pa. 37, 12 A.2d 299 (1940). Cf. In re Grand River Dam Authority, 484 P.2d 505 (Okl.1971). See generally 26 Am.Jur.2d Eminent Domain § 212 (1966).

granting of franchises to street railroads, since these are considered a particularly extreme interference with other uses of the streets.[17]

Except as limited by the above-described constitutional provisions, the power to grant street franchises within, as well as outside, municipalities rests with the state.[18] The granting of such franchises is a matter of statewide concern, and thus state law will prevail over conflicting city laws on the subject even where the city has its own home-rule charter.[19] Where the state constitution does contain the above-described requirement of local consent, state law prevails as to the manner in which the consent is to be granted.[20] Further, the city acquires no power from such a constitutional provision to regulate the rates of utilities operating within the city—a matter that is normally left to the control of the state.[21]

Even where the state constitution does not prohibit the granting of franchises within a municipality without local consent, control over granting and denying such franchises is often delegated by statute (or occasionally, to some extent, by constitutional provision) to the municipalities, since this is obviously an area of great local interest.[22]

---

[17] See Fordham, Local Government Law 64 (2d rev. ed. 1986). Such a limited provision may be taken as meaning that local consent is *not* necessary to the state's granting of franchises other than for street railroads even though local streets are to be used. City of Tulsa v. Southwestern Bell Telephone Co., 75 F.2d 343 (10th Cir.1935), cert. denied 295 U.S. 744, 55 S.Ct. 656, 79 L.Ed. 1690 (1935) (doctrine of expressio unius leads to conclusion that Oklahoma constitutional requirement applies only to street railroads since only they are mentioned). But Oklahoma constitutional and statutory provisions on the method of awarding *all* franchises have been treated by that *state's* courts as always requiring local consent. See State ex rel. Williamson v. Garrison, 348 P.2d 859 (Okl.1959); In re Okmulgee Gas Co., 141 Okl. 98, 284 P. 70 (1930); Oklahoma Natural Gas Corp. v. State, 141 Okl. 80, 284 P. 40 (1930). See generally, with a list of the various "franchise" provisions of state constitutions, Stason & Kauper, Municipal Corporations 26 (3d ed. 1959).

[18] Elizabeth City v. Banks, 150 N.C. 407, 64 S.E. 189 (1909) (city cannot grant franchise without state legislative authority). See Water, Light & Gas Co. v. Hutchinson, 207 U.S. 385, 28 S.Ct. 135, 52 L.Ed. 257 (1907) (statutes granting cities power to award franchises are strictly construed). See generally 2 McQuillin, Municipal Corporations § 4.155 (3d rev. ed. 1996) & 12 McQuillin, Municipal Corporations §§ 34.13–.14 (3d rev. ed. 1995).

[19] Overholser v. Oklahoma Interurban Traction Co., 29 Okl. 571, 119 P. 127 (1911) (city may not violate state laws on voter approval of franchise and limit on duration, but mere enlargement of facility did not require voter approval). See City of Sapulpa v. Oklahoma Natural Gas Co., 79 Okl. 196, 192 P. 224 (1920), error dism'd, 258 U.S. 608, 42 S.Ct. 316, 66 L.Ed. 788 (1922) (city acts as agent of state in granting franchise); Henry v. Bartlesville Gas & Oil Co., 33 Okl. 473, 126 P. 725 (1912) (franchise void where violated state law limiting such grants to domestic pipeline companies); Nugent v. City of East Providence, 103 R.I. 518, 238 A.2d 758 (1968) (city has no inherent power to grant right to use streets). Cf. Subriar v. City of Bakersfield, 59 Cal.App.3d 175, 130 Cal.Rptr. 853 (Dist.Ct.1976) (authority of city to grant exclusive franchise for specific period of time does not exist unless authorized by state statute or city charter); St. Joe Natural Gas Co. v. City of Ward Ridge, 265 So.2d 714 (Fla.App.1972) (city cannot grant exclusive franchise except as authorized by state legislature); City of Tyler v. Television Cable Service, Inc., 493 S.W.2d 322 (Tex.Civ.App.1973), ref'd n. r. e. (under state statute, only city commission had power to grant franchise).

[20] City of Tyler v. Television Cable Service, Inc., *supra* note 19 (city charter provisions requiring voter approval of franchise were void where they conflicted with state statutes giving power of approval to governing authorities of city). As to the procedure for granting franchises, see generally 36 Am.Jur.2d Franchises § 15, at 737–38 (1968).

[21] See City of Kalamazoo v. Titus, 208 Mich. 252, 175 N.W. 480 (1919); City of Kalamazoo v. Kalamazoo Circuit Judge, 200 Mich. 146, 166 N.W. 998 (1918). The subject of utility rate regulation is one of statewide concern, and thus one on which state law will prevail over conflicting laws of even home-rule cities; and sometimes, sole power as to such regulation has been vested in the state, with the cities then having *no* regulatory powers in this regard. See City of Jackson v. Consumers Power Co., 312 Mich. 437, 20 N.W.2d 265 (1945).

[22] See 36 Am.Jur.2d Franchises § 11 (1968). Cf. Blair v. City of Chicago, 201 U.S. 400, 26 S.Ct. 427, 50 L.Ed. 801 (1906); Mobile v. Louisville & Nashville Railroad Co., 84 Ala. 115, 4 So. 106 (1888) (municipality

§ 5.3 Prohibition of State Interference with Local Streets

Somewhat similar to, but broader in nature than, the constitutional limits on state franchises mentioned *supra*, are provisions found in several state constitutions forbidding state interference with local streets and highways. Most such prohibitions apply to vacation or alteration of local streets by the state government; in a few states, the restriction extends also to the establishment of local streets. And in some states, the restriction is now merely one part of the general proscription on "special" legislation,[23] discussed *infra*.

In the absence of constitutional limitations, control of municipal streets, even in home-rule cities, rests with the state legislature. While state control is paramount, some of this power is very often delegated by the state legislature to the various cities and towns.[24] The delegated power, however, is generally interpreted as not exclusive against the state; and in cases of conflict, state law will still prevail over that of the municipality as to control of major traffic arteries.[25] Clearly, a city's delegated power in this regard is also subject to constitutional requirements that the municipality must always act for the public benefit and cannot vacate a street merely for the benefit of a private individual.[26]

While the idea of some local control of streets dates at least to the early 1800's in this country, it is entirely consistent with modern concepts of local planning. Thus, the power to *establish* streets is often expressly conferred and may be readily inferred from more general grants of municipal power;[27] is sometimes held, in the case of home-rule cities, to be exclusive of any state power in this regard;[28] and has been held to include

---

acts as agent for state); Albuquerque Bus Co. v. Everly, 53 N.M. 460, 211 P.2d 127 (1949); People v. O'Brien, 111 N.Y. 1, 18 N.E. 692 (1888) (constitution confers on municipalities the power to grant franchises); Salt Lake on Track v. Salt Lake City, 939 P.2d 680 (Utah 1997) (state statutes empower city to permit a third party to install a railroad on city streets, either by granting a franchise by ordinance or by granting "use rights" for rapid transit by a resolution); State ex rel. Attorney General v. Madison Street Railway Co., 72 Wis. 612, 40 N.W. 487 (1888). Some state constitutions require local consent to the *operation* of a utility within municipal limits, even if a street franchise is not needed by the utility. See Alabama Power Co. v. Citizens of Alabama, 527 So.2d 678 (Ala.1988), interpreting such a provision and finding that a statewide system of assigning territories to electric suppliers did not violate the cities' right to consent.

[23] See 2 McQuillin, Municipal Corporations § 4.35 (3d rev. ed. 1996). Cf. Stason & Kauper, Municipal Corporations 27 (3d ed. 1959) (with list of constitutional provisions).

[24] See Martin v. Rowlett, 185 Okl. 431, 93 P.2d 1090 (1939) (municipality has only such control as delegated by the state). See generally 2 McQuillin, *supra* note 23, pointing out, at § 4.147, that the delegation of control over streets to the municipalities is sometimes made by the state constitution itself. But a delegation of this power will not be inferred merely from general constitutional provisions granting rights of local self-government and home rule to municipalities. Whalen v. Wagner, 2 Misc.2d 89, 152 N.Y.S.2d 386 (1956), aff'd 3 A.D.2d 936, 163 N.Y.S.2d 225, aff'd 4 N.Y.2d 575, 176 N.Y.S.2d 616, 152 N.E.2d 54.

[25] Allen v. State Highway Commissioner, 338 Mich. 407, 61 N.W.2d 625 (1953) (parking regulation of state as applied to "trunk highway" prevailed over city's authorization of parking). Sometimes, city and state regulations may be found not to conflict and may co-exist. Lincoln Park Coach Co. v. City of Detroit, 295 Mich. 189, 294 N.W. 149 (1940) (though state had given inter-city bus carrier a permit to use city streets, city could make a reasonable designation of the route that the carrier must follow). And the power of a home-rule city to *establish, lay out,* and *improve* city streets is often held superior to the state's. See Section 6.5, note 71 and accompanying text, *infra*.

[26] City of Stillwater v. Lovell, 159 Okl. 214, 15 P.2d 12 (1932).

[27] See 10A McQuillin, Municipal Corporations § 30.31 (3d rev. ed. 1999).

[28] City of San Jose v. Lynch, 4 Cal.2d 760, 52 P.2d 919 (1935); Village of Perrysburg v. Ridgway, 108 Ohio St. 245, 140 N.E. 595 (1923); Wilson v. City of Medford, 107 Or. 624, 215 P. 184 (1923).

the power to change the grade of a street.[29] *Improvement* of city streets is also a power readily inferred in favor of the cities, and may be considered exclusive in a city that has a home-rule charter.[30] Regulation of traffic (as by speed limits, etc.) is, on the other hand, generally a matter of statewide concern; any municipal power is shared with the state, and state law will prevail in situations of conflict.[31]

Whatever title the municipality holds to public streets and ways, it holds in trust for public use.[32] Very often the city will not have full fee title to a street or other way, but only an easement for limited purposes.[33] This is the usual result where the city has, by eminent domain, condemned land for street purposes. But if land is otherwise conveyed to the city, the city *will* normally acquire fee ownership despite any recitation in the deed that the property is conveyed for use as a street or for other public purposes.[34] In any case, the city's interest in the street or way—whatever the extent of that interest—is held subject to state supervision, limited only by specific constitutional restrictions on the state's power.[35]

§ 5.4 Requirement of Local Election or Appointment of Local Officers

A third limitation on state power over municipalities found in some state constitutions requires local election or appointment of local officers.[36] Such a provision

---

[29] See Edwards v. Thrash, 26 Okl. 472, 109 P. 832 (1910). Cf. City of Los Angeles v. Central Trust Co., 173 Cal. 323, 159 P. 1169 (1916) (opening, laying out, and regulating streets are matters of much greater concern to local inhabitants than to people of state-at-large and are thus municipal affairs).

[30] Blake v. City of Eureka, 201 Cal. 643, 258 P. 945 (1927); Salsbury v. City of Lincoln, 117 Neb. 465, 220 N.W. 827 (1928). See Gadd v. McGuire, 69 Cal.App. 347, 231 P. 754 (Dist.Ct.1924) (street improvement is purely municipal affair if special benefits therefrom are limited to city inhabitants or property owners, but not otherwise). Cf. Ambrister v. City of Norman, 344 P.2d 665 (Okl.1959) (traffic arteries serving a dual purpose as both streets within city and as portions of state highway system may be improved by either city or state independently, or by both jointly).

[31] Ex parte Daniels, 183 Cal. 636, 192 P. 442 (1920); City & County of Denver v. Pike, 140 Colo. 17, 342 P.2d 688 (1959); People v. Interstate Dress Carriers, Inc., 203 Misc. 883, 120 N.Y.S.2d 370 (Ct. of Spec.Sess.1953). See Pipoly v. Benson, 20 Cal.2d 366, 125 P.2d 482 (1942); Bruce v. Ryan, 138 Minn. 264, 164 N.W. 982 (1917). Cf. Opinion to House of Representatives, 79 R.I. 277, 87 A.2d 693 (1952) (state may legislate concerning parking meters even on purely local street of home-rule municipality). It has been observed that though regulation of street traffic may once have been of only local concern, this situation changed—and the matter became of more general concern—with the advent of the automobile. Mervynne v. Acker, 189 Cal.App.2d 558, 11 Cal.Rptr. 340 (Dist.Ct.1961); Omaha Parking Authority v. City of Omaha, 163 Neb. 97, 77 N.W.2d 862 (1956) (alleviation of street congestion, as by off-street parking, is of statewide concern).

[32] Bond v. City of Pasadena, 6 Cal.2d 139, 56 P.2d 946 (1936); Hirsh v. Oklahoma City, 94 Okl.Cr. 249, 234 P.2d 925 (1951); Industrial Co. v. Tompkins, 27 S.W.2d 343 (Tex.Civ.App.1930), error ref'd. See 2 McQuillin, Municipal Corporations § 4.148 (3d rev. ed. 1996).

[33] Woodville v. United States, 152 F.2d 735 (10th Cir. 1946), cert. denied 328 U.S. 842, 66 S.Ct. 1021, 90 L.Ed. 1617 (1946). Cf. City of Norman v. Ballard, 202 Okl. 93, 210 P.2d 340 (1949). See generally 10A McQuillin, Municipal Corporations § 30.32 (3d rev. ed. 1999).

[34] McClain v. Oklahoma City, 192 Okl. 4, 133 P.2d 198 (1943).

[35] People v. Kerr, 27 N.Y. 188 (1863).

[36] See 1 Antieau, Municipal Corporation Law § 2.12 (1998). 2 McQuillin, Municipal Corporations § 4.118–.119 (3d rev. ed. 1996); Stason & Kauper, Municipal Corporations 26–27 (3d ed. 1958), all containing lists of the relevant provisions. Good discussions of a typical provision are found in New York cases: Bareham v. City of Rochester, 246 N.Y. 140, 158 N.E. 51 (1927), modifying 221 App.Div. 36, 222 N.Y.S. 141 (1927), which modified 128 Misc. 642, 220 N.Y.S. 66 (1927); People ex rel. Town of Pelham v. Village of Pelham, 215 N.Y. 374, 109 N.E. 513 (1915); People ex rel. Metropolitan Street Railway Co. v. State Board of Tax Commissioners, 174 N.Y. 417, 67 N.E. 69 (1903), aff'd 199 U.S. 1, 25 S.Ct. 705, 50 L.Ed. 65, 199 U.S. 48, 25 S.Ct. 713, 50 L.Ed. 79, and 199 U.S. 53, 25 S.Ct. 715, 50 L.Ed. 85.

has been said to be intended to preserve the principle of local self-government.[37] The rule is said in some states to apply only to local offices that existed at the time the state constitution, containing this provision, was adopted.[38] Such a constitutional provision does not preclude the state legislature from creating local offices and boards, defining their duties, and providing for their method of selection, so long as the actual selection is left to electors or officials of the local unit.[39] Indeed, it may be said that in general the *method* of selection of all local officers is a subject properly left to state legislative action.[40] In some states, however, the power to prescribe methods of selection of certain officers and boards is delegated, often by the state constitution itself, to the city council or some other local body.[41]

The actual selection of local officers is clearly a subject that should appropriately be handled by the local unit even if the method for such selection is specified by the state. Thus, where constitutional language does not specifically require election or appointment by local electors or authorities, such a right of local selection may still sometimes be inferred.[42] Similarly, it may be inferred that an elected officer must be, and remain, a resident of the unit he purports to serve or represent.[43] Such rules are

---

[37] Kerr v. City of Louisville, 271 Ky. 335, 111 S.W.2d 1046 (1937); Covington Bridge Commission v. City of Covington, 257 Ky. 813, 79 S.W.2d 216 (1934). See State v. Lafayette Fire Insurance Co., 134 La. 78, 63 So. 630 (1913) (act unconstitutional where it provided for local fire marshall to be appointed by governor). Cf. State ex rel. Burke v. Cervantes, 423 S.W.2d 791 (Mo.1968); Chase v. Burns, 114 R.I. 485, 335 A.2d 334 (1975); State ex rel. Wannemaker v. Alder, 87 Wis. 554, 58 N.W. 1045 (1894); Jones v. Kolb, 56 Wis. 263, 14 N.W. 177 (1882).

[38] This is true in New York. People ex rel. Williamson v. McKinney, 52 N.Y. 374, 378 (1872). Cf. People ex rel. Bolton v. Albertson, 55 N.Y. 50, 56 (1873).

Several jurisdictions have also recognized an exception for state appointment of local officers to serve temporarily, as in an emergency or where a provisional government has to be established for a limited time. State ex rel. Gibbs v. Couch, 139 Fla. 353, 190 So. 723 (1939) (temporary appointment of municipal officers when legislature had abolished former municipal government); Moreland v. Millen, 126 Mich. 381, 85 N.W. 882 (1901) (rule applies only if is necessity for provisional appointment); Stewart v. City of Cheyenne, 60 Wyo. 497, 154 P.2d 355 (1944). See Lambert v. Norman, 119 Ga. 351, 46 S.E. 433 (1904) (legislative act incorporated town and also designated persons to hold certain of the new municipality's offices until successors could be elected). Cf. Daley v. St. Paul, 7 Minn. 390 (1862) (legislature allowed to appoint officers for temporary, specified purpose of laying out street and assessing benefits and damages).

[39] State ex rel. Porterie v. Walmsley, 183 La. 139, 162 So. 826 (1935), appeal dism'd 296 U.S. 540, 56 S.Ct. 141, 80 L.Ed. 384, reh. denied 296 U.S. 663, 56 S.Ct. 246, 80 L.Ed. 473; State v. Voorhies, 169 La. 626, 125 So. 737 (1929). Cf. Mayor of Americus v. Perry, 114 Ga. 871, 40 S.E. 1004 (1902); Vineyard v. City Council, 15 Idaho 436, 98 P. 422 (1908); State ex rel. Faxon v. Owsley, 122 Mo. 68, 26 S.W. 659 (1894). See also Schlientz v. City of North Platte, 172 Neb. 477, 110 N.W.2d 58 (1961) (legislature could subject residents of area outside city to jurisdiction of city officers in whose selection they had no voice).

[40] In re Senate Bill Providing for Board of Public Works, 12 Colo. 188, 21 P. 481 (1889); Bryan v. Landis ex rel. Reeve, 106 Fla. 19, 142 So. 650 (1932); People ex rel. Peterson v. Pollock, 306 Ill. 358, 137 N.E. 820 (1922); Walsh v. City Council, 117 N.J.L. 64, 186 A. 818 (1936). Cf. People v. Chicago Transit Authority, 392 Ill. 77, 64 N.E.2d 4 (1945); Oren ex rel. Maybury v. Bolger, 128 Mich. 355, 87 N.W. 366 (1901).

[41] See Scheafer v. Herman, 172 Cal. 338, 155 P. 1084 (1916) (constitution allows cities to provide in charters for method of selecting local officers); State ex rel. Canada v. Phillips, 168 Ohio St. 191, 151 N.E.2d 722 (1958); State ex rel. Haffner v. Green, 160 Ohio St. 189, 115 N.E.2d 154 (1953); Fitzgerald v. City of Cleveland, 88 Ohio St. 338, 103 N.E. 512 (1913); Cole v. President of the Village of Black River Falls, 57 Wis. 110, 14 N.W. 906 (1883). Cf. People v. Raymond, 37 N.Y. 428 (1868).

[42] People ex rel. Le Roy v. Hurlbut, 24 Mich. 44 (1871). Cf. Scofield v. Strain, 142 Ohio St. 290, 51 N.E.2d 1012 (1943).

[43] Baughman v. Weicker, 136 Okl. 33, 276 P. 208 (1929) (council member who moved out of ward from which elected could not continue to serve). Cf. Franks v. Ponca City, 170 Okl. 134, 38 P.2d 912 (1934) (charter provision that city official must be qualified elector means qualified elector of city). See as to residency requirements Section 13.4 *infra*.

consistent with modern notions of equality in representation of voters, responsibility of officers to those they serve, and local handling of local problems.

§ 5.5 Prohibition of Taxes for Local Purposes

A number of state constitutions either expressly or impliedly prohibit the legislature from levying taxes for local purposes.[44] These again reflect the idea that local problems, and in this case local expenditures, should be dealt with locally, not by the state.[45] Some of these provisions merely say that the state shall not levy taxes on the inhabitants or property in any municipality for municipal purposes, while others include more positive terminology declaring that the state legislature may authorize the municipalities themselves to assess and collect taxes for local (or "corporate") purposes.[46] In either case, the interpretation is generally the same: the state legislature is prevented from levying taxes for functions performed voluntarily by municipalities under their permissive powers, but the legislature may levy taxes for the financing of tasks as to which the municipality acts governmentally and hence as mere agent of the state,[47] such as the paying of jury fees[48] or of penalties for failing to suppress mobs or riots.[49] But where the prohibition applies, it prevents the legislature from burdening municipalities with debts or obligations that necessitate resort to additional taxation.[50]

These state constitutional provisions vary as to the local units to which they apply. Municipalities are covered by all such statements, but some do not cover counties[51] or special function districts.[52] Where the limitation is relevant, it may be used to strike down such state legislation as that requiring the city to support a board of park

---

[44] See, with lists of relevant provisions, 1 Antieau, Municipal Corporation Law § 2.09 (1998); Stason & Kauper, Municipal Corporations 27–78 (3d ed. 1958). Cf. 2 McQuillin, Municipal Corporations § 4.161 (3d rev. ed. 1996).

[45] Walker v. Bedford, 93 Colo. 400, 26 P.2d 1051 (1933). Cf. Obitz v. Airport Authority, 181 Neb. 410, 149 N.W.2d 105 (1967) (airport authority can take property within city so long as no taxes imposed on city, its inhabitants or property for corporate purposes).

[46] See 1 Antieau, Municipal Corporation Law § 2.09 (1998). These latter type provisions, permitting the legislature to authorize municipal taxation for local purposes, have been held not to be self-executing but to require legislation to carry them into effect. King County v. City of Algona, 101 Wash.2d 789, 681 P.2d 1281 (1984).

[47] People ex rel. Cannon v. Chicago, 351 Ill. 396, 184 N.E. 610 (1933); District Board v. Lexington, 227 Ky. 7, 12 S.W.2d 348 (1928); Furlong v. Darnaby, 206 Ky. 63, 257 S.W. 707 (1923); Rogers v. Bass & Harbour Co., 64 Okl. 321, 168 P. 212 (1917).

[48] People ex rel. Chicago v. Board of Commissioners, 355 Ill. 244, 189 N.E. 26 (1934).

[49] Sturges v. Chicago, 237 Ill. 46, 86 N.E. 683 (1908), aff'd 222 U.S. 313, 32 S.Ct. 92, 56 L.Ed. 215.

[50] Darcy v. City of San Jose, 104 Cal. 642, 38 P. 500 (1894); People v. Mayor of Chicago, 51 Ill. 17 (1869). See Metropolitan Utilities District v. Omaha, 112 Neb. 93, 198 N.W. 858 (1924). Cf. Helena Consolidated Water Co. v. Steele, 20 Mont. 1, 49 P. 382 (1897). Such clauses may also, of course, be used to invalidate attempts by a state legislature to delegate the power to tax for municipal purposes to a group not subject to municipal control. People ex rel. Gallenbach v. Franklin, 388 Ill. 560, 58 N.E.2d 555 (1944) (attempt to establish pension plan for city employees, with control in board not chosen by city voters or by method approved by such voters). See Idaho County v. Fenn Highway District, 43 Idaho 233, 253 P. 377 (1926); Hinze v. People ex rel. Halbert, 92 Ill. 406 (1879).

[51] Los Angeles County v. Riley, 6 Cal.2d 625, 59 P.2d 139 (1936) (county not within meaning of "municipal corporations").

[52] Shoshone Highway District v. Anderson, 22 Idaho 109, 125 P. 219 (1912) (highway district); Fenton v. Ada County, 20 Idaho 392, 119 P. 41 (1911) (school district).

commissioners,[53] pay the expenses of a county court,[54] or pay the cost of lowering gas and water mains and relocating hydrants where the work is considered necessary by an independent gas and water authority.[55] But the state may require the local unit to levy a tax for *general* public purposes in which the state as an entirety is interested.[56]

§ 5.6 Prohibition of Commissions to Supervise Local Government

A fifth type of restriction on state power prohibits the legislature from appointing commissions to interfere with or supervise local government. This type of provision originated in Pennsylvania in 1873, after the city of Philadelphia felt it had been mistreated by a legislature-appointed board, and similar prohibitions have since been adopted in several other states.[57] These provisions have been said to reflect a continuing belief in the right of local self-government,[58] and a desire to prevent undue state interference in local affairs.[59] Under such a restriction, courts have invalidated statutes attempting to establish commissions to improve city streets,[60] control municipal buildings,[61] supervise public morals in the cities,[62] or regulate municipally owned utilities.[63] There must generally be found some state attempt to interfere with or control

---

53 State ex rel. Gerry v. Edwards, 42 Mont. 135, 111 P. 734 (1910).

54 Campbell County v. Newport, 174 Ky. 712, 193 S.W. 1 (1917). Cf. McDonald v. City of Louisville, 113 Ky. 425, 68 S.W. 413 (1902) (requiring tax to support disabled firemen).

55 Metropolitan Utilities District v. City of Omaha, 112 Neb. 93, 198 N.W. 858 (1924). Cf. Kenton Water Co. v. City of Covington, 156 Ky. 569, 161 S.W. 988 (1913) (forcing cities to purchase private utilities).

56 Fox v. Board for Louisville & Jefferson County Children's Home, 244 Ky. 1, 50 S.W.2d 67 (1932) (with list); Littell v. City of Peoria, 374 Ill. 344, 29 N.E.2d 533 (1940); Tobin v. La Guardia, 290 N.Y. 119, 48 N.E.2d 287 (1943), motion denied 290 N.Y. 743, 49 N.E.2d 1009 (state may compel city to maintain armory for housing regiment). See Essex County v. City of Newburyport, 254 Mass. 232, 150 N.E. 234 (1926) (city can be required to pay part of cost of county hospital); State ex rel. Helena Housing Authority v. City Council, 108 Mont. 347, 90 P.2d 514 (1939) (city may be required to pay costs of housing authority). Cf. Housing Authority v. City Council, 208 Cal.App.2d 599, 25 Cal.Rptr. 493 (Dist.Ct. 1962) (city, when functioning under Housing Authorities Law, is agency of state).

57 See, with citations to relevant provisions, 1 Antieau, Municipal Corporation Law § 2.11 (1998); Fordham, Local Government Law 63 (2d rev. ed. 1986); Stason & Kauper, Municipal Corporations 28 (3d ed. 1958). The history of these provisions, sometimes called "ripper clauses," is thoroughly discussed in Porter, The Ripper Clause in State Constitutional Law: An Early Urban Experiment—Parts I & II, 1969 Utah L. Rev. 287, 450.

58 Logan City v. Public Utilities Commission, 72 Utah 536, 271 P. 961 (1928). See County Water System v. Salt Lake City, 3 Utah 2d 46, 278 P.2d 285 (1954) (this provision precludes state utility commission regulation of municipal utility even as to sale of surplus water outside city limits).

59 People v. City of Los Angeles, 179 Cal.App.2d 558, 4 Cal.Rptr. 531 (Dist.Ct.1960), appeal dism'd 364 U.S. 476, 81 S.Ct. 243, 5 L.Ed.2d 221, reh. denied 365 U.S. 805, 81 S.Ct. 466, 5 L.Ed.2d 462. In some jurisdictions, the invalidating of state commissions to handle municipal problems was once achieved through use of the "inherent home rule" doctrine, discussed in Chapter 4 *supra*. See Board of Park Commissioners v. Common Council, 28 Mich. 228 (1873). But that doctrine is no longer in favor. While the use of state commissions to handle municipal matters may no longer be so great a problem as it once was, the state of New York in 1971 named a commission to study the finances and operations of New York City and its sub-agencies (and Mayor Lindsay of New York City responded by appointing a commission to study the efficiency of the state government). See N.Y.Times, Aug. 3, 1971, at 1, col. 5.

60 Mellon v. City of Pittsburgh, 31 L.I. 212 (Pa.Dist.Ct.Allegheny Co.1874). Cf. City of Philadelphia v. Spangler, 9 Pa.D. & C. 577 (1927) (commission to operate city parks).

61 Perkins v. City of Philadelphia, 156 Pa. 554, 27 A. 356 (1893).

62 Moll v. Morrow, 253 Pa. 442, 98 A. 650 (1916).

63 Stewart v. City of Cheyenne, 60 Wyo. 497, 154 P.2d 355 (1944). See Logan City v. Public Utilities Comm'n, 72 Utah 536, 271 P. 961 (1928). Cf. City & County of Denver v. Public Utilities Comm'n, 181 Colo. 38, 507 P.2d 871 (1973); People v. City of Loveland, 76 Colo. 188, 230 P. 399 (1924); Holyoke v. Smith, 75 Colo.

municipal property, funds, or functions before a statute will be struck down on this ground.[64]

But despite this kind of restriction, statutes have been upheld if they create an agency that is under the control of *municipal* authorities, since such an agency is not considered within the constitutional intent of preventing interference with local autonomy.[65] And if an agency or commission is charged with the performance of "governmental" or statewide affairs, as opposed to "municipal" matters, the provision is considered inapplicable, as where water, drainage, or sanitation districts are created within the territory of a municipality.[66] Also, if the powers delegated by statute to an agency or commission are considered merely administrative in nature—that is, such as to involve only carrying out an established policy rather than determining policy—, then it is likely that the constitutional prohibition will not be found to have been violated.[67] Under this reasoning, state laws have been upheld that provide for cities to engage in compulsory bargaining with police and fire officers,[68] or that create agencies to supervise the implementation of low-cost housing or urban renewal plans.[69]

§ 5.7 Restrictions on Special Legislation

A sixth limitation on state power over municipalities is one that is found, in some form or other, in most state constitutions—a restriction on special legislation.[70] While

---

286, 226 P. 158 (1924) (Colorado allows state commission to regulate municipal utilities but only as to their operations outside city limits). In Montana and Pennsylvania, these constitutional provisions have been held inapplicable to actions of the state public utility commissions. Public Service Comm'n v. City of Helena, 52 Mont. 527, 159 P. 24 (1916); Borough of Wilkinsburg v. Public Service Comm'n, 72 Pa.Super. 423 (1919).

[64] See Backman v. Salt Lake County, 13 Utah 2d 412, 375 P.2d 756 (1962). Cf. Uhls v. State, 429 P.2d 74 (Wyo.1967).

[65] In re Senate Bill Providing for a Board of Public Works in Denver, 12 Colo. 188, 21 P. 481 (1889); State ex rel. Quintin v. Edwards, 38 Mont. 250, 99 P. 940 (1909) (police commission under control of municipal officials); Belovsky v. Redevelopment Authority, 357 Pa. 329, 54 A.2d 277 (1947). Cf. Walnut & Quince Streets Corp. v. Mills, 303 Pa. 25, 154 A. 29 (1931), appeal dism'd, 284 U.S. 573, 52 S.Ct. 16, 76 L.Ed. 498 (art jury to approve highway structures).

[66] City of Pasadena v. Chamberlain, 204 Cal. 653, 269 P. 630 (1928) (water district); Pixley v. Saunders, 168 Cal. 152, 141 P. 815 (1914) (sanitation district); People ex rel. Rogers v. Letford, 102 Colo. 284, 79 P.2d 274 (1938) (water district); Billings Sugar Co. v. Fish, 40 Mont. 256, 106 P. 565 (1910) (drainage district); Lehi City v. Meiling, 87 Utah 237, 48 P.2d 530 (1935) (water district); Sullivan v. Blakesley, 35 Wyo. 73, 246 P. 918 (1926) (irrigation district). In City of West Jordan v. Utah State Retirement Bd., 767 P.2d 530 (Utah 1988), a statute delegating to the State Retirement Board the responsibility for operating a retirement program covering municipal employees was held not to delegate a "municipal function" to a special commission in violation of the constitutional prohibition. Cf. Winslow Constr. Co. v. City & County of Denver, 960 P.2d 685 (Colo.1998) (Executive Director of state Department of Revenue was not performing "municipal function" within constitutional prohibition when he decided taxpayer's appeal from decision by city's manager of revenue); Utah Associated Municipal Power Systems v. Public Serv. Comm'n, 789 P.2d 298 (Utah 1990) (Interlocal Co-Operation Act did not delegate "municipal function" to Public Service Commission when it required that before political subdivision of state proceeded with construction of electric transmission line it must obtain certificate of public convenience and necessity from Commission).

[67] Uhls v. State, 429 P.2d 74 (Wyo.1967). Cf. Evans v. West Norriton Township Municipal Authority, 370 Pa. 150, 87 A.2d 474 (1952).

[68] State v. Laramie, 437 P.2d 295 (Wyo.1968).

[69] Dornan v. Philadelphia Housing Authority, 331 Pa. 209, 200 A. 834 (1938). See Housing Authority v. Dockweiler, 14 Cal.2d 437, 94 P.2d 794 (1939) (housing authority for slum clearance). Cf. Belovsky v. Redevelopment Authority, 357 Pa. 329, 54 A.2d 277 (1947); Appeal of Ward, 289 Pa. 458, 137 A. 630 (1927) (board of zoning appeals).

[70] See 1 Antieau, Municipal Corporation Law §§ 2.14–.15 (1998); 2 McQuillin, Municipal Corporations 4.30–.76 (3d rev. ed. 1996); Cloe & Marcus, Special and Local Legislation, 24 Ky.L.J. 351 (1936); Hubbard,

such constitutional provisions have possible relevance to a wide variety of topics, they have been of particular importance in limiting legislative attempts to accord different treatment to different cities and towns within the same state. They became especially common during the latter half of the 19th century, and they remain important and are still often involved in litigation. They were designed to prevent state legislatures from granting preferences to some local units or areas within the state, thus creating an irregular system of laws, lacking state-wide uniformity. It was noted that if "special laws" were permitted, the result would often be a situation in which it became customary for members of the legislature to vote for the local bills of others in return for comparable cooperation from them (a practice often termed "logrolling"); in which members of the legislature would be reelected or defeated mainly on the basis of their proficiency in gaining special favors for the districts they represented; and in which much legislative time would be consumed in passing a wilderness of very limited laws, lacking symmetry or overall plan.[71] The restrictions on special laws may be said to rest partly on the distinction often drawn between the proper role of the legislative branch under our system of government, and the proper tasks of the judiciary: the legislature is intended, and presumably better equipped, to draft uniform plans and general policies; the judiciary is designed to decide specific cases involving the particular problems of individuals.

The restrictions on special legislation that are found in the various state constitutions take three main forms[72] though some states have two, or even all three, of these kinds of limitation scattered through their constitutions. One type of provision forbids special legislation as to certain listed subjects, and those subjects often include the incorporating of cities and towns, changing the charters of municipalities, locating or changing county seats, laying out or maintaining roads and streets, and/or regulating the affairs of municipalities and other local units. Thus, this type of restriction obviously has relevance as to many statutes that might be passed dealing with local governments. A second type of provision commonly declares that all general laws shall have uniform application throughout the state and that no special law shall be passed where a general law could be made applicable. This in effect amounts to a nearly total prohibition of "special" laws.[73] A third type of provision merely requires that special legislation must

---

Special Legislation for Municipalities, 18 Harv.L.Rev. 588 (1905). For historic background, see Dillon, Municipal Corporations ch. 5 (5th ed. 1911); McBain, The Law and Practice of Home Rule ch. 2 (1916).

[71] Anderson v. Board of Commissioners, 77 Kan. 721, 95 P. 583 (1908). See 1 Antieau, Municipal Corporation Law § 2.14, at 2–46 (1978). Cf. State v. Circuit Court, 50 N.J.L. 585, 15 A. 272 (1888) (limitations on special laws are not intended to bring complete uniformity but to prevent vesting of a power of local self-government in one municipality but not another). The object of these constitutional provisions has been said to be the substitution of general laws for local ones in every situation in which this is possible. Conlin v. Board of Supervisors, 114 Cal. 404, 46 P. 279 (1896); Columbia Trust Co. v. Lincoln Institute, 138 Ky. 804, 129 S.W. 113 (1910). Sometimes, the constitutional limitation is limited in application to laws that regulate the internal affairs of municipalities. See State ex rel. Dempsey v. Mayor of Newark, 53 N.J.L. 4, 20 A. 886 (1890).

[72] See Stason & Kauper, Municipal Corporations 28–30 (3d ed. 1958). Cf. Fordham, Local Government Law 65–69 (2d rev. ed. 1986).

[73] See Conlin v. Board of Supervisors, *supra* note 2; Eckerson v. City of Des Moines, 137 Iowa 452, 115 N.W. 177 (1908); Barker v. Kansas City, 149 Kan. 696, 88 P.2d 1071 (1939); Rambo v. Larrabee, 67 Kan. 634, 73 P. 915 (1903); Bryan v. Voss, 143 Ky. 422, 136 S.W. 884 (1911); Hixson v. Burson, 54 Ohio St. 470, 43 N.E. 1000 (1896); State ex rel. v. Bargus, 53 Ohio St. 94, 41 N.E. 245 (1895). Cf. Miller v. Kister, 68 Cal. 142, 8 P. 813 (1885). See generally 1 Antieau, Municipal Corporation Law § 2.16, at 2–48 (1978), noting that a law might be general, and thus avoid a proscription of special laws, and yet not be of uniform application throughout the state, as where a law applies only within a restricted geographic area of the state, or favors one class of municipalities over another. See State ex rel. Keefe v. McInerney, 63 Wyo. 280, 182 P.2d 28 (1947).

undergo a specified procedure before it is considered, or at least before it is passed, by the state legislature. Often the procedure consists mostly of publication requirements, such as that the bill be published a designated number of times in a newspaper of general circulation within the state.[74] Such requirements are normally presumed to have been met; and the burden is on anyone challenging the legislation, after its passage, to show that some such requirement was not fulfilled.[75] Occasionally, the special requirements have to do with the proportion of the legislature that must vote for the "special" law in order for it to be passed.[76]

All such limitations apply only to "special" laws, and thus a definition of these is needed. A comprehensive one says that a law "is special if by reason of some intrinsic limitation on its scope of application, it is arbitrarily made to apply to some particular thing, location, person, or group and thereby grants privileges or imposes burdens which, but for the limitation, would apply to a larger class, each member bearing the same relationship to the subject matter of the law in question; more specifically, a law is special if by reason of its being made applicable to a particular municipality or group thereof, it arbitrarily grants privileges or imposes burdens on less than all the

---

Nonetheless, decisions under the constitutional requirements that general laws be of uniform application, and that special laws not be used where general are possible, have tended to use much the same tests as where the other types of limitation on special laws are found. See Webb v. Adams, 180 Ark. 713, 23 S.W.2d 617 (1929) (law found special because did not have uniform operation throughout state); Masto v. Gypsum Resources, LLC, 294 P.3d 404 (Nev. 2013) (statute regulating land adjacent to conservation area held invalid because it fell within constitutional prohibition of local or special laws if they operated over a particular locality rather than over the whole territory of the state). But cf. Cummings v. City of Chicago, 144 Ill. 563, 33 N.E. 854 (1893) (constitutional prohibition of special laws does not mean all laws must have uniform operation throughout state). In Tafalier v. Lead-Impacted Communities Relocation Assistance Trust, 237 P.3d 181 (Okla. 2010), it is stated that the test to be applied under constitutional provisions requiring enactments of a general, as opposed to a special, law wherever possible is whether the legislative objective can be achieved by a general law or whether the statute addresses a special situation possessing characteristics impossible of treatment by general law. *Id.* at 194. In this instance of a statute governing eligibility for relocation assistance, the special situation of those landowners in a high risk area, along with damages from tornadoes, did not allow for a general law to be enacted to address the situation, and therefore was held not to be a special law. *Id.*

[74] See Middleton v. City of St. Augustine, 42 Fla. 287, 29 So. 421 (1900); Annot., Construction & Application of Constitutional Provisions Prescribing Requisites or Conditions of Passage of Local or Special Law Relating to Property, Affairs, or Government of Municipality, 106 A.L.R. 1471 (1937). On interpretation of the Florida publication requirement in particular, see Chavous v. Goodbred, 158 Fla. 826, 30 So.2d 370 (1947); State ex rel. Pierce v. Gustafson, 127 Fla. 741, 174 So. 12 (1937). On interpretation of the Louisiana requirement, see City of New Orleans v. Borey, 52 So.2d 728 (La.App.1951); State ex rel. Grosch v. City of New Orleans, 211 La. 241, 29 So.2d 778 (1947); Federal Land Bank v. John D. Nix, Jr., Enterprises, 166 La. 566, 117 So. 720 (1928). Alabama requires publication of special laws relating to subjects as to which such laws are not totally forbidden. Ala.Const. Art. 4, § 106.

[75] Cravens v. State, 57 Tex.Cr.R. 135, 122 S.W. 29 (1909). In North Carolina, the court took the position that it would not under any circumstances look behind the face of an enacted law to determine whether publication had been made. Brodnax v. Groom, 64 N.C. 244 (1870). This led to considerable legislative ignoring of the publication requirement where laws aimed at particular localities were passed. See Matthews v. Town of Blowing Rock, 207 N.C. 450, 177 S.E. 429 (1934). The North Carolina Constitution no longer lists the organization and powers of units of local government among the subjects as to which local laws are forbidden. N.C.Const. Art. 2, § 23. See Plemmer v. Matthewson, 281 N.C. 722, 190 S.E.2d 204 (1972) (legislature may create, and enlarge boundaries of, town by special act). But see City of New Bern v. New Bern–Craven County Bd. of Educ., 338 N.C. 430, 450 S.E.2d 735 (1994) (legislative acts shifting responsibility for enforcing building code from city to county, but applying only to one particular county, invalidated as unconstitutional local law).

[76] This is true under the New York Constitution. N.Y.Const. Art. 9, § 2. See Burke v. Krug, 161 Misc. 687, 291 N.Y.S. 897 (1936), aff'd 272 N.Y. 575, 4 N.E.2d 744; Osborn v. Cohen, 272 N.Y. 55, 4 N.E.2d 289 (1936) (statute on city fire department not special); New York Steam Corp. v. New York, 268 N.Y. 137, 197 N.E. 172 (1935) (taxes for unemployment relief not special). Cf. Di Prima v. Wagner, 27 Misc.2d 380, 215 N.Y.S.2d 687 (1961) modif'd 14 A.D.2d 36, 215 N.Y.S.2d 705, aff'd 10 N.Y.2d 728, 219 N.Y.S.2d 272, 176 N.E.2d 839.

municipalities to which the particular law would naturally apply in the absence of the limitation."[77] This boils down to saying that a law dealing with municipalities is "special" if it *arbitrarily* includes some and excludes others from its coverage. The key is the "arbitrariness" of the legislation—its drawing distinctions among the potential subjects of its application without good reason. If a statute applies to New York City and not to Albany, it becomes suspect as possibly special; but the further question must be asked: is the distinction—the difference in application—arbitrary?

Much of the legislation questioned as possibly special is legislation that places cities in various *categories*, usually with the result that the legislation then applies to some categories but not others, or applies differently to the various categories. A law is not invalidly special merely because no cities, or very few, fit a particular classification; but on the other hand, a mere scheme of classification, with each class treated separately, does not prevent legislation from being found special.[78] Older authority tended to require that statutes, in order not to be found special, must base any differentiations on necessity;[79] but more recent cases tend to look only for a rational purpose behind the classifications.[80] Population is often a valid basis on which to distinguish categories, as with legislation that makes it easier to initiate urban renewal projects in larger cities of the state, since they normally have the more severe problems of urban blight.[81] But a

[77] Winters, Classification of Municipalities, 57 Nw.U.L.Rev. 279 (1962). See McLaughlin v. Ford, 168 Ark. 1108, 273 S.W. 707 (1925). A few authorities indicate that a law is not special so long as it relates to a subject in which the people of the state at large are interested. See Sullins v. Roma, 336 S.W.2d 814 (Tex.Civ.App.1959). Compare State v. Christi, 149 Ariz. 323, 718 P.2d 487 (App. 1986), defining a "special law" as one applying only to certain members of a class or to an arbitrarily defined class which is not rationally related to a legitimate legislative purpose, and defining a "local law" (likewise forbidden by the state constitution) as a law which arbitrarily singles out one locality in the jurisdiction for special treatment. Cf. City of New Bern v. New Bern-Craven County Bd. of Educ., 338 N.C. 430, 450 S.E.2d 735 (1994) (statutes granting one particular county, instead of the city, power to conduct building inspections at specified places invalidated as local law); City of Brookfield v. Milwaukee Metropolitan Sewerage Dist., 144 Wis.2d 896, 426 N.W.2d 591 (1988) (statutes applicable to only one sewer district in the state found invalid as local legislation). On Arkansas cases applying the "local and special" restriction, see Comment, Streight Curve: The Knuckleball Interpretation of "Local and Special Acts," 66 Ark. L. Rev. 705 (2013).

[78] Appeal of Ayars, 122 Pa. 266, 16 A. 356 (1889). Thus, a statute classifying according to population may be upheld as non-special though there is only one city currently qualifying for a particular category. City of Indianapolis v. Navin, 151 Ind. 139, 47 N.E. 525 (1897), reh. denied 151 Ind. 139, 51 N.E. 80; Parker-Washington Co. v. Kansas City, 73 Kan. 722, 85 P. 781 (1906); Ladd v. Holmes, 40 Or. 167, 66 P. 714 (1901). Cf. Gaca v. City of Chicago, 411 Ill. 146, 103 N.E.2d 617 (1952) (statute requiring cities over 500,000 population to indemnify policemen for certain judgments against them; applicable only to Chicago). But where only one city in the state can *ever* qualify for coverage under the statute, the legislation will often be found special. See New York Steam Corp. v. New York, 268 N.Y. 137, 197 N.E. 172 (1935); Brown v. State ex rel. Merland, 120 Ohio St. 297, 166 N.E. 214 (1929). Cf. City of Topeka v. Gillett, 32 Kan. 431, 4 P. 800 (1884). See also Pennsylvania Turnpike Comm'n v. Commonwealth of Pennsylvania, 587 Pa. 347, 899 A.2d 1085 (2006), noted 45 Duquesne L. Rev. 97 (2006) (Pennsylvania Constitution requires that state laws promote a legitimate state interest or public value, and any classification must be reasonably related to accomplishing that articulated state interest or public value).

[79] State ex rel. Cone v. Bauman, 120 Neb. 77, 231 N.W. 693 (1930); Appeal of Ayars, c.

[80] Webb v. Adams, 180 Ark. 713, 23 S.W.2d 617 (1929) (reasonable classification permissible); State ex rel. Welsh v. Darling, 216 Iowa 553, 246 N.W. 390 (1933); Hunt v. Rosenbaum Grain Corp., 355 Ill. 504, 189 N.E. 907 (1934); Board of Aldermen v. Dwyer, 120 N.J.Super. 184, 293 A.2d 460 (1972) (no logical reason for classification; law special); In the Matter of the Incorporation of the Village of Loch Arbour, 25 N.J. 258, 135 A.2d 663 (1957) (distinction between villages and other types of local government valid); Admiral Realty Co. v. City of New York, 206 N.Y. 110, 99 N.E. 241 (1912); Roberts v. Ledgerwood, 134 Okl. 152, 272 P. 448 (1928).

[81] Lindauer v. Oklahoma City Urban Renewal Authority, 320 F.Supp. 332 (W.D.Okl.1970), aff'd 452 F.2d 117 (10th Cir.), cert. denied 405 U.S. 1017, 92 S.Ct. 1293, 31 L.Ed.2d 479, reh. denied 406 U.S. 911, 92 S.Ct. 1607, 31 L.Ed.2d 823; Kansas City v. Robb, 183 Kan. 834, 332 P.2d 520 (1958); Lindauer v. Oklahoma City Urban Renewal Authority, 496 P.2d 1174 (Okl.1972). Cf. State ex rel. Pentzer v. Malone, 74 Neb. 645, 105

point may be reached at which so great a number of separate categories is created that differences among them become meaningless and thus the reason for the differentiation ceases to exist.[82]

One leading and oft-cited case laid down five requirements that any legislation classifying cities must meet in order *not* to be declared special:[83] (1) the classification must be based on substantial differences that make one category really different from another; (2) the scheme of classification must be germane to the purpose of the law—for instance, if population is used as the basis of distinguishing various classes, size of population must be relevant to the act's subject matter, as with the above-described urban renewal laws; (3) the law must apply equally to every member of a class so that there is no unjustified discrimination within the various categories created; (4) the

---

N.W. 893 (1905) (provision for election of aldermen not special legislation merely because, due to its population limitations, it currently applied to only one city); Williams v. Smith, 94 N.J.Super. 341, 228 A.2d 349 (1967), aff'd 51 N.J. 161, 238 A.2d 457 (if population was at all relevant to granting of tenure to building inspectors, statute must stand; statute held valid). Compare Williams v. Starr, 534 P.2d 29 (Okl. App. 1975) (law authorizing planning commissions in counties containing less than 100,000 inhabitants and containing a city with a population of 5000 or more held not special), with Elias v. City of Tulsa, 408 P.2d 517 (Okl.1965) (law empowering city of no less than 180,000 population nor more than 240,000 population to zone some territories outside its limits invalidated as special). See generally 2 McQuillin, Municipal Corporations §§ 4.60, 4.68–.76 (3d rev. ed. 1996); Annot., Validity of Statutory Classifications Based on Population—Zoning, Building, and Land Use Statutes, 98 A.L.R.3d 679 (1980). See also City of Enid v. Public Employees Relations Bd., 133 P.3d 281 (Okla. 2006) (statute upheld which classified municipal employers as municipalities with populations greater than 35,000; good review of cases and of reasons for using population as basis for classification).

[82] Appeal of Ayars, *supra* note 78. See State ex rel. Knisely v. Jones, 66 Ohio St. 453, 64 N.E. 424 (1902); Pittsburg, Fort Worth & Chicago Railway v. Martin, 53 Ohio St. 386, 41 N.E. 690 (1895) (act granted certain powers to cities with not less than 5750 and not more than 5800 people); City of Fort Worth v. Bobbitt, 121 Tex. 14, 36 S.W.2d 470 (1931), aff'd 121 Tex. 14, 41 S.W.2d 228 (figure based on particular census). Cf., finding a lack of rational relationship between the classification by population and the legislation's purpose, Gangemi v. Rosengard, 44 N.J. 166, 207 A.2d 665 (1965); Elias v. City of Tulsa, 408 P.2d 517 (Okl.1965). Cf. People ex rel. Adamowski v. Wilson, 20 Ill.2d 568, 170 N.E.2d 605 (1960). The Ohio Constitution no longer permits classification on the basis of population, beyond that specified by the Constitution itself. See Sanzere v. City of Cincinnati, 157 Ohio St. 515, 106 N.E.2d 286 (1952), noted 21 U.Cin.L.Rev. 506 (1952), interpreting Ohio Const. Art. 18. But classification is permitted on the basis of whether a city is a charter or non-charter municipality. Sanzere v. City of Cincinnati, *supra*. For a good discussion of whether a classification based on population involves a "real and substantial distinction," see Kinney v. Board of County Comm'rs of Tulsa County, 894 P.2d 444 (Okla. App. 1995) (statute provided that any county with population of less than 550,000 which contained a metropolitan area with a population of 250,000 or more could adopt or amend county home rule charter invalidated; no rational basis for the 550,000 population cap).

Statutes classifying cities according to their form of government—for instance, whether or not they have the commission form—have sometimes been struck down as unreasonable or lacking in sufficient relation to the legislation's purpose. Mankin v. Dean, 228 Ark. 752, 310 S.W.2d 477 (1958) (statute limiting work-week of firemen in cities having commission form; no logical connection to statute's purpose); In re Struck, 41 Ill.2d 574, 244 N.E.2d 176 (1969) (recall statute applicable only to cities with commission form struck down); People ex rel. Hoeinghaus v. Campbell, 285 Ill. 557, 121 N.E. 183 (1918); Hueston v. Atwater, 97 N.J.L. 414, 118 A. 209 (1922). But cf. Whittaker v. Carter, 238 Ark. 1074, 386 S.W.2d 498 (1965). No doubt many statutes on qualifications for and powers of city officers are valid despite being limited in application to particular forms of city government since the limitation is often then appropriate.

The whole classification problem is exhaustively discussed in Bally v. Guilford Township School Corp., 234 Ind. 273, 126 N.E.2d 13 (1955), where a classification of townships based on population was upheld.

[83] Federal Paving Corp. v. Prudisch, 235 Wis. 527, 293 N.W. 156 (1940). Cf. Le Tourneau v. Hugo, 90 Minn. 420, 97 N.W. 115 (1903); Johnson v. City of Milwaukee, 88 Wis. 383, 60 N.W. 270 (1894). The *Federal Paving* case, *supra*, dealt with a situation as to which possibly special legislation is often applied: municipal action (in that case, entering into a contract) that is invalid because of failure to comply with some technical requirements. The legislature may then often attempt to pass a bill giving relief in the form of validation of the action. These acts are often upheld because they are sufficiently general in application or because the situation is one to which a general law could not be made applicable; but in several cases, they have been invalidated as special. See 2 McQuillin, Municipal Corporations § 4.–51 (3d rev. ed. 1996).

characteristics of each class must be so far different from those of other classes as reasonably to suggest the propriety of the differing treatment under the legislation; and (5) the classification cannot be based on existing circumstances.

The last of those requirements is more narrow in application than might appear from the language. It is simply taken to mean that the legislation cannot create "closed classes," with no provision for cities moving from one class to another, *if* the factor on which the classification is based is one that is subject to change. For example, population is obviously subject to change. Thus, if a system of classification employed in a statute is based on the population of various cities, the statute must provide that the cities can change categories as their population moves up or down.[84] If the legislation classifies cities according to some particular census, such as the 2010 Federal census, the classification will be a frozen one with no room for change in the law's application even though the population of cities changes; and the law will then be special.[85] Classification on the basis of some *permanent* condition, such as geographic location, is normally assumed not to make the legislation special even if there is no provision for cities moving from one category to another; since change in the factor underlying the classification is generally impossible, no provision for change in classification is needed.[86]

There has been some difficulty over "option legislation"—legislation under which a city may choose to bring itself (as by vote of the people or by action of the city council) or decline to bring itself. Thus, what if a law allows cities to adopt a particular form of city government but only if the qualified electors of the city so vote? Such legislation almost inevitably creates different categories of cities within the state, but is normally held valid since the categories are not closed—that is, a city may adopt or reject the statutory form at any time.[87] But if the legislation sets a deadline by which the option must be exercised or else the choice is forever lost, then closed categories are created, and the legislation is special.[88]

---

[84] City of Atlanta v. Gower, 216 Ga. 368, 116 S.E.2d 738 (1960). See Barge v. Camp, 209 Ga. 38, 70 S.E.2d 360 (1952); Dearborn v. Board of Supervisors, 275 Mich. 151, 266 N.W. 304 (1936); City of Fort Worth v. Fire Department, 213 S.W.2d 347 (Tex.Civ.App.1948), aff'd in part, rev'd in part 147 Tex. 505, 217 S.W.2d 664. See Sherman v. City of Tempe, 202 Ariz. 339, 45 P.3d 336 (2002) (general law, as opposed to prohibited special law, must be elastic, or open, not only to admit entry of additional subjects but also to enable others to exit the statute's coverage when they no longer have the required characteristics).

[85] State ex rel. West v. Des Moines, 96 Iowa 521, 65 N.W. 818 (1896); State ex rel. Gray v. Swigert, 59 Or. 132, 116 P. 440 (1911); Fleming v. City of Memphis, 126 Tenn. 331, 148 S.W. 1057 (1912). Cf. Heckler v. Conter, 206 Ind. 376, 187 N.E. 878 (1933); State v. Pugh, 43 Ohio St. 98, 1 N.E. 439 (1885). See generally Note, Municipal Corporations—Constitutionality of Local or Special Laws, 10 Tex.L.Rev. 108 (1931).

[86] Higgins v. Johnson County Commissioners, 153 Kan. 560, 112 P.2d 128 (1941); State ex rel. Bowker v. Wright, 54 N.J.L. 130, 23 A. 116 (1891) (limitation to cities on the ocean valid). Cf. Albright v. Sussex County Lake & Park Commission, 68 N.J.L. 523, 53 A. 612 (1902) (classification of counties valid where based on size of fresh-water lakes therein); Madison Metropolitan Sewerage District v. Committee on Water Pollution, 260 Wis. 229, 50 N.W.2d 424 (1951). But cf. State ex rel. Alexander v. City of Elizabeth, 56 N.J.L. 71, 28 A. 51 (1894) (statute invalid as creating closed categories when based on whether or not municipality already has a racetrack; since this is a factor that can change, provision must be made for change).

[87] Opinion of the Justices, 249 Ala. 509, 31 So.2d 717 (1947); Town of San Mateo City v. State ex rel. Landis, 117 Fla. 546, 158 So. 112 (1934); People v. Hoffman, 116 Ill. 587, 5 N.E. 596 (1886); State ex rel. Elsas v. Missouri Workmen's Compensation Commission, 318 Mo. 1004, 2 S.W.2d 796 (1928); State ex rel. Paul v. Circuit Court, 50 N.J.L. 585, 15 A. 272 (1888); State ex rel. Hunt v. Tausick, 64 Wash. 69, 116 P. 651 (1911). But cf. State ex rel. Childs v. Copeland, 66 Minn. 315, 69 N.W. 27 (1896). See generally 2 McQuillin, Municipal Corporations § 4.–49 (3d rev. ed. 1996).

[88] State ex rel. Christie v. Mayor of Bayonne, 64 N.J.L. 191, 44 A. 887 (1899); De Hart v. Atlantic City, 63 N.J.L. 223, 43 A. 742 (1899). Even where the statute contained a time limitation, it had been upheld in an

If a state does not have any constitutional limitation on special laws, all such legislation may be valid. But it may often be subject to challenge as violating the equal protection clauses of state and federal constitutions.[89] It may end up being struck down for much the same reasons as under a "special legislation" prohibition, but the "equal protection" tests that have been developed by the courts—such as the "compelling interest" and "rational basis" tests of the U.S. Supreme Court—will be employed. In a few cases, broad constitutional prohibitions of laws conferring special powers or privileges on "corporations" have been held applicable to laws dealing with municipal corporations,[90] and thus have also served much the same functions as "special law" prohibitions.

When a "special law" prohibition is adopted as part of a state constitution, an exception for existing laws is often provided, since otherwise, due process questions might be raised if private property rights were destroyed or adversely affected without compensation.[91]

Limits on special legislation remain of some importance since they are contained in the constitutions of so many states. But an increasing number of attacks on state legislation are made on the basis of broader constitutional provisions, such as due process and equal protection. It may be contended also that the need for the constitutional restrictions on local laws is less nowadays. The situations of legislative abuse that led to their passage have perhaps lessened in number and seriousness, and a countervailing need has increasingly been recognized to accord separate treatment to separate areas of many states.

---

earlier New Jersey case, In re Cleveland, 51 N.J.L. 319, 18 A. 67 (1889), aff'd 52 N.J.L. 188, 19 A. 17 (1890). There is a good review of the New Jersey cases in Albright v. Sussex County Lake & Park Commission, 68 N.J.L. 523, 53 A. 612 (1902) (law can be sustained if time for submission is merely directory, not mandatory). Cf. Cole v. Dorr, 80 Kan. 251, 101 P. 1016 (1909). See also Long v. Napolitano, 203 Ariz. 247, 53 P.3d 172 (App. 2002) (requirement that county call election by certain date was a trigger to activate provisions of legislation rather than a criterion for class membership, and thus legislation was sufficiently elastic so as not to constitute a special law).

[89] Thus in Branson v. City & County of Denver, 707 P.2d 338 (Colo.1985), the court dealt with a statutory classification denying benefits to firefighters' widows in cities over 100,000 population if marriage occurred after firefighters' retirement, while providing benefits to such widows in cities of less than 100,000 population regardless of the time of marriage, and to police officers' widows regardless of the size of city or time of marriage. Applying the rational basis test under Equal Protection, the court invalidated that law, finding no rational connection with the purported governmental goal of maintaining fiscal certainty. See Fleming v. City of Memphis, 126 Tenn. 331, 148 S.W. 1057 (1912); Hincks v. City of Milwaukee, 46 Wis. 559, 1 N.W. 230 (1879); Durkee v. City of Janesville, 28 Wis. 464 (1871). But see Section 5.1, note 9 *supra* and accompanying text (federal equal protection clause does not apply to state action affecting municipalities except where rights of third persons are involved).

[90] Commercial National Bank v. Iola, 154 U.S. 617, 14 S.Ct. 1199, 22 L.Ed. 463 (1875); School District v. St. Joseph Fire & Marine Insurance Co., 103 U.S. 707, 26 L.Ed. 601 (1881); Sarlls v. State ex rel. Trimble, 201 Ind. 88, 166 N.E. 270 (1929); Town of Longview v. City of Crawfordsville, 164 Ind. 117, 73 N.E. 78 (1905); State v. Pugh, 43 Ohio St. 98, 1 N.E. 439 (1885); Terry v. King County, 43 Wash. 61, 86 P. 210 (1906). Cf. State ex rel. Godard v. Downs, 60 Kan. 788, 57 P. 962 (1899). But see Sun Printing & Publishing Association v. Mayor of New York, 152 N.Y. 257, 46 N.E. 499 (1897).

[91] See Ayars Appeal, 122 Pa. 266, 16 A. 356 (1889) (fact that some special laws are in effect when constitutional prohibition is adopted and that those laws are not affected by the prohibition does not justify substitution of other special laws in their stead). Due Process Clauses have limited application to the rights of cities against the parent-state; see Section 5.1, notes 10–12 *supra* and accompanying text. But a violation of due process might be found if legislation were invalidated under which a municipality, in its proprietary capacity, had property rights, or under which third parties had vested rights.

§ 5.8 Miscellaneous Limitations on State Control of Municipalities

A number of other limitations on state action regarding municipalities are found in various constitutions. Many of these limits relate to local finances and are discussed in the chapters relating to that topic *infra*. For instance, some constitutions contain a prohibition of the state lending its credit in aid of private persons or corporations *or* municipal corporations; as applied to municipalities, this rule has been termed "anachronistic."[92] Similar limitations on lending credit may apply to the municipalities themselves—that is, the state may be forbidden to authorize any city or town to become a stockholder in any private corporation or to loan its credit to any private individual or corporation.[93] State constitutions often contain a provision—to be discussed in connection with city officers and employees *infra*—that no additional compensation is to be paid any public officer or employee after services have been rendered by, or a contract made with, such an agent; and these prohibitions frequently apply to state legislative action as well as other action—the state legislature cannot authorize any such payment.[94]

Bans on payment of unauthorized claims are also sometimes encountered in state constitutions. Typically, these provide that the state may not authorize payment of any claim against the state or a municipal corporation if that claim is based on an agreement made without express legal authority. These act as a prohibition of validating, or "curative," statutes that attempt to cure contractual defects.[95] Constitutional provisions in several states including New York forbid the state from imposing any contracts or debts on municipalities without their consent,[96] and the same result was reached by a court decision in Vermont.[97] But, as with the ban on imposing taxes for municipal purposes, these provisions have been held inapplicable to legislative imposition of debts or contracts in areas where the municipality acts as mere agent of the state.[98]

In addition to the broad limitations on special legislation discussed in the preceding section, there are sometimes separate constitutional provisions forbidding special laws

---

[92] Fordham, Local Government Law 61 (2d rev. ed. 1986), discussing the typical provision found in Missouri. On a modern method of lending state credit to cities by means of the state's guaranteeing payment of municipal securities, see generally Minge, Guarantying Municipal Bonds, 1974 Wis. L.Rev. 89.

[93] See Fordham, *supra* note 92, at 61–62.

[94] See *id.* at 62. Cf. 1 Antieau, Municipal Corporation Law § 2.16, at 2–69 (1998), noting the Alabama law.

[95] See Fordham, *supra* note 92, at 63–64. Often such laws are, in any case, invalidated as special legislation, since they frequently relate only to past transactions and thus create closed categories. *Id.* A few state constitutions specifically prohibit the state from releasing or extinguishing any municipal indebtedness. See 2 McQuillin, Municipal Corporations § 4.26 (3d rev. ed. 1996).

[96] See 1 Antieau, Municipal Corporation Law § 2.10 (1998), citing N.Y.Const. Art. 8, § 3. Cf. Albany Port District Commission v. National Commercial Bank & Trust Co., 259 App.Div. 1115, 21 N.Y.S.2d 267 (1940), aff'd 283 N.Y. 768, 28 N.E.2d 977; Sleight v. People for Use of Weller Township, 74 Ill. 47 (1874).

[97] Atkins & Co. v. Town of Randolph, 31 Vt. 226 (1858). The New York Court of Appeals reached a similar decision even prior to the specific prohibition being added to that state's constitution. People ex rel. Dunkirk Railway v. Batchellor, 53 N.Y. 128 (1873).

[98] Board of Park Comm'rs v. Common Council, 28 Mich. 228 (1873).

on certain limited subjects, such as incorporation of municipalities.[99] There may be such provisions as to removal of county seats or consolidation of counties, or there may be special constitutional requirements, usually involving voter approval, before these things can be done.[100] Counties are, indeed, often dealt with in considerable detail in state constitutions, with their form of government and the duties of their various offices spelled out.[101]

As to financial matters also, some state constitutions expressly forbid certain specific state acts, such as the state using its public funds for works of local improvement,[102] or the state making any kind of gift to a municipality.[103]

---

[99] *E.g.*, Okl.Const. Art. 18, § 1, specifically providing that municipal corporations shall not be created by special laws, though this is also covered by the list of subjects as to which special laws are forbidden in the more general prohibition of Okl.Const. Art. 5, § 46.

[100] See Fordham, Local Government Law 64–65 (2d rev. ed. 1986), citing Mo. Const. Art. 6, §§ 3–6.

[101] See Sato & Van Alstyne, State and Local Government Law 133–34 (2d ed. 1977), noting the difficulties presented by the rigid requirements for counties set forth in some state constitutions. See Winters, State Constitutional Limitations on Solutions of Metropolitan Area Problems 50 (1961).

[102] Sato & Van Alstyne, *supra* note 101. Such provisions may not apply to state-financed public improvements used for *governmental* purposes, as opposed to local corporate purposes. See Visina v. Freeman, 252 Minn. 177, 89 N.W.2d 635 (1958).

[103] Sato & Van Alstyne, *supra* note 101, at 133. See Mallon v. City of Long Beach, 44 Cal.2d 199, 282 P.2d 481 (1955), interpreting such a provision in the California constitution. That constitution was subsequently amended to allow state funds to be given to local governments for local purposes. Cal. Const. Art. 13, § 24.

In addition to the state constitutional limitations discussed in this text, a few additional ones are mentioned in 1 Antieau, Municipal Corporation Law § 2.16 (1998).

Chapter 6

LIMITS ON STATE CONTROL OF MUNICIPALITIES: CONSTITUTIONAL AND STATUTORY HOME RULE

Analysis

§ 6.1 History and Purposes of Home Rule

Since the doctrine of inherent home rule, discussed in Chapter 4 *supra*, is generally rejected in the United States today, and since the specific constitutional limitations on state control over municipalities, discussed in Chapter 5 *supra*, are of limited scope and value, is there any other doctrine in our legal system that gives municipalities independence and control as to their own affairs? Yes, there is the doctrine of municipal home rule, not perceived as an inherent right, but granted by constitution and/or statute in most states. This doctrine is sometimes traced to the powers and privileges enjoyed by some localities in England, even prior to Magna Charta, either through grant from the crown or simply through long use.[1] But the codified form of home rule as we today know it in the United States is usually said to have started with a Missouri

[1] See People ex rel. Metropolitan Street Railway Co. v. State Board of Tax Commissioners, 174 N.Y. 417, 67 N.E. 69 (1903). (For subsequent history of case, see Section 5.4, note 36.) See generally Bebout, An Ancient Partnership—Local Government, Magna Carta, and the National Interest 33–39 (1966).

constitutional amendment in 1875.[2] The codified form of home rule serves both as a grant of power to cities and as a limitation on state control of these same cities.[3]

Home rule in the United States was sometimes envisioned in its early days as giving the cities to whom such rule was granted full-fledged sovereignty over local affairs, thus bringing about dual state and local sovereignty along the national plan of federal and state governments.[4] But such local sovereignty has never developed, nor have any clear-cut distinctions between state and local power.[5] Home-rule arrangements vary from state to state and are everchanging.[6] But most arrangements rest on vague constitutional or statutory language granting powers of "local self-government" to qualifying municipalities; most are judicially interpreted to give home-rule municipalities at least sufficient power so that municipal laws prevail over state laws as to matters of "purely municipal concern" (but not as to matters of state-wide concern); and thus in most instances, the gist of the home-rule problem becomes the determination of what are local matters and what are state matters.[7]

There are great variations from place to place as to the zeal with which home-rule powers have been utilized; but it has been noted that this seems to vary more according to the state-of-mind of local officials than according to differences in the form of state authorization of home rule.[8] Recently, there have been especially notable attempts to increase the exercise of home-rule powers, and to undercut arguments for restrictive judicial interpretation of home rule, by providing in constitutions or statutes that local action is valid wherever the state legislature could have authorized the action and has not affirmatively forbidden it.[9]

---

[2] See 1 Antieau, Municipal Corporation Law § 3.00 (1998), with list of constitutional and statutory provisions. Cf. Fordham, Local Government Law 73 n. 1 (2d rev. ed. 1986) (with list of state constitutional provisions on municipal and county home rule); Stason & Kauper, Municipal Corporations 44 (3d ed. 1958). On the history of home rule, see generally McBain, The Law and Practice of Municipal Home Rule (1916); McGoldrick, The Law and Practice of Municipal Home Rule, 1916–1930 (1933). See also Chicago Dep't of Law, The Number One Municipal Law Problem—Home Rule (1940), with extensive bibliography.

[3] See 1 Antieau, Municipal Corporation Law §§ 3.01–.20 (1998), with detailed discussion of home rule as a source of municipal power, and as a limitation on state control, in various states. Cf., on home rule as a curb on state legislative power, 2 McQuillin, Municipal Corporations § 4.28 (3d rev. ed. 1996). See generally Note, Home Rule: A Solution for Municipal Problems?, 16 Wyo.L.J. 47 (1962). On the place of home-rule municipalities within the general American governmental structure, see Macdonald, American City Government 89 (1929); Reed, Municipal Government in the United States 140 (1934 rev. ed.).

[4] See City of St. Louis v. Western Union Telegraph Co., 149 U.S. 465, 468, 13 S.Ct. 990, 991, 37 L.Ed. 810 (1893), where Mr. Justice Brewer referred to local home rule as involving "imperium in imperio."

[5] See Valente & McCarthy, Local Government Law 110 (4th ed. 1992). For a critical view of home rule, see Fordham, The West Virginia Municipal Home Rule Proposal, 38 W.Va.L.Q. 235 (1932).

[6] See United States Advisory Comm'n on Intergovernmental Relations, 14th Annual Report 50 (1973). For an extensive list of studies of home rule as it exists in individual states, see generally 2A McQuillin, Municipal Corporations §§ 903, 907–08 (3d rev. ed. 1996) (with case cites from many jurisdictions). Cf. Stason & Kauper, Municipal Corporations 44–45 n. 9 (3d ed. 1958).

[7] See Vanlandingham, Municipal Home Rule in the United States, 10 Wm. & Mary L.Rev. 269, 291–92 (1968). Cf. Grad, The State's Capacity to Respond to Urban Problems, in The States and the Urban Crisis 27 (Am.Assembly 1970). See generally Mott, Home Rule for America's Cities (Amer. Mun.Ass'n 1949); Bromage, The Home Rule Puzzle, 46 Nat'l Mun.Rev. 119 (1957); Fordham & Asher, Home Rule Powers in Theory and Practice, 9 Ohio St. L.J. 18 (1948).

[8] Vanlandingham, *supra* note 7, at 282–83 & 294–96. Cf. Fordham & Asher, *supra* note 7, at 20.

[9] American Municipal Ass'n (Nat'l League of Cities), Model Constitutional Provision for Home Rule § 6 (1953); National Municipal League, Model State Constitution § 8.02 (1963). See United States Advisory Comm'n on Intergovernmental Relations, State Legislative Program 185–86 (1963). The American Municipal Association's Model Constitutional Provisions for Municipal Home Rule are set forth in their entirety in

Attempts are often made to distinguish between constitutional home rule and statutory home rule, with the former said to exist where a self-executing state constitutional provision directly confers home rule on certain cities, and the latter said to exist where the constitution merely authorizes state laws on home rule and the actual delegation of power to the cities takes the form of such legislation.[10] There are obvious differences flowing from the two approaches as to whether the constitutional provisions or state statutes are considered the ultimate source of the home-rule power, and differences in interpretation of the extent of such power may occasionally result.[11] But the labels may be considered really more confusing than helpful: legislative home rule is not necessarily more restrictive than its constitutional counterpart, and the main source of powers under either system is often considered to be the municipality's own charter.[12]

Home rule has been said to be intended to allow localities to decide for themselves the form of local government that they desire and the scope of its powers.[13] Proponents have put forth 5 main arguments in favor of home rule:[14] (1) It prevents too much state

---

Fordham, Local Government Law 76–86 (1975 rev. ed.). On proposals and constitutional amendments that incorporate this concept of expanded home rule, see Hyman, Home Rule in New York 1941–1965, Retrospect and Prospect, 15 Buff. L.Rev. 335, 360–64 (1965); Vanlandingham, *supra* note 7, at 305–08; Westbrook, Municipal Home Rule: An Evaluation of the Missouri Experience, 33 Mo.L.Rev. 45, 70 (1968).

The National Municipal League proposal, *supra*, for constitutional home-rule provisions states that a home-rule locality may perform any function not denied it by its charter, not denied to such localities generally, and within the limitations the state legislature has established by general law. This is intended to shift the task of defining home-rule powers away from the courts and to the legislatures. See Grad, *supra* note 7, at 49. Cf. Sharp, Home Rule in Alaska: A Clash Between the Constitution and the Court, 3 UCLA—Alaska L.Rev. 1 (1973). But see Vaubel, Toward Principles of State Restraint Upon the Exercise of Municipal Power in Home Rule, 20 Stetson L. Rev. 5 (1990), urging that the power of municipalities to take action within their territorial limits ought to be co-extensive with the interests of local citizens.

10 1 Antieau, Municipal Corporation Law § 3.01, at 3–8 (1998). Cf. Stason & Kauper, Municipal Corporations 42–43 (3d ed. 1958). See generally Sato & Van Alstyne, State and Local Government Law 135–36 (2d ed. 1977). For a good analysis of one example of constitutional home rule, see Comment, Constitutional Home Rule in Rhode Island, 11 Roger Williams U. L. Rev. 677 (2006). See also Symposium, Home Rule, 86 Denver U.L. Rev. 1239–1473 (2009), especially Baker & Rodriquez, Constitutional Home Rule and Judicial Scrutiny, *id.* at 1337.

11 See Grad, *supra* note 7, at 42–43. See generally, as to possible differences between constitutional and legislative home rule, 1 Antieau, Municipal Corporation Law §§ 3.03, 3.07, 3.08, 3.10, 3.14, 3.16, 3.17 (1998). On the various forms of home rule, and the differences among them, see Krane, Rigos & Hill, Home Rule in America 10–14 (2001); Sandalow, The Limits of Municipal Power Under Home Rule: A Role for the Courts, 48 Minn. L. Rev. 643, 661–68 (1964), both reprinted in Baker & Gillette, Local Government Law (3d ed. 2004), at 274–81.

12 See Vanlandingham, *supra* note 7, at 277. On the confusion created by the "constitutional" and "legislative" labels, see Sandalow, The Limits of Municipal Power Under Home Rule: A Role for the Courts, 48 Minn.L.Rev. 643, 699 (1964). Cf. Fordham, Local Government Law 72 (1975 rev. ed.). Another way of classifying home-rule charters is according to whether the charter operates as a grant of powers or as a limitation on powers. See Home Builders Ass'n v. City of Lincoln, 271 Neb. 353, 711 N.W.2d 871, 876–79 (2006) (a charter that grants specifically enumerated municipal powers is to be strictly construed, while a charter authorizing the municipality to act without specific legislative authorization wherever no limitation is expressed will be more broadly construed; Lincoln, Nebraska, found to have the latter type of charter and thus to have authority to impose development impact fees).

13 City of La Grande v. Public Employees Retirement Bd., 281 Or. 137, 576 P.2d 1204 (1978), reaffirmed 284 Or. 173, 586 P.2d 765. See Farha v. City of Wichita, 284 Kan. 507, 161 P.3d 717 (2007) (home rule ensures that cities have the power to determine local public policy and regulation, and authorizes cities to adopt ordinances of any type on subjects not addressed by the legislature).

14 See 1 Antieau, Municipal Corporation Law § 3.01 (1998), citing Fragley v. Phelan, 126 Cal. 383, 58 P. 923 (1899); Kalodimos v. Village of Morton Grove, 103 Ill.2d 483, 83 Ill.Dec. 308, 470 N.E.2d 266 (1984). See generally 56 Am.Jur.2d Municipal Corporations § 126 (1971). See generally Briffault, Home Rule and Local Political Innovation, 22 J.L. & Pol. 1 (2006).

legislative interference with local affairs. (2) It prevents control of urban affairs by the rural interests that in the past often dominated state legislatures. (3) By placing much of the power of local governance in local hands, home rule encourages in city residents a sense of responsibility and ongoing familiarity with city affairs. (4) The citizens of each locality are in the best position to understand that locality's particular problems and needs; therefore, these should be handled by those citizens. (5) Home rule allows qualifying municipalities to serve as testing grounds or "pilot projects" for experiments in new forms of government, and such experiments can best be conducted at a limited, local level. Thus, municipalities have sometimes utilized such devices as initiative and referendum as to legislation, and recall as to elected officers, before these were used at the state level.[15]

§ 6.2 Procedure for Obtaining Home Rule; Extent of Adoption

The procedure by which a municipality may obtain home rule is commonly set forth in considerable detail in constitutional or statutory provisions. Fundamental to the process is the drafting of a document usually called a "city charter" or "home-rule charter," which becomes the organic law of that municipality and is often considered analogous to a constitution.[16] Five requirements may have to be met before a municipality can obtain home rule, though not all of these are found in all jurisdictions. (1) A municipality desiring home rule must be incorporated as some form of local government. Occasionally, it may be specified or implied that it must be a "city," as defined in that state; but usually incorporation as a town or village will suffice.[17] (2) Generally, some minimum population is required, with most such minimums between 2000 and 10,000.[18] Though it may not be required by law, the practice is that a city once having obtained home rule will be allowed to retain it though its population subsequently falls below this minimum. For instance, Tombstone, Arizona, remains a home-rule

---

[15] See 42 Am.Jur.2d Initiative & Referendum §§ 1, 2, 7 (1969). See generally Briffault, Home Rule and Local Political Innovation, 22 J.L. & Pol. 1 (2006). Compare Symposium, States as Laboratories for Social Change, 17 Temple Pol. & Civ. Rts. L. Rev. 341 (2008).

[16] See 56 Am.Jur.2d Municipal Corporations § 127 (1971). Cf. Brummell v. Clark, 31 Or.App. 405, 570 P.2d 671 (1977) (county charter bears same relation to county ordinances as constitution of state bears to state statutes). See generally 2A McQuillin, Municipal Corporations § 9.03 (3d rev. ed. 1996), noting numerous authorities calling a city charter the fundamental organic law of the city, but arguing that legislative charters—as opposed to those adopted by the electors of the community—are just grants of power or recognitions of rights and should not be termed constitutions or organic laws. See generally as to construction of charters *id.* § 9.22. See also County of Kaua'i v. Baptiste, 115 Hawai'i 15, 165 P.3d 916 (2007) (charter said to be in effect a local constitution, providing a broad organizational framework establishing the form and structure of government in pursuance of which the political subdivision is to be governed and local laws enacted).

[17] See Hudson Motor Car Co. v. City of Detroit, 282 Mich. 69, 275 N.W. 770 (1937) (electors of a city or village may adopt charter as organic law thereof); Bleck v. Monona Village, 34 Wis.2d 191, 148 N.W.2d 708 (1967) (home rule applies only to local governments validly organized under state law). See generally Fordham, Decision-Making in Expanding Urban Life, 21 Ohio St. L.J. 274 (1960), noting, at 278, that there was then no concept of home rule for an entire metropolitan region. But see Section 2.14 *supra* on city-county consolidation.

In many jurisdictions, it is specifically provided that incorporated towns, as well as cities, may obtain home rule. See, *e.g.*, Mass.Const. Art. 2, §§ 1–6; 11 Okl.Stat. 1981, § 13–101; Penn.Const. Art. 9, §§ 2, 3, 14. Cf. 56 Am.Jur.2d Municipal Corporations §§ 126–27 (1971). See generally Council of State Governments, Report of the Committee on State-Local Regulations 168, 172–74 (1946), praising the Wisconsin law allowing home rule for cities and villages.

[18] See Fordham, Local Government Law 72 (2d rev. ed. 1986). At least one state, Ohio, has no population minimum. *Id.*

municipality, though its population is now well below the 3500 minimum in Arizona.[19] (3) The city charter must be prepared—a document specifying the municipality's powers and responsibilities. Often the law provides that this preparation is to be the task of an elected board of qualified voters within the municipality.[20] Historically, it was sometimes provided that the board members must be "freeholders"—literally meaning owners of realty. Requirements of property ownership have largely disappeared and would now likely be found unconstitutional.[21] But the terminology lingers, and the board that drafts the charter is still occasionally called a "board of freeholders," while its product may be termed a "freeholders' charter."[22] (4) The charter drafted by the board or committee must then be approved by the voters—usually by majority vote of those qualified electors of the municipality who vote at a special election. (5) In some jurisdictions, but by no means all, there must be some state approval of the home-rule charter, either by signature of the governor or vote of the legislature.[23] With the process thus completed, the municipality then is supposed to enjoy full powers of local self-government.[24] A similar procedure is generally specified for amendment or repeal of the home-rule charter.[25]

---

[19] See Ariz.Rev.Stat. § 9–281. On the government and powers of Tombstone, see City of Tombstone v. Macia, 30 Ariz. 218, 245 P. 677 (1926); Valley Bank v. Brodie, 9 Ariz. 17, 76 P. 617 (1904).

[20] See Fordham, Local Government Law 73 (2d rev. ed. 1986); Michelman & Sandalow, Government in Urban Areas 303–04 (1970); 56 Am.Jur.2d Municipal Corporations § 126 (1971). On the procedures for obtaining home rule, see generally Harper & Savage, Procedures in Home Rule Charter Making, 9 Ohio St. L.J. 127 (1948). See also Mendelson, Paths to Constitutional Home Rule for Municipalities, 6 Vand.L.Rev. 66 (1952).

[21] In Quinn v. Millsap, 491 U.S. 95, 109 S.Ct. 2324, 105 L.Ed.2d 74 (1989), on remand 785 S.W.2d 82 (Mo.1990), a requirement that a person own real property in order to be eligible for appointment to a "board of freeholders" appointed to reorganize the governments of the city of St. Louis and St. Louis County was held violative of equal protection. See City of Phoenix v. Kolodziejski, 399 U.S. 204, 90 S.Ct. 1990, 26 L.Ed.2d 523 (1970); Cipriano v. City of Houma, 395 U.S. 701, 89 S.Ct. 1897, 23 L.Ed.2d 647 (1969); Kramer v. Union Free School District, 395 U.S. 621, 89 S.Ct. 1886, 23 L.Ed.2d 583 (1969).

[22] See Strode v. Sullivan, 72 Ariz. 360, 236 P.2d 48 (1951) (freeholders' charter of city of Phoenix); Stohl v. Hortsmann, 64 Cal.App.2d 316, 148 P.2d 697 (Dist.Ct.1944) (freeholders' charter of city of Oakland); 2 McQuillin, Municipal Corporations §§ 9.07–.08 (3d ed. 1966 rev.). Cf. City of Sapulpa v. Land, 101 Okl. 22, 223 P. 640 (1924).

[23] See 56 Am.Jur.2d Municipal Corporations § 126 (1971). Cf. Michelman & Sandalow, Government in Urban Areas 303 (1970), discussing the California method of requiring legislative approval of home-rule charters, the Michigan method of requiring submission to the governor, and the West Virginia method of requiring an opinion from the state Attorney General as to the proposed charter's consistency with state laws. On the utility of legislative approval, see McGoldrick, The Law and Practice of Municipal Home Rule 49–50 (1933). In many states, no state approval is necessary in order for the electors of a municipality to frame and adopt their own charter. See City & County of Denver v. New York Trust Co., 229 U.S. 123, 33 S.Ct. 657, 57 L.Ed. 1101 (1913); St. Louis v. Western Union Telegraph Co., 149 U.S. 465, 13 S.Ct. 990, 37 L.Ed. 810 (1893); People ex rel. Elder v. Sours, 31 Colo. 369, 74 P. 167 (1903).

[24] 2A McQuillin, Municipal Corporations § 9.02, at 162 (3d rev. ed. 1996). Cf. City of Beaumont v. Fall, 116 Tex. 314, 291 S.W. 202 (Com.App.1927) (city free to act for itself so long as state has not acted). The charter serves as a kind of "mini-constitution" for the municipality, and municipal ordinances must conform to the charter and cannot change its effect. See Harris v. DeSoto, 80 Hawai'i 425, 911 P.2d 60 (Hawaii 1996). Cf. Olson v. Hillside Community Church SBC, 124 P.3d 874 (Colo. App. 2005), cert. denied 2005 WL 3742159 (Colo. 2005) (charter of a home-rule city is in effect its constitution, and city's ordinances may not conflict with its charter); Homeowners for Fair Zoning v. City of Tulsa, 123 P.3d 67 (Okla.Civ.App. 2005) (city charter is an authority superior to a city ordinance, and the council cannot by ordinance divest itself of power conferred on it by the charter).

[25] See 2A McQuillin, Municipal Corporations § 9.24–.30 (3d rev. ed. 1996). On charter reform, see generally Lane, Lessons on City Charter Reform, 11 Urban, State & Local L. Newsletter, No. 3, at 1 (Summer 1988).

Most home-rule states, whether they have so-called "constitutional" home rule or "legislative" home rule, do have a state constitutional provision that at least *authorizes* home rule in municipalities. The difference between the two systems is simply that in the "constitutional" states, the constitutional provision is largely self-executing, while in the "legislative" states additional legislation is needed, and the actual delegation of home-rule power is then made by statute.[26] But there is authority that no constitutional provision on home rule is needed at all and that the *entire* delegation *may* be made by statute, without constitutional authorization.[27] This has been done in Delaware and Indiana.[28]

The home-rule movement in the United States, which began in the 1870's and which had great momentum through the early decades of the 20th century, continues to have considerable strength today. Several states adopted municipal home rule in the latter half of the twentieth century.[29] Nonetheless, the movement has not been without its critics. It has been noted that home rule tends to emphasize self-determination of relatively small local units with fixed geographic boundaries, while many contemporary urban problems cry out for flexibility in governmental arrangements and for co-operation cutting across rigid boundaries and traditional divisions of responsibility.[30]

---

[26] See notes 10–12 *supra* and accompanying text. Cf. 2 McQuillin, Municipal Corporations § 4.28, at 71 (3d rev. ed. 1996). See generally Note, Municipal Corporations: Home Rule—The Power of Local Self-Government and the Effect of State Enabling Legislation, 30 Washburn L.J. 554 (1991), discussing Blevins v. Hiebert, 247 Kan. 1, 795 P.2d 325 (1990) (county exceeded its home-rule powers when it issued general obligation bond to finance highway construction without holding statutorily required referendum).

[27] See McBain, Delegation of Legislative Powers to Cities, 32 Pol.Sci.Quar. 276 (1917), citing pro and con cases. Cf. Town of Abbeville v. Police Jury, 207 La. 779, 22 So.2d 62 (1945).

[28] 22 Del.Code Ann. § 802; Ind.Stat. 18–1–1.5–1–30. Ohio, on the other hand, has constitutional provisions which confer some home-rule powers even on cities that do not adopt home-rule charters. Ohio Const. Art. 18, § 3. Charter-making authority is also conferred, however. *Id.* § 7. See Leavers v. City of Canton, 1 Ohio St.2d 33, 203 N.E.2d 354 (1964). The lack of a charter is generally considered undesirable as leaving too many unanswered questions on division of power within city government and the relationship between state and city law. See American Municipal Association, Model Constitutional Provisions for Municipal Home Rule 19 (1953); McBain, The Law and Practice of Municipal Home Rule 668–69 (1916).

[29] In 1966, Massachusetts adopted home rule (Mass.Const. Art. 2), as did North Dakota (N.D.Const. § 130). In 1968, Florida adopted home rule (Fla.Const. Art. 8, §§ 1, 2) and so did Iowa (Iowa Const. Art. 3. § 40) and Pennsylvania (Penn. Const. Art. 9, § 2). And in 1970, Illinois (Ill.Const. Art. 7, § 6) and Montana (Mont. Const. Art. 11, § 6) provided for home rule. Forty-eight states now provide some form of home rule for municipalities. Hovey, State Policy and Local Governments, 12 State Policy Rep., Issue 1, Jan., 1994, at 15; McCarthy, Local Government Law in a Nutshell 19 (4th ed. 1995). See generally Barron, Reclaiming Home Rule, 116 Harv. L. Rev. 2255 (2003), arguing that the debate over "sprawl" often wrongly equates home rule with local legal autonomy, when in reality what now passes for home rule frustrates cities and suburbs in their efforts to reduce sprawl. The author proposes that municipal powers be expanded so that city and suburbs can more adequately address regional problems like sprawl. *Id.* at 2334–86. As to "sprawl," see generally Section 21.1, note 6 *infra*, and Section 21.5, note 61, *infra*, and accompanying texts. As to the continuing need for home rule, plus suggestions for its possible improvement, see Briffault, Home Rule for the Twenty-first Century, 36 Urban Law. 253 (2004). The attitude of the courts in some states has been criticized as not really providing the desirable powers to municipalities that supposedly have home rule. See in Macdonald & Papez, Over 100 Years Without True "Home Rule" Idaho: Time for Change, 46 Idaho L. Rev. 587 (2010) (Idaho courts have recognized municipal home-rule power only as to police powers). See also Note, The Inconsistent State of Municipal Home Rule in Iowa, 57 Drake L. Rev. 263 (2008); Note, Up in Smoke: Home Rule City Authority Diminished by the Nebraska Special Legislation Provision, 88 Neb. L. Rev. 612 (2010). Compare Kaplan, New York City Taxis and the New York State Legislature: What Is Left of the State Constitution's Home Rule Clause After the Court of Appeals Decision in the HAIL Act Case?, 77 Alb. L. Rev. 113 (2013–14).

[30] See Fordham, Local Government Law 73–74 (2d rev. ed. 1986), admitting, however, that interest in home rule has increased, not waned, in recent years. See generally Fordham, The West Virginia Municipal Home Rule Proposal, 38 W.Va.L.Q. 235 (1932).

Especially notable, so far as home-rule expansion is concerned, has been the authorization in close to half the states of home rule by the counties.[31] Such rule in the counties clearly changes their traditional status as little more than sub-agencies of the states, and it may aggravate problems of overlapping governments and division of authority.[32] But it has been considered a necessity in some areas if increasingly urban counties are to be able to cope with ever-increasing, ever-more complex problems.[33] Not nearly all the counties in which home rule is authorized have availed themselves of the chance for greater self-government,[34] possibly due to intra-county rivalries and political inertia.[35] The movement may, however, gain speed as part of the general trend toward regionalism, and could eventually result in consolidation of some existing local units.

Sometimes state statutes or constitutions specify the provisions that may be included in the charters of localities. Charters in the past were sometimes granted individual cities by special acts of the legislature. These would today often run afoul of constitutional prohibitions of special legislation; but municipal charters are still created by *general* laws in several states. These charter provisions are sometimes found in the statutes on incorporation of cities, so that by virtue of incorporating under a particular set of statutes, the city automatically receives the relevant provisions as its charter.[36]

---

[31] See Fordham, Local Government Law 73 n. 2 (2d rev. ed. 1986), with list of state provisions for county home rule. See generally Valente & McCarthy, Local Government Law 155 (4th ed. 1992). At least thirty-seven states now allow county home rule. Hoover, Home Is the Rule—County Home Rule Is the Norm in Most of the U.S., Tulsa World, Jan. 11, 1999, at A-1. See generally DeSantis, County Government: A Century of Change, in The Municipal Year Book 55 (Int'l City Mgmt. Ass'n 1989). For good discussions of specific experiences with county home rule, see Note, The Role of County Government in the New York State Land Use System, 18 Pace L. Rev. 311 (1998); Timmons, Grant, Popp & Westby, County Home Rule Comes to Minnesota, 19 Wm. Mitchell L. Rev. 822 (1993). See also Ward, The Charter Form of County Government: Wayne County, 25 Years Later, 54 Wayne L. Rev. 1791 (2008). Home rule for school districts has also been proposed in a number of states and has been authorized in Texas. See Goldner, Home Rule School Districts: An Opportunity for Meaningful Reform or Simple Window Dressing?, 21 S. Ill. U.L.J. 255 (1997).

[32] See Fordham, Local Government Law 101 (2d rev. ed. 1986). Cf. City of West Allis v. County of Milwaukee, 39 Wis.2d 356, 159 N.W.2d 36 (1968), cert. denied 393 U.S. 1064, 89 S.Ct. 717, 21 L.Ed.2d 707. County home rule, where adopted, results in a situation analogous to that under municipal home rule: county enactments prevail over state law as to matters of basically county concern, but state law remains preeminent in matters of statewide concern. See Buchanan v. Wood, 79 Or.App. 722, 720 P.2d 1285 (1986), review denied 302 Or. 158, 727 P.2d 128 (1986). But see Dibb v. County of San Diego, 8 Cal.4th 1200, 36 Cal.Rptr.2d 55, 884 P.2d 1003 (1994), finding that a home-rule county had authority to create a civilian review board, but stating that in California home-rule counties have less expansive powers than do home-rule cities.

[33] Glauberman, County Home Rule: An Urban Necessity. 1 Urban Lawyer 170 (1969). Cf. Note, County Home Rule: An Approach to Metropolitan Problems in Michigan, 6 U.Mich.J.Law Reform 232 (1972).

[34] Bollens, American County Government 74–76 (1969). Cf. Etter, County Home Rule in Oregon, 46 Or.L.Rev. 251 (1967).

[35] See Valente & McCarthy, Local Government Law 156 (4th ed. 1992). On problems in connection with adopting county home rule, see generally Freilich, Robards, & Wilson, Home Rule for the Urban County: Observations on the New Jackson County Constitutional Charter, 39 U.M.K.C.L.Rev. 297 (1971). See also Comment, Still Afraid of "Negro Domination"?: Why County Home Rule Limitations in the Alabama Constitution of 1901 Are Unconstitutional, 57 Ala. L. Rev. 545 (2005).

[36] See 2A McQuillin, Municipal Corporations § 9.07 (3d rev. ed. 1996), distinguishing "legislative charters" (those created by statute) from "constitutional" or "freeholders' charters" (those created and adopted by the voters of a municipality under constitutional, and sometimes statutory, authorization). In some states, charters may be created either by statute or by act of the city voters. Thus, in Texas, certain cities and towns may be chartered by general law under Tex.Const. Art. 11, § 4 (five thousand or less in population), while others may adopt a charter by vote of the electors under Tex.Const. Art. 11, § 5 (more than 5000 population). "Legislative charters" do not necessarily grant any great amount of home rule, while "freeholders' charters" normally do; so the latter alone are sometimes referred to as "home rule charters." See 2 McQuillin, Municipal Corporations § 9.08 (3d rev. ed. 1996).

Nowadays when some state statutes set forth possible charter provisions, they provide a variety of possible forms of government. Such legislation is called "optional charter legislation" and permits a locality to make its choice among the offerings, usually by means of a vote of the local electors.[37]

§ 6.3 General Effects of Home Rule

When a city obtains a home-rule charter, what powers are obtained by the city and what limitations are imposed on the state? Certain generalizations may be made.[38] (1) Under constitutional home rule, the constitution itself, by means of a charter obtained thereunder, grants the locality all necessary powers for the government and administration of *local* affairs. (2) Under constitutional home rule, the qualifying city may legislate even on matters of *general* or statewide concern unless specifically forbidden by general state law or by the locality's own charter. (3) Under legislative home rule, the home-rule city has at least such powers as are included in its own charter and authorized by the state statutes.[39] (4) Under either form of home rule, state legislative acts must yield to local laws when those acts deal with basically *local* concerns *and* are in conflict with laws of the municipality. On the other hand, since even home-rule cities are subject to *general* state laws, state law prevails, in cases of conflict between state and city law, as to matters of *statewide* concern.[40] (5) In a few states, home rule is deemed to terminate *all* state control over basically municipal affairs, and state laws on these matters become inapplicable to home-rule cities even where there is no conflict with local law, or even no local law at all on the matter.[41] (6) In a few other states, the state legislature retains limited power to pass local laws (that is, laws on matters of basically

---

[37] See Fordham, Local Government Law 69–70 (2d rev. ed. 1986); 2A McQuillin, Municipal Corporations § 9.14 (3d rev. ed. 1996). The validity of such plans has been upheld. Adams v. City of Beloit, 105 Wis. 363, 81 N.W. 869 (1900) (no unconstitutional delegation of legislative power but merely a way of determining the facts on which laws will operate). Cf. City of Paterson v. The Society for Establishing Useful Manufactures, 24 N.J.L. 385 (1854). But if the legislature simply delegates to municipalities the power to make their own charters and no guidance is given, this can be declared an unconstitutional delegation of legislative authority. State ex rel. Mueller v. Thompson, 149 Wis. 488, 137 N.W. 20 (1912). In modern cases, the option plan has also withstood attack based on the allegation that the authorizing statutes are special legislation. See State ex rel. Benson v. Peterson, 180 Minn. 366, 230 N.W. 830 (1930); Commonwealth ex rel. James v. Woodring, 289 Pa. 437, 137 A. 635 (1927). This option method of dealing with the organization of cities is considered a compromise between mere city organization under general state laws, with perhaps no charter at all, and home rule under a legislative or freeholders' charter.

[38] See 1 Antieau, Municipal Corporation Law §§ 3.03, 3.07, 3.08, 3.10, 3.11, 3.14, 3.16–.18, 3.20 & 3.21 (1998).

[39] See *supra* note 38 § 3.10, at 3–31 & –32, where it is noted that under legislative home rule, mere incorporation of a city and the obtaining of a home-rule charter *may* give little power, but that statutes in some legislative home-rule states do grant broad general powers to cover situations not specifically mentioned in the statutes.

[40] See 1 Antieau, *supra* note 38 § 3.17. See City of Thornton v. Farmers Reservoir & Irrigation Co., 194 Colo. 526, 575 P.2d 382 (1978) (operation of water works a purely local matter). The home-rule city's law will prevail as to local matters whether that law is in the city charter itself or in legislation enacted thereunder. Cf. Save Sunset Beach Coalition v. City & County of Honolulu, 102 Hawai'i 465, 78 P.3d (2003) (if a city ordinance conflicts with a state statute that is of statewide concern, then the ordinance is necessarily invalid because it violates the state constitution and the state's supremacy provisions).

[41] 1 Antieau, *supra* note 38 § 3.16, noting opinions from California, Colorado, Ohio, Oklahoma, and Oregon that contain language adopting or indicating such a view.

local, rather than statewide, concern) applicable to home-rule cities but only if those cities consent to or approve of such legislation.[42]

Questions relating to powers of cities—as derived from state constitutions and statutes and local charters—are considered in Chapter 8, *infra*. But questions of limitations on state control of localities, and of the relationship of state and municipality, are those raised by points 4, 5, and 6 in the above paragraph. All these turn on the question of what matters are of statewide concern and what are of purely, or basically, local concern. Here too, some generalizations are possible.[43] A city's form of government and method of enacting and publishing ordinances are, so long as no basic constitutional provisions are violated, of purely local concern, and the law of a home-rule city will prevail over state law. The home-rule city may determine the make-up of its own government, establish any kinds of boards and commissions, provide the means for nomination, election, or appointment of local officials, and provide (or not provide) for initiative and referendum—and on all these matters, city law will normally prevail even if there is state law in conflict. But the state has a sovereign and supreme interest in enforcing the laws on liquor, gambling, prostitution—areas where uniform, statewide enforcement is necessary to effectiveness. As to these matters, and such others as annexation and method of appealing a criminal conviction (even a conviction in municipal court), uniformity is needed; and in case of conflict, state law will prevail over that of a home-rule city.

Aside from looking to the need for uniformity and consistency, courts will also sometimes apply the governmental-proprietary test as a rule of thumb: If matters are of governmental nature, they are likely to be classed as of statewide, general concern. If they are proprietary ("business-like" in nature, such as operation of a utility), they are likely to be considered of basically local concern.[44]

§ 6.4 Conflicts Between State Laws and Laws of Home-Rule Cities—Municipal Government, Officers and Employees

Much of the litigation regarding home rule has centered on situations of conflict between state and city law. In such situations, it must be determined what matters are of statewide, or general, concern and what matters are of purely, or—as sometimes

---

[42] See 1 Antieau, *supra* note 38 § 3.18 (1998), especially noting such provisions in New York and Rhode Island.

[43] See 1 Antieau, *supra* note 38 §§ 3.20–.40 (1998).

[44] Tucson v. Tucson Sunshine Climate Club, 64 Ariz. 1, 164 P.2d 598 (1945); Green v. City of Amarillo, 244 S.W. 241 (Tex.Civ.App.1922), aff'd 267 S.W. 702. See Ruud, Legislative Jurisdiction of Texas Home Rule Cities, 37 Tex.L.Rev. 682, 687 n. 24 (1959). Cf. Ex parte Hitchcock, 34 Cal.App. 111, 166 P. 849 (Dist.Ct.1917) (basically municipal affairs are those that relate to the internal business affairs of a municipality).

But any such tests often merely add to the confusion of classification. See 1 Antieau, Municipal Corporation Law § 3.21, at 3–64 (1998), citing Oregon ex rel. Heinig v. City of Milwaukie, 231 Or. 473, 373 P.2d 680 (1962) (fire protection is usually classified as of state concern, but kind of uniforms to be worn by city firefighters is of local concern). Cf. City of Tucson v. Arizona Alpha of Sigma Alpha Epsilon, 67 Ariz. 330, 195 P.2d 562 (1948), noting that there is a twilight zone where it is difficult to differentiate matters of statewide concern from those of local concern. See generally Merrill, Constitutional Home Rule for Cities—Oklahoma Version, 5 Okl.L.Rev. 139, 159–61 (1952), saying it can't simply be concluded that "general" matters are those that affect the state or people at large, since in our mobile society, *any* function of a local government may have some such effect; the author endorses a "wider public interest" test as focusing attention, not on any single factor, but on all factors surrounding a particular exercise of power. Compare Ohio (1976–1995), 22 Ohio N.U.L. Rev. 143 (1995), discussing the tests applied in Ohio.

said—"basically," local concern. In the situations of statewide concern, state law will prevail to the extent of the conflict. In situations of purely local concern, the city law prevails. Various tests and rules-of-thumb have been suggested but have proved of limited use in deciding the statewide-v.-local question. The cases are decided on a largely ad hoc basis, but with certain precedential patterns having been established over the years.[45] Within the limits of basic constitutional guarantees, a city's form of government—such as whether it employs the commission form or the city-manager form, etc.—is often held to be of purely municipal concern.[46] So are the establishment, qualifications, and powers of municipal boards and commissions;[47] the method prescribed for election or nomination of municipal officers;[48] and municipal adoption of such devices as initiative, referendum, and recall.[49] In general, any matters relating to

---

[45] See Shean v. Edmonds, 89 Cal.App.2d 315, 200 P.2d 879 (Dist.Ct.1948); Omaha Parking Authority v. City of Omaha, 163 Neb. 97, 77 N.W.2d 862 (1956); State ex rel. Mueller v. Thompson, 149 Wis. 488, 137 N.W. 20 (1912). See generally, on tests sometimes used to distinguish local affairs from those of statewide concern, 1 Antieau, Municipal Corporation Law § 3.21 (1978); 2 McQuillin, Municipal Corporations § 4.85 (3d ed. 1966 rev.). See also Note, Conflicts Between State Statutes and Municipal Ordinances, 72 Harv.L.Rev. 737 (1959) (a matter is considered purely local if it concerns the administrative and procedural aspects of the local government and has no effect on those living outside the municipality); Appellate Decisions 1979–80, Part IX—Zoning Law, 22 Ariz.L.Rev. 1177, 1182–84 (1980) (summary of Arizona cases). Note also the tests discussed in note 44 *supra*.

[46] People ex rel. Moore v. Perkins, 56 Colo. 17, 137 P. 55 (1913); Moore v. Oklahoma City, 122 Okl. 234, 254 P. 47 (1927) (Oklahoma City changed from commission to city-manager form of government); Lackey v. State, 29 Okl. 255, 116 P. 913 (1911) (Oklahoma City had adopted commission form of government). In Farmer v. City of Sapulpa, 645 P.2d 518 (Okl.1982), the court, in upholding the mayor's power to restrict water usage within the city during a shortage, held that the form of government of a charter city is a matter of local concern and that the charter will therefore control as to the distribution of powers and duties within the government. See Boatman v. Waddle, 264 P.2d 730 (Okl.1953) (initiative petition for change from commission form of government to council-manager form pertained to matters within province of people of the municipality, as reserved to them by state constitution). But some authority takes the view that a municipality's form of government is initially a matter of state concern and that municipalities derive their control of this only by state delegation (often made in the state constitution itself). See Mayor of Gloucester v. City Clerk, 327 Mass. 460, 99 N.E.2d 452 (1951); Bucino v. Malone, 12 N.J. 330, 96 A.2d 669 (1953). Cf. Opinion of the Justices, 328 Mass. 674, 105 N.E.2d 565 (1952). See generally 2 McQuillin, Municipal Corporations § 4.97 (3d rev. ed. 1996).

[47] State ex rel. Freeman v. Zimmerman, 86 Minn. 353, 90 N.W. 783 (1902) (board of health); City of Tulsa v. Langley, 196 Okl. 680, 168 P.2d 116 (1946) (water commission); Bussell v. Gill, 58 Wash. 468, 108 P. 1080 (1910) (municipal plans commission). Cf. State ex rel. Bindas v. Andrish, 165 Ohio St. 441, 136 N.E.2d 43 (1956) (election of school teacher to city council; governed by city law). See also Comment, Constitutional Law—Bailey v. County of Shelby: Can County Charter Governments Set Qualifications for Members of the County Legislative Body?, 37 U. Memphis L. Rev. 839 (2007), noting Bailey v. County of Shelby, 188 S.W.3d 539 (Tenn. 2006) (statute authorizing county to establish qualifications for county legislative body upheld as not an unconstitutional delegation of legislature's authority to establish qualifications of local officials; term limits provision upheld).

[48] See People ex rel. Moore v. Perkins, *supra* note 46; Fitzgerald v. City of Cleveland, 88 Ohio St. 338, 103 N.E. 512 (1913). In State ex rel. Short v. Callahan, 96 Okl. 276, 221 P. 718 (1923), it was held that even a state constitutional provision on a mandatory primary-election system had no application to a home-rule city's election of local officers, since the election was a purely local matter. See City of Tucson v. State of Arizona, 229 Ariz. 172, 273 P.3d 624 (2012) (city's method and manner of conducting city council elections was of strictly local concern; need for compliance with federal Voting Rights Act did not render city's elections a matter of statewide concern so as to be governed by state statute prohibiting partisan city elections), further proceedings, 333 P.3d 761 (Ariz. App. 2014) (statute mandating municipal candidate elections be held on even-numbered years intruded on area of purely or solely local interest and was thus superseded by provisions of city charter). Cf. Johnson v. Bradley, 4 Cal.4th 389, 14 Cal.Rptr.2d 470, 841 P.2d 990 (1992) (state law prohibiting any candidate from accepting public funds did not preclude home-rule city from adopting a partial public financing measure).

[49] In re Pfahler, 150 Cal. 71, 88 P. 270 (1906) (initiative and referendum); Hilzinger v. Gillman, 56 Wash. 228, 105 P. 471 (1909) (recall). But if the city charter is silent on such subjects as initiative and referendum, any relevant state statutes will govern in most states. See Shelton v. Lambert, 399 P.2d 467 (Okl.1965). Cf. Sharp v. Lee, 201 Okl. 49, 200 P.2d 756 (1948). In Clapsaddle v. Blevine, 66 P.3d 352 (Okla.

the selection, hiring, and firing of municipal officers and employees, as well as the tasks assigned them and compensation paid them, are of purely local concern;[50] and so is the conducting of elections at which only municipal issues and/or offices are involved.[51] But state law governs the conduct of any elections at which state or county offices and/or issues are at stake.[52]

1998), the court held that the setting of special municipal elections for the possible recall of city officials was not a matter of purely local concern; therefore, state statutes prevailed over the city charter.

[50] City of Pasadena v. Charleville, 215 Cal. 384, 10 P.2d 745 (1932) (compensation); Adams v. Wolff, 84 Cal.App.2d 435, 190 P.2d 665 (Dist.Ct.1948) (selection and hiring); State ex rel. Mullin v. Mansfield, 26 Ohio St.2d 129, 269 N.E.2d 602 (1971), cert. denied 404 U.S. 985, 92 S.Ct. 452, 30 L.Ed.2d 369 (number of employees to be hired in department); City of Mansfield v. Endly, 38 Ohio App. 528, 176 N.E. 462 (1931), aff'd 124 Ohio St. 652, 181 N.E. 886 (compensation); Lorain Street Railroad Co. v. Public Utilities Commission, 113 Ohio St. 68, 148 N.E. 577 (1925) (tasks of municipal employees); State ex rel. Frankenstein v. Hillenbrand, 100 Ohio St. 339, 126 N.E. 309 (1919) (civil service law); State ex rel. Trimble v. City of Moore, 818 P.2d 889 (Okl.1991) (compensation paid mayor and council); Greenberg v. City of Bradford, 432 Pa. 611, 248 A.2d 51 (1968) (compensation of police and fire officers). But a residency requirement has been held of state concern. Mosebar v. Moore, 41 Wn.2d 216, 248 P.2d 385 (1952). Cf. City of Pasadena v. Charleville, *supra* at 398–400, 10 P.2d at 750–51, (employment of aliens is of state concern); Reed v. City of Tulsa, 569 P.2d 451 (Okl.1977) (statute encouraging municipal employees to participate in militia is of state concern). But see City & County of Denver v. State, 788 P.2d 764 (Colo.1990) (state law prohibiting municipalities from imposing residency requirements on their employees held an unconstitutional interference with home-rule powers of local governments). Minimum wage laws may also be found of state concern. City of Phoenix v. Kidd, 54 Ariz. 75, 92 P.2d 513 (1939), aff'd 54 Ariz. 123, 94 P.2d 428; City of Phoenix v. Drink-water, 46 Ariz. 470, 52 P.2d 1175 (1935); State v. Jaastad, 43 Ariz. 458, 32 P.2d 799 (1934); Wholesale Laundry Board of Trade, Inc. v. City of New York, 17 A.D.2d 327, 234 N.Y.S.2d 862 (1962), aff'd 12 N.Y.2d 998, 239 N.Y.S.2d 128, 189 N.E.2d 623 (1963). But see State Building & Constr. Trades Council v. City of Vista, 143 Cal. Rptr. 3d 529, 295 P.3d 480 (2012) (no statewide concern shown that would justify state's regulation of wages that home-rule cities require their contractors to pay workers hired to construct locally funded public works; local ordinances governed, not state Prevailing Wage Law); Bishop v. City of San Jose, 1 Cal.3d 56, 81 Cal.Rptr. 465, 460 P.2d 137 (1969); City of Baltimore v. Sitnick, 254 Md. 303, 255 A.2d 376 (App.1969), noted 2 Urban Lawyer 116 (1970). Cf. Greenberg v. City of Bradford, *supra*. Regulation of the hours of work may also be found of statewide concern. See State v. Tibbetts, 21 Okl. Cr. 168, 205 P. 776 (1922). As may the rules regarding unemployment compensation. City of Colorado Springs v. Industrial Comm'n, 749 P.2d 412 (Colo.1988) (unemployment compensation for former employees of city). Cf. New Mexicans for Free Enterprise v. City of Santa Fe, 138 N.M. 785, 126 P.3d 1149 (App. 2005) (state's Minimum Wage Act is a general law of concern to workers across the state, though home-rule city was free to enact a higher minimum wage applicable within municipality). See generally Comment, Madison's Minimum-Wage Ordinance, Section 104.001, and the Future of Home Rule in Wisconsin, 2007 Wis. L. Rev. 151 (2007). See also Lurie, Enforcement of State Minimum Wage and Overtime Laws: Resources, Procedures, and Outcomes, 15 Employee Rights & Employment Pol'y J. 411 (2011).

Marriage has been held a matter of statewide concern. Lockyer v. City & County of San Francisco, 33 Cal.4th 1055, 17 Cal.Rptr.3d 225, 95 P.3d 459 (2004) (city mayor exceeded his authority by requesting that county clerk and county recorder determine what changes were necessary to render marriage licensing forms nondiscriminatory as to gender and sexual orientation). But the extension of benefits to domestic partners in same-sex relationships has been held a matter of local rather than statewide concern. Heinsma v. City of Vancouver, 144 Wash.2d 556, 29 P.3d 709 (2001). See Leskovar v. Nickels, 140 Wash.App. 770, 166 P.3d 1251 (2007) (mayor's executive order requiring city employees to recognize same-sex marriages of city employees in same manner as opposite-sex marriages for purposes of employee benefits held not to conflict with state's Defense of Marriage Law; employee benefits said to be of local concern).

[51] Strode v. Sullivan, 72 Ariz. 360, 236 P.2d 48 (1951); Rees v. Layton, 6 Cal.App.3d 815, 86 Cal.Rptr. 268 (Dist.Ct.1970); Scheafer v. Herman, 172 Cal. 338, 155 P. 1084 (1916); State ex rel. Sherrill v. Brown, 155 Ohio St. 607, 99 N.E.2d 779 (1951); Mitchell v. Carter, 31 Okl. 592, 122 P. 691 (1912). Cf. Triano v. Massion, 109 Ariz. 506, 508, 513 P.2d 935, 937 (1973); Mackey v. Thiel, 262 Cal.App.2d 362, 68 Cal.Rptr. 717 (Dist.Ct.1968). But see State ex rel. Flynn v. McCaughey, 81 R.I. 143, 99 A.2d 482 (1953) (Rhode Island constitution reserves full power over elections to state legislature).

[52] Fitzgerald v. City of Cleveland, 88 Ohio St. 338, 103 N.E. 512 (1913). See Strode v. Sullivan, *supra* note 51. Cf. State ex rel. Automatic Registering Machine Co. v. Green, 121 Ohio St. 301, 168 N.E. 131 (1929). In addition, basic constitutional guarantees, such as the one-person one-vote principle and related matters involving fair representation, are of statewide concern even when such principles are applied to the election of purely local governing bodies. See Casuse v. City of Gallup, 106 N.M. 571, 746 P.2d 1103 (1987) (statute

Many problems have arisen over the operation of municipal police and fire departments. Since the peace and safety of citizens is of general concern, the traditional majority view has been that the selection, hiring, firing, etc. of police officers, and the general operation of police departments, are matters on which state law will prevail over home-rule city law in cases of conflict.[53] This has generally been the rule applied to the pay received by police officers.[54] But there is authority that pensions and "fringe benefits," being less matters of routine and more matters of discretion than are salaries, are of purely municipal concern.[55] And there has long been a minority view, now verging on becoming the majority, that *all* matters of police personnel—such as hiring and pay—are, like city personnel matters in general, of basically local concern.[56]

Under the majority view, the operation and administration of municipal *courts* are treated as matters of state concern as to which state law must prevail over local in cases

requiring members of municipal governing bodies to be elected from single-member districts invalidated city charter provision allowing at-large election). Cf. State ex rel. Haynes v. Bonem, 114 N.M. 627, 845 P.2d 150 (1992) (statute mandating single-member districting reflects matter of statewide concern and is thus "general law" limiting legislative power of home-rule municipalities).

53 Fox v. McDonald, 101 Ala. 51, 13 So. 416 (1893); State ex rel. Reynolds v. Jost, 265 Mo. 51, 175 S.W. 591 (1915); Van Gilder v. City of Madison, 222 Wis. 58, 267 N.W. 25 (1936), reh. denied 222 Wis. 58, 268 N.W. 108. Cf. People ex rel. Le Roy v. Hurlbut, 24 Mich. 44 (1871). It has been said that police functions are of general, statewide concern, while fire-fighting functions are of only local concern. Von Walter v. City of Canby, 19 Or.App. 60, 526 P.2d 599 (1974). But cf. Jones v. Bayless, 208 Okl. 270, 255 P.2d 506 (1953) (city charter provisions on removal of police officers would prevail over general laws, but charter provision did not apply to demotions).

54 Van Gilder v. City of Madison, *supra* note 9. See Luhrs v. City of Phoenix, 52 Ariz. 438, 83 P.2d 283 (1938) (state controls minimum wages and pensions of policemen). Cf. State ex rel. Reynolds v. Jost, *supra* note 9 (state can provide metropolitan police force and compel city to finance it adequately). But cf. People ex rel. Seal Beach Police Officers Ass'n v. City of Seal Beach, 36 Cal.3d 591, 205 Cal.Rptr. 794, 685 P.2d 1145 (1984) (police salaries are municipal affairs, but process by which salaries are fixed is of statewide concern).

55 See Ebald v. City of Philadelphia, 387 Pa. 407, 128 A.2d 352 (1957); Annot., Matters Pertaining to Police Department as Within Exclusive Control of Municipalities Under Home-Rule Charters, 105 A.L.R. 259, 263–64 (1936). Cf. Bruckshaw v. Paolino, 557 A.2d 1221 (R.I.1989) (court ruled in general terms that regulation of city's pension plan is of local concern). But see City of Cincinnati v. Gamble, 138 Ohio St. 220, 34 N.E.2d 226 (1941). Cf. Conrad v. City of Thornton, 191 Colo. 444, 553 P.2d 822 (1976). See generally 2 McQuillin, Municipal Corporations § 4.106 (3d rev. ed. 1996) (pensions may in some respects be a municipal affair and in other respects a state affair).

56 Popper v. Broderick, 123 Cal. 456, 56 P. 53 (1899); Dinan v. Superior Court, 6 Cal.App. 217, 91 P. 806 (Dist.Ct.1907) (removal of police chief); Fraternal Order of Police v. City & County of Denver, 926 P.2d 582 (Colo.1996) (qualifications for municipal deputy sheriffs); State ex rel. Brownlee v. Broadview Heights, 10 Ohio Misc. 254, 227 N.E.2d 424 (1967); Leavers v. City of Canton, 1 Ohio St.2d 33, 203 N.E.2d 354 (1964) (retirement of police officers); State ex rel. Canada v. Phillips, 168 Ohio St. 191, 151 N.E.2d 722 (1958) (promotions within police department); State ex rel. Lynch v. City of Cleveland, 164 Ohio St. 437, 132 N.E.2d 118 (1956) (method of selecting police chief); Ex parte Tracey, 93 S.W. 538 (Tex.Cr.App.1905). Cf. Klench v. Board of Pension Fund Commissioners, 79 Cal.App. 171, 249 P. 46 (Dist.Ct.1926) (pensions); Hawaii Government Employees' Association v. County of Maui, 59 Hawaii 65, 576 P.2d 1029 (1978) (administration of police has become of local concern).

of conflict.[57] Clearly, this is true as to the extent of the jurisdiction of municipal courts,[58] but the same rule has even been applied to the pay of judicial officers,[59] though there is some authority that this is of only local concern.[60]

Where the operation of a fire department is involved, most authority has followed the general rule as to municipal employees and departments, holding that the law of a home-rule city prevails over state law.[61] But there seems obvious inconsistency in holding that police departments are of statewide concern (as they are under the traditional view) while fire departments are of purely local concern. Thus, a number of cases—on such matters as hiring, pay, and pensions of fire department personnel—have held that state law prevails.[62] It now appears that authority on the matter is almost evenly divided.

---

[57] Matter of Siracusa, 125 Misc. 882, 212 N.Y.S. 400 (1925); State ex rel. Cherrington v. Hutsinpiller, 112 Ohio St. 468, 147 N.E. 647 (1925) (home-rule cities cannot even establish municipal courts; must be done by state law); Fossett v. State, 34 Okl.Cr.App. 106, 245 P. 668 (1926) (appeal from conviction in municipal court); City of La Grande v. Municipal Court, 120 Or. 109, 251 P. 308 (1926) (same). See Hardamon v. City of Boulder, 178 Colo. 271, 497 P.2d 1000 (1972) (state can require jury trials in municipal courts). Cf. Villanazul v. City of Los Angeles, 37 Cal.2d 718, 235 P.2d 16 (1951) (determination of whether there shall be a municipal court is left to city, but operation of any such court is governed by state). But cf. Lee v. Norick, 447 P.2d 1015 (Okl.1968) (removal of municipal judge governed by municipal charter—but state statutes were silent). In Town of Frisco v. Baum, 90 P.3d 845 (Colo. 2004), it was held that in Colorado, a home-rule city has constitutional and statutory power to create a municipal court and define its jurisdiction, as long as the court's jurisdiction is limited to matters of local and municipal concern.

[58] Ex parte Boalt, 123 Or. 1, 260 P. 1004 (1927). Cf. Matter of Siracusa, *supra* note 57 (judge's power to issue search warrants). Of course, the jurisdiction of *state* courts is a matter of state concern. City of Atlanta v. Landers, 212 Ga. 111, 90 S.E.2d 583 (1955); Civil Service Commission v. Engel, 187 Mich. 83, 153 N.W. 358 (1915); State ex rel. City of Minot v. Gronna, 79 N.D. 673, 59 N.W.2d 514 (1953) (juvenile court is of state concern).

[59] See Nicholl v. Koster, 157 Cal. 416, 108 P. 302 (1910) (appointment and pay of probation officer). Cf. Jett v. City of Tucson, 180 Ariz. 115, 882 P.2d 426 (1994) (removal of city magistrate); State ex rel. Dann v. Hutchinson, 206 Minn. 446, 288 N.W. 845 (1939) (removal of justice of peace); Underwood v. Isham, 61 Ohio App. 129, 22 N.E.2d 468 (1939), appeal dism'd, 135 Ohio St. 320, 20 N.E.2d 719 (city could not apply its civil service to employees of municipal court).

[60] Kansas City v. Brouse, 468 S.W.2d 15, 17 (Mo.1971) (pay of judges), noted in 1 Antieau, Municipal Corporation Law § 3.35 (1998).

[61] Popper v. Broderick, 123 Cal. 456, 56 P. 53 (1899) (pay of firemen); State ex rel. Fischer v. City of Lincoln, 137 Neb. 97, 288 N.W. 499 (1939) (discharge); Osborn v. Cohen, 272 N.Y. 55, 4 N.E.2d 289 (1936) (hours of work); City of Wewoka v. Rodman, 172 Okl. 630, 46 P.2d 334 (1935) (discharge); State ex rel. Heinig v. City of Milwaukee, 231 Or. 473, 373 P.2d 680 (1962) (establishment of civil service for firemen). See Leavers v. City of Canton, 1 Ohio St.2d 33, 203 N.E.2d 354 (1964); Oliver v. City of Tulsa, 654 P.2d 607 (Okl.1982) (longevity pay of city firefighters said to be of local concern, but no conflict with state law found anyway). Cf. State ex rel. Burke v. Cervantes, 423 S.W.2d 791 (Mo.1968) (legislature could not force mayor to appoint firemen's arbitration board). See generally 37 Am.Jur.2d Municipal Corporations § 110 (1971). See also Cohen, The Burning Question, Time magazine, Nov. 1, 2010, at 73, discussing the history of firefighting in America and stating "To this day, firefighting remains largely a local matter." *Id.* at 74.

[62] See Luhrs v. City of Phoenix, 52 Ariz. 438, 83 P.2d 283 (1938) (state control of pensions and minimum wages); Huff v. Colorado Springs, 182 Colo. 108, 512 P.2d 632 (1973) (pensions of fireman); Board of Trustees of Firemen's Pension Fund v. People ex rel. Behrman, 119 Colo. 301, 203 P.2d 490 (1949) (pensions); Grosse Pointe Fire Fighters Association v. Village of Grosse Pointe Park, 303 Mich. 405, 6 N.W.2d 725 (1942) (maximum hours); Axberg v. City of Lincoln, 141 Neb. 55, 2 N.W.2d 613 (1942) (pensions); City of Cincinnati v. Gamble, 138 Ohio St. 220, 34 N.E.2d 226 (1941). Cf. Professional Fire Fighters, Inc. v. City of Los Angeles, 60 Cal.2d 276, 32 Cal.Rptr. 830, 384 P.2d 158 (1963) (labor relations of fire department are of state concern); State ex rel. Benson v. Peterson, 180 Minn. 366, 230 N.W. 830 (1930) (civil service of state concern); Billings Firefighters Local 521 v. City of Billings, 214 Mont. 481, 694 P.2d 1335 (1985) (home-rule city could not pass ordinances superseding state law regarding municipal fire department); State ex rel. Strain v. Houston, 138 Ohio St. 203, 34 N.E.2d 219 (1941) (platoon system); Salt Lake City v. International Association of Firefighters, 563 P.2d 786 (Utah 1977) (state could withdraw delegation to municipalities of control over wages, etc.).

§ 6.5 Conflicts Between State Laws and Laws of Home-Rule Cities—Exercises of Police Power

What of exercises of the police power by home-rule cities—actions undertaken to protect public safety, health, morals, or general welfare? The police power, to the extent it resides in municipal governments, is delegated from the state; and most "police-power matters" are considered of statewide concern. The following generalizations can be made: (1) Wherever a state criminal law exists, the state law defining the crime, providing for its suppression or prosecution, providing a penalty for its violation, and in general protecting the public from the forbidden act, prevails over any municipal laws.[63] In some areas of criminal activity—such as liquor, gambling, and prostitution—, the need for statewide uniformity of rules and enforcement procedures is cited as a reason.[64] But even as to criminal activities where that need might not be considered so great, there is an obvious general interest in anything that the state has defined as criminal conduct. (2) Because of the clear effect of conditions in one city on the rest of the state, matters affecting public health are nearly always considered of statewide concern. This applies to laws on such subjects as sanitation standards for businesses, sewage disposal, regulation of dairy products, and licensing of doctors.[65] Occasionally—partly because the

---

[63] See Van Gilder v. City of Madison, 222 Wis. 58, 267 N.W. 25 (1936) (suppression of crime is of statewide concern). See generally 1 Antieau, Municipal Corporation Law § 3.34 (1998). See also 2 McQuillin, Municipal Corporations § 4.107 (3d rev. ed. 1996) (on police powers of municipalities). In Colorado, home-rule cities cannot punish conduct made criminal by state law; thus as to all such crimes, the state has effectively pre-empted the field. See Gazotti v. City & County of Denver, 143 Colo. 311, 352 P.2d 963 (1960).

[64] Mayor of Prescott v. Randall, 67 Ariz. 369, 196 P.2d 477 (1948) (liquor control); In re Iverson, 199 Cal. 582, 250 P. 681 (1926) (liquor control); Farmer v. Behmer, 9 Cal.App. 773, 100 P. 901 (Dist.Ct.1909) (prostitution); State ex rel. Smith v. City of International Falls, 132 Minn. 298, 156 N.W. 249 (1916) (liquor control); State v. Linn, 49 Okl. 526, 153 P. 826 (1915) (gambling). Cf. Canon City v. Merris, 137 Colo. 169, 323 P.2d 614 (1958) (driving while intoxicated is of state concern); Neil House Hotel Co. v. City of Columbus, 144 Ohio St. 248, 58 N.E.2d 665 (1944). See also Fancy's Entertainment L.L.C. v. City of Enid, 171 P.3d 928 (Okla. App. 2007) (underage drinking, while a matter of legitimate concern to local officials, is not exclusively a local matter). In Beseler v. Freier, 258 P.3d 720 (Wyo. 2011), the court observed that "whereas municipalities may to some extent police the sale and consumption of alcoholic beverages at the local level, they may not by ordinance establish a negligence standard of care different from that chosen by the legislature." *Id.* at 725. Compare the dissent of Justice Kits, finding nothing in state statutes that would preclude cities and towns from exercising home rule with respect to alcohol. *Id.* at 728–29. But cf. Hawaii Government Employees' Association v. County of Maui, 59 Haw. 65, 576 P.2d 1029 (Hawaii 1978) (such matters as administration of police, and liquor control, have become matters of local concern under county home rule). In Kansas, even if a matter is of statewide concern, a city may exempt itself from the pertinent state statute if that statute is not uniformly applicable to all cities. See Junction City v. Griffin, 227 Kan. 332, 607 P.2d 459 (1980) (ordinances prohibited solicitation for prostitution and provided mandatory jail sentence upon conviction; held valid). Indeed the Kansas rule allowing home-rule cities by ordinances to exempt themselves from a statute with statewide effect (known as "charter ordinance") is subject to four potentially overlapping exceptions in all: (1) enactments of statewide concern uniformly applicable to all cities, (2) other enactments uniformly applicable to all cities, (3) enactments uniformly applicable to all cities of the same class that prohibit or limit the levying of any tax, excise, fee, charge, or other exaction; and (4) enactments prescribing limits of indebtedness. See Farha v. City of Wichita, 284 Kan. 507, 161 P.3d 717 (2007). Cf. Laramie Citizens for Good Government v. City of Laramie, 617 P.2d 474 (Wyo.1980) (municipal legislation must not conflict with state statutes that are uniformly applicable to cities and towns).

[65] City of Phoenix v. Breuninger, 50 Ariz. 372, 72 P.2d 580 (1937) (dairy products); Ex parte Maki, 56 Cal.App.2d 635, 133 P.2d 64 (Dist. Ct. 1943) (licensing of doctors); Ex parte Hoffman, 155 Cal. 114, 99 P. 517 (1909) (sale of milk); Smith v. Zimmermann, 268 N.Y. 491, 198 N.E. 369 (1935); Robertson v. Zimmermann, 268 N.Y. 52, 196 N.E. 740 (1935); State ex rel. Mowrer v. Underwood, 137 Ohio St. 1, 27 N.E.2d 773 (1940). See 1 Antieau, Municipal Corporation Law § 3.33 (1998). Cf. City & County of Denver v. Eggert, 647 P.2d 216 (Colo.1982) (location of waste disposal facility is of statewide concern and thus a home-rule city is subject to the state legislation); DuHamel v. People ex rel. City of Arvada, 42 Colo.App. 491, 601 P.2d 639 (1979) (system of emergency medical care was of statewide concern; city could not require operator of ambulance service,

particular activities are considered "proprietary" or "business-like" in nature—, the operation of sewer systems has been classified as of purely local concern.[66] (3) All laws and provisions on education are normally considered to deal with matters of general, not local, concern.[67] This is almost universally true as to operation of the school system, but the operation of public libraries may occasionally be considered a local matter.[68] (4) Normally, matters related to public safety, morality, and welfare are also of statewide concern. This principle has usually encompassed traffic controls such as speed limits.[69] But a couple qualifications must be made: (a) In a few states, traffic regulations applying to a city's own streets are characterized as of purely local concern.[70] This rule may be

---

already licensed by county, to obtain city license); State v. Johnson, 175 Neb. 498, 122 N.W.2d 240 (1963) (storm sewer bonds are of state concern because such sewers affect public health); Hofer v. Carson, 102 Or. 545, 203 P. 323 (1922) (keeping of dogs). But the impounding of stray animals is often classified as municipal. 2 McQuillin, Municipal Corporations § 4.40 (3d rev. ed. 1996) (health is usually a matter of state concern). See generally on public health *id.* § 4.99.

Air-pollution control is clearly an area of statewide concern, but broad home-rule power has been recognized as long as there is no conflict with state law. See Oriental Boulevard Co. v. Heller, 27 N.Y.2d 212, 316 N.Y.S.2d 226, 265 N.E.2d 72 (1970), appeal dism'd 401 U.S. 986, 91 S.Ct. 1234, 28 L.Ed.2d 527, noted 22 Syracuse L.Rev. 1173 (1972). See generally Comment, Local Government and Air Pollution, 33 Ohio St. L.J. 924 (1972).

66 See Westerly Residents for Thoughtful Development, Inc. v. Brancato, 565 A.2d 1262 (R.I.1989) (establishment and operation of sewer systems is purely local function, and home-rule municipality had inherent authority to expand sewer system). See generally 2 McQuillin, Municipal Corporations § 4.109 (3d rev. ed. 1996) (construction and maintenance of sewers and drains). In California, it would appear that the entire subject of operation of sewers is left to the control of home-rule cities. Cramer v. City of San Diego, 164 Cal.App.2d 168, 330 P.2d 235 (Dist.Ct.1958). Cf. City of Grass Valley v. Walkinshaw, 34 Cal.2d 595, 212 P.2d 894 (1949) (collection and treatment of garbage are of purely local concern).

67 Lanza v. Wagner, 11 N.Y.2d 317, 229 N.Y.S.2d 380, 183 N.E.2d 670 (1962), appeal dism'd 371 U.S. 74, 83 S.Ct. 177, 9 L.Ed.2d 163, cert. denied 371 U.S. 901, 83 S.Ct. 205, 9 L.Ed.2d 164 (terms of Board of Education members subject to state control); Niehaus v. State ex rel. Board of Education, 111 Ohio St. 47, 144 N.E. 433 (1924) (school buildings must be approved in conformity with state law); Harbach v. Mayor of Milwaukee, 189 Wis. 84, 206 N.W. 210 (1925) (state can change tax limit for educational purposes). Cf. Board of Education v. Houghton, 181 Minn. 576, 233 N.W. 834 (1930) (schools erected by board of education not subject to city planning commission); Carlberg v. Metcalfe, 120 Neb. 481, 234 N.W. 87 (1930) (establishment of municipal university). But there is doubt as to the law of California on this point. Compare Law v. City of San Francisco, 144 Cal. 384, 77 P. 1014 (1904) (bonds for new schools are a municipal affair), and Stern v. City Council, 25 Cal.App. 685, 145 P. 167 (Dist. Ct.App.1914) (compensation of school officials is of local concern), with Hancock v. Board of Education, 140 Cal. 554, 74 P. 44 (1903) (school system said to be of general concern).

68 State ex rel. Brown v. Dunnaway, 207 Okl. 144, 248 P.2d 232 (1952). Cf. City of Pasadena v. Paine, 126 Cal.App.2d 93, 271 P.2d 577 (Dist.Ct.1954) (necessity for, and location of, branch libraries). Contra, State ex rel. Carpenter v. City of St. Louis, 318 Mo. 870, 2 S.W.2d 713 (1928). If library employees, commissions, etc. are involved, it would seem the decision on such a matter should turn on whether the court found the interests of the employees or board members (usually local matters) to dominate the issue, or the interest in public education (usually a state matter).

69 Pipoly v. Benson, 20 Cal.2d 366, 125 P.2d 482 (1942). See Atlas Mixed Mortar Co. v. City of Burbank, 202 Cal. 660, 262 P. 334 (1927). Cf. Phoenix Respirator & Ambulance Service, Inc. v. McWilliams, 12 Ariz.App. 186, 468 P.2d 951 (1970) (state statutes control operation of emergency vehicles on streets); Webb v. City of Black Hawk, 295 P.3d 480 (Colo. 2013) (ordinance prohibiting bicycles from outside municipality on streets within municipality was not a matter of purely local concern; state statute governed). In City of Greenwood Village ex rel. State v. Fleming, 643 P.2d 511 (Colo.1982), provisions of a home-rule city's speeding ordinance classifying some traffic offenses as noncriminal, permitting conviction on a preponderance of the evidence, and not allowing the accused the privilege against self-incrimination were struck as in violation of state law. See City of Rio Rancho v. Young, 119 N.M. 324, 889 P.2d 1246 (App. 1995) (statute limiting authority of municipality to enforce its traffic ordinances on private property applied to all municipalities, including home-rule cities). But see Haney v. City Court ex rel. City of Empire, 779 P.2d 1312 (Colo.1989) (municipality had authority to adopt Model Traffic Code to regulate traffic within municipality).

70 Wiggins v. McAuliffe, 144 Colo. 363, 356 P.2d 487 (1960). Cf. Lorain Street Railroad Co. v. Public Utilities Commission, 113 Ohio St. 68, 148 N.E. 577 (1925) (but majority of Ohio court stopped short of holding that local law would prevail in case of conflict). There is also a split of authority on what governs the weight of

considered to receive some support from the often-applied doctrine that the opening, laying out, and improving of city streets are purely local matters.[71] (b) Occasionally, zoning restrictions on very specific matters, even if enacted partly for reasons of safety, are classified as of purely local concern—as where a city ordinance imposes restrictions on the location of oil or gas wells,[72] or sets height or setback limits on buildings.[73]

§ 6.6 Conflicts Between State Laws and Laws of Home-Rule Cities—Financial Matters

Finances—including the levy and collection of taxes—represent another area in which the activities of one governmental unit have substantial effect on those of others.

---

loads that may be carried through home-rule cities. Compare in this regard Atlas Mixed Mortar Co. v. City of Burbank, *supra* note 69 (state), with Union Sand & Supply Corp. v. Fairport, 172 Ohio St. 387, 176 N.E.2d 224 (1961), and Froelich v. City of Cleveland, 99 Ohio St. 376, 124 N.E. 212 (1919) (home-rule city's law prevails). Cf. Perkins v. Quaker City, 165 Ohio St. 120, 133 N.E.2d 595 (1956) (city can compel truckers to stay on state highways when going through city).

[71] See Civic Center Association v. Railroad Commission, 175 Cal. 441, 166 P. 351 (1917); Salsbury v. City of Lincoln, 117 Neb. 465, 220 N.W. 827 (1928); Massa v. City of Cincinnati, 110 N.E.2d 726 (Ohio Com.Pl.1953), appeal dism'd 160 Ohio St. 254, 115 N.E.2d 689. But state highways can be built through, or relocated in, home-rule cities without city permission. City of Lakewood v. Thormyer, 171 Ohio St. 135, 168 N.E.2d 289 (1960). And control of outdoor advertising signs located within a home-rule municipality but along roads of the state highway system has been held a subject governed by state, rather than municipal, law where there is a conflict between the two. National Advertising Co. v. Department of Highways of Colorado, 751 P.2d 632 (Colo.1988) (treated as matter of mixed state and local concern). And railroad crossings may be considered a matter of statewide concern, and are in at least one state—California—subject to control by the Public Utilities Commission. See Union City v. Southern Pacific Co., 261 Cal.App.2d 277, 67 Cal.Rptr. 816 (Dist.Ct.1968); Jones, Is the Regulation of Railroad Crossings a Municipal Affair?, 5 Cal.L.Rev. 292 (1917). Provision of off-street parking has also been held of local concern. City of Ponca City v. Edwards, 460 P.2d 418 (Okl.1969).

[72] See Van Meter v. Westgate Oil Co., 168 Okl. 200, 32 P.2d 719 (1934); Courter Oil Co. v. Oklahoma City, 167 Okl. 633, 31 P.2d 596 (1934); Gant v. Oklahoma City, 150 Okl. 86, 6 P.2d 1065 (1931), appeal dism'd 284 U.S. 594, 52 S.Ct. 203, 76 L.Ed. 512. As to the home-rule status of hydraulic fracturing, see Nearpass & Brenner, High Volume Hydraulic Fracturing and Home Rule: The Struggle for Control, 76 Alb. L. Rev. 167 (2012–13). See also Note, Embracing Federalism or: How I Learned to Stop Worrying and Love Fracking, 4 Geo. Wash. J. Energy & Envt'l. L. 121 (2013). Some few cases have said in general terms that zoning is a purely local matter; but it seems clear that it is actually of state concern to at least the extent that it is controlled by the state constitution. See McQuillin, Municipal Corporations § 4.112a (3d ed. 1966 rev.). Cf. State ex rel. Thelen v. City of Missoula, 168 Mont. 375, 543 P.2d 173 (1975) (power of state over zoning is supreme). State law also prevails as to preservation of historic landmarks. State v. City of Seattle, 94 Wash.2d 162, 615 P.2d 461 (1980). Occasionally, it is stated that zoning, and land-use planning in general, are simply areas where some matters covered by the laws are of statewide concern and some matters are predominantly local. Allison v. Washington County, 24 Or.App. 571, 548 P.2d 188 (1976). See Comment, Land-Use Controls, Externalities, and the Municipal Affairs Doctrine: A Border Conflict, 8 Loyola U. (L.A.) L.Rev. 432 (1975). See generally Comment, The Gray Zone in the Power of Local Municipalities: Where Zoning Authority Clashes With State Law, 5 J. Bus. Entrepreneurship & L. 215 (2012). But the majority view would seem to remain that zoning and land-use matters are of statewide concern. See Turnpike Woods v. Town of Stony Point, 70 N.Y.2d 735, 519 N.Y.S.2d 960, 514 N.E.2d 380 (1987) (towns may not restrict development of land in a manner inconsistent with state law unless this power is expressly conferred); State ex rel. Baker v. Strange, 960 P.2d 1016 (Wyo.1998) (authority of municipality to adopt zoning ordinance is limited by state statute, and statute limiting time for appeal from city agency decision on zoning matter controlled over inconsistent city law). Cf. City of Fort Collins v. Root Outdoor Advertising, Inc., 788 P.2d 149 (Colo.1990) (city sign ordinance which provided for amortization of outdoor advertising signs did not comply with compensation requirement of state law; state law prevailed).

[73] Ekern v. City of Milwaukee, 190 Wis. 633, 209 N.W. 860 (1926) (maximum height of buildings is local affair; local affairs said to be those that grow out of the existence of a city or village, as distinguished from a rural or pastoral community). Cf. Board of County Commissioners v. City of Thornton, 629 P.2d 605 (Colo.1981) (home rule city not inferior to state legislature with respect to such local matters as preservation of value of city property; city here had standing to attack amendment to county master plan).

Further, the tax power, like the police power, is one that initially resides in the states but not the municipalities; the latter enjoy only such power as delegated by the state. And there is considered to be a need for some statewide uniformity and supervision. Therefore, financial matters in general, and taxes in particular, are classified as matters of state concern.[74] This applies to laws on budgets,[75] debt limitations,[76] and the issuance and redemption of municipal bonds.[77]

There are four necessary qualifications here: (1) Special assessments for *local* improvements, such as improvements to local streets, are usually agreed to be of purely local concern.[78] (2) Most authority takes the view that where a license tax is imposed by a locality on a business or occupation for purely *revenue* purposes, and not for purposes of regulation, this is entirely a matter of local concern.[79] (3) In a few states, bond issues

---

[74] 1 Antieau, Municipal Corporation Law § 3.30–.31 (1998). See generally City of Tulsa v. State of Oklahoma ex rel. Oklahoma Tax Comm'n, 278 P.3d 602 (Okla. 2012) (streamlining sales and use tax collection was matter of state concern); Coulter v. City of Rawlins, 662 P.2d 888 (Wyo.1983) (levying of taxes, excises, fees or other charges is an area of statewide concern). See also Walgreen Co. v. Charnes, 819 P.2d 1039 (Colo.1991), where the court held that the appellate process accompanying contested municipal taxes was a matter of statewide concern subject to uniform statewide regulation in light of the importance of uniformity in the appellate process. It has been stated that a chief failure of home rule has been its general inability to provide municipalities with financial autonomy. Cohn, Municipal Revenue Powers in the Context of Constitutional Home Rule, 51 Nw.U.L.Rev. 27, 30 (1956). But a local tax measure will generally not conflict with state legislation which merely *regulates* the same subject matter. Pines v. City of Santa Monica, 29 Cal.3d 656, 175 Cal.Rptr. 336, 630 P.2d 521 (1981) (city's condominium tax ordinance upheld).

[75] American–La France & Foamite Corp. v. City of Phoenix, 47 Ariz. 133, 54 P.2d 258 (1936); City of Portland v. Welch, 154 Or. 286, 59 P.2d 228 (1936). See State ex rel. Spink v. Kemp, 365 Mo. 368, 283 S.W.2d 502 (1955). But cf. City of Tucson v. Tucson Sunshine Climate Club, 64 Ariz. 1, 164 P.2d 598 (1945) (home-rule city could spend money on advertising in excess of amount allowed by state law).

[76] Phillips on Behalf of Lima v. Hume, 122 Ohio St. 11, 170 N.E. 438 (1930). But cf. State ex rel. Cronin v. Wald, 26 Ohio St.2d 22, 268 N.E.2d 581 (1971) (state legislature cannot prescribe manner local government must follow in setting amount of expenditures that can be made without council authorization).

[77] City of Tulsa v. Dabney, 133 Okl. 54, 270 P. 1112 (1928); Burton v. Gibbons, 148 Or. 370, 36 P.2d 786 (1934).

[78] Board of Commissioners v. City of Colorado Springs, 66 Colo. 111, 180 P. 301 (1919); State ex rel. Kansas City v. Field, 99 Mo. 352, 12 S.W. 802 (1889); State ex rel. Martin v. Cunningham, 158 Neb. 708, 64 N.W.2d 465 (1954) (rate of interest on delinquent assessments); Moore Funeral Homes, Inc. v. City of Tulsa, 552 P.2d 702 (Okl.1976); Nix v. Reynolds, 193 Okl. 15, 141 P.2d 86 (1943); Berry v. McCormick, 91 Okl. 211, 217 P. 392 (1923); Wilson v. City of Medford, 107 Or. 624, 215 P. 184 (1923). Cf. Stanton v. Thompson, 234 Mo. 7, 136 S.W. 698 (1911). But see Saginaw School District v. School District No. 6, 231 Mich. 664, 204 N.W. 737 (1925); City of Portland v. Welch, 154 Or. 286, 59 P.2d 228 (1936). Since the construction of a major thoroughfare within a locality is of statewide concern, this concern extends to the method of financing construction of such a facility. See Committee of Seven Thousand v. Superior Court, 45 Cal.3d 491, 247 Cal.Rptr. 362, 754 P.2d 708 (1988).

[79] See Union Transportes de Nogales v. City of Nogales, 195 Ariz. 166, 985 P.2d 1025 (Ariz. 1999) (occupational license tax on motor carrier activity is of local concern unless state has pre-empted the field); State Farm Mutual Automobile Insurance Co. v. Temple, 176 Colo. 537, 491 P.2d 1371 (1971) (where tax strictly for revenue, home-rule city could impose occupation tax on insurers despite general statute indicating that state tax was exclusive). Cf. City of Mesa v. Home Builders Association, 111 Ariz. 29, 523 P.2d 57 (1974) (city could tax contractors despite general state tax on them). See generally Annot., Home Rule Charter as Affecting Power of Legislature in Respect of Municipal Taxation, 106 A.L.R. 1202, 1205 (1937). See also Red Slipper Club, Inc. v. Oklahoma City, 599 P.2d 406 (Okl.1979) (where licensing ordinance is merely *regulatory*, fee should not exceed expense of regulation; but a license fee may also be used to gain revenue). Thus, a home-rule city may impose a license tax on lawyers if the tax is for revenue only, despite the thorough regulation of the practice of law by the state. Russo v. City of Tucson, 20 Ariz.App. 401, 513 P.2d 690 (1973); Salt Lake City v. Robbins, 550 P.2d 730 (Utah 1976). Cf. People v. Williams, 207 Cal.App.2d Supp. 912, 24 Cal.Rptr. 922 (Dist.Ct.1962) (city may impose occupational tax on attorneys, though state has pre-empted field of regulation). But cf. Silverman v. Mayor of Savannah, 125 Ga.App. 41, 186 S.E.2d 447 (1971), where the court did not find the measure to be purely for revenue purposes; Harlen v. City of Helena, 208 Mont. 45, 676 P.2d 191 (1984), where a city ordinance requiring all businesses to apply for a license and pay an annual fee was held invalid

to provide funds for purely local projects are considered municipal matters, as to which local law will prevail.[80] (4) There is some authority that the *manner* of levying and assessing any municipal taxes—at least so long as the revenue is to be used for local purposes—is of purely local concern.[81] The latter two qualifications appear still to be minority views, but may indicate a trend toward allowing home-rule municipalities greater autonomy over raising money for their own local activities.

§ 6.7 Conflicts Between State Laws and Laws of Home-Rule Cities—Miscellaneous Matters; Generalities

Another important power generally delegated by states to municipalities is the power of eminent domain: the power to condemn private property and take it for public uses upon the payment of fair compensation. But as with the police and tax powers of municipalities, this power *does* initially reside in the state; municipalities have only such power as the state delegates. For that reason, and because the taking of property in one location may be thought to have a "ripple" effect on other places, eminent domain is usually classified as an area of statewide concern—one in which state law prevails over that of a home-rule city.[82] This has been thought to be especially true of a city's exercise of this power as to property *outside* city limits, since any such extraterritorial power that the city may enjoy is usually exceptional and limited, and obviously is not solely the concern of the people of the city.[83] But the same rule has normally been applied where the taking has been of property within city limits.[84] There is a minority view on this

---

with respect to attorneys as it infringed on the constitutional authority of the state supreme court to exercise exclusive supervision and regulation over attorneys.

[80] City of Redondo Beach v. Taxpayers, Property Owners, Citizens and Electors, 54 Cal.2d 126, 5 Cal.Rptr. 10, 352 P.2d 170 (1960); Fladung v. City of Boulder, 165 Colo. 244, 438 P.2d 688 (1968); Berman v. City & County of Denver, 156 Colo. 538, 400 P.2d 434 (1965). See City of Santa Monica v. Grubb, 245 Cal.App.2d 718, 54 Cal.Rptr. 210 (Dist.Ct.1966) (home-rule city does not need grant of power from legislature to issue bonds); Denver Urban Renewal Authority v. Byrne, 618 P.2d 1374 (Colo.1980) (issuance of tax allocation bonds for urban renewal purposes; city had standing to challenge validity of state statute due to city's right of home rule). But it seems that bond issues for *state* purposes are always state matters. See City of Santa Clara v. Von Raesfeld, 3 Cal.3d 239, 90 Cal.Rptr. 8, 474 P.2d 976 (1970).

[81] West Coast Advertising Co. v. City and County of San Francisco, 14 Cal.2d 516, 95 P.2d 138 (1939); Eppley Hotels Co. v. City of Lincoln, 133 Neb. 550, 276 N.W. 196 (1937), cert. denied 304 U.S. 576, 58 S.Ct. 1045, 82 L.Ed. 1540. This rule is approved at 1 Antieau, Municipal Corporation Law § 3.30, at 3–85 (1998). Cf. Town of Avon v. Weststar Bank, 151 P.3d 631 (Colo. App. 2006) (tax lien of home-rule town was superior to lien and security interest of bank in the proceeds of a tax sale conducted by state, where state constitution furnished the authority for town to create a lien to enforce its tax sale, and the priority established by Uniform Commercial Code in favor of bank was specifically made inapplicable to town's tax lien). But see McWilliams v. City of Long Beach, 56 Cal. 4th 613, 155 Cal. Rptr. 3d 817, 300 P.3d 886 (2013) (state's Government Claims Act provides the necessary legislative authorization for class claims of taxpayer refunds against local governmental entities and is not precluded by local charters or ordinances).

[82] Wilson v. Beville, 47 Cal.2d 852, 306 P.2d 789 (1957); City of Los Angeles v. Koyer, 48 Cal.App. 720, 192 P. 301 (Dist.Ct.1920); State ex rel. Nelson v. Butler, 145 Neb. 638, 17 N.W.2d 683 (1945); Thurber v. City of McMinnville, 63 Or. 410, 128 P. 43 (1912); Lamasco Realty Co. v. City of Milwaukee, 242 Wis. 357, 8 N.W.2d 372 (1943), reh. denied 242 Wis. 357, 8 N.W.2d 865. See 2 McQuillin, Municipal Corporations § 4.94 (3d rev. ed. 1996).

[83] See Ramsey v. Leeper, 168 Okl. 43, 31 P.2d 852 (1933). Cf. City of McMinnville v. Howenstine, 56 Or. 451, 109 P. 81 (1910).

[84] See City of Pryor Creek v. Public Service Co., 536 P.2d 343 (Okl.1975). Cf. Sublett v. City of Tulsa, 405 P.2d 185 (Okl.1965).

subject, reasoning that since municipalities normally exercise eminent domain for their own local purposes and projects, the whole subject is one of purely local concern.[85]

The regulation of utilities is also considered to be of statewide concern. This is clearly true of transportation utilities[86] and communication utilities[87] since there is a definite interdependence among the various parts of such a system and a need for uniformity in service and regulation. But the same holding has resulted where the case has involved regulation of other utilities, such as gas and water companies.[88] If the state delegates some of its regulatory power to its municipalities, it may subsequently rescind the delegation since the state interest remains paramount.[89] Even as to the granting of street franchises (that is, the right to use public streets for pipes, wires, tracks, etc.) within home-rule cities, the state interest is paramount, and state law prevails in the absence of specific constitutional limitations.[90] Where the city itself operates a utility,

---

[85] Northern Pacific Railway Co. v. City of Duluth, 153 Minn. 122, 189 N.W. 937 (1922); State ex rel. Ryan v. District Court, 87 Minn. 146, 91 N.W. 300 (1902); Lockhart v. Kansas City, 351 Mo. 1218, 175 S.W.2d 814 (1943); Kansas City v. Marsh Oil Co., 140 Mo. 458, 41 S.W. 943 (1897); Simmons v. Cleveland Heights, 160 N.E.2d 677 (Ohio Com.Pl.1959). See State ex rel. St. Louis County v. Campbell, 498 S.W.2d 833 (Mo.App.1973).

[86] Northeast Rapid Transit Co. v. City of Phoenix, 41 Ariz. 71, 15 P.2d 951 (1932) (motor carriers); People v. Willert, 37 Cal.App.2d Supp. 729, 93 P.2d 872 (1939); Lorain Street Railroad Co. v. Public Utilities Commission, 113 Ohio St. 68, 148 N.E. 577 (1925) (street railroad). But cf. Sylvania Busses v. City of Toledo, 118 Ohio St. 187, 160 N.E. 674 (1928) (city could prohibit intra-city service by inter-city buses licensed by state).

[87] City of Englewood v. Mountain States Telephone & Telegraph Co., 163 Colo. 400, 431 P.2d 40 (1967) (city cannot deny permission to operate to a company having such permission from the state); Public Utilities Comm'n v. Mountain States Tel. Co., 125 Colo. 167, 243 P.2d 397 (1952) (regulation of rates and service). See City of Tulsa v. Southwestern Bell Tel. Co., 75 F.2d 343 (10th Cir. 1935), cert. den., 295 U.S. 744, 55 S.Ct. 656, 79 L.Ed. 1690 (1935) (statutory authorization of use of city streets by telephone company prevails over municipal law).

[88] City of Kalamazoo v. Titus, 208 Mich. 252, 175 N.W. 480 (1919) (rates of gas company); Galbreath v. Oklahoma Natural Gas Co., 130 Okl. 34, 264 P. 878 (1928) (water utility's charges to city). See Chugach Elec. Ass'n v. City of Anchorage, 476 P.2d 115 (Alaska 1970) (state certification of electric utility's service area governs); State ex rel. Klapp v. Dayton Power & Light Co., 11 Ohio App.2d 64, 228 N.W.2d 673 (1962), aff'd 10 Ohio St.2d 14, 225 N.E.2d 230 (1967) (city cannot oust utility from its streets without state permission). Cf. Givigliano v. Veltri, 180 Colo. 10, 501 P.2d 1044 (1972) (trash hauling is of statewide concern; city could not pass ordinance in conflict with state regulation). See generally Vaubel, Of Concern to Painesville—Or Only to the State?—Home Rule in the Context of Utilities Regulation, 33 Ohio St.L.J. 257 (1972), noting Cleveland Electric Illuminating Co. v. Painesville, 15 Ohio St.2d 125, 239 N.E.2d 75 (1968) (ordinance requiring underground installation of electric lines void as contrary to state statute). Cf. Union Elec. Co. v. City of Crestwood, 499 S.W.2d 480 (Mo.1973) (underground installation ordinance void). A state law requiring a city to purchase an existing utility before the city itself may engage in similar utility service has also been found of statewide concern. City of Tucson v. Polar Water Co., 76 Ariz. 404, 265 P.2d 773 (1954).

[89] See Southwestern Bell Telephone Co. v. City of Kountze, 543 S.W.2d 871 (Tex.Civ.App.1976), upholding Texas statute conferring on state Public Utilities Commission exclusive jurisdiction over regulation of telephone utilities. Plaintiff City of Kountze was a general-law, not a home-rule, city; but Texas law formerly delegated much of the regulation of utilities to municipalities, whether home-rule or not. The situation was modified by the Public Utility Regulatory Act, Tex.Rev.Civ.Stat.Ann. art. 1446c (1962 Supp.1978), applied in the *Kountze* case *supra*. As to the prior law under which municipalities had broad delegations of exclusive regulatory power, see Tuck v. Texas Power & Light Co., 543 S.W.2d 214 (Tex.Civ.App.1976), ref'd n. r. e.; Kousal v. Texas Power & Light Co., 142 Tex. 451, 179 S.W.2d 283 (1944).

[90] City of Tulsa v. Southwestern Bell Telephone Co., 75 F.2d 343 (10th Cir.1935), cert. denied 295 U.S. 744, 55 S.Ct. 656, 79 L.Ed. 1690; Henry v. Bartlesville Gas & Oil Co., 33 Okl. 473, 126 P. 725 (1912); Overholser v. Oklahoma Interurban Traction Co., 29 Okl. 571, 119 P. 127 (1911); City of Jacksonville v. Entex, Inc., 538 S.W.2d 250 (Tex.Civ.App.1976), ref'd n. r. e.; City of Tyler v. Television Cable Service, Inc., 493 S.W.2d 322 (Tex.Civ.App.1973), ref'd n. r. e. See City of Chickasha v. Arkansas Louisiana Gas Co., 625 P.2d 638 (Okl.App.1981) (rules promulgated by state commission prevail over city ordinances as to franchised utility's duty to repair, maintain, or install its equipment).

the state interest in regulating rates, service, etc. would still seem to be supreme. But often, municipally owned and operated utilities are specifically exempted by statute from state regulation, at least as to their operation within city limits.[91] The theory is that the city residents who are the utility's customers are also, by virtue of their status as voters, the utility's owners and can "vote out" the management if they don't like the way the utility is operating. Obviously, those residing outside the city, however, have no such protection and are in need of state regulation for protection.

Annexation—the extension of city boundaries—necessarily involves land that, prior to the city's action, is outside city limits. Further, the annexations of one city affect possible such actions by others. Thus, annexation has been held a matter of statewide concern.[92] The same has been held true of detachment of territory from a city—variously called "deannexation" or "disannexation."[93] Consolidation or merger of cities is also a statewide matter.[94] As to all these subjects, there is need for a uniform procedure and general planning. But the change of ward boundaries—that is, the boundaries determining the districts of various members of the city council—within a home-rule city is of purely local concern.[95]

There is authority that the method of enacting ordinances is of statewide concern, since all the people of the state have some interest in the laws made by its various governments.[96] But this would seem a minority view; and in any case, much of the control

---

91 As to state power, see City of Logansport v. Public Service Commission, 202 Ind. 523, 177 N.E. 249 (1931) (municipal utility); City of Woodburn v. Public Service Commission, 82 Or. 114, 161 P. 391 (1916). Cf. Kansas City Southern Railway Co. v. Wood, 126 Okl. 275, 259 P. 262 (1927) (state law might apply to bonds of city-owned utility but inapplicable to municipality under 2000 population). As to the exemption of municipal utilities from state control—but only as to their operations *within* the municipality—, see City of Loveland v. Public Utilities Comm'n, 195 Colo. 298, 580 P.2d 381 (1978); City & County of Denver v. Public Utilities Commission, 181 Colo. 38, 507 P.2d 871 (1973) (mass transit system). Cf. Chastain v. Oklahoma City, 208 Okl. 604, 258 P.2d 635 (1953) (neither Constitution nor statutes prescribe rates of municipally operated utility nor for what purpose profits may be used). See generally 56 Am.Jur.2d Municipal Corporations § 135 (1971). In some states, the home-rule provision of the state constitution specifically authorizes municipalities to operate public utilities and is held to preclude any state restrictions. See 1 Antieau, Municipal Corporation Law § 3.23 (1998). Cf. City of Albuquerque v. New Mexico State Corporation Commission, 93 N.M. 719, 605 P.2d 227 (1979) (city had authority to establish limousine service; municipal transit law governed over state law on same subject because municipal law more specific). See generally Brown, The Administration of Municipally Operated Utilities, 14 Okl.L.Rev. 176 (1961). In City & County of Denver ex rel. Board of Water Comm'rs v. Colorado River Water Conservation Dist., 696 P.2d 730 (Colo.1985), the court declared that the municipality had authority to appropriate and supply water to users outside its boundaries, in the absence of any conflicting state legislation or charter provision. The matter was treated as not exclusively of either local or statewide concern but as concerning both levels of government. Similarly, a city ordinance establishing the right to a lien in favor of the city for unpaid utility charges was upheld in Sant v. Stephens, 753 P.2d 752 (Colo.1988), the court finding this a matter of local concern—though possibly also of state concern—and finding no conflict with state statutes.

92 Los Angeles County v. City Council of Lawndale, 202 Cal.App.2d 20, 20 Cal.Rptr. 363 (Dist.Ct.1962); People v. City of Long Beach, 155 Cal. 604, 102 P. 664 (1909); Independent School District v. City of Duluth, 284 Minn. 279, 170 N.W.2d 116 (1969); St. Louis County v. Florissant, 406 S.W.2d 281 (Mo.1966); New York City v. Lawrence, 250 N.Y. 429, 165 N.E. 836 (1929); Barton v. Stuckey, 121 Okl. 226, 248 P. 592 (1926); In re Baldwin Township Annexation, 305 Pa. 490, 158 A. 272 (1931); State ex rel. Wilkinson v. Self, 191 S.W.2d 756 (Tex.Civ.App.1945). Cf. City of Beloit v. Kallas, 76 Wis.2d 61, 250 N.W.2d 342 (1977).

93 Beachwood v. Board of Elections, 167 Ohio St. 369, 148 N.E.2d 921 (1958).

94 See Douglas v. City of Juneau, 484 P.2d 1040 (Alaska 1971); State ex rel. Tongue v. Gilbert, 66 Or. 434, 134 P. 1038 (1913).

95 Baldwin v. City of Buffalo, 6 N.Y.2d 168, 189 N.Y.S.2d 129, 160 N.E.2d 443 (1959).

96 See 2 McQuillin, Municipal Corporations § 4.101 (3d rev. ed. 1996). A state Open Meetings Act has been held to deal with a matter of statewide concern and thus to prevail over a conflicting municipal law. City

over determining the procedure for ordinance-making is frequently delegated by the state constitution to the home-rule cities themselves.[97] The method of *publication* of municipal ordinances is generally considered a purely municipal affair.[98]

At one time or another, numerous other matters have had to be classified as "of statewide concern" or "of purely municipal concern" by the courts.[99] What tests appear to be generally used by the courts in making these somewhat ad hoc determinations? One leading authority has suggested four generalizations:[100] (1) If uniform regulation throughout the state appears necessary or desirable, as with traffic regulations and utility rate regulation, the matter is likely to be classified as of statewide concern. (2) Courts are likely to look somewhat to the roles that have historically been played, and the services traditionally furnished, by state and local governments. Thus, municipalities have historically furnished firefighting and fire-prevention service, while states have often supplied educational needs. (3) The effect of the particular matter on those *outside* the municipality must be considered of great importance. Thus, annexation by a city necessarily affects persons outside the city and may be considered a matter of general interest, while salaries paid local officials are of little concern to those outside the locality. (4) Where cooperation between locality and state, or among governmental units within the state, is needed, the matter is generally classified as of state concern.

---

of Kingfisher v. State, 958 P.2d 170 (Okl. App. 1998) (home-rule charter required all meetings to be public, but state statute allowed executive sessions for some purposes).

[97] See Inland Development Co. v. Oklahoma City, 9 F.Supp. 96 (W.D.Okl.1934), appeal dism'd, 82 F.2d 1011 (10th Cir. 1936); Adler v. City Council of Culver City, 184 Cal.App.2d 763, 7 Cal.Rptr. 805 (Dist.Ct.1960). Cf. In re Pfahler, 150 Cal. 71, 88 P. 270 (1906) (municipality may provide for enactment of ordinances by initiative and referendum). Similarly, the method for amending a city charter is of statewide concern. People ex rel. Seal Beach Police Officers Ass'n v. City of Seal Beach, 36 Cal.3d 591, 205 Cal.Rptr. 794, 685 P.2d 1145 (1984); City of Ecorse v. People's Community Hospital Authority, 336 Mich. 490, 58 N.W.2d 159 (1953). Cf. Bard v. City of Minneapolis, 256 Minn. 581, 99 N.W.2d 468 (1959) (legislature can establish percentage of vote needed to amend charters). But by constitutional or statutory provision, authority to determine the method of amendment is often delegated to the city itself. See In re Initiative Petition, City of Okmulgee, 89 Okl. 134, 214 P. 186 (1923). A city charter has been held to prevail over state statute as to the mayor's veto power. Trentham v. Isaacs, 324 P.3d 425 (Okla. Civ. App. 2013).

[98] Oklahoma Journal Publishing Co. v. Oklahoma City, 620 P.2d 452 (Okl.App.1979); Goodall v. City of Clinton, 196 Okl. 10, 161 P.2d 1011 (1945). See 2 McQuillin, Municipal Corporations § 4.102 (3d rev. ed. 1996).

The public nature of municipal documents may be considered of general, not local, concern. See Oklahoma Publishing Co. v. City of Moore, 682 P.2d 754 (Okl.1984) (public nature of city police department records of arrests and incarcerations is of general concern, but since state law was silent on the subject, city charter controlled).

[99] See 1 Antieau, Municipal Corporation Law § 3.39 ("Miscellaneous matters") (1998); 2 McQuillin, Municipal Corporations § 4.113 (3d rev. ed. 1996). A good number of "miscellaneous matters" have been found of statewide concern. See Humphrey v. City of Phoenix, 55 Ariz. 374, 102 P.2d 82 (1940) (slum clearance); Edward Brown & Sons v. City & County of San Francisco, 36 Cal.2d 272, 223 P.2d 231 (1950) (tort liability of municipalities); Michelson v. City of Grand Island, 154 Neb. 654, 48 N.W.2d 769 (1951) (sewage disposal); Adler v. Deegan, 251 N.Y. 467, 167 N.E. 705 (1929) (slum clearance and public housing); State ex rel. Martin v. City of Juneau, 238 Wis. 564, 300 N.W. 187 (1941) (water pollution).

[100] 1 Antieau, Municipal Corporation Law § 3.40 (1998). Some Colorado cases list similar factors: the need for statewide uniformity of regulation; impact of municipal regulation on persons living outside the municipal limits; historical considerations, such as whether the matter is traditionally controlled by the state or by local government; and whether the state constitution specifically commits the matter to state or local regulation. Commerce City v. State, 40 P.3d 1273 (Colo. 2002) (statutes governing automated vehicle identification systems superceded conflicting provisions of home-rule cities' ordinances); City & County of Denver v. QWest Corp., 18 P.3d 748 (Colo. 2001). Cf. City & County of Denver v. Board of Assessment Appeals, 30 P.3d 177 (Colo. 2001) (local functions affect only those residing within boundaries of a local governmental unit, while functions of statewide interest affect the larger statewide public).

This is true of matters involving health care and protection. With these considerations kept in mind by the courts, cases must be decided individually, without, it is hoped, blind allegiance to precedent or to labels.[101]

§ 6.8 Conflicts Between State Laws and Laws of Home-Rule Cities—When Is a Conflict Present?

As is evident from the preceding sections, many cases have faced and decided the issue of whether a particular matter is of statewide or of purely local concern. But in most jurisdictions, this question need not be reached unless there is a *conflict* between the state law on the matter and the law of the home-rule city.[102] It might often be well for the courts first to address the question of whether or not the state and local laws are in conflict, and then, only if such conflict is found, reach the determination of state matters vs. local matters, in order to decide which law (state or municipal) prevails to the extent of the conflict. In practice, the conflict sometimes seems assumed with little discussion; or the courts go ahead and classify a matter as state or local even before addressing the conflict question.

A conflict is usually said to exist where a local ordinance prohibits an act that a state statute permits, or permits an act that a state statute prohibits.[103] Since even home-rule municipalities are subject to the general laws of the state, if there is, as to a matter of general concern, a conflict between state law and the law of the home-rule city, the state law must prevail.[104] But local laws prevail as to local matters.

---

[101] See *id.* at 3–108–09. See generally, finding that no reliable criteria have been developed by the courts in distinguishing local from statewide matters, Sato, "Municipal Affairs" in California, 60 Cal.L.Rev. 1055 (1972).

[102] See Billings Associated Plumbing, Heating & Cooling v. State Board of Plumbers, 184 Mont. 249, 602 P.2d 597 (1979) (dual regulation of plumbing permitted so long as municipal regulation not in conflict with state's). Colorado often expresses the rule a little differently: Local laws govern matters of purely local concern; state laws govern matters of statewide concern; in matters of mixed state and local concern, state law prevails to the extent of conflict. See City & County of Denver v. Board of County Comm'rs, 760 P.2d 656 (Colo.App.1988), aff'd 782 P.2d 753 (Colo.1989), citing Denver & Rio Grande R.R. v. City & County of Denver, 673 P.2d 354 (Colo.1983). Inconsistency with state law has been called the most basic inquiry used to determine whether a statute evinces an intent to negate a home-rule city's ordinance. Protection & Advocacy System v. City of Albuquerque, 145 N.M. 156, 195 P.3d 1, 17 (App. 2008).

If a municipality is exempt from a state law, or is free to reject it and does reject it, the municipality may then adopt legislation, even on matters of statewide concern, that is inconsistent with state provisions. See Anchorage Municipal Employees Association v. Municipality of Anchorage, 618 P.2d 575 (Alaska 1980) (state statute on collective bargaining). There are a few states in which *all* state control over *municipal* affairs is deemed to be terminated when home rule is obtained. This means that state law on local matters will have no effect on the home-rule city even if the state law is not in conflict with any city law, and even if the city has no law at all on the subject. There are also a few states where local laws governing home-rule cities may be passed, but only with consent from the city. See notes 40–41 *supra* and accompanying text.

[103] Junction City v. Lee, 216 Kan. 495, 532 P.2d 1292 (1975). See 37 Am.Jur.2d Municipal Corporations §§ 127–28 (1971). But see Simpson v. Municipality of Anchorage, 635 P.2d 1197 (Alaska Ct.App.1981) (question is not whether there is a discrepancy between state and local law but whether any discrepancy impedes policy expressed by state law). See generally Note, Conflicts Between State Statutes and Municipal Ordinances, 72 Harv.L.Rev. 737 (1959). See also Stennis v. City of Santa Fe, 143 N.M. 320, 176 P.3d 309 (2008) (municipal ordinance conflicts with state law when state law specifically allows activities that the ordinance forbids or when state law is of such a character that local prohibitions on those activities would be inconsistent with or antagonistic to that state law or policy).

[104] See 56 Am.Jur.2d Municipal Corporations § 128 (1971).

Under the above test, a conflict will exist if state law expressly permits Sunday sales of beer and the city prohibits them.[105] (This being a statewide concern, state law will govern.) If state law expressly allows persons with a designated kind of permit to serve alcoholic beverages at all hours, a city ordinance forbidding liquor sales after midnight will be found to conflict and thus be declared invalid.[106] But the specific language is highly important here. If a law of the state simply prohibits serving alcohol after 3 a.m., but does not expressly *permit* its being served until that hour, then the home-rule city may set a higher standard and order the serving of alcohol to cease at 1:30 a.m.[107] The city, it is often said, may move in the same direction as the state but not counter thereto.[108] It may set higher standards, as for the sale of milk,[109] than those set by the state, so long as it does not permit milk to be sold where the state forbids this, or forbid the sale in situations where the state expressly allows it.

Where the state merely forbids carrying a concealed knife with intent to use it unlawfully against another, the home-rule city may declare it a crime to carry any dangerous knife on one's person—regardless of concealment or intent.[110] Such stricter

---

[105] Sparger v. Harris, 191 Okl. 583, 131 P.2d 1011 (1942). Cf. Town of Warren v. Hazardous Waste Facility Site Safety Council, 392 Mass. 107, 466 N.E.2d 102 (1984) (town bylaws providing that no hazardous waste facility could be located in certain areas conflicted with state statutes allowing such a facility to be constructed in any location presently zoned for industrial use if procedural requirements were met). Compare Fondessy Enterprises, Inc. v. City of Oregon, 23 Ohio St.3d 213, 492 N.E.2d 797 (1986) (no conflict found between state and municipal laws regulating hazardous waste landfills; concurrent authority of state and city recognized).

[106] Neil House Hotel Co. v. City of Columbus, 144 Ohio St. 248, 58 N.E.2d 665 (1944). See Noey v. City of Saginaw, 271 Mich. 595, 261 N.W. 88 (1935).

[107] Leavenworth Club Owners Association v. Atchison, 208 Kan. 318, 492 P.2d 183 (1971).

[108] Johnson v. City of Tulsa, 97 Okl.Cr.85, 258 P.2d 695 (1953); Sparger v. Harris, *supra* note 105. See City of Coral Gables v. Seiferth, 87 So.2d 806 (Fla.1956); Arrow Club, Inc. v. Nebraska Liquor Control Commission, 177 Neb. 686, 131 N.W.2d 134 (1964); Eastern Carolina Tastee-Freez, Inc. v. City of Raleigh, 256 N.C. 208, 123 S.E.2d 632 (1962). See Schaefer v. City & County of Denver, 973 P.2d 717 (Colo.App.1998) (home-rule city could pass ordinance extending dependent health care benefits to "spousal equivalents" of its employees, though state statute limited term "dependent" to spouse or child); Rabon v. City of Seattle, 135 Wash.2d 278, 957 P.2d 621 (1998) (city ordinance forbidding possession of dangerous dogs did not irreconcilably conflict with state statute providing that local authorities should issue certificate of registration for dangerous dogs). Cf. Billings Firefighters Local 521 v. City of Billings, 293 Mont. 41, 973 P.2d 222 (1999) (pre-suspension hearing requirement in collective bargaining agreement between city and firefighters' union did not conflict with statute's post-suspension hearing requirement).

[109] Beatrice Foods Co. v. City of Okmulgee, 381 P.2d 863 (Okl.1963) (city may prescribe higher sanitation standards for milk than set by state and may charge reasonable inspection fee). But cf. City of Grand Haven v. Grocer's Co-op. Dairy Co., 330 Mich. 694, 48 N.W.2d 362 (1951) (state found to have assumed plenary control over pasteurization). Cf. Lizotte v. Conservation Comm'n, 216 Conn. 320, 579 A.2d 1044 (1990) (town's regulation containing setback requirements for sewer systems does not run counter to state legislation merely because town's regulation was more stringent). See also Steffes v. City of Lawrence, 284 Kan. 380, 160 P.3d 843 (2007) (where both ordinance and statute are prohibitory and the only difference is that the ordinance goes further in its prohibition, there is no conflict; no conflict found where smoking ordinance generally prohibited smoking in public places and places of employment, while state statute authorized persons in charge of public places to designate areas in which smoking was permitted).

[110] Junction City v. Lee, 216 Kan. 495, 532 P.2d 1292 (1975). Cf. City & County of Denver v. Howard, 622 P.2d 568 (Colo. 1981) (ordinance on interference with peace officer was broader and more inclusive than statute; no conflict); Dillon v. City of Tulsa, 273 P.2d 145 (Okl.Cr.App.1954) (ordinance prohibiting carrying of concealed weapon in car and statute prohibiting carrying of concealed weapon on or about the person not in conflict). Where state statutes restrict the offer for sale, or use, of the larger, more powerful kinds of fireworks, a city may prohibit the offer for sale, or use, of smaller, less powerful ones. Haddenham v. City of Laramie, 648 P.2d 551 (Wyo.1982) (statute specifically authorized such further restriction by city, but court says city would have had the power anyway). Cf. City of Portland v. Jackson, 316 Or. 143, 850 P.2d 1093 (1993) (where state statute prohibited display of genitalia for purposes of sexual arousal, city could prohibit such display for any

municipal standards are often justified as being required by more crowded, more dangerous urban conditions—but regardless of any such justification, there is simply no conflict. The city may act to regulate areas left untouched by the state—as nude dancing in bars where the state has only regulated the serving and consumption of liquor,[111] or driving on shopping-center parking lots where state laws apply only to public streets.[112] Traffic control is an area where municipalities often impose broader regulations than the state, and where such regulations are upheld as not in conflict with the state law.[113] Utility regulation by a municipality is possible as to areas not touched by state law.[114] Again, there is clearly no conflict. But if a state statute specifically permits resistance to an unlawful arrest, a city ordinance prohibiting resistance is invalid.[115] It sets no higher

---

purpose). Where a state "dog-bite" statute applies only to the "owner" of a dog, a city may enact an ordinance imposing liability on anyone who harbors or maintains a dog, and the city legislation will simply be interpreted as broader than the state law, not in conflict therewith. See Hampton v. Hammons, 743 P.2d 1053 (Okl.1987). A city's sex offender registration law may be stricter than the state's law. American Civil Liberties Union v. City of Albuquerque, 139 N.M. 761, 137 P.3d 1215 (App. 2006) (city's law included convictions as far back as 1970, while state's law had a later cut-off date). And a city's criminal ordinance may validly omit elements required by the state's law on the same offense. Salt Lake City v. Newman, 2006 Utah 69, 148 P.3d 931 (2006) (city's battery ordinance did not conflict with state law although ordinance lacked state statute's injury element).

[111] Moore v. City of Tulsa, 561 P.2d 961 (Okl.1977). See generally, on regulation of nude dancing, City of Erie v. Pap's A.M., 529 U.S. 277, 120 S.Ct. 1382, 146 L.Ed.2d 265 (2000) (ban on nudity in public places valid as applied to nude erotic dancing); California v. LaRue, 409 U.S. 109, 93 S.Ct. 390, 34 L.Ed.2d 342, reh. denied 410 U.S. 948, 93 S.Ct. 1351, 35 L.Ed.2d 615 (1973).

[112] See Laughlin v. City of Tulsa, 492 P.2d 1131 (Okl.Cr.App.1972). Any motor-vehicle statute or ordinance is generally assumed to apply to both public and private property unless it is clearly limited to public streets. Henig v. District of Columbia, 213 A.2d 824 (D.C.App.1965); Farley v. State, 251 Miss. 497, 170 So.2d 625 (1965); Valentine v. County of Brunswick, 202 Va. 696, 119 S.E.2d 486 (1961). See also State ex rel. Lightfield v. Village of Indian Hill, 69 Ohio St.3d 441, 633 N.E.2d 524 (1994) (charter contained general language regarding police officers' employment but nothing referring specifically to their promotion by examination; so no conflict found with state statute); Oliver v. City of Tulsa, 654 P.2d 607 (Okl.1982) (law on collective bargaining was of statewide concern but did not pertain to longevity pay of firefighters; so no conflict found). But occasionally a matter may be found inappropriate for municipal legislation even though state laws are silent on the particular point. See In re Public Serv. Elec. & Gas Co., 35 N.J. 358, 173 A.2d 233 (1961) (ordinance requiring underground transmission lines void; some matters need uniform treatment and are not proper subjects of municipal legislation even though state has not spoken).

[113] See City of Wichita v. Hackett, 275 Kan. 848, 69 P.3d 621 (2003) (city's DUI ordinances included operation of bicycle, while state's regulation did not). Compare Hansen v. Eyre, 205 Utah 29, 116 P.3d 290 (2005) (city ordinance permitting bicyclists to ride in any marked bicycle lane, whether lane was located on the right or left side of the roadway, conflicted with state law which expressly required bicyclists to ride on the right-hand side of the road, and thus ordinance was invalid). Cf. Webb v. City of Black Hawk, 295 P.3d 480 (Colo. 2013) (municipal ordinance prohibiting bicyclists from riding on local roads conflicts with state law allowing prohibition only if there is an alternate bicycle path provided). See also Lawson v. City of Pasco, 144 Wash.App. 203, 181 P.3d 896 (2008) (city ordinance prohibiting the placement of recreational vehicles in residential mobile home parks did not irrevocably conflict with state statute, which encompassed landlord-tenant relationships arising from rental of lot spaces for recreational vehicles used as primary residences; Act did not require a landlord to rent a mobile home park lot for placement of a recreational vehicle in any or every particular place within the state, and statute and ordinance could stand together and each operate distinctly without inconsistency).

[114] See Springfield Util. Bd. v. Emerald People's Util. Dist., 191 Or.App. 536, 84 P.3d 167 (2004), aff'd 339 Or. 631, 125 P.3d 740 (2005) (city had authority to exclude a people's utility district from operating within city's limits as to area that was not within territory the state commission had allocated; statutes did not apply to unallocated territory, and thus city's home-rule authority there was undiminished).

[115] Bennion v. City & County of Denver, 180 Colo. 213, 504 P.2d 350 (1972). Cf. City of Junction City v. Cadoret, 263 Kan. 164, 946 P.2d 1356 (Kan. 1997) (city could not prosecute defendant for third driving-under-the-influence violation under ordinance that did not make such offense a "nonperson felony," as state statute did make the offense a "nonperson felony").

standard; it does not move in the same direction as the statute; instead, it moves counter to the statute and therefore conflicts with it.

Activities that are made criminal by the state may also be made criminal by the city (unless, as discussed in the following section, the state has pre-empted the field), and the city may impose a harsher or a less severe penalty than that imposed by the state.[116] It used to be true that a person could then be prosecuted for the same act under either city or state law, or both.[117] Now, however, a person can only be prosecuted under one or the other. In 1970, the U.S. Supreme Court ruled that the state and a city therein are not dual and separate sovereigns but constitute the same sovereign. The protection against double jeopardy was then held applicable to the states, and it was held that to be prosecuted both in state and city court for the same act—in that case, removing a canvas mural from city hall—would be a violation of the accused person's right to be free

---

[116] See City of Aurora v. Martin, 181 Colo. 72, 507 P.2d 868 (1973) (offense of assault and battery is matter of "mixed" state *and* local concern, and both may legislate thereon); State ex rel. Franklin v. City of Topeka, 266 Kan. 385, 969 P.2d 852 (1998) (city anti-discrimination ordinance and state anti-discrimination statute could stand together, city could enforce its ordinance, which to a large extent paralleled the state law). In the *City of Aurora* case, *supra*, the *state* penalty was greater. Other cases upholding municipal ordinances imposing lesser punishments than those provided by the state include City of Chicago v. Union Ice Cream Manufacturing Co., 252 Ill. 311, 96 N.E. 872 (1911); City of Duluth v. Evans, 158 Minn. 450, 197 N.W. 737 (1924); State ex rel. Department of Rev. & Taxation v. McNeese, 718 P.2d 38 (Wyo.1986) (municipal ordinance need not provide for revocation of driver's license for failure to stop and render aid at scene of accident even though such revocation was provided under state statute dealing with same offense). But ordinances imposing greater penalties than those prescribed by state statutes have also been upheld. City of Fort Scott v. Arbuckle, 165 Kan. 374, 196 P.2d 217 (1948); Kalita v. City of Detroit, 57 Mich.App. 696, 226 N.W.2d 699 (1975). But cf. City of Bellingham v. Schampera, 57 Wn.2d 106, 356 P.2d 292 (1960) (city could not impose penalty in excess of those provided by state statute, but since penalties here actually imposed were within the permissible limits, conviction affirmed). See generally, 62 C.J.S. Municipal Corporations § 174, at 296 (1999). Oregon follows the general rule that both the state and the municipality may enact laws in the same area of criminal conduct, but holds that a city ordinance may not increase either the minimum or maximum penalty authorized by state law for the same criminal conduct unless there is evidence of legislative acquiescence. See City of Portland v. Dollarhide, 300 Or. 490, 714 P.2d 220 (1986) (city's mandatory minimum penalty in prostitution ordinance invalid where it established harsher minimum than state's for same offense). In Texas, the general rule is followed that a municipality may by ordinance make an act an offense against the municipality though it is also an offense against the state. Ex parte Mooney, 106 Tex.Cr.R. 156, 291 S.W. 246 (1927). Cf. Young v. City of Seagoville, 421 S.W.2d 485 (Tex.Civ.App.1967) (city ordinance allowing pool halls void as conflicting with statute prohibiting them; subsequent statute allowing pool halls under certain conditions couldn't give life to the ordinance). But where the state has specifically defined an offense and fixed a penalty for its violation, any ordinance penalizing the same conduct must—in Texas, contrary to the general rule—conform to state law as to definition and penalty. Young v. State, 160 Tex.Cr.R. 67, 267 S.W.2d 423 (1954) (municipal ordinance invalid due to different penalty for Sunday sale of beer); Brewer v. State, 113 Tex.Cr.R. 522, 24 S.W.2d 409 (1930); Ex parte Farley, 65 Tex.Cr.R. 405, 144 S.W. 530 (1912). See City of Fort Worth v. McDonald, 293 S.W.2d 256 (Tex.Civ.App.1956) ref'd n. r. e.; Cannon v. City of Dallas, 263 S.W.2d 288 (Tex.Civ.App.1953), ref'd n. r. e. For a good review of the several New Mexico cases in which ordinances were upheld though they provided a lesser penalty than that provided for the same offense by state statute, see City of Rio Rancho v. Mazzei, 148 N.M. 553, 239 P.3d 149 (App. 2010).

Might a city ordinance imposing a greater penalty than a state law imposes for the same offense constitute a violation of equal protection? See City of Seattle v. Hogan, 53 Wash.App. 387, 766 P.2d 1134 (1989), where such a violation was found.

[117] Village of Struthers v. Sokol, 108 Ohio St. 263, 140 N.E. 519 (1923); Ex parte Simmons, 4 Okl.Cr. 662, 112 P. 951 (1911), reh. denied 5 Okl.Cr. 399, 115 P. 380; Annot., Limitations Under Double Jeopardy Clause of Fifth Amendment Upon State Criminal Prosecutions—Supreme Court Cases, 25 L.Ed.2d 968 (1971). See Gross, Successive Prosecutions by City and State, 43 Or.L.Rev. 281 (1964). It is still possible, as a matter of constitutional law, for a person to be prosecuted in both federal and state courts for the same act. But there is a longstanding federal *policy*, not required by the constitution, against multiple prosecutions for the same conduct or transaction. See Rinaldi v. United States, 434 U.S. 22, 98 S.Ct. 81, 54 L.Ed.2d 207 (1977); Petite v. United States, 361 U.S. 529, 80 S.Ct. 450, 4 L.Ed.2d 490 (1960).

from double jeopardy.[118] Of course, separate offenses may be committed within the same general transaction, and the state may then prosecute for one offense and the city for another. Thus, where a person spits in a police officer's face, the officer then attempts to arrest the offender, and the offender struggles with the officer and kicks him, the state may prosecute for the kicking even though the city has already prosecuted, and convicted, for the spitting.[119]

The change in the law of double jeopardy left unchanged the basic rule of municipal law: The city and state may both forbid the same conduct, or regulate the same area, and both the state law and the city law may validly operate, so long as there is no conflict between the two. Of course, there will be no conflict where one or the other has not legislated.[120] Thus, where there is no city law on a subject, the state law (if any) will necessarily govern (except that in a few states, state law has no application at all to home-rule cities where purely local matters are concerned[121]). And where there is no state law, city law will inevitably govern, assuming the law is within the city's charter powers.

§ 6.9 State Pre-Emption of Certain Fields

Home-rule cities enjoy certain advantages over other cities. (1) Through home-rule provisions in the state constitution and statutes and through the municipality's own charter, powers are often granted such a city that are not enjoyed by other municipalities of the state. The interpretation of such powers is discussed in more detail in Chapter 8, *infra*. Other cities must depend on general state statutes for all their powers. (2) Where purely local matters are involved, the law of the home-rule city will ordinarily prevail over state law in cases of conflict. Other cities are subject to all statutes of the state, whether general or local in nature; in case of conflict with local law, the state law will *always* prevail—not just, as with home-rule cities, where the statute involves a matter of statewide concern.

But there is one exception to the second above-stated advantage of home-rule cities. In certain areas, the state may by legislation have pre-empted (or "occupied") a particular field of activity or regulation. When the state has done this, there is no room for city law on the matter, whether law of a home-rule city or a non-home-rule city. In effect, *any* city legislation, whether by city charter itself or city ordinance, will be considered to conflict with the state statute, whether or not the usual tests of "conflict" are met. And by virtue of the state's pre-emption (assuming the state legislation is valid), the area covered by the legislation will be considered of statewide concern. So the state

---

[118] Waller v. Florida, 397 U.S. 387, 90 S.Ct. 1184, 25 L.Ed.2d 435 (1970), reh. denied 398 U.S. 914, 90 S.Ct. 1684, 26 L.Ed.2d 79, appeal after remand 270 So.2d 26, cert. denied 414 U.S. 945, 94 S.Ct. 256, 38 L.Ed.2d 168. Cf. Robinson v. Neil, 409 U.S. 505, 93 S.Ct. 876, 35 L.Ed.2d 29 (1973), reh. denied 410 U.S. 959, 93 S.Ct. 1423, 35 L.Ed.2d 694, on remand 366 F.Supp. 924 (E.D.Tenn.), giving *Waller* retroactive effect. See generally Annot., Limitations Under Double Jeopardy Clause of Fifth Amendment Upon State Criminal Prosecutions—Supreme Court Cases, 67 L.Ed.2d 831 (1982). But cf. United States v. Lara, 541 U.S. 193, 124 S.Ct. 1628, 158 L.Ed.2d 420 (2004) (Double Jeopardy Clause does not bar federal prosecution of defendant for assaulting a federal officer after Indian tribe's prosecution and punishment of him for violence to the policeman, absent any showing that the source of the tribal prosecution was federal power).

[119] Walker v. State, 513 P.2d 1309 (Okl.Cr.App.1973).

[120] See Ray v. City & County of Denver, 109 Colo. 74, 121 P.2d 886 (1942); Clemons v. Wilson, 151 Kan. 250, 98 P.2d 423 (1940). Cf. Consumers' Coal Co. v. City of Lincoln, 109 Neb. 51, 189 N.W. 643 (1922).

[121] See note 41 *supra*, and accompanying text.

law will prevail—not just to the extent of actual conflict with the city law, but to the extent of completely wiping out the city law. The state is taken to have said, expressly or impliedly, that there is no room for city legislation in this field.

What areas are often pre-empted by the state; and how can we tell whether, in a particular jurisdiction, a field has been so pre-empted? It is generally agreed that state pre-emption is never assumed merely from the fact of state legislation or regulation. Thus, if the state licenses an occupation or activity, it is assumed that the municipality may also license the same work or activity to the extent it is carried on within the city's boundaries.[122] Pre-emption may occasionally be expressly stated in legislation, but more often it is only implied—and the courts are left with determining when the implication is present. Two important considerations are: (1) The comprehensiveness and pervasiveness of the state regulation. Has the state legislation thoroughly covered all likely activities and objects of regulation within the general subject matter? (2) The need for uniform treatment throughout the state. Is this an area where it is desirable to have a single, all-encompassing scheme of regulation, so that local laws—not just local laws that conflict with the state's, but *any* local laws—would unduly complicate the picture? Using such tests, a court may well find that criminal liability for sexual intercourse outside marriage is an area pre-empted by sweeping state regulation.[123] The same may

---

[122] See Mogolefsky v. Schoem, 50 N.J. 588, 236 A.2d 874 (1967) (both state and municipality can regulate real-estate brokers) and Boulevard Apts., Inc. v. Borough of Hasbrouck Heights, 111 N.J.Super. 408, 268 A.2d 359 (1970) (distinguishing *Mogelefsky* and narrowly interpreting exclusion in pre-emption statute). But the state may expressly forbid municipalities from requiring further licenses or fees of those licensed by the state; so held in the *Boulevard Apts.* case, *supra.* Cf. Tamiami Trail Tours, Inc. v. City of Orlando, 120 So.2d 170 (Fla.1960) (statute said state tax was in lieu of all other taxes and fees; precluded city tax for revenue purposes). In general, express pre-emption will not be found unless clearly stated in the legislation. See State of Kansas v. Jenkins, 284 P.3d 1037 (Kan. 2012) (home-rule power does not authorize cities to act where the state has clearly pre-empted the subject with a uniformly applicable enactment, but legislative intent to reserve exclusive jurisdiction to regulate to the state must be clearly apparent in the statute); San Pedro Mining Corp. v. Board of County Comm'rs, 121 N.M. 194, 909 P.2d 754 (N.M.App.1995) (state mining law was ambiguous concerning its effect on local mining ordinances; so no pre-emption found).

[123] In re Carol Lane, 58 Cal.2d 99, 22 Cal.Rptr. 857, 372 P.2d 897 (1962). See City of Spokane v. Portch, 92 Wn.2d 342, 596 P.2d 1044 (1979) (state had pre-empted criminalization of obscenity). Cf. Lancaster v. Municipal Court, 6 Cal.3d 805, 100 Cal.Rptr. 609, 494 P.2d 681 (1972) (regulation of massage parlors). But see Colorado Springs Amusement, Ltd. v. Rizzo, 524 F.2d 571 (3d Cir.1975), cert. denied 428 U.S. 913, 96 S.Ct. 3228, 49 L.Ed.2d 1222 (regulation of massage parlors; no preemption). Compare Smith v. Municipality of Anchorage, 652 P.2d 499 (Alaska App.1982) (statewide uniformity not a significant purpose of state law on concealment of merchandise; thus no preemption found). Where statewide environmental concerns are involved, uniformity is often considered desirable and thus pre-emption will be inferred from a state regulation. See City of Shelton v. Commissioner of Dep't of Environmental Protection, 193 Conn. 506, 479 A.2d 208 (1984) (state operation of regional landfill not subject to local zoning). Cf. Albany Area Builders Ass'n v. Town of Guilderland, 74 N.Y.2d 372, 547 N.Y.S.2d 627, 546 N.E.2d 920 (1989) (state had enacted comprehensive and detailed regulatory scheme as to highway funding; found to have pre-empted field). See also O'Connell v. City of Stockton, 41 Cal.4th 1061, 63 Cal.Rptr.3d 67, 162 P.3d 583 (2007) (whenever the legislature adopts a general scheme for the regulation of a particular subject, the entire control over whatever phases of the subject are covered by state legislation ceases as far as local legislation is concerned; ordinance found pre-empted by statute concerning seizure of vehicles as nuisances when used in connection with prostitution); American Financial Services Assn. v. City of Oakland, 34 Cal.4th 1239, 23 Cal.Rptr.3d 453, 104 P.3d 813 (2005) (city ordinance regulating predatory lending practices was pre-empted by state legislation, which was extensive in scope, clearly indicating state's implicit intent to occupy field of regulation of predatory lending tactics in home mortgages, a subject historically regulated at the state, not local, level); City of Northglenn v. Ibarra, 62 P.3d 151 (Colo. 2003) (home-rule city ordinances prohibiting unrelated or unmarried registered sex offenders from living together in a single-family residence were pre-empted by state law; state's interest in placing and supervising adjudicated delinquent children in foster homes, pursuant to uniform, statewide criteria, overrode any home-rule city's interest in controlling land uses within its borders).

be true as to regulation of liquor sales and consumption.[124] But if, as is sometimes true with regulation of gambling, some forms of a particular activity are forbidden by the state but others are left unrestricted, the way seems open for additional regulation by the cities.[125]

Where a statute contains exceptions—as where it applies to some but not all the cities of the state—, a court is likely to find that the state has not pre-empted the field; the necessary uniformity is not present.[126] If a statute imposing taxes declares that these are to be the exclusive taxes on a business or activity, or are in lieu of all other taxation, this may well be considered a state occupation of the field of taxation of that business or activity.[127] Since pre-emption is not readily to be inferred, the courts proceed with caution here and sometimes find a partial, or "selective," pre-emption. Thus, state regulation of gambling may be found to have pre-empted restrictions on certain types of games but not others,[128] or on all games in which the element of "chance" predominates, but not games in which skill predominates.[129] The intent of the state legislature should

---

[124] 7–Eleven, Inc. v. McClain, 422 P.2d 455 (Okl.1967) (zoning regulation on beer sales invalid; state has pre-empted field except as it expressly allows city control). See as to the development of Oklahoma law on liquor regulation Note, Exorcising the Ghosts of the Past: An Exploration of Alcoholic Beverage Regulation in Oklahoma, 37 Okla. City U.L. Rev. 289 (2012) (state law now provides a system of local option on a county level). See generally Note, Bringing Down the Walls of State Pre-emption: California Cities Fight for Local Control of Alcohol Outlets, 3 African-American L. & Pol'y Rep. 295 (1997).

[125] See Cossack v. City of Los Angeles, 11 Cal.3d 726, 114 Cal.Rptr. 460, 523 P.2d 260 (1974) (state pre-empted regulation of games of chance but not games of skill); In re Hubbard, 62 Cal.2d 119, 41 Cal.Rptr. 393, 396 P.2d 809 (1964), noted 53 Cal.L.Rev. 902 (1965). Implied pre-emption will not be found when the legislature has indicated an intent to permit local regulations or when the statutory scheme recognizes local regulations. See People ex rel. Deukmejian v. Mendocino County, 36 Cal.3d 476, 204 Cal.Rptr. 897, 683 P.2d 1150 (1984) (legislation on pesticides indicated intent to allow local regulation). Compare Borough of McAdoo v. Lawn Specialties, 120 Pa.Cmwlth. 120, 547 A.2d 1297 (1988), where a state law concerning the registration of companies using and applying pesticides indicated that it was to control the field; this was held to pre-empt local ordinances. Pre-emption will not ordinarily be found if the state and municipal law can be regarded as furthering the same goals in the same general way. See Foreman v. Anchorage Equal Rights Comm'n, 779 P.2d 1199 (Alaska 1989) (antidiscrimination laws). Cf. State v. Long, 106 Or.App. 389, 807 P.2d 815 (1991) (ordinance may complement field not expressly occupied by state law; state statute defining offense of possession of concealed firearm did not preempt municipal ordinance defining offense of carrying loaded firearm in public). Sometimes the state statutes are found not so *extensive* as to show a legislative intent to occupy the field. See City of Tucson v. Grezaffi, 200 Ariz. 130, 23 P.3d 675 (App. 2001) (city ordinance forbidding smoking in restaurants was not pre-empted by state laws). The state may also be found not to have pre-empted a field if its regulations leave a term undefined, thus allowing the municipality to define it. See Heinsma v. City of Vancouver, 144 Wash.2d 556, 29 P.3d 709 (2001) (state legislature did not define the term "dependents" in statute authorizing city to provide medical benefits to its employees and their dependents; city not pre-empted from providing a reasonable definition).

[126] See Claflin v. Walsh, 212 Kan. 1, 509 P.2d 1130 (1973) (control of memorial buildings; state statute not uniformly applicable to all cities because of exception for county-seat city).

[127] City of Tempe v. Prudential Ins. Co., 109 Ariz. 429, 510 P.2d 745 (1973), appeal dism'd 414 U.S. 1088, 94 S.Ct. 717, 38 L.Ed.2d 546 (city had pre-empted field of taxation of insurance companies).

[128] DeLong v. Downes, 175 Mont. 152, 573 P.2d 160 (1977) (legislature had preempted field to extent of authorizing certain forms of gambling). Also, where the state requires a certain element for liability, it may be found to have pre-empted any local ordinances that do not include that element. See Holt's Cigar Co. v. City of Philadelphia, 608 Pa. 146, 10 A.3d 902 (2011) ("strict liability" ordinance banning the sale of drug-related paraphernalia regardless of seller's mental state is pre-empted by state statute requiring *mens rea*).

[129] Cossack v. City of Los Angeles, *supra* note 4. Some states also recognize a doctrine of "operational pre-emption," where a local law is totally or partially pre-empted when its operational effect conflicts with the application of the state law—that is, where effectuation of a local interest would materially impede or destroy the state interest. See Town of Carbondale v. GSS Properties, LLC, 169 P.3d 675 (Colo. 2007). County ordinances, in states where counties are empowered to enact legislation, are subject to state pre-emption based on the same standards used for pre-emption of municipal ordinances. See Colorado Mining Ass'n v. Board of

always be the underlying question, though various factors may have to be weighed in ascertaining that intent. Has the legislature indicated an intent to exercise plenary control over the matter?[130] Did the legislature intend to cover the matter fully, to the exclusion of any other control?[131]

County Comm'rs of Summit County, 199 P.3d 718 (Colo. 2009) (county ordinance banning use of cyanide or other toxic-acidic chemicals in certain mining operations pre-empted by state statute).

[130] See City of Grand Haven v. Grocer's Co-op. Dairy Co., 330 Mich. 694, 48 N.W.2d 362 (1951) (state legislation indicated intent to exercise plenary control over pasteurization of dairy products). Cf. Allstate Insurance Co., Inc. v. Municipality of Anchorage, 599 P.2d 140 (Alaska 1979) (statute reserved to state the exclusive power to regulate insurance industry; city commission could *investigate* alleged discrimination by insurance company but could issue no orders or rules affecting insurance business). See also Bishop v. City of San Jose, 1 Cal.3d 56, 81 Cal.Rptr. 465, 460 P.2d 137 (1969), emphasizing legislative intent in determining whether a matter was of statewide concern. If a state statute does not indicate an intent to occupy a field of regulation *fully*, no state pre-emption will generally be found. See Idaho Dairymen's Ass'n v. Gooding County, 148 Idaho 653, 227 P.3d 907 (2010) (state regulation of water quality at confined animal feeding operations did not call for a uniform regulatory scheme).

[131] See Pipoly v. Benson, 20 Cal.2d 366, 125 P.2d 482 (1942) (regulation of pedestrian traffic was intended to be fully covered by act of legislature); Dempsey v. City & County of Denver, 649 P.2d 726 (Colo.App.1982) (comprehensive and pervasive nature of state regulation evinced intent by legislature to pre-empt field of personnel compensation within social services system); Caesar v. State, 101 Idaho 158, 610 P.2d 517 (1980) (regulation of state-owned buildings fully covered by state law). Cf. Prendergast v. City of Tempe, 143 Ariz. 14, 691 P.2d 726 (App. 1984) (legislature had "appropriated" field of compensation of law enforcement personnel); Abbott v. City of Los Angeles, 53 Cal.2d 674, 3 Cal.Rptr. 158, 349 P.2d 974 (1960) (whether state has pre-empted field depends not only on statutory language but also on purpose and scope of legislative scheme); City of Green River v. Debernardi Constr. Co., 816 P.2d 1287 (Wyo.1991) (state statute establishing 5% preference for letting public contracts to contractors who were state residents pre-empted field of residential preference). But in D & F Sanitation Serv. v. City of Billings, 219 Mont. 437, 713 P.2d 977 (1986), the court held that a statute allowing private garbage haulers serving an area prior to municipal annexation a limited right to continue such service after annexation did not show an intent by the state to pre-empt the entire field of garbage regulation. Cf. Jett v. City of Tucson, 180 Ariz. 115, 882 P.2d 426 (1994) (no state pre-emption of authority to discharge municipal magistrates where no indication that legislature had meant to occupy entire field; city council could remove magistrate, though state law also gave commission on judicial conduct that power); City of Riverside v. Inland Empire Patients & Wellness Center, Inc., 56 Cal. 4th 729, 156 Cal. Rptr. 3d 409, 300 P.3d 494 (2013) (pre-emption by state law is not lightly presumed as to appropriate uses of land within a local jurisdiction's borders; California's medical marijuana statutes held not to pre-empt a local ban on facilities that distribute medical marijuana); Candid Enterprises, Inc. v. Grossmont Union High School Dist., 39 Cal.3d 878, 218 Cal.Rptr. 303, 705 P.2d 876 (1985) (state statute permitting local measures imposing school-impact fees on developers of new residential developments in order to finance new school facilities found not to have preemptive effect). On state pre-emption, see generally Symposium, 17 Hastings L.J. 425–581 (1966). On the conflict between home-rule powers of cities and the state's power to pre-empt a field, see Note, Municipal Home Rule's Narrow Escape from the Morass of Implicit Preemption, 57 Me. L. Rev. 613 (2005), discussing Smith v. Town of Pittston, 2003 Me, 46, 820 A.2d 1200 (2003) (town ordinance imposing future limits on sewer usage did not violate home-rule statute). Compare Note, Preemption Hogwash: North Carolina's Judicial Repeal of Local Authority to Regulate Hog Farms, 80 N.C. L. Rev. 2121 (2002), noting Craig v. County of Chatham, 356 N.C. 40, 565 S.E.2d 172 (2002) (state law pre-empted county swine ordinance). See generally on North Carolina law, Bluestein, Do North Carolina Local Governments Need Home Rule?, 84 N.C. L. Rev. 1983 (2006). Cf. State of Washington v. Kirwin, 165 Wash. 2d 818, 203 P.3d 1044 (2009) (city ordinance prohibiting littering not pre-empted by state statute notwithstanding that both prohibit same behavior, since statute says its intent is to add to and coordinate existing recycling and litter control and removal efforts, not to terminate or supplement them). See also Lawson v. City of Pasco, 168 Wash. 2d 675, 230 P.3d 1038 (2010) (Manufactured/Mobile Home Landlord-Tenant Act conferred concurrent jurisdiction on local governments to regulate conduct of mobile-home park landlords and tenants).

Similarly, some opinions emphasize the strong judicial policy to seek to reconcile the operation of both state and local laws rather than to find state pre-emption. See Thunderbird Mobile Club, LLC v. City of Wilsonville, 234 Or. App. 457, 228 P.3d 650 (2010) (ordinances regulating conversion of mobile-home parks to other uses not pre-empted). Some courts are extremely reluctant to infer pre-emption in the absence of an express statement to that effect in the statute. See Zimmerman v. Board of County Comm'rs, 289 Kan. 926, 218 P.3d 400 (2009), saying that Kansas has routinely, though not always clearly and consistently, rejected implied pre-emption.

§ 6.10 Power of City to Enact Private Law

The very act of obtaining its own home-rule charter enables a city to enjoy certain powers delegated by the charter itself, and also by state statutes relevant to home-rule cities.[132] But does a home-rule city have any power to enact its own body of "private law"—that is, law on such matters as torts and contracts, governing the relationships among private individuals? It has generally been said that even a home-rule city has no such power.[133] Certainly any such laws adopted by the city would seem to be in areas of statewide concern and thus would have to yield to state law to the extent of conflict. But arguments based on the need for certainty and predictability as to the law, as well as on fairness, have been put forth tending to the conclusion that the home-rule city should have no power *at all* to enact private laws; in effect, the state should be found to have pre-empted this field.[134]

Distinguishing private law from public law is not always easy. A Model State Constitution promulgated some years ago suggested a provision that home-rule power not include the power to enact laws governing civil relationships except as an incident to some independent power.[135] But this can lead to further problems of interpretation—what is an independent power?,—and its helpfulness has been questioned.[136] Under such a provision, courts may still have difficulty determining, for instance, whether a municipality has power to enact a rent control measure.[137]

Where the tort liability of the city itself is concerned, state law is usually agreed to prevail in cases of *conflict*.[138] But within the limits of state law, either exemptions from tort liability or waivers of immunity may be upheld.[139]

As to state pre-emption of regulation of hydraulic fracking, see Nolon and Gavin, Hydrofracking: State Preemption, Local Power and Cooperative Governance, 63 Case W. Res. L. Rev. 795 (2013); Note, Implied Preemption and Its Effect on Local Hydrofracking Bans in New York, 21 J.L & Pol'y 631 (2013).

[132] Dawley v. Ingham, Circuit Judge, 242 Mich. 247, 218 N.W. 766 (1928) (city had authority under state statute to enact zoning ordinance though charter silent on the matter).

[133] McBain, The Law and Practice of Municipal Home Rule 673–74 (1918). See Fordham, Local Government Law 96–99 (2d rev. ed. 1986). See generally Diller, The City and the Private Right of Action, 64 Stan. L. Rev. 1109 (2012); Serkin, Public Entrenchment Through Private Law: Binding Local Governments, 78 U. Chi. L. Rev. 879 (2011).

[134] See Comment, The Power of Ohio Municipalities to Enact Private Law, 9 Ohio St. L.J. 152 (1948).

[135] National Municipal League, Model State Constitution § 8.02 (6th ed. 1963).

[136] Sandalow, The Limits of Municipal Power under Home Rule: A Role for the Courts, 48 Minn.L.Rev. 643, 674 (1964). But cf., taking a more favorable view of the Model Constitution's provision, Schwartz, The Logic of Home Rule and the Private Law Exception, 20 U.C.L.A.L.Rev. 671 (1973).

[137] It was held that they do not in Marshal House, Inc. v. Rent Review & Grievance Board, 357 Mass. 709, 260 N.E.2d 200 (1970). Accord, under a somewhat different home-rule provision, City of Miami Beach v. Fleetwood Hotel, Inc., 261 So.2d 801 (Fla. 1972), criticized in Note, 27 U.Miami L.Rev. 518 (1973). Rent control ordinances have often been upheld, sometimes without any serious objection that they amount to "private law". See Inganamort v. Borough of Fort Lee, 62 N.J. 521, 303 A.2d 298 (1973), appeal after remand 72 N.J. 412, 371 A.2d 34; Warren v. City of Philadelphia, 382 Pa. 380, 115 A.2d 218 (1955).

[138] See 2 McQuillin, Municipal Corporations § 4.112 (3d rev. ed. 1996).

[139] See Taylor v. Prince George's County, 377 F.Supp. 1004 (D.Md.1974) (waiver of immunity in county home-rule charter); Fuller v. City of Mankato, 248 Minn. 342, 80 N.W.2d 9 (1956) (charter provision limiting municipal liability to situations in which notice given within prescribed time upheld). But cf. Stevens v. Lycan & Co., 259 Minn. 106, 105 N.W.2d 889 (1960) (municipal exemption didn't apply to city officials). Minnesota's state law now contains provisions that may circumscribe the sort of limitation of liability that was upheld in the Fuller case *supra*, Minn.Stat.Ann. § 466.05 (1977).

Of course, home-rule cities do have powers to enact penal ordinances, and even non-home-rule cities usually have some such power by state statute. And these ordinances may help establish the standard of care applicable in tort litigation between private parties, despite any objection that this indirectly allows the city to enact private laws.[140]

---

140 See Borum v. Graham, 4 Cal.App.2d 331, 40 P.2d 866 (Dist.Ct.1935) (city ordinance governs as to pedestrian's rights within crosswalk where state law silent); City and County of Denver v. Henry, 95 Colo. 582, 38 P.2d 895 (1934); Leis v. Cleveland Railway Co., 101 Ohio St. 162, 128 N.E. 73 (1920). See generally Comment, Municipal Home Rule Power: Impact on Private Legal Relationships, 56 Iowa L.Rev. 631 (1971). In tort litigation, the violation of a penal safety ordinance, like the violation of such a statute, usually amounts to negligence per se in the absence of justification or excuse. See Greyhound Terminal v. Thomas, 307 Ky. 44, 209 S.W.2d 478 (1947), overruling prior authority that the violation was merely evidence of negligence and adopting the majority view. See generally James, Statutory Standards and Negligence in Accident Cases, 11 La.L.Rev. 95 (1950); Morris, The Role of Criminal Statutes in Negligence Actions, 49 Colum.L.Rev. 21 (1949), reprinted in Morris, Studies in the Law of Torts 141 (1952).

Chapter 7

RELATIONSHIP OF MUNICIPALITIES TO FEDERAL GOVERNMENT

Analysis

§ 7.1 Extent of Federal-Local Relations

Municipal corporations in the United States are largely under the control of the states and are not under the direct control of the federal government. The creation of municipalities has largely been left to the states. State control, and responsibility for establishment, is even greater where public quasi-corporations, such as counties, are concerned, since these are basically arms of the state. But in recent decades, the federal government, through a great variety of activities and programs, has exerted a considerable and increasing influence on local governments, particularly municipalities. The federal government, in spending for the general welfare, has stimulated, controlled, and sometimes terminated large-scale programs in such areas as public housing, urban renewal, and crime control.[1] The federal aid has often been financially necessary to the

[1] Bromage, Introduction to Municipal Government and Administration 142–59 (2d ed. 1957); Foley, Recent Developments in Federal-Municipal Relationships, 86 U.Pa.L.Rev. 485 (1938); Hanks, Neglected Cities turn to the United States, 35 Nat'l Mun.Rev. 172 (1946). See generally Gelfand, A Nation of Cities—The Federal Government and Urban America, 1933–65 (Oxford Univ. Press 1975); Mandelker, Netsch, Salsich & Wegner, State and Local Government in a Federal System (4th ed. 1996), earlier edition reviewed in Martineau, The Status of State Government Law in Legal Education, 53 U. Cinc. L. Rev. 511 (1984). A later edition of the State and Local Government in a Federal System casebook, cited *supra*, is Mandelker, Netsch, Salsich & Wegner, State and Local Government in a Federal System: Cases and Materials (5th ed. 2002). On trends toward shifting more functions away from the federal government and toward state and local governments, see Freilich, Frye & Carpenter, The New Federalism—American Urban Policy in the 1980's: Trends and Directions in Urban, State and Local Government Law, 15 Urban Law. 159 (1983); Kmiec & Diamond, New Federalism Is Not Enough: The Privatization of Nonpublic Goods, 7 Harv. J. L. & Pub. Pol. 321 (1984). See also Macchiarola & Bailey, Equity and Federalism: The Role of the Local Education Administrator, 15 Urban Law. 3 (1983). On changes in the balance of power between federal and local governments, see Griffith (ed.), Federalism—The Shifting Balance (American Bar Ass'n 1989); Symposium, Federalism, 28 Urban Law. 401–547 (1996). On the law of federal grants, see Cappalli, Federal Grants and Cooperative Agreements—Law, Policy and Practice (1982); Mason, Federal Grant Law (American Bar Ass'n 1982); Brown, Federalism from the "Grant Law" Perspective, 15 Urban Law. ix (Fall, 1983); Cappalli, Federal Grant Disputes: The Lawyer's Next Domain, 11 Urban Law. 377 (1979). On prohibition of discrimination in the awarding of federal grants, see Bakken & Van Zandt, Discrimination and Federal Grants: An Overview of Recent Decisions Concerning the Rehabilitation Act, 15 Urban Law. 805 (1983). On the "explosion" in the number and amount of federal grants in the 1960's and 1970's and the cutbacks in subsequent years, see Casino, Federal Grants-in-Aid: Evolution, Crisis, and Future, 20 Urban Law. 25 (1988). For historical perspective on federal grants and programs, see Tretter, Public Housing Finance, 54 Harv. L. Rev. 1325 (1941).

undertaking or the possible success of such programs, and thus the aid has been much sought, and conditions attached to the grants or loans have been accepted.

Occasionally, in entering into dealings with the federal government, a municipal corporation or public quasi-corporation may run afoul of state laws that prescribe and limit the nature of the local government. The city exists to serve the needs of its inhabitants and provide them with a local government; it cannot agree to put the federal government's interests ahead of those of its own citizens or allow its own government to be controlled by the federal. Thus, where a city in accepting a license from the Federal Power Commission for construction of a hydro-electric project agreed to complete domination by the federal agency, this was held to exceed the city's powers.[2] And it has been said, as to other contractual arrangements between cities and the United States, that a city cannot give over or delegate its governmental authority to agencies of the federal government.[3]

There has been much debate over the extent to which the federal government can regulate relations between state and local governments, on the one hand, and their

---

An area in which participation by the federal government in state and local programs has increasingly been proposed is the study of climate change. See Salkin, Cooperative Federalism and Climate Change: New Meaning to "Think Globally—Act Locally," 40 Envtl. L. Rep. News & Analysis 10562 (2010); Note, Putting the Pieces Together: How Cooperative Federalism Can Help Solve the Climate Change Puzzle, 39 Boston Coll. Envtl. Aff. L. Rev. 391 (2012). See also Dernback, McKinstry & Peterson, Making the States Full Partners in a National Climate Change Effort: A Necessary Element for Sustainable Economic Development, 40 Envtl. L. Rep. News & Analysis 10597 (2010). Partnership between the federal government and the *states* has often occurred in federal grants-in-aid programs designed to remedy poverty, such as Medicare, but has been subject to criticism that this "poverty industry" helps states increase claims for federal aid and the additional funding is then often diverted from its intended purpose. See Hatcher, Poverty Revenue: The Subversion of Fiscal Federalism, 52 Ariz. L. Rev. 675 (2010). As to federal-state-local disputes, see generally Laurie Reynolds, A Role for Local Government in Federal-State-Local Disputes, 43 Urban Law. 977(2011), urging that the U.S. Supreme Court not overlook the space for localism in the law and also take a more nuanced view of state sovereignty.

On "localism" in the law, see the leading articles by Briffault, Our Localism: Part I—The Structure of Local Government Law, 90 Colum. L. Rev. 1 (1990) & Our Localism: Part II—Localism and Legal Theory, 90 Colum. L. Rev. 346 (1990). See also Davison, Cooperative Localism: Federal-Local Collaboration in an era of State Sovereignty, 93 Va. L. Rev. 959 (2007), examining numerous instances of "cooperative localism": interactions of three willing partners—state, federal, and local—in an enterprise. Compare Comment, The Dual-Faceted Federalism Framework and the Derivative Constitutional Status of Local Governments, 2012 B.Y.U.L. Rev. 1585. See also Martin, Federalism and Municipal Innovation: Lessons From the Fight Against Vacant Properties, 46 Urban Law. 361 (2014).

[2] McGuinn v. City of High Point, 217 N.C. 449, 8 S.E.2d 462 (1940).

[3] See City of Middlesboro v. Kentucky Utilities Co., 284 Ky. 833, 146 S.W.2d 48 (1940); Aquamsi Land Co. v. City of Cape Girardeau, 346 Mo. 524, 142 S.W.2d 332 (1940). See generally, on the historical development of local surrenders of power in order to obtain federal aid, Annot., Power of Municipality to Agree to Abide by Conditions or Regulations Imposed by Federal Authority in Respect of Construction, Maintenance, or Operation of a Municipal Public Utility Plant or Enterprise, 128 A.L.R. 620 (1940). Just as local governments should not surrender their basic governmental powers to the federal government, the federal should, via the "comity doctrine," recognize that the nation will fare best if the states and their institutions are left free to perform their separate functions in separate ways. See Levin v. Commerce Energy, Inc., 560 U.S. 413, 130 S.Ct. 2323, 176 L.Ed.2d 1131 (2010) (federal tribunals lack authority to remand to the state court system an action initiated in federal court; complaint of discriminatory state taxation should proceed in state court). But see Haywood v. Drown, 556 U.S. 729, 129 S.Ct. 2108, 173 L.Ed.2d 920 (2009) (state, as well as federal, courts are entrusted with providing forum for vindication of federal rights violated by state or local officials). See generally Logan, Contingent Constitutionalism: State and Local Criminal Laws and the Applicability of Federal Constitutional Rights, 51 Wm. & Mary L. Rev. 143 (2009). See also Comment, Between a Rock and a Hard Place: Legal and Practical Issues Regarding Municipal Power to Address Federal Mandates, 50 Idaho L. Rev. 27 (2014).

employees, on the other hand. In the celebrated *National League of Cities* case,[4] the U.S. Supreme Court struck down the federal government's attempt to extend the minimum-wage and maximum-hour provisions of the Fair Labor Standards Act to state and local governmental employees. This was declared a federal intrusion that might threaten the separate and independent existence of the states, and thus in excess of Congress's power under the Commerce Clause. In a subsequent case, however, the Court upheld application of the Age Discrimination in Employment Act to state and local governments.[5] The court declared that the commerce power is exceeded due to interference with state power only if (1) Congress has attempted to regulate the states as states, (2) the regulation addresses matters that are indisputably attributes of state sovereignty, and (3) the states' compliance with the federal law would directly impair their ability to structure integral operations in areas of traditional governmental functions. Here, no direct impairment of the states' ability was found. Then in 1985, the Court overruled *National League of Cities*, upheld application of the minimum-wage and overtime requirements of the Fair Labor Standards Act to local government employees, and indicated that the commerce power is not exceeded unless a law is destructive of state sovereignty or violative of some constitutional provision.[6]

---

[4] National League of Cities v. Usery, 426 U.S. 833, 96 S.Ct. 2465, 49 L.Ed.2d 245 (1976), on remand 429 F.Supp. 703 (D.D.C. 1977).

[5] Equal Employment Opportunity Comm'n v. Wyoming, 460 U.S. 226, 103 S.Ct. 1054, 75 L.Ed.2d 18 (1983). See Comment, When the Walls Come Tumbling Down: What Remains of *National League of Cities?*, 53 U. Cinc. L. Rev. 625 (1984). See also Freilich, Acconcia & Martin, Judicial Federalism and State Sovereignty, 16 Urban Law. 539 (1984).

[6] Garcia v. San Antonio Metropolitan Transit Auth., 469 U.S. 528, 105 S.Ct. 1005, 83 L.Ed.2d 1016 (1985), reh. denied 471 U.S. 1049, 105 S.Ct. 2041, 85 L.Ed.2d 340 (1985). For later proceedings in this litigation, see Garcia v. San Antonio Metropolitan Transit Auth., 838 F.2d 1411 (5th Cir.1988), cert. denied 488 U.S. 889, 109 S.Ct. 221, 102 L.Ed.2d 212 (1988). The background of the *Garcia* case, which involved employees of a public mass transit authority that had received substantial federal financial assistance, is described in "States' Rights: A Landmark Decision Is in the Making," Bus. Week, Sept. 14, 1984, at 130. In 1985, amendments were enacted to the Fair Labor Standards Act mitigating the effect of that law on local governments. Pub. L. 99–150, Act of Nov. 4, 1985, 99 Stat. 787, 29 U.S.C.A. §§ 201–03 (1985). The underlying rationale of the *Garcia* case was, however, not affected. For interpretation of the 1985 amendments, see Moreau v. Klevenhagen, 508 U.S. 22, 113 S.Ct. 1905, 123 L.Ed.2d 584 (1993) (public employer in a state that prohibits public sector collective bargaining may provide compensatory time-off pursuant to individual agreements). Cf. Christensen v. Harris County, 529 U.S. 576, 120 S.Ct. 1655, 146 L.Ed.2d 621 (2000) (section of Fair Labor Standards Act requiring public employer to honor employee's reasonable request to use compensatory time did not prohibit employer from forcing employees to use accrued compensatory time). For history of the amendments, see Lee, The Political Safeguards of Federalism? Congressional Responses to Supreme Court Decisions on State and Local Liability, 20 Urban Law. 301 (1988). On the Fair Labor Standards Act, cf. Alden v. Maine, 527 U.S. 706, 119 S.Ct. 2240, 144 L.Ed.2d 636 (1999) (in suit brought against state for violation of overtime provisions of Act, Court held that Congress could not subject state to suit in state court without its consent; applying Eleventh Amendment). See also Kimel v. Florida Bd. of Regents, 528 U.S. 62, 120 S.Ct. 631, 145 L.Ed.2d 522 (2000), finding that the Age Discrimination in Employment Act could not validly abrogate the states' Eleventh Amendment immunity from suit by private individuals (applying Seminole Tribe of Fla. v. Florida, 517 U.S. 44, 116 S.Ct. 1114, 134 L.Ed.2d 252 (1996)). On proposals to reinstate the *National League of Cities* rule, see Comment, Restoring the Tenth Amendment: A Call to Overrule *United States v. Darby* and Reinstate *National League of Cities v. Usery*, 25 T.M. Cooley L. Rev. 555 (2008). See generally Hickok, *National League of Cities* and the Ephemeral Nature of Significant Supreme Court Cases, 34 J. Sup. Ct. History 303 (2009).

In Federal Maritime Comm'n v. South Carolina State Ports Auth., 535 U.S. 743, 122 S.Ct. 1864, 152 L.Ed.2d 962 (2002), the Supreme Court held that the Eleventh Amendment immunized states from having to submit to adjudication of private parties' complaints before federal administrative agencies. This holding, along with the *Alden* case *supra*, largely rendered obsolete the *Garcia* case *supra*, though *Garcia* has not been overruled. See Greenhouse, The Last Days of the Rehnquist Court: The Rewards of Patience and Power, 45 Ariz. L. Rev. 251, 259–62 (2003). Other leading cases applying the Eleventh Amendment include Tennessee Student Assistance Corp. v. Hood, 541 U.S. 440, 124 S.Ct. 1905, 158 L.Ed.2d 764 (2004) (under Eleventh

§ 7.2 Federal-Local Relations as to Eminent Domain and Police Power

Problems of the relationship of the various levels of government—federal, state, and local—have sometimes arisen in connection with some government's assertion of the power of eminent domain, or the police power, against another government. For instance, the United States enjoys the power of eminent domain in connection with its control of navigable streams. It has been recognized that the federal government can grant its power in this regard to municipalities.[7] But can the municipality then exercise this delegated power against its parent state? In a case in which a city with such delegated power condemned a state fish hatchery, the city's power was upheld in federal courts.[8] Clearly, the United States could condemn the state property itself. But clearly also, the city could not, apart from the federally delegated power, condemn the state property without state permission. Not surprisingly then, even after the initial federal court decision upholding city power, the state supreme court enjoined the taking of the fish

---

Amendment, unconsenting state is immune from suits by its own citizens as well as by citizens of another state; but Bankruptcy Court's exercise of its in rem jurisdiction to discharge state-held student loan does not infringe state sovereignty, and thus debtor's initiation of adversary proceeding seeking hardship determination is not suit against state under Eleventh Amendment); Nevada Dept. of Human Resources v. Hibbs, 538 U.S. 721, 123 S.Ct. 1972, 155 L.Ed.2d 953 (2003) (Congress may abrogate Eleventh Amendment immunity in federal court if it makes its intention unmistakably clear and acts pursuant to a valid exercise of its power under the enforcement section of the Fourteenth Amendment, as where Congress acted to abrogate Eleventh Amendment immunity for purposes of the Family and Medical Leave Act). Cf. Middleton v. Hartman, 45 P.3d 721 (Colo. 2002) (state employees do not enjoy sovereign immunity when they are sued in individual capacities and relief is sought from these personally; thus, dean and dean's assistant were not protected by immunity on Fair Labor Standards Act claim, even though state would be required to indemnify them for costs of defense if employee did not prove willful and wanton conduct).

Other important cases on federal/local relations include Printz v. United States, 521 U.S. 898, 117 S.Ct. 2365, 138 L.Ed.2d 914 (1997) (provisions of federal Brady Handgun Violence Prevention Act of 1993 that required local officers to conduct background checks on prospective handgun purchasers invalidated as imposing unconstitutional burden on state officers to execute federal laws); United States v. Lopez, 514 U.S. 549, 115 S.Ct. 1624, 131 L.Ed.2d 626 (1995) (federal Gun-Free School Zones Act exceeded Congress's power under Commerce Clause); New York v. United States, 505 U.S. 144, 112 S.Ct. 2408, 120 L.Ed.2d 120 (1992) (federal regulation directed only at the states, commandeering state regulatory mechanisms to federal ends, is invalid). See Kelly, Federalism: While the Stewards Slept . . . *New York v. United States*, 29 Urban Law. 529 (1997); Vile, Truism, Tautology or Vital Principle? The Tenth Amendment Since *United States v. Darby*, 27 Cumberland L. Rev. 445 (1997). On continuing trends in this area, see generally Freilich, Connet & Walters, Federalism in Transition: The Emergence of New State and Local Strategies in the Face of the Vanishing Tenth Amendment, 20 Urban Law. 863 (1988); O'Brien, The Supreme Court and Intergovernmental Relations: What Happened to "Our Federalism"?, 9 J.L. & Pol. 609 (1993). Several excellent articles on this subject are found in Symposium, State and Local Issues Before the Supreme Court and Federal Courts, 20 Urban Law. 233–365 (1988). See also Berger, Federalism: The Founders' Design (Univ. of Okla. Press 1987); Freilich, Wyker & Harris, Federalism at the Millennium: A Review of U.S. Supreme Court Cases Affecting State and Local Government, 31 Urban Law. 683 (1999); Freilich, Francis & Popejoy, State and Local Government at the Crossroads: A Bitterly Divided Supreme Court Reevaluates Federalism in the Bicentennial Year of the Constitution, 19 Urban Law. 791 (1987); Symposium, Federalism in the Bicentennial Year of Our Constitution, 19 Urban Law. 431–741 (1987).

On local animosity to the federal government and its ownership of public lands, as evidenced by the "county supremacy movement," see Southwell, The County Supremacy Movement: The Federalism Implications of a 1990's States' Rights Battle, 32 Gonzaga L. Rev. 417 (1996).

[7] See City of Davenport v. Three-Fifths of an Acre of Land, 147 F.Supp. 794 (S.D.Ill.1957), aff'd 252 F.2d 354 (7th Cir.).

[8] Washington Department of Game v. Federal Power Commission, 207 F.2d 391 (9th Cir.1953), cert. denied 347 U.S. 936, 74 S.Ct. 626, 98 L.Ed. 1087. Cf. City of Davenport v. Three-Fifths of an Acre of Land, 252 F.2d 354 (7th Cir.1958) (municipality, under power from federal government, could condemn land owned by another municipality in another state).

hatchery on the ground that the state had not granted the city this power.[9] But the U.S. Supreme Court reversed the granting of the injunction, finding the state bound by the decision in the earlier federal-court litigation.[10] Thus, it seems that the city can take by eminent domain even the property of its parent state, though the parent state hasn't consented, if the city is exercising a grant of power from the United States government.

But in some situations, local authorities, instead of having their powers expanded through dealings with the federal government, may find their power curtailed by the United States. For instance, federal aid has often been given for the construction of major highways, but this may cause greater judicial scrutiny of the *necessity* for the taking of particular property than would otherwise occur. In one leading case, the United States Supreme Court noted that the Secretary of Transportation is prohibited from authorizing the use of federal funds to construct a road through park lands unless there is no feasible alternative route and all planning to minimize harm to the park has occurred.[11] The case was sent back for further determinations of the possible harm to the park and possible use of other routes. Eventually, the Secretary of Transportation

---

[9] City of Tacoma v. Taxpayers of Tacoma, 49 Wn.2d 781, 307 P.2d 567 (1957), rev'd 357 U.S. 320, 78 S.Ct. 1209, 2 L.Ed.2d 1345.

[10] City of Tacoma v. Taxpayers of Tacoma, 357 U.S. 320, 78 S.Ct. 1209, 2 L.Ed.2d 1345 (1958), where the Court held that (1) the authority of the Federal Power Commission to delegate the eminent-domain power and the competence of the city to carry out the power were reviewable only in federal court, (2) the state of Washington had been a party to the earlier federal-court proceedings, *supra* note 8, and was therefore bound by them, and (3) the Washington State Supreme Court thus lacked jurisdiction to relitigate the questions, already settled in federal court, in a proceeding involving the same parties as the prior litigation. For continuing developments before the same courts on similar matters, see Public Utility District No. 1 v. Federal Power Commission, 308 F.2d 318 (D.C.Cir.1962), cert. denied 372 U.S. 908, 83 S.Ct. 719, 9 L.Ed.2d 716, reh. denied 375 U.S. 871, 84 S.Ct. 29, 11 L.Ed.2d 101; Beezer v. City of Seattle, 62 Wn.2d 569, 383 P.2d 895 (1963), rev'd on other grounds 376 U.S. 224, 84 S.Ct. 709, 11 L.Ed.2d 656 (1964); Beezer v. City of Seattle, 60 Wn.2d 239, 373 P.2d 796 (1962), appeal dism'd 60 Wn.2d 652, 375 P.2d 256.

[11] Citizens to Preserve Overton Park, Inc. v. Volpe, 401 U.S. 402, 91 S.Ct. 814, 28 L.Ed.2d 136 (1971), on remand 335 F.Supp. 873 (W.D.Tenn.) supplemented 357 F.Supp. 846, rev'd 494 F.2d 1212 (6th Cir.) cert. denied 421 U.S. 991, 95 S.Ct. 1997, 44 L.Ed.2d 481, interpreting 23 U.S.C.A. § 138. See Note, Citizens to Preserve Overton Park v. Volpe: Environmental Law and the Scope of Judicial Review, 24 Stan. L.Rev. 1117 (1972); Comment, The Road to Overton Park: "Parklands Statutes" in Federal Highway Legislation, 39 Tenn. L.Rev. 433 (1972). Cf. Named Individual Members of San Antonio Conservation Society v. Texas Highway Department, 446 F.2d 1013 (5th Cir.1971), cert. denied 406 U.S. 933, 92 S.Ct. 1775, 32 L.Ed.2d 136, appeal after remand 496 F.2d 1017 (5th Cir.), cert. denied 420 U.S. 926, 95 S.Ct. 1123, 43 L.Ed.2d 396. See generally Annot., Construction and Application of § 4(f) of Department of Transportation Act of 1966 and § 18(a) of Federal-Aid Highway Act of 1968 Requiring Secretary of Transportation to Determine that All Possible Planning for Highways Has Been Done to Minimize Harm to Public Park and Recreation Lands, 19 A.L.R.Fed. 904 (1974). See also Gray, Environmental Requirements of Highway and Historic Preservation Legislation, 20 Catholic U.L.Rev. 45 (1970).

In Maryland Conservation Council, Inc. v. Gilchrist, 808 F.2d 1039 (4th Cir.1986), it was held that construction of a highway through a state park, built with substantial federal funds, was a "federal action" that required filing and approval of an environmental impact statement and that required approval of the Secretary of Interior for the conversion of the park land to other uses. Cf. Audubon Soc'y v. Dailey, 977 F.2d 428 (8th Cir.1992), in which an environmental organization obtained an injunction against the Army Corps of Engineers' issuance of a permit for a road extension that would increase vehicular traffic through a park; the court found that the Corps' decision that the road extension would not significantly affect the human environment was arbitrary and capricious and that the Corps should be prohibited from issuing the necessary permit until an environmental impact statement was issued. On environmental cases involving informal actions of government agencies (such as involved in the *Overton Park* case *supra*), see generally Sive, Judicial Review of Administrative Actions, Trial, Oct., 1989, at 58. On the federal government's power of eminent domain, see generally Gelin & Miller, The Federal Law of Eminent Domain (Michie 1982), with discussion of the *Overton Park* case at 34–35.

rejected plans to build the interstate highway through park land, despite the urgings of state and local officials.[12]

While a state or locality may not condemn federal land without the United States' permission, the federal government may condemn state or municipal property, even if it is being put to public use. But since the states are not mere creatures of the federal government, fair compensation must be paid.[13] In condemning property, the federal government is not limited by state statutes that may ordinarily preclude the taking of certain types of property, such as cemetery land,[14] though a Congressional intention to abide by local restrictions may sometimes be inferred.[15] In return for giving aid to state

---

[12] See Preservation News, Feb., 1973, at 1. See generally, as to experiences under the provision limiting use of parkland for highway purposes, Netherton, Transportation Planning and the Environment, 1970 Urban L.Ann. 65. In 1978, an effort to force the Secretary of Transportation to approve a tunnel through the park failed in a vote of the U.S. Senate Committee on the Environment and Public Works. Preservation News, June, 1978, at 1. In 1981, state officials totally abandoned the idea of a highway through the park; some former residents of the area sought to repurchase their former land from the state at the prices for which they had sold the properties to the state. See Gray, Bitter Memories Mar Overton Park Residents' Plans to Return, The (Nashville) Tennessean, Feb. 15, 1981, at 18-D, col. 1.

[13] See United States v. Carmack, 329 U.S. 230, 67 S.Ct. 252, 91 L.Ed. 209 (1946), reh. denied 329 U.S. 834, 67 S.Ct. 627, 91 L.Ed. 706 (federal power supreme over state and local uses as well as private uses). Cf. United States v. 50 Acres of Land, 469 U.S. 24, 105 S.Ct. 451, 83 L.Ed.2d 376 (1984) (reference to "private property" in takings clause of Fifth Amendment covers property of state and local governments, and same principles of just compensation presumptively apply as with private condemnees); Minnesota v. United States, 125 F.2d 636 (8th Cir.1942) (state held land for reforestation and wild-life control; United States could take for use as Indian reservation). Once land becomes public land of the United States, Congressional control of its disposition is exclusive. See Utah Power & Light Co. v. United States, 243 U.S. 389, 37 S.Ct. 387, 61 L.Ed. 791 (1917).

[14] Eden Memorial Park Association v. Department of Public Works, 59 Cal.2d 412, 29 Cal.Rptr. 790, 380 P.2d 390 (1963). See United States v. Certain Parcels of Land, 209 F.Supp. 483 (S.D.Ill.1962), aff'd sub nom. United States v. Pleasure Driveway & Park Dist., 314 F.2d 825 (7th Cir.1963). Generally, the land needed for federal-aid highways is acquired by the states; but a federal statute—23 U.S.C.A. § 107a—authorizes federal exercise of eminent domain when the Secretary of Transportation determines that the state is unable to acquire necessary lands or interests therein. See generally Baude, Rethinking the Federal Eminent Domain Power, 122 Yale L. J. 1738 (2013).

[15] See Maun v. United States, 347 F.2d 970 (9th Cir.1965), where the Atomic Energy Commission undertook to condemn an easement for a high-power transmission line through Woodside, California. The court concluded that Congress intended that the AEC comply with local regulations on the transmission of electricity, which required placing the lines underground. Later, however, Congress approved the use of an overhead line. See Miller, Electric Transmission Lines—To Bury, Not to Praise, 12 Vill.L.Rev. 497 (1967).

Under the Intergovernmental Relations Act of 1968, 40 U.S.C.A. § 533(b), when the federal government acquires property in an urban area for a public building, the General Services Administrator shall, to the extent possible, consider and comply with local zoning and planning laws. Cf. Maryland–National Capital Park & Planning Commission v. United States Postal Service, 487 F.2d 1029 (D.C.Cir.1973). Clearly, the federal government, because of its immunity from state and local exercises of the police power, does not *have* to comply with local zoning regulations. Town of Groton v. Laird, 353 F.Supp. 344 (D.Conn.1972). Cf. Ventura County v. Gulf Oil Corp., 601 F.2d 1080 (9th Cir.1979), aff'd 445 U.S. 947, 100 S.Ct. 1593, 63 L.Ed.2d 782 (1980) (lessee of federal government could not be required to obtain "open space use permit" from county planning commission; oil lease of national forest land was involved). But it has been suggested that courts should not *assume* the immunity to apply, especially where the government has leased the property to others, unless a federal statute specifically exempts a particular parcel. See Comment, Preemption of Local Zoning by Federal Lessee, 1971 Urban L.Ann. 200. Mere governmental authorization to engage in an activity does not normally confer immunity from zoning laws, as where authority to operate a radio station at a particular location is obtained from the Federal Communications Commission. Kroeger v. Stahl, 248 F.2d 121 (3d Cir.1957). Cf. O'Banion v. State ex rel. Shively, 146 Ind.App. 223, 253 N.E.2d 739 (1969). But cf. New York State Natural Gas Corp. v. Town of Elma, 182 F.Supp. 1 (W.D.N.Y.1960) (federal licensee—a gas company—held not compelled to abide by local zoning ordinance where particular site was reasonably necessary).

and local projects, the United States may attach reasonable conditions—such as speed limits to be placed on roads—, and the locality may agree to these without being held to have impermissibly granted away its governmental authority—at least if the conditions are reasonable and limited.[16]

What of assertions of the police power or safety standards by one government against another? These are limitations on the use of property less sweeping than an actual taking of the property. It has been held that the state and city cannot assert their police powers against the United States. Thus, they cannot enforce their safety requirements as to a federally built housing project unless the United States agrees.[17] But where a state or city operation comes within the scope of federal powers, as with a state-operated railroad engaging in interstate and foreign commerce, the United States may apply its safety standards against the state or locality.[18] Similarly, state and local operations are subject to federal rent-control laws[19] and federal price controls.[20] So the supremacy of the federal government over state and local governments in the eminent-domain and police-power areas seems clear.

§ 7.3 Federal-Local Relations as to Taxation and Revenue

In regard to finances, particularly taxation, the different positions of the different levels of government are of great importance. The federal government's property and

---

An attempt by a municipality to regulate location of electric lines may also conflict with *state* legislation, or simply be considered an encroachment on an area of exclusive state power. See In re Public Service Electric & Gas Co., 35 N.J. 358, 173 A.2d 233 (1961).

16 See Bidlingmeyer v. City of Deer Lodge, 128 Mont. 292, 274 P.2d 821 (1954); Vap v. City of McCook, 178 Neb. 844, 136 N.W.2d 220 (1965), both concerning speed limits on federal-aid highways.

17 Oklahoma City v. Sanders, 94 F.2d 323 (10th Cir. 1938) (city ordinances as to licenses, bonds, and inspections inapplicable). See United States v. City of Philadelphia, 56 F.Supp. 862 (E.D.Pa.1944), aff'd 147 F.2d 291 (3d Cir.), cert. denied 325 U.S. 870, 65 S.Ct. 1410, 89 L.Ed. 1989 (city laws inapplicable to federal construction of permanent buildings for wartime housing). Cf. Johnson v. Maryland, 254 U.S. 51, 41 S.Ct. 16, 65 L.Ed. 126 (1920) (state cannot compel federal employee to obtain state driver's license where he uses state highways on federal business). But cf. Wood Marine Serv., Inc. v. City of Harahan, 858 F.2d 1061 (5th Cir.1988) (city zoning ordinance designed to curtail further commercial development along banks of Mississippi River within city limits upheld as not interfering with interstate commerce). On the problems of enforcing state and local zoning laws and other police-power enactments against Indian-reservation land, see Section 2.11 *supra*, and authorities cited therein.

18 United States v. California, 297 U.S. 175, 56 S.Ct. 421, 80 L.Ed. 567 (1936) (California's belt railway on San Francisco waterfront had to comply with federal safety laws or pay penalty). Similarly, a contract between a state and a rail carrier is subject to federal regulations under the commerce clause. State of New York v. United States, 257 U.S. 591, 42 S.Ct. 239, 66 L.Ed. 385 (1922) (intrastate rates). And the federal commerce power extends to state and municipal operation of radio stations. City of New York v. Federal Radio Commission, 36 F.2d 115 (D.C.Cir.1929), cert. denied 281 U.S. 729, 50 S.Ct. 246, 74 L.Ed. 1146.

19 City of Dallas v. Bowles, 152 F.2d 464 (U.S.Emerg.App.1945).

20 Case v. Bowles, 327 U.S. 92, 66 S.Ct. 438, 90 L.Ed. 552 (1946) (auction of public lands). See the companion case of Hulbert v. Twin Falls County, Idaho, 327 U.S. 103, 66 S.Ct. 444, 90 L.Ed. 560 (1946) (county's sale of tractor subject to Emergency Price Control Act). Federal anti-trust legislation has been held inapplicable to actions of *state* governments. Parker v. Brown, 317 U.S. 341, 63 S.Ct. 307, 87 L.Ed. 315 (1943) (Sherman Act). But the immunity does not extend to actions of municipal corporations unless the state has authorized or directed the municipality to act as it did. City of Lafayette, Louisiana v. Louisiana Power & Light Co., 435 U.S. 389, 98 S.Ct. 1123, 55 L.Ed.2d 364 (1978) (the authorization or direction must be based on state policy to displace competition with regulation and monopoly), noted 11 Urban Law. vii (1979). For background, see generally Note, Antitrust Law and Municipal Corporations: Are Municipalities Exempt from Sherman Act Coverage Under the Parker Doctrine?, 65 Geo.L.J. 1547 (1977).

activities are immune from state and local taxation.[21] But the federal government may tax state and local revenues, at least if they are not ones uniquely capable of being earned only by a government and if the state or locality is not so heavily burdened that it cannot conduct governmental affairs.[22] In addition to its constitutional immunity from local taxation, the federal government may remove other subjects from state or local taxation,

---

[21] United States v. Allegheny County, 322 U.S. 174, 64 S.Ct. 908, 88 L.Ed. 1209 (1944); Mayo v. United States, 319 U.S. 441, 63 S.Ct. 1137, 87 L.Ed. 1504 (1943), reh. denied 320 U.S. 810, 64 S.Ct. 27, 88 L.Ed. 489; John K. & Katherine S. Mullen Benevolent Corp. v. United States, 290 U.S. 89, 54 S.Ct. 38, 78 L.Ed. 192 (1933). Cf. Graves v. People of State of New York ex rel. O'Keefe, 306 U.S. 466, 59 S.Ct. 595, 83 L.Ed. 927 (1939). But cf. First Nat'l Bank of Atlanta v. Bartow County Bd. of Tax Assessors, 470 U.S. 583, 105 S.Ct. 1516, 84 L.Ed.2d 535 (1985), where the Court held that when federal obligations are acquired by incurring liabilities, a pro rata method of allocating a fair share of the obligations to liabilities for purposes of property taxation does not infringe on the immunity from taxation of the federal obligations.

In United States v. New Mexico, 455 U.S. 720, 102 S.Ct. 1373, 71 L.Ed.2d 580 (1982), the Court held that contractors having contracts with the federal government to manage government-owned atomic laboratories were not constituent parts of the federal government and that a state use tax could thus be validly imposed on property purchased by them. But a state's tax laws may not discriminate against contractors or others who deal with the federal government. See Washington v. United States, 460 U.S. 536, 103 S.Ct. 1344, 75 L.Ed.2d 264 (1983), on remand 707 F.2d 381 (9th Cir.1983) (Washington State sales tax was generally imposed on owner of project but in case of a federal project was imposed on contractor; no discrimination found since federal contractor was not required to pay more than contractor on a private project). Compare Memphis Bank & Trust Co. v. Garner, 459 U.S. 392, 103 S.Ct. 692, 74 L.Ed.2d 562 (1983) (Tennessee bank excise tax invalidated as discriminating in favor of securities issued by Tennessee and its political subdivisions and against federal obligations, thus discriminating against federal government and those with whom it deals).

In general, state and local government may not, under the U.S. Constitution, directly tax federal property or impose a tax that has an adverse effect on the federal government's borrowing ability. See Rockford Life Ins. Co. v. Illinois Dep't of Rev., 482 U.S. 182, 107 S.Ct. 2312, 96 L.Ed.2d 152 (1987) (federal guarantee of loan does not preclude state taxation of obligation). And not only will state or local taxes be invalidated if they discriminate against the federal government or those with whom it deals (as in the *Garner* case *supra*), but such taxation cannot discriminate against interstate commerce. See Amerada Hess Corp. v. Director, Division of Taxation, 490 U.S. 66, 109 S.Ct. 1617, 104 L.Ed.2d 58 (1989) (provision of New Jersey Business Corporation Tax denying deduction by crude oil producers of federal windfall profit tax held not to discriminate against interstate commerce). Cf. Goldberg v. Sweet, 488 U.S. 252, 109 S.Ct. 582, 102 L.Ed.2d 607 (1989) (Illinois tax on interstate telecommunications which taxed only those calls originated or terminated in Illinois and charged to Illinois service address did not discriminate against interstate commerce). In addition to these constitutionally based exemptions, statutory immunity may also be provided by the federal government; but the statutory immunity now codified at 31 U.S.C.A. § 3142(a) has been treated as largely a statement of the constitutional doctrine of intergovernmental immunity. See Rockford Life Ins. Co. v. Illinois Dep't of Rev., *supra* at 186, 107 S.Ct. at 2315. See generally Hartman, Federal Limitations on State and Local Taxation (Lawyers Co-operative 1981), with Supp. by Trost (West Pub. 1999).

It has been held that a locality's hotel/motel room rental tax can be imposed on rooms contracted for by the United States government. United States v. Montgomery County, 761 F.2d 998 (4th Cir.1985).

[22] See Massachusetts v. United States, 435 U.S. 444, 98 S.Ct. 1153, 55 L.Ed.2d 403 (1978) (registration tax on aircraft does not unduly interfere with traditional governmental functions of state and thus can be applied to state); New York v. United States, 326 U.S. 572, 66 S.Ct. 310, 90 L.Ed. 326 (1946) (sale by state of mineral water subject to federal tax). Four of the majority justices in the New York v. United States case indicated that a federal tax applied to the state was permissible if it did not unduly burden the conduct of state affairs; two majority justices said the United States could tax any state revenues not uniquely capable of being earned only by a state. Cf. United States v. Wells Fargo Bank, 485 U.S. 351, 108 S.Ct. 1179, 99 L.Ed.2d 368 (1988) (state and local public housing agency obligations issued pursuant to the Housing Act of 1937 are not exempt from federal estate taxation).

It is generally agreed that a municipality may not tax the operations of the state or of its subdivisions or of another municipality without express statutory authorization. See Salt River Project Agricultural Imp. & Power Dist. v. City of Phoenix, 129 Ariz. 398, 631 P.2d 553 (App. 1981). See generally Sands & Libonati, Local Government Law § 5.14 (2000). Some authority, however, indicates that a city can tax the *proprietary* activities of the state, its subdivisions or another municipality to the same extent that private businesses may be thus taxed. See King County v. City of Algona, 101 Wash.2d 789, 681 P.2d 1281 (1984) (county's waste disposal operation was governmental in nature and thus could not be taxed by municipality without express statutory authorization).

such as the stock of banks owned by a government-supported corporation.[23] Some federal projects, such as the Tennessee Valley Authority, have removed large amounts of property from the scope of local taxation. Often, the United States, when engaging in such projects, has made "in lieu" payments to the localities involved.[24] And occasionally, the United States simply waives its tax immunity.

When federal immunity applies, it extends to any tax that rests upon instrumentalities of the United States, such as U.S. military installations.[25] But it has been held that a local property tax may be imposed on a lessee or licensee of federally owned property, and may be imposed for the full value of the property, not just the value of the lease or license.[26] Any discrimination against the United States or its property would, however, invalidate any such tax.[27]

Immunity of governmental employees from income taxes has, after a period of shaky recognition, long ago been terminated. This applies to federal taxation of the income of a state or local employee,[28] and state or local taxation of the earnings of a federal worker.[29] But again, some inequality enters the picture: for the United States can compel state and local governments to make federal tax withholdings from the wages of their employees,[30] while the states and localities cannot make the United States withhold for them.[31]

---

[23] Maricopa County v. Valley National Bank, 318 U.S. 357, 63 S.Ct. 587, 87 L.Ed. 834 (1943). See Federal Land Bank v. Bismarck Lumber Co., 314 U.S. 95, 62 S.Ct. 1, 86 L.Ed. 65 (1941); Pittman v. Home Owners' Loan Corp., 308 U.S. 21, 60 S.Ct. 15, 84 L.Ed. 11 (1939).

[24] See 31 U.S.C.A. §§ 1601–07. See generally Guandolo, Federal Payments to States and Local Governments Respecting Property of the United States, 101 U.Pa. L.Rev. 509 (1953), urging general legislation providing "in lieu" payments as to all federal properties. The "in lieu" payments are a type of gift and may not be subject to all the controls that apply to tax money. See Edelmann, The T.V.A. and Intergovernmental Relations, 37 Am.Pol.Sci.Rev. 455 (1943).

[25] See United States v. State Tax Commission, 421 U.S. 599, 95 S.Ct. 1872, 44 L.Ed.2d 404 (1975), striking down a sales tax collected from military installations. Cf. First Agricultural National Bank v. State Tax Commission, 392 U.S. 339, 88 S.Ct. 2173, 20 L.Ed.2d 1138 (1968); Kern-Limerick, Inc. v. Scurlock, 347 U.S. 110, 74 S.Ct. 403, 98 L.Ed. 546 (1954), conformed to 223 Ark. 464, 266 S.W.2d 298; Alabama v. King & Boozer, 314 U.S. 1, 62 S.Ct. 43, 86 L.Ed. 3 (1941).

[26] United States v. City of Detroit, 355 U.S. 466, 78 S.Ct. 474, 2 L.Ed.2d 424 (1958) (Michigan tax).

[27] See Phillips Chemical Co. v. Dumas Independent School District, 361 U.S. 376, 80 S.Ct. 474, 4 L.Ed.2d 384 (1960), conformed to 160 Tex. 599, 334 S.W.2d 779, reh. denied 362 U.S. 937, 80 S.Ct. 749, 4 L.Ed.2d 751.

[28] Helvering v. Gerhardt, 304 U.S. 405, 58 S.Ct. 969, 82 L.Ed. 1427 (1938) (federal taxation of state employee).

[29] Graves v. People of State of New York ex rel. O'Keefe, 306 U.S. 466, 59 S.Ct. 595, 83 L.Ed. 927 (1939) (New York State taxation of federal employee). See United States v. County of Fresno, 429 U.S. 452, 97 S.Ct. 699, 50 L.Ed.2d 683 (1977) (state may tax federal employees on their possessory interests in housing supplied them by federal government). Cf. Jefferson County v. Acker, 527 U.S. 423, 119 S.Ct. 2069, 144 L.Ed.2d 408 (1999) (under federal Public Salary Tax Act, county could impose occupational taxes on federal district judges); Barker v. Kansas, 503 U.S. 594, 112 S.Ct. 1619, 118 L.Ed.2d 243 (1992) (under statute authorizing states to tax federal employees' compensation, military retirement benefits are treated as deferred pay, not current compensation). See generally Annot., State Income Tax as Violating Immunity of United States, 103 L.Ed.2d 1027 (1991).

[30] See Sims v. United States, 359 U.S. 108, 79 S.Ct. 641, 3 L.Ed.2d 667 (1959) (United States could levy on salary of state employee to satisfy federal income-tax claim).

[31] See Fordham, Local Government Law 137 (2d rev. ed. 1986), but noting that under what is now 5 U.S.C.A. § 84b, Congress has *consented* to withholding in the case of state income taxes, and more recently, under 5 U.S.C.A. § 5520, to withholding of income taxes of units of general local government.

A much-debated area of remaining inter-governmental immunity is the immunity under the federal income tax of income from state and local securities. The immunity was broadly applied and treated as essential to our federal system in some old cases,[32] but seems out-of-line with the modern idea that income may be taxed even if its source cannot be.[33] The immunity provides lower net interest costs to states and cities and has been called essential to local borrowing power—and thus, ultimately, to local autonomy.[34] There are, however, some qualifications to the immunity: (1) It does not cover capital gains realized on the sale of "immune" securities.[35] (2) With limited exceptions, the immunity does not now cover industrial revenue bonds at all, nor so-called "arbitrage" bonds[36] (ones issued where the proceeds are to be used to acquire other securities that are expected to yield more than the bonds—sometimes called "refunding bonds").

On the other hand—whatever inroads may have occurred against *income*-tax immunity of local securities—property tax immunity of state and local bonds seems secure.[37] And the states and localities as purchasers continue to enjoy statutory immunity from many federal excise taxes.[38]

---

[32] Pollock v. Farmers' Loan & Trust Co., 158 U.S. 601, 15 S.Ct. 912, 39 L.Ed. 1108 (1895). Cf. Commissioner of Internal Revenue v. Shamberg's Estate, 144 F.2d 998 (2d Cir.1944), cert. denied 323 U.S. 792, 65 S.Ct. 433, 89 L.Ed. 631 (interest on bonds of Port of New York Authority exempt).

[33] See People of State of New York ex rel. Cohn v. Graves, 300 U.S. 308, 57 S.Ct. 466, 81 L.Ed. 666 (1937), upholding state taxation of rents from out-of-state realty and declaring that income from a source does not necessarily enjoy the source's immunity.

[34] Epstein, Self-Government versus Federal Taxation of Your Local Securities, 6 Leg.Notes on Local Gov't 187 (1941), noting that those who buy exempt securities pay, in effect, a tax to the issuer by accepting a lower rate of interest. *Id.* at 190. Views of opponents of the immunity were published in Department of Justice, Taxation of Government Bondholders and Employees (1938).

[35] Willcuts v. Bunn, 282 U.S. 216, 51 S.Ct. 125, 75 L.Ed. 304 (1931). See Boehm, Taxing Refunded Municipals, 26 Taxes 787 (1948). On the possibility of holding local governments liable for fraud under the Securities Exchange Act and regulations issued thereunder, see Sachs, Are Local Governments Liable Under Rule 10b–5? Textualism and Its Limits, 70 Wash. U.L.Q. 19 (1992).

[36] 26 U.S.C.A. § 103. See Fordham, Local Government Law 139 (2d rev. ed. 1986). The Tax Reform Act of 1984, P.L. 98–369, 98 Stat. 494 (1984), placed a ceiling, or "cap," on the amount of tax-exempt "private activity bonds" that may be issued in any year. A "private activity bond" is defined as including all industrial development bonds and student loan bonds, with limited exceptions. See Arkuss, New Federal Tax Legislation Affecting Tax-Exempt Obligations, 16 Urban Law. 805 (1984). On the effects of the Tax Reform Act of *1986* on municipal bonds, see generally Arey & O'Connor, Tax-Exempt Obligations After the Tax Reform Act of 1986—A Brief Guide for the Local Government Attorney, 19 Urban Law. 1051 (1987) (tax exemption of many classes of municipal bonds left untouched).

Section 310(b)(1) of the Tax Equity and Fiscal Responsibility Act of 1982 removed federal income tax exemption for interest earned on publicly offered long-term bonds issued by state and local governments unless the bonds were issued in registered form. 26 U.S.C.A. § 103(j)(1) (1982). The validity of this provision was upheld in State of South Carolina v. Baker, 485 U.S. 505, 108 S.Ct. 1355, 99 L.Ed.2d 592 (1988), reh. denied 486 U.S. 1062, 108 S.Ct. 2837, 100 L.Ed.2d 937 (1988), the Court holding that state bond interest is not immune from a nondiscriminatory federal tax. Some analysts believe that total elimination of the federal income tax exemption for state and local government bonds will eventually occur. See Peers & Herman, Growing Municipal Bond Mess Underscores Wall Street's Woes, Wall St. J., April 25, 1989, at C-1, C-17, quoting Edward Armendariz, director of finance at the Metropolitan Transportation Authority in New York; Spain, Developments in the Area of Tax-Exempt Obligations, 21 Urban Law. 959 (1989).

[37] Department of Justice, *supra* note 34, at 30. But local property taxation of an unliquidated claim due from the United States to a contractor was upheld in Smith v. Davis, 323 U.S. 111, 65 S.Ct. 157, 89 L.Ed. 107 (1944), discussed in Powell, The Remnant of Intergovernmental Tax Immunities, 58 Harv.L.Rev. 757, 788 (1945).

[38] See Fordham, Local Government Law 140 (2d rev. ed. 1986), noting 26 U.S.C.A. § 4221(a)(4).

Federal legislation concerning municipal bankruptcy once was invalidated as interfering unduly with state control of municipalities.[39] But more modern legislation,—providing for what was found to be state cooperation, rather than abdication of its supervisory responsibilities—was upheld.[40] Such legislation is further discussed in connection with local finances, *infra.*

Federal spending to help localities is further discussed in connection with various programs, such as urban renewal. It is safe to generalize that there is increased recognition of the great impact that federal spending has on regional and local economies and of the potential of federal spending for guiding growth and development of particular geographic areas.[41]

§ 7.4 Federal Pre-Emption of Certain Fields

Occasionally, a city may find that some area of law-making has been pre-empted (or "occupied") by the federal government so as to make any local regulation impossible, just as such pre-emption sometimes occurs through *state* action. Of course, Congress in legislating for the federal government is limited to areas of constitutionally recognized power—but some such areas, as that covered by the Commerce Clause, have proven broad. Assuming that the requisite power is present, a Congressional intent to occupy a field of possible regulation will still not be assumed, but will be found if any one of three conditions exists:[42] (1) an *express* legislative provision of pre-emption,[43] (2) a scheme of

---

[39] Ashton v. Cameron County Water Improvement District, 298 U.S. 513, 56 S.Ct. 892, 80 L.Ed. 1309 (1936), reh. denied 299 U.S. 619, 57 S.Ct. 5, 81 L.Ed. 457.

[40] United States v. Bekins, 304 U.S. 27, 58 S.Ct. 811, 82 L.Ed. 1137 (1938), reh. denied 304 U.S. 589, 58 S.Ct. 1043, 82 L.Ed. 1549. See generally Patterson, Municipal Debt Adjustments under the Bankruptcy Act, 90 U.Pa.L.Rev. 520 (1942). The present provisions on municipal bankruptcy are a permanent part of the Bankruptcy Act; 11 U.S.C.A. § 401–04. See Carolina Pipeline Co. v. York County Natural Gas Auth., 388 F.2d 297 (4th Cir.1967), cert. denied 393 U.S. 824, 89 S.Ct. 83, 21 L.Ed.2d 95; Mozingo v. York County Natural Gas Authority, 352 F.2d 78 (4th Cir.1965), cert. denied 383 U.S. 970, 86 S.Ct. 1277, 16 L.Ed.2d 310.

On state control over insolvent municipalities during the period when there was no federal legislation, see Faitoute Iron & Steel Co. v. City of Asbury Park, 316 U.S. 502, 62 S.Ct. 1129, 86 L.Ed. 1629 (1942). See generally, on state control of financially troubled local units, Note, 46 Harv.L.Rev. 1317 (1933).

[41] See "A Push to Tie Federal Spending to Area Needs," Bus. Week, Jan. 30, 1978, at 66. See generally Page, Who Gets What from Government (Univ. of Calif. Press 1984).

[42] See City of Burbank v. Lockheed Air Terminal Inc., 411 U.S. 624, 93 S.Ct. 1854, 36 L.Ed.2d 547 (1973), noted 8 Urban L.Ann. 229 (1974). On the subject of *state* pre-emption of various fields of regulation, see Chapter 6 *supra.*

[43] An example of express pre-emption is found in Exxon Corp. v. Hunt, 475 U.S. 355, 106 S.Ct. 1103, 89 L.Ed.2d 364 (1986), appeal after remand 109 N.J. 110, 534 A.2d 1 (1987), where a federal environmental statute provided that no person may be required to contribute to a fund for any damages or claims that are compensated under the federal statute. This was held to pre-empt any state fund intended, in whole or in part, to pay for the same type of expenses. Cf. Vango Media, Inc. v. City of New York, 34 F.3d 68 (2d Cir.1994) (ordinance requiring that public health messages warning of dangers of smoking be displayed found pre-empted by federal statute on cigarette advertising since federal statute stated that no requirement based on smoking and health should be imposed under state law with respect to advertising or promotion of cigarettes). Compare Note, ERISA's Preemption of State Tax Laws, 61 Fordham L. Rev. 401 (1992), discussing the express federal pre-emption of regulation of employee benefit plans found in the Employment Retirement Income Security Act of 1974 (ERISA) and problems of statutory interpretation thereunder. See generally Hutchinson & Ifshin, Federal Preemption of State Law Under the Employee Retirement Income Security Act of 1974, 46 U. Chi. L. Rev. 23 (1978). See also National Meat Ass'n v. Harris, 565 U.S. ___, 132 S.Ct. 965, 181 L.Ed.2d 950 (2012) (Federal Meat Inspection Act expressly pre-empts application against federally inspected swine slaughterhouses of California Penal Code provision prohibiting sale of meat or meat product of "nonambulatory" animals for human consumption and requiring euthanization of nonambulatory animals).

federal regulation so pervasive as to lead to the reasonable inference that Congress left no room for additional regulation, or (3) Congressional legislation touching a field in which federal interest is so dominant that the federal system is assumed to preclude state or local laws on the subject. In the first instance, *express* pre-emption has occurred, and in the second and third instances, *implied* pre-emption. Even where there is the possibility of finding express federal pre-emption, a presumption against pre-emption applies if there are questions of interpretation of the statutory language.[44]

Examples of federal pre-emption are actually rather few in number and limited in scope. Often, situations of *implied* pre-emption involve interstate commerce. The federal government has been found to have impliedly pre-empted the field of control over aircraft noise so as to preclude municipalities from enforcing "curfews" on the taking-off and landing of jet aircraft.[45] The same is true of the establishing of minimum altitudes for

---

Compare Fatale, Common Sense: Implicit Constitutional Limitations on Congressional Preemptions of State Tax, 2012 Mich. St. L. Rev. 41.

[44] Mid-Con Freight Systems, Inc. v. Michigan Pub. Serv. Com'n, 545 U.S. 440, 125 S.Ct. 2427, 162 L.Ed.2d 418 (2005) (Michigan statute, imposing $100 registration fee on Michigan-plated trucks operating entirely in interstate commerce, was not pre-empted by federal statute; pre-emption clause of federal statute applied only to those state registration requirements that concerned the subject matter of the federal statute and that were in excess of registration requirements imposed by that statute); City of Columbus v. Ours Garage and Wrecker Serv., Inc., 536 U.S. 424, 122 S.Ct. 2226, 153 L.Ed.2d 430 (2002) (Congress's use of phrase "State (or) political subdivision of a state" in purporting to pre-empt any law enacted by state or its subdivisions relating to price, route or service of any motor carrier transporting property was not sufficiently clear to pre-empt local safety laws). But cf. Engine Manufacturers Ass'n v. South Coast Air Quality Management Dist., 541 U.S. 246, 124 S.Ct. 1756, 158 L.Ed.2d 529 (2004) (state air quality management district rules requiring fleet operators to purchase or lease only vehicles that met state motor vehicle pollution standards was pre-empted by federal Clean Air Act provision prohibiting adoption or attempted enforcement of any state or local standard relating to emissions from new motor vehicles or new motor vehicle engines); City of Seattle v. Burlington Northern R. Co., 145 Wash.2d 661, 41 P.3d 1169 (2002) (Congress clearly gave exclusive jurisdiction over railroad switching activities to federal Surface Transportation Board; city ordinances pre-empted). See generally Young, The Ordinary Diet of the Law": The Presumption Against Preemption in the Roberts Court, 2011 Sup. Ct. Rev. 253. But see Arizona v. Inter-Tribal Council of Arizona, ___ U.S. ___, 133 S.Ct. 2247 (2013) (Elections Clause of U.S. Constitution imposes on States the time, place and manner of electing Representatives and Senators, but also confers on Congress the power to alter or supplant those regulations; Arizona's evidence-of-citizenship requirement held pre-empted by National Voter Registration Act of 1993).

[45] City of Burbank v. Lockheed Air Terminal, Inc., *supra* note 42; American Airlines, Inc. v. Town of Hempstead, 272 F.Supp. 226 (E.D.N.Y.1967), aff'd 398 F.2d 369 (2d Cir.), cert. denied 393 U.S. 1017, 89 S.Ct. 620, 21 L.Ed.2d 561. See Reports, Airport Law, 8 Urban Law. 653, 654 (1976), 10 Urban Law. 371 (1978), discussing litigation over flights of the *Concorde* aircraft in and out of New York's Kennedy Airport. (In British Airways Board v. Port Authority, 564 F.2d 1002 (2d Cir.1977), the Court declared the New York Port Authority's ban on operations of the *Concorde* aircraft at Kennedy Airport discriminatory and thus invalid.) But see Greater Westchester Homeowners Association v. City of Los Angeles, 26 Cal.3d 86, 160 Cal.Rptr. 733, 603 P.2d 1329 (1979) (federal pre-emption did not bar nuisance suit for noise from city-owned airport), discussed at 12 Urban Law. 617–20 (1980) (portion of Annual Review of Local Government Law). See generally Aurbach, Aviation Noise Abatement Policy: The Limits on Federal Intervention, 9 Urban Law. 559 (1977).

For a summary of developments in the controversy involving the Concorde's use of New York's Kennedy Airport, see Note, The Concorde and Local Control of Airport Noise: Federal Preemption?, 13 New Eng. L.Rev. 473 (1978). See also Chicago and North Western Transportation Co. v. Kalo Brick & Tile Co., 450 U.S. 311, 101 S.Ct. 1124, 67 L.Ed.2d 258 (1981) (authority of Interstate Commerce Commission to regulate abandonment of railroad lines is exclusive). The federal pre-emption rule of the *City of Burbank* case, *supra* note 42, may apply only against local regulation of a *privately* owned airport, not where the locality is proprietor of an airport. See Note, The Concorde and Local Control of Airport Noise: Federal Preemption?, *supra* at 487 & 492–503. See generally Lesser, The Aircraft Noise Problem: The Past Decade—Still Federal Power and, at Least for a While Longer, Local Liability, 13 Urban Law. 285 (1981).

In City of Atlanta v. Owen, 248 Ga. 299, 282 S.E.2d 906 (1981), cert. denied 456 U.S. 972, 102 S.Ct. 2235, 72 L.Ed.2d 846 (1982), it was held that nuisance and trespass claims against the city for its airport operation were not barred by federal pre-emption; the lower court's holding that plaintiffs' damage claim was pre-empted under the *City of Burbank* case *supra* was held error. See also Krueger v. Mitchell, 112 Wis.2d 88, 332 N.W.2d

aircraft approaching airports.[46] But not all matters touching aviation are outside the scope of local restrictions; municipalities may be allowed to regulate the establishment and operation of "heliports" and other helicopter landing areas.[47] Nor are all matters touching on interstate communications pre-empted by federal regulation: It has been

---

733 (1983), in which the Wisconsin court, in a nuisance action against a private airport, distinguished between a municipality's exercise of its police power to regulate aircraft noise and an airport proprietor's power to control noise levels. Since only the latter was involved in the *Krueger* case, the court found the *City of Burbank* case not in point. But cf. National Helicopter Corp. v. City of New York, 137 F.3d 81 (2d Cir.1998) (city could not restrict the use of certain sightseeing routes by helicopters).

A presumption of *implied* federal pre-emption will ordinarily be found only where there is conspicuous federal intent to exclude state law. See Todd v. Frank's Tong Serv. Inc., 784 P.2d 47 (Okla.1989) (Federal Surface Transportation Assistance Act's "whistleblower" provision does not pre-empt state court claims for wrongful termination based on implied duty of good faith in employment contracts). See generally Annot., Federal Pre-emption of Whistleblower's State Law Action for Wrongful Retaliation, 99 A.L.R. Fed. 775 (1990). See also Bronco Wine Co. v. Jolly, 33 Cal.4th 943, 17 Cal.Rptr.3d 180, 95 P.3d 422 (2004) (presumption against federal pre-emption applied to California statute restricting use on wine labels of geographic brand names; protection from misleading brand names and labels of food and beverages in general, and of wine in particular, has traditionally been regulated by states).

[46] Allegheny Airlines v. Village of Cedarhurst, 238 F.2d 812 (2d Cir.1956). Cf. Aloha Airlines, Inc. v. Director of Taxation of Hawaii, 464 U.S. 7, 104 S.Ct. 291, 78 L.Ed.2d 10 (1983) (Hawaii statute imposing a tax on annual gross income of airlines operating in that state found pre-empted by federal law prohibiting state from levying tax on gross receipts derived from sale of air transportation); Banner Advertising, Inc. v. City of Boulder, 868 P.2d 1077 (Colo. 1994) (city ordinance prohibiting commercial signs towed by aircraft was pre-empted by federal law). See also Rowe v. New Hampshire Motor Transport Ass'n, 552 U.S. 364, 128 S.Ct. 989, 169 L.Ed.2d 933 (2008) (Federal Aviation Administration Authorization Act pre-empts state enforcement actions and laws having connection with or reference to carrier rates, routes or services, and thus pre-empts state requirement that tobacco shipper utilize delivery service providing verification of buyer's legal age, and pre-empts state's imposing on carrier constructive knowledge that packages originating from specified types of senders contained tobacco); Morales v. Trans World Airlines, Inc., 504 U.S. 374, 112 S.Ct. 2031, 119 L.Ed.2d 157 (1992) (Airline Deregulation Act of 1978 pre-empts state consumer-fraud statutes against deceptive airline-fare advertisements; pre-emption may occur even if state law has only an indirect effect on airline rates, routes, or services).

Many cases finding federal pre-emption emphasize the need for uniformity in the area being regulated. See Aetna Health Inc. v. Davila, 542 U.S. 200, 124 S.Ct. 2488, 159 L.Ed.2d 312 (2004) (clear purpose of federal Employee Retirement Security Act is to provide uniform regulatory regime over employee benefit plans); Beneficial Nat'l Bank v. Anderson, 539 U.S. 1, 123 S.Ct. 2058, 156 L.Ed.2d 1 (2003) (uniform rules limiting the liability of national banks and prescribing exclusive remedies for their overcharges are needed).

Some cases finding no federal pre-emption emphasize that the federal legislation does not involve uniquely federal areas of interest. See Chamber of Commerce of the U.S. v. Whiting, 563 U.S. 582, 131 S.Ct. 1968, 179 L.Ed.2d 1031 (2011) (provision of Arizona law allowing suspension and revocation of business licenses not impliedly pre-empted; regulating in-state businesses through licensing laws is not an area of uniquely federal interest). Other cases simply rely on evidence of the federal statute's intended objectives. See Williamson v. Mazda Motors of America, Inc., 562 U.S. 323, 131 S.Ct. 1131, 179 L.Ed.2d 75 (2011) (Federal Motor Vehicle Safety Standard giving auto manufacturers choice of installing lap belts or lap-and-shoulder belts on rear inner seats did not pre-empt California tort claims law seeking to hold manufacturer liable for installing mere lap belt on rear inner seat of minivan; providing manufacturers with seat belt choice was not significant objective of federal law). Cf. John v. Douglas County School Dist., 125 Nev. 746, 219 P.3d 1276 (2009) (Anti-Strategic Lawsuits Against Public Participation (anti-SLAPP) statute was not a state sovereign immunity statute and thus not pre-empted by Federal Civil Rights Act; unlike sovereign laws, anti-SLAPP statute was not an absolute bar to liability). As to anti-SLAPP statutes, see generally Section 21.4, note 42, para. 2.

Basically, federal pre-emption should be found only if the text and structure of the federal legislation demonstrate an affirmative intent to leave the subject matter untouched by state law and local regulation. See California Grocers Ass'n v. City of Los Angeles, 52 Cal. 4th 177, 127 Cal. Rptr. 3d 726, 254 P.3d 1019, 1037 (2011) (ordinance generally requiring grocery stores to retain their former staff for 90 days after a change in ownership was not pre-empted by National Labor Relations Act).

[47] See Thomson Industries, Inc. v. Incorporated Village of Port Washington North, 55 Misc.2d 625, 286 N.Y.S.2d 187 (1967), aff'd on other grounds 32 A.D.2d 1072, 304 N.Y.S.2d 83, 27 N.Y.2d 537, 313 N.Y.S.2d 117, 261 N.E.2d 260 (village could prohibit plaintiff from using part of property for helicopter landing area).

held that municipalities may restrict the height of antennas constructed by amateur radio operators licensed by the Federal Communications Commission, since the federal agency's main concern is the competency of the operator.[48]

In areas of environmental concern, federal regulation *may* preclude regulations of state and local governments—even consistent regulations aimed at a problem such as oil spills.[49] But federal statutes on billboard control along highways not only envision state

---

[48] Matter of Presnell v. Leslie, 3 N.Y.2d 384, 165 N.Y.S.2d 488, 144 N.E.2d 381 (1957). Cf. Guschke v. City of Oklahoma City, 763 F.2d 379 (10th Cir. 1985) (city's zoning restriction on the height of radio towers was a matter of local concern that was not pre-empted by federal statutes or Federal Communications Commission regulations); La Salle National Bank v. County of Cook, 34 Ill.App.3d 264, 340 N.E.2d 79 (1975) (upholding a municipal zoning ordinance restricting building heights around a military airport to heights below those authorized by the Federal Aviation Administration). But cf. Thernes v. City of Lakeside Park, Ky., 779 F.2d 1187 (6th Cir.1986) (lower court's judgment upholding city's zoning that prohibited the construction of amateur radio towers within the city vacated and remanded in light of Federal Communications Commission ruling that a limited federal pre-emption in this area was warranted). See also Capital Cities Cable, Inc. v. Crisp, 467 U.S. 691, 104 S.Ct. 2694, 81 L.Ed.2d 580 (1984), holding that state regulation of retransmission by cable television systems had been pre-empted by the federal government and that a state could thus not require cable television operators to delete all advertisements for alcoholic beverages contained in the out-of-state signals they retransmit by cable to their subscribers.

In Nixon v. Missouri Municipal League, 541 U.S. 125, 124 S.Ct. 1555, 158 L.Ed.2d 291 (2004), it was held that a provision of the federal Telecommunications Act authorizing pre-emption of state and local laws expressly or effectively prohibiting the ability of "any entity" to provide telecommunications services did not pre-empt a state statute barring political subdivisions from providing telecommunications services. The words "any entity" were held to refer only to private entities. See also Note, Reasonable Accommodation of Amateur Radio Communications by Zoning Authorities: The FCC's PRB–1 Pre-emption, 37 Conn. L. Rev. 321 (2004).

[49] See Ray v. Atlantic Richfield Co., 435 U.S. 151, 98 S.Ct. 988, 55 L.Ed.2d 179 (1978). Cf. City of Philadelphia v. New Jersey, 437 U.S. 617, 98 S.Ct. 2531, 57 L.Ed.2d 475 (1978) (state regulation of solid waste was not pre-empted, but struck down as invading federal commerce power). But cf. Pennsylvania Environmental Council, Inc. v. Bartlett, 315 F.Supp. 238 (M.D.Pa.1970), aff'd 454 F.2d 613 (3d Cir.) (federal law on relocation of highways allows delegation to state of assessment of environmental impact of such relocation). See generally Note, State Environmental Protection Legislation and the Commerce Clause, 87 Harv.L.Rev. 1762 (1974).

In Silkwood v. Kerr-McGee Corp., 464 U.S. 238, 104 S.Ct. 615, 78 L.Ed.2d 443 (1984), reh. denied 465 U.S. 1074, 104 S.Ct. 1430, 79 L.Ed.2d 754 (1984), it was held that federal pre-emption of the safety aspects of nuclear energy did not extend to state-authorized awards of punitive damages for conduct related to radiation hazards and that such awards were thus permissible. Cf. English v. General Elec. Co., 496 U.S. 72, 110 S.Ct. 2270, 110 L.Ed.2d 65 (1990), on remand 765 F.Supp. 293 (E.D.N.C.1991), aff'd 977 F.2d 572 (4th Cir.1992) (nuclear fuel production facility employee's state law claim for intentional infliction of emotional distress, based on alleged retaliation for reporting safety violations, was not pre-empted by federal legislation). But the federal Nuclear Regulatory Commission *does* have exclusive authority regarding construction and operation of nuclear facilities, pre-empting any state or local regulation except as specifically provided by federal law. See County of Suffolk v. Long Island Lighting Co., 728 F.2d 52 (2d Cir.1984), later proceedings, Long Island Lighting Co. v. County of Suffolk, 628 F.Supp. 654 (E.D.N.Y.1986). Cf. Jersey Cent. Power & Light Co. v. Township of Lacey, 772 F.2d 1103 (3d Cir.1985), cert. denied 475 U.S. 1013, 106 S.Ct. 1190, 89 L.Ed.2d 305 (1986) (township's ban on importation and storage of nuclear waste materials held pre-empted by federal statutes). Compare Rollins Environmental Serv., Inc. v. Parish of St. James, 775 F.2d 627 (5th Cir.1985) (ordinance that effectively precluded the locating within parish boundaries of a toxic waste facility held pre-empted by federal law); Borough of Maywood v. United States, 679 F.Supp. 413 (D.N.J.1988) (federal law pre-empted decisions of local planning boards denying approval of toxic waste cleanup sites). But see Pacific Gas & Elec. Co. v. State Energy Resources Conservation & Dev. Comm'n, 461 U.S. 190, 103 S.Ct. 1713, 75 L.Ed.2d 752 (1983) (state moratorium on certification of new nuclear plans not pre-empted by Atomic Energy Act). Cf. Wisconsin Pub. Intervenor v. Mortier, 501 U.S. 597, 111 S.Ct. 2476, 115 L.Ed.2d 532 (1991) (Federal Insecticide, Fungicide, and Rodenticide Act did not pre-empt local regulation of pesticide use); Central Maine Power Co. v. Town of Lebanon, 571 A.2d 1189 (Me. 1990) (no federal or state pre-emption of town's ordinance regulating herbicides); Sharon Steel Corp. v. City of Fairmont, 175 W.Va. 479, 334 S.E.2d 616 (1985), appeal dism'd 474 U.S. 1098, 106 S.Ct. 875, 88 L.Ed.2d 912 (1986) (ordinance prohibiting permanent disposal of hazardous wastes in city held not pre-empted by federal or state law). See generally Mandelker, NEPA Law and Litigation (Callaghan & Co. 1984), describing federal environmental policies and procedures. See also Andreen, Of Fables and Federalism: A Re-examination of the Historical Rationale for Federal Environment

legislation on the subject but also allow state rules *inconsistent* with the federal.[50] Requirements on selection of public housing sites issued by the federal government have been found not to preclude state and local restrictions.[51] And, though power to regulate immigration into the United States is exclusively a federal power, even state and local laws on treatment of aliens—such as regulation of employment of aliens illegally within the country—are not always precluded by the relevant federal legislation.[52]

Regulation, 42 Envtl. L. 627 (2012); Babcock, Can Vermont Put the Nuclear Genie Back in the Bottle? A Test of Congressional Preemptive Power, 39 Ecology L.Q. 691 (2012).

[50] See Markham Advertising Co. v. State, 73 Wn.2d 405, 439 P.2d 248 (1968) (no federal pre-emption because federal billboard control provision was optional, with state losing some federal aid if it failed to comply). But see Opinion of Acting Attorney-General Ramsey Clark, 42 Op.Atty. Gen. 246 (1966). On federal regulation of federally owned land and the effect on nearby communities, see generally Freyfogle, Federal Lands and Local Communities, 27 Ariz. L. Rev. 653 (1985).

[51] Ranjel v. City of Lansing, 417 F.2d 321 (6th Cir.1969), cert. denied 397 U.S. 980, 90 S.Ct. 1105, 25 L.Ed.2d 390, reh. denied 397 U.S. 1059, 90 S.Ct. 1352, 25 L.Ed.2d 680, noting that the requirement that public housing sites be outside areas of racial concentration appeared only in federal regulations, not in the statutes. But state and local provisions for referenda on openhousing laws have sometimes been struck down as violative of Equal Protection. Hunter v. Erickson, 393 U.S. 385, 89 S.Ct. 557, 21 L.Ed.2d 616 (1969) (mandatory referendum for open housing); Reitman v. Mulkey, 387 U.S. 369, 87 S.Ct. 1627, 18 L.Ed.2d 830 (1967) (constitutional amendment adopted by referendum prohibiting open-housing statutes). But see James v. Valtierra, 402 U.S. 137, 91 S.Ct. 1331, 28 L.Ed.2d 678 (1971), upholding a California constitutional amendment requiring a local referendum on any low-rent public housing project, not just those occupied by minorities. See generally Freilich & Seidel, Recent Trends in Housing Law: Prologue to the '70's, 2 Urban Lawyer 1 (1970). See also Fullilove v. Klutznick, 448 U.S. 448, 100 S.Ct. 2758, 65 L.Ed.2d 902 (1980), upholding the "minority business enterprises" provision of the Public Works Employment Act of 1977, requiring that at least 10% of federal funds granted for local public works projects must be used to procure services or supplies from business owned by minority citizens.

[52] DeCanas v. Bica, 424 U.S. 351, 96 S.Ct. 933, 47 L.Ed.2d 43 (1976), saying preemption is required to be found only where the nature of the subject matter permits no other conclusion or Congress has unmistakably ordained pre-emption. Cf. Skafte v. Rorex, 191 Colo. 399, 553 P.2d 830 (1976), appeal dism'd 430 U.S. 961, 97 S.Ct. 1638, 52 L.Ed.2d 352 (no federal pre-emption of state statute denying aliens the right to vote in school elections). An example of a state or local law that would be found pre-empted because of the dominant federal interest is any law that interferes with the President's conduct of foreign affairs. See American Ins. Ass'n v. Garamendi, 539 U.S. 396, 123 S.Ct. 2374, 156 L.Ed.2d 376 (2003) (California's Holocaust Victim Insurance Relief Act requiring any insurer that did business in California and that sold insurance policies in Europe which were in effect during the Holocaust-era to disclose certain information about those policies or risk losing its license held pre-empted). As to immigration, see Note, Is Immigration Still Exclusively a Federal Power? A Preemption Analysis on Legislation by Hazelton, Pennsylvania, Regulating Illegal Immigration, 52 Villanova Envtl. L.J. 331 (2007). See generally McKanders, Welcome to Hazleton! "Illegal" Immigrants Beware: Local Immigration Ordinances and What the Federal Government Must Do About It, 39 Loyola U. Chicago L.J. 1 (2007); Olivas, Immigration-related State and Local Ordinances: Preemption, Prejudice, and the Proper Role for Enforcement, 2007 U. Chicago Legal F. 27 (2007); Rodriguez, The Significance of the Local Immigration Regulation, 106 Mich. L. Rev. 567 (2008). See also Engle, The Political Economy of State and Local Immigration Regulation: Comments on Olivas and Hollifield, Hunt & Tichenor, 61 SMU L. Rev. 159 (2008).

As a general rule, the laws on immigration are made by the federal government, which, however, can and does call on state and local governments for *enforcement* of those laws. See Fandl, Immigration Passes U.S. Immigration Law and Local Enforcement Practices, 34 J. Legis. 16 (2008); Kim, The Limits of State and Local Immigration Enforcement Regulation, 3 Albany Gov't L. Rev. 242 (2010); Motomura, The Discretion that Matters: Federal Immigration Enforcement, State and Local Arrests, and the Civil-Criminal Line, 58 U.C.L.A. L. Rev. 1819 (2011); Parra-Chico, An Up-Close Perspective: The Enforcement of Federal Immigration Laws by State and Local Police, 7 Seattle J. for Soc. Just. 321 (2008); Stumpf, States of Confusion: The Rise of State and Local Power Over Immigration, 86 N.C.L. Rev. 1557 (2008); Su, Police Discretion and Local Immigration Policymaking, 79 U.M.K.C. L. Rev. 901 (2011); Note, With a Little Help from My Friends: The Federal Government's Reliance on Cooperation from the States in Enforcing Immigration Policy, 31 Wash. U.J.L. & Pol'y 193 (2009).

States and local governments have increasingly passed legislation that *touches* the immigration area. See Symposium, Breaching Borders: State Encroachment into the Federal Immigration Domain?, 51 Washburn L. J. 189–347 (2012). Sometimes the touching relates only to the enforcement of federal law by the state and local government, as is usually allowed; but even this may have limits. See Bach, State Law to the Contrary? Examining Potential Limits on the Authority of State and Local Law Enforcement to Enforce Federal Immigration Law, 22 Temple Political & Civ. Rts. L. Rev. 67 (2012).

Municipal legislation regarding immigration and aliens has often taken the form of restrictions on *housing* of aliens, but has frequently been found to have been pre-empted by federal law. See Note, Municipal Overreaching: Federal Preemption as It Applies to Town Ordinances Outlawing the Rental of Housing to Undocumented Aliens, 14 Tex. Hispanic J.L. & Pol'y 69 (2008). See generally Staddor & Rippson, State and Local Governments and Immigration Law, 41 Urban Law. 387 (2009); Symposium, Local Dimensions of Immigration: Challenges and Opportunities in Our Changing Communities, 36 Hofstra L. Rev. 1227–1338 (2008). See also Oliveri, Between a Rock and a Hard Place: Landlords, Latinos, Anti-illegal Immigrant Ordinance and Housing Discrimination, 62 Vand. L. 105, Rev. 55 (2009); Note, The Constriction of Rights: A Property Law Approach to City-Based Immigration Initiatives that Place Rental Bans on City Ballots, 12 Scholar 291 (2010).

On state or local limits on *employment or recruitment* of aliens, see Lozano v. City of Hazleton, 620 F.3d 170 (3d Cir. 2010), invalidating, on the basis of federal pre-emption, city ordinances making it illegal to recruit, hire or continually recruit illegal immigrants. See generally Shannon, Regulating Immigration at the State Level: A Focus on Employment, 3 Albany Gov't L. Rev. 218 (2010); Comment, The Legal Arizona Workers Act: A Threat to Federal Supremacy Over Immigration, 42 Ariz. St. L. J. 411 (2010); Note, The Legal Legal Arizona Workers Act and Preemption Doctrine, 15 Mich. J. Race & L. 417 (2010). Some such state and local laws, however, have been upheld as with the Arizona unauthorized alien employment law, which allowed the suspension and revocation of business licenses for employing unauthorized aliens and required every employer to verify the employment eligibility of hired employees through a specific Internet-based system. The law was upheld in Chamber of Commerce of the U.S. v. Whiting, 563 U.S. 582, 131 S.Ct. 1968, 179 L.Ed.2d 1031 (2011), noted 57 Loyola L. Rev. 673 (2011).

Then in Arizona v. United States, ___ U.S. ___, 132 S.Ct. 2492, ___ L.Ed.2d ___ (2012), an Arizona law making it a misdemeanor for an unauthorized alien to seek or engage in work in Arizona and making failure to comply with federal alien registration requirements a state misdemeanor was struck down as pre-empted by federal law, though a preliminary injunction against a provision of the Arizona law requiring police conducting a stop, detention, or arrest to verify the person's status with the federal government if the officer suspected the person was unlawfully in the United States was ruled improper. See Symposium, Immigration in the Wake of *Arizona v. United States*, 3 Wake Forest J.L. & Pol'y 231–395 (2013). See also Note, A "Right Without a Remedy": An Analysis of the Sovereign Immunity Issues Implicated by State Power (or the Lack Thereof) Over Immigration Following *Arizona v. United* States, 26 Geo. Immigration L. J. 629 (2012). Some state and local legislators have even attempted to deport illegal aliens. See Ruddell, Champion, and Norris, The Ethical Dilemma of Local Ordinances that Purport to Deport Illegal Aliens, 89 U. Detroit Mercy L. Rev. 299 (2012). Such state and local efforts may be viewed as an attack on federalism. See Comment, Emma Lazarus Weeps: State-Based Anti-Immigration Initiatives and the Federalism Challenge, 80 U.M.K.C. L. Rev. 905 (2012). Some writers have, however, emphasized the need for a re-working of our immigration rules and standards, including greater cooperation among the levels of government. See Gulasekaram and Ramakrishnan, Immigration Federalism: A Reappraised, 88 N.Y.U.L. Rev. 2074 (2013); Note, State Power to Regulate Immigration: Searching for a Workable Standard in Light of *United States v. Arizona* and *Keller v. City of Fremont*, 91 Neb. L. Rev. 530 (2012); Note, Arizona's S.B. 1070 and Federal Preemption of State and Local Immigration Laws: A Case for a More Cooperative and Streamlined Approach to Judicial Review of Subnational Immigration Laws, 85 So. Cal. L. Rev. 955 (2012). See generally Johnson, Immigration and Civil Rights: State and Local Efforts to Regulate Immigration, 46 Ga. L. Rev. 609 (2012); Shapiro, States Can't Regulate Immigration, But They Can Regulate Illegal Immigrants, 6 Charleston L. Rev. 585 (2012) (remarks at symposium); Comment, Aliens in a Foreign Field: Examining Whether States Have the Authority to Pass Legislation in the Field of Immigration Law, 63 Mercer L. Rev. 1077 (2012).

On *local attempts to limit immigration*, see generally Bartlett, Grass Roots Immigration Reform, 69 La. L. Rev. 989 (2009); Kobach, Reinforcing the Rule of Law: What States Can and Should Do to Reduce Illegal Immigration, 22 Georgetown Immigr. L. J. 459 (2008); Comment, "Mi Casa No Es Su Casa": How Far Is Too Far When States and Localities Take Immigration Matters Into Their Own Hands, 29 Chicana/o-Latina/o L. Rev. 103 (2010); Comment, Testing the Borders: The Boundaries of State and Local Power to Regulate Illegal Immigration, 34 Pepperdine L. Rev. 483 (2012). See also Note, From 287(g) to SB 1070: The Decline of the Federal Immigration Partnership and the Rise of State-Level Immigration Enforcement, 52 Ariz. L. Rev. 1083 (2010); Note Cooperative Noncooperation: A Proposal for an Effective Uniform Noncooperation Immigration Policy for Local Governments, 77 Geo. Wash. L. Rev. 740 (2009); Note, Divided We Stand, United We Fall: A Public Policy Analysis of Sanctuary Cities' Role in the "Illegal Immigration" Debate, 42 Ind. L. Rev. 165 (2009). See also Section 8.4, note 90, *infra*.

Control over Indian reservations and Indian lands and affairs is another area in which the federal government is often found to have pre-empted state and local controls. See Ramah Navajo School Bd., Inc. v.

It has been observed that no single test can be used to determine pre-emption, but that the chief concern must be whether the state or local law is an obstacle to Congressional objectives.[53] There has been a growing tendency in the Supreme Court to avoid striking down state legislation on federal pre-emption grounds.[54] This is illustrated by a case[55] in which a Florida statute allowing recovery for the cost of cleaning-up oil spills was held not pre-empted by federal legislation that dealt with the same subject but differed somewhat as to degree of fault required and amount of liability. A similar attempt at reconciling state or local laws with federal statutes has been made by some lower federal courts when local rent-control ordinances and federal rent controls (in connection with programs to subsidize low- and moderate-income housing) have been

---

Bureau of Rev. of New Mexico, 458 U.S. 832, 102 S.Ct. 3394, 73 L.Ed.2d 1174 (1982) (federal law pre-empted state tax imposed on gross receipts that a non-Indian construction company received from tribal school board for construction of school for Indian children on reservation, since federal regulation of construction and financing of Indian schools is comprehensive and pervasive). Cf. New Mexico v. Mescalero Apache Tribe, 462 U.S. 324, 103 S.Ct. 2378, 76 L.Ed.2d 611 (1983) (application of state's hunting and fishing laws to reservation preempted). But cf. State ex rel. May v. Seneca-Cayuga Tribe of Oklahoma, 1985 OK 54, 711 P.2d 77 (1985) (state regulation of bingo games on Indian tribal lands not pre-empted by federal law). See also Section 2.11 *supra.*

[53] See Hines v. Davidowitz, 312 U.S. 52, 67, 61 S.Ct. 399, 404, 85 L.Ed. 581 (1941), holding Pennsylvania's Alien Registration Act pre-empted by the federal Alien Registration Act. Cf. Commonwealth of Pennsylvania v. Nelson, 350 U.S. 497, 76 S.Ct. 477, 100 L.Ed. 640 (1956) (federal law prohibiting the knowing advocacy of overthrow of United States government by force and violence had effect of pre-empting state sedition law). Compare Dan's City Used Cars, Inc. v. Pelkey, 569 U.S. ___, 133 S.Ct. 1769, 185 L.Ed.2d 909 (2013) (New Hampshire statute regulating the removal, storage, and disposal of abandoned motor vehicles was not the kind of state economic regulation Congress sought to pre-empt under the Federal Aviation Administration Authorization Act). See generally Zimmerman, Federal Preemption: The Silent Revolution (Iowa State Univ. Press 1991), analyzing numerous cases dealing with the question of Congressional intent to pre-empt state and local laws.

[54] See Medtronic, Inc. v. Lohr, 518 U.S. 470, 116 S.Ct. 2240, 135 L.Ed.2d 700 (1996) (historic police powers of state are not superseded by federal act unless this is clearly the Congressional intent; federal Medical Device Amendments held not to pre-empt state or local requirements that are equal or substantially identical to federal requirements); Cipollone v. Liggett Group, Inc., 505 U.S. 504, 112 S.Ct. 2608, 120 L.Ed.2d 407 (1992) (Congress's enactment of provision defining pre-emptive reach of statute implies that matters beyond that reach are not pre-empted; amended Federal Cigarette Labeling and Advertising Act did not pre-empt state claims based on express warranty, intentional fraud and misrepresentation, or conspiracy). Cf. Hillsborough County v. Automated Med. Labs., Inc., 471 U.S. 707, 105 S.Ct. 2371, 85 L.Ed.2d 714 (1985), on remand 767 F.2d 748 (11th Cir.1985), where a county ordinance regulating blood plasma centers was held not pre-empted by federal law. The Court concluded that any concern that state and local laws might impose such stringent requirements as to present an obstacle to the federal goal of assuring an adequate plasma supply was too speculative to support a finding of pre-emption. See generally Mandelker, Netsch, Salsich & Wegner, State and Local Government in a Federal System 595–606 (4th ed. 1996); Catz & Lenard, The Demise of the Implied Federal Pre-emption Doctrine, 4 Hastings Con. L.Q. 295 (1977); Stern, Preemption Doctrine and the Failure of Textualism in *Cipollone v. Liggett Group*, 80 Va. L. Rev. 979 (1994); Note, The Preemption Doctrine: Shifting Perspectives on Federalism and the Burger Court, 75 Colum. L. Rev. 623 (1975).

Courts will usually be reluctant to find state common-law actions precluded merely because a federal statute provides a remedy for a particular wrong. See Integrity Management Internat'l, Inc. v. Tombs & Sons, Inc., 836 F.2d 485 (10th Cir.1987) (state common-law actions seeking remedies against bidders who violate Small Business Act standards are not pre-empted by the Act or its regulations).

[55] Askew v. American Waterways Operators, Inc., 411 U.S. 325, 93 S.Ct. 1590, 36 L.Ed.2d 280, reh. denied 412 U.S. 933, 93 S.Ct. 2746, 37 L.Ed.2d 162 (1973). Cf. Huron Portland Cement Co. v. Detroit, 362 U.S. 440, 80 S.Ct. 813, 4 L.Ed.2d 852 (1960), upholding Detroit's smoke abatement code as applied to ships cruising in navigable waters and inspected and licensed under federal acts.

allowed to co-exist.[56] An administrative regulation, however, has been taken to indicate a federal intent to pre-empt rent regulation of subsidized housing.[57]

Even if Congress has not actually pre-empted a particular area of the law, a state or local law may nonetheless be invalidated under the Supremacy Clause—Article 6,

---

[56] Columbia Plaza Limited Partnership v. Cowles, 403 F.Supp. 1337 (D.D.C. 1975), remanded 551 F.2d 466 (D.C.Cir.); Helmsley v. Borough of Fort Lee, 362 F.Supp. 581 (D.N.J.1973). See Kargman v. Sullivan, 552 F.2d 2 (1st Cir.1977), reh. denied 558 F.2d 612 (Boston rent control ordinance not preempted by federal housing legislation; local ordinance had not impaired solvency of federally insured rental housing). Cf. Baker v. Donovan, 112 R.I. 411, 311 A.2d 278 (1973) (rent freeze statute did not prevent increases in public housing rents).

[57] Levin-Sagner-Orange v. Rent Leveling Board of City of Orange, 142 N.J.Super. 429, 361 A.2d 616 (1976), aff'd 147 N.J.Super. 303, 371 A.2d 302, applying 24 C.F.R. § 403.9 (1975). Cf. City of Boston v. Hills, 420 F.Supp. 1291 (D.Mass.1976).

There was formerly authority that a mere administrative regulation would not normally be taken by itself as establishing federal pre-emption. See Ranjel v. City of Lansing, *supra* note 51. But it has now been established by the U.S. Supreme Court that federal regulations can have as great a pre-emptive effect as do federal statutes. Capital Cities Cable, Inc. v. Crisp, 467 U.S. 691, 104 S.Ct. 2694, 81 L.Ed.2d 580 (1984) (Federal Communications Commission regulation). See Fidelity Fed. Sav. and Loan Ass'n v. de la Cuesta, 458 U.S. 141, 102 S.Ct. 3014, 73 L.Ed.2d 664 (1982), dealing with a regulation of the Federal Home Loan Bank Board that was contrary to state law. Cf. City of New York v. Federal Communications Comm'n, 486 U.S. 57, 108 S.Ct. 1637, 100 L.Ed.2d 48 (1988) (FCC did not exceed authority in pre-empting state and local technical standards governing quality of cable television signals; phrase "Laws of the United States" in supremacy clause said to encompass both federal statutes and federal regulations); Nantahala Power & Light Co. v. Thornburg, 476 U.S. 953, 106 S.Ct. 2349, 90 L.Ed.2d 943 (1986), on remand 318 N.C. 277, 347 S.E.2d 460 (1986) (order of North Carolina Utility Commission pre-empted by decision of Federal Energy Regulatory Commission); Van Meter v. Township of Maplewood, 696 F.Supp. 1024 (D.N.J.1988) (order by FCC regulating satellite dish reception pre-empted zoning ordinance attempting to regulate placement of such devices). But cf. California Coastal Comm'n v. Granite Rock Co., 480 U.S. 572, 107 S.Ct. 1419, 94 L.Ed.2d 577 (1987) (Forest Service regulations did not pre-empt state regulatory authority where they did not specifically express pre-emptive intent); Louisiana Pub. Serv. Comm'n v. Federal Communications Comm'n, 476 U.S. 355, 106 S.Ct. 1890, 90 L.Ed.2d 369 (1986) (dual regulatory system established by Communications Act of 1934 bars pre-emption by Federal Communications Commission of state regulation of depreciation methods used in setting rates for intrastate telephone service). See generally Project: The Role of Preemption in Administrative Law, 45 Admin. L. Rev. 107 (1993). On regulation of cable television, see generally Sinel & Ryerson, Regulating Cable Television in the 1990's, 17 Stetson L. Rev. 607 (1988). See also Parsons v. Comcast of California/Colorado/Washington I, Inc., 150 Wash. App. 721, 208 P.3d 1261 (2009) (cable television subscribers living in annexed area of city brought action alleging cable company violated franchise agreement with city as to rates charged; federal pre-emption over rate regulation held total, with the only venue for challenges being the Federal Communications Commission). As to pre-emption of drug labels and warnings by the federal Food and Drug Administration's regulation, see Wyeth v. Levine, 555 U.S. 555, 129 S.Ct. 1187, 173 L.Ed.2d 51 (2009) (federal drug labeling laws did not pre-empt the field or prevent state law claims against drug manufacturer; preamble to FDA regulations, which asserted that state laws contrary to the regulations were pre-empted, held not entitled to deference). See generally Note, Warning, This Decision Will Increase the Cost of Prescription Drugs, 63 Okla. L. Rev. 553 (2011). It has been suggested that federal pre-emption would be desirable as to electrical transmission. See Note, Power to the People: Why We Need Full Federal Preemption of Electrical Transmission Regulation, 48 U. Mich. J.L. Reform 1361 (2013). As to pre-emption by a federal compact with several states, see Tarrant Regional Water Dist. v. Herrmann, ___ U.S. ___, 133 S.Ct. 2120 (2013) (a state's statutes governing water rights are not pre-empted by federal water compact among several states when the compact does not grant cross-border water rights in the signatory states and the state statutes do not violate the Dormant Commerce Clause).

President Reagan dealt with the question of federal regulatory pre-emption by issuing Executive Order 12612, 3 C.F.R. § 253 (1987), directing federal agencies to treat federal statutes as pre-empting state law only when (1) the statute expressly so provided, or (2) when there was firm and palpable evidence that Congress so intended, or (3) when exercise of state authority directly conflicted with federal authority. Further, federal agencies were instructed to issue pre-emptive regulations only when expressly or clearly authorized and were asked to keep such pre-emption to a minimum.

clause 2 of the U.S. Constitution—if it is in conflict with federal law or stands as an obstacle to accomplishment of Congressional objectives.[58]

[58] See Lawrence County v. Lead-Deadwood School Dist. No. 40–1, 469 U.S. 256, 105 S.Ct. 695, 83 L.Ed.2d 635 (1985), on remand 367 N.W.2d 207 (S.D.1985), where a South Dakota statute requiring local units of government to spend monies received under the federal Payment in Lieu of Taxes Act in the same manner as they distributed general tax revenues was invalidated under the Supremacy Clause on the ground that Congress clearly intended local governments to have more discretion in spending this money than the state was allowing them. Cf. United States v. State of Connecticut, 566 F.Supp. 571 (D.Conn.1983), aff'd 742 F.2d 1443 (2d Cir.1983), where a state statute prohibiting tandem trailers on highways within its borders was struck down under the Supremacy Clause as in conflict with an act of Congress allowing such trucks on certain federally funded highways. On federal pre-emption of state truck regulations, see generally Friedman & Collins, Recent Developments in Highways and Public Transportation, 20 Urban Law. 1105, 1114–17 (1989). See also Forbes, Inc. v. Department of Finance of City of New York, 66 N.Y.2d 243, 496 N.Y.S.2d 394, 487 N.E.2d 251 (1985), cert. denied 475 U.S. 1109, 106 S.Ct. 1517, 89 L.Ed.2d 915 (1986) (city's corporation tax, which discriminated against investments in federal obligations, violated Supremacy Clause).

Cases of *conflict* between federal and state or local laws are, strictly speaking, different from cases of federal pre-emption, as pre-emption cases do not require a conflict so long as there is Congressional intent to occupy the field. But conflict cases are often also called cases of "pre-emption." See Pliva, Inc. v. Mensing 564 U.S. ___, 131 S.Ct. 2567, 180 L.Ed.2d 580 (2011) (federal drug regulations held to conflict directly with state laws and therefor to pre-empt those laws). See generally Adoption of A.B. & D.T., 245 P.3d 711 (Utah 2010), discussing and distinguishing "express pre-emption" (where an explicit statement clearly delivered by Congress is present); "field pre-emption" (when the scope of the statute indicates the intent of Congress to occupy the field exclusively, as where the federal regulation is so pervasive as to indicate Congress intended no room for state supplementation); and "conflict pre-emption" (where it is impossible to comply with both federal and state requirements or where state law stands as an obstacle to the purposes and objectives of Congress). See also State ex rel. Johnson v. Reliant Energy, Inc., 289 P.3d 1186 (Nev. 2012) (under Supremacy Clause of U.S. Constitution, federal law pre-empts state law when Congress expressly so provides or when state law conflicts with terms or purposes behind federal law).

For an example of a state law that was found an obstacle to achievement of Congressional objectives, see International Paper Co. v. Ouellette, 479 U.S. 481, 107 S.Ct. 805, 93 L.Ed.2d 883 (1987), on remand 823 F.2d 545 (2d Cir.1987), where the Supreme Court held that the federal Clean Water Act precluded Vermont courts from applying that state's nuisance law so as to impose liability on an out-of-state source, as such liability would interfere with the methods by which the federal statute was designed to reach its goals. See generally Lininger, Narrowing the Preemptive Scope of the Clean Water Act as a Means of Enhancing Environmental Protection, 20 Harv. Envtl. L. Rev. 165 (1996). Compare Golden State Transit Corp. v. City of Los Angeles, 475 U.S. 608, 106 S.Ct. 1395, 89 L.Ed.2d 616 (1986), on remand 791 F.2d 1383 (9th Cir.1986) (municipal action conditioning renewal of taxi franchise on settlement of ongoing labor dispute held pre-empted by National Labor Relations Act because action interferes with collective bargaining process); Michigan Canners and Freezers Ass'n, Inc. v. Agricultural Marketing & Bargaining Bd., 467 U.S. 461, 104 S.Ct. 2518, 81 L.Ed.2d 399 (1984), on remand 422 Mich. 862, 365 N.W.2d 760 (1985) (Michigan Agricultural Fair Practices Act must yield to federal law even though federal government, had not entirely displaced state regulation in this area); Biotechnology Industry Organization v. District of Columbia, 496 F.3d 1362 (Fed. Cir. 2007), reh. denied 505 F.3d 1343 (Fed. Cir. 2007) (state or local law prohibiting any patented drug from being sold at an excessive price held pre-empted as an obstacle to federal patent law's intent to give patentee full exercise of power over its patented drug). But cf. Hayfield Northern R. Co., Inc. v. Chicago & N.W. Transp. Co., 467 U.S. 622, 104 S.Ct. 2610, 81 L.Ed.2d 527 (1984) (post-abandonment condemnation of railroad under Minnesota statute was not pre-empted by federal act providing expedited abandonment process, even though state procedure may have frustrated economically optimal use of rail assets).

Chapter 8

POWERS OF MUNICIPALITIES

Analysis

§ 8.1 Charter as Source of Municipal Powers: Dillon's Rule for Interpreting Charter

Quite aside from any problems of conflicts and relationships between municipalities, on the one hand, and state and federal government, on the other hand,—the question must be asked: What powers does a municipality possess, and what is the source of these powers? Basically, the answer is that a municipality has such powers as are granted by its charter—and, obviously then, the charter is the source of municipal powers.

Despite some lack of historical accuracy,[1] the theory in the United States has been that the state pre-dates the municipal corporation and that the state, in granting a charter to a municipality, thereby delegates, for purposes of local self-government, a portion of the state's powers.[2] A city charter has been said to have the force and effect of an act of the legislature[3]—and indeed, has at times been called a state, as opposed to a municipal, law.[4] The *majority* view is that a municipal charter is a *grant* of power to the locality.[5] This means that a municipality will have only those powers expressed or

---

[1] See 1 McQuillin, Municipal Corporations § 1.09 (3d rev. ed. 1999).

[2] See 2A McQuillin, Municipal Corporations § 9.01 (3d rev. ed. 1996).

[3] Platt v. City & County of San Francisco, 158 Cal. 74, 110 P. 304 (1910); State ex rel. Freeman v. Zimmerman, 86 Minn. 353, 90 N.W. 783 (1902); Giers Improvement Corp. v. Investment Service, 361 Mo. 504, 235 S.W.2d 355 (1950); Wiget v. City of St. Louis, 337 Mo. 799, 85 S.W.2d 1038 (1935). See Adams v. Wolff, 84 Cal.App.2d 435, 190 P.2d 665 (Dist.Ct.1948) (home-rule charter is supreme law of state with respect to government of city). Cf. L Street Investments v. Municipality of Anchorage, 307 P.3d 965 (Alaska 2013) (in interpreting municipal charters, court uses rules of statutory construction); State ex rel. Duniway v. City of Portland, 65 Or. 273, 133 P. 62 (1913) (charter adopted by city has same effect as one granted directly by legislature).

[4] Ex parte Sparks, 120 Cal. 395, 52 P. 715 (1898); Mitchell v. City of St. Paul, 228 Minn. 64, 36 N.W.2d 132 (1949) (charter is comparable to a local statute); In re Addison, 385 Pa. 48, 122 A.2d 272 (1956).

[5] Utley v. City of St. Petersburg, 106 Fla. 692, 144 So. 53 (1932); Philson v. City of Omaha, 167 Neb. 360, 93 N.W.2d 13 (1958); Consumers' Coal Co. v. City of Lincoln, 109 Neb. 51, 189 N.W. 643 (1922); Harder v. City of Springfield, 192 Or. 676, 236 P.2d 432 (1951). See City of La Grande v. Municipal Court, 120 Or. 109, 251 P. 308 (1926) (municipality cannot enact legislation simply because it is not expressly forbidden). Cf. State

implied in its charter, or that somehow can be derived therefrom. It also means that in cases of conflict between state and local law, state law will prevail on statewide matters, local on local questions. Where there is no conflict between state and local law on a subject, both laws will stand together. And where one level of government (that is, the state *or* the locality) has enacted law on a subject but the other level hasn't, that law, if validly enacted, will govern the matter, regardless of whether the matter is of statewide concern or merely local.

But there is a *minority* view which says that, as to local affairs, a municipal charter is a *limitation* on powers and not a grant—that as to matters of local concern, a city can do anything its charter does not forbid.[6] This means that a city is, as to local matters, not dependent on any express or implied power in its charter in order to engage in a particular activity. So long as the matter is (1) local, and (2) not forbidden by the charter, the city may do whatever it wishes.

Municipal powers actually come not only from the home-rule charter itself but also from relevant state statutes or constitutional provisions, so that in a broad sense all these taken together may be considered the "charter."[7] And, of course, there are many local governments that have no home-rule document at all—most public quasi-corporations (such as counties, townships, etc.) still do not; and a great many municipal corporations do not, often not even meeting the requirements for attaining home-rule. These non-home-rule localities are then *entirely* controlled by state laws and constitutional provisions; those are their sole sources of power. These laws and provisions might, in such cases, be considered *analogous* to a city charter; but clearly, the locality then really has no charter at all—for instance, the inhabitants cannot amend the state statutes applicable to them in the same way that inhabitants of a home-rule city can amend their city charter.[8]

All cities—whether or not having home-rule—do have one thing in common: They are creatures of the law established for special purposes, and their powers must be

---

ex rel. Ekern v. City of Milwaukee, 190 Wis. 633, 209 N.W. 860 (1926), discussing municipal power to set height limitations for buildings. See generally 2A McQuillin, Municipal Corporations §§ 9.03, 9.08 (3d rev. ed. 1996).

6 City of Glendale v. Trondsen, 48 Cal.2d 93, 308 P.2d 1 (1957); Wiley v. City of Berkeley, 136 Cal.App.2d 10, 288 P.2d 123 (Dist.Ct.1955) (city charter silent on change in use of park land; city has power); State ex rel. McClure v. Hagerman, 155 Ohio St. 320, 98 N.E.2d 835 (1951) (city charter did not authorize or prohibit using public funds for cost of membership in municipal finance officers' association; city had power). See Domar Elec. Inc. v. City of Los Angeles, 9 Cal.4th 161, 36 Cal.Rptr.2d 521, 885 P.2d 934 (1994), on remand 41 Cal.App.4th 810, 48 Cal.Rptr.2d 822 (1995) (mere failure of city charter to grant express power to require bidders to conduct subcontractor outreach program did not render such program void); City of Marysville v. Boyd, 181 Cal.App.2d 755, 5 Cal.Rptr. 598 (Dist. Ct. 1960); D & F Sanitation Serv. v. City of Billings, 219 Mont. 437, 713 P.2d 977 (1986) (home-rule city has all local powers except those specifically prohibited; overruling prior authority); Clopton v. Madison County Comm'n, 216 Mont. 335, 701 P.2d 347 (1985) (home-rule city may exercise any power not prohibited by its charter or by state constitution or law); Waksman v. City of Albuquerque, 102 N.M. 41, 690 P.2d 1035 (1984) (home-rule municipality need look to legislative enactments only for express limitations on its power, not for grant of power); Apodaca v. Wilson, 86 N.M. 516, 525 P.2d 876 (1974) (city charter and general state laws are limitations on, not grants of, city power; city could levy water and sewer charges though not authorized by general state law). Cf. Stennis v. City of Santa Fe, 143 N.M. 320, 176 P.3d 309 (2008) (home-rule municipalities need not look to the legislature for a grant of power to act, but need only look for limitations on their power to act).

7 See Stason & Kauper, Municipal Corporations 105 (3d ed. 1959). Cf. 2A McQuillin, Municipal Corporations § 10.03 (3d rev. ed. 1996). On statutory grants of power, see Etter, General Grants of Municipal Power in Oregon, 26 Or.L.Rev. 141 (1947).

8 Morehead v. Dyer, 518 P.2d 1105 (Okl.1973).

granted by law: in the case of home-rule governments, by the home-rule charter *or* by state statutes and constitutional provisions; in the case of non-home-rule entities, by state statutes or constitutional provisions alone.[9] There is a famous rule of interpretation known as Dillon's Rule[10] that has traditionally been applied, and is still often used, to determine the total scope of power of local governments. This says that such governments have (1) those powers *expressly* conferred by state constitution, state statutes, and (where applicable) home-rule charter, (2) those powers necessarily or fairly *implied* in, or incident to, the powers expressly granted, and (3) those powers *essential* to the declared objects and purposes of the municipality or quasicorporation.[11] Under the

---

[9] See Cripe Baking Co. v. City of Bethany, 64 F.2d 755 (8th Cir.1933); New Haven Water Co. v. City of New Haven, 152 Conn. 563, 210 A.2d 449 (1965); City of Midway v. Midway Nursing & Convalescent Center, Inc., 230 Ga. 77, 195 S.E.2d 452 (1973); Branigar v. Village of Riverdale, 396 Ill. 534, 72 N.E.2d 201 (1947); James v. City of Pittsburg, 195 Kan. 462, 407 P.2d 503 (1965); Birge v. Town of Easton, 274 Md. 635, 337 A.2d 435 (1975); Itzen & Robertson, Inc. v. Board of Health, 89 N.J.Super. 374, 215 A.2d 60 (1965), aff'd 92 N.J.Super. 241, 222 A.2d 769; Seaman v. Fedourich, 16 N.Y.2d 94, 262 N.Y.S.2d 444, 209 N.E.2d 778 (1965); High Point Surplus Co. v. Pleasants, 264 N.C. 650, 142 S.E.2d 697 (1965); Fetzer v. Minot Park District, 138 N.W.2d 601 (N.D.1965); Barnes v. City of Dayton, 216 Tenn. 400, 392 S.W.2d 813 (1965); Faulk v. City of Tyler, 389 S.W.2d 706 (Tex.Civ.App.1965), ref'd n. r. e.; State ex rel. Bowen v. Kruegel, 67 Wash.2d 673, 409 P.2d 458 (1965); Toler v. City of Huntington, 153 W.Va. 313, 168 S.E.2d 551 (1969). See generally Stevens v. City of Missoula, 205 Mont. 274, 667 P.2d 440 (1983) (powers of non-home-rule city should be liberally construed, just as are those of a home-rule city). Acts performed with no legal authority are ultra vires and totally void even if proper procedural requirements are followed. But authorized acts done without following proper procedure may be held valid where there is no fraud or collusion but only mistake. See, with good review of Washington State authorities involving state or local government, South Tacoma Way, LLC v. State of Washington, 169 Wash. 2d 118, 233 P.3d 871 (2010) (failure to notify abutting landowners of intent to sell state land did not render sale to purchaser ultra vires). See generally International Ass'n of Firefighters Local Union v. City of Cheyenne, 316 P.3d 1162 (Wyo. 2013) (city official, like city itself, has only powers expressly granted by legislature or necessarily implied in those powers granted; city council held to be only party having authority to negotiate with firefighters on wages and working conditions).

[10] Taking its name from Dillon, Municipal Corporations § 55 (1st ed. 1872). See 2A McQuillin, Municipal Corporations § 10.09 (3d rev. ed. 1996). Doubt has been expressed that the authorities cited by Dillon supported his "rule". See Mandelker, Managing Our Urban Environment 97 (2d ed. 1971). But the rule is still often cited even where no longer strictly applied.

[11] City of York, Nebraska v. Iowa–Nebraska Light & Power Co., 109 F.2d 683 (8th Cir.1940), cert. denied 309 U.S. 690, 60 S.Ct. 893, 84 L.Ed. 1032; Cincinnati, Newport & Covington Railway v. City of Cincinnati, 71 F.2d 124 (6th Cir.1934), cert. denied 293 U.S. 612, 55 S.Ct. 142, 79 L.Ed. 702 (1934); City of Osceola v. Whistle, 241 Ark. 604, 410 S.W.2d 393 (1966); Douglass v. City of Los Angeles, 5 Cal.2d 123, 53 P.2d 353 (1935); Cook v. City of Delta, 100 Colo. 7, 64 P.2d 1257 (1937); Asbell v. Green, 159 Fla. 702, 32 So.2d 593 (1947); People ex rel. Schlaeger v. Bunge Bros. Coal Co., 392 Ill. 153, 64 N.E.2d 365 (1945); Southern Railway v. Harpe, 223 Ind. 124, 58 N.E.2d 346 (1944); Gritton v. City of Des Moines, 247 Iowa 326, 73 N.W.2d 813 (1955); Louisville & Nashville Railroad Co. v. City of Hazard, 304 Ky. 370, 200 S.W.2d 917 (1947); Town of Pineville v. Vandersypen, 212 La. 521, 33 So.2d 56 (1947); White v. Treasurer of Wayland, 273 Mass. 468, 173 N.E. 701 (1930); Skutt v. City of Grand Rapids, 275 Mich. 258, 266 N.W. 344 (1936); Sutton v. Fox Missouri Theatre Co., 336 S.W.2d 85 (Mo.1960); Ronnow v. City of Las Vegas, 57 Nev. 332, 65 P.2d 133 (1937); New Jersey Good Humor, Inc. v. Board of Commissioners, 124 N.J.L. 162, 11 A.2d 113 (1940); Whittaker v. Village of Franklinville, 265 N.Y. 11, 191 N.E. 716 (1934), aff'd 239 App.Div. 881, 265 N.Y.S. 977, reargument denied 266 N.Y. 505, 195 N.E. 174; Brumley v. Baxter, 225 N.C. 691, 36 S.E.2d 281 (1945); Worley v. French, 184 Okl. 116, 85 P.2d 296 (1938); Ex parte Jones, 4 Okl.Cr. 74, 109 P. 570 (1910); Pederson v. City of Portland, 144 Or. 437, 24 P.2d 1031 (1933); In re Valley Deposit & Trust Co., 311 Pa. 495, 167 A. 42 (1933); Buckhout v. City of Newport, 68 R.I. 280, 27 A.2d 317 (1942); Bean v. City of Knoxville, 180 Tenn. 448, 175 S.W.2d 954 (1943); Foster v. City of Waco, 113 Tex. 352, 255 S.W. 1104 (1923); Nance v. Mayflower Tavern, Inc., 106 Utah 517, 150 P.2d 773 (1944); Hopkins v. City of Richmond, 117 Va. 692, 86 S.E. 139 (1915); Pacific First Federal Savings & Loan Association v. Pierce County, 27 Wn.2d 347, 178 P.2d 351 (1947); Pugnier v. Ramharter, 275 Wis. 70, 81 N.W.2d 38 (1957). Cf. Miller v. Burch, 32 Tex. 208 (1869) (town ordinance authorized removal of building in which nuisance conducted; found to exceed charter powers and thus to give no protection to officers acting thereunder). The authorities supporting the basic principle have been called too numerous for citation. City of Leavenworth v. Norton, 1 Kan. 432 (1863). For a more thorough list, see 2 McQuillin, Municipal Corporations § 10.09 ns. 6, 7 (3d rev. ed. 1996). See also 1 Antieau, Municipal Corporation Law § 3.01–.13 (1998). When a power is not mentioned in the home-rule document, or when there is no such document, Dillon's Rule may be

above-stated majority view as to local powers,[12] a municipality will have only powers that can be found to exist under some one or more of Dillon's three-part test. Under the minority view,[13] a municipality will have only those same powers as to matters of statewide concern—but as to local matters, will have authority to do anything not forbidden by general state law or home-rule charter, and thus need not bother with Dillon's Rule as to local matters.

Under the majority view, Dillon's Rule is an exclusive enumeration of powers; no others exist.[14] Sometimes, certain matters that may be included in home-rule charters are enumerated in the state constitution[15] or a state statute.[16] But such lists are not always all-inclusive, and in any case leave considerable room for interpretation as to what powers can be inferred from those specifically stated.[17] It is generally agreed that the powers that may be granted by the home-rule charter (or for that matter, by state statute) cannot contravene provisions of the state constitution.[18]

Questions of municipal power often boil down to applications of the second part of Dillon's Rule. Express powers by themselves lead to few arguments. The "essential powers" referred to in the third portion of Dillon's Rule have not been of great importance. But what are the implied powers? Here, much room for judicial interpretation is found.

---

applied to relevant state statutes to determine whether a municipality has a particular power. See Development Industries, Inc. v. City of Norman, 412 P.2d 953 (Okl.1966).

Louisiana has now squarely rejected Dillon's Rule and has held that a home-rule charter empowers a city to enforce any ordinances not inconsistent with the Louisiana Constitution. City of New Orleans v. Board of Comm'rs, 640 So.2d 237 (La.1994), noted 69 Tulane L. Rev. 809 (1995). Cf. City of Port Angeles v. Our Water-Our Choice, 170 Wash. 2d 1, 239 P.3d 589 (2010), where the majority find that a state statute grants code cities broad, though specific, powers notwithstanding Dillon's Rule. *Id.* at 596 & n.7. Sometimes Dillon's Rule is applied but not by name. See State of Arizona v. Britton, 226 Ariz. 457, 250 P.3d 234 (App. 2011), upholding a city's authority to regulate parking.

The history of Dillon's Rule and the criticisms of it are well summarized in "From Dillon's Rule to Home Rule," in Briffault & Reynolds, State and Local Government Law 266–69 (6th ed. 2004). See generally Swiney, John Forrest Dillon Goes to School: Dillon's Rule in Tennessee Ten Years After *Southern Constructors*, 79 Tenn. L. Rev. 103 (2011) (Dillon's Rule has, over past 10 years, regained importance in Tennessee law, particularly in contractual situations where local government attempts to repudiate terms of a contract; also, Rule has been applied to a county board of education).

[12] See note 5 *supra* and accompanying text.

[13] See note 6 *supra* and accompanying text.

[14] See City of Bessemer v. Huey, 247 Ala. 12, 22 So.2d 325 (1945); Clinton G. Cauldwell, Inc. v. Patterson, 133 Ind.App. 138, 177 N.E.2d 490 (1961); In re Public Serv. Elec. & Gas Co., 35 N.J. 358, 173 A.2d 233 (1961); Safe Way Motor Coach Co. v. City of Two Rivers, 256 Wis. 35, 39 N.W.2d 847 (1949). See City of San Antonio v. Whitten, 161 Tex. 150, 338 S.W.2d 119 (1960). Cf. Kansas Public Service Co. v. State Corporation Commission, 199 Kan. 736, 433 P.2d 572 (1967); Toms River Pub. Co. v. Borough of Manasquan, 127 N.J.Super. 176, 316 A.2d 719 (1974); Novak v. Town of Poughkeepsie, 63 Misc.2d 385, 311 N.Y.S.2d 393 (1970).

[15] See Adams v. Wolff, 84 Cal.App.2d 435, 190 P.2d 665 (Dist.Ct.1948).

[16] See People v. Sell, 310 Mich. 305, 17 N.W.2d 193 (1945).

[17] City Commission v. Hirschman, 253 Mich. 596, 235 N.W. 265 (1931). See Sandalow, Limits of Municipal Power Under Home Rule: A Role for the Courts, 48 Minn. L.Rev. 643 (1964).

[18] See Georgia Power Co. v. City of Decatur, 281 U.S. 505, 50 S.Ct. 369, 74 L.Ed. 999 (1930); Laird Norton Yards v. City of Rochester, 117 Minn. 114, 134 N.W. 644 (1912). Cf. In re Cloherty, 2 Wash. 137, 27 P. 1064 (1891). But occasionally, even a matter covered by the state constitution may be found of purely local concern, such as the use of partisan primaries for the election of officers; in such a case, the city law will prevail over that of the state. See State ex rel. Short v. Callahan, 96 Okl. 276, 221 P. 718 (1923).

§ 8.2 Interpreting Municipal Charters—Implied Powers: Generalizations and Trends

The area of municipal activity touching on the prevention, detection, and punishment of crime is one in which Dillon's Rule has often received a rather strict application. It has been reasoned that crime control is basically a function of the state, not of any locality or subdivision of the state, and thus that delegations of powers and duties to municipalities in this area will not be readily assumed.[19] Thus, unless there is express authority in its home-rule document or a relevant statute, a city has often been held to lack authority to offer a reward for the apprehension or conviction of a criminal suspect.[20] An occasional exception has been recognized in situations of arson, which is sometimes treated as a matter of special local concern.[21]

Where—as is common—power is expressly conferred on a city to preserve the public peace, this implies the authority to employ a regular police force, but not, in the absence of exceptional circumstances, to hire private detectives.[22] However, where there is adequate reason to suspect covert criminal activities, circumstances may warrant an inference of power to allow city officials to hire detectives as needed;[23] and power may be implied on the city's part to appoint investigative committees to look into such alleged activities.[24]

Strict construction of Dillon's Rule, while still encountered as to some matters, has been the subject of criticism;[25] and as to some municipal activities, the trend is

---

[19] See City of Los Angeles v. Gurdane, 59 F.2d 161 (9th Cir.1932); Brite v. Siskiyou County, 21 Cal.App.2d 233, 68 P.2d 1007 (Dist.Ct.1937) (county had no authority to offer reward); Griffin v. City of Los Angeles, 134 Cal.App. 763, 26 P.2d 655 (Dist.Ct.1933); Hanger v. City of Des Moines, 52 Iowa 193, 2 N.W. 1105 (1879); Patton v. Stephens, 77 Ky. (14 Bush) 324 (1878) (embezzlement of city funds); Madry v. Town of Scotland Neck, 214 N.C. 461, 199 S.E. 618 (1938). Authority to offer rewards is sometimes granted municipalities or counties by state statute. See People ex rel. Attorney General v. Holly, 119 Mich. 637, 78 N.W. 665 (1899); Lewis v. Petroleum County, 92 Mont. 563, 17 P.2d 60 (1932).

[20] Crofut v. City of Danbury, 65 Conn. 294, 32 A. 365 (1894) (no power to offer reward for detection of an "incendiary"); Hanger v. City of Des Moines, *supra* note 19. Abel v. Pembroke, 61 N.H. 357 (1881); City of Winchester v. Redmond, 93 Va. 711, 25 S.E. 1001 (1896); Butler v. City of Milwaukee, 15 Wis. 493 (1862). Cf. Murphy v. City of Jacksonville, 18 Fla. 318 (1881).

[21] See Shaub v. City of Lancaster, 156 Pa. 362, 26 A. 1067 (1893); Choice v. City of Dallas, 210 S.W. 753 (Tex.Civ.App.1919), both finding authority to offer a reward for the apprehension of an arsonist. See generally 67 Am.Jur.2d Rewards § 8 (1985).

[22] See Bridgeman v. Derby, 104 Conn. 1, 132 A. 25 (1926) (no implied power in city attorney, though might be found in council); Flannagan v. Buxton, 145 Wis. 81, 129 N.W. 642 (1911). Cf. Chapman v. City of Fullerton, 90 Cal.App. 463, 265 P. 1035 (Dist.Ct.1928); State ex rel. Crouse v. Holdren, 128 W.Va. 365, 36 S.E.2d 481 (1945). See generally Annot., Power of Municipal Corporation or Authorities to Employ Detective, 45 A.L.R. 737 (1926).

[23] See State ex rel. Balser v. Bowen, 111 Ohio St. 561, 146 N.E. 108 (1924). Cf. Bridgeman v. Derby, *supra* note 22. See generally Annot., Power of Municipal Corporation or Authorities to Employ Detective, *supra* note 22. See also National Council of Railway Patrolmen's Unions v. Sealy, 152 F.2d 500 (5th Cir.1945) (special police officer has same authority as regular officer; federal regulation would usually not cover).

[24] Du Bois v. Gibbons, 2 Ill.2d 392, 118 N.E.2d 295 (1954). See Eggers v. Kenny, 15 N.J. 107, 104 A.2d 10 (1954).

[25] See Winter, Municipal Home Rule, A Progress Report?, 36 Neb.L.Rev. 447 (1957). An Iowa statute attempts largely to eliminate Dillon's Rule, providing instead that a city shall have the powers needed for protection of its property and inhabitants and for the preservation of peace and good order where not inconsistent with state statutes. Iowa Code Ann. § 368.2. See Richardson v. City of Jefferson, 257 Iowa 709, 134 N.W.2d 528 (1965); Wilson v. City of Council Bluffs, 253 Iowa 162, 110 N.W.2d 569 (1961) (upholding power to require fluoridation of municipal water supply). Cf. Iowa City v. Muscatine Development Co., 258

increasingly to find implied power. For instance, older cases held that express authorization was needed for a city to employ legal counsel.[26] But in more recent times, most cases have inferred, from general grants of power to manage city affairs, etc., the authority to hire attorneys, as reasonably needed, to draft documents for the city and represent it in litigation.[27] The modern tendency is to say that such authority is necessarily incidental to the capacity to sue and be sued and that the power is one that *should* be found unless expressly forbidden. Most larger municipalities now employ a full-time city attorney who, with his staff, handles regular legal matters and ordinary litigation; but special counsel may also be hired to assist the regular staff when special circumstances warrant.[28] Thus, where the permanent city attorney is ill, absent, or disqualified, implied power in the city is readily found to employ persons to render temporary legal services.[29]

Even without express authorization, a city has been found to have power to employ counsel to handle the municipality's legal interests in another state;[30] or to employ an attorney on a contingent fee basis;[31] or to hire an attorney to represent the city in litigation in which its rights are involved although the city is not itself a party, as where the city's right to license liquor sales is called into question.[32] And where suits are filed against municipal officers for acts done in discharge of their official duties, the city has

---

Iowa 1024, 141 N.W.2d 585 (1966), saying that even the earlier rule of strict construction of municipal powers applied only to the determination of whether a power was granted, not to the method of exercising powers.

[26] See City of Birmingham v. Wilkinson, 239 Ala. 199, 194 So. 548 (1940).

[27] Dianis v. Waenke, 29 Ill.App.3d 133, 330 N.E.2d 302 (1975) (implied authority to employ village attorney; state statute did not establish an exclusive method); Vicksburg Waterworks Co. v. Mayor of Vicksburg, 99 Miss. 132, 54 So. 852 (1911); Meeske v. Baumann, 122 Neb. 786, 241 N.W. 550 (1932); Cahn v. Town of Huntington, 29 N.Y.2d 451, 328 N.Y.S.2d 672, 278 N.E.2d 908 (1972) (express *or* implied authority needed to employ attorney); Fleischmann v. Graves, 118 Misc. 214, 193 N.Y.S. 816 (1922), aff'd without opinion 202 App.Div. 825, 194 N.Y.S. 934, aff'd 235 N.Y. 84, 138 N.E. 745; Treeman v. City of Perry, 11 Okl. 66, 65 P. 923 (1901); Cheesebrew v. Point Pleasant, 71 W.Va. 199, 76 S.E. 424 (1912). Cf. City of Moorhead v. Murphy, 94 Minn. 123, 102 N.W. 219 (1905); McClintic v. Cavender, 75 W.Va. 36, 83 S.E. 78 (1914). But cf. Pechous v. Slawko, 64 Ill.2d 576, 2 Ill.Dec. 701, 357 N.E.2d 1144 (1976) (under statute, *council* in city manager government has no authority to appoint and remove city attorney—any such power is in manager). See generally Annot., Power of Municipal Corporation to Employ Attorney, 83 A.L.R. 135 (1933).

[28] See State ex rel. Burmedez v. Heath, 20 La.Ann. 172 (1868); City Council v. Sakai, 58 Hawaii 390, 570 P.2d 565 (1977); Village of Farmingdale v. Karp, 54 Misc.2d 714, 283 N.Y.S.2d 267 (1967) (village board had implied power to employ and pay additional legal counsel as needed); Cheesebrew v. Point Pleasant, *supra* note 27.

[29] See Meeske v. Baumann, *supra* note 27; City of South Houston v. Sears, 488 S.W.2d 169 (Tex.Civ.App.1972) (city's corporate counsel could secure special counsel when needed); Wiley v. City of Seattle, 7 Wash. 576, 35 P. 415 (1894) (emergency warranted mayor's employing special counsel, though council action usually required). Cf. Turner v. Cook, 502 S.W.2d 824 (Tex. Civ.App.1973) (county commissioners' court could employ private counsel to assist county attorney in defending suit).

[30] City of Memphis v. Adams, 56 Tenn. (9 Heisk.) 518 (1872).

[31] Miles v. Cheyenne County, 96 Neb. 703, 148 N.W. 959 (1914); Town of Mannford v. Watson, 394 P.2d 506 (Okl.1964). But cf. Darnell v. City of Broken Bow, 139 Neb. 844, 299 N.W. 274 (1941) (contract to pay attorney percentage of all delinquent taxes collected, or of taxes collected on property that had escaped assessment, may be void as against public policy). See generally Annot., Validity of Contract Between Governmental Unit and Attorney Which Makes Compensation Contingent Upon Results Accomplished, 136 A.L.R. 101 (1942).

[32] Cheesebrew v. Point Pleasant, *supra* note 27. But cf. City of Purcell v. Wadlington, 43 Okl. 728, 144 P. 380 (1914), where it was held the city could not employ an attorney to appear before the state Corporation Commission to resist an application of the telephone company to raise its rates. In State ex rel. Steilacoom Town Council v. Volkmer, 73 Wash.App. 89, 867 P.2d 678 (1994), it was held the town council lacked legal authority to hire private legal counsel to represent it in a dispute with the mayor over a variance issue where no reason was shown that the town attorney was unable to represent the council.

implied authority to provide those officers with legal counsel.[33] Ordinarily, however, expenses incurred in defending, even successfully, against *criminal* charges are considered to be for private purposes; and in the absence of express authorization, public money cannot be used to cover these.[34] There is some contrary authority, however, where clearly groundless or frivolous charges have been brought against public officers.[35] Where a lawsuit is brought over who is entitled to a municipal office, the view has been taken that a city has implied authority to utilize a city attorney's services and spend public funds in the matter if, but only if, the city can be shown to have an interest in the litigation so that any expenditures are for the public benefit.[36]

Other areas in which there is a trend toward more easily inferring municipal power are the employment of lobbyists; advertisement and promotion of the city to attract business and tourism; and activities of an educational, cultural, or recreational nature. Thus, some older cases took the view that, without express provision in its home-rule document or state law, the city could not employ a lobbyist to represent the city before the state legislature and could not otherwise spend public money to obtain favorable legislation.[37] But Connecticut has long taken a contrary view;[38] many cities now employ lobbyists not only in their respective state capitals but also in Washington, D.C.; and the trend seems to be toward inferring from the municipality's powers in connection with general welfare or other matters, authority to employ lobbyists.[39]

---

[33] See Cullen v. Town of Carthage, 103 Ind. 196, 2 N.E. 571 (1885); State ex rel. Crow v. City of St. Louis, 174 Mo. 125, 73 S.W. 623 (1903); Errington v. Mansfield Township Board of Education, 100 N.J.Super. 130, 241 A.2d 271 (1968) (allegedly libelous resolution passed by board; under statute, members who were individually sued could recover legal expenses); State ex rel. Bradley v. Council of Hammonton, 38 N.J.L. 430 (1876). Cf. City of Birmingham v. Wilkinson, *supra* note 26. See generally Annot., Payment of Attorneys' Services in Defending Action Brought Against Officials Individually as Within Power or Obligation of Public Body, 47 A.L.R.5th 553 (1997); Annot., Power of Municipal Corporation to Employ Attorney, 83 A.L.R. 135, 139 (1933).

[34] See City of Birmingham v. Wilkinson, *supra* note 26. Cf. Thorndike v. Inhabitants of Camden, 82 Me. 39, 19 A. 95 (1889); Roberts v. City of St. Louis, 242 S.W.2d 293 (Mo.App.1951); Chapman v. City of New York, 168 N.Y. 80, 61 N.E. 108 (1901). See generally 56 Am.Jur.2d Municipal Corporations § 208 (1971).

[35] See City of Birmingham v. Wilkinson, *supra* note 26. Statutes, or provisions in home-rule charters, sometimes specifically authorize the use of public funds to pay expenses incurred by municipal officers in the defense of criminal charges, or in defending against attempts to remove them from office; and the constitutionality of these has usually been upheld. See Deuel v. Gaynor, 141 App.Div. 630, 126 N.Y.S. 112 (1910); Kane v. McClellan, 110 App.Div. 44, 96 N.Y.S. 806 (1905).

[36] See Estes v. City of North Miami Beach, 227 So.2d 33 (Fla.1969) (council could hire special legal counsel where losing candidate sued council members individually). Cf. Maricopa County v. Biaett, 21 Ariz.App. 286, 518 P.2d 1003 (1974) (county recorder could hire attorney, and charge the county with the expense, where recorder himself was suing county board of supervisors, charging them with usurping his office).

[37] Valentine v. Robertson, 300 F. 521 (9th Cir.1924); Minot v. Inhabitants of West Roxbury, 112 Mass. 1 (1873) (legislation would have brought about territorial changes in municipality). Cf. State ex rel. Port of Seattle v. Superior Court, 93 Wash. 267, 160 P. 755 (1916) (municipality could not spend public funds to influence passage of referendum nullifying state's debt limitation law).

[38] See Farrel v. Town of Derby, 58 Conn. 234, 20 A. 460 (1889) (counsel employed to oppose division of town).

[39] See Powell v. City & County of San Francisco, 62 Cal.App.2d 291, 144 P.2d 617 (Dist.Ct.1944) (payment to delegation sent to Congress to lobby); Meehan v. Parsons, 271 Ill. 546, 111 N.E. 529 (1916) (reimbursement to mayor for lobbying); Reilly v. Ozzard, 33 N.J. 529, 166 A.2d 360 (1960) (local government has right to lobby as to legislation affecting its interests, but this is not part of municipal attorney's job). Cf. City Affairs Committee v. Board of Commissioners, 134 N.J.L. 180, 46 A.2d 425 (Err. & App.1946); In re Carrick, 127 N.J.L. 316, 22 A.2d 561 (1941), both upholding the power of a municipality to advertise for or against legislation. See also Annot., Right of Political Division to Challenge Acts or Proceedings by Which its

Some authorization in home-rule document or statutes has been held necessary to a municipality's making expenditures for advertising or promotion of the locality,[40] and courts have sometimes refused to infer this power from provisions concerning the general welfare or the general power to tax.[41] But it has been indicated that the power to advertise the city might be inferred from charter provisions authorizing ordinances or expenditures for purposes of trade or commerce.[42]

Since home-rule charters or state statutes usually contain some reference to municipal action for public health or education, courts have long been able to find authority in the city to provide exhibits at fairs or expositions,[43] and increasingly have inferred the power to spend for various educational and recreational purposes, such as

---

Boundaries or Limits Are Affected, 86 A.L.R. 1367, 1369 (1933), noting the split of authority as to employing lobbyists to defeat legislation that would change municipal boundaries. As to state and municipal regulation of lobbying, see Fischer & Gullahorn, The Advent of State and Local Lobby Regulations and the Legal and Ethical Considerations for Attorneys, 3 St. Mary's J. Legal Malpractice & Ethics 32 (2013).

[40] Loeb v. City of Jacksonville, 101 Fla. 429, 134 So. 205 (1931); Moreland v. City of San Antonio, 116 S.W.2d 823 (Tex.Civ.App.1938), error ref'd. See Annot., Power of Municipality to Make Expenditures for Advertising or Other Forms of Publicity, 79 A.L.R. 466 (1932). Calling attention to the advantages of a community, for purposes of trade, tourism, etc., has been called a public purpose for which express authorization of the use of public funds *may* be given. See Anderson v. City of San Antonio, 123 Tex. 163, 67 S.W.2d 1036 (1934) (but no *implied* power found); Davis v. City of Taylor, 123 Tex. 39, 67 S.W.2d 1033 (1934).

[41] Anderson v. City of San Antonio and Davis v. City of Taylor, *supra* note 40.

[42] See Sacramento Chamber of Commerce v. Stephens, 212 Cal. 607, 299 P. 728 (1931) (construction and leasing of convention facilities); Ruggeri v. City of St. Louis, 441 S.W.2d 361 (Mo.1969) (city could establish convention-and-tourism bureau, financing it by tax on receipts of hotels, motels, and restaurants).

[43] See Daggett v. Colgan, 92 Cal. 53, 28 P. 51 (1891); Norman v. Kentucky Board of Managers, 93 Ky. 537, 20 S.W. 901 (1892); State ex rel. Douglas County v. Cornell, 53 Neb. 556, 74 N.W. 59 (1898); Capen v. City of Portland, 112 Or. 14, 228 P. 105 (1924).

providing parks,[44] golf course[45] and public concerts.[46] Two qualifications should be recognized, however: (1) Basic constitutional limitations must be obeyed; and thus displays in city parks and buildings may sometimes be ruled to violate the constitutional rule on separation of church and state.[47] The U.S. Supreme Court has, however, upheld

---

[44] Booth v. City of Minneapolis, 163 Minn. 223, 203 N.W. 625 (1925). See Board of Assessors v. Cunningham Foundation, 305 Mass. 411, 26 N.E.2d 335 (1940) (corporation to beautify town could own park partly in that town and partly in another); Vrooman v. City of St. Louis, 337 Mo. 933, 88 S.W.2d 189 (1935) (city contribution for park was for public purpose; was statutory authorization). See generally 59 Am.Jur.2d Parks, Squares, and Playgrounds §§ 5–6 (1971). Where the state specifically authorizes or requires the municipality to levy taxes for park purposes, the state action may be invalidated as in conflict with state constitutional provisions forbidding state taxation for local or municipal purposes. See State ex rel. Gerry v. Edwards, 42 Mont. 135, 111 P. 734 (1910). See generally Chapter 5 *supra*. The creation of Druid Hill Park in Baltimore has been noted as involving several aspects of the police power: the fostering of community among an increasingly heterogeneous urban population; the increase in land value of the surrounding area; the providing of open recreation space removed from the bulk of the urban population; and the providing of an area for shaping perception and defining hopes for urban development. See Schley, Landscape and Politics: The Creation of Baltimore's Druid Hill Park, 1860, 103 Md. Historical Mag. 292 (Fall, 2008). A monument within a city park has also been recognized as serving a public purpose. See Pleasant Grove City v. Summum, 555 U.S. 460, 129 S.Ct. 1125, 172 L.Ed.2d 853 (2009), well discussed in Casenote, Constitutional Law—The First Amendment—The City Exercised Government Speech by Allowing Placement of a Donated Permanent Monument in a Public Park and Therefore Was Not Subject to Strict Scrutiny Under the Free Speech Clause, 40 Cumb. L. Rev. 965 (2009–10). But see the cases on possible violations of church/state separation in notes 47–49 *infra*.

On the importance of London's Hyde Park to the history of public parks, see Foreman, Park of Ages, 82 American Scholar 44 (Summer 2013). On the effects of the U.S. civil rights movement of the 1940's and 1950's on public parks and sports facilities, see Patenaude, Playing Fair: The Fight for Interracial Athletics in Baltimore, 107 Md. Historical Mag. 175 (Summer, 2012) (all public parks and playgrounds in Baltimore were integrated in 1955).

[45] State v. North Palm Beach, 133 So.2d 641 (Fla.1961); Booth v. City of Minneapolis, *supra* note 44 (power to establish parks includes power to establish golf courses). Cf. Capen v. City of Portland, *supra* note 43 (golf course found to be within statutory authority on public utilities). But see Bradentown v. State, 88 Fla. 381, 102 So. 556 (1924), where the court refused to infer the power to establish golf courses from the powers expressly given in the particular charter. Cf. City of Daytona Beach v. King, 132 Fla. 273, 181 So. 1 (1938). See generally Annot., Power of Municipal Corporation to Establish and Maintain Golf Course, 36 A.L.R. 1301 (1925). See also Annot., Power of County or Municipality to Exempt from Taxation or Otherwise Aid or Subsidize Private Enterprises Conducted for Recreational, Exhibition, or Entertainment Purposes, 116 A.L.R. 889 (1938). As to other sports and entertainment facilities, see Panel Discussion, Constructing and Operating Sports and Entertainment Facilities, 19 Seton Hall J. Sports & Entertainment L. 382 (2009). See also Comment, Going for It on Fourth and Long: Gambling Public Funds on a New Vikings Stadium, 7 U. St. Thomas J.L. & Pub. Pol'y 240 (2013).

[46] See City of Tombstone v. Macia, 30 Ariz. 218, 245 P. 677 (1926) (dictum); Egan v. City & County of San Francisco, 165 Cal. 576, 133 P. 294 (1913); Green v. Thomas, 37 Ohio App. 489, 175 N.E. 226 (1930), petition in error dism'd, 123 Ohio St. 669, 177 N.E. 766. Cf. Lewis v. La Guardia, 172 Misc. 82, 14 N.Y.S.2d 463 (1939), aff'd without opinion 258 App.Div. 713, 14 N.Y.S.2d 991, aff'd 282 N.Y. 757, 27 N.E.2d 44 (municipal radio station); Meyer v. City of Cleveland, 35 Ohio App. 20, 171 N.E. 606 (1930). See generally Annots., Scope and Effect of Express Constitutional Provisions Prohibiting Legislature from Imposing Taxes for County or Corporate Purposes, or Providing that the Legislature May Invest Power to Levy Such Taxes in the Local Authorities, 106 A.L.R. 906, 918 (1937), 46 A.L.R. 609, 709 (1927) (on public buildings, etc.).

While implied power to provide certain cultural and educational activities may be found, the function of educating children and other students is basically one that resides in the state, and municipalities have only such authority in this matter as the state delegates. See Robinson v. Cahill, 62 N.J. 473, 303 A.2d 273 (1973), cert. denied 414 U.S. 976, 94 S.Ct. 292, 38 L.Ed.2d 219, reh. supplemented 69 N.J. 133, 351 A.2d 713 (municipality has no implied power to tax for education). Cf. Moses Lake School District v. Big Bend Community College, 81 Wn.2d 551, 503 P.2d 86 (1972), appeal dism'd 412 U.S. 934, 93 S.Ct. 2776, 37 L.Ed.2d 393. As to public libraries and the effects thereon of modern technology, see Note, An American Tragedy: E-books, Licenses, and the End of Public Lending Libraries?, 66 Vand. L. Rev. 615 (2013).

[47] Lowe v. City of Eugene, 254 Or. 518, 463 P.2d 360 (1969), appeal dism'd and cert. denied 397 U.S. 591, 1042, 90 S.Ct. 1366, 25 L.Ed.2d 597 reh. denied 398 U.S. 944, 90 S.Ct. 1838, 26 L.Ed.2d 283 (1970) (Latin cross in city park ordered removed). Cf. Fox v. City of Los Angeles, 22 Cal.3d 792, 150 Cal.Rptr. 867, 587 P.2d 663 (1978) (city could not display lighted cross on city hall). But see Meyer v. Oklahoma City, 496 P.2d 789

a city's construction of a Christmas display, including a nativity scene, in a park, where there was no surreptitious effort to express governmental advocacy of a particular religious message, there were legitimate secular purposes for the scene, and any benefit to religion was indirect, remote and incidental.[48] On the other hand, a public school's

---

(Okl.1972), cert. denied 409 U.S. 980, 93 S.Ct. 314, 34 L.Ed.2d 244 (cross in secular environment—on fair grounds—could be maintained with city money). Cf. Paul v. Dade County, 202 So.2d 833 (Fla. Dist.App.1967), cert. denied 207 So.2d 690, cert. denied 390 U.S. 1041, 88 S.Ct. 1636, 20 L.Ed.2d 304 (cross on courthouse, but no public funds involved); Eugene Sand & Gravel, Inc. v. City of Eugene, 276 Or. 1007, 558 P.2d 338 (1976), cert. denied 434 U.S. 876, 98 S.Ct. 226, 54 L.Ed.2d 155 (display of cross as veterans war memorial does not violate establishment-of-religion clause). The *Eugene Sand & Gravel* case is a later development in the dispute dealt with in the *Lowe v. City of Eugene* case *supra*.

In Salazar v. Buona, 559 U.S. 700, 130 S.Ct. 1803, 176 L.Ed.2d 634 (2010), plaintiff had obtained an injunction prohibiting the U.S. Government, on Establishment Clause grounds, from permitting display on public land of a Latin cross honoring fallen soldiers in World War I. A federal statute was enacted, after the injunction was entered, authorizing transfer of the land and cross to a private party. The Supreme Court remanded, finding the district court had failed to consider the context in which the statute was enacted and the reasons for its passage and had failed to acknowledge the statute's significance as a substantial change in circumstances bearing on the propriety of the injunction. Compare American Atheists, Inc. v. Duncan, 616 F.3d 1145 (10th Cir. 2010) (privately funded crosses on public land as memorials to fallen state highway officers held to violate Establishment Clause). See generally Note, A Cross to Bear: The Need to Weigh Context in Determining the Constitutionality of Religious Symbols on Public Land, 7 U. Maryland L. J. Race, Religion, Gender & Class 377 (2008). See also Dolan, The Cross National Memorial: At the Intersection of Speech and Religion, 61 Case Res. L. Rev. 117 (2011).

As to *hilltop* crosses, see generally Comment, A Cross-Examination of the Establishment Clause and Boise's Table Rock Cross, 45 Idaho L. Rev. 651 (2009); Comment, Mt. Soledad in the Supreme Court's Crosshairs: Why Legislative Recognition Should Be Considered in Public Displays of Religion, 40 McGeorge L. Rev. 973 (2009). As to *roadside* crosses, see Note, Courts Mistakenly Cross-Out Memorials: Why the Establishment Clause Is Not Violated by Roadside Crosses, 39 Hofstra L. Rev. 723 (2011). See generally Reid, Private Memorials on Public Space: Roadside Crosses at the Intersection of the Free Speech Clause and the Establishment Clause, 92 Neb. L. Rev. 124 (2013). See also, as to possible changes in attitude and in the law regarding religious symbols, Comment, An Inconsistent Truth: The Various Establishment Clause Tests as Applied in the Context of Public Displays of (Allegedly) "Religious" Symbols and Their Applicability Today, 34 N. Ill. U.L. Rev. 431 (2014).

In Friedman v. Board of County Comm'rs, 781 F.2d 777 (10th Cir.1985), cert. denied 476 U.S. 1169, 106 S.Ct. 2890, 90 L.Ed.2d 978 (1986), a county government's use of a seal—used on documents, stationery, motor vehicles, etc.—bearing a Latin cross and the Spanish motto "con esta vencemos" was held to convey the impression of an endorsement of Christianity and thus to violate the Establishment Clause. The court noted that, unlike a seasonal display, use of the seal pervaded the daily lives of residents and conveyed the impression that county officers might not provide even-handed treatment. Accord, Robinson v. City of Edmond, 68 F.3d 1226 (10th Cir.1995), cert. denied 517 U.S. 1201, 116 S.Ct. 1702, 134 L.Ed.2d 801 (1996) (city seal violated Establishment Clause due to Christian cross). But see Murray v. City of Austin, 744 F.Supp. 771 (W.D.Tex.1990), aff'd in part, vac'd in part 947 F.2d 147 (5th Cir.1991), cert. denied 505 U.S. 1219, 112 S.Ct. 3028, 120 L.Ed.2d 899 (1992) (city's seal, containing depiction of a Latin cross, held not to violate constitution). See generally Spain, The Flags and Seals of Texas, 33 S. Tex. L. Rev. 215 (1992). See also Patrick, Church, State and Charter: Canada's Hidden Establishment Clause, 14 Tulsa J. Comp. & Int'l L. 25 (2006).

[48] Lynch v. Donnelly, 465 U.S. 668, 104 S.Ct. 1355, 79 L.Ed.2d 604 (1984), reh. denied 466 U.S. 994, 104 S.Ct. 2376, 80 L.Ed.2d 848 (1984) (no violation of Establishment Clause; park was owned by a nonprofit corporation). In McCreary v. Stone, 739 F.2d 716 (2d Cir.1984), aff'd by equally divided Court sub nom. Board of Trustees of Scarsdale v. McCreary, 471 U.S. 83, 105 S.Ct. 1859, 85 L.Ed.2d 63 (1985), a village's neutral accommodation to permit display of a creche in a village park during the Christmas season was held not a violation of the Establishment Clause. But cf. American Civil Liberties Union v. City of Birmingham, 588 F.Supp. 1337 (E.D.Mich.1984), judgment aff'd 791 F.2d 1561 (6th Cir.1986), cert. denied 479 U.S. 939, 107 S.Ct. 421, 93 L.Ed.2d 371 (1986), where a nativity scene on public property was found violative of the Establishment Clause, no secular purpose being shown. The Supreme Court's decisions on nativity scenes are sometimes referred to as establishing a "reindeer rule": a partially religious scene on public property is constitutional so long as it also contains secular objects, such as a Santa's house and reindeer, but otherwise is unlawful. See "Is the Court Hostile to Religion?," Time, July 17, 1989, at 80. Cf. Chabad–Lubavitch of Vermont v. City of Burlington, 936 F.2d 109 (2d Cir.1991), cert. denied 505 U.S. 1218, 112 S.Ct. 3026, 120 L.Ed.2d 897 (1992) (Chanukah menorah in city park would violate Establishment Clause); American Jewish Congress v. City of Chicago, 827 F.2d 120 (7th Cir.1987) (nativity scene inside city's government center would

violate Establishment Clause); Burelle v. City of Nashua, 599 F.Supp. 792 (D.N.H.1984) (nativity scene with no secular purpose would violate Establishment Clause). But cf. Capitol Square Review & Advisory Bd. v. Pinette, 515 U.S. 753, 115 S.Ct. 2440, 132 L.Ed.2d 650 (1995) (permitting private party to erect Latin cross on state capitol grounds lawful); Lubavitch Chabad House v. City of Chicago, 917 F.2d 341 (7th Cir.1990) (Christmas trees in city airport lawful); Doe v. City of Clawson, 915 F.2d 244 (6th Cir.1990) (creche in Christmas display on city hall lawn lawful). See generally Comment, Private Religious Displays in Public Fora, 61 U. Chi. L. Rev. 253 (1994); Comment, Government, the Holiday Season, and the Establishment Clause: A Perspective on the Issues, 20 Stetson L. Rev. 217 (1990). On the constitutionality of governmental observances of Good Friday, see Note, The Constitutionality of the Good Friday Holiday, 73 N.Y.U.L. Rev. 193 (1998).

As to the posting of the Ten Commandments on public land or facilities, compare McCreary County v. American Civil Liberties Union, 545 U.S. 844, 125 S.Ct. 2722, 162 L.Ed.2d 729 (2005) (posting of Ten Commandments at courthouses violated First Amendment; counties' purpose was to emphasize and celebrate the Commandments' religious message), with Van Orden v. Perry, 545 U.S. 677, 125 S.Ct. 2854, 162 L.Ed.2d 607 (2005) (monument inscribed with Ten Commandments on grounds of Texas State Capitol did not violate First Amendment; display simply acknowledged religion's historical role in American life). Accord with Van Orden, ACLU v. Grayson County, 591 F.3d 837 (6th. Cir.2010) (historical display which includes copy of Ten Commandments does not violate Establishment Clause). See Finkelman, The Ten Commandments on the Courthouse Lawn and Elsewhere, 73 Fordham L. Rev. 1477 (2005); Note, Context Is King: A Perception-Based Test for Evaluating Government Displays of the Ten Commandments, 51 Vill. L. Rev. 379 (2006). Compare Irons, Curing a Monumental Error: The Presumptive Unconstitutionality of Ten Commandments Displays, 63 Okla. L. Rev. 1 (2010), arguing that any permanent display of the Ten Commandments on public property is presumptively unconstitutional as a violation of the Establishment Clause. But see ACLU v. Grayson County, 591 F.3d 837 (6th Cir. 2010) (county court's approval of historical display which includes copy of Ten Commandments does not violate Establishment Clause). See generally Summum v. Pleasant Grove City, 345 P.3d 1188 (Utah 2015) (religious liberty clause of Utah Constitution did not require city to install a second religious monument in a public park where a Ten Commandments monument was already situated); Sinsheimer, The Ten Commandments as a Secular Historic Artifact or Sacred Religious Text: Using *Modrovick v. Allegheny County* to Illustrate How Words Create Reality, 5 U. Md. L.J. Race, Religion, Gender & Class 325 (2005). See also Abbott, Chemerinsky, Manion, Sekulow & Van Alstyne, An Analysis of the Ten Commandments Cases, 14 Wm. & Mary Bill of Rts. J. i, 1–72 (series of articles); Note, Passive Acknowledgment or Active Promotion of Religion? Neutrality and the Ten Commandments, 2010 B.Y.U.L. Rev. 3. As to what is a lack of neutrality and a favoring of religion, see Freedom From Religion Foundation, Inc. v. City of Warren, 707 F.3d 686 (6th Cir.2013) (city's decision to exclude sign saying "religion is but myth and superstition" from its holiday display, and mayor's letter defending the exclusion, do not violate Establishment Clause or free speech rights; city's civic center held not a public forum).

A number of cases applying the doctrine of church-state separation have involved the public schools. See Board of Educ. of Kiryas Joel v. Grumet, 512 U.S. 687, 114 S.Ct. 2481, 129 L.Ed.2d 546 (1994) (statute creating special school district including only the property owned and inhabited by practitioners of strict form of Judaism violated Establishment Clause); School Dist. of City of Grand Rapids v. Ball, 473, U.S. 373, 473 U.S. 373, 105 S.Ct. 3216, 87 L.Ed.2d 267 (1985) (school district's shared time and community education programs, which provided classes to nonpublic school students at public expense in classrooms located in and leased from nonpublic schools, had primary effect of advancing religion and therefore violated Establishment Clause). But see Agostini v. Felton, 521 U.S. 203, 117 S.Ct. 1997, 138 L.Ed.2d 391 (1997) (public schools could send their teachers into parochial schools to provide remedial education to disadvantaged children; no violation of Establishment Clause, overruling prior authority); Lamb's Chapel v. Center Moriches Union Free School Dist., 508 U.S. 384, 113 S.Ct. 2141, 124 L.Ed.2d 352 (1993) (allowing church access to school premises to exhibit film on family and child-rearing issues would not violate Establishment Clause; school district violated free speech clause when it denied church such access). Cf. Mitchell v. Helms, 530 U.S. 793, 120 S.Ct. 2530, 147 L.Ed.2d 660 (2000) (state and federal aid programs could be applied to parochial schools). For discussion of the *Kiryas Joel* case *supra*, see Failer, The Draw and Drawbacks of Religious Enclaves in a Constitutional Democracy: Hasidic Public Schools in Kiryas Joel, 72 Ind. L.J. 383 (1997); Greene, *Kiryas Joel* and Two Mistakes About Equality, 96 Colum. L. Rev. 1 (1996); Note, The Curious Case of *Kiryas Joel*, 63 U. Cinc. L. Rev. 1947 (1995). For proceedings after the U.S. Supreme Court decision in the *Kiryas Joel* case, see Grumet v. Cuomo, 90 N.Y.2d 57, 659 N.Y.S.2d 173, 681 N.E.2d 340 (N.Y.Ct. App.1997) (statute allowing Kiryas Joel to form own school district invalidated). For discussion of the *Agostini* case *supra* and its place in the law, see Lugg, Providing Title I Services on Parochial School Grounds: *Aguilar v. Felton* Is No Longer the Law, 31 Urban Law. 2149 (1999). As to the ongoing controversy about prayer in the public schools, see Santa Fe Independent School Dist. v. Doe, 530 U.S. 290, 120 S.Ct. 2266, 147 L.Ed.2d 295 (2000) (student-led, student-initiated prayers before public-school football games violated Establishment Clause; with review of authorities). See generally, noting the Supreme Court's tendency toward applying a neutrality standard in Establishment Clause cases, Note, Life Without *Lemon*: The Status of Establishment Clause Jurisprudence After *Rosenberger v. University of Virginia*, 17 N. Ill. U.L. Rev. 123 (1996).

exclusion of a children's Christian club from meeting after hours at the school, based on its religious nature, was held unconstitutional viewpoint discrimination.[49] (2) It has been held, often partly on the basis of state constitutional prohibitions of municipal aid to private groups, that a city may not aid or subsidize private enterprises conducting fairs or exhibitions or providing cultural facilities such as museums.[50] Increasingly, though, this second qualification is being narrowed or terminated, and it has often now been held that the city has implied authority to spend for cultural purposes if there is public benefit even if the agency operating the facility is private.[51]

Celebration of historic events and of holidays has long been recognized as of public benefit, and a proper municipal activity where specifically authorized.[52] Here too, the trend is to say that a municipality has *implied* authority to spend public money for fireworks, various displays, entertainment, and other things reasonably necessary for celebration of an appropriate occasion.[53]

A final area in which powers of municipalities are increasingly inferred is that of procuring insurance. It has been held that from the power to hire and pay employees may be inferred the power to enter into group insurance arrangements for their benefit;[54]

---

[49] Good News Club v. Milford Central School, 533 U.S. 98, 121 S.Ct. 2093, 150 L.Ed.2d 151 (2001). See Schweitzer, The Supreme Court Rules in Favor of Religious Club's Right to Meet on Public School Premises: Is This "Good News" for First Amendment Rights?, 18 Touro L. Rev. 127 (2001). The Court in the *Good News* case, *supra*, found no violation of the Establishment Clause in allowing groups presenting any viewpoints to use the public facilities, even though only groups presenting a religious viewpoint had opted to take advantage of the facilities at a particular time. Cf. Zelman v. Simmons–Harris, 536 U.S. 639, 122 S.Ct. 2460, 153 L.Ed.2d 604 (2002) (school voucher program, enacted for valid secular purpose of providing educational assistance to poor children in failing public school system, did not violate Establishment Clause, even though majority of participating students had enrolled in religious affiliated schools; program was in all respects neutral toward religion). See generally Comment, "No Christian Child Left Behind": The Supreme Court's Jurisprudence in Establishment Clause Cases Involving Schoolchildren, 42 Houston L. Rev. 197 (2005). See also Note, The Future of the *Lemon* Test: A Sweeter Alternative for Establishment Clause Analysis, 40 Ga. L. Rev. 1171 (2006).

[50] See City of Daytona Beach v. King, *supra* note 45. Cf. Meriwether v. Garrett, 102 U.S. 472, 513, 26 L.Ed. 197 (1880). See generally Annot., Power of County or Municipality to Exempt from Taxation or Otherwise Aid or Subsidize Private Enterprises Conducted for Recreational, Exhibition, or Entertainment Purposes, 116 A.L.R. 889, 894–98 (1938).

[51] See McGuire v. City of Cincinnati, 22 O.O. 334, 40 N.E.2d 435 (1941), appeal dism'd 139 Ohio St. 218, 38 N.E.2d 1023 (city operated zoo through nonprofit corporation). See generally Annot., Power of County or Municipality, *supra* note 50, at 891–94, 897–98.

[52] See Annot., Use of Public Funds or Exercise of Taxing Power to Promote Patriotism, 30 A.L.R. 1035, 1039–43 (1924). Cf. State ex rel. American Legion 1941 Convention Corp. v. Smith, 235 Wis. 443, 293 N.W. 161 (1940) (state appropriation to American Legion national convention upheld; patriotic purpose). But cf. Southern Railway Co. v. Claiborne County, 157 Tenn. 71, 291 S.W. 837 (1927) (statute authorizing county to appropriate money for war memorial didn't authorize borrowing for this purpose). See also Hutcheson v. Atherton, 44 N.M. 144, 99 P.2d 462 (1940), striking down a statute authorizing public indebtedness for buildings, etc., to be used for commemoration of 400th anniversary of exploration of state.

[53] Stegmaier v. Goeringer, 218 Pa. 499, 67 A. 782 (1907). Cf. State ex rel. John Tague Post, American Legion v. Klinger, 114 Ohio St. 212, 151 N.E. 47 (1926) (county could appropriate for Memorial Day observance; was statutory authorization). See generally Annot., Use of Public Funds, *supra* note 50, at 1036–39, 1041–42. But see Love v. City of Raleigh, 116 N.C. 296, 21 S.E. 503 (1895) (no power to appropriate public money for celebrations in absence of express authorization). Cf. Marth v. City of Kingfisher, 22 Okl. 602, 98 P. 436 (1908) (no implied power found for Fourth of July celebration). As to Fourth of July celebrations, see generally Heintze, When in the Course of Human Events It Became Necessary to Celebrate July 4th, Phi Kappa Phi Forum, Summer, 2009, at 4, saying it is Americans' patriotic duty to celebrate July 4. See also Heintze, The Fourth of July Encyclopedia (McFarland & Co. 2007).

[54] Nohl v. Board of Education, 27 N.M. 232, 199 P. 373 (1921); State ex rel. Thompson v. City of Memphis, 147 Tenn. 658, 251 S.W. 46 (1923). See Bussie v. McKeithen, 259 So.2d 345 (La.App.1971), writ ref'd 261 La. 451, 259 So.2d 910 (insurance on state employees). Cf. Maryland Casualty Co. v. Wilson, 6 Ariz.App.

from the power to own property may be inferred the power to take out insurance to cover possible damage to, or destruction of, the property;[55] and from the power to engage in activities that may lead to tort liability may be inferred the authority to take out liability insurance.[56]

§ 8.3 Interpreting Municipal Charters—Business Powers

Older authorities often took the view that even with specific authorization, a municipality should not engage in a business of a private nature,[57] or sell commodities that are commonly sold on the open market.[58] Today, however, such authorizations are usually held valid if the business can be justified as contributing to the public welfare and any profits are put to public purposes.[59]

470, 433 P.2d 650 (1967) (state can provide insurance for its employees injured by uninsured motorist). See generally Annot., Right to Use Public Funds to Carry Insurance for Public Officers or Employees, 27 A.L.R. 1257 (1923).

[55] Struble v. Nelson, 217 Minn. 610, 15 N.W.2d 101 (1944); French v. Mayor of Millville, 66 N.J.L. 392, 49 A. 465 (1901), aff'd without opinion 67 N.J.L. 349, 51 A. 1109 (city can carry insurance on its building and can take out such insurance with a mutual company); State ex rel. King County v. Murrow, 199 Wash. 685, 93 P.2d 304 (1939). Cf. Clark School Township v. Home Insurance & Trust Co., 20 Ind.App. 543, 51 N.E. 107 (1898) (school trustees). See generally Libby v. City of Portland, 105 Me. 370, 74 A. 805 (1909) (city may own and manage farm but is liable for negligence in its operation). On problems faced by municipalities due to insurance companies' insertion (largely since the terrorist attacks of September 11, 2001) into their policies of exclusions of liability for terrorist acts, see Thomas, Insurance Implications of September 11 and Possible Responses, 34 Urban Law. 727 (2002).

[56] Travelers' Insurance Co. v. Wadsworth, 109 Ohio St. 440, 142 N.E. 900 (1924). See Annot., Power of Municipal Corporation to Take Out Liability Insurance, 33 A.L.R. 717 (1924). Cf. Sullivan v. Midlothian Park District, 51 Ill.2d 274, 281 N.E.2d 659 (1972) (liability insurance by local public entities authorized by statute); City of Spencer for Use of Spencer Municipal Utilities v. Hawkeye Security Insurance Co., 216 N.W.2d 406 (Iowa 1974); Medlar v. Aetna Insurance Co., 127 Vt. 337, 248 A.2d 740 (1968) (statute authorized but did not compel liability insurance on employees). The effect of a local government's taking out liability insurance, as well as the effect of legislative authorization of such insurance on municipal tort immunity, is discussed in connection with municipal liability in tort, *infra.*

[57] Union Ice & Coal Co. v. Town of Ruston, 135 La. 898, 66 So. 262 (1914); Opinion of Justices, 204 Mass. 607, 91 N.E. 405 (1910); Opinion of Justices (In re Municipal Fuel Plants), 182 Mass. 605, 66 N.E. 25 (1903); Opinion of Justices (In re House Bill No. 519), 155 Mass. 598, 30 N.E. 1142 (1892); Rippe v. Becker, 56 Minn. 100, 57 N.W. 331 (1894) (warehouse for storage of grain); Feldman & Co. v. City Council of Charleston, 23 S.C. 57 (1885). See Lowell v. City of Boston, 111 Mass. 454 (1873) (deficit might have to be made up by taxation; thus, a statute authorizing a city to go into private business could lead to taxation for nonpublic purposes); State ex rel. City of Toledo v. Lynch, 88 Ohio St. 71, 102 N.E. 670 (1913) (motion picture theatre), disapproved in part in Village of Perrysburg v. Ridgway, 108 Ohio St. 245, 140 N.E. 595 (1923).

[58] Laughlin v. City of Portland, 111 Me. 486, 90 A. 318 (1913); Baker v. City of Grand Rapids, 142 Mich. 687, 106 N.W. 208 (1906). See In re Opinion of Justices, 211 Mass. 624, 98 N.E. 611 (1912); Opinion of Justices (In re Municipal Fuel Plants), 182 Mass. 605, 66 N.E. 25 (1903).

[59] See Seattle Gas Co. v. Seattle, 291 U.S. 638, 54 S.Ct. 550, 78 L.Ed. 1037 (1934); Puget Sound Power & Light Co. v. Seattle, 291 U.S. 619, 54 S.Ct. 542, 78 L.Ed. 1025 (1934), rehearing denied 292 U.S. 603, 54 S.Ct. 712, 78 L.Ed. 1466; Huesing v. City of Rock Island, 128 Ill. 465, 21 N.E. 558 (1889) (public slaughterhouse); Standard Oil Co. v. Lincoln, 114 Neb. 243, 207 N.W. 172 (1926), aff'd 275 U.S. 504, 48 S.Ct. 155, 72 L.Ed. 395 (municipal charter authorized city to sell gas and oil at retail and wholesale); Moore v. City of Greensboro, 191 N.C. 592, 132 S.E. 565 (1926) (slaughterhouse). See State v. City of Tallahassee, 142 Fla. 476, 195 So. 402 (1940) (city may erect property for rental purposes where legislature has found a public purpose); Albritton v. City of Winona, 181 Miss. 75, 178 So. 799 (1938), appeal dism'd 303 U.S. 627, 58 S.Ct. 766, 82 L.Ed. 1088 (1938) (upholding statute authorizing city to own and operate manufacturing plants). Cf. Faulconer v. City of Danville, 313 Ky. 468, 232 S.W.2d 80 (1950) (city could issue bonds for construction of industrial building); Harrison v. Claybrook, 372 P.2d 602 (Okl.1962) (city could create municipal authority to obtain industrial development). On municipal power to enter into contracts, see generally the chapter on municipal contracts *infra.*

Where it is necessary to *infer*, from some other power, the municipality's legal authority to engage in a business enterprise, a policy of strict construction has sometimes been encountered.[60] Thus, it has been held that the power to construct and maintain public streets does not give rise to authority to operate a stone quarry to furnish paving material for the streets,[61] and the power to maintain an exhibition hall does not confer power to operate a private garage business therein.[62] But, as is true generally, a trend toward greater liberality in finding implied powers can be seen in many cases. There are cases—contrary to those in note 61 *supra*—holding that the authority to operate a stone quarry *can* be found implied in the power to pave and maintain streets.[63] And it has been held that the power to operate a nursery and greenhouse may be inferred from the express power to provide and maintain parks.[64] Such city enterprises as the quarry and the nursery, of course, exist mainly to supply goods to the city government itself; but there has long been authority that any surplus or by-products may be sold on the open market for a profit, even without express authorization.[65] What of a business operation that *primarily* serves the public? The power of a municipality to operate a utility—such as gas, electric, or water company—often is expressly granted[66] and can even be found implied in the "general welfare" provision of the delegated police power.[67] The power of a municipality to engage in business outside the traditional utility fields presents

---

[60] See, indicating strict construction of grants that might be interpreted as allowing commercial activity by municipalities, MacRae v. Selectmen of Concord, 296 Mass. 394, 6 N.E.2d 366 (1937); Mauldin v. City Council of Greenville, 33 S.C. 1, 11 S.E. 434 (1890). Cf. Webb v. City of Demopolis, 95 Ala. 116, 13 So. 289 (1892) (city on navigable river cannot erect wharves and charge public for their use unless power is conferred by special legislative act); Taylor v. Dimmitt, 336 Mo. 330, 78 S.W.2d 841 (1934) (municipality had no power under state law to construct and maintain electric transmission line to serve consumers outside municipality).

[61] City of Radford v. Clark, 113 Va. 199, 73 S.E. 571 (1912); Donable's Administrator v. Town of Harrisonburg, 104 Va. 533, 52 S.E. 174 (1905). Cf. Attorney General v. Common Council of Detroit, 150 Mich. 310, 113 N.W. 1107 (1907) (no implied power to build municipal paving-brick plant for manufacture of brick to pave public streets). In Heckert Constr. Co. v. City of Fort Scott, 278 Kan. 223, 91 P.3d 1234 (2004), a state statute was applied that allowed a city or county governing body to sell paving materials to private entities if such materials were not readily available from a nongovernmental entity. But asphalt was found to be readily available from nongovernmental sources.

[62] City of Cleveland v. Ruple, 130 Ohio St. 465, 200 N.E. 507 (1936). See People ex rel. Busching v. Ericsson, 263 Ill. 368, 105 N.E. 315 (1914).

[63] Schneider v. Menasha, 118 Wis. 298, 95 N.W. 94 (1903). Cf. Colwell v. Waterbury, 74 Conn. 568, 51 A. 530 (1902).

[64] People ex rel. Sweitzer v. City of Chicago, 363 Ill. 409, 2 N.E.2d 330 (1936).

[65] City of Tucson v. Sims, 39 Ariz. 168, 4 P.2d 673 (1931); Public Service Co. v. City of Loveland, 79 Colo. 216, 245 P. 493 (1926); Town of Hamden v. City of New Haven, 91 Conn. 589, 101 A. 11 (1917); Carroll v. City of Cedar Falls, 221 Iowa 277, 261 N.W. 652 (1935); Milligan v. Miles City, 51 Mont. 374, 153 P. 276 (1915); Light v. City of Danville, 168 Va. 181, 190 S.E. 276 (1937).

[66] See Travelers' Ins. Co. v. Village of Wadsworth, 109 Ohio St. 440, 142 N.E. 900 (1924); Lone Star Gas Co. v. City of Fort Worth, 128 Tex. 392, 98 S.W.2d 799 (Com. App.1936). Cf. Ruth v. Oklahoma City, 143 Okl. 62, 287 P. 406 (1930) (hospital); City National Bank v. Town of Kiowa, 104 Okl. 161, 230 P. 894 (1924) (municipality may itself engage in any business for which it could grant a franchise). On interpreting an express grant of power to operate a utility, see City of Tacoma v. Taxpayers of Tacoma, 108 Wash.2d 679, 743 P.2d 793 (1987) (city had implied power to pay for installation of energy conservation devices in residential and commercial structures; held not to be an unconstitutional gift of public funds).

[67] Ellinwood v. City of Reedsburgh, 91 Wis. 131, 64 N.W. 885 (1895). Cf. City of Albuquerque v. New Mexico Pub. Serv. Comm'n, 115 N.M. 521, 854 P.2d 348 (1993), (municipal power to contract for utility rates on behalf of municipal inhabitants can be inferred from municipal powers to contract, to regulate use of streets, and to grant franchises to public utilities). But cf. Okeson v. City of Seattle, 159 Wash.2d 436, 150 P.3d 556 (2007) (municipal utility attempted to mitigate effects of its greenhouse gas emissions by paying public and private entities to reduce those entities' emissions; held that utility lacked power to use ratepayer money for these offset contracts since this program did not serve a proprietary utility purpose).

somewhat more difficulty but is now usually upheld also, though often where some fairly specific authorization can be found.[68]

When municipal powers, especially to engage in commercial types of activity, are inferred, the inference is often drawn from the police power: the municipality's power, usually delegated by state statute and/or home-rule document, to act for the public safety, health, morals; *and* general welfare. While some courts hesitate to employ the general welfare clause, with its obviously very broad potential, to add significantly to powers that are expressly enumerated,[69] it has been noted that over the years, the "welfare grant" has often been liberally construed so as to give local governments considerable discretion in their exercises of the police power.[70] Many times, an implication can be found not only in the general welfare clause, but also in other portions of the police power. For instance, the fluoridation of the city's water supply has been

---

[68] See Jones v. City of Portland, 245 U.S. 217, 38 S.Ct. 112, 62 L.Ed. 252 (1917); Shaffer v. Allt, 25 Ariz.App. 565, 545 P.2d 76 (1976) (authority to purchase liquor license inferred from authority to operate places of recreation); Holton v. City of Camilla, 134 Ga. 560, 68 S.E. 472 (1910) (ice plant); Laughlin v. City of Portland, 111 Me. 486, 90 A. 318 (1914) (fuel yard). Cf. Interstate Power Co. v. City of Cushing, 12 F.Supp. 806 (W.D.Okl.1935), appeal dism'd 82 F.2d 1012; City of Blackwell v. Lee, 178 Okl. 338, 62 P.2d 1219 (1936) (municipality may operate airport and hangar where charter doesn't prohibit); Capen v. City of Portland, 112 Or. 14, 228 P. 105 (1924) (golf links held "public utility"). On municipal operation of businesses, see generally Chapter 16 *infra*.

[69] See City of Stuttgart v. Strait, 212 Ark. 126, 205 S.W.2d 35 (1947) (general welfare clause does not authorize establishing setback lines for property); Wood v. Peckham, 80 R.I. 479, 98 A.2d 669 (1953) (municipality not authorized by general welfare clause to regulate trailer parks).

[70] Adams v. City of New Kensington, 357 Pa. 557, 55 A.2d 392 (1947). See Ex parte Johnson, 77 Okl.Cr. 360, 141 P.2d 599 (1943); Etter, General Grants of Municipal Powers in Oregon, 26 Or.L.Rev. 141 (1947). Cf. Huff v. City of Des Moines, 244 Iowa 89, 56 N.W.2d 54 (1952) (city regulation of trailer parks authorized by general welfare clause). Legislative grants of the welfare power may be held to authorize city regulation of many businesses. See Summer v. Township of Teaneck, 53 N.J. 548, 251 A.2d 761 (1969), applying a New Jersey statute so as to uphold city regulation of real-estate brokers. Cf. Chicago Real Estate Board v. City of Chicago, 36 Ill.2d 530, 224 N.E.2d 793 (1967), upholding city licensing of real-estate brokers under a statute authorizing municipal "regulation" of such brokers. See generally Siegel, Chicago's Power to License and Regulate (1965). On the limitations that may be found inherent in legislative grants of general-welfare powers, see Wagner v. Mayor & Municipal Council of Newark, 24 N.J. 467, 132 A.2d 794 (1957) (grant relates only to matters of local concern, not those of statewide concern).

upheld under the welfare *and* public-health headings,[71] while ordinances against violent or abusive language may be held valid under the welfare *and* public-morals headings.[72]

§ 8.4 Interpreting Municipal Charters—Tests That Have Been Developed

Jurisdictions vary in the liberality with which their courts are willing to infer municipal powers from general grants, and cases within any given jurisdiction are likely to show varying attitudes, also. For instance, the Utah court refused to infer, from the power to regulate streets and the parking of vehicles thereon for a fee, the power to establish a rule of evidence that the presence of a vehicle on a public street in violation of parking ordinances made a prima facie case that the person in whose name the vehicle was registered had committed or authorized the violation.[73] But at other times, that court has exhibited greater willingness to find implied powers—as where it inferred from general city powers the authority to prohibit drunken driving.[74]

---

[71] Dowell v. City of Tulsa, 273 P.2d 859 (Okl.1954), cert. denied 348 U.S. 912, 75 S.Ct. 292, 99 L.Ed. 715. See Annot., Validity, Construction, and Effect of Statute, Ordinance, or Other Measure Involving Chemical Treatment of Public Water Supply, 43 A.L.R.2d 453 (1955). Cf. Wilson v. City of Council Bluffs, 253 Iowa 162, 110 N.W.2d 569 (1961). But cf. McGurren v. City of Fargo, 66 N.W.2d 207 (N.D.1954). See generally George, Municipal Power and Fluoridation, 1 Kan.L.Rev. 156 (1953); Note, Municipal Corporations—Constitutional Law—Validity of Fluoridation of Public Water Supply, 20 Brooklyn L.Rev. 298 (1954); Note, Municipal Corporations: Constitutional Law: Validity of Fluoridation of Public Water Supply, 8 Okl.L.Rev. 472 (1955). See also Antieau, The Power of Municipal Corporations to Protect Public Health and Safety, 1951 Wash.U.L.Q. 358. But the U.S. Supreme Court has never ruled on the constitutionality of fluoridating municipal water supplies, and some controversy continues over this question. See Note, Fluoridation of Public Water Systems: Valid Exercise of State Police Power or Constitutional Violation?, 14 Pace Envtl. L. Rev. 645 (1997). See generally Roosevelt, Not in My Water Supply, Time, Oct. 24, 2005, at 62 (despite evidence that fluoridation hardens teeth and prevents cavities, it still meets resistance). The federal government in 2011 lowered its recommended limit on the amount of fluoride in drinking water for the first time in 50 years, saying that spots on some children's teeth showed they were receiving too much of the mineral. Martin, Government Advises Less Fluoride in Water, Wall St. J., Jan. 8–9, 2011, at A3.

Another type of activity that might be justified under both the welfare and public-health headings of the police power is adjusting to the results of climate change. See Long, From Warranted to Valuable Belief: Local Government, Climate Change, and Giving Up the Pickup to Save Bangladesh, 49 Nat. Resources J. 743 (2009); Silveira da Rocka Sampaio, Regulation of Climate Change Risk at the Local Level—The Denver Experience: Greenprint or Greenwash?, 17 Mo. Envtl. L. & Pol'y Rev. 356 (2010). See also Section 18.4, note 106, *infra.*

Similarly, municipal preparation for possible disasters and emergencies, such as New Orleans experienced with Hurricane Katrina, may be justified as exercises of the public-health and welfare portions of the police power. See Symposium, Katrina's Wake: Emergency Preparedness With Response From the Bayou to the Beltway, 12 U. District of Columbia L. Rev. 3–133 (2009), particularly Morin, A Tale of Two Cities: Lessons Learned From New Orleans to the District of Columbia for the Protection of Vulnerable Populations From the Consequences of Disaster, *id.* at 45.

As to the possible justifications for local regulation of hydrofracking, see Note, Local Government Fracking Regulations: A Colorado Case Study, 33 Stan. Envtl. L. J. 61 (2014).

[72] Oney v. Oklahoma City, 120 F.2d 861 (10th Cir. 1941).

An area in which municipal power is sometimes found implied—in the expressly provided general welfare power or other powers—is protection of human rights. See Note, Diffusion of Local Regulatory Innovations: The San Francisco CEDAW Ordinance and the New York City Human Rights Initiative, 104 Colum. L. Rev. 768 (2004).

[73] Nasfell v. Ogden City, 122 Utah 344, 249 P.2d 507 (1952), noted 3 Utah L.Rev. 382 (1953). Colorado also sometimes indicates an attitude of strict construction. See City of Sheridan v. City of Englewood, 199 Colo. 348, 609 P.2d 108 (1980) (statute authorizing tax on amusement or place of amusement did not authorize tax on persons gaining admission to public place or event; rule of strict construction stated).

[74] Salt Lake City v. Kusse, 97 Utah 113, 93 P.2d 671 (1938). See Triangle Oil, Inc. v. North Salt Lake Corp., 609 P.2d 1338 (Utah 1980) (under legislative grant of power to "regulate or prohibit" sale of beer, city could limit number of retail outlets). Cf. Utah Power & Light Co. v. Provo City, 94 Utah 203, 74 P.2d 1191

A number of tests and rules have developed for possible use by the courts in determining whether or not to find a particular municipal power implied in home-rule documents or statutes. A rule that used to be encountered with great frequency, and to which at least lip service is still often paid, is the rule of strict construction: This declares that charters are special grants of power, and thus whatever power is not expressly given, or necessary to the fulfillment of express powers, must be deemed withheld.[75] Under this rule of interpretation, it is often said that doubts or ambiguities in statutes or home-rule documents should be resolved against the existence of any municipal power.[76] Sometimes it has been said that municipal powers should not be extended by unauthorized or unduly liberal definitions of words.[77] But the trend seems away from strict construction. In some jurisdictions, this rule of strict interpretation has been

---

(1937), cert. denied 305 U.S. 628, 59 S.Ct. 92, 83 L.Ed. 402 (express authority to build power plant implies authority to issue revenue bonds to finance construction); Salt Lake City v. Bennion Gas & Oil Co., 80 Utah 530, 15 P.2d 648 (1932) (authority to pass inspection ordinances implies power to charge fee to pay for inspections). In one case in 1981, the Utah court repudiated Dillon's Rule to the extent it requires strict construction of local governmental powers. State v. Hutchinson, 624 P.2d 1116 (Utah 1981) (upholding ordinance requiring financial disclosure by candidates for public office; grant of general welfare power said to provide local governments with independent authority apart from specific grants). But cf. Redwood Gym v. Salt Lake County Commission, 624 P.2d 1138 (Utah 1981) (upholding county's "massage parlor" ordinance but saying local governments have no inherent police power but only such as is expressly or impliedly granted them or is essential to their fundamental objectives). Dillon's Rule was also applied (though not by name) in Provo City v. Ivie, 2004 Utah 30, 94 P.3d 206 (2004) (city not authorized to condemn property outside municipal borders for purposes of constructing a road and bike path).

[75] Hoskins v. City of Orlando, 51 F.2d 901 (5th Cir.1931); City of Flagstaff v. Associated Dairy Products Co., 75 Ariz. 254, 255 P.2d 191 (1953); City of Los Angeles v. Keck, 14 Cal.App.3d 920, 92 Cal.Rptr. 599 (Dist.Ct.1971); Martin v. Board of Public Instruction, 42 So.2d 712 (Fla.1949); City of Midway v. Midway Nursing & Convalescent Center, Inc., 230 Ga. 77, 195 S.E.2d 452 (1973); City of Chicago Heights v. Western Union Telegraph Co., 406 Ill. 428, 94 N.E.2d 306 (1950); Dolan v. Louisville Water Co., 295 Ky. 291, 174 S.W.2d 425 (1943); Philson v. City of Omaha, 167 Neb. 360, 93 N.W.2d 13 (1958); City of Clovis v. Crain, 68 N.M. 10, 357 P.2d 667 (1960); In re Smith, 146 N.Y. 68, 40 N.E. 497 (1895); Cain's Coffee Co. v. City of Muskogee, 171 Okl. 635, 44 P.2d 50 (1935); City of LaGrande v. Municipal Court; 120 Or. 109, 251 P. 308 (1926); Willman v. City of Corsicana, 213 S.W.2d 155 (Tex.Civ.App.1948), aff'd 147 Tex. 377, 216 S.W.2d 175. Cf. Harden v. Superior Court, 44 Cal.2d 630, 284 P.2d 9 (1955); Stine v. Kansas City, 458 S.W.2d 601 (Mo.App.1970); City of Richmond v. Confrere Club of Richmond, 239 Va. 77, 387 S.E.2d 471 (1990) (Virginia said to subscribe to Dillon's Rule of strict construction; statute expressly gave city council alone the authority to suspend bingo permits, and this power could thus not be delegated by the council). Strict construction of charter powers is sometimes said justified because charters are special grants under which any power not expressly given, or necessary to executing powers that are expressly given, must be deemed intentionally withheld. See State v. Smith, 67 Conn. 541, 35 A. 506 (1896); Bear v. City of Cedar Rapids, 147 Iowa 341, 126 N.W. 324 (1910); Brackman's Inc. v. City of Huntington, 126 W.Va. 21, 27 S.E.2d 71 (1943). Cf. Ex parte Higgs, 97 Okl.Cr. 338, 263 P.2d 752 (1953). See also Biggers v. City of Bainbridge Island, 169 P.3d 14, 162 Wash.2d 683 (2007) (where there is doubt as to the existence of the state's delegation of some of its power to a local government, the court will construe the question against the local government's having the claimed power; city's police power held not to include authority to issue moratoria on shoreline development where the state constitution gave that power to the state).

[76] City of Ottawa v. Carey, 108 U.S. 110, 2 S.Ct. 361, 27 L.Ed. 669 (1883); Whitmore v. Brown, 207 Cal. 473, 279 P. 447 (1929); City of Miami v. Kayfetz, 158 Fla. 758, 30 So.2d 521 (1947); City of Chicago v. Barnett, 404 Ill. 136, 88 N.E.2d 477 (1949); In re Piers Old Nos. 8, 9, 10 & 11, 228 N.Y. 140, 126 N.E. 809 (1920); City of Purcell v. Wadlington, 43 Okl. 728, 144 P. 380 (1914) (denying city the power to employ attorney to appear before regulatory commission to resist telephone rate increase). See Oregon Short Line Railroad Co. v. Village of Chubbuck, 83 Idaho 62, 357 P.2d 1101 (1960); In re Valley Deposit & Trust Co., 311 Pa. 495, 167 A. 42 (1933); Wilson v. City of Seattle, 122 Wash.2d 814, 863 P.2d 1336 (1993) (if there is any doubt as to whether power is granted, the power must be denied).

[77] City of Jackson v. Freeman–Howie, Inc., 239 Miss. 84, 121 So.2d 120 (1960); City of Brookfield v. Kitchen, 163 Mo. 546, 63 S.W. 825 (1901); Dotson v. Town of Gilbert, 129 W.Va. 130, 39 S.E.2d 108 (1946). See City of Portland v. Portland Railway, Light & Power Co., 80 Or. 271, 156 P. 1058 (1916).

clearly abrogated by constitutional or statutory provision,[78] and in a number of other states, the courts themselves have rejected the doctrine.[79] Certainly, it is now generally agreed—and often emphasized—that powers should not be so strictly construed as to defeat legislative intent[80] or to hinder reasonable exercise of the city's general powers.[81] Beyond that, some cases are now saying or indicating that where a power is fairly inferable, it should be inferred rather than rejected.[82]

Another common rule of construction distinguishes between municipal powers that are legislative or governmental in nature and those that are "proprietary" (*i.e.*, corporate or private or "businesslike") in nature. As this differentiation is generally applied, it results in governmental powers being strictly construed[83] while proprietary powers, once granted, are more leniently interpreted in favor of the municipal authority.[84] The theory

---

[78] An example of a statutory provision is Iowa Code Ann. § 362.8 (1999) (city code to be liberally construed to effectuate its purposes). Cf., interpreting the New Jersey constitution, Chrinko v. South Brunswick Township Planning Bd., 77 N.J.Super. 594, 187 A.2d 221 (1963); Greggio v. City of Orange, 69 N.J.Super. 453, 174 A.2d 390 (1961), aff'd 37 N.J. 462, 181 A.2d 751; Fred v. Mayor & Council of Old Tappan, 10 N.J. 515, 92 A.2d 473 (1952).

[79] See City of Grass Valley v. Walkinshaw, 34 Cal.2d 595, 212 P.2d 894 (1949); Tousley v. Leach, 180 Minn. 293, 230 N.W. 788 (1930); State v. Hutchinson, *supra* note 74. Cf. Northern Pacific Railway Co. v. Weinberg, 53 F.Supp. 133 (D.Minn.1943) (municipalities retained power to determine number and qualifications of persons who must serve on a locomotive at railroad crossings within corporate limits). On the question of whether it is the courts or the legislature that should change the law as to the use of Dillon's Rule, see Csoka, The Dream of Greater Municipal Autonomy: Should the Legislature or the Courts Modify Dillon's Rule, a Common Law Restraint on Municipal Power?, 29 N.C. Central L.J. 194 (2007).

[80] See Robia Holding Corp. v. Walker, 257 N.Y. 431, 178 N.E. 747 (1931); Seafeldt v. Port of Astoria, 141 Or. 418, 16 P.2d 943 (1932). Cf. Burns v. City of Watertown, 126 Misc. 140, 213 N.Y.S. 90 (1925).

[81] Reams v. McMinnville, 155 Tenn. 222, 291 S.W. 1067 (1927). See Fullerton v. City of Des Moines, 147 Iowa 254, 126 N.W. 159 (1910).

[82] Liberis v. Harper, 89 Fla. 477, 104 So. 853 (1925); State ex rel. Ellis v. Tampa Waterworks Co., 56 Fla. 858, 47 So. 358 (1908); Kirkwood Drug Co. v. City of Kirkwood, 387 S.W.2d 550 (Mo.1965). Cf. Kyle v. Malin, 8 Ind. 34 (1856) (municipal corporations are to be favored by the courts). Many cases, of course, state that a city charter must be given a sensible, reasonable construction. See Salinas v. Pacific Telephone & Telegraph Co., 72 Cal.App.2d 494, 164 P.2d 905 (Dist.Ct.1946); Cochrane v. Mayor of Frostburgh, 81 Md. 54, 31 A. 703 (1895); In re Village of Kenmore, 59 Misc. 388, 110 N.Y.S. 1008 (1908); West v. Lysle, 302 Pa. 147, 153 A. 131 (1931).

[83] Certain Lots v. Town of Monticello, 159 Fla. 134, 31 So.2d 905 (1947); Higgins v. City of Galesburg, 401 Ill. 87, 81 N.E.2d 520 (1948); Rose v. Port of Portland, 82 Or. 541, 162 P. 498 (1917). Cf. State ex rel. City of Memphis v. Hackman, 273 Mo. 670, 202 S.W. 7 (1918); Pressel v. Ferris, 148 Misc. 910, 266 N.Y.S. 517 (1933).

[84] Indiana Service Corp. v. Town of Warren, 206 Ind. 384, 189 N.E. 523 (1934); City of Des Moines v. Horrabin, 204 Iowa 683, 215 N.W. 967 (1927); Dolan v. Louisville Water Co., 295 Ky. 291, 174 S.W.2d 425 (1943); State ex rel. White v. City of Cleveland, 125 Ohio St. 230, 181 N.E. 24 (1932). Cf. Mines v. Del Valle, 201 Cal. 273, 257 P. 530 (1927); City of Bowling Green v. Kirby, 220 Ky. 839, 295 S.W. 1004 (1927); Wilke v. City of Duluth, 172 Minn. 374, 215 N.W. 511 (1927); Butler v. Karb, 96 Ohio St. 472, 117 N.E. 953 (1917); Municipality of Metropolitan Seattle v. Division 587, Amalgamated Transit Union, 118 Wash.2d 639, 826 P.2d 167 (1992) (when municipality acts as a business, its powers are broadly construed; thus, power to enter into binding wage agreements with employees, including agreement to submit labor disputes to interest arbitration, was found). Washington State has been particularly inclined to apply the governmental-proprietary distinction. See Pacific Northwest Shooting Park Ass'n v. City of Sequim, 158 Wash.2d 342, 144 P.3d 276 (2006) (municipality acts in a proprietary capacity when it acts as proprietor of a business enterprise for private advantage of the municipality); Branson v. Port of Seattle, 152 Wash.2d 862, 101 P.3d 67 (2004) (acts of setting airport fees and entering into contracts are generally considered proprietary); Okeson v. City of Seattle, 150 Wash.2d 540, 78 P.3d 1279 (2003) (provision of streetlights through electric utility was a governmental function, even though operation of utility itself was proprietary). (After remand of the *Okeson* case *supra*, it was held that art projects funded with the electric utility's funds were properly limited to such projects that benefited the utility. Okeson v. City of Seattle, 130 Wash.App. 814, 125 P.3d 172 (2005).) In City of Tacoma v. City of Bonney Lake, 173 Wash.2d 584, 269 P.3d 1017 (2012), the court held that a city's decision to operate a utility is proprietary, including its right to contract for any lawful condition, while a city's decision

is that when a city acts as a business, it should be readily assumed to have the powers that private businesses enjoy.[85] However, the distinction is sometimes rejected;[86] some cases have observed that business powers not *usual* to the operation of a government should not be easily assumed to exist;[87] and there are even cases applying the governmental-proprietary distinction in a manner opposite that of the majority view: It can be reasoned that proprietary powers of a municipality are exceptional, or at least outside the scope of the government's primary purpose, and therefore should be strictly construed, while governmental powers, connected with the locality's main reasons for existence, should be liberally construed.[88]

Where courts are making a strict construction of municipal powers, they also sometimes seize on the general principle that an express enumeration of powers is assumed exclusive, at least to the exclusion of powers not necessarily implied.[89] And sometimes, even if the state has not totally pre-empted the field or even if there is no substantial inconsistency with state law, courts may be less willing to infer powers in areas where the state itself has legislated.[90]

---

to grant a franchise is governmental. Cf. Skagit County Public Hospital Dist. No. 304 v. Skagit County Public Hospital Dist. No. 1, 305 P.3d 1079 (Wash. 2013) (whether a municipal act is governmental or proprietary depends largely on whether the act is for the common good or for the specific benefit or profit of the corporate entity; rural public hospital district operates in a governmental capacity when providing health care).

[85] See Nelson–Johnston & Doudna v. Metropolitan Utilities District, 137 Neb. 871, 291 N.W. 558 (1940) (city operating municipal gas plant has implied power to sell gas appliances). Cf. Burns v. City of Seattle, 161 Wash.2d 129, 164 P.3d 475 (2007) (power to grant a franchise is a governmental power, but power of city to form an electric utility is a proprietary power, which the city may exercise very much in the same way as a private individual; city's municipal electric utility had power to enter agreement promising to pay other cities a percentage of revenues received from other cities' power customers in exchange for other cities' promise to forbear from establishing their own municipal electric utilities).

[86] See MacRae v. Selectmen of Concord, 296 Mass. 394, 6 N.E.2d 366 (1937).

[87] Fort Scott v. W. G. Eads Brokerage Co., 117 F. 51 (8th Cir.1902), cert. denied 187 U.S. 647, 23 S.Ct. 846, 47 L.Ed. 348; Richards v. Wheeler, 10 Cal.App.2d 108, 51 P.2d 436 (Dist.Ct.1935); City of Rockford v. Hey, 366 Ill. 526, 9 N.E.2d 317 (1937). Cf. Williams v. Town of Dunnellon, 125 Fla. 114, 169 So. 631 (1936); City of Somerville v. Dickerman, 127 Mass. 272 (1879) (where city takes land for street, agreement to submit assessment of damages to arbitration is void).

[88] See Southern Utilities Co. v. City of Palatka, 86 Fla. 583, 99 So. 236 (1923), aff'd 268 U.S. 232, 45 S.Ct. 488, 69 L.Ed. 930. Cf. Arnold v. City of Chicago, 387 Ill. 532, 56 N.E.2d 795 (1944); Shreveport v. Southwestern Gas & Electric Co., 151 La. 864, 92 So. 365 (1922); Bull v. McQuie, 342 Mo. 851, 119 S.W.2d 204 (1938). In City of Grangeville v. Haskin, 116 Idaho 535, 777 P.2d 1208 (1989), the court noted that the general rule in Idaho is to construe proprietary powers of municipalities more strictly than governmental and thus held that a city had no implied power to impose a lien for overdue charges for city utility services. Cf. Chemical Bank v. Washington Pub. Power Supply Sys., 99 Wash.2d 772, 666 P.2d 329 (1983), appeal after remand 102 Wash.2d 874, 691 P.2d 524 (1984), cert. denied 471 U.S. 1065, 105 S.Ct. 2140, 85 L.Ed.2d 497 (1985) (implied power of municipality to pledge revenues to pay for electric generating facilities did not include implied power to agree, in exchange for a share of power generated by contemplated nuclear power plants, that municipalities would unconditionally guarantee payments on revenue bonds secured by pledge of utility revenues). See also Plummer v. City of Fruitland, 140 Idaho 1, 89 P.3d 841 (2003) (rule that if a power is in doubt, the doubt must be resolved against the city is especially applicable to proprietary functions, such as garbage collection services).

[89] Canavan v. Messina, 31 Conn.Sup. 447, 334 A.2d 237 (1973); City of Pensacola v. Fillingim, 46 So.2d 876 (Fla.1950); Village of Lombard v. Illinois Bell Telephone Co., 405 Ill. 209, 90 N.E.2d 105 (1950); City of Humboldt v. Knight, 255 Iowa 22, 120 N.W.2d 457 (1963); George v. City of Raceland, 279 Ky. 316, 130 S.W.2d 825 (1939); Sebewaing Industries, Inc. v. Village of Sebewaing, 337 Mich. 530, 60 N.W.2d 444 (1953); Edwards v. Mayor & Council of Moonachie, 3 N.J. 17, 68 A.2d 744 (1949).

[90] See Allen v. City of Norfolk, 196 Va. 177, 83 S.E.2d 397 (1954), striking down a city anti-lottery ordinance. One provision of the ordinance *was* found inconsistent with state law, but the entire ordinance was initially held invalid. On rehearing, the portions of the ordinance not inconsistent with state law were upheld. See Note, Municipal Corporations—Section of City Ordinance Making Possession of Certain Indicia of a

While many of these traditional rules help justify strict constructions against cities, the current trend is clearly toward more liberal interpretations, as municipalities feel called upon to perform an increasing array of activities.

Where express powers of a municipality are concerned, questions of interpretation, of course, can still arise. But usual rules of statutory construction are normally applied,[91] and the problems are less complex than those connected with implied powers. What, however, of that third and final part of Dillon's Rule, dealing with powers essential to the municipality's objects and purposes? This has not been of great use, but has occasionally been employed in recognizing municipal power to do something considered necessary to the effective operation of a government, such as removing an officer guilty of official misconduct,[92] or something necessary to the security of local residents, such as providing fire and police protection.[93] It has been said that while the first two parts of Dillon's Rule can be applied also in determining the powers of public *quasi*-corporations (such as counties, townships, etc.), the *third* part of Dillon's Rule does not apply to those entities, whose powers (since those governments are only arms of the state) are to be more strictly limited.[94] But some cases have applied the third part of Dillon's Rule even to such quasi-corporate entities as school districts and counties.[95]

Lottery Prima Evidence of Guilt Held Invalid Because Inconsistent with State Statute, 40 Va.L.Rev. 966 (1954). Cf. Commonwealth v. Wolbarst, 319 Mass. 291, 65 N.E.2d 552 (1946) (state had pre-empted field of regulation of gambling). See also City of Seattle v. Hogan, 53 Wash.App. 387, 766 P.2d 1134 (1989) (city ordinance imposing greater penalty for misdemeanor of attempted vehicle prowling than was imposed under state law found to violate equal protection). As to state and municipal regulation of the largely *federal* field of immigration, see Comment, Emma Lazarus Weeps: State-Based Anti-Immigration Initiatives and the Federalism Challenge 80 U.M.K.C. L. Rev. 905 (2012). See generally Marzen, Hispanics in the Heartland: The Fremont Nebraska Immigration Ordinance and the Future of Latino Civil Rights, 29 Harv. J. Racial & Ethnic Just. 69 (2013); Varley & Snow, Don't You Dare Live Here: The Constitutionality of the Anti-Immigrant Employment and Housing Ordinances at Issues in *Keller v. City of Fremont*, 45 Creighton L. Rev. 503 (2012). See also Section 7.4, note 52, *supra*.

[91] See 2A McQuillin, Municipal Corporations §§ 10.10, 10.18–.26 (3d rev. ed. 1996).

[92] Hawkins v. Common Council of Grand Rapids, 192 Mich. 276, 158 N.W. 953 (1916).

[93] Ellinwood v. City of Reedsburgh, 91 Wis. 131, 64 N.W. 885 (1895). Cf. Denver & Salt Lake Railway Co. v. Moffat Tunnel Improvement District, 35 F.2d 365 (D.Colo. 1929); Morley Bros. v. Carrollton Township, 305 Mich. 285, 9 N.W.2d 543 (1943); Palisades Properties, Inc. v. Brunetti, 44 N.J. 117, 207 A.2d 522 (1965); Y & Y Cab Service v. Oklahoma City, 167 Okl. 134, 28 P.2d 551 (1933); Huff v. City of Wichita Falls, 121 Tex. 281, 48 S.W.2d 580 (1932); State ex rel. Hunter v. Superior Court, 34 Wn.2d 214, 208 P.2d 866 (1949). Cf. Nance v. Mayflower Tavern, Inc., 106 Utah 517, 150 P.2d 773 (1944). But cf. Public Serv. Co. v. Town of West Newbury, 835 F.2d 380 (1st Cir.1987) (issuance of permits allowing nuclear power plant to erect emergency warning sirens on utility poles held not within town's inherent authority).

[94] Wilson v. School District, 328 Pa. 225, 195 A. 90 (1937). See SDI, Inc. v. Pivotal Parker Commercial, LLC, 339 P.3d 672 (Colo. 2014) (as creatures of statute, special districts possess only those powers expressly conferred on them by constitution or statute, as well as the incidental implied powers reasonably necessary to perform the express powers).

[95] See Seattle High School Chapter No. 200 v. Sharples, 159 Wash. 424, 293 P. 994 (1930). Cf. Goodman v. School District No. 1, 32 F.2d 586 (10th Cir. 1929) (school district could operate restaurant); Commonwealth v. Fayette County, 239 Ky. 485, 39 S.W.2d 962 (1931) (county could purchase fire truck). The "essential powers" portion of Dillon's Rule was held applicable to a public utility district, which was treated as a form of municipal corporation, in Hite v. Public Util. Dist. No. 2, 112 Wash.2d 456, 772 P.2d 481 (1989) (lien to secure payment of electricity charges was within district's power; proprietary nature of activity stressed by court, which followed majority view that proprietary powers are to be construed more liberally than governmental).

§ 8.5 Exercise of Municipal Powers—"Reasonableness" Limitation

Assuming that a municipality has a particular power, how is it to be exercised? It is usually said that unless the power's exercise is clearly limited by some law, the method of exercise is left to the reasonable discretion of local officials.[96] Any "appropriate" mode of execution may be employed,[97] and there is a presumption of the correctness and validity of actions taken by municipal authorities under any grant of power.[98] There is a vague, general standard of reasonableness that the actions of local governments must meet; but seldom is it applied so as to strike down any actions. Thus, where such a government acts in a legislative capacity, as by passing an ordinance, the action will not be found "ultra vires" (*i.e.*, outside the scope of the government's authority) so long as it is "fairly debatable" whether or not the government is acting properly.[99] It has been said that municipal *legislation* will be invalidated as unreasonable only if it is found an arbitrary fiat or whimsical in nature.[100] Where *non*-legislative actions of the locality are concerned, as with the internal administration of a city's government, much is also left to the discretion of officials, and conduct will be declared invalid only if malicious,

---

[96] Walker v. Jameson, 140 Ind. 591, 37 N.E. 402 (1894); Webb v. City of Meridian, 195 So.2d 832 (Miss.1967); City of Flordell Hills v. Hardekopf, 271 S.W.2d 256 (Mo.App.1954); Page v. Town of Gallup, 26 N.M. 239, 191 P. 460 (1920); Matter of Assessment of Improvement of Lateral Sewer, 24 Misc.2d 618, 194 N.Y.S.2d 279 (1959); Lakota Oil & Gas Co. v. City of Casper, 57 Wyo. 329, 116 P.2d 861 (1941). See Red River Construction Co. v. City of Norman, 624 P.2d 1064 (Okl.1981) (if reasonableness is fairly debatable, action comes within ambit of legislative discretion even if compliance with edict is burdensome—but ordinance restricting weight of sand trucks here found unreasonable).

[97] Kindricks v. Machin, 135 Ark. 459, 205 S.W. 815 (1918); Heman v. Schulte, 166 Mo. 409, 66 S.W. 163 (1901), aff'd 189 U.S. 507, 23 S.Ct. 852, 47 L.Ed. 922; Lower Colorado River Authority v. Chemical Bank & Trust Co., 185 S.W.2d 461 (Tex.Civ.App.1945), aff'd 144 Tex. 326, 190 S.W.2d 48. Cf. Meyers v. New York State Division of Housing & Community Renewal, 36 A.D.2d 166, 319 N.Y.S.2d 522 (1971).

[98] Austin Western Road Machinery Co. v. City of New Madrid, 185 S.W.2d 850 (Mo.App.1945); Philippi v. Tygarts Valley Water Co., 99 W.Va. 473, 129 S.E. 465 (1925).

[99] See City of Miami Beach v. Ocean & Inland Co., 147 Fla. 480, 486, 3 So.2d 364, 366 (1941). See King v. City of Tulsa, 415 P.2d 606 (Okl.Cr.1966).

It has been held that where a municipal ordinance is expressly authorized by statute or by city charter provision, there can be no attack on its reasonableness, apart from constitutional arguments (such as the due process requirement that penal ordinances be reasonably definite and certain, and the equal protection argument that classification be based on reasonable differences). See Standard Oil Co. v. City of Charlottesville, 42 F.2d 88 (4th Cir.1930); Hagerty v. City of Chicago, 360 Ill. 97, 195 N.E. 652 (1935); People ex rel. Doyle v. Atwell, 232 N.Y. 96, 133 N.E. 364 (1921), error dism'd 261 U.S. 590, 43 S.Ct. 410, 67 L.Ed. 814; Bungalow Amusement Co. v. City of Seattle, 148 Wash. 485, 269 P. 1043 (1928). Cf. State v. Rice, 158 N.C. 635, 74 S.E. 582 (1912). But municipal legislation enacted under general or implied grants of power is often said to be subject to a test of reasonableness in addition to the test of constitutionality. The test of reasonableness, however, usually amounts only to a requirement that the ordinance appear fair, general, and not unduly oppressive. See Yick Wo v. Hopkins, 118 U.S. 356, 6 S.Ct. 1064, 30 L.Ed. 220 (1886); Klever Shampay Karpet Kleaners, Inc. v. City of Chicago, 323 Ill. 368, 154 N.E. 131 (1926); Commonwealth v. Kimball, 299 Mass. 353, 13 N.E.2d 18 (1938); People v. Kuc, 272 N.Y. 72, 4 N.E.2d 939 (1936); State ex rel. Carter v. Harper, 182 Wis. 148, 196 N.W. 451 (1923). Even where an ordinance *is* expressly authorized by statute or charter, the *details* of the ordinance, if not themselves specifically authorized, may be challenged as an unreasonable exercise of power. People ex rel. Busching v. Ericsson, 263 Ill. 368, 105 N.E. 315 (1914).

[100] Brae Burn, Inc. v. City of Bloomfield Hills, 350 Mich. 425, 432, 86 N.W.2d 166, 170 (1957). See McConnell v. Town Clerk of Tipton, 704 P.2d 479 (Okl.1985) (only legitimate basis for judicial interference with the legislative functions of a municipality occurs when the municipality has acted unreasonably, arbitrarily, or in such a way as to violate Equal Protection or Due Process); City of Healdton v. Beall, 341 P.2d 583 (Okl.1959). Cf. Homes Unlimited, Inc. v. City of Seattle, 90 Wn.2d 154, 579 P.2d 1331 (1978).

capricious, or corrupt.[101] Of course, even if action is found reasonable so as not to be ultra vires, it still may be challenged on constitutional grounds of due process and equal protection, under which standards of reasonableness are also often employed; thus, the "reasonableness" test used in the "ultra vires" sense of determining whether the exercise of a power is within the scope of local authority blends sometimes with "reasonableness" as applied under constitutional requirements.[102]

One area in which the "reasonableness" (in the "ultra vires" sense) of city action is often called into question is the city's entering into contracts the performance of which extends into the future. The city, it has been said, cannot bind itself perpetually or for an unreasonable length of time.[103] But members of a city council, or other governing board, must often act so as to secure leases, utility service, etc. for a municipality well into the future; so what is the test of such members' power to bind their successors? A distinction is drawn between the governmental and the proprietary activities of the locality. Where the local unit acts in a governmental or legislative capacity, or a matter of policy-making "discretion" is involved, the rule of thumb is that the council cannot, in the absence of some express grant of power, bind the city beyond the present council's own term.[104] But where the council acts in a business-type or proprietary area of activity,

---

[101] Wolgamood v. Village of Constantine, 302 Mich. 384, 4 N.W.2d 697 (1942). Cf. Atlas Life Insurance Co. v. Board of Education, 83 Okl. 12, 200 P. 171 (1921). See also Johnson v. Central Valley School Dist. No. 356, 97 Wash.2d 419, 645 P.2d 1088 (1982), cert. denied 459 U.S. 1107, 103 S.Ct. 732, 74 L.Ed.2d 955 (1983), distinguishing the ultra vires acts of a municipality that are done wholly without legal authorization or in direct violation of statute from those acts which are merely performed in an irregular manner or through unauthorized procedures. An example of municipal action that was held arbitrary and unreasonable is found in Lane Ranch Partnership v. City of Sun Valley, 145 Idaho 87, 175 P.3d 776 (2007), where a city had misinterpreted its ordinances by unnecessarily requiring design review or subdivision approval in order for a landowner to construct a private road. The city's actions were found to be an abuse of discretion because the city had acted without a reasonable basis in fact or law, entitling the landowner to attorney's fees.

[102] See Petstel, Inc. v. County of King, 77 Wn.2d 144, 459 P.2d 937 (1969), stating various "ultra vires" and constitutional criteria of "reasonableness" by which legislation should be judged. Cf. Montgomery v. Oklahoma City, 195 Okl. 312, 157 P.2d 454 (1945) (ordinance regulating a business will be declared invalid only if passes beyond limits of police power and infringes on basic rights). See generally Stason & Kauper, Municipal Corporations 123–24 n. 4 (1959).

[103] See Flynn v. Little Falls Electric & Water Co., 74 Minn. 180, 77 N.W. 38 (1898), aff'd 74 Minn. 180, 78 N.W. 106 (city could not enter into 30-year contract with company that was to furnish and maintain fire hydrants). See also Section 25.3.

[104] See Omaha Water Co. v. City of Omaha, 147 F. 1 (8th Cir.1906), appeal dism'd 207 U.S. 584, 28 S.Ct. 262, 52 L.Ed. 351; Illinois Trust & Savings Bank v. Arkansas City, 76 F. 271 (8th Cir. 1896); City of Riviera Beach v. Witt, 286 So.2d 574 (Fla. App.1973) (employment of city prosecutor); Westminster Water Co. v. Mayor of Westminster, 98 Md. 551, 56 A. 990 (1904); Columbus Gaslight & Coke Co. v. City of Columbus, 50 Ohio St. 65, 33 N.E. 292 (1893). See Edsall v. Wheler, 29 A.D.2d 622, 285 N.Y.S.2d 306 (1967) (retention of engineers; contract void). Cf. Town of Tempe v. Corbell, 17 Ariz. 1, 147 P. 745 (1915); East St. Louis & Interurban Water Co. v. City of Belleville, 360 Ill. 490, 196 N.E. 442 (1935) (annual rental for fire hydrants); Hansen v. City of Havre, 112 Mont. 207, 114 P.2d 1053 (1941) (no discretion left council to make up deficiency; so contract binding successors is valid); Sherman v. City of Picher, 201 Okl. 229, 204 P.2d 535 (1949). But see Bowley v. City of Omaha, 181 Neb. 515, 149 N.W.2d 417 (1967) (contract granting use of park to city valid though related to governmental function and extended beyond term of city officials). See generally Griffith, Local Government Contracts: Escaping from the Governmental/Proprietary Maze, 75 Iowa L. Rev. 277 (1990).

Where members of the municipal legislative body are serving *staggered* terms, it is possible to uphold a governmental contract extending beyond the term of some or all of the members by applying the theory that the legislative body is a continuing one. See Daly v. Stokell, 63 So.2d 644 (Fla.1953). But where the existing *majority* may be ousted in an upcoming election, *most* cases invalidate a governmental contract extending beyond the current terms of the majority. See Board of Education v. Gulick, 398 S.W.2d 483 (Ky.1966); Duggan v. City of Taunton, 360 Mass. 644, 277 N.E.2d 268 (Mass. 1971); Thomas v. Board of Education, 89 N.J.Super. 327, 215 A.2d 35 (1965), aff'd 46 N.J. 581, 218 A.2d 630. Cf. Independent School District v. Pennington, 181 Iowa 933, 165 N.W. 209 (1917) (contract invalid where it was totally within term of succeeding board). But see

it is governed by basically the same rules that would control those operating a private business,[105] and a valid and binding contract may be made for any reasonable period of time.[106] Thus, a local governing body has been allowed to enter into leases of property extending beyond the term of any present member of the council.[107] The appointment and removal of officers is generally held a governmental function as to which contractual commitments may not be made beyond the term of those presently on the council.[108] But where the hiring of mere "employees" such as schoolteachers is concerned (that is, the hiring of persons not vested with any of the governing authority), it is usually held that no governmental power is being exercised in such appointment, and a contract may be made for any reasonable period.[109]

Since contracts involving utility service are of a proprietary nature and must only meet the "reasonableness" test as to length of time, contracts for water or sewer service have been upheld though the city had committed itself for 30 years[110] or some other

---

King City Union High School District v. Waibel, 2 Cal.App.2d 65, 37 P.2d 861 (Dist.Ct.1934). Cf. Board of Education v. Finne, Lyman & Finne, 88 N.J.Super. 91, 210 A.2d 794 (1965) (rejecting idea that school board with staggered terms is continuous body but applying rule of reasonableness to uphold an architect's contract).

In Brunick v. Clatsop County, 204 Or.App. 326, 129 P.3d 738 (2006), it was held that an elected governing body of finite tenure which enters into a contract involving a governmental function cannot bind a subsequently elected body; and thus, where an elected body or officer makes "just cause" the termination standard for an employee who performs governmental functions, the "just cause" standard does not bind a subsequently elected body or officer because, even if that standard becomes part of the employment contract, the subsequently elected body or officer is not bound by the contract.

[105] See City of Walla Walla v. Walla Walla Water Co., 172 U.S. 1, 19 S.Ct. 77, 43 L.Ed. 341 (1898); McBean v. City of Fresno, 112 Cal. 159, 44 P. 358 (1896); City of Vincennes v. Citizens' Gaslight Co., 132 Ind. 114, 31 N.E. 573 (1892); Boerth v. Detroit City Gas Co., 152 Mich. 654, 116 N.W. 628 (1908); Picket Publishing Co. v. Board of Commissioners, 36 Mont. 188, 92 P. 524 (1907) (public printing). But cf. Shelden v. Butler County, 48 Kan. 356, 29 P. 759 (1892) (public printing; contract could not extend beyond term of present council).

[106] City of Detroit v. Detroit Citizens' Street Railway Co., 184 U.S. 368, 22 S.Ct. 410, 46 L.Ed. 592 (1902); City of Valparaiso v. Gardner, 97 Ind. 1 (1884). Occasionally, this rule of reasonableness is applied even to contracts that may be of a *governmental* nature. See Board of Education v. Finne, Lyman & Finne, *supra* note 104 (rejecting governmental-proprietary distinction and upholding contract for planning and constructing a new school). But see Uintah Basin Med. Center v. Hardy, 2002 Utah 92, 54 P.3d 1165 (2002) (court declined to repudiate governmental/proprietary test and held that contract for pathology services between doctor and county hospital involved a proprietary function and therefore was enforceable against successor boards of trustees if it was of a reasonable duration).

[107] Lease of city property to others: City of Biddeford v. Yates, 104 Me. 506, 72 A. 335 (1908); Baily v. City of Philadelphia, 184 Pa. 594, 39 A. 494 (1898). Cf. Macon Ambulance Service, Inc. v. Snow Properties, Inc., 218 Ga. 262, 127 S.E.2d 598 (1962) (five-year exclusive franchise to operate ambulance service found unreasonably long). (Franchise contracts—especially those granting exclusive rights—may be subject to especially strict scrutiny, and are often subject to statutory or constitutional length limitations. See generally Section 5.2 *supra*.) Lease of property from others by city: Gale v. Village of Kalamazoo, 23 Mich. 344 (1871); Ambrozich v. City of Eveleth, 200 Minn. 473, 274 N.W. 635 (1937).

[108] Millikin v. Edgar County, 142 Ill. 528, 32 N.E. 493 (1892); Board of Commissioners v. Taylor, 123 Ind. 148, 23 N.E. 752 (1890); Water Commissioners v. Cramer, 61 N.J.L. 270, 39 A. 671 (1898); Bergeron v. Jackson, 94 Vt. 91, 108 A. 912 (1920). Cf. Serna v. Pima County, 185 Ariz. 380, 916 P.2d 1096 (Ariz.App.1995) (county could not enter into contract with county manager extending beyond political life of county's governing board where contract was for personal or professional services for board itself). But if a contract is not for services to be rendered during a particular period but for the performance of a specific task, the contract may be valid though the performance is likely to extend, and does extend, beyond the term of the council members who make the contract. See Denio v. City of Huntington Beach, 22 Cal.2d 580, 140 P.2d 392 (1943).

[109] Gates v. School-District, 53 Ark. 468, 14 S.W. 656 (1890); Manley v. Scott, 108 Minn. 142, 121 N.W. 628 (1909). See Annot., Power of Board to Appoint Officer or Make Contract Extending Beyond Its Own Term, 70 A.L.R. 794, 802 (1931).

[110] Little Falls Electric & Water Co. v. City of Little Falls, 102 F. 663 (C.C. Minn. 1900), upholding as reasonable the same contract that, on demurrer, was declared unreasonably long in the *Flynn* case decided by

substantial period,[111] or even indefinitely.[112] Such contracts are especially likely to be upheld if the city has received, in return for the service it provides, some substantial and equally long-lasting benefit.[113]

§ 8.6 Exercise of Municipal Powers—Territorial Limitation

Assuming that a municipality possesses a specific power and exercises it reasonably, within what territory does the municipality have authority to act? We start with the general rule that a local government has no extraterritorial powers and cannot, without express authorization from the state, extend its regulations or the force of its laws outside its own boundaries.[114] But it must be noted that (1) statutes often do expressly authorize municipalities to exercise specified police powers, and the power of eminent domain for certain purposes, outside city limits, at least within a certain radius of the city,[115] and (2) it has been held that if a power expressly granted a municipality

---

the Minnesota Supreme Court, *supra* note 103. Cf. Gillam v. City of Fort Worth, 287 S.W.2d 494 (Tex.Civ.App.1956), ref'd n. r. e. (ten-year contract to supply water to another city).

[111] Creston Waterworks Co. v. City of Creston, 101 Iowa 687, 70 N.W. 739 (1897); Oconto City Water–Supply Co. v. City of Oconto, 105 Wis. 76, 80 N.W. 1113 (1899). See City of Phoenix v. Long, 158 Ariz. 59, 761 P.2d 133 (App. 1988) (agreement between six cities and two public utilities granting the utilities options, good for 67 years, to purchase sewage effluent upheld). See generally Annot., Power of Board to Make Appointment to Office or Contract Extending Beyond Its Own Term, 149 A.L.R. 336 (1944); Annot., Power of Board to Appoint Officer or Make Contract Extending Beyond Its Own Term, 70 A.L.R. 794 (1931).

[112] City of Des Moines v. City of West Des Moines, 239 Iowa 1, 30 N.W.2d 500 (1948), noted 34 Iowa L.Rev. 121 (1948) (contract of indefinite duration to supply water to another city at a set price).

[113] See City of Gainesville v. Board of Control, 81 So.2d 514 (Fla.1955), noted 35 Neb.L.Rev. 140 (1956), upholding a contract under which the city agreed to furnish water free to the University of Florida; the court interpreted this to mean the free service would last so long as the University remained in Gainesville.

[114] City of Sedalia ex rel. Ferguson v. Shell Petroleum Corp., 81 F.2d 193 (8th Cir.1936); Jones v. Hines, 157 Ala. 624, 47 So. 739 (1908); City of Wichita v. Clapp, 125 Kan. 100, 263 P. 12 (1928); Summit Township v. City of Jackson, 154 Mich. 37, 117 N.W. 545 (1908); Taylor v. Dimmitt, 336 Mo. 330, 78 S.W.2d 841 (1934); Light v. City of Danville, 168 Va. 181, 190 S.E. 276 (1937). See City of Pueblo v. Flanders, 122 Colo. 571, 225 P.2d 832 (1950); Capital Elec. Line Builders, Inc. v. Lennen, 232 Kan. 379, 654 P.2d 464 (1982), modified 232 Kan. 652, 658 P.2d 365 (1983) (statute governing local retailers' sales tax construed as referring to place where services were actually performed, thus avoiding an interpretation that would have unconstitutionally granted local units power to collect the tax on services outside their jurisdiction). Cf. McClain v. City of South Pasadena, 155 Cal.App.2d 423, 318 P.2d 199 (Dist.Ct.1957). But cf. Butler v. City of Little Rock, 231 Ark. 834, 332 S.W.2d 812 (1960) (city planning commissions given jurisdiction over land within 5 miles of municipal limits; act upheld).

Generally, a police officer's authority (to make arrests, searches, etc.) does not extend beyond the boundaries of the officer's jurisdiction, with three often-recognized exceptions: (1) when the officer is in hot pursuit of a suspect or escapee, (2) when one municipality or other governmental unit has asked for assistance from another, pursuant to a statute, and (3) when an officer is serving an arrest warrant. See United States of America v. Sawyer, 92 P.3d 707 (Okla. Crim. App. 2004) (police officers acting outside their jurisdiction under color of law cannot legally obtain consent to search). As to *state* jurisdiction, see Florey, State Courts, State Territory, State Power: Reflections on the Extraterritoriality Principle in Choice of Law and Legislation, 84 Notre Dame L. Rev. 1057 (2009).

[115] See White v. City of Decatur, 225 Ala. 646, 144 So. 873 (1932); Smeltzer v. Messer, 311 Ky. 692, 225 S.W.2d 96 (1949); State v. Rice, 158 N.C. 635, 74 S.E. 582 (1912); Salt Lake City v. Young, 45 Utah 349, 145 P. 1047 (1915); Kelley v. County of Brunswick, 200 Va. 45, 104 S.E.2d 7 (1958); Haddenham v. City of Laramie, 648 P.2d 551 (Wyo. 1982) (city found to have statutory authorization to restrict sale, offer for sale, or use, of fireworks within two miles of city limits). Cf. City of Naperville v. Wehrle, 340 Ill. 579, 173 N.E. 165 (1930). See generally Maddox, Extraterritorial Powers of Municipalities in the United States (1955); Anderson, The Extraterritorial Power of Cities, 10 Minn.L.Rev. 475, 564 (1926); Hemingway, The Extraterritorial Powers of a Municipality, 24 Ky.L.J. 107 (1936); Note, Extraterritorial Powers of Municipalities, 41 Harv.L.Rev. 894 (1928). See also Twin Falls County v. Hettinga, 151 Idaho 209, 254 P.3d 510 (App. 2011) (county code designated area bordering city as city impact area and stated that area of impact was to be governed by city's zoning ordinances). But cf. Hatman v. City of Mission, 43 Kan. App.2d 867, 233 P.3d 755 (2010) (under state

cannot be exercised without its going outside its corporate boundaries, the authority to act extraterritorially may even be implied.[116] Thus, where a city has express power to provide sewers and drains and it is essential to the well-being of city inhabitants that drainage be removed from city limits, an implied power can be found in the city government to contract for the construction of the necessary plants outside the municipal borders.[117]

A municipality's laws ordinarily extend only to its own boundaries. Thus, a city cannot impose against a non-resident its charter's requirement that a certain amount of notice be given before suit is filed against the city;[118] nor does a city, without express state authorization, have power to license and regulate businesses carried on outside the city.[119] But extraterritorial businesses often affect city residents, as where a dairy operated outside city limits sells its milk products within the city. The city may then have an obvious interest in protecting its residents against unwholesome products sold by such a concern. Three main generalizations may be made.

(1) A city may, despite the indirect effect of regulating extraterritorial operations, impose reasonable conditions and limitations on the sale of goods and offering of services within its own limits. Thus, in reasonably exercising its police power for protection of public health, safety, and welfare, it may require that milk sold in the city, whatever the milk's place of production, be pasteurized, that the seller be licensed, and that the

---

law, only residents of city may sign a petition seeking a referendum election in the city or vote in any such election; mere property owners or business owners have no such rights).

In Holt Civic Club v. City of Tuscaloosa, 439 U.S. 60, 99 S.Ct. 383, 58 L.Ed.2d 292 (1978), the Court upheld statutes which subjected areas near, but outside, city limits to city police, sanitary, and licensing laws, even though residents of the areas could not vote in city elections. Cf. May v. Town of Mountain Village, 969 P.2d 790 (Colo. App.1998) (extension of voting franchise to nonresident property owners did not violate state constitution or home-rule statute).

[116] Austin v. Shaw, 235 N.C. 722, 71 S.E.2d 25 (1952) (power implied to spend money on overpasses and underpasses outside city limits); Schneider v. Menasha, 118 Wis. 298, 95 N.W. 94 (1903) (power implied to acquire land outside city for manufacturing crushed rock to use on city streets). See Howard v. City of Atlanta, 190 Ga. 730, 10 S.E.2d 190 (1940). On the problem of whether or not a city, expressly authorized to operate an airport outside city limits, may zone the surrounding extraterritorial property, see Yara Engineering Corp. v. City of Newark, 132 N.J.L. 370, 40 A.2d 559 (1945) (no such power). See generally Note, Municipal Power Arising from the Ownership of Extraterritorial Property, 1957 U.Ill.L. Forum 99.

[117] Langley v. City Council of Augusta, 118 Ga. 590, 45 S.E. 486 (1903); City of Evansville v. Decker, 84 Ind. 325 (1882); City of Coldwater v. Tucker, 36 Mich. 474 (1877). See McBean v. City of Fresno, 112 Cal. 159, 44 P. 358 (1896). Cf. Cales v. State, 648 P.2d 838 (Okl. Crim. App. 1982) (firemen acting outside city limits while engaged in official firefighting duties were within protection of state statute prohibiting interference with firefighters). A municipal police officer is generally held to have power to act extraterritorially only if in hot pursuit of a person reasonably suspected of having committed an unlawful act within the officer's jurisdiction, or if in response to another municipality's request for assistance, or where—if authorized by statute—serving an arrest warrant. See Staller v. State, 932 P.2d 1136 (Okl. Crim. App. 1996) (peace officer outside his jurisdiction acts as private citizen, but evidence seized by such officer can be used in establishing probable cause for arrest warrant); Graham v. State, 560 P.2d 200 (Okl. Crim. App. 1977). But cf. Molan v. State, 614 P.2d 79 (Okl. Crim. App. 1980) (no power to make extraterritorial arrest where crime had occurred outside officer's jurisdiction, making "hot pursuit" rule inapplicable). See generally State v. Ross, 247 Kan. 191, 795 P.2d 937 (1990) (city police officer may exercise powers outside city limits when in fresh pursuit of suspect or where request for assistance made by officers of neighboring jurisdiction).

[118] City of Collinsville v. Brickey, 115 Okl. 264, 242 P. 249 (1925). Cf. City of Rockford v. Hey, 366 Ill. 526, 9 N.E.2d 317 (1937); Sproles v. City of Tulsa, 730 P.2d 9 (Okl. Crim. App. 1986) (to prevent reversal of municipal court conviction, city must establish that violation of city ordinance occurred within municipal limits; insufficient that witnesses merely provided street names and name of a building).

[119] See State v. Nelson, 66 Minn. 166, 68 N.W. 1066 (1896); City of Norfolk v. Flynn, 101 Va. 473, 44 S.E. 717 (1903).

pasteurization plant and/or sources of supply be inspected and approved by the city's own officials.[120] Where any substantial amount of extraterritorial regulation, or complex licensing procedure, is involved, express authorization—or at least authorization that can be clearly implied—may be required by some courts; but state authorization, by statute or through home-rule document, will, where clearly granted, be universally upheld against constitutional attack.[121]

(2) The extraterritorial effects of the city's laws must be for purposes of regulation, not revenue. Even with state authorization, a city cannot impose a tax on trades or occupations carried on outside city limits,[122] as this would amount to taxation without representation and to a taking of private property without due process of law.[123] Of course, once a business is carried on inside city limits, its sales and activities can be taxed even if the business's "home base" is elsewhere. And a license fee or tax may be imposed on such an "extraterritorial" business if this charge is not for revenue but to cover the cost of permissible regulation.[124] Thus, this limitation often means little more than that a city must have some territorial connection with a business in order to tax it, such as income earned or sales made within the city.

(3) Any distinctions drawn by the city between extraterritorial businesses and those conducted entirely within the city must be reasonable; there usually can be no flat prohibition of goods or services coming into the city from outside; and there can be no undue burden on interstate commerce. Thus, requirements that only milk pasteurized *within* the city be sold therein may be found unnecessarily and unreasonably strict,[125]

---

[120] State v. Nelson, *supra* note 119; Korth v. City of Portland, 123 Or. 180, 261 P. 895 (1927); Hill v. Fetherolf, 236 Pa. 70, 84 A. 677 (1912). See Otto Milk Co. v. Rose, 375 Pa. 18, 99 A.2d 467 (1953), noted 27 Temp. L.Q. 361 (1954). Cf. Wright v. Richmond County Department of Health, 182 Ga. 651, 186 S.E. 815 (1936) (upholding county regulation forbidding shipment of ice cream into a city within the county from points outside the inspection area of board of health, which covered area within radius of 60 miles from the city).

[121] See Jourdan v. City of Evansville, 163 Ind. 512, 72 N.E. 544 (1904). Cf. Standard Chemical & Oil Co. v. City of Troy, 201 Ala. 89, 77 So. 383 (1917); Chicago Packing & Provision Co. v. City of Chicago, 88 Ill. 221 (1878) (upholding statute allowing city to regulate packing houses within one mile of its borders—even if packing house was within another municipality). But there are limits to the amount of extraterritorial power that may be constitutionally conferred on a city. Thus, a city cannot be authorized to exercise all governmental control over outlying areas. See Malone v. Williams, 118 Tenn. 390, 103 S.W. 798 (1907). Cf. Brown v. City of Cle Elum, 145 Wash. 588, 261 P. 112 (1927) (city cannot be authorized to pass penal ordinance regarding lake outside city limits). See generally Annot., Extension of Police Power of Municipal Corporation Beyond Territorial Limits, 55 A.L.R. 1182 (1928).

[122] St. Charles v. Nolle, 51 Mo. 122 (1872) (charter only authorized licensing and taxing of wagons used within city; ordinance applied to wagons carrying goods from points in city to points outside, and vice versa); Western Union Telegraph Co. v. Fremont, 39 Neb. 692, 58 N.W. 415 (1894), reh. denied 43 Neb. 499, 61 N.W. 724. See generally Vigdor, Other People's Taxes: Nonresident Voters and Statewide Limitation of Local Government, 47 J.L. & Econ. 453 (2004).

[123] Robinson v. City of Norfolk, 108 Va. 14, 60 S.E. 762 (1908). See City of Argenta v. Keath, 130 Ark. 334, 197 S.W. 686 (1917). Cf. City of Sedalia ex rel. Ferguson v. Shell Petroleum Corp., 81 F.2d 193 (8th Cir.1936); Madden v. Governing Body of City of Lenexa, 239 Kan. 397, 721 P.2d 261 (1986) (without statutory authorization, municipality cannot assess land outside its boundaries for a local improvement). See also MeadWestvaco Corp. v. Illinois Dept. of Revenue, 553 U.S. 16, 128 S.Ct. 1498, 170 L.Ed.2d 404 (2008) (Due Process and Commerce Clauses bar states from taxing extraterritorial values, but state may tax an apportioned share of value generated by intrastate and extrastate activities of multistate enterprise, if those activities form part of a unitary business).

[124] White v. City of Decatur, 225 Ala. 646, 144 So. 873 (1932); Standard Chemical & Oil Co. v. City of Troy, *supra* note 121.

[125] State ex rel. Larson v. City of Minneapolis, 190 Minn. 138, 251 N.W. 121 (1933). Cf. Buckler v. City of Geary, 174 Okl. 533, 51 P.2d 271 (1935) (ordinance prohibiting baker outside city from delivering products at wholesale to retail merchants of city is not within city's power); Prescott v. City of Borger, 158 S.W.2d 578

as may a policy of inspecting only milk produced within or near the city and labeling all other milk "uninspected."[126] Where unbridled discretion is given some officer to decide what products are allowed to be sold in the city and what are not, a municipal ordinance will also be invalidated as unreasonable.[127]

With a 1951 decision of the U.S. Supreme Court,[128] much of the law as to extraterritorial effect of municipal regulation came to depend on interpretation of the Commerce Clause of the federal Constitution. It was there held that a city ordinance limiting inspection of pasteurization plants to those within 5 miles of the city square, and generally prohibiting the sale of milk from uninspected facilities, was invalid as a discriminatory burden on interstate commerce. But a municipal ordinance is not invalid merely because it has some incidental effect on an interstate business so long as no unreasonable burden is imposed,[129] and so long as there is no discrimination against interstate commerce.[130] For example, Michigan statutes prohibiting out-of-state

---

(Tex.Civ.App.1942), error ref'd (striking down ordinance prohibiting sale within city of milk pasteurized outside county in which city located). But see Lang's Creamery, Inc. v. City of Niagara Falls, 224 App.Div. 483, 231 N.Y.S. 368 (1928), aff'd 251 N.Y. 343, 167 N.E. 464, upholding a requirement that only milk pasteurized in the city be sold therein.

[126] Dean Milk Co. v. City of Aurora, 404 Ill. 331, 88 N.E.2d 827 (1949). Cf. Higgins v. City of Galesburg, 401 Ill. 87, 81 N.E.2d 520 (1948), noted 44 Ill.L.Rev. 241 (1949).

[127] City of Wewoka v. Rose Lawn Dairy, 202 Okl. 286, 212 P.2d 1056 (1949).

[128] Dean Milk Co. v. City of Madison, 340 U.S. 349, 71 S.Ct. 295, 95 L.Ed. 329 (1951). Cf. Great Atlantic & Pacific Tea Co. v. Cottrell, 424 U.S. 366, 96 S.Ct. 923, 47 L.Ed.2d 55 (1976), striking down a Mississippi regulation that milk from another state could be sold in Mississippi only if the other state accepted milk produced and processed in Mississippi on a reciprocal basis. For earlier cases raising the interstate commerce implications of restrictive milk laws, see Baldwin v. G.A.F. Seelig, Inc., 294 U.S. 511, 55 S.Ct. 497, 79 L.Ed. 1032 (1935); Miller v. Williams, 12 F.Supp. 236 (D.Md. 1935).

[129] See City of Chicago v. Willett Co., 344 U.S. 574, 73 S.Ct. 460, 97 L.Ed. 559 (1953); Richard v. City of Mobile, 208 U.S. 480, 28 S.Ct. 372, 52 L.Ed. 581 (1908); Phillips v. City of Mobile, 208 U.S. 472, 28 S.Ct. 370, 52 L.Ed. 578 (1908); Atlantic & Pacific Telegraph Co. v. City of Philadelphia, 190 U.S. 160, 23 S.Ct. 817, 47 L.Ed. 995 (1903); Wiggins Ferry Co. v. East St. Louis, 107 U.S. 365, 2 S.Ct. 257, 27 L.Ed. 419 (1883). But cf. Harmon v. City of Chicago, 147 U.S. 396, 13 S.Ct. 306, 37 L.Ed. 216 (1893) (ordinance requiring license fee of tugboats involved in interstate and foreign commerce invalid).

[130] Under the Commerce Clause of the U.S. Constitution, a state may not discriminate between transactions on the basis of an interstate element, as by taxing a transaction or incident more heavily because it has crossed state lines. See Armco Inc. v. Hardesty, 467 U.S. 638, 104 S.Ct. 2620, 81 L.Ed.2d 540 (1984), reh. denied 469 U.S. 912, 105 S.Ct. 285, 83 L.Ed.2d 222 (1984) (West Virginia's wholesale gross receipts tax unconstitutionally discriminated against interstate commerce by exempting local manufacturers from tax). (The *Armco* decision *supra* was applied retroactively in National Mines Corp. v. Caryl, 497 U.S. 922, 110 S.Ct. 3205, 111 L.Ed.2d 740 (1990)). Cf. C & A Carbone, Inc. v. Town of Clarkstown, 511 U.S. 383, 114 S.Ct. 1677, 128 L.Ed.2d 399 (1994), on remand 208 A.D.2d 612, 617 N.Y.S.2d 482 (1994) (town ordinance requiring that all solid waste processed or handled within town be processed or handled at town's transfer station discriminated against interstate commerce and was thus invalid); Oregon Waste Systems, Inc. v. Department of Environmental Quality, 511 U.S. 93, 114 S.Ct. 1345, 128 L.Ed.2d 13 (1994), on remand 319 Or. 251, 876 P.2d 749 (1994) (Oregon placed higher surcharge on disposal of out-of-state waste than imposed on in-state waste; held discriminatory on its face and thus violative of Commerce Clause). See generally Turner, The Flow Control of Solid Waste and the Commerce Clause: *Carbone* and Its Progeny, 7 Villanova Envtl. L.J. 203 (1996); Note, Solid Waste Flow Control and the Commerce Clause: Circumventing *Carbone*, 7 Albany L.J. Sci. & Tech. 185 (1996); Note, Environmental Law—Solid Waste Disposal: The Dormant Commerce Clause and Traditional Governmental Functions, 14 Temple Envtl. L. & Tech. J. 77 (1995); Note, The Need for a Rational State and Local Response to *Carbone*: Alternate Means to Responsible, Affordable Municipal Solid Waste Management, 18 Va. Envtl. L.J. 129 (1999). See also McCray, Commerce Clause Sanctions Against Taxation on Mail Order Sales: A Re-Evaluation, 17 Urban Law. 529 (1985), noting that most seller's and buyer's states do not impose a sales tax on interstate sales due to the Commerce Clause prohibitions laid down by the U.S. Supreme Court. For discussion of cases concerning imposition of state sales tax on mail order sales, see Politi and Karl, Recent Developments in State and Local Taxation, 19 Urban Law. 1067, 1067–81 (1987), which favors the overruling of National Bellas Hess, Inc. v. Department of Rev., 386 U.S. 753, 87 S.Ct. 1389, 18 L.Ed.2d 505 (1967), the

leading case holding that a state may not require collection of taxes on mail order sales made by an out-of-state company to residents of that state. See generally McCray, Overturning *Bellas Hess*: Due Process Considerations, 1985 B.Y.U.L. Rev. 265 (1985); Comment, The Imposition of Use Tax Collection Liability on Mail-Order Retailers: What Happens When the *Bellas Hess* Barrier Is Removed?, 23 Conn. L. Rev. 1087 (1991). In Quill Corp. v. North Dakota, 504 U.S. 298, 112 S.Ct. 1904, 119 L.Ed.2d 91 (1992), the Court further defined the nexus required between a mail order retailer and a state in order for the state to assert use tax jurisdiction and held that due process does not bar enforcement of state use tax collection statutes against mail order sellers merely because the seller lacks a physical presence in the state. But *Bellas Hess* was not overruled, and the physical presence requirement was retained for Commerce Clause purposes. See Note, *National Bellas Hess*, Inc.: Obsolescent Precedent or Good Law After *Quill Corp. v. North Dakota?*, 49 Wash. & Lee L. Rev. 1183 (1992).

Even when Congress has been silent on a matter, the Supreme Court has sometimes interpreted the Commerce Clause as forbidding state taxation of interstate commerce; this involves application of the so-called "dormant" Commerce Clause. Compare Camps Newfound/Owatonna, Inc. v. Town of Harrison, 520 U.S. 564, 117 S.Ct. 1590, 137 L.Ed.2d 852 (1997) (property tax exemption statute that favored institutions that served mostly state residents held invalid under dormant Commerce Clause; discrimination against interstate commerce found), with Oklahoma Tax Comm'n v. Jefferson Lines, Inc., 514 U.S. 175, 115 S.Ct. 1331, 131 L.Ed.2d 261 (1995), noted 34 Duquesne L. Rev. 139 (1995) (sales tax on interstate bus tickets not prohibited). Cf. Comptroller of Treasury of Maryland v. Wynne, ___ U.S. ___, 135 S.Ct. 1787 (2015) (Maryland's income tax scheme violated dormant Commerce Clause by imposing double taxation on income earned by Maryland residents out of state, thus favoring intrastate commerce); American Trucking Ass'ns, Inc. v. Michigan Pub. Serv. Comm'n, 545 U.S. 429, 125 S.Ct. 2419, 162 L.Ed.2d 407 (2005) (dormant Commerce Clause prevents state from jeopardizing welfare of nation as a whole by placing burdens on flow of commerce across its borders that commerce wholly within those borders would not bear; but Michigan imposition of flat annual fee on trucks engaging in intrastate commercial hauling did not violate dormant Commerce Clause where fee was imposed only on intrastate transactions and did not reflect effort to tax activity taking place outside of state). See generally Zelinsky, Restoring Politics to the Commerce Clause: The Case for Abandoning the Dormant Commerce Clause Prohibition of Discriminatory Taxation, 29 Ohio N.U. L. Rev. 29 (2002); Note, State Taxation on Interstate Transactions and How to Comply with the Dormant Commerce Clause, 49 S.D. L. Rev. 341 (2004). See also Firestone, Does a Commuter's Choice of Where to Reside Implicate the Dormant Commerce Clause?, 49 N.Y.U. Sch. L. Rev. 943 (2004–05); Comment, Interstate Commerce and the Future of State Sales and Use Taxes, 54 Ala. L. Rev. 1393 (2003). It has been suggested that the dormant Commerce Clause may also come into play when local governments attempt to limit the size of retail stores, since the desire to protect local enterprises from competition is often one reason for the legislation. See Denning & Lary, Retail Store Size-Capping Ordinances and the Dormant Commerce Clause Doctrine, 37 Urban Law. 907 (2005). See also Monk, Are Public Facilities Different from Private Ones?: Adopting a New Standard of Review of the Dormant Commerce Clause, 60 SMU L. Rev. 157 (2007), arguing that a law that does not discriminate between local and foreign private firms is presumptively non-discriminatory, and that if a substantial majority of the law's burdens fall on local residents, there should be a presumption of non-discrimination. Compare Day, The Expanded Concept of Facial Discrimination in the Dormant Commerce Clause Doctrine, 40 Creighton L. Rev. 497 (2007). As to the purpose of the dormant Commerce Clause, see Douglas Disposal, Inc. v. Wee Haul, LLC, 170 P.3d 508 (Nev.2007) (Clause does not protect any particular interstate business interest; it protects the flow of commerce between the states so that no single business interest, intrastate or interstate, unduly burdens that flow; county's exclusive franchise agreement upheld).

While state or local laws that discriminate against interstate commerce are subject to strict judicial scrutiny and are generally invalid, a law that merely burdens interstate commerce will normally be upheld if it burdens local and interstate commerce equally and if the local benefits outweigh the burden on commerce. See Farber, State Regulation and the Dormant Commerce Clause, 18 Urban Law. 567 (1986). Cf. Department of Revenue of Kentucky v. Davis, 553 U.S. 328, 128 S.Ct. 1801, 170 L.Ed.2d 685 (2008) (state's exempting interest on bonds issued by state or its subdivisions from state income tax, while taxing interest on bonds from other states and their subdivisions, did not run afoul of dormant Commerce Clause; the exemption favored traditional government function without any differential treatment favoring local entities over substantially similar out-of-state interests); Goldberg v. Sweet, 488 U.S. 252, 109 S.Ct. 582, 102 L.Ed.2d 607 (1989) (Illinois tax on interstate telecommunications which taxed only those calls originated or terminated in Illinois and charged to Illinois service address did not violate Commerce Clause since tax was fairly apportioned, didn't discriminate against interstate commerce, and was fairly related to services which state provided taxpayer); National Paint & Coatings Ass'n v. City of Chicago, 45 F.3d 1124 (7th Cir.1995), cert. denied 515 U.S. 1143, 115 S.Ct. 2579, 132 L.Ed.2d 829 (1995) (no undue burdening of interstate commerce found in anti-graffiti ordinance that forbade sale or possession of spray paint or indelible jumbo magic markers); Shell Oil Co. v. City of Santa Monica, 830 F.2d 1052 (9th Cir.1987), cert. denied 487 U.S. 1235, 108 S.Ct. 2901, 101 L.Ed.2d 934 (1988) (no discrimination against interstate commerce, or subjection of such commerce to inconsistent regulation, found in city's oil pipeline franchise fee). Compare American Trucking Ass'n v. Scheiner, 483 U.S.

wineries from shipping wine directly to in-state consumers, but permitting in-state wineries to do so if licensed, was held to discriminate impermissibly against interstate commerce.[131]

266, 107 S.Ct. 2829, 97 L.Ed.2d 226 (1987), on remand 528 Pa. 212, 596 A.2d 784 (1991) (Pennsylvania statutes imposing lump-sum annual taxes on out-of-state trucks held to discriminate against interstate commerce and thus contradict purpose of Commerce Clause). It has been held that Congress may authorize state regulations that burden or discriminate against interstate commerce, but any such authorizations must be clearly expressed. Hillside Dairy Inc. v. Lyons, 539 U.S. 59, 123 S.Ct. 2142, 156 L.Ed.2d 54 (2003). As to the effect that *Department of Revenue of Kentucky v. Davis, supra,* has had, see Recent Development Note, To Form a More Perfect Union: Taxation, Economic Efficiency, and the Dormant Commerce Clause, 88 N.C.L. Rev. 311 (2009); Note, The Dormant Commerce Clause: Adopting a New Standard and a Return to Principle, 17 Wm. & Mary Bill Rights J. 1243 (2009). See generally Mank, The Supreme Court's New Public-Private Distinction Under the Dormant Commerce Clause: Avoiding the Traditional Versus Nontraditional Classification Trap, 37 Hastings Const. L.Q. 1 (2009). A good summary of Dormant Commerce Clause litigation is found in Zimmerman v. Hudson, 293 Kan. 332, 264 P.3d 989 (2011) (zoning amendment that prohibited development of commercial wind farms held not facially violative of that Clause; case was remanded to determine outcome of balancing of the burden and benefits).

For criticism of the *Department of Revenue of Kentucky* case, *supra*, see Zelinsky, The False Modesty of *Department of Revenue of Kentucky v. Davis*: Disrupting the Dormant Commerce Clause Through the Traditional Public Function Doctrine, 29 Va. Tax Rev. 407 (2010). See generally Comment, Rethinking the Dormant Commerce Clause: The Supreme Court as Catalyst for Spurring Legislative Gridlock in State Income Tax Reform, 2013 B.Y.U. L. Rev. 1021. In Rousso v. State, 239 P.3d 1084 (Wash. 2010), it was held that a statute that in effect banned Internet gambling does not violate the Dormant Commerce Clause because it does not discriminate against out-of-state versus in-state economic interests, serves a legitimate state purpose, and does not impose a clearly excessive burden on interstate commerce.

It has been held that one state's laws may not be applied to commerce that takes place wholly outside that state's borders even if the commerce has effects within that state. Healy v. Beer Institute, Inc., 491 U.S. 324, 109 S.Ct. 2491, 105 L.Ed.2d 275 (1989) (Connecticut beer-price affirmation statute held violative of Commerce Clause).

The federal government's powers under the Commerce Clause have traditionally been construed as quite broad, but the majority opinion of the U.S. Supreme Court on the federal health-care laws indicated a more restrictive reading of that Clause in National Federation of Independent Business v. Sebelius, ___ U.S. ___, 132 S.Ct. 2566, 2587–91, 183 L.Ed.2d 450 (2012) (Affordable Health Care Act not sustainable under Commerce Clause, though upheld under Taxing Clause).

[131] Granholm v. Heald, 544 U.S. 460, 125 S.Ct. 1885, 161 L.Ed.2d 796 (2005), noted 75 Miss. L.J. 619 (2006). But see United Haulers Assn., Inc. v. Oneida–Herkimer Solid Waste Management Auth., 550 U.S. 330, 127 S.Ct. 1786, 167 L.Ed.2d 655 (2007) (county flow control ordinances that favored state-created public benefit corporation but that treated every private business, whether in-state or out-of-state, in exactly the same way, did not discriminate against interstate commerce in violation of dormant aspect of Commerce Clause). Cf. Cherry Hill Vineyard, LLC v. Baldacci, 505 F.3d 28 (1st Cir. 2007) (Maine statute permitting farm wineries to sell directly to consumers only when they conduct the transaction face-to-face does not violate the dormant Commerce Clause). For a summary of U.S. Supreme Court treatment of the dormant Commerce Clause, including the *Carbone* case, *supra* note 130, and the *United Haulers* case, *supra*, see Shanske, The Supreme Court and the New Old Public Finance: A New Old Defense of the Court's Recent Dormant Commerce Clause Jurisprudence, 43 Urban Law. 659 (2011) (praising the "sensible and administrable analysis that *United Haulers* indicates should be applied in the majority of cases likely to arise"; *id.* at 721). See also Bobrowski, The Regulation of Formula Businesses and the Dormant Commerce Clause Doctrine, 44 Urban Law. 227 (2012) ("formula businesses" being those, generally including franchise outlets, that sell standardized merchandise from standardized stores, restaurants, etc.; see *id.*, at 233–37).

Chapter 9

DELEGATION OF POWERS

Analysis

§ 9.1 Delegations by the State

The state legislative power—that is, the exercise of the policymaking judgment and discretion on state matters that state constitutions vest and recognize in the legislature—cannot be delegated to some other person or body but must rest with the legislature itself. Thus, the legislature cannot delegate to a commission the power to determine the form of government, powers, and functions of proposed municipalities since these matters require legislative judgment.[1] But the details of organization of its own government can be left to a municipality, limited only by general state law; and such basic state powers as the police power, taxing power, and power of eminent domain can be, and almost always are, delegated to local governments for their use for local purposes.[2] The rule against delegation of state legislative authority is no barrier to the delegation of powers of *local* self-government to local units.[3] Some state constitutions even allow the legislature to delegate to local governments powers that the legislature itself cannot directly exercise, and/or to allow localities (through a "local-option system")

---

1 State ex rel. Mueller v. Thompson, 149 Wis. 488, 137 N.W. 20 (1912). Cf. Town of Chino Valley v. State Land Department, 119 Ariz. 243, 580 P.2d 704 (1978); Oklahoma City v. State ex rel. Oklahoma Dept. of Labor, 918 P.2d 26 (Okl.1995) (state legislature could not delegate power to determine prevailing hourly rate of wages within state to federal Department of Labor). See generally Annot., Permissible Limits of Delegation of Legislative Power, 79 L.Ed. 474, 553 (1935).

2 See Barrow v. Bradley, 190 Ky. 480, 227 S.W. 1016 (1921); O'Brien v. Town of Greenburgh, 239 App.Div. 555, 268 N.Y.S. 173 (1933), aff'd 266 N.Y. 582, 195 N.E. 210. See generally City of Jacksonville v. Bowden, 67 Fla. 181, 64 So. 769 (1914); Cleveland v. City of Watertown, 222 N.Y. 159, 118 N.E. 500 (1917). On delegation of the power of local taxation to municipal corporations, see Schreck, Local Taxation and the Nondelegation Principle, 25 Idaho L. Rev. 13 (1988).

3 See People ex rel. Adamowski v. Public Building Commission, 11 Ill.2d 125, 147, 142 N.E.2d 67, 79 (1957); Fish Creek Park Co. v. Village of Bayside, 274 Wis. 533, 537, 80 N.W.2d 437, 439–40 (1957). Thus, in Cogswell v. Sherman County, 238 Kan. 438, 710 P.2d 1331 (1985), the court noted that the constitutional maxim against delegation of legislative power to any body or authority other than the state legislature is not violated by vesting cities and counties with powers of legislation as to matters of purely local concern. Such delegation was said to recognize that local governments are better judges of their immediate needs than is the state legislature. Cf. State ex rel. Tomasic v. Kansas City, 230 Kan. 404, 636 P.2d 760 (1981) (statutes authorizing cities and counties to create local port authorities properly delegates powers of local legislation). But municipalities have only those powers that they derive from their respective states—even in those states of the East where many municipalities existed before the state government did. See Buckhout v. City of Newport, 68 R.I. 280, 27 A.2d 317 (1942). Cf. Hart v. Teaneck Township, 135 N.J.L. 174, 50 A.2d 856 (1947).

to decide whether or not to be bound by certain state laws.[4] Of course, state legislatures also delegate tasks to many persons and groups unconnected with local governments, such as the great variety of agencies and commissions found in most states. So long as the delegation is not a lawmaking or discretionary power, but only a delegation of the power to *implement* policies in light of legislatively supplied guidelines (or, as sometimes said, so long as the delegation is only one of "administrative" authority), the delegation is proper.[5]

Subject to the limitation on delegating away the state law-making power, the generalization has been made that whatever the state may do directly, it may also delegate to its municipalities.[6] On the other hand, constitutional limitations apply to delegations of authority by the state legislature the same as they apply to other acts of the legislature, and that body cannot, in the absence of express constitutional authorization, circumvent constitutional prohibitions by allowing a municipality to do an act that is forbidden to the state.[7] In some jurisdictions, a provision of the state constitution expressly forbids certain delegations of control over municipal matters to special commissions or private groups.[8]

§ 9.2 Delegations by Municipalities—General Power and Limitations

Municipal corporations, and other units of local government, are often said to perform certain acts. But obviously this means that those acts are performed by agents of the government. Like a private corporation, a municipal corporation can only act through its various officers and employees.[9] Thus, if it is to function at all, a municipal government must delegate different tasks to its agents. Basically the same restrictions that limit delegations by the state legislature also apply to delegations by the municipal

---

4 See Bucino v. Malone, 12 N.J. 330, 96 A.2d 669 (1953); Locke's Appeal, 72 Pa. 491 (1873).

5 See Belovsky v. Redevelopment Authority, 357 Pa. 329, 54 A.2d 277 (1947) (legislature had prescribed general rules and standards for urban redevelopment; preparation of plans and specifications for each locality left to administrative bodies); Roehl v. Public Utility District No. 1, 43 Wn.2d 214, 261 P.2d 92 (1953) (statute allowed public utility districts to delegate powers to engineer and board). Cf. New York Central Securities Corp. v. United States, 287 U.S. 12, 24, 53 S.Ct. 45, 48, 77 L.Ed. 138 (1932); State ex rel. Interstate Air–Parts, Inc. v. Minneapolis–St.Paul Metropolitan Airports Commission, 223 Minn. 175, 25 N.W.2d 718 (1947) (delegation of power to approve airports within metropolitan area upheld). See generally Winters, State Constitutional Limitations 124–27 (1961), concluding that attempts to invalidate legislation for metropolitan areas on grounds of an unconstitutional delegation of power have usually been unsuccessful.

6 See Norfolk & Western Railway Co. v. Sims, 191 U.S. 441, 24 S.Ct. 151, 48 L.Ed. 254 (1903); Guthrie National Bank v. Guthrie, 173 U.S. 528, 19 S.Ct. 513, 43 L.Ed. 796 (1899); Read v. City of Plattsmouth, 107 U.S. 568, 2 S.Ct. 208, 27 L.Ed. 414 (1883).

7 Valenciano v. Bateman, 323 F.Supp. 600 (D.Ariz.1971); Phenix City v. Alabama Power Co., 239 Ala. 547, 195 So. 894 (1940); Village of Ashley v. Ashley Lumber Co., 40 N.D. 515, 169 N.W. 87 (1918); State ex rel. Bayer v. Funk, 105 Or. 134, 209 P. 113 (1922); McClintock v. Richlands Brick Corp., 152 Va. 1, 145 S.E. 425 (1928). Cf. Allen v. Axford, 285 Ala. 251, 231 So.2d 122 (1969); Wiley v. Harrison, 105 Okl. 280, 232 P. 816 (1925). But, as noted in the text accompanying note 4 *supra*, some state constitutions specifically allow the state legislature to delegate to municipalities certain tasks that the legislatures are not allowed to perform themselves.

8 See Valente & McCarthy, Local Government Law 98 (4th ed. 1992), citing several such provisions. Cf. the discussions of such provisions in Chapter 5 *supra*.

9 See Clark v. Council of Washington, 25 U.S. (12 Wheat.) 40, 6 L.Ed. 544 (1827); Scott v. City of Tampa, 62 Fla. 275, 55 So. 983 (1911).

corporation.[10] The entire police power or lawmaking power cannot be delegated away to some city official but must rest ultimately with the city's legislative body, whether that is called a city "council," "commission," or whatever.[11]

Since delegation of authority by local governments is essential but since such delegation cannot encompass the whole governmental power, rules of limitation have been developed by the courts. Three basic ones may be stated: (1) There can be no delegation to private individuals (meaning those who are not agents of the city) of any of the governmental (as opposed to the proprietary or "business-type") powers. (2) A delegation of power, even to a city agent, will be allowed only where that power is administrative, executive, or ministerial in nature; the lawmaking and policy-formulating powers must remain in the city legislative body. (3) Any delegation of power by the city's legislative body must be accompanied with adequate standards to guide the exercise of power by the agent or body to whom that delegation is made. The third of these rules may be considered actually a corollary of the second: If adequate guidelines do not accompany a delegation of authority, then the person or body to whom this is delegated is left to formulate the necessary standards and limitations—and such formulation is really a law-making chore, not mere administration.

§ 9.3 Delegations by Municipalities—Application of Limitations

The first of these limitations—against delegating governmental power to private persons—has been applied to invalidate an ordinance permitting the manager of a railroad station to allow vehicles to stand on the streets in front of the station,[12] and a delegation to bankers of the right to determine who should perform engineering and legal services for the city,[13] and even a statute requiring the city council to change a street name on petition of 60% of the owners of property abutting the street.[14] Similarly, city legislation has been invalidated where it made the amount of pay to local policemen and firemen depend on the wages paid various *private* workers in the community,[15] or

---

[10] City of Chicago v. Stratton, 162 Ill. 494, 44 N.E. 853 (1896); Automobile Club of Missouri v. City of St. Louis, 334 S.W.2d 355 (Mo.1960). Cf. Dean Milk Co. v. City of Aurora, 404 Ill. 331, 88 N.E.2d 827 (1949) (city cannot delegate to an administrative officer the power to determine what the law is and to whom it shall be applied).

[11] Tighe v. Osborne, 149 Md. 349, 131 A. 801 (1925). See Curran Bill Posting & Distributing Co. v. City of Denver, 47 Colo. 221, 107 P. 261 (1910); People ex rel. Healy v. Clean Street Co., 225 Ill. 470, 80 N.E. 298 (1907); City of New Orleans v. Sanford, 137 La. 628, 69 So. 35 (1915). Cf. City of Jacksonville v. Ledwith, 26 Fla. 163, 7 So. 885 (1890) (public duty entrusted to discretion of city council cannot be left to others to perform).

[12] City of Cincinnati v. Cook, 107 Ohio St. 223, 140 N.E. 655 (1923). See Automobile Club of Missouri v. City of St. Louis, *supra* note 10 (regulation of traffic, including establishment of parking zones, is legislative function that cannot be delegated). Cf. Toussaint v. State Bd. of Medical Examiners, 285 S.C. 266, 329 S.E.2d 433 (1985) (statute requiring appointees to State Board of Medical Examiners to be drawn from membership of private medical association unconstitutionally delegates power of appointment to private organization).

[13] Mayor of Natchez v. Engle, 51 So.2d 564 (1951).

[14] People ex rel. Chicago Dryer Co. v. City of Chicago, 413 Ill. 315, 109 N.E.2d 201 (1952). Cf. Lowery v. City of Lexington, 116 Ky. 157, 75 S.W. 202 (1903). See generally Note, Delegation of Legislative Power by Municipal Corporations, 8 Va.L.Rev. 450 (1922).

[15] Schryver v. Schirmer, 84 S.D. 352, 171 N.W.2d 634 (1969). See Glidewell v. Hughey, 314 S.W.2d 749 (Mo.1958) (duty of setting wages and hours of city employees is legislative in nature and not a proper subject for contract with labor union). Cf. Oglesby v. Fort Smith, 105 Ark. 506, 152 S.W. 145 (1912) (city promised to pay its attorney the same fee its adversary paid its counsel; invalid); Green v. City of Atlanta, 162 Ga. 641, 135 S.E. 84 (1926) (ordinance provided automatic pay raises for firemen whenever mail carriers' wages were increased; invalid). But see State ex rel. Pinzone v. City of Cleveland, 34 Ohio St.2d 26, 295 N.E.2d 408 (1973)

made the maximum work week of firefighters depend on a vote of the firefighters' association.[16]

On the other hand, a city can enlist the aid of members of the real estate community to bring compliance with rent-control laws where no power to enact or change any laws is given the realtors;[17] and contracts between local governments and developers have usually been upheld where the developer agrees to pay for certain improvements to a tract (such as street improvements) if the area is rezoned for his desired use.[18] Considerable litigation has involved so-called "consent provisions" in land-use laws under which certain uses of property are permitted or denied according to whether or not neighboring property-owners give their consent. The automatic imposition of restrictions on property, without any action of the local governing body, on the mere signature of a petition by a designated number or percentage of neighbors has been held clearly invalid.[19] A number of cases have said in general terms that ordinances making the use of property depend on the consent of neighbors is an unlawful delegation of governmental power.[20] Some cases have relied partly on the lack of adequate standards being supplied those who are to give or withhold consent.[21] Where the matter has been

---

(city charter requires governing body to establish wage rates in accord with those prevailing for such services in the area; held valid).

On the basis of unlawful delegation, courts often used to strike down collective bargaining agreements between municipalities and labor unions. See Glidewell v. Hughey, *supra.* Cf. Transit Auth. of Lexington–Fayette Urban County Gov't v. Amalgamated Transit Union, 698 S.W.2d 520 (Ky. 1985) (binding interest arbitration clause in collective bargaining agreement between transit authority and union invalidated as unconstitutional delegation of policy-making function of transit authority). Or the adoption by a municipality of a union wage scale. Wagner v. City of Milwaukee, 177 Wis. 410, 188 N.W. 487 (1922), noted 8 Va.L.Rev. 450 (1922). Or agreements by municipalities to withhold ("check-off") union dues from the salaries of municipal employees who are union members. Mugford v. Mayor & City Council of Baltimore, 185 Md. 266, 44 A.2d 745 (1945); Hagerman v. City of Dayton, 147 Ohio St. 313, 71 N.E.2d 246 (1947). But the trend—sometimes with the aid of legislation—is in favor of allowing all these actions. See Westbrook, The Use of the Nondelegation Doctrine in Public Sector Labor Law: Lessons from Cases that Have Perpetuated an Anachronism, 30 St. Louis U.L.J. 331 (1986). See generally Chapter 14 *infra.*

16 City of Alexandria v. Alexandria Fire Fighters Association, 220 La. 754, 57 So.2d 673 (1952).

17 8200 Realty Co. v. Lindsay, 27 N.Y.2d 124, 313 N.Y.S.2d 733, 261 N.E.2d 647 (1970) appeal dism'd 400 U.S. 962, 91 S.Ct. 367, 27 L.Ed.2d 381. Cf. State v. Clarke Plumbing & Heating Co., 238 Minn. 192, 56 N.W.2d 667 (1952) (ordinance sustained requiring permit for installation of heating equipment with provision that permit wouldn't be granted unless plans prepared by professional engineer).

18 See State ex rel. Myhre v. City of Spokane, 70 Wn.2d 207, 422 P.2d 790 (1967), with list of cases. The problem is further discussed in Chapter 21 *infra.*

19 Eubank v. City of Richmond, 226 U.S. 137, 33 S.Ct. 76, 57 L.Ed. 156 (1912). It has generally also been held that a city cannot contract away, or leave to the control of private parties, its power of eminent domain. See Pennsylvania Hospital v. City of Philadelphia, 245 U.S. 20, 38 S.Ct. 35, 62 L.Ed. 124 (1917); City of Moberly v. Hogan, 317 Mo. 1225, 298 S.W. 237 (1927). But cf. Southern Indiana Gas & Electric Co. v. Boonville, 252 Ind. 385, 248 N.E.2d 343 (1969).

20 State of Washington ex rel. Seattle Trust Co. v. Roberge, 278 U.S. 116, 49 S.Ct. 50, 73 L.Ed. 210 (1928) (home for aged); State ex rel. Foster v. City of Minneapolis, 255 Minn. 249, 97 N.W.2d 273 (1959); Concordia Collegiate Institute v. Miller, 301 N.Y. 189, 93 N.E.2d 632 (1950) (private school); City of Glens Falls v. Standard Oil Co., 127 Misc. 104, 215 N.Y.S. 354 (1926) (owners of four-fifths of frontage in a block could determine allowable structures); Wilcher v. Sharpe, 236 N.C. 308, 72 S.E.2d 662 (1952) (feed mill); Willis v. Woodruff, 200 S.C. 266, 20 S.E.2d 699 (1942) (filling station); Spann v. City of Dallas, 111 Tex. 350, 235 S.W. 513 (1921) (place of business in residential area). See State ex rel. Nehrbass v. Harper, 162 Wis. 589, 156 N.W. 941 (1916). Cf. Schulte v. Garnett, 186 Kan. 117, 348 P.2d 629 (1960), invalidating an ordinance requiring the consent of neighbors for establishment of gas stations on the ground that the neighbors might refuse to agree merely because of whim or caprice.

21 Williams v. Whitten, 451 S.W.2d 535 (Tex.Civ.App.1970) (trailer park could not be located within 200 feet of property line unless all owners of property within 200 feet consented). Cf. Yanow v. Seven Oaks Park, 18 N.J.Super. 411, 87 A.2d 454 (1952), rev'd on other grounds 11 N.J. 341, 94 A.2d 482; Levy v. Mravlag,

pressed, however, many—probably most—courts have drawn a distinction between imposing restrictions based on the protests of neighbors (almost uniformly forbidden) and *lifting* restrictions based on the permission of neighbors. It has been held that a prohibition *may* be lifted if those who are presumably most affected by the lifting give their consent.[22] This is considered in the nature of merely allowing a limited exception, not making a basic change in the law, though it seems this practice may destroy comprehensive planning at times—and some ordinances are disturbingly unclear as to the duration of such consensual "liftings." Some cases have indicated they would allow the consensual lifting only where the land-use was a nuisance or something close to a nuisance.[23] But this distinction has been criticized as involving an illogical, perhaps impossible differentiation between "nuisance-like" and "non-nuisancelike" uses and as not supported by the U.S. Supreme Court language on which it has supposedly been based.[24]

While governmental powers such as power to control zoning or the sewer system cannot be delegated away to private persons,[25] contracts can validly be made turning over proprietary activities to private entities.[26] The test in all cases of delegations to private persons is whether the municipality has surrendered any of its *governmental* power. Thus, it has been held that a city, in connection with the issuance of revenue

---

96 N.J.L. 367, 115 A. 350 (1921) (consent procedure results in lack of uniformity of treatment); City of Utica v. Hanna, 202 App.Div. 610, 195 N.Y.S. 225 (1922) (actions taken could be inconsistent with master plan).

[22] Thomas Cusack Co. v. City of Chicago, 242 U.S. 526, 37 S.Ct. 190, 61 L.Ed. 472 (1917) (signs); In re Petersen, 51 Cal.2d 177, 331 P.2d 24 (1958), appeal dism'd 360 U.S. 314, 79 S.Ct. 1294, 3 L.Ed.2d 1259 (cab stands with consent of owner of adjacent property); Cross v. Bilett, 122 Colo. 278, 221 P.2d 923 (1950) (filling station); Smolensky v. City of Chicago, 282 Ill. 131, 118 N.E. 410 (1918) (junk shop); Huff v. City of Des Moines, 244 Iowa 89, 56 N.W.2d 54 (1952); People v. Gottlieb, 337 Mich. 276, 59 N.W.2d 289 (1953); Epstein v. Weisser, 278 App.Div. 668, 102 N.Y.S.2d 678 (1951), aff'd 302 N.Y. 916, 100 N.E.2d 186 (gas station); State ex rel. Standard Oil v. Combs, 129 Ohio St. 251, 194 N.E. 875 (1935); City of Muskogee v. Morton, 128 Okl. 17, 261 P. 183 (1927) (gas station); In re Perrin, 305 Pa. 42, 156 A. 305 (1931) (gas station); Shepard v. City of Seattle, 59 Wash. 363, 109 P. 1067 (1910), error dism'd 223 U.S. 749, 32 S.Ct. 534, 56 L.Ed. 641. See Downey v. Sioux City, 208 Iowa 1273, 227 N.W. 125 (1929) (dictum). Cf. Chief Petroleum Corp. v. City of Walla Walla, 10 Wn.2d 297, 116 P.2d 560 (1941) (no business use in residential area unless approved by 75% of property owners within 400 feet *or* approved by city commission).

[23] Austin v. Thomas, 96 W.Va. 628, 123 S.E. 590 (1924). See Epstein v. Weisser, *supra* note 22; Concordia Collegiate Institute v. Miller, 301 N.Y. 189, 93 N.E.2d 632 (1950).

[24] 1 Antieau, Municipal Corporation Law § 5.27, at 5–122–23 (1998). See Leighton v. City of Minneapolis, 16 F.Supp. 101 (D.Minn.1936). The Supreme Court language suggesting the possible "nuisance distinction" is found at State of Washington ex rel. Seattle Trust Co. v. Roberge, 278 U.S. 116, 122, 49 S.Ct. 50, 52, 73 L.Ed. 210 (1928), quoted in Antieau, *supra* at 5–122.

[25] See Houston Petroleum Co. v. Automotive Products Credit Association, 9 N.J. 122, 87 A.2d 319 (1952); Fidelity Land & Trust Co. v. City of West University Place, 496 S.W.2d 116 (Tex.Civ.App.1973) ref'd n. r. e. (city, in return for grant of easement for sewer, contracted to let grantor make connections to sewer system without charge; invalid as allowing private control of sewer system). Cf. Larkin v. Grendel's Den, Inc., 459 U.S. 116, 103 S.Ct. 505, 74 L.Ed.2d 297 (1982) (statute vesting in the governing bodies of churches and schools the power to veto liquor licenses within 500-foot radius of the church or school delegates governmental power to private entities and violates Establishment Clause of First Amendment); Jones v. Eads, 97 Okl. Cr. 225, 261 P.2d 633 (1953) (application for building permit submitted to private individual for approval; ordinance as thus applied amounted to unconstitutional delegation). On contracting-out the authority to make arrests to a private agency, see People v. Robinson, 344 Mich. 353, 74 N.W.2d 41 (1955) (defendant didn't sustain burden of showing that person who arrested him, employee of a private corporation that city had engaged to enforce traffic laws, was not a deputy sheriff), noted 54 Mich.L.Rev. 1016 (1956).

[26] Stason & Kauper, Municipal Corporations 133 n. 7 (3d ed. 1959).

bonds, may covenant to maintain parking meters as a source of the needed revenue so long as there is no surrender of control over the streets.[27]

But most often, a municipal delegation of authority is not made to a private person but to some municipal officer or agent. In these cases, the distinction is employed between "legislative" or "discretionary" tasks on the one hand (which may not be delegated) and "ministerial" tasks on the other hand (which may be delegated).[28] The adoption of rules is, for instance, a legislative matter, and thus a police officer cannot be given the authority to adopt rules as to the zones in which parking shall be forbidden on city streets and the length of time parking shall be allowed in other zones.[29] But such an officer can be given authority to direct traffic on a day-by-day basis, including authority to order a motorist not to make a left turn, due to congestion, where turns are usually allowed.[30] Where the holder of a somewhat higher office is involved—that is, an office the duties of which normally include some planning or adjudicative functions—, even greater delegations have been allowed. Thus, a director of traffic has been permitted to designate which city streets are "through" streets and which are "stop" ones,[31] and to set speed limits for city streets.[32] It has been recognized that certain areas and situations may give rise to the need for greater-than-usual amounts of power being delegated. For example, effective health-control programs may require considerable flexibility in allowing administrators to promulgate rules,[33] and war-time or other emergency conditions may necessitate the exercise of much administrative discretion in establishing price controls.[34]

There is apparent in the cases a general trend over the past decades to allow increasingly greater delegations of authority to local administrators. It is felt that otherwise city councils will become mired in the details of routine operations when they should instead be concerned with setting basic priorities and policies. Thus, a holding that the city council itself must inspect the soil in which a sewer would be constructed

---

[27] Skidmore v. City of Elizabethtown, 291 S.W.2d 3 (Ky.1956). See Poole v. City of Kankakee, 406 Ill. 521, 94 N.E.2d 416 (1950); State ex rel. Bibb v. Chambers, 138 W.Va. 701, 77 S.E.2d 297 (1953). But see Sammons v. City of Beaufort, 225 S.C. 490, 83 S.E.2d 153 (1954), noted 53 Mich.L.Rev. 896 (1955).

In Winkenwerder v. City of Yakima, 52 Wn.2d 617, 328 P.2d 873 (1958), the court upheld contracts made by the city for private advertising on curb-side parking meters. Cf. Starrett v. City of Portland, 196 Or.App. 534, 102 P.3d 728 (2004) (city could validly lease public property to radio station for celebration under terms that permitted station to prohibit attendees from possessing firearms; ordinance allowing city to lease public property to private parties on terms that permitted lessee to prohibit carrying weapons did not involve exercise of governmental authority).

[28] See State ex rel. Taylor v. City of Tallahassee, 130 Fla. 418, 177 So. 719 (1937); City of Elkhart v. Murray, 165 Ind. 304, 75 N.E. 593 (1905); Poggel v. Louisville Ry., 225 Ky. 784, 10 S.W.2d 305 (1928); In re Wilson, 32 Minn. 145, 19 N.W. 723 (1884); Librizzi v. Plunkett, 126 N.J.L. 17, 16 A.2d 280 (1940). See generally 1 Antieau, Municipal Corporation Law § 5.32 (1998).

[29] City of Shreveport v. Herndon, 159 La. 113, 105 So. 244 (1925).

[30] City of Chicago v. Marriotto, 332 Ill. 44, 163 N.E. 369 (1928).

[31] Staley v. Vaughn, 92 Colo. 6, 17 P.2d 299 (1932).

[32] Pressman v. Barnes, 209 Md. 544, 121 A.2d 816 (1956).

[33] See Givner v. Commissioner of Health, 207 Md. 184, 113 A.2d 899 (1955) (commissioner authorized to make regulations to improve health of city); Goodall v. City of Clinton, 196 Okl. 10, 161 P.2d 1011 (1945) (board of health could declare places nuisances); Richards v. City of Columbia, 227 S.C. 538, 88 S.E.2d 683 (1955) (commission and/or officer could determine whether dwelling was unfit for human habitation—but part of ordinance was invalidated due to inadequate standards).

[34] See People v. Sell, 310 Mich. 305, 17 N.W.2d 193 (1945); People v. Lewis, 295 N.Y. 42, 64 N.E.2d 702 (1945). But see City of Cleveland v. Piskura, 145 Ohio St. 144, 60 N.E.2d 919 (1945), noted U.Det.L.J. 43 (1945).

before authorizing the construction[35] has given way to the conclusion that a city engineer must often be permitted to determine what materials must be used, and where, in the construction of an improvement.[36] There still may be reluctance, however, to allow an administrator the authority to fix fees charged residents for services,[37] or to hire teachers and set their wages,[38] or to bring about the repeal of laws considered to conflict with the city charter.[39]

The rule that ministerial functions can be delegated but discretionary functions cannot be is often found to overlap the rule that any delegation of authority must be circumscribed by adequate standards—particularly in cases of delegations of power to grant or deny licenses to carry on certain trades or activities. The need for standards is here considered necessary not only to prevent arbitrary governmental action and allow for adequate judicial review, but also to inform citizens of what is needed in order for them to obtain the permit or approval they seek.[40] Thus, unconstitutional delegations have been found where the granting of a license is left to the uncontrolled discretion of

---

[35] Bolton v. Gilleran, 105 Cal. 244, 38 P. 881 (1894), invalidating assessments on private property to pay for sewers. This case was followed in a number of later ones: San Jose Improvement Co. v. Auzerais, 106 Cal. 498, 39 P. 859 (1895); Perine Contracting & Paving Co. v. City of Pasadena, 116 Cal. 6, 47 P. 777 (1897); Stansbury v. White, 121 Cal. 433, 53 P. 940 (1898); Chase v. City Treasurer, 122 Cal. 540, 55 P. 414 (1898); Haughawout v. Hubbard, 131 Cal. 675, 63 P. 1078 (1901). Cf. City of St. Louis v. Clemens, 52 Mo. 133 (1873), invalidating an ordinance allowing the city engineer to determine the dimensions of sewers that were to be built.

[36] McCaleb v. Dreyfuss, 156 Cal. 204, 103 P. 924 (1909), overruling Bolton v. Gilleran, *supra* note 35. See Harrison v. Snyder, 217 Ark. 528, 231 S.W.2d 95 (1950), noting the impossibility of a city council deciding all details of municipal action. Cf. State v. McCarthy, 126 Fla. 433, 171 So. 314 (1936) (city officials can be given the authority to locate parking meters); Hendricks v. City of Minneapolis, 207 Minn. 151, 290 N.W. 428 (1940) (same); American Baseball Club v. City of Philadelphia, 312 Pa. 311, 167 A. 891 (1933), appeal dism'd 290 U.S. 595, 54 S.Ct. 128, 78 L.Ed. 524 (authority can be delegated to establish fees for police protection at baseball games). On the delegations of authority in the parking meter cases, see generally Grimes, The Legality of Parking Meter Ordinances and Permissible Use of Parking Meter Funds, 35 Cal.L.Rev. 235, 241–42 (1947).

[37] See City of Harrison v. Snyder, *supra* note 36. Cf. Automobile Club v. City of St. Louis, 334 S.W.2d 355 (Mo.1960) (establishment of parking zones and fees cannot be delegated).

[38] Big Sandy School Dist. v. Carroll, 164 Colo. 173, 433 P.2d 325 (1967). Cf. City of Los Angeles v. Superior Court, 158 Cal. Rpt. 3d 1, 302 P.3d 194 (2013) (public agencies and officers may not surrender or delegate to subordinates any powers to set salaries and fix the budget).

[39] Hialeah v. Hill, 79 So.2d 658 (Fla. 1955). Cf. Rusignuolo v. Orechio, 126 N.J.Super. 106, 312 A.2d 883 (1973), aff'd in part, rev'd in part 70 N.J. 330, 360 A.2d 326 (only the city council can establish general rules and regulations, such as one requiring all police officers to have phones in their homes); Albrecht Grocery v. Overfield, 32 Ohio App. 512, 168 N.E. 386 (1929) (limiting rule-making power of police departments).

[40] 1 Antieau, Municipal Corporation Law § 5.33, at 5–145 (1998). See Melbourne Corp. v. Hearing Board for Nursing Homes, 14 Ill.App.3d 589, 302 N.E.2d 729 (1973), aff'd 59 Ill.2d 409, 322 N.E.2d 481; Mister Softee v. City of Hoboken, 77 N.J.Super. 354, 186 A.2d 513 (1962); State ex rel. Humble Oil & Refining Co. v. Wahner, 25 Wis.2d 1, 130 N.W.2d 304 (1964). Cf. Griswold v. City of Homer, 252 P.3d 1020 (Alaska 2010) (city could delegate to city clerk authority to reject land use appeals where power given was not arbitrary but limited by specific criteria).

an official;[41] it is not enough that the official must be "satisfied."[42] There must be some specific standards to guide the administrator's judgment,[43] and he cannot be left unaided to determine what is a "hazard,"[44] or what property is located within a "residence district."[45] There has, however, here too been a tendency toward flexibility—away from the insistence on detailed or definite standards.[46] This is especially true when prompt action is considered necessary[47] or when personal fitness of applicants for licenses is regarded as highly relevant.[48] There is increased emphasis on the impossibility, and undesirability, of spelling-out rules that will govern every situation and on the use of judicial review to curb possibilities of arbitrary and capricious action.[49]

What of delegations of authority by the city council to one of its own committees? Basically the same rules apply as with other delegations, and ministerial tasks can be

---

[41] In re Petersen, 51 Cal.2d 177, 331 P.2d 24 (1958), appeal dism'd 360 U.S. 314, 79 S.Ct. 1294, 3 L.Ed.2d 1259; Northern Boiler Co. v. David, 157 Ohio St. 564, 106 N.E.2d 620 (1952). See Town of Windham v. LaPointe, 308 A.2d 286 (Me.1973) (officials given arbitrary power to approve or disapprove location of trailer parks). Cf. State v. Defiance, 99 Ohio App. 398, 133 N.E.2d 392 (1955).

In City of Lakewood v. Plain Dealer Publishing Co., 486 U.S. 750, 108 S.Ct. 2138, 100 L.Ed.2d 771 (1988), a statute giving a mayor unbridled discretion over whether to permit newsracks on public property was held unconstitutional. Cf. Gannett Satellite Information Network v. Berger, 894 F.2d 61 (3d Cir. 1990) (port authority rule granting standardless discretion to regulate written expression referring to commercial activity poses real and substantial threat of undetectable censorship, violating First Amendment); News Printing Co. v. Borough of Totowa, 211 N.J.Super. 121, 511 A.2d 139 (1986) (where ordinance regulating newsracks set forth no standards for issuance or denial of permit, this was invalid as giving unfettered discretion to city officials and as a prior restraint on free speech); City of Burlington v. New York Times Co., 148 Vt. 275, 532 A.2d 562 (1987) (ordinance requiring permit and fee before anyone may obstruct city streets or sidewalks invalidated as giving city authorities unlimited discretion in issuing permits). See generally Comment, The First Amendment and Newspaper Vending Machine Regulation, 69 U. Colo. L. Rev. 223 (1998).

[42] City of Rockford v. Hey, 366 Ill. 526, 9 N.E.2d 317 (1937). See Itzen & Robertson, Inc. v. Borough of Oakland, 89 N.J.Super. 374, 215 A.2d 60 (1965), aff'd 92 N.J.Super. 241, 222 A.2d 769. Cf. Schloss Poster Advertising Co. v. Rock Hill, 190 S.C. 92, 2 S.E.2d 392 (1939) (no standards set for administrator's decision on whether to allow erection of billboards).

[43] Gross v. Allan, 37 N.J.Super. 262, 117 A.2d 275 (1955) (license ordinance). Cf. Isola v. Borough of Belmar, 34 N.J.Super. 544, 112 A.2d 738 (1955) (police officers could not have outside employment unless they obtained permission of board; no standards to guide board). Compare Stevens v. State Alcoholic Beverage Control Bd., 257 P.3d 1154 (Alaska 2011) (borough could delegate its power to protest bar owner's continued operation under liquor license to borough's director of planning and land use where director could protest only if license was out of compliance with conditional use permit requirements).

[44] City of Saginaw v. Budd, 381 Mich. 173, 160 N.W.2d 906 (1968). Cf. City of Kankakee v. New York Central Railroad Co., 387 Ill. 109, 55 N.E.2d 87 (1944) (smoke abatement ordinance didn't set adequate standards); City of Columbus v. Dollings, 113 Ohio App. 134, 177 N.E.2d 545 (1961) (placing of traffic control markers).

[45] State ex rel. Srigley v. Woodworth, 33 Ohio App. 406, 169 N.E. 713 (1929).

[46] Pressman v. Barnes, 209 Md. 544, 121 A.2d 816 (1956). See Lydy, Inc. v. City of Chicago, 356 Ill. 230, 190 N.E. 273 (1934); Roland Electric Co. v. City of Baltimore, 210 Md. 396, 124 A.2d 783 (1956); Hiscox v. Levine, 31 Misc.2d 151, 216 N.Y.S.2d 801 (1961). Cf. City of Santa Fe v. Gamble-Skogmo, Inc., 73 N.M. 410, 389 P.2d 13 (1964).

[47] Lux v. Milwaukee Mechanics Insurance Co., 322 Mo. 342, 15 S.W.2d 343 (1929). Cf. Ward v. Scott, 11 N.J. 117, 93 A.2d 385 (1952).

[48] Milgram Food Stores v. Ketchum, 384 S.W.2d 510 (Mo.1964), cert. dism'd 382 U.S. 801, 86 S.Ct. 10, 15 L.Ed.2d 55; Ex parte Williams, 345 Mo. 1121, 139 S.W.2d 485 (1940), cert. denied sub nom. Williams v. Golden, 311 U.S. 675, 61 S.Ct. 42, 85 L.Ed. 434 (1940); Borough of Brielle v. Zeigler, 73 N.J.Super. 352, 179 A.2d 789 (1962); Moyant v. Borough of Paramus, 30 N.J. 528, 154 A.2d 9 (1959). Cf. Florka v. City of Detroit, 369 Mich. 568, 120 N.W.2d 797 (1963).

[49] See Iscoff v. Police Commission, 222 Cal.App.2d 395, 35 Cal.Rptr. 189 (Dist.Ct. 1963); In re Dawson, 136 Okl. 113, 277 P. 226 (1928) (upholding board of adjustment to hear zoning appeals; noted that there could be further appeal to the courts).

delegated—such as the negotiation of details in a contract into which the city enters.[50] The actual task of enacting legislation is obviously a legislative one—and one that is not delegable, because city voters are entitled to the exercise of the judgment and discretion of those they have elected to perform this job.[51] But the council may create committees to obtain actual information bearing on the need for legislation, to investigate possible methods of handling problems, and to make reports and recommendations.[52] A committee of the council may be given authority to decide whether or not to lease city property to certain persons, and to determine the terms of any such lease.[53]

In general, delegation to a board or committee—whether this is composed of council members or merely of other city officers or private citizens—is more likely to be upheld than a delegation to a single person.[54] Thus, a council-appointed committee has been allowed to manage a municipal water system,[55] and a committee has been permitted to regulate rates charged by city water and electric utilities.[56] Where a delegation to an individual is involved, it may more likely be upheld if the individual is the mayor or some other high-ranking city officer. Thus, a mayor has been allowed to grant or deny permits to set off fire crackers with little to guide him except general considerations of public safety;[57] and to order dogs muzzled whenever there is danger of hydrophobia.[58] And a

---

[50] See Hitchcock v. Galveston, 96 U.S. 341, 24 L.Ed. 659 (1877). Cf. Krumpelman v. Louisville & Jefferson County Metropolitan Sewer District, 314 S.W.2d 557 (Ky. 1958) (job of letting sewer construction contract and issuing appointment warrants could be delegated to sewer district); Kramrath v. City of Albany, 127 N.Y. 575, 28 N.E. 400 (1891).

[51] See Robinson v. City of Detroit, 107 Mich. 168, 65 N.W. 10 (1895); City of Cincinnati v. Cook, 107 Ohio St. 223, 140 N.E. 655 (1923). On the other hand, deciding whether or not facts exist such as to make an ordinance applicable is normally an administrative task and can be delegated. See People v. Grand Trunk Western Railway, 232 Ill. 292, 83 N.E. 839 (1908).

[52] Schumacher v. City of Bozeman, 174 Mont. 519, 571 P.2d 1135 (1977); City of Scranton v. Hollenberg, 152 Pa.Super. 138, 31 A.2d 437 (1943). See 2A McQuillin, Municipal Corporations § 10.40 (3d rev. ed. 1996). Cf. Walls v. Guntersville, 253 Ala. 480, 45 So.2d 468 (1950); State ex rel. Moock v. City of Cincinnati, 120 Ohio St. 500, 166 N.E. 583 (1929), cert. denied 280 U.S. 578, 50 S.Ct. 31, 74 L.Ed. 628 (issuing permits under specified circumstances). But see City of Elkhart v. Murray, 165 Ind. 304, 75 N.E. 593 (1905), striking down an ordinance that required street cars to have certain fenders, or ones "equally good" that were approved by the council or its street committee.

[53] City of Biddeford v. Yates, 104 Me. 506, 72 A. 335 (1908). But cf. Prezeau v. City of Whitefish, 198 Mont. 416 646 P.2d 1186 (1982) (under statute, sale or lease of land held in trust by a municipality for a specific purpose required electoral approval even if the sale or lease would not interfere with the public use).

[54] Fischer v. City of St. Louis, 194 U.S. 361, 24 S.Ct. 673, 48 L.Ed. 1018 (1904). See Haggerty v. City of Oakland, 161 Cal.App.2d 407, 326 P.2d 957 (Dist.Ct.1958); City of Oakland v. Hogan, 41 Cal.App.2d 333, 106 P.2d 987 (Dist.Ct.1940). But see PRB Enterprises, Inc. v. South Brunswick Planning Bd., 105 N.J. 1, 518 A.2d 1099 (1987) (undue delegation to municipal planning board to determine what were "low-traffic generating uses," which were the only ones allowable in particular district; no objective standards provided to measure traffic generation).

[55] State ex rel. Excelsior Springs v. Smith, 336 Mo. 1104, 82 S.W.2d 37 (1935).

[56] City of Mayfield v. Phipps, 203 Ky. 532, 263 S.W. 37 (1924). Cf. Ex parte White, 56 Okl.Cr. 418, 41 P.2d 488 (1935) (upholding ordinance prohibiting solicitation for charitable funds without obtaining permit from committee appointed by mayor).

[57] City of Centralia v. Smith, 103 Mo.App. 438, 77 S.W. 488 (1903). Cf. Tower Realty, Inc. v. City of East Detroit, 196 F.2d 710 (6th Cir.1952) (mayor could license amusement park if it was in a safe and proper place).

[58] Walker v. Towle, 156 Ind. 639, 59 N.E. 20 (1901). Cf. Farmer v. City of Sapulpa, 645 P.2d 518 (Okl.1982) (delegation to mayor of power to restrict water usage during shortage upheld). But delegations even to high officials such as mayors will be closely scrutinized where First Amendment freedoms are involved. See City of Lakewood v. Plain Dealer Publishing Co., *supra* note 41 (statute giving mayor discretion over whether or not to allow newsracks on public property found unconstitutional).

city finance officer has been allowed to make rules for administration of an occupational license tax where the council delegated him this task.[59]

In general also, delegations (or "adoptions") are likely to be upheld where they involve some other governmental entity, as an ordinance basing the pay of fire fighters on the amount paid such workers in a nearby city or surrounding county.[60] Thus, no improper delegation has been found where a price ceiling set by a federal agency or administrator has been adopted by a city.[61]

There may seem inconsistency in the "delegation" cases in that they sometimes indicate that discretion cannot be delegated, and then turn around and say that any discretion that *is* delegated must be limited by adequate standards. The net result seems to be that some exercise of judgment must necessarily be delegated, but that this should not, particularly in the case of lower-echelon agents, be *unbridled* judgment but should be circumscribed by reasonable legislative guidelines.

---

59 Kohler v. Benckart, 252 S.W.2d 854 (Ky.1952).

60 Kugler v. Yocum, 69 Cal.2d 371, 71 Cal.Rptr. 687, 445 P.2d 303 (1968). Cf. Fuldauer v. City of Cleveland, 32 Ohio St.2d 114, 290 N.E.2d 546 (1972) (charter provided that council should pay police officers and fire fighters a wage 3% above that paid comparable employees in any other Ohio city with more than 50,000 population; upheld).

61 See cases cited note 34 *supra*.

Chapter 10

MUNICIPAL LEGISLATION: REQUIREMENT OF DEFINITENESS AND CERTAINTY

Analysis

§ 10.1 Tests of Definiteness and Certainty: Their Application

If a municipality possesses a particular power, adheres to any relevant limits as to time and territory in exercising the power, and does not make a delegation of unbridled discretion to any agent or employee, is there any other limitation on the municipality's use of the power? There is one other rule of particular importance: Any municipal law must "set forth with clarity some norm or standard by which all persons may know their rights and obligations thereunder."[1] This is often referred to as the requirement of reasonable definiteness and certainty and applies to any municipal legislation affecting the lives, liberties, or property of citizens.[2] It applies in the licensing ordinances because a person wishing to obtain a license must be reasonably informed of the standards he must meet.[3] It applies to zoning ordinances and other restrictions on businesses because

[1] Sea Isle City v. Vinci, 34 N.J.Super. 273, 274, 112 A.2d 18, 19 (1955).

[2] See Winters v. New York, 333 U.S. 507, 68 S.Ct. 665, 92 L.Ed. 840 (1948); Application of Laiolo, 83 Nev. 186, 426 P.2d 726 (1967); People v. Caswell-Massey Co., 6 N.Y.2d 497, 190 N.Y.S.2d 649, 160 N.E.2d 895 (1959); State v. Furio, 267 N.C. 353, 148 S.E.2d 275 (1966). See generally Collings, Unconstitutional Uncertainty—An Appraisal, 40 Cornell L.Q. 195 (1955). Different tests are, however, sometimes applied in determining whether or not the constitutional requirement of definiteness and certainty is met, according to whether the legislation being tested is criminal or civil in nature. See Paul v. Department of Transp., 115 Hawai'i 416, 168 P.3d 546 (2007) (revocation of license of motor vehicles safety inspector was civil, rather than penal, in nature, and thus mere uncertainty is not enough for the relevant laws to be held unconstitutionally vague; rather the laws must be substantially incomprehensible—that is, so vague as really to be no rule or standard at all). Cf. Terrazas v. Blaine County, 147 Idaho 193, 207 P.3d 169 (2009) (greater tolerance is permitted in a civil statute as opposed to a criminal statute under the void-for-vagueness doctrine; mountain overlay district ordinance held not void for vagueness).

[3] See Village of Hoffman Estates v. Flipside, Hoffman Estates, Inc., 455 U.S. 489, 102 S.Ct. 1186, 71 L.Ed.2d 362 (1982), reh. denied 456 U.S. 950, 102 S.Ct. 2023, 72 L.Ed.2d 476 (1982) (ordinance requiring any retailer who sells "any items, effect, paraphernalia, accessory or thing which is designed or marketed for use with illegal cannabis or drugs" to obtain a license held not unconstitutionally vague): City of Eau Gallie v. Holland, 98 So.2d 786 (Fla.1957); State ex rel. Ohio Oil Co. v. City of Defiance, 99 Ohio App. 398, 133 N.E.2d 392 (1955). But cf. City of Mesquite v. Aladdin's Castle, Inc. 455 U.S. 283, 102 S.Ct. 1070, 71 L.Ed.2d 152 (1982), on remand 713 F.2d 137 (5th Cir.1983), reh. denied 713 F.2d 137 (5th Cir.1983), where the Court held that the federal Constitution does not preclude a city from giving vague or ambiguous directions to officials who are merely authorized to make investigations and recommendations if the ultimate granting or denying of a license is not to be based on those directions. Thus, a section of a city licensing ordinance governing coin-operated amusement establishments and directing the police chief to consider whether a license applicant had any "connections with criminal elements" was upheld where the police chief only made a recommendation. The

the person wanting to operate a business is entitled to know the applicable restrictions.[4] And the requirement applies with particular force to all measures of a penal nature because legislation forbidding an act in terms so indefinite that people of common intelligence cannot understand what is forbidden violates the first essential of due process of law.[5] An unequivocal warning as to what conduct is prohibited has been called necessary to due process before a citizen can be fined or imprisoned for such conduct.[6] At least four reasons have been cited as supporting the need for reasonable definiteness and certainty in penal ordinances:[7] (1) to prevent trapping citizens who try to be law-abiding, (2) to ensure that a defendant accused of violating an ordinance can make a reasonable effort to defend himself against the charge, (3) to prevent arbitrary enforcement of the law against some citizens but not others, and (4) to make judicial review possible.

What test is used to determine if an ordinance is sufficiently definite and certain? Sometimes it is merely said that "reasonable" definiteness and certainty are required.[8] But more often the requirement is declared to be that the average person—the person of average intelligence and understanding—can, when reading the ordinance, tell what conduct is regulated or forbidden.[9] Applying such tests, courts have invalidated ordinances prohibiting people from appearing on the street in other than "customary

---

final decision was then made by the city manager, and this was not based on any existence of "connections with criminal elements."

4 See Wasem v. City of Fargo, 49 N.D. 168, 190 N.W. 546 (1922), invalidating, as too indefinite, an ordinance providing that no undertaking establishment be maintained in those parts of the municipality occupied mainly by residences. See generally Wilson, Recent Void for Vagueness Challenges to Zoning Ordinances: "How High the Active Element of the Antenna Array?", 44 Urban Law. 589 (2012).

5 City of Cleveland v. Baker, 167 N.E.2d 119 (Ohio App.1960). Cf. Olympic Drive-in Theatre v. Pagedale, 441 S.W.2d 5 (Mo.1969). See Note, Due Process Requirements of Definiteness in Statutes, 62 Harv. L.Rev. 77 (1948). See generally Freund, The Supreme Court and Civil Liberties, 4 Vand. L.Rev. 533, 539–40 (1951); Note, Constitutional Law, Void for Vagueness: An Escape from Statutory Interpretation, 23 Ind.L.J. 272 (1948).

6 People v. Scott, 26 N.Y.2d 286, 309 N.Y.S.2d 919, 258 N.E.2d 206 (1970). See Scott, Constitutional Limitations on Substantive Criminal Law, 29 Rocky Mt. L.Rev. 275, 287–89 (1957). Cf. City of Seattle v. Shepherd, 93 Wn.2d 861, 613 P.2d 1158 (1980) (ordinance must provide defendant with fair warning of criminality of his conduct and must not present danger, due to inadequate guidelines, of ad hoc determinations of guilt).

7 1 Antieau, Municipal Corporation Law § 5.17, at 5–62 (1998), citing Dunn v. City of Wilmington, 58 Del. (8 Storey) 569, 212 A.2d 596 (1965).

8 See City of Chicago v. Chicago & North Western Railway, 275 Ill. 30, 113 N.E. 849 (1916); Town of Jonesboro v. Kincheloe, 148 Tenn. 688, 257 S.W. 418 (1923).

9 Duplantis v. Bonvillain, 675 F.Supp. 331 (E.D.La.1987) (terms "junk, trash, garbage, or other ugly materials" held to have clear definitions and to be understandable to persons of ordinary intelligence); State v. Clarke, 69 Conn. 371, 37 A. 975 (1897); State v. New Orleans City & Lake Railroad, 49 La.Ann. 1571, 22 So. 839 (1897); People v. Derose, 230 Mich. 180, 203 N.W. 95 (1925); Diemer v. Weiss, 343 Mo. 626, 122 S.W.2d 922 (1938); Eaves v. Board of Clark County Commissioners, 96 Nev. 921, 620 P.2d 1248 (1980) ("men of common intelligence" must be able to understand meaning; ordinance prohibiting persons from working as "escort" or "social companion," or from conducting escort business, held void); Staub v. City of Knoxville, 161 Tenn. 663, 33 S.W.2d 415 (1930); Ex parte Bell, 32 Tex.Crim.R. 308, 32 Tex.Crim. 308, 22 S.W. 1040 (1893); Village of Wonewoc v. Taubert, 203 Wis. 73, 233 N.W. 755 (1930).

street attire,"[10] but have upheld an ordinance forbidding "any fighting" in the city.[11] An ordinance making it a misdemeanor thereunder to commit any act that is a misdemeanor under state statutes or the common law has been struck down,[12] as has an ordinance prohibiting the establishment of a lumberyard within 150 feet of "any inhabited portion" of any residence district but not defining "inhabited portion" or "residence district."[13] In general, a penal ordinance does not meet the test of certainty if it requires that an act be done in a "suitable" manner but supplies no test of suitableness.[14]

Many anti-loitering ordinances have been voided because of the vagueness of such terms as "loiter" or "lounge"—and because these terms seem clearly to cover perfectly innocent conduct as well as some conduct that might be reasonably calculated to cause harm.[15] The term "presence," as in an ordinance forbidding persons to be present at certain events, is too vague to satisfy due process.[16] Sometimes even fairly specific

---

[10] People v. O'Gorman, 274 N.Y. 284, 8 N.E.2d 862 (1937) (ordinary member of society couldn't know how to comply with the requirements). See Comment, "No Saggy Pants": A Review of the First Amendment Issues Presented by the State's Regulation of Fashion in Public Streets, 113 Penn. St. L. Rev. 329 (2008). Cf. City of Lincoln Center v. Farmway Co-op, Inc., 316 P.3d 707 (Kan. 2013) (noise ordinance lacked sufficiently objective standards to prevent its arbitrary enforcement); Ex parte Westellison, 38 Okl.Cr. 207, 259 P. 873 (1927), saying an ordinance won't be invalidated unless so uncertain as to deceive the ordinary mind, but finding that an ordinance forbidding people from selling newspapers in a "loud" voice must be struck down under this test. Anti-noise ordinances are often upheld if they prohibit disturbances that "unreasonably" bother other persons. See City of Farmington v. Wilkins, 106 N.M. 188, 740 P.2d 1172 (App.1987), cert. denied 106 N.M. 174, 740 P.2d 1158 (1987) (ordinance upheld making it a misdemeanor to create unreasonably loud, disturbing or unnecessary noise so as to be detrimental to the repose, life, or health of others, despite lack of reference to decibel levels); City of Seattle v. Eze, 111 Wash.2d 22, 759 P.2d 366 (1988) (ordinance prohibiting "loud or raucous behavior" on a public bus if such behavior "unreasonably disturbs others" upheld). Cf. Howard v. City of Tulsa, 712 P.2d 797 (Okl. Crim. App. 1986) (ordinance prohibiting the playing of radios, phonographs, or musical instruments at such volume that the peace and quiet of another person in his residence is disturbed upheld).

[11] City of Stoughton v. Powers, 264 Wis. 582, 60 N.W.2d 405 (1953) (part of general ordinance against "disorderly conduct"). Cf. People ex rel. City of Arvada v. Nissen, 650 P.2d 547 (Colo.1982) (battery ordinance making it unlawful to intentionally or recklessly strike or hit another held not unconstitutionally vague either because of failure to require intent to injure or because of failure separately to define "intentionally" and "recklessly").

[12] Kreulhaus v. City of Birmingham, 164 Ala. 623, 51 So. 297 (1909).

[13] City of St. Paul v. Schleh, 101 Minn. 425, 112 N.W. 532 (1907). See Harris Books, Inc. v. City of Santa Fe, 98 N.M. 235, 647 P.2d 868 (1982) (ordinance forbidding location of adult bookstore within 1,000 feet of residential area held unconstitutionally vague where no clear definition given of "residential area"); City of Cherokee v. Tatro, 636 P.2d 337 (Okl. 1981) (zoning unconstitutional where no way to tell whether particular property lay within "residence district"). Cf. District of Columbia v. Keen, 31 App.D.C. 541 (1908) (ordinance restricting keeping of live fowls unless neighbors consented void as not making clear what neighbors must consent).

[14] See State v. Clarke, *supra* note 9. But cf. Fowler v. Board of Educ., 819 F.2d 657 (6th Cir.1987), cert. denied 484 U.S. 986, 108 S.Ct. 502, 98 L.Ed.2d 501 (1987) (statute proscribing conduct unbecoming a schoolteacher held not unconstitutionally vague as applied to teacher who was discharged for showing students a controversial film).

A city ordinance authorizing a penalty for "unsightly" accumulation of refuse has been held unconstitutionally vague on the ground that the term "unsightly" is purely subjective and qualitative and could thus lead to arbitrary enforcement of the law. City of Independence v. Richards, 659 S.W.2d 795 (Mo.App.1983).

[15] See People v. Diaz, 4 N.Y.2d 469, 176 N.Y.S.2d 313, 151 N.E.2d 871 (1958); Switzer v. City of Tulsa, 598 P.2d 247 (Okl. Crim.App.1979) (ordinance making it an offense to "frequent" or "loiter" in "any place" where gambling was occurring was unconstitutionally vague). Cf. State v. Pocras, 166 Neb. 642, 90 N.W.2d 263 (1958), voiding for lack of certainty an ordinance forbidding persons to dispose of obscene or lewd publications.

[16] State v. Abellano, 50 Hawaii 384, 441 P.2d 333 (1968), invalidating an ordinance that made it unlawful to be present at a cockfight.

requirements are voided as not sufficiently definite, as in a case involving an ordinance requiring chimneys to be covered with "heavy wire netting of a mesh fine enough to arrest the passage of sparks."[17]

The requirement of definiteness and certainty in penal ordinances *does* extend to the portion of the legislation prescribing the penalty or punishment for violations.[18] But a considerable margin for variation can here be left to the discretion of the sentencing authority, since there is need to vary the penalty according to many surrounding circumstances.[19] Provisions setting both a minimum and a maximum penalty have normally been upheld,[20] but an ordinance establishing only a minimum punishment, and leaving the maximum totally open-ended, may be struck down for uncertainty.[21]

Courts often strive to uphold ordinances if some reasonable construction can be given them that will *not* render them unduly vague.[22] It has been recognized that it is often impossible to spell out in detail every act that might constitute a violation of an ordinance; general terminology must sometimes be used.[23] And an ordinance that is unclear if read by itself may still be upheld if it incorporates by reference some other ordinance or some statute that supplies sufficient clarity.[24]

---

[17] Oregon Box & Manufacturing Co. v. Jones Lumber Co., 117 Or. 411, 244 P. 313 (1926).

[18] In re Ah You, 88 Cal. 99, 25 P. 974 (1891), finding the penalty also unreasonably severe. See Arnett v. Cardwell, 135 Ky. 14, 121 S.W. 964 (1909); Town of Jonesboro v. Kincheloe, 148 Tenn. 688, 257 S.W. 418 (1923).

[19] See In re Ah You, *supra* note 18; Atkins v. Philips, 26 Fla. 281, 8 So. 429 (1890).

[20] See Bills v. City of Goshen, 117 Ind. 221, 20 N.E. 115 (1889); Arnett v. Cardwell, *supra* note 18.

[21] Sconyers v. Town of Coffee Springs, 230 Ala. 12, 160 So. 552 (1934), cert. denied 230 Ala. 206, 160 So. 554. See Arnett v. Cardwell, *supra* note 18.

[22] See Oney v. Oklahoma City, 120 F.2d 861 (10th Cir. 1941) (ordinance against profane, violent, abusive, or insulting language, etc. upheld as furnishing sufficiently ascertainable standard of guilt). Cf. Town of Clyde Hill v. Roisen, 48 Wash.App. 769, 740 P.2d 378 (1987), dec. aff'd 111 Wash.2d 912, 767 P.2d 1375 (1989), where an ordinance prohibiting naturally grown fences exceeding 8 feet in height was upheld on the ground that "fence" as defined in the ordinance meant essentially the same thing as under the common definition of "fence": a barrier intended to mark a boundary or to prevent escape or intrusion.

An ordinance is not necessarily void in its entirety merely because *some* of its wording is unconstitutionally vague, so long as the vague words can be severed in such a way as to leave the remaining legislation meaningful and reasonably clear. See City of Farmington v. Phillips, 92 N.M. 304, 587 P.2d 451 (App.1978) (words "common" and "ill-governed" are too vague, but "disorderly house" is sufficiently clear). Similarly, a law will not be invalidated for vagueness merely because it shows a potential for arbitrary enforcement; there must be evidence of a history of actual arbitrary application. See Haggblom v. City of Dillingham, 191 P.3d 991 (Alaska 2008) (city ordinance providing that an animal that bites a person without provocation is to be euthanized held not void for vagueness); State of Arizona v. Putzi, 223 Ariz. 578, 225 P.3d 1154 (App. 2010) (ordinance not rendered unconstitutionally vague because there is a theoretical potential for arbitrary enforcement and some assessment by a law enforcement officer may be required; ordinance prohibiting urinating in public upheld). But cf. United States v. Stevens, 559 U.S. 460, 130 S.Ct. 1577, 176 L.Ed.2d 435 (2010) (under canon of *noscitur a sociis*, an ambiguous term in a statute may be given more precise content by its neighboring words, but Supreme Court won't uphold an unconstitutional statute merely because the Government promises to use it responsibly and won't rewrite a law to conform it to constitutional requirements; statute criminalizing depictions of animal cruelty held substantially overbroad).

[23] State v. Cherry, 185 Neb. 103, 173 N.W.2d 887 (1970) (upholding disorderly conduct ordinance). Cf. State v. Koo, 647 P.2d 889 (Okl. Crim. App. 1982), cert. denied 459 U.S. 1036, 103 S.Ct. 447, 74 L.Ed.2d 602 (1982) (statute defining commercial gambling in part as "receiving bets" not unconstitutionally vague).

[24] City of Tucson v. Stewart, 45 Ariz. 36, 40 P.2d 72 (1935) (ordinance may be made valid by incorporation of a statute, a pre-existing ordinance of the same municipality, or any public record already established by law); Southern Operating Co. v. City of Chattanooga, 128 Tenn. 196, 159 S.W. 1091 (1913). Cf. Baumgartner v. Hasty, 100 Ind. 575 (1884).

§ 10.2 Recent Use of Definiteness and Certainty Rules; Overlap with Other Rules

The certainty and definiteness requirement is derived from the basic constitutional guaranty of due process. And often the certainty rule has come to overlap other rules of due process—and additional constitutional guarantees—in modern cases. Quite aside from the need for definiteness and certainty, due process also has been held to require that ordinances be, in general, reasonable measures and have a reasonable tendency to protect the public interest.[25] This means that ordinances cannot be arbitrary nor can they make unwarranted interferences in citizens' exercises of rights.[26] But the burden is on a party asserting the unreasonableness of an ordinance,[27] and all doubts on this score will be resolved in favor of the ordinance's validity.[28]

Another ground for attacks on legislation is violation of the equal protection clause of Federal and/or state constitutions. These clauses require at least that (1) any legislative classifications bear a rational relationship to the purpose that the legislation is intended to serve, and (2) that any statutory classifications be related to permissible purposes and not result in unjustified discrimination against some persons.[29]

---

[25] See Nelson v. State ex rel. Gross, 157 Fla. 412, 26 So.2d 60 (1946); Brookdale Homes v. Johnson, 123 N.J.L. 602, 10 A.2d 477 (1940), aff'd 126 N.J.L. 516, 19 A.2d 868. Normally, the question of due process reasonableness, where raised, is brought up in regard to regulatory ordinances enacted under a municipality's police power. See Senefsky v. Lawler, 307 Mich. 728, 12 N.W.2d 387 (1943) (reasonableness of exercises of police power is always subject to judicial review). Theoretically, the reasonableness requirement in the "due process sense" can be distinguished from the reasonableness requirement in the "ultra vires sense." The latter is discussed in Section 8.2 *supra*, and means that municipal actions must be reasonably related to some municipal power (Often it is the police power that is at issue.) or else they will be outside the scope of corporate authority ("ultra vires"), hence void. In the due-process sense, reasonableness requires that the ordinance not be arbitrary or unsupported by any need or rational purpose. In practice, the two senses of "reasonableness" are hopelessly intermingled. See Stason & Kauper, Municipal Corporations 123–24 n. 4 (3d ed. 1959).

[26] Harrigan & Reid Co. v. Burton, 224 Mich. 564, 195 N.W. 60 (1923). See S.S. Kresge Co. v. Couzens, 290 Mich. 185, 287 N.W. 427 (1939). Cf. Hurvitch v. City of Birmingham, 35 Ala.App. 341, 46 So.2d 577 (1950) (must be reasonable relationship with object sought to be accomplished).

[27] City & County of San Francisco v. Market Street Railway, 98 F.2d 628 (9th Cir.1938), cert. denied 306 U.S. 667, 59 S.Ct. 460, 83 L.Ed. 1062 (1939). See Chicago Motor Coach Co. v. Budd, 346 Ill.App. 385, 105 N.E.2d 140 (1952). It is often said that the arbitrary or otherwise unreasonable nature of the ordinance must be shown by clear and convincing evidence. See Hart v. City of Columbus, 125 Ga.App. 625, 188 S.E.2d 422 (1972); Lang v. Chicago & North Western Railroad, 208 Mich. 487, 295 N.W. 57 (1940); Mitchell v. City of Roswell, 45 N.M. 92, 111 P.2d 41 (1941).

[28] Jones v. City of Chicago, 348 Ill.App. 310, 108 N.E.2d 802 (1952); West Springs v. Bernhagen, 326 Ill. 100, 156 N.E. 753 (1927); State ex rel. Howard v. Village of Roseville, 244 Minn. 343, 70 N.W.2d 404 (1955); McBriety v. City of Baltimore, 219 Md. 223, 148 A.2d 408 (1959); C.C. Julian Oil & Royalties Co. v. Oklahoma City, 167 Okl. 384, 29 P.2d 952 (1934); Rapid City v. Rensch, 77 S.D. 242, 90 N.W.2d 380 (1958). Cf. City of Madison v. Chicago, Milwaukee, St. Paul & Pacific Railroad, 2 Wis.2d 467, 87 N.W.2d 251 (1958) (ordinance will be found constitutional unless the contrary is shown beyond a reasonable doubt); Town of West Orange v. Jordan Corp., 52 N.J.Super. 533, 146 A.2d 134 (1958) (ordinance not unreasonable merely because other communities in the area don't have a comparable one).

[29] See Parr v. Municipal Court, 3 Cal.3d 861, 92 Cal.Rptr. 153, 479 P.2d 353 (1971), cert. denied 404 U.S. 869, 92 S.Ct. 46, 30 L.Ed.2d 113, striking down a municipal ordinance of Carmel-by-the-Sea that purported to prohibit all persons from sitting on grass and misusing public property but that contained a "Declaration of Urgency" making clear that the ordinance was aimed at "unsanitary visitors" known as "hippies." It is sometimes said that civil laws are held to a less strict vagueness standard under due process principles than criminal laws because the consequences of imprecision are less severe. See Carrigan v. Commission on Ethics, 313 P.3d 880 (Nev. 2013) (conflict of interest recusal provisions held not to violate city council member's right of association though it posed problems of application that required case-by-case elaboration). See also note 2 *supra*.

Where the requirement of certainty and definiteness has been applied in recent decades, the traditional rules of interpretation have continued to be employed. Thus, it has been held that the use of the word "habit," in an ordinance against keeping in the city a dog that is in the habit of barking or howling, does not make an ordinance unduly vague since the person of common intelligence would understand the meaning—and it is difficult to find any other word to express the intended meaning.[30] The definiteness-and-certainty rule has had particular importance in the U.S. Supreme Court's striking down vagrancy ordinances of kinds that were quite common in the past: The Court has ruled unconstitutionally vague penal laws against "vagrancy" and "loitering"[31] and against wandering about without any visible or lawful business.[32] State and lower federal court cases have produced similar holdings,[33] though occasionally an ordinance

---

[30] State v. Cole, 18 Ariz.App. 237, 501 P.2d 413 (1972). Cf. City of Choteau v. Joslyn, 208 Mont. 499, 678 P.2d 665 (1984) (ordinance forbidding any person from owning, harboring, keeping, or having control of an unlicensed dog upheld against arguments that terms "harbor" and "keep" were unconstitutionally vague). But cf. City of Spokane v. Fischer, 110 Wash.2d 541, 754 P.2d 1241 (1988), where an ordinance making it a nuisance for a dog owner, or the occupant of premises on which a dog was kept, to allow the dog to disturb or annoy any other person by frequent or habitual howling, yelping, or barking was held not to provide adequate notice of the forbidden conduct and thus to be void for vagueness. The *Cole* case *supra* was distinguished as only dealing with the term "habit," while the ordinance here in question contained other terms of questionable meaning such as "disturb or annoy." See generally Aigler, Legislation in Vague or General Terms, 21 Mich.L.Rev. 831 (1923); Freund, The Use of Indefinite Terms in Statutes, 30 Yale L.J. 437 (1921).

[31] Papachristou v. City of Jacksonville, 405 U.S. 156, 92 S.Ct. 839, 31 L.Ed.2d 110 (1972). The Court there invalidated an ordinance of Jacksonville that provided for the punishment of "rogues and vagabonds, or dissolute persons who go about begging, common gamblers, persons who use juggling or unlawful games or plays, common drunkards, common night walkers," etc. *Id.* at 156 n. 1. See Timmons v. City of Montgomery, 658 F.Supp. 1086 (M.D.Ala.1987); Waters v. McGuriman, 656 F.Supp. 923 (E.D.Pa.1987), both invalidating ordinances that prohibited loitering on public streets on the grounds they were unconstitutionally vague and permitted arrests without probable cause in violation of the Fourth Amendment of the U.S. Constitution. Cf. State v. Stallman, 519 N.W.2d 903 (Minn. App.1994) ("anti-cruising ordinance," prohibiting a motorist from passing a control point in a non-cruising zone three or more times in a five-hour period, declared unconstitutionally vague and violative of fundamental right to travel; "cruising" not a term of art, and public was not sufficiently notified of the proscribed behavior); Profit v. City of Tulsa, 617 P.2d 250 (Okl.Crim.App.1980) (ordinance punishing loitering held void as overbroad). See generally Gofman, Car Cruising: One Generation's Innocent Fun Becomes the Next Generation's Crime, 41 Brandeis L.J. 1 (2002).

In City of Chicago v. Morales, 527 U.S. 41, 119 S.Ct. 1849, 144 L.Ed.2d 67 (1999), an ordinance authorizing police to order dispersal of persons loitering in public places who were reasonably believed to be "criminal street gang members" was invalidated as vague, both because it failed to provide fair notice of the prohibited conduct and because it failed to establish minimal guidelines for enforcement. See generally Strosnider, Anti-gang Ordinances After *City of Chicago v. Morales*: The Intersection of Race, Vagueness Doctrine, and Equal Protection in the Criminal Law, 39 Am. Crim. L. Rev. 101 (2002); Note, Gang Loitering Ordinances Post-*Morales*: Has Vagueness Been Remedied?, Somerville, Massachusetts, Says Yes, 32 New Eng. J. on Crim. & Civ. Confinement 161 (2006); Note, Street Gangs, Public Spaces, and the Limits of Police Discretion, 5 Tex. Hispanic J.L. & Pol'y 105 (2001); "Note, The Sheriff Knows Who the Troublemakers Are, Just Let Him Round Them Up": Chicago's New Gang Loitering Ordinance, 2002 U. Ill. L. Rev. 729. See also Note, Striking a Balance: The Efforts of One Massachusetts City to Draft an Effective Anti-loitering Law Within the Bounds of the Constitution, 39 Suffolk U. L. Rev. 1069 (2006).

[32] Palmer v. City of Euclid, 402 U.S. 544, 91 S.Ct. 1563, 29 L.Ed.2d 98 (1971), striking down an ordinance that subjected to a possible fine and jail sentence a person who wandered about the streets or was found abroad at late or unusual hours in the night without any visible or lawful business and who did not give a satisfactory account of himself. Cf. Kolender v. Lawson, 461 U.S. 352, 103 S.Ct. 1855, 75 L.Ed.2d 903 (1983), where a statute requiring persons who loiter or wander on the streets to provide a "credible and reliable" identification was held unconstitutionally vague as leaving to the judgment of the police officer on the beat the determination of what was "credible and reliable." Compare Hiibel v. Sixth Judicial Dist. Court of Nev., 542 U.S. 177, 124 S.Ct. 2451, 159 L.Ed.2d 292 (2004) (Nevada statute upheld where state supreme court had interpreted it as requiring only that suspect disclose his name; *Kolender* case, *supra*, distinguished).

[33] Arnold v. City & County of Denver, 171 Colo. 1, 464 P.2d 515 (1970); State v. Grahovac, 52 Hawaii 527, 480 P.2d 148 (1971); State v. Caez, 81 N.J.Super. 315, 195 A.2d 496 (1963); City of Akron v. Effland, 112 Ohio App. 15, 174 N.E.2d 285 (1960); Hayes v. Municipal Court, 487 P.2d 974 (Okl.Crim.App.1971); City of

is "saved" by a court's reading it as covering only certain clearly defined and potentially harmful conduct. Thus, an anti-loitering ordinance was upheld where it was interpreted to apply only to one whose conduct gave rise to a reasonable suspicion of criminal conduct and who refused to identify himself to a peace officer.[34] And "loitering" with some specified intent—such as intent to commit an act of prostitution—may be considered a sufficiently well-defined overt act.[35]

The certainty-and-definiteness rule has also been employed to invalidate ordinances against assemblages that cause "annoyance,"[36] and against "disorderly" conduct.[37] Legislation can be invalidated as unclear if it, *as interpreted and applied* by the courts, did not give a defendant fair notice of its meaning, as where a statute against exhibiting obscene movies is applied to showings at a drive-in theatre though it would not be applied against screenings at an indoor theatre.[38] A line must always be clearly drawn between those forms of an activity, such as nonceremonial treatments of the U.S. flag,

---

Seattle v. Drew, 70 Wash.2d 405, 423 P.2d 522 (1967); State v. Starks, 51 Wis.2d 256, 186 N.W.2d 245 (1971). See note 15 *supra* and accompanying text. Cf. In re John Doe, 54 Hawaii 647, 513 P.2d 1385 (1973), invalidating an ordinance that prohibited persons under 18 from loitering in public places between 10 P.M. and sunrise unless accompanied by a parent, legal guardian, or spouse; Alegata v. Commonwealth, 353 Mass. 287, 231 N.E.2d 201 (1967), invalidating an ordinance making it a crime for persons to be abroad at night without giving a satisfactory account of themselves.

Among the numerous cases in lower federal courts invalidating anti-loitering and anti-vagrancy ordinances are Ricks v. District of Columbia, 414 F.2d 1097 (D.C.Cir. 1968); Hawaii v. Anduha, 48 F.2d 171 (9th Cir.1931); Scott v. District Attorney, 309 F.Supp. 833 (E.D.La.1970), aff'd 437 F.2d 500 (5th Cir.). Cf. Baker v. Bindner, 274 F.Supp. 658 (W.D.Ky.1967), invalidating an ordinance requiring a loiterer to give a satisfactory account of himself.

[34] Salt Lake City v. Savage, 541 P.2d 1035 (Utah 1975), cert. denied 425 U.S. 915, 96 S.Ct. 1514, 47 L.Ed.2d 766.

[35] City of Seattle v. Jones, 79 Wash.2d 626, 488 P.2d 750 (1971) (as to validity of prostitute-loitering ordinance, loitering is an overt act). See State v. Cook, 139 Ariz. 406, 678 P.2d 987 (App. 1984) (ordinance declaring it a misdemeanor to be in any public place "for the purpose of inducing, enticing or procuring another to commit an act of lewdness, fornication or unlawful sexual intercourse" upheld as clearly prohibiting solicitation for prostitution); City of Junction City v. White, 2 Kan.App.2d 403, 580 P.2d 891 (1978) (upholding ordinance against soliciting for prostitution). Cf. City of Tacoma v. Luvene, 118 Wash.2d 826, 827 P.2d 1374 (1992) ("drug loitering" ordinance, which prohibited remaining in public while intentionally soliciting, enticing, inducing, or procuring another person to exchange, sell, buy, or use illegal drugs or drug paraphernalia, upheld). Compare State of Oregon v. Krueger, 208 Or.App. 166, 144 P.3d 1007 (2006) (city ordinance prohibiting prostitution upheld; each of the terms objected to was clear and definite when viewed in context: "linger," "prostitution procurement activities," and "repeatedly circling"); with City of Spokane v. Neff, 152 Wash.2d 85, 93 P.3d 158 (2004) (city anti-prostitution ordinance was unconstitutionally vague for failure to define term "known prostitute").

The word "during" has been held sufficiently definite and certain as meaning "at any time," not "throughout." See Denning v. Kansas Public Employees Retirement System, 285 Kan. 1045, 180 P.3d 564 (2008) (statute provided an annual-earnings cap for a retiree receiving retirement benefits under Kansas Police and Firemen's Retirement System who returns to work for any employer that paid his or her wages *during* the preceding two years; law upheld as not unconstitutionally vague).

[36] Coates v. City of Cincinnati, 402 U.S. 611, 91 S.Ct. 1686, 29 L.Ed.2d 214 (1971) (ordinance was unconstitutionally vague as subjecting right of assembly to an unascertainable standard, and unconstitutionally broad as authorizing punishment of constitutionally protected rights of assembly and association).

[37] Marks v. City of Anchorage, 500 P.2d 644 (Alaska 1972). Cf. Edwards v. South Carolina, 372 U.S. 229, 83 S.Ct. 680, 9 L.Ed.2d 697 (1963), striking down a statute against breaches of the peace as applied to persons who demonstrated on the grounds of the state legislature. See generally Note, Breach of the Peace and Disorderly Conduct Laws: Void for Vagueness?, 12 How.L.J. 318 (1966).

[38] Rabe v. State of Washington, 405 U.S. 313, 92 S.Ct. 993, 31 L.Ed.2d 258 (1972).

that are being made criminal and those that are not.[39] At times, a criminal defendant has even been allowed to raise such objections as vagueness and/or overbreadth of the legislation as applied to others though these objections did not relate to the legislation's application to defendant himself.[40]

The overbreadth doctrine is another constitutional argument that is not always separable from the void-for vagueness doctrine but is actually based on separate constitutional grounds: the principle of substantive due process that forbids legislatures from interfering with constitutionally guaranteed freedoms even though *some* applications of particular legislation would not infringe on any such freedoms.[41] Thus,

---

[39] See Smith v. Goguen, 415 U.S. 566, 94 S.Ct. 1242, 39 L.Ed.2d 605 (1974), striking down a Massachusetts statute subjecting to criminal liability anyone who publicly treated the United States flag contemptuously. See generally Annot., Supreme Court's Views as to Constitutionality of Laws Prohibiting, or of Criminal Convictions for, Desecration, Defiance, or Misuse of American Flag, 105 L.Ed.2d 809 (1991).

[40] See Plummer v. City of Columbus, 414 U.S. 2, 94 S.Ct. 17, 38 L.Ed.2d 3 (1973) (invalidating an ordinance providing that no persons shall abuse another by using menacing, insulting, slanderous, or profane language); Gooding v. Wilson, 405 U.S. 518, 92 S.Ct. 1103, 31 L.Ed.2d 408 (1972). Vagueness of the law as applied to third persons, though the law clearly does apply to the defendant, can successfully be raised only if the law applies to pure speech, not conduct. Similarly, the overbreadth argument can be raised as to third persons if pure speech is restricted or if the overbreadth is real and substantial, judged in relation to the legislation's plainly legitimate sweep; but if conduct and not pure speech is restricted and there is no substantial overbreadth, an accused person cannot raise the issue of overbreadth as to other persons. See Houston v. Hill, 482 U.S. 451, 107 S.Ct. 2502, 96 L.Ed.2d 398 (1987) (municipal ordinance punishing intentional verbal interruptions of police officers in the performance of their duties held substantially overbroad and thus invalid on its face under First Amendment); City of Englewood v. Hammes, 671 P.2d 947 (Colo.1983) (good review of cases; court says in the vagueness cases, the emphasis as to standing is on the risk of standardless enforcement, while in the overbreadth cases the emphasis as to standing is on the possible chilling effect of the law on third persons). Cf. Seeley v. State, 134 Ariz. 263, 655 P.2d 803 (App.1982) (unless constitutionally protected rights are involved, defendant claiming overbreadth must have standing to claim constitutional protection for himself; court upholds ordinance prohibiting lying, sleeping, or sitting on public rights-of way as not unduly vague or overbroad); Hearn v. City of Overland Park, 244 Kan. 638, 772 P.2d 758 (1989), cert. denied 493 U.S. 976, 110 S.Ct. 500, 107 L.Ed.2d 503 (1989) (legislation unconstitutionally vague on its face only if no standard at all is specified and law is thus vague in all its applications). Courts, including the U.S. Supreme Court, have not always been consistent in their application of the requirements for standing in vagueness and overbreadth cases. See Young v. American Mini Theatres, Inc., 427 U.S. 50, 96 S.Ct. 2440, 49 L.Ed.2d 310 (1976), reh. denied 429 U.S. 873, 97 S.Ct. 191, 50 L.Ed.2d 155 (1976), where theatres were not allowed to challenge the vagueness of a zoning ordinance as applied to others despite the involvement of free speech issues.

[41] Marks v. City of Anchorage, *supra* note 37; Conchito v. City of Tulsa, 521 P.2d 1384 (Okl.Crim.App.1974). Cf. Lazarus v. Faircloth, 301 F.Supp. 266 (S.D.Fla.1969). On the overbreadth doctrine, see Cameron v. Johnson, 390 U.S. 611, 88 S.Ct. 1335, 20 L.Ed.2d 182, reh. denied 391 U.S. 971, 88 S.Ct. 2029, 20 L.Ed.2d 887 (1968); Zwickler v. Koota, 389 U.S. 241, 88 S.Ct. 391, 19 L.Ed.2d 444, on remand 290 F.Supp. 244 (D.N.Y.), rev'd 394 U.S. 103, 89 S.Ct. 956, 22 L.Ed.2d 113 (1969); Kirkwood v. Ellington, 298 F.Supp. 461 (W.D.Tenn.1969). Cf. Jaynes v. Commonwealth of Virginia, 276 Va. 443, 666 S.E.2d 303 (2008) (Virginia anti-spam statute that prohibits the anonymous transmission of unsolicited bulk e-mails containing political and religious speech found overbroad in its prohibition of protected speech). See generally Note, The First Amendment Overbreadth Doctrine, 83 Harv.L.Rev. 844 (1970). See also Amsterdam, Federal Constitutional Restriction on the Punishment of Crimes of Status, Crimes of General Obnoxiousness, Crimes of Displeasing Police Officers and the Like, 3 Crim.L.Bull. 205, 224–26 (1967). On the distinction between the overbreadth rule and the vagueness doctrine, see Note, The Void-for-Vagueness Doctrine in the Supreme Court, 109 U.Pa. L.Rev. 67, 110–13 (1960). See generally Quigley & Shank, The Invalidity of an Overbroad Statute, 40 U. Kan. L. Rev. 45 (1991).

In Virginia v. Hicks, 539 U.S. 113, 123 S.Ct. 2191, 156 L.Ed.2d 148 (2003), the Court, in upholding a city housing authority policy authorizing police to arrest those who returned to a low-income housing development after receiving a barment notice, recognized that rarely, if ever, will an overbreadth challenge succeed against a law or regulation that is not specifically addressed to speech or to conduct necessarily associated with speech, such as picketing or demonstrating. But cf. State of Hawaii v. Beltran, 116 Hawai'i 146, 172 P.3d 458 (2007) (ordinance imposing criminal penalties for camping without a permit was unconstitutionally overbroad when read in conjunction with rule that defined "camping" as the use of public park for living accommodation

an ordinance that would curtail constitutionally protected free speech can be invalidated for overbreadth although much of its effect is the curtailment of speech that is not so protected. Often, ordinances aimed against profane, or otherwise offensive, speech are attacked on grounds of both overbreadth and vagueness—sometimes with success.[42]

purposes; court says that in determining for overbreadth purposes whether a substantial amount of protected, innocent conduct is affected, the court should consider the ambiguous as well as the unambiguous scope of the enactment, thus making the vagueness of the law affect the overbreadth analysis).

[42] Conchito v. City of Tulsa, *supra* note 41. See Cohen v. California, 403 U.S. 15, 91 S.Ct. 1780, 29 L.Ed.2d 284 reh. denied 404 U.S. 876, 92 S.Ct. 26, 30 L.Ed.2d 124 (1971). Cf. Lewis v. City of New Orleans, 415 U.S. 130, 94 S.Ct. 970, 39 L.Ed.2d 214 (1974); Williams v. District of Columbia, 419 F.2d 638 (D.C.Cir.1969). But cf. Profit v. City of Tulsa, 574 P.2d 1053 (Okl.Crim.App.1978) (upholding ordinance—challenged on grounds of vagueness and overbreadth—that prohibited soliciting another person to commit an act of lewdness or prostitution); Patty v. State, 491 P.2d 300 (Okl.Crim.App.1971) (upholding statute against outraging public decency). See also Bates v. City of Little Rock, 361 U.S. 516, 80 S.Ct. 412, 4 L.Ed.2d 480 (1960). In State of Idaho v. Doe, 148 Idaho 919, 231 P.3d 1016 (2010), a curfew ordinance forbidding minors to "loiter, idle, wander, stroll, play, or otherwise be upon" public places at certain hours was upheld as not unconstitutionally vague and not facially overbroad.

Chapter 11

MUNICIPAL LEGISLATION: FORMS AND PROCEDURES FOR ENACTMENT

Analysis

§ 11.1 The Parts of Municipal Enactments

Assuming that a municipality has power to act as to a particular subject, and is willing to observe all constitutional and other limits on its exercise of such power, what form can the municipal action take? Very often legislation will be a necessary ingredient in any course of conduct. There is authority that, apart from requirements found in statutes and city charters, municipal legislation need not take any particular form and may be an ordinance, resolution, motion, or order.[1] But most commonly, municipal enactments of importance are referred to as "ordinances"; traditionally, these have four main parts: (1) title, (2) preamble, (3) ordaining clause, and (4) purview.[2] But again, apart from statutory or charter requirements, not all of these are necessary to an ordinance's validity, and some or all of the first three parts are frequently missing.[3]

The *title* of an ordinance is intended to indicate the nature of the subject matter involved. To prevent concealment and to discourage log-rolling, there are often statutory and charter requirements that there be a title. Lack of compliance will then normally

---

1 See Sylvestre v. St. Landry Parish School Board, 164 La. 204, 113 So. 818 (1927) (ordinance creating school district could be repealed by simple motion); Colby v. City of Medford, 85 Or. 485, 167 P. 487 (1917); Northern Texas Utilities Co. v. Community Natural Gas Co., 297 S.W. 904 (Tex.Civ.App.1927) error ref'd. Cf. Western & Atlantic Railroad v. Swigert, 57 Ga.App. 274, 195 S.E. 230 (1938); Fidelity & Deposit Co. v. Commonwealth, 252 Ky. 476, 67 S.W.2d 719 (1934) (sufficient if intention of the governing body is clear). On interpretation of municipal legislation, see City of Puyallup v. Pacific Northwest Bell Tel. Co., 98 Wash.2d 443, 656 P.2d 1035 (1982) (same rules of construction apply to municipal ordinances as to state statutes; to extent possible, all provisions harmonized). Cf. Pinecrest Homeowners Ass'n v. Glen A. Cloninger & Assocs., 151 Wash.2d 279, 87 P.3d 1176 (2004) (state supreme court's review of any claimed error of law in the city council's interpretation of city ordinances is de novo and must accord deference to city council's expertise).

2 Fordham, Local Government Law 352 (2d rev. ed. 1986). Cf. Duquesne Light Co. v. City of Pittsburgh, 251 Pa. 557, 97 A. 85 (1916), discussing the nature of a title and a preamble.

3 See Colby v. City of Medford, *supra* note 1. Cf. Hirsch v. City & County of San Francisco, 143 Cal.App.2d 313, 300 P.2d 177 (1956) (need for protection against a particular evil and intention to provide the protection need not be expressed in ordinance, as both will be presumed).

invalidate the ordinance,[4] but it has been held sufficient if the title indicates the tenor of the legislation to a reader with a reasonably inquiring mind.[5] The title can be quite general in nature,[6] and, unless otherwise required by law or city charter, the ordinance need not be strictly limited to subjects mentioned in the title.[7] Often, however, statutes and charters *do* state that ordinances must be limited to only one subject, and this is generally agreed to be mandatory.[8]

A *preamble,* while not essential, often is useful in indicating the occasion for and purpose of the enactment. Sometimes, a factual basis for the legislation is spelled out in the preamble; but more often now, this is included in a "policy section" within the purview. The preamble has been defined as a prefatory statement, explanation, or finding of facts, stating the reason or occasion for the particular legislation—expounding on powers conferred but not itself actually creating them.[9]

The *ordaining clause* states the intention that the measure take effect as law: "Be it enacted that . . ." or similar words.[10]

Statutory or charter provisions usually allow certain measures to be passed as "emergency measures" and then take effect more speedily than other enactments. An emergency ordinance is often required to contain, somewhere in the enactment, a statement of the special necessity; and a failure to comply will cause the measure to be treated as only regular, not emergency, legislation.[11]

---

[4] Stone v. City of Wichita, 145 Kan. 377, 65 P.2d 595 (1937); Brooklyn Apartments v. Mayor and City Council of Baltimore, 189 Md. 201, 55 A.2d 500 (1947); Village of Deshler v. Southern Nebraska Power Co., 133 Neb. 778, 277 N.W. 77 (1938); Heffner v. City of Toledo, 75 Ohio St. 413, 80 N.E. 8 (1907). But cf. Lappas v. Board, 23 N.J.Super. 553, 93 A.2d 406 (1952) (title requirements merely directory, not mandatory); Prince v. W.H. Cothrum & Co., 227 S.W.2d 863 (Tex.Civ.App.1950).

[5] See Pittman v. Nix, 152 Fla. 378, 11 So.2d 791 (1943); Webber v. City of Scottsbluff, 155 Neb. 48, 50 N.W.2d 533 (1951); Fallon Florist v. City of Roanoke, 190 Va. 564, 58 S.E.2d 316 (1950). Cf. Dodd v. City of Jackson, 238 Miss. 372, 118 So.2d 319 (1960); Richards v. Magnolia, 100 Miss. 249, 56 So. 386 (1911); City of Harrisburg v. Pass, 372 Pa. 318, 93 A.2d 447 (1953).

[6] See Kansas City v. Robb, 183 Kan. 834, 332 P.2d 520 (1958).

[7] Jackson v. City of Prichard, 24 Ala.App. 532, 137 So. 469 (1931); Lappas v. Board, *supra* note 4; Northern Texas Utilities Co. v. Community Natural Gas Co., *supra* note 1.

[8] Glaser v. City of Burlington, 231 Iowa 670, 1 N.W.2d 709 (1942); Missouri Pacific Railway v. Wyandotte, 44 Kan. 32, 23 P. 950 (1890); Heffner v. City of Toledo, 75 Ohio St. 413, 80 N.E. 8 (1907). But limitations to one subject are satisfied if matters included in an ordinance all have a logical connection to one another. Miller v. City of Cleveland, 146 N.E.2d 178 (Ohio Com.Pl.1957). Cf. Garbade v. City of Portland, 188 Or. 158, 214 P.2d 1000 (1950). And a constitutional provision that "legislation" must be limited to a single subject has been held applicable only to state statutes, not municipal ordinances. McBriety v. City of Baltimore, 219 Md. 223, 148 A.2d 408 (1959). See generally Comment, Washington's Title Match: The Single-Subject and Subject-in-Title Rules of Article II, Section 19 of the Washington State Constitution, 81 Wash. L. Rev. 595 (2006).

[9] Continental Oil Co. v. City of Santa Fe, 25 N.M. 94, 177 P. 742 (1918). Cf. Calve Brothers v. City of Norwalk, 143 Conn. 609, 124 A.2d 881 (1956).

[10] The ordaining clause generally uses language such as "be it ordained" or "be it enacted." See State ex rel. Fleck v. Dalles City, 72 Or. 337, 143 P. 1127 (1914). But the exact form is often prescribed by statute or charter. Such prescriptions are often held directory, not mandatory. Glenn v. Prattville, 14 Ala.App. 621, 71 So. 75 (1916); City of Napa v. Easterby, 76 Cal. 222, 18 P. 253 (1888); Elliott v. Texas Pacific Coal & Oil Co., 19 S.W.2d 442 (Tex.Civ.App.1929), aff'd 29 S.W.2d 982. But see Liberty National Bank v. Metrick, 410 Ill. 429, 102 N.E.2d 308 (1951); Noonan v. O'Leary, 206 Misc. 175, 132 N.Y.S.2d 726 (1954), aff'd 284 A.D. 646, 133 N.Y.S.2d 167. See generally 5 McQuillin, Municipal Corporations § 16.27 (3d rev. ed. 1996). See also Kepner v. Commonwealth, 40 Pa. 124, 129 (1861), on meaning of "ordain."

[11] City of Youngstown v. Aiello, 156 Ohio St. 32, 100 N.E.2d 62 (1951). Cf. Miller v. City of Cleveland, *supra* note 8. But see Colorado Auto Auction Serv. Corp. v. Commerce City, 800 P.2d 998 (Colo.1990) (factual

The *purview* contains the real substance of the ordinance—the actual rules being enacted. Also included therein may be a definition section, a short title (by which the enactment can be conveniently called, rather than having to use the more cumbersome official title), a policy section, administrative provisions, a separability clause (stating that if part of the ordinance is found invalid, this shall not affect the remainder), temporary provisions, a duration clause, etc.[12]

Ordinances, it is often said, must conform to the municipal charter. If an ordinance conflicts with charter provisions, the ordinance is void.[13] However, it is generally held as to penal ordinances that if the penalty exceeds that authorized by the charter, but the enactment is otherwise valid, then the penalty may be enforced to the extent it does not exceed the lawful limit.[14] But where the excessive penalty violates a state statute or constitutional provision, the enactment is sometimes treated as in excess of municipal authority and hence totally void.[15] This assumes that the state statutory or constitutional provision is—as is normally true of penal matters—one of statewide concern, in which case the state law prevails, to the extent of conflict, over that of any city, even a home-rule city. In the case of such cities, their laws *will* prevail over state enactments as to matters of purely *local* concern. Non-home-rule cities enjoy no such power, and state laws, in cases of conflict, prevail over *all* of their enactments.[16]

§ 11.2 Ordinances and Resolutions; Compilations and Codes

There is a considerable body of case-law on the question of whether particular municipal enactments must take the form of ordinances or may instead be validly enacted as mere "resolutions." This law has developed because statutes and charters often have detailed provisions on the form and manner of passage for ordinances.[17]

---

basis for emergency need not be stated unless city charter so requires). See generally 1 Antieau, Municipal Corporation Law § 4.38 (1978); Annot., Conclusiveness of Declaration of Emergency in Ordinance, 35 A.L.R.2d 586 (1954).

12 See Fordham, *supra* note 2. On the need for ordinances or resolutions to be signed by the mayor or some other official, see Davies v. Village of Madelia, 205 Minn. 526, 287 N.W. 1 (1939). As to the mayor's signature and power of veto, see generally 1 Antieau, Municipal Corporation Law § 4.37 (1998).

13 Bredice v. City of Norwalk, 152 Conn. 287, 206 A.2d 433 (1964) (charter and ordinance conflicted as to how city was to provide for its legal services; charter controls); Brady v. City of Detroit, 353 Mich. 243, 91 N.W.2d 257 (1958); Philson v. City of Omaha, 167 Neb. 360, 93 N.W.2d 13 (1958) (conflict between charter and ordinance as to letting of city contracts; charter governs). See Parrack v. City of Phoenix, 84 Ariz. 382, 329 P.2d 1103 (1958); Reed v. City of Youngstown, 173 Ohio St. 265, 181 N.E.2d 700 (1962) (makes no difference whether charter granted by state legislature or adopted by city voters). Cf. Town of West Miami v. Durrance, 107 So.2d 797 (Fla.App.1958) (charter gave mayor power to remove municipal employees; power could not be terminated by ordinance). See generally 1 Antieau, Municipal Corporation Law § 5.43 (1998).

14 Sconyers v. Town of Coffee Springs, 230 Ala. 12, 160 So. 552 (1934), cert. denied 230 Ala. 206, 160 So. 554; City of Cartersville v. McGinnis, 142 Ga. 71, 82 S.E. 487 (1914); Norwood v. Wiseman, 141 Md. 696, 119 A. 688 (1922); Continental Oil Co. v. City of Santa Fe, 36 N.M. 343, 15 P.2d 667 (1932); City of Greenville v. Pridmore, 86 S.C. 442, 68 S.E. 636 (1910).

15 See Commonwealth v. Maletsky, 203 Mass. 241, 89 N.E. 245 (1909); Brannon v. City of Wilmington, 31 Ohio App. 307, 165 N.E. 311 (1928), writ dism'd 119 Ohio St. 652, 166 N.E. 199. But see Kist v. Butts, 71 N.D. 436, 1 N.W.2d 612 (1942) (penalty in excess of that provided by statute; sentence enforceable to extent it was within limit). See generally Annot., Unreasonableness, or Variance from Constitutional, Charter, or Statutory Provision, of Penalty Prescribed by Ordinance, 138 A.L.R. 1208 (1942).

16 See Chapter 6 *supra*.

17 See 1 Antieau, Municipal Corporation Law §§ 4.16–.17 & 4.19–.21 (1998). Even as to the passage of ordinances, it is somEtimes said that exactness in following a prescribed form is unnecessary and that the main requirement is that the will of the municipal legislative body be made clear. See Western & Atlantic Railroad v. Swigert, 57 Ga.App. 274, 195 S.E. 230 (1938); Fidelity & Deposit Co. v. Commonwealth, 252 Ky.

Resolutions, on the other hand, may usually be passed with little formality and with no heed being paid the requirements that govern the passage of ordinances.[18] So the question arises—what happens if a municipal legislative body tries to enact law without following the procedure or format required for a valid ordinance? What if, for instance, the city council attempts to avoid the mayor's power to veto an ordinance (which he has in many communities) by enacting a "resolution"?[19] The question is really one of when an ordinance *must* be used and when some other form of enactment (a "non-ordinance"—but usually called a "resolution") is equally valid.

Three main distinctions between "ordinances" and "resolutions" have been noted.[20] (1) An ordinance is an act of legislation, while a resolution is a mere expression of the sense or will of the local legislative body—often a declaration of opinion, as when it honors, or expresses appreciation for, some citizen.[21] (2) An ordinance usually prescribes a continuing rule or restriction, while a resolution more often is utilized to deal with a temporary matter—a special occasion in the city's history, the city's taking an appeal in a particular lawsuit, etc.[22] (3) Ordinances deal mostly with legislative matters, while

---

476, 67 S.W.2d 719 (1934). But failure to make *substantial* compliance with *procedures* specified in statute or city charter will usually invalidate any ordinance passed. See Schultz v. City of Philadelphia, 385 Pa. 79, 122 A.2d 279 (1956) (statute required public hearing on a proposed ordinance; measure was considerably amended after the hearing, then passed with the amendments; held void); Lancaster City Ordinance Case, 383 Pa. 471, 119 A.2d 307 (1956) (ordinance void because of lack of compliance with statutory requirement that 3 days elapse between introduction and passage of ordinance). Cf. Ex parte Higgs, 97 Okl.Cr. 338, 263 P.2d 752 (1953). But if a long time goes by before an ordinance is challenged, it may be held that attacks on procedural defects are then precluded. Handler v. City & County of Denver, 102 Colo. 53, 77 P.2d 132 (1938).

Public documents, such as a contract between the city and another party, may be made part of an ordinance, even though statutory or charter rules on the form of ordinances usually make no reference to such incorporation. The document may be incorporated by reference so long as it is adequately identified and there is no uncertainty as to what was adopted. See Scott Paper Co. v. City of Anacortes, 90 Wn.2d 19, 578 P.2d 1292 (1978).

As to validation of ordinances that are defective as originally passed, see 1 Antieau, Municipal Corporation Law § 4.27 (1998).

[18] Sawyer v. Lorenzen & Weise, 149 Iowa 87, 127 N.W. 1091 (1910); New Orleans & North Eastern Railroad v. Picayune, 164 Miss. 737, 145 So. 101 (1933) (resolution need not contain the formalities required of an ordinance); City of Spokane v. Ridpath, 74 Wash. 4, 132 P. 638 (1913). See generally 1 Antieau, Municipal Corporation Law § 4.18 (1998).

The terms "resolution" and "motion" are usually treated as synonymous where applied to enactments of local legislative bodies; both mean mere expressions of will. See Pepin v. City of North Bend, 198 F.Supp. 644 (D.Or.1961). Cf. Keyport Sewerage Authority v. Granata, 52 N.J.Super. 76, 144 A.2d 811 (1958) (mere fact that appointments made by motion did not invalidate the appointments, though statute prescribed a resolution).

[19] See Benson v. City of De Soto, 212 Kan. 415, 510 P.2d 1281 (1973) (city may by resolution authorize taking an appeal in a civil action).

[20] 1 Antieau, Municipal Corporation Law § 4.14 (1998). Cf. Jewett v. Luau-Nyack Corp., 31 N.Y.2d 298, 338 N.Y.S.2d 874, 291 N.E.2d 123 (1972).

[21] Joiner v. City of Dallas, 380 F.Supp. 754 (N.D.Tex.1974) aff'd 419 U.S. 1042, 95 S.Ct. 614, 42 L.Ed.2d 637, reh. denied 419 U.S. 1132, 95 S.Ct. 818, 42 L.Ed.2d 831; Shaw v. WaKeeney, 187 Kan. 301, 356 P.2d 832 (1960); Evans v. City of Jackson, 202 Miss. 9, 30 So.2d 315 (1947). Cf. Baker v. City of Milwaukie, 17 Or.App. 89, 520 P.2d 479 (1974), mod. 271 Or. 500, 533 P.2d 772 (resolution is not a law but an expression of opinion).

[22] See Town of Walkerton v. New York, Chicago & St. Louis Railroad, 215 Ind. 206, 18 N.E.2d 799 (1939), cert. denied 308 U.S. 556, 60 S.Ct. 75, 84 L.Ed. 467 (1939); Collins v. City of Schenectady, 256 App.Div. 389, 10 N.Y.S.2d 303 (1939); Campbell v. City of Cincinnati, 49 Ohio St. 463, 31 N.E. 606 (1892); Dunlap v. Williamson, 369 P.2d 631 (Okl.1962). Cf. LaMon v. City of Westport, 22 Wn.App. 215, 588 P.2d 1205 (1978).

In Council of Holladay City v. Larkin, 204 UT 24, 89 P.3d 164 (2004), it was held that the city council could enact a resolution authorizing an election on reorganization of the city government without any formal participation of the mayor; ordinances and resolutions were referred to (at 169) as "entirely different statutory species."

resolutions concern matters of administrative detail or of a ministerial nature, such as the city council's own rules of internal procedure.[23] It has been said that, in the absence of a statutory or charter requirement to the contrary, any administrative or ministerial power of a local government may be exercised through a resolution.[24]

Even where a matter is not administrative or ministerial in nature, there is authority that, in the absence of contrary statute or charter provision, a resolution may be used instead of an ordinance and will be equally valid.[25] Certainly there should be no magic in the *name* by which an enactment is called, and a measure called a "resolution" but passed with all the formality of an ordinance will be valid even if the situation is one in which an "ordinance" is found to be required.[26] Often statutes or charters *do* require that certain matters, such as the creation of municipal offices, be handled by ordinances, and in that case any measure not enacted in the *manner* prescribed for ordinances will not be valid.[27] Beyond that, a number of courts have indicated they will require

---

[23] Owensboro v. Board of Trustees, 301 Ky. 113, 190 S.W.2d 1005 (1945); Kij v. Aszkler, 163 Misc. 63, 296 N.Y.S. 351 (1937). But cf. Chapman v. Bordelon, 242 La. 637, 138 So.2d 1 (1962), noting that the term "ordinance" is sometimes used to cover all municipal enactments, whether administrative or legislative in nature.

[24] Read v. City of Scottsbluff, 139 Neb. 418, 297 N.W. 669 (1941). See Coal District Power Co. v. Booneville, 169 Ark. 1065, 278 S.W. 353 (1925); Kleiber v. City & County of San Francisco, 18 Cal.2d 718, 117 P.2d 657 (1941); Rule v. City of Stamford, 121 Conn. 447, 185 A. 178 (1936); Allen v. Wise, 204 Ga. 415, 50 S.E.2d 69 (1948); Kalamazoo Municipal Utility Association v. City of Kalamazoo, 345 Mich. 318, 76 N.W.2d 1 (1956); Hecker v. Congregation B'Nai Israel, 75 N.J.Super. 84, 182 A.2d 172 (1962). See International Ass'n of Firefighters Local 1596 v. City of Lawrence, 14 Kan.App.2d 788, 798 P.2d 960 (1990) (use of resolution held proper to establish procedure for obtaining agreements between a city and its employees on working conditions; court noted that negotiating employment agreements comes within city's administrative or proprietary business). Cf. State ex rel. Morrison v. City of Seattle, 6 Wn.App. 181, 492 P.2d 1078 (1971) (ministerial or administrative actions not having a general legislative purpose may be handled by resolution).

Resolutions are often used to specify such details as the size of pipe to use in a waterline. See Utility Supply Co. v. City of Broken Arrow, 539 P.2d 740 (Okl.1975) (resolution upheld as not being capricious or unreasonable). But resolutions have been upheld when used even for such matters as levying special assessments and declaring the forfeiture of a franchise. See 56 Am.Jur.2d Municipal Corporations § 152 (1971).

[25] See Board of Education v. De Kay, 148 U.S. 591, 13 S.Ct. 706, 37 L.Ed. 573 (1893); City of Batesville v. Ball, 100 Ark. 496, 140 S.W. 712 (1911) (resolution used to submit question to vote of people); People ex rel. Sweitzer v. City of Chicago, 363 Ill. 409, 2 N.E.2d 330 (1936); City of Crawfordsville v. Braden, 130 Ind. 149, 28 N.E. 849 (1891); Wheelock v. City of Lowell, 196 Mass. 220, 81 N.E. 977 (1907); Cimarron Utility Co. v. City of Guymon, 171 Okl. 344, 43 P.2d 143 (1935); Hicks v. City of Houston, 524 S.W.2d 539 (Tex.Civ.App.1975) ref'd n. r. e.; Giesecke v. Gayle, 129 S.W.2d 334 (Tex.Civ.App.1939); Wisconsin Gas & Electric Co. v. City of Ft. Atkinson, 193 Wis. 232, 213 N.W. 873 (1927). See Snake River Homebuilders Association v. City of Caldwell, 101 Idaho 47, 607 P.2d 1321 (1980) (city could increase water rates by resolution).

[26] Crowe v. Boyle, 184 Cal. 117, 193 P. 111 (1920); Massey v. City of Bowling Green, 206 Ky. 692, 268 S.W. 348 (1925). See O'Rourke v. Graul, 261 App.Div. 87, 24 N.Y.S.2d 819 (1941), aff'd 285 N.Y. 755, 34 N.E.2d 908; Wisconsin Gas & Electric Co. v. City of Ft. Atkinson, *supra* note 25.

[27] Dearmont v. Mound City, 278 S.W. 802 (Mo.App.1925); Coast Co. v. Mayor of Spring Lake, 56 N.J.Eq. 615, 36 A. 21 (1896), aff'd per curiam 58 N.J.Eq. 586, 47 A. 1131 (1897); Shaub v. City of Lancaster, 156 Pa. 362, 26 A. 1067 (1893); Masterson v. Town of Hedley, 265 S.W. 406 (Tex.Civ.App.1924). Donivan v. Dallastown Borough, 835 F.2d 486 (3d Cir.1987), cert. denied 485 U.S. 1035, 108 S.Ct. 1596, 99 L.Ed.2d 910 (1988) (abolishment of local police force by mere vote rather than by enactment of an ordinance held improper under state statutes and thus did not entitle local council members to absolute legislative immunity under Federal Civil Rights Act); Cf. O'Connor v. Union City, 117 N.J.Super. 575, 285 A.2d 270 (1971), appeal dism'd 409 U.S. 1031, 93 S.Ct. 524, 34 L.Ed.2d 481 (offices can only be created by ordinances, not resolutions).

Merely because a matter is required by law to be dealt with by ordinance does not mean that matter will be deemed "legislative" for all purposes. Thus, in Campbell v. City of Eugene, 116 Or. 264, 240 P. 418 (1925), it was held that a city charter provision requiring the passage of 30 days before an ordinance "enacting municipal legislation" could become effective did not apply to an ordinance calling a special election to vote on a charter amendment—even though the call of the election had to be made by ordinance.

ordinances to be used as to "legislative" (as opposed to "administrative") matters even if no statute or charter provision expressly requires this.[28] So the "ordinance route" is clearly the safer one for a legislative body to use when in doubt.

Sometimes in this ordinance-v.-resolution area, as in so many areas of local government law, a distinction is made between governmental activities of a municipality and proprietary (or corporate or "business-like") activities. Where proprietary functions are involved, a city's use of a resolution, as in selling an electric plant or other utility, is more likely to be upheld than where governmental functions are concerned.[29]

One special principle is sometimes applied to the ordinance-v.-resolution debate, and is called the "equal dignity rule." This generally accepted principle states that an ordinance cannot be repealed or amended by a mere resolution, or by any other legislation of less dignity than the ordinance itself. The repeal or amendment must be brought about by another ordinance.[30] Indeed, it has been held that, in the absence of contrary rules in the statutes or charter, a city must exercise exactly the same formalities and procedures (such as the several readings of the legislation that are sometimes required) in repealing an ordinance as have to be followed in passing such an ordinance.[31]

Where does a person go to look for municipal ordinances and other enactments of local legislative bodies? Until the 1940's, it was often difficult to find any record of these except in the minutes of city council meetings,[32] or perhaps in newspapers that had

---

[28] Woods v. Babcock, 185 F.2d 508 (D.C.Cir.1950); Sullivan v. Mortensen, 132 Conn. 289, 43 A.2d 731 (1945); Carlton v. Jones, 117 Fla. 622, 158 So. 170 (1934); Chicago & North Pacific Railroad v. City of Chicago, 174 Ill. 439, 51 N.E. 596 (1898); Prell v. McDonald & Files, 7 Kan. 426 (1871); Thompson Scenic Railway v. McCabe, 211 Mich. 133, 178 N.W. 662 (1920); Chasis v. Tumulty, 8 N.J. 147, 84 A.2d 445 (1951); Collins v. City of Schenectady, 256 App.Div. 389, 10 N.Y.S.2d 303 (1939); Southwestern Bell Telephone Co. v. Gohmert, 222 S.W.2d 644 (Tex.Civ.App.1949). See Wuebker v. Hopkins, 29 Ohio App. 386, 163 N.E. 566 (1928). Cf. Food, Beverage & Express Drivers Local Union v. City of Shelton, 147 Conn. 401, 161 A.2d 587 (1960) (city charter required that collective bargaining agreement be made by ordinance).

[29] Kalamazoo Municipal Utilities Association v. City of Kalamazoo, 345 Mich. 318, 76 N.W.2d 1 (1956) (sale of municipal light plant); Yarbrough v. Donaldson, 67 Okl. 318, 170 P. 1165 (1918) (sale of electric plant). Cf. People ex rel. Sweitzer v. City of Chicago, 363 Ill. 409, 2 N.E.2d 330 (1936) (operation of municipal nursery to provide shrubs for city parks was ministerial in nature and thus could be brought about by resolution).

[30] Harrison v. Snyder, 217 Ark. 528, 231 S.W.2d 95 (1950); City of Coral Gables v. City of Miami, 138 Fla. 881, 190 So. 427 (1939); Paxton v. Bogardus, 201 Ill. 628, 66 N.E. 853 (1903); Hibbard v. City of Chicago, 173 Ill. 91, 50 N.E. 256 (1898); Swindell v. State ex rel. Maxey, 143 Ind. 153, 42 N.E. 528 (1895); Glaser v. City of Burlington, 231 Iowa 670, 1 N.W.2d 709 (1942); City of Saginaw v. Consumers' Power Co., 213 Mich. 460, 182 N.W. 146 (1921); Eichenlaub v. City of St. Joseph, 113 Mo. 395, 21 S.W. 8 (1893); Nugent v. City Commission, 461 S.W.2d 678 (Tex.Civ.App.1970); Hukle v. City of Huntington, 134 W.Va. 249, 58 S.E.2d 780 (1950); City of Tacoma v. Lillis, 4 Wash. 797, 31 P. 321 (1892). See Bubb v. Barber, 295 So.2d 701 (Fla.App.1974); In re Annexation of Certain Territory to City of Salem, 120 Ind.App. 247, 91 N.E.2d 648 (1950); Mollner v. City of Omaha, 169 Neb. 44, 98 N.W.2d 33 (1959); State ex rel. Hunzicker v. Pulliam, 168 Okl. 632, 37 P.2d 417 (1934) (interpreting city charter); Wynne v. Township of Lower Merion, 181 Pa.Super. 524, 124 A.2d 487 (1956). Cf. Reiff v. City Council of Hamilton, 32 Ohio App.2d 224, 289 N.E.2d 358 (1972) (absent contrary statute, a new ordinance is needed for express repeal of existing ordinance). But cf. City of Fort Smith v. Taylor, 228 Ark. 722, 310 S.W.2d 13 (1958), suggesting that in cities with the commission form of government, a resolution could modify an ordinance; Sylvestre v. St. Landry Parish School Bd., 164 La. 204, 113 So. 818 (1927) (ordinance creating school board could be repealed by simple motion); Yarbrough v. Donaldson, *supra* note 29 (dictum that ordinance could be repealed by resolution).

[31] Swindell v. State ex rel. Maxey, 143 Ind. 153, 42 N.E. 528 (1895). Cf. Hibbard v. City of Chicago, *supra* note 30.

[32] See National Institute of Municipal Officers, Codification of Municipal Ordinances 3 (Report No. 95 1943).

published the legislation at the time of, or prior to, its passage.[33] Increasingly, most major municipalities have at least brought their laws together into compilations: collections of all laws currently in force. Many municipalities have adopted codes: publications organizing all currently valid laws under various subject headings, as has been done with most state and federal statutes. Frequent revision is, of course, necessary to keep any compilation or code up-to-date, and this problem is often handled by use of a loose-leaf form of publication.

Since a *compilation* does not change existing law, an ordinance is not repealed if it is inadvertently omitted from such a collection.[34] But a *code* is an enactment in and of itself; and anything omitted is likely to be held repealed, even if the omission was unintended.[35] The enactment of a code has been held not to violate a requirement that every law must have a single subject which is expressed in its title.[36] In connection with adoption of a code, there may be practical problems as to requirements of newspaper publication of all enactments, since the code may be quite lengthy. Sometimes such statutory or charter requirements may be held inapplicable to codes, especially building, or comparable, codes;[37] statutes in a number of states expressly except even general codes of ordinances from publication requirements;[38] and there is authority that, in any case, publication of an entire code can be dispensed with if the code is made a public record and then adopted by reference.[39] Over the years, the accessibility of municipal ordinances has increased, due in part to federal financial aid for codification projects and to the development of ordinance revision and codification services.

---

[33] See Fordham, Local Government Law 353 (2d rev. ed. 1986). Publication of municipal enactments is not necessary except as required by statute or city charter. Houston v. Kirschwing, 117 Colo. 92, 184 P.2d 487 (1947); City of Paducah v. Ragsdale, 122 Ky. 425, 92 S.W. 13 (1906); Forbes v. Woburn, 306 Mass. 67, 27 N.E.2d 733 (1940). But requirements that publication occur either during the enactment process or immediately after enactment are extremely common and are usually considered mandatory. See 1 Antieau, Municipal Corporation Law § 4.21 (1998).

Statutes or charters sometimes require that publication of ordinances, official notices, etc. occur in a newspaper that is "published" within the particular locality. This has been held to mean that the newspaper must maintain its main office within that locality, rather than to refer to the place where the paper is printed or to the paper's area of circulation. Express Publishing, Inc. v. City of Ketchum, 114 Idaho 114, 753 P.2d 1260 (1988) (newspaper not published within city where it had only branch office, not its principal office); Oklahoma Journal Publishing Co. v. Oklahoma City, 620 P.2d 452 (Okl.App.1979). Cf. City of Plainfield v. Courier-News, 72 N.J. 171, 369 A.2d 513 (1976) (place of publication is at headquarters). As to the often-encountered requirement that notice be published in a newspaper of "general circulation," see City of St. Mary's v. St. Mary's Native Corp., 9 P.3d 1002 (Alaska 2000) (statute required notice of public hearing to be published in newspaper of general circulation; newspaper qualifies for this designation if it contains news of general interest to the community and reaches a diverse readership).

[34] Gallaher v. City of Jefferson, 125 Iowa 324, 101 N.W. 124 (1904). Cf. Town of Crowley v. Rucker, 107 La. 213, 31 So. 629 (1902) (failure to enter ordinance in "ordinance book" does not affect validity). See also Boardman v. Davis, 231 Iowa 1227, 3 N.W.2d 608 (1942) (zoning ordinance not recorded; still valid).

[35] See Ex parte City of Albany, 213 Ala. 371, 106 So. 200 (1925).

[36] Central of Georgia Railway v. State, 104 Ga. 831, 31 S.E. 531 (1898). On codes, see generally Lamm, Zollner & MacKenzie, Recent Developments on Ordinances and Administrative Regulations, 14 Urban Law. 855, 857–61 (1982).

[37] See Magnolia Petroleum Co. v. Beck, 41 S.W.2d 488 (Tex.Civ.App.1931), error dism'd (publication requirement inapplicable to existing code of building ordinances).

[38] See American Municipal Association, Requirements for Publication of Municipal Ordinances and Adoption of Codes by Reference (Report No. 141 1940).

[39] City of Tucson v. Stewart, 45 Ariz. 36, 40 P.2d 72 (1935). Cf. City of Hazard v. Collins, 304 Ky. 379, 200 S.W.2d 933 (1947).

§ 11.3 Requirements for Enactments—Meetings

How are the law-making and other powers of a municipal legislative body to be exercised? These powers must be exercised at a lawfully called meeting of the body and cannot be exercised otherwise, as through a poll taken or informal agreement obtained outside a meeting.[40] If the place of meeting is not fixed by statute or city charter, the members have reasonable discretion in selecting a site;[41] but a meeting held outside the corporate limits of the locality—and any action taken there—has been held invalid.[42] A local governing body is considered continuous in nature, so where several readings of proposed legislation are required before it can be passed, the reading requirement is satisfied even if there are changes in the membership of the body between the first reading and the last.[43]

Statutes or charters usually specify that regular meetings of a municipal legislative body shall be held at certain times. Provision is often made for special meetings at the call of the mayor or other presiding officer, or sometimes at the call of a specified number of members.[44] Where the mayor is authorized to call special meetings, the acting mayor may perform this act in his absence—but "absence" is interpreted to mean lack of capacity to perform the act, not literal physical absence from the city.[45] Notice of regularly scheduled meetings does not necessarily have to be given either to members or

---

[40] Dunfield v. School District No. 72, 138 Kan. 800, 28 P.2d 987 (1934); City of Tulsa v. Melton, 175 Okl. 581, 54 P.2d 159 (1936); Murphy v. City of Albina, 22 Or. 106, 29 P. 353 (1892); City of Fort Worth v. First Baptist Church, 268 S.W. 1016 (Tex.Civ.App.1924). Cf. Zottman v. City and County of San Francisco, 20 Cal. 96 (1862). See also, involving application of an open-meeting law, Right to Know Committee v. City Council of Honolulu, 117 Hawai'i 1, 175 P.3d 111 (Intermediate App. 2007) (city council members were not permitted to engage in serial communications involving a quorum of council members in deliberating resolution that sought to reorganize the council's standing committees). As to legislating via e-mail, see DuVivier, E-legislating, 92 Or. L. Rev. 9 (2013).

[41] See In re Borough Council of Frackville, 308 Pa. 579, 162 A. 835 (1932) (meeting held at home of ill member).

[42] See Town of Paradise Valley v. Acker, 100 Ariz. 62, 411 P.2d 168 (1966) (meeting violated requirement that council meetings be public); Anderson v. Municipality of South Vancouver, 45 Can.S.C. 425 (1911). Cf. Motes v. Putnam County, 143 Fla. 134, 196 So. 465 (1940) (county board of bond trustees met outside county seat; resolution passed at such meeting held invalid).

[43] Breternitz v. City of Arvada, 174 Colo. 56, 482 P.2d 955 (1971); Reuter v. Meacham Contracting Co., 143 Ky. 557, 136 S.W. 1028 (1911). Cf. Rogers v. Concord, 104 N.H. 47, 178 A.2d 509 (1962). Both the *Breternitz* and *Reuter* cases *supra* dealt with situations where the entire council membership had changed between readings of the proposed legislation. Of course, the procedure can even more easily be held valid if only a portion of the membership has changed, as where the terms of the members are staggered. See McGraw v. Whitson, 69 Iowa 348, 28 N.W. 632 (1886); Zeo v. Lester, 241 Mass. 340, 135 N.E. 458 (1922). See also McGrain v. Daugherty, 273 U.S. 135, 47 S.Ct. 319, 71 L.Ed. 580 (1927) (U.S. Senate is a continuing body).

[44] See Stow v. Wyse, 7 Conn. 214 (1828) (incorporated company); City of Knoxville v. Knoxville Water Co., 107 Tenn. 647, 64 S.W. 1075 (1901), aff'd 189 U.S. 434, 23 S.Ct. 531, 47 L.Ed. 887 (1903) (officer designated to call special meeting must be judge of the necessity for such).

[45] See Gelinas v. Fugere, 55 R.I. 225, 180 A. 346 (1935), where the acting mayor, without any indication of an emergency, called a special meeting as soon as the mayor left town.

In Riggins v. Richards, 97 Tex. 229, 77 S.W. 946 (1904), it was held that the president pro tem—a council member elected to preside in case of the mayor's "failure, refusal, or inability"—should preside where the mayor was disqualified due to a personal interest in the subject matter.

to the general public.[46] But notice to the public is sometimes required by statute or charter before certain types of enactment—such as zoning ordinances—can occur.[47]

Notice *does* ordinarily have to be given all members of a local legislative body before a special meeting of such body is held.[48] But the giving of notice to a particular member may be excused if highly impracticable, as where the member is out of state and unavailable at the time the call is issued.[49] And the requirement of notice to *members* may be considered waived if all members attend and consent to the transaction of any business undertaken[50] (though there still may be problems if notice to the public is required and hasn't been given). The notice to members regarding special meetings must usually give reasonable indication of the business to be considered, and action on any unspecified matter will then be invalid.[51] Often this requirement of notice to members—

---

[46] See Sullivan v. Credit River Township, 299 Minn. 170, 217 N.W.2d 502 (1974). Cf. State ex rel. State Board of Milk Control v. Newark Milk Co., 118 N.J.Eq. 504, 179 A. 116 (1935) (due process does not require notice to the public of regular meetings). But notice of regular, as well as special, meetings is sometimes required by open meeting statutes; see generally Section 11.4 *infra.*

[47] Saks & Co. v. City of Beverly Hills, 107 Cal.App.2d 260, 237 P.2d 32 (Dist.Ct.1951); Pollard v. City of Norwalk, 108 Conn. 145, 142 A. 807 (1928); Oehlert Tractor & Equipment Co. v. Board of Highway Commissioners, 137 Kan. 286, 20 P.2d 527 (1933); Drowne v. Lovering, 93 N.H. 195, 37 A.2d 190 (1944); Village of Mill Neck v. Nolan, 233 App.Div. 248, 251 N.Y.S. 533 (1931), aff'd 259 N.Y. 596, 182 N.E. 196 (1932); Peters v. Gough, 86 S.W.2d 515 (Tex.Civ.App.1935), all holding that notice requirements in statutes or charters must be strictly followed. See Jennings v. Suggs, 180 Ga. 141, 178 S.E. 282 (1935). Cf. Sullivan v. Credit River Township, *supra* note 46, holding that a statute requiring open meetings implied that the public must be given notice of such meetings. See also Low v. City of Monticello, 2004 UT 90, 103 P.3d 130 (2004) (in context of legislative changes by a municipality, voters must be given adequate notice so that they may institute referendum procedures promptly).

Notice to the public *is* customarily required for all New England town meetings, regular or special. See Tilden, Some Fundamentals of Town Meetings, 46 Mass.L.Q. 165 (1961); see generally Johnson, The City Lawyer and the Town Meeting, 55 Mass. L.Q. 363 (1970). The notice must often be fairly elaborate and must give detailed information on the matters to be considered. See Nelson v. Town of Belmont, 274 Mass. 35, 174 N.E. 320 (1931); Opinion of the Justices, 101 N.H. 544, 134 A.2d 281 (1957). And requirements as to posting of the notice are strictly applied. See Pollard v. City of Norwalk, *supra*; Drowne v. Lovering, *supra.*

[48] Rogers v. Slonaker, 32 Kan. 191, 4 P. 138 (1884); Donough v. Dewey, 82 Mich. 309, 46 N.W. 782 (1890); People ex rel. Loew v. Batchelor, 22 N.Y. 128 (1860).

[49] Burrows v. Keebaugh, 120 Neb. 136, 231 N.W. 751 (1930); City of Knoxville v. Knoxville Water Co., 107 Tenn. 647, 64 S.W. 1075 (1901), aff'd 189 U.S. 434, 23 S.Ct. 531, 47 L.Ed. 887 (1903). Cf. Crook v. Clark Township, 74 N.J.Super. 148, 180 A.2d 715 (1962). And where not all members are notified of a special meeting, action taken at such meeting may be ratified at a later regular meeting. Simpson v. City of Highwood, 372 Ill. 212, 23 N.E.2d 62 (1939).

[50] Town of Jonesboro v. Gentrey, 165 La. 1003, 116 So. 488 (1928); Giesel v. City of Broadview Heights, 14 Ohio Misc. 70, 236 N.E.2d 222 (1968). Cf. Knickerbocker v. Redlands High School District, 49 Cal.App.2d 722, 122 P.2d 289 (Dist.Ct.1942) (defect in notice of special meeting held waived); William v. City of Evansville, 121 Ind.App. 185, 98 N.E.2d 219 (1951); Bluff City v. Western Light & Power Corp., 137 Kan. 169, 19 P.2d 478 (1933); Beaver Creek v. Hastings, 52 Mich. 528, 18 N.W. 250 (1884); Brechner v. Lake Success, 25 Misc.2d 920, 208 N.Y.S.2d 365 (1960), motion denied 12 A.D.2d 621, 210 N.Y.S.2d 757, aff'd 14 A.D.2d 567, 218 N.Y.S.2d 1017, appeal dism'd 11 N.Y.2d 929, 228 N.Y.S.2d 678 183 N.E.2d 81; Tandy & Fairleigh Tobacco Co. v. Hopkinsville, 174 Ky. 189, 192 S.W. 46 (1917). And the presence of a member at a special meeting cures the defect of a failure to notify *him.* Crook v. Clark Township, *supra* note 49.

[51] Baumgardner v. Hawthorne, 104 Cal.App.2d 512, 231 P.2d 864 (Dist.Ct. 1951); Scott v. Paulen, 15 Kan. 162 (1875); Russell v. Wellington, 157 Mass. 100, 31 N.E. 630 (1892) (substantial compliance required); Burns v. Stenholm, 310 Mich. 639, 17 N.W.2d 781 (1945) (member objected to action being taken on matter not specified in notice; action invalid); State v. Smith, 22 Minn. 218 (1875); Okolona v. Chickashaw County, 171 Miss. 424, 157 So. 690 (1934). See Wilson v. Lexington, 155 Miss. 157, 124 So. 268 (1929); State ex rel. Oil Operators' Trust v. Hellman, 120 Tex. 282, 36 S.W.2d 1002 (1931) (notice may be oral but must specify nature of business to be transacted). In Mills v. City of San Antonio, 65 S.W. 1121 (Tex.Civ.App.1901), error ref'd, it was held that legislation enacted at a special meeting was invalid where the subject matter was not specifically included in the meeting's call, and the passage of the legislation could not be ratified at a later meeting—at least, not by mere approval of the minutes of the prior meeting. But there is some authority that if all members

and of taking action only on matters listed in the notice—is now codified in statutes or city charters; and again, under such provisions, actions on other matters will be invalid.[52] If the law does not specify otherwise, the notice of a special meeting must simply be given a "reasonable" time in advance.[53] Usually nowadays, statutes or city charters require that notice to the public must also be given, in some reasonable manner, before any special meetings of the local governing body can validly be held.[54] Such notice will normally have to include an indication of the business to be transacted, and action on other matters will not be lawful.[55] This notice is often achieved by publication, in a newspaper of general circulation in the locality, of the same announcement that is sent the council members.

§ 11.4 Requirements for Enactments—Procedures at Meetings

The legislative body of a municipality is said to have inherent power to make its own rules of procedure so long as these are not violative of the constitution, state statutes, or the municipality's own charter.[56] Once adopted, such rules are presumed

---

of the local legislative body attend a special meeting and consent to the transaction of certain business that is within the body's general area of authority, action may be valid though that business was not specified in the call for the meeting. See City of Vicksburg v. Melsheimer, 183 Miss. 517, 184 So. 68 (1938); City of Knoxville v. Knoxville Water Co., *supra* note 49. See generally 2 Dillon, Municipal Corporations § 505 (5th ed. 1911). And some statutory or charter requirements that notice of special meetings specify the matters to be transacted may be found directory, not mandatory. See Holden v. Boerne, 252 S.W.2d 474 (Tex.Civ.App.1952), ref'd n. r. e. Cf. Lewick v. Glazier, 116 Mich. 493, 74 N.W. 717 (1898) (notice need not be written nor need it state object of meeting); 28 Del. 235 (Pa.Quarter Sessions 1939).

[52] Barile v. City Comptroller, 56 Misc.2d 190, 288 N.Y.S.2d 191 (1968).

[53] See Green v. Jones, 144 W.Va. 276, 108 S.E.2d 1 (1959) (reasonable time means sufficient time for preparations and for attendance at the specified time and place).

[54] See Sullivan v. Credit River Township, *supra* note 46. See generally 1 Antieau, Municipal Corporation Law § 4.06 (1998).

[55] See Fordham, Local Government Law 329 (2d rev. ed. 1986), saying that where notice of a special meeting must be given the public, and must include a list of the business to be transacted, the council should not, even by unanimous consent, be able to take action on an unlisted matter.

[56] See Murdoch v. Strange, 99 Md. 89, 57 A. 628 (1904); Zeiler v. Central Ry., 84 Md. 304, 35 A. 932 (1896). The use of a prayer to start a council meeting has been held not necessarily a violation of the First Amendment. Marsa v. Wernik, 86 N.J. 232, 430 A.2d 888 (1981). See Marsh v. Chambers, 463 U.S. 783, 103 S.Ct. 3330, 77 L.Ed.2d 1019 (1983), where the practice of the Nebraska legislature in opening each session with a prayer by a chaplain paid from public funds was held not to violate the Establishment Clause, even though the same clergyman had been selected for this job for 16 years and the prayers were customarily in the Judeo-Christian tradition. The Court relied heavily on historical evidence and said that the practice of opening legislative sessions with prayer has become part of the fabric of our society. Cf. Lincoln v. Page, 109 N.H. 30, 241 A.2d 799 (1968), upholding town-meeting invocations given by guest clergymen on a rotating basis.; Society of Separationists, Inc. v. Whitehead, 870 P.2d 916 (Utah 1993) (city council's practice of permitting prayer to be given during portion of city council meeting set aside for opening remarks did not violate state constitution's prohibition of expenditure of public money to support religion). But cf. Rasul v. District of Columbia, 680 F.Supp. 436 (D.D.C.1988) (city's policy of hiring prison chaplains on a denominational basis held a prima facie violation of Federal Civil Rights Act). See also Snyder v. Murray City Corp., 2003 UT 13, 73 P.3d 325 (2003) (city's rejection of prayer that individual requested to read at opening ceremony of municipal council meeting, based on prayer's content and council's disagreement with the beliefs expressed therein, was discriminatory and thus violated provision of state constitution requiring that use of public money or property to benefit religious exercise be on a neutral basis; distinguishing *Society of Separationists* case, *supra*, where the neutrality requirement was found satisfied). In Hinrichs v. Bosma, 440 F.3d 393 (7th Cir. 2006), the *Marsh* case, *supra*, was held to allow legislative prayer only so long as it is nonsectarian and does not proselytize or disparage any faith; sectarian prayers before official Indiana House of Representative meetings were thus held to violate the U.S. Constitution. See also County of Allegheny v. American Civil Liberties Union, 492 U.S. 573, 109 S.Ct. 3086, 106 L.Ed.2d 472 (1989), dealing with the constitutionality of holiday displays on government property, and the general discussion of such displays in Section 8.2, notes 47–48, *supra*, and accompanying text. Compare Pleasant Grove City v. Summum, 555 U.S. 460, 129 S.Ct. 1125, 172 L.Ed.2d 853 (2009)

valid;[57] but since the rules are an internal matter, they may also be waived or suspended at the council's pleasure so long as no constitutional or statutory rights are violated.[58] It has been held that even an ordinance prescribing a mere rule of procedure for the city council, such as a requirement of oral reading of proposed legislation, may be waived by unanimous consent of council members present.[59] The city council has been recognized as having inherent power to set rules for election of its own officers where these rules are not established by statute or the city charter[60]—as well as inherent power to establish rules necessary to the orderly conduct of meetings.[61]

(government has a right to speak for itself, and when so speaking, it is exempt from First Amendment scrutiny and can discriminate on content and viewpoint; thus a city could accept some facially religious monuments and reject others). See Gaylord, When the Exception Becomes the Rule: *Marsh* and Sectarian Legislative Prayer Post-*Summum*, 79 U. Cinc. L. Rev. 1017 (2011). See generally Lund, Legislative Prayer and the Secret Costs of Religious Endorsements, 94 Minn. L. Rev. 972 (2010); Lund, The Congressional Chaplaincies, 17 Wm. & Mary Bill Rts. J. 1171 (2009). Some city councils have taken the attitude that prayer before legislative meetings is appropriate so long as the prayer occurs before the opening gavel, does not promote a specific religion or try to convert anyone, and/or so long as atheists are also invited to speak. See Wollan & McKinley, City Decides to Continue Pre-Meeting Invocation, N.Y. Times, Oct. 2, 2009, at A15 (National Edition), describing the practices of the Lodi, California, city council. See also Note, Hold That Line!: The Proper Establishment Clause Analysis for Military Public Prayers, 22 Regent U.L. Rev. 209 (2009–10).

In Town of Greece v. Galloway, ___ U.S. ___,134 S.Ct. 1811 (2014), the U.S. Supreme Court abrogated the *County of Allegheny* case, *supra*, and ruled that prayers opening town board meetings did not have to be nonsectarian in order to comply with the Establishment Clause so long as they lended gravity to the occasion and reflected values that have long been part of the nation's heritage. See generally Rohr, Can the City Council Praise the Lord? Some Ruminations About Prayers at Local Government Meetings, 36 Nova L. Rev. 481 (2012). See also Note, Solemn School Boards: Limiting *Marsh v. Chambers* to Make School Board Prayer Unconstitutional, 101 Geo. L. J. 839 (2013).

On requirements that meetings must be conducted and laws passed in English, see Yniguez v. Arizonans for Official English, 69 F.3d 920 (9th Cir.1995), noted 30 U. Calif. Davis L. Rev. 277 (1996) (Arizona requirement invalidated on First Amendment grounds), opinion vacated for lack of standing 520 U.S. 43, 117 S.Ct. 1055, 137 L.Ed.2d 170 (1997), vacated on remand 118 F.3d 667 (9th Cir.1997); Ruiz v. Hill, 191 Ariz. 441, 957 P.2d 984 (1998) ("English only" amendment of Arizona Constitution violated equal protection and First Amendment). See generally Note, English-Only Laws and the Fourteenth Amendment: Dealing with Pluralism in a Nation Divided by Xenophobia, 29 U. Miami Inter-Am. L. Rev. 349 (1998). See also Comment, Patriotism or Prejudice: Alabama's Official English Amendment, 34 Cumberland L. Rev. 253 (2003–04). As to the possible conflict between English-only requirements and voting rights, see Zuckerman, Constitutional Clash: English-Only Meets Voting Rights, 28 Yale L. & Pol'y Rev. 353 (2010).

[57] Thorne v. Squier, 264 Mich. 98, 249 N.W. 497 (1933) (rules of procedure printed in manual are presumed validly adopted). On procedures of municipal legislative bodies, see generally Evans, Municipal Councils Compared with Legislatures, 17 Mo.L.Rev. 139 (1952); Shaft, Powers and Procedures of City and Village Governing Boards, 31 N.D.L.Rev. 137 (1955). See also Ebel, Investigatory Powers of City Councils, 38 Marq. L.Rev. 223 (1955); Annot., Power of Municipal Council to Correct Its Minutes, 3 A.L.R. 1308 (1919).

[58] Rutherford v. City of Nashville, 168 Tenn. 499, 79 S.W.2d 581 (1935) (council waived usual rule as to reconsidering action taken at the previous meeting).

[59] Jefferson v. City of Anchorage, 513 P.2d 1099 (Alaska 1973) (rule could be waived by unanimous consent; such consent presumed, without actual vote, where waiver of oral reading was usual practice). Cf. City of Pasadena v. Paine, 126 Cal.App.2d 93, 271 P.2d 577 (Dist.Ct.1954); Coleman v. Louison, 296 Mass. 210, 5 N.E.2d 46 (1936).

[60] State ex rel. Reed v. De Mairoibus, 131 Ohio St. 201, 2 N.E.2d 506 (1936). But state statutes or city charters sometimes prescribe methods for election of certain council officers, and then these methods are deemed mandatory. See Mack v. Polonko, 118 N.J.L. 133, 191 A. 844 (1937); In re Heafy, 247 App.Div. 277, 285 N.Y.S. 188 (1936), aff'd 270 N.Y. 616, 1 N.E.2d 357.

[61] See Gigler v. City of Klamath Falls, 21 Or.App. 753, 537 P.2d 121 (1975) (city council could adopt rule prohibiting nonresidents of city from speaking at meeting without prior notice and permission, and could eject an individual who attempted to speak in violation of rule and disrupted meeting). Cf. State v. Smith, 46 N.J. 510, 218 A.2d 147 (1966), cert. denied 385 U.S. 838, 87 S.Ct. 85, 17 L.Ed.2d 71 (1966). See generally Wilson & Alcarez, But It's My Turn to Speak! When Can Unruly Speakers at Public Hearings Be Forced to Leave or Be Quiet?, 41 Urban Law. 579 (2009). See also Wright, The Lighter Side of Local Government, ch. 3

With increasing frequency, one important requirement for city council meetings *is* established by state constitution, statute, or city charter, rather than being left to the discretion of council members: the requirement that meetings be open to the public. Most states now have laws imposing this requirement.[62] Called "Sunshine Laws" or "open-meeting laws," these are intended to foster public awareness of the local legislative process and deter official misconduct or secretive actions.[63] The laws customarily apply to the "governing bodies" of designated entities, including municipalities. The laws sometimes apply even to "executive sessions," though there are often exceptions for discussion of specified matters, such as personnel decisions.[64] A meeting does not

---

("The Council and Its Committees") (George Allen & Unwin, Ltd. 1935), quoting Sir Alfred Zimmern (at p. 50) as saying "No one likes to sit for hours listening to other men talk." Where an ordinance on orderly conduct at meetings contains overly broad or unduly vague language that is ruled unconstitutional, it is sometimes possible to apply the remaining, constitutional portion of the ordinance. See Acosta v. City of Costa Mesa, 694 F.3d 960 (9th Cir. 2012) (prohibition of "insolent" behavior was overly broad, but other reasonable and viewpoint-neutral regulations on right-to-speak upheld).

[62] Fordham, Local Government Law 330–31 (2d rev. ed. 1986) ("nearly three-fourths of the states"). There is generally held to be no common-law right, nor any implied right under U.S. or state constitutions, for members of the public or of newsgathering organizations to attend governmental meetings. Abood v. League of Women Voters, 743 P.2d 333 (Alaska 1987). See Watkins, Open Meetings Under the Arkansas Freedom of Information Act, 38 Ark. L. Rev. 268 (1984).

[63] See Duncan, Open Meeting Statutes in the United States, 12 Local Government Law Service Letter No. 9, at 1 (1962); Note, Open Meeting Statutes: The Press Fights for the Right to Know, 75 Harv.L.Rev. 1199 (1962). For a critical look at open-meeting laws, see Statler, Let the Sunshine In?, 67 A.B.A.J. 573 (1981). For a more favorable view, compare McSwain, The Sun Rises on the Florida Legislature: The Constitutional Amendment on Open Legislative Meetings, 19 Fla. St. U.L. Rev. 307 (1991). See generally Crowder, "Ain't No Sunshine": Examining Informality and State Open Meetings Acts as the Anti-Public Norm in Inner-City Redevelopment Deal Making, 74 Tenn. L. Rev. 623 (2007). As to the application of open-meeting laws to land-use deliberations, see Baker, Exploring How Municipal Boards Can Settle Appeals of Their Land Use Decisions Within the Framework of the Massachusetts Open Meeting Law, 44 Suffolk U. L. Rev. 455 (2011); Crowder, "Ain't No Sunshine": Examining Informality and State Open Meeting Acts as the Anti-Public Norm in Inner-City Redevelopment Deal Making, 18 J. Affordable Housing & Commun. Dev. L. 113 (2008). Cf. Noble v. Kootenai County, 148 Idaho 937, 231 P.3d 1034 (2010) (site visit by County Board of Commissioners to property that was the subject of landowners' subdivision application violated open meeting laws, though this did not require reversal of Board's rejection of application).

[64] See Minn.Stat.Ann. § 471.705, (except as otherwise provided, all meetings, including executive sessions, must be open to public). Contra, Oklahoma Association of Municipal Attorneys v. State, 577 P.2d 1310 (Okl.1978), applying 25 Okl.Stat.1981, §§ 301–14, and holding that a public body may hold executive sessions, closed to the public, for purposes of consultations with the body's attorney. But see Neu v. Miami Herald Publishing Co., 462 So.2d 821 (Fla. 1985) (open meeting law applied to meeting between city council and attorney concerning pending litigation to which city was a party). Cf. Booth Newspapers, Inc. v. Wyoming City Council, 168 Mich.App. 459, 425 N.W.2d 695 (1988) (city council sessions with attorney were not privileged and violated open meetings law). Mere negotiations between public bodies and labor organizations, or other groups, often fall outside the scope of open meeting laws. See International Ass'n of Firefighters, Local 2479 v. Thorpe, 632 P.2d 408 (Okl.1981) (negotiations between city manager and firefighters' union). Cf. SJL of Montana Associates Limited Partnership v. City of Billings, 263 Mont. 142, 867 P.2d 1084 (1993) (open meeting statutes did not require that meeting of city public works director, city engineer, and individuals representing private contractor and private engineering company to discuss problems surrounding delays in public construction project be open to public); Taylor v. Borough Council, 721 A.2d 388 (Pa.Commwlth.1998) (open meetings law does not apply to council's taking testimony in investigation of police chief). But some open meetings laws have been interpreted to cover every step of the deliberative and decision-making process. See Brookwood Area Homeowners Ass'n v. Municipality of Anchorage, 702 P.2d 1317 (Alaska 1985) (meeting between municipal assembly and developer to discuss developer's application for rezoning came within open meeting law, even though public hearing on the rezoning was scheduled for one week later).

Some open meetings laws contain an express exception as to discussion of strategy to be followed with respect to collective bargaining or to litigation. See Jarussi v. Board of Trustees, 204 Mont. 131, 664 P.2d 316 (1983), where such an exception was held not to apply to a school board's deliberations regarding the request of a high-school principal and teacher for a salary increase. Other open meetings laws specifically provide that they *do* apply to collective bargaining negotiations. See City of Fort Myers v. News–Press Publishing Co., 514

necessarily violate such a law because it is held in a normally private place, such as a private home, so long as the public *is* allowed access to the meeting itself.[65] But the law is violated if the public is not given adequate notice of a meeting that is required by the law to be "open."[66]

So.2d 408 (Fla.App.1987) (post-impasse meetings between the city's representatives and an employees' bargaining unit held covered by law). Where there is an exception for "personnel decisions," courts may be influenced in their interpretation by the risk that an officeholder's or applicant's reputation could be compromised by admission of the public. See City of Kenai v. Kenai Peninsula Newspapers, Inc., 642 P.2d 1316 (Alaska 1982) (exception applied, and public barred, though court recognizes than an applicant's reputation won't ordinarily be damaged by public discussion of his or her qualifications).

Courts sometimes carve out exceptions to open-meeting laws where no exceptions are specified in the law itself. See Comment, Government in the Sunshine: Another Cloud on the Horizon, 25 U.Fla.L.Rev. 603 (1973). See also Hunt v. Nuclear Regulatory Commission, 611 F.2d 332 (10th Cir.1979), cert. denied 445 U.S. 906, 100 S.Ct. 1084, 63 L.Ed.2d 322 ("Sunshine Act" inapplicable to in camera hearings of Atomic Safety and Licensing Board). But the term "meeting," in provisions requiring any meeting of certain groups to be open, is usually construed broadly. See Times Publishing Co. v. Williams, 222 So.2d 470 (Fla.App.1969); People ex rel. Difanis v. Barr, 78 Ill.App.3d 842, 34 Ill.Dec. 223, 397 N.E.2d 895 (1979), aff'd 83 Ill.2d 191, 46 Ill.Dec. 678, 414 N.E.2d 731 (1980) (caucus of city council members belonging to a particular party was within Open Meetings Act). But cf. Adler v. City Council, 184 Cal.App.2d 763, 7 Cal.Rptr. 805 (Dist.Ct. 1960) (dinner at which zoning problems discussed was not "meeting"). On the provision often found in open meetings laws that limits their application to "public" or "governmental" bodies, see Prescott Newspapers, Inc. v. Yavapai Community Hosp. Ass'n, 163 Ariz. 33, 785 P.2d 1221 (App. 1989) (community hospital association was not "public body," since it was creation of group of private individuals acting together as authorized by statutes governing creation of private nonprofit corporations); Poughkeepsie Newspaper v. Mayor's Intergovernmental Task Force, 145 A.D.2d 65, 537 N.Y.S.2d 582 (1989) (task force formed to study future water needs of New York City and surrounding counties held not a "public body," which must perform a governmental function and must be required to have a quorum in order to do business); Salmon For All v. Department of Fisheries, 118 Wash.2d 270, 821 P.2d 1211 (1992) (Columbia River Compact held not a "governing body"). In Dewey v. Redevelopment Agency of Reno, 119 Nev. 87, 64 P.3d 1070 (2003), private briefings which lacked a quorum of the city redevelopment agency's members were held not "meetings" within the meaning of the state Open Meeting Law, although the briefings were designed to permit the agency members to gather information and discuss the highly complex redevelopment proposal. Compare Cheyenne Newspaper, Inc. v. Building Code Bd. of Appeal, 222 P.3d 158 (Wyo. 2010) (quorum of members of city's building code board of appeals, which met to discuss and deliberate the appeal from action of the city's historic preservation board, qualified as "meeting" under Public Meetings Act, but no action of the board would be nullified since *final* action came at a public meeting).

On coverage of, and exceptions under, open-meeting laws, see generally Wickham, Let the Sun Shine In! Open-Meeting Legislation Can Be Our Key to Closed Doors in State and Local Government, 68 Nw. U.L.Rev. 480 (1973); Note, Administrative Law—Freedom of Information, 49 Tex.L.Rev. 764 (1971); Annot., Validity, Construction and Application of Statutes Making Public Proceedings Open to the Public, 38 A.L.R.3d 1070 (1971). Open meeting laws that are general in wording may prove unworkable and may have to be amended to provide more detail. See Note, Legislation: Sunshine in the Sunbelt: Oklahoma's New Open Meeting Act, 34 Okl.L.Rev. 362 (1981), discussing amendments to the Oklahoma statute. See also Cloud Over Florida's Sunshine Laws, 23 U. Fla. J. L. & Pub. Pol'y 73 (2012); Note, Transparency Trumps Technology: Reconciling Open Meeting Laws With Modern Technology, 55 Wm. & Mary L. Rev. 2287 (2014).

[65] Smith v. Gilbertsville, 309 S.W.2d 162 (Ky.1958). Cf. Gutierrez v. City of Albuquerque, 96 N.M. 398, 631 P.2d 304 (1981) (fact that city council chambers were not large enough to accommodate all of the crowd that wanted to attend meeting did not render meeting invalid). But cf. City of Lexington v. Davis, 310 Ky. 751, 221 S.W.2d 659 (1949), where a meeting at the mayor's home was held to have violated the law. As to the extent that open-meeting laws apply to electronic communications among legislators, see Comment, Sunshine in Cyberspace? Electronic Deliberation and the Reach of Open Meeting Laws, 48 St. Louis U. L.J. 755 (2004).

[66] See Green v. Beste, 76 N.W.2d 165 (N.D.1956). Cf. Carefree Imp. Ass'n v. City of Scottsdale, 133 Ariz. 106, 649 P.2d 985 (App.1982) (even though notices of a special city council meeting to be held on a Monday had been posted at the places required by statute on the prior Saturday, these were insufficient to satisfy the open meetings law since the public had very limited access to those places over the weekend); Sonstelie v. Board of Trustees, 202 Mont. 414, 658 P.2d 413 (1983) (even though open meetings law did not specifically require notice by publication as to special school board meeting, school board has duty to insure that public has ample opportunity to participate in board decision). See also Town of Paradise Valley v. Acker, 100 Ariz. 62, 411 P.2d 168 (1966) (meeting outside town limits violates requirement that council meetings be public). It has been held

Enforcement of open meetings laws can prove difficult. Criminal penalties and injunctive relief are sometimes provided but seldom prove useful.[67] Invalidity of legislation passed at meetings held in violation of the law is another possible enforcement device, but courts may be reluctant to impose this where not clearly provided by the open-meeting provision and/or where the violation of the law is considered inadvertent.[68]

City legislative bodies would seem to have power at common law to exclude filming and recording devices from their proceedings.[69] But open-meeting laws may sometimes curtail such power.[70]

---

that in determining whether public notice of a meeting is a sufficiently "full" notice within a statutory requirement, the court should apply an objective standard—that is, notice should be interpreted in light of the knowledge of an ordinary member of the community to whom it is directed. Town of Marble v. Darien, 181 P.3d 1148 (Colo. 2008) (where notice listed "Committee Update" on a matter as part of agenda, this was sufficient notice that the matter might be acted upon).

[67] See Note, Administrative Law—Freedom of Information, *supra* note 64, at 772–80 (with proposed amendment to Texas statute). An example of a situation in which members of a city legislative body were convicted of violating an open meeting law is found in Hilliary v. State, 630 P.2d 791 (Okl.Crim.App.1981) (willful violation; no criminal intent required since crime is malum prohibitum; convictions affirmed). It has been held that violations of an open meeting law may be sufficient grounds for holding a recall election as to the officials who committed the violations. See Dona Ana County Clerk v. Martinez, 138 N.M. 575, 124 P.3d 210 (2005).

[68] See Sullivan v. Credit River Township, 299 Minn. 170, 217 N.W.2d 502 (1974) (statute did not specify that actions taken in violation of Open Meeting Law were invalid); Carter v. City of Nashua, 113 N.H. 407, 308 A.2d 847 (1973). An example of a case in which action *was* invalidated because taken in violation of an "open meetings law" is Gray v. City of Manitou Springs, 43 Colo.App. 60, 598 P.2d 527 (Colo.App.1979) (city council request that acting city manager fire police chief). Cf. In re Order Declaring Annexation Dated June 28, 1978, 637 P.2d 1270 (Okl.App.1981) (annexation resolution by school board). Compare Van Hooser v. Warren County Bd. of Educ., 807 S.W.2d 230 (Tenn.1991) (school board's failure to observe open meetings law when a teacher's employment was discussed did not entitle teacher to reinstatement). Cf. Stoldt v. City of Toronto, 234 Kan. 957, 678 P.2d 153 (1984) (only the attorney general, district attorneys, and county attorneys had standing to seek voidance of governmental actions taken in violation of open meetings law; therefore an employee dismissed by city council in alleged violation of such law did not have standing to seek voidance of his dismissal but was limited to remedies of injunction or writ of mandamus, or obtaining help of a public prosecutor).

Even where invalidation of action is possible due to violation of an open meetings law, it has been held that violation at a meeting where the matter is merely discussed does not taint final action taken at a meeting that does comply with the law. State v. City of Hailey, 102 Idaho 511, 633 P.2d 576 (1981). Cf. Fox v. City of Lakewood, 39 Ohio St.3d 19, 528 N.E.2d 1254 (1988), reh. denied 39 Ohio St.3d 726, 534 N.E.2d 359 (1988) (adoption of amendment to city charter by electorate cured illegality created by city council's holding meeting on the proposed amendment in private); Ward v. Richfield City, 798 P.2d 757 (Utah 1990) (even if city council meeting at which police chief was discharged violated the agenda and notice provisions of the open meetings law, the council cured any violations by subsequently holding a fully publicized meeting on the discharge). See also Zunski v. Frenchtown Rural Fire Dep't, 309 P.3d 21 (Mont. 2013) (governing body can remedy illegality of a meeting by making a new decision that is not based on anything from the illegal meeting); Allen v. Lakeside Neighborhood Planning Committee, 371 Mont. 310, 308 P.3d 956 (2013) (neighborhood planning committee was not an agency but was an advisory committee; consequently, while the open meeting law applied to its proceedings, the statutes pertaining to the voiding of agency decisions did not). But see Brookwood Area Homeowners Ass'n v. Municipality of Anchorage, *supra* note 64.

On enforcement of open meetings laws, see generally Davis, Rivera-Sanchez & Chamberlin, Sunshine Laws and Judicial Discretion: A Proposal for Reform of State Sunshine Law Enforcement Provisions, 28 Urban Law. 41 (1996).

[69] Davidson v. Common Council, 40 Misc.2d 1053, 244 N.Y.S.2d 385 (1963) (self-powered tape recorder could be excluded).

[70] See Nevens v. City of Chino, 233 Cal.App.2d 775, 44 Cal.Rptr. 50 (Dist.Ct. 1965) (council's action arbitrary, capricious, too restrictive).

Open-meeting laws normally apply only to entities exercising some real governmental authority, not to mere advisory bodies.[71] Committees that determine the admission of candidates to state or municipal colleges and universities are, however, often within the purview of the open-meeting laws.[72]

§ 11.5 Requirements for Enactments—Quorums and Voting

A number of cases have raised issues as to what number constitutes a quorum for a municipal legislative body, and what number of votes is needed to take certain action. At common law, a quorum is a majority of the council members.[73] The council itself normally has no power to vary the quorum requirement;[74] and action taken with less than a quorum present is void,[75] except that some authority has upheld the power of less than a quorum (usually a simple majority of those present) to adjourn a meeting.[76] Where a vacancy exists on the council, the generally accepted rule is that a majority of the full membership, not merely a majority of the remaining members, is necessary to a quorum.[77] A presiding officer—such as a mayor—is counted as part of the membership for quorum and all other purposes, if such officer has full-fledged voting rights. But if the officer votes only in case of a tie (*i.e.*, can only make a tie-breaking or "casting" vote),

---

[71] See Washington School District No. 6 v. Superior Court, 112 Ariz. 335, 541 P.2d 1137 (1975) (advisory committee of teachers and laypersons to evaluate school textbooks did not come within law); McLarty v. Board of Regents, 231 Ga. 22, 200 S.E.2d 117 (1973) (faculty-student committee formed to review student government's proposed allocation of funds; not within law); Sanders v. Benton, 579 P.2d 815 (Okl.1978) (citizens' advisory committee to recommend possible locations for treatment center not within law). But cf. Town of Palm Beach v. Gradison, 296 So.2d 473 (Fla.1974); IDS Properties v. Town of Palm Beach, 279 So.2d 353 (Fla.Dist.Ct.App.1973), both finding a citizens' planning committee within the scope of the Florida law.

[72] See Carl v. Board of Regents, 577 P.2d 912 (Okl.1978). Cf. Greene v. Athletic Council, 251 N.W.2d 559 (Iowa 1977) (council directing athletic programs for state university and determining the athletes who would receive scholarships and awards was within law).

[73] Penton v. Brown-Crummer Inv. Co., 222 Ala. 155, 131 So. 14 (1930); Seiler v. O'Maley, 190 Ky. 190, 227 S.W. 141 (1921); Lawrence v. Ingersoll, 88 Tenn. 52, 12 S.W. 422 (1889); Herring v. Mexia, 290 S.W. 792 (Tex.Civ.App.1926), error ref'd. See Heiskell v. Mayor of Baltimore, 65 Md. 125, 4 A. 116 (1886). But as to New England town meetings, the common-law rule is that if the meeting is correctly called, less than a majority of the whole do have power to act. 2 Dillon, Municipal Corporations § 520 (5th ed. 1911). Cf. E. B. & A. C. Whiting Co. v. City of Burlington, 106 Vt. 446, 175 A. 35 (1934).

[74] See Zeiler v. Central Railway Co., 84 Md. 304, 35 A. 932 (1896); Heiskell v. City of Baltimore, *supra* note 73. But the power to set a quorum may be delegated to the council by statute. See Seiler v. O'Maley, *supra* note 73.

[75] See Penton v. Brown-Crummer Inv. Co., *supra* note 73; Clark v. Waltham City Council, 328 Mass. 40, 101 N.E.2d 369 (1951); Ellison v. Mayor of Haverhill, 309 Mass. 350, 35 N.E.2d 202 (1941); Baker v. Police Commissioners of Port Huron, 62 Mich. 327, 28 N.W. 913 (1886); Reynolds County Tel. Co. v. Piedmont, 152 Mo.App. 361, 133 S.W. 141 (1911); People ex rel. O'Neill v. Hill, 260 App.Div. 111, 20 N.Y.S.2d 874 (1940), aff'd 283 N.Y. 766, 28 N.E.2d 977; Commonwealth ex rel. Park v. Kaiserman, 330 Pa. 196, 199 A. 143 (1938); Gaskin v. Jones, 198 S.C. 508, 18 S.E.2d 454 (1942).

[76] City of Rolla v. Schuman, 189 Mo.App. 252, 175 S.W. 241 (1915); Kimball v. Marshall, 44 N.H. 465 (1863); O'Neil v. Tyler, 3 N.D. 47, 53 N.W. 434 (1892). This seems clearly the better view, avoiding the confusion of a meeting that remains unadjourned; but there is some contrary authority. Pennsylvania Co. v. Cole, 132 F. 668 (C.C.Ind.1904); State ex rel. Parker v. Smith, 22 Minn. 218 (1875). See generally 4 McQuillin, Municipal Corporations § 13.38.10 (3d rev. ed. 1992).

[77] Pimental v. City of San Francisco, 21 Cal. 351 (1863); McLean v. City of East St. Louis, 222 Ill. 510, 78 N.E. 815 (1906) (with discussion of differing views); Clark v. North Bay Village, 54 So.2d 240 (Fla.1951). Contra, People v. Wright, 30 Colo. 439, 71 P. 365 (1902); Ross v. Miller, 115 N.J.L. 61, 178 A. 771 (1935) (dictum). Cf. State ex rel. Attorney General v. Orr, 61 Ohio St. 384, 56 N.E. 14 (1899). These latter cases take the view that a quorum is a majority of the remaining members. What if members of a council or board whose terms have expired continue to take part in the body's actions? See Smyers v. City of Albuquerque, 140 N.M. 198, 141 P.3d 542 (App. 2006) (validity of action not affected by the expirations).

he or she is generally not counted for quorum purposes.[78] If a member is disqualified from voting because of an interest in the subject matter under consideration, the member is not counted for quorum purposes either.[79] (This may seem inconsistent with the rule that where a seat on the council is vacant, a majority of the whole membership is still required to constitute a quorum. But in the situation of vacancy, the empty position can eventually be filled, and thus no long-lasting stalemate due to lack of a quorum is likely to result, even if there should be several vacancies, while if a number of members are personally interested in a matter and thus disqualified from voting, a quorum as to that matter might become unobtainable for as long as those members remained on the council.) If a quorum is once obtained, it may nonetheless subsequently fail if sufficient members leave.[80] Of course, all the above-stated quorum requirements are sometimes now varied by particular statutory or charter provisions.[81]

If a quorum is present, by the *common-law rule* a measure can be passed by a simple majority of those voting.[82] Silence or inaction can be, and frequently is, taken as voting in accord with the majority of votes actually cast,[83] thus helping avoid stalemates where some members attend but refuse to take any part in the proceedings. The same

---

[78] Bybee v. Smith, 22 Ky.L.Rep. 1684, 61 S.W. 15 (1901); McLean v. City of East St. Louis, *supra* note 77; Griffin v. Messenger, 114 Iowa 99, 86 N.W. 219 (1901). See Cate v. Martin, 70 N.H. 135, 46 A. 54 (1900) (dictum that mayor who presides at council meetings is not to be counted in determining quorum). See generally Annot., Constitutionality and Effect of Statute Relating to Deadlock or Tie Vote in Governmental Body, 40 A.L.R. 808, 817 (1926). See also City of Centerville v. Adkisson, 291 S.W.2d 798 (Tex.Civ.App.1956) (mayor had only a "casting vote"; this means a deciding vote in case of a tie, and his vote could not be counted where a two-thirds vote was needed). On the mayor's (or other presiding officer's) eligibility to vote, see 1 Antieau, Municipal Corporation Law § 4.08 (1998).

[79] Woodward v. City of Wakefield, 236 Mich. 417, 210 N.W. 322 (1926); Smith v. City of Centralia, 55 Wash. 573, 104 P. 797 (1909). On conflicts of interest on the part of municipal officers, see generally Chapter 13 *infra*.

[80] See Gaskins v. Jones, 198 S.C. 508, 18 S.E.2d 454 (1942) (county governing board). Cf. State ex rel. Walden v. Vanosdal, 131 Ind. 388, 31 N.E. 79 (1892).

[81] See Attorney General v. Shepard, 62 N.H. 383 (1882); Dombal v. Garfield, 129 N.J.L. 555, 30 A.2d 579 (1943); Morris v. Cashmore, 253 App.Div. 657, 3 N.Y.S.2d 624 (1938), aff'd 278 N.Y. 730, 17 N.E.2d 143. See generally 4 McQuillin, Municipal Corporations § 13.27.10 (3d rev. ed. 1992).

[82] Martin v. Ballenger, 25 Cal.App.2d 435, 77 P.2d 888 (Dist.Ct.1938); Ross v. Miller, *supra* note 77; Peter's Garage, Inc. v. City of Burlington, 121 N.J.L. 523, 3 A.2d 634 (1939), aff'd per curiam 123 N.J.L. 227, 8 A.2d 910. See Ellison v. Haverhill, *supra* note 75. Cf. Laconia Water Co. v. City of Laconia, 99 N.H. 409, 112 A.2d 58 (1955) (majority of those voting can pass proposition at town meeting). This is often expressed by saying that a majority of the quorum is necessary for a measure to carry, since most authority requires that in order for a majority of the votes cast to suffice for passing a measure, this number must also constitute a majority of a quorum. See Reynolds, Voting Requirements in Municipal Governing Bodies: Minority Rule or Legislative Stalemate?, 27 Urban Law. 87, 90–92 (1995). See Manno v. City of Clifton, 14 N.J.Super. 100, 81 A.2d 368 (1951). Cf. Rushville Gas Co. v. City of Rushville, 121 Ind. 206, 23 N.E. 72 (1889); Chamberlain v. Inhabitants of Dover, 13 Me. 466 (1836); State ex rel. Burdick v. Tyrrell, 158 Wis. 425, 149 N.W. 280 (1914).

[83] Somers v. City of Bridgeport, 60 Conn. 521, 22 A. 1015 (1891); Pierson-Trapp Co. v. Knippenberg, 387 S.W.2d 587 (Ky.1965) (abstainers will be considered as voting with those otherwise in the majority); Napier v. Gay, 264 Ky. 359, 94 S.W.2d 682 (1936) (silence can be taken as voting affirmatively); State v. Gruber, 231 Or. 494, 373 P.2d 657 (1962) (members not voting will be taken as acquiescing in action of majority). See State ex rel. Cole v. Chapman, 44 Conn. 595 (1878); State ex rel. Miller v. Marshall, 135 Fla. 214, 184 So. 870 (1938); Launtz v. People ex rel. Sullivan, 113 Ill. 137 (1885); Attorney General v. Shepard, 62 N.H. 383 (1882); State v. Green, 37 Ohio St. 227 (1881). But cf. Miller v. Rapides Parish School Board, 209 La. 877, 25 So.2d 623 (1946) (majority of full membership, not just of those attending meeting, held necessary to discharge bus driver in light of statutory policy to protect drivers); Kozusko v. Garretson, 102 N.J.L. 508, 134 A. 614 (1926); Lawrence v. Ingersoll, 88 Tenn. 52, 12 S.W. 422 (1889). See generally Annot., Abstention from Voting of Member of Municipal Council Present at Session as Affecting Requisite Voting Majority, 63 A.L.R.3d 1072 (1975).

presumption of voting with the majority has been applied to an abstention due to a conflict of interest.[84]

Statutes and city charters are replete with provisions that action on certain matters—often zoning questions—can be taken only upon the obtaining of a majority of the *whole council,* or some "supermajority," such as two-thirds or three-fourths, of the whole council.[85] These provisions are usually strictly construed as meaning that the required number or percentage of the full membership must vote for the action. Thus, absence or abstention of a member, or a vacancy on the council, does *not* then lessen the number of votes required.[86] Similarly an "affirmative vote of the majority" means a majority of the total possible membership, and the common-law presumption that

---

[84] Northwestern Bell Telephone Co. v. Board of Commissioners of City of Fargo, 211 N.W.2d 399 (N.D.1973), discussing the authorities. A slightly different approach was taken in Alamo Heights v. Gerety, 264 S.W.2d 778 (Tex.Civ.App.1954), ref'd n. r. e. where an abstention from voting, due to a personal interest in the matter, was held to reduce the total number of members of the council for purposes of that question, so that the requisite number of votes for approval was calculated on the basis of a reduced total membership. (A statute required affirmative votes by three-fourths of the whole membership; this was held to mean the whole membership eligible to vote.) Cf. Board of Commissioners v. Wachovia Loan & Trust Co., 143 N.C. 110, 55 S.E. 442 (1906); Nalle v. City of Austin, 41 Tex.Civ.App. 423, 93 S.W. 141 (1906), error ref'd (where one member of council has died, vacant position is not counted as to what is the majority or required fraction). On problems raised by conflicts of interest, see generally Chapter 13 *infra.*

[85] See, as to statutes and charter provisions requiring a majority of the whole council, People ex rel. Anderson v. City of Chicago & North Western Railway, 396 Ill. 466, 71 N.E.2d 701 (1947) (appropriations); Tucker v. Raney, 145 Kan. 256, 65 P.2d 329 (1937) (construction of power plant; statute required "majority of all members elect" of council); Settle v. Jones, 306 Ky. 9, 206 S.W.2d 59 (1947) (establishing salaries); Tennant v. Crocker, 85 Mich. 328, 48 N.W. 577 (1891) (general requirement); Melita v. Nolan, 126 Misc. 345, 213 N.Y.S. 674 (1926) (zoning ordinance); Russell v. Murphy, 177 Okl. 255, 58 P.2d 560 (1936) (amendment to zoning law); Summergrade v. Rees, 102 Ohio App. 335, 132 N.E.2d 645 (1956); State ex rel. Doyle v. Torrence, 203 Tenn. 175, 310 S.W.2d 425 (1958) (pension program). Statutory or charter provisions requiring a majority (or greater proportion) of "the members" of the council to vote for a measure have also generally been interpreted as requiring the designated fraction of the full council membership. See Illinois Trust & Savings Bank v. Arkansas City, 76 F. 271 (8th Cir.1896); City of Anniston v. Davis, 98 Ala. 629, 13 So. 331 (1893); Newbold v. City of Stuttgart, 145 Ark. 544, 224 S.W. 993 (1920); City of Haven v. Gregg, 244 Kan. 117, 766 P.2d 143 (1988) (statute provided that no ordinance is valid unless a majority of the members of the city council vote in its favor; held to mean that passage requires the affirmative votes of a majority of the entire membership, modifying the common-law rule that abstention counts as an affirmative vote); State ex rel. Peterson v. Hoppe, 194 Minn. 186, 260 N.W. 215 (1935). Cf. Hawaii Elec. Light Co. v. Department of Land & Natural Resources, 102 Hawai'i 257, 75 P.3d 160 (2003) (statute required a simple majority of the members to take any action and made four members a quorum to do business; this provision held to modify common-law rule by requiring a majority vote of the entire board of six, regardless of the number present and voting).

As to statutory or charter provisions requiring a "super-majority" of the whole council, see Application of Reynolds, 328 P.2d 441 (Okl.Crim.App.1958). (statute required three-fourths vote to pass zoning ordinance). Where a super-majority vote is required merely by a rule of the city council, that body can change the requirement by simple majority vote. See Roti v. Washington, 148 Ill.App.3d 1006, 102 Ill.Dec. 570, 500 N.E.2d 463 (1986) (council could by simple majority change its rule that had required a two-thirds vote to make rule changes, and mayor's tie-breaking vote establishing the majority was properly cast).

[86] Pollasky v. Schmid, 128 Mich. 699, 87 N.W. 1030 (1901); State ex rel. Peterson v. Hoppe, *supra* note 85; Smithtown v. Howell, 31 N.Y.2d 365, 339 N.Y.S.2d 949, 292 N.E.2d 10 (1972) (vacancy). Cf. City of Jacksonville v. Ledwith, 26 Fla. 163, 7 So. 885 (1890) (ordinance "passed" with less than prescribed number of votes is invalid). But see Nalle v. City of Austin, *supra* note 84. In Palmer v. Municipality of Anchorage, 65 P.3d 832 (Alaska 2003), it was held that a requirement of an affirmative vote of 5 of the sitting members of the police and fire retirement board for approval of any claim for occupational disability benefits, rather than a majority of a quorum present, did not deny the petitioning officer due process. But cf. Southern Nev. Homebuilders Ass'n v. Clark County, 121 Nev. 446, 117 P.3d 171 (2005) (county zoning ordinance's supermajority approval requirement for non-conforming zone change applications violated county's enabling statute and was thus invalid).

abstention is a vote with the majority does not apply in the face of such a specific and stringent requirement.[87]

The general rule is that municipal bodies may reconsider their actions—adopting measures previously defeated and rescinding measures earlier passed—either at the same meeting as the original action or a subsequent meeting,[88] but only if no rights of third persons have vested as a result of the action.[89] Once an appointment of a municipal officer is completed, it cannot be reconsidered; the proper procedures for removal of the officer must then be followed.[90]

Often, statutes or charters require that a roll call vote be taken and the votes yea and nay recorded in the council's journal in order for certain actions to be taken. Such a requirement is deemed mandatory, and a failure to comply invalidates the action.[91]

§ 11.6 Relationship of Municipal Legislative Body to Other Branches of City Government

The tripartite division of the federal and state governments into independent branches is not reflected in the set-up of a great many cities. The mayor of a city is, for instance, generally not an exclusively executive officer and does not enjoy immunity from

---

[87] Mann v. Housing Authority, 20 N.J.Super. 276, 89 A.2d 725 (1952). But if a statute or charter requires a "unanimous vote" (or similar words) and does not indicate that this must be of the whole council or of all members, the unanimous vote of those at the meeting (assuming a quorum is present) has usually been held to suffice. San Christina Inv. Co. v. City & County of San Francisco, 167 Cal. 762, 141 P. 384 (1914); Strain v. Mims, 123 Conn. 275, 193 A. 754 (1937); Atkins v. Philips, 26 Fla. 281, 8 So. 429 (1890). And the same is true where a certain percentage is required, but no mention of the "whole council" or "all members" or "the members" is made. See Gumm v. City of Lexington, 247 Ky. 139, 56 S.W.2d 703 (1933); Zeiler v. Central Railroad, 84 Md. 304, 35 A. 932 (1896). See generally 4 McQuillin, Municipal Corporations § 13.31.15 (3d rev. ed. 1992). The rules—both common-law and statutory—on quorums and on voting requirements are summarized in Reynolds, Voting Requirements in Municipal Governing Bodies: Minority Rule or Legislative Stalemate?, 27 Urban Law. 87 (1995).

[88] State v. Hettinger, 134 Kan. 405, 5 P.2d 862 (1931) (any time prior to publication); Dal Maso v. Board of County Commissioners, 182 Md. 200, 34 A.2d 464 (1943); Frost v. Hoar, 85 N.H. 442, 160 A. 51 (1932); Decker v. City of Toledo, 56 Ohio App. 344, 10 N.E.2d 955 (1937); Edwards Realty & Finance Co. v. City of Superior, 250 Wis. 472, 27 N.W.2d 370 (1947). See McConoughey v. Jackson, 101 Cal. 265, 35 P. 863 (1894); People ex rel. MacMahon v. Davis, 284 Ill. 439, 120 N.E. 326 (1918); Tuell v. Meacham Contracting Co., 145 Ky. 181, 140 S.W. 159 (1911); Hall v. City of Seattle, 24 Wn.App. 357, 602 P.2d 366 (1979) (municipal civil service commission could set new hearing to correct own error). See generally Annot., At What Stage Does a Statute or Ordinance Pass Beyond the Power of Legislative Body to Reconsider or Recall?, 96 A.L.R. 1309, 1313 (1935).

[89] See State v. Bentley, 96 Kan. 344, 150 P. 218 (1915); Kay Construction Co. v. County Council, 227 Md. 479, 177 A.2d 694 (1962) (by ordinance, zoning could be reconsidered for good cause). Cf. State ex rel. Fatzer v. Salome, 169 Kan. 585, 220 P.2d 192 (1950). If a measure can no longer be "reconsidered," it can nonetheless be repealed—but the prescribed formalities must be followed. See Section 11.2, notes 30–31 *supra* and accompanying text.

[90] Ekonomon v. Milford, 21 Conn.Sup. 123, 145 A.2d 381 (1958) (appointee could only be removed for cause; vote could not be rescinded); DeWoody v. Underwood, 66 Ohio App. 367, 34 N.E.2d 263 (1940) (once received by appointee, appointment is irrevocable). See State ex rel. Coogan v. Barbour, 53 Conn. 76, 22 A. 686 (1885); Hadley v. Mayor of Albany, 33 N.Y. 603 (1865) (council having once legally canvassed the votes for mayor cannot reverse its decision at subsequent meeting); State ex rel. Calderwood v. Miller, 62 Ohio St. 436, 57 N.E. 227 (1900); State ex rel. Pierce v. Hardin, 163 Tenn. 471, 43 S.W.2d 924 (1931). See generally Annot., Reconsideration of Appointment, or Confirmation of Appointment, to Office, 89 A.L.R. 132, 155 (1934), discussing when an appointment becomes completed so that it may not be "reconsidered."

[91] People ex rel. Ballance v. Chicago & E. I. Ry., 314 Ill. 352, 145 N.E. 716 (1924); Missouri Public Service Co. v. Barton County Electric Cooperative, 353 S.W.2d 818 (Mo.App.1962).

the subpoena powers of the legislative branch.[92] There is much overlapping of administrative, legislative, and even judicial functions among municipal organs—and ideally, much cooperation.

The question often arises as to whether municipal courts will take judicial notice of the ordinances of their own municipality, or will require these to be proven as facts. The general rule is that a municipal court does take judicial notice of the municipality's ordinances,[93] and this rule can also be applied in state appellate courts hearing appeals from a municipal court.[94] In other state-court cases, as where the matter is initially tried in state court or is appealed from any court other than that of the municipality whose ordinance is involved, the ordinance must be pleaded and proved as a fact.[95]

---

[92] LaGuardia v. Smith, 288 N.Y. 1, 41 N.E.2d 153 (1942), appeal denied 262 A.D. 726, 28 N.Y.S.2d 705. See generally on the lack of three independent branches of government at the municipal level State ex rel. Wilkinson v. Lane, 181 Ala. 646, 62 So. 31 (1913); Sarlls v. State ex rel. Trimble, 201 Ind. 88, 166 N.E. 270 (1929); State ex rel. Simpson v. City of Mankato, 117 Minn. 458, 136 N.W. 264 (1912); Walker v. City of Spokane, 62 Wash. 312, 113 P. 775 (1911). On the investigative powers of a municipal council, see generally 1 Antieau, Municipal Corporation Law § 4.07 (1998).

Occasionally, however, the action of a city mayor of other executive officer is invalidated as a usurpation of legislative power. See Under 21, Catholic Home Bureau for Dependent Children v. City of New York, 65 N.Y.2d 344, 492 N.Y.S.2d 522, 482 N.E.2d 1 (1985) (mayor without authority to issue executive order prohibiting discrimination against homosexuals and bisexuals by city contractors). Cf. Prospect v. Cohalan, 65 N.Y.2d 867, 493 N.Y.S.2d 293, 482 N.E.2d 1209 (1985), reargument denied 65 N.Y.2d 1026, 494 N.Y.S.2d 306, 484 N.E.2d 669 (1985) (order issued by county's chief executive directing county officials to review an emergency response plan developed by a nuclear power company held a usurpation of legislative function). See also Hollins v. Powell, 773 F.2d 191 (8th Cir.1985), cert. denied 475 U.S. 1119, 106 S.Ct. 1635, 90 L.Ed.2d 181 (1986) (mayor who ordered arrest of members of city commission when they refused to adjourn a regularly scheduled meeting abused his authority; city was rendered liable under Federal Civil Rights Act). As to limits on the power of a city manager, see Nottingham v. City of Yukon, 766 P.2d 973 (Okl.1988) (power to compromise claim against city rests with legislative branch and cannot be exercised by city manager).

[93] See Ex parte Luening, 3 Cal.App. 76, 84 P. 445 (Dist.Ct.1906); Jackman v. Hamersley, 72 Idaho 301, 240 P.2d 829 (1952); Solomon v. Hughes, 24 Kan. 211 (1880); Orose v. Hodge Drive-It-Yourself Co., 132 Ohio St. 607, 9 N.E.2d 671 (1937), noted 11 U.Cin.L.Rev. 535 (1937); Mayhew v. City of Eugene, 56 Or. 102, 104 P. 727 (1909); City of Moundsville v. Velton, 35 W.Va. 217, 13 S.E. 373 (1891); City of Racine v. Smith, 272 Wis. 374, 75 N.W.2d 454 (1956).

[94] Warren v. State, 162 Neb. 623, 76 N.W.2d 728 (1956). But see Goomda v. Oklahoma City, 506 P.2d 991 (Okl.Crim. App.1973) (municipal court will take judicial notice of ordinance, but appellate court will not); Patton v. State, 112 Tex.Cr.R. 351, 16 S.W.2d 1072 (1929).

[95] As to cases initially heard in state court, see Old Colony Trust Co. v. Merchant Enterprises, 332 Mass. 484, 126 N.E.2d 112 (1955); City of Rolla v. Riden, 349 S.W.2d 255 (Mo.App.1961); Schulte v. Johnson, 106 Ohio St. 359, 140 N.E. 116 (1922); Jones v. State, 172 Tex.Cr.R. 100, 354 S.W.2d 160 (1962); State v. Pelletier, 123 Vt. 271, 185 A.2d 456 (1962). Cf. Carter v. City of Gadsden, 264 Ala. 544, 88 So.2d 689 (1955); Pankey v. Wyandotte Cab, Inc., 174 Kan. 17, 254 P.2d 305 (1953); Sprout v. Oklahoma Railway, 207 Okl. 118, 247 P.2d 972 (1952); City of Sweetwater v. Foster, 37 S.W.2d 799 (Tex.Civ.App.1931). But cf. Taylor v. Jennison, 335 S.W.2d 902 (Ky.1960) (ordinance introduced as to issue of negligence will be judicially noticed). See generally Wigmore, Evidence § 2572 (3d ed. 1940).

As to the knowledge that citizens are expected to have of city ordinances, see City of Chicago v. Atkins, 19 Ill.App.2d 177, 153 N.E.2d 302 (1958) (city ordinances presumed known by city inhabitants and by others dealing with city).

Chapter 12

TERRITORIAL COMPOSITION OF MUNICIPALITIES

Analysis

---

§ 12.1 Introduction

A municipal corporation, or other entity of local government, normally needs three things in order to engage in effective action: (1) territory over which the government has some control, (2) people to perform the functions of government, and (3) money with which to pay the costs of activities. This chapter will consider the first of these requisites: the territorial make-up of local units. First, we will consider the process by which local units and their boundaries are established—generally called "incorporation"—and then consider the processes by which territorial boundaries may be expanded ("annexation") and other methods of changing or terminating the territorial control of local governments (de-annexation, consolidation, dissolution, etc.).[1]

§ 12.2 Incorporation of Municipalities—Substantive Requirements

State legislatures normally have plenary power to prescribe the method by which units of local government may be organized, subject only to any limitations contained in the state constitution.[2] The prescribed method need not, and sometimes does not, require

---

[1] As to the differences among incorporation and annexation laws within the various states, see Zeinemann, Overlooked Linkages Between Municipal Incorporation and Annexation Laws: An In-Depth Look at Wisconsin's Experience, 39 Urban Law. 257 (2007), focusing on the laws of Wisconsin.

[2] State ex rel. Consol. School District No. 8 v. Smith, 343 Mo. 288, 121 S.W.2d 160 (1938); Atlantic Beach Hotel v. Larkin, 25 Misc.2d 511, 202 N.Y.S.2d 769 (1960). See Burton v. City of Tucson, 88 Ariz. 320,

consent of a majority, or any specified percentage, of the inhabitants or voters within the affected area.[3] The task of establishing requirements for incorporation is considered a strictly legislative task.[4] Statutes that might be interpreted as according discretion to some administrative body to allow or deny incorporation will be construed against the delegation of such discretion wherever possible;[5] and where delegation of such discretion is unavoidably found in a statute's terms, the statute may be held unconstitutional.[6] But here, as elsewhere, the trend is to allow the legislature more leniency than in the past to delegate tasks of a basically fact-finding nature. Thus, most cases say that if the legislature establishes the general requisites for incorporation, the job of determining whether or not particular areas meet the requirements may validly be delegated to a judicial or administrative body.[7] Similarly, statutory provisions that *do* (even though this is not constitutionally required) make incorporation depend on consent of the electorate in the affected area have been upheld as not involving unconstitutional delegations.[8]

---

356 P.2d 413 (1960) (power of legislature over incorporation is plenary). Similarly, the state legislature may modify or terminate previously established methods for incorporation of localities. Becker v. Adams, 37 N.J. 337, 181 A.2d 349 (1962). See City of Fort Lauderdale v. Town of Hacienda Village, Inc., 172 So.2d 451 (Fla.1965). And limitations on incorporation—such as prohibitions of new municipal incorporations within a certain radius of an existing city or town—have been sustained. Vernon v. State ex rel. City of San Antonio, 406 S.W.2d 236 (Tex.Civ.App.1966), ref'd n. r. e. See People ex rel. DuPage County v. Lowe, 67 Ill.App.2d 369, 214 N.E.2d 593 (1966), rev'd 36 Ill.2d 372, 224 N.E.2d 1; State ex rel. Dawson v. City of Victoria, 97 Kan. 638, 156 P. 705 (1916); In re Village of Oconomowoc Lake, 270 Wis. 530, 72 N.W.2d 544 (1955).

The possible advantages and problems of incorporation are well discussed in Lazega & Fletcher, The Politics of Municipal Incorporation in South Florida, 12 J. Land Use & Envtl. L. 215 (1997). See also Ihn, The Long Road to Self-Determination: A Critique of Municipal Incorporation Through the East Los Angeles Cityhood Movement, 13 Harv. Latino L. Rev. 67 (2010).

3 Berlin v. Gorham, 34 N.H. 266 (1856); Paterson v. Society for Establishing Useful Manufacturers, 24 N.J.L. 385 (1854). But state constitutions sometimes provide that the consent of inhabitants of the affected area must in some manner be obtained prior to incorporation. See State ex rel. Davis v. Town of Lake Placid, 109 Fla. 419, 147 So. 468 (1933). And state constitutions or statutes often now require an election as one step in the incorporation process. See note 33 *infra* and accompanying text.

4 See State ex rel. Mercer v. Town of Crestwood, 248 Iowa 627, 80 N.W.2d 489 (1957), supplemented 248 Iowa 627, 81 N.W.2d 452; State ex rel. Higgins v. Aicklen, 167 La. 456, 119 So. 425 (1929); Carolina-Virginia Coastal Highway v. Coastal Turnpike Authority, 237 N.C. 52, 74 S.E.2d 310 (1953); In re North Milwaukee, 93 Wis. 616, 67 N.W. 1033 (1896).

5 Attwood v. Wayne County, 349 Mich. 415, 84 N.W.2d 708 (1957). See State ex rel. Behrens v. Crismon, 354 Mo. 174, 188 S.W.2d 937 (1945); State ex rel. Williams v. Second Judicial District Court, 30 Nev. 225, 94 P. 70 (1908). Cf. State ex rel. Brunette v. Sutton, 71 N.D. 530, 3 N.W.2d 106 (1942) (approving authority has little discretion).

6 State ex rel. Luly v. Simons, 32 Minn. 540, 21 N.W. 750 (1884); In re Petition for Fond du Lac Metropolitan Sewerage District, 42 Wis.2d 323, 166 N.W.2d 225 (1969) (unconstitutional delegation of legislative authority where court was given discretion to decide whether creation of sewerage district would serve the interests of the parties). Questions of incorporation have been called ones of policy rather than of either law or fact—thus making them matters for the legislature, not the courts. See City of Galesburg v. Hawkinson, 75 Ill. 152 (1874).

7 People ex rel. Rhodes v. Fleming, 10 Colo. 553, 16 P. 298 (1887); Boone County v. Verona, 190 Ky. 430, 227 S.W. 804 (1921); People ex rel. Shumway v. Bennett, 29 Mich. 451 (1874); Board of Directors v. Kelly, 171 Or. 691, 137 P.2d 295 (1943). See Lyon v. City of Payette, 38 Idaho 705, 224 P. 793 (1924). The finding, by an administrative agency or lower court, of the requisite facts for incorporation is subject to possible judicial review. See Burnett v. Greene, 97 Fla. 1007, 122 So. 570 (1929). Cf. Parnell v. State ex rel. Wilson, 68 Ariz. 401, 206 P.2d 1047 (1949) (determination of whether an area is a city or town is a judicial task).

8 St. Paul Gaslight Co. v. Village of Sandstone, 73 Minn. 225, 75 N.W. 1050 (1898); State ex rel. Normandy Fire Protection District v. Smith, 358 Mo. 572, 216 S.W.2d 440 (1948). In Adams v. Beloit, 105 Wis. 363, 81 N.W. 869 (1900), a provision allowing inhabitants to vote on proposed incorporation of their area was held not to violate the constitutional prohibition of special laws.

Four substantive requirements for incorporation are commonly encountered, though seldom will all four of these be present in a particular statute. (1) Often, there is a *minimum population* prescribed that must reside within the designated area.[9] The minimum may vary, of course, according to the type of local unit that is to be formed—with, for instance, greater population required for incorporation as a city than for incorporation as a town. Sometimes the basic population requirement may be coupled with a requirement that there be at least a prescribed degree of density of population within the area.[10] Occasionally, a minimum permissible area is designated.[11] (2) Sometimes, there are rather vague requirements that the incorporation be *"right"* or *"reasonable."*[12] While appearing largely meaningless on their face, these provisions may allow reviewing courts to develop additional standards, as by considering whether the incorporation will benefit residents of the area.[13] (3) A number of statutes require—at least for incorporation of a city or town—that there be a *"community"* within the designated area, or that incorporation be for the good of the community, or even that there be a "city or town" (presumably in the everyday sense of those terms—even though the city or town is not yet incorporated as such) within the area. In a few states, the courts have ruled that there is an implied constitutional limitation on the legislature's power to provide for incorporation to the effect that this can only be authorized as to a "community." Such an implication may be drawn either from the general purpose of incorporation and the minimum population requirements,[14] or from constitutional language authorizing the legislature to allow incorporation of a "city," "town," etc.[15] In any case, without need for resort to constitutional language, requirements of a

---

9 See State ex rel. Smith v. Island Lake, 130 Minn. 100, 153 N.W. 257 (1915); State ex rel. Little v. Board of County Commissioners, 182 Neb. 419, 155 N.W.2d 351 (1967); Ellis v. State, 383 S.W.2d 635 (Tex.Civ.App.1964). Cf. State ex rel. Corbin v. Sabel, 138 Ariz. 253, 674 P.2d 316 (App. 1983) (county board lacks jurisdiction to incorporate town which does not contain population required by statute; official census data has exceptional reliability and is admissible through judicial notice, but may be rebutted by competent evidence).

10 An example is found in Vernon's Ann.Tex.Civ.Stat. art. 971, which provides that no city or town having a superficial area of more than 2 square miles shall incorporate if it has less than 2000 inhabitants; no city or town having a superficial area of more than 4 square miles shall incorporate if it has more than 2000 but less than 5000 inhabitants; and no city or town with more than 9 square miles of superficial area shall incorporate if it has more than 5000 but less than 10,000 inhabitants. This has been held applicable also in annexation proceedings, so that a city or town cannot after incorporation increase its superficial area, for instance, by annexation of additional territory where the result would be a superficial land area of more than 2 square miles holding less than 2000 inhabitants. City of Deer Park v. State ex rel. Shell Oil Co., 259 S.W.2d 284 (Tex.Civ.App.1953), aff'd 154 Tex. 174, 275 S.W.2d 77 (1954). See generally Mandelker, Standards for Municipal Incorporations on the Urban Fringe, 36 Tex.L.Rev. 271, 276 (1958).

11 See Fenton v. Ryan, 140 Wis. 353, 122 N.W. 756 (1909).

12 See Mandelker, *supra* note 10, at 286–80.

13 Thus, in Hoye v. Schaefer, 109 Ohio App. 489, 157 N.E.2d 140 (1959), a statute providing that incorporation could be invalidated if not "right" or "just" was used by court to strike down an attempt to incorporate a U-shaped area surrounding much of the city of Columbus.

14 State ex rel. Landis v. Boynton Beach, 129 Fla. 528, 177 So. 327 (1937) (territory must be sufficiently populated and industrialized to make incorporation necessary or desirable); State ex rel. Davis v. Lake Placid, 109 Fla. 419, 147 So. 468 (1933) (are inherent limits to the legislature's power to provide for incorporation, and population is essential to a municipal corporation). See, following these earlier authorities, State ex rel. Tropical Audubon Society v. Islandia, 224 So.2d 427 (Fla.App.1969).

15 See In re Village of Chubbuck, 71 Idaho 60, 226 P.2d 484 (1950); In re Incorporation of Elmwood Park, 9 Wis.2d 592, 101 N.W.2d 659 (1960); In re Incorporation of Village of Oconomowoc Lake, 7 Wis.2d 400, 97 N.W.2d 189 (1959); State ex rel. Holland v. Lammers, 113 Wis. 398, 86 N.W. 677 (1902). But cf. State v. Odell, 61 Wash.2d 476, 378 P.2d 932 (1963), where the statute merely specified a population requirement (300 inhabitants) and the court refused to read into the law any requirement of a "community."

"community" are often specified in state statutes,[16] or are "read-in" by judicial interpretation.[17] The "community" requirement is said to be satisfied if the area is reasonably homogeneous and compact, with a developed community center.[18]

(4) Overlapping the community requirement, a requirement is generally found—usually by implication rather than express provision—that areas to be incorporated into a single entity must be *contiguous.* Thus, totally detached tracts of land cannot be incorporated under a single government,[19] nor tracts separated by a body of water half a mile wide,[20] nor tracts connected only by a short strip, such as a road 40 feet wide and 2,640 feet long.[21] An irregular shape does not necessarily prevent an incorporation from being valid,[22] though the overall effect of the population, community, and contiguity requirements is that most validly incorporated areas will have to be reasonably compact units. Additional requirements for incorporation are occasionally included by the process of judicial construction,[23] and it is generally assumed—even if not specified—that land already included within an incorporated municipality is not subject to inclusion by a newly incorporating city or town.[24] From the "community" and other requirements, an

---

[16] See, interpreting such requirements, Parnell v. State ex rel. Wilson, 68 Ariz. 401, 206 P.2d 1047 (1949) (attempted incorporation of mostly unoccupied range and desert land held void); State ex rel. Northern Pump Co. v. So-Called Village of Fridley, 233 Minn. 442, 47 N.W.2d 204 (1951).

[17] People ex rel. County of DuPage v. Lowe, 67 Ill.App.2d 369, 214 N.E.2d 593 (1966) (village-in-fact must exist before incorporation of a village can occur); Petition to Incorporate the City of Duquesne, 322 S.W.2d 857 (Mo.1959) (incorporation should include only a compact center of population and any suburban areas connected therewith). See 1000 Friends of Oregon v. Wasco County Court, 68 Or.App. 765, 686 P.2d 375 (1984) (incorporation of city on rural land outside established urban growth boundary held a per se violation of statewide planning goals). See also People ex rel. Snowden v. Hurst, 401 Ill. 158, 81 N.E.2d 491 (1948), where a community was held necessary for the creation of a school district.

[18] See Scharping v. Johnson, 32 Wis.2d 383, 145 N.W.2d 691 (1966). See generally Note, Municipal Corporations: Formation: Judicial Review of Necessity for Urban Character, 3 Okl.L.Rev. 449 (1950) (concluding that an urban character was a prerequisite to incorporation as a city, but not as a town, under Oklahoma statutes).

Where a community is required for incorporation, an implication may also sometimes be found that the *entire* community should be included in the incorporation. See Harang v. State ex rel. West Columbia, 466 S.W.2d 8 (Tex.Civ.App.1971). But see State ex rel. Cole v. City of Hendersonville, 223 Tenn. 365, 445 S.W.2d 652 (1969) (incorporation of small part of densely settled area upheld).

[19] Larkin v. Bontatibus, 145 Conn. 570, 145 A.2d 133 (1958); Hillman v. City of Pocatello, 74 Idaho 69, 256 P.2d 1072 (1953). See Leatherman v. Alta Cliff Co., 114 Fla. 305, 153 So. 845 (1934); Enterprise v. State, 29 Fla. 128, 10 So. 740 (1892).

[20] Ocean Beach Heights v. Brown-Crummer Investment Co., 302 U.S. 614, 58 S.Ct. 385, 82 L.Ed. 478 (1938), reh. denied 303 U.S. 666, 58 S.Ct. 608, 82 L.Ed. 1123 (statute forbade incorporation of disconnected tracts).

[21] City of Springfield v. Bedolli, 85 Ill.App.2d 191, 228 N.E.2d 755 (1967). Cf. Wild v. People ex rel. Stephens, 227 Ill. 556, 81 N.E. 707 (1907) (not sufficient that a narrow strip one-and-a-half miles long was included merely to make two tracts contiguous). But cf. In re Village of Buffalo Grove, 128 Ill.App.2d 261, 261 N.E.2d 746 (1970) (sufficient for contiguity required by *annexation* statute where tract was joined to municipality by strip 675 feet long and 300 feet wide).

[22] People ex rel. Magnuson v. Kramer, 21 Ill.2d 392, 172 N.E.2d 757 (1961).

[23] See Mandelker, Standards for Municipal Incorporations on the Urban Fringe, 36 Tex.L.Rev. 271, 276–80 (1958). Cf. Town of Quita v. Heidgen, 247 Ark. 943, 448 S.W.2d 631 (1970), where an incorporation was invalidated because it was found to have been solely for the purpose of preventing annexation by another city.

[24] See State ex rel. Northern Pump Co. v. So-Called Village of Fridley, 233 Minn. 442, 47 N.W.2d 204 (1951). Cf. Incorporation of Town of Eastridge v. City of Aurora, 198 Colo. 440, 601 P.2d 1374 (1979) (area completely encircled by, and encompassed within, the exterior limits of city cannot be incorporated under Colorado law). And in some jurisdictions, statutes provide that incorporation cannot occur within a specified distance of already incorporated municipalities—in effect giving the existing municipalities a protected zone around them, for their possible subsequent annexation. See Burns v. City of Carrollton, 421 S.W.2d 758 (Tex.Civ.App.1967), interpreting a Texas statute forbidding incorporation within a certain distance of another

inference can often be drawn that large tracts of agricultural or unsettled land are not to be included within an incorporating municipality,[25] but such an inference often proves no great limitation: tracts, though rural in nature themselves, may be included if they are surrounded by or connected with more developed areas or are likely to be developed in the near future.[26]

§ 12.3 Incorporation of Municipalities—Procedure

Apart from the substantive requirements for incorporation, certain procedural steps are usually specified by state law. Five such steps are commonly found: (1) Incorporation is most often initiated by a *petition* signed by a specified percent of residents, electors, or owners of land—or the owners of a specified percentage of the land—within the area proposed for incorporation.[27] The petition must usually at least include a designation of the boundaries of the proposed entity, and often maps and surveys must accompany the petition.[28] (2) It is usually provided by statute that, before or when an incorporation petition is filed with the appropriate authority, *notice* must be given the public—as by publication in a newspaper of general circulation in the area, or by other designated means.[29] (3) Sometimes—though by no means always—statutes provide that a *period for*

---

city unless that city consents. Cf. Application for Incorporation as City of Sherwood, 241 Kan. 396, 736 P.2d 875 (1987) (statute upheld, against constitutional attacks, requiring a unanimous vote of board of county commissioners for a proposed incorporation of an area within 5 miles of an existing city); City of Sunland Park v. Santa Teresa Concerned Citizens Ass'n, 110 N.M. 95, 792 P.2d 1138 (1990) (under New Mexico statutes, residents seeking to incorporate area within "urbanized territory" of another city must present "conclusive proof" that city is unable to provide municipal services to area within same period of time that proposed incorporated municipality could provide those services).

[25] State ex rel. Richardson v. Larkin, 41 Tex.Civ.App. 253, 90 S.W. 912 (1905), error refused.

[26] See State ex inf. Rosenberger v. Bellflower, 129 Mo.App. 138, 108 S.W. 117 (1908) (agricultural lands were connected with lands used for town purposes; incorporation valid); State ex rel. Burchill v. City of Polytechnic, 194 S.W. 1136 (Tex.Civ.App.1917) (inclusion of undeveloped land permitted if it may benefit from the municipal government within a reasonable time). Cf. State ex rel. Perrin v. Hoard, 94 Tex. 527, 62 S.W. 1054 (1901) (couldn't be said as a matter of law that inclusion of 205 acres of farm land in town of 475 acres rendered incorporation invalid). It has been held that Indian lands may be included within an incorporating municipality. Agua Caliente Band v. Palm Springs, 347 F.Supp. 42 (C.D.Cal.1972).

[27] See, applying such laws, Cooper v. Town of Valley Head, 212 Ala. 125, 101 So. 874 (1924); Booth v. Copley, 283 Ky. 23, 140 S.W.2d 662 (1940). In Bridges v. City of Biloxi, 250 Miss. 717, 168 So.2d 40 (1964), it was held that once such a petition was filed with the designated authority, additional names could not be placed thereon.

[28] See Taylor v. Pile, 154 Colo. 516, 391 P.2d 670 (1964) (requirement of accurate map is mandatory; not sufficient that map "almost accurate"); Hoye v. Schaefer, 148 N.E.2d 532 (Ohio C.P.1957), aff'd 109 Ohio App. 489, 157 N.E.2d 140 (1959) (requirement of map mandatory); State ex rel. Brunette v. Sutton, 71 N.D. 530, 3 N.W.2d 106 (1942). In State ex rel. City of Azle v. City of Sanctuary, 467 S.W.2d 211 (Tex.Civ.App.1971), it is observed that only an incorporated municipality has definite metes and bounds and that an unincorporated municipality has no defined boundaries.

On the acquisition and use of a corporate name for a municipality, see 2 McQuillin, Municipal Corporations Chapter 5 (3d rev. ed. 1996). On the acquisition and use of a corporate seal, see 2 McQuillin *supra* Chapter 6.

[29] See, applying provisions for such notice, State ex rel. Galloway v. Roberts, 200 La. 36, 7 So.2d 607 (1942); Petition for Incorporation of Borough of Eden Park, 158 Pa.Super. 40, 43 A.2d 529 (1945). Cf. People v. Walker, 59 Ill.App.3d 192, 16 Ill.Dec. 736, 375 N.E.2d 843 (1978) (due process requires notice to all landowners in incorporating district where incorporation is begun by petition rather than legislative action); Matter of Incorporation of City of Mesa Vista, 104 Nev. 516, 762 P.2d 879 (1988) (incorporation petition, taking the place of an election, must be scrutinized closely; petition here held invalid where notice had not been given residents of other towns that those towns would, under the proposal, be incorporated into the new municipality). But see Board of County Commissioners v. Sims, 252 Ind. 531, 251 N.E.2d 9 (1969) (legislature need not give notice to anyone when incorporating municipalities or providing for such incorporation); Thorpe v. King, 248 Ind. 275, 221 N.E.2d 895 (1966) (no constitutional right to notice); Cherry v. Hayti Heights, 563 S.W.2d 72, 87 (Mo.1978)

possible protests shall follow the public notice of the petition. Such a period allows residents, or electors, or property-owners within the designated area to protest—usually by petition—the proposed incorporation. It is generally provided that a petition signed by a particular percentage of those eligible to sign will halt the incorporation effort.[30]

(4) The petition of those proposing the incorporation must be *filed* with, and *approved* by, a designated officer or body. Most often this is the county governing body or chief executive officer; occasionally it is a local judge or court. Often the approving authority has little if any discretion in deciding whether or not to proceed with the proposed incorporation: if the statutory requirements are met, the procedure must be allowed to continue, and the approving authority can be compelled, by writ of mandamus, to act.[31] In a few states, however, the approving authority is now given discretion to approve or deny a petition after weighing such factors as present cost and adequacy of government services in the area and the effect of the proposed incorporation on neighboring communities.[32] (5) After approval by the designated authority, the incorporation must also, in most states, be approved at an *election* held within the area designated for incorporation.[33] Those eligible to vote for state offices are usually eligible to vote in the incorporation election, and a majority of votes cast in favor of incorporation at the election will normally bring about that result.[34]

(power to incorporate is not subject to due process requirements of notice). Cf. State v. Zimmerschied, 559 S.W.2d 178 (Mo.1977) (requirements of notice and hearing as to incorporation of ambulance district were merely directory, not mandatory).

30 See 1 Antieau, Municipal Corporation Law § 1.11 (1998).

31 Application of Tarter, 18 Misc.2d 617, 185 N.Y.S.2d 277 (1959), aff'd 8 A.D.2d 943, 190 N.Y.S.2d 639 (1959) aff'd 8 N.Y.2d 718, 200 N.Y.S.2d 823, 167 N.E.2d 459 (1960); McManus v. Skoko, 255 Or. 374, 467 P.2d 426 (1970); Harley v. Town Board of Delafield, 7 Wis.2d 303, 96 N.W.2d 363 (1959). Any findings of the approving authority are subject to judicial review. Denny v. Des Moines County, 143 Iowa 466, 121 N.W. 1066 (1909); Shreves v. Gibson, 76 Kan. 709, 92 P. 584 (1907); Wooten v. Hickahala Drainage District, 116 Miss. 787, 77 So. 795 (1918). But the reviewing court should only determine whether the requisite facts were established and the correct procedures followed. Kenney v. Bank of Miami, 19 Ariz. 338, 170 P. 866 (1918). Thus, a decision to allow incorporation will not be reversed if the evidence indicates all requirements are met. See Board of County Commissioners v. Sims, 252 Ind. 531, 251 N.E.2d 9 (1969) (sufficient evidence to justify decision). Sometimes, the approving authority is required to hold a hearing before making a decision on incorporation. On judicial participation in the processes of incorporation and annexation, see generally Cox, Application of "Sunset" Principles to State Judicial Functions: Judges as Fact Finders, 33 Okl. L.Rev. 681, 690–96 (1980).

32 See, as an example, West's Ann.Cal.Gov.Code §§ 54793, 54796. Cf. City of Wichita v. Board of County Comm'rs of Sedgwick County, 232 Kan. 149, 652 P.2d 717 (1982), saying that advisability of incorporation in Kansas is left to legislative wisdom of board of county commissioners, who are not bound by weight of the evidence and may grant or deny incorporation even though evidence favors a contrary result. A reviewing court in Kansas is then limited to determining whether the board acted fraudulently, arbitrarily, or capriciously, whether the board's order is supported by substantial evidence, and whether the board's order is within the scope of its authority. Appeal of City of Lenexa, 232 Kan. 568, 657 P.2d 47 (1983).

33 See Cooper v. Town of Valley Head, *supra* note 27. Proper notice of the election to those eligible to vote is often required. See State ex rel. Pope v. Shields, 140 So.2d 144 (Fla.App.1962); People v. Snedeker, 160 N.Y. 350, 54 N.E. 659 (1899). On election requirements and procedures, see generally Mandelker, Municipal Incorporation on the Urban Fringe: Procedures for Determination and Review, 18 La.L.Rev. 628 (1958). Where a recent attempt at incorporation has unsuccessfully been made, some states forbid another attempt within a legislatively prescribed period of time, *if* the area involved is substantially the same. See Central Manufacturing District v. Board of Supervisors, 176 Cal.App.2d 850, 1 Cal.Rptr. 733 (Dist.Ct.1960).

34 See Bray v. Stewart, 239 Mich. 340, 214 N.W. 193 (1927). But in Clay v. Thornton, 253 S.C. 209, 169 S.E.2d 617 (1969), appeal dism'd 397 U.S. 39, 90 S.Ct. 814, 25 L.Ed.2d 40, the state constitution was held to require that incorporation be approved by a majority of those residing within the area, not just a majority of those voting in the election.

Two trends as to municipal incorporations are apparent: (1) While requirements relating to incorporation petitions and protests have in the past often been rather "undemocratic" in nature, as where they were framed in terms of the owners of a designated percentage of the property within the region, such "property-holding" restrictions are now often being eliminated or struck down as unconstitutional.[35] (2) Increasing state supervision of local incorporations is found, as where state "boundary commissions" or comparable bodies are established to approve or reject proposed municipalities.[36] The required approval of such a body may be in addition to, but often is now instead of, that of the county or other authority that formerly had power to approve petitions for incorporation; and some state bodies may initiate incorporation proceedings without the need for a petition by local residents. The state control is intended to bring better planning and coordination to urban development.

§ 12.4 Annexation by Municipalities—Substantive Requirements

The original boundaries of a municipality are established at the time of incorporation, as described in the prior section. Expansion of those boundaries occurs by the process called "annexation." Control over expansion of municipal boundaries resides initially in the state. Non-home rule cities ordinarily have only such power to annex

---

[35] See Curtis v. Board of Supervisors, 7 Cal.3d 942, 104 Cal.Rptr. 297, 501 P.2d 537 (1972), striking down as violative of equal protection a law that provided for incorporation proceedings to be terminated if a written protest was filed by signers representing 51% of the assessed valuation of the land within the boundaries of the proposed incorporation. Compare Sacramento County Bd. of Supervisors v. Local Agency Formation Comm'n, 3 Cal.4th 903, 13 Cal.Rptr.2d 245, 838 P.2d 1198 (1992), cert. denied 507 U.S. 988, 113 S.Ct. 1588, 123 L.Ed.2d 154 (1993) (statute precluding county residents from voting in election to confirm municipal incorporation within county unless they reside in territory to be incorporated does not violate equal protection clauses of U.S. or California Constitutions). See generally Hagman & Disco, One-Man One-Vote as a Constitutional Imperative for Needed Reform of Incorporation and Boundary Change Laws, 2 Urban Lawyer 459 (1971). See also Hagman, The Unconstitutionality of Incorporation and Boundary Change Laws as an Impetus for Needed Reform (Institute of Government & Public Affairs, U.C.L.A.1970). The decisions invalidating property-owner requirements as to eligibility to vote in bond elections would seem sound authority for the invalidity of any comparable requirements for voting in incorporation elections. See Chapter 15 *infra*.

[36] See, discussing the activities of such commissions, Mobil Oil Corp. v. Local Boundary Commission, 518 P.2d 92 (Alaska 1974) (agency action in approving formation of a borough will be upheld if it has a reasonable basis); Incorporation of Indian Hills, 8 N.C.App. 564, 174 S.E.2d 850 (1970); Pleasant Prairie v. Johnson, 34 Wis.2d 8, 148 N.W.2d 27 (1967) (petitions for incorporation referred to Director of Planning, who may approve or deny; his decisions will be upheld if supported by substantial evidence). Some of the commissions also rule on petitions for annexation (*i.e.*, enlargement of municipalities, discussed in the next couple sections *infra*). See Rockwood v. State Boundary Commission, 45 Mich.App. 265, 206 N.W.2d 530 (1973) (commission passes on petitions for annexation and incorporation); City of Wood Village v. Portland Metropolitan Area Local Government Boundary Commission, 48 Or.App. 79, 616 P.2d 528 (1980) (in considering petition for annexation, boundary commission erred in failing to consider effect the annexation would have on "island" area surrounded by annexing city). A review board's decision on a proposed incorporation or annexation will normally be upheld if supported by substantial evidence. See In re Northwest Pasco Annexation, 100 Wash.2d 864, 676 P.2d 425 (1984); Spokane County Fire Protection Dist. No. 9 v. Spokane County Boundary Review Bd., 97 Wash.2d 922, 652 P.2d 1356 (1982) ("substantial evidence" standard for reviewing county boundary review board decision said to be significantly narrower in scope than the "clearly erroneous" standard). See generally 1 Antieau, Municipal Corporation Law § 1.16 (1998).

On general trends as to incorporation in the past, see Advisory Comm'n on Inter-governmental Relations, Urban America and the Federal System 77 (Oct., 1969) (fewer incorporations during the 1960's than in prior decades); Schmandt, The Municipal Incorporation Trend (1961) (most incorporations in the 1950's were in West, South, and North Central regions; few in the East; many incorporations were within metropolitan areas).

territory as is specifically given them by state statute.[37] Home-rule cities in some states are accorded the power of annexation by the state constitution; otherwise, they also acquire this power only by statute—in any case, this is considered an area of "state-wide" (as opposed to purely local) concern, so that state law will prevail over municipal law in situations of conflict.[38] Annexation is a legislative function; so if an act of annexation is challenged in the courts, the role of the judiciary is normally limited to determining whether or not the conditions prescribed by the state legislature (and the constitution, where relevant) have been met.[39] But a few states, by specific statutory provision or by judicial interpretation of the statutes, allow the courts a greater role in ruling on the wisdom of annexation—as in Virginia, where the need and expediency of annexation may be judicially considered.[40]

---

[37] See Pittsburgh, C., C. & St. L. Ry. Co. v. City of Anderson, 176 Ind. 16, 95 N.E. 363 (1911); Atchison & Nebraska Railroad v. Maquilkin, 12 Kan. 301 (1873); City of New York v. Lawrence, 250 N.Y. 429, 165 N.E. 836 (1929). Cf. Oregon Short Line Railroad v. Chubbuck, 83 Idaho 62, 357 P.2d 1101 (1960) (municipality can annex territory only within the limitations set by state legislature).

[38] See People ex rel. Scholler v. Long Beach, 155 Cal. 604, 102 P. 664 (1904); Wheeler v. City of Brownsville, 148 Tex. 61, 220 S.W.2d 457 (1949); State ex rel. Bowen v. Kruegel, 67 Wn.2d 673, 409 P.2d 458 (1965). For cases interpreting state constitutional provisions giving the power of annexation directly to home-rule cities, see City of Hannibal v. Winchester, 391 S.W.2d 279 (Mo.1965) (constitutional method is the exclusive one for annexation by charter cities); City of Irving v. Dallas County Flood Control District, 383 S.W.2d 571 (Tex.1964); Pelly v. Harris County Water Control & Improvement District, 145 Tex. 443, 198 S.W.2d 450 (1946) (home-rule cities can annex under constitutional authority).

On annexation, see generally Sengstock, Annexation: A Solution to the Metropolitan Area Problem (Mich.Legal Publications 1960); Recent Legislation Comment, New Control over Municipal Formation and Annexation, 4 Santa Clara Law. 125 (1964); Comment, Annexation by Municipal Corporations, 37 Wash.L.Rev. 404 (1962). On trends regarding annexations in recent years, see Mandelker, Netsch, Salsich, & Griffith, State and Local Government in a Federal System 85–86 (7th ed. 2010) (most annexations now occur in suburban areas). See generally, Tyson, Annexation and the Mid-size Metropolis: New Insights in the Age of Mobile Capital, 73 U. Pitt. L. Rev. 505 (2012). See also Comment, Bargain Basement Annexation: How Municipalities Subvert the Intent of North Carolina Annexation Laws, 29 N.C. Cent. L.J. 77 (2006).

[39] City of Decorah v. Peterson, 203 N.W.2d 629 (Iowa 1973); City of Cedar Falls v. Sieglaff, 259 Iowa 263, 144 N.W.2d 116 (1966); State ex rel. Kreamer v. City of Overland Park, 192 Kan. 654, 391 P.2d 128 (1964). See Fairview Public Utility District v. City of Anchorage, 368 P.2d 540 (Alaska 1962), appeal dism'd 371 U.S. 5, 83 S.Ct. 39, 9 L.Ed.2d 49 (determination of what parts of state should be within a city is a political matter for the legislature); City of Greenwood Village v. Petitioners for Proposed City of Centennial, 3 P.3d 427 (Colo. 2000) (role of judiciary is to respect and carry out the statutes on incorporation and annexation). A number of cases have invalidated statutes that delegated to the court the task of determining *what* conditions must be satisfied for annexation to occur, rather than merely the task of determining *whether* certain legislatively established prerequisites had been met. Auburndale v. Adams Packing Association, 171 So.2d 161 (Fla.1965) (separation of powers violated); City of Louisville v. Kraft, 297 S.W.2d 39 (Ky.1956), cert. denied 359 U.S. 953, 79 S.Ct. 740, 3 L.Ed.2d 761; Town of Beloit v. City of Beloit, 37 Wis.2d 637, 155 N.W.2d 633 (1968). See Botsford v. City of Norman, 226 F.Supp. 258 (W.D.Okl.1964), aff'd 354 F.2d 491, 494 (10th Cir.1965) (annexation called a purely legislative function); State ex rel. Klise v. Riverdale, 244 Iowa 423, 57 N.W.2d 63 (1953) (courts and other approving agencies are limited to determining whether standards set by the legislature are met); Goethal v. Board of Supervisors, 361 Mich. 104, 104 N.W.2d 794 (1960) (political and economic advisability of annexation are for legislature to determine). Cf. Dillon Real Estate Co. v. City of Topeka, 284 Kan. 662, 163 P.3d 298 (2007) (power of annexation is vested exclusively in legislatures, and failure to comply with legislation nullifies attempted annexation). See generally Note, Municipal Annexation in North Carolina: The Pros, the Cons, and the Judiciary, 27 N.C. Cent. L.J. 224 (2005).

[40] See County of Fairfax v. Town of Fairfax, 201 Va. 362, 111 S.E.2d 428 (1959), listing a number of factors that the court should weigh in determining whether annexation is needed and expedient. The Virginia statutory language was held not unconstitutionally vague in Citizens Committee v. Lynchburg, 400 F.Supp. 68 (W.D.Va.1975), aff'd in part and vac'd in part 528 F.2d 816, application denied 423 U.S. 1043, 96 S.Ct. 766, 46 L.Ed.2d 632. Cf., under an earlier statute, Henrico County v. City of Richmond, 106 Va. 282, 55 S.E. 683 (1906) (court may necessarily have to decide some legislative questions in giving its judgment). For cases from other jurisdictions where the court considers, to some extent, the wisdom of annexation, see Smith v. Town of Culver, 140 Ind.App. 508, 224 N.E.2d 59 (1967) (court can deny annexation if not in best interests of territory

Under almost all statutes, and with usually only a few designated exceptions, there is one clear requirement for municipal annexation of land: *contiguity* of the territory to the existing municipality.[41] This is ordinarily taken to mean that the annexed area must be adjacent to the annexing city or town—that, at a minimum, the annexed tract must touch the city or town at some point.[42] But the contiguity requirement is usually not taken to preclude the annexation of long strips of land touching the annexing municipality only at some rather narrow point;[43] nor to preclude annexation of

---

to be annexed); Common Council v. Town Board, 23 A.D.2d 381, 261 N.Y.S.2d 144 (1965) (sustaining law under which court can determine whether annexation is in public interest). Cf. City of St. Joseph v. Hankinson, 312 S.W.2d 4 (Mo.1958) (upholding statute under which courts can refuse annexation if not reasonable and necessary); Village of Wakefield v. Utecht, 90 Neb. 252, 133 N.W. 240 (1911) (courts approve annexations that are just and equitable); State ex rel. Loofbourrow v. Board of County Commissioners, 104 Ohio App. 541, 150 N.E.2d 498 (1957), aff'd 167 Ohio St. 156, 146 N.E.2d 721 (1957) (board of county commissioners has much discretion in granting or denying petitions for annexation). But cf. City of Claremore v. Town of Verdigris, 50 P.3d 208 (Okla. 2001), where the court invalidated a statute authorizing the court to consider the "substantial government interest" in an annexation because this involved a political, not a judicial, consideration.

[41] Kalb v. West Helena, 249 Ark. 1123, 463 S.W.2d 368 (1971); Clark v. Holt, 218 Ark. 504, 237 S.W.2d 483 (1951); People ex rel. Hamilton v. City of Santa Barbara, 205 Cal.App.2d 501, 23 Cal.Rptr. 240 (Dist.Ct.1962); City of Denver v. Coulehan, 20 Colo. 471, 39 P. 425 (1894); Hillman v. City of Pocatello, 74 Idaho 69, 256 P.2d 1072 (1953); People ex rel. Henderson v. City of Bloomington, 38 Ill.App.2d 9, 186 N.E.2d 159 (1962); Spaulding School District v. Waukegan, 18 Ill.2d 526, 165 N.E.2d 283 (1960); State ex rel. Meek v. Kansas City, 93 Kan. 420, 144 P. 218 (1914); Niobrara v. Tichy, 158 Neb. 517, 63 N.W.2d 867 (1954); In Re Lancaster City Ordinance, 374 Pa. 546, 98 A.2d 34 (1953); City of Arlington v. City of Grand Prairie, 451 S.W.2d 284 (Tex.Civ.App.1970); City of Irving v. Callaway, 363 S.W.2d 832 (Tex.Civ.App.1962), ref'd n. r. e. See Guthrie v. City of Bloomington, 143 Ind.App. 615, 242 N.E.2d 37 (1968) (no compact area found); Ridings v. City of Owensboro, 383 S.W.2d 510 (Ky.1964).

[42] Common Council v. Town Board, 37 A.D.2d 459, 327 N.Y.S.2d 28 (1971) ("adjoining" means touching or contiguous); Watson v. Doolittle, 10 Ohio App.2d 143, 226 N.E.2d 771, 39 O.O.2d 267 (1967) ("adjacent," "adjoining," and "contiguous" are synonymous words); City of Houston v. Houston Endowment, Inc., 428 S.W.2d 706 (Tex.Civ.App.1968), motion denied 438 S.W.2d 935, ref'd n. r. e. ("adjacent" means in the vicinity of, and contiguous to, the annexing city). See City of Safford v. Town of Thatcher, 17 Ariz.App. 25, 495 P.2d 150 (1972), listing various definitions of "contiguous"; Goodin v. Board of Education, 601 P.2d 88 (Okl.1979), defining both "annexation" and "contiguous" in regard to question of school-district annexation. Cf. Cesario v. City of Colorado Springs, 200 Colo. 459, 616 P.2d 113 (Colo.1980) (statute allowed annexation of property having two-thirds boundary contiguity with city; measurements must be confined solely to perimeter of area proposed to be annexed); City of Ada v. Whitaker, 202 Okl. 249, 212 P.2d 482 (1949) ("adjacent" means abutting on). But cf. Cox v. Municipal Boundary Comm'n, 120 N.M. 703, 905 P.2d 741 (N.M. App. 1995) ("contiguous" means in physical contact or close proximity); Lyons v. Lake Geneva, 56 Wis.2d 331, 202 N.W.2d 228 (1972) (property can be contiguous though not touching, if it is near the municipality). See generally Annot., What Land is Contiguous or Adjacent to Municipality so as to be Subject to Annexation, 49 A.L.R.3d 589 (1973). See also 56 Am.Jur.2d Municipal Corporations, Counties, and Other Political Subdivisions § 65 (1971). As made clear by most of the above-cited authorities, contiguity is a question of law for the court. Because of this, judicial review is generally de novo. See Board of County Comm'rs v. City of Aurora, 62 P.3d 1049, 1052 (Colo. App. 2002).

In Costco Wholesale Corp. v. City of Beaverton, 206 Or.App. 380, 136 P.3d 1219 (2006), it was held that Oregon statutes require complete contiguity for annexation to occur; the statutory phrase "surrounded by" requires that the territory annexed has to be completely enclosed by and contiguous with the corporate boundaries of the city, or the corporate boundaries of the city and a body of water. While that view seems unusually strict, it is generally agreed that statutory requirements of contiguity require some actual touching, not merely that the annexed territory be "nearby" the annexing municipality. See Board of County Comm'rs v. City of Cheyenne, 2004 WY 16, 85 P.3d 999, 1005–09 (2004) (subdivision that was separated from city by approximately one-quarter of a mile was not contiguous or adjacent and thus could not be annexed).

[43] Botsford v. City of Norman, 226 F.Supp. 258 (W.D.Okl.1964), aff'd 354 F.2d 491 (10th Cir.1965); Bierschenk v. City of Omaha, 178 Neb. 715, 135 N.W.2d 12 (1965); Saranac Lake v. Gillispie, 261 App. Div. 854, 24 N.Y.S.2d 403 (1941); Sharp v. Oklahoma City, 181 Okl. 425, 74 P.2d 383 (1937); Fox Development Co. v. City of San Antonio, 468 S.W.2d 338 (Tex.1971); Wichita Falls v. Bowen, 143 Tex. 45, 182 S.W.2d 695 (1944). See People ex rel. Forde v. Corte Madera, 115 Cal.App.2d 32, 251 P.2d 988 (1952). But cf. Ridings v. Owensboro, *supra* note 41 (annexation of a long corridor not necessarily void but may be struck down by court as abuse of discretion); State ex rel. City of West Orange v. City of Orange, 300 S.W.2d 705 (Tex.Civ.App.1957) (annexation

irregularly shaped areas,[44] or very small areas.[45] And where a number of tracts are annexed at once, it is not necessary that each tract adjoin the annexing municipality, so long as the tracts are contiguous to one another and one of them adjoins the municipality.[46] Thus, it would seem that the weight of authority supports the view that contiguity is the key to the validity of annexation, and that compactness—of either the territory annexed or of the resulting municipality after the annexation is complete—is irrelevant. However, a minority view followed in several states requires that the annexed territory must have a "substantial" common boundary, or a common boundary of "reasonable length," with the annexing municipality.[47] In a few states, the authorizing

---

of corridor may be attacked as abuse of power). Annexation of long, narrow strips is often referred to as "strip," "shoestring," or "corridor" annexation. Sometimes, the shape is more like that of an hourglass. See Donohue v. Village of Fox Point, 275 Wis. 182, 81 N.W.2d 521 (1957), cert. denied, 355 U.S. 867, 78 S.Ct. 115, 2 L.Ed.2d 74, rehearing denied, 355 U.S. 920, 78 S.Ct. 337, 2 L.Ed.2d 280. Statutes in a few states forbid "strip annexation." See Salt River Project Agricultural Imp. & Power Dist. v. City of St. Johns, 149 Ariz. 282, 718 P.2d 184 (1986), discussing such a statute. Cf. City of Middletown v. McGee, 39 Ohio St.3d 284, 530 N.E.2d 902 (1988) (annexation of roadway extending outward from city would amount to a strip or gerrymandered annexation of the type generally disapproved as violating contiguity and territorial integrity requirements).

Where the bulk of the annexed property is connected to the annexing city by a narrow "stem," the annexation is sometimes referred to as the "cherry stem" variety, which, like other annexations of irregularly shaped parcels, is usually held not per se unreasonable or invalid. See Morsman v. City of Madras, 191 Or.App. 149, 81 P.3d 711 (2003). (For subsequent history of the *Morsman* case, see Morsman v. City of Madras, 203 Or.App. 546, 126 P.3d 6 (2006), in which the annexation was again upheld.) Some jurisdictions require that the "stem" or corridor that is used to provide the connection to the otherwise discontinguous tracts of land must itself have a tangible municipal value or purpose at the time of annexation. See In re De-Annexation of Certain Real Property from the City of Seminole, 102 P.3d 120, 130 (Okla. 2004), applying Oklahoma statutes. Cf. Griffin v. City of Robards, 990 S.W.2d 634, 640 (Ky. 1999) (if only a barren corridor exists, there is no contiguity). Compare City of Claremore v. Town of Verdigris, 50 P.3d 208 (Okla. 2001) (two intervening strips of land between the annexing town's strip and the annexed property could be ignored for purposes of determining contiguity).

[44] See People ex rel. Averna v. City of Palm Springs, 51 Cal.2d 38, 331 P.2d 4 (1958); Burlingame v. San Mateo County, 90 Cal.App.2d 705, 203 P.2d 807 (1949) (horseshoe-shaped territory); Tovey v. City of Charleston, 237 S.C. 475, 117 S.E.2d 872 (1961). Cf. Rivergate Residents Ass'n v. Portland Metropolitan Area Local Gov't Boundary Comm'n, 70 Or.App. 205, 689 P.2d 326 (1984), review denied 298 Or. 553, 695 P.2d 49 (1985), where the court said that annexation of an irregularly shaped parcel raises a red flag as to the reasonableness of the action, but nonetheless upheld an annexation that created an "island" of certain unannexed territory. But cf. Snohomish County v. Hinds, 61 Wash.App. 371, 810 P.2d 84 (1991) ("flag pole shape" of annexed territory found abnormally irregular; county boundary review board's decision to deny annexation upheld). See also Costco Wholesale Corp. v. City of Beaverton, 343 Or. 18, 161 P.3d 926 (2007) (city had statutory authority to annex property without consent of owners if the city boundaries completely and contiguously surround the property that was annexed—often called "island" annexation; but this did not give the city the authority to annex only a portion of the "island").

[45] City of Sherwood v. Hardin, 230 Ark. 762, 325 S.W.2d 75 (1959).

[46] Hendricks v. City of Nampa, 93 Idaho 95, 456 P.2d 262 (1969); Huff v. City of Lafayette, 108 Ind. 14, 8 N.E. 701 (1886); Bettendorf v. Abeln, 261 Iowa 404, 154 N.W.2d 836 (1967); McGraw v. Merryman, 133 Md. 247, 104 A. 540 (1918); State ex inf. Taylor v. North Kansas City, 360 Mo. 374, 228 S.W.2d 762 (1950); In re Sadler, 142 Pa. 511, 21 A. 978 (1891); Tovey v. City of Charleston, *supra* note 44; Lefler v. City of Dallas, 177 S.W.2d 231 (Tex.Civ.App.1943). See City of Leawood v. City of Overland Park, 245 Kan. 283, 777 P.2d 830 (1989) (annexation of multiple contiguous tracts under one hearing and one ordinance was proper where owners had consented and part of annexed land adjoined city). But see Banzer v. City of Wichita, 237 Kan. 798, 703 P.2d 812 (1985) (statute which allows annexation of land that adjoins city does not allow municipality to use multiple sequential annexation ordinances for tracts that do not adjoin city when the annexation is commenced).

[47] People ex rel. Cherry Valley Fire Protection District v. Rockford, 122 Ill.App.2d 272, 258 N.E.2d 577 (1970); People ex rel. Cherry Valley Fire Protection District v. Rockford, 120 Ill.App.2d 275, 256 N.E.2d 653 (Ill.App.1970); Morgan Park v. City of Chicago, 255 Ill. 190, 99 N.E. 388 (1912); Township of Owosso v. City of Owosso, 25 Mich.App. 460, 181 N.W.2d 541 (1970), aff'd 385 Mich. 587, 189 N.W.2d 421 (1971); Town of Mount Pleasant v. City of Racine, 24 Wis.2d 41, 127 N.W.2d 757 (1964). See Potvin v. Chubbuck, 76 Idaho 453, 284 P.2d 414 (1955) (land 3 miles from annexing municipality was to be connected only by five-foot strip; no

statutes now establish minimum requirements as to the length of the common boundary between the annexed and the annexing territory.[48] Under either statutory or common-law rules, an annexation is not necessarily voided by the contiguity requirement if a stream separates the annexed territory from the municipality, so long as the stream is not too wide and is spanned by bridges.[49] Sometimes, statutes remove the contiguity requirement as to annexations for certain limited purposes (as for a city's annexing a water supply) or in certain limited situations (as where the annexed territory is separated from the municipality only by a road or a railroad right-of-way).

The only other substantive requirement of importance as to annexation is the requirement that the annexed territory be suitable for urban purposes or development. At common law, a standard of reasonableness is here applied,[50] and the annexation will be upheld so long as there are possibilities of developing the land for urban uses in the foreseeable future, plus reasonable possibilities of the city providing governmental services within that time.[51] While annexation is subject to challenge as resulting in a

---

contiguity); City of Pasadena v. State ex rel. City of Houston, 442 S.W.2d 325 (Tex.1969). Compare BJ Hough, LLC, v. City of Cheyenne, 287 P.3d 761 (Wyo. 2012) (degree of contact between ranch property and city, the location, and the character of the ranch parcel were sufficient to support finding that annexed ranch property touched city "to a substantial degree," as statute required for annexation). Cf. Reafsnyder v. Warsaw, 155 Ind.App. 455, 293 N.E.2d 540 (1973) (if alleged contiguity is a mere subterfuge for expanding boundaries and resulting city would have little unity, annexation can be held invalid).

[48] See, applying such requirements, People ex rel. Hamilton v. City of Santa Barbara, *supra* note 41; Williams v. Town of Grifton, 19 N.C.App. 462, 199 S.E.2d 288 (1973).

[49] Garner v. Benson, 224 Ark. 215, 272 S.W.2d 442 (1954) (area to be annexed separated from city by a creek); Vestal v. City of Little Rock, 54 Ark. 321, 15 S.W. 891 (1891), adhered to, 54 Ark. 321, 16 S.W. 291 (1891); Hendricks v. City of Nampa, *supra* note 46; People ex rel. Redford v. City of Burley, 86 Idaho 519, 388 P.2d 996 (1964); Blanchard v. Bissell, 11 Ohio St. 96 (1860). See Vogel v. City of Little Rock, 54 Ark. 335, 15 S.W. 836 (1891), aff'd 55 Ark. 609, 19 S.W. 13; McGraw v. Merryman, *supra* note 46; Pinckney v. City of Beaufort, 296 S.C. 142, 370 S.E.2d 909 (App. 1988) (annexation of tract upheld despite its location across the tidal arm of a river from the annexing city, with the only access via a road across unannexed county property). But cf. Re Lancaster City Ordinance, *supra* note 41, where the court in dictum suggested that land separated from a city by a lake would not be contiguous. Compare Williams v. Town of Salina, 114 P.3d 482 (Okla. Civ. App. 2005) (a genuine issue of material fact existed as to whether annexed property, which was more than a mile away from the annexing city across a lake, but was connected by a bridge, met the contiguity requirement). As to the relevance on the contiguity issue of a road or right-of-way between the annexing municipality and the land to be annexed, see Town of Erie v. Town of Frederick, 251 P.3d 500 (Colo. App. 2010) (contiguity not affected by existence of public right-of-way).

[50] See City of Fulton v. Dawson, 325 S.W.2d 505 (Mo.App.1959); Town of Brookfield v. City of Brookfield, 274 Wis. 638, 80 N.W.2d 800 (1957) (annexation can be upheld though most of the territory is agricultural land).

[51] See Woodson Terrace v. Herklotz, 349 S.W.2d 446 (Mo.App.1961). While courts are not inclined to inquire into the motives for annexation, an annexation may be struck down if it appears to have been initiated by the city solely in order to obtain additional revenue and if there is no reasonable prospect of substantial city services being extended to the area. See United States v. City of Bellevue, 474 F.2d 473 (8th Cir.1973), cert. denied 414 U.S. 827, 94 S.Ct. 46, 38 L.Ed.2d 60 (attempted annexation of Strategic Air Command base); Chevron U.S.A., Inc. v. City of North Salt Lake, 711 P.2d 228 (Utah 1985) (applying Utah statutes, court invalidates attempted annexation of land owned by Chevron Company on ground that city's sole purpose was acquisition of revenue, with no accompanying ability to render municipal services). Cf. United States v. McGee, 432 F.Supp. 557 (S.D.Ohio 1977) (city enjoined from annexing air base). Compare Chidester v. City of Hobart, 631 N.E.2d 908 (Ind.1994), appeal after remand 631 N.E.2d 908 (Ind.1994), where a city's annexation ordinance was upheld because the city had plans to provide services to the annexed area equivalent to those being offered within the rest of the city. Under statutes in Oklahoma, certain rural lands, though they can be annexed, cannot be taxed by the annexing city unless municipal services are furnished the residents thereof. See In the Matter of Assessment of Certain Property, 519 P.2d 482 (Okl.1974).

Land is not ineligible for annexation merely because it is owned by some government. Howard v. Commissioners of the Sinking Fund, 344 U.S. 624, 73 S.Ct. 465, 97 L.Ed. 617 (1953) (U.S. naval ordinance plant annexed to city); Jarl Co. v. Village of Croton-on-Hudson, 148 Misc. 150, 265 N.Y.S. 271 (1932), aff'd 238

violation of equal protection and/or of civil-rights statutes, the courts seem reluctant to find such violation, even where relatively undeveloped areas are annexed, so long as statutory methods for annexation have been followed and a valid municipal purpose for the annexation exists.[52] By statute, some states now specifically forbid the annexation of rural, or undeveloped, or unplatted lands.[53]

App.Div. 865, 263 N.Y.S. 956 (1933), aff'd 262 N.Y. 551, 188 N.E. 60 (1933) (county-owned parklands); Day v. City of Salem, 65 Or. 114, 131 P. 1028 (1913) (state property); Wichita Falls v. Bowen, *supra* note 43 (U.S. military reservation). But see Nilson Enterprises, Inc. v. City of Great Falls, 190 Mont. 341, 621 P.2d 466 (Mont.1980) (city could not annex state-owned land without state's consent). A municipality may annex federal land without the federal government's consent. Surplus Trading Co. v. Cook, 281 U.S. 647, 50 S.Ct. 455, 74 L.Ed. 1091 (1930). But see Your Food Stores, Inc. v. Village of Espanola, 68 N.M. 327, 361 P.2d 950 (1961), cert. denied 368 U.S. 915, 82 S.Ct. 194, 7 L.Ed.2d 131 (1961), disallowing annexation of Indian lands. Cf. Board of County Comm'rs v. Junction City, 233 Kan. 947, 667 P.2d 868 (1983), giving retrospective application to a statute prohibiting annexation of any territory of a United States military reservation. Compare City of Hopewell v. County of Prince George, 239 Va. 287, 389 S.E.2d 685 (1990), where a state statute provided immunity from annexation to areas already being provided with "urban-type" services and such immunity was held to exist where the services were largely being furnished by a federal military installation.

At common law, one municipality may not annex territory that is already within another incorporated municipality. State ex rel. Village of Fridley v. City of Columbia Heights, 237 Minn. 124, 53 N.W.2d 831 (1952); Village of North Fargo v. City of Fargo, 49 N.D. 597, 192 N.W. 977 (1923); City of West University Place v. City of Bellaire, 198 S.W.2d 766 (Tex.Civ.App.1946); Sandy City v. City of South Jordan, 652 P.2d 1316 (Utah 1982) (attempt by one municipality to annex territory within another is void ab initio). But by statute in some jurisdictions, certain municipalities are allowed to annex territories within others. See Smalley v. City of Fort Smith, 239 Ark. 39, 386 S.W.2d 944 (1965); State ex rel. Nelson v. City of Anoka, 240 Minn. 350, 61 N.W.2d 237 (1953); City of Portsmouth v. City of Chesapeake, 205 Va. 259, 136 S.E.2d 817 (1964). Cf. Griffin v. City of Canon City, 147 Colo. 15, 362 P.2d 200 (1961) (annexation of entire other municipality).

[52] See City of Richmond, Virginia v. United States, 422 U.S. 358, 95 S.Ct. 2296, 45 L.Ed.2d 245 (1975) (annexation did not violate Voting Rights Act of 1965 if were legitimate reasons for annexation even though result was to reduce Negro proportion of population from 52% to 42%); Holt v. City of Richmond, 459 F.2d 1093 (4th Cir.1972), cert. denied 408 U.S. 931, 92 S.Ct. 2510, 33 L.Ed.2d 343 (1972) (annexation not invidiously motivated). Cf. Cunningham v. King County Boundary Review Board, 6 Wn.App. 385, 493 P.2d 811 (1972), appeal dism'd 409 U.S. 972, 93 S.Ct. 311, 34 L.Ed.2d 236 (no violation of equal protection though annexation could occur on petition of owners of 60% of land in area). But see City of Pleasant Grove v. United States, 479 U.S. 462, 107 S.Ct. 794, 93 L.Ed.2d 866 (1987) (city's failure to annex black areas at same time it was annexing nonblack areas was of great significance in demonstrating that its annexations were for discriminatory purposes forbidden by Voting Rights Act of 1965; finding of such purposes here upheld). See generally City of Rome v. United States, 446 U.S. 156, 100 S.Ct. 1548, 64 L.Ed.2d 119 (1980), reh. denied 447 U.S. 916, 100 S.Ct. 3003, 64 L.Ed.2d 865 (1980) (annexation constitutes a change in standard, practice, or procedure with respect to voting, and is thus within Voting Rights Act of 1965); Symposium (Hagman, ed.), The White Curtain: Racially Disadvantaging Local Government Boundary Practices, 54 U.Detroit J.Urban L. 681–1073 (1977). But some cases have found a denial of equal protection when *property owners* within an area are given an exclusive right to prevent annexation. Levinsohn v. City of San Rafael, 40 Cal.App.3d 656, 115 Cal.Rptr. 309 (Dist.Ct.1974) (property owners could prevent holding of annexation election). Or when votes are weighted according to property ownership. Kelley v. Mayor & Council of Dover, 314 A.2d 208 (Del.Ch.1973), aff'd 327 A.2d 748 (property owner had one vote for each $100 of assessed valuation; no compelling state interest found). But cf. Weber v. City Council of Thousand Oaks, 9 Cal.3d 950, 109 Cal.Rptr. 553, 513 P.2d 601 (1973) (election required if area to be annexed had 12 or more registered voters, but not otherwise; no violation of equal protection); Forks v. City of Warsaw, 257 Ind. 237, 273 N.E.2d 856 (1971), cert. denied 409 U.S. 841, 93 S.Ct. 39, 34 L.Ed.2d 80 (protest allowed only by real property owners; upheld as against equal protection attack; court required only rational basis, not compelling state interest). See generally Note, The Right to Vote in Municipal Annexations, 88 Harv.L.Rev. 1571 (1975). See also State ex rel. Jordan v. City of Overland Park, 215 Kan. 700, 527 P.2d 1340 (1974) (manner of annexation entirely beyond power of courts if statutes are followed; statutes providing alternative methods, mostly involving geographical conditions, are not unduly vague).

[53] See, applying such statutes, Finucane v. Village of Hayden, 86 Idaho 199, 384 P.2d 236 (1963); Sullivan v. City of Omaha, 183 Neb. 511, 162 N.W.2d 227 (1968); Shields v. Kearney, 179 Neb. 49, 136 N.W.2d 174 (1965) (determining what is rural land and what is urban); Southern Railway v. Hook, 261 N.C. 517, 135 S.E.2d 562 (1964) (interpreting statute requiring annexed land to be developed for urban purposes). Cf. State ex rel. Town of White Bear v. City of White Bear Lake, 255 Minn. 28, 95 N.W.2d 294 (1959), interpreting state

§ 12.5 Annexation by Municipalities—Procedure

The *procedure* for annexation is laid down by state statutes (and, sometimes, state constitutions). Three main methods are used: (1) Almost universally, annexation may be initiated by petition of residents of the area for which annexation is sought.[54] The petition will need to contain a designated number of signatures,[55] and must usually also designate with reasonable definiteness the boundaries of the affected territory.[56] The sufficiency of the petition and other required documents will be judged by the "substantial compliance" test—*i.e.*, have the statutory requirements been substantially met?[57] The petition will ordinarily have to be presented to a county or state board for a determination of the petition's sufficiency. But the board has power *only* to determine the legal sufficiency of the petition; if the petition is valid and satisfies all requirements, the board must order the requested annexation, and can be compelled by mandamus to do so.[58]

(2) In many states, a municipality may itself, through its city council or other governing body, initiate the annexation process by applying to a county board,[59] a state

---

laws as requiring that annexation only occur where the annexed land could be properly subjected to municipal government.

[54] See City and County of Denver v. Holmes, 156 Colo. 586, 400 P.2d 901 (1965); People v. Forest View, 21 Ill.2d 384, 172 N.E.2d 780 (1961) (requirement of a petition is jurisdictional); County of Chesterfield v. Berberich, 199 Va. 500, 100 S.E.2d 781 (1957). See generally 2 McQuillin, Municipal Corporations §§ 7.16 & 7.30 (3d rev. ed. (1996)). But residents of an area bordering a municipality have no common-law right to compel annexation. Rockville v. Brookeville Turnpike Construction Co., 246 Md. 117, 228 A.2d 263 (1967). The constitutionality of the petition method of annexation was upheld against attack based on the privileges and immunities clause of the state constitution in Grant County Fire Protection Dist. v. City of Moses Lake, 150 Wash.2d 791, 83 P.3d 419 (2004).

On the basic nature of the various methods of annexation, see Dugger v. City of Santa Fe, 114 N.M. 47, 834 P.2d 424 (App.1992) (petition method is considered legislative in nature; other methods provided by New Mexico law, involving boundary commission or arbitration, are administrative). See generally Note, Municipal Annexation in Ohio: Putting an End to the Bitter Battle, 41 Cleveland St. L. Rev. 345 (1993), discussing annexation procedures in Ohio and concluding that annexations could solve some of the state's urban problems if interjurisdictional rivalries and conflicts could only be avoided.

[55] See County of Clark v. North Las Vegas, 89 Nev. 10, 504 P.2d 1326 (1973), cert. denied 414 U.S. 1003, 94 S.Ct. 358, 38 L.Ed.2d 239 (failure to obtain requisite number of signatures will invalidate annexation). Generally, it is held that a person who has signed an annexation petition may withdraw his signature prior to the petition's being acted on by the authority to whom it is presented. D. H. Willey Lumber Co. v. Flick, 146 N.E.2d 167 (Ohio C.P.1957), aff'd 169 Ohio St. 425, 160 N.E.2d 239 (1959); Jensen v. Bountiful City, 20 Utah 2d 159, 435 P.2d 284 (1967). And the withdrawal may be revoked, and the signature reinstated, during that same period of time. See McAlmond v. City of Bremerton, 60 Wn.2d 383, 374 P.2d 181 (1962). See generally 1 Antieau, Municipal Corporation Law § 1A.13 (1998).

[56] See Dallas Borough Annexation Case, 169 Pa.Super. 129, 82 A.2d 676 (1951).

[57] In re Annexation of Portion of South Pymatuning Township, 409 Pa. 324, 186 A.2d 13 (1962) (minor errors in description of area may be disregarded); Miller v. City of Mercedes, 361 S.W.2d 464 (Tex.Civ.App.1962) ref'd n. r. e. (charter required that notice of hearing give description of territory; substantial compliance found though territory described in notice was 3 miles larger than that described in annexation ordinance); Miller v. Town of Mills, 590 P.2d 378 (Wyo.1979) (petition met minimum-compliance rule even though description of entire area was not contained therein; each petitioner had adequately described his or her lot). See Scottsdale v. State ex rel. Pickrell, 98 Ariz. 382, 405 P.2d 871 (1965) (no substantial compliance where signatures were made conditionally).

[58] See Watkins v. Town Board, 8 Misc.2d 251, 169 N.Y.S.2d 753 (Sup.Ct.1957). Cf. Pennington v. City of Corpus Christi, 363 S.W.2d 502 (Tex.Civ.App.1962) ref'd n. r. e., cert. denied 375 U.S. 439, 84 S.Ct. 507, 11 L.Ed.2d 471 (city council had ordered annexation election; this necessarily means they found petition was legally sufficient, and the finding can be overturned only with a showing of abuse of discretion or bad faith).

[59] See City of Salina v. Thompson, 169 Kan. 579, 220 P.2d 147 (1950) (county board upheld); Cox v. City of Albuquerque, 53 N.M. 334, 207 P.2d 1017 (1949) (temporary board); City of Fargo v. Annexation Review

commission,[60] or a court.[61] The powers of the agency to which application is made are usually here greater than they are under the first method; the agency has considerable discretion to consider the reasonableness of the proposed annexation; and its decision will be upheld, if there is a judicial appeal, so long as not unlawful or totally unsupported by the evidence.[62] (3) In several states, a municipality may annex territory merely by passage of an ordinance,[63] if any state statutory requirements on publication of the ordinance are complied with,[64] and if the territory to be annexed is described with reasonable accuracy in the ordinance.[65]

Under *any* of the three above-mentioned methods, there are often provisions for an election to be held in the area to be annexed. Generally, the effect of a protest by a

---

Commission, 123 N.W.2d 281 (N.D.1963) (appeal to annexation review commission); River Road Water District v. City of Eugene, 8 Or.App. 290, 492 P.2d 812 (1972) (boundary commissions at county level).

[60] See Fairview Public Utility District v. City of Anchorage, 368 P.2d 540 (Alaska 1962) appeal dism'd, cert. denied 371 U.S. 5, 83 S.Ct. 39, 9 L.Ed.2d 49 (state commission considers, and may recommend to legislature, any proposed changes in boundaries of local units); In re Town of White Bear, 268 Minn. 383, 129 N.W.2d 560 (1964) (state commission approves or disapproves of proposed annexations). In some jurisdictions, an individual landowner may apply to a state commission to have that landowner's property annexed to a city. But see City of Albuquerque v. State Municipal Boundary Comm'n, 131 N.M. 665, 41 P.3d 933 (App. 2002), holding that the state's Municipal Boundary Commission could not approve such annexation over the city's reasonable objection.

[61] See In re City of Forest, 247 Miss. 340, 153 So.2d 688 (1963) (city files application with court and has burden of establishing the reasonableness of the requested expansion); City of Liberty v. Dealers Transport Co., 343 S.W.2d 40 (Mo.1961); City of Portsmouth v. County of Norfolk, 198 Va. 247, 93 S.E.2d 296 (1956).

[62] See City of Ames v. Olson, 253 Iowa 983, 114 N.W.2d 904 (1962) (petition presented to court; court was to grant request only if city met burden of showing its capability to provide services to annexed area); City of Glencoe v. Beneke, 288 Minn. 190, 179 N.W.2d 279 (1970) (request made to commission, which had broad discretion to grant or deny); Meyer v. Waite Park, 278 Minn. 20, 152 N.W.2d 778 (1967). But see Planque v. Eureka Springs, 243 Ark. 361, 419 S.W.2d 788 (1967) (court must grant city's petition for annexation, following a favorable vote on the matter, unless complaint is filed by property owners who prove that annexation is unreasonable).

The Iowa procedure described in the *Ames* case *supra* has since been modified. Iowa Code Ann. §§ 368.9–.22.

[63] See Burton v. City of Tucson, 88 Ariz. 320, 356 P.2d 413 (1960); State ex rel. Kreamer v. City of Overland Park, 192 Kan. 654, 391 P.2d 128 (1964) (land laid off into blocks or lots can be annexed by ordinance); In re Annexation Ordinances, 253 N.C. 637, 117 S.E.2d 795 (1961) (sustaining validity of such ordinances); State ex rel. Balsinger v. Madisonville, 222 Tenn. 272, 435 S.W.2d 803 (1968); Morton v. Johnson City, 206 Tenn. 411, 333 S.W.2d 924 (1960) (finding no unconstitutional delegation of legislative power); State ex rel. American Manufacturing Co. v. City of Fort Worth, 339 S.W.2d 707 (Tex.Civ.App.1960), ref'd n. r. e. Cf. Hammonds v. Corpus Christi, 226 F.Supp. 456, 459 (S.D.Tex.1964), aff'd 343 F.2d 162 (5th Cir.), cert. denied 382 U.S. 837, 86 S.Ct. 85, 15 L.Ed.2d 80, commenting on the power of Texas municipalities in this regard.

[64] Vincent v. Bowling Green, 349 S.W.2d 694 (Ky.1961) (failure to publish invalidates annexation). See Town of Goldsby v. City of Purcell, 233 P.3d 409 (Okla. Civ. App. 2010) (city and town had both attempted annexation of area, but city's notice of annexation was not published in "legal newspaper of the county" in which the area was located; thus city's attempt to annex was void). There is generally held, however, to be no constitutional requirement that legal notice be given those in the area to be annexed. See Freeman v. Centerville City, 600 P.2d 1003 (Utah 1979).

[65] St. Matthews v. Beechwood Village, 373 S.W.2d 427 (Ky.1963). But a reasonably accurate description *will* suffice. See McCune v. City of Phoenix, 83 Ariz. 98, 317 P.2d 537 (1957) (minor deviations won't invalidate if borders of the area can be accurately determined); People ex rel. Rogers v. City of Park Ridge, 86 Ill.App.2d 82, 230 N.E.2d 289 (1967) (description of land in annexation ordinance need not be so exact as required for a deed); TCD North, Inc. v. City Council of Greenwood Village, 713 P.2d 1320 (Colo.App.1985) (annexation not rendered invalid by publication of two slightly differing descriptions of property to be annexed, one including the streets and rights-of-way in the description and the other not including them). But cf. City of Lenexa v. City of Olathe, 233 Kan. 159, 660 P.2d 1368 (1983), where publication of an incorrect land description of the first tract in an annexation ordinance was found not to "substantially comply" with the statutory requirement, thus invalidating the attempted subsequent annexation of additional tracts adjoining the first one.

designated number of persons is the halting of further annexation proceedings.[66] But occasionally, state statutes provide that a protest by the requisite number of persons will simply require the proposed annexation to be submitted to a popular referendum,[67] or that the protests will allow the annexation to occur only if the municipality goes into court and establishes the fairness of, and need for, the proposed expansion.[68] Protests are sometimes limited to owners (as opposed to renters) of property, or to resident owners as opposed to nonresident owners; and so far, the courts have tended to uphold these limitations.[69]

Often—particularly under the above-described second and third methods of annexation—the annexation cannot occur until approved by a vote of the people—at least a majority vote of those in the affected area, but more often a majority vote both in the affected area and in the annexing municipality.[70] The state statutes may validly require an election under some annexation procedures and not allow the election under other procedures—if the distinction has a reasonable basis.[71] But due process has

---

[66] See American Distilling Co. v. City Council of Sausalito, 34 Cal.2d 660, 213 P.2d 704 (1950); State ex rel. Konen v. City of Butte, 144 Mont. 95, 394 P.2d 753 (1964).

[67] See Rheinhardt v. Yancey, 241 N.C. 184, 84 S.E.2d 655 (1954), interpreting the North Carolina statutes to this effect.

[68] See City of Danville v. Wilson, 395 S.W.2d 583 (Ky.1965); City of Greenville v. Gossett, 355 S.W.2d 311 (Ky.1962); Smith v. Incorporated Town of Culver, 249 Ind. 665, 234 N.E.2d 494 (1968); City of Aurora v. Bryant, 240 Ind. 492, 165 N.E.2d 141 (1960).

[69] Forks v. City of Warsaw, 257 Ind. 237, 273 N.E.2d 856 (1971), cert. denied 409 U.S. 841, 93 S.Ct. 39, 34 L.Ed.2d 80 (only those owning, not merely renting, property in the area may protest); Burritt v. City of Butte, 161 Mont. 530, 508 P.2d 563 (1973) (in first-class cities, only resident freeholders may protest, though in smaller cities, all freeholders, without regard to residence, may protest). See Pitts v. Mills, 165 Ind.App. 646, 333 N.E.2d 897 (1975) (statute may validly limit protests to owners of real property). Cf. Goodyear Farms v. City of Avondale, 148 Ariz. 216, 714 P.2d 386 (1986), upholding against equal protection attack a statute requiring a petition requesting annexation to be signed by the owners of not less than one-half in value of the real and personal property subject to taxation in the area proposed for annexation. Since no infringement on the right to vote or other fundamental right was found, the court stated that only a rational basis for the classification need be present. It would seem, as with some restrictions often found in incorporation laws, these limitations might be struck down as violative of equal protection. See City of Seattle v. State, 103 Wash.2d 663, 694 P.2d 641 (1985) (property owners within area proposed for annexation, could block the annexation; violation of equal protection found since no compelling state interest existed in granting greater rights to property owners even if property taxes would be affected by the annexation). Compare the cases cited in note 35 *supra* and accompanying text. Cf. Kelley v. Mayor and Council of Dover, 314 A.2d 208 (Del.Ch.1973), aff'd 327 A.2d 748 (voiding statute giving each real-estate owner one vote for each $100 of real estate assessed to him). On who are "interested parties" to annexation proceedings, see generally City of Lenexa v. City of Olathe, 228 Kan. 773, 620 P.2d 1153 (Kan.1980) (as to annexation of land *adjoining* city, only interested parties are city and owner of land proposed for annexation; but under statute allowing limited annexation of *non-adjacent* land, rights of another incorporated city in county must be considered). On "annexation rivalries" between municipalities, see also Section 12.6 *infra*.

[70] See City of Batesville v. Ball, 100 Ark. 496, 140 S.W. 712 (1911); Perry v. City of Denver, 27 Colo. 93, 59 P. 747 (1899); Dees v. City of Lake Charles, 50 La.Ann. 356, 23 So. 382 (1898); St. Louis County v. City of Florissant, 406 S.W.2d 281 (Mo.1966); Lutterloh v. City of Fayetteville, 149 N.C. 65, 62 S.E. 758 (1908); Forest Acres v. Forest Lake, 226 S.C. 349, 85 S.E.2d 192 (1954); Sitton v. City of Lindale, 455 S.W.2d 939 (Tex.1970); Wheeler School District No. 152 v. Hawley, 18 Wn.2d 37, 137 P.2d 1010 (1943). Cf. City of Bridgeton v. Ford Motor Credit Co., 788 S.W.2d 285 (Mo.1990) (state statutes required majority vote of residents in both annexing municipality and area sought to be annexed; held to preclude annexation of areas having no residents). A statute limiting the franchise to residents of the territory to be annexed, and excluding residents of the annexing municipality, has been upheld. Citizens Against Forced Annexation v. Local Agency Formation Comm'n of Los Angeles County, 32 Cal.3d 816, 187 Cal.Rptr. 423, 654 P.2d 193 (1982) (court noted that areas with a low tax base or high cost of providing services might otherwise be unable to gain admission to any adjoining municipality).

[71] Adams v. Colorado Springs, 308 F.Supp. 1397 (D.Colo.1970), aff'd 399 U.S. 901, 90 S.Ct. 2197, 26 L.Ed.2d 555, reh. denied 400 U.S. 855, 91 S.Ct. 25, 27 L.Ed.2d 93. Cf. Weber v. City Council of Thousand Oaks,

uniformly been held not to require any election at all in order for annexation to be valid.[72] The municipality may, so long as it complies with relevant statutes, expand its boundaries without seeking or obtaining the consent of those annexed or of those who, even prior to the annexation, resided within its borders.

§ 12.6 Incorporation and Annexation: Priority Among Competing Units; Other Inter-Relationships

What happens in the situation where two or more municipalities are trying to annex the same territory at the same time? Priority will be accorded the proceeding first instituted—that is, the one in which the "first step" was validly taken at the earlier time.[73] The same rule is applied where the conflict is between an attempt to annex

---

9 Cal.3d 950, 109 Cal.Rptr. 553, 513 P.2d 601 (1973) (right to vote on annexation given those in "inhabited" areas but not those in "uninhabited" areas); Town of Wilson v. City of Sheboygan, 230 Wis. 483, 283 N.W. 312 (1939) (statute provided for referendum in detachment proceedings, but held to have no application to annexation proceedings).

[72] See People ex rel. Strong v. City of Whittier, 133 Cal.App. 316, 24 P.2d 219 (Dist.Ct.1933) (discretion with legislature whether or not to provide for annexation vote); Board of County Commissioners v. City and County of Denver, 150 Colo. 198, 372 P.2d 152 (1962) (territory could be detached from county jurisdiction without vote in county); McGraw v. Merryman, 133 Md. 247, 104 A. 540 (1918); Mid-County Future Alternatives Comm. v. City of Portland, 310 Or. 152, 795 P.2d 541 (1990), cert. denied 498 U.S. 999, 111 S.Ct. 558, 112 L.Ed.2d 564 (1990) (no constitutional right to vote on municipal annexations; boundary commission's approval of boundary change did not violate home rule); Smallwood v. City of Dallas, 216 S.W.2d 272 (Tex.Civ.App.1948); City of Seattle v. State, 103 Wash.2d 663, 694 P.2d 641 (1985) (residents of municipality have no constitutional right to vote on annexation decisions; state has wide discretion in establishing boundaries). Cf. Slack v. City of Colorado Springs, 655 P.2d 376 (Colo.1982) (city council could use its emergency power to enact an annexation ordinance a few days before passage of a constitutional amendment allowing residents of the area to be annexed to vote on the proposed annexation); Sampson v. Treasurer & Receiver General, 282 Mass. 119, 184 N.E. 465 (1933) (incorporation of sewer district effective on vote of town meeting; subsequent referendum ineffective); Pieper v. Health Division, 288 Or. 551, 606 P.2d 1145 (1980) (annexation could, under state statutes, occur without vote of electorate of annexed area if conditions in area found to constitute danger to public health). See generally Laurie Reynolds, Rethinking Municipal Annexation Powers, 24 Urban Law. 247 (1992), urging the use of "involuntary" municipal annexation—*i.e.*, annexation without vote or consent of residents of the annexed area—as a means of ensuring orderly urban growth and equitable provision of services. As to "involuntary" annexations, see Tyson, Localism and Involuntary Annexation: Reconsidering Approaches to New Regionalism, 87 Tulane L. Rev. 297 (2012). See also Comment, Municipal Manifest Destiny: Constitutionality of Unilateral Municipal Annexations, 2013 B.Y.U. L. Rev. 619.

It has often been stated that, except as limited by the state constitution, the state legislature may change municipal boundaries even against the will of the affected areas and without the consent of local authorities. See De Lano v. City of Tulsa, 26 F.2d 640 (8th Cir.1928), cert. denied 278 U.S. 654, 49 S.Ct. 179, 73 L.Ed. 564; Barnes v. Kansas City, 359 Mo. 519, 222 S.W.2d 756 (1949); Adriaansen v. Board of Education, 222 App.Div. 320, 226 N.Y.S. 145 (1927), aff'd 248 N.Y. 542, 162 N.E. 517 (1928); City of Bethany v. District Court, 200 Okl. 49, 191 P.2d 187 (1948); City of Pelly v. Harris County Water Control and Improvement District, 145 Tex. 443, 198 S.W.2d 450 (1946); City of Houston v. State ex rel. City of West University Place, 142 Tex. 190, 176 S.W.2d 928 (1943), appeal dism'd 322 U.S. 711, 64 S.Ct. 1159, 88 L.Ed. 1554; School District No. 3 v. Callahan, 237 Wis. 560, 297 N.W. 407 (1941). Cf. City of Fort Worth v. State ex rel. Ridglea Village, 186 S.W.2d 323 (Tex.Civ.App.1945), ref'd w. m. (city could annex land without submitting question to vote of those in territory to be annexed).

[73] McCune v. City of Phoenix, 83 Ariz. 98, 317 P.2d 537 (1957); Garden Grove v. Santa Ana, 187 Cal.App.2d 533, 9 Cal.Rptr. 920 (1960); City of Cupertino v. City of San Jose, 186 Cal.App.2d 29, 8 Cal.Rptr. 525 (1960); Countryside v. LaGrange, 24 Ill.2d 163, 180 N.E.2d 488 (1962); School District v. School District No. 2, 318 Mich. 363, 28 N.W.2d 265 (1947); Emerson Electric Manufacturing Co. v. Ferguson, 376 S.W.2d 643 (Mo.App.1964); Landis v. City of Roseburg, 243 Or. 44, 411 P.2d 282 (1966); State ex rel. City of Everman v. City of Fort Worth, 363 S.W.2d 500 (Tex.Civ.App.1962), ref'd n. r. e.; In re Incorporation of Village of St. Francis, 208 Wis. 431, 243 N.W. 315 (1932). See Daytona Beach v. Port Orange, 165 So.2d 768 (Fla.App.1964); Couch v. Fort Worth, 287 S.W.2d 255 (Tex.Civ.App.1956); Town of Ruston v. City of Tacoma, 90 Wash.App. 75, 951 P.2d 805 (1998) (municipality that was first to incorporate disputed territory prevails in boundary dispute

unincorporated territory and an attempt to incorporate that area.[74] The "first step" is usually defined as the first *public procedural* step,[75] such as the introduction of an ordinance or the filing of a petition.

If allowed by statute, an annexing municipality may attach conditions, such as the payment of fees by residents of the annexed area, to its annexation.[76] And a city may make a valid, enforceable contract that it will annex certain territory.[77]

---

with neighboring municipality). See generally Wegner, North Carolina's Annexation Wars: Whys, Wherefores, and What Next, 91 N.C.L. Rev. 165 (2012).

[74] Fuller v. San Bernardino Valley Municipal Water District, 242 Cal.App.2d 66, 51 Cal.Rptr. 130 (Dist.Ct.1966); Borghi v. Board of Supervisors, 133 Cal.App.2d 463, 284 P.2d 537 (1955); East St. Louis v. Touchette, 14 Ill.2d 243, 150 N.E.2d 178 (1958); State ex rel. Harrier v. Spring Lake Park, 245 Minn. 302, 71 N.W.2d 812 (1955); In re Incorporation of Forest Hills, 280 So.2d 837 (Miss.1973), cert. denied 414 U.S. 1130, 94 S.Ct. 869, 38 L.Ed.2d 755; Baumhardt v. Mitchell, 107 Ohio App. 209, 157 N.E.2d 898 (1958); City of Cincinnati v. Rosi, 92 Ohio App. 8, 109 N.E.2d 290 (1952), appeal dism'd 158 Ohio St. 180, 107 N.E.2d 113; State ex rel. City of Fort Worth v. Lakeside, 328 S.W.2d 245 (Tex.Civ.App.1959); El Paso v. Tuck, 282 S.W.2d 764 (Tex.Civ.App.1955).

[75] Lincolnshire v. Highbaugh Realty Co., 278 S.W.2d 636 (Ky.1955). See City of Joplin v. Shoal Creek Drive, 434 S.W.2d 25 (Mo.1968) (introduction of ordinance before city council gives priority). Cf. Davis County Solid Waste Management Dist. v. City of Bountiful, 2002 UT 60, 52 P.3d 1174 (2002) (annexation of land by city occurred when annexation resolution and plat were filed with county recorder's office, rather than when annexation resolution was passed). If the first-initiated attempt proves void, the later proceedings can prevail. Slack v. City of Colorado Springs, 655 P.2d 376 (Colo.1982) (petition for annexation election held ineffective; therefore, city council could commence and prosecute unilateral proceedings for annexation of same area); Town of Clive v. Colby, 255 Iowa 483, 123 N.W.2d 331 (1963). And if an earlier attempt is rejected by voters, or some other group that must approve the action, it seems that the later attempt may then succeed. See Landis v. City of Roseburg, 243 Or. 44, 411 P.2d 282 (1966). It is also true that a first-initiated attempt to take jurisdiction over territory may fail if the municipality taking such first step subsequently delays, for an unreasonable time, any further action. See People ex rel. Village of Worth v. Ihde, 23 Ill.2d 63, 177 N.E.2d 313 (1961); Village of Brown Deer v. City of Milwaukee, 16 Wis.2d 206, 114 N.W.2d 493 (1962), cert. denied 371 U.S. 902, 83 S.Ct. 205, 9 L.Ed.2d 164. Five and a half years has been held unreasonable. Arterburn v. City of St. Matthews, 512 S.W.2d 505 (Ky.1974).

In People ex rel. City of Prospect Heights v. Village of Arlington Heights, 171 Ill.App.3d 766, 121 Ill.Dec. 663, 525 N.E.2d 970 (1988), appeal denied 122 Ill.2d 592, 125 Ill.Dec. 234, 530 N.E.2d 262 (1988), the filing of a statutory notice of contemplated annexation was held to commence the annexation process and thereby prevent another city from similar proceedings as to the same area. But see City of Des Moines v. City Dev. Bd., 473 N.W.2d 197 (Iowa 1991), where a voluntary annexation of land by one municipality was approved over a previously filed competing attempt at involuntary annexation by another municipality.

[76] City of Aurora v. Andrew Land Co., 176 Colo. 246, 490 P.2d 67 (1971); Child v. Spanish Fork, 538 P.2d 184 (Utah 1975) (property owners required to transfer irrigation water to city as condition to annexation). Cf. Adams v. Colorado Springs, 178 Colo. 241, 496 P.2d 1005 (1972) (legislature may authorize municipalities to annex upon certain conditions).

[77] See Housing Authority v. City of Los Angeles, 40 Cal.2d 682, 256 P.2d 4 (1953) (city had agreed to annex land for housing authority; compelled to do so); Elm Lawn Cemetery Co. v. Northlake, 94 Ill.App.2d 387, 237 N.E.2d 345 (1968). Cf. Perl-Mack Enterprises Co. v. City and County of Denver, 194 Colo. 4, 568 P.2d 468 (1977) (annexation agreement between city and developer upheld). But cf. Bell v. City of Corvallis, 25 Or.App. 821, 551 P.2d 125 (1976) (city cannot bind itself to annex an area, but can contract to provide water and sewer services, and to consider annexation in due course). See City of Leeds v. Town of Moody, 294 Ala. 496, 319 So.2d 242 (1975).

In Pitzer v. City of Abilene, 323 S.W.2d 623 (Tex.Civ.App.1959), a city having received benefits under an agreement by which it promised *not* to annex certain territory was held estopped to deny the agreement's validity during the period set by the agreement. But it seems that a city cannot permanently contract away its power to annex certain territory. See Safety Harbor v. Clearwater, 330 So.2d 840 (Fla.App.1976). Cf. American Bemberg Corp. v. City of Elizabethton, 180 Tenn. 373, 175 S.W.2d 535 (1943) (state could annex land to city despite city's agreement not to annex).

Modern planning laws can be expected to have increased effect on annexation proceedings. Some annexation statutes, for instance, now require that an annexing city have a comprehensive plan for future development.[78]

Once territory is annexed by a municipality, it is thereafter treated the same as other parts of that municipality. For instance, property within the area is subject to taxation by the annexing city,[79] including taxation to pay debts incurred prior to the annexation.[80] And once the annexation is complete, property in the territory is freed from taxation by any local unit of which it was formerly part, but from which it became separated at the time of the annexation.[81] The annexed territory, and persons therein, become immediately subject to the laws of the annexing governmental unit;[82] but there

---

[78] See Rivergate Residents Association v. Land Conservation and Development Commission, 38 Or.App. 149, 590 P.2d 1233 (1979) (annexation not precluded though city lacked comprehensive plan of its own, where it had agreed to use county's comprehensive plan until another was developed). Cf. York v. Town of Carmel, 166 Ind.App. 672, 337 N.E.2d 511 (1975) (statute could require that annexing town develop fiscal plan, plus plan to furnish services to annexed area); Clarke v. City of Wichita, 218 Kan. 334, 543 P.2d 973 (1975) (statute may require bona fide plan covering services to be furnished annexed area); Dunn v. City of Charlotte, 284 N.C. 542, 201 S.E.2d 873 (1974) (same).

Note that annexation statutes sometimes require that, if an unsuccessful attempt at annexation of an area has been made by a municipality, it must wait a certain length of time before attempting annexation of that area again. *E.g.*, Ohio Rev.Code § 709.17 (five years).

Another limitation occasionally encountered is a prohibition of the annexation of land in a county other than that in which the annexing municipality is located. See 1 Antieau, Local Government Law § 3.08[3] (2d ed. 2000).

On the need for greater consideration of the intergovernmental effects of annexations, see Murphy, Commentary: The Intergovernmental Dynamics of Annexation and Deannexation: The *Richmond* Case, 31 Admin.L.Rev. 385 (1979). On the possible use of annexation to achieve a more regional government and lessen intergovernmental conflicts, see generally Sengstock, Annexation: A Solution to the Metropolitan Area Problem (Mich. Legal Publications 1985).

[79] Corpus Christi v. Arnold, 424 S.W.2d 492 (Tex.Civ.App.1968), ref'd n. r. e.

[80] Smith v. Mayor of Saginaw, 81 Mich. 123, 45 N.W. 964 (1890); Wilcox v. County of Olmsted, 258 Minn. 281, 104 N.W.2d 297 (1960).

[81] People v. Downey County Water District, 202 Cal.App.2d 786, 21 Cal.Rptr. 370 (Dist.Ct.1962). But it has been suggested that if the unit of which the newly annexed territory is no longer a part proved unable to pay off its obligations without help from its "lost" territory, a court might order taxation of that annexed territory, so as to protect the claims of creditors. 1 Antieau, Local Government Law § 3.09[2], at 3–77 (2d ed. 2000).

In some states, the law permits rural cooperatives to continue serving customers in a previously rural area that has been annexed if the cooperative had been serving the particular property prior to the annexation. See Missouri Pub. Serv. Co. v. Platte-Clay Elec. Cooperative, Inc., 700 S.W.2d 838 (Mo.1985).

[82] Bush v. City of Gainesville, 105 Ga.App. 381, 124 S.E.2d 667 (1962) (city obtains immediate jurisdiction over newly annexed land); Duke Power Co. v. Blue Ridge Electric Membership Corp., 253 N.C. 596, 117 S.E.2d 812 (1961) (city ordinances apply in the city's newly acquired territory); Hoops v. Burlington Northern, Inc., 83 Wn.2d 396, 518 P.2d 707 (1974). Once annexation occurs, a public highway within the annexed territory becomes ipso facto a street of the municipality. See 39 Am.Jur.2d Highways § 238 (1999). Cf. Northwestern Industries, Inc. v. City of Seattle, 33 Wash.App. 757, 658 P.2d 24 (1983) (city which had annexed area containing county roads was not limited to procedures for vacating roads that were applicable to counties). By statute, a municipality that annexes some or all of a special function district's territory may be required to pay just compensation to the district. See Rural Water Dist. #2 v. City of Louisburg, 288 Kan. 811, 207 P.3d 1055 (2009) (statute required city to pay rural water district "reasonable value" of water distribution facilities; this is held equivalent to just compensation required under U.S. Constitution and should include "going concern" value). But cf. David W. v. Paramount Homes, LLC, 360 Mont. 421, 253 P.3d 903 (2011) (city's annexation of property within which road over which homeowners' association had easement rights was located did not extinguish association's easement rights). On the "vested rights doctrine" that allows land developers to proceed with their developments under the laws that existed at the time they acquired title to property, despite subsequent incorporation or annexation of the property, see Vashon Island Comm. for Self-Government v. Washington State Boundary Rev. Bd., 127 Wash.2d 759, 903 P.2d 953 (Wash.1995) (committee

is a special problem as to zoning laws since the zoning rules of the annexing municipality cannot be applied automatically—classification of property is necessary—and the zones established (if any) by the former government of the area may not mesh with the patterns of the new government. Therefore, the majority rule is that the annexed territory comes into the annexing municipality as unzoned land—and remains such until the annexing municipality establishes zones therein.[83] A minority view allows the prior zoning to remain in effect until modified by the annexing government.[84]

§ 12.7 Defective Incorporations and Annexations; Challenges and Cures

If an attempted incorporation or annexation is in some manner defective, how can it be challenged, and how may the defect be cured? Considerable instability would obviously result if efforts at incorporation and annexation could be easily overturned; thus, the law has developed several doctrines to protect good-faith attempts at creating municipalities and/or at expanding their boundaries.

In the case of incorporations, at least four methods or theories may be pursued by one seeking to uphold, or remedy, defective attempts: (1) the rule of prescription, (2) the possibility of validation, (3) the rules limiting the persons by whom, and methods by which, an incorporation may be legally challenged, and (4) the doctrine of de facto

---

for incorporation did not have vested right to have its application for incorporation of city evaluated under law existing at time it filed application).

As to the effect of annexation on a franchise to provide utility service to the annexed area, see Dahl–Smyth, Inc., v. City of Walla Walla, 148 Wash.2d 835, 64 P.3d 15 (2003) (if a city annexes territory covered by a garbage hauler's certificate, the city may retain the hauler's service or choose to provide its own solid waste collection service; but if the city takes over the service, it must, under Washington State law, compensate the holder of the certificate). Cf. Public Serv. Co. v. Northeastern Okla. Elec. Cooperative, Inc., 49 P.3d 80 (Okla. 2002) (rural electric cooperative had standing to challenge an ordinance that annexed an industrial park to the municipality, which would allow a public service company then to provide electric service to that area instead of the rural cooperative).

[83] South San Francisco v. Berry, 120 Cal.App.2d 252, 260 P.2d 1045 (Dist.Ct.1953); Ben Lomond, Inc. v. Idaho Falls, 92 Idaho 595, 448 P.2d 209 (1968); Taylor v. Bowen, 272 N.C. 726, 158 S.E.2d 837 (1968). See State ex rel. Holiday Park, Inc. v. City of Columbia, 479 S.W.2d 422 (Mo.1972) (land comes into annexing city unzoned unless an ordinance provides for interim zoning; interim zoning not here authorized). Cf. Burt v. City of Idaho Falls, 105 Idaho 65, 665 P.2d 1075 (1983) (annexed territory came into city as unzoned land but amendment of the comprehensive plan and of the zoning ordinance concurrently with or immediately following the annexation was required). Compare Highlands Dev. Corp. v. City of Boise, 145 Idaho 958, 188 P.3d 900 (2008) (county zoning ordinance ceased to apply to two parcels once the parcels were removed from county's jurisdiction through annexation by city). But cf. Davidson v. City of Clinton, Mississippi, 826 F.2d 1430 (5th Cir.1987) (zoning ordinance prohibiting sale of alcoholic beverages within 500 feet of a public school could validly be applied to nightclub in a newly annexed area). See generally Note, Municipal Corporations: Effect of Zoning Ordinances on Annexed Lands, 7 Okl.L.Rev. 355 (1954).

Nonconforming uses that existed prior to the annexation will be protected to the same extent that the annexing municipality protects other nonconforming uses. Muttontown v. Friscia, 60 Misc.2d 1014, 304 N.Y.S.2d 664 (Sup.Ct.1969). On such uses, see generally Chapter 18 *infra*.

[84] See Highland Village Land Co. v. City of Jackson, 243 Miss. 34, 137 So.2d 549 (1962) (county zoning ordinance remained in effect); Kligler v. City of Elyria, 2 Ohio App.2d 181, 207 N.E.2d 389 (1965) (township zoning law remained in effect). Cf. Crumbaker v. Hunt Midwest Mining, Inc., 275 Kan. 872, 69 P.3d 601 (2003) (quarry land, used by mining company, did not lose its county zoning classification upon annexation by city, but rather maintained classification until city took affirmative action through zoning process). Sometimes the annexing government will rezone the property as part of the annexation process. See Barton v. City of Lebanon, 193 Or.App. 114, 88 P.3d 323 (2004) (city properly rezoned property as part of its annexation process, and separate actions were not required). But cf. Interlake Sporting Assn. v. Washington State Boundary Review Bd. for King County, 158 Wash.2d 545, 146 P.3d 904 (2006) (boundary review board could not impose city's pre-annexation indebtedness or zoning on property owners outside the petition area).

incorporation. Though there is not a great deal of authority on prescription in this regard, several courts have declared that a presumption—generally conclusive—of proper incorporation arises after a municipality has, with acquiescence of the state and populace, exercised municipal powers for many years.[85] Validating acts passed by the state legislature may also be used to cure defects in incorporation, often even if the defects would, if unremedied, be serious enough to void the incorporation.[86] To be safe, the legislative validation should be in the form of a general law, as *special* acts on these matters may sometimes be voided as unconstitutional.[87]

Where there has been no validation, the validity of a municipal corporation can be questioned in a quo warranto proceeding by the state in which the municipality is located.[88] This has been said in general to place the burden of proving the incorporation's validity on the municipality.[89] But even in these quo warranto actions, long acquiescence by the state in the municipality's existence has been held, under the prescription doctrine, to preclude successful attack on the municipality's legitimacy.[90] Attacks on incorporation are rarely successful when those attacks are brought by parties *other* than the state. While the incorporation is pending but not yet complete, residents of the area proposed for incorporation may pursue remedies given them by statute, or may bring equitable proceedings to halt the incorporation if statutory methods are not being

---

[85] See People ex rel. Gridley v. Farnham, 35 Ill. 562 (1864) (municipal corporation had been recognized by legislative enactment); Bow v. Allenstown, 34 N.H. 351 (1857) (2-years exercise of municipal powers). Cf. Balock v. Town of Melstone, 186 Mont. 303, 607 P.2d 545 (1980) (long acquiescence between parties as to municipal boundaries eventually establishes those boundaries; property found within city for property-tax purposes); Robie v. Sedgwick & Hardenbrook, 35 Barb. (N.Y.) 319 (Sup. Ct.1861) (long user of power overrides lack of any record of original organization). But cf. Gregory v. City of Forsyth, 187 Mont. 132, 609 P.2d 248 (1980) (doctrine of acquiescence inapplicable to boundaries that are easily or clearly defined). The prescriptive rule is codified in Florida. West's Fla.Stat. Ann. § 165.23.

[86] Osann v. Purported Town of Portage, 132 Ind.App. 695, 177 N.E.2d 666 (1961); Perkins v. State, 367 S.W.2d 140 (Tex.1963). See Jennison v. Oyster River Co-op. School District, 99 N.H. 424, 113 A.2d 117 (1955); State ex rel. Carroll v. Bastian, 66 Wn.2d 546, 403 P.2d 896 (1965). See generally 1 Dillon, Municipal Corporations § 68 (5th ed. 1911); Fordham, Local Government Law 216 (2d rev. ed. 1986).

[87] See Town of Enterprise v. State ex rel. Attorney General, 29 Fla. 128, 10 So. 740 (1892). Cf. Thorpe v. King, 248 Ind. 283, 227 N.E.2d 169 (1967) (after court had ruled incorporation invalid, legislation validating the incorporation was void as an intrusion on role of judiciary). But the tendency of most courts in the twentieth century has been to uphold validating laws as non-special, often on the ground that general laws are not here appropriate. See State ex rel. Johnson v. Eddy, 95 Fla. 978, 117 So. 377 (1928); Lane v. Johnson, 283 N.Y. 244, 28 N.E.2d 705 (1940); State ex rel. Richardson v. Larkin, 41 Tex.Civ.App. 253, 90 S.W. 912 (1905) error ref'd (ban on incorporation by special law doesn't prevent validation of incorporation by special law). On special laws, see generally Chapter 5 *supra*.

[88] Parnell v. State ex rel. Wilson, 68 Ariz. 401, 206 P.2d 1047 (1949); South Miami v. State ex rel. Gibbs, 143 Fla. 524, 197 So. 109 (1940); People ex rel. Mohlenbrock v. Pike, 197 Ill. 449, 64 N.E. 393 (1902); State ex rel. Tolle v. Shufford, 77 Kan. 263, 94 P. 137 (1908); Hempel v. Rogers, 313 Mich. 1, 20 N.W.2d 787 (1945); State ex rel. Eagleton v. Champ, 393 S.W.2d 516 (Mo.1965); State ex rel. Carroll v. Bastian, 66 Wn.2d 546, 403 P.2d 896 (1965) (prosecuting attorney of county brings quo warranto action). See State ex rel. Cox v. Consolidated Independent School District, 246 Iowa 566, 68 N.W.2d 305 (1955).

[89] See People ex rel. Moran v. Teolis, 20 Ill.2d 95, 169 N.E.2d 232 (1960) (but motives of the incorporators are not relevant); Town of Enterprise v. State ex rel. Attorney General, *supra* note 87.

[90] State v. Leatherman, 38 Ark. 81 (1881) (a leading case); People ex rel. Lindsey v. Board of Education, 3 Ill.2d 159, 120 N.E.2d 887 (1954); Jameson v. People, 16 Ill. 257 (1855); State ex rel. West v. Des Moines, 96 Iowa 521, 65 N.W. 818 (1896); People v. Maynard, 15 Mich. 463 (1867); State ex rel. Eagleton v. Champ, *supra* note 88; Independent School District v. State Board of Education, 451 P.2d 684 (Okl.1969). See People ex rel. Mohlenbrock v. Pike, *supra* note 88; Annot., Estoppel to Question Validity of Proceedings Extending Boundaries of Municipality, 101 A.L.R. 581 (1936). But a few courts refuse to apply doctrines such as laches or acquiescence against the state. See City of Coral Gables v. State ex rel. Watson, 38 So.2d 48 (Fla.1948). Cf. State ex rel. Carroll v. Bastian, *supra* note 88 (applying statute).

followed by the incorporators.[91] Generally, *direct* attacks by residents of the incorporated area on the validity of incorporation, once that process is completed, are not allowed by the courts;[92] this means, for instance, that a declaratory judgment action questioning the validity of the incorporation cannot be brought by such residents.[93] But a few courts have allowed declaratory judgment or quo warranto proceedings to be brought by private citizens,[94] and a few states now prescribe by statute certain methods of direct attack that can be used by private persons to challenge incorporations.[95] It is even more widely held that a *collateral* attack on a municipality's incorporation—as by a taxpayer who refuses to pay municipal taxes because he claims the municipality was not properly formed—will not be allowed.[96] And the rule against collateral attack has also been applied where the attack was attempted by another municipality or unit of local government.[97]

---

[91] See Taylor v. Nieusma, 374 Mich. 393, 132 N.W.2d 80 (1965) (equitable relief by residents of area is possible if correct method for incorporation is not being followed). But see Cole v. Langford, 221 Tenn. 458, 427 S.W.2d 562 (1968), where a taxpayer was unsuccessful in an attempt to enjoin an incorporation election.

[92] See Burns v. District Court, 144 Colo. 259, 356 P.2d 245 (1960); St. Joseph & Grand Island Railway v. School District, 114 Kan. 67, 217 P. 296 (1923); State ex rel. Wah-We-Yea-Cuming v. Olson, 107 Minn. 136, 119 N.W. 799 (1909). Cf. Crimmins v. Horseshoe Creek Watershed Joint Dist., 25 Kan.App.2d 63, 956 P.2d 1355 (Kan.App.1998) (private citizens lacked standing to challenge incorporation of municipal watershed district).

[93] Bean v. Town of Vidor, 440 S.W.2d 676 (Tex.Civ.App.1969) ref'd n. r. e.; Harrison v. Bunnell, 420 S.W.2d 777 (Tex.Civ.App.1967). See Enos v. District Court, 124 Colo. 335, 238 P.2d 861 (1951).

[94] Cooper v. Town of Valley Head, 212 Ala. 125, 101 So. 874 (1924) (private citizens can bring quo warranto actions); Richmond v. Town of Largo, 155 Fla. 226, 19 So.2d 791 (1944) (citizens can bring declaratory judgment action); Crabtree v. Stephens, 198 Tenn. 149, 278 S.W.2d 672 (1955) (declaratory judgment).

[95] Daytona Beach Shores v. Foster, 135 So.2d 903 (Fla.App.1961) (statute allows private individual to bring quo warranto action where attorney-general refuses); City of Cincinnati v. Rosi, 92 Ohio App. 8, 109 N.E.2d 290 (1952), appeal dism'd 158 Ohio St. 180, 107 N.E.2d 113 (residents of area allowed by statute to attack incorporation, but nearby municipality could not). See Port Valdez Co. v. City of Valdez, 522 P.2d 1147 (Alaska 1974).

[96] Town of Maysville v. Magnolia Petroleum Co., 272 F.2d 806 (10th Cir.1959) (municipality acting under color of law; its existence cannot be collaterally attacked by private parties); Coe v. City of Los Angeles, 42 Cal.App. 479, 183 P. 822 (Dist.Ct.1919); Burns v. District Court, 144 Colo. 259, 356 P.2d 245 (1960) (de facto corporation could not be collaterally attacked); Wellman v. Burr Oak, 124 Kan. 780, 262 P. 607 (1928) (suit to enjoin collection of taxes not allowed); Mendenhall v. Burton, 42 Kan. 570, 22 P. 558 (1889); Atchison, Topeka & Santa Fe Railroad v. Wilson, 33 Kan. 223, 6 P. 281 (1885); Saylor v. Wallins, 220 Ky. 651, 295 S.W. 993 (1927); People v. Smith, 131 Mich. 70, 90 N.W. 666 (1902); Coe v. Gregory, 53 Mich. 19, 18 N.W. 541 (1884); Sage v. City of Plattsmouth, 48 Neb. 558, 67 N.W. 455 (1896); Northern Pacific Railway v. John Day Irrigation District, 106 Or. 140, 211 P. 781 (1923); Bute v. League City, 390 S.W.2d 811 (Tex.Civ.App.1965). See MacDonell v. North Atlanta, 216 Ga. 559, 118 S.E.2d 460 (1961); DeForest v. Herbert, 204 Kan. 516, 464 P.2d 265 (1970). But there is authority that if not even a de facto municipality exists and if there is no acquiescence or unreasonable delay, a collateral attack by private persons on an incorporation is permitted. See Town of Maysville v. Magnolia Petroleum Co., *supra*; Arnold v. McCarroll, 200 Ark. 1094, 143 S.W.2d 35 (1940); West v. Town of Lake Placid, 97 Fla. 127, 120 So. 361 (1929); Booth v. Copley, 283 Ky. 23, 140 S.W.2d 662 (1940); Fox v. Personnel Appeal Board, 99 R.I. 566, 209 A.2d 447 (1965), motion denied 99 R.I. 566, 210 A.2d 50.

[97] City of Bethany v. Mason, 202 Okla. 66, 210 P.2d 353 (1949); Gladwater v. Pelphrey, 309 S.W.2d 472 (Tex.Civ.App.1957), ref'd n. r. e. (incorporation not totally void; could not be attacked in declaratory judgment proceeding by another municipality); State ex rel. Town of Mercer Island v. City of Mercer Island, 58 Wn.2d 141, 361 P.2d 369 (1961). See Sour Lake v. Branch, 6 F.2d 355 (5th Cir.1925), cert. denied 269 U.S. 565, 46 S.Ct. 24, 70 L.Ed. 414 (1925); Schatzman v. Greenfield, 273 Wis. 277, 77 N.W.2d 511 (1956) (another city not allowed to interplead in action challenging validity of incorporation). Cf. Matter of Incorporation of Fernan Lake Village, 80 Idaho 412, 331 P.2d 278 (1958) (adjacent city not an "aggrieved party" within statute allowing attacks on incorporation); City of Cincinnati v. Rosi, *supra* note 95 (statute allowed residents of area to attack incorporation, but this didn't include nearby municipality). A municipality cannot challenge the validity of its own incorporation, as in an action attempting to avoid one of its own obligations. St. Paul Gaslight Co. v. Sandstone, 73 Minn. 225, 75 N.W. 1050 (1898).

Finally, courts in the United States have applied the rule that where a municipality has not achieved de jure incorporation, it may nonetheless be treated as a de facto municipal corporation whose acts are given validity. Application of this doctrine requires: (1) a statute under which this type of municipal corporation *could* have been organized; (2) a good faith attempt to incorporate under that statute; (3) substantial (or, as sometimes said, "colorable") compliance with the statute; and (4) exercise of municipal powers by the corporation.[98] A couple matters are not entirely clear under this doctrine: the extent to which it will be applied to uphold a municipality's existence even where that existence is attacked by the *state*, and the results that follow where a corporation was so defectively formed that it cannot be held to have even de facto existence, as where no constitutional statute existed under which the incorporation could have occurred or where the entity attempted is one for which there was absolutely no authorization in the state statutes. But courts are extremely reluctant to rule invalid a functioning municipality, and thus it seems the de facto doctrine could be applied even against the state.[99] And it seems that even a totally defective "incorporation" might be treated as a legal entity for purposes of holding it liable on its otherwise lawfully contracted debts.[100]

But if an attempted incorporation lacks even de facto existence, a collateral attack by another municipality might be allowed. Couch v. Fort Worth, 287 S.W.2d 255 (Tex.Civ.App.1956). Cf. Walling v. North Central Texas Municipal Water Authority, 162 Tex. 527, 348 S.W.2d 532 (1961) (if authorizing statute is unconstitutional, there is not even a de facto corporation, and collateral attack is possible). And a city that has already begun annexation proceedings as to an area may be allowed to challenge an incorporation subsequently undertaken in that area. Matter of the Incorporation of the Town of Waconia, 248 Iowa 863, 82 N.W.2d 762 (1957). And finally, other municipal corporations may by statute be given authority to attack an attempted incorporation. See San Ysidro Irrigation District v. Superior Court, 56 Cal.2d 708, 16 Cal.Rptr. 609, 365 P.2d 753 (1961).

[98] Tulare Irrigation District v. Shepard, 185 U.S. 1, 22 S.Ct. 531, 46 L.Ed. 773 (1902); Jefferson v. State, 527 P.2d 37 (Alaska 1974); Waldrop v. Kansas City Southern Railway, 131 Ark. 453, 199 S.W. 369 (1917); Back v. Carpenter, 29 Kan. 349 (1883); Bowman v. City of Moorhead, 228 Minn. 35, 36 N.W.2d 7 (1949); Starbuck v. Havelock, 252 N.C. 176, 113 S.E.2d 278 (1960); City of Guthrie v. Wylie, 6 Okl. 61, 55 P. 103 (1896); Gilkey v. How, 105 Wis. 41, 81 N.W. 120 (1899) (a leading case). See Ocean Beach Heights, Inc. v. Brown-Crummer Investment Co., 302 U.S. 614, 58 S.Ct. 385, 82 L.Ed. 478 (1938), reh. denied 303 U.S. 666, 58 S.Ct. 608, 82 L.Ed. 1123; Cooper v. Town of Valley Head, *supra* note 94. Cf. Rothkopf v. City of Danbury, 156 Conn. 347, 242 A.2d 771 (1968) (merger of cities; de facto doctrine applied). See generally Tooke, De Facto Municipal Corporations under Unconstitutional Statutes, 37 Yale L.J. 935 (1928).

The *Jefferson* case, *supra*, emphasizes, in applying the de facto doctrine, that Alaska broadly construes the powers of its home rule cities, following the theory that home-rule municipalities have those powers not prohibited by state law, rather than the theory that state law prevails over local law in cases of inconsistency except where purely local matters are involved. See Sharp, Home Rule in Alaska: A Clash Between the Constitution and the Court, 3 U.C.L.A.-Alaska L.Rev. 1 (1973). On the different theories as to powers of home-rule municipalities, see generally Chapter 6 *supra*.

De facto corporations are usually said to have the same rights and liabilities as de jure ones. Universal City v. City of Selma, 514 S.W.2d 64 (Tex.Civ.App.1974), ref'd n. r. e. See Blue Summit Landfill, Inc. v. Jackson County, 532 S.W.2d 484 (Mo.App.1975) (permit issued by de facto government is valid even though the incorporation is later invalidated). See generally 1 McQuillin, Municipal Corporations §§ 3.45–.55 (3d rev. ed. 1999); Rhyne, Municipal Law § 2–21 (1957).

[99] See State v. Leatherman, *supra* note 90 (state may be precluded from attacking de facto incorporation); People ex rel. Fitzgerald v. Boyd, 132 Ill. 60, 23 N.E. 342 (1890); State ex rel. West v. Des Moines, *supra* note 90; State ex rel. Brown v. Town of Westport, 116 Mo. 582, 22 S.W. 888 (1893). But cf. City of Carthage v. Burton, 51 Tex.Civ.App. 195, 111 S.W. 440 (1908), saying that if a municipality has been illegally constituted, the state alone *can* take advantage of this.

[100] See Shapleigh v. San Angelo, 167 U.S. 646, 17 S.Ct. 957, 42 L.Ed. 310 (1897) (where incorporation held void, this does not avoid municipality's contract; on reincorporation of area, obligations devolve on new corporation). Cf. Chicot County Drainage District v. Baxter State Bank, 308 U.S. 532, 60 S.Ct. 84, 84 L.Ed. 449 (1939) (bonds of district valid though district was organized under an unconstitutional statute); Blue Summit Landfill v. Jackson County, *supra* note 98 (permit issued by de facto government valid). See generally

The same reluctance to void good-faith actions is found where challenges to annexation are concerned. The three last-mentioned methods used for defending incorporation have also been used where annexations are subject to challenge. Thus, curative statutes have been ruled effective to remedy defects in attempted annexation, so long as no constitutional rights are violated.[101] Attacks on the validity of annexation may be made, by quo warranto action, by the state in which the annexed territory is located.[102] But *collateral* attacks by private individuals—as an attack by an annexed taxpayer who refuses to pay taxes to the municipality that annexed him, claiming the annexation was invalid—are not allowed.[103] There is, however, one difference here from

---

Field, The Status of a Municipal Corporation Organized Under an Unconstitutional Statute, 27 Mich.L.Rev. 523 (1929); Fordham, Local Government Law 256 (1975 rev. ed.), both indicating that collateral attacks on municipal corporations, based on alleged unconstitutionality of the statute under which the corporation was organized, are generally not permitted. It has been concluded that if a statute is found unconstitutional, it could not be taken *by itself* as sufficient color of authority to uphold a unit of local government as a de facto creation, but that sufficient color of authority may be supplied by the recognition of the potential existence of such units by the general laws or constitution of the state. See Tooke, *supra* note 98.

It is true, however, that if even a de facto municipal corporation cannot be found to exist (as where there is *no* color of authority for the corporation's organization), collateral attacks may sometimes be allowed where they would not be permitted if de facto existence were present. See notes 96 & 97 *supra*. Thus, the rule on de facto existence and the rule limiting those persons who may attack corporate existence often go hand-in-hand.

101 Sacramento Municipal Utility District v. All Parties and Persons, 6 Cal.2d 197, 57 P.2d 506 (1936); City of Sebring v. Harder Hall, Inc., 150 Fla. 824, 9 So.2d 350 (1942); Steger v. Traveling Men's Building & Loan Association, 208 Ill. 236, 70 N.E. 236 (1904); United States Mortgage Co. v. Gross, 93 Ill. 483 (1879), aff'd 108 U.S. 477, 2 S.Ct. 940, 27 L.Ed. 795 (1883); Hufstedler v. City of Lubbock, 40 S.W.2d 982 (Tex.Civ.App.1931). But such validating acts have been said to be for the purpose of curing technical or procedural defects, and not capable of legalizing annexations for which there could be no possible legal basis. See People ex rel. Forde v. Town of Corte Madera, 115 Cal.App.2d 32, 251 P.2d 988 (1952); Town of Davie v. Hartline, 199 So.2d 280 (Fla.1967) (annexation under unconstitutional statute); Beaty v. Inlet Beach, Inc., 151 Fla. 495, 9 So.2d 735 (1942), motion denied and opinion modified 152 Fla. 276, 10 So.2d 807. Cf. Gray County Production Co. v. Christian, 231 S.W.2d 901 (Tex.Civ.App.1950) (curative act didn't validate annexation of more land than was needed for town purposes). And a mere act of the legislature cannot validate an act that contravenes the state constitution. See 1 McQuillin, Municipal Corporations § 3.47, at 379 (3d rev. ed. 1999). But even an unconstitutional annexation could, it seems, be validated by an amendment to the constitution. Oakwood Independent School District v. Liberty Common School District, 10 S.W.2d 174 (Tex.Civ.App.1928), error ref'd. And at least one case has held that even a totally void annexation can be validated by mere act of the legislature, where there is no constitutional prohibition. City of Arlington v. City of Grand Prairie, 451 S.W.2d 284 (Tex.Civ.App.1970), ref'd n. r. e. As to curative statutes that create a presumption of validity as to annexations, see generally Davis v. Provo City Corp., 193 P.3d 86 (Utah 2008) (area annexed to a municipality is conclusively presumed to have been validly annexed if two conditions are met: the municipality has levied, and taxpayers within the area have paid, property taxes for more than a year, and no resident of the area contested the annexation during that year; this is not a statute of limitations but a substantive rule of law affecting the ability of a party successfully to challenge an annexation).

102 People ex rel. Averna v. City of Palm Springs, 51 Cal.2d 38, 331 P.2d 4 (1958); People ex rel. Peck v. City of Los Angeles, 154 Cal. 220, 97 P. 311 (1908); Levitt v. Wilson, 72 Kan. 160, 83 P. 397 (1905); Lincoln v. Village of Robbins, 15 Ill.App.2d 293, 146 N.E.2d 216 (1957); Town of Luther v. State, 425 P.2d 986 (Okl.1967); City of San Antonio v. State ex rel. Town of Olmos Park, 195 S.W.2d 421 (Tex.Civ.App.1946); State ex rel. Thigpen v. City of Kent, 64 Wn.2d 823, 394 P.2d 686 (1964).

103 Burton v. City of Tucson, 88 Ariz. 320, 356 P.2d 413 (1960); Burton v. Kautenburger, 88 Ariz. 319, 356 P.2d 412 (1960); Lincoln v. Village of Robbins, *supra* note 102 (declaratory judgment action); Smith v. City of Emporia, 168 Kan. 187, 211 P.2d 101 (1949); Gardner v. Benn, 81 Kan. 442, 105 P. 435 (1909) (suit to enjoin tax collection); City of Topeka v. Dwyer, 70 Kan. 244, 78 P. 417 (1904) (suit to resist enforcement of city ordinances); Phillips v. City of Odessa, 287 S.W.2d 518 (Tex.Civ.App.1956), ref'd n. r. e. (declaratory judgment); Lefler v. City of Dallas, 177 S.W.2d 231 (Tex.Civ.App.1943); Tod v. City of Houston, 276 S.W. 419 (Tex.Com.App.1925) (suit to enjoin tax collection); Harris v. City of Port Arthur, 267 S.W. 349 (Tex.Civ.App.1924), error dism'd (suit to enjoin sale of improvement bonds); Dixon v. City of Bremerton, 25 Wn.2d 508, 171 P.2d 243 (1946). See North Miami Beach v. Bernay, 117 So.2d 863 (Fla.App.1960) (declaratory judgment); City of Blackwell v. City of Newkirk, 31 Okla. 304, 121 P. 260 (1912), error dism'd 232 U.S. 718, 34 S.Ct. 479, 58 L.Ed. 813 (1914). Some courts, though following this general rule, will nonetheless allow collateral

the situation as to challenges to incorporations: by statute or court-made rule, other governmental entities affected by annexation are now being allowed to bring direct attacks (as by declaratory judgment proceedings) against the annexation,[104] and have even been allowed in some cases to make a collateral attack.[105] And private persons directly affected by annexation (such as residents or property-owners within the annexed area) are now generally being allowed to make *direct* attacks on that annexation, as by declaratory judgment proceedings, actions to enjoin the annexation, and mandamus actions.[106] Finally, the above-described "de facto" doctrine has been applied to annexations, as well as incorporations, so that a good faith attempt to annex, coupled

---

attacks on annexation if the proceedings are not yet final. See Colquhoun v. City of Tucson, 55 Ariz. 451, 103 P.2d 269 (1940); American Distilling Co. v. City Council, 34 Cal.2d 660, 213 P.2d 704 (1950). Cf. In re De-Annexation of Certain Real Property from City of Seminole, 143 P.3d 228 (Okla. Civ. App. 2006) (ordinance annexing territory to a city which on its face recites the jurisdictional facts giving the city jurisdiction to annex the territory may not be collaterally attacked by a private individual; but ordinance which fails to give the jurisdictional facts *is* subject to collateral attack).

[104] Johnson v. City of San Pablo, 132 Cal.App.2d 447, 283 P.2d 57 (Dist.Ct.1955) (municipality competing for annexation of same territory); Jefferson Union School District v. City Council of Sunnyvale, 129 Cal.App.2d 264, 277 P.2d 104 (Dist.Ct.1954) (school district which would lose territory if annexation succeeded); Elkins v. City and County of Denver, 157 Colo. 252, 402 P.2d 617 (1965) (statute authorized attack by county); Town of Burnsville v. City of Bloomington, 264 Minn. 133, 117 N.W.2d 746 (1962) (declaratory judgment action allowed); St. Louis County v. Village of Champ, 438 S.W.2d 205 (Mo.1969) (statute authorized attack by county); In re Annexation of Portion of South Pymatuning Township, 409 Pa. 324, 186 A.2d 13 (1962) (statute authorized attack by township); Town of Fond du Lac v. City of Fond du Lac, 22 Wis.2d 533, 126 N.W.2d 201 (1964) (declaratory judgment allowed); Town of Blooming Grove v. City of Madison, 275 Wis. 328, 81 N.W.2d 713 (1957) (statute authorized attack by town). But see State ex rel. Kreamer v. City of Overland Park, 192 Kan. 654, 391 P.2d 128 (1964) (one city not allowed to attack another city's annexation). See generally Annot., Right of One Government Subdivision to Challenge Annexation Proceedings by Another Such Subdivision, 17 A.L.R. 5th 195 (1994).

[105] Galena Park v. City of Houston, 133 S.W.2d 162 (Tex.Civ.App.1939); Town of Griffing Park v. City of Port Arthur, 36 S.W.2d 593 (Tex.Civ.App.1931); Town of Wauwatosa v. City of Milwaukee, 259 Wis. 56, 47 N.W.2d 442 (1951).

[106] Hubbell v. City of Los Angeles, 142 Cal.App.2d 1, 297 P.2d 724 (Dist.Ct.1956) (mandamus allowed); Gavend v. City of Thornton, 165 Colo. 182, 437 P.2d 778 (1968); Julian v. City of Liberty, 427 S.W.2d 300 (Mo. App.1968) (suit to enjoin annexing municipality from exercising jurisdiction over annexed territory); Stoltman v. City of Clayton, 205 Mo.App. 568, 226 S.W. 315 (1920) (action to set annexation aside); City of Pasadena v. Houston Endowment, Inc., 438 S.W.2d 152 (Tex.Civ.App.1969), ref'd n. r. e. (suit to enjoin exercise of jurisdiction); City of Irving v. Callaway, 363 S.W.2d 832 (Tex.Civ.App.1962) ref'd n. r. e. (suit to enjoin proposed annexation); Schatzman v. Town of Greenfield, 273 Wis. 277, 77 N.W.2d 511 (1956). See Sullivan v. City of Omaha, 183 Neb. 511, 162 N.W.2d 227 (1968); Red River Valley Brick Co. v. City of Grand Forks, 27 N.D. 8, 145 N.W. 725 (1914) (suit to enjoin annexation); Lutien v. City of Kewaunee, 143 Wis. 242, 126 N.W. 662 (1910), reh. denied 143 Wis. 242, 127 N.W. 942. Cf. Citizens for Cold Springs v. City of Reno, 125 Nev. 625, 218 P.3d 847 (2009) (under Nevada law, any person or city claiming to be adversely affected by an annexation decision may challenge it). The time limits for any such attacks are often short, and strictly enforced. See Village of Brown Deer v. City of Milwaukee, 2 Wis.2d 441, 86 N.W.2d 487 (1957). Cf. Schanz v. City of Billings, 182 Mont. 328, 597 P.2d 67 (1979) (developers estopped to deny that annexation of their property was valid where they had initiated the annexation proceedings and had enjoyed benefits for 3 years). Such attacks are not allowed by the owners of land that is merely adjacent to, not within, the area purported to be annexed. See Knudsen v. Ereaux, 275 Mont. 146, 911 P.2d 835 (Mont. 1996) (plaintiffs who did not own property within proposed annexation could not directly or collaterally attack the annexation). And if a statute authorizes a particular form of attack by private persons, it may well be held that this is an exclusive remedy. See Schurman v. City of Holland, 355 Mich. 406, 94 N.W.2d 808 (1959). Cf. Santa Fe County Bd. of County Comm'rs v. Town of Edgewood, 136 N.M. 301, 97 P.3d 633 (App. 2004) (statute limiting appeal of annexation to persons "owning land" within the annexed territory applies only to those having an interest in real property that amounts to an equitable or fee title).

with substantial compliance with relevant statutes, will cause the annexation to be upheld, despite failure to comply with some technical requirements.[107]

During the time that annexation is being challenged, the territory in question will be treated as part of the municipality which has attempted the annexation; thus, the disputed area will be subject to municipal taxes, and entitled to receive municipal services, during this period.[108]

In this area of disputed incorporations and annexations, there is a general tendency of the courts away from flat rules, and toward a weighing, in each case, of such factors as whether the challenge is direct or collateral (with direct attacks more likely to succeed), whether the attempted annexation or incorporation was performed under some color of authority (with such authority making the attempt more likely to be held valid), the length of time that has passed without prior challenge to the alleged incorporation or annexation (with the chances of the incorporation or annexation being overthrown becoming progressively less with each passing year), and the possible effect of any validating legislation.

§ 12.8 "De-Annexation" or "Severance"

The terms "de-annexation," "disannexation," "detachment," "severance," and "exclusion" are all used to refer to the severing of territory from a municipality to which that territory had formerly been attached. In the absence of statutory authority, it is usually agreed that a municipality cannot detach areas from its territory;[109] nor can courts order such detachment without legislative authorization.[110] But it is generally

---

107 Port Valdez Co. v. City of Valdez, 522 P.2d 1147 (Alaska 1974); Skinner v. City of Phoenix, 54 Ariz. 316, 95 P.2d 424 (1939); Hazelton v. City of San Diego, 183 Cal.App.2d 131, 6 Cal.Rptr. 723 (Dist.Ct.1960), cert. denied 366 U.S. 910, 81 S.Ct. 1084, 6 L.Ed.2d 235, reh. denied 368 U.S. 870, 82 S.Ct. 25, 7 L.Ed.2d 71 (1961); Griffin v. City of Canon City, 147 Colo. 15, 362 P.2d 200 (1961); Petition of Kansas City, 190 Kan. 308, 374 P.2d 35 (1962); Saylor v. Town of Wallins, 220 Ky. 651, 295 S.W. 993 (1927); White v. City of Columbia, 461 S.W.2d 806 (Mo.1970); Kuhn v. City of Port Townsend, 12 Wash. 605, 41 P. 923 (1895). See Gorman v. City of Phoenix, 70 Ariz. 59, 216 P.2d 400 (1950); Cooper v. Leslie Salt Co., 70 Cal.2d 627, 75 Cal.Rptr. 766, 451 P.2d 406 (1969), cert. denied 396 U.S. 821, 90 S.Ct. 62, 24 L.Ed.2d 72. It seems the doctrine can even be applied against the state. See People ex rel. Knaus v. Village of Hinsdale, 111 Ill.App.2d 368, 250 N.E.2d 309 (1969) (village had exercised jurisdiction over the area for more than 40 years). Cf. People ex rel. Lindsey v. Board of Education, 3 Ill.2d 159, 120 N.E.2d 887 (1954) (quo warranto denied because of laches, and because of great inconvenience that would result from ouster); State ex rel. Dawson v. City of Harper, 94 Kan. 478, 146 P. 1169 (1915) (state estopped due to its acquiescence). Thus, though there is very little authority, it seems that even the doctrine of acquiescence or prescription (the "first-mentioned doctrine," *supra* note 85 and accompanying text), used to uphold incorporations, can also be used to uphold annexations.

108 City Council v. Board of Directors, 181 Colo. 334, 509 P.2d 317 (1973).

109 Atchison & E. Bridge Co. v. Atchison County, 150 Kan. 24, 91 P.2d 34 (1939); City of New York v. Village of Lawrence, 250 N.Y. 429, 165 N.E. 836 (1929). See generally Note, Losing Ground: *Seminole* and the Annexation Power of Municipalities in Oklahoma, 58 Okla. L. Rev. 527 (2005), noting In re De-Annexation of Certain Real Property from the City of Seminole, 102 P.3d 120 (Okla. 2004).

110 Littleton v. Wagenblast, 139 Colo. 346, 338 P.2d 1025 (1959); Woolverton v. Albany, 152 Ind. 77, 52 N.E. 455 (1899). See Richards v. City of Tustin, 225 Cal.App.2d 97, 37 Cal.Rptr. 124 (Dist.Ct.1964) (city withheld consent to deannexation; court was without power to order such, even though city was not providing sewage services to area); Punke v. Village of Elliott, 364 Ill. 604, 5 N.E.2d 389 (1936); City of Hastings v. Hansen, 44 Neb. 704, 63 N.W. 34 (1895); Consolidated Gray-Fordtown-Colonial Heights Utility District v. O'Neill, 209 Tenn. 342, 354 S.W.2d 63 (1962). Cf. In re De-Annexation of Certain Real Property, 662 P.2d 1375 (Okl.1983) (court invalidated statute under which district court was to declare a requested de-annexation, or annexation, if it found that this could be granted without injustice to the inhabitants or other interested persons; this was found an improper delegation of legislative power to the courts). Compare Kel-Kan Inv. Corp. v. Village of Greenwood, 428 So.2d 401 (La.1983) (court exceeded its authority in ordering de-annexation where were no overriding public policy considerations or countervailing interests of an adjoining municipality). See

recognized that areas not being served by a unit of local government, and with no reasonable prospect of being served in the foreseeable future, should not be subject to the burdens of taxation and regulation by that government.[111] Therefore, general statutes in most states now provide methods by which detachment of land—particularly undeveloped land located along the border of a municipality—can be detached; and the validity of such statutes has been upheld even where the consent of the inhabitants of the disconnected area need not be obtained.[112] The method usually provided by statute involves (1) the signing of a petition for detachment by a specified number or percentage of residents (or property owners) in the area concerned, or the drafting of a request by the city legislative body, (2) the presentation of this petition or request to some judicial or administrative body specified by statute,[113] (3) the review of the petition by the designated judicial or administrative authority to determine whether there is

---

generally Annot., Power to Detach Land from Municipal Corporations, Towns, or Villages, 117 A.L.R. 267, 272 (1938). McQuillin states flatly that courts have no power, absent statutory authorization, to detach territory from municipalities. 2 McQuillin, Municipal Corporations § 7.24, at 401 (3d rev. ed. 1996). But a few cases have actually held that courts have equity power to order detachment of territory where no municipal services are being provided. See State ex rel. Attorney General v. City of Avon Park, 108 Fla. 641, 149 So. 409 (1933), reh. denied 117 Fla. 556, 151 So. 701, modified 117 Fla. 565, 158 So. 159; Sole v. City of Geneva, 106 Neb. 879, 184 N.W. 900 (1921); Plutus Mining Co. v. Orme, 76 Utah 286, 289 P. 132 (1930). See generally Note, Secession in the Garden State: The Secession Movement in Essex County, New Jersey, and the Law of Deannexation, 57 Rutgers L. Rev. 1417 (2005). Some statutes limit de-annexation, or certain methods thereof, to *non*-home-rule municipalities. See Allely v. City of Evans, 124 P.3d 911 (Colo. App. 2005) (definition of "city" in de-annexation statute excluded home-rule municipalities).

[111] See Metropolitan Sanitary District v. Palos Heights, 30 Ill.App.2d 336, 174 N.E.2d 574 (1961) (purpose of disconnection is to provide relief to taxpayers in the area); Pittsburgh-Des Moines Steel Co. v. Clive, 249 Iowa 1346, 91 N.W.2d 602 (1958) (purpose is to give relief where area included in municipality only for revenue purposes); Hunter v. City of Tracy, 104 Minn. 378, 116 N.W. 922 (1908). Cf. McKeon v. Council Bluffs, 206 Iowa 556, 221 N.W. 351 (1928) (river changed course by avulsion, leaving state boundary unchanged by cutting city of Council Bluffs in two; equity procedure for severance applied under statute). Though the *McKeon* case *supra* relied on a statute, it also contains a strong statement of the general obligation of a city to provide equal services to all its parts and of the right of an area not so treated to be severed from the city. Cf. Johnson v. Town of Suwannee River, 336 So.2d 122 (Fla.App.1976) (tract receiving no municipal services may properly be deannexed).

Another possible remedy for a portion of a municipality that is victim to discrimination is an action under the Federal Civil Rights Act to require equalization of services. See Hawkins v. Town of Shaw, 437 F.2d 1286 (5th Cir.1971) (municipal policy had resulted in black neighborhoods receiving substantially inferior services), noted 37 Brooklyn L.Rev. 568 (1971) (calling this a landmark decision in civil rights), 1971 Utah L.Rev. 397 (saying case adds little to established principles, though it illustrates importance of statistical evidence in equal protection cases). See generally Haar & Fessler, The Wrong Side of the Tracks (Simon & Schuster 1986), reviewed 19 Urban Law. 176 (1987), discussing possible legal remedies for inequality in provision of municipal services and noting that the value of the *Hawkins* case *supra* was largely destroyed by Washington v. Davis, 426 U.S. 229, 96 S.Ct. 2040, 48 L.Ed.2d 597 (1976), requiring discriminatory intent, not merely discriminatory effect, for the invalidation of a law under equal protection.

[112] Hunter v. Pittsburgh, 207 U.S. 161, 28 S.Ct. 40, 52 L.Ed. 151 (1907); Gewecke v. Niles, 368 Ill. 463, 14 N.E.2d 482 (1938); Kingsford v. Cudlip, 258 Mich. 144, 241 N.W. 893 (1932); Adriansen v. Board of Education, 248 N.Y. 542, 162 N.E. 517 (1928); Oneida v. Pearson Hardwood Flooring Co., 169 Tenn. 449, 88 S.W.2d 998 (1935). See Town of Malabar v. State, 195 So.2d 43 (Fla.App.1967); Hickory Lane Land & Dev. Co. v. Novi, 372 Mich. 219, 125 N.W.2d 487 (1964). But a statute intended to be used for disenfranchising a particular racial group can, of course, be ruled unconstitutional. Gomillion v. Lightfoot, 364 U.S. 339, 81 S.Ct. 125, 5 L.Ed.2d 110 (1960). See generally Bickley, Annexation and Disannexation, 24 S.W.L.J. 202 (1970). Some statutes disallow de-annexation where it would mar the symmetry of the municipality. See Williamson v. City of McCall, 135 Idaho 452, 19 P.3d 766 (2001) (evidence supported finding that symmetry of city would be materially marred by detachment of property).

[113] McCombs v. West, 155 F.2d 601 (5th Cir.1946). See In re Mathews, 59 App.Div. 159, 69 N.Y.S. 203 (1901); Petition of Parks, 71 S.D. 401, 24 N.W.2d 919 (1946). Cf. Howard v. North Salt Lake, 3 Utah 2d 189, 281 P.2d 216 (1955) (petition not signed by majority of real property owners as required; proceedings set aside).

substantial compliance with the statutory conditions,[114] and (4) the granting or denial of the petition by the judicial or administrative authority, depending on the reasonableness and equity of the request, with particular attention to whether or not the area in question is receiving any substantial benefits from the local unit and whether there are reasonable prospects for such benefits in the near future.[115] It is agreed that a municipality cannot retain undeveloped land merely for revenue purposes.[116]

Any bonds or other obligations of the unit from which the territory has been detached remain, of course, binding on the still-existing unit and all its remaining property; therefore, bondholders or creditors of the unit cannot prevent detachment

---

[114] Independent Amusements, Inc., v. Village of Milan, 348 Ill.App. 258, 109 N.E.2d 238 (1952); Temple v. Fulton, 430 S.W.2d 737 (Tex.Civ.App.1968) ref'd n. r. e. See Metropolitan Sanitary District v. Palos Heights, *supra* note 111 (favoring liberally allowing deannexation); Enderson v. Hildenbrand, 52 N.D. 533, 204 N.W. 356 (1925) (court merely determines whether the factual conditions set by the legislature have been met). Cf. LaSalle National Bank v. Burr Ridge, 81 Ill.App.2d 209, 225 N.E.2d 33 (1967) (in Illinois, court *must* order detachment where conditions met). Among the factual conditions often specified for deannexation are geographic location (usually along the border of the municipality) and/or inadequate municipal services. The reviewing court or authority can always consider whether or not these conditions have been met. See Enderson v. Hildenbrand, *supra*. Sometimes a minimum area is set by statute below which the municipality cannot be reduced by de-annexation. See Vernon's Ann.Tex.Civ.Code art. 975 (cannot be reduced to lesser area than one square mile or one mile in diameter around center of original corporate limits). See also Harvey v. Cedar Hills City, 227 P.3d 256 (Utah 2010), applying Utah statute that required court to consider whether a proposed disconnection would leave the municipality with a residual area for which the cost, requirements, or other burdens of municipal services would materially increase over previous years or for which it would become economically or practically unreasonable to administer as a municipality.

[115] See Town of Medley v. Seminole Rock Products, Inc., 138 So.2d 534 (Fla.App.1962); Klemm v. Winter Haven, 114 So.2d 11 (Fla. App.1959); Van Allen v. Town of Ocean Ridge, 46 So.2d 452 (Fla.1950); Evans v. Council Bluffs, 65 Iowa 238, 21 N.W. 584 (1884) (test of reasonableness emphasized); Secord v. Village of Leonard, 307 Mich. 134, 11 N.W.2d 833 (1943) (test is whether detachment would be inequitable to municipality); Marshall v. Mayor & Board of Selectmen of McComb City, 251 Miss. 750, 171 So.2d 347 (1965), cert. denied 382 U.S. 836, 86 S.Ct. 83, 15 L.Ed.2d 79 (test is whether area receiving substantial benefits); West Point Island Civic Association v. Dover Township, 97 N.J.Super. 549, 235 A.2d 507 (1967), aff'd 54 N.J. 339, 255 A.2d 237 (1969) (township could be ordered to consent to detachment of territory from it where it had no reasonable grounds to refuse); Brooks v. South Sioux Falls, 76 S.D. 114, 73 N.W.2d 339 (1955) (exclusion refused where much of area was reasonably needed by city for residential use); Klosterman v. City of Elkton, 53 S.D. 324, 220 N.W. 910 (1928) (test of reasonableness); Zajicek v. Wessington, 53 S.D. 315, 220 N.W. 913 (1928). Cf. Iowa Power & Light Co. v. Pleasant Hill, 253 Iowa 532, 112 N.W.2d 304 (1961) (test is whether municipality incapable of extending services into territory); Shelton Grain & Supply Co. v. Village of Shelton, 178 Neb. 695, 134 N.W.2d 815 (1965) (upholding statute authorizing detachment where justice and equity require); Davidson v. City of Ravenna, 153 Neb. 652, 45 N.W.2d 741 (1951) (test is whether is community of interest between territory to be detached and the territory as an entirety); In re Matter of Disconnection of Territory of City of Draper, 646 P.2d 699 (Utah 1982) (judicial order of de-annexation found supported by "justice and equity" where city would not be prejudiced other than by loss of property taxes from the de-annexed land and where the disconnection did not create "islands" or "peninsulas" that would increase the city's cost of providing services to unreasonable levels). See generally In re Disconnection of Certain Territory from Highland City, 668 P.2d 544 (Utah 1983), listing factors the court should consider in ruling on a de-annexation petition and holding that the court did not err in refusing to consider the concerns and desires of city residents for their life-style. Compare, applying the Utah statute, Bluffdale Mountain Homes, LC v. Bluffdale City, 2007 UT 57, 167 P.3d 1016 (2007), where it was held that the issues of whether disconnection from a municipality would materially increase the costs to the municipality of providing services and the issue of whether a disconnection would make it economically or practically unfeasible for the municipality to continue to function are questions of fact, on which the Supreme Court will not reverse unless clearly erroneous, while the issue of whether justice and equity require that the territory be disconnected is a mixed question of fact and law, subject to substantial deference but not so much deference that the court will reverse only when a determination is clearly erroneous.

[116] Hustead v. Village of Phillips, 131 Neb. 303, 267 N.W. 919 (1936); Runyan v. Ong, 154 Neb. 127, 47 N.W.2d 97 (1951); Thiel v. City of Alexandria, 41 S.D. 427, 171 N.W. 209 (1919). It would seem that a municipality shouldn't retain even *developed* land merely for revenue purposes. See McKeon v. Council Bluffs, *supra* note 111.

unless they show that their security is being substantially weakened.[117] Does the detached territory remain subject to taxation or assessment for obligations incurred prior to the detachment? Most authority says that in the absence of statutory provision to the contrary, it does not.[118] There is a certain inequity in this, since property owners in the detached area may have benefited, and may be continuing to benefit, from improvements for which they are no longer obligated to pay. Thus, at least one jurisdiction has ruled that detached lands are not released from taxation for payment of obligations incurred by a municipality while those lands were part of that municipality.[119]

§ 12.9 "Division"

The term "division" refers to the splitting of some territory of one municipal corporation between that corporation and another (as opposed to the above-discussed situation of "de-annexation" where land is merely taken out from under one municipal corporation *without* being placed under the jurisdiction of another). Except as limited by the constitution, the legislature may engage in division of territory among local units and may apportion the property and burdens in any reasonable manner.[120] Unless clearly provided otherwise, each unit remains liable for all its debts existing at the time of the division, even where some debt was incurred for the benefit of land that is now under the control of another unit.[121] It seems, however, that the legislature must, in

---

[117] See Von Hoffman v. City of Quincy, 71 U.S. 535, 4 Wall. 535, 18 L.Ed. 403 (1866) (bondholders have contractual relationship with local units that is protected by Contract Clause of U.S. Constitution; legislative acts unreasonably weakening security can be unconstitutional); City of Fort Myers v. State, 129 Fla. 166, 176 So. 483 (1937); Hardin v. Pavlat, 130 Neb. 829, 266 N.W. 637 (1936) (bondholders don't have lien on property within municipality to secure their payments; normally, bondholders should have constructive knowledge that municipal boundaries might be changed); Metcalf v. State, 49 Ohio St. 586, 31 N.E. 1076 (1892). See generally, Case Comment, Municipal Corporations—Effect of Disannexation on Rights of Bondholders, 21 Fla.L.J. 22 (1947).

[118] Miller v. Pineville, 121 Ky. 211, 89 S.W. 261 (1905); Ocoee v. Bell, 108 So.2d 766 (Fla.App.1959). See Punke v. Village of Elliott, 364 Ill. 604, 5 N.E.2d 389 (1936) (applying statute). As to control over public roads following de-annexation, see Martini v. Smith, 42 P.3d 629 (Colo. 2002) (upon de-annexation, county took control of road).

[119] Certain Lands v. Town of Lake Placid, 49 So.2d 542 (Fla.1950). Cf. Hardin v. Pavlat, *supra* note 117 (disconnecting of lands from village so as not to render such lands subject to payment of bonds did not impair bondholder's contract). It has been held that if a property owner's land has been subjected to assessments for an improvement, he can continue to utilize that improvement even though his land is subsequently detached from the local unit responsible therefor. Catholic Foreign Mission Society v. Glen Ellyn, 339 Ill.App. 565, 90 N.E.2d 653 (1950).

[120] See Laramie County v. Albany County, 92 U.S. 307, 23 L.Ed. 552 (1875); Corby v. City of Detroit, 180 Mich. 208, 146 N.W. 670 (1914); State ex rel. Behrens v. Crismon, 354 Mo. 174, 188 S.W.2d 937 (1945); Graham v. Township of Edison, 35 N.J. 537, 173 A.2d 403 (1961); Town of Cassian v. Town of Nokomis, 254 Wis. 94, 35 N.W.2d 408 (1948) (applying statute). Cf. Hustead v. Village of Phillips, 131 Neb. 303, 267 N.W. 919 (1936) (legislature has absolute power to change boundaries of municipal corporations); City of New York v. Village of Lawrence, 250 N.Y. 429, 165 N.E. 836 (1929) (special law upheld); Metcalf v. State, 49 Ohio St. 586, 31 N.E. 1076 (1892) (same).

[121] See Laramie County v. Albany County, *supra* note 120; Turnbull v. Alpena School District, 45 Mich. 496, 8 N.W. 65 (1881); Schriber v. Town of Langlade, 66 Wis. 616, 29 N.W. 547 (1886). Cf. O'Connor v. Memphis, 74 Tenn. 730 (1881), recognizing a possible exception where a municipality is so reduced in population and territory by detachment that it could not meet its liabilities. See also City of Jeffersonville v. Jeffersonville School Township, 77 Ind.App. 32, 130 N.E. 879 (1921) (title to public property annexed to municipal corporation passes to municipal corporation without payment of compensation to governmental unit from which taken); Custer County Bank v. Custer County, 18 S.D. 274, 100 N.W. 424 (1904) (legislature transferred to a town all that part of a road district that was within the town; county, not town, liable on road warrants issued by county prior to transfer).

engaging in division, exercise care not to weaken substantially the security of creditors of any local unit; any such substantial weakening can cause the legislative act to be struck down as an unconstitutional infringement on the obligation of contracts.[122]

§ 12.10 Merger and Consolidation

State legislatures also have plenary power to merge and to consolidate municipal corporations.[123] Technically, "merger" occurs when one corporation swallows another (*A* absorbs *B; A* continues in existence, while *B* becomes defunct), and "consolidation" occurs when a new corporation is formed by two or more previously existing units (*A* and *B* form *C*, and neither *A* nor *B* any longer exists). But in municipal law, the terms are frequently used inexactly; in any particular state, there is often only one procedure that is called either "merger" or "consolidation"—or that is sometimes called by one name and sometimes by the other; and the requirements and results depend more on the governing statutes than on the terminology used.[124] The traditional distinction between terms does, however, have some relevance here: merger, unless otherwise provided by statute, causes the larger (in population) municipal corporation to succeed to the property, contracts, and debts of the smaller corporation,[125] while in consolidation the new corporation succeeds to the property, contracts, and debts of *all* the absorbed units.[126]

---

[122] See Brewis v. Duluth, 13 F. 334 (C.C.Minn.1882); Winter Haven v. A.M. Klemm & Son, 132 Fla. 334, 181 So. 153 (1938), reh. denied 133 Fla. 525, 182 So. 841; Humphreys v. State ex rel. Palm Beach Co., 108 Fla. 92, 145 So. 858 (1933). Cf. American Bemberg Corp. v. City of Elizabethton, 180 Tenn. 373, 175 S.W.2d 535 (1943) (where contracting of municipal boundaries occurs in such manner as to interfere with bond payments of the municipality, might be subject to constitutional objection).

[123] Hunter v. Pittsburgh, 207 U.S. 161, 28 S.Ct. 40, 52 L.Ed. 151 (1907); Douglas v. City and Borough of Juneau, 484 P.2d 1040 (Alaska 1971) (consolidation can be ordered by legislature even though home-rule municipalities are involved); Brown Deer v. Milwaukee, 2 Wis.2d 441, 86 N.W.2d 487 (1957). Much recent "consolidation" has involved the unifying of county government with the governments of cities within the county. See Bollens & Schmandt, The Metropolis 303–04 (1970); Note, Decentralization of Metropolitan Government: Reform in Indianapolis, 4 *J.* Law Reform 310 (1970); 61 Nat'l Civic Rev. 417–19 (1972). See generally Chapter 2 *supra*. The constitutionality of these consolidations has been upheld. Jackson v. Consolidated Government of Jacksonville, 225 So.2d 497 (Fla.1969); Dortch v. Lugar, 255 Ind. 545, 266 N.E.2d 25 (1971) (act consolidating Indianapolis and Marion County upheld); Frazer v. Carr, 210 Tenn. 565, 360 S.W.2d 449 (1962) (legislative act authorizing consolidation of Nashville and Davidson County upheld; government had two districts—one covering the whole area, and one covering only the former city limits—with differing tax rates). A slightly differing response, with limited use so far, to the problems of metropolitan areas is the creation of "metropolitan special districts"—multiple function districts to provide most of the local government needed in large urban centers. See Tobin, The Legal and Governmental Status of the Metropolitan Special District, 13 U.Miami L.Rev. 129 (1958); Note, Special Districts and Deficient Local Government in Salt Lake Metropolitan Area, 7 Utah L.Rev. 229 (1960). See generally Pock, Independent Special Districts: A Solution to the Metropolitan Area Problem (1962); Tobin, The Metropolitan Special District: Inter-County Metropolitan Government of Tomorrow, 14 U.Miami L.Rev. 333 (1960).

The consolidation or merger discussed here in Section 75 generally requires the participation of at least two municipalities. See Mid-County Future Alternatives Comm. v. Portland Metropolitan Area Local Gov't Boundary Comm'n, 300 Or. 14, 706 P.2d 924 (1985) (consolidation could not be used to bring unincorporated territory into a municipality).

[124] See Fordham, Local Government Law 202–03 (2d rev. ed. 1986).

[125] Mount Pleasant v. Beckwith, 100 U.S. 514, 25 L.Ed. 699 (1879); Ensley v. Simpson, 166 Ala. 366, 52 So. 61 (1909); Fuller v. Consolidated Rural High School District, 138 Kan. 881, 28 P.2d 750 (1934); Thompson v. Abbott, 61 Mo. 176 (1875). See People ex rel. City of Downey v. Downey County Water District, 202 Cal.App.2d 786, 21 Cal.Rptr. 370 (Dist.Ct.1962). The ordinances of the larger unit are often treated, by statute or common law, as effective throughout the area following the merger. The ordinances of the smaller unit become inoperative—except that zoning ordinances may remain in effect till superseded by later laws. See generally Fordham, *supra* note 124, at 203.

[126] State v. Miami, 103 Fla. 54, 137 So. 261 (1931); Kocsis v. Chicago Park District, 362 Ill. 24, 198 N.E. 847 (1935); Peterson v. Swan, 231 Iowa 745, 2 N.W.2d 70 (1942); Wilson v. School District, 233 Mich. 581, 207

The procedure for either merger or consolidation is usually specified by general statute of the state and generally provides either for a petition of voters (or property holders), *or* a vote of the municipal governing body, in each of the affected municipalities, *plus* in any case, an election in each of the affected municipalities.[127] Substantial compliance with all statutory requirements is needed.[128] In some states, consolidations or mergers must now be approved by a state administrative body.[129]

Occasionally, merger has been held to have occurred by operation of law. This happens where all the territory of a special function district, or other local unit of limited powers, such as a fire protection district, is annexed by a municipality with power to exercise the same function(s).[130] The doctrine is applied in order to prevent unnecessary duplication of functions.

N.W. 810 (1926); Troop v. City of Pittsburgh, 254 Pa. 172, 98 A. 1034 (1916). By statute or common law, the ordinances of both cities are generally treated in this situation as applicable to the whole territory following the consolidation. See Pittsburgh v. Pennsylvania Railroad, 394 Pa. 58, 145 A.2d 700 (1958) (statute so provided). Cf. Ratliff v. Lexington-Fayette Urban County Government, 540 S.W.2d 8 (Ky.1976), cert. denied 429 U.S. 1096, 97 S.Ct. 1113, 51 L.Ed.2d 544 (charter may provide that ordinances of one or both units shall be effective).

[127] See Bouldin v. Homewood, 277 Ala. 665, 174 So.2d 306 (1965) (proper elections must be held); Wolf v. Petty, 414 S.W.2d 539 (Tex.Civ.App.1967) (mandamus can be used to compel official action where petitions properly filed). But there is no constitutional right to an election in such situations unless the state constitution clearly so provides; otherwise, the legislature may order consolidation without holding elections in the affected localities. Long Beach Resort v. Collins, 261 So.2d 498 (Fla.1972); Smith v. Mayor of Saginaw, 81 Mich. 123, 45 N.W. 964 (1890). Cf. State ex rel. Cutlip v. North Bend, 171 Or. 329, 137 P.2d 607 (1943) (mandamus required a joint meeting of city councils of two cities proposed for consolidation; meeting had to choose members of a charter commission to prepare a home-rule document for the new unit in case the consolidation occurred).

[128] Smith v. Mayor of Saginaw, *supra* note 127. Where two or more consolidation (or merger) proceedings, or a consolidation (or merger) proceeding and an annexation proceeding, occur at the same time relative to the same territory, the first-in-time rule applies: priority is given the proceeding in which the first valid step was earlier taken. State ex rel. City of Jackson v. Grimm, 555 S.W.2d 643 (Mo.App.1977); Mayor of Liberty v. Dealers Transport Co., 343 S.W.2d 40 (Mo.1961) (irrelevant which unit *completes* its proceedings first).

[129] As under Minn.Stat.Ann. § 414.041, an earlier, somewhat different version of which (Minn.Stat.Ann. § 414.021) was applied in Doyle v. Minnesota Municipal Commission, 340 F.Supp. 841 (D.Minn.1972), aff'd 468 F.2d 620 (8th Cir.) (Minnesota Municipal Commission must pass on proposed consolidations; held to have authority to approve consolidation though residents of area were not given opportunity to vote on the matter); Farmington v. Minnesota Municipal Commission, 284 Minn. 125, 170 N.W.2d 197 (1969) (Commission's order can be invalidated by courts if not in best interest of entire area). See generally Honadle, The Barriers to Citizen-Led Municipal Consolidations: An Analysis of Minnesota's Municipal Boundary Adjustment Law, 17 Hamline J. Pub. L. & Pol'y 63 (1995), noting the difficulty of achieving voter-led consolidation.

[130] People v. Downey County Water District, *supra* note 125 (sufficient for merger to occur if the unit into which the other is merged is *capable* of performing the function involved, even if not presently performing it; when county water district was annexed by city, water district merged into city, and district ceased to exist). See In re Sanitary Board of East Fruitvale Sanitary District, 158 Cal. 453, 111 P. 368 (1910) (dissolution of sanitary district upon annexation of its territory to adjacent municipality). But see Lake Worth Util. Auth. v. City of Lake Worth, 468 So.2d 215 (Fla.1985) (statute providing for creation of utilities authorities held a constitutional enactment of power specifically reserved to the state legislature; city's home-rule powers held not to authorize city to dissolve utilities authority and take over its offices and bank accounts). Sometimes, the special district is treated as automatically ousted from any annexed territory, whether or not that territory constitutes the *whole* of the district. See State ex rel. Flaxel v. Chandler, 180 Or. 28, 175 P.2d 448 (1946); Weatherwax v. Grays Harbor County, 116 Wash. 212, 199 P. 303 (1921). By law (usually statute) in some states, an annexing municipality can oust a special function district from territory annexed by the municipality if, but only if, the municipality compensates the district for its facilities within the area. See City of Mesa v. Salt River Project Agricultural Improvement & Power District, 92 Ariz. 91, 373 P.2d 722 (1962), appeal dismissed 372 U.S. 704, 83 S.Ct. 1018, 10 L.Ed.2d 124; Morgan County Rural Electric Membership Corp. v. Public Service Co., 253 Ind. 541, 255 N.E.2d 822 (1970), superseded 261 Ind. 323, 302 N.E.2d 776; Franklin Power & Light Co. v. Middle Tennessee Electric Membership Corp., 222 Tenn. 182, 434 S.W.2d 829 (1968). But

§ 12.11 Dissolution of Local Units

How is a municipal corporation dissolved? Most authority agrees that dissolution does not occur merely because of the corporation's long non-user of its powers; permission of the state legislature is needed.[131] The legislature has been held competent to dissolve municipal corporations at will;[132] but today, legislatures generally do not pass laws dissolving specific corporations, but instead pass general statutes that provide a means by which municipal corporations can be dissolved (or "disincorporated") for particular reasons, such as long failure to exercise corporate powers.[133] The procedure most often provided involves (1) a petition for dissolution by a specified number, or percentage, of the voters of the local unit, (2) presentation of the petition to a specified court, agency, or official, and (3) if the petition substantially complies with statutory requirements, an election within the unit in question.[134] Statutes often provide for disposition of the

---

some states specifically provide by statute for concurrent existence of a municipality and a special district. See City of Aurora v. Aurora Sanitation District, 112 Colo. 406, 149 P.2d 662 (1944). See generally Note, Problems Created by Municipal Annexation of Special District Territory, 1967 Wash.U.L.Q. 560.

Special districts may sometimes be dissolved, or "merged" with the new local unit, when the territory they cover becomes part of a newly *incorporated* municipality. See Airport Authority v. City of Omaha, 185 Neb. 623, 177 N.W.2d 603 (1970).

Annexation *by* special districts is usually subject to the same rules and limitations as apply to annexation by municipalities. See Pock, *supra* note 123, at Chapter 9. And consolidation by such districts is usually also possible under statutes the same as, or similar to, those governing municipal consolidations; but consolidations by most types of special function districts are rare. See *Id.* at 175–76. Many consolidations of school districts have occurred, however, since the 1930's. See Bollens, Special District Governments in the United States 197–277 (1957).

[131] United States Bank v. City of Kendall, 179 F. 914 (D.Kan.1910); Treadwell v. Oak Hill, 175 So.2d 777 (Fla.1965); People ex rel. Petty v. Thomas, 361 Ill. 448, 198 N.E. 363 (1935); People ex rel. Gauen v. Niebruegge, 244 Ill. 82, 91 N.E. 115 (1910); Riddle v. Howard, 357 S.W.2d 705 (Ky.1962); Hill v. Anderson, 122 Ky. 87, 90 S.W. 1071 (1906); Cain v. Brown, 111 Mich. 657, 70 N.W. 337 (1897); County of Platte v. James, 489 S.W.2d 216 (Mo.1973); Snortland v. Nelson County, 123 N.W.2d 288 (N.D.1963); Beale v. Pankey, 107 Va. 215, 57 S.E. 661 (1907). Cf. Goodloe v. Baesler, 539 S.W.2d 298 (Ky.1976) (consolidated city and county government cannot be abolished, and former local governments reinstated, without legislative authorization). But see Cincinnati, New Orleans & Texas Pacific Railway v. Baughman, 116 Ky. 479, 76 S.W. 351 (1903) (city failed for 17 years to exercise any of its rights and powers under its act of incorporation; held dissolved by non-user). Cf. Butler v. Walker, 98 Ala. 358, 13 So. 261 (1893), applying a statute, such as exist in a few states, under which a municipal corporation is automatically dissolved by nonuser of its powers for a specified time. This, of course, can be considered a kind of legislative authorization, given in advance of the particular case. See generally Anderson, Dissolving Cities, 121 Yale L. J. 1364 (2012).

[132] Allen v. Board of Trustees of Bakersfield, 157 Cal. 720, 109 P. 486 (1910); State ex rel. Bradford v. Hamilton, 40 Kan. 323, 19 P. 723 (1888); La Guardia v. Smith, 288 N.Y. 1, 41 N.E.2d 153 (1942); Town of Highlands v. Hickory, 202 N.C. 167, 162 S.E. 471 (1932); Leuhrman v. Taxing District, 70 Tenn. 425 (1879); Brackman's, Inc. v. Huntington, 126 W.Va. 21, 27 S.E.2d 71 (1943); Mullens v. Town of Corinne, 112 W.Va. 371, 164 S.E. 408 (1932). See Meriwether v. Garrett, 102 U.S. 472, 511, 26 L.Ed. 197 (1880) (concurring opinion of Mr. Justice Field). The municipal charter, if there is one, is no barrier to dissolution, as it does not constitute a contract with the state within the meaning of the Contract Clause of the U.S. Constitution. Hunter v. Pittsburgh, 207 U.S. 161, 28 S.Ct. 40, 52 L.Ed. 151 (1907); Ensley v. Simpson, 166 Ala. 366, 52 So. 61 (1909).

[133] Olds v. State ex rel. Cole, 101 Fla. 218, 133 So. 641 (1931); Sizemore v. Commonwealth, 285 Ky. 142, 147 S.W.2d 56 (1941) (dissolution not automatic; official action by state officer needed); State v. Mustian, 243 N.C. 564, 91 S.E.2d 696 (1956). Cf. Ensley v. Simpson, *supra* note 132 (disincorporation by special act of legislature).

[134] See Boone County v. Town of Verona, 190 Ky. 430, 227 S.W. 804 (1921) (petition made to designated agency); Couch v. City of Fort Worth, 287 S.W.2d 255 (Tex.Civ.App.1956) (election held; if vote favors dissolution, order should be issued accordingly). It has been held that names may be withdrawn from the petition prior to its being considered by the designated court or agency. Town of Gulf Shores v. Coggin, 269 Ala. 233, 112 So.2d 793 (1959). Under modern authority, it may be unconstitutional in a dissolution election to restrict the vote, as often done in the past, to property owners. See City of La Grulla v. Rodriguez, 415 S.W.2d 701 (Tex.Civ.App.1967), ref'd n. r. e. (restriction of vote to those owning taxable property would be

property of a dissolved unit, and the handling of its debt. In the absence of statutory provision, the assets, and the debts, pass to any successor corporation; and if there is no successor, the assets pass to the state, and creditors must look to the state legislature for compensation.[135]

It has been held that mere changes in classification of a local unit—as from a town to a city because of an increase in population—have no effect on corporate identity, property, or obligations.[136]

---

improper, but election would not be invalidated unless evidence showed that election officials had in fact restricted voting to property owners and that there were sufficient non-property-owning, otherwise-eligible voters to affect outcome). See generally note 35 *supra* and accompanying text.

[135] See Meriwether v. Garrett, 102 U.S. 472, 26 L.Ed. 197 (1880) (assets become property of successor corporation or of the state); Barkley v. Levee Commissioners, 93 U.S. 258, 23 L.Ed. 893 (1876) (if no other provision made, creditors of dissolved corporation can only seek relief from state legislature). An effort is made to find a successor corporation that can be held responsible for the dissolved entity's debts. See Broughton v. Pensacola, 93 U.S. 266, 23 L.Ed. 896 (1876) (when new form is given to old corporation, it will be assumed responsible for its predecessor's obligations). Cf. Port of Mobile v. Watson, 116 U.S. 289, 6 S.Ct. 398, 29 L.Ed. 620 (1886) (Port of Mobile was successor by legislative act to City of Mobile; held liable for City's debts); Humphreys v. State ex rel. Palm Beach Co., 108 Fla. 92, 145 So. 858 (1933) (bondholders of dissolved municipality could continue to assert all rights given them by statutes in effect when bonds sold). See generally Flournoy, The Rights of Creditors of a Municipal Corporation When the State has Passed a Law to Abolish or Alter It, 12 Va.L.Reg. 175 (1906).

Statutes now often make provision for the handling of property of a dissolved municipality. See Pepin Tp. v. Sage, 129 F. 657 (8th Cir.1904); Highland Grove Township v. Village of Winnipeg Junction, 125 Minn. 280, 146 N.W. 974 (1914); Schwan v. New York, 173 N.Y. 32, 65 N.E. 774 (1902), all applying such statutes. And statutes also often provide a method for dealing with the defunct municipality's debts. See Board of Commissioners v. Pierce, 6 N.M. 324, 28 P. 512 (1892). Some statutes *condition* the dissolution of a municipality on its prior settlement of all obligations. See Branch v. City of Sour Lake, 9 F.2d 971 (E.D.Tex. 1924), aff'd 6 F.2d 355; National Tax & Mortgage Co. v. Cartwright, 90 Colo. 16, 5 P.2d 878 (1931); Matz v. City of Newport, 265 Ky. 126, 95 S.W.2d 1071 (1936).

As a last resort, it seems a court of equity could take over the property of a defunct municipal corporation and manage it for the creditors, where other provision wasn't made by statute. See Broughton v. Pensacola, *supra* at 268–69; City of Decatur v. Thames Bank & Trust Co., 84 F.2d 105 (5th Cir.1936); Chalstran v. Board of Education, 244 Ill. 470, 91 N.E. 712 (1910); People v. O'Brien, 111 N.Y. 1, 18 N.E. 692 (1888) (applying statute). See generally 2A McQuillin, Municipal Corporations § 8.15 (3d rev. ed. 1996).

[136] City of Oakwood v. Hartford Accident & Indemnity Co., 81 F.2d 717 (6th Cir.1936). See Hill v. Selectmen of Easthampton, 140 Mass. 381, 4 N.E. 811 (1886); Smith v. Mayfield Heights, 108 N.E.2d 861 (Ohio C.P.1952) (police chief could remain in office despite change in municipality's classification); Trustees of Erie Academy v. Erie, 31 Pa. 515 (1858) (ordinances remain in effect despite change in classification). Cf. Bates v. Gregory, 89 Cal. 387, 26 P. 891 (1891) (change in name doesn't affect municipal obligations). But in some states, a city will move from one category to another, under the statutory scheme of classification, as its population changes; and its powers may change accordingly. See State ex rel. Clark v. Board of Education, 148 Kan. 632, 84 P.2d 507 (1938).

Chapter 13

PUBLIC OFFICERS

Analysis

§ 13.1 Definition of "Public Officer" and "Office"

Besides having territory over which to exercise jurisdiction, a municipality must have people to maintain the government and perform its work. These people are referred to as "officers" and "employees," though the distinction between these two categories is far from clear-cut—and a person who qualifies as an "officer" for some purposes may for other purposes be categorized as an "employee." Nonetheless, under many constitutional, statutory, and common-law rules, it is necessary—as when dealing with the problem of the same person holding two or more governmental positions, discussed *infra*—to draw a line between an "officer" and an "employee"; thus, this is a basic distinction with which discussions of local government personnel must deal.

The classic definition of a "public office" (the holder of which will be, of course, an officer, as opposed to an employee) is found in a 1927 Montana case[1] which states: (1) an office is created by law; that is, by the constitution, by statute, or by authority conferred on some body (such as a city council) by statute; (2) an office has delegated to it, and its

1 State ex rel. Barney v. Hawkins, 79 Mont. 506, 257 P. 411 (1927). See, applying much the same factors, People ex rel. Chapman v. Rapsey, 16 Cal.2d 636, 107 P.2d 388 (1940); State v. Taylor, 260 Iowa 634, 144 N.W.2d 289 (1966); Commonwealth v. Howard, 379 S.W.2d 475 (Ky.1964); Eads v. Boulder City, 94 Nev. 735, 587 P.2d 39 (1978) (director of public works was officer, and thus not within civil service); State ex rel. McIntosh v. Hutchinson, 187 Wash. 61, 59 P.2d 1117 (1936). Cf. Moore v. Panish, 32 Cal.3d 535, 186 Cal.Rptr. 475, 652 P.2d 32 (1982) (public office said to have two essential elements: a position which is not transient, occasional, or incidental but which is itself an entity in which incumbents succeed one another, and delegation to the position of some portion of the sovereign functions of government; position of member of county central committee of a political party held not an office). See generally Annot., Distinction Between Office and Employment, 53 A.L.R. 595 (1928). The distinction between "officer" and "employee" has been criticized as illusory and as inappropriate in many of the contexts in which it has been used. See Glasser, A New Jersey Municipal Law Mystery: What Is a "Public Office"?, 6 Rutgers L.Rev. 503 (1952).

holder thus can exercise, a portion of the sovereign power of government; (3) the powers and duties of an office are defined by the legislature, or by some authority to whom the legislature has delegated the task of definition; (4) the duties are performed without control of a superior power except the power of the law, and (sometimes) the general control of a superior officer or body to whom the control is given by the legislature; and (5) the duties are continuing in nature, not occasional or intermittent, so that the position can be said to have some permanence and continuity. Other factors are mentioned by various authorities—for instance, a fixed tenure is a common characteristic of an office, not of mere employment.[2] The holder of an office is often required to take a public oath and/or to post an official bond.[3] Typically, the holder of an office in the past has often been required to be a resident of the area served[4]—but residency requirements are now under considerable attack, as discussed *infra*. In the case of local government personnel, the status of "officer" is more likely to be found if the salary for the position is fixed by statute or charter,[5] and if the salary is paid out of the local government's treasury, not from the funds of an individual.[6]

It is usually agreed that the language of constitutions, statutes, and ordinances is not determinative of whether a position is an office, but is merely one factor that may be weighed.[7] Where, however, a position is not expressly or impliedly created by constitution or legislation but only arises from contract, this is strong evidence the position is not an office.[8] And where a position is not referred to by relevant statutes as an "office," there is a tendency to resolve doubts against its being such.[9] An officer normally has responsibilities of considerable gravity and importance,[10] and often has power of supervision over other persons, plus liability as a "public offender" in case of malfeasance on the job.[11]

---

[2] See Bredice v. City of Norwalk, 152 Conn. 287, 206 A.2d 433 (1964).

[3] See Coulter v. Pool, 187 Cal. 181, 201 P. 120 (1921) (fixed tenure of position, exaction of oath and bond mentioned as factors); Mosby v. Board of Commissioners, 134 Ind.App. 175, 186 N.E.2d 18 (1962); City of Lexington v. Thompson, 250 Ky. 96, 61 S.W.2d 1092 (1933).

[4] See Seals v. State ex rel. Matthews, 164 Ala. 582, 51 So. 337 (1910); State ex rel. Shea v. Cocking, 66 Mont. 169, 213 P. 594 (1923). Cf. State ex rel. Goodell v. McGeary, 69 Vt. 461, 38 A. 165 (1897) (actual inhabitancy required, not merely building a house within the municipality).

[5] City & County of Denver v. Rinker, 148 Colo. 441, 366 P.2d 548 (1961); People ex rel. Adamowski v. Wilson, 20 Ill.2d 568, 170 N.E.2d 605 (1960).

[6] See Stevens v. Truman, 127 Cal. 155, 59 P. 397 (1899); State ex rel. Clark v. Stanley, 66 N.C. 59 (1872).

[7] See Rand v. Collins, 214 Cal. 168, 4 P.2d 529 (1931) (title is unimportant; the duties and powers of the job are determinative); Mosby v. Board of Commissioners, *supra* note 3. But see Brown v. Turner, 70 N.C. 93, 100 (1874), indicating that the legislative designation of a position as an "office" will be controlling.

[8] Main v. Claremont Unified School District, 161 Cal.App.2d 189, 326 P.2d 573 (1958); Shelby v. Alcorn, 36 Miss. 273 (1858); Riddlestorffer v. City of Rahway, 82 N.J.Super. 423, 197 A.2d 883 (1964); State v. Small, 103 Ohio App. 214, 145 N.E.2d 200 (1956) (teacher is employee).

[9] See People ex rel. Adamowski v. Wilson, 20 Ill.2d 568, 170 N.E.2d 605 (1960).

[10] See Logan v. Shields, 190 Cal. 661, 214 P. 45 (1923) (regulating traffic involves exercising part of state's sovereign power; thus, job is an office); State ex rel. Clyatt v. Hocker, 39 Fla. 477, 22 So. 721 (1897); LaPolla v. Board of Chosen Freeholders, 71 N.J.Super. 264, 176 A.2d 821 (1961); State v. Hord, 264 N.C. 149, 141 S.E.2d 241 (1965); Hamlin v. Kassafer, 15 Or. 456, 15 P. 778 (1887).

[11] See Mosby v. Board of Commissioners, *supra* note 3. Cf. State ex rel. Attorney General v. Jennings, 57 Ohio St. 415, 49 N.E. 404 (1898) (an officer has independent public duties rather than being under direction and control of someone else).

Examples of those usually classified as "officers" are mayors,[12] members of the municipal council or other legislative body,[13] city managers,[14] and city attorneys.[15] Judges of all types are normally classified as officers.[16] A superintendent of schools may be an officer,[17] but a teacher is ordinarily classified as an employee.[18] A police chief is usually considered an officer,[19] and what is probably the weight of authority supports the view that other policemen and policewomen are officers as well.[20] But there is

---

[12] State ex inf. Ellis v. Ferguson, 333 Mo. 1177, 65 S.W.2d 97 (1933), cert. denied 291 U.S. 682, 54 S.Ct. 559, 78 L.Ed. 1070 (1934); Riddlestorffer v. City of Rahway, *supra* note 8.

[13] See Akers v. State ex rel. Witcher, 283 Ala. 248, 215 So.2d 578 (1968) (alderman); In re Bruno's Case, 340 Mass. 420, 165 N.E.2d 93 (1960) (town selectman); Van Cleve v. Wallace, 216 Minn. 500, 13 N.W.2d 467 (1944) (council members); Bernstein v. Krom, 108 N.J.Super. 176, 260 A.2d 269 (1969); O'Keefe v. Dunn, 89 N.J.Super. 383, 215 A.2d 66 (1965), aff'd 47 N.J. 210, 219 A.2d 872; Commonwealth v. Witman, 217 Pa. 411, 66 A. 986 (1907) (council members); In re Newport Charter, 14 R.I. 655 (1883) (council members); State ex rel. Ralich v. Millsop, 138 W.Va. 599, 76 S.E.2d 737 (1953) (council members). Cf. Commonwealth v. Howard, 379 S.W.2d 475 (Ky.1964) (commissioner of water district). A position on an elected school board has been held a public office. See Sallee v. Oklahoma City, 247 P.3d 750 (Okla. Civ. App. 2010) (holder of public office forbidden by city charter from being a firefighter). But see Diffie v. Cowan, 56 S.W.2d 1097 (Tex.Civ.App.1932) ("officers" covers executives, not legislators; city alderman not "any officer"). Cf. Bilger v. State, 63 Wash. 457, 116 P. 19 (1911) (commissioners appointed to assess benefits were not officers).

[14] McClendon v. Board of Health, 141 Ark. 114, 216 S.W. 289 (1919); City of Lexington v. Thompson, 250 Ky. 96, 61 S.W.2d 1092 (1933); State ex rel. Diers v. Sheldon, 29 Wyo. 233, 213 P. 92 (1923). But see Bowers v. City of Albuquerque, 27 N.M. 291, 200 P. 421 (1921) (manager had no term of office; held not an officer within statute banning salary increase for officers during their term).

[15] People ex rel. Chapman v. Rapsey, 16 Cal.2d 636, 107 P.2d 388 (1940). Cf. Reilly v. Ozzard, 33 N.J. 529, 166 A.2d 360 (1960) (township attorney); Snyderwine v. Craley, 434 Pa. 349, 254 A.2d 16 (1969) (township solicitor). See Rhyne, Municipal Law § 8–2, at 118 (1957). See also City of Tulsa v. Oklahoma State Pension & Retirement Bd., 674 P.2d 10 (Okl.1983) (relationship between municipal attorney and city is analogous to that of private attorney and client). Similarly, a city auditor has been held an "officer." Ross v. City of Garfield, 126 N.J.L. 462, 19 A.2d 818 (1941). As has a county clerk. Alachua County v. Powers, 351 So.2d 32 (Fla.1977). See also Whalley, Elected Versus Appointed Policy Makers: Evidence From City Treasurers, 56 J. L. & Econ. 39 (2013).

[16] See Franklin v. Westfall, 273 Ill. 402, 112 N.E. 974 (1916) (under election statute); Candelaria v. Valencia County, 77 N.M. 458, 423 P.2d 982 (1967) (election judge not covered by workmen's compensation). Even court stenographers and clerks may be classified as "officers." See City of Louisville v. Wilson, 99 Ky. 598, 36 S.W. 944 (1896) (within provision forbidding changing of salary during term).

[17] Smith v. Board of Education, 111 F.2d 573 (6th Cir.1940) (Kentucky law). But see Board of Education of Graves County v. De Weese, 343 S.W.2d 598 (Ky.1961), holding a superintendent of schools not to be an officer within a constitutional limitation on salaries.

[18] Main v. Claremont Unified School District, 161 Cal.App.2d 189, 326 P.2d 573 (1958); Duncan v. Koustenis, 260 Md. 98, 271 A.2d 547 (1970) (with review of authorities); State v. Small, 103 Ohio App. 214, 145 N.E.2d 200 (1956); State ex rel. Board of Directors v. Preston, 120 Wash. 569, 208 P. 47 (1922). Cf. Shlakman v. Board of Higher Education, 282 App.Div. 718, 122 N.Y.S.2d 286 (1953), appeal denied 282 App.Div. 841, 124 N.Y.S.2d 349, aff'd 306 N.Y. 532, 119 N.E.2d 373 (college professor not officer); Tilley v. Rogers, 405 S.W.2d 220 (Tex.Civ.App.1966) (college professor).

[19] State v. Carey, 241 Ind. 692, 175 N.E.2d 354 (1961) (statute on prosecution of municipal officers); Turner v. Cole, 559 S.W.2d 170 (Ky.App.1977); State v. Hord, 264 N.C. 149, 141 S.E.2d 241 (1965) (statute on misconduct in office); Broyles v. State, 207 Tenn. 571, 341 S.W.2d 724 (1960) (statute banning from public office those who have been convicted of a misdemeanor in office). See Bunt v. Garden City, 118 Idaho 427, 797 P.2d 135 (1990) (police chief was an appointed officer, not an employee, and could thus be removed without notice or hearing). Compare Smith v. City & County of Denver, 789 P.2d 442 (Colo.App.1989) (even if police chief was not an "officer" of city, charter provision requiring every "officer or person" receiving funds, other than salary, for services performed in his official capacity to deliver those funds to city applied to divisional police chief). But see Vega v. Borough of Burgettstown, 394 Pa. 406, 147 A.2d 620 (1958) (with dissent by Justice Musmanno).

[20] McNichols v. People ex rel. Cook, 95 Colo. 235, 35 P.2d 863 (1934); Maudsley v. City of North Lauderdale, 300 So.2d 304 (Fla.App.1974) (officer not required to "set off" wages earned during a period of wrongful discharge, though *employee* must mitigate damages); Hayes v. City of Dalton, 209 Ga. 286, 71 S.E.2d 618 (1952) (quo warranto could be used to try title to office); Edwards v. Mayor & Aldermen of Milledgeville,

considerable authority, particularly under legislation relating to salaries, residence requirements, and civil service, that members of the police force are employees.[21] Similarly, firefighters have, more often than not, been ruled officers;[22] but there is contrary authority.[23]

The method of creating local offices is often specified by statute or charter, with a common requirement being that an *ordinance* must be used by the locality in creating an office.[24] If an office or other post is unlawfully created, no holder of the job can be protected in his occupancy of the position.[25]

§ 13.2 De Facto Officers

What happens in the situation in which an office has been lawfully created but the person holding the office turns out not to have valid title thereto? That office-holder's acts may nonetheless be held valid under the doctrine of "de facto officers." A "de facto officer" is one who, even though it turns out he was not legally appointed or elected to office, (1) has taken and held office under "color of law"—that is, with an apparent right

---

52 Ga.App. 288, 183 S.E. 130 (1935) (under dismissal statutes); Calabrese v. Policemen's Benevolent Association, 157 N.J.Super. 139, 384 A.2d 579 (1978); Dunn v. Froehlich, 155 N.J.Super. 249, 382 A.2d 686 (1978) (under statute banning incompatible offices); Mercadante v. City of Paterson, 111 N.J.Super. 35, 266 A.2d 611 (1970), aff'd 58 N.J. 112, 275 A.2d 440; Canteline v. McClellan, 282 N.Y. 166, 25 N.E.2d 972 (1940) (under statute requiring officers to waive privilege against self-incrimination); State v. Stogner, 264 N.C. 163, 141 S.E.2d 248 (1965) (under statute providing punishment for those who corruptly neglect their office); Cornett v. City of Chattanooga, 165 Tenn. 563, 56 S.W.2d 742 (1933) (officer so far as workmen's compensation concerned); State v. Shores, 48 Utah 76, 157 P. 225 (1916) (statute requiring officers to be qualified electors of city); Matczak v. Mathews, 265 Wis. 1, 60 N.W.2d 352 (1953) (statute providing for payment of judgments against public officers). See Estrada v. Indemnity Insurance Co., 158 Cal.App.2d 129, 322 P.2d 294 (1958) (policeman held city "official" under terms of insurance policy).

[21] Smith v. City and County of Denver, 39 Colo.App. 421, 569 P.2d 329 (1977); Newport v. Schindler, 449 S.W.2d 17 (Ky.1969) (residency requirement); City of Jackson v. Little, 248 So.2d 795 (Miss.1971); Mangam v. City of Brooklyn, 98 N.Y. 585 (1885) (ban on changing compensation during term of office); State ex rel. Randel v. Scott, 95 Ohio App. 197, 118 N.E.2d 426 (1952) (civil service law); Wise v. City of Knoxville, 194 Tenn. 90, 250 S.W.2d 29 (1952); Heffernan v. City of Janesville, 248 Wis. 299, 21 N.W.2d 651 (1946) (policeman not officer within rule entitling officer to full compensation during period of wrongful suspension or discharge). See Walck v. City of Albuquerque, 117 N.M. 651, 875 P.2d 407 (App.1994) (wrongfully terminated police officer was public employee, not officer, for purposes of computing back pay to be awarded). Cf. Stoops v. Department of Retirement Systems, 91 Wash.App. 898, 963 P.2d 189 (Wash.App.1998) ("special policeman" whose duties were those of a park security guard or park ranger did not meet definition of "law enforcement officer" under retirement statutes). See generally Comment, When Is a Police Officer an Officer of the Law? The Status of Police Officers in Schools, 99 J. Crim. L. & Criminology 541 (2009).

[22] Padden v. New York City, 45 Misc. 517, 92 N.Y.S. 926 (Sup.Ct.1904) (within provision that officers need not "set off" earnings made elsewhere during time of wrongful suspension or discharge); State ex rel. Beck v. Carter, 2 Wn.App. 974, 471 P.2d 127 (1970); Nelson v. City of Superior, 109 Wis. 618, 85 N.W. 412 (1901) (within provision that salaries of officers could not be reduced during their term). See Jackson v. Wilde, 52 Cal.App. 259, 198 P. 822 (1921) (came within rule that salaries of officers continue during disability); Mercadante v. City of Paterson, *supra* note 20.

[23] Mason v. City of Los Angeles, 130 Cal.App. 224, 20 P.2d 84 (1933) (noting that firefighters are subject to much supervision); Barfield v. City of Atlanta, 53 Ga.App. 861, 187 S.E. 407 (1936) (could waive part of compensation); Devillier v. City of Opelousas, 247 So.2d 412 (La.App.1971).

[24] See Holcombe v. Grota, 129 Tex. 100, 102 S.W.2d 1041 (1937) (creation of municipal offices is legislative matter; office could be created by ordinance); 2A Antieau, Municipal Corporation Law § 22.07 (1998). See generally 3 McQuillin, Municipal Corporations § 12.39 (3d rev. ed. 1990) (on creation of municipal offices, departments, boards, etc.) On the difference between an ordinance and other forms of municipal legislation, see generally Chapter 11 *supra*.

[25] See Keenan v. Essex County, 105 N.J.Super. 271, 251 A.2d 785 (1969) (appointment to nonexistent office).

to the office,[26] (2) has been in unobstructed possession of office under such circumstances that the reasonable citizen would, if no investigation were made, consider the occupant's holding of the office to be lawful,[27] and (3) has discharged, or is discharging, the duties of the office.[28] There can be no de facto officer where the true de jure officer is occupying the position.[29]

It has often been indicated that there is a fourth requirement for a person to be a de facto officer: the existence of a de jure *office*.[30] Under this view, there can be no de facto officer in an office that was not lawfully created—as where the position was created by an unconstitutional statute. But the weight of authority favors the view that since there can be a reasonable appearance of proper authority even where it later turns out that an office was not validly created, the requirements of a "de facto officer" can be met despite the lack of a legally established position for the officer to fill.[31]

---

[26] See Waite v. Santa Cruz, 184 U.S. 302, 22 S.Ct. 327, 46 L.Ed. 552 (1902); In re Bunker Hill Urban Renewal Project, 61 Cal.2d 21, 37 Cal.Rptr. 74, 389 P.2d 538 (1964), cert. denied 379 U.S. 899, 85 S.Ct. 185, 13 L.Ed.2d 174; State v. Carroll, 38 Conn. 449 (1871); People ex rel. Hess v. Wheeler, 353 Ill. 147, 187 N.E. 146 (1933); Grooms v. LaVale Zoning Board, 27 Md.App. 266, 340 A.2d 385 (1975) (de facto officer can't be mere usurper); Hallgrene v. Campbell, 82 Mich. 255, 46 N.W. 381 (1890) (must hold under color of law); Jersey City v. Department of Civil Service, 57 N.J.Super. 13, 153 A.2d 757 (1959); State ex rel. Witten v. Ferguson, 148 Ohio St. 702, 76 N.E.2d 886 (1947); Borough of Pleasant Hills v. Jefferson, 359 Pa. 509, 59 A.2d 697 (1948) (invalid election); Country Clubs, Inc. v. City of Knoxville, 217 Tenn. 104, 395 S.W.2d 789 (1965); Heard v. Elliott, 116 Tenn. 150, 92 S.W. 764 (1906); Schoonover v. City of Viroqua, 245 Wis. 239, 14 N.W.2d 9 (1944). It has been held that a nominee for office whose appointment requires approval of the State Senate and whose nomination has been rejected by the Senate cannot be a de facto officer, as there is then no appearance or color of authority. Sierra Club v. Castle & Cooke Homes Hawaii, Inc., 320 P.3d 849 (Hawaii 2013).

[27] See People ex rel. Hess v. Wheeler, *supra* note 26; Kone v. Baltimore County, 231 Md. 466, 190 A.2d 800 (1963); State v. Franks, 7 Wn.App. 594, 501 P.2d 622 (1972). Often, the de facto officer is one who failed to perform some required act such as posting a bond or taking an oath. See Longobardi v. Oakley, 51 Misc.2d 424, 273 N.Y.S.2d 367 (1966); State v. Porter, 272 N.C. 463, 158 S.E.2d 626 (1968). Cf. City of Christine v. Johnson, 255 S.W. 629 (Tex.Civ.App.1923) (election held on wrong day). The doctrine has even been applied to persons who lack some requisite, such as age, residency, or other qualification, for the office. See In re Danford, 157 Cal. 425, 108 P. 322 (1910); Riggs v. Beloit, 199 Kan. 425, 429 P.2d 821 (1967) (non-resident when appointed; later became resident); McFadden v. Cedar County, 95 Neb. 318, 145 N.W. 639 (1914) (failed to take oath). And the doctrine has been applied to one who "holds over" in office after his term has really expired. Andrulis v. First National Bank, 4 Ill.App.3d 436, 281 N.E.2d 417 (1972), cert. denied 410 U.S. 931, 93 S.Ct. 1373, 35 L.Ed.2d 593; Gillson v. Heffernan, 40 N.J. 367, 192 A.2d 577 (1963); State ex rel. Stain v. Christensen, 84 Utah 185, 35 P.2d 775 (1934).

[28] Hallgrene v. Campbell, *supra* note 26; State v. Franks, *supra*, note 27. See Gambill v. City of Denton, 215 S.W.2d 389 (Tex.Civ. App.1948) (city attorney "held over" after resignation accepted, but not entitled to salary as de facto officer since services not then used by city). Cf. People v. Sherrod, 204 P.3d 466 (Colo. 2009) (lack of proper documentation found for county judge's appointment as acting district judge, but his pretrial actions when presiding over a felony action in district court could be upheld under de facto officer doctrine, as he was otherwise qualified and acting under color of authority).

[29] Fee v. Bornhorn, 251 S.W.2d 230 (Ky.1952); Stowers v. Blackburn, 141 W.Va. 328, 90 S.E.2d 277 (1955).

[30] See Ex parte Giambonini, 117 Cal. 573, 49 P. 732 (1897); Miller v. County Commissioners, 226 Md. 105, 172 A.2d 867 (1961); Wagner v. Borough of Lodi, 56 N.J.Super. 204, 152 A.2d 389 (1959). It seems agreed that there can be no de facto officer if there is absolutely *no* office to fill—as where the legislation purporting to create the office is a nullity. Norton v. Shelby County, 118 U.S. 425, 6 S.Ct. 1121, 30 L.Ed. 178 (1886) (legislation creating Board of Commissioners had been declared unconstitutional). See note 25 *supra* and accompanying text. The more difficult problem arises when, as in the first 3 cases cited in this note and in the cases cited in note 7 *infra*, there has been an attempt to create an office but the attempt proves invalid, often because of some technicality.

[31] City of Lampasas v. Talcott, 94 F. 457 (5th Cir.1899), cert. denied 178 U.S. 612, 20 S.Ct. 1029, 44 L.Ed. 1215 (local government not properly organized); Platte v. Dortch, 255 Ind. 157, 263 N.E.2d 266 (1970); Thompson v. Couch, 144 Mich. 671, 108 N.W. 363 (1906); Lang v. Mayor of City of Bayonne, 74 N.J.L. 455, 68 A. 90 (1907); Demarest v. New York, 147 N.Y. 203, 41 N.E. 405 (1895). See Jersey City v. Department of Civil

The doctrine of "de facto officers" is intended to assure the stability of community governance—to guarantee that actions taken will not be overthrown or reversed merely because it turns out that the person who took the action lacked, perhaps because of some technicality such as failure to post the proper bond, valid title to his office. Thus, the chief result of this "de facto" doctrine is that the acts of the de facto officer will be held valid and binding.[32] Bonds issued by de facto officers will, for instance, be treated as valid obligations.[33] But, since by definition de facto officers do not have fully valid title to their offices, they can be removed by proper means—usually a quo warranto action brought by the state or by such officials as are designated by state statute to bring a quo warranto action.[34]

Service, *supra* note 26. When a de facto officer appoints another officer (and the appointment is valid except for the merely de facto status of the appointing person), some authority treats the appointed officer as also de facto. See Board of Education v. Nevels, 551 S.W.2d 15 (Ky.1977) (appointment made by body that included de facto member whose vote was necessary to make the appointment); Reed v. President & Commissioners of North East, 226 Md. 229, 172 A.2d 536 (1961); Von Nieda v. Bennett, 117 N.J.L. 231, 187 A. 629 (1936), noted 50 Harv.L.Rev. 990 (1937). Cf. State ex rel. Roush v. Board of Education, 128 W.Va. 150, 35 S.E.2d 850 (1945) (as against one claiming title to office, a person appointed by a de facto officer is charged with knowledge of defect in his title, even though his acts may be binding as to the public). But *much* authority takes the view that the appointed person is a fully de jure officer. State ex rel. James v. Deakyne, 44 Del. 217, 58 A.2d 129 (Super. 1948) (one council member who voted for appointment was only a de facto officer). See Robinson v. Kreischer, 97 N.J.Super. 104, 234 A.2d 496 (1967), aff'd 101 N.J.Super. 482, 244 A.2d 699 (appointment of magistrate by acting mayor was valid); State ex rel. Roush v. Board of Education, 128 W.Va. 150, 35 S.E.2d 850 (1945). It would seem that the view that the appointed officer must *at least* be treated as de facto is in accord with the general rule recognizing as de facto an officer appointed by a person or board that in fact didn't have the power of appointment. See State v. Carroll, *supra* note 26; Beattie v. Passaic County Board of Taxation, 96 N.J.L. 72, 114 A. 798 (1921). See generally Annot., Status as De Jure Public Officer of One Appointed by a De Facto Officer or by a Body Which Included a De Facto Member Whose Vote or Consent was Necessary to the Appointment, 106 A.L.R. 1324 (1937).

[32] Waite v. Santa Cruz, *supra* note 26; People v. Hecht, 105 Cal. 621, 38 P. 941 (1895); State v. Johnson, 249 La. 950, 192 So.2d 135 (1966); Wattles v. Upjohn, 211 Mich. 514, 179 N.W. 335 (1920); Boggess v. Pence, 321 S.W.2d 667 (Mo.1959); Wolfgram v. Hall, 79 N.D. 138, 54 N.W.2d 896 (1952) (ordinances passed by de facto officers were valid); Country Clubs Inc. v. City of Knoxville, *supra* note 26; Stowers v. Blackburn, *supra* note 29. See Susanville v. Long, 144 Cal. 362, 77 P. 987 (1904); Hagood v. Hamrick, 223 Ga. 600, 157 S.E.2d 429 (1967); Fruit v. Metropolitan School District, 241 Ind. 621, 172 N.E.2d 864 (1961); Petrey v. City of Hazard, 346 S.W.2d 534 (Ky.1961); Reed v. President & Commissioners of North East, 226 Md. 229, 172 A.2d 536 (1961); Huff v. Sauer, 243 Minn. 425, 68 N.W.2d 252 (1955); Burt v. Winona & St. Paul Railway, 31 Minn. 472, 18 N.W. 285 (1884); Galloway v. Township of Clark, 94 N.J.Super. 527, 229 A.2d 279 (1967); State v. Porter, 272 N.C. 463, 158 S.E.2d 626 (1968); State v. Gambrell, 814 P.2d 1136 (Utah App.1991) (the filing of an information instituting proceedings against a defendant was a valid act and conferred jurisdiction on the court even though the county attorney filing the information had not filed an acceptable bond and was thus only a de facto officer). An acting judge may qualify to be a de facto officer whose acts are legally binding on the public and on third persons if done within the scope and apparent authority of his or her office, even though the judge's actual authority suffers from a procedural defect. See Vroman v. City of Soldotna, 111 P.3d 343 (Alaska 2005). Cf. Marine Forests Soc'y v. California Coastal Comm'n, 36 Cal.4th 1, 30 Cal.Rptr.3d 30, 113 P.3d 1062 (2005), cert. denied 546 U.S. 979, 126 S.Ct. 577, 163 L.Ed.2d 463 (2005) (de facto officer doctrine barred challenges to decisions of California Coastal Commission even if statutory provisions under which members of the commission were appointed violated separation of powers provision of state constitution).

[33] Platte v. Dortch, *supra* note 31; Wrenn v. Kure Beach, 235 N.C. 292, 69 S.E.2d 492 (1952). Cf. People ex rel. Chillicothe Township v. Board of Review, 19 Ill.2d 424, 167 N.E.2d 553 (1960) (property assessments valid though set by de facto board).

[34] See Tadlock v. Smith, 38 N.M. 288, 31 P.2d 708 (1934). Injunctions restraining de facto officers from performing the duties of an office, or from collecting their pay, will usually not succeed. See Purviance v. Compton, 94 Cal.App. 277, 271 P. 120 (1928) (title to office of licensing-board member will not be tried in injunctive proceeding brought by person whose license was being revoked). And mandamus will ordinarily not be used to remove a de facto officer, though it may be available against an intruder with *no* claim on an office. See Keeler v. Deo, 117 Mich. 1, 75 N.W. 145 (1898); Adair v. Caney, 169 Okl. 587, 38 P.2d 493 (1934). Either in actions to remove de facto officers or in other actions, a collateral attack can generally not be brought against the validity of actions taken by those officers. See Detroit Edison Co. v. East China Tp. School District, 366

Where a de facto officer occupies a position for a time but is then ousted and the rightful holder enters the office, who is entitled to the compensation for the time that the de facto officer held the job? The generally accepted view is that the de jure officer may recover the salary from the de facto officer who has received it.[35] In the alternative, the de facto officer can be forced to return his compensation to the municipality so that it can then be paid the rightful holder of the office, or put to other proper use.[36] But it seems the municipality has no *duty* to recover this money; and by most authority, the de jure officer's exclusive legal remedy, where he finds that his salary has been paid a de facto officer, is to proceed against that officer. In order to protect the municipality from possibly having to pay twice for the same services, the municipality that has in good faith paid a de facto officer won't be held liable to the de jure officer for the salary—the de jure officer's remedy is to sue the de facto office-holder, not the city.[37]

§ 13.3 Qualifications for Local Office—General Principles

Qualifications for local offices are occasionally set by the state constitution; and where this is done, those qualifications may be deemed exclusive—*i.e.*, the legislature or

---

Mich. 638, 115 N.W.2d 298 (1962) (annexations undertaken by de facto members of school board could not be invalidated merely because board members were not de jure officers).

[35] Albright v. Sandoval, 216 U.S. 331, 30 S.Ct. 318, 54 L.Ed. 502 (1910) (indicating that de facto officer has offset for his reasonable expenses in earning the salary); Cooper v. Hawkins, 234 Ala. 636, 176 So. 329 (1937); Walker v. Hughes, 42 Del. 447, 36 A.2d 47 (1944); People ex rel. Benoit v. Miller, 24 Mich. 458 (1872). See Jarrett, De Facto Public Officers: The Validity of Their Acts and Their Right to Compensation, 9 S.Cal.L.Rev. 199, 231 (1936). But see Davenport v. Teeters, 315 S.W.2d 641 (Mo.App.1958) (officer who was declared elected did not have to turn salary over to person who, upon recount, turned out to be actual winner). See generally Annots., Right of De Facto Officer to Salary or Other Compensation Annexed to Office, 151 A.L.R. 952 (1944); 93 A.L.R. 258 (1934).

The de jure officer's suit against the de facto officer is in the nature of an equitable action and can be barred by laches. See Newland v. City of Richmond, 293 F.Supp. 862 (E.D.Ky.1968).

[36] Gracey v. City of St. Louis, 213 Mo. 384, 111 S.W. 1159 (1908); State ex rel. Cutts v. Hart, 56 Mont. 571, 185 P. 769 (1919) (de facto officer—even one wrongly appointed by governor—cannot recover the compensation annexed to the office). See Maricopa County v. Rodgers, 52 Ariz. 19, 78 P.2d 989 (1938) (all local officers and employees can be compelled to return compensation improperly received). But cf. Miller v. County Commissioners, 226 Md. 105, 172 A.2d 867 (1961) (de facto officer who rendered services in good faith should be allowed to keep compensation). See generally Annot., Right of De Facto Officer to Salary or Other Compensation Annexed to Office, 93 A.L.R. 258, 270, 272 (1934); Annot., Right to Salary of One Illegally Elected or Appointed to Legislature, 7 A.L.R. 1678 (1920).

If a local government *hasn't* paid a de facto officer, he will often be unable to recover the compensation from it. See Longobardi v. Oakley, *supra* note 27; Cooke v. Roberts, 335 Pa. 561, 7 A.2d 357 (1939). But some cases have allowed such recovery if there is no de jure claimant to the office. Drach v. Leckenby, 64 Colo. 546, 172 P. 424 (1918); Gershon v. Kansas City, 240 Mo.App. 418, 215 S.W.2d 771 (1948).

[37] Smith v. Board of Education, 111 F.2d 573 (6th Cir.1940); McKinley v. City of Chicago, 369 Ill. 268, 16 N.E.2d 727 (1938); Ryan v. City of Chicago, 369 Ill. 59, 15 N.E.2d 708 (1938); Glenn v. Chambers, 244 Iowa 750, 56 N.W.2d 892 (1953) (emphasizing the need to protect the public against paying twice); Ashland v. Barney's Administrator, 231 Ky. 835, 22 S.W.2d 255 (1929); Scott v. Crump, 106 Mich. 288, 64 N.W. 1 (1895); State ex rel. Gallagher v. Kansas City, 319 Mo. 705, 7 S.W.2d 357 (1928); State ex rel. Cox v. Hooper, 137 Ohio St. 222, 28 N.E.2d 598 (1940). But if a local government knows of a de jure officer's claim and nonetheless makes payments to the de facto officer, there is authority that the government can be held liable to the de jure officer. See Ratajczak v. Board of Education, 118 N.J.L. 311, 192 A. 591 (1937), aff'd 89 N.J.Eq. 203, 103 A. 912; City of Tulsa v. Coker, 181 Okl. 291, 73 P.2d 443 (1937); State ex rel. Byrd v. Scott County, 181 Tenn. 665, 184 S.W.2d 20 (1944). Similarly, where there has been any bad faith on the locality's part in paying the de facto officer. See State ex rel. Ham v. Hulley, 192 Ind. 547, 137 N.E. 177 (1922). Or where payments have been made by the locality to the de facto officer after an ouster action against him has succeeded. People ex rel. Trapp v. Tanner, 19 Ill.App.2d 138, 153 N.E.2d 246 (1958); Morten v. City of Aurora, 96 Ind.App. 203, 182 N.E. 259 (1932). Cf. People ex rel. Swinburne v. Nolan, 101 N.Y. 539, 5 N.E. 446 (1886) (claimant could recover damages, against usurper of office, in same action in which he established his right to the office).

local government cannot add further requirements.[38] With that limitation, qualifications for local offices can be established by state statute, and the statute will prevail over any conflicting local rules of *non*-home-rule cities. As to home-rule cities, local rules (established by city charter or city ordinance, for instance) will generally prevail, in cases of conflict with state law, as to qualifications of officers.[39] In any case, state statutes frequently delegate to municipalities, whether home-rule or not, the task of setting the qualifications for the municipality's own officers and employees.[40] Of course, all statutory, charter, or ordinance requirements for local office are subject to challenge under state and federal constitutional principles. Filing fee requirements that make payment of a fee an absolute prerequisite for a candidate for elective office to be listed on the ballot have, for instance, been voided as violative of Equal Protection under the U.S. Constitution.[41] But a "semiclosed" primary system, under which a political party

---

[38] See Wilson v. Newell, 223 So.2d 734 (Fla.1969).

[39] See Chapter 6 *supra*. But state law will often prevail as to residency requirements. See Mosebar v. Moore, 41 Wash.2d 216, 248 P.2d 385 (1952) (state statute saying was no city-residency requirement as to city firemen governed over city ordinance to the contrary).

[40] See Doyle v. City of Dearborn, 370 Mich. 236, 121 N.W.2d 473 (1963) (home-rule city); State ex rel. Patterson v. Lee, 218 So.2d 434 (Miss.1969) (general rule is that municipalities may set qualifications for their officers so long as not inconsistent with state statutes); Hellyer v. Pendergast, 176 App.Div. 383, 162 N.Y.S. 788 (1917); Surry v. City of Seattle, 14 Wn.2d 350, 128 P.2d 322 (1942).

[41] Lubin v. Panish, 415 U.S. 709, 94 S.Ct. 1315, 39 L.Ed.2d 702 (1974) (no reasonable alternative provided); Bullock v. Carter, 405 U.S. 134, 92 S.Ct. 849, 31 L.Ed.2d 92 (1972) (same; compelling state interest required because of appreciable impact on franchise and because this impact is related to resources of voters supporting a particular candidate; no such interest found). On regulation of state and local political campaigns, see Brown v. Hartlage, 456 U.S. 45, 102 S.Ct. 1523, 71 L.Ed.2d 732 (1982), invalidating a Kentucky ban on public statements regarding the willingness of candidates to serve in public office without remuneration; this was found a restriction on First Amendment rights and unsupported by any compelling state interest. On prohibitions on anonymous campaign literature, see McIntyre v. Ohio Elections Comm'n, 514 U.S. 334, 115 S.Ct. 1511, 131 L.Ed.2d 426 (1995), noted 29 Conn. L. Rev. 459 (1996), 74 N.C.L. Rev. 553 (1996), 63 U. Chi. L. Rev. 1211 (1996) (statutory prohibition on distribution of any anonymous campaign literature violated First Amendment). On legislation that regulates the speech of those seeking public office, see generally Note, Judicial Campaign Speech Regulation: Integrity or Incentives? 19 Geo. J. Legal Ethics 769 (2006). See also notes 95–97 *infra* and accompanying text. On public financing of political campaigns, see Peck & McDowell, Dollar Democracy: An Analysis of Public Financing of State Politics, 15 Urban Law. 921 (1983). See generally Note, Full Public Funding: An Effective and Legally Viable Model for Campaign Finance Reform in the States, 92 Corn. L. Rev. 733 (2007). On the use of mail ballots and other developments in municipal elections, see generally Peck, Warhurst & McDowell, Recent Developments in Election Law, 16 Urban Law. 765 (1984). On the use of absentee ballots, see generally Note, Elderly Electors Go Postal: Ensuring Absentee Ballot Integrity for Older Voters, 13 Elder L.J. 453 (2005).

Restrictions on political campaign contributions have sometimes been upheld. See Federal Election Comm'n v. Beaumont, 539 U.S. 146, 123 S.Ct. 2200, 156 L.Ed.2d 179 (2003) (such restrictions treated as merely marginal restrictions on speech because contributions lie closer to the edges than to the core of political expression, and *corporate* contributions are furthest from the core of political expression); McConnell v. Federal Election Comm'n, 540 U.S. 93, 124 S.Ct. 619, 157 L.Ed.2d 491 (2003) (Bipartisan Campaign Reform Act of 2002 banning state and local political parties from using unregulated "soft" money for federal election activities did not violate parties' free speech/free association rights, as the ban was closely drawn to address governmental interest in preventing actual or apparent corruption of federal candidates and officeholders). But see Federal Election Comm'n v. Wisconsin Right to Life, 551 U.S. 449, 127 S.Ct. 2652, 168 L.Ed.2d 329 (2007) (Bipartisan Campaign Reform Act's prohibition on use of corporate funds to finance "electioneering communications" during periods preceding federal elections violated free speech rights of nonprofit ideological advocacy corporation when applied to corporation's issue-advocacy advertisements opposing filibustering of President's judicial candidates in U.S. Senate); Randall v. Sorrell, 548 U.S. 230, 126 S.Ct. 2479, 165 L.Ed.2d 482 (2006) (Vermont campaign finance statute's limits on amounts candidates for state office could spend on their campaigns violated First Amendment free speech protections, as statute was not closely drawn to meet valid objectives). See generally DeVier, Full of Surprises—and More to Come: Randall v. Sorrell, the First Amendment, and Campaign Finance Regulation, 2006 Sup. Ct. Rev. 173. See also Davis v. Federal Election Comm'n, 554 U.S. 724, 128 S.Ct. 2759, 171 L.Ed.2d 737 (2008) (disclosure requirements under "Millionaires'

Amendment" of Bipartisan Campaign Reform Act requiring self-financed candidate for U.S. House of Representatives to disclose to his opponent that he intended to spend more than $350,000 in personal funds on his campaign violated First Amendment right to free exercise of political speech). On the *Randall* case, *supra*, see generally Note, Constitutional Law—Campaign Finance Law & the First Amendment—Can You See the Light?: Illuminating Precedent and Creating a New Tier of Judicial Scrutiny for Campaign Finance Laws, 30 U. Ark. Little Rock L. Rev. 149 (2007). See also Arizona Free Enterprise Club's Freedom Club PAC v. Bennett, 564 U.S. ___, 131 S.Ct. 2806, 180 L.Ed.2d 664 (2011) (matching funds provision of Arizona Citizens Clean Election Act, pursuant to which, after privately-financed candidate has raised or spent threshold amount, each dollar spent by privately-financed candidate triggered direct payment of public money of almost one additional dollar to publicly-financed opponents, substantially burdened political speech and was thus subject to strict scrutiny; no compelling state interest found and law thus ruled unconstitutional). As to the effects of the *Arizona Free Enterprise* case, *supra,* see Note, "Leveling the Playing Field": Reconsidering Campaign Finance Reform in the Wake of *Arizona Free Enterprise Club PAC v. Bennett*, 32 St. Louis U. Pub. L. Rev. 487 (2013). See generally Marshall, The Constitutionality of Campaign Finance Regulation: Should Differences in a State's Political History and Culture Matter?, 74 Mont. L. Rev. 79 (2013); Symposium, Campaign Finance, 40 Fordham Urb. L. J. 587–799 (2012). Compare Hunker, Elections Across the Pond: Comparing Finance Regimes in the United States and United Kingdom, 36 Harv. L. J. & Pub. Pol'y 1099 (2013). Campaign finance laws sometimes contain different treatment of judicial offices from that provided for executive and legislative positions. See Note, A Horse of a Different Color: Distinguishing the Judiciary From the Political Branches in Campaign Financing, 115 W. Va. L. Rev. 401 (2012).

In Citizens United v. Federal Election Commission, 558 U.S. 310, 130 S.Ct. 876, 175 L.Ed.2d 753 (2010), the Court ruled that a federal law severely limiting corporate expenditures for electioneering communications violated the First Amendment. On the effects of this decision, see Bezanson, No Middle Ground? Reflections on the *Citizens United* Decision, 96 Iowa L. Rev. 649 (2011); Garden, Citizens, united and *Citizens United*: The Future of Labor Speech Rights?, 53 Wm. & Mary L. Rev. 1 (2011); Hasen, *Citizens United* and the Illusion of Coherence, 109 Mich. L. Rev. 581 (2011); Symposium, An Intersection of Laws: *Citizens United v. FEC*, 27 Ga. St. U. L. Rev. 887–1168 (2011); Symposium, *Citizens United* at Age One, 26 J. L. & Politics 531–96 (2011); Symposium, Money, Politics and the Constitution: Beyond *Citizens United*, 35 N.Y.U. Rev. L. & Soc. Change 497–705 (2011).

As to the future of campaign financing after *Citizens United*, see Symposium, Democracy, Inc.?: *Citizens United*, Corporate Expenditures, and the Future of Campaign Finance Law, 46 U. San Francisco L. Rev. 281–579 (2011). The *Citizens United* decision was reaffirmed by the Supreme Court in American Tradition Partnership, Inc. v. Bullock, ___ U.S. ___, 132 S.Ct. 2490, 183 L.Ed.2d 448 (2012), holding a Montana statute violative of First Amendment political speech rights.

There has been much speculation on the extent to which *Citizens United* affects various areas of the law and of corporate politics. See Coates, Corporate Politics, Governance, and Value Before and After *Citizens United*, 9 J. Empirical Legal Stud. 657 (2012); Ghoshray, Examining *Citizens United*'s Expansive Reach: Looking Through the Lens of Marketplace of Ideas and Corporate Personhood, 57 Wayne L. Rev. 373 (2011); Magpantay, Associational Rights and Standing: Does *Citizens United* Require Constitutional Symmetry Between the First Amendment and Article III?, 15 N.Y.U. J. Legis. & Pub. Pol'y 667 (2012); Murray, Friends With Benefits: Measuring Corruption in Politics After *Citizens United*, 36 N.C. Cent. L. Rev. 1 (2013); Tillman, *Citizens United* and the Scope of Professor Teachout's Anti-Corruption Principle, 107 N.W. U. L. Rev. 399 (2012); Vogel, Clinton, Campaigns, and Corporate Expenditures: The Supreme Court's Recent Decision in *Citizens United* and Its Impact on Corporate Political Influence, 86 St. John's L. Rev. 183 (2012); Note, *Citizens United*, Tax Policy, and Corporate Governance, 12 Fla. Tax Rev. 589 (2012). And the case continues to generate much questioning and adverse reaction. See Langvardt, The Sorry Case for *Citizens United*, 6 Charleston L. Rev. 569 (2012); Note, The Real Error in *Citizens United*, 69 Wash. & Lee L. Rev. 2171 (2012); Symposium, Democracy Realized or Defeated?, 96 Minn. L. Rev. 1639 (2012). The entire body of law on campaign financing has even been attacked. See Levinson, The Original Sin of Campaign Finance Law: Why *Buckley v. Valeo* Is Wrong, 47 U. Rich. L. Rev. 881 (2013), discussing Buckley v. Valeo, 424 U.S. 1, 96 S.Ct. 612, 46 L.Ed.2d 659 (1976), in which the Court upheld Congress's power to regulate campaign contributions to protect against corruption or the appearance of corruption. The *Buckley* opinion dealt mainly with base limits—that is, limits on how much money a donor may contribute to a particular candidate or committee—and only briefly considered aggregate limits—limits on how much money a donor may contribute in total to all candidates or committees. When validity of aggregate limits—as set by the Federal Election Campaign Act of 1971, § 315(a)(3), 2 U.S.C.A. § 441a(a)(3)—again came before the Court in McCutcheon v. Federal Election Committee, ___ U.S. ___, 134 S.Ct. 1434 (2014), the Court struck down the aggregate limits as not sufficiently closely drawn to achieve the governmental objective of preventing corruption or the appearance of corruption. Compare Arizona Citizens Clean Elections Comm'n v. Brain, 322 P.3d 139 (Ariz. 2014) (voter-passed initiative interpreted as allowing state legislature to adjust campaign contribution limits through simple majority vote), discussed in Note, Last Rites for Clean Elections, 56 Ariz. L. Rev. 1243 (2014).

Limitations on the number of terms for which a person may hold public office have in general been upheld. See Bates v. Jones, 131 F.3d 843 (9th Cir.1997), cert. denied 523 U.S. 1021, 118 S.Ct. 1302, 140 L.Ed.2d 468 (1998) (lifetime term limits for state legislators did not violate First or Fourteenth Amendments); Legislature of California v. Eu, 54 Cal.3d 492, 286 Cal.Rptr. 283, 816 P.2d 1309 (1991), cert. denied 503 U.S. 919, 112 S.Ct. 1292, 117 L.Ed.2d 516 (1992), noted 105 Harv. L. Rev. 953 (1992), upholding a limitation imposed by a voter-passed initiative. Cf. Lowe v. Kansas City Bd. of Election Comm'rs, 752 F.Supp. 897 (W.D.Mo.1990) (city charter amendment limiting terms of office of council members, thus making some ineligible for reelection, did not violate Voting Rights Act of 1965). But cf. State of Nevada Employees Ass'n v. Lau, 110 Nev. 715, 877 P.2d 531 (1994), applying a constitutional amendment imposing term limits on the office of governor but stating that such limitations must be liberally construed against disqualification and in favor of voters' rights to exercise their electoral choice. And it has been held that state laws attempting to impose limits on the number of terms that may be served by members of the U.S. Senate or House are void as violative of the qualification clauses of Article I of the U.S. Constitution. United States Term Limits, Inc. v. Thornton, 514 U.S. 779, 115 S.Ct. 1842, 131 L.Ed.2d 881 (1995), noted 22 J.L. & Politics 521 (1996), 24 Pepperdine L. Rev. 649 (1997) (power to set additional qualifications is not reserved to the states by the Tenth Amendment). See Swan, The Political Economy of Congressional Term Limits: *U.S. Term Limits, Inc. v. Thornton*, 47 Ala. L. Rev. 775 (1996); Wellington, Term Limits: History, Democracy and Constitutional Interpretation, 40 N.Y.L. School L. Rev. 833 (1996). Compare Cottrell v. Santillanes, 120 N.M. 367, 901 P.2d 785 (N.M.App.1995) (New Mexico Constitution does not allow home-rule municipality to impose eligibility requirements for municipal elected office beyond those set forth in qualifications clause and elsewhere in state constitution). Cf. Cook v. Gralike, 531 U.S. 510, 121 S.Ct. 1029, 149 L.Ed.2d 44 (2001) (states may regulate the incidents of election to Congress only within the exclusive delegation of power under the Elections Clause of U.S. Constitution; amendment to Missouri Constitution requiring that any failure of U.S. Senators or Representatives, or nonincumbent candidates for those offices, to support term limit provision be noted on ballot was not a valid regulation under Elections Clause); Van Valkenburgh v. Citizens for Term Limits, 135 Idaho 121, 15 P.3d 1129 (2000) (provisions of term-limit pledge statute requiring Secretary of State to identify on the ballot candidates who had signed or broken term-limit pledge infringe on fundamental right to vote and were unconstitutional); Cathcart v. Meyer, 2004 WY 49, 88 P.3d 1050 (2004) (if no person can be elected to an office who does not possess constitutional qualifications, it follows that any person who does possess them can be elected; therefore, constitutionally prescribed qualifications are exclusive, and term-limit law is invalid). See generally Huefner, Term Limits in State Legislative Elections: Less Value for More Money?, 79 Ind. L.J. 427 (2004). See also Gibbons v. Cenarrusa, 140 Idaho 316, 92 P.3d 1063 (2002) (legislators could immediately repeal voter-enacted term-limits act). As to interpretation of term-limit legislation, see Municipality of Anchorage v. Mjos, 179 P.3d 941 (Alaska 2008) (court, noting presumption in favor of candidate eligibility, held that an assemblyman who had served two full terms and one partial term could run for re-election under municipal charter providing that a person who had served on municipal assembly for three consecutive terms could not be re-elected to assembly until after one full term had intervened). See also Herbst Gaming, Inc. v. Heller, 122 Nev. 877, 141 P.3d 1224 (2006), discussed in Cathcart, Campaigns Halt as Nevada Court Upholds Term Limits, N.Y. Times, July 26, 2008, at A9 (a day before the start of early voting, some incumbents found their re-election bids were ended by state supreme court's upholding of term limits, but limits could not apply retroactively to those who had begun their terms before the limits took effect). But cf. Miller v. Burk, 124 Nev. 579, 188 P.3d 1112 (2008) (application of 12-year term limits under state constitution to candidates for reelection to state office or local governing body who were elected prior to provision's effective date but whose terms did not commence until after that date did not constitute an impermissible retrospective application). Cf. on Nevada's 12-year term limits, Lorton v. Jones, 322 P.3d 1051 (Nev. 2014) (city council members who had served 12 years precluded from being elected mayor, since mayor also served as a member of the council).

The U.S. Supreme Court has upheld a state ban on write-in voting as not violative of the First or Fourteenth Amendment of the federal Constitution. Burdick v. Takushi, 504 U.S. 428, 112 S.Ct. 2059, 119 L.Ed.2d 245 (1992) (ban imposed only limited burden on voters' rights and therefore had only to further important regulatory interests, not compelling state interest, to be upheld; adequate ballot access was afforded under Hawaii's election code). Contra, Canaan v. Abdelnour, 40 Cal.3d 703, 221 Cal.Rptr. 468, 710 P.2d 268 (1985) (city's prohibition of write-in voting in municipal general elections held to violate Equal Protection under both federal and state constitutions). See generally Note, The Dimensions of the Right to Vote: The Write-in Vote, Donald Duck, and Voting Booth Speech Written-Off, 58 Mo. L. Rev. 945 (1993); Annot., Elections: Validity of State or Local Legislative Ban on Write-in Votes, 69 A.L.R.4th 948 (1989). See also Kennedy v. Lodge, 288 P.3d 108 (Ariz. 2012) (statute prohibiting the filing of nominating petitions for write-in candidate for the general election if the candidate filed a nomination petition for the current primary election for the office sought and failed to provide a sufficient number of valid petition signatures barred incumbent judge's write-in candidacy in general election).

It has been recognized that states do have a compelling interest in limiting access to the ballot to candidates who can demonstrate at least a modicum of support, and thus reasonable restrictions aimed at granting access only to such persons have been upheld against First Amendment attack despite the substantial burden thus imposed on freedom of association. See American Party of Texas v. White, 415 U.S. 767, 94 S.Ct. 1296, 39 L.Ed.2d 744 (1974), reh. denied 416 U.S. 1000, 94 S.Ct. 2414, 40 L.Ed.2d 777 (1974) (candidates of minor political parties required to demonstrate support by persons numbering at least 1% of total vote cast for governor at last preceding general election; upheld on basis that preservation of integrity of electoral process and avoidance of voter confusion are compelling objectives); Munro v. Socialist Workers Party, 479 U.S. 189, 107 S.Ct. 533, 93 L.Ed.2d 499 (1986) (minor party candidate for partisan office required to receive at least 1% of all votes cast for that office in state's primary election before the candidate's name would be placed on the general election ballot). Cf. Storer v. Brown, 415 U.S. 724, 94 S.Ct. 1274, 39 L.Ed.2d 714 (1974), reh. denied 417 U.S. 926, 94 S.Ct. 2635, 41 L.Ed.2d 230 (1974) (ballot access denied an independent candidate if that person had been affiliated with any political party within one year prior to the immediately preceding primary election); Constitution Party of Kansas v. Kobach, 695 F.3d 1140 (10th Cir. 2012) (requirement of specified member of signatures in order to become a recognized political party upheld); Libertarian Political Organization of Oklahoma v. Clingman, 162 P.3d 948 (Okla.Civ.App. 2007) (restrictions in state election law that affected an unrecognized political party's ability to appear on ballot upheld as justified by state's important regulatory interest in orderly elections). But the compelling state interest in maintaining the integrity of the political process and preventing voter confusion has been held insufficient to support a statute mandating closed primaries where a political party within the state wishes to open its primary to unaffiliated voters. Tashjian v. Republican Party of Connecticut, 479 U.S. 208, 107 S.Ct. 544, 93 L.Ed.2d 514 (1986). Cf. Norman v. Reed, 502 U.S. 279, 112 S.Ct. 698, 116 L.Ed.2d 711 (1992), on remand 154 Ill.2d 77, 180 Ill.Dec. 685, 607 N.E.2d 1198 (1992) (statute which effectively required new political party to gain more signatures on ballot petitions in multidistrict subdivision of state than were required to obtain place on statewide ballot violated First and Fourteenth Amendment rights of members of new party). Compare California Democratic Party v. Jones, 530 U.S. 567, 120 S.Ct. 2402, 147 L.Ed.2d 502 (2000) (California proposition converting state's primary election from closed to blanket primary, in which voter could vote for any candidate regardless of voter's or candidate's party affiliation, invalidated as violating political parties' First Amendment right of association). See generally Freilich, Vaskov & Ernst, 1991–92 Supreme Court Review: The Court's New Path—The Middle Ground, 24 Urban Law. 669, 753–57 (1992). A state may, however, prohibit candidates from appearing on a ballot as the candidate of more than one political party. Timmons v. Twin Cities Area New Party, 520 U.S. 351, 117 S.Ct. 1364, 137 L.Ed.2d 589 (1997) ("antifusion statute" upheld as not violative of First and Fourteenth Amendment associational rights).

A state law requiring government-issued identification to vote has been held not violative of either the Fourteenth Amendment right to vote or the federal Voting Rights Act; the state's interests were found sufficiently weighty to justify the limitation imposed on voters. Crawford v. Marion County Election Bd., 553 U.S. 181, 128 S.Ct. 1610, 170 L.Ed.2d 574 (2008). See Note, The Missouri Photo-ID Requirement for Voting: Ensuring Both Access and Integrity, 72 Mo. L. Rev. 651 (2007). See generally Symposium, Emerging Issues in Election Law, 27 N. Ill. U. L. Rev. 313–443 (2007). As to possible challenges to voter-identification laws, see Kern, As-Applied Constitutional Challenges, Class Actions, and Other Strategies: Potential Solutions to Challenging Voter Identification Laws, 42 Loyola L.A.L. Rev. 629 (2009). See generally Note, *Crawford v. Marion County Election Board:* A Picture Is Worth a Thousand Words and Exactly One Vote, 9 U. Md. L. J. Race, Religion, Gender & Class 373 (2009). Voter-identification laws are sometimes attacked as disenfranchising minority groups. See Comment, May I See Your ID? How Voter Identification Laws Disenfranchise Native Americans' Fundamental Right to Vote, 37 Am. Indian L. Rev. 597 (2012–13). It has been suggested that attacks on such laws brought under Section 2 of the Voting Rights Act might succeed. See Note, A New Approach to Voter ID Challenges: Section 2 of the Voting Rights Act, 81 Geo. Wash. L. Rev. 292 (2013); Note, Changing Focus and Exposing a Solution: Using Section 2 of the Voting Rights Act to Defeat Tennessee's Voter Photo ID Law, 44 U. Memphis L. Rev. 229 (2013). The 24th Amendment to the U.S. Constitution provides another possible line of attack. See Note, The Forgotten Amendment and Voter Identification: How the New Wave of Voter Identification Laws Violate the Twenty-Fourth Amendment, 42 Hofstra L. Rev. 343 (2013). See generally Note, A Tale of Two States: Challenge to Voter ID Ballot Measures in Missouri and Minnesota, 42 Wash. U. J. L. & Pol'y 203 (2013). See also Note, The Legislative Lawyer as Voting Rights Advocate: The Role of Public Interest Attorneys in the Debate on Voter Photo Identification, 20 Georgia J. on Poverty L. & Pol'y 397 (2013). As to the role of *state* constitutions in right-to-vote cases, see generally Douglas, The Right to Vote Under State Constitutions, 67 Vand. L. Rev. 89 (2014). See also Comment, Better Safe Than Sorry: How Strong Voter Identification Laws Can Protect Louisianans Against the Double-Sided Coin of Voter Disenfranchisement, 74 La. L. Rev. 1227 (2014).

can invite only its own registered members and voters registered as Independents to vote in its primary election, has been held not to violate First Amendment right to freedom of political association.[42]

There is a split of authority as to whether an officer must possess the required qualifications at the time of election or appointment, or need only possess them at the time of taking office. Holdings vary, partly on the basis of particular statutory language, but the weight of authority seems to support the view that the officer must meet the requirements when elected or appointed, and is ineligible if he meets such requirements only after the election or appointment, even though prior to actually assuming office.[43] What if the officer does meet the requirements at the time of election or appointment but *ceases* to meet the requirements (as by moving his residence outside the municipality, in a case where residence is required) by the time of taking office? The requirements are generally deemed continuing unless there is clear legislative indication to the contrary, and thus such an officer would also be disqualified from assuming the position.[44] And an officer who, during his term, ceases to possess the necessary qualifications will be deemed to have forfeited his office.[45] When it turns out that an

---

[42] Clingman v. Beaver, 544 U.S. 581, 125 S.Ct. 2029, 161 L.Ed.2d 920 (2005). Cf. Washington State Grange v. Washington State Republican Party, 552 U.S. 442, 128 S.Ct. 1184, 170 L.Ed.2d 151 (2008) (speculation that voters might possibly misinterpret candidates' designation, on whatever ballot form was ultimately developed to implement Washington's newly established blanket primary system, of their party of preference as indicating that the candidate had been endorsed by that party was not legitimate basis for striking down Washington law establishing this primary system as facially violative of political parties' associational rights).

Although a state may constitutionally choose a primary election system for selecting candidates for political office, this does not render the use of a convention system of selection unconstitutional. See New York State Bd. of Elections v. Lopez Torres, 552 U.S. 196, 128 S.Ct. 791, 169 L.Ed.2d 665 (2008). See generally Schleicher, Why Is There No Partisan Competition in City Council Elections?: The Role of Election Law, 23 J.L. & Politics 419 (2007).

It has been held that use of a uniform direct recording electronic (DRE) voting system does not violate citizens' equal protection rights nor deny citizens the fundamental right to vote. Favorito v. Handel, 285 Ga. 795, 684 S.E.2d 257 (2009) (court rejected argument that voters who used the DRE system were treated differently from those who completed a paper absentee ballot in that procedures for recount differed between the two voting methods).

[43] Sheehan v. Scott, 145 Cal. 684, 79 P. 350 (1905); State ex rel. McKelvie v. Wait, 95 Neb. 806, 146 N.W. 1048 (1914); State ex rel. Morrison v. Freeland, 139 W.Va. 327, 81 S.E.2d 685 (1954) (new election had to be called where council members elected were not freeholders, as required by law, at time of election; requirement not satisfied by removal of disqualification after election). See Chapa v. Whittle, 536 S.W.2d 681 (Tex.Civ.App.1976) (eligibility for office determined at time of general election; but holder of another office can be disqualified on that ground only if terms of the two offices would overlap). But see State ex rel. Dostert v. Riggleman, 155 W.Va. 808, 187 S.E.2d 591 (1972) (eligibility of officer can be determined as of time his term begins; candidate for prosecuting attorney was not licensed attorney but could remove this ineligibility before next general election or commencement of next term of office). Cf. Reale v. Board of Real Estate Appraisers, 880 P.2d 1205 (Colo.1994) (bond and oath requirements traditionally not considered qualifications for eligibility to office but rather are requirements necessary to "qualify" to take office under constitutional provisions). Some states have statutes requiring that a candidate for office meet certain requirements, such as being a registered voter, at the time of filing a petition for candidacy. See Smith v. Brito, 2007 WY 191, 173 P.3d 351 (2007) (winning candidate in town council election was not legally eligible to hold municipal office where he was not a registered voter on day he filed his petition for candidacy, even though his mistake was honest, and when he discovered it, he promptly registered and was allowed to vote).

[44] State ex rel. Willis v. Larson, 539 P.2d 352 (Wyo.1975).

[45] See Ketcham v. Wagner, 90 Mich. 271, 51 N.W. 281 (1892); State ex rel. Cooper v. Roth, 140 Ohio St. 377, 44 N.E.2d 456 (1942). But cf. May v. Edwards, 258 Ark. 871, 529 S.W.2d 647 (1975) (office not automatically vacated when officeholder convicted of crime; this merely furnishes ground for removal).

ineligible person has been elected to office, he should not, of course, be allowed to assume the position—a new election for the post should be called.[46]

§ 13.4 Qualifications for Local Office—Age, Residency, Freedom from Conflicts, etc.

Any qualifications for office or other employment must be free from unreasonable discrimination.[47] Discrimination based on race or color is generally invalidated.[48]

---

[46] See Saunders v. Haynes, 13 Cal. 145 (1859) (fairer to hold new election than to declare the runner-up elected); Sheridan v. City of St. Louis, 183 Mo. 25, 81 S.W. 1082 (1904); Haack v. Ranieri, 83 N.J.Super. 526, 200 A.2d 522 (1964) (candidate having second highest total should not be declared elected).

[47] See Turner v. Fouche, 396 U.S. 346, 90 S.Ct. 532, 24 L.Ed.2d 567 (1970) (citizens have federal constitutional right to be considered for public service without having invidiously discriminatory requirements imposed); Andrews v. Drew Municipal Separate School District, 507 F.2d 611 (5th Cir.1975); Wilson v. City of Los Angeles, 54 Cal.2d 61, 4 Cal.Rptr. 489, 351 P.2d 761 (1960); Landes v. Town of North Hempstead, 20 N.Y.2d 417, 284 N.Y.S.2d 441, 231 N.E.2d 120 (1967). But cf. Escamilla v. Cuello, 282 P.3d 403 (Ariz. 2012) (no general constitutional right to seek or hold public office; disqualification of candidate for her inability to comprehend the English language upheld), noted 22 J. L. & Pol'y 305 (2013).

[48] See Reynolds v. Board of Public Instruction, 148 F.2d 754 (5th Cir.1945), cert. denied 326 U.S. 746, 66 S.Ct. 53, 90 L.Ed. 446 (1945); Crockett v. Green, 388 F.Supp. 912 (D.Wis.1975), aff'd 534 F.2d 715 (7th Cir.) (locality has burden of justifying qualifications that are shown to exclude disproportionate number of minority persons); Boston Chapter, NAACP v. Beecher, 371 F.Supp. 507 (D.Mass.1974), aff'd 504 F.2d 1017 (1st Cir.); Vulcan Society v. Civil Service Commission, 360 F.Supp. 1265 (S.D.N.Y.1973), aff'd in part, cause remanded 490 F.2d 387 (2d Cir.) (use of racially discriminatory tests enjoined). See generally Annot., Racial Discrimination in the Hiring, Retention, or Assignment of Teachers—Federal Cases, 3 A.L.R.Fed. 325 (1970). The general rule against racial discrimination is, however, subject to one exception: a government employer may validly implement an "affirmative action" program of hiring to remedy the effects of past discrimination. Detroit Police Officers' Association v. Young, 608 F.2d 671 (6th Cir.1979) (Federal Civil Rights Act does not prevent public entity which receives federal funds from establishing race-conscious preference program to remedy past discrimination); Price v. Civil Service Commission, 26 Cal.3d 257, 161 Cal.Rptr. 475, 604 P.2d 1365 (1980) (government employer may implement a reasonable race-conscious hiring program to remedy effects of its own past discrimination). See Portland Police Ass'n v. Civil Serv. Bd., 292 Or. 433, 639 P.2d 619 (1982) (affirmative action program upheld as not invalid on its face, but judgment reserved as to validity of application to particular situations; would be conflict with city charter if minority status or gender found not to be job-related characteristics as to particular groups of personnel); Chmill v. City of Pittsburgh, 488 Pa. 470, 412 A.2d 860 (1980), noted 26 Vill. L. Rev. 167 (1980) (incidental statutory conflict outweighed by public purpose). Cf. Regents of University of California v. Bakke, 438 U.S. 265, 98 S.Ct. 2733, 57 L.Ed.2d 750 (1978) (state medical school could consider race in judging applicants for admission but could not set racial quotas). See generally Freilich, White-Wasson, & Cofer, 1979–1980 Annual Review of Local Government Law: Municipal Liability and Other Certain Uncertainties, 12 Urban Lawyer 577, 657–60 (1980); Jacobs, Justice Out of Balance: Voluntary Race-Conscious Affirmative Action in State and Local Government, 17 Urban Law. 1 (1985). The U.S. Supreme Court has held that a state university's race-conscious admission policy, using race as a plus factor in law-school admissions decisions, is narrowly tailored to serve the compelling interest in obtaining the educational benefits that flow from a diverse student body and thus does not violate equal protection. Grutter v. Bollinger, 539 U.S. 306, 123 S.Ct. 2325, 156 L.Ed.2d 304 (2003). But in another decision on that same day, the Court found that a state university's policy of automatically awarding 20 points, or one-fifth of those needed to guarantee admission, to every single "underrepresented minority" applicant solely because of race was not narrowly tailored to a compelling state interest and thus violated equal protection. Gratz v. Bollinger, 539 U.S. 244, 123 S.Ct. 2411, 156 L.Ed.2d 257 (2003). Cf. Malabed v. North Slope Borough, 70 P.3d 416 (Alaska 2003) (borough's hiring preference favoring Native Americans violated state's equal protection clause). And in Parents Involved in Community Schools v. Seattle School Dist., 551 U.S. 701, 127 S.Ct. 2738, 168 L.Ed.2d 508 (2007), the U.S. Supreme Court found that school districts had failed to show that use of racial classifications in their student assignment plans was necessary to achieve their stated goal of racial diversity, though the Court reaffirmed the principle that local school districts have a compelling interest in racially diverse schools and do not have to ignore race in their effort to achieve that goal. As to implications in the *Parents Involved* case, *supra*, see Note, New Limits on the Use of Race in Public School Student Assignment Plans, 33 S. Ill. U. L. J. 279 (2009). See generally Foley, From Comparing Plus Factors to Context Review: The Future of Affirmative Action in Higher Education, 39 J. L. & Educ. 183 (2010).

The U.S. Supreme Court has continued to endorse the broad goals of affirmative action. See Local No. 93, International Ass'n of Firefighters v. City of Cleveland, 478 U.S. 501, 106 S.Ct. 3063, 92 L.Ed.2d 405 (1986) (voluntary consent decree that set quotas for promotions was not, under the Federal Civil Rights Act, an impermissible remedy for past discrimination within city's fire department; such voluntary action between city and minority firefighters might include benefits to individuals who had not themselves been victims of discrimination); Local No. 28, Sheet Metal Workers' Internat'l Ass'n v. Equal Employment Opportunity Comm'n, 478 U.S. 421, 106 S.Ct. 3019, 92 L.Ed.2d 344 (1986) (district court's appointment of administrator to supervise union's compliance with court's orders to establish an affirmative action program with a specified non-white membership upheld as a remedy for past discrimination). But a school board's policy of extending preferential protection against layoffs to some employees because of their race, during an economic crunch, was held to violate the Fourteenth Amendment. Wygant v. Jackson Bd. of Educ., 476 U.S. 267, 106 S.Ct. 1842, 90 L.Ed.2d 260 (1986), reh. denied 478 U.S. 1014, 106 S.Ct. 3320, 92 L.Ed.2d 728 (1986). Cf. Firefighters Local Union No. 1784 v. Stotts, 467 U.S. 561, 104 S.Ct. 2576, 81 L.Ed.2d 483 (1984), on remand 762 F.2d 1011 (6th Cir.1985) (district court exceeded powers in ordering that white employees be laid off during a financial crunch before black employees were dismissed where seniority system ordinarily used would have called for layoff of blacks with less seniority than whites; bona fide seniority system said to be protected by Federal Civil Rights Act unless it is intentionally discriminatory or unless minority group members can show they were individually the victims of discrimination). And the U.S. Supreme Court has also held that all racial classifications, including affirmative action programs—whether imposed by the federal government or by state or local governments—, must be judicially reviewed under strict scrutiny standards and are thus constitutional only if narrowly tailored to further a compelling governmental interest, such as remedying past discrimination. Adarand Constructors, Inc. v. Pena, 515 U.S. 200, 115 S.Ct. 2097, 132 L.Ed.2d 158 (1995), noted 1996 Brigham Young U.L. Rev. 301, 29 Creighton L. Rev. 771 (1996), 5 Kansas J.L. & Pub. Pol'y 31 (Spring, 1996). See generally Comment, Affirmative Action: An Idea Whose Time Has Gone, 27 Seton Hall L. Rev. 1579 (1997). Examples of cases where an affirmative action plan *has* been found narrowly tailored to remedy past discrimination include United States v. Paradise, 480 U.S. 149, 107 S.Ct. 1053, 94 L.Ed.2d 203 (1987) (district court required that 50% of promotions in Alabama Department of Public Safety go to blacks until either 25% of each rank of state troopers were black or a new promotion plan was implemented; found narrowly tailored to remedy past discrimination against blacks becoming state troopers); Peightal v. Metropolitan Dade County, 26 F.3d 1545 (11th Cir.1994) (county's affirmative action plan for its fire department upheld). But in City of Richmond v. J.A. Croson Co., 488 U.S. 469, 499, 109 S.Ct. 706, 724, 102 L.Ed.2d 854 (1989), where a city required prime contractors awarded city construction contracts to subcontract at least 30% of the dollar amount of each contract to one or more "Minority Business Enterprises," this quota system was held not realistically tied to any injury that had been suffered by anyone and thus not narrowly tailored to remedy past wrongs; evidence of general past discrimination against black-owned businesses in awarding public contracts did not suffice. See Duncan, *Croson* Revisited: A Legacy of Uncertainty in the Application of Strict Scrutiny, 26 Colum. Human Rights L. Rev. 679 (1995); Note, Looking Back at *City of Richmond v. J.A. Croson Co.*: Its Effects on State and Local Set-Aside Programs, 1991 Brigham Young U.L. Rev. 1633; Note, The Aftermath of *Croson*: A Blueprint for a Constitutionally Permissible Minority Set-Aside Program, 53 Ohio St. L.J. 555 (1992); Comment, Walking a Tightrope: Local Government Minority Business Enterprise Programs Since *City of Richmond v. J.A. Croson*, 40 U. Kan. L. Rev. 257 (1991). Cf. Michigan Road Builders Ass'n v. Milliken, 834 F.2d 583 (6th Cir.1987), judgment aff'd 489 U.S. 1061, 109 S.Ct. 1333, 103 L.Ed.2d 804 (1989) (law setting aside a portion of state contracts for minority- and women-owned businesses violates equal protection); J. Edinger & Son, Inc. v. City of Louisville, 802 F.2d 213 (6th Cir.1986) (city ordinance according minority group preferential status in bidding for contracts is unconstitutional as denying equal protection unless is sufficient evidence of past intentional discrimination). See generally Symposium: Post-*Croson*, 26 Urban Law. 381–540 (1994). See also, discussing the effect of the *Croson* case in New York State, Note, The Constitutionality of New York State's Affirmative Action Law, 21 Fordham Urban L.J. 1107 (1994).

In Ricci v. DeStefano, 557 U.S. 557, 129 S.Ct. 2658, 174 L.Ed.2d 490 (2009), the Supreme Court held that before an employer can engage in intentional discrimination for the asserted purpose of avoiding unintentional disparate racial impact—in this case, the refusal to certify the results of a promotional examination given white firefighters and one Hispanic firefighter—the employer must have evidence to believe it will be subject to disparate-impact liability if it fails to take race-conscious action; no such basis existed here. See Rutherglen, *Ricci v. DeStafano*: Affirmative Action and the Lessons of Adversity, 2009 Sup. Ct. Rev. 83. See generally as to the limits now placed on affirmative action, Baker, After the Gold Rush: Grutter, Sander, and 'Affirmative Action', "On the Run" in the Twenty-First Century, 36 J. College & University L. 249 (2009). See also Carter, Affirmative Action as Government Speech, 59 U.C.L.A. L. Rev. 1 (2011). In Fisher v. University of Texas at Austin, ___ U.S. ___, 133 S.Ct. 2411 (2013), the Court further narrowed the use of race as a means to achieve student-body diversity, holding that the university must establish that it could not achieve sufficient diversity without using racial classifications.

On the question of who may challenge "affirmative action" employment decisions made pursuant to consent decrees, see Martin v. Wilks, 490 U.S. 755, 109 S.Ct. 2180, 104 L.Ed.2d 835 (1989), reh. denied 492 U.S. 932, 110 S.Ct. 11, 106 L.Ed.2d 626 (1989) (white firefighters could challenge promotion of blacks as "reverse discrimination" violative of Federal Civil Rights Act even though the whites had not intervened in the earlier employment discrimination proceedings in which consent decrees were entered).

California voters in 1996 passed a law banning race- or gender-based preferences in public hiring, contracting, and school admission; and the ban survived initial equal-protection and supremacy-clause challenges in the courts. Coalition for Economic Equity v. Wilson, 122 F.3d 692 (9th Cir.1997), cert. denied 522 U.S. 963, 118 S.Ct. 397, 139 L.Ed.2d 310 (1997). See Purdum, Supreme Court Declines to Hear Challenge to California's Ban on Affirmative Action, N.Y. Times, Nov. 4, 1997, at A-13. Cf. Schuette v. Coalition to Defend Affirmative Action, ___ U.S. ___, 134 S.Ct. 1623 (2014) (no authority in U.S. Constitution would allow judiciary to set aside amendment to Michigan Constitution, adopted by Michigan voters through initiative, prohibiting affirmative action in public education, employment and contracting).

Discrimination on the basis of sex will be invalidated unless it bears some close and substantial relationship to important government objectives. Personnel Administrator v. Feeney, 442 U.S. 256, 99 S.Ct. 2282, 60 L.Ed.2d 870 (1979), on remand 475 F.Supp. 109 (veterans' preference law upheld as *not* a pretext for gender discrimination). See United States v. Virginia, 518 U.S. 515, 116 S.Ct. 2264, 135 L.Ed.2d 735 (1996), noted Signaling A New Direction In Gender Classification Scrutiny: United States v. Virginia 29 Conn. L. Rev. 521 (1996) (state failed to show exceedingly persuasive justification for excluding women from citizen-soldier program offered at state military college; thus, violation of equal protection found). See generally Annot., Validity, Under Equal Protection Clause of Fourteenth Amendment, of Gender-Based Classification Arising by Operation of State Law—Federal Cases, 60 L.Ed.2d 1188 (1980). See also Rostker v. Goldberg, 453 U.S. 57, 101 S.Ct. 2646, 69 L.Ed.2d 478 (1981), upholding the Military Selective Service Act against due process attack despite its providing only for the registration of men. At one time, it seemed the U.S. Supreme Court would invalidate, on equal protection grounds, discrimination based on gender unless a *compelling* government interest were shown, since sex was considered a "suspect classification." Frontiero v. Richardson, 411 U.S. 677, 93 S.Ct. 1764, 36 L.Ed.2d 583 (1973). But more recent cases have upheld sex-based distinctions if a rational purpose and a substantial relationship to government objectives are shown. See Weinberger v. Wiesenfeld, 420 U.S. 636, 95 S.Ct. 1225, 43 L.Ed.2d 514 (1975) (no rational purpose found); Schlesinger v. Ballard, 419 U.S. 498, 95 S.Ct. 572, 42 L.Ed.2d 610 (1975), reh. denied 420 U.S. 966, 95 S.Ct. 1363, 43 L.Ed.2d 446 (women in military service received more lenient time-limit before being discharged for lack of promotion; upheld); Geduldig v. Aiello, 417 U.S. 484, 94 S.Ct. 2485, 41 L.Ed.2d 256 (1974), noted 75 Colum.L.Rev. 441 (1975) (state's disability insurance covered medical expenses except those related to pregnancy; upheld). Cf. O'Connor v. Board of Education, 449 U.S. 1301, 101 S.Ct. 72, 66 L.Ed.2d 179 (1980) (gender-based classification in junior high competitive contact sports upheld); Wengler v. Druggists Mutual Insurance Co., 446 U.S. 142, 100 S.Ct. 1540, 64 L.Ed.2d 107 (1980), on remand 601 S.W.2d 8 (gender-based discriminations must serve important governmental objectives; workers' compensation law discriminated against widowers, held invalid); Hardy v. Stumpf, 21 Cal.3d 1, 145 Cal.Rptr. 176, 576 P.2d 1342 (1978) (physical performance test could be upheld if it had rational relationship to job qualifications; no fundamental right to be police officer; so no compelling interest need be shown). Statutes may, of course, prohibit discrimination that would not be invalidated under equal protection. See Dothard v. Rawlinson, 433 U.S. 321, 97 S.Ct. 2720, 53 L.Ed.2d 786 (1977) (height requirement for state prison guards; prima facie case of sex discrimination found under statute); Marshall v. City of Sheboygan, 577 F.2d 1 (7th Cir.1978) (federal legislation could validly prohibit local government discrimination between men and women as to compensation for equal work). Cf. Los Angeles Department of Water & Power v. Manhart, 435 U.S. 702, 98 S.Ct. 1370, 55 L.Ed.2d 657 (1978), on remand 577 F.2d 98 (women live longer than men; so had to make larger contribution to pension fund than men; invalidated under civil rights legislation—even a true generalization can't be used to disqualify an individual as to whom the generalization is untrue); Nashville Gas Co. v. Satty, 434 U.S. 136, 98 S.Ct. 347, 54 L.Ed.2d 356 (1977) (maternity leave policy could violate civil rights laws). See generally Annot., Sexual Advances by Employee's Superior as Sex Discrimination Within Title VII of Civil Rights Act of 1964, 46 A.L.R.Fed. 224 (1980).

Case law affords relief, in general, to employees who suffer sexual harassment from superiors if submission to demands for sexual favors becomes a condition of employment. Submission will be found a condition of employment if the employee complains about the situation and the employer makes no effort to investigate or to remedy the matter. Tomkins v. Public Service Electric & Gas Co., 568 F.2d 1044 (3d Cir.1977). But an employer can escape liability if it demonstrates a policy of discouraging such conduct and a functioning procedure for handling complaints. See Miller v. Bank of America, 418 F.Supp. 233 (N.D.Cal.1976). Cf. Klink v. Ramsey County, 397 N.W.2d 894 (Minn.App.1986) (no sexual harassment of woman employee found where men allegedly used coarse language among themselves and kept sexually explicit material in their desks; conduct was not directed at the woman employee). But where severe or pervasive sexual harassment *is* found, this may constitute a violation of the Equal Protection Clause of the Federal Constitution and be the basis for a suit under the Federal Civil Rights Act. See Bohen v. City of East Chicago, 799 F.2d 1180 (7th Cir.1986), on remand 666 F.Supp. 154 (N.D.Ind.1987) (governmental employee has constitutional right to be free from sexual harassment at hand of employer). But see Patterson v. McLean Credit Union, 491 U.S. 164, 109 S.Ct. 2363, 105 L.Ed.2d 132 (1989), on remand 887 F.2d 484 (4th Cir.1989) (sexual harassment claim not actionable under Section 1981 of Federal Civil Rights Act, which covers only conduct at initial formation of contract and conduct which impairs right to enforce contractual obligations through legal process). A good summary of the rules on sexual harassment is found in B.E. Griffith, Sexual Harassment in the Public Workplace (Section of State & Local Government Law, American Bar Assn. 2001), reviewed 33 Urban Law. 1111 (2001). An example of hostile work-environment sexual harassment justifying dismissal of a police officer is found in Jurgens v. City of North Pole, 153 P.3d 321 (Alaska 2007).

On sex discrimination, see also Davis v. Passman, 442 U.S. 228, 99 S.Ct. 2264, 60 L.Ed.2d 846 (1979) (alleged that U.S. Congressman had discriminated against staff member on basis of her sex; damages available if violation of *constitutional* rights shown, even though civil rights statute inapplicable). On what *constitutes* discrimination-based-on-sex, see Lorance v. AT&T Technologies, Inc., 490 U.S. 900, 109 S.Ct. 2261, 104 L.Ed.2d 961 (1989) (seniority system violates Title VII of Federal Civil Rights Act only if actual intent to discriminate on statutorily proscribed grounds is found); Anderson v. Bessemer City, 470 U.S. 564, 105 S.Ct. 1504, 84 L.Ed.2d 518 (1985), on remand 762 F.2d 347 (4th Cir.1985) (district court's finding that female applicant for city recreation director was discriminated against on account of gender upheld); Smith v. Troyan, 520 F.2d 492 (6th Cir.1975), cert. denied 426 U.S. 934, 96 S.Ct. 2646, 49 L.Ed.2d 385 (1976) (height requirement as to police sustained, but weight requirement invalidated as in conflict with legislation; requirements disqualified disproportionate number of women). See generally Callis, Minimum Height and Weight Requirements as a Form of Sex Discrimination, 25 Labor L.J. 736 (1974). On the extent of coverage by federal statutes, see Grove City College v. Bell, 465 U.S. 555, 104 S.Ct. 1211, 79 L.Ed.2d 516 (1984), where the Supreme Court ruled that (1) a private college some of whose students received federal financial assistance was subject to federal statutes prohibiting sex discrimination in education programs, even though the college itself received no direct federal financial assistance, but (2) the receipt of federal assistance by some students did not trigger institution-wide coverage by the anti-discrimination statutes but only coverage of the financial aid program. See generally Annot., Application of Title IX of the Education Amendments of 1972 to Sex Discrimination in Educational Employment, 54 A.L.R. Fed. 522 (1981). The *Grove City College* case's holding that receipt of financial assistance by some students did not result in institution-wide coverage by the anti-discrimination statutes was legislatively overruled by 1988 amendments found at 20 U.S.C.A. 1687 (1988), broadly defining such relevant terms as "program or activity." On the effect of affirmative action programs on sex discrimination cases, see Johnson v. Transportation Agency, 480 U.S. 616, 107 S.Ct. 1442, 94 L.Ed.2d 615 (1987) (county did not violate Title VII of Federal Civil Rights Act by taking female employee's gender into account and promoting her over male employee with higher test score where this was done pursuant to affirmative action plan designed to remedy underrepresentation of women and minorities in traditionally segregated job categories such as road dispatcher). See generally Woodside & Marx, Walking the Tightrope Between Title VII and Equal Protection: Public Sector Voluntary Affirmative Action After *Johnson* and *Wygant*, 20 Urban Law. 367 (1988).

As to discrimination due to homosexuality or other matters of sexual preference, see National Gay Task Force v. Board of Educ. of Oklahoma City, 729 F.2d 1270 (10th Cir.1984), aff'd by equally divided Court, 470 U.S. 903, 105 S.Ct. 1858, 84 L.Ed.2d 776 (1985) (Tenth Circuit ruled that classification based on sexual preference is not subject to strict scrutiny under Equal Protection); Norton v. Macy, 417 F.2d 1161 (D.C.C.1969) (would be absurd to disqualify all those who have had some homosexual experience). Cf. Stephens v. Board of Educ., 230 Neb. 38, 429 N.W.2d 722 (1988), upholding a school board's termination of a teacher's contract due to incidents of aggressive and unsolicited homosexual advances by him. See generally Annot., Refusal to Hire, or Dismissal from Employment, on Account of Plaintiff's Sexual Lifestyle or Sexual Preference as Violation of Federal Constitution or Federal Civil Rights Statutes, 42 A.L.R.Fed. 189 (1979). A number of cities have ordinances protecting the rights of homosexuals, though a few cities have repealed such ordinances. See Peirce, Gay Activism: New Force in Grassroots Politics, Albuquerque Journal, Aug. 3, 1980, at B3. See also Under 21, Catholic Home Bureau for Dependent Children v. City of New York, 65 N.Y.2d 344, 492 N.Y.S.2d 522, 482 N.E.2d 1 (1985) (mayor was without authority to issue an executive order prohibiting discrimination against homosexuals and bisexuals by city contractors as the order amounted to a usurpation of legislative power). As to the tests used to determine what amounts to impermissible discrimination based on sexual preference, see Tumeo, Civil Rights for Gays and Lesbians and Domestic Partner Benefits: How Far Could an Ohio Municipality Go?, 50 Clev. St. L. Rev. 165 (2002–03); Comment, Protecting Laws Designed to Remedy Anti-Gay Discrimination From Equal Protection Challenges: The Desirability of Rational Basis Scrutiny, 8 U. Pa. J. Const. L. 513 (2006). As to the effect on this entire area of the law exerted by Lawrence v. Texas, 539 U.S. 558, 123 S.Ct. 2472, 156 L.Ed.2d 508 (2003) (invalidating criminal laws against sodomy), see generally Tribe, *Lawrence v. Texas*: The "Fundamental Right" that Dare Not Speak Its Name, 117 Harv. L. Rev. 1893 (2004).

In Romer v. Evans, 517 U.S. 620, 116 S.Ct. 1620, 134 L.Ed.2d 855 (1996), a voter-approved amendment to the Colorado Constitution that prohibited all legislative, executive, or judicial action designed to protect homosexuals from discrimination (such as municipal ordinances banning such discrimination in housing, employment, etc.) was declared unconstitutional as violative of equal protection. See Rosenthal, *Romer v. Evans* as the Transformation of Local Government Law, 31 Urban Law. 257 (1999). But cf. Boytano v. Fritz,

Discrimination based on alienage—that is, a requirement that the officeholder be a United States citizen—can, when it primarily affects economic interests, be justified only if a *compelling* public interest is thereby served, and when it serves a primarily political function, only if a *rational* purpose is found.[49] Minimum-age requirements are

---

321 Or. 498, 901 P.2d 835 (1995), allowing the placing on the ballot of an initiative measure to amend a city charter so as to prohibit the city from granting minority or special class status to homosexuals. See generally Student Article, *Romer v. Evans* and the Amendment 2 Controversy: The Rhetoric and Reality of Sexual Orientation Discrimination in America, 6 Tex. F. on C.L. & C.R. 261 (2002). See also, on Wisconsin's attempt to deal legislatively with the problem of sexual-orientation discrimination, Turner, The Gay Rights State: Wisconsin's Pioneering Legislation to Prohibit Discrimination Based on Sexual Orientation, 22 Wis. Women's L.J. 91 (2007). Since same-gender marriage is now constitutionally protected, any discrimination on the basis of gender-preference is now of doubtful validity. See Obergefell v. Hodges, ___ U.S. ___, 135 S.Ct. 2584 (2015) (right to marry held fundamental, states must allow same-sex marriage and must recognize such lawful marriages performed in other states).

Disqualifications based on conviction of crime, or conviction of specified crimes, have usually been upheld. See Upshaw v. McNamara, 435 F.2d 1188 (1st Cir.1970) (provision that convicted felons could not be police officers upheld); People v. Gualano, 97 Ill.App.2d 248, 240 N.E.2d 467 (1968); Ross v. Crane, 291 Mass. 28, 195 N.E. 884 (1935); Connelly v. Municipal Employees Pension Commission, 130 N.J.L. 101, 31 A.2d 488 (1943); Beck v. Finegan, 254 App. Div. 110, 3 N.Y.S.2d 1009 (1938); Broyles v. State, 207 Tenn. 571, 341 S.W.2d 724 (1960) (conviction of even a misdemeanor results in disqualification for life; upheld). See State ex rel. Woods v. Thrower, 272 Ala. 344, 131 So.2d 420 (1961) (conviction required for disqualification; plea of nolo contendere did not result in disqualification—but some disqualification statutes do cover such pleas). Cf. Sandlin v. Criminal Justice Standards & Training Comm'n, 531 So.2d 1344 (Fla.1988) (after convicted felon has been granted a full pardon, he is eligible for certification as a law enforcement officer, but certifying party may consider the pardoned conviction in determining whether applicant has the required good character). See generally Annot., What Constitutes Conviction Within Statutory or Constitutional Provision Making Conviction of Crime Ground of Disqualification for, Removal from, or Vacancy in, Public Office, 10 A.L.R.5th 139 (1993).

Disqualification merely on the basis of use of drugs is likely to be held arbitrary and unreasonable. Spruils v. New York City Transit Authority, 61 A.D.2d 1014, 402 N.Y.S.2d 623 (1978). And disqualification (in either public or private employment) on the basis of physical handicaps, while sometimes justified, is often limited by statute. See Annot., Construction and Effect of State Legislation Forbidding Job Discrimination on Account of Physical Handicap, 90 A.L.R.3d 393 (1979).

It is sometimes observed that any provisions on disqualification should be strictly construed, with every doubt resolved in favor of eligibility. See Chapa v. Whittle, *supra* note 41.

[49] See Cabell v. Chavez-Salido, 454 U.S. 432, 102 S.Ct. 735, 70 L.Ed.2d 677 (1982) (peace officers could be required to be citizens; restriction sufficiently tailored to meet political goals); Sugarman v. Dougall, 413 U.S. 634, 93 S.Ct. 2842, 37 L.Ed.2d 853 (1973) (general ban on public employment by aliens void as violative of equal protection); Purdy & Fitzpatrick v. State, 71 Cal.2d 566, 79 Cal.Rptr. 77, 456 P.2d 645 (1969) (prohibition on employment of aliens violated equal protection and infringed on Congress's exclusive control of immigration); Hsieh v. Civil Service Commission, 79 Wn.2d 529, 488 P.2d 515 (1971) (limitation of civil service exams to citizens unconstitutional). Cf. In re Griffiths, 413 U.S. 717, 93 S.Ct. 2851, 37 L.Ed.2d 910 (1973), on remand 165 Conn. 807, 309 A.2d 689 (prohibition of aliens becoming attorneys invalidated); People ex rel. Holland v. Bleigh Construction Co., 61 Ill.2d 258, 335 N.E.2d 469 (1975) (preferences against resident aliens and against residents who had resided in state less than a year preceding employment held violative of equal protection, but preference for those who were residents at time of employment upheld). A prohibition on aliens becoming members of the state police force was upheld in Foley v. Connelie, 435 U.S. 291, 98 S.Ct. 1067, 55 L.Ed.2d 287 (1978). And in Ambach v. Norwich, 441 U.S. 68, 99 S.Ct. 1589, 60 L.Ed.2d 49 (1979), it was held that aliens could be denied the opportunity to be public-school teachers (who are usually classified as "employees" rather than "officers") since teachers are able to influence the attitude of students toward government, etc. (five-to-four opinion). Cf. Heim v. McCall, 239 U.S. 175, 36 S.Ct. 78, 60 L.Ed. 206 (1915) (aliens could be denied work on public works projects). See generally Maltz, The Burger Court and Alienage Classifications, 31 Okl.L.Rev. 671 (1978); Comment, Alienation: Congressional Authorization of State Discrimination Against Immigrants, 31 Loyola L.A.L. Rev. 1033 (1998); Comment, Alienage as a Suspect Class: Nonimmigrants and the Equal Protection Clause, 10 Seton Hall Circuit Rev. 199 (2013). In McBurney v. Young, 569 U.S. ___, 133 S.Ct. 1709, 185 L.Ed.2d 758 (2013), Virginia's Freedom of Information Act, which grants Virginia citizens access to all public records but grants no such right to non-Virginians, was upheld against attacks based on the Privileges and Immunities Clause and the dormant Commerce Clause of the U.S. Constitution.

sometimes considered necessary and valid, but they can be sustained only if there is a rational basis for the distinction.[50] The same is true of maximum-age limits;[51] and discrimination against older persons is now forbidden, under many circumstances, by federal statutes.[52]

---

[50] See Manson v. Edwards, 482 F.2d 1076 (6th Cir.1973) (rational basis test is to be used in reviewing minimum-age requirement; no "suspect" classification involved); Blassman v. Markworth, 359 F.Supp. 1 (N.D.Ill.1973) (requirement that school board members must be at least 21 sustained); Canavan v. Messina, 31 Conn.Sup. 447, 334 A.2d 237 (1973) (striking down, as in conflict with state law, a requirement that elected town officers must be at least 28); Landsberg v. Board of Examiners, 129 Kan. 196, 281 P. 908 (1929); Opatz v. St. Cloud, 293 Minn. 379, 196 N.W.2d 298 (1972) (state constitutional provision setting minimum age for all offices did not violate equal protection). See generally Note, Constitutional Law—Equal Protection—Minimum Age Requirement, 71 Mich. L.Rev. 854 (1973) noting lower-court opinion in *Manson, supra*; Annot., Validity of Age Requirement for State Public Office, 90 A.L.R.3d 900 (1979). See also General Dynamics Land Sys., Inc. v. Cline, 540 U.S. 581, 124 S.Ct. 1236, 157 L.Ed.2d 1094 (2004) (employer did not impermissibly discriminate against workers age 40–49 in violation of Age Discrimination in Employment Act by implementing collective bargaining agreement that eliminated retiree health benefits program for workers then under 50 but retained program for workers then over 50; Act's prohibition against age discrimination targeted discrimination against the relatively old, not the relatively young).

[51] United States ex rel. Just v. Simon, 62 F.2d 879 (D.C.Cir.1933) (reasonable maximum-age requirement will be upheld); Cawley v. Board of Trustees, 138 W.Va. 571, 76 S.E.2d 683 (1953) (same). See Civil Serv. Bd. v. Bureau of Labor & Industries, 298 Or. 307, 692 P.2d 569 (1984), where a city's refusal to hire persons over the age of 32 as firefighters was invalidated as not reasonably necessary to normal operation of the fire department; the city was unable to show that persons over 32 would be unable to function safely and efficiently as firefighters or that it would be highly impractical to distinguish applicants who were physically qualified from those who were not. Cf. Link v. City of Lewistown, 253 Mont. 451, 833 P.2d 1070 (1992) (where plaintiff had been employed by city as part-time firefighter before he reached the maximum age, he was eligible for full-time position despite having then passed the maximum). See generally Kirby v. City of Tacoma, 124 Wash.App. 454, 98 P.3d 827 (2004) (to establish prima facie case of employment discrimination based on age, employee must show that he was within the statutorily protected group; that he applied, and was qualified, for an available promotion; that he was not offered the position; and that the promotion went to a significantly younger person). As to *when* a person passes a maximum-age limit, see Bailey v. City of Lawrence, 972 F.2d 1447 (7th Cir.1992) (police officer was not beyond the maximum age at time of his appointment the day prior to his birthday).

[52] 29 U.S.C.A. §§ 621–34 (the Age Discrimination in Employment Act of 1967), prohibiting discrimination, except as based on bona fide occupational qualifications, against most workers and job applicants over age 40. See Oscar Mayer & Co. v. Evans, 441 U.S. 750, 99 S.Ct. 2066, 60 L.Ed.2d 609 (1979), on remand 602 F.2d 183 (under Age Discrimination Act, suit may not be brought in federal court until state administrative remedies, where available, are attempted). A requirement that police officers be between 18 and 35 has been upheld as not violative of equal protection, and was held not violative of the Age Discrimination in Employment Act *if* part of bona fide occupational qualifications. Arritt v. Grisell, 567 F.2d 1267 (4th Cir.1977) (rationality standard applied under equal protection—but legislation can prohibit practices which would pass equal-protection muster). Cf. Ross v. City of Great Falls, 291 Mont. 377, 967 P.2d 1103 (1998) (statute requiring that city police officers be between 18 and 35 when hired was not impliedly repealed by statutes setting general prohibitions on age discrimination). But see Equal Employment Opportunity Comm'n v. City of Linton, Indiana, 623 F.Supp. 724 (S.D.Ind.1985) (law preventing the hiring as a municipal police officer of an applicant who had reached his or her 36th birthday found to violate the Age Discrimination in Employment Act and not to be reasonably necessary to promotion of public safety). Cf. Public Employees Retirement Sys. v. Betts, 492 U.S. 158, 109 S.Ct. 2854, 106 L.Ed.2d 134 (1989), on remand 897 F.2d 1380 (6th Cir.1990), cert. denied 498 U.S. 963, 111 S.Ct. 397, 112 L.Ed.2d 407 (1990) (regulation which construed exemption in Age Discrimination in Employment Act as protecting age-based distinctions in employee benefit plans only when justified by increased cost benefits for older workers held invalid). In Kimel v. Florida Bd. of Regents, 528 U.S. 62, 120 S.Ct. 631, 145 L.Ed.2d 522 (2000), the U.S. Supreme Court held that Congress under the Age Discrimination in Employment Act could not validly abrogate the states' Eleventh Amendment immunity from suit by private individuals. Thus, state employees who are the victims of age discrimination by their employers cannot sue for such discrimination under the federal Act, but must look to state laws for protection and remedies. See also the discussion of mandatory retirement in Section 14.3 *infra*. As to the relationship of state age protection laws to the federal statute, see Lahey, State Age Protection Laws and the Age Discrimination in Employment Act, 51 J. L. & Econ. 433 (2008). For application of a state constitution's equal protection clause in invalidating a state statute, see Jaksha v. Butte-Silver Bow County, 352 Mont. 46,

What of residency requirements, stipulating that an officer or employee must live within the locality being served? All residency requirements must at least meet the general test of being reasonable, not arbitrary, or else they will be struck down as violating *due process*.[53] Beyond that, two types of residency requirements must be distinguished for purposes of "equal protection" scrutiny: *simple* residency requirements, which merely state that the officer or employee must reside within the locality, and *durational* residency rules, which require that the officer or employee have resided within the locality a stated period of time, such as one year. If there is some rational purpose behind them (and this can usually be found), simple residency requirements will be upheld as against equal protection attack.[54] In the case of members of the city council

---

214 P.3d 1248 (2009) (statutory provision that those hired as firefighters shall not be more than 34 years of age at time of original appointment invalidated, using rational basis test).

[53] See Hanson v. Unified School District, 364 F.Supp. 330 (D.Kan.1973); Local Union v. Highland Park, 363 Mich. 79, 108 N.W.2d 898 (1961).

[54] McCarthy v. Philadelphia Civil Service Commission, 424 U.S. 645, 96 S.Ct. 1154, 47 L.Ed.2d 366 (1976) (per curiam) (simple residency requirement for firemen does not violate constitutional right to travel); Wright v. City of Jackson, 506 F.2d 900 (5th Cir.1975) (employees must live within city); Petty v. City of Pine Bluff, 239 Ark. 49, 386 S.W.2d 935 (1965); Denton v. City & County of San Francisco, 119 Cal.App.2d 369, 260 P.2d 83 (1953); Lines v. City of Topeka, 223 Kan. 772, 577 P.2d 42 (1978) ("management employees" must reside within city); Detroit Police Officers Association v. City of Detroit, 385 Mich. 519, 190 N.W.2d 97 (1971), dismissed, 405 U.S. 950, 92 S.Ct. 1173, 31 L.Ed.2d 227 (1972) (residency requirement for police officers upheld); Hattiesburg Firefighters Local 184 v. City of Hattiesburg, 263 So.2d 767 (Miss.1972); Skolski v. Woodcock, 149 N.J.Super. 340, 373 A.2d 1008 (1977); Mandelbaum v. Department of Civil Service, 142 N.J.Super. 323, 361 A.2d 560 (1976) (per curiam; residency requirement upheld but doubt expressed as to exemptions for police and fire officers); Abrahams v. Civil Service Commission, 65 N.J. 61, 319 A.2d 483 (1974); Bland v. City of Wilmington, 278 N.C. 657, 180 S.E.2d 813 (1971) (residency requirement upheld as to fire officials); Loiselle v. East Providence, 116 R.I. 585, 359 A.2d 345 (1976); City of Memphis v. International Brotherhood of Electric Workers Union, 545 S.W.2d 98 (Tenn.1976) (Memphis charter provision that city employees must live within Shelby County upheld); Jackson v. City of Galveston, 466 S.W.2d 412 (Tex.Civ. App.1971) (residency requirement as to firemen upheld). Cf. Tiffany v. City of Payette, 121 Idaho 396, 825 P.2d 493 (1992) (city requirement that employees live within a certain area during their employment was not a durational requirement, did not impact the fundamental right to travel, and thus was governed by rational basis standard, not strict scrutiny); Clinton Police Dep't Bargaining Unit v. City of Clinton, 464 N.W.2d 875 (Iowa 1991) (certain public employees required to live within ten miles of their employment; upheld as reasonably related to legitimate purposes such as enhanced community safety and improved employee performance). But see Hanson v. Unified School District, 364 F.Supp. 330 (D.Kan.1973) (requirement that teachers live within county violated equal protection); State, County & Municipal Employees Local 339 v. City of Highland Park, 363 Mich. 79, 108 N.W.2d 898 (1961) (residency requirement invalidated as unreasonable); Angwin v. City of Manchester, 118 N.H. 336, 386 A.2d 1272 (1978) (ordinance requiring teachers to live in city held unconstitutional); Mosebar v. Moore, *supra* note 39 (same). Occasionally a residency requirement may be invalidated as unconstitutionally vague. See Bastian v. Personnel Bd. of Chicago, 108 Ill.App.3d 672, 64 Ill.Dec. 213, 439 N.E.2d 142 (1982) (residence requirement for civil servants constitutionally permissible, but requirement that such servants be "actual residents" was, as applied, not reasonably definite and certain).

A number of municipalities now have laws providing that a certain percentage of workers on city-funded construction projects be city residents. Such a policy was upheld against Commerce Clause attack in White v. Massachusetts Council of Constr. Employers, Inc., 460 U.S. 204, 103 S.Ct. 1042, 75 L.Ed.2d 1 (1983) (city or state not subject to restraints of Commerce Clause when entering the market as a participant, nor when actions are specifically authorized by Congress). See Barbash, Court Upholds Cities' Rules on Job Residency, Wash. Post, March 1, 1983, at A-1, noting that such hiring preferences for residents are often used to improve job opportunities for minorities and the tax bases and economies of large cities. Doubt was cast on the validity of some such preferences by United Bldg. & Constr. Trades Council v. Mayor & Council of Camden, 465 U.S. 208, 104 S.Ct. 1020, 79 L.Ed.2d 249 (1984), where a municipal ordinance requiring that at least 40% of employees of contractors and subcontractors working on city construction projects be city residents was found possibly violative of the Privileges and Immunities Clause of the U.S. Constitution. The Court ruled that the ordinance could survive such attack only if a substantial reason was shown for the discrimination against citizens of other states, and the case was remanded for determination of whether the ordinance was carefully tailored, as the city contended, to counteract grave economic and social ills involving unemployment of city residents and a sharp decline in the city's population. Other residency requirements are now being attacked

or other governing body, these requirements may validly stipulate that the member be a resident of the district or ward which he or she represents.[55] *Durational* residency requirements are on much shakier ground, with some courts finding them an infringement on the right to travel,[56] or striking down particular requirements as unreasonably long.[57] But if not ruled unduly long, most of even these requirements have been upheld—though only if they are supported by a compelling public interest.[58]

---

under the Privileges and Immunities Clause also. See Supreme Court of New Hampshire v. Piper, 470 U.S. 274, 105 S.Ct. 1272, 84 L.Ed.2d 205 (1985) (state supreme court rule limiting bar admission to state residents found unsupported by a substantial relationship to a state objective and thus violative of Privileges and Immunities). Cf. Barnard v. Thorstenn, 489 U.S. 546, 109 S.Ct. 1294, 103 L.Ed.2d 559 (1989) (Virgin Islands bar admission rule requiring applicant to live in Virgin Islands for one year before applying to district court and to declare intention to reside in Virgin Islands invalidated under Privileges and Immunities Clause); Supreme Court of Virginia v. Friedman, 487 U.S. 59, 108 S.Ct. 2260, 101 L.Ed.2d 56 (1988) (requirement that applicant for admission to Virginia bar "on motion" be permanent resident of Virginia violated Privileges and Immunities Clause). See generally Note, The Revival of "Privileges or Immunities" and the Controversy Over State Bar Admission Requirements: The Makings of a Future Constitutional Dilemma?, 11 Wm. & Mary Bill Rts. J. 1239 (2003). As to the general program of community revival that was involved in the *United Bldg. & Constr. Trades Council* case, *supra*, see generally Note, Solving Camden's Crisis: Makeover or Takeover?, 33 Rutgers L.J. 185 (2001).

Sometimes residency requirements apply only to officers, as opposed to employees, or only to certain employees and not others. Such distinctions can be upheld if based on a rational difference. See Municipal Civil Service Commission v. Myers, 348 So.2d 1334 (La.App.1977) (upholding distinction between municipal employees, who were required to live in city, and policemen and firemen, who were not so required). See generally Comment, Not in Your Backyard: Ohio's Prohibition on Residency Requirements for Police Officers, Firefighters, and Other Municipal Employees, 37 U. Dayton L. Rev. 351 (2012).

The distinction between mere residency requirements and durational residency requirements is well stated in Memorial Hospital v. Maricopa County, 415 U.S. 250, 254–55, 94 S.Ct. 1076, 39 L.Ed.2d 306 (1974); Shapiro v. Thompson, 394 U.S. 618, 636, 89 S.Ct. 1322, 22 L.Ed.2d 600 (1969).

[55] State ex rel. Repay v. Fodeman, 30 Conn.Sup. 82, 300 A.2d 729 (1972) (council member can be ousted from office if moves from district); Horwitz v. Reichenstein, 15 N.J. 6, 103 A.2d 881 (1954); League of Women Voters v. Board of Commissioners, 451 Pa. 26, 301 A.2d 797 (1973).

[56] Wellford v. Battaglia, 485 F.2d 1151 (3d Cir.1973) (five-year residency requirement for mayor invalidated; no compelling public interest); Green v. McKeon, 468 F.2d 883 (6th Cir.1972) (2-year residency requirement invalidated as not supported by compelling state interest; right to run for public office is not fundamental, but right to travel is). See also Saenz v. Roe, 526 U.S. 489, 119 S.Ct. 1518, 143 L.Ed.2d 689 (1999) (state's one-year limitation on welfare eligibility held unsupported by compelling state interest and thus violative of Fourteenth Amendment right to travel; good review of cases).

[57] See Alexander v. Kammer, 363 F.Supp. 324 (E.D.Mich.1973) (five-year residency requirement—plus two-year *district* residency requirement—for city commissioner invalidated); Bolanowski v. Raich, 330 F.Supp. 724 (E.D.Mich.1971) (three-year residency requirement for mayor invalid); Peloza v. Freas, 871 P.2d 687 (Alaska 1994) (court, applying strict scrutiny, invalidated three-year residency requirement for city council as violative of equal rights clause of Alaska Constitution; periods longer than one year said to be "problematic" and "generally viewed with skepticism," and three-year period found "an unacceptably long time." *Id.* at 691 & n. 8); Thompson v. Mellon, 9 Cal.3d 96, 107 Cal.Rptr. 20, 507 P.2d 628 (1973) (two-year requirement for council members invalid); Zeilenga v. Nelson, 4 Cal.3d 716, 94 Cal.Rptr. 602, 484 P.2d 578 (1971) (five-year requirement for county commissioner invalid); Cowan v. City of Aspen, 181 Colo. 343, 509 P.2d 1269 (1973) (three-year residency requirement for mayor and council members struck down, but court indicated approval of the state's one-year requirement); Bird v. City of Colorado Springs, 181 Colo. 141, 507 P.2d 1099 (1973) (five-year requirement for council members and mayor invalid).

[58] Woodward v. City of Deerfield Beach, 538 F.2d 1081 (5th Cir.1976) (candidates for city commissioner must have resided in city for 6 months prior to election; valid); Daves v. City of Longwood, 423 F.Supp. 503 (M.D.Fla.1976) (one-year residency requirement for candidates for city council; upheld); Brandenberg v. McClellan, 427 F.Supp. 943 (E.D.Mo.1977) (same as to requirement for alderman); Triano v. Massion, 109 Ariz. 506, 513 P.2d 935 (1973) (one-year residency requirement for city council upheld); Lawrence v. Cleveland, 13 Cal.App.3d 127, 91 Cal.Rptr. 863 (1970) (five-year residency requirement for council members sustained); Cahnmann v. Eckerty, 40 Ill.App.3d 180, 351 N.E.2d 580 (1976), appeal dismissed 431 U.S. 934, 97 S.Ct. 2644, 53 L.Ed.2d 252 (one-year residency requirement for alderman sustained); Lawrence v. City of Issaquah, 84 Wn.2d 146, 524 P.2d 1347 (1974) (one-year residency requirement for council members upheld; compelling state interest found). See Castner v. City of Homer, 598 P.2d 953 (Alaska 1979) (even under strict scrutiny,

Residency requirements may be considered to help ensure that public workers are available to those they serve, live near enough their place of work so that they could be called upon for emergency service at "off-hours," and partake of the local facilities and services for which they are partially responsible (thus making them, presumably, more interested in local conditions); *durational* residency requirements increase the odds that public workers will be familiar with the local environment. All residency requirements are, however, less popular—in our increasingly mobile society—than they used to be, and are often considered inappropriate when applied to many employees, such as teachers. Thus, there is some tendency to eliminate such requirements from city charters and other laws.[59] Requirements that officeholders (and perhaps employees—but these requirements are usually applied only to officeholders) be *electors* of the municipality, or have been electors a certain length of time, have been sustained.[60] But again, the durational requirements may have some doubt cast on their validity now, and can be

---

one-year residency requirement for city council was constitutional; court says trend is to invalidate residency requirements of *longer* than one year). The *McCarthy* case, note 54 *supra*, upholding a *mere* residency requirement for public employees, may be taken as indicating that the U.S. Supreme Court would *not* uphold a *durational* residency requirement in this context. See O'Neil, The Rights of Government Employees 30 (American Civil Liberties Union Handbook (1978)) (government would probably have to show strong interests to uphold waiting period). A *preference* in public employment for longer-term residents may be valid. *Id.* at 31, citing Town of Milton v. Civil Service Comm'n, 365 Mass. 368, 312 N.E.2d 188 (1974). See People ex rel. Holland v. Bleigh Constr. Co., 61 Ill.2d 258, 335 N.E.2d 469 (1975). In Hayes v. Municipality of Anchorage, 46 P.3d 971 (Alaska 2002), a municipal charter provision establishing a one-year residency requirement for municipal candidates was held to require residency for at least one year before the election within the geographical boundaries of the election district as drawn at the time of election; thus a candidate who had lived for 20 years at the same residence that fell within a newly drawn district satisfied the residency requirement. But cf. Chachas v. Miller, 120 Nev. 51, 83 P.3d 827 (2004) (candidate for mayor who purchased home outside city limits and resided there, but considered rented room within city limits his legal domicile, was not a bona fide resident of city under statute requiring that candidates reside in city for at least one year prior to election).

Durational residency requirements are, like simple residency requirements (discussed in , note 54 *supra*), increasingly vulnerable to attack under the Privileges and Immunities Clause of the U.S. Constitution. See Barnard v. Thorstenn, *supra* note 54, where a bar admission requirement that the applicant live in the jurisdiction one year before applying for admission, and declare the intention to live in the jurisdiction, was struck as unconstitutional under Privileges and Immunities. Any residency requirement may also be attacked on vagueness grounds, but such attack is not likely to succeed. See In re Contested Election of Schoessler, 140 Wash.2d 368, 998 P.2d 818 (2000) (lack of definition of term "resident" in statute under which person is ineligible to hold city office unless he or she has been city resident at least one year held not unconstitutionally vague).

[59] See City of Atlanta v. Myers, 240 Ga. 261, 240 S.E.2d 60 (1977), applying a Georgia statute that prohibits localities from requiring residency as a condition of governmental employment; Bjorseth v. City of Seattle, 15 Wash.App. 797, 551 P.2d 1372 (1976) (state statute may eliminate nonresidency as ground for discharge of local employee). Where *employees*, such as schoolteachers, are the object of residency requirements (as opposed to such requirements being applied only to officers), the requirements are especially vulnerable to attack as irrational and unnecessary. See Angwin v. Manchester, *supra* note 54 (requirement that teachers live in the locality held unconstitutional). See generally Annot., Validity, Construction, and Effect of Municipal Residency Requirements for Teachers, Principals, and Other School Employees, 75 A.L.R. 4th 272 (1990); "Residency Idea Unpopular," Dallas Morning News, Feb. 21, 1977. Although the laws of home-rule cities on qualifications of their officers and employees are often held to prevail over state laws in situations of conflict, it seems an exception to this is frequently applied where residency requirements are concerned—state law then prevails. See Mosebar v. Moore, *supra* note 39. But cf. Triano v. Massion, *supra* note 58, stating that local elections are of purely local concern—but there was no conflict with state law anyway, since the locality simply imposed a stricter rule.

[60] See State v. Macias, 162 Ariz. 316, 783 P.2d 255 (App. 1989) (mayor who was disqualified from office because she was not a qualified elector of city preceding her election could not cure disqualification by becoming qualified elector by the time she took office). But cf. Arthur v. Payne County Election Bd., 964 P.2d 213 (Okl.1998) (neither change in candidate's voting registration less than 6 months before he filed for office nor his failure to vote for several years disqualified him from being "qualified elector"). See generally 3 McQuillin, Municipal Corporations § 12.61 (3d rev. ed. 1990).

upheld only if supported by a compelling public interest. Requirements that an officer must own property—or, as such requirements are usually framed, own property *within* the locality—are today almost always struck down as violative of equal protection.[61]

In general, a person is disqualified from a particular public job—whether office or employment—by any substantial conflict of interest.[62] Thus, a tenant in a housing project may not be allowed to serve on the governing body of the authority operating the project.[63] Under this general principle, an officer with appointing power is usually considered ineligible for any office to which he can appoint.[64] Close relatives of the person with appointing power are also often considered ineligible even under common-law principles. But the practice of appointing one's relatives to public office or hiring them as public employees—a practice known as "nepotism"—is now widely regulated by statutory and charter provisions. Most such provisions ban appointment or hiring of anyone related to the appointing (or hiring) authority within a specified degree of affinity or consanguinity; any appointments made in violation of such a provision are void.[65]

---

61 Quinn v. Millsap, 491 U.S. 95, 109 S.Ct. 2324, 105 L.Ed.2d 74 (1989), on remand 785 S.W.2d 82 (Mo.1990) (invalidating requirement that a person own real property in order to be eligible for appointment to a "board of freeholders" appointed to reorganize the governments of the city of St. Louis and St. Louis County); Chappelle v. Greater Baton Rouge Airport District, 431 U.S. 159, 97 S.Ct. 2162, 52 L.Ed.2d 223 (1977); Turner v. Fouche, 396 U.S. 346, 90 S.Ct. 532, 24 L.Ed.2d 567 (1970) (school board membership cannot be limited to freeholders); Stapleton v. City of Inkster, 311 F.Supp. 1187 (E.D.Mich.1970); Gonzales v. City of Sinton, 319 F.Supp. 189 (S.D.Tex.1970) (persons cannot be kept from running for city council because they own no property or are delinquent in paying property taxes); Sadler v. Connolly, 175 Mont. 484, 575 P.2d 51 (1978) (freeholder requirement for city council membership is unconstitutional); Landes v. Town of North Hempstead, *supra* note 47. Cf. State ex rel. Piccirillo v. City of Follansbee, 160 W.Va. 329, 233 S.E.2d 419 (1977) (candidates for local governing body cannot be limited to those who paid more than a certain amount in property taxes). As to a requirement that candidates for office not be delinquent on their taxes, compare Corrigan v. City of Newaygo, 55 F.3d 1211 (6th Cir.1995), cert. denied 516 U.S. 943, 116 S.Ct. 379, 133 L.Ed.2d 303 (1995), upholding an ordinance preventing citizens who are delinquent on local taxes or water and sewer fees from appearing on a local election ballot, with Deibler v. City of Rehoboth Beach, 790 F.2d 328 (3d Cir.1986), on remand 659 F.Supp. 159 (1987), invalidating a requirement that no candidate for the city governing body owe back city taxes as not rationally related to any legitimate governmental interest and thus violative of Equal Protection.

62 See Raymond v. Bartlett, 77 Cal.App.2d 283, 175 P.2d 288 (1946); Commonwealth ex rel. Gast v. Kelly, 255 Pa. 475, 100 A. 272 (1917). Whether there is a sufficient conflict is a factual question in each case, but a person can be disqualified though no dishonesty or wrongful intent on his part is shown. See Township Committee v. Morales, 119 N.J.Super. 29, 289 A.2d 563 (1972). Cf. Keckeisen v. Independent School District, 509 F.2d 1062 (8th Cir.1975), cert. denied 423 U.S. 833, 96 S.Ct. 57, 46 L.Ed.2d 51, upholding a school board's rule against employing one spouse as an administrator in the district and the other spouse as a teacher.

63 Brown v. Kirk, 64 Ill.2d 144, 355 N.E.2d 12 (1976). Similarly, a school teacher cannot serve on the school board of the district in which he or she teaches. See Annot., Right of School Teacher to Serve as Member of School Board in School District Where Employed, 70 A.L.R.3d 1188 (1976). See also note 73 *infra.*

64 Ehlinger v. Clark, 117 Tex. 547, 8 S.W.2d 666 (1928); Cotlar v. Warminster Township, 8 Pa.Cmwlth. 163, 302 A.2d 859 (1973) (against public policy for officer to appoint himself to another public office). When a person who is a member of an appointing *group* votes in favor of his own appointment to another office, his appointment may be held void only if his vote was controlling, unless legislation provides a stricter rule. Township Committee v. Morales, *supra* note 62 (vote was controlling; so appointment void).

Some state constitutions contain provisions (modeled on a similar provision in the U.S. Constitution) forbidding a member of the state legislature during the term for which he was elected from being elected to any office in the state the emoluments of which have been increased during his term of office. See, upholding such provisions, Fair v. State Election Bd., 879 P.2d 1223 (Okl.1994); State ex rel. Anderson v. Chapman, 86 Wash.2d 189, 543 P.2d 229 (1975).

65 See Town of Hallett v. Stephens, 125 Okla. 157, 256 P. 921 (1927); State ex rel. Atkin v. City of Knoxville, 203 Tenn. 622, 315 S.W.2d 115 (1958) (appointment in violation of law was invalid). Cf. State ex rel. Robinson v. Keefe, 111 Fla. 701, 149 So. 638 (1933), defining nepotism, but finding the anti-nepotism statutes inapplicable to certified teachers, whose qualifications were established by other general state laws. Exceptions are also sometimes "read into" the statutes for very small localities, where it might be impossible to find persons to serve who were not related to other officers or employees. Baillie v. Town of Medley, 262 So.2d 693

Many laws also provide for loss of office by, and possible criminal penalties against, anyone who engages in nepotism.[66]

§ 13.5 Plural Office-Holding

At common law, there is no rule against a person holding two or more positions in the same government, or with various governments, so long as there is no conflict of

---

(Fla.App.1972). See Backman v. Bateman, 1 Utah 2d 153, 263 P.2d 561 (1953) (statute unconstitutional insofar as it affected principal and teacher who had been employed many years before their brothers were elected to school board and who would lose interests in retirement funds if they lost their positions). Anti-nepotism laws often apply to the appointing or hiring of either officers or employees.

Anti-nepotism laws have generally been ruled constitutional. See Parks v. City of Warner Robins, 43 F.3d 609 (11th Cir.1995) (city's anti-nepotism rule held constitutional as applied to a police sergeant who would be required to leave the department if she married her fiancé, a captain in that department). Cf. McCabe v. Sharrett, 12 F.3d 1558 (11th Cir.1994) (transfer of police chief's secretary to allegedly less desirable position because of her marriage to officer in department did not violate her constitutional rights). See generally Annot., Validity, Construction, and Effect of State Constitutional or Statutory Provision Regarding Nepotism in the Public Service, 11 A.L.R. 4th 826 (1982), noting that most laws have been upheld but that due process problems are presented if a law has the effect of penalizing someone hired prior to its enactment, or prior to the appointment or election of a relative whose hiring allegedly triggered the violation.

Some anti-nepotism laws apply even to *candidacy* for public office. See Sharp v. Tulsa County Election Bd., 890 P.2d 836 (Okl.1994), upholding a statute that prohibited anyone closely related to an employee of a school district from being a candidate for the school board. And some anti-nepotism policies apply to persons who are cohabiting even if they are not married or otherwise related to one another. See Kukla v. Village of Antioch, 647 F.Supp. 799 (N.D.Ill.1986), upholding a police department rule against department employees cohabiting with one another and holding that two cohabiting employees could be discharged since their conduct would have a significant negative impact on their job performance and on department operations; the court indicated that such relationships outside marriage are entitled to less protection than marital relationships.

If an officer is appointed in violation of an anti-nepotism law, he will usually nonetheless be a de facto officer, and thus his official actions will be valid. See Jackson v. Maypearl Independent School District, 392 S.W.2d 892 (Tex.Civ.App.1965).

Some localities go beyond mere anti-nepotism laws and apply a policy of not hiring spouses or close relatives of present officers or employees—regardless of what person does the hiring. See Espinoza v. Thomas, 580 F.2d 346 (8th Cir.1978), upholding such a policy. But cf. Voichahoske v. City of Grand Island, 194 Neb. 175, 231 N.W.2d 124 (1975) (employee could not be dismissed for marrying another city employee unless compelling state interest shown for such policy).

[66] See State ex inf. Ellis v. Ferguson, 333 Mo. 1177, 65 S.W.2d 97 (1933), cert. denied 291 U.S. 682, 54 S.Ct. 559, 78 L.Ed. 1070; State ex inf. McKittrick v. Whittle, 333 Mo. 705, 63 S.W.2d 100 (1933) (school-board officer forfeited office by hiring relative); Haislip v. White, 124 W.Va. 633, 22 S.E.2d 361(1942).

At one time, "loyalty oaths"—affirmations of loyalty to state and federal government, etc.—were required of many public officers and employees, and the use of such oaths was upheld. See Adler v. Board of Education, 342 U.S. 485, 72 S.Ct. 380, 96 L.Ed. 517 (1952); Garner v. Board of Public Works, 341 U.S. 716, 71 S.Ct. 909, 95 L.Ed. 1317 (1951), reh. denied 342 U.S. 843, 72 S.Ct. 21, 96 L.Ed. 637; Gerende v. Board of Supervisors, 341 U.S. 56, 71 S.Ct. 565, 95 L.Ed. 745 (1951), reh. denied 341 U.S. 923, 71 S.Ct. 741, 95 L.Ed. 1356. It was held that one who advocated, or knowingly was a member of a group that advocated, violent overthrow of the government could be barred from government positions. Scales v. United States, 367 U.S. 203, 81 S.Ct. 1469, 6 L.Ed.2d 782 (1961), reh. denied 366 U.S. 978, 81 S.Ct. 1912, 6 L.Ed.2d 1267. See generally Comment, Loyalty Oaths, Conscience, and the Constitution, 5 Ariz.L.Rev. 254 (1964) (noting the Arizona case of Elfbrandt v. Russell, subsequently reversed by the U.S. Supreme Court—see *infra*). But this era ended with the invalidation of such loyalty oaths in Elfbrandt v. Russell, 384 U.S. 11, 86 S.Ct. 1238, 16 L.Ed.2d 321 (1966), noted 52 A.B.A.J. 579 (1966); Loyalty Oaths For State Employees, 80 Harv.L.Rev. 198 (1966); 12 Villanova L.Rev. 363 (1967). The Court in *Elfbrandt* pointed out that discharge and criminal penalties could, under the invalidated Arizona system, apply even to those who did not subscribe to a "subversive" group's unlawful ends but who were merely members of a group having the purpose of overthrowing the government, if such members had knowledge of the purpose. Cf. Keyishian v. Board of Regents, 385 U.S. 589, 87 S.Ct. 675, 17 L.Ed.2d 629 (1967) (statute banning state employment of anyone advocating overthrow of government invalidated as too vague).

interest and no incompatibility in the positions.[67] State constitutional provisions or statutes, however, often declare that a person cannot hold more than one office with the state and/or with local governments within the state.[68] Even at common law, a doctrine of incompatibility is recognized: a person cannot hold two or more public offices if such offices are incompatible with one another. Offices are, of course, incompatible if it is physically impossible for the same person to perform the duties of both.[69] But beyond that, positions are incompatible if their *duties* are inconsistent, as where one office has supervisory power over the other, or power to review actions taken by the holder of the other.[70] Generally, offices are incompatible if the holder of one office has power to appoint, remove, or discipline the holder of the other.[71] Clearly, the offices of city judge

---

[67] See City of Everett v. Curnane, 329 Mass. 490, 109 N.E.2d 135 (1952) (welfare department employee could also serve on school committee). Cf. Shepherd v. Platt, 177 Ariz. 63, 865 P.2d 107 (App. 1993) (members of Navajo tribal council or tribe employees could also serve as elected members of county board of supervisors since functions of the positions were not inconsistent and it was not physically impossible to perform the duties of both positions); Jarnagin v. Harris, 138 Ga.App. 318, 226 S.E.2d 108 (1976) (county registrar could be elected to municipal office); State v. Villeza, 85 Hawai'i 258, 942 P.2d 522 (1997) (duties of offices of circuit court judge and administrative director not incompatible); Jarnagin v. Harris, 138 Ga.App. 318, 226 S.E.2d 108 (1976) (county registrar could be elected to municipal office); Chalfin v. Specter, 426 Pa. 464, 233 A.2d 562 (1967) (district attorney could *run* for mayor without resigning).

[68] See Smith v. State ex rel. Mayor of Citronelle, 276 Ala. 378, 162 So.2d 473 (1964) (constitution prohibits person from holding more than one public office for profit at same time); State ex rel. Scarl v. Small, 103 Ohio App. 214, 145 N.E.2d 200 (1956); State ex rel. Ralich v. Millsop, 138 W.Va. 599, 76 S.E.2d 737 (1953). Cf. Matter of Sawyer, 286 Or. 369, 594 P.2d 805 (1979) (state constitutional provision prohibits officials of one department of state government from exercising functions of another). Sometimes, home-rule *charter* provisions also limit municipal office-holders to a single office. See Doyle v. City of Dearborn, 370 Mich. 236, 121 N.W.2d 473 (1963). Any such legislative or charter provisions often apply only to situations where plural *office*-holding is involved, and not to the situation of an officer or employee accepting another position where that second position is not an "office" but mere employment. See McCutcheon v. City of St. Paul, 298 Minn. 443, 216 N.W.2d 137 (1974) (legislator barred from holding "any other office" under state; could nonetheless be policeman or deputy police chief); Ruiz v. State of Texas, 540 S.W.2d 809 (Tex.Civ.App.1976) (teacher is employee and thus not within constitutional prohibition of dual office-holding; in any case, the prohibition expressly excepted the other position here involved, justice of peace). Cf. Kereiakes v. Graham, 458 S.W.2d 162 (Ky.1970) (member of municipal governing body could also be member of municipal electric plant board despite constitutional prohibition of plural office-holding). On the development of legislative and common-law limitations on plural office-holding, see generally Conklin, Plural Office Holding, 28 Or.L.Rev. 332 (1949). *On judicial* officers holding additional offices, see Cox, Application of "Sunset" Principles to State Judicial Functions: The Ex Officio Role, 33 Okl.L.Rev. 459, 463–509 (1980).

[69] Attorney General ex rel. Moreland v. Detroit Common Council, 112 Mich. 145, 70 N.W. 450 (1897); Pistole v. Wiltshire, 90 O.L.A. 525, 189 N.E.2d 654 (Com.Pl.1961). See Perkins v. Manning, 59 Ariz. 60, 122 P.2d 857 (1942); Marini v. Holster, 91 N.J.Super. 4, 218 A.2d 887 (1966).

[70] Welsch v. Wilson, 218 Ga. 843, 131 S.E.2d 194 (1963) (mayor cannot also serve as city manager); Russell v. Worcester County, 323 Mass. 717, 84 N.E.2d 123 (1949); State ex rel. Hover v. Wolven, 175 Ohio St. 114, 191 N.E.2d 723 (1963) (member of local school board could not simultaneously serve on county board that supervised the former). See Byrd v. State, 240 Ark. 743, 402 S.W.2d 121 (1966) (incompatibility found where one office subordinate to the other); State ex rel. Schenck v. Barrett, 121 Conn. 237, 184 A. 379 (1936); State v. Thompson, 193 Tenn. 395, 246 S.W.2d 59 (1952). But it has been said that the mere *possibility* of future conflicts of interest does not make offices incompatible. Anderson v. City of Parsons, 209 Kan. 337, 496 P.2d 1333 (1972); Reilly v. Ozzard, 33 N.J. 529, 166 A.2d 360 (1960). See Marini v. Holster, *supra* note 69 (offices not necessarily incompatible merely because one is ordinarily subordinate to the other); People ex rel. Ryan v. Green, 58 N.Y. 295 (Ct.App.1874); McCabe v. Kane, 101 R.I. 119, 221 A.2d 103 (1966). See generally Lillich & Linton, Incompatible Municipal Offices in New York, 28 Fordham L.Rev. 463 (1959); Annot., Incompatibility, Under Common-Law Doctrine, of Office of State Legislator and Position or Post in Local Political Subdivision, 89 A.L.R.2d 632 (1963).

[71] See State ex rel. Doherty v. Finnegan, 25 Conn.Sup. 390, 206 A.2d 477 (1964); State ex rel. Schenck v. Barrett, *supra* note 70.

and city attorney are incompatible,[72] as are the jobs of teacher and member of the board of education in the same district.[73] Sometimes, the office of mayor has been ruled incompatible with such other positions as council member or municipal judge.[74] But the mayor's office has, at least as often, been found not incompatible with other public office—particularly if the other office is of a judicial or educational nature, and particularly where a small community is involved.[75] The doctrine of incompatibility, except as given more specific form by some legislation, may be considered just one application of the general rule against conflicts of interest. As such, the doctrine may be

---

[72] People ex rel. Chapman v. Rapsey, 16 Cal.2d 636, 107 P.2d 388 (1940); State ex rel. Stark v. Hines, 194 Wis. 34, 215 N.W. 447 (1927). Cf. Moore v. Wesley, 125 Kan. 22, 262 P. 1035 (1928) (county attorney and district-court clerk); Russell v. Worcester County, *supra* note 70 (county commissioner and district-court clerk); In re F___ C___, 484 S.W.2d 21 (Mo.App.1972) (simultaneously serving as prosecuting attorney and juvenile officer; found repugnant to statutes and to due process). There is a split of authority as to whether a conflict of interest exists, preventing effective assistance of counsel, where a city attorney is appointed to represent an indigent defendant being tried in the city in which the attorney acts as prosecutor. Some courts have found no denial of effective assistance. State v. Mitchell, 356 So.2d 974 (La.1978), cert. denied 439 U.S. 926, 99 S.Ct. 310, 58 L.Ed.2d 319 (1978); State v. Hamblin, 448 S.W.2d 603 (Mo.1970). See Dawson v. Commonwealth, 498 S.W.2d 128 (Ky.1973) (no conflict of interest necessarily found merely because defendant's trial counsel was also city attorney). Some courts have found no conflict but have cautioned against the general use of municipal attorneys to represent indigent criminal defendants. Karlin v. State, 47 Wis.2d 452, 177 N.W.2d 318 (1970). See Jones v. Baker, 406 F.2d 739 (10th Cir.1969) (one of defendant's trial counsels was city magistrate). But there is a trend toward finding a conflict of interest to exist in any such case, and thus a denial of the constitutional right to effective assistance of counsel. See People v. Rhodes, 12 Cal.3d 180, 115 Cal.Rptr. 235, 524 P.2d 363 (1974); People v. Washington, 101 Ill.2d 104, 77 Ill.Dec. 770, 461 N.E.2d 393 (1984), cert. denied 469 U.S. 1181, 105 S.Ct. 941, 83 L.Ed.2d 953 (1985). Compare Petition for Review of Opinion 552, 102 N.J. 194, 507 A.2d 233 (1986), holding that a municipal attorney may represent both the municipality and officers or employees of the municipality when all are sued in a civil rights action.

[73] Visotcky v. City of Garfield, 113 N.J.Super. 263, 273 A.2d 597 (1971); Haskins v. State ex rel. Harrington, 516 P.2d 1171 (Wyo.1973). See Doebler v. Mincemoyer, 446 Pa. 130, 285 A.2d 159 (1971). See generally Annot., Right of School Teacher to Serve as Member of School Board in School District Where Employed, 70 A.L.R.3d 1188 (1976). Note that this is an application of the *common-law* rule that persons should not hold incompatible public positions even though at least one of those positions is clearly that of an employee and not an officer. School teachers are almost always classified as employees—and thus are often not within *constitutional* or *legislative* bans on plural office-holding. See Ruiz v. State of Texas, *supra* note 68. See generally Annot., Status of Teacher as an Officer or Employee, 75 A.L.R. 1352 (1931).

[74] See Davis v. Doyle, 230 Ark. 421, 323 S.W.2d 202 (1959) (mayor could not be manager of municipal water and sewer system); State ex rel. Crawford v. Anderson, 155 Iowa 271, 136 N.W. 128 (1912) (mayor and justice of peace incompatible); Lesieur v. Lausier, 148 Me. 500, 96 A.2d 585 (1953) (mayor could not be municipal judge); Howard v. Harrington, 114 Me. 443, 96 A. 769 (1916) (mayor and police-court judge); Engle v. Sorrentino, 116 N.J.Super. 300, 282 A.2d 69 (1971) (mayor could not also serve as council member). Cf. Attorney General ex rel. Moreland v. Detroit Common Council, 112 Mich. 145, 70 N.W. 450 (1897) (mayor could not also be governor). See also Commonwealth ex rel. MacElree v. Legree, 530 Pa. 381, 609 A.2d 155 (1992) (council member could not also serve as city constable; interpreting statutes).

[75] Poynter v. Walling, 54 Del. 409, 177 A.2d 641 (1962) (mayor could also be judicial officer); Ahto v. Weaver, 39 N.J. 418, 189 A.2d 27 (1963) (mayor could be on legal staff of county); Brown v. Healey, 76 N.J.Super. 371, 184 A.2d 666 (1962), aff'd 80 N.J.Super. 1, 192 A.2d 589 (mayor could be county purchasing agent); People v. Czajka, 11 N.Y.2d 253, 228 N.Y.S.2d 809, 183 N.E.2d 216 (1962) (mayor could be justice of peace); Corsall v. Gover, 10 Misc.2d 664, 174 N.Y.S.2d 62 (1958) (mayor could be teacher and bowling coach in public schools). Cf. City of Glasgow v. Burchett, 419 S.W.2d 544 (Ky.1967) (police-court judge could act as legal adviser to another city).

State legislators have also been allowed to hold a municipal office unless clearly prohibited by statute or constitution. See Reilly v. Ozzard, *supra* note 70 (township attorney and member of state legislature); Stewart v. Mayor of New York, 15 App.Div. 548, 44 N.Y.S. 575 (1897); People ex rel. Ryan v. Green, *supra* note 70; but see Weza v. Auditor General, 297 Mich. 686, 298 N.W. 368 (1941) (member of legislature could not also be county school commissioner because commissioner's post was subordinate to legislature).

applied to positions regardless of whether their occupants are considered officers or employees.[76]

What happens when a holder of one position attempts also to assume another position that is incompatible with the first? The *general* rule is that acceptance of the second position will be deemed a surrender of the first.[77] This seems clearly to be the majority view where offices are merely incompatible; but much authority distinguishes from this the situation of "forbidden offices"—*i.e.*, the situation where by legislation the second office is specifically forbidden to a holder of the first office. In this "forbidden" situation, the doctrine works the *opposite* way: the first office will be retained, while the second remains vacant, since the person presuming to take the second office is by law ineligible for it.[78]

In the incompatibility situation a minority view—instead of declaring the first office vacated by acceptance of the second—allows the person to *choose* the office he will retain.[79] Even where the majority view is followed in incompatibility situations, exceptions are sometimes recognized. Thus, the first office cannot be considered to have been vacated where there is a legislative mandate that the first office cannot be abandoned, or where the first office exists under a different sovereign (such as the federal government).[80] If the first office is a seat in a legislative body, it can be argued that that body's power to determine the qualifications of its members is final, and thus that a member's subsequent attempt to accept an incompatible office is nugatory.[81] Wherever any of these exceptions is applied, the rule will (as in the "forbidden" situation, *supra*) be the *opposite* of the usual: the first office will here be retained and the second position remain open.

---

[76] Knuckles v. Board of Education, 272 Ky. 431, 114 S.W.2d 511 (1938) (with list of authorities); Cummings v. Godin, 119 R.I. 325, 377 A.2d 1071 (1977); Haskins v. State ex rel. Harrington, *supra* note 73. See O'Connor v. Calandrillo, 117 N.J.Super. 586, 285 A.2d 275 (1971), aff'd, 121 N.J.Super. 135, 296 A.2d 326, cert. denied, 412 U.S. 940, 93 S.Ct. 2775, 37 L.Ed.2d 399 (1973). But it has been observed that some statements of the incompatibility doctrine—especially statements in older authorities—limited its application to situations of dual or plural *offices*. See Fordham, Local Government Law 234 (2d rev. ed. 1986). And legislative statements of the rule are often limited to "offices." See also notes 68 & 73 *supra*.

[77] Butera v. Lombardi, 146 Conn. 299, 150 A.2d 309 (1959); Millard v. Guy, 334 Mich. 694, 55 N.W.2d 210 (1952); People v. Harris, 294 N.Y. 424, 63 N.E.2d 17 (1945); People ex rel. Kelly v. Common Council, 77 N.Y. 503 (1879) (no judicial proceeding necessary to end tenure in first office); State ex rel. Hover v. Wolven, *supra* note 70. But cf. Haskins v. State ex rel. Harrington, *supra* note 73, rejecting automatic application of the rule that the first office is vacated by acceptance of the second. See generally Annot., Effect of Election to or Acceptance of One Office by Incumbent of Another Where Both Cannot Be Held by Same Person, 100 A.L.R. 1162, 1170 (1936).

[78] Shelby v. Alcorn, 36 Miss. 273 (1858) (constitution provided that member of legislature could not be appointed to another public office; any such appointment held void); State v. Thompson, *supra* note 70. See Fyfe v. Kent County Clerk, 149 Mich. 349, 112 N.W. 725 (1907) (office-holder ineligible to assume an office that is incompatible with his present position). See generally on the distinction between "incompatible" offices and "forbidden" offices, Conklin, Plural Office Holding, 28 Or.L.Rev. 332, 346–47, 358 (1949).

[79] McDonough v. Roach, 35 N.J. 153, 171 A.2d 307 (1961); Commonwealth ex rel. Crow v. Smith, 343 Pa. 446, 23 A.2d 440 (1942). See McCue v. Antisell, 105 N.J.Super. 128, 251 A.2d 308 (1969).

[80] State ex rel. Welty v. Outland, 149 Ohio St. 13, 77 N.E.2d 245 (1948) (person cannot qualify for state post until has surrendered federal position). See Annot., Effect of Election to or Acceptance of One Office by Incumbent of Another, *supra* note 77, at 1183. See generally Conklin, *supra* note 78.

[81] This argument was successful in State ex rel. Ezzell v. Shumate, 172 Tenn. 451, 113 S.W.2d 381 (1938), but the usual rule of vacation of the first office appears to have been applied in most of the cases even when the "first office" involved is a seat in the legislature.

Problems may arise when a local government officer or employee is also an officer in the United States armed forces. Exceptions are sometimes specified in, or "read into," relevant legislation forbidding dual "office-holding," and the common-law rule may be considered inapplicable if no incompatibility is found, as where the person is not on active military duty.[82]

It is usually held at common law that a public officer or employee may retain his position while *seeking* another office, even if the job being sought would be incompatible with that already held.[83] The surrender of the first office does not result from mere candidacy for, or even election to, the second office, but only when (provided the majority view is applied) the second office is actually assumed.[84]

---

[82] See Annot., Induction or Voluntary Enlistment in Military Service as Creating a Vacancy in, or as Ground for Removal from, Public Office or Employment, 157 A.L.R. 1456 (1945). A leave-of-absence is sometimes granted public officers or employees for the time they are in military service. See In re Advisory Opinion to Governor, 151 Fla. 44, 9 So.2d 172 (1942); Note, Public Officers: Can State or Municipal Officers Hold Office Under the United States?, 30 Cal.L.Rev. 99 (1941). See generally Annot., Incompatibility of Offices in the Military and in the Civil Service, 140 A.L.R. 1499 (1942).

Typical provisions exempting military officers from the usual dual-office-holding prohibition are found in Tex.Const. art. 16, §§ 33, 40 (1955 Supp.1979).

In Schlesinger v. Reservists Committee to Stop the War, 418 U.S. 208, 94 S.Ct. 2925, 41 L.Ed.2d 706 (1974), it was alleged that the armed forces reserve membership of a member of Congress violated the incompatibility clause of the federal Constitution—Art. 1, § 6, cl. 2, providing that no person holding any office under the United States shall be a member of either House of Congress. The Court found that plaintiffs as citizens lacked standing to sue for declaratory relief. See generally Note, An Officer and a Congressman: The Unconstitutionality of Congressmen in the Armed Forces Reserve, 97 Geo. L. J. 1739 (2005).

In Home v. Rothschild, 227 Ariz. 119, 253 P.3d 1242 (2011), it was held that membership in the state bar did not disqualify a person from being a candidate for mayor since—although members of the bar are technically officers of the court—mere membership in the bar conveys no judicial power.

[83] Schloer v. Moran, 482 N.E.2d 460 (Ind.1985) (police officer was eligible to run for city council even though if elected he could not serve as both a council member and a police officer at same time); Wilson v. Niesse, 251 Ind. 639, 244 N.E.2d 436 (1969); Burton v. Graham, 242 S.W.2d 855 (Ky.1951); Kelly v. Reed, 76 Nev. 389, 355 P.2d 969 (1960). Cf. Rattray v. Lindsay, 61 Misc.2d 39, 304 N.Y.S.2d 645 (1969) (mayor's campaigning for re-election held not to violate ban on outside employment). But see Klein v. Doll, 777 S.W.2d 602 (Ky.App.1989) (once candidate had filed for nomination for county judge executive, he could not file for post of mayor, an incompatible position). Cf. State ex rel. White v. Franklin County Bd. of Elections, 65 Ohio St.3d 45, 600 N.E.2d 656 (1992) (candidate could not run for two incompatible county offices at same time, but this rule did not apply where he withdrew his candidacy for one office before seeking the other).

[84] See People ex rel. Kraemer v. Bagshaw, 55 Cal.App.2d 155, 130 P.2d 243 (1942) (first office not vacated by merely filing oath or bond for second office but only upon actual assumption of duties); City of Somerset v. Caylor, 241 S.W.2d 990 (Ky.1951) (first office not vacated merely by becoming candidate for second office); McCue v. Antisell, *supra* note 79 (winner of election is not incumbent until qualifies for the office won); Nesbitt v. Apple, 891 P.2d 1235 (Okl.1995) (actual acceptance of second office required in order for first office to be vacated). In Mancuso v. Taft, 476 F.2d 187 (1st Cir.1973), a city ordinance prohibiting continuance in the classified service of the city after becoming a candidate for public office was struck down as violative of equal protection. But a similar ordinance was upheld (though the case was remanded for consideration of an overbreadth argument) by the same court in Magill v. Lynch, 560 F.2d 22 (1st Cir.1977), cert. denied 434 U.S. 1063, 98 S.Ct. 1236, 55 L.Ed.2d 763, the court finding that the U.S. Supreme Court has ruled political candidacy not to be a "fundamental" interest.

There are now a number of statutory or charter provisions that, at least in certain situations, candidacy for one office results in vacation of a public office already held. See Oklahoma State Election Board v. Coats, 610 P.2d 776 (Okl.1980) (district attorney could not, by statute, run for any office having a term that overlapped the term for which he was elected district attorney). Such provisions have been held constitutional. See Willis v. City of Fort Worth, 380 S.W.2d 814 (Tex.Civ.App.1964) (home-rule charter provided for forfeiture of city council membership by becoming candidate for other public office; provision upheld). The validity of the "resign-to-run" or "automatic resignation" provisions of the Texas Constitution was upheld, against equal protection attack, in Clements v. Fashing, 457 U.S. 957, 102 S.Ct. 2836, 73 L.Ed.2d 508 (1982), reh. denied 458 U.S. 1133, 103 S.Ct. 20, 73 L.Ed.2d 1404 (1982) (wide range of state and county officeholders automatically

§ 13.6 Title to Local Offices

The usual way to try title to a local government office is the action of quo warranto, which is brought by the state or a designated official thereof.[85] In most jurisdictions, quo warranto has been held the *exclusive* means of trying title to most or all offices;[86] but considerable authority also allows the use of mandamus actions for this purpose in appropriate circumstances—usually by a person who himself claims the office.[87]

---

resign if they become a candidate for another office at a time when the unexpired term of their present office exceeds one year; Court noted that right to run for office has not been classified as "fundamental" and that strict scrutiny was thus not applicable to this case). Cf. Laos v. Arnold, 141 Ariz. 46, 685 P.2d 111 (1984), holding that a resign-to-run provision of the state constitution applied to all salaried elected officials in the state, including those of charter cities. The federal "Hatch Act" prohibits state and local officers and employees of federally funded agencies from becoming candidates for elective office (with an exception for nonpartisan candidacies). 5 U.S.C.A. §§ 1502–03. See generally Annot., Prohibiting Public Employee from Running for Elective Office as Violation of Employee's Federal Constitutional Rights, 44 A.L.R.Fed. 306 (1979); Minge, Federal Restrictions on the Political Activities of State and Local Employees, 57 Minn.L.Rev. 493 (1973). Until 1974, the "Hatch Act" more broadly prohibited political activity by state and local employees. See Annot., What Acts Amount to Violation of Hatch Act Prohibiting Political Activity of Certain State and Local Employees, 8 A.L.R.Fed. 343 (1971). Some authorities believe that the Hatch Act, though much less sweeping than it once was, is still undesirable. See Miller, The Unwise and Unconstitutional Hatch Act: Why State and Local Government Employees Should Be Free to Run for Public Office, 34 S. Ill. U.L.J. 313 (2010). See also the discussion of the Hatch Act *infra* note 95, in fifth paragraph (part of the discussion of limits on political activities).

[85] See Hayes v. City of Dalton, 209 Ga. 286, 71 S.E.2d 618 (1952); People v. Scheffler, 381 Ill. 173, 45 N.E.2d 36 (1942); Millard v. Guy, 334 Mich. 694, 55 N.W.2d 210 (1952); Boggess v. Pence, 321 S.W.2d 667 (Mo.1959); State ex rel. Ethell v. Hendricks, 165 Ohio St. 217, 135 N.E.2d 362 (1956); State ex rel. Walker v. Ramaker, 57 Wn.2d 767, 359 P.2d 813 (1961). Generally the action can be brought only by the attorney general or other designated officials. See Jenkins v. Congleton, 242 Ky. 46, 45 S.W.2d 456 (1932); Lund ex rel. Wilbur v. Pratt, 308 A.2d 554 (Me.1973). But occasionally, citizens are allowed to bring the action if they have first applied to the appropriate official, who has refused or neglected to act. See State ex rel. Genz v. Thomas, 185 Neb. 637, 177 N.W.2d 607 (1970) (relief can be denied plaintiff if his interests are outweighed by public policies, as where he participated or acquiesced in election irregularity). In Florida, a citizen claiming the office *or* authorized by the attorney general may bring quo warranto. See Butterworth v. Espey, 523 So.2d 1278 (Fla.App.1988), review denied 531 So.2d 167 (Fla.1988) (person not claiming right to office may not bring quo warranto unless authorized by attorney general). In Montana, private citizens have a general right to bring quo warranto. See State ex rel. Morales v. City of Helena, 174 Mont. 237, 570 P.2d 887 (1977).

The quo warranto action has been said to place the burden on the defendant to show his right to the office. See State ex rel. Gaski v. Basile, 174 Conn. 36, 381 A.2d 547 (1977); State ex rel. Doherty v. Finnegan, *supra* note 71.

[86] Hallinan v. Mellon, 218 Cal.App.2d 342, 32 Cal.Rptr. 446 (Dist.Ct.1963); McCamant v. City & County of Denver, 31 Colo.App. 287, 501 P.2d 142 (1972) (exclusive remedy except where a plaintiff is himself asserting right to the office in question); City of McKeesport v. Fullard, 26 Pa.Cmwlth. 393, 364 A.2d 739 (1976); Mayer v. Hemphill, 411 Pa. 1, 190 A.2d 444 (1963) (quo warranto is exclusive remedy whether right challenged is that of a de facto or a de jure officer; action can only be brought by appropriate official or a person with a special interest in the office); Country Clubs, Inc. v. City of Knoxville, 217 Tenn. 104, 395 S.W.2d 789 (1965); Saenz v. Lackey, 522 S.W.2d 237 (Tex.Civ.App.1975), ref'd n. r. e.; Board of Trustees v. District Boundary Board, 489 P.2d 1393 (Wyo.1971). It is generally agreed that an occupant's title to office cannot be collaterally attacked—*i.e.*, attacked in a proceeding in which the occupant is not a party or which was not instituted specifically to determine the title to the office. See Blatchford v. Mayor of Gloucester, 331 Mass. 6, 116 N.E.2d 695 (1954); Smith v. Landsden, 212 Tenn. 543, 370 S.W.2d 557 (1963); Smith v. Baughman, 194 Wash. 78, 76 P.2d 1022 (1938).

Sometimes, provisions in statutes or charters make a municipal governing body the exclusive judge of the right to office of its own members. These provisions have been upheld, and interpreted to mean there is no judicial review, even by quo warranto. Witten v. Sternberg, 475 S.W.2d 496 (Ky.1971); Crossman v. Hanson, 4 Mich.App. 98, 143 N.W.2d 783 (1966); Houston v. McKinlay, 4 Mich.App. 94, 143 N.W.2d 781 (1966); Harrington v. Carroll, 428 Pa. 510, 239 A.2d 437 (1968). But cf. State v. Quickstad, 66 N.D. 689, 268 N.W. 683 (1936), where such a provision was held not to preclude judicial review.

[87] Housing Authority v. City Council, 208 Cal.App.2d 599, 25 Cal.Rptr. 493 (Dist.Ct.1962) (mandamus available to a public officer seeking reinstatement); Forami v. Reynolds, 248 Md. 246, 236 A.2d 20 (1967);

Equitable actions, as for an injunction, are not here allowed, nor are declaratory judgment actions.[88] Injunctions, however, have occasionally been used to prevent undue *interference* with an officeholder's continuance in office or performance of duties, just as they may be used to prevent interference with other legal rights.

Thus, it may be said that (1) quo warranto lies wherever a person is wrongfully kept out of office, and in general to try title to office; (2) mandamus lies, in a *minority* of jurisdictions, if a person has wrongfully been ousted from office—and occasionally has been found to lie where a person has been wrongfully kept from ever taking office in the first place; but most jurisdictions require the use of quo warranto in both these situations rather than the use of mandamus; (3) injunctive relief lies to prevent interference with proper continuance in office.

Where terms of local office are set by state constitution or statute, such provision will generally govern over any city law to the contrary.[89] But considerable power to set terms of office is often delegated to the localities themselves. To the extent they enjoy this power, the local governing bodies can reduce or extend terms, or even abolish the position altogether.[90] It is usually held that an officeholder may remain in office, and validly exercise the powers thereof, until his successor qualifies for the position, even though the fixed term of the incumbent has expired.[91]

§ 13.7 Restrictions on Holders of Local Offices—Other Employment and Political Activities

Aside from the restrictions on the holding of plural positions with the government, discussed *supra*, there are often bans on outside employment, and on political activity,

---

Blatchford v. Mayor of Gloucester, *supra* note 86; Hertzog v. Fox, 141 W.Va. 849, 93 S.E.2d 239 (1956) (mandamus can be used by a person seeking admission or restoration to office). See Note, Procedure to Test Title to Public Office in Maryland, 6 Md.L.Rev. 186 (1942). But see State ex rel. Kay v. Nixon, 82 Ohio App. 264, 81 N.E.2d 399 (1947) (title to office cannot be tried in mandamus); 3 McQuillin, Municipal Corporations § 12.90 (3d rev. ed. 1990), concluding that quo warranto, not mandamus, is the proper remedy to try title to office.

[88] Hallinan v. Mellon, *supra* note 86 (taxpayer's action to enjoin payment of salary improper); Doyle v. Yudkin, 22 Conn.Supp. 10, 158 A.2d 261 (1960) (declaratory judgment action cannot be used to try title to office); Hayes v. Dalton, *supra* note 85 (injunctive action not appropriate for trying title to office); Crawford v. City of Sheridan, 392 P.2d 519 (Wyo.1964) (resort to injunction inappropriate where quo warranto is adequate remedy). See Hampson v. State ex rel. Buckson, 233 A.2d 155 (Del.1967) (quo warranto remedy is exclusive; so even attorney general cannot bring declaratory judgment action to try title). But cf. Saenz v. Lackey, *supra* note 86 (injunction could be used to restrain payment of unearned benefits where city had made allegedly void agreement to pay former acting tax collector).

[89] See Clark v. State ex rel. Graves, 177 Ala. 188, 59 So. 259 (1912) (localities cannot change the term set by state law); Bottone v. Madison Township, 92 N.J.Super. 564, 224 A.2d 333 (1966); Newman v. Fair Lawn, 31 N.J. 279, 157 A.2d 314 (1960) (appointment for term longer than authorized by statute; appointment valid only for the statutory term).

[90] Sueppel v. Iowa City, 257 Iowa 1350, 136 N.W.2d 523 (1965). Cf. Higginbotham v. City of Baton Rouge, 306 U.S. 535, 59 S.Ct. 705, 83 L.Ed. 968 (1939), reh. denied 307 U.S. 649, 59 S.Ct. 831, 83 L.Ed. 1529, holding that an officeholder's office can be abolished, and thus swept away from him, at mid-term without violating any constitutional rights. Similar power is enjoyed by the state where the state has retained this authority rather than delegating it to localities. See New Castle County Council v. State, 698 A.2d 401 (Del.Super.1996), upholding a statute shortening the terms of county council members. An employee may often have more security in this regard than does an officer; but even an employee's rights are largely based on contract or statute, such as civil-service laws. See Chapter 14 *infra*.

[91] Youngblood v. Marr, 253 Ind. 412, 254 N.E.2d 868 (1970) (applying constitutional provision); Reed v. President & Commissioners of North East, 226 Md. 229, 172 A.2d 536 (1961). See De Woody v. Underwood, 66 Ohio App. 367, 34 N.E.2d 263 (1940) (no vacancy in office until successor qualifies).

by those holding governmental positions. Where otherwise valid, these can apply to both officers and employees—and frequently they do so apply. Bans on outside employment will be sustained if they have a reasonable relation to the fitness of the officers or employees to perform their public work.[92] Thus, the outside employment of police officers and firefighters can be restricted in an effort to ensure that they will be alert for their public duties.[93] Any prohibitions or limitations will be invalidated if they go beyond what

---

[92] Bell v. District Court, 314 Mass. 622, 51 N.E.2d 328 (1943) (general ban on outside employment by municipal officers and employees sustained); Flood v. Kennedy, 12 N.Y.2d 345, 239 N.Y.S.2d 665, 190 N.E.2d 13 (1963) (with review of cases); People ex rel. Masterson v. Police Commissioners, 110 N.Y. 494, 18 N.E. 133 (1888) (police can be barred from outside employment); Cox v. McNamara, 8 Or.App. 242, 493 P.2d 54 (1972), cert. denied 409 U.S. 882, 93 S.Ct. 169, 34 L.Ed.2d 137 (ban on most outside employment by police held reasonable); Willard v. Civil Service Board, 75 S.D. 297, 63 N.W.2d 801 (1954) (limitation on outside employment by police officers); Lombardino v. City of San Antonio, 310 S.W.2d 651 (Tex.Civ.App.1958), ref'd n. r. e.; Huhnke v. Wischer, 271 Wis. 66, 72 N.W.2d 915 (1955) (ban on outside employment by fire department members). See Calfapietra v. Walsh, 183 Misc. 6, 49 N.Y.S.2d 829 (1944), aff'd 269 App.Div. 734, 54 N.Y.S.2d 231, aff'd 294 N.Y. 867, 62 N.E.2d 490 (ordinance imposing general ban). In State ex rel. Richardson v. Morrow, 276 Ala. 385, 162 So.2d 480 (1964), the court upheld a ban on local government officers being employed by utilities or having franchises from the local government. But see Wadsworth v. State, 275 Mont. 287, 911 P.2d 1165 (Mont. 1996) (state had no compelling interest in infringing on state employee's fundamental right to pursue employment, and therefore could not adopt rule restricting ability of Department of Revenue real estate appraisers from pursuing certain outside employment).

Even regulations governing the dress and hair-style of municipal officers and employees will be upheld if not unreasonable and arbitrary. Kelley v. Johnson, 425 U.S. 238, 96 S.Ct. 1440, 47 L.Ed.2d 708 (1976), on remand 543 F.2d 465 (hair regulation for police not arbitrary; could contribute to similarity of appearance, fostering recognizability to public plus "espirit de corps" among police); Burback v. Goldschmidt, 17 Or.App. 181, 521 P.2d 5 (1974) (regulation of hair length of police upheld). See Cooper v. Eugene School Dist. No. 4J, 301 Or. 358, 723 P.2d 298 (1986), appeal dismissed 480 U.S. 942, 107 S.Ct. 1597, 94 L.Ed.2d 784 (1987) (religious dress statute, prohibiting public school teacher from wearing religious dress while engaged in teaching duties, valid if limited to actual incompatibility with teaching function; certificate of tenured teacher was revoked for wearing Sikh dress). Cf. Goldman v. Weinberger, 475 U.S. 503, 106 S.Ct. 1310, 89 L.Ed.2d 478 (1986) (First Amendment did not prohibit application of Air Force regulation to prevent wearing of yarmulke while Orthodox Jew was on duty and in uniform; decision based on need for military discipline); Fitzpatrick v. City of Atlanta, 2 F.3d 1112 (11th Cir.1993) (summary judgment approved in favor of city fire department's policy prohibiting facial hair). See also Note, Trans Employee and Personal Appearance Standards Under Title VII, 50 Ariz. L. Rev. 939 (2008), discussing appearance standards as to transgender and transsexual individuals under Title VII of the Federal Civil Rights Act, which prohibits gender discrimination. As to situations of discrimination against obese persons, see Comment, A Fatter Butt Equals a Skinnier Wallet: Why Workplace Wellness Programs Discriminate Against the Obese and Violate Federal Employment Law, 11 Wyo. L. Rev. 639 (2011). See generally Note, The Looking-Glass Window: Appearance-based Discrimination in the Workplace, 19 Cardozo J.L. & Gender 683 (2013). On the scope of the constitutionally protected privacy interest of government employees, see O'Connor v. Ortega, 480 U.S. 709, 107 S.Ct. 1492, 94 L.Ed.2d 714 (1987), on remand 817 F.2d 1408 (9th Cir.1987) (standard of reasonableness applies to public employer's search of employee's desk and office; whether employer's search of hospital supervisor's office was here unreasonable was factual question precluding summary judgment). See generally Baird, Kadue & Sulzer, Public Employee Privacy—A Legal and Practical Guide to Issues Affecting the Workplace (American Bar Ass'n 1995). See also Koster, Workplace Searches by Public Employers and the Fourth Amendment, 39 Urban Law. 75 (2007).

As to the possible discrimination and resulting constitutional claims presented by restrictions on public officers and employees who display tattoos and other bodily decorations, see generally Kramer, Generation Y: Tattoos, Piercings, and Other Issues for the Private and Public Employer, 38 Urban Law. 593 (2006).

[93] See Jurgens v. Davenport Railway, 249 Iowa 711, 88 N.W.2d 797 (1958); Hopwood v. City of Paducah, 424 S.W.2d 134 (Ky.1968) (limitation on outside working time of police upheld); Board of County Commissioners v. Milstead, 258 Md. 477, 265 A.2d 879 (1970) (firemen prohibited from also serving with volunteer fire departments). Cf. Long Beach Police Officers Ass'n v. City of Long Beach, 46 Cal.3d 736, 250 Cal.Rptr. 869, 759 P.2d 504 (1988) (statute prohibiting police officers and other city employees from engaging in collateral activities that conflict with official duties did not limit police department's power to impose additional restrictions on off-duty activities of its officers); Fraternal Order of Police v. City of Evansville, 559 N.E.2d 607 (Ind.1990) (regulation prohibiting city police officers from accepting off-duty employment in places where alcoholic beverages were served held valid); Allison v. City of Southfield, 172 Mich.App. 592, 432 N.W.2d 369 (1988) (rule barring police officers from secondary employment without approval held not

is reasonably necessary, and thus total bans on all outside work—as opposed to bans that merely limit the type or hours of such work—will sometimes be struck down.[94]

Similarly, bans on specified political activities, such as solicitation and/or contribution of funds for political candidates, have been sustained.[95] But total bans on

---

unconstitutionally vague nor violative of due process or equal protection). *Cox v. McNamara*, *supra* note 92, notes some of the valid reasons for limiting off-duty employment by police officers: ensuring availability of police officers 24 hours a day; increasing efficiency of the officers during their off-duty hours; avoiding possible conflicts of interest; and preventing possible detrimental effects on the image of the police force.

[94] See City of Crowley Firemen v. City of Crowley, 280 So.2d 897 (La.1973) (total ban is invalid); Mobley v. City of Evansville, 130 Ind.App. 575, 167 N.E.2d 473 (1960) (unreasonable restriction invalidated; arbitrarily prohibited all members of fire department from selling alcoholic beverages). Cf. Cox v. McNamara, *supra* note 92 (limited exceptions to ban on outside employment upheld). See also Natilson v. Hodson, 289 N.Y. 842, 47 N.E.2d 442 (1943) (unreasonable restriction on outside employment of social welfare workers; outside work did not interfere with civil service duties). If permission to hold outside employment must be obtained from some officer or board, adequate standards must be provided to guide the granting or denial of the permission, or else the rule is unconstitutional. See Isola v. Borough of Belmar, 34 N.J.Super. 544, 112 A.2d 738 (1955). On the delegation of such authority, see generally Chapter 9 *supra*. See also McDaniel v. Paty, 435 U.S. 618, 98 S.Ct. 1322, 55 L.Ed.2d 593 (1978) (ministers and priests cannot be barred from political posts).

[95] Mining v. Wheeler, 378 F.Supp. 1115 (W.D.Mo.1974); Paulos v. Breier, 371 F.Supp. 523 (E.D.Wis.1974), aff'd 507 F.2d 1383 (8th Cir.); Commonwealth v. McCarthy, 281 Mass. 253, 183 N.E. 495 (1932) (ban on soliciting or receiving political funds upheld); State v. Kirby, 349 Mo. 988, 163 S.W.2d 990 (1942); Salt Lake City Fire Fighters Local v. Salt Lake City, 22 Utah 2d 115, 449 P.2d 239 (1969), cert. denied 395 U.S. 906, 89 S.Ct. 1748, 23 L.Ed.2d 220. See Wachsman v. Dallas, 704 F.2d 160 (5th Cir.1983), cert. denied 464 U.S. 1012, 104 S.Ct. 537, 78 L.Ed.2d 717 (1983) (broad restrictions on political activity by municipal employees constitutional in every respect except when they prohibited employees from endorsing candidates at private or nonpolitical gatherings; city found to have compelling interest in protecting efficiency and independence of its employees by prohibiting specified political activities); Kilburn v. Colwell, 396 S.W.2d 803 (Ky.1965) (police officer who solicited political funds could be discharged). Cf. Broadrick v. Oklahoma, 413 U.S. 601, 93 S.Ct. 2908, 37 L.Ed.2d 830 (1973), upholding, against charges of undue vagueness and overbreadth, a state statute prohibiting political activities by state employees; United States Civil Service Commission v. National Association of Letter Carriers, 413 U.S. 548, 93 S.Ct. 2880, 37 L.Ed.2d 796 (1973) (federal legislation against political activity, and regulations under such legislation, not unconstitutionally overbroad or vague). In Pollard v. Board of Police Comm'rs, 665 S.W.2d 333 (Mo.1984), cert. denied 473 U.S. 907, 105 S.Ct. 3534, 87 L.Ed.2d 657 (1985), a state statute prohibiting officers or employees of the Kansas City Police Department from making campaign contributions to candidates for public office was held not pre-empted by the federal legislation in the area and not violative of Equal Protection or the First Amendment. In Reeder v. Kansas City Bd. of Police Comm'rs, 796 F.2d 1050 (8th Cir.1986), cert. denied 479 U.S. 1065, 107 S.Ct. 951, 93 L.Ed.2d 1000 (1987), the statute was again upheld against Equal Protection attack in light of Kansas City's past experiences with political corruption.

In Republican Party of Minn. v. White, 536 U.S. 765, 122 S.Ct. 2528, 153 L.Ed.2d 694 (2002), the Court, in a 5–to–4 opinion, invalidated as violative of the First Amendment a Minnesota Supreme Court canon of judicial conduct that prohibited candidates for judicial election from announcing their views on disputed legal or political issues. See Sparling, Attorneys Un-muzzled: Does *Republican Party of Minnesota v. White* Invalidate the Use of an Objective Standard in Cases Involving Extrajudicial Speech Criticizing a Judge?, 30 Hamline L. Rev. 59 (2007); Note, The First Amendment Allows a Candidate for Judicial Election to Announce His or Her Views on Disputed Legal or Political Issues, 41 Duq. L. Rev. 425 (2003); Note, Bought Elections, 11 Geo. Mason L. Rev. 765 (2003); Note, *Republican Party of Minnesota v. White* Threatens Judicial Impartiality in Texas, 41 Houston L. Rev. 201 (2004); Note, Are There Any Limits on Judicial Candidates' Political Speech After *Republican Party v. White*?, 33 N.M.L. Rev. 449 (2003); Comment, Judicial Campaign Speech Restrictions in Light of *Republican Party of Minn. v. White*, 24 N. Ill. U. L. Rev. 295 (2004). On limitations on judges' campaign speeches, see generally Belmas & Shepard, Speaking From the Bench: Judicial Campaigns, Judges' Speech, and the First Amendment, 58 Drake L. Rev. 709 (2010); Griffen, Judicial Elections, Campaigning, and the First Amendment: Looking Past the Hype and Hysteria to Democracy, 64 Ark. L. Rev. 77 (2011); Hertz-Bungi, Pledge, Promise or Commit: New York's Tenuous Limitations on Judicial Campaign Speech, 29 Touro L. Rev. 569 (2013).

As to when a judge, because of contributions made to his campaign, should recuse himself from hearing a case involving one of his contributors, see Caperton v. A.T. Massey Coal Co., 556 U.S. 868, 129 S.Ct. 2252, 173 L.Ed.2d 1208 (2009) (state Supreme Court of Appeals judge who had received three million dollar campaign contribution from CEO of corporation should have recused himself in case against corporation). See

all political activities are usually invalidated as unduly broad, unnecessarily infringing on rights of free speech and association.[96] Bans on government officers and employees running for election to other public posts will be upheld if supported by a rational purpose.[97]

---

generally Brill, Campaign Contributions, Campaign Involvement, and Judicial Recusal, 64 Ark. L. Rev. 103 (2011). In Williams-Yulee v. Florida Bar, ___ U.S. ___, 135 S.Ct. 1656 (2015), a state's judicial conduct rule prohibiting judicial candidates from personally soliciting campaign funds was upheld, applying strict scrutiny, as narrowly tailored to protect the integrity of the judiciary and maintain the public's confidence in an impartial judiciary. On the possible effect of the *Republican Party v. White* case on judicial selection, see Schultz, *Minnesota Republican Party v. White* and the Future of State Judicial Selection, 69 Albany L. Rev. 985 (2006); Note, The Increasing Politicization of the American Judiciary: *Republican Party of Minnesota v. White* and Its Effects on Future Judicial Selection in State Courts, 12 Wm. & Mary Bill Rts. J. 577 (2004). See generally Lambert, Contestable Judicial Elections: Maintaining Respectability in the post-*White* Era, 94 Ky. L.J. 1 (2006). See also as to legislation or regulations that restrict the speech of those seeking public office note 41 *supra*, and accompanying text. For a full history of the development of the law on free speech in public employment, see Oluwole, Eras in Public Employment—Free Speech Jurisprudence, 32 Vt. L. Rev. 317 (2007). On criminalization of false statements made about candidates during political campaigns, see Susan B. Anthony List v. Driehaus, ___ U.S. ___, 134 S.Ct. 2334 (2014) (finding that advocacy organizations' challenge to Ohio statute criminalizing such statements was ripe for judicial review). See generally Hasen, A Constitutional Right to Lie in Campaigns and Elections?, 74 Mont. L. Rev. 53 (2013).

Though most of the above-cited cases involved bans imposed by state statutes or city ordinances, such bans are sometimes imposed merely by departmental regulations. These too have been upheld. Lecci v. Looney, 33 A.D.2d 916, 307 N.Y.S.2d 594 (1970) (police department rule against participation in political campaigns). Cf. Swinney v. Untreiner, 272 So.2d 805 (Fla.1973), cert. denied 413 U.S. 921, 93 S.Ct. 3064, 37 L.Ed.2d 1043 (County Civil Service Act imposing *criminal* penalty for political activity went beyond what was necessary to public interest, but provisions on dismissal for political activity upheld).

Federal legislation (the "Hatch Act") which once prohibited political activity by employees of federally financed local agencies now has been amended so as only to prohibit such employees from becoming candidates for public office. 5 U.S.C. § 1502(a)(3) (1977). Even such candidacy is allowed where it is non-partisan. 5 U.S.C.A. § 1503. See generally Vaughn, Restrictions on the Political Activities of Public Employees: The Hatch Act and Beyond, 44 Geo.Wash.L.Rev. 516 (1976). For interpretation of the Hatch Act where it does still apply, as to federal employees, see Blaylock v. United States Merit Systems Protection Bd., 851 F.2d 1348 (11th Cir.1988) (president of union of public employees did not violate Hatch Act prohibition against actively participating in political campaigns by his publication of a series of columns in the union newsletter highly critical of one U.S. Presidential candidate and supportive of the other). See generally Bloch, The Judgment of History: Faction, Political Machines, and the Hatch Act, 7 U. Pa. J. Lab. & Emp. L. 225 (2005). See also the discussion of the Hatch Act as related to plural office-holding, *supra* note 84, para. 2.

[96] Fort v. Civil Service Commission, 61 Cal.2d 331, 38 Cal.Rptr. 625, 392 P.2d 385 (1964) (ban on both partisan and non-partisan political activities too broad); City of Miami v. Sterbenz, 203 So.2d 4 (Fla.1967) (ban on all solicitation for political purposes too broad); De Stefano v. Wilson, 96 N.J.Super. 592, 233 A.2d 682 (1967) (complete ban on political activities violates First Amendment rights). Cf. Bellevue Fire Fighters Local 1604 v. City of Bellevue, 100 Wash.2d 748, 675 P.2d 592 (1984), cert. denied 471 U.S. 1015, 105 S.Ct. 2017, 85 L.Ed.2d 299 (1985) (city ordinance forbidding city employees from actively participating in nonpartisan political campaigns invalidated as in conflict with state law giving such employees the right to participate in even partisan campaigns).

[97] Clements v. Fashing, 457 U.S. 957, 102 S.Ct. 2836, 73 L.Ed.2d 508 (1982), reh. denied 458 U.S. 1133, 103 S.Ct. 20, 73 L.Ed.2d 1404 (1982) (candidacy for office does not involve fundamental right; strict scrutiny unnecessary, and therefore rational purpose will suffice to uphold law). See Willis v. City of Fort Worth, 380 S.W.2d 814 (Tex. Civ. App. 1964), ref'd n.r.e. (forfeiture of city council post by becoming candidate for any other public office; upheld as rational). Cf. Magill v. Lynch, 560 F.2d 22 (1st Cir.1977), cert. denied 434 U.S. 1063, 98 S.Ct. 1236, 55 L.Ed.2d 763 (1978) (ban on city employees being candidates in municipal elections upheld; court says that Supreme Court does not treat political candidacy as a "fundamental interest"); Laos v. Arnold, 141 Ariz. 46, 685 P.2d 111 (1984) (resign-to-run provision of state constitution held applicable to all salaried elected officials in state, including those of home-rule cities). Prior to the *Clements* case *supra*, some authority upheld bans on government officers and employees running for other posts only if a *compelling* governmental interest was shown. See Kinnear v. City & County of San Francisco, 61 Cal.2d 341, 38 Cal.Rptr., 631, 392 P.2d 391 (1964). See generally Annot., Prohibiting Public Employee from Running for Elective Office as Violation of Employee's Federal Constitutional Rights, 44 A.L.R. Fed. 306 (1979). See also Section 13.5 *supra*. On potential ramifications for taking adverse actions against public employees because of their political

§ 13.8 Restrictions on Holders of Public Offices—Avoiding Conflicts of Interest

It is universally agreed that local government officers owe their government, and the people of their locality, a fiduciary duty of the highest possible fidelity—and of the greatest skill and diligence, as to their work, of which they are capable.[98] While this fiduciary duty is usually stated as applicable to *officers,* it is clear that employees as well as officers have an obligation to avoid conflicts of interest and to be influenced, in their public work, solely by considerations of the public good.[99] The general principles are augmented in most jurisdictions by specific statutory and/or charter provisions prohibiting conflicts of interest by either officers or employees.[100] Violation of such provisions is usually a ground for removal,[101] and criminal penalties are often provided—though the criminal laws can be applied only if the rule is unambiguous and the violation is clear beyond a reasonable doubt.[102]

Conflicts of interest may initially disqualify a person from government work, as discussed *supra.* But even where this does not occur (for instance, where any possible conflicts are mere matters of speculation as to the future), an officer or employee may subsequently be disqualified from participation in a particular item of business. Such disqualification occurs whenever the officer or employee is placed in a situation of temptation to serve his own interests to the possible detriment of the public interest.[103]

---

candidacies, see Koster, Election Battles and Their Impact on the Public Employer, 38 Urban Law. 1187 (2006), examining candidacy-related claims alleging violation of First Amendment rights and/or of due process.

[98] Terry v. Bender, 143 Cal.App.2d 198, 300 P.2d 119 (Dist.Ct.1956); People v. Sullivan, 113 Cal.App.2d 510, 248 P.2d 520 (Dist.Ct.1952) (officers accountable for breaches of good faith); Katz v. Brandon, 156 Conn. 521, 245 A.2d 579 (1968); Place v. Board of Adjustment, 42 N.J. 324, 200 A.2d 601 (1964); State v. Weleck, 10 N.J. 355, 91 A.2d 751 (1952) (public officers are under obligation to serve with highest fidelity); State v. McKelvey, 12 Ohio St.2d 92, 232 N.E.2d 391 (1967).

[99] See Newton v. Demas, 107 N.J.Super. 346, 258 A.2d 376 (1969); State v. Weleck, *supra* note 98.

[100] See Bourne v. Sullivan, 104 N.H. 348, 186 A.2d 834 (1962); Buss, The Massachusetts Conflict-of-Interest Statute, An Analysis, 45 Boston U.L.Rev. 299 (1965); Kaplan v. Lillich, Municipal Conflicts of Interest: Inconsistencies and Patchwork Prohibitions, 58 Colum.L.Rev. 157 (1958); Comment, Legislative Conflicts of Interest—An Analysis of the Pennsylvania Code of Ethics, 19 Vill.L.Rev. 82 (1973).

Systems under which the pay of judicial officers depends on the amount of fines the officers themselves assess give rise to an obvious conflict-of-interest and may violate the due process of defendants appearing before the courts. See Ward v. Village of Monroeville, 409 U.S. 57, 93 S.Ct. 80, 34 L.Ed.2d 267 (1972); Tumey v. Ohio, 273 U.S. 510, 47 S.Ct. 437, 71 L.Ed. 749 (1927).

[101] See Hussey v. Petito, 25 A.D.2d 449, 267 N.Y.S.2d 244 (1966), aff'd 18 N.Y.2d 963, 277 N.Y.S.2d 826, 224 N.E.2d 337, cert. denied 386 U.S. 1031, 87 S.Ct. 1482, 18 L.Ed.2d 594.

[102] See Bourne v. Sullivan, *supra* note 100. Bribery of public officials, and officials' solicitation and acceptance of bribes, are crimes everywhere. See Winckler, Drafting an Effective Bribery Statute, 1 Am. J.Crim.L. 210 (1972). See generally Annots., Furnishing Public Official with Meals, Lodging, or Travel, or Receipt of Such Benefits, as Bribery, 67 A.L.R.3d 1231 (1975) (corrupt intent usually required for bribery); Criminal Liability of Corporation for Bribery or Conspiracy to Bribe Public Official, 52 A.L.R.3d 1274 (1973); Validity and Construction of Statutes Punishing Commercial Bribery, 1 A.L.R.3d 1350 (1965); Solicitation or Receipt of Funds by Public Officer or Employee for Political Campaign Expenses or Similar Purposes as Bribery, 55 A.L.R.2d 1137 (1957). See also Annots., Criminal Offense of Bribery as Affected by Lack of Authority of State Public Officer or Employee, 73 A.L.R.3d 374 (1976); Criminal Offense of Bribery as Affected by Lack of Legal Qualification of Person Assuming or Alleged to Be an Officer, 115 A.L.R. 1263 (1938).

[103] See Josephson v. Planning Board, 151 Conn. 489, 199 A.2d 690 (1964) (member of board could not rule on zoning application of party represented by realtor who had given free desk space and telephone service to member); Warren v. City of Leesburg, 203 So.2d 522 (Fla.App.1967) (voiding conveyance by city to one of its own officials); S & L Associates, Inc. v. Washington Township, 61 N.J.Super. 312, 160 A.2d 635 (App.Div.1960) (no actual proof of dishonesty needed to establish conflict of interest). But cf. City of Coral Gables v. Weksler,

Thus, public officers and employees are in violation of the common-law rule of disqualification (and often in violation of specific legislative provisions) when they *vote*, as part of the performance of their public work, on matters in which they have any substantial interest that might conflict with that of the public.[104] For instance, members of planning or zoning boards cannot vote on the zoning of property they own, or property owned by an organization to which they belong.[105]

---

164 So.2d 260 (Fla.App.1964) (upholding city lease to one of its employees). It is often stated, and occasionally held, that a conflict of interest disqualifies a particular officer or employee from participation in a matter only if he has a direct, pecuniary interest in that matter. See Atherton v. City of Concord, 109 N.H. 164, 245 A.2d 387 (1968); Wilson v. Long Branch, 27 N.J. 360, 142 A.2d 837 (1958), cert. denied 358 U.S. 873, 79 S.Ct. 113, 3 L.Ed.2d 104 (interest found too remote and contingent to disqualify). But where pressed on the matter, most courts hold that a "temptation to serve his own purposes" suffices for disqualification and that the officer or employee does not have to have a direct or pecuniary interest. See United States v. Mississippi Valley Generating Co., 364 U.S. 520, 81 S.Ct. 294, 5 L.Ed.2d 268 (1961), reh. denied 365 U.S. 855, 81 S.Ct. 798, 5 L.Ed.2d 820; Schaefer v. Berinstein, 140 Cal.App.2d 278, 295 P.2d 113 (1956); Griggs v. Borough of Princeton, 33 N.J. 207, 162 A.2d 862 (1960) (action by council members invalid where they were employed by Princeton University and the action affected land owned by Princeton); Delta Electric Construction Co. v. City of San Antonio, 437 S.W.2d 602 (Tex.Civ.App.1969), ref'd n. r e. Sometimes, the possibility of personal benefit to an officer or employee is treated as merely one factor to weigh in determining if there is a conflict of interest. See Katz v. Brandon, *supra* note 98. Cf. Randolph v. City of Brigantine Planning Bd., 405 N.J. Super. 215, 963 A.2d 1224 (Ct. App. Div. 2009) (municipal official should have recused herself from considering matter in which she had a personal interest that *may* influence her action in the matter; *appearance* of impropriety is what most concerns the courts in cases of alleged conflict of interest). See generally Eisenberg, Conflicts of Interest Situations and Remedies, 13 Rutgers L.Rev. 666 (1959); Feinberg & Porro, Ethics, Incompatibility and Conflict of Interests of Public Officials, 7 Current Municipal Problems 393 (1966); Note, Conflicts of Interest of State and Local Legislators, 55 Iowa L.Rev. 450 (1969); Note, The Doctrine of Conflicting Interests Applied to Municipal Officials in New Jersey, 12 Rutgers L.Rev. 582 (1958).

[104] Baker v. Marley, 8 N.Y.2d 365, 208 N.Y.S.2d 449, 170 N.E.2d 900 (1960); Reckner v. School District of German Township, 341 Pa. 375, 19 A.2d 402 (1941) (school district voted on own salary increase). See Atherton v. City of Concord, *supra* note 103, saying an officer is disqualified where he has a direct personal and pecuniary interest in a matter; Piggott v. Borough of Hopewell, 22 N.J.Super. 106, 91 A.2d 667 (1952). But cf. City of Miami Beach v. Schauer, 104 So.2d 129 (Fla.App.1958), cert. discharged 112 So.2d 838 (personal interest did not serve to disqualify council member from voting on matter unless legislation so provided).

[105] Singewald v. Minneapolis Gas Co., 274 Minn. 556, 142 N.W.2d 739 (1966) (member of village council could not participate in granting franchise to company of which he was an employee); Zell v. Borough of Roseland, 42 N.J.Super. 75, 125 A.2d 890 (1956) (planning board member could not vote on zoning change in favor of church of which he was a member). But see Katz v. Brandon, *supra* note 98, where a council member who served as union agent in a company interested in a redevelopment project was held entitled to vote on the project. In Anderson v. City of Parsons, 209 Kan. 337, 496 P.2d 1333 (1972), it was held that city commissioners who owned land in a general urban renewal area were entitled to vote on a project so long as they owned no property within the territory covered by that specific project. Cf. Hantges v. City of Henderson, 121 Nev. 319, 113 P.3d 848 (2005) (redevelopment agency advisory commission members' private interest in property being considered for a city redevelopment plan did not create conflict of interest that tainted adoption of plan by city council, as members of the advisory committee were not "public officers" subject to conflict of interest rules and since members recused themselves from discussion and voting on plan). See Anderson & Sass, Is the Wheel Unbalanced? A Study of Bias on Zoning Boards, 36 Urban Law. 447 (2004). See generally Anderson & Luebbering, Zoning Bias II: A Study of Oregon's Zoning Commission Composition Restrictions, 38 Urban Law. 63 (2006). On procedures for enacting and amending zoning laws, see Sections 18.6 & 18.7, *infra*. See also Johnson, Ethics in Government at the Local Level, 36 Seton Hall L. Rev. 715 (2006).

Sometimes laws require, in addition to or instead of disqualification, *disclosure* by public officials or employees of any interest they have in matters coming before them; reports on their assets are also required of some public workers. But see City of Carmel-by-the-Sea v. Young, 2 Cal.3d 259, 85 Cal.Rptr. 1, 466 P.2d 225 (1970), striking down as overbroad a statute directing that every public officer and candidate for public office file a statement as to his investments and those of certain family members.

A city officer whose activities present a conflict of interest with his public duties may also be subject to removal from office. See Price v. City of San Marcos, 744, S.W.2d 349 (Tex. Civ. App. 1988), appeal dism'd, cert. denied 488 U.S. 961, 109 S.Ct. 485, 102 L.Ed.2d 522 (1988) (official removed, under city code of ethics, for appearance before zoning board on his own behalf).

What happens when a "disqualified" officer or employee does nonetheless vote on a matter of personal interest? The majority view is that the proceedings are rendered void.[106] The interested person's participation in the matter casts a cloud on the action taken, and thus that action should be rendered nugatory. A few jurisdictions follow a minority view that the disqualified person's vote renders the action taken void only if the disqualified vote was controlling.[107]

§ 13.9 Responsibility for Public Funds and Property

Local government officers and employees can be held liable for any public funds or property they appropriate for their own use, and the suit to establish such liability can be brought either by the local government or any taxpayer thereof.[108] The public worker who has misappropriated to his own use is liable not only for the return to the locality of what was misappropriated, but also for interest.[109] Criminal actions will usually be available against such a wrongdoer as well.[110]

What if a public officer or employee makes an unlawful disbursement of public funds, but the disbursement is not for his own benefit? At common law, the majority rule is that the public worker, here too, is liable to the government for the funds, which can be reclaimed in a suit brought either by the local government itself or by a taxpayer thereof.[111] A few courts have refused to apply this harsh rule of strict liability in

---

[106] Daly v. Town Plan & Zoning Commission, 150 Conn. 495, 191 A.2d 250 (1963); Wilson v. Iowa City, 165 N.W.2d 813 (Iowa 1969) (with review of cases); S & L Associates, Inc. v. Washington Township, *supra* note 103; Pyatt v. Mayor of Dunellen, 9 N.J. 548, 89 A.2d 1 (1952); Baker v. Marley, *supra* note 104. Cf. Thomson v. Call, 38 Cal.3d 633, 214 Cal.Rptr. 139, 699 P.2d 316 (1985), cert. denied 474 U.S. 1057, 106 S.Ct. 796, 88 L.Ed.2d 773 (1986) (city council member's sale of property to city, using a corporation as a conduit, was void; city could retain land and at same time recover purchase price plus interest). See generally Nevada Comm'n on Ethics v. Carrigan, 564 U.S. ___, 131 S.Ct. 2343, 180 L.Ed.2d 150 (2011) (recusal provision of state ethics law, prohibiting city council member from voting on a proposal and/or from advocating its passage or defeat in situations where the member has a conflict, upheld as not violating member's freedom of speech).

[107] Eways v. Reading Parking Authority, 385 Pa. 592, 124 A.2d 92 (1956). See Anderson v. City of Parsons, *supra* note 105; Singewald v. Minneapolis Gas Co., *supra* note 105. Cf. Griswold v. City of Homer, 55 P.3d 64 (Alaska 2002) (if member of zoning authority with a conflict of interest cast the decisive vote, ordinance is invalid; but if not, the court examines three factors: (1) whether the member disclosed the interest, or the other members were fully aware of it; (2) the extent of the member's participation in the decision; (3) the magnitude of the member's interest).

[108] Fransham v. McDowell, 202 Kan. 604, 451 P.2d 131 (1969); McWhorter v. Richmond, 514 S.W.2d 678 (Ky.1974); Grudnosky v. Bislow, 251 Minn. 496, 88 N.W.2d 847 (1958); Roundup v. Liebetrau, 134 Mont. 114, 327 P.2d 810 (1958); State v. McKelvey, 12 Ohio St.2d 92, 232 N.E.2d 391 (1967) (improper travel funds); City of Fort Worth v. Pippen, 439 S.W.2d 660 (Tex.1969). See Borough of Totowa v. American Surety Co., 39 N.J. 332, 188 A.2d 586 (1963) (surety of public official liable). Local government officials are often described as fiduciaries, subject to a fiduciary's duty of loyalty. See Lawrence, Local Government Officials as Fiduciaries: The Appropriate Standard, 71 U. Detroit Mercy L. Rev. 1 (1993).

Accountings can be required by the local government where there is reason to believe government funds or properties have been misappropriated. Town of Myrtle Beach v. Suber, 225 S.C. 201, 81 S.E.2d 352 (1954). Taxpayers can also force an accounting. See Brooker v. Smith, 108 So.2d 790 (Fla.App.1959).

[109] See Borough of Totowa v. American Surety Co., *supra* note 108 (interest is part of the damages, not a penalty).

[110] See People v. Nathanson, 134 Cal.App.2d 43, 284 P.2d 975 (Dist.Ct. 1955). Cf. Stark v. Superior Court, 52 Cal. 4th 368, 128 Cal. Rptr.3d 611, 257 P.3d 41 (2011) (embezzlement statute criminalizing the appropriation of public funds to oneself or another without authority of law does not require proof of defendant's actual knowledge of the legal requirements underlying the statute but rather only requires proof that defendant knew, or was criminally negligent in failing to know, those legal requirements).

[111] City of Princeton v. Baker, 237 Ky. 325, 35 S.W.2d 524 (1931); Lowell v. Massachusetts Bonding & Insurance Co., 304 Mass. 153, 23 N.E.2d 91 (1939); Bay City, 26 Mich. 44 (1872); Burns v. Essling, 163 Minn. 57, 203 N.W. 605 (1925); Pugnier v. Ramharter, 275 Wis. 70, 81 N.W.2d 38 (1957) (town official who made

situations where no wrongful intent was shown.[112] Statutes sometimes codify the common-law rule of strict liability;[113] in addition, criminal penalties for misapplication of funds are generally provided, with some wrongful intent or criminal negligence usually required.[114]

Finally, what if a local government officer or employee is responsible for the *loss* of public funds or property entrusted to his care? Again, the common-law rule is one of strict liability.[115] The strict liability has even been applied to losses caused by the act of a subordinate of the public worker who is sued.[116] A minority view holds that the public official or employee is liable only if negligence is shown; this treats the situation as similar to an ordinary bailment, with the bailee held to the standard of care of the reasonably prudent person.[117]

---

unauthorized payments to charities was liable in taxpayer action to recover the money). See Osburn v. Stone, 170 Cal. 480, 150 P. 367 (1915); Burt v. Blumenauer, 299 Or. 55, 699 P.2d 168 (1985), appeal after remand 84 Or.App. 144, 733 P.2d 462 (1987) (public official personally liable for improperly expended funds to promote measure during election period when that issue was before the voters); Webster v. Douglas County, 102 Wis. 181, 77 N.W. 885 (1899), motion granted 102 Wis. 181, 78 N.W. 451. This doctrine has been supported by a long line of Wisconsin cases and thus is sometimes called the "Wisconsin doctrine." See Burns v. Essling, *supra.*

[112] Adams v. Bryant, 236 Ark. 859, 370 S.W.2d 432 (1963). See McCarty v. City of St. Paul, 279 Minn. 62, 155 N.W.2d 459 (1967), distinguishing earlier Minnesota cases (see note 111 *supra*) and holding that officials who made wrongful expenditures should not be liable therefor in a taxpayers' suit where the officials made no personal profit and the locality received value for what was spent. It seems that even in states that usually impose strict liability here, reliance on advice of legal counsel may be a defense. Cannon v. Taylor, 88 Nev. 89, 493 P.2d 1313 (1972). See Burns v. Essling, *supra* note 111. But the reliance must be reasonable. See Leskinen v. Pucelj, 262 Minn. 461, 115 N.W.2d 346 (1962).

[113] See Porter v. Tiffany, 11 Or.App. 542, 502 P.2d 1385 (1972), applying such a statute. Some statutes require that defendants have actually made a misappropriation, not merely approved of such. See Paine v. Matthews, 213 Miss. 506, 57 So.2d 148 (1952).

[114] People v. Dillon, 199 Cal. 1, 248 P. 230 (1926). See Crider v. Commonwealth, 206 Va. 574, 145 S.E.2d 222 (1965).

[115] American Surety Co. v. Thomasville, 73 F.2d 584 (5th Cir.1934); City of St. Louis v. Whitley, 283 S.W.2d 490 (Mo.1955); Bird v. McGoldrick, 277 N.Y. 492, 14 N.E.2d 805 (1938) (rule called too well established to be changed by the courts); State v. Engen, 60 Wash.2d 52, 371 P.2d 638 (1962) (only excuses for loss are act of God and act of public enemy); City of Shelton v. Clapper, 23 Wash.2d 811, 162 P.2d 445 (1945) (with review of cases). A public officer has even been held liable where he has deposited funds in a bank that fails, despite a lack of negligence on the officer's part. See Annot., Liability of Public Officer or his Bond for Loss of Public Funds Due to Insolvency of Bank in Which They Were Deposited, 155 A.L.R. 436 (1945); 93 A.L.R. 819 (1934).

[116] United States Fidelity & Guarantee Co. v. Davis, 32 N.J.Super. 115, 107 A.2d 819 (1954); State v. Engen, *supra* note 115. But some authority has indicated the vicarious liability extends only to acts of persons in the public officer or employee's *private* service, not to acts of other public officers or employees. See Robertson v. Sichel, 127 U.S. 507, 8 S.Ct. 1286, 3 L.Ed. 203 (1888). Even under such a restrictive rule, an officer or employee could, of course, be liable for his own negligence in hiring incompetent subordinates or failing to supervise subordinates carefully. See Fernelius v. Pierce, 22 Cal.2d 226, 138 P.2d 12 (1943) (city officials could be found negligent in failing to take steps after receiving reports of police brutality).

Sheriffs are now generally held liable for acts of their deputies committed within the scope of employment. See Chaudoin v. Fuller, 67 Ariz. 144, 192 P.2d 243 (1948); Marshall v. County of Los Angeles, 131 Cal.App.2d 812, 281 P.2d 544 (1955).

[117] Jordon v. Baker, 252 Ky. 40, 66 S.W.2d 84 (1933); Edwards v. Hylbert, 146 W.Va. 1, 118 S.E.2d 347 (1960) (ordinary diligence required); Ball v. Toler, 109 W.Va. 61, 153 S.E. 238 (1930) (diligence of ordinarily prudent man required). See City of Healdsburg v. Mulligan, 113 Cal. 205, 45 P. 337 (1896) (city treasurer not liable when funds taken in bank robbery). Cf. City of Scranton v. Aetna Casualty & Surety Co., 11 F.Supp. 986 (M.D.Pa.1935), aff'd 94 F.2d 941 (3d Cir. 1938) (officer required by law to deposit funds in specified banks; held to modify rule as to officer's strict liability).

Even under the rule of strict liability, an officer or employee is usually not liable for shortages caused by a predecessor. See City of Fairview v. Norris, 234 F.2d 199 (10th Cir. 1956). Cf. City of Bessemer v. Korpi, 282

§ 13.10 Right to Compensation

Any right to compensation for a local government officer or employee must be based on some valid legislation authorizing the payment.[118] Without such authorization, local government workers have no claim to pay, and the rendition of services by them will be considered gratuitous. Often, statutes or charters require that there have been an appropriation prior to hiring certain personnel, in order to ensure that adequate funds are available for compensating these workers. Where no such appropriation has been made, the person hired in violation of these provisions cannot recover pay.[119] This is based partly on the idea that everyone—here including the worker hired in violation of legal requirements—is held to know the law.

Except as qualified by legislation and/or by the common-law rule against holding incompatible offices (discussed *supra*), a person may receive compensation for two or more government posts—even when they are both within the same government.[120]

Mich. 190, 275 N.W. 815 (1937) (city funds already on deposit in bank, and bank insolvent, when city treasurer took office; she was held not liable for loss due to bank's insolvency).

[118] Gavagan v. Marshall, 160 Fla. 154, 33 So.2d 862 (1948); Gallagher v. Clinton, 247 Ind. 668, 221 N.E.2d 350 (1966); Espinos v. Township of Monroe, 81 N.J.Super. 283, 195 A.2d 478 (1963); Adams v. Plainfield, 110 N.J.L. 377, 166 A. 164 (1933); Tomlinson v. New York City, 50 Misc.2d 977, 271 N.Y.S.2d 1019 (Civ.Ct.1966); Stetler v. McFarlane, 230 N.Y. 400, 130 N.E. 591 (1921) (claimant must show some statute that permits payment).

An attempt by the federal government to extend the minimum-wage and maximum-hour provisions of the Fair Labor Standards Act to employees of state and local governments was once struck down as in excess of Congress's power under the commerce clause. National League of Cities v. Usery, 426 U.S. 833, 96 S.Ct. 2465, 49 L.Ed.2d 245 (1976), on remand 429 F.Supp. 703 (would have impaired states' ability to function in a federal system). But the Supreme Court subsequently upheld application of the Age Discrimination in Employment Act to state and local governments. Equal Employment Opportunity Comm'n v. Wyoming, 460 U.S. 226, 103 S.Ct. 1054, 75 L.Ed.2d 18 (1983). See Comment, When the Walls Come Tumbling Down: What Remains of *National League of Cities*?, 53 U. Cinc. L. Rev. 625 (1984). Then in 1985, the Court overruled *National League of Cities*, upheld application of the minimum-wage and overtime requirements of the Fair Labor Standards Act to local government employees, and indicated that the commerce power is not exceeded unless a law is destructive of state sovereignty or violative of some constitutional provision. Garcia v. San Antonio Metropolitan Transit Auth., 469 U.S. 528, 105 S.Ct. 1005, 83 L.Ed.2d 1016 (1985), reh. denied 471 U.S. 1049, 105 S.Ct. 2041, 85 L.Ed.2d 340 (1985). See generally Section 7.1 *supra*. Any federal laws forbidding pay discrimination would thus now seem clearly applicable to local government employees also. See Maxwell v. City of Tucson, 803 F.2d 444 (9th Cir.1986) (municipality that pays disparate wages to some employees due to their gender is in violation of federal Equal Pay Act unless a statutorily designated affirmative defense is proven). On the *Garcia* case's implications as to municipal liability for wages, see generally Yuhas & Fluker, Recent Developments in Government Liability, 17 Urban Law. 765, 775–83 (1985); Walters, Hesslink & Spencer, Recent Developments in Public Employee Relations, 17 Urban Law. 961 (1985). See also Freilich, Greenhagen & Lamkin, The Demise of the Tenth Amendment: An Analysis of Supreme Court Decisions Affecting Constitutional Federalism, 17 Urban Law. 651 (1985).

Amendments to the Fair Labor Standards Act were enacted in 1985 mitigating the effect of that law on local governments. 29 U.S.C.A. § 203 (1985). But the basic principles of the *Garcia* case were not affected.

[119] Gavett v. City of Hoboken, 47 N.J.Super. 596, 136 A.2d 448 (1957). Cf. Sagarese v. Board of Health of Morristown, 31 N.J.Super. 526, 107 A.2d 351 (1954) (compensation had to be fixed by ordinance; no ordinance had been passed).

[120] Raymond v. Bartlett, 77 Cal.App.2d 283, 175 P.2d 288 (Dist.Ct.1946); City of Texarkana v. Floyd, 59 S.W.2d 449 (Tex. Civ.App.1933), error ref'd. But cf. Vestal v. City of St. Joseph, 413 S.W.2d 537 (Mo.App.1967) (contrary to public policy for one person to receive salaries from *three* local government posts).

By statute, public officers and employees are often entitled to all or part of their normal pay during leave for active duty in the federal military reserve forces. See Comment, A Survey and Comparative Analysis of State Statutes Entitling Public Employees to Paid Military Leave, 68 Gonzaga L. Rev. 67 (1994–95).

Within any limitations set by constitution or statute, the local governing body can set salaries for all its officers and employees.[121] Similarly, the governing body can change salaries, or even abolish a particular position altogether.[122] The power of council members to change salaries extends to changes in their own compensation so long as they act in good faith.[123] But most jurisdictions do have some constitutional or statutory bans on increasing (and sometimes also on decreasing) salaries for officers during their term of office. These are to prevent an officer from attempting to use his influence to obtain a salary raise at a time when he is not vulnerable to being turned out of office by the voters or appointing authority.[124] Often the provisions apply only to officers, not

---

[121] City and County of San Francisco v. Cooper, 13 Cal.3d 898, 120 Cal.Rptr. 707, 534 P.2d 403 (1975) (courts will normally not review the amount of compensation established); San Francisco Chamber of Commerce v. City and County of San Francisco, 275 Cal.App.2d 499, 79 Cal.Rptr. 915 (1969) (same); Burton v. City of Detroit, 190 Mich. 195, 156 N.W. 453 (1916); City of San Antonio v. Kneupper, 161 Tex. 153, 338 S.W.2d 121 (1960); City of San Antonio v. Whitten, 161 Tex. 150, 338 S.W.2d 119 (1960); Dandoy v. Milwaukee County, 214 Wis. 586, 254 N.W. 98 (1934) (compensation of officer or employee can be increased or diminished during his term or employment, except as limited by statute or constitution). See Council of City of Saginaw v. Board of Estimates, 256 Mich. 624, 239 N.W. 872 (1932) (some salaries established by charter; others left to discretion of council, with board of estimate having power to reduce some items).

[122] City of Augusta v. Angelo, 225 Ark. 884, 286 S.W.2d 321 (1956) (extreme reduction in salary); Williams v. City of New Bedford, 303 Mass. 213, 21 N.E.2d 265 (1939) (abolition of office); Town of Waveland v. Dufour, 212 Miss. 884, 56 So.2d 70 (1952) (change in salary); Moser v. Board of Commissioners, 10 N.J.Misc. 315, 159 A. 630 (Sup.Ct. 1932) (abolition of office). See Crawford v. Hunt, 41 Ariz. 229, 17 P.2d 802 (1932). But *employees* (as opposed to officers) often have contractual rights which the government cannot impair. See Sonoma County Organization of Public Employees v. County of Sonoma, 23 Cal.3d 296, 152 Cal.Rptr. 903, 591 P.2d 1 (1979), holding that a statute which voided certain local governments' agreements to pay cost-of-living increases was an unconstitutional impairment of contractual obligation. But see Proksa v. Arizona State Schools for the Deaf & Blind, 205 Ariz. 627, 74 P.3d 939 (2003) (two management employees at school did not have an employment contract with the state, and thus the legislature could statutorily change the terms of their employment without providing for offer, acceptance or assent, and without consideration).

[123] Alexander v. Edwards, 220 Miss. 699, 71 So.2d 785 (1954). This is an exception to the general rule against officers voting on matters in which they have a personal interest. But cf. Reckner v. School District of German Township, *supra* note 104 (school district director could not vote on own salary increase).

[124] See, applying such provisions, Rutledge v. Eureka, 195 Cal. 404, 234 P. 82 (1925) (discussing reasons for rule); Board of Education of Graves County v. De Weese, 343 S.W.2d 598 (Ky.1960); Pressman v. D'Alesandro, 211 Md. 50, 125 A.2d 35 (1956); Schurtz v. Grand Rapids, 205 Mich. 102, 171 N.W. 463 (1919); Darnell v. City of Broken Bow, 139 Neb. 844, 299 N.W. 274 (1941); Bowers v. City of Albuquerque, 27 N.M. 291, 200 P. 421 (1921); Presley v. Board of County Comm'rs, 981 P.2d 309 (Okl.1999) (upholding ban on mid-term salary increase against equal protection attack); Turner v. Ramsey, 63 Okl. 199, 163 P. 712 (1917); Delardas v. County Court, 155 W.Va. 776, 186 S.E.2d 847 (1972). See also Annot., Validity of Contract Between Governmental Unit and Attorney Which Makes Compensation Contingent Upon Results Accomplished, 136 A.L.R. 101 (1942).

This type of restriction has been applied to changes in fringe benefits. State ex rel. Parsons v. Ferguson, 46 Ohio St.2d 389, 348 N.E.2d 692 (1976). The ban cannot be avoided by naming an officer to an additional position. See Dalton v. City of Moline, 48 Ill.App.3d 494, 3 Ill.Dec. 861, 359 N.E.2d 500 (1977), appeal after remand 56 Ill.App.3d 859, 14 Ill.Dec. 524, 372 N.E.2d 720 (attempt to pay mayor extra salary as liquor control commissioner); State ex rel. Mikus v. Roberts, 15 Ohio St.2d 253, 239 N.E.2d 660 (1968) (county attempted to give county engineer second title with extra compensation).

To the extent some of these provisions forbid salary *decreases* during terms, they are designed to discourage attempts at political revenge through salary cuts.

A variation on these provisions is the sometimes-encountered restriction prohibiting a legislator's appointment to an office created, or the salary of which was increased, while he was a member of the legislature. See Warwick v. State ex rel. Chance, 548 P.2d 384 (Alaska 1976), applying such a rule.

And some states prohibit payment of "extra compensation" after services have been rendered. McElveen v. Callahan, 309 So.2d 379 (La.App.1975), writ denied 313 So.2d 602. See the discussion of pensions (which have generally not been held to violate these provisions) in the next chapter.

employees.[125] And they do not apply to an increase that goes into effect only at the start of the following term, even though the present incumbent may be re-elected and subsequently receive the higher salary.[126] The prohibition refers only to the current term, and means that a change cannot be made so as to affect the salary paid during that term.

---

[125] See Morgan v. Du Page County, 371 Ill. 53, 20 N.E.2d 40 (1939) (assistant superintendent of schools); Moody v. Duerson, 280 Ky. 527, 133 S.W.2d 712 (1939); Wiley, Attorney General v. Board of Education, 225 Mich. 237, 196 N.W. 417 (1923) (provision inapplicable to school teachers); Hammitt v. Gaynor, 144 N.Y.S. 123 (Sup.Ct.1913), complaint dism'd 82 Misc. 196, 144 N.Y.S. 127; Morris v. Mayor of New York, 99 N.Y. 645, 1 N.E. 671 (1885). Such a provision is often held inapplicable to deputies. State ex rel. Rusch v. Board of County Commissioners, 121 Mont. 162, 191 P.2d 670 (1948); Wilkins v. Trimbur, 86 N.E.2d 503 (Ohio Com.Pl.1949); Dandoy v. Milwaukee County, 214 Wis. 586, 254 N.W. 98 (1934). The same is true as to police officers. Haack v. Banish, 287 Mich. 592, 283 N.W. 700 (1939); Jordan v. Kane, 389 Pa. 1, 131 A.2d 364 (1957). Cf. Little v. Porter, 67 S.W.2d 624 (Tex.Civ.App.1934) (town marshal).

[126] Storke v. Goux, 129 Cal. 526, 62 P. 68 (1900); Schanke v. Mendon, 250 Iowa 303, 93 N.W.2d 749 (1958); Thornsberry v. City of Campbell, 218 Mo.App. 357, 274 S.W. 847 (1925); State ex rel. Emmons v. Farmer, 271 Mo. 306, 196 S.W. 1106 (1917); State ex rel. Wyrick v. City of Ritzville, 16 Wash.2d 36, 132 P.2d 737 (1942). See McKesson v. Lowery, 51 Cal.2d 660, 335 P.2d 662 (1959) (ban does not apply to increase voted during term of office but prior to individual's appointment to fill unexpired term). Cf. Barton v. Derryberry, 500 P.2d 281 (Okl.1972) (ban would not apply to salary increase effective during term but resulting from operation of statute enacted prior to office-holder's election). On the numerous complicated situations that may arise under these provisions, see generally 4 McQuillin, Municipal Corporations § 12.198 (3d rev. ed. 1992).

Chapter 14

PUBLIC EMPLOYEES

Analysis

---

§ 14.1 General Trends in Public Employment

Over recent decades, government has grown into the largest business in the United States, with one out of every six working Americans on a government payroll. And the greatest growth in government employment has been at the state and local levels. Increasingly, this large work force has made its presence felt in our economy, and its members have sought fairer methods of selection and promotion of government employees, increased pay and greater job benefits, and more security.[1] Their efforts have been felt in four major areas: (1) the development of civil service, or "merit," systems to govern selection, retention, and promotion of government workers; (2) the growth of retirement and other benefits—and sometimes, a fight against mandatory retirement; (3) the development of statutory and constitutional limits on the grounds for which, and methods by which, government workers may be dismissed from their jobs; and (4) the growth of unions, and the appearance of collective bargaining and strikes, in the public sector of the work force.

---

[1] See "Public Workers and Public on a Collision Course," U.S. News and World Rep., March 14, 1977, at 82; "Public Employees vs. the Cities," Bus. Week, July 21, 1975, at 50. As to changes in the entitlements of public employees in modern times, see generally O'Neil, The Rights of Public Employees (American Civil Liberties Union Handbook 2d ed. 1993).

The early 1980's brought a slow-down in the growth of public employment in some areas, necessitated by economic downturns and tax cuts. See "Now the Belt Tightens on Public Employees, Too," U.S. News & World Rep., July 26, 1982, at 59; "The Pinch on Public Employees," Bus. Week, June 23, 1980, at 71. But in general, the number of state and local government employees continued to soar during the last decades of the twentieth century, though the number of federal employees remained stable. See "Local Government's Deceptive Charm," Bus. Week, May 1, 1995, at 166. State and local governments employ over 1 out of 8 of all U.S. workers, with 53% of those state and local employees working (as of 1995) in education services. Holmes, United States Population—A Profile of America's Diversity—The View from the Census Bureau, 1998, in World Almanac and Book of Facts 373, 374 (1999).

§ 14.2 Selection of Government Personnel—Merit and Civil-Service Systems

Three types of systems for selecting government personnel have existed in America. One is the method of political appointments, under which jobs are passed out as rewards for political or other service performed by the job-recipient or by some friend or relative of his. But increasingly, this system has been replaced by one of the two others, both of which can be put under the general heading of "merit systems." One type of merit system is often called "career service" and involves recruitment of people very soon after their education is complete. Entrance requirements are usually fairly stringent; examinations are normally part of the selection process, and are intended to indicate an applicant's lifetime potential. Promotions generally come as a matter of course following the initial assignment if work is performed satisfactorily. The other type of merit system is called "civil service." It, too, makes use of examinations for initial selection—and sometimes for later promotions. But here the recruitment is of people of all levels of education and any age, with the requirements simply varying according to the particular jobs for which people are currently being sought. Here, applicants are sought for specific positions, rather than for a lifetime of service in various positions. And here, once a person is hired for a particular job, there is not necessarily any assurance of promotion or advancement even though the job is satisfactorily performed.[2] This latter is perhaps the more common merit system now found, but the "career" and "civil service" systems are sometimes found co-existing; and the term "civil service" is often now used to indicate either one.

The first Civil Service Act was enacted by the United States government in 1883 as part of a reform movement to limit the old "spoils system" of political appointments. Over 90% of federal workers now occupy positions that are classified under civil service.[3] Also in 1883, New York enacted the first merit system on the state level, and this move was followed by Massachusetts the next year.[4] Today, most of the states—though not all—have civil-service coverage of most of their employee positions,[5] and most of the major cities have some type of merit system.[6]

---

[2] See Mosher, Careers and Career Services in the Public Service, Public Personnel Rev. 47–48 (1963). For a critical look at the functioning of merit systems in American municipalities, see Gottfried, The Merit System and Municipal Civil Service: A Fostering of Social Inequality (Greenwood Press 1988).

[3] See Kaplan, The Law of Civil Service 8–14 (1958).

[4] *Id.* at 22–27.

[5] See Mitau, State and Local Government 154 (1966). See generally Hounshell v. White, 220 Ariz. 1, 202 P.3d 466 (App. 2008) (merit systems are designed to ensure that the hiring, retention, and dismissal of public employees is based on the employees' merit and competence, not on political considerations). See also McGregor, Arizona's Merit Selection System: Improving Public Participation and Increasing Transparency, 59 Syracuse L. Rev. 383 (2009).

[6] See Phillips, Municipal Government and Administration in America 387 (1960), reporting that by 1960, three-fourths of the cities having populations of 10,000 and over had adopted merit systems—and *all* the cities with populations of a quarter million or more had such systems. On the purposes of merit systems, see Pima County v. Pima County Law Enforcement Merit Sys. Council, 211 Ariz. 224, 119 P.3d 1027 (2005) (merit systems principles of public employment embrace the notion that hiring, retention, and dismissal of public employees should be based on employees' merit and competence, not on political considerations; right to treatment based on merit and to a hearing by neutral board before discipline becomes final are the central merit-system principles of public employment). For a critical view of some civil service laws, see Note, The Massachusetts Civil Service Law: Is It Necessary to Destroy the Current System in Order to Save It?, 40 New Eng. L Rev. 1103 (2006). See also Hounshell v. White, 217 Ariz. 407, 175 P.3d 65 (App. 2008) (merit systems are designed to ensure that the hiring, retention, and dismissal of public employees is based on employees'

The merit system in effect in most municipalities involves the classification of the various positions by a local civil service commission. This commission has great discretion in classifying the various kinds of municipal employment, and its designations will be judicially overturned only upon a strong showing of arbitrary or capricious action.[7] But certain government workers are exempt from the civil service: elected officials necessarily are exempt, and so in general are most workers who are considered officers rather than employees.[8] Certainly, the civil service provisions are inapplicable to all officers who have a definite term of office,[9] or who are heads of departments.[10] Professional persons, and persons given temporary appointments (as during an emergency situation), are commonly exempt, also.[11]

The civil service commission customarily prepares and administers competitive examinations for the various positions of local employment that are to be filled. As with the classifying of positions, the commission is here allowed great discretion as to the type of exam given, the questions asked, and the weight accorded various parts of the examining process. Commission actions will not be overturned unless shown to have

---

merit and competence, not on political considerations; county sheriff held to be sole "appointing authority" for purposes of statute providing that any officer or employee in classified civil service may be dismissed, suspended or reduced in rank by the appointing authority).

7 Mullin v. Ringle, 27 N.J. 250, 142 A.2d 216 (1958) (strong showing of arbitrariness required); Manko v. City of Buffalo, 181 Misc. 143, 44 N.Y.S.2d 829 (Sup.Ct.1943), aff'd 266 App.Div. 1061, 45 N.Y.S.2d 727, appeal denied 267 App.Div. 854, 47 N.Y.S.2d 292; Whisted v. City of Philadelphia, 385 Pa. 213, 122 A.2d 723 (1956). Cf. Oklahoma Public Employees Ass'n v. Oklahoma Military Dept., 330 P.3d 497 (Okla. 2014) (Public Employees Association established sufficient irreparable harm to support a temporary injunction to prevent Oklahoma Military Department from making certain pay increases for classified employees dependent on their declassification since the declassification would cause them to lose the protections of the merit system).

8 See City and County of Denver v. Rinker, 148 Colo. 441, 366 P.2d 548 (1961); Chapman v. Frobisher, 123 N.J.L. 127, 8 A.2d 76 (1939); Civil Service Technical Guild v. LaGuardia, 181 Misc. 492, 44 N.Y.S.2d 860 (Sup.Ct.1943), aff'd 267 App. Div. 860, 47 N.Y.S.2d 114, aff'd 292 N.Y. 586, 55 N.E.2d 49 (awarding of architectural and engineering contracts does not create employment relationship; civil service lists need not be used). Cf. Webb v. Village of Ruidoso Downs, 117 N.M. 253, 871 P.2d 17 (App. 1994) (state statute authorizing municipalities to enact merit system for municipal employees does not authorize such a system to cover municipal *officers,* such as municipal clerk-treasurer).

9 White v. City of Hopkinsville, 280 Ky. 661, 134 S.W.2d 236 (1939); Riley v. Holland, 362 Mo. 682, 243 S.W.2d 79 (1951); Woodbridge Township v. Civil Service Commission, 4 N.J.Super. 111, 66 A.2d 448 (1949); Browne v. Hagen, 91 N.J.L. 544, 104 A. 207 (1918) (health inspector with fixed term). See Black v. Sutton, 301 Ky. 247, 191 S.W.2d 407 (1945).

10 Robertson v. Commissioner of Civil Service, 259 Mass. 447, 156 N.E. 536 (1927); Riley v. Holland, *supra* note 9 (director of public safety not within civil service); Milton v. Department of Civil Service, 71 N.J.Super. 135, 176 A.2d 492 (1961) (superintendent of public properties); Kropp v. Common Council of North Tonawanda, 26 Misc.2d 127, 207 N.Y.S.2d 411 (1960); see Fagen v. Morris, 83 N.J.L. 3, 84 A. 1067 (1912), aff'd 84 N.J.L. 759, 86 A. 1102 (clerk found to be head of department); Dellecese v. Burke, 60 Misc.2d 572, 303 N.Y.S.2d 282 (1969), aff'd 36 A.D.2d 566, 317 N.Y.S.2d 1022 (commissioner of assessment and taxation).

11 See City and County of San Francisco v. Boyd, 17 Cal.2d 606, 110 P.2d 1036 (1941) (engineer hired for 5 years to advise on traffic problems; not within civil service); Civil Service Technical Guild v. LaGuardia, *supra* note 8 (architectural and engineering services); Burrell v. City of Portland, 61 Or. 105, 121 P. 1 (1912) (consulting engineer to aid city engineer); Commonwealth ex rel. Attorney General v. Fitler, 147 Pa. 288, 23 A. 568 (1892). See DeWoody v. Underwood, 136 Ohio St. 575, 27 N.E.2d 240 (1940) (assistant legal directors and police prosecutors held not within classified service); State ex rel. Ryan v. Kerr, 126 Ohio St. 26, 183 N.E. 535 (1932) (assistant police prosecutor not within classified service). But see Turel v. Delaney, 285 N.Y. 16, 32 N.E.2d 774 (1941) (physician within classified service). Judges are generally excepted from the classifications and examinations of civil service systems, but may be part of a "merit selection" process that includes retention elections. See Symposium, Mulling Over the Missouri Plan: A Review of State Judicial Selection and Retention Systems, 74 Mo. L. Rev. 473–800 (2009), particularly Fitzpatrick, The Politics of Merit Selection, *id.* at 675, and, Tarr, Do Retention Elections Work? *id.* at 605.

been capricious and without any reasonable basis.[12] Actions are likely to be reversed only if (1) the commission has failed to abide by its own rules in administering an exam,[13] or (2) there has been a violation of an applicant's constitutional rights, such as the right of privacy,[14] or (3) a clearly unreasonable amount of weight has been attached by the commission to some factor, such as personality or experience, that can be judged only quite subjectively.[15]

Courts have occasionally invalidated the use of oral examinations or interviews as not sufficiently capable of objective evaluation.[16] But most courts have reasoned that oral exams are sometimes necessary, particularly where supervisory, management, or public-relations skills are needed for a job. Thus, the majority view approves the use of oral exams at least where (1) personality traits are relevant to the position to be filled, (2) standards are provided the examiners so as to provide some uniformity in testing, and (3) records are kept to show a basis for any rating given.[17]

Basic requirements for eligibility to take a civil-service exam are usually established by the commission. Once the exam is taken and passed by some of the applicants, the

---

[12] See Short v. Kissinger, 184 Neb. 491, 168 N.W.2d 917 (1969) (commission has broad discretion in deciding type of exam to give); Zicherman v. Department of Civil Service, 40 N.J. 347, 192 A.2d 566 (1963) (courts won't nullify civil service exam unless abuse of discretion by administering agency is shown); Ankner v. Lang, 33 Misc.2d 341, 225 N.Y.S.2d 161 (1962); Application of Pearl, 8 Misc.2d 712, 169 N.Y.S.2d 847 (1957), aff'd 4 N.Y.2d 828, 173 N.Y.S.2d 804, 150 N.E.2d 234; Stoor v. City of Seattle, 44 Wn.2d 405, 267 P.2d 902 (1954).

[13] See State ex rel. Mulkey v. Auburn, 60 Wn.2d 728, 375 P.2d 499 (1962) (chief examiner not present, as civil service regulations required, when exam given).

[14] Resnick v. Civil Service Commission, 156 Conn. 28, 238 A.2d 391 (1968) (examiners asked about applicant's religious and political affiliations). The use of civil-service exams was upheld against Equal Protection attack in Washington v. Davis, 426 U.S. 229, 96 S.Ct. 2040, 48 L.Ed.2d 597 (1976), despite evidence that more black persons than white persons were thereby disqualified. The Court ruled that since no discriminatory purpose was shown, the discriminatory effect of the tests, which were neutral on their face, did not make their use impermissible. But see Bridgeport Guardians, Inc. v. City of Bridgeport, 933 F.2d 1140 (2d Cir.1991), cert. denied 502 U.S. 924, 112 S.Ct. 337, 116 L.Ed.2d 277 (1991) (city's selection process, which had a substantial disparate impact on minorities, held to violate Title VII of Federal Civil Rights Act). See generally Lewis v. City of Chicago, 560 U.S. 205, 130 S.Ct. 2191, 176 L.Ed.2d 967 (2010) (if African-American applicants could prove that city used written-examination requirement that caused a disparate impact, they could prevail on their Federal Civil Rights Act claims; disparate impact does not require proof of discriminatory intent).

[15] See Cowen v. Reavy, 283 N.Y. 232, 28 N.E.2d 390 (1940), motion denied 284 N.Y. 596, 29 N.E.2d 670, where the court invalidated a procedure under which applicants for the position of unemployment insurance referee were rated 60% on their experience and 40% on a written test. Cf. Swearer v. Karoleski, 128 Pa.Cmwlth. 335, 563 A.2d 586 (1989) (use of psychological test score to deny employment to police officer applicant violated city personnel regulations and required reconsideration). Civil-service rules normally provide that exams are to be competitive, and this has often been held to mean that some objective standards must be employed to judge those in the competition. See Elliott v. Hoberman, 61 Misc.2d 411, 306 N.Y.S.2d 627 (Sup.Ct.1969), aff'd 33 A.D.2d 753, 305 N.Y.S.2d 969; Mark v. Lang, 52 Misc.2d 469, 276 N.Y.S.2d 512 (Sup.Ct. 1967) (objective measure that is capable of being challenged and reviewed must be employed); Fink v. Finegan, 270 N.Y. 356, 1 N.E.2d 462 (1936).

[16] Civil Service Board v. Warren, 74 Ariz. 88, 244 P.2d 1157 (1952) (answers not capable of objective evaluation); Bridgman v. Kern, 282 N.Y. 375, 26 N.E.2d 299 (1940) (oral exam for educators; responses solicited were too vague for objective evaluation). Cf. Gilbert v. City of Little Rock, 799 F.2d 1210 (8th Cir.1986), on remand 709 F.Supp. 856 (E.D.Ark.1987) (oral examination portion of city police department's *promotional* process held to violate Federal Civil Rights Act).

[17] See Almassy v. Los Angeles County Civil Service Commission, 34 Cal.2d 387, 210 P.2d 503 (1949) (portion of exam may be oral; recording of examiner's findings on appraisal sheet suffices for oral record); Kelly v. Civil Service Commission, 37 N.J. 450, 181 A.2d 745 (1962) (with review of cases; use of oral exams here approved in testing for police inspector and captain); Application of Pearl, *supra* note 12 (position in insurance department); Sloat v. Board of Examiners, 274 N.Y. 367, 9 N.E.2d 12 (1937) (oral exams permissible in hiring teachers); Stoor v. City of Seattle, *supra* note 12 (same).

commission certifies to the appointing board of officers a list of eligible persons (the "eligibility list"). Thus, the commission does not itself make appointments; it merely participates in the process by screening the applicants and eliminating some of them. Appointments then must be made by the proper authority from the names on the list.[18]

There has been considerable litigation over the preference given veterans (of U.S. military service) under many civil-service systems. Provisions completely exempting veterans from examinations have been declared unconstitutional since they don't require that veterans meet the usual qualifications.[19] The same is true of systems that add points to the scores of veterans, thus enabling some of them to pass who otherwise wouldn't.[20] But where the system simply provides that among applicants all of whom have passed the qualifying exam a preference shall be given veterans, the priority has been upheld.[21] Here the courts reason that (1) all applicants are required to meet the same basic minimum standard; (2) a preference for veterans, as among those meeting that standard, is justified since veterans have presumably acquired qualities of industry, obedience, and discipline that are desirable in public service; and (3) any hardship against women brought about by this preference is an incidental effect and not the result of any intended discrimination based on sex. Veterans' preferences are, of course, not a matter of right

---

[18] See, discussing the procedures, Bloodworth v. Suggs, 60 So.2d 768 (Fla.1952); Timmins v. Civil Service Commissioners, 276 Mass. 142, 177 N.E. 1 (1931); Lawlor v. City of Dearborn, 309 Mich. 168, 14 N.W.2d 822 (1944). Sometimes a specified number of the highest candidates on the list are all eligible for appointment under civil-service rules. See Hellum v. Johnson, 51 Wash.2d 326, 317 P.2d 1073 (1957). Passing a civil-service exam does not automatically entitle an applicant to a job but only makes him or her eligible for such—for so long as a particular "eligible list" is used. See Schroder v. Kiss, 74 N.J.Super. 229, 181 A.2d 41 (1962).

[19] Yates v. Rezeau, 62 So.2d 726 (Fla.1952); McNamara v. Director of Civil Service, 330 Mass. 22, 110 N.E.2d 840 (1953); Brown v. Russell, 166 Mass. 14, 43 N.E. 1005 (1896); Matter of Keymer, 148 N.Y. 219, 42 N.E. 667 (1896).

[20] State ex rel. Higgins v. Civil Service Commission, 139 Conn. 102, 90 A.2d 862 (1952); Carney v. Lowe, 336 Pa. 289, 9 A.2d 418 (1939); Commonwealth ex rel. Graham v. Schmid, 333 Pa. 568, 3 A.2d 701 (1938) (state privileges and immunities clause violated). But see Arthur v. City & County of Denver, 198 P.3d 1285 (Colo. App. 2008) (applicant for city firefighter position who had served in military during "period of undeclared war or other armed hostilities" was entitled to five-point preference on entrance exam; interpreting state constitutional provision establishing hiring preference for veterans).

[21] Personnel Administrator v. Feeney, 442 U.S. 256, 99 S.Ct. 2282, 60 L.Ed.2d 870 (1979), on remand 475 F.Supp. 109 (qualifying veterans given priority over qualifying nonveterans; no denial of equal protection to women); Rios v. Dillman, 499 F.2d 329 (5th Cir.1974) (preference for veterans who served in the field); Jones v. O'Toole, 190 Cal. 252, 212 P. 9 (1923); Dennis v. Bennet, 258 Iowa 664, 140 N.W.2d 123 (1966); Babcock v. City of Des Moines, 180 Iowa 1120, 162 N.W. 763 (1917); Commissioner v. Director of Civil Service, 348 Mass. 184, 203 N.E.2d 95 (1964); Mayor of Lynn v. Commissioner of Civil Service, 269 Mass. 410, 169 N.E. 502 (1929); State ex rel. Kangas v. McDonald, 188 Minn. 157, 246 N.W. 900 (1933); Crabtree v. Montana State Library, 204 Mont. 398, 665 P.2d 231 (1983) (absolute preference to veterans who met minimal qualifications for public employment upheld; no conflict found with state's merit system nor any impermissible discrimination against women). See Swantush v. City of Detroit, 257 Mich. 389, 241 N.W. 265 (1932). Veterans' preferences have also been sustained as to positions *not* within the civil service. Shaw v. Marshalltown, 131 Iowa 128, 104 N.W. 1121 (1905); Phelps v. Byrne, 36 S.D. 369, 154 N.W. 825 (1915). But veterans' preference provisions often contain exclusions, as for judicial positions. See Krohn v. Judicial Magistrate Appointing Commission, 239 N.W.2d 562 (Iowa 1976) (statute according preference to veterans held inapplicable to county magistrates). And some veterans' preference provisions apply only for a certain length of time after an applicant's having left the armed services. See Davis v. Civil Service Board, 39 Or.App. 695, 593 P.2d 1209 (1979) (preference points had to be used within 15 years after release from service). In Attorney General of New York v. Soto-Lopez, 476 U.S. 898, 106 S.Ct. 2317, 90 L.Ed.2d 899 (1986), a New York veterans' preference law that applied only to veterans who entered the armed forces while residing in New York was invalidated as violating the constitutionally protected right to travel.

and can be withdrawn by a change in legislation at any time.[22] Furthermore, such preferences ordinarily apply to initial hiring but give no priority as to subsequent retention, which will be determined by the same rules applicable to all other employees.[23] In some jurisdictions, veterans' preferences don't apply to promotions either;[24] but often they *do,* and their use in connection with promotions has been upheld.[25]

§ 14.3 Retirement of Government Personnel—Pensions; Mandatory Retirement

Increasingly, local governments provide some form of pension or other retirement program for their employees. These are considered to serve the valid public purpose of inducing competent persons to enter, and remain in, public service, and thus have been upheld against attacks alleging that they amount to the spending of public funds for private purposes.[26] They have also been upheld against charges that they violate constitutional provisions against payment of additional compensation for services already rendered,[27] and usually these provisions are held not to be violated even where pensions are increased for those already retired.[28] (Sometimes, pensions and other

---

[22] State ex rel. Dolan v. City of St. Paul, 293 Minn. 477, 197 N.W.2d 711 (1972). See Nick v. Montana Dep't of Highways, 219 Mont. 168, 711 P.2d 795 (1985) (statute revoking veterans' preference upheld against Equal Protection attack; preference said to be gratuity, not contractual right). On the new veterans' (and handicapped persons') preference law adopted by Montana, see Olson v. State Dep't of Rev., 235 Mont. 31, 765 P.2d 171 (1988) (absolute preference abolished; is now preference for veterans and handicapped persons over others with "substantially equal qualifications").

[23] People ex rel. Hansen v. Collins, 351 Ill. 551, 184 N.E. 641 (1933) (no preference for veterans when suspensions are necessary); Smith v. City Commission, 258 Mich. 698, 242 N.W. 814 (1932) (no preference when dismissals necessary for economic reasons). See Moresh v. Board of Education, 52 N.J.Super. 105, 144 A.2d 897 (1958) (position held by veteran can be abolished). Cf. Clancy v. Halleran, 263 N.Y. 258, 188 N.E. 746 (1934) (position held by veteran can be abolished, but he enjoys a degree of priority as to being re-hired). In a number of states, statutes *do* give some preference to veterans so far as retention is concerned. See Koch v. Yunich, 533 F.2d 80 (2d Cir. 1976) (such legislation has been sustained); Barkus v. Sadloch, 20 N.J. 551, 120 A.2d 465 (1956) (statute held applicable to de facto as well as de jure officers).

[24] State ex rel. Schmidt v. Harter, 43 Ohio App. 503, 183 N.E. 389 (1932). See Commonwealth ex rel. Maurer v. O'Neill, 368 Pa. 369, 83 A.2d 382 (1951), commenting that the value of service in the armed forces decreases with the lapse of time and it becomes more important to consider on-the-job performance.

[25] Rios v. Dillman, *supra* note 21; State ex rel. Higgins v. Civil Service Commission, 139 Conn. 102, 90 A.2d 862 (1952); McNamara v. Director of Civil Service, *supra* note 19. As to the general use of merit systems in regard to *promotion* of public employees, see Seattle Police Officers Guild v. City of Seattle, 151 Wash.2d 823, 92 P.3d 243 (2004), where a city ordinance allowing the police chief to choose for promotion from among the top five candidates on the civil-service register was upheld as substantially accomplishing the purpose of state statutes governing public-safety civil service, which was to ensure that officers received promotions based on merit.

[26] Snyder v. City of Alameda, 58 Cal.App.2d 517, 136 P.2d 857 (Dist.Ct. 1943); Olivier v. City of Fall River, 306 Mass. 376, 28 N.E.2d 228 (1940); Fellows, Attorney General v. Connolly, 193 Mich. 499, 160 N.W. 581 (1916). Cf. City of Marysville v. State, 101 Wash.2d 50, 676 P.2d 989 (1984) (state constitutional provision prohibiting a gift or loan of the city's credit held not to preclude payment of retirement pensions by the city in connection with the prior service rendered to a golf course by employees who continued their employment at the golf course after its purchase by the city). In some states, local governments are under a statutory duty to establish pension funds for certain of their workers, and mandamus can then be used to force establishment of such a fund. See Taylor v. Abernathy, 422 Pa. 629, 222 A.2d 863 (1966).

[27] State v. Love, 89 Neb. 149, 131 N.W. 196 (1911); Retirement Board v. McGovern, 316 Pa. 161, 174 A. 400 (1934) (county retirement plan); State ex rel. O'Neil v. Blied, 188 Wis. 442, 206 N.W. 213 (1925). See State ex rel. Watson v. Lee, 157 Fla. 62, 24 So.2d 798 (1946).

[28] See Luders v. City of Spokane, 57 Wn.2d 162, 356 P.2d 331 (1960), applying a constitutional amendment which specifically allows increases in pensions to those already retired, thus in effect overruling the earlier case of Sonnabend v. City of Spokane, 53 Wn.2d 362, 333 P.2d 918 (1958). But cf. State ex rel. Thomson v. Giessel, 262 Wis. 51, 53 N.W.2d 726 (1952) (under constitutional prohibition of "extra

retirement payments are now specifically exempted from such constitutional bans on "added compensation.") Under one view—the "Illinois view"—the amount of a pension is set as of the date of retirement, and if based on a percentage of the employee's salary, does not increase even though there are later increases in the salary of employees having the same rank or grade that the pensioner had.[29] But under another method—the "California view"—such subsequent raises in the salary of employees with the rank that the pensioner had, result in increases in the pension also.[30]

Older authority tended to treat pensions as gratuities and to hold that a retired employee could not compel payment of the promised amount.[31] But the modern view is that pension plans involve contractual relationships and that an employee acquires vested rights as to a pension as soon as his employment, with a government employer having such a plan, begins.[32] There may, of course, be reasonable conditions attached to the payment of the pension, and reasonable grounds on the basis of which the right to the payment may be lost—but the payment can only be denied for reasons that were

---

compensation" after services rendered, statute providing additional retirement benefits for previously retired teachers could not be sustained). See generally 2A Antieau, Municipal Corporation Law § 22.119 (1998), arguing that increases in pensions to those already retired should definitely be allowed.

[29] O'Neil v. Harding, 314 Ill. 516, 145 N.E. 593 (1924). See Board of Trustees v. Burns, 348 P.2d 1067 (Okl.1959).

[30] See Jones v. Cooney, 82 Cal.App. 265, 255 P. 536 (1927); Board of Trustees v. Schupp, 223 Ky. 269, 3 S.W.2d 606 (1928). Cf. Donnelly v. Board of Trustees of Fire Retirement Sys., 403 N.W.2d 768 (Iowa 1987), applying a state statute providing that on certain dates a pension shall be adjusted by the appropriate percentage of any raise in salary given an active worker of the same rank as the retiree.

[31] Tomlinson v. Kansas City, 391 S.W.2d 850 (Mo.1965). See Robinson v. Police Pension Board, 85 Ariz. 384, 339 P.2d 739 (1959); Keegan v. Board of Trustees, 412 Ill. 430, 107 N.E.2d 702 (1952); Mell v. State ex rel. Fritz, 130 Ohio St. 306, 199 N.E. 72 (1935); City of Dallas v. Trammell, 129 Tex. 150, 101 S.W.2d 1009 (1937).

[32] Yeazell v. Copins, 98 Ariz. 109, 402 P.2d 541 (1965); Carman v. Alvord, 31 Cal.3d 318, 182 Cal.Rptr. 506, 644 P.2d 192 (1982) (by entering public service, an employee obtains vested contractual rights to earn a pension on terms substantially equivalent to those then offered by the employer; voter-approved tax to fund city's retirement pensions held exempt from California's Proposition 13); Abbott v. City of San Diego, 165 Cal.App.2d 511, 332 P.2d 324 (Dist.Ct.1958); Hanson v. Idaho Falls, 92 Idaho 512, 446 P.2d 634 (1968); Bardens v. Board of Trustees, 22 Ill.2d 56, 174 N.E.2d 168 (1961) (where pension plan voluntary); Mulholland v. City of Tacoma, 83 Wn.2d 782, 522 P.2d 1157 (1974) (only changes that can be made are those necessary to keep plan flexible and maintain its integrity); Bowen v. Statewide City Employees Retirement System, 72 Wn.2d 397, 433 P.2d 150 (1967). Cf. Moorhouse v. City of Wichita, 259 Kan. 570, 913 P.2d 172 (Kan.1996) (public employee who has contributed to retirement fund over a period of years and who has performed substantial services for employer acquires a right or interest in the retirement plan that cannot be whisked away by stroke of legislative or executive pen, regardless of whether employee's contribution is voluntary or mandatory); Lauderdale v. Eugene Water & Electric Bd., 217 Or.App. 551, 177 P.3d 13 (2008) (city public utility board employees' right to free or low-cost retirement health care benefits vested when the employees began working for the board; thus, board did not have authority to unilaterally modify the benefits, where board induced employees to accept employment by promising the benefits). But see Wylie v. Chesser, 173 P.3d 64 (Okla. 2007) (general rule is that pension vests at time one becomes eligible to receive that pension; but where it is unclear whether a surviving spouse was intended to be benefitted by pension, the pension must be denied). When a person is hired by a governmental entity not having a pension plan, that person's rights nonetheless vest as soon as such a plan is adopted. See Police Pension & Relief Board v. Bills, 148 Colo. 383, 366 P.2d 581 (1961); Hickey v. Pension Board, 378 Pa. 300, 106 A.2d 233 (1954). But some courts speak of an employee's rights in a pension vesting only when all the conditions for retirement have been met. See Pennie v. Reis, 132 U.S. 464, 10 S.Ct. 149, 33 L.Ed. 426 (1889); Eberle v. LaGuardia, 285 N.Y. 247, 33 N.E.2d 692 (1941), rearg. denied 286 N.Y. 584, 35 N.E.2d 931. Cf. Hickey v. Pension Board, 378 Pa. 300, 106 A.2d 233 (1954) (new conditions cannot be imposed once employee has completed the required period of service). An employee having vested rights in a pension has been held to have a due process right to a hearing on his or her application for the pension. Ostlund v. Bobb, 825 F.2d 1371 (9th Cir.1987), cert. denied 486 U.S. 1033, 108 S.Ct. 2016, 100 L.Ed.2d 603 (1988).

valid conditions governing the pension at the time the employment was commenced.[33] Some courts have said that no change can be made in a government's pension plan to the detriment of a participant unless he consents.[34] But most courts reason that the employee's vested right is only a right to a substantial and reasonable pension, not to a particular amount, and that reasonable changes may be made prior to the claimant's retirement.[35] Once an employee has, however, fulfilled the conditions for the pension and has actually retired, courts will generally hold that his rights are perfected and that later changes in the program cannot affect him to his detriment.[36] Thus, it seems that various degrees of vesting are recognized where pension rights are concerned: under much authority, there is some degree of vested right as soon as the employment relationship begins; but the final vesting does not occur until retirement takes place. Although women on the average have greater longevity than men, any requirement that women contribute

---

[33] See Wallace v. City of Fresno, 42 Cal.2d 180, 265 P.2d 884 (1954) (city could not terminate pensions, because of commission of felony, at time employment began; couldn't then do so on that basis after employment began). See generally Note, Post-Retirement Employment Restrictions on Public Employment in Kansas, 5 Kansas J.L. & Pub. Pol'y 199 (Spring, 1996).

[34] See Smith v. City of Dothan, 279 Ala. 571, 188 So.2d 532 (1966); City of Phoenix v. Boerger, 5 Ariz.App. 445, 427 P.2d 937 (1967); Terry v. City of Berkeley, 41 Cal.2d 698, 263 P.2d 833 (1953). Cf. City of Aurora v. Ackman, 738 P.2d 796 (Colo.App.1987) (even though pension rights not yet fully vested because employee hasn't met length-of-service requirements, employee who has performed under contract promising a pension is normally entitled to receive benefits pursuant to that program; requirement of additional 5 years of service held invalid despite corollary addition of new benefits). See generally McAllister v. City of Bellevue Firemen's Pension Bd., 166 Wash. 2d 623, 210 P.3d 1002 (2009) (although a public employee may have vested contractual pension rights, the pension may be modified prior to an employee's retirement in order to keep the system flexible enough to permit adjustments for changing conditions and at the same time maintain the integrity of the system).

[35] Police Pension Board v. Denney, 84 Ariz. 394, 330 P.2d 1 (1958); Henry v. City of Los Angeles, 201 Cal.App.2d 299, 20 Cal.Rptr. 440 (Dist.Ct.1962); Kern v. City of Long Beach, 29 Cal.2d 848, 179 P.2d 799 (1947); Sweesy v. Los Angeles Retirement Bd., 17 Cal.2d 356, 110 P.2d 37 (1941); Day v. Mruk, 307 N.Y. 349, 121 N.E.2d 362 (1954) (no taking without due process if employee can, in event of changes in plan before his retirement, quit the plan and obtain back all his own contributions); Vallet v. City of Seattle, 77 Wn.2d 12, 459 P.2d 407 (1969). See Betts v. Board of Administration, 21 Cal.3d 859, 148 Cal.Rptr. 158, 582 P.2d 614 (1978). Cf. Duncan v. Retired Pub. Employees of Alaska, Inc., 71 P.3d 882 (Alaska 2003) (employee's right to benefits vests on employment and enrollment in the system, meaning that in general the benefits to an employee may not be diminished or impaired during his tenure; reasonable modifications are permissible, but to be reasonable, changes that result in disadvantages to employees must be accompanied by comparable new advantages). See generally McAllister v. City of Bellevue Firemen's Pension Bd., 166 Wash. 2d 623, 210 P.3d 1002 (2009) (although a public employee may have vested contractual pension rights, the pension may be modified prior to an employee's retirement in order to keep the system flexible enough to permit adjustments for changing conditions and at the same time maintain the integrity of the system).

[36] Police Pension & Relief Bd. v. McPhail, 139 Colo. 330, 338 P.2d 694 (1959). See Atchison v. Retirement Bd., 343 S.W.2d 25 (Mo.1960) (changes in pension plans will be assumed inapplicable to those retired unless clear contrary intent); Board of Trustees of Police Pension & Retirement Sys. v. Weed, 719 P.2d 1276 (Okl.1986) (police officer's pension rights became vested when he contributed to retirement fund for 20 years, as required by his contract, and he met requirement of meritorious service at time of his retirement; pension could not be forfeited as consequence of his felony conviction 4 years after retirement). Cf. Deonier v. State Public Employee Retirement Bd., 114 Idaho 721, 760 P.2d 1137 (1988) (statute requiring that amount of disability retirement benefits received by firemen be offset by amount of worker's compensation benefits they are entitled to receive held unconstitutional as impairment of right of contract); Alldredge v. Oklahoma Firefighters Pension & Retirement Bd., 816 P.2d 580 (Okl. App.1991) (firefighters' pension rights were controlled by statutes in effect at time they were eligible to retire). But cf. Woods v. City of Lawton, 845 P.2d 880 (Okl.1992) (former city employee could be denied pension benefits upon conviction of embezzlement from city if criminal acts were committed before retirement; right to pension had not vested). See generally Bordwine v. Oklahoma Firefighters Pension & Retirement Sys., 99 P.3d 703 (Okla. App. 2004) (retired city firefighter's right to retirement benefits attaches and becomes fixed at time of retirement, and statute of limitations for breach of retirement benefits contract begins to run when pensioner knew or should have known that employer failed to pay the benefits required to be paid at time of retirement).

more than men to retirement funds (so as to make more money available for the women's longer periods of retirement) is likely to be invalidated as in violation of civil rights legislation.[37] It is unfortunate but true that many retirement pension plans have not been adequately funded; that in some cases, such plans have not been funded at all, with payments to retired workers having to come from current tax revenues; and that payment of pensions is now adding to the already serious financial problems of many cities.[38]

Mandatory retirement at a certain age has been under attack in recent years, sometimes on equal protection grounds. Such policies have traditionally been upheld where necessary to protect the efficiency of governmental operations.[39] Mandatory retirement at an age as low as 60 has even been sustained as to police officers and firefighters;[40] and the U.S. Supreme Court has upheld forced retirement at 60 for U.S. foreign service officers.[41] Where challenged on equal protection grounds, mandatory retirement rules will be upheld if rationally related to a legitimate public purpose.[42] But

---

[37] See City of Los Angeles Dep't of Water v. Manhart, 435 U.S. 702, 98 S.Ct. 1370, 55 L.Ed.2d 657 (1978), applying 42 U.S.C.A. § 2000e–2(a)(1). Discrimination on the basis of gender, violating the Federal Civil Rights Act, has also been found in a retirement plan under which women make the same contributions as men but are, upon retirement, paid lower monthly benefits. Arizona Governing Comm. v. Norris, 463 U.S. 1073, 103 S.Ct. 3492, 77 L.Ed.2d 1236 (1983), appeal after remand 796 F.2d 1119 (9th Cir.1986) (state employees had option of receiving retirement benefits from one of several companies, all of which paid women lower monthly retirement benefits; invalidated). See generally Developments in the Law: Employment Discrimination and Title VII of the Civil Rights Act of 1964, 84 Harv.L.Rev. 1109 (1971); Annot., Variations or Inequalities in Retirement, Pension, or Death Benefit Plans as Violation of 42 U.S.C.A. § 2000e–2(a), 35 A.L.R.Fed. 15 (1977).

[38] See "The Hidden Cost that May Break the Cities," Nation's Business, Sept., 1971, at 30. See generally Zakaria, Why We Need Pension Reform, Time magazine, June 25, 2012, at 28, calling the costs of public-sector retirees "the single biggest threat to the U.S.'s fiscal health." See also Comment, Solving Insolvent Public Pensions: The Limitations of the Current Bankruptcy Option, 28 Emory Bankr. Dev. J. 89 (2011). A good article on New York City's growing pension debt is Chen & Walsh, New York City's Public Pension Jam Grows Worse, N.Y. Times, Aug. 5, 2014, at 17 (Internatl.Ed.).

Among the articles suggesting solutions to the pension-debt problem are Digou, A View of the Rhode Island Pension Landscape: The Potential Reform of Local Pension Plans Under the Preemption Doctrine, 19 Roger Williams U. L. Rev. 740 (2014); Dorocak & Estes, State and Local Government Funding of Health and Retirement Benefits for Employees: Current Problems and Possible Solutions With California Health Benefits as an Example, 62 Syracuse L. Rev. 303 (2012); Surowiecki, Deadbeat Governments, The New Yorker, Dec. 23 & 30, 2013, at 46 (saying governments should be legally bound to make pension contributions every year); Note, Making Sausage No One Wants to Eat: Options for Restructuring Illinois's Pension Debt, 2013 U. Ill. L. Rev. 1251. See generally Symposium, Public Employment in Times of Crisis, 27 A.B.A. J. Labor & Employment L. 149–328 (2012), particularly Madiar, Public Pension Benefits Under Siege: Does State Law Facilitate or Block Recent Efforts to Cut the Pension Benefits of Public Servants?, *id.* at 179. See also Note, Pension Plans in Distress: A Case Study of Cincinnati, 82 U. Cin. L. Rev. 1271 (2014).

[39] Fabio v. City of St. Paul, 267 Minn. 273, 126 N.W.2d 259 (1964); Boyle v. City of Philadelphia, 338 Pa. 129, 12 A.2d 43 (1940); Fox v. City of Columbia, 491 S.W.2d 353 (Tenn.1973) (with review of authorities). See Firing v. Kephart, 18 Pa.Cmwlth. 578, 336 A.2d 470 (1975), aff'd 466 Pa. 560, 353 A.2d 833 (justice of the peace could be mandatorily retired at 70 though the term for which he was elected extended beyond that); Power v. City of Providence, 582 A.2d 895 (R.I. 1990) (statute providing for mandatory retirement at age 60 of city's police officers upheld as not conflicting with general law against age discrimination).

[40] Peters v. City of Springfield, 57 Ill.2d 142, 311 N.E.2d 107 (1974); Heminger v. Police Commission, 161 Ind.App. 72, 314 N.E.2d 827 (1974); Gardner v. Nation, 522 P.2d 1281 (Wyo.1974).

[41] Vance v. Bradley, 440 U.S. 93, 99 S.Ct. 939, 59 L.Ed.2d 171 (1979).

[42] Massachusetts Bd. of Retirement v. Murgia, 427 U.S. 307, 96 S.Ct. 2562, 49 L.Ed.2d 520 (1976) (standard of rationality, not strict scrutiny, applies). See Nelson v. Miwa, 56 Hawaii 601, 546 P.2d 1005 (1976), where a violation of equal protection *was* found. See generally Kaplan, Too Old to Work: The Constitutionality of Mandatory Retirement Plans, 44 S.Cal.L.Rev. 150 (1971); McHugh, The Constitutional Challenge to Mandatory Retirement Statutes, 49 St. Johns L.Rev. 748 (1975). See also Borelho, Cain, & Friedman, Mandatory Retirement: The Law, the Courts, and the Broader Social Context, 11 Willamette L.J. 398 (1975);

three limitations should be noted: (1) Specific retirement orders as to an individual will be overturned if it is shown that the person was singled out for intentional discrimination.[43] (2) Reductions in the age of mandatory retirement will be held invalid as to present employees or officers who would thereby lose vested rights in pensions or other compensation.[44] (3) In the case of some government workers, particularly those who do not depend greatly on physical skills in their work, it may be difficult to find a rational basis for automatic termination at a certain age.[45] Beyond the above-noted developments in the courts, the federal Age Discrimination in Employment Act[46] now

---

Kovarsky & Kovarsky, Economic, Medical and Legal Aspects of the Age Discrimination Laws in Employment, 7 Vand. L.Rev. 839 (1974). It has been argued that the low scrutiny applied to mandatory retirement rules in the *Murgia* case *supra* is now inappropriate and should be modified. Comment, Age Classifications and the Fourteenth Amendment: Is the *Murgia* Standard Too Old to Stand?, 6 Constitutional L.J. 263 (1995).

[43] State ex rel. Mulhern v. McHenry, 31 Conn.Sup. 172, 326 A.2d 132 (Super.Ct.1974). Cf. Nelson v. Miwa, *supra* note 42, where a violation of equal protection was found when an individual performance evaluation was supposedly provided for each employee on reaching age 65, and retention of such employees was theoretically possible—but in fact, the system really foreclosed the possibility of retention beyond 65 despite a good evaluation.

It has been held that an officer or employee who is mandatorily retired is not entitled to notice and a hearing prior to retirement, unless some statute or regulation clearly so provides. See Appeal of Wallington, 390 Pa. 416, 135 A.2d 744 (1957).

[44] Eagan v. Spellman, 90 Wn.2d 248, 581 P.2d 1038 (1978) (county employee acquired vested right to a potential date of retirement, and to a pension potential, when she became a member of the Public Employees' Retirement System). See also Annot., Validity of Legislation Providing for *Additional* Retirement or Disability Allowances for Public Employees Previously Retired or Disabled, 27 A.L.R.2d 1442 (1953) (emphasis added); Annot., Constitutionality, Construction, and Application of Statute or Ordinance Providing for Reduction of Pension or Retirement Benefit of Public Officer or Employee Because of Independent Income, 7 A.L.R.2d 692 (1949).

[45] See Gault v. Garrison, 569 F.2d 993 (7th Cir.1977), cert. denied 440 U.S. 945, 99 S.Ct. 1421, 59 L.Ed.2d 633, dealing with a school board's policy as to public school teachers and observing that the physical demands of teaching don't approach those of some activities, such as serving as a police officer.

[46] 29 U.S.C.A. §§ 621(b), 623(a)(1) & (f)(2), 626(d), 631. In Equal Employment Opportunity Comm'n v. Wyoming, 460 U.S. 226, 103 S.Ct. 1054, 75 L.Ed.2d 18 (1983), the Age Discrimination in Employment Act's coverage of state and local governments was upheld as a valid exercise of Congress's power under the Commerce Clause. See generally as to the Act's effects Findley, Over 65? This Law Is for You, Parade, June 24, 1979, at 4. While the law contains an exception for an age limit that is a bona fide occupational qualification, this may be difficult to show. See Aaron v. Davis, 414 F.Supp. 453 (E.D.Ark.1976), reconsideration denied 424 F.Supp. 1238 (no "special relevance" of age 62 justified the forced retirement of firemen at that age). See generally Note, The BFOQ in Law Enforcement: Guardian of Public Safety or Conduit for Arbitrary Discrimination?, 17 Stetson L. Rev. 787 (1988), noting E.E.O.C. State Dep't of Highway Safety & Motor Vehicles, 660 F.Supp. 1104 (N.D.Fla.1986), where it was ruled that the Florida Highway Patrol failed to prove that its mandatory retirement age of 62 was a bona fide occupational qualification.

The federal statute originally forbade discharge of most workers on the basis of age only if the workers were between 40 and 70, but the age-70 cap was eliminated by amendments effective January 1, 1987, and the statute now broadly makes it unlawful for an employer to fail or refuse to hire, or to discharge, any person, or otherwise discriminate against any person, because of that person's age. 29 U.S.C. § 623(a)(1). See Kurtz & Ruben, Recent Developments in Public Employee Relations, 19 Urban Law. 1021, 1022–23 (1987), discussing Age Discrimination in Employment Amendments of 1986. The federal statute does allow mandatory retirement of elected officials where provided by state or local law. See E.E.O.C. v. Commonwealth of Massachusetts, 858 F.2d 52 (1st Cir.1988); Apkin v. Treasurer, 401 Mass. 427, 517 N.E.2d 141 (1988), both interpreting the law as allowing mandatory retirement of appointed, as well as elected, judges. And in Gregory v. Ashcroft, 501 U.S. 452, 111 S.Ct. 2395, 115 L.Ed.2d 410 (1991), the Supreme Court specifically held that appointed state judges constituted appointees "on a policymaking level" within an exclusion to the Age Discrimination in Employment Act and thus that Missouri's mandatory retirement law as to such judges was void. However, in Kimel v. Florida Bd. of Regents, 528 U.S. 62, 120 S.Ct. 631, 145 L.Ed.2d 522 (2000), the U.S. Supreme Court held that the Age Discrimination in Employment Act could not validly abrogate the states' Eleventh Amendment immunity from suit by private individuals, since Congress can abrogate that immunity only under the enforcement clause of the Fourteenth Amendment, while the Age Discrimination in Employment Act was enacted under Congress's Article I powers, not its Fourteenth Amendment authority.

forbids discharge, with limited exceptions, of any person because of that person's age; and this has been supplemented by a great deal of state legislation—much of it also forbidding any mandatory retirement rules based on age.[47] It has been held, however, that the federal law was not intended to eliminate retirement plans instituted in good faith prior to enactment of that law.[48]

§ 14.4 Disability Leaves and Benefits

At common law, sickness or other disability usually does not deprive an officer of his salary,[49] but does deprive an employee of his.[50] But provisions for disability leaves or pensions for employees of local governments are now quite common and have been upheld.[51] It has been held that such programs create contractual obligations on the part

---

Thus, employees of the state and its entities who are subjected to age discrimination by their employers must now look to state statutes for protection and relief.

[47] See "The Ax for Forced Retirement," Bus. Week, Sept. 19, 1977, at 38. See generally Annot., Application of State Law to Age Discrimination in Employment, 96 A.L.R.3d 195 (1980). It has been held that federal legislation on age discrimination has not pre-empted the field. Simpson v. Alaska State Commission for Human Rights, 423 F.Supp. 552 (D.Alaska 1976). And the mere fact that the federal Age Discrimination in Employment Act contains an exception allowing mandatory retirement of a certain category of federal workers does not establish that mandatory retirement at the same age, or even a higher age, is a valid exception under state or local laws as to nonfederal workers in the same general line of work. Johnson v. Mayor & City Council of Baltimore, 472 U.S. 353, 105 S.Ct. 2717, 86 L.Ed.2d 286 (1985), on remand 637 F.Supp. 903 (D.Md.1986), judgment aff'd 829 F.2d 35 (4th Cir.1987) (law requiring most federal firefighters to retire at age 55 did not establish that age 55 was a bona fide occupational qualification for nonfederal firefighters). A list of state statutes protecting against age discrimination, and providing remedies therefor, is found in the footnote to the opinion of the Court in Kimel v. Florida Bd. of Regents, 528 U.S. 62, 120 S.Ct. 631, 650, 145 L.Ed.2d 522 (2000).

[48] United Air Lines, Inc. v. McMann, 434 U.S. 192, 98 S.Ct. 444, 54 L.Ed.2d 402 (1977). See de Loraine v. MEBA Pension Trust, 499 F.2d 49 (2d Cir.1974), cert. denied 419 U.S. 1009, 95 S.Ct. 329, 42 L.Ed.2d 284.

[49] Cavanee v. City of Milan, 99 Mo.App. 672, 74 S.W. 408 (1903) (city marshal); O'Leary v. Board of Education, 93 N.Y. 1 (1883); Webb v. City of Hugo, 169 Okl. 438, 37 P.2d 621 (1934) (mayor disabled; could still draw salary). Cf. Bolger v. City of San Diego, 239 Cal.App.2d 888, 49 Cal.Rptr. 204 (Dist.Ct.1966) (police officer suffered heart attack while on duty; entitled to injury-leave under municipal code).

[50] Neal v. City of New Haven, 83 Conn. 151, 76 A. 543 (1910); Flournoy v. City of Shreveport, 170 So. 264 (La.App.1936); Furnia v. Murphy, 31 N.Y.S.2d 875 (Sup.Ct.1941), modified 264 App.Div. 809, 35 N.Y.S.2d 460; Rogers v. City of New York, 120 App.Div. 513, 105 N.Y.S. 172 (1907). See Donoghue v. Holyoke St. Ry., 246 Mass. 485, 141 N.E. 278 (1923) (applying civil service law).

[51] See Hawthorn v. City of Beverly Hills, 111 Cal.App.2d 723, 245 P.2d 352 (Dist.Ct.1952) (firemen and police officers disabled by injuries arising from duty); Rogers v. City and County of Denver, 121 Colo. 484, 217 P.2d 865 (1950) (same); Birmingham v. Mirrington, 204 Misc. 821, 123 N.Y.S.2d 72 (1953) (fire fighters injured in performance of work); White v. West Norriton Township, 158 Pa.Super. 375, 45 A.2d 401 (1946) (work-connected injury of police and fire officers); See City of Orange v. Chance, 325 S.W.2d 838 (Tex.Civ.App.1959) (accumulated sick leave was paid on termination of employment; upheld against contention this violated rule against payment of extra salary). Cf. Frederick v. City of Peoria, 203 Ill.App. 486 (1916) (withholding salary of police officer due to absences caused by illness was not allowed by relevant laws); Manchester Education Association v. City of Manchester, 114 N.H. 83, 314 A.2d 662 (1974) (city could contract for *greater* sick-leave benefits than those provided by city charter). There is a split of authority as to whether a municipality may, without violating fundamental constitutional rights of its employees, require that an employee on injury or sick leave remain in his or her residence at all times except for matters relating to the injury or illness. Compare Crain v. Board of Police Comm'rs, 920 F.2d 1402 (8th Cir.1990) (police department's sick leave regulation prohibiting officer from leaving his residence except to obtain medical care upheld), and Korenyi v. Department of Sanitation, 699 F.Supp. 388 (E.D.N.Y.1988) (municipal sick leave policy requiring employees to remain at home while recuperating held not facially violative of right to travel or other constitutional rights), with Pienta v. Village of Schaumburg, 536 F.Supp. 609 (N.D.Ill.1982), aff'd 710 F.2d 1258 (7th Cir.1983) (rule invalidated as violative of constitutional rights). See generally Note, Defending Paid Sick Leave in New York City, 19 J.L. & Pol'y 973 (2011).

Under some programs, higher disability-pension benefits are received if the employee's disability was caused by performance of his or her employment duties. See Annot., Determination Whether Peace Officer's Disability Is Service-Connected for Disability Pension Purposes, 12 A.L.R. 4th 1158 (1982). And some funds

of local governments so that rights thereunder cannot be abridged by subsequent legislative action.[52]

There has been considerable litigation over maternity leaves and benefits. It has been held that mandatory rules requiring a teacher to take a leave at a designated time during her pregnancy violate due process, since any such cut-off dates are arbitrary; the facts of each case, and each teacher's individual abilities, must be given consideration.[53] But the exclusion of pregnancy from programs providing disability benefits or income protection was upheld as not violative of the Fourteenth Amendment,[54] or even, until amendments in 1978, of civil rights legislation.[55] What if accumulated seniority leave is

---

provide benefits *only* where an employee is injured, killed or made ill in the line of duty. See Kramer v. State, Peace Officers Benefit Fund, 380 N.W.2d 497 (Minn.1986) (former police officer died from heart attack suffered a year and a half after retirement; widow not entitled to benefits). Cf. Woldrich v. Vancouver Police Pension Bd., 84 Wash.App. 387, 928 P.2d 423 (Wash.App.1996) (stress reaction to disciplinary demotion was not a disability in line of duty for purposes of police disability retirement benefits). Some sick-leave programs now provide such leave where necessary to care for an ill member of the employee's family. See Ross v. Denver Dep't of Health & Hosps., 883 P.2d 516 (Colo. App.1994), holding that "immediate family" under such a program did not include the employee's same sex domestic partner. But see Alaska Civil Liberties Union v. State of Alaska, 122 P.3d 781 (Alaska 2005) (state and municipal programs offered valuable benefits to employees' spouses that they did not offer to unmarried employees' domestic partners; violation of equal protection found).

[52] State ex rel. Evans v. Fire Dep't Relief Ass'n, 138 Mont. 172, 355 P.2d 670 (1960). Cf. Lynn v. Kootenai County Fire Protective District, 97 Idaho 623, 550 P.2d 126 (1976) (statute that would have lessened, in particular case, benefits to be paid held to violate equal protection).

[53] Cleveland Bd. of Educ. v. LaFleur, 414 U.S. 632, 94 S.Ct. 791, 39 L.Ed.2d 52 (1974). See, finding a violation of civil rights laws by a private employer, Burwell v. Eastern Air Lines, Inc., 458 F.Supp. 474 (E.D.Va.1978), aff'd in part, rev'd in part 633 F.2d 361 (4th Cir.). See generally Annot., Mandatory Maternity Leave Rules for Policies for Public School Teachers as Constituting Violation of Equal Protection Clause of Fourteenth Amendment, 17 A.L.R.Fed. 768 (1973). On the continuing significance of the *Cleveland* case, see Note, What Employees Say, or What Employers Do: How Post-*Cleveland* Decisions Continue to Obscure Discrimination, 62 Vand. L. Rev. 1245 (2009).

[54] Geduldig v. Aiello, 417 U.S. 484, 94 S.Ct. 2485, 41 L.Ed.2d 256 (1974), upholding California's "self-support" program despite its exclusion of pregnancy. But cf. Zichy v. City of Philadelphia, 392 F.Supp. 338 (E.D.Pa.1975) (disability because of pregnancy deserves same treatment as other disability; sick leave must be allowed—applying civil rights laws), reversed but remanded for possible amendment, 559 F.2d 1210 (3d Cir.1977), motion to amend denied, 444 F.Supp. 344 (E.D.Pa.1977), reversed for possible showing of discriminatory intent, 590 F.2d 503 (3d Cir.1979).

Under amendments effective in 1978, the Civil Rights Act of 1964 forbids an employer, as to leave policies and fringe-benefit programs, from discriminating against women disabled by pregnancy, childbirth, or related conditions. 42 U.S.C.A. § 2000–e(k). See Matthies, The New Rules on Pregnancy, 50 Okl.B.J. 907 (1979).

A law requiring employers covered by the Federal Civil Rights Act to allow pregnant employees up to four months leave has been upheld against charges it impermissibly discriminates against males. California Fed. Sav. & Loan Ass'n v. Guerra, 758 F.2d 390 (9th Cir.1985), aff'd 479 U.S. 272, 107 S.Ct. 683, 93 L.Ed.2d 613 (1987). See Note, After *California Federal Savings & Loan Association v. Guerra*: The Parameters of the Pregnancy Discrimination Act, 31 Ariz. L. Rev. 141 (1989). See generally "Expectant Moms, Office Dilemma," U.S. News & World Rep., March 10, 1986, at 52. But cf. AT&T v. Hultsen, 556 U.S. 701, 129 S.Ct. 1962, 173 L.Ed.2d 898 (2009) (employer does not necessarily violate the Pregnancy Discrimination Act when it pays, pursuant to a seniority system, pension benefits calculated in part under an accrual rule—applied only prior to the Pregnancy Discrimination Act—that gave less retirement credit for pregnancy than for medical leave generally). Compare Equal Employment Opportunity Comm'n v. Houston Funding II, Ltd., 717 F.3d 425 (5th Cir. 2013) (employers engage in sex discrimination under Federal Civil Rights Act by discharging female employees who are lactating or expressing breast milk as these are protected by Pregnancy Discrimination Act).

[55] General Electric Co. v. Gilbert, 429 U.S. 125, 97 S.Ct. 401, 50 L.Ed.2d 343 (1976), reh. denied 429 U.S. 1079, 97 S.Ct. 825, 50 L.Ed.2d 799 (private employer excluded pregnancy-related disability from benefit program; no violation of civil rights laws if no discriminatory intent). See Wetzel v. Liberty Mut. Ins. Co., 511 F.2d 199 (3d Cir.1975), vacated and remanded with instructions to dismiss appeal 424 U.S. 737, 96 S.Ct. 1202, 47 L.Ed.2d 435 (1976). See generally French, Liberty Mutual Insurance Company v. Wetzel: An Analysis, 8

denied women who return from pregnancy leaves but accorded others who return from leaves? Here a possible violation of civil rights laws was found even prior to the 1978 amendments, which clearly forbid such discrimination.[56]

§ 14.5 Dismissal of Government Personnel

The grounds for discharge of local government personnel are usually stated in legislation: the state constitution, statutes, city charter, and local ordinances. The grounds thus specified are generally held to be exclusive,[57] and even these grounds will be sustained only if reasonable.[58] In general, a local government's arbitrary dismissal of an officer or employee will violate the due process clause of the 14th Amendment to the U.S. Constitution.[59] A leading case[60] held that a government worker could not be

---

Urban Law. 899 (1976); Annot., Pregnancy Leave or Maternity Leave Policy, or Lack Thereof, as Unlawful Employment Practice Violative of Title VII of the Civil Rights Act of 1964, 27 A.L.R.Fed. 537 (1976). See also Wimberly v. Labor & Indus. Relations Comm'n, 479 U.S. 511, 107 S.Ct. 821, 93 L.Ed.2d 909 (1987), where the Court held that the Federal Unemployment Tax Act does not prohibit a state from disqualifying unemployment-compensation applicants who leave their jobs due to pregnancy if the state denies the claims of *all* persons who leave their jobs voluntarily for reasons not associated with their work or employer. But see, as to discrimination against pregnancy-related disabilities in leave policies, the amendments to the Federal Civil Rights Act cited in note 54 *supra*.

[56] Nashville Gas Co. v. Satty, 434 U.S. 136, 98 S.Ct. 347, 54 L.Ed.2d 356 (1977) (exclusion of pregnancy-related absences from sick-leave plan was not a per se violation of 1964 Civil Rights Act, as it then existed, but would be violation if shown that exclusion of pregnancy was mere pretext aimed at achieving invidious discrimination). On the effect of the 1978 amendments to the civil rights laws, see Matthies, *supra* note 54. See generally Rabin, Women, Careers, Babies: An Issue of Timing?, 13 U.C.L.A. Women's L.J. 293 (2005).

[57] State ex rel. Cosson v. Baughn, 162 Iowa 308, 143 N.W. 1100 (1913); Pettit v. Reitzell, 202 La. 12, 11 So.2d 13 (1942); Dick v. Melvindale, 271 Mich. 419, 261 N.W. 68 (1935); City of Natchez v. McGehee, 157 Miss. 225, 127 So. 902 (1930). See Roberts v. Fredrick, 295 Ala. 281, 328 So.2d 277 (1976) (causes for removal specified in constitution were exclusive). But see Wilson v. West Haven, 142 Conn. 646, 116 A.2d 420 (1955); Hunter v. Quick, 183 Okl. 19, 79 P.2d 590 (1938).

[58] Jepsen v. Board of Educ., 19 Ill.App.2d 204, 153 N.E.2d 417 (1958); State ex rel. McGinnis v. Police Civil Service Comm'n, 253 Minn. 62, 91 N.W.2d 154 (1958). See Alexander v. Scattergood, 51 Cal.App.2d 127, 124 P.2d 151 (Dist.Ct.1942); Ferdinand v. Moses, 26 N.Y.S.2d 382 (Sup.Ct.1941), aff'd 262 App.Div. 1001, 30 N.Y.S.2d 842 (1941), appeal denied 263 App.Div. 706, 31 N.Y.S.2d 666; Riggins v. City of Waco, 40 Tex.Civ.App. 569, 90 S.W. 657 (1905), error ref'd.

[59] Wieman v. Updegraff, 344 U.S. 183, 73 S.Ct. 215, 97 L.Ed. 216 (1952). See Hunter v. City of Ann Arbor, 325 F.Supp. 847 (D.Mich.1971), saying that all government employees are entitled to (1) protection from arbitrary or discriminatory discharge, or discharge based on unnecessary limitation of constitutional rights, and (2) a procedure that will show whether discharge has been arbitrary or discriminatory. Cf. Lindsey v. State ex rel. Department of Corrections, 593 P.2d 1088 (Okl.1979), striking down an attempt to demote an employee for his refusal to obey his superior's instructions to falsify a record.

[60] Pickering v. Board of Educ., 391 U.S. 563, 88 S.Ct. 1731, 20 L.Ed.2d 811 (1968). On the reasons for the general rule of *Pickering* that a government employee cannot be dismissed for exercising rights of free speech, and for the exceptions and qualifications to that general rule, see Note, Public Employee Free Speech: The Policy Reasons for Rejecting a Per Se Rule Precluding Speech Rights, 46 Boston College L. Rev. 893 (2005); Note, The Exception to the Rule: Government Employers' Right to Restrict Free Speech of Employees, 29 J. College & University L. 719 (2003).

Accord with *Pickering*, Givhan v. Western Line Consolidated School Dist., 439 U.S. 410, 99 S.Ct. 693, 58 L.Ed.2d 619 (1979) (teacher could not be dismissed for expressing criticisms of school district practices and policies); Belshaw v. City of Berkeley, 246 Cal.App.2d 493, 54 Cal.Rptr. 727 (1966) (disciplinary proceedings improper where based on violation of rule against public expressions of disapproval of departmental policies); Klein v. Civil Service Comm'n, 260 Iowa 1147, 152 N.W.2d 195 (1967). Compare City of St. Petersburg v. Pfeiffer, 52 So.2d 796 (Fla.1951) (dangerous to discipline an employee for criticizing a superior). See Bagley v. Washington Township Hospital District, 65 Cal.2d 499, 55 Cal.Rptr. 401, 421 P.2d 409 (1966), holding that a government agency cannot, as a condition of employment, require waiver of constitutional rights, unless it shows (1) that the political restraints relate to the improvement of public service, (2) that the benefits the public gains by the restraints outweigh the impairment of constitutional rights, and (3) that no alternatives less restrictive of constitutional rights are available. See generally Bogacki v. Board of Supervisors, 5 Cal.3d

dismissed for making critical comments about the local entity for which she worked, since this would violate the worker's right of free speech. A number of qualifications were, however, expressed; the prohibition was stated not to apply (1) where the statements were made with knowledge of their falsity, or in reckless disregard of their truth; (2) where the statements were so without foundation as to call into question the worker's fitness for the position; (3) where there was a breach of confidentiality involved, and the position is such as to justify a need for confidentiality; (4) where the position is such as to require the maintaining of discipline by superiors or harmony among co-workers, and the comments of the worker-in-question were such as to jeopardize that discipline or harmony; or (5) where the worker had failed to follow a required grievance procedure before making public a complaint. In general, it may be said that a local government officer or employee may not be dismissed for making statements that do not impede either that worker's performance of duty or the general operation of government, and may not be dismissed for the exercise of *any* of his or her constitutional rights unless such a restriction serves some compelling public interest which could not be protected by any reasonable alternative without infringing on constitutional rights.

771, 97 Cal.Rptr. 657, 489 P.2d 537 (1971), cert. denied 405 U.S. 1030, 92 S.Ct. 1301, 31 L.Ed.2d 488 (1972). See also Bertot v. School Dist. No. 1, 613 F.2d 245 (10th Cir. 1979) (nonrenewal of teacher's contract in retaliation for her exercise of First Amendment rights; violation of civil rights found, and teacher entitled to back pay from district and school-board members in their official capacities despite their claim of good faith). As to damages awardable, see Annot., Award of Back Pay in Suit Under Title VII as Amended by Equal Employment Practices, 21 A.L.R. Fed. 472 (1974). See generally Annot., Award of Compensatory Damages, Aside from Backpay or Frontpay, for Violation of Title VII of Civil Rights Act of 1964, 48 A.L.R. Fed. 338 (1980). The *Pickering* case has often been applied in cases involving free-speech rights of public school teachers. See Gee, Establishing a Constitutional Standard that Protects Public School Teacher Classroom Expression, 38 J. L. & Educ. 409 (2009); Comment, *"Pick"ering* the Speech Rights of Public School Teachers: Arguing for a Movement by Courts Toward the *Hazelwood-Tinker* Standard Under the First Amendment, 3 Fla. A.& M. U. L. Rev. 41 (2008); Comment, Tinkering With Restrictions on Educator Speech: Can School Boards Restrict What Educators Say on Social Networking Sites?, 36 U. Dayton L. Rev. 115 (2010). The area of public school teachers' freedom of speech was also much affected by the *Garcetti v. Ceballos* case; see notes 63 & 64 *infra* and accompanying text. See also Note, Compelled Investigatory and Testimonial Speech: An Overdue Clarification of the Public Employee Speech Doctrine That Rehabilitates "All of the Values at Stake," 101 Ky. L. J. 403 (2012).

Although a public employee enjoys the Fifth Amendment right not to be compelled to respond to potentially incriminating questions and not to have his refusal to speak used against him in a subsequent criminal proceeding, such refusal may be treated as insubordination and may justify disciplinary action by the employer. Lybarger v. City of Los Angeles, 40 Cal.3d 822, 221 Cal.Rptr. 529, 710 P.2d 329 (1985). See Comment, Should Public Employers Be Forced to Warn Their Employees of Their Immunity and Duty to Answer Questions Before Demanding Answers and Taking Adverse Action?, 56 Catholic U.L. Rev. 1069 (2007). As to an employee's refusal to take a polygraph test, see note 71 *infra*.

The *Pickering* case remains good law but has been affected by three later Supreme Court cases—*Connick v. Myers* in 1983,[61] *Rankin v. McPherson* in 1987,[62] and, most

---

[61] Connick v. Myers, 461 U.S. 138, 103 S.Ct. 1684, 75 L.Ed.2d 708 (1983), the Court declared that when a public employee speaks on matters of merely personal or intra-office interest, not as a citizen on matters of public concern, a federal court is ordinarily not the appropriate forum in which to review the wisdom of a personnel decision. Here, where an assistant district attorney had allegedly been discharged for making critical comments about the office's transfer policy, morale, the need for a grievance committee, the level of confidence that officeworkers felt in their superiors, and pressure to participate in political campaigns, the discharge was held not to offend the First Amendment since the matters on which the discharged employee had expressed her views related (with the exception of pressure to participate in political campaigns) to questions of personal or internal office concern, not matters of public concern. See Waters v. Churchill, 511 U.S. 661, 114 S.Ct. 1878, 128 L.Ed.2d 686 (1994), noted 61 Brooklyn L. Rev. 1055 (1995), 24 Capital U.L. Rev. 893 (1995), 4 Widener J. Pub. L. 581 (1995) (public employee could be discharged for portion of her speech that was either on a matter not of public concern or was disruptive; issue of fact here existed as to basis of firing); Shockey v. City of Portland, 313 Or. 414, 837 P.2d 505 (1992), cert. denied 507 U.S. 1017, 113 S.Ct. 1813, 123 L.Ed.2d 444 (1993) (municipal employee's circulation of petition protesting city policy that employees be clean-shaven did not raise matter of public concern protected by First Amendment). See generally Note, Public Employees' Freedom of Association: Should *Connick v. Myers'* Speech-Based Public-Concern Rule Apply?, 61 Fordham L. Rev. 473 (1992).

[62] Rankin v. McPherson, 483 U.S. 378, 107 S.Ct. 2891, 97 L.Ed.2d 315 (1987), reh. denied 483 U.S. 1056, 108 S.Ct. 31, 97 L.Ed.2d 819 (1987), where it was held that a clerical employee in a constable's office could not be fired for saying, upon hearing of the assassination attempt on Pres. Reagan, "If they go for him again, I hope they get him." This was held to be a purely private statement on a matter of public concern and thus within an area of protected free speech, where expression will rarely, if ever, justify discharge. See United States v. National Treasury Employees Union, 513 U.S. 454, 115 S.Ct. 1003, 130 L.Ed.2d 964 (1995), invalidating—as to lower-level executive branch employees—the portion of Ethics in Government Act that prohibited receipt of honoraria by government employees; this was found to impose a significant burden on expressive activity on matters of public concern. Cf. Moore v. City of Kilgore, Texas, 877 F.2d 364 (10th Cir. 1989), cert. denied 493 U.S. 1003, 110 S.Ct. 562, 107 L.Ed.2d 557 (1989) (First Amendment rights of a firefighter who spoke to the press concerning departmental conditions and injuries suffered by members of the department were violated by disciplinary measures taken against him; expressions found to encompass areas of vital public concern); Koch v. City of Hutchinson, 814 F.2d 1489 (10th Cir.1987), aff'd en banc 847 F.2d 1436 (10th Cir.1988) (fire marshall's arson investigation reports, used as basis for his demotion, held to address matters of public concern and thus to be protected speech under First Amendment). But cf. Smith v. Fruin, 28 F.3d 646 (7th Cir.1994), cert. denied 513 U.S. 1083, 115 S.Ct. 735, 130 L.Ed.2d 638 (1995) (public employer's complaints about his office's noncompliance with smoke-free workplace ordinances not a matter of public concern when made for purely personal reasons); Kinsey v. Salado Independent School Dist., 950 F.2d 988 (5th Cir.1992), cert. denied 504 U.S. 941, 112 S.Ct. 2275, 119 L.Ed.2d 201 (1992) (no violation of school superintendent's free speech rights where suspended for support of slate of candidates for school board); Dennison v. County of Frederick, 921 F.2d 50 (4th Cir.1990), cert. denied 501 U.S. 1218, 111 S.Ct. 2828, 115 L.Ed.2d 998 (1991) (personal grievances about working conditions and about level of building code enforcement held not to qualify as matters of public concern). Even where a matter of public concern is involved, an employee's speech may validly be the basis of dismissal, as recognized in *Pickering*, if the speech is disruptive of the department's operations. See Acevedo v. City of Muskogee, 897 P.2d 256 (Okl.1995) (detective dismissed from police department for making allegations of corruption in the law enforcement and legal community). Cf. Bishop v. Municipality of Anchorage, 899 P.2d 149 (Alaska 1995) (city employee's refusal to obey employer's order to exchange work stations was just cause for dismissal; termination found not to have been in retaliation for employee's letters to newspaper criticizing employer). See generally Estlund, Free Speech and Due Process in the Workplace, 71 Ind. L.J. 101 (1995); Hiers, First Amendment Speech Rights of Government Employees: Trends and Problems in Supreme Court and Fifth Circuit Decisions, 45 Sw. L.J. 741 (1991); Rynard, The Public Employee and Free Speech in the Supreme Court: Self-Expression, Public Access to Information, and the Efficient Provision of Governmental Services, 21 Urban Law. 447 (1989); Schoen, *Pickering* Plus Thirty Years: Public Employees and Free Speech, 30 Tex. Tech. L. Rev. 5 (1999); Note, Don't Tip the Scales! The Actual Malice Standard Unjustifiably Eliminates First Amendment Protection for Public Employees' Recklessly False Statements, 80 Minn. L. Rev. 911 (1996); Note, Recklessly False Statements in the Public-Employment Context, 63 U. Chi. L. Rev. 1277 (1996); Annot., First Amendment Protection for Law Enforcement Employees Subjected to Discharge, Transfer, or Discipline Because of Speech, 109 A.L.R. Fed. 9 (1992); Annot., First Amendment Protection for Publicly Employed Firefighters Subjected to Discharge, Transfer, or Discipline Because of Speech, 106 A.L.R. Fed. 396 (1992); Annot., Public Employee's Right of Free Speech Under Federal Constitution's First Amendment—Supreme Court Cases, 97 L.Ed.2d 903 (1989).

importantly, *Garcetti v. Ceballos* in 2006.[63] In *Garcetti*, the Court noted that two inquiries guide interpretation of the constitutional protection accorded public employees' speech: the first requires determining whether the employee spoke as a citizen on a matter of public concern. If not, he has no First Amendment cause of action based on the government's dismissal or discipline of him. If the answer to the first inquiry is in the affirmative, there is a possible First Amendment claim, and the question then becomes whether the government had adequate justification for its treatment of the employee. Here, a deputy district attorney alleged that he was subject to adverse treatment due to his writing a memorandum recommending dismissal of a case on the basis of purported governmental misconduct. The Court ruled that the district attorney was not speaking as a citizen when he wrote the memorandum and thus was not protected by the First Amendment.[64]

An elected official's vote on public issues is protected speech under the First Amendment. See Carrigan v. Commission on Ethics, 236 P.3d 616 (Nev. 2010) (failure to abstain from voting on matter due to potential conflict of interest is protected speech). Cf. Denke v. Shoemaker, 347 Mont. 322, 198 P.3d 284 (2008) (claims by city clerk that city council retaliated against her for bringing sexual harassment charges against city by failing to control the particular viewpoints expressed at council meeting were barred by First Amendment; once a meeting was opened for public discussion, city could not impose restrictions that discriminated among the viewpoints expressed). As to free speech rights of public employees when off-duty, see Papandrea, The Free Speech Rights of Off-Duty Government Employees, 2010 B.Y.U.L. Rev. 2117. As to the right to a jury trial in public employee free-speech cases, see Comment, Preserving the Right to a Jury Trial in Public Employee Free Speech Litigation: The Protected Status of Speech Must Be Labeled a Mixed Question of Law and Fact, 79 U. Cinc. L. Rev. 375 (2010). As to the possible use of authorities other than the First Amendment to protect employee speech, see Note, *Huppert*, *Reilly*, and the Increasing Futility of Relying on the First Amendment to Protect Employee Speech, 19 Wm. & Mary Bill Rts. J. 449 (2010). As to government "whistleblowers" and their protection, or lack thereof, from dismissal or other retaliatory actions, see Comment, Whistleblowers in the Workplace: The Government Employee's "Official Duty" to Tell the Truth, 65 SMU L. Rev. 685 (2012).

[63] Garcetti v. Ceballos, 547 U.S. 410, 126 S.Ct. 1951, 164 L.Ed.2d 689 (2006).

[64] See City of San Diego v. Roe, 543 U.S. 77, 125 S.Ct. 521, 160 L.Ed.2d 410 (2004) (speech of police officer, who video-taped himself stripping off generic police uniform and engaging in acts of masturbation and who offered home-made videos for sale on online auction site, did not touch on matter of public concern and thus was not subject to the possible protection of the *Pickering* case). Cf. Dew v. City of Scappoose, 208 Or.App. 121, 145 P.3d 198 (2006) (former city police chief brought Federal Civil Rights action against city and city councilor, asserting they retaliated against her for exercising her free speech rights; to prevail, employee must show that she was speaking on a matter of public concern and that the speech was a substantial or motivating factor for the adverse employment action; the government may then escape liability by showing that it would have taken the same action even in the absence of the protected free-speech conduct or that the termination was justified by a sufficiently strong countervailing government interest).

It has been noted that the precise meaning of the *Garcetti* case, *supra* note 63, has been much debated—and probably will continue to be debated far into the future. See Kramer, Recent Developments in Government Operations and Liability: *Garcetti v. Ceballos*: The Battle Has Just Begun, 39 Urban Law. 983 (2007). See generally Bice, Tough Talk from the Supreme Court on Free Speech: The Illusory Per Se Rule in *Garcetti* as Further Evidence of *Connick*'s Unworkable Employee/Citizen Speech Partition, 8 J.L. in Soc'y 45 (2007). As to the effect of the *Garcetti* case on the speech of public school educators, see Griffin, Academic Freedom and Professional Speech in the Post-*Garcetti* World, 37 Seattle U.L. Rev. 1 (2013); McCarthy & Eckes, Silence in the Hallways: The Impact of *Garcetti v. Ceballos* on Public School Educators, 17 Boston U. Pub. Interest L.J. 209 (2008); Note, Reconciling the Public Employees Speech Doctrine and Academic Speech After *Garcetti v. Ceballos*, 94 Minn. L. Rev. 1202 (2010); Note, Pursing Academic Freedom After *Garcetti v. Ceballos*, 91 Tex. L. Rev. 1253 (2013).

As to the relation of the *Garcetti* case and open meeting laws, see Note, Open Meetings and Closed Mouths: Elected Officials' Free Speech Rights After *Garcetti v. Ceballos*, 61 Case W. Res. L. Rev. 551 (2010).

In Lane v. Franks, ___ U.S. ___, 134 S.Ct. 2369 (2014), a former director of a community college's program gave sworn testimony at criminal corruption trials of a former program employee, who was also a state representative. The director's testimony was held to be citizen speech eligible for First Amendment protection, not unprotected employee speech, since the testimony concerned matters of public concern (corruption in a public program and misuse of state funds) and the government lacked any interest justifying the allegedly

Some local government employees are not within civil-service provisions and do not have any other statutory or charter rights in their jobs. They can be dismissed without cause—meaning for any reason the local governing body, or other appointing authority, thinks adequate.[65] But even here—and even if the statutes or home-rule charter

---

retaliatory termination of the director. See generally Spurgeon, The Endangered Citizen Servant: *Garcetti v.* the Public Interest and Academic Freedom, 39 J. College & University L. 405 (2013); Note, Policeman, Citizen, or Both? A Civilian Analogue Exception to *Garcetti v. Ceballos*, 111 Mich. L. Rev. 789 (2013). See also Note, Rescuing the Union Grievance From the Shoals of *Garcetti*: A Call for the Return to Reason in Public Workplace Speech Jurisprudence, 57 N.Y. Law School L. Rev. 905 (2012–13). On the question of when to apply the tests of *Pickering, supra* note 60, to determine First Amendment protection and when to apply *Garcetti*, see Demers v. Austin, 729 F.3d 1011 (9th Cir. 2013) (*Garcetti* applies to academic writing on matters of public concern).

On the related topic of the free-speech rights of students in public schools, see Morse v. Frederick, 551 U.S. 393, 127 S.Ct. 2618, 168 L.Ed.2d 290 (2007) (principal did not violate students' right to free speech by confiscating banner she reasonably viewed as promoting illegal drug use), with citations to prior authorities; Tinker v. Des Moines Independent Community School Dist., 393 U.S. 503, 89 S.Ct. 733 (1969) (describing student free speech rights within the context of public schools). For criticism of *Morse, supra*, see Comment, Student Rights Up in Smoke: The Supreme Court's Clouded Judgment in *Morse v. Frederick*, 25 Touro L. Rev. 739 (2009). As to students' free speech rights, see generally Goldman, Student Speech and the First Amendment: A Comprehensive Approach, 63 Fla. L. Rev. 395 (2011); Moss, The Overhyped Path From *Tinker* to *Morse*: How the Student Speech Cases Show the Limits of Supreme Court Decisions, for the Law and for the Litigants, 63 Fla. L. Rev. 1407 (2011); Note, Getting Past the Schoolhouse Gate: Rethinking Student Speech in the Digital Age, 71 Ohio St. L. J. 611 (2010); Symposium, One Generation Under *Hazelwood*: A 25-year Retrospective on Student First Amendment Rights, 11 First Amend. L. Rev. 291–440 (2013). Compare Note, Rehabilitating *Tinker*: A Modest Proposal to Protect Public-School Students in the Digital Age, 98 Iowa L. Rev. 1309 (2013). See also Crawford, When Student Off-Campus Cyberspeech Permeates the Schoolhouse Gate: Are There Limits to *Tinker's* Reach?, 45 Urban Law. 235 (2013).

[65] Brown v. Hirst, 443 F.2d 899 (4th Cir.1971); Metropolitan Dade County v. Peterson, 311 So.2d 119 (Fla.App.1975) (employee has no vested rights in his position and may be dismissed without cause); Ray v. Mayor of Everett, 328 Mass. 305, 103 N.E.2d 269 (1952); Adamczyk v. Town of Caledonia, 52 Wis.2d 270, 190 N.W.2d 137 (1971). See Bishop v. Wood, 426 U.S. 341, 96 S.Ct. 2074, 48 L.Ed.2d 684 (1976) (police officer had no property interest in continued employment; could be dismissed at pleasure of city, without a hearing); Doyle v. Miller, 114 Cal.App.2d 347, 250 P.2d 324 (Dist.Ct.1952) (some employees can be removed without cause); Barnes v. Mendonsa, 110 Ga.App. 464, 138 S.E.2d 914 (1964) (power to appoint carries with it the power to remove without cause, unless restricted by statute or charter); Potts v. School Board, 177 La. 1103, 150 So. 290 (1933); City of Muskogee v. Landry, 567 P.2d 988 (Okl.1977) (city clerk could suspend deputy for failing to comply with proper directive); Jordan v. City of Oakville, 106 Wash.2d 122, 720 P.2d 824 (1986) (temporary member of police force, not covered by civil service, could be dismissed at will). Cf. Blanton v. Housing Auth. of Norman, 794 P.2d 412 (Okl.1990) (requirement of good cause before discharging employee is not implicit in at-will contract); Dew v. City of Florence, 279 S.C. 155, 303 S.E.2d 664 (1983), cert. denied 464 U.S. 936, 104 S.Ct. 345, 78 L.Ed.2d 312 (1983) (dismissal of "at will" city employee by city manager valid despite city manager's failure to comply strictly with warning provisions in municipal handbook). But an employee—even an at-will employee—discharged in violation of his or her constitutional rights may have an action for wrongful dismissal. See Vannerson v. Board of Regents, 784 P.2d 1053 (Okl.1989) (if at-will state employee was discharged for going over his supervisor's head in complaining of an illegal disposition of state property, this would support claim for wrongful dismissal). Probationary employees can normally be terminated without cause during or at the end of the probationary period. See Douglas v. O'Grady, 51 Misc.2d 518, 273 N.Y.S.2d 496 (Sup.Ct.1966). Cf. City of Jenks v. Stone, 321 P.3d 179 (Okla. 2014) (probationary employee, such as a trainee in the police department, is an at-will employee and lacks the full panoply of employment rights enjoyed by those who have completed their initial training). See also note 74 *infra*.

On the question of when an employee has property rights in a job, see Rains v. City of Stillwater, 817 P.2d 753 (Okl. App. 1991) (employee had no property rights in job when charter allowed his removal by city manager "when deemed necessary for the good of the service"). But the *Rains* case was overruled in City of Durant v. Cicio, 50 P.3d 218 (Okla. 2002), where a police officer was held entitled to review of the decision to terminate his employment, since a statute specifically provided that the officer was protected from discharge "except for cause" and was granted an appeal to a board of review. This controlled over the statute, relied on in the *Rains* case, authorizing the city manager to exercise discretion in appointing and removing officers and employees for the good of the service, except as otherwise provided by law. See Barnthouse v. City of Edmond, 73 P.3d 840 (Okla. 2003), cert. denied Cochran v. Barnthouse, 540 U.S. 981, 124 S.Ct. 464, 157 L.Ed.2d 371 (2003) (police officers had a property interest in their employment and rank, which could not be denied without due process, including a hearing, where employer's discretion to demote employees was restricted to demotions

specifically provide for dismissal without cause—there can be no dismissal based on an employee's exercise of constitutional rights.[66]

---

for cause; in Federal Civil Rights action, genuine issue of material fact existed as to whether chief of police violated police officers' due process and whether such violation took place in his official capacity).

[66] Rosenfield v. Malcolm, 65 Cal.2d 559, 55 Cal.Rptr. 505, 421 P.2d 697 (1967) (discharge of assistant health officer, without tenure, for membership in a labor organization was violation of freedom of association). See Brown v. Hirst, *supra* note 65; Johnson v. Branch, 364 F.2d 177 (4th Cir. 1966), cert. denied 385 U.S. 1003, 87 S.Ct. 706, 17 L.Ed.2d 542 (1967) (even a probationary employee cannot be terminated for exercise of his or her constitutional rights); Jervey v. Martin, 336 F.Supp. 1350 (W.D.Va.1972) (same); Ball v. City Council, 252 Cal.App.2d 136, 60 Cal.Rptr. 139 (Dist. Ct.1967) (dismissal of police chief for membership in labor union where statute specifically allowed such membership).

It has been held that public employees cannot be discharged solely because of their political affiliation unless the hiring authority can demonstrate that party affiliation is an appropriate job requirement. Branti v. Finkel, 445 U.S. 507, 100 S.Ct. 1287, 63 L.Ed.2d 574 (1980), noted 34 Okl.L.Rev. 93 (1981); 25 St. Louis U.L.J. 189 (1981); 35 Sw.L.J. 675 (1981); 55 Tulane L.Rev. 576 (1981) (continued employment of an assistant public defender cannot properly be conditioned on his allegiance to the political party in control of the county government); Elrod v. Burns, 427 U.S. 347, 96 S.Ct. 2673, 49 L.Ed.2d 547 (1976) (discharge of non-civil-service employee for non-affiliation with new sheriff's political party held violative of First Amendment). See Shakman v. Democratic Organization of Cook County, 481 F.Supp. 1315 (N.D.Ill.1979) (hiring or firing of employees for political reasons discriminated against independent candidates and voters and could not be justified in absence of compelling state interests), noted 66 A.B.A.J. 664 (1980). Earlier proceedings in the *Shakman* litigation, *supra*, are found at 435 F.2d 267 (7th Cir.1970) (complaint by resident taxpayer-voters as to operation of patronage system was justiciable), injunction issued by district court on remand aff'd 533 F.2d 344 (7th Cir.1976). The *Shakman* litigation finally ended June 16, 2014, when a federal judge lifted the 42-year-old court order that had placed Chicago's city hall under federal supervision. See Time magazine, June 30, 2014, at 18 ("The Rundown—Patronage"). As to retaliatory actions against an employee for political activities, see Note, Constitutional Law—The First Amendment Retaliation Doctrine, 81 Tenn. L. Rev. 367 (2014). For a situation where discharging a public employee was found justified on the basis of that employee's political views, see Carlson v. Bratton, 681 P.2d 1333 (Wyo.1984) (mayor entitled to have someone in the position of chief of police who concurs in mayor's policies and with whom the mayor can work toward the goal of implementing those policies). Cf. Soderstrum v. Town of Grand Isle, 925 F.2d 135 (5th Cir.1991) (termination of police chief's secretary was lawful even if done for political reasons); Williams v. City of River Rouge, 909 F.2d 151 (6th Cir.1990) (city attorney does not enjoy protection from politically motivated dismissal); Freeman v. Poling, 175 W.Va. 814, 338 S.E.2d 415 (1985) (deputies who were discharged by a new sheriff were not denied protection of their liberty interests; but anyway, they failed to establish that the sheriff's actions were politically motivated). See also Shondel v. McDermott, 775 F.2d 859 (7th Cir. 1985) (firing of city employee allegedly due to her being related to a supporter of the losing mayoral candidate did not violate her First Amendment rights). The *Elrod* case *supra* indicated that discharge of an employee for political reasons is likely to be upheld if the employee held a policy-making position. See Ray v. City of Leeds, 837 F.2d 1542 (11th Cir.1988) (politically motivated discharge of a policy-making employee who directed city's senior citizens department held not to violate free speech or due process); Phillips v. Wiseman, 857 P.2d 50 (Okl.1993) (political affiliation was appropriate requirement for deputy commissioner of labor; dismissal based on such affiliation justified). Cf. Powers v. Richards, 549 F.3d 505 (7th Cir. 2008) (where party loyalty is necessary for the effective execution of a government job, the First Amendment does not prohibit an administration from firing an employee based on the employee's political affiliation; Executive Secretary of Illinois Civil Service Commission found to be such a job).

In Rutan v. Republican Party of Illinois, 497 U.S. 62, 110 S.Ct. 2729, 111 L.Ed.2d 52 (1990), noted 11 N. Ill. L. Rev. 375 (1991), the rule of the *Elrod* case *supra* was extended to hiring, as well as firing, decisions, with the Court holding broadly, in a case involving low-level government positions, that hiring, promotions, transfers, and recalls (after layoffs) based on political affiliation or support are impermissible infringements on public employees' First Amendment rights. See generally Martin, Patronage Employment Decisions After *Rutan*, 23 U. Toledo L. Rev. 68 (1991).

In O'Hare Truck Serv., Inc. v. City of Northlake, 518 U.S. 712, 116 S.Ct. 2353, 135 L.Ed.2d 874 (1996), the rule of the *Elrod* case *supra* was again extended by the Supreme Court—this time so as to afford independent contractors the same protections against being discharged for political reasons as have been afforded public employees. See Welch v. Goldstein, The First Amendment and Independent Contractors: The Supreme Court Expands Governmental Liability, 29 Urban Law. 341 (1997). Cf. Umbehr v. McClure, 44 F.3d 876 (10th Cir. 1995), cert. denied 515 U.S. 1161, 115 S.Ct. 2616, 132 L.Ed.2d 859 (1995), judgment aff'd and remanded by 518 U.S. 668, 116 S.Ct. 2342, 135 L.Ed.2d 843 (1996) (contractor could maintain action against county for having been terminated in retaliation for exercising rights of free speech).

As for removal of officers and employees *for* cause, this has been recognized as an essential and inherent power of local governments.[67] Generally, local governing bodies can exercise this power even as to elected officials.[68] Where officers are accorded, either by statute or charter, a definite term of office, dismissal is normally possible *only* for cause,[69] and this is also usually one of the results of inclusion of an employee under civil-service rules: once the employee qualifies and serves any probationary period that is required, removal is only for cause. Wherever "cause"—or its equivalent terms "just cause," "good cause," or "substantial cause"—is required for removal of an officer or employee, this means (1) the removal must be based on a substantial fault or shortcoming of the dismissed worker,[70] and (2) the fault or shortcoming must bear a substantial relation to the impairment of public service.[71] Being absent from work

---

[67] State ex rel. McMahon v. City Council of New Orleans, 107 La. 632, 32 So. 22 (1902); Healey v. Jones, 152 Pa.Super. 18, 30 A.2d 732 (1943); Richards v. Town of Clarksburg, 30 W.Va. 491, 4 S.E. 774 (1887). See Hawkins v. Common Council of Grand Rapids, 192 Mich. 276, 158 N.W. 953 (1916). The power to remove for cause cannot be limited by contract. Potts v. Morehouse Parish School Board, *supra* note 62; State ex rel. City of St. Paul v. Oehler, 218 Minn. 290, 16 N.W.2d 765 (1944).

[68] McComb v. City of Lansing, 264 Mich. 609, 250 N.W. 326 (1933); Richards v. Town of Clarksburg, *supra* note 64. But cf. Legault v. Board of Trustees, 161 Cal. 197, 118 P. 706 (1911) (governing body of locality cannot remove elected official where legislature has provided judicial proceedings for such removal). There are sometimes express or implied limitations on removing an officer for misconduct during a prior term, when he has subsequently been re-elected or re-appointed. See Annot., Removal of Public Officer for Misconduct During Previous Term, 42 A.L.R.3d 691 (1972).

[69] Day v. Andrews, 279 Ala. 563, 188 So.2d 523 (1966); Staheli v. Redondo Beach, 131 Cal.App. 71, 21 P.2d 133 (Dist.Ct.1933); Field v. Malster, 88 Md. 691, 41 A. 1087 (1898); Hallgrene v. Campbell, 82 Mich. 255, 46 N.W. 381 (1890); Riccio v. Town Council of Bristol, 109 R.I. 431, 286 A.2d 881 (1972); Rutter v. Burke, 89 Vt. 14, 93 A. 842 (1915). See Winter v. Coor, 144 Ariz. 56, 695 P.2d 1094 (1985) (town magistrates, who serve a term of office, cannot be removed at will of council); Boca Raton v. Cassady, 167 So.2d 886 (Fla.App.1964).

[70] Downs v. Conway School District, 328 F.Supp. 338 (E.D.Ark.1971); Civil Service Commission of City of Tucson v. Livingston, 22 Ariz.App. 183, 525 P.2d 949 (1974); Williams v. Dent, 207 Ark. 440, 181 S.W.2d 29 (1944); Molino v. Torrington, 154 Conn. 368, 225 A.2d 805 (1966); Coursey v. Board of Fire and Police Commissioners, 90 Ill.App.2d 31, 234 N.E.2d 339 (1967); Bole v. Civil City of Ligonier, 130 Ind.App. 362, 161 N.E.2d 189 (1959); Roth v. State ex rel. Kurtz, 158 Ind. 242, 63 N.E. 460 (1902); McCallister v. Priest, 422 S.W.2d 650 (Mo.1968); State ex rel. Rockwell v. State Board of Education, 213 Minn. 184, 6 N.W.2d 251 (1942); State ex rel. Hart v. Common Council of Duluth, 53 Minn. 238, 55 N.W. 118 (1893); Paulson v. Civil Service Commission, 90 Nev. 41, 518 P.2d 148 (1974); State ex rel. Bowlin v. Welliver, 60 Nev. 154, 104 P.2d 188 (1940); Walker v. Village of Belpre, 171 Ohio St. 177, 168 N.E.2d 535 (1960); Layne v. Hayes, 141 W.Va. 289, 90 S.E.2d 270 (1955). Very often the grounds on which a teacher or other employee is dismissed involve "incompetency," "inefficiency," or "insubordination." See What Constitutes "Insubordination" as Ground for Dismissal of Public School Teacher, 78 A.L.R.3d 83 (1977); Annot., What Constitutes "Incompetency" or "Inefficiency" as a Ground for Dismissal or Demotion of Public School Teacher, 4 A.L.R.3d 1090 (1965). See generally Jacobsen, Sperry & Jensen, The Dismissal and Non-Reemployment of Teachers, 1 J.L. & Educ. 435 (1972). See also Annot., Right to Dismiss Public School-Teacher on Ground that Services Are No Longer Needed, 100 A.L.R.2d 1141 (1965); Annot., Dismissal or Rejection of Public Schoolteacher Because of Disloyalty, 27 A.L.R.2d 487 (1953).

Courts have recognized an "economic exception" to the general rule of dismissal-only-for-good-cause—*i.e.*, an employee may be dismissed despite lack of fault or shortcoming on his or her part if the dismissal is a matter of economic necessity. See Small v. Board of Safety, 513 N.E.2d 196 (Ind.App.1987) (town could dismiss police officer where town would be unable to obtain liability insurance if that officer remained on the force). Cf. Hennessey v. City of Bridgeport, 213 Conn. 656, 569 A.2d 1122 (1990) (officer appointed for fixed term may be dismissed by city before expiration of term if extraordinary financial conditions require such dismissal).

[71] Brickman v. New Orleans Aviation Board, 236 La. 143, 107 So.2d 422 (1958); Gersh v. Tuckahoe, 23 A.D.2d 258, 260 N.Y.S.2d 75 (1965); People ex rel. Van Tine v. Purdy, 221 N.Y. 396, 117 N.E. 609 (1917) (cause must relate to fitness of person to discharge duty properly). There has been considerable litigation over whether the sexual behavior of a person, or the general moral character, is relevant to the person's performance of public work. See Gaylord v. Tacoma School District No. 10, 88 Wn.2d 286, 559 P.2d 1340 (1977), cert. denied 434 U.S. 879, 98 S.Ct. 234, 54 L.Ed.2d 160 (avowed homosexuality held to constitute immorality for which high-school teacher could be dismissed). See generally Annot., Sexual Conduct as Ground for Dismissal of Teacher or Denial or Revocation of Teaching Certificate, 78 A.L.R.3d 19 (1977); Annot.,Tests of Moral

Character or Fitness as Requisite to Issuance of Teacher's License or Certificate, 96 A.L.R.2d 536 (1964). See also Annot., Use of Illegal Drugs as Ground for Dismissal of Teacher, or Denial or Cancellation of Teacher's Certificate, 47 A.L.R.3d 754 (1973).

It is sometimes said in general terms that what a public officer or employee does in his or her private life is no cause for dismissal. See Anderson v. Board, 227 Iowa 1164, 290 N.W. 493 (1940); Wilson v. Highland Park, 284 Mich. 96, 278 N.W. 778 (1938); Jarvella v. Willoughby-Eastlake School District, 12 Ohio Misc. 288, 233 N.E.2d 143 (1967). But as the *Jarvella* case *supra* recognizes, private conduct becomes relevant when it affects the individual's quality of public service. And it is often considered relevant if it brings the public service into disrepute or undermines public confidence in the government. See Lilley v. City of Carmel, 527 N.E.2d 224 (Ind.App.1988) (firefighter could be discharged for off-duty intoxication on ground this was unbecoming conduct for a fire official); Nodes v. City of Hastings, 284 Minn. 552, 170 N.W.2d 92 (1969) (with discussion of authorities; police officer's negligent and inexcusable failure to pay his private debts can impair his usefulness as an officer); Herbert v. Atlantic City, 87 N.J.L. 98, 93 A. 80 (1915). And conviction of a crime—at least one involving moral turpitude—is always recognized as a possible basis for removal. See City of Colorado Springs v. Givan, 897 P.2d 753 (Colo.1995) (city could discharge employee who pled guilty to felony incest). Cf. Brown v. Department of Justice, 715 F.2d 662 (D.C.Cir.1983), on remand Charest v. Department of Justice, I.N.S., 20 M.S.P.R. 254 (1984), (U.S. Border Guards indicted for conspiring to defraud U.S. government by interfering with functions of Border Patrol and violating civil rights of suspected illegal aliens; held to furnish reasonable cause to believe employees had committed work-related crime and thus to justify suspension; court noted that termination might be justified even if employees acquitted, as public employer may nonetheless be able to establish misconduct by preponderance of evidence); Hoflin v. City of Ocean Shores, 121 Wash.2d 113, 847 P.2d 428 (1993) (city employee dismissed for "just cause" where at time of dismissal city reasonably believed that employee had been convicted of federal felony). See generally Annot., Elections: Effect of Conviction under Federal Law, or Law of Another State or Country, on Right to Vote or Hold Public Office, 39 A.L.R.3d 303 (1971); Annots., What Constitutes Conviction Within Statutory or Constitutional Provision Making Conviction of Crime Ground of Disqualification for, Removal From, or Vacancy in, Public Office, 71 A.L.R.2d 593 (1960); What Is an Infamous Crime or One Involving Moral Turpitude Constituting Disqualification to Hold Public Office, 52 A.L.R.2d 1314 (1957). On statutory developments regarding discharge of a public employee due to handicap or illness, see School Bd. of Nassau County v. Arline, 480 U.S. 273, 107 S.Ct. 1123, 94 L.Ed.2d 307 (1987), reh. denied 481 U.S. 1024, 107 S.Ct. 1913, 95 L.Ed.2d 519 (1987) (school teacher afflicted with contagious tuberculosis was "handicapped individual" within meaning of federal Rehabilitation Act of 1973; federally funded state program could not discriminate against such individual solely by reason of handicap).

There is a split of authority as to whether a public employee can be discharged for refusal to take a polygraph test concerning possible improprieties in his or her work. Compare Rivera v. City of Douglas, 132 Ariz. 117, 644 P.2d 271 (App. 1982) (employee can be dismissed; use of polygraph proper if questions relate narrowly and specifically to performance of official duties, answers cannot be used against employee in any subsequent criminal proceeding, and penalty for refusal to answer is dismissal), and Fichera v. State Personnel Bd., 217 Cal.App.2d 613, 32 Cal.Rptr. 159 (1963) (same as to police officer), with Farmer v. City of Fort Lauderdale, 427 So.2d 187 (Fla.1983), cert. denied 464 U.S. 816, 104 S.Ct. 74, 78 L.Ed.2d 86 (1983) (police officer's refusal to take polygraph did not justify his dismissal); Kaske v. City of Rockford, 96 Ill.2d 298, 70 Ill.Dec. 841, 450 N.E.2d 314 (1983), cert. denied, 464 U.S. 960, 104 S.Ct. 391, 78 L.Ed.2d 335 (1983) (same); Engel v. Township of Woodbridge, 124 N.J.Super. 307, 306 A.2d 485 (1973) (same), and Stape v. Civil Serv. Comm'n of Philadelphia, 404 Pa. 354, 172 A.2d 161 (1961) (same). See generally Note, Police Officers—Officers May Not Be Compelled to Undergo Polygraph Examination: Polygraph Results Inadmissible in Administrative Proceedings, 1984 S. Ill. U.L.J. 205, noting the *Kaske* case *supra*. The trend apart from statute would seem to be toward upholding a public employer's right to threaten an employee with discharge for refusal to take a polygraph examination so long as minimal safeguards are provided to ensure the examination's fairness and relevance and so long as the employee is not required to waive the privilege against self-incrimination. See Erwin v. Price, 778 F.2d 668 (11th Cir.1985); Hester v. City of Milledgeville, 777 F.2d 1492 (11th Cir.1985), reh. denied 782 F.2d 180 (11th Cir.1986). But the area is much affected by statutes. The California rule stated in the *Fichera* case *supra* was later changed by statute; West's Ann. Cal. Gov't Code § 3307 (no action may be taken against public safety officer for refusal to take polygraph test). In Long Beach City Employees Ass'n v. City of Long Beach, 41 Cal.3d 937, 227 Cal.Rptr. 90, 719 P.2d 660 (1986), it was held that polygraph examinations impinge on the fundamental right of privacy and that therefore the statutory scheme that protected public safety officers (and also private employees) from compulsory polygraph tests but did not so protect public officials or employees *other* than public safety officers was valid only if supported by a compelling governmental interest. No such interest was found, and injunctive relief was thus held proper against an order requiring certain city employees to submit to polygraph tests as a condition of employment. In 1988, Congress enacted the Employee Polygraph Protection Act, making it unlawful for most employers to require any employee to submit to a lie detector test. 29 U.S.C.A. §§ 2001–09. But the Act does not apply to state or local governments. *Id.* § 2006. See O'Hartigan v. Department of Personnel, 118 Wash.2d 111, 821 P.2d 44 (1991) (applicant for State Patrol could be required to submit to polygraph exam in light of strong interest in ensuring that prospective law enforcement employees are of highest moral and ethical character). Cf. Pearson v. Hope Lumber & Supply Co., 820 P.2d 443 (Okl.1991) (federal Act, which was not in effect at the time this case arose, held not to express a public policy against discharging employees who refuse a polygraph exam). See generally Annot., Validity and Construction of Statute Prohibiting Employers from Suggesting or Requiring Polygraph or Similar Tests as Condition of Employment or Continued Employment, 23 A.L.R. 4th 187 (1983).

Mandatory drug testing for public employees is frequently proposed and sometimes implemented on the federal, state, and local levels. See "Rolling Out the Big Guns," Time, Sept. 22, 1986, at 25, 26. See generally Bensinger, Drugs in the Workplace: A Commentary, 3 Behavioral Sci. & L. 441 (1985); Bishop, Drug Testing Comes to Work, 6 Cal. Law. 29 (1986); Rothstein, Screening Workers for Drugs: A Legal and Ethical Framework, 11 Employee Relations L.J. 422 (1985). The leading case is National Treasury Employees Union v. Von Raab, 489 U.S. 656, 109 S.Ct. 1384, 103 L.Ed.2d 685 (1989), on remand 876 F.2d 376 (5th Cir.1989), where the Supreme Court held that in the case of public employees seeking positions involving interdiction of illegal drugs or requiring them to carry firearms, drug testing could be required by the employer without the need for a warrant or for any individualized suspicion as to the particular person's use of drugs. Customs Service employees seeking promotions were there involved and were held subject to warrantless drug testing even in the absence of individualized suspicion. The same was held true as to railroad employees in Skinner v. Railway Labor Executives' Ass'n, 489 U.S. 602, 109 S.Ct. 1402, 103 L.Ed.2d 639 (1989) (government's interest in safe operation of railroads presents special needs justifying departures from usual warrant and probable cause requirements for searches). See Jones v. McKenzie, 833 F.2d 335 (D.C.Cir.1987), cert. granted, judgment vac'd 490 U.S. 1001, 109 S.Ct. 1633, 104 L.Ed.2d 149 (1989), on remand 878 F.2d 1476 (D.C.Cir.1989), amended by 878 F.2d 1476 (C.A.D.C. 1989) (drug testing of school bus attendants upheld); McCloskey v. Honolulu Police Dep't, 71 Haw. 568, 799 P.2d 953 (1990) (drug testing of police officer not an unreasonable search under Hawaii Constitution); O'Connor v. Police Comm'r of Boston, 408 Mass. 324, 557 N.E.2d 1146 (1990) (drug testing of police academy cadets held reasonable where cadets agreed to testing before accepting employment); Middlebrooks v. Wayne County, 446 Mich. 151, 521 N.W.2d 774 (1994) (drug testing of provisional county worker whose job involved operating equipment on and near public ways); Caruso v. Ward, 72 N.Y.2d 432, 534 N.Y.S.2d 142, 530 N.E.2d 850 (1988) (random drug testing of elite drug investigation unit upheld). Cf. Fraternal Order of Police v. City of Miami, 609 So.2d 31 (Fla.1992), noted 23 Stetson L. Rev. 237 (1993) (drug testing of police officers suspected of off-duty drug use was not a subject of mandatory collective bargaining because such testing fell within the managerial prerogative of employer-city).

See also Vernonia School Dist. 47J v. Acton, 515 U.S. 646, 115 S.Ct. 2386, 132 L.Ed.2d 564 (1995), on remand 66 F.3d 217 (9th Cir.1995), noted 29 Creighton L. Rev. 861 (1996), 19 Harv. J.L. & Pub. Pol'y 209 (1995), 56 La. L. Rev. 959 (1996), 75 Neb. L. Rev. 151 (1996), 49 Rutgers L. Rev. 551 (1997), 27 Seton Hall L. Rev. 230 (1996), 35 U. Louisville J. Fam. L. 379 (1996–97), 3 Villanova Sports & Ent. L.J. 325 (1996), 71 Wash. L. Rev. 797 (1996), 17 Whittier L. Rev. 527 (1996), 1996 Wis. L. Rev. 1101 (public school district's student athlete drug policy, which authorized random urinalysis of students who participated in its athletic programs, did not violate students' federal or state constitutional right to be free from unreasonable searches). But see Chandler v. Miller, 520 U.S. 305, 117 S.Ct. 1295, 137 L.Ed.2d 513 (1997), noted 23 S. Ill. U.L.J. 781 (1999) (Georgia's statutory requirement that candidates for state office pass drug test did not fit within closely guarded category of constitutionally permissible suspicionless searches); Horsemen's Benevolent & Protective Ass'n v. Massachusetts Racing Comm'n, 403 Mass. 692, 532 N.E.2d 644 (1989) (regulation of State Racing Commission authorizing random testing of owners, trainers, jockeys, etc. violates Massachusetts Constitution; probable cause needed for such testing). Cf. Loder v. City of Glendale, 14 Cal.4th 846, 59 Cal.Rptr.2d 696, 927 P.2d 1200 (1997) (suspicionless drug testing of all current employees who were offered promotion was not reasonable under Fourth Amendment, though suspicionless drug testing of all job *applicants* was reasonable). In Board of Educ. of Independent School Dist. No. 92 v. Earls, 536 U.S. 822, 122 S.Ct. 2559, 153 L.Ed.2d 735 (2002), it was held that a school district's policy requiring *all* students—not only student athletes, as involved in the *Vernonia* case, *supra*—who participated in competitive extracurricular activities to submit to drug testing was a reasonable means of furthering the district's important interest in preventing and deterring drug use among schoolchildren and therefore did not violate the Fourth Amendment. See Comment, Shedding Their Rights: The Fourth Amendment and Suspicionless Drug Testing of Public School Student Participating in Extracurricular Activities, 51 Cath. U.L. Rev. 951 (2002). Compare Comment, Tiny Glimmer of Hope for Student Athletes Affected by Suspicionless Drug Testing Policies Rests in the States, 13 Seton Hall J. Sport L. 261 (2003) (discussing reasons why suspicionless drug-testing policies are not in the best interest of students and proposing that students' only hope of retaining their privacy rests in interpretations of state constitutions; *id.* at 289–96). In Board of Educ. of Independent School Dist. No. 92 v. Earls, 536 U.S. 822 122 S.Ct. 2559, 153 L.Ed.2d 735 (2002), it was held that a school district's policy requiring *all* students—not only student athletes, as involved in the *Vernonia* case, *supra*—who participated in competitive extracurricular activities to submit to drug testing was a reasonable means of furthering the district's important interest in preventing and deterring drug use among schoolchildren and therefore did not violate the Fourth Amendment. See Comment, Shedding Their Rights: the Fourth Amendment and Suspicionless Drug Testing of Public School Student Participating in Extracurricular Activities, 51 Cath. U.L. Rev. 951 (2002). In Hamm, Mandatory Drug Testing:

without obtaining leave, or being habitually tardy, have been upheld as adequate "causes."[72] Where, upon judicial review, a lack of adequate cause is found for the dismissal of an officer or employee who can be dismissed only for cause, the courts will order reinstatement of that worker, with back pay.[73]

Employees who have no statutory, charter, or contract rights may be dismissed without notice or hearing, and this is not considered a violation of procedural due process.[74] But if by statute, charter, or contract, either an officer or an employee has

---

Balancing the Interests, 30 Ariz. L. Rev. 297 (1988), the author (at 318) concludes that where there is no reasonable suspicion of an individual's drug use, mandatory testing should be limited to critical positions where drug-related impairment would pose a significant threat to fellow workers and/or the public; in these critical positions, a compelling state interest that justifies even random testing can be found. But see City & County of Denver v. Casados, 862 P.2d 908 (Colo.1993), cert. denied 511 U.S. 1005, 114 S.Ct. 1372, 128 L.Ed.2d 48 (1994) (provision requiring testing of those who did not hold public safety or security sensitive positions was not facially invalid in light of primary focus on detection and prevention of on-duty drug and alcohol use). See generally Weeks, Public Employee Drug Testing Under the Fourth Amendment After *Skinner* and *Von Raab*, 24 Urban Law. 515 (1992); Weeks, Public Employee Drug Testing Under the Fourth and Fifth Amendments: Where Are We Now and Where Are We Going Under Federal Decisions?, 20 Urban Law. 445 (1988); Note, Mandatory Drug Testing in the Public Work Sector: Erosion of Fourth Amendment Protections, 12 U. Bridgeport L. Rev. 293 (1991). See also Hoffman, Steal This Urine Test (Viking Penguin, Inc. 1987); Gottfredson & Uihlein, Drug Testing in the Workplace: A View from the Data, 33 Wm. & M.L. Rev. 127 (1991); Halbert, Coming up Dirty: Testing at the Workplace, 32 Villanova L. Rev. 691 (1987). Some cases have emphasized that a school's role is "custodial and tutelary" as to students, thus permitting a degree of supervision and control over drugs that could not ordinarily be exercised as to adults. See Hageman v. Goshen County School Dist. No. 1, 256 P.3d 487, 496 (Wyo. 2011), quoting the *Vernonia* case, *supra.* Cf. Note, Constitutional Law—"Can't Touch This": The Falling Standard of *New Jersey v. T.L.O.* in School Searches, 10 Wyo. L. Rev. 575 (2010), discussing Safford Unified School Dist. No. 1 v. Redding, 557 U.S. 364, 129 S.Ct. 2633, 174 L.Ed.2d 354 (2009). Some school searches have, however, included drug testing of *teachers*. See Cooley, Fleming & McFadden-Wade,The Constitutional and Contractual Controversy of Suspicionless Drug Testing of Public School Teachers, 63 Okla. L. Rev. 421 (2011).

[72] See Annot., Dismissal of Public School-Teacher Because of Unauthorized Absence or Tardiness, 78 A.L.R.3d 117 (1977). See also Annot., Right of Employer to Terminate Contract Because of Employee's Illness or Physical Incapacity, 21 A.L.R.2d 1247 (1952). It is generally said that "substantial evidence" must support a dismissal in order for a reviewing court to affirm. See Brown v. Personnel Bd. for City of Kenai, 327 P.3d 871 (Alaska 2014) (city employee engaged in sexual harassment); Wadsworth v. Board of Trustees of Lincoln County School Dist., 316 P.3d 541 (Wyo. 2014).

[73] Glenn v. Chambers, 242 Iowa 760, 48 N.W.2d 275 (1951); Cullen v. Mayor of Newton, 308 Mass. 578, 32 N.E.2d 201 (1941); Parker v. Township of West Bloomfield, 60 Mich.App. 583, 231 N.W.2d 424 (1975); Lilienthal v. Wyandotte, 286 Mich. 604, 282 N.W. 837 (1938); Thompson v. Civil Service Commission, 103 Utah 162, 134 P.2d 188 (1943); Schultz v. City of Pasco, 39 Wn.2d 262, 235 P.2d 168 (1951). An officer may be entitled to reinstatement if an office is abolished merely as a pretext for removing him, and then recreated for another person. See Mattia v. City of Newark, 122 N.J.L. 557, 6 A.2d 662 (1939); State ex rel. Thein v. City of Milwaukee, 229 Wis. 12, 281 N.W. 653 (1938). A reinstated employee is not necessarily entitled to exactly the same position and duties as he or she had prior to dismissal. See Maupin v. Independent School Dist. No. 26, 632 P.2d 396 (Okl.1981) (failure to reinstate teacher to coaching position did not result in failure to provide, as required, full employment status and benefits). Cf. Gelenter v. Greenville Municipal Separate School Dist., 644 So.2d 263 (Miss.1994) (school board's order to renew principal's contract but in a different position held proper).

Statutes sometimes now provide remedies for wrongful discharge, but these do not necessarily abrogate common-law actions for breach of covenant. See Reed v. Municipality of Anchorage, 782 P.2d 1155 (Alaska 1989) (statute created remedy for retaliatory discharge, but fired employee retained common-law cause of action for breach of contract). Tort actions, such as wrongful discharge, may be barred by the sovereign immunity of state and local governments. See Rouse v. Grand River Dam Auth., 326 P.3d 1139 (Okla. 2014) (discharged employee of state agency had no claim for wrongful termination except under Whistleblower Act). As to tort immunity, see Chapter 26 *infra*.

[74] Hodgin v. Noland, 435 F.2d 859 (4th Cir.1970), cert. denied 408 U.S. 942, 92 S.Ct. 2846, 33 L.Ed.2d 766; Sevina v. Hickok, 113 Cal.App. 301, 298 P. 116 (1931); In re Carter, 141 Cal. 316, 74 P. 997 (1903); Lentz v. City of Augusta, 48 Ga.App. 555, 173 S.E. 406 (1934); Riffe v. Finsby, 103 Ky. 631, 45 S.W. 1046 (1898); Williams v. City Manager of Haverhill, 330 Mass. 14, 110 N.E.2d 851 (1953); Perrella v. Board of Education,

property rights in his position, then he is entitled to procedural due process—meaning adequate notice and hearing.[75] These due process requirements ordinarily apply to (1)

---

51 N.J. 323, 240 A.2d 417 (1968); Ocean Hill-Brownsville Governing Board v. Board of Education, 30 A.D.2d 447, 294 N.Y.S.2d 134 (1968), aff'd 23 N.Y.2d 483, 297 N.Y.S.2d 568, 245 N.E.2d 219; Kropp v. North Tonawanda, 26 Misc.2d 127, 207 N.Y.S.2d 411 (Sup.Ct.1960); State ex rel. Wickline v. Jenkinson, 9 Ohio App.2d 39, 222 N.E.2d 825 (1966); Town of Davis v. Filler, 47 W.Va. 413, 35 S.E. 6 (1900). See Bishop v. Wood, 426 U.S. 341, 96 S.Ct. 2074, 48 L.Ed.2d 684 (1976) (policeman's liberty was not infringed when he was dismissed without a pretermination hearing, even though reasons publicly given for his dismissal probably weren't true); People ex rel. Gersch v. City of Chicago, 242 Ill. 561, 90 N.E. 259 (1909); Martin v. Aldermen of Newton, 337 Mass. 544, 150 N.E.2d 545 (1958); Sponenburgh v. Gillespie, 203 Mich. 379, 168 N.W. 1031 (1918); Scott v. Philadelphia Parking Authority, 402 Pa. 151, 166 A.2d 278 (1960) (ordinary employee takes subject to summary removal; is an employee-at-will). Probationary employees may be dismissed either during their probation or at the end thereof without notice or hearing. See Cooner v. Board of Educ., 136 Ariz. 11, 663 P.2d 1002 (App. 1982) (probationary teacher whose contract is not renewed is not entitled to hearing before board of education; court will review the non-renewal only if reason given is unreasonable, arbitrary or capricious); Clark v. City of Manchester, 113 N.H. 270, 305 A.2d 668 (1973); Edell v. Municipal Broadcasting System, 9 Misc.2d 220, 169 N.Y.S.2d 993 (Sup.Ct.1958). Cf. City of Jenks v. Stone, 321 P.3d 179 (Okla. 2014) (probationary employee is an at-will employee). See also note 65 *supra*. On the decline of at-will employment in both the public and private sectors, see Markowitz, The Demise of At-Will Employment and the Public Employee Conundrum, 27 Urban Law. 305 (1995).

Even an employee who has constitutionally protected rights in his or her position may be *suspended,* without pay, without notice and hearing. Gilbert v. Homar, 520 U.S. 924, 117 S.Ct. 1807, 138 L.Ed.2d 120 (1997) (state university employee suspended without pay following his arrest on drug-related charges; held not entitled under due process to notice and hearing prior to the suspension).

[75] See Perry v. Sindermann, 408 U.S. 593, 92 S.Ct. 2694, 33 L.Ed.2d 570 (1972); Board of Regents v. Roth, 408 U.S. 564, 92 S.Ct. 2701, 33 L.Ed.2d 548 (1972); Russell v. Hodges, 470 F.2d 212 (2d Cir.1972). See generally Toman, Practical Guidelines for Liberty Interest Hearings in Public Employee Dismissals, 14 Urban Law. 325 (1982), particularly discussing the *Roth* case *supra.*

In Cleveland Bd. of Educ. v. Loudermill, 470 U.S. 532, 105 S.Ct. 1487, 84 L.Ed.2d 494 (1985), on remand 763 F.2d 202 (6th Cir.1985), it was held that Due Process requires that any public employee having a constitutionally protected property interest in his employment be given some kind of a hearing *prior* to his discharge. Such pretermination hearing does not have to resolve definitively the propriety of the discharge but should serve as an initial check against mistaken decisions—a determination of whether there are reasonable grounds to believe the charges against the employee are true and support his discharge. See City of North Pole v. Zabek, 934 P.2d 1292 (Alaska 1997) (city's failure to give employee opportunity to be heard prior to her termination denied due process); Danielson v. City of Seattle, 108 Wash.2d 788, 742 P.2d 717 (1987) (pretermination hearing should serve as initial check against mistaken decisions, to determine whether there are reasonable grounds to believe charges against employee are true and support the proposed action). See generally Tans, Due Process and Pre-Termination Hearing, 2 Alaska Municipal Adviser, No. 4, at 3 (July, 1988). A good discussion of the *Loudermill* case, and its place in the law, is found at Note, Employment Law: Classification in Oklahoma Public Employment: Does It Really Matter?,53 Okla. L. Rev. 143, 146–47 (2000).

Whether or not statements in an employee handbook constitute an express or implied contract, giving the employee property rights in his job, is a question on which opinion is divided. Compare Farthing v. City of Shawnee, 39 F.3d 1131 (10th Cir. 1994) (provision in city manual did not give rise to property interest in municipal employment for due process purposes), and Williams v. West Jordan City, 714 F.2d 1017 (19th Cir. 1983) (mere distribution of personnel manual, listing grounds for dismissal and establishing grievance procedure, created no property rights in employees), with Vinyard v. King, 655 F.2d 1016 (10th Cir.1981), later proceedings 728 F.2d 428 (10th Cir.1984) (handbook amounted to contract where both employer and employee signed the last page, which contained an express statement that the employee could be discharged only for cause). A majority of state court opinions appear to hold that an employee manual may amount to a binding contract, though most of the cases have involved private employers. See Cleary v. American Airlines, Inc., 111 Cal.App.3d 443, 168 Cal.Rptr. 722 (1980); Kaiser v. Dixon, 127 Ill.App.3d 251, 82 Ill.Dec. 275, 468 N.E.2d 822 (1984); Weiner v. McGraw-Hill, Inc., 57 N.Y.2d 458, 457 N.Y.S.2d 193, 443 N.E.2d 441 (1982); Hammond v. North Dakota State Personnel Bd., 345 N.W.2d 359 (N.D.1984); Russell v. Board of County Comm'rs, 952 P.2d 492 (Okl.1997) (employee handbook may form basis of implied contract where competent parties, consent, legal object, and consideration are all present). Cf. Piacitelli v. Southern Utah State College, 636 P.2d 1063 (Utah 1981) (appellate court accepts as res judicata unappealed lower court finding that handbook amounts to contract). See also Cabaness v. Thomas, 232 P.3d 486 (Utah 2010) (employee manual created an implied contract that foreman would be protected from abusive and coercive conduct).

employees covered by civil-service laws,[76] (2) elected officials,[77] (3) officers appointed for a fixed term,[78] and (4) any officers or employees who are specified as holding their positions for "good behavior."[79] In addition, all officers and employees, whether or not within the civil-service system, are generally held entitled to procedural due process if they can, under a relevant law or contract, be dismissed only for "cause."[80]

Where procedural due process does have to be accorded an officer or employee prior to dismissal, such process must include three things: (1) an adequate notice to the worker, indicating (with particularity as to time and place) the specific acts or failures that are cited as grounds for the proposed dismissal, and also apprising the worker that a hearing will be held on this matter;[81] (2) a full and fair hearing at which the officer or

---

In Skeets v. Johnson, 805 F.2d 767 (8th Cir.1986), reh. granted 808 F.2d 1278 (8th Cir.1986), a grievance procedure provided in an employee manual of a state highway department was held to create a property interest in continued employment until a final dismissal decision was made. Cf. Howell v. Town of Carolina Beach, 106 N.C.App. 410, 417 S.E.2d 277 (1992) (personnel manual did not amount to employment agreement but did create reasonable expectation of employment within due process clause so that police officer could not be fired without receiving grievance hearing). But cf. Pittman v. Wilson County, 839 F.2d 225 (4th Cir.1988) (in absence of evidence that a "personnel resolution" in a county employee's handbook was a formally enacted ordinance, an employee had no property right in her employment, and her dismissal without a hearing was not a denial of due process). Apart from the question of whether a handbook is part of an employee's contract, it is certainly the general rule that if termination procedures *are* specified in an employee's contract or in a relevant ordinance, failure of an employer-government to follow those procedures will invalidate a discharge. See Anderson v. City of Lawton, 748 P.2d 53 (Okl. App. 1987).

[76] See Hanley v. Murphy, 40 Cal.2d 572, 255 P.2d 1 (1953) (civil service employee had to be given notice and opportunity to be heard; where he wasn't, dismissal could be set aside); State ex rel. Gibbs v. Bloodworth, 134 Fla. 369, 184 So. 1 (1938); Ervin v. Triplett, 236 Iowa 272, 18 N.W.2d 599 (1945); Ture v. Ecorse, 331 Mich. 380, 49 N.W.2d 339 (1951); Darmstatter v. Passaic, 81 N.J.L. 162, 79 A. 545 (1911); State ex rel. Ness v. City of Fargo, 63 N.D. 33, 245 N.W. 887 (1932). Cf. Civil Service Association v. City & County of San Francisco, 22 Cal.3d 552, 150 Cal.Rptr. 129, 586 P.2d 162 (1978) (suspended civil-service employees entitled to notice, with reasons, either during suspension or within a reasonable time thereafter); Umholtz v. City of Tulsa, 565 P.2d 15 (Okl.1977) (reasons for suspension must be given, but pre-suspension notice and hearing unnecessary).

[77] Dullam v. Willson, 53 Mich. 392, 19 N.W. 112 (1884); State ex rel. Ballmer v. Strever, 93 Neb. 762, 141 N.W. 820 (1913).

[78] State ex rel. Loeb v. Jordan, 149 La. 312, 89 So. 15 (1921); Hallgren v. Campbell, *supra* note 69; Gracey v. City of St. Louis, 213 Mo. 384, 111 S.W. 1159 (1908); Rosetty v. Township Committee, 82 N.J.Super. 340, 197 A.2d 600 (1964), aff'd 96 N.J.Super. 66, 232 A.2d 455. But see Bailen v. Board of Assessors, 241 Mass. 411, 135 N.E. 877 (1922); Smith v. Mayor & Board of Woonsocket, 127 A. 562 (R.I.1925).

[79] Shira v. State ex rel. Ham, 187 Ind. 441, 119 N.E. 833 (1918).

[80] See Farish v. Young, 18 Ariz. 298, 158 P. 845 (1916); Walton v. Davis, 188 Ga. 56, 2 S.E.2d 603 (1939); Will v. Herington, 201 Kan. 627, 443 P.2d 667 (1968); Board of Street Commissioners v. Williams, 96 Md. 232, 53 A. 923 (1903); Ham v. Board of Police, 142 Mass. 90, 7 N.E. 540 (1886); Rowell v. City of Battle Creek, 169 Mich. 19, 135 N.W. 79 (1912); Larson v. Bunch, 208 Okl. 278, 255 P.2d 486 (1953); Riccio v. Town Council of Bristol, 109 R.I. 431, 286 A.2d 881 (1972). Cf. Becker v. Sunset City, 309 P.3d 223 (Utah 2013) (police officer could only be discharged for cause and thus held a property interest in employment that is protected by due process, including adequate notice and a hearing; termination here upheld).

[81] See Olson v. Regents of University of Minnesota, 301 F.Supp. 1356 (D.Minn.1969); Civil Service Commission v. Mills, 23 Ariz.App. 499, 534 P.2d 430 (1975) (notice not sufficiently specific); Burklin v. Willis, 97 So.2d 129 (Fla.App.1957); Jones v. Mayor of Athens, 105 Ga.App. 86, 123 S.E.2d 420 (1961); Mills v. City of Winchester, 130 Ind.App. 397, 162 N.E.2d 97 (1959); Robbins v. New Orleans Public Library, 208 So.2d 25 (La.App.1968); State ex rel. Denison v. City of St. Louis, 90 Mo. 19, 1 S.W. 757 (1886); Owens v. Ackerman, 72 O.L.A. 552, 136 N.E.2d 93 (Ct.App.1955); In re Johnston Appeal, 181 Pa.Super. 448, 124 A.2d 652 (1956); Ridgway v. City of Fort Worth, 243 S.W. 740 (Tex.Civ.App.1922), error dism'd. Cf. State ex rel. Felthoff v. Richards, 203 Ind. 637, 180 N.E. 596 (1932) (notice must indicate that hearing will be held, and also the reasons asserted for dismissal). In Lovelace v. Ingram, 518 P.2d 1102 (Okl.1973), a notice to a dismissed school teacher was held inadequate where it stated as the reasons for dismissal: "1. System of grading. 2. Partial to certain students. 3. Complaints of some parents on method of teaching." It is often stated as a rule-of-thumb that notice must be sufficiently specific that a dismissed officer or employee can prepare a defense against the reasons alleged for the dismissal. See Breeden v. City of Nome, 628 P.2d 924 (Alaska 1981); Sudduth v. Board

employee has a reasonable opportunity to present evidence,[82] and (3) a decision supported by the evidence.[83] In some states, statutes provide administrative review of dismissals.[84] In any case, there is the possibility of a dismissed officer or employee obtaining *judicial* review, but this is ordinarily very limited. The judicial review is usually obtained by certiorari, and is limited to a determination of whether there is *some* valid evidence to support the action taken; the evidence is not weighed to determine where a preponderance lies.[85]

Aside from dismissal of an officer or employee by the authority that has power to hire and fire for that position, there are several other means of removing *officers*—most of these methods generally apply *only* to officers, not employees. *Recall* of local officers by the voters is possible in many states—and is discussed *infra*, along with methods used for popular initiation and passage of legislation. *Impeachment* of local officers is

---

of Fire and Police Commissioners, 48 Ill.App.2d 194, 198 N.E.2d 705 (1964); Town of West New York v. Bock, 38 N.J. 500, 186 A.2d 97 (1962); Brassard v. McCarthy, 83 R.I. 479, 120 A.2d 325 (1956). Cf. City of Washington v. Boger, 132 Ind.App. 192, 176 N.E.2d 484 (1961) (not enough that notice gives the conclusions drawn by the dismissing authorities). See generally Annot., Sufficiency of Notice of Intention to Discharge or Not to Rehire Teacher, Under Statutes Requiring Such Notice, 52 A.L.R.4th 301 (1987). See also Gray v. Board of Higher Educ., 692 F.2d 901 (2d Cir.1982) (absent a statement of reasons for refusing to grant tenure to university instructor, instructor is entitled to discover how individual faculty members voted in order for him to obtain evidence of possible discrimination). Municipal ordinances sometimes reiterate, or elaborate on, statutory and constitutional guarantees. See Town of Evansville Police Dept. v. Porter, 256 P.3d 476 (Wyo. 2011) (town ordinance specified that pretermination procedural due process required written notice and a taped record of any informal hearing).

[82] See Rockefeller v. Hogue, 244 Ark. 1029, 429 S.W.2d 85 (1968) (officer or employee entitled to public hearing if desires it); Conley v. Board of Education, 143 Conn. 488, 123 A.2d 747 (1956) (right to hearing includes right to hear local government's evidence in support of the dismissal). The right to a hearing also usually includes the right of the officer or employee to be represented by legal counsel at that hearing. See Fusco v. Moses, 304 N.Y. 424, 107 N.E.2d 581 (1952). And the right to have a stenographer present at the hearing to make an accurate record. Johnson v. Cohasset, 263 Minn. 425, 116 N.W.2d 692 (1962).

On the right of non-probationary federal employees to a hearing prior to dismissal, and the kind of hearing necessary, see Arnett v. Kennedy, 416 U.S. 134, 94 S.Ct. 1633, 40 L.Ed.2d 15 (1974), reh. denied 417 U.S. 977, 94 S.Ct. 3187, 41 L.Ed.2d 1148, in which the Court was badly split—but six Justices did agree that some hearing was necessary to satisfy due process. It is agreed that the hearing must be before a fair and impartial tribunal. See Phillips v. Board of Fire and Police Commissioners, 24 Ill.App.3d 242, 320 N.E.2d 355 (1974); Guido v. City of Marion, 151 Ind.App. 435, 280 N.E.2d 81 (1972); State ex rel. Beam v. Fulwiler, 76 Wn.2d 313, 456 P.2d 322 (1969) (members of body that originally investigated charges should not sit in judgment at the hearing on those charges).

[83] See Will v. Herington, *supra* note 80; Auge v. Anderson, 112 R.I. 296, 309 A.2d 17 (1973).

[84] See Tennant v. Finane & Vicksburg, 227 Miss. 410, 86 So.2d 453 (1956); Borough of Park Ridge v. Salimone, 21 N.J. 28, 120 A.2d 721 (1956); Cassese v. Lindsay, 51 Misc.2d 59, 272 N.Y.S.2d 324 (Sup.Ct.1966) (civilian review board for police department upheld despite charges its creation involved an unlawful delegation of power). Cf. Daytona Beach v. Civil Service Board, 314 So.2d 168 (Fla.App.1975) (charter provided that hearing had to be held within specified time if requested by employee, or board's jurisdiction would be lost; court held that board did not have to *complete* the hearing within the specified time). Where administrative review is provided, the protesting employee or officer must exhaust the administrative remedies before seeking judicial review. Blake v. Public Utilities Comm'n, 120 Cal.App.2d 671, 261 P.2d 773 (Dist.Ct.1953); Sullivan v. Roe, 18 N.J. 156, 113 A.2d 1 (1955); City of Corpus Christi v. Stowe, 338 S.W.2d 767 (Tex.Civ.App.1960).

[85] See Walker v. Dunham, 78 Ariz. 419, 281 P.2d 125 (1955) (court won't weigh evidence on certiorari); McKenzie v. Board of Educ., 1 Cal.App. 406, 82 P. 392 (Dist.Ct.1905); Aurora v. Schoberlein, 230 Ill. 496, 82 N.E. 860 (1907); In re Fredericks, 285 Mich. 262, 280 N.W. 464 (1938); Lewis v. City of Omaha, 153 Neb. 11, 43 N.W.2d 419 (1950). Increasingly, statutes lay down the precise method(s) to be used by a public officer or employee appealing a dismissal, and such specified methods are usually exclusive. See Tennant v. Finane & Vicksburg, *supra* note 84.

authorized by a number of state constitutions, and sometimes by statute or charter.[86] Often the local legislative body will try cases involving impeachment of local officers, and it has been held this body may act even on impeachment of one of its own members.[87]

Quo warranto or *ouster* proceedings are also authorized by many constitutions, statutes, or charters. These proceedings are initiated by the state attorney-general or other designated officer and must be based on grounds specified in the relevant legislation, such as conviction of a crime of moral turpitude.[88] Miscellaneous methods of removal are allowed under the statutes of various states. Sometimes the governor can remove local officials for neglect of duty;[89] and in a few states, citizens can initiate removal proceedings against a local officer by filing a complaint with a local judge.[90]

§ 14.6 Resignations

An officer or employee of local government can resign the position, either by formal act of resignation or by some act that clearly implies resignation.[91] Two things are needed: (1) an intention to surrender the position (which, of course, can be inferred from actions), and (2) a positive act of relinquishment.[92] Controversy exists over whether there is a third requirement: acceptance of the resignation by the local government. The majority view is that such acceptance is necessary before the resignation takes effect, since a position of public trust is being surrendered.[93] The acceptance, like the resignation itself, may be either by formal act or by any action implying agreement.[94] Until the resignation is accepted by the local government, it can, according to most

---

86 See Wallace v. State, 58 Del. 521, 211 A.2d 845 (1965), applying the impeachment provision of the Delaware Constitution.

87 Poirier v. Martineau, 86 R.I. 473, 136 A.2d 814 (1957).

88 See People ex rel. Ward v. Tomek, 54 Ill.App.2d 197, 203 N.E.2d 744 (1964) (applying the Illinois statute, which provides for ouster on conviction of an infamous crime; conspiracy held to be such a crime); McDonald v. Brooks, 215 Tenn. 535, 387 S.W.2d 803 (1965) (ouster not justified; proceedings could be enjoined); State ex rel. Schroeder v. McAllister, 365 S.W.2d 696 (Tex.Civ.App.1963) (ouster is penal in nature; statute will be strictly construed).

89 See Frederick v. Combs, 354 S.W.2d 506 (Ky.1962), applying the Kentucky statute on gubernatorial removal of local officers.

90 See State ex rel. Stokes v. Probate Court, 17 Ohio App.2d 247, 246 N.E.2d 607 (1969), appeal dism'd 22 Ohio St.2d 120, 258 N.E.2d 594, applying the Ohio statute providing for complaints about local officers to be filed with the county judge.

91 Warner v. Selectmen of Amherst, 326 Mass. 435, 95 N.E.2d 180 (1950). An officer's abandonment of his office may be treated as a resignation. State ex rel. Schaub v. Scottsbluff, 169 Neb. 525, 100 N.W.2d 202 (1960); City of Tulsa v. Johnson, 196 Okl. 213, 163 P.2d 993 (1945). Similarly, accepting an incompatible office. See Chapter 13 *supra*. On the effect of a resignation on tenure rights, see Annot., Termination of Teacher's Tenure Status by Resignation, 9 A.L.R.4th 729 (1981), saying that resignation by a tenured teacher usually terminates any rights to tenure, but noting some contrary authority.

92 See State ex rel. Reeder v. Municipal Civil Service Commission, 82 O.L.A. 225, 165 N.E.2d 490 (Com.Pl. 1958).

93 Green v. Jones, 144 W.Va. 276, 108 S.E.2d 1 (1959). See Campbell v. City of Boston, 337 Mass. 676, 151 N.E.2d 68 (1958) (once resignation tendered and accepted, is immediate severance from office). Under this view, the officers remain in office unless and until the resignation is accepted by the proper authority. See Haine v. Googe, 248 F.Supp. 349 (S.D.N.Y.1965) (officer responsible for duties of office until resignation accepted). But see Meeker v. Reed, 70 Cal.App. 119, 232 P. 760 (Dist.Ct.1924), applying the view that a resignation takes effect immediately on the date mentioned in the resignation itself, if it is filed as provided by law.

94 Sawyer v. City of San Antonio, 149 Tex. 408, 234 S.W.2d 398 (1950) (a formal declaration or something tantamount to an acceptance will suffice). See Kidder v. Mayor of Cambridge, 304 Mass. 491, 24 N.E.2d 151 (1939); Crouch v. Texas City, 459 S.W.2d 491 (Tex.Civ.App.1970), ref'd n. r. e.

authority, be withdrawn.[95] A resignation will be thrown out by the courts and treated as a nullity if it is shown to have been given under duress or because of undue influence.[96]

§ 14.7 Unionization of Government Personnel; Strikes and Other Labor-Organization Activities

Officers and employees of local governments often attempt to assert their collective rights through unionization, and increasingly this is being allowed. In the past, legislative bans on unionization by police officers and firefighters were very common and were generally sustained.[97] Bans on unionization of other local government workers were often upheld also.[98] But the great weight of authority now recognizes the right of public workers to unionize,[99] and holds that union membership cannot be made a ground for discharge of such workers.[100] Occasionally, state statutes now specifically *recognize* the right of local officers and employees to unionize, and city laws to the contrary are then invalidated simply on the basis of the conflict with state law.[101] But even in the

---

[95] Haine v. Googe, *supra* note 93; City of Dothan v. Lucas, 47 Ala.App. 336, 254 So.2d 341 (1971); Commonwealth ex rel. Wootton v. Berninger, 255 Ky. 451, 74 S.W.2d 932 (1934); Greene v. Freeholders of Hudson County, 44 N.J.L. 388 (1882); Garcia v. Angelini, 412 S.W.2d 949 (Tex.Civ.App.1967). But where the view is applied that the resignation is effective as soon as filed with the proper authorities, withdrawal after such filing is usually not permitted. See Amy v. Watertown, 130 U.S. 301, 9 S.Ct. 530, 32 L.Ed. 946 (1889); Allen v. Powell, 42 Ill.2d 66, 244 N.E.2d 596 (1969); State ex rel. Kleinsteuber v. Kotecki, 155 Wis. 66, 144 N.W. 200 (1913). Cf. City of Amarillo v. Mendenhall, 276 S.W.2d 868 (Tex.Civ.App.1955), ref'd n. r. e. (police officer had given resignation to chief, who had given it to civil service commission; too late to withdraw).

[96] Keithley v. Civil Service Bd., 11 Cal.App.3d 443, 89 Cal.Rptr. 809 (Dist.Ct.1970); Crouch v. Texas City, *supra* note 94; Willborn v. Deans, 240 S.W.2d 791 (Tex.Civ.App.1951), ref'd n. r. e. See Odorizzi v. Bloomfield School Dist., 246 Cal.App.2d 123, 54 Cal.Rptr. 533 (Dist.Ct.1966), defining undue influence.

[97] See Fraternal Order of Police v. Harris, 306 Mich. 68, 10 N.W.2d 310 (1943), cert. denied 321 U.S. 784, 64 S.Ct. 781, 88 L.Ed. 1076 (1944); Hutchinson v. Magee, 278 Pa. 119, 122 A. 234 (1923); San Antonio Fire Fighters' Local v. Bell, 223 S.W. 506 (Tex.Civ.App.1920), error ref'd; McNatt v. Lawther, 223 S.W. 503 (Tex.Civ.App.1920); Carter v. Thompson, 164 Va. 312, 180 S.E. 410 (1935). Cf. Local No. 201 v. City of Muskegon, 369 Mich. 384, 120 N.W.2d 197 (1963), cert. denied 375 U.S. 833, 84 S.Ct. 54, 11 L.Ed.2d 64 (police officers could not accept membership in a union if people other than members of the police department belonged to that union).

[98] See Hayman v. City of Los Angeles, 17 Cal.App.2d 674, 62 P.2d 1047 (Dist.Ct.1936) (garbage collectors); Congress of Industrial Organizations v. City of Dallas, 198 S.W.2d 143 (Tex.Civ.App.1946) (city ordinance prohibiting city employees from joining labor union upheld). See generally Note, 54 Harv.L.Rev. 1360 (1941).

[99] American Federation of State, County, and Municipal Employees v. Woodward, 406 F.2d 137 (8th Cir.1969); McLaughlin v. Tilendis, 398 F.2d 287 (7th Cir.1968); Atkins v. City of Charlotte, 296 F.Supp. 1068 (W.D.N.C.1969). See Lontine v. VanCleave, 483 F.2d 966 (10th Cir.1973) (deputy sheriff could join union); Hagan v. Picard, 171 Misc. 475, 12 N.Y.S.2d 873 (1939), aff'd 258 App.Div. 771, 14 N.Y.S.2d 706. See generally Annot.,Right of Public Employees to Form or Join a Labor Organization Affiliated with a Federation of Trade Unions or Which Includes Private Employees, 40 A.L.R.3d 728 (1971). As with membership in labor unions in general, such membership by government personnel has declined or grown very slightly in recent decades. See Trottman, Union Membership Stagnates Around 11%, Wall St. J., Jan. 24–25, 2015, at A-3, stating "Membership rate in the public sector was once a bright spot for union growth, but has taken a hit in recent years."

[100] Norwalk Teachers' Association v. Board of Education, 138 Conn. 269, 83 A.2d 482 (1951). See Ohland v. Dubay, 133 Vt. 300, 336 A.2d 203 (1975) (alleged wrongful discharge of police officer because of his union activity).

[101] See Stearns v. Commission of Public Docks, 246 Or. 36, 423 P.2d 748 (1967); Beverly v. City of Dallas, 292 S.W.2d 172 (Tex.Civ.App.1956), ref'd n. r. e. (Texas statute held to allow unionization of public employees). Cf. State ex rel. Missey v. City of Cabool, 441 S.W.2d 35 (Mo.1969) (employer, refusing to recognize union, violated statute). Major impetus to the movement toward statutory authorization of unionization by government employees was provided by President Kennedy's issuing, in 1962, of Executive Order 10988, allowing many federal employees to unionize and bargain.

absence of legislative authorization, bans on unions of public workers are generally invalidated now on some one or more of three possible grounds: (1) The ban is usually now considered to violate the First Amendment's guarantee of freedom of association.[102] (2) The prohibition may occasionally be considered unduly broad and thus a violation of Fourteenth Amendment due process.[103] (3) In states having "right-to-work laws," any ban on unionization of public workers may be considered in violation of those laws, since the "right-to-work" provisions declare that no one shall be denied employment because of union membership or non-membership.[104]

But though unionization of public officers and employees is now allowed, the law in many states has not gone beyond mere legal recognition of such unions. Where the *activities* of unions of public workers are concerned, four important limitations are often applied:

(1) The *closed or union shop* arrangement, under which workers are required to join a union in order to acquire a job (or, in the case of the union shop, retain the job), has not been allowed in public employment.[105] Such arrangements have been considered

---

[102] See Lontine v. Van Cleave, *supra* note 99; American Federation of State, County, and Municipal Employees v. Woodward, *supra* note 99; Atkins v. City of Charlotte, *supra* note 99. Cf. Texas State Teachers Ass'n v. Garland Independent School Dist., 777 F.2d 1046 (5th Cir.1985), judgment aff'd 479 U.S. 801, 107 S.Ct. 41, 93 L.Ed.2d 4 (1986) (public employees such as teachers could not be deprived of all opportunities to discuss matters relating to employee organizations, though teachers could be restricted to having such discussions during nonclass time). But cf. Smith v. Arkansas State Highway Employees, 441 U.S. 463, 99 S.Ct. 1826, 60 L.Ed.2d 360 (1979) (public employer can validly require that employee submit a grievance to employer in writing before it will be considered).

[103] Melton v. City of Atlanta, 324 F.Supp. 315 (N.D.Ga.1971). Even bans that merely prohibit police and/or fire officers from joining unions are now usually invalidated as violations of freedom of association or due process. See Lontine v. Van Cleave, *supra* note 99. Cf. Escanaba v. Michigan Labor Mediation Board, 19 Mich.App. 273, 172 N.W.2d 836 (1969) (applying Michigan statute). But see Elk Grove Firefighters Local v. Willis, 400 F.Supp. 1097 (N.D.Ill.1975), aff'd 539 F.2d 714 (7th Cir.) (fire department captains and lieutenants could be prohibited from joining unions).

[104] Levasseur v. Wheeldon, 79 S.D. 442, 112 N.W.2d 894 (1962). See Potts v. Hay, 229 Ark. 830, 318 S.W.2d 826 (1958); Miami Water Works Local v. City of Miami, 157 Fla. 445, 26 So.2d 194 (1946); Beverly v. City of Dallas, *supra* note 101.

[105] See City of Los Angeles v. Los Angeles Building & Constr. Trades Council, 94 Cal.App.2d 36, 210 P.2d 305 (Dist.Ct.1949); Mugford v. City of Baltimore, 185 Md. 266, 44 A.2d 745 (1945); Benson v. School Dist., 136 Mont. 77, 344 P.2d 117 (1959); Petrucci v. Hogan, 5 Misc.2d 480, 27 N.Y.S.2d 718 (1941).

In Abood v. Detroit Bd. of Educ., 431 U.S. 209, 97 S.Ct. 1782, 52 L.Ed.2d 261 (1977), reh. denied 433 U.S. 915, 97 S.Ct. 2989, 53 L.Ed.2d 1102, the Court upheld as to public employment the so-called "agency shop" arrangement under which employees don't have to join the union but if they don't join must pay the union a service-charge equal to regular dues. The Court ruled that such service-charges can only be used to support such union activities as collective bargaining, contract administration, and grievance adjustment procedures, which benefit all employees, and may not be used to support political causes or candidates that an individual non-member does not favor. See Lehnert v. Ferris Faculty Ass'n, 500 U.S. 507, 111 S.Ct. 1950, 114 L.Ed.2d 572 (1991) (state could not compel public employees under agency shop arrangement to subsidize legislative lobbying or other political activity of union outside the limited context of contract ratification or implementation). In Harris v. Quinn, ___ U.S. ___, 134 S.Ct. 2618 (2014), the *Abood* case's requirement that state employees pay an agency fee to support union work that is related to the collective-bargaining process was held inapplicable to Medicaid-funded home-care personal assistants in Illinois, who were state employees under Illinois law only for collective-bargaining purposes and were otherwise regarded as private-sector employees. The *Abood* Court's analysis was called questionable, but the case was not overruled. See Walsh, Division of Labor, A.B.A.J., Sept., 2014, at 20. On the "agency shop," cf. Chicago Teachers Union, Local No. 1 v. Hudson, 475 U.S. 292, 106 S.Ct. 1066, 89 L.Ed.2d 232 (1986), on remand 117 F.R.D. 413 (N.D.Ill.1987), aff'd 922 F.2d 1306 (7th Cir.1991), cert. denied 501 U.S. 1230, 111 S.Ct. 2852, 115 L.Ed.2d 1020 (1991), cert. denied 501 U.S. 1230, 111 S.Ct. 2852, 115 L.Ed.2d 1020 (1991) (nonunion employee whose First Amendment rights are affected by an agency shop arrangement and who bears burden of agency fee is entitled to be given sufficient information to determine propriety of fee and is entitled to have objections addressed in an

discriminatory, inconsistent with civil-service laws, and violative of the principle that public employment should not depend on membership in a private organization.

(2) Considerable authority has struck down, often as an undue delegation of governmental authority to a private group, arrangements by which a local government "*checks off*" (*i.e.*, automatically deducts from workers' paychecks, and pays directly to the union) the amount of union dues.[106] The U.S. Supreme Court has upheld a city's refusal to "check off" union dues even where the city made deductions from workers' paychecks for charitable and various other purposes.[107] But there is now some trend to *allow* union "checkoffs" where cities are willing to perform them, so long as they are done on a nondiscriminatory basis for other purposes as well, and so long as each worker whose wages are "checked off" has consented to this.[108]

(3) At common law, most courts have held that local governments may not validly enter into *collective bargaining agreements* with their workers.[109] Such agreements have been invalidated as an abdication of the continuing responsibility of the legislative

---

expeditious, fair, and objective manner). See generally on agency-fee litigation Kurtz & Ruben, Recent Developments in Public Employment Relations, 19 Urban Law. 1021, 1033–37 (1987). See generally on the "agency shop," Comment, Impact of the Agency Shop on Labor Relations in the Public Sector, 55 Cornell L.Q. 547 (1970). Compare Board of Regents of Univ. of Wis. Sys. v. Southworth, 529 U.S. 217, 120 S.Ct. 1346, 146 L.Ed.2d 193 (2000) (First Amendment allows a public university to charge its students an activity fee used to fund a program facilitating extracurricular student speech, provided allocation of funding support is viewpoint neutral; *Abood* case *supra* distinguished). In Knox v. Service Employees Internatl. Union, ___ U.S. ___, 132 S.Ct. 2277, 183 L.Ed.2d 281 (2012), the Court held that the First Amendment requires a union to provide nonmembers with a fresh "*Hudson* notice"—as required in the *Hudson* case *supra*—whenever the union imposes a special assessment or dues increase, whether or not the assessment or increase is imposed for political purposes. See generally Note, Public Employees at the School of Hard *Knox*: How the Supreme Court Is Turning Public-Sector Unions Into a History Lesson, 39 Wm. Mitchell L. Rev. 1404 (2013).

See also Seidemann v. Bowen, 499 F.3d 119 (2d Cir. 2007) (union's agency fee procedure, which requires nonunion employees to file annual objections to expenditures and to specify percentages of expenditures in dispute to obtain arbitration, violates the nonunion employees' First Amendment rights by placing an unnecessary burden on those employees).

As to "fair share" arrangements, see American Federation of State, County & Municipal Employees v. City of Phoenix, 213 Ariz. 358, 142 P.3d 234 (2006) ("fair share" proposal of union representing city employees, which would have required all workers, including non-union workers, to contribute to union for services performed for workers' benefit, violated state constitution and "right to work" statutes; although the "fair share" may have been less than full union dues, it was the compulsion rather than the amount that was significant).

[106] Foltz v. City of Dayton, 22 Ohio Misc. 27, 254 N.E.2d 395 (Com.Pl.1969); Hagerman v. City of Dayton, 147 Ohio St. 313, 71 N.E.2d 246 (1947); City of Cleveland v. Division 268, 15 Ohio Supp. 76, 30 O.O. 395 (C.P.1945).

[107] City of Charlotte v. Local 660, 426 U.S. 283, 96 S.Ct. 2036, 48 L.Ed.2d 636 (1976).

[108] Kirkpatrick v. Reid, 193 Misc. 702, 85 N.Y.S.2d 378 (Sup.Ct.1968). See Mugford v. City of Baltimore, *supra* note 105 (dues could be collected by city on individual request), noted 9 Md.L.Rev. 70 (1948).

[109] Nutter v. City of Santa Monica, 74 Cal.App.2d 292, 168 P.2d 741 (Dist.Ct.1946); Fellows v. LaTronica, 151 Colo. 300, 377 P.2d 547 (1962) (with review of cases); Dade County v. Amalgamated Association, 157 So.2d 176 (Fla.App.1963), cert. denied 379 U.S. 971, 85 S.Ct. 642, 13 L.Ed.2d 563; Cook County Police Association v. Harvey, 8 Ill.App.3d 147, 289 N.E.2d 226 (1972); City of Springfield v. Clouse, 356 Mo. 1239, 206 S.W.2d 539 (1947); International Brotherhood of Electrical Workers v. City of Hastings, 179 Neb. 455, 138 N.W.2d 822 (1965); Weakley County Municipal Electric System v. Vick, 43 Tenn.App. 524, 309 S.W.2d 792 (1957); Amalgamated Transit Union v. Dallas Public Transit Board, 430 S.W.2d 107 (Tex.Civ.App.1968), ref'd n. r. e., cert. denied 396 U.S. 838, 90 S.Ct. 99, 24 L.Ed.2d 89. Cf. Shelofsky v. Helsby, 32 N.Y.2d 54, 343 N.Y.S.2d 98, 295 N.E.2d 774 (1973), appeal dism'd, 414 U.S. 804, 94 S.Ct. 60, 38 L.Ed.2d 41 (supervisory personnel have no right to bargain collectively). See generally Ripley, Meet Your Government Workers, Time magazine, March 7, 2011, at 40, noting some movement toward eliminating collective bargaining in the public sector but commenting: "Eliminating collective-bargaining rights will not fix the main problem, which is a lack of healthy incentives." *Id.* at 44.

governing body; as inconsistent with the civil-service system; as not reasonably necessary because the dangers of exploitation of labor and undue profit-seeking that are found in the private sector of the economy don't exist in the public sphere; and as involving an undue delegation of governmental power, thus leading to a government of people and not of laws. A few cases at common law, generally involving transit or utility workers, have upheld collective bargaining by local entities.[110] Some authority now allows collective bargaining with public workers—but this is largely brought on by the legislatures, not the courts. Statutes in many states now authorize collective bargaining with some or all local-government workers.[111] But some topics—such as, in the case of

[110] Local 266, International Brotherhood of Electrical Workers v. Salt River Project Agricultural Improvement and Power District, 78 Ariz. 30, 275 P.2d 393 (1954) (utility workers); International Brotherhood of Electrical Workers v. Town of Farmington, 75 N.M. 393, 405 P.2d 233 (1965) (same); Civil Service Forum v. New York City Transit Authority, 4 A.D.2d 117, 163 N.Y.S.2d 476 (1957), aff'd 4 N.Y.2d 866, 174 N.Y.S.2d 234, 150 N.E.2d 705 (1958) (transit workers); City of Alcoa v. International Brotherhood of Electrical Workers, 203 Tenn. 12, 308 S.W.2d 476 (1957), noted 25 Tenn.L.Rev. 511 (1958); Christie v. Port of Olympia, 27 Wn.2d 534, 179 P.2d 294 (1947); State ex rel. Fire Fighters Local No. 946 v. City of Laramie, 437 P.2d 295 (Wyo.1968). See Richmond Education Association v. Crockford, 55 F.R.D. 362 (E.D.Va.1972).

[111] See City & County of Denver v. Denver Firefighters Local No. 858, 663 P.2d 1032 (Colo.1983) (grievance arbitration under a collective bargaining agreement ruled constitutional and desirable under authorizing statutes; undue-delegation-of-authority argument rejected); City of Detroit v. Detroit Police Officers Association, 408 Mich. 410, 294 N.W.2d 68 (1980) (no unlawful delegation of powers); Roseville v. Local No. 1614, 53 Mich.App. 547, 220 N.W.2d 147 (1974), sustaining such legislation; City of Anadarko v. Fraternal Order of Police, Lodge No. 118, 934 P.2d 328 (Okl.1997) (statute permitting binding interest arbitration between municipalities and their police and firefighters did not deny access to courts in violation of state constitution and did not violate public policy of state); Fraternal Order of Police, Lodge No. 165 v. City of Choctaw, 933 P.2d 261 (Okl.1996) (statute providing for binding interest arbitration between municipality and its police and firefighters did not improperly delegate power to arbitrator and did not violate "home rule" doctrine); City of Bethany v. Public Employees Relations Bd., 904 P.2d 604 (Okl.1995) (statute on collective bargaining between municipalities and their police and firefighters does not violate state constitutional prohibition of special laws); City of Roseburg v. Roseburg City Firefighters, 292 Or. 266, 639 P.2d 90 (1981), holding that state legislation prevailed over conflicting municipal ordinance. Mandamus was held the appropriate remedy to use in challenging a city's refusal to honor an arbitral award in Garner v. City of Tulsa, 651 P.2d 1325 (Okl.1982). See generally Baird & Walters, Recent Developments in Public Sector Labor Law, 14 Urban Law. 869, 869–81 (1982); Annot., Validity and Construction of Statutes Providing for Arbitration of Labor Disputes Involving Public Employees, 68 A.L.R.3d 885 (1976); 2A Antieau, Municipal Corporation Law § 22.46 (1998). See also Ritter, The Duty to Bargain Under Education Labor Relations Acts, 17 Urban Law. 571 (1985), stating that over 30 states have comprehensive collective bargaining statutes that cover most public employees. A good symposium on collective bargaining by public employers and employees is Collective Bargaining in the Public Sector, 1 Okla. C.U.L. Rev. 1–155 (1976). An excellent refutation of the argument that statutes mandating collective bargaining by governmental units, and authorizing collective bargaining agreements by such units, constitute an undue delegation of governmental authority is found in Westbrook, The Use of the Nondelegation Doctrine in Public Sector Labor Law: Lessons from Cases That Have Perpetuated an Anachronism, 30 St. Louis U.L.J. 331 (1986). But cf. County of Riverside v. Superior Court, 30 Cal.4th 278, 132 Cal.Rptr.2d 713, 66 P.3d 718 (2003) (statute requiring counties to submit to binding arbitration of economic issues that arise during negotiations with unions representing firefighters or law enforcement officers violates state constitutional prohibition of legislature's delegating to a private body the function of establishing compensation for county employees). See generally Comment, Stealing the Public Purse: Why Washington's Collective Bargaining Law for State Employees Violates the State Constitution, 81 Wash. L. Rev. 159 (2006). As to the controversy in Wisconsin and elsewhere regarding termination of collective-bargaining rights of public employees, see Murphy, The Real Stakes in Wisconsin, Time magazine, March 14, 2011, at 24, noting that collective bargaining for public employees didn't gain strength till the 1960's and was, at the time of the article, adopted in 26 states but had not been largely adopted as to federal workers. *Id.* See generally Kramer, High "C's" Ahead: Public Employer Collective Bargaining, Contractual and Constitutional Hurdles in Concessionary Bargaining, 42 Urban Law. 739 (2010), commenting that "There are numerous decisions where courts have found state attempts to impair rights under collective bargaining agreements violate the Contract Clause" of the U.S. Constitution. *Id.* at 757. See also Rosenthal, Public Sector Collective Bargaining, Majoritarianism, and Reform, 91 Or. L. Rev. 673 (2013). Compare Befort, The Constitutional Dimension of Unilateral Change in Public-Sector Collective Bargaining, 27 A.B.A.J. Labor & Employment L. 165 (2012) (part of Symposium on Public Employment in Times of Crisis).

teachers, matters of academic freedom and questions of the creation and consolidation of academic departments—are generally held outside the scope of collective bargaining, even under statutes specifically allowing such bargaining.[112]

(4) Finally, at common law, *strikes* by public officers or employees have almost universally been condemned as not within the rights of such workers[113] and have been

---

Some statutes merely require a public body to "meet and confer" with the labor organization, with any proposals coming from the meetings being submitted to the local governing body for acceptance or rejection, while other statutes provide for binding agreements to be made by representatives of the public employer and the union. See Edwards, The Emerging Duty to Bargain in the Public Sector, 71 Mich.L.Rev. 885, 895 (1973). Cases interpreting the "meet and confer" type of statute include Glendale City Employees' Association v. City of Glendale, 15 Cal.3d 328, 124 Cal.Rptr. 513, 540 P.2d 609 (1975), cert. denied 424 U.S. 943, 96 S.Ct. 1411, 47 L.Ed.2d 349 (agreement binding once it is approved by city council); State ex rel. Missey v. City of Cabool, 441 S.W.2d 35 (Mo.1969) (no obligation to accept the agreement). Note that some of the same objections made to collective bargaining at common law—such as the bargaining being an undue delegation of governmental authority—may still exist where there is an authorizing statute. See generally Troy, Are Municipal Collective Bargaining and Municipal Governance Compatible?, 5 U. Pa. J. Lab. & Emp. L. 453 (2003). See also Symposium, Public Sector Collective Bargaining and the Distortion of Democracy: Do Public Sector Unions Have "Too Much" Power?, 34 Comparative Labor L. & Pol'y J. 245–555 (2013). The economic background to efforts to end public-sector collective bargaining is well described in Clark, Public Sector Collective Bargaining at the Crossroads, 44 Urban Law. 185, 188–99 (2012).

On problems of determining the appropriate bargaining unit for public employees, see Shaw & Clark, Determination of Appropriate Bargaining Units in the Public Sector: Legal and Practical Problems, 51 Ore. L.Rev. 152 (1971); Rock, The Appropriate Unit Question in the Public Service; The Problem of Proliferation, 67 Mich.L.Rev. 1001 (1969).

[112] See Glidewell v. Hughey, 314 S.W.2d 749 (Mo.1958) (interpreting charter); Dunellen Board of Education v. Dunellen Education Association, 64 N.J. 17, 311 A.2d 737 (1973) (consolidation of chairmanships of departments not subject to collective bargaining). Cf. Central State Univ. v. American Ass'n of University Professors, 526 U.S. 124, 119 S.Ct. 1162, 143 L.Ed.2d 227 (1999) (imposition of a faculty workload policy that was exempt from collective bargaining held valid against equal protection attack as a rational step toward increasing time spent by faculty in classroom); Midwest City v. Cravens, 532 P.2d 829 (Okl.1975) (Public Employees Relation Board had no authority to adjudicate charge of unfair labor practices since legislature had granted Board absolute discretion, and this constituted an undue delegation of legislative power). But cf. Mount Clemens Fire Fighters Union Local 838 v. City of Mount Clemens, 58 Mich.App. 635, 228 N.W.2d 500 (1975) (change in computing benefits under city pension plan held a "grievable" matter). In Portland Fire Fighters Ass'n v. City of Portland, 305 Or. 275, 751 P.2d 770 (1988), it was held that a statute identifying certain subjects as proper ones for mandatory collective bargaining removed those subjects from the scope of the usual judicial review as to the appropriateness of particular topics for such bargaining. Cf. Minnesota State Bd. for Community Colleges v. Knight, 465 U.S. 271, 104 S.Ct. 1058, 79 L.Ed.2d 299 (1984) (Minnesota statute required public employers to engage in official exchanges of views only with their professional employees' exclusive representatives on policy questions relating to employment even if those questions were outside the scope of mandatory collective bargaining; Court upheld statute as supporting state's legitimate interest in assuring that its public employers hear one, and only one, voice presenting the majority view of its professional employees). See generally Anderson, The Impact of Public Sector Bargaining, 1973 Wis.L.Rev. 986, 998–1005. See also National Labor Relations Board v. Yeshiva University, 444 U.S. 672, 100 S.Ct. 856, 63 L.Ed.2d 115 (1980) (private university's full-time faculty members exercised managerial functions and were thus not entitled to benefits of collective bargaining under National Labor Relations Act).

On the importance of the budgeting process in employee relations, including collective bargaining, see Allshouse, The Role of the Appropriations Process in Public Sector Bargaining, 17 Urban Law. 165 (1985). On dispute-solving procedures such as mediation, see Perez, Dispute Resolution Procedures in Public Employee Bargaining, 17 Urban Law. 199 (1985).

A public employer may attach reasonable conditions to its willingness to negotiate labor matters. See Smith v. Arkansas State Highway Employees, *supra* note 102 (grievances must be submitted in writing).

[113] Pinellas County Classroom Teachers Association v. Pinellas County Board of Public Instruction, 214 So.2d 34 (Fla.1968); Fletcher v. Civil Service Commission, 6 Ill.App.3d 593, 286 N.E.2d 130 (1972); Anderson Federation of Teachers v. School City of Anderson, 252 Ind. 558, 251 N.E.2d 15 (1969), reh. denied 252 Ind. 558, 254 N.E.2d 329 (1970), cert. denied 399 U.S. 928, 90 S.Ct. 2243, 26 L.Ed.2d 794 (1970); McAleer v. Jersey City Incinerator Authority, 79 N.J.Super. 142, 190 A.2d 891 (1963); Donevero v. Jersey City Incinerator Authority, 75 N.J.Super. 217, 182 A.2d 596 (1962); Weinstein v. New York City Transit Authority, 49 Misc.2d 170, 267 N.Y.S.2d 111 (Sup.Ct.1966) (transit workers); New York City v. Social Service Employees Union, 48

recognized as a valid ground for the discharge of a participating worker.[114] Such strikes have been called inconsistent with public workers' obligation to make government operate efficiently and economically, as a denial of governmental authority by the very persons entrusted with some of the sovereignty of the state, as in contravention of public welfare and possibly detrimental to public health and safety, and as improper coercion on the public and on the legislative branch of government. Statutes specifically outlawing strikes, slowdowns, and comparable actions by government workers, and providing criminal penalties for violations, have been upheld.[115] Nonetheless, strikes by police officers, transit workers, school teachers, sanitation workers, and other public employees do sometimes occur,[116] and it has been suggested that the possibility of strikes, at least by some public personnel, should be recognized as a necessary part of the collective bargaining process.[117] A few statutes now recognize a limited right to strike by certain public employees.[118] The California court has rejected the common-law

---

Misc.2d 820, 266 N.Y.S.2d 277 (Sup.Ct.1965); City of Cleveland v. Division 268, 84 Ohio App. 43, 81 N.E.2d 310 (1948) further opinion, 85 Ohio App. 153, 85 N.E.2d 811. See City of Detroit v. Division 26, 332 Mich. 237, 51 N.W.2d 228 (1952). But see Local 266 v. Salt River Project District, 78 Ariz. 30, 275 P.2d 393 (1954) (strike by employees of water district lawful since district was essentially a business organization). See generally Annot., Labor Law: Right of Public Employees to Strike or Engage in Work Stoppage, 37 A.L.R.3d 1147 (1971).

[114] See Hortonville Joint School District No. 1 v. Hortonville Education Association, 426 U.S. 482, 96 S.Ct. 2308, 49 L.Ed.2d 1 (1976) (teachers who took part in illegal strike could be dismissed by school board); Newmarker v. Regents of University of Cal., 160 Cal.App.2d 640, 325 P.2d 558 (Dist.Ct.1958) (observing that the common-law rule is that participation in a strike terminates employment). Cf. Wagner v. Office of Personnel Management, 783 F.2d 1042 (Fed.Cir.1986), cert. denied 477 U.S. 906, 106 S.Ct. 3276, 91 L.Ed.2d 566 (1986) (those who participate in strike against federal government may be barred indefinitely from government employment).

[115] Zeluck v. Board of Education, 62 Misc.2d 274, 307 N.Y.S.2d 329 (Sup.Ct.1970), aff'd 36 A.D.2d 615, 319 N.Y.S.2d 409 (statute ruled not a bill of attainder); City of New York v. De Lury, 23 N.Y.2d 175, 295 N.Y.S.2d 901, 243 N.E.2d 128 (1968), application denied 23 N.Y.2d 766, 296 N.Y.S.2d 958, 244 N.E.2d 472, appeal dism'd 394 U.S. 455, 89 S.Ct. 1223, 22 L.Ed.2d 414 (with review of authorities). See Annot., Criminal Prosecution of Federal Employees Participating in Illegal Strike, 61 A.L.R.Fed. 701 (1983). On the coverage of prohibitions against strikes, see Annot., Who Are Employees Forbidden to Strike Under State Enactments or State Common-Law Rules Prohibiting Strikes by Public Employees or Stated Classes of Public Employees, 22 A.L.R. 4th 1103 (1983) (police officers and firefighters universally included within such bans; teachers now normally included also; some split of authority over nonteaching school personnel, though they are generally included). Under some of the statutes outlawing strikes, public employees can be held liable in tort for damages caused the public employer by an illegal strike. See State ex inf. Ashcroft v. Kansas City Firefighters Local No. 42, 672 S.W.2d 99 (Mo.App.1984), where, however, the suit was allowed only against named union officers, not all union members, in light of evidence that many members were opposed to the strike. But see City & County of San Francisco v. United Ass'n of Journeymen & Apprentices of the Plumbing & Pipefitting Industry, 42 Cal.3d 810, 230 Cal.Rptr. 856, 726 P.2d 538 (1986) (in absence of statutory provision, illegal strike by public employees is not a tort for which employer may recover damages).

[116] See Anderson, Strikes and Impasse Resolution in Public Employment, 67 Mich. L.Rev. 943 (1969); "Strike Troubles Pile Up for Cities and States," U.S. News & World Rep., April 6, 1970, at 69; "New York—Shortage of Blue," Time, Jan. 25, 1971, at 23. See generally Ziskind, One Thousand Strikes of Government Employees (1940).

[117] See Kheel, Strikes and Public Employment, 67 Mich.L.Rev. 931 (1969). See generally Belasco, Resolving Dispute over Contract Terms in the State Public Service: An Analysis, 16 Lab.L.J. 533 (1965); Cornell, Collective Bargaining by Public Employee Groups, 107 U.Pa.L.Rev. 43 (1958). See also Little, Arbitrating Public Employment Disputes, 68 A.B.A.J. 1100 (1982).

[118] See Los Angeles Metropolitan Transit Authority v. Brotherhood of Railroad Trainmen, 54 Cal.2d 684, 8 Cal.Rptr. 1, 355 P.2d 905 (1960), interpreting a statute, authorizing concerted activities by employees for the purpose of collective bargaining or other mutual aid, as allowing strikes. Cf. Board of Education v. Public School Employees' Union, 233 Minn. 144, 45 N.W.2d 797 (1951) (statute forbade injunction against labor stoppage). See also City of Fairmont v. Retail, Wholesale, and Department Store Union, 166 W.Va. 1, 283 S.E.2d 589 (W.Va.1980) (public employer has no common-law right to damage for peaceful work stoppage by public employees who have no employment contract).

prohibition against strikes in the public sector and has held that such strikes are lawful at common law unless or until it is demonstrated that a particular strike creates a substantial and imminent threat to the health and safety of the public.[119]

Picketing is usually treated as within the same ban on disruptive activities that covers strikes, and thus it has been held that government workers have no right to picket government facilities.[120] But there is a minority view that picketing does not necessarily interfere with government operations—and should be considered lawful so long as it does not.[121]

Montana by statute grants many public employees a broad right to engage in economic strikes and does not even provide, as some state statutes do, that a lawful strike of public employees may be enjoined if a clear and present danger to the public health or welfare is found. See Comment, Defining Appropriate Criteria for the Public Employee Strike Injunction in Montana, 53 Montana L. Rev. 317 (1992).

[119] County Sanitation Dist. No. 2 v. Los Angeles County Employees Ass'n, 38 Cal.3d 564, 214 Cal.Rptr. 424, 699 P.2d 835 (1985), cert. denied 474 U.S. 995, 106 S.Ct. 408, 88 L.Ed.2d 359 (1985). See generally Malin, Public Employees' Right to Strike: Law and Experience, 26 U. Mich. J.L. Reform 313 (1993).

[120] See Board of Education v. Redding, 32 Ill.2d 567, 207 N.E.2d 427 (1965) (because strike was illegal, so was picketing, and could be enjoined); City of Alcoa v. International Brotherhood of Electrical Workers, *supra* note 110 (no right to picket local government facilities). Cf. Hunter v. City of Eugene, 309 Or. 298, 787 P.2d 881 (1990) (striking teachers did not have private right of action under state constitution for damages allegedly caused by city police officers interfering with their picketing, though they might have common-law, equitable, or statutory remedies).

[121] Peters v. South Chicago Community Hospital, 107 Ill.App.2d 460, 246 N.E.2d 840 (1969) (picketing of hospital would be enjoined only if it disrupted hospital activities); City of Rockford v. Local No. 413, 98 Ill.App.2d 36, 240 N.E.2d 705 (1968).

Chapter 15

FINANCES OF LOCAL GOVERNMENTS

Analysis

§ 15.1 Sources of Local Revenue—In General

In addition to territory to govern and personnel to perform the work of governing, a local government needs funds in order to carry out its public functions.[1] In recent decades, many local governments have been hard pressed by spiraling costs and wage demands, on one hand, and by, on the other hand, increasing reluctance of taxpayers to supply additional revenue. Thus, the "budget crunch" has become one of the most serious of municipal problems—just at a time when urban areas have been faced with an increasingly high proportion of modern America's social and economic problems.[2]

---

1 See United States v. New Orleans, 98 U.S. 381, 25 L.Ed. 225 (1878).

2 See Abbott, The New Barbarians 134–47 (1925) (on the cost of bureaucracy); Capes, The Modern City and Its Government 223–34 (1922) (cost of municipal government compared to other costs); Drexler, The Four Causes of the State and Local Budget Crisis and Proposed Solutions, 26 Urban Law. 563 (1994); Hobhouse, Social Evolution and Political Theory 167 (1911) (democratic element in politics brings the development of increased public activity); Lutz, Public Finance 64–93 (1924) (discussing the increase in municipal expenses, and blaming some of the costs on administrative inefficiency); "The Crunch on City and State Budgets," Bus. Week, March 10, 1975, at 78 (discussing the revenue short-falls faced by many cities and the cutbacks thus necessitated in services). See generally, on the increase in expenditures, Tax Foundation, Inc., Fiscal Outlook for State and Local Government to 1975, at 1–3 (1966). See also Colloquium, Big Problems, Small Government: Assessing the Recent Financial Crisis's Impact on Municipalities, 39 Fordham Urb. L.J. 577–803 (2012).

From what sources can a local government derive revenue?[3] Ordinarily the two most important sources are (1) taxes and special assessments and (2) loans to the city, often obtained through the issuance of bonds. In addition, revenue is obtained through the issuing of licenses, as for various businesses carried on in the city, and through general exercise of the police power, as by fees charged for building permits and fines levied for the violation of ordinances. These varied sources are the subject of this chapter. Municipalities often try to improve their tax-base, and generally increase their revenue, by the inducement of additional private business into the community. And many local governments make money from utilities—by granting franchises to privately owned utility companies and/or by entering the utility business themselves. Those activities are discussed in following chapters.

§ 15.2 Local Taxation—The Basic Power

Although a number of authorities have spoken broadly of an inherent power of taxation in municipalities,[4] the great weight of authority supports the views that local governments have only such power to tax as is given them by state constitution, state statute, or their own home-rule charter.[5] The power must be derived from the state, and a grant of it will be strictly construed,[6] with doubts resolved against the existence of any

---

[3] See 15 McQuillin, Municipal Corporations § 39.03 (3d rev. ed. 1995). See generally United States Advisory Comm'n on Intergovernmental Relations, State-Local Revenues (1972); United States Advisory Comm'n on Intergovernmental Relations, Tax Overlapping in the United States (1964); 4 United States Bureau of the Census, 1967 Census of Governments (Government Finances). On the continuing search for new methods of financing city services and improvements, see Mudge & Jakubiak, Financing Infrastructure: Innovations at the Local Level (National League of Cities 1987). See also Makowsky & Stratmann, More Tickets, Fewer Accidents: How Cash-Strapped Towns Make for Safer Roads, 54 J. L. & Econ. 863 (2011).

[4] See United States v. New Orleans, *supra* note 1, at 393; Taylor v. McFadden, 84 Iowa 262, 50 N.W. 1070 (1892); Oconto City Water-Supply Co. v. Oconto, 105 Wis. 76, 80 N.W. 1113 (1899).

[5] See Hackleburg v. Northwest Alabama Gas District, 277 Ala. 355, 170 So.2d 792 (1964) (no inherent power of taxation); State ex rel. Bennett v. Glynn, 154 Conn. 237, 224 A.2d 711 (1966); Village of Lombard v. Illinois Bell Telephone Co., 405 Ill. 209, 90 N.E.2d 105 (1950); Clark v. City of Des Moines, 222 Iowa 317, 267 N.W. 97 (1936); Carter Carburetor Corp. v. City of St. Louis, 356 Mo. 646, 203 S.W.2d 438 (1947); State ex rel. Emerson v. Mound City, 335 Mo. 702, 73 S.W.2d 1017 (1934); People ex rel. Metropolitan Street Railway v. State Board of Tax Commissioners, 174 N.Y. 417, 67 N.E. 69 (1903) (for subsequent history, see section 30, n. 1); In re Earned Income Tax Ordinance, 208 Pa.Super. 424, 222 A.2d 499 (1966); Bates v. Bassett, 60 Vt. 530, 15 A. 200 (1888); Chesapeake & Potomac Telephone Co. v. Morgantown, 143 W.Va. 800, 105 S.E.2d 260 (1958). Even in jurisdictions recognizing the inherent right of home-rule (See Chapter 4 *supra*.), no inherent power to tax has been recognized. See Zoercher v. Agler, 202 Ind. 214, 172 N.E. 186 (1930). Cf. Arborwood Idaho, L.L.C. v. City of Kennewick, 151 Wash.2d 359, 89 P.3d 217 (2004) (constitutional provisions which permit the legislature to grant municipal authorities the power to levy and collect taxes are not self-executing, and constitutional grant of police powers to local governments does not include power to tax; municipalities must have express authority, either constitutional or legislative, to levy taxes). See generally Karayan, Swenson, Gupta & Neff, State and Local Taxation—Principles and Planning (J. Ross Publishing 2d ed. 2003). In some jurisdictions, taxes can only be imposed by elected bodies or officials. See McSweeney & Russell, *Marshall v. Northern Virginia Transportation Authority*: The Supreme Court of Virginia Rules that Taxes Can Be Imposed by Elected Bodies Only, 42 U. Rich. L. Rev. 51 (2008).

As to the very wide-ranging power of the *federal* government to tax, see National Federation of Independent Business v. Sebelius, ___ U.S. ___, 132 S.Ct. 2566, 2593–2600, 183 L.Ed.2d 450 (2012), upholding the Affordable Care Act under the Taxing Clause.

[6] See State ex rel. Woodruff v. Centanne, 265 Ala. 35, 89 So.2d 570 (1956); Gotlieb v. City of Birmingham, 243 Ala. 579, 11 So.2d 363 (1943); City of Tampa v. Birdsong Motors, 261 So.2d 1 (Fla.1972); State v. City of Wichita, 184 Kan. 196, 335 P.2d 786 (1959); McCarthy v. Marcellus, 32 Mich.App. 679, 189 N.W.2d 80 (1971); Mastrangelo v. Buckley, 433 Pa. 352, 250 A.2d 447 (1969); Price v. Tax Review Board of Philadelphia, 409 Pa. 479, 187 A.2d 280 (1963); Eugene Theatre Co. v. City of Eugene, 194 Or. 603, 243 P.2d 1060 (1952); Williams v. City of Richmond, 177 Va. 477, 14 S.E.2d 287 (1941); Walker v. Morgantown, 137 W.Va. 289, 71 S.E.2d 60 (1952). But exemption statutes are often strictly construed also. See City of Detroit v.

particular aspect of the power.[7] In a number of states, municipalities—or at least home-rule municipalities—derive power to tax from constitutional provisions, usually authorizing, in rather sweeping terms, taxation for municipal affairs and purposes.[8] But more often, the power to tax is derived, not from the state constitution, but merely from state statutes. This is particularly true as to taxing powers of (1) non-home-rule localities (including, of course, all localities in those states not recognizing home rule), and (2) home-rule localities in most states having "legislative," as opposed to "constitutional,"

General Foods Corp., 39 Mich.App. 180, 197 N.W.2d 315 (1972). And occasionally, a court will say that a statute conferring the taxing power should be given a reasonable, not a strict, construction. See Neal v. City of Huntington, 151 W.Va. 1051, 158 S.E.2d 223 (1967). The general rule is that estoppel cannot be successfully asserted against a local government in a tax matter, just as it cannot against a state government. See Annot., Estoppel of State or Local Government in Tax Matters, 21 A.L.R. 4th 573 (1983).

On a taxpayer's standing to question the validity of a tax or the expenditure of tax monies, see Butte-Silver Bow Local Gov't v. State, 235 Mont. 398, 768 P.2d 327 (1989) (standing exists when issues presented directly affect constitutional validity of collection and use of proceeds of tax by state or local government). Cf. In re Objections & Defenses to Real Property Taxes for 1985 Assessment, 410 N.W.2d 321 (Minn.1987) (owners' association responsible for managing condominiums has standing to bring action in tax court, challenging tax assessment, whenever it asserts its own rightful claim or can bring a claim on behalf of two or more owners who have their own rightful claim). But cf. Gallagher v. State of Idaho, 141 Idaho 665, 115 P.3d 756 (2005) (smoker lacked standing to challenge cigarette tax paid by wholesaler; to have standing, a taxpayer must establish a peculiar or personal injury that is different from that suffered by the public). See generally Marks, Adhere Resolutely to a Mistake: The Florida Taxpayer-Standing Cases, 33 Stetson L. Rev. 401 (2004). See also Note, Denying State Taxpayers Standing in Federal Court: Are Municipal Taxpayers Next?,38 U. Toledo L. Rev. 1241 (2004), noting DaimlerChrysler Corp. v. Cuno, 547 U.S. 332, 126 S.Ct. 1854, 164 L.Ed.2d 589 (2006) (Ohio taxpayers lacked standing to challenge award of state franchise tax credit to automobile manufacturer to induce it to remain in city). In Arizona Christian School Tuition Organization v. Winn, 563 U.S. 125, 131 S.Ct. 1436, 179 L.Ed.2d 523 (2011), taxpayers brought an action alleging that an Arizona statute which granted tuition tax credits to income taxpayers who contributed money to "student tuition organizations" that used the money to provide scholarships to students attending private schools, including religious schools, violated the First Amendment's Establishment Clause. But the Court ruled 5 to 4 that the taxpayers lacked standing to make this challenge to the tax credits since they sustained no injury therefrom. The majority reasoned that since the state was merely declining to impose a tax, rather than making an expenditure, any financial injury to the taxpayer was speculative.

[7] Consolidated Diesel Electric Corp. v. City of Stamford, 156 Conn. 33, 238 A.2d 410 (1968); Fischer v. City of Pittsburgh, 383 Pa. 138, 118 A.2d 157 (1955). See Miller v. Standard Nut Margarine Co., 284 U.S. 498, 52 S.Ct. 260, 76 L.Ed. 422 (1932) (tax laws to be construed against government and in favor of taxpayers); Xerox Corp. v. City of Pittsburgh, 15 Pa.Cmwlth. 411, 327 A.2d 206 (1974). Under the rule of statutory construction known as "expressio unius est exclusio alterius," a grant of power to levy a particular tax will be deemed a denial of the power to levy other taxes as to which a grant is not elsewhere made. Decatur Transit v. City of Gadsden, 249 Ala. 314, 31 So.2d 339 (1947); Carter Carburetor Corp. v. City of St. Louis, 356 Mo. 646, 203 S.W.2d 438 (1947) (city was granted power to levy property tax; couldn't impose earnings tax); Dixon, 138 Pa.Super. 385, 11 A.2d 169 (1940). Cf. Phillips, 64 Okl. 276, 167 P. 221 (1917) (grant of power to impose occupation tax eliminates possibility of license tax on automobiles). And courts are reluctant to find any municipal power to tax *implied* in municipal powers that are expressly given. See Green v. Mayor of Milledgeville, 112 Ga.App. 130, 144 S.E.2d 225 (1965), rev'd 221 Ga. 498, 145 S.E.2d 507, conf. to 112 Ga.App. 653, 145 S.E.2d 720 (power to tax is separate, and not to be inferred from other powers); Corbett v. City of Portland, 31 Or. 407, 48 P. 428 (1897) (no doubtful inferences will be made). Thus, the power to regulate does not give the power to charge license fees for revenue. City of Chicago v. R. & X. Restaurant, 369 Ill. 65, 15 N.E.2d 725 (1938); Salomon v. Jersey City, 12 N.J. 379, 97 A.2d 405 (1953). See Idaho Bldg. Contractors Ass'n v. City of Coeur d'Alene, 126 Idaho 740, 890 P.2d 326 (1995) (if fee or charge is imposed by municipality primarily for revenue purposes, it is in essence a tax and can only be upheld under some grant of the power of taxation).

[8] See Ainsworth v. Bryant, 34 Cal.2d 465, 211 P.2d 564 (1949); In re Braun, 141 Cal. 204, 74 P. 780 (1903); Hampton v. City of Wichita, 192 Kan. 534, 389 P.2d 757 (1964); G. Andrews Espy Realty v. Burton-Rodgers, Inc., 94 Ohio App. 417, 116 N.E.2d 14 (1952), all applying such constitutional provisions.

home rule.[9] Statutory grants to local governments of the power to tax have been upheld against constitutional challenges.[10]

Delegations of the taxing power, whether in constitution, statute, or charter, are often limited to grants of power as to particular types of tax—such as ad valorem property taxes, sales taxes, etc. In determining whether or not a particular tax is within the power granted a local government, the courts will look to the basic nature of that tax—its operation and effect—rather than merely to the label given it by the taxing locality.[11] But if the courts find that the power does exist, they will not look into the wisdom of a particular tax or its method of assessment. Thus, the amount or rate of tax is, within any limits prescribed by the basic authorization, left to the discretion of local officials.[12]

Some subject matters—such as the sale of liquor or the operation of real-estate businesses—are, in various jurisdictions, held to be outside the scope of local taxation because the state has pre-empted the field of such taxation. In a few states, the state is held to have pre-empted a field simply by imposing a tax itself on a particular subject, such as corporate property or corporate income.[13] But in most states, the usual rules on state pre-emption are applied in the tax field, and the state is *not* found to have pre-empted taxation of a subject matter simply because it has levied a tax on it, or because it has pre-empted the *regulation* of that subject.[14]

---

[9] See Appeal of School District of Allentown, 370 Pa. 161, 87 A.2d 480 (1952) (municipal power to tax comes only from legislature); Glens Falls Insurance Co. v. City of Columbia, 242 S.C. 237, 130 S.E.2d 573 (1963); Walker v. Morgantown, *supra* note 6.

[10] English v. Robinson Township School District, 358 Pa. 45, 55 A.2d 803 (1947). See Hackleburg v. Northwest Alabama Gas District, *supra* note 5.

[11] City of Columbus v. Atlanta Cigar Co., 111 Ga.App. 774, 143 S.E.2d 416 (1965); Franklin v. Harrison, 153 N.E.2d 467, 5 O.O.2d 97 (Ohio Mun.1957), aff'd 112 Ohio App. 423, 160 N.E.2d 15, aff'd 171 Ohio St. 329, 170 N.E.2d 739.

[12] Lurie v. City of Indianapolis, 245 Ind. 457, 198 N.E.2d 755 (1964); Eugene Theatre Co. v. City of Eugene, *supra* note 6.

[13] See Panama City v. Jackson's Minit Markets, 193 So.2d 189 (Fla.App.1966) (liquor license taxes precluded); East Ohio Gas Co. v. City of Akron, 7 Ohio St.2d 73, 218 N.E.2d 608 (1966) (gross receipts tax on utilities); City of Cincinnati v. Queen City Petroleum Products Co., 123 Ohio St. 448, 175 N.E. 699 (1931) (tax on gas stations); Murray v. City of Philadelphia, 364 Pa. 157, 71 A.2d 280 (1950) (tax on corporate income); A.E. Dick Contracting Co. v. Hazle Township School District, 362 Pa. 387, 65 A.2d 381 (1949) (tax on corporate property). Cf. City of Tempe v. Prudential Insurance Co., 109 Ariz. 429, 510 P.2d 745 (1973), appeal dism'd 414 U.S. 1088, 94 S.Ct. 717, 38 L.Ed.2d 546 (state had preempted field of taxation of insurance companies, with designated exceptions); City of Hot Springs v. Vapors Theatre Restaurant, Inc., 298 Ark. 444, 769 S.W.2d 1 (1989) (city could not impose additional tax on mixed drinks where state law already provided for complete taxation on alcoholic beverages).

[14] See Willingham Bus Lines v. Municipal Court, 66 Cal.2d 893, 59 Cal.Rptr. 618, 428 P.2d 602 (1967) (state regulation does not preclude city from imposing license tax for revenue); Ainsworth v. Bryant, *supra* 5 (municipal purchase-and-use tax may be imposed on liquor distributors despite exclusive state control over sale of liquor); American National Building & Loan Association v. City of Baltimore, 245 Md. 23, 224 A.2d 883 (1966). But cf. Parker v. City of Silverton, 109 Or. 298, 220 P. 139 (1923) (intercity carrier subject to state regulation could not be subjected to city license tax). On state pre-emption, see generally Chapter 6 *supra*. Some taxes are used for purposes of regulation as well as for revenue—for instance, high sales taxes on commodities whose purchase the government desires to discourage, such as tobacco. See generally Note,Taxes as Regulatory Tools: An Argument for Expanding New York City's Taxing Authority, 86 N.Y.U.L. Rev. 1556 (2011). See also note 29, para. 2, *infra*, on "excise taxes."

Often, state constitutional provisions or statutes conferring the taxing power on localities prohibit certain kinds of taxation and/or exempt certain property from taxation. And property of the state and its subdivisions is usually expressly or impliedly declared exempt from municipal taxation. See City of Phoenix v. Elias, 64 Ariz. 95, 166 P.2d 589 (1946) (applying constitutional provision); County of Westchester v. Town of

§ 15.3 Local Taxation—The Property Tax

Six taxes are of particular importance to local governments in the United States (though not all are permitted to localities in all states): the property tax (assessed against real and/or personal property within the locality); the sales tax; admissions and amusement taxes; income taxes; gross receipts taxes; and license taxes. Traditionally, the property tax—and in particular, the tax on real property—has been the mainstay of municipal revenue-gathering—the largest single source of municipal revenue. But real-property taxes have been under increasing criticism. Measures such as California's "Proposition 13" (adopted by the voters of that state in 1978) limiting property-tax levies have been adopted or proposed in many jurisdictions. The property tax has been criticized as often excessively high, as discriminating against those who own land, as contributing to urban blight and the "flight to the suburbs," and as creating inequality in educational and other services provided to different areas within a state.[15] A number

---

Harrison, 201 Misc. 211, 114 N.Y.S.2d 492 (Sup.Ct.1951) (county property exempt); Weaverville v. Hobbs, 212 N.C. 684, 194 S.E. 860 (1938). Property of other *local* governments (such as other municipalities) within a city or town is usually exempt if used for "public" or "governmental" purposes, but not exempt (in the absence of specific legislative exemption) if used for "business" or "proprietary" purposes. See City of Phoenix v. Bowles, 65 Ariz. 315, 180 P.2d 222 (1947); Collector of Taxes v. City of Boston, 278 Mass. 274, 180 N.E. 116 (1932); Port of New York Authority v. City of Newark, 20 N.J. 386, 120 A.2d 18 (1956) (port authority's truck terminal); Redevelopment Commission v. Guilford County, 274 N.C. 585, 164 S.E.2d 476 (1968). See generally Gunning, Into and Out of the Bog: The Intergovernmental Tax Immunity Doctrine, 41 Willamette L. Rev. 151 (2005). As to municipal immunity from taxation by the state and its agencies, see Bittick, Department of Revenue v. City of Gainesville: The Florida Supreme Court Attempts to Define the Scope of Municipal Exemption from Ad Valorem Taxation, 36 Stetson L. Rev. 457 (2007).

[15] See "The Coming Change in the Property Tax," Bus. Week, Feb. 12, 1972, at 50. See generally Note, Tax Assessments of Real Property: A Proposal for Legislative Reform, 68 Yale L.J. 335 (1958), with a good review of the issues surrounding the property tax. See also Lackman, Value-Added Tax vs. the Property Tax: A Case Study, 8 Real Estate L.J. 34 (1979).

On some of the effects of California's approval of the measure designed to limit property taxation—"Proposition 13"—see Chase, California's Public Services Suffer from Tax-Revolt Spending Cuts, Wall St. J., Feb. 16, 1982, at 23, cols. 5–6; Rader & Lang, Proposition 13 and the Poor: The New Alchemy in the Golden State, 12 Clearinghouse Rev. 681 (1979). The constitutionality of this measure was upheld in Nordlinger v. Hahn, 505 U.S. 1, 112 S.Ct. 2326, 120 L.Ed.2d 1 (1992); Amador Valley Joint Union High School v. State Board of Equalization, 22 Cal.3d 208, 149 Cal.Rptr. 239, 583 P.2d 1281 (1978) (no violation of equal protection, of federal contract clause, etc.). See generally Rappaport,The Constitutionality of Proposition 13 Under the Equal Protection Clause, 26 Real Prop. Prob. & Tr. J. 235 (1991). The measure's adoption led to proposal and/or adoption of similar limitations in a number of other states. See Review of Local Government Law, 11 Urban Lawyer 576–83 (1979); The Annual Survey of Local Government Law, 1977–78, 10 Urban Lawyer 584–91 (1978); "Tax-Cut Fever—Suddenly It's Spreading," U.S. News & World Rep., July 30, 1979, at 63: "A Wave of Tax Cuts Hits the States," U.S. News & World Rep., March 12, 1979, at 92, col. 2. See generally Kuttner, Revolt of the Haves (1980), reviewed Bus. Week, Nov. 3, 1980, at 15. Some of the tax cuts in California have necessitated increased use of special fees for certain services (trash collection, use of recreational facilities, etc.) by some local governments. See "Californians Discover Tax-Cut Mania Has a Corollary: Fee Fever," Wall St. J., June 1, 1979, at 1, col. 1. California gave a limited application to the provision of Proposition 13 that required a two-thirds vote of qualified electors in order for a city, county, or special district to impose "special taxes." This was held to apply only to such "special districts" as are empowered to levy property taxes. Los Angeles County Transp. Comm'n v. Richmond, 31 Cal.3d 197, 182 Cal.Rptr. 324, 643 P.2d 941 (1982) (transportation commission could impose retail transaction and use tax with consent of bare majority of voters). See Huntington Park Redev. Agency v. Martin, 38 Cal.3d 100, 211 Cal.Rptr. 133, 695 P.2d 220 (1985) (since community redevelopment agency was not empowered by law to levy property taxes, it was not subject to requirement of approval by two-thirds of electors before imposing sales and use tax). But in 1986, California voters approved another statutory initiative—Proposition 62—that required all new local taxes to be approved by a vote of the local electorate. See Santa Clara County Local Transp. Auth. v. Guardino, 11 Cal.4th 220, 45 Cal.Rptr.2d 207, 902 P.2d 225 (Cal. 1995) (sales tax imposed by county transportation authority required two-thirds approval of electorate). See generally Note, Prisoners of Proposition 13: Sales Taxes, Property Taxes, and the Fiscalization of Municipal Land Use Decisions, 71 S. Cal. L. Rev. 183 (1997). Subsequent "tax revolts"

of courts have struck down, usually as violative of equal protection, state school-financing laws under which public education was financed largely by real-property taxation.[16] But the U.S. Supreme Court, noting that education is not a right expressly

---

have sometimes failed in California. See "Revolt R.I.P.?," Time, June 16, 1980, at 17 (plan to cut state personal income taxes rejected by voters). And in other states. See "Referendums: Rising Impatience," Time, Nov. 17, 1980, at 73, noting defeat of "Proposition 13" type tax-cutting proposals in several states, though adoption of such a measure by Massachusetts voters. In the 1984 and 1988 elections, most "Proposition 13-type" tax reforms were rejected by the voters, and the electorate's revolt against the property tax subsided. See "Suddenly, Voters Look at Taxes and See Schools and Roads," Bus. Week, Nov. 28, 1988, at 33; "Taking Matters into Their Own Hands," Time, Nov. 19, 1984; at 95. See generally O'Sullivan, Sexton & Sheffrin, Property Taxes and Tax Revolts: The Legacy of Proposition 13 (Cambridge Univ. 1995). For a good historical treatment of the property tax revolt of the 1970's, particularly in California, see Lo, Small Property Versus Big Government: Social Origins of the Property Tax Revolt (Univ. of Calif. Press 1990). See also Powell, A Historical Perspective on Montana Property Tax: 25 Years of Statewide Appraisal and Appeal Practice, 70 Mont. L. Rev. 21 (2009).

The argument has been made that, due to allegedly improper implementation, California's Proposition 13 has never achieved the intended goal of equity in property taxes. See Note, In Pursuit of Equity in Property Tax Allocation: Discussing the Flawed Implementation of Proposition 13, 30 Va. Tax Rev. 761 (2011). That Proposition certainly increased California's dependence on income-tax revenue and thus led to budget problems when incomes dropped during the 2008–10 recession. See Suddath & O'Leary, Spotlight-California's Budget Crisis, Time magazine, July 27, 2009, at 16, commenting "California's system of governance seems designed to thwart any solution its lawmakers propose. With a two-thirds majority required to raise taxes or pass a judgment, 40% of public funds earmarked for public schools, and no method of overriding voter initiatives, California seems stymied by a complex puzzle that no one can solve." *Id.*

On the definition of "property tax," see Knapp v. City of Jacksonville, 342 Or. 268, 151 P.3d 143 (2007) (public safety surcharge on persons responsible for paying sewer and water bills was not a property tax since fees were not based on ownership but were instead imposed on occupants of property, including those who had no corporeal interest in property). See generally C. Goodall & (student) S.A. Goodall, Property Tax: A Primer and a Modest Proposal for Maine, 57 Me. L. Rev. 585 (2005). See also Robinson, Difficulties in Achieving Coherent State and Local Fiscal Policy at the Intersection of Direct Democracy and Republicanism: The Property Tax as a Case in Point, 35 U. Mich. J.L. Reform 511 (2002). As to the effects of California's "Proposition 13" and subsequent developments in that state, as well as tax-limitation measures adopted in Colorado, see Johnson, Beck and Hoyt, State Constitutional Tax Limitations: The Colorado and California Experiences, 35 Urban Law. 817 (2003). See also Garvey, Resolving Boundary Disputes in California: A Radical Reassessment in Light of Proposition 13, 43 U. San Francisco L. Rev. 829 (2009).

[16] Van Dusartz v. Hatfield, 334 F.Supp. 870 (D.Minn.1971); Serrano v. Priest, 5 Cal.3d 584, 96 Cal.Rptr. 601, 487 P.2d 1241 (1971) (a famous case); Horton v. Meskill, 172 Conn. 615, 376 A.2d 359 (1977) (fashioning of a constitutional system was for legislature); Robinson v. Cahill, 118 N.J.Super. 223, 287 A.2d 187 (1972), suppl. 119 N.J.Super. 40, 289 A.2d 569, mod. 62 N.J. 473, 303 A.2d 273, rearg. 63 N.J. 196, 306 A.2d 65, cert. denied 414 U.S. 976, 94 S.Ct. 292, 38 L.Ed.2d 219. See Goldstein, Interdistrict Inequalities in School Financing: A Critical Analysis of *Serrano v. Priest* and Its Progeny, 120 U.Pa.L.Rev. 504 (1972). See generally Karst, *Serrano v. Priest*: A State Court's Responsibilities and Opportunities in the Development of Federal Constitutional Law, 60 Cal.L.Rev. 720 (1972); Note, The Evolution of Equal Protection: Education, Municipal Services, and Wealth, 7 Harv. Civ. Rights-Civ. Lib. L.Rev. 103 (1972). See also 1 Levin, Muller, Scanlon, & Cohen, Public School Finance: Present Disparities and Fiscal Alternatives (1972). On the *Serrano* case, *supra*, and its effect, compare Stark & Zasloff, Tiebout and Tax Revolts: Did *Serrano* Really Cause Proposition 13?, 50 U.C.L.A. L. Rev. 801 (2003), with Fischel, Did John Serrano Vote for Proposition 13? A Reply to Stark and Zasloff's "Tiebout and Tax Revolts: Did *Serrano* Really Cause Proposition 13?,"51 U.C.L.A. L. Rev. 887 (2004).

For a discussion of the historical development of reliance on the property tax to fund public education, see Comment, An Historical Analysis of Property Taxes as a Method of Funding Public Education, 10 St. Louis U. Pub. L. Rev. 615 (1991). In Lobato v. State of Colorado, 218 P.3d 358 (Colo. 2009), the court held that whether the public school financing system violated the state constitutional mandate for a "thorough and uniform" system of public schools was a justiciable issue and should be decided on a rational-basis analysis. See generally Viteritti, The Inadequacy of Adequacy Guarantees: A Historical Commentary on State Constitutional Provisions that Are the Basis for School Finance Litigation, 7 U. Md. L.J. Race, Religion, Gender & Class 58 (2007).

The U.S. Supreme Court has upheld the power of federal courts to force local officials to raise taxes in order to remedy school desegregation. Missouri v. Jenkins, 495 U.S. 33, 110 S.Ct. 1651, 109 L.Ed.2d 31 (1990). See Whitten, *Missouri v. Jenkins*: Taxation Without Representation or Remedy of Last Resort?, 14 Urban, State & Local L. Newsletter, No. 1, at 1 (Fall, 1990); Note, Judicial Taxation as a Means of Remedying Public

or implicitly protected by the federal Constitution, has upheld use of the property tax for financing educational services despite some inequality in taxable base, and thus in the education provided, among school districts.[17]

School Segregation Under *Missouri v. Jenkins*: Boldly Gone Where No Federal Court Has Gone Before, 12 Whittier L. Rev. 551 (1991). See generally *Yonkers/Jenkins* Symposium, 24 Urban Law. 589–651 (1992).

[17] San Antonio Independent School District v. Rodriguez, 411 U.S. 1, 93 S.Ct. 1278, 36 L.Ed.2d 16, reh. denied 411 U.S. 959, 93 S.Ct. 1919, 36 L.Ed.2d 418 (1973). See Note, San Antonio Independent School District v. Rodriguez: A Study of Alternatives Open to State Courts, 8 Univ. San Francisco L.Rev. 90 (1973). See generally, supporting much the same view as taken by the majority in the *Rodriguez* case, Carrington, On Egalitarian Overzeal: A Polemic Against the Local School Property Tax Cases, 1972 Ill.L.F. 232.

The *Rodriguez* decision temporarily slowed but did not halt the movement away from the property tax as the main source of financing for education and other local services. On the search for alternative methods of financing, see *Serrano* Symposium—The Death Knell to Ad Valorem School Financing, 5 Urban Lawyer 83 (1973) (particularly Fordham, Part IV, at 110); Grubb, The First Round of Legislative Reforms in the Post-Serrano World, 38 Law & Contemp. Prob. 459 (1974); Ruvoldt, Educational Financing in New Jersey:*Robinson v. Cahill* And Beyond, 5 Seton Hall L.Rev. 1 (1973). See also Serrano v. Priest, 18 Cal.3d 728, 135 Cal.Rptr. 345, 557 P.2d 929 (1976) (decision after remand for trial), reaffirming the invalidity of the property-tax school-financing system that had been used.

It has been observed that the *Rodriguez* decision rests on the Court's ruling that education is not a fundamental interest under the federal Constitution, while many state constitutions do make education a fundamental interest. Thus, under state constitutional law principles, inequalities among school districts are subject to strict scrutiny and often cannot survive legal challenge. See Spring, 1982, Newsletter, American Bar Ass'n Section on Local Government, reporting Jan., 1982, business meeting of that Section.

In Edgewood Independent School Dist. v. Kirby, 777 S.W.2d 391 (Tex.1989), the court ruled that the Texas public school system's heavy reliance on the property tax, resulting in wide disparities between school districts, violated the Texas Constitution's guarantee of an efficient school system committed to the general diffusion of knowledge. Other state cases after *Rodriguez* (besides the California case cited in note 16 *supra* and the Texas case *supra*) that have invalidated property-tax-based school financing include DuPree v. Alma School Dist. No. 30, 279 Ark. 340, 651 S.W.2d 90 (1983); Horton v. Meskill, 172 Conn. 615, 376 A.2d 359 (1977); Rose v. Council for Better Educ., Inc., 790 S.W.2d 186 (Ky.1989); Helena Elementary School Dist. No. 1 v. State, 236 Mont. 44, 769 P.2d 684 (1989), opinion amended 236 Mont. 44, 784 P.2d 412 (1990); Brigham v. State, 166 Vt. 246, 692 A.2d 384 (Vt. 1997); Seattle School Dist. No. 1 v. State, 90 Wash.2d 476, 585 P.2d 71 (1978); Washakie County School Dist. No. 1 v. Herschler, 606 P.2d 310 (Wyo.1980), cert. denied 449 U.S. 824, 101 S.Ct. 86, 66 L.Ed.2d 28 (1980). Cf. Hull v. Albrecht, 192 Ariz. 34, 960 P.2d 634 (Ariz. 1998) (state statutory plan for financing school system invalidated as causing substantial disparities among school districts, though court says that school districts may seek local sources of revenue, such as property taxes, in order to surpass minimum state standards); Pauley v. Kelly, 162 W.Va. 672, 255 S.E.2d 859 (1979) (recognizing cause of action under state constitution and remanding for determination of possible violation). In addition, the New Jersey *Robinson v. Cahill* litigation, *supra* note 16, continued after *Rodriguez*: Robinson v. Cahill (Robinson II), 63 N.J. 196, 306 A.2d 65 (1973), cert. denied 414 U.S. 976, 94 S.Ct. 292, 38 L.Ed.2d 219 (1973); Robinson v. Cahill (Robinson III), 67 N.J. 35, 335 A.2d 6 (1975); Robinson v. Cahill (Robinson IV), 67 N.J. 333, 339 A.2d 193 (1975), reprinted in corrected form, 69 N.J. 133, 351 A.2d 713 (1975), cert. denied 423 U.S. 913, 96 S.Ct. 217, 46 L.Ed.2d 141 (1975); Robinson v. Cahill (Robinson V), 69 N.J. 449, 355 A.2d 129 (1976); Robinson v. Cahill (Robinson VI), 70 N.J. 155, 358 A.2d 457 (1976); Robinson v. Cahill (Robinson VII), 70 N.J. 464, 360 A.2d 400 (1976). See generally Reed, Twenty-Five Years After Rodriguez: School Finance Litigation and the Impact of the New Judicial Federalism, 32 Law & Soc'y Rev. 175 (1998); Note, Education Finance Reform Litigation and Separation of Powers: Kentucky Makes Its Contribution, 80 Ky. L.J. 309 (1991); Comment, The Constitutionality of Property Tax Based School Financing Schemes: Is Illinois' System Next to Fail?, 16 S. I11. U.L.J. 157 (1991); Note, State Constitutional Analysis of Public School Finance Reform Cases: Myth or Methodology?,45 Vand. L. Rev. 129 (1992); Note, To Render Them Safe: The Analysis of State Constitutional Provisions in Public School Finance Reform Litigation, 75 Va. L. Rev. 1639 (1989); Comment, The Exception to the Rule, Wisconsin's Fundamental Right to Education and Public School Financing, 1995 Wis. L. Rev. 1387 (Wisconsin regards education as a fundamental right and applies strict scrutiny to most issues related to education but not to education finance). As of 1994, twenty-eight states had ruled on school financing suits under their state constitutions, with about half upholding their existing system and half finding that greater equity was needed. See Reed, The People v. The Court: School Finance Reform and the New Jersey Supreme Court, 4 Cornell J.L. & Pub. Pol. 137 (1994), discussing efforts in New Jersey to equalize expenditures for public education among school districts and noting (*id.* at 189) that one state—Michigan—has taken the extreme step of eliminating the local property tax as a funding mechanism for public education. See generally "School Funding: Reforms Add Up," Bus. Week, April 5, 1999, at 28. On local control of school finances, see

Regardless of the U.S. Supreme Court's upholding of the property tax as the chief means of financing public education, reliance on this tax, either to finance education or to finance other activities of local government, has decreased some in light of the stream of criticism. But the tax has numerous advantages that may keep it in use to a considerable extent: (1) Property, especially real property, is directly benefited by many municipal services, such as fire protection and garbage collection. Thus, there is a certain fairness in assessing the costs of these services on the basis of the value of property benefited thereby. (2) It is fairly easy to forecast in advance the amount of revenue that the real-property tax in a particular locality will produce, thus facilitating the budget process. (3) The real-property tax is not likely to be used by the federal government; it is thus one of the few potential sources of municipal income that is untapped by the U.S. government. And the full potential of the real-property tax has not been realized, since much urban property is assessed, and thus taxed, at substantially less than its current fair-market value.[18]

The basic limit on municipal use of the property tax is territoriality—*i.e.*, a local government can only tax property within its boundaries.[19] Generally, the locality can tax only property that was within its boundaries on the date set by law for completion of the tax assessment rolls for a particular year, not property subsequently annexed.[20] Beyond

---

Brown, Deconstructing Local Control: Ohio's Contribution, 25 Capital U.L. Rev. 1 (1996); Gillette, Reconstructing Local Control of School Finance: A Cautionary Note, 25 Capital U.L. Rev. 225 (1996). For discussion of school finance litigation in two particular states, compare Apter, Institutional Constraints, Policies and Good Faith: A Case Study of School Reform in Massachusetts, 17 Cornell J. L. & Pub. Pol'y 621 (2008), with Kauffman, The Texas School Finance Litigation Saga: Great Progress, Then Near Death by a Thousand Cuts, 40 St. Mary's L.J. 511 (2008).

On the effects of school-finance litigation on other areas of the law, see Wadhwani, Achieving Greater Inter-local Equity in Financing Municipal Services: What We Can Learn From School Finance Litigation, 7 Tex. F. on C.L. & C.R. 91 (2002).

What if limitations on the property tax, such as a two-thirds vote requirement, come into conflict with the Legislature's duty to finance public schools? See Note, Appropriations—Legislature's Duty to Fund Primary Schools Trumps Recent Amendment to the Constitution Requiring Two-thirds Majority for Tax Revenue Increases, 35 Rutgers L.J. 1393 (2004), noting Guinn v. Legislature of Nevada, 119 Nev. 277, 71 P.3d 1269 (2003) & 119 Nev. 460, 76 P.3d 22 (2004), cert. denied 541 U.S. 957, 124 S.Ct. 1662, 158 L.Ed.2d 392 (2004).

A good summary of the Texas cases that have dealt with school-finance issues is found in "A Recent History of Texas School Financing," Dallas Morning News, Jan. 28, 2008, at 8A.

[18] See as to these advantages of the property tax 2A Antieau, Municipal Corporation Law § 21.62 (1998). Recent cases have sometimes required that property be assessed at "full" or "actual" value—see note 25 *infra*, and accompanying text. Natural disasters sometimes cause large decreases in property values. See Cowan, Towns' Next Hit From Hurricane Is to Tax Bases, N.Y. Times, Jan. 25, 2013, at A1, describing the devastating losses to some municipalities due to the damage from Hurricane Sandy in 2012. See also Hayashi, Property Taxes and Their Limits: Evidence From New York City, 25 Stan. L. & Pol'y Rev. 33 (2014).

[19] Klich v. Miami Land & Development Co., 139 Fla. 794, 191 So. 41 (1939); Standard Oil Co. v. City of Barbourville, 274 Ky. 742, 120 S.W.2d 397 (1938). But specific legislative grants of power to a municipality can be made to tax property outside municipal limits, if the tax is for some limited purpose that involves benefit to the extraterritorial property or subject-matter. See Chadwick v. Town of Hammondville, 270 Ala. 618, 120 So.2d 899 (1960) (businesses outside city but within its police jurisdiction); Lurie v. City of Indianapolis, *supra* note 12 (city could tax land outside city limits but within park district if revenue was used solely for park purposes). Some authorities have proposed expanding property taxes to include services rendered. See Hurley, Curing the Structural Defect in State Tax Systems: Expanding the Tax Base to Include Services, 61 Mercer L. Rev. 491 (2010).

[20] Koch v. City of Detroit, 236 Mich. 338, 210 N.W. 239 (1926). Cf. Oneida v. Pearson Hardwood Flooring Co., 169 Tenn. 449, 88 S.W.2d 998 (1935) (de-annexed land could not be taxed). But cf. Lynch v. Howell, 165 Neb. 525, 86 N.W.2d 364 (1957) (city could tax property that was within city on date tax was levied even though it was not within city on date of assessment; had been earlier assessed by locality in which previously located).

that limitation, however, the property-tax power is usually interpreted as quite broad. It encompasses, for instance, the power to tax both legal and equitable interests in land.[21] And except as specifically exempted by constitutional or legislative provision, property is subject to the tax though it has not particularly benefited from the municipal services financed thereby.[22]

The key prerequisite to imposition of a property tax is assessment of the taxable property. The assessment consists of two steps: (1) preparation of a list of properties subject to the tax, and (2) valuation of the property in the manner prescribed by applicable statutes. The courts entertain a strong presumption that assessments are correct,[23] and a particular assessment will not be overturned because of improprieties in method unless the taxpayer seeking the relief shows specific injury to him from the

---

[21] Bancroft Investment Corp. v. City of Jacksonville, 157 Fla. 546, 27 So.2d 162 (1946). Where it is necessary to determine for tax purposes what property is "real" and what is "personal," the usual rules of property law are applied. See Franklin v. Metcalfe, 307 Mass. 386, 30 N.E.2d 262 (1940).

[22] See Moore v. Town of Stamford, 134 Conn. 65, 54 A.2d 588 (1947); Kelly v. Pittsburgh, 85 Pa. 170 (1878), aff'd 104 U.S. 78, 26 L.Ed. 658 (1881); Atherton v. Essex Junction, 83 Vt. 218, 74 A. 1118 (1910). Cf. Mitchell v. Negaunee, 113 Mich. 359, 71 N.W. 646 (1897) (except as specifically exempted, farm lands may be taxed by municipality). But where lands are not receiving services from the municipality of which they are a part, a proceeding for de-annexation may be justified; see Chapter 12 *supra*.

[23] See Alfred J. Sweet, Inc. v. City of Auburn, 134 Me. 28, 180 A. 803 (1935). See generally Annot., Original Cost of Construction or Reproduction Cost as Proper Factors in Assessing Real Property for Taxation, 104 A.L.R. 784 (1936). But a method of assessment will be set aside by the courts if it is found fundamentally erroneous. See Texas & Pacific Ry. v. City of El Paso, 126 Tex. 86, 85 S.W.2d 245 (1935); Republic Insurance Co. v. Highland Park Indep. School District, 57 S.W.2d 627 (Tex.Civ. App.1933) (irregularity not waived by taxpayer's paying amount he considered fair). On discrimination in property tax assessment against low-income areas, see Baar, Property Tax Assessment Against Low-Income Neighborhoods, 13 Urban Law. 333 (1981). On the influence of race in property tax assessments, see Lee, "Assessing" Discrimination: The Influence of Race in Residential Property Tax Assessments, 20 J. Land Use & Envtl. L. 1 (2004). On exemption for property held by charities, see Note, Tennessee's Charitable Property Tax Exemption: A Legally and Economically Unwieldy Tool for Achieving Charitable Policy Objectives, 37 U. Memphis L. Rev. 149 (2006). As to the exemptions or deductions sometimes given the elderly, see Note, Property Tax Relief for the Elderly: A Survey of the Nation, 6 Marquette Elder's Advisor 325 (2005). As to possible relief of a similar nature to low-income owners of property, see Note, Circuit Breakers: Implementing a Property Tax Credit to Help Low-Income Households, 19 Georgetown J. on Poverty L. & Pol'y 111 (2012).

When property belonging to senior citizens or veterans is exempt or treated more favorable under state statutes, this favorable treatment may be challenged as violative of equal protection. See State of Alaska v. Schmidt, 323 P.3d 647 (2014) (exemption program for senior citizens and disabled veterans discriminated between married and same-sex couples in violation of equal protection).

Property of religious institutions is usually exempt if used for religious purposes. See Cedar Lake Conference Ass'n v. Lake County Property Tax Assessment Bd. of Appeals, 887 N.E. 2d 205 (Ind. Tax 2008) (if property is predominantly used for religious purposes, state property tax assessment will apply even though property is sometimes used for non-religious purposes).

State or local governments may divide different kinds of property into categories and assign a different tax burden to each class; such a classification will be upheld against equal protection attack so long as it rests on reasonable differences and is not arbitrary or capricious. See Williams Natural Gas Co. v. State Bd. of Equalization, 891 P.2d 1219 (Okla.1994), cert. denied 516 U.S. 816, 116 S.Ct. 70, 133 L.Ed.2d 31 (1995) (public service property of railroads and airlines was assessed at lower ratio than was applied to property of other public service corporations; upheld against equal protection attack as neither arbitrary nor irrational). For examples of state methods of assessment and proposals for improvement, see (as to New York) Melnik & Cendella, Tax Assessment in New York State, 4 Albany Gov't L. Rev. 427 (2011), & Melnik & Cendella, Real Property Taxation and Assessment Processes: A Case for a Better Model, 12 N.Y.U. J. Legis. & Pub. Pol'y 259 (2008–09); and (as to Pennsylvania) Note, Pennsylvania's Assessment Laws Permitting the Use of a Base Year Method in Property Taxation Are Not Facially Unconstitutional, But Are Unconstitutionally Non-Uniform as Applied in Allegheny County, 48 Duquesne L. Rev. 651 (2010), noting Clifton v. Allegheny County, 600 Pa. 662, 969 A.2d 1197 (2009).

irregularity.[24] The legislation governing property-tax assessment usually declares that property is to be assessed at its "value," "actual value," or something similar—and any such words and phrases are generally taken to mean fair market value.[25] This, in turn, is defined as the highest price that a willing buyer would pay a willing seller.[26]

---

[24] See Billingsley v. City of Fort Worth, 278 S.W.2d 869 (Tex.Civ.App.1955) error ref. On the adequacy of property-tax refund procedures, see Rosewell v. LaSalle National Bank, 450 U.S. 503, 101 S.Ct. 1221, 67 L.Ed.2d 464 (1981), reh. denied 451 U.S. 1011, 101 S.Ct. 2349, 68 L.Ed.2d 864 (1981) (fact that interest not paid on refunds did not mean that remedy wasn't adequately speedy and efficient). On reassessment of property, see Sterk & Engler, Property Tax Reassessment: Who Needs It?, 81 Notre Dame L. Rev. 1037 (2006). As to some of the problems with property tax assessment appeals, see Note, Welcome Home, Suckers—Constitutional Problems With the Pennsylvania Property Tax Assessment Appeals System, 4 Pitt. Tax Rev. 85 (2006). As to the relief possible in a property tax appeal, see Maracay, LLC v. Maricopa County, 224 Ariz. 385, 231 P.3d 389 (Tax 2010) (two forms of relief possible: retrospective, where there is a refund of excessive taxes already collected, and prospective, involving an order that the assessor correct the value of the property on the tax roll; objection to assessor's valuation of real property for certain tax year is not lost due to subsequent sale of property).

[25] United States Steel Corp. v. Bucks County, 422 Pa. 463, 223 A.2d 92 (1966) (interpreting "actual value"). See Johnson v. State, 245 Ala. 499, 17 So.2d 662 (1944); Negaunee v. State Tax Commission, 337 Mich. 169, 59 N.W.2d 136 (1953) (interpreting "cash value"); Redmond v. Town of Tarboro, 106 N.C. 122, 10 S.E. 845 (1890). In some jurisdictions, constitutional or statutory language declares that property is to be assessed at a specified *percentage* of its value. See State ex rel. Barlow v. Kinnear, 70 Wn.2d 482, 423 P.2d 937 (1967). And in some states, a state board or other authority is given supervisory powers to equalize property-tax assessments made by local authorities throughout the state. See, for example, Okl. Const. Art. 10, § 21, providing the duties of the Oklahoma State Board of Equalization. Constitutional and statutory provisions sometimes specifically require uniformity of assessment throughout the state—but in any event, requirements that assessments be "at value" (or similar language) are usually interpreted as being intended to secure uniformity and equality. See Pullman Car & Mfg. Corp. v. Hamilton, 229 Ala. 184, 155 So. 616 (1934). Cf. City of Fort Worth v. Fort Worth Radiator Manufacturing Co., 278 S.W.2d 184 (Tex.Civ.App.1955), ref'd n. r. e. (proof of wrongful discrimination voids assessment). But cf. Adair v. Clay, 780 P.2d 650 (Okl.1988), cert. denied 493 U.S. 1076, 110 S.Ct. 1125, 107 L.Ed.2d 1032 (1990) (uniformity clause in state constitution does not apply to valuation of property but to rate of taxation).

In Board of County Comm'rs v. City of Muskogee, 820 P.2d 797 (Okl.1991), it was held that a state statute could validly impose the duty on a municipality to pay its proportionate share of the costs of an ad valorem property tax revaluation program since the city was one of the statutory beneficiaries of ad valorem levies.

A number of cases in recent years have required assessors to evaluate property, in accord with constitutional or statutory standards, at "true" or "full" value. See State ex rel. Beggrow v. Atkisson, 170 So.2d 455 (Fla.App.1964); Russman v. Luckett, 391 S.W.2d 694 (Ky.1965); Bettigole v. Assessors of Springfield, 343 Mass. 223, 178 N.E.2d 10 (1961); Village of Ridgefield Park v. Bergen County Board of Taxation, 31 N.J. 420, 157 A.2d 829 (1960) (the leading case); Hellerstein v. Assessor of Islip, 37 N.Y.2d 1, 371 N.Y.S.2d 388, 332 N.E.2d 279 (1975) (town must assess in accord with statutory standard of full value); State ex rel. Park Investment Co. v. Board of Tax Appeals, 175 Ohio St. 410, 195 N.E.2d 908 (1964), cert. denied 379 U.S. 818, 85 S.Ct. 35, 13 L.Ed.2d 29; Union Pacific Railroad v. Hoefke, 232 Or. 521, 376 P.2d 80 (1962); State ex rel. Barlow v. Kinnear, 70 Wn.2d 482, 423 P.2d 937 (1967). On the reaction (subsequent legislative proposals, etc.) to New York's *Hellerstein* decision *supra*, see Beebe & Sinnott, In the Wake of *Hellerstein*: Whither New York?, 43 Albany L.Rev. 203, 411, 777 (1979). In the past, "full" (or "true") value requirements were ignored in many states. See C. Bird, The General Property Tax: Findings of the 1957 Census of Governments 40 (1957). See generally Kilmar, The Legal Requirements for Equality in Tax Assessments, 25 Albany L.Rev. 203, 210 (1961); Note, Inequality in Property Tax Assessments: New Cures for an Old Ill, 75 Harv. L.Rev. 1374 (1962); Comment, Tax Assessments of Real Property: A Proposal for Legislative Reform, 68 Yale L.J. 335, 336–41 (1958). See also Barker, The Three Faces of Equality: Constitutional Requirements in Taxation, 57 Case W.L. Rev. 1 (2006); Laurie Reynolds, Uniformity of Taxation and the Preservation of Local Control in School Finance Reform, 40 U. Cal. Davis L. Rev. 1835 (2007).

[26] See Blackstone Manufacturing Co. v. Blackstone, 200 Mass. 82, 85 N.E. 880 (1908); City of New Brunswick v. State Division of Tax Appeals, 39 N.J. 537, 189 A.2d 702 (1963). Cf. Washington Beef, Inc. v. County of Yakima, 143 Wash.App. 165, 177 P.3d 162 (2008) (for purposes of property tax appraisal, the phrase "true and fair value in money" means "fair market value," which is what a willing buyer with no obligation to buy would pay a willing seller under no obligation to sell). See generally Comment, Twenty-five Years of Debate: Is Acquisition-Value Property Taxation Constitutional? Is It Fair? Is It Good Policy?, 53 Emory L.J.

In some jurisdictions, personal property is taxed instead of, or in addition to, real property. This tax is generally imposed on personal property permanently situated within the taxing locality,[27] and any personal property generally kept within that locality (even if temporarily outside the locality on the date the tax is assessed).[28]

§ 15.4 Local Taxation—Sales, Income, and Other Taxes; Methods of Enforcement

In 1934, New York City became the first major local unit in the United States to impose the sales tax on retail sales. Since that time, the sales tax has become a major revenue producer—often second only to the real-property tax—for many U.S. cities, particularly cities that are relatively large in population. But this tax remains controversial, often being criticized as "regressive," since it falls with disproportionate effect on the poorer members of the community. The regressive nature can be somewhat alleviated by exemptions for food and other necessities, but such exemptions may be difficult to administer—and may be struck down if the authorizing legislation stipulates that uniformity of taxation is necessary.[29] Where the sales tax is used, private

---

587 (2004), concluding that jurisdictions practicing acquisitions-value taxation should try to prevent extreme disparities between similar property owners. See *id.* at 615–25.

[27] See Church v. City of Los Angeles, 96 Cal.App.2d 89, 214 P.2d 550 (Dist.Ct.1950) (city cannot tax property just because it is within city on tax day, if it is permanently stationed in another municipality). Cf. Detroit Trust Co. v. City of Detroit, 248 Mich. 612, 227 N.W. 715 (1929) (locality could not tax personal property that came into local taxpayer's possession after day set for completion of assessment rolls). See also Polar Tankers, Inc. v. City of Valdez, 557 U.S. 1, 129 S.Ct. 2277 174 L.Ed.2d 1 (2009) (city's ad valorem property tax on large vessels docking at city's ports violated Tonnage Clause of U.S. Constitution—Art. 1, § 10, cl.3—where tax applied to no other form of personal property except large vessels; purpose of the Clause is to prevent states from nullifying the constitutional prohibition on import and export duties by taxing the vessels transporting merchandise), discussed in Cofer, Supreme Court Strikes Down Personal Property Tax on Vessels Under Tonnage Clause, 34 Tulane Maritime L. J. 153 (2009).

[28] See Liquid Carbonic Corp. v. Michigan Tax Comm'n, 4 Mich.App. 488, 145 N.W.2d 278 (1966); Annis Furs v. City of Detroit, 336 Mich. 527, 58 N.W.2d 907 (1953). Sometimes, state statutes define what will be considered the situs of personal property for purposes of local taxation. See City of Dallas v. Texas Prudential Insurance Co., 156 Tex. 36, 291 S.W.2d 693 (1956).

[29] See Butcher v. City of Philadelphia, 333 Pa. 497, 6 A.2d 298 (1938). Cf. Dow Jones & Co. v. State ex rel. Oklahoma Tax Comm'n 787 P.2d 843 (Okl.1990) (sales and use taxes exempting "sales of newspapers and periodicals where any individual transaction does not exceed 75 cents" invalidated as imposing an impermissible burden on the right to disseminate information). But cf. Oklahoma Ass'n for Equitable Taxation v. Oklahoma City, 901 P.2d 800 (Okl.1995) (city could create classes of taxpayers for purposes of collection of municipal sales taxes, and thus sales tax refunds to persons 65 and over did not violate equal protection). A Model City Tax Code has now been promulgated in an effort to provide greater uniformity in local sales and use taxes. See Kalson & Swain, Municipal Sales and Use Taxes—Highlights of the New Model City Tax Code, 23 Ariz. B.J. 12 (June/July 1987).

On the application of sales and use taxes to electronic commerce, see McLure, Sales and Use Taxes on Electric Commerce: Legal, Economic, Administrative, and Political Issues, 34 Urban Law. 487 (2002); Note, Capturing Tax Revenue on Internet Sales: Abandoning the Streamlined Agreement for Origin Sourcing, 56 Ariz. L. Rev. 249 (2014); Note, Much Ado About Nexus: The States Struggle to Impose Sales Tax Obligations on Out-of-State Sellers Engaged in E-Commerce, 24 Fordham Intellectual Prop. Media, & Entertainment L. J. 263 (2013); Comment, The Enigma of Sales Taxation Through the Use of State or Federal "Amazon" Laws: Are We Getting Anywhere?, 49 Idaho L. Rev. 121 (2012); Note, Online Retailers Battle With Sales Tax: A Physical Rule Living in a Digital World, 46 Suffolk U. L. Rev. 673 (2013); Note, The "Amazon Tax" Issue: Washing Away the Requirement of Physical Presence for Sales Tax Jurisdiction Over Internet Businesses, 2013 U. Ill. J. L. Tech. & Pol'y 231. On the requirements and desirability of sales and use taxes, see generally Roberts, A History of the Wyoming Sales Tax and How Lawmakers Chose It From Among Severance Taxes, an Income Tax, Gambling, and a Lottery, 4 Wyo. L. Rev. 157 (2004); Swain, State Sales and Use Tax Jurisdiction: An Economic Nexus Standard for the Twenty-first Century, 38 Ga. L. Rev. 343 (2003); Varyani, Taxing Electronic Commerce: The Efforts of Sales and Use Tax to Evolve With Technology, 39 Okla. City U. L. Rev. 151 (2014).

individuals—the sellers of goods—become in effect the tax collectors, but this system has been sustained against allegations that it is an undue delegation of governmental authority.[30]

In such major cities as New York, Chicago, Philadelphia, and in the municipalities of Washington State, taxes on admissions (to theatres, etc.) and amusements are large revenue-producers. These, too, remain controversial; they are alleged to have driven entertainment facilities into the suburbs of some major cities, thus contributing to the decline of city-centers. But they have produced less litigation than most other taxes. The usual rule of strict construction of the municipal taxing power is much in evidence, here, however: The power to levy admissions and amusement taxes will not be found to exist unless clearly granted by the state, and will not be inferred from a grant of power to levy license taxes on businesses and occupations.[31]

On interstate cooperation as to sales and use taxes, see Galle, Designing Interstate Institutions: The Example of the Streamlined Sales and Use Tax Agreement ("SSUTA"), 40 U. Cal. Davis L. Rev. 1381 (2007).

"Excise taxes" are similar to sales taxes; but while sales taxes are imposed on the sale of all commodities except those specifically exempted, excise taxes are applicable only to certain specified commodities, such as cigarettes or gasoline. See Rastgoufard, Too Much Smoke and Not Enough Mirrors: The Case Against Cigarette Excise Taxes and for Gasoline Taxes, 36 Urban Law. 411, 414 (2004), noting that while sales taxes are generally designed to raise revenue, excise taxes are often designed not only for that purpose but also to exert social control. *Id.* Both sales and excise taxes are considered regressive in nature. *Id.* at 412. For other, more direct methods of restricting smoking, see Section 23.8 *infra*. "Use taxes" are imposed on the exercise of a right or power over tangible personal property, as opposed to being imposed on a *sale* of tangible personal property or services as is the sales tax. See the discussion of the distinction in Gracie, LLC v. Idaho State Tax Comm'n, 149 Idaho 570, 237 P.3d 1196 (2010) (under the "resale exemption," any sale to a purchaser who leases, rents or resells the purchased item prior to making any significant use of it is exempt from the Idaho use tax; but purchases here found to be outside the exemption). See generally Comment, Use It or Lose It: State Approaches to Increasing Use-Tax Revenue, 60 U. Kan. L. Rev. 649 (2012).

30 Blauner's v. City of Philadelphia, 330 Pa. 342, 198 A. 889 (1938). See Ainsworth v. Bryant, 34 Cal.2d 465, 211 P.2d 564 (1949) (retail liquor dealer would be made to collect sales tax for city though state had exclusive regulatory power over retail sales). Cf. Kesbec, Inc. v. McGoldrick, 278 N.Y. 293, 16 N.E.2d 288 (1938), rearg. denied, 278 N.Y. 716, 17 N.E.2d 136 (dealer cannot legally challenge validity of tax or sue for refunds illegally collected). On the possible personal liability of a retail dealer for sales taxes he should have collected, see City of New York v. Bernstein, 90 N.Y.S.2d 759 (Sup.Ct.1949) (personal liability of corporate officer sustained, with little discussion, applying local law). See generally Cragan, Methods of Collecting Sales Taxes Effectively, 2 Alaska Municipal Adviser, No. 4, at 2 (July 1988). On "enhanced sales tax incentive programs"—under which local retailers invest in public and public-related improvements at their establishments in return for which the city agrees to share some fraction of its incremental increase in municipal sales taxes received after the retailer completes the improvements—, see Hayes & Godec, Taxation Innovations: Enhanced Sales Tax Incentive Programs, 22 Urban Law. 143 (1990).

31 City of St. Petersburg v. Florida Coastal Theatres, 43 So.2d 525 (Fla.1949); Eugene Theatre Co. v. City of Eugene, 194 Or. 603, 243 P.2d 1060 (1952). See Central City Opera House Ass'n v. City of Central, 650 P.2d 1349 (Colo.App.1982) (city charter provision authorizing council to license, tax, and regulate theatrical and other exhibitions, shows, and amusements held not to authorize an ordinance levying an excise tax on persons who pay to gain admission to such events, since the charter authorized taxes on businesses, not on their customers); Paramount-Gulf Theatres v. City of Pensacola, 62 So.2d 431 (Fla.1951) (power to charge admissions tax must be clearly shown). Cf. Wilderness World, Inc. v. Department of Rev., 182 Ariz. 196, 895 P.2d 108 (1995) (taxpayer's business of providing guided rafting trips did not fall within scope of amusement as to which amusements tax was authorized); Kansas City Renaissance Festival Corp. v. City of Bonner Springs, 269 Kan. 670, 8 P.3d 701 (2000) (city could not use ordinary ordinance to exempt itself from state statute prohibiting city excise taxes on services, such as amusements). See generally Annot., Validity of License Tax or Fee on Show or Place of Amusement, 58 A.L.R. 1340 (1929), supplemented 111 A.L.R. 778 (1937). See also Annot., Validity of Municipal Admission Tax for College Football Games or Other College-Sponsored Public Events, 60 A.L.R.3d 1027 (1974) (municipal admissions tax may validly be applied to tickets sold to university football games, though may be invalid as applied to events that are part of the educational process of the university); Annot., Admission Charges or Other Receipts from Extracurricular Activities of Schools as Subject to Taxation, 115 A.L.R. 1411 (1938).

In 1938, Philadelphia imposed an income tax on its residents—the first major American city to do so. The municipal income tax is now of great importance to many cities in Pennsylvania, as well as major cities in Ohio, and to such other metropolises as New York City and St. Louis. Of course, as with other taxes, no inherent power exists in a local government to levy an income tax,[32] but statutory authorizations of such taxes have withstood challenges to their constitutionality.[33] Many such taxes have been applied to the income earned within the city by non-residents of the city, making the tax a so-called "commuter tax." The constitutionality of such an application has been upheld,[34] even where the non-resident thus taxed was an employee of the state or federal

---

Admissions and amusement taxes have often survived constitutional challenges. See Friends of Chamber Music v. City & County of Denver, 696 P.2d 309 (Colo.1985) (ordinance authorizing admission tax on events at all city-owned facilities in order to retire municipal bonds issued by city for improvements to stadium held not violative of due process); Denver Center for the Performing Arts v. Briggs, 696 P.2d 299 (Colo.1985) (admissions tax imposed on patrons attending events held in municipal facility found not to violate the due process or equal protection rights of the patrons); Forbes v. City of Seattle, 113 Wash.2d 929, 785 P.2d 431 (1990) (ordinance levying admissions tax on patrons of motion picture theaters and exempting patrons of nonprofit tax-exempt organizations upheld against First Amendment and equal protection attack).

Related in nature to the admissions and amusements taxes are the taxes now imposed by a number of municipalities on occupancy of hotel and motel rooms. See Cournoyer, Hotel, Restaurant and Travel Law 12–21 (1978); Gelfand & Salsich, State and Local Taxation and Finance 68 (1985). Cf. Youngblood v. State, 259 Ga. 864, 388 S.E.2d 671 (1990), upholding a statute authorizing special taxing districts to impose hotel and motel taxes. But cf. Britt v. City of Pomona, 223 Cal.App.3d 265, 272 Cal.Rptr. 724 (1990) (municipal tax on occupants of hotels and like accommodations which house transient guests held invalid as denial of equal protection and due process). As with other tax revenues, the proceeds must ordinarily be used for public benefit, not for the benefit of a particular private group. See Allegheny County v. Monzo, 509 Pa. 26, 500 A.2d 1096 (1985), invalidating a county's hotel room rental tax adopted to finance a single downtown convention center. The court found that the tax in effect subsidized downtown hotels and businesses, which would benefit from increased convention business, at the expense of others in the taxed class. It has been held that a hotel/motel room rental tax can be imposed on rooms contracted for by the United States government. United States v. Montgomery County, 761 F.2d 998 (4th Cir.1985) (tax falls on occupant, not government, even though U.S. agency reimburses the occupant). See also Comment, Unconventional Decisions: Challenging the Use of Hotel Taxes in Convention Center Projects, 7 U. Pa. J. Const. L. 533 (2004). As to the increase in hotel taxes—both in their use and, where used, in their rate—in recent times, see "Taxed Out," Travel & Leisure magazine, June, 2012, at 77, saying that they are "one of the easiest targets in town" and that "many of these taxes support projects only tangentially related to tourism." *Id.* As to taxation of online travel companies, see Note, *Pitt County v. Hotels.com*: The Dormant Commerce Clause and State Taxation of Online Travel Companies, 64 Tax Law. 223 (2010).

[32] Carter Carburetor Corp. v. City of St. Louis, 356 Mo. 646, 203 S.W.2d 438 (1947). See generally Schlunk, Why Every State Should Have an Income Tax (and a Retail Sales Tax, Too), 78 Miss. L.J. 637 (2009).

[33] See City of Louisville v. Sebree, 308 Ky. 420, 214 S.W.2d 248 (1948); Walters v. City of St. Louis, 364 Mo. 56, 259 S.W.2d 377 (1953), aff'd 347 U.S. 231, 74 S.Ct. 505, 98 L.Ed. 660 (1954) (upholding ordinance levying income tax on *gross salaries* of employed persons but only on net *profits* of self-employed persons and of businesses); Angell v. City of Toledo, 153 Ohio St. 179, 91 N.E.2d 250 (1950); Butcher v. City of Philadelphia, *supra* note 29. See generally Fordham & Mallison, Local Income Taxation, 11 Ohio St. L.J. 217 (1950); Hartman, Municipal Income Taxation, 31 Rocky Mtn. L.Rev. 123 (1958); Muchnick, A Municipal Income Tax for Boston: Discourse in Possibilities, 5 Suffolk U.L.Rev. 1 (1970); Note, An Analysis of the Philadelphia Income Tax Ordinance, 27 Temple L.Q. 453 (1954). See also Januta, The Municipal Revenue Crisis: California Problems and Possibilities, 56 Cal.L.Rev. 1525 (1968); Note, The Uniform Municipal Income Tax Act, 18 Ohio St.L.J. 489 (1957). On the use of an increased income tax to stimulate economic growth in Columbus, Ohio, see Foroohar, The Columbus Comeback, Time magazine, Oct. 8, 2012, at 23.

[34] American Commuters Association v. Levitt, 279 F.Supp. 40 (S.D.N.Y.1967), aff'd 405 F.2d 1148 (2d Cir.1969); Dooley v. City of Detroit, 370 Mich. 194, 121 N.W.2d 724 (1963);Kansas City v. Querry, 511 S.W.2d 790 (Mo.1974); Arnold v. Berra, 366 S.W.2d 321 (Mo.1963) (Illinois resident who worked in St. Louis could be charged income tax by St. Louis; no violation of due process or commerce clause, and irrelevant that taxpayer also paid taxes in state of residence); Thompson v. City of Cincinnati, 2 Ohio St.2d 292, 208 N.E.2d 747, 31 O.O.2d 563 (1965); McConnell v. City of Columbus, 172 Ohio St. 95, 173 N.E.2d 760, 15 O.O.2d 168 (1961); Angell v. City of Toledo, *supra* note 33; Kiker v. City of Philadelphia, 346 Pa. 624, 31 A.2d 289 (1943), cert. denied 320 U.S. 741, 64 S.Ct. 41, 88 L.Ed. 439 (1943). See Shaffer v. Carter, 252 U.S. 37, 40 S.Ct. 221, 64 L.Ed.

government.[35] The application of the city income tax to the non-resident can be justified since a non-resident who works in the city will almost invariably benefit from city streets and from such city services as police and fire protection.[36] A resident of a municipality may be taxed on all his income by that municipality, even though part of it was earned outside municipal limits.[37]

A gross receipts tax on the total revenues of businesses and individuals can be imposed by municipalities under authorizing statutes that exist in about half the states. In a few jurisdictions, the tax can only be levied on certain designated businesses, such as public utilities. These taxes have been upheld even in their application to professional persons such as attorneys.[38]

---

445 (1920) (state could tax income earned within its borders by nonresident). On the similarity between state and municipal taxes on non-residents, see County of Alameda v. City of San Francisco, 19 Cal.App.3d 750, 97 Cal.Rptr. 175 (Dist. Ct.1971). On municipal income taxes on the wages of non-residents, see generally Merz, Municipal Personal Income Taxation of Nonresidents, 31 Ohio St. L.J. 770 (1970); Comment, Suburbia Lost—Constitutional and Other Challenges Regarding the Municipal Income Tax on Nonresidents, 5 Willamette L.J. 295 (1968); Note, The Validity of San Francisco's Commuter Tax, 20 Hastings L.J. 813 (1969); Annot., Validity of Municipal Ordinance Imposing Income Tax or License Upon Nonresidents Employed in Taxing Jurisdiction (Commuter Tax), 48 A.L.R.3d 343 (1973).

[35] McConnell v. City of Columbus, *supra* note 34 (nonresident who worked for the state on state-owned property within city); Kiker v. City of Philadelphia, *supra* note 34 (services were performed by worker for federal government). See Application of Thompson, 157 F.Supp. 93 (E.D.Pa.1957), aff'd sub nom. United States ex rel. Thompson v. Lennox, 258 F.2d 320 (3d Cir.1958), cert. denied 358 U.S. 931, 79 S.Ct. 317, 3 L.Ed.2d 303 (1959), reh. denied 359 U.S. 921, 79 S.Ct. 579, 3 L.Ed.2d 584. Cf. Marson v. City of Philadelphia, 342 Pa. 369, 21 A.2d 228 (1941) (state employee residing in city liable for city income tax).

[36] See Kiker v. City of Philadelphia, *supra* note 34. See generally Gillette, Who Should Authorize a Commuter Tax?, 77 U. Chi. L. Rev. 223 (2010), a part of the Symposium, Reassessing the State & Local Government Toolkit, 77 Chi. L. Rev. 1–366 (2010).

[37] See Glen Alden Coal Co. v. Thomas, 165 Pa.Super. 199, 67 A.2d 754 (1949) (worker had residence in two localities; had to pay full income tax in both; state law usually allowed credit, against tax paid where wages earned, for tax paid at residence, but no such credit here).

[38] Franklin v. Peterson, 87 Cal.App.2d 727, 197 P.2d 788 (1948) (attorney). Cf. Steinbeck v. Gerosa, 4 N.Y.2d 302, 175 N.Y.S.2d 1, 151 N.E.2d 170 (1958), appeal dism'd 358 U.S. 39, 79 S.Ct. 64, 3 L.Ed.2d 45 (gross receipts tax could be applied to earnings of resident writer). While public utility earnings are usually a prime, and valid, object of these taxes, occasionally it may be found that the state has pre-empted public utility taxation. See Haefner v. City of Youngstown, 147 Ohio St. 58, 68 N.E.2d 64 (1946); Youngstown Municipal Railway v. City of Youngstown, 154 Ohio St. 311, 95 N.E.2d 585 (1950). A gross receipts tax has been upheld as applied to the business of publishing newspapers. Times Mirror Co. v. City of Los Angeles, 192 Cal.App.3d 170, 237 Cal.Rptr. 346 (1987), appeal dism'd 484 U.S. 1022, 108 S.Ct. 743, 98 L.Ed.2d 756 (1988). Cf. Tucson Newspapers, Inc. v. City of Tucson, 172 Ariz. 378, 837 P.2d 180 (App. 1992) ("business privilege tax" on 2% of gross income of newspaper upheld). Cf. Moss v. City of Dunwoody, 750 S.E.2d 326 (Ga. 2013) (city ordinance requiring attorneys with offices in the city to register their business location with the city, obtain an occupation tax certificate and pay a tax does not amount to an unconstitutional precondition on the practice of law so long as the tax is merely a means to generate revenue and is not a regulatory fee). But cf. Montana–Dakota Utilities Co. v. City of Billings, 318 Mont. 862, 80 P.3d 1247 (2003) (city ordinance which imposed gross-revenue fee for use of public right-of-way amounted to an impermissible tax on goods or services where utilities had occupied the rights-of-way for years prior to enactment of the ordinance and the fee was not tied to the utilities' use or occupancy of the right-of-way). Compare Ford Motor Co. v. City of Seattle, 160 Wash.2d 32, 156 P.3d 185 (2007), cert. denied 128 S.Ct. 1224, 170 L.Ed.2d 61 (2008) (upholding cities' imposition of business and occupation tax on taxpayer's gross receipts on wholesale auto sales to independent dealers within cities).

In City of Pittsburgh v. Alco Parking Corp., 417 U.S. 369, 94 S.Ct. 2291, 41 L.Ed.2d 132 (1974), the Court sustained a very high tax on gross receipts of nonresidential parking facilities despite evidence that operators of such facilities could, under such a tax arrangement, make little if any profit and that such operators faced competition from a public parking authority. The Court reasoned that the city was entitled to put automobile drivers to the choice of paying the parking tax (through higher parking fees) or using other transportation.

A "license tax" is one imposed on the doing of business or engaging in an occupation within the taxing locality.[39] Though the power to impose a license tax must be clearly granted a municipality and will not be inferred from other powers,[40] such a tax—where clearly authorized—may be levied even though *regulation* of the particular business or occupation has been completely pre-empted by the state government.[41] The tax can validly be applied to non-residents of the taxing locality,[42] and it is generally agreed that its amount may vary according to the volume of business done by the particular taxpayer.[43]

Methods of enforcing the payment of taxes levied by local governments are such as are specified by state constitution and/or statute. Usually the relevant legislation will provide for the existence of liens against real property when the property taxes thereon are not paid. Upon proper notice being given, foreclosure of the lien and subsequent sale of the property will occur—but the statutory methods must be strictly followed.[44] Other

---

[39] City of St. Petersburg v. Florida Coastal Theaters, *supra* note 31. See Miles v. City Council of Augusta, Georgia, 710 F.2d 1542 (11th Cir. 1983) (promotion of "talking cat" (Blackie the Talking Cat) was "occupation" or "business" within city ordinance requiring license fee; activity came within legitimate exercise of city's taxing power).

[40] Viquesney v. Kansas City, 305 Mo. 488, 266 S.W. 700 (1924); Eugene Theater Co. v. City of Eugene, *supra* note 31. See Coos Bay v. Order of Eagles, 179 Or. 83, 170 P.2d 389 (1946) (authority to impose business tax must be strictly construed against municipality). Cf. Pierce v. Stephenville, 206 S.W.2d 848 (Tex.Civ.App.1947) (municipalities given power by Texas Constitution to levy occupation taxes up to half the amount of *state* occupation taxes; no power found by court to levy tax on occupations untaxed by state).

[41] Post v. City of Grand Junction, 118 Colo. 434, 195 P.2d 958 (1948) (city has authority to impose occupational excise taxes purely for revenue); Coos Bay v. Order of Eagles, *supra* note 40. See note 13 *supra* and accompanying text. But cf. Beierle v. City of Newport, 305 Ky. 477, 204 S.W.2d 806 (1947) (occupation tax on games of chance invalid where such games *illegal* under state law).

Where the state has *not* pre-empted the field of regulation, a municipality may, of course, impose a license *fee* for regulatory purposes. Such a fee should not—under the city's *regulatory* power—exceed the cost of regulation; but acting under its *revenue* powers, the city may also make a reasonable profit on issuance of licenses. See Red Slipper Club, Inc. v. Oklahoma City, 599 P.2d 406 (Okl.1979). See also Section 15.12, note 141 *infra* and accompanying text.

[42] See Annot., Discrimination as Regards License or Occupation Tax Between Persons or Concerns Engaged in Same Line of Business, Based on Maintenance or Nonmaintenance of Plants or Places of Business Within City Limits, 109 A.L.R. 903 (1937). See generally Annot., Validity of Municipal Ordinance Imposing Income Tax or License Upon Nonresidents, *supra* note 34.

[43] See City of Louisville v. Sebree, 308 Ky. 420, 214 S.W.2d 248 (1948). There is a general test of reasonableness that all license taxes must meet, and such taxes will be invalidated if arbitrary, or if they contain unjust classifications. See 508 Chestnut Inc. v. City of St. Louis, 389 S.W.2d 823 (Mo.1965), appeal dism'd 382 U.S. 203, 86 S.Ct. 400, 15 L.Ed.2d 271 (tax will not be invalidated unless clearly shown to be arbitrary); Gooch Food Products Co. v. Rothman, 131 Neb. 523, 268 N.W. 468 (1936); Federal Drug Co. v. City of Pittsburgh, 358 Pa. 454, 57 A.2d 849 (1948); Forest Lake v. Forest Acres, 227 S.C. 163, 87 S.E.2d 587 (1955) (business tax invalid if not graduated justly). See also LCM Enterprises, Inc. v. Town of Dartmouth, 14 F.3d 675 (1st Cir.1994) (town could charge higher harbor fee to nonresidents when goal was to make up for unequal contribution to harbor expenses).

[44] See City of Auburn v. Mandarelli, 320 A.2d 22 (Me.1974), appeal dism'd, 419 U.S. 810, 95 S.Ct. 25, 42 L.Ed.2d 37 (1974). Cf. Borough of Paramus v. Block, 42 N.J.Super. 369, 126 A.2d 660 (1956) (notice requirements of statutes are mandatory). On the due-process requirement of giving notice to all interested parties in connection with foreclosing a tax lien, see Robinson v. Hanrahan, 409 U.S. 38, 93 S.Ct. 30, 34 L.Ed.2d 47 (1972); Schroeder v. New York City, 371 U.S. 208, 83 S.Ct. 279, 9 L.Ed.2d 255 (1962); Walker v. Hutchinson, 352 U.S. 112, 77 S.Ct. 200, 1 L.Ed.2d 178 (1956); Nelson v. New York, 352 U.S. 103, 77 S.Ct. 195, 1 L.Ed.2d 171 (1956); Covey v. Town of Somers, 351 U.S. 141, 76 S.Ct. 724, 100 L.Ed. 1021 (1956); Mullane v. Central Hanover Bank & Trust Co., 339 U.S. 306, 70 S.Ct. 652, 94 L.Ed. 865 (1950). In Pruitt v. Ferguson, 224 Va. 507, 297 S.E.2d 714 (1982), it was held that notice of a tax sale was valid where given under the name listed in the records, even though, due to a scrivener's mistake, the deed had been recorded under the wrong name and thus the true owner of the property never received notice of the tax sale. Where the property is subject to a mortgage, the mortgagee, having a legally protected and substantial property interest, is constitutionally entitled to

common methods of enforcing payment of taxes to local governments are (1) seizure of personal property and its subsequent sale, for non-payment of real-property taxes, and sometimes for non-payment of personal-property taxes, (2) liens on personal property for non-payment of taxes thereon, (3) personal judicial actions against the delinquent taxpayer for non-payment of taxes *other than* property taxes (and, where clearly authorized by statute, for non-payment of real-property taxes), and (4) under the laws of some states, the placing into receivership of properties on which taxes have not been paid.[45]

§ 15.5 State Revenue-Sharing

The subject of federal revenue-sharing with local governments is discussed later in this chapter. But *state* sharing of tax revenues with local governments has existed for many years in some jurisdictions, and often involves substantial sums of money. Such programs of state sharing are thought to prevent too heavy a burden from falling on owners of properties and businesses within municipal boundaries, to enable the state-as-a-whole to aid poorer communities, and to spread out among all state residents the costs of cultural and other facilities that are customarily (and most conveniently) located in the centers of population. But it has been argued, on the other hand, that the use of state taxation to aid local governments may lessen the sense of political responsibility of the residents of the cities, and weaken their ability to make effective protests when they feel taxes are too high or the revenues are improperly used.[46]

---

notice of a tax sale reasonably calculated to apprise him of the pending event. Mennonite Bd. of Missions v. Adams, 462 U.S. 791, 103 S.Ct. 2706, 77 L.Ed.2d 180 (1983) (notice as required under Indiana statute—by posting and publishing announcement of tax sale and mailing notice to *mortgagor* by certified mail—did not meet due process requirements of Fourteenth Amendment). Cf. Franks v. Noble, 159 P.3d 302 (Okla. Civ. App. 2007) (county treasurer failed to mail the statutorily required notice of tax sale to two persons owning partial interests in property, whose ownership interests were not included in the tax rolls; tax sale of the property held invalid as to those two owners). But see M & M Investment Group, LLC v. Ahlemeyer Farms, Inc., 994 N.E.2d 1108 (Ind. 2013) (state statute that requires a mortgagee to opt-in annually to request notice that a parcel of land is eligible for a prospective tax sale does not violate Due Process); In re Foreclosure of Liens for Delinquent Land Taxes by Action in Rem Collector of Revenue v. Bhatti, 334 S.W.3d 444 (Mo. 2011) (notice provisions of Missouri law as applied to property owner facing a tax sale of his home do not violate property owner's Due Process when notice is given only by first-class mail sent to address provided by the owner, and city had no reason to know that owner could not receive mail at that address). On the economic effects of foreclosure on the community, see Comment, Making Debt Pay: Examining the Use of Property Tax Delinquency as a Revenue Source, 62 Emory L. J. 217 (2012); Comment, Tax Foreclosure: A Drag on Community Vitality or a Tool for Economic Growth?, 81 U. Cin. L. Rev. 1615 (2013). See also Comment, Saving Alabama's Urban Neighborhoods: Revisions to Alabama's Property Tax Sale Laws, 44 Cumberland L. Rev. 497 (2013–14). On the special problems regarding notice to elderly homeowners, see Comment, Redeeming What Is Lost: The Need to Improve Notice for Elderly Homeowners Before and After Tax Sales, 25 Geo. Mason U. Civil Rights L. J. 85 (2014). On the government's duty when the notice of tax sale is returned unclaimed, see Jones v. Flowers, 547 U.S. 220, 126 S.Ct. 1708, 164 L.Ed.2d 415 (2006) (when mailed notice of tax sale is returned unclaimed, state, as a matter of due process, must take additional reasonable steps to attempt to provide notice to property owner before selling property, if it is practicable to do so). On tax liens and their foreclosure, see generally 2A Antieau, Municipal Corporation Law §§ 21.86–.87 (1998). On the priority between tax liens and other interests, see Oklahoma City v. Habana Inn, 753 P.2d 400 (Okl. App. 1987) (liens for ad valorem property tax must be afforded priority and paid ahead of all other competing interests; but hotel tax is personal, not ad valorem, and lien for it ceases to exist when mortgagee with prior, recorded mortgage foreclosed on property).

[45] See Antieau, *supra* note 44, §§ 21.88–.94. As noted in § 21.93, fines and other criminal penalties for non-payment of taxes are also authorized in most jurisdictions.

[46] See 2A Antieau, *supra* note 44, § 21.102. See also File, Financial Responsibility of West Virginia Municipalities, 52 W.Va.L.Rev. 208 (1950). On typical amounts of state payments to local governments for various activities, see United States Bureau of the Census, Chartbook of Governmental Data 12 (1978).

§ 15.6 Special Assessments

Sometimes a local government will make a particular improvement—such as paving or widening a street—and pay for it by assessing the property that is thought to be specially benefited by the improvement—such as property bordering, or within a certain distance of, the street that is paved or widened. The use of such "special assessments" has a long history in the United States.[47] It is often held to be within the legislative discretion of the local governing authorities as to when to use general tax funds for a particular improvement or project, and when to use special assessments against particular properties.[48]

Of course, as with the taxing power, the power to levy special assessments is not inherent and must be found in some grant from the state.[49] There is one broad

---

[47] See People ex rel. Griffin v. Mayor of Brooklyn, 4 N.Y. 419, 438 (1851), noting a 1691 New York statute on assessments in New York City, and other early authorities on the subject. On the beneficial effects of special assessments in curbing political corruption in the mid-1800's, see "Robin Einhorn Rewrites Urban History," 32 Pub. Affairs Rep., March, 1991, No. 2, at 5. See generally Antieau, The Special Assessments of Municipal Corporations, 35 Marq.L.Rev. 315 (1952).

On the definition of "special assessments," see Knox v. City of Orland, 4 Cal.4th 132, 14 Cal.Rptr.2d 159, 841 P.2d 144 (1992) ("special assessment" is compulsory charge levied against real property within a predetermined district and made for purpose of deferring the expense of a permanent public improvement, whereas a "tax" can be levied without reference to particular benefits to particular property); Zelinger v. City & County of Denver, 724 P.2d 1356 (Colo.1986) (assessments are charges imposed for purposes of financing local improvements; must be directed against users of improvement, and revenue must be applied only to maintenance, operation, or development of the improvement; are not included in constitutional provision requiring uniformity of taxation); Appeal of Boeing Co., 261 Kan. 508, 930 P.2d 1366 (Kan. 1997) ("general taxes" are exactions placed on citizens by taxing authorities for support of government while "special assessments" are imposed on property within a limited area for payment of special or local improvements). Cf. Salt Lake County v. Board of Educ., 808 P.2d 1056 (Utah 1991) (drainage fee was not "local assessment" within meaning of school district's statutory exemption from paying local assessments).

[48] See Memphis & Charleston Ry. v. Pace, 282 U.S. 241, 51 S.Ct. 108, 75 L.Ed. 315 (1931) (federal Constitution does not limit discretion of municipal authorities on whether an improvement is paid for by taxes or assessments); Valley Farms Co. v. County of Westchester, 261 U.S. 155, 43 S.Ct. 261, 67 L.Ed. 585 (1923) (state legislature levied sewer assessments); Houck v. Little River Drainage District, 239 U.S. 254, 36 S.Ct. 58, 60 L.Ed. 266 (1915). Cf. Kansas City Southern Railway v. Road Improvement District No. 3, 266 U.S. 379, 45 S.Ct. 136, 69 L.Ed. 335 (1924) (act of state legislature assessing cost of public road against private lands, and determining what lands to assess and in what amounts, does not offend due process unless determination is palpably arbitrary); O'Flynn v. Village of East Rochester, 292 N.Y. 156, 54 N.E.2d 343 (1944) (taxes to pay electric plant bonds were not discriminatory merely because applied to all village property on ad valorem basis). See generally Board of Directors v. Reconstruction Finance Corp., 170 F.2d 430 (8th Cir.1948) (Congress can consent to special assessments on federal property, but mere consent to "taxation" of such property doesn't cover assessments; good discussion of difference between taxes and assessments). On possible expanded use of assessments to pay for such projects as environmental cleanups and the construction of mass transit, see Melnick, New Avenues for Special Assessment Financing, 25 Urban Law. 539 (1993).

[49] See Fordham, Local Government Law 513 (2d rev. ed. 1986). See generally Tooke, Construction and Operation of Municipal Powers, 7 Temp.L.Q. 267 (1933). On the nature of assessments, see Wasson v. Hogenson, 196 Colo. 183, 583 P.2d 914 (1978) (not taxes in the strict sense, but are in the nature of taxes); Krumpelman v. Louisville & Jefferson County Metropolitan Sewer District, 314 S.W.2d 557 (Ky.1958) (assessments are for fixed amount and are assessed with reference to special benefit to property; taxes are for general revenue, are levied periodically, have no relation to direct benefit to person or property taxed). Cf. St. Lucie County-Fort Pierce Fire Prevention & Control District v. Higgs, 141 So.2d 744 (Fla.1962) (levy for fire protection service was property tax, not assessment, because no parcel of land was specially benefited in proportion to its value). On the difference between assessments and taxes, see Martin v. City of Tigard, 335 Or. 444, 72 P.3d 619 (2003) (charge for street improvement project was an assessment for a local improvement, not a tax, within meaning of constitutional provision limiting real property taxes); Cary v. Mason County, 132 Wash.App. 495, 132 P.3d 157 (2006) (special assessments are a distinctive form of user charge which allocates the cost of public improvements that increase the value of property to the owner of that asset; assessments must relate directly to the cost of the improvements, relate to the value of the improvements to the property

requirement that is generally applied: special assessments can only be used where there is some "special benefit" to the property assessed. This can usually be found, for instance, where public parking facilities are being created in a business area—the neighboring businesses are specially benefited.[50] But such special benefit may be found lacking even as to nearby properties where the facility is a library to be used by an entire community,[51] or a viaduct or tunnel on a major thoroughfare.[52]

---

assessed, and be deposited in special accounts for the particular improvements). On application of the Equal Protection of the U.S. Constitution to assessments, see Armour v. City of Indianapolis, 566 U.S. ___, 132 S.Ct. 2073, 182 L.Ed.2d 998 (2012), where a city, in transitioning from one system of funding sewer improvement projects to another, chose to forgive all assessments still owed, but declined to pay a refund to homeowners who had already paid their assessments. The Court found this distinction justified by administrative considerations and thus to have a rational basis that satisfied Equal Protection.

[50] See City of Whittier v. Dixon, 24 Cal.2d 664, 151 P.2d 5 (1944); Thomson v. City of Dearborn, 349 Mich. 685, 85 N.W.2d 122 (1957); Northern Pacific Railway v. City of Grand Forks, 73 N.W.2d 348 (N.D. 1955); Duncan Development Corp. v. Crestview Sanitary District, 22 Wis.2d 258, 125 N.W.2d 617 (1964) (water tank and appurtenances could be considered a local improvement, and paid for by special assessments). See generally Annot., Parking Place as Public Improvement Which May Be Established or Supported in Whole or Part by Special Assessment, 153 A.L.R. 961 (1944). Determining the area benefitted by an improvement is generally held to be a legislative function; and the legislative determination, unless clearly unjust, is usually conclusive and not subject to judicial interference unless arbitrariness, abuse, or unreasonableness is shown. See Wood v. City of Lewiston, 138 Idaho 218, 61 P.3d 575 (2002) (competent evidence supported findings that construction of water main in area to west of local improvement district boundaries did not reflect impermissible westward expansion of project, but was effective means of connecting local improvement district system to city system). But cf. Silicon Valley Taxpayers Assn. v. Santa Clara County Open Space Auth., 44 Cal. 4th 431, 79 Cal. Rptr. 3d 312, 187 P.3d 37 (2008) (enhanced recreational opportunities, expanded access to recreational areas, protection of views, the scenery, and the other environmental benefits were "general benefits" that could not be funded by special assessment). See generally Note, *Silicon Valley Taxpayers Association*: Local Voters, State Propositions, and the Fate of Property Assessments, 97 Cal. L. Rev. 1899 (2009).

It has been stated by some courts that an assessment must specially benefit or enhance the value of the assessed property in an amount at least equal to the burden imposed and that if no special benefit is conferred on the assessed property, the assessment amounts to a taking of the property without due process. Reams v. City of Grand Junction, 676 P.2d 1189 (Colo.1984). Cf. Tocci v. City of Three Forks, 216 Mont. 159, 700 P.2d 171 (1985) (city's assessment must be in proportion to benefits conferred, but city's judgment as to what property to assess is ordinarily conclusive absent proof of fraud or mistake). The benefit to the assessed property from the improvement need not, however, be immediate but may lie in the future. City of Wasilla v. Wilsonoff, 698 P.2d 656 (Alaska 1985) (presumption of correctness is accorded assessment). See Kerr v. Hallett, 67 Or.App. 324, 677 P.2d 1098 (1984), review denied 297 Or. 272, 683 P.2d 92 (1984) (landowner's present use of property not determinative of whether special benefit has accrued; any reasonably anticipated future uses of the land could be considered by city council). The question of whether a property has been specially benefitted by an improvement for purposes of determining the validity of a special assessment has been held a question of fact. Bellevue Associates v. City of Bellevue, 108 Wash.2d 671, 741 P.2d 993 (1987). The improvements for which the assessments are made need not be physical additions but can consist of services. See City of Seattle v. Rogers Clothing for Men, 114 Wash.2d 213, 787 P.2d 39 (1990) (advertising and maintenance services designed to benefit the businesses assessed). See generally Stevens, The Ever-Expanding Use of Special-Benefit Assessments, 25 Urban Law. 567 (1993).

[51] Heavens v. King County Rural Library District, 66 Wash.2d 558, 404 P.2d 453 (1965). But cf. St. Joseph Township v. Municipal Finance Commission, 351 Mich. 524, 88 N.W.2d 543 (1958) (special assessment district for fire department purposes upheld).

[52] Hinman v. Temple, 133 Neb. 268, 274 N.W. 605 (1937) (viaduct eliminating grade crossing where highway crossed railroad tracks). See City of Waukegan v. De Wolf, 258 Ill. 374, 101 N.E. 532 (1913) (special assessments improper for constructing viaduct on principal thoroughfare). But see Bauer v. City of Olathe, 257 Kan. 540, 894 P.2d 823 (Kan. 1995) (designation of road as main traffic way did not preclude city from financing part of costs by special assessment). See generally Annot., Elimination of Railroad Grade Crossing as Local Improvement for Which Property Specially Benefited May Be Assessed, 111 A.L.R. 1222 (1937). As to assessments for street curbs, see Note, Curb Appeal: Municipal Special Assessments, 57 S. D. L. Rev. 443 (2012), discussing Hubbard v. City of Pierre, 784 N.W. 2d 499 (S.D. 2010).

Pennsylvania has the unusual rule that special assessments may be used only to defray the original cost of an improvement, not for maintenance, restoration, or renewal—such as repaving a street when the original paving deteriorates.[53] Other jurisdictions have no such flat rule; and while regular day-to-day maintenance of streets and other facilities is usually paid for from general tax funds, restoration—including repaving of streets—is commonly, and validly, financed by special assessments.[54] It is generally agreed that such restoration and renewal may just as appropriately be considered a local improvement as the original building of the road or other facility.

Any legislatively determined method as to apportionment of a special assessment—based on frontage of a property on a street being improved, for example, or based on valuation or area of the property—will be upheld so long as reasonable.[55] There is great

---

In the case of In re Indian Trail Trunk Sewer, 35 Wash.App. 840, 670 P.2d 675 (1983), expert testimony that the fair market value of assessed land was either not affected or else was diminished by building the trunk sewer system for which the assessment was made was held to overcome the presumption in favor of the assessment's validity. The ultimate burden of showing special benefit was said to rest with the city; here, the trunk sewer was too remote to confer such benefit. Cf. Dixon Road Group v. City of Novi, 426 Mich. 390, 395 N.W.2d 211 (1986) (where assessment to properties was approximately 2.6 times the increase in the values of the property, assessment invalid). Courts may also set aside individual special assessments due to irrational discrepancies between the amounts of assessments established for similarly situated landowners. Alberty v. City of Henderson, 106 Nev. 299, 792 P.2d 390 (1990).

As to the circumstances under which separate lots may be considered together for purposes of applying the "special benefit" standard, see Doolittle v. City of Everett, 114 Wash.2d 88, 786 P.2d 253 (1990) (generally each parcel should be assessed separately, but different rule applies where owner has actually combined several lots and put them to unified use). On the "special benefit" principle, see generally Rollow v. City of Ada, 794 P.2d 1211 (Okl.1990) (property cannot be included within assessment district if it will not benefit from the improvements, nor can property that is directly benefitted be excluded while rates are increased on the included property).

[53] See Supervisors of Manheim Township v. Workman, 350 Pa. 168, 38 A.2d 273 (1944) (street-light assessment invalidated, though service fees might be validated); City of Harrisburg v. Segelbaum, 151 Pa. 172, 24 A. 1070 (1892); Appeal of The Protestant Orphan Asylum, 111 Pa. 135, 3 A. 217 (1886). It is said that an assessment for special benefits should be imposed only once as to any particular improvement and that after the improvement is once created, its upkeep is an ordinary duty of the municipality for the public good.

[54] See Clayton v. City of Farmington, 102 N.M. 340, 695 P.2d 490 (App. 1985) (repaving of street is continuation of paving power and may properly be paid for by special assessments); Holswade v. City of Huntington, 96 W.Va. 124, 122 S.E. 449 (1924) (with review of authorities). Cf. Bloom v. City of Fort Collins, 784 P.2d 304 (Colo.1989), where a "transportation utility fee," varying according to a lot's street frontage and estimated street usage, was upheld when imposed on owners or occupants of developed lots or parcels of land within the city for the purpose of providing revenues for maintenance of city streets. See also Baker, Using Special Assessments as a Tool for Smart Growth: Louisville's New Metro Government as a Potential Example, 45 Brandeis L.J. 1 (2006).

[55] See Roberts v. Richland Irrigation Dist., 289 U.S. 71, 53 S.Ct. 519, 77 L.Ed. 1038 (1933); Conyers v. City of Prescott, 182 Ariz. 336, 897 P.2d 638 (Ariz.App.1994) (city's method of apportioning sewer system assessment based on number of units into which landowner could divide his property held valid); Simmons v. City of Moscow, 111 Idaho 14, 720 P.2d 197 (1986) (assessments based on square footage of property and on zones, which were based on proximity to the improvements, held valid); Ward v. Ada County Highway Dist., 106 Idaho 889, 684 P.2d 291 (1984) (county highway district did not err in basing assessments on front foot method); Board of Educ. v. City of Topeka, 214 Kan. 811, 522 P.2d 982 (1974) (square-foot method of apportionment not unjust as to property put to educational use); Hagmann v. City of New Orleans, 190 La. 796, 182 So. 753 (1938) (square footage can be used in apportioning street paving costs); South Ferry Street Project v. City of Schenectady, 72 Misc.2d 134, 338 N.Y.S.2d 730 (1972) (cost of street widening assessed according to zones of benefit); Time Oil Co. v. City of Port Angeles, 42 Wash.App. 473, 712 P.2d 311 (1985) (front foot method of assessment will be presumed correct where record shows that city council determined that this method more fairly reflected the special benefits to properties being assessed than would other methods). Cf. Donaldson's Heirs v. City of New Orleans, 166 La. 1059, 118 So. 134 (1927) (front-footage rule as to paving assessment may be applied even to irregularly shaped (triangular) lot); Emery v. City of Rawlins, 596 P.2d 675 (Wyo.1979) (classification used in computing square footage of properties upheld). See generally on the history of methods of apportionment, 4 Dillon, Municipal Corporations § 1436 (5th ed. 1911).

legislative discretion both in determining the property that is specially benefited (and that can thus be assessed) and in determining the division of the assessment among properties within the general, particularly benefited area. No hearing or prior notice need be accorded the assessed persons before the assessment is levied against their property.[56]

Property owners are frequently given an option of paying the full amount of the assessment within a prescribed period of time, such as a month, or of electing to pay in installments over a period of years.[57] Where assessments are not paid on time, the usual method of enforcement is a lien on the property benefited. Personal liability of *resident* owners is also sometimes provided, and has been declared valid despite contrary authority in the past.[58] Personal liability of *non-resident* owners has in the past often been considered beyond the scope of a local government's authority, but the trend is to allow this liability also, if there is express statutory authorization and if personal jurisdiction of the non-resident is obtained in any enforcement proceedings.[59]

Lands owned by the state or federal government will ordinarily be exempt from liability for assessments unless the owning government has consented, or waived its immunity. And the immunity often applies to "restricted lands" of Indians. See Powell v. City of Ada, 61 F.2d 283 (10th Cir. 1932), where the Indian-owner had petitioned for annexation by the city, consented to the city improvement and accepted its benefits—but nonetheless was able to avoid an assessment for the improvement.

[56] See Tonawanda v. Lyon, 181 U.S. 389, 21 S.Ct. 609, 45 L.Ed. 908 (1901); Wight v. Davidson, 181 U.S. 371, 21 S.Ct. 616, 45 L.Ed. 900 (1901); French v. Barber Asphalt Paving Co., 181 U.S. 324, 21 S.Ct. 625, 45 L.Ed. 879 (1901), and companion cases. But if a municipality acts without jurisdiction in making a contract for an improvement, the municipality cannot assess the costs of the contract against property owners. See Butler v. City of Blackfoot, 102 Idaho 608, 635 P.2d 1231 (1981).

[57] See City of Salisbury v. Arey, 224 N.C. 260, 29 S.E.2d 894 (1944), where it was held that the municipality could elect the installment plan as to a property owner who did nothing during the election period. Cf. Texaco, Inc. v. Oklahoma City, 619 P.2d 869 (Okl.1980) (interpreting statute as allowing landowner to discharge his obligation by payment in full of assessment, plus interest accrued as of next succeeding payment date).

[58] Werninger v. Stephenson, 82 W.Va. 367, 95 S.E. 1035 (1918). See Davidson v. City of New Orleans, 96 U.S. (6 Otto) 97, 24 L.Ed. 616 (1878). But most authority has denied personal liability where this is not clearly provided by statute; and a considerable body of authority (formerly the majority of cases) has even invalidated attempts at legislative authorization of such liability on the grounds it amounts to a taking of property without compensation and/or it violates the "special benefits" theory of assessments and/or it conflicts with constitutional requirements of equality and uniformity of taxation. See Annot., Personal Liability of Property Owner to Pay Assessments for Local Improvements, 127 A.L.R. 551 (1940). A considerable number of cases, especially in more recent decades, have, however, sustained, expressly or impliedly, the validity of legislative authorization of personal liability for assessments. *Id.* at 572–83. And it is usually now recognized that property owners may be held personally liable on assessments for public improvements where the property owners have promised to pay the costs of the improvements. See Annot., Validity and Effect of Agreement by Property Owners or Occupants to Pay Cost of, or Assessment Against Property for, Local Improvement, 167 A.L.R. 1030 (1947).

[59] See Rubin, Collection of Delinquent Real Property Taxes by Action in Personam, 3 Law & Contemp. Prob. 410, 422 (1936).

In Dewey v. City of Des Moines, 173 U.S. 193, 19 S.Ct. 379, 43 L.Ed. 665 (1899), an attempt to hold a non-resident owner personally liable for an assessment was invalidated; there had been no personal service on the owner, but the Court spoke in general terms. However, an attachment of property other than that taxed was allowed in Nickey v. Mississippi, 292 U.S. 393, 54 S.Ct. 743, 78 L.Ed. 1323 (1934), where the nonresident owner was delinquent as to his ad valorem real-property taxes. And most states now have "long-arm statutes" under which personal service is allowed on nonresidents who have engaged in various activities, usually including owning real estate, within the jurisdiction. But cf. Bloom v. City of Oakley, 33 Kan.App.2d 538, 104 P.3d 1007 (2005) (city lacked statutory authority to levy an assessment for improvement of boundary line road located entirely within city against property located outside city boundaries, where city failed to enter into an interlocal agreement with county prior to assessing property outside its boundaries).

Assessments are sometimes employed by at least one unit of government involved in projects undertaken through intergovernmental cooperation among various units—for instance, where a public authority or special-function district uses revenue-bond financing to supply its part of the needed money, and a cooperating city or other general-function unit of government uses assessments to provide its share of payments for the project.[60]

The type of assessments here being discussed differ, it should be noted, from the tax levies (sometimes called "assessments" also) of incorporated special-function districts—those districts are described in Chapter 2 *supra*. In the special-function district, the levy is usually an annual tax imposed to meet the principal and interest demands of bonds issued to finance the project or projects which the district has created and maintains. Thus, instead of a single sum, the obligation is for continuing support of projects—with the "assessments" often coming in the form of taxes apportioned according to the value or size of the taxpayer's property. The obligation is little different from that for ordinary real-property taxes, though here the levy is by a unit of government that has very limited functions and powers, rather than by a general-function unit.[61] There is similarity, however, in the theories underlying assessments by general-function units and underlying the creation of special-assessment districts: the property specially benefited by an improvement is, in either case, supposedly burdened with paying for that improvement.

Distinctions in this area have been clouded by loose use of language. As accurately used, "special function district" means a unit of local government organized for some limited purpose or purposes, such as providing fire protection to an area or building a particular improvement, with the above-described, continuing "assessments" on property owners in the district paying the original cost and upkeep. "Assessment district" means territory delineated by some unit of local government (usually a general-function unit) as that on which lump-sum assessments for a particular project should

---

[60] See Griffith v. McCandless Township, 366 Pa. 309, 77 A.2d 430 (1951), where this arrangement was used to secure a water supply.

[61] See City of Pasadena v. Chamberlain, 204 Cal. 653, 269 P. 630 (1928) (special district has same powers of levying and collecting taxes for its limited purposes as municipal corporations have for their more general purposes); People ex rel. Rogers v. Letford, 102 Colo. 284, 79 P.2d 274 (1938); Patterick v. Carbon Water Conservancy District, 106 Utah 55, 145 P.2d 503 (1944) (water conservancy district can levy general taxes). Cf. Norris v. Montezuma Valley Irrigation District, 248 F. 369 (8th Cir.1918), cert. denied 248 U.S. 569, 39 S.Ct. 10, 63 L.Ed. 425 (1918) (statutory power of irrigation district to issue bonds imposes obligation to levy sufficient taxes to pay bonds).

In California Portland Cement Co. v. Picture Rocks Fire Dist., 143 Ariz. 170, 692 P.2d 1019 (App. 1984), it is observed that property cannot be included in a assessment district unless it is specially benefitted by the service or facility for which it is assessed, but a true special function district—as, in this case, a fire district—can tax property within the district even if that specific property receives no special benefit. Cf. Teter v. Clark County, 104 Wash.2d 227, 704 P.2d 1171 (1985) (in operating sewer system, city had statutory authority to impose charge under police power without "special benefit" rule applying). The difference, however, may not be of great significance since decisions on what property to include within an assessment district are seldom overturned, the courts generally saying that they will overturn them only if arbitrary or fraudulent conduct is shown, or a clear mistake. See Garvey Elevators, Inc. v. City of Wichita, 238 Kan. 682, 714 P.2d 956 (1986) (exclusion of various properties from assessment district for construction of drainage system upheld as not arbitrary or capricious). And the inclusion of property in a special district, while not requiring special benefit to that specific property, is based on the underlying theory that the included property does, at least in a general way, benefit from the district's activities. See Public Serv. Co. of Okla. v. Northwest Rogers County Fire Protection Dist., 675 P.2d 134 (Okl.1983) (levies for creation of fire protection district said to be based on benefit to the assessed property).

fall; the so-called "district" is not a separate unit of government at all. But the terms (discussed in more detail in Chapter 2 *supra*) are sometimes used interchangeably—with various special-function districts (such as road districts or conservation districts) often being loosely called "assessment districts."

§ 15.7 Local Powers to Spend and Borrow Money

The spending of money by municipalities, and the incurring of indebtedness by such units, are both governed by the same two general principles: (1) Authority either to spend money or to incur indebtedness for a particular purpose must be based on an express or clearly implied grant of power—found in the state constitution or statutes or a home-rule charter.[62] It has been said that any grant of power to incur indebtedness must be strictly construed;[63] but in modern times, indebtedness has become so commonplace and so necessary that the rule of strict construction seems little impediment to municipal actions. Thus, it is agreed that from an express power to purchase, implied power to incur indebtedness to make the purchase may be found.[64] (2) Any expenditures of public money by a unit of local government must be made for *public* purposes, and any indebtedness created by such units must be incurred for public purposes.[65] A

---

[62] See Wilson v. City of Shreveport, 29 La.Ann. 673 (1877) (city cannot incur indebtedness unless expressly or impliedly given the power); Gregg v. Town of Bourbonnais, 327 Ill.App. 253, 64 N.E.2d 106 (1945) (incurring debts is not an incidental power of incorporated towns); Du Toit v. Village of Belview, 94 Minn. 128, 102 N.W. 216 (1905) (express power under statute; statute not too vague); Green v. Kitchin, 229 N.C. 450, 50 S.E.2d 545 (1948) (municipality has implied power to spend money for instruction of its police force); Georges Township v. Union Trust Co., 293 Pa. 364, 143 A. 10 (1928). Cf. Montgomery v. State, 228 Ala. 296, 153 So. 394 (1934) (county funds could not be expended without express or implied authorization); Hoffman v. Pawnee County Commissioners, 3 Okl. 325, 41 P. 566 (1895) (municipality has implied power to incur indebtedness where necessary to carrying out its powers and where the indebtedness is not forbidden by statute or charter). Sometimes it is said that municipalities have implied or incidental power to spend, and incur indebtedness, for *necessities*. See Hightower v. City of Raleigh, 150 N.C. 569, 65 S.E. 279 (1909).

[63] Ex parte Simms, 40 Fla. 432, 25 So. 280 (1898); Bogart v. Township of Lamotte, 79 Mich. 294, 44 N.W. 612 (1890). See, indicating strict construction of all financial powers of municipalities, including powers of expenditure, City of Phoenix v. Michael, 61 Ariz. 238, 148 P.2d 353 (1944); Village of Monsanto v. Touchette, 63 Ill.App.2d 390, 211 N.E.2d 471 (1965); Andrello v. Dulan, 49 Misc.2d 17, 266 N.Y.S.2d 738 (1966) (city's purchase of bus line held proper); City of Cleveland v. Artl, 62 Ohio App. 210, 23 N.E.2d 525 (1939).

[64] See Allen v. Intendant & Councilmen of La Fayette, 89 Ala. 641, 8 So. 30 (1890) (power to maintain schools includes power to buy school property on credit); City of Richmond v. McGirr, 78 Ind. 192 (1881) (power to purchase realty includes power to purchase it on credit); Ketchum v. City of Buffalo, 21 Barb. 294 (1855), aff'd 14 N.Y. 356 (1856) (city had power to purchase market grounds). And the power to borrow includes the power to create a debt to that extent. See Harman v. Alabama College, 235 Ala. 148, 177 So. 747 (1937). There is some authority that mere power to buy or build property does not give power to borrow money for these purposes. See Rushe v. Town of Hyattsville, 116 Md. 122, 81 A. 278 (1911). But the trend has long seemed clearly to the contrary. See Forrest City v. Bank of Forrest City, 116 Ark. 377, 172 S.W. 1148 (1915) (power to provide water supply includes power to borrow money for moving expenses). Cf. Glucose Sugar Refining Co. v. Marshalltown, 153 F. 620 (C.C.S.D.Iowa 1907) (power to construct sewers includes power to borrow money to build plant to dispose of sewage). See generally Gelfand (ed.), State and Local Government Financing (Callaghan & Co. 1985) (2 vols.), reviewed 18 Urban Law. 753 (1986).

[65] See The Liberty Bell, 23 F. 843 (C.C.E.D.La.1885) (appropriation of tax money for purposes beyond purview of municipal government is wrongful and can be enjoined); State v. Town of North Miami, 59 So.2d 779 (Fla.1952); Opinion of the Justices of the Supreme Judicial Court Given Under the Provisions of Section 3 of Article VI of the Constitution, 152 Me. 440, 131 A.2d 904 (1957); McLean v. City of Boston, 327 Mass. 118, 97 N.E.2d 542 (1951) (public purpose found in acquiring housing sites for those displaced by expansion of rapid transit system); Hays v. City of Kalamazoo, 316 Mich. 443, 25 N.W.2d 787 (1947); Arens v. Village of Rogers, 240 Minn. 386, 61 N.W.2d 508 (1953), appeal dism'd 347 U.S. 949, 74 S.Ct. 680, 98 L.Ed. 1096; Dysart v. City of St. Louis, 321 Mo. 514, 11 S.W.2d 1045 (1928); Ennis v. Kansas City, 321 Mo. 536, 11 S.W.2d 1054 (1928); State ex rel. Beck v. City of York, 164 Neb. 223, 82 N.W.2d 269 (1957); City of Clovis v. Southwestern Public Service, 49 N.M. 270, 161 P.2d 878 (1945); Hesse v. Rath, 224 App.Div. 344, 230 N.Y.S. 676 (1928), aff'd 249

municipality has no power to donate money for private uses,[66] and the obligation to spend only for public purposes applies even where the government has express power authorizing the spending of a certain sum without specification as to the purpose of the expenditure.[67]

Within the limits imposed by these general principles, the power to spend money is necessarily entrusted to the proper municipal authorities with little additional restriction. But the power to borrow *is* surrounded by other limitations—including very often the requirement of voter approval. Under the varying requirements of constitutions, statutes, and charters in the different states, electoral approval must sometimes be obtained by a municipality in order to incur any indebtedness at all; or in

---

N.Y. 436, 164 N.E. 342 (1928); State ex rel. McClure v. Hagerman, 155 Ohio St. 320, 98 N.E.2d 835 (1951); Protest of Reid, 160 Okl. 3, 15 P.2d 995 (1932); Heimerl v. Ozaukee County, 256 Wis. 151, 40 N.W.2d 564 (1949). Cf. People ex rel. Schlaeger v. Bunge Brothers Coal Co., 392 Ill. 153, 64 N.E.2d 365 (1945) (purchase of works of art by local artists held not a public purpose); Wheelock v. City of Lowell, 196 Mass. 220, 81 N.E. 977 (1907) (if money used for other than public purposes, would be taking of private property for private use). A purpose may be public though it involves an activity of a business-like, or "proprietary," nature. See Bazell v. City of Cincinnati, 13 Ohio St.2d 63, 233 N.E.2d 864 (1968), appeal dism'd and cert. denied 391 U.S. 601, 88 S.Ct. 1865, 20 L.Ed.2d 845. Of course, the power to tax—like the power to spend public money and the power to borrow—is also limited to public purposes. See also Chapter 16.1, notes 1 & 2 *infra* and accompanying text. The subject of whether "public purpose" should have different meanings in different areas of the law is well discussed in Note, The Different Faces of "Public Purpose": Shouldn't It Always Mean the Same Thing?, 30 Fla. St. U.L. Rev. 529 (2003). On the question of whether or not the influencing of an election is a "public purpose" for which public funds may be expended, see Ameritel Inns, Inc. v. Greater Boise Auditorium Dist., 141 Idaho 849, 119 P.3d 624 (2005) (auditorium district could not use public funds to influence contested election on issuance of bonds to fund construction of district's convention center). See generally Note, *Kromko v. City of Tucson*: Use of Public Funds to Influence the Outcome of Elections, 46 Ariz. L. Rev. 423 (2004), noting Kromko v. City of Tucson, 202 Ariz. 499, 47 P.3d 1137 (App. 2002) (interpreting Arizona statute as violated only if city engaged in "express advocacy," which court defined as communication unambiguously urging a person to vote in a particular manner). As to the use of public funds for private suburban developments, see Note, Public Tax Dollars for Private Suburban Development: A First Report on a National Phenomenon, 26 Va. Tax Rev. 709 (2007).

[66] On what are private, and what are public, uses, see City of Ojai v. Chaffee, 60 Cal.App.2d 54, 140 P.2d 116 (Dist.Ct.1943) (gift from city to county); City of Chicago v. Pittsburgh, Cincinnati, Chicago & St. Louis Railway, 244 Ill. 220, 91 N.E. 422 (1910) (release by municipality to private company from liability held *not* donation, however, where company performed certain acts in return); Love v. City of Des Moines, 210 Iowa 90, 230 N.W. 373 (1930); Quinlan v. City of Cambridge, 320 Mass. 124, 68 N.E.2d 11 (1946); State ex rel. Brown v. City of Warr Acres, 946 P.2d 1140 (Okl.1997) (city's economic development plan to induce retailer to relocate facility to city satisfied public purpose requirement); Burkhardt v. City of Enid, 771 P.2d 608 (Okl.1989) (expenditure of public funds to acquire private university's campus, and to lease campus back to university for sum below market rate, was for public purpose since city was attempting to keep university economically afloat and thus preserve jobs for city residents); State ex rel. Lacy v. Jackson, 682 P.2d 218 (Okl.1983) (municipality could *not* lawfully pay costs of printing and distributing a newspaper published by private company; not for a public purpose, which court said is basically synonymous with a governmental purpose); Harbold v. City of Reading, 355 Pa. 253, 49 A.2d 817 (1946); CLEAN v. City of Spokane, 133 Wash.2d 455, 947 P.2d 1169 (Wash. 1997) (parking ramp project for business district met public purpose test under state constitutional provision on taxes); City of Seattle v. State, 100 Wash.2d 232, 668 P.2d 1266 (1983) (city-funded contributions to candidates in city elections served an underlying public interest and did not amount to a subsidy forbidden by state constitution). On the use of public funds to build sports and entertainment facilities, see Comment, Building New Stadiums with Your Money Whether You Like It or Not: The Pennsylvania Constitution Does Not Prohibit the Use of Public Funds to Construct New Stadiums, 37 Duquesne L. Rev. 423 (1999). Cf. Board of Educ. v. City of Corbin, 301 Ky. 686, 192 S.W.2d 951 (1946) (municipality could not supplement salaries of teachers in independent school district that was coterminous with city). But cf. Maxcy v. City of Oshkosh, 144 Wis. 238, 128 N.W. 899 (1910) (if donation made to city for a municipal purpose, municipality could make donation in return).

[67] See Castner v. City of Minneapolis, 92 Minn. 84, 99 N.W. 361 (1904); State ex rel. McClure v. Hagerman, *supra* note 65.

order to incur debt for certain purposes or above a certain limit; or in order to issue bonds. But the rules as to elections for all these varied purposes tend to be the same.

Within statutory limits, the governing authorities, such as the city council, are entrusted with the decision on whether to hold a bond election or indebtedness election; their motives for calling such an election are not subject to judicial inquiry; and an election will not be enjoined by the courts on the basis of alleged improper motives.[68] But an election that would be invalid, and hence a nullity, can be enjoined.[69] And where an election is *required* by law prior to indebtedness being incurred or bonds being issued, the indebtedness or bond issue can be enjoined until the proper approval is obtained.[70] Apart from constitutional, statutory, and charter requirements, municipal authorities can, on their own volition and without an election, incur indebtedness and issue bonds.[71]

---

[68] See Sublett v. City of Tulsa, 405 P.2d 185 (Okl.1965). In some jurisdictions, an "advisory" election on the issuance of bonds may be held—that is, though no election is required by law, the question of the bond issue may be submitted to the voters for their non-binding expression of opinion. See Muscatine Lighting Co. v. City of Muscatine, 205 Iowa 82, 217 N.W. 468 (1928) (advisory election on whether to issue lighting and power bonds); Swanker v. City of Amsterdam, 5 Misc.2d 932, 161 N.Y.S.2d 932 (1957) (city council not required to issue bonds even if election favorable).

[69] See Coleman v. Board of Education, 131 Ga. 643, 63 S.E. 41 (1908); Swanker v. Amsterdam, *supra* note 68. See generally, on the enjoining of bond elections and elections on expenditures, de Funiak, Equitable Protection of Personal or Individual Rights, 36 Ky.L.J. 7, 28 (1947); Note, Injunction—Equity's Jurisdiction to Enjoin Election, 32 Colum.L.Rev. 138 (1932); Note, Equity: Taxpayer's Bill to Enjoin an Election, 18 Corn.L.Q. 278 (1933); Annot., Power to Enjoin Holding of an Election, 33 A.L.R. 1376, 1384 (1924).

[70] See Coleman v. Town of Eutaw, 157 Ala. 327, 47 So. 703 (1908) (constitution forbids issuance of bonds without approval of voters; equity can enjoin issuance if bonds not properly approved); City of St. Petersburg v. English, 54 Fla. 585, 45 So. 483 (1907) (absent intervening rights of third parties, legislature can arrest issuance of bonds until approved by voters, even if bonds have already been physically issued under legislation not requiring electoral approval of such a bond issue). Cf. Hill v. Memphis, 134 U.S. 198, 10 S.Ct. 562, 33 L.Ed. 887 (1890) (where constitution requires vote of people, legislature cannot dispense with this); Easterlin v. City of New Port Richey, 105 So.2d 361 (Fla.1958) (issuance of bonds required election; city could not avoid election requirement by issuing certificates of indebtedness). If a statutory or constitutional provision requires a vote *only* on the issue of indebtedness, another election does not have to be held on the issuance of the bonds therefor. Hammond v. City of Charlotte, 206 N.C. 604, 175 S.E. 148 (1934); In re Initiative Petition No. 2, 205 Okl. 160, 236 P.2d 247 (1951). See State ex rel. Houston v. Hillsborough County, 136 Fla. 503, 183 So. 157 (1938) (vote on adoption of voting machines was in effect a vote to use credit to purchase them; no further vote needed to issue certificates of indebtedness); Carlson v. City of Helena, 39 Mont. 82, 102 P. 39 (1909) (two elections on bond issuance unnecessary).

[71] Starmount Co. v. Ohio Savings Bank & Trust Co., 55 F.2d 649 (4th Cir. 1932); Ashland Waterworks Co. v. Ashland, 251 F. 492 (6th Cir.1918) (election required only where indebtedness exceeds that otherwise permitted); Newton v. City of Fort Collins, 78 Colo. 380, 241 P. 1114 (1925) (home-rule city could issue bonds for waterworks without election unless constitution provided otherwise); Callahan v. City of Berkley, 307 Mich. 701, 12 N.W.2d 431 (1943) reh. denied 307 Mich. 701, 14 N.W.2d 87 (no election required for special assessment bonds of village); Tennessee Electric Power Co. v. City of Chattanooga, 172 Tenn. 505, 114 S.W.2d 441 (1937) (statute authorized issuance of bonds; vote of people unnecessary). See Collins v. City of Phoenix, 54 F.2d 770 (9th Cir.1931); Weisfield v. City of Seattle, 180 Wash. 288, 40 P.2d 149 (1935). Cf. People ex rel. Carr v. Chicago Heights Terminal Transfer Railway, 319 Ill. 389, 150 N.E. 262 (1925) (to authorize bond issue without submission to vote of people, ordinance authorizing the issue must specify that indebtedness is for purpose for which election not needed); Mayor & City Council of Baltimore v. Board of Supervisors, 156 Md. 196, 143 A. 800 (1928) (legislature must authorize creation of debt before question may be submitted to voters). But cf. Busse v. City of Golden, 73 P.3d 660 (Colo. 2003) (in addition to any constitutional and charter requirements, city must observe several requirements to issue bonds and expend proceeds: question submitted to voters must be specific and apprise them of particular purpose for which bonds are to be issued; purpose must not be misleading; and proceeds must be spent for the purpose for which they were voted; if city expends proceeds for the approved purpose, the judgment and discretion concerning the expenditures are reserved for city officials, not the courts).

In some states, the approval of a state agency is needed before a local unit can issue bonds. Sometimes, the state agency has power to review the *wisdom* of a bond issue. La.Const. Art. 7, § 8; N.C.Gen.Stat. §§ 159–

To vote in an election on bonds or indebtedness, a person must ordinarily be a qualified voter of the locality concerned.[72] But the U.S. Supreme Court has struck down restrictions, frequently encountered in the past, that only property-owning, or property-taxpaying, persons within the locality could vote on the issuance of bonds. Such limitations have been invalidated, under the equal protection clause, as to both elections dealing with the issuance of revenue bonds[73] (*i.e.*, those payable only from revenues produced by the facility built from the proceeds of the bond sale) and elections concerning the issuance of general obligation bonds[74] (*i.e.*, those that are payable out of general tax funds of the issuing government). An exception that so far appears fairly narrow has been recognized: a local unit with a special limited purpose may limit the vote (at least as to electing officers, and presumably also to issuing bonds, where that activity is possible) to landowners if the unit's activities have, as in the case of an irrigation district, a disproportionately greater effect on landowners than on other residents.[75] Aside from

---

52, 53. In other states, the agency's review does not extend to policy questions but only to legal authority and regularity of the bond issue. 53 Pa.Stat. §§ 6780–351–60.

On the extent to which federal securities law applies to sales of municipal securities, see Doty & Peterson, The Federal Securities Laws and Transactions in Municipal Securities, 71 Nw.L.Rev. 283 (1976); Comment, Amended SEC Rule 15C2–12: An Attempt to Improve Disclosure Practices in the Municipal Securities Market, 45 DePaul L. Rev. 1117 (1996); Comment, Federal Regulation of Municipal Securities: A Constitutional and Statutory Analysis, 1976 Duke L.J. 1261; Note, Federal Regulation of Municipal Securities, 60 Minn.L.Rev. 567 (1976). See also Note, Creditors' Remedies in Municipal Default, 1976 Duke L.J. 1363.

[72] See Price v. Hodges, 172 Ga. 871, 159 S.E. 241 (1931) (election held without required registration of voters is void); Hannah v. District Court, 33 N.M. 533, 271 P. 469 (1928) (attempt to purge registration list); Miller v. Trinner, 224 App.Div. 411, 231 N.Y.S. 230 (1928); Trotter v. City of Maryville, 191 Tenn. 510, 235 S.W.2d 13 (1950); Wingo v. Seale, 212 S.W.2d 968 (Tex.Civ.App.1948). Cf. Holmer v. State ex rel. Stewart, 158 Fla. 397, 28 So.2d 586 (1947) (qualification to vote determined as of date of election); State ex rel. Davis v. Ryan, 118 Fla. 42, 151 So. 416 (1933), reh. denied 118 Fla. 42, 158 So. 62 (1934) (local law on voting qualifications prevails over inconsistent general law). The right to vote in bond elections can be limited to *registered* voters. See People ex rel. Chicago & Rock River Railroad v. Dutcher, 56 Ill. 144 (1870) (elections held at town meetings in townships). Cf. Foster v. Mayor & Council of College Park, 153 Ga. 112, 112 S.E. 361 (1922), applying constitutional prohibition of special registration for bond elections. And *residency* requirements for voters have been upheld. See McKenzie v. City of De Witt, 196 Ark. 1115, 121 S.W.2d 71 (1938) (non-resident who owned property in city not eligible to vote on city bonds). See generally Annot., Validity, Under Federal Constitution, of State Residency Requirements for Voting in Elections, 31 L.Ed.2d 861 (1973).

[73] Cipriano v. Houma, 395 U.S. 701, 89 S.Ct. 1897, 23 L.Ed.2d 647 (1969).

[74] City of Phoenix v. Kolodziejski, 399 U.S. 204, 90 S.Ct. 1990, 26 L.Ed.2d 523 (1970). See Fair v. Fair, 317 F.Supp. 859 (M.D.Fla.1970); Spencer v. Rayburn, 483 P.2d 735 (Okl.1971); Cypert v. Washington County School District, 24 Utah 2d 419, 473 P.2d 887 (1970). Cf. Pike v. School District No. 11, 172 Colo. 413, 474 P.2d 162 (1970) (in election to authorize increase in school-district budget, limitation of right to vote to taxpaying electors was unconstitutional); Weber v. City of Helena, 89 Mont. 109, 297 P. 455 (1931) (elector could not be required to pay taxes as condition to eligibility to vote on increase in municipal indebtedness). On the reasons for the old provisions limiting the vote to property-owners or taxpayers, see Hanson v. Jordan, 145 Tex. 320, 198 S.W.2d 262 (1946) (induces owners of property to place it on tax rolls). See generally Note, The Equal Protections Clause v. Restriction of the Franchise to Property Owners in Texas, 22 Baylor L.Rev. 594 (1970); Comment, Constitutional Law—Equal Protection—Property Ownership Qualifications on the Right to Vote in Special Municipal Elections, 67 Mich.L.Rev. 1260 (1969); Comment, The Last Bastion Crumbles: All Property Restrictions on The Franchise Are Unconstitutional, 1 N.M.L.Rev. 403 (1971); Comment, Ownership of Land as a Prerequisite to the Right to Vote: Equal or Unequal Protection?, 117 U.Pa.L.Rev. 594 (1969); Note, Property Ownership Versus The Right to Vote, A Question of Equal Protection, 25 Sw.L.J. 633 (1971); Note, Voting Rights—Ownership of Property No Longer a Valid Qualification, 23 Sw.L.J. 964 (1969); Note, Constitutional Law—Voting Rights—Limitation of the Franchise on the Basis of Property Ownership, 44 Tul.L.Rev. 575 (1970); Annot., Validity, Under Federal Constitution, of State or Local Provision Making Right to Vote Dependent Upon Ownership of, or Payment of Taxes Upon, Property, 35 L.Ed.2d 843 (1974).

[75] Salyer Land Co. v. Tulare Lake Basin Water Storage District, 410 U.S. 719, 93 S.Ct. 1224, 35 L.Ed.2d 659 (1973), where the limitation of the franchise to landowners within the district was upheld. But cf., both invalidating such limitations for lack of a sufficiently greater interest on the property-owners' part, Burrey v.

that, the U.S. Supreme Court has said that any classifications restricting the franchise on grounds other than residence, age, and citizenship are not valid unless they serve a compelling state interest.[76] Statutes often prescribe the form of the ballot to be used in indebtedness and bond elections, but substantial compliance will suffice to make the election valid.[77] Even without a specific statutory requirement on the matter, it has been said that the ballot must clearly state the amount of indebtedness, or the amount of the bond issue, on which the vote is being taken.[78]

§ 15.8 Limitations on Debt of Local Units

In most states, there are some debt limitations applicable to most or all units of local government; at a minimum, these limitations generally apply to the more populous municipalities. Such restrictions originated in Iowa in 1857, with Illinois following in 1870; financial difficulties in the 1870's led to widespread adoptions of such limits in other states. They are designed to maintain municipal solvency, to protect municipalities and their citizens from abuse of their credit, and to protect residents from the overburdensome taxation that would likely follow from unrestrained spending and indebtedness.[79] There are two main types of debt limitation: (1) Some are set in terms of

---

Embarcadero Municipal Improvement District, 5 Cal.3d 671, 97 Cal.Rptr. 203, 488 P.2d 395 (1971); Lippe v. Jones, 59 Misc.2d 843, 300 N.Y.S.2d 396 (1969). (Note, however, that the *Burrey* and *Lippe* cases, *supra*, were both decided *before* the *Salyer* case's clear enunciation of the conditions under which a limitation of the franchise to property-owners could be upheld.)

[76] Hill v. Stone, 421 U.S. 289, 95 S.Ct. 1637, 44 L.Ed.2d 172, reh. denied 422 U.S. 1029, 95 S.Ct. 2617, 45 L.Ed.2d 686 (1975). But cf. Snead v. City of Albuquerque, 663 F.Supp. 1084 (D.N.M.1987), judgment aff'd 841 F.2d 1131 (10th Cir.1987), cert. denied 485 U.S. 1009, 108 S.Ct. 1475, 99 L.Ed.2d 704 (1988) (constitutional provision and statute giving nonresident property owners the right to vote on creation of municipal indebtedness upheld against equal protection attack; court rejected claim that state, having extended right to vote to some county residents, must extend it to all such residents unless a compelling state interest was shown). See generally Annot., Validity of Statute Requiring Information as to Age, Sex, Residence, etc., as Condition of Registration or Right to Vote, 14 A.L.R. 260 (1921). The system invalidated in the *Hill* case, *supra*, involved use of a "dual box procedure," by which persons owning taxable property voted in one box in bond elections, and other registered voters voted in another box; the bond issue passed only if it received a majority of all votes cast *and* a majority of votes cast by the property owners, thus giving the property owners a veto power.

[77] See City of Florence v. State ex rel. Burtwell, 211 Ala. 617, 101 So. 462 (1924); Allen v. Fuller, 332 Ill. 304, 163 N.E. 675 (1928); Harding v. Board of Supervisors, 213 Iowa 560, 237 N.W. 625 (1931); Davidson v. Board of Education, 225 Ky. 165, 7 S.W.2d 1056 (1928); Michigan Public Service Co. v. City of Cheboygan, 324 Mich. 309, 37 N.W.2d 116 (1949); City of Raytown v. Kemp, 349 S.W.2d 363 (Mo.1961); Sexton v. Lee, 100 W.Va. 389, 130 S.E. 437 (1925) (form of ballot sufficient if permits voter to make clear indication of his vote on the question involved). Cf. Douty v. Mayor & City Council of Baltimore, 155 Md. 125, 141 A. 499 (1928) (whole ordinance need not be printed on ballot); Schuck v. Borough of Stone Harbor, 87 N.J.L. 484, 95 A. 133 (1915) (separate ballots, instead of a blanket ballot, could be used on bond issue). Compare Moore v. City of Page, 148 Ariz. 151, 713 P.2d 813 (App. 1986) (allegations that county recorder failed to purge from registration list voters who should legally have been purged and that city called for bond election after registration had closed and included misleading information on ballot held sufficient to challenge validity of bond election). As to recounts in bond elections, see State ex rel. Lydick v. Brown, 516 P.2d 239 (Okl.1973) (voter not entitled to recount absent allegation of fraud, misconduct, or mistake).

[78] See In re Common Council of Lackawanna, 158 App.Div. 263, 143 N.Y.S. 198 (1913); Kerlin v. City of Devils Lake, 25 N.D. 207, 141 N.W. 756 (1913); Fairfax County Taxpayers Alliance v. Board of County Supervisors, 202 Va. 462, 117 S.E.2d 753 (1961). But cf. Quinn v. City of Tulsa, 777 P.2d 1331 (Okl.1989) (mere omission from ballot title in bond election of fact that additional funding was anticipated to complete the listed projects did not make question invalidly deceptive, misleading, or indefinite). See generally Annot., Statement Regarding Cost of Proposed Public Improvement in Ballot for Special Election in that Regard, 117 A.L.R. 892 (1938).

[79] On the purposes, history, and types of debt limitations, see 15 McQuillin, Municipal Corporations §§ 41.01–.07 (3d rev. ed. 1995); Sato & Van Alstyne, State and Local Government Law 561–62 (2d ed. 1977).

a percentage of the value of taxable property, or of all real and personal property, within the locality. This type of restriction obviously necessitates regular assessments of property value. (2) Some are set in terms of the income and revenue of the locality for a given period, as where they provide that indebtedness incurred in any year cannot exceed the income and revenue provided. A few debt limitations contain both these kinds of restriction. Most debt limitations are found in state constitutions and statutes, but some home-rule cities include such limits in their own charters. Some debt limitations are absolute, with no possible authorization of greater indebtedness; but often, a higher indebtedness (which sometimes must be within a set *absolute* maximum) can be authorized by vote of a designated majority of the voters.[80] Debts incurred for public utilities operated by the local unit are within the debt limitation unless clearly excepted therefrom.[81] But a number of state debt limitations for local units *do* contain a clear exception for debts incurred for utility expenses, or for certain utilities such as sewers.[82]

See generally Bowmar, The Anachronism Called Debt Limitation, 52 Iowa L.Rev. 863 (1967); Note, Municipal Debt Limitations in Pennsylvania, 15 Vill.L.Rev. 612 (1970). See also McBean v. City of Fresno, 112 Cal. 159, 164, 44 P. 358, 359 (1896), explaining the reasons for the type of debt limitation that restricts indebtedness in any year to the income for that year. On the status of debt limitations in modern times, see Amdursky & Gillette, Municipal Debt Finance Law—Theory and Practice ch. 4 (Debt Limits and Their Avoidance) (Little, Brown & Co, 1992, with 1999 Supp.). See generally Krishnakumar, In Defense of the Debt Limit Statute, 42 Harv. J. on Legis. 135 (2005). See also Gillette, Can Public Debt Enhance Democracy?, 50 Wm. & Mary L. Rev. 937 (2008). As to the entities covered by debt limits, see Urban Renewal Agency of Rexburg v. Hart, 148 Idaho 299, 222 P.3d 467 (2009) (urban renewal agency was not alter ego of city, and thus debt limitations applicable to cities did not apply to agency).

[80] Often, some "super-majority" (such as a 60% affirmative vote of those voting) is required in bond election. Such a requirement was declared constitutional in Gordon v. Lance, 403 U.S. 1, 91 S.Ct. 1889, 29 L.Ed.2d 273 (1971) (60% vote requirement in school bond case). Where the debt limitation is exceeded only if the debt to be incurred exceeds a percentage of the "aggregate tax valuation," this has been held to mean the specified percentage of the *assessed* valuation of all property within the local unit, not the appraised valuation of the property. See Limtiaco v. Camacho, 549 U.S. 483, 127 S.Ct. 1413, 167 L.Ed.2d 212 (2007) (phrase "tax valuation" in proscription of public indebtedness exceeding 10% of "aggregate tax valuation of the property in Guam" referred to assessed valuation).

The Pennsylvania Constitution now establishes a system somewhat different from the usual for setting debt limits for local governments: The Legislature sets limits based on percentages of total revenues of the units. Pa.Const. Art. 9 § 10 (1994).

[81] City of Chicago v. McDonald, 176 Ill. 404, 52 N.E. 982 (1898); Hurst v. City of Millersburg, 220 Ky. 108, 294 S.W. 788 (1927); Zachary v. City of Wagoner, 146 Okl. 268, 292 P. 345 (1930); Hoffman v. Kline, 300 Pa. 485, 150 A. 889 (1930) (bonds for extension and repair of municipal water system); State ex rel. Marinette, Tomahawk & Western Railway v. Common Council of Tomahawk, 96 Wis. 73, 71 N.W. 86 (1897). See City of Tulsa v. Langley, 196 Okl. 680, 168 P.2d 116 (1946).

[82] See City of Jerseyville v. Connett, 49 F.2d 246 (7th Cir.1931); Buntman v. City of Phoenix, 32 Ariz. 18, 255 P. 490 (1927); O. T. Johnson Corp. v. City of Los Angeles, 198 Cal. 308, 245 P. 164 (1926); Town of Meredith v. State Board of Health, 94 N.H. 123, 48 A.2d 489 (1946) (because of imperative necessity of sewers, their cost not included in debt limitation); City of Truth or Consequences v. Robinson, 58 N.M. 111, 266 P.2d 356 (1954) (sewers and water refunding); Sharp v. Hall, 198 Okl. 678, 181 P.2d 972 (1947) (sewers); Williams v. City of Norman, 85 Okl. 230, 205 P. 144 (1921) (electric light plant); McCarthy v. City of Kelso, 129 Wash. 121, 223 P. 151 (1924) (water-filtration plant); Payne v. City of Racine, 217 Wis. 550, 259 N.W. 437 (1935) (sewage disposal system). Cf. Kendrick v. City of Birmingham, 242 Ala. 112, 5 So.2d 82 (1941) (waterworks within exception whether furnished water for industrial or domestic purposes); Bollenbacher v. Harris, 196 Ind. 657, 148 N.E. 417 (1925) (purchase of stock of water company by city and issuing bonds therefor; not within debt limit); Williams v. Village of Kenyon, 187 Minn. 161, 244 N.W. 558 (1932) (purchase of generating equipment for electric plant not within debt limit); Williamson v. City of High Point, 213 N.C. 96, 195 S.E. 90 (1938) (bond issue for construction of electric plant not within debt limit); Ennis v. Town of Herndon, 168 Va. 539, 191 S.E. 685 (1937) (bonds for construction of water and sewer system were within exceptions to debt limits).

What constitutes "indebtedness" within the meaning of limits thereon? Definitions vary, but a debt is usually said to involve an unconditional promise to pay a fixed sum at some specified time.[83] Five types of obligation are often excepted from debt-limitation provisions, either because they are not considered "debts" within the meaning of these limits, or because an express exception is provided for them. (1) *Current expenses*—such as rent payments and payment of salaries to officers and employees—are sometimes expressly excepted from debt limits.[84] But even where there is no such specific exception, the prevailing view is that current expenditures do not create "indebtedness" *if* the local unit has money on hand to pay these, or provides a present means of raising the necessary money (other than by loan).[85] The theory is that if obligations of the local unit do not exceed its present revenues, there is no obligation extending beyond the means of immediate payment—thus no debt.

(2) Overlapping the first-mentioned exception for current expenses is an exception for *debts in anticipation of collection of revenues.* By constitutional provision in several

---

[83] Saleno v. City of Neosho, 127 Mo. 627, 30 S.W. 190 (1895). See Oppenheim v. City of Florence, 229 Ala. 50, 155 So. 859 (1934) (debt is pecuniary liability, or charge against general credit); First National Bank v. City of Jackson, 199 Ky. 94, 250 S.W. 795 (1923) (an obligation of which there is no present means of payment); Stone v. City of Hobbs, 54 N.M. 237, 220 P.2d 704 (1950); Levy v. McClellan, 196 N.Y. 178, 89 N.E. 569 (1909); Duane v. City of Philadelphia, 322 Pa. 33, 185 A. 401 (1936); McGuire v. City of Philadelphia, 245 Pa. 287, 91 A. 622 (1914) (indebtedness includes whatever city can be called on to pay). See generally Southern Corrections Systems, Inc. v. Union City Pub. Schools, 64 P.3d 1083 (Okla. 2002) (state constitutional provision preventing school districts from becoming indebted, in any matter or for any purpose, by an amount exceeding the income and revenue provided for a fiscal year, without the assent of three-fifths of the voters, forces school districts to operate on a cash basis, and prevents indebtedness out of tax revenues from extending beyond one year; provision serves as a restriction on both the school district and the legislature).

[84] See Smith v. Town of Guin, 229 Ala. 61, 155 So. 865 (1934); McHenry v. City of Lawrence, 295 Mass. 119, 3 N.E.2d 262 (1936). See generally 1 Dillon, Municipal Corporations § 195 (5th ed. 1911); 15 McQuillin, Municipal Corporations § 41.24 (3d rev. ed. 1995). Some state constitutions contain exceptions for ordinary, normal, or necessary expenses. See Wickey v. Muscatine County, 242 Iowa 272, 46 N.W.2d 32 (1951), applying such a provision (hospital not necessary expense). Cf. Koch v. Canyon County, 145 Idaho 158, 177 P.3d 372 (2008), interpreting a state constitutional provision prohibiting counties from incurring indebtedness, other than for ordinary and necessary expenses, in excess of their income and revenue for the year unless voter approval is obtained. In North Carolina, an election must be held as to any local government expense that is *not* "necessary." N.C. Const. Art. 5, § 4(2). And as to any tax imposed by a local government for other than "necessary" expenses. N.C. Const. Art. 5, § 2(5).

[85] See Collins v. City of Phoenix, 54 F.2d 770 (9th Cir.1931) (cost of street improvement was not indebtedness where was to be assessed against district benefited); Federal Deposit Insurance Corp. v. Sugarcreek Township, 53 F.Supp. 732 (W.D.Pa. 1944); Chesnutt v. Yates, 177 Ark. 894, 9 S.W.2d 37 (1928); Arthur v. City of Petaluma, 175 Cal. 216, 165 P. 698 (1917); People ex rel. Toman v. B. Mercil & Sons Plating Co., 378 Ill. 142, 37 N.E.2d 839 (1941); Meyers v. City of Louisville, 310 Ky. 348, 220 S.W.2d 852 (1949); McGrath v. Grout, 171 N.Y. 7, 63 N.E. 547 (1902); Ward v. City of Pittsburgh, 321 Pa. 414, 184 A. 240 (1936); Andrus v. Crystal City, 253 S.W. 557 (Tex.Civ.App.1923), aff'd 265 S.W. 550 (no tax levy needed for amounts payable out of funds for current year); Camden Clay Co. v. Town of New Martinsville, 67 W.Va. 525, 68 S.E. 118 (1910). Cf. State v. City of Miami, 150 Fla. 270, 7 So.2d 146 (1942) (contract for payment of county or municipal expenses, such as hospital care for charity patients, doesn't come within limitations if revenues available annually to meet these expenses). Cf. Fleming & Gandall, PLLC v. Town of Cashion, 167 P.3d 975 (Okla. Civ. App. 2007) (amount due from town to accounting firm for preparation of financial statements was not a debt within state constitutional provision limiting indebtedness of public entities where the town had the funds available to pay for the services rendered when the invoice was presented for payment). But see People ex rel. Adamowski v. Public Building Commission, 11 Ill.2d 125, 142 N.E.2d 67 (1957) (lease creates present debt for aggregate of all rentals for term of lease); Schnell v. City of Rock Island, 232 Ill. 89, 83 N.E. 462 (1907). See generally Cameron County Water Improvement District v. Western Metal Manufacturing Co., 125 S.W.2d 650 (Tex.Civ.App.1939), error dism'd (test of whether "debt" is created is whether burden created on revenues for future years). See also State of Kansas ex rel. Hecht v. City of Topeka, 293 P.3d 713 (Kan. 2013) ("cash-basis" statute prohibits municipalities from creating indebtedness in excess of funds actually on hand in the municipality's treasury; contracts in violation of the law are void).

states, debts are not within the debt limitation if they are incurred in anticipation of collection of revenue by the local unit for the current year.[86] This is based on the theory that, just as the government is really not "in debt" for a particular amount if it has cash on hand to pay that sum, so the government is not in debt if it anticipates having tax-money or other revenue on hand within the current year to pay the amount. Thus, even where not included in the constitution or in some statute, this exception has been adopted by the courts of many states.[87] The exception, it has been said, can only apply to normal or ordinary expenses during the current fiscal year.[88] And where tax moneys are those relied upon to supply the revenue, the tax must have been actually levied,[89] and the obligation must be only to pay out of the revenue thus produced.[90]

(3) *Contingent obligations* are usually treated as not within debt limitations. This is true, for instance, of unliquidated property-damage claims against a city[91] and of contractual obligations where the amount to be paid depends on the supply furnished.[92]

---

[86] See City of Florence v. Anderson, 95 F.2d 777 (4th Cir.1938); City of Georgetown v. Elliott, 95 F.2d 774 (4th Cir.1938); Blood v. Beal, 100 Me. 30, 60 A. 427 (1905); Gibson v. Knapp, 21 Misc. 499, 47 N.Y.S. 446 (1897); Haddon v. Cheatham, 161 S.C. 384, 159 S.E. 843 (1931). Cf. Taylor v. Lovett, 184 Ga. 295, 191 S.E. 113 (1937) (anticipated income from state highway board not within debt limit). See generally City of Stillwater v. International Assn. of Fire Fighters, 238 P.3d 926 (Okla. 2010) (purpose of constitutional prohibition on city becoming indebted in amount exceeding the income and revenue provided for a year is to force municipalities to operate on cash basis and to prevent indebtedness from extending beyond one year). Some state constitutional limits of this nature contain exceptions where electoral approval is obtained. See City of Idaho Falls v. Fuhriman, 149 Idaho 574, 237 P.3d 1200 (2010) ("proviso clause" as to voter approval is an exception to general rule that cities are barred from debts or liabilities in excess of income and revenue provided for debts and liabilities in such year, though no public vote is required if the expenditures constitute ordinary and necessary expenses authorized by general laws of the state).

[87] Holmgren v. City of Moline, 269 Ill. 248, 109 N.E. 1031 (1915); Callahan v. City of Berkley, 307 Mich. 701, 12 N.W.2d 431 (1943), reh. denied 307 Mich. 701, 14 N.W.2d 87 (bonds issued in anticipation of special assessments); Pittsburgh Paving Co. ex rel. Iron & Glass Dollar Savings Bank v. City of Pittsburgh, 332 Pa. 563, 3 A.2d 905 (1938); Williamson v. Aldrich, 21 S.D. 13, 108 N.W. 1063 (1906). See Chicago & Northwestern Railway Co. v. Faulk County, 15 S.D. 501, 90 N.W. 149 (1902) (warrants in anticipation of uncollected revenue are debts only in a limited sense). Cf. Arthur v. City of Stillwater, 611 P.2d 637 (Okl.1980) (where city not obligated to pay revenue to trust for period beyond current year's revenue was not a forbidden indebtedness of city). But see Burt v. Municipal Council of Taunton, 275 Mass. 535, 176 N.E. 511 (1931) (order to purchase pumping engine invalid where cost was to be charged to future unexpended balances). Cf. State v. Spring City, 123 Utah 471, 260 P.2d 527 (1953) (bonds invalid where issued in anticipation of income of *future* years).

[88] See Wickey v. Muscatine County, 242 Iowa 272, 46 N.W.2d 32 (1951) (payment of deficit of county hospital would not be ordinary or essential expense, and thus *would* be within constitutional debt limit); Windsor v. City of Des Moines, 110 Iowa 175, 81 N.W. 476 (1900) (necessity for electric plant is not justification for exceeding debt limit); Sawyer v. Jefferson County Fiscal Court, 438 S.W.2d 531 (Ky. 1969) (Kentucky statute held unconstitutional to extent it authorized appropriations to be received in future to be pledged to payment of debts); Brown v. City of Corry, 175 Pa. 528, 34 A. 854 (1896) (indebtedness exists though payments for waterworks construction to be made only from current revenues).

[89] People ex rel. Seely v. May, 9 Colo. 404, 12 P. 838 (1886); City of Springfield v. Edwards, 84 Ill. 626 (1877). See City of Ottumwa v. City Water Supply Co., 119 F. 315 (8th Cir.1902) (order for levy to be made in future is not actual levy).

[90] See Fuller v. City of Chicago, 89 Ill. 282 (1878) (warrant must be against, and to be paid out of, taxes levied for that particular fund); Law v. People ex rel. Huck, 87 Ill. 385 (1877); Hamilton Test Sys., Inc. v. City of Albuquerque, 103 N.M. 226, 704 P.2d 1102 (1985) (any agreement by which a municipality obligates itself to pay out of tax revenues, and commits itself beyond revenues for the current fiscal year, falls within the constitutional debt restriction). Cf. People ex rel. Seeley v. May, *supra* note 89 (warrant must be made payable out of incoming revenue for current year).

[91] See Boise Dev. Co. v. City of Boise, 26 Idaho 347, 143 P. 531 (1914) (claims for property damage against city are not debts until city liquidates or settles the claim and fixes a definite amount of indebtedness, after which the amount thus fixed is a new debt).

[92] See Lamar Water & Electric Light Co. v. City of Lamar, 140 Mo. 145, 39 S.W. 768 (1897). It is often stated in general terms that incurring a contingent future liability does not create indebtedness. Quill v. City

It has been observed that there really is no contingency, and thus there *is* "debt" within the limitations, when the so-called "contingency" is something certain to take place.[93] But it seems that if the *amount* is totally unliquidated—as in the property-damage and supply-furnished cases mentioned *supra*—the obligation will still be treated as "contingent" and not within the debt limitation, by most authority, even though *some* liability seems virtually certain. There is simply no sum that can, with any justification, be treated as representing the amount of the obligation.

(4) An exception is recognized, to varying extents, by most jurisdictions for *involuntary obligations*. Within this exception are usually found two sub-categories: (a) Obligations that are strictly essential to the continued existence of the municipality or other local unit, such as fire service.[94] An obligation does not come within this part of the

---

of Indianapolis, 124 Ind. 292, 23 N.E. 788 (1890); City of Lebanon v. Schneider, 349 Mo. 712, 163 S.W.2d 588 (1942); Davidson v. City of Elmira, 180 Misc. 1052, 44 N.Y.S.2d 302 (1943), aff'd 267 App.Div. 797, 46 N.Y.S.2d 655, appeal denied 267 App.Div. 926, 47 N.Y.S.2d 604 (city's guaranty of debt incurred by Housing Authority not a city debt since liability was contingent on Authority's default); Pearson v. Salt Lake County, 9 Utah 2d 388, 346 P.2d 155 (1959); Banner v. City of Laramie, 74 Wyo. 429, 289 P.2d 922 (1955). See Wheeler v. Board of Commissioners of Hopkinsville, 245 Ky. 388, 53 S.W.2d 740 (1932) (city had right to use sewerage system, paying for such use as it made; no debt); Homebuilders Association v. Kansas City, 431 S.W.2d 111 (Mo.1968), appeal after remand 509 S.W.2d 134 (contract for reimbursement from revenues derived from water-main extensions not debt); Conrad v. City of Pittsburgh, 421 Pa. 492, 218 A.2d 906 (1966) (city would pay from its revenues any amount by which Stadium Authority was deficient in servicing its debt; if payment insufficient, obligation would be carried over to subsequent years to be paid from current revenues of city in later years; no city debt, since was not to exceed current revenues—unnecessary to decide whether a contingent liability is a debt, but many cases cited holding it is not). But see Smith v. Town of Guin, 229 Ala. 61, 155 So. 865 (1934) (contingent liabilities included in debt limit); Austin v. Healy, 376 Ill. 633, 35 N.E.2d 78 (1941) (debts payable in future and debts payable on contingency *are* within constitutional debt limitation); Rivers v. City of Owensboro, 287 S.W.2d 151 (Ky. 1956) (obligations within debt limit where city would be personally liable whenever special assessments proved insufficient). Cf. Button v. Day, 205 Va. 629, 139 S.E.2d 91 (1964) (city's agreement to assume payment of amount to port authority not exceeding rental paid by railroad lessee; found within debt limit). See generally City of Stillwater v. International Assn. of Fire Fighters, 238 P.3d 926 (Okla. 2010) (purpose of constitutional prohibition on city becoming indebted in amount exceeding the income and revenue provided for a year is to force municipalities to operate on cash basis and to prevent indebtedness from extending beyond one year). Some state constitutional limits of this nature contain exceptions where electoral approval is obtained. See City of Idaho Falls v. Fuhriman, 149 Idaho 574, 237 P.3d 1200 (2010) ("proviso clause" as to voter approval is an exception to general rule that cities are barred from debts or liabilities in excess of income and revenue provided for debts and liabilities in such year, though no public vote is required if the expenditures constitute ordinary and necessary expenses authorized by general laws of the state).

[93] See Burlington Water Co. v. Woodward, 49 Iowa 58 (1878) (if obligation assumed which, without further action on municipality's part, creates indebtedness at some future date, this is within limitation; but if the indebtedness depends on some further volitional act of municipality, is no debt). The *Burlington* case, *supra*, indicated that even if the obligation was initially contingent and thus not within the debt limit, the debt limit would apply once the contingency was met and the obligation became firm. But in American Co. v. City of Lakeport, 220 Cal. 548, 32 P.2d 622 (1934), the court held that even when the contingency occurs, the debt remains outside the limit, reasoning that the validity of a debt must be determined when it is incurred; otherwise, the security of transactions would be defeated. See, in accord with the *American Co.* case, note 104 *infra* and accompanying text. But cf. In re Bond Issuance of Greater Wenatchee Regional Events Center Public Facilities Dist., 287 P.3d 567 (Utah. 2012) (even if municipality's liability is contingent on the failure of payment by an intervening agency, such contingent liability is subject to the constitutional debt limits if the ultimate risk of loss falls upon the municipality).

[94] Weisfield v. City of Seattle, 180 Wash. 288, 40 P.2d 149 (1935) (fire service for large city). See Jefferson County v. State ex rel. Carmichael, 233 Ala. 148, 170 So. 70 (1936); Wakem v. Inhabitants of Van Buren, 137 Me. 127, 15 A.2d 873 (1940); Le Cocq Motors, Inc. v. Whatcom County, 4 Wn.2d 601, 104 P.2d 475 (1940) (mandatory duty on county to assist the unemployed); State ex rel. Peterkin v. City Council of Parkersburg, 95 W.Va. 502, 121 S.E. 489 (1924) (expenses of election were essential). Cf. Ballard v. Adair County, 268 Ky. 347, 104 S.W.2d 1100 (1937) (saying that county may pay necessary governmental expenses even if claims exceed revenue for year); City of Covington v. O. F. Moore Co., 218 Ky. 102, 290 S.W. 1066 (1927) (necessary expenses not limited to fixed charges).

exception merely because it involves an authorized expenditure, or the obtaining of some useful services, such as the hiring of a "handyman" to work in various city departments.[95] To come within this portion of the exception, the expenditure must be for something without which the government could not continue to function for the public benefit. (b) Obligations made mandatory by the constitution or state law, as a fine or assessment levied against the city under state law.[96] Thus, if state law requires that a municipality pay some or all of the expense of a school bond election, the amount thus spent is not within the debt limit.[97] Note that the two sub-parts of this exception may sometimes overlap: State law may require that the municipality provide certain health- and safety-related services, for instance, and that the municipality pay the cost of these; arguably, the expenses would then relate to matters essential to the municipality's existence, and would also be expenses imposed on the locality by mandatory provision of law. (In some cases, the obligation might, in addition, qualify as "contingent," and thus within the third exception.) Because of the mandatory-obligation exception, it is usually said in broad terms that debt limitations do not apply to municipal tort liability.[98] Of course, until a judgment is entered or a settlement reached, the amount would clearly be contingent and thus within the third exception anyway. But the "mandatory" exception has sometimes been applied though agreement has been reached as to the tort liability and its amount.[99]

(5) Another exception concerns *obligations payable only out of a special fund,* not out of general revenues. Thus, if bonds are issued to finance the construction of a

---

[95] Goff v. City of Seattle, 197 Wash. 665, 86 P.2d 222 (1939). See Patterson v. Edmonds, 72 Wash. 88, 129 P. 895 (1913).

[96] See Lake County v. Rollins, 130 U.S. 662, 9 S.Ct. 651, 32 L.Ed. 1060 (1889); Rochlin v. State, 112 Ariz. 171, 540 P.2d 643 (1975) (retirement system); Los Angeles County v. Byram, 36 Cal.2d 694, 227 P.2d 4 (1951); Los Angeles Gas & Electric Corp. v. City Council, 18 Cal.App.2d 97, 63 P.2d 326 (Dist.Ct.1936); Hancock v. Village of Hazel Crest, 318 Ill.App. 170, 47 N.E.2d 557 (1943); Knepfle v. City of Morehead, 301 Ky. 417, 192 S.W.2d 189 (1946) (applying Kentucky constitution and citing many cases); Martin v. Territory, 5 Okl. 188, 48 P. 106 (1897); Rauch v. Chapman, 16 Wash. 568, 48 P. 253 (1897) (limit on county indebtedness does not include expenses made mandatory by constitution or statute). Cf. Los Angeles County v. Payne, 8 Cal.2d 563, 66 P.2d 658 (1937) (poor relief found mandatory); Lewis v. Widber, 99 Cal. 412, 33 P. 1128 (1893) (salary of public officer was fixed by statute; found to be mandatory). But cf. Del City v. Fraternal Order of Police, 869 P.2d 309 (Okl.1993) (obligations imposed by the legislature or by voluntary contract come within debt limitation; only obligations that are imposed by federal or state constitution do not come within such limit); Baylis v. City of Tulsa, 780 P.2d 686 (Okl.1989) (claims of city employees under provisions in city manual stating that they were entitled to 5% pay raise were not expenses incurred in performance of constitutionally required governmental function and thus came within statute requiring proof of municipality's ability to pay claim in order that any judgment not exceed debt limits).

[97] State ex rel. McCormick v. Bentley, 98 Kan. 442, 157 P. 1197 (1916). See State ex rel. Peterkin v. City Council of Parkersburg, *supra* note 94. Cf. Liberty Nat'l Bank v. County Excise Bd., 175 Okl. 245, 52 P.2d 51 (1936) (requirement of voter consent not needed where expense imposed by state law).

[98] See Wichita Finance & Thrift Co. v. City of Lawton, 131 F.Supp. 788 (W.D.Okl. 1955); Indiana Harbor Belt Railroad Co. v. Calumet City, 391 Ill. 280, 63 N.E.2d 369 (1945) (wrongful handling of trust fund by city agents); State ex rel. Pyle v. University City, 320 Mo. 451, 8 S.W.2d 73 (1928); Barker v. State ex rel. Napoleon, 39 N.M. 434, 49 P.2d 246 (1935); Evans v. Berry, 262 N.Y. 61, 186 N.E. 203 (1933) (damages to persons injured by police in making arrests); Raynor v. King County, 2 Wn.2d 199, 97 P.2d 696 (1940). Cf. Town of Flagstaff v. Gomez, 29 Ariz. 481, 242 P. 1003 (1926) (bonds issued for payment of tort judgment were not within debt limit); Metropolitan Life Insurance Co. v. Deasy, 41 Cal.App. 667, 183 P. 243 (Dist.Ct.1919) (exceeding of debt limit is no defense in action against city for tort); Banta v. Clarke County, 219 Iowa 1195, 260 N.W. 329 (1935) (limit inapplicable to expenses made necessary by embezzlement or misappropriation by officers).

[99] See G. W. Jones Lumber Co. v. City of Marmarth, 67 N.D. 309, 272 N.W. 190 (1937) (bonds issued to judgment creditor in amount of compromise settlement reached under statute, held not a "debt").

particular project, such as a stadium, and are payable only out of revenue produced by that facility (so-called "revenue bonds"), the bonds are not an obligation against the general credit of the locality and thus not within its debt limit.[100] Similarly, contracts for local improvements the whole cost of which is to be paid by assessments against the property benefited (the "special assessments" discussed *supra*) do not create debts within the debt limitations.[101]

Beyond all these exceptions, there are certain obligations that may not, at a given time, come within the debt limits because (although the obligation is not contingent either as to liability or amount) they are not yet due to be paid. Thus, interest on an out-

---

[100] See United States v. City of Charleston, 149 F.Supp. 866 (S.D.W.Va.1957); Lyon v. Shelby County, 235 Ala. 69, 177 So. 306 (1937) (warrants for highway improvement were payable out of gas fund); City of Tucson v. Corbin, 128 Ariz. 83, 623 P.2d 1239 (App.1980) (but obligations payable from ad valorem taxes are within debt limit; good discussion of cases); Switzer v. City of Phoenix, 86 Ariz. 121, 341 P.2d 427 (1959); Garrett v. Swanton, 216 Cal. 220, 13 P.2d 725 (1932); De Leuw, Cather & Co. v. City of Joliet, 327 Ill.App. 453, 64 N.E.2d 779 (1945) (obligation payable out of fund created by federal loan and grant); Department of Public Sanitation v. Solan, 229 Ind. 228, 97 N.E.2d 495 (1951); Grimm v. Moloney, 358 S.W.2d 496 (Ky.1962); Ronnow v. City of Las Vegas, 57 Nev. 332, 65 P.2d 133 (1937); Adams v. City of Durham, 189 N.C. 232, 126 S.E. 611 (1925) (debt incurred for public auditorium was payable solely from proceeds of sale of lot; no popular vote needed); Morris v. Oklahoma City, 299 P.2d 131 (Okl.1956); Eddins v. Wasco County, 189 Or. 184, 219 P.2d 159 (1950); Clarke v. South Carolina Public Service Authority, 177 S.C. 427, 181 S.E. 481 (1935); City of Waco v. McCraw, 127 Tex. 268, 93 S.W.2d 717 (1936) (bonds could not become claim against tax funds of city; not "debt"). Cf. City of Redondo Beach v. Taxpayers of Redondo Beach, 54 Cal.2d 126, 5 Cal.Rptr. 10, 352 P.2d 170 (1960) (municipality not liable to maintain special fund from general taxes even if the special fund proved insufficient for intended purpose; so not within debt limit); Laverents v. City of Cheyenne, 67 Wyo. 187, 217 P.2d 877 (1950) (same; with review of many authorities). *Bonds* payable out of special funds do not create "debt" within most debt limitations. See Baisden v. City of Greenville, 215 Ala. 512, 111 So. 2 (1927) (improvement bonds not general obligations of city, not within limit; thus valid); Shainwald v. City of Portland, 153 Or. 167, 55 P.2d 1151 (1936); State ex rel. Roddey v. Byrnes, 219 S.C. 485, 66 S.E.2d 33 (1951). Cf. Hansen v. City of Havre, 112 Mont. 207, 114 P.2d 1053 (1941) (possibility that portion of bonds would have to be paid out of loan from tax funds, but this was a contingency—no debt within debt limit); Conrad v. City of Pittsburgh, *supra* note 92 (possibility that city would have to make up deficit of authority; but was a contingency—and amount was never to exceed current revenue of city for a given year; not within debt limit).

In DeFazio v. Washington Pub. Power Supply Sys., 296 Or. 550, 679 P.2d 1316 (1984), it was held that the "special fund" exception is not limited to self-liquidating projects, nor to situations where the persons who provide the special fund are the direct beneficiaries of the expenditure—indeed, there need be no quid pro quo. But some jurisdictions do not recognize the "special fund" doctrine as to municipal obligations. See Note, Public Finance: State and Municipal Revenue: Special Fund Doctrine in Oklahoma, 3 Okla. L. Rev. 333 (1950) (doctrine accepted in most jurisdictions, but Oklahoma only applies it to the state, not to municipal revenue bond projects). Cf. Asson v. City of Burley, 105 Idaho 432, 670 P.2d 839 (1983), cert. denied 469 U.S. 870, 105 S.Ct. 219, 83 L.Ed.2d 149 (1984) (under constitutional provision limiting county and municipal indebtedness, approval of voters necessary whether indebtedness is against general fund of city or limited to special fund of project-generated revenues).

[101] See Collins v. City of Phoenix, 54 F.2d 770 (9th Cir.1931); City of Mankato v. Barber Asphalt Paving Co., 142 F. 329 (8th Cir.1905); Cyr & Evans Contracting Co. v. Graham, 2 Ariz.App. 196, 407 P.2d 385 (1965); City of Pasadena v. McAllaster, 204 Cal. 267, 267 P. 873 (1928); Griffin v. Clay County, 304 Ky. 592, 201 S.W.2d 733 (1947); State ex rel. Webster Groves Sanitary Sewer District v. Smith, 342 Mo. 365, 115 S.W.2d 816 (1938); Robertson v. Zimmermann, 268 N.Y. 52, 196 N.E. 740 (1935); City of Perry v. Johnson, 106 Okl. 32, 233 P. 679 (1925); Henning v. City of Casper, 50 Wyo. 1, 57 P.2d 1264 (1936), reh. denied 50 Wyo. 1, 62 P.2d 304. Cf. Wall v. Chicago Park District, 378 Ill. 81, 37 N.E.2d 752 (1941) (lake shore improvement payable out of special assessments; not within debt limit); Coke v. Dowell, 281 Ky. 362, 136 S.W.2d 3 (1940) (street improvement expense payable by abutting owners; not within debt limit); State ex rel. Gentry v. Curtis, 319 Mo. 316, 4 S.W.2d 467 (1928) (bonds financed by assessments within sewer district; not indebtedness under state laws). This rule was applied to a sewer and water district in Mann v. Granite Reeder Water & Sewer Dist., 143 Idaho 248, 141 P.3d 1117 (2006) (statute requiring voter approval of any indebtedness exceeding income and revenue provided for the year did not include special assessments; improvement projects for sewer treatment facilities were to be paid for by assessments on benefitted property amounting to 58% of cost, and remaining costs were to be paid from grant funds and loans).

standing obligation is not a debt until due and payable.[102] And where a contract is made by the municipality for a term of years—as a contract to receive services each year and pay for them annually—the amount that will be owed over the entire term is not considered the current debt for debt-limit purposes, but only the amount that will be due within the current year.[103]

In deciding whether or not contracts are valid so far as debt limitations are concerned, the determination must be made when the contract is made. If at that time, the contract does not create an indebtedness exceeding the limit for the locality, then subsequent events cannot bring the obligation over the limit and thus invalidate it.[104] This is necessary to preserve the security of transactions. Otherwise, a person might make a contract, apparently valid, with a municipality—only to find the agreement later invalidated because of unrelated local expenses. Thus, where an installment contract is made by a municipality, it will be valid if the amount due and payable thereon during the current year does not create an obligation in excess of the debt limit (applying the rule mentioned *supra* that only amounts currently due and owing are within the limit)—and will be binding as to installments due in future years as well.[105] In the case of bonds,

---

[102] See Thom v. Mayor & City Council of Baltimore, 154 Md. 273, 141 A. 125 (1928); State ex rel. Helena Waterworks Co. v. City of Helena, 24 Mont. 521, 63 P. 99 (1900); Schieber v. City of Mohall, 66 N.D. 593, 268 N.W. 445 (1936); Kurn v. Helm, 182 Okl. 260, 77 P.2d 552 (1938) (interest which is due and payable counts toward allowed debt; unmatured interest is not debt); Herman v. City of Oconto, 110 Wis. 660, 86 N.W. 681 (1901). See generally Annot., Interest on Indebtedness of Municipality as Part of Debt Within Constitutional or Statutory Debt Limitation, 100 A.L.R. 604 (1936).

[103] City of Walla Walla v. Walla Walla Water Co., 172 U.S. 1, 19 S.Ct. 77, 43 L.Ed. 341 (1898); Hillard v. City of Mobile, 253 Ala. 676, 47 So.2d 162 (1950); City of Los Angeles v. Offner, 19 Cal.2d 483, 122 P.2d 14 (1942); Protsman v. Jefferson-Craig Consolidated School Corp., 231 Ind. 527, 109 N.E.2d 889 (1953); Salisbury Water Supply Co. v. Town of Salisbury, 341 Mass. 42, 167 N.E.2d 320 (1960); Oakland County Drain Commissioner v. City of Royal Oak, 306 Mich. 124, 10 N.W.2d 435 (1943); Kansas City Power & Light Co. v. Town of Carrollton, 346 Mo. 802, 142 S.W.2d 849 (1940); Robbins v. Rapid City, 71 S.D. 171, 23 N.W.2d 144 (1946); Allison v. City of Chester, 69 W.Va. 533, 72 S.E. 472 (1911) (sum of all installments is *not* the current debt). But see Public Market Co. v. City of Portland, 171 Or. 522, 130 P.2d 624 (1942), amplif'd 171 Or. 522, 138 P.2d 916. Cf. East St. Louis & Interurban Water Co. v. City of Belleville, 360 Ill. 490, 196 N.E. 442 (1935) (contract does create debt for aggregate of all installments).

Under the majority view, a present indebtedness is not created for all payments of rent that will become due under a lease, but only for the payment due during the present year. City of Los Angeles v. Offner, *supra*; Hall v. Mayor & City Council of Baltimore, 252 Md. 416, 250 A.2d 233 (1969). See King v. City of Mobile, 273 Ala. 109, 134 So.2d 746 (1961) (one dollar per annum rent for lease of state tunnel). See generally Annot., Aggregate of Rent for Entire Period of Lease of Property to Municipality as Present Indebtedness for Purposes of Condition of Incurring, or Limitation of Amount of, Municipal Debt, 112 A.L.R. 278 (1938).

[104] See City of Winchester v. Winchester Bank, 306 Ky. 45, 205 S.W.2d 997 (1947); Opinion of the Justices, 150 Me. 362, 134 A.2d 511 (1957); Davidson v. City of Elmira, 180 Misc. 1052, 44 N.Y.S.2d 302 (1943), aff'd 267 App.Div. 797, 46 N.Y.S.2d 655, appeal denied 267 App.Div. 926, 47 N.Y.S.2d 604; Board of Education v. State Board of Education, 217 N.C. 90, 6 S.E.2d 833 (1940); Murrell v. City of Sapulpa, 148 Okl. 16, 297 P. 241 (1931); Addyston Pipe & Steel Co. v. City of Corry, 197 Pa. 41, 46 A. 1035 (1900) (debt was intended to be partially paid by assessments; debt not increased, within constitutional prohibition, when it was later determined that some assessments couldn't be enforced); Zimmerman v. Town of New Martinsville, 117 W.Va. 752, 188 S.E. 124 (1936). Cf. City of Richmond v. Durham, 260 Ky. 95, 83 S.W.2d 879 (1935) (debt valid when incurred cannot be rendered invalid by incurring other indebtedness not indispensable to maintenance of government).

[105] *No* debt is incurred until an installment is due and payable. See Ambrozich v. City of Eveleth, 200 Minn. 473, 274 N.W. 635 (1937); Kansas City Power & Light Co. v. Town of Carrollton, *supra* note 103; Wade v. Borough of Oakmont, 165 Pa. 479, 30 A. 959 (1895); City of Tyler v. L. L. Jester & Co., 97 Tex. 344, 78 S.W. 1058 (1904); Fjeldsted v. Ogden City, 83 Utah 278, 28 P.2d 144 (1933); Herman v. City of Oconto, 110 Wis. 660, 86 N.W. 681 (1901) (if nothing due on contract when contract made, is no debt at that time). And if the contract is within the debt limit when made, it will not become invalid though the limit is later exceeded. See City of Cincinnati v. Cameron, 33 Ohio St. 336 (1878); City of Tulsa v. Langley, 196 Okl. 680, 168 P.2d 116 (1946).

the debt is usually considered to have been incurred at the time of sale, not at the time when the sale was authorized (by vote of the people or otherwise).[106] Therefore, a bond election may validly be held though the indebtedness on which the vote is taken would currently exceed the debt limit; the bonds will nonetheless be valid if the debt limit is not exceeded when the bonds are *sold*.[107]

What if a contract is made that *does* in fact exceed the debt limit? With certain exceptions as to bonds (discussed *infra* under "recitals"), such contract or indebtedness is invalid to the extent of the excess.[108] All persons dealing with a local government are on notice as to debt limitations.[109] And a debt that is invalid because it exceeds the limit cannot be ratified by any action of the local government.[110] But the majority view is that the contract or indebtedness is invalid only to the extent that it *does* exceed the debt limit; to the extent that it is within the limit, it is valid and enforceable.[111] Where a bond issue occurs and the bonds are delivered at different dates, they are valid, and payable in full, until the debt limit is reached; any that are delivered after the debt limit is reached are nullities.[112] If the bonds are all delivered at the same time, then a different

---

106 Thompson-Houston Electric Co. v. City of Newton, 42 F. 723 (C.C.S.D. Iowa 1890); Boll v. City of Ludlow, 234 Ky. 812, 29 S.W.2d 547 (1930); Sublett v. City of Tulsa, 405 P.2d 185 (Okl.1965); Redding v. Esplen Borough, 207 Pa. 248, 56 A. 431 (1903); Town of Freeport v. Sellers, 144 Tex. 389, 190 S.W.2d 813 (1945); Crogster v. Bayfield County, 99 Wis. 1, 74 N.W. 635 (1898). See Jaeger v. City of Hillsboro, 164 Kan. 533, 190 P.2d 420 (1948). But see Bordes v. East Jefferson Waterworks District, 186 La. 249, 172 So. 8 (1936); Fisher v. City of Philadelphia, 382 Pa. 607, 116 A.2d 735 (1955).

107 See Howard v. Town of Loyall, 284 Ky. 233, 144 S.W.2d 502 (1940); Frost v. Central City, 134 Ky. 434, 120 S.W. 367 (1909); Hecker v. McKernan, 105 N.H. 195, 196 A.2d 38 (1963). Cf. Prickett v. City of Marceline, 65 F. 469 (C.C.W.D.Mo.1895), aff'd 69 F. 462 (8th Cir.) (date of registration of bond was not date on which indebtedness incurred).

108 See Oklahoma Utilities Co. v. City of Hominy, 2 F.Supp. 849 (N.D.Okl.1933); County Board of Education v. Elba, 273 Ala. 151, 135 So.2d 812 (1961); Chicago Heights v. Public Service Co., 345 Ill.App. 393, 103 N.E.2d 519 (1952); Maffit v. City of Decatur, 322 Ill. 82, 152 N.E. 602 (1926); Fulton v. City of Lockwood, 269 S.W.2d 1 (Mo.1954); McMurtry v. City of Raton, 64 N.M. 117, 325 P.2d 707 (1958); First National Bank v. City of Norman, 182 Okl. 7, 75 P.2d 1109 (1938); Innes v. School District, 342 Pa. 433, 20 A.2d 225 (1941); Hatley v. Bexar County, 144 S.W.2d 695 (Tex.Civ.App.1940), modif'd 136 Tex. 354, 150 S.W.2d 980; McCoy v. Town of Riverside, 109 W.Va. 670, 158 S.E. 539 (1930). No recovery is usually possible on such a debt. See American La France Fire Engine Co. ex rel. American La France & Foamite Industries, Inc. v. Borough of Shenandoah, 30 F.Supp. 251 (E.D.Pa.1939), aff'd 115 F.2d 866 (3d Cir.); Woodside Water Co. v. Long Island City, 23 App.Div. 78, 48 N.Y.S. 686 (1897), aff'd without opinion 159 N.Y. 558, 54 N.E. 1095; Haskins & Sells v. Oklahoma City, 36 Okl. 57, 126 P. 204 (1912).

109 See Toomey v. City of Bridgeport, 79 Conn. 229, 64 A. 215 (1906); Green v. Hutsonville Township High School District, 356 Ill. 216, 190 N.E. 267 (1934); Winchester v. Winchester Bank, *supra* note 104; Protest of Carter Oil Co., 148 Okl. 1, 296 P. 485 (1931).

110 Schooley v. City of Chehalis, 84 Wash. 667, 147 P. 410 (1915); Balch v. Beach, 119 Wis. 77, 95 N.W. 132 (1903). See In re Town of Afton, 43 Okl. 720, 144 P. 184 (1914) (statute could not validate indebtedness that was in excess of that authorized by constitution). But where the debt limit is fixed by statute, not by the constitution, a subsequent statute may ratify the excess. Callahan v. City of Berkley, *supra* note 87. And if the excess could have originally been approved by the electorate, it can be ratified by subsequent vote of the electorate. Bell v. Burgess & Town Council of Waynesboro, 195 Pa. 299, 45 A. 930 (1900).

111 Oppenheim v. City of Florence, 229 Ala. 50, 155 So. 859 (1934); Trepp v. Independent School District, 213 Iowa 944, 240 N.W. 247 (1932); Southern Bitulithic Co. v. Detreville, 156 Ky. 513, 161 S.W. 560 (1913); Pittsburgh Paving Co. ex rel. Iron & Glass Dollar Sav. Bank v. City of Pittsburgh, *supra* note 87; McGillivray v. Joint School District No. 1, 112 Wis. 354, 88 N.W. 310 (1901). To the extent of the excess, there is no recovery even though goods or services have been furnished the locality. See Black v. Common Council of Detroit, 119 Mich. 571, 78 N.W. 660 (1899) (laches inapplicable to taxpayer's objection to city resolution unless he had actual notice or knowledge of resolution).

112 City of Columbus v. Woonsocket Institution of Savings, 114 F. 162 (5th Cir. 1902); Meyer v. City & County of San Francisco, 150 Cal. 131, 88 P. 722 (1907); Citizens' Bank v. City of Terrell, 78 Tex. 450, 14 S.W. 1003 (1890).

method of apportionment must be used: the bonds should be paid pro rata to the extent they do not exceed the debt limit.[113]

§ 15.9 Power of Local Units to Issue Bonds

The power to issue bonds is one not easily found apart from express grant of authority. There is clearly no inherent power in a local government to issue bonds, and it is often said that express authorization is necessary.[114] Some authority has said that the power may be inferred where absolutely necessary to the carrying-out of other powers expressly given.[115] But the power cannot ordinarily be inferred merely from a grant of the police power (as to public health, safety, etc.),[116] and thus a locality cannot

---

[113] See McPherson v. Foster Bros., 43 Iowa 48 (1876) (bonds void only to extent of excess); Towe v. City of Scottsville, 269 Ky. 486, 107 S.W.2d 326 (1937); Johnson v. Sewerage District No. 2, 239 La. 840, 120 So.2d 262 (1960); City of Laredo v. Looney, 108 Tex. 119, 185 S.W. 556 (1916).

[114] Brenham v. German-American Bank, 144 U.S. 173, 12 S.Ct. 559, 36 L.Ed. 390 (1892), modif'd 144 U.S. 549, 12 S.Ct. 975, 36 L.Ed. 399; City of Juneau v. Hixson, 373 P.2d 743 (Alaska 1962); Miehls v. City of Independence, 249 Iowa 1022, 88 N.W.2d 50 (1958) (city had no power to issue "electric revenue bonds"); Dietrich v. City of Deer Lodge, 124 Mont. 8, 218 P.2d 708 (1950); Schnoerr v. Miller, 4 Ohio App.2d 99, 212 N.E.2d 671 (1963), aff'd 2 Ohio St.2d 121, 206 N.E.2d 902 (municipality may issue bonds only for purposes enumerated in statute); Fullerton v. Central Lincoln People's Utility District, 185 Or. 28, 201 P.2d 524 (1948); Lakota Oil & Gas Co. v. City of Casper, 57 Wyo. 329, 116 P.2d 861 (1941). See Merrill v. Town of Monticello, 14 F. 628 (C.C.D.Ind.1882), aff'd 138 U.S. 673, 11 S.Ct. 441, 34 L.Ed. 1069 (no general power to issue commercial paper); Van Eaton v. Town of Sidney, 211 Iowa 986, 231 N.W. 475 (1930); Tierney v. Cohen, 268 N.Y. 464, 198 N.E. 225 (1935), aff'd 246 App.Div. 511, 282 N.Y.S. 944. On municipal bonds, see generally Chung, Municipal Securities: The Crisis of State and Local Government Indebtedness, Systemic Costs of Low Default Rates, and Opportunities for Reform, 34 Cardozo L. Rev. 1455 (2013); A. G. White, Municipal Bonding and Taxation (Garland Publ. 1979). On the preparation of official municipal statements to be used in the sale of municipal securities (as often required by state law), see Daley, A Guide to Municipal Official Statements (Harcourt Brace Jovanovich 1980). On the functions of bond counsel, see National Ass'n of Bond Lawyers Committee on Professional Responsibility, The Function and Professional Responsibilities of Bond Counsel, 16 Urban Law. 489 (1984).

[115] See State v. City of Key West, 153 Fla. 226, 14 So.2d 707 (1943) (charter authorized acquisition of electric utility; this implies all means necessary to carry out the power); State ex rel. Miller v. Kansas City, 60 Kan. 518, 57 P. 118 (1899) (dictum); Kruesel v. Collin, 171 Wash. 200, 17 P.2d 854 (1933) (power to borrow money implies power to issue bonds where a function imposed by the state is involved). Cf. Hill v. Elizabeth City, 291 F. 194 (E.D.N.C.1923) aff'd 298 F. 67 (4th Cir.) (power to construct and operate various utilities implies power to issue bonds therefor); State ex rel. City of Norfolk v. Babcock, 22 Neb. 614, 35 N.W. 941 (1888) (power to construct sewers implies power to issue bonds for needed sewers); Salt Lake City Corp. v. Jordan River Restoration Network, 299 P.3d 990 (Utah 2012) (city enjoys plenary power to develop parks and associated facilities, such as regional sports, recreation, and education complex; court affirms validation of bonds approved by voters 8 years earlier).

[116] See People ex rel. City of Rock Island v. Rudgren, 378 Ill. 408, 38 N.E.2d 723 (1941); Hostetter v. Muskingum Watershed Conservancy District, 58 Ohio App. 161, 12 O.O. 26, 16 N.E.2d 428 (1938). See Byer v. Rural High School District No. 4, 169 Kan. 351, 219 P.2d 382 (1950) (no implied statutory authority to issue bonds to cover cost of moving schoolhouse). But cf. Heilbron v. Mayor of Cuthbert, 96 Ga. 312, 23 S.E. 206 (1895) (power to contract debts indicates power to issue bonds). *Some* decisions have found the power to issue bonds implied in the power to purchase property or erect buildings. See Desmond v. City of Jefferson, 19 F. 483 (C.C.W.D.Tex.1883) (since city had power to organize fire department, it could purchase fire engine and issue bonds for that purpose); State v. Babcock, *supra* note 115. (Cf. other cases cited note 115 *supra*.) But *most* authority is to the contrary. Farr v. City of Grand Rapids, 112 Mich. 99, 70 N.W. 411 (1897); City of Hazlehurst v. Mayes, 96 Miss. 656, 51 So. 890 (1910) (authorization to buy and hold parklands did not imply authorization to issue bonds therefor); City of Bayonne v. Marburger, 100 N.J.Super. 87, 241 A.2d 248 (1968); Whipps v. Town of Greybull, 56 Wyo. 355, 109 P.2d 805 (1941).

It is doubtful that municipalities have power to issue bonds solely or primarily to make a profit from the proceeds. See State v. City of Orlando, 576 So.2d 1315 (Fla. 1991) (revenue bonds issued primarily for reinvestment of proceeds for profit lacked proper municipal purpose and would be invalid).

act with certainty in this area unless the power is expressly stated in the constitution, statutes, or home-rule charter.

If bonds are approved by the electorate (or by the necessary authorities when electoral approval is not needed), when should they be issued? Unless legislation provides a specific time-limit, the general rule is that the bonds need not be issued at any particular time, but only within a reasonable time.[117] The reasonableness of the time-period must be determined under the facts of each case. Usually the bonds will be issued within a year or so of approval; but there is considerable discretion in this regard in the local authorities, and delays of even 18 or 19 years have been found reasonable where there was some justification for the time-lag.[118]

§ 15.10 Rights of Local-Unit Bondholders

What are the rights of holders of bonds issued by local governments? Many of the principles here applied are drawn from the general law on bills and notes. Thus, if the bonds are negotiable, a bona fide purchaser will take free from any equities as between the original parties[119] (though if the bonds are *non*-negotiable, any defense that would have been good against the original purchaser remains good against subsequent purchasers, even bona fide ones[120]). A bona fide purchaser is one who takes the bonds, from the original purchaser or a subsequent one, (1) for value, (2) in good faith, (3) before maturity of the bonds, and (4) without notice of defects.[121] But while a bona fide

---

[117] Hager v. Board of Education, 254 Ky. 791, 72 S.W.2d 475 (1934) (4 years' delay was reasonable); Hitchins v. Mayor & City Council of Cumberland, 215 Md. 315, 138 A.2d 359 (1958); Quaid v. City of Detroit, 319 Mich. 268, 29 N.W.2d 687 (1947) (mere lapse of time does not cause forfeiture of right to issue bonds). See Sparks v. Sparks, 300 Ky. 392, 189 S.W.2d 354 (1945) (25-year delay was unreasonable). A bond issue, though approved as an entirety by the electorate, need not be issued in a single installment. See Baugham v. Willacy County Water Control & Improvement District, 112 S.W.2d 318 (Tex.Civ.App.1938), error ref'd.

[118] Petition of City of St. Louis, 363 S.W.2d 612 (Mo.1963) (18 years); Quaid v. City of Detroit, *supra* note 117 (19 years). See Jonson v. Fiscal Court, 272 Ky. 9, 113 S.W.2d 453 (1938) (11 years not unreasonable); Runyon v. Simpson, 270 Ky. 646, 110 S.W.2d 440 (1937) (8 years not unreasonable); Brewery Arts Center v. State Bd. of Examiners, 108 Nev. 1050, 843 P.2d 369 (1992) (two-year delay in issuance of general obligation bonds to fund cultural projects was a reasonable and appropriate exercise of discretion and did not warrant the issuance of a writ of mandamus). But in Sparks v. Sparks, *supra* note 117, a delay of 25 years as to a road and bridge bond issue was found unreasonable. Whenever the bonds are issued, their proceeds must be expended for the purpose(s) indicated at the time of the election. See Inverness Forest Improvement Dist. v. Hardy Street Investors, 541 S.W.2d 454 (Tex.Civ.App.1976), ref'd n. r. e. (absent showing that voters who approved bond issue relied on statements by officials that proceeds would be used only for certain improvements, city could not be enjoined from using funds on other projects).

[119] See Christmas v. City of Asbury Park, 10 F.Supp. 22 (D.N.J.1935); State v. Board of Public Instruction, 126 Fla. 142, 170 So. 602 (1936) (some of school bonds were in hands of innocent purchasers for value; validity couldn't be questioned); Driscoll v. Burlington-Bristol Bridge Co., 8 N.J. 433, 86 A.2d 201 (1952), cert. denied 344 U.S. 838, 73 S.Ct. 25, 97 L.Ed. 652, reh. denied 344 U.S. 888, 73 S.Ct. 181, 97 L.Ed. 687; Citizens' Sav. Bank v. Greenburgh, 173 N.Y. 215, 65 N.E. 978 (1903); State ex rel. Leecraft v. Hoffman, 127 Okl. 101, 260 P. 12 (1927) (purchaser for value of municipal bonds, without notice of their invalidity as between antecedent parties, takes free from all infirmities); Royce v. Public Utility District, 26 Wn.2d 733, 175 P.2d 624 (1946). Cf. Getz v. City of Harvey, 118 F.2d 817 (7th Cir.1941), cert. denied 314 U.S. 628, 62 S.Ct. 59, 86 L.Ed. 504 (latent defenses arising after issuance of bonds not available to city as against bona fide purchaser); Armstrong v. City of South Fulton, 169 Tenn. 54, 82 S.W.2d 862 (1935) (innocent purchaser of bonds could recover thereon despite invalidity of underlying assessments; bonds certified their compliance with relevant laws).

[120] See City of Sterling v. Commercial Savings Bank, 116 Colo. 369, 181 P.2d 361 (1947). Cf. Jones v. American Savings Bank & Trust Co., 139 Wash. 598, 247 P. 1017 (1926) (non-negotiable bonds; purchaser from thief had no title).

[121] See Shelby County v. Provident Savings Bank & Trust Co., 54 F.2d 602 (5th Cir.1932), cert. denied 287 U.S. 604, 53 S.Ct. 9, 77 L.Ed. 526; Prange v. City of Marion, 319 Ill.App. 136, 48 N.E.2d 980 (1943);

purchaser may be protected against defects in the original *sale* from the locality to the first purchaser,[122] he is not necessarily protected against a failure of the issuing locality to perform conditions precedent, established by law, to the *issue* of the bonds. Unless estoppel is found, a failure of the locality to perform a condition precedent to the issue of the bonds *is* a valid defense even against bona fide purchasers.[123] This applies, for instance, to a failure of the issuing locality to obtain required approval of the electorate prior to issuing the bonds.[124] Where such a condition is not performed, the bonds are in effect void—and their invalidity cannot be cured by any transfer to an innocent party.

Sometimes, however, an issuing locality may be estopped from denying the validity of bonds it has issued. This estoppel is usually based on "recitals" in the bonds themselves. Recitals are defined as statements that something has been done—that, in the case of municipal bonds, certain specific conditions precedent (such as electoral approval) have been fulfilled, or that in general all necessary conditions have been performed.[125] A municipality may be estopped to deny the truth of such recitals as against, and only as against, bona fide purchasers[126]—but only if the officers issuing the

---

Montvale v. People's Bank, 74 N.J.L. 464, 67 A. 67 (1907) (applying statute); Bankers' Trust Co. v. City of Statesville, 203 N.C. 399, 166 S.E. 169 (1932); Eaton v. St. Louis-San Francisco Railway Co., 122 Okl. 143, 251 P. 1032 (1925); Fannin-Lamar-Delta Improvement District v. State, 73 S.W.2d 1101 (Tex.Civ.App.1934) error dism'd. Cf. Toon v. Wapinitia Irrigation Co., 117 Or. 374, 243 P. 554 (1926) (municipal coupon bond; statute applied). But a purchaser of bonds *after* their maturity does not usually qualify as a bona fide purchaser. See Edwards v. Bates County, 117 F. 526 (C.C.W.D.Mo.1902) (purchaser after maturity is not bona fide purchaser unless he acquired title through a prior holder who had taken title, as a bona fide purchaser, before maturity). And there can be no bona fide purchaser of bonds that are totally void. See Richmond v. Town of Largo, 155 Fla. 226, 19 So.2d 791 (1944) (saying that purchaser of bonds which have not been adjudicated to be valid takes them subject to subsequent adjudication as to validity); State v. Town of Belleair, 125 Fla. 669, 170 So. 434 (1936) (no such thing as bona fide holder of bonds issued in contravention of constitutional provision against issuing bonds to benefit private company).

[122] For instance, a failure of consideration in the original sale is no defense against a bona fide purchaser. Inhabitants of Bernards Township v. Morrison, 133 U.S. 523, 10 S.Ct. 333, 33 L.Ed. 766 (1890); City of Cripple Creek v. Adams, 36 Colo. 320, 85 P. 184 (1906). See Town of Ontario v. Union Bank, 21 Misc. 770, 47 N.Y.S. 927 (1897), modif'd sub. nom. Town of Ontario v. Hill, 31 App. Div. 324, 52 N.Y.S. 328 (1898). (But the lack of consideration in original sale *is* a good defense if the bonds are non-negotiable. Flagg v. School Dist. No. 70, 5 N.D. 191, 65 N.W. 674 (1895). See generally note 120 *supra* and accompanying text.) And fraud in the original sale is no defense against a bona fide purchaser. See Pulaski County v. Eichstaedt, 110 F.2d 79 (6th Cir.1940) (county bonds); Town of Fletcher v. Hickman, 136 F. 568 (8th Cir.1905). Note that a purchaser *from* a bona fide purchaser is *always* protected, even if this subsequent purchaser himself has notice of defects. Board of Comm'rs of Gunnison County v. E.H. Rollins & Sons, 173 U.S. 255, 19 S.Ct. 390, 43 L.Ed. 689 (1899).

[123] See Lehman v. City of San Diego, 83 F. 669 (9th Cir.1897); First Wisconsin National Bank v. Bessemer Township, 286 Mich. 426, 282 N.W. 203 (1938) (note issued in violation of statutory regulations). Cf. Silk v. City of Louisville, 299 Ky. 736, 187 S.W.2d 286 (1945) (recognizing general rule, but finding that all prerequisites to issuance of flood control bonds had been met; an appropriation by Congress was unnecessary).

[124] Board of Education v. Taft, 7 Ill.App. 571 (1880). See Crayton v. City of Charlotte, 175 N.C. 17, 94 S.E. 689 (1917).

[125] See 15 McQuillin, Municipal Corporations § 43.97 (3d rev. ed. 1995), distinguishing general and special recitals.

[126] Divide Creek Irrigation District v. Hollingsworth, 72 F.2d 859 (10th Cir. 1934); Board of Educ. v. James, 49 F.2d 91 (10th Cir. 1931); Chemical Bank & Trust Co. v. Oakland County, 264 Mich. 673, 251 N.W. 395 (1933). See Knott County v. Aid Association for Lutherans, 140 F.2d 630 (6th Cir.1944) (recitals not binding when purchaser knows they are untrue, as where recitals false on their face); St. Paul Fire & Marine Ins. Co. v. Town of Monongah, 209 F.Supp. 514 (N.D.W.Va.1962); State ex rel. Havana State Bank v. Rodes, 115 Fla. 259, 151 So. 289 (1934). See generally Annot., Estoppel of Municipal Corporation or Other Public Subdivision by Recitals in its Bonds to Dispute Their Validity as Affected by the Character of the Owner of Bonds as an Original Holder or a Transferee, 86 A.L.R. 1101 (1933); Annot., Estoppel by Recitals in Municipal Bonds as to Lawfulness of Issue, 86 A.L.R. 1057 (1933).

bonds had the authority to make the recitals in question.[127] In most jurisdictions, recitals that conditions precedent have been performed or that the bonds are issued pursuant to certain legislation—even if the recitals are only general in nature, not specifying the exact conditions that have been fulfilled—are conclusive as against bona fide purchasers.[128] That is, against such purchasers, the issuing locality is estopped from denying the truth of the statements, and the purchaser can recover on the bonds though in fact the statements are false.

Does the doctrine of estoppel by recital (described in the above paragraph) protect a bona fide purchaser who buys bonds that exceed the issuing locality's debt limitation? It does to a limited extent. The rules have been summarized[129] as follows: (1) The estoppel applies despite the bonds exceeding the debt limitation if there is an express recital that the debt limit is not exceeded, *and* if the bonds don't show on their face the total amount of the bond issue.[130] (2) There is no estoppel, however, if the bonds show on their face that the limit is exceeded, as simply by showing the total amount of the issue (since this is considered to give notice of the violation),[131] or where the recital is merely a general statement of compliance with legal requirements.[132] (3) There is some old, and

---

127 Bloomfield Village Drain District v. Keefe, 119 F.2d 157 (6th Cir.1941), cert. denied 314 U.S. 649, 62 S.Ct. 95, 86 L.Ed. 520, motion denied 314 U.S. 709, 62 S.Ct. 133, reh. denied 315 U.S. 830, 62 S.Ct. 910, 86 L.Ed. 1224 (officers were without power to issue bonds or make recitals); Starmount Co. v. Ohio Savings Bank and Trust Co., 55 F.2d 649 (4th Cir.1932); George A. Eyer & Co. v. Mercer County, 292 F. 292 (E.D.Ky. 1923), aff'd 1 F.2d 609 (6th Cir.); City of Highland Park v. Clark, 300 Mich. 501, 2 N.W.2d 479 (1942); Bolton v. Wharton, 163 S.C. 242, 161 S.E. 454 (1931).

128 Board of Comm'rs v. Aspinwall, 62 U.S. (21 How.) 539, 16 L.Ed. 208 (1858) (the leading case); Board of County Comm'rs v. Board of Finance of Methodist Episcopal Church, 100 F.2d 766 (10th Cir. 1938); Henderson County v. Sovereign Camp, 12 F.2d 883 (6th Cir.1926), cert. denied 273 U.S. 721, 47 S.Ct. 111, 71 L.Ed. 858; Baxter v. Vineland Irrigation District, 136 Cal. 185, 68 P. 601 (1902); Thompson v. Village of Mecosta, 127 Mich. 522, 86 N.W. 1044 (1901); St. Paul Gaslight Co. v. Village of Sandstone, 73 Minn. 225, 75 N.W. 1050 (1898); Driscoll v. Burlington-Bristol Bridge Co., *supra* note 119; Southwest Securities Co. v. Board of Education, 40 N.M. 59, 54 P.2d 412 (1936); Wilson v. Board of Education, 12 S.D. 535, 81 N.W. 952 (1900), aff'd 15 S.D. 317, 89 N.W. 480; Nolan County v. State, 83 Tex. 182, 17 S.W. 823 (1891). But Missouri rejects the usual rule and holds that recitals in municipal bonds do *not* estop the municipality as against bona fide purchasers. See Evans v. McFarland, 186 Mo. 703, 85 S.W. 873 (1905). And a few other states accept the general rule only with qualifications. See Newberry Library v. Board of Education, 390 Ill. 48, 60 N.E.2d 552 (1945) (estoppel only as to questions of fact, not questions of law); Montpelier Savings Bank & Trust Co. v. School District No. 5, 115 Wis. 622, 92 N.W. 439 (1902) (minutes of meeting at which bonds were authorized showed they were not refunding bonds, as they appeared to be; no estoppel).

On the nature of the recitals necessary, under the majority view, to estop an issuing locality, see Independent School District v. Stone, 106 U.S. 183, 1 S.Ct. 84, 27 L.Ed. 90 (1882) (general recital that bonds issued in pursuance of a named statute will suffice); Caldwell v. Guardian Trust Co., 26 F.2d 218 (8th Cir.1928).

129 See 15 McQuillin, Municipal Corporations § 43.114 (3d rev. ed. 1995).

130 State ex rel. Ohio National Bank v. Village of Hudson, 134 Ohio St. 150, 11 O.O. 577, 16 N.E.2d 266 (1938). See Gunnison County v. E. H. Rollins & Sons, *supra* note 122.

131 Board of Comm'rs of Chaffee County v. Potter, 142 U.S. 355, 12 S.Ct. 216, 35 L.Ed. 1040 (1892); Dixon County v. Field, 111 U.S. 83, 4 S.Ct. 315, 28 L.Ed. 360 (1884). Cf. Sutliff v. Lake County Comm'rs, 147 U.S. 230, 13 S.Ct. 318, 37 L.Ed. 145 (1893) (public record prescribed by statute as determinative of amount of authorized issue; showed that debt limit was exceeded). As to possible constructive notice of the amount of a bond issue, see Rathbone v. Board of Comm'rs, 83 F. 125 (8th Cir.1897), cert. denied 170 U.S. 705, 18 S.Ct. 940, 42 L.Ed. 1218.

132 Lake County v. Graham, 130 U.S. 674, 9 S.Ct. 654, 32 L.Ed. 1065 (1889); Independent School Dist. v. Stone, *supra* note 128; Geer v. School District No. 11, 97 F. 732 (8th Cir. 1899). See generally Nesbit v. Riverside Independent Dist., 144 U.S. 610, 12 S.Ct. 746, 36 L.Ed. 562 (1892). But general recitals in funding or refunding bonds, which do not themselves actually create indebtedness, have been said to bar the defense that the debt limit is exceeded. See Gillespie v. Yell County, 124 F.2d 632 (8th Cir.1942); City of Pierre v. Dunscomb, 106 F. 611 (8th Cir.1901), cert. denied 181 U.S. 621, 21 S.Ct. 925, 45 L.Ed. 1032.

now doubtful, authority that a general recital that bonds were issued under a specified *statute* works an estoppel as to exceeding a statutory debt limit[133] (though clearly not a debt limit set by constitution).

§ 15.11 Types of Bonds Issued by Local Units

There are two main types of bonds issued by local governments: general obligation bonds and revenue bonds. General obligation bonds are payable from the general revenues of the locality, while revenue bonds are payable only from a specified fund—often a fund consisting of amounts earned by the facility (a stadium, for instance) that the bonds were issued to finance. Bonds will be assumed to be general obligation unless they themselves contain a clear promise to pay *only* out of a special fund.[134] Revenue bonds are often issued to finance the cost of building public improvements, and of building and/or operating utilities. Sometimes, municipalities are given express statutory authority to pledge the proceeds of designated taxes—such as municipal license taxes or franchise taxes—as security for revenue bonds. But in the absence of express authority, a locality may not pledge to the payment of its revenue bonds any income other than that from the improvement the bonds were issued to finance.[135]

---

[133] See Humboldt Township v. Long, 92 U.S. 642, 23 L.Ed. 752 (1875); Marcy v. Township of Oswego, 92 U.S. 637, 23 L.Ed. 748 (1875).

[134] See City of Deland v. State ex rel. Bond Realization Corp., 120 Fla. 402, 162 So. 892 (1935); Mutual Benefit Life Insurance Co. v. City of Elizabeth, 42 N.J.L. 235 (1880) (general obligation bond cannot be converted into promise to pay out of particular fund). Cf. Beaulieu & Allen v. City of Pleasant Hill, 14 F. 222 (C.C.W.D.Mo.1882) (holders of general obligation bonds may not insist on payment from sources other than yearly revenue of city, but may insist on proper exercise of city's taxing power). On the definition and operation of revenue bonds, see Wayland v. Snapp, 232 Ark. 57, 334 S.W.2d 633 (1960); In re Cherokee County, Kansas Health Care Facility Revenue Bonds, 262 Kan. 941, 946 P.2d 83 (Kan. 1997) (revenue bonds are distinguished by single source of payment, as opposed to general obligation bonds, which pledge full faith and credit of issuer); McKinney v. City of Owensboro, 305 Ky. 254, 203 S.W.2d 24 (1947); Castle Farms Dairy Stores v. Lexington Market Authority, 193 Md. 472, 67 A.2d 490 (1949) (statute declaring revenue bonds not a debt of city was constitutional); City of El Campo v. South Texas National Bank, 200 S.W.2d 252 (Tex.Civ.App.1946), error ref'd (distinguishing feature of revenue bonds is that holders have no claim on funds raised by taxation).

By the last decades of the twentieth century, close to 70% of bonds issued by municipalities were revenue, as opposed to general obligation, bonds—almost a complete reversal of the situation in the 1960's. See Godwin, The New Look of Municipal Bonds, 68 A.B.A.J. 1580 (1982).

[135] City of Treasure Island v. State, 117 So.2d 721 (Fla.1960); City of West Palm Beach v. State, 113 So.2d 374 (Fla.1959); Britt v. City of Wilmington, 236 N.C. 446, 73 S.E.2d 289 (1952) (revenue from on-street parking could not be pledged to pay bonds for off-street parking facility). See Public Util. Dist. No. 1 v. Washington Pub. Power Supply Sys., 104 Wash.2d 353, 705 P.2d 1195 (1985), opinion modified 713 P.2d 1109 (1986) (loans in connection with proposed construction of nuclear plants were repayable only from two specific nuclear plants involved, not from revenue from other projects). Cf. City of Spokane v. Taxpayers of City of Spokane, 111 Wash.2d 91, 758 P.2d 480 (1988) (ordinance requiring a popular vote approving capital expenditures "requiring indebtedness of the taxpayers and property owners" did not apply to a project financed by the sale of revenue bonds).

A special category of bonds is that of "arbitrage" or "refunding" bonds: bonds issued for the purpose of funding a valid, already existing debt. Generally the proceeds from such a bond issue are used to acquire other securities that are expected to yield more than the bonds. See also Section 7.3 *supra*. By the majority view, the issuance of such bonds does not create a new indebtedness within debt-limitation laws. See Taxpayers & Citizens of Shelby County v. Shelby County, 246 Ala. 192, 20 So.2d 36 (1944) (with review of cases). Cf. City of Tucson v. Commissioner of Internal Revenue, 820 F.2d 1283 (D.C.Cir.1987), ruling that a Department of the Treasury regulation that classified municipal sinking funds, established for the payment of principal or interest on municipal bonds, as "arbitrage bonds" rather than tax-exempt municipal bonds was invalid as beyond the scope of the relevant statute. See generally Panico & Peterson, Survey of the Final Arbitrage Regulations, 25 Urban Law. 1013 (1993), discussing the Internal Revenue Code's arbitrage regulations. On taxation of interest on arbitrage bonds, see Amdursky & Gillette, Municipal Debt Finance Law—Theory and Practice § 7.14 (Little, Brown & Co. 1992), noting that interest on such bonds has not been exempt from federal

Municipal bonds have often been popular investments in modern times, particularly because of the exemption from federal income tax of interest paid on long-term (maturing in over one-year) state and local fixed-income bonds.[136] But the experiences of default, or near default, on bonds by New York City and other municipalities have at times caused investors to buy municipal bonds only if high yields seemed possible, and have scared away some of the more conservative investors.[137] In times when the stock market appears shaky, municipal bonds—and in general, most long-term bonds—are still, however, considered relatively safe and desirable investments.[138]

§ 15.12 Miscellaneous Sources of Local Revenue: Fines, License Fees, etc.

A number of miscellaneous sources of revenue—*i.e.*, sources other than taxes and borrowing—are of importance to local governments. Fines imposed for violation of municipal ordinances are considered in the chapter on crime-control activities of municipalities, *infra*. Revenues from utility operations are discussed in the chapter on utilities.

Local governments often require licenses in order for certain occupations and activities to be carried on within the limits of the locality, and permits in order for buildings to be erected, subdivisions (of homes) to be constructed, etc. In this way, the local licensing agency can review the legality of the proposed activity and try to assure the competence of those involved. Periodic re-inspections and re-licensing are often required. Where there is power to regulate such businesses (and this can usually be found in grants of the police power, if not in any more specific grant), there is clearly power to charge fees (license fees, etc.) to finance the regulatory program. If the revenue

---

income tax since 1969. *Id.* at 483. An excellent summary of the law, including tax regulations, applicable to arbitrage bonds, is Ballard, ABCs of Arbitrage: Tax Rules for Investment of Bond Proceeds by Municipalities (American Bar Assn. 2011). On "tax-exempt derivatives"—bonds structured to provide tax-exempt income to investors—see Conlon & Aquilino (principal authors & coeds.), Tax-Exempt Derivatives (American Bar Ass'n Section of Urban, State & Local Gov't Law 1994).

[136] See Burrus, Clarke, & Gottsfield, What Clients Want Lawyers to Know About Municipal Bonds, Ariz.B.J., April, 1979, at 8; "Another Munificent Year for Munis," Bus. Week, Dec. 27, 1993, at 118; "Why Muni Bonds Are Ripe for Picking," Bus. Week, Nov. 4, 1985, at 83; "The Surge in Municipal Bonds," Bus. Week, June 8, 1974, at 47. See generally Hardy, Guidelines to Earning Tax-Free Income from Municipal Bonds,63 A.B.A.J. 1241 (1977). On the effects of the Tax Reform Act of 1986 on the federal tax exemption enjoyed by municipal bonds, see Holzschuh, Urban Issues, American West magazine, Jan., 1987, at 12 (many classes of municipal bonds left untouched). Some observers believe that the federal income tax exemption for state and local government bonds will eventually be totally eliminated. See Peers & Herman, Growing Municipal Bond Mess Underscores Wall Street's Woes, Wall St. J., April 25, 1989, at C-1, C-17.

[137] See "Municipal Bonds: High Yields, High Risk," Bus. Week, Dec. 29, 1975, at 114. In 1989, it was reported that municipal bonds were regarded as riskier investments than in the past due to the more than 500 municipal defaults that had occurred since 1983. See "Munis Are Evolving into More Dangerous Animals," Bus. Week, June 19, 1989, at 106. The increased rate of defaults continued into the 1990's. See "The Muni Mine Field—Defaults Are Up, and May Get Worse," Bus. Week, Sept. 23, 1991, at 34, noting that many defaults were occurring in relatively prosperous Sunbelt cities that had acquired large debts in the 1980's to fund high-risk projects such as convention centers, apartment complexes, and jails. See generally "The Trouble with Munis," Bus. Week, Sept. 6, 1993, at 44. On the possibility of holding local governments liable for fraud under the Securities Exchange Act and regulations issued thereunder, see Sachs, Are Local Governments Liable Under Rule 10b–5? Textualism and Its Limits, 70 Wash. U.L.Q. 19 (1992).

[138] See "Why Municipal-Bond Yields Are Plunging," Bus. Week, Sept. 19, 1977, at 43. See generally Foust, So You Think Munis Are Safe?, Bus. Week, Aug. 5, 2002, at 88, saying, at 89, "Many investors are still desperately seeking a safe haven from the misery of the stock market. But the public sector can only offer so much succor."

earned from such fees is not disproportionate to the licensing and regulatory expenses, the fee will be upheld.[139] But the police power, or related powers of regulation, cannot justify taxation; and thus if the amount charged is clearly out of line with the direct and indirect costs of the licensing and regulatory program, the fee will be invalidated.[140] The desired revenue would have to be collected by the locality under its taxing powers, if at all. A "fee" is regarded as a charge for a direct public service rendered to a particular customer, while a "tax" is a forced contribution by the public at large to meet public needs.[141] Further discussion of licensing is found in the chapter on trade regulation.

User charges, or service fees, are also employed by some local governments to defray the costs of providing certain services—such as garbage and waste collection. Such fees have been upheld if reasonable, and differentials in the fees charged will be upheld if based on real differences in type or amount of service.[142] The theory behind these charges

---

[139] See Vernor v. Secretary of State, 179 Mich. 157, 146 N.W. 338 (1914) (automobile licensing fee levied by state statute).

[140] Merrelli v. City of St. Clair Shores, 355 Mich. 575, 96 N.W.2d 144 (1959) (fees for building permits invalidated). See Weber Basin Home Builders Association v. Roy City, 26 Utah 2d 215, 487 P.2d 866 (1971) (residential building fee exceeded cost of regulation, but could be justified since statute authorized license fee or tax, and this was a hybrid of both; but invalidated as discriminatory); Airwick Industries, Inc. v. Carlstadt Sewerage Authority, 57 N.J. 107, 270 A.2d 18 (1970), cert. denied 402 U.S. 967, 91 S.Ct. 1666, 29 L.Ed.2d 132 (schedule of sewage service fees). Cf. Brewster v. City of Pocatello, 115 Idaho 502, 768 P.2d 765 (1988) (ordinance imposing street restoration and maintenance fee on city residents invalidated as having no necessary relationship to regulation of travel; was revenue-raising measure and thus required voter approval). On the meaning of "fee," see State v. Medeiros, 89 Hawai'i 361, 973 P.2d 736 (1999) (charge for costs of prosecution automatically imposed by city-county on criminal defendants following their convictions was not a "fee" within meaning of statute allowing counties to fix fees for services but was an unauthorized tax).

[141] See Potts Constr. Co. v. North Kootenai Water Dist., 141 Idaho 678, 116 P.3d 8 (2005) (in addition to having a regulatory purpose, a municipal fee must be reasonably related to that purpose); Holmes Harbor Sewer Dist. v. Frontier Bank, 123 Wash.App. 45, 96 P.3d 442 (2004) (three questions determine whether an amount charged is a fee or tax: whether primary purpose is to regulate fee payers or to collect revenue to finance broad-based public improvements; whether the money collected is allocated solely to regulating the entity or activity being assessed; and whether there is a direct relationship between the rate charged and either a service received by the fee payers or a burden to which they contribute). Cf. Storedahl Properties, LLC v. Clark County, 143 Wash.App. 489, 178 P.3d 377 (2008) (primary purpose of clean water charge which county imposed based on storm water runoff was not to raise money for the general welfare but rather was to fund activities directly related to the public health and safety impacts of storm water runoff; thus, charge was akin to a regulatory fee rather than a tax). It has been said that a "fee" is a charge for a direct public service rendered to the particular customer, while a "tax" is a forced contribution by the public at large to meet public needs"; a fee's purpose is regulation, while taxes are imposed primarily to raise revenue. North Idaho Building Contractors Assn. v. City of Hayden, 343 P.3d 1086 (Idaho 2015) (city's sewer connection "fee" was not based on service rendered and thus was an unauthorized tax); Lewiston Independent School Dist. No. 1 v. City of Lewiston, 151 Idaho 800, 264 P.3d 907 (2011) (city's stormwater "fee" was actually an unauthorized tax, as it was used for the non-regulatory function of repairing, maintaining, and expanding the city's pre-existing stormwater system and streets). Cf. Barber v. Ritter, 196 P.3d 238 (Colo.2008) (transfer of fees from cash funds to state's general fund did not alter their essential character as fees so as to transform them into taxes, which would require voter approval; but statutory charge, even though called a "fee," *may* in effect be a tax if the amount charged is unreasonably in excess of cost of the services the charge is designed to defray); Tooele Associates Limited Partnership v. Tooele City Corp., 247 P.3d 371 (Utah 2011) (city's civil inspection fee was enacted to compensate city for costs of civil inspections and was reasonably related to inspection costs and thus constitutional); Cedar River Water & Sewer Dist. v. King County, 178 Wash. 2d 763, 315 P.3d 1065 (2013) (state constitutional provision declaring that every law imposing a tax shall state distinctly the object to which it applies is applicable only to taxes, not fees such as sewage treatment fees). See generally Spitzer, Taxes vs. Fees: A Curious Confusion, 38 Gonzaga L. Rev. 335 (2002–03). See also Laurie Reynolds, Taxes, Fees, Assessments, Dues, and the "Get What You Pay For" Model of Local Government, 56 Fla. L. Rev. 373 (2004).

[142] See McCoy v. City of Sistersville, 120 W.Va. 471, 199 S.E. 260 (1938) (charges varied according to assessed valuation; differential found justified only as to fire protection). Lower rates for charitable and educational institutions have been upheld. See Fort Collins Motor Homes, Inc. v. City of Fort Collins, 30 Colo.App. 445, 496 P.2d 1074 (1972) (no minimum charge assessed against state university). But statutory

is similar to that underlying special assessments, discussed *supra*: Those who benefit should bear the cost of providing the benefit. But again, as with license and permit fees, the amount charged is not supposed to return an overall profit to the locality but only cover the cost of providing the service (except as localities are allowed a reasonable return on their utility operations, discussed *infra*). Practical difficulties of administration and enforcement have made the use of service fees less popular with municipalities than the use of general taxation.

Hard-pressed for revenue, a number of *state* governments now sponsor lotteries—following the lead of New Hampshire, which initiated a lottery in 1964;[143] and legalization of other forms of gambling (such as long found in Nevada) has now occurred in many states.[144] Taxation of profits of gambling operations—and the increase in property values in areas where gambling is allowed, with resulting increases in property tax assessments—are often pointed to as potential benefits from gambling. Atlantic City, New Jersey, legalized casino gambling, and tax revenues and property values increased—but so has criminal activity, which some people allege is related to the gambling.[145] It has been suggested that New York City should take over the "numbers

exemptions from property taxes and/or special assessments don't, in themselves, give immunity from user charges. Young Men's Christian Association v. Rochester Pure Waters District, 44 A.D.2d 219, 354 N.Y.S.2d 201 (1974), aff'd 37 N.Y.2d 371, 372 N.Y.S.2d 633, 334 N.E.2d 586. On the possible use of user fees to avoid constitutional limits on taxes, see Zielke, User Fees in Lieu of Taxes: Avoiding Constitutional Limitations, 23 Urban Law 439 (1991).

143 On the revenue raised by state lotteries, see "State Lotteries," Parade magazine, Dec. 20, 1981, at 9. On the popularity of state lotteries and of legalized gambling in general, see "America's Gambling Fever," Bus. Week, April 24, 1989, at 112. Proposals have been made that Congress authorize a national lottery. See "A National Lottery—How Soon?," Parade magazine, April 13, 1985, at 16. See generally Leacock, Lotteries and Public Policy in the United States and Commonwealth Caribbean Law: Scrutinizing the Success of Lotteries as a Voluntary and "Painless" Tax, 45 U. Miami Inter-Am. L. Rev. 91 (2013); Leacock, Lotteries and Public Policy in American Law, 46 J. Marshall L. Rev. 37 (2012).

144 See "More States Turn to Gambling to Raise Money in Hard Times," U.S. News & World Rep, June 30, 1975, at 22. On discussion of the involvement of organized crime in legalized gambling and the effects of such gambling on American economy and society, see Roberts, The National Gambling Debate: Two Defining Issues, 18 Whittier L. Rev. 579 (1997). For interpretation of statutes that in some states restrict or forbid certain types of gambling, see Ecumenical Ministries of Oregon v. Oregon State Lottery Comm'n, 318 Or. 551, 871 P.2d 106 (1994) (use of video lottery games did not violate constitutional prohibition against casinos); Roberts, The Constitutionality of Gaming in Tennessee, 61 Tenn. L. Rev. 675 (1994) (state constitution forbids "lotteries" in Tennessee, but state supreme court has not made clear what comes within this prohibition). See also Thompson & Prentice, Should Casinos Exist as Monopolies or Should Casinos Be in Open Markets?, 4 U.N.L.V. Gaming L. J. 39 (2013). As to casinos on Indian lands, see Section 14, note 11, paragraphs 1 & 2.

On state-sanctioned sports wagering at casinos, racetracks, etc., see Hudson, Losing to the Spread, A.B.A.J., Nov., 2014, at 17, noting the federal Professional & Amateur Sports Protection Act, which was passed in 1992 and which disallows sports gambling in all states except Delaware, Montana, Nevada and Oregon. So far, that law has been upheld against attacks based on the 10th Amendment and the equal sovereignty doctrine.

145 See Satchell, Atlantic City's Great Gold Rush, Parade, June 10, 1979, at 8. The legalization of gambling did not prevent continuing problems with unemployment. See Janson, Atlantic City Jobless Rate Is Rising Despite Casinos, N. Y. Times, Oct. 19, 1979, at B2. On the situation in Atlantic City eleven years after the arrival of casino gambling, see Painton, Boardwalk of Broken Dreams, Time, Sept. 25, 1989, at 64, noting the continued mix of prosperity and decay. See generally Sternliev & Hughes, The Atlantic City Gamble (Center for Urban Policy Research 1983). In 2015, the New Jersey governor appointed an emergency manager to take over the day-to-day operations and troubled finances of Atlantic City—a step that was "an unprecedented extension of state control over a New Jersey municipality." Haddon & Dawsey, State Manager Will Oversee Atlantic City, Wall St. J., Jan. 22, 2015, at A-13. On the initiation of casino gambling in New Orleans and its effects, see Medley, Big Gamble in the Big Easy, Historic Preservation magazine, July/Aug., 1994, at 26. On the pros and cons of gambling being legalized in a state or city, see Becker, Gambling's Advocates Are Right—But for the Wrong Reasons, Bus. Week, Sept. 6, 1993, at 14 (gambling will add only a

racket" and operate it as a legalized form of gambling, comparable to state lotteries.[146] But so far, either legalization of gambling, or actual government operation of gambling activities, has (apart from a few of the highly successful *state* lotteries) not contributed greatly to the coffers of most state and local governments.

§ 15.13 Federal Financial Assistance to Local Units: Grants, Revenue-Sharing, etc.

Local-government expenditures have been increasing in recent times at an even faster pace than those of state and federal government. As more and more activities have been undertaken by local units and as an ever greater concentration of economic and social difficulty has occurred in urban areas, municipalities have often turned to the federal government for financial help. Federal transfers of funds to state and local governments increased more than four-fold just in the period from 1965 to 1974.[147] Until 1972, most of the federal transfers took the form of "categorical grants"—so called, because they were issued for various categories of programs, such as urban renewal, law-enforcement activities, etc. Each program of federal assistance was largely separate from all other such programs; each had its own requirements and conditions (often including requirements that localities receiving federal aid contribute a certain amount of financial support themselves to the program); and most involved considerable "red tape"—planning, applications, approvals.[148] The categorical-grant programs have been, in one

---

modest amount to government revenues, but will enable many people to satisfy their urge to gamble without having to patronize illegal establishments or facilities controlled by criminals); Note, Legalized Gambling and Public Corruption: Removing the Incentive to Act Corruptly, or, Teaching an Old Dog New Tricks, 13 J.L. & Pol. 453 (1997). See also Kindt, Legalized Gambling Activities as Subsidized by Taxpayers, 48 Ark. L. Rev. 889 (1995). For a discussion of the ways in which many state and local governments have legalized various forms of gambling, see Verchick, Loving Las Vegas, 37 Urban Law. 619 (2005), stating that "States and local governments are consciously imitating the Las Vegas formula of a gambling-dependent economy, whether based on casinos, race tracks, lotteries, or some combination." *Id.* at 619–20. On legalized gambling on Indian lands, see Section 2.11 *supra*.

As for the effects of legalized gambling on a community smaller than Atlantic City or other gambling meccas, see the description of Tunica, Mississippi's experiences in Kilborn, Casinos Revive a Town, but Poverty Persists, N.Y. Times, Oct. 20, 2002, at 1 (Tunica has become the nation's third largest gambling center, after Las Vegas and Atlantic City, but the black neighborhood north of downtown has seen little development, and the county as a whole remains poor.) As to favoritism toward gambling on riverboats, see Fitzgerald v. Racing Ass'n of Central Iowa 539 U.S. 103, 123 S.Ct. 2156, 156 L.Ed.2d 97 (2003) (Iowa statute taxed revenues from slot machines on riverboats at maximum rate of 20 per cent, while taxing slot machines at racetracks at 36 per cent; upheld against Equal Protection attack). See generally on taxation of gambling profits Thompson & Stream, Casino Taxation and Revenue Sharing: A Budget Game, or a Game for Economic Development?, 22 T.M. Cooley L. Rev. 515 (2005).

As to the implications of casinos and horse racing tracks for land use control by local governments, see McClenathan, Land Use Implications of Casinos and Racinos on Local Governments in New York State, 39 Urban Law. 111 (2007).

As to proposals for establishing a land-based casino in Chicago, see Comment, A Winner for the Windy City: A Comment in Support of Establishing a Land-based Casino in the City of Chicago, 40 John Marshall L. Rev. 1391 (2007). See generally Symposium on Gaming Law, 40 John Marshall L. Rev. 1123–1316 (2007).

[146] See Penn, More Public Officials Eye Legal Gambling as Source of Revenue, Wall St.J., Nov. 7, 1972, at 1.

[147] United States Bureau of the Census, 1974 Statistical Abstract 249 (1974). On federal aid to state and local governments, see generally United States Department of Commerce, 1976 Pocket Data Book, Table 284 (1976).

[148] See United States Advisory Comm'n on Intergovernmental Relations, Special Revenue Sharing: An Analysis of the Administration's Grant Consolidation Proposals (1971).

excellent analysis,[149] sub-divided into three types: (1) *Functional grants,* which are payments from the federal to the local level for which the recipient undertakes activities agreed upon by the grantor and grantee; these have often been used in connection with educational activities, public welfare, and highway construction. (2) *Equalizing grants,* which are designed to bring facilities, such as housing, or general fiscal resources in a particular locality up to an established minimum standard. Sometimes, these grants are given *only* to localities whose present facilities or resources are below the minimum, but often functional grants that are given to a wide range of localities have equalizing *components* in their allocation formula, so that those localities having the poorest conditions (and thus the greatest need) receive the largest grants.[150] (3) *Block grants,* which are simple cash transfers from the federal to the local government; the recipient has wide discretion as to how to spend these funds, though under the categorical-grant approach, the funds are still usually ear-marked for some general areas of activity, such as housing or pollution-control. Block grants can also be made solely to *state* governments, with the state then exercising control of any disbursements to local units. *This* block-grant system, unlike that in which the grants are made directly to the municipalities, is not always popular with cities and towns since it leaves them at the discretion of state officials.

The State and Local Fiscal Assistance Act of 1972[151] was a departure from the traditional categorical-grant approach; in a sense, it involves an expansion on the above-described "block grants." The Act provided for the distribution of over $30 billion to approximately 39,000 state and local governments, with the state government receiving one-third of the total allocation for each state, and the remaining two-thirds being divided among the local governments within that state. Allocations to the states were based on formulas employing such factors as population, relative income in that state, and the general tax effort of the state. Lump-sum payments were made to the states and localities; and broad discretion was accorded recipients as to how the money was to be spent, though reports concerning use of the funds had to be filed periodically with the federal government.[152] The Act established certain "priority expenditure" categories on which general revenue funds received were to be spent, but it was noted that there was little machinery with which to enforce the supposed "priorities."[153] One study indicated that older, larger, and more financially hard-pressed localities tended to use the federal money as a substitute for tax revenues, thus giving citizens some tax relief, rather than to undertake new activities, while new, smaller, and more prosperous communities

---

149 Grove & Bish, Financing Government 356–59 (1973).

150 See United States Advisory Comm'n on Intergovernmental Relations, The Role of Equalization in Federal Grants (1964).

151 31 U.S.C.A. §§ 1221–28, 1241–45, 1261–65.

152 See Watt, The Goals and Objectives of General Revenue Sharing, 419 Annals Am.Acad.Pol. & Soc.Sci. 13–17 (1975). See generally Calaba, The Analysis and Application of the State and Local Fiscal Assistance Act of 1972, 28 Tax L.Rev. 377 (1973); Stolz, Revenue Sharing—New American Revolution or Trojan Horse?, 58 Minn. L.Rev. 1 (1973).

Although discretion is given local officials as to how to spend revenue-sharing funds, an attempt to use those funds to pay the salaries of firefighters and to divert general funds, relieved from the salary payments, to lower the water and sewer rates was struck down in Mathews v. Massell, 356 F.Supp. 291 (N.D.Ga.1973). The court indicated that revenue-sharing funds could be used to provide relief to taxpayers, but not just to water and sewer users.

153 See Comment, The Revenue Sharing Act of 1972: Untied and Untraceable Dollars from Washington, 10 Harv. J.Legisl. 276 (1973).

tended to use the money to expand their activities.[154] While the affluent community of Redding, Connecticut, was reported to have trouble deciding how to spend its share of the "revenue sharing"—debating such possibilities as tennis courts and dog kennels—the amount received by New York City did little to relieve its financial woes.[155] Many communities used some of the money to improve outdated equipment, or buy new, for such functions as fire-fighting.[156] Although the possibility existed under such legislation that communities could lose their share of the federal revenue if they did not comply with certain minimum federal standards (as on affirmative action, for instance),[157] the program was criticized as not adequately providing for central cities or for minority groups and for not providing allocation and use of funds on the basis of nationwide priorities.[158] Some local governments came to depend on the funds, and the revenue-sharing program was for a time extended.[159] The program was, however, terminated as to the states in 1981 and as to the cities in 1986.[160]

§ 15.14 Municipal Financial Crises: Bankruptcy

In mid-1975, the country's largest city, New York, faced an unprecedented financial crisis in which it appeared the city would be unable to meet payments on its bonds, could not obtain further loans, and would at all events have to decrease many city services. The crisis was variously blamed on soaring salaries and benefits for officers and employees, proliferating services and welfare payments for residents, and the narrowing tax base resulting from movement of many businesses, and affluent citizens, to the suburbs and an influx of poorer persons to the city.[161] It was noted that many other cities might soon face financial problems nearly as severe as New York's and that in general most municipalities would not be able to continue piling up debt, especially short-term debt, as they had done in the past.[162] The immediate New York crisis was averted, first

---

[154] Nathan, The Uses of Shared Revenue, 30 J.Finance 557 (1975). Cf. Reagan, The Pro and Con Arguments, 419 Annals Am.Acad.Pol. & Soc.Sci. 23 (1975) (part of a symposium on revenue sharing; Reagan notes that many cities have been unable, despite revenue sharing, to initiate new projects since the funds have been consumed by the increasing cost of existing services); N.Y. Times, April 4, 1974, at 27, col. 3, noting a Brookings Institution report that local governments were spending only 31.4% of revenue-sharing funds on new programs. In 1977, the Census Bureau reported that the largest part of revenue-sharing funds was spent on education and police protection. See "Around the Nation—Revenue Sharing Spent on Education and Police," N.Y. Times, July 7, 1980, at A12. See generally Macbeth & Sofaer, Recent Developments in Local Government Law, 7 Urban Law. 1–7 (1975). Though revenue sharing programs have been popular with local governments, the fear was expressed that such programs may undermine local control of some activities. See Stolz, Revenue Sharing—New American Revolution or Trojan Horse?, 55 Minn.L.Rev. 1 (1973).

[155] See Adams, Can Uncle Sam Bail Out New York?, Wall St. J., Feb. 23, 1973.

[156] A Red-Hot Season for Fire-Equipment Manufacturers, Bus.Week, Sept. 8, 1975, at 46.

[157] See Hartford's Suburban Crunch, Bus.Week, May 10, 1975, at 75, reporting that 4 Connecticut towns, suburbs of Hartford, were in danger of losing revenue sharing funds because of alleged failure to comply with federal standards on housing, minority employment, and delivery of services.

[158] See Reuss, Should We Abandon Revenue Sharing?, 419 Annals Am.Acad.Pol. & Soc.Sci. 88, 96 (1975). Cf. Reagan, *supra* note 154. See generally Comment, 33 Cong.Q.Weekly Rep. 2055 (1975).

[159] 31 U.S.C.A. § 1224. On the debate over federal revenue-sharing with the cities, see "The Drive to Kill Revenue Sharing," Time, March 11, 1985, at 30.

[160] See "The Crumbling of America: A New Crisis in Public Works," Bus. Week, Dec. 1, 1986, at 62; "One More Blow for America's Cities," U.S. News & World Rep., Sept. 29, 1986, at 31 (program officially terminated Sept. 30, 1986; new block grants were initiated, but many cities suffered a financial blow).

[161] See "How New York City Lurched to the Brink," Time, June 16, 1975, at 16. See generally C. Morris, The Cost of Good Intentions—New York City and the Liberal Experiment (1980).

[162] See "Borrowing Too Much to Keep Running," Bus. Week, Sept. 22, 1975, at 84. Short-term borrowing by municipalities often comes within exceptions, discussed *supra*, to debt-limitation laws such as the exception

by a moratorium on bond payments, which was, however, subsequently declared unconstitutional,[163] and then by a plan to redeem from the city's own resources the short-term notes that had been frozen by the moratorium, and the resulting renewal of credit and extension of loans by the city's two traditional sources of credit—the federal government and the municipal pension systems. A state agency was created in 1975 to help finance the city's continuing needs, and city officials eventually concluded that they could get along without further long-term financing by the federal government.[164] In August, 1978, a federal law provided loan guarantees, but no new money, from the United States government to help New York put into effect its own plans to achieve, over a several-year period, a balanced budget.[165] It was noted that the city's plans included

---

for amounts payable out of current revenues. See Swanson v. City of Ottumwa, 118 Iowa 161, 91 N.W. 1048 (1902). Consequently, there are often few if any controls over short-term municipal debts. See United States Advisory Comm'n on Intergovernmental Relations, City Financial Emergencies 6 (1973). On the amount of short- v. long-term borrowing of municipalities for some representative years, see Tax Foundation, Inc., Facts and Figures on Government Finance 242 (16th ed. 1971). See generally Maxwell, Financing State & Local Governments (1969 rev. ed.).

Wayne County, Michigan, was another local entity that faced periodic financial crises in the 1970's and 1980's. See Peterson, County Embracing Detroit Unable to Meet Payroll, N.Y. Times, Oct. 19, 1979, at A14. Financial difficulties forced considerable layoffs of personnel at times in Philadelphia. See "Philadelphia Catches Fiscal Flu," Bus. Week, Feb. 25, 1980, at 53. And Cleveland, Ohio, in 1978 became the first American city since the Great Depression to default on its obligations—but later was able to bring about a recovery. See "Running a City Like a Business," Bus.Week, June 2, 1980, at 100. See generally "A First Step to Raise Cleveland from Default," June 23, 1980, at 37. See also "Economic Diary—Cleveland vs. Cincinnati: A Lesson for Older Cities," Bus.Week, May 5, 1980, at 26 (comparing Cincinnati's healthy financial condition with Cleveland's financial difficulties). As to municipal financial problems after 1990, see note 165 *infra*.

[163] Flushing National Bank v. Municipal Assistance Corp., 40 N.Y.2d 731, 390 N.Y.S.2d 22, 358 N.E.2d 848 (1976), on remand 88 Misc.2d 1047, 391 N.Y.S.2d 969, motion granted 40 N.Y.2d 1088, 392 N.Y.S.2d 392, 360 N.E.2d 1075, on remand 89 Misc.2d 342, 393 N.Y.S.2d 873, subsequent opinion 90 Misc.2d 204, 397 N.Y.S.2d 662, striking down McKinney's N.Y.Unconsol. Laws ch. 24–A, §§ 1–7. See Note, Municipal Corporations—A State's Police Power Does Not Allow the Alteration of the Payment Terms of Short Term Municipal Notes, 81 Dick.L.Rev. 866 (1977); Note, The Limits of State Intervention in a Municipal Fiscal Crisis, 4 Fordham Urban L.J. 545, 559–62 (1976).

[164] See "Why New York Faces the Same Old Prospect: Bankruptcy", Bus. Week, Jan. 16, 1978, at 86. On the use of state agencies, often called "financial control boards," to oversee municipal finances during a fiscal crisis, see Note, Missed Opportunity: Urban Fiscal Crises and Financial Control Boards, 110 Harv. L. Rev. 733 (1997). On state assistance to financially troubled municipalities, see generally Jarik, Ansani, Morris & Schraidt, Municipal Financial Distress: A Case Study of a Partnership Between the Village of Maywood and the Illinois Development Finance Authority, 25 Urban Law. 995 (1993).

[165] New York City Loan Guarantees Act, 31 U.S.C.A. §§ 1521–31. Earlier provision for federal loans to New York City was contained in the New York City Seasonal Financing Act of 1975, 31 U.S.C.A. §§ 1501–10. See, on the legislative history, 1975 U.S. Code Cong. & Ad.News 1509. On subsequent improvements in New York City's financial picture, see Gargan, Surplus Forecast of $243 Million in New York City, N.Y. Times, May 11, 1981, at 1, col. 1; Haberman, Mayor Koch Submits $14.7 Billion Budget, N.Y.Times, May 13, 1981, at 1, col. 5. New York achieved a balanced budget in 1981, and subsequently enjoyed a financial comeback and new-found prosperity. See "The New York Colossus," Bus. Week, July 23, 1984, at 98. See generally "New York—The American Dream, the American Nightmare," The Economist, Oct. 7, 1989. Some difficulty in balancing New York's budget did occur again in the early 1990's. See Roberts, New York Rushing to Fiscal Deadline, N.Y. Times, June 27, 1991, at A-1.

Several other cities experienced serious financial difficulties in the 1990's and into the 21st century, including *Philadelphia.* See "The City of Brotherly Love Keeps Taking It on the Chin," Bus. Week., Sept. 10, 1990, at 80; Gevelin & Goel, Philadelphia's Mayor Has Failed to Deliver on High Expectations, Wall St. J., Sept. 21, 1990, at 1. On the financial crisis in 1995 in *Washington, D.C.,* see Ritter, Capital's Survival in Congress' Hands, U.S.A. Today, March 29, 1995, at 3A; Schneider & Vise, GAO Report Declares District to be "Insolvent"; Council Votes for 6 Percent Cut in Union Salaries, Wash. Post., Feb. 22, 1995, at A1. This crisis resulted in the creation of a Presidentially appointed board to oversee the finances of the District of Columbia. See Janofsky, Congress Creates Board to Oversee Washington, D.C., N.Y. Times, April 18, 1995, at 1. See generally Section 2.11 *supra.* In June, 1991, *Bridgeport, Connecticut,* filed a petition for bankruptcy—the largest municipality then to do so and the first American city to do this since the great depression. In re City

cuts in municipal employment and services that are difficult to make,[166] and fear continues that other cities will experience financial shortages that they will be able to overcome only if they find new sources of income, or receive substantial aid from other levels of government.

---

of Bridgeport, 128 B.R. 688 (Bkrtcy. D.Conn.1991). See Incantalupe, Conn. City Seeks Refuge in Bankruptcy Court, Newsday, June 8, 1991, at 15. But the bankruptcy court found Bridgeport to be solvent and thus dismissed the petition. In re City of Bridgeport, 129 B.R. 332, 339 (Bkrtcy. D.Conn.1991). See Brown, Fiscal Distress and Politics: The Bankruptcy Filing of Bridgeport as a Case Study in Reclaiming Local Sovereignty, 11 Bankruptcy Developments J. 625 (1995). See generally, discussing the Bridgeport situation and other instances of municipal financial problems, Note, Municipal Bankruptcy: Will Labor Be Forced to Take the Proverbial Haircut?, 26 Ga. L. Rev. 959 (1992). On the filing for bankruptcy in 1994 of *Orange County, California*, see "The California Wipeout—Orange County Files for Bankruptcy After Losing Big on High-Risk Investments," Time, Dec. 19, 1994; Jereski, How a Rescue Mission Failed, Just Barely, in Orange County, Wall St. J., Dec. 22, 1994, at A1. For subsequent developments in Orange County, see Sterngold, Orange County Bankruptcy: The Poor Feel the Most Pain, N.Y. Times, Dec. 5, 1995, at A1 (Orange County said to be stumbling through a fiscal recovery after having shifted much of the burden to the county's growing numbers of poor people); Sterngold, Orange County Creditors Said to Accept Plan, N.Y. Times, May 6, 1996, at B1 (bankruptcy proceedings were nearing a conclusion with the announcement that creditors had accepted a recovery plan); Reed, 5 Years Later, Bankruptcy Still Toxic, Orange County Sunday Register, Dec. 5, 1999, at News 1 (county assumed $1 billion in additional debt in order to pull itself out of bankruptcy). As to the effect that the Orange County bankruptcy had on California's municipal bankruptcy law, see Tung, After Orange County: Reforming California Municipal Bankruptcy Law, 53 Hastings L.J. 885 (2002). *Vallejo, California,* in 2008 filed for bankruptcy. Its unfunded pension liabilities were reported a few years later to have reached $195 million. See Zielenziger, Bankrupt!, 52 AARP Bulletin No. 4, May 2011, at 20. Then in July, 2012, three other California cities filed for bankruptcy—*Stockton, Mammoth Lakes,* and *San Bernardino,* using a newly passed California law under which cities must hire a third-party mediator to negotiate with employee unions and creditors before the city files for Chapter 9 bankruptcy under the federal law—but the city can avoid the mediation process by declaring a fiscal emergency. (As to Chapter 9, see note 167 *infra* and accompanying text.) See Lovett, Third City in California Votes to Seek Bankruptcy, N. Y. Times, July 12, 2012, at A14 (Natl. Edition). Some local governments in *Rhode Island* have also struggled with financial problems. See Comment, Preserving Local Autonomy in the Face of Municipal Financial Crisis: Reconciling Rhode Island's Response to the Central Falls Financial Crisis With the State's Home Rule Tradition, 16 Roger Williams U. L. Rev. 348 (2011). *Detroit, Michigan*: In 2013, Detroit became the largest city in U.S. history to file for bankruptcy. See Cassidy, Motown Down, The New Yorker, Aug. 5, 2013, at 19 (saying "decades of deindustrialization are the main culprit"); Foroohur, Broken City—How Detroit's Epic Bankruptcy Could Help the Rest of the Country, Time magazine, Aug. 5, 2013, at 22 (saying, at 25, that Detroit's problems may lead other cities to take control of their economies). As to the plan for Detroit's future proposed by a task force, see Davey, $1.85 Billion Renewal Plan for Bankrupt Detroit, N. Y. Times, May 28, 2014, at A1. See generally Colloquium, Legacy Liabilities and Municipal Financial Distress, 41 Fordham Urb. L. J. 771–1040 (2014), especially Chung, Zombieland/The Detroit Bankruptcy, *id.* at 771; Jacoby, The Detroit Bankruptcy Pre-Eligibility, *id.* at 849. See also Kimhi, A Tale of Four Cities—Models of State Intervention in Distressed Localities Fiscal Affairs, 80 U. Cin. L. Rev. 881 (2012); Moringiello, Goals and Governance in Municipal Bankruptcy, 71 Wash. & Lee L. Rev. 403 (2014); Note, Municipal Bankruptcy and Public Pensions: Detroit's Eligibility for Chapter 9 Relief and Legal Restraints on the City's Actions as a Debtor, 89 Notre Dame L. Rev. 2299 (2014). See also Section 1.1, note 6, *supra.* As to the effects of bankruptcy and other remedies on municipal independence, see Note, Examining the Conflict Between Municipal Receivership and Local Autonomy, 98 Va. L. Rev. 1109 (2012).

As to *state* bankruptcy, see Schwarez, A Minimalist Approach to State "Bankruptcy," 59 UCLA L. Rev. 322 (2011). See also Gillette, Fiscal Federalism, Political Will, and Strategic Use of Municipal Bankruptcy, 79 U. Chi. L. Rev. 281 (2012). On the history of bankruptcy legislation, see Section 7.3, notes 39–40 and accompanying text, *supra.* As to financing of distressed government units, see generally Symposium, Distressed Municipal Financing, 33 Rev. Banking & Fin. L. 567–794 (2013–14).

[166] See "The Flaws in New York's Recovery Plan," Bus. Week, Aug. 28, 1978, at 89. See generally J. Weitzman, City Workers and the Fiscal Crisis: Cut-Backs, Give-Backs and Survival, A Study of the New York City Experience (Rutgers Institute of Management 1979). On the personnel cuts that were actually made by New York City, see "Koch Says Layoffs of City Employees Will Be Necessary," N.Y. Times, Nov. 8, 1982, at 1, col. 6. See generally the excerpts from the Citizens Budget Commission's report on New York City's fiscal prospects, N.Y. Times, Nov. 9, 1982, at 13. See also "New York State Joins the City on the Ailing List," Bus. Week, Nov. 19, 1979, at 154.

As a last resort, bankruptcy procedures for municipalities are provided by federal law, and have been used by some of the local governments discussed in notes 162 and 165.[167]

[167] These provisions are found in Chapter IX of the Bankruptcy Law, 11 U.S.C.A. §§ 401–18. Their constitutionality was upheld in United States v. Bekins, 304 U.S. 27, 58 S.Ct. 811, 82 L.Ed. 1137 (1938). (An earlier version was declared unconstitutional in Ashton v. Cameron County Water Improvement Dist. No. 1, 298 U.S. 513, 56 S.Ct. 892, 80 L.Ed. 1309 (1936).) The law is discussed in Greenberg, Municipal Bankruptcy: Some Basic Aspects, 10 Urban Lawyer 266 (1978); King, Municipal Insolvency: The New Chapter IX of the Bankruptcy Act, 1976 Duke L.J. 1157 (discussing procedural rules promulgated for Chapter IX). See generally Biern, A Survey of Municipal Bankruptcy Law and Procedure, 38 Brooklyn L.Rev. 478 (1971); Hempel, An Evaluation of Municipal "Bankruptcy" Laws and Procedures, 28 J.Finance 1339 (1973); King, Municipal Insolvency: Chapter IX, Old and New; Chapter IX Rules, 50 Am. Bankr.L.J. 55 (1976). On rejection of executory contracts, including labor agreements, under the bankruptcy laws, see Note, Bankruptcy and Rejection of Collective Bargaining Agreements, 51 Notre Dame Lawyer 819 (1976). On remedies of creditors in cases of municipal default, see Note, Creditors' Remedies in Municipal Default, 1976 Duke L.J. 1363.

A number of amendments were made to the municipal bankruptcy statute in 1988. See Amdursky, The 1988 Municipal Bankruptcy Amendments: History, Purposes, and Effects, 22 Urban Law. 1 (1990). See generally on the current status of municipal bankruptcy law and its shortcomings Dubrow, Chapter 9 of the Bankruptcy Code: A Viable Option for Municipalities in Fiscal Crisis?, 24 Urban Law. 539 (1992); Kupetz, Municipal Debt Adjustment Under the Bankruptcy Code, 27 Urban Law. 531 (1995); McConnell & Picker, When Cities Go Broke: A Conceptual Introduction to Municipal Bankruptcy, 60 U. Chi. L. Rev. 425 (1993). See also Skeel (with commentaries by Gelpern & Gillette), The Seventeenth Annual Frankel Lecture: Is Bankruptcy the Answer for Troubled Cities and States?, 50 Houston L. Rev. 1063 (2013); Skeel, States of Bankruptcy, 79 U. Chi. L. Rev. 677 (2012); Comment, The Next Financial Hurricane? Rethinking Municipal Bankruptcy in Louisiana, 72 La. L. Rev. 555 (2012). As to the effects of the 2008–10 recession on cities, including causing some of them to resort to Chapter 9 bankruptcy, see Curriden, The Next Chapter, 97 A.B.A.J. 50 (2011). See generally Gillette, Dictatorships for Democracy: Takeovers of Financially Failure Cities, 114 Colum. L. Rev. 1373 (2014).

Chapter 16

LOCAL INDUCEMENTS TO BUSINESS AND INDUSTRY

Analysis

§ 16.1 Encouraging Business to Enter a Community

One solution to the financial problems of urban areas is the increasing of the tax base through encouragement of businesses to settle in the community. Such encouragement has been much discussed, and sometimes actually undertaken, in the past—and is increasing today as the need for a solution to urban economic problems becomes more urgent. The encouragement has taken four main forms: (1) direct donations and/or lending of credit from state or local government to businesses; (2) advertising and promotions to convince people of a locality's desirability for business and tourism; (3) tax exemptions, or favorable tax rates, for businesses—or at least "new businesses"—within a locality; and (4) the construction of facilities by the government for lease to private business. Related to these activities—though not always done as an inducement to other business—is the direct entry of a local government itself into business activities.

It has long been held that a tax may be levied only for public purposes. This notion may be based either on general concepts of the purpose of government,[1] or on the more specific idea that to tax for private benefit amounts to a taking of property without due process of law.[2] On this basis, attempts by municipalities to provide financial aid directly from municipal revenues to private businesses, or to lend municipal credit to such businesses, have been struck down.[3] Some state constitutions specifically prohibit

---

[1] See Citizens' Savings & Loan Association v. Topeka, 87 U.S. (20 Wall.) 655, 22 L.Ed. 455 (1874); Sharpless v. Mayor of Philadelphia, 21 Pa. 147 (1853).

[2] Fallbrook Irrigation District v. Bradley, 164 U.S. 112, 17 S.Ct. 56, 41 L.Ed. 369 (1896). But the use of municipal funds to aid a utility, including a railroad, can be sustained on the principle that the enterprise is of special benefit to the municipal unit. See United States v. Baltimore & Ohio Railroad Co., 84 U.S. (17 Wall.) 322, 21 L.Ed. 597 (1873).

[3] City of Parkersburg v. Brown, 106 U.S. 487, 1 S.Ct. 442, 27 L.Ed. 238 (1883) (direct aid to non-utility business not allowed). See Cole v. La Grange, 113 U.S. 1, 5 S.Ct. 416, 28 L.Ed. 896 (1885) (state legislature can not authorize city to issue its bonds for purpose of donation to private manufacturing company). See also Zobel v. Williams, 457 U.S. 55, 102 S.Ct. 2309, 72 L.Ed.2d 672 (1982) (dividend distribution plan, rewarding Alaska residents according to the number of years of their residency in state and intended to encourage persons to establish and maintain residency in Alaska, struck down as violative of Equal Protection). But see City of Aurora v. Public Util. Comm'n, 785 P.2d 1280 (Colo.1990) (under Colorado Constitution's provision prohibiting a city from making "any donation" to public or private company, city could nonetheless confer monetary benefit

governmental aid, by donation, lending of credit, or investment in stock, to private enterprise.[4]

What of municipal expenditures to advertise the benefits of a city? An express grant of such power will clearly be upheld today as being for a public purpose.[5] Two statements of caution should be added, however: (1) It is clearly desirable for a city wishing to engage in such activities to *have* express statutory or home-rule charter power, since the *implication* of such authority from general city powers has sometimes been denied.[6] The trend, however, is to find an implication of the power to advertise in express powers concerning the commerce or general welfare of the city.[7] (2) In connection with its advertising efforts, the municipality should, at least where express authority does not exist, avoid direct donations to private organizations, which may be struck down as unconstitutional.[8] It has been held, however, that a city may, in connection with its advertising powers, *employ* a person to help bring about the location of industry within municipal limits.[9]

---

on private company in consideration for company's undertaking a project, even though the company might have been required to undertake the project without such benefit). Cf. King County v. Taxpayers of King County, 133 Wash.2d 584, 949 P.2d 1260 (1997) (lease of stadium to baseball team did not violate constitutional prohibition of making gift of public funds). As to the use of economic incentives to help, or prevent harm to, the environment, see Holloway, The Effectiveness and Environmental Impact of Economic Development Incentives as Measures to Respond to Environmental Harm, 24 Vill. Envtl. L. J. 225 (2013).

4 See Schuler v. Board of Education, 370 Ill. 107, 18 N.E.2d 174 (1938). Cf. Cole v. La Grange, *supra* note 3 (constitutional limitation only required electoral approval; constitutional provisions held restrictive, not enabling; legislature had no power to authorize city to issue bonds by way of donation to private enterprise).

5 Sacramento Chamber of Commerce v. Stephens, 212 Cal. 607, 299 P. 728 (1931). See City of Jacksonville v. Oldham, 112 Fla. 502, 150 So. 619 (1933); Davis v. City of Taylor, 123 Tex. 39, 67 S.W.2d 1033 (1934).

6 See Loeb v. City of Jacksonville, 101 Fla. 429, 134 So. 205 (1931); State v. City of Cape May, 66 N.J.L. 544, 49 A. 584 (1901).

7 See Annot, Power of Municipality to Make Expenditures for Advertising or Other Forms of Publicity, 79 A.L.R. 466 (1932). Cf. Ruggeri v. City of St. Louis, 441 S.W.2d 361 (Mo.1969) (city could establish convention and tourism bureau, and could impose additional tax on gross receipts of hotels, motels, and restaurants to finance bureau's activities); In re Carrick, 127 N.J.L. 316, 22 A.2d 561 (1941) (city could advertise against bills that were before state legislature where bills considered disadvantageous to city citizens); Bland v. City of Taylor, 37 S.W.2d 291 (Tex.Civ.App.1931), aff'd 123 Tex. 39, 67 S.W.2d 1033, noted 10 Tex. L.Rev. 516 (1932) (tax to maintain board of city development, which would advertise city, upheld). See generally Note, Legal Limitations on Public Inducements to Industrial Location, 59 Colum.L.Rev. 618, 643 (1959) (promotional advertising is valid public purpose); Chapter 8 *supra* on express and implied powers of municipalities. See also Lewis v. La Guardia, 172 Misc. 82, 14 N.Y.S.2d 463 (1939), aff'd 258 App.Div. 713, 14 N.Y.S.2d 991, aff'd 282 N.Y. 757, 27 N.E.2d 44 (city may spend its money for broadcast over municipal radio station of programs of general interest).

8 See Atlanta Chamber of Commerce v. McRae, 174 Ga. 590, 163 S.E. 701 (1932) (county made outright appropriations to chamber of commerce, freight bureau, and tourist bureau; struck down as donations to private parties). Cf. Stone v. State ex rel. Mobile Broadcasting Corp., 223 Ala. 426, 136 So. 727 (1931) (county's contracting with broadcasting corporation was invalid, and could not constitutionally be authorized by statute, where primary purpose was to establish station, not to advertise county).

9 City of Fernandina v. State, 143 Fla. 802, 197 So. 454 (1940) (public purpose found in expenditure; also found to be authorized by general welfare clause of city charter). In such a case, there is, of course, no "donation" involved, since substantial services are rendered by the person employed.

Some cities have come to recognize the advantages of what has been called "community personality planning": the process of identifying the unique features of a municipality's personality and then planning to preserve or enhance these in order to promote tourism and make the municipality an attractive place in which to live. See Rosenow & Pulsipher, Tourism: The Good, the Bad, and the Ugly (Century Three Press 1981). See also Jacobs, It Takes More Than a Village: Community Economic Development Clinics as a Mechanism for Meaningful Public Participation in an Adversarial Planning Landscape, 13 Conn. Pub. Int. L.J. 301 (2013–14).

Although taxes may not be levied for private (as opposed to public) benefit, *exemptions* from property taxes may validly be authorized by state law except as such exemptions are prohibited by the state constitution.[10] The device of exempting from property taxation new businesses or industries that enter a community, and often also exempting additions or extensions to existing businesses, has been used with some success in several states—chiefly in the South—and has been upheld.[11] In a few states,

---

On the special efforts that some communities make during hard financial times to lure additional businesses, see "We're Your Kind of Town," Time, Sept. 6, 1982, at 24. On the efforts of small communities in particular, see Quintanilla & Rose, Some Tiny Towns Find a Way to Create Jobs: Attract Manufacturers, Wall St. J., Sept. 16, 1996, at 1, col. 6.

[10] See New Jersey v. Wilson, 11 U.S. (7 Cranch) 164, 3 L.Ed. 303 (1812) (state can abdicate taxing power by contract granting exemption). See generally Cooley, Taxation § 705 (4th ed. 1924). Some state constitutions specify the classes of property that may be granted exemptions. See Mo.Const. Art. 10, § 6; Tenn.Const. Art. 2, § 28. On the increasing adoption in almost every state of widespread tax incentives for business, see Enrich, Business Tax Incentives: A Status Report, 34 Urban Law. 415 (2002). See generally Griffith, State and Local Revenue Enhancement and Taxation Policies in a Digital Age: E-Commerce Taxation, Business Tax Incentives, and Litigation Generated Revenues, 34 Urban Law. 429 (2002); Comment, Tax Incentives for the Biotechnology Industry: Should Tennessee Offer Sales Tax Exemptions and Net Operating Loss Extensions?, 70 Tenn. L. Rev. 567 (2003).

See also Alboher, Mission Beyond Profit for Venture Financiers, N.Y. Times, July 24, 2008, at C5, noting that "another option is gaining currency in old manufacturing cities looking to prop up their struggling economies—homegrown nonprofit groups that nurture new businesses from the ground up."

In General Motors Corp. v. Oklahoma County Bd. of Equalization, 678 P.2d 233 (Okl.1983), cert. denied 466 U.S. 909, 104 S.Ct. 1689, 80 L.Ed.2d 163 (1984), a tax abatement agreement between the State Industries Authority and General Motors, which had constructed an assembly plant in Oklahoma in reliance on the agreement, was held void as unauthorized by the state constitution. General Motors was held, despite the agreement, subject to ad valorem taxation. Subsequently, Oklahoma voters approved an amendment to the state constitution authorizing exemption of certain new or expanding manufacturing plants from ad valorem taxation for a period of 5 years. Okl. Const. Art. X, § 6B. In DaimlerChrysler Corp. v. Cuno, 547 U.S. 332, 126 S.Ct. 1854, 164 L.Ed.2d 589 (2006), the Court held that Ohio taxpayers lacked standing to challenge an award of state tax credit to an automobile manufacturer to induce it to remain in a city. See Note, The Debate Over Kentucky's Tax Incentives: Do They Have a Future in the Commonwealth if State Courts Follow the Coercive Pre-existing Tax Liability Test?, 45 Brandeis L.J. 809 (2007); Note, the Supreme Court Hits the Brakes on Determining the Constitutionality of Investment Incentives Given by States to Corporate America, 58 Mercer L. Rev. 1411 (2007). See generally Garman, The New War Between the States: A Look at the Incentives to Recruit Foreign Automakers to the South, *DaimlerChrysler Corp. v. Cuno*, and the European Union's Prohibition Against State Aid, 24 T.M. Cooley L. Rev. 313 (2007); Symposium *DaimlerChrysler v. Cuno* and the Constitutionality of State Tax Incentives for Economic Development, 4 Geo. J.L. & Pub. Pol'y 15–131 (2006). See also Vey, Restoring Prosperity: The State Role in Revitalizing America's Older Industrial Cities (Brookings Institutions 2007). Compare Note, Giving State Tax Incentives to Corporations: How Much Is Too Much?, 7 South Car. J. Int'l L. & Bus. 257 (2011).

[11] See Pullman Car & Manufacturing Corp. v. Hamilton, 229 Ala. 184, 155 So. 616 (1934) (legislation granting industrial exemptions upheld). Cf. Green v. City of Mount Pleasant, 256 Iowa 1184, 131 N.W.2d 5 (1964) (industrial property acquired for leasing exempt under statute exempting property devoted to public use); City of Houston v. Houston Endowment, Inc., 428 S.W.2d 706 (Tex.Civ.App.1968), motion for stay of order dissolving injunction denied, 438 S.W.2d 935, ref'd N.R.E. (validity of industrial-district program, involving special tax rate for land outside city limits, upheld). See generally Mulligan, Economic Development Incentives and North Carolina Local Governments: A Framework for Analysis, 91 N.C.L. Rev. 2021 (2013).

"Enterprise zones" have been proposed or created in some large cities: economically depressed areas as to which reduced taxes and relief from some government regulations would be used to induce new businesses. See "How 'Enterprise Zones' in Cities Will Work," U.S. News & World Rep., March 15, 1982, at 66; "New Tax Plan to Overhaul Decaying Cities," U.S.News & World Rep., Nov. 3, 1980, at 52. See generally Callies & Tamashiro, Enterprise Zones: The Redevelopment Sweepstakes Begins, 15 Urban Law. 231 (1983); Silverman, Enterprise Zones and Fundamental Issues, 14 Urban Law. 751, in Fernsler & Tuttle, Recent Developments in Housing and Community Development, 14 Urban Law. 745 (1982). On possible judicial attacks on enterprise zones, see Callies, Land Use Controls: Of Enterprise Zones, Takings, Plans and Growth Controls, 14 Urban Law. 781, 782–89 (1982); Comment, Enterprise Zones in the Courts: Legal Challenges to State Economic Redevelopment Legislation, 30 U. Richmond L. Rev. 877 (1996). On the operation of enterprise zones, see Rubin & Trawinski, New Jersey's Urban Enterprise Zones: A Program That Works, 23 Urban Law, 461 (1991);

constitutional or statutory provisions themselves exempt designated categories of businesses from property taxation. More often, the relevant constitution or statute merely *authorizes* local governments to create categories of exempt businesses, or to contract with certain businesses regarding exemptions or more favorable tax treatment.[12] Exemptions granted by local governments are generally held valid only where authorized by state law; otherwise, exemptions are likely to be struck down as in violation of the principles of equality and uniformity of taxation.[13] While tax exemptions can be justified as serving a public purpose by, in the long run, increasing the wealth and taxable base of a community, they are subject to attack as inequitable, granting favored treatment to entities that may make heavy use of community facilities, and as less important in the attracting of businesses than are sound overall tax policy and administration.

From early times in this country, local governments have often provided for the use of private businesses such facilities as marketplaces, wharves, and docks. A markethouse has been held a "necessary" municipal expense.[14] Typically, these facilities, or portions thereof, are leased to private enterprise. Beginning with Mississippi in 1936,

---

Wolf, An "Essay in Re-Plan": American Enterprise Zones in Practice, 21 Urban Law. 29 (1989). See generally Thompson, Can Free Enterprise Cure Urban Ills?: Lost Opportunities for Business Development in Urban, Low-income Communities Through the New Markets Tax Credit Program, 37 U. Mem. L. Rev. 659 (2007). See also Clay & Jones, A Brief History of Community Economic Development, 18 J. Affordable Housing & Commun. Dev. L. 257 (2009). Similar to enterprise zones are "business improvement districts," which usually are a kind of assessment district within which businesses are assessed for the cost of a local improvement or facility within or near the district. See Bacon & Son, Inc. v. City of Tulsa, 297 P.3d 428 (Okla. Civ. App. 2013) (assessment of property owners in a business improvement district for a municipal sports stadium upheld). See generally Symposium, Business Improvement Districts and the Evolution of Urban Governance, 3 Drexel L. Rev. 1–372 (2010) (with introduction by Richardson Dilworth). See also MacDonald *et. al,* The Privatization of Public Safety in Urban Neighborhoods: Do Business Improvement Districts Reduce Violent Crime Among Adolescents?, 47 Law & Soc. Rev. 621 (2013). Compare with enterprise zones the special districts that in some jurisdictions focus on *residential* development, as described in Mitchell & Gyden, State Legislatures and Residential Development Districts, 35 Urban Law. 813 (2003).

On the history of business inducements in the Southern states, see generally Cobb, The Selling of the South: The Southern Crusade for Industrial Development, 1936–1980 (1982). On attempts by a number of states to lure Japanese and other foreign businesses, see Green, State Investment in Mid-America, 22 Urban Law. 245 (1990). On the trend toward states "getting tough" with businesses that accept incentives to locate therein but subsequently fail to keep their end of the bargain, see "States Now Want a Money-Back Guarantee," Bus. Week, Sept. 21, 1992, at 35. Many states have passed legislation requiring accountability of the businesses lured by state and local governments. See Gilbert, Selling the City Without Selling Out: New Legislation on Development Incentives Emphasizes Accountability, 27 Urban Law. 427 (1995). On the particular problem of businesses that are attracted by governmental incentives but that stay only a short time before moving elsewhere, see Note, Take the Money and Stay: Industrial Location Incentives and Relational Contracting, 70 N.Y.U.L. Rev. (1995).

On the questionable wisdom of luring businesses to a community by giving tax breaks, particularly at times of revenue shortfalls in the local government, see McFarlane, Local Economic Development Incentives in an Era of Globalization: The Exploitation of Decentralization and Mobility, 35 Urban Law. 305 (2003).

[12] See Note, Legal Limitations, *supra* note 7, at 625–27. See generally Zelinsky, Tax Incentives for Economic Development: Personal (and Pessimistic) Reflections, 58 Case W. Res. L. Rev. 1145 (2008). Compare Kaye, The Gentle Art of Corporate Seduction: Tax Incentives in the United States and the European Union, 57 U. Kan. L. Rev. 93 (2008).

[13] See Halbert v. Helena-West Helena Industrial Development Corp., 226 Ark. 620, 291 S.W.2d 802 (1956) (statute exempted bonds issued by nonprofit development corporations; invalid as not authorized by constitution). Cf. Opinion of the Justices, 161 Me. 182, 210 A.2d 683 (1965) (exemption of industrial facilities held by municipality was unconstitutional since facilities not used for governmental purposes). See also Hellerstein & Coenon, Commerce Clause Restraints on State Business Development Incentives, 81 Corn. L. Rev. 789 (1996).

[14] Swinson v. Town of Mt. Olive, 147 N.C. 611, 61 S.E. 569 (1908).

many states in recent times have authorized local bond issues to finance the building of industrial plants, or comparable private business facilities, which are then leased or sold to private industry. The validity of the Mississippi statute was upheld.[15] Since then, financial aid of this general type has taken at least four main forms:[16] (1) Sometimes, as under the original Mississippi plan, *general obligation bonds* are issued, and the proceeds used to construct industrial facilities, which are then turned over to private businesses, usually under leases. (2) More often—as under the present Mississippi arrangement—*revenue bonds* (payable solely from the lease revenues) are issued to finance the construction of the industrial facilities. As under the first form of aid, the facilities are normally leased to private businesses—but title to those facilities is here often conveyed to the private businesses after the bonds are paid. This second form of aid is perhaps now the most common of all inducements to local businesses (aside from mere advertising of a community), and is especially often used to aid in construction of pollution-control facilities.[17] (3) Under a third form, the state, or some other governmental entity, may make loans, secured by a second mortgage, to local nonprofit corporations created to aid industrial development. The loans are made from current revenues of the state. (4) Another form, employed in some New England states, involves the state's insuring of loans that are incurred by nonprofit development corporations, which then use the loan money to build industrial facilities that, again, are sold or leased to private enterprise.

Two main lines of attack have been directed at the four above-mentioned forms of providing industrial or business facilities. (1) The issuing of the bonds, or other governmental action, has been challenged as purely or substantially for the benefit of private parties and thus not for a public purpose, as governmental actions must be. This argument has occasionally been successful.[18] But most courts have rather easily found

---

[15] Albritton v. City of Winona, 181 Miss. 75, 178 So. 799 (1938), appeal dism'd 303 U.S. 627, 58 S.Ct. 766, 82 L.Ed. 1088. See Note, Municipal Subsidies and the Industrialization of the South, 47 Yale L.J. 1412 (1938). See generally Annot., Constitutionality of Statute Authorizing State to Loan Money or Engage in Business of a Private Nature, 115 A.L.R. 1436 (1938). The particular Mississippi legislation upheld in the *Albritton* case *supra* was repealed in 1940.

[16] See Pinsky, State Constitutional Limitations on Public Industrial Financing: An Historical and Economic Approach, 111 U.Pa.L.Rev. 265 (1963).

[17] See, all upholding the use of revenue bonds to finance pollution-control or various other facilities, Ginsberg v. City and County of Denver, 164 Colo. 572, 436 P.2d 685 (1968) (acquisition of stadium by city; no requirement found that issuance of bonds must be first approved by voters); Green v. City of Mount Pleasant, 256 Iowa 1184, 131 N.W.2d 5 (1964); City of Gaylord v. Beckett, 378 Mich. 273, 144 N.W.2d 460 (1966); State ex rel. Brennan v. Bowman, 89 Nev. 330, 512 P.2d 1321 (1973); Carruthers v. Port of Astoria, 249 Or. 329, 438 P.2d 725 (1968); Allen v. Tooele County, 21 Utah 2d 383, 445 P.2d 994 (1968); State ex rel. County Court v. Demus, 148 W.Va. 398, 135 S.E.2d 352 (1964); Uhls v. State ex rel. City of Cheyenne, 429 P.2d 74 (Wyo.1967). But see, rejecting revenue-bond financing of pollution-control facilities as involving a lending of state credit for private purposes, Port of Longview v. Taxpayers of Port of Longview, 85 Wash.2d 216, 527 P.2d 263 (1974), opinion modif'd 85 Wn.2d 216, 533 P.2d 128. Cf. State ex rel. Beck v. City of York, 164 Neb. 223, 82 N.W.2d 269 (1957) (purchase of building to be financed by sale of revenue bonds, with building then being leased to private company, held invalid); State ex rel. Saxbe v. Brand, 176 Ohio St. 44, 197 N.E.2d 328 (1964) (sale of revenue bonds by state commission, and use of proceeds to make loan to private borrower, is prohibited loan of state's credit). Compare CLEAN v. City of Spokane, 133 Wash.2d 455, 947 P.2d 1169 (Wash. 1997) (use of revenue bonds upheld to finance parking garage near downtown shopping area); CLEAN v. State, 130 Wash.2d 782, 928 P.2d 1054 (1996) (public development of major league baseball stadium upheld).

[18] See State v. Town of North Miami, 59 So.2d 779 (Fla.1952) (destruction of private-enterprise system feared); Stanley v. Department of Conservation and Development, 284 N.C. 15, 199 S.E.2d 641 (1973) (revenue bonds could not be used to finance either pollution abatement *or* the building of industrial facilities); State ex rel. Beck v. City of York, *supra* note 17.

sufficient public purpose in the inducement of business into a community since this results in a decrease in unemployment, stabilization of the local economy, and a halting of any existing or potential exodus of businesses from the area.[19] (2) Providing of facilities for private business has also been attacked as involving a prohibited lending of public credit to private enterprise. In several cases involving the issuance of revenue bonds, this attack has prevailed.[20] But more often, this argument is successfully answered by the same reasoning used in response to the first line of attack: There is a public purpose, and thus the evils envisioned by the prohibition are not present.[21] Where revenue bonds are involved, the further response can be given that there is no obligation on the issuing government and thus no "lending of credit" occurs.[22] If the state or its agency is purchasing the bonds of a local development corporation, it can also be noted that the state is becoming a creditor, not a debtor.[23] Finally—though all of the four above-mentioned methods of providing industrial facilities *may* be upheld even in the absence of specific constitutional authorization—state constitutional provisions in a number of jurisdictions now do specifically authorize some ways of financing the development of business facilities.[24]

---

19 Opinion of Justices, 54 Del. 366, 177 A.2d 205 (1962) (state guaranteed bonds issued by local development corporation); State v. Jacksonville Port Authority, 266 So.2d 1 (Fla.1972); People ex rel. City of Salem v. McMackin, 53 Ill.2d 347, 291 N.E.2d 807 (1972) (revenue-bond financing for construction of industrial projects, which were then to be leased to private industry, upheld); Industrial Development Authority v. Eastern Kentucky Regional Planning Comm'n, 332 S.W.2d 274 (Ky.1960) (state loan to local nonprofit development corporations); Dyche v. City of London, 288 S.W.2d 648 (Ky.1956) (general obligation bonds upheld); City of Frostburg v. Jenkins, 215 Md. 9, 136 A.2d 852 (1957) (general obligation bonds); State ex rel. Brennan v. Bowman, *supra* note 17; Gripentrog v. City of Wahpeton, 126 N.W.2d 230 (N.D.1964) (revenue bonds); Basehore v. Hampden Industrial Development Authority, 433 Pa. 40, 248 A.2d 212 (1968) (revenue bonds); McConnell v. City of Lebanon, 203 Tenn. 498, 314 S.W.2d 12 (1958); State ex rel. Hammermill Paper Co. v. La-Plante, 58 Wis.2d 32, 205 N.W.2d 784 (1973). Cf. State v. Ocean Highway & Port Authority, 217 So.2d 103 (Fla.1968) (public authority can issue revenue bonds to finance construction of pulp-and-paper plant to be leased to private company). See generally Mumford, The Past, Present and Future of Industrial Development Bonds, 1 Urban Law. 147 (1969); Comment, The "Public Purpose" of Municipal Financing for Industrial Development, 70 Yale L.J. 789 (1961).

A good discussion of the general distinction between public and private purposes—and the shifting meaning of "public purpose"—is found in Mitchell v. North Carolina Industrial Development Financing Authority, 273 N.C. 137, 159 S.E.2d 745 (1968), sustaining bond-issue financing of industrial development.

On the *operation* of bond financing to support the building of industrial facilities, see 64 Am.Jur.2d Public Securities and Obligations § 109 (1972).

Because of the success of Scranton, Pennsylvania, in public financing of the construction of industrial facilities, such programs are sometimes called "Scranton Plans."

20 See Village of Moyie Springs v. Aurora Manufacturing Co., 82 Idaho 337, 353 P.2d 767 (1960); York, *supra* note 17; State v. City of Port of Longview v. Taxpayers of Port of Longview, *supra* note 17 (financing of pollution-control facilities). See generally Pinsky, *supra* note 16, at 304–05.

21 State ex rel. Farmers' Electric Cooperative, Inc. v. State Environmental Improvement Auth., 518 S.W.2d 68 (Mo.1975); Kennecott Copper Corp. v. Town of Hurley, 84 N.M. 743, 507 P.2d 1074 (1973); McConnell v. City of Lebanon, *supra* note 19. See State v. City of Pittsburg, 188 Kan. 612, 364 P.2d 71 (1961) (particular constitutional language on lending of credit found not violated); Gripentrog v. City of Wahpeton, *supra* note 19 (same.).

22 Newberry v. City of Andalusia, 257 Ala. 49, 57 So.2d 629 (1952). See Green v. City of Mount Pleasant, *supra* note 17.

23 See Industrial Development Auth. v. Eastern Kentucky Regional Planning Commission, *supra* note 19. Cf. Halbert v. Helena-West Helena Industrial Development Corp., *supra* note 13 (state agency authorized to purchase bonds of development corporation; constitutional restriction inapplicable since state merely investing in bonds).

24 See Ga.Const. Art. 7, § 2–4705 (authorizing creation of a state commission to make loans to development authorities, using tax money for this purpose); Me.Const. Art. 9, § 8–A (authorizing municipalities

For many years, interest earned on local industrial development bonds was exempt from federal income tax, just like interest on municipal bonds in general. But criticism to this exemption mounted as the amounts paid on such bonds grew;[25] and in 1968, the Internal Revenue Code was amended to terminate the exemption except as to bonds issued for the financing of limited kinds of facilities (such as pollution-control facilities, which still come within an exemption).[26] Moreover, though industrial development bonds are not within the Securities Act of 1933 and thus not fully subject to the jurisdiction of the Securities and Exchange Commission,[27] that Commission has now issued regulations requiring registration of some such bonds, thus providing a degree of federal control over financing arrangements.[28] Though the use of industrial development bonds and other devices to provide business facilities has, in some communities, not proven so successful as had been hoped,[29] it would seem that the validity of such devices is now recognized in most jurisdictions.

§ 16.2 Governmental Entry into Business

Sometimes, rather than merely aiding financially the construction of business and industry, a local government attempts to enter the business world itself, as by constructing and operating a hotel. Here, of course, there is a degree of competition with comparable local businesses (if any), and to that extent the government is not necessarily aiding, but may actually be harming, local private enterprise. But the local government

---

to issue bonds to finance industrial facilities); Okl.Const. Art. 10, §§ 34–35 (state may sell bonds and make loans to development agencies; municipalities and counties may issue bonds for development of industry in or near municipality, or within the county).

25 See Armstrong, "Municipal Inducements"—The New Mexico Commercial and Industrial Project Revenue Bond Act, 48 Calif.L.Rev. 58 (1960); Spiegel, Financing Private Ventures with Tax-Exempt Bonds: A Developing "Truckhole" in the Tax Law, 17 Stan. L.Rev. 224 (1965). On the growth in amount of industrial development bonds, see 26 Cong.Q.W.Rep.No. 21, at 1197 (1968).

26 Internal Rev.Code § 103(c) (1968). See, criticizing the amended provisions, Note, The Limited Tax-Exempt Status of Interest on Industrial Development Bonds Under Subsection 103(c) of the Internal Revenue Code, 85 Harv.L.Rev. 1649 (1972). See generally McDaniel, Federal Income Taxation of Industrial Bonds: The Public Interest, 1 Urban Lawyer 157 (1969). The exemption as to financing of pollution-control facilities is discussed in Port of Longview v. Taxpayers of Port of Longview, *supra* note 17. Where public financing is used to construct business facilities which are then leased to private parties, the lessee is generally subject to property taxation (on his leasehold) the same as anyone else. See Opinion of the Justices, *supra* note 13 (private party's interest made taxable by statute); Village of Deming v. Hosdreg Co., 62 N.M. 18, 303 P.2d 920 (1956) (leasehold remains taxable under general tax law).

The Tax Reform Act of 1984, 98 Stat. 494 (1984), placed a ceiling, or "cap," on the amount of tax-exempt "private activity bonds" that may be issued in any year. A "private activity bond" is defined as including all industrial development bonds and student loan bonds, with limited exceptions. See Arkuss, New Federal Tax Legislation Affecting Tax-Exempt Obligations, 16 Urban Law. 805 (1984). On changes regarding the industrial development bonds that remain free from federal income taxation, see Friel & Arkuss, Recent Developments on Tax Exemptions, 14 Urban Law. 899, 907–15 (1982).

27 15 U.S.C.A. § 77c(a)(2).

28 See Definition of security issued under governmental obligations, 17 CFR 230.131 (1979), providing that any part of an obligation evidenced by bonds, etc. payable from payments to be made in respect of property or money which is or will be used under lease, sale, or loan arrangement by or for industrial enterprise shall be considered a separate security, thus subject to registration requirements. Cf. County of Yellowstone, Blue Sky L.Rep. para. 80,719 (S.E.C.1976), ruling that although the proposed issue and sale of industrial revenue bonds may be effected without compliance with the registration requirements of the Securities Act, *guarantees* on the bonds may be deemed separate securities and thus within the registration requirements. See generally Lyons, SEC Registration Requirements for Taxable Municipal Securities, 21 Urban Law. 223 (1989).

29 See Comment, Financing Industrial Development with Municipal Revenue Bonds, 1967 Ill.L.F. 331; Note, The Proliferation of Industrial Revenue Bond Financing: Ban the Bond?, 41 Temp.L.Q. 289 (1968). See generally Abbey, Municipal Industrial Development Bonds, 19 Vand. L.Rev. 25 (1965).

may contend—particularly where businesses of the type involved are scarce in the vicinity—that it is improving the local economic base by providing a needed facility. Thus, a municipality's operation of a hotel may surely stimulate the tourist and convention trade in that area.[30] In the past, some courts nonetheless struck down local-government operation of businesses as not for a public purpose—and specifically as using tax money for private purposes.[31] But it is clear that there is no federal constitutional objection to a local government's conducting an enterprise merely because that business is often carried on by private persons.[32] The trend is toward allowing municipalities, and other units of local government, to operate businesses, at least where specific charter authorization is found.[33]

---

[30] See Note, Power of Municipality to Construct and Operate a Hotel, 16 Geo. Wash.L.Rev. 394 (1948); Note, Municipal Corporation—Proposed Expenditure by Town for Construction and Operation of Hotel Not a Public Purpose, 34 Va.L.Rev. 99 (1948).

[31] See Union Ice & Coal Co. v. Town of Ruston, 135 La. 898, 66 So. 262 (1914) (ice plant not a public purpose); Nash v. Town of Tarboro, 227 N.C. 283, 42 S.E.2d 209 (1947) (city could not lawfully operate hotel despite statutory authorization; legislature was without power to authorize use of tax money for such purpose), *criticized in* Note, Municipal Corporation—Proposed Expenditure, *supra* note 30. The *Union Ice* case *supra* was in effect overruled by the adoption of a constitutional amendment, La. Const. Art. 14, § 18, authorizing municipal ice plants; but such a specific provision is not found in the present Louisiana Constitution. It *is* provided therein that legislation may authorize political subdivisions to aid local industry (Art. 6 § 27) and to issue bonds to construct or acquire public utilities or works or public improvements (Art. 6 § 37). See generally Kean, Local Government and Home Rule—1974 Constitution, 21 La.L.Rev. 63 (1975).

[32] See Standard Oil Co. v. City of Lincoln, 275 U.S. 504, 48 S.Ct. 155, 72 L.Ed. 395 (1927) (municipal gas station); Green v. Frazier, 253 U.S. 233, 40 S.Ct. 499, 64 L.Ed. 878 (1920) (legislation upheld authorizing state to manufacture and sell farm products); Jones v. City of Portland, 245 U.S. 217, 38 S.Ct. 112, 62 L.Ed. 252 (1917) (municipal taxation upheld for coal and fuel yard). Cf. Denton v. Denton Home Ice Co., 119 Tex. 193, 27 S.W.2d 119 (Com.App.1930) (municipal ice plant upheld as public utility).

[33] See Seattle Gas Co. v. City of Seattle, 291 U.S. 638, 54 S.Ct. 550, 78 L.Ed. 1037 (1934); Puget Sound Power & Light Co. v. City of Seattle, 291 U.S. 619, 54 S.Ct. 542, 78 L.Ed. 1025 (1934) reh. denied 292 U.S. 603, 54 S.Ct. 712, 78 L.Ed. 1466 (city can engage in furnishing electric light and power in competition with private company); Huesing v. City of Rock Island, 128 Ill. 465, 21 N.E. 558 (1889) (public slaughterhouse); Moore v. City of Greensboro, 191 N.C. 592, 132 S.E. 565 (1926) (same); Haesloop v. City Council of Charleston, 123 S.C. 272, 115 S.E. 596 (1923) (hotel); Ferrell v. Doak, 152 Tenn. 88, 275 S.W. 29 (1925) (manufacturing plant to be leased for private use). Cf. Albritton v. City of Winona, *supra* note 15 (municipality can issue general obligation bonds to finance construction of facilities to be leased to private businesses); Dickinson v. Salt Lake City, 57 Utah 530, 195 P. 1110 (1921) (public funds can be expended on municipal construction and maintenance of bath house); Hudson v. City of Wenatchee, 94 Wash.App. 990, 974 P.2d 342 (1999) (city policy of allowing its police officers to assist citizens who are locked out of their vehicles does not result in gift of public funds in violation of state constitution). See generally Annot., Constitutionality of Statute Authorizing State to Loan Money or Engage in Business of a Private Nature, 115 A.L.R. 1456, 1459 (1938). But express or clearly implied authority is often required before a municipality can validly enter into a non-utility business, and the principle of strict construction of any such power is still sometimes applied. See Laughlin v. City of Portland, 111 Me. 486, 90 A. 318 (1914) (municipality could be authorized to establish fuel-yard—but only because fuel is a necessity); Mac Rae v. Selectmen of Concord, 296 Mass. 394, 6 N.E.2d 366 (1937) (statute construed *not* to grant power to city to sell electrical appliances or do installation and repair work). The operation of *utilities* is, of course, a much more generally recognized municipal power; see Chapter 17 *infra*. The powers to acquire, construct, and maintain utilities have often been inferred from the "general welfare" clause of the police power, which is usually delegated to municipalities. See City of Greenville v. Greenville Waterworks Co., 125 Ala. 625, 27 So. 764 (1900); Osburn v. Stone, 170 Cal. 480, 150 P. 367 (1915); Overall v. Madisonville, 125 Ky. 684, 102 S.W. 278 (1907) (electric power plant); City of Eau Claire v. Eau Claire Water Co., 137 Wis. 517, 119 N.W. 555 (1909) (waterworks).

Even where a rule of strict construction of municipal powers is applied to power to engage in businesses or other activities, the strict construction usually applies only to the existence and extent of the power, not the means of executing it once it is found to exist. See James v. Young, 77 N.D. 451, 43 N.W.2d 692 (1950). On municipal powers, see generally Chapter 8 *supra*.

On the trend toward more governmental entry into business, and toward more aid to existing businesses, see generally Herbers, State Roles Grow in Aid to Business, N.Y. Times, Dec. 9, 1985, at 1. Another trend that has developed, somewhat contrary to that of municipal governments engaging in private business, is the turning-over by municipalities of some formerly public services to private enterprise. Such "privatization" often allows municipalities to cut their payrolls and save money. See Gold, The Privatization of Prisons, 28 Urban Law. 359 (1996); "Want to Buy a Fire Dept.?," Newsweek, April 25, 1983, at 55, stating, "Faced with shrinking revenues and rising prices, local governments are increasingly turning to businessmen to provide fire and police protection, collect garbage, run airports and operate libraries." As to the possible privatization of airports that were formerly government operated, see Saulny, In Chicago, Private Firm Is to Run Midway Airport, N. Y. Times, Oct. 1, 2008, at A16 (Natl. Edition). See also "Schools for Profit," Time, Oct. 17, 1994, at 48, on Hartford, Connecticut's experiment with turning public education over to a private company. Such private enterprises may not enjoy the immunity from tort liability that has traditionally (though now to a lesser extent; see chapter on Liability in Tort *infra*) been enjoyed by municipalities. See Fleming, The Privatization Precedent Set by the Lord Chancellor in *Iolanthe*: An Analysis of *Walker v. McKnight*, 30 Urban Law. 233 (1998), commenting on Walker v. McKnight, 521 U.S. 399, 117 S.Ct. 2100, 138 L.Ed.2d 540 (1997), where the Court held that prison guards employed by a private firm were not entitled to qualified immunity from suit under Section 1983 of the Federal Civil Rights Act. Compare Comment, State Sovereign Immunity and Privatization: Can Eleventh Amendment Immunity Extend to Private Entities?, 5 FIU L. Rev. 209 (2009). Cf. Volokh, Privatization and the Elusive Employee-Contractor Distinction, 46 U. C. Davis L. Rev. 133 (2012). See generally Fitzgerald, When Government Goes Private: Successful Alternatives to Public Services (Universe Books 1988), reviewed 24 Urban Law. 417 (1992); Mays, Privatization of Municipal Services: A Contagion in the Body Politic, 34 Duq. L. Rev. 41 (1995); Note, The Local Baker-Local Bureaucrat Dilemma: Privatization and Power in New York City, 42 N.Y.L. School L. Rev. 1163 (1998); Note, The Due Process Failure of America's Prison Privatization Statutes, 21 Seton Hall Legis. J. 371 (1997); Comment, A Legal Roadmap to Privatizing Government Services in Washington State, 72 Wash. L. Rev. 153 (1997). See also Jones, Tandon & Vogelsang, Selling Public Enterprise: A Cost Benefit Methodology (MIT Press 1991), reviewed 25 Urban Law. 475 (1993); Osborne & Gaebler, Reinventing Government: How the Entrepreneurial Spirit Is Transforming the Public Sector (Addison-Wesley Pub. 1992), reviewed 25 Urban Law. 683 (1993) & (as published in paperback by Penguin Books) 31 Urban Law. 1037 (1999).

As to the continuing expansion of privatization into other parts of the public sphere, see Callies & Suarez, Privatization and the Providing of Public Facilities Through Private Means, 21 J.L. & Pol. 477 (2005); Finegan, Watching the Watchers: The Growing Privatization of Criminal Law Enforcement and the Need for Limits on Neighborhood Watch Associations, 8 U. Mass. L. Rev. 88 (2013); Current Development, Privatization of Public Education: An Examination of U.S. and Canadian Policy and Trends Utilizing Vouchers that Indirectly Aid Sectarian Schools, 12 New England J. Int'l & Comp. L. 327 (2006). See also Reynolds & Ball, Exactions and the Privatization of the Public Sphere, 21 J.L. & Pol. 451 (2005). On the effects on the community of privatization, see Franzese, Does It Take a Village? Privatization, Patterns of Restrictiveness and the Demise of Community, 47 Vill. L. Rev. 553 (2002). See generally Symposium, Michigan in Transition: The Restructuring of Governance Through Privatization and Corporatization, 14 J. L. Soc'y 167–243 (2013), particularly Grant, Water Privatization Overview: A Public Interest Perspective on For-Profit, Private Sector Provision of Water and Sewer Services in the United States, *id.* at 167.

On the use of privatization as to public parks in particular, see Murray, Private Management of Public Spaces: Nonprofit Organizations and Urban Parks, 34 Harv. Envtl. L. Rev. 179 (2010).

As to the effect of privatization on tax revenues, see Robin, Privatization and the Sale of Tax Revenues, 95 Minn. L. Rev. 1965 (2011). On the effects of privatization on land use controls and planning, see Emerson, Merging Public and Private Governances: How Disney's Reedy Creek Improvement District "Re-imagined" the Traditional Division of Local Regulatory Powers, 36 Fla. St. U. L. Rev. 177 (2009). As to the role that privatization may play in urban renewal, see Batchie, Business Improvement Districts and the Constitution: The Troubling Necessity of Privatized Government for Urban Revitalization, 38 Hastings Const. J. Q. 91 (2010).

Such popular types of housing as condominiums, cooperatives, planned, walled, or gated communities may be considered an extension of privatization, in that they often involve turning many traditional government services over to private persons or organizations. See Mashaw, Panel Discussion: Living with Privatization: At Work and in the Community, 28 Fordham Urban L.J. 1397, 1398 (2001), describing privatization as the "private contractual arrangement for the provision of formerly publicly-provided services." See generally Franzese, Privatization and Its Discontents: Common Interest Communities and the Rise of Government for "the Nice," 37 Urban Law. 335 (2005), part of Symposium, Common Interest Communities, 37 Urban Law. 325–69 (2005). Compare Michaels, Privatization's Pretensions, 77 U Chi. L. Rev. 727 (2010). On condominiums and cooperatives, see also Section 20.9, note 117, *infra*.

§ 16.3 Questioning the Wisdom of Inducements to Business

Some questions have been raised over the years about the wisdom of inducing more and bigger businesses into municipalities. It has been noted that an influx of businesses does raise property values—but this in turn has sometimes resulted in increases in property taxes that have driven large numbers of homeowners out of a city into the suburbs. Some business properties—in particular, high-rise office buildings—cost a city considerably more for services than they produce in tax revenue, while other businesses—in particular, many factories—bring pollution and other environmental problems with them.[34] The whole "bigger is better" philosophy is increasingly being challenged, as it has been shown that after a certain point, economies of scale don't occur as to the providing of municipal services—*i.e.*, it costs more, not less, per capita to provide police and other services in cities of half a million population than in cities of 100,000 population.[35] It has also been observed that so large an exodus of people and business has already occurred from some cities that reversing the tide may now be impossible—and can surely not be achieved by efforts obviously aimed at luring back citizens and industries merely so that they can help carry the tax load.[36] Any effort at rejuvenation of depressed urban centers can be successful, it would seem, only if it includes efforts at improving municipal environments in general, and municipal educational systems in particular.

---

[34] See Brugmann & Sletteland, The Ultimate Highrise (1971); von Hoffman, Book Review (of The Ultimate Highrise), 24 Historic Preservation, April-June, 1972, at 44. Cf. Manchester Environmental Coalition v. Stockton, 184 Conn. 51, 441 A.2d 68 (1981) (group opposed to development of industrial park had standing to sue merely by showing possibility of injury).

For a critical view of state and local economic development incentives, asserting their ineffectiveness in improving local economies, see Weber, Why Local Economic Development Incentives Don't Create Jobs: The Role of Corporate Governance, 32 Urban Law. 97 (2000) (R. Marlin Smith Student Writing Competition Award Winner). See generally Symposium on Community Economic Development, 8 J. Small & Emerging Bus. L. 131–272 (2004); Symposium: Issues in Community Economic Development, 29 W. New England L. Rev. 1–191 (2006). See also Ellis, Hayden & Rogers, A Game Changer for the Political Economy of Economic Development Incentives, 56 Ariz. L. Rev. 953 (2014), considering whether the duty of care standard used in corporate governance should be applied to public decision-making on economic development incentives.

When municipalities use incentives to attract new businesses, pre-existing businesses are sometimes harmed, understandably angering owners of the older enterprises. See Scaggs, One Firm's Perk Is Another's Slap, Wall St. J., Jan 29, 2015, at B-6.

[35] See Lamm, Is Bigger Also Better?, The New Republic, June 5, 1971, at 17.

[36] See Patterson, Commentary: The Prospect of a Nation with No Important Cities, Bus.Week, Feb. 2, 1976, at 66.

On laws passed recently in some states to restrict the closing of industrial plants or their ceasing production in the state and moving elsewhere, see Leary, Deindustrialization, Plant Closing Laws, and the States, 58 State Gov't 113 (1985).

Chapter 17

LOCAL OPERATION OF UTILITIES

Analysis

---

§ 17.1 Relationship of Local Governments to Privately Owned Public Utilities

"Utilities" or "public utilities" are the terms applied to those businesses that offer such essential services as natural gas, electricity, and water; as broadly used, the terms also encompass businesses supplying transportation and/or communication. Many "public utilities" are actually *privately* owned companies, ranging in size from American Telephone and Telegraph to electric companies in small communities. But some utilities are operated by a governmental entity, generally a municipality, as in the case of municipal water companies. When a privately owned utility operates within a municipality, that locality's dealings with the utility often are chiefly concerned with granting the utility a franchise: the right to use public streets and ways for the laying of the utility's pipes and mains, stringing of its wires, etc.[1] A franchise from the city must be obtained by the utility, however, only if the utility needs, in its operations, to make use of the city's public ways.[2] And since those ways are primarily under the control of the *state*, the municipality has only such power to grant—and deny—franchises as is

---

1 See State ex rel. York v. Board of Com'rs of Walla Walla County, 28 Wn.2d 891, 184 P.2d 577 (1947). See generally Annot., Use of Streets and Highways by Co-operative Utility, 172 A.L.R. 1020 (1948). On franchises and local control thereover, see generally Chapter 5 *supra*. As to the problems involved in granting franchises for cable television, see Note, Statewide Cable Franchising: Expand Nationwide or Cut the Cord?, 64 Fed. Comm. L.J. 199 (2011).

2 Oklahoma Gas & Electric Co. v. Total Energy, Inc., 499 P.2d 917 (Okl.1972) (company did not need franchise to generate electricity within municipality where it made no use of public streets). On the nature of franchise agreements, cf. B-C Cable Co., Inc. v. City & Borough of Juneau, 613 P.2d 616 (Alaska 1980) (franchise agreements not "enactments"; when franchise expires, implied contract arises). See also City of Bisbee v. Arizona Water Co., 214 Ariz. 368, 153 P.3d 389 (App. 2007) (city could require water utility to obtain a franchise to continue using city streets even though city had allowed water utility to operate without a franchise in the past and had granted temporary permits in the past).

In some communities—Gainesville, Florida, for instance—such traditional "municipal services" as trash collection, and maintenance of city vehicles, are now being performed by private businesses, operating under contract with the city. On this trend toward "privatization" of public services, see Section 16.2, note 33 *supra*. See also Benson, To Serve and Protect: Privatization and Community in Criminal Justice (New York Univ. Press 1998) (urging greater privatization in the criminal justice system), reviewed 32 Urban Law. 167 (2000).

conferred by state law.[3] Very often, though, state constitutions and statutes *do* confer on municipalities the power to award franchises, following prescribed limitations (as to length of the franchise) and procedures (as to electoral approval, etc.).[4] A number of state constitutions specify that the state may not grant a franchise within a municipality without obtaining local approval.[5] Subject to these requirements and any other limitations laid down by state law, the municipality may, in granting a franchise, attach to the grant any conditions that are not against public policy,[6] such as the payment of compensation by the utility.[7] When a utility is granted a franchise, this constitutes a property right that cannot be destroyed or damaged by the government without compensation—though the utility accepts its rights subject to an implied obligation to

---

[3] See City of Owensboro v. Cumberland Telephone & Telegraph Co., 230 U.S. 58, 33 S.Ct. 988, 57 L.Ed. 1389 (1913); Water, Light & Gas Co. v. City of Hutchinson, 207 U.S. 385, 28 S.Ct. 135, 52 L.Ed. 257 (1907); Blair v. City of Chicago, 201 U.S. 400, 26 S.Ct. 427, 50 L.Ed. 801 (1906); Walla Walla v. Walla Walla Water Co., 172 U.S. 1, 19 S.Ct. 77, 43 L.Ed. 341 (1898); Port of Mobile v. Louisville & Nashville R.R., 84 Ala. 115, 4 So. 106 (1888); City of Mesa v. Salt River Project Agricultural Improvement & Power District, 92 Ariz. 91, 373 P.2d 722 (1962), appeal dism'd 372 U.S. 704, 83 S.Ct. 1018, 10 L.Ed.2d 124; Lasher v. People, 183 Ill. 226, 55 N.E. 663 (1899). Cf. Care Ambulance Co. v. Multnomah County, 97 Or.App. 618, 777 P.2d 997 (1989), review denied 309 Or. 231, 785 P.2d 1057 (1990) (prohibition in city charter against granting exclusive franchise did not apply to city/county agreement on ambulance service; regulation of ambulance service was county function, governed by state law); K N Energy, Inc. v. City of Casper, 755 P.2d 207 (Wyo.1988) (statute permitting municipalities to grant franchises to public utilities did not authorize municipality to adopt ordinance imposing penalty on utility that operated therein without license or franchise).

[4] See State ex rel. McKittrick v. Missouri Utilities Co., 339 Mo. 385, 96 S.W.2d 607 (1936); City National Bank v. Town of Kiowa, 104 Okl. 161, 230 P. 894 (1924), both applying laws requiring electoral approval. Cf. Oklahoma Electric Cooperative, Inc. v. Oklahoma Gas and Electric Company, 982 P.2d 512 (Okl.1999) (city was required to obtain voter approval before granting a franchise allowing public utility, which prior to city's annexation of area had provided electric service to a few customers living therein, to expand its service beyond the annexed area).

[5] See Chapter 5 *supra* on this and other constitutional limitations on state control over municipalities.

[6] Chicago General Ry. v. City of Chicago, 176 Ill. 253, 52 N.E. 880 (1898); Southern Public Utilities Co. v. City of Charlotte, 179 N.C. 151, 101 S.E. 619 (1919). See Southern Pacific Co. v. City of Portland, 227 U.S. 559, 33 S.Ct. 308, 57 L.Ed. 642 (1913) (conditions become part of franchise contract); City of Indianapolis v. Consumers' Gas Trust Co., 140 Ind. 107, 39 N.E. 433 (1895); City of Louisville v. Louisville Home Telephone Co., 149 Ky. 234, 148 S.W. 13 (1912); Chrysler Light & Power Co. v. City of Belfield, 58 N.D. 33, 224 N.W. 871 (1929); City of Portsmouth v. Virginia Ry. & Power Co., 141 Va. 54, 126 S.E. 362 (1925). The granting of franchises is a matter of state-wide concern, and thus state law will prevail, in cases of conflict, over the law of a city—even a home-rule city. See Chapter 6 *supra*.

[7] Chrysler Light & Power Co. v. Belfield, *supra* note 6; Nashville Gas & Heating Co. v. City of Nashville, 177 Tenn. 590, 152 S.W.2d 229 (1941). See Group W Cable, Inc. v. City of Santa Cruz, 679 F.Supp. 977 (N.D.Cal.1988) (cable television operator's use of utility poles was not within the city franchise granted to utilities, and thus city could independently charge the operator for use of its easements and rights of way); City of Salem v. Anson, 40 Or. 339, 67 P. 190 (1902) (requirement of bond in specified sum, conditioned on prompt completion of structures; sum construed as liquidated damages). Cf. De Motte v. City of Valparaiso, 161 Ind. 319, 67 N.E. 985 (1903) (requirement that grantee agree to sell to municipality); State ex rel. City of Tacoma v. Sunset Telephone & Telegraph Co., 86 Wash. 309, 150 P. 427 (1915) (franchise could not be transferred without consent of municipality). See also City of Detroit v. Public Utilities Commission, 288 Mich. 267, 286 N.W. 368 (1939) (under Michigan Constitution, city can by franchise-contract set reasonable rates as a condition to use of its streets by utility, even though city has no governmental power otherwise to regulate rates); City of St. Mary's v. Hope Natural Gas Co., 71 W.Va. 76, 76 S.E. 841 (1912) (same under West Virginia law). On franchise charges as a revenue-raising device, see Colton & Sheehan, Raising Local Government Revenue Through Utility Franchise Charges: If the Fee Fits, Foot It, 21 Urban Law. 55 (1989).

In Golden State Transit Corp. v. City of Los Angeles, 475 U.S. 608, 106 S.Ct. 1395, 89 L.Ed.2d 616 (1986), on remand 791 F.2d 1383 (9th Cir.1986), a city's action of conditioning renewal of a franchise on settlement of a labor dispute by a certain date was held pre-empted by the National Labor Relations Act.

relocate its facilities at its own expense when necessary to proper governmental use of the streets or ways.[8]

While municipalities often enjoy the above-described power to grant franchises to privately owned utilities operating within municipal limits, most control over such utilities resides exclusively in the state government. In most jurisdictions, the setting of rates, and the establishing of rules of operation, for such utilities are completely within the power of the state;[9] state laws on such utilities' rates and practices will prevail over the laws of a city, even a home-rule city;[10] and, apart from franchise requirements, a city

---

[8] Southern California Gas Co. v. City of Los Angeles, 50 Cal.2d 713, 329 P.2d 289 (1958) cert. denied 359 U.S. 907, 79 S.Ct. 583, 3 L.Ed.2d 572; U.S. West Communications, Inc. v. City of Longmont, 948 P.2d 509 (Colo.1997) (city ordinance requiring owners and operators of existing overhead electric and communications facilities to relocate facilities underground at their own cost did not constitute uncompensated "taking" of property, as carrier locating its facilities above ground was on notice that city might require relocation under city's police powers); City & County of Denver v. Mountain States Tel. & Tel. Co., 754 P.2d 1172 (Colo.1988) (utility must pay cost of relocating its facilities from a public street whenever municipality requires this in order to protect public health, safety, or convenience; relocation of underground telephone lines necessitated by sewer construction held to be for protection of public health and welfare); Mountain States Tel. & Tel. Co. v. Boise Redevelopment Agency, 101 Idaho 30, 607 P.2d 1084 (1980); Consolidated Edison Co. v. Lindsay, 24 N.Y.2d 309, 300 N.Y.S.2d 321, 248 N.E.2d 150 (1969). Northwest Natural Gas Co. v. City of Portland, 300 Or. 291, 711 P.2d 119 (1985) (municipality could order telephone and power utilities to relocate without compensation in order to accommodate construction of rail transit system). See Northeast Sacramento County Sanitation Dist. v. Northridge Park County Water Dist., 247 Cal.App.2d 317, 55 Cal.Rptr. 494 (Dist.Ct.1966). Meadowbrook-Fairview Metropolitan Dist. v. Board of County Comm'rs, 910 P.2d 681 (Colo.1996) (board of county commissioners could compel water and sanitation districts to assume costs of relocation of water lines necessitated by roadway improvements initiated by board). Cf. Norfolk Redev. & Housing Auth. v. Chesapeake & Potomac Tel. Co., 464 U.S. 30, 104 S.Ct. 304, 78 L.Ed.2d 29 (1983) (telephone company required to relocate its transmission facilities because of urban renewal project was not entitled to relocation benefits under federal statutes; those statutes leave unchanged the common-law rule that a utility forced to relocate from a public right-of-way must do so at its own expense). But cf. General Telephone Company v. City of Bothell, 105 Wash.2d 579, 716 P.2d 879 (1986) (common-law duty of utility to relocate facilities at own expense may be changed by contract or statute). See generally City of Albuquerque v. New Mexico Pub. Regulation Comm'n, 134 N.M. 472, 79 P.3d 297 (2003) (utility locates its facilities above, on or under a public way at the risk they might be, at some future time, disturbed, and a municipality's police power in this regard extends to the subsurface of the streets; but the common-law rule of imposing expenses of relocation on the utility applies only if the improvement is necessitated by public health and safety). Where the utility line is in place *before* the dedication of the street or the acquisition of the road by the public body making a road improvement, the public utility will have superior rights, and the public body—not the utility—will then have to bear the cost of relocating the utility's lines, mains, etc. See City of Chandler v. Arizona Dept. of Transportation, 224 Ariz. 400, 231 P.3d 932 (App. 2010). The general principle that a utility's location of its facilities on public roads is subject to the public interest has been said to date, in the United States, to the Post Road Act of 1856. Qwest Corp. v. City of Chandler, 222 Ariz. 474, 217 P.3d 424 (App. 2009) (franchise granted a public utility is at all times subject to the police power of the sovereign, and the utility must, at its own expense, generally make such changes as the public convenience and necessity require if the franchise agreement is silent on the issue of payment of relocation cost).

[9] See Union Electric Co. v. City of Crestwood, 499 S.W.2d 480 (Mo.1973) (city could not require that all future electric power lines be placed underground, as this invaded an area reserved to state regulatory commission); In re Public Service Electric & Gas Co., 35 N.J. 358, 173 A.2d 233 (1961). But a state legislature, or a local unit acting under legislative authorization, may *abdicate* its regulatory powers. See City of Detroit v. Detroit Citizens' Street Railway, 184 U.S. 368, 22 S.Ct. 410, 46 L.Ed. 592 (1902).

A number of communities have in recent years attempted, as in the *Union Electric Co.* case *supra*, to require "undergrounding" of electric and other wires, and sometimes the authority to do this may be upheld. See Maun v. United States, 347 F.2d 970 (9th Cir.1965), holding that the Atomic Energy Commission had to comply with a local undergrounding requirement. Subsequently, however, Congress gave the Commission approval to proceed with overhead lines. See Miller, Electric Transmission Lines, 12 Villanova L.Rev. 497 (1967).

[10] See State ex rel. Guthrie v. City of Richland, 80 Wn.2d 382, 494 P.2d 990 (1972) (city charter provision allowing referendum on any legislative ordinance was in conflict with, and must yield to, state

cannot even deny a utility the right to operate within that city if the appropriate state commission has given the utility that right.[11] Regulation of such utilities is entrusted to federal and state bodies. The appropriate state body is usually called the Public Utilities Commission (or, in some jurisdictions, the Corporation Commission, or comparable name)—though special bodies may sometimes be established to regulate particular aspects of utility operation, such as air pollution control.[12]

§ 17.2 Operation of Utilities by Municipalities Themselves: Relationship of Such Utilities to the State

What about utilities that are operated by localities themselves, such as the aforementioned municipally owned and operated water company? While there is considerable variation in the degree of state control over these utilities,[13] and while such

---

statute establishing procedure for municipal acquisition of or additions to utility). On conflicts between state laws and laws of home-rule cities, see generally Chapter 6 *supra*.

[11] Chugach Electric Ass'n v. City of Anchorage, 476 P.2d 115 (Alaska 1970) (city could not deny electric cooperative a building permit to extend service to bowling alley where state commission had determined that the cooperative could serve that area). But cf. City Transportation Co. v. Pharr, 186 Tenn. 217, 209 S.W.2d 15 (1948) (statute authorizing the city to charter public carriers found to have divested the state commission of any jurisdiction over city).

[12] See Orange County Air Pollution Control District v. Public Utilities Commission, 4 Cal.3d 945, 95 Cal.Rptr. 17, 484 P.2d 1361 (1971) (air pollution control district could regulate the emissions of public utilities). As to judicial review of public utility commission decisions, see Note, Note, Judicial Review of Public Utility Commissions, 86 Ind. L. J. 1163 (2011), noting Northern Indiana Pub. Serv. Co. v. United States Steel Corp., 907 N.E. 2d 1012 (Ind. 2009), where the court stated that a utility regulatory commission's orders are reviewed by the following standards: basic facts for substantial evidence, legal propositions for correctness, and ultimate facts or "mixed questions" for reasonableness. *Id.* at 1018. Federal control, based on the power over interstate commerce, has, of course, spread for decades through much of the utility field. See Rhyne, Municipal Interest in the Work of the Federal Power Commission, 14 Geo.Wash.L.Rev. 247 (1945).

Federal legislation largely covers the regulation of cable television but specifically leaves some matters to municipal control. See Ciamporcero, Is There Any Hope for Cities? Recent Developments in Cable Television Law, 18 Urban Law. 369 (1986). It has been held that a municipality may not deny a cable television company access to public facilities, such as utility poles and conduits, when those facilities are physically capable of accommodating the company, as such denial would infringe the company's First Amendment rights. Preferred Communications, Inc. v. City of Los Angeles, 754 F.2d 1396 (9th Cir.1985), aff'd and remanded for determination of fact questions 476 U.S. 488, 106 S.Ct. 2034, 90 L.Ed.2d 480 (1986). And the U.S. Supreme Court has ruled that federal regulations have pre-empted any state or local controls over the signals carried by cable television systems, thus precluding a state or locality from banning commercials for alcoholic beverages on out-of-state cable television transmissions. Capital Cities Cable, Inc. v. Crisp, 467 U.S. 691, 104 S.Ct. 2694, 81 L.Ed.2d 580 (1984). See Witt, Cable Television Regulation after *Crisp*: Is There Anything Left? 17 Urban Law. 277 (1985). Cf. City of New York v. Federal Communications Comm'n, 486 U.S. 57, 108 S.Ct. 1637, 100 L.Ed.2d 48 (1988) (FCC did not exceed authority in pre-empting state and local technical standards governing quality of cable television signals).

[13] See Kneier, State Supervision Over Municipally Owned Utilities, 49 Colum.L.Rev. 180 (1949); Reese, State Regulation of Municipally Owned Electric Utilities, 7 Geo.Wash.L.Rev. 557 (1939); 12 McQuillin, Municipal Corporations ch. 35 (3d rev. ed. 1995). See generally Note, Municipal Utilities: Jurisdiction of State Commissions, 33 Colum.L.Rev. 338 (1933); Note, Municipal Operation of Public Utilities, 41 Yale L.J. 116 (1931); Annot., Power of State or Public Service Commission to Regulate, or of Court to Pass Upon Reasonableness of Rates, of Municipally Owned or Operated Public Utility, 127 A.L.R. 94 (1940); Annot., Power of State or Public Service Commission to Regulate Rates of Municipally Owned or Operated Public Utility, 76 A.L.R. 851 (1932); Annots., Applicability of Public Utility Acts to Municipal Corporations Owning or Operating a Public Utility, 18 A.L.R. 946 (1922); 10 A.L.R. 1432 (1921). See also Bibikos, "Municipal Corporations" and Public Utility Service in Pennsylvania, 13 Widener L.J. 879 (2004). As to forcing a local water utility to produce recycled water, see Comment, Out of the Mud: Moving Past *Environmental Defense Fund v. East Bay Municipal Utility District* Toward Finding a Duty to Produce Recycled Water, 46 U. San Francisco L. Rev. 1125 (2012).

utilities are generally agreed to be subject to state regulatory power *if* the state should choose to exercise such power, these utilities are commonly excepted from the state commission's regulation, at least as to their operation within the territorial limits of the owning city.[14] The theory is that the customers of the utility are then also, as voters in the community, the owners of that utility, and if dissatisfied with utility rates or service, the customer-owners have the remedy of the ballot box. Occasionally, this hands-off policy of the state is applied even to operations by the municipal utility outside city limits.[15] But obviously, the ballot-box remedy for dealing with dissatisfaction is not available to those who live outside the city. Thus, the relevant state law often provides—or is interpreted to provide—that state regulation *does* apply to a municipal utility's *extraterritorial* operation (*i.e.*, its operation outside the limits of the owning locality) but *not* to its activities within the confines of the owning locality.[16] This would seem the majority view today. Occasionally, it is ruled in general terms that *all* operations of municipal utilities—inside or outside the locality—should be subject to state regulatory control, since the premise underlying any such control is that rates and standards should be equitably and uniformly set, by a body of experts, for the entire jurisdiction.[17] But the trend view would seem to allow state regulatory control, wherever relevant statutes permit such an interpretation, only as to extraterritorial operations; as to those

---

It has been held that such local governmental activities as operation of a utility may come within federal antitrust laws. City of Lafayette v. Louisiana Power & Light Co., 435 U.S. 389, 98 S.Ct. 1123, 55 L.Ed.2d 364 (1978). See generally Section 26.7 *infra*.

[14] Kitchens v. City of Paragould, 191 Ark. 940, 88 S.W.2d 843 (1935); Georgia Public Service Commission v. City of Albany, 180 Ga. 355, 179 S.E. 369 (1935); Logan City v. Public Utilities Commission, 72 Utah 536, 271 P. 961 (1928). See City of Durango v. Durango Transp., Inc., 807 P.2d 1152 (Colo.1991), on remand 824 P.2d 48 (Colo.App.1991) (county exempt from regulation by state Public Utilities Commission when providing mass transit within county boundaries; court notes that similar exemption has long been applied to municipal utilities operating within municipal boundaries); City of Wichita v. State Corp. Comm'n, 225 Kan. 524, 592 P.2d 880 (1979) (state required approval of state commission before city could issue revenue bonds for a utility where a privately owned utility in the city already supplied the same product; held not in conflict with general exemption of municipally owned utilities from state control). See generally Township of Morris v. Town of Morristown, 49 N.J. 194, 229 A.2d 516 (1967) (municipal residents have adequate political control over municipally owned utility; state control generally unneeded; but *is* needed when municipality sells water *outside* its boundaries). See also In re Residents of Struthers, Ohio, 45 Ohio St.3d 227, 543 N.E.2d 794 (1989) (Ohio Public Utilities Commission lacks jurisdiction to review contract entered into between public utility and a municipality). Many states require that a city that has been providing utility service must obtain permission from the state regulatory commission before going out of the business of providing such service. See Swetzof v. Philemonoff, 192 P.3d 992 (Alaska 2008) (city could not simply stop selling electricity but was required to seek state regulatory commission's permission).

[15] See City of Colorado Springs v. Public Utilities Comm'n, 126 Colo. 265, 248 P.2d 311 (1952) (extraterritorial municipal water service not subject to state commission's jurisdiction). Cf. City of Georgetown v. Public Service Comm'n, 516 S.W.2d 842 (Ky.1974) (state commission has no jurisdiction over city-owned utilities even when they extend service beyond city limits; overruling prior authority).

[16] See City of Fort Morgan v. Colorado Pub. Utilities Comm'n, 159 P.3d 87 (Colo. 2007) (under Colorado Constitution, a municipally owned utility operating outside its boundaries is subject to Public Utilities Commission regulation, and a non-municipal utility operating within municipal boundaries is subject to such regulation); Regional Transp. Dist. v. Colorado Department of Labor & Employment, 830 P.2d 942 (Colo.1992) (when a city supplies utility services outside its municipal boundaries, regulation by state commission is constitutionally permissible); Township of Morris v. Town of Morristown, *supra* note 14; Borough of Phoenixville v. Pennsylvania Public Utility Comm'n, 3 Pa.Cmwlth. 56, 280 A.2d 471 (1971). See generally Rhyne, Municipal Law 502 (1957), with lists of jurisdictions in which state regulation of municipal utilities' intramural and extramural service is allowed, and those in which only regulation of *extra*-mural service is allowed.

[17] See Public Service Comm'n v. City of Helena, 52 Mont. 527, 159 P. 24 (1916) (city water system subject to control of state commission); State ex rel. City of Wheeling v. Renick, 145 W.Va. 640, 116 S.E.2d 763 (1960); Pabst Corp. v. City of Milwaukee, 190 Wis. 349, 208 N.W. 493 (1926).

operations, the situation (from the customers' point of view) is similar to that in which service is provided by a privately owned company.[18]

A locality may enter the utility business by original construction of a plant, by purchase of existing facilities, or by condemnation of an existing plant. Some states provide by constitution or statute that a city granting a franchise must, or may, reserve an option to purchase the utility as a condition of granting the franchise. And some states have statutory requirements that a locality *must* purchase or condemn any already-operating utility facilities of the same nature before it can enter that line of utility operation itself—*e.g.*, must purchase or condemn an existing electric utility in the city before setting-up a city-run electric company.[19] Where municipal condemnation of a utility occurs, the amount of compensation to be paid is usually set by the courts, as in other eminent domain situations;[20] but occasionally, a state law will entrust the fixing of compensation to the commission that regulates public utilities in that jurisdiction.[21]

§ 17.3 Rates and Revenues of Municipally Operated Utilities

For what reasons does a local unit of government enter the utility business? Municipal operation of a utility provides, of course, a service to municipal residents—and thus relates to the following chapters on activities of cities and towns. But the operation may also result in revenue for the municipality—and thus relates to the prior chapters on municipal finances. It is generally held that a municipality is entitled to earn a fair return on its utility investment the same as would a privately owned utility company.[22] There is, however, one important difference: while the rates of the privately

---

[18] See Public Utilities Comm'n v. City of Loveland, 87 Colo. 556, 289 P. 1090 (1930); Lamar v. Town of Wiley, 80 Colo. 18, 248 P. 1009 (1926); Town of Holyoke v. Smith, 75 Colo. 286, 226 P. 158 (1924).

[19] See Mohave Disposal, Inc. v. City of Kingman, 186 Ariz. 343, 922 P.2d 308 (Ariz. 1996) (private garbage collector provided "public utility service" within meaning of statute requiring municipality which provides competing service in area already being adequately provided with such service to acquire facilities and business already serving the area). See generally Note, Municipal Acquisition of Public Utilities, 34 Colum.L.Rev. 534 (1934). See also Washington Fruit & Produce Co. v. City of Yakima, 3 Wn.2d 152, 100 P.2d 8 (1940), adhered to 3 Wn.2d 152, 103 P.2d 1106 (*charter* requirements on purchase of overhead street lighting from utility by city; held not to be a "franchise" so as to require electoral approval). On the trend at the turn of the nineteenth century for municipalities to assume the providing of water service, see Troesken and Geddes, Municipalizing American Waterworks, 1897–1915, 19 J.L. Economics & Organization 373 (2003).

[20] See City of Tucson v. Tucson Gas, Electric Light & Power Co., 152 F.2d 552 (9th Cir.1945), cert. denied 327 U.S. 799, 66 S.Ct. 901, 90 L.Ed. 1024.

[21] See Sacramento Municipal Utility Dist. v. Pacific Gas & Electric Co., 72 Cal.App.2d 638, 165 P.2d 741 (Dist.Ct.1946).

[22] City of Logansport v. Public Service Comm'n, 202 Ind. 523, 177 N.E. 249 (1931) (state has power to regulate rates of municipal utilities). But see Holton Creamery Co. v. Brown, 137 Kan. 418, 20 P.2d 503 (1933) (rates of municipal utility subject to control of city government, not of state; applying Kansas statute). See generally Annot., Power of State or Public Service Commission to Regulate Rates of Municipally Owned or Operated Public Utility, 76 A.L.R. 851 (1932), noting a split of authority. Municipally operated utilities may be subject to state taxes on their income. See Department of Treasury v. City of Linton, 223 Ind. 363, 60 N.E.2d 948 (1945). Occasionally, such state taxation has been criticized as putting a premium on inefficiency and rendering the municipal utility that operates at a loss immune from taxation. See Comment, Public Utilities Under Home Rule, 9 Ohio St.L.J. 141, 147–49 (1948).

A municipality operating its own utility may include a fair and reasonable amount for capital improvements in its connection charges or operating charges. See Meglino v. Township Comm., 103 N.J. 144, 510 A.2d 1134 (1986). On the law of utility ratesetting, see generally Pond, The Law Governing the Fixing of Public Utility Rates: A Response to Recent Judicial and Academic Misconceptions, 41 Admin. L. Rev. 1 (1989). On the use of the public utility concept to fund such traditionally "nonutility" functions as stormwater management programs and road improvement and maintenance, see Schoettle & Richardson, Nontraditional Use of the Utility Concept to Fund Public Utilities, 25 Urban Law. 519 (1993).

owned utility must be approved by the appropriate state or federal commission, the municipally owned utility is (as noted *supra*) often free from such regulatory control, at least as to its operation within the municipality. Some authority has taken the view that the rates charged by such a utility are simply a matter of contract—*i.e.*, they are set by the contract between the utility and its customer, and any such agreement, if valid under general rules of contract law, is enforceable.[23] But most authority takes the position that while the rates of a municipal utility are largely within the legislative discretion of the city, they *are* subject to review by the *courts* and can be invalidated if clearly unreasonable or discriminatory.[24] Thus, classification of customers into different categories, with differing rates, must not be unjust but is permissible only if based on substantial differences among the categories.[25] Classification of apartments and mobile home parks, and of hotels and motels, in the same category as "single-family residences" rather than in the same category as "commercial businesses" has often been upheld against attack.[26] On the other hand, charging higher fees to nonresidents of the

---

[23] City of Phoenix v. Kasun, 54 Ariz. 470, 97 P.2d 210 (1939); Childs v. City of Columbia, 87 S.C. 566, 70 S.E. 296 (1911) (city under no duty to furnish water to nonresident at reasonable rates, or to furnish it at all). See generally Annot., Power of State or Public Service Commission to Regulate, or of Court to Pass Upon Reasonableness of, Rates of Municipally Owned or Operated Public Utility, 127 A.L.R. 94, 96 (1940), particularly noting cases involving rates for service beyond city limits.

The city generally has broad discretion in determining the amount, time, and method of a bond issuance to raise money for the operation and expansion of municipal utilities. See Board of Public Utilities v. Kansas City, 227 Kan. 194, 605 P.2d 151 (1980) (decision rests with city, not with board of public utilities, which is merely an administrative agency of city).

[24] See Knotts v. Nollen, 206 Iowa 261, 218 N.W. 563 (1928); Oklahoma City Hotel & Motor Hotel Association, Inc. v. Oklahoma City, 531 P.2d 316 (Okl.1974); Shirk v. Lancaster City, 313 Pa. 158, 169 A. 557 (1933); American Aniline Products, Inc. v. City of Lock Haven, 288 Pa. 420, 135 A. 726 (1927) (city operating legalized monopoly cannot be allowed to discriminate unjustly; to give water away free would be unfair discrimination). Cf. RR Village Ass'n v. Denver Sewer Corp., 826 F.2d 1197 (2d Cir.1987) (homeowners paying established rate for sewer services have property right in receiving *past* services at that rate and must be afforded procedural due process before rates can be retroactively increased by local governing body). See generally 12 McQuillin, Municipal Corporations § 34.158–.164 (3d rev. ed. 1995); Rhyne, Municipal Law § 23–7 through –9 (1957). As to enforcement of charges for municipal utility services, see City of Grangeville v. Haskin, 116 Idaho 535, 777 P.2d 1208 (1989) (without statutory authority, city could not impose liens for delinquent water, sewer, and garbage charges; court takes minority view that proprietary powers of municipality are to be more strictly construed than governmental powers—see Section 8.4 *supra*).

[25] Oklahoma City Hotel & Motor Hotel Association, Inc. v. Oklahoma City, *supra* note 24; Kliks v. Dalles City, 216 Or. 160, 335 P.2d 366 (1959). The *Kliks* case *supra* indicates that the cost of providing service is the only valid basis for classification, but the *Oklahoma City* case *supra* holds that other factors—such as the identity of the ultimate consumer or user of the service—may also be used in establishing classifications. *Accord* with the Oklahoma view, Oradell Village v. Township of Wayne, 98 N.J.Super. 8, 235 A.2d 905 (1967), aff'd 101 N.J.Super. 403, 244 A.2d 513, aff'd 53 N.J. 496, 251 A.2d 441; Kermit v. Rush, 351 S.W.2d 598 (Tex.Civ.App.1961). See "Laramie Citizens for Good Government" v. City of Laramie, 617 P.2d 474 (Wyo.1980) (classification of water-users must be reasonable and based on such factors as amount of water received, type of service, time of use, cost of service, etc.). Clearly, race discrimination by municipally operated utilities is unlawful. See Note, Thirsting for Equal Protection: The Legal Implications of Municipal Water Access in *Kennedy v. City of Zanesville* and the Need for Federal Oversight of Governments Practicing Unlawful Race Discrimination, 59 Cath. U.L. Rev. 587 (2010), noting Kennedy v. City of Zanesville, 505 F. Supp. 2d 456 (S. D. Ohio 2007).

[26] Fort Collins Motor Homes, Inc. v. City of Fort Collins, 30 Colo.App. 445, 496 P.2d 1074 (1972); Knotts v. Nollen, *supra* note 24; Lewis v. Mayor of Cumberland, 189 Md. 58, 54 A.2d 319 (1947); Land v. City of Grandville, 2 Mich.App. 681, 141 N.W.2d 370 (1966); Oradell Village v. Township of Wayne, *supra* note 25; Caldwell v. City of Abilene, 260 S.W.2d 712 (Tex.Civ.App.1953), error ref'd. See Loup-Miller Constr. Co. v. City & County of Denver, 676 P.2d 1170 (Colo.1984) (distinction between apartment buildings and commercial buildings as to city's sewer fees held not to violate Equal Protection; distinction between new and old customers also upheld where requiring new customers to pay a facilities development fee for new connections was rationally related to need to develop increased capacity occasioned by those new connections). But see Kliks v. Dalles City, *supra* note 25. In Oklahoma City Hotel & Motor Hotel Association v. Oklahoma City, *supra* note

municipality has been declared illegally discriminatory unless some relevant ground for the distinction is established.[27]

It is usually held that revenue from a municipal utility—that is, the profit made on the utility operation by the city—belongs to the city the same as any other revenue and may be put to any municipal purpose.[28] Thus, where one municipal utility makes a profit, this money may be used to pay the bonds or other obligations of another municipal utility or operation.[29] These authorities following the general view have, however, indicated that the obligations of the utility itself should be paid off before its revenues are diverted to other uses. And a few jurisdictions have taken the view that, even after a utility's own debts are fully paid, its profits should be employed only in that utility enterprise itself, not in other municipal endeavors.[30]

25, the court held that apartments and mobile home parks could be classified with residences, rather than with commercial users, but that hotels and motels should be placed in the same category as other volume commercial users. See generally Annot., Validity and Construction of Regulation by Municipal Corporation Fixing Sewer-Use Rates, 61 A.L.R.3d 1236 (1975). It has been held that a landlord may be held liable for utility fees unpaid by a tenant. See Coffinberry v. Town of Thermopolis, 183 P.3d 1136 (Wyo. 2008) (interpreting state statute).

[27] See City of Texarkana v. Wiggins, 151 Tex. 100, 246 S.W.2d 622 (1952) (higher charges discriminatory). But higher charges to those outside the municipality are justified if based on some financial reason, such as greater cost of service, or tax contributions to the utility operation by residents but not by non-residents. See Durant v. City of Beverly Hills, 39 Cal.App.2d 133, 102 P.2d 759 (Dist.Ct.1940) (presumption that city council acted reasonably and fairly in setting rates); Barr v. First Taxing District, 151 Conn. 53, 192 A.2d 872 (1963); Faxe v. City of Grandview, 48 Wn.2d 342, 294 P.2d 402 (1956) (burden of proving discrimination is on consumers). Cf. Burba v. City of Vancouver, 113 Wash.2d 800, 783 P.2d 1056 (1989) (inclusion of city gross receipts tax levied against utility revenues received for water and sewer services from resident and nonresident customers in rates charged nonresidents upheld as constitutional even though nonresidents did not have right to vote in municipality's elections); City of Bremerton v. Kitsap County Sewer District, 71 Wn.2d 689, 430 P.2d 956 (1967) (reasonable discrimination as to replacement of facilities). See generally Annot., Power of Municipality to Charge Nonresidents Higher Fees than Residents for Use of Municipal Facilities, 57 A.L.R.3d 998 (1974). It has been suggested that, in situations where unfairly higher charges to nonresidents are alleged, the burden of showing discrimination should be on the nonresident consumers but the municipal utility should have a burden of producing cost information for the items used in determining rates. Sax, Municipal Water Supply for Nonresidents: Recent Developments and A Suggestion for the Future, 5 Natural Resources J. 54, 60 (1965).

[28] This *majority* view is taken by Mitchell v. City of Mobile, 244 Ala. 442, 13 So.2d 664 (1943); Johnson v. Dermott, 189 Ark. 830, 75 S.W.2d 243 (1934); Niles v. Union Ice Corp., 133 Ohio St. 169, 12 N.E.2d 483 (1938); Killion v. Paris, 192 Tenn. 446, 241 S.W.2d 524 (1951); Crouch v. McKinney, 47 Tex.Civ.App. 54, 104 S.W. 518 (1907), error ref'd. See Fretz v. City of Edmond, 66 Okl. 262, 168 P. 800 (1916) (city may put resources of its utilities to any public uses; held that city utility could donate water to state school). See generally Annots, Disposition of Revenues from Operation of Revenue-Producing Enterprise Owned by Municipal Corporation, 165 A.L.R. 854 (1946); 103 A.L.R. 579 (1936).

Statutory or charter provisions sometimes impose limits on use of general tax revenues to support a municipal utility. See Cleveland Elec. Illuminating Co. v. City of Cleveland, 37 Ohio St.3d 50, 524 N.E.2d 441 (1988), reh. denied 38 Ohio St.3d 704, 532 N.E.2d 1321 (1988), where a charter provision that a municipally owned utility must be "non-tax-supported" was held to prevent a city from advancing money out of tax-generated revenue to such a utility without a repayment requirement.

[29] City of Harrison v. Braswell, 209 Ark. 1094, 194 S.W.2d 12 (1946). See Annot., Disposition of Revenues, 165 A.L.R. 845, *supra* note 28.

[30] This *minority* view is taken by Uhl v. Badaracco, 199 Cal. 270, 248 P. 917 (1926); Wilkins v. Leeds, 216 Ind. 508, 25 N.E.2d 442 (1940); Freeland v. City of Sturgis, 248 Mich. 190, 226 N.W. 897 (1929); Fjeldsted v. Ogden City, 84 Utah 302, 35 P.2d 825 (1934). See Annots., Disposition of Revenues, *supra* note 28. See generally 56 Am. Jur.2d Municipal Corporations §§ 583–84 (1971). It is usually now agreed that revenue from a municipal utility may *at least* be used for the maintenance, extension, and improvement of that utility enterprise. See George v. City of Asheville, 80 F.2d 50 (4th Cir.1935) (gross revenues from city waterworks may be used in maintaining and extending system but not for other purposes); Barsaloux v. City of Chicago, 245 Ill. 598, 92 N.E. 525 (1910) (net earnings of traction companies). See also Annot., Permissible Use of Funds

§ 17.4 Rights and Obligations of Municipal Utilities to Serve Particular Customers

If a municipality undertakes to supply a particular utility service to its residents, must it offer the service to *all* residents? Considerable discretion is here allowed the governing authorities, since it is recognized that an extension of pipes, mains, etc. to a relatively isolated resident might prove highly unprofitable. Thus, where town or city officials have reasonably exercised their judgment, a court will refrain from ordering them to extend facilities and supply service, even within the municipal limits, to additional persons,[31] or to extend service to a new subdivision being developed on the urban fringe.[32] But again, as with rates, unreasonable discrimination is forbidden. A city cannot ordinarily supply utility service, without special assessments, to all sections of the city but one, and then agree to supply that one remaining area only if the residents pay a special assessment.[33] So long as all portions of the city are treated equitably, the city may provide the necessary facilities (pipes, etc.) for utility service entirely at municipal expense, *or* may assess the costs of each improvement against residents of the area benefited, *or* may require that the work be done by the developer of the area, with or without reimbursement to him.[34] The general rule, both as to the municipality's duty to supply service to its residents and as to the method of paying for any extensions of service, is that residents in substantially similar positions must be treated similarly.[35]

---

from Parking Meters, 83 A.L.R.2d 625 (1962) (some uses of parking-meter revenues held impermissible if not sufficiently related to parking regulation; revenue measures may not be passed in guise of regulation).

[31] City of Greenwood v. Provine, 143 Miss. 42, 108 So. 284 (1926) (city resident living in remote corner could not compel extension of water mains to his premises regardless of cost); Rose v. Plymouth Town, 110 Utah 358, 173 P.2d 285 (1946). See Lawrence v. Richards, 111 Me. 95, 88 A. 92 (1913) (not every inhabitant of water district entitled to have mains extended to his residence). Cf. Lehman v. City of Shaker Heights, 418 U.S. 298, 94 S.Ct. 2714, 41 L.Ed.2d 770 (1974) (city bus system could allow some advertising on its vehicles but preclude political advertising).

Where a city utility has already laid a main or other facility on a prospective customer's street, however, that prospective customer may, if ready and able to accept and pay for service, compel the city to allow him to make a connection to the system since no further, substantial expenditure of city funds is involved. See Home Owners' Loan Corp. v. Logan City, 97 Utah 235, 92 P.2d 346 (1939). See generally McLawhorn, Where Will You Go When the Well Runs Dry? Local Government Ownership and Water Allocation in North Carolina, 32 Campbell L. Rev. 51 (2009). See also Grainey, Global Warming and Its Impact on Water Supply—The Energy Implications of Climate Change and the Effects of Our Energy Choices, 47 Willamette L. Rev. 593 (2011).

[32] See Reid Development Corp. v. Parsippany-Troy Hills Township, 31 N.J.Super. 459, 107 A.2d 20 (1954) (uncertainty as to whether the subdivision would provide sufficient consumer demand in the reasonably near future). Cf. Srail v. Village of Lisle, 588 F.3d 940 (7th Cir. 2009) (using a rational basis test, rather than strict scrutiny, court found no violation of equal protection in municipality's decision not to extend water services to a subdivision within the city). See generally Note, Sometimes There's Nothing Left to Give: The Justification for Denying Water Service to New Customers to Control Growth, 44 Stan. L. Rev. 429 (1992). See also Johnson, Sub-dividing the Waters: The Need for an Adequate and Sustainable Water Supply in Ex-urban Subdivisions, 14 Wyo. L. Rev. 473 (2014).

[33] Rutan Estates, Inc. v. Town of Belleville, 56 N.J.Super. 330, 152 A.2d 853 (1959). Cf. Johnson v. Reasor, 392 S.W.2d 54 (Ky.1965) (city could not charge subdivider for extension of utility service where it made no such charge to those who built their own houses). See also Mikeska v. City of Galveston, 451 F.3d 376 (5th Cir. 2006) (city refusing to reconnect utilities to houses located along public beaches, which have become disconnected due to tropical storms, must provide a rational basis for not reconnecting).

[34] See Deerfield Estates, Inc. v. Township of East Brunswick, 60 N.J. 115, 286 A.2d 498 (1972), setting forth these alternatives.

[35] See Nolte v. City of Olympia, 96 Wash.App. 944, 982 P.2d 659 (1999) (city that was exclusive provider of water and sewer service to urban growth area located adjacent to but outside city boundary owed public duty to serve all land within the area, subject to reasonable conditions). See generally Annots., Right to Compel Municipality to Extend its Water System, 48 A.L.R.2d 1222 (1956); 45 A.L.R. 829 (1926); 78 Am.Jur.

In addition, any rules or conditions as to service must meet the test of rationality.[36] Any irrational distinctions will be invalidated; and ones based on suspect classifications such as race—as where "white" and "black" neighborhoods of a city are treated unequally—will be struck down unless a compelling state interest is involved.[37]

Since a municipally operated utility is often allowed to supply some city residents but not supply others, it comes as no surprise that such a utility is ordinarily held under no duty to serve those *outside* municipal limits.[38] But here, too, the utility, as a government agency, cannot engage in unreasonable discrimination: if service is extended to *some* persons in a particular area outside the city, service can be ordered to other, similarly situated residents of that area.[39] Since a municipality may usually refuse service to those outside its limits, it may, as a fairly obvious corollary of this rule, condition its extension of service on annexation of the area concerned.[40]

Waterworks §§ 18–22 (1975). See also Front Royal & Warren County Industrial Park Corp. v. Town of Front Royal, 749 F.Supp. 1439 (W.D.Va.1990) (property owners had been subjected to a "taking" by town's wrongful failure to furnish sewer and water service; owners were thus entitled to compensation measured by difference between fair market value of their land with and without the service), vac'd 945 F.2d 760 (4th Cir.1991) (abstention by federal court was appropriate since state remedies might be available), cert. denied 503 U.S. 937, 112 S.Ct. 1477, 117 L.Ed.2d 620 (1992).

[36] See Davis v. Weir, 359 F.Supp. 1023 (N.D.Ga.1973), aff'd in part, modif'd in part 497 F.2d 139 (5th Cir.) (city could not refuse service because bill incurred by another person on same premises remained unpaid); Oliver v. Hyle, 14 Or.App. 302, 513 P.2d 806 (1973). It has been held that a municipal utility may not terminate service for nonpayment without meeting due process requirements of adequate notice, including advising the customer of a procedure for protesting the termination and providing an opportunity for the customer to present any complaints he may have about being overcharged. Memphis Light, Gas & Water Division v. Craft, 436 U.S. 1, 98 S.Ct. 1554, 56 L.Ed.2d 30 (1978). Cf. Sterling v. Village of Maywood, 579 F.2d 1350 (7th Cir.1978), cert. denied 440 U.S. 913, 99 S.Ct. 1227, 59 L.Ed.2d 462 (cause of action stated for utility's wrongful refusal to reinstate service).

[37] See Hawkins v. Town of Shaw, 437 F.2d 1286 (5th Cir.1971), reaff'd on reh. 461 F.2d 1171. See also Selmont Improvement Association v. Dallas County Commission, 339 F.Supp. 477 (S.D.Ala.1972) (prima facie case of discrimination against black area as to paving of roads by city).

[38] See Mongiello v. Borough of Hightstown, 17 N.J. 611, 112 A.2d 241 (1955) (incidental service to some nonresidents does not give rise to duty to render additional non-resident service); Penn-York Lanes, Inc. v. Village of Waverly, 26 Misc.2d 150, 205 N.Y.S.2d 689 (Sup.Ct.1960); State ex rel. Indian Hill Acres, Inc. v. Kellogg, 149 Ohio St. 461, 79 N.E.2d 319 (1948). But a state regulatory commission may order a municipal utility—if it has jurisdiction over it, as a few state commissions do—to continue and expand service outside the municipality where the commission finds that the municipality has "dedicated" itself to such service. City of Milwaukee v. Public Service Comm'n, 268 Wis. 116, 66 N.W.2d 716 (1954). See Mayor of Rockville v. Goldberg, 257 Md. 563, 264 A.2d 113 (1970) (city may be compelled to extend service beyond its boundaries only if it has held itself out as a public utility in such area). Cf. Harberd v. City of Kettle Falls, 120 Wash.App. 498, 84 P.3d 1241 (2004) (in the absence of express or implied contract, a municipality generally cannot be compelled to supply water or sewer service outside its corporate limits; municipality may be under a general duty to provide such service if it is the exclusive supplier in a region extending beyond borders of the city, but even that duty is not absolute, as the municipality may deny water or sewer services if it lacks the needed capacity).

[39] Delmarva Enterprises, Inc. v. Mayor of City of Dover, 282 A.2d 601 (Del.1971). See Mayor of Rockville v. Goldberg, *supra* note 38. But see Denby v. Brown, 230 Ga. 813, 199 S.E.2d 214 (1973), specifically refusing to order extraterritorial service even under these circumstances. Cf. Mongiello v. Borough of Hightstown, *supra* note 38 (service to a few non-residents does not create obligation to serve others).

[40] State ex rel. McCann v. City of Defiance, 105 Ohio App. 280, 152 N.E.2d 152 (1957), aff'd 167 Ohio St. 313, 148 N.E.2d 221 (city had constitutional authority to provide service outside its borders, but this also allowed it to demand annexation before providing service). See City of Colorado Springs v. Kitty Hawk Development Co., 154 Colo. 535, 392 P.2d 467 (1964), cert. denied 379 U.S. 647, 85 S.Ct. 612, 13 L.Ed.2d 551 (city could refuse utility service to subdivision unless it was annexed and subdivider paid a sum to the city). Cf. Yakima County Fire Protection Dist. No. 12 v. City of Yakima, 122 Wash.2d 371, 858 P.2d 245 (1993) (city requirement that extraterritorial landowners sign agreement promising to support future annexation efforts upheld as reasonable condition of city providing sewer services, though portion of agreement requiring

Sometimes the problem is not whether a municipal utility can be *compelled* to provide service outside its limits, but whether, where the utility is willing and able to provide such service, it will be *allowed* to do so. At common law, courts have occasionally enjoined such extraterritorial service on the ground that the municipality's primary obligation is to serve its own residents and the fulfillment of this obligation might be jeopardized by extraterritorial service.[41] But today, most jurisdictions have statutes specifically allowing at least some municipal utilities to provide their services outside municipal limits.[42] The situation is complicated somewhat if the extraterritorial area that a municipal utility proposes to serve is already being supplied the same kind of service by another utility—often, though not necessarily, one operated by another governmental entity. Under such circumstances, most courts will issue an injunction against the proposed competition, if, but only if, irreparable damage to the existing supplier is threatened.[43] A few courts are more lenient in granting injunctions and do not require the threat of *irreparable* harm, since they assume a general policy against competition in utility operations, at least within a territory that is already being supplied its utility service by some governmental unit.[44] Where a special function district (for

---

landowners actually to promote annexation violated First Amendment and was unenforceable). But cf. MT Development, LLC, v. City of Renton, 140 Wash.App. 422, 165 P.3d 427 (2007) (while a municipality may impose reasonable conditions on its agreement to provide service outside its borders, such conditions do not include mandatory compliance with residential density limits in municipality's comprehensive land use plan, even where the proposed service location is within the municipality's potential annexation area, because such a requirement amounts to zoning, and a municipality may not zone property outside its borders).

[41] City of Sweetwater v. Hamner, 259 S.W. 191 (Tex.Civ.App.1923), error dism'd. Cf. Yancey v. City of Searcy, 213 Ark. 673, 212 S.W.2d 546 (1948) (city had statutory authority to provide extraterritorial service, but court construed this to apply only when surplus supply existed; city not allowed to purchase a water company and continue that company's service inside and outside city); City of Ceres v. City of Modesto, 274 Cal.App.2d 545, 79 Cal.Rptr. 168 (Dist.Ct.1969) (taxpayer's suit entertained to prevent city's extension of sewers into unincorporated area; court reasoned the extension might be of no benefit to city). But see City of Henderson v. Young, 119 Ky. 224, 83 S.W. 583 (1904), where the court allowed a city to supply electricity outside its limits, reasoning that when acting in its proprietary or business capacity, a city should be treated the same as a private company.

[42] See Lumbee River Elec. Membership Corp. v. City of Fayetteville, 309 N.C. 726, 309 S.E.2d 209 (1983) (service to new subdivision four miles outside city limits found to be "within reasonable limitations," thus allowing municipal utility to provide service under relevant statute). See generally Sengstock, Extraterritorial Powers in the Metropolitan Area 19–20 (1962). In some jurisdictions, this right to provide extraterritorial service is granted by the state constitution. See Colorado Open Space Council, Inc. v. City & County of Denver, 190 Colo. 122, 543 P.2d 1258 (1975), interpreting such a provision. Sometimes, a municipality cannot, under these provisions, offer utility service within another municipality without the latter's consent. *E.g.*, West's Ann.Cal.Const. Art. 11 § 9 (provision added to constitution in 1970). But cf. Morgan v. Town of Hertford, 70 N.C.App. 725, 321 S.E.2d 170 (1984) (municipality that had been sole provider of electric service to unincorporated area could continue to provide such service to that area where it was annexed by another municipality so long as statutory requirement of area being "within reasonable limitations" was met). See also Central Rural Elec. Cooperative v. City of Stillwater, 146 P.3d 811 (Okla.Civ.App. 2006) (city electric utilities that "opted in" to Electric Restructuring Act were not in violation of the Act by providing service to consumers outside their borders where they were not previously or currently served by another utility, the customers either requested the service or were owned by the municipality, and references in the Act to fixing of territories was to future action that would not occur until enabling legislation for the Act was passed).

[43] See Jackson County Public Water Supply Dist. No. 1 v. Ong Aircraft Corp., 409 S.W.2d 226 (Mo.App.1966), cert. denied, 387 U.S. 919, 87 S.Ct. 2033, 18 L.Ed.2d 973, reh. denied 389 U.S. 890, 88 S.Ct. 17, 19 L.Ed.2d 200, where such an injunction was denied because of lack of evidence of irreparable damage. Cf. City of Corpus Christi v. Continental Bus Systems, Inc., 445 S.W.2d 12 (Tex.Civ.App.1969), ref'd n. r. e., 453 S.W.2d 470, where a private bus company was denied an injunction against a city bus company's competition on roads outside city limits.

[44] See Alderwood Water District v. Pope & Talbot, Inc., 62 Wn.2d 319, 382 P.2d 639 (1963) (one water district should not be allowed to "raid" another). Cf. Domestic Electric Service, Inc. v. City of Rocky Mount,

example, a water district) is the governmental unit that has been supplying utility service to a particular area, it may be judicially ruled that the district has been dissolved if its entire territory has been annexed to a general-function unit of government (such as a city or town) that is now able to supply the same service.[45] And if *some*, but not all, of the special function district's territory is annexed by a general-function unit, the special district will often be prevented from providing future service to the annexed area.[46]

Where a municipal utility does provide service outside city limits—though under no obligation to provide such service in the first place—it cannot unreasonably discriminate among customers as to rates or service. It cannot, for instance, charge higher water rates to customers who do not also purchase their electricity from the city,[47] nor refuse service

---

285 N.C. 135, 203 S.E.2d 838 (1974) (city does not have authority to serve area outside its boundaries if such area is already served by a privately owned public utility). But see City of Covington v. Board of Commissioners, 371 S.W.2d 20 (Ky.1963), where the court overturned a ruling of the State Public Utility Commission that water districts should not be allowed to serve areas already served by the city; the court noted that it had no jurisdiction, under Kentucky law, over the city and thus would be powerless if the city discontinued service—thus, there was a need for another source of supply. Cf. People ex rel. Chicago Title & Trust Co. v. Mission Brook Sanitary District, 76 Ill.App.2d 423, 222 N.E.2d 8 (1966) (water district did not have exclusive rights to supply water to area); City of Cold Spring v. Campbell County Water District, 334 S.W.2d 269 (Ky.1960) (same).

[45] In re Sanitary Board of East Fruitvale Sanitary Dist., 158 Cal. 453, 111 P. 368 (1910). See People ex rel. City of Downey v. Downey County Water District, 202 Cal.App.2d 786, 21 Cal.Rptr. 370 (1962). But this judicial rule of "merger" or "automatic dissolution" is sometimes now qualified by statute. See City of Aurora v. Aurora Sanitation District, 112 Colo. 406, 149 P.2d 662 (1944), interpreting such a provision as allowing concurrent existence of a municipality and a special function district. And California, subsequent to the *Fruitvale* and *Downey* cases *supra*, adopted a statute leaving it to the county board of supervisors in each instance to determine whether a utility district should continue to exist following its annexation by a municipality. See generally Note, Problems Created by Municipal Annexation of Special District Territory, 1967 Wash.U.L.Q. 560. On special function districts and their providing of utility and other services, see generally Chapter 2 *supra*. On annexation and consolidation, see generally Chapter 12 *supra*.

[46] Cox v. Otay Municipal Water Dist., 200 Cal.App.2d 672, 19 Cal.Rptr. 595 (Dist.Ct.1962) (finding statutory support for conclusion that water district could no longer provide service to annexed area). See State on Information of Flaxel v. Chandler, 180 Or. 28, 175 P.2d 448 (1946); Weatherwax v. Grays Harbor County, 116 Wash. 212, 199 P. 303 (1921). In several states, an annexing municipality may at its option oust a utility district from the annexed territory if, but only if, the municipality compensates the district for its facilities serving that area. See City of Mesa v. Salt River Project Agricultural Improvement & Power District, 92 Ariz. 91, 373 P.2d 722 (1962), appeal dism'd 372 U.S. 704, 83 S.Ct. 1018, 10 L.Ed.2d 124; Morgan County Rural Electric Membership Corp. v. Public Service Co., 253 Ind. 541, 255 N.E.2d 822 (1970); Franklin Power & Light Co. v. Middle Tennessee Electric Membership Corp., 222 Tenn. 182, 434 S.W.2d 829 (1968). See also Airport Authority v. City of Omaha, 185 Neb. 623, 177 N.W.2d 603 (1970) (when city which had established airport authority was annexed by metropolitan city, debts and obligations of authority become those of metropolitan city).

Some special function districts, including utility districts, are created so as to coincide with the limits of other units of government, usually municipalities or counties. The district will then normally expand if the other unit expands its boundaries. See Pock, Independent Special Districts: A Solution to the Metropolitan Area Problems 171 (1962). This is sometimes provided by statute. *E.g.*, Wash.Rev.Stat. § 35.61.020.

[47] Hicks v. City of Monroe Utilities Comm'n, 237 La. 848, 112 So.2d 635 (1959). See Schroeder v. City of Grayville, 166 Ill.App.3d 814, 117 Ill.Dec. 681, 520 N.E.2d 1032 (1988) (although a city is not obligated to provide water or other utility service to nonresidents, if it does choose to serve them, it may not discriminate unreasonably in rates or manner of service). Cf. Eudora Dev. Co. of Kan. v. City of Eudora, 276 Kan. 626, 78 P.3d 437 (2003) (discrimination in municipal water and sewer rates is lawful unless unjust and unreasonable; if there is a rational basis for distinguishing between owners of multi-unit buildings having only one water meter and other users who have a meter in each domestic unit, for purposes of setting municipal water and sewer rates, the classification must be upheld). Some authority upholds in general terms a municipality's charging of higher rates to customers who live outside city limits. See Mitchell v. City of Wichita, 270 Kan. 56, 12 P.3d 402 (2000) (no statutory impediment to city's charging higher rate for water or sewer service to customers who live outside city limits).

altogether to prospective customers who refuse to obtain their other utility services from the city.[48] Reasonable requirements, justified, for instance, by reasons of health or efficiency, may, however, be attached to a municipal utility's willingness to serve either residents or nonresidents of the municipality.[49]

---

[48] Edris v. Sebring Utilities Comm'n, 237 So.2d 585 (Fla.Dist.Ct.1970), cert. denied 240 So.2d 643 (Fla.1970). See People ex rel. Chicago Title & Trust Co. v. Mission Brook Sanitary District, *supra* note 44 (water district could not refuse sewage service to developer because of his refusal to take water service from the district). But see Sebring Utils. Comm'n v. Home Sav. Ass'n, 508 So.2d 26 (Fla.App.1987), review denied 515 So.2d 230 (1987), noted 17 Stetson L. Rev. 807 (1988), where it was held that a municipality could lawfully tie-in the provision of water service with the provision of electric service as to customers residing outside municipal limits so long as the municipality applied the policy uniformly to all potential out-of-city customers and the policy was supported by justifiable economic reasons.

[49] See Hutchinson v. City of Valdosta, 227 U.S. 303, 33 S.Ct. 290, 57 L.Ed. 520 (1913) (no violation of resident's Fourteenth Amendment rights found in city's requirement that resident connect to public sewer rather than use septic tank; so held despite evidence that appellant's house was in thinly settled area and was not a health hazard); Town of Ennis v. Stewart, 247 Mont. 355, 807 P.2d 179 (1991) (municipality could require by ordinance that all residents be connected to town water system); Rupp v. Grantsville City, 610 P.2d 338 (Utah 1980) (city could condition water service to residents on hook-up to municipal sewer system). But cf. City of Midway v. Midway Nursing & Convalescent Center, Inc., 230 Ga. 77, 195 S.E.2d 452 (1973) (customer could not be required to connect with city water system rather than extract his own groundwater where the groundwater was fit for human consumption). Much attention in the utility field has been concentrated on the development of additional sources of energy, such as the wind. See Prescott, Ridgelines and National Security Implications of Commercial Wind Energy Development in Vermont, 13 Vt. J. Envtl. L. 651 (2012); Note, Stifling the Wind: California Environmental Quality Act and Local Permitting, 38 Colum. J. Envtl. L. 163 (2013); Note, Second Wind: A Legal and Policy-based Evaluation of the Block Island Wind Farm and the Legislation That Saved It, 45 Conn. L. Rev. 1457 (2013); Note, A Right to Wind? Promoting Wind Energy by Limiting the Possibility of Nuisance Litigation, 3 Geo. Wash. J. Energy & Envtl. L. 256 (2012); Comment, You Don't Need a Weatherman to Know Which Way the Wind Blows: An Argument for Offshore Wind Development in the Gulf of Mexico, 50 Houston L. Rev. 899 (2013); Note, Windy City Heat: How Wind Energy Can Help Lower Illinois into the Future, 2012 U. Ill. J.L. Tech. & Policy 167. See also Note, The Future of Energy: Lunar Resource Management and the Common Heritage of Mankind, 24 Geo. Int'l Envtl. L. Rev. 221 (2012); Comment, The New Wave of Florida Energy: The Regulatory Path to Harnessing Marine Hydrokinetic Power, 34 Public Land & Resources L. Rev. 191 (2013).

Chapter 18

LOCAL CONTROL OF THE USE OF PROPERTY: ZONING AND RELATED METHODS

Analysis

§ 18.1 Private and Public Nuisance

Control over, and planning of, the uses made of land within a community are among the chief functions of local government. Prior to the twentieth century, the tort action of nuisance had already developed as one means of land-use control; and this remedy for bothersome uses of property still exists. A private nuisance action will lie where defendant's unreasonable use of his property interferes, unreasonably and substantially, with the reasonable use and enjoyment of plaintiff's real property, as where lights, noise, dust, etc. from defendant's premises disturb plaintiff's dwelling or business. The possible remedies include monetary damages and/or an injunction against the continuance of the nuisance.[1] Public nuisance has a dual life: *Criminal* liability is possible, since by definition this type of nuisance involves violation of some criminal statute. And public authorities may take action to have the public nuisance abated or enjoined. But without regard to whether or not public officials have acted, a private individual may seek a *tort* remedy for public nuisance if that individual can show violation of a criminal statute, an interference with a "public right" (or, as some modern cases say, with the "general

[1] See Prosser & Keeton, Law of Torts 637–43 (5th ed. 1984). See generally 1 Antieau, Municipal Corporation Law §§ 6.–04–.20 (1998). Cities with constitutional home rule are granted powers by the state constitutions to define and abate public nuisances, while other municipalities frequently have such power under state statutes. See Antieau, *supra*, §§ 6.08–.09. When a city legislative body declares certain activities or structures nuisances, the courts normally accept that declaration unless it is clearly arbitrary or unreasonable. See Horbach v. Butler, 135 Neb. 394, 281 N.W. 804 (1938) (city council finding is conclusive unless power abused); Boden v. City of Milwaukee, 8 Wis.2d 318, 99 N.W.2d 156 (1959). And where the state gives localities power over nuisances, this usually includes the power to abate, as by demolition, a nuisance—if adequate notice, and opportunity to rectify the condition, are given the owner. See Antieau, *supra*, §§ 6.13–.20. On enjoining *threatened* nuisances, see Annots., Right to Enjoin Threatened or Anticipated Nuisances, 55 A.L.R. 880 (1928); 32 A.L.R. 724 (1924); 26 A.L.R. 937 (1923); 7 A.L.R. 749 (1920).

public"—or at least with "a considerable number of people"), and some special injury to plaintiff, differing in kind (not just in degree) from the injury to the public.[2] Again, the chief remedies are damages and/or an injunction.[3]

---

[2] See Reynolds, Public Nuisance: A Crime in Tort Law, 31 Okl.L.Rev. 318 (1978). Also sometimes included as elements of the tort action are a substantial interference with plaintiff (not necessarily with plaintiff's use of his real property) and some basis of liability: intent, negligence, or strict liability (such as for an abnormally dangerous activity). See *id.* at 337–42. See generally Prosser, Private Action for Public Nuisance, 52 Va.L.Rev. 997 (1966). The differences between public and private nuisance are well summarized in Comment, "Feed the Hungry, but Not on Our Block,"—Armory Park Neighborhood Association v. Episcopal Community Services in Arizona, 28 Ariz. L. Rev. 121, 123 (1986). Cf. People ex rel. Gallo v. Acuna, 14 Cal.4th 1090, 60 Cal.Rptr.2d 277, 929 P.2d 596 (1997) ("community aspect" of public nuisance said to distinguish it from its cousin private nuisance; court upholds preliminary injunction against alleged criminal street gang members appearing in public with any other gang member). See generally Antolini, Modernizing Public Nuisance: Solving the Paradox of the Special Injury Rule, 28 Ecology L.Q. 755 (2001). See also the classic article on nuisance by Calabresi & Melamed, Property Rules, Liability Rules, and Inalienability: One View of the Cathedral, 85 Harv. L. Rev. 1089 (1972), discussed in Godsil, Viewing the Cathedral from Behind the Color Line: Property Rules, Liability Rules, and Environmental Racism, 53 Emory L.J. 1807, 1810–11 (2004). As to the differences between nuisance tort claims and trespass tort claims, see Anderson, Subsurface "Trespass": A Man's Subsurface Is Not His Castle, 49 Washburn L.J. 247 (2010), noting, at 248, that nuisance law has the desirable flexibility to resolve many land-use cases but that "when one intentionally injects a substance" into a neighbor's property, "money damages should be recoverable for any actual and substantial damage caused without having to engage in the uncertainty of balancing whether the gravity of harm to the landowner outweighs the utility of the defendant's conduct," as is often done in private nuisance law, and that trespass may thus be a more appropriate remedy.

In the *tort* action for nuisance (that is, the *private* nuisance action), it is sometimes emphasized that there must be either evidence of physical injury to property or of interference with use and enjoyment of property. See Smith v. Kansas Gas Service Co., 285 Kan. 33, 169 P.3d 1052 (2007) (to maintain tort action for nuisance, plaintiff must establish an interference with owner's use and enjoyment of the property which is separate and distinct from claim that property's value has diminished because of marketplace fear or stigma).

There is a trend toward eliminating from public nuisance the traditional requirement of violation of some criminal (*i.e.*, penal) law. Restatement (Second) of Torts § 821B (1977) lists violation of a criminal law as merely one of several factors to be assessed in determining the unreasonableness of the conduct that is a requisite for liability, and the defendant need not be found criminally responsible. *Id.* & Comment d, at 89 (1977). See Armory Park Neighborhood Ass'n v. Episcopal Community Services, 148 Ariz. 1, 712 P.2d 914 (1985) (regardless of presence of criminal statute, liability for public nuisance depends on whether conduct is unreasonable; plaintiff's complaint, seeking injunction, should not be dismissed merely for failure to allege criminal violation). Compare Lange v. Minton, 303 Or. 484, 738 P.2d 576 (1987) (ordinance declaring it a public nuisance to keep an animal found running at large held to imply some element of fault—knowledge, consent, willingness, or negligence—on part of animal's keeper).

[3] See Prosser & Keeton, *supra* note 1, at 643–52. Public nuisance statutes generally give government officials broad powers to shut down public nuisances even if private individuals have not filed criminal complaints or tort actions. See Mackey v. State ex rel. Harris, 495 P.2d 105 (Okl.1972). On the use of nuisance closure laws to abate a First Amendment use of property, see Arcara v. Cloud Books, Inc., 478 U.S. 697, 106 S.Ct. 3172, 92 L.Ed.2d 568 (1986), on remand 68 N.Y.2d 553, 510 N.Y.S.2d 844, 503 N.E.2d 492 (1986) (adult bookstore could be closed for one year due to illicit sexual activities on the premises). On a government's power to abate a public nuisance without committing a compensable "taking" of property, see Bearden v. City of Tulsa, 821 P.2d 394 (Okl. App. 1991) (where removal of property was in connection with abatement of public nuisance, no inverse condemnational taking found). See generally on the validity of forfeitures to the government Bennis v. Michigan, 516 U.S. 442, 116 S.Ct. 994, 134 L.Ed.2d 68 (1996), upholding forfeiture of property used in connection with criminal activity and finding it not a compensable taking. Cf. Gold Vein Limited Liability Co. v. City of Cripple Creek, 973 P.2d 1286 (Colo.App. 1999) (city had authority to provide for abatement of public nuisance caused by dangerous buildings and to impose lien on property for sums expended). On the effect of governmental authorization on public nuisance status, see State ex rel. Village of Los Ranchos de Albuquerque v. City of Albuquerque, 119 N.M. 150, 889 P.2d 185 (N.M. 1994) (if a public works project, such as a bridge, is in existence and poses a present nuisance, due authorization is a qualified defense; but if project has yet to be completed and is challenged as an anticipatory nuisance, due authorization is complete defense). On the process for administering public nuisance law, see generally Comment, Due Process and Local Administrative Hearings Regulating Public Nuisances: Analysis and Reform, 43 St. Mary's L.J. 619 (2012). See also Note, Climate Change and Public Nuisance Law: *AEP v. Connecticut* and Its Implications for

But nuisance has obvious limitations as a land-use control device: The private nuisance action depends entirely on the initiative of private citizens; and the public nuisance also will, as a practical matter, often not be curtailed unless action is taken, or at least complaint made, by some private individual. The very existence of a private nuisance depends on a balancing of the rights of the persons involved; and relief of an injunctive nature, particularly as to private nuisance, always involves a further "balancing of the equities" to determine whether this extreme remedy is justified.[4] In one celebrated modern case, the developer of a retirement community obtained an injunction against continuance of a cattle feedlot (which had been in existence before the retirement community)—but the injunction was conditioned on the plaintiff's indemnifying defendant-feedlot for the reasonable cost of moving or shutting-down the

---

State Common Law Actions, 36 Wm. & Mary Envtl. L. & Pol'y Rev. 865 (2012), noting Connecticut v. American Elec. Power Co., 582 F.3d 309 (2d Cir. 2009), rev'd, 564 U.S. ___, 131 S.Ct. 2527, 180 L.Ed.2d 435 (2011).

[4] See, for instance, the cases cited in Annot., Children's Playground as Nuisance, 32 A.L.R.3d 1127 (1970), many of which consider such factors as the amount of annoyance to neighboring property-owners from noise, dust, lights, etc. Courts have usually held or indicated that a total enjoining of a children's playground is unlikely to be granted; but an injunction may occasionally be drawn so as to eliminate or mitigate the particular annoyances of which complaint is made. See Kasala v. Kalispell Pee Wee Baseball League, 151 Mont. 109, 439 P.2d 65 (1968); Lieberman v. Saddle River, 37 N.J.Super. 62, 116 A.2d 809 (1955). On "balancing the equities" in nuisance cases, see generally Prosser & Keeton, note 1, at 630–32. On developing areas in which private nuisances might be found, see *e.g.,* Sowers v. Forest Hills Subdivision, 294 P.3d 427 (Nev. 2013) (residential wood turbine may be or become a nuisance due to improper or negligent manner in which it is conducted or due to its location); Alden, Declaring Solar Access Interference a Private Nuisance, 10 Temple Envtl. L. & Tech. J. 93 (1991); Note, The Role of Nuisance in the Developing Common Law of Hydraulic Fracturing, 41 Boston Coll. Envtl. Aff. L. Rev. 265 (2014); Annot., Computer as a Nuisance, 45 A.L.R. 4th 1212 (1986).

On the uses of nuisance law nowadays as a land-control tool, see Ellickson, Alternatives to Zoning: Covenants, Nuisance Rules and Fines as Land Use Controls, 40 U.Chi. L.Rev. 681, 719–24 (1973). On regulating the keeping of animals within municipal limits, and the use of municipal power to define and abate public nuisances as a means of exercising such power, see C.J.S. Municipal Corporations §§ 212–13 (1949). Cf. *Id.* § 214 (on use of police power to prevent animals from running at large), § 215 (on control over, and removal of, dead animals), § 216 (suppression of diseases of animals), § 217 (preventing cruelty to animals), § 218 (regulating possession of dogs), and § 219 (regulating the slaughtering of animals). Cf. Barnes v. Board of Adjustment of Bartlesville, 987 P.2d 430 (Okl.Civ.App. 1999) (Vietnamese pot-bellied pig found to be nuisance). A municipality may impose special restrictions on the ownership of pit bull dogs. See State v. Peters, 534 So.2d 760 (Fla.App.1988) (owners must maintain insurance or have other proof of financial responsibility). Under express power from the state, municipalities may even regulate the keeping and treatment of animals within a specified distance outside municipal boundaries. See State v. Rice, 158 N.C. 635, 74 S.E. 582 (1912) (within a quarter mile). On the use of public nuisance law to *protect* animals, see O'Keefe, Using Public Nuisance Law to Protect Wildlife, 6 Buffalo Envtl. L.J. 85 (1998). Cf. Hood River County v. Mazzara, 193 Or.App. 272, 89 P.3d 1195 (2004) (statute granting immunity to farmers in certain nuisance cases applied where dog that was guarding sheep barked for six hours; evidence indicated that dogs would protect herd by barking at predator, and thus dog's owner was following a legitimate and recommended farming practice). See also Klass, Bees, Trees, Preemption, and Nuisance: A New Path to Resolving Pesticide Land Use Disputes, 32 Ecology L.Q. 763 (2005). As to nuisance liability for wind farms and other wind energy projects, see Comment, Headwinds to a Clean Energy Future: Nuisance Suits Against Wind Energy Projects in the United States, 97 Cal. L. Rev. 1337 (2009); Comment, Social and Regulatory Control of Wind Energy—An Empirical Survey of Texas and Kansas, 4 Tex. J. Oil, Gas & Energy L. 89 (2008–09); Comment, A Don Quixote Tale of Modern Renewable Energy: Counties and Municipalities Fight to Ban Commercial Wind Power Across the United States, 79 UMKC L. Rev. 717 (2011). As to climate-change litigation, see generally Comment, Preserving Legal Avenues for Climate Justice in Florida Post-*American Electric Power*, 64 U. Fla. L. Rev. 295 (2012), discussing American Elec. Power Co. v. Connecticut (AEP), 564 U.S. ___, 131 S.Ct. 2527, 180 L.Ed.2d 435 (2011), which held that the Federal Clean Air Act and the regulatory actions it authorizes displace any *federal* common-law right to seek abatement of fired power plants, thus foreclosing the use of federal common-law rights of action in climate-change litigation but leaving unanswered whether the Clean Air Act also displaces *state* common-law tort actions. This suggests that state-based public nuisance could play a part in future climate-change litigation. See *id.* at 2537. But the Court indicates a preference for confining climate-change litigation to agency- and regulatory-focused actions, as opposed to common-law tort actions. *Id.* at 2540.

operation.[5] Finally, nuisance is at best a piecemeal remedy to particular problems, not a method by which comprehensive planning of land uses can be achieved.

§ 18.2 Zoning—Pre-1926 Development

Some device for controlling land uses on a comprehensive, planned, area-wide basis was needed; and the answer developed for this need was zoning: an exercise of the police power by which the nature and extent of the use of land is regulated—and sometimes also the architectural and structural requirements for buildings erected on the land.[6] The development of zoning laws and their varied forms and application are the subjects of a rich literature.[7] While some laws limiting the types of buildings that could be erected

---

[5] Spur Industries, Inc. v. Del E. Webb Development Co., 108 Ariz. 178, 494 P.2d 700 (1972), noted 26 Vand.L.Rev. 193 (1973). See Comment, Indemnification of a Nuisance Defendant for Costs Incurred by Complying With an Injunction, 15 Ariz. L.Rev. 1004 (1973); Recent-Case Note, Remedies—Enjoining a Nuisance—Damages to the Defendant as a Condition of Granting the Injunction, 38 Mo.L.Rev. 135 (1973); Note, Land Use and Environmental Policy: Litigation of Nuisances As a Land Use Control: The Spur Industries Case, 26 Okla.L.Rev. 583 (1973); Annot., Nuisance: Right of One Compelled to Discontinue Business or Activity Constituting Nuisance to Indemnity from Successful Plaintiff, 53 A.L.R.3d 873 (1973). For an up-date on the *Spur Industries* case, see Reynolds, Of Time and Feedlots: The Effect of *Spur Industries* on Nuisance Law, 41 Wash. U.J. Urban & Contemp. L. 75 (1992). Compare Payne v. Skaar, 127 Idaho 341, 900 P.2d 1352 (1995) (court not required to grant permanent injunction against feedlot which had been declared private nuisance where complaining citizens did not show that only total closure or relocation would abate nuisance and entirely closing feedlot would be momentous invasion of owner's property rights). Cf. Boomer v. Atlantic Cement Co., 26 N.Y.2d 219, 309 N.Y.S.2d 312, 257 N.E.2d 870 (1970) (injunction would be vacated on payment by defendant of permanent damages to plaintiffs). As to the significance of plaintiff's having "moved to" an existing nuisance, see Annot., "Coming to Nuisance" as a Defense or Estoppel, 42 A.L.R.3d 344 (1972). See generally Prosser & Keeton, *supra* note 1, at 634; 58 Am.Jur.2d Nuisances §§ 216–17 (1971). As to aesthetics in nuisance law, see Section 118, note 51, para. 3.

[6] See 1A Antieau, Municipal Corporation Law § 7.00 (1998). On what is regarded in the law as a "land use decision," see Westside Neighborhood Quality Project, Inc. v. School Dist. 4J Bd. of Directors, 58 Or.App. 154, 647 P.2d 962 (1982), review denied 294 Or. 78, 653 P.2d 999 (1982) (decision to close elementary school not a "land use decision" and thus not reviewable by state's Land Use Board of Appeals). Compare Heritage Enterprises v. City of Corvallis, 300 Or. 168, 708 P.2d 601 (1985) (determination of whether a proposed annexation is in accord with comprehensive plans is "land use decision"): 1000 Friends of Oregon v. Wasco County Court, 299 Or. 344, 703 P.2d 207 (1985) (incorporation of new city is "land use decision").

On past developments, and probable future developments, in the zoning and planning field, see generally Planning and Zoning Symposium Part I, 32 Urban Law. 447–611 (2000) & Planning and Zoning Symposium Part II, 32 Urban Law. 939–1038 (2000). On model laws for land use planning and regulation, see Mandelker, Model Legislation for Land Use Decisions, 35 Urban Law. 635 (2003), reviewing American Planning Association, Growing Smart Legislative Guidebook: Model Statutes for Planning and Management of Change 10–3 (Stuart Meck ed. 2002). See also Sax, Land Use Regulation: Time to Think About Fairness, 50 Nat. Resources J. 455 (2010).

On appropriate pedagogy in land-use courses, see Salkin & Nolan, Practically Grounded: Convergence of Land Use Law Pedagogy and Best Practices, 60 J. Legal Educ. 519 (2011), concluding that today "the traditional casebook method is not sufficient to fully prepare law students for the interdisciplinary and multi-faceted practice of land use and community development law."

[7] See Anderson, American Law of Zoning (5 vols. 3d ed. 1986 & 4th ed. 1995–97); Freilich & Stuhler, The Land Use Awakening (American Bar Ass'n 1981) (series of articles originally published in The Urban Lawyer); Metzenbaum, Law of Zoning (3 vols. 2d ed. 1955); Rathkopf, The Law of Zoning & Planning (5 vols. 4th ed. 1995); Williams, American Land Planning Law (6 vols. 1985–89, with annual supps.); Yokley, Zoning Law and Practice (6 vols. plus Table & Index 1980); Stalcup & Williams, Zoning, 24 Sw.L.J. 41 (1970). As to land-use terms and definitions, see Endres, Bioenergy, Resource Scarcity and the Rising Importance of Land Use Definitions, 88 North Dak. L. Rev. 559 (2012). An excellent analysis of zoning in operation is Babcock, The Zoning Game—Municipal Practices & Policies (U. of Wisconsin Press 1969). See also Mandelker, The Zoning Dilemma (1971); Peterson & McCarthy, Handling Zoning and Land Use Litigations: A Practical Guide, (Michie Co. 1982). A valuable historical source is Bassett, Zoning: The Laws, Administration and Court Decisions During the First Twenty Years (Russell Sage Foundation 1936). For a discussion of land-use patterns in pre-zoning days, see Cappel, A Walk Along Willow: Patterns of Land Use Coordination in Pre-Zoning New Haven (1870–1926), 101 Yale L.J. 617 (1991). For an entertaining account of an early case invalidating zoning actions

on particular pieces of land appeared as early as the 1600's, modern American zoning is usually said to have started with an ordinance passed in 1916 by New York City.[8] It resembled much of the zoning still found today in that it was comprehensive (*i.e.*, it covered all the city except areas specifically designated as unrestricted); it classified various uses of property (residential, commercial, etc.) and created zones for these uses; and it also included restrictions on the height and bulk of structures. Some early attempts at zoning relied not on the police power, but on the power of eminent domain: certain uses would be forbidden as to certain properties upon the payment of compensation to the owners of those properties, the theory being that some of their rights

---

of a municipality, see Power, Pyrrhic Victory: Daniel Goldman's Defeat of Zoning in the Maryland Court of Appeals, 82 Md. Hist. Mag. 275 (Winter, 1987). An analysis of where and how the modern concept of zoning developed is Kosman, Toward an Inclusionary Jurisprudence: A Reconceptualization of Zoning, 43 Catholic U.L. Rev. 59 (1993). For a treatment of land-use controls as collective property rights, see Fischel, The Economics of Zoning Laws: A Property Rights Approach to American Land Use Controls (John Hopkins Univ. Press 1987), reviewed 22 Urban Law. 345 (1990). On land-use controls in general, see Mandelker, Land Use Law (5th ed. 2003); Moss (ed.), Land Use Controls in the United States (Natural Resources Defense Council, Inc. 1977). See also Burchell & Listokin, Future Land Use (Center for Urban Policy Research 1975) (collection of papers); Symposium; Land Use in the 21st Century: The New Frontier for Environmental Law, 23 Wm. & M. Envtl. L. & Pol'y R. 705–855 (1999). Other outstanding books in the land-use area include: Juergensmeyer & Roberts, Hornbook on Land Use Planning & Development Regulation Law (3d ed. 2013); Mandelker, Payne, Salsich & Stroud, Planning and Control of Land Development: Cases and Materials (6th ed. LexisNexis 2005); Nolon & Salkin, Land Use in a Nutshell (2006). See generally Glicksman & Coggins, Modern Public Land Law in a Nutshell (3d ed. 2006); Salkin, Trends in Land Use Law from A to Z: Adult Uses to Zoning (American Bar Ass'n Section of State and Local Government Law 2002). For a comparison of trends in the United States land law with those in other countries, see Nolon, Comparative Land Use Law: Patterns of Sustainability, 37 Urban Law. 807 (2005). See also Lewyn, Land Use Regulation: It Just Gets Worse, 2 U. Baltimore J. Land & Development 1 (2012), reviewing Talen, City Rules: How Regulations Affect Urban Form (2011); Tarlock, Land Use Regulation: The Weak Link in Environmental Protection, 82 Wash. L. Rev. 651 (2007).

[8] Lefcoe, An Introduction to American Land Law 218–19 (1974) (with summary of the New York ordinance). See Juergensmeyer & Roberts, Land Use Planning & Control Law 42 (1998). See generally Hagman & Juergensmeyer, Urban Planning & Land Development Control Law (2d ed. 1986). Even before the New York ordinance (which was upheld in Lincoln Trust Co. v. Williams Building Corp., 229 N.Y. 313, 128 N.E. 209 (1920), and which remains on the books today in somewhat amended form), height restrictions on buildings had been imposed by some localities; and the constitutionality of such a restriction was upheld in Welch v. Swasey, 214 U.S. 91, 29 S.Ct. 567, 53 L.Ed. 923 (1909). And one authority reports that a system similar to modern zoning had been initiated in Germany in the late 1800's. Lefcoe, *supra* at 218. On the history of American zoning, see generally Toll, Zoned American (1969). See also Maltbie, The Legal Background of Zoning, 22 Conn.B.J. 2 (1948). For a study of the impact of zoning on placement of social activities, see Willhelm, Urban Zoning and Land-Use Theory (Free Press of Glencoe 1962). One major American city—Houston, Texas—developed with hardly any zoning restrictions, and some feel that its experience proves that such restrictions are neither necessary nor desirable. See Siegan, Land Use Without Zoning (Heath & Co. 1972), particularly Ch. 2. In 1993, Houston voters, for the third time in 45 years, rejected a proposed zoning law, thus retaining Houston's distinction as the nation's largest city without zoning. See generally Comment, Land Use Regulation in Houston Contradicts the City's Free Market Reputation, 34 Envtl. L. Rep. News & Analysis 10003 (2004).

Height restrictions on buildings, which were among the first types of zoning laws, have once again become popular in recent times, in an effort to alleviate the congestion, noise, and darkness attributed to the proliferation of skyscrapers in many cities. See "Outlawing the Modern Skyscraper," Time, July 22, 1985, at 56, noting the rules governing development in downtown San Francisco. On early height restrictions, see also Power, High Society: The Building Height Limitation on Baltimore's Mt. Vernon Place, 79 Md. Hist. Mag. 197 (Fall, 1984). On the unusual history of height restrictions in Philadelphia (where there was long an unwritten agreement that no structure should be higher than the statue of William Penn atop City Hall—an agreement that was finally breached in 1986), see Gerber, "No-Law" Urban Height Restrictions: A Philadelphia Story, 38 Urban Law. 111 (2006). As to the development of land-use controls in New York, see Salkin & Bacher, Modernization of New York's Land Use Laws Continues to Meet Growing Challenges of Sustainability, 29 Pace L. Rev. 563 (2009). See generally Anderson, Zoning and Land Use, 64 SMU L. Rev. 617 (2011); Iovine, Zoning Laws Grow Up, N.Y. Times, Jan 19, 2012, at D6, stating that in New York City, "zoning has assumed a more activist role than ever before."

were being "taken." Such zoning is still possible, and has been used and upheld in Missouri;[9] but it has the obvious practical difficulty of being expensive to the zoning community. Thus, more and more communities in the early decades of the 20th century began experimenting with zoning as an exercise of the *police power*: legislative restrictions imposed on use and development of property, with no compensation being paid in return for the restriction.

The validity of such zoning remained in doubt until 1926. Up to that time, the main zoning issue dealt with by the U.S. Supreme Court was that of whether or not certain uses of property—as for a billboard, a home for older persons, etc.—could be made dependent on the consent of neighboring property-owners. Gradually, the law as to this problem has developed: imposition of particular zoning restrictions cannot be made to depend on the consent of neighbors, as this is an unlawful delegation of governmental authority.[10] This is subject to two qualifications: (1) Adoption or amendment of zoning ordinances may validly require, as a prerequisite to the legislative action, the consent of a designated percentage of near-by property owners.[11] (2) Many courts—perhaps most that have ruled on the question in recent times—have upheld zoning ordinances that permit the *lifting* of restrictions if the consent of a designated percentage of neighbors is obtained.[12]

---

[9] See Kansas City v. Kindle, 446 S.W.2d 807 (Mo.1969). See generally 1A Antieau, Municipal Corporation Law § 7.03 (1998). See also Berger, A Policy Analysis of the Taking Problem, 49 N.Y.U.L.Rev. 165 (1974).

[10] See Washington ex rel. Seattle Title Trust Co. v. Roberge, 278 U.S. 116, 49 S.Ct. 50, 73 L.Ed. 210 (1928) (ordinance prohibiting old people's homes in certain areas unless neighbors consented; invalidated); Marta v. Sullivan, 248 A.2d 608 (Del.1968) appeal after remand 256 A.2d 736 (apartments permitted in neighborhood only if 75% of residents within radius of one-eighth of a mile approved; invalidated); State ex rel. Foster v. City of Minneapolis, 255 Minn. 249, 97 N.W.2d 273 (1959); Concordia Collegiate Institute v. Miller, 301 N.Y. 189, 93 N.E.2d 632 (1950); Roman Catholic Archbishop v. Baker, 140 Or. 600, 15 P.2d 391 (1932). Cf. Eubank v. Richmond, 226 U.S. 137, 33 S.Ct. 76, 57 L.Ed. 156 (1912) (invalidating delegation of authority to neighbors to establish "setback" line from street).

[11] See City of Stockton v. Frisbie & Latta, 93 Cal.App. 277, 270 P. 270 (Dist.Ct. 1928); Building Inspector v. Stoklosa, 250 Mass. 52, 145 N.E. 262 (1924); O'Brien v. City of St. Paul, 285 Minn. 378, 173 N.W.2d 462 (1969).

[12] Thomas Cusack Co. v. Chicago, 242 U.S. 526, 37 S.Ct. 190, 61 L.Ed. 472 (1917) (signs prohibited in residential neighborhoods unless neighbors consented); Downey v. Sioux City, 208 Iowa 1273, 227 N.W. 125 (1929); East Lansing v. Smith, 277 Mich. 495, 269 N.W. 573 (1936); State ex rel. Standard Oil Co. v. Combs, 129 Ohio St. 251, 194 N.E. 875 (1935). Cf. Gorieb v. Fox, 274 U.S. 603, 47 S.Ct. 675, 71 L.Ed. 1228 (1927) (setback provision that house could be no closer to street than the average of 60% of houses on a block; upheld). But cf. Drovers Trust & Savings Bank v. City of Chicago, 16 Ill.2d 589, 158 N.E.2d 620 (1959) (consent provisions in zoning ordinances may be valid, but particular provision struck down as unreasonable). The *Cusack* case, *supra*, was distinguished in the *Roberge* case, *supra* note 10, on the ground that *Cusack* dealt with signs, which may be considered quasi-nuisances and as to which greater restrictions are thus allowed. See Havinghurst, Property Owners' Consent Provisions in Zoning Ordinances, 36 W.Va. L.Q. 175 (1930). Another frequently encountered type of provision in zoning laws stipulates that where a proposed amendment is protested (usually through signing a petition) by a designated percentage of the property owners in the affected area (or within a certain distance of that area), the amendment can only be adopted by a specified supermajority vote (usually three-fourths) of the city governing body. Such provisions have nearly always been held valid. See Annot., Zoning: Validity and Construction of Provisions of Zoning Statute or Ordinance Regarding Protest by Neighboring Property Owners, 7 A.L.R.4th 732 (1981).

Because zoning is a legislative function, zoning laws are presumed constitutional and otherwise valid. See 1 Rathkopf, The Law of Zoning and Planning § 5.02 (1988). But it has been noted that zoning laws are, in practice, often subjected to intense judicial review. See Mandelker & Tralock, Shifting the Presumption of Constitutionality in Land-Use Law, 24 Urban Law. 1 (1992).

§ 18.3 Zoning—Development from 1926 Until Today

In the celebrated 1926 case of *Village of Euclid v. Ambler Realty Co.*, the U.S. Supreme Court upheld zoning as a potentially constitutional exercise of the police power.[13] Specifically, the Court found no violation of due process in reasonable restrictions on the use of land; the system there upheld was of the type that has come to be called "Euclidean zoning": the community was divided into a geometric pattern of use districts (usually of three kinds: residential, commercial, and industrial or unrestricted), with all land being placed in one of the categories. This early type of zoning was usually also cumulative: only the highest use was exclusive, and residential use was considered the highest. Thus, in a residential zone, no other uses would be permitted. But in the "loweruse" zones, the "higher" uses would also be allowed—a residence could, for instance, be established in a commercial or an industrial zone.

In a 1928 case, the Supreme Court invalidated a zoning ordinance as applied to a particular parcel of land because it had the result of making part of the parcel of little possible value and because the public good was found not to be promoted by this particular zoning.[14] This case seemed to indicate that the Court would readily and carefully scrutinize challenged zoning laws. But the Court then fell silent on the subject; and with scarcely any exceptions,[15] it did not speak again on the matter until cases in

---

[13] 272 U.S. 365, 47 S.Ct. 114, 71 L.Ed. 303 (1926), noted 40 Harv.L.Rev. 644 (1927), 25 Mich.L.Rev. 907 (1927), 13 Va. L.Rev. 321 (1927), 36 Yale L.J. 427 (1927). See Note, Zoning Texas Cities—Constitutionality of Comprehensive City Plan Ordinances, 5 Tex.L.Rev. 307 (1927). The Court may have been influenced toward the Village of Euclid ordinance by the brief filed by Alfred Bettman as Counsel for the National Conference on City Planning and various other groups that appeared in the case as *amici curiae*. The brief is reprinted in Bettman, City and Regional Planning Papers 157–93 (1946). A sidelight on the Court's deliberations in the *Euclid* case (which was argued to the Court twice before it was decided) appears in McCormack, A Law Clerk's Recollections, 46 Col.L.Rev. 710, 712 (1946) (Justice Sutherland changed his mind—and thus the decision). On the subsequent healthy growth of the municipality of Euclid, see 1 Metzenbaum, The Law of Zoning 60 (2d ed. 1955); Oyaski, Economic Erosion: The Case Against Urban Sprawl, 22 State & Local L. News, No. 3, at 5 (Spring, 1999) (discussing the development of Euclid and urging growth controls). On the place of the Village of Euclid case in modern law, see Wolf, Euclid at Threescore Years and Ten: Is This the Twilight of Environmental and Land-Use Regulation?, 30 U. Richmond L. Rev. 961 (1996) (part of a symposium on The Future of Environmental and Land-Use Regulation). See generally (in the same symposium) Haar, The Twilight of Land-Use Controls: A Paradigm Shift?, 30 U. Richmond L. Rev. 1011 (1996).

The *Euclid* case has continued to be recognized as an important landmark in the law of land use control. See Claeys, *Euclid* Lives? The Uneasy Legacy of Progressivism in Zoning, 73 Fordham L. Rev. 731 (2004) & response by Haar & Wolf, Yes, Thankfully, *Euclid* Lives, 73 Fordham L. Rev. 771 (2004); Symposium on the Seventy-Fifth Anniversary of *Village of Euclid v. Amber Realty Co.*, 51 Case W. Res. L. Rev. 593 (2001). It has been observed that the influence of the *Euclid* case has not always been beneficial. See Note, Divide and Sprawl, Decline and Fall: A Comparative Critique of Euclidean Zoning, 68 U. Pitt. L. Rev. 915 (2007). See generally Wolf, The Zoning of America: *Euclid v. Ambler* (University Press of Kansas 2008). See also Batchis, Enabling Urban Sprawl: Revisiting the Supreme Court's Seminal Zoning Decision—*Euclid v. Ambler* in the 21st Century, 17 Va. J. Soc. Pol'y & L. 373 (2010).

[14] Nectow v. City of Cambridge, 277 U.S. 183, 48 S.Ct. 447, 72 L.Ed. 842 (1928), noted 3 U.Cin.L.Rev. 319 (1928), 7 Tex. L.Rev. 157 (1928). See Comment, Zoning—Restrictions in Particular Cases Limited to a Reasonable Exercise of Power, 8 Bost. U.L.Rev. 330 (1928).

[15] A couple of cases touched on zoning-type issues: In Berman v. Parker, 348 U.S. 26, 75 S.Ct. 98, 99 L.Ed. 27 (1954), the Court upheld the use of eminent domain in connection with urban-renewal projects and spoke of the government's legitimate concern in making cities attractive. In Goldblatt v. Town of Hempstead, 369 U.S. 590, 82 S.Ct. 987, 8 L.Ed.2d 130 (1962), an ordinance prohibiting excavations below water level in the town, and requiring excavations already below that level to be filled, was upheld, despite the resulting near-exclusion of quarries from the area—but there was no showing the land involved lacked other profitable uses. On the Court's silence on land-control cases during this period, see Johnson, Constitutional Law and Community Planning, 20 Law & Contemp. Prob. 199 (1955).

the 1970's dealing largely with attempts to exclude multi-family dwellings and other "undesirable" uses from neighborhoods[16] or with the question of standing to object to zoning ordinances.[17]

But the basic principles had been established by the *Euclid* case and its predecessors: (1) Zoning can be constitutional if it is reasonable, and bears a reasonable relationship to community health, safety, morality, or general welfare.[18] (2) Zoning is a legislative, not a judicial, function.[19] Municipalities were thus free to engage in this form

---

A notable case of this period was Arverne Bay Construction Co. v. Thatcher, 278 N.Y. 222, 15 N.E.2d 587 (1938), in which a zoning amendment classifying plaintiff's vacant lot as residential was struck down as leaving him no profitable use for the property. Compare Consolidated Rock Products Co. v. City of Los Angeles, 57 Cal.2d 515, 20 Cal.Rptr. 638, 370 P.2d 342 (1962) appeal dism'd 371 U.S. 36, 83 S.Ct. 145, 9 L.Ed.2d 112, where the court upheld a zoning law that prohibited a rock quarry on plaintiff's property even though there was evidence the property had no appreciable value for other purposes. The U.S. Supreme Court dismissed the appeal for want of substantial federal question. See generally, discussing the *Goldblatt* and *Consolidated Rock* cases *supra*, Sax, Takings and the Police Power, 74 Yale L.J. 36, 42–44 (1964). See also Dodrill, In Defense of "Footnote 4": A Historical Analysis of the New Deal's Effect on Land Use Regulation in the U.S. Supreme Court, 72 Law & Contemp. Probs. 191 (2009).

[16] Moore v. City of East Cleveland, 431 U.S. 494, 97 S.Ct. 1932, 52 L.Ed.2d 531 (1977) (invalidating ordinance that limited occupancy of dwelling unit to a single family and narrowly defined "family"); Young v. American Mini Theatres, Inc., 427 U.S. 50, 96 S.Ct. 2440, 49 L.Ed.2d 310 (1976) reh. denied 429 U.S. 873, 97 S.Ct. 191, 50 L.Ed.2d 155 (upholding ordinance that confined "adult" movie theatres, bookstores, etc. to certain areas); Village of Belle Terre v. Boraas, 416 U.S. 1, 94 S.Ct. 1536, 39 L.Ed.2d 797 (1974) (upholding ordinance that limited occupancy of one-family dwellings to traditional family-groups or groups of not more than two unrelated persons). Cf. Village of Arlington Heights v. Metropolitan Housing Development Corp., 429 U.S. 252, 97 S.Ct. 555, 50 L.Ed.2d 450 (1977), saying that refusal to change zoning laws to permit low rent housing projects is unconstitutional only if there is proof the refusal is motivated by racial or other illegal discrimination. All these cases are discussed later in this chapter in connection with the purposes of zoning laws.

[17] Warth v. Seldin, 422 U.S. 490, 95 S.Ct. 2197, 45 L.Ed.2d 343 (1975), laying down the standards as to who may attack exclusionary zoning practices.

[18] City of New Orleans v. La Nasa, 230 La. 289, 88 So.2d 224 (1956); Town of Lexington v. Simeone, 334 Mass. 127, 134 N.E.2d 123 (1956); Fass v. City of Highland Park, 321 Mich. 156, 32 N.W.2d 375 (1948). See Krom v. City of Elmhurst, 8 Ill.2d 104, 133 N.E.2d 1 (1956); Granger v. City of Des Moines, 241 Iowa 1356, 44 N.W.2d 399 (1950); State ex rel. Cooper v. Cowan, 307 S.W.2d 676 (Mo.App.1957); Roselle v. Wright, 37 N.J.Super. 507, 117 A.2d 661 (1955) aff'd 21 N.J. 400, 122 A.2d 506. It is often added that zoning ordinances will be set aside only if arbitrary, confiscatory, or discriminatory. See Nelson v. County Council, 214 Md. 587, 136 A.2d 373 (1957); Buckley v. City of Bloomfield Hills, 343 Mich. 83, 72 N.W.2d 210 (1955); Fowler v. City of Hattiesburg, 196 So.2d 358 (Miss.1967). Usually, courts say that the reasonableness and general validity of zoning must be judged according to circumstances at the time of the decision. See Gust v. Township of Canton, 342 Mich. 436, 70 N.W.2d 772 (1955). But it has been recognized that a regulation that is reasonable at one time may subsequently become unreasonable due to changed circumstances—and may then be invalidated. See Skalko v. City of Sunnyvale, 14 Cal.2d 213, 93 P.2d 93 (1939); Miami Beach v. First Trust Co., 45 So.2d 681 (Fla.1949). And at least one opinion has said that a court, in judging the reasonableness of zoning, can look to the future and consider the betterment of an area that local officials, in enacting the zoning, are envisioning. Vickers v. Township Committee, 37 N.J. 232, 181 A.2d 129 (1962), cert. denied and appeal dism'd 371 U.S. 233, 83 S.Ct. 326, 9 L.Ed.2d 495. As to zoning for purposes of public health, see generally Wooten, McLaughlin, Chen, Fry, Mongeon & Graff, Zoning and Licensing to Regulate the Retail Environment and Achieve Public Health Goals, 5 Duke Forum for L. & Social Change 65–96 (2013). Compare as to trade regulations enacted for public health and/or other police-power purposes Section 23.2 *infra*.

[19] See City of Miami Beach v. Wiesen, 86 So.2d 442 (Fla.1956); Roll v. Troy, 370 Mich. 94, 120 N.W.2d 804 (1963). Thus, if a trial court attempts to tell a locality specifically how to zone, the decision is likely to be reversed on appeal. See Addis v. Smith, 225 Ga. 157, 166 S.E.2d 361 (1969). And if a statute purports to grant the judiciary the power to zone, it is likely to be ruled an unconstitutional delegation of legislative power. Coe v. City of Albuquerque, 76 N.M. 771, 418 P.2d 545 (1966). See Schwartz v. City of Flint, 426 Mich. 295, 395 N.W.2d 678 (1986) (procedures under which courts rezoned property after a zoning ordinance was found unconstitutional were ruled invalid as violative of the separation of judicial and legislative powers). Cf. Fiore v. Highland Park, 76 Ill.App.2d 62, 221 N.E.2d 323 (1966), cert. denied 393 U.S. 1084, 89 S.Ct. 867, 21 L.Ed.2d 776 (courts shouldn't usurp legislative function of making zoning classifications).

of land-use control—though only to the extent the state had delegated them this power, since the police power resides initially in the states and is not inherent in municipalities.[20] But delegations to municipal governments of the power to zone are today found, to varying extents, in all states. And certain corollaries, and rules of interpretation, have come to be generally accepted. For instance, when a particular use is allowed in a zone, accessory (or "incidental") uses are also allowed—*i.e.*, those that are customarily associated with the principal use and either necessary to it or at least commonly to be expected along with it.[21] Thus, tennis courts, swimming pools and comparable facilities for the use of a dwelling's occupants will be allowed in a residential zone—though these accessory uses may sometimes be excluded from the *front* yards of the dwellings.[22] Another generally accepted rule is that federal and state government

---

[20] See Boozer v. Johnson, 33 Del.Ch. 554, 98 A.2d 76 (1953); State v. Owen, 242 N.C. 525, 88 S.E.2d 832 (1955); Miller v. City of Memphis, 181 Tenn. 15, 178 S.W.2d 382 (1944). Thus, it has customarily been said that grants of power to zone will be strictly construed. See Livingston v. Davis, 243 Iowa 21, 50 N.W.2d 592 (1951). But like most such rules of strict construction, this is often now given little more than "lip service." See Himebaugh, Tie Goes to the Landowner: Ambiguous Zoning Ordinances and the Strict Construction Rule, 43 Urban Law. 1061 (2011), arguing that the strict construction rule, under which ambiguous zoning laws should be construed in favor of property owners, is in many courts overshadowed by judicial deference to zoning controls.

Of course, simply because a locality *does* possess the power to zone, it does not *have* to exercise such power. See Zopfi v. City of Wilmington, 273 N.C. 430, 160 S.E.2d 325 (1968). But zoning quickly gained in popularity after the *Village of Euclid* case, *supra* note 13, and it is said that by the late 1920's, over 800 municipalities—and 58 of the 68 cities over 100,000 in population—were zoned. Lefcoe, An Introduction to American Land Law 219 (1974).

On model state legislation on zoning, see Babcock, Krasnowiecki & McBride, The Model State Statute, 114 U.Pa.L.Rev. 140 (1965). For discussion of the typical state zoning enabling statute and proposed changes to such legislation, see Babcock, The Zoning Game 160–66 (1966); Liebmann, The Modernization of Zoning: Enabling Act Revision as a Means to Reform, 23 Urban Law. 1 (1991). For an example of revision of a state zoning enabling act, see Chase, Primer on the New Zoning Enabling Act, 26 Suffolk U.L. Rev. 333 (1992), discussing the law enacted in Rhode Island in 1991.

[21] Town of Bloomfield v. Parizot, 88 N.J.Super. 181, 211 A.2d 230 (1965); State v. Mair, 39 N.J.Super. 18, 120 A.2d 487 (1956) (owner used part of premises for clinical laboratory, leased the rest for residential purposes; laboratory not accessory to residence); Wiley v. County of Hanover, 209 Va. 153, 163 S.E.2d 160 (1968). See Town of Needham v. Winslow Nurseries, 330 Mass. 95, 111 N.E.2d 453 (1953) (accessory use is dependent on or pertains to the main use). Cf. Town of Alta v. Ben Hame Corp., 836 P.2d 797 (Utah App.1992) (commercial lodging facility held not necessary to main residential use). See generally Annot., Zoning: What Constitutes "Incidental" or "Accessory" Use of Property Zoned, and Primarily Used, for Business or Commercial Purposes, 60 A.L.R. 4th 907 (1988). As to "accessory dwelling units" (often called "ADU") that are often permitted in residential zones, see Brinig & Garnett, Room of One's Own? Accessory Dwelling Unit Reforms and Local Parochialism, 45 Urban Law. 519 (2013). See also Anderson v. Provo City Corp., 205 UT 5, 108 P.3d 701 (2005) (ordinance governing residential area near university allowed only those homeowners who resided in their homes to rent out "accessory" apartments; upheld as reasonably necessary to protect city's justifiable and legitimate interest in preserving single-family residential character of neighborhoods).

[22] See Hardy v. Calhoun, 383 S.W.2d 652 (Tex.Civ.App.1964) (private tennis court); Thomas v. Zoning Board, 241 S.W.2d 955 (Tex.Civ.App.1951) (private swimming pool). On the validity of restrictions on locating tennis courts and comparable facilities in front yards, see Town of Atherton v. Templeton, 198 Cal.App.2d 146, 17 Cal.Rptr. 680 (Dist.Ct.1961), upholding such a restriction. See generally Schindler, Banning Lawns, 82 Geo. Wash. L. Rev. 394 (2014); Annot., Application of Zoning Regulations to Golf Courses, Swimming Pools, Tennis Courts, or the Like, 32 A.L.R.3d 424 (1970). See also Annot., Statutes, Ordinances, or Regulations Relating to Private Residential Swimming Pools, 92 A.L.R.2d 1283 (1963); Annot., Construction and Application of Provision of Zoning Ordinance Which Permits Use for Accessory or Incidental Purposes, 150 A.L.R. 494 (1944). See also Friends of Eugene v. City of Eugene, 196 Or.App. 771, 103 P.3d 643 (2004) (ordinance allowing hospitals in residential zone was inconsistent with city's comprehensive plan; hospital might qualify as "auxiliary" to residential use in some circumstances, but nothing in ordinance ensured that proposed hospital would qualify as such use); City of Woodinville v. Northshore United Church of Christ, 139 Wash.App. 639, 162 P.3d 427 (2007) (permanent homelessness encampment was not a permissible accessory use of church

enjoy exemption from municipal zoning laws, while units of local government enjoy such immunity only as to their governmental (not their proprietary) functions.[23] Thus, public

---

property under city zoning code, as use was not incidental to a residence and was not an accessory use inside a church building).

Private garages are generally considered accessory to residential premises. Olson v. Zoning Board of Appeal, 324 Mass. 57, 84 N.E.2d 544 (1949); Schack v. Trimble, 28 N.J. 40, 145 A.2d 1 (1958) (even though garage was on adjacent lot). Cf. People v. Firestone, 48 Misc.2d 480, 265 N.Y.S.2d 179 (1965) (parking of school buses, but not repair thereof, was accessory use to a private school). But use of a garage in a residential neighborhood for commercial vehicles or for commercial purposes is not an accessory use. See Piper v. Moore, 163 Kan. 565, 183 P.2d 965 (1947); Borough of Northvale v. Blundo, 85 N.J.Super. 56, 203 A.2d 721 (1964) (commercial vehicles). Compare Smith v. Board of County Comm'rs, 137 N.M. 280, 110 P.3d 496 (2005) (amateur radio towers held incidental to residential use).

[23] Federal immunity unless Congress consents: United States v. Chester, 144 F.2d 415 (3d Cir.1944); Ann Arbor Township v. United States, 93 F.Supp. 341 (E.D.Mich.1950). State immunity unless otherwise provided by statute: State ex rel. Ohio Turnpike Commission v. Allen, 158 Ohio St. 168, 107 N.E.2d 345 (1952), cert. denied 344 U.S. 865, 73 S.Ct. 107, 97 L.Ed. 671; Rutgers, The State University v. Piluso, 60 N.J. 142, 286 A.2d 697 (1972) (state university); Charleston v. Southeastern Construction Co., 134 W.Va. 666, 64 S.E.2d 676 (1950) (state office building). See Note, Municipal Power to Regulate Building Construction and Land Use by Other State Agencies, 49 Minn.L.Rev. 284 (1964). Cf. State v. City of Seattle, 94 Wn.2d 162, 615 P.2d 461 (1980) (city ordinance allowing board to designate historic sites could not constitutionally be applied to state-owned structures). Counties, townships, and comparable units immune from municipal zoning unless statute provides otherwise: County of Los Angeles v. City of Los Angeles, 212 Cal.App.2d 160, 28 Cal.Rptr. 32 (Dist.Ct.1963); Appelbaum v. Saint Louis County, 451 S.W.2d 107 (Mo.1970) (county incinerator and landfill operation immune); Opinion of the Justices, 113 N.H. 217, 304 A.2d 872 (1973) (county courthouse immune); Green County v. City of Monroe, 3 Wis.2d 196, 87 N.W.2d 827 (1958) (city could not restrict building of county jail—jail is governmental function). There is some authority that counties enjoy the immunity only as to their governmental operations, not their proprietary. See Jefferson County v. City of Birmingham, 256 Ala. 436, 55 So.2d 196 (1951) (operation of sewage disposal plant by county was proprietary and thus subject to city zoning); County of Tompkins v. Powers, 43 Misc.2d 736, 252 N.Y.S.2d 206 (1964) (highway maintenance is governmental and thus not subject to local zoning). Cf. Sherman v. Town of Brentwood, 112 N.H. 122, 290 A.2d 47 (1972) (possible merit in argument of county hospital's immunity from local zoning, but issue found moot and not ruled on here). Governmental immunity from zoning laws generally does not continue to attach once a property is conveyed to a non-governmental owner. See Pima County v. Clear Channel Outdoor, Inc., 212 Ariz. 48, 127 P.3d 64 (App. 2006) (state's governmental function exemption from local zoning and building regulations did not transfer to outdoor advertising company when state transferred real property to it as just compensation in a condemnation action; county zoning regulation thus applied).

One local government is not, in its governmental activities, subject to the zoning of another local government: City of Scottsdale v. Municipal Court, 90 Ariz. 393, 368 P.2d 637 (1962) (sewage disposal plant; strong dissent); City of Bloomfield v. Davis County Community School District, 254 Iowa 900, 119 N.W.2d 909 (1963) (school district's gasoline storage tank and pump); Village of Larchmont v. Town of Mamaroneck, 208 App.Div. 812, 203 N.Y.S. 957 (1924), aff'd as modified per curiam 239 N.Y. 551, 147 N.E. 191 (village water works). But one local government may be subject to the zoning of another locality where the former is acting in its proprietary capacity. City of Treasure Island v. Decker, 174 So.2d 756 (Fla.App.1965) (toll gate on causeway). Cf. Wilmette Park Dist. v. Village of Wilmette, 112 Ill.2d 6, 96 Ill.Dec. 77, 490 N.E.2d 1282 (1986) (park district held not immune from village's zoning laws regarding the kind of lighting permitted, since there was no clear statutory immunity). These are the rules usually applied to one municipality acting within another, or to a school district or other special function district acting within a municipality. Some authorities seem willing, however, to grant *complete* immunity from zoning laws to any such local government acting within another's territory. See People ex rel. Scott v. North Shore Sanitary District, 132 Ill.App.2d 854, 270 N.E.2d 133 (1971) (sanitary district not subject to city zoning); Aviation Services v. Board of Adjustment of Hanover Tp., 20 N.J. 275, 119 A.2d 761 (1956).

Zoning ordinances are often held inapplicable to *all* properties of the municipality enacting those ordinances. Sometimes such exemptions are specifically provided by the ordinances themselves, and such an exemption will be sustained as reasonable. See McCarter v. Beckwith, 247 App.Div. 289, 285 N.Y.S. 151 (1936), aff'd 272 N.Y. 488, 3 N.E.2d 882, cert. denied 299 U.S. 601, 57 S.Ct. 194, 81 L.Ed. 443; City of Cincinnati v. Wegehoft, 119 Ohio St. 136, 162 N.E. 389 (1928). Sometimes the exemption is "read in." See Sunny Slope Water Co. v. City of Pasadena, 1 Cal.2d 87, 33 P.2d 672 (1934) (water wells and pumps); Decatur Park District v. Becker, 368 Ill. 442, 14 N.E.2d 490 (1938) (public parks); Thornton v. Village of Ridgewood, 17 N.J. 499, 111 A.2d 899 (1955). Cf. Glascock v. Baltimore County, Maryland, 321 Md. 118, 581 A.2d 822 (1990) (county has immunity from its own zoning regulations when there is no specific restriction made by the legislature requiring adherence to the ordinance). But where the exemption is not specified by the applicable ordinances, what is probably the *majority* of authority states that the exemption applies only to governmental properties of the enacting municipality, not proprietary ones. See Lauderdale County Board of Education v. Alexander, 269 Ala. 79, 110 So.2d 911 (1959); Taber v. Benton Harbor, 280 Mich. 522, 274 N.W. 324 (1937) (municipality could not erect water tower in violation of its own height limitation); O'Brien v. Town of Greenburgh, 239 App.Div. 555, 268 N.Y.S. 173 (1933), aff'd without opinion 266 N.Y. 582, 195 N.E. 210 (1935) (garbage disposal plant proprietary, subject to zoning); Kedroff v. Town of Springfield, 127 Vt. 624, 256 A.2d 457 (1969) (sewage treatment plant ruled governmental, thus allowed in residential zone). In some jurisdictions, one government is not subject to the zoning of the other if the former could take property within the other by eminent domain. See City of Scottsdale v. Municipal Court, *supra*; Aviation Services v. Board of Adjustment of Hanover, *supra*. But the Minnesota court rejected this in favor of a "balancing-of-the-public-interests" test. Town of Oronoco v. City of Rochester, 293 Minn. 468, 197 N.W.2d 426 (1972). See generally Note, Governmental Immunity from Local Zoning Ordinances, 84 Harv.L.Rev. 869 (1971) (noting criticisms of governmental-proprietary test and discussing other tests); Comment, The Inapplicability of Municipal Zoning Ordinances to Governmental Land Uses, 19 Syracuse L.Rev. 698 (1968); Comment, The Applicability of Zoning Ordinances to Governmental Land Use, 39 Texas L.Rev. 316 (1961); Annot., Applicability of Zoning Regulations to Governmental Projects or Activities, 62 A.L.R.2d 970 (1958).

There is a trend, in the area of intergovernmental immunity from zoning, away from flat rules and toward a "balancing" approach, such as taken in the *Town of Oronoco* case *supra*. See City of Crown Point v. Lake County, 510 N.E.2d 684 (Ind. 1987) (local land-use decision, while initially binding on other governmental unit, is subject to judicial review by balancing the public interests involved; city could enforce its zoning laws against county buildings); City of Ames v. Story County, 392 N.W.2d 145 (Iowa 1986) (with review and rejection of tests previously used); Independent School Dist. No. 89 v. Oklahoma City, 722 P.2d 1212 (Okl.1986) (school districts not automatically immune from city zoning; court should consider legislative intent, which, if unclear, is to be determined by weighing such factors as nature of instrumentality seeking immunity, kind of function or planned use involved, extent of public interest to be served, effect the local land-use regulation would have on enterprise concerned, and impact on legitimate local interests). Cf. Native Village of Eklutna v. Alaska R.R., 87 P.3d 41 (Alaska 2004) (state legislature did not clearly exempt state-operated railroad from local zoning laws, so "balancing of interests" test was proper to use for determining legislative intent; but balancing test would not be used until railroad made good faith effort to comply with local regulations). See generally Lehavi, Intergovernmental Liability Rules, 92 Va. L. Rev. 929 (2006). See also Taylor & Wyckoff, Intergovernmental Zoning Conflicts Over Public Facilities Siting: A Model Framework for Standard State Acts, 41 Urban Law. 653 (2009).

Zoning laws are sometimes held inapplicable to public utilities, even where the utilities are not owned by any level of the government. See Freight, Inc. v. Board of Township Trustees, 107 Ohio App. 288, 158 N.E.2d 537 (1958). But there is contrary authority. See Porter v. Southwestern Public Service Co., 489 S.W.2d 361 (Tex.Civ. App.1972), ref'd n. r. e. (not automatically exempt even though have power of eminent domain). It seems the immunity will at least exist where utilities would otherwise be totally excluded from the municipality. See Annot., Applicability of Zoning Regulations to Projects of Nongovernmental Public Utility as to Which Utility Has Power of Eminent Domain, 87 A.L.R.3d 1265 (1978). Or where the state is found to have preempted the field of utility regulation. See Note, Application of Local Zoning Ordinances to State-Controlled Public Utilities and Licensees: A Study in Preemption, 1965 Wash.U.L.Q. 195. See generally Note, Municipal Corporations—Control Over Public Utilities Through Zoning Ordinances, 42 N.C.L.Rev. 761 (1964). See also Note, Zoning and the Expanding Public Utility, 13 Syracuse L.Rev. 581 (1962).

Where a lessee of government-owned land is involved, the courts often apply—regardless of the levels of government involved—the governmental-proprietary test, finding immunity as to governmental uses of land but not as to proprietary. See Annot., Applicability of Zoning Regulation to Nongovernmental Lessee of Government-Owned Property, 84 A.L.R.3d 1187 (1978). See also Annot., Application of Zoning Regulation to Radio or Television Facilities, 81 A.L.R.3d 1086 (1977) (zoning usually applicable to such facilities despite federal licensing).

schools are commonly exempt from zoning ordinances,[24] while private and parochial schools are not.[25]

---

[24] See Note, Immunity of Schools from Zoning, 14 Syracuse L.Rev. 644 (1963); Annot., Zoning Regulations as Applied to Public Elementary and High Schools, 74 A.L.R.3d 136 (1976); Annot., Zoning Regulations as Applied to Colleges, Universities, or Similar Institutions for Higher Education, 64 A.L.R.3d 1138 (1975). See generally Annot., What Constitutes "School," "Educational Use," or the Like Within Zoning Ordinance, 64 A.L.R.3d 1087 (1975). See also Annot., Application of Zoning Regulations to College Fraternities or Sororities, 25 A.L.R.3d 921 (1969). On what is a "public school," see City of Little Rock v. Infant-Toddler Montessori School, Inc., 270 Ark. 697, 606 S.W.2d 743 (1980) (Montessori school not a "public school"). As to the effect that U.S. Supreme Court cases on school desegregation and diversity have had on zoning, see Note, A Narrow Path to Diversity: The Constitutionality of Rezoning Plans and Strategic Site Selection of Schools after *Parents Involved in Cmty. Sch. v. Seattle Sch. Dist. No. 1,* 107 Mich. L. Rev. 501 (2008).

[25] See Annot., Zoning Regulations as Applied to Private and Parochial Schools Below the College Level, 74 A.L.R.3d 14 (1976). But problems of unequal treatment and undue discrimination may sometimes arise if zoning laws do in fact apply differently to public and private schools. Thus, an exclusion of *all* schools—public and private—from a residential area may be upheld. Roman Catholic Diocese v. Borough of Ho-Ho-Kus, 42 N.J. 556, 202 A.2d 161 (1964), later appeal 47 N.J. 211, 220 A.2d 97. But laws allowing public but not private schools within residential areas are likely to be struck down as unreasonable and/or capricious. See Roman Catholic Welfare Corp. v. Piedmont, 45 Cal.2d 325, 289 P.2d 438 (1955); Catholic Bishop of Chicago v. Kingery, 371 Ill. 257, 20 N.E.2d 583 (1939). See generally 1A Antieau, Municipal Corporation Law § 7.76 (1980); Reynolds, Zoning Private and Parochial Schools—Could Local Government Restrict Socrates and Aquinas?, 24 Urban Law. 305 (1992).

Churches and religious bodies are not necessarily exempt altogether from zoning regulations, but ordinances totally excluding such uses from municipalities have been uniformly invalidated—and most cases have invalidated ordinances totally excluding such uses from residential zones. Islamic Center of Mississippi, Inc. v. City of Starkville, Mississippi, 840 F.2d 293 (5th Cir. 1988) (city's denial of permit to use residentially zoned building as Islamic center violated free exercise clause of First Amendment). See Note, Churches and Zoning, 70 Harv.L.Rev. 1428 (1957); Annot., What Constitutes "Church," "Religious Use," or the Like Within Zoning Ordinance, 62 A.L.R.3d 197 (1975). See generally 1A Antieau, Municipal Corporation Law § 7.75 (1980); Annot., Zoning Regulations as Affecting Churches, 74 A.L.R.2d 377 (1960); Annot., Building Restrictions, By Covenant or Condition in Deed or by Zoning Regulation, as Applied to Religious Groups, 148 A.L.R. 367 (1944). On what land uses are accessory to religious or educational institutions, see Annot., What Constitutes Accessory or Incidental Use of Religious or Educational Property Within Zoning Ordinance, 11 A.L.R. 4th 1084 (1982). There is a split of authority as to whether a school is an accessory use as to a permitted religious use of property. Compare City of Las Cruces v. Huerta, 102 N.M. 182, 692 P.2d 1331 (App. 1984), cert. denied 102 N.M. 225, 693 P.2d 591 (1984) (full-time parochial schools not among ancillary uses encompassed by zoning permits for churches), with Diocese of Rochester v. Planning Bd. of Brighton, 1 N.Y.2d 508, 154 N.Y.S.2d 849, 136 N.E.2d 827 (1956) (a school and a meeting room are accessory to permitted church use). Cf. Western Presbyterian Church v. Board of Zoning Adjustment, 862 F.Supp. 538 (D.D.C.1994) (church's feeding program for homeless persons was religious conduct which could not be substantially burdened by zoning laws in absence of compelling interest). Cemeteries have been held not "accessory" to religious uses of property; and rather severe restrictions or exclusions as to cemeteries have sometimes been upheld. See Annot., Zoning Regulations in Relation to Cemeteries, 96 A.L.R.3d 921 (1980). Even where specific religious facilities are permitted by a zoning law, problems of interpretation may arise. See City of Minneapolis v. Church Universal & Triumphant, 339 N.W.2d 880 (Minn.1983) (organization could qualify as "monastery" even though residents held jobs or attended schools in the community and otherwise participated in community life).

In Grace United Methodist Church v. City of Cheyenne, 427 F.3d 775 (10th Cir. 2005), it was held that while a church has a right to build and operate a day care center, it cannot choose to exercise that right wherever it pleases and could thus be validly barred by an ordinance, applicable to a low-density residential zone, that prohibited a day care center with more than 12 children.

Use of land for religious purposes may validly be found in violation of a *restrictive covenant* that does not permit such use. See Voice of the Cornerstone Church Corp. v. Pizza Property Partners, 160 S.W.3d 657 (Tex. Ct. App. 2005) (church's use of land for religious purposes violated restrictive covenant limiting land's use to commercial/light industry purposes; enforcement of the facially neutral covenant by injunction does not unconstitutionally burden church's freedom of religious expression). Cf. Utah Gospel Mission v. Salt Lake City Corp., 425 F.3d 1249 (10th Cir. 2005) (government relinquishment of an easement to a private religious group, and subsequent free speech restrictions on the religious group's privately owned land, did not violate the Establishment Clause).

Within the limits laid down by the *Euclid* case, zoning can occur. If the limits—as of reasonableness, for instance—are overstepped, the police power is then being exceeded; and the governmental action can be justified—if at all—only as a "taking" under the power of eminent domain.[26] The "takings" problem is often framed as involving drawing a line between valid regulatory exercises of the police power (which are not "takings" and do not require compensation by the government) and exercises of the power of eminent domain (which are "takings" and do require compensation).[27] It has been observed that zoning laws usually do not rise to the level of a taking of property, but that if the zoning interferes significantly with the use or enjoyment of property, the government has overstepped its police power and the law is no longer a land use regulation but does amount to a taking.[28] Changes have, of course, occurred in the typical zoning patterns since the *Euclid* case was decided. For example: (1) Many more types of zones—not just the basic three of residential, commercial, and industrial—are now commonly employed, as where "agricultural" zones are designated. And there are often sub-categories within zones: residential zones where only single-family dwellings are permitted, ones where multiple-family dwellings are allowed, ones where professional offices are also allowed, etc. (2) Cumulative zoning is no longer so fashionable as it once was; zones may now be designated "exclusively industrial," for instance, and the so-called "higher uses" will not then be allowed in that area. (3) The number of uses permitted in a zone as a matter of *right* has often decreased; many more uses are permitted if, and only if, some special permit is obtained—usually from a zoning or planning commission. Zoning has become less a matter of sweeping regulations, and more a matter of *ad hoc* restrictions, with numerous special exceptions, variances, etc. being recognized. (4) Zoning has grown from being largely a creature of the big cities and

---

[26] See Comment, "Takings" Under the Police Power—The Development of Inverse Condemnation as a Method of Challenging Zoning Ordinances, 30 Sw.L.J. 723 (1976), noting various cases in which governmental "takings" have been found, and suggesting a possible "inverse condemnation" action for monetary damages by a landowner whose property is severely restricted and/or lessened in value by zoning. In Lomarch Corp. v. Mayor and Common Council, 51 N.J. 108, 237 A.2d 881 (1968), a one-year freeze on construction in a proposed subdivision was held constitutional only if compensation was paid those damaged. In Peacock v. County of Sacramento, 271 Cal.App.2d 845, 77 Cal.Rptr. 391 (Dist.Ct.1969), compensation was held required for restrictive regulation around an airport. See generally Badler, Municipal Zoning Liability in Damages—A New Cause of Action, 5 Urban Lawyer 25 (1973); Kanner, Developments in Eminent Domain: A Candle in the Dark Corner of the Law, 52 U.Det.J.Urban L. 861 (1975); Comment, Inverse Condemnation: Its Availability in Challenging the Validity of a Zoning Ordinance, 26 Stan.L.Rev. 1439 (1974); Comment, Compensable Regulation: Outlines of a New Land Use Planning Tool, 10 Willamette L.J. 451 (1974).

On "takings" and "inverse condemnation" in general, see Chapter 19 *infra*.

An unusual instance in which a taking was found is McKinney v. City of High Point, 237 N.C. 66, 74 S.E.2d 440 (1953), where a city erected a water tower in violation of its own zoning ordinances. It was held that the city was immune from the zoning law in this governmental endeavor—see note 23 *supra*—but that the city would be held liable to a neighboring property-owner on the theory that his property had been so lessened in value as to have been "taken."

[27] See Keene, When Does a Regulation "Go Too Far"?—The Supreme Court's Analytical Framework for Drawing the Line Between an Exercise of the Police Power and an Exercise of the Power of Eminent Domain, 14 Penn St. Envtl. L. Rev. 397 (2006).

[28] See In re Initiative Petition No. 382, 142 P.3d 400, 406–07 (Okla. 2006). On the original intent of the "takings clause" in Article 5 of the U.S. Constitution, see Hart, Land Use Law in the Early Republic and the Original Meaning of the Takings Clause, 94 Nw. U.L. Rev. 1099 (2000). A good summary of subsequent interpretations of the "takings clause" is found in Note, Takings Jurisprudence and Complex Schemes of Land Use Regulation: What the Supreme Court Could Learn from the States, 33 Rutgers L.J. 457 (2002), noting Good v. United States, 189 F.3d 1355 (Fed. Cir. 1999) (requirement that a claimant have investment-backed expectations in order to demonstrate a regulatory taking limits recovery to owners who can demonstrate that they bought their property in reliance on the nonexistence of the challenged regulation).

suburbs into a common-place type of regulation even in smaller communities and rural areas. (5) Finally—and definitely contrary to the traditional *Euclidean* zoning—zoning permitting a mixture of uses (residential, commercial, etc.) within a given area is now frequently encountered. This is often called "planned unit development." Somewhat similar in nature—and also directly contrary to "*Euclidean* ideas"—is the concept of a "floating zone": a zone not immediately effective but which will apply, to an area yet to be determined, when certain changes have occurred or specified conditions have been met.[29] Both "planned unit development" and "floating zones" have been much endorsed by writers and generally upheld; they are often thought to introduce much-needed elements of flexibility into the rigid classifications found under more traditional zoning techniques.[30]

§ 18.4 Zoning—Valid Purposes

Assuming a municipality is given the basic power to zone by state law, what are the purposes for which the municipality may validly zone? At least six main purposes may be mentioned[31] though in some instances, one such purpose may not be enough to uphold

---

[29] See Sheridan v. Planning Board, 159 Conn. 1, 266 A.2d 396 (1969); Chatham Corp. v. Beltram, 243 Md. 138, 220 A.2d 589 (1966). See generally 1A Antieau, Municipal Corporation Law § 7.61 (1998); Reno, Non-Euclidean Zoning: The Use of the Floating Zone, 23 Md.L.Rev. 105 (1963); Annot., Zoning: Regulations Creating and Placing "Floating Zones," 80 A.L.R.3d 95 (1977). At one time, the validity of floating zones was in doubt. See Eves v. Zoning Bd. of Adjustment, 401 Pa. 211, 164 A.2d 7 (Pa. 1960) (not in accord with a comprehensive plan, as required by statute). But the validity today is established in most states. See Rodgers v. Village of Tarrytown, 302 N.Y. 115, 96 N.E.2d 731 (1951); State ex rel. Zupancic v. Schimenz, 46 Wis.2d 22, 174 N.W.2d 533 (1970). See generally Selmi & Kushner, Land Use Regulation—Cases and Materials 100–01 (Aspen 1999). On the difference between a floating zone and a fixed zone, see Bellemeade Co. v. Priddle, 503 S.W.2d 734, 738 (Ky.1973) (boundaries of floating zone are undefined until it becomes anchored).

[30] See Bigenho v. Montgomery County Council, 248 Md. 386, 237 A.2d 53 (1968), approving "floating zones." See generally Report, Planned Unit Developments and Floating Zones, 7 Real Property, Probate & Trust J. 61 (1972); Annot., Zoning: Planned Unit, Cluster, or Green Belt Zoning, 43 A.L.R.3d 888 (1972). On planned unit developments in particular, see Hanke, Planned Unit Development and Land Use Intensity, 114 U.Pa.L.Rev. 15 (1965); Krasnowiecki, Planned Unit Development: A Challenge to Established Theory and Practice of Land Use Control, 114 U.Pa.L.Rev. 47 (1965). See also Goldston & Scheur, Zoning of Planned Residential Developments, 73 Harv.L.Rev. 241 (1959); Note, Non-Euclidean "Zoning": Its Theoretical Validity and Practical Desirability in Undeveloped Areas, 30 U.Cin.L.Rev. 297 (1961). On possible problems created by a "planned unit development," see Kenart & Associates v. Skagit County, 37 Wash.App. 295, 680 P.2d 439 (1984) (board of county commissioners denied permit, finding that development would contribute to loss of agricultural lands, increase traffic levels and school population, and aggravate drainage problems; court remands for clarification of these findings). On planned unit developments and the related concept of "cluster zoning," see generally Section 21.5 *infra.*

Some communities have tried to achieve flexibility by making the whole municipality a single-use district and then granting numerous variances, special permits, etc. But this method has sometimes been invalidated as not providing adequately for various uses. See Rockhill v. Township of Chesterfield, 23 N.J. 117, 128 A.2d 473 (1957); Town of Hobart v. Challe, 3 Wis.2d 182, 87 N.W.2d 868 (1958). See generally Goldman, Zoning Change: Flexibility v. Stability, 26 Md. L.Rev. 48 (1966) (saying the *Rockhill* and *Hobart* cases *supra* are attempts at wholesale creation of floating zones); Haar & Hering, The Lower Gwynedd Township Case: Too Flexible Zoning or an Inflexible Judiciary?, 74 Harv.L.Rev. 1552 (1961) (saying the cases represent a move altogether away from Euclidean zoning *and* from floating zones, toward the English system of zoning by special permit). On the distinction between "floating zones" and "special permits" (the latter of which are discussed in this chapter *infra*), see Summ v. Zoning Commission, 150 Conn. 79, 186 A.2d 160 (1962); Sieber v. Laawe, 33 N.J.Super. 115, 109 A.2d 470 (1954). On trends in, and the possible future development of, zoning law, see generally Symposium, Post-Zoning: Alternative Forms of Public Land Use Controls, 78 Brooklyn L. Rev. 305–623 (2013).

[31] See Hagman & Juergensmeyer, Urban Planning & Land Development Control Law 51–52 (2d ed. 1986); Juergensmeyer & Roberts, Land Use Planning & Control Law 45–59 (1998), both noting that zoning must (1) be within valid police-power purposes, and (2) be within the purposes for which zoning is authorized by the relevant state law—usually the zoning enabling act. See also the purposes mentioned in Section 1 of

a zoning law's validity: for instance, it is sometimes said that aesthetics alone cannot support a zoning ordinance, but only when coupled with some other purpose as well. (All these purposes, it should be noted, flow from the police power and the basic desire to exclude harmful uses from various neighborhoods.)[32]

One purpose usually recognized as proper is the conserving and maintaining of property values in a community. It has been said that local authorities, in enacting zoning laws, may consider the resulting increase in property valuations and the other economic advantages to the municipality.[33] Certainly the sum total of real property values in a community should be increased by the orderly development that will hopefully flow from zoning laws—as opposed to the haphazard development that might otherwise occur. But it must be emphasized that it is the welfare of the community as a whole with which the zoning authorities should be concerned,[34] and that zoning may be valid though it actually depresses (as it frequently will) the value of some parcels of land. Thus, it has often been held that zoning as applied to particular property is not necessarily unreasonable simply because the property would be more valuable if zoned so as to allow different or additional uses.[35] Mere financial loss, such as lessening of profits, does not, even though directly attributable to the zoning classification of the property, invalidate the zoning restrictions.[36] Still, a loss in value as to particular property will be weighed as *one factor* in determining the reasonableness of the zoning

---

the Standard State Zoning Enabling Act, reprinted at 5 Anderson, American Law of Zoning § 32.01 (5th ed. 1997); Hagman & Juergensmeyer, *supra* at 55; Juergensmeyer & Roberts, *supra* at 46; 5 Rathkopf, The Law of Zoning and Planning Appendix A (4th ed. 1995). See 1 Anderson, American Law of Zoning §§ 2.21–.28 (4th ed. 1995), summarizing the Standard Act.

[32] See Kaplan v. City of Boston, 330 Mass. 381, 113 N.E.2d 856 (1953) (primary purpose is preservation of neighborhoods against deleterious uses).

[33] See Addison-Wesley Publishing Co. v. Town of Reading, 354 Mass. 181, 236 N.E.2d 188 (1968). But cf. Glassey v. County of Tazewell, 11 Ill.App.3d 1087, 297 N.E.2d 235 (1973) (a use may not be denied merely because it might increase governmental costs; application for mobile home park). In many jurisdictions, zoning is now enacted by counties as well as municipalities. See Motta v. Granite County Comm'rs, 304 P.3d 720 (Mont. 2013) (zoning districts within county could be established either by citizen petition or directly by board of county commissioners); Wilson Advisory Committee v. Board of County Comm'rs, 292 P.3d 855 (Wyo. 2012) (broad grant of authority to county commissioners to promulgate zoning ordinances includes both express power to enact zoning and implied power to do what is necessary to make exercises of the express power meaningful in the unincorporated areas of the county). See generally Section 6.2, notes 31–35 and accompanying text, *supra*, on home rule in counties. See also Section 2.5 on counties, *supra*.

[34] See Save a Valuable Environment v. City of Bothell, 89 Wn.2d 862, 576 P.2d 401 (1978) (zoning invalid if doesn't serve welfare of community as a whole). Cf. Southern Burlington County N.A.A.C.P. v. Township of Mount Laurel, 67 N.J. 151, 336 A.2d 713 (1975), appeal dism'd, cert. denied 423 U.S. 808, 96 S.Ct. 18, 46 L.Ed.2d 28 (bedroom restriction designed to limit number of families with children in community, and thus reduce education costs, is contrary to general welfare and hence void).

[35] Leventhal v. District of Columbia, 100 F.2d 94 (D.C.Cir.1938); City and County of Denver v. American Oil Co., 150 Colo. 341, 374 P.2d 357 (1962); Town of Surfside v. Abelson, 106 So.2d 108 (Fla.App.1958), cert. denied 111 So.2d 40 (Fla.1959); Elmhurst National Bank v. City of Chicago, 22 Ill.2d 396, 176 N.E.2d 771 (1961); Reiskin v. County Council, 229 Md. 142, 182 A.2d 34 (1962) (land would have been more profitable if zoned to allow multiple-family dwellings); Ulmer Park Realty Co. v. City of New York, 270 App.Div. 1044, 63 N.Y.S.2d 143 (1946), aff'd 297 N.Y. 788, 77 N.E.2d 797. See State National Bank v. Trumbull, 156 Conn. 99, 239 A.2d 528 (1968) (maximum enrichment of property owner is not the purpose of zoning); Turner v. City of Atlanta, 257 Ga. 306, 357 S.E.2d 802 (1987), cert. denied 485 U.S. 934, 108 S.Ct. 1108, 99 L.Ed.2d 269 (1988) (refusal to rezone not unconstitutional merely because property would be more valuable if rezoned).

[36] See Samp Mortar Lake Co. v. Town Plan and Zoning Commission, 155 Conn. 310, 231 A.2d 649 (1967); Dixon v. County of Kane, 77 Ill.App.2d 338, 222 N.E.2d 354 (1966); Levitt v. Incorporated Village of Sands Point, 6 N.Y.2d 269, 189 N.Y.S.2d 212, 160 N.E.2d 501 (1959). Cf. City of Baltimore v. Borinsky, 239 Md. 611, 212 A.2d 508 (1965) (no relief just because property owners show substantial loss from zoning law).

law as applied to that property;[37] and the zoning *will* be invalidated if the point is reached at which all otherwise legal or all beneficial uses of the property are forbidden,[38] or at which the only uses permitted are physically impossible given the nature of the property.[39] Most courts go somewhat farther than this and say that if all *reasonable* uses of the property are prohibited, the zoning is invalid as applied to that land.[40] The modern

---

[37] Herzog v. City of Pocatello, 83 Idaho 365, 363 P.2d 188 (1961); Ervin Acceptance Co. v. City of Ann Arbor, 322 Mich. 404, 34 N.W.2d 11 (1948); Pearce v. Village of Edina, 263 Minn. 553, 118 N.W.2d 659 (1962) (also saying zoning invalid if enacted to protect enterprises from competition or to carry out aesthetic ideas of planning commission). Thus, where zoning results in extreme differentials in the resulting value of various pieces of property, this may be evidence the law is arbitrary. Pearce v. Village of Edina, *supra.* Or where property would be worth many times as much if zoned less restrictively. Town of Surfside v. Normandy Beach Development Co., 57 So.2d 844 (Fla. 1952) (property had little value for residential use, for which zoned, but had business value of $20,000).

[38] New Products Corp. v. City of North Miami, 271 So.2d 24 (Fla.App.1972) (land owned by private party zoned for use only as public park). See Morris County Land Improvement Co. v. Township of Parsippany-Troy Hills, 40 N.J. 539, 193 A.2d 232 (1963); Chase v. City of Glen Cove, 41 Misc.2d 889, 246 N.Y.S.2d 975 (1964); Greenhills Home Owners Corp. v. Village of Greenhills, 202 N.E.2d 192 (Ohio App. 1964), cert. denied 385 U.S. 836, 87 S.Ct. 82, 17 L.Ed.2d 70 (protective belt of forest-land park created; amounted to a taking without just compensation). But the corporation in the *Greenhills* case, *supra,* was subsequently held "estopped" from attacking the zoning restriction as a taking, and the earlier judgment was reversed. Greenhills Home Owners Corp. v. Village of Greenhills, 5 Ohio St.2d 207, 215 N.E.2d 403 (1966), cert. denied 385 U.S. 836, 87 S.Ct. 82, 17 L.Ed.2d 70.

[39] See Robyns v. City of Dearborn, 341 Mich. 495, 67 N.W.2d 718 (1954). Cf. City of Evansville v. Reis Tire Sales, Inc., 165 Ind.App. 638, 333 N.E.2d 800 (1975) (natural ravine and resulting construction costs prevented any reasonable use of the property as zoned); Beachland Glass Co. v. Woodmansee, 11 Ohio Misc. 262, 230 N.E.2d 360 (1967) (if no economic use can be made of property, classification is arbitrary and unreasonable unless it promotes general welfare of community).

[40] See State ex rel. Taylor v. City of Jacksonville, 101 Fla. 1241, 133 So. 114 (1931); Northwest Merchants Terminal, Inc. v. O'Rourke, 191 Md. 171, 60 A.2d 743 (1948); City of Pittsfield v. Oleksak, 313 Mass. 553, 47 N.E.2d 930 (1943); Bassey v. City of Huntington Woods, 344 Mich. 701, 74 N.W.2d 897 (1956); Stevens v. Town of Huntington, 20 N.Y.2d 352, 283 N.Y.S.2d 16, 229 N.E.2d 591 (1967); Mary Chess, Inc. v. City of Glen Cove, 18 N.Y.2d 205, 273 N.Y.S.2d 46, 219 N.E.2d 406 (1966); Baronoff v. Zoning Board, 385 Pa. 110, 122 A.2d 65 (1956); Sundlun v. Zoning Board of Review, 50 R.I. 108, 145 A. 451 (1929); Chrome Plating Co. v. City of Milwaukee, 246 Wis. 526, 17 N.W.2d 705 (1945). Courts usually refer to such zoning as "confiscatory" or as a "taking" or "regulatory taking," and thus invalid, where the zoning permits no reasonable use to be made of the property. See Frankel v. City of Baltimore, 223 Md. 97, 162 A.2d 447 (1960); City of Plainfield v. Borough of Middlesex, 69 N.J.Super. 136, 173 A.2d 785 (1961); Mary Chess, Inc. v. City of Glen Cove, *supra.* Cf. Keystone Bituminous Coal Ass'n v. DeBenedictis, 480 U.S. 470, 107 S.Ct. 1232, 94 L.Ed.2d 472 (1987) (Pennsylvania statute requiring that 50% of coal beneath certain structures be kept in place to provide surface support held not a "taking" of coal mines where there was no evidence that any mining operations or mines had been rendered unprofitable by the regulation); Griffin Dev. Co. v. City of Oxnard, 39 Cal.3d 256, 217 Cal.Rptr. 1, 703 P.2d 339 (1985) (land-use measure, such as limitation on conversion of apartments to condominiums, is invalid only if it deprives owner of substantially all reasonable use of his property). Compare State v. Johnson, 265 A.2d 711 (Me.1970) (Wetlands Act deprived owners of reasonable use of property and was thus a "taking"). The Supreme Court has ruled that where a zoning regulation deprives a landowner, even temporarily, of all reasonable use of his property, he is entitled not only to a judicial declaration of the invalidity of the zoning law but to compensation for the "taking" that occurred while the regulation was in effect. Lucas v. South Carolina Coastal Council, 505 U.S. 1003, 112 S.Ct. 2886, 120 L.Ed.2d 798 (1992); First English Evangelical Lutheran Church v. County of Los Angeles, 482 U.S. 304, 107 S.Ct. 2378, 96 L.Ed.2d 250 (1987), on remand 210 Cal.App.3d 1353, 258 Cal.Rptr. 893 (1989), cert. denied 493 U.S. 1056, 110 S.Ct. 866, 107 L.Ed.2d 950 (1990). Accord, Corrigan v. City of Scottsdale, 149 Ariz. 538, 720 P.2d 513 (1986). On the test used in determining whether a taking has occurred, see Cope v. City of Cannon Beach, 317 Or. 339, 855 P.2d 1083 (1993) (zoning ordinance prohibiting transient occupancy did not deny property owners all economically viable use of their property and thus did not effect a facial taking); Dodd v. Hood River County, 317 Or. 172, 855 P.2d 608 (1993) (test is whether the challenged ordinance allows landowners some substantial beneficial use of their property; forest zoning ordinance prohibiting landowners from building a dwelling on their property held not to constitute a taking); Margola Associates v. City of Seattle, 121 Wash.2d 625, 854 P.2d 23 (1993) (rent regulation found not a "total taking" because it didn't deny all economically viable use of owner's land). For background on the *Dodd* case *supra,* see Carlton, 'Takings' Cases Don't Always Favor Takers, Wall St. J., Nov. 10, 1992, at B1. For analysis of the *Lucas* case, *supra,* see Note, Unintended Consequences: *Lucas,* the Public

law in this area is usually said to have originated in the *Penn Central* case,[41] setting forth—in order to determine whether a governmental regulation amounted to "taking"—a complex of factors including the regulation's economic effect on the landowner, the extent to which the regulation interferes with reasonable investment-back expectations, and the character of the government action. The *Penn Central* test was clearly extended to cases of *temporary* regulation in the *Tahoe-Sierra* case,[42] where a moratorium on development imposed during the process of devising a comprehensive land-use plan was held not to constitute a per se taking of property, requiring compensation, but to depend on the particular circumstances of the case.[43] Constitutional provisions are generally

---

Trust Doctrine, and the Erosion of Private Property Rights Under the Takings Clause, 2013 Utah L. Rev. 1687, and authorities cited in Section 125, note 25, para. 2. See also Pagano, Where's the Beach? Coastal Access in the Age of Rising Tides, 42 SW. L. Rev. 1 (2012). On Supreme Court development of the law on regulatory takings, see Delaney, What Does it Take to Make a Take? A Post-*Dolan* Look at the Evolution of Regulatory Takings Jurisprudence in the Supreme Court, 27 Urban Law. 55 (1995). See generally § 125 *infra*. See also Eagle, "Economic Impact" in Regulatory Takings Law, 19 Hasting W.-Nw. J. Envtl. L. & Pol'y 407 (2013); Siegel, Evaluating Economic Impact in Regulatory Takings Cases, 19 Hastings W.-Nw. J. Envtl. L. & Pol'y 373 (2013); both articles are part of the Symposium from the 15th Annual Conference on Litigating Takings Challenges to Land Use & Environmental Regulations, 19 Hastings W.-NW. J Envtl. L. & Pol'y 337–545 (2013).

On the effect that cases such as the *First Evangelical* case, *supra*, have had on government regulations, see Merriam, Reengineering Regulation to Avoid Takings, 33 Urban Law. 1 (2001), stating that almost all governmental takings, both regulatory and physical, are avoidable. As to the differences between regulatory takings and regulatory exactions, see Comment, Confusing Regulatory Takings With Regulatory Exactions: The Supreme Court Gets Lost in the Swamp, 41 Boston Coll. Envtl. Affairs L. Rev. 555 (2014), commenting on Koontz v. St. Johns River Water Management Dist., ___ U.S. ___, 133 S.Ct. 2586 (2013). See also Section 19.2, note 24, *infra,* and accompanying text.

The present law of "takings" and its origins are well summarized in Karkkainen, The Police Power Revisited: Phantom Incorporation and the Roots of the Takings "Muddle," 90 Minn. L. Rev. 826 (2006).

[41] Penn Central Transp. Co. v. New York City, 438 U.S. 104, 98 S.Ct. 2646, 57 L.Ed.2d 631 (1978). At issue in that case was regulation for the purpose of historic preservation; see notes 83–85 *infra* and accompanying text.

[42] Tahoe-Sierra Preservation Council, Inc. v. Tahoe Regional Planning Agency, 535 U.S. 302, 122 S.Ct. 1465, 152 L.Ed.2d 517 (2002).

[43] See Kahn, Lake Tahoe Clarity and Takings Jurisprudence: The Supreme Court Advances Land Use Planning in *Tahoe-Sierra*, 26 Environs 33 (2002); Comment, After *Tahoe-Sierra*, One Thing Is Clearer: There Is Still a Fundamental Lack of Clarity, 46 Ariz. L. Rev. 353 (2004); Comment, Temporary Moratoria and Regulatory Takings Jurisprudence After *Tahoe-Sierra*, 27 Harv. Envtl. L. Rev. 277 (2003); Note, Taking Shape: Temporary Takings and the *Lucas* Per Se Rule in *Tahoe-Sierra Preservation Council, Inc. v. Tahoe Regional Planning Authority,* 82 Or. L. Rev. 189 (2003) (noting the effect that *Tahoe-Sierra* had on the law of the *Lucas* case, *supra*); Comment, Land Use Moratoria and Temporary Takings Redefined After Lake Tahoe?, 30 Pepperdine L. Rev. 273 (2003); Note, Will Regulations Keep Tahoe Blue? Searching for Stewardship in Property Law and Regulatory Takings Analysis, 27 Thomas Jefferson L. Rev. 187 (2004). See generally Note, Caught in the Toils of Regulation: *Tahoe-Sierra*, Ripeness, Permit Requirements, and a Measure of Relief, 79 Notre Dame L. Rev. 2079 (2004).

On the effect that the *Tahoe-Sierra* case, *supra*—as well as the decision in Brown v. Legal Foundation of Wash., 538 U.S. 216, 123 S.Ct. 1406, 155 L.Ed.2d 376 (2003) (often called the IOLTA case), dealing with clients' property rights in interest earned on lawyer trust accounts—has had on regulatory takings law, see Roberts, Regulatory Takings in the Wake of *Tahoe-Sierra* and the IOLTA Decision, 35 Urban Law. 759 (2003).

On a landowner's possible *damages* action where a governmental zoning or planning body has been judicially declared to have arbitrarily and capriciously denied a permit to develop land, or has denied such permission in violation of the landowner's due process or equal protection rights, see Wilson, Congratulations, You've Won a Steak Dinner: Recent Constitutional Claims for Damages in Land Use Litigation, 38 Urban Law. 713 (2006) (state court findings do not necessarily result in damages liability in federal court proceedings).

In McCarran Internatl. Airport v. Sisolak, 122 Nev. 645, 137 P.3d 1110 (2006) cert. denied 549 U.S. 1206, 127 S.Ct. 1260, 167 L.Ed.2d 76 (2007), it was held that county ordinances limiting building height on property adjacent to an airport constituted a *regulatory taking per se* (as opposed to the *Penn Central*-type takings cases) since the ordinances permitted the presence of aircraft over the owner's property at altitudes below 500 feet, authorized the permanent physical invasion of the owner's airspace, and excluded the owner from using his

held not to guarantee that each landowner will be allowed to make the most profitable use of his or her land.[44] Though courts occasionally speak of invalidating zoning laws when those laws do not encourage the most appropriate use of property,[45] it seems that the invalidation actually occurs only if the courts find that (1) the particular property is lessened in value because the zoning laws do not allow it to be put to its highest or best use, *and* (2) there is no counterbalancing benefit to public health, safety, morality, or general welfare from such zoning.[46]

The stabilizing and homogenizing of areas may be considered another purpose behind zoning. Zoning classifications are ideally the outgrowth of an orderly plan for community development, with only certain uses, or certain mixes of uses, allowed in any particular zone. Indeed, statutes often require that zoning in each community be in accord with a "comprehensive plan" for the community: a plan relating to the present and reasonably foreseeable needs of the whole municipality.[47] Conformity to such a plan

---

property. Regulatory per se takings were said to be relatively rare and easily identified, and usually to cause a greater affront to individual property rights then do *Penn Central*-type takings. *Id.* at 1124.

44 Madis v. Higginson, 164 Colo. 320, 434 P.2d 705 (1967); Baum v. City and County of Denver, 147 Colo. 104, 363 P.2d 688 (1961); Cobble Close Farm v. Middletown Township, 10 N.J. 442, 92 A.2d 4 (1952); Scuteri v. Incorporated Village of Bayville, 120 N.Y.S.2d 794 (Sup.Ct.1953). See West Bloomfield Township v. Chapman, 351 Mich. 606, 88 N.W.2d 377 (1958), indicating that effective zoning would be impossible if each landowner were allowed to make the best possible use of his or her land. Cf. First National Bank v. County of Lake, 7 Ill.2d 213, 130 N.E.2d 267 (1955) (effect of zoning on land immediately involved is one factor to consider, but so is effect on other land in area); Dodge Mill Land Corp. v. Town of Amherst, 61 A.D.2d 216, 402 N.Y.S.2d 670 (1978) (only a showing that land as zoned cannot be properly used, leased or sold will entitle plaintiffs to have zoning invalidated). See generally Meltz, Merriam & Frank, The Takings Issue—Constitutional Limits on Land-Use Control & Environmental Regulation (Island Press 1999).

45 See McGiverin v. City of Huntington Woods, 343 Mich. 413, 72 N.W.2d 105 (1955); Raskin v. Town of Morristown, 21 N.J. 180, 121 A.2d 378 (1956); Vernon Park Realty, Inc. v. City of Mount Vernon, 307 N.Y. 493, 121 N.E.2d 517 (1954) (right to attack validity of zoning ordinance not waived by purchase with knowledge of restriction, or by unsuccessful application for variance, or by *failure* to seek variance).

46 See La Salle National Bank v. City of Chicago, 5 Ill.2d 344, 125 N.E.2d 609 (1955). Cf. Dawson Enterprises, Inc. v. Blaine County, 98 Idaho 506, 567 P.2d 1257 (1977) (zoning ordinance may be valid though it restricts development of property to other than the most suitable use).

47 Fairlawns Cemetery Association v. Bethel, 138 Conn. 434, 86 A.2d 74 (1952); Grooms v. LaVale Zoning Board, 27 Md.App. 266, 340 A.2d 385 (1975). See, applying a similar standard of "comprehensive plan," Ward v. Montgomery Township, 28 N.J. 529, 147 A.2d 248 (1959). It has been observed that Maryland does not by statute specify that zoning must be in accord with a comprehensive plan; but the courts have applied similar standards in requiring some overall organization. See Nottingham Village, Inc. v. Baltimore County, 266 Md. 339, 292 A.2d 680 (1972) (also noting that a "comprehensive plan" need not conform to a master plan). Where a "comprehensive plan" *is* specifically required by statute, this does not necessarily mean a written plan, or master plan, based on a comprehensive study; the ordinances themselves may reveal sufficient orderly planning. Toole v. May-Day Realty Corp., 101 R.I. 379, 223 A.2d 545 (1966). The basic requirement is that there be proof that consideration has been given, in drafting the specific ordinances, to the needs of the community as an entirety. See Udell v. Haas, 21 N.Y.2d 463, 288 N.Y.S.2d 888, 235 N.E.2d 897 (1968). Cf. Lazy Mtn. Land Club v. Matanuska-Susitna Borough Bd. of Adjustment & Appeals, 904 P.2d 373 (Alaska 1995) (comprehensive plan need not be integrated into a single document, and the various parts need not have been enacted at the same time). Whether a zoning ordinance is "in accord with a comprehensive plan" has been held a question of fact. Love v. Board of County Comm'rs of Bingham County, 108 Idaho 728, 701 P.2d 1293 (1985) (governing body charged with zoning "in accord with a comprehensive plan" must make factual inquiry to determine whether requested ordinance or amendment reflects goals of, and takes into account the factors in, comprehensive plan in light of present factual circumstances; court should not overturn governing body's decision unless clearly erroneous). On the differing attitudes of various states as to what satisfies a "comprehensive plan" requirement for zoning, see Sullivan & Kressel, Twenty Years After: Renewed Significance of the Comprehensive Plan Requirement, 9 Urban L.Ann. 33 (1975). See generally Haar, "In Accordance with a Comprehensive Plan," 68 Harv.L.Rev. 1154 (1955), taking the view that the use of a comprehensive plan should be a separate requisite to the validity of zoning laws, not just a part of the "reasonableness" requirement. The author also advocates the requirement that such a comprehensive plan be

is thought to ensure that the zoning classifications will, at least in most instances, be free from arbitrariness or unreasonable discrimination.[48] It is because of the lack of conformity with a comprehensive plan that zoning is often struck down as "spot" or "piecemeal" zoning.[49] Such zoning is usually said to exist when small areas are given a different classification from that assigned neighboring parcels that are similarly situated.[50] It is invalid *if* arbitrary or otherwise unreasonable,[51] or if it was enacted

---

evidenced by an actual "master plan," though he notes the courts' tendency not to require the latter. See also Sullivan, Report of the Subcommittee on the Plan as Law, 23 Urban Law. 845 (1991). For further discussion of the planning process in land use, see Chapter 21 *infra*, particularly Section 143, dealing with master plans. As to stabilization as a goal of zoning, see also Note, Potholes in the Motor City: How Vacant Properties and Neighborhood Stabilization Can Subject Detroit and Similarly Situated Municipalities to Liability, 47 New Eng. L. Rev. 714 (2013).

Note that typical "Euclidean zoning" is "cumulative" and thus achieves only a rather loose homogenizing of areas, since "higher uses" are allowed in a "lower use" zone—a residence, for instance, in a commercial or industrial zone. Some courts insist on such zoning. See Katobimar Realty Co. v. Webster, 20 N.J. 114, 118 A.2d 824 (1955) (shopping center could not be prohibited in industrial zone). But there is a tendency now to allow "non-cumulative zoning," in which even "lower-use zones" may also be exclusive, just as "higher-use zones" have traditionally been. See People ex rel. Skokie Town House Builders, Inc. v. Village of Morton Grove, 16 Ill.2d 183, 157 N.E.2d 33 (1959). See generally Madsen, Noncumulative Zoning in Illinois, 37 Chi.-Kent L.Rev. 108 (1960); Comment, Industrial Zoning to Exclude Higher Uses, 32 N.Y.U.L.Rev. 1261 (1957). On possible drawbacks to non-cumulative zoning, see Hills & Schleicher, The Steep Costs of Using Non-cumulative Zoning to Preserve Land for Urban Manufacturing, 77 U. Chi. L. Rev. 249 (2010), part of Symposium, Reassessing the State and Local Government Toolkit 77 U. Chi. L. Rev. 1–366 (2010). On trends in zoning laws, see also Section 18.3 *supra*.

[48] See Miller v. Town Planning Comm'n, 142 Conn. 265, 113 A.2d 504 (1955). Cf. Women's Kansas City St. Andrew Society v. Kansas City, 58 F.2d 593 (8th Cir.1932) (restriction against use of property as "old ladies' home" without special permission of zoning board; held void as not essential to general plan). See generally Mandelker, The Role of the Local Comprehensive Plan in Land Use Regulation, 74 Mich. L. Rev. 899 (1976). On the growing importance of the comprehensive plan over the years, see Sullivan & Pelham, The Evolving Role of the Comprehensive Plan, 29 Urban Law. 363 (1997). See also Section 21.3 *infra*.

[49] Chapman v. City of Troy, 241 Ala. 637, 4 So.2d 1 (1941); Guerriero v. Galasso, 144 Conn. 600, 136 A.2d 497 (1957); Schadlick v. City of Concord, 108 N.H. 319, 234 A.2d 523 (1967) (spot zoning invalid if not in accord with comprehensive planning for good of community); Santmyers v. Town of Oyster Bay, 10 Misc.2d 614, 169 N.Y.S.2d 959 (Sup.Ct.1957); Spann v. City of Dallas, 111 Tex. 350, 235 S.W. 513 (1921). See Davis v. City of Omaha, 153 Neb. 460, 45 N.W.2d 172 (1950); Conlon v. Board of Public Works, 11 N.J. 363, 94 A.2d 660 (1953); Blumberg v. City of Yonkers, 21 A.D.2d 886, 251 N.Y.S.2d 750 (1964), motion gr. 15 N.Y.2d 547, 254 N.Y.S.2d 363, 202 N.E.2d 906. But it has been said that merely because statutes require that zoning be in accord with a comprehensive plan, the entire community does not have to be zoned all at once—authorities may begin by zoning only part of the locality. See Connell v. Town of Granby, 12 A.D.2d 177, 209 N.Y.S.2d 379 (1961) (some areas may be left open for future development and evolution but evidence must show that relationship of the part to the whole was considered; not shown here). See generally Citizen Advocates for a Livable Missoula, Inc. v. City Council, 331 Mont. 269, 130 P.3d 1259 (2006), listing the factors for determining whether "spot zoning" exists: (1) whether the requested use is significantly different from the prevailing use in the area, (2) whether the area that is differently zoned, or proposed for such different zoning, is small and looks to benefit a small number of persons, and (3) whether the zoning of the small area appears to be in the nature of special legislation, designed to benefit a few landowners at the expense of the surrounding landowners or the general public.

[50] Appeal of Mulac, 418 Pa. 207, 210 A.2d 275 (1965). See Cassel v. City of Baltimore, 195 Md. 348, 73 A.2d 486 (1950); Leahy v. Inspector of Buildings, 308 Mass. 128, 31 N.E.2d 436 (1941); Linden Methodist Episcopal Church v. City of Linden, 113 N.J.L. 188, 173 A. 593 (1934); Perkins v. Marion County, 252 Or. 313, 448 P.2d 374 (1968) (many persons in neighborhood had signed petition protesting the singling-out of a particular spot by the zoning ordinance); Appeal of Glorioso, 413 Pa. 194, 196 A.2d 668 (1964); Weaver v. Ham, 149 Tex. 309, 232 S.W.2d 704 (1950); Anderson v. City of Seattle, 64 Wn.2d 198, 390 P.2d 994 (1964). Cf. Lavitt v. Pierre, 152 Conn. 66, 203 A.2d 289 (1964) (inappropriate use of land must be provided by ordinance in order for invalid "spot zoning" to be found). See generally Reynolds, "Spot Zoning"—A Spot That Could Be Removed from the Law, 48 J. Urban & Contemp. L. 117 (1995), criticizing use of the term "spot zoning."

[51] See Eden v. Town Plan and Zoning Commission, 139 Conn. 59, 89 A.2d 746 (1952); Smith v. Board of Appeals, 313 Mass. 622, 48 N.E.2d 620 (1943) (67-foot wide strip designated "funeral home district" for benefit of one land-owner; held invalid "spot zoning"); Page v. City of Portland, 178 Or. 632, 165 P.2d 280

mainly for the purpose of advancing certain private interests, not for the public good.[52] (Note that "spot zoning" has become such a pejorative term that is often used to indicate invalidity—but the term as technically used means only a kind of zoning that is *potentially* invalid.) Sometimes, such zoning might be invalidated not only as in violation of due process because unreasonable or arbitrary, but also as in violation of equal protection. Clearly, zoning laws *can* be struck down if in violation of the equal protection clause of the U.S. Constitution and comparable state constitutional provisions. Mostly, these clauses have been utilized in situations where it is shown that certain activities are banned from a particular district while similar activities—not reasonably to be differentiated—are allowed in that district.[53] On the equal-protection basis and/or due

---

(1946); Salvitti v. Kennedy Township, 429 Pa. 330, 240 A.2d 534 (1968); Cleaver v. Board of Adjustment, 414 Pa. 367, 200 A.2d 408 (1964). Cf. Taco Bell v. City of Mission, 234 Kan. 879, 678 P.2d 133 (1984) (rezoning four fast-food restaurant properties to office use found arbitrary and capricious).

[52] Hermann v. City of Des Moines, 250 Iowa 1281, 97 N.W.2d 893 (1959); Thomas v. Town of Bedford, 11 N.Y.2d 428, 230 N.Y.S.2d 684, 184 N.E.2d 285 (1962); Appeal of Lieb, 179 Pa.Super. 318, 116 A.2d 860 (1955); Putney v. Township of Abington, 176 Pa.Super. 463, 108 A.2d 134 (1954). See Zandri v. Zoning Commission, 150 Conn. 646, 192 A.2d 876 (1963) (spot zoning may be result of effort to aid owner or owners of one small area); Guerriero v. Galasso, *supra* note 49 (spot zoning disturbs overall planning of neighborhood); McQuail v. Shell Oil Co., 40 Del.Ch. 396, 183 A.2d 572 (1962). Often, spot zoning has been invalidated in situations where a particular small area is given unreasonably *favorable* treatment, but invalidation can also occur if an area is singled-out for unreasonably *unfavorable* treatment. See Helena Sand & Gravel, Inc. v. Lewis & Clark County Planning & Zoning Comm'n, 290 P.3d 691 (Mont. 2012) (both "spot zoning"—where the spot is treated favorably—and "reverse spot zoning"—where the spot is treated unfavorably—may be found illegal); Appeal of Glorioso, *supra* note 50. See generally Note, Spotty Behavior or Good Precedent: The Rebirth of the Inverse Spot Zoning Doctrine, 35 Seton Hall Legis. J. 516 (2011) ("inverse spot zoning" treats a particular property *less* favorably than other property in the area and can thus potentially be invalidated as discriminatory when challenged by the owner of the "spot"; most spot zoning cases deal with small areas that are treated more favorably than other properties in the area, thus causing neighbors to challenge the "spot"). Spot zoning has usually been invalidated in situations where a rather small area—such as a single city lot—has been treated differently from the surrounding neighborhood; such invalid zoning can be found even where a sizable tract is treated discriminatorily. See Wilcox v. City of Pittsburgh, 121 F.2d 835 (3d Cir.1941); Keppy v. Ehlers, 253 Iowa 1021, 115 N.W.2d 198 (1962) (zoning of twenty-acre tract invalidated); Evanns v. Gunn, 177 Misc. 85, 29 N.Y.S.2d 368 (1940), aff'd 262 App.Div. 865, 29 N.Y.S.2d 150. Cf. Reskin v. City of Northlake, 55 Ill.App.2d 184, 204 N.E.2d 600 (1965) (zoning of two lots). Conversely, zoning is not necessarily invalid spot zoning simply because a single small parcel is treated differently from the surrounding area. Bucholz v. City of Omaha, 174 Neb. 862, 120 N.W.2d 270 (1963). See Partain v. City of Brooklyn, 138 N.E.2d 180 (Ohio Com.Pl.1955), aff'd 101 Ohio App. 279, 133 N.E.2d 616 (1956); Pollock v. Zoning Board of Adjustment, 20 Pa.Cmwlth. 641, 342 A.2d 815 (1975) (rezoning of small area for use different from rest of neighborhood is not invalid if is in accord with comprehensive plan and is for reasonable purpose); Schubach v. Silver, 461 Pa. 366, 336 A.2d 328 (1975) (rezoning to permit nursing home on four-acre tract upheld). Indeed, it is sometime stated in general terms that different zoning classifications for small tracts *are* valid if the zoning is in accord with an overall plan and is directed primarily at the public good, not private advantage. See Penn v. Metropolitan Plan Comm'n, 141 Ind.App. 387, 228 N.E.2d 25 (1967); Kozesnik v. Montgomery Township, 24 N.J. 154, 131 A.2d 1 (1957) (zoning not necessarily invalid because private interests are incidentally benefited thereby); Twenty-One White Plains Corp. v. Village of Hastings-on-Hudson, 14 Misc.2d 800, 180 N.Y.S.2d 13 (Sup.Ct.1958), aff'd 9 A.D.2d 934, 196 N.Y.S.2d 562.

[53] Village of University Heights v. Cleveland Jewish Orphan's Home, 20 F.2d 743 (6th Cir.1927), cert. denied 275 U.S. 569, 48 S.Ct. 141, 72 L.Ed. 431; Miami Beach v. State ex rel. Lear, 128 Fla. 750, 175 So. 537 (1937); Catholic Bishop of Chicago v. Kingery, 371 Ill. 257, 20 N.E.2d 583 (1939); James S. Holden Co. v. Connor, 257 Mich. 580, 241 N.W. 915 (1932). See City of Chicago v. Sachs, 1 Ill.2d 342, 115 N.E.2d 762 (1953). Some cases have also found a violation of equal protection in situations where zoning has been administered by a local government for spiteful reasons, or out of ill will, rather than for any proper purpose. See Wilson, Nasty Motives Visit the Supreme Court: A Consideration of Recent Land-Use Damages Cases, 32 Urban Law. 787 (2000).

On the increased tendency of landowners to sue for damages, often successfully, where a municipality violates equal protection and/or due process in its treatment of plaintiff's land, see Wilson, When Sending Flowers Is Not Enough: Development in Landowner Civil Rights Lawsuits Against Municipal Officials, 34 Urban Law. 981 (2002), noting (at 981–82) the importance of Village of Willowbrook v. Olech, 528 U.S. 562,

process grounds, zoning ordinances can be struck down where they lack uniformity in application *within* a particular district—as where public garages are allowed in parts of a district but not in all.[54] Such discrimination obviously defeats the purpose of homogenizing of areas. But as with other "spot zoning," it seems the lack of uniformity within a district is invalid only if *not* based on relevant differences among the parts of the area that are treated differently.[55]

A third legitimate purpose of zoning is the limiting of density of population. Though a community has an obvious interest in preventing over-crowding and in limiting population growth so that it will not overwhelm the community's ability to offer needed services to its residents, zoning aimed, partly or entirely, at controlling population has been a subject of much controversy. It has been called "snob" or "exclusionary" zoning. It often has taken the form of requirements in residential areas that lots, or floor space of homes, have a designated minimum size. In practice, it is alleged to have frequently excluded certain racial and/or economic groups from many communities.[56] Occasionally

---

120 S.Ct. 1073, 145 L.Ed.2d 1060 (2000), in allowing equal protection claims, but also noting (at 982–91) that municipalities have done surprisingly well at defending against equal protection claims, while (at 991–94) landowners have done surprisingly well under due process claims. Cf. Village of Willowbrook v. Olech, 528 U.S. 562, 120 S.Ct. 1073, 145 L.Ed.2d 1060 (2000), where a claim for relief under traditional equal protection analysis was found to be stated by a property owner's allegation that a village had engaged in arbitrary and capricious action in zoning his property differently from its zoning of similarly situated land. The Supreme Court, however, did not reach the question involving the alternative theory that the village had acted out of subjective ill will, which had been the basis of the Seventh Circuit's granting relief for violation of equal protection. Olech v. Village of Willowbrook, 160 F.3d 386, 387 (7th Cir. 1998), aff'd 528 U.S. 562, 120 S.Ct. 1073, 145 L.Ed.2d 1060 (2000). See generally Tassinary, Jourdan & Parsons, Equal Protection and Aesthetic Zoning: A Possible Crack and a Preemptive Repair, 42 Urban Law. 375, 377–78 (2010).

[54] Henry v. White, 194 Tenn. 192, 250 S.W.2d 70 (1952). See Clements v. McCabe, 210 Mich. 207, 177 N.W. 722 (1920); Raskin v. Morristown, 21 N.J. 180, 121 A.2d 378 (1956); Olean v. Conkling, 157 Misc. 63, 283 N.Y.S. 66 (1935); Blankenship v. City of Richmond, 188 Va. 97, 49 S.E.2d 321 (1948). Often, the requirement of uniformity within a district is found in enabling state legislation on the municipal zoning power; but the requirement may be considered basic to all zoning. See Schmidt v. Board of Adjustment, 9 N.J. 405, 88 A.2d 607 (1952). A lack of uniformity, possibly violating equal protection, can also be found where large businesses and small businesses are treating differently within the same zone; but a reasonable basis for the differentiation is generally sufficient for it to be upheld. See Hernandez v. City of Hanford, 41 Cal.4th 279, 59 Cal.Rptr.3d 442, 159 P.3d 33 (2007) (equal protection challenge to city's zoning ordinance that allowed department stores with 50,000 or more square feet of floor space to sell furniture in specific commercial district, while denying that right to smaller retailers, was subject to rational relationship or rational basis standard of judicial review; ordinance upheld).

[55] Borough of West Caldwell v. Zell, 22 N.J.Super. 188, 91 A.2d 763 (1952). Cf. Bogert v. Washington Township, 25 N.J. 57, 135 A.2d 1 (1957) (uniformity is ultimate end of zoning; too great an amount of nonconformance will make area less attractive).

[56] See Marcus, Exclusionary Zoning: The Need for a Regional Planning Context,16 N.Y.L.F. 732 (1970); Note, Exclusionary Zoning and Equal Protection, 84 Harv. L.Rev. 1645 (1971); "Battle to Open the Suburbs: New Attack on Zoning Laws," U.S. News & World Rep., June 22, 1970, at 39. Compare Papke, Keeping the Underclass in Its Place: Zoning the Poor, and Residential Segregation, 41 Urban Law. 787 (2009). Cf. Gallese, Housing for the Poor Blocked Despite Curb on "Snob Zoning" Laws, Wall St. J., Oct. 17, 1972, at 1 (describing efforts—not always successful—to circumvent "snob zoning" laws in order to establish low- and moderate-income housing, and housing for the elderly, in some areas). See generally Kushner, Apartheid in America: An Historical and Legal Analysis of Contemporary Racial Segregation in the United States (Carrollton Press 1980); Jorgensen, Tearing Down the Walls: The Federal Challenge to Exclusionary Land Use Laws, 13 Urban Lawyer 201 (1981); Annot., Validity of Zoning Regulations Prescribing Minimum Area for House Lots or Requiring an Area Proportionate to Number of Families to be Housed, 95 A.L.R.2d 716 (1964). See also Freilich & Bass, Exclusionary Zoning: Suggested Litigation Approaches, 3 Urban Lawyer 344 (1971); Yannacone, Rahenkamp & Cerchione, Impact Zoning: Alternative to Exclusion in the Suburbs, 8 Urban Lawyer 417 (1976), urging zoning that takes into account regional demands and the prospects of local growth. On planning for future growth, see generally Chapter 21 *supra*.

zoning is invalidated if its aim is the exclusion of a particular group of persons, such as children.[57] But the Supreme Court has refused to infer discriminatory intent against racial minorities from mere refusal to rezone property to allow a low-cost housing project

---

On the *legitimate* use of zoning to control population density, see Hukle v. Kansas City, 212 Kan. 627, 512 P.2d 457 (1973) (city could deny rezoning for townhouse complex that would put burden on city services).

[57] See Molino v. Borough of Glassboro, 116 N.J.Super. 195, 281 A.2d 401 (1971), invalidating an ordinance which required that in any particular garden-apartment-complex, at least 70% of all the units must have not more than one bedroom, no more than 25% could have two bedrooms, and no more than 5% could have 3 bedrooms. The provision was admittedly designed to keep children out of the community and thus lower taxes, since fewer schools would be required. Cf. Kirsch Holding Co. v. Borough of Manasquan, 59 N.J. 241, 281 A.2d 513 (1971) (invalidating ordinance prohibiting "group rentals" of seashore residences). See also State ex rel. Thelen v. City of Missoula, 168 Mont. 375, 543 P.2d 173 (1975) (state law providing that homes for the *disabled* must be allowed in all residential areas governed over any local zoning laws to the contrary).

Many landlords refuse to rent to persons who have children living with them, but a few states and a number of cities now have bans on such discrimination. See "No Children Allowed," Parade magazine, Oct. 5, 1980, at 21. On the constitutionality of laws proscribing age discrimination in housing, see Metropolitan Dade County Fair Housing & Employment Appeals Bd. v. Sunrise Village Mobile Home Park, 511 So.2d 962 (Fla.1987), noted 17 Stetson L. Rev. 915 (1988), upholding a county's power to enact such a law but holding unconstitutional an ordinance that authorized awards of damages for humiliation, embarrassment, and mental distress.

Amendments to the federal Fair Housing Act, which were passed in 1988 and took effect in 1989, forbid discrimination against persons with children in the selling and leasing of most housing. Exceptions are provided for retirement or "adults only" communities. Eighty per cent of the units in a complex must contain at least one occupant who is 55 years of age or older in order for the complex to qualify for the exemption. In addition, facilities or services specifically designed to meet the needs of older persons must be provided, and the complex must publish and adhere to policies showing an intent to provide housing for those 55 or older. 42 U.S.C.A. §§ 3601–17, 3631 (1988). See Brooks, New Law Likely to Have a Major Impact on Condos, N.Y. Times, Jan. 15, 1989, at 29; Coan & Salmon, The Fair Housing Act and Seniors' Housing, 27 Urban Law. 826 (1995). See generally Lewin, Children as Neighbors? Elderly Bar the Door, N.Y. Times, Nov. 28, 1989, at 1; Note, The Enforceability of Age Restrictive Covenants in Condominium Developments, 54 S. Cal. L. Rev. 1397 (1981). See also Dwyer, No Place for Children: Addressing Urban Plight and Its Impact on Children Through Child Protection Law, Domestic Relations Law, and "Adult-only" Residential Zoning, 62 Ala. L. Rev. 887 (2011).

Historically, retirement or "adult," communities have often been successful in excluding, or limiting the number of, younger residents—through the use of zoning, restrictive covenants, and/or exclusionary marketing policies. See Doyle, Retirement Communities: The Nature and Enforceability of Residential Segregation by Age, 76 Mich.L.Rev. 64 (1977) (trend is to uphold age-restrictive zoning by such communities). Cf. Comment, Neither Seen Nor Heard: Keeping Children Out of Arizona's Adult Communities under Arizona Revised Statutes Section 33–1317B, 1975 Ariz.St. L.J. 813. See generally Note, Housing Discrimination Against Children: The Legal Status of a Growing Social Problem, 16 J.Family L. 559 (1978). See also Brown, Housing for the Elderly: Federal Subsidy Policy and Its Effect on Age-Group Isolation, 57 U.Detroit J. Urban L. 257 (1980). On the history and development of Sun City, Arizona, the first major retirement community, see Loh, Sun City—The Next Generation, Arizona (Tucson) Daily Star, May 29, 1990, at C-1. On the changing nature of retirement communities because of the increasing youthfulness of many retirees, see Kadlec, Farewell to Bingo, Time magazine, Nov. 26, 2007, at 56. As to zoning practices and policies relating to nursing homes for the elderly, see Hoffman & Landon, Zoning and the Aging Population: Are Residential Communities Zoning Elder Care Out?, 44 Urban Law. 629 (2012).

Minimum-age restrictions for retirement communities or districts will be upheld against equal-protection attack if the restrictions are supported by a *rational purpose;* unlike the situation with racial discrimination, a compelling state interest need not be found. See Taxpayers Association v. Weymouth Township, 80 N.J. 6, 364 A.2d 1016 (1976), cert. denied 430 U.S. 977, 97 S.Ct. 1672, 52 L.Ed.2d 373 (ordinance limited occupancy of mobile home parks to those 52 and over, and those over 18 who belonged to a family the head of which—or whose spouse—was 52 or over; upheld); Shepard v. Woodland Township Committee and Planning Board, 71 N.J. 230, 364 A.2d 1005 (1976) (senior citizen communities authorized as special uses; persons under 52 mostly excluded; upheld); Maldini v. Ambro, 36 N.Y.2d 481, 369 N.Y.S.2d 385, 330 N.E.2d 403 (1975), appeal dism'd 423 U.S. 993, 96 S.Ct. 419, 46 L.Ed.2d 367 (town created "retirement community district" for subsidized housing for the elderly; sustained). Cf. Riley v. Stoves, 22 Ariz.App. 223, 526 P.2d 747 (1974) (portion of mobile-home subdivision set aside for persons 21 and older; no violation of equal protection).

therein.[58] Generally, minimum-lot-size restrictions have been upheld as having a reasonable relationship to public health, safety, and/or general welfare.[59] Minimums as

---

[58] Village of Arlington Heights v. Metropolitan Housing Development Corp., 429 U.S. 252, 97 S.Ct. 555, 50 L.Ed.2d 450 (1977) (no discriminatory intent shown, though had discriminatory effect). The case was then remanded to the Court of Appeals to determine whether the village's refusal to rezone violated the Fair Housing Act, 42 U.S.C.A. §§ 3601–31. That court held the village did have a *statutory* obligation to refrain from zoning policies that effectively foreclosed any low-cost housing within its boundaries, and the case was remanded to the district court for a determination of whether the defendant had done so. Metropolitan Housing Development Corp. v. Village of Arlington Heights, 558 F.2d 1283 (7th Cir.1977), cert. denied 434 U.S. 1025, 98 S.Ct. 752, 54 L.Ed.2d 772 (1978). The court of appeals listed various factors to be examined in determining possible violations of the Fair Housing Act; 558 F.2d 1283, 1290–93 (7th Cir.1977). See, adopting similar standards, United States v. City of Black Jack, 508 F.2d 1179 (8th Cir.1974), cert. denied 422 U.S. 1042, 95 S.Ct. 2656, 45 L.Ed.2d 694, reh. denied 423 U.S. 884, 96 S.Ct. 158, 46 L.Ed.2d 115 (1975) (statutory violation found in incorporation of community, followed by rezoning so as to exclude subsidized housing project); Otero v. New York City Housing Authority, 484 F.2d 1122 (2d Cir.1973). Cf. Town of Huntington v. Huntington Branch, N.A.A.C.P., 488 U.S. 15, 109 S.Ct. 276, 102 L.Ed.2d 180 (1988), reh. denied 488 U.S. 1023, 109 S.Ct. 824, 102 L.Ed.2d 813, where the Court found that a town's refusal to amend its zoning ordinance, which restricted private multifamily housing projects to a largely minority urban renewal area, was a violation of the Fair Housing Act; the sole justification offered—that the ordinance encouraged developers to invest in a deteriorated and needy section of town—was found inadequate. But cf. Joseph Skillken & Co. v. City of Toledo, 528 F.2d 867 (6th Cir.1975), vacated and remanded 429 U.S. 1068, 97 S.Ct. 800, 50 L.Ed.2d 786, aff'd on remand 558 F.2d 350 (6th Cir.) (refusal to rezone to permit low-income housing found not to discriminate against minorities). See generally American Bar Ass'n Advisory Comm'n on Housing & Urban Growth, Housing for All Under Law (1977); Moskowitz, Exclusionary Zoning Litigation (Ballinger Publ.1977); Hyson, The Problem of Relief in Developer-Initiated Exclusionary Zoning Litigation, 12 Urban L.Ann. 21 (1976); Mandelker, Racial Discrimination and Exclusionary Zoning: A Perspective on *Arlington Heights*, 55 Tex.L.Rev. 1217 (1977); Sussna, Remedying Exclusionary Zoning Practices in Suburbia, 28 U.Fla.L.Rev. 671 (1976). See also Kmiec, Exclusionary Zoning and Purposeful Racial Segregation in Housing: Two Wrongs Deserving Separate Remedies, 18 Urban Law. 393 (1986), stating that racially motivated exclusionary zoning can be rectified under the federal Constitution and Fair Housing Act but concluding that enactment of a Proposed Model State Land Use Enabling Statute (set forth at *id.* 420–22) by the states is needed to put an end to exclusionary zoning that is *not* racially motivated; Note, Anti-Snob Zoning in Massachusetts: Assessing One Attempt at Opening the Suburbs to Affordable Housing, 78 Va. L. Rev. 535 (1992).

Blacks and other minority groups do now live, of course, in many suburbs; but few suburbs are truly integrated, with a mixture of races. Many suburbs in which blacks reside in considerable numbers are, for instance, spillovers from older ghettos or enclaves into areas abandoned by whites. See H. Rose, Black Suburbanization (1976). See generally Connolly, Black Movement into the Suburbs, 9 Urban Aff.Q.91 (1973). See also Comment, Breaking the Color Line: Zoning and Opportunity in America's Metropolitan Areas, 8 J. Gender Race & Just. 667 (2005).

On the use of "fair housing laws"—at the federal, state, and local level—to "open up" communities to all racial and ethnic groups, see Chapter 27 *infra*. Cf. Gladstone, Realtors v. Village of Bellwood, 441 U.S. 91, 99 S.Ct. 1601, 60 L.Ed.2d 66 (1979) (area residents and village alleged that real-estate brokers and sales personnel "steered" prospective home buyers to different residential areas according to race; village and individual residents of described area held to have standing to complain under Fair Housing Act and Civil Rights Act of 1866).

[59] See Clemons v. City of Los Angeles, 36 Cal.2d 95, 222 P.2d 439 (1950) (minimum of 5000 square feet); Chucta v. Planning and Zoning Comm'n of Seymour, 154 Conn. 393, 225 A.2d 822 (1967); First National Bank of Skokie v. City of Chicago, 25 Ill.2d 366, 185 N.E.2d 181 (1962); J. D. Construction Corp. v. Township of Freehold, 119 N.J.Super. 140, 290 A.2d 452 (1972) (control of population density specifically said to be a valid zoning objective); State v. Gallop Building, 103 N.J.Super. 367, 247 A.2d 350 (1968); Clary v. Eatontown, 41 N.J.Super. 47, 124 A.2d 54 (1956) (minimum of 20,000 square feet upheld); Fulling v. Palumbo, 21 N.Y.2d 30, 286 N.Y.S.2d 249, 233 N.E.2d 272 (1967) (is legitimate interest in preserving character of area and in preventing too great a density for municipal facilities to handle). See generally Symposium, Exclusionary Zoning, 22 Syracuse L.Rev. 465 (1971); Annot., Construction and Application of Zoning Laws Setting Minimum Lot Size Requirements, 2 A.L.R. 5th 553 (1992); Annot., Exclusionary Zoning, 48 A.L.R.3d 1210 (1973). Minimums for the front-width of residential properties are also sometimes established by zoning ordinances, and these have also been sustained if reasonable. See Di Salle v. Giggal, 128 Colo. 208, 261 P.2d 499 (1953); Bilbar Construction Co. v. Board of Adjustment, 393 Pa. 62, 141 A.2d 851 (1958) (150 feet). See generally Annot., Validity and Construction of Zoning Regulations Prescribing a Minimum Width or Frontage for Residence Lots, 96 A.L.R.2d 1367 (1964). The concern for assuring adequacy of municipal services prior to allowing population growth has also led some communities to adopt limits on building permits for new

large as ten acres have been sustained.[60] But there are also now a number of cases striking down such minimums, usually on the ground they are unreasonably large to achieve the supposed purposes;[61] and there is some evidence that courts are becoming increasingly unfavorable to this type of restriction.[62] Similarly, minimum-floor-space requirements for residences in particular areas have often been sustained as reasonably related to public health or other police-power purposes.[63] But there has been much

---

residential construction, to require the developers to wait a certain length of time and/or themselves provide certain public services before constructing or expanding residential subdivisions, etc. ("timed" or "sequential" growth); see Chapter 21 *infra.*

[60] Rodgers v. Village of Tarrytown, 302 N.Y. 115, 96 N.E.2d 731 (1951) (minimum of ten acres in one class of residential zone). Cf. Rubi v. 49'er Country Club Estates, 7 Ariz.App. 408, 440 P.2d 44 (1968) (one acre); De Mars v. Zoning Commission, 142 Conn. 580, 115 A.2d 653 (1955) (increase in minimum dimensions of lots challenged; upheld); Honeck v. Cook County, 12 Ill.2d 257, 146 N.E.2d 35 (1957) (5 acres); County Com'rs of Queen Anne's County v. Miles, 246 Md. 355, 228 A.2d 450 (1967) (five acres); Fischer v. Bedminster Township, 11 N.J. 194, 93 A.2d 378 (1952) (five acres); Levitt v. Incorporated Village of Sands Point, 6 N.Y.2d 269, 189 N.Y.S.2d 212, 160 N.E.2d 501 (1959) (two acres); Franmor Realty Corp. v. Village of Old Westbury, 280 App.Div. 945, 116 N.Y.S.2d 68 (1952) (two acres); State ex rel. Grant v. Kiefaber, 114 Ohio App. 279, 181 N.E.2d 905 (1960), aff'd 171 Ohio St. 326, 170 N.E.2d 848 (80,000 square feet); Jones v. Woodway, 70 Wn.2d 977, 425 P.2d 904 (1967) (one acre). In Flora Realty & Investment Co. v. City of Ladue, 362 Mo. 1025, 246 S.W.2d 771 (1952), a minimum-lot-size of three acres was upheld, and the U.S. Supreme Court dismissed an appeal for want of a substantial federal question. 344 U.S. 802, 73 S.Ct. 41, 97 L.Ed. 626 (1952).

[61] See Hamer v. Town of Ross, 59 Cal.2d 776, 31 Cal.Rptr. 335, 382 P.2d 375 (1963) (one acre); Cherry Hills Village v. Trans-Robles Corp., 181 Colo. 356, 509 P.2d 797 (1973); (2½ acres); Aronson v. Town of Sharon, 346 Mass. 598, 195 N.E.2d 341 (1964) (100,000 square feet); Christine Building Co. v. City of Troy, 367 Mich. 508, 116 N.W.2d 816 (1962) (21,780 square feet); Appeal of Kit-Mar Builders, 439 Pa. 466, 268 A.2d 765 (1970) (two acres); National Land & Investment Co. v. Kohn, 419 Pa. 504, 215 A.2d 597 (1965) (four acres). Cf. Morris v. City of Los Angeles, 116 Cal.App.2d 856, 254 P.2d 935 (Dist.Ct. 1953) (other houses in area were on smaller lots and thus restriction inappropriate; zoning regulation said to have come 50 years too late). There is also the possibility that if the allowed density is reduced, as by increasing the minimum lot size (or wherever the law is changed so that only less intense uses are now allowed—for instance, only residential uses where commercial used to be permitted), a property-owner may have an action for "taking" or "inverse condemnation," or may be able to have the change in the law declared invalid. But courts tend to apply the same standard of reasonableness to such changes as they apply to the original law—and thus most such changes have been upheld, and no relief granted. See Williamson, Constitutional and Judicial Limitations on the Community's Power to Downzone, 12 Urban Lawyer 157 (1980). (Changes that reduce the allowed density or intensiveness of use are often called "downzoning.") On "takings" and "inverse condemnation," see generally Chapter 19 *infra.* Relief under the Federal Civil Rights Act, 42 U.S.C. § 1983 (1974), is also a possibility where minimum-lot requirements are increased. This was recognized in Steel Hill Development, Inc. v. Sanbornton, 335 F.Supp. 947 (D.N.H. 1971); but in a subsequent proceeding, the court held the amendments, and minimum sizes thus established, not so unreasonable or arbitrary as to deprive plaintiffs of constitutional rights. 338 F.Supp. 301 (D.N.H. 1972), aff'd 469 F.2d 956 (1st Cir.). See generally Annot., Right of Real Property Owner to Relief Under Federal Civil Rights Acts Against Amendment of Zoning Ordinance Increasing Minimum Lot Requirements, 25 A.L.R. Fed. 850 (1975); Annot., Rezoning or Amendment of Zoning Regulations as Affecting Persons Who Have Purchased or Improved Property in Reliance Upon Original Regulations, 138 A.L.R. 500 (1942). See also Annot., Purchaser of Real Property as Precluded from Attacking Validity of Zoning Regulations Existing at the Time of the Purchase and Affecting the Purchased Property, 17 A.L.R.3d 743 (1968). On the use of large minimum-lot-size restrictions to preserve rural environments, see Note, Protection of Environmental Quality in Nonmetropolitan Regions by Limiting Development, 57 Iowa L.Rev. 126 (1971).

[62] See Appeal of Kit-Mar Builders, *supra* note 58; National Land & Investment Co. v. Kohn, 419 Pa. 504, 215 A.2d 597 (1965), both rejecting minimum-lot-size restrictions and other exclusionary zoning in fairly general terms; Sager, Tight Little Islands: Exclusionary Zoning, Equal Protection, and the Indigent, 21 Stan.L.Rev. 767 (1969). See generally Note, Removing the Bar of Exclusionary Zoning to a Decent Home, 32 Ohio State L.J. 373 (1971). See also Haar, Housing the Poor in Suburbia (Ballinger Publ.1974).

[63] Hitchman v. Oakland Township, 329 Mich. 331, 45 N.W.2d 306 (1951); Dundee Realty Co. v. City of Omaha, 144 Neb. 448, 13 N.W.2d 634 (1944) (1000 square feet for one-story dwellings; 1200 for more-than-one-story dwelling); Lionshead Lake, Inc. v. Wayne Township, 10 N.J. 165, 89 A.2d 693 (1952), appeal dism'd 344 U.S. 919, 73 S.Ct. 386, 97 L.Ed. 708 (the leading case; sustained ordinance requiring 786 square feet for one-story residence, 1000 square feet for two-story dwellings with attached garages, 1200 square feet for two-story residences without attached garages). See Flower Hill Building Corp. v. Village of Flower Hill, 199 Misc.

discussion, and increasing controversy, about them;[64] and some have been invalidated as unreasonably small, or as simply not sufficiently related to the alleged objectives.[65]

Another type of "exclusionary" zoning is that in which only single-family residences are permitted in a particular zone. This type of provision has usually been upheld,[66] and the U.S. Supreme Court has even sustained the zoning of an entire (though small) village for one-family dwellings, to the exclusion of apartment houses, boarding houses, etc.[67]

344, 100 N.Y.S.2d 903 (1950) (minimum of 1800 square feet not invalid on its face); Thompson v. City of Carrollton, 211 S.W.2d 970 (Tex.Civ.App. 1948) (900 square-foot minimum in certain district sustained). Cf. Harris v. State ex rel. Ball, 23 Ohio App. 33, 155 N.E. 166 (1926) (set-back line of 25 feet from street for residences upheld). But cf. Comer v. City of Dearborn, 342 Mich. 471, 70 N.W.2d 813 (1955) (minimum floor area of 640 square feet in each unit of multiple dwelling invalid as applied to motel). See generally McCrory, The Undersized House: A Municipal Problem, 27 Chi.-Kent L.Rev. 142 (1948); Note, Municipal Corporations—Zoning—Validity of Minimum Floor Space Requirements, 21 Geo.Wash.L.Rev. 500 (1953); Annot., Validity and Construction of Zoning Laws Setting Minimum Requirements for Floorspace or Cubic Footage Inside Residence, 87 A.L.R. 4th 294 (1991). For analysis of the *Wayne Township* case, *supra*, see Haar, Wayne Township: Zoning for Whom?—In Brief Reply, 67 Harv.L.Rev. 986 (1954); Haar, Zoning for Minimum Standards: The Wayne Township Case, 66 Harv.L.Rev. 1051 (1953).

[64] See Nolan & Horack, How Small a House?—Zoning for Minimum Space Requirements, 67 Harv.L.Rev. 967 (1954); Note, Constitutional Law—Equal Protection—Zoning—Snob Zoning: Must a Man's Home Be a Castle?, 69 Mich.L.Rev. 339 (1970). See generally Williams & Wacks, Segregation of Residential Areas Along Economic Lines: Lionshead Lake Revisited, 1969 Wis.L.Rev. 827. See also Clark, Blacks in Suburbs: A National Perspective (Center for Urban Policy Research 1979). Because of limited space and high costs of land, planners in some cities now try to increase, rather than limit, the density of population in residential areas. See Wentling & Bookout (eds.), Density by Design (Urban Land Institute 1988), reviewed 25 Urban Law. 693 (1993).

[65] See Senefsky v. Lawler, 307 Mich. 728, 12 N.W.2d 387 (1943); Appeal of Medinger, 377 Pa. 217, 104 A.2d 118 (1954) (1000 square feet required in some areas, 1800 in others; if 1000 square-foot dwellings don't impair health in some areas, why require 1800 square feet in other areas?). Cf. City of North Miami v. Newsome, 203 So.2d 634 (Fla.App.1967) (unreasonable as to business premises); Comer v. City of Dearborn, *supra* note 63 (usual restriction for multiple dwellings invalid as applied to motel); Ridgeview Co. v. Board of Adjustment, 57 N.J.Super. 142, 154 A.2d 23 (1959) (unreasonable as to business premises); Frischkorn Construction Co. v. Lambert, 315 Mich. 556, 24 N.W.2d 209 (1946) (house met square footage requirement but not cubic foot requirement; ordinance held invalid).

[66] See Wilcox v. City of Pittsburgh, 121 F.2d 835 (3d Cir.1941); Koch v. City of Toledo, 37 F.2d 336 (6th Cir.1930); City of Miami Beach v. Lachman, 71 So.2d 148 (Fla.1953) appeal dism'd 348 U.S. 906, 75 S.Ct. 292, 99 L.Ed. 711; Jacobson v. Wilmette, 403 Ill. 250, 85 N.E.2d 753 (1949); Antrim v. Hohlt, 122 Ind.App. 681, 108 N.E.2d 197 (1952); Leigh v. City of Wichita, 148 Kan. 607, 83 P.2d 644 (1938) (apartment house enjoined as in violation of zoning, which was for one- and two- family dwellings; city not estopped by prior failure to enforce); Brett v. Building Commissioner, 250 Mass. 73, 145 N.E. 269 (1924); Pascack Association, Ltd. v. Mayor and Council, 74 N.J. 470, 379 A.2d 6 (1977); Fanale v. Borough of Hasbrouck Heights, 26 N.J. 320, 139 A.2d 749 (1958); Repp v. Shahadi, 132 N.J.L. 24, 38 A.2d 284 (1944). But see Britton v. Town of Chester, 134 N.H. 434, 595 A.2d 492 (1991) (town ordinance severely restricting multifamily housing held contrary to state's zoning enabling statute, the court finding that the welfare of the entire affected region must be considered in determining whether the law promoted valid police-power purposes); Dowsey v. Village of Kensington, 257 N.Y. 221, 177 N.E. 427 (1931) (village contiguous to big city zoned all property almost exclusively for one-family-dwelling use; unreasonable as to property just within village boundary and fronting on a main highway). On power to *change* single-family zoning to less restrictive zoning, see Note, Zoning—Municipal Corporations—Due Process—Restrictions on the Power to Change Zoning Ordinances, 8 U.Pitt.L.Rev. 69 (1941). See generally Boyd, Zoning for Apartments: A Study of the Role of Law in the Control of Apartment Houses in New Haven, Connecticut 1912–32, 33 Pace L. Rev. 600 (2013); Annot., Supreme Court's Views as to Constitutionality of Residential Zoning Restrictions, 52 L.Ed.2d 863 (1978). See also Annot., Use of Property for Multiple Dwellings as Violating Restrictive Covenant Permitting Property to Be Used for Residential Purposes Only, 99 A.L.R.3d 985 (1980); Annot., Change of Neighborhood as Affecting Restrictive Covenants Precluding Use of Land for Multiple Dwelling, 53 A.L.R.3d 492 (1973).

[67] Village of Belle Terre v. Boraas, 416 U.S. 1, 94 S.Ct. 1536, 39 L.Ed.2d 797 (1974). See Note, Zoning—Equal Protection—Right of Privacy, 60 Corn.L.Rev. 299 (1975); Comment, Boraas: A Warning to Industry and Land Developers, 12 Houston L.Rev. 253 (1974); Note, Constitutional Law—Zoning, 19 Vill.L.Rev. 819 (1974); Comment, Property: Zoning and the Rational Basis Test: Foundation for New Use of an Old Power, 14 Washburn L.J. 182 (1975); "New Privacy Problems," Time, April 15, 1974, at 104. Cf. Guaclides v. Borough of

But the Supreme Court has struck down as violative of due process an ordinance limiting occupancy of a dwelling to a "single family" and then very *narrowly* defining what constitutes such a "family."[68] And some state courts have now found a duty in

---

Englewood Cliffs, 11 N.J.Super. 405, 78 A.2d 435 (1951) (ordinance upheld despite its practically excluding multiple-family dwellings from borough); Fountain Gate Ministries v. City of Plano, 654 S.W.2d 841 (Tex.App. 1983) (operation of college enjoined as in violation of single-family zoning ordinances; court stated that operation of college is not protected as a First Amendment exercise of speech or religion). Though the U.S. Supreme Court in the *Belle Terre* case *supra* sustained a restriction against more than two unrelated persons living together, a number of state courts have invalidated such limitation. While the U.S. Supreme Court required only a "rational purpose" in order for such law to pass Equal Protection muster, some of these state tribunals have, due to the restriction on freedom of association, applied a stricter test and required a substantial relationship to a state objective. Other state court cases have simply distinguished *Belle Terre* on the ground that the group of unrelated persons there involved—6 college students—did not in any real sense constitute a single housekeeping unit but were merely temporarily residing together. See Annot., Validity of Ordinance Restricting Number of Unrelated Persons Who Can Live Together in Residential Zone, 12 A.L.R. 4th 238 (1982). Even applying a "rational purpose" test, a state court may invalidate a restriction on related persons living together as violative of Due Process under the *state* constitution. See Charter Township of Delta v. Dinolfo, 419 Mich. 253, 351 N.W.2d 831 (184) (ordinance not reasonably related to legitimate objective of maintaining residential nature of neighborhood). But see City of Ladue v. Horn, 720 S.W.2d 745 (Mo.App.1986) (zoning designating certain zones as "one family residential" could validly prevent an unmarried man and woman from living together; held rationally related to police power purposes). Cf. Zavala v. City of County of Denver, 759 P.2d 664 (Colo. 1988) (unmarried, unrelated homeowners failed to establish discriminatory enforcement of ordinance restricting use to single-family dwellings and failed to establish violation of due process or equal protection). See generally Frame & Scorza, Village of Belle Terre v. Boraas: Property Rights, Personal Rights and The Liberal Regime, 2 Hast.Con.L.Q.935 (1975); Note, *Belle Terre* and Single-Family Home Ordinances: Judicial Perceptions of Local Government and the Presumption of Validity, 74 N.Y.U. L. Rev. 447 (1999). Local governments have sometimes temporarily lifted bans on multiple-family dwellings, or have granted variances, because of housing shortages; such relief has usually been upheld. See Lamarre v. Commissioner of Public Works, 324 Mass. 542, 87 N.E.2d 211 (1949); Hendlin v. Fairmount Construction Co., 8 N.J.Super. 310, 72 A.2d 541 (1950); Gedney v. City of White Plains, 99 N.Y.S.2d 111 (Sup.Ct. 1950). Cf. City of Miami Beach v. First Trust Co., 45 So.2d 681 (Fla.1949) (court ordered zoning restrictions removed because of changed conditions). But see Polk v. Axton, 306 Ky. 498, 208 S.W.2d 497 (1948); Clifton Hills Realty Co. v. City of Cincinnati, 60 Ohio App. 443, 21 N.E.2d 993 (1938). See generally Comment, The Effect of the Housing Shortage on the Single-Family Residential Zone, 46 Ill.L.Rev. 745 (1951). See also Babcock & Bosselman, Suburban Zoning and the Apartment Boom, 111 U.Pa.L.Rev. 1040 (1963); Note, The Battle for Apartments in Benign Suburbia: A Case of Judicial Lethargy, 59 Nw. U.L.Rev. 345 (1964).

The *Village of Belle Terre* case, *supra*, was cited with approval in Sustainable Growth Initiative Committee v. Jumpers, LLC, 122 Nev. 53, 128 P.3d 452 (2006), where the court held that material issues of fact precluded summary judgment as to the validity of a county's sustainable growth initiative. The court recognized that, as the Court in *Belle Terre* said, the police power is not limited to the elimination of filth, stench and unhealthy conditions but includes the promotion of family values, youth values, and the advantages of quiet seclusion and clear air. *Id.* at 466, quoting *Belle Terre*, 416 U.S. at 9, 94 S.Ct. at 1536, 39 L.Ed.2d at 804.

[68] Moore v. City of East Cleveland, 431 U.S. 494, 97 S.Ct. 1932, 52 L.Ed.2d 531 (1977) (would have been crime under ordinance for homeowner to have living with her a son and grandson, plus second grandson who was cousin of first). See City of Santa Barbara v. Adamson, 27 Cal.3d 123, 164 Cal.Rptr. 539, 610 P.2d 436 (1980) (invalidating ordinance creating single-family zone and defining "family" as individual, or 2 or more persons related by blood, marriage, or adoption living together as single housekeeping unit, or group of not more than 5 persons living together as single unit—discriminated against groups of more than 5 unrelated persons); Incorporated Village of Freeport v. Association for the Help of Retarded Children, 94 Misc.2d 1048, 406 N.Y.S.2d 221 (1977), aff'd 60 A.D.2d 644, 400 N.Y.S.2d 724 (zoning regulation limited a district to single-family units and defined "family" as only including persons related by blood, marriage, or adoption; invalid as applied to residence in which 8 mentally retarded persons lived with house-parents); City of White Plains v. Ferraioli, 34 N.Y.2d 300, 357 N.Y.S.2d 449, 313 N.E.2d 756 (1974). Compare Saunders v. Clark County Zoning Department, 66 Ohio St.2d 259, 421 N.E.2d 152 (1981) (family-based, group foster home could constitute "family"), with Garcia v. Siffrin Residential Association, 63 Ohio St.2d 259, 407 N.E.2d 1369 (1980) (8 or fewer mentally retarded persons not "family"). Cf. Costley v. Caromin House, Inc., 313 N.W.2d 21 (Minn.1981) (group home for 6 retarded adults and 2 house parents was single-family unit); State ex rel. Ellis v. Liddle, 520 S.W.2d 644 (Mo.App. 1975) ("Achievement House" for boys living as family-type group could be allowed in zone for single-family dwellings without rezoning or special permit); YWCA v. Board of Adjustment, 134 N.J.Super. 384, 341 A.2d 356 (1975) (those who live together as a family, though not related by blood or marriage, cannot

municipalities to provide an appropriate variety of housing.[69] The finding of such a duty has been generally approved by the writers, who often urge municipalities to take a more

---

be discriminated against by community); Saunders v. Clark County Zoning Dep't, 66 Ohio St.2d 259, 421 N.E.2d 152 (1981) (group home for delinquent boys constituted a "family" for zoning purposes and was permissible in residential district); Jackson v. Williams, 714 P.2d 1017 (Okl.1985) (use of residence as a group home for five mentally retarded women and their housekeeper constituted a "single-family dwelling" within a zoning ordinance); Citizens for a Safe Neighborhood v. City of Seattle, 67 Wash.App. 436, 836 P.2d 235 (1992) (housing examiner's decision that house for homeless, low-income women recovering from alcohol and/or chemical dependency was a single-family residence, not a "halfway house," upheld). But see Maryland Comm'n on Human Relations v. Greenbelt Homes, Inc., 300 Md. 75, 475 A.2d 1192 (1984) (Maryland statute prohibiting marital-status discrimination in housing did not preclude a housing cooperative from enforcing a contract restricting occupancy to a cooperative member's immediate family and thus precluding a member from living there with her boyfriend); Open Door Alcoholism Program, Inc. v. Board of Adjustment of New Brunswick, 200 N.J.Super. 191, 491 A.2d 17 (1985) (halfway house for recovering alcoholics did not create functional equivalent of family unit for purposes of single-family zoning). Cf. Agins v. City of Tiburon, 447 U.S. 255, 100 S.Ct. 2138, 65 L.Ed.2d 106 (1980) (open-space zoning restricting use of land to single-family residences and open space upheld). See generally Note, "Burning the House to Roast the Pig:" Unrelated Individuals and Single-Family Zoning's Blood Relation Criterion, 58 Corn.L.Rev. 138 (1972); Note, Excluding The Commune from Suburbia: The Use of Zoning for Social Control, 23 Hast.L.J. 1459 (1972). See also Annot., What Constitutes a "Family" Within Meaning of Zoning Regulation or Restrictive Covenant, 71 A.L.R.3d 693 (1976). It has been held that the terms "family" and "dwelling unit" in a zoning ordinance are not unconstitutionally vague. Douglass v. City of Spokane, 25 Wn.App. 823, 609 P.2d 979 (1980), review denied 94 Wash.2d 1006 (1980), involving an ordinance that defined "family" as "an individual or two or more persons related by blood, marriage or legal adoption, or a group of not more than five persons unrelated . . . , living together as a single housekeeping unit and doing their own cooking on the premises in a dwelling unit." See also, on the meaning of "family," Norwalk CORE v. David Katz & Sons, Inc., 410 F.2d 532 (2d Cir.1969), determining that a mother and father, their son, the son's wife and baby, were a "family" within statutory provisions requiring rents for relocation housing to be within the means of the family displaced. On the history of family-based zoning restrictions, see Note, ". . . Not Related by Blood, Marriage, or Adoption": A History of the Definition of "Family" in Zoning Law, 16 J. Affordable Housing & Commun. Dev. L. 144 (2007); Comment, The Definition of "Family" in Missouri Local Zoning Ordinances: An Analysis of the Justifications for Restrictive Definitions, 52 St. Louis U.L.J. 631 (2008).

Alabama once construed its zoning statutes so as to allow municipalities to prohibit group homes for the mentally disabled in certain residential areas. Indian Rivers Community Health Center v. City of Tuscaloosa, 443 So.2d 894 (Ala.1983). This was reversed by a statute expressly abolishing any zoning law that prevents or prohibits the mentally ill from living in multi-family-zoned residential areas. Regulation as to Housing of Mentally Retarded or Mentally Ill Persons in Multi-Family Zone, Ala. Code §§ 11.52–75.1 (1986). See generally Steinman, The Effect of Land-Use Restrictions on the Establishment of Community Residences for the Disabled: A National Study, 19 Urban Law. 1 (1987); Note, Zoning the Mentally Retarded Into Single-Family Residential Areas: A Grape of Wrath or a Fermentation of Wisdom, 1979 Ariz. St. L.J. 385; Case Comment, Community Commitment: To Accept or Reject the Mentally Ill?, 5 Whittier L. Rev. 417 (1983). On group residences for the elderly, see generally Pollack, Zoning Matters in a Kinder, Gentler Nation: Balancing Needs, Rights and Political Realities for Shared Residences for the Elderly, 10 St. Louis U. Pub. L. Rev. 501 (1991).

In City of Edmonds v. Oxford House, Inc., 514 U.S. 725, 115 S.Ct. 1776, 131 L.Ed.2d 801 (1995), it was held that a single-family zoning ordinance, defining a "family" as persons related by genetics, adoption, or marriage, or group of 5 or fewer unrelated persons, was not automatically exempt from the federal Fair Housing Act's prohibition of housing discrimination against the handicapped. To justify the single-family restriction, local officials must show that their particular application of their laws reasonably accommodates the needs of the handicapped. See Barrett, High Court Ruling Favors Group Homes, Wall St., J., May 16, 1995, at B12, concluding that the Court's ruling makes it harder for local governments to exclude many kinds of group homes from single-family neighborhoods. See generally Davis & Gaus, Protecting Group Homes for the Non-Handicapped: Zoning in the Post-*Edmonds* Era, 46 U. Kan. L. Rev. 777 (1998); Note, Civil Rights—Closing a Loophole in the Fair Housing Act—*City of Edmonds v. Oxford House, Inc.*, 70 Temple L. Rev. 369 (1997).

[69] Oakwood at Madison, Inc. v. Township of Madison, 72 N.J. 481, 371 A.2d 1192 (1977) (local governments must provide their fair-share of regional housing needs, including housing for low- and moderate-income groups); Urban League v. Mayor and Council of Carteret, 142 N.J.Super. 11, 359 A.2d 526 (1976), rev'd 170 N.J.Super. 461, 406 A.2d 1322 (eleven municipalities ordered by lower court to rezone so that each provided a fair share of its own and the county's low-and moderate-income housing needs, but appellate court held no relevant region shown); Southern Burlington County N.A.A.C.P. v. Township of Mount Laurel, 67 N.J. 151, 336 A.2d 713 (1975), cert. denied 423 U.S. 808, 96 S.Ct. 18, 46 L.Ed.2d 28 (1975) (the leading, and a famous, case; ordinance zoning most of township for single-family detached dwellings on 20,000 square-foot lots held invalid as contrary to general welfare and outside statutory powers), noted 61 A.B.A.J. 975 (1975), 59

"regional" approach to their zoning decisions; and a trend may be seen toward requiring each locality to provide its "fair share" of low-and moderate-income housing.[70] The state of New Jersey has held that a municipality which zones for industrial uses must also zone so as to allow a "fair share" of lower income housing and that this obligation must be satisfied on an objective basis—a bona fide attempt is not sufficient.[71]

Marq.L.Rev. 211 (1976), 7 U.Ind.L.Rev. 341 (1975); Surrick v. Zoning Hearing Board, 476 Pa. 182, 382 A.2d 105 (1977) (exclusion of multiple-family residences from most of township was unconstitutional; township must accept its fair share of all categories of persons desiring to live in area); Board of Supervisors of Willistown Township v. Walsh, 20 Pa.Cmwlth. 275, 341 A.2d 572 (1975); Township of Willistown v. Chesterdale Farms, Inc., 462 Pa. 445, 341 A.2d 466 (1975) (apartment construction allowed on only 80 acres out of total of over 11,000; township is not putting a fair share of its land area to proper housing purposes). See Berenson v. Town of New Castle, 38 N.Y.2d 102, 378 N.Y.S.2d 672, 341 N.E.2d 236 (1975) (local desire to maintain status quo must be balanced against greater public interest that *regional* needs be met); Appeal of Girsh, 437 Pa. 237, 263 A.2d 395 (1970) (failure to provide for apartments was unconstitutional, though apartments not explicitly prohibited). But cf. Nigito v. Borough of Closter, 142 N.J.Super. 1, 359 A.2d 521 (1976), holding that even after the *Mt. Laurel* case, *supra*, an ordinance in New Jersey that does not provide for multi-family housing is not necessarily invalid; such an ordinance was thus upheld in a small, almost fully-developed borough. See also Rose, *Oakwood at Madison*: A Tactical Retreat to Preserve the *Mt. Laurel* Principle, 13 Urban L.Ann. 38 (1979), emphasizing that the New Jersey court, in the *Oakwood at Madison* case *supra*, stated that courts, in determining whether communities have provided for their "fair share" of low- and moderate-income housing, need not adopt fair share housing *quotas* or make findings in reference thereto. On the future of the "*Mt. Laurel* obligations," see Kinsey, The Growth Share Approach to *Mount Laurel* Housing Obligations: Origins, Hijacking, and Failure, 63 Rutgers L. Rev. 867 (2011); Mallach, The *Mount Laurel* Doctrine and the Uncertainties of Social Policy in a Time of Retrenchment, 63 Rutgers L. Rev. 849 (2011). See generally Holmes, The Clash of Home Rule and Affordable Housing: The Mount Laurel Story Continues, 12 Conn. Pub. Interest L. J. 325 (2013).

On laws that attempt to impose on builders and developers, in return for their being granted the necessary permits, an obligation to construct a certain amount of low-and/or moderate-income housing, see Chapter 21 *infra*.

In Fernley v. Board of Supervisors of Schuylkill Township, 509 Pa. 413, 502 A.2d 585 (1985), the court held that an ordinance totally prohibiting multifamily dwellings was unconstitutional. Since a total prohibition of an ordinarily legitimate use was shown, the burden shifted to the municipality to establish a police-power purpose, and a more substantial relationship to such a purpose had to be shown than where the regulation merely confined a use to a particular area. No such purpose was here shown. A "fair-share" analysis had been misapplied by the lower court, it was ruled, where that court had used the analysis to reach the conclusion that that no one had been excluded because the municipality was not a logical area for development; the "fair-share" formula might be used where there was partial, or de facto, exclusion of a use, but not where there was by law a total exclusion. On what are legitimate public purposes that might overcome the Pennsylvania presumption that a total prohibition of an ordinarily lawful use is unconstitutional, see Appeal of Marple Gardens, Inc., 99 Pa.Cmwlth. 485, 514 A.2d 216 (1986), appeal denied 514 Pa. 650, 524 A.2d 496 (1987).

[70] See Rose, Fair Share Housing Allocation Plans: Which Formula Will Pacify the Contentious Suburbs?, 12 Urban L.Ann. 3 (1976); Williams & Doughty, Studies in Legal Realism: *Mount Laurel, Belle Terre*, and *Berman*, 29 Rutgers L.Rev. 73 (1975); Note, Land Use Planning—Zoning Regulations That Exclude Segments of the Region's Population on the Basis of Wealth Are Presumptively Invalid, 7 Texas Tech. L.Rev. 182 (1975); Note, The Mount Laurel Case: A Question of Remedies, 37 U.Pitt.L.Rev. 442 (1975); Comment, Calling a Halt to Exclusionary Zoning in New Jersey, 15 Washburn L.J. 180 (1975). See generally Note, The Inadequacy of Judicial Remedies in Cases of Exclusionary Zoning, 74 Mich.L.Rev. 760 (1976) (most satisfactory answer to problems concerning low-cost housing lies in comprehensive legislation).

Following its general rule that total prohibitions of ordinarily lawful uses are presumed invalid (see note 69 *supra*), Pennsylvania has held unconstitutional a zoning ordinance totally excluding apartments from a community. Appeal of Girsh, *supra* note 69. Cf. Township of Willistown v. Chesterdale Farms, Inc., *supra* note 69 (fair share of township must be usable for apartment construction). See generally Comment, Do *Girsh* and *Mt. Laurel* Compel the Zoning of a Fair Share of Acreage for Apartment Use? Pennsylvania Says Yes, 13 Urban L.Ann. 277 (1977).

[71] Southern Burlington County N.A.A.C.P. v. Township of Mount Laurel, 92 N.J. 158, 456 A.2d 390 (1983), on remand 207 N.J.Super. 169, 504 A.2d 66 (1984). This case (which is often called "Mount Laurel II", distinguishing it from the earlier litigation, "Mount Laurel I", cited in note 69 *supra*) also held that apparently exclusionary devices, such as low density limits on population, serve as evidence of facial invalidity of the zoning laws in which they are contained, but that this presumption of invalidity can be rebutted by the

A related question is the *standing* of various persons and organizations, particularly non-residents of a community that has "exclusionary" zoning laws, to challenge zoning rules. Obviously, the exclusionary practices of one community may have an effect on the entire area. But the U.S. Supreme Court, in a case in which plaintiffs—non-residents of the excluding community, though all residents of the metropolitan area involved—alleged violation of their rights under the U.S. constitution and federal civil rights laws, announced a rather strict standard for standing: plaintiff must allege specific, concrete facts showing that the challenged practice harms him and that he would benefit, personally and in a tangible way, from the courts' intervention.[72] State statutes, however, usually provide merely that a party challenging a zoning law must be an "aggrieved person" (or similar language), and there is a tendency in many courts now to hold that municipal boundaries do not pose an absolute obstacle to a person's being "aggrieved" by the zoning practices of a neighboring community.[73]

---

locality's showing of compliance, elsewhere in the community, with the obligation to provide a "fair share" of opportunity for low- and moderate-income housing. Thus, in New Jersey, "exclusionary" zoning does not enjoy the presumption of validity that has traditionally attached to this type, as well as other types, of zoning law; the presumption as to "exclusionary" zoning is now one of *invalidity*. On *Mt. Laurel II*, see generally Buchsbaum, No Wrong Without a Remedy: The New Jersey Supreme Court's Effort to Bar Exclusionary Zoning, 17 Urban Law. 59 (1985); Freilich, Donovan & Ralls, Anti-Trust Liability and Preemption of Authority: Trends and Developments in Urban, State and Local Government Law, 15 Urban Law. 705, 747–50 (1983); Rose, The Mount Laurel II Decision: Is It Based on Wishful Thinking?, 12 Real Estate L.J. 115 (1983). See also Rose & Rothman, After Mount Laurel: The New Suburban Zoning (1977) (written between the two *Mount Laurel* decisions). On the trend, as represented by *Mt. Laurel II*, toward undermining the favored position once enjoyed by "single-family zoning," see Burch & Ryals, Land Use Controls: Requiem for Zoning and Other Musings on the Year 1982, 15 Urban Law. 879 (1983).

In response to the *Mt. Laurel* holdings, the New Jersey legislature enacted a Fair Housing Act, which established a Council on Affordable Housing with the responsibility of designating housing regions, estimating needs, and adopting criteria and guidelines for determining a municipality's fair share of those needs. The legislation was held facially constitutional in Morris County Fair Housing Council v. Boonton Township, 209 N.J.Super. 393, 507 A.2d 768 (1985), and was subsequently upheld against a wide range of constitutional attacks in Hills Dev. Co. v. Township of Bernards, 103 N.J. 1, 510 A.2d 621 (1986) (sometimes called "Mt. Laurel III"), which praised the legislative approach as providing more consistency than a judicial approach. See generally Haar, Suburbs Under Siege: Race, Space, and Audacious Judges (Princeton Press 1996) (reviewed 30 U. Richmond L. Rev. 1093 (1996)) and Kirp, Dwyer & Rosenthal, Our Town: Race, Housing, and the Soul of Suburbia (Rutgers Press 1995), both reviewed 85 Geo. L. J. 2265 (1997); Colloquium, *Mount Laurel* and the Fair Housing Act: Success or Failure?, 19 Fordham Urban L.J. 59 (1991). See also Berger, Inclusionary Zoning Devices as Takings: The Legacy of the Mount Laurel Cases, 70 Neb. L. Rev. 186 (1991); Connerly & Smith, Developing a Fair Share Housing Policy for Florida, 12 J. Land Use & Envtl. L. 63 (1996); Comment, From Mt. Laurel to Montgomery: The Creation of Affordable Housing in Alabama, 23 Cumberland L. Rev. 197 (1993) (examining the possible creation of "*Mt. Laurel* obligations" in Alabama). On judicial attempts to develop "urban policy" in this area, see Rose, Waning Judicial Legitimacy: The Price of Judicial Promulgation of Urban Policy, 20 Urban Law. 801, 814–35 (1988). On the effects of *state* growth-control policies on exclusionary zoning, see generally Note, State-Sponsored Growth Management as a Remedy for Exclusionary Zoning, 108 Harv. L. Rev. 1127 (1995).

[72] Warth v. Seldin, 422 U.S. 490, 95 S.Ct. 2197, 45 L.Ed.2d 343 (1975). See Blum, The New Criteria for Standing in Exclusionary Zoning Litigation, 11 Suffolk U.L.Rev. 1 (1976); Note, Standing to Challenge Exclusionary Land-Use Devices in Federal Courts After Warth v. Sedlin, 29 Stan.L.Rev. 323 (1977). See generally Comment, Exclusionary Zoning and a Reluctant Supreme Court, 13 Wake Forest L.Rev. 107, 121 (1977). See also Scott, Standing in the Supreme Court—A Functional Analysis, 86 Harv.L.Rev. 645 (1973); Sedler, Standing to Assert Constitutional Jus Tertii in the Supreme Court, 71 Yale L.J. 599 (1962).

[73] See Stokes v. City of Mishawaka, 441 N.E.2d 24 (Ind.App.1982) (property owners who resided outside city limits on property adjacent to a rezoned tract within city limits had standing to seek declaratory relief as to the rezoning); Jefferson Landfill Comm. v. Marion County, 297 Or. 280, 686 P.2d 310 (1984); Annot., Standing of Owner of Property Adjacent to Zoned Property, but Not Within Territory of Zoning Authority, to Attack Zoning, 69 A.L.R.3d 805 (1976) (such persons often held to have standing); Annot., Standing of Municipal Corporation or Other Governmental Body to Attack Zoning of Land Lying Outside Its Borders, 49 A.L.R.3d 1126 (1973). But cf. Evans v. Lynn, 376 F.Supp. 327 (S.D.N.Y.1974), affirmed 537 F.2d 571 (2d Cir.—

Broader than the question of zoning a locality entirely for single-family residences is the question of zoning the entire municipality for any single use. For instance, what about zoning the community exclusively for residences—though not necessarily single-family residences? There are a number of cases upholding such zoning, often with the argument that a community is entitled to preserve its essentially residential character so long as needs for business and other uses are adequately supplied elsewhere in the region.[74] But this again puts an obvious burden on the rest of an area—though a less extreme burden than where a community is zoned only for *single-family* dwellings. Here too, there are occasional cases finding such exclusive zoning unreasonable under the circumstances or beyond the statutory powers of the municipality.[75]

---

final decision on rehearing), cert. denied sub nom. Evans v. Hills, 429 U.S. 1066, 97 S.Ct. 797, 50 L.Ed.2d 784 (1977) (non-residents had no standing to challenge federal grants to a community by showing that its zoning discriminates against racial minorities where the non-residents did not complain that they had unsuccessfully sought housing in area or that the community had arbitrarily rejected housing proposals of benefit to them), discussed (prior to the final decision) in "Another Crack in the Suburban Zoning Wall," Bus. Week, July 21, 1975, at 41; Earth Movers of Fairbanks, Inc. v. Fairbanks North Star Borough, 865 P.2d 741 (Alaska 1993) (business competitor whose only alleged injury results from competition lacks standing to challenge land use decision; standing in this area is limited by statute). See generally Ayer, The Primitive Law of Standing in Land Use Disputes: Some Notes from a Dark Continent, 55 Iowa L.Rev. 344 (1969); Comment, Standing to Appeal Zoning Determinations: The "Aggrieved Person" Requirement, 64 Mich. L.Rev. 1070 (1966); Note, Nonresidents Permitted to Protest Proposed Zoning Change, 38 N.Y.U. L. Rev. 161 (1963), noting Koppel v. City of Fairway, 189 Kan. 710, 371 P.2d 113 (1962); Note, Extending Standing to Non-Residents—A Response to the Exclusionary Effects of the Zoning Fragmentation, 24 Vand.L.Rev. 341 (1971); Note, Zoning: Looking Beyond Municipal Boundaries, 1965 Wash.U.L.Q. 107 (1965); Note, The "Aggrieved Person" Requirement in Zoning, 8 Wm. & M. L. Rev. 294 (1967). As to regional approaches to zoning and the persons who are allowed to challenge such zoning, see also Note, Crossing the Home-Rule Boundaries Should Be Mandatory: Advocating for a Watershed Approach to Zoning and Land Use in Ohio, 58 Clev. St. L. Rev. 463 (2010).

It has been held that residents of a community cannot be denied standing to protest that community's exclusionary zoning practices merely because those residents own no real property. Suffolk Housing Services v. Town of Brookhaven, 91 Misc.2d 80, 397 N.Y.S.2d 302 (Sup.Ct.1977), aff'd and mod. 63 A.D.2d 731, 405 N.Y.S.2d 302 (low-income persons protesting ordinance that excluded multi-family developments; they had standing, as did civil-rights organizations). On property-owning limitations on the right to vote, see generally the materials on bond elections in Chapter 15 *supra*, especially Section 15.7.

On the standing of *groups* of property owners to challenge zoning laws, see Annot., Standing of Civic or Property Owners' Association to Challenge Zoning Board Decision (as Aggrieved Party), 8 A.L.R. 4th 1087 (1981) (such associations are now usually recognized as having standing even though the association itself owns no property). See generally Douglaston Civic Ass'n, Inc. v. Galvin, 36 N.Y.2d 1, 364 N.Y.S.2d 830, 324 N.E.2d 317 (1974), listing the factors to be weighed in determining a homeowners' association's standing.

As to standing to protest *violations* of a zoning ordinance, see Rose v. Chaikin, 187 N.J.Super. 210, 453 A.2d 1378 (Ch.Div. 1982) (test for standing is not a stringent one; plaintiff must merely show that he or she is an "interested party" due to being denied reciprocal benefits of a common zoning plan; neighbors granted injunction against operation of windmill). Cf. HD Dunn & Son LP v. Teton County, 140 Idaho 808, 102 P.3d 1127 (2004) (neighbor who owned land adjacent to landowners had standing to challenge landowners' act of subdividing their land without complying with county ordinances).

[74] Valley View Village v. Proffett, 221 F.2d 412 (6th Cir.1955) (not necessarily unreasonable for small community to be zoned entirely residential); Cadoux v. Planning and Zoning Commission, 162 Conn. 425, 294 A.2d 582 (1972), cert. denied 408 U.S. 924, 92 S.Ct. 2496, 33 L.Ed.2d 335 (1972); City of Richlawn v. McMakin, 313 Ky. 265, 230 S.W.2d 902 (1950), cert. dism'd 340 U.S. 945, 71 S.Ct. 531, 95 L.Ed. 682. See generally Annot., Validity of Ordinance Zoning Entire Municipality for Residential Use, 54 A.L.R.3d 1282 (1974). See also Annot. Exclusion from Municipality of Industrial Activities Inconsistent With Residential Character, 9 A.L.R.2d 683 (1950).

[75] See Gundersen v. Bingham Farms, 372 Mich. 352, 126 N.W.2d 715 (1964) (beyond power given by enabling statute); Moline Acres v. Heidbreder, 367 S.W.2d 568 (Mo.1963) (single-use zoning beyond municipal power in Missouri); Dowsey v. Village of Kensington, *supra* note 66 (unreasonable to zone almost all of village exclusively for *one-family* dwellings); Town of Hobart v. Collier, 3 Wis.2d 182, 87 N.W.2d 868 (1958) (some lands in town not fit for any purpose allowed under the ordinance). Cf. Hamilton Co. v. Louisville & Jefferson County Planning & Zoning Commission, 287 S.W.2d 434 (Ky.1955) (where neighboring land had commercial

What of zoning that singles-out for exclusion mobile homes and/or trailer parks? Historically, these were even less popular in many communities than were multi-unit dwellings, and total exclusions of such homes from a community have been upheld.[76] But the tendency is to be more favorable toward such uses,[77] though clearly mobile homes can still be excluded from most residential zones.[78]

---

structures and applicants' land was not suitable for residential purposes, rejecting reclassification of land from single-family residential to commercial found unwarranted).

[76] Vickers v. Township Committee, 37 N.J. 232, 181 A.2d 129 (1962), cert. denied and appeal dism'd 371 U.S. 233, 83 S.Ct. 326, 9 L.Ed.2d 495; Stoddard v. Town of Marilla, 60 A.D.2d 771, 400 N.Y.S.2d 637 (1977); Davis v. McPherson, 58 O.O. 253, 132 N.E.2d 626 (1955), appeal dism'd 164 Ohio St. 375, 58 O.O. 157, 130 N.E.2d 794 (1955). See Hohl v. Township of Readington, 37 N.J. 271, 181 A.2d 150 (1962); State ex rel. Cunagin Construction Corp. v. Creech, 23 Ohio App.2d 13, 52 O.O.2d 8, 260 N.E.2d 617 (1969). See generally Annot., Validity and Application of Zoning Regulations Relating to Mobile Home or Trailer Parks, 42 A.L.R.3d 598 (1972). See also Annot., Use of Trailer or Similar Structure for Residence Purposes as Within Limitation of Restrictive Covenant, Zoning Provision, or Building Regulation, 96 A.L.R.2d 232 (1964); Annot., Classification, as Real Estate or Personal Property, of Mobile Homes or Trailers for Purposes of State or Local Taxation, 7 A.L.R. 4th 1016 (1981).

[77] Thus, several cases have now struck down total, or near-total, exclusions of mobile homes from communities. Smith v. Building Inspector, 346 Mich. 57, 77 N.W.2d 332 (1956); Gust v. Canton Township, 342 Mich. 436, 70 N.W.2d 772 (1955); Jackson & Perkins Co. v. Martin, 12 N.Y.2d 1082, 240 N.Y.S.2d 29, 190 N.E.2d 422 (1963); Hunter v. Richter, 9 Pa.D. & C.2d 58 (C.P.1957) (but upholding portion of ordinance requiring trailers staying in town beyond a certain length of time to meet standards for "dwellings"). See Southern Burlington County N.A.A.C.P. v. Township of Mount Laurel, 92 N.J. 158, 456 A.2d 390 (1983), on remand 207 N.J.Super. 169, 504 A.2d 66 (1984) (the "Mt. Laurel II" case discussed in note 71 *supra*) (changed circumstances regarding the structural soundness, safety, and attractiveness of mobile homes have rendered absolute bans on such homes no longer justifiable on the ground of adverse effect on real estate values); Koston v. Town of Newburgh, 45 Misc.2d 382, 256 N.Y.S.2d 837 (1965) (statute did not give town the power to prohibit trailer camps); Robinson Township v. Knoll, 410 Mich. 293, 302 N.W.2d 146 (1981) (exclusion of mobile homes from all areas not designated as mobile-home parks was unreasonable and thus unconstitutional; overruling prior authority); Roddick v. Lower Macungie Zoning Board, 39 Pa. D. & C.2d 529 (C.P.1966) (trailer camps could be regulated by township but not totally prohibited). See generally Bartke & Gage, Mobile Homes: Taxation and Zoning, 55 Cornell L.J. 491 (1970).

Sometimes, exclusion of mobile homes has been achieved somewhat indirectly by ordinances declaring that such homes must—if they remain in the community a certain length of time, or if they have a permanent foundation, etc.—meet building code requirements for structures—which are often difficult for mobile homes to meet. See Morin v. Zoning Board of Review, 102 R.I. 457, 232 A.2d 393 (1967) (trailer with permanent foundation held to be structure). Cf. Lower Merion Township v. Gallup, 158 Pa.Super. 572, 46 A.2d 35 (1946) (citing cases), appeal dism'd 329 U.S. 669, 67 S.Ct. 92, 91 L.Ed. 591 (if house trailer was used for living or sleeping purposes within township for aggregate of more than 30 days, it became subject to building code rules on light, air, sanitation, and safety), noted 45 Mich.L.Rev. 225 (1946).

[78] See Jensen's, Inc. v. Town of Plainville, 146 Conn. 311, 150 A.2d 297 (1959); Cook v. Bandeen, 356 Mich. 328, 96 N.W.2d 743 (1959); State ex rel. Howard v. Village of Roseville, 244 Minn. 343, 70 N.W.2d 404 (1955); Stevens v. Stillman, 18 Misc.2d 274, 186 N.Y.S.2d 327 (1959); City of Raleigh v. Morand, 247 N.C. 363, 100 S.E.2d 870 (1957), appeal dism'd 357 U.S. 343, 78 S.Ct. 1369, 2 L.Ed.2d 1367. See Adams v. Cowart, 224 Ga. 210, 160 S.E.2d 805 (1968) (ordinance prohibited mobile homes in single-family residence; upheld); Stevens v. Smolka, 11 App.Div.2d 896, 202 N.Y.S.2d 783 (1960) (ordinance prohibited any new trailer camp in any residential or agricultural district; upheld). Cf. Hohl v. Township of Readington, *supra* note 76 (trailers could be excluded even from business zone). But see City of Eau Gallie v. Holland, 98 So.2d 786 (Fla.1957) (ordinance unconstitutional because it delegated legislative authority without adequate standards); Clark v. Joslin, 348 Mich. 173, 82 N.W.2d 433 (1957). On what constitutes a "trailer house" within the meaning of zoning regulations, see Clackamas County v. Dunham, 282 Or. 419, 579 P.2d 223 (1978). Sometimes, ordinances prohibit the outdoor storage of trailers, motor homes, etc.; and the validity of such regulations has usually been upheld. See Annot., Validity of Zoning Ordinances Prohibiting or Regulating Outside Storage of House Trailers, Motor Homes, Campers, Vans, and the Like, in Residential Neighborhoods, 95 A.L.R.3d 378 (1979). Laws restricting mobile homes to established parks have also usually been upheld. See Annot., Validity of Zoning or Building Regulations Restricting Mobile Homes or Trailers to Established Mobile Home or Trailer Parks, 17 A.L.R. 4th 106 (1982).

As to restrictions on prefabricated dwellings, see Your Home, Inc. v. City of Portland, 483 A.2d 735 (Me.1984), appeal after remand 499 A.2d 145 (Me.1985), where it was held that a city cannot deny a permit

Undoubtedly, one reason that there used to be considerable opposition to mobile homes in many neighborhoods was that they were considered unsightly. As their appearance has greatly improved so has the willingness to admit them to more and more zones. But this raises the general question of the validity of zoning for aesthetic purposes. Traditionally, aesthetic grounds were considered not sufficient in themselves to uphold the constitutionality of zoning—and this may still be the majority view.[79] But it was said by a case in the 1920's that when an aesthetic purpose was served by a zoning restriction, only a little more—something in the nature of a more practical reason—was needed to support the restriction.[80] Today the *trend* is toward holding that aesthetic reasons may even be enough in themselves to support the validity of otherwise-reasonable zoning,[81] and thus aesthetics may now be listed as the fourth purpose of

---

for construction of prefabricated homes merely because of the mobility of such structures if the applicants demonstrate compliance with building ordinances. The denial of applicant's permit was, however, ultimately upheld, the court finding valid an ordinance prohibiting erection of single-unit manufactured housing in a residential zone outside of manufactured housing developments. Your Home, Inc. v. City of Portland, 501 A.2d 1300 (Me.1985). But cf. Tyrone Township v. Crouch, 426 Mich. 642, 397 N.W.2d 166 (1986) (township ordinance establishing minimum standards for prefabricated mobile homes in residential zones unfairly discriminated against mobile homes and was thus invalid); Geiger v. Zoning Hearing Bd. of North Whitehall, 510 Pa. 231, 507 A.2d 361 (1986) (ordinance that excluded mobile homes manufactured in one piece while permitting dwellings manufactured in two or more sections, or constructed on the site, held to make an arbitrary and capricious distinction and thus to violate Equal Protection).

Ordinances have been passed in some communities precluding or restricting condominiums in certain residential zones. See Annot., Zoning or Building Regulations as Applied to Condominiums, 71 A.L.R.3d 866 (1976). See generally Rohan, Condominium Housing: A Purchaser's Perspective, 17 Stan.L.Rev. 842 (1965); Rosenstein, Inadequacies of Current Condominium Legislation—A Critical Look at the Pennsylvania Unit Property Law, 47 Temple L.Q. 655 (1974); Note, Cooperative Apartment Housing, 61 Harv.L.Rev. 1407 (1948); Symposium on Practical Problems of Condominiums, 11 Practical Lawyer 35–64 (Jan., 1965); Symposium on the Law of Condominiums, 47 St. John's L.Rev. 677 (1974). On the Uniform Condominium Act, see Jackson & Colgan, The Uniform Condominium Act from a Local Government Perspective, 10 Urban Law. 429 (1978).

[79] Detroit Edison Co. v. Wixom, 382 Mich. 673, 172 N.W.2d 382 (1969); Wolverine Sign Works v. City of Bloomfield Hills, 279 Mich. 205, 271 N.W. 823 (1937); State ex rel. Magidson v. Henze, 342 S.W.2d 261 (Mo.App.1961); Baker v. Somerville, 138 Neb. 466, 293 N.W. 326 (1940); Youngstown v. Kahn Brothers Building Co., 112 Ohio St. 654, 148 N.E. 842 (1925); Norris v. Bradford, 204 Tenn. 319, 321 S.W.2d 543 (1958); Niday v. City of Bellaire, 251 S.W.2d 747 (Tex.Civ.App.1952). See Women's Kansas City St. Andrew Society v. Kansas City, 58 F.2d 593 (8th Cir.1932); Jackson v. Bridges, 243 Miss. 646, 139 So.2d 660 (1962); Dowsey v. Village of Kensington, *supra* note 66; City of Euclid v. Fitzthum, 48 Ohio App.2d 297, 357 N.E.2d 402 (1976) (saying Ohio treats zoning for purely aesthetic reasons as unconstitutional). See generally Annot., Aesthetic Objectives or Considerations as Affecting Validity of Zoning Ordinance, 21 A.L.R.3d 1222 (1968); 82 Am.Jur.2d Zoning §§ 41–42 (1976).

[80] People v. Sterling, 128 Misc. 650, 220 N.Y.S. 315 (1927), aff'd 222 App.Div. 849, 226 N.Y.S. 881. See Trust Co. v. City of Chicago, 408 Ill. 91, 96 N.E.2d 499 (1951) (it's no *objection* to zoning ordinance that it tends, in addition to other effects, to promote aesthetics). Cf. United Advertising Corp. v. Borough of Metuchen, 42 N.J. 1, 198 A.2d 447 (1964) (aesthetics relevant when they bear on questions of land utilization). See also Berman v. Parker, 348 U.S. 26, 75 S.Ct. 98, 99 L.Ed. 27 (1954), upholding the use of eminent domain for urban renewal and noting that the legislature may determine that a community should be beautiful as well as healthy. For discussion of *Berman v. Parker* and its importance to the laws of zoning, eminent domain, public housing, and urban renewal, see Lavine, Urban Renewal and the Story of *Berman v. Parker*, 42 Urban Law. 423 (2010). As to the case's particular importance in urban renewal, see Section 20.2, *infra*.

[81] See State v. Diamond Motors, 50 Hawaii 33, 429 P.2d 825 (1967) (upholding zoning controls on location and size of billboards; noting power under Hawaiian constitution); Lamar Corp. v. City of Twin Falls, 133 Idaho 36, 981 P.2d 1146 (1999) (city may regulate the construction and placement of billboards for purpose of preserving aesthetics); Westfield Motor Sales Co. v. Town of Westfield, 129 N.J.Super. 528, 324 A.2d 113 (1974); Cromwell v. Ferrier, 19 N.Y.2d 263, 279 N.Y.S.2d 22, 225 N.E.2d 749 (1967) (holding limits on location of billboards); Oregon City v. Hartke, 240 Or. 35, 400 P.2d 255 (1965) (total exclusion of automobile wrecking yards from city upheld; a leading case); Racine County v. Plourde, 38 Wis.2d 403, 157 N.W.2d 591 (1968). Cf. Highway 100 Auto Wreckers, Inc. v. City of West Allis, 6 Wis.2d 637, 96 N.W.2d 85 (1959) reh. denied 6 Wis.2d 637, 97 N.W.2d 423 (upholding ordinances that prohibited burning of automobile bodies and parts). See generally Agnor, Beauty Begins a Comeback: Aesthetic Considerations in Zoning, 11 J. Pub. L. 230 (1962);

zoning. This purpose has been especially important in cases involving bans on automobile-wrecking yards and junkyards,[82] and has been relied on in many cases

---

Dukeminier, Zoning for Aesthetic Objectives: A Reappraisal, 20 Law & Contemp. Prob. 218 (1955); Rodda, Accomplishment of Aesthetic Purposes Under the Police Power, 27 S.Cal.L.Rev. 149 (1954); Sayre, Aesthetics and Property Values: Does Zoning Promote the Public Welfare?, 35 A.B.A.J. 471 (1949); Note, Zoning for Aesthetics—A Problem of Definition, 32 U.Cin.L.Rev. 367 (1963); Note, Aesthetic Control of Land Use: A House Built Upon the Sand?, 59 Nw.U.L.Rev. 372 (1964); Note, Aesthetic Considerations in Land Use Regulation, 2 Willamette L.J. 420 (1963); Note, The Aesthetic as a Factor Considered in Zoning, 15 Wyo.L.J. 77 (1960). Aesthetics may now be held sufficient justification for zoning that restricts development on some properties in order to preserve the scenic view enjoyed by owners of other properties. See Landmark Land Co. v. City & County of Denver, 728 P.2d 1281 (Colo.1986), appeal dism'd 483 U.S. 1001, 107 S.Ct. 3222, 97 L.Ed.2d 729 (1987) (ordinance extending mountain view protection to a greater area of land held reasonably related to legitimate public purpose of protection of aesthetics). But any ordinances promoting aesthetics are vulnerable to attack on vagueness and overbreadth grounds. See Note, Beauty and the Well-Drawn Ordinance: Avoiding Vagueness and Overbreadth Challenges to Municipal Aesthetic Regulations, 6 J.L. & Pol'y 853 (1998). As to the extent to which additional states are becoming more receptive to aesthetic regulations, compare Bufford, Beyond the Eye of the Beholder: A New Majority of Jurisdictions Authorize Aesthetic Regulation, 48 U.M.K.C.L. Rev. 125 (1980) (the number of jurisdictions accepting aesthetics as a basis for land use regulation found to be increasing), with the later response of Pearlman, Linville, Phillips & Prosser, Beyond the Eye of the Beholder Once Again: A New Review of Aesthetic Regulation, 38 Urban Law. 1119 (2006) (there has been an increase in the number of jurisdictions that allow aesthetics alone to justify a land use regulation, but the increase has not been dramatic).

In People v. Stover, 12 N.Y.2d 462, 240 N.Y.S.2d 734, 191 N.E.2d 272 (1963), appeal dism'd 375 U.S. 42, 84 S.Ct. 147, 11 L.Ed.2d 107, an ordinance banning clotheslines in front yards or side yards facing a street was upheld despite a protesting citizen's claim that the ordinance interfered with his free speech: he was demonstrating his objection to city property taxes by putting tattered rags on the clothesline in front of his house. But more serious freedom-of-speech issues are raised by many of the cases dealing with aesthetic restrictions on billboards and signs; see note 79 *infra*.

The law of nuisance—especially private nuisance—has also played a role in attempts to eliminate "eyesores." See McVicars v. Christensen, 320 P.3d 948 (Idaho 2014) (landowner does not have the right under nuisance law to prohibit the erection on adjoining land of structures he or she considers not aesthetically pleasing, though nuisance law does prohibit erection of a structure that serves no useful purpose and is only erected to injure a neighbor); Noel, Unaesthetic Sights as Nuisance, 25 Corn. L.Q. 1 (1939). See generally Prosser & Keeton, Law of Torts 626 n. 3 (5th ed. 1984).

[82] Oregon City v. Hartke, *supra* note 81, where a total ban on automobile wrecking yards was upheld solely on aesthetic grounds. See Texas Co. v. City of Tampa, 100 F.2d 347 (5th Cir.1938); Leary v. Adams, 226 Ala. 472, 147 So. 391 (1933); Radco v. Zoning Commission, 27 Conn.Sup. 362, 238 A.2d 799 (Com.Pl.1967) (with review of cases); Howden v. City of Savannah, 172 Ga. 833, 159 S.E. 401 (1931); Highland Oil Corp. v. Lathrup Village, 349 Mich. 650, 85 N.W.2d 185 (1957); Slater v. City of River Oaks, 330 S.W.2d 892 (Tex.Civ.App. 1959). Cf. City of Baltimore v. Muller, 242 Md. 269, 219 A.2d 91 (1966) (denial of permit to allow filling station in residential area held justified; station would be traffic hazard and unwarranted commercial intrusion); City of Jackson v. McPherson, 162 Miss. 164, 138 So. 604 (1932) (noting importance of preserving desirable home surroundings in predominantly residential areas). But cf. City of St. Louis v. Friedman, 358 Mo. 681, 216 S.W.2d 475 (1948), upholding an exclusion of junkyards but saying that aesthetics are definitely not enough reason for such a ban. A stronger case for exclusion of junkyards or automobile wrecking yards may be established if the zoning authority does not rely on aesthetics alone but relies largely or entirely on health concerns. See Schuster v. Plumstead Township Zoning Hearing Bd., 69 Pa.Cmwlth. 271, 450 A.2d 799 (1982) (township's water supply came from well, which could be polluted by plaintiff's proposed automobile wrecking and recycling center). See generally Comment, Municipal Regulation of Junk Yards, 12 Syracuse L.Rev. 79 (1960); Annot., Validity, Construction, and Application of Zoning Ordinance Relating to Operation of Junkyard or Scrap Metal Processing Plant, 50 A.L.R.3d 837 (1973). See also Annot., Automobile Wrecking Yard or Place of Business as Nuisance, 84 A.L.R.2d 653 (1962).

Sometimes, bans on junk yards and comparable uses have been found unreasonable where the law's effect was to exclude such uses from a municipality entirely. See Deshler v. Hoops, 196 N.E.2d 476, 26 O.O.2d 30 (Com.Pl.1963). Cf. Shatz v. Phillips, 225 Tenn. 519, 471 S.W.2d 944 (1971) (ban of junkyards from business zones found unreasonable). See also Comment, Can a City Declare That All Pickup Trucks Are Legally Ugly? A Florida Case Tests the Limits of Aesthetic Regulation, 9 Fla. Intl. U.L. Rev. 83 (2013), commenting on Kuvin v. City of Coral Gables, 64 So. 3d 118 (Fla. 2011).

dealing with restrictions on billboards and signs.[83] Many ordinances forbidding or restricting advertising signs contain an exception for signs advertising the business

---

[83] See Valley View Village v. Proffett, 221 F.2d 412 (6th Cir.1955) (ban on signs in residential areas); Grant v. City of Baltimore, 212 Md. 301, 129 A.2d 363 (1957) (removal of billboards from residential areas within 5 years); United Advertising Corp. v. Borough of Metuchen, 42 N.J. 1, 198 A.2d 447 (1964) (total ban on advertising signs in all districts); United Advertising Corp. v. Borough of Raritan, 11 N.J. 144, 93 A.2d 362 (1952) (same). But cf. Metromedia, Inc. v. City of San Diego, 453 U.S. 490, 101 S.Ct. 2882, 69 L.Ed.2d 800 (1981) (city could not limit contents of billboards to commercial messages, or permit some noncommercial signs but not others); Stoner McCray System v. City of Des Moines, 247 Iowa 1313, 78 N.W.2d 843 (1956) (immediate removal of nonconforming billboards could not be required). See generally Annot., Validity and Construction of Ordinance Prohibiting Roof Signs, 76 A.L.R.3d 1162 (1977); Annot., Power of Municipality as to Billboards and Outdoor Advertising, 72 A.L.R. 465 (1931), supplemented, 58 A.L.R.2d 1314 (1958). See also Annot., Billboards and Other Outdoor Advertising Signs as Civil Nuisance, 38 A.L.R.3d 647 (1971).

The *Metromedia* case *supra* was remanded to the California Supreme Court. Noting that the U.S. Supreme Court had found that the ordinance-in-question violated the First Amendment to the extent it prohibited noncommercial billboards, the California court ruled that the ordinance could not be fairly construed so as to preserve its constitutionality. Limiting the ordinance's scope to prohibiting only commercial signs would, the court held, be clearly contrary to the language of the law and the intent of its drafters, and would invite constitutional difficulties with respect to distinguishing between commercial and noncommercial signs. Metromedia, Inc. v. City of San Diego, 32 Cal.3d 180, 185 Cal.Rptr. 260, 649 P.2d 902 (1982).

Subsequently, the U.S. Supreme Court gave strong endorsement to the protection of aesthetics as a valid ground for restrictions on signs in Members of City Council v. Taxpayers for Vincent, 466 U.S. 789, 104 S.Ct. 2118, 80 L.Ed.2d 772 (1984), on remand 738 F.2d 353 (9th Cir.1984). The Court there upheld, as reasonably necessary to the goal of avoiding visual clutter, an ordinance banning the affixing of handbills or signs to utility poles and other designated objects in public places. The Court relied heavily on its decision in the *Metromedia* case, *supra*, where seven Justices had indicated that a content-neutral prohibition on outdoor signs would be upheld. Cf. Temple Baptist Church, Inc. v. City of Albuquerque, 98 N.M. 138, 646 P.2d 565 (1982) (ordinance restricting, for aesthetic reasons, the size, number, and location of signs upheld). But see City of Ladue v. Gilleo, 512 U.S. 43, 114 S.Ct. 2038, 129 L.Ed.2d 36 (1994), where the Court invalidated (as applied to an 8.5-by-11-inch sign displayed during the Persian Gulf War in the second-story window of a house and proclaiming "For Peace in the Gulf") an ordinance banning all residential signs (with limited exceptions) for the purpose of minimizing visual clutter. The ordinance was found broader than necessary to achieve its goal and thus violative of residents' right of free speech. See generally Kramer, Members of the City Council v. Taxpayers for Vincent, A Step Backward for Political Campaigning, 17 Urban Law. 91 (1985); McPherson, Municipal Regulation of Political Signs: Balancing First Amendment Rights Against Aesthetic Concerns, 45 Drake L. Rev. 767 (1997).

In general, since the *Members of City Council v. Taxpayers for Vincent* case, *supra*, sign ordinances have been upheld *if* found to advance governmental interest in aesthetics, to be narrowly tailored to achieve that governmental interest, and to leave open ample alternative communication channels. See Salib v. City of Mesa, 212 Ariz. 446, 133 P.3d 756 (App. 2006); City of Seattle v. Mighty Movers, Inc., 152 Wash.2d 343, 96 P.3d 979 (2004) (also holding that utility poles are a nonpublic forum and that regulations as to them need only be reasonable, not the most reasonable or the only reasonable limitation). As to what constitutes the "visual clutter" that the *Members of City Council v. Taxpayers for Vincent* case declared subject to reasonable government regulation, see Note, Scylla or Charybdis: Navigating the Jurisprudence of Visual Clutter, 103 Mich. L. Rev. 1877 (2005). Because of the difficulty of drafting ordinances that are reasonably designed to prevent visual clutter or otherwise advance governmental interests in aesthetics, as illustrated by the above-cited *Metromedia* litigation and the *City of Ladue* case, some commentators believe that sign regulations will increasingly be found unconstitutional. See Menthe, Writing on the Wall: The Impending Demise of Modern Sign Regulation Under the First Amendment and State Constitutions, 18 George Mason U. Civ. Rights L.J. 1 (2007). Cf. Reed v. Town of Gilbert, ___ U.S. ___, 135 S.Ct. 2218 (2015) (town's sign code that subjected signs to varying restrictions according to content was subject to strict scrutiny and thus not sustainable).

As to bans on portable signs, see Don's Porta Signs, Inc. v. City of Clearwater, 829 F.2d 1051 (11th Cir.1987), cert. denied 485 U.S. 981, 108 S.Ct. 1280, 99 L.Ed.2d 491 (1988) (ban on portable signs in beach community upheld largely on aesthetic grounds); Lindsay v. City of San Antonio, 821 F.2d 1103 (5th Cir.1987), reh. denied 829 F.2d 1124 (5th Cir.1987), noted 17 Stetson L. Rev. 829 (1988) (ordinance banning portable signs furthered city's aesthetic interest and did not violate First Amendment). Cf. Mobile Sign, Inc. v. Town of Brookhaven, 670 F.Supp. 68 (E.D.N.Y. 1987), upholding against First Amendment attack an ordinance restricting the time a mobile sign could remain at a given location. See also Kitsap County v. Mattress Outlet/Kevin Gould, 153 Wash.2d 506, 104 P.3d 1280 (2005) (raincoat-clad workers used as offsite advertisements constituted "use of signs" within county's sign ordinances, but ordinances held

conducted on that very premise. These latter signs can be considered an accessory use of the property, and the distinction in their favor is normally upheld.[84]

---

unconstitutional as failing to serve county's asserted interest in aesthetics and safety and as being more extensive than necessary).

Some authority takes the view that total bans on signs or billboards are unconstitutional, though lesser restrictions may not be. See Bell v. Township of Stafford, 110 N.J. 384, 541 A.2d 692 (1988) (ordinance outlawing both commercial and noncommercial billboards found patently unconstitutional where no adequate alternative means of like communication was afforded). But cf. Outdoor Systems, Inc. v. City of Mesa, 169 Ariz. 301, 819 P.2d 44 (1991), where the court upheld on aesthetic grounds an ordinance prohibiting all off-premises advertising signs and conditioning issuance of new construction permits on removal of any nonconforming signs located on the parcel for which the permits were sought.

Bans on signs advertising tobacco products and/or liquor may be upheld even if more general bans would not be. See Penn Advertising v. Mayor of Baltimore, 63 F.3d 1318 (4th Cir.1995) (cigarette billboards); Anheuser-Busch, Inc. v. Schmoke, 63 F.3d 1305 (4th Cir.1995), cert. granted, judgment vacated 517 U.S. 1206, 116 S.Ct. 1821, 134 L.Ed.2d 927 (1996) (outdoor advertising of liquor), both discussed in Note, Over the *Edge*: The Fourth Circuit's Commercial Speech Analysis in *Penn Advertising* and *Anheuser-Busch*, 74 N.C.L. Rev. 2086 (1996). See generally Marshall, Regulation of Signs and Outdoor Advertising, 28 Urban Law. 701 (1996).

[84] Board of Adjustment v. Osage Oil & Transportation, Inc., 258 Ark. 91, 522 S.W.2d 836 (1975), appeal dism'd, cert. denied 423 U.S. 941, 96 S.Ct. 350, 46 L.Ed.2d 273 (signs advertising goods and services offered on the premises were merely restricted in size, while others were totally prohibited); Schloss v. Jamison, 262 N.C. 108, 136 S.E.2d 691 (1964) (with review of cases); Silver v. Zoning Board of Adjustment, 381 Pa. 41, 112 A.2d 84 (1955). See John Donnelly & Sons, Inc. v. Outdoor Advertising Board, 369 Mass. 206, 339 N.E.2d 709 (1975) (local government could limit size and location of non-accessory (off-premises) advertising signs and require their removal within 5 years). Cf. Burk v. Municipal Court, 229 Cal.App.2d 696, 40 Cal.Rptr. 425 (Dist.Ct. 1964) (upholding ban on "for sale" or "for rent" signs by brokers in residential areas, but permitting property-owner to so advertise); Murphy, Inc. v. Town of Westport, 131 Conn. 292, 40 A.2d 177 (1944) (upholding validity of ordinance prohibiting off-premises advertising structures in certain zones; but noting that as to visibility, there is no essential difference between using the premises to advertise the owner's business and using it to advertise the business of another). See generally Jourdan, Hurd, Hawkins & Winson-Geideman, Evidence-Based Sign Regulation: Regulating Signage on the Basis of Empirical Wisdom, 45 Urban Law. 327 (2013), discussing local government regulation of on-premises signage; Annot., Validity and Construction of State or Local Regulation Prohibiting Off-Premises Advertising Structures, 81 A.L.R.2d 486 (1977). Annot., Advertising Rights on Leased Premises, 20 A.L.R.2d 940 (1951). See also Annot., Validity of Regulations Restricting Size of Freestanding Advertising Signs, 56 A.L.R.3d 1207 (1974). Some cases have invalidated bans on off-premises advertising signs where such bans applied throughout an entire municipality, township, etc., finding such a sweeping prohibition unreasonable. See Metromedia, Inc. v. City of Des Plaines, 26 Ill.App.3d 942, 326 N.E.2d 59 (1975) (ordinance prohibited all off-premises outdoor advertising within city limits—held facially unconstitutional; court says aesthetic considerations alone cannot justify exercise of police power); Daikeler v. Zoning Board of Adjustment, 1 Pa.Cmwlth. 445, 275 A.2d 696 (1971) (ban throughout township unreasonable); Norate Corp. v. Zoning Board, 417 Pa. 397, 207 A.2d 890 (1965) (saying courts are inclined to invalidate a ban on off-site advertising if it applies everywhere in city or township; review of cases). Cf. City of Naples v. Polk, 346 So.2d 1076 (Fla.App.1977) (ban on all "non-point-of-sale advertising" invalid). On the other hand, a ban on off-premises signs that applies throughout an historic district is likely to be upheld. See Messer v. City of Douglasville, 975 F.2d 1505 (11th Cir.1992), cert. denied 508 U.S. 930, 113 S.Ct. 2395, 124 L.Ed.2d 296 (1993) (aesthetics considered a sufficiently compelling government interest, especially in an historic area; since ban did not apply to other areas of city, there were plenty of other places for signs). As to the application to *non*commercial advertising of bans on off-site signs, see Forsling, After *Southlake Property*: Settling the Confusion Over the Location of Billboards Containing Noncommercial Speech, 28 Stetson L. Rev. 721 (1999), discussing and advocating the traditional view that noncommercial signs are off-site unless placed on premises relating to the message conveyed.

Special problems of constitutional rights may be presented where a ban applies to political advertising. See Farrell v. Township of Teaneck, 126 N.J.Super. 460, 315 A.2d 424 (1974), holding unconstitutional a ban on such signs in residential areas; Peltz v. South Euclid, 11 Ohio St.2d 128, 228 N.E.2d 320 (1967), holding unconstitutional as violative of the First Amendment an ordinance banning all political signs. More lenient treatment of political signs is thus often upheld. See Montana Media, Inc. v. Flathead County, 314 Mont. 121, 63 P.3d 1129 (2003) (city ordinance's exemption of political signs from permit requirements upheld as not unconstitutionally vague). But see West Coast Media, LLC v. City of Gladstone, 192 Or.App. 102, 84 P.3d 213 (2004) (city code provision violated state constitutional right to free expression by permitting campaign signs and public service information billboards in both on-premises and off-premises circumstances, while prohibiting off-premises commercial advertising). See generally 3d para., note 83, *supra*. See also Fox, Smut,

What of zoning that attempts not only to exclude unsightly uses but that attempts to control the architecture of those structures that are erected? Such controls are obviously aimed to a large extent at creating aesthetically pleasing areas—but the controls also may contribute to the homogeneity of a zone, may improve property values in the zone and the community, etc. Thus, such restrictions relate to a number of the purposes for zoning, and may be considered to have given birth to a separate, and fifth, ground recognized as a valid purpose for zoning: control of architecture.[85] Often, such control is achieved by allowing some commission or board to grant or refuse building permits according to whether or not the proposed structure will be in conformity with existing buildings and features of the neighborhood. Such delegations will be upheld if definite and reasonable standards are established for the administering body to apply.[86]

Sixth, zoning is increasingly being used to preserve—in substance as well as appearance—historic districts, such as the French Quarter of New Orleans, the historic buildings of Nantucket, and the historical district of Santa Fe.[87] Creation of an "historic

---

Smokes and Spirits: The First Amendment Re-examined, 32 Urban Law. 449 (2000); Note, Regulation of Political Signs in Private Homeowner Associations: A New Approach, 59 Vand. L. Rev. 571 (2006).

[85] See State ex rel. Stoyanoff v. Berkeley, 458 S.W.2d 305 (Mo.1970) (noting stabilizing and protecting of property values, and finding that sufficient standards had been given the architectural board that had to decide whether a proposed structure would be permitted); City of Santa Fe v. Gamble-Skogmo, Inc., 73 N.M. 410, 389 P.2d 13 (1964); State ex rel. Saveland Park Holding Corp. v. Wieland, 269 Wis. 262, 69 N.W.2d 217 (1955), cert. denied 350 U.S. 841, 76 S.Ct. 81, 100 L.Ed. 750 (building permit would not be issued if building was so at variance with existing structures as to cause substantial depreciation in property values). See generally Annot., Validity and Construction of Zoning Ordinance Regulating Architectural Style or Design of Structure, 41 A.L.R.3d 1397 (1972). See also Note, Wish You Were Here: A Cross-cultural Analysis of Architectural Preservation, Reconstruction, and the Contemporary Built Environment, 30 Syracuse J. Int'l L. & Com. 395 (2003). On the various methods that a city may use to achieve uniformity and beauty in its buildings, see Tappendorf, Architectural Design Regulations: What Can a Municipality Do to Protect Against Unattractive, Inappropriate, and Just Plain Ugly Structures?, 34 Urban Law. 961 (2002).

[86] See State ex rel. Stoyanoff v. Berkeley, *supra* note 85; Reid v. Architectural Board of Review, 119 Ohio App. 67, 192 N.E.2d 74 (1963) (board had denied permit to single-story, ten-foot high, U-shaped house in area of stately, older, two-and-a-half story homes). On possible First Amendment problems with the use of zoning to control architecture, see Poole, Architectural Appearance Review Regulations and the First Amendment: The Good, the Bad, and the Consensus Ugly, 19 Urban Law. 287 (1987). Uniformity of architectural appearance in many neighborhoods has been achieved by restrictive covenants. See Annot., Validity and Construction of Restrictive Covenant Controlling Architectural Style of Buildings to Be Erected on Property, 47 A.L.R.3d 1232 (1973).

[87] On New Orleans: Maher v. City of New Orleans, 371 F.Supp. 653 (E.D.La. 1974), aff'd 516 F.2d 1051 (5th Cir.) reh. denied 521 F.2d 815, cert. denied 426 U.S. 905, 96 S.Ct. 2225, 48 L.Ed.2d 830; City of New Orleans v. Levy, 223 La. 14, 64 So.2d 798 (1953); City of New Orleans v. Pergament, 198 La. 852, 5 So.2d 129 (1941); City of New Orleans v. Impastato, 198 La. 206, 3 So.2d 559 (1941). On Nantucket: Opinion of the Justices, 333 Mass. 773, 128 N.E.2d 557 (1955) (emphasizing importance of tourism to the community, and importance to the tourism of preserving the old buildings). (Cf. Opinion of the Justices to the Senate, 333 Mass. 783, 128 N.E.2d 563 (1955), upholding creation of an historic district for the Beacon Hill area of Boston; Attorney General v. Williams, 174 Mass. 476, 55 N.E. 77 (1899), upholding historic district around Copley Square in Boston; compensation was provided, but the court commented that the police power might have been used.) On Santa Fe: See City of Santa Fe v. Gamble-Skogmo, Inc., *supra* note 85. An historic district somewhat smaller in scale has been upheld as created around the home of Abraham Lincoln in Springfield, Illinois: M & N Enterprises v. City of Springfield, 111 Ill.App.2d 444, 250 N.E.2d 289 (1969); Rebman v. City of Springfield, 111 Ill.App.2d 430, 250 N.E.2d 282 (1969). See generally Preservation Law Symposium, Re-inventing the Past, 8 Widener L. Symposium J. i-vi, 163–483 (2002). For a critique of historic-district ordinances in a number of municipalities, see Tipson, Putting the History Back in Historic Preservation, 36 Urban Law. 289 (2004), concluding that "Historic district ordinances and guidelines suffer today from an untenable degree of theoretical incoherence." *Id.* at 316. See also Byrne, Hallowed Ground: The Gettysburg Battlefield in Historic Preservation Law, 22 Tulane Envtl. L. J. 203 (2009).

It has been observed that historic-preservation zoning started with Charleston, South Carolina, in 1924, and New Orleans, in 1925, with at least 39 municipalities now having districts zoned as "historic." Note, The

zone," and restriction on uses and changes permitted therein, is a fairly easy process if buildings of particular significance are conveniently grouped together, as in the above examples. But many structures of historic (or architectural) importance are scattered throughout various regions of our country. Thus, some local governments have established "landmark commissions" (or similarly named bodies) to identify and designate important landmarks; these structures may then not be demolished or substantially altered unless it is shown the structure cannot, in its existing state, earn a fair return.[88] There have sometimes been problems with declaring churches and other

---

Police Power, Eminent Domain, and the Preservation of Historic Property, 63 Colum.L.Rev. 708, 713–14 (1963). On Charleston's program, see Hosmer, The Charleston Ordinance, Preservation News, March, 1981, at 5. See generally Comment, Legal Methods of Historic Preservation, 19 Buffalo L.Rev. 611 (1970); Note, Land Use Controls in Historic Areas, 44 Notre Dame Lawyer 379 (1969). See also Thoresen, Historic Districts Aren't Obsolete, But . . . , Historic Preservation, July/Aug., 1981, at 46. On recent developments in New Orleans's preservation efforts, see "Builders Take on Old New Orleans," Business Week, Jan. 27, 1973, at 60. In City of New Orleans v. Dukes, 427 U.S. 297, 96 S.Ct. 2513, 49 L.Ed.2d 511 (1976), the U.S. Supreme Court upheld, per curiam, a prohibition on street vendors in the New Orleans French Quarter, containing an exception ("grandfather clause") for those who had continually operated the same business in the same locality 8 years or more. On trade restrictions, see generally Chapter 23 *infra.*

Though the creation of an "historic district" means that restrictions will be imposed on changes that can be made, residents of an area are sometimes anxious to obtain the designation for their area, believing it will ensure property values and physical appearance. See Tatum, A City Cornerstone Discovers Salvation, Dallas Morning News, Nov. 14, 1976, § E, at 1. On a notable effort to allow low-income residents to remain in an historic district, while the historic character of the area is also preserved, see McMillan, Staying Home in Savannah, Historic Preservation magazine, March/April, 1980, at 10. See generally Note, By What We Have Destroyed: Historic Preservation and the Preservation of Individual Property Rights, 52 U. Louisville L. Rev. 153 (2013); Comment, Historic Districts and the Imagined Community: A Study of the Impact of the Old Georgetown Act, 24 Seton Hall J. Sports & Entertainment L. 81 (2014). On the popularity of the preservationist movement and resulting rejuvenation of some downtown areas, see Collins, Waters & Dotson, America's Downtowns: Growth, Politics and Preservation (Preservation Press 1991); "Spiffing Up the Urban Heritage," Time, Nov. 23, 1987, at 72. As to historic preservation in rural areas, see Note, Confronting the Appalachian Breakdown: Historic Preservation Law in Appalachia and the Potential Benefits of Historic Preservation for Rural Communities, 110 W. Va. L. Rev. 1303 (2008).

Some municipalities have "Heritage Tree" ordinances, providing that trees over a certain size cannot be removed or altered without permission from a local commission. Such ordinances protect both the heritage and the beauty of a community. See "Sacramento's Shady Side," American Way magazine, Oct., 1980, at 31 (Sacramento protects trees that are 100 inches or more in girth and in good health). See generally Shea, A Shorter Cut to Forestation: The Constitutionality of Local Tree Ordinances, 20 State & Local L. News, No. 4, at 3 (Summer, 1997). See also "Braverman, Everybody Loves Trees": Policing American Cities Through Street Trees, 19 Duke Envtl. L. & Pol'y F. 81 (2008); Braverman, Governing Certain Things: The Regulation of Street Trees in Four North American Cities, 22 Tulane Envtl. L. J. 35 (2008); Buckley, America's Conservation Impulse: A Century of Saving Trees in the Old Line State (Maryland) (Center for American Places at Columbia College Chicago 2010), reviewed by Bergman, 107 Md. Hist. Mag. 390 (Fall 2012).

[88] See Note, Urban Landmarks: Preserving Our Cities' Aesthetic and Cultural Resources, 39 Albany L.Rev. 521 (1974); Note, Landmark Preservation Laws: Compensation for Temporary Taking, 35 U.Chi. L.Rev. 362 (1968) (urging that the laws be found unconstitutional *unless* the owner is reimbursed for losses caused by the restrictions); "A National Surge of Preservationist Power," Bus. Week, April 21, 1980, at 157. See generally Twentieth Century Task Force on Urban Preservation Policies (O. Lehman, Chair), Living Cities (Center for Urban Policy Research 1985) (with background paper by D. Listokin). On the constitutional issues in historic-preservation zoning, see generally Bowers, Historic Preservation Law Concerning Private Property, 30 Urban Law. 405, 424–36 (1998); Fleming, Back to the Future: The Role of Historic Preservation in Assigning a Minor Part to the Taking Issue in the Land Use Drama, 17 Stetson L. Rev. 689 (1988); Netherton, The Due Process Issue in Zoning for Historic Preservation, 19 Urban Law. 77 (1987). Legislation establishing historic districts may sometimes be invalidated as denying due process or equal protection if it allows selected property owners within the district to enter into contracts with the city that other affected property owners are not allowed to enter. See Native American Rights Fund, Inc. v. City of Boulder, 97 P.3d 283 (Colo. App. 2004), cert. denied 2004 WL 1814003 (Colo.2004) (provision in ordinance establishing historic district that allowed city to enter into privately negotiated contracts with selected property owners in district deprived other affected property owners of due process and was invalid). See generally Note, Living History: How Homeowners in a New Local Historic District Negotiate Their Legal Obligations, 116 Yale L.J. 768 (2007). See also Note, What's

religious structures to be historical landmarks, thus making them subject to special restrictions, in light of the "free exercise of religion" clause of the U.S. Constitution.[89] One attempt by Congress to protect religious institutions from historic preservation laws that substantially burden those institutions was held unconstitutional.[90] Congress

---

It to You? Citizen Challenges to Landmark Preservation Decisions and the Special Damage Requirement, 113 Colum. L. Rev. 447 (2013).

[89] The Washington Supreme Court once ruled than an historic preservation ordinance allowing designation of a church's exterior as an historic landmark, thus requiring the church to obtain governmental approval before making structural changes thereto, violated the "free exercise" clause of the First Amendment of the U.S. Constitution. First Covenant Church v. City of Seattle, 114 Wash.2d 392, 787 P.2d 1352 (1990). But the judgment was vacated and the case remanded by the U.S. Supreme Court. 499 U.S. 901, 111 S.Ct. 1097, 113 L.Ed.2d 208 (1991), on remand 120 Wash.2d 203, 840 P.2d 174 (1992) (vacated and remanded in light of Employment Div., Dep't of Human Resources v. Smith, 494 U.S. 872, 110 S.Ct. 1595, 108 L.Ed.2d 876 (1990), reh. denied 496 U.S. 913, 110 S.Ct. 2605, 110 L.Ed.2d 285 (1990) (free exercise clause of First Amendment doesn't prohibit application of state drug laws to ceremonial ingestion of peyote)). Cf. Rector, Wardens, and Members of St. Bartholomew's Church v. City of New York, 914 F.2d 348 (2d Cir.1990), cert. denied 499 U.S. 905, 111 S.Ct. 1103, 113 L.Ed.2d 214 (1991) (municipality's application of its landmarks law to require preservation of a church's auxiliary services building was not an unconstitutional infringement on free exercise of religion nor an unlawful taking of property); Open Door Baptist Church v. Clark County, 140 Wash.2d 143, 995 P.2d 33 (2000) (requiring church to apply for conditional use permit in rural estate zoning district was not an impermissible burden on free exercise of religion). But cf. Society of Jesus v. Boston Landmarks Comm'n, 409 Mass. 38, 564 N.E.2d 571 (1990) (designation of interior of church as historic landmark held to violate *state* constitution's guarantee of free exercise of religion). See generally Carmella, Houses of Worship and Religious Liberty: Constitutional Limits to Landmark Preservation and Architectural Review, 36 Villanova L. Rev. 401 (1991): Kelster, Supreme Court Rules for Preservation, Historic Preservation News, April, 1991, at 1; Weinstein, The Myth of Ministry vs. Mortar: A Legal and Policy Analysis of Landmark Designation of Religious Institutions, 65 Temple L. Rev. 91 (1992); White & Keatings, Report of the Subcommittee on Historic Preservation and Architectural Control Law, 23 Urban Law. 699, 727–32 (1991); Note, Fire and Brownstone: Historic Preservation of Religious Properties and the First Amendment, 33 Boston C.L.Rev. 93 (1991); Note, Religious Landmarks, Guidelines for Analysis: Free Exercise, Takings and Least Restrictive Means, 53 Ohio St. L.J. 211 (1992); Comment, For Whom the Bell Tolls: Religious Properties as Landmarks Under the First Amendment, 8 Pace Envtl. L. Rev. 579 (1991); Comment, Landmarking Religious Institutions: The Burden of Rehabilitation and the Loss of Religious Freedom, 28 Urban Law. 327 (1996). See also Note, Landmarks as Cultural Property: An Appreciation of New York City, 44 Rutgers L. Rev. 427 (1992). Compare Comment, An Empirical Look at Churches in the Zoning Process, 116 Yale L.J. 859 (2007). The *Open Door Baptist Church* case, *supra*, is well-analyzed in Note, Religious Land Use Jurisprudence, 26 Seattle U.L. Rev. 365 (2002). For an alternative approach, see Monk (student) & Tyler, The Application of Prior Restraint: An Alternative Doctrine for Religious Land Use Cases, 37 U. Toledo L. Rev. 747 (2006). As to zoning of religious uses in general, see Giaimo & Lucero, Religious Land Uses, Zoning, and the Courts (American Bar Assn. Section of State & Local Govt. 2009); Symposium, God and the Land: Conflicts Over Land Use and Religious Freedom, 2 Albany Gov't L. Rev. 354–652 (2009). See also Note, Direct Government Grants to Churches for Façade Improvements, 86 U. Detroit Mercy L. Rev. 509 (2009). As to the basic power to zone educational and religious institutions, see Section 117, notes 12–13, and accompanying text.

[90] On the unsuccessful attempt by Congress to provide protection to religious institutions from application of historic preservation, or other, laws that substantially burden free exercise of religion, see Drinan, Reflections on the Demise of the Religious Freedom Restoration Act, 86 Geo. L.J. 101 (1997), noting City of Boerne v. Flores, 521 U.S. 507, 117 S.Ct. 2157, 138 L.Ed.2d 624 (1997), in which the Supreme Court invalidated the Religious Freedom Restoration Act, 42 U.S.C. 2000bb (1994). See generally Williamson, *City of Boerne v. Flores* and the Religious Freedom Restoration Act: The Delicate Balance Between Religious Freedom and Historic Preservation, 13 J. Land Use & Envtl. L. 107 (1997); Symposium on *City of Boerne v. Flores*, 39 Wm. & M.L. Rev. 597–960 (1998). See also Comment, Why Free Exercise Jurisprudence in Relation to Zoning Restrictions Remains Unsettled After *Boerne v. Flores*, 52 SMU L. Rev. 305 (1999); Comment, The Free Exercise Clause and Historic Preservation Law: Suggestions for a More Coherent Free Exercise Analysis, 72 Tulane L. Rev. 1767 (1998). For discussion of what the Religious Freedom Restoration Act was intended to do, see Comment, Zoning and Religion: Will the Religious Freedom Restoration Act of 1993 Shift the Line Toward Religious Liberty?, 45 Am. U.L. Rev. 199 (1995). On the place of the *City of Boerne case, supra*, in the law, see Colker, *City of Boerne* Revisited, 70 U. Cin. L. Rev. 455 (2002). See generally McAward, The Scope of Congress's Thirteenth Amendment Enforcement Power After *City of Boerne v. Flores*, 88 Wash. U.L. Rev. 77 (2010). See also Lee, The Trouble With *City of Boerne* and Why It Matters for the Fifteenth Amendment as Well, 90 Denver U.L. Rev. 483 (2012).

responded with another statute providing more limited protection to religious uses.[91] In an opinion that, in general terms, recognizes the power of a city to preserve its desirable

---

[91] In 2000, Congress adopted the Religious Land Use and Institutionalized Persons Act (RLUIPA) in an attempt to respond to concerns raised by the Supreme Court in the *Boerne* case *supra* note 90, but still provide protections for religious uses. 42 U.S.C. § 2000cc (2005). The Act prohibits local land-use regulations from imposing a "substantial burden" on religious land use absent a compelling reason, and forbids treating religious activities on "less than equal terms" than their secular counterparts.

As to the "substantial burden" proviso, see Note, Abandoning the Use of Abstract Formulations in Interpreting RLUIPA's Substantial Burden Provision in Religious Land Use Cases, 36 Colum. J. L. & Arts 283 (2013); Note, A Defining Case for the Substantial Burden Test Under RLUIPA, 23 Pace Envtl. L. Rev. 263 (2005–06). For discussion of the "equal terms" provision of the Act, see Mosley, Zoning Religion Out of the Public Square: Constitutional Avoidance and Conflicting Interpretations of RLUIPA's Equal Terms Provision, 55 Ariz. Rev. 465 (2013); Comment, Equally Confused: Constructing RLUIPA's Equal Terms Provision, 41 Ariz. St. L. J. 1139 (2009); Note, Restoring RLUIPA's Equal Terms Provision, 58 Duke L. J. 1071 (2009); Note, A Circuit Split: Interpretation of the Equal Terms Provision of the Religious Land Use and Institutionalized Persons Act, 34 Seton Hall Legis. J. 57 (2009); Note, We're on a Mission From God: Properly Interpreting RLUIPA's "Equal Terms" Provision, 86 St. John's L. Rev. 715 (2012); Comment, Equal Terms: What Does It Mean and How Does It Work, 80 U. Cin. L. Rev. 179 (2011); Comment, Zoned Secular: Seattle's Prohibition of New Religious Facilities in Industrial Zones Violates the RLUIPA's "Equal Terms" Rule, 81 Wash. L. Rev. 191 (2006). See generally Note, The Role of Economics in the Discourse on RLUIPA and Nondiscrimination in Religious Land Use, 53 Boston Coll. L. Rev. 1089 (2012). See also Wallwork, Legislating the Free Exercise Clause: Congressional Power and the Religious Land Use and Institutionalized Persons Act of 2000, 5 Faulkner L. Rev. 1 (2013–14).

As to the possible effect of the RLUIPA on eminent domain actions, see Serkin & Tebbe, Condemning Religion: RLUIPA and the Politics of Eminent Domain, 85 Notre Dame L. Rev. 1 (2009); Comment, RLUIPA and Eminent Domain: Probing the Boundaries of Religious Land Use Protection, 2008 B.Y.U. L. Rev. 1213; Note, Taking the Temple: Eminent Domain and the Limits of RLUIPA, 96 Geo. L. J. 2057 (2008). On the effects the RUILPA may have on special relief—such as variances and special use permits—in zoning cases, see Comment, RLUIPA and the Individualized Assessment: Special Use Permits and Variances Under Strict Congressional Scrutiny, 31 U. Hawaii L. Rev. 257 (2008). On RUILPA's effects on land use in general, see Lennington, Thou Shall Not Zone: The Overbroad Applications and Troubling Implications of RLUIPA's Land Use Provisions, 29 Seattle U.L. Rev. 805 (2006); Silverberg, The Application of RLUIPA to Land Use Regulation, 28 State & Local L. News, Summer, 2005 at 1; Weinstein, The Effects of RLUIPA's Land Use Provisions on Local Governments, 39 Fordham Urb. L. J. 1221 (2012); Note, Individualized vs. Generalized Assessments: Why RLUIPA Should Not Apply to Every Land-Use Request, 62 Duke L. J. 79 (2012); Juergensmeyer & Roberts, Land Use Planning & Development Regulation Law 477–78 (West Hornbook Series 2003). As to possible application of RLUIPA to liquor regulation, see Comment, Land, Libations, and Liberty: RLUIPA and the Specter of Liquor Control Laws, 49 Idaho L. Rev. 157 (2012). See also generally on RLUIPA, Santoro, Section Five of the Fourteenth Amendment and RLUIPA, 24 Whittier L. Rev. 493 (2002); Note, RLUIPA: What's the Use?, 17 Mich. J. Race & L. 359 (2012); Comment, The Religious and Institutionalized Persons Act of 2000: Congress' New Twist on "Speak Softly and Carry a Big Stick," 34 Urban Law. 829 (2002). See also Goldfien, Thou Shalt Love Thy Neighbor: RLUIPA and the Mediation of Religious Land Use Disputes, 2006 J. Disp. Resol. 435; Salkin & Lavine, The Genesis of RLUIPA and Federalism: Evaluating the Creation of a Federal Statutory Right and Its Impact on Local Government, 40 Urban Law. 195 (2008). As to doubts on the constitutionality of RLUIPA, see Note, RLUIPA's Land Use Provisions: Congress' Unconstitutional Response to *City of Boerne*, 28 Environs 155 (2004).

Some states have enacted statutes—often modeled on the Religious Freedom Restoration Act of the federal government that was ruled unconstitutional in the *Boerne* case, *supra* note 90—relevant to zoning of religious uses. See Note, The Constitutional Standard for Zoning Cases Under the Texas Religious Freedom Restoration Act, 6 Tex. Forum on Civ. Liberties & Civ. Rights 365 (2002). Some state constitutions contain provisions forbidding state and local governments from imposing a substantial burden on a religious body. See City of Woodinville v. Northshore United Church of Christ, 166 Wash. 2d 633, 211 P.3d 406 (2009) (city's moratorium on all land use permit applications placed a substantial burden on church in violation of church's right to religious freedom under state constitution). See also Comment, The California Missions Preservation Act: Safeguarding Our History or Subsidizing Religion?, 55 Am. U.L. Rev. 1523 (2006). For a *state* court application of the *federal* Religious Land Use and Institutionalized Persons Act of 2000, discussed *supra*, see Corporation of Presiding Bishop of the Church of Jesus Christ of Latter-Day Saints v. City of West Linn, 192 Or.App. 567, 86 P.3d 1140 (2004), aff'd, 338 Or. 453, 111 P.3d 1123 (2005) (federal act does not provide that religious entities are entirely exempt from land-use regulations but only precludes imposition or implementation of land-use regulations in a way that imposes a substantial burden on the entity, unless the government demonstrates that the burden is the least restrictive means of furthering a compelling

aesthetic and cultural features, the U.S. Supreme Court has upheld designation and preservation of landmarks through zoning restrictions, so long as the owners are not prevented from earning a reasonable rate of return on their investment.[92]

---

governmental interest). It has been suggested that the Religious Land Use and Institutionalized Persons Act of 2000 revives the bifurcated approach to judicial review of zoning regulations that the U.S. Supreme Court applied in the early years of zoning, with facial challenges being viewed under *Village of Euclid's* highly deferential rational basis standard, and as-applied challenges being more strictly scrutinized, as in the *Nectow* case, note 14 *supra*. Ostrow, Judicial Review of Local Land Use Decisions: Lessons from RLUIPA, 31 Harv. J.L. & Public Pol'y 717 (2008).

[92] Penn Central Transportation Co. v. City of New York, 438 U.S. 104, 98 S.Ct. 2646, 57 L.Ed.2d 631 (1978) reh. denied 439 U.S. 883, 99 S.Ct. 226, 58 L.Ed.2d 198. See Preservation News, Aug., 1978, at 1, col. 1 (hailing the victory, which involved historic-landmark status for Grand Central Station); Preservation News, March, 1975, at 1, noting earlier setbacks in the effort to designate Grand Central Station a landmark. See generally Lang, *Penn Central Transportation Co. v. New York City*: Fairness and Accommodation Show the Way Out of the Takings Corner, 13 Urban Law. 89 (1981). Compare Wade, *Penn Central's* Ad Hocery Yields Inconsistent Takings Decisions, 42 Urban Law. 549 (2010). As to the eventual preservation and renovation of Grand Central Station, see Haberman, Looking Out on Grand Central, and Looking Back on Saving It, N.Y. Times, Jan. 28, 2013, at 415. See generally 2011 Fitch Forum, 45 Years of Preservation Law: New York City and the Nation, the Past, and the Future, 18 Widener L. Rev. 123 (2012). It seems that a "taking" will still be found if the "landmark" designation results in an owner's being unable to put his property to any profitable use. See Benenson v. United States, 548 F.2d 939 (Ct.Cl. 1977) (Willard Hotel in Washington, D.C.); Lutheran Church in America v. City of New York, 35 N.Y.2d 121, 359 N.Y.S.2d 7, 316 N.E.2d 305 (1974). Of course, a governmental authority may always, if it can afford to, purchase historical property in order to preserve it; it has been said that the historical movement in America got its start in 1850 when the State of New York purchased Hasbrouck House—the Newburgh, New York, headquarters of George Washington during the Revolutionary War. See Note, Urban Landmarks, *supra* note 88, at 521, citing Lutheran Church in America v. City of New York, *supra*. And the power of eminent domain has been upheld where used for the purpose of preserving historical property. United States v. Gettysburg Electric Railway, 160 U.S. 668, 16 S.Ct. 427, 40 L.Ed. 576 (1896) (federal taking of Gettysburg battlefield); State ex rel. Smith v. Kemp, 124 Kan. 716, 261 P. 556 (1927) (condemnation of historic Shawnee Mission); Flaccomio v. Mayor and City Council, 194 Md. 275, 71 A.2d 12 (Ct.App.1950) (condemnation of Baltimore's Star-Spangled Banner Flag House upheld though was to be operated by private association; house is where the flag was made that flew at Ft. McHenry, inspiring Francis Scott Key to write the national anthem); Attorney General v. Williams, *supra* note 87. See Application of Department of Archives and History, 246 N.C. 392, 98 S.E.2d 487 (1957), saying the state legislature could declare restoration of Tyron's Palace to have a public purpose and could authorize use of eminent domain therefor. See generally Montague, Planning for Preservation in Virginia, 51 Va.L.Rev. 1214 (1965); Wilson & Winkler, The Response of State Legislation to Historic Preservation, 36 Law & Contemp. Prob. 309 (1971).

Federal legislation, the National Historic Preservation Act of 1966, 16 U.S.C.A. § 470, provides for a National Register of Historic Places, as to which matching grants-in-aid can be made available for preservation efforts (§ 470a), and as to which limits are imposed regarding federal projects affecting the listed properties (§ 470f). See Shull & Shull, New Inroads for Historic Preservation, 26 Ad.L.Rev. 357 (1974). As of amendments in 1980 to the National Registry legislation, a private property can be listed only if the owner does not object. See "Register Closed to Private Sites," Preservation News, March, 1981, at 1. For 11 months, the Register was closed to private properties altogether, while new regulations were drafted; it was reopened in November, 1981. See Preservation News, Dec., 1981, at 1. On the 1980 legislation, see generally "'Lame Ducks' Compromise, Pass 3 Major Bills," Preservation News, Jan., 1981, at 1. As to how the National Register of Historic Places is operated—including its history and how the correct name for it is Register, not Registry—see "What Is the National Register?," Preservation magazine, May/June, 2011, at 38. Some states also now have a register of historic properties and encourage state agencies to rent office space in such buildings. See Leccese, New York Succeeds Second Time Around, Preservation News, Sept., 1980, at 1.

On the effects that the *Penn Central* case, *supra*, had on the general law of regulatory takings, see Claeys, The *Penn Central* Test and Tensions in Liberal Property Theory, 30 Harv. Envtl. L. Rev. 339 (2006); Hubbard, Do Owners Have a Fair Chance of Prevailing Under the Ad Hoc Regulatory Takings Test of *Penn Central Transportation Company?*, 14 Duke Envtl. L. & Pol'y F. 121 (2003); Comment, Substantially Advancing *Penn Central*: Sharpening the Remaining Arrow in the Property Advocate's Quiver for the New Age of Regulatory Takings, 30 Nova L. Rev. 445 (2006). For a critique of the *Penn Central* case, see Echeverria, Is the Penn Central Three-Factor Test Ready for History's Dustbin?, 1 Land Use L. & Zoning Digest 3 (2000). On the use of the concept of "investment-backed expectations" to determine whether or not a taking has occurred, see Eagle, The Rise and Rise of "Investment-Backed Expectations," 32 Urban Law. 437 (2000). As noted in this article, the concept originated in Michelman, Property, Utility, and Fairness: Comments on the Ethical

Foundations of "Just Compensation" Law, 80 Harv. L. Rev. 1165 (1967), and became part of constitutional jurisprudence in the *Penn Central* case, *supra*. See generally on the *Penn Central* test note 41, *supra*, and accompanying text. See also Breemer, Playing the Expectations Game: When Are Investment-Backed Land Use Expectations (Un)reasonable in State Courts?, 38 Urban Law. 81 (2006). As to transferrable-development rights, see generally paragraph 6 of this note, *infra*.

Many private groups have also, of course, performed outstanding work in preserving historic properties; an early example was provided by the Mount Vernon Ladies' Association, which purchased George Washington's home in 1859. See Note, Urban Landmarks, *supra* note 88, at 521 & note 3. See generally Johnson, How the Girls Saved Mount Vernon, Sat. Eve. Post, Feb. 21, 1953, at 24. See also Balzer, The Savannah Spectrum, Travel/Holiday, Oct., 1980, at 48, 51, describing how seven Savannah women initiated efforts that led to today's large-scale preservation of that city's historic sites. On the work of the National Trust for Historic Preservation—particularly the Endangered Properties Program—, see Anthony, Last Hope for Landmarks, Historic Preservation magazine, March/April, 1981, at 22. On the National Trust's Main Street Program, aimed at revitalizing historic downtown areas in towns and small cities, see Keister, Main Street Makes Good, Historic Preservation, Sept./Oct., 1990, at 44. Compare Note, Historic Preservation in Southeast Asia: The Role of Public-Private Partnerships, 39 Vanderbilt J. Transnat'l L. 1013 (2006). See also Note (R. Marlin Smith Student Writing Competition Winner), Preservation of Historic Properties' Environs, 36 Urban Law. 137 (2004).

An excellent symposium on historic preservation is found in 12 Urban Lawyer 3–101 (1980). The significance of that symposium, the efforts of the American Bar Association Committee on Housing and Urban Development Law, and the nature of future programs likely to be undertaken in the area of historic preservation are discussed in Waters & Scott, The Need for Expanded Initiatives: An Overview of the ABA Special Symposium on Preserving, Conserving, and Re-Using Historic Properties, 12 Urban Law. 413–28 (1980).

Transferrable-development-rights programs, allowing certain property owners to convey to other property owners the formers' unused potential under the zoning laws (such as unused potential for maximum building size, height, etc.) have been employed in some communities to encourage historic preservation. For instance, under the Denver program, owners of historic buildings have been able to sell their unused development rights and have thus obtained funds for renovation of their own structures. See Reichhardt, Will New Denver Zoning Become National Model?, Preservation News, Feb., 1983, at 1. See generally Been & Infranca, Transferrable Development Rights Programs: "Post-zoning"?, 78 Brooklyn L. Rev. 435 (2013); Delaney, Kominers & Gordon, TDR Redux: A Second Generation of Practical Legal Concerns, 15 Urban Law. 593 (1983); Miller, Transferrable Development Rights in the Constitutional Landscape: Has Penn Central Failed to Weather the Storm?, 39 Nat. Resources J. 459 (1999); Williams, Coastal TDRs and Taking in a Changing Climate, 46 Urban Law. 139 (2014); Note, Transferrable Development Rights and the Deprivation of All Economically Beneficial Use: Can TDRs Salvage Regulations That Would Otherwise Constitute a Taking?, 34 Idaho L. Rev. 679 (1998); Note, Caught Between Scalia and the Deep Blue Lake: The Takings Clause and Transferrable Development Rights Programs, 83 Minn. L. Rev. 815 (1999); Comment, Transferring Development Rights: Purpose, Problems, and Prospects in New York, 17 Pace L. Rev. 319 (1996); Comment, Past, Present, and Future Constitutional Challenges to Transferrable Development Rights, 74 Wash. L. Rev. 825 (1999). See also Juergensmeyer, Nicholas & Leebrick, Transferrable Development Rights and Alternatives after *Suitum*, 30 Urban Law. 441 (1998), commenting particularly on Suitum v. Tahoe Regional Planning Agency, 520 U.S. 725, 117 S.Ct. 1659, 137 L.Ed.2d 980 (1997), which involved transferrable development rights but was decided on narrow ripeness grounds. A good discussion of the history of transferrable development rights in New York City is found in Kruse, Constructing the Special Theater Subdistrict: Culture, Politics, and Economics in the Creation of Transferrable Development Rights, 40 Urban Law. 95 (2008) (24th Smith–Babcock–Williams Student Writing Competition Winner). As to the Miami program, see Note, Preserving Miami: An Evaluation of Miami's Transferrable Development Rights Program, 24 U. Fla. J. L. & Pub. Pol'y 271 (2013). See also Scro, Navigating the Takings Maze: The Use of Transfers of Development Rights in Defending Regulations Against Takings Challenges, 19 Ocean & Coastal L. J. 219 (2014).

Tax incentives have been much discussed, and sometimes employed, as a method of encouraging historic preservation. See Powers, Tax Incentives for Historic Preservation, 12 Urban Lawyer 103 (1980). See also Costonis, The Chicago Plan: Incentive Zoning and the Preservation of Urban Landmarks, 85 Harv.L.Rev. 574 (1972). On the historical development of tax incentives for historic preservation, see Listokin, Landmarks Preservation and the Property Tax (Center for Urban Policy Research 1982). On the particular provisions of the Economic Recovery Tax Act of 1981 that provide incentives for the rehabilitation of older and historic buildings, see Schulman, The Certified Historic Structure: An Aid to Neighborhood Conservation and Low-Income Housing, 14 Urban Law. 765 (1982), in Fernsler & Tuttle, Recent Developments in Housing and Community Development 14 Urban Law. 745 (1982). On the lessening of incentives toward historic preservation under the Tax Reform Act of 1986, see "Rehab Takes a Fall," Historic Preservation, Sept./Oct., 1990, at 51. See also Roddewig, Preservation Easement Law: An Overview of Recent Developments, 18 Urban

A few other grounds are occasionally cited as legitimate reasons for zoning, or as adding weight to the arguments for a particular zoning ordinance's validity. Preserving scenic beauty, in areas of natural attractiveness, is sometimes cited; and the trend is to allow this as a sufficient reason, in accord with the general trend on aesthetics.[93] Enhancing the tax base of a community is clearly *not* a valid purpose by itself for zoning, but is occasionally mentioned as a "make-weight" or additional argument for validity

---

Law, 229 (1986); Williams, Historic Preservation Easements—The Benefits and Burdens Associated With the Donation of an Easement on an Historic Structure, 57 Okla. B.A.J. 749 (1986), discussing the tax benefits of donating historic preservation easements. On preservation easements in general, see Phelps, Preserving Preservation Easements?: Preservation Easements in an Uncertain Regulatory Future, 91 Neb. L. Rev. 121 (2012).

On the development of the law concerning air rights, a subject involved in the *Penn Central* litigation *supra*, see Schnidman & Roberts, Municipal Air Rights: New York City's Proposal to Sell Air Rights over Public Buildings and Public Spaces, 15 Urban Law. 347 (1983). On developments as to the air rights over Grand Central Terminal, see Horsley, Air Rights Bought at Grand Central, N.Y. Times, Nov. 26, 1983, at 1, col. 1. On the significant contributions to land-use and historic-preservation law—in particular the *Penn Central* decision *supra*—made by Justice William Brennan during his years on the U.S. Supreme Court, see Haar & Kayden, Landmark Justice: The Influence of William J. Brennan on America's Communities (Preservation Press 1989). For an interesting contrast to the *Penn Central* case, see United Artists Theater Circuit, Inc. v. City of Philadelphia, 528 Pa. 12, 595 A.2d 6 (1991), where the court invalidated—as a "taking" without compensation—provisions of a municipal code which authorized historic landmark designation of private property and accompanying restrictions on use without consent of the owner. But the Pennsylvania court subsequently reversed itself on rehearing and ruled that historic designation is a valid use of government powers and does not necessarily effect a taking. United Artists' Theater Circuit, Inc. v. City of Philadelphia, 535 Pa. 370, 635 A.2d 612 (1993). See generally White & Keatings, Recent Developments in Historic Preservation and Architectural Control Law, 26 Urban Law. 777, 790–93 (1994), discussing both of the *United Artists'* opinions. See also Wade, *Penn Central's* Economic Failings Confounded Takings Jurisprudence, 31 Urban Law. 277 (1999). On the attempts sometimes now made to undo landmark designations, see Yelin, Routes to Landmark "De-Designation": An Analysis of Selected Cases, 22 Urban Law. 307 (1990).

An excellent summary of the background of, and litigation over, historic preservation laws is found in Annot., Validity and Construction of Statute or Ordinance Protecting Historical Landmarks, 18 A.L.R.4th 990 (1982), noting, at 995, that all 50 states and more than 500 municipalities have enacted laws to encourage or require preservation of historic or aesthetic buildings and areas. A good article specifically dealing with *local* efforts at historic preservation over the years, and judicial challenges to those efforts, is Smith, Judicial Review of Historic and Landmark Preservation Ordinances, 15 Urban Law. 555 (1983). On a particularly successful effort at rehabilitating and reusing historic structures, see Freeman, Lessons from Lowell, Historic Preservation, Nov./Dec., 1990, at 32, discussing rehabilitation in Lowell, Massachusetts. See generally Martin, Adaptive Use (Urban Law Institute 1980), reviewed 25 Urban Law. 695 (1993); Murtagh, Keeping Time: The History and Theory of Preservation in America (Main Street Press 1988). On the vagueness problems that sometimes plague historic preservation legislation, see Comment, Florida's Local Historic Preservation Ordinances: Maintaining Flexibility While Avoiding Vagueness Claims, 25 Fla. St. U.L. Rev. 1017 (1998).

On possible conflicts between historic preservation efforts and disability access, see Comment, A Comparative Analysis of the Tension Created by Disability Access and Historic Preservation Laws in the United States and England, 22 Conn. J. Int'l L. 379 (2007). Regarding other exceptions to, or conflicts with, the law, see Note, Engineering Exceptions to Historic Preservation Law: Why the Army Corps of Engineers' Section 106 Regulations Are Invalid, 40 Wm. Mitchell L. Rev. 1580 (2014).

[93] See National Advertising Co. v. County of Monterey, 211 Cal.App.2d 375, 27 Cal.Rptr. 136 (1962) (sign-control case); Opinion of Justices, 103 N.H. 268, 169 A.2d 762 (1961) (maintenance of natural beauty along highways can be considered by legislature). Cf. L.C. Canyon Partners v. Salt Lake County, 266 P.3d 797 (Utah 2011), recognizing legitimate government objectives in protecting the foothills and canyon areas of a county; *id.* at 800. The Federal Highway Beautification Act of 1965, 23 U.S.C.A. § 131, provides incentives for states which prohibit advertising structures (other than those advertising goods or services offered on the premises where the sign is located) near interstate highways. See generally Williams, Legal Techniques to Protect and to Promote Aesthetics Along Transportation Corridors, 17 Buff.L.Rev. 701 (1968). See also Lamm & Yosinow, The Highway Beautification Act of 1965: A Case Study in Frustration, 46 Denver L.J. 437 (1969). As to environmental concerns in land-use law, see generally Colburn, Localism's Ecology: Protecting and Restoring Habitat in the Suburban Nation, 33 Ecology L.Q. 945 (2006); Symposium, The Intersection of Environmental and Land Use Law: A Special Edition of the Pace Environmental Law Review, 23 Pace Envtl. L. Rev. 671–1018 (2006).

where other purposes, such as improving property values and promoting homogeneity, are present.[94] The promotion of morals was mentioned in some older cases regarding regulation of billboards—because immoral activities were thought to take place behind them;[95] and in more recent times, it has been held that promotion of morality may justify "spacing" requirements as to the location of adult movie theatres, liquor establishments, etc.[96] Set-back ordinances (which require that structures be located a certain distance

---

[94] See Gruber v. Raritan Township, 39 N.J. 1, 186 A.2d 489 (1962). A zoning ordinance cannot be justified merely on the ground it will reduce taxes, as by lowering expenses for education, unless it is supported by some other valid ground. See Southern Burlington County N.A.A.C.P. v. Township of Mount Laurel, 67 N.J. 151, 336 A.2d 713 (1975), appeal dism'd cert. denied 423 U.S. 808, 96 S.Ct. 18, 46 L.Ed.2d 28, (bedroom restriction attempting to limit number of families with children in community). See also, on attempts to exclude children, note 68 *supra* and accompanying text. Compare, as to the effects that tax law may have on land development, McElfish, Taxation Effects on Land Development and Conservation, 22 Temple Envtl. L. & Tech. J. 155 (2004).

[95] See Thomas Cusack Co. v. City of Chicago, 242 U.S. 526, 529, 37 S.Ct. 190, 191, 61 L.Ed. 472 (1917) (noting that billboards shield immoral practices); General Outdoor Advertising Co. v. City of Indianapolis, 202 Ind. 85, 172 N.E. 309 (1930). Cf. Hav-A-Tampa Cigar Co. v. Johnson, 149 Fla. 148, 5 So.2d 433 (1941) (regulation of signboards along highways held constitutional as promoting public safety and general welfare). Massachusetts has held that, under state constitutional authority, advertising in public places and within public view may be regulated on grounds of taste and fitness. General Outdoor Advertising Co. v. Department of Public Works, 289 Mass. 149, 193 N.E. 799 (1935), appeals dism'd 296 U.S. 543, 56 S.Ct. 95, 80 L.Ed. 385, 297 U.S. 725, 56 S.Ct. 495, 80 L.Ed. 1008, interpreting Mass.Const. art. 50 (1979). See Gardner, The Massachusetts Billboard Decision, 49 Harv.L.Rev. 869 (1936). See generally Wilson, Billboards and the Right to Be Seen from the Highway, 30 Geo.L.J. 723 (1942); Annot., Validity and Construction of State or Local Regulation Prohibiting the Erection or Maintenance of Advertising Structures Within a Specified Distance of Street or Highway, 81 A.L.R.3d 564 (1977). As to morality as a proper purpose of zoning laws, see generally Smith & Bailey, Regulating Morality Through the Common Law and Exclusionary Zoning, 60 Catholic U. L. Rev. 403 (2011).

[96] See Young v. American Mini Theatres, 427 U.S. 50, 96 S.Ct. 2440, 49 L.Ed.2d 310 (1976), reh. denied 429 U.S. 873, 97 S.Ct. 191, 50 L.Ed.2d 155 (upholding, against First and Fourteenth Amendment attacks, ordinances prohibiting operation of any "adult" movie theatre, bookstore, etc. within 1000 feet of any other such establishment, or within 500 feet of a residential area); Mazo v. City of Detroit, 9 Mich.App. 354, 156 N.W.2d 155 (1968) (ordinance prohibiting establishment of a bar within 1000 feet of another upheld). But see Schad v. Borough of Mount Ephraim, 452 U.S. 61, 101 S.Ct. 2176, 68 L.Ed.2d 671 (1981) (ordinance excluding live entertainment, including nude dancing, *throughout* a borough could not be justified against First Amendment attack); Pringle v. City of Covina, 115 Cal.App.3d 151, 171 Cal.Rptr. 251 (Dist.Ct.1981) (ordinance barred exhibition within 500 feet of residential area of material characterized by emphasis on certain sexual activities, etc.; but court refused to ban such films completely, as would irreparably injure owners of theatre—occasional showings would be allowed). Cf. Williams v. City & County of Denver, 198 Colo. 573, 607 P.2d 981 (1979) (lower court had struck down restrictions on adult bookstores and theatres; court here holds those portions not severable from rest of ordinance). See generally Annot., Validity of "War Zone" Ordinances Restricting Location of Sex-Oriented Businesses, 1 A.L.R. 4th 1297 (1980). In City of Los Angeles v. Alameda Books, Inc., 535 U.S. 425, 122 S.Ct. 1728, 152 L.Ed.2d 670 (2002), the Court upheld an ordinance barring more than one adult entertainment business in the same building. As to the application of motive review to zoning restrictions on adult businesses, see Swiney, Applying Legal Expressivism to Motive Review of Adult-Use Zoning, 36 Capital U. L. Rev. 769 (2008).

While in the *Young* and *Los Angeles* cases *supra*, the Court upheld an attempt to *disperse* adult uses, attempts by a community to *concentrate* such uses in limited areas have also been found valid. City of Renton v. Playtime Theatres, Inc. 475 U.S. 41, 106 S.Ct. 925, 89 L.Ed.2d 29 (1986), reh. denied 475 U.S. 1132, 106 S.Ct. 1663, 90 L.Ed.2d 205 (1986) (ordinance prohibited adult motion picture theaters from locating within 1000 feet of any residential zone, single- or multiple-family dwelling, church, park or school; upheld as valid time, place and manner restriction on speech); Pangaea Cinema, LLC, 310 P.3d 604 (N.M. 2013) (cities may use zoning to disperse adult businesses or to concentrate them, consistent with the right to free speech). Thus, it is left to the political judgment of the community whether to use the dispersal or concentration method, if any method is used at all. But any type of "spacing" restriction is subject to challenge on grounds of vagueness. See Harris Books, Inc. v. City of Santa Fe, 98 N.M. 235, 647 P.2d 868 (1982) (ordinance forbidding location of adult bookstore within 1000 feet of residential area unconstitutionally vague where "residential area" not defined). Or on the ground of delegating governmental power to private individuals or entities. See Larkin v. Grendel's Den, Inc., 459 U.S. 116, 103 S.Ct. 505, 74 L.Ed.2d 297 (1982) (statute vesting in the governing bodies

from public streets, ways, etc.), off-street parking requirements, and other zoning or quasi-zoning restrictions, are sometimes justified partly on the ground of promoting the

---

of churches and schools the power to veto liquor licenses within 500-foot radius of the church or school delegates governmental power to private entities and violates Establishment Clause of First Amendment). Or on the ground of overbroadly infringing on free speech. See Pensack v. City & County of Denver, 630 F.Supp. 177 (D.Colo.1986) (city's application of adult bookstore ordinance to bakery offering cakes with sexually explicit themes held unconstitutional). But the general validity of "spacing" restrictions now seems well established. See 15192 Thirteen Mile Road, Inc. v. City of Warren, 626 F.Supp. 803 (E.D.Mich.1985) (ordinance upheld that limited location of adult businesses to no closer than 500 feet from any residence and at least 1000 feet from any other adult use and that required location along a major thoroughfare; protection of quality of residential life held a sufficient justification for "spacing" restriction). Cf. National City v. Wiener, 3 Cal.4th 832, 12 Cal.Rptr.2d 701, 838 P.2d 223 (1992), cert. denied 510 U.S. 824, 114 S.Ct. 85, 126 L.Ed.2d 53 (1993) (ordinance effectively limiting adult bookstores to enclosed malls upheld). See generally Brody, When First Amendment Principles and Local Zoning Regulations Collide, 12 N. Ill. L. Rev. 671 (1992); Pearlman, Zoning and the First Amendment, 16 Urban Law. 217 (1984). See also Mandelker & Rubin (eds.), Protecting Free Speech and Expression—The First Amendment and Land Use Law (Section of State and Local Government, American Bar Ass'n 2002) (a collection of essays detailing various land-use topics and their interrelationship with the First Amendment), reviewed 35 Urban Law. 391 (2003).

For interpretation of the *Renton* case *supra*, see SDJ, Inc. v. City of Houston, 837 F.2d 1268 (5th Cir.1988), aff'd on rehearing 841 F.2d 107 (5th Cir.1988) (city only needs to prove that ordinance is narrowly tailored to serve a substantial interest and leaves open alternative channels of communication). Cf. Town of Islip v. Caviglia, 141 A.D.2d 148, 532 N.Y.S.2d 783 (1988) (applying *Renton* test, court upholds ordinance restricting adult businesses to industrial zones, though "special exception" provision is invalidated for lack of adequate standards).

Some courts will uphold "spacing" restrictions applied to businesses protected by the First Amendment only if there is a showing of a real and immediate threat of substantial harm to the particular neighborhood. See City of Portland v. Tidyman, 306 Or. 174, 759 P.2d 242 (1988) (city ordinance imposing location and spacing restrictions on adult bookstores held an invalid restraint on free expression where ordinance did not specify the adverse effects that constituted nuisance attributable to sale of adult materials and therefore did not necessarily apply only where those adverse effects were shown to occur or imminently threaten to occur). See generally Roeseler, Regulating Adult Entertainment Establishments Under Conventional Zoning, 19 Urban Law. 125 (1987); Annot., Validity of Ordinances Restricting Location of "Adult Entertainment" or Sex-Oriented Businesses, 10 A.L.R.5th 538 (1993). See also Gerard, Local Regulation of Adult Businesses (West Group 1998). For critical examinations of "spacing" requirements, see Eckert, The Incoherence of the Zoning Approach to Regulating Pornography: The Exclusion of Gender and a Call for Category Refinement in Free Speech Doctrine, 4 Geo. J. Gender & L. 863 (2003); Note, Are We Losing the First Amendment, or Just Adult Businesses?, 12 Villanova Sports & Ent. L.J. 227 (2005).

In Arcara v. Cloud Books, Inc., 478 U.S. 697, 106 S.Ct. 3172, 92 L.Ed.2d 568 (1986), on remand 68 N.Y.2d 553, 510 N.Y.S.2d 844, 503 N.E.2d 492 (1986), the U.S. Supreme Court held constitutional the enforcement of a nuisance closure law to shut down an adult bookstore at its present location for a one-year period due to illicit sexual activities on the premises. But see World Wide Video, Inc. v. City of Tukwila, 117 Wash.2d 382, 816 P.2d 18 (1991), cert. denied 503 U.S. 986, 112 S.Ct. 1672, 118 L.Ed.2d 391 (1992), finding that adult businesses with predominantly take-home merchandise do not necessarily have the same harmful secondary effects traditionally associated with adult movie theaters and peep shows and therefore cannot, under the First Amendment, be subjected to the same severe zoning restrictions. See generally Cramer, Zoning Adult Businesses: Evaluating the Secondary Effects Doctrine, 86 Temple L. Rev. 577 (2014); Hudson, The Secondary Effects Doctrine: "The Evisceration of First Amendment Freedoms," 37 Washburn L.J. 55 (1997); Comment, Preventing the Secondary Effects of Adult Entertainment Establishments: Is Zoning the Solution?, 12 J. Land Use & Envtl. L. 383 (1997). In Stringfellow's of New York, Ltd. v. City of New York, 91 N.Y.2d 382, 671 N.Y.S.2d 406, 694 N.E.2d 407 (1998), the court upheld zoning ordinances that treated adult uses differently from other commercial uses due to the differing secondary effects. See Note, New York City's Restrictive Zoning of Adult Businesses: A Constitutional Analysis, 23 Fordham U.L.J. 187 (1995). See generally Note, Adult Uses and the First Amendment: The *Stringfellow's* Decision and Its Impact on Municipal Control of Adult Businesses, 15 Touro L. Rev. 241 (1998). As to secondary effects, see also Daniel, An Examination of the Assumption that Adult Businesses Are Associated with Crime in Surrounding Areas: A Secondary Effects Study in Charlotte, North Carolina, 38 Law & Soc'y Rev. 69 (2004). As to the creation of "anti-prostitution zones" in some cities, see Comment, Anti-prostitution Zones: Justifications for Abolition, 91 J. Crim. L. & Criminology 1101 (2001), discussing laws enacted or proposed in some Florida communities making mere presence in a "prostitution free zone" a probation violation for repeat offenders.

speedy and safe movement of traffic.[97] Other safety considerations are among the reasons for two common types of specialized zoning: Flood-plain zoning is designed to prevent building of residences and other structures in areas subject to periodic or seasonal flooding, and this is upheld where reasonably necessary to protect the health or safety of those who would use the buildings.[98] "Airport zoning" can validly limit the

---

[97] Set-back requirements: See Moore v. City of Pratt, 148 Kan. 53, 79 P.2d 871 (1938); Wulfsohn v. Burden, 241 N.Y. 288, 150 N.E. 120 (1925); State ex rel. Cataland v. Birk, 97 Ohio App. 299, 125 N.E.2d 748 (1953); Appeal of Kerr, 294 Pa. 246, 144 A. 81 (1928). See generally Note, Municipal Corporations—Validity of Set-Back Ordinance, 27 Mich.L.Rev. 959 (1929). Set-back ordinances may also be justified on aesthetic and economic grounds. See Weiner v. City of Los Angeles, 68 Cal.2d 697, 68 Cal.Rptr. 733, 441 P.2d 293 (1968) ("greenbelt" created; value of homes increased). See generally Matter of Schrader, 660 P.2d 135 (Okl. 1983) (setback ordinance as applied to owner of residential carport upheld against allegations that words "building" and "structure" in the ordinance were unduly vague).

Off-street parking requirements: Chambers v. Zoning Board of Adjustment, 250 N.C. 194, 108 S.E.2d 211 (1959) (necessary in order to protect children from traffic). See Citizens Association of Georgetown, Inc. v. District of Columbia Board of Zoning Adjustment, 337 A.2d 495 (D.C.1975) (ordinance required additional parking spaces to be provided by owner if another building added; terrace on restaurant held not a "building"). But see Ronda Realty Corp. v. Lawton, 414 Ill. 313, 111 N.E.2d 310 (1953) (improper classification found where off-street parking requirement applied to apartment houses but not to hotels or rooming houses). Cf. Stroud v. City of Aspen, 188 Colo. 1, 532 P.2d 720 (1975) (off-street parking requirements entitled to same presumption of validity as applies to any other zoning ordinances; but a requirement that property owner provide parking spaces himself or lease them from city, but which does not require city actually to provide such spaces, is overbroad).

Regulation of signs and advertising structures may also be justified on the ground of eliminating traffic hazards and promoting highway safety. See Perlmutter v. Greene, 259 N.Y. 327, 182 N.E. 5 (1932) (highway authorities proposed putting screen in front of distracting billboard near curve of road; injunction denied). See generally Annot., Validity and Construction of State or Local Regulation Prohibiting the Erection of Maintenance of Advertising Structures Within a Specified Distance of Street or Highway, 81 A.L.R.3d 564 (1977). Safety considerations may also justify restrictions on signs overhanging public streets or walks. See Annot., Validity and Construction of State or Local Regulation Prohibiting or Regulating Advertising Sign Overhanging Street or Sidewalk, 80 A.L.R.3d 687 (1977). See also Pittsford Plaza Assoc. v. Spiegel, 66 N.Y.2d 717, 496 N.Y.S.2d 992, 487 N.E.2d 902 (1985) (town board had authority to reject proposal for 7-screen movie theater on basis, among others, that the proposed use would create traffic problems).

In Mobil Oil Co. v. Township of Westtown, 21 Pa.Cmwlth. 295, 345 A.2d 313 (1975), a zoning ordinance requiring spacing of gasoline stations along highways in order to reduce traffic accidents was upheld. Various safety considerations have been cited in a number of other cases sustaining spacing requirements as to gasoline stations. Stone v. City of Maitland, 446 F.2d 83 (5th Cir.1971) (requirement that there be at least 350 feet between proposed filling station and any existing station, and between proposed station and any existing church, hospital, school, etc.); City of Boca Raton v. Tradewind Hills, Inc., 216 So.2d 460 (Fla.App.1968) (minimum distance of 750 feet between filling stations); Harvard Enterprises v. Board of Adjustment, 56 N.J. 362, 266 A.2d 588 (1970). Cf. Rasmussen v. Village of Bensenville, 56 Ill.App.2d 119, 205 N.E.2d 631 (1965) (upholding ban on storage of flammable liquids within 200 feet of schools, hospitals, churches, and theatres). But see Buck v. Kilgore, 298 A.2d 107 (Me.1972) (ordinance banning gasoline stations within 2000 feet of schools, churches, etc. held unreasonable). See generally Mosher, Proximity Regulations of the Modern Service Station, 17 Syracuse L.Rev. 1 (1965).

[98] See Turnpike Realty Co. v. Town of Dedham, 362 Mass. 221, 284 N.E.2d 891 (1972), cert. denied 409 U.S. 1108, 93 S.Ct. 908, 34 L.Ed.2d 689 (1973). Cf. Cappture Realty Corp. v. Board of Adjustment, 133 N.J.Super. 216, 336 A.2d 30 (1975) (moratorium on construction in flood plain for specified period; upheld). But a number of specific regulations have been found unreasonable as applied to the particular property, or otherwise so extreme as to be "takings." See Dooley v. Town Plan and Zoning Commission of Town of Fairfield, 151 Conn. 304, 197 A.2d 770 (1964); State v. Johnson, 265 A.2d 711 (Me.1970); MacGibbon v. Board of Appeals, 356 Mass. 635, 255 N.E.2d 347 (1970). See generally Dunham, Flood Control via the Police Power, 107 U.Pa.L.Rev. 1098 (1959); Annot., Local Use Zoning of Wetlands or Flood Plain as Taking Without Compensation, 19 A.L.R.4th 756 (1983) (such zoning generally held not to constitute a "taking without compensation").

uses and heights of structures near airports and/or within the approach pattern to such facilities.[99]

Restrictions on use of properties near the shore of lakes and streams ("shore-lands zoning") can be sustained if reasonably necessary to preservation of the natural environment.[100] Similarly, "greenbelt zoning" has been used to preserve woodlands and

---

[99] See Baggett v. City of Montgomery, 276 Ala. 166, 160 So.2d 6 (1963); Waring v. Peterson, 137 So.2d 268 (Fla.App.1962); Village of Willoughby Hills v. Corrigan, 29 Ohio St.2d 39, 278 N.E.2d 658 (1972), cert. denied 409 U.S. 919, 93 S.Ct. 218, 34 L.Ed.2d 181. In Harrell's Candy Kitchen v. Sarasota-Manatee Airport Authority, 111 So.2d 439 (Fla.1959), the adoption in an airport zoning ordinance of the airport-approach standards of the Civil Aeronautics Administration was held reasonable. But rules differing from the federal standards may also be valid, if there is no actual conflict and no federal pre-emption as to the particular matter. See LaSalle National Bank v. County of Cook, 34 Ill.App.3d 264, 340 N.E.2d 79 (1975).

Again, a number of cases have found a "taking," at least of an easement, under the particular circumstances. See Peacock v. County of Sacramento, 271 Cal.App.2d 845, 77 Cal.Rptr. 391 (Dist.Ct.1969); Roark v. Caldwell, 87 Idaho 557, 394 P.2d 641 (1964); Indiana Toll Road Commission v. Jankovich, 244 Ind. 574, 193 N.E.2d 237 (1963) cert. dism'd 379 U.S. 487, 85 S.Ct. 493, 13 L.Ed.2d 439; Jackson Municipal Airport Authority v. Evans, 191 So.2d 126 (Miss.1966); Yara Engineering Corp. v. City of Newark, 132 N.J.L. 370, 40 A.2d 559 (1945). Cf. Hageman v. Wayne Township, 20 Ohio App.2d 12, 251 N.E.2d 507 (1969) (if regulation amounts to taking, court can issue injunction against the regulation or direct the institution of eminent domain proceedings). See generally Annot., Zoning Regulations Limiting Use of Property Near Airport as Taking of Property, 18 A.L.R.4th 542 (1982), containing citations to a number of cases in which "airport zoning" has been found to result in a taking for which compensation is required.

[100] See Just v. Marinette County, 56 Wis.2d 7, 201 N.W.2d 761 (1972), where it is noted that the county has power to zone shorelands in Wisconsin, and if the county does not enact an ordinance complying with state standards, the state may enact an ordinance applicable to that county. In some jurisdictions, the state may have *preempted* the field of shorelands zoning. See Lauricella v. Planning and Zoning Board of Appeals, 32 Conn.Sup. 104, 342 A.2d 374 (Com.Pl.1975) (state has pre-empted authority over tidal wetlands). Again, a taking requiring compensation will be found if the zoning restriction leaves the wetlands or shorelands property with no reasonable use—or by some authority may be found if the owner is deprived of a substantial part of the economic use or value. See Florida Rock Industries, Inc. v. United States, 18 F.3d 1560 (Fed.Cir.1994), cert. denied 513 U.S. 1109, 115 S.Ct. 898, 130 L.Ed.2d 783 (1995), noted 2 George Mason U.L. Rev. 245 (1995); 14 Temple Envtl. L. & Tech. J. 55 (1995).

On the interpretation of shorelands legislation, see Clam Shacks of America, Inc. v. Skagit County, 109 Wash.2d 91, 743 P.2d 265 (1987) (state statute was to be liberally construed so as to regulate uses as well as development; as thus construed, statute, and county shoreline master program enacted thereunder, applied to clam-harvesting operation). On zoning along ocean coasts, see Berke, San Francisco Bay: A Successful Case of Coastal Zone Planning Legislation and Implementation, 15 Urban Law. 487 (1983). On the Coastal Zone Management Act of 1972, 16 U.S.C.A. 1451–54, providing federal funds for states to develop coastal management programs, see Mandeleker & Sherry, The National Coastal Zone Management Act of 1972, 7 Urban L. Ann. 120 (1974). See generally California v. Watt, 683 F.2d 1253 (9th Cir.1982) (major purpose of Coastal Zone Management Act is to avoid conflict and encourage cooperation between federal and state governments in developing a comprehensive plan for long-term management of resources in coastal zone), rev'd on other grounds 464 U.S. 312, 104 S.Ct. 656, 78 L.Ed.2d 496 (1984) (Department of Interior's sale of oil and gas leases on outer continental shelf doesn't directly affect coastal zone so as to require a consistency determination under Coastal Zone Management Act); Malone, The Coastal Zone Management Act and the Takings Clause in the 1990's: Making the Case for Federal Land Use to Preserve Coastal Areas, 62 U. Colo. L. Rev. 711 (1991); Rychlak, Coastal Zone Management and the Search for Integration, 40 DePaul L. Rev. 981 (1991). On the lack of enforcement of many provisions of the National Coastal Zone Management Act, see Archer & Knecht, The U.S. National Coastal Zone Management Program—Problems and Opportunities in the Next Phase, 15 Coastal Mgt. 103 (1987). See also Salvesen, Wetlands: Mitigating and Regulating Development Impacts (Urban Land Institute 1990); McKinstry, Constraints Upon Development in Environmentally Sensitive Areas: Regulation of Wetlands, Streams, and Floodplains in Pennsylvania, 2 Villanova Envtl. L.J. 333 (1991).

For a summary of legislative and U.S. Supreme Court authority on wetlands regulation, see Minan, Wetlands Regulation and the United States Supreme Court, 38 Urban Law. 523 (2006). See generally Comment, A Historical Perspective on the Recent Decline in "Judicial Pioneering" in Wetlands Regulation, 33 Wm. Mitchell L. Rev. 1225 (2007), noting Rapanos v. United States, 547 U.S. 715, 126 S.Ct. 2208, 165 L.Ed.2d 159 (2006) (only those wetlands with a continuous surface connection to bodies that are waters of the United States in their own right are covered by federal Clean Water Act). See also, on the possible use of local laws to

open areas around some cities, and also to create a "buffer" between residences and other uses.[101] Originally the Supreme Court, in the *Agins* case, applied a two-prong test to determine whether a taking had occurred when a city zoned land as open space: In order to avoid "taking" liability, the government's action must substantially advance legitimate state interests *and* must not deny the landowner all economically viable use of the property.[102] In the *Lingle* case in 2005,[103] the *Agins* case was partially overruled by the Court's elimination of the first prong of the test for determining whether the land-use measure was a proper and noncompensable exercise of the police power or was a regulatory taking: whether the measure in question substantially advanced legitimate governmental interests. At issue in *Lingle* was a rent-control ordinance. Because the party arguing that a taking of its property had occurred (Chevron) had relied on the "substantially advances" language of *Agins*, it was not entitled to summary judgment on its claim.[104]

---

provide habitat protection, Colburn, Localism's Ecology: Protecting and Restoring Habitat in the Suburban Nation, 33 Ecology L.Q. 945 (2006). As to creating and/or protecting a healthy environment via land-use law, see generally Mudd, A "Constant and Difficult Task": Making Local Land Use Decisions in States With a Constitutional Right to a Healthful Environment, 38 Ecology L. Q. 1 (2011).

[101] See Agins v. City of Tiburon, 447 U.S. 255, 100 S.Ct. 2138, 65 L.Ed.2d 106 (1980) (city's open-space zoning upheld; compensation not required); State v. Gallop Building, 103 N.J.Super. 367, 247 A.2d 350 (1968). See generally Humbach, Land and a New Land Ethic, 74 Minn. L. Rev. 339 (1989). As to the validity of zoning that restricts development of "substandard" lots—*i.e.*, lots not meeting minimum area requirements—, see Tekoa Constr., Inc. v. City of Seattle, 56 Wash.App. 28, 781 P.2d 1324 (1989), review denied 114 Wash.2d 1005, 788 P.2d 1079 (1990) (upholding ordinance restricting development of such lots in common ownership). On planning of green belts and open areas, see also Sections 21.1 and 21.5 *infra.*

[102] Agins v. City of Tiberon, *supra* note 101. For a critique of this test, see Sullivan, Emperors and Clothes: The Genealogy and Operation of the *Agins* Tests, 33 Urban Law. 343 (2001). See also, criticizing Supreme Court cases partially based on *Agins*, Sullivan, Return of the Platonic Guardians: *Nollan* and *Dolan* and the First Prong of *Agins*, 34 Urban Law. 39 (2002).

[103] Lingle v. Chevron U.S.A., Inc., 544 U.S. 528, 125 S.Ct. 2074, 161 L.Ed.2d 876 (2005).

[104] See Jacobs, Indigestion for Eating Crow: The Impact of *Lingle v. Chevron, U.S.A., Inc.,* on the Future of Regulatory Takings Doctrine, 38 Urban Law. 451 (2006) ("very little upheaval in case law is seen within federal and state jurisprudence"; *id.* at 479); Radford, Just a Flesh Wound? The Impact of *Lingle v. Chevron* on Regulatory Takings Law, 38 Urban Law. 437 (2006) ("the same facts that previously led to takings liability under the substantial advancement test will simply be pled under a different legal theory in the future, arriving at the same result that would have pertained pre-*Lingle*"; *id.* at 438). As to rent control, see generally Section 23.2, notes 13–14, *infra,* and accompanying text. See also Baron, Winding Toward the Heart of the Takings Muddle: *Kelo, Lingle*, and Public Discourse About Private Property, 34 Fordham Urban L.J. 613 (2007); Curtin, Gowder & Wenter, Exactions Update: The State of Development Exactions After *Lingle v. Chevron U.S.A., Inc.*, 38 Urban Law. 641 (2006), concluding "As land use exactions continue to be employed by local governments as a means to require that new development pay its own way, *Nollan* and *Dolan*'s 'nexus' and 'rough proportionality' rules will continue to be applied and shaped through litigation in state courts. *Id.* at 655.

Excellent analysis of the *Lingle* case and its effect on earlier cases is found in several articles in a Real Estate Symposium in John Marshall Law Review: Callies & Goodin, The Status of *Nollan v. California Coastal Commission* and *Dolan v. City of Tigard* After *Lingle v. Chevron U.S.A., Inc.*, 40 John Marshall L. Rev. 539 (2007); Epstein, From *Penn Central* to *Lingle*: The Long Backwards Road, *id.* at 593; and Whitman, Deconstructing *Lingle*: Implications for Takings Doctrine, *id.* at 573.

On possible relinquishment of the right to attach open-space and related requirements to permits for subdivisions, see Wilson v. Board of County Comm'rs of Teton County, 153 P.3d 917 (Wyo. 2007) (developers relinquished their right to contest validity and constitutionality of conditions imposed on their subdivision, requiring them to set aside portions of the subdivision as mandatory open space and for affordable housing, when they did not challenge the conditions until after subdivision had been approved and all but four lots in the subdivision had been sold, gifted, or reserved for their business).

Some states have enacted land-use laws designating certain areas as "agricultural lands" and providing for their conservation.[105] Preserving and protecting the environment is increasingly recognized as a valid purpose in land-use law, as is dealing with and containing air pollution.[106] Though in general the regulation of economic

---

[105] See Lewis County v. Western Wash. Growth Management Hearings Bd., 157 Wash.2d 488, 139 P.3d 1096 (2006), applying the Washington State statute and defining "agricultural land" under the Act as land that is not already characterized by urban growth and that is primarily devoted to the commercial production of agricultural products, including land in areas used or capable of being used for production based on land characteristics. The court said that land should be designated as "agricultural" based not only on soil and land characteristics but also on farm industry's projected needs. The county's exclusion of "farm centers" and farm homes for agricultural-land designation was held erroneous, as was the allowing of residential subdivisions and other non-farm uses within the designated areas. Compare Seward County v. Navarro, 35 Kan.App.2d 744, 133 P.3d 1283 (2006) (training of horses for racing purposes was not agricultural use). Cf. Wetherell v. Douglas County, 342 Or. 666, 160 P.3d 614 (2007) (in determining whether land is suitable for farm use, local government may not be precluded from considering the costs or expenses of engaging in those activities). See generally Chumbler, Negro & Bechler (eds.), Urban Agriculture—Policy, Law, Strategy and Implementation (ABA Section of State and Local Government Law 2015); Heckler, A Right to Farm in the City: Providing a Legal Framework for Legitimizing Urban Farming in American Cities, 47 Valparaiso U. L. Rev. 217 (2012); Witt, Urban Agriculture and Local Government Law: Promises, Realities, and Solutions, 16 U. Pa. J. L. & Soc. Change 221 (2013); Note, The Intersection Between Urban Agriculture and Form-Based Zoning: A Return to Traditional Planning Techniques, 19 Hastings W.-N.W. J. Envtl. L. & Pol'y 83 (2013); Note, Putting Paradise in the Parking Lot: Using Zoning to Promote Urban Agriculture, 88 Notre Dame L. Rev. 2551 (2013). Much writing on urban agriculture has focused on experiments and experiences in particular localities: *Baltimore*: Note, Farming the Slums: Using Eminent Domain and Urban Agriculture to Rebuild Baltimore's Blighted Neighborhoods, 38 Wm. & Mary Envtl. L. & Pol'y Rev. 479 (2014); *Detroit*: Note, Securing the Momentum: Could a Homestead Act Help Sustain Detroit Urban Agriculture?, 16 Drake J. Agri. L. 241 (2011); Note, Growing in the D: Revising Current Laws to Promote a Model of Sustainable City Agriculture, 89 U. Detroit Mercy L. Rev. 181 (2012); *Florida*: Cossey & student, Protecting Equine Rescue From Being Put Out to Pasture: Whether Ranches Dedicated to Abused, Abandoned, and Aging Horses May Qualify for "Agricultural" Classifications Under Florida's Greenbelt Law, 16 Drake J. Agri. L. 69 (2011); *Trenton and Newark, New Jersey*: Note, Encouraging the Growth of Urban Agriculture in Trenton and Newark Through Amendments to the Zoning Codes: A Proven Approach to Addressing the Persistence of Food Deserts, 14 Vt. J. Envtl. L. 71 (2012). See also, as to *Hawaii*, Comment, Avoiding the Next Hakulia: The Debate Over Hawaii's Agricultural Subdivisions, 27 U. Hawaii L. Rev. 441 (2005).

As to what is "agricultural land," see City of Arlington v. Central Puget Sound Growth Management Hearings Bd., 164 Wash. 2d 768, 193 P.3d 1077 (2008) ("agricultural land" is, among other characteristics, land that has long-term commercial significance for agricultural production). See generally La Croix, Urban Agriculture and Other Green Uses: Remaking the Shrinking City, 42 Urban Law. 225 (2010). Some have urged caution in the creation of agricultural zones. See Note, The Rise of Urban Agriculture: A Cautionary Tale—No Rules, Big Problems, 4 Wm. & Mary Bus. L. Rev. 241 (2013). Cf., Note, Applying Sustainable Land Use Development Studies to Sustainable Agriculture: Are the Conditions Ripe for a Successful Movement Toward Sustainable Agriculture?,78 Brooklyn L. Rev. 1033 (2013). See generally Symposium, Safety and Sustainability in the Era of Food Systems: Reaching a More Integrated Approach, 2014 Wis. L. Rev. 199–469, particularly Schindler, Unpermitted Urban Agriculture: Transgressive Actions, Changing Norms, and the Local Food Movement, *id.* at 369. One activity that may be affected by urban agriculture is the keeping of bees. See Peters, Keeping Bees in the City? Disappearing Bees and the Explosion of Urban Agriculture Inspire Urbanites to Keep Honeybees, 17 Drake J. Agri. L. 597 (2012). Some commentators see urban agriculture as a way of helping revive cities. See Comment, Bringing Food Back Home: Revitalizing the Postindustrial City Through State and Local Policies Promoting Urban Agriculture, 92 Or. L. Rev. 783 (2014). As to environmental issues presented by urban agriculture, see La Croix, Urban Agriculture and the Environment, 46 Urban Law. 227 (2014). The history of urban agriculture in the United States from the 19th century to the present is well summarized in Pollans & Roberts, Setting the Table for Urban Agriculture, 46 Urban Law. 199 (2014).

[106] See generally Comment, Recreating the Western City in a Post-Industrialized World: European Brownfield Policy and an American Comparison, 53 Buffalo L. Rev. 1273 (2005). "Brownfields," as discussed in the above-cited comment, are real estate on which there is contamination by hazardous materials, or at least the perception of possible contamination. *Id.* at 1274. Such areas have been a major problem in the development of many urban areas in the United States. See Appex, The Brownfield Manifesto, 37 Urban Law. 163 (2005); Eison, Brownfields at 20: A Critical Reevaluation, 34 Fordham Urban L.J. 721 (2007). See also Comment, Fighting Uncertainty: Municipal Partnerships With Redevelopment Agencies Can Mitigate Uncertainty to Encourage Brownfield Redevelopment, 1 Golden Gate Envtl. L.J. 267 (2007). Among the

competition is *not* a legitimate purpose of zoning, such regulation may be permissible if it promotes other police-power purposes, including the protection of a downtown business district.[107]

---

suggested remedies for brownfields is using them to promote urban agriculture. See Note, Utilizing Michigan Brownfield Policies to Incentivize Community-Based Urban Agriculture in Detroit, 3 Mich. J. Envtl. & Admin. L. 421 (2014). Or using them as part of mixed use projects. See Laitos & student, The Role of Brownfields as Sites for Mixed Use Development Projects in America and Britain, 40 Denver J. Int'l L. & Pol'y 492 (2011–12). Or using them as energy havens. See Scholtes, From Trash to Treasure: Converting America's Contaminated Land Into Renewable Energy Havens, 47 Suffolk U. L. Rev. 1 (2014). See generally American Bar Ass'n Section of Environment, Energy & Resources, Brownfields: A Comprehensive Guide to Redeveloping Contaminated Property (3d ed. 2013); Edwards (ed.), Implementing Institutional Controls at Brownfields and Other Contaminated Sites (2d ed. ABA Books 2012).

It has been suggested that climate change may make necessary some changes in local zoning laws, perhaps making desirable a revamping of our entire zoning system since federal involvement may now be needed in that system, though historically the federal government has not participated there. Flatt, Adapting Laws for a Changing World: A Systemic Approach to Climate Change Adaptation, 64 U. Fla. L. Rev. 269, 292 (2012). See Heinzerling, Climate, Preemption, and the Executive Branches, 50 Ariz. L. Rev. 925 (2008), and Stewart, States and Cities as Actors in Global Climate Regulation, 50 Ariz. L. Rev. 681 (2008), both parts of Symposium, Federalism and Climate Change: The Role of the States in a Future Federal Regime, 50 Ariz. L. Rev. 673–938 (2008). See generally Sussman, Climate Change Adaptation: Fostering Progress Through Law and Regulation, 18 N.Y.U. Envtl. L. Rev. 55 (2010); Trisolini, What Local Climate Change Plans Can Teach Us About City Power, 36 Fordham Urb. L. J. 863 (2009); Trisolini, All Hands on Deck: Local Governments and the Potential for Bidirectional Climate Change Regulation, 62 Stan. L. Rev. 669 (2010); Colloquium, Cities and Climate Change, 36 Fordham Urb. L. J. 159 (2009).

Dealing with climate change has been suggested as coming within the police power and thus being an appropriate purpose for zoning. See Dellinger, Localizing Climate Change Action, 14 Minn. J. L., Science & Technology 603 (2013); Nolon, Land Use and Climate Change: Lawyers Negotiating Above Regulation, 78 Brooklyn L. Rev. 521 (2013); Osofsky, Suburban Climate Change Efforts: Possibilities for Small and Nimble Cities Participating in State, Regional, National, and International Networks, 22 Cornell J. L. & Pub. Pol'y 395 (2012); Comment, Quantifying an Uncertain Future: The Demands of the California Environmental Quality Act and the Challenge of Climate Change Analysis, 43 McGeorge L. Rev. 1065 (2012). Cf. Craig, Ocean Governance for the 21st Century: Making Marine Zoning Climate Change Adaptable, 36 Harv. Envtl. L. Rev. 305 (2012); Negro, Recent Development in Coastal Adaptation to Climate Change, 45 Urban Law. 991 (2013). See also Burkett, Duty and Breach in an Era of Uncertainty: Local Government Liability for Failure to Adapt to Climate Change, 20 George Mason L. Rev. 775 (2013); Symposium, Climate Change Justice, 13 Chicago J. Int'l L. 345–614 (2013).

It has also been recognized that the police power covers regulation of hydraulic fracturing by the oil and gas industry and thus may be subject to regulation by local governments *if* the state has not pre-empted the field. See Note, Moving Past Preemption: Enhancing the Power of Local Governments Over Hydraulic Fracturing, 98 Minn. L. Rev. 385 (2013); Comment, Regulating Hydraulic Fracturing Through Land Use: State Preemption Prevails, 85 U. Colo. L.Rev. 817 (2014). See generally Symposium, Legal Aspects of Hydraulic Fracturing, 49 Idaho L. Rev. 241–517 (2013). On the situation in New York State, see Note, Zoning Out Fracking: Zoning Authority Under New York State's Oil, Gas, and Solution Mining Law, 40 Fordham Urb. L. J. 869 (2012); Note, Drawing Lines in the Shale: Local Zoning Bans, the Taking Clause, and the Clash to Come If New York State Promulgates Hydrofracking Regulations, 64 Syracuse L. Rev. 489 (2014); Symposium, Fractured Communities: Hydraulic Fracturing and the Law in New York State, 77 Albany L. Rev. 643 (2013–14).

As to whether hydrofracking is most appropriately regulated at the federal, state, or local level—or some combination of these—, compare Freilich & Popowitz, Oil and Gas Fracking: State and Federal Regulation Does Not Preempt Needed Local Government Regulation, 44 Urban Law. 533 (2012), with Burford, The Need for Federal Regulation of Hydraulic Fracturing, 44 Urban Law. 577 (2012). See generally Nolon & Polidoro, Hydrofracking: Disturbances Both Geological and Political: Who Decides?, 44 Urban Law. 507 (2012). See also Burger, The (Re)federalization of Fracking Regulation, 2013 Mich. St. L. Rev. 1484; Wegemer, Drilling Down: New York Hydraulic Fracturing, and the Dormant Commerce Clause, 28 B.Y.U. J. Pub. L. 351 (2014).

[107] See Hernandez v. City of Hanford, 41 Cal.4th 279, 59 Cal.Rptr.3d 442, 159 P.3d 33 (2007) (zoning ordinance restricting furniture sales was drafted so as to protect city's unique downtown commercial district, which was known for its furniture retailers; upheld). See also, on restrictions on "big box" stores, Lefcoe, The Regulation of Superstores: The Legality of Zoning Ordinances Emerging from the Skirmishes Between Wal–Mart and the United Food and Commercial Workers Union, 58 Ark. L. Rev. 833 (2006). As to the validity and

§ 18.5 Zoning—Nonconforming Uses

One limitation commonly found on the effect of zoning ordinances is that they don't apply to nonconforming uses. Such a use has been defined as one lawfully in existence at the time the zoning ordinance took effect and continuing to exist since that time.[108] The exception for such uses developed early in the history of American zoning[109] because (1) zoning was considered mainly a matter of prospective control, not a tool to change existing development; (2) "Euclidean" zoners felt that a few nonconforming uses wouldn't harm the overall plan—especially since early zoning was nearly always cumulative, not exclusive (*i.e.*, so-called "higher uses" were allowed in "lower-use zones"); (3) political opposition to zoning in the early years was strong enough that zoning laws often could not be passed unless exception was made for existing land uses; and (4) the constitutionality of zoning laws was in doubt for some time, and if nonconforming uses are not allowed, the arguments against this use of the police power are greatly strengthened.[110] Most zoning ordinances specifically provide for nonconforming uses,[111] but occasionally an exception for such uses is "read in" where the language of an ordinance is unclear, or even seems not to allow these uses.[112]

---

effect of zoning to protect small local businesses, as opposed to large chain and discount stores, see Botwinick, Effron & Huang, Saving Mom and Pop: Zoning and Legislating for Small and Local Business Retention, 18 J. L. & Pol'y 607 (2010). See also, as to efforts to limit "formula" businesses, such as franchise outlets, through zoning laws, Bobrowski, The Regulation of Formula Businesses and the Dormant Commerce Clause Doctrine, 44 Urban Law. 227 (2012).

[108] Arsenault v. City of Keene, 104 N.H. 356, 187 A.2d 60 (1962); Town of Highland Park v. Marshall, 235 S.W.2d 658 (Tex.Civ.App. 1950), ref'd n.r.e.; Rhod-A-Zalea & 35th, Inc. v. Snohomish County, 136 Wash.2d 1, 959 P.2d 1024 (1998). See Annot., Classification and Maintenance of Advertising Structures as Nonconforming Use, 80 A.L.R.3d 630 (1977). See generally 82 Am. Jur.2d Zoning and Planning § 178 (1976). A change in ownership of the nonconforming use does not necessarily terminate the right to the use, but a zoning ordinance *may* validly provide for such termination upon change in ownership. See Annot., Zoning: Change in Ownership of Nonconforming Business or Use as Affecting Right to Continuance Thereof, 9 A.L.R.2d 1039 (1950). Cf. Iazzetti v. Village of Tuxedo Park, 145 Misc.2d 78, 546 N.Y.S.2d 295 (1989) (landowner had non-conforming business use of property and subsequently transferred the business, but not the land, to son and grandson; held that this did not constitute a change in use so as to permit termination). See generally Serkin, Existing Uses and the Limits of Land Use Regulations, 84 N.Y.U. L. Rev. 1222 (2009).

[109] See Juergensmeyer & Roberts, Land Use Planning & Control Law 149 & n. 3 (1998), noting that some early cases sustained retroactive applications of zoning-like restrictions—but doubt remained as to the validity of retroactive effect, since those cases involved nuisances or near-nuisances. (Citing Hadacheck v. Sebastian, 239 U.S. 394, 36 S.Ct. 143, 60 L.Ed. 348 (1915) (brickyard); Reinman v. City of Little Rock, 237 U.S. 171, 35 S.Ct. 511, 59 L.Ed. 900 (1915) (stables).) On the history of nonconforming uses, see generally Krause, Nonconforming Uses in Illinois, 43 Chi.-Kent L.Rev. 153 (1966); Strong, Nonconforming Uses: The Black Sheep of Zoning, 7 Institute on Planning & Zoning 25 (1968). Non-conforming uses are sometimes referred to as "grandfather" uses or rights. See Lawrence v. City of Rawlins, 224 P.3d 862, 865 note 1 (Wyo. 2010), citing Snake River Brewing Co. v. Town of Jackson, 39 P.3d 397 (Wyo. 2002).

[110] Occasionally, zoning ordinances that don't permit nonconforming uses have been declared unconstitutional. See Jones v. City of Los Angeles, 211 Cal. 304, 295 P. 14 (1930). Or outside the scope of the power granted by state statutes. Bane v. Township of Pontiac, 343 Mich. 481, 72 N.W.2d 134 (1955). But the trend is toward upholding ordinances that eliminate such uses, at least if a sufficient period of "amortization" is allowed before termination must occur. See note 128 *infra* and accompanying text.

[111] See Edmonds v. City of Los Angeles, 40 Cal.2d 642, 255 P.2d 772 (1953) (provision exempting nonconforming uses is usually included in zoning ordinances because otherwise there is hardship, and doubt about the ordinance's constitutionality); State ex rel. Covenant Harbor Bible Camp v. Steinke, 7 Wis.2d 275, 96 N.W.2d 356 (1959).

[112] See Amereihn v. Kotras, 194 Md. 591, 71 A.2d 865 (1950) (zoning regulation cannot eliminate pre-existing use since would amount to confiscation of vested right). Cf. Township of Orion v. Weber, 83 Mich.App. 712, 269 N.W.2d 275 (1978), where an attempt to allow nonconforming uses only if they did not significantly interfere with the community's master plan was invalidated.

As to the initial existence of a nonconforming use, there are two main requirements: the use must be *actual* and *lawful* at the time the zoning control goes into effect. Thus, it has been held that the nonconforming utilization of the premises must be actually in operation at the time of the new zoning law; it is not enough that the property had been purchased when it was free of such restrictions and/or that the nonconforming use had been contemplated at the time of purchase and/or that plans had actually been drawn up for such a use.[113] And the use must, when the zoning ordinance takes effect, be in violation of no other laws; it must, aside from the new zoning restriction, be a "lawful use" of the premises.[114] This is sometimes, though not always, said to require that the user has even obtained all permits necessary to the conducting of the nonconforming business or other use.[115] Clearly, if the alleged nonconforming use could not have *qualified* to obtain the necessary permit (as opposed to the situation where the permit was obtainable but simply had not been procured), there should be no doubt that the use

---

[113] See Sherman-Colonial Realty Corp. v. Goldsmith, 155 Conn. 175, 230 A.2d 568 (1967); Fairlawns Cemetery Association v. Bethel, 138 Conn. 434, 86 A.2d 74 (1952); Bolduc v. Pinkham, 148 Me. 17, 88 A.2d 817 (1952) (purchaser had bought land in order to build bakery, was unable to do so because of wartime economic conditions and shortages; nonetheless, zoning law passed before he began his use could validly prohibit the bakery); Chayt v. Board of Zoning Appeals, 177 Md. 426, 9 A.2d 747 (1939); City of Harrisburg v. Pass, 372 Pa. 318, 93 A.2d 447 (1953); Talbot v. Myrtle Beach, 222 S.C. 165, 72 S.E.2d 66 (1952). Cf. O'Rourke v. Teeters, 63 Cal.App.2d 349, 146 P.2d 983 (Dist.Ct.1944) (large investment in city lot with intent to use for business does not prevent city from subsequently zoning the property for residential use only); Weber v. Pieretti, 72 N.J.Super. 184, 178 A.2d 92 (1962), aff'd 77 N.J.Super. 423, 186 A.2d 702 (nonconforming use could not be enlarged; building permit purporting to allow enlargement was invalid and created no estoppel); Mahler v. City of Seabrook, 538 S.W.2d 870 (Tex.Civ.App. 1976) (city could enforce ordinance against nonconforming use even though it had allegedly permitted such uses on other tracts). If only part of a tract is actually utilized for the nonconforming use, the right to continue the use has been said to extend to the rest of the tract only if there has been an appropriation of the entire area for nonconforming purposes. Conway v. City of Greenville, 254 S.C. 96, 173 S.E.2d 648 (1970). But usually the expansion of nonconforming use is restricted anyway. See note 120 *infra* and accompanying text. On the sufficiency of activity to establish "use," see Fredal v. Forster, 9 Mich.App. 215, 156 N.W.2d 606 (1967) (removal of 50,000 cubic yards of stone was substantial enough to establish a quarry).

[114] See State v. Stonybrook, Inc., 149 Conn. 492, 181 A.2d 601 (1962), appeal dism'd, cert. denied 371 U.S. 185, 83 S.Ct. 265, 9 L.Ed.2d 227, (violation of building code); 12701 Shaker Boulevard Co. v. City of Cleveland, 31 Ohio App.2d 199, 287 N.E.2d 814 (1972); Botchlett v. City of Bethany, 416 P.2d 613 (Okl.1966); Town of Scituate v. O'Rourke, 103 R.I. 499, 239 A.2d 176 (1968); King County, Dept. of Dev. & Environmental Services v. King County, 305 P.3d 240 (Wash. 2013) (component of establishing a non-conforming use is that the use be lawfully established); David A. Ulrich, Inc. v. Town of Saukville, 7 Wis.2d 173, 96 N.W.2d 612 (1959). Cf. Universal Holding Co. v. Township of North Bergen, 55 N.J.Super. 103, 150 A.2d 44 (1959) (if in violation of zoning laws when use begins, cannot later claim non-conforming use). But it has been held that merely because a property-owner is in violation of a restrictive covenant, his use does not become illegal, since this is a contractual matter between private parties. Gauthier v. Village of Larchmont, 30 App. Div.2d 303, 291 N.Y.S.2d 584 (1968).

[115] See Mang v. County of Santa Barbara, 182 Cal.App.2d 93, 5 Cal.Rptr. 724 (Dist.Ct.1960) (owner was without legal right to obtain permit for gasoline station where zoning prohibiting such use became effective prior to his application for permit); Scavone v. Mayor and Council of Totowa, 49 N.J.Super. 423, 140 A.2d 238 (1958) (owner had valid nonconforming use where had necessary license, though had not obtained certificate of occupancy, which was supposedly also required—law on such certificates not strictly enforced); Smalls v. Board of Standards and Appeals, 28 Misc.2d 147, 211 N.Y.S.2d 212 (1961), aff'd 14 A.D.2d 548, 218 N.Y.S.2d 1005, aff'd 11 N.Y.2d 698, 225 N.Y.S.2d 765, 180 N.E.2d 917 (no certificate of occupancy had been obtained; no right to nonconforming use). Cf. City of Raleigh v. Fisher, 232 N.C. 629, 61 S.E.2d 897 (1950) (business not a valid nonconforming use if carried on under an illegally issued permit). See generally Annot., Rights of Permittee Under Illegally Issued Building Permit, 6 A.L.R.2d 960 (1949). Under the vested rights doctrine, it has been said that an owner's permit applications should be processed under the regulations in effect at the time a complete permit application is filed. Town of Woodway v. Snohomish County, 322 P.3d 1219 (Wash. 2014).

is not "lawful."[116] What if the real-property owner has obtained all necessary building permits and has begun construction for an intended use, but the zoning law is then changed so that the proposed use is no longer permitted? Neither the application for,[117] nor the actual obtaining of,[118] the building permit suffices to establish a nonconforming use. But the general rules are bent a little in one situation: If the owner has, in good faith and in reliance on a valid building permit (if such permit is necessary), begun substantial construction on his proposed use, *or* incurred substantial expenses directly related to construction, he will usually be deemed to have a nonconforming use, despite the lack of actual operation.[119]

---

[116] See Eggert v. Board of Appeals, 29 Ill.2d 591, 195 N.E.2d 164 (1963); Heimerle v. Village of Bronxville, 168 Misc. 783, 5 N.Y.S.2d 1002 (1938), aff'd 256 App.Div. 993, 11 N.Y.S.2d 367 (1939).

[117] National Amusements v. Commissioner of Inspectional Services Dep't, 26 Mass.App.Ct. 80, 523 N.E.2d 789 (1988), review denied 403 Mass. 1101, 526 N.E.2d 1295 (1988) (zoning amendment may supersede and thus frustrate a building permit application). See Annot., Retroactive Effect of Zoning Regulation, in Absence of Saving Clause, on Pending Application for Building Permit, 50 A.L.R.3d 596 (1973) (a newly adopted law will apply to bar issuance of a building permit that was duly applied for prior to adoption of effective date of the law). Cf. City of Aspen v. Marshall, 912 P.2d 56 (Colo.1996) (municipality may properly refuse building permit for land use repugnant to pending zoning ordinance, even though application was made when intended use conformed to existing regulations). But Washington State takes a different view. Twin Bridge Marine Park, L.L.C. v. Washington Dep't of Ecology, 162 Wash.2d 825, 175 P.3d 1050 (2008) (doctrine of vested rights entitles developers to have a land development proposal processed under the regulations in effect at time a complete building permit is filed, regardless of subsequent changes in zoning or other land use regulations); Noble Manor Co. v. Pierce County, 133 Wash.2d 269, 943 P.2d 1378 (1997) (filing of complete application for subdivision vested in developer the right to develop property under land use laws in effect on date of application); Erickson & Associates, Inc. v. McLerran, 123 Wash.2d 864, 872 P.2d 1090 (1994) (developer entitled to have proposal processed under regulations in effect at time building permit application is filed, regardless of subsequent changes in regulations); Valley View Industrial Park v. City of Redmond, 107 Wash.2d 621, 733 P.2d 182 (1987) (property owner has vested right to use his property according to applicable zoning ordinances in effect at time he applies for building permit). Accord, Lauer v. Pierce County, 173 Wash. 2d 242, 267 P.3d 988 (2011). For a good discussion of the vested right doctrine, see WCHS, Inc. v. City of Lynnwood, 120 Wash.App. 668, 86 P.3d 1169 (2004). Compare KOB–TV, L.L.C. v. City of Albuquerque, 137 N.M. 388, 111 P.3d 708 (App. 2005) (term "vested right" may be used to describe a non-conforming use, but the vested-rights *doctrine* applies to an ongoing development or project which has been approved and on which substantial investment has been made; regardless of whether property owner's operation of helipad was non-conforming use or vested right, city had right to impair that use by enacting ordinance regulating placement of helicopters within city limits). If the permit is initially denied, a reviewing court will generally apply the law in effect at the time of its decision, not that in effect when the permit was denied. See Selby Realty Co. v. City of San Buenaventura, 10 Cal.3d 110, 109 Cal.Rptr. 799, 514 P.2d 111 (1973).

Some zoning ordinances contain "saving clauses" that protect the rights of persons who have applied for and/or received building permits prior to an ordinance's taking effect. See Annot., Zoning Provisions Protecting Landowners Who Applied for or Received Building Permit Prior to Change in Zoning, 49 A.L.R.3d 1150 (1973).

[118] See Franchise Realty Interstate Corp. v. City of Detroit, 368 Mich. 276, 118 N.W.2d 258 (1962); County of Saunders v. Moore, 182 Neb. 377, 155 N.W.2d 317 (1967). But see Ben Lomond, Inc. v. City of Idaho Falls, 92 Idaho 595, 448 P.2d 209 (1968) (zoning ordinance adopted after application made for permit to build service station held inapplicable to that application). See generally Annot., Retroactive Effect of Zoning Regulation, in Absence of Saving Clause, on Validly Issued Building Permit, 49 A.L.R.3d 13 (1973).

[119] See Dobbins v. Los Angeles, 195 U.S. 223, 25 S.Ct. 18, 49 L.Ed. 169 (1904) (purchase of lands, contract for erection of gasworks, and construction of foundation); Kissinger v. City of Los Angeles, 161 Cal.App.2d 454, 327 P.2d 10 (Dist.Ct.1958); Graham Corp. v. Board of Zoning Appeals, 140 Conn. 1, 97 A.2d 564 (1953); Fitzgerald v. Merard Holding Co., 110 Conn. 130, 147 A. 513 (1929), cert. denied 281 U.S. 732, 50 S.Ct. 247, 74 L.Ed. 1148 (1930); Renieris v. Village of Skokie, 85 Ill.App.2d 418, 229 N.E.2d 345 (1967); Perkins v. Joint City-Council Planning Commission, 480 S.W.2d 166 (Ky.1972); Stow v. Pugsley, 349 Mass. 329, 207 N.E.2d 908 (1965); Expert Steel Treating Co. v. Clawson, 368 Mich. 619, 118 N.W.2d 815 (1962); Kiges v. City of St. Paul, 240 Minn. 522, 62 N.W.2d 363 (1953); State ex rel. Great Lakes Pipe Line Co. v. Hendrickson, 393 S.W.2d 481 (Mo.1965); Donadio v. Cunningham, 58 N.J. 309, 277 A.2d 375 (1971); Reichenbach v. Windward at Southampton, 80 Misc.2d 1031, 364 N.Y.S.2d 283 (1975), aff'd 48 A.D.2d 909, 372 N.Y.S.2d 985, appeal dism'd 38 N.Y.2d 912, 382 N.Y.S.2d 757, 346 N.E.2d 557; Herskovits v. Irwin, 299 Pa. 155, 149 A. 195 (1930); City of Dallas v. Meserole, 155 S.W.2d 1019 (Tex.Civ.App.1941) error ref'd; State ex rel. Morehouse v. Hunt,

Expansion of nonconforming uses is generally not allowed,[120] nor are substantial alterations,[121] but only the normal repair and maintenance, plus minor improvements,

---

235 Wis. 358, 291 N.W. 745 (1940). Cf. Bankoff v. Board of Adjustment, 875 P.2d 1138 (Okla. 1994) (landowner entitled to operate a nonconforming landfill and not have a zoning amendment applied to him retroactively where he had obtained a trial court ruling that the county board should have issued the necessary permit, where $800,000 had been spent on the project, and where the landfill would have been in actual use at the time of the zoning application but for the automatic stay when the county appealed the trial court order); Penn Township v. Yecko Brothers, 420 Pa. 386, 217 A.2d 171 (1966), cert. denied 385 U.S. 826, 87 S.Ct. 60, 17 L.Ed.2d 63 (person who obtained permit and made substantial change of position before change in law may be entitled to nonconforming use—but must show good faith, including that he didn't race to get permit before a proposed change was made in the law). If a permit and/or construction performed thereunder *does* entitle a person to proceed with his nonconforming use, he may nonetheless be held obligated to pursue the remaining construction diligently in order to keep his rights. See Boyd v. Donelon, 193 So.2d 291 (La.App.1966), writ ref'd 250 La. 366, 195 So.2d 643. See generally Annot., Zoning: Building in Course of Construction as Establishing Valid Nonconforming Use or Vested Right to Complete Construction for Intended Use, 89 A.L.R.3d 1051 (1979). As to the desirability of having legislation that creates certainty and fairness in this area of "vested rights," see Hall, State Vested Rights Statutes: Developing Certainty and Equity and Protecting the Public Interest, 40 Urban Law. 451 (2008).

[120] Dienelt v. Monterey County, 113 Cal.App.2d 128, 247 P.2d 925 (Dist.Ct. 1952); Rehfeld v. City of San Francisco, 218 Cal. 83, 21 P.2d 419 (1933); Yuba City v. Cherniavsky, 117 Cal.App. 568, 4 P.2d 299 (Dist.Ct.1931) (non-conforming grocery could not expand); Anderson v. Board of Adjustment, 931 P.2d 517 (Colo.App.1996) (city ordinance did not permit expansion of non-conforming filling station to include similarly non-conforming automated car wash); Mercer Lumber Cos. v. Village of Glencoe, 390 Ill. 138, 60 N.E.2d 913 (1945); Jahnigen v. Staley, 245 Md. 130, 225 A.2d 277 (1967); Seekonk v. Anthony, 339 Mass. 49, 157 N.E.2d 651 (1959); Austin v. Older, 283 Mich. 667, 278 N.W. 727 (1938); County of Freeborn v. Claussen, 295 Minn. 96, 203 N.W.2d 323 (1972); Pisicchio v. Board of Appeals, 165 Misc. 156, 300 N.Y.S. 368 (1937); State ex rel. City Ice & Fuel Co. v. Stegner, 120 Ohio St. 418, 166 N.E. 226 (1929) (was proper to deny permit for ice manufacturers where premises previously used only for storage); State ex rel. Miller v. Cain, 40 Wn.2d 216, 242 P.2d 505 (1952). Cf. Beerwort v. Zoning Board of Appeals, 144 Conn. 731, 137 A.2d 756 (1958) (aim is to lessen and eventually abolish nonconforming uses); Town of Hampton v. Brust, 122 N.H. 463, 446 A.2d 458 (1982) (expansion of non-conforming penny arcade into different area within same building disallowed, though held that arcade operator could not be prevented from replacing an attendant-operated game area with coin-operated machines); City of Keene v. Blood, 101 N.H. 466, 146 A.2d 262 (1958) (denials by zoning authorities of permission to expand nonconforming uses will generally be upheld on appeal); State ex rel. Carter v. Harper, 182 Wis. 148, 196 N.W. 451 (1923) (application for permit to expand dairy denied; upheld on appeal). But cf. Stagecoach Trails MHC, L.L.C. v. City of Benson, 307 P.3d 989 (Ariz. App. 2013) (replacing a mobile home in a mobile home park is a reasonable alteration and does not extinguish park's status as a non-conforming use); City of Okoboji v. Okoboji Barz, Inc., 746 N.W.2d 56 (Iowa 2008) (sale and service of alcoholic beverages by restaurant held not an expansion of non-conforming use). See generally Note, Municipal Corporations—Police Power and Regulations—Whether or Not Provision in Zoning Ordinance Restricting Extension of Nonconforming Uses Is Arbitrary and Unreasonable, 23 Chi.-Kent L.Rev. 349 (1945); Annot., Construction of New Building or Structure on Premises Devoted to Nonconforming Use as Violation of Zoning Ordinance, 56 A.L.R.4th 769 (1987).

In Pennsylvania, the courts have not totally prohibited expansion of nonconforming uses but have allowed "normal" growth. See Jackson v. Pottstown Zoning Board of Adjustment, 426 Pa. 534, 233 A.2d 252 (1967); William Chersky Joint Enterprises v. City of Pittsburgh, 426 Pa. 33, 231 A.2d 757 (1967); Appeal of Heidorn, 412 Pa. 570, 195 A.2d 349 (1963). But cf. Silver v. Zoning Board of Adjustment, 435 Pa. 99, 255 A.2d 506 (1969), saying a municipality may impose reasonable restrictions on expansion of a nonconforming use.

[121] See City of Earle v. Shackleford, 177 Ark. 291, 6 S.W.2d 294 (1928) (structural alterations not allowed); Piccolo v. Town of West Haven, 120 Conn. 449, 181 A. 615 (1935) (refusal to allow rebuilding of structure destroyed by fire where new building would have greater frontage on street); Selligman v. Von Allmen Brothers, Inc., 297 Ky. 121, 179 S.W.2d 207 (1944); Commercial Club v. Chicago, St. Paul, Minneapolis, & Omaha Railway, 142 Minn. 169, 171 N.W. 312 (1919) (ordinance forbidding enlargement of wooden structures in area); State ex rel. Euclid-Doan Building Co. v. Cunningham, 97 Ohio St. 130, 119 N.E. 361 (1918). It is sometimes said that alterations are so "substantial" that they will be disallowed if the structure would be converted to a markedly different one. See Town of Guilford v. Landon, 146 Conn. 178, 148 A.2d 551 (1959); Goodrich v. Selligman, 298 Ky. 863, 183 S.W.2d 625 (1944). Cf. Wechter v. Board of Appeals, 3 Ill.2d 13, 119 N.E.2d 747 (1954) (tinsmith and woodworking shop could not be converted to spray-paint business); Pross v. Excelsior Cleaning & Dyeing Co., 110 Misc. 195, 179 N.Y.S. 176 (1919) (structural change is determined by considering whether it affects a vital and substantial portion of the premises, whether it changes appearance of the use, whether change is extraordinary in scope or unusual in amount of expenditure,

made necessary or desirable by the passage of time and by continued use.[122] Where extraction of mineral resources is involved, continued working of the site is usually allowed, even if it entails deepening or enlarging pits or deepening wells, but the drilling of new wells or opening of new mines is likely to be held forbidden.[123]

Zoning ordinances generally provide, or are interpreted as providing, that a nonconforming use is terminated, and there is no right to resume it, when it is abandoned. But abandonment cannot be found from mere discontinuance; it requires a

---

etc.). If substantial alterations are forbidden, so are new buildings devoted to the nonconforming use. See Hanna v. Board of Adjustment, 408 Pa. 306, 183 A.2d 539 (1962). See generally Young, Regulation and Removal of Nonconforming Uses, 12 W.Res.L.Rev. 681 (1961); Annot., Alteration, Extension, Reconstruction, or Repair of Nonconforming Structure or Structure Devoted to Nonconforming Use as Violation of Zoning Ordinance, 63 A.L.R.4th 275 (1988). See also Annot., Change in Area or Location of Nonconforming Use as Violation of Zoning Ordinance, 56 A.L.R.4th 769 (1987).

[122] City of Madison Heights v. Manto, 359 Mich. 244, 102 N.W.2d 182 (1960). See Morin v. Board of Appeals, 352 Mass. 620, 227 N.E.2d 466 (1967) (new, improved instrumentalities can be acquired); Horwitz v. Dearborn Township, 332 Mich. 623, 52 N.W.2d 235 (1952) (aluminum covering could be used to replace canvas); 440 East 102nd Street Corp. v. Murdock, 285 N.Y. 298, 34 N.E.2d 329 (1941); Zoning Board v. Lawrence, 309 S.W.2d 883 (Tex.Civ.App. 1958), ref'd n. r. e. In Dienelt v. County of Monterey, *supra* note 120, it was held that replacing a flagstone patio with a concrete slab patio went beyond mere repair and amounted to a forbidden change. But cf. Endara v. Culver City, 140 Cal.App.2d 33, 294 P.2d 1003 (Dist.Ct.1956) (manufacture of tile ceramics allowed on premises as nonconforming use; permission for expansion of operations properly granted). Accord, Eddins v. City of Lewiston, 150 Idaho 30, 244 P.3d 174 (2010) (replacement of recreational vehicles in manufactured home park constituted a continuation of non-conforming use protected by due process). See generally Babcock, What Should and Can Be Done With Nonconforming Uses, 1972 Planning, Zoning, & Eminent Domain Institute 23; Annot., Zoning: Right to Repair or Reconstruct Building Operating as Nonconforming Use, After Damage or Destruction by Fire or Other Casualty, 57 A.L.R.3d 419 (1974). Some zoning ordinances forbid even repairs, at least if they are extensive in nature. See Fratcher, Constitutional Law: Zoning Ordinances Prohibiting Repair of Existing Structures, 35 Mich.L.Rev. 642 (1937).

[123] See Beverly Oil Co. v. City of Los Angeles, 40 Cal.2d 552, 254 P.2d 865 (1953) (nonconforming use does not give right to sink new wells or deepen old ones); De Felice v. Zoning Board of Appeals, 130 Conn. 156, 32 A.2d 635 (1943) (change not allowed in method of extraction); Town of Billerica v. Quinn, 320 Mass. 687, 71 N.E.2d 235 (1947) (new pit cannot be opened on another part of land); Fredal v. Forster, 9 Mich.App. 215, 156 N.W.2d 606 (1967) (owner could continue to work the present site but not open new sites). But cf. McCaslin v. City of Monterey Park, 163 Cal.App.2d 339, 329 P.2d 522 (Dist.Ct.1958) (once operation is established, nonconforming use protected as to entire deposit); Hawkins v. Talbot, 248 Minn. 549, 80 N.W.2d 863 (1957) (owner even allowed to develop new gravel beds, beyond those actually excavated at time of ordinance). Regulations under the police power requiring the termination of mining activities have sometimes been upheld. See Goldblatt v. Town of Hempstead, 369 U.S. 590, 82 S.Ct. 987, 8 L.Ed.2d 130 (1962) (excavations below water level prohibited, and those already below such level had to be filled); Tulsa Rock Co. v. Board of County Commissioners, 531 P.2d 351 (Okl.App.1974) (further quarrying in limestone quarry prevented, but owner found to have suffered no great or unpreventable hardship). Cf. Marblehead Land Co. v. City of Los Angeles, 47 F.2d 528 (9th Cir.1931), cert. denied 284 U.S. 634, 52 S.Ct. 18, 76 L.Ed. 540 (upholding ordinance declaring oil-well drilling operations in residential zone illegal—repealed ordinance which had previously excluded certain land from residential district and had allowed drilling thereon); Seherr-Thoss v. Teton County Bd. of County Comm'rs, 329 P.3d 936 (Wyo. 2014) (applying statute, court allows expansion of gravel quarry under doctrine of diminishing assets).

showing of intent to abandon.[124] And the act of abandonment must be a voluntary one;[125] thus, a temporary discontinuance due to fire, act of God, or governmental activities will

---

[124] See Grushkin v. Zoning Board, 26 Conn.Sup. 457, 227 A.2d 98 (1967); Auditorium, Inc. v. City of Wilmington, 47 Del. 373, 91 A.2d 528 (1952) (abandonment not found from mere discontinuance of activity); Union Quarries v. Johnson County, 206 Kan. 268, 478 P.2d 181 (1970); Stieff v. Collins, 237 Md. 601, 207 A.2d 489 (1965); Schack v. Trimble, 28 N.J. 40, 145 A.2d 1 (1958); City of Las Cruces v. Neff, 65 N.M. 414, 338 P.2d 731 (1959); Tigard Sand & Gravel, Inc. v. Clackamas County, 149 Or.App. 417, 943 P.2d 1106 (Or.App.1997) (non-conforming quarry use abandoned where quarrying activity had virtually stopped for 7 years and where for last 2 of those 7 years, site was used for business activity totally unrelated to quarrying); City of Dallas v. Fifley, 359 S.W.2d 177 (Tex.Civ. App.1962), ref'd n. r. e. Thus, a temporary discontinuance of the nonconforming use for a brief period will usually not be found to show abandonment. See Lehmaier v. Wadsworth, 122 Conn. 571, 191 A. 539 (1937); Paul v. Selectmen of Scituate, 301 Mass. 365, 17 N.E.2d 193 (1938); Civic Association v. Horowitz, 318 Mich. 333, 28 N.W.2d 97 (1947); City of Binghampton v. Gartell, 275 App.Div. 457, 90 N.Y.S.2d 556 (1949) (junk business; little activity for 4 years but no abandonment). In Maryland, it has even been said that nonuser is no evidence of abandonment unless it lasts for the statutory period of limitations for actions to recover real property. Landay v. MacWilliams, 173 Md. 460, 196 A. 293 (1938). Cf. Feldstein v. LaVale Zoning Board, 246 Md. 204, 227 A.2d 731 (1967) (clear evidence of inattention or inaction for a reasonable period of time required). A Pennsylvania case once found that discontinuance of a use for twelve years did not, under the particular ordinance, bring about an abandonment. Null v. Power, 391 Pa. 51, 137 A.2d 316 (1958) (mere passage of time not enough). But usually, abandonment can be readily inferred from a lengthy discontinuance—such as several years—unless there is some convincing explanation. See Holloway Ready Mix Co. v. Monfort, 474 S.W.2d 80 (Ky.1968) (quarry was not used for ten years); Attorney General v. Johnson, 355 S.W.2d 305 (Ky.1962) (nonconforming grocery store had ceased 5 years ago; owner wanted to establish nonconforming laundry, and ordinance allowed shift from one nonconforming business to another, but abandonment here found); Longo v. Eilers, 196 Misc. 909, 93 N.Y.S.2d 517 (1949). Ordinances sometimes indicate that non-use for a prescribed period of time shall be determinative of abandonment; some courts still tend to find abandonment only if the requisite intent is established. See Smith v. Howard, 407 S.W.2d 139 (Ky.1966) (intent or such lack of diligence as to amount to abandonment required); Dusdal v. City of Warren, 387 Mich. 354, 196 N.W.2d 778 (1972). But it is usually held that such legislation *can* remove the intent requirement if this is made sufficiently clear. See Franmor Realty Corp. v. LeBoeuf, 201 Misc. 220, 104 N.Y.S.2d 247 (1951), aff'd 279 App.Div. 795, 109 N.Y.S.2d 525, appeal denied 279 App. Div. 874, 110 N.Y.S.2d 910; State ex rel. Peterson v. Burt, 42 Wis.2d 284, 166 N.W.2d 207 (1969). Ordinances forbidding resumption after a designated period of discontinuance have also been generally upheld if found reasonable. Wilson v. Edgar, 64 Cal.App. 654, 222 P. 623 (Dist.Ct.1923); Marchese v. Norristown Borough Zoning Board of Adjustment, 2 Pa.Cmwlth. 84, 277 A.2d 176 (1971) (with list of cases); State ex rel. Brill v. Mortenson, 6 Wis.2d 325, 96 N.W.2d 603 (1959) (discontinuance for one year; not necessary under this ordinance that owner *voluntarily* relinquish nonconforming use in order for abandonment to occur). Cf. Kootenai County v. Harriman-Sayler, 293 P.3d 637 (Idaho 2012) (applying ordinance that provided non-conforming use that is discontinued for 6 consecutive months, or for 18 months in a 3-year period, is terminated); State ex rel. Harris v. Zoning Board of Appeal and Adjustment, 221 La. 941, 60 So.2d 880 (1952) (where ordinance forbids resumption after property has been vacant for six months, board of adjustment cannot authorize revival of nonconforming use); Bither v. Baker Rock Crushing Co., 249 Or. 640, 438 P.2d 988 (1968), mod'd 249 Or. 640, 440 P.2d 368 (ordinance prohibiting resumption after 6 months' discontinuance assumed valid, but no discontinuance here found). In Rogers v. West Valley City, 2006 UT App. 302, 142 P.3d 554 (2006), it was held that a city zoning ordinance providing that discontinuance of a non-conforming use for a period of more than a year constituted abandonment of such use precluded consideration of the landowner's intent.

Where the premises are *used,* but for a purpose that conforms to the zoning law, much the same rules apply as where the property is not utilized at all: A temporary change to a *conforming* use does not indicate abandonment. State ex rel. Morehouse v. Hunt, *supra* note 119. But a lengthy utilization of the premises for a conforming purpose is strong evidence of abandonment of the nonconforming use. See Branch v. Powers, 210 Ark. 836, 197 S.W.2d 928 (1946) (use of garage for conforming purpose for 2 years prior to passage of zoning ordinance and 9 years thereafter).

What of a change from one nonconforming use to another? This may be dealt with under the rules on alterations, abandonment, etc. See Blake v. City of Phoenix, 157 Ariz. 93, 754 P.2d 1368 (App. 1988) (where prior owner of non-conforming use had run quiet business of growing orchids in greenhouses while current owners ran busy retail nursery trade, this was found an abandonment of non-conforming use). But even aside from such rules, it has sometimes been stated that a change from one nonconforming use to another causes a loss of the right. See Town of Montclair v. Bryan, 16 N.J.Super. 535, 85 A.2d 231 (1951); Parks v. Board of County Commissioners, 11 Or.App. 177, 501 P.2d 85 (1972); 2 Metzenbaum, The Law of Zoning 1241 (2d ed. 1955). Some ordinances, however, allow, or can be read as allowing, a change in the direction of conformity. See Hagman, Larson, & Martin, California Zoning Practice § 9.22 (1969). Cf. Baker v. Town of Sullivan's

not work a surrender of the nonconforming use[126] unless a statute or ordinance clearly so provides. But what if the relevant legislation *does* so provide? A considerable number of zoning ordinances now state that nonconforming uses damaged or destroyed, even through no fault of the owner, cannot be re-built as nonconforming structures. In other words, the right to the nonconformity is lost by statute, despite the lack of voluntary action or intent. Such limitations on right to rebuild usually apply where the buildings, improvements, etc. have been totally or substantially destroyed; and legislation so providing has been upheld.[127] Indeed, such provisions can be looked upon as part of a general trend toward the gradual elimination of all nonconforming uses. A number of zoning ordinances now provide for "amortization" of such uses: the nonconformity with the zoning ordinance is allowed to remain a specified length of time after the ordinance goes into effect—say, ten years—, but then the nonconforming use must be terminated. This may be considered to grant the user a period of relative monopoly—since presumably, uses of the same nonconforming type won't be allowed to "start up" in the area if they don't pre-date the zoning ordinance—in return for which the eventual termination of the use is being required. Such amortization ordinances have been upheld

---

Island, 279 S.C. 581, 310 S.E.2d 433 (App. 1983) (conversion of apartment building to condominiums not so substantial a change as to amount to a switch from one non-conforming use to another). See generally Annot., Change in Type of Activity of Nonconforming Use as Violation of Zoning Ordinance, 61 A.L.R.4th 902 (1988); Annot., Zoning—Change in Volume, Intensity, or Means of Performing Nonconforming Use as Violation of Zoning Ordinances, 61 A.L.R.4th 806 (1988). See also Triangle Fraternity v. City of Norman, 63 P.3d 1 (Okla. 2003) (proposed use of house as fraternity house was same as church's use of house as a retired women's boarding house, and thus fraternity was entitled to extension of church's non-conforming use).

It has been held that failure to obtain a city license for a non-conforming use is not in itself abandonment of the use. Mayor & City Council of Baltimore v. Dembo, Inc., 123 Md.App. 527, 719 A.2d 1007 (1998).

[125] See Green v. Copeland, 286 Ala. 341, 239 So.2d 770 (1970); Navin v. Early, 56 N.Y.S.2d 346 (1945); Empire City Racing Association v. City of Yonkers, 132 Misc. 816, 230 N.Y.S. 457 (1928) (race meets held twice a year; no intent to abandon use as race track; building destroyed by fire could be rebuilt); Rowton v. Alagood, 250 S.W.2d 264 (Tex.Civ.App.1952). See generally Strauss & Giess, Elimination of Nonconformities: The Case of Voluntary Discontinuance, 25 Urban Law. 159 (1993).

[126] See Annot., Zoning: Right to Repair or Reconstruct Building Operating as Nonconforming Use, After Damage or Destruction by Fire or Other Casualty, 57 A.L.R.3d 419 (1974); Annot., Zoning: Right to Resume Nonconforming Use of Premises After Involuntary Break in the Continuity of Nonconforming Use Caused by Governmental Activity, 56 A.L.R.3d 138 (1974); Annot., Right to Resume Nonconforming Use of Premises After Involuntary Break in the Continuity of Nonconforming Use Caused by Difficulties Unrelated to Governmental Activity, 56 A.L.R.3d 14 (1974). But if the discontinuance appears voluntary or is unexplained, an abandonment will often be found. See Annot., Zoning: Right to Resume Nonconforming Use of Premises After Voluntary or Unexplained Break in the Continuity of Nonconforming Use, 57 A.L.R.3d 279 (1974).

[127] See A. H. Jacobson Co. v. Commercial Union Assurance Co., 83 F.Supp. 674 (D.Minn.1949); State v. Hillman, 110 Conn. 92, 147 A. 294 (1929); D'Agostino v. Jaguar Realty Co., 22 N.J.Super. 74, 91 A.2d 500 (1952) (total destruction; not entitled to rebuild); Jetter v. Hofheins, 190 Misc. 99, 70 N.Y.S.2d 808 (1947); Koeber v. Bedell, 254 App.Div. 584, 3 N.Y.S.2d 108 (1938), aff'd 280 N.Y. 692, 21 N.E.2d 200; Appeal of Berberian, 351 Pa. 475, 41 A.2d 670 (1945); Haase v. City of Memphis, 149 Tenn. 235, 259 S.W. 545 (1924); State ex rel. Covenant Harbor Bible Camp v. Steinke, 7 Wis.2d 275, 96 N.W.2d 356 (1959) (right to nonconforming use lost if use is accidentally destroyed in large measure). Some ordinances provide that a nonconforming use cannot be repaired or rebuilt if destroyed to the extent of a specified percentage of its former value; such legislation has been upheld. Moffatt v. Forrest City, 234 Ark. 12, 350 S.W.2d 327 (1961) (if destroyed to extent of 60% of value); Baird v. Bradley, 109 Cal.App.2d 365, 240 P.2d 1016 (Dist.Ct.1952) (50% of value and 60% of physical proportion); Bobandal Realties, Inc. v. Worthington, 21 App.Div.2d 784, 250 N.Y.S.2d 575 (1964), aff'd 15 N.Y.2d 788, 257 N.Y.S.2d 588, 205 N.E.2d 685 (1965) (50% of value). Cf. O'Mara v. City Council, 238 Cal.App.2d 836, 48 Cal.Rptr. 208 (Dist.Ct.1965) (market value must be considered in determining degree of destruction).

if the period provided is found a reasonable one, considering the amount of investment involved in the particular use.[128]

§ 18.6 Zoning—Procedure for Enactment

Procedures for the enactment of municipal zoning laws are laid down by state statute and/or home-rule charter. It has often been stated that these procedures must be

---

[128] Village of Oak Park v. Gordon, 32 Ill.2d 295, 205 N.E.2d 464 (1965) (entitled to presumption of reasonableness, like other zoning ordinances); Spurgeon v. Board of Commissioners, 181 Kan. 1008, 317 P.2d 798 (1957); Grant v. City of Baltimore, 212 Md. 301, 129 A.2d 363 (1957) (billboards had to be removed from residential areas within 5 years; upheld); McKinney v. Riley, 105 N.H. 249, 197 A.2d 218 (1964); Village of Larchmont v. Sutton, 30 Misc.2d 245, 217 N.Y.S.2d 929 (1961) (nonconforming signs had to be removed within 15 months). Cf. Harbison v. City of Buffalo, 4 N.Y.2d 553, 176 N.Y.S.2d 598, 152 N.E.2d 42 (1958) (junkyard in residential zone had to be removed within 3 years; case remanded for determination of reasonableness of length of time). See generally Fell, Amortization of Nonconforming Uses, 24 Md. L.Rev. 323 (1964); Koegel, Elimination of Nonconforming Uses, 35 Va.L.Rev. 348 (1949); Moore, Termination of Nonconforming Uses, 6 Wm. & M. L. Rev. 1 (1965); Norton, Elimination of Nonconforming Uses and Structures, 20 L. & Contemp. Prob. 305 (1955); Sussna, Abatement of Nonconforming Uses and Structures, 44 Conn.B.J. 589 (1970); Whitnall, Abatement of Nonconforming Uses, 2 Institute on Planning and Zoning 131 (1962); Note, Regulation of Urban Nonconforming Uses in Arkansas: Limitation and Termination, 16 Ark.L.Rev. 270 (1962); Note, The Abatement of Pre-Existing Nonconforming Uses Under Zoning Laws: Amortization, 57 Nw. U.L.Rev. 323 (1962); Note, Termination of Nonconforming Uses: *Harbison* to the Present, 14 Syracuse L.Rev. 62 (1962).

It has been noted that early authorities on zoning expected that nonconforming uses would be few in number and would rather quickly disappear but that this has not proven true: nonconforming uses, having a degree of monopoly in their neighborhoods, often thrive and become more firmly entrenched with time. Note, Nonconforming Uses: A Rationale and an Approach, 102 U.Pa.L.Rev. 91, 94 (1953). Thus, pressure to eliminate such uses has grown. See Bartholomew, Non-Conforming Uses Destroy the Neighborhood, 1 J. Land & P. U. Econ. 96 (1939); Mandelker, Prolonging the Nonconforming Use: Judicial Restriction of the Power to Zone in Iowa, 8 Drake L.Rev. 23 (1958); Comment, The Elimination of the Nonconforming Use in California, 8 Hastings L.J. 64 (1956). It is often stated in general terms that nonconforming uses are not favored and that the law encourages their elimination. See Farr v. Town of Manchester, 139 Conn. 577, 95 A.2d 792 (1953) (nonconforming uses should be reduced as rapidly as law allows); Attorney General v. Johnson, *supra* note 124 (law ordains the gradual elimination of such uses); Hay v. Board of Adjustment of Fort Lee, 37 N.J.Super. 461, 117 A.2d 650 (1955) (policy of law is to restrict nonconforming uses closely and not allow their expansion); Hanna v. Board of Adjustment, 408 Pa. 306, 183 A.2d 539 (1962) (nonconforming uses should be reduced as speedily as law and constitution allow). Cf. City of Tucson v. Clear Channel Outdoor, Inc., 218 Ariz. 172, 181 P.3d 219 (App. 2008) (in order to support the public policy of eliminating non-conforming uses, courts do not follow the customary rule of construing zoning regulations in favor of property owners).

Amortization has been applied with particular frequency in situations involving non-conforming signs. See Durden, Sign Amortization Laws: Insight into Precedent, Property, and Public Policy, 35 Capital U.L. Rev. 891 (2007). On constitutional limits on elimination of nonconforming uses, see generally O'Reilly, The Non-conforming Use and Due Process of Law, 23 Geo.L.J. 218 (1935); Annot., Validity of Provisions for Amortization of Nonconforming Uses, 8 A.L.R.5th 391 (1992). On the special situation in Pennsylvania, see PA Northwestern Distributors, Inc. v. Zoning Hearing Bd. of Township of Moon, 526 Pa. 186, 584 A.2d 1372 (1991), noted 37 Villanova L. Rev. 161 (1992) (amortization of lawful nonconforming use is per se confiscatory and violative of Pennsylvania Constitution). On the reasonableness of the time period allowed for amortization, see Reynolds, The Reasonableness of Amortization Periods for Nonconforming Uses—Balancing the Private Interest and the Public Welfare, 34 Wash. U.J. Urban & Contemp. L. 99 (1988). See generally Lawrence, A Proposal to Amend the Michigan Zoning Enabling Act to Allow Amortization of Nonconforming Uses, 1998 Detroit C.L. Mich. St. U.L. Rev. 653. A good review of the authorities on the constitutionality of amortization provisions is found in Note, A Taking Without Just Compensation? The Constitutionality of Amortization Provisions for Nonconforming Uses, 109 W. Va. L. Rev. 225 (2006). For a summary of state court cases on the constitutionality of amortization legislation, see Michaels, Amortization and the Constitutional Methodology for Terminating Non-conforming Uses, 41 Urban Law. 807 (2009), finding that only 3 states—Missouri, Ohio, and Pennsylvania—have ruled that amortization is a per se unconstitutional taking; that the law in one of these—Ohio—is in doubt; and that all the rulings of unconstitutionality have been based on *state* constitutional provisions, not the U.S. Constitution. *Id.* at 813–14, concluding that "In the vast majority of states, amortization provisions have been held valid where reasonable."

A few states have special provisions for the condemning of nonconforming uses under the power of eminent domain. See, *e.g.*, Mich. Compiled Laws Ann. § 125.583a; Minn.Stat.Ann. § 462.12.

strictly followed in order for the intended legislation to be valid.[129] Generally, municipal zoning laws must take the form of ordinances, not mere resolutions.[130] Besides the usual requirements for enactment of ordinances, three special requirements for *zoning* ordinances must often be met: (1) It is frequently provided—usually by city charters—that municipalities must submit proposed legislation to local (or occasionally, county-wide) planning commissions before the legislation is finally approved by the governing body. Occasionally, the planning commission's *approval* must be obtained; or if it is not obtained, the legislation can be passed only by some super-majority of the city governing body. But most often, the planning commission has authority only to *recommend* passage or non-passage of the legislation. Nonetheless, the requirement of submission to the planning commission—for its recommendation or whatever action it is empowered to take—is nearly always treated as mandatory.[131]

(2) Statutes and/or charters usually now provide that a public hearing must be held prior to the passage of zoning laws and amendments, and that proper notice be given of such hearing. It is often specified that the notice must be to the general public (as through newspaper publication, etc.) and/or to specified, affected property owners (as by mailing of notice to those within the affected area and a certain distance therefrom). These requirements are, like the above-mentioned requirement of submission to a planning commission, treated as mandatory; and a zoning ordinance passed without the

---

[129] Manning v. Reilly, 2 Ariz.App. 310, 408 P.2d 414 (1965) (if there isn't substantial compliance with statutory rules, legislation is void); Bowling Green-Warren County Airport Board v. Long, 364 S.W.2d 167 (Ky. 1962); Stevens v. Madison Heights, 358 Mich. 90, 99 N.W.2d 564 (1959); Schroeppel v. Spector, 43 Misc.2d 290, 251 N.Y.S.2d 233 (1963) (procedures must be strictly adhered to); State v. Thomasson, 61 Wn.2d 425, 378 P.2d 441 (1963) (map not included in zoning resolution). See Grantwood Lumber Co. v. Schweitzer, 7 N.J.Misc. 1016, 147 A. 741 (1929) (ordinance not read in final form before passage as required by statute; held void). But cf. Hopping v. Cobb County Fair Association, 222 Ga. 704, 152 S.E.2d 356 (1966) (rezoning action was prolonged 8 days past time limit; valid where no harm shown from delay); Rossi v. Township of Richfield, 60 Mich.App. 34, 230 N.W.2d 553 (1975) (publication without the required zoning map; but other requirements were met; held valid).

[130] City of Hutchins v. Prasifka, 450 S.W.2d 829 (Tex.1970). On the difference between "ordinances" and "resolutions," see Chapter 11 *supra*.

[131] Kissinger v. City of Los Angeles, 161 Cal.App.2d 454, 327 P.2d 10 (Dist.Ct.1958); Florida Tallow Corp. v. Bryan, 237 So.2d 308 (Fla.App.1970); Davis v. Imlay Township, 7 Mich.App. 231, 151 N.W.2d 370 (1967) (county zoning authority). Of course, if the power of the planning commission is only to *recommend*, its recommendation need not be followed by the local legislative body. See Fleetwood Development Corp. v. Vestavia Hills, 282 Ala. 439, 212 So.2d 693 (1968). Cf. McVeigh v. City of Battle Creek, 350 Mich. 214, 86 N.W.2d 279 (1957) (zoning board has only the powers given it by statute, charter, or ordinance). The final decision on zoning matters must rest with the city governing body, not with a planning or zoning commission; otherwise there is an unlawful delegation of authority. See Jackson v. Guilford County Board of Adjustment, 275 N.C. 155, 166 S.E.2d 78 (1969). See generally Anderson, Brees & Reninger, A Study of American Zoning Board Composition and Public Attitudes Toward Zoning Issues, 40 Urban Law. 689 (2008), noting that these local administrative bodies go by various designations, including Planning & Zoning Commission, Board of Zoning Adjustment, or Board of Zoning Appeals. *Id.* at 689.

But even though a planning or zoning commission's power is thus limited, members should not participate in a matter in which they have a pecuniary or other personal interest; and passage of a recommended measure may be invalidated if such a vote is cast. See Buell v. City of Bremerton, 80 Wn.2d 518, 495 P.2d 1358 (1972) (chairman of planning commission had possibility of interest in rezoned property). Cf. Narrowsview Preservation Association v. City of Tacoma, 84 Wn.2d 416, 526 P.2d 897 (1974) (presence on planning commission of member whose employer was bank to which property sought to be rezoned was pledged as collateral held to violate "appearance of fairness" doctrine). In some states, the presence on a legislative or quasi-legislative body of a person with a personal interest in a matter will, however, invalidate action taken thereon only if that person voted and his or her vote was determinative. See generally Chapter 11 *supra*.

required and properly noticed hearing will be void.[132] (3) Often it is provided by statute or charter that, in addition to any required public hearing and notice thereof, or even where no hearing is required—, there must be notice given the community of the proposed zoning legislation itself, as through newspaper publication thereof. Again, such a requirement is mandatory in order for the legislation to be valid.[133]

If zoning laws are properly passed, a presumption of their reasonableness, validity, and constitutionality then attaches to them in any subsequent judicial or administrative challenge.[134] The burden of proof is on anyone who asserts the unreasonableness or lack

---

[132] Saks & Co. v. City of Beverly Hills, 107 Cal.App.2d 260, 237 P.2d 32 (Dist.Ct. 1951); Hurst v. City of Burlingame, 207 Cal. 134, 277 P. 308 (1929); Hutchinson v. Board of Zoning Appeals, 138 Conn. 247, 83 A.2d 201 (1951); Moon v. Smith, 138 Fla. 410, 189 So. 835 (1939); Whittemore v. Town Clerk of Falmouth, 299 Mass. 64, 12 N.E.2d 187 (1937); Krajenke Buick Sales v. Kopkowski, 322 Mich. 250, 33 N.W.2d 781 (1948); Wippler v. Hohn, 341 Mo. 780, 110 S.W.2d 409 (1937); Sackett Lake Property Owners Association v. Levine, 268 App.Div. 809, 48 N.Y.S.2d 490 (1944), appeal denied 268 App.Div. 934, 51 N.Y.S.2d 748; Voight v. Saunders, 206 Okl. 318, 243 P.2d 654 (1952); State ex rel. Gulf Refining Co. v. De France, 89 Ohio App. 334, 101 N.E.2d 782 (1950); Fierst v. William Penn Memorial Corp., 311 Pa. 263, 166 A. 761 (1933); State ex rel. Lightman v. City of Nashville, 166 Tenn. 191, 60 S.W.2d 161 (1933); Bolton v. Sparks, 362 S.W.2d 946 (Tex.1962). See Hart v. Bayless Investment & Trading Co., 86 Ariz. 379, 346 P.2d 1101 (1959) (no formal hearing after requisite notice; zoning commission and county board lacked jurisdiction to adopt measure).

Even if the proper hearing is held, zoning legislation subsequently passed can be voided on the ground that proper notice of such hearing was not given. See Anderson v. Judd, 158 Colo. 46, 404 P.2d 553 (1965); Carson v. McDowell, 203 Kan. 40, 452 P.2d 828 (1969) (notice not given sufficiently far in advance). Cf. Hart v. Bayless Investment & Trading Co., *supra* (news article did not suffice as an official notice). And once the required hearing is held, the legislation therein discussed must be passed within a reasonable time, or else it cannot be passed at all without *another* properly announced hearing being held. See Gricus v. Superintendent of Buildings, 345 Mass. 687, 189 N.E.2d 209 (1963) (more than 5 years was unreasonable length of time). The hearing, and notice thereof, are usually treated as being required only by legislation, but there is some argument that due process requires that affected property-owners be given a reasonable opportunity to be heard. See Masters v. Pruce, 290 Ala. 56, 274 So.2d 33 (1973).

On the purposes intended to be served by hearings on zoning legislation, see Pate v. City of Bethany, 672 P.2d 677 (Okl. App. 1983) (intended to protect a protestant's right to be heard and to afford protestants a chance to explain how they think their interests are affected by proposed changes and how public at large is affected, and to bring to attention of legislative body any relevant fact that might have been overlooked). Cf. Lai Chun Chan Jin v. Board of Estimate, 115 Misc.2d 774, 454 N.Y.S.2d 601 (1982), judgment rev'd 92 A.D.2d 218, 460 N.Y.S.2d 28 (1983) (community must be given adequate notice of hearing so that public can participate in decision-making).

[133] See Gendron v. Borough of Naugatuck, 21 Conn.Sup. 78, 144 A.2d 818 (1958) (information was carried in news stories in newspaper; held insufficient notice). Again, the requirement has usually been treated as legislatively, not constitutionally, imposed. See Lawton v. City of Austin, 404 S.W.2d 648 (Tex.Civ.App.1966), ref'd n. r. e. (notice provisions of statutes found constitutionally adequate and valid). But some authority now holds that notice to affected persons is required by due process. Tolman v. Salt Lake County, 20 Utah 2d 310, 437 P.2d 442 (1968). See Masters v. Pruce, *supra* note 132.

Notice requirements, relating either to notice of hearings or notice of the legislation itself, will be held fulfilled if there has been substantial compliance. See Nesbit v. City of Albuquerque, 91 N.M. 455, 575 P.2d 1340 (1977) (notice must fairly apprise average citizen as to general purpose of what is contemplated; here found inadequate). See generally 1A Antieau, Municipal Corporation Law §§ 7.06–.07 (1998).

[134] Zahn v. Board of Public Works, 274 U.S. 325, 47 S.Ct. 594, 71 L.Ed. 1074 (1927); American Wood Products Co. v. City of Minneapolis, 35 F.2d 657 (8th Cir.1929); McCarthy v. City of Manhattan Beach, 41 Cal.2d 879, 264 P.2d 932 (1953), cert. denied 348 U.S. 817, 75 S.Ct. 29, 99 L.Ed. 644 (1954); City of Miami v. Rosen, 151 Fla. 677, 10 So.2d 307 (1942) (good discussion of nature of municipalities and municipal ordinances); Krom v. City of Elmhurst, 8 Ill.2d 104, 133 N.E.2d 1 (1956); City of Louisville v. Bryan S. McCoy Inc., 286 S.W.2d 546 (Ky.1955); Schertzer v. City of Somerville, 345 Mass. 747, 189 N.E.2d 555 (1963); Bzovi v. City of Livonia, 350 Mich. 489, 87 N.W.2d 110 (1957); Bogert v. Township of Washington, 25 N.J. 57, 135 A.2d 1 (1957); Bond v. Cooke, 237 App.Div. 229, 262 N.Y.S. 199 (1932); Midgarden v. City of Grand Forks, 79 N.D. 18, 54 N.W.2d 659 (1952); Cleveland Trust Co. v. Village of Brooklyn, 92 Ohio App. 351, 110 N.E.2d 440 (1952), appeal dism'd 158 Ohio St. 258, 108 N.E.2d 679 (same presumption of validity that applies to other legislative acts). See Dawson Enterprises, Inc. v. Blaine County, 98 Idaho 506, 567 P.2d 1257 (1977) (zoning ordinances sometimes said to have strong presumption of validity); Pierce v. Town of Wellesley, 336 Mass. 517,

of valid purpose.[135] One frequent method of stating this general rule is by saying that if the zoning law is "fairly debatable," it will be upheld.[136] That is, if there could be debate over the reasonableness of the ordinance, if there is room for legitimate difference of opinion, then the courts will yield to the legislative determination.[137] This deference

---

146 N.E.2d 666 (1957) (judgment of municipal legislative body assumed reasonable); Dodge Mill Land Corp. v. Town of Amherst, 61 A.D.2d 216, 402 N.Y.S.2d 670 (1978) (if zoning ordinance enacted in accord with comprehensive plan, is entitled to strongest possible presumption of validity). On challenges to local land-use decisions, see generally Nelson, Comparative Judicial Land-Use Appeals Processes, 27 Urban Law. 251 (1995), noting that most judicial systems in the United States are not well equipped to handle zoning appeals but discussing innovative methods that had been tried in Florida, New Jersey and Oregon.

It has been stated that the presumption of validity extends to the zoning body's application and interpretation of its own zoning ordinances. Crown Point Dev., Inc. v. City of Sun Valley, 144 Idaho 72, 156 P.3d 573 (2007) (city council had denied plat application for subdivision; court says that zoning agency's action should be affirmed unless court finds that agency's findings or decisions are in violation of constitutional or statutory provisions, are in excess of agency's statutory authority, are made upon unlawful procedure, are not supported by substantial evidence, *or* are arbitrary, capricious, or an abuse of discretion). As to when "abuse of discretion" can be found, see Botz v. Bridge Canyon Planning & Zoning Comm'n, 289 P.3d 180 (Mont. 2012) (abuse of discretion occurs when the information upon which the municipal entity based its decision is so lacking in fact and foundation that it is clearly unreasonable).

[135] See Board of County Commissioners v. Simmons, 177 Colo. 347, 494 P.2d 85 (1972) (person alleging invalidity must prove it beyond a reasonable doubt); State ex rel. Prats v. City Planning & Zoning Commission, 59 So.2d 832 (La.App.1952); State v. Mundet Cork Corp., 8 N.J. 359, 86 A.2d 1 (1952), 344 U.S. 819, 73 S.Ct. 14, 97 L.Ed. 637; Fra-Nat Builders Inc. v. Town of Oyster Bay, 16 Misc.2d 851, 183 N.Y.S.2d 830 (1959) (person attacking ordinance must show unreasonableness beyond a reasonable doubt); Smith v. City of Brookfield, 272 Wis. 1, 74 N.W.2d 770 (1956). But see Pinellas County v. Dynamic Investments, Inc., 279 So.2d 97 (Fla.App.1973) (burden for sustaining restrictions is on zoning authority). Certainly the burden may *shift* to the zoning authorities once the presumption of validity is overcome. See Cole-Collister Fire Protection District v. City of Boise, 93 Idaho 558, 468 P.2d 290 (1970). And some observers feel that the presumption of validity often is allowed to disappear very readily. See 1A Antieau, Municipal Corporation Law § 7.23, at 7–61 (1998). See Yurczyk v. Yellowstone County, 319 Mont. 169, 83 P.3d 266 (2004), as an example of a case carefully considering all the possible police-power grounds for sustaining the law, and then rejecting all those grounds. The case involved a modular home that violated a zoning ordinance requiring on-site construction of dwellings. The court found that no health and only minimal safety concerns were addressed by the law and found that no welfare concern that the law promoted property values or aided residents' ability to control their environment was addressed by the law.

[136] See City of Miami Beach v. Wiesen, 86 So.2d 442 (Fla.1956); Eckes v. Board of Zoning Appeals, 209 Md. 432, 121 A.2d 249 (1956); Thomas v. Bedford, 11 N.Y.2d 428, 230 N.Y.S.2d 684, 184 N.E.2d 285 (1962); Partain v. City of Brooklyn, 101 Ohio App. 279, 133 N.E.2d 616 (1956); Mid-Continent Life Ins. Co. v. Oklahoma City, 701 P.2d 412 (Okl.1985) (zoning is legislative function and if the validity of a zoning ordinance is fairly debatable, municipality's legislative judgment must stand); Heisler v. Thomas, 651 P.2d 1330 (Okl.1982) (role of judiciary in reviewing zoning classification is to determine if it is unreasonable, arbitrary or an unconstitutionally unequal exercise of police power; decision to retain a single-family zoning classification will be upheld so long as it is fairly debatable); McNair v. Oklahoma City, 490 P.2d 1364 (Okl.1971) (validity of amendment to zoning ordinance challenged). Cf. O'Rourke v. City of Tulsa, 457 P.2d 782 (Okl.1969) (aggrieved person may challenge zoning by petition for injunction without first applying for variance; but where city governing body has refused to rezone, its decision won't be overturned if it is fairly debatable). The "fairly debatable" rule is applied to original zoning and classifications *and* to rezoning or denials thereof. See Bradley v. Payson City Corp., 2003 UT 16, 70 P.3d 47 (2003) (municipal land use decisions as a whole are generally entitled to a great deal of deference; city council's denial of zoning change would not be overturned where decision was reasonably debatable).

[137] Trust Co. v. City of Chicago, 408 Ill. 91, 96 N.E.2d 499 (1951). See Mueller v. C. Hoffmeister Undertaking & Livery Co., 343 Mo. 430, 121 S.W.2d 775 (1938) (if zoning classification is doubtful, judgment of municipal authorities must be respected). Cf. Spencer v. Kootenai County, 180 P.3d 487 (Idaho 2008) (planning and zoning decisions are entitled to a strong presumption of validity on review, including a county zoning board's application and interpretation of its own zoning ordinances). See also Sterk & Brunelle, Zoning Finality: Reconceptualizing Res Judicata Doctrine in Land Use Cases, 63 Fla. L. Rev. 1139 (2011).

Since the decision of the governing body on how to zone (or rezone) property is a legislative determination (not a judicial or quasi-judicial one), it cannot be appealed to the state courts, but can be attacked in such courts by means of a suit for mandamus or injunction. Gregory v. Board of County Commissioners, 514 P.2d 667 (Okl. 1973). Cf. Garrett v. Oklahoma City, 594 P.2d 764 (Okl.1979) (persons aggrieved by zoning may seek

occurs because municipal authorities are assumed to be familiar with local conditions and thus in the best position to plan the development of their community.[138] The courts will supposedly not "second-guess" the legislative body as to the *wisdom* of zoning ordinances, but will only determine whether, at least debatably, there is some reasonable connection with a police-power purpose and reasonable exercise of the power.

Zoning ordinances are most often passed by municipal legislative bodies in basically the same form as other ordinances are passed, and by the same procedures—with the addition of those steps above noted.[139] But some municipalities have provisions, in state

---

injunction). Mandamus may be used not only to attempt to compel municipal action to change zoning regulations but also to compel enforcement of existing zoning regulations. See Annot., Mandamus to Compel Zoning Officials to Cancel Permit Granted in Violation of Zoning Regulation, 68 A.L.R.3d 166 (1976), noting a split of authority as to whether mandamus is available to *cancel* building permits. Clearly, mandamus is available to compel *issuance* of building permits where such issuance is dictated by law. But mandamus is always considered an extraordinary remedy, and a strong case of dereliction of duty must be established before the writ will issue. See generally 52 Am.Jur.2d Mandamus §§ 4, 160, 216 (on compelling issuance of building permits) (1970). On mandamus, see also chapter on extraordinary remedies *infra*. Statutes frequently designate the methods of challenging zoning amendments, and such methods are likely to be considered exclusive. See Bischoff v. Hennessy, 251 S.W.2d 582 (Ky. 1952). But unless a statute prescribes other methods that are deemed exclusive, a declaratory judgment action is generally recognized as a possible means of attacking amendments. See Holdredge v. City of Cleveland, 218 Tenn. 239, 402 S.W.2d 709 (1966).

It is usually held that a party challenging a zoning ordinance need not exhaust legislative remedies prior to the challenge but must exhaust administrative remedies, such as applying for a variance. This is subject to the qualifications that (1) if legislative remedies have not been pursued, the courts will assume the ordinance would be applied in the manner most generous, consistent with its terms, to the protestant's wishes, and (2) the courts will not require that clearly futile administrative remedies be pursued. See Note, Exhausting Administrative and Legislative Remedies in Zoning Cases, 48 Tulane L. Rev. 665 (1974). On the complicated situation in Illinois regarding the exhaustion issue, see Babcock, The Unhappy State of Zoning Administration in Illinois, 26 U. Ill. L. Rev. 509, 522–32 (1959). As to who has standing to challenge the validity or application of zoning laws under which a land-use permit is granted or denied, see Wilson, "I Don't Live Next Door, But I Do Drive by on the Nearby Highway": Recent Developments in the Law of Standing in Court Cases Challenging Land Use Permits, 39 Urban Law. 711 (2007), analyzing opinions in five states, all purporting to apply the standard that the plaintiff must show "particularized injury" or the potential thereof. Cf. Johnson v. Blaine County, 146 Idaho 916, 204 P.3d 1127 (2009) (adjoining landowner was affected person as to approval of planned unit development and thus could seek judicial review of the approval); Weber Coastal Bells Limited Partners v. Metro, 352 Or. 122, 282 P.3d 822 (2012) (citizen group had standing to challenge Land Use Board of Appeals decision). See generally on standing in zoning cases, notes 72–73, *supra*, and accompanying text.

On the legislative nature of zoning, see also note 19 of this chapter and accompanying text *supra*.

[138] Luery v. Zoning Board, 150 Conn. 136, 187 A.2d 247 (1962) (municipal judgment will not be overridden unless is definite breach of duty); Montgomery County Council v. Shiental, 249 Md. 194, 238 A.2d 912 (1968) (courts won't substitute their judgment for the expertise of the zoning authorities); Burnham v. Board of Appeals, 333 Mass. 114, 128 N.E.2d 772 (1955) (much weight must be given the judgment of the local legislative body since it is familiar with local conditions). Cf. City of Miami Beach v. Schauer, 104 So.2d 129 (Fla.App. 1958), aff'd 112 So.2d 838 (Fla.1959) (amendment of zoning ordinance is legislative act; court won't ordinarily scrutinize motives of city council).

While the *wisdom* of the legislative decision will not be questioned by the court, it should be noted that votes on zoning matters may sometimes be invalidated if someone with a personal interest in the matter has participated in the decision. See note 129 *supra*. See generally Note, Municipal Corporations—Zoning—Disqualification of Councilman for Personal Interest, 57 Mich. L.Rev. 423 (1959); Annot., Motive of Members of Municipal Authority Approving or Adopting Zoning Ordinance or Regulation as Affecting its Validity, 71 A.L.R.2d 568 (1960). And it has been held that one who claims fraud or corruption in the enactment or administration of zoning ordinances must only prove his or her claim by a preponderance of the evidence. Wyman v. Popham, 252 Ga. 247, 312 S.E.2d 795 (1984). As to the possible need for more training for those involved is making zoning decisions, see Comment, A Proposal to Implement Mandatory Training Requirements for Home Rule Zoning Officials, 2008 Mich. St. L. Rev. 879.

[139] See notes 131–133 *supra* and accompanying text. For a "model" set of administrative provisions for use in zoning ordinances, see American Society of Planning Officials, The Text of a Model Zoning Ordinance (3d ed. 1966).

statutes or home-rule charters, for popular enactment of legislation through the process known as "initiative." This usually entails a designated number of voters signing a petition in order to have a proposed measure placed on the ballot at some election; the measure then becomes law if approved by a majority, or some designated super-majority, of those voting on the question at that election. Related in nature is the process known as "referendum," under which legislation passed by the governing body is (through action of that body itself or by petition of the voters) submitted to the electorate for final approval or rejection.[140] Can these processes be used to pass or reject zoning ordinances? Traditionally, it has often been held that the initiative cannot be used to pass or amend zoning laws, frequently on the ground that a specific and *exclusive* method has been provided by statute or charter, or that requirements generally applied to zoning ordinances (such as hearing and notice) are not met when the initiative method is used.[141] But the California court has stated in general terms that there is no valid objection to zoning legislation being passed by the initiative process.[142] And several jurisdictions have now adopted what seems the "trend view": policy-setting zoning laws can be adopted by the initiative method, though specific, administrative-type decisions on particular land-uses cannot be made in this fashion.[143] This distinction is also often

---

[140] On initiative and referendum, see generally Chapter 27 *infra*.

[141] See Moon v. Smith, 138 Fla. 410, 189 So. 835 (1939); City Council of Augusta v. Irvin, 109 Ga.App. 598, 137 S.E.2d 82 (1964); Deans v. West, 189 Neb. 518, 203 N.W.2d 504 (1973); Williston Park v. Israel, 191 Misc. 6, 76 N.Y.S.2d 605 (1948), aff'd 276 App.Div. 968, 94 N.Y.S.2d 921, appeal denied 276 App.Div. 1013, 95 N.Y.S.2d 602, aff'd 301 N.Y. 713, 95 N.E.2d 208; State v. Town of Tumwater, 66 Wn.2d 33, 400 P.2d 789 (1965). Cf. Transamerica Title Ins. Co. v. City of Tucson, 157 Ariz. 346, 757 P.2d 1055 (1988) (initiative process cannot be used to amend city and county zoning ordinances so as to create "buffer zones" as this would violate due process and contravene provisions of state law delegating zoning powers to governing bodies of counties and cities); Whatcom County v. Brisbane, 125 Wn.2d 345, 884 P.2d 1326 (1994) (county's land planning ordinance not subject to referendum). See generally Comment, Land Use by, for, and of the People: Problems with the Application of Initiatives and Referenda to the Zoning Process, 19 Pepperdine L. Rev. 99 (1991). Compare Freilich & Guemmer, Removing Artificial Barriers to Public Participation in Land-Use Policy: Effective Zoning and Planning by Initiative and Referenda, 21 Urban Law. 511 (1989).

[142] Associated Home Builders v. City of Livermore, 18 Cal.3d 582, 135 Cal.Rptr. 41, 557 P.2d 473 (1976), noted 66 Cal.L.Rev. 373 (1978); Builders Association v. City of San Jose, 13 Cal.3d 225, 118 Cal.Rptr. 158, 529 P.2d 582 (1974) (initiative ordinance provided that land couldn't be rezoned for residential development within certain areas of city unless party seeking rezoning agreed to provide satisfactory alternative to permanent school construction); San Diego Building Contractors Association v. City Council, 13 Cal.3d 205, 118 Cal.Rptr. 146, 529 P.2d 570 (1974), appeal dism'd 427 U.S. 901, 96 S.Ct. 3184, 49 L.Ed.2d 1195 (initiative ordinance established a uniform height limitation for buildings erected along city's coastline in the future). Earlier California cases had tended to allow zoning measures to be originated by initiative where the initiative power was granted the city electors by the city's own home-rule charter, but not where the power was granted by the general state statutes on initiative. See Annot., Adoption of Zoning Ordinance or Amendment Thereto Through Initiative Process, 72 A.L.R.3d 991, § 8 (1976). See generally Aperin & King, Ballot Box Planning: Land Use Planning Through the Initiative Process in California, 21 Sw. U.L. Rev. 1 (1992); Hayes & Smith, Report of the Subcommittee on Zoning Process, 23 Urban Law. 855, 858–63 (1991).

[143] See Arnel Development Co. v. City of Costa Mesa, 28 Cal.3d 511, 169 Cal.Rptr. 904, 620 P.2d 565 (1980) (zoning, or rezoning, ordinance—but not administrative decisions—can be enacted by initiative); Redevelopment Agency v. City of Berkeley, 80 Cal.App.3d 158, 143 Cal.Rptr. 633 (Dist.Ct. 1978) (initiative could not be used to amend city's development plan; administrative powers of redevelopment agency were involved); Storegard v. Board of Elections, 22 Ohio Misc. 5, 255 N.E.2d 880, 50 O.O.2d 228 (1969); Drockton v. Board of Elections, 16 Ohio Misc. 211, 240 N.E.2d 896, 45 O.O.2d 171 (1968); Russell v. Linton, 115 N.E.2d 429, 52 O.O. 228 (Ohio Com.Pl.1953). Cf. Meridian Development Co. v. Edison Township, 91 N.J.Super. 310, 220 A.2d 121 (1966) (with review of cases; voters could amend zoning ordinance by initiative and referendum); Allison v. Washington County, 24 Or.App. 571, 548 P.2d 188 (1976) (state constitution gave authority to legislate locally on zoning matters by initiative and referendum—a referendum was here involved). See generally Oren, The Initiative and Referendum's Use in Zoning, 64 Cal.L.Rev. 74 (1976); Annot., Adoption of Zoning Ordinance, *supra* note 142.

now employed in determining whether, assuming the general availability of the referendum method, a zoning measure may be submitted to the voters in a referendum.[144] (This is in accord with the legislative-v.-administrative distinction often drawn whenever questions arise of the availability of the initiative and referendum processes, as discussed in the chapter on extraordinary remedies *infra*.) The U.S. Supreme Court has found no federal Constitutional objection to the use of a popular referendum on zoning questions.[145]

Attempts are occasionally made to "condition" a particular zoning classification— one desired by the property-owner(s), as by the executing of a restrictive covenant limiting further uses of the land. This is known as "contract" or "conditional" zoning[146]

---

[144] See Yost v. Thomas, 36 Cal.3d 561, 205 Cal.Rptr. 801, 685 P.2d 1152 (1984) (adoption of land-use plan for coastal zone was a legislative act and thus subject to referendum); Johnston v. City of Claremont, 49 Cal.2d 826, 323 P.2d 71 (1958); City of Coral Gables v. Carmichael, 256 So.2d 404 (Fla.App.1972), cert. dism'd per curiam 268 So.2d 1; Anne Arundel County v. McDonough, 277 Md. 271, 354 A.2d 788 (1976) (referendum available as to comprehensive zoning plan *if* a clear, understandable statement of the issues is presented); Denney v. City of Duluth, 295 Minn. 22, 202 N.W.2d 892 (1972) (amendments changing boundaries of districts entitled to as much dignity as original enactment, and are thus also subject to referendum provisions of city charter); Forman v. Eagle Thrifty Drugs & Markets, Inc., 89 Nev. 533, 516 P.2d 1234 (1973) (whether or not to embark on a zoning plan is a legislative question and proper subject for referendum, but changing of areas and granting of exceptions are administrative, and thus not subject to referendum); Hilltop Realty, Inc. v. City of South Euclid, 110 Ohio App. 535, 164 N.E.2d 180, 13 O.O.2d 348 (1960), appeal dismissed 170 Ohio St. 581, 11 O.O.2d 423, 166 N.E.2d 924, cert. denied sub nom. Crahan v. Ohio, 364 U.S. 842, 81 S.Ct. 82, 5 L.Ed.2d 66 (rezoning ordinance subject to referendum); State ex rel. Hunzicker v. Pulliam, 168 Okl. 632, 37 P.2d 417 (1934) (city ordinance extending zone for oil and gas drilling was legislative in nature and thus subject to referendum). Cf. West v. City of Portage, 392 Mich. 458, 221 N.W.2d 303 (1974) (amendment changing zoning as to particular property not subject to referendum). On the procedure to be used and factors to be weighed in determining whether a zoning change is legislative in nature, and thus subject to referendum, or is administrative, and thus not so subject, see Citizen's Awareness Now v. Marakis, 873 P.2d 1117 (Utah 1994). But see Westgate Families v. County Clerk of Los Alamos County, 100 N.M. 146, 667 P.2d 453 (1983) (New Mexico Zoning Enabling Act, by expressly providing for zoning by representative bodies, denied exercise of this power by referendum regardless of legislative or administrative nature of the matter). The Nebraska court seemed to adopt the legislative-v.-administrative test in Kelley v. John, 162 Neb. 319, 75 N.W.2d 713 (1956), where it was held that a referendum could not be conducted as to a particular zoning change. But in Hoover v. Carpenter, 188 Neb. 405, 197 N.W.2d 11 (1972) (not a zoning case), the court disapproved of any such test and said that whether or not a referendum can be held as to a particular matter must depend on the governing statutory language as to referenda and the facts of each case. See generally Reber & Mika, Democratic Excess in the Use of Zoning Referenda, 29 Urban Law. 277 (1997) (arguing that mandatory zoning referenda are often unnecessary and thwart zoning legislation); Rosenberg, Referendum Zoning: Legal Doctrine and Practice, 53 U. Cinc. L. Rev. 381 (1984); Annot., Adoption of Zoning Ordinance or Amendment Thereto as Subject of Referendum, 72 A.L.R.3d 1030 (1976).

With little or no reliance on the legislative-v.-administrative test, some cases have found zoning ordinances subject to a referendum under the relevant state law. See Witkin Homes, Inc. v. City & County of Denver, 31 Colo.App. 410, 504 P.2d 1121 (1972) (under charter, city council could submit "any ordinance" to referendum); Reva v. Portage Township, 356 Mich. 381, 96 N.W.2d 778 (1959); State ex rel. Wahlmann v. Reim, 445 S.W.2d 336 (Mo.1969) (zoning enabling act did not prohibit referendum on comprehensive zoning ordinance).

[145] City of Eastlake v. Forest City Enterprises, Inc., 426 U.S. 668, 96 S.Ct. 2358, 49 L.Ed.2d 132 (1976) (due process of landowner applying for zoning change not violated though referendum required to ratify the change, and change had to be approved by 55% in the referendum). Cf. Arthur v. City of Toledo, 782 F.2d 565 (6th Cir.1986) (city referendum barring sewer extensions did not violate civil rights of public housing applicants). A referendum may even be validly required on the issue of locating low- or moderate-income housing projects in a municipality. See Annot., Referendum Relating to Low- or Moderate-Income Housing Projects as Constituting Racial Discrimination in Violation of Federal Constitution, 15 A.L.R.Fed. 613 (1973). Of course, legal requirements for the referendum must, as in all cases, be strictly obeyed. See In re Referendum Petitions of City of Norman, 155 P.3d 841 (Okla. Civ. App. 2006) (referendum petition as to rezoning ordinances held invalid for failure to include exact copies of the rezoning ordinances). See generally Chapter 27 *infra*.

[146] A distinction is sometimes drawn between these terms, with "contract zoning" then used to cover the situation in which the property owner provides consideration to the local governing body (usually in the form

and has usually been struck down as violative of equal protection, or of rules against "contracting away" governmental authority, or of other constitutional provisions.[147] But this is subject to an exception: Requirements that a propertyowner (often a subdivider) must, in order to take advantage of new zoning classifications, dedicate some of his property for public uses (streets, parks, etc.) have been upheld if they are equally and fairly applied.[148]

§ 18.7 Zoning—Amendments

Amendments to zoning ordinances can be proposed by the municipal governing body itself, by the municipal planning board (where there is one), or by petition of affected

---

of a promise to do or not do certain things) in return for requested rezoning or an enforceable promise of such rezoning. "Conditional zoning" is then used to indicate situations in which zoning legislation is passed on condition that a landowner perform a certain act prior to, simultaneous with, or after passage of the ordinance. In the latter cases, there is no promise enforceable against the landowner, but passage or effectiveness of the legislation is conditioned on the landowner's act. See Annot., Validity, Construction, and Effect of Agreement to Rezone, or Amendment to Zoning Ordinance, Creating Special Restrictions or Conditions Not Applicable to Other Property Similarly Zoned, 70 A.L.R.3d 125, 131 (1976). On the possible validity of "conditional zoning" even in a jurisdiction where "contract zoning" is invalid, see Ellickson & Tarlock, Land-Use Controls 245–50 (1981); Wright & Gitelman, Land Use in a Nutshell 189–90 (4th ed. 2000) (finding the attempt to distinguish conditional zoning from contract zoning "obviously tenuous"; *id.* at 190). See generally Note, Contract and Conditional Zoning: A Tool for Zoning Flexibility, 23 Hastings L.J. 825 (1972). See also Trager, Contract Zoning, 23 Md.L.Rev. 121 (1963); Comment, The Use and Abuse of Contract Zoning, 12 U.C.L.A.L.Rev. 897 (1965).

[147] See Haas v. City of Mobile, 289 Ala. 16, 265 So.2d 564 (1972); Bartsch v. Planning & Zoning Comm'n, 6 Conn.App. 686, 506 A.2d 1093 (1986) (zoning commission's attempt to condition a rezoning on the filing of a restrictive covenant limiting use of premises to a medical office building and requiring the creation of a green-belt buffer area invalidated as violating statutory requirements of uniformity); Hartnett v. Austin, 93 So.2d 86 (Fla.1956); Cederberg v. City of Rockford, 8 Ill.App.3d 984, 291 N.E.2d 249 (1972) (promise to execute restrictive covenant); Baylis v. City of Baltimore, 219 Md. 164, 148 A.2d 429 (1959); Houston Petroleum Co. v. Automotive Products Credit Association, 9 N.J. 122, 87 A.2d 319 (1952). Cf. Board of County Comm'rs v. H. Manny Holtz, Inc., 65 Md.App. 574, 501 A.2d 489 (1985) (statute interpreted as not authorizing "conditional use zoning"). But Washington State allows such zoning subject, by and large, to the same restrictions that apply to other zoning. See State ex rel. Myhre v. City of Spokane, 70 Wn.2d 207, 422 P.2d 790 (1967) (agreement with private person valid if zoning agreed to is reasonable and not solely for benefit of private persons). Cf. Di Salle v. Giggal, 128 Colo. 208, 261 P.2d 499 (1953) (defendant-developer had agreed to comply with population-density restrictions at termination of war-emergency situation, could not repudiate agreement); Bucholz v. City of Omaha, 174 Neb. 862, 120 N.W.2d 270 (1963) (rezoning to permit shopping center valid even though property-owner, at direction of council, executed and recorded protective covenant agreement requiring that property be developed in accord with plan presented to council in support of the rezoning, and even though agreement was approved by council and was an inducement for the rezoning). See generally Shapiro, The Case for Conditional Zoning, 41 Temple L.Q. 267 (1968); Contract and Conditional Zoning Without Romance: A Public Choice Analysis, 81 Fordham L. Rev. 1923 (2013).

On the relationship between zoning ordinances and restrictive covenants, see generally Berger, Conflicts Between Zoning Ordinances and Restrictive Covenants: A Problem in Land Use Policy, 43 Neb.L.Rev. 449 (1964) (noting that most courts simply conclude that the restrictive covenant is not abrogated or affected by the zoning ordinance). See also Comment, The Effect of Private Restrictive Covenants on the Exercise of the Public Powers of Zoning and Eminent Domain, 1963 Wis.L.Rev. 321. On the effect that changed conditions in an area may have on restrictive covenants, see Note, Real Property—Restrictive Covenants—Effect of Change in Neighborhood on Enforceability, 44 Or. L. Rev. 157 (1964); Annot., Change of Neighborhood as Affecting Restrictive Covenants Precluding Use of Land for Multiple Dwelling, 53 A.L.R.3d 492 (1973).

[148] See Haas v. City of Mobile, *supra* note 147; Funger v. Mayor & Council of Somerset, 249 Md. 311, 239 A.2d 748 (1968); City of Greenbelt v. Bresler, 248 Md. 210, 236 A.2d 1 (1967) (city agreed to recommend rezoning to county, in return for developer's promise to limit density and to donate park to city); State ex rel. Zupancic v. Schimenz, 46 Wis.2d 22, 174 N.W.2d 533 (1970) (with review of cases). But cf. Pressman v. City of Baltimore, 222 Md. 330, 160 A.2d 379 (1960) (planning commission found to have no authority to impose conditions).

property owners.[149] Amendments may involve changes in the zone applied to a particular parcel of land (often called "rezoning" or "reclassification") or zoning-text amendments: a change in the language as to what is allowed within a particular zone. In either case, the same requirements, such as hearing and notice, will ordinarily apply to amendments as apply to initial adoption of zoning laws;[150] in most jurisdictions, the same presumption of reasonableness attaches once the amendment is adopted;[151] and the "fairly debatable"

---

[149] See Shellburne, Inc. v. Roberts, 43 Del.Ch. 276, 224 A.2d 250 (1966); Pitman v. City of Medford, 312 Mass. 618, 45 N.E.2d 973 (1942). Amendments that reduce the permitted uses of a piece of property or reduce the permitted intensity of use are often referred to as "downzoning." See Tiffany, Downzoning—What Does it Mean?. 25 Ariz. Attorney, No. 7, at 19 (March, 1989).

[150] See Holly Development, Inc. v. Board of County Comm'rs, 140 Colo. 95, 342 P.2d 1032 (1959) (notice must be intelligible to average citizen to be effective); Board of County Comm'rs v. McNally, 168 Neb. 23, 95 N.W.2d 153 (1959) (notice requirements must be rigidly followed for rezoning to be valid); Bruno v. Borough of Shrewsbury, 2 N.J.Super. 550, 65 A.2d 131 (1949) (purpose of notice requirement is to allow parties and citizens to present their views on the matter); Kelly v. City of Philadelphia, 382 Pa. 459, 115 A.2d 238 (1955). Cf. Commerce Oil Refining Corp. v. Miner, 170 F.Supp. 396 (D.R.I.1959), cert. denied 364 U.S. 910, 81 S.Ct. 274, 5 L.Ed.2d 225 (original zoning ordinance invalid for lack of proper notice on hearing; amendment was therefore also invalid); National Transportation Co. v. Toquet, 123 Conn. 468, 196 A. 344 (1937) (change in zoning invalid where notice of hearing on change not given in compliance with statute requiring 15 days' notice).

As with notice required as to original zoning, notices of amendments and/or of meetings concerning proposed amendments will suffice if they show substantial compliance with any statutory or charter requirements and give a reasonably clear indication of the contemplated action. See Ciaffone v. Community Shopping Corp., 195 Va. 41, 77 S.E.2d 817 (1953). And notice of a hearing on a proposed amendment does not become invalid because the wording of the amendment, as stated in the notice, is changed as a result of the meeting itself. Neuger v. Zoning Board, 145 Conn. 625, 145 A.2d 738 (1958).

On the degree of compliance with statutory or charter requirements that is required for zoning amendments, see generally State v. Payne, 131 Conn. 647, 41 A.2d 908 (1945); Howell v. Liebowitz, 116 N.Y.S.2d 537 (1952); Brachfeld v. Sforza, 114 N.Y.S.2d 722 (1952), all indicating that rather strict compliance is needed.

In some jurisdictions, there are provisions that if a designated percentage of the landowners within (or within a certain distance of) an affected area protest a proposed amendment to a zoning law, the law can only be passed by some designated super-majority vote of the local governing body. Such provisions have almost universally been held valid. See Annot., Zoning: Validity and Construction of Provisions of Zoning Statute or Ordinance Regarding Protest by Neighboring Property Owners, 7 A.L.R.4th 732 (1981).

[151] See Ruben v. City of Pittsburgh, 142 F.Supp. 787 (W.D.Pa.1956); Wolfpit-Villa Crest Association, Inc. v. Zoning Comm'n of Norwalk, 144 Conn. 560, 135 A.2d 732 (1957); Kinney v. City of Joliet, 411 Ill. 289, 103 N.E.2d 473 (1952); Cohen v. City of Lynn, 333 Mass. 699, 132 N.E.2d 664 (1956) (not necessary to find change in locus to support change in zoning); Miller v. Kansas City, 358 S.W.2d 100 (Mo.App. 1962); Moody v. City of University Park, 278 S.W.2d 912 (Tex.Civ.App.1955), ref'd n.r.e. But the "Maryland Rule" is that amendments to zoning ordinances will *only* be sustained if it is shown that the original zoning was mistaken or that there have been changed circumstances. Board of County Commissioners v. Turf Valley Associates, 247 Md. 556, 233 A.2d 753 (1967); Zinn v. Board of Zoning Appeals, 207 Md. 355, 114 A.2d 614 (1955). This rule is criticized in Hirokawa, Making Sense of a "Misunderstanding of the Planning Process": Examining the Relationship Between Zoning and Rezoning Under the Change-or-Mistake Rule, 44 Urban Law. 295 (2012). Oregon has sometimes shown a willingness to go along with this rule. See Cunningham v. City of Brookings, 11 Or.App. 579, 504 P.2d 760 (1972); Roseta v. County of Washington, 254 Or. 161, 458 P.2d 405 (1969). Cf. the Oregon cases cited in next paragraph of this footnote. As has Mississippi. Moore v. Madison County Board of Supervisors, 227 So.2d 862 (Miss. 1969). New Mexico follows a similar rule. See Davis v. City of Albuquerque, 98 N.M. 319, 648 P.2d 777 (1982) (before a zoning ordinance can be validly amended, the municipality must show either a mistake in the original zoning or a substantial change in the character of the area). But cf. Albuquerque Commons Partnership v. City Council of Albuquerque, 144 N.M. 99, 184 P.3d 411 (2008) ("change or mistake" rule ordinarily requires that proponent of a piecemeal zoning change show that the change is justified by a change in conditions in the community or a mistake in the original zoning, but municipality may also be able to justify an amendment that downzones a particular property by showing that the change is advantageous to the community, as articulated in the city's comprehensive or master plan). Washington State has usually required a change in circumstances to justify an amendment. See Woods v. Kittitas County, 162 Wash.2d 597, 174 P.3d 25 (2007) (proposed rezoning is not presumed valid, can be justified only by a showing of a change of circumstances since the original zoning, and must have a substantial relationship to public

rule—that the ordinance will be treated as reasonable and otherwise valid wherever the matter is at least fairly debatable—will be applied in judicial challenges of the zoning.[152] But it has been observed both by courts and writers that there is considerable tendency of the courts to apply mere lip service to the presumptions of validity where amendments in the original law are concerned; after all, if the original law is presumed to have been reasonable and otherwise valid, can the same presumption logically apply once that law is changed?[153]

§ 18.8 Building Codes

Building codes—and such specific sets of laws as fire codes, electrical codes, health codes, etc.—are often enacted by municipalities under their police power from the state. Building codes are designed to ensure safe construction, adequate means of handling possible disasters, and a reasonably healthful environment. A specific type of such a code is a housing code, designed to assure fitness of housing for human occupancy, and often containing standards for particular buildings such as limits on number of occupants and requirements as to services and maintenance. In general, many of the same standards of reasonableness and rules of procedure apply to such codes as apply to zoning laws. Three important differences may be noted: (1) As new methods and materials are regularly developed within the building trades, there is a special need for flexibility,

---

health, safety, morals, or general welfare). And occasional authorities in other states apply this rule. See Zygmont v. Planning & Zoning Commission, 152 Conn. 550, 210 A.2d 172 (1965) (*ordinarily* a change of zone must be justified by some new condition, changing the character of the area). Cf. Miller v. Kansas City, *supra* (original business district extended; amendment held reasonable, court saying a change in conditions is not *always* necessary to justify change in zone). On Connecticut law, see generally Andrew C. Petersen, Inc. v. Town of Bloomfield, 154 Conn. 638, 228 A.2d 126 (1967), saying a change of zone may occasionally be allowed without proof of changed conditions.

In a notable 1973 decision concerning a zoning change, Oregon announced a new rule of review: legislative land-use actions, which establish general policies, will be overturned only if capricious or arbitrary action is shown; but quasi-judicial decisions, involving application of policies to particular property, will be more strictly scrutinized. Fasano v. Board of County Commissioners, 264 Or. 574, 507 P.2d 23 (1973). See, applying the distinctions, South of Sunnyside Neighborhood League v. Board of Commissioners, 280 Or. 3, 569 P.2d 1063 (1977) (zone changes affected large areas; held legislative).

152 See Trust Co. v. City of Chicago, 408 Ill. 91, 96 N.E.2d 499 (1951); Sandenburgh v. Michigamme Oil Co., 249 Mich. 372, 228 N.W. 707 (1930); McNair v. Oklahoma City, 490 P.2d 1364 (Okl.1971); Kenny v. Kelly, 254 S.W.2d 535 (Tex.Civ.App.1953). Cf. Garrett v. Oklahoma City, 594 P.2d 764 (Okl.1979) (decision *not* to rezone judged by "fairly debatable" rule). See generally, listing factors to weigh in determining the validity of zoning amendments, Garner v. City of Carmi, 28 Ill.2d 560, 192 N.E.2d 816 (1963). An amendment may be invalidated as unreasonable if it unduly depreciates the value of nearby properties. Clifton Hills Realty Co. v. City of Cincinnati, 60 Ohio App. 443, 21 N.E.2d 993 (1938), noted 38 Mich.L.Rev. 431 (1940). And an amendment is invalid if made only to accommodate certain private interests. Page v. City of Portland, 178 Or. 632, 165 P.2d 280 (1946) (saying power to amend exists where there has been a substantial change of conditions and the amendment furthers the public interest).

153 See American Smelting & Refining Co. v. City of Chicago, 347 Ill.App. 32, 105 N.E.2d 803 (1952) (amendments will be carefully examined by court, especially if no change in the area is shown and if classification is changed after a purchase in reliance on the former zoning); City of Baltimore v. National Association for Advancement of Colored People, 221 Md. 329, 157 A.2d 433 (1960) (is presumption amendment reasonable, but this faces the counter-presumption that original zoning was reasonable); D'Angelo v. Knights of Columbus Building Association, 89 R.I. 76, 151 A.2d 495 (1959) (presumption of amendment's reasonableness has no application when evidence of arbitrary "spot zoning" is introduced). Cf. Roseta v. County of Washington, *supra* note 151 (usual presumption of legislative regularity doesn't apply to amendments). See generally 1A Antieau, Municipal Corporation Law § 7.159, at 7–259 (1998). See also Appleman, Can Florida's Legislative Standard of Review for Small-scale Land Use Amendments Be Justified?, 24 U.C.L.A.J. Envtl. L. & Pol'y 305 (2005–06).

and/or fairly frequent changes, in building codes.[154] (2) There is generally no right to a nonconforming use under building and housing codes. Such laws can constitutionally be made applicable to existing structures, and often are.[155] (3) There are special problems

---

[154] See Thompson, The Problem of Building Code Improvement, 12 Law & Contemp. Prob. 95 (1947). See generally Kelly, Fair Housing, Good Housing or Expensive Housing? Are Building Codes Part of the Problem or Part of the Solution?, 29 John Marshall L. Rev. 349 (1996); Comment, Building Codes, Housing Codes and the Conservation of Chicago's Housing Supply, 31 U.Chi.L.Rev. 180 (1963), urging that building codes not be made too strict. See also Valletta, Regulation of Building Materials and Appliances in New York City, 18 Urban Law. 209 (1986). On the effects of federal legislation mandating design standards for many structures so as to allow access to disabled persons, see Andersen, Architectural Barriers Legislation and the Range of Human Ability: Of Civil Rights, Missed Opportunities, and Building Codes, 28 Willamette L. Rev. 525 (1992). On the history of building codes and the effects that certain tragic events have had on the creation of them, see Stein, Doomed to Re-repeat History: The Triangle Fire, the World Trade Center Attack, and the Importance of Strong Building Codes, 21 St. John's J. Legal Comment. 767 (2007), reviewing Von Drehle, Triangle: The Fire that Changed America (2003), and Dwyer & Flynn, 102 Minutes: The Untold Story of the Fight to Survive Inside the Twin Towers (2005).

As to the effect that "green movements" have had on building codes, see Hirokawa, At Home With Nature: Early Reflections on Green Building Laws and the Transformation of the Built Environment, 39 Envtl. L. 507 (2009); Schindler, Following Industry's LEED ®: Municipal Adoption of Private Green Building Standards, 62 Fla. L. Rev. 285 (2010). See generally Abair, Green Buildings: What It Means to Be "Green" and the Evolution of Green Building Laws, 40 Urban Law. 623 (2008). See also Circo, Will Green Building Contracts Transform Construction and Design Law?, 43 Urban Law. 483 (2011).

As to the possibility of federal pre-emption of local "green building" laws, see Hupp, Recent Trend in Green Buildings Laws: Potential Preemption of Green Buildings and Whether Retrofitting Existing Buildings Will Reduce Greenhouse Gases and Save the Economy, 41 Urban Law. 489 (2009).

As to the problems attending the most common form of "green zoning"—the incorporation of privately generated standards into public law –, see Wolf, A Yellow Light for "Green Zoning": Some Words of Caution About Incorporating Green Building Standards into Local Land Use Law, 43 Urban Law. 949 (2011), discussing how the highly popular LEED (Leadership in Energy and Environmental Design) ratings systems have been a major force in the "green" movement. See generally Schindler, *supra*. As to the desirability of such ratings systems, compare Note, LEED Locally: How Local Governments Can Effectively Mandate Green Building Standards, 2013 U. Ill. L. Rev. 1211, with Note, LEEDing in the Wrong Direction: Addressing Concerns With Today's Green Building Policy, 85 S. Cal. L. Rev. 1377 (2012). See also Comment, Incorporating Third Party Green Building Rating Systems Into Municipal Building and Zoning Codes, 31 Pace Envtl. L. Rev. 832 (2014); Note, Legal Impediments to Sustainable Architecture and Green Building Design, 14 Vt. J. Envtl. L. 611 (2013); Howe & Gerrard (eds.), The Law of Green Buildings: Regulatory and Legal Issues in Design, Construction, Operations, and Financing (American Bar Assn. Section of Environment, Energy & Resources 2012); Kahn, Green Cities—Urban Growth and the Environment (Brookings Institution Press 2006).

As to the need to have building laws that will help prevent damages in disasters, see Baldridge, Disaster Resilience: A Study of San Francisco's Soft-Story Building Problem, 44 Urban Law. 465 (2012). (Soft-story residential buildings are defined as "multi-story, wood-frame structures with inadequately braced lower stories." *Id.* at 466 note 10). Many current building codes may be inadequate in disaster situations. See *id.* at 470. See also Comment, Green Efficiency at Its Finest: Shifting the Building Permit Process to Promote Sustainable Buildings, 48 U. San. Francisco L. Rev. 533 (2014).

[155] Queenside Hills Realty Co. v. Saxl, 328 U.S. 80, 66 S.Ct. 850, 90 L.Ed. 1096 (1946), upheld the constitutionality of the retroactive application of a sprinkler-system requirement—*i.e.*, application to structures existing before the code was passed. See Fordham & Upson, Constitutional Status of Housing Codes 54 (National Ass'n of Housing & Redevelopment Officials 1961). Cf. Third & Catalina Associates v. City of Phoenix, 182 Ariz. 203, 895 P.2d 115 (Ariz.App. 1994) (ordinance that required retrofitting of commercial high-rise buildings with sprinkler systems held not an unconstitutional "taking" without compensation); Building Industry Ass'n v. City of Livermore, 45 Cal.App.4th 719, 52 Cal.Rptr.2d 902 (1996) (statute upheld authorizing municipality to require sprinkler systems in all new or substantially remodeled construction). Sometimes courts have been unwilling—because of defendant's good faith, the effect of changed conditions, etc.—to order a builder to *remove* a structure built in violation of building codes; but even this extreme relief has probably been granted in a majority of the cases where sought and where less extreme relief was not possible. See Van Hecke, Injunctions to Remove or Remodel Structures Erected in Violation of Restrictions, 32 Tex.L.Rev. 521 (1954). Of course, building code provisions, like zoning laws, may be struck down if the requirements bear no reasonable relationship to a police-power purpose. See Safer v. City of Jacksonville, 237 So.2d 8 (Fla.App.1970); Kaukas v. City of Chicago, 27 Ill.2d 197, 188 N.E.2d 700 (1963), appeal dism'd 375 U.S. 8, 84 S.Ct. 67, 11

in enforcement of building and housing codes, since violations often cannot be detected without close inspection of the premises. It has been held that local authorities may obtain warrants for searches of premises if they have probable cause to suspect violations in the general area, even if they lack specific knowledge of the condition of the particular building.[156]

§ 18.9 Special Relief from Zoning: Exceptions, Variances, Conditional Use Permits

Earlier sections of this chapter have indicated some ways in which a property owner may escape the normal effect of zoning ordinances: The owner may be able to establish that he has a nonconforming use—a use ordinarily not permitted by the ordinance but allowed as to his property because the use was lawfully in existence when the ordinance took effect. Or the owner may be able to have the local legislative body amend the zoning ordinance—as, for instance, by reclassifying his property, or by redefining the uses allowed in his zone. Or the owner may be able to show that the zoning as applied to his property would amount to an unconstitutional "taking"—as where the owner can show he is left with no possible, or at least no reasonable, uses under the law. But what if the owner's situation is not so extreme as to show a taking, and the owner does not qualify as having a nonconforming use, and lacks the political clout or other ability to get an amendment passed—is all hope gone? Not necessarily; the owner might consider the possibilities of three kinds of special relief that may be available; the exception; the variance; and the special (or conditional) use permit.

As so often in the law, these terms are not always used precisely—and are sometimes used as if they were interchangeable, even though each really has a distinct meaning of its own. As accurately used, "exception" means a deviation from the generally permitted zoning that is specifically provided by the legislative body when the zoning law is enacted.[157] Thus, the law may specify that no non-residential uses are allowed, or

---

L.Ed.2d 40 (is for court to decide whether challenged provisions bear reasonable relationship to public welfare); Gates Co. v. Housing Appeals Board of City of Columbus, 10 Ohio St.2d 48, 225 N.E.2d 222 (1967).

[156] See Camara v. Municipal Court, 387 U.S. 523, 87 S.Ct. 1727, 18 L.Ed.2d 930 (1967). Cf. Community Renewal Foundation, Inc. v. Chicago Title & Trust Co., 44 Ill.2d 284, 255 N.E.2d 908 (1970), upholding a statute allowing the court to appoint a receiver to cause structures to conform to city ordinances, with power in the receiver to create a lien on real estate, etc. Building codes sometimes provide that if a building owner fails to make ordered improvements within a certain length of time, the municipality may contract for the repairs and assess the cost, plus a municipal service charge, against the owner. See Vande Bunte v. City of Lansing, 140 Mich.App. 60, 362 N.W.2d 889 (1985), ruling that such an assessment is not a property tax but an exercise of the city's police power. See generally Gribtz & Grad, Housing Code Enforcement: Sanctions and Remedies, 66 Colum.L.Rev. 1254 (1966). See also Howe, Code Enforcement in Three Cities: An Organizational Analysis, 13 Urban Law. 65 (1981).

In extreme cases, courts can even issue orders to vacate or to demolish buildings not conforming to building codes; but the structures must present a grave and imminent danger to the public—and usually will, where such means are justified, be nuisances. See City of Chicago v. Busch, 132 Ill.App.2d 486, 270 N.E.2d 249 (1971) (destruction not proven necessary); City of Danville v. Hartley, 101 Ill.App.2d 31, 241 N.E.2d 460 (1968); City of Pittsburgh v. Kronzek, 2 Pa.Cmwlth. 660, 280 A.2d 488 (1971) (demolition order upheld).

[157] See Piscitelli v. Township of Scotch Plains, 103 N.J.Super. 589, 248 A.2d 274 (1968). Unlike variances, exceptions can be allowed without any showing of undue hardship. See Mitchell Land Co. v. Planning & Zoning Board, 140 Conn. 527, 102 A.2d 316 (1953); Moriarty v. Pozner, 21 N.J. 199, 121 A.2d 527 (1956); Application of Devereux Foundation, 351 Pa. 478, 41 A.2d 744 (1945), appeal dism'd 326 U.S. 686, 66 S.Ct. 89, 90 L.Ed. 403. But an occasional authority treats exceptions and variances the same, and requires undue hardship for even an exception to be justified. See Marino v. City of Baltimore, 215 Md. 206, 137 A.2d

that only residential uses are allowed, *except* . . . (certain designated uses—for instance, hospitals or schools). Once the owner establishes that he is within the terms of such an exception, the owner is usually considered to be entitled to the exceptional use as a matter of right.[158] But two qualifications on this "right" sometimes exist—and may help account for the fact that the "exception" so often becomes confused with the variance and with the special use permit: (1) Since factual questions, and questions of interpretation may exist, as to whether or not a proposed use actually comes within an exception, a property owner does often have to apply to the local zoning board or other administrative body to establish his right to the exception.[159] Adequate standards must be provided the administrative body—standards that are reasonably definite and certain—in order for it to be able validly to grant and deny the exceptions.[160] Often, statutes or zoning laws provide that notice must be given nearby property owners—as by posting in the neighborhood, or through newspaper publication—and that such neighbors must be given an opportunity to be heard if they desire it; any such provisions are normally mandatory.[161] (2) Conditions may be imposed, as on the method of operation of the specially permitted used, by the ordinance that authorizes the exception.[162] Again, it is the zoning commission or a comparable administrative body that will decide whether the conditions are met; but the commission has no authority to impose additional conditions of its own unless, as is sometimes the case, this is clearly allowed by state statute or the local zoning ordinances.[163]

---

198 (1957). On all the forms of exceptional relief from zoning laws, see generally Dallstream & Hunt, Variances, Exceptions and Conditional Use Permits in California, 5 U.C.L.A.L.Rev. 179 (1958).

[158] Graves v. Bloomfield Planning Board, 97 N.J.Super. 306, 235 A.2d 51 (1967) (no necessary hardship need be shown; exception, like rest of zoning ordinance, will be upheld if reasonable). Exceptions exist only where clearly provided by legislation. See Bellings v. Township of Denville, 96 N.J.Super. 351, 233 A.2d 73 (1967). But since zoning is in derogation of rights of private property, some authorities urge a liberal construction of exceptions. See Application of Rea Construction Co., 272 N.C. 715, 158 S.E.2d 887 (1968). "Exceptions" are also sometimes called "special exceptions" or "exemptions."

[159] Miklus v. Zoning Board of Appeals, 154 Conn. 399, 225 A.2d 637 (1967) (exceptions could be granted by local boards for hospitals in residential areas). See generally Annot., Construction and Application of Provisions for Variations in Application of Zoning Regulations and Special Exceptions Thereto, 168 A.L.R. 13 (1947).

[160] See Jackson v. Guilford County Board of Adjustment, 275 N.C. 155, 166 S.E.2d 78 (1969) (ordinance providing that exception could be granted if it would not adversely affect the public interest was void as too indefinite); Lauder v. Westerly, 101 R.I. 623, 226 A.2d 135 (1967); Williams Estates Inc. v. Zoning Board of Review, 94 R.I. 490, 182 A.2d 314 (1962) (sustaining ordinance); Lund v. City of Tumwater, 2 Wash.App. 750, 472 P.2d 550 (1970), review denied 78 Wash.2d 995 (1970). Cf. O'Boyle v. Coe, 155 F.Supp. 581 (D.D.C. 1957) (noting findings that must be made before gasoline station could be allowed in commercial zone of District of Columbia); In re Long Island Lighting Co. v. Horn, 49 Misc.2d 717, 268 N.Y.S.2d 366 (1964), aff'd 24 A.D.2d 840, 263 N.Y.S.2d 696 (1965) (setting forth standards listed in a New York ordinance on exceptions); Appeal of Moreland, 497 P.2d 1287 (Okl.1972) (ordinance found not to delegate legislative power to board of adjustment). See generally Annot., Attack on Validity of Zoning Statute, Ordinance, or Regulation on Ground of Improper Delegation of Authority to Board or Officer, 58 A.L.R.2d 1083 (1958).

[161] See Maher v. Town Planning & Zoning Commission, 154 Conn. 420, 226 A.2d 397 (1967) (requirements of posting in neighborhood).

[162] Montgomery County v. Mossburg, 228 Md. 555, 180 A.2d 851 (1962) (conditions imposed must be reasonable). See Creative Country Day School v. Montgomery County Board of Appeals, 242 Md. 552, 219 A.2d 789 (1966) (if conditions authorized by law and are reasonable, exception will be denied until they are met); Borough of North Plainfield v. Perone, 54 N.J.Super. 1, 148 A.2d 50 (1959). Cf. Tarver v. City of Sheridan Bd. of Adjustments, 327 P.3d 76 (Wyo. 2014) (board of adjustment had power to impose parking restrictions on bed and breakfast as condition of granting "special exemption").

[163] Beckish v. Planning & Zoning Commission, 162 Conn. 11, 291 A.2d 208 (1971) (conditions must be found in the zoning regulations or laws); Parish of St. Andrew's Protestant Episcopal Church v. Zoning Board

A variance is a special relaxing of the rules as to particular property because of the unusual nature of that property—an administratively granted dispensation because the burden on the particular property would otherwise be disproportionate to any public benefit.[164] Unlike the situation with exceptions, the obtaining of a variance is not a matter of right.[165] Since the awarding of the variance requires that the specific property have some unique characteristics, this is not an appropriate remedy where the zoning creates hardships as to all owners in an area—the appropriate relief in the latter case would be a legislatively enacted amendment to the zoning law.[166] Under statutes, charters, or zoning ordinances themselves, there is usually some provision for the granting of variances, and usually the task of deciding on these is given the zoning or planning commission, or some special board of zoning "appeals" or "adjustments;" such a grant does not carry with it the authority to change boundaries of zones, as that is a legislative task that must be left with the local governing body.[167] Reasonably definite

---

of Appeals, 155 Conn. 350, 232 A.2d 916 (1967). But cf. Borough of North Plainfield v. Perone, 54 N.J.Super. 1, 148 A.2d 50 (1959) (inherent power found in zoning board to limit grant of exception).

[164] Arcadia Development Corp. v. City of Bloomington, 267 Minn. 221, 125 N.W.2d 846 (1964); Rosedale-Skinker Improvement Association v. Board of Adjustment, 425 S.W.2d 929 (Mo.1968); Moriarty v. Pozner, 21 N.J. 199, 121 A.2d 527 (1956). The granting of a variance does not constitute invalid "spot zoning" since the latter involves an *arbitrary* zoning of a small area, while variances should only be granted for good reason. See Life of the Land, Inc. v. City Council, 61 Hawaii 390, 606 P.2d 866 (1980) (approval of variance was non-legislative act and did not here single-out a particular parcel for a use inconsistent with comprehensive zoning plan). On spot zoning, see generally ns. 16–19, section 118 and accompanying text. On variances and similar devices, see generally Arnebergh, Variances in Zoning, 24 U.Kan.City L.Rev. 240 (1956); Note, Variance Law in New York: An Examination and Proposal, 44 Albany L.Rev. 781 (1980); Note, Zoning Variances, 74 Harv.L.Rev. 1396 (1961); Note, "Use" Variances: An Attempt to Eliminate Confusion, 17 Rutgers L.Rev. 789 (1963); Annot., Construction and Application of Provisions for Variations in Application of Zoning Regulations and Special Exceptions Thereto, *supra* note 159; Annot., Attack Upon Validity of Zoning Statute or Ordinance as Affected by Provisions for Variations, Permits, etc., 136 A.L.R. 1378 (1942).

Variances are also sometimes called "variations."

[165] See Poster Advertising Co. v. Zoning Board, 408 Pa. 248, 182 A.2d 521 (1962); Magrann v. Zoning Board, 404 Pa. 198, 170 A.2d 553 (1961) (applicant for variance must show substantial and compelling reasons); Richman v. Philadelphia Zoning Board, 391 Pa. 254, 137 A.2d 280 (1958) (evidence of grants of similar variances in similar zones establishes no right in applicant and is irrelevant to his case); Pistachio v. Zoning Board of Review, 88 R.I. 285, 147 A.2d 461 (1959) (one seeking variance has burden of showing it would not be contrary to public interest and that literal enforcement of law would cause him unnecessary hardship). Cf. Bartlett v. City of Corpus Christi, 359 S.W.2d 122 (Tex.Civ.App.1962), distinguishing exceptions and variances.

But once a variance is granted, it is not merely personal to the then-owner, but becomes a right that passes with the land to any new owner(s). See State ex rel. Parker v. Konopka, 119 Ohio App. 513, 200 N.E.2d 695 (1963) (with review of cases); Nuckles v. Allen, 250 S.C. 123, 156 S.E.2d 633 (1967) (if person purchases property in reliance on variance that has previously been granted, he acquires a vested property right). Cf. Sandenburgh v. Michigamme Oil Co., 249 Mich. 372, 228 N.W. 707 (1930) (local government estopped to revoke variance where property owner has made a substantial change of position in reliance thereon); Jones v. Zoning Board of Pittsburgh, 423 Pa. 416, 224 A.2d 205 (1966) (same). But in New Jersey, a new owner is not necessarily entitled to a variance granted a prior owner. See Smith v. Paquin, 77 N.J.Super. 138, 185 A.2d 673 (1962); Ardolino v. Board of Adjustment, Florham Park, 24 N.J. 94, 130 A.2d 847 (1957).

[166] State ex rel. Killeen Realty Co. v. City of East Cleveland, 108 Ohio App. 99, 153 N.E.2d 177 (1958), aff'd 169 Ohio St. 375, 160 N.E.2d 1. See Jasy Corp. v. Board of Adjustment, 413 Pa. 563, 198 A.2d 854 (1964) (if parcel not unique but is disadvantaged equally with rest of area, variance improper). But cf. Ench v. Mayor & Council of Pequannock Township, 47 N.J. 535, 222 A.2d 1 (1966), indicating either an amendment or a variance might be appropriate where local government wishes to allow a use formerly forbidden; but a mere resolution cannot be used.

[167] See Bray v. Beyer, 292 Ky. 162, 166 S.W.2d 290 (1942); Sugar v. North Baltimore Methodist Protestant Church, 164 Md. 487, 165 A. 703 (1933); Farah v. Sachs, 10 Mich.App. 198, 157 N.W.2d 9 (1968) (board may not, in guise of granting variance, amend or disregard zoning ordinance); Staller v. Cranston Zoning Board, 100 R.I. 340, 215 A.2d 418 (1965); Allan v. Zoning Board of Review, 79 R.I. 413, 89 A.2d 364

and certain standards must be legislatively established—by statute, charter, or ordinance—for the administrative body to apply in granting and denying variances; otherwise, the body's actions are invalid because of the unconstitutional delegation of legislative authority.[168] The basic test laid down by much legislation is that the variance can be granted upon a showing of "practical difficulty and unnecessary (or undue) hardship," and such language has almost universally been held to be a sufficiently definite guideline.[169] Much modern legislation, however, goes beyond those broad terms and specifies standards with somewhat more particularity; generally, these standards include some or all of four possible factors: (1) the grant will not be injurious to the general welfare of the community or interfere with the overall comprehensive plan; (2) the grant will not be substantially detrimental to nearby property owners; (3) the need for the variance arises from some conditions peculiar to the specific land involved, not

---

(1952); Driskell v. Board of Adjustment, 195 S.W.2d 594 (Tex.Civ.App. 1946) ref'd n. r. e. (zoning board of adjustment cannot be given power to create zoning districts; that power must be exercised by city authorities). Cf. Board of Adjustment v. Stovall, 218 S.W.2d 286 (Tex.Civ. App.1949) (ordinance which attempts to confer legislative functions on board of adjustment would be invalid delegation of legislative powers). But cf. Bradley v. Board of Zoning Adjustment, 255 Mass. 160, 150 N.E. 892 (1926) (statute conferring on board of zoning adjustment the power to change boundaries does not delegate legislative power in violation of constitution). Some jurisdictions have statutes requiring that any local government wishing to exercise zoning power have a board of adjustment. See Town of Wellston v. Wallace, 152 P.3d 284 (Okla. Civ. App. 2006) (municipality must have both a zoning commission and a board of adjustment in order to exercise zoning authority).

For critical assessments of the work of zoning boards of adjustment, see Dukeminier & Stapleton, The Zoning Board of Adjustment: A Case Study in Misrule, 50 Ky. L.J. 273 (1962); Note, Board of Zoning Appeals Procedure: Informality Breeds Contempt, 16 Syracuse L.Rev. 568 (1965). On the appealing of zoning decisions of boards of adjustment, and challenges to zoning decisions of local legislative bodies, see generally Note, Trial Practice: Procedure for Appealing Decisions of a Municipal Zoning Agency, 18 Okla.L.Rev. 111 (1965); Note, Exhaustion of Remedies in Zoning Cases, 1964 Wash.U.L.Q. 368 (complainant attacking specific zoning as applied to his property must exhaust the available administrative remedies before resorting to courts, but challenge to constitutionality of zoning ordinance in entirety may be made in courts without recourse to administrative remedies).

[168] See Sugar v. North Baltimore Methodist Protestant Church, *supra* note 167; Tighe v. Osborne, 149 Md. 349, 131 A. 801 (1925); Concordia Collegiate Institute v. Miller, 301 N.Y. 189, 93 N.E.2d 632 (1950); State ex rel. Selected Properties v. Gottfried, 163 Ohio St. 469, 127 N.E.2d 371 (1955); Root v. City of Erie, 180 Pa.Super. 38, 118 A.2d 297 (1955); Flynn v. Zoning Board of Review, 77 R.I. 118, 73 A.2d 808 (1950); Texas Consolidated Theatres v. Pittillo, 204 S.W.2d 396 (Tex.Civ.App.1947). See Note, Municipal Corporations—Excessive Delegation of Powers by Municipality to Board of Adjustment, 1 Baylor L.Rev. 228 (1948).

[169] See Appeal of Blackstone, 38 Del. 230, 190 A. 597 (1937); Freeman v. Board of Adjustment, 97 Mont. 342, 34 P.2d 534 (1934); City of Lincoln v. Foss, 119 Neb. 666, 230 N.W. 592 (1930); Sundeen v. Rogers, 83 N.H. 253, 141 A. 142 (1928); Sheldon v. Board of Appeals, 234 N.Y. 484, 138 N.E. 416 (1923); L & M Investment Co. v. Cutler, 125 Ohio St. 12, 180 N.E. 379 (1932); In re Dawson, 136 Okl. 113, 277 P. 226 (1928); Spencer-Sturla Co. v. City of Memphis, 155 Tenn. 70, 290 S.W. 608 (1927). But see Welton v. Hamilton, 344 Ill. 82, 176 N.E. 333 (1931) (law authorizing board of appeals to modify zoning ordinance in cases of practical difficulties or unnecessary hardship is unconstitutional delegation of legislative power). See generally Note, Zoning—Power of Board to Vary, 26 Ill. L.Rev. 575 (1932); Note, Discretionary Powers of Zoning Boards of Adjustment in Pennsylvania, 97 U.Pa.L.Rev. (1948).

It has been held that the phrases "unnecessary hardship" and "practical difficulties"—each of which is used in some of the relevant legislation—have the same meaning here. Snyder v. Waukesha County Zoning Board of Adjustment, 74 Wis.2d 468, 247 N.W.2d 98 (1976). See McKnight v. Mitchell, 144 Ga.App. 109, 240 S.E.2d 313 (1977) (owner entitled to variance when he shows practical difficulty or unnecessary hardship). See generally Note, Zoning Variances: The "Unnecessary Hardship" Rule, 8 Syracuse L.Rev. 85 (1956). But in some jurisdictions the terms "unnecessary hardship" and "practical difficulties" are differentiated, with the former—the more rigorous standard—applied to applications for *use* variances, and the latter—a more easily met requirement—applied to *area* variances. See Matthew v. Smith, 707 S.W.2d 411 (Mo.1986).

Even where the local legislative body itself determines whether or not a variance should be granted, it has been held that adequate standards must be provided by legislation. See City of Homestead v. Schild, 227 So.2d 540 (Fla.App.1969); Appeal of Clements, 2 Ohio App.2d 201, 207 N.E.2d 573 (1965).

because of general conditions in the region or neighborhood; and (4) literal application of the ordinance would create "unnecessary," "undue," or "unusual" hardship for the owner of the property as to which the variance is sought.[170]

Some degree of financial detriment, it is often emphasized, does not by itself justify the grant of a variance,[171] but if a literal application of the law would mean that no economic or beneficial use of the property could reasonably be made, then a variance is justified.[172] A strong case for a variance may be presented if the particular property has peculiar physical characteristics, such as unusual subsoil conditions, an unusual shape or configuration (as with a triangular lot, as to which the usual setback restrictions might operate harshly), or an unusual physical feature such as a ravine; but even in these situations, the requirement that the conditions be unique to the specific property must be met.[173] It is generally agreed that the location of a property on or near the boundary-line of a zone does not in itself make out a case of "unnecessary or undue

[170] See, all applying criteria similar to those mentioned, Metropolitan Board of Zoning Appeals v. Rumple, 261 Ind. 214, 301 N.E.2d 359 (1973), applying Ind.Stat. Ann. § 18–7–2–71 and finding a denial of a variance legal; Frank v. Russell, 160 Neb. 354, 70 N.W.2d 306 (1955); Otto v. Steinhilber, 282 N.Y. 71, 24 N.E.2d 851 (1939), rearg. denied 282 N.Y. 681, 26 N.E.2d 811; Pelican Production Corp. v. Mize, 573 P.2d 703 (Okl.1977); Brown v. Fraser, 467 P.2d 464 (Okl.1970). Cf. Kohl v. Mayor & Council of Fair Lawn, 50 N.J. 268, 234 A.2d 385 (1967) (variances can be granted where there are special reasons and there won't be public detriment; applying statute, and upholding the statutory standard); Vinson v. Medley, 737 P.2d 932 (Okl.1987) (variance justified where there is otherwise some degree of interference with ordinary legal property rights from which hardship would arise, the hardship is peculiar to the landowner's situation, the degree of hardship imposed by the ordinance is not essential to carrying out its spirit, and substantial deprivation results to landowners). See generally Note, Hardship and the Granting of Zoning Variances, 89 Neb. L. Rev. 1171 (2011).

[171] Baccante v. Zoning Board, 153 Conn. 44, 212 A.2d 411 (1965); Makar v. Zoning Board, 150 Conn. 391, 190 A.2d 45 (1963); Culinary Institute v. Board of Zoning Appeals, 143 Conn. 257, 121 A.2d 637 (1956); Piccirillo v. Board of Appeals, 139 Conn. 116, 90 A.2d 647 (1952); Marino v. City of Baltimore, 215 Md. 206, 137 A.2d 198 (1957) (pecuniary loss does not suffice; some arbitrary and capricious interference with property rights must be shown); Poster Advertising Co. v. Zoning Board of Adjustment, 408 Pa. 248, 182 A.2d 521 (1962) (fact that increase or decrease in property value will result from grant or refusal of variance does not show the required hardship); Spadaro v. Zoning Board of Adjustment, 394 Pa. 375, 147 A.2d 159 (1959) (economic hardship does not justify variance). Cf. Walker v. Board of County Commissioners, 208 Md. 72, 116 A.2d 393 (1955) cert. denied 350 U.S. 902, 76 S.Ct. 180, 100 L.Ed. 792 (variance won't be granted merely because property would then be more profitable); Blackman v. Board of Appeals, 334 Mass. 446, 136 N.E.2d 198 (1956) (variance cannot be granted solely on basis of economic hardship); Puritan-Greenfield Improvement Association v. Leo, 7 Mich.App. 659, 153 N.W.2d 162 (1967) (variance won't be granted just because applicant's property could then be more profitably used); Beirn v. Morris, 14 N.J. 529, 103 A.2d 361 (1954) (disadvantages to use of lot for purposes for which zoned were not peculiar to that lot; denial of variance affirmed).

[172] Mischiara v. Board of Adjustment, 77 N.J.Super. 288, 186 A.2d 141 (1962) (sufficient ground if property cannot be put to any practical economic use unless variance granted); Burke v. Board of Adjustment, 52 N.J.Super. 498, 145 A.2d 790 (1958); Charles Land Co. v. Zoning Board, 99 R.I. 161, 206 A.2d 453 (1965) (variance should not be granted unless owner would otherwise be deprived of all beneficial use of property); Cole v. Zoning Board, 97 R.I. 220, 197 A.2d 166 (1964). Cf. Poster Advertising Co. v. Zoning Board of Adjustment, *supra* note 171 (reasons for granting variance must be substantial, serious, and compelling; economic hardship not sufficient in itself).

[173] See Broadway, Laguna, Vallejo Association v. Board of Permit Appeals, 66 Cal.2d 767, 59 Cal.Rptr. 146, 427 P.2d 810 (1967) (subsoil conditions not a sufficiently "exceptional circumstance" to justify variance—profit motive not adequate ground for variance). If property is legally indistinguishable from surrounding lands, and is disadvantaged by zoning laws only to the same extent as other property in the area, a variance should not be granted. See Clark v. Board of Zoning Appeals, 301 N.Y. 86, 92 N.E.2d 903 (1950), motion denied 301 N.Y. 681, 95 N.E.2d 44, cert. denied 340 U.S. 933, 71 S.Ct. 498, 95 L.Ed. 673 (variance improperly granted to allow funeral parlor in residential zone); Jasy Corp. v. Board of Adjustment, 413 Pa. 563, 198 A.2d 854 (1964). For an argument that the "unique circumstances" requirement for variances should be more strictly applied by the courts, see Reynolds, The "Unique Circumstances" Rule in Zoning Variances—An Aid in Achieving Greater Prudence and Less Leniency, 31 Urban Law. 127 (1999).

hardship," though it is one factor that may be weighed.[174] If, however, the property—particularly if having a rather small area—is bisected by zoning lines—so that, for instance, part is in an exclusively residential zone and part in a commercial zone—, a strong case for a variance is shown.[175] It is usually agreed that an "unnecessary" hardship will not be found where the detriment has occurred through the voluntary act of the owner of the property—as his own development of the land;[176] and this rule of "self-induced hardship" has often been applied to deny a variance to a person who purchased the property with actual or constructive knowledge of the zoning restrictions.[177] But it seems that the unique nature of the property and other general requirements for the variance may sometimes be met in situations where the present owner "purchased with knowledge," and the trend now is to hold that this situation is not necessarily one in which the variance should be denied.[178]

---

[174] Bellamy v. Board of Appeals, 32 Misc.2d 520, 223 N.Y.S.2d 1017 (1962) (property adjacent to area zoned for business; not a unique circumstance justifying a variance).

[175] Or sometimes zoning that results in such a splitting of property may be ruled unreasonable and thus invalid. See generally Annot., Validity and Construction of Zoning Regulation Respecting Permissible Use as Affected by Division of Lot or Parcel by Zone Boundary Line, 58 A.L.R.3d 1241 (1974). See also Comment, Use District Boundary Lines, 17 Syracuse L.Rev. 714 (1966). On the need for reasonably definite boundary lines, see Annot., Validity of Zoning Regulations, with Respect to Uncertainty and Indefiniteness of District Boundary Lines, 39 A.L.R.2d 766 (1955).

[176] M. & R. Enterprises v. Town of Southington, 155 Conn. 280, 231 A.2d 272 (1967); Highland Park, Inc. v. Zoning Board of Appeals, 155 Conn. 40, 229 A.2d 356 (1967); Green v. City of Miami, 107 So.2d 390 (Fla.App.1958), cert. denied 114 So.2d 617; Salisbury Board of Zoning Appeals v. Bounds, 240 Md. 547, 214 A.2d 810 (1965); Deer-Glen Estates v. Board of Adjustment & Appeal, 39 N.J.Super. 380, 121 A.2d 26 (1956); Sherwood Realty Corp. v. Feriola, 193 Misc. 194, 82 N.Y.S.2d 505 (1948); Stratford Arms v. Zoning Board of Adjustment, 429 Pa. 132, 239 A.2d 325 (1968) (where hardship results from applicant's willful violation of zoning laws, variance cannot be granted). Cf. Banks v. City of Bethany, 541 P.2d 178 (Okl.1975) (hardship self-imposed where applicant needed to use additional area for display and storage of merchandise; also, condition creating hardship was not unique to his property); City of Pittsburgh v. Zoning Bd. of Adjustment, 522 Pa. 44, 559 A.2d 896 (1989) (hardship experienced by property owners as result of subdividing building into apartments in reliance on building permits was hardship of own making and didn't justify a variance where the building permits were based on false information provided by the property owners).

[177] See Minney v. City of Azusa, 164 Cal.App.2d 12, 330 P.2d 255 (Dist.Ct.1958), appeal dism'd 359 U.S. 436, 79 S.Ct. 941, 3 L.Ed.2d 932; Spalding v. Board of Zoning Appeals, 144 Conn. 719, 137 A.2d 755 (1957); Allstate Mortgage Corp. v. City of Miami Beach, 308 So.2d 629 (Fla.App.1975), cert. denied 317 So.2d 763 (Fla.1975) (applicant had purchased land that was already subject to set-back restriction); Elwyn v. City of Miami, 113 So.2d 849 (Fla.App. 1959), cert. denied 116 So.2d 773 (Fla.1959) (variance should not be granted for alleged "hardship" where owner had purchased property while it was in a certain zoning classification, and then applied for the variance); Podmers v. Village of Winfield, 39 Ill.App.3d 615, 350 N.E.2d 232 (1976) (property owner chargeable with knowledge of zoning restrictions when selling portion of tract); Clark v. Board of Zoning Appeals, 301 N.Y. 86, 92 N.E.2d 903 (1950), motion denied 301 N.Y. 681, 95 N.E.2d 44, cert. denied 340 U.S. 933, 71 S.Ct. 498, 95 L.Ed. 673 (applying the majority rule, denying a variance to a purchaser; this is sometimes called the "New York rule"); In re, McClure's Appeal, 415 Pa. 285, 203 A.2d 534 (1964). Cf. Richards v. Turner, 336 A.2d 581 (Del.Super.1975), aff'd 366 A.2d 833 (hardship self-inflicted where applicant could have avoided it by declining to exercise an option on the property). It has been suggested that a purchaser hopeful of using the property for a purpose forbidden by current zoning laws should condition the contract upon the securing of a use variance. See Salsbery v. District of Columbia Board of Zoning Adjustment, 357 A.2d 402 (D.C.App.1976). It seems that a variance may often be denied a "purchaser with knowledge" simply on the basis that variances are exceptional and somewhat discretionary, and one who purchased with knowledge usually does not have the equities on his side.

"Undue" or "unnecessary" hardship will not be found from the fact that applicant owned the property prior to the imposition of zoning restrictions, though this may qualify the owner for a non-conforming use. See Holman v. Board of Adjustment, 78 N.J.Super. 74, 187 A.2d 605 (1963).

[178] See Board of Adjustment v. Shanbour, 435 P.2d 569 (Okl.1967); Borough of Ingram v. Sinicrope, 8 Pa.Cmwlth. 448, 303 A.2d 855 (1973). The Oklahoma Supreme Court seemed about to overturn the *Shanbour* holding, *supra*, in Bailey v. Uhls, 43 Okl.B.A.J. 1337 (1972); but that opinion was vacated (42 Okl.B.A.J. 3285

Power is often expressly given, or is readily inferred, for the administrative body that rules on variances to attach reasonable conditions to the granting thereof.[179] The entire procedure for seeking variances is normally laid down by charter or ordinance, and generally now includes mandatory provisions for notice to neighboring owners or to the general public, plus some public hearing on the application.[180] Actions taken on applications for variances can be challenged in the courts, but this possibility contains two limitations: (1) The grant of a variance can only be challenged by a person showing peculiar damage therefrom—for instance, a neighbor who will be bothered by the noise resulting from the specially allowed use. The protesting person must show harm that is different-in-kind from that suffered by the general community.[181] (2) Neither the grant nor denial of a variance will be overturned by the courts unless the action is shown to be clearly unreasonable, arbitrary, or an abuse of discretion, as where clearly against the weight of the evidence.[182] In recent years, courts often emphasize that the power to grant

---

(1972)), and the court ultimately affirmed a denial of variance on the grounds there was inadequate showing of unnecessary hardship and the board of adjustment's denial was not clearly against the weight of evidence. Bailey v. Uhls, 503 P.2d 877 (Okl.1972). See generally Reynolds, Self-Induced Hardship in Zoning Variances: Does a Purchaser Have No One But Himself to Blame?, 20 Urban Law. 1 (1988), stating that purchase-with-knowledge is not now, and should not be, grounds in itself for denial of a variance; since a variance will, once obtained, pass with the land, so should the right to obtain the variance.

[179] See Houdaille Construction Materials, Inc. v. Board of Adjustment, 92 N.J.Super. 293, 223 A.2d 210 (1966); Alperin v. Middletown Township, 91 N.J.Super. 190, 219 A.2d 628 (1966). Cf. Cornell Uniforms, Inc. v. Township of Abington, 8 Pa.Cmwlth. 317, 301 A.2d 113 (1973) (local governing body can condition grant of variance).

[180] See Aurora v. Zoning Board of Appeals, 153 Conn. 623, 220 A.2d 277 (1966); Winslow v. Zoning Board, 143 Conn. 381, 122 A.2d 789 (1956); Walker v. Board of County Commissioners, 208 Md. 72, 116 A.2d 393 (1955); Radick v. Zoning Board, 83 R.I. 392, 117 A.2d 84 (1955). Cf. Slagle v. Zoning Board, 144 Conn. 690, 137 A.2d 542 (1957) (81-hours' notice of hearing held inadequate). But there are two qualifications as to notice requirements: (1) It has been held that, where *not* provided by legislation, no right to notice exists in neighboring property owners. Nagel v. Kummerow, 51 Misc.2d 659, 273 N.Y.S.2d 726 (1966). (2) Where notice is ordinarily required as to a hearing, it may be held that lack of such notice is waived by objectors who personally appear at the hearing. See Phil Anthony Homes, Inc. v. City of Anaheim, 175 Cal.App.2d 268, 346 P.2d 231 (Dist.Ct.1959). But see Slagle v. Zoning Board, *supra* (objectors who appeared at meeting not estopped to deny inadequacy of notice). It would seem the objectors should still be allowed to protest the inadequacy of notice where they can reasonably allege they weren't given adequate time to *prepare* for the meeting.

[181] Marquis Who's Who, Inc. v. Ohio-St. Clair Garage Corp., 95 Ill.App.2d 73, 238 N.E.2d 74 (1968); Kennerly v. Mayor & City of Baltimore, 247 Md. 601, 233 A.2d 800 (1967); Stickelber v. Board of Zoning Adjustment, 442 S.W.2d 134 (Mo.App.1969). See Hawkins v. Bonneville County Bd. of Comm'rs, 151 Idaho 228, 254 P.3d 1224 (2011) (neighbor had standing to petition for judicial review of order granting property owners variances to build houses on agricultural land). Statutes or ordinances often now specify that persons "aggrieved" or "substantially affected" may attack the grant of a variance; but these provisions are usually interpreted as also requiring a showing of special injury. See Mabank Corp. v. Board of Zoning Appeals, 143 Conn. 132, 120 A.2d 149 (1956); Scott v. Board of Adjustment, 405 S.W.2d 55 (Tex.1966). Cf. Victoria Corp. v. Atlanta Merchandise Mart, 101 Ga.App. 163, 112 S.E.2d 793 (1960), interpreting statute requiring that protestant have "substantial interest." See generally Foss, Interested Third Parties in Zoning, 12 U.Fla.L.Rev. 16, 35 (1959).

[182] Ames v. City of Pasadena, 167 Cal.App.2d 510, 334 P.2d 653 (Dist.Ct.1959); San Diego County v. McClurken, 37 Cal.2d 683, 234 P.2d 972 (1951); Bailey v. Uhls, *supra* note 178; In re Upper St. Clair Township Grange, 397 Pa. 67, 152 A.2d 768 (1959); O'Neill v. City of Philadelphia, 384 Pa. 379, 120 A.2d 901 (1956); Tripp v. Zoning Board, 84 R.I. 262, 123 A.2d 144 (1956). Where the variance has been denied, courts have the power to order it awarded. See City of Baltimore v. Sapero, 230 Md. 291, 186 A.2d 884 (1962); Beardsley v. Evangelical Lutheran Bethlehem Church, 261 Mich. 458, 246 N.W. 180 (1933); Jersey Triangle Corp. v. Board of Adjustment, 127 N.J.L. 194, 21 A.2d 845 (1941); Application of Shadid, 205 Okl. 462, 238 P.2d 794 (1951); In re Blanarik, 375 Pa. 209, 100 A.2d 58 (1953); Morin v. Zoning Board, 89 R.I. 406, 153 A.2d 149 (1959). But a denial will generally be reversed only upon *extremely* strong proof of abuse of discretion. See Coleman v. Board of Appeal, 281 Mass. 112, 183 N.E. 166 (1932); Hickox v. Griffin, 298 N.Y. 365, 83 N.E.2d 836 (1949); Appeal of Kerr, 294 Pa. 246, 144 A. 81 (1928); Denelle v. Zoning Board, 89 R.I. 456, 153 A.2d 143 (1959). Compare Lindy's Restaurant, Inc. v. Zoning Board of Appeals, 143 Conn. 620, 124 A.2d 918 (1956) (power to

variances should be sparingly exercised, as otherwise there is danger of gradual erosion of the comprehensive plan that should be the basis of any orderly pattern of zoning.[183]

"Special (or conditional) use permits" are similar to exceptions in that the authority for granting them is spelled-out in legislation: state statutes, home-rule charters, or the zoning ordinances; and no undue hardship need be shown in order for them to be granted. Again, the granting or denial is left to some administrative body, which must be given reasonably definite guidelines to control its exercise of judgment.[184] But the

---

grant variance must be sparingly exercised; grant of variance merely on basis of financial hardship will be overturned). In Shelton v. City of College Station, 780 F.2d 475 (5th Cir. 1986) (en banc), cert. denied 477 U.S. 905, 106 S.Ct. 3276, 91 L.Ed.2d 566 (1986), the court went even farther than usual in deferring to the judgment of the zoning board of adjustment, holding that variance decisions are quasi-legislative and thus reviewable only for arbitrary and capricious action.

It has been held that where a board of adjustment's decision on a variance is overturned by the trial court, the presumption initially attaching to the correctness of the board ruling is to be regarded as having been overcome by the trial court's decision. Red Dog Saloon v. Board of Adjustment, 791 P.2d 112 (Okl. App. 1989) (denial of variance had been reversed by trial court). As to who may appeal the granting of a variance, see Hacker v. Sedgwick County, 286 P.3d 222 (Kan. App. 2012) (zoning statute allowed appeal by "any person aggrieved" by a final decision of a city or county; held to cover neighbors dissatisfied by grant of variance).

[183] See Celentano, Inc. v. Board of Zoning Appeals, 149 Conn. 671, 184 A.2d 49 (1962); Wil-Nor Corp. v. Zoning Board of Appeals, 146 Conn. 27, 147 A.2d 197 (1958) (power should be sparingly exercised); Carney v. City of Baltimore, 201 Md. 130, 93 A.2d 74 (1952); Kohl v. Mayor & Council of Fair Lawn, 50 N.J. 268, 234 A.2d 385 (1967) (variances tend to impair sound zoning); In re Riccardi's Appeal, 393 Pa. 337, 142 A.2d 289 (1958); Bliss v. City of Fort Worth, 288 S.W.2d 558 (Tex.Civ.App.1956), ref'd n. r. e. Cf. Blackman v. Board of Appeals, 334 Mass. 446, 136 N.E.2d 198 (1956) (district has to end somewhere, and boundaries should not be pared down by granting of variances). Thus, it is sometimes stressed that *exceptional* circumstances must exist for a variance to be justified. See Hasage v. Philadelphia Zoning Board, 415 Pa. 31, 202 A.2d 61 (1964). This attitude no doubt helps explain the extreme deference given by courts to *denials* by local zoning bodies of variances, as discussed note 182 *supra*. See Cummins v. Board of Adjustment, 39 N.J.Super. 452, 121 A.2d 405 (1956) (more is to be feared from grants of variances than from denials). See generally Annot., Requirement that Zoning Variances or Exceptions Be Made in Accordance with Comprehensive Plan, 40 A.L.R.3d 372 (1971) (is need to develop standards that courts could use to determine whether particular variance, or other change, conforms to comprehensive plan of community). See also Owens, The Zoning Variance: Reappraisal and Recommendations for Reform of a Much-Maligned Tool, 29 Columbia J. Envtl. L. 279 (2004). As to whether the legal standards for granting or denying variances are really used in practice, see Sampson, Theory and Practice in the Granting of Dimensional Land Use Variances: Is the Legal Standard Conscientiously Applied, Consciously Ignored, or Something in Between?, 39 Urban Law. 877 (2007), examining the decisions of the variance-granting boards of three Denver-area municipalities as to applications for "area" or "dimensional" (as opposed to "use") variances.

[184] See Schultz v. Board of Adjustment, 258 Iowa 804, 139 N.W.2d 448 (1966). But see State ex rel. Standard Mining & Development Corp. v. City of Auburn, 82 Wash.2d 321, 510 P.2d 647 (1973) (standards need not be legislatively set for imposing the *conditions* under which special use permit will be issued). Special or conditional uses are often provided because it is thought this device introduces a needed element of flexibility into zoning plans. See State ex rel. Skelly Oil Co. v. Delafield, 58 Wis.2d 695, 207 N.W.2d 585 (1973). But the flexibility should not be allowed to go too far; thus, one court found that where an entire township was zoned for agricultural and residential uses, with other uses allowed only upon obtaining a special permit, this was the antithesis of zoning and was invalid. Rockhill v. Township of Chesterfield, 23 N.J. 117, 128 A.2d 473 (1957). This desire for flexibility may, however, help justify greater delegations of authority to administrative bodies or exercises of broad power by legislative bodies—as to what conditions to attach, exactly how to frame the permit, etc.—than could be justified where exceptions or variances are concerned. See Bollinger v. Board of Supervisors, 217 Va. 185, 227 S.E.2d 682 (1976) (local governing body may reserve right to issue special use permits without specifying standards for issuance in ordinance); Gerla v. City of Tacoma, 12 Wash.App. 883, 533 P.2d 416 (1975), review denied 85 Wash.2d 1011 (1975) (local governments have inherent power to impose reasonable conditions on special use permit even though such conditions not guided by specific standards); State ex rel. Standard Mining & Development Corp. v. City of Auburn, *supra*.

Special use permits may be required as to certain uses which are considered undesirable and which it is therefore thought should be allowed only under unusual circumstances. See Arizona Public Service Co. v. Town of Paradise Valley, 125 Ariz. 447, 610 P.2d 449 (1980) (utility poles and wires had to be placed underground unless special permit obtained; ordinance upheld, court noting that town, as part of its zoning powers, could

special or conditional use, almost by definition, always requires the obtaining of a special permit, to which reasonable conditions can be attached; and there is often less right to such permit than there is to an exception: The empowered authority can consider the possible detrimental effects on the neighborhood and community, the need for the proposed use in the area, the possible existence of an adequate number of other such uses, and various factors connected with the public welfare.[185] The grant or denial will, as with the variance, be overturned by the courts only if clearly arbitrary or capricious action is shown.[186] This procedure is often used where some uses other than those for

---

require undergrounding of all utility wires, etc.). Cf. Alaska R.R. v. Native Village of Eklutna, 43 P.3d 588 (Alaska 2002) (conditional use is a use that is generally inappropriate for area in which it is situated but that is permitted after additional controls and safeguards are instituted to ensure its compatibility with permitted principal uses). In general, special use permits and conditional permits are "essentially one and the same." See Gardiner v. Boundary County Bd. of Comm'rs, 148 Idaho 764, 229 P.3d 369, 372 (2010) (interpreting Idaho statutes).

[185] See Kotrich v. County of Du Page, 19 Ill.2d 181, 166 N.E.2d 601 (1960), appeal dism'd 364 U.S. 475, 81 S.Ct. 243, 5 L.Ed.2d 221, reh. denied 365 U.S. 805, 81 S.Ct. 466, 5 L.Ed.2d 463 (special or conditional zoning utilized for infrequent types of land use which are sometimes necessary and desirable); S. Volpe & Co. v. Board of Appeals, 4 Mass.App. 357, 348 N.E.2d 807 (1976) (zoning board has considerable discretion to deny special use permit where would be injurious to neighborhood or community); Anderson v. Peden, 284 Or. 313, 587 P.2d 59 (1978) (landowner not entitled as a matter of right to special permit for mobile home); Christian Retreat Center v. Board of County Commissioners, 28 Or.App. 673, 560 P.2d 1100 (1977) (conditional use permit could be denied where granting it would result in increased congestion and noise in area). Cf. Marcia T. Turner, L.L.C. v. City of Twin Falls, 144 Idaho 203, 159 P.3d 840 (2007) (council could deny application for special use permit for television transmission tower even if nobody testified against application at public hearing and could consider aesthetics when making its decision). See generally Manly v. City of Shawnee, 287 Kan. 63, 194 P.3d 1 (2008), upholding a city's grant of a special use permit for an illuminated softball complex and stadium; listing 8 factors to be considered by governing bodies in zoning matters. But in some jurisdictions, a special or conditional use permit is similar to an exception: a right to the use may be found to exist if the required standards are met. See Hay v. Township of Grow, 296 Minn. 1, 206 N.W.2d 19 (1973) (where ordinance specifies standards for permit and applicant fully complies, denial of permit is arbitrary as a matter of law).

In *all* jurisdictions, it is generally agreed that a denial of a permit *can* be overturned, at least where the denial is found arbitrary and unreasonable. See Pioneer Trust & Savings Bank v. County of McHenry, 41 Ill.2d 77, 241 N.E.2d 454 (1968); Cove Pizza, Inc. v. Hirshon, 61 A.D.2d 210, 401 N.Y.S.2d 838 (1978). Cf. Taylor v. County of Peoria, 30 Ill.App.3d 685, 333 N.E.2d 726 (1975) (fear of overcrowding of schools was not sufficient reason to deny permit to mobile home park); LaSalle National Bank v. County of Lake, 27 Ill.App.3d 10, 325 N.E.2d 105 (1975) (denial of special use permit for a planned unit development—variety of housing, commercial area, etc.—was unreasonable where developer had substantially met all requirements). Compare Uintah Mt. RTC, L.L.C. v. Duchesne County, 2005 UT App 565, 127 P.3d 1270 (2005) (denial of conditional use permit is arbitrary only if it is not supported by substantial evidence; denial here was not so supported and thus is overturned). Cf. Laughter v. Board of County Comm'rs for Sweetwater County, 2005 WY 54, 110 P.3d 875 (2005) (while discretion of officials may not be unbridled in deciding whether to issue conditional use permit, officials must be allowed to act with a certain amount of discretion, exercised reasonably, not arbitrarily or capriciously). See also cases cited note 186 *infra*. But the *issuance* of a special or conditional use permit creates vested property rights in the owner, particularly where relied on in the expenditure of money, and a permit cannot ordinarily be rescinded except as specifically provided by its terms. Schulman v. Fulton County, 249 Ga. 852, 295 S.E.2d 102 (1982) (permit for outdoor aerial lighting system).

A special permit, once granted, ordinarily runs with the land. See County of Imperial v. McDougal, 19 Cal.3d 505, 138 Cal.Rptr. 472, 564 P.2d 14 (1977), application denied 434 U.S. 899, 98 S.Ct. 294, 54 L.Ed.2d 187.

[186] See Columbus Park Congregation of Jehovah's Witnesses v. City of Chicago, 25 Ill.2d 65, 182 N.E.2d 722 (1962) (denial must bear substantial relation to some police-power purpose). Cf. State ex rel. Rochester Association of Neighborhoods v. City of Rochester, 268 N.W.2d 885 (Minn.1978) (special use permit's grant or denial is subject to stricter judicial review than is amendment of zoning ordinance—which is a legislative act and must be upheld if supported by any rational basis). See also cases cited in 2d paragraph of note 185 *supra*. Compare Hargrave v. Tulsa Bd. of Adjustment, 55 P.3d 1088 (Okla. 2002) (district court has same power and authority as city board of adjustment to grant or deny a zoning variance or special permit).

Conditions in a special permit, or an ordinance allowing such permits, are also presumed valid, but can be invalidated if shown unreasonable. See County of Cook v. Priester, 62 Ill.2d 357, 342 N.E.2d 41 (1976). Cf.

which an area is basically zoned are needed or desired in the vicinity—as some hospitals or medical facilities, or some schools, in a residential area.

What trends are apparent as to these qualifications—the exception, the variance, and the conditional use permit—on basic zoning patterns? (1) The overall trend since the 1920's has been toward more *ad hoc* zoning—*i.e.*, greater use of all these modifying devices. But in recent years, some courts and commentators have become increasingly concerned that the proliferation of these devices is resulting in less orderly, less comprehensive planning. Thus, some tightening of standards can be noted. (2) "Exceptions" and "conditional use permits" have moved closer together, as conditions are often now attached to exceptions, just as they always have been to conditional use permits, and as some courts even treat the use permits as being deserved as a matter of right where the prescribed conditions are met. In some jurisdictions, these two devices may now be virtually indistinguishable. (3) While amendments to zoning ordinances (being legislative in nature) won't be overturned unless no rational purpose is found, the granting or denial of an exception, variance, or use permit can be overturned if the decision is clearly against the weight of evidence—to such an extent as to be arbitrary or otherwise unreasonable. While in theory, the standard of review may be somewhat less stringent in the latter situations (*i.e.*, an overturning is easier to achieve), in practice the rules work out much the same. The review of *grants* of exceptions (and in some jurisdictions, conditional use permits) is qualified by the basic principle that there is a *right* to such relief upon the meeting of certain definitions or standards. And the review

---

J.L. Storedahl & Sons, Inc. v. Cowlitz County, 125 Wash.App. 1, 103 P.3d 802 (2004) (if conditions imposed are reasonably calculated to achieve protection of homeowners, public, and adjacent land, they cannot be set aside on appeal; conditions here imposed with issuance of special use permit for expansion of surface mine found reasonably calculated to achieve such protection).

If there is no legitimate reason for requiring a special permit for a particular use—as where, for instance, other similar uses are allowed without the need for such permit—a violation of Equal Protection may be found. See City of Cleburne, Texas v. Cleburne Living Center, 473 U.S. 432, 105 S.Ct. 3249, 87 L.Ed.2d 313 (1985) (requiring special use permit for group home for mentally retarded violated Equal Protection where no rational basis shown in the record for believing such a home would pose any special threat to city's legitimate interest, and requirement thus appeared to rest on irrational prejudice against the mentally retarded). Compare J.W. v. City of Tacoma, 720 F.2d 1126 (9th Cir.1983), where the court ruled that an ordinance requiring a special use permit for a group home for recently released mental patients was subject to "heightened scrutiny" and could be upheld only if it rationally furthered some substantial municipal goal; the ordinance in that case was found discriminatory and invalid. But "heightened scrutiny" was specifically rejected in *Cleburne*, *supra*, at 473 U.S. 441–46, 105 S.Ct. 3255–58. Cf. Baxter v. Belleville, Illinois, 720 F.Supp. 720 (S.D.Ill.1989) (injunction issued restraining city from refusing to allow special use permit for facility to care for persons in late stages of HIV); Love Church v. City of Evanston, 671 F.Supp. 515 (N.D.Ill.1987) (ordinance requiring churches to obtain special use permits involved classification based on religion since other similar uses, such as community centers and schools, did not need special permit; such classification permissible only if ordinance is narrowly tailored to serve a compelling governmental interest, which was not found here); Application of Volunteers of America, Inc., 749 P.2d 549 (Okl.1988) (special exception for prison prerelease center in commercial high intensity zone could not be denied merely because of fear, not necessarily having a basis in fact, of adverse effect on future development of area). See also Board of County Comm'rs of Leavenworth County v. Whitson, 281 Kan. 678, 132 P.3d 920 (2006) (statute prohibiting municipalities from requiring special use permits for group homes for disabled persons if such permits were not required for single-family residences within the same zoning classification did not apply to group homes for disabled, transitioning sexually violent predators). As to views regarding the *Cleburne* case, *supra*, and its results, see Comment, Conceptualizing *Cleburne*, 41 Golden Gate U.L. Rev. 121 (2010). Cf. Centro Familiar Cristiano Buenas Neuvas v. City of Yuma, 651 F.3d 1163 (9th Cir. 2011) (municipal ordinance that allows "religious organizations" to operate in an entertainment district only if they obtain a conditional use permit, but grants permits as of right for similarly situated secular groups, violates the "equal terms" provision of the Religious Land Use and Institutionalized Persons Act; see note 91, *supra*, and accompanying text).

of *denials* of variances is qualified by the increasingly adverse attitude of courts toward variances—so that a denial will seldom be reversed.

Chapter 19

MUNICIPAL ACQUISITION OF PROPERTY: EMINENT DOMAIN AND OTHER METHODS

Analysis

§ 19.1 Municipal Use of Eminent Domain—In General

In addition to the police power—which is exercised in a variety of ways, including through zoning, as discussed in the prior chapter—municipalities ordinarily enjoy the power of eminent domain—the power to acquire property by condemnation. Where municipal action against private property is found to have exceeded the limits of mere police power regulation and to have become a full-fledged "taking" of property, the action may nonetheless be sustained—but only under the eminent domain power, with such limitations (including the compensation requirement) as are attached to that power. The power of eminent domain is not inherent in municipalities and exists in them only to the extent it has been delegated by the state—through state constitution, statute, or home-rule charter.[1] Any grant of this authority to local governments is often said to be strictly

[1] Harden v. Superior Court, 44 Cal.2d 630, 284 P.2d 9 (1955); In re Armory Site in Kansas City, 282 S.W.2d 464 (Mo.1955); City of Tacoma v. Welcker, 65 Wn.2d 677, 399 P.2d 330 (1965). Eminent domain is generally considered a matter of state-wide concern; so in cases of conflict between state and city law, state law will prevail; see Chapter 6 *supra*. Not even all *state* agencies have the power of eminent domain—only those to which the legislature has given such power. See State of Texas v. City of Denton, 542 S.W.2d 224 (Tex.Civ.App.1976), refused n. r. e. (North Texas State University lacked power of eminent domain). See generally Epstein, Private Property and the Power of Eminent Domain (Harvard Univ. Press 1985). See also Symposium, Litigating Takings, 34 Ecology L.Q. 291–754 (2007); Symposium, Judicial Takings, 21 Widener L.J. 621–887 (2012); Malloy (ed.), Private Property, Community Development, and Eminent Domain (Ashgate Publ. 2008).

Public utilities often enjoy rights of eminent domain, but—as with municipalities—only those rights granted by statute. See Chalk & Harrison-Fincher, Eminent Domain Power Granted to Private Pipeline Companies Meets With Greater Resistance From Property Owners in Urban Rather Than Rural Areas, 16 Tex. Wesleyan L. Rev. 17 (2009); Kent, Public Utilities, Eminent Domain, and Local Land Use Regulations: Has Texas Found the Proper Balance?, 16 Tex. Wesleyan L. Rev. 29 (2009).

construed;[2] and it is particularly true that a municipality has only such power to condemn land *outside* municipal borders as is *clearly* conferred by the state.[3] Where the municipal power of eminent domain does exist, three main areas of problems may be encountered: (1) When has a taking of some property interest occurred? (2) If such a taking has occurred, have the substantive requirements been met? These requirements are (a) that the taking be for a public use or purpose, (b) that the taking be a matter of necessity, and (c) that the taking be accompanied by payment of fair compensation to the owners of the interest(s) taken. (3) Has the correct procedure—usually prescribed by state constitution and/or statutes—been followed?

§ 19.2 Municipal Use of Eminent Domain—When Does a "Taking" Occur?

Courts have, over the past several decades, been increasingly inclined to find a "taking" of property in various disturbances to the use of that property, so long as the disturbances are substantial in nature. "Taking," it has been observed, includes but is not limited to the *destruction* of property rights.[4] Repeated low-level flights over private land by government aircraft,[5] or governmental acts causing an unnatural amount of

---

As to the history of eminent domain in the United States, see generally Scheiderich, Fraser & Callies (eds.), Eminent Domain: A Handbook of Condemnation Law (State & Local Govt. Section of American Bar Assn. 2011). See also Note, Taking the Courts: A Brief History of Takings Jurisprudence and the Relationship Between State, Federal, and the United States Supreme Courts, 35 Hastings Const. L.Q. 897 (2008).

[2] See Town of Eaton v. Bouslog, 133 Colo. 130, 292 P.2d 343 (1956) (power can never be implied from doubtful language); Beth Medrosh Hagodol v. City of Aurora, 126 Colo. 267, 248 P.2d 732 (1952); Baycol, Inc. v. Downtown Development Authority, 315 So.2d 451 (Fla.1975); Inhabitants of Town of Holliston v. Holliston Water Co., 306 Mass. 17, 27 N.E.2d 194 (1940); City of Des Moines v. Hemenway, 73 Wn.2d 130, 437 P.2d 171 (1968). Even if the power of eminent domain exists in local governments, it is often subject to limitations: a local government, for instance, usually cannot condemn property already being put to some public use. See 26 Am.Jur.2d Eminent Domain §§ 88–96 (1966); Annot., Eminent Domain: Right to Condemn Property Owned or Used by Private Educational, Charitable, or Religious Organization, 80 A.L.R.3d 833 (1977), noting that the limitation on taking property already put to public use generally applies only against local units, not against the state, and that private educational and charitable institutions are usually found *not* to be devoting their property to "public use" in this sense. *Id.* at 838.

[3] See City of Des Moines v. Hemenway, *supra* note 2. Cf. City of Phoenix v. Harnish, 214 Ariz. 158, 150 P.3d 245 (App. 2006) (city was not authorized by statute to exercise its eminent domain power outside its boundaries solely to establish nature preserve). But see Town of Telluride v. San Miguel Valley Corp., 185 P.3d 161 (Colo. 2008) (home rule article of Colorado constitution grants home rule municipalities the authority to condemn property for open space and park purposes, including property outside their boundaries; statute attempting to take away this power was unconstitutional). See generally Note, E.T., Take Home: The Out-of-This-World Rationale for Extraterritorial Takings and Ignoring Their Inherent Conflict with the Fifth Amendment, 75 U.M.K.C. L. Rev. 943 (2007).

[4] Abend, Federal Liability for Takings and Torts: An Anomalous Relationship, 31 Fordham L.Rev. 481, 491 (1963). See United States v. General Motors Corp., 323 U.S. 373, 378, 65 S.Ct. 357, 89 L.Ed. 311 (1945) ("taking" does not require acquisition of title, or actual occupancy, so long as owner is deprived of some interest or right). See generally Epstein, Takings: Private Property and the Power of Eminent Domain (Harvard Univ. Press 1985), reviewed in Balkin, Learning Nothing and Forgetting Nothing: Richard Epstein and the Takings Clause, 18 Urban Law. 707 (1986). For historical background, see Ely, "That Due Satisfaction May Be Made"—The Fifth Amendment and the Origins of the Compensation Principle, 36 Am. J. Legal History 1 (1992). Compare Ostler, Bills of Attainder and the Formation of the American Takings Clause at the Founding of the Republic, 32 Campbell L. Rev. 227 (2010). See also Christie, A Tale of Three Takings: Taking Analysis in Land Use Regulation in the United States, Australia, and Canada, 32 Brooklyn J. Int'l L. 343 (2007).

[5] Griggs v. Allegheny County, 369 U.S. 84, 82 S.Ct. 531, 7 L.Ed.2d 585 (1962) reh. denied 369 U.S. 857, 82 S.Ct. 931, 8 L.Ed.2d 16 (1962) (flights in and out of government-operated airport); United States v. Causby, 328 U.S. 256, 66 S.Ct. 1062, 90 L.Ed. 1206 (1946) (low-level flights over private land by government aircraft). See Town of East Haven v. Eastern Airlines, Inc., 470 F.2d 148 (2d Cir.1972), cert. denied 411 U.S. 965, 93 S.Ct. 2144, 36 L.Ed.2d 685 (compensation awarded for taking of easements for flights over plaintiffs'

foraging of the land by wildlife,[6] may be held to constitute a taking. Some appropriation *or* destruction of a property interest is required, not merely an expense or injury to the owner.[7] But the courts have also expanded what is considered a "property interest" for the taking of which compensation must be paid. Such a compensable interest has been found to have been taken where a person has lost an equitable servitude or restrictive

---

property in connection with operation of city-owned airport; on payment, city would acquire permanent easements for operation of similar number of flights by planes such as were in use at time of trial). For a "taking" to be found, the traditional view requires some actual "trespass" to the air-space directly *over* the property allegedly taken by the governmental flights or airport operations. Batten v. United States, 306 F.2d 580 (10th Cir.1962), cert. denied 371 U.S. 955, 83 S.Ct. 506, 9 L.Ed.2d 502, reh. denied 372 U.S. 925, 83 S.Ct. 718, 9 L.Ed.2d 731; Louisville & Jefferson County Air Board v. Porter, 397 S.W.2d 146 (Ky.1965); Ferguson v. City of Keene, 108 N.H. 409, 238 A.2d 1 (1968). But a few courts have now allowed "inverse condemnation" actions where there were no direct overflights but there were flights sufficiently close to create a nuisance. Thornburg v. Port of Portland, 233 Or. 178, 376 P.2d 100 (1962); Martin v. Port of Seattle, 64 Wn.2d 309, 391 P.2d 540 (1964), cert. denied 379 U.S. 989, 85 S.Ct. 701, 13 L.Ed.2d 610. It may be generalized that there can be recovery for disturbances by aircraft if (1) there are flights directly over plaintiff's property, and (2) there is substantial interference with plaintiff's property interests. And in some jurisdictions, requirement no. (1) is eliminated if the disturbances are sufficient to constitute a legal "nuisance." See Baxter, Legal Aspects of Airport Noise, 15 J.L. & Econ. 1 (1972). See generally Netherton, Implementation of Land Use Policy: Police Power v. Eminent Domain, 3 Land & Water L.Rev. 33 (1968). See also Berger, You Know I Can't Hear You When the Planes Are Flying, 4 Urban Law. 1 (1972); Comment, Air Law, The Federal Aviation Act of 1958, 57 Mich.L.Rev. 1214 (1959). In Air Pegasus of D.C., Inc., v. United States, 424 F.3d 1206 (Fed. Cir. 2005), it was held that a heliport operation does not have a cognizable property interest in the navigable airspace above its business sufficient to support a Fifth Amendment takings claim. The plaintiff here did not own or operate any helicopters of its own, but derived its income from letting owners and operators of helicopters use the airspace above the heliport. Therefore, the court determined that plaintiff was asking for compensation for the taking of other people's property in the right to use the heliport, not the taking of its own property.

On "inverse condemnation," see generally notes 13–24 *infra* and accompanying text.

[6] State v. Herwig, 17 Wis.2d 442, 117 N.W.2d 335 (1962). Cf. Arkansas Game & Fish Comm'n v. United States, 568 U.S. ___, 133 S.Ct. 511, 184 L.Ed.2d 417 (2012) (recurrent floodings by U.S. government, even if of finite duration, may be compensable "takings" if they require property owner to sacrifice all economically beneficial uses of land; temporary government-induced flooding enjoys no automatic exemption from Takings Clause of U.S. Constitution); Sharp v. Drainage District, 164 Ark. 306, 261 S.W. 923 (1924) (flooding of property is a taking); H.A. Bosworth & Son, Inc. v. Tamiola, 24 Conn.Sup. 328, 190 A.2d 506 (1963) (draining of plaintiff's land onto defendant's would be a taking); State v. Johnson, 265 A.2d 711 (Me.1970) (restricting the filling of wetlands); Bino v. Hurley, 273 Wis. 10, 76 N.W.2d 571 (1956) (preventing owners of lakeside property from bathing in lake). But cf. Jackson v. United States, 230 U.S. 1, 33 S.Ct. 1011, 57 L.Ed. 1363 (1913) (no taking where Mississippi River flooded land, allegedly due to increased overflow caused by levees built by state and federal authorities); Rowe v. City of Temple, 510 S.W.2d 173 (Tex.Civ.App.1974) (disconnection of sewer line caused backup of sewage into house; no taking because no intent—was only negligence).

[7] See More-Way North Corp. v. State Highway Commission, 44 Wis.2d 165, 170 N.W.2d 749 (1969) (no taking where lowering the grade of highway necessitated plaintiff's reconstructing parking lot and losing some parking places). Cf. Goldblatt v. Town of Hempstead, 369 U.S. 590, 82 S.Ct. 987, 8 L.Ed.2d 130 (1962) (no taking where ordinance regulated amount of dredging and excavating, even though this might prevent continuation of previously lawful business); Wisconsin Power & Light Co. v. Columbia County, 3 Wis.2d 1, 87 N.W.2d 279 (1958) (no taking where gravel deposited close to tower, causing it to tilt). See also Brown v. Town of Corinth, 515 S.W.2d 722 (Tex.Civ.App.1974) (loss of business cannot be sole item of damage, must be some taking of property right—recovery denied for "inverse condemnation").

covenant through governmental action,[8] or has lost water rights[9] or paving assessment liens.[10] There is a property right of ingress to, and egress from, one's real property; and thus if access is cut off by governmental action, compensation must be paid.[11] Even if

---

[8] The majority view requires compensation where such an interest is taken. See United States v. Certain Land, 220 F.Supp. 696 (D.Me.1963); City of Phoenix v. South Bank Corp., 133 Ariz. 90, 649 P.2d 293 (App.1982) (compensation must be paid for taking right of entry coupled with right to remove sand and gravel and right to have equipment on the property); Comment, Real Property—Compensation for Abrogation of a Restrictive Covenant by Public Authority, 53 Mich.L.Rev. 451 (1955). Cf. Castor v. City of Minneapolis, 429 N.W.2d 244 (Minn.1988) (compensation must be paid where government has destroyed property owner's easement of air, light, and view, as by construction of public skyway over alley). See generally Annot., Eminent Domain—Restrictive Covenant or Right to Enforcement Thereof as Compensable Property Right, 4 A.L.R.3d 1137 (1965). See also Annot., Existence of Restrictive Covenant as Element in Fixing Value of Property Condemned, 22 A.L.R.3d 961 (1968). A possible problem under the majority view is that a landowner might enter into a restrictive agreement as soon as a government project in his area was announced, and the owner of the servitude could then claim compensation from the government. See Arkansas State Highway Commission v. McNeill, 238 Ark. 244, 381 S.W.2d 425 (1964). The minority view is illustrated by Friesen v. City of Glendale, 209 Cal. 524, 288 P. 1080 (1930). Where compensation is awarded for property subject to a restrictive covenant or comparable interest, the value of the entire fee simple is normally determined first and this amount is then apportioned among the owners of the fee, covenant, etc. See Morley v. Jackson Redev. Auth., 632 So.2d 1284 (Miss.1994). Cf. Leigh v. Village of Los Lunas, 137 N.M. 119, 108 P.3d 525 (App. 2004) (landowners in subdivision found to have action against village for decline in the value of their property where village built drainage pond that violated subdivision's restrictive covenants). The owner of a tenancy-at-will has been held to have no right to share in the lessor-property-owner's condemnation award. Oklahoma Transp. Auth. v. Tulsa Kampground, Inc., 57 P.3d 141 (Okla.Civ.App. 2002). But see Ward v. Downtown Dev. Auth., 786 F.2d 1526 (11th Cir. 1986) (where tenancy-at-will is recognized as a property interest under state law, a taking of the interest is compensable when tenants are displaced by the redevelopment). On compensation for tenancies in general, see note 98 *infra* (compensation usually allowed).

[9] See City & County of Denver v. Sheriff, 105 Colo. 193, 96 P.2d 836 (1939) (under appropriation system of water rights); City of New Britain v. Sargent, 42 Conn. 137 (1875) (under riparian system of water rights). Cf. Frost v. Ponca City, 541 P.2d 1321 (Okl.1975) (right to capture hydrocarbons underlying land held a valuable property interest; city must account to landowners when it removed the hydrocarbons and sold them). But cf. In re The Adjudication of the Water Rights of Upper Guadalupe Segment, 642 S.W.2d 438 (Tex.1982) (termination of rights of riparian owners, on notice and reasonable terms, to water not beneficially used during any one of the 5 years of the test period, is not an unconstitutional taking). See generally Note, Acquisition of a Water Supply by Right of Eminent Domain, 58 L.R.A. 240 (1903). See also Shepard, The Unbearable Cost of Skipping the Check: Property Rights Takings Compensation & Ecological Protection in the Western Water Law Context, 17 N.Y.U. Envtl. L.J. 1063 (2009); Report of 13th Annual Conference on Litigating Regulatory Takings Challenges to Land Use and Environmental Regulations, 38 Ecology L.J. 619–748 (2011); Annot., Diversion: Propriety of Injunctive Relief Against Diversion of Water by Municipal Corporation or Public Utility, 42 A.L.R.3d 426 (1972).

[10] Swatek v. Board of Regents, 535 P.2d 295 (Okl.1975). The holder of a mortgage has a compensable interest therein. See Western Fertilizer & Cordage Co. v. City of Alliance, 244 Neb. 95, 504 N.W.2d 808 (1993) (mortgagee could assert inverse condemnation claims).

Trade secrets have been held, despite their intangible nature, to be protected against takings without compensation. Ruckelshaus v. Monsanto Co., 467 U.S. 986, 104 S.Ct. 2862, 81 L.Ed.2d 815 (1984). Cf. Palm Beach County v. Cove Club Investors Ltd., 734 So.2d 379 (Fla.1999) (country club's right to collect recreational fee is compensable property right).

[11] State ex rel. State Highway Department v. 14.69 Acres of Land, 226 A.2d 828 (Del.1967). But cf. Osborne v. City of Manhattan, 244 Kan. 107, 765 P.2d 1100 (1988) (landowner has right of reasonable access to an adjoining road or street but not a right to access at every point where the land touches the right-of-way; owners who had been using the street right-of-way as an extension of their own property were not entitled, on city's condemnation of their right of access, to compensation for loss of access at every point but only for loss of reasonable access). See generally Stoebuck, The Property Right of Access Versus the Power of Eminent Domain, 47 Tex.L.Rev. 733 (1969). See also Kau Take Home No. 1 v. City of Wichita, 281 Kan. 1185, 135 P.3d 1221 (2006), cert. denied 549 U.S. 1265, 127 S.Ct. 1495, 167 L.Ed.2d 229 (2007) (when the government actually blocks or takes away existing access to and from property, the landowner is generally entitled to compensation; but the mere regulation of traffic flow does not involve a taking if it furthers a police-power purpose). Compare, as to a situation involving physical damage to property, Estate of Kirkpatrick v. City of Olathe, 289 Kan. 554, 215 P.3d 561 (2009) (city's building of roundabout allegedly caused flooding and cracking of landowner's

access remains but is materially reduced, compensation is often now required for the burden of circuitous travel if this substantially affects the land value.[12]

Increasingly—either under statutory provisions or judicial expansion of the concept of "takings of property interests"—compensation is being required, in suits brought by property owners, wherever there is a substantial *"invasion"* of property rights of such

---

basement; such damage can amount to a "taking" under Kansas law and is thus compensable in inverse condemnation action).

If a landowner is required to dedicate a right-of-way to the government as a condition of obtaining a building permit, there is authority that compensation must be paid or else an unconstitutional "taking" occurs. See Roberts v. City of Bethany, 668 P.2d 350 (Okl.App. 1977), opinion modified 668 P.2d 332 (Okl.1979). See generally note 24 *infra* and accompanying text.

[12] See Breidert v. Southern Pacific Co., 61 Cal.2d 659, 39 Cal.Rptr. 903, 394 P.2d 719 (1964). Palm Beach County v. Tessler, 538 So.2d 846 (Fla.1989) (owners of commercial property located on major public roadways were entitled to compensation where county blocked access to these properties from the major roadway); Department of Transp. v. Harkey, 308 N.C. 148, 301 S.E.2d 64 (1983) (landowner entitled to compensation for loss of direct access to abutting highway, even though alternative routes to the highway remained available). Cf. McCracken v. City of Philadelphia, 69 Pa.Cmwlth. 492, 451 A.2d 1046 (1982) (cumulative effect of street closings, removal of street lights, constant presence of heavy-duty vehicles, etc. found to be a de facto taking). See generally Note, The Landowner's Right of Access to the Abutting Street—A Damaging for the Public Use, 20 Sw.L.J. 393 (1966); Annot., Abutting Owner's Right to Damages for Limitation of Access Caused by Traffic Regulation, 15 A.L.R.5th 821 (1993). But compensation has been denied in many such cases because of lack of substantial harm and/or because the circuitry of travel is considered not a special burden, but one shared by the general public. See State of Idaho Transp. Bd. v. HI Boise, LLC, 282 P.3d 595 (Idaho 2012) (no compensable taking where right of access to public streets is not destroyed or substantially impaired); Cavanaugh v. Gerk, 313 Mo. 375, 280 S.W. 51 (1926); Lindley v. Oklahoma Turnpike Authority, 262 P.2d 159 (Okl.1953). Thus, if an owner abuts two streets, it may be ruled that there is no taking where access to one street is cut off, but reasonable access via the other street remains. See City of San Antonio v. Pigeonhole Parking, 158 Tex. 318, 311 S.W.2d 218 (1958). Cf. State v. Kimco of Evansville, Inc. 902 N.E.2d 206 (Ind. 2009), cert. denied, 558 U.S. 1147, 130 S.Ct. 1136, 175 L.Ed.2d 971 (2010) (street reconfigurations that affected the traffic flow through a shopping center and prevented expansion of the existing points of ingress and egress but left the existing points in place did not constitute a compensable taking); City of Salem v. Merritt Truax, Inc., 70 Or.App. 138, 688 P.2d 120 (1984) (closing of one of three driveways leading to service station held not a compensable taking even though it was a permanent change and made access to the station less convenient); Boese v. City of Salem, 40 Or.App. 381, 595 P.2d 822 (1979) (owners had adequate access to their property from another street). See generally Comment, Eminent Domain—Damages—Recovery for Interference with the Right of Access, 18 S.Cal. L.Rev. 42 (1944). It is also usually agreed that compensation need not be paid for interference-with-access that is of short duration, as during construction on a public road. See Hill v. State Highway Commission, 85 N.M. 689, 516 P.2d 199 (1973) (no compensation since interference not shown to have been unnecessary, unreasonable, arbitrary, or unduly prolonged). See generally Annot., Damages Resulting from Temporary Conditions Incident to Public Improvements or Repairs as Compensable Taking, 23 A.L.R.4th 674 (1983). On the tendency of some courts to make it difficult for landowners to receive compensation for loss of access, see Montague, The Circuitous Route Taken to Deny Property Owners Damages in Access Cases: Where Has All the Fairness Gone?, 32 Urban Law. 523 (2000).

magnitude that the owner is deprived of practical enjoyment of his property.[13] This is the so-called doctrine of "inverse condemnation" or "reverse condemnation."[14]

---

[13] See Holtz v. Superior Court, 3 Cal.3d 296, 90 Cal.Rptr. 345, 475 P.2d 441 (1970) (excavations made by city and county caused damage to plaintiffs' property); Albers v. County of Los Angeles, 62 Cal.2d 250, 42 Cal.Rptr. 89, 398 P.2d 129 (1965) (landslide caused by county's construction of road); Rose v. State, 19 Cal.2d 713, 123 P.2d 505 (1942); Kirkpatrick v. City of Jacksonville, 312 So.2d 487 (Fla.App.1975) (cause of action in inverse condemnation stated where plaintiff's buildings demolished); Albert v. City of Mountain Home, 81 Idaho 74, 337 P.2d 377 (1959) (building demolished as public nuisance; this determination later found to be mistaken); Alevizos v. Metropolitan Airports Commission, 298 Minn. 471, 216 N.W.2d 651 (1974) (property owner could maintain inverse condemnation action against government operating airport if could show deprivation of enjoyment of property and loss in market value). But cf. HFH, Ltd. v. Superior Court of Los Angeles County, 15 Cal.3d 508, 125 Cal.Rptr. 365, 542 P.2d 237 (1975), cert. denied 425 U.S. 904, 96 S.Ct. 1495, 47 L.Ed.2d 754 (1976) (zoning regulation not a taking; property owner's interest in his land is subordinate to interests of society, and some uncompensated hardships are price of living in a modern, enlightened, and progressive community); Nestle v. City of Santa Monica, 6 Cal.3d 920, 101 Cal.Rptr. 568, 496 P.2d 480 (1972) (city's operation of airport alleged to cause bothersome noise; inverse condemnation remedy rejected because of lack of evidence of reduction in property values, but possible nuisance action recognized); Fred F. French Investing Co. v. City of New York, 39 N.Y.2d 587, 385 N.Y.S.2d 5, 350 N.E.2d 381 (1976), cert. denied 429 U.S. 990, 97 S.Ct. 515, 50 L.Ed.2d 602 (no taking where government merely regulates land; only remedy is to have the regulation declared invalid); Brown v. Town of Corinth, *supra* note 7 (no recovery for inverse condemnation merely because city began offering water and sewer services in competition with plaintiffs' business). See generally Meltz, Merriam & Frank, The Takings Issue—Constitutional Limits on Land-Use Control and Environmental Regulation (Island Press 1999). See also Vokoun v. City of Lake Oswego, 335 Or. 19, 56 P.3d 396 (2002) (plaintiff in a taking action is not required to show the government deprived him of *all* use and enjoyment of property; a substantial interference with use and enjoyment suffices, but there also must have been intent to take the property). As to pleadings and procedure in "takings" cases, see Comment, Rethinking the Facial Takings Claim, 120 Yale L.J. 967 (2011). See generally Symposium, Litigating Takings and Other Legal Challenges to Land Use and Environmental Regulation, 28 Stan. Envtl. L.J. 397–612 (2009).

[14] See Agins v. City of Tiburon, 447 U.S. 255, 100 S.Ct. 2138, 65 L.Ed.2d 106 (1980), noted 12 Urban Lawyer 608–12 (1980). This remedy is based on the Just Compensation Clause of the Fifth Amendment of the United States Constitution, which applies to the states through the 14th Amendment. The requirement of compensation is regarded as self-executing, thus authorizing suit by the person whose property-interest is invaded. In addition, most state constitutions have similar provisions forbidding the taking of property without just compensation—and sometimes going farther and providing for compensation where property is merely "damaged" by the state. The "inverse condemnation" action avoids problems of governmental immunity that may arise if a tort action is brought against the state or a local unit. The action is called "inverse" or "reverse" because it is brought by the private person who alleges his interest has been invaded, rather than being initiated by the governmental unit in an avowed effort to take the property—the owner alleges that the government has in effect "taken" his property but without initiating the condemnation proceedings necessary to such action. See United States v. Clarke, 445 U.S. 253, 100 S.Ct. 1127, 63 L.Ed.2d 373 (1980), discussing nature of inverse condemnation and holding that state or local government could not acquire by inverse condemnation lands allotted to Indians; Mattoon v. City of Norman, 617 P.2d 1347 (Okl.1980) (question of whether there has been sufficient interference with landowner's use and enjoyment to constitute a "taking" is one of fact). See generally Mandelker, Inverse Condemnation: The Constitutional Limits of Public Responsibility, 1966 Wis.L.Rev. 3; Van Alstyne, Inverse Condemnation: Unintended Physical Damage, 20 Hastings L.J. 431 (1969); Van Alstyne, Statutory Modification of Inverse Condemnation: The Scope of Legislative Power, 19 Stan.L.Rev. 727 (1967); Note, Property—Inverse Condemnation: A Growing Problem, 3 Tulsa L.J. 169 (1966). See also Foster, Tort Liability Under Damage Clauses, 5 Okl.L.Rev. 1 (1952). On the difference between the compensation requirement in cases of actual "taking" and the requirement in situations of mere damage, see Note, Air Easement: Oklahoma Adopts the Trespass-Nuisance Dichotomy, 8 Tulsa L.J. 138, 140 (1972). See generally Shearer, The Measure of Damages in "Inverse Condemnation" Cases, 25 Urban Law. 841 (1993). See also Regency Outdoor Advertising, Inc., v. City of Los Angeles, 39 Cal.4th 507, 46 Cal.Rptr.3d 742, 139 P.3d 119 (2006) (inverse condemnation plaintiff does not establish a "taking" merely by showing that government action has somewhat decreased the market value of property; thus, mere impairment of visibility of advertising company's billboards from street, caused by city's planting of palm trees along roadway, was not compensable); Material Serv. Corp. v. Rogers County Comm'rs, 136 P.3d 1063 (Okla.Civ.App. 2006) (inverse condemnation requires a substantial impairment of property's usefulness, resulting from overt governmental act amounting to an assertion of dominion and control over property; whether annexation and

zoning of land substantially impaired mining company's lease so as to amount to a taking of private property was genuine issue of fact).

Compensation has generally not been required where governmental destruction of property has occurred under emergency conditions, such as war or natural disaster. United States v. Caltex, Inc., 344 U.S. 149, 73 S.Ct. 200, 97 L.Ed. 157 (1952), reh'g denied 344 U.S. 919, 73 S.Ct. 345, 97 L.Ed. 708 (1953) (oil terminal and storage facilities destroyed in face of advancing enemy army); Miller v. Schoene, 276 U.S. 272, 48 S.Ct. 246, 72 L.Ed. 568 (1928) (statute required destruction of infected cedar trees to prevent spread of rust to apple orchards; upheld despite lack of compensation); Brewer v. State of Alaska, 341 P.3d 1107 (Alaska 2014) (under doctrine of necessity, no right to compensation to landowners whose property was set on fire by firefighters to prevent spread of wildfire); House v. Los Angeles County Flood Control District, 25 Cal.2d 384, 153 P.2d 950 (1944). On the cases arising from warfare, see Note, Constitutional Law—Under the Fifth Amendment, the Government Is Not Obliged to Pay for Property Destroyed to Prevent Its Use to the Enemy, 41 Geo.L.J. 422 (1953); Note, Constitutional Law—Eminent Domain—War Claims, 27 N.Y.U.L.Rev. 503 (1952). See generally Van Alstyne, Statutory Modification of Inverse Condemnation: Deliberately Inflicted Injury or Destruction, 20 Stan.L.Rev. 617 (1968). Cases denying compensation where the government has destroyed property because of an emergency often rely on the "public necessity" defense of tort law, but this has been criticized as inappropriate to such cases and out-of-line with the general trend toward compensation for all government "takings." See Reynolds, Is "Public Necessity" Necessary?, 29 Okl.L.Rev. 861 (1976). See generally Mandelker, Inverse Condemnation, *supra* at 7–8. See also Inama v. Boise County, 138 Idaho 324, 63 P.3d 450 (2003) (provision of state Disaster Preparedness Act granting immunity to political subdivisions for damage to property resulting from disaster relief operations was intended by legislature to codify a version of public necessity doctrine).

Some jurisdictions are reluctant to recognize inverse condemnation actions unless the government has actually taken possession of plaintiff's property. See State ex rel. Department of Highways v. Cook, 542 P.2d 1405 (Okl.1975) (no action if no physical taking of property). Compare State ex rel. Department of Transportation v. Hoebel, 594 P.2d 1213 (Okl.1979) (flooding may justify action in inverse condemnation). Cf., all finding possible inverse condemnation actions for flooding, Marty v. State, 117 Idaho 133, 786 P.2d 524 (1989), appeal after remand 122 Idaho 766, 838 P.2d 1384 (1992) (possible inverse condemnation claim stated by owners of flooded farmland); Corbell v. State ex rel. Department of Transp., 856 P.2d 575 (Okla.App. 1993) (Department of Transportation's actions in replacing culvert, causing flooding, constituted taking of property); Hawkins v. City of La Grande, 315 Or. 57, 843 P.2d 400 (1992) (test for inverse condemnation does not involve counting the number of floods but determining whether there has been flooding that destroys or materially decreases value of private property; livestock killed and crops destroyed by government action are permanently "taken" so as to require compensation). But it is now generally agreed that physical occupation is not essential to an inverse condemnation action. See Martino v. Santa Clara Valley Water Dist., 703 F.2d 1141 (9th Cir.1983), cert. denied 464 U.S. 847, 104 S.Ct. 151, 78 L.Ed.2d 141 (1983) (physical invasion is not necessary for a "taking" to occur when public entity excessively delays in a condemnation proceeding or otherwise acts unreasonably); Oxley v. City of Tulsa, 794 P.2d 742 (Okl.1989), cert. denied 493 U.S. 1077, 110 S.Ct. 1128, 107 L.Ed.2d 1034 (1990) (jury question whether interference with property by noise, odors, and fumes from airport was sufficiently substantial to constitute fee simple taking).

It has been held that a governmental agency may be liable in inverse condemnation for a "taking" even though it lacks the power of eminent domain. Fountain v. Metropolitan Atlanta Rapid Transit Auth., 678 F.2d 1038 (11th Cir.1982). A "taking" does require some direct governmental action against the property and has not been found, for instance, where a city orders tenants temporarily to vacate their leaseholds due to housing code violations if the uninhabitability of the premises has resulted from either landlord or tenant action, not state action. Devines v. Maier, 728 F.2d 876 (7th Cir.1984), cert. denied 469 U.S. 836, 105 S.Ct. 130, 83 L.Ed.2d 71 (1984). In general, inverse condemnation is the appropriate remedy wherever a condemning authority takes or harms property without paying just compensation or without initiating the proper proceedings to condemn; but if the condemner simply takes more land than is reasonably necessary, or causes excessive damage by the manner in which the taking occurs, a trespass action may lie. See North v. Public Serv. Co. of New Mexico, 101 N.M. 222, 680 P.2d 603 (App. 1983), cert. quashed 101 N.M. 11, 677 P.2d 624 (1984). Compare McCracken v. City of Lawton, 648 P.2d 18 (Okl.1982) (immunity from tort liability attaches to city's legislative actions, but city is nonetheless liable for takings of property). Cf. Sullivant v. Oklahoma City, 940 P.2d 220 (Okl.1997) (takings claim cannot be used to recover for tortious actions of government employees, and proper exercise of police power is not a "taking").

It has been held that a claim for inverse condemnation accrues after the full extent of the impairment of plaintiff's use and enjoyment of the property becomes apparent and that it is not necessary for the landowner to seek a variance before pursuing the inverse condemnation claim. See City of Coeur D'Alene v. Simpson, 142 Idaho 839, 136 P.3d 310 (2006). Cf. Smith v. Board of County Comm'rs of Park County, 291 P.3d 947 (Wyo. 2013) (period of limitations for bringing inverse condemnation action is general limitations period for civil actions other than actions for recovery of real property). As to whether a purchaser may challenge a land use

The line between mere police-power restrictions on property (which are noncompensable) and eminent-domain takings of property (which are compensable) can be hard to draw, and various tests have been proposed. Some early authority required compensation only if a substantial interference with property interests occurred.[15] Later, the amount of diminution in property value was considered all-important;[16] building on this idea, most modern cases look to the amount of economic harm and find a taking if property values are greatly diminished[17] but not if the harm is slight—at least if there

---

restriction as a "taking" when the purchaser's property was already impaired by the restriction at the time of purchase, see Brown, Taking the Takings Claim: A Policy and Economic Analysis of the Survival of Takings Claims After Property Transfers, 36 Conn. L. Rev. 7 (2003) ("although the event of the property transfer should not limit or eliminate the takings claim, the determination of compensation will undoubtedly consider the amount paid by the successive interest holder for the property"; *id.* at 73).

Inverse condemnation may be a remedy where a zoning ordinance results in substantial damage to property. See Comment, "Takings" Under the Police Power—The Development of Inverse Condemnation as a Method of Challenging Zoning Ordinances, 30 Sw.L.J. 723 (1976). Under such a remedy, a landowner alleges his property was "taken" due to the zoning law and thus that he was entitled to compensation—rather than simply alleging the zoning law was *invalid* as beyond the scope of the police power. See generally the discussion of regulatory taking *infra* this section.

[15] See Martin v. Port of Seattle, 64 Wash.2d 309, 391 P.2d 540 (1964), cert. denied 379 U.S. 989, 85 S.Ct. 701, 13 L.Ed.2d 610 (1965) (with review of authorities). See also Freund, The Police Power, Public Policy, and Constitutional Rights 546–47 (1904), suggesting that the police power is exercised where a use of property is found harmful to the public, and eminent domain is exercised where the property may be beneficial to the public.

[16] See Pennsylvania Coal Co. v. Mahon, 260 U.S. 393, 43 S.Ct. 158, 67 L.Ed. 322 (1922) (state statute prohibited the mining of coal in a manner that would cause the subsidence of land on which certain structures were located; statute invalidated as an unconstitutional taking without compensation of mine owners' property rights). But in Keystone Bituminous Coal Ass'n v. DeBenedictis, 480 U.S. 470, 107 S.Ct. 1232, 94 L.Ed.2d 472 (1987), noted 21 Creighton L. Rev. 213 (1987–88), 11 Harv. J.L. & Pub. Policy 227 (1988), 33 Wash. U.J. Urban & Contemp. L. 169 (1988), the Court upheld as not a "taking" a Pennsylvania statute requiring that 50% of the coal beneath certain structures be kept in place to provide surface support. The Court stated that the test for a regulatory taking involves comparing the value that has been taken from the property with the value that remains. Here, it was found that the amount of coal required to be left represented only 2% of the coal in the mines, that the evidence indicated that only about 75% of underground coal can be profitably mined anyhow, and that there was no evidence that petitioners' mining operations, or even any specific mines, had been rendered unprofitable by the regulation. The *Pennsylvania Coal Co. v. Mahon* case *supra* was distinguished on the grounds that (1) the statute there involved was enacted solely for the benefit of private parties, while this statute served genuine public interests, and (2) the record in the earlier case had indicated, unlike the record here, that the statute there challenged made it impossible for petitioners to engage profitably in their mining business. It has also been suggested that compensation should be paid whenever a governmental act enhances the economic value of government enterprises to the detriment of private interests. Sax, Takings and the Police Power, 74 Yale L.J. 36 (1964). But the author later modified this view somewhat. Sax, Takings, Private Property and Public Rights, 81 Yale L.J. 149 (1971). The question of whether or not a taking has occurred has often arisen in connection with subdivision controls. See Reps & Smith, Control of Urban Land Subdivision, 14 Syracuse L.Rev. 405 (1963). See generally Heyman & Gilhool, The Constitutionality of Imposing Increased Community Costs on New Suburban Residents Through Subdivision Exactions, 73 Yale L.J. 1119 (1964). See also Section 21.4 *infra*.

[17] See Nectow v. City of Cambridge, 277 U.S. 183, 48 S.Ct. 447, 72 L.Ed. 842 (1928) (zoning ordinance struck down as beyond scope of police power where plaintiff's land found to have comparatively little value for the uses that would have been permitted); Arverne Bay Construction Co. v. Thatcher, 278 N.Y. 222, 15 N.E.2d 587 (1938). Cf. Benners v. City of University Park, 477 S.W.2d 326 (Tex.Civ.App.1972) (amortization provision invalid where property would be greatly reduced in value after termination of nonconforming use, was thus unreasonable exercise of city's police power). But cf. Consolidated Rock Prod. Co. v. City of Los Angeles, 57 Cal.2d 515, 20 Cal.Rptr. 638, 370 P.2d 342 (1962), appeal dism'd 371 U.S. 36, 83 S.Ct. 145, 9 L.Ed.2d 112 (1962); West Brothers Brick Co. v. City of Alexandria, 169 Va. 271, 192 S.E. 881 (1937), appeal dism'd 302 U.S. 658, 58 S.Ct. 369, 82 L.Ed. 508, reh. denied, 302 U.S. 781, 58 S.Ct. 480, 82 L.Ed. 603 (1938), both sustaining zoning ordinances that prohibited certain mining operations on the property involved, despite considerable resulting loss (especially in the former case) in property value. Some authority clearly endorses the view that a land-use regulation amounts to an unconstitutional taking *only* if its effect is to deprive the landowner of substantially all reasonable use of his property, not if it merely reduces the value of the property. See Griffin

is also an absence of actual physical invasion.[18] Some states have broader requirements as to when, and how much, compensation must be paid for harm done by land regulations. For instance, in 2004, voters in Oregon approved "Measure 37," which requires either payment of "lost value" of real property due to land regulations or, alternatively, waiver of those regulations, if the regulations were enacted after acquisition of the property by the "present owner."[19] The constitutionality of "Measure 37" was upheld by the Oregon Supreme Court.[20] Similar ballot measures requiring compensation for regulatory takings and, often, for less extreme situations of "lost value" have now appeared in other states.[21] Such zoning-type restrictions as ordinances against building on flood-plains will be held not to give rise to an obligation to compensate if the property's usefulness and value (though perhaps reduced) remain to some considerable degree intact.[22] But if no practical use for the property is left, a "taking" has occurred for which compensation must be paid.[23]

Dev. Co. v. City of Oxnard, 39 Cal.3d 256, 217 Cal.Rptr. 1, 703 P.2d 339 (1985) (city's denial of a special use permit for conversion of apartments to condominiums was not a confiscatory taking since building owner was free to continue renting-out the apartments, and this was a reasonable use of the property). Compare Hall v. City of Santa Barbara, 797 F.2d 1493 (9th Cir.1986), cert. denied 485 U.S. 940, 108 S.Ct. 1120, 99 L.Ed.2d 281 (1988) (mobile home rent-control ordinance could constitute a taking).

[18] Sayre v. City of Cleveland, 493 F.2d 64 (6th Cir.1974), cert. denied 419 U.S. 837, 95 S.Ct. 65, 42 L.Ed.2d 64. See Goldblatt v. Town of Hempstead, *supra* note 7. It has also been observed that courts are less likely to require compensation if restrictions are imposed on land uses that are often considered nuisances or quasi-nuisances—and courts are also less likely to require payment where restrictions are part of a regional plan. Bosselman, et al., The Taking Issue 322–23 (Council on Environmental Quality 1973). See also Michaelman, Property, Utility, and Fairness: Comment on Ethical Foundations of "Just Condemnation" Law, 80 Harv.L.Rev. 1165 (1967).

[19] See Sullivan, Year Zero: The Aftermath of Measure 37, 38 Urban Law. 237 (2006). See generally Clune, Government Hardly Could Go on: Oregon's Measure 37, Implications for Land Use Planning and a More Rational Means of Compensation, 38 Urban Law. 275 (2006), advocating a system in which land use regulations which *increase* property values would allow the legislating government to recapture the value of the increase, which would otherwise be a windfall to the property owner. This would then create a fund from which payments, such as required by Measure 37 or similar measures, could be paid for *decreases* in value caused by land regulations. Compare, analyzing a voter-passed initiative enacted in Arizona (Proposition 207) that is similar to Oregon's "Measure 37," Sparks, Land Use Regulation in Arizona After the Private Property Rights Protection Act, 51 Ariz. L. Rev. 211 (2009).

[20] MacPherson v. Department of Administrative Servs., 340 Or. 117, 130 P.3d 308 (2006). In 2007, Oregon voters approved "Measure 49," which altered the remedies and procedures available under "Measure 37." As to the changes made by this initiative, see State ex rel. English v. Multnomah County, 348 Or. 417, 238 P.3d 980 (2010), affirming 231 Or. App. 286, 219 P.3d 594 (2009). See generally Potapov, Making Regulatory Takings Reform Work: The Lessons of Oregon's Measure 37, 39 Envtl. L. Rep. News & Analysis 10516 (2009).

[21] See Salkin & Lavine, Measure 37 and a Spoonful of *Kelo*: A Recipe for Property Rights Activists at the Ballot Box, 38 Urban Law. 1065 (2006), giving a national overview of these ballot initiatives and noting that the broad judicial view of governmental power of eminent domain—as exemplified by the *Kelo* case, discussed in Section 12.6, note 17, *infra*—has helped fuel this movement. See also Jacobs, The Future of the Regulatory Takings Issue in the United States and Europe: Divergence or Convergence?, 40 Urban Law. 51 (2008), predicting (at 64) that courts will continue to be hesitant to provide a clear test for delineating regulation that goes too far (and becomes a compensable "taking") from regulation that does not, though property rights advocates will continue to seek a bright-line test.

[22] See Candlestick Properties, Inc. v. San Francisco Bay Conservation & Development Commission, 11 Cal.App.3d 557, 89 Cal.Rptr. 897 (1970); Turnpike Realty Co. v. Town of Dedham, 362 Mass. 221, 284 N.E.2d 891 (1972), cert. denied 409 U.S. 1108, 93 S.Ct. 908, 34 L.Ed.2d 689 (1973); Fifth Avenue Corp. v. Washington County, 282 Or. 591, 581 P.2d 50 (1978) (owner still had some substantial beneficial use of his property). Cf. Just v. Marinette County, 56 Wis.2d 7, 201 N.W.2d 761 (1972) (shoreline zoning ordinance prohibited changing natural character of land within designated distance from lakes or rivers; not confiscatory).

[23] Dooley v. Town Plan & Zoning Commission, 151 Conn. 304, 197 A.2d 770 (1964). See MacGibbon v. Board of Appeals, 356 Mass. 635, 255 N.E.2d 347 (1970). Cf. Morris County Land Improvement Co. v.

It seems clearly established that when a physical intrusion by the government reaches the extreme form of a permanent physical occupation, a Fifth Amendment taking, for which compensation must be paid, has occurred, regardless of the size of the occupation.[24] An unsettled question for a long time was whether a compensable taking

---

Parsippany-Troy Hills Township, 40 N.J. 539, 193 A.2d 232 (1963) (compensation required if restrictions are for sole benefit of government, at expense of the zoned land). See generally Annot., Supreme Court's Views as to What Constitutes "Taking" Within Meaning of Fifth Amendment's Command That Property Not Be Taken for Public Use Without Just Compensation, 57 L.Ed.2d 1254 (1979). On the various tests used or proposed over the years to determine whether or not a "taking" has occurred, see Humbach, Economic Due Process and the Takings Clause, 4 Pace Envtl. L. Rev. 311 (1987); Lawrence, Regulatory Takings: Beyond the Balancing Test, 20 Urban Law. 389 (1988). See generally Eagle, Regulatory Takings (Michie 1996). A good review of the regulatory-taking cases through 2001 is found in Podolsky, *Palazzolo v. Rhode Island*: Revival of *Penn Central* and Implications for Environmental Regulation, 35 Urban Law. 353 (2003), noting that since the *Palazzolo* ruling, "in the absence of a *per se* taking, the status of investment-back expectations is not dispositive" of regulatory-taking cases. *Id.* at 353. See Section 18.4, notes 33–46, *supra*, and accompanying text. As to the *Palazzolo* case, see note 31, *infra*. As to the need to establish definite standards regarding when a "taking" has occurred, see Holloway & Guy, Weighing the Need to Establish Regulatory Takings Doctrine to Justify Takings Standards of Review and Principles, 34 Wm. & Mary Envtl. L. & Pol'y Rev. 315 (2010). Cf. Moongate Water Co. v. City of Las Cruces, 302 P.3d 405 (N.M. 2013) (in evaluating takings claims under state constitution, court turns to both federal and state cases for guidance; city's provision of water to area previously served by utility did not constitute regulatory taking of utility's property).

[24] Loretto v. Teleprompter Manhattan CATV Corp., 458 U.S. 419, 102 S.Ct. 3164, 73 L.Ed.2d 868 (1982), on remand 58 N.Y.2d 143, 459 N.Y.S.2d 743, 446 N.E.2d 428 (1983), reargument denied 59 N.Y.2d 761, 463 N.Y.S.2d 1030, 450 N.E.2d 254 (1983) (New York law requiring landlord to permit installation of cable television facilities on his rental property held to effect a "taking"). See Howard, Real Property Issues in CATV Use of Public Rights-of-Way and Easements Dedicated for Compatible Use, 23 Urban Law, 413 (1991); Milligan, *Loretto v. Teleprompter Manhattan CATV Corporation*: Another Excursion into the Takings Dilemma, 17 Urban Law. 109 (1985). See generally on "taking" in such situations of government regulations and requirements Franck & Bredesen, Recent Developments in Condemnation Law, 17 Urban Law. 751, 755–63 (1985); Freilich, Solving the "Taking" Equation: Making the Whole Equal the Sum of Its Parts, 15 Urban Law. 447 (1983); Newton & Slattery, The Changing Areas in Condemnation Law, 15 Urban Law. 791 (1983). See also Riva, Regulatory Takings in American Law and "Material Expropriation" in Swiss Law—A Comparison of the Applicable Standards, 16 Urban Law. 425 (1984).

Just as physical occupation, as in the *Loretto* case *supra*, requires compensation, so may a governmentally imposed requirement that a landowner convey to the government or to the public some of the owner's rights in the land. See Nollan v. California Coastal Comm'n, 483 U.S. 825, 107 S.Ct. 3141, 97 L.Ed.2d 677 (1987), noted 17 Golden Gate U.L. Rev. 197 (1987), 11 Harv. J.L. & Pub. Policy 265 (1988), 39 Mercer L. Rev. 1033 (1988), where a state commission imposed, as a condition of approval of a rebuilding permit, the requirement that landowners provide access to the public to pass across their property. This was held to be a taking that required compensation under the Fifth Amendment. See generally Acton, Much Ado About *Nollan*: The Supreme Court Addresses the Complex Network of Property Rights, Land Use Regulations, and Just Compensation in the *Keystone*, *Nollan*, and *First English* Cases, 17 Stetson L. Rev. 727 (1988); Anderson, Takings and Expectations: Toward a "Broader Vision" of Property Rights, 37 Kan. L. Rev. 529 (1989); Callies, Property Rights: Are There Any Left?, 20 Urban Law, 597 (1988); Wenar, The Concept of Property and the Takings Clause, 97 Colum. L. Rev. 1923 (1997) (good review of other writings).

See also Mongeau, Public Beach Access: An Annotated Bibliography, 95 Law Lib. J. 515 (2003): Thompson, Property Theory and Owning the Sandy Shore: No Firm Ground to Stand On, 11 Ocean & Coastal L.J. 47 (2005–06); Comment, Laying Out an "Unwelcome Mat" to Public Beach Access, 18 J. Land Use & Envtl. L. 331 (2003); Comment, The "Public Access Doctrine": Our Constitutional Right to Sun, Surf, and Sand, 11 Ocean & Coastal L.J. 73 (2005–06). Compare Comment, What About My Beach House? A Look at the Takings Issue as Applied to the Texas Open Beaches Act, 40 Houston L. Rev. 119 (2003).

The *Nollan* case *supra* may be looked upon as recognizing a limited exception to the *Loretto* case *supra*: *Nollan* indicates that the state may physically occupy an owner's land without compensation as a condition to granting a development permit if the occupation advances the same purpose as would denial of the permit. But this "nexus" requirement was not satisfied in *Nollan*. See Note, Taking a Step Back: A Reconsideration of the Takings Test of *Nollan v. California Coastal Commission*, 102 Harv. L. Rev. 448 (1988). See generally Kayden, Land-Use Regulations, Rationality, and Judicial Review: The RSVP in the *Nollan* Invitation (Part I), 23 Urban Law. 301 (1991). But *Nollan* may also be more broadly viewed as indicating the Court will apply heightened scrutiny to determine whether the takings clause of the Fifth Amendment requires compensation for reduction in property value caused by a regulation. See Lawrence, Means, Motives, and Takings: The Nexus

---

Test of *Nollan v. California Coastal Commission,* 12 Harv. Envtl. L. Rev. 231 (1988); Sallet, Court Expands "Takings" Clause, Legal Times, Sept. 14, 1987 at 25, col. 1. Cf. Blue Jeans Equities West v. City & County of San Francisco, 3 Cal.App.4th 164, 4 Cal.Rptr.2d 114 (1992), cert. denied, 506 U.S. 866, 113 S.Ct. 191, 121 L.Ed.2d 135 (1992) (*Nollan* heightened scrutiny test applies only to possessory, not regulatory, takings). See generally Eagle, Regulatory Takings (Michie 1996), reviewed 30 Urban Law. 497 (1998). See also Biddle, Justice Stevens' Pro-Land Use Planning Views and Recent Regulatory Takings, 21 Urban Law, 579 (1989). For descriptions of the likely effects of the *Nollan* case, see Crew, Development Agreements After *Nollan v. California Coastal Commission,* 22 Urban Law. 23 (1990); Haar & Kayden, Private v. Public Use, N.Y. Times, July 29, 1987, at A-23, col. 2; "Beach Property Owners Win High Court Ruling," N.Y. Times, June 27, 1987, at A-33, col. 5. With the *Loretto* and *Nollan* cases *supra*, compare Smith v. City of Owatonna, 450 N.W.2d 309 (Minn.1990) (divided court holds that property owners required by a municipally-owned gas company to pay the cost of installing new high-pressure service lines did not have property interests which could be the subject of a due process or inverse condemnation claim).

The Supreme Court amplified the *Nollan* ruling in Dolan v. City of Tigard, 512 U.S. 374, 114 S.Ct. 2309, 129 L.Ed.2d 304 (1994), on remand 319 Or. 567, 877 P.2d 1201 (1994), noted 24 Capital U.L. Rev. 861 (1995), 71 N.Y.U.L. Rev. 1301 (1996), 74 Or. L. Rev. 1105 (1995), 63 U. Chi. L. Rev. 199 (1996). The Court here dealt with a city's attempt to require a landowner, as a condition of the city's permitting her to develop her property commercially, to dedicate a portion of the property lying within a flood plain for improvement of the storm drainage system, dedicate property adjacent to the flood plain as a bicycle-pedestrian pathway, and dedicate a portion of the property in the flood plain as a possible greenway. The Court stated that it would first have to determine whether an essential nexus, as required under *Nollan,* existed between the conditions imposed and a legitimate state interest, and then if such nexus was found, would have to decide whether the *degree* of the exactions bore the required relationship to the development: a "rough proportionality," which essentially means a reasonable relationship. Here, flood prevention and the reduction of traffic congestion were found to be legitimate public purposes, but no reasonable relationship was shown between Dolan's proposed development and the need for the floodplain easement or the pathway easement. On the background of this case, see Barrett, A Store Owner's Squabble With a City Tests Government's Right to Private Land, Wall St. J., March 23, 1994, at B1; Eagle, Private Property Rights vs. Public Works, Wall St. J., March 2, 1994, at A15. See generally Cholewa & Edmonds, Federalism and Land Use After *Dolan*: Has the Supreme Court Taken Takings from the States?, 28 Urban Law. 401 (1996); Davidson, Rosenberg & Spåta, "Where's *Dolan?*" Exactions Law in 1998, 30 Urban Law. 683 (1998); Delaney, What Does It Take to Make a Take? A Post-*Dolan* Look at the Evolution of Regulatory Takings Jurisprudence in the Supreme Court, 27 Urban Law. 55 (1995); Freilich & Bushek, Thou Shalt Not Take Title Without Adequate Planning: The Takings Equation After *Dolan v. City of Tigard,* 27 Urban Law. 187 (1995); Note, A Newly-Minted Hurdle for City Planners: *Dolan v. City of Tigard,* 28 Creighton L. Rev. 559 (1995). On continued development of the *Nollan* and *Dolan* rules, see Curtin & Davidson, Life After *Dolan*: Review of the Cases, 27 Urban Law. 874 (1995); Curtin, Davidson & Lindgren, *Nollan/Dolan*: The Emerging Wing in Regulatory Takings Analysis, 28 Urban Law. 789 (1996); Davidson & Lindgren, Exactions and Impact Fees—*Nollan/Dolan*: Show Me the Findings!, 29 Urban Law. 427 (1997); Freis & Reynoak, Putting Takings Back Into the Fifth Amendment: Land Use Planning After *Dolan v. City of Tigard,* 21 Colum. J. Envtl. L. 103 (1996); Stroud & Trevarthen, Defensible Exactions After *Nollan v. California Coastal Commission* and *Dolan v. City of Tigard*, 25 Stetson L. Rev. 719 (1996); Sullivan, *Dolan* and Municipal Risk Assessment, 12 J. Envtl. L. & Litig. 1 (1997); Note, How Much Is Enough? Assessing the Impact of *Dolan v. City of Tigard,* 46 Case Western Res. L. Rev. 193 (1995); Note, *Dolan v. City of Tigard*: Rough Proportionality as the Supreme Court's Next Step in Takings Jurisprudence, 12 Ga. St. U.L. Rev. 553 (1996); Note, *Dolan v. City of Tigard*: A Heightened Scrutiny of the Takings Clause of the First Amendment, 32 Houston L. Rev. 1153 (1995); Note, *Dolan v. City of Tigard*: Judicial Panacea to the Takings Clause?, 31 Tulsa L.J. 181 (1995); Note, *Dolan v. City of Tigard*: Exalting Private Economic Rights in Land Use Over the "Legitimate Public Interest," 4 Widener J. Pub. L. 617 (1995). An excellent symposium dealing with *Nollan* and *Dolan* is Discretionary Limits in Local Land-Use Control, 15 N. Ill. U.L. Rev. 477–670 (1995). It has been noted that the problems of *Nollan* and *Dolan* could probably be avoided if a municipality uses the power of eminent domain rather than the police power to obtain easements, etc. See "Kendall & Ryan, Paying" for the Change: Using Eminent Domain to Secure Exactions and Sidestep *Nollan* and *Dolan,* 81 Va. L. Rev. 1801 (1995). See generally Coyle, Property Rights and the Constitution—Shaping Society Through Land Use Regulation (State Univ. of N.Y. Press 1993). See also Comment, Exacting Public Beach Access: The Viability of Permit Conditions and Florida's State Beach Access Laws After *Dolan v. City of Tigard,* 12 J. Land Use & Envtl. L. 303 (1997); Note, Exactions for Transportation Corridors After *Dolan v. City of Tigard,* 29 Loyola L.A.L. Rev. 247 (1995).

On the importance of constitutional interpretations in "takings" cases such as *Dolan*, see Rosenberg & Stroud, When *Lochner* Met *Dolan*: The Attempted Transformation of American Land-Use Law by Constitutional Interpretation, 33 Urban Law. 663 (2001).

should be found in situations where a police power regulation is invalidated. Traditionally, the courts in such situations merely struck down the regulation as beyond the scope of the police power and awarded no compensation; but the argument was frequently made that during the time the regulation was in effect, the owner's property was "taken," particularly if the owner could show that the regulation substantially lessened the value of the property, and certainly if the regulation had left the owner during that time with no reasonable use of the property.[25] For a time, the U.S. Supreme Court avoided the question of the need for compensation in such situations—first in a case in which the appeal to the Supreme Court was dismissed for lack of a final

---

On whether the *Dolan* case can, and should, be explained in terms of administrative v. legislative exactions, see Haskins, Closing the *Dolan* Deal—Bridging the Legislative/Adjudicative Divide, 38 Urban Law. 487 (2006) (arguing that *Dolan* should apply to legislative as well as adjudicative decisions); Comment, *Dolan v. City of Tigard* and the Distinction Between Administrative and Legislative Exactions: "A Distinction Without a Constitutional Difference," 28 U. Hawaii L. Rev. 139 (2005). See generally Baker, Much Ado About *Nollan/Dolan*: The Comparative Nature of the Legislative-Adjudicative Distinction in Exactions, 43 Urban Law. 171 (2010) (26th Smith-Babcock-Williams Student Writing Competition Winner). As to the interplay between the rules of the *Dolan* and *Nollan* cases, see Curtin & Gowder, Exactions Update: When and How Do the *Dolan/Nollan* Rules Apply?, 35 Urban Law. 729 (2003).

Since the *Dolan* case, there has been much uncertainty as to whether its rule of "rough proportionality" applies to all types of infrastructure financing and as to whether it applies to impact fees set legislatively or only to those that, as in *Dolan*, are imposed adjudicatively. See Sullivan & Lester, The Role of the Comprehensive Plan in Infrastructure Financing, 37 Urban Law. 53 (2005). As to impact fees, see also Section 21.4, note 50 *infra*, and accompanying text. In Koontz v. St. Johns River Water Management Dist., ___ U.S. ___, 133 S.Ct. 2586 (2013), it was held that the government's demand for property from a land-use permit applicant must satisfy the *Nollan/Dolan* requirement even when the government's demand is for money, not land. The case has been criticized for treating exactions the same as takings. Comment, Confusing Regulatory Takings With Regulatory Exactions: Lost in the Swamp, 41 Boston Coll. Envtl. Affairs L. Rev. 555 (2014). See Note, The New Per Se Takings Rule: *Koontz*'s Implicit Revolution of the Regulatory State, 63 Am. U.L. Rev. 919 (2014). See generally Freilich & Popowitz, How Local Governments Can Resolve *Koontz*'s Prohibitions on Ad Hoc Land Use Restrictions, 45 Urban Law. 971 (2013); Kamprath, A Look at *Koontz v. St. Johns Water Management Dist.*, 45 Urban Law. 953 (2013); Note, Monetary Exactions Not Just Compensation? The Expansion of *Nollan* and *Dolan* in *Koontz*, 25 Vill. Envtl. L.J. 465 (2014); Litigating Takings Challenges to Land Use and Environmental Regulations, 36 Vt. L. Rev. 503–807 (2012). As to the implementation of the *Koontz* case's expansion of the law on land-use conditions, see Eagle, *Koontz* in the Mansion and the Gatehouse, 46 Urban Law. 1 (2014). Compare Comment, The Post-*Koontz* Landscape: *Koontz*'s Shortcomings and How to Move Forward, 64 Emory L.J. 129 (2014). See also Clodfelter & Sullivan, Substantive Due Process Through the Just Compensation Clause: Understanding *Koontz*'s "Special Application" of the Doctrine of Unconstitutional Conditions by Tracing the Doctrine's History, 46 Urban Law. 569 (2014); Herman, The Continuing Struggle Against Government Extortion and Why the Time Is Now Right to Employ Heightened Scrutiny to All Exactions, 46 Urban Law. 655 (2014). As to the right to breach access, see Wright v. Incline Village General Improvement Dist., 665 F.3d 1128 (9th Cir. 2011) (beach access based on property ownership or residency may be constitutionally denied where the beach is not a traditional public forum, the restrictions are reasonable and viewpoint neutral, and the restrictions are rationally related to a legitimate governmental interest and do not treat similarly situated persons differently).

[25] See Comment, "Takings" Under the Police Power—The Development of Inverse Condemnation as a Method of Challenging Zoning Ordinances, 30 Sw. L.J. 723 (1976). Cf. Nemmers v. City of Dubuque, 764 F.2d 502 (8th Cir.1985) (landowner entitled to compensation for temporary taking of his property effected by rezoning, which had subsequently been invalidated by court); Burrows v. City of Keene, 121 N.H. 590, 432 A.2d 15 (1981) (landowner entitled to interim damages until offending regulation repealed). See generally Rankin, The First Bite at the Apple: State Supreme Court Takings Jurisprudence Antedating *First English*, 22 Urban Law. 417 (1990). Actions alleging that a "taking" has been effected, under guise of the police power, by government action are often brought under the Federal Civil Rights Act's Section 1983. See Bley, Use of the Civil Rights Act to Recover Money Damage for the Overregulation of Land, 14 Urban Law. 223 (1982). See generally the material on Section 1983 actions in the chapter on Local Governmental Liability in Tort and Related Theories *infra*. The history of the regulatory takings doctrine is well described in Power, Regulatory Takings: A Chronicle of the Construction of a Constitutional Concept, 23 B.Y.U. J. Pub. L. 221 (2009).

judgment,[26] and then in a case in which it was found that the claimant had not shown that state inverse condemnation proceedings were unavailable or inadequate and had not applied for a variance from the allegedly invalid laws.[27] But in 1987, the Court ruled that where regulation of property leaves the owner, even temporarily, with no reasonable use, the owner *is* entitled to compensation for this "regulatory taking"—*i.e.*, damages for the time that the regulation was in effect and the owner's property rights were thus

---

[26] San Diego Gas & Elec. Co. v. City of San Diego, 450 U.S. 621, 101 S.Ct. 1287, 67 L.Ed.2d 551 (1981), where a site acquired by plaintiff for a nuclear power plant was rezoned by the city, reducing the acreage for industrial use and designating much of the area for open space. Compare Suitum v. Tahoe Regional Planning Agency, 520 U.S. 725, 117 S.Ct. 1659, 137 L.Ed.2d 980 (1997) (landowners' claim that regional planning agency had committed a regulatory taking was ripe for review as agency had made final determination that land was in area that rendered it ineligible for development).

[27] Williamson County Regional Planning Comm'n v. Hamilton Bank, 473 U.S. 172, 105 S.Ct. 3108, 87 L.Ed.2d 126 (1985), on remand 779 F.2d 50 (6th Cir.1985), where, after a developer had obtained approval for development of a tract, the county zoning ordinance was changed to reduce the allowable density of dwelling units. For analysis of the *Williamson* case, *supra*, see Whitcomb & Huett, Recent Developments in Regulatory Takings Jurisprudence, 41 Urban Law. 445 (2009), noting that 25 years after the *Williamson* case was decided, courts and property owners were continuing "to struggle with federal court jurisdiction over regulatory takings claims." *Id.* at 445. Cf. Breemer, Ripeness Madness: The Expansion of *Williamson County's* Baseless "State Procedures" Takings Ripeness Requirement to Non-Takings Claims, 41 Urban Law. 615 (2009). On the need to seek a variance before challenging a zoning ordinance as a taking (also noted in Section 18.6, note 137 *supra*), see Annot., Seeking of Variance as Prerequisite for Ripeness of Challenge to Zoning Ordinance Under Due Process Clause of Federal Constitution's Fifth and Fourteenth Amendments—Post-*Williamson* Cases, 111 A.L.R. Fed. 483 (1993). Cf. MacDonald, Sommer & Frates v. Yolo County, 477 U.S. 340, 106 S.Ct. 2561, 91 L.Ed.2d 285 (1986), reh. denied 478 U.S. 1035, 107 S.Ct. 22, 92 L.Ed.2d 773 (1986), on remand 77 Or.App. 440, 714 P.2d 229 (1986), review denied 300 Or. 722, 717 P.2d 630 (1986) (Court could not determine whether "taking" had occurred as result of county's rejection of subdivision proposal in absence of final and authoritative determination by county planning commission as to how it would apply challenged regulations to property in question). Accord, Lake Nacimiento Ranch Co. v. County of San Luis Obispo, 841 F.2d 872 (9th Cir.1987), cert. denied 488 U.S. 827, 109 S.Ct. 79, 102 L.Ed.2d 55 (1988) (to establish that regulation has gone too far, plaintiff must show that government has made a final and authoritative determination concerning type and intensity of development legally permitted on subject property). Compare Pennell v. City of San Jose, 485 U.S. 1, 108 S.Ct. 849, 99 L.Ed.2d 1 (1988), where the Court declined to consider a "takings" challenge to a "tenant hardship clause" in a rent-control ordinance on the ground that there was no evidence the clause had ever been used to reduce a landlord's rent. See Hill, Reflections, Refractions, and Regulations: Variations on the Takings Theme, 12 Urban, State & Local L. Newsletter No. 3, at 1 (Summer, 1989). On cases declining to find that a regulatory "taking" has occurred, see Mixon, Compensation Claims Against Local Governments for Excessive Land-Use Regulations: A Proposal for More Efficient State Level Adjudication, 20 Urban Law. 675 (1988). See generally Kanner, Hunting the Snark, Not the Quark: Has the U.S. Supreme Court Been Competent in Its Effort to Formulate Coherent Regulatory Takings Law?, 30 Urban Law. 307 (1998); Whitman, The Ripeness Doctrine in the Land Use Context: The Municipality's Ally and the Landowner's Nemesis, 29 Urban Law. 13 (1997). On whether federal courts should be able to hear federal takings cases without initial state court litigation, see Delaney & Desiderio, Who Will Clean Up the "Ripeness Mess"? A Call for Reform So Takings Plaintiffs Can Enter the Federal Courthouse, 31 Urban Law. 195 (1999). See generally Meacham, The *Williamson* Trap, 32 Urban Law. 239 (2000). See also Berger & Kanner, Shell Game: You Can't Get There from Here: Supreme Court Ripeness Jurisprudence in Takings Cases at Long Last Reaches the Self-parody Stage, 36 Urban Law. 671 (2004).

effectively taken.[28] Subsequently, in the *Lucas* case,[29] the Court elaborated on its test for a "taking," holding that where the government forbids all economically viable use of

---

[28] First English Evangelical Lutheran Church v. Los Angeles County, 482 U.S. 304, 107 S.Ct. 2378, 96 L.Ed.2d 250 (1987), on remand 210 Cal.App.3d 1353, 258 Cal.Rptr. 893 (1989), cert. denied 493 U.S. 1056, 110 S.Ct. 866, 107 L.Ed.2d 950 (1990), noted 24 Cal. W.L.Rev. 33 (1987–88), 63 Ind. L.J. 649 (1988), 48 La. L. Rev. 947 (1988), 7 Stan. Envtl. L.J. 49 (1987–88), 48 U. Pitt. L. Rev. 1215 (1987), 27 Washburn L.J. 382 (1988) (regulatory ordinance prohibited construction on property, denying landowner all use thereof; mere invalidation of ordinance without payment of fair value for period that landowner was denied use would be constitutionally insufficient remedy for the taking). The Court stated that the government retained a range of options as to its future conduct: It could amend or withdraw the invalidated regulation, or it could condemn the property under its power of eminent domain; but no subsequent action could remove the necessity of paying compensation for the taking that had already occurred. *Id.* at 2389. On reaction to the case, see "No Taking Without Paying," Time, June 22, 1987, at 64. On this and other notable "takings" cases of that period, see Berger, Happy Birthday, Constitution: The Supreme Court Establishes New Ground Rules for Land-Use Planning, 20 Urban Law. 735 (1988); Bozung & McRoberts, Land Use Planning and Zoning in 1987; A National Survey, 19 Urban Law. 899 (1989); Franck & Morgan, Recent Developments in Condemnation Law, 19 Urban Law. 867 (1987). Cf. Wheeler v. City of Pleasant Grove, Alabama, 833 F.2d 267 (11th Cir.1987), reh. denied 844 F.2d 794 (11th Cir.1988) (landowner and developer who were damaged by temporary regulatory taking resulting from unconstitutional ordinance were entitled to damages). But cf. Berrios v. City of Lancaster, 798 F.Supp. 1153 (E.D.Pa.1992) (renters who were forced to vacate when premises condemned as unfit for habitation were not entitled to recover damages as they could not have reasonably expected to continue to occupy them); McCuskey v. Canyon County Comm'rs, 128 Idaho 213, 912 P.2d 100 (1996) (zoning ordinance which downgrades economic value of property does not constitute unconstitutional taking without compensation where some residual value remains in property; in any case, taking claim was here barred by statute of limitations). See generally Note, Constitutional Law: Where Does *First English Evangelical Lutheran Church v. County of Los Angeles* Fit Into the Regulatory Takings Law Puzzle?, 41 Okla. L. Rev. 726 (1988).

[29] Lucas v. South Carolina Coastal Council, 505 U.S. 1003, 112 S.Ct. 2886, 120 L.Ed.2d 798 (1992), on remand 309 S.C. 424, 424 S.E.2d 484 (1992). See Humbach, "Taking" the Imperial Judiciary Seriously: Segmenting Property Interests and Judicial Revision of Legislative Judgments, 42 Catholic U.L. Rev. 771 (1993); Note, This Land Is My Land: The Clash Between Private Property and the Public Interest in Lucas v. South Carolina Coastal Council, 33 Boston C.L. Rev. 797 (1992); Note, A House Built on Sand: *Lucas v. South Carolina Coastal Council*, 71 N.C.L. Rev. 928 (1993). See generally Callies (ed.), Takings: Land-Development Conditions and Regulatory Takings after *Dolan* and *Lucas* (American Bar Ass'n State & Local Gov't Law Section 1995), reviewed 28 Urban Law. 357 (1996). On the nature of a regulatory taking claim, cf. City of Monterey v. Del Monte Dunes at Monterey, Ltd., 526 U.S. 687, 119 S.Ct. 1624, 143 L.Ed.2d 882 (1999) (jury trial is available to plaintiff in regulatory taking case brought under Section 1983 of Federal Civil Rights Act since the claim is analogous to a tort action for monetary damages), discussed at length in Symposium: *City of Monterey v. Del Monte Dunes at Monterey, Ltd.*, 31 Urban Law. 361–92 (1999). On whether a regulatory taking claim passes with ownership of the property, see Drabek v. City of Norman, 946 P.2d 658 (Okl.1996) (property owner could bring inverse condemnation suit based on city's installation of water main on land even though installation occurred before owner purchased the property, as seller had transferred to purchaser the right to recover from city). See generally Windfalls or Windmills: The Right of a Property Owner to Challenge Land Use Regulations (A Call to Critically Reexamine the Meaning of *Lucas*), 13 J. Land Use & Envtl. L. 161 (1997). For a proposal that would largely end the requirement of compensation for regulatory takings, see Rubenfeld, Usings, 102 Yale L. 1077 (1993), arguing that property is "taken" by the government only when the government productively uses it. For criticism of this argument, see Abraham, *Landgate*—Taken But Not Used, 31 Urban Law. 18 (1999). On cases and developments after *Lucas supra*, see generally Drees, Do State Legislatures Have a Role in Resolving the "Just Compensation" Dilemma? Some Lessons from Public Choice and Positive Political Theory, 66 Fordham L. Rev. 787 (1997); Eagle, The 1997 Regulatory Takings Quartet: Retreating from the "Rule of Law," 42 N.Y.L. School L. Rev. 345 (1998); Note, Georgia Nuisance Law and the Takings Clause After *Lucas v. South Carolina Coastal Council,* 12 Ga. St. U.L. Rev. 601 (1996); Note, Defining the Relevant Property in Regulatory Takings Claims, 17 J. Land Resources & Envtl. L. 403 (1997). For a discussion of how the *Del Monte Dunes* case, *supra*, fits into the pattern established by earlier regulatory taking cases, see Ziegler, Development Exactions and Permit Decisions: *Nollan, Dolan*, and *Del Monte Dunes*, 34 Urban Law. 155 (2002).

In Tahoe-Sierra Preservation Council, Inc. v. Tahoe Regional Planning Agency, 535 U.S. 302, 122 S.Ct. 1465, 152 L.Ed.2d 517(2002), the Court held that a moratorium on development of land that was temporarily imposed during the process of devising a comprehensive land-use plan does not constitute a *per se* taking of land, requiring compensation. See Alperin, *Tahoe-Sierra*—The Supreme Court Again Rejects Per Se Rules for Regulatory Takings Claims, 34 Urban Law. 811 (2002); Peterson, The False Dichotomy Between Physical and Regulatory Takings Analysis: A Critique of *Tahoe-Sierra*'s Distinction Between Physical and Regulatory

land, it must pay compensation unless the proscription merely makes explicit restrictions that had already existed against the property under principles of the state's property and nuisance law.[30] But where regulations permitted a landowner to build a substantial residence on his tract, leaving him with $200,000 in development value, the Court held that the landowner was not deprived of all economic use of his tract and thus was not entitled to compensation for a "taking."[31]

The recent U.S. Supreme Court "takings" cases, which have all been discussed in the text, can be divided into three categories: (1) those dealing with the test for regulatory takings, (2) those dealing with the damages remedy in regulatory takings, and (3) those in which the taking involves some degree of actual physical intrusion or invasion of rights. There are four cases in the first category: Penn Central Transp. Co., v. City of New York[32] (listing a complex of factors to determine whether a regulatory

---

Takings, 34 Ecology L.Q. 381 (2007). On the effect of the *Tahoe-Sierra* case on temporary takings, see generally Roberts (ed.), Taking Sides on Takings Issues (American Bar Ass'n Publ. 2002), reviewed 35 Urban Law. 387 (2003); Note, Reconsidering *Tahoe-Sierra*: Temporary Takings Under the Nuisance Exception, 43 Tex. Envtl. L.J. 337 (2013). See also Section 18.4, notes 138–141, *supra*, and accompanying text.

As to the possibility of a *partial* regulatory taking where some, but not all, of the possible uses of a property are denied and compensation is sought for diminution in the property's value, see Boise Cascade Corp. v. Oregon Board of Forestry, 216 Or.App. 338, 174 P.3d 587 (2007) (no per se regulatory taking occurred with respect to Board of Forestry's refusal to permit landowner to conduct logging operations on property on which a spotted owl nesting site had been located; landowner did not plead or prove that Board's regulation denied it use of the entire parcel but sought compensation for deprivation of only one "stick" in bundle of rights he had in land); Coffey, High Hopes, Hollow Harvest: State Remedies for Partial Regulatory Takings, 39 Urban Law. 619 (2007), concluding that this problem has received "many statutory nods but no meaningful compensation for property owners" (at 631) and that "The time has come to recognize that the question of how to provide compensation for partial regulatory takings is a riddle that cannot be answered" (at 632). See generally Homsy, The Land Use Planning Impacts of Moving "Partial Takings" from Political Theory to Legal Reality, 37 Urban Law. 269 (2005) (2004 R. Marlin Smith Student Writing Competition Award Winner), where it is noted that the Supreme Court does recognize the need for compensation for partial takings that involve a physical appropriation of part of a parcel of land, however small, but that there is very little authority on partial takings that reduce a property's value but fall short of causing a complete loss of economic value. *Id.* at 272. See also Comment, Making Landowners Whole Without Putting Holes in Zoning: Personal Waivers as the Solution to the Partial Regulatory Takings Compensation Issue, 15 George Mason L. Rev. 513 (2008).

30 As to the effect of the *Lucas* case on the law of nuisance, see Humbach, Evolving Thresholds of Nuisance and the Takings Clause, 18 Columbia J. Envtl. L. 1 (1993), noting that "The constitutional scope of the legislative power has become, at least for total takings of land, a matter of state common law." *Id.* at 2. See generally Huffman, Background Principles and the Rule of Law: Fifteen Years After *Lucas*, 35 Ecology L.Q. 1 (2008).

31 In Palazzolo v. Rhode Island, 533 U.S. 606, 121 S.Ct. 2448, 150 L.Ed.2d 592 (2001), regulations which precluded use of fill on wetlands and subsequent development of a beach club on the wetlands portion of an 18-acre tract, but which permitted the landowner to build a substantial residence on the uplands portion of the tract, leaving the parcel with $200,000 in development value, were held not to deprive the landowner of all economic use of the entire parcel, and thus did not, under the *Lucas* case *supra*, present a takings claim for deprivation of all economic use. See Comment, *Palazzolo v. Rhode Island*: Preserving a Constitutional Safety Valve in the Murky Waters of the Self-Imposed Hardship Rule, 107 Dickinson L. Rev. 919 (2003). Cf. Coast Range Conifers, LLC v. State, 339 Or. 136, 117 P.3d 990 (2005) (regulation prohibiting the economic use of a section of a parcel of land did not result in a taking under either the Oregon or United States Constitution). For discussion of the *Palazzolo* decision, *supra*, and changes it made in the law, see Alperin, *Palazzolo*—The Supreme Court's Decision Departs from Accepted Doctrine, 34 Urban Law. 297 (2002); Power, *Palazzolo v. Rhode Island*: Regulatory Takings, Investment-Backed Expectations, and Slander of Title, 34 Urban Law. 313 (2002). Compare Hatcher, The Odyssey of *Palazzolo*: Public Rights Litigation and Coastal Change, 36 Fordham Urban L.J. 849 (2009). See generally Echeverria, From a "Darkling Plain" to What?: The Regulatory Takings Issue in U.S. Law and Policy, 30 Vermont L. Rev. 969 (2006). See also Wade & Bunting, Average Reciprocity of Advantage: "Magic Words" or Economic Reality—Lessons from *Palazzolo*, 39 Urban Law. 319 (2007).

32 438 U.S. 104, 98 S.Ct. 2646, 57 L.Ed.2d 631 (1978), reh'g denied 439 U.S. 883, 99 S.Ct. 226, 58 L.Ed.2d 198 (1978). For further analysis of the *Penn Central* case, see Echeverria, Making Sense of *Penn*

taking has occurred, including economic effect on the landowner, character of the government action, and extent of damage to or interference with investment-backed expectations); Agins v. City of Tiburon[33] (to avoid "taking" liability of the government when restricting use of land, government action must substantially advance legitimate state interests *and* must not deny landowner all economically viable use of property); Tahoe-Sierra Preservation Council, Inc., v. Tahoe Regional Planning Agency[34] (*Penn Central's* test as to "taking" extended to temporary regulations); and Lingle v. Chevron, U.S.A., Inc.[35] (first prong of *Agins* test, as to advancing legitimate state interests, eliminated).

In the second category, there are also four cases: First English Evangelical Lutheran Church of Glendale v. Los Angeles County[36] (if landowner is deprived, even temporarily, of all reasonable use of his property by a land-use restriction, he is entitled not only to a declaration that the law exceeds the police power and is thus invalid as it stands, but is also entitled to compensation for the time the law has been in operation); Lucas v. South Carolina Coastal Council[37] (reiterates *First English* case and declares that where the government forbids all economically viable use of land, it must pay compensation unless the proscription merely makes explicit restrictions that already existed—for instance, under the law of nuisance); City of Monterey v. Del Monte Dunes at Monterey, Ltd.[38] ("taking" claim under Section 1983 of Federal Civil Rights Act is analogous to a tort action for damages, and jury trial is thus available to plaintiff); Palazzolo v. Rhode Island[39] ("investment-backed expectations" portion of *Penn Central* test largely eliminated).

Finally, the third category has three cases: Loretto v. Teleprompter Manhattan CATV Corp.[40] (when physical intrusion by government reaches extreme form of permanent physical occupation, there is always a taking, requiring compensation); Nollan v. California Coastal Comm'n[41] (governmentally imposed requirement that a landowner convey to government or the people some rights to the land, such as access across the property, amounts to a taking, requiring compensation, unless it is imposed as a condition that advances the same legitimate purpose as would denial of permission to develop the land—the "nexus" requirement); and Dolan v. City of Tigard[42] (conditions

---

Central, 39 Envtl. L. Rep. News & Analysis 10471 (2009); Miller, *Penn Central* for Tomorrow: Making Regulatory Takings Predictable, 39 Envtl. L. Rep. News & Analysis 10457 (2009).

[33] 447 U.S. 255, 100 S.Ct. 2138, 65 L.Ed.2d 106 (1980).

[34] 535 U.S. 302, 122 S.Ct. 1465, 152 L.Ed.2d 517 (2002).

[35] 544 U.S. 528, 125 S.Ct. 2074, 161 L.Ed.2d 876 (2005). See Note, Regulatory Takings: The Supreme Court Eliminates the Substantially Advances Test from Takings Jurisprudence, 14 Mo. Envtl. J. & Pol'y Rev. 339 (2006). See generally Note, Derailing *Penn Central*: A Post-*Lingle*, Cost-Basis Approach to Regulatory Takings, 78 Geo. Wash. L. Rev. 870 (2010). For a comparison of United States regulatory takings law with the laws of other countries, see Alterman, The U.S. Regulatory Takings Debate Through an International Lens, 42/43 Urban Law. 331 (2010–11).

[36] 482 U.S. 304, 107 S.Ct. 2378, 96 L.Ed.2d 250 (1987).

[37] 505 U.S. 1003, 112 S.Ct. 2886, 120 L.Ed.2d 798 (1992).

[38] 526 U.S. 687, 119 S.Ct. 1624, 143 L.Ed.2d 882 (1999).

[39] 533 U.S. 606, 121 S.Ct. 2448, 150 L.Ed.2d 592 (2001).

[40] 458 U.S. 419, 102 S.Ct. 3164, 73 L.Ed.2d 868 (1982).

[41] 483 U.S. 825, 107 S.Ct. 3141, 97 L.Ed.2d 677 (1987).

[42] 512 U.S. 374, 114 S.Ct. 2309, 129 L.Ed.2d 304 (1994). As to the effects on the law of impact fees that have occurred due to the *Nollan* case, *supra* note 41, and the *Dolan* case, see Note, *Nollan* and *Dolan*: Providing

imposed on granting a development permit must, in order to avoid liability for taking, have not only a reasonable nexus to a legitimate state interest, but the degree of the exactions imposed must bear a reasonable relationship ("rough proportionality") to the proposed development).

Sometimes it is clear that a government intends *eventually* to "take" property under the power of eminent domain, as when that government announces that land is to be cleared and a highway built thereon. But the question may still arise: at what moment in time has the taking actually happened so that compensation must be paid—when the plan is announced, when buildings on the land are razed, etc.? A mere announcement of plans for a project in a particular area is usually said not to constitute a taking.[43] But little more may be required: a denial of building permits, or other actions hindering sale or development of the property, may, when coupled with the announcement of a government project in the area, suffice for a taking.[44] A "taking" requires some direct legal restraint on use.[45] Actual governmental use or invasion need not yet have occurred

---

a Roadmap for Adopting a Uniform System to Determine Transportation Impact Fees, 25 B.Y.U. J. Pub. L. 143 (2011).

[43] See April v. City of Broken Arrow, 775 P.2d 1347 (Okl.1989) (city's future plans for inclusion of property in flood control plan did not give rise to inverse condemnation action); Empire Construction, Inc. v. City of Tulsa, 512 P.2d 119 (Okl.1973), cert. denied 414 U.S. 1094, 94 S.Ct. 725, 38 L.Ed.2d 551 (no overt act after announcement of plan). Cf. Wendy's Internat'l Inc. v. City of Birmingham, 868 F.2d 433 (11th Cir.1989) (mere enactment of legislation authorizing condemnation cannot be considered a taking); Calhoun v. City of Durant, 970 P.2d 608 (Okl.Civ.App. 1997), cert. denied 526 U.S. 1065, 119 S.Ct. 1456, 143 L.Ed.2d 543 (1999) (voters' authorization of issuance of bonds to expand water treatment system and passing of ten years since announcement of proposed expansion did not constitute a taking); Gorham v. Public Bldg. Auth., 612 A.2d 708 (R.I.1992) (taking requires actual intrusion; mere passage of legislation does not normally suffice); E & J Inc. v. Redevelopment Agency of Woonsocket, 122 R.I. 288, 405 A.2d 1187 (R.I.1979) (condemnation of *adjacent* land plus closure of some streets in area, but no interference with plaintiff's possession, only a decrease in value; no taking found). See generally Annot., Eminent Domain—Plotting or Planning in Anticipation of Improvement as Taking or Damaging of Property Affected, 37 A.L.R.3d 127 (1971).

Anticipatory changes in land-use planning, and in redevelopment projects, have also been treated as irrelevant to the amount of condemnation awards, where such changes have not actually been undertaken at the time of taking. See Jersey City Redevelopment Agency v. Kugler, 58 N.J. 374, 277 A.2d 873 (1971) (depreciating threat of, or inflationary reaction to, the proposed public project may be disregarded).

[44] Grosso v. Board of Adjustment, 137 N.J.L. 630, 61 A.2d 167 (1948); Suess Builders Co. v. City of Beaverton, 294 Or. 254, 656 P.2d 306 (1982), on remand 77 Or.App. 440, 714 P.2d 229 (1986) (mere designation of property as a park in comprehensive plan does not suffice for a taking, but other elements in the dealings between the owners and the governmental entities, such as the governments' negotiating for purchase at less than market value, might make out a taking). See Note, Problems of Advance Land Acquisition, 52 Minn. L. Rev. 1175 (1968). Cf. Foster v. City of Detroit, 254 F.Supp. 655 (E.D.Mich.1966), aff'd 405 F.2d 138 (6th Cir.1968), motion denied 423 F.2d 660 (condemnation proceedings commenced, abandoned ten years later, reinstituted still later—"taking" occurred when threat of condemnation caused property-value decline to be accelerated); Washington Market Enterprises, Inc. v. City of Trenton, 68 N.J. 107, 343 A.2d 408 (1975) ("taking" occurs when threat of condemnation destroys beneficial use of property). See generally Adams, Eminent Domain, Police Power, and Urban Renewal: Compensation for Interim Depreciation in Land Values, 7 Ga.L.Rev. 226 (1973); Comment, Delay, Abandonment of Condemnation, and Just Compensation, 41 So.Cal. L.Rev. 862 (1968); Note, The Condemnor's Liability for Damages Arising Through Instituting, Litigating, or Abandoning Eminent Domain Proceedings, 1967 Utah L.Rev. 548. See also Mandelker, Planning the Freeway: Interim Controls in Highway Programs, 1964 Duke L.J. 439.

[45] City of Buffalo v. J.W. Clement Co., 28 N.Y.2d 241, 321 N.Y.S.2d 345, 269 N.E.2d 895 (1971), reargument denied by 29 N.Y.2d 640, 324 N.Y.S.2d 462, 273 N.E.2d 315, appeal after remand 40 A.D.2d 753, 337 N.Y.S.2d 642, appeal dism'd 31 N.Y.2d 958, 341 N.Y.S.2d 104, 293 N.E.2d 252, appeal after remand 41 A.D.2d 41, 342 N.Y.S.2d 89, appeal after remand 45 A.D.2d 620, 360 N.Y.S.2d 362 (intent to condemn does not suffice for "taking," though physical entry not essential). Some intent to put the property to public use normally accompanies a "taking," though the use may not yet have occurred. See Note, Constitutional Law—Eminent Domain—Destruction of Private Property to Prevent Enemy Capture, 51 Mich.L.Rev. 739 (1953). See generally Jenkins, Recent Constitutional Developments on Eminent Domain, 4 Vand.L.Rev. 673 (1951).

if there is a substantial interference with the private use and enjoyment of the property.[46]

§ 19.3 Municipal Use of Eminent Domain—"Public Use" or "Public Purpose"

The first requirement for any taking by eminent domain traditionally was that the property must be taken for some "public use." This is still the requirement applied in a few states,[47] though it has been noted that a "public use" defies firm definition[48] and that the meaning of the term has shifted according to surrounding circumstances.[49] The requirement has sometimes caused problems when local governments have attempted to acquire land for industrial or other business development, with the ultimate purpose of turning this over to private enterprise.[50] While the term was often given a broad meaning in the early decades of our history—so as to require nothing more than some furthering of the public good—by the mid-1800's, many courts, worried that the eminent-domain power was being abused, required actual use by the public. In the 20th century, however, there was a gradual liberalization of the term once again, leading to some suggestion that the public-use requirement poses little obstacle to most programs that

---

[46] See Cayon v. City of Chicopee, 360 Mass. 606, 277 N.E.2d 116 (1971) (character of invasion, not amount of damage, is determinative). Note that the question of *when* a "taking" has occurred is important not only in deciding whether certain property has been "taken" at all by the government, but also—assuming a "taking"—in deciding the amount of compensation, since this should equal the value at the moment of taking. In State ex rel. Department of Transp. v. Post, 125 P.3d 1183 (Okla. 2005), it was held that, where state law provided that commissioners determined the amount of the condemnation award, it was the date on which the condemning agency paid this award into court that was the date of the taking, whether or not the agency took possession of the property on that date. On the theories for deciding the time-of-taking for purposes of valuation, see Comment, Date of Valuation in Eminent Domain: Irreverence for Unconstitutional Practice, 30 U.Chi.L.Rev. 319 (1963); Annot., Valuation at Time of Original Wrongful Entry by Condemnor or at Time of Subsequent Initiation of Condemnation Proceedings, 2 A.L.R.3d 1038 (1965). See generally the discussion of condemnation damages in Section 19.5, *infra*.

[47] See People ex rel. Tuohy v. City of Chicago, 394 Ill. 477, 68 N.E.2d 761 (1946) (listing requirements); Opinion of the Justices, 231 A.2d 431 (Me.1967). See generally Nichols, The Meaning of "Public Use" in the Law of Eminent Domain, 20 Boston U.L.Rev. 615 (1940).

[48] Barnes v. City of New Haven, 140 Conn. 8, 98 A.2d 523 (1953); McSorley v. Fitzgerald, 359 Pa. 264, 59 A.2d 142 (1948).

[49] Fallbrook Irrigation Dist. v. Bradley, 164 U.S. 112, 17 S.Ct. 56, 41 L.Ed. 369 (1896). It is usually agreed that a "public use" does not have to be one that the entire public, or any large portion thereof, actually enjoys, so long as the use is open to the general public on equal terms and the use affects the community, not merely certain individuals. See In re Opinion of the Justices, 297 Mass. 567, 8 N.E.2d 753 (1937). As to the possibility of employing the term "public use" in the area of government accountability, see Note, Maintaining Government Accountability: Calls for a "Public Use" Beyond Eminent Domain, 83 Ind. L.J. 1097 (2008).

[50] See City of Little Rock v. Raines, 241 Ark. 1071, 411 S.W.2d 486 (1967) (use of eminent domain for industrial-development project invalid); Adams v. Housing Authority, 60 So.2d 663 (Fla.1952); Opinion of the Justices, 152 Me. 440, 131 A.2d 904 (1957) (acquiring land for industrial sites invalid); Edens v. City of Columbia, 228 S.C. 563, 91 S.E.2d 280 (1956) (use of eminent domain invalid under redevelopment plan where plan was not intended to provide better low-cost housing to occupants of area but to transform low-cost housing area into commercial area). Cf. Kessler v. City of Indianapolis, 199 Ind. 420, 157 N.E. 547 (1927) (local government cannot secure right-of-way to a municipal street for a private individual). At one time, the Georgia court struck down a redevelopment project as not involving a public use. Housing Authority v. Johnson, 209 Ga. 560, 74 S.E.2d 891 (1953). But a contrary result was reached after the state constitution was amended so as to allow the use of eminent domain for slum clearance and redevelopment. Bailey v. Housing Authority, 214 Ga. 790, 107 S.E.2d 812 (1959), applying Ga.Const. Art. 16, § 2–8501, now § 2–6104, and statutes passed thereunder.

any government would be likely to undertake.[51] Though historically a use has not been considered "public" merely because it benefited the community to a greater extent than the property's pre-condemnation use,[52] some modern cases have come close to defining "public use" as little more than a "higher and better" method of utilizing the property from the point of view of the general community.[53]

Most courts now do not require that a taking be for a "public use" so long as a public *purpose* is involved. This slight shift in language makes it easier for courts to rule that some incidental private purpose or benefit involved in a taking does not invalidate the action,[54] and this in turn facilitates the upholding of industrial-development parks and

---

[51] See Comment, The Public Use Limitation on Eminent Domain: An Advance Requiem, 58 Yale L.J. 599 (1949). On the liberalization in recent times of the public use requirement, see Franck & Bredesen, Recent Developments in Condemnation Law, 17 Urban Law. 751 (1985). See generally Annot., When Is Taking of Property for "Public Use" So as to Be Permissible under Federal Constitution if Just Compensation Is Provided—Supreme Court Cases, 81 L.Ed.2d 931 (1987).

[52] See Hogue v. Port of Seattle, 54 Wn.2d 799, 341 P.2d 171 (1959) (authority was trying to achieve better industrial balance in area; use of eminent domain invalidated).

[53] See Courtesy Sandwich Shop, Inc. v. Port of New York, 12 N.Y.2d 379, 240 N.Y.S.2d 1, 190 N.E.2d 402 (1963), appeal dism'd 375 U.S. 78, 84 S.Ct. 194, 11 L.Ed.2d 141, reh. denied 375 U.S. 960, 84 S.Ct. 440, 11 L.Ed.2d 318 (upholding constitutionality of condemnation for World Trade Center to facilitate flow of commerce; public purpose found). See generally Note, Condemnation Friendly or Land Use Wise? A Broad Interpretation of the Public Use Requirement Works Well for New York City, 76 Fordham L. Rev. 1121 (2007). It has been recognized that a municipality might lawfully condemn a private business, including a sports franchise, that was attempting to move out of that city if the city could show that the business would be put to a public use that requires its condemnation. See. City of Oakland v. Oakland Raiders, 32 Cal.3d 60, 183 Cal.Rptr. 673, 646 P.2d 835 (1982), appeal after remand 136 Cal.App.3d 565, 186 Cal.Rptr. 326 (1982), dealing with the attempt of Oakland, California, to prevent a privately owned professional football team from moving its National Football League franchise to Los Angeles. The court remanded the case to the trial level for determination of whether the property rights involved were within the territorial limits of the municipality, as required by statute, and of whether the condemnation was for a valid public use. On remand, the trial court found that the condemnation would entail an extraterritorial taking for which there was no statutory authorization and that the evidence did not support the contention that the taking was necessary to the public interest; therefore, the eminent domain proceedings were dismissed. City of Oakland v. Oakland Raiders, Case No. 76044 (Cal. Super. Ct., Monterey County, July 22, 1983). In subsequent proceedings, it was held that the city's attempt to acquire the franchise by eminent domain was invalid under the Commerce Clause of the U.S. Constitution. City of Oakland v. Oakland Raiders, 174 Cal.App.3d 414, 220 Cal.Rptr. 153 (1985), cert. denied 478 U.S. 1007, 106 S.Ct. 3300, 92 L.Ed.2d 714 (1986). Cf. Mayor & City Council of Baltimore v. Baltimore Football Club, Inc., 624 F.Supp. 278 (D.Md.1985) (professional football team that had moved its business operation and most of its tangible property to another state was not subject to eminent domain power of state from which it had moved; and team's former home city, which had paid no compensation to the franchise owner, lacked power to condemn the franchise). See also Olesker, The Colts' Baltimore—A City and Its Love Affair in the 1950's (Johns Hopkins Univ. Press 2008).

As to whether taking property for a sports facility such as a stadium, involves taking for a public use or purpose, see Comment, Taking Private Property to Build an Urban Sports Arena: A Valid Exercise of Eminent Domain Powers?, 69 Albany L. Rev. 1135 (2006). Compare Note, Take Some Land for the Ball Game: Sports Stadiums, Eminent Domain, and the Public Use Doctrine, 19 Sports Law J. 173 (2012); Note, For the Public's Use? Eminent Domain in Stadium Construction, 15 Sports Law J. 173 (2008). See also Note, Whether Building a New Sports Area Will Revitalize Downtown and Make the Team a Winner, 17 U. Miami Bus. L. Rev. 269 (2009).

[54] See Kansas City v. Liebi, 298 Mo. 569, 252 S.W. 404 (1923) (incidental private purpose does not prevent taking by eminent domain); Waldo's, Inc. v. Village of Johnson City, 74 N.Y.2d 718, 544 N.Y.S.2d 809, 543 N.E.2d 74 (1989) (village's condemnation for purpose of widening intersection was supported by useful public purpose despite incidental benefit to private property owners); State ex rel. Washington State Convention & Trade Center v. Evans, 136 Wash.2d 811, 966 P.2d 1252 (Wash. 1998) (state could condemn property for expansion of state convention center though private developer would partially fund project and would acquire fee simple title to ground-level property on which expansion would sit). Compare City of Lansing v. Edward Rose Realty, Inc., 442 Mich. 626, 502 N.W.2d 638 (1993) (asserted public interest in mandatory access to rental properties by franchised cable services did not justify taking by city). See generally, on public

other projects that are eventually leased or sold to private persons.[55] Similarly, a public purpose—such as slum clearance and/or provision of public housing—can be found in urban renewal and redevelopment projects.[56] Indeed, the law in this area has gone through stages of finding the public purpose in removal of slums, then in preventing blight to developed property, then in removing blight from or preventing its spread to *un*developed property, and finally (sometimes) to improving the appearance of neighborhoods.[57] But even under the "public purpose" test, a taking cannot be upheld if the *primary* purpose is one of private benefit (although there may be some incidental public benefit),[58] and thus the task of a reviewing court on this issue is to determine the principal purpose of the proposed project. Though the task of deciding "public use" has been called ultimately a judicial task,[59] great deference will here be accorded legislative findings of such use, and eminent-domain takings are seldom overturned for lack of this

---

purpose, Kessler v. City of Indianapolis, *supra* note 50 (purpose of eminent domain must be public, not private); In re Opinion of the Justices, *supra* note 49.

[55] See Poole v. City of Kankakee, 406 Ill. 521, 94 N.E.2d 416 (1950). See generally Ross, Transferring Land to Private Entities by the Power of Eminent Domain, 51 Geo. Wash. L. Rev. 356 (1983). Good reviews of the industrial-development cases are found in Note, Some Legal and Economic Aspects of Industrial Development Financing, 22 Vand. L. Rev. 159 (1958); Annot., Eminent Domain—Industrial Park or Similar Development as Public Use Justifying Condemnation of Private Property, 62 A.L.R.4th 1183 (1988).

[56] Chicago Land Clearance Commission v. White, 411 Ill. 310, 104 N.E.2d 236 (1952), cert. denied 344 U.S. 824, 73 S.Ct. 23, 97 L.Ed. 641 (1952); Bowker v. City of Worcester, 334 Mass. 422, 136 N.E.2d 208 (1956); Cannata v. New York City, 24 Misc.2d 694, 204 N.Y.S.2d 982 (Sup.Ct.1960), modified 14 A.D.2d 813, 221 N.Y.S.2d 457, aff'd 11 N.Y.2d 210, 227 N.Y.S.2d 903, 182 N.E.2d 395, appeal dism'd 371 U.S. 4, 83 S.Ct. 28, 9 L.Ed.2d 48 (slum clearance is in public interest); Murray v. La Guardia, 291 N.Y. 320, 52 N.E.2d 884 (1943), cert. denied 321 U.S. 771, 64 S.Ct. 530, 88 L.Ed. 1066; Redevelopment Commission of Greensboro v. Security National Bank, 252 N.C. 595, 114 S.E.2d 688 (1960); Foeller v. Housing Authority, 198 Or. 205, 256 P.2d 752 (1953) (eventual sale to private persons does not prevent use of eminent domain); Schenck v. City of Pittsburgh, 364 Pa. 31, 70 A.2d 612 (1950); Davis v. City of Lubbock, 160 Tex. 38, 326 S.W.2d 699 (1959); Miller v. City of Tacoma, 61 Wn.2d 374, 378 P.2d 464 (1963). See Paulk v. Housing Authority, 195 So.2d 488 (Miss.1967) (fact that land will be leased to private persons does not defeat power of eminent domain). Cf. State ex rel. Allerton Parking Corp. v. City of Cleveland, 4 Ohio App.2d 57, 211 N.E.2d 203 (1965), aff'd 6 Ohio St.2d 165, 216 N.E.2d 876 (1966) (resale to private developers, for purposes of urban redevelopment and under restrictions as to use, was part of continuing public benefit and not improper); City of Seattle v. Mall, Inc., 104 Wash.2d 621, 707 P.2d 1348 (1985) (condemnation of land for park did not unconstitutionally mix public and private uses where city had divested itself of any interest in private retail functions of retail project bordering park). See also Note, Property: Eminent Domain and Restoring Access to Parcels Isolated by Highway Reconstruction: Finding the Public Use, 39 Wm. Mitchell L. Rev. 336 (2012).

[57] See Mandelker, Public Purpose in Urban Redevelopment, 28 Tul.L.Rev. 96 (1953). Cf. Berman v. Parker, 348 U.S. 26, 75 S.Ct. 98, 99 L.Ed. 27 (1954) (a leading case upholding the use of eminent domain for urban redevelopment; whole area could be redesigned, not merely the blighted parts); Housing & Redevelopment Authority v. Greenman, 255 Minn. 396, 96 N.W.2d 673 (1959). See also Mount Laurel Township v. Mipro Homes, L.L.C., 379 N.J.Super. 358, 878 A.2d 38 (App. Div. 2005), where the township's acquisition of land to preserve open space, even if not directly in accordance with a master plan, was upheld.

[58] See Baycol, Inc. v. Downtown Development Authority, 315 So.2d 451 (Fla.1975) (eminent domain proceedings will be invalidated if public purpose only incidental to a private one); Grubstein v. Urban Renewal Agency, 115 So.2d 745 (Fla.1959); Adams v. Housing Auth., 60 So.2d 663 (Fla.1952) (incidental benefit to public does not suffice for public purpose); Burger v. City of Beatrice, 181 Neb. 213, 147 N.W.2d 784 (1967) (right to condemn will be denied if private purpose is substantial rather than merely incidental); Stratford v. City of Greensboro, 124 N.C. 127, 32 S.E. 394 (1899); City of Jamestown v. Leevers Supermarkets, 552 N.W.2d 365 (N.D.1996) (city's condemnation for construction of retail facility was for public use, but remand required to determine whether primary benefit was public or private).

[59] See City of Cincinnati v. Vester, 281 U.S. 439, 50 S.Ct. 360, 74 L.Ed. 950 (1930); University of Southern California v. Robbins, 1 Cal.App.2d 523, 37 P.2d 163 (1934), cert. denied 295 U.S. 738, 55 S.Ct. 650, 79 L.Ed. 1685; Poole v. City of Kankakee, *supra* note 55; Auburn v. Hawkins, 65 Wn.2d 560, 398 P.2d 723 (1965). See generally Holmberg, Municipal Powers and the Public Purpose Doctrine, 21 Rocky Mt. L.Rev. 277 (1949).

requirement.[60] In a few cases involving the development of off-street parking facilities, courts have found a lack of public purpose—usually because of a lack of any continuing government control over the operation.[61] But most courts—whether employing the "public purpose" or even the "public use" test—have upheld takings for such projects.[62] The U.S. Supreme Court has taken a very broad view of the "public use" requirement in eminent domain, indicating that it is coterminous with the scope of governmental police powers and holding that even a state program for reducing concentration of land ownership may meet the public use requirement.[63]

In 2005, the Supreme Court decided the celebrated *Kelo* case, in which it upheld, as supported by a sufficient public purpose, the use of eminent domain by a city as part of an economic rejuvenation plan that the city believed would provide appreciable benefits to the community, including, but not limited to, new jobs and increased revenue.[64] The city had determined that the geographic area involved was sufficiently distressed to justify this program, including the taking of the land at issue, though there was no plan to open the condemned land—at least in its entirety—to use by the general public.[65] The

---

[60] See Anaheim Union High School District v. Vieira, 241 Cal.App.2d 169, 51 Cal.Rptr. 94 (1966) (public purpose cannot be disputed in absence of fraud or bad faith; where fraud or bad faith is pleaded, court must review); In re Madera Irrigation District, 92 Cal. 296, 28 P. 272 (1891) (will of legislature must prevail over any doubts of courts as to public use); Tate v. Malden, 334 Mass. 507, 136 N.E.2d 188 (1956); City of Tacoma v. Welcker, 65 Wn.2d 677, 399 P.2d 330 (1965). As to cases involving bad faith, see generally Oswald, Public Uses and Non-Uses: Sinister Schemes, Improper Motives, and Bad Faith in Eminent Domain Law, 35 Boston College Envtl. Aff. L. Rev. 45 (2008).

[61] City & County of San Francisco v. Ross, 44 Cal.2d 52, 279 P.2d 529 (1955); Denihan Enterprises, Inc. v. O'Dwyer, 277 App.Div. 407, 100 N.Y.S.2d 512 (1950), aff'd 302 N.Y. 451, 99 N.E.2d 235 (1951). But see Larsen v. City & County of San Francisco, 152 Cal.App.2d 355, 313 P.2d 959 (Dist.Ct.1957), distinguishing the *Ross* case *supra* and finding a sufficient public purpose in the building of a parking facility to be leased to a private party, since the government was retaining considerable control over rates and operation.

A few cases not directly dealing with the eminent-domain issue have found a lack of public purpose in proposed parking facilities. See Price v. Philadelphia Parking Authority, 422 Pa. 317, 221 A.2d 138 (1966). The factors that courts sometimes find objectionable, and indicative of a lack of sufficient public purpose, in such projects include little or no government retention of control over rates to be charged and rules of operation, too much floor-area not used for the parking operations, and/or a contract for a building, or a lease of a building, having specifications peculiar to the needs of a particular prospective lessee.

[62] See Wilmington Parking Authority v. Ranken, 34 Del.Ch. 439, 105 A.2d 614 (1954) (off-street parking facility with 40% of space devoted to commercial uses; upheld); Allright Auto Parks, Inc. v. City of Atlanta, 257 Ga. 315, 357 S.E.2d 797 (1987) (condemnation of parking lot for development of parking facility to be leased to a private company; held to be for public use); Foltz v. City of Indianapolis, 234 Ind. 656, 130 N.E.2d 650 (1955); Opinion of the Justices, 231 A.2d 431 (Me.1967); Club Jolliet, Inc. v. Manchester, 110 N.H. 172, 262 A.2d 844 (1970) (part of urban renewal project); Opinion of the Justices, 109 N.H. 396, 254 A.2d 273 (1969); Ogden City v. Stephens, 21 Utah 2d 336, 445 P.2d 703 (1968) (acquisition of private parking lot). Cf. City of Arlington v. Golddust Twins Realty Corp., 41 F.3d 960 (5th Cir.1994) (condemnation for parking lot and subsequent land exchange was for public use).

[63] Hawaii Housing Auth. v. Midkiff, 467 U.S. 229, 104 S.Ct. 2321, 81 L.Ed.2d 186 (1984), on remand 740 F.2d 15 (9th Cir.1984) (title to real property could be taken from lessors and sold to lessees; regulating oligopoly and the evils associated with it said by Court to be a classic exercise of state's police powers). See Newton & Sha, Recent Developments in Condemnation Law, 16 Urban Law. 645 (1984). See generally Burch, Bozung, Miller & Hill, Land Use Controls: Public Use and Private Beneficiaries, 16 Urban Law. 713 (1984).

[64] Kelo v. City of New London, 545 U.S. 469, 125 S.Ct. 2655, 162 L.Ed.2d 439 (2005), reh. denied 545 U.S. 1158, 126 S.Ct. 24, 162 L.Ed.2d 922 (2005).

[65] See the summary of the opinions in this case at Martinez, 16 Summary of U.S. Supreme Court Cases in State and Local Government: The 2004–2005 Term, No. 1, at 1 (Nov., 2005). See generally Perspectives on *Kelo v. City of New London*, 38 McGeorge L. Rev. 369–459 (2007). See also Comment, Two Tales of the City: Eminent Domain Post-Katrina and a Response to *Kelo*, 53 Loyola L. Rev. 115 (2007). For discussion of the background of the *Kelo* case, see Lefcoe, Jeff Benedict's Little Pink House: The Back Story of the *Kelo* Case, 42 Conn. L. Rev. 925 (2010), reviewing Benedict, Little Pink House: A True Story of Defiance and Courage (2009).

Kelo case has been the subject of much analysis and commentary, a lot of it adversely critical.[66] The case clearly has possible repercussions not only in the area of economic development,[67] but also as to takings for urban renewal[68] or for environmental reform.[69] Some jurisdictions have held that eminent-domain takings for economic development are violative of *state* constitutional and/or statutory provisions.[70] In many states, legislation, citizen-initiated ballot measures, or constitutional amendments have been

---

66 See Kanner, *Kelo v. New London*: Bad Law, Bad Policy, and Bad Judgment, 38 Urban Law. 201 (2006); Schultz, What's Yours Can Be Mine: Are There Any Private Takings After *Kelo v. City of New London*?, 24 U.C.L.A.J. Envtl. L. & Pol'y 195 (2006); Note, That Land Is Your Land, This Land Is My Land . . . Until the Local Government Can Turn It for a Profit: A Critical Analysis of *Kelo v. City of New London*, 20 B.Y.U.J. Pub. L. 139 (2005); Comment, "Don't Know What a Slide Rule Is For": The Need for a Precise Definition of Public Purpose in North Carolina in the Wake of *Kelo v. City of New London*, 28 Campbell L. Rev. 291 (2006); Note, Constitutional Law—Public Use Clause—Use of Eminent Domain to Promote Economic Development Held Constitutional, 36 Cumberland L. Rev. 407 (2006); Note, Breaking New Ground: Using Eminent Domain for Economic Development, 73 Fordham L. Rev. 1837 (2005); Note, Restraining Eminent Domain Through Just Compensation, 29 Harv. J.L. & Pub. Pol'y 759 (2006); Note, What's the Use? The Court Takes a Stand on the Public Use Doctrine in *Kelo v. City of New London*, 57 Mercer L. Rev. 689 (2006); Note, *Kelo v. City of New London*, 32 Ohio N.U.L. Rev. 381 (206); Comment, Take It or Leave It: Eminent Domain for Economic Development—Statutes, Ordinances & Politics, Oh My!, 12 Tex. Wesleyan L. Rev. 523 (2006). See generally Dowling, How to Think About *Kelo* After the Shouting Stops, 38 Urban Law. 191 (2006); Lopez, Weighing and Reweighing Eminent Domain's Political Philosophies Post-*Kelo*, 41 Wake Forest L. Rev. 237 (2006); Symposium, *Kelo v. City of New London*, 46 Santa Clara L. Rev. 767–888 (2006); Merriam & Ross, Eminent Domain Use and Abuse: *Kelo* in Context (American Bar Ass'n Section of State & Local Government Law 2005); Vermont Law School's Land Use Institute & Vermont J. of Envtl. Law, The Supreme Court and Takings: Four Essays (2005). See also Roosevelt, This Land Is My Land, Time, Nov. 6, 2006, at 41; Note, Private Business as Public Good: Hotel Development and *Kelo v. City of New London*, 24 Yale L. & Pol'y Rev. 363 (2006). As to the public outcry in response to the *Kelo* decision, see Somin, The Limits of Backlash: Assessing the Political Response to *Kelo*, 93 Minn. L. Rev. 2100 (2009); Woodyard & Boggs, Public Outcry: *Kelo v. City of New London*—A Proposed Solution, 39 Envtl. L. 431 (2009). Cf. Note, Intermediate Scrutiny for Economic Development Takings: Proposing a New Test Based on Justice Kennedy's *Kelo* Concurrences, 31 T. Jefferson L. Rev. 431 (2009). As to whether the outcry over *Kelo* will be lasting, see Seidenberg, Where's the Revolution?, 95 A.B.A.J. 50 (April, 2009), noting that municipalities have been making less frequent use of eminent domain in recent years, but concluding that "It is possible, however, that the movement against eminent domain has peaked." *Id.* at 56. See generally Somin, The Grasping Hand—*Kelo v. City of New London* and the Limits of Eminent Domain (Univ. of Chicago Press 2015).

67 See Mihaly, Living in the Past: The *Kelo* Court and Public-Private Economic Redevelopment, 34 Ecology L.Q. 1 (2007); Somin, Controlling the Grasping Hand: Economic Development Takings After *Kelo*, 15 Sup. Ct. Econ. Rev. 183 (2007); Comment, Public Use or Private Purpose?: The Ever-changing Role of the Courts and the Legislature in Interpreting the Public Use Clause in Deciding Whether a State Can Take Private Property in Eminent Domain Proceedings for the Purpose of Promoting Private Economic Development, 44 Duq.L.Rev. 709 (2006). See generally Stark, How Do You Solve a Problem Like in *Kelo*?, 40 John Marshall L. Rev. 609 (2007) (part of a Real Estate Law Symposium).

68 See Blais, Urban Revitalization in the Post-*Kelo* Era, 34 Fordham Urb. L.J. 657 (2007); Pearce, Recent Development—Forcing Urban Redevelopment to Proceed "Building by Building": North Carolina's Flawed Response to *Kelo*, 85 N.C. L. Rev. 1784 (2007).

69 See Comment, Is This the Start of a Silent Spring? *Kelo v. New London*'s Effect on Environmental Reforms, 56 Catholic U.L. Rev. 1107 (2007).

70 See City of Norwood v. Horney, 110 Ohio St.3d 353, 853 N.E.2d 1115 (2006) (public use requirement of Ohio Constitution is not satisfied by showing of economic benefit to the government and community); Board of County Comm'rs of Muskogee County v. Lowery, 136 P.3d 639 (Okla. 2006) (economic development alone is not a public use or purpose sufficient to justify eminent domain as a matter of Oklahoma constitutional law, nor does it satisfy the public purpose requirement of state eminent-domain statute). See generally Sandefur, Don't Mess with Public Rights in Texas: How the State Constitution Protects Property Owners in the Wake of *Kelo*, 41 Real Prop. Prob. & Tr. J. 227 (2006); Comment, Eminent Domain, Regulatory Takings and Legislative Responses in the Post-*Kelo* Northwest, 43 Idaho L. Rev. 539 (2007); Note, Quieting the Clang: *Hathcock* as a Model of the State-based Protection of Property Which *Kelo* Demands, 14 Wm. & Mary Bill of Rights J. 351 (2005) (noting County of Wayne v. Hathcock, 471 Mich. 445, 684 N.W.2d 765 (2004), discussed at Section 20.2, note 8, *infra*).

enacted in reaction to *Kelo*[71] These measures, which have been enacted in one form or another in at least 42 states, have limited, or outright prevented, the use of condemnation to acquire property for economic development, and many have also re-defined what constitutes "blight" for purposes of condemning property for urban renewal.[72] Federal legislation modifying the effect of *Kelo* has also been suggested.[73]

§ 19.4 Municipal Use of Eminent Domain—"Necessity"

A second requirement often encountered in eminent domain is that the taking be a matter of necessity. This means that the particular property taken must be necessary for the public project intended. But the importance of this "necessity" rule is diminished by three facts: (1) In several states, there is no constitutional or statutory requirement that local governments condemn property only in cases of necessity; in these states, it has been held that no judicial review of "necessity" should occur.[74] (2) In those states that *do* require, constitutionally or legislatively, that takings be "necessary," the term is taken to mean only a *reasonable* necessity, not an absolute one.[75] It will often be true, of course, that the specific area taken is not absolutely essential to a project; other property might serve the intended purpose as well or nearly as well, but a certain amount of discretion must be accorded governing authorities—which raises the third limitation on

---

[71] See Scheiderich, Post-Post-*Kelo* Urban Renewal Legislation, 30 State & Local L. News, No. 4, at 5 (Summer 2007); Note, Michigan's Proposed Constitutional Amendment in Response to *Kelo*: Adequate Protection Against Eminent Domain Abuse or False Hope to Private Property Owners?, 84 U. Detroit Mercy L. Rev. 187 (2007). See generally Cavazos, Beware of Wooden Nickels: The Paradox of Florida's Legislative Overreaching in the Wake of *Kelo*, 13 U. Pa. J. Bus. L. 685 (2011); Note, *Kelo* Six Years Later: State Responses, Ramifications, and Solutions for the Future, 31 Boston Coll. Third World L.J. 311 (2011); Comment, More Than Just a Plot of Land: Ohio's Rejection of Economic Development Takings, 38 Capital U.L. Rev. 79 (2009); Symposium, Post-*Kelo* Reform, 17 Sup. Ct. Econ. Rev. 1–278 (2009). See also Comment, Closing Pandora's Box: Proposing a Statutory Solution to the Supreme Court's Failure to Adequately Protect Private Property, 2012 B.Y.U. L. Rev. 1331. Reaction to the *Kelo* case can have some unforeseen consequences. See Robson, *Kelo v. City of New London*: Its Ironic Impact on Takings Authority, 44 Urban Law. 865 (2012) (saying "policy responses to *Kelo* have so substantially restricted takings authority as to negate and indeed reverse the net effect of *Kelo* on takings authority," *id.* at 899); Vars, Irregular *Kelo* Takings: A Potential Response to Natural Disasters, 44 Urban Law. 853 (2012) (legislation passed to undo *Kelo* may have the effect of foreclosing the otherwise valid "squaring" the shape of lots following a flood or other natural disaster).

[72] See Eagle & Smart, America's Ongoing Property Rights Debate Reinvigorated: Legislative and Judicial Responses to *Kelo*, 31 State & Local L. News, No. 1, at 1 (Fall 2007). As to the "blight" requirement for condemning property for urban-renewal projects, see generally Section 20.4 *infra*. On blight and decline within cities as a possible justification for eminent domain, see Thomas, Recent Developments in Condemnation Law: Public Use, Private Property, 43 Urban Law. 877 (2011). For interesting speculation on what-might-have-been (and still might if the Supreme Court decides to re-visit *Kelo*), see Somin, What If *Kelo v. City of New London* Had Gone the Other Way?, 45 Ind. L. Rev. 21 (2011).

[73] See Bell, Legislatively Revising *Kelo v. City of New London*: Eminent Domain, Federalism, and Congressional Powers, 32 J. Legis. 165 (2006). See generally Cohen, Eminent Domain After *Kelo v. City of New London*: An Argument for Banning Economic Development Takings, 29 Harv. J.L. & Pub. Pol'y 491 (2006); Johnson, Correcting for *Kelo*: Social Capital Impact Assessments and the Re-balancing of Power Between "Desperate" Cities, Corporate Interests, and the Average Joe, 16 Cornell J.L. & Pub. Pol'y 187 (2006). See also Zeiner, Establishing a Leasehold Through Eminent Domain: A Slippery Slope Made More Treacherous by *Kelo*, 56 Catholic U.L. Rev. 503 (2007).

[74] Starr v. Nashville Housing Authority, 145 F.Supp. 498 (M.D.Tenn.1956), aff'd 354 U.S. 916, 77 S.Ct. 1378, 1 L.Ed.2d 1432; Anaheim Union High School District v. Vieira, *supra,* note 60; Embry v. Caneyville, 397 S.W.2d 141 (Ky.1965). See McAuliffe & Burke Co. v. Boston Housing Authority, 334 Mass. 28, 133 N.E.2d 493 (1956) (necessity for taking rests with discretion of governing authority).

[75] See City of Hawthorne v. Peebles, 166 Cal.App.2d 758, 333 P.2d 442 (Dist.Ct.1959); State v. Pinson, 66 Nev. 227, 207 P.2d 1105 (1949); Luccock v. City of Norman, 578 P.2d 1204 (Okl.1978); Latchis v. State Highway Board, 120 Vt. 120, 134 A.2d 191 (1957); City of Tacoma v. Welcker, *supra,* note 60; Klump v. Cybulski, 274 Wis. 604, 81 N.W.2d 42 (1957).

"necessity." (3) Great deference—even considerably greater than that accorded on the "public purpose" question—is given a legislative finding of necessity, and such a finding will ordinarily be overturned only if a reviewing court is convinced of arbitrary, capricious, or fraudulent conduct, or some gross abuse of discretion.[76] An example of such an abuse of discretion is the situation in which a local government attempts to condemn land because the governing officials want to rid the community of the landowner, or because they find his use of his land undesirable.[77] But courts will not, assuming a public purpose is present, look into the expediency or desirability of the proposed governmental project,[78] nor even weigh the environmental effects of taking the particular land.[79]

In two respects, the courts may exercise somewhat greater than usual scrutiny over the "necessity" for taking particular land: as to the *timing* of the acquisition (*i.e.*, is the property needed *now*?) and as to the *amount* of property taken (*i.e.*, is this *much* property needed?). But even as to the timing of a condemnation, it is again recognized that a considerable amount of discretion must be allowed governing officials—they need the flexibility, for instance, to try to buy when the market is best even though the property is not needed for immediate use. A condemnation of land for use 30 years in the future as a school site has been struck down as unnecessary,[80] as have a few other takings for remote or conjectural purposes.[81] But if there are plans to utilize the property in the reasonably foreseeable future, and the condemning authority intends in good faith to

---

[76] See Ermels v. Webster City, 246 Iowa 1305, 71 N.W.2d 911 (1955); In re Armory Site in Kansas City, 282 S.W.2d 464 (Mo.1955); Burlington City Board of Education v. Allen, 243 N.C. 520, 91 S.E.2d 180 (1956) (selection of site for school and condemning land therefor); Board of Education v. Park District, 70 N.W.2d 899 (N.D.1955); Rueb v. Oklahoma City, 435 P.2d 139 (Okl.1967); Luby v. City of Dallas, 396 S.W.2d 192 (Tex.Civ.App.1965), ref'd n. r. e.; Housing Authority v. Higginbotham, 135 Tex. 158, 143 S.W.2d 79 (1940). Cf. Delhi Gas Pipeline Corp. v. Swanson, 520 P.2d 670 (Okl.1974) (exceptions to necessity of taking were overruled and not appealed; held to have been waived). See generally North, The Element of Necessity in Washington Eminent Domain Proceedings, 18 Gonzaga L. Rev. 665 (1982–83). See also Yakima County v. Evans, 135 Wash.App. 212, 143 P.3d 891 (2006) (court would defer to county commissioners' determination that road modifications were necessary and as minimal as feasible, where property owners did not prove fraud or capricious conduct).

[77] See In re Real Property of Hewlett Bay Park, 48 Misc.2d 833, 265 N.Y.S.2d 1006 (Sup.Ct.1966).

[78] See Poole v. City of Kankakee, *supra* note 55. Cf. Ermels v. Webster City, *supra* note 76 (question of necessity not ordinarily subject to collateral attack; cannot be raised in independent suit to enjoin condemnation). The public use or purpose and the necessity of condemnation can be questioned in a suit brought either by owners of the property being taken or by taxpayers of the condemning authority. See Adams v. Housing Auth., 60 So.2d 663 (Fla.1952). A collateral attack can be made only on the ground of lack of jurisdiction or the ground of fraud. Carlor v. City of Miami, 62 So.2d 897 (Fla.1953), 346 U.S. 821, 74 S.Ct. 37, 98 L.Ed. 347.

[79] Ragland v. State Department of Transportation, 242 So.2d 475 (Fla.App.1970) (environmental objections to building highway through petitioner's land). See generally Note, Eminent Domain and the Environment, 56 Cornell L.Q. 651 (1971); Annot., Propriety of Court's Consideration of Ecological Effects of Proposed Project in Determining Right of Condemnation, 47 A.L.R.3d 1267 (1973). In some jurisdictions, property already being put to some use of benefit to the public can be condemned for another public use or purpose only if that use or purpose is found "more necessary" than the previous one. In such cases, of course, judicial scrutiny of the "necessity" of the proposed new use is likely to be more stringent than usual. See State ex rel. Smart v. City of Big Timber, 165 Mont. 328, 528 P.2d 688 (1974) (applying statute).

[80] Board of Educ. v. Baczewski, 340 Mich. 265, 65 N.W.2d 810 (1954).

[81] State ex rel. Sun Oil Co. v. City of Euclid, 164 Ohio St. 265, 130 N.E.2d 336 (1955). See Rueb v. Oklahoma City, *supra* note 76 (hope based on speculation is not proper basis for condemnation, but government may consider demands that are to be fairly anticipated in future).

make the public use as soon as reasonably practicable, an advance acquisition will normally be upheld.[82]

Technically, a condemning government should take no greater interest in land than is necessary for the intended public use or purpose.[83] But again, it is usually said that much discretion must be allowed local authorities in determining the quantum of property needed,[84] and that in the absence of a showing of fraud or clear abuse of discretion, the courts will not overturn those authorities' decision as to the legal interest to be taken in property (fee simple v. term for years or easement; title to land or only to buildings thereon, etc.),[85] or as to the physical amount of land to be condemned.[86] The question of the amount of land to acquire may overlap with the question, discussed in the prior paragraph *supra*, of the timing of eminent domain, because sometimes not *all* the property condemned is needed immediately even if *some* is required right away. If there is evidence that all the property taken will be needed within the reasonably foreseeable future, the courts will allow the taking of all of it.[87] The condemning local government may engage in reasonable anticipation of future increased demand for the public use to which the property will be devoted.[88] But what if the government goes beyond this and takes more property than is now needed or than can reasonably be foreseen to be needed in the near future? This is so-called "excess condemnation," and it is now sometimes authorized by constitutional provisions or statutes—which are usually

---

[82] See Sellors v. Town of Concord, 329 Mass. 259, 107 N.E.2d 784 (1952). Cf. In re Opinion of the Justices, 297 Mass. 567, 8 N.E.2d 753 (1937) (condemnation upheld though condemning authority intended to turn property over in near future to another governmental unit). See generally Note, Problems of Advance Land Acquisition, 52 Minn.L.Rev. 1175 (1968); Annot., Validity of Appropriation of Property for Anticipated Future Use, 80 A.L.R.3d 1085 (1977). See also Davis v. Brown, 221 Ill.2d 435, 303 Ill.Dec. 773, 851 N.E.2d 1198 (2006), cert. denied, 549 U.S. 995, 127 S.Ct. 510, 166 L.Ed.2d 369 (2006) (Illinois statute which authorized the state Department of Transportation to prepare and record maps that establish approximate locations and widths of rights-of-way for future additions to state highway system held constitutional; no regulatory taking found).

[83] See A.L. Kornman Co. v. Metropolitan Government, 216 Tenn. 205, 391 S.W.2d 633 (1965), on remand 57 Tenn.App. 230, 417 S.W.2d 793.

[84] See Poremba v. City of Springfield, 354 Mass. 432, 238 N.E.2d 43 (1968); State ex rel. Tacoma School Dist. No. 10 v. Stojack, 53 Wn.2d 55, 330 P.2d 567 (1958).

[85] See Berman v. Parker, 348 U.S. 26, 75 S.Ct. 98, 99 L.Ed. 27 (1954) (redevelopment agency could take full title to property if it considered this necessary). Cf. Elliott v. City of Guthrie, 725 P.2d 861 (Okl.1986) (fee simple title will be assumed taken by a condemning government if that appears to have been the legislative intent, such title was reasonably requisite to the designated use, and suitable proceedings were prosecuted for that purpose). See also Bogart v. Caprock Communications Co., 69 P.3d 266 (Okla. 2003) (where company was authorized by statute to lay cable within road easements, installation of cable by telecommunications company within the confines of a public right-of-way or easement did not impose any increased servitude on the land which would entitle the landowner to additional compensation).

[86] See City of Phoenix v. McCullough, 24 Ariz.App. 109, 536 P.2d 230 (1975). As to whether condemnation of land includes subsurface rights, see Department of Transportation v. Gypsum Ranch Co., LLC, 244 P.3d 127 (Colo. 2010) (interpreting state statute that prohibited government from acquiring mineral rights beneath real property that is condemned for highway purposes except to the extent necessary for subsurface support).

[87] *Id.* On the overlap between the problems of excess condemnation and condemnation for future needs, see Matheson, Excess Condemnation in California: Proposals for Statutory and Constitutional Change, 42 So.Cal.L.Rev. 421 (1969); Note, Excess Condemnation—To Take or not to Take—A Functional Analysis, 15 N.Y.L.F. 119 (1969). Cf. State ex rel. Thomson v. Giessel, 265 Wis. 185, 60 N.W.2d 873 (1953), distinguishing municipal power to sell excess lands *after* they've proven unnecessary from power in the first instance to sell land the municipality knows won't be needed. See generally Mandelker, Controlling Land Values in Areas of Rapid Urban Expansion, 12 U.C.L.A.L.Rev. 734 (1965).

[88] City of Chicago v. Newberry Library, 7 Ill.2d 305, 131 N.E.2d 60 (1955).

limited to specific situations, as where an uneconomic or odd-shaped remnant of land would otherwise be left.[89] Any such authorization is strictly construed; under Ohio constitutional provisions allowing excess condemnation, the state supreme court ruled that the condemning local government must still show reasonable need for the property in furtherance of some public use.[90] And in the *absence* of specific constitutional or legislative authority, courts generally invalidate attempts at excess condemnation.[91] Where the only purpose for the excess taking is the condemning government's hope of recouping some of its expenses by selling the extra land after the planned government project is completed, courts are likely to be especially unwilling to find any authorization for such taking.[92]

§ 19.5 Municipal Use of Eminent Domain—"Just Compensation"

The third requirement by which local governments must abide in exercising the power of eminent domain is that of just compensation.[93] Such compensation is defined

---

[89] *E.g.*, Mass.Const. Art. 10, Pt. 1; N.Y.Const. Art. 9, § 1(e); Ohio Const. Art. 18, § 10; 27 Okl.Stat. § 13. See People ex rel. Department of Public Works v. Superior Court, 68 Cal.2d 206, 65 Cal.Rptr. 342, 436 P.2d 342 (1968) (statute interpreted to allow excess taking in cases where excessive severance damages would otherwise have to be paid—and only in such cases); State v. Buck, 94 N.J.Super. 84, 226 A.2d 840 (1967) (excess condemnation found to be authorized by statute when the additional land could not otherwise be lawfully used). But cf. State ex rel. State Highway Department v. 9.88 Acres of Land, 253 A.2d 509 (Del.1969) (a worthless remnant might be condemned, but here the remnant had market value). Cf. State Highway Commission v. Chapman, 152 Mont. 79, 446 P.2d 709 (1968) (statute provided for taking whole parcel whenever condemnation of part would leave remainder in such shape or condition as to give rise to litigation over damages; statute held inapplicable—remainder too large to be a "physical remnant," and it was not rendered valueless; so was not a "financial remnant"). Among the reasons sometimes offered for excess condemnation are (1) protection of the land surrounding a public improvement for aesthetic or land-use purposes, (2) preventing the leaving of unusable and/or odd-shaped remnants of land which the public agency may condemn in order to prevent hardship or in order to combine the remnant with other land to make a usable parcel, and (3) recoupment of some of the cost of the public improvement by sale of the excess land. But the last reason is still generally considered an improper ground for condemnation. See note 92 *infra* and accompanying text. See generally Mandelker, Managing Our Urban Environment 670–71 (2d ed. 1971).

[90] East Cleveland v. Nau, 124 Ohio St. 433, 179 N.E. 187 (1931). Cf. City of Richmond v. Carneal, 129 Va. 388, 106 S.E. 403 (1921), invalidating a statute that would have allowed cities, in widening streets, to take all the property that would be injuriously affected.

[91] See Opinion of the Justices, 204 Mass. 607, 91 N.E. 405 (1910); Pennsylvania Mutual Life Insurance Co. v. City of Philadelphia, 242 Pa. 47, 88 A. 904 (1913); City of Seattle v. Faussett, 123 Wash. 613, 212 P. 1085 (1923). But see City of Tacoma v. Welcker, 65 Wn.2d 677, 399 P.2d 330 (1965) (city could condemn land bordering river from which it took its water supply; needed for protection of watershed). Cf. Pearl River Valley Water Supply District v. Brown, 248 Miss. 4, 156 So.2d 572 (1963), motion overruled 248 Miss. 4, 158 So.2d 694, cert. denied 376 U.S. 970, 84 S.Ct. 1136, 12 L.Ed.2d 84 (by statute, land could be condemned for public use within quarter-mile perimeter area; condemnation in such area valid where was for pollution control, control of access, etc.).

[92] See City of Cincinnati v. Vester, 281 U.S. 439, 50 S.Ct. 360, 74 L.Ed. 950 (1930), aff'g 33 F.2d 242 (6th Cir.1929).

[93] See Chicago, Burlington & Quincy Railroad Co. v. City of Chicago, 166 U.S. 226, 17 S.Ct. 581, 41 L.Ed. 979 (1897) (Fourteenth Amendment requires compensation when local government takes property). On compensation, see generally 3, 4, 4A and 5 Nichols, Eminent Domain (Sackman 3d rev. ed. 1982). A good review of the rules and arguments on "just compensation" is contained in Gruen, Takings, Just Compensation, and the Efficient Use of Land, Urban, and Environmental Resources, 33 Urban Law. 517 (2001), particularly Sections III & IV, at 523–46.

On the "collision course" that exists between the principle of sovereign immunity that bars suits against an unconsenting government for money and the principle of just compensation that requires a government to pay for property taken for public use, see Seamon, The Asymmetry of State Sovereign Immunity, 76 Wash. L. Rev. 1067 (2001), noting (at 1068) that the U.S. Supreme Court has never answered the question whether a person can sue a State for taking that person's property for public use without paying for it.

as market value, which in turn is generally said to mean the price which would be paid by a willing buyer to a willing seller under ordinary circumstances, with neither party under any compulsion to act.[94] The price paid at a recent voluntary sale of the very property that is now being condemned is ordinarily admissible as strong evidence of the

---

[94] City of Wilmington v. State, 251 A.2d 341 (Del.1969); In re Armory Site in Kansas City, 282 S.W.2d 464 (Mo.1955); City of Alexandria v. Jones, 236 La. 612, 108 So.2d 528 (1959). If the property does not have fair-market value in the usual sense—as may be true of religious properties, schools, cemeteries, etc.—the value for the uses to which it is being put and to which it is adaptable may be shown. See Graceland Park Cemetery Co. v. City of Omaha, 173 Neb. 608, 114 N.W.2d 29 (1962). Cf. United States v. 564.54 Acres of Land, 441 U.S. 506, 99 S.Ct. 1854, 60 L.Ed.2d 435 (1979) (U.S. condemned property of nonprofit organization, used for summer camps; held that fair-market value could be awarded rather than replacement cost). See generally Annot., Measure of Damages Payable on Condemnation of Real Property by Federal Government—Supreme Court Cases, 60 L.Ed.2d 1107 (1980). Where the property of one public agency is condemned by another government for some other public purpose, the cost of providing "substitute facilities" is often used as the measure of damages. See Wichita v. Unified School District, 201 Kan. 110, 439 P.2d 162 (1968), appeal after remand 205 Kan. 701, 472 P.2d 253 (condemnee ought to be placed in as good a position as if property had not been taken). But this "substitute facilities" test was rejected in the United States v. 564.54 Acres case *supra*. On the power of one level of government to condemn property of another level, see generally Chapter 7 *supra*.

The fair-market value is, generally speaking, to be determined as of the date of condemnation—but without any increases or decreases that may have been caused by public knowledge of the proposed governmental project for the area. See United States v. Miller, 317 U.S. 369, 377, 63 S.Ct. 276, 281, 87 L.Ed. 336 (1943), reh. denied 318 U.S. 798, 63 S.Ct. 557, 87 L.Ed. 1162 (the leading case); United States v. 85.11 Acres of Land, 243 F.Supp. 423 (N.D.Okl.1965); Jones v. Oklahoma City Urban Renewal Authority, 514 P.2d 661 (Okl.1973). Cf. Wohl v. City of Missoula, 369 Mont.108, 300 P.3d 1119 (2013) (damages measured by value of land at time of taking). See generally Annot., Eminent Domain: Right of Owner of Land Not Originally Taken or Purchased as Part of Adjacent Project to Recover, on Enlargement of Project to Include Adjacent Land, Enhanced Value of Property by Reason of Proximity to Original Project—State Cases, 95 A.L.R.3d 752 (1979) (condemnee entitled, under *Miller* case *supra*, to enhanced value *if* adjacent land was *not* within scope of project from time the condemnor was committed to it). On the problems created when the value of property is affected by the prospect of future condemnation, see Editor's Comment, Planning Blight: The Anglo-American Experience, 29 Urban Law. vii (1997). On the effect, in determining fair-market value, of the condemnor's delay in initiating condemnation proceedings, see Washington Metropolitan Area Transit Auth. v. One Parcel of Land in Fairfax County, 780 F.2d 467 (4th Cir.1986) (where transit authority waited to initiate condemnation proceedings, it must pay for enhancement in value of condemned property caused by its ongoing construction of nearby station).

An owner of condemned land may recover compensation for improvements made thereon in good faith, even if made with knowledge of impending condemnation. See Annot., Eminent Domain: Recovery of Value of Improvements Made with Knowledge of Impending Condemnation, 98 A.L.R.3d 504 (1980). But cf. City of Wichita v. Denton, 294 P.3d 207 (Kan. 2013) (billboard structure was personal property or a "trade fixture," not part of the realty, and lessee was not entitled to compensation for it). As to billboards and other improvements on land, see generally note 98 *infra*.

In general, the owner of condemned property is *not* entitled to the cost of acquiring a substitute facility but only to market value if that amount is ascertainable. See United States v. 50 Acres of Land, 469 U.S. 24, 105 S.Ct. 451, 83 L.Ed.2d 376 (1984). Cf. DeSambourg v. Board of Comm'rs, 621 So.2d 602 (La.1993), cert. denied 510 U.S. 1093, 114 S.Ct. 925, 127 L.Ed.2d 218 (1994) (state could deny compensation for land considered "batture": the portion of a river that is annually covered by ordinary high water). For a good argument that "market value" is only one possible means of reaching the goal of "just compensation," see Montague, Market Value and All That Jazz: The Proof of the Pudding Is in the Eating, 30 Urban Law. 631 (1998). Cf. Gergen, Why Fair Market Value Fails as Just Compensation, 14 Hamline J. Pub. L. & Pol'y 181 (1993), arguing that the fair-market-value standard often fails to compensate adequately. See also Bell & Parchomovsky, The Hidden Function of Takings Compensation, 96 Va. L. Rev. 1673 (2010). Compare Chen, Economic Value or Fair Market Value: What Form of Takings Compensation Is Efficient?, 20 Sup. Ct. Econ. Rev. 35 (2012); Williams, Restitution, Eminent Domain, and Economic Development: Moving to a Gains-Based Conception of the Takings Clause, 41 Urban Law. 183 (2008) (25th Smith-Babcock-Williams Student Writing Competition Winner), noting that many commentators believe that the recent debate on what is a public purpose in eminent-domain law could better focus on the amount of compensation provided. *Id.* at 183–84 & note 5, citing in particular Gillette, *Kelo* and the Local Political Process, 34 Hofstra L. Rev. 13, 20–21 (2005), which endorsed the views of Prof. Thomas Merrill.

property's market value;[95] and the prices paid at recent sales of comparable properties, at least if in the same general geographic area, are usually admissible in evidence also.[96] Offers to purchase—even if recent offers to purchase the very property under consideration—are usually not allowed in evidence, being considered unreliable indicators of value.[97] Other factors that may be weighed in determining fair-market value include rental income; cost, or replacement cost, of improvements, less depreciation; and the value of any business that has been conducted on the property.[98]

---

[95] Epstein v. City & County of Denver, 133 Colo. 104, 293 P.2d 308 (1956). It rests largely in the discretion of the trial judge to determine whether a particular sale was recent enough to be relevant. See City of Baltimore v. Schreiber, 243 Md. 546, 221 A.2d 663 (1966). But cf. Miller v. Glacier Development Co., L.L.C., 284 Kan. 476, 161 P.3d 730 (2007), cert. denied 552 U.S. 1258, 128 S.Ct. 1657, 170 L.Ed.2d 355 (2008) (court's exercise of discretion in admitting and excluding evidence of value of condemned property is circumscribed by governing law, which provides that prior sale is relevant only if shown to have occurred recently and if it is shown that values in that area have not changed since prior sale or purchase).

[96] See City of Alexandria v. Jones, *supra* note 94; Township of Moorestown v. Slack, 85 N.J.Super. 109, 204 A.2d 23 (1964) (property must be similar). Cf. United States v. 75.13 Acres of Land, 693 F.2d 813 (8th Cir.1982) (sales of comparable land in the area, with consideration given the condition of the properties and their use at the time of taking, properly weighed as evidence); Barlow Ranch Limited Partnership v. Greencore Pipeline Co., LLC, 301 P.3d 75 (Wyo. 2013) (natural gas pipeline easements could be viewed as comparables when determining fair market value of carbon dioxide pipeline easement). But cf. United States v. 0.161 Acres of Land, 837 F.2d 1036 (11th Cir.1988), holding that evidence presented by a qualified expert witness to establish the value of property is admissible even if not based on comparable sales. Again, the trial judge has great discretion in deciding whether or not the other property is sufficiently comparable for its sale-price to be relevant. See Weeden v. Beloit, 29 Wis.2d 662, 139 N.W.2d 616 (1966). This is also true as to whether the sale was recent enough to be relevant—and, of course, the more recent the sale, the more weight it may be given. See City of St. Louis v. Vasquez, 341 S.W.2d 839 (Mo.1960). Cf. Oklahoma Transp. Auth. v. George Abdo Trust Dated 10-15-74, 130 P.3d 751 (Okla.Civ.App. 2005) (evidence of sale of land, which was adjacent to the subject property, was inadmissible when the contract for sale of the land was not closed until over 6 months after the date of taking of the subject property).

[97] See McAlester Urban Renewal Authority v. Watts, 516 P.2d 261 (Okl.1973); Lower Nueces River Water Supply District v. Sellers, 323 S.W.2d 324 (Tex.Civ.App.1959), ref'd n. r. e. See generally Annot., Unaccepted Offer for Purchase of Real Property as Evidence of Its Value, 25 A.L.R.4th 571 (1983). See also Annot., Unaccepted Offer to Sell or Listing of Real Property as Evidence of Its. Value, 25 A.L.R.4th 983 (1983) (offer to *sell* is self-serving statement lacking reliability and is thus generally inadmissible on question of value); 29 Am. Jur. 2d Evidence § 768 (1994) (unaccepted offer to sell may be admissible *against* offeror landowners but not in favor of a landowner or offeror).

[98] See Gleghorn v. City of Wichita Falls, 545 S.W.2d 446 (Tex.1976) (all factors that would reasonably be given weight in negotiations between willing buyer and willing seller should be weighed). See generally 2A Antieau, Municipal Corporation Law § 20.06, at 20–28 (1998). The taking of real property usually includes an appropriation of all permanent improvements, structures, and fixtures affixed to the land (though not of personal property found on the premises); the improvements are usually compensable to the extent they enhance the value of the land as a whole. See Annot., Eminent Domain: Determination of Just Compensation for Condemnation of Billboards or Other Advertising Signs, 73 A.L.R.3d 1122 (1976); Annot., Eminent Domain: Valuation of Land and Improvements and Fixtures Thereon Separately or as Unit, 1 A.L.R.2d 878 (1948); Annot., Eminent Domain: Cost of Repairs and Improvements on Property Taken, as Evidence of its Value, 172 A.L.R. 236 (1948). Where a leasehold is condemned, or is part of the total interest condemned, the lessee is entitled to compensation measured by what a willing private buyer would have paid for the lease interest. See Beaverton Urban Renewal Agency v. Koning, 53 Or.App. 842, 632 P.2d 1359 (1981), review denied 291 Or. 893, 642 P.2d 309 (1981) (where estate in fee simple is condemned, a lease on the property thereupon terminates and lessee is entitled to share in condemnation award unless the lease provides otherwise). Cf. Ward v. Downtown Dev. Auth., 786 F.2d 1526 (11th Cir.1986) (tenancy-at-will is a property interest under state law and is subject of a compensable taking where tenants displaced by redevelopment); Utah Dept. of Transportation v. FPA West Point, LLC, 304 P.3d 810 (Utah 2012) (value of respective interests, including leasehold, in condemned property must be individually assessed). This award to the lessee may include most of the compensation paid for the improvements on the land where the improvements were placed thereon by the lessee, had a life expectancy exceeding the lease-term, and were subject to removal by the lessee. See Almota Farmers Elevator & Warehouse Co. v. United States, 409 U.S. 470, 93 S.Ct. 791, 35 L.Ed.2d 1 (1973). If an option to purchase is part of the lease agreement and there is reason to suppose the tenant would exercise that option, then loss of this right should be figured as part of the tenant's damages in his condemnation award.

In deciding the fair-market value, courts will consider not only the use to which the property is currently being put but also other uses to which it might be readily put.[99] It

---

State v. Jan-Mar, Inc., 236 N.J.Super. 28, 563 A.2d 1153 (1989); Spokane School Dist. v. Parzybok, 96 Wash.2d 95, 633 P.2d 1324 (1981). See Note, Property—Condemnation—Option to Purchase Held Compensable, 1 Okla. C.U.L. Rev. 203 (1976), noting County of San Diego v. Miller, 13 Cal.3d 684, 119 Cal.Rptr. 491, 532 P.2d 139 (1975). See generally Annot., Eminent Domain: Measure and Elements of Lessee's Compensation for Condemnor's Taking or Damaging of Leasehold, 17 A.L.R.4th 337 (1982) (market value of leasehold is measure of damages, but this is sometimes difficult to determine since leaseholds are not often sold, frequently cannot be assigned without the landlord's consent, and vary significantly in term, rent, and other particulars); Annot., Elements and Measure of Lessee's Compensation for Taking Leasehold in Eminent Domain—Federal Cases, 94 L.Ed. 826 (1950). As to eminent-domain compensation for an option to purchase that stands alone, apart from any lease, see Mount Juneau Enterprises, Inc. v. City & Borough of Juneau, 923 P.2d 768 (Alaska 1996), cert. denied 520 U.S. 1168, 117 S.Ct. 1431, 137 L.Ed.2d 539 (1997) (option to purchase creates compensable interest in property, but no compensation awarded here, in inverse condemnation action, where owner of option failed to introduce evidence of diminution of option's value); Sterling Park, L.P. v. City of Palo Alto, 163 Cal. Rptr. 2, 310 P.3d 925 (2013) (purchase option is sufficiently strong interest in property to require compensation where government takes it in eminent domain). See also City of Roeland Park v. Jasan Trust, 281 Kan. 668, 132 P.3d 943 (2006) (lease agreement providing that sublessee was entitled to a portion of lessee's condemnation award to compensate sublessee for lost profits was enforceable).

Loss of business profits and other income, even though stemming directly from the move necessitated by the condemnation, is usually not compensated, since such a loss is considered too remote and speculative. See Arizona Water Co. v. City of Yuma, 7 Ariz.App. 53, 436 P.2d 147 (1968); Ace Ambulance Service Inc. v. City of Augusta, 337 A.2d 661 (Me.1975). Nor are the good will and general value of a business compensable when its place of business is condemned. See Auraria Businessmen Against Confiscation, Inc. v. Denver Urban Renewal Auth., 183 Colo. 441, 517 P.2d 845 (1974); Restaurants, Inc. v. City of Wilmington, 274 A.2d 137 (Del.1971); Verzani v. State Department of Roads, 188 Neb. 162, 195 N.W.2d 762 (1972). But see In re Fifth Ave. Coach Lines, Inc., 18 N.Y.2d 212, 273 N.Y.S.2d 52, 219 N.E.2d 410 (1966), remittitur amended 18 N.Y.2d 741, 274 N.Y.S.2d 349, 221 N.E.2d 174, appeal dism'd 386 U.S. 778, 87 S.Ct. 1480, 18 L.Ed.2d 524, where compensation for "going concern value" was held necessary when a business capable of profitable operation was condemned. See generally Aloi & Goldberg, A Reexamination of Value, Goodwill, and Business Losses in Eminent Domain, 53 Cornell L.Rev. 604 (1968); Newton & Slattery, The Changing Areas in Condemnation Law 791, 800–02 (1983), noting some trend toward allowing recovery for loss of business good-will when a business premises is condemned; Risinger, Direct Damages: The Lost Key to Constitutional Just Compensation When Business Premises Are Condemned, 15 Seton Hall L. Rev. 483 (1985); 27 Am.Jur.2d Eminent Domain § 335 (1996). There is usually no compensation for attorneys' fees, moving expenses, etc. See Dohany v. Rogers, 281 U.S. 362, 50 S.Ct. 299, 74 L.Ed. 904 (1930). Cf. United States v. Bodcaw Co., 440 U.S. 202, 99 S.Ct. 1066, 59 L.Ed.2d 257 (1979), on remand 594 F.2d 169 (5th Cir.) (appraisal expenses not part of just compensation); Luby v. City of Dallas, 396 S.W.2d 192 (Tex.Civ.App.1965), ref'd n. r. e. (expense of moving tenant's personal property not compensable). But occasionally, some of these items are specifically allowed by statute. See Auraria Businessmen Against Confiscation, Inc. v. Denver Urban Renewal Auth., *supra* (relocation expenses of those displaced by urban renewal made compensable); City of Muskegon v. Slater, 2 Mich.App. 235, 139 N.W.2d 346 (1966), aff'd 379 Mich. 466, 152 N.W.2d 652. In general, the courts are reluctant, unless required by statute, to compensate for *any* intangible items. See United States v. Fuller, 409 U.S. 488, 93 S.Ct. 801, 35 L.Ed.2d 16 (1973) (no compensation for value added to lands by grazing permits). But see City of McCall v. Seubert, 142 Idaho 580, 130 P.3d 1118 (2006) (businesses that were located on property subject to city's eminent domain proceeding could recover relocation costs as business damages where businesses had no choice but to relocate). Cf. State. ex rel. Department of Transp. v. Little, 100 P.3d 707 (Okla. 2004) (property owners were not required to exhaust administrative remedies before seeking relocation expenses as part of just compensation).

While such items as engineering costs incurred on the land by the condemnee prior to condemnation, and costs of moving personal property, are not (except as otherwise specified by statute) separately included in the condemnation award, they may be considered to the extent they are reflected in the land's market value—what the willing seller would accept and the willing buyer pay. See Rustcon Developers, Inc. v. State, 33 A.D.2d 582, 304 N.Y.S.2d 287 (1969).

On the relevance of loss of value caused by fears due to the proximity of power lines, see Schutt, The Power Line Dilemma: Compensation for Diminished Property Value Caused by Fear of Electromagnetic Fields, 24 Fla. St. U.L. Rev. 125 (1996). See generally Bolton & Sick, Power Lines and Property Values: The Good, The Bad, and the Ugly, 31 Urban Law. 331 (1999) (Part I of Symposium); Comment, The Psychological Cost of Eminent Domain Takings and Just Compensation, 30 Law & Psychol. Rev. 215 (2006).

[99] See United States ex rel. TVA v. Powelson, 319 U.S. 266, 63 S.Ct. 1047, 87 L.Ed. 1390 (1943), conformed to 138 F.2d 343 (4th Cir.), cert. denied 321 U.S. 773, 64 S.Ct. 612, 88 L.Ed. 1067 (uses to which

is often said that the property's "highest and best use" should be considered—*i.e.*, the most profitable use to which the property could be put.[100] Of course, zoning laws and restrictive covenants may limit the property's lawful uses, and thus these restrictions should also be considered.[101] But the majority view allows, in addition, consideration of any *changes* in zoning laws or in other restrictions if these changes are *reasonably probable* in the near future.[102]

Where only a portion of a landowner's property is taken, that owner is, in most jurisdictions, entitled not only to compensation for the part taken but to "severance damages" for the harm to the remainder. Severance damages should cover harm to any uses to which the property is lawfully devoted,[103] and the total of these damages should

---

property presently devoted and those to which could be readily converted); Tharp v. City of Paducah, 389 S.W.2d 453 (Ky.1965) (uses for which land adapted and available).

[100] Caldwell v. Roark, 92 Idaho 99, 437 P.2d 615 (1968); Andrews v. Kingsbury General Improvement District, 84 Nev. 88, 436 P.2d 813 (1968). See Graceland Park Cemetery Co. v. City of Omaha, *supra* note 94. See generally Sussna, The Concept of Highest and Best Use Under Takings Theory, 21 Urban Law. 113 (1989).

[101] See Staninger v. Jacksonville Expressway Authority, 182 So.2d 483 (Fla.App.1966) (restrictive covenants); City of Honolulu v. Bishop Trust Co., 48 Haw. 444, 404 P.2d 373 (1965); State ex rel. Lord v. Pahl, 254 Minn. 349, 95 N.W.2d 85 (1959) (zoning ordinances). Cf. State Dep't of Transp. v. Lundberg, 312 Or. 568, 825 P.2d 641 (1992), cert. denied 506 U.S. 975, 113 S.Ct. 467, 121 L.Ed.2d 374 (1992) (evidence of city's ordinance requiring sidewalk dedication in connection with development of property was relevant in determining fair market value even though property owners had not applied for any land use approvals that would invoke the dedication requirement).

[102] Moschetti v. City of Tucson, 9 Ariz.App. 108, 449 P.2d 945 (1969); Long Beach City High School District v. Stewart, 30 Cal.2d 763, 185 P.2d 585 (1947) (effect of probable change on minds of willing purchasers should be considered).

[103] United States v. Grizzard, 219 U.S. 180, 31 S.Ct. 162, 55 L.Ed. 165 (1911). See City of Charlotte v. Spratt, 263 N.C. 656, 140 S.E.2d 341 (1965); Williams Natural Gas Co. v. Perkins, 952 P.2d 483 (Okl.1997) (severance damages cover harm, if any, caused by separation of part taken from remaining property, loss or impairment of right of access, and damage caused by construction or use of project on property being taken). Cf. City of Phoenix v. Garretson, 302 P.3d 640 (Ariz. App. 2013) (severance damages are available when government condemns a portion of an aggrieved party's property but are not available when there is merely a loss of access rights); City of Texarkana v. Kitty Wells, Inc., 539 S.W.2d 205 (Tex.Civ.App.1976), holding that although the cost of relocating improvements is not a separate item in condemnation cases, it can be considered to the extent it depreciates the value of the land in situations where *part* of the tract is taken and improvements must be moved because of this. See generally Comment, The Price of Protection: Compensation for Partial Takings Along the Coast, 30 Touro L. Rev. 861 (2014).

"Aesthetic loss" is compensable if it diminishes the market value of the remaining property. See Annot., Unsightliness of Power Line or Other Wire, or Related Structure, as Element of Damages in Easement Condemnation Proceeding, 97 A.L.R.3d 587 (1980). See generally Bockrath, Aesthetics and Condemnation Awards: Problems in Preserving the Aesthetic Environment Through Eminent Domain, 7 Natural Resources Lawyer 621 (1974).

If there is unity of use among physically separate tracts of land, or if it can otherwise be established that the tracts constituted a "single parcel," severance damages are required for the taking of one, or less than all, of several tracts despite their lack of contiguity. See State v. McDonald, 98 Wash.2d 521, 656 P.2d 1043 (1983) (whether three parcels that had constituted hop farm were inseparably connected in their use, so that taking of one tract destroyed the farm as an economic unit and rendered all three parcels worthless, was jury question). Cf. City of San Diego v. Neumann, 6 Cal.4th 738, 25 Cal.Rptr.2d 480, 863 P.2d 725 (1993) (commonly owned but separately utilized parcels could be aggregated for purposes of severance damages upon a showing of reasonable probability that all of the parcels would be foreseeably available for development as a common unit); Clarmar Realty Co. v. Redevelopment Auth. of Milwaukee, 129 Wis.2d 81, 383 N.W.2d 890 (1986) (where most advantageous use of condemned parcel was in an integrated use with another parcel and where assemblage of the parcels was reasonably probable, property's value as integrated, less cost of acquiring the other parcel, was an acceptable method of calculating fair market value). Compare City of Salem v. H.S.B., 302 Or. 648, 733 P.2d 890 (1987), where unity of ownership with the condemned parcel was not established by the corporate landowner seeking compensation and the landowner was thus held not entitled to recover for injury to its separate parcel.

represent the loss in value of the remaining property, for sale or rental, between the time immediately *before* and the time immediately *after* the taking.[104]

What if the remaining land, instead of being harmed—or in addition to being in some respects harmed—, is actually *benefited* by the taking, as where some land is condemned for a highway and the remaining property, now bordering the road, becomes much more valuable for business uses? There is considerable controversy over whether, in awarding damages to a property-owner, an "offset" should be made for these benefits. Some states allow no such offset, or allow it only against the severance damages; but most hold that at least the "special" benefits (those accruing to this particular property and not accruing to the general public or to all property in the area) should be offset against the total damages awarded—and several states hold that *all* benefits, whether special or general, should be offset against the total award.[105]

---

[104] See City of Alexandria v. Jones, *supra* note 94; Southwestern Bell Telephone Co. v. Ramsey, 542 S.W.2d 466 (Tex.Civ.App.1976), ref'd n. r. e. (landowner has right to claim severance damages to entire remainder, but may waive damages as to part and claim them only as to other part of remainder). Cf. City of Albuquerque v. Chapman, 76 N.M. 162, 413 P.2d 204 (1966); Board of Trustees of Town of Farmington v. Spencer, 75 N.M. 636, 409 P.2d 269 (1965) ("before and after" rule applies to partial takings—owner recovers total amount by which his property depreciated; court must consider both benefits and detriments to remaining land). Note that if none of a landowner's property is taken in eminent domain but he is nonetheless harmed by a nearby government project (for instance, by noise and vibrations from a highway), he must recover, if at all, in a tort suit (often limited by government immunity) or in "inverse condemnation" (see Section 19.2 *supra*); but if some of a person's land is taken for the government project, he may recover for the harm to the remainder as part of his severance damages. See Annot., Traffic Noise and Vibration from Highway as Element of Damages in Eminent Domain, 51 A.L.R.3d 860 (1973). Thus, in State ex rel. Miller v. J.R. Norton Co., 158 Ariz. 50, 760 P.2d 1099 (App.1988), it was held that allowing the jury to consider the proximity of a new roadway to a landowner's property and the consequent noise was proper in determining severance damages in a condemnation action based on the state's taking a portion of the land for a freeway ramp. Similarly, where part of a person's land is taken, that person is entitled to compensation for loss of view to the remaining property, even though no damages might be awardable due to an interference with view that did not involve a physical taking of any of the person's land. See Annot., Eminent Domain: Compensability of Loss of View from Owner's Property—State Cases, 25 A.L.R.4th 671 (1983). Cf. State ex rel. Humphrey v. Strom, 493 N.W.2d 554 (Minn.1992) (in case of partial taking of land, evidence of construction related interferences and loss of visibility may be taken into account in determining compensation to extent these affect market value of the property). See also Annot., Eminent Domain: Compensability of Loss of Visibility of Owner's Property, 7 A.L.R.5th 113 (1992). But see County of Anoka v. Blaine Bldg. Corp., 566 N.W.2d 331 (Minn.1997) (commercial property owner subjected to partial taking could not recover severance damages due to reduced access of traffic to property).

[105] See Los Angeles County, Metropolitan Transp. Auth. v. Continental Dev. Corp., 16 Cal.4th 694, 66 Cal.Rptr.2d 630, 941 P.2d 809 (1997) (both special and general benefits to remainder may be offset against severance damages, overruling prior authority); Commonwealth v. Sherrod, 367 S.W.2d 844 (Ky.1963). The rules applied in the various states were set forth in In re Water Front, 190 N.Y. 350, 83 N.E. 299 (1907). See generally Annot., Eminent Domain, Deduction of Benefits in Determining Compensation or Damages in Proceedings Involving Opening, Widening, or Otherwise Altering Highway, 13 A.L.R.3d 1149 (1967); Lewis, Eminent Domain (Michie ed. 1953). See also Haar & Hering, The Determination of Benefits in Land Acquisition, 51 Cal. L.Rev. 833 (1963). Where a distinction is made between "general" and "special" benefits, the meaning of these terms is not always clear, and a number of definitions are possible. See Juergensmeyer & Roberts, Land Use Planning & Control Law 702–03 (1998), defining "special benefits"; Palmore, Damages Recoverable in a Partial Taking, 21 S.W. L.J. 740 (1967); Peacock, The Offset of Benefits Against Losses in Eminent Domain Case in Texas, 44 Tex. L. Rev. 1564 (1966).

§ 19.6 Municipal Use of Eminent Domain—Procedural Requirements

The procedures for condemnation of property are prescribed by constitution, statute, or (occasionally) home-rule charter, and must be strictly followed.[106] There is at least one procedural requirement under the U.S. Constitution: Timely notice, reasonably calculated to inform interested parties of the proceedings, must be given those whose property interests are being taken.[107] Where, as often, a jury is employed to set eminent-domain awards, an award will be set aside by the court only if a clear error is shown, or the verdict is shown to have been the result of passion or prejudice.[108] The award will, however, be set aside if it either exceeds the maximum amount justified by the evidence or is lower than the lowest figure suggested by the evidence.[109] In appealing a condemnation award, a property owner must strictly follow statutory and charter

---

[106] See McAuliffe & Burke Co. v. Boston Housing Authority, 334 Mass. 28, 133 N.E.2d 493 (1956) (if essential steps in condemnation procedure were omitted, landowner may challenge the taking); State ex rel. Sun Oil Co. v. City of Euclid, 164 Ohio St. 265, 130 N.E.2d 336 (1955); Roehl v. City of Milwaukee, 141 Wis. 341, 124 N.W. 400 (1910). On the nature of eminent domain condemnation proceedings, see generally City of Tahlequah v. Lake Region Elec. Cooperative, Inc., 47 P.3d 467 (Okla. 2002) (condemnation proceeding is a special statutory proceeding designed to determine in a single action the damages for property taken from private persons for public use). If delays ensue because of the need for legal proceedings to determine fair-market value, the property owner is entitled to interest from the date of taking to the date of payment, or some comparable reimbursement for use of his money during this time. See Smyth v. United States, 302 U.S. 329, 58 S.Ct. 248, 82 L.Ed. 294 (1937); United States v. Highsmith, 255 U.S. 170, 41 S.Ct. 282, 65 L.Ed. 569 (1921); Tillson v. United States, 100 U.S.(10 Otto) 43, 25 L.Ed. 543 (1879); Russian Orthodox Greek Catholic Church v. Alaska State Housing Authority, 498 P.2d 737 (Alaska 1972). See generally 3 Nichols, Eminent Domain § 8.63 (Sackman 3d rev. ed. 1965).

[107] Walker v. Hutchinson, 352 U.S. 112, 77 S.Ct. 200, 1 L.Ed.2d 178 (1956). But cf. Fifth Ave. Coach Lines v. City of New York, *supra* note 98, holding that notice is not necessary prior to condemnation but only prior to the determination of questions of public use and fair compensation. Cf. Campbell v. Edinger, 607 P.2d 697 (Okl.1980) (condemnor is only required to join owners, parties who assert claims, etc. if condemnor has actual knowledge of their claims). Even if a citizen does not receive proper notice of a condemnation hearing, he cannot be heard to complain of this failure if he actually appears at the hearing. See M.R.D. Corp. v. City of Bellevue, 195 Neb. 722, 240 N.W.2d 46 (1976). Cf. City of Stigler v. Crumley, 99 P.3d 253 (Okla.Civ.App. 2004) (city's failure to notify individual designated heirs of intention to condemn decedent's land did not deprive heirs of due process where city had notified estate's personal representative, who stood in position of condemnee).

[108] See City of Chicago v. Exchange National Bank, 64 Ill.App.2d 455, 212 N.E.2d 494 (1965); Steck v. City of Wichita, 179 Kan. 305, 295 P.2d 1068 (1956) (jury verdict will not be disturbed if there is any evidence to support it); City of Jackson v. Landrum, 217 Miss. 10, 63 So.2d 391 (1953). Cf. In re Civic Center in Detroit, 335 Mich. 528, 56 N.W.2d 375 (1953); In re Widening of Michigan Ave., 280 Mich. 539, 273 N.W. 798 (1937) (trial judge should not disturb jury verdict if it is supported by the evidence). See generally Comment, The Jury's Role in Eminent Domain Compensation, 22 J. Natural Resources & Envtl. L. 219 (2008–09), explaining Metropolitan Water Dist. of So. California v. Campus Crusade for Christ, Inc., 41 Cal. 4th 954, 62 Cal. Rptr. 3d 623, 161 P.3d 1175 (2007).

[109] Redevelopment Agency v. Modell, 177 Cal.App.2d 321, 2 Cal.Rptr. 245 (Dist.Ct.1960); City of Los Angeles v. Frew, 139 Cal.App.2d 859, 294 P.2d 1073 (1956); City of Chicago v. Koff, 341 Ill. 520, 173 N.E. 666 (1930); Avins v. Commonwealth, 379 Pa. 202, 108 A.2d 788 (1954).

It has been held that a jury's averaging of two separate and entirely different approaches to value in an eminent domain case is analogous to use of a quotient verdict and is reversible error. Times Square Realty, Inc. v. City of Grenada, 421 So.2d 1053 (Miss. 1982). On "quotient verdicts," see generally State ex rel. Department of Transp. v. Davis, 134 P.3d 899 (Okla.Civ.App. 2006) ("quotient verdict doctrine" generally applies to vitiate jury verdict where, before deliberation, members of jury agree to assess damages by quotient, without consideration of all facts and circumstances).

requirements.[110] And although condemnation proceedings are contemplated or actually commenced, a local government may abandon them; even after a jury award, it cannot be compelled to proceed.[111]

§ 19.7 Municipal Acquisition of Property by Purchase, Gift, and Lease

The exercise of eminent domain by local governments receives considerable attention because of the limitations surrounding, and litigation arising from, this method of acquisition—and because eminent domain has been much utilized in connection with such recent, and sometimes controversial, municipal activities as urban renewal. But local governments may acquire real property in three other principal ways: by purchase, by gift, and by lease.

Like any person or corporation, municipalities may *purchase* property, on the open market or otherwise, so long as relevant statutory and charter provisions allow the municipalities this power.[112] The power to purchase property is usually inferred readily from other powers and is broadly interpreted.[113] But there are three limitations: (1) Any procedural requirements of statutes or home-rule charters must be honored.[114] (2) Municipal action can be voided by the courts upon strong proof of malicious or capricious

---

[110] See Savannah, Augusta & Northern Railway Co. v. Williams, 133 Ga. 679, 66 S.E. 942 (1909); City of Austin v. Wright, 262 Minn. 301, 114 N.W.2d 584 (1962) (right to review lost when property owner failed to file written objections as required by charter).

[111] Lord Calvert Theatre v. City of Baltimore, 208 Md. 606, 119 A.2d 415 (1956). But statutes in some jurisdictions require the government that has commenced eminent-domain proceedings to pay certain costs (counsel and witness fees, etc.) of the landowner if the government discontinues the proceedings. See City of Jackson v. Lee, 234 Miss. 502, 106 So.2d 892 (1958). Even without statute, a government that dismisses a condemnation action *after trial* may be held liable for the property owner's costs unless it can establish that its refusal to accept the trial-court award was due to circumstances it could not reasonably have foreseen. Whitestone v. Town of South Tucson, 2 Ariz.App. 494, 410 P.2d 116 (1966). And in other situations, some courts may now find that a government's long delay in pursuing an announced condemnation has resulted in a "taking" having occurred, or has entitled the landowner to interest or other damages. See Foster v. City of Detroit, 405 F.2d 138 (6th Cir.1968), motion denied 423 F.2d 660 (damages for loss of value of property during 10-year period between commencement of condemnation proceedings by city and city's discontinuance of the action). See generally Section 19.2 *supra*.

On the question of possible regaining of property by the condemnee if the condemnor ceases to use it for a public purpose, see Oswald, Can a Condemnee Regain Its Property If the Condemnor Abandons the Public Use?, 39 Urban Law. 671 (2007) (at common law, the condemnee may not regain the property if the condemnor acquired a fee simple absolute in it, but if the condemnor took only a lesser estate (such as an easement), the property may be regained; statutes now often expand the condemnee's right to regain).

[112] See Borough of Fenwick v. Town of Old Saybrook, 133 Conn. 22, 47 A.2d 849 (1946); Henry H. Stambaugh Auditorium Association v. City of Youngstown, 73 Ohio App. 234, 55 N.E.2d 672 (1943).

[113] Thus, power has been found in a municipality to purchase real property located in another state. Sabaugh v. City of Dearborn, 16 Mich.App. 182, 167 N.W.2d 826 (1969), aff'd 384 Mich. 510, 185 N.W.2d 363 (1971) (Michigan city could purchase property in Florida for home for city's senior citizens). See Birge v. Town of Easton, 274 Md. 635, 337 A.2d 435 (1975) (purchase of property in another state for use in operation of municipal electric system).

Courts have, however, occasionally said that a *general* statutory authorization to acquire property gives a local government only the power to purchase properties for "municipal" or "corporate" purposes. See Lewis v. Shreveport, 108 U.S. 282, 2 S.Ct. 634, 27 L.Ed. 728 (1883); State v. Town of North Miami, 59 So.2d 779 (Fla.1952).

[114] Hoskins v. City of Orlando, 51 F.2d 901 (5th Cir.1931); Scarborough Properties Corp. v. Village of Briarcliff Manor, 278 N.Y. 370, 16 N.E.2d 369 (1938); City of Beaumont v. Matthew Cartwright Land & Improvement Co., 224 S.W. 589 (Tex.Civ. App.1920), error ref'd.

conduct by local officials.[115] (3) Most important—the acquisition must be for a public purpose.[116] In determining the presence or absence of public purpose, courts have weighed a number of factors, including how many residents will be benefited, the prospect of making a profit, and the *need* for the proposed municipal undertaking for which the property is desired, in light of present economic conditions and the sufficiency of similar undertakings in the private sector.[117] The trend over recent decades has definitely been toward finding the required public purpose in more and more activities, even those often conducted by private enterprises also.[118]

Local governments usually have express, or clearly implied, power to accept *gifts* of either personal[119] or real[120] property, though occasionally there are requirements that must be met, such as approval by local planning commissions of the acceptance of realty.[121] One of the most common forms of donation to local governments is *dedication:* the appropriation of property (usually land) to some public use, made by the owner of the fee, accompanied by public acceptance of the property for such use.[122] Dedication exists at common law;[123] and though there are now numerous statutes governing the

---

[115] See Moran v. Leadbetter, 334 Mich. 234, 54 N.W.2d 310 (1952).

[116] State ex rel. City of Toledo v. Lynch, 88 Ohio St. 71, 102 N.E. 670 (1913). See Barnes v. City of New Haven, 140 Conn. 8, 98 A.2d 523 (1953) (promotion of public safety and welfare suffices for public purpose; some benefit to certain individuals does not negate such public purpose); State ex rel. Fatzer v. Urban Renewal Agency, 179 Kan. 435, 296 P.2d 656 (1956) (public purpose must be broadly interpreted); McSorley v. Fitzgerald, 359 Pa. 264, 59 A.2d 142 (1948). Cf. Wheelock v. City of Lowell, 196 Mass. 220, 81 N.E. 977 (1907) (if dominating motive for erection of hall is public use, use of public funds is proper though hall will occasionally be devoted to non-public purposes).

[117] 2A Antieau, Municipal Corporation Law § 20.10, at 20–44, –45 (1998). See Allydonn Realty Corp. v. Holyoke Housing Authority, 304 Mass. 288, 23 N.E.2d 665 (1939), also listing factors. Cf. Borgelt v. City of Minneapolis, 271 Minn. 249, 135 N.W.2d 438 (1965) (chief factor is whether enterprise is in active competition with private business).

[118] See Standard Oil Co. v. Lincoln, 114 Neb. 243, 207 N.W. 172 (1926), aff'd 275 U.S. 504, 48 S.Ct. 155, 72 L.Ed. 395 (gas station); Green v. Frazier, 253 U.S. 233, 40 S.Ct. 499, 64 L.Ed. 878 (1920) (grain elevator); Newberry v. City of Andalusia, 257 Ala. 49, 57 So.2d 629 (1952) (industrial plant); Jones v. City of Portland, 113 Me. 123, 93 A. 41 (1915) (coal yard); State ex rel. City of Excelsior Springs v. Smith, 336 Mo. 1104, 82 S.W.2d 37 (1935) (health spring); Moore v. City of Greensboro, 191 N.C. 592, 132 S.E. 565 (1926) (slaughter-house); McConnell v. City of Lebanon, 203 Tenn. 498, 314 S.W.2d 12 (1958) (factory building); Schneider v. City of Menasha, 118 Wis. 298, 95 N.W. 94 (1903) (stone quarry). But see Toebe v. City of Munising, 282 Mich. 1, 275 N.W. 744 (1937) (no public purpose in municipal acquisition of coal yard); Nash v. Town of Tarboro, 227 N.C. 283, 42 S.E.2d 209 (1947) (same as to municipal construction and operation of hotel); State ex rel. City of Toledo v. Lynch, *supra* note 116 (same as to movie theatre). Cf. John Wright & Associates v. City of Red Wing, 254 Minn. 1, 93 N.W.2d 660 (1958), mandamus denied 256 Minn. 101, 97 N.W.2d 432 (operation of movie theatre is not valid municipal purpose). See generally, as to municipal operation of businesses, Chapter 16 *supra.*

[119] See Moss v. Youngblood, 187 Ga. 188, 200 S.E. 689 (1938) (bequest); State ex rel. Singelmann v. Morrison, 57 So.2d 238 (La. App.1952); Ash v. City of Omaha, 152 Neb. 393, 41 N.W.2d 386 (1950), reh. denied 152 Neb. 699, 42 N.W.2d 648; Warm v. City of Cincinnati, 1 Ohio Supp. 273 (Com.Pl.1937), aff'd 57 Ohio App. 43, 11 N.E.2d 281 (contract among state, city, and railroad for elimination of railroad crossings, with federal and city funds, did not involve advancement of city credit for railroad's benefit).

[120] City of Bangor v. Merrill Trust Co., 149 Me. 160, 99 A.2d 298 (1953); Van Reuth v. City of Baltimore, 165 Md. 651, 170 A. 199 (1934).

[121] See Ash v. City of Omaha, *supra* note 119.

[122] Elias Bros., Inc. v. City of Hazel Park, 1 Mich.App. 30, 133 N.W.2d 206 (1965); Alton v. Meeuwenberg, 108 Mich. 629, 66 N.W. 571 (1896). On the theory of dedication, see Dugan v. Zurmuehlen, 203 Iowa 1114, 211 N.W. 986 (1927). See generally Note, The American Extension of the Doctrine of Dedication, 16 Harv.L.Rev. 128 (1902).

[123] See City of Cincinnati v. White's Lessee, 31 U.S. (6 Pet.) 431, 8 L.Ed. 452 (1832) (the leading case); Cooper v. City of Great Bend, 200 Kan. 590, 438 P.2d 102 (1968).

matter, a dedication that is ineffective under the statutes may nonetheless be valid by the common law.[124] The requisites at common law are (1) an intention to donate on the part of the owner, (2) an actual transfer of control to a public body, and (3) acceptance of the dedication on behalf of the public.[125] The owner's intent may be either express or implied.[126] The acceptance requires some official action indicating the property is being treated as dedicated to public use.[127] At common law, the offer to dedicate can be

---

[124] See 3 Dillon, Municipal Corporations § 1071 (5th ed. 1911); 11A McQuillin, Municipal Corporations § 33.03 (3d rev. ed. 2000). A common-law dedication ordinarily conveys only an easement to the government, with the fee remaining in the grantor—though more may be conveyed if such intention is clear. Certainly the fee can, and often does, pass to the public under *statutory* methods of dedication. On the difference between common-law and statutory dedication in this regard, see Town of Reydon v. Anderson, 649 P.2d 541 (Okl.1982).

[125] See Flack v. Village of Green Island, 122 N.Y. 107, 25 N.E. 267 (1890) (must be surrender by grantor and acceptance by grantee). Cf. Chandler v. Independent School District No. 12, 625 P.2d 620 (Okl.1981) (common-law dedication is founded on equitable estoppel; such dedication requires assent of owner and use of premises for purpose intended).

[126] See McIntosh v. City of Joplin, 486 S.W.2d 287 (Mo.App.1972); Village of Hicksville v. Lantz, 153 Ohio St. 421, 92 N.E.2d 270 (1950); Township of Millcreek v. A Piece of Land, 181 Pa.Super. 214, 124 A.2d 448 (1956) (any act clearly indicating intent will suffice). Cf. Gion v. City of Santa Cruz, 2 Cal.3d 29, 84 Cal.Rptr. 162, 465 P.2d 50 (1970) (common-law dedication may be proved either by showing acquiescence of owner under circumstances negating existence of a license or by showing open and continuous use by public for the prescriptive period).

But it is often said that evidence of the intent to dedicate must be very clear and convincing. See City & County of San Francisco v. Grote, 120 Cal. 59, 52 P. 127 (1898) (intention not sufficiently manifest where public had been allowed to travel over the land for 8 years); Pocock v. Town of Medley, 89 So.2d 162 (Fla.1956); DeGrilleau v. Frawley, 48 La.Ann. 184, 19 So. 151 (1896) (proof of intent to dedicate must exclude any other reasonable hypothesis); Town of Paden City v. Felton, 136 W.Va. 127, 66 S.E.2d 280 (1951). Cf. Stacy v. Glen Ellyn Hotel & Springs Co., 223 Ill. 546, 79 N.E. 133 (1906) (mere non-assertion of right does not establish intent to dedicate).

As the *Gion* case *supra* indicates, acquisition of property by municipalities through dedication often overlaps the possibility of acquisition of the property by prescription. It has been said that the latter theory is better suited to acquisition of *private* easements, and that the courts would do well to stick consistently to the dedication theory in regard to public ways. Fordham, Local Government Law 972 (1975 rev. ed.) But there *are* a number of cases recognizing that a local government may acquire property by adverse possession, just as an individual may. See City of Bowling Green v. Board of Education, 278 S.W.2d 726 (Ky.1955); Terry v. City of Independence, 388 S.W.2d 769 (Mo.1965); New York v. Carleton, 113 N.Y. 284, 21 N.E. 55 (1889); Polanski v. Town of Eagle Point, 30 Wis.2d 507, 141 N.W.2d 281 (1966). And may acquire an easement by prescription. See Town of Paden City v. Felton, *supra*.

[127] Hames v. City of Marietta, 212 Ga. 331, 92 S.E.2d 534 (1956); Parish of Jefferson v. Doody, 167 So.2d 489 (La.App.1964); Moseley v. Searcy, 363 S.W.2d 561 (Mo.1962) (must be acceptance, though sometimes shown by long public use); Spiegle v. Borough of Beach Haven, 116 N.J.Super. 148, 281 A.2d 377 (1971) (acceptance may be by any official action treating the property as dedicated to public use). See City of Northglenn v. City of Thornton, 193 Colo. 536, 569 P.2d 319 (1977) (both intent to dedicate and acceptance of dedication must be shown by unambiguous actions of parties); Phillips v. City of Stamford, 81 Conn. 408, 71 A. 361 (1908) (discussing the degree of user that may show acceptance). Moore v. City of Lawrence, 232 Kan. 353, 654 P.2d 445 (1982) (subdivision plat filed with register of deeds and approved by planning commission constituted acceptance by city of dedicated lands). See generally Annot., Implied Acceptance, by Public Use, of Dedication of Beach or Shoreline Adjoining Public Waters, 24 A.L.R.4th 294 (1983). Some courts will assume acceptance under certain circumstances. See McKernon v. City of Reno, 76 Nev. 452, 357 P.2d 597 (1960) (where dedication is beneficial to municipality and imposes no burden, acceptance can be presumed as of date of dedication). On the need for acceptance, see generally Mighill v. Rowley, 224 Mass. 586, 113 N.E. 569 (1916). Sometimes municipal action may suffice as acceptance for dedication purposes but may not be sufficient to make the municipality responsible, and potentially liable, for condition of the premises. See Downing v. Coatesville Borough, 214 Pa. 291, 63 A. 696 (1906).

withdrawn at any time until the acceptance has occurred, but this rule is sometimes modified under statutory methods.[128]

Dedication was originally found in cases involving highways and public walks, but has now been found in situations involving parks, docks, and schools—even though in some of these instances, the use would not really be by the general public. Thus, as with the "public use" requirement for eminent domain discussed *supra*, a strict requirement of "public use" seems to have given way to mere requisites of "public purpose" or "public benefit." In recent times, dedications have often been found to have occurred where a subdivider's plat shows certain areas of the subdivision to be streets, parks, etc. and where lots in the area are then sold with reference to that plat.[129] Sometimes a local government is spoken of as "dedicating" its own property to a particular use;[130] but this is loose terminology and has been criticized as misleading, since the usual requisites and results of dedication are not present in such situations.[131]

Municipal power to acquire an interest in property by *lease* is often accorded by state constitutions, statutes, or home-rule documents; but in any case, such power is generally inferred quite readily from express power to acquire property.[132]

§ 19.8 Municipal Use of Property: Change in Use; Lease, Sale

When a local government has acquired property by means other than dedication, the use to which the property is put may be changed without ordinarily affecting the government's rights in the property.[133] This is subject to three qualifications: (1) As with other property owners, a locality may acquire property subject to a possibility of reverter

---

[128] See Shoreline Builders Co. v. City of Park Ridge, 60 Ill.App.2d 282, 209 N.E.2d 878 (1965) (statute may set limits on offeror's right to retract offer to dedicate); Doyle v. Babcock, 182 Minn. 556, 235 N.W. 18 (1931).

[129] Edmiston v. City of Harlingen, 347 S.W.2d 742 (Tex.Civ.App.1961) ref'd n.r.e. See State ex rel. Kincaid v. Hamilton, 109 Tenn. 276, 70 S.W. 619 (1902); Huddleston v. Deans, 124 W.Va. 313, 21 S.E.2d 352 (1942). See generally Note, Unity Plan in Dedication of Ways, 49 W.Va.L.Q. 88 (1942).

Where a subdivider records a plat and sells lots with reference thereto, some authority indicates that acceptance of the dedication becomes unnecessary—and certainly this may be true under some modern statutes. See 4 Tiffany, Real Property § 1106 (3d ed. 1975).

[130] See City Council v. Newsome, 211 Ga. 899, 89 S.E.2d 485 (1955); Norton v. City of Gainesville, 211 Ga. 387, 86 S.E.2d 234 (1955); Koch v. Borough of Seaside Heights, 40 N.J.Super. 86, 122 A.2d 250 (1956), aff'd 22 N.J. 218, 125 A.2d 402; Petition of Acchione, 425 Pa. 23, 227 A.2d 816 (1967). Cf. Anderson v. Mayor & Council of Wilmington, 37 Del.Ch. 74, 137 A.2d 521 (1958) (park lands had been dedicated to public use, could not be used for school purposes); Bedford-Nugent Co. v. Argue, 281 Ky. 827, 137 S.W.2d 392 (1939) (local government had dedicated its own lands for park use, could not devote land to other purposes); City of Louisville v. Hull, 292 So.2d 177 (Miss.1974) (city could dedicate its own property for a park, but change of use would be allowed absent clear, unequivocal proof of dedication for this purpose). See also Paepcke v. Public Building Commission, 46 Ill.2d 330, 263 N.E.2d 11 (1970) (state had dedicated land for park purposes, but adjoining property owners not allowed to prevent change in use).

[131] 2A Antieau, Municipal Corporation Law § 20.14, at 20–62, & § 20.24, at 20–87 (1998).

[132] See City of San Francisco v. Boyle, 195 Cal. 426, 233 P. 965 (1925); Ambrozich v. City of Eveleth, 200 Minn. 473, 274 N.W. 635 (1937) (the greater power to purchase property necessarily includes the lesser power to acquire property by lease); American-LaFrance, Inc. v. City of Philadelphia, 183 Miss. 207, 184 So. 620 (1938). See generally Mardikes, Cone & Van Horn, Governmental Leasing: A Fifty State Survey of Legislation and Case Law, 18 Urban Law. 1 (1986). On implied powers of municipalities, see generally Chapter 8 *supra*.

[133] See Carlor Co. v. City of Miami, 62 So.2d 897 (Fla.1953), cert. denied 346 U.S. 821, 74 S.Ct. 37, 98 L.Ed. 347; Hames v. City of Marietta, 212 Ga. 331, 92 S.E.2d 534 (1956); Phillips v. Ober, 197 Md. 167, 78 A.2d 630 (1951); Moore v. City of Beaumont, 195 S.W.2d 968 (Tex.Civ.App.1946), aff'd 146 Tex. 46, 202 S.W.2d 448. Thus if property is condemned for a particular purpose but not put to that use, it does not ordinarily revert to the former owners. Marsh v. Hot Springs, 241 Ark. 159, 406 S.W.2d 714 (1966).

or power of termination in the grantor; often, such possibilities or powers take effect upon a specified change in the property's use, as where land is no longer used for park purposes. Under such circumstances, an abandonment of the specified use can cause ownership of the property to revert to the grantor.[134] (2) It is possible that a local government, as well as other owners, may so totally surrender all dominion over property that it will be treated as "abandoned"; but this requires a showing of intent to abandon, which is not established by mere non-use.[135] (3) Statutes and charters often specify procedures by which streets—and sometimes other properties held for public use—may be "vacated."[136] This results in the property being restored to the owner of the fee, no

---

[134] See Moseley v. Searcy, 363 S.W.2d 561 (Mo.1962); Scarborough Properties Corp. v. Village of Briarcliff Manor, 278 N.Y. 370, 16 N.E.2d 369 (1938); Trustees of Union College v. New York, 173 N.Y. 38, 65 N.E. 853 (1903); Ward v. Klamath County, 108 Or. 574, 218 P. 927 (1923). But courts will, where a government is a grantee, be even more than usually inclined to treat possible reverter clauses and conditions subsequent as mere declarations of intention that a property is to be put to a particular use, thus avoiding the grantee's loss of the property upon discontinuance of the use. See Wright v. Morgan, 191 U.S. 55, 24 S.Ct. 6, 48 L.Ed. 89 (1903) (phrase interpreted as only a statement of the intended use, no legal effect); Briggs v. City of Grand Rapids, 261 Mich. 11, 245 N.W. 555 (1932); Board of Education v. Brophy, 90 N.J.Eq. 57, 106 A. 32 (1919); Miller v. Village of Brookville, 152 Ohio St. 217, 89 N.E.2d 85 (1949); Cf. Sharp v. City of Guthrie, 49 Okl. 213, 152 P. 403 (1915) (patent conveyed lands for parks, schools, and other public purposes; absolute title held conveyed).

[135] See Dade County v. North Miami Beach, 69 So.2d 780 (Fla.1953) (non-use of park for 17 years did not show abandonment); Ford v. City of Detroit, 273 Mich. 449, 263 N.W. 425 (1935) (dedicated land—no abandonment, thus no reverter); Goode v. City of St. Louis, 113 Mo. 257, 20 S.W. 1048 (1892); DeVoe v. State, 281 Mont. 356, 935 P.2d 256 (Mont. 1997) (evidence insufficient to establish that state abandoned easement acquired for use as public highway despite removal of roadway surface); Baertsch v. County of Lewis & Clark, 256 Mont. 114, 845 P.2d 106 (1992) (county could claim title to full 100-foot right-of-way to a county road even though a portion of that right-of-way had not been used for public benefit in over 90 years and the county had accepted and approved subdivision plats showing a right-of-way of less than 100 feet); A.L. Kornman Co. v. Metropolitan Government, 57 Tenn.App. 230, 417 S.W.2d 793 (1967) (intent to abandon must be shown external act); Hicks v. City of Houston, 524 S.W.2d 539 (Tex.Civ.App.1975), rev'd n. r. e. (circumstances must show intention to abandon). Cf. Clark v. City of Grand Rapids, 334 Mich. 646, 55 N.W.2d 137 (1952) (sale to another local government was not abandonment, where was for purpose of carrying out original intent of dedication); Skrmetta v. Moore, 227 Miss. 119, 86 So.2d 46 (1956) (local government has not abandoned merely by accepting payment of taxes on property by a private claimant; court seems almost to require that property have been adversely possessed by another in order to have been abandoned by locality). But see In re Real Property at Moiliili, 49 Haw. 537, 425 P.2d 83 (1967) (abandonment found from non-user). Cf. Anson v. Arnett, 250 S.W.2d 450 (Tex.Civ.App.1952), ref'd n.r.e. (long and unexplained non-user may give rise to inference of intention to abandon). But it should be noted that (1) much authority supports the view that, with the possible exception of easements by prescription, there is no such thing—by *any* owner—as abandonment of *real* property. See Simonton, Abandonment of Interests in Land, 25 Ill.L.Rev. 261 (1930). (2) Many of the cases discussing municipal "abandonment" of property deal with situations where the municipality acquired the property subject to a possibility of reverter or power of termination relating to use, or where an easement was dedicated to the municipality for a particular use. The question in such cases is simply whether the *use* has been abandoned and the property has thus possibly reverted to the grantor (or his heirs) or dedicator (or his heirs). (3) Some of the cases on "abandonment" deal with possible acquisition of property *from* a local government by adverse possession. It is generally agreed at common law that property held in a proprietary capacity by a municipality may be acquired by adverse possession, but property held in a governmental capacity may not be so acquired. See City of Oakland v. Burns, 46 Cal.2d 401, 296 P.2d 333 (1956); Engleman v. City of Kalamazoo, 229 Mich. 603, 201 N.W. 880 (1925). The rule is sometimes changed by statute so that *no* loss of property can occur to a municipality through adverse possession. See Southern Pacific Co. v. City & County of San Francisco, 62 Cal.2d 50, 41 Cal.Rptr. 79, 396 P.2d 383 (1964), applying such a statute. The rules on governmental abandonment are also sometimes modified by statute. See City of Reno v. Estate of Wells, 110 Nev. 1218, 885 P.2d 545 (1994) (statute provided that governing body could abandon property if public would not be materially injured). But cf. State of Montana v. Fisher, 317 Mont. 49, 75 P.3d 338 (2003) (statute provided that all county roads continue as such unless abandoned or vacated; neither non-use of road nor state's building a highway created an abandonment, nor did the combination of these two acts).

[136] See Buck v. City of Winona, 271 Minn. 145, 135 N.W.2d 190 (1965); Zakutansky v. City of Bayonne, 88 N.J.Super. 516, 212 A.2d 852 (1965), applying the procedures for vacation. On what happens to a street or public way after it is abandoned or vacated, see Carney v. Heinson, 133 Idaho 275, 985 P.2d 1137 (1999)

longer subject to any public claims. If the locality itself owns the fee, it, of course, remains the owner, but with the prior use of the land (for a street, or whatever) having been terminated.

Where rights in property are acquired by a locality through dedication, there is more limitation on change of use. Some changed use, or additional use, will be permitted if sufficiently within the spirit of the original dedication, as where park land is utilized for a library or recreational building.[137] But uses farther afield from the original intent of the dedicator, such as use of park land for a court house or town hall, can be enjoined[138]—and conceivably could result in a reversion of ownership to the dedicator if the terms of the conveyance so provide, or if the dedication was merely of an easement on the land.

Local governments may lease their "proprietary" properties to others without specific statutory or charter authority, so long as there is no interference with public needs.[139] The traditional view is that express authorization is needed for the locality to

---

(vacated alley became part of adjoining properties); Herreid v. Hauck, 254 Mont. 496, 839 P.2d 571 (1992) (title to center line transferred to abutting landowners); Ahluwalia v. Davis, 964 P.2d 217 (Okl.Civ.App. 1997) (when street is vacated, ownership ordinarily reverts to owners on each side in proportion to their frontage).

137 See Spires v. City of Los Angeles, 150 Cal. 64, 87 P. 1026 (1906) (park land used for library); City of Bangor v. Merrill Trust Co., 149 Me. 160, 99 A.2d 298 (1953) (park land used for recreation building). Cf. Los Angeles Athletic Club v. City of Long Beach, 128 Cal.App. 427, 17 P.2d 1061 (1933) (auditorium in park); City of Wichita v. Clapp, 125 Kan. 100, 263 P. 12 (1928) (airport in park); Aquamsi Land Co. v. City of Cape Girardeau, 346 Mo. 524, 142 S.W.2d 332 (1940) (recreation building, community center, and fair grounds in park); Biglin v. Town of West Orange, 46 N.J. 367, 217 A.2d 135 (1966) (swimming pool in park); Priory v. Borough of Manasquan, 39 N.J.Super. 147, 120 A.2d 625 (1956) (comfort station on beach); Bernstein v. City of Pittsburgh, 366 Pa. 200, 77 A.2d 452 (1951) (open-air auditorium in park). But see Carstens v. City of Wood River, 332 Ill. 400, 163 N.E. 816 (1928) (swimming pool not allowed in park); Cooper v. City of Great Bend, 200 Kan. 590, 438 P.2d 102 (1968) (parking area not allowed in park); City of Hopkinsville v. Jarrett, 156 Ky. 777, 162 S.W. 85 (1914) (library in park not allowed); Hill v. Borough of Belmar, 3 N.J.Misc. 254, 127 A. 789 (Sup.Ct.1925) (swimming pool in park not allowed); Miller v. City of Columbia, 138 S.C. 343, 136 S.E. 484 (1927) (stadium not allowed in park).

138 McIntyre v. El Paso County, 15 Colo.App. 78, 61 P. 237 (1900) (courthouse not allowed in park); Village of Princeville v. Auten, 77 Ill. 325 (1875) (town hall not allowed in park); Church v. City of Portland, 18 Or. 73, 22 P. 528 (1889) (city hall and jail not allowed in park). Cf. Lord v. City of Wilmington, 332 A.2d 414 (Del.Ch.1975), aff'd 378 A.2d 635 (water tower not allowed in park); Flaten v. City of Moorhead, 51 Minn. 518, 53 N.W. 807 (1892) (jail not allowed in park); Miller v. New York City, 15 N.Y.2d 34, 255 N.Y.S.2d 78, 203 N.E.2d 478 (1964) (golf driving-range, operated by private concession, not allowed in park). Similarly, land dedicated for a public square cannot be used for a courthouse. McBride v. Rockwall County, 195 S.W. 926 (Tex.Civ.App.1917), error ref'd. Cf. Melin v. Community Consolidated School District, 312 Ill. 376, 144 N.E. 13 (1924) (school not allowed in public square); Porter v. International Bridge Co., 200 N.Y. 234, 93 N.E. 716 (1910) (bridge approach not allowed on open area). But a library has sometimes been allowed in a public square. See Riggs v. Board of Education, 27 Mich. 262 (1873). Cf. Summit County Historical Society v. City of Akron, 115 Ohio App. 555, 183 N.E.2d 634 (1961) (skating rink allowed in public square); Knoerr v. Crews, 246 S.C. 174, 143 S.E.2d 120 (1965) (parking facilities allowed in open square). The special limitations on changes in the use of dedicated land should apply only where a true common-law or statutory dedication of the property has occurred—not where a municipality has simply put ("dedicated") property to a particular use; but some opinions fail to draw the distinction. See 2A Antieau, Municipal Corporation Law § 20–24 (1998).

Changes in the use of dedicated property are usually said to be allowable where the dedicator consents to the change—or if he is deceased, all his heirs consent. See Griffith v. City of Los Angeles, 175 Cal.App.2d 331, 346 P.2d 49 (Dist.Ct.1959); Headley v. City of Northfield, 227 Minn. 458, 35 N.W.2d 606 (1949). On who may maintain actions to halt diversions of dedicated property, see Annot., Right of Abutting Owner to Complain of Misuse of Public Park or Violation of Rights or Easements Appurtenant Thereto, 60 A.L.R. 770 (1929); Annot., Special Injury to Property Interest as Condition of Right to Enjoin Diversion of Dedicated Property, 41 A.L.R. 1410 (1926).

139 Bailey v. City of Philadelphia, 184 Pa. 594, 39 A. 494 (1898) (gas works); Winkenwerder v. City of Yakima, 52 Wn.2d 617, 328 P.2d 873 (1958); State ex rel. Charleston v. Coghill, 156 W.Va. 877, 207 S.E.2d 113 (1973) (space in parking facility); S.D. Realty Co. v. Sewerage Commission, 15 Wis.2d 15, 112 N.W.2d 177 (1961). See Dothan Area Chamber of Commerce v. Shealy, 561 So.2d 515 (Ala.1990) (unused portion of property

lease property it holds in its *governmental* capacity.[140] But many modern cases have found such power implied in the locality's authority to own and dispose of property, or in other general powers, so long as there is no serious interference with governmental operations.[141] The limitation of the traditional rule has also often been avoided by holdings that concessions on city property (as for a restaurant in a city park) don't amount to leases,[142] and that local governments clearly have implied power to "lease out" property that was once used for governmental purposes but is no longer needed for such.[143]

---

acquired by condemnation for electric power substation could be leased to chamber of commerce); Clarey v. City of Philadelphia, 311 Pa. 11, 166 A. 237 (1933) (convention hall); King County v. Taxpayers of King County, 133 Wash.2d 584, 949 P.2d 1260 (1997), cert. denied 522 U.S. 1076, 118 S.Ct. 854, 139 L.Ed.2d 754 (1998) (lease of stadium to baseball team upheld as not violating constitutional prohibition against making gifts of public funds). But Kansas has required specific legislative authority for leasing of even proprietary property. State ex rel. Mitchell v. Coffeyville, 127 Kan. 663, 274 P. 258 (1929) (airport); State ex rel. Griffith v. City of Independence, 123 Kan. 766, 256 P. 799 (1927) (memorial building). Cf. Dancliff Realty Corp. v. Miller, 101 R.I. 478, 225 A.2d 52 (1966) (beach).

[140] See Norton v. City of Gainesville, 211 Ga. 387, 86 S.E.2d 234 (1955); Lake George Steamboat Co. v. Blais, 30 N.Y.2d 48, 330 N.Y.S.2d 336, 281 N.E.2d 147 (1972); Buckhout v. City of Newport, 68 R.I. 280, 27 A.2d 317 (1942). In several cases, the rule against leasing without express authority is stated in broad terms and applied even to leases of what might well be termed "proprietary" properties. See Daytona Beach v. Dygert, 146 Fla. 352, 1 So.2d 170 (1941) (airport); Nebraska City v. Nebraska City Speed & Fair Association, 107 Neb. 576, 186 N.W. 374 (1922) (lease of park area for race track). Cf. City of Bessemer v. Huey, 247 Ala. 12, 22 So.2d 325 (1945) (lease of city hall and auditorium for theatre); Derr v. City of Fairview, 121 Okl. 23, 247 P. 45 (1926) (lease of park for swimming pool). See generally Miller v. New York City, 15 N.Y.2d 34, 255 N.Y.S.2d 78, 203 N.E.2d 478 (1964) (park impressed with trust for public could not be subjected to anything but a revocable permit).

[141] See Corning v. Patton, 236 Ala. 354, 182 So. 39 (1938); Inland Waterways Co. v. City of Louisville, 227 Ky. 376, 13 S.W.2d 283 (1929); Jones v. Inhabitants of Sanford, 66 Me. 585 (1877) (town hall leased to dramatic company); Murphy v. Erie County, 28 N.Y.2d 80, 320 N.Y.S.2d 29, 268 N.E.2d 771 (1971); Merryman v. School District, 43 Wyo. 376, 5 P.2d 267 (1931) (school house rented for dances). But cf. Prezeau v. City of Whitefish, 198 Mont. 416, 646 P.2d 1186 (1982) (where statute commanded that municipal property held in trust for a specific purpose could only be sold or leased with electoral approval, such approval was needed in order to build an indoor rifle range in a public park even if there would be no substantial interference with the public-park use of the property). It is sometimes stated in general terms that a municipality can lease its premises for private purposes when they are not needed for public uses. See Hansen v. Kootenai County Board of County Commissioners, 93 Idaho 655, 471 P.2d 42 (1970) (county could lease fair grounds to racing association); Center v. City of Benton, 414 Ill. 107, 110 N.E.2d 223 (1953) (land purchased for reservoir, later considered for park use, finally leased for use as drive-in theatre). But many of the cases so stating have involved proprietary properties of the local government. See note 139 *supra* and accompanying text. And/or they have involved situations in which the property is no longer needed, and won't be needed in the foreseeable future, for public use. See note 143 *infra* and accompanying text.

[142] See Warren v. City of Topeka, 125 Kan. 524, 265 P. 78 (1928); Bailey v. City of Topeka, 97 Kan. 327, 154 P. 1014 (1916).

[143] See Corning v. Patton, *supra* note 141 (abandoned courthouse—governmental property can be leased when use abandoned); Woodward v. Fox West Coast Theaters, 36 Ariz. 251, 284 P. 350 (1930) (lease of former city hall); Davis v. Inhabitants of Rockport, 213 Mass. 279, 100 N.E. 612 (1913) (common land not needed for government use); Big Prairie Township v. Big Prairie Township Grange, 286 Mich. 268, 282 N.W. 143 (1938) (township could lease unneeded portion of town hall); Anderson v. City of Montevideo, 137 Minn. 179, 162 N.W. 1073 (1917) (building once used as city hall but no longer needed for such; could be leased as theatre). Cf. Robinson v. Hal Johnson & Co., 206 Okl. 397, 243 P.2d 657 (1952) (abandoned airport). Some opinions go farther and find implied authority to lease properties not presently needed for governmental purposes, though such a need might someday arise. See Ballantine v. Town of Falmouth, 363 Mass. 760, 298 N.E.2d 695 (1973) (municipality could take, for public parking purposes, land already in use for public parking and lease it to private individuals). Cf. Opinion of the Justices, 109 N.H. 396, 254 A.2d 273 (1969) (legislature could authorize lease of air rights not presently needed for municipal purposes).

The rules on *sale* of property by local governments are similar to the rules on leases: Express authority is not ordinarily needed for the sale of "proprietary" properties,[144] but is needed for the sale of governmental.[145] Where the specific authority is needed, it must be found in state constitution, statutes, or home-rule charter. But there is authority that if property is *condemned* for a public purpose and not actually put to that use, it may be sold without express authorization, even where the property's proposed use had been a governmental one.[146] And, on the other hand, property acquired by the locality through *dedication* cannot be conveyed at all, even *with* specific authorization, regardless of the governmental or proprietary nature of the use to which dedicated.[147]

---

[144] City of Fort Wayne v. Lake Shore & Michigan Southern Railway Co., 132 Ind. 558, 32 N.E. 215 (1892); Palmer v. City of Albuquerque, 19 N.M. 285, 142 P. 929 (1914); Seafeldt v. Port of Astoria, 141 Or. 418, 16 P.2d 943 (1932) (dredge); Williamsburg v. Lyell, 132 Va. 455, 112 S.E. 666 (1922). See Moore v. City of Beaumont, 195 S.W.2d 968 (Tex.Civ.App.1946), aff'd 146 Tex. 46, 202 S.W.2d 448 (mineral rights under city airport). Cf. Kalamazoo Municipal Utilities Association v. City of Kalamazoo, 345 Mich. 318, 76 N.W.2d 1 (1956) (upholding use of resolution, rather than ordinance, for sale of city utility).

[145] Anderson v. Adams, 291 Ala. 523, 283 So.2d 416 (1973); Gritton v. City of Des Moines, 247 Iowa 326, 73 N.W.2d 813 (1955); McRobie v. Mayor & Commissioners of Westernport, 260 Md. 464, 272 A.2d 655 (1971); Curry v. City of Highland Park, 242 Mich. 614, 219 N.W. 745 (1928). See City of Rochester v. Carnahan, 57 Misc.2d 704, 293 N.Y.S.2d 479 (Sup.Ct.1967) (park lands could not be conveyed without approval of legislature); Valley View Tenant's Association v. Doorley, 112 R.I. 465, 312 A.2d 209 (1973). Some courts, as in the *Valley View* case *supra*, generalize that no municipal property actually devoted to public use can be sold without specific authorization. See Commercial Waterway District v. Permanente Cement Co., 61 Wn.2d 509, 379 P.2d 178 (1963) (land held in trust for public cannot be alienated unless legislature so provides).

Under the generally accepted view, a broad grant of power to sell property will not be held to imply authority to sell "governmental" properties, and "governmental" will usually be interpreted to include park lands. See City of New Orleans v. Louisiana Society for Prevention of Cruelty to Animals, 229 La. 246, 85 So.2d 503 (1955).

[146] Kirkland v. Johnson, 209 Ga. 824, 76 S.E.2d 396 (1953); Skelly Oil Co. v. Kelly, 134 Kan. 176, 5 P.2d 823 (1931) (park land); Kings County Fire Insurance Co. v. Stevens, 101 N.Y. 411, 5 N.E. 353 (1886); Beach v. Haynes, 12 Vt. 15 (1840). This rule can be used to justify sale of condemned land that is found to be in excess of what is actually needed for a project. See Vilbig v. Housing Authority, 287 S.W.2d 323 (Tex. Civ.App.1955), ref'd n.r.e. (housing authority could sell excess land).

Statutes often expressly authorize sale of land found to be in excess of what is needed, or found to be no longer needed. See Nordine v. Illinois Power Co., 32 Ill.2d 421, 206 N.E.2d 709 (1965); Young v. City of Dayton, 12 Ohio St.2d 71, 232 N.E.2d 655 (1967); Pullen v. Oregon Industrial Development Corp., 240 Or. 583, 402 P.2d 240 (1965), applying such statutes.

[147] Moore v. City of Fairhope, 277 Ala. 380, 171 So.2d 86 (1965); Warren v. Mayor of Lyons, 22 Iowa 351 (1867); Cummings v. City of St. Louis, 90 Mo. 259, 2 S.W. 130 (1886). See State ex rel. Johnston v. City of Manhattan, 115 Kan. 794, 225 P. 85 (1924); Beverly Wood Associates v. City of Albuquerque, 78 N.M. 334, 431 P.2d 67 (1967). Dedicated property cannot ordinarily be reconveyed even to the original dedicator. Ash v. City of Omaha, 152 Neb. 393, 41 N.W.2d 386 (1950), reh. denied 152 Neb. 699, 42 N.W.2d 648. But there are two possible exceptions to the general rule: (1) If property is dedicated merely for the use and/or benefit of the public, and not dedicated for any *particular* use or uses, then the property may be freely disposed of for the public good. See Gering v. Jones, 175 Neb. 626, 122 N.W.2d 503 (1963). (2) A court with equity powers may occasionally allow a sale of dedicated property where changed circumstances make continued use of the property for the dedicated purpose impossible or extremely difficult. See City of Aurora ex rel. Egan v. Y.M.C.A., 9 Ill.2d 286, 137 N.E.2d 347 (1956); Loechel v. School District, 369 Pa. 132, 85 A.2d 81 (1952) (applying statute allowing sale of public land where court approval is obtained). But there is also the possibility that where the dedicated purpose is no longer possible, the property will be returned to the dedicator or his successors. See Gaskins v. Williams, 235 Mo. 563, 139 S.W. 117 (1911) (land dedicated for county court house; county seat located elsewhere). This certainly should be the result where the dedication has been merely of an easement, not the fee. In any case, courts are generally reluctant to find that the dedicated purpose is no longer possible. See McAlpine v. Chicago Great Western Railway Co., 68 Kan. 207, 75 P. 73 (1904).

Gifts of property by local governments—at least to private individuals—are generally banned by statute or as a matter of common law;[148] any transfer of municipal property must be supported by some reasonable compensation or benefit in return.

---

[148] See Solow v. City of New York, 25 A.D.2d 442, 266 N.Y.S.2d 823 (1966), aff'd 20 N.Y.2d 960, 286 N.Y.S.2d 852, 233 N.E.2d 855; Brumley v. Baxter, 225 N.C. 691, 36 S.E.2d 281 (1945). But courts often find quite readily that there has been some consideration for the transfer made by the municipal government and thus that the transaction is not really a "gift." See Hill v. City of Summit, 64 N.J.Super. 522, 166 A.2d 610 (1960) (grant of municipal property to veterans' organization); Haesloop v. City of Charleston, 123 S.C. 272, 115 S.E. 596 (1923). On what constitutes a "gift," see Hama Realty Co. v. New York City, 52 Misc.2d 192, 274 N.Y.S.2d 392 (Sup.Ct.1966), aff'd 27 A.D.2d 988, 281 N.Y.S.2d 974, cross motion dism'd 20 N.Y.2d 794, 284 N.Y.S.2d 451, 231 N.E.2d 128. Furthermore, transfers of even governmental property from one local government to another governmental unit or public institution have sometimes been upheld despite an apparent lack of consideration—either on the theory that this is an exception to the general rule or on the basis that some public benefit has actually been received in return by the grantor. See People ex rel. Illinois Armory Board v. Kelly, 369 Ill. 280, 16 N.E.2d 693 (1938); Sinas v. City of Lansing, 382 Mich. 407, 170 N.W.2d 23 (1969) (city made land available to community college at less than fair-market value; was legislative authorization); Sommers v. City of Flint, 355 Mich. 655, 96 N.W.2d 119 (1959) (park transferred to federal government for use as armory). See generally Norene v. Municipality of Anchorage, 704 P.2d 199 (Alaska 1985) (in land exchange between city and hospital, consideration of problems with the properties the city was acquiring and of varying estimates of value of land that city was giving-up was for municipal legislative body in determining whether to approve transaction, not for courts in taxpayers' action challenging validity of transaction).

Chapter 20

URBAN RENEWAL AND PUBLIC HOUSING

Analysis

§ 20.1 Urban Renewal: The Early Years

The middle decades of the twentieth century saw much federal aid, great efforts of local authorities, and increasing amounts of private money and effort devoted to attempts to rejuvenate American cities—especially the downtowns or "city centers" that have been faced with the competition of the suburbs and have often come upon hard times. The efforts were born of housing shortages (especially in the post-World War II years), concern over substandard or "slum" housing, and a desire to prevent the growth of areas that were considered "blighted" and regarded as breeding grounds for criminal activities. Gradually many programs expanded so as to include, for instance, the planned development of previously undeveloped areas, and the attempted beautification of the cities.

Modern "urban renewal" is usually thought to have started with a New York State program in 1941 that involved the use of eminent domain to acquire slum dwellings, which were then turned over for redevelopment to limited-dividend corporations that would eventually sell or lease the properties to private persons.[1] Under the New York law, redevelopment agencies could be established to administer the programs in participating cities; and these agencies were empowered to issue tax-exempt bonds and to take advantage of such federal aid as was available for public housing projects. But such federal aid was limited, and programs in New York and other states were thus not

1 Laws of April 29, 1941, ch. 892, (1941) N.Y.Laws 2039, now found in 41 McKinney's Consolidated Laws of New York, Priv.Hous.Fin.Law § 200–21 (1976). See Hagman, Urban Planning and Land Development Control Law 369 (1971); Comment, Urban Redevelopment, 54 Yale L.J. 116 (1944). On modern state legislation on urban renewal, see Hagman, *supra* at 413–19, particularly discussing the Wisconsin law. See generally Rosenthal, ed., Urban Revitalization (Sage Publications 1980); Sundby, The Elimination and Prevention of Urban Blight, 1959 Wis.L.Rev. 73.

too active, until the Housing Act of 1949.[2] This federal legislation noted the housing shortage and the need for elimination of substandard housing, and it provided possible financial assistance to local public bodies (which could be states, counties, municipalities, or other governmental entities authorized by state law to undertake redevelopment projects) that had programs of building, planning, and land-use controls designed to lower housing costs and prevent slums from developing. The financial assistance under this pioneering legislation took two main forms: (1) Forty-year *loans* were provided to cover the expense of local public agencies for the assembly, clearance, preparation, sale and/or lease of land for redevelopment. (2) Capital *grants* from the federal government were available to local agencies for the redevelopment projects (other than openland projects), and the formula for determining the amount was one that continued in use for many years: the grant could be up to two-thirds of the net cost of the project, with the locality financing the other third. Advances were also made available (payable out of the funds later received) so the localities could make surveys and plans for preparation of projects; and it was provided that obligations issued by localities to fund the redevelopment, and any income of localities from the projects, would be exempt from federal taxes.[3]

Six main conditions were attached to the federal aid: (1) A redevelopment plan, approved by the local government unit (usually a municipality), was required, showing what specific activities were to be undertaken and what were the eventual goals. (2) A showing had to be made that the particular plan conformed to a general plan for the locality. (3) It had to be demonstrated that the financial aid was necessary, and was consistent with the needs of the locality as an entirety. (4) Purchasers and lessees had to agree to devote the land to the uses specified in the redevelopment plan, and had to begin building within a reasonable time. (5) The local authorities had to provide a feasible method for relocation of displaced persons in equally desirable, though not necessarily the same, areas. (6) A public hearing was held before any land was actually acquired, through eminent domain or otherwise, for the project.[4]

The overall administration—including decisions on what localities qualified for the aid—was left to the Housing and Home Finance Administrator of the U.S. That administrator could specify covenants to run with the project land, including provisions that would assure that excessive prices were not paid for the land so as to preclude speculation in land-holding; and he could pay state and local taxing authorities for any losses in real-property taxes caused by acquisition of the land.[5] The project areas were to be deteriorating ones, and predominantly residential; but if the area was

---

[2] 42 U.S.C.A. §§ 1441–90. See generally Johnstone, The Federal Urban Renewal Program, 25 U.Chi.L.Rev. 301 (1958); Comment, Urban Renewal—Essentials of the Federal Program, 48 Ky.L.J. 262 (1960). A symposium on the federal urban renewal program is at 25 Law & Contemp. Prob. 631–812 (1960) and 26 Law & Contemp. Prob. 1–77 (1961). A good review of the past and present federal role in public housing and urban renewal efforts is found in Salsich, Saving Our Cities: What Role Should the Federal Government Play?, 36 Urban Law. 475 (2004).

[3] 42 U.S.C.A. § 1452(a) (on the 40-year loans), (b) (on the ten-year loans), (d) (on the advances), (g) (on the tax exemption for obligations) (1978); 42 U.S.C.A. §§ 1453–54 (on the federal grants).

[4] These conditions are set forth in 42 U.S.C.A. § 1455.

[5] 42 U.S.C.A. § 1460(c).

predominantly residential, tracts largely devoted to other uses—even open land necessary to sound community growth—could be included.[6]

Where public improvements constituted part of the locality's share, those improvements might, of course, sometimes serve not only the project area, but other areas of the locality as well—so a system of prorating the facility's cost, to determine the locality's resulting contribution to the project, was provided.[7] The local public agency could be a state, county, municipality, or other governmental entity authorized to undertake redevelopment projects.

In the 1940's and '50's, constitutional and statutory measures were adopted in most states specifically authorizing urban renewal authorities and allowing them to take

---

6 42 U.S.C.A. § 1460(c).

7 42 U.S.C.A. § 1450(d).

On the use of "tax increment financing" to support urban renewal, see Muskogee Urban Renewal Auth. v. Excise Bd., 899 P.2d 624 (Okl.1995) (legislation authorizing tax increment financing held constitutional on its face); Dennehy v. Department of Rev., 305 Or. 595, 756 P.2d 13 (1988), on remand 11 Or. Tax 191 (1989), judgment aff'd in part, rev'd in part 308 Or. 423, 781 P.2d 346 (1989) (constitutionality of statute authorizing such financing upheld). This financing is a statutory mechanism by which municipalities may dedicate future ad valorem tax revenues to be obtained from the increased property values in a redevelopment area to pay the expenditures incurred for the redevelopment project. See generally Michel, Brother, Can You Spare a Dime: Tax Increment Financing in Indiana, 71 Ind. L.J. 457 (1996); Winter, Tax Increment Financing: A Potential Redevelopment Financing Mechanism for New York Municipalities, 18 Fordham Urban L.J. 655 (1991). See also Suggs, Bringing Small Business Development to Urban Neighborhoods, 30 Harv. Civ. Rights/Civ. Liberties L. Rev. 487 (1995), proposing the use of tax increment credits to aid minority business activity in deteriorating urban neighborhoods. Compare Note, Protecting Low Income Residents During Tax Increment Financing Redevelopment, 36 Wash. U.J. L. & Pol'y 203 (2011).

In Harvey v. Oklahoma City, 111 P.3d 239 (Okla. 2005), it was held that so long as city ordinances regarding tax increment financing comply with constitutional requirements authorizing this device, the ordinances do not violate the general state constitutional requirement that a city may not incur long-term debt without three-fifths assent of the city's voters and without a determination that the new debt, combined with existing debt, does not exceed 5% of the valuation of all taxable property in the city. Cf. City of Guymon v. Butler, 92 P.3d 80 (Okla. 2004) (economic development project and tax increment district were public rather than private project and thus did not violate state constitution). As to whether tax increment financing bonds come within state debt limits, see generally Geheb, Tax Increment Financing Bonds as "Debt" Under State Constitutional Debt Limitations, 41 Urban Law. 725 (2009). On the purpose of tax increment financing, see In re Application of Oklahoma Dev. Fin. Auth., 94 P.3d 87 (Okla. 2004) (objective of such financing is to use increased ad valorem property tax revenue generated by a project to pay the principal and interest on tax increment bonds issued to finance the project). See generally Note, Tax Increment Financing: Public Use or Private Abuse?, 90 Minn. L. Rev. 213 (2005); Note, The Use of Tax Increment Financing to Attract Private Investment and Generate Redevelopment in Virginia, 20 Va. Tax Rev. 777 (2001). See also Comment, Detroit's Renaissance Zones: The Economics of Tax Incentives in Metropolitan Location Decisions, the Results of the Zones to Date, and Thoughts on the Future, 83 U. Detroit Mercy L. Rev. 329 (2006). As to the interrelationship of tax increment financing and government grants, see Woolever, Tax Increment Financing, Government Grants, and Developer Tax Consequences: An Analysis of Statutes, Regulations, Case Law and Related Policy Considerations, 40 Urban Law. 299 (2008). See also Johnson, How Tax Increment Financing (TIF) Districts Correlate With Taxable Properties, 34 N. Ill. U.L. Rev. 39 (2013).

For an example of how tax increment financing can be used successfully in urban renewal, see Bassett, Tax Increment Financing as a Tool for Redevelopment: Attracting Private Investment to Serve a Public Purpose—The Example of Michigan, 41 Urban Law. 755 (2009). As to the wisdom, or lack thereof, of using tax increment financing for urban renewal and business development, see Lefcoe, Competing for the Next Hundred Million Americans: The Uses and Abuses of Tax Increment Financing, 43 Urban Law. 427 (2011); Note, Fields of Dreams: The Expectation and Common Reality of Tax Increment Financing, 79 U.M.K.C. L. Rev. 791 (2011). See generally as to tax increment financing and its alternatives, Collies & Gowder, Tax Increment Financing (American Bar Assn. Section of State & Local Govt. Law 2012). Tax increment financing has not always been successful. See Comment, Still as Moonlight: Why Tax Increment Financing Stalled in North Carolina, 91 N.C. L. Rev. 661 (2013). As to possible changes in the law, see Comment, Specificity, Blight, and Two Tiers of TIF: A Proposal for Reform of Tax Increment Financing Law, 33 St. Louis U. Pub. L. Rev. 255 (2013).

advantage of the federal aid programs. Typically, the governing body of the municipality is authorized to establish such an authority. At the same time or soon thereafter, the governing body generally requests an appropriate municipal agency—such as a planning board or commission—to make investigations and hold hearings to determine whether a particular area of the city is slum or blighted.[8] Once a determination of "slum" or "blight" is reported to the governing body, that body reviews the finding. If the finding is approved, the authority then proceeds to define the precise boundaries of the project area and to prepare a redevelopment plan. The plan must ordinarily be approved by the local governing body—and sometimes by a state agency—before the authority can begin acquiring property.[9]

§ 20.2 Constitutionality of Urban Renewal

A number of constitutional attacks have been leveled at urban renewal legislation, but the statutes have usually survived. Arguments of violation of due process[10] and of equal protection[11] have always been rejected. Similarly, it seems agreed that the legislation does not involve an unlawful delegation of legislative authority.[12] Arguments have been made that urban redevelopment projects do not involve a sufficient public use or purpose to justify the exercise of the eminent-domain power; but these arguments have usually failed,[13] as have those alleging there was not a sufficiently "public purpose"

---

[8] See Wilson v. City of Long Branch, 27 N.J. 360, 142 A.2d 837 (1958), cert. denied 358 U.S. 873, 79 S.Ct. 113, 3 L.Ed.2d 104 (the required hearing is legislative in character, not judicial). Where the *statute* specifies a hearing and/or presentation of a redevelopment plan to a municipal planning commission, a program will be void if attempted without these steps. See Sheehan v. Altschuler, 148 Conn. 517, 172 A.2d 897 (1961). And where federal aid is involved, the federal statute does require a public hearing before land is acquired. 42 U.S.C.A. § 1455(d). See note 4 *supra* and accompanying text. But *due process* does not necessarily require a hearing, or notice to property-owners in the area if a hearing is held, prior to condemnation for a redevelopment project.

[9] See Sheehan v. Atlschuler, *supra* note 8. Once a finding of "blight" or "slum" is approved as required by the local and state legislative bodies, it will be overturned by the courts only if shown to be arbitrary and capricious. Housing Authority v. Nunn, 292 Ala. 60, 288 So.2d 775 (1974); Allright Missouri, Inc. v. Civic Plaza Redevelopment Corp., 538 S.W.2d 320 (Mo.1976), cert. denied 429 U.S. 941, 97 S.Ct. 358, 50 L.Ed.2d 311. Cf. Parking Systems, Inc. v. Kansas City Downtown Redevelopment Corp., 518 S.W.2d 11 (Mo.1974) (legislative determination of blight will be disturbed only if fraud, collusion, bad faith, or exceeding of city power is shown). On what is "blight," see generally the material in Section 133 on blight-determination as a condition precedent to the exercise of eminent domain, and Section 135 on whether particular property has to be "blighted" in order to be condemned for urban renewal.

[10] Berman v. Parker, 348 U.S. 26, 75 S.Ct. 98, 99 L.Ed. 27 (1954); Redevelopment Agency v. Hayes, 122 Cal.App.2d 777, 266 P.2d 105 (Dist.Ct.1954); Cremer v. Peoria Housing Authority, 399 Ill. 579, 78 N.E.2d 276 (1948); Sorbino v. City of New Brunswick, 43 N.J.Super. 554, 129 A.2d 473 (1957).

[11] See Redevelopment Agency v. Hayes, *supra* note 10; Sorbino v. City of New Brunswick, *supra* note 10. Cf. State ex rel. Tomasic v. Unified Government of Wyandotte County/Kansas City, 265 Kan. 779, 962 P.2d 543 (1998) (statutory classification in urban redevelopment statute limiting "major tourism area of the state" to the development of automobile race track facilities did not violate equal protection).

[12] See City of Sparks v. Best, 96 Nev. 134, 605 P.2d 638 (1980) (no grant of uncontrolled discretionary power was given the community redevelopment agency); Miller v. City of Tacoma, 61 Wn.2d 374, 378 P.2d 464 (1963).

[13] Berman v. Parker, *supra* note 10. See cases cited notes 15–20 *infra* and accompanying text (on "public use" or "public purpose" requirement of eminent domain and how it is satisfied by various factors). Cf. City of Seattle v. Loutsis Investment Co., 16 Wn.App. 158, 554 P.2d 379 (1976), review denied 88 Wash.2d 1016 (1977) (government contributes its power of eminent domain to assemble the land and private enterprise does the redeveloping). See generally Mandelker, Public Purpose in Urban Development, 28 Tul. L.Rev. 96 (1953); Note, Urban Renewal—The Evolving Concept of "Public Use," 39 Miss.L.J. 341 (1968).

to justify the spending of public money.[14] In 2005, the U.S. Supreme Court held, in the celebrated *Kelo* case, that a city's economic rejuvenation plan, designed to bring new jobs and increased revenue to the city, provided sufficient public purpose to justify the use of eminent domain.[15] There *is* contrary authority in Michigan, where the court had at one time, in the *Poletown* case, found public purpose in an economic development corporation's condemnation of a large tract of land to be conveyed to a private corporation as the site for construction of an assembly plant,[16] but subsequently overruled the *Poletown* case and found insufficient public purpose in the condemnation of property for private economic benefit.[17] Of course, in the *eminent-domain cases*, the degree of "public purpose" can vary according to the nature of each particular project. But it is well established that slum clearance is such a purpose,[18] as is the construction of low-cost

---

[14] Crommett v. City of Portland, 150 Me. 217, 107 A.2d 841 (1954); Velishka v. City of Nashua, 99 N.H. 161, 106 A.2d 571 (1954); Foeller v. Housing Auth., 198 Or. 205, 256 P.2d 752 (1953). See cases cited notes 21–22 *infra* and accompanying text.

[15] Kelo v. City of New London, 545 U.S. 469, 125 S.Ct. 2655, 162 L.Ed.2d 439 (2005), reh. denied 545 U.S. 1158, 126 S.Ct. 24, 162 L.Ed.2d 922 (2005), discussed in Section 19.3, notes 64–73, *supra* and accompanying text.

[16] Poletown Neighborhood Council v. City of Detroit, 410 Mich. 616, 304 N.W.2d 455 (1981). See City of Detroit v. Vavro, 177 Mich.App. 682, 442 N.W.2d 730 (1989), where the court felt constrained by stare decisis to uphold a condemnation by a municipality for the purpose of transferring the property to an automobile manufacturer, but cited with approval the dissenting opinions in *Poletown*.

[17] County of Wayne v. Hathcock, 471 Mich. 445, 684 N.W.2d 765 (2004). See Agneti, Are You Still Master of Your Domain? Abuses of Economic Development Takings, and Michigan's Return to "Public Use" in *County of Wayne v. Hathcock*, 79 St. John's L. Rev. 1259 (2005); Mogk, Eminent Domain and the "Public Use": Michigan Supreme Court Legislates an Unprecedented Overruling of *Poletown* in *County of Wayne v. Hathcock*, 51 Wayne L. Rev. 1331 (2005). It has been suggested that the *Hathcock* case's use of state law to overturn economic-development takings of private property may be employed as a remedy to the U.S. Supreme Court's extremely broad interpretation of the "public use" requirement in eminent domain. See Note, Reconsidering *Poletown*: In the Wake of *Kelo*, States Should Move to Restore Private Property Rights, 48 Ariz. L. Rev. 369 (2006); Note, Quieting the Clang: *Hathcock* as a Model of the State-based Protection of Property Which *Kelo* Demands, 14 Wm. & Mary Bill of Rights J. (2005). See generally Note, The Public Use Clause, Common Sense and Takings, 10 Boston U.L. Pub. Int. L.J. 335 (2001). As to the U.S. Supreme Court's broad interpretation of the public use clause of the federal Constitution, and as to possibly narrower interpretations of that requirement as found in state law, see Section 19.3, notes 64–73, *supra* including discussion of the *Kelo* case. See also Ross, Does *County of Wayne v. Hathcock* Signal a Revival of the Public Use Limit to the Taking of Private Property?, 37 Urban Law. 243 (2005); Salkin & Lucero, Community Redevelopment, Public Use, and Eminent Domain, 37 Urban Law. 201 (2005).

[18] Berman v. Parker, *supra* note 10; Schneider v. District of Columbia, 117 F.Supp. 705 (D.D.C.1953), mod. 348 U.S. 26, 75 S.Ct. 98, 99 L.Ed. 27; Rowe v. Housing Auth., 220 Ark. 698, 249 S.W.2d 551 (1952); People ex rel. Adamowski v. Chicago Land Clearance Commission, 14 Ill.2d 74, 150 N.E.2d 792 (1958); Chicago Land Clearance Commission v. White, 1 Ill.2d 69, 115 N.E.2d 337 (1953); People ex rel. Gutknecht v. City of Chicago, 414 Ill. 600, 111 N.E.2d 626 (1953); People ex rel. Tuohy v. City of Chicago, 399 Ill. 551, 78 N.E.2d 285 (1948); In re Slum Clearance in Detroit, 331 Mich. 714, 50 N.W.2d 340 (1951); Kaskel v. Impellitteri, 306 N.Y. 73, 115 N.E.2d 659 (1953); Murray v. LaGuardia, 291 N.Y. 320, 52 N.E.2d 884 (1943); Eikenbary v. City of Dayton, 3 Ohio App.2d 295, 210 N.E.2d 402 (1964); Belovsky v. Redevelopment Authority, 357 Pa. 329, 54 A.2d 277 (1947); Isaacs v. Oklahoma City, 437 P.2d 229 (Okl.1966), cert. denied 389 U.S. 825, 88 S.Ct. 63, 19 L.Ed.2d 79. Much judicial deference is paid a legislative finding that an area is "slum" or blighted, and thus in need of clearance and redevelopment. See State v. Land Clearance for Redev. Authority, 364 Mo. 974, 270 S.W.2d 44 (1954). See generally Opinion to the Governor, 76 R.I. 249, 69 A.2d 531 (1949) (public use found in elimination of conditions inimical to public health, safety, welfare). See also Kotlyarevskaya, "Public Use" Requirement in Eminent Domain Cases Based on Slum Clearance, Elimination of Urban Blight, and Economic Development, 5 Conn. Pub. Interest L.J. 197 (2006); Pritchett, The "Public Menace" of Blight: Urban Renewal and the Private Uses of Eminent Domain, 21 Yale L. & Pol'y Rev. 1 (2003).

For historical material on the validity of slum-clearance legislation, see generally Annots., Constitutionality, Construction, and Application of Statutes or Governmental Projects for Improvement of Housing Conditions (Slum Clearance), 172 A.L.R. 966 (1948); 130 A.L.R. 1069 (1941).

housing.[19] Even the provision of moderate-cost housing, where more is needed in the community, can be found supported by a public purpose,[20] as can the building of such public facilities as a coliseum or a parking garage.[21] At least where the elimination of slum or blight was also involved, courts have upheld the redevelopment of land for private industrial or commercial use.[22] And where land is unmarketable, it has often been considered actually or potentially "blighted" so that its taking can be justified even if the land is actually vacant when taken.[23] Similarly, the presence or absence of "public purpose," in cases where the *spending of government money* is challenged, can vary somewhat with the nature of the particular activity; but courts have found the clearance of slums[24] and the providing of housing[25] to be definitely of a sufficiently public benefit to satisfy this requirement.

Perhaps the two strongest constitutional arguments mounted against urban renewal legislation have been (1) that too much unbridled discretion is given authorities to determine what areas are "blighted" or "slum" and thus eligible for redevelopment; and (2) that there is a lack of sufficient "public purpose" (either for eminent-domain

---

[19] Keyes v. United States, 119 F.2d 444 (D.C.1941), cert. denied 314 U.S. 636, 62 S.Ct. 70, 86 L.Ed. 510; Blumenschein v. Housing Authority, 379 Pa. 566, 109 A.2d 331 (1954) (under Pennsylvania statute, redevelopment, with use of eminent domain, can occur to provide low-cost housing, as well as for the elimination of slums and blighted areas). See generally Note, Ensuring Proper Land Re-Use in Urban Renewal: An Analysis of Present Federal and Local Policies and Practices, 37 N.Y.U.L.Rev. 882 (1962); Note, Suburban Renewal in Pennsylvania, 111 U.Pa.L.Rev. 61 (1962).

[20] See People ex rel. Gutknecht v. City of Chicago, *supra* note 19; Cremer v. Peoria Housing Authority, *supra* note 10. Cf. Yonkers Community Development Agency v. Morris, 37 N.Y.2d 478, 373 N.Y.S.2d 112, 335 N.E.2d 327 (1975), appeal dism'd 423 U.S. 1010, 96 S.Ct. 440, 46 L.Ed.2d 381 (urban renewal need not be limited to slums; removal of economic underdevelopment and stagnation also serves a public purpose).

[21] Club Jolliet, Inc. v. City of Manchester, 110 N.H. 172, 262 A.2d 844 (1970) (public parking facility; applying state statute); Kaskel v. Impellitteri, *supra* note 18 (coliseum); Campbell v. Bethlehem Parking Authority, 20 Pa.Cmwlth. 445, 342 A.2d 114 (1975) (parking garage; any private gain said to be incidental).

[22] Dalton v. Land Clearance for Redev. Authority, 364 Mo. 974, 270 S.W.2d 44 (1954); Levin v. Township Committee, 57 N.J. 506, 274 A.2d 1 (1971), appeal dism'd 404 U.S. 803, 92 S.Ct. 58, 30 L.Ed.2d 35; Cannata v. New York City, 11 N.Y.2d 210, 227 N.Y.S.2d 903, 182 N.E.2d 395 (1962), appeal dism'd 371 U.S. 4, 83 S.Ct. 28, 9 L.Ed.2d 48. See In re Bunker Hill Urban Renewal Project, 61 Cal.2d 21, 37 Cal.Rptr. 74, 389 P.2d 538 (1964), cert. denied 379 U.S. 899, 85 S.Ct. 185, 13 L.Ed.2d 174, appeal dism'd, cert. denied 379 U.S. 28, 85 S.Ct. 190, 13 L.Ed.2d 173; Housing & Redevelopment Authority v. Minneapolis Metropolitan Co., 259 Minn. 1, 104 N.W.2d 864 (1960); Ferreira v. City of Asbury Park, 237 N.J.Super. 142, 567 A.2d 233 (1989), cert. denied 121 N.J. 627, 583 A.2d 324 (1990) (municipality could sell oceanfront land to private developer who intended to use it for residential and commercial purposes); Schenck v. City of Pittsburgh, 364 Pa. 31, 70 A.2d 612 (1950). Cf. People ex rel. City of Urbana v. Paley, 68 Ill.2d 62, 11 Ill.Dec. 307, 368 N.E.2d 915 (1977) (redevelopment project can be used to stimulate an economically stagnant downtown area).

[23] See People ex rel. Gutnecht v. City of Chicago, *supra* note 18 (applying Illinois statute and upholding legislative determination that unmarketable areas may be a blight on communities); Levin v. Township Committee, *supra* note 22 (sustaining condemnation of unmarketable vacant land under New Jersey statute); Cannata v. New York City, *supra* note 22.

The exact determinations of the redevelopment site and its boundaries are always subjects left largely to legislative determination. See Sherman v. Haddington Leadership Organization, 8 Pa.Cmwlth. 309, 302 A.2d 919 (1973) (judiciary will intervene only if local authority acts outside its power or abuses its discretion). Cf. Schweig v. City of St. Louis, 569 S.W.2d 215 (Mo.App.1978) (court will not inquire into motives of city legislative body in designating blighted area). But cf. City of Helena v. DeWolf, 162 Mont. 57, 508 P.2d 122 (1973), where the court denied the city power to condemn land at the edge of the redevelopment project, finding the city failed to show it was reasonably necessary to clearance of the blighted area.

[24] Allydonn Realty Corp. v. Holyoke Housing Authority, 304 Mass. 288, 23 N.E.2d 665 (1939). See Redevelopment Agency v. Hayes, *supra* note 10.

[25] Watkins v. Fugazzi, 394 S.W.2d 594 (Ky.1965). See People ex rel. Gutknecht v. City of Chicago, *supra* note 18.

purposes or to justify spending of public money) because the property will often end up in the hands of private redevelopers. But the first argument has consistently been rejected because adequate standards of what is "blighted" or "slum" are found to have been provided by legislation and/or because decisions of the local authority are usually subject to approval or rejection by the local governing body itself.[26] As to the second argument—The transfer to private developers has been ruled incidental to the primary public purposes,[27] the courts often being influenced in this determination by the considerable control over permissible land uses generally retained by the local government.[28] Thus, it has been said in broad terms that sale or lease of property within the project to private persons is valid so long as those persons agree to respect the redevelopment plan.[29] Even if the redevelopment authority sells the land at less than what it had to pay for acquisition and clearance, this does not amount to a forbidden donation to private parties if the sale was at no less than current "use value" and the

---

[26] See Berman v. Parker, *supra* note 10; Belovsky v. Redevelopment Authority, *supra* note 18; David Jeffrey Co. v. City of Milwaukee, 267 Wis. 559, 66 N.W.2d 362 (1954). Cf. Johnson v. Redevelopment Agency of Salt Lake County, 913 P.2d 723 (Utah 1995) (Utah Neighborhood Development Act requires that finding that redevelopment project area is blighted be made by redevelopment agency at time preliminary plan is prepared and by legislative body prior to adopting plan, and this finding is subject to property owner's right of de novo review, though right of de novo review held here not to apply to preliminary vote of county commission concluding that property was blighted). On the standards as to what is "blighted" or "slum," see generally the material in this chapter on blight-determination as a pre-requisite to the exercise of eminent domain, *infra*.

The usual rules on disqualification will apply to a member of the municipal, or urban-renewal authority, governing body where such member has a conflict of interest. See Anderson v. City of Parsons, 209 Kan. 337, 496 P.2d 1333 (1972) (city commissioner disqualified from voting only where his property-interest exists in property included, or planned to be included, in a specific urban-renewal project on which action is being taken; not disqualified because owns property in the general urban renewal area). On conflicts of interest, see generally Chapter 13 *supra*.

[27] See Gohld Realty Co. v. City of Hartford, 141 Conn. 135, 104 A.2d 365 (1954); Holloway v. Lakeland Downtown Dev. Auth., 417 So.2d 963 (Fla.1982) (eliminating blighted condition of a portion of downtown involved sufficient public purpose to justify issuance of revenue bonds, and the public purpose was not defeated by the area's being resold to a private entity for construction of a regional shopping center); Papadinis v. City of Somerville, 331 Mass. 627, 121 N.E.2d 714 (1954) (primary objective of taking property is slum clearance, and disposition of land thereafter is incidental to that purpose); Housing & Redevelopment Auth. v. Coleman's Service, 281 Minn. 63, 160 N.W.2d 266 (1968); Housing & Redevelopment Auth. v. Greenman, 255 Minn. 396, 96 N.W.2d 673 (1959); Wheeler v. Town of Islip, 51 Misc.2d 386, 273 N.Y.S.2d 399 (1966); Cannata v. New York City, *supra* note 22. Cf. Dilley v. City of Des Moines, 247 N.W.2d 187 (Iowa 1976) (rejecting contention that special privileges were being accorded private developer); City of Charlottesville v. DeHaan, 228 Va. 578, 323 S.E.2d 131 (1984) (city's role in development of a hotel-convention center in a redevelopment area held not to violate state constitution's prohibition of lending the city's credit to a private entity since city's involvement was primarily for public purpose, not to benefit the private developer). But cf. Morley v. Jackson Redev. Auth., 632 So.2d 1284 (Miss.1994) (insufficient showing of public use where was mere legislative declaration of such use and where primary objective seemed to be the sale of the property to another developer). See generally Annot., Validity, Construction, and Effect of Statutes Providing for Urban Redevelopment by Private Enterprise, 44 A.L.R.2d 1414 (1955).

[28] See Rowe v. Housing Authority, *supra* note 18; Gohld Realty Co. v. City of Hartford, *supra* note 27; Foeller v. Housing Authority, *supra* note 14; Miller v. City of Tacoma, *supra* note 12.

[29] In re Slum Clearance in Detroit, *supra* note 18. Cf. Opinion of the Justices, 254 Ala. 343, 48 So.2d 757 (1950) (sale of land to private redevelopers at fair price does not violate constitutional prohibition on special privileges to private parties). See generally Scheuer, Goldston & Sogg, Disposition of Urban Renewal Land—A Fundamental Problem in the Rebuilding of Our Cities, 62 Colum.L.Rev. 959 (1962).

It has been held that redevelopment authorities can sell land to churches and other religious organizations at use value without violating constitutional provisions on separation of church and state. Fishman v. City of Stamford, 159 Conn. 116, 267 A.2d 443 (1970), cert. denied 399 U.S. 905, 90 S.Ct. 2197, 26 L.Ed.2d 560 (sale to church at a fair "use value"); Kintzele v. City of St. Louis, 347 S.W.2d 695 (Mo.1961) (sale to Catholic university); 64th Street Residences, Inc. v. New York City, 4 N.Y.2d 268, 174 N.Y.S.2d 1, 150 N.E.2d 396 (1958), cert. denied sub nom. Harris v. New York City, 357 U.S. 907, 78 S.Ct. 1152, 2 L.Ed.2d 1157 (same).

purchaser agrees to redevelop in accord with the plan.[30] Contractual provisions—often involving covenants running with the land—can bind the redevelopers and/or purchasers to abide by the plan, thus assuring a degree of continued governmental control; and upon non-performance of the contractual obligations, courts can order a reconveyance of the property to the local government or its redevelopment authority.[31]

§ 20.3 Urban Renewal Programs in the 1950's and 1960's

From the early 1950's through the late '60's, extensive programs of redevelopment—generally with federal aid—were undertaken in many U.S. cities. Meantime, the federal legislation underwent some changes. For one thing, the name of the program was changed from "urban redevelopment" to "urban renewal"—to emphasize that rehabilitation and conservation features were included and that the activities were not limited to tearing down old buildings but were to include rejuvenation of areas.[32]

Besides the change in name—and some change in emphasis indicated thereby—, four major areas of modification and expansion during the '50's and '60's can be detected: (1) *Additional loans and advances* were made available. Loans were made available to prevent the *spread* of slums and of deterioration, and to help provide rehabilitation and conservation. Also, to provide for "starting costs" and to stimulate localities into action, new provisions for advances were added to the legislation; the advances, from the federal government to qualifying localities, could be made for studies on the feasibility of possible projects, for the creation of plans for voluntary repair and rehabilitation in some

---

[30] Cremer v. Peoria Housing Auth., *supra* note 10; Dalton v. Land Clearance for Redev. Authority, 364 Mo. 974, 270 S.W.2d 44 (1954); Club Jolliet v. City of Manchester, *supra* note 21.

It has been said that invitations to bid on redevelopment property cannot be unreasonably limited and that specifications "need not be as precise as when buying a fire truck." Eikenbary v. City of Dayton, 3 Ohio App.2d 295, 310, 210 N.E.2d 402, 412 (1964). Cf. Ott v. West New York, 92 N.J.Super. 184, 222 A.2d 541 (1966) (redevelopment property need not always be sold the highest bidder; other factors can be considered, such as qualifications and financial capability of redeveloper, and court won't interfere unless is bad faith, corruption, or gross abuse of discretion). It is provided by federal legislation that opportunities for employment and contracts for work should, to the greatest extent feasible, be awarded persons residing in the redevelopment area, since this furthers the purpose of stimulating the local economy. 12 U.S.C.A. § 1701u. See generally the annotation on this statute, 40 A.L.R.Fed. 836 (1978).

[31] Feldman v. Urban Commercial, Inc., 70 N.J.Super. 463, 175 A.2d 683 (1961). A governmental authority may also be liable to a redeveloper for breach of contract if it fails to fulfill its part of the urban renewal agreement. See West Haven Sound Dev. Corp. v. City of West Haven, 207 Conn. 308, 541 A.2d 858 (1988) (city held liable for loss of value of business after a referendum halted an urban renewal project).

[32] See 42 U.S.C.A. §§ 1450–69(c), containing what is titled the "Slum Clearance and Urban Renewal" program. The 1954 amendments, which included a number of the changes discussed *infra*, made up what was called the Slum Clearance and *Urban Renewal* Act of 1954 (italics supplied). On the shift in emphasis in the early 1950's, see generally Note, Conservation of Dwellings: The Prevention of Blight, 29 Ind.L.J. 109 (1953). Recommendations that the program be expanded are found in M. Colean, Renewing Our Cities (1953); President's Advisory Comm'n on Gov't Housing Policies and Programs, A Report to the President of the United States (1953). Others have also recommended that emphasis be placed on improvement of municipal services and rehabilitation of existing structures. See Report of the President's Task Force on Urban Renewal, Urban Renewal: One Tool Among Many (May, 1970) (M. Colean, chair). See also Vider, The City That Said "No," Historic Preservation, Sept.-Oct., 1980, at 48, discussing the decision of Waterbury, Connecticut, civic leaders to revise the city's urban-renewal plan to emphasize rehabilitation, especially of historically or architecturally significant structures, as well as new development. In 1984, the U.S. Department of Housing and Urban Development published regulations concerning its Rental Rehabilitation Grant Program, which was another effort to shift the emphasis away from new construction and toward upgrading existing structures—in this case, rental housing in particular. See 16 Urban Law. 504 (1984).

areas, and for plans for more effective enforcement of such land use controls as zoning laws.[33]

(2) *Additional grants* were made available, and these fell into four main groups. (a) By amendments in 1954 and subsequent years, larger grants were made available for "demonstration projects" for the prevention and elimination of urban blight. These were available both to public bodies and to nonprofit organizations, and could be at 90%, rather than two-thirds, of the net project costs. Such special incentives were intended to induce localities to develop improved methods for the elimination and prevention of slums and to result in some "model projects" that could serve as guides for others.[34] (b) Grants were also made available for development of *open* land *if* it was redeveloped for public low- or moderate-income housing—in an effort to encourage more of such housing to be built.[35] (c) As a further inducement to urban renewal in smaller cities, the size of grants was increased from two-thirds to three-fourths of net project costs in municipalities of less than 50,000 population.[36] (d) As of 1964 amendments, rehabilitation grants could be made directly to property owners to assist them in making the repairs necessary to put their properties into safe and sanitary condition, and demolition and code enforcement grants were made available to local governments.[37]

---

[33] 42 U.S.C.A. § 1452 is the loan section of the legislation and has been often amended. See Hagman, Urban Planning and Land Development Control Law 373–74 (1971). On urban-renewal loans and grants, see generally 40 Am.Jur.2d Housing Laws and Urban Redevelopment §§ 6–7 (1968).

[34] The original legislation was found at 42 U.S.C.A. § 1452(a), repealed by Pub.L. 91–609 (1970), effective July 1, 1971. This concept of "Model projects" was also employed in the Demonstration Cities and Metropolitan Development Act of 1966, 42 U.S.C.A. §§ 3301–13. The 1966 legislation applied to selected cities a new approach involving greater co-ordination of federal, state, and local programs; grants could be as much as 80% of aggregate costs. See Annot., Validity, Construction, and Application of "Model Cities" Provisions of Demonstration Cities and Metropolitan Development Act of 1966, as Amended, 10 A.L.R.Fed. 802 (1972). See generally Hetzel & Pinsky, The Model Cities Program, 22 Vand.L.Rev. 727 (1969). On changes in emphasis that occurred in the "model cities" program, see Mandelker, Managing Our Urban Environment 877–78 (2d ed. 1971).

[35] See 42 U.S.C.A. § 1453(a)(1); United States Dep't of Housing & Urban Development, Urban Renewal Handbook RHA 7205.1, ch. 2, at 607 (Supp. 1969).

[36] 42 U.S.C.A. § 1453(a).

The allegation has sometimes been made that federal programs paid insufficient attention to the problems of smaller cities. See Reinhold, Small-City Officials Say Their Needs Are Neglected, N.Y. Times, Dec. 8, 1977, at A-18. And the revitalization of downtowns in smaller cities has proved a continuing problem. In 1980, the National Trust for Historic Preservation, aided by a federal grant and by the cooperation of several federal agencies, opened the National Main Street Center—to provide technical assistance to older, small municipalities seeking to revitalize their downtowns. See Knight, U.S. Grant Will Open Main Street Center, Preservation News, June, 1980, at 1. *Privately* financed urban renewal projects have sometimes occurred in small or medium-size cities. See "Bringing Urban Glitter to Smaller Cities," Bus. Week., July 23, 1984, at 140, describing urban developer James Rouse's projects in Norfolk, Va.; Toledo, Ohio; and Flint, Mich. But some of Rouse's "festival marketplaces" in these smaller cities did not enjoy the success that his developments had in such larger cities as Baltimore and Boston. See "Jim Rouse May Be Losing His Touch," Bus. Week, April 4, 1988, at 33, noting problems with his developments in Toledo, Flint, and Richmond, Va. On Rouse's efforts to revitalize American cities, see generally Carter, "Whatever Ought to Be, Can Be," Parade magazine, May 12, 1991, at 4; Zoglin, The Urban Renewer—James W. Rouse: 1914–1996, Time, April 22, 1996, at 97 (an obituary that credits Rouse with bringing hope and renewed vitality to many American cities but that notes his lack of success in such smaller cities as Richmond and Toledo).

[37] 42 U.S.C.A. § 1452b (rehabilitation loans to owners and tenants; to qualify, a *tenant* must occupy under a lease having a period to run of not less than the term of the loan); 42 U.S.C.A. § 1466 (Housing and Urban Development can authorize rehabilitation grants, by a local public agency, to families and individuals). See Hagman, *supra* note 33, at 395–96. Housing and Urban Development can also make grants to local governments to assist programs to aid areas planned for *later* clearance or rehabilitation, but which are in need of some immediate relief of a more limited nature. 42 U.S.C.A. § 1468a.

(3) The *conditions* attached to federal aid were increased, particularly with regard to requirements for relocation of persons and businesses displaced by urban renewal projects. As of 1959, relocation requirements were clearly made applicable to individuals and businesses, not just families. And since many communities were alleged not to be providing adequately for relocation, a relocation assistance program was specifically required for each project in order to determine the needs for relocation, to provide information and assistance to those being "relocated," and to assure coordination with governmental construction of low-rent housing projects.[38] As of amendments in 1969, relocation plans for each project had to be reviewed every two years by the Secretary of Housing and Urban Development; and prior to any demolition or removal of residential structures, replacement housing had to be made available, unless it was shown there was a high residential vacancy rate in the area.[39] Other conditions show a desire on the part of federal legislators to emphasize rehabilitation rather than demolition in urban renewal projects. For instance, amendments to the original law provide that before the Secretary of Housing and Urban Development can make a capital grant for demolition or removal, he or she must make a finding that the objectives of the urban renewal plan for the area could not be accomplished by rehabilitation.[40]

(4) Finally, some changes *require* that *more housing*—particularly low- and moderate-income housing—be provided in urban renewal areas than had often been occurring in the past. Since 1954, it has been provided that air rights over highways, railroads, etc. can be acquired by urban renewal agencies for development of low- and moderate-income housing—or if unsuitable for such use, for industrial or educational facilities.[41] And since too much non-residential development was thought by many critics to be occurring, it was provided that urban renewal areas must, in general, be predominantly residential both before and after redevelopment—and that, in any case, not more than 35% of all capital grants could be made to projects not primarily residential.[42] But amendments provided an exception to the "predominantly residential" requirements where an educational institution or hospital is built in, or within a mile of, the project area.[43] A 1961 amendment also removed the "primarily residential" requirements as to areas found economically depressed.[44] To encourage more low-cost housing, a provision was added in 1966 that at least half the housing in each

---

38 42 U.S.C.A. § 1455(c). Since 1969, it has been required that local relocation plans be reviewed every two years by the Secretary of Housing and Urban Development. 42 U.S.C.A. § 1455(c)(3).

39 42 U.S.C.A. § 1455(h). See generally Note, Family Relocation in Urban Renewal, 82 Harv.L.Rev. 864 (1969). See also the discussion, *infra* this chapter, on court cases dealing with challenges to allegedly discriminatory or inadequate relocation programs.

40 42 U.S.C.A. § 1460(c).

41 42 U.S.C.A. § 1460(c)(1)(iv). An urban-renewal project can include the construction of foundations and platforms necessary to utilize air rights. 42 U.S.C.A. § 1460(c)(7). On ownership and development of air space, see generally Comment, The Creation of Estates in Airspace, 25 Rocky Mt.L.Rev. 354 (1953); Note, Airspace: A New Dimension in Property Law, 1960 U.Ill.L.F. 303. See also Bell, Air Rights, 23 Ill.L.Rev. 250 (1928); Brennan, Lots of Air—A Subdivision in the Sky, Title News, Feb., 1957, at 6.

42 42 U.S.C.A. § 1460(c). Since allegations had been made that too much urban renewal area was being devoted to luxury hotels, it was also provided that a specific determination of a need for hotels must be made, and affirmed by the federal administrator, before hotels could be included in future urban-renewal developments. 42 U.S.C.A. § 1456(g).

43 42 U.S.C.A. § 1463 (exceptions where educational institution or hospital within vicinity).

44 42 U.S.C.A. § 1464. Many of the usual requirements for urban-renewal projects can also be relaxed (as of 1956 amendments) when the President has declared a project-area to be a disaster-area (because of some such catastrophe as a flood, fire, earthquake, etc.). 42 U.S.C.A. § 1462.

community's urban renewal projects must be for low- and moderate-income families or individuals, and 20% must be for *low*-income families or individuals.[45]

Another important change occurred in 1967, when, as part of governmental reorganization, the Secretary of Housing and Urban Development was made chief federal administrator of the program.[46]

§ 20.4 Acquisition of Property for Urban Renewal Projects

How does urban renewal "work" so far as acquiring property is concerned? It has been noted[47] that urban renewal combines the state power of eminent domain—as delegated to municipalities and other units—with federal and local contributions of money in order to buy up property, which is then turned over to private parties for redevelopment. The eminent-domain procedures are basically those provided by state law.[48] But federal requirements have at times imposed some important limitations. These fall into three main categories: (1) Federal assistance is available only if the owner of condemned property does not have to surrender possession until paid—or, if only the amount of payment is in dispute, until the owner is paid at least 75% of the appraised value.[49] (2) There may be requirements of warning, and/or of prior attempts to purchase the property, before condemning it. The federal statutes for a time required that an occupant of condemned property must be given at least 90 days' warning before being required to surrender possession, in order for federal aid to be available.[50] That particular provision was repealed; it remained true that attempts at negotiated *purchase* of urban-renewal land were encouraged, the hope being that much land can be purchased without its ever having to be condemned. (3) Generally speaking, federal aid is available only as to "slum" or "blighted" areas and only these can be condemned with the help of federal aid.[51] *State* statutes also often limit redevelopment to such areas, and it has been

---

[45] 42 U.S.C.A. § 1455(f). Cf. Zoning Bd. of Appeals of Wellesley v. Housing Appeals Comm., 385 Mass. 651, 433 N.E.2d 873 (1982), applying requirements of the Massachusetts Housing Finance Agency that a certain amount of the housing in projects funded by that agency be rented to low-income tenants.

[46] See 42 U.S.C.A. § 1460(j).

[47] See Brown, Urban Redevelopment, 29 Boston U.L.Rev. 318 (1949). Cf. City of Seattle v. Loutsis Investment Co., 16 Wn. App. 158, 554 P.2d 379 (1976), review denied 88 Wash.2d 1016 (1977) (urban renewal and redevelopment involve cooperation between government and private enterprise to remedy blight or decay; government contributes power of eminent domain to assemble needed land while private enterprise does actual redevelopment work). See generally Comment, The Concept and Objectives of Urban Renewal, 37 S.Cal.L.Rev. 55 (1964).

[48] See 42 U.S.C.A. § 1460. See generally Morris, The Quiet Legal Revolution: Eminent Domain and Urban Redevelopment, 52 A.B.A.J. 355 (1966).

[49] See United States Dep't of Housing & Urban Development, Urban Renewal Handbook RHA 7208, I, ch. 4, § 2 (1968). A taking of property for urban renewal can often occur quite speedily since both the federal government and most state governments have "quick taking" laws, providing for the transfer of title upon *commencement* of condemnation proceedings. The federal law is found at 40 U.S.C.A. § 258a. On a typical state law, see Taylor, Possession Prior to Final Judgment in California Condemnation Procedure, 7 Santa Clara Law. 37 (1966).

[50] 42 U.S.C.A. § 3072, repealed by Pub.L. 91–646 (1971). The procedure, timing, and interest-payment requirements are now governed by the general provisions of 40 U.S.C.A. § 258a; see note 49 *supra*. On the basic policy of encouraging a negotiated purchase rather than condemnation wherever possible, see United States Dep't of Housing & Urban Development, Urban Renewal Handbook RHA 7208.1, ch. 1 (1968).

[51] 42 U.S.C.A. § 1460(c). See United States Dep't of Housing & Urban Development, Urban Renewal Handbook RHA § 7205.1, ch. 1 (1968), setting forth standards for "blight". See generally Hagman & Juergensmeyer, Urban Planning & Land Development Control Law 542–43 (2d ed. 1986); Annot., What Constitutes "Blighted Area" Within Urban Renewal and Redevelopment Statutes, 45 A.L.R.3d 1096 (1972). See also Rukab v. City of Jacksonville Beach, 811 So.2d 727 (Fla. App. 2002) (where government has power to

held that an urban-renewal authority then has no power to acquire property unless the area thus qualifies.[52] In order for a renewal authority validly to find that an area is "slum" or "blighted" and for the local governing body to approve the finding, facts establishing such condition should relate to the public health, safety, morals, and/or welfare.[53] The authority's finding of such conditions is, once affirmed by the local governing body, reviewable by the courts; but a presumption of correctness then attaches to the finding,[54] and it will be overturned only if shown to be arbitrary, capricious, or made in bad faith.[55]

---

rid city of urban blight by using its power of eminent domain, property owners may challenge the eminent domain action as not for public purpose and/or not necessary even where an owner has not previously challenged the "blighted" destination). As to the general use of eminent domain to rid a community of blight, see Eagle, Does Blight Really Justify Condemnation?, 39 Urban Law. 833 (2007) ("blackletter law" is that the presence of blight justifies condemnation, but author finds that "blight condemnation is dubious at best"; *id.* at 833). See also note 15, *supra,* and accompanying text. Some state eminent-domain statutes require that in order for an area to be condemned on the basis of blight, it must be shown that the area is an economic and social liability, and this requirement may be harder to satisfy than other statutory standards. See Centene Plaza Redevelopment Corp. v. Mint Properties, 225 S.W.3d 431 (Mo. 2007) (under such a requirement, the area must be a menace injurious to public health, safety, morals and welfare).

[52] Bristol Redevelopment & Housing Authority v. Denton, 198 Va. 171, 93 S.E.2d 288 (1956). See 40 Am.Jur.2d Housing Laws and Urban Redevelopment § 15 (1968). Cf. W. & G. Co. v. Redevelopment Agency, 802 P.2d 755 (Utah App.1990) (to enact redevelopment plan under Utah statutes, legislative body must make a finding, supported by sufficient evidence, that project area is blighted). Compare City of Midwest City v. House of Realty, Inc., 100 P.3d 678 (Okla. 2004) (city did not possess authority pursuant to its general eminent domain powers to condemn property for purposes of economic redevelopment and blight removal; therefore, city had to comply with specific statutes governing removal of blighted property and economic redevelopment). See also Note, Raze the Dead: Urban Blight, Private Universities, and the Path Towards Revitalization, 74 U. Pitt. L. Rev. 85 (2012).

[53] See Crommett v. City of Portland, 150 Me. 217, 235, 107 A.2d 841, 851 (1954). Cf. Apostle v. City of Seattle, 70 Wn.2d 59, 422 P.2d 289 (1966) (city not allowed to condemn property as "blighted" without stating facts to show specifically how it was "blighted"). See generally, on the causes and effects of urban "blight," Steiner, Report on Urban Renewal in the United States, in Miller, New Life for Cities Around the World (Supp. No. 4 1959). See also Weiss, Is the Power of Eminent Domain Dangerous Under the Urban Redevelopment Act?, 57 Dick.L.Rev. 326 (1953). As to the problems of defining "blight" for the purposes of urban renewal as well as for other purposes, see Note, Balancing Blight: Using the Rules Versus Standards Debate to Construct a Workable Definition of Blight, 45 Colum. J.L. & Soc. Probs. 45 (2011).

[54] See In re Bunker Hill Urban Renewal Project, 61 Cal.2d 21, 37 Cal.Rptr. 74, 389 P.2d 538 (1964), cert. denied 379 U.S. 899, 85 S.Ct. 185, 13 L.Ed.2d 174, appeal dism'd, 379 U.S. 28, 85 S.Ct. 190, 13 L.Ed.2d 173; Warren v. Waterville Urban Renewal Authority, 161 Me. 160, 210 A.2d 41 (1965); Despatchers' Cafe v. Somerville Housing Authority, 332 Mass. 259, 124 N.E.2d 528 (1955); Levin v. Township Committee, 57 N.J. 506, 274 A.2d 1 (1971), appeal dism'd 404 U.S. 803, 92 S.Ct. 58, 30 L.Ed.2d 35; Stahl v. Board of Finance, 69 N.J.Super. 242, 174 A.2d 238 (1961); Grisanti v. City of Cleveland, 89 O.L.A. 1, 181 N.E.2d 299 (Ct.App.1962), appeal dism'd 173 Ohio St. 386, 182 N.E.2d 568, appeal dism'd 371 U.S. 68, 83 S.Ct. 111, 9 L.Ed.2d 119. Cf. Lyons v. City of Camden, 52 N.J. 89, 243 A.2d 817 (1968) (determination of blight is entrusted to discretion of local authorities); Wilson v. City of Long Branch, 27 N.J. 360, 142 A.2d 837 (1958), cert. denied 358 U.S. 873, 79 S.Ct. 113, 3 L.Ed.2d 104 (hearing on blight is legislative, not judicial). Compare Tucson Community Dev. & Design Center, Inc. v. City of Tucson, 131 Ariz. 454, 641 P.2d 1298 (App. 1981) (no requirement that mayor and council hold hearing or receive evidence at time they make findings of necessity for redevelopment of blighted area).

[55] Katz v. Brandon, 156 Conn. 521, 245 A.2d 579 (1968) (court will only consider whether agency has acted unreasonably or in bad faith or has exceeded its powers); Housing & Redevelopment Authority v. Coleman's Service, Inc., 281 Minn. 63, 160 N.W.2d 266 (1968); Housing & Redevelopment Authority v. Minneapolis Metropolitan Co., 259 Minn. 1, 104 N.W.2d 864 (1960) (findings won't be overturned unless is fraudulent or capricious action or unless findings are against overwhelming evidence); Miller v. City of Tacoma, 61 Wn.2d 374, 378 P.2d 464 (1963) (determination of blight won't be overturned unless is strong proof it was arbitrary, capricious, or unsupported by the evidence). See Berggren v. Moore, 61 Cal.2d 347, 38 Cal.Rptr. 722, 392 P.2d 522 (1964) (trial court is not to exercise independent judgment on evidence upon which city council acted in adopting redevelopment plan). Cf. Schenck v. City of Pittsburgh, 364 Pa. 31, 70 A.2d 612 (1950) (certification by City Planning Commission that area is blighted is not subject to judicial review except on

Does particular property have to be "blighted" or "slum" in order to be validly taken for urban renewal? It has been held that it does not, so long as the general *area* qualifies for that description.[56] It is sometimes added that the taking of the particular property must be necessary to accomplishing the main purposes of the project.[57] Thus, the urban renewal authority and local governing body are free to treat a basically deteriorated area as a unit and condemn property therein that is not itself "blighted." Even undeveloped airspace can be validly taken under this theory.[58] Are the terms "blighted" and "slum" synonymous within the context of urban renewal? Both words are used in most urban-renewal legislation, and it has been said the term "blighted" is broader than "slum" and brings within the reach of the legislation properties not, for instance, in such state of

---

grounds of fraud or bad faith). See generally Weinstein, Judicial Review of Urban Renewal, 21 Fed.B.J. 318 (1961); Note, Blight Elimination Takings as Eminent Domain Abuse: The Great Lakes States in *Kelo's* Public Use Paradigms, 5 Ave Maria L. Rev. 299 (2007). Cf. City of Las Vegas Downtown Redevelopment Agency v. Pappas, 119 Nev. 429, 76 P.3d 1 (2003), cert. denied 54 U.S. 912, 124 S.Ct. 1603, 158 L.Ed.2d 260 (2004) (judicial review was barred as to whether substantial evidence supported the city redevelopment agency's determination that an area was blighted, and the fact that the protesting property owners' land did not itself suffer blight did not prohibit the agency from taking the property). In Midwest City v. House of Realty, Inc., 198 P.3d 886 (Okla. 2008), it was held that a city's determination of "blight" under urban renewal statutes is legislative, not judicial, and will be overturned by a court only if the city acted arbitrarily or capriciously. Cf. Goldstein v. New York State Urban Dev. Corp., 13 N.Y.3d 511, 893 N.Y.S.2d 472, 921 N.E.2d 164 (2009) (judges will not interfere with a reasonable finding of blight by a designated legislative entity, nor does redevelopment of the property constitutionally require the construction of low-income housing when the cause for redevelopment was not the eradication of slums).

Similarly, courts will not reverse local authorities' decisions on the boundary lines of urban-renewal areas unless fraudulent, capricious, or clearly unreasonable action is shown. See Gibson & Perin Co. v. City of Cincinnati, 480 F.2d 936 (6th Cir.1973), cert. denied 414 U.S. 1068, 94 S.Ct. 577, 38 L.Ed.2d 473; Watkins v. Fugazzi, 394 S.W.2d 594 (Ky.1965); Wilson v. City of Long Branch, *supra* note 54; Eikenbary v. City of Dayton, 3 Ohio App.2d 295, 210 N.E.2d 402 (1964). Cf. Woodland Market Realty Co. v. City of Cleveland, 426 F.2d 955 (6th Cir.1970) (person outside urban-renewal area held to have no 14th Amendment action against city for depreciation of his property). See also note 9 *supra* and accompanying text.

Determinations by local authorities on where to locate a public housing project are reviewable only by a similarly narrow standard. See Varnadoe v. Housing Authority, 221 Ga. 467, 145 S.E.2d 493 (1965); Philbrook v. Chapel Hill Housing Authority, 269 N.C. 598, 153 S.E.2d 153 (1967); Blumenschein v. Housing Authority, 379 Pa. 566, 109 A.2d 331 (1954), appeal dism'd 350 U.S. 806, 76 S.Ct. 68, 100 L.Ed. 724. In some jurisdictions, public housing projects need not be located only in areas that have been cleared because of having been "slum" or "blighted" but may be located in other neighborhoods. See Riggin v. Dockweiler, 15 Cal.2d 651, 104 P.2d 367 (1940); In re Housing Authority of Charlotte, 233 N.C. 649, 65 S.E.2d 761 (1951).

[56] Stockus v. Boston Housing Authority, 304 Mass. 507, 24 N.E.2d 333 (1939); Miller v. City of Tacoma, *supra* note 55. See Berman v. Parker, 348 U.S. 26, 75 S.Ct. 98, 99 L.Ed. 27 (1954); State ex rel. Bruestle v. Rich, 159 Ohio St. 13, 110 N.E.2d 778 (1953) (buildings and vacant land may be taken when reasonably necessary to clear slum-area and prevent recurrence). Cf. Urban Renewal Agency v. Iacometti, 79 Nev. 113, 379 P.2d 466 (1963) (court won't consider the issue of taking or leaving of specific buildings if designation of *area* is valid). See generally Vestal, Planning for Urban Areas: The Fight for Coherency, 56 Iowa L.Rev. 19 (1970); Note, The Regional Approach to Planning, 50 Iowa L.Rev. 582 (1965). See also the material on "blight" determinations in Sections 132 & 133.

[57] Paulk v. Housing Authority, 195 So.2d 488 (Miss.1967). See Velishka v. City of Nashua, 99 N.H. 161, 106 A.2d 571 (1954) (sufficient that taking as a whole is reasonably necessary to clearance of blighted areas and prevention of their recurrence); Miller v. City of Tacoma, *supra* note 55 (taking of some vacant lands, and of inoffensive or innocuous structures, can be justified as a necessary concomitant of taking the blighted structures). See generally Sundby, The Elimination and Prevention of Urban Blight, 1959 Wis.L.Rev. 73 (1959); Note, Urban Renewal: Problems of Eliminating and Preventing Urban Deterioration, 72 Harv.L.Rev. 504 (1958).

[58] Jersey City Chapter of Property Owner's Protective Association v. City Council, 55 N.J. 86, 259 A.2d 698 (1969). But cf. Prestonia Area Neighborhood Ass'n v. Abramson, 797 S.W.2d 708 (Ky.1990) (evidence in support of urban renewal ordinances did not justify finding that neighborhoods were sufficiently blighted to authorize project; mere recitation of statutory criteria will not suffice, and fact that some property might be affected by airport noise was insufficient).

disrepair that they could be considered nuisances, and areas not so depressed as to be called "slums".[59] In some jurisdictions, an area qualifies for urban renewal not merely by being "blighted" or "slum"; it must also be "substandard" and/or "unsanitary."[60]

§ 20.5 Procedures Involved in Federal Aid for Urban Renewal

Under the basic pattern established by the legislation of the 1940's, '50's, and '60's, urban renewal projects involving federal aid proceed through four main steps:[61] (1) As a prerequisite to any federal financial assistance, the governing body of the locality must adopt a "workable program" for community improvement. This is a broad statement of local goals and is concerned with community-wide, not merely project, activities. (2) An application for federal funds must include an "urban renewal plan" conforming to the general plan of the locality as a whole and to the above-mentioned workable program; the urban renewal plan should designate the area of the project and the steps to be undertaken therein. (3) Before any project is approved for actual execution, the local governing body must hold a public hearing on the project, and must officially adopt the urban-renewal plan, detailing the improvements planned for the renewal area itself; the renewal agency must approve this plan, too. The designation of the renewal area must, of course, be supported by findings that the area is "slum" or "blighted," and this must be supported by data on the buildings and environmental conditions therein.[62] Where, as is usual, the renewal agency is a separate corporate body (generally taking the form of a "public authority"),[63] the obligations of the local government (city, county, etc.) are often set forth in a cooperation agreement between it and the renewal agency. (4) Then comes the actual execution of the project: acquisition of the property, by purchase or condemnation; surveys to determine the needed items of improvement, where

---

[59] Rabinoff v. District Court of Denver, 145 Colo. 225, 360 P.2d 114 (1961). See generally Annot., What Constitutes "Blighted Area," *supra* note 51, at 1103.

[60] See Kaskel v. Impellitteri, 306 N.Y. 73, 115 N.E.2d 659 (1953) (area must be "substandard and unsanitary"; courts will give great weight to determination of local authorities). Cf. Stockus v. Boston Housing Authority, *supra* note 56 (applying statute that requires area to be "substandard").

[61] See Hagman & Juergensmeyer, Urban Planning and Land Development Control Law 531–34 (2d ed. 1986), discussing 42 U.S.C.A. §§ 1451–64. See generally Note, Citizen Participation in Urban Renewal, 66 Colum.L.Rev. 485 (1966), particularly noting requirements of citizen participation in the first step—preparation of a "workable program." The regulations governing the preparation of a "workable program" are well summarized in 3 CCH, Urban Affairs Reporter § 18,103 (1969). The planning required in urban renewal is well discussed in Mandelker, The Comprehensive Planning Requirement in Urban Renewal, 116 U.Pa.L.Rev. 25 (1967). See also Rhyne, The Workable Program—Challenge for Community Improvement, 25 Law & Contemp. Prob. 685 (1960). There is a good summary of all the planning and other steps required for urban renewal in Krasnowiecki, Housing and Urban Development 440–41 (1969).

[62] See notes 51–55 *supra* and accompanying text. See generally Note, Urban Renewal: Problems of Eliminating and Preventing Urban Deterioration, 72 Harv.L.Rev. 504 (1959).

In Tucson Community Dev. & Design Center, Inc. v. City of Tucson, 131 Ariz. 454, 641 P.2d 1298 (App. 1981), it was held that the mayor and council did not have to conduct a hearing or receive evidence at the time they made findings of the necessity for redevelopment of a blighted area. The court noted that a stricter standard of judicial review is applied where findings are made by an administrative, rather than legislative, body. But a hearing is normally required prior to adoption of the actual urban renewal *plan*. See East Grand County School Dist. No. 2 v. Town of Winter Park, 739 P.2d 862 (Colo.App.1987) (town council's submission of proposed urban renewal plan to voters did not excuse compliance with Colorado statutory requirement of a public hearing on the plan).

[63] See Hagman & Juergensmeyer, Urban Planning & Land Development Control Law 530 (2d ed. 1986), noting 42 U.S.C.A. § 1460(h), under which the local public agency can include any public body authorized to undertake a project.

rehabilitation of existing structures is involved; removal of structures and preparation of the site (all usually done under contract with a private contractor), etc.

One of the areas of greatest controversy has been the relocating of displaced families, individuals, and businesses. Since amendments to the federal legislation in 1969, standard housing must be provided for low-and moderate-income displaced persons on a one-to-one basis for every unit of housing demolished; and the Secretary of Housing and Urban Development must review the effectiveness of relocation programs in each locality every two years.[64] Payments to those displaced by renewal and redevelopment projects are also provided by the statutes.[65]

Despite the requirement in federal (and many state) statutes of relocation programs, persons displaced by urban renewal were generally unsuccessful until 1968 in getting any judicial review of the relocation arrangements of local agencies: no provision for their standing was found in the federal statutes; it was noted that they were not themselves parties to the loan and grant contracts; and state courts noted that they lacked jurisdiction to review exercises of discretion by federal officials acting under federal law.[66] But a celebrated decision in 1968 held that individuals displaced by a renewal project had standing to allege that they, as members of minority groups, were being denied equal protection under the Fourteenth Amendment when relocation efforts for them were not equal to those for white persons.[67] It has also now been ruled that residents of a renewal area, apart from any discrimination argument, have standing to

---

[64] 42 U.S.C.A. §§ 1453, 1455. See "Changes in Housing Law: What They Mean," U.S. News & World Rep., Dec. 29, 1969, at 20.

[65] Uniform Relocation Assistance and Real Property Acquisition Policies Act, 42 U.S.C.A. §§ 4601–55, noted 3 Urban Lawyer 290 (1971). See Annot., Uniform Relocation Assistance and Real Property Acquisition Policies Act of 1970, 33 A.L.R. Fed. 9 (1977). See generally Leary & Turner, The Injustice of "Just Compensation" to Fixed Income Recipients—Does Recent Relocation Legislation Fill the Void?, 48 Temple L.Q. 1 (1974); Lucke, Relocation Assistance Advisory Programs: A Need for Early Judicial Review, 27 Ad.L.Rev. 17 (1975); Comment, The Uniform Relocation Act: A Viable Solution to the Plight of the Displaced, 25 Catholic U.L.Rev. 552 (1976); Special Research Study, Relocation—The Uniform Relocation Assistance and Real Property Acquisition Policies Act of 1970—An Empirical Study, 26 Mercer L.Rev. 1329 (1975).

As to who are "displaced persons," and thus entitled to benefits, under the Relocation Assistance Act, see Alexander v. United States Department of Housing & Urban Development, 441 U.S. 39, 99 S.Ct. 1572, 60 L.Ed.2d 28 (1979) (tenants in public housing project that fails, forcing them to move, are not such persons).

[66] See Note, Judicial Review of Displacee Relocation in Urban Renewal, 77 Yale L.J. 966 (1968); Annot., Who Is Entitled to Attack Urban Renewal Projects Undertaken Pursuant to Federal Housing Act of 1949, as Amended, 8 A.L.R. Fed. 415 (1971). See generally Hartman, Relocation: Illusory Promises and No Relief, 57 Va.L.Rev. 745 (1971).

[67] Norwalk CORE v. Norwalk Redevelopment Agency, 395 F.2d 920 (2d Cir.1968) (plaintiffs were Negro and Puerto Rican families and agencies representing them), noted 1968 Duke L.J. 994; 82 Harv.L.Rev. 691 (1969); 43 N.Y.U.L.Rev. 1257 (1968); 10 Wm. & M.L.Rev. 482 (1968). See Garrett v. City of Hamtramck, 503 F.2d 1236 (6th Cir.1974) (urban-renewal program which displaced Negro residents violated equal protection). See generally Tondro, Urban Renewal Relocation: Problems in Enforcement of Conditions on Federal Grants to Local Agencies, 117 U.Pa.L.Rev. 183 (1968). See also Davis, The Liberalized Law of Standing, 37 U.Chi.L.Rev. 450 (1970); Note, The Federal Courts and Urban Renewal, 69 Colum.L.Rev. 472 (1969).

Doubt was cast on much of the reasoning of the *Norwalk CORE* case, *supra*, by Washington v. Davis, 426 U.S. 229, 96 S.Ct. 2040, 48 L.Ed.2d 597 (1976), where it was held that an equal protection violation is shown only if there is proof of discriminatory purpose—discriminatory impact or effect is not enough, the Supreme Court said, whereas the *Norwalk CORE* case said it *was* sufficient.

An offshoot of the *Norwalk CORE* case, *supra*, was Norwalk CORE v. David Katz & Sons, Inc., 410 F.2d 532 (2d Cir.1969), where it was determined that a particular group—mother and father, their son, son's wife, and baby—constituted a "family" within statutory provisions requiring rents for relocation housing to be within the means of the family displaced—thus, the son's income was properly to be included in determination of the group's ability to pay.

enjoin a project until the renewal agency has submitted a satisfactory relocation plan to the Housing and Urban Development Department.[68]

§ 20.6 Urban Renewal over the Years: Changes, Successes, Failures

Urban renewal programs have changed over the years since their inception. Three main areas of change can be noted: (1) Increasingly, most urban renewal projects are being undertaken with little or no government aid. For example, the Crown Center project in Kansas City, Missouri, was privately financed altogether, except that the developer did take advantage of tax abatements offered under Missouri land

---

[68] Western Addition Community Organization v. Weaver, 294 F.Supp. 433 (N.D.Cal.1968), motion gr. 320 F.Supp. 308. See English v. Town of Huntington, 335 F.Supp. 1369 (E.D.N.Y.1970) (individuals and township committee had standing to bring action against township and federal officials claiming failure of officials to comply with replacement-housing requirements of urban-renewal law). The injunction issued in the first Western Addition case, *supra*, was dissolved in Western Addition Community Organization v. Romney, 320 F.Supp. 308 (N.D.Cal.1969), where the court held that an unqualified expression of satisfaction by the Secretary of Housing and Urban Development with the local agency's relocation plan was not shown to be arbitrary or without a factual basis and thus satisfied the statutory requirements. Tenants of a demolished building may also have a *tort* claim against an urban-renewal authority if adequate provision is not made for their relocation. See Urban Renewal Agency v. Lackey, 275 Or. 35, 549 P.2d 657 (1976) (claim is subject to notice requirement of tort claims act; but counterclaim filed by tenants—in agency's suit for rent—satisfied the notice requirement). Cf. Battison v. City of Niles, 445 F.Supp. 1082 (N.D.Ohio 1977) (local authorities cannot act out of political motivation in refusing to relocate businessman in desired location). But cf. Tober's, Inc. v. Portsmouth Housing Authority, 116 N.H. 660, 367 A.2d 603 (1976) (businesses not entitled to compensation in tort for interruption of their business when they had been given proper notice of condemnation for redevelopment).

A controversial decision, relevant to standing to raise relocation issues, was that in which the city of Hartford, Connecticut, was denied standing to complain of an alleged lack of reasonable housing assistance plans in the block grant applications for funds for community development (specifically, a lack of an accurate estimate of the number of low-income persons expected to reside in the community) made by communities surrounding Hartford. City of Hartford v. Town of Glastonbury, 561 F.2d 1032 (2d Cir.1976), cert. denied 434 U.S. 1034, 98 S.Ct. 766, 54 L.Ed.2d 781 (1978). See Warren, The Housing and Community Development Act: Two Years After Hartford, 30 Ad.L.Rev. 549 (1978). Later developments relating to the *City of Hartford* problems, and clarifying the Department of Housing and Urban Development's enforcement powers over communities applying for grants, are discussed in Freilich, White-Wasson & Cofer, 1979–1980 Annual Review of Local Government Law: Municipal Liability and Other Certain Uncertainties, 12 Urban Law. 577, 645–47 (1980).

The Housing and Community Development Act of 1987, which reauthorized federal housing and community development programs, provided aid to those displaced by development projects only if they were displaced by luxury housing developments or commercial and industrial projects that do not principally benefit low-and moderate-income households. The aid was also provided only in situations of direct displacement, not to those indirectly displaced. 42 U.S.C.A. §§ 4601, 4621–22 (1987). See generally Durham & Sheldon, Mitigating the Effects of Private Revitalization on Housing for the Poor, 70 Marq. L. Rev. 1 (1986). See also Hartman, Keating & Le Gates, Displacement: How to Fight It (National Housing Law Project 1982).

Utilities are sometimes left "on their own" to relocate their wires, pipes, mains, etc., and pay the expenses of the relocation, when urban renewal necessitates any move. Norfolk Redev. & Housing Auth. v. Chesapeake & Potomac Tel. Co., 464 U.S. 30, 104 S.Ct. 304, 78 L.Ed.2d 29 (1983) (telephone company required to relocate its transmission facilities because of an urban renewal project was not entitled to relocation benefits under federal statutes; the statutes left unchanged the common-law rule that a utility forced to relocate from a public right-of-way must do so at its own expense). See Consolidated Edison Co. v. Lindsay, 24 N.Y.2d 309, 300 N.Y.S.2d 321, 248 N.E.2d 150 (1969); Urban Renewal Agency v. Pacific Northwest Bell Telephone Co., 23 Or.App. 384, 542 P.2d 908 (1975). Cf. Northwest Natural Gas Co. v. City of Portland, 300 Or. 291, 711 P.2d 119 (1985) (construction of mass transit system involved). But state statutes now sometimes specify that tax money may be used by the redevelopment agency to pay the relocation expenses, and it has been held that such legislation is valid. See Housing Authority v. Arkansas Louisiana Gas Co., 257 Ark. 867, 520 S.W.2d 215 (1975) (housing authority, having required gas company to adjust its lines in connection with urban-renewal project, was liable to company for costs).

redevelopment laws.[69] With hardly any government aid, five local companies undertook a "new town in town" development—Franklin Town—in central Philadelphia.[70] Some major insurance companies have made substantial financial commitments to the rehabilitation of old housing units and building of new ones in several American cities.[71] Private efforts of a different sort are shown by the neighborhood associations in some areas: groups of persons and/or businesses residing or owning property in an area who form an organization for the redevelopment of the area. Some state legislation makes such associations eligible to receive limited power of eminent domain and other forms of state aid.[72]

(2) Where federal aid has been granted, it is often not in the form of the old "categorical grants"—grants for various categories of activity, such as urban renewal, sewer lines, etc. Instead, money has been distributed to localities under "block grants"—the locality simply applies for a share of the appropriated funds and is largely free to spend what it receives however it wants, so far as the U.S. government is concerned.[73] Some of this money was distributed in the form of so-called "action grants": grants

---

[69] See "Lifting the Face of Kansas City," Bus. Week, May 20, 1972, at 95. Some criticism was leveled at the Crown Center Development since it is located a little distance from the "older downtown" and was alleged to be competitive therewith. *Id.* On Missouri's tax abatement program, see generally Board of Educ. v. City of St. Louis, 879 S.W.2d 530 (Mo.1994) (city could grant additional periods of ad valorem tax relief to blighted property without running afoul of 25-year maximum provided in state constitution).

[70] See "An Old City's New Town," Time, June 14, 1971, at 62. On the use of a combination of public and private funds to provide low- and middle-income housing in a Chicago urban-renewal area, see "Bringing Hope Back to the Hood," Bus. Week, Aug. 19, 1996, at 70. On cooperative public/private arrangements for urban redevelopment and the drafting of the agreements necessary to such ventures, see generally Froelich, Practical Considerations in Negotiating and Drafting Development and Redevelopment Agreements, 26 Urban Law. 973 (1994). Some privately financed urban renewal projects have occurred in smaller cities. See note 35 *supra* and accompanying text.

[71] See Peirce, Insurers Helping Out Inner Cities, Wash. Post, May 10, 1980, at E-37, noting particularly the grants made by Aetna Life & Casualty Co., and the agreement of Aetna and some other companies not to "redline" inner-city neighborhoods—*i.e.*, not to adopt a company rule against insuring property therein. On such "redlining" by insurance companies, see Comment, Insurance Redlining and the Future of the Urban Core, 16 Colum.J.L. & Soc. Prob. 1 (1980).

[72] See, sustaining such legislation in Illinois, Zisook v. Maryland-Drexel Neighborhood Redevelopment Corp., 3 Ill.2d 570, 121 N.E.2d 804 (1954); Zurn v. City of Chicago, 389 Ill. 114, 59 N.E.2d 18 (1945). On the renewal efforts of neighborhood associations, see generally Graham, Our Restored Cities, Where the Living Is Easier, Parade magazine, April 25, 1999, at 4, particularly discussing the success of urban renewal in Chattanooga, Tennessee.

Important developments of recent years—sometimes undertaken with federal grants, sometimes with purely private funds—have also included the "recycling" of old buildings (*e.g.*, trolley-car barns in Salt Lake City turned into an entertainment center; a torpedo factory in Alexandria, Virginia, turned into an arts center; cotton warehouses in Savannah turned into retail shops, etc.) and the restoration of old marketplaces, such as Quincy Market, near Faneuil Hall in Boston.

On the various nonprofit and nongovernmental institutions—community development organizations, limited equity cooperatives, etc.—working to achieve urban redevelopment, see Simon, The Community Economic Development Movement: Law, Business, and the New Social Policy (Duke University Press 2001), reviewed by Barron, The Community Economic Development Movement: A Metropolitan Perspective, 56 Stan. L. Rev. 701 (2003). See also Sections 16.1–16.3, *supra,* on local government incentives to business.

[73] See "Who Wins in the New Federal Grant Game," Bus. Week, March 24, 1975, at 136. Block grants may also, however, be given directly to the *state* government, which then controls the distribution; this system has increased in use in recent years but is often, of course, less popular with cities. See generally Howells, Looking for the Butterfly Effect: An Analysis of Urban Economic Development Under the Community Development Block Grant Program, 16 St. Louis U. Pub. L. Rev. 383 (1997).

awarded if the locality shows that the money is needed to trigger private investment in the project(s) for which it will be used.[74]

(3) A program that has had some degree of success in a few cities is known as "urban homesteading." Under this type of program, cities (such as Wilmington, Delaware; Philadelphia; and Baltimore) that have become the owners of deteriorated houses (usually because the prior owners defaulted on property-tax payments) offer the houses free of charge (or for a nominal rent) to persons willing to agree to live there a certain length of time and make specified improvements.[75] The initially great amount of enthusiasm for such projects faded in some cities after a while.[76] But such a program—

---

[74] "More Action in Action Grants," Bus. Week, Nov. 5, 1979, at 172, noting, "Cities have wide latitude in how they use action grants. They may spend the funds on land acquisition or infrastructure improvements or they may lend it at low interest rates to push along a privately financed development or a neighborhood revitalization project. Generally cities must show that the money is needed to trigger the commitment of private investment in a project." During most of the Carter administration, emphasis was placed on the Department of Housing and Urban Development's Urban Development Action Grant (UDAG) program—a complement to the Community Development Block Grant program. 42 U.S.C.A. §§ 5301–17. See Ellison, The Urban Action Grant Program: Using Federal Funds to Leverage Private Investment in Distressed Communities, 11 Urban Law. 424 (1979). This action-grant program (UDAG program) continued to be utilized during Pres. Reagan's administration to finance industrial parks, factory expansions, and downtown developments. Each federal dollar was reportedly matched by about $6 in private financing, and mayors across the country eagerly competed for the grants. But critics charged that the grants amounted to a glorified subsidy for downtown developers, created few new jobs, and resulted only in projects that would have been built anyhow. Kurtz, '83 Version of Urban Renewal Sports a Touch of Luxury, Wash. Post, April 2, 1983, at A4. The Urban Development Grants were totally eliminated by legislation passed in 1989. N.Y. Times, Feb. 5, 1990, at A-18, col. 1. Redevelopment grants and tax breaks have, however, still been awarded under HUD programs to designated urban and rural "empowerment zones" that are considered particularly needy and likely candidates for rejuvenation. See "White House Lists Recipients of Funds for Redevelopment," Wall St. J., Dec. 22, 1994, at A14.

Sometimes attempts have been made to stimulate inner-city growth by a combination of federal, state, and local *exemptions* from taxes and regulatory controls. This is often called the "enterprise zone" approach. On tax exemptions for businesses, see generally Chapter 16 *supra*. On the use of tax increment financing to achieve downtown revitalization in particular, see Mead, Incentives for Downtown Revitalization: Tax Increment Districts, Chapter 380, and Other Tools, 32 Urban Law. 1013 (2000), concentrating on Texas law.

[75] See "Using Homesteaders to Restore the Cities," Bus. Week, Sept. 1, 1973, at 22, describing the Philadelphia and Wilmington programs. See generally Chamberlain, Homesteading Offers Antidote for Urban Blight, Am. City, Jan., 1974, at 60; Maloney, Homesteading: 20th-Century Style; Program Begun in Wilmington, Del., Am. City, March, 1974, at 41; Newberg, Anatomy of a Housing Program: Urban Homesteading in Theory and Practice, 8 J.L. & Pol. 731 (1992) (concluding that urban homesteading programs have been neither a great success nor a failure but are good programs needing improvement); Winslow, Urban Homesteading: Little to Lose and a Lot to Gain, Am. City, Oct., 1974, at 71.

In Section 810 of the Housing and Community Development Act of 1974, federal recognition is given to the possibilities of "urban homesteading": The Secretary of Housing and Urban Development is authorized to transfer, without payment, to local or state governments or public authorities the title to unoccupied residential property of which the Secretary holds title and which the state or local unit requests for use in an urban-homestead program. 12 U.S.C.A. § 1706e.

[76] See Comment, Philadelphia's Urban Homestead Ordinance: A Poor Beginning Toward Reoccupying the Urban Ghost Town, 23 Buffalo L.Rev. 735 (1974); King, Urban Homesteading Faltering in Fight Against Blight of Cities, N.Y. Times, May 30, 1975, at 1, col. 6. See generally—with particular reference to problems and possible solutions in Detroit—Comment, Property Abandonment in Detroit, 20 Wayne L.Rev. 845 (1974). See also Holsendolph, H.U.D. Plans Test of Homesteading, N.Y. Times, May 31, 1975, at 13, col. 5. On mortgage failures as to properties involved in homestead and similar programs, see Pinkston, In the Weeds: Homeowners Falling Behind on Their Mortgages, Lenders Playing the Foreclosure Game, and Cities Left Paying the Price, 34 S. Ill. U.L.J. 621 (2010).

together with substantial involvement, of private interests in urban renewal—played a considerable role in the rejuvenation of downtown Baltimore.[77]

Overall, it may be noted also that the trend—evident even in the early '50's at times—toward conservation, toward renewal rather than destruction of existing structures, has continued to gain strength. This is illustrated by the formation in some jurisdictions of local "conservation boards" to deal with areas that may be on their way to becoming slums or blighted, though not yet qualifying as such;[78] by the tendency to preserve old housing that in earlier decades was being destroyed;[79] and by efforts to combine preservation of historic properties with urban renewal.[80]

What has been the overall success of urban renewal? It had considerable success in rejuvenating downtowns in a few American cities. Starting with a project in Pittsburgh (which began in 1949 and was completed 20 years later), urban renewal has contributed to a city-center "comeback" in other cities such as Los Angeles.[81] In the bicentennial year of 1976, it was reported that among the nation's most impressive sights were the new skyscrapers of Atlanta and Denver and the Renaissance Center in Detroit; the skywalks (indoor walkways between buildings) of Spokane and Minneapolis; the modernistic sculptures and buildings of New York, Chicago, and San Francisco; and the riverfront developments of Omaha and Louisville.[82] A boom in downtown construction has touched

---

77 See "What Is Reviving Baltimore," Bus. Week, Aug. 15, 1977, at 122, 123. See also Hummel, East Side Story: The Redevelopment of East Baltimore, 15 U. Baltimore J. Envtl. L. 97 (2008).

78 See People ex rel. Gutknecht v. City of Chicago, 3 Ill.2d 539, 121 N.E.2d 791 (1954), upholding the constitutionality of the Illinois statute providing for creation of local conservation boards and granting them power of eminent domain and power to resell property to private parties agreeing to follow a conservation plan.

79 See "Fading St. Louis Area Has a Partial Revival," N.Y. Times, Dec. 9, 1979, at 79, discussing revival of a "predominantly black neighborhood near downtown St. Louis."

80 See "HUD Clarifies Preservation Stance," Preservation News, Jan., 1979, at 1, noting fears at one time that, under community-development block grants from the federal government (See notes 73–74 *supra* and accompanying text.), historic preservation—no longer aided by a separate categorical grant program—would lose out to other objectives, but also noting a reassuring memo from Housing and Urban Development to its regional staff, stressing support for historic preservation. But fears continue to surface that urban-renewal projects will result in destruction of some historic areas. See Satterthwaite, Is It the New Urban Renewal?, Preservation News, Dec., 1979, at 1. See generally, as to preservation and renewal in Louisiana, Brand & Villaviso, Revisiting *Palermo*: The Twentieth Anniversary of Louisiana's Landmark Land Use Rights and Zoning Decision and Its Legacy for Planning in Louisiana, 57 Loyola L. Rev. 113 (2011), discussing the effects of Palermo Land Co. v. Planning Comm'n of Calcasieu Parish, 561 So. 2d 482 (La. 1990). See also Comment, Rebuilding New Orleans: How the Big Easy Can Be the Next Big Example, 55 Loyola L. Rev. 353 (2009).

81 See "Comeback Starts for Big-City Downtowns," U.S. News & World Rep., Aug. 3, 1970, at 17, noting developments in Los Angeles, San Francisco, Atlanta, Chicago, St. Louis, Detroit, Houston, and Newark. The Gateway Center in Newark, completed in 1971, was sometimes cited as an example of both the success and limitations of urban renewal: It included a covered glass bridge to Penn Station so that commuters could get to their offices without having to set foot in the streets. On later attempts at urban renewal in Newark, see "Been Down So Long It Looks Like Up in Newark," Bus. Week, Oct. 3, 1988, at 70. On successes and shortcomings of urban renewal in Los Angeles, see Goldberger, Los Angeles Tries, But Its Heart Isn't in Downtown, N.Y. Times, April 11, 1982, at 13, noting that Los Angeles is a city that does not have—and despite efforts of urban planners may never have—a single "downtown" center. See generally Comment, The Concept and Objectives of Urban Renewal, 37 S. Cal. L. Rev. 55 (1964).

82 "Downtown Is Looking Up," Time, July 5, 1976, at 54. On waterfront developments, see Note, Waterfront Redevelopment as an Urban Revitalization Tool: Boston's Waterfront Redevelopment Plan, 23 Harv. Envtl. L. Rev. 471 (1999). See generally the National Academy of Sciences publication, Urban Waterfront Lands (Environmental Studies Board, National Research Council 1980). See also Note, Land Banking as a Tool for the Economic Redevelopment of Older Industrial Cities, 3 Drexel L. Rev. 607 (2011). "Land banking" is a land management technique used by local governments to purchase tax-delinquent, tax-reverted, foreclosed, or abandoned properties; these properties are then "banked" for future use or resale. See

a considerable number of communities.[83] But a great deal of this "boom" has been caused by the building of additional *office* space. All too many deteriorated areas—particularly residential areas—remain at the core of numerous U.S. cities; and the move to the suburbs by former city residents (and also, in many cases, businesses) was certainly not halted in a number of metropolitan areas.[84] Suburban shopping centers continue to lure customers, and eventually additional businesses, away from many "downtowns." However, bold new plans continue to be put into effect in some cities,[85] and urban

---

Tappendorf & Denzine, Turning Vacant Properties into Community Assets Through Land Banking, 43 Urban Law. 801 (2011). These "land banks" differ from "land trusts," where land is held for the purpose of preserving it in perpetuity; see Section 21.5, note 22, *infra.*

On the redevelopment of New York City's Times Square area—undertaken partly in the hope of "cleaning up" this area that had become notorious for its prostitution, pornography, and other vice—see "A Happy Step Backward for Times Square," U.S. News & World Rep., Sept. 27, 1982, at 53. Critics pointed out that Times Square was not a slum in which people were forced by economic conditions to live, but a place where people voluntarily congregated to partake of "undesirable" uses, which, if eliminated here, were likely to spring up elsewhere. See Terry, Raw and Bawdy, 42nd Street Awaits a Big Change, N.Y. Times, Dec. 11, 1989, at A1. Cf. "Renewal But a Loss of Funk," Time, Feb. 29, 1988, at 102, noting that urban renewal could cause the Times Square area some loss of "the reasonable scale, the special romance and the sense of celebration." But the eventual result of the renewal of Times Square was a truly revitalized area, with a shift in emphasis from commerce toward tourism and entertainment, that surprised and pleased nearly everyone. See Goldberger, The New Times Square: Magic That Surprised the Magicians, N.Y. Times, Oct. 15, 1996, at B1. For the full history of the background, deterioration and redevelopment of the Times Square area, see Traub, The Devil's Playground: A Century of Pleasure and Profit in Times Square (Random House 2004), discussed in Lacayo, The Great Washed Way, Time, March 29, 2004, at 67. On the general trend toward revitalizing areas with viable uses, not merely "slum" areas, see Buchsbaum, Old Wine in New Bottles: Redevelopment Tales of a City, a Suburb, and a State, 30 Urban Law. 745 (1998).

[83] See "A Towering Rise in Downtown Construction," Bus. Week, March 5, 1979, at 91. On increased use of skywalks between buildings in many downtown areas, see "Fast Life Along the Skywalks," Time, Aug. 1, 1988, at 72. Construction of a public skywalk may sometimes result in a compensable impairment of the implied easement of air, light, and view enjoyed by neighboring property owners. See Castor v. City of Minneapolis, 429 N.W.2d 244 (Minn.1988) (inverse condemnation action for skywalk built over alley). For an adverse view on skywalks, see "Contrary to Previous Reports, Cities Are Not Dead," Time, Aug. 7 1989, at 9, discussing William H. Whyte's book *City*, which challenges many orthodox views of city planning, praises free-floating urban congestion, and criticizes skywalks as contributing to the decline of downtowns by sapping them of pedestrian traffic.

[84] See, discussing the Washington, D.C., experience in particular, Richards, The New Suburbs, Wash. Post, May 10, 1980, at A-19. For a good summary of the problems of central cities, see Lassar, Carrots and Sticks: New Zoning Downtown (Urban Law Institute 1989), reviewed 25 Urban Law. 694 (1993). See generally Sternlieb & Hughes, "The Uncertain Future of the Central City," in Sternlieb, Patterns of Development 109–21 (1986).

See also, on problems of urban decline in the United States and elsewhere and on some hopeful signs that the "flight to the suburbs" is slowing, Chapter 1 *supra.*

[85] See as to Oklahoma City, for instance, Bagby, Lakes and Towers—New Plan Maps a Bold Future for Downtown Oklahoma City, Sunday (Oklahoma City) Oklahoman, Orbit Magazine section, Feb. 23, 1975, at 16; Money, Canal Landscaping Ready for City OK, Daily Oklahoman, July 27, 2000, at 1-A. On development of an urban renewal district in Dallas that centers on its Museum of Art, see "The Art World—Dallas," The New Yorker, June 13, 1983, at 92. On the degree of success enjoyed by efforts to revitalize declining city centers in four U.S. cities (Boston, Louisville, Pittsburgh, and St. Louis), see Levitt (ed.), Cities Reborn (Urban Land Institute 1987). See generally Frieden & Sagalyn, Downtown, Inc.: How America Rebuilds Cities (MIT Press 1989) (noting the failures of many federal urban renewal projects but the success of some more recent efforts); Porter & Sweet (eds.), Rebuilding America's Cities—Roads to Recovery (Center for Urban Policy Research 1984); Symposium, Revitalizing America's Cities, 27 U. Mich. J.L. Reform 613–875 (1994). See also Teaford, The Rough Road to Renaissance: Urban Revitalization in America 1940–1985 (Johns Hopkins Univ. Press 1990). On a successful effort to revive a big-city downtown in another country, see Hoge, For Brazilians, Curitiba Serves As a Model City, N.Y. Times, March 8, 1981, § 1, at 5. See also Note, Revitalization From the Inside Out: The Attempts to Move Towards an Urban Renaissance in the Cities of the United States and the United Kingdom, 19 Conn. J. Int'l L. 159 (2003); Note, Incentivizing Local Reform and Urban Renewal During an Economic Crisis, 88 Notre Dame L. Rev. 1491 (2013).

renewal represents an ongoing fight, in many populous regions, against blight and decay. It has surely been demonstrated that glossy new buildings are not alone the answer to deterioration; but perhaps if other problems can be solved—if city finances can be kept healthy, if the educational system can be maintained at a level of competence, if racial conflicts can be settled, if the citizens have faith in law-enforcement—then rehabilitation and rebuilding of structures can contribute a share to preserving an active life in urban centers. Experience has shown (1) a need to confront root causes, including poverty and educational deficiencies, of city decay, not just such symptoms as rotting and abandoned buildings; (2) a need for a broad-based attack on urban problems, not an isolated effort against a single problem; and (3) the need to attract residents—not merely people who work in the city by day and leave at night—to central areas, if those areas are to be revived.

§ 20.7 Adequate Housing for All Citizens: The Basic Problems

A detailed study in 1973 concluded that at least one out of every five American households was living in substandard or overcrowded conditions or was forced to spend an excessive part of its income on housing.[86] At times in our recent history, severe

---

It has been recognized that urban-renewal efforts, to be effective, should not result merely in isolated projects scattered through a community but in overall development and rejuvenation of the community; each project should be based on area-wide planning and on desired changes in social and political conditions. See Editorial, 27 J. Housing 468 (1970); "Second City Puts Locus on Finding a Star Role," Financial Times, March 11, 2013 at Business Section 1.

[86] See Fried, 13 Million Families Are Held "Housing-Deprived," N.Y. Times, Dec. 12, 1973, at 64, reporting on a study by the Joint Center for Urban Studies of Harvard University and the Massachusetts Institute of Technology. On the bleak housing picture as of 1980 (low supply of rental housing, high mortgage interest rates, continued discrimination, etc.), see Freilich, White-Wasson & Cofer, 1979–1980 Annual Review of Local Government Law: Municipal Liability and Other Certain Uncertainties, 12 Urban Law. 577, 635–36 (1980). On developments in the 1980's and 1990's, see Note, Homeless Families from 1980–1996: Casualties of Declining Support for the War on Poverty, 70 S. Cal. L. Rev. 1141 (1997). As to the continued lack of adequate housing, and possible solutions to the problem, in the 21st century, see Kushner, Affordable Housing as Infrastructure in the Time of Global Warming, 42/43 Urban Law. 179 (2010–11). See also Ponce, Affordable Housing as Urban Infrastructure: A Comparative Study From a European Perspective, 42/43 Urban Law. 223 (2010–11). See generally Zarembka, The Urban Housing Crisis: Social, Economic and Legal Issues and Proposals (Greenwood Press 1990). See also Keenan, The Political Economy of Housing, 16 J. Affordable Housing & Community Development L. 107 (2007), reviewing criticisms of United States housing policy. On efforts to increase the density of population in residential areas, see Wentling & Bookout (eds.), Density by Design (Urban Land Institute 1988), reviewed 25 Urban Law. 693 (1993). On the extent to which existing laws—zoning, building codes, subdivision regulations, etc.—may have contributed to the shortage of affordable housing, see Note, Breaking the Exclusionary Land Use Regulation Barrier: Policies to Promote Affordable Housing in the Suburbs, 82 Geo. L.J. 2039 (1994), stating (at 2042): "The answer to the housing shortage for all income groups lies in a tailored set of regulatory reforms that would allow the market to meet the needs of 'moderate income' households, thereby satisfying a major segment of the overall housing market." Compare Note, State-Sponsored Growth Management as a Remedy for Exclusionary Zoning, 108 Harv. L. Rev. 1127 (1995), urging state growth-management plans as a means to curtail suburban power to exclude affordable housing and as a way of assuring that such housing is actually built.

For analysis of the housing shortage in a particular jurisdiction, see Delaney, Addressing the Workforce Housing Crisis in Maryland and Throughout the Nation, 33 U. Baltimore L. Rev. 153 (2004). For predictions of housing trends in this century, see De Haan, Essay: Housing Trends for the 21st Century, 5 Marq. Elder's Advisor 201 (2004). See generally Articles, A Place to Call Home? Affordable Housing Issues in America, 42 Wake Forest L. Rev. 333–593 (2007). See also Iglesias, Housing Impact Assessments: Opening New Doors for State Housing Regulation While Localism Persists, 82 Or. L. Rev. 433 (2003), saying that only the states have the power to impose comprehensive regulation of local governments' exercise of discretion in land use decisions affecting housing, and recommending that each state adopt a housing impact assessment regime. Examples of *state* programs designed to provide adequate housing are discussed in Harsch, Initiatives and Tools for the Preservation of Affordable Housing in Illinois, 18 J. Affordable Housing & Commun. Dev. L. 403 (2009); Note Massachusetts's Chapter 40R: A Model for Incentive-Based Land Use Planning and Affordable Housing

housing shortages—particularly shortages of housing for low- and moderate-income groups—have afflicted the nation;[87] and such housing as is available, often is not equally available—*i.e.*, certain minority groups have been effectively excluded from many areas, especially suburban communities.[88] A three-pronged attack has been mounted by some municipalities against these housing problems: (1) housing codes, which have already been mentioned,[89] and which are designed to assure reasonably safe and sanitary

---

Development, 10 Vt. J. Evtl. L. 181 (2008). For an example of a program designed to provide adequate housing for a particular event, see Note, Hosting the Games for All and by All: The Right to Adequate Housing in Olympic Host Cities, 36 Brooklyn J. Int'l L. 1111 (2011).

[87] See "The Breakdown in Our Cities" (interview with then-Secretary of Housing and Urban Development George Romney), U.S. News & World Rep., July 28, 1969, at 48, noting that the housing shortage in 1969 was—due to deterioration of many units and because of the population increase—the most severe since World War II. On the plight of the homeless in America, see Collin, Homelessness: The Policy and the Law, 16 Urban Law. 317 (1984). See also Baxter & Hopper, Private Lives/Public Spaces: Homeless Adults on the Streets of New York (1981). Laws in many jurisdictions discriminate against homeless persons. See Note, We Can Do Better: Anti-Homeless Ordinances as Violations of State Substantive Due Process Law, 59 Vand. L. Rev. 1413 (2006); Comment, Adding Insult to Injury: Criminalization of Homelessness in Los Angeles, 29 Whittier L. Rev. 515 (2007). See also Comment, "I Lost My Home, Don't Take My Voice!": Ensuring the Voting Rights of the Homeless Through Negotiated Rulemaking, 2009 J. Disp. Resol. 175; Note, Ordinances Targeting the Homeless: Constitutional or Cost Effective?, 19 Wash. & Lee J. Civil Rights & Social Justice 437 (2013). For a description of what it's like to be homeless and living on the street, see Walther, Homeless in the City, American Scholar, Winter, 2014, at 48. See also Farida, Limiting the Poor's Right to Public Space: Criminalizing Homelessness in California, 21 Geo. J. on Poverty L. & Pol'y 197 (2014).

The problem of homelessness has remained substantial even in relatively prosperous times. See "Homelessness: The Policy Failure Haunting America," Bus. Week, April 25, 1988, at 132, concluding that the main cause of the crisis is a shortage of housing that poor persons can afford. In the 1990's, many cities adopted a less tolerant attitude toward the homeless, sweeping them off the streets at night and requiring that all able-bodied homeless persons work in order to be eligible for city-provided shelter. See More, Cracking Down on the Homeless, Time, Dec. 20, 1999, at 69. See generally Erickson & Wilhelm, Housing the Homeless (Center for Urban Policy Research 1986); Savela, Homelessness and the Affordable Housing Shortage: What Is to Be Done? 9 Law & Inequality 279 (1991). See also Salins, Housing America's Poor (Univ. of North Carolina Press 1987); Simon, Towns Without Pity: A Constitutional and Historical Analysis of Official Efforts to Drive Homeless Persons from American Cities, 66 Tulane L. Rev. 631 (1992); Symposium on Homelessness: Problems and Solutions, 36 Villanova L. Rev. 1019–1149 (1991). As to additional possible solutions to the homelessness problem, see Note, Financing Homelessness Prevention Programs With Social Impact Bonds, 31 Rev. Banking & Fin. L. 987 (2011–12). Compare Loveland, Legal Rights and Political Realities: Governmental Responses to Homelessness in Britain, 16 Law & Soc. Inquiry 249 (1991). See also Ponce, Land Use Law, Liberalization, and Social Cohesion Through Affordable Housing in Europe: The Spanish Case, 36 Urban Law. 317 (2004).

A survey in 2005 estimated that one in 400 Americans had no home. See Kasindorf, National Count of Homeless Puts Issue in Human Terms, USA Today, Oct. 12, 2005, at 1. It has been noted that one cause of the homelessness problem is the increasing scarcity of land available for home building. See Barta, Growing Scarcity of Land Alters Home Economics, Wall St. J., April 15, 2003, at A1. See generally Homelessness as a Property Problem, 36 Urban Law. 273 (2004); Hopper, Reckoning with Homelessness (Cornell Univ. Cross 2003), reviewed by Baron, The "No Property" Problem: Understanding Poverty by Understanding Wealth, 102 Mich. L. Rev. 1000 (2004). See also Kloch, The Virtue of Home Ownership and the Vice of Poorly Secured Lending, 45 Ariz. St. L.J. 135 (2013); Ruiz, In Defense of Low-income Homeownership, 5 Ala. Civil Rights & Civil Liberties L. Rev. 107 (2013).

[88] See the material on "exclusionary zoning," Chapter 18 *supra*. Cf. note 84 *supra*, discussing the "flight to the suburbs" by whites, and the exclusion of minorities from the suburbs. See generally United States Comm'n on Civil Rights, Equal Opportunity in Suburbia 1, 72 (1974). See also Wolf, Participation in the Right of Access to Adequate Housing, 14 Tulsa J. Comparative & Int'l L. 269 (2007).

[89] See discussion in Chapter 18 *supra*. In a number of major cities and populous counties, "housing courts" (or similar tribunals) now exist, both to enforce (through criminal penalties, etc.) housing-code violations and to provide a forum for civil disputes between landlords and tenants—where grievances can be aired and a judicial determination of rights made. See Greaney, Praetz, & Modzelewski, Hampden County Housing Court: A Product of Citizen Initiative, 58 Am. Judicature 277 (1975); Keating, Judicial Approaches to Urban Housing Problems: A Study of the Cleveland Housing Court, 19 Urban Law. 345 (1987). See generally on the work of housing courts in a number of American cities Symposium, The New York City Housing Court in the 21st Century: Can It Better Address the Problems Before It?, 3 Cardozo Pub. L. Pol. & Ethics J. 591

housing construction and maintenance; (2) fair housing legislation, designed to eliminate racial and other invidious discrimination in the sale and rental of housing; and (3) public housing projects, in which housing complexes are built with public financing and in which units are then leased (or, occasionally, sold) to lower-income persons. These housing projects have often formed a key part of urban-renewal activities, discussed in the earlier parts of the chapter; but increasingly, there is a trend toward other ways of aiding those in need of financial help for housing.

§ 20.8 Attacking Discrimination in Housing

A federal statute passed in 1968 broadly prohibits discrimination on the basis of race, creed, color, etc. in the sale and rental of housing;[90] but the U.S. Supreme Court

---

(2006); Symposium: Housing Courts and Housing Justice, 17 Urban L. Ann. 3–398 (1979) (including bibliography). See also Ramsey & Zolna, A Piece in the Puzzle of Providing Adequate Housing: Court Effectiveness in Code Enforcement, 18 Fordham Urban L.J. 605 (1991). But housing codes, even properly enforced, do not assure the availability of adequate housing for the poor. See generally Ackerman, Regulating Slum Housing Markets on Behalf of the Poor: Of Housing Codes, Housing Subsidies and Income Redistribution Policy, 80 Yale L.J. 1093 (1971).

Sometimes if repairs are ordered by public authorities in order to bring dwelling units into line with housing codes, tenants are then allowed to claim constructive eviction if the repairs are not promptly made. See Annot., Failure of Landlord to Make, or Permit Tenant to Make, Repairs or Alterations Required by Public Authority as Constructive Eviction, 86 A.L.R.3d 352 (1978). It has also been held that tenants of a federally owned housing project may sue the Department of Housing and Urban Development for breach of contract if there is a failure to comply with the warranty of habitability in their leases. Mann v. Pierce, 803 F.2d 1552 (11th Cir.1986).

[90] Federal Fair Housing Law, 42 U.S.C.A. §§ 3533, 3535, 3601–19, 3631. See generally Symposium, The Fair Housing Act After 40 Years: Continuing the Mission to Eliminate Housing Discrimination and Segregation, 41 Ind. L. Rev. 507–816 (2008). See also Comment, Racial Dimensions of Property Value Protection Under the Fair Housing Act, 101 Cal. L. Rev. 1437 (2013). The Supreme Court has held that disparate-impact claims are cognizable under the Fair Housing Act; discriminatory intent need not be established. Texas Dep't of Housing and Community Affairs v. The Inclusive Communities Project, Inc., ___ U.S. ___, 135 S.Ct. 2507 (2015).

The federal goal of integrated housing was further emphasized by the provisions of the Housing and Community Development Act of 1974, 42 U.S.C.A. §§ 5301–19. See Fishman, Title I of the Housing and Community Development Act of 1974: New Federal and Local Dynamics in Community Development, 7 Urban Law. 189 (1975). The 1974 law emphasized "block grants" to communities, with the communities left much discretion on how to use funds, rather than the old project-by-project system of funding. See Freilich, White-Wasson & Cofer, 1979–80 Annual Review of Local Government Law: Municipal Liability and Other Certain Uncertainties, 12 Urban Law. 577, 645 (1980). See generally Goering (ed.), Housing Desegregation and Federal Policy (Univ. of North Carolina Press 1986). See also Note, Enforcing the Fair Housing Act: Can Agency Interpretations Override Congressional Intent in Anti-discrimination Legislation?, 9 N.Y.U.J. Legis. & Pub. Pol'y 535 (2005–06); Note, Making Exclusionary Zoning Remedies Work: How Courts Applying Title VII Standards to Fair Housing Cases Have Misunderstood the Housing Market, 24 Yale L. & Pol'y Rev. 437 (2006). For discussion of the fair housing movement as an important part of the civil rights movement, see Pritchett, Where Shall We Live? Class and the Limitations of Fair Housing Law, 35 Urban Law. 399 (2003). As to the testing performed to determine how various categories of people are treated by a particular housing program in an effort to discover and eliminate discrimination, see Symposium, Fair Housing Testing, 41 Urban Law. 229–337 (2009), particularly Freiberg, A Test of Our Fairness, *id.* at 239. For discussion of the relationship of fair housing laws to efforts to fight urban sprawl, see Prebble, Anti-sprawl Initiatives: How Complete Is the Convergence of Environmental, Desegregationist, and Fair Housing Interests?, 30 Buffalo Pub. Interest L.J. 197 (2011–12).

The U.S. Housing and Urban Development Department has, through its regulations, tried at times to disperse federally assisted housing—which is often occupied by large numbers of minority persons—throughout the community, rather than have it concentrated in existing "ghettos." See "Pressure to Build Outside the Ghettos," Bus. Week, Oct. 9, 1971, at 24. Cf. notes 91–100 *infra* and accompanying text. See generally Comment, The Perpetuation of Residential Racial Segregation in America: Historical Discrimination, Modern Forms of Exclusion, and Inclusionary Remedies, 14 J. Land Use & Envtl. L. 89 (1998).

has also found that racial discrimination in private housing was outlawed by an 1866 statute, passed to implement the Thirteenth Amendment.[91] The modern federal statute has a limited exception, applying to sale or rental of a single-family dwelling by an owner;[92] and the earlier legislation also has some exceptions and gaps. But there is also much state and local legislation designed to assure reasonably equal access to housing, and the federal statute of 1968 specifically recognizes such legislation and declares that the federal law is to have no adverse effect on such other laws protecting the same rights as it does.[93]

Two means have, however, continued to be used with considerable success—and with judicial recognition of their possible legitimacy—to exclude low-income housing projects, and thus effectively to exclude many minority persons, from some communities. (1) The U.S. Supreme Court has refused to infer discriminatory intent against minorities from mere refusal to rezone property to allow a low-cost housing project therein, ruling that the mere presence of discriminatory effect does not show discriminatory intent in

---

A notable dispute over attempts to place public housing in "white neighborhoods" occurred in Yonkers, New York. See United States v. Yonkers Bd. of Educ., 837 F.2d 1181 (2d Cir.1987), cert. denied 486 U.S. 1055, 108 S.Ct. 2821, 100 L.Ed.2d 922 (1988) (city liable for racial segregation of housing; both city and school board liable for racial segregation of Yonkers public schools). On that dispute, and on changes in the federal Fair Housing Act designed to make it easier for the federal government to assist victims of discrimination in public housing, see "A House Divided," Time, Aug. 15, 1988, at 14. See generally *Yonkers/Jenkins* Symposium, 24 Urban Law. 589–651 (1992). On the argument that the threat of court-ordered public housing in a predominantly white neighborhood may deny the white residents equal protection, see Werner, NIMBY: Is There Room in *Paradise* for Public Housing?, 30 Urban Law. 477 (1998). See generally Hendrickson, Racial Desegregation and Income Deconcentration in Public Housing, 9 Geo. J. on Poverty L. & Pol'y 35 (2002); Thomas, Fixing Up Fair Housing Laws: Are We Ready for Reform?, 53 So. Carolina L. Rev. 7 (2001).

[91] Jones v. Alfred H. Mayer Co., 392 U.S. 409, 88 S.Ct. 2186, 20 L.Ed.2d 1189 (1968). Cf. Hurd v. Hodge, 334 U.S. 24, 68 S.Ct. 847, 92 L.Ed. 1187 (1948) (courts of District of Columbia cannot—because of statutory law and public policy—enforce racially discriminatory covenants as to sale or rental of real estate); Shelley v. Kraemer, 334 U.S. 1, 68 S.Ct. 836, 92 L.Ed. 1161 (1948) (violative of equal protection for state courts to enforce private agreements excluding persons of designated race or color from use or occupancy of real estate for residential purposes). See generally Block v. Hirsh, 256 U.S. 135, 41 S.Ct. 458, 65 L.Ed. 865 (1921) (public control of housing justified; Holmes opinion; rent-control case). See also Note, Circumvention of the Rule Against Enforcement of Racially Restrictive Covenants, 37 Cal.L.Rev. 493 (1949). The historical importance of *Shelley v. Kraemar, supra*, is noted in Hodah, Precedents—*Shelley v. Kraemer* Decided, 96 A.B.A.J. 72 (May 2010).

[92] 42 U.S.C.A. § 3604(b). This applies only if facilities or services of brokers or salespeople are *not* used and only if there is no advertisement or written notice such as is forbidden by the general terms of the Act. See United States v. Hunter, 459 F.2d 205 (4th Cir.1972), cert. denied 409 U.S. 934, 93 S.Ct. 235, 34 L.Ed.2d 189, reh. denied 413 U.S. 923, 93 S.Ct. 3046, 37 L.Ed.2d 1045 (provision applies to classified ads in newspapers; section held constitutional and found violated by ad stating that apartment for rent was in "white home").

[93] 42 U.S.C.A. § 3615. See United States v. Wisconsin, 395 F.Supp. 732 (W.D.Wis.1975). On statutes and cases dealing with discrimination in housing, see generally Schwemm, Housing Discrimination Law (Bur. of Nat'l Affairs 1983). On *gender*-based discrimination in housing, see generally Annot., State Civil Rights Legislation Prohibiting Sex Discrimination in Housing, 81 A.L.R. 4th 205 (1990). On *age* discrimination, see generally Section 18.4, notes 57–58 *supra*. On discrimination against home buyers from foreign countries, see Crespi, Green Cards for Foreign Home Buyers: A Way to Stabilize Housing Prices, 45 Tulsa L. Rev. 471 (2010). See generally "Note, There Be No Shelter Here": Anti-Immigrant Housing Ordinances and Comprehensive Reform, 20 Cornell J.L. & Pub. Pol'y 399 (2010); Note, "Not the Place for You": Anti-immigrant Housing Ordinances, Federal Preemption, and Keller v. City of Fremont, 719 F.3d 931 (2013), cert. denied, 134 S.Ct. 2140 (2014), 93 Neb. L. Rev. 226 (2014). As to screening of a prospective tenant's criminal background, see Note, Do Not (Re)enter: The Rise of Criminal Background Tenant Screening as a Violation of the Fair Housing Act, 15 Mich. J. Race & L. 181 (2009).

violation of constitutional rights.[94] But there *is* authority that a local government does have a *statutory* obligation, under the federal fair-housing laws, to refrain from zoning policies that effectively foreclose *any* low-cost housing within its borders.[95] And in lower federal courts, there have been a few successful attacks on zoning and other regulations directly aimed at excluding low-income housing or minority groups.[96] (2) No violation of the U.S. Constitution was found in a requirement that low-income housing projects in a community be approved at a popular referendum, the theory being that the public has a

---

[94] Village of Arlington Heights v. Metropolitan Housing Development Corp., 429 U.S. 252, 97 S.Ct. 555, 50 L.E.2d 450 (1977), on remand 558 F.2d 1283, cert. denied 434 U.S. 1025, 98 S.Ct. 752, 54 L.Ed.2d 772, on remand 469 F.Supp. 836, aff'd 616 F.2d 1006.

[95] Metropolitan Housing Development Corp. v. Village of Arlington Heights, 558 F.2d 1283 (7th Cir.1977), cert. denied 434 U.S. 1025, 98 S.Ct. 752, 54 L.Ed.2d 772 (1978), on remand 469 F.Supp. 836, aff'd 616 F.2d 1006 (case remanded to district court for determination of whether defendant-village had effectively foreclosed low-cost housing within its borders). See United States v. City of Black Jack, 508 F.2d 1179 (8th Cir.1974), cert. denied 422 U.S. 1042, 95 S.Ct. 2656, 45 L.Ed.2d 694 (1975), reh. denied 423 U.S. 884, 96 S.Ct. 158, 46 L.Ed.2d 115; Otero v. New York City Housing Authority, 484 F.2d 1122 (2d Cir.1973) (fact issues existed as to whether non-white concentration in housing project would have "tipping" effect which housing authority, in exercise of its duty to integrate, could avoid, and as to whether certain transfer had been made for safety reasons or on impermissible religious grounds). Cf. Robinson v. 12 Lofts Realty, Inc., 610 F.2d 1032 (2d Cir.1979) (black purchaser sought injunction to enable him to buy a cooperative apartment; his claim could not be defeated by merely hypothetical reasons). See generally American Bar Ass'n Advisory Comm'n on Housing and Urban Growth, Housing for All Under Law (R. Risham ed. 1978); Sussna, Remedying Exclusionary Zoning Practices in Suburbia, 28 U.Fla. L.Rev. 671 (1976). See also the discussion of "exclusionary zoning," Section 18.4 *supra*. In a later proceeding in the *Black Jack* dispute, *supra*, the court held that, where a racially integrated town-house development, had been blocked by a discriminatory zoning ordinance, intervening economic factors did not relieve the city of liability, and the city should be required by district court to take affirmative steps to bring low-cost housing to the city. Park View Heights Corp. v. City of Black Jack, 605 F.2d 1033 (8th Cir.1979), cert. denied 445 U.S. 905, 100 S.Ct. 1081, 63 L.Ed.2d 321 (1980). A brief summary of all litigation and developments in the *Black Jack* case is found in American Civil Liberties Union Newsletter, Nov., 1980, at 4. A good, concise summary of many cases and developments is found in Freilich, White-Wasson & Cofer, 1979–1980 Annual Review, *supra* note 90, at 635–39 (1980). On the limitations of fair housing legislation at all levels of government, see generally S.G. Meyer, As Long as They Don't Move Next Door: Segregation and Racial Conflict in American Neighborhoods (Rowman & Littlefield 2000), reviewed 33 Urban Law. 189 (2001).

[96] See Kennedy Park Homes Association v. City of Lackawanna, 436 F.2d 108 (2d Cir.1970), cert. denied 401 U.S. 1010, 91 S.Ct. 1256, 28 L.Ed.2d 546 (1971) (racially discriminatory actions found where city council, after low-income housing project was planned, declared moratorium on new subdivisions and zoned proposed project's site as open space and park area); Crow v. Brown, 332 F.Supp. 382 (N.D.Ga.1971), aff'd 457 F.2d 788 (5th Cir.1972) (county could not deny building permits for apartment houses because they didn't want blacks to live in them; here, the land was already zoned for apartments). Cf. United States v. West Peachtree Tenth Corp., 437 F.2d 221 (5th Cir.1971) (failure to notify black applicants of requirement of security deposit before application for housing would be processed).

It is doubtful, however, that allegedly racially discriminatory zoning regulations, as applied to low-cost housing, can be attacked by anyone other than developers of federally subsidized housing who are seeking specific relief from the zoning restriction. See Mandelker, Cunningham & Payne Planning and Control of Land Development 415 (4th ed. 1995), citing Warth v. Seldin, 422 U.S. 490, 95 S.Ct. 2197, 45 L.Ed.2d 343 (1975) (Rochester, New York, area residents, taxpayers, and groups denied standing to challenge exclusionary zoning of a Rochester suburb where these plaintiffs showed no specific harm to themselves), discussed in Chapter 18 *supra*. See generally Note, Alternatives to *Warth v. Seldin*: The Potential Resident Challenger of an Exclusionary Zoning Scheme, 11 Urban L.Ann. 223 (1976). An example of a case against racially discriminatory zoning that *was* brought by a developer seeking specific relief, and would thus meet the *Warth* test, is Dailey v. City of Lawton, 425 F.2d 1037 (10th Cir.1970) (actions of planning commission and city council in denying building permit and zoning change to construct low-income housing project found racially motivated). On standing to sue for discrimination in public housing, see Jaimes v. Toledo Metropolitan Housing Auth., 758 F.2d 1086 (6th Cir.1985), appeal after remand 833 F.2d 1203 (6th Cir.1987) (plaintiffs must show injury caused by defendant, plus substantial probability that the relief sought would benefit them personally; uncertain here whether housing authority caused plaintiffs' inability to move to suburbs).

legitimate interest in such a commitment of public funds.[97] The Supreme Court *did* invalidate a city charter provision requiring that fair-housing legislation pass a popular referendum, where other legislation was not so treated.[98] These two means of blocking housing projects, though seemingly rather narrow, are broad enough to exclude many minority persons from many communities. Since housing and zoning are generally matters of state-wide concern, one possible solution is state legislation creating a state body with power to override local land-use regulations that hinder low- and moderate-income housing. This has been tried and upheld in Massachusetts,[99] but has proven difficult and time-consuming to implement.[100] Efforts at racial desegregation of communities and efforts to provide public housing thus often go together—and in the past, have often failed together.

§ 20.9 Providing Low-Cost Housing

The providing of low-cost housing has been recognized as a valid use of public funds,[101] and as a sufficiently public purpose to justify exercise of the power of eminent

---

[97] James v. Valtierra, 402 U.S. 137, 91 S.Ct. 1331, 28 L.Ed.2d 678 (1971). See Mahaley v. Cuyahoga Metropolitan Housing Authority, 500 F.2d 1087 (6th Cir.1974), cert. denied 419 U.S. 1108, 95 S.Ct. 781, 42 L.Ed.2d 805 (1975) (suburban cities simply refused to answer inquiries from metropolitan housing authority on whether they would agree to have public housing within their limits; held that community can decide for itself whether it wants low-cost housing); Southern Alameda Spanish Speaking Organization v. Union City, 424 F.2d 291 (9th Cir.1970), aff'd 314 F.Supp. 967 (N.D.Cal.) (voters in a referendum rejected zoning change that would have allowed low- and moderate-income housing in community; lower court had not acted improperly in refusing to convene three-judge court). Cf. Ranjel v. City of Lansing, 417 F.2d 321 (6th Cir.1969), cert. denied 397 U.S. 980, 90 S.Ct. 1105, 25 L.Ed.2d 390 (1970), reh. denied 397 U.S. 1059, 90 S.Ct. 1352, 25 L.Ed.2d 680 (refusing to enjoin referendum on zoning change for low-income housing). See generally Bosselman, Commentary on *James v. Valtierra*, 23 Zoning Digest 117 (1971); Comment, *James v. Valtierra*: Housing Discrimination by Referendum?, 39 U.Chi.L.Rev. 115 (1971); Note, The Equal Protection Clause and Exclusionary Zoning After *Valtierra* and *Dandridge*, 81 Yale L.J. 611 (1971).

In City of Cuyahoga Falls, Ohio, v. Buckeye Community Hope Foundation, 538 U.S. 188, 123 S.Ct. 1389, 155 L.Ed.2d 349 (2003), note 26 Hamline L. Rev. 631 (2003), the city submitted to voters a facially neutral referendum petition calling for repeal of a municipal housing ordinance authorizing construction of a low-income housing complex, and refused to issue building permits while the petition was pending. The Court held that neither the city's submission of the petition to voters nor its refusal to issue building permits reflected the discriminatory intent required to support equal protection liability.

[98] Hunter v. Erickson, 393 U.S. 385, 89 S.Ct. 557, 21 L.Ed.2d 616 (1969). See Reitman v. Mulkey, 387 U.S. 369, 87 S.Ct. 1627, 18 L.Ed.2d 830 (1967) (constitutional amendment adopted by voters invalidated, as violating federal equal protection, where it repealed fair housing laws and prohibited all legislative infringement on right of persons to sell and lease property to whomever they chose).

[99] Board of Appeals v. Housing Appeals Committee, 363 Mass. 339, 294 N.E.2d 393 (1973).

[100] See Gallese, Housing for the Poor Blocked Despite Curb on "Snob Zoning" Laws, Wall St. J., Oct. 17, 1972, at 1, noting that "suburbs in Massachusetts have managed to completely frustrate the first state law in the U.S. designed to open the suburbs to the poor." See generally Witten, Adult Supervision Required: The Commonwealth of Massachusetts' Reckless Adventures With Affordable Housing and the Anti-Snob Zoning Act, 35 Boston College Envtl. Affairs L. Rev. 217 (2008).

[101] See People ex rel. Gutknecht v. City of Chicago, 414 Ill. 600, 111 N.E.2d 626 (1953); Watkins v. Fugazzi, 394 S.W.2d 594 (Ky.1965). On government programs to assure adequate low-cost housing, see generally Fernsler, Tuttle, Kessler, Kogan, Simons & Walsh, Historical Perspectives, Current Trends, and Future Roles in Housing and Community Development, 16 Urban Law. 683 (1984). On the history of public-housing involvement by the federal government in particular, see generally Symposium, Bringing Economic & Social Rights Home: The Right to Adequate Housing in the United States, 45 Columbia Human Rts. L. Rev. 732–895 (2014); Mitchell (ed.), Federal Housing Policy and Programs: Past and Present (Center for Urban Policy Research 1985). On one city's attempts to provide additional low-cost housing, see Note, $1 Per Lot for Affordable Housing in Detroit: Non-monetary Benefits Can Constitute Fair Value in the Sale of City-owned Surplus Property to Community Development Corporations, 48 Wayne L. Rev. 1191 (2002). On Baltimore's efforts to provide affordable housing through a program of public/private cooperation to those who qualify for

domain.[102] And local authorities ordinarily have wide discretion in selecting the site for such housing projects; their selection will be judicially overturned only if shown to have been arbitrary, capricious, in bad faith, or in excess of their power.[103] But this is subject to three qualifications that may be applicable where the question of racial balance, or location of minority groups, touches the matter of housingsite selection: (1) Federal legislation indicates that, where federal aid for housing projects is granted, there is an intent to reduce the isolation of income groups within communities, and a purpose of promoting diversity and vitality of neighborhoods by spreading low-income housing opportunities throughout an area.[104] (2) There is authority that the U.S. Department of Housing and Urban Development has an affirmative *duty* to take into account the effect of federally aided projects—in particular, low-income housing projects—on racial concentration.[105] It thus seems that this effect is one factor that should be weighed in

---

"workforce housing," see Kroopnick, Affording Baltimore: Public-Private Approaches to Workforce Housing, 40 Urban Law. 331 (2008).

In light of City of Lafayette v. Louisiana Power & Light Co., 435 U.S. 389, 98 S.Ct. 1123, 55 L.Ed.2d 364 (1978)—which held that local governmental activities may be within the scope of federal antitrust laws—, some concern was expressed over whether cities and housing authorities could regulate the resale prices of dwellings originally built for low- and moderate-income purchasers. A discussion of the problem, plus a proposed ordinance argued to be valid, is found in Strauss & Stegman, Moderate-Cost Housing After *Lafayette:* A Proposal, 11 Urban Law. 209 (1979). On anti-trust problems and legislative relief from them, see the chapter on Liability in Torts and Related Theories *infra.* Aside from any antitrust problems, a court may sometimes enjoin diversion to other uses of a project built for public housing. See Tenants for Justice v. Hills, 413 F.Supp. 389 (E.D.Pa.1975) (private purchaser of property previously held by Housing and Urban Development enjoined from evicting tenants; HUD sale said to be of questionable validity because adequate consideration had not been given to means of disposition that would have preserved the original status of the project).

[102] See Keyes v. United States, 119 F.2d 444 (D.C.App.1941), cert. denied 314 U.S. 636, 62 S.Ct. 70, 86 L.Ed. 510 (1941); Schneider v. District of Columbia, 117 F.Supp. 705 (D.D.C.1953) mod. 348 U.S. 26, 75 S.Ct. 98, 99 L.Ed. 27; Blumenschein v. Housing Authority, 379 Pa. 566, 109 A.2d 331 (1954).

[103] See Thompson v. Housing Authority, 251 F.Supp. 121 (S.D.Fla.1966) (with review of cases); In re Bunker Hill Urban Renewal Project, 61 Cal.2d 21, 37 Cal.Rptr. 74, 389 P.2d 538 (1964), cert. denied 379 U.S. 899, 85 S.Ct. 185, 13 L.Ed.2d 174, appeal dism'd 379 U.S. 28, 85 S.Ct. 190, 13 L.Ed.2d 173; Varnadoe v. Housing Authority, 221 Ga. 467, 145 S.E.2d 493 (1965); Kaskel v. Impellitteri, 306 N.Y. 73, 115 N.E.2d 659 (1953); Philbrook v. Chapel Hill Housing Authority, 269 N.C. 598, 153 S.E.2d 153 (1967); Blumenschein v. Housing Authority, *supra* note 102. Cf., overturning a site selection as arbitrary, In re Housing Authority of Salisbury, 235 N.C. 463, 70 S.E.2d 500 (1952). See generally, on selection of urban-renewal locations, Chapter 20 *supra.* Of course, housing authority officials must also satisfy requirements of the National Environmental Policy Act of 1969, 42 U.S.C.A. §§ 4321–61. See Strycker's Bay Neighborhood Council, Inc. v. Karlen, 444 U.S. 223, 100 S.Ct. 497, 62 L.Ed.2d 433 (1980) (requirements found satisfied where HUD had considered environmental consequences of its decisions to redesignate proposed site for low-income housing).

[104] See Housing & Community Development Act, 42 U.S.C.A. § 1441a ("National Housing Goals"). Cf. on U.S. housing policy 42 U.S.C.A. §§ 1437 ("Declaration of policy") and 1441 ("Congressional declaration of national housing policy"). See generally Coan, The Housing and Urban Development Act of 1968: Landmark Legislation for the Urban Crisis, I Urban Law. 1 (1969).

As with many urban problems, a more regional approach to their solution has sometimes been suggested. See Note, Democratizing the American Dream: The Role of a Regional Housing Legislature in the Production of Affordable Housing, 37 U. Mich. J.L. Reform 599 (2004). As to regional planning, see generally Sections 142 & 145. As to the possible use of "inclusionary zoning" to solve shortages of affordable housing, see Sections 142 & 145.

[105] See Shannon v. United States Department of Housing & Urban Development, 436 F.2d 809 (3d Cir.1970), applying provisions of the Civil Rights Act of 1968—42 U.S.C.A. §§ 3601, 3608(d). See generally Recent Case Note, Administrative Law—Urban Renewal—HUD Has Affirmative Duty to Consider Low Income Housing's Impact Upon Racial Concentration, 85 Harv.L.Rev. 870 (1972). On the race discrimination that has often existed in federally subsidized housing programs, see Adams, Separate and (Un)Equal: Housing Choice, Mobility, and Equalization in the Federally Subsidized Housing Program, 71 Tulane L. Rev. 413 (1996).

Racial quotas—so-called "benign quotas," generally favoring whites—have sometimes been utilized to achieve integration of public housing. See Otero v. New York City Housing Authority, *supra* note 95. See generally Ackerman, Integration for Subsidized Housing, in Integration for Subsidized Housing and the

the Secretary of Housing and Urban Development's decision on whether or not to approve, and authorize federal aid for the carrying out of, local plans. (3) It has been held that site selection should definitely be reversed by the courts when used to perpetuate patterns of racial segregation; the selection must not be tainted by any design of concentrating one racial group in a particular area to the exclusion of other groups.[106]

In matters of selection and eviction of tenants, rent increases, etc., it is clear that action of a public housing authority, and/or the municipality with which it is associated, are governmental actions; the federal constitutional guarantees, such as due process, apply to matters involving the tenants' rights to adequate notice and opportunity to be heard.[107] It has been ruled that these same due process requirements apply even against

---

Question of Racial Occupancy Controls, 26 Stan.L.Rev. 245 (1974); Note, Benign Quotas—Fair Housing—Affirmative Action Permits the Granting of Preference to Whites in Admission to Public Housing to Insure Racial Integration, 20 Wayne L.Rev. 1109 (1974). But the use of quotas was rejected by the U.S. Supreme Court in connection with medical school admissions policies, and is thus of doubtful validity in other contexts. See Regents of University of California v. Bakke, 438 U.S. 265, 98 S.Ct. 2733, 57 L.Ed.2d 750 (1978) (race may be one of a number of factors considered as to admission to medical school, but racial quotas may not be set).

On racial discrimination in building, and assigning tenants to, public housing (concentrating on Chicago's experiences), see generally L.S. Rubinowitz & J.E. Roenbaum, Crossing the Class and Color Lines: From Public Housing to White Suburbia (Univ. of Chicago Press 2000), reviewed 33 Urban Law. 209 (2001). See also Swan, The Law and Economics of Affirmative Action in Housing: The Diversity Impulse, 15 U. Miami Bus. L. Rev. 133 (2006). As to the *Bakke* case, *supra*, and the consideration of race in determining college admissions, compare Grutter v. Bollinger, 539 U.S. 306, 123 S.Ct. 2325, 156 L.Ed.2d 304 (2003), reh. denied 539 U.S. 982, 124 S.Ct. 35, 156 L.Ed.2d 694 (2003) (use of race or ethnicity as one factor among many in an overall flexible selection process does not violate the Equal Protection Clause of the U.S. Constitution), with Gratz v. Bollinger, 539 U.S. 244, 123 S.Ct. 2411, 156 L.Ed.2d 257 (2003) (university admissions policy that automatically allocates points to underrepresented minority applicants solely because of their race violates the Equal Protection Clause).

[106] Hills v. Gautreaux, 425 U.S. 284, 96 S.Ct. 1538, 47 L.Ed.2d 792 (1976) (federal district court could, in exercising its equitable power to remedy de jure racial segregation committed by Chicago Housing Authority, grant metropolitan relief—*i.e.*, relief extending into suburban areas, outside Chicago city limits—though Supreme Court noted it was not compelling the district court to order relief in this particular form). See generally Marks, Fair Housing Desegregation Policy: Recent Developments and Proposed Site Selection Safe Harbors, 22 J. Affordable Housing & Community Dev. L. 67 (2013); Comment, The Limits of Litigation: Public Housing Site Selection and the Future of Injunctive Relief, 122 U.Pa.L.Rev. 1300 (1974).

[107] See Note, Procedural Due Process in Government-Subsidized Housing, 86 Harv. L.Rev. 880 (1973), summarizing the rules on procedural due process in public housing. See generally Smyers, High Noon in Public Housing: The Showdown Between Due Process Rights and Good Management Practices in the War on Drugs and Crime, 30 Urban Law. 573 (1998). In Department of Housing & Urban Dev. v. Rucker, 535 U.S. 125, 122 S.Ct. 1230, 152 L.Ed.2d 258 (2002), the Court held that the Anti-Drug Abuse Act required lease terms that give public housing authorities the discretion to terminate the lease of a tenant when a member of the household or a guest engaged in drug-related activity, regardless of whether the tenant knew, or should have known, of the drug-related activity. See generally Note, Protecting the Innocent: The Future of Mentally Disabled Tenants in Federal Subsidized Housing After *Department of Housing & Urban Dev. v. Rucker*, 40 Harv. Civ. Rights L. Civ. Liberties L. Rev. 197 (2005).

On the standing of housing-project tenants to challenge payments to housing-authority officials, see Housing Authority v. State ex rel. Velasquez, 539 S.W.2d 911 (Tex.Civ.App.1976) ref'd n.r.e. (tenants had standing to challenge monthly lump-sum expense payments to each commissioner).

On the establishing of rent levels for tenants in public housing, see Garvey v. Worcester Housing Authority, 629 F.2d 691 (1st Cir.1980), cert. denied 450 U.S. 925, 101 S.Ct. 1379, 67 L.Ed.2d 356 (minors' social security benefits included in family income for purpose of establishing rent levels; no violation of statutes or of equal protection). Public-housing tenants have a possible cause of action under the Federal Civil Rights Act if they are charged higher rent than allowed under federal housing legislation. Wright v. City of Roanoke Redev. & Housing Auth., 479 U.S. 418, 107 S.Ct. 766, 93 L.Ed.2d 781 (1987) (alleged overbilling for utilities in violation of rent ceiling established by amendment to federal Housing Act and implementing regulations). Statutes, often applicable to all rental housing, sometimes now provide that if a landlord does not properly maintain rental apartments, the tenant may pay his or her rent into a court-maintained escrow account where

a nonprofit redevelopment corporation organized to build and operate a housing project.[108]

In the 1970's, much dissatisfaction existed over federal aid-to-housing programs. A number of public housing authorities experienced economic difficulties; some had difficulty finding tenants; and one part of a large St. Louis public-housing complex was actually dynamited out of existence because it proved economically unworkable.[109] The celebrated "Sections 235 and 236" of the Housing Act of 1968 had attempted to stimulate housing supply by subsidy payments to lenders: Section 235 allowed a low-income family to pay $200 down on a house, with a mortgage of up to 40 years on which the government would pay interest charges down to 1%; Section 236 gave similar help to the renter, whose rent might be as low as $75 a month because the government would pay most of the mortgage-interest charges, allowing the building owner to pass along the savings in the form of lower rent.[110] But these programs resulted in huge commitments of funds by the federal government; and Washington officials—also worried over incidents of fraud in the program—soon perceived that a more direct form of aid to housing purchasers and renters might be more workable.[111] Thus, the "housing allowance"—an idea also much discussed in the 1930's—was proposed: an amount given low-income families or individuals toward housing, with the recipients then left to shop for themselves in the open market.[112] Eventually, a compromise was achieved in Congress: Modest experiments were conducted with housing allowances, but more emphasis was put on "Section 8" of the Housing and Community Development Act of 1974: under this, once an eligible family has paid up to 25% of its annual income in rent, Housing and Urban Development pays the difference between that amount and the "fair market" rent.[113] The

---

the money will be kept until proper repairs are made. See Chernin v. Welchans, 844 F.2d 322 (6th Cir.1988), upholding such a statute against due process attack.

[108] Lopez v. Henry Phipps Plaza South, Inc., 498 F.2d 937 (2d Cir.1974).

[109] See "A Threat to Dump Public Housing," Bus. Week, Nov. 18, 1972, at 18, noting that 5 major public-housing authorities then faced imminent bankruptcy. As to destruction of *abandoned* housing, see Note, One Nail at a Time: Building Deconstruction Law as a Tool to Demolish Abandoned Housing Problems, 45 Ind. L.J. 547 (2012).

[110] National Housing Act of 1968, §§ 235–36, 12 U.S.C.A. §§ 1715z, 1715z–1. See Krooth & Spragens, The Interest Assistance Programs—A Successful Approach to Housing Problems, 39 Geo.Wash.L.Rev. 789 (1971). See generally Brincefield, The Low Rent Public Housing Program: Some Observations, Suggestions and Predictions, 3 Urban Law. 31 (1971).

[111] "The Bankruptcy of Subsidized Housing," Bus. Week, May 27, 1972, at 42. On causes of some of the problems with subsidized housing, see "Money Cuts, New Rules—Hard Times for Public Housing," U.S. News & World Rep., March 26, 1973, at 87. On the moratorium declared on subsidies for housing in 1972, see "Housing Subsidies Reel from an Icy Slap," Bus. Week, Jan. 13, 1973, at 16. See generally Downs, Are Subsidies the Best Answer for Housing Low and Moderate Income Households?, 4 Urban Law. 405 (1972).

[112] See "Housing Money that Goes to the People," Bus. Week, Jan. 8, 1972, at 51.

[113] "Will the New Housing Law Work?," Bus. Week, March 31, 1975, at 78, noting. "The absence of loan guarantees insures that HUD will not end up owning a lot of housing, as happened earlier. But construction-oriented critics charge that the program will not stimulate new housing." Regarding problems under this program, see Huntington Branch, NAACP v. Town of Huntington, 689 F.2d 391 (2d Cir.1982), cert. denied 460 U.S. 1069, 103 S.Ct. 1523, 75 L.Ed.2d 947 (1983) (plaintiff, who was attempting to obtain funding under Section 8 for a lower-income housing project, had standing to claim that city's zoning ordinance against such project was discriminatory, even though was doubt as to availability of funds for plaintiff's project). Several changes were made in 1981 to the "Section 8" program: A mandatory minimum lease term of one year was imposed; the owner of a Section 8 unit was allowed to terminate a tenancy only for "good cause"; and it was provided that eviction notices could be sent by the private landlord, not just by the public housing authority. See Sarshik, The Effect of Statutory Changes Upon the Rights of Section 8 Tenants, 14 Urban Law. 749 (1982), in Fernsler & Tuttle, Recent Developments on Housing and Community Development, 14 Urban Law. 745 (1982). The amount that tenants in the Section 8 program had to pay was also raised from 25% to an eventual ceiling of

payments go to landlords; but the program allows the individual or family the choice of where to live; and the subsidies are not linked to construction of housing. Subsidies to cut home-buyers' mortgage payments were also available under the 1974 legislation.[114] Since passage of that original legislation, there has been some renewed provision of federal loans for construction of public housing projects, especially for the elderly; but the main emphasis has remained on direct aid to housing purchasers and renters.[115]

30%. On the method of making rent adjustments under the Section 8 program, see Cisneros v. Alpine Ridge Group, 508 U.S. 10, 113 S.Ct. 1898, 123 L.Ed.2d 572 (1993), on remand 995 F.2d 948 (9th Cir.1993) (contracts between private landlords and HUD did not prohibit use of comparability studies to impose cap on rent adjustments, as authorized by 1989 legislation).

Tenants in public housing may be required to comply with reasonable certification standards, such as annually certifying their income and family composition, and if they fail to meet these requirements, the housing authority may raise their rent above the usual statutory limits. See Beckham v. New York City Housing Auth., 755 F.2d 1074 (2d Cir.1985), noting that appropriate rent cannot be calculated without income and family composition information since it is impossible to calculate a percentage of an unknown quantity. Of course, the lease of a tenant who fails to meet certification requirements can be terminated; but since this remedy does not satisfy the objectives of the housing program or the needs of the tenants, the authority may elect instead to raise the rent temporarily. *Id.* See generally Annot., Tenants' Procedural Rights Prior to Eviction or Termination of Benefits Under § 8 of Housing Act of 1937 (42 U.S.C.A. § 1437f), 81 A.L.R. Fed. 844 (1987), discussing under what circumstances tenants who come within the housing assistance payments program may be evicted or deprived of assistance benefits. As to termination, see also Turner, The Elephant in the Hearing Room: Colorblindness in Section 8 Voucher Termination Hearings, 13 Berkeley J. Afr.-Am. L. & Pol'y 45 (2011); Note, Procedural Due Process and Hearsay Evidence in Section 8 Housing Voucher Termination Hearings, 49 Boston Coll. L. Rev. 517 (2010).

As to changes made to the Federal Fair Housing Law by Congressional legislation in 2008, see Note, Housing and Economic Recovery Act of 2008, 46 Harv. J. on Legis. 585 (2009). The statute is criticized in Note, Federal Housing Help Falls Short: The Housing and Economic Recovery Act of 2008, 21 Loyola Consumer L. Rev. 249 (2008). (As to changes made in 1989, see note 115 *infra*.)

It has been noted that federal policy has shifted away from supply-side subsidy programs and toward a more demand-side orientation, in which the government concentrates less on construction of housing projects and more on subsidizing tenants; but local jurisdictions, including New York City, have not always joined in this shift. See Zeidel, Affordable Housing: The Case for Demand-Side Subsidies in Superstar Cities, 42 Urban Law. 135 (2010).

[114] See "Tandem: Housing Aid that Didn't Help," Bus. Week, May 3, 1976, at 43, saying that the housing recovery at that time owed little to this governmental program, which was criticized as "dishing-out" aid to those who need it *and* those who don't.

[115] See "A Big Boost for Housing," U.S. News & World Rep., March 14, 1977, at 42; "Congress Reinvents the Housing Subsidy," Bus. Week, Aug. 9, 1976, at 16 (discussing a bill subsequently signed into law by Pres. Ford). There have also been efforts on the government's part to make private mortgage money more available for financing public housing and urban development. See "Spurring S & L Loans for the Inner City," Bus. Week, April 25, 1977.

Beginning with the administration of George H.W. Bush, attempts have been made to sell-off public housing to tenants, rather build more units, and to spur investment in inner cities through tax breaks rather than provide direct governmental aid. See "The 'Reverend Jack' Believes—Now He Has to Deliver," Bus. Week, June 12, 1989, at 86, discussing the efforts of Housing and Urban Development Secretary Jack Kemp. See generally Glasheen & Hornig, Public Housing Authorities and HOPE 1: May HUD Give Away What It Doesn't Own?, 25 Urban Law, 69 (1993). But see Bratt, Hartman & Myerson (eds.), Critical Perspectives on Housing (Temple Univ. Press 1986), taking the position that government-sponsored housing development is the only means likely to achieve safe and decent housing for all persons. Cf. Note, Public Housing: Abandon HOPE, But Not Privatization, 103 Yale L.J. 961 (1994), criticizing Secretary Kemp's program (known as Homeownership and Opportunity for People Everywhere, or HOPE) but favoring privatization. See generally Stegman, Housing Finance and Public Policy: Cases and Supplementary Readings (Van Nostrand Reinhold Co. 1986); Newman & Feola, Housing Incentives: A National Perspective, 21 Urban Law. 307 (1989); Wolf, HUD and Housing in the 1990's: Crisis in Affordability and Accountability, 18 Fordham Urban L.J. 545 (1991). On changes made in federal housing legislation in 1989, including the creation of firm criteria for housing grants and new aid for low-income families desiring to become homeowners, see "A New Direction for Housing?" in Freilich, Marshall & Flick, Urban Problems Regenerated: A Twenty-Year View, 22 Urban Law. 537, 547–51 (1990). On trends in public housing near the start of the 21st century, see Becker, Housing Projects and Rent Control Should

With the increased use of "block grants" from the federal government to local units (instead of the old "categorical grants" for specified purposes),[116] more leeway has been created for the local units themselves to determine how much federal-aid money should be devoted to public housing construction, and exactly how such money should be spent. Thus, some cities have had some success in providing incentives for rehabilitation of existing housing, rather than construction of new units.[117] This has proven one of the

---

Crumble, Bus. Week, Aug. 4, 1997, at 20 (favoring the providing of housing vouchers to renters rather than the building of public housing); Levy, Housing Projects Face Big Changes as U.S. Aid Shrinks, N.Y. Times, Feb. 24, 1997, at A1 (noting cuts in federal aid and the possibility of turning over some developments to private management); "How Green Is My Alley," Bus. Week, April 19, 1999, at 123 (noting the decline of federal subsidies and increases in use of tax credits for private investment in housing). On continuing problems with public housing, see Schill, Distressed Public Housing: Where Do We Go from Here?, 60 U. Chi. L. Rev. 497 (1993).

[116] See notes 73–74 *supra* and accompanying text.

[117] See "Why St. Louis is Tops in Rehab," Bus. Week, April 21, 1980, at 163, noting, "For years, housing officials have argued that in cities with a substantial stock of run-down but still usable housing, rehabilitation programs tended to lag behind. Now, the Housing & Urban Development Dep't is encouraging housing rehabilitation as part of overall neighborhood development." See generally Listokin, Housing Rehabilitation—Economic, Social and Policy Perspectives (Center for Urban Policy Research 1983). Some commentators have proposed that—and some have questioned if—we should recognize a right to housing. See Adams, Do We Need a Right to Housing?, 9 Nev. L.J. 275 (2009). And some have suggested that we have put too high a priority on home ownership, noting that in many areas of the United States, "Renters are zoned out." Kiviat, The Case Against Home Ownership, Time magazine, Sept. 6, 2010, at 40, 46. See generally Chase, Rethinking the Homeownership Society: Rental Stability Alternative, 28 J.L. & Pol'y 1–293 (2009). Tent cities have even been suggested as a temporary solution to both the homelessness problem and the problem of affordable housing shortages. See Comment, Tent Cities: An Interim Solution to Homelessness and Affordable Housing Shortages in the United States, 99 Cal. L. Rev. 1037 (2011).

The housing situation for much of the world's population is, of course, far worse than that in the United States, despite the above-noted difficulties in this country. In 1976, a United Nations Conference on Human Settlement (known as the "Habitat Conference") was held in Vancouver, British Columbia, Canada. It was there reported that as much as 50% of the population of many "third-world cities" lives in squatter slums and that third-world governments have tended to withhold the support necessary for low-cost housing. See N.Y. Times, April 18, 1976, § viii, at 1, col. 4. For other accounts of preparations for, and discussions occurring at, this conference, see N.Y. Times, May 30, 1976, § iv, at 7, col. 4; May 31, 1976, at 3, col. 1; June 1, 1976, at 11, col. 1 (reporting opening of the conference); June 2, 1976, at 33, col. 7; June 6, at 24, col. 3 (describing conference exhibits); June 7, 1976, at 5, col. 1; June 9, 1976, at 4, col. 4; June 12, 1976, at 1, col. 6 (describing end of conference); June 13, at 21, col. 1.

A notable development of recent times in the United States has been the growth in the share of the housing market made up of condominium apartments. See generally Barton & Silverman, Common Interest Communities, Private Governments and the Public Interest (Univ. of Calif. Press 1994). reviewed 27 Urban Law. 631 (1995); Comment, Areas of Dispute in Condominium Law, 12 Wake Forest L.Rev. 979 (1976); Note, Living in a Condominium: Individual Needs versus Community Interests, 46 U.Cin.L.Rev. 523 (1977). On the Uniform Condominium Act, see Jackson & Colgan, Uniform Condominium Act from a Local Government Perspective, 10 Urban Lawyer 429 (1978); Judy & Wittie, Uniform Condominium Act: Selected Key Issues, 13 Real Prop. Prob. & Trust J. 437 (1978). The creation of condominiums and cooperatives may be considered a part of the general trend toward "privatization"—the turning over of traditionally governmental services to private organizations. See Section 16.2, note 33, *supra*. See generally Symposium, Common Interest Communities, 37 Urban Law. 325–69 (2005), particularly Franzese, Privatization and Its Discontents: Common Interest Communities and the Rise of Government for "the Nice," 37 Urban Law. 335 (2005). See also Note, First-Aid for Housing the Low- and Fixed-Income Elderly: The Case for Resuscitating Cooperative Housing, 15 Elder L.J. 293 (2007).

Some communities have attempted to set limits on the conditions under which housing can be converted into condominiums. See Note, Validity of Ordinances Limiting Condominium Conversion, 78 Mich.L.Rev. 124 (1979), concluding that some of these conversion regulations may improperly delegate governmental power to tenants. But the validity of most such ordinances has been upheld against a variety of constitutional attacks. See Troy Ltd. v. Renna, 727 F.2d 287 (3d Cir.1984) (retroactive condominium-conversion law prohibiting eviction of certain tenants for up to 40 years after date of conversion did not violate the impairment-of-contract and taking clauses of U.S. Constitution); Griffin Dev. Co. v. City of Oxnard, 39 Cal.3d 256, 217 Cal.Rptr. 1, 703 P.2d 339 (1985) (condominium-conversion ordinance upheld against argument it constituted an

most successful ways so far devised of combining the objectives that have so often—not always with success—been combined in the past: providing of low-cost housing on a basis free from invidious discrimination, and rejuvenation of decaying center-cities.

---

unconstitutional taking of property); Hornstein v. Barry, 560 A.2d 530 (D.C.App.1989) (statute conditioning condominium-conversion on approval by majority of tenants did not deny property owners due process nor impermissibly delegate legislative authority). Cf. Edgewater Inv. Associates v. Borough of Edgewater, 103 N.J. 227, 510 A.2d 1178 (1986), upholding retroactive application of a law protecting the tenancies of senior citizens and disabled persons from condominium-conversion evictions. But see Greater Boston Real Estate Bd. v. City of Boston, 397 Mass. 870, 494 N.E.2d 1301 (1986) (ordinance regulating condominium and cooperative housing conversions held invalid as not authorized by relevant statute). Cf. Angleton v. Pierce, 574 F.Supp. 719 (D.N.J.1983), aff'd without opinion 734 F.2d 3 (3d Cir.1984), cert. denied 469 U.S. 880, 105 S.Ct. 245, 83 L.Ed.2d 183 (1984), reh. denied 469 U.S. 1067, 105 S.Ct. 551, 83 L.Ed.2d 438 (1984) (landlord's conversion of conventional rent controlled units to cooperative ownership did not violate National Housing Act or due process when mortgage was insured by Department of Housing and Urban Development). See generally Feldman, Regulating Condominium Conversions: The Constitutionality of Tenant Approval Provisions, 21 Urban Law. 85 (1989); Annot., Validity and Construction of Law Regulating Conversion of Rental Housing to Condominiums, 21 A.L.R. 4th 1083 (1983). Despite controversy, condominiums have constituted a large part of the housing market since the 1970's and have offered a partial solution to the problem of inadequate supply of moderate-income housing. On the history and development of condominiums, see generally Berger, Condominium: Shelter on a Statutory Foundation, 63 Colum. L. Rev. 987 (1963); Cribbet, Condominium—Home Ownership for Megalopolis?, 61 Mich. L. Rev. 1207 (1963); Recent Statute Note, Property—Condominiums—Massachusetts Passes Condominium Enabling Legislation, 77 Harv. L. Rev. 777 (1964). On the difference between condominiums and cooperatives, see Note, Community Apartment: Condominium or Stock Cooperative?, 50 Cal. L. Rev. 299 (1962). On cooperatives, see Haar, Middle-Income Cooperative Apartments: The Cooperative Snare? 29 Land Econ. 289 (1953); Note, Federal Assistance in Financing Middle-Income Cooperative Apartments, 68 Yale L.J. 542 (1959). See generally Wilcox, Cooperative Techniques and Effective Reduction in Housing Costs, 29 Land Econ. 295 (1953).

There have also been notable attempts to use factory-built housing to fill the need for affordable urban homes. See Schmidt, A Factory-Built Answer to Housing's High Cost, N.Y. Times, Dec. 5, 1988, at A16. See also Sellman, Equal Treatment of Housing: A Proposed Model State Code for Manufactured Housing, 20 Urban Law. 73 (1988). On problems arising from the possible application to manufactured housing of bans on mobile homes, see Brown & Sellman, Manufactured Housing: The Invalidity of the "Mobility" Standard, 19 Urban Law. 367 (1987). On the development of "co-housing communities," in which the emphasis is on communal living rather than single-family detached dwellings, see Giese, A Communal Type of Life With Dinner for All and Day Care, Too, N.Y. Times, Sept. 27, 1990, at B1.

Chapter 21

"PLANNING" AT THE LOCAL LEVEL

Analysis

§ 21.1 Definition and History of Local Planning

"Planning" at the local level has been defined as "a systematic development of a municipality to promote the general welfare and prosperity of its people with the greatest efficiency and economy."[1] It is primarily concerned with the physical

---

[1] Forest Construction Co. v. Planning and Zoning Commission, 155 Conn. 669, 236 A.2d 917 (1967). See Kiska v. Skrensky, 145 Conn. 28, 138 A.2d 523 (1958); Seligman v. Belknap, 288 Ky. 133, 155 S.W.2d 735 (1941). See generally A. A. Altshuler, The City Planning Process (1965) (noted analysis of the planning process and its political implications); T. Kent, The Urban General Plan (1964); Mandelker & Cunningham, Planning and Control of Land Development (1979) (cases and materials); Rosenbaum, Citizen Involvement in Land Use Governance (1976); Gans, From Urbanism to Policy-Planning, 36 J.Am.Inst.Planners 223 (1970). See also Chapin, Urban Land Use Planning (2d ed. 1965); Mandelker, Environmental and Land Controls Legislation (1976 Supp.1980). For a good description of the planning process within a typical state, see G. Isberg, Local and Regional Planning in Minnesota (1975). For an excellent description of a program involving extensive citizen participation in planning (in Fairfax County, Virginia), see G. Dawson, No Little Plans (1977). For a good description of the process used by city planners, see D.B. Lee, Models and Techniques for Urban Planning (1968). On the historical development of city planning, see Choay, The Modern City: Planning in the 19th Century (1969); Churchill, The City Is the People (1945); Perloff, Education for Planning (1957); Gaus, The Education of Planners, 21 J. Land & Pub. Util. Econ. 307 (1945). See also Goodman & Goodman, Communitas (1947), reviewed 57 Yale L.J. 173 (1947). Modern urban planning has been said to have started with the writings of Ebenezer Howard in Great Britain, particularly his self-published book in 1898. See Kunzig, Cities Are the Solution, Natl. Geographic, Dec., 2011, at 124, 132. The most influential *casebook* in the field of land-use planning has been Haar & Wolf, Land Use Planning: A Casebook on the Use, Misuse, and Re-use of Urban Land (Little Brown & Co. 1958).

On the relationship of law and planning, see Brooks, Millstone Two and the Rainbow: Planning Law and Environmental Protection, 4 Conn.L.Rev. 54 (1971). See generally Salkin (ed.), 2009 Zoning and Planning Law Handbook (29th ed. 2009), reviewed by Freilich, 42 Urban Law. 205 (2010).

As to the importance to society of planners, see Liberty, Rising to the Land Use Challenge: How Planners and Regulators Can Help Sustain Our Civilization, 38 Vt. L. Rev. 251 (2013). As to an early failure of city planning in the United States, see Brady, The Failure of America's First City Plan, 46 Urban Law. 507 (2014), describing the first comprehensively planned grid in the American colonies, adopted in New Haven, Connecticut. Though the plan has often been praised, Brady contends it "ultimately failed its residents and stunted New Haven's growth." *Id.* at 509. Aside from more direct legal efforts to encourage land-use planning and regulate land uses, taxes are often employed as an indirect method of land-use control. See Delogu, Taxing Power as a Land Use Control Device, 45 Denver L.J. 279 (1968). On constitutional limits on the planning process, see Blaesser & Weinstein (eds.), Land Use and the Constitution: Principles for Planning Practice

development of the community in an orderly fashion.[2] It has been observed[3] that planning, in general, should have 5 main features: (1) it is future-oriented, in that it involves establishing goals, aiming for achievements not yet reached; (2) it is, ideally at least, a continuous process—the goals are being constantly revised; (3) it requires a determination of present and projected conditions within the area covered by the plan—and indeed, the process usually starts with an inventory of pertinent information, followed by pressure for continual updating; (4) it is fair; and (5) it is comprehensive, involving a knowledge of all relevant data and the various alternative goals that may be achieved. At meetings held in Athens in 1933 and in Peru in 1977, planners, architects, and students of urban development from around the world recognized the need for all levels of government to establish guidelines for growth, particularly in metropolitan areas.[4] In Europe, there has been a great deal of orderly planning of urban growth in recent decades: planning that is often handled by a single national office, subject to approval of plans for a particular locality by the local governing body. The pattern favored by many planners on the Continent is an eventual urban layout like a round flower (the center-city), with slender petals radiating from it (the major developed areas, generally built along transit lines), and with undeveloped areas between the petals (parks, natural preserves, and farms).[5]

(Planners Press 1989), reviewed 24 Urban Law. 659 (1992). See also Lai, Law in Urban Design and Planning: The Invisible Web (Van Nostrand Reinhold Co. 1988), reviewed 24 Urban Law. 663 (1992).

Increasingly, planning activities have spread to smaller communities. See H. J. Bryce, Planning Smaller Cities (Joint Center for Political Studies 1979). See generally H. J. Bryce (ed.), Small Cities in Transition: The Dynamics of Growth and Decline (Ballinger Pub. 1977).

[2] See Angermeier v. Borough of Sea Girt, 27 N.J. 298, 142 A.2d 624 (1958); Shelton v. City of Bellevue, 73 Wn.2d 28, 435 P.2d 949 (1968). As to whether planning can be considered a public use, see Garnett, Planning as Public Use?, 34 Ecology L.Q. 443 (2007).

[3] Juergensmeyer & Roberts, Land Use Planning & Development Regulation Law 27–29 (2003).

[4] See McGrath & Zevallos, A Silence Broken, Americas magazine, Feb., 1979, at 16, discussing the Town Planning Chart of 1933 (known as the Charter of Athens) and the 1977 document known as the Charter of Machu Picchu. The latter was signed at the Inca ruins of Machu Picchu in Peru—a site chosen because that ancient "lost city" displays many enlightened principles of urban planning and design.

[5] See "Cities of the Future as Europe Sees Them," U.S. News & World Rep., Dec. 2, 1968, at 80. Some planning efforts in the United States have also aimed at the concentration of development along transit lines. See Callies, Land Use Controls: Of Enterprise Zones, Takings, Plans and Growth Controls, 14 Urban Law. 781, 819–24 (1982); Cervero, Growing Smart by Linking Transportation and Urban Development, 19 Va. Envtl. L.J. 357 (2000). Compare Ellickson, Boundaries—The Law and Economics of Street Layouts: How a Grid Pattern Benefits a Downtown, 64 Ala. L. Rev. 463 (2013). See also Baltruzak, The Core Plan or How I Learned to Stop Worrying and Love the Central City: Shifting Control of Regional Mass Transit to the Central City, 5 Pierce L. Rev. 271 (2007); Seuffert, Caught in a Cement Spider Web: Proposed Suburban Transportation Policies to Architecting Less Automobile Reliant Communities, 15 Penn St. Envtl. L. Rev. 295 (2007). A good work on planning efforts in urban areas of various countries is Lefcoe, Land Development in Crowded Places: Lessons from Abroad (1979), reviewed 53 S. Cal. L. Rev. 1129 (1980). On planning in Europe, see Hansen, French Regional Planning (Indiana Univ. Press 1971); Young, The Law of Planning in Scotland (Wm. Hodge 1978); Calavita, Urbanization, Public Control of Land Use and Private Ownership of Land: The Development of Italian Planning Law, 16 Urban Law. 459 (1984); Kushner, Growth for the Twenty-First Century: Tales from Bavaria and the Vienna Woods: Comparative Images of Planning in Munich, Salzburg, Vienna, and the United States, 29 Urban Law. 911 (1997); Kushner, A Tale of Three Cities: Land Development and Planning for Growth in Stockholm, Berlin, and Los Angeles, 25 Urban Law. 197 (1993); Note, Different Ideas of the City: Origins of Metropolitan Land-Use Regimes in the United States, Germany, and Switzerland, 24 Yale J. Int'l L. 577 (1999). See generally Beatley, Green Urbanism—Learning from European Cities (Island Press 2000); Garner & Gravells (eds.), Planning Law in Western Europe (Elsevier Science Publ. Co. 1986). On planning in Canada, see Cullingworth, Urban and Regional Planning in Canada (Center for Urban Policy Research 1987). On planning in China, see Ziegler, China's Cities, Globalization and Sustainable Development: Comparative

In the United States, there has been increased interest in recent years in better planning of urban development, especially in light of the savings of money and energy possible from such planning.[6] But the U.S. lacks the agencies for centralized planning at the national level that are found in some countries; and even at the local level, planning efforts are often fragmented among offices of traffic control, housing, zoning, etc. There *was* an experiment with central planning in this country from 1934 until 1943, under the National Resources Committee, later called the National Resources Planning Board.[7] This was a committee that presented to the President plans and recommendations for development of land and natural resources, and that consulted with—and attempted to coordinate efforts of—other federal, state, and local bodies concerned with planning. But the committee met resistance from other agencies as to what they considered interference in their projects, and this effort at centralized planning was allowed to die. There have been some modern attempts to revive national planning: The Intergovernmental Cooperation Act of 1968 provides in general for coordination of federal programs with state and local planning;[8] in particular, Title VIII of that act requires federal agencies to coordinate land acquisition, disposal, and changes in plans

---

Thoughts on Urban Planning, Energy, and Environmental Policy, 5 Wash. U. Global Studies L. Rev. 295 (2006).

6 See "The Costs of Sprawl," Time, Nov. 4, 1974, at 63. See generally Juergensmeyer & Roberts, *supra* note 3, at 28. On urban sprawl and efforts to contain it, see Lewyn, The Law of Sprawl: A Road Map, 25 Quinnipiac L. Rev. 147 (2006); Ziegler, Urban Sprawl, Growth Management and Sustainable Development in the United States: Thoughts on the Sentimental Quest for a New Middle Landscape, 11 Social Pol'y & L. 26 (2003). See generally Bruegmann, Sprawl: A Compact History (Univ. of Chicago Press 2006), reviewed in Zimmerman, Not New or Bad?, Historic Preservation, May/June, 2006, at 67. See also Lewyn, Sprawl in Canada and the United States, 44 Urban Law. 85 (2012). "Sprawl" is often contrasted with "smart growth," as to which see notes 17 and 57, *infra,* and accompanying texts. As to "sprawl," see also note 57, *infra.*

On the history of city planning in the United States, see Krueckeberg (ed.), Introduction to Planning History in the United States (Center for Urban Policy Research 1983): McClendon & Quay, Mastering Change: Winning Strategies for Effective City Planning (Planners Press—American Planning Ass'n 1988) (with advice based on past experiences). On planning developments in recent times, see Clavel, The Progressive City: Planning and Participation, 1969–84 (Rutgers Univ. Press 1986); Forester, Planning in the Face of Power (Univ. of Calif. Press 1989); Fulton, Guide to California Planning (Solano Press Books 1991), reviewed 15 Urban Law. 473 (1993). See generally Williams, Planning Law in the 1990's, 31 Ariz. L. Rev. 471 (1989), describing the development of American land-use law through various periods and in different states and discussing the prevailing rules of law. On the need for making efficient use of space in planning, see Trancik, Finding Lost Space (Van Nostrand Reinhold Co. 1986). On the need for comprehensiveness in city planning, see Gallion, The Urban Pattern: City Planning and Design (Van Nostrand Reinhold Co. 1986). See generally Anderson, Guidelines for Preparing Urban Plans (Planners Press—American Planning Ass'n 1995). On the extent to which the beliefs of planners and architects—that cars are bad, density is good, etc.—have often put them at odds with most of the American public, see Rybczynski, "Edge Cities": The People's Answer to Planners, N.Y. Times, Nov. 17, 1991, at H36. On the ethical responsibilities of urban planners, see Beatley, Ethical Land Use: Principles of Policy and Planning (John Hopkins Univ. Press 1994); Wachs (ed.), Ethics in Planning (Center for Urban Policy Research 1985); Salkin, Legal Ethics and Land-Use Planning, 30 Urban Law. 383 (1998). Cf. Salkin, Failure to Articulate Clear Ethics Rules and Standards at the Local Level Continues to Haunt Local Land Use Decision Makers, 43 Urban Law. 757 (2011). See also Salkin & Ince, It's a "Criming Shame": Moving From Land Use Ethics to Criminalization of Behavior Leading to Permits and Other Zoning Related Acts, 46 Urban Law. 249 (2014). On the possible use of local land-use planning as an environmental justice strategy, see Arnold, Planning Milagros: Environmental Justice and Land Use Regulation, 76 Denver U.L. Rev. 1 (1998). On the respective roles of lawyers and planners, see Bobrowski, Planners and Lawyers: Toward a Division of Labor, 22 Urban Law. 431 (1990). On the role of politics in planning, see Johnson, Urban Planning and Politics (Planners Press 2d ed. 1997).

7 The agency charged with national planning was originally called the National Resources Board and was created by Executive Order in 1934. Its name was changed in 1935 to National Resources Committee. Later, it was called the National Resources Planning Board. It was abolished by Congress in 1943. See Hagman, Urban Planning & Land Development Control Law 54 (2d ed. 1980).

8 Intergovernmental Cooperation Act of 1968, 42 U.S.C.A. §§ 4201–44.

by such agencies, with local plans and activities.[9] Bills have been introduced at various times in Congress that would have established more thorough-going programs of national land-use planning, but they have not passed.[10]

Housing and urban-renewal legislation passed in the 1950's does make federal *aid* available for local planning efforts: The Housing Act of 1954 contains provisions allowing grants to municipalities, counties, and regional and state bodies, under which two-thirds of the cost of urban planning can be financed.[11] Under the "Community Renewal Program" created in 1959, local public agencies can receive federal funds for specified planning activities—identifying slum and deteriorating areas, formulating programs for renewal of these areas, etc.[12] But delays, inadequate funding, and intense competition for available funds have often limited the importance of these federal aid activities.

§ 21.2 State and Regional Planning

State planning agencies now exist in most jurisdictions; many were started in the 1930's, and there was revived interest in the 1950's and '60's. These state bureaus provide information to local agencies and help them obtain federal aid—and sometimes they help coordinate local efforts, implement planning systems, and even exercise control over local annexations and incorporations.[13] But three limits on their powers may be

---

[9] Federal Urban Land-Use Act, 40 U.S.C.A. §§ 531–35.

[10] See Bosselman, The Twilight of National Land Use Policy, 45 John Marshall L. Rev. 237 (2012). Hagman, *supra* note 7, at 62. A measure creating a Council on Urban Growth, which makes reports to Congress every-other year in order to help formulate national urban growth policy, did become law at the close of 1970, as part of the Urban Growth and New Community Development Act. 42 U.S.C.A. § 4503. Some general goals are also set forth in the National Urban Policy, 42 U.S.C.A. §§ 4501–03, and Pres. Carter in 1978 signed four executive orders dealing with urban policy and sent a report thereon to Congress. See generally Hagman *supra* note 7, at 63–74. See also Krannich, A Modern Disaster: Agricultural Land, Urban Growth, and the Need for a Federally Organized Comprehensive Land Use Planning Model, 16 Cornell J.L. & Pub. Pol'y 57 (2006).

In June, 1974, the House of Representatives defeated a bill that would have called for federal grants to the states, over an 8-year period, to assist them in comprehensive land-use planning. But some federal aid for local planning has been authorized; notes 11 & 12 *infra* and accompanying text.

[11] 40 U.S.C.A. § 461. This planning assistance is sometimes called the "701 program"—named for the section of the National Housing Act in which it first appeared. As amended in 1974, the statute requires planning agencies receiving federal funds to include housing and land-use elements in their plans. 40 U.S.C.A. § 461(c). A definition of "comprehensive planning"—as that term is used in this legislation—is found in 40 U.S.C.A. § 461(m)(4). See generally Mandelker Cunningham & Payne, Planning and Control of Land Development 20 (1995).

[12] 42 U.S.C.A. § 1453(d) (grants for preparation and completion of community renewal programs).

[13] See generally Hagman & Juergensmeyer, Urban Planning & Land Development Control Law 52–53 (2d ed. 1986). Federal aid for state planning was made available in 1959 under § 701 of the Housing Act of 1954. 40 U.S.C.A. § 461. On state-city cooperation in the planning process, see Buckwalter, State-City Connections: A Now Imperative, 58 State Gov't 124 (1986). See generally on state planning DeGrove & Stroud, New Developments and Future Trends in Local Government Comprehensive Planning, 17 Stetson L. Rev. 573 (1988), particularly examining the Florida experience. Further discussion of developments in Florida planning law is found in Davidson, Plan-Based Land Development and Infrastructure Controls: New Directives for Growth Management, 2 J. Land Use & Envtl. L. 151 (1986); Pelham, Hyde & Banks, Managing Florida's Growth: Toward an Integrated State, Regional, and Local Comprehensive Planning Process, 13 Fla. St. U.L. Rev. 515 (1985); Pelham, Florida's New Approach to Intergovernmental Coordination, 18 State & Local L. Newsletter, No. 3, at 1 (Spring, 1995). On multicounty planning within a state, see Freilich & Ragsdale, Land Use Control in the Minneapolis-St. Paul Metropolitan Region, 58 Minn. L. Rev. 1009 (1974), discussing the work of the Metropolitan Council that participates in the governing of the 7-county Twin Cities area of Minnesota. On Growth Management Acts and the role of the state agencies that apply them, see Lloyd, Accommodating Growth or Enabling Sprawl? The Role of Population Growth Projections in Comprehensive Planning Under the Washington State Growth Management Act, 36 Gonzaga L. Rev. 73 (2001). See generally Mandelker, Implementing State Growth Management Programs: Alternatives and Recommendations, 45 John

noted:[14] (1) The state agencies often have little power unless directly attached to the governor's office—and even then, little may be accomplished in states where the governor has only a two-year term. (2) Money and power at the state level are much less than at the federal. (3) State lines often cut across metropolitan and other economically united regions, making the state an inappropriate level at which to engage in planning for some urban areas.

What then of interstate and regional planning? This is surely possible through interstate compacts; and some of these have been adopted, with approval of Congress. A notable experience involved the Appalachian region, covered by the Appalachian Regional Development Act of 1965,[15] encompassing all or part of 13 states. But states are seldom willing to delegate much power to such bodies, and they have largely been limited to making studies, giving advice, and attempting coordination.[16]

Marshall L. Rev. 307 (2012). See also Warner, Growth Management Acts' "Land Supply Mandate," Or, Why the Growth Monster Eats the Leftover Meatloaf in the Refrigerator, 42 Urban Law. 395 (2010), adversely criticizing the "adequate land supply" mandate found in some states' growth management legislation. These mandates are intended to require jurisdictions to adjust comprehensive land use plans periodically to accommodate future population increases, but may preclude affected areas from achieving an optimal, sustainable population level. *Id.* As to comprehensive (or "master") plans, see Section 21.3, *infra.* As to the powers of state agencies to rule on proposed incorporations of municipalities, see Section 12.3, note 36, *supra*, and accompanying text.

As to land use law in Hawaii, which has a history of unusually centralized control and of zoning at the state level, see Callies, Regulating Paradise: Land Use Controls in Hawaii (2d ed. 2010), reviewed by Salkin, 43 Urban Law. 1107 (2011). See generally Callies, It All Began in Hawaii, 45 John Marshall L. Rev. 317 (2012), part of Symposium, 40th Anniversary of the Quiet Revolution in Zoning and Land Use Revolution, *id.* at 237–434, which also contains articles on planning laws in Florida (*id.* at 397), Oregon (*id.* at 357), and Vermont (*id.* at 417).

[14] See Hagman & Juergensmeyer, *supra* note 13. See also Note, This Land Is Whose Land? The Feasibility of Extraterritorial Jurisdiction in West Virginia's Land Use Planning Laws, 109 W. Va. L. Rev. 929 (2007).

[15] 40 Appendix U.S.C.A. §§ 1–405. Most of this legislation expired Oct. 1, 1979. *Id.* § 405. But further expenditures to carry out most programs under the Act were authorized by the Energy and Water Development Appropriation Act of 1980, 93 Stat. 448, 40 Appendix U.S.C.A. §§ 1, 105. Substantial cuts in the grants to the Appalachian Regional Commission were made under the Reagan administration. See Gregory, $10 Million in Grants to State May Be Lost, The (Nashville) Tennessean, Feb. 15, 1981, at 1. When the program died out in the early 1980's, it could be said to have had only limited effect. See Carey, As Help for Appalachia Trails Off, Some Places Seem as Needy as Ever, Wall St. J., July 6, 1982, at 1, col. 1. On the need for more state and regional planning, see Symposium, State and Regional Land Use Planning: An Idea Whose Time Has Come, 73 St. John's L. Rev. 1007 (1999). See generally Symposium on Regionalism, 48 Buffalo L. Rev. 1–82 (2000). Regionalism in planning has increasingly emphasized environmental issues in metropolitan areas. See McKinney, The Realities of Regional Stewardship: From Urban Issues to Natural Landscape, 29 Pub. Land & Resources L. Rev. 123 (2008); Ziegler, The Case for Metropolitan Growth Management in the 21st Century: Regional Urban Planning and Sustainable Development in the United States, 41 Urban Law. 147 (2009); Note, Bioregionalism and Environmental Regulation: A Policy Consideration for Future Environmental Reforms, 17 U. Baltimore J. Envtl. L. 1 (2009).

[16] See Hagman & Juergensmeyer, *supra* note 13. See generally Calthorpe & Fulton, The Regional City—Planning for the End of Sprawl (Island Press 2000); Clavel (ed.), Urban and Regional Planning in an Age of Austerity (Pergamon Press 1980). On recent developments in regional planning, see Davidson & Foster, The Mobility Case for Regionalism, 47 U.Cal. Davis L. Rev. 63 (2013); Gottlieb, Regional Land Use Planning: A Collaborative Solution for the Conservation of Natural Resources, 29 J. Envtl. L. & Litigation 35 (2014); Note, A New Regionalist Perspective on Land Use and Environment, 56 How. L.J. 207 (2012); J. Barnett, Planning for a New Century—The Regional Agenda (Island Press 2001), reviewed 33 Urban Law. 1122 (2001). On regionalism in planning, see also Section 21.5 *infra* as to recent developments. For a case study of a particular urban area in which some degree of regional planning has been employed in order to prevent unwanted sprawl, see Jackson, The Need for Regional Management of Growth: Boulder, Colorado, as a Case Study, 37 Urban Law. 299 (2005), where it is suggested that "Because of the impact of growth mechanisms on

§ 21.3 Urban Planning: The Master Plan

This brings us to the local level, where the bulk of urban planning is done. Zoning may be considered the most prevalent form of municipal planning; but it is also true that "planning" for the orderly development of the community involves much more than zoning.[17] But the two functions are surely intermingled, and sometimes indistinguishable, in many municipalities—especially since the local planning body (often called the "planning commission") is sometimes entrusted with some zoning powers: recommending to the city legislative body the boundaries of, and permitted uses, in various zones, and hearing protests to existing zoning, and requests for changes.[18] Whatever powers local planning boards have must be derived from state statute, home-rule charter, or city ordinance.[19] The task most frequently assigned local planning boards

---

surrounding communities, growth, particularly in crowded metropolitan areas, should be managed by a *regional* form of government." *Id.* at 300–01. As to such governments, see generally Section 2.14 *supra.*

[17] 1A Antieau, Municipal Corporation Law § 8.00, at 8–3 (1998). Cf. Baker v. City of Milwaukie, 271 Or. 500, 533 P.2d 772 (1975) (comprehensive plan is the planning instrument; zoning is the means by which the comprehensive plan is effectuated). See generally Juergensmeyer & Roberts, Land Use Planning & Control Law 24–25 (1998), listing such city plans (besides the zoning plan) as a plan for streets, a plan for public transit, and a plan for parks and recreation. On techniques for simplifying and coordinating the administration of zoning laws and other planning devices, see Vranicar, Sanders & Mosena, Streamlining Land Use Regulation (American Planning Ass'n 1982). On the clash between those who favor planning for continued growth and development in a community and those who urge curbs on development in order to protect the environment, see the excellent discussion of San Diego's situation in Witt & Sammartino-Gardner, Growth Management v. Vested Rights: One City's Experience, 20 Urban Law. 647 (1988). See generally Freilich, From Sprawl to Smart Growth—Successful Legal, Planning, and Environmental Systems (American Bar Ass'n Section of State & Local Gov't Law 2000); Kushner, Smart Growth: Urban Growth Management and Land-Use Regulation Law in America, 32 Urban Law. 211 (2000); Ohm, Reforming Land Planning Legislation at the Dawn of the 21st Century—The Emerging Influence of Smart Growth and Livable Communities, 32 Urban Law. 181 (2000) (describing smart growth as "an evolving approach to development that balances economic development with environmental protection and a better quality of life"; *id.* at 189). On "smart growth," see also Davidson & Trevarthan, Land Use Mediation: Another Smart Growth Alternative, 33 Urban Law. 705 (2001). As to the origins and development of the "smart growth" movement, see Section 21.5, note 57, *infra.* See also note 6, *supra.* For discussion of a proposal that presents another alternative to traditional zoning and "smart growth," see Ketcham, The Alexandrian Planning Process: An Alternative to Traditional Zoning and Smart Growth, 41 Urban Law. 339 (2009), suggesting an approach based on the work of architect Christopher Alexander.

[18] See, on the various functions of planning commissions, City Plan Commission v. Pielet, 167 Ind.App. 324, 338 N.E.2d 648 (1975) (plan commission's recommendation to rezone was not a "decision" reviewable by certiorari). Cf. Melemanu Woodlands Community Association, Inc. v. Koga, 56 Hawaii 235, 533 P.2d 867 (1975) (advisory opinion of planning commission was not an appealable final order). On the various procedures for appealing zoning decisions, and the boards and commissions to which they may be appealed, see Note, Trial Practice: Procedure for Appealing Decisions of a Municipal Zoning Agency, 18 Okl.L.Rev. 111 (1965); Note, Board of Zoning Appeals Procedure—Informality Breeds Contempt, 16 Syracuse L.Rev. 568 (1965). Cf. Note, Exhaustion of Remedies in Zoning Cases, 1964 Wash.U.L.Q. 368 (property owner attacking zoning ordinance provisions as applied to his property must exhaust administrative remedies before seeking judicial relief, though need not exhaust such remedies if challenging constitutionality of entire ordinance; difficulties of the exhaustion rule shown). See generally on zoning practices Chapter 18 *supra.* See also Williams, Planning Law and Democratic Living, 20 Law & Contemp. Prob. 317 (1955).

In some states, counties, as well as municipalities, have statutory authority to adopt master plans. See Muzzy Ranch Co. v. Solano County Airport Land Use Comm'n, 41 Cal.4th 372, 60 Cal.Rptr.3d 247, 160 P.3d 116 (2007) (county airport commission's land use compatibility plan can operate like a multijurisdictional general plan to trump the land use planning authority that affected jurisdictions might otherwise exercise through plans or zoning); Droste v. Board of County Comm'rs, 159 P.3d 601 (Colo. 2007) (county had authority under Local Government Land Use Control Enabling Act to adopt ordinances imposing a temporary moratorium on land-use application reviews while county prepared its master plan).

[19] Shanbour v. Oklahoma City, 422 P.2d 444 (Okl.1967). See Reid Development Corp. v. Parsippany-Troy Hills Township, 10 N.J. 229, 89 A.2d 667 (1952) (city could not deny water service to subdivider in order

is the preparation and revision of the city's master plan. The master plan shows the board's expectations and recommendations as to the community's future development and growth: the uses that will be made of land in different areas (residential, commercial, etc.); the services that will be offered (water, sewers, sometimes electricity and gas), and (sometimes) how soon; projected transportation facilities (streets and their location, parking, public transit, airports, etc.); public facilities (parks, schools, libraries, civic centers, etc.); and predictions as to municipal growth, population density, etc.[20] The plan is usually a composite of maps and of written proposals and predictions, and its purpose is to guide future development in a coordinated manner.

The master plan is prepared by the planning commission; statutes sometimes specify exactly what it is to include, or what the commission is to consider in preparing it. Once it is finally approved by the commission itself, it is generally recommended to the local governing body for adoption. Until adopted by that body, the plan is nothing

---

to force him to agree to lot-size that the city wanted; planning powers can only be exercised as prescribed by statute). Cf. In re Environmental Planning Commission, 87 N.M. 215, 531 P.2d 949 (1974) (environmental planning body has only such powers as granted by legislation). Occasionally, a state may pre-empt the field of creation of planning boards. See Del Duca v. Town Administrator, 368 Mass. 1, 329 N.E.2d 748 (1975) (town could not, in replacing an elected board with an appointed one, remove elected members during their terms of office by failing to appoint them to new board). On state enabling legislation as to planning by local units, see generally Mandelker, The Role of the Local Comprehensive Plan in Land Use Regulation, 74 Mich. L.Rev. 799, 951–56 (1976). Most state enabling acts are derived from one or the other of two model acts promulgated by the U.S. Department of Commerce in the 1920's. United States Dep't of Commerce, A Standard City Planning Enabling Act (1928). No state followed the models exactly, however, and some of the language of the Acts may seem confusing and, today, outdated. See Black, The Comprehensive Plan, in Principles and Practice of Urban Planning 349–55 (W. Goodmean & E. Freund, eds. 1968). Another suggested model is found in American Law Institute, A Model Land Development Code (1976). On questions raised in New York City about the role of the City Planning Commission, particularly in regard to privately financed developments, see Purnick, Early History of a Luxury Complex: Classic Case of New York City Politics, N.Y. Times, Nov. 8, 1982, at 16. On planning for New York City, see generally Goldberger, A Helluva Towne—Finding the Future in Old New York, The New Yorker, Nov. 30, 1998, at 120 (emphasizing the importance for New York City's future development of the adoption in 1811 of the Commissioners' Plan, which mapped Manhattan's streets in a huge grid).

[20] See Haar, The Master Plan: An Impermanent Constitution, 20 Law & Contemp. Prob. 353 (1955); Haar, In Accordance With a Comprehensive Plan, 68 Harv. L. Rev. 1154 (1955). It has been said that these two articles were "Professor's Haar's most original works" and were the "seminal law review articles on the comprehensive plan." Freilich, A Tribute to Charles M. Haar, 44 Urban Law. 291 (2012). See generally M. Branch, Planning Urban Environment ch. 7 (1974); Dunham, An Analysis of the Content of the Master Plan, 1 J. Law & Econ. 170 (1958); Sullivan, The Role of the Comprehensive Plan, 31 Urban Law. 915 (1999); Sullivan, The Evolving Role of the Comprehensive Plan, 30 Urban Law. 699 (1998). A leading work on city planning in the twentieth century was Kent, The Urban General Plan (Planners Press 1964), reviewed 25 Urban Law. 192 (1993). On the successes enjoyed because of the use of master plans, see Comment, Planning Ahead: Consistency With a Comprehensive Land Use Plan Yields Consistent Results for Municipalities, 60 Okla. L. Rev. 73 (2007). Compare Comment, The Role of the Comprehensive Plan in Ohio: Moving Away from the Traditional View, 17 U. Dayton L. Rev. 207 (1991).

For a good summary of the varying weight given a master plan in the various states, see Sullivan, The Evolving Role of the Master Plan, 32 Urban Law. 813 (2000), which updates the earlier articles of the same name by Sullivan, *supra*. Some cases in recent years have reflected a growing deference to the municipality's comprehensive, or master, plan. See Sullivan, 2001 Comprehensive Planning Law Update 713 (2001). See generally Sullivan, Recent Developments in Comprehensive Planning Law, 38 Urban Law. 685 (2006).

As to the authority of the various parts of a comprehensive plan, see Staus v. City of Corvallis, 199 Or.App. 217, 111 P.3d 759 (2005) (text of city's comprehensive plan controlled over ambiguous coloring on comprehensive plan map). Cf. Town of Woodway v. Snohomish, 291 P.3d 278 (Wash. App. 2013) (local governments have broad discretion in developing comprehensive plans tailored to local circumstances, but such discretion is bounded by state's Growth Management Act). See also Mudd, A Next, Big Step for the West: Model Legislation to Create a Water-Climate Element in Local Comprehensive Plans, 3 Wash. J. Envtl. L. & Pol'y 1 (2013).

more than a proposal, and it is clear that a property-owner within the community cannot yet protest the plan's designations.[21] Statutes or charters usually require that the governing body give some kind of notice (as through newspaper publication) to the community prior to adoption of a master plan, and hold a public hearing thereon; such provisions are mandatory.[22] Once adopted, the plan can be modified in the same manner: notice and hearing are required, and the local governing body then votes on the proposed amendments.[23] Any changes will normally be upheld against judicial challenge unless found arbitrary, unreasonable, or designed primarily for the benefit of private parties rather than the community.[24] Even after the master plan has been adopted, most authority treats it as only a declaration of policy and intention, not having regulatory or other legal effect; and therefore, a property-owner attacking the plan will usually have his suit dismissed.[25] The attack at such point is considered premature, if based solely on the plan; only when implemented by zoning or other concrete legislation does the plan become more than a guideline. Since a master plan does indicate expectations as to future zoning and development, it can, of course, sometimes lessen the value of property; but this does not entitle the owner to compensation unless (1) an eventual governmental taking of the land is indicated, *and* in the meantime, any economically feasible use of the property is effectively precluded, *or* (2) a governmental intrusion inflicting

---

[21] See Cochran v. Planning Board, 87 N.J.Super. 526, 210 A.2d 99 (1965). Indeed, in some jurisdictions—including New Jersey—, the master plan is merely a proposal for future guidance and need not ever necessarily be adopted by the local governing body as an overall plan, though parts of it will presumably be adopted in particular zoning ordinances. See Cervase v. Kawaida Towers, Inc., 124 N.J.Super. 547, 308 A.2d 47 (1973), aff'd 129 N.J.Super. 124, 322 A.2d 477 (housing project need only comply with zoning ordinance, not master plan). On the other hand, a development plan in England is considered sufficiently definite and concrete that it can cause blight (referred to as "planning blight")—that is, it can cause affected properties to be depressed in value, sometimes necessitating the purchase of the property by the public entity involved. See Hagman, Planning (Condemnation) Blight, Participation and Just Compensation: Anglo-American Comparisons, 4 Urban Law. 434 (1972) (noting that in America, a master plan is treated as a mere guide).

[22] Lordship Park Association v. Board of Zoning Appeals, 137 Conn. 84, 75 A.2d 379 (1950) (plan unconstitutional because adopted without notice and hearing). But persons who actually appear at a hearing may be held to have thus waived any right to protest inadequate notice of the hearing. Schwartz v. Town of Hamden, 168 Conn. 8, 357 A.2d 488 (1975).

[23] See Dalton v. City and County of Honolulu, 51 Hawaii 400, 462 P.2d 199 (1969) (amendment must be enacted in same manner as required for adoption of plan); Brozowski v. City of Detroit, 351 Mich. 10, 87 N.W.2d 114 (1957) (council had made additions, deletions, and modifications to plan over the years); Tierney v. Duris, 21 Or.App. 613, 536 P.2d 435 (1975) (plan may be amended though the change affects only one tract). It has been noted that an amendment affecting only a single small area is a "judicial" action requiring a "judicial-type hearing," while an amendment affecting a large area is legislative action. Marggi v. Ruecker, 20 Or.App. 669, 533 P.2d 1372 (1975). Cf. Roy v. City of Woonsocket, 116 R.I. 745, 360 A.2d 565 (1976) (charter requirement of hearing prior to amendment of plan does not apply to implementation of plan, as in selecting specific sites for municipal improvements).

[24] See Rosenberg v. Planning Board, 155 Conn. 636, 236 A.2d 895 (1967) (persons directly affected by change may protest, but amendment is valid if predominant purpose is benefit of whole community, although individual will receive incidental benefit).

[25] See Cervase v. Kawaida Towers, Inc., *supra* note 21. Compare Township of Orion v. Weber, 83 Mich.App. 712, 269 N.W.2d 275 (1978) (invalid attempt to zone according to master plan found where nonconforming use allowed only if it created no significant obstacle to plan), with State ex rel. Kearns v. Ohio Power Co., 163 Ohio St. 451, 127 N.E.2d 394 (1955) (local governing body gave permission for utility to locate in area not designated for utilities by master plan; upheld), and Giltner Dairy, LLC v. Jerome County, 181 P.3d 1238 (Idaho 2008) (landowner challenging amendment to map was not entitled to judicial review under statute permitting review by an applicant denied a permit or aggrieved by a decision; plan serves as a guide to making zoning decisions but is not a legally controlling zoning law). See also Sustainable Growth Initiative Committee v. Jumpers, LLC, 122 Nev. 53, 128 P.3d 452 (2006), saying that a master plan is a standard that commands deference but is not a legislative mandate from which no leave can be taken; Tarlock, Consistency with Adopted Land Use Plans as a Standard of Review: The Case Against, 9 Urban Law Ann. 69 (1975).

irreversible damage can be shown.[26] Similarly, since the master plan is only a general guideline and not a binding restriction (and is intended to apply primarily in the future, not immediately), a zoning law will prevail over the master plan where there is a conflict.[27]

What purposes does the master plan serve? First, it is a limitation on *public* building and development. Generally, once the master plan is adopted by the local government's legislative body, that local government must submit any proposals regarding *its own* public buildings, streets, parks, etc. to the local planning commission for that commission's determination of whether or not the proposed action conforms to the master plan. For instance, a proposal to open a new street, or close an old one, must be so submitted. If the planning commission disapproves an action that had been proposed by municipal officials, those officials can appeal to the local governing body itself. That governing body then makes the final determination—which will not be reversed by the courts unless arbitrary action or an abuse of discretion is shown.[28] However, a local

---

[26] Fifth Avenue Corp. v. Washington County, 282 Or. 591, 581 P.2d 50 (1978) (damages for inverse condemnation might be awarded if, but only if, the stated conditions were met). Cf. Comment, Official Maps and the Regulatory Takings Problem: A Legislative Solution, 2011 B.Y.U. L. Rev. 2251.

[27] Stones v. Plattsmouth Airport Authority, 193 Neb. 552, 228 N.W.2d 129 (1975); Marracci v. Scappoose, 26 Or.App. 131, 552 P.2d 552 (1976). Cf. Bone v. City of Lewiston, 107 Idaho 844, 693 P.2d 1046 (1984) (court refused issuance of mandamus to compel city to rezone property in accordance with comprehensive plan; plan said only to indicate projected land uses for the future, not the presently appropriate uses); State by Rochester Association of Neighborhoods v. City of Rochester, 268 N.W.2d 885 (Minn.1978) (city need not amend land-use plan before adopting inconsistent zoning ordinance; ordinance may nonetheless be valid); Pohrman v. Klamath County Commissioners, 25 Or.App. 613, 550 P.2d 1236 (1976) (plan adopted by county was less restrictive than zoning law adopted by local government; local government need not immediately make ordinance consistent with plan).

Washington State has been particularly strong in declaring that zoning laws prevail over a comprehensive plan in cases of conflict. See Cingular Wireless, LLC v. Thurston County, 131 Wash.App. 756, 129 P.3d 300 (2006) (if a comprehensive plan prohibits a use that the zoning code permits, the use is permitted); Timberlake Christian Fellowship v. King County, 114 Wash.App. 174, 61 P.3d 332 (2002) (where there is a conflict between comprehensive plan and zoning regulations, the regulations must prevail). See generally Citizens for Mount Vernon v. City of Mount Vernon, 133 Wash.2d 861, 947 P.2d 1208 (1997). Oklahoma is in accord. Holtzen v. Tulsa County Bd. of Adjustment, 97 P.3d 1150 (Okla. Civ. App. 2004) (as a general rule, a comprehensive plan is considered a guide and advisory in nature, not the equivalent of a zoning law). But cf. Flathead Citizens for Quality Growth, Inc. v. Flathead County Bd. of Adjustment, 341 Mont. 1, 175 P.3d 282 (2008) (provisions of district land use plan that were more restrictive than county zoning regulations controlled when county board was determining whether to issue a conditional use permit).

One authority has divided the cases of conflict between zoning laws and a comprehensive plan into three categories: those that attach no special significance to the comprehensive plan, if there is one (called "the Unitary view"); those that attach some significance to the plan (the "Planning Factor view"); and those that give the plan dispositive significance as a law (the "Plan-As-Law view"). Sullivan, Comprehensive Planning, 36 Urban Law. 541 (2004). The author notes that Connecticut is a state that "is aggressive in placing the zoning ordinance at the top of the land use hierarchy," but finds that in the year prior to this article, there was not a single published appellate case in any state in which a zoning regulation was explicitly held to trump a comprehensive plan. *Id.* at 542–43. See generally Sullivan, Recent Developments in Comprehensive Planning Law, 43 Urban Law. 823 (2011); Sullivan, Recent Developments in Comprehensive Planning Law, 38 Urban Law. 685 (2006). Connecticut thus adheres to the Unitary view that a comprehensive plan can be found in the zoning ordinances and maps and that there is no need for a separate plan. This was once considered the majority view but is now found in very few states. See Sullivan & Bragar, Recent Developments in Comprehensive Planning, 45 Urban Law. 727, 728–30 (2013). Accord, Sullivan & Bragar, Recent Developments in Comprehensive Planning, 46 Urban Law. 685, 687–89 (2014).As to the increased deference accorded comprehensive plans in some jurisdictions, see also this section note 20, *supra*, and note 34, *infra*, and accompanying text.

[28] See Passaic Junior Chamber of Commerce, Inc. v. Housing Authority of Passaic, 45 N.J.Super. 381, 132 A.2d 813 (1957). Cf. Dry Creek Partners, LLC v. Ada County Comm'rs, 148 Idaho 11, 217 P.3d 1282 (2009) (court affirms county's denial of request for second extension of time to obtain approval of final subdivision

master plan is not binding on the *state* and its agencies, as to *their* building of public improvements, unless state law so provides.[29]

Second, in many jurisdictions, plats for new subdivisions within a community must be approved by the planning commission—which, of course, is to give its approval only if it finds the proposed subdivision conforms to the master plan.[30] Third and finally, statutes and home-rule charters generally provide that zoning must be in accord with a "*comprehensive* plan."[31] It has been noted that this does not necessarily require an actual *master* plan; the requirement may be taken as indicating merely that the zoning must be in accord with some overall, orderly system of development, and the master plan may not be devised until after zoning ordinances have been adopted.[32] Sometimes, the

---

plat). Those with a personal stake in the case may seek judicial review; Heffernan v. Missoula City Council, 360 Mont. 207, 255 P.3d 80 (2011) (adjacent landowner and neighborhood association had standing to challenge city council's approval of subdivision plat). But cf. Mills v. Alta Vista Ranch, LLC, 344 Mont. 212, 187 P.3d 627 (2008) (act of county recorder in recording survey did not constitute a decision by a "governing body" approving or denying a subdivision plat for purposes of state statute allowing aggrieved parties 30 days to appeal governing body's decision).

[29] See Kunimoto v. Kawakami, 56 Hawaii 582, 545 P.2d 684 (1976) (state university not subject to charter requirement that any public improvement must conform to development plan for area). Cf. Department of Transp. v. Lopez-Torres, 526 So.2d 674 (Fla. 1988) (state Department of Transportation may place bridge in location that conflicts with municipality's comprehensive growth plan). Though there is little authority, it would seem that much the same limitations, as far as governmental immunity is concerned, would apply to the master plan as apply to zoning controls. As to the latter, see generally Chapter 18 *supra*.

[30] See Kiska v. Skrensky, 145 Conn. 28, 138 A.2d 523 (1958). There is often a time prescribed by statute or charter within which the planning commission is supposed to act on subdividers' requests for approval; and if no action is taken within that time, the plan is customarily treated as approved. See State ex rel. Lozoff v. Board of Trustees of Hartland, 55 Wis.2d 64, 197 N.W.2d 798 (1972) (tabling of consideration did not amount to taking action on plat). Mandamus has also been held available to compel the planning body to take action. Maricopa County v. Anzwool, Inc., 19 Ariz.App. 242, 506 P.2d 282 (1973); Ayres v. City Council of Los Angeles, 34 Cal.2d 31, 207 P.2d 1 (1949); People ex rel. American National Bank & Trust Co. v. City of Park Ridge, 25 Ill.App.2d 424, 166 N.E.2d 635 (1960); Allen v. Stockwell, 210 Mich. 488, 178 N.W. 27 (1920); Hilbol Realty, Inc. v. Barnhart, 205 Misc. 187, 126 N.Y.S.2d 865 (1953); State ex rel. Pelham Development Corp. v. Cerny, 11 Ohio St.2d 228, 228 N.E.2d 309 (1967). If there is no planning commission, subdivision applications go directly to the city or county governing body for approval or denial. See MM&I, LLC v. Board of County Comm'rs of Gallatin County, 358 Mont. 420, 246 P.3d 1029 (2010) (county commission's denial of subdivision application upheld as supported by the evidence). A denial of an application will generally be upheld by the courts unless found arbitrary and capricious. See Richards v. County of Missoula, 288 P.3d 175 (Mont. 2012) (denial of application for rural subdivision upheld). Rules of administrative law—such as appeal to the courts being allowed only where a final decision has been made and only when administrative remedies, unless futile, have been exhausted—will be applied. See Kellberg v. Yuen, 319 P.3d 432 (Hawaii 2014). Approval of a subdivision application is sometimes required as to any residential "development." See Pacific Palisades Bowl Mobile Estates, LLC v. City of Los Angeles, 149 Cal. Rptr. 3d 383, 288 P.3d 717 (2012) (mobile home park conversion from tenant occupancy to resident ownership was a "development" within statutory permit requirement).

[31] See Baker v. City of Milwaukie, 271 Or. 500, 533 P.2d 772 (1975) (comprehensive plan is the planning instrument for a city, and zoning is the means by which this is effectuated). See generally "Haar, In Accordance With a Comprehensive Plan," 68 Harv.L.Rev. 1154 (1955). See also the discussion of zoning requirements Chapter 18 *supra*.

[32] See Kozesnik v. Montgomery Township, 24 N.J. 154, 131 A.2d 1 (1957) (plan can be revealed in the zoning ordinance); Juergensmeyer & Roberts, Land Use Planning & Control Law § 2.11 (1998). Cf. Sweetman v. Town of Cumberland, 117 R.I. 134, 364 A.2d 1277 (1976) (zoning need not conform with the master plan; the "comprehensive plan" requirement only means that zoning must bear a reasonable relationship to public health, safety, and welfare); Cougar Mountain Associates v. King County, 111 Wash.2d 742, 765 P.2d 264 (1988) (density requirement set forth in zoning code prevailed over conflicting requirements in county comprehensive plan since plan is only a general policy guide). Idaho has emphasized with regularity the general view that a master, or comprehensive, plan is only a guide as to possible future action. See Martin v. Camas County, 150 Idaho 508, 248 P.3d 1243 (2011) (comprehensive plan creates no present right or enforceable expectation); Krempasky v. Nez Perce County Planning & Zoning Comm'n, 150 Idaho 231, 245 P.3d 983 (2010) (comprehensive plan does not operate as a legally controlling zoning law but merely as a guide).

"comprehensive plan" requirement is taken only to mean that zoning ordinances and amendments must be reasonable and cannot lawfully result in "spot zoning."[33] But under a few legislative or charter provisions, at least as interpreted by the courts, zoning may be required to conform to the master plan itself.[34] Even then, a general harmony between the zoning ordinances and the plan would seem to suffice; there need not be conformity in every detail.[35] A planning commission, as has been noted, often makes recommendations to the local legislative body on zoning or rezoning of property; certainly in performing this task, the planning commission should strive to bring the municipality's zoning into line with the master plan.

Since the planning commission thus performs a number of tasks dealing with project-approval, plat-approval, and zoning-recommendations, the delegation of these powers to the commission has occasionally been challenged. But the delegation of authority over approval of public buildings has been upheld,[36] as has the delegation of control over subdivision plats,[37] so long as reasonably clear standards are provided the commission by state or local legislation.[38] The delegation of authority to recommend zoning laws, and changes therein, is seldom even challenged, and will clearly be upheld—even without the need for standards other than those supplied by the master plan itself or other very general guidelines.[39]

---

[33] See Kuehne v. Town Council of East Hartford, 136 Conn. 452, 72 A.2d 474 (1950) (town council's action could not be sustained where not in furtherance of any general plan). Cf. Southwest Ranches Homeowners Ass'n, Inc. v. County of Broward, 502 So.2d 931 (Fla.App.1987), review denied 511 So.2d 999 (Fla.1987) (in reviewing reasonableness of zoning changes, court should consider consistency with comprehensive plan).

[34] Rosenberg v. Planning Board, 155 Conn. 636, 236 A.2d 895 (1967) (applying city-charter provision and holding that zoning ordinance could not be amended to permit a use not allowed by the master plan). See Sullivan, The Plan as Law, 24 Urban Law. 881 (1992) & 26 Urban Law. 753 (1994), noting the trend in a number of states to give greater deference to a comprehensive plan. This trend is illustrated by Mendota Golf, LLP v. City of Mendota Heights, 708 N.W.2d 162 (Minn. 2006), noted 33 Wm. Mitchell L. Rev. 627 (2007). See generally Sullivan, Recent Developments in Comprehensive Planning Law 681 (2007), stating (at 694) that "the comprehensive plan is gradually gaining more credence, through state legislation and court decisions." In many jurisdictions, master plans must conform to the requirements of state growth management acts, and often must be approved by state growth management agencies. See generally as to growth management goals Juergensmeyer & Nicholas, Loving Growth Management in the Time of Recession, 42/43 Urban Law. 417 (2010–11); Weitz, The New Wave in Growth Management, 42/43 Urban Law. 407 (2010–11). See also Basse, Urbanization and Growth Management in Europe, 42/43 Urban Law. 385 (2010–11). Growth management acts are discussed in note 13 *supra*.

[35] See Pecora v. Zoning Commission, 145 Conn. 435, 144 A.2d 48 (1958) (zoning ordinances should be in general harmony with comprehensive plan). Cf. Citizen Advocates for a Livable Missoula, Inc. v. City Council, 331 Mont. 269, 130 P.3d 1259 (2006) (under Montana statutes, zoning bodies should substantially comply with the master plan or growth policy). See generally Sullivan & Bragar, Recent Developments in Comprehensive Planning, 44 Urban Law. 615 (2012).

[36] City of Chicago v. Central National Bank, 5 Ill.2d 164, 125 N.E.2d 94 (1955).

[37] Gore v. Hicks, 115 N.Y.S.2d 187 (Sup.Ct.1952).

[38] See Beach v. Planning and Zoning Commission, 141 Conn. 79, 103 A.2d 814 (1954); Borough of Oakland v. Roth, 28 N.J.Super. 321, 100 A.2d 698 (1953). Some of the "standards" provided are rather broad and general, and courts have nonetheless tended to presume them reasonable and adequate. See Florka v. City of Detroit, 369 Mich. 568, 120 N.W.2d 797 (1963).

[39] Hopkins v. MacCulloch, 35 Cal.App.2d 442, 95 P.2d 950 (Dist.Ct.1940).

§ 21.4 Subdivision Restrictions

The above-mentioned power of planning commissions to approve or disapprove of subdivision plats[40] clearly opens the door for imposing conditions and regulations on proposed subdivisions within the community. The local government has a legitimate interest in seeing that the community in general enjoys a balanced growth, and that new subdivisions in particular are adequately provided with essential facilities and services.[41] Thus, it has been recognized that the police power of the state includes the power to regulate subdivisions and that this power may be delegated to the municipalities,[42] as it generally has been by state legislation. The range of possible regulations is often defined by the statutes, and usually includes provisions assuring proper arrangement of streets, adequate provision for utilities, and sufficient light and air. The precise regulations are then generally adopted by the municipal governing body itself; but that body must abide by procedures established by state law—which may include requirements that the regulations be in the form of an ordinance,[43] and/or the

---

[40] See note 30 *supra* and accompanying text.

[41] See Bluett v. County of Cook, 19 Ill.App.2d 172, 153 N.E.2d 305 (1958) (plat-approving authority has no power to grant variances from zoning laws); Mansfield & Swett v. Town of West Orange, 120 N.J.L. 145, 198 A. 225 (1938). See generally Turner & Herring, Planning, Zoning and Subdivision Law, 25 U. Richmond L. Rev. 841 (1991).

As to the difference between zoning laws and subdivision regulations, see Boone v. Board of County Comm'rs, 107 P.3d 1114 (Colo. App. 2004) (zoning and subdivision regulations are distinct types of controls that serve different purposes: zoning limits the current use of land, while subdivision regulations generally restrict transferability and plan for future use involving a platted subdivision); Shoptaugh v. Board of County Commissioners, 37 Colo. App. 39, 543 P.2d 524 (1975) (both are exercises of the police power, but they are separate regulations serving separate purposes; subdivider must comply with both, including subdivision regulations issued, as here, by state and county). On problems that may occur when subdivisions are not subject to regulation, see Robichaux, Arizona's Rural Sprawl: Fast Growth Spawns "Wildcat" Subdivisions, Wall St. J., Jan. 30, 2001, at A1. See also note 42 *infra*.

[42] Stoker v. Town of Irvington, 71 N.J.Super. 370, 177 A.2d 61 (1961). See generally Yokley, The Law of Subdivisions (1963 Supp.1980). On what is a "subdivision" within the meaning of state laws subjecting subdivisions to municipal regulation, see Planning Bd. of Naples v. Michaud, 444 A.2d 40 (Me.1982) (vendor's plan for conveying his interests in campsites came within subdivision regulations). See generally Comment, State Regulation of Subdivisions: Defining the Boundary Between State and Local Land Use Jurisdiction in Vermont, Maine, and Florida, 19 Boston C. Envtl. Affairs L. Rev. 385 (1991).

A disturbing development late in the twentieth century was the filing of frivolous lawsuits by developers against those who expressed opposition to the developers' planned projects. Thus, at least 20 states have passed laws, commonly called Anti-SLAPP statutes (an acronym for Strategic Lawsuit Against Public Participation), allowing special motions to dismiss that can bring about speedy dismissal of these frivolous lawsuits, by those who are sued because of their participation in public permitting processes, such as by circulating petitions, testifying at public hearings, and filing appeals of zoning decisions. See Wilson, Of Sexy Phone Calls and Well-Aimed Golf Balls: Anti-SLAPP Statutes in Recent Land-Use Damages Litigation, 36 Urban Law. 375 (2004). See generally Wilson, "A Large Fortune or a Small Fortune" to Drop That Appeal: Developers Charge Project Opponents with Illicit Motives in Recent Land Use Damage Litigation, 36 Urban Law. 571 (2004). These statutes are credited with helping reduce frivolous litigation while allowing genuine grievances to be heard. See Note, Reducing Uncertainty in Anti-SLAPP Protection, 71 Ohio St. L.J. 845 (2010); Note, Paris Hilton Avoids Getting Slapped: The Application of California's Anti-SLAPP Statute to a Right of Publicity Claim, 18 Villanova Sports & Ent. L.J. 289 (2011); Comment, A Cure for a "Public Concern": Washington's New Anti-SLAPP Law, 86 Wash. L. Rev. 663 (2011). As to the scope of Anti-SLAPP statutes, see Wilson & Shaw, Robber Barons, Back-Stabbers and Extortionists: How Far Does Anti-SLAPP Protection Go?, 43 Urban Law. 745 (2011). As to experiences in one jurisdiction, see Note, The Dark Side of Direct Democracy: Protecting Political Speech From the Use of SLAPPs in North Dakota's Political Process, 89 North Dakota L. Rev. 181 (2013).

[43] In re Lower Moreland Township Ordinance, 81 Pa.D. & C. 387 (Pa.Quar.Sess.1951). On the difference between ordinances and resolutions, see generally Chapter 11 *supra*. In some jurisdictions, considerable power to adopt particular regulations is granted by statute or home-rule charters to the planning commission itself. See Forest Constr. Co. v. Planning & Zoning Commission, 155 Conn. 669, 236 A.2d 917

requirement that public notice be given and a public hearing be held before the regulations are adopted.[44] The planning commission of the locality must then apply these regulations, as well as the more general master plan if there is one, in ruling on applications for subdivision approval.[45] Conditions may be imposed by the planning commission on the subdividers—but the power to impose the particular conditions or "exactions" must be expressed or implied in state constitution or statute or in local home-rule charter,[46] and the conditions must meet the usual test, as with all exercises of the police power, of being neither arbitrary nor unreasonable.[47]

(1967). See generally Listokin & Walker. The Subdivision and Site Plan Handbook (Center for Urban Policy Research 1989) (with a model subdivision and site-plan ordinance).

[44] See Beach v. Planning & Zoning Commission, 141 Conn. 79, 103 A.2d 814 (1954). But cf. Hopkins v. MacCulloch, *supra* note 39, where, in a situation not involving plat approval, it was held that protesting persons who had actual notice of the hearing, and appeared there themselves, could not subsequently challenge the lack of legally sufficient notice of the meeting.

[45] See J & M Realty Co. v. City of Norwalk, 156 Conn. 185, 239 A.2d 534 (1968); South East Property Owners & Residents Association v. City Plan Commission, 156 Conn. 587, 244 A.2d 394 (1968); Jeffrey v. Platting Board of Review, 103 R.I. 578, 239 A.2d 731 (1968) (planning board has no discretion to disapprove a plat that conforms to the rules the board has adopted). Even the "precise" regulations for subdivisions are sometimes rather vague and not too detailed—and this condition has been recognized as necessary because of the many variables that may arise as to individual subdivisions. See Forest Construction Co. v. Planning and Zoning Commission, *supra* note 43. Some states require that a public hearing be held on each application for subdivision-plat approval.

[46] Avonside Inc. v. Zoning and Planning Commission of Avon, 153 Conn. 232, 215 A.2d 409 (1965); Rosen v. Village of Downers Grove, 19 Ill.2d 448, 167 N.E.2d 230 (1960); Baltimore Planning Commission v. Victor Development Co., 261 Md. 387, 275 A.2d 478 (1971); Castle Estates, Inc. v. Park and Planning Board, 344 Mass. 329, 182 N.E.2d 540 (1962); Longridge Builders v. Princeton Township, 92 N.J.Super. 402, 223 A.2d 640 (1966), aff'd 98 N.J.Super. 67, 236 A.2d 154, aff'd 52 N.J. 348, 245 A.2d 336 (finding no authority in township to order subdivider to pave a road outside his development); Midtown Properties, Inc. v. Township of Madison, 68 N.J.Super. 197, 172 A.2d 40 (1961), aff'd 78 N.J.Super. 471, 189 A.2d 226 (1963) (finding that municipality could not require subdivider to pay for construction of schools since this was not authorized by state); Sanchez v. City of Santa Fe, 82 N.M. 322, 481 P.2d 401 (1971); In re Lake Secor Development Co., 141 Misc. 913, 252 N.Y.S. 809 (1931), aff'd 235 App.Div. 627, 255 N.Y.S. 853 (1932); State ex rel. Kahler-Ellis Co. v. Cline, 69 O.L.A. 305, 125 N.E.2d 222 (Com.Pl.1954); City of Corpus Christi v. Unitarian Church, 436 S.W.2d 923 (Tex.Civ.App.1968), ref'd n.r.e. See Coronado Development Co. v. City of McPherson, 189 Kan. 174, 368 P.2d 51 (1962) (municipality could not impose fee, based on appraised value of subdivision, where was not authorized by statute); Battaglia v. Wayne Township Planning Board, 98 N.J.Super. 194, 236 A.2d 608 (1967) (requiring landowner to grant 50-foot easement, post bond to cover cost of improving it as a road and ultimately dedicate road to township constituted taking of property); Skinner v. Gilcrease Hills Development Corp., 548 P.2d 679 (Okl.App.1976) (planning commission cannot authorize developer to use land other than its own).

On the scope of implications in this area, see Ayres v. City Council of Los Angeles, 34 Cal.2d 31, 207 P.2d 1 (1949); Frank Ansuini, Inc. v. City of Cranston, 107 R.I. 63, 264 A.2d 910 (1970) (authority to require dedication of park-land could be inferred, though the specific condition here imposed was ruled unreasonable); Prudential Trust Co. v. City of Laramie, 492 P.2d 971 (Wyo.1972) (right to approve plat necessarily carries with it the right to set reasonable pre-requisites).

As with the master plan itself (see note 29 *supra* and accompanying text), subdivision regulations will usually be found inapplicable to land owned or controlled by the state or federal government. See Sangre de Cristo Development Corp. v. City of Santa Fe, 84 N.M. 343, 503 P.2d 323 (1972), cert. denied 411 U.S. 938, 93 S.Ct. 1900, 36 L.Ed.2d 400 (planning controls could not be imposed on Indian lands; control had been pre-empted by the federal government).

[47] See Gordon v. City of Warren, 29 Mich.App. 309, 185 N.W.2d 61 (1971), aff'd 29 Mich.App. 309, 185 N.W.2d 61 (1971); State ex rel. Noland v. St. Louis County, 478 S.W.2d 363 (Mo.1972); Harris v. Salem County Planning Board, 123 N.J.Super. 304, 302 A.2d 552 (1973) (subdivider could be required to install off-site improvements, and pay part of the cost, if improvements bore a reasonable connection to needs of subdivision); Deerfield Estates v. Township of East Brunswick, 60 N.J. 115, 286 A.2d 498 (1972); Brazer v. Borough of Mountainside, 55 N.J. 456, 262 A.2d 857 (1970) (costs that subdivider is forced to assume must bear reasonable relationship to needs created by, and benefits conferred upon, the subdivision); Westchester Reform Temple v. Brown, 22 N.Y.2d 488, 293 N.Y.S.2d 297, 239 N.E.2d 891 (1968). If the conditions are reasonable, they will normally be upheld as not amounting to a "taking" of property without due process, even though no

Requirements that subdividers dedicate land within the proposed subdivision for public streets are among the most common conditions and have generally been upheld.[48] Courts have also upheld some more far-reaching requirements, such as that the subdivider pave and improve the streets within the subdivision,[49] and that the subdivider dedicate land for school and recreational purposes.[50] Three new types of

---

compensation is paid the subdivider. See Associated Home Builders v. City of Walnut Creek, 4 Cal.3d 633, 94 Cal.Rptr. 630, 484 P.2d 606 (1971), appeal dism'd 404 U.S. 878, 92 S.Ct. 202, 30 L.Ed.2d 159 (1971); Pioneer Trust and Savings Bank v. Village of Mount Prospect, 22 Ill.2d 375, 176 N.E.2d 799 (1961) (ordinance requiring dedication for recreational and educational facilities in subdivision invalid where need for such facilities not specifically attributable to subdivision). Cf. Ayres v. City Council of Los Angeles, *supra* note 46, indicating that a municipality may require a developer to provide streets necessitated by activity within the subdivision but not to provide a major thoroughfare the need for which arises from the activity of the whole community. It is sometimes said that the developer is not being forced to meet the required conditions, but is only making a voluntary improvement in return for being given the requested approval. See Ridgefield Land Co. v. City of Detroit, 241 Mich. 468, 217 N.W. 58 (1928). As to the possibility of a governmental "taking" (requiring compensation) being found, see also Section 19.2, note 24, and accompanying text.

[48] See Bellefontaine Neighbors v. J.J. Kelley Realty & Building Co., 460 S.W.2d 298 (Mo.App.1970); Kligman v. Lautman, 91 N.J.Super. 488, 221 A.2d 231 (1966); McKain v. Toledo City Plan Commission, 26 Ohio App.2d 171, 270 N.E.2d 370 (1971) (but municipality cannot compel dedication of street outside the development and unrelated to the planned subdivision). But cf. Schwing v. City of Baton Rouge, 249 So.2d 304 (La.App.1971), application denied 259 La. 770, 252 So.2d 667 (dedication requirement confiscatory where primary benefit would be to general public). Courts often say that there must be a reasonable nexus between the exaction imposed on the subdivider and the proposed subdivision. See Howard County v. JJM, Inc., 301 Md. 256, 482 A.2d 908 (1984) (developer could not be required to set aside land for highway where there was no showing of nexus between the highway project and the developer's subdivision). Cf. Roberts v. City of Bethany, 668 P.2d 350 (Okl. App. 1977), opinion modified 668 P.2d 332 (1979), where a requirement that an individual landowner, in return for a building permit to remodel and enlarge his house, dedicate a right-of-way to the city was invalidated as an unconstitutional taking without compensation.

[49] See Pratt v. Adams, 229 Cal.App.2d 602, 40 Cal.Rptr. 505 (Dist.Ct.1964); Allen v. Stockwell, 210 Mich. 488, 178 N.W. 27 (1920); Blevens v. City of Manchester, 103 N.H. 284, 170 A.2d 121 (1961); Noble v. Chairman and Members of Township Committee, 91 N.J.Super. 111, 219 A.2d 335 (1966), cert. denied 48 N.J. 120, 223 A.2d 497 (1966); Application of Se-Frank Developers v. Gibson, 5 A.D.2d 687, 169 N.Y.S.2d 136 (1957); Brous v. Smith, 304 N.Y. 164, 106 N.E.2d 503 (1952). But cf. Longridge Builders, Inc. v. Planning Board of Princeton Township, 92 N.J.Super. 402, 223 A.2d 640 (1966), aff'd 98 N.J.Super. 67, 236 A.2d 154, aff'd 52 N.J. 348, 245 A.2d 336 (subdivider could not be compelled to construct or improve streets beyond his subdivision).

[50] See Aunt Hack Ridge Estates, Inc. v. Planning Commission of Danbury, 160 Conn. 109, 273 A.2d 880 (1970); Admiral Development Corp. v. Maitland, 267 So.2d 860 (Fla.App.1972); Billings Properties v. Yellowstone County, 144 Mont. 25, 394 P.2d 182 (1964); Midtown Properties, Inc. v. Township of Madison *supra* note 46; Jenad, Inc. v. Village of Scarsdale, 18 N.Y.2d 78, 271 N.Y.S.2d 955, 218 N.E.2d 673 (1966); Jordan v. Village of Menomonee Falls, 28 Wis.2d 608, 137 N.W.2d 442 (1965), appeal dism'd 385 U.S. 4, 87 S.Ct. 36, 17 L.Ed.2d 3. See generally Pioneer Trust & Savings Bank v. Village of Mount Prospect, *supra* note 47, where a requirement that a developer dedicate land for a school site was found an unconstitutional taking and the court laid down a strict standard: If the requirement imposed on a developer is within statutory grants of power and if the burden is specifically attributable to the developer's activity, the requirement is permissible; otherwise, it is not. Requirements that developers provide water and/or sewer facilities as a condition of receiving plat approval have been upheld. See Mefford v. City of Tulare, 102 Cal.App.2d 919, 228 P.2d 847 (Dist.Ct.1951); Lake Intervale Homes, Inc. v. Parsippany-Troy Hills Township, 43 N.J.Super. 220, 128 A.2d 300 (1956). Cf. Willow Wind, Inc. v. City of Midwest City, 790 P.2d 1067 (Okl.1989), appeal after remand 873 P.2d 1029 (Okl.1994), upholding an ordinance requiring developers to pay the cost of connecting sewer and water lines to existing city lines, with subsequent developers making payments on a per lot and per acre basis to be used to reimburse the initial developers. As have requirements that they pay for fire hydrants. Town of Wheatland v. Allison, 577 P.2d 1006 (Wyo.1978). Cf. Crownhill Homes, Inc. v. City of San Antonio, 433 S.W.2d 448 (Tex.Civ.App.1968) (subdivision developers had to pay entire cost of local on-site water main extensions into new area; upheld). Typical cases of required dedications or fee-payments for recreational purposes include Fielder v. Board of County Comm'rs, 337 Mont. 256, 162 P.3d 67 (2007) (county commissioners, considering developer's preliminary subdivision plat for possible approval, could accept cash-in-lieu payment to satisfy parks dedication requirements, as land proposed for dedication by developer was not suitable for use as parkland); Trimen Dev. Co. v. King County, 124 Wash.2d 261, 877 P.2d 187 (1994) (imposition of park development fees in lieu of dedication of land upheld as reasonably necessary as a direct result of developer's proposed project); View Ridge Park Assoc. v. Mountlake Terrace, 67 Wash.App. 588, 839 P.2d 343 (1992)

(ordinance requiring dedication of recreational facilities in connection with multiple-unit housing construction, and allowing payments in lieu thereof, held not facially invalid); Coulter v. City of Rawlins, 662 P.2d 888 (Wyo.1983) (city found to have implied power to require developer to pay a sum in lieu of parkland dedication in order to lessen the pressure on park facilities resulting from the influx of inhabitants caused by his development). See generally Kaiser & Mertes, Acquiring Parks and Recreation Facilities Through Mandatory Dedication—A Comprehensive Guide (Venture Publ. 1986).

Some of the cases cited in notes 47–50 *supra* will be observed to involve requirements that the developer make a dedication or improvement outside his immediate development. It seems such requirements can be upheld (1) if there is express or clearly implied statutory or city-charter authorization (which often is found lacking), *and* (2) if the required dedication or improvement has direct relevance to the subdivision—*i.e.*, will be used extensively by its residents, etc. And, of course, the overall requirement of reasonableness also applies.

It is often stated that *any* dedications, improvements, *or* exactions required of a developer must be limited to needs created as a direct consequence of the particular development for which the requirement is imposed. See New Jersey Builders Ass'n v. Mayor of Bernards Township, 108 N.J. 223, 528 A.2d 555 (1987) (street, water, and sewage or drainage facility improvements must have direct causal relationship with the development, and a need for the improvement must be shown); Squires Gate, Inc. v. County of Monmouth, 247 N.J.Super. 1, 588 A.2d 824 (App.Div.1991) (county could condition approval of development on developer's contributing toward necessary offsite improvements, such as bridge). Cf. Nollan v. California Coastal Comm'n, 483 U.S. 825, 107 S.Ct. 3141, 97 L.Ed.2d 677 (1987), where the Court invalidated a state commission's conditioning a building permit for a beach house on the property owner's granting the public an easement across their beach. The Court found a lack of any nexus between the state interests involved (such as protecting public views of the beach) and the condition attached to the desired development. See generally Keenan, The *Nollan* Decision Amidst Land-Use Exactions and Impact Fees, 25 Urban Law. 817 (1993); Note, Municipal Development Exactions, the Rational Nexus Test, and the Federal Constitution, 102 Harv. L. Rev. 992 (1989). For further development of this "nexus" requirement, see Dolan v. City of Tigard, 512 U.S. 374, 114 S.Ct. 2309, 129 L.Ed.2d 304 (1994), on remand 319 Or. 567, 877 P.2d 1201 (1994). As to *Nollan, Dolan* and the literature thereon, see also Section 19.2 *supra*. On the rights of an applicant for a building permit, see Littlefield v. City of Afton, 785 F.2d 596 (8th Cir.1986) (applicant has constitutionally protected property interest where state law and city ordinance require issuance conditioned only on compliance with reasonable requirements). As to the various tests sometimes used for determining whether there is a sufficiently close relationship between a proposed development and the need for an improvement, see Callies, Property Rights: Are There Any Left? 20 Urban Law. 597, 632–37 (1988). See generally Frank & Rhodes (eds.), Development Exactions (Planners Press—American Planning Ass'n 1987).

On the assessment of "impact fees" on developers to pay the costs of improvements, services, etc. necessitated by their development, see Nelson, Development Impact Fees: Policy Rationale, Practice, Theory and Issues (Planners Press 1988), reviewed 25 Urban Law. 193 (1993); Keenan, Report of the Subcommittee on Exactions and Impact Fees, 26 Urban Law. 741 (1994); Nelson, Development Impact Fees: The Next Generation, 26 Urban Law. 541 (1994); Note, Conscripting Private Resources to Meet Urban Needs: The Statutory and Constitutional Validity of Affordable Housing Impact Fees in New York, 20 Fordham Urban L.J. 911 (1993). See also Note, Local Government Environmental Mitigation Fees: Development Exactions, The Next Generation, 45 Fla. L. Rev. 835 (1993). As to the reasonableness of impact fees, see Home Builders Ass'n v. City of North Logan, 983 P.2d 561 (Utah 1999) (city's imposition of park impact fee only on residential developments, not commercial developments, held reasonable since city could assume that residential growth placed the primary burden on park facilities); Banberry Dev. Corp. v. South Jordan City, 631 P.2d 899 (1981) (listing factors for determining the reasonableness of impact fees; *id.* at 903–04). Cf. B.A.M. Dev., L.L.C. v. Salt Lake County, 2006 UT 2, 128 P.3d 1161 (2006) (exactions are conditions imposed by the government on developers for issuance of a building permit or subdivision plat approval; they may take the form of mandatory dedications, water or sewer connection fees, or impact fees, and they may be invalidated as regulatory takings if so onerous as to amount to a direct appropriation or ouster); City of Olympia v. Drebick, 156 Wash.2d 289, 126 P.3d 802 (2006), cert. denied 549 U.S. 988, 127 S.Ct. 436, 166 L.Ed.2d 330 (2006) (under Washington statute, legislature clearly intended that impact fees are to be proportionate share of costs of improvements that are reasonably related to and reasonably benefit the particular development seeking approval). See generally Estill, Powell & Stringham, Taxing Development: The Law and Economics of Traffic Impact Fees, 16 Boston U. Pub. Int. L.J. 1 (2006); Rosenberg, The Changing Culture of American Land Use Regulation: Paying for Growth with Impact Fees, 59 SMU.L. Rev. 177 (2006). On the possible effects of Supreme Court cases, such as the *Nollan* and *Dolan* cases, *supra*, on exactions, possibly including impact fees, see Sullivan & Lester, The Role of the Comprehensive Plan in Infrastructure Financing, 37 Urban Law. 53 (2005). See generally Note, Escaping the Takings Maze: Impact Fees and the Limits of the Taking Clause, 62 Vand. L. Rev. 1315 (2009). As to the use of impact fees to encourage "green" developments, see Note, Making It Easy to Be Green: Using Impact Fees to Encourage Green Building, 83 N.Y.U. L. Rev. 532 (2008). Impact fees have been used to finance schools. See Roessler, Public Education, Local Authority, and Democracy: The Implied

requirement have appeared in recent decades: (1) In some states, subdividers are now required to prepare environmental impact statements, since it is reasoned that subdivisions will often have a substantial effect on the surrounding environment.[51] (2) Some states have experimented with ordinances—sometimes called "inclusionary zoning"—requiring developers, as a condition of plat approval, to include a certain amount of lowcost housing in their residential developments.[52] One court has ruled such a requirement unconstitutional as amounting to a taking of the developer's property

---

Power of North Carolina Counties to Impose School Impact Fees, 33 Campbell L. Rev. 239 (2011). See generally Gowder & Wenter, Recent Developments in Exactions and Impact Fees, 40 Urban Law. 587 (2008) (also exploring the effects of the U.S. Supreme Court's *Nollan* and *Dolan* cases on the law of required dedications of land, commonly called "exactions"). Impact fees are very often used to pay for roads. See Buckskin Properties, Inc. v. Valley County, 300 P.3d 18 (Idaho 2013). As to opposition to impact fees, see Weinstein, The Ohio Supreme Court's Perverse Stance on Development Impact Fees and What to Do About It, 60 Clev. St. L. Rev. 655 (2012). See also on impact fees Section 19.2, note 24 *supra*, and accompanying text.

Impact fees have been held to be a form of tax and thus invalid unless the locality imposing the fee has statutory authority from the state. Mayor of Ocean Springs v. Homebuilders Ass'n of Miss., Inc., 932 So.2d 44 (Miss. 2006) (municipality had no power to assess impact fees in absence of enabling legislation). On the extent of local governmental power to impose impact fees, see generally Gowder & Wenter, Exactions and Impact Fees 2007: The Limits of Local Authority, 39 Urban Law. 645 (2007).

[51] See Mont.Code Ann. 76–3–504 (with exception in 76–3–210); N.C.Gen.Stat. § 113A–9(3). California statutes, West's Ann.Cal.Pub.Res.Code §§ 21060–69, include local government approval of subdivisions within the projects (as defined in § 21065) for which government agencies must prepare an environmental impact report before granting the approval—if the project may have a significant effect on the environment. But the State Resources Agency is authorized to grant exemptions to certain classes of project. West's Ann.Cal.Pub.Res.Code §§ 21084–86. See generally California Supreme Court Report § 10B, Duty of Private Parties to File Environmental Statement, 61 Cal.L.Rev. 559 (1973). In a number of jurisdictions, *state* agencies must now, under statutory requirements, prepare environmental impact statements before taking numerous actions, and a few of these requirements apply to certain activities of local governments as well. See West's Wash.Rev.Code Ann. §§ 43.21.010–.060. See generally Moviematic Industries Corp. v. Dade County, 349 So.2d 667 (Fla.App.1977) (ecological considerations are legitimate zoning objectives—with review of cases).

[52] See Fox & Davis, Density Bonus Zoning to Provide Low and Moderate Cost Housing, 3 Hastings Con.L.Q. 1015 (1976) (surveying ordinances in several localities); Kleven, Inclusionary Ordinances—Policy and Legal Issues in Requiring Private Developers to Build Low Cost Housing, 21 U.C.L.A.L.Rev.1432 (1974), noting experiments in Fairfax County, Virginia (invalidated by the courts—see note 53 *infra*) and Montgomery County, Maryland. See generally Franklin, Falk, & Lavin, In-Zoning: A Guide for Policy-Makers on Inclusionary Land Use Programs 131–40 (1974); Mallach, Inclusionary Housing Programs—Policies and Practices (Center for Urban Policy Research 1984); "Fairfax County Experiment," New Republic, July 24, 1971, at 11 (praising the Fairfax County plan); "Inclusionary Zoning," Parade magazine, May 25, 1980, at 17, discussing attempts at inclusionary zoning in California, Maryland, New Jersey, and Oregon. The term "inclusionary zoning" is here used to indicate the contrast with the much-criticized but widely found practice of "exclusionary zoning"—zoning that requires minimum lot sizes in residential areas, etc. and that often effectively excludes lower-income groups, and thus many members of racial minorities. See generally Section 18.4 *supra*. Some jurisdictions have required *non*residential developers, as a condition precedent to approval of their developments (such as office and commercial projects), to construct low- or moderate-income housing elsewhere in the community. This is called "linkage." See Taub, Exactions, Linkages, and Regulatory Takings: The Developer's Perspective, 20 Urban Law. 515 (1988), particularly discussing such linkage programs in Boston, Seattle, San Francisco, and Miami. *Id.* at 534–49. Often the obligation of either a residential or nonresidential developer can be satisfied by paying fees—called "housing linkage fees"—to be used in funding low- and moderate-income housing. See Holmdel Builders Ass'n v. Township of Holmdel, 121 N.J. 550, 583 A.2d 277 (1990) (ordinances required developers to pay a fee based on number of dwelling units, or square footage of residential space, that they desired to develop; fees upheld by court). See generally Alterman, Evaluating Linkage, and Beyond (1989); Collin & Lytton, Linkage: An Evaluation and Exploration, 21 Urban Law. 413 (1989); Keenan & Buchsbaum, Report of the Subcommittee on Exactions and Impact Fees, 23 Urban Law. 627 (1991); Schukoske, Housing Linkage: Regulating Development Impact on Housing Costs, 76 Iowa L. Rev. 1011 (1991). See also Merrill & Lincoln, Linkage Fees and Fair Share Regulations: Law and Method, 25 Urban Law. 223 (1993). For a study of the economics involved in inclusionary zoning, see Powell & Stringham, "The Economics of Inclusionary Zoning Reclaimed": How Effective Are Price Controls?, 33 Fla. St. U.L. Rev. 471 (2005). See generally Comment, Cracking the Foundation: Highlighting and Criticizing the Shortcomings of Mandatory Inclusionary Zoning Practices, 37 Pepperdine L. Rev. 1039 (2010).

without just compensation,[53] but it has been suggested that some courts would likely uphold the requirement as a reasonable condition in light of community needs to deal with housing problems.[54] (3) Developers of new subdivisions have in many instances been required—in order to receive necessary plat approval, building permits, etc.—to create community associations to operate and maintain the subdivision in lieu of the municipality providing traditional services therein, including street maintenance, sewer service, and water supply.[55]

---

[53] Board of Supervisors v. DeGroff Enterprises, Inc., 214 Va. 235, 198 S.E.2d 600 (1973), invalidating the Fairfax County plan, cited note 52 *supra*. See generally Annot., Validity and Construction of Zoning Ordinance Requiring Developer to Devote Specified Part of Development to Low and Moderate Income Housing, 62 A.L.R.3d 880 (1975). On inclusionary zoning as a "taking," see Berger, Inclusionary Zoning Devices as Takings: The Legacy of the Mount Laurel Cases, 70 Neb. L. Rev. 186 (1991). See generally Note, The Need for Affordable Housing: The Constitutional Viability of Inclusionary Zoning, 26 John Marshall L. Rev. 75 (1992), saying that the "not in my backyard" syndrome evidenced by the views of many voters and politicians may be a greater obstacle to inclusionary zoning than any constitutional objections. As to the problems created for urban planning and rejuvenation by the "not in my backyard" syndrome (NIMBY), see generally Marguilies, Building Communities of Virtue: Political Theory, Land Use Policy, and the "Not in My Backyard" Syndrome, 43 Syracuse L. Rev. 945 (1992). See also Ellickson, The Irony of "Inclusionary" Zoning, 54 S. Cal. L. Rev. 1167 (1981).

[54] Franklin, Falk, & Levin, In-Zoning, *supra* note 52, at 107–08. See Taxpayers Association v. Weymouth Township, 80 N.J. 6, 364 A.2d 1016 (1976), cert. denied 430 U.S. 977, 97 S.Ct. 1672, 52 L.Ed.2d 373; Maldini v. Ambro, 36 N.Y.2d 481, 369 N.Y.S.2d 385, 330 N.E.2d 403 (1975), appeal dism'd, cert. denied 423 U.S. 993, 96 S.Ct. 419, 46 L.Ed.2d 367, both upholding the creation of special zoning district for elderly persons and indicating a favorable view toward "inclusionary zoning." See generally American Bar Ass'n Advisory Comm'n on Housing & Urban Growth, Housing for All Under Law 589–92 (R. Rishman ed. 1978). See also Comment, Making Room: Why Inclusionary Zoning Is Permissible Under Washington's Tax Preemption Statute and Takings Framework, 88 Wash. L. Rev. 591 (2013); Note, Municipalities and the Increasing Need for Low and Moderate Income Housing, 28 Wash. & Lee L.Rev. 408 (1971), discussing such possibilities as a requirement that developers dedicate some of their land to the community for housing, or that payments (in lieu of low-income developments) be required of the developers to be used toward low-income housing, or that an incentive mechanism be created, whereby developers who *did* construct low-income housing would receive cash bonuses from the community.

A California court has upheld a 10% inclusionary housing ordinance on new development, imposed by the city of Napa. Home Builders Ass'n of Northern Calif. v. City of Napa, 108 Cal.Rptr.2d 60, 90 Cal.App.4th 188 (2001), cert. denied 535 U.S. 954, 122 S.Ct. 1356, 152 L.Ed.2d 353 (2002) (ten per cent of all newly constructed units must be "affordable," as defined in ordinance). See Curtin & Naughton, Inclusionary Housing Ordinance Is Not Facially Invalid and Does Not Result in a Taking, 34 Urban Law. 913 (2002).

For a general discussion of the possible use of "inclusionary zoning" to deal with housing problems, see Note, Mandatory Inclusionary Zoning—The Answer to the Affordable Housing Problem, 33 Boston College Envtl. Aff. L. Rev. 383 (2006). See also Note, Inclusionary Zoning in Westchester County, New York: Is It a Viable Tool to Reduce a County-wide Housing Crisis?, 27 Pace L. Rev. 89 (2006). On the increasing use of "inclusionary zoning," see Talbert & Costa, Current Issues in Inclusionary Zoning, 36 Urban Law. 557 (2004), listing the benefits of such programs and noting that "hundreds of communities nationwide have implemented" them. *Id.* at 558. See generally Talbert, Costa & Krumbein, Recent Developments in Inclusionary Zoning, 38 Urban Law. 701 (2006), noting that while inclusionary zoning remains a popular means of providing a sufficient supply of affordable housing, other methods are also being used, often on a more regional basis: "the use of dedicated revenue sources, programs requiring localities to provide for affordable housing, and statutes that limit the ability of localities to reject or condition housing projects in a manner that makes them infeasible." *Id.* at 701–02. See also Dickinson, Inclusionary Eminent Domain, 45 Loyola U. Chi. L.J. 845 (2014).

[55] See Siegel, The Public Role in Establishing Private Residential Communities: Towards a New Formulation of Local Government Land Use Policies That Eliminates the Legal Requirements to Privatize New Communities in the United States, 38 Urban Law. 859 (2006), noting that the increase in "gated communities" has brought about some of the rise in the number of community associations since the gated communities are necessarily managed by community associations. *Id.* at 868. As to "gated communities," see generally Section 24.1, note 10, *infra*. On the general trend toward privatization of government services, see also Section 16.2, note 33, *supra*. Homeowners' associations often play an important role in enforcing restrictive covenants against landowners. See Note, The House of the Rising Sun: Homeowners' Associations, Restrictive Covenants, Solar Panels, and the Contract Clause, 50 Nat. Resources J. 721 (2010). The associations' activities,

§ 21.5 "Timed Growth" and Other Modern Developments in Urban Planning

Besides the above-mentioned requirements imposed on subdividers, American planning law in recent decades has witnessed four developments of particular importance: (1) A number of communities have attempted to limit their growth through methods often called "timed (or phased) growth" devices. (2) "Planned unit developments," mentioned in the chapter on zoning *supra*,[56] have become common, as has the use of the closely related, less far-reaching concept of "cluster zoning." (3) Planning and zoning have increasingly been employed to achieve "green belts" around urban areas—and in general to assure adequate open space and recreational land—, and the use of zoning for such a purpose has been judicially approved. (4) Often, planning now occurs at the metropolitan or regional level, not merely on the municipal level.

The leading case on "timed growth" is *Golden v. Planning Board of Ramapo*, a New York opinion holding that the deferral of residential development until the establishment of specified public services within an area—sewers, drainage facilities, roads, etc.—was a valid exercise of the zoning power.[57] This decision has been hailed as opening a whole new era in American planning law and as marking the greatest advance in zoning since the 1926 case of *Village of Euclid v. Ambler Realty Co.*[58] Under the

---

including the providing of recreational facilities for the common use of members, are generally financed by assessments against the property owners, which can be enforced as liens on the property and can ultimately result in foreclosures. See generally Note, Collecting Unpaid Assessments: The Homeowner Association's Dilemma When Foreclosure Is No Longer a Viable Option, 19 J. L. & Pol'y 751 (2011).

56 On this subject—and also the topic of "floating zones"—see Section 18.3, notes 27–29 *supra* and accompanying text.

57 30 N.Y.2d 359, 334 N.Y.S.2d 138, 285 N.E.2d 291 (1972), appeal dism'd 409 U.S. 1003, 93 S.Ct. 436, 34 L.Ed.2d 294, and 409 U.S. 1003, 93 S.Ct. 440, 34 L.Ed.2d 294. Cf. Schenck v. City of Hudson, 997 F.Supp. 902 (N.D.Ohio 1998), aff'd 208 F.3d 215 (6th Cir.2000) (annual limit on allotments for residential development, based on level of city's infrastructure, upheld). See generally Annot., Validity of Zoning Ordinance Deferring Residential Development Until Establishment of Public Services in Area, 63 A.L.R.3d 1184 (1975). Legislation in Florida now provides that the infrastructure necessary to support real estate development must be concurrent with the development. See Levy, Living with Growth Management—Florida in the 1990's, 13 Urban, State & Local L. Newsletter, No. 3, Spring, 1990, at 9. See generally Symposium on growth management, 20 Nova. L. Rev. 585–1015 (1996), particularly Grosso, Florida's Growth Management Act: How Far We Have Come, and How Far We Have Yet to Go, at 589. Washington State has somewhat more limited requirements, applicable mainly in the more urban and urbanizing counties. See Lassar, Land Use Committee Explores Washington State Revolution, 14 Urban, State & Local L. Newsletter, No. 4, Summer, 1991, at 4. See also Thomas, Comment: Municipal Land Use Control in British Columbia, 14 Urban Law. 847 (1982). An exhaustive summary of growth-control techniques is found in Kushner, Subdivision Law and Growth Management (Clark Boardman Callaghan 1991, with annual supplements), reviewed 27 Urban Law. 173 (1995).

58 Editor's Comments, Golden v. Town of Ramapo: Establishing a New Dimension in American Planning Law, 4 Urban Lawyer ix (1972) (by Freilich). See Note, Golden v. Planning Board: Time Phased Development Control Through Zoning Standards, 38 Albany L.Rev. 142 (1973); Note, Growth Restrictions—Town Ordinance Conditioning Approval of Residential Subdivision Plan on the Availability of Necessary Municipal Services Held Valid, 1 Fordham Urban L.J. 516 (1973); Comment, *Golden v. Planning Bd. of Ramapo* Revisited: Old Lessons for New Problems, 12 Pace L. Rev. 107 (1992). See generally Elliott & Marcus, From Euclid to Ramapo: New Directions in Land Development Controls, 1 Hofstra L.Rev. 56 (1973); Comment, The Limits of Permissible Exclusion in Fiscal Zoning, 53 Boston U.L.Rev. 453 (1973) (noting the objectives of timing controls); Note, Phased Zoning: Regulation of the Tempo and Sequence of Land Development, 26 Stan. L.Rev. 585 (1974). See also Fredland, Environmental Performance Zoning: An Emerging Trend?, 12 Urban Lawyer 678 (1980), noting the tendency toward land-use controls that test the permissibility of any development by its anticipated effect on the environment of an area. The *Village of Euclid* case, cited as a landmark in several of these articles, is found at 272 U.S. 365, 47 S.Ct. 114, 71 L.Ed. 303 (1926) and is discussed in Chapter 18 *supra*. For perspectives in Urban Planning on the *Golden v. Planning Board of*

Ramapo plan, subdivision development was not permitted until, according to scheduled completion dates in the town's 18-year master plan, the availability of the designated services reached a specified level; but a prospective developer could advance the date of subdivision approval by himself providing the required services for the area.

The "smart growth" movement in modern American planning law is often thought to have received much of its impetus from the *Golden* case.[59] "Smart growth" has been described as development that balances economic expansion with environmental protection and improvement in quality of life.[60] "Smart growth" is often contrasted with "sprawl": growth that is uncontrolled and disorganized. But it has been noted that there can be benefit as well as harm from "urban sprawl."[61] The device of imposing a

---

Ramapo case from the vantage point of 30 years afterward, see the excellent collection of articles in The 30th Anniversary of *Golden v. Ramapo*: A Tribute to Robert H. Freilich, 36 Urban Law. 1–202 (2003), particularly Sullivan & Michel, *Ramapo* Plus Thirty: The Changing Role of the Plan in Land Use Regulation, *id.* at 75; and Callies, Franzese & Guth, *Ramapo* Looking Forward: Gated Communities, Covenants, and Concerns, *id.* at 177. See generally Nolon, The Contemporary Relevance of *Golden v. Ramapo*, 26 State & Local L. News, Fall, 2002, at 1.

59 See Nolon, *Golden* and Its Emanations: The Surprising Origins of Smart Growth, 36 Urban Law. 15 (2003). On the "smart growth" movement, see generally Bolen, Brown, Kiernan & Konschnik, Smart Growth: A Review of Programs State by State, 8 Hastings W.-Nw. J. Envtl. L. & Pol'y 145 (2002); Kushner, Smart Growth, New Urbanism and Diversity: Progressive Planning Movements in America and Their Impact on Poor and Ethnic Populations, 21 U.C.L.A.J. Envtl. L. & Pol'y 45 (2002–03); Symposium, Getting Bigger Better, 43 Idaho L. Rev. 323–538 (2007) (particularly Callies & Sonoda, Providing Infrastructure for Smart Growth: Land Development Conditions, *id.* at 351; and Knapp & Frece, Smart Growth in Maryland: Looking Forward and Looking Back, *id.* at 445); Symposium, Saving Spaces, Smart Growth and Beyond, 23 Temple Envtl. L. & Tech. J. 1–82 (2004) (particularly Salkin, Smart Ethics: Ethical Considerations in Promoting Smart Growth Principles, *id.* at 63). See also Section 21.3, note 17, *supra.* As to "smart growth" in a particular area of the United States, see Articles, Sustainable Growth: Evaluating Smart Growth Efforts in the Southeast, 35 Wake Forest L. Rev. 509–727 (2000). As to the role that legislation has played in the "smart growth" movement, see Zovanyi, The Role of Initial Statewide Smart-Growth Legislation in Advancing the Tenets of Smart Growth, 39 Urban Law. 371 (2007). As to the use of "smart growth" to combat urban sprawl, see Note, Halting Urban Sprawl: Smart Growth in Vancouver and Seattle, 30 Boston Coll. Int'l & Comp. L. Rev. 43 (2010). See generally Lewyn, Sprawl in Canada and the United States, 44 Urban Law. 85 (2012). See also note 61, *infra,* and Section 21.1, note 6, *supra,* and accompanying text.

60 Ohm, Reforming Land Planning Legislation at the Dawn of the 21st Century—The Emerging Influence of Smart Growth and Livable Communities, 32 Urban Law. 181, 189 (2000). See Note, Growing Pains: Maryland's Struggle to Introduce Smart Growth to a Growing Population, 18 U. Baltimore J. Envtl. L. 79 (2010); Note, Vermont's Act 183: Smart Growth Takes Root in the Green Mountain State, 32 Vt. L. Rev. 583 (2008). See generally Sullivan & Yeh, Smart Growth: State Strategies in Managing Sprawl, 45 Urban Law. 349 (2013). See also Stohr, The Local Identity of Smart Growth: How Species Preservation Efforts Promote Culturally Relevant Comprehensive Planning, 43 Envtl. L. Rep. News & Analysis 10024 (2013).

61 Buzbee, Sprawl's Political-Economy and the Case for a Metropolitan Green Space Initiative, 32 Urban Law. 367 (2000), noting that sprawl, while much criticized, does sometimes result in the creation of desirable open space; Lundgren, Beyond Zoning: Dynamic Land Use Planning in the Age of Sprawl, 11 Buffalo Envtl. L.J. 101 (2004). See generally Lewyn, Five Myths About Sprawl, 23 Harv. BlackLetter L.J. 81 (2007), reviewing Bruegmann, Sprawl: A Compact History (2005); McElfish, New Paths in Existing Law: Opportunities for Pennsylvania to Avoid Sprawl, 16 Widener L.J. 853 (2007); Welch, Containing Urban Sprawl: Is Reinvigoration of Home Rule the Answer?, 9 Vt. J. Envtl. L. 131 (2008); Comment, Rocking the Suburbs: Incentive Zoning as a Tool to Eliminate Sprawl, 22 BYU J. Public L. 255 (2007). See also on sprawl Section 21.1, note 6, *supra,* and accompanying text. As to "sprawl" versus "smart growth" and "sustainability," see generally Freilich, Sitkowski & Mennillo, From Sprawl to Sustainability: Smart Growth, New Urbanism, Green Development, and Renewable Energy (ABA Book Publishing 2d ed. 2010). "Sprawl" is generally regarded as a threat to a clean, healthy environment. See Note, Highway to the Danger Zone: Urban Sprawl, Land Use, and the Environment, 22 Geo. Int'l Envtl. L. Rev. 707 (2010). Cf. Thurston County v. Western Wash. Growth Management Hearings Bd., 164 Wash. 2d 329, 190 P.3d 38 (2008) (a goal of the state Growth Management Act is the reducing of sprawl). See generally Lewyn, Sprawl in Europe and America, 46 San Diego L. Rev. 85 (2009). Various proposals have been put forth for reducing sprawl. See Davis, A (Radical) Way to Fix Suburban Sprawl, Time magazine, June 22, 2009, at 54, mentioning construction of taller buildings,

"residential development tax"—to pay for services necessitated by such development—on all who construct a dwelling unit within a municipality has also been sustained.[62] These measures may, of course, be considered only logical outgrowths of the more traditional forms of subdivision control and of municipal taxation—but what of a moratorium on further residential development? Such moratoria—on residential development or even on building in general—have been sustained in a number of cases where the restriction was for a limited and reasonable period of time (generally two years or less) and was supported by some valid reason—such as the need to develop a comprehensive zoning plan[63] or to provide adequate flood controls.[64] A zoning ordinance prohibiting further residential building permits until "double sessions" and overcrowded classrooms in the schools were eliminated, and until sewer and water facilities met specified standards, has survived an attack based on its alleged vagueness.[65] And in the celebrated case of *Construction Industry Ass'n v. City of Petaluma*, an absolute limit of 500 new housing units per year (applying only to projects containing five or more units) was found a reasonable exercise of the police power and not an undue burden on interstate commerce.[66] Thus, it seems that growth limits of reasonable duration, and

---

increase in public mass transit, increased building of walkways, etc. As to "sustainability," see Section 21.6, note 85.

As to the occurrence of sprawl in rural areas, see Anderson, Sprawl's Shepherd: The Rural County, 100 Cal. L. Rev. 365 (2012). See also Batchis, Urban Sprawl and the Constitution: Educational Inequality as an Impetus to Low Density Living, 42 Urban Law. 95 (2010), contending that U.S. Supreme Court decisions have contributed to educational inequality, which in turn has been a factor in causing urban sprawl.

[62] City of Mesa v. Home Builders Association, 111 Ariz. 29, 523 P.2d 57 (1974) (tax imposed on dwelling units, including mobile homes and trailer spaces).

[63] See Collura v. Town of Arlington, 367 Mass. 881, 329 N.E.2d 733 (1975) (two-year moratorium); Almquist v. Town of Marshan, 308 Minn. 52, 245 N.W.2d 819 (1976) (six-month moratorium; case remanded for consideration of possible injustice in denying building permit to property owner who had applied for permit before the moratorium was adopted). Cf. Naylor v. Township of Hellam, 717 A.2d 629 (Pa.Cmwlth.Ct. 1998) (one-year moratorium, later extended for additional two months, upheld while municipality was revising its subdivision and land development ordinances). See generally Greenbaum, Land Use Interim Zoning Controls and Planning Moratoria: An Analysis Update, 18 Urban Law. 247 (1986). Some moratoria have imposed a freeze on major additions to existing houses, such as apartments built over garages. See Reinhold, Broad Limit on Growth Passes in San Francisco, N.Y. Times, Dec. 8, 1987, at B20, discussing a 120-day freeze imposed in San Francisco to give the city time to frame new zoning and open-space rules and to implement a slow-growth referendum.

[64] Cappture Realty Corp. v. Elmwood Park, 126 N.J.Super. 200, 313 A.2d 624 (1973), aff'd 133 N.J.Super. 216, 336 A.2d 30 (two-year moratorium would be reasonable). Cf. Bayshore Sewerage Co. v. Department of Environmental Protection, 122 N.J.Super. 184, 299 A.2d 751 (1973), aff'd 131 N.J.Super. 37, 328 A.2d 246 (moratorium may be justified where sewage facilities are inadequate); Sun Ridge Dev., Inc. v. City of Cheyenne, 787 P.2d 583 (Wyo.1990) (municipal moratorium on building construction in a subdivision was imposed because of unresolved drainage problems; held valid exercise of police power). But cf. Charles v. Diamond, 41 N.Y.2d 318, 392 N.Y.S.2d 594, 360 N.E.2d 1295 (1977) (moratorium on building permits or sewer attachments is valid if reasonably limited as to time, *but* dilatory tactics really designed to frustrate all private uses of property are unjustified). On the use of limitations on utility expansion to control urban growth, see Briggs, No Drip, No Flush, No Growth: How Cities Can Control Growth Beyond Their Boundaries by Refusing to Extend Utility Services, 22 Urban Law. 285 (1990); Stone, The Prevention of Urban Sprawl Through Utility Extension Control, 14 Urban Law. 357 (1982). See generally Note, Sometimes There's Nothing Left to Give: The Justification for Denying Water Service to New Consumers to Control Growth, 44 Stan. L. Rev. 429 (1992); Note, Control of the Timing and Location of Government Utility Extensions, 26 Stan. L. Rev. 945 (1974); Comment, Utility Extensions: An Untested Control on Wisconsin's Sprawl, 1977 Wis. L. Rev. 1132.

[65] Associated Home Builders v. City of Livermore, 18 Cal.3d 582, 135 Cal.Rptr. 41, 557 P.2d 473 (1976).

[66] Construction Industry Association v. City of Petaluma, 522 F.2d 897 (9th Cir.1975), cert. denied 424 U.S. 934, 96 S.Ct. 1148, 47 L.Ed.2d 342 (finding that the plaintiffs—construction association and landowners—lacked standing to raise the issue of possible interference with third parties' right to travel), reversing 375 F.Supp. 574 (N.D.Cal.) (which found an unconstitutional violation of the right to travel). See Note, Zoning

involving a reasonable amount of restriction, will be upheld. A stronger case for validity is probably presented if, as in the *Ramapo* case, the limitation is tied directly to the providing of specified services—but even an absolute numerical limit on annual growth, as in the *Petaluma* case, *can* be sustained if related to the community's basic nature and prior growth pattern.

The control of the density of population has long been recognized as a legitimate object of zoning laws. Often, such control now takes the form of "cluster zoning" or "planned unit development zoning," under either of which the municipal legislative body determines the percentage of a particular area to be devoted to open space and the percentage that can be used for dwelling units.[67] Under cluster zoning, the goal is

---

Growth Controls for the General Welfare, 55 Neb.L.Rev. 523 (1976); Note, The Petaluma Decision: Another Indication that Federal Courts Want to Avoid Land Use Litigation, 30 Sw.L.J. 794 (1976); Comment, Property: Zoning—Preservation of a Small Town Character, 16 Washburn L.J. 225 (1976) (noting that it was the comprehensiveness of the Petaluma Plan that helped it survive due process challenge—it did not attempt to provide for only a certain type of growth). See generally Hoffman & Killefer, So You Want to Move to the Suburbs: Policy Formulation and the Constitutionality of Municipal Growth-Restricting Plans, 3 Hastings Con.L.J. 803 (1976). On the lower-court opinion in *Petaluma*, see Note, 60 A.B.A.J. 1436 (1974). Boulder, Colorado, is another city that has successfully imposed a sharp limit on construction of new residential units. But see Beck v. Town of Raymond, 118 N.H. 793, 394 A.2d 847 (1978) (invalidating town's limit on the number of building permits to be issued each year—found not within the police powers delegated to town). Cf. Stoney-Brook Dev. Corp. v. Town of Fremont, 124 N.H. 583, 474 A.2d 561 (1984) (ordinance limited building permits to three per developer and limited growth to 3%; invalidated since it did not provide for ultimately relaxing or terminating the controls). On difficulties with, and criticisms of, timed growth laws, see generally Buchsbaum, Timed Growth Ordinances Rejected in New Jersey, 31 Urban Law. 823 (1999), noting Toll Bros., Inc. v. West Windsor Township, 312 N.J.Super. 540, 712 A.2d 266 (App.Div.1998), cert. denied 157 N.J. 543, 724 A.2d 803 (1998), where an intermediate appellate court panel rejected a timed growth plan as inconsistent with state statutory restrictions on moratoria.

A provision of the California evidence code requires that local governments, in enacting growth-control ordinances, balance the need for such ordinances against the need for new housing opportunities, and shifts the burden to the locality to show that an ordinance is reasonably related to protection of the public health, safety, or general welfare; and a provision of the government code relating to zoning requires a local government to consider the effect of ordinances on local housing needs and to balance those needs against the public-service needs and the available fiscal and environmental services. In Building Industry Ass'n v. City of Camarillo, 41 Cal.3d 810, 226 Cal.Rptr. 81, 718 P.2d 68 (1986), the first-mentioned section was held applicable to zoning measures enacted by the initiative process. See generally Note, Zoning: Exclusionary Zoning as a Reasonable Exercise of the Police Power, 1 Okla. C.U.L. Rev. 243 (1976); Comment, A Constitutionally Valid Justification for the Enactment of No-Growth Ordinances: Integrating Concepts of Population Stabilization and Sustainability, 19 U. Hawaii L. Rev. 93 (1997). See also Myren, Growth Control as a Taking, 25 Urban Law. 385 (1993) (posing a hypothetical growth-control ordinance and discussing its constitutional validity in the face of arguments that it amounts to a "taking"); Comment, Sedona's Sustainable Growth Ordinance: Testing the Parameters of *Dolan v. City of Tigard,* 28 Ariz. St. L.J. 1297 (1997).

A notable controversy has existed over whether government programs should attempt to stimulate growth of relatively rural regions, in order to discourage further concentration of people in thickly settled centers; or whether the government should only encourage natural growth patterns, and not create "artificial" incentives to rural growth. Compare Forrester, Urban Dynamics (M.I.T. Press 1969) (proposing improvement of rural areas in order to draw people away from urban areas), with Hansen, Rural Poverty and the Urban Crisis: A Strategy for Regional Development (Indiana Univ. Press 1971) (2 volumes; advocating natural growth patterns). See generally Gappert, Can We Help Our Cities by Leaving Them?, New Republic, May 29, 1971, at 27. Some commentators believe, of course, that growth of *world* population and industry must be halted in the near future or economic and environmental disaster will befall us. See Meadows, The Limits of Growth (1972); "Meadows: Curbing Growth," Bus. Week, May 12, 1975, at 58.

[67] The uses of "cluster zoning" and "planned unit developments" are well stated in McCarthy& Laurie Reynolds, Local Government Law in a Nutshell 231–34 (5th ed. 2003). Cf. Burroughs v. Board of County Commissioners, 88 N.M. 303, 540 P.2d 233 (1975) ("planned unit development" would not ordinarily include an overnight campground). See generally Hanke, Planned Unit Development and Land Use Intensity, 114 U.Pa.L.Rev. 15 (1965); Krasnowiecki, Planned Unit Development: A Challenge to Established Theory and Practice of Land Use Control, 114 U.Pa.L.Rev. 47 (1965); Mumford, Mother Jacobs' Home Remedies, New Yorker, Dec. 1, 1962, at 160 (noting the possible desirability, so far as crime prevention is concerned, of a

residential density no greater than that of the basic minimum-lot-size zoning district. Planned unit development zoning is more far-reaching and aims at a self-contained community or neighborhood (within the general metropolitan area) that includes a mixture of uses: residential, commercial, open-space, etc. Generally, a minimum percentage of land that must be devoted to open space is set, and maximums are established as to the percentage of the area that can be put to residential uses and to various specified commercial uses. Further provisions usually limit the number of residential units per acre and the height and proximity of residential structures. The validity of planned unit development zoning was upheld in a leading case from Pennsylvania—which, as many authorities do, seemed to use the terms "cluster zoning" and "planned unit development zoning" interchangeably.[68] Sometimes a combination of cluster zoning and subdivision controls is found: developers may be allowed to reduce the minimum-lot-size requirement that would ordinarily apply to them if they donate a certain amount of land for recreational use or open space; such a system has been found a legitimate means of preventing overcrowding and of promoting the general welfare.[69]

Even apart from density limitations, the preservation of "buffer zones" or "green belts"—around certain land uses, such as factories, or around urbanized areas in general—may be considered desirable. In Europe, the idea has long been advanced, and widely accepted, that urban development should radiate from the city-center in "lobes" or "petals," separated from one another by parks, natural preserves, or agricultural areas.[70] In recent times, increased emphasis has been placed on the providing of green spaces and gardens within such cities as Paris.[71] While United States planners have

---

mixture of uses within an area); Note, The Public Trust Doctrine and Mixed-Use Development: The Proposed Golden State Warriors Arena and the Implications for Future Development on the San Francisco Bay, 20 Hastings W.-Nw. J. Envtl. L. & Pol'y 461 (2014). See also, on planned unit development and the concept of "floating zones," Section 18.3, notes 27–29, *supra* and accompanying text.

[68] Cheney v. Village 2 at New Hope, Inc., 429 Pa. 626, 241 A.2d 81 (1968) (considerable delegations of power to planning commission—as to how to fill-in the particular districts created by the legislative body—sustained). See generally Annot., Zoning: Planned Unit, Cluster, or Green Belt Zoning, 43 A.L.R.3d 888 (1972). A number of buildings constructed in the late 20th century included residences, offices and stores, making it possible for some people to live, work, and shop all in the same place, as, for instance, the Watergate complex in Washington, D.C. See Moore, PUDs in Practice (Urban Law Institute 1985). On the growth of, and planning for, planned unit developments, see generally Langdon, A Good Place to Live, Atlantic Monthly, March, 1988, at 39, 50–55. As to the relationship between planned unit developments and local governments, see Board of County Comm'rs of Boulder County v. Hygiens Fire Protection Dist., 221 P.3d 1063 (Colo. 2009). (state's Planned Unit Development Act allows for a unified plan of development as an alternative to traditional zoning requirements; fire protection district could not be prohibited by county from locating fire station in planned unit development). See also Nelson, The Mass Market for Suburban Low-Density Development Is Over, 44 Urban Law. 811 (2012), noting the trend toward "more compact, mixed-use, walkable neighborhoods." *Id.* at 811.

[69] Chrinko v. South Brunswick Township Planning Board, 77 N.J.Super. 594, 187 A.2d 221 (1963).

[70] See "Cities of the Future as Europe Sees Them," U.S. News & World Rep., Dec. 2, 1968, at 80. While the United States has not engaged in so much, or such centralized, planning of urban areas as have many European countries, some U.S. cities exhibit a degree of good planning—for instance, Washington, D.C., Savannah, Ga., and Portland, Ore. Savannah has been called our first planned city. On Savannah, see Balzer, The Savannah Spectrum, Travel/Holiday, Oct., 1980, at 48, 50; Berke, The Ideal City, Preservation magazine, July/Aug., 1998, at 36 (calling the plan of Savannah "an urban masterwork"); Williams, Savannah, Sat. Rev., Aug. 21, 1976, at 16; "Planned Lighting for a Planned City," Am. City, Jan., 1972, at 76. On Washington, D.C., see Haar & Wolf, Land-Use Planning—A Casebook on the Use, Misuse, and Re-Use of Urban Land 39–44 (4th ed. 1989); D. Lewis, District of Columbia: A Bicentennial History (The States and the Nation Series 1976). On Portland, Ore., see Ortega, Portland, Ore., Shows Nation's City Planners How to Guide Growth, Wall St. J., Dec. 26, 1995, at Al (noting the regional approach regarding land use that Portland has taken).

[71] See "The Greening of Paris," Time, Nov. 4, 1974, at 63.

sometimes lagged behind those of Europe in the designation of any open spaces, "green belts" around cities have now been created in many areas. The use of zoning to provide green belts and buffer zones has been sustained, when reasonably related to police-power purposes, by the U.S. Supreme Court,[72] and by other courts.[73]

One problem in the creation of open spaces around cities has been that most zoning in the United States has traditionally been done separately by each municipality (though such an approach does not, of course, hinder the creation of green belts around certain uses *within* each municipality). But increasingly, counties and other such units of government have been given zoning powers that can be exercised on a wider level, and even as to land that is primarily rural in nature. A number of states have now conferred on municipalities the power to zone within a certain distance of municipal limits. Statutes conferring such power have been upheld since an obvious effect on the municipality itself—and on its growth—is exercised by the land-uses found near, though outside, city boundaries.[74] The basic need is clearly for zoning and planning on a metropolitan or regional level—particularly in areas containing a large number and variety of communities—, and the need exists not just so that some open spaces can be preserved, but also in order that overall development of a region may occur in organized fashion. Such regional planning is, in many areas, coming about in three main ways: (1) Statutes sometimes authorize local planning commissions to draw plans for surrounding areas, though the plans usually have no binding effect unless and until incorporated into

---

[72] See Agins v. City of Tiburon, 447 U.S. 255, 100 S.Ct. 2138, 65 L.Ed.2d 106 (1980) (city's open-space zoning ordinance which restricted land to single-family residences and open-space use, was valid, and not a "taking"), discussed 12 Urban Law. 608 (1980). See generally Markeson, Comment, A Tale of Two Greenways: A Comparative Study of Greenway Projects, 34 Fordham Urban L.J. 1489 (2007). As to the use of land use law to prevent and contain contamination (the "Brownfields" problem), see Section 18.4, note 106, *supra*.

Another means—with a long history, but enjoying greater popularity under recent tax laws—for preserving open spaces is the "land trust": a private, charitable organization that acquires and holds interests in land for the purpose of conserving the land in perpetuity. See Fenner, Land Trusts: An Alternative Method of Preserving Open Space, 33 Vand.L.Rev. 1039 (1980). On preservation of open space, see generally Eveleth, An Appraisal of Techniques to Preserve Open Space, 9 Vill.L.Rev. 559 (1964); Moore, The Acquisition and Preservation of Open Lands, 23 Wash. & Lee L.Rev. 274 (1966); Schroder, Preservation and Control of Open Space in Metropolitan Areas, 5 Ind. Legal F. 345 (1972); Note, Techniques for Preserving Open Spaces, 75 Harv.L.Rev. 1622 (1962).

[73] See State v. Gallop Building, 103 N.J.Super. 367, 247 A.2d 350 (1968). It has been noted that open space preservation is well rooted in American tradition and that "The creation of green, civic open spaces was recognized as an important design concept in the formation of a number of the country's early cities." Griffith, Green Infrastructure: The Imperative of Open Space Preservation, 42/43 Urban Law. 259 (2010–11), discussing Philadelphia, Savannah, and New Haven as examples. See generally Reps, The Zoning of Undeveloped Areas, 3 Syracuse L.Rev. 292 (1952). See also Hallman, Growth Control: A Proposal for Handling Scattered Metropolitan Growth, 33 Land Econ. 80 (1957).

[74] See Plebst v. Barnwell Drilling Co., 243 La. 874, 148 So.2d 584 (1963); City of Syracuse v. Farmers Elevator, Inc., 182 Neb. 783, 157 N.W.2d 394 (1968); Bucholz v. City of Omaha, 174 Neb. 862, 120 N.W.2d 270 (1963); City of Raleigh v. Morand, 247 N.C. 363, 100 S.E.2d 870 (1957); Walworth Co. v. City of Elkhorn, 27 Wis.2d 30, 133 N.W.2d 257 (1965). But cf. Elias v. City of Tulsa, 408 P.2d 517 (Okl.1965) (statute found to violate ban on special laws as it applied only to cities within certain counties). When there is no constitutional or statutory authorization, however, municipalities do *not* have power to zone extraterritorially. Roberson v. City of Montgomery, 285 Ala. 421, 233 So.2d 69 (1970); City of Carlsbad v. Caviness, 66 N.M. 230, 346 P.2d 310 (1959). See State v. Owen, 242 N.C. 525, 88 S.E.2d 832 (1955) (ordinance zoning extraterritorial property was invalid under enabling statute existing at time of its enactment and was not validated by mere amendment of statute). On territorial limits on municipal powers, see generally Section 8.6 *supra*. On possible use of a "regional" or "landscape" approach to metropolitan development in order to promote green space within urban areas, see "Encountering the Countryside-I," The New Yorker, Aug. 21, 1989, at 40, 52–69. On regional planning as to commercial developments, see Saxer, Local Autonomy or Regionalism?: Sharing the Benefits and Burdens of Suburban Commercial Development, 30 Ind. L. Rev. 659 (1997).

zoning legislation by the authority having zoning power over the area.[75] (2) In states where counties are authorized to zone land, representation on the county zoning body is usually provided for municipalities within that county, and municipal participation in zoning decisions for the entire county is often extensive.[76] Thus, a considerable degree of county-wide co-ordination can be achieved. (3) In a number of states, legislation authorizes the preparation of regional master plans, and often the implementation of zoning in accord with such plans, for large areas.[77] As with county-wide zoning, such

---

[75] See Sanders v. Snyder, 113 Ohio App. 370, 178 N.E.2d 174 (1960) (applying Ohio statute—Ohio Rev.Code Ann. § 713.02).

[76] See Ohio Rev.Code Ann. § 713.22, providing for the organization of county planning commissions on application of the planning commissions of a majority of the municipalities in the county. Other Ohio provisions authorize municipal planning commissions to cooperate with the planning commissions of other municipalities and of counties to form a regional planning commission; allow municipal planning commissions to adopt regional or county plans; and provide that such plans, if adopted, become the same as a regular municipal plan. Ohio Rev.Code Ann. §§ 713.23–.25. See State ex rel. Kearns v. Ohio Power Co., 163 Ohio St. 451, 127 N.E.2d 394 (1955) (upholding provision that no public improvement can be erected in violation of a regional plan once that plan is adopted by a municipality). See generally Kancler, Litigating the Zoning Case in Ohio: Suggestions to Fill the Textbook Void, 24 Clev.St.L.R. 33 (1975). In New York, proposed zoning changes of local units must be referred to county or regional planning commissions—whose disapproval can, however, be overridden by a supermajority vote of the local commission. N.Y.Gen.Mun.Law § 239–m. Any modifications made by the county or regional planning body are supposed to be set forth in the adoptive resolution, but noncompliance with the provision has been held not to invalidate rezoning. Bloom v. Town Board, 102 Misc.2d 938, 424 N.Y.S.2d 983 (1980), judgment modified by 80 A.D.2d 823, 436 N.Y.S.2d 355 (1981).

Some city-county planning bodies are merely advisory in nature. See Williams v. Starr, 534 P.2d 29 (Okl.App.1975) (statute authorized city-county "metropolitan area planning commission" in counties within certain population limits; upheld as not special legislation).

[77] See West's Ann.Cal.Gov.Code § 65060–65069.5 (state planning board divides state into regional planning districts); Conn.Gen.Stat.Ann. § 8.31–a; Ill.Rev.Stat. 1960, 1980 Supp., ch. 34, § 3001–88 (county may create regional planning commission, though its plans are advisory until adopted by the municipal corporations within the region); Vernon's Ann.Mo.Stat. § 251.150; N.J.Stat.Ann. 40:55D–77–82, –84, –88 (municipal corporations and counties may form regional planning boards; all powers of municipal planning boards can then be delegated to these); 53 Pa.Stat.Ann. §§ 491–99; West's Wash.Rev.Code Ann. 35.63.070. See, with emphasis on the California provisions, Marks & Taber, Prospects for Regional Planning, 4 Pacific L.J. 117 (1973); Perry, Local "General Plan" in California, 9 San Diego L.Rev. 1 (1971). For emphasis on the Illinois law, see Bowe, Regional Planning v. Decentralized Land-Use Controls; Zoning for Megalopolis, 18 De Paul L.Rev. 144 (1968). In Oregon, land-use planning has now been undertaken on a state-wide basis. Or.Rev.Stat. 197.030–.430. See Morgan & Shonwilker, Statewide Land Use Planning in Oregon with Special Emphasis on Housing Issues, 11 Urban Law. 1 (1979). See generally Leonard, Managing Oregon's Growth: The Politics of Development Planning (Conservation Foundation 1983), reviewed 15 Urban Law. 684 (1983). See also on Oregon's regional problem-solving process, Ainsworth & Sullivan, Regional Problem Solving in Action: Lessons From the Greater Bear Creek Valley RPS Process, 46 Urban Law. 269 (2014). Hawaii also has statewide land-use regulations, administered by a state commission. See Callies, Regulating Paradise: Land Use Controls in Hawaii (Univ. of Hawaii Press 1984). On past problems and future prospects of the Hawaii system, see generally Lowry, Evaluating State Land Use Control: Perspectives and Hawaii Case Study, 18 Urban L Ann. 85 (1980); Mandelker & Kolis, Whither Hawaii?, 1 U. Hawaii L. Rev. 48 (1979). On the statewide land-use restrictions adopted in Vermont, see McCullough, Historic Preservation and Land Use Control at the State Level—Vermont's Act 250, 14 Brit. Col. Envtl. Affairs L. Rev. 1 (1986). Vermont's law provides for direct state-level control of large building projects. See In re Wal-Mart Stores, Inc., 167 Vt. 75, 702 A.2d 397 (Vt. 1997), where a land-use permit for a Wal-Mart Store was invalidated due to potential adverse effects on other businesses and on the environment. See generally Note, Staving Off the Pillage of the Village: Does *In re Wal-Mart Stores, Inc.* Offer Hope to Small Merchants Struggling for Economic Survival Against Box Retailers?, 54 J. Urban & Contemp. L. 323 (1998). Washington State has also adopted some statewide planning procedures. See Comment, Administrative Forces in Oregon's Land Use Planning and Washington's Growth Management, 12 J. Envtl. L. & Litig. 115 (1997), comparing the Oregon and Washington approaches. On the increased emphasis on regionalism in Florida's growth-management law, see Van Rooy, The Development of Regional Impact in Florida's Growth Management Scheme: The Changing Role in Regionalism, 19 J. Land Use & Envtl. L. 255 (2004). It has been observed that the increasing importance of regionalism may lead to conflicts between home-rule principles, on the one hand, and, on the other, the role of regional governance. See Alexander, Inherent Tensions Between Home Rule and Regional Planning, 35 Wake Forest L. Rev. 539 (2000). But a

regional zoning generally involves considerable participation by municipalities within the area. The validity of regional planning and zoning has been upheld;[78] and there is increasing recognition that control of land-use must often occur, if it is to be effective and orderly, on a wide-area basis.

§ 21.6 Future of Urban Planning

What does the future hold for urban planning? Technology has made new tools available to planners; for instance, data from spaceflights can be used in projecting population trends and planning transportation systems for urban areas.[79] Increasingly, the impact of urban developments on the environment must, in light of modern ecological concerns, be weighed;[80] housing developments must be planned with an eye to energy-

---

regional approach may help in the control of urban sprawl. See Calthorpe & Fulton, The Regional City: Planning for the End of Sprawl (2001), reviewed in Miller, Developing Regionalism, 11 N.Y.U. Envtl. L.J. 842 (2003). On regionalism in land-use control, see also Section 21.2 *supra*.

[78] See State ex rel. Kearns v. Ohio Power Co., *supra* note 23; State ex rel. Ohio Power Co. v. Regional Planning Commission, 158 Ohio St. 496, 110 N.E.2d 415 (1953). See generally Note, Regional Development and the Courts, 16 Syracuse L.Rev. 600 (1965); Note, Zoning: Looking Beyond Municipal Borders, 1965 Wash.U.L.Q. 107. See also Danielson & Doig, New York: The Politics of Urban Regional Development (Univ. of Calif. Press 1982). On the use of statewide and regional limitations on growth, see Curtin & Danforth, Looking Beyond the City Limits: Regional Approaches to the Growth Crisis, 22 Urban Law. 701 (1990). See also Freilich & Ragsdale, Timing and Sequential Controls—The Essential Basis for Effective Regional Planning: An Analysis of the New Directions for Land Use Control in the Minneapolis-St. Paul Metropolitan Region, 58 Minn. L. Rev. 1009 (1974).

[79] See "Data for Urban Planning Taken in NASA Flights," Houston Post, Aug. 9, 1970, at 5A. Cf. Callison v. Land Conservation & Dev. Comm'n, 145 Or.App. 277, 929 P.2d 1061 (1996) (city's use of aerial photographs to locate watershed areas held reasonable). See also Note, Use of Computers and Technology in Land Use Control, 18 Rutgers Computer & Tech. L.J. 403 (1992).

As to the future of cities in general, and city planning in particular, see R. Rogers & A. Power, Cities for a Small Country (Cambridge Univ. Press 2000). As to the importance of water supply in future urban planning, see Hanak, Show Me the Water Plan: Urban Water Management Plans and California's Water Supply Adequacy Laws, 4 Golden Gate U. Envtl. L. J. 69 (2010); Moose, The Relationship Between Water Supply and Land Use Planning: Leading Cases Under the California Environmental Quality Act, 4 Golden Gate U. Envtl. L. J. 27 (2010). See also Brook, A History of Future Cities (Norton 2013), reviewed The New Yorker, March 18, 2013, at 81; Schleicher, City Unplanning, 122 Yale L. J. 1670 (2013)

[80] See Yannacone, Rahenkamp, & Cerchione, Impact Zoning: Alternative to Exclusion in the Suburbs, 8 Urban Lawyer 417 (1976). Some municipalities have passed ordinances requiring "impact statements" before major public or private projects are undertaken. See Macbeth & Sofaer, Recent Developments in Local Government Law, 7 Urban Lawyer 1, 34 (1975), noting examples of such ordinances in Bowie, Maryland, and Modesto, California. It has been held that such statements could, under state law in California, be required even of the state government itself. City of Orange v. Valenti, 37 Cal.App.3d 240, 112 Cal.Rptr. 379 (Dist.Ct.1974) (suit filed by city). But state and local requirements will generally be inapplicable to federal land. See Ventura County v. Gulf Oil Corp., 601 F.2d 1080 (9th Cir.1979), aff'd, 445 U.S. 947, 100 S.Ct. 1593, 63 L.Ed.2d 782 (1980) (lessee of federal government could not be required to obtain "open space use permit" from county planning commission; oil lease of national forest land was involved). See generally Frelich, White-Wasson, & Cofer, 1979–1980 Annual Review of Local Government Law: Municipal Liability and Other Certain Uncertainties, 12 Urban Lawyer 577, 615–16 (1980); "Justices Narrow Zoning Powers for Localities," Wall St. J., June 11, 1980, at 10, col. 1. See also Chapter 7 *supra* on federal-local relations.

It should also be noted that much "environmental legislation" merely requires that certain government agencies *consider* environmental factors in deciding on whether, when, and where to undertake projects. Other factors may nonetheless be found by an agency to outweigh the environmental ones. See Strycker's Bay Neighborhood Council, Inc. v. Karlen, 444 U.S. 223, 100 S.Ct. 497, 62 L.Ed.2d 433 (1980) (H.U.D. had considered environmental consequences of its decision to redesignate site for low-income housing; nothing more required). CompareSpyke, Charm in the City: Thoughts on Urban Ecosystem Management, 16 J. Land Use & Envtl. L. 153 (2001).

efficiency in supplying heat and cooling, and in satisfying other needs of residents.[81] Inevitably, much future development will be guided by prevailing forms of transportation—many of which may still be on the drawingboards, and many of which may utilize underground or aboveground spaces.[82] As indicated by the popularity of suburban shopping centers, many urban areas may no longer be centered around a single core, or "downtown," but will consist of a number of residential areas, each clustered around its own commercial center.[83] Probably there will be continued outcries against the proliferation of "high-rise" buildings—with their high densities and obstruction of air circulation[84]—, and perhaps such protests will eventually affect building trends. Certainly there will be continued efforts to bring the public (governmental) and private

---

[81] Thus, Italian-born architect Paolo Soleri has coined the term "arcology"—a combination of architecture and ecology—to describe his concepts for new urban environments. See Soleri, Arcology: The City in the Image of Man (M.I.T. Press 1969); "Arcology: An Answer for the Years Ahead," Parks & Recreation, May, 1970, at 41. Soleri is putting his ideas into effect in the city—Arcosanti—he is erecting north of Phoenix, Arizona. See Davis, Arcosanti: Dream City, Newsweek, Aug. 16, 1976, at 78; Karp, Designer in the Desert, Horizon, Autumn, 1970, at 30; "Spacious Living in a Heap—Cities that Climb into the Sky," Life, Dec. 5, 1969, at 102; "In Arizona: A City Has to Be Built," Time, Aug. 18, 1980, at 6. On the financing of Arcosanti, see Simington, A City of the Future Blossoms in the Desert, American Way, Sept., 1980, at 120 (most revenue is generated by the project itself—tour donations, sale of souvenirs, etc.; the project has also received a few grants; all funding is channeled through a foundation). But Arcosanti has had financial difficulties. See "A Dream City, Or a Ghost Town?," Newsweek, March 23, 1981, at 14. Development has proceeded much more slowly than had originally been anticipated. See Severson, Back to the Future—Arcosanti Vision Still Evolving, (Tucson) Arizona Daily Star, June 27, 1997, at D14 (population in 1997 was only about 55, instead of the previously projected 7000). Paolo Soleri died in 2013. One obituary described Arconsanti at that time as "an unfinished community north of Phoenix intended to maximize quality of life while minimizing ecological damage." Time magazine, April 22, 2013, at 18.

[82] See Young, What's to Come, Life, Dec. 24, 1965, at 143–67, discussing—and providing illustrations of—possible designs for cities of the future. See generally Lynch, The Image of the City (M.I.T. Press 1960). See also Sternlieb & Schwartz, New Jersey Growth Corridors—Site Selection and Locational Satisfaction of New Firms: A Survey of Industrial Location (Center for Urban Policy Research 1986), discussing the effect of highways on site selection for industrial facilities. On the effect that transportation should have on urban planning, see generally Cervero, Growing Smart by Linking Transportation and Urban Development, 19 Va. Envtl. L.J. 357 (2000); Pollard, Follow the Money: Transportation Investments for Smarter Growth, 22 Temple Envtl. L. & Tech. J. 155 (2004).

[83] See "A Model City on Indian Lands," U.S. News & World Rep., June 23, 1969, at 96, discussing a proposed development in the Four Corners region of the Southwestern United States. The community, according to some proposals, would be divided into "clusters" without any specific downtown. *Id.* at 98. This seems the direction some long-existing cities are taking—unless efforts to revive traditional "downtowns" are successful.

[84] See Brugmann & Sletteland (eds.), The Ultimate Highrise: San Francisco's Mad Rush Toward the Sky (1971); Doxiades, The Great Urban Crimes that We Permit by Law (World Peace Through Law Center 1973) (citing many sources). On restrictions enacted in San Francisco to limit building of skyscrapers (particularly because of their contributing to congestion and noise), see "Outlawing the Modern Skyscraper," Time, July 22, 1985, at 56. On the wind problems created by "high-rise" buildings and on efforts of architects and city planners to alleviate those problems, see Zuckerman & Seligman, Working to Tame Urban Gusts, USA Today, Feb. 17, 1984, at 3A. Also notable are measures taken in New York City and San Francisco to "ban blank walls"—*i.e.,* zone so as to allow only retail uses at street level in commercial buildings, in an effort to revitalize city centers and stop the proliferation of blank walls, which have become the dominant feature of some downtowns. See "Drawing a Blank Downtown," Time, April 4, 1983, at 61.

On general trends in urban architecture and design, see "Whatever Became of the Future?," Time, June 27, 1983, at 58, reporting on the 33rd annual International Design Conference at Aspen, Colorado, and noting that the popularity of historic preservation is, in part, a rebellion against "modern" designs. See generally Mansfield, Cosmopolis: Yesterday's Cities of the Future (Center for Urban Policy Research 1990), describing plans for urban "utopias" that were put forth in the past but never fulfilled. For a modern proposal of a utopia, see Lynch, Good City Form (MIT Press 1984). On what the "city of the future" will be like, see Matthews, 2050: A Place Odyssey, Preservation magazine, Sept./Oct., 1999, at 62.

(business) sectors of the community together in joint efforts at mapping plans for the physical, cultural, and economic rejuvenation of troubled urban areas.[85]

---

[85] See "Toward a Master Plan to Meet City Ills," U.S. News & World Rep., Dec. 23, 1968, at 24. On the efforts of Partners for Livable Places, a nonprofit coalition of about 300 groups ranging from the American Council for the Arts to the National Trust for Historic Preservation, see "Toward More Livable Cities," Time, Nov. 2, 1981, at 109. The coalition has attempted to shift the trend in urban architecture and design away from monumental construction toward historic restoration, preservation of local tradition, and creation of humble touches. On the increased popularity of historic preservation and the resulting rejuvenation of some downtown areas, see "Spiffing Up the Urban Heritage," Time, Nov. 23, 1987, at 72. On the use of old buildings for new purposes, see Martin, Adaptive Use (Urban Land Institute 1980), reviewed 25 Urban Law. 695 (1993). On the return to some town-planning traditions of the early 20th century and prior periods, see Langdon, A Good Place to Live, Atlantic Monthly, March, 1988, at 39. See generally as to trends in planning Bozung & Alessi, Recent Developments in Environmental Preservation and the Rights of Property Owners, 20 Urban Law. 969 (1988).

On the "New Urbanism" movement, which emerged in the late 1970s and early 1980s and which seeks to reform conventional planning and real estate development in many areas, such as urban and suburban infill development, see Braun, Growth Management and New Urbanism: Legal Implications, 31 Urban Law. 817 (1999); Sitkowski & Ohm, Enabling the New Urbanism, 34 Urban Law. 935 (2002) (New Urbanist developments are intended to reflect techniques popular prior to World War II, such as more compact, pedestrian friendly, mixed-use communities). See generally Ohm & Sitkowski, The Influence of New Urbanism on Local Ordinances—The Twilight of Zoning?, 35 Urban Law. 783 (2003). See also Ohm & Sitkowski, Integrating New Urbanism and Affordable Housing Tools, 36 Urban Law. 857 (2004), noting that despite New Urbanism's supposed emphasis on diversity of housing, "observers have criticized traditional neighborhood developments and other New Urbanist-influenced projects for not meeting diversity of housing needs." *Id.* On the relationship of "New Urbanism" to other movements in planning, see Blaesser & Cody (eds.), Redevelopment Planning, Law, and Project Implementation: A Guide for Practitioners (ABA Section of State & Local Government 2d ed. 2011); the first edition was reviewed by Gowder, 32 State & Local News, No. 2, at 5 (Winter, 2009), noting "The convergence of three movements, in particular—Smart Growth, New Urbanism, and Green Building—has profoundly influenced government land use and development policies, and the minds of the consuming public." *Id.* As to the effect of New Urbanism on regional planning, see Note, How Localism's Rationales Limit New Urbanism's Success and What New Regionalism Can Do About It, 41 Fordham Urb. L. J.1085 (2014). .

The key ingredient in many modern planning efforts and proposals is "sustainability." See Foy, Complexities of Urban Sustainability: Using Local Land-Use Authority to Achieve Environmental Goals, 3 Charlotte L. Rev. 23 (2011); Long, Sustainability Starts Locally: Untying the Hands of Local Governments to Create Sustainable Communities, 10 Wyo. L. Rev. 1 (2010). As to the importance of considering possible climate change as a component of sustainability, see Farber, Adaptation Planning and Climate Impact Assessments: Learning From NEPA's Flaws, 39 Envtl. L. Rep. News & Analysis 10605 (2009); Symposium, It's Not Easy Building Green: Legal and Political Issues in Sustainable Development, 34 Wm. & Mary Envtl. L. & Pol'y Rev. 1–279 (2009), especially Salkin, Sustainability and Land Use Planning: Greening State and Local Land Use Plans and Regulations to Address Climate Change Challenges and Preserve Resources for Future Generations, *id.* at 121. See generally on sustainability Bryant, Red, White and Green: A Federal Sustainability Vision for the National Capital, 37 Wm. & Mary Envtl. L. & Pol'y Rev. 1 (2012); Peck, Sustainable Development and the Reconciliation of Opposites, 57 St. Louis U. L. J. 151 (2012); Symposium, Sustainable Cities: Harnessing Urbanization to Achieve Social and Environmental Goals, 43 Envtl. L. Rep. News & Analysis 10083–10094 (2013); Symposium, Saving the Cities: How to Make America's Urban Core Sustainable in the Twenty-First Century, 33 St. Louis U. Pub. L. Rev. 1–190 (2013); Frieders, Foundations of Sustainable Development Law, Regulation, and Planning (ABA Section of Real Property, Trust, and Estate Law 2013). See also Norton, Agenda 21 and Its Discontents: Is Sustainable Development a Global Imperative or Globalizing Conspiracy?, 46 Urban Law. 325 (2014), discussing the United Nations Environmental Program's 1992 Agenda 21 supporting the sustainability movement.

As to the "green movement" and its effect on urban planning, see Millan, Green Buildings and Plugging the Gaps in Environmental Laws, 27 Tulane Envtl. L. J. 43 (2013); Freilich, Sitkowski & Mennillo, Greening Local Government: Legal Strategies for Promoting Sustainability, Efficiency, and Fiscal Savings (ABA Section of State & Local Government 2013).

See generally on the future of urban planning, Symposium on Urban Development in the 21st Century, 24 Notre Dame J. L. Ethics & Pub. Pol'y 1–284 (2010), especially Carrion, A New Urban Vision for a New Urban Reality, *id.* at 1. See also Freilich & Popowitz, The Umbrella of Sustainability: Smart Growth, New Urbanism, Renewable and Green Development in the 21st Century, 42 Urban Law. 1 (2010). Compare Fitzgerald, Emerald Cities: Urban Sustainability and Economic Development (Oxford Univ. Press 2010), reviewed by Freilich & Popowitz, 42 Urban Law. 759 (2010). As to the use of "community benefits agreements" to make the land use decision-making processes more responsive to otherwise underserved communities, see Seigal, Community Benefit Agreements in a Union City: How the Structure of CBAs May Result in Inefficient, Unfair Land Use Decisions, 46 Urban Law. 419 (2014). See also Section 2.13, note 111 *supra*.

Chapter 22

EFFORTS TO ESTABLISH "NEW TOWNS"

Analysis

§ 22.1 History of "New Town" Movement

"Urban renewal," discussed *supra*,[1] attempts to rejuvenate existing, though often decayed, city centers. But another approach to urban problems—one that received considerable attention in the 1960's and '70's—is the development of whole new communities—municipalities designed to be free from the problems of pollution, congestion, and disorderly growth that have plagued older communities. As envisioned in recent times in the United States, "new towns" are large-scale developments constructed under a single or unified management; they are built according to a precise plan and include a variety of land-uses: different types of housing, commercial uses, and cultural facilities.[2] Ideally, a new town is intended to be a self-contained facility that includes not only sufficient businesses to serve the needs of its residents, but also enough businesses to provide jobs for those residents—*i.e.*, it is not merely a "bedroom community" for some larger city.[3] The development of new towns, with help sometimes supplied by government financing, allows planners and government officials to use public investment to stimulate growth where it is *wanted*, rather than to allow growth to occur in haphazard fashion.[4] And such towns give planners an opportunity to put into effect modern ideas for city planning. Thus, planned unit developments—single

---

1 See Chapter 20 *supra*.

2 See Hagman & Juergensmeyer, Urban Planning and Land Development Control Law 506 (2d ed. 1986). See generally F. Osborn & A. Whittick, The New Towns (rev. ed. 1969); Dames & Greco, A Survey of New Town Planning Considerations, 11 Current Mun. Problems 265 (1970). See also M.C. Branch, Selected Annotated Bibliography on New Town Planning and Development (Vance Bibliographies 1980); C. Moe, New Towns and Utopias (Vance Bibliographies 1980).

3 See "The City: Starting from Scratch," Time, March 7, 1969, at 25. See generally Hagman & Juergensmeyer, *supra* note 2, at 511. On successful new towns in other countries (exhibiting a variety of land uses), see E. Spiegal, New Towns in Israel: Urban and Regional Planning and Development (A. Rockwood transl. 1967); McFarland, The Administration of Alberta New Towns Program, 5 Duquesne U.L.Rev. 377 (1967); McFarland, The Administration of the English New Towns Program, 1965 Wash.U.L.Q. 17. See generally United Nations, Planning of Metropolitan Areas and New Towns (1967). See also notes 5 and 7 *infra*.

4 See "The Need to Set Priorities for National Growth," Bus. Week, Aug. 26, 1972, at 48.

developments containing a mixture of residential, commercial, and other uses—have been constructed in some new towns of recent years.[5]

Precedent for, or at least predecessors of, the recent new towns can be found in the "company towns" built as residential and shopping areas for company workers by many U.S. corporations—particularly in the period from 1830 to 1900. Examples are Pullman, Illinois; Gary, Indiana; Lowell, Massachusetts; and Kohler, Wisconsin.[6] Later decades—especially from the 1950's on—saw the development of retirement communities by private enterprises—such as Sun City and Green Valley in Arizona, and several such communities in California and Florida. But the words "new towns" in the middle part of the twentieth century came to indicate communities the development of which was, at least in part, financially supported by the federal government. Even such governmental involvement was not really new: During World War I, the United States Housing Corporation built some 25 developments (subsequently sold), including Yorkship Village, New Jersey, and Hilton, Virginia; the New Deal years of the Franklin Roosevelt administration brought efforts by the Resettlement Administration to establish several model communities, notably Greenbelt, Maryland; Greenhills, Ohio; and Greendale, Wisconsin; and during World War II, the Atomic Energy Commission established, as places of residence for those working on the atom-bomb project, the towns of Oak Ridge, Tennessee, and Los Alamos, New Mexico (which were later sold).[7] Further, there have for many years been federal statutes providing for the possible use of certain national

---

[5] See Hagman & Juergensmeyer, *supra* note 2, at Section 16, 7. See generally Babcock, An Introduction to the Model Enabling Act for Planned Residential Development, 114 U.Pa.L.Rev. 136 (1965); Comment, Planned Unit Development, 35 Mo. L.Rev. 27 (1970). See also, on planned unit developments and the related concept of "floating zones," footnotes 15–16, § 117 of Chapter 18 *supra*, and accompanying text. On planned unit developments and "cluster zoning," see generally Section 21.5, notes 64–66 *supra*, and accompanying text.

An interesting attempt to plan and construct a new community in Peru, using modern planning techniques and providing low-cost housing, is described in "Students, Faculty Will Design a New City in the Andes," Stanford Observer (Stanford University, California), June, 1971, at 4. On the development of Brazil's capital, Brasilia, in a former wilderness, also using many modern planning techniques, see Shoumatoff, Profiles—The Capital of Hope, The New Yorker, Nov. 3, 1980, at 59.

[6] See Hagman & Juergensmeyer, *supra* note 2, at 507. See generally R. Knight, Work Camps and Company Towns in Canada and the U.S.: An Annotated Bibliography (New Star Book 1975). See also J. Allen, The Company Town in the American West (1966). Different in nature, but also forerunners of more recent "planned communities," were the "utopian" communities—such as Robert Owen's New Harmony, Indiana—developed by some philanthropists and philosophers in the 1800's. Also such religious communities as Ocean Grove, New Jersey—organized under a special New Jersey law in 1869. But the New Jersey Supreme Court in modern times has ruled that the Ocean Grove legislation was unconstitutional, violating the doctrine of separation of church and state. State v. Celmer, 80 N.J. 405, 404 A.2d 1 (1979), overruling Schaad v. Ocean Grove Camp Meeting Association, 72 N.J. 237, 370 A.2d 449 (1977), and other cases. See Ryan, Ocean Grove: The Town That Made Time Stand Still, Parade magazine, June 1, 1980, at 4. See generally Arredondo, Toward a Viable Policing Model for Closed Religious Communities, 35 Am. J. Crim. L. 107 (2008).

During the early decades of the twentieth century, a notable example of a privately financed planned community, similar to later "new towns," was Coral Gables, Florida. See Wilkins, Coral Gables: 1920s New Town, Historic Preservation, Jan./March, 1978, at 6.

[7] See Hagman & Juergensmeyer, *supra* note 2, at 507–08. On the development of Greenbelt, Maryland, before, during, and after World War II, see Hunter, Greenbelt, Maryland: A City on a Hill, 63 Md. Hist. Magazine 105 (1968). See generally Knepper, Greenbelt, Maryland: A Living Legacy of the New Deal (Johns Hopkins Univ. Press 2001), reviewed 97 Md. Historical Magazine 248 (Summer, 2002).

A number of European countries have had great success with planned communities in recent decades. The "garden cities" of Britain (See McFarland, The Administration of the English New Towns Program, *supra* note 3.) and new towns in The Netherlands, Sweden, and the Soviet Union are examples. Tapiola, Finland, not far from Helsinki, has been hailed as the new town coming closest to the ideal. See "The City: Starting from Scratch," *supra* note 3; see also the other authorities cited in note 3 *supra*.

forest lands as new-town sites;[8] and since 1906, certain reclamation lands have also been available for such sites.[9]

§ 22.2 Governing a "New Town"

While there have long been examples of various kinds of "new towns," there have also been problems in their development as true model communities—particularly problems concerning their government and financing. Indeed, there may be problems in the establishment, in the first place, of any such communities since incorporation may be made difficult by population and election requirements of relevant state laws.[10] Once the community is started, the developer—or anyone with a substantial financial involvement—will surely want to retain some control over the town's continued growth; such persons will not, for instance, want the community's residents to be able, by the electoral process or otherwise, to prevent completion of the developer's plan, thus perhaps jeopardizing the investment. But state and local governments—and residents of the community—will also want a "say" in the area's development. One authority has suggested three methods by which local governments might exercise some planning control over new towns:[11] (1) If a governmental agency is undertaking the town's development, a system may be borrowed from urban-renewal projects, with the continued planning and control made a responsibility of the participating local government. (2) Or—again if a public agency is developing the community—a special public authority may be established to carry out the planning and development of the town, with a state agency given powers to supervise and review the authority's work. (3) A third method can be used where private enterprise, not the government, develops a new community. The developer first prepares a generalized plan, which is then submitted for discussion at a public hearing and for approval by a county—or other local—legislative body. After such approval of the general plan, further government control would be left largely to the local government's planning commission, which would consider—and approve or reject—the developer's more detailed "final development plan." This final plan could be considered and approved in stages rather than all at once; it would include some zoning-like restrictions on land use.[12]

But what of protecting the *developer's* continued interest—what of giving the developer some continuing control while also supplying the area with a form of municipal government? A non-profit corporation has often been established to manage privately financed new towns—with most members of the controlling board being chosen initially by the developer, but with power to select such members gradually passing to the residents as the town is completed. This corporation—often called a "homeowners' (or homes) association"—serves as a kind of local government, providing such services as

---

[8] 7 U.S.C.A. § 1012a; 6 U.S.C.A. § 478a.

[9] 43 U.S.C.A. § 561.

[10] See Hagman & Juergensmeyer, *supra* note 2, at 514–15. Cf. State ex rel. Davis v. Town of Lake Placid, 109 Fla. 419, 147 So. 468 (1933), holding that the legislature's power to establish communities does not extend to the incorporation of towns in rural, unoccupied areas. On problems—and possible solutions—regarding incorporation of new towns, see generally Mullarkey, Evolution of a New Community, 6 Harv.J.Legis. 462 (1969). Following the article is a proposed statute, designed to solve many of the problems of incorporating a new town. A New Community Local Government Act, 6 Harv.J.Legis. 484 (1969).

[11] See Hagman & Juergensmeyer, *supra* note 2, at 522–23.

[12] See, discussing possible legislation that would incorporate this method, Christensen, Land Use Control for the New Community, 6 Harv.J.Legis. 496 (1969), with proposed ordinance at 536.

utilities, road construction and maintenance, and cultural activities. Some services, such as police protection and education, may be provided at the county (or equivalent) level, while neighborhood associations are also sometimes formed to provide services—such as the maintenance of neighborhood parks and other common areas—on a *very* local level. The homeowners' association is given power to enforce restrictive covenants, servitudes, etc.[13] Numerous variations on these methods are possible; one of the advantages of new communities is that they offer a chance for experimenting with new forms of local governance—with, for instance, increased participation in government by neighborhood-level associations and by various groups of social planners.[14]

§ 22.3 Financing a "New Town"

Whatever system of government may be devised for a new community, the problem of financing remains. Large amounts of "patient money" will be needed—*i.e.*, money that cannot be repaid—and on which no substantial profit is likely to be earned—for a considerable length of time. Without government aid, few private sources could make the necessary investments. Federal governmental support for new towns was foreshadowed by 1966 legislation which provided mortgage insurance for privately financed land developments—including new-community developments.[15]

The mortgage-insurance legislation of 1966 was little utilized, and in 1968 it was replaced by a statute known as the New Communities Act.[16] This declared a national policy of encouraging the development of new communities which (1) have a full range of urban activities, (2) develop various land uses in a well-balanced and harmonious fashion, and (3) have a favorable effect on the area in which located—in terms of economic development, minimization of transportation needs, conservation of land, and provision of housing. It was stated by the new legislation that a "new community" could

---

[13] See Hagman & Juergensmeyer, *supra* note 2, at 521–22; Comment, Democracy in the New Towns: The Limits of Private Government, 36 U.Chi.L.Rev. 379 (1969). This method has been used, for instance, in the widely praised new towns of Reston, Virginia, and Columbia, Maryland. See Wedemeyer, New Towns Creating a Utopia, Houston Chronicle, Aug. 16, 1970, § 2, at 2. See generally Reichman, Residential Private Governments, 43 U.Chi.L.Rev. 253 (1976). An excellent suggestion for the use of *special districts* to supply many of the governmental needs of new towns is found in Note, New Community Development Districts: A Proposal to Aid New Town Developers, 9 Houston L.Rev. 1032 (1972). See generally Hagman & Juergensmeyer, *supra* note 2, at 516–19. Any special function districts should be subject to statutory safeguards to protect members of the public who buy property or bonds. California had bad experiences with districts of this nature which were not adequately safeguarded. See Willoughby, The Quiet Alliance, 38 S.Cal. L.Rev. 72 (1965); Comment, The Use of Special Assessment Districts as Aids in Financing Private Land Development, 53 Cal. L.Rev. 364 (1965). On special districts, see generally Chapter 2 *supra*. See also Perrenod, Special Districts, Special Purposes: Fringe Governments and Urban Problems in the Houston Area (Texas A. & M. Univ. Press 1984), reporting on suburban special districts in the Houston metropolitan area, including districts utilized for the governing of new communities in that area.

Columbia, Maryland, has been the subject of considerable writing. See H. Gans, People and Plans 183 (1968); Rouse, A Garden for People to Grow In, 45 Title News 88 (1966); Tannenbaum, Planning Determinants for Columbia, Urban Land, April, 1965, at 3.

[14] See Kraemer, Developing Governmental Institutions in New Communities, 1 Urban Law. 268, 272 (1969).

[15] Demonstration Cities & Metropolitan Development Act of 1966, 12 U.S.C.A. §§ 1749aa–11 (Title IV, "Mortgage Insurance for Land Development and New Communities"). See particularly the standards set for "new communities"; *id.* § 1749cc.–1. See generally 1966 U.S.Code Congressional & Administrative News 3999, 4023–26.

[16] 42 U.S.C.A. §§ 3901–14. See generally Keegan & Rutzick, Private Developers and the New Communities Act of 1968, 57 Geo.L.J. 1119 (1969).

be located in an urban, urbanizing, *or* rural area, but must be integrated with any existing developments. Such a community need not be totally self-sufficient, but should tend in that direction—it should not be a "single-purpose" development—including *only* housing, or *only* commercial uses, etc. The federal aid was provided in the form of guarantees of the obligations of a new-community developer. A number of new communities were promptly undertaken with the help of the federal guarantees; and the Urban Growth and New Community Development Act of 1970—signed into law in 1971[17]—broadened the program by bringing state land development agencies, and other public bodies, within the provisions for guarantees, and by increasing the size of the federal guarantee.

Within the Department of Housing and Urban Development, a Community Development Agency was created to administer the program; and provision was made for the development by this agency of new community "demonstration projects" on federal lands if the President specifically authorized such.[18] In a few states—notably New York[19]—, legislation was passed authorizing state development of new towns and/or state aid (such as loan guarantees) to private developers of new communities. But most of the "new town" activity of the 1960's and '70's was at the federal level. The federal legislation of 1970–71, it should be noted, provided possible assistance for *four* types of new communities;[20] (1) economically balanced communities within metropolitan areas—as alternatives to urban sprawl; (2) additions to existing smaller towns and cities—to convert these into growth centers and prevent their decline; (3) "new-town-in-town" developments—to help renew central cities; and (4) freestanding, "frontier" communities, particularly where needed to accommodate population growth in the general region. Thus, the definition of "new town" had broadened by the time this legislation was passed, as only the fourth category fits the more traditional notion of a new community.

§ 22.4 Successes and Failures of "New Towns"

What success did this mid-century experiment in new towns have? Much of the program was a failure—financially a disaster—out of which the main hope to emerge was that knowledge and experience may have been gained to aid future planning. The program began with high hopes of helping start 300 new communities by the year 2000—hopes that were encouraged by the success of the privately financed new towns of Reston, Virginia, and Columbia, Maryland.[21] Federal aid was concentrated on communities to be developed in areas of anticipated population growth and economic boom, such as the

---

17 42 U.S.C.A. §§ 4501–32.

18 See 42 U.S.C.A. § 4524. See generally Hagman & Juergensmeyer, *supra* note 2, at 512–13.

19 McKinney's N.Y. Unconsol. Laws § 6254 created the New York State Urban Development Corporation to aid the development of new towns. See Hagman & Juergensmeyer, *supra* note 2, at 519–20; Reilly & Schulman, The State Urban Development Corporation: New York's Innovation, 1 Urban Law. 129 (1969). On the Corporation's role in aiding the development of two towns in upstate New York, see Khies, State Starts Plans for 2 "New Towns," N.Y. Times, Aug. 4, 1969, § 1, at 26, col. 2. See generally "City," The 1970 World Book Year Book (Annual supplement to World Book Encyclopedia) 274, 276 (1970). On *state* participation in the new-town program in general, see Scott, Urban Growth Challenges New Towns, 48 Public Management 253 (1966).

20 See 1970 U.S. Code Congressional & Administrative News 5586, 5587–88, discussing Urban Growth & New Community Development Act of 1970, (Part B—Development of New Communities).

21 See Wedemeyer, New Towns Creating a Utopia, *supra* note 13.

area near the Dallas-Ft. Worth regional airport.[22] By 1973, fifteen projects had been approved for federal assistance—but critics were noting that the developments might in some instance have unfavorable effects on the ecology of the surrounding areas,[23] and a study had revealed that such problems as air pollution could quickly come to plague the new communities, just as they've long bothered older settlements.[24] In the mid-1970's, inflation and a sagging housing market were raising doubts that the federally aided new communities could survive; officials of Housing and Urban Development began negotiating refinancing deals, involving new federal guarantees for more bonds to be issued by the new-town developers.[25] The Department of Housing and Urban Development closed the door to further "new community" applications in January, 1975. As the downturn in the economy worsened in 1975, the developers found themselves caught in a squeeze between spiraling building costs on the one side and dwindling mortgage-money supplies on the other—and the homes that had been completed in many of the new towns were not selling well.[26] The problems were not limited to the federally aided projects—New York State's Urban Development Corporation had grave economic difficulties and had to be "rescued" in 1975 by a loan of $275 million from savings banks.[27]

The situation brightened somewhat in late 1975 as sales improved and as refinancing plans were worked out for the federal projects.[28] But by April, 1976, it was reported that Housing and Urban Development was having to fulfill the promise of its guarantees by paying the bond interest for eight of the new towns.[29] Thirteen of the projected, federally assisted new towns were actually built, at least in part; but by late 1976, four of them had been fully taken over by Housing and Urban Development and three others were in deep difficulty; only two were any longer making their own interest

---

[22] See "The Land Boom at a Texas Airport," Bus. Week, March 11, 1972, at 116, discussing the new town of Flower Mound, which was one of those whose financing was guaranteed by the U.S. government.

[23] See "The Big Troubles at San Antonio Ranch," Bus. Week, Nov. 3, 1973, at 78, discussing fears of water pollution raised by a proposed new town north of San Antonio.

[24] See Newhouse, Futuristic Model City Plagued by Pollution Problems of the Past, Arizona (Tucson) Daily Star, July 4, 1971 (Associated Press article), noting a three-year study which had concluded that air pollution had developed in the new town of Columbia, Maryland. On Columbia, see generally Rosenthal, A Tale of One City, N.Y. Times, Dec. 26, 1971, § VI, at 4. See also Kneeland, The Outer City: There Is No Firm Stereotype, N.Y. Times, May 31, 1971, at 1, col. 8.

[25] See "Can 'New Towns' Survive the Economic Crunch?," Bus. Week, Feb. 10, 1975, at 43.

[26] See "New Towns in Trouble," Time, March 24, 1975, at 70.

[27] See "What's Behind the UDC Debacle," Bus. Week, March 24, 1975, at 118. One of the New York Urban Development Corporation's projects, the Roosevelt Island community in New York City's East River, experimented with some interesting, innovative devices, such as an aerial tramway providing transportation to and from Manhattan and a pneumatic waste-disposal system to whisk garbage from homes to a central collection ground. See generally "New Towns in Trouble," *supra* note 26. The Roosevelt Island development was discussed in articles found in N.Y. Times, May 2, 1976, § VIII, at 1, col. 1; May 20, 1977, § 11, at 4, col. 1; Jan. 25, 1979, § 11, at 8, col. 1.

Though unusual because of its physical separation from Manhattan Island, the Roosevelt Island development illustrates the concept of a "new town in town"—*i.e.*, within an existing urban area. This concept has been much discussed by planners. See Perloff, New Towns in Town, 32 J. Am. Institute of Planners 155 (1966). Cf. "An Old City's New Town," Time, June 14, 1971, at 62 (on privately financed Franklin Town development in Philadelphia). The "Model Cities Program" of the Demonstration Cities and Metropolitan Development Act of 1966 encompassed aid for "new towns in town." 42 U.S.C.A. §§ 3301–74. On locations for new towns, see generally Ricks, New Town Development and the Theory of Location, 46 Land Economics 5 (1970).

[28] "A Shot in the Arm for New Towns," Bus. Week, Sept. 22, 1975, at 32.

[29] "The New Towns that Haunt HUD," Bus. Week, April 12, 1976, at 36.

payments on their bonds.[30] The fast-rising cost of borrowed money and the needs of the projects for large amounts of money for long periods had caught developers and the government by surprise; and it was estimated in late '76 that the federal government might lose $150 million on the program.[31] In 1978, the Secretary of Housing and Urban Development announced that federal involvement in the projects was being, to the extent possible, terminated: HUD would try to sell, or at least transfer the financing of, seven of the towns and would dissolve the Community Development Agency, which had been overseeing the program; but federal money would still be spent on 6 of the communities that it was thought had a good chance of survival.[32] In effect, the program was largely a failure—but some rays of hope could be seen: It was noted that many of the developments could not possibly achieve their full potential for 20 years or more and that those that were continued might yet prove successful.[33] The success of Reston, Virginia, and Columbia, Maryland, could be noted as hopeful signs, as could the experiences of England's new-town program. It has been suggested that in the future, a U.S. program—better planned and financed than the prior experiment, and with appropriate legal regulations—may yet show that "new communities" can be a partial solution to problems of growth and congestion.[34]

---

30 See "Picking up the Pieces of HUD's New Towns," Bus. Week, Aug. 23, 1976, at 30. The two that were reported as still making their own interest payments were St. Charles, near Baltimore, Maryland; and Soul City, North Carolina. The other eleven of the new towns were Maumelle, Arkansas; Shenandoah, Georgia; Park Forest South, Illinois; Cedar-Riverside, Minnesota; Jonathan, Minnesota; Ganada, New York; Riverton, New York; Newfields, Ohio; Harbison, South Carolina; Flower Mound, Texas; and The Woodlands, Texas.

31 See Stuart, Government and Private Backers Face Huge Losses on New Towns, N.Y. Times, Dec. 12, 1976, at 1.

32 See "New Town Blues," Time, Oct. 16, 1978, at 84.

33 See Farrell, "New Towns" Facing Growing Pains, N.Y. Times, June 13, 1976, at 1, col. 1. Cf. Oser, U.S. Re-Evaluating "New Towns" Program, N.Y. Times, July 23, 1976, at 11, col. 1.

34 See Brooks, The Policy Issues of New Towns: One Failure of Law to Guide Planning in America, 8 Urban Lawyer 94 (1976). The author of this article has been much concerned with the relationship of law and planning. See Brooks, Millstone Two and the Rainbow: Planning Law and Environmental Protection, 4 Conn.L.Rev. 54 (1971).

As with urban-renewal projects, there is a trend toward increased *private* development of "new towns." Irvine Ranch, California, 40 miles south of Los Angeles, is considered the nation's largest planned community and has been developed by the Irvine Company, owned by a development consortium. See Hollis, N.Y. Times, May 4, 1980, § 8, at 1, col. 1. See generally Eichler, Why New Communities, in Shaping an Urban Future: Essays in Memory of Catherine Bauer Wurster (B. Frieden & W. Nash, Jr., eds. 1968); Kneeland, The Outer City: There Is No Firm Stereotype, N.Y. Times, May 31, 1971, at 1, col. 8, comparing the Irvine development with other types of suburban and urban-fringe developments. In the mid-1990's, the Disney Corporation built the model village of Celebration, Florida, a self-contained town, modeled after pre-World War II Southeastern towns, featuring various architectural styles. See "A Theme Park You Can Live In," Bus. Week, Sept. 25, 1995, at 57. Since 1981, the Miami-based architectural firm of Andres Duany and Elizabeth Plater-Zyberk has designed several dozen new communities around the United States, all attempting to create the ambience of old-fashioned villages. See Goldberger, It Takes a Village, The New Yorker, March 27, 2000, at 128, reviewing the book by Duany & Plater-Zyberk (with Speck), Suburban Nation: The Rise of Sprawl and the Decline of the American Dream (North Point 2000). On the success of the privately financed master-planned community of Las Colinas, Texas, between Dallas and Fort Worth, see La Tour, Design of the Times, American Way magazine, Jan., 1983, at 31, containing a good summary of the history of "new towns." See generally Ewing, Developing Successful New Communities (Urban Land Institute 1991), reviewed 25 Urban Law. 469 (1993), analyzing 58 new communities throughout the United States and presenting an in-depth study of 5 of them. See also Section 21.6, note 81, *supra* on architect Paolo Soleri's development north of Phoenix, Arizona.

"Gated communities" may be considered a relative of new towns, though the former are often considered neighborhoods rather than self-contained, separate communities and often exist mainly as a crime-control device. See Section 24.1, note 10, *infra*. See also the material on "community associations," formed (often as required by law in order to receive the necessary plot approval, building permits, etc.) by private developers to provide traditional municipal services, Section 21.4, note 50, *supra*; and the material on the general trend toward privatization of many municipal services, Section 16.2, note 33, *supra*.

Chapter 23

LOCAL REGULATION OF TRADE, BUSINESS, AND OTHER ENTERPRISES

Analysis

§ 23.1 Trade Regulation—Basic Principles

Along with controlling the use of property, and attempting to rejuvenate decaying areas, one of the most important activities of local government is the regulation of trades and businesses. As with land-use control, trade regulation usually involves an exercise of the police power. Overall, four main limitations on municipal regulation of trades and businesses may be noted: (1) The municipality can only exercise power that is expressly or impliedly delegated to the municipality by the state;[1] thus, the police power, some other general power, or some specific delegated power will normally have to justify any regulation of business. (2) The power must then be exercised in a reasonable manner; there must be a rational connection between the restriction and some legitimate end of government policy. (3) Due-process standards must be met; there must be no "taking" of property interests (including a license to do business) without fair compensation, and no penalties assessed without according the penalized person all rights of procedural and substantive due process. (4) Any classifications made and distinctions drawn—by which, for instance, one category of businesses is treated differently from another—must at least be reasonable, and must meet all applicable requirements of equal protection. A complete prohibition of a business activity may often be found so severe as to be

[1] See Priddy v. City of Tulsa, 882 P.2d 81 (Okl.Cr.1994) (ordinances required all sign painters to be licensed and to obtain permit for each sign painted; held unconstitutional as unsupported by any local power). Compare Thomas v. Oklahoma City, 955 P.2d 747 (Okl. Civ. App. 1998) (home rule city had power to regulate taxi drivers; by granting all municipalities limited authority to regulate taxicabs, state statute did not impliedly prohibit home-rule cities from also regulating them under their general police powers). See generally Chapter 8 *supra*.

unreasonable (thus not meeting the second-mentioned test);[2] classifications or exceptions must then necessarily be created, and these will generally be upheld if based on some rational distinction—as in a U.S. Supreme Court case upholding a New Orleans ordinance that banned the sale of foodstuffs from pushcarts in the French Quarter, *except* by vendors who had continually operated the same business within the Quarter 8 years or more.[3]

§ 23.2 Trade Regulation—Valid Purposes

Much municipal regulation of business is attempted under the police-power purposes of promoting public safety or health (or a combination of these two), or under the "catch-all" purpose of promoting the general welfare. Such terms as "safety" and "welfare," of course, cover a wide area, and can include protecting the public from fraudulent activity or price-gouging. Thus, rather strict licensing, or other, requirements for pawnbrokers have often been sustained due to fear of criminal activity by such persons.[4] The prospective pawnbroker can be required by the city to furnish proof of good character and to photograph every person who does business with him.[5] But regulation of business is normally an area of statewide concern, and municipal pawnbroking

---

[2] Thus, in Good Humor Corp. v. City of New York, 290 N.Y. 312, 49 N.E.2d 153 (1943), a nearly total prohibition of street vending was invalidated as not reasonably necessary. See New Jersey Good Humor v. Board of Commissioners, 124 N.J.L. 162, 11 A.2d 113 (1940). But prohibitions of peddling, curb service, etc. in particular areas, such as those with heavy traffic, may be upheld. See People v. Dmytro, 280 Mich. 82, 273 N.W. 400 (1937) (prohibition of curb service on public streets in commercial areas). As to prohibitions of and limitations on door-to-door solicitation, see Section 23.6, notes 82–99 *infra* and accompanying text.

[3] City of New Orleans v. Dukes, 427 U.S. 297, 96 S.Ct. 2513, 49 L.Ed.2d 511, on remand 537 F.2d 856 (5th Cir.1976). See Riley v. Rhode Island, 941 A. 2d 198 (R. I. 2008) (fishing regulations prohibited only *new* fishermen from access to depleted species of fish; statute found to have rational basis and not to violate the Due Process and Equal Protection clauses of either the U.S. or Rhode Island Constitution). Compare Reed, Pro-business or Anti-gay? Disguising LGBT Animus as Economic Legislation, 9 Stan. J. Civil Rights & Civil Liberties 153 (2013). See generally Annot., Governmental Regulation of Place of Amusement, Entertainment, or Recreation as Violating Rights of Owner or Operator Under Equal Protection Clause of Federal Constitution's Fourteenth Amendment—Supreme Court Cases, 104 L.Ed.2d 1078 (1991). Certain "suspect" classifications can, under U.S. Supreme Court authority, be justified only if a compelling state interest is shown, while most classification can be justified merely by a showing of rational purpose. See Houle, Compelling State Interest vs. Mere Rational Classification: The Practitioner's Equal Protection Dilemma, 3 Urban Law. 375 (1971). If a business is singled-out for enforcement of a municipal ordinance against it when similarly situated businesses are not required to comply with the ordinance, the "victim" of the law's enforcement may have a claim against the city for discrimination, based on violation of Equal Protection. See Brander's Club, Inc. v. City of Lawton, 918 P.2d 69 (Okl.1996) (city found to have no immunity for constitutional violations; court indicates relief could be granted under Federal Civil Rights Act).

Some cases, without even referring to "equal protection," declare in general that discrimination is fatal to trade-regulation ordinances. See Crawford's Clothes, Inc. v. Board of Commissioners, 131 N.J.L. 97, 35 A.2d 38 (1944) (invalidating restriction on hours that certain businesses could stay open, but with exceptions for a number of businesses); Siciliano v. Neptune Township, 83 N.J.L. 158, 83 A. 865 (1912).

[4] See Provident Loan Soc. v. City & County of Denver, 64 Colo. 400, 172 P. 10 (1918); Medias v. City of Indianapolis, 216 Ind. 155, 23 N.E.2d 590 (1939) (sustaining ordinance requiring pawnbrokers to take thumbprints of all persons from whom they purchased or received goods); City of Wichita v. Wolkow, 110 Kan. 127, 202 P. 632 (1921); City of Hobbs v. Biswell, 81 N.M. 778, 473 P.2d 917 (1970), cert. denied 81 N.M. 772, 473 P.2d 911; Solof v. City of Chattanooga, 180 Tenn. 296, 174 S.W.2d 471 (1943), reh. denied 180 Tenn. 296, 176 S.W.2d 816 (sustaining regulation of pawnshop hours). Cf. Holsman v. Thomas, 112 Ohio St. 397, 147 N.E. 750 (1925) (upholding ordinance restricting jewelry auctions to sixty days in one year and imposing restrictions on jewelry auctioneers). See generally Annot., Validity of Statutes or Ordinances Which Impose Duties Upon Pawnbrokers as Regards Identity of Persons With Whom They Deal or Other Means of Enforcing Criminal Law Against Theft, 125 A.L.R. 598 (1940).

[5] Liberman v. Cervantes, 511 S.W.2d 835 (Mo.1974) (photographs of customers had to be made available to police on request).

ordinances may be invalidated if in conflict with state statutes;[6] they also will be struck down if they provide for revocation of a license, or imposition of other penalty, without providing such "due process rights" as notice of specific charges and opportunity to cross-examine witnesses.[7]

Similarly, municipal licensing and regulation of sellers of secondhand goods is usually sustained because of the need to protect the public from fraudulent sales.[8] The scope of permissible regulation extends to used car dealers;[9] and here, additional safety and health considerations may also be relied upon, as in justifying a requirement that all open lots for the sale of cars be enclosed with a fireproof fence.[10] The prevention of fraud has also been an important factor in justifying state and local restrictions on astrologers and fortune-tellers.[11] Where short supply, a monopoly situation, or other

---

6 See Lakewood Pawnbrokers, Inc. v. City of Lakewood, 183 Colo. 370, 517 P.2d 834 (1973), invalidating portions of a statutory city's ordinance that were in conflict with state law—but finding the ordinance a reasonable exercise of the police power and declaring that the valid portions of the ordinance would remain in effect. Cf. Asakura v. City of Seattle, 265 U.S. 332, 44 S.Ct. 515, 68 L.Ed. 1041 (1924), invalidating—as in conflict with a treaty between the U.S. and Japan—an ordinance which excluded Japanese nationals from pawn broking.

7 See Wolfenbarger v. Hennessee, 520 P.2d 809 (Okl.1974).

8 See Iscoff v. Police Commission, 222 Cal.App.2d 395, 35 Cal.Rptr. 189 (Dist.Ct.1963) (police chief had power to issue licenses for pawnbrokers—adequate standards provided); City of Grand Rapids v. Braudy, 105 Mich. 670, 64 N.W. 29 (1895); Sherman, Clay & Co. v. Brown, 142 Wash. 37, 252 P. 137 (1927). But cf. City of Guthrie v. Pike & Long, 206 Okl. 307, 243 P.2d 697 (1952), invalidating as discriminatory an ordinance regulating the sale of distressed goods or damaged merchandise.

In order to prevent gambling, fraud, etc., statutes and ordinances restricting or prohibiting businesses from conducting lotteries and other promotional games have generally been sustained also. See Bullock, Merchandising Through Use of Lotteries, 19 Clev.St.L.Rev. 620 (1970); Note, Promotional Games and the Ohio Lottery Laws, 39 U.Cin.L.Rev. 163 (1970); Annot., Validity and Construction of Statute or Ordinance Prohibiting Promotional Games in Connection with Sale of Gasoline, 57 A.L.R.3d 1288 (1974). See generally Annot., Promotion Schemes of Retail Stores as Criminal Offense Under Antigambling Laws, 29 A.L.R.3d 888 (1970); Annot., Scheme for Advertising or Stimulating Legitimate Business as a Lottery, 113 A.L.R. 1121 (1938) (citing prior annotations on same subject). See also Annot., Advertising of "Free Gifts" and Representations as to Price of Goods as Unfair Method of Competition or Practice Within § 5(a) of the Federal Trade Commission Act, 15 L.Ed.2d 865 (1966). Statutes and ordinances have occasionally regulated the use of trading stamps, too. See Annot., Constitutionality of Statutes Prohibiting Giving of Premiums or Trading Stamps, 133 A.L.R. 1087 (1941) (citing prior annotations on same subject).

To provide protection against fraud, municipalities may even enact general "consumer protection" laws, though much enactment of such legislation has been at the *state* level. See McClellan v. Kansas City, 379 S.W.2d 500 (Mo.1964). Cf. Blackman v. County Court, 169 Colo. 345, 455 P.2d 885 (1969) (municipal regulation of weights and measures sustained).

9 See Vaughn v. City of Los Angeles, 59 Cal.App.2d 771, 140 P.2d 130 (Dist.Ct.1943) appeal dism'd 321 U.S. 751, 64 S.Ct. 639, 88 L.Ed. 1052; People v. Sturgeon, 272 Mich. 319, 262 N.W. 58 (1935); State v. H.J. Minar Co., 249 Minn. 116, 81 N.W.2d 268 (1957) (specifying written statement that dealer must give each purchaser); Ring v. Mayor & Council of North Arlington, 136 N.J.L. 494, 56 A.2d 744 (1948) aff'd 1 N.J. 24, 61 A.2d 508, appeal dism'd 335 U.S. 889, 69 S.Ct. 250, 93 L.Ed. 427.

10 See Chaiet v. City of East Orange, 136 N.J.L. 375, 56 A.2d 599 (1948) (city could require license though state did also; fence was justified in order to keep cars from driving across sidewalk except at designated entrances and exits). Municipal prohibitions of self-service gas stations have been sustained on safety grounds. Shell Oil Co. v. City of Revere, 383 Mass. 682, 421 N.E.2d 1181 (1981); Town of North Hempstead v. Exxon Corp., 53 N.Y.2d 747, 439 N.Y.S.2d 342, 421 N.E.2d 834 (1981). See cases cited note 38 *infra*.

11 See Annot., Regulation of Astrology, Clairvoyancy, Fortunetelling, and the Like, 91 A.L.R.3d 766 (1979), noting that restrictions on these practices have usually been upheld—the courts believing that many such practices are inherently deceptive. A leading case is Davis v. State, 118 Ohio St. 25, 160 N.E. 473 (1928), error dism'd per curiam, 277 U.S. 571, 48 S.Ct. 432, 72 L.Ed. 993. But see Spiritual Psychic Science Church of Truth, Inc. v. City of Azusa, 39 Cal.3d 501, 217 Cal.Rptr. 225, 703 P.2d 1119 (1985) (city ordinance prohibiting fortune-telling for consideration ruled an unconstitutional restriction on free speech; court declared that other

special circumstances make price-gouging a real danger, municipal price controls can be sustained;[12] and reasonable ceilings on rent charged tenants will similarly be upheld,[13]

---

methods of preventing fraudulent fortune-telling were available that would impose less drastic restrictions on protected speech). Cf. Argello v. City of Lincoln, 143 F.3d 1152 (8th Cir.1998) (ordinance prohibiting practices such as clairvoyancy, fortune-telling, and mind—reading invalidated as a content-based regulation that was not supported by a compelling state interest). And an occasional law has been struck down as discriminatory. See Daniel v. Cruz, 268 S.C. 11, 231 S.E.2d 293 (1977) (state statute requiring licenses for itinerant fortunetellers). Cf. Canale v. Steveson, 224 Tenn. 578, 458 S.W.2d 797 (1970) (state statute forbidding fortunetelling in certain counties invalidated as class legislation). Many restrictions in this field have been at the state level.

[12] See Anthony v. City of Atlanta, 66 Ga.App. 506, 18 S.E.2d 82 (1941). Cf. People v. Cook, 34 N.Y.2d 100, 356 N.Y.S.2d 259, 312 N.E.2d 452 (1974) (city could regulate retail price of cigarettes in order to require price differential between brands with high tar-and-nicotine content and those with lower such content). Wartime conditions have been held to justify municipal price controls. See People v. Sell, 310 Mich. 305, 17 N.W.2d 193 (1945); People v. Lewis, 295 N.Y. 42, 64 N.E.2d 702 (1945). A few cases—mostly in the 1930's or before—invalidated municipal price controls in broad terms, finding a lack of power. City of Mobile v. Rouse, 27 Ala.App. 344, 173 So. 254 (1937), cert. denied 233 Ala. 622, 173 So. 266; Duncan v. City of Des Moines, 222 Iowa 218, 268 N.W. 547 (1936). And an occasional ordinance has been invalidated as involving an unlawful delegation of power. City of Cleveland v. Piskura, 145 Ohio St. 144, 60 N.E.2d 919 (1945). See Note, Municipal Corporations—Price Control—Invalid Delegation of Municipal Legislative Power to Federal Agency, 9 U.Det.L.J. 43 (1945). See generally, on delegation of power, Chapter 9 *supra*.

Municipal minimum-wage ordinances are valid if they do not conflict with state laws but merely supplement any existing state measures. See City of Atlanta v. Associated Builders & Contractors, 240 Ga. 655, 242 S.E.2d 139 (1978).

[13] See Stoneridge Apartments Co. v. Lindsay, 303 F.Supp. 677 (S.D.N.Y.1969); Lifschitz v. City of Miami Beach, 339 So.2d 232 (Fla.App.1976); Gardens v. City of Passaic, 130 N.J.Super. 369, 327 A.2d 250 (1974); Inganamort v. Borough of Fort Lee, 62 N.J. 521, 303 A.2d 298 (1973), appeal after remand 72 N.J. 412, 371 A.2d 34; 8200 Realty Corp. v. Lindsay, 27 N.Y.2d 124, 313 N.Y.S.2d 733, 261 N.E.2d 647 (1970), appeal dism'd 400 U.S. 962, 91 S.Ct. 367, 27 L.Ed.2d 381; Plaza Management Co. v. City Rent Agency, 25 N.Y.2d 630, 306 N.Y.S.2d 11, 254 N.E.2d 227 (1969); Matter of Hartley Holding Corp. v. Gabel, 13 N.Y.2d 306, 247 N.Y.S.2d 97, 196 N.E.2d 537 (1963); Warren v. City of Philadelphia, 382 Pa. 380, 115 A.2d 218 (1955). Cf. Kennedy v. City of Seattle, 94 Wash.2d 376, 617 P.2d 713 (1980) (rent-control provisions of city's houseboat ordinance upheld though eviction provisions found unconstitutionally confiscatory). But cf. Meyerstein v. City of Aspen, 282 P.3d 456 (Colo. App. 2011) (property owner could pursue rent-control challenge by way of declaratory judgment action; amended *anti*-rent control statute was remedial in nature and could be applied retroactively); Property Owners Association v. Township of North Bergen, 74 N.J. 327, 378 A.2d 25 (1977) (ordinance invalidated as in effect requiring that either landlords or other tenants subsidize needy senior citizens). Some rent-control ordinances have been invalidated as not authorized by state law. City of Miami Beach v. Fleetwood Hotel, Inc., 261 So.2d 801 (Fla.1972) (no power in absence of legislative enactments); Marshal House, Inc. v. Rent Review & Grievance Board, 357 Mass. 709, 260 N.E.2d 200 (1970); Tietjens v. City of St. Louis, 359 Mo. 439, 222 S.W.2d 70 (1949). Or as inconsistent with state law. Heubeck v. City of Baltimore, 205 Md. 203, 107 A.2d 99 (1954). Cf. Old Colony Gardens v. City of Stamford, 147 Conn. 60, 156 A.2d 515 (1959) (contrary to public policy of state as declared in legislation). See also Action Apartment Ass'n, Inc. v. City of Santa Monica, 41 Cal.4th 1232, 63 Cal.Rptr.3d 398, 163 P.3d 89 (2007) (city's "tenant harassment" ordinance, addressing a landlord's malicious efforts to terminate a tenancy through legal proceedings, found pre-empted by state law). Or as pre-empted by federal regulations. See Hill Manor Apartments v. Stokes, 154 N.J.Super. 496, 381 A.2d 1224 (1977) (regulation of Department of Housing and Urban Development exempting all unsubsidized insured housing projects from local rent control).

It is agreed that any rent-control measure must allow landlords the possibility of a reasonable rate of return, or the measure will be invalidated as confiscatory. See Hall v. City of Santa Barbara, 797 F.2d 1493 (9th Cir.1986), cert. denied 485 U.S. 940, 108 S.Ct. 1120, 99 L.Ed.2d 281 (1988) (rent-control ordinance applied to mobile home park would amount to a taking if owners not allowed to obtain reasonable return on their investment); Troy Hills Village v. Township Council, 68 N.J. 604, 350 A.2d 34 (1975); Brunetti v. Borough of New Milford, 68 N.J. 576, 350 A.2d 19 (1975); Hutton Park Gardens v. Town Council, 68 N.J. 543, 350 A.2d 1 (1975). But see Sandpiper Mobile Village v. City of Carpinteria, 10 Cal.App.4th 542, 12 Cal.Rptr.2d 623 (1992), cert. denied 507 U.S. 1032, 113 S.Ct. 1850, 123 L.Ed.2d 473 (1993) (mobile-home-park rent-control ordinance upheld as not a taking). Cf. Kavanau v. Santa Monica Rent Control Bd., 16 Cal.4th 761, 66 Cal.Rptr.2d 672, 941 P.2d 851 (Sup.Ct.1997), cert. denied 522 U.S. 1077, 118 S.Ct. 856, 139 L.Ed.2d 755 (1998) (even where rent ceiling violated landlord's due process rights, he had no taking action as he had not been deprived of all economically beneficial or productive use of property or suffered interference with investment-backed expectations). See generally Radford, Regulatory Takings Law in the 1990's: The Death of Rent Control?, 21

with only some rational basis for the regulation, not necessarily a true emergency, being required by reviewing courts.[14]

Sw. U.L. Rev. 1019 (1992). In Galland v. City of Clovis, 24 Cal.4th 1003, 103 Cal.Rptr.2d 711, 16 P.3d 130 (2001), cert. denied 534 U.S. 826, 122 S.Ct. 65, 151 L.Ed.2d 32 (2001), owners of a rent-controlled mobile home park filed an action seeking damages under Section 1983 of the Federal Civil Rights Act for alleged due process violations. The court held that costs associated with obtaining rent increases could be the basis of a Section 1983 claim if a landlord suffers confiscation as a result of such costs, thus answering a question left open in the *Kavanau* case, *supra*. But cf. Cacho v. Boudreau, 40 Cal.4th 341, 53 Cal.Rptr.3d 43, 149 P.3d 473 (2007), holding that the California Mobilehome Residency Law, unlike the city ordinances involved in the *Galland* and *Kavanau* cases, *supra*, was not a rent control law. See generally Note, It's the End of the World as We Know It (and I Feel Fine): Rent Regulation in New York City and the Unanswered Questions of Market and Society, 72 Fordham L. Rev. 1125 (2004).

A rent-control ordinance may validly provide a method by which a hearing officer or body is allowed to consider a tenant's hardship, or lack thereof, in fixing a reasonable rent. Pennell v. City of San Jose, 485 U.S. 1, 108 S.Ct. 849, 99 L.Ed.2d 1 (1988), aff'g 42 Cal.3d 365, 228 Cal.Rptr. 726, 721 P.2d 1111 (1986). (The U.S. Supreme Court did not, however, reach the merits of the claim that the "tenant hardship clause" constituted a "taking" of property in violation of the landlord's due process, since there was no evidence that the clause had ever been used to reduce the rent owed a landlord. See Hill, Reflections, Refractions, and Regulations: Variation on the Takings Theme, 12 Urban, State & Local L. Newsletter, No. 3, at 1 (Summer, 1989).) Cf. Yee v. City of Escondido, 503 U.S. 519, 112 S.Ct. 1522, 118 L.Ed.2d 153 (1992) (rent-control ordinance as applied to mobile home park owners did not amount to physical taking of property, but issues of whether ordinance violated due process or constituted a regulatory taking found not properly before Court). See generally Baar, The Right to Sell the "Im" mobile Manufactured Home in Its Rent Controlled Space in the "Im" mobile Home Park: Valid Regulation or Unconstitutional Taking?, 24 Urban Law. 157 (1992).

[14] See Birkenfeld v. City of Berkeley, 17 Cal.3d 129, 130 Cal.Rptr. 465, 550 P.2d 1001 (1976) (also upholding use of the initiative process to enact rent-control amendment to city charter, but voiding the particular procedure as not providing for prompt and adequate adjustments). Cf. Troy Hills Village v. Township Council, *supra* note 13 (judicial review of rent control is limited to determining if rational basis exists). Rent control legislation purely for the benefit of *elderly* tenants has also been upheld. See Annot., Validity and Construction of Statute or Ordinance Establishing Rent Control Benefit or Rent Subsidy for Elderly Tenants, 5 A.L.R. 4th 922 (1981).

A "rent-holdback" ordinance—allowing tenants to hold back rent and pay the amount into escrow until the landlord has remedied building deficiencies or ordinance violations—can also be upheld if a reasonable need exists. See State ex rel. Michalek v. LeGrand, 77 Wis.2d 520, 253 N.W.2d 505 (1977). Cf. Small Property Owners v. City of San Francisco, 141 Cal.App.4th 1388, 47 Cal. Rptr. 3d 121 (Dist.Ct. 2006) (ordinance requiring landlords to pay tenants interest on security deposits at a rate exceeding then-existing money market rates did not constitute an unconstitutional taking of property).

In Fisher v. City of Berkeley, 37 Cal.3d 644, 209 Cal.Rptr. 682, 693 P.2d 261 (1984), reh. denied 475 U.S. 1150, 106 S.Ct. 1806, 90 L.Ed.2d 350 (1986), a rent-control ordinance was upheld against the claim it conflicted with the Sherman Anti-Trust Act. The court found the ordinance to be rationally related to police power purposes and held that plaintiff-landlords had not demonstrated that the municipality's purposes could be achieved as effectively by a means having a less intrusive impact on federal anti-trust policies. The U.S. Supreme Court affirmed on the ground that the rent controls lacked the concerted action required for a per se violation of Section 1 of the Sherman Act. Fisher v. City of Berkeley, 475 U.S. 260, 106 S.Ct. 1045, 89 L.Ed.2d 206 (1986), reh. denied 475 U.S. 1150, 106 S.Ct. 1806, 90 L.Ed.2d 350 (1986). But cf. South Hamilton Assoc. v. Mayor & Council of Morristown, 99 N.J. 437, 493 A.2d 523 (1985) (rent-control ordinance could not be applied retroactively so as to impair contract rights).

The municipal power to control rent has been held separate and distinct from the power to regulate land use by zoning. All Peoples Congress of Jersey City v. Mayor of Jersey City, 195 N.J.Super. 532, 480 A.2d 948 (1984) (rent-control ordinance exempting large, new apartment complexes built in redevelopment areas did not come within restrictions on exclusionary zoning that had been established by New Jersey Supreme Court). See generally Downs, Residential Rent Controls: An Evaluation (Urban Land Institute 1988). See also Drobak, Constitutional Limits on Price and Rent Control: The Lessons of Utility Regulation, 64 Wash. U.L.Q. 107 (1986).

Rent control remains highly controversial. In 1982, a Presidential Commission on Housing recommended that local regulations on rent be ended as quickly as possible and that the federal government pre-empt rent controls on all rental housing financed by insured institutions or by federally insured mortgages. See "Presidential Panel Calls for Ban on Rent Control," 68 A.B.A.J. 903 (1982). See also Comment, San Francisco's Owner Move-In Legislation: Rent Control or Out of Control?, 34 U. San Francisco L. Rev. 537 (2000). Rent regulation has also sometimes been applied to mobile homes. See Equity Lifestyle Properties, Inc. v. County

Protection of public *health* is the strongest ground on which regulation of purveyors of food and drink can be justified. If not in conflict with state law,[15] most municipal restrictions on such purveyors have been upheld—including inspection[16] and licensing[17] requirements. Thus, local health regulations as to meat markets and butcher shops, with provision for regular inspections, have been sustained,[18] as have such regulations as applied to groceries.[19] *Specific* restrictions will be upheld if reasonable, as, for example,

---

of San Luis Obispo, 548 F.3d 1184 (9th Cir. 2008) (property owner's "as applied" takings claim challenging mobile home rent control ordinance was barred where claimant failed to avail itself of possible remedy of just compensation under state law).

Another type of charge that has been considered appropriate for possible regulation is the surcharge often imposed by banks on ATM transactions. As to whether such surcharges can, and should, be regulated by cities, see Note, The Legality of Local ATM Surcharge Bans: The Case for the Cities of Santa Monica and San Francisco, 74 So. Cal. L. Rev. 1353 (2001). See also Note, Payday Loan Regulation: Any Interest?, 11 DePaul Bus. & Commercial L. J. 417 (2013).

Some local governments have imposed minimum wage limitations, which can be valid if not pre-empted by, or in conflict with, state law. See Gillette, Local Redistribution, Living Wage Ordinances, and Judicial Intervention, 101 N.W.U.L. Rev. 1057 (2007).

[15] See Town of Honea Path v. Flynn, 255 S.C. 32, 176 S.E.2d 564 (1970) (void if conflict with state law). Cf. Application of Tenny v. Sainsbury, 7 A.D.2d 514, 184 N.Y.S.2d 185 (1959) (void if state has preempted the field); 7-Eleven, Inc. v. McClain, 422 P.2d 455 (Okl.1967) (regulation of beer-sales pre-empted by state except where municipalities expressly given power).

On the effect that fear of bioterrorism has had on municipal use of power to control public health (especially since the terrorist attacks of September 11, 2001), see Richards, O'Brien & Rathbun, Bioterrorism and the Use of Fear in Public Health, 34 Urban Law. 685 (2002). On municipal food ordinances based on public health, see generally Comment, The Real Toy Story: The San Francisco Board of Supervisors Healthy Food Incentives Ordinance, 8 J. Food L. & Pol'y 347 (2012). See also Note, Food Ordinances: Encouraging Eating Local, 37 Wm. & Mary Envtl. L. & Pol'y Rev. 511 (2013).

[16] City of Dayton v. Jacobs, 120 Ohio St. 225, 165 N.E. 844 (1929). This includes the power to charge inspection fees, but only if they are reasonable in amount. See City of Chicago v. R. & X. Restaurant, 369 Ill. 65, 15 N.E.2d 725 (1938). See generally Annot., Reasonableness of Fee Required of Places Where Food Is Served for Consumption Upon the Premises, and Basis for Fixing Amount, 117 A.L.R. 1313 (1938).

[17] Arms v. City of Chicago, 314 Ill. 316, 145 N.E. 407 (1924). This includes power to charge a reasonable license fee. See Larson v. City of Rockford, 371 Ill. 441, 21 N.E.2d 396 (1939). But if the fee is levied under the municipal power of regulation, rather than the power to raise revenue, the amount must bear a reasonable relationship to the regulatory expenses involved. See Crackerjack Co. v. City of Chicago, 330 Ill. 320, 161 N.E. 479 (1928).

[18] Trigg v. Dixon, 96 Ark. 199, 131 S.W. 695 (1910); Ex parte Banta, 25 Cal.App.2d 622, 78 P.2d 243 (Dist.Ct.1938); Cosby v. City of Washington, 72 Ga.App. 146, 33 S.E.2d 446 (1945) (holding that permit from U.S. did not exempt from municipal requirements); Kinsley v. City of Chicago, 124 Ill. 359, 16 N.E. 260 (1888); Cronin v. People, 82 N.Y. 318 (1880). Cf. Ex parte Lowenthal, 92 Cal.App. 200, 267 P. 886 (Dist.Ct.1928) (regulation of sale of uncooked meats allowed). The power to inspect includes, as is usual, the power to charge reasonable inspection fees, but unreasonable ones will be held invalid. See City of Baton Rouge v. Sanchez, 161 La. 320, 108 So. 552 (1926) (city exceeded power in assessing inspection fee clearly in excess of expenses of inspection). Cf. Hoefling v. City of San Antonio, 85 Tex. 228, 20 S.W. 85 (1892) (tax on butchers invalidated where collected only from those selling meat at private stalls, not from those renting stalls from city).

Municipalities have also been found to have power to inspect and mark canned meat products. City of Baltimore v. Bloecher & Schaff, 149 Md. 648, 132 A. 160 (1926), aff'd per curiam 275 U.S. 490, 48 S.Ct. 33, 72 L.Ed. 389. And regulations of slaughterhouses have long been upheld. See City of Albany v. Newhof, 256 N.Y. 661, 177 N.E. 183 (1931) (forbidding slaughterhouses in certain districts of city); Simon v. Cleveland Heights, 46 Ohio App. 234, 188 N.E. 308 (1933) (inspection of slaughterhouses); Sitterle v. Victoria Cold Storage Co., 33 S.W.2d 546 error dism'd (Tex.Civ. App.1931).

[19] Justesen's Food Stores, Inc. v. City of Tulare, 43 Cal.App.2d 616, 111 P.2d 424 (Dist.Ct.1941). See Natal v. Louisiana, 139 U.S. 621, 11 S.Ct. 636, 35 L.Ed. 288 (1891) (license can be required). But cf. Brown v. City of Seattle, 150 Wash. 203, 272 P. 517 (1928) mod. 150 Wash. 203, 278 P. 1072 (hours regulation of meat market held unconstitutional as not promoting public health or safety).

Wholesale dealers in groceries can also be regulated by municipalities. See Ritter v. City of Pontiac, 276 Mich. 416, 267 N.W. 641 (1936); American Grocery Co. v. Board of Commissioners of New Brunswick, 126 N.J.L. 367, 19 A.2d 696 (1941).

requirements of adequate refrigeration[20] and of adequate protection of foodstuffs from dirt and insects.[21] Licensing and inspection of restaurants by municipalities is ordinarily sustained,[22] as are such specific requirements as that drinking glasses be sterilized by restaurants[23] or that employees be required to pass regular medical examinations.[24] The

---

[20] City of Chicago v. Arbuckle Brothers, 344 Ill. 597, 176 N.E. 761 (1931); State v. Witt's Market House, Inc., 191 Minn. 425, 254 N.W. 596 (1934); S. H. Cranston v. Department of Health, 168 Misc. 749, 6 N.Y.S.2d 275 (1938).

[21] State ex rel. Bacigalupo v. O'Connor, 115 Minn. 339, 132 N.W. 303 (1911). Cf. DeCarlo v. Jefferson County Board of Health, 274 Ala. 506, 150 So.2d 374 (1963) (ordinance required that passage from living or sleeping quarters into area where food was handled could only be via outside; upheld).

[22] See Western Pennsylvania Restaurant Association v. City of Pittsburgh, 366 Pa. 374, 77 A.2d 616 (1951); Nance v. Mayflower Tavern, 106 Utah 517, 150 P.2d 773 (1944). Cf. Del Vecchio v. Mayor & Township Committee of South Hackensack, 49 N.J.Super. 44, 138 A.2d 839 (1958) (upholding ordinance requiring windows, doors, etc. of restaurants to be certain distance from property line); City of Rochester v. Schonleber, 9 Misc.2d 160, 168 N.Y.S.2d 412 (1957) (reasonable controls on catering businesses allowed). See generally Note, Constitutional Law—Municipal Corporations—Restaurant Licensing and Grading, 12 U.Pitt.L.Rev. 623 (1951). See also Annot., Discrimination as Between Restaurants or Eating Places in Statute or Ordinances Respecting Them, 169 A.L.R. 976 (1947); Annot., What Constitutes a Restaurant, 122 A.L.R. 1399 (1939). A number of local governments—such as New York City, Philadelphia, and Montgomery County, Maryland—, as well as the state of California, have enacted laws banning trans fats in restaurants. See Steinhauer, California Bars Restaurant Use of Trans Fats, N.Y. Times, July 26, 2008, at A1. In New York State Restaurant Ass'n v. New York City Bd. Of Health, 509 F. Supp. 2d 351 (S.D.N.Y. 2007), aff'd, 556 F.3d 114 (2d Cir. 2009), the courts upheld a law that required all restaurants that voluntarily disclose nutritional information and all chain restaurants that sell standardized meals in 15 or more locations nationwide to post the calorie content of their menu items. See Note, Cheeseburger in Paradise? An Analysis of How *New York State Restaurant Association v. New York City Board of Health* May Reform Our Fast Food Nation, 59 DePaul L. Rev. 733 (2010), noting that the law was intended to encourage healthful eating and to fight obesity. See generally McCann, Economic Efficiency and Consumer Choice Theory in Nutritional Labeling, 2004 Wis. L. Rev. 1161 (discussing, at 1233–44, various nutritional disclosure methods); Comment, Fast Food: Oppression Through Poor Nutrition, 95 Cal. L. Rev. 2221 (2007); Note, Putting Calorie and Fat Counts on the Table: Should Mandatory Nutritional Disclosure Laws Apply to Restaurant Foods?, 73 Geo. Wash. L. Rev. 377 (2005) (proposing federal legislation requiring restaurants to make various nutritional items of information available to customers, though not necessarily on the menu). National legislation does now require retailers with more than 20 locations to post calorie counts. See Park, Health—The Big Gulp, Time magazine, June 18, 2012, at 20.

Limits on the size of sweetened beverages that may be sold have been attempted in some municipalities including New York City. See Note, The New York City Sugar-Sweetened Beverage Portion Cap Rule: Lawfully Regulating Public Enemy Number One in the Obesity Epidemic, 46 Conn. L. Rev. 807 (2013); Note, Large-sized Soda Ban as an Alternative to Soda Tax, 23 Cornell J. L. & Pub. Pol'y 187 (2013). As to increasing taxes on sweetened beverages, see DeSantis, Formulating a Soda Tax Fit for Consumption: A Pragmatic Approach to Implementing the Failed New York Soda Tax, 16 Mich. St. U. J. Med. & L. 363 (2012). See generally Fry, Zimmerman & Kappagoda, Healthy Reform, Healthy Cities: Using Law and Policy to Reduce Obesity Rates in Underserved Communities, 40 Fordham Urb. L. J. 1265 (2013). See also Hsu, A Cost-Benefit Analysis of Sugary Drink Regulation in New York City, 10 J. Food L. & Pol'y 73 (2014); Comment, Big Brother Takes a Bite Out of the Big Apple and Gets a Worm: Can *Any* Government Body Regulate Portions?, 55 S. Tex. L. Rev. 553 (2014).

Regulation of bakeries has also been sustained. Jay Burns Baking Co. v. Bryan, 264 U.S. 504, 44 S.Ct. 412, 68 L.Ed. 813 (1924); Ward Baking Co. v. City of Chicago, 340 Ill. 212, 172 N.E. 171 (1930). As has regulation of manufacturers and sellers of candy. See People v. Greenberg, 134 App.Div. 599, 119 N.Y.S. 325 (1909) (adulterated food law applied to middleman). And of soft drinks. City of Chicago v. Chicago Beverage Co., 372 Ill. 33, 22 N.E.2d 708 (1939). And municipalities can regulate and inspect vending machines selling products for human consumption. Larson v. City of Rockford, 371 Ill. 441, 21 N.E.2d 396 (1939).

[23] Donahue v. City of Portland, 137 Me. 83, 15 A.2d 287 (1940).

[24] Langley v. City of Dallas, 252 S.W. 203 (Tex.Civ.App.1923).

regulation of dairy facilities[25] and of local distributors of milk[26] is similarly justifiable on grounds of protecting public health. As to containers for beverages, one type of law has become common: a requirement that return-deposits be made on such containers. This type of restriction has been generally upheld, mainly as necessary to prevention of litter and as thus promoting a clean environment.[27] A combination of health and

---

[25] See Natural Milk Producers Association v. City of San Francisco, 20 Cal.2d 101, 124 P.2d 25 (1942); Koy v. City of Chicago, 263 Ill. 122, 104 N.E. 1104 (1914); Nelson v. City of Minneapolis, 112 Minn. 16, 127 N.W. 445 (1910) (tuberculin test required); Stephens v. Oklahoma City, 150 Okl. 199, 1 P.2d 367 (1931). The power extends to regulation and inspection of dairy herds. See Carpenter v. City of Little Rock, 101 Ark. 238, 142 S.W. 162 (1911); City of Norfolk v. Flynn, 101 Va. 473, 44 S.E. 717 (1903). This necessarily involves some extraterritorial exercise of the city's regulation, and extraterritorial power has been found in this regard if expressly or impliedly conferred by statute or charter, but not otherwise. See Dean Milk Co. v. City of Waukegan, 403 Ill. 597, 87 N.E.2d 751 (1949) (city could not prohibit sale of milk other than that produced and pasteurized in that county); City of Rockford v. Hey, 366 Ill. 526, 9 N.E.2d 317 (1937) (extraterritorial effect of ice cream ordinance held void). See generally, on extraterritorial exercise of city powers, Chapter 8 *supra*.

A municipality may regulate the temperature at which milk can be transported into the city. City of Chicago v. Chicago & Northwestern Railway, 275 Ill. 30, 113 N.E. 849 (1916).

[26] Dean Milk Co. v. City of Aurora, 404 Ill. 331, 88 N.E.2d 827 (1949); Kansas City v. Henre, 96 Kan. 794, 153 P. 548 (1915); City of Newport v. Hiland Dairy Co., 291 Ky. 561, 164 S.W.2d 818 (1942); City of St. Louis v. Kellmann, 295 Mo. 71, 243 S.W. 134 (1922), error dism'd 263 U.S. 679, 44 S.Ct. 132, 68 L.Ed. 503 (city may require milk sellers to take out permits—no defense to failure to obtain permit that milk was clean and sanitary); Stracquadanio v. Department of Health, 285 N.Y. 93, 32 N.E.2d 806 (1941). Clearly, the municipal regulation can extend to the requirement that all milk sold in the city be pasteurized. See Koy v. City of Chicago, *supra* note 25. As to regulation of unpasteurized ("raw") milk, see Ozersky, Taste of America—Got Raw?, Time magazine, Sept. 20, 2010, at 69 (under federal law, it's illegal to sell consumers unpasteurized milk that has been transported across state lines; ten states forbid such milk from being sold at all, and 30 others restrict such sales). See generally Note, Striking a Balance: Regulation of Raw Milk and a New Approach for Indiana, 11 Ind. Health L. Rev. 399 (2014). See also Note, Township Makes "Moo"ves Against Dairy: The Nebraska Supreme Court Recognizes Local Government Regulation of Agriculture in Butler County Dairy, L.L.C. v. Butler County, 827 N.W. 2d 267 (2013), 93 Neb. L. Rev. 196 (2014). And the city can impose restrictions on the method of pasteurization allowed. Pacific Coast Dairy v. City of San Francisco, 214 Cal. 668, 8 P.2d 140 (1932). See generally Note, Constitutional Law—Municipal Corporations—Police Power, 16 St. John's L.Rev. 124 (1941); Annot., Constitutionality of Regulations as to Milk, 80 A.L.R. 1225 (1932). The processing and distribution of other dairy products can also be regulated. See Simco Sales Service v. Brackin, 344 Pa. 628, 26 A.2d 323 (1942) (ice cream); City of Spokane v. Arnold, 73 Wash. 256, 131 P. 815 (1913) (butter).

A leading U.S. Supreme Court case—Nebbia v. State of New York, 291 U.S. 502, 54 S.Ct. 505, 78 L.Ed. 940 (1934)—upheld sweeping state restrictions on the milk business, including regulation of retail prices. The dairy industry is one of the most thoroughly regulated of all businesses in America. See Note (on state-court decision in *Nebbia*), Constitutional Law—Public Utilities—Police Power—Emergency, 2 Geo. Wash.L.Rev. 96 (1933); Recent Case (on state-court decision in *Nebbia*), Note, Constitutional Law—Due Process of Law—Fixing of Minimum Milk Prices, 47 Harv.L.Rev. 130 (1933); Comment, Constitutional Law—Regulation of the Price of Milk in Interstate Commerce, 1 Mo.L.Rev. 64 (1936); Legislation Note, Milk Regulation: A Problem in Economics, Legislation, and Administration, 40 W.Va.L.Q. 247 (1934). See generally Note, Nebbia v. People: A Milestone, 82 U.Pa.L.Rev. 619 (1934).

[27] Bowie Inn, Inc. v. City of Bowie, 274 Md. 230, 335 A.2d 679 (1975) (requirement held not arbitrary); American Can Co. v. Oregon Liquor Control Commission, 15 Or.App. 618, 517 P.2d 691 (1973) (no violation of commerce clause); Anchor Hocking Glass Corp. v. Barber, 118 Vt. 206, 105 A.2d 271 (1954) (reasonable relation to a police-power purpose found). See Gargan, New York's New Deposit Law on Bottles and Cans Will Take Effect Tomorrow, N.Y. Times, Sept. 11, 1983, at A19, noting that New York was becoming the ninth state to adopt a return deposit law. The most discussed law of this nature is the Oregon statute requiring beverage retailers to accept empty beverage containers and pay the consumer the statutory refund value, and requiring distributors to accept the empty containers from the retailer for the refund value. See Beals, Comment: Oregon's Bottle Law: A Model for Comparable Legislation?, 11 Cal.West. L.Rev. 537 (1975); Note, American Can: Judicial Response to Oregon's Nonreturnable Container Legislation, 4 Ecology L.Q. 145 (1974); Note, The Oregon Bottle Bill, 54 Or.L.Rev. 175 (1975). See generally Greef & Martin, Beverage Container Legislation: A Policy and Constitutional Evaluation, 52 Tex.L.Rev. 351 (1974); Gudger & Walters, Beverage Container Regulation: Economic Implications and Suggestions for Model Legislation, 5 Ecology L.Q. 265 (1976); Slade, Wilson & Wilson, State and Local Regulation of Nonreturnable Beverage Containers, 1972 Wis.L.Rev. 536; "A Stepped-up Drive to Smash Bottle Bills," Bus. Week, July 12, 1982, at 30 (noting the efforts of the container

environmental factors have also been cited by courts in sustaining municipal regulation of junkyards and wrecking yards, which are considered potentially dangerous sources of fire and disease.[28] It is also sometimes noted that such places are often used for the disposition of stolen goods.[29] For these reasons, licensing requirements as to such yards have been sustained,[30] as have requirements that records be kept of all purchases.[31] Fencing requirements as to junkyards have been sustained as providing protection to children in the neighborhood and minimizing the dangers of vandalism.[32] Increasingly, aesthetic reasons are being accepted as legitimate grounds for fencing requirements and even for exclusion of junk yards from entire areas.[33]

Some businesses are recognized as posing special dangers to customers, to persons in the neighborhood, or to both such groups; and thus strict regulation is justified. Laundries, for instance, may be made subject to licensing requirements,[34] and may be

---

and beverage industries to defeat or repeal return-deposit laws); Annot., Validity and Construction of Statute or Ordinance Requiring Return Deposits on Soft Drink or Similar Containers, 73 A.L.R.3d 1105 (1976). See also Minnesota v. Clover Leaf Creamery Co., 449 U.S. 456, 101 S.Ct. 715, 66 L.Ed.2d 659 (1981), upholding a statute banning retail sale of milk in plastic non-returnable, non-refillable containers, though permitting sale of milk in *non*-plastic, non-returnable, non-refillable containers; Wisconsin Association of Food Dealers v. City of Madison, 89 Wis.2d 311, 278 N.W.2d 481 (1979), upholding an ordinance requiring retailers of milk to offer this product in returnable containers. On problems of garbage disposal, see generally Section 23.5, notes 73–81 of this chapter *infra*, and accompanying text.

[28] See Vermont Salvage Corp. v. Village of St. Johnsbury, 113 Vt. 341, 34 A.2d 188 (1943); Lerner v. Delavan, 203 Wis. 32, 233 N.W. 608 (1930). See generally State ex rel. Keener v. Serr, 53 Ohio App.2d 143, 372 N.E.2d 360 (1976); City of Enid v. Ramer, 556 P.2d 646 (Okl.App.1976) (with review of cases), both noting the sustaining of many local restrictions on junkyards and salvage yards.

[29] See City of Grand Rapids v. Braudy, 105 Mich. 670, 64 N.W. 29 (1895); Bologno v. O'Connell, 7 N.Y.2d 155, 196 N.Y.S.2d 90, 164 N.E.2d 389 (1959). Cf. Mansbach Scrap Iron Co. v. City of Ashland, 235 Ky. 265, 30 S.W.2d 968 (1930) (owner can be required to let police search the premises); State v. Wybierala, 305 Minn. 455, 235 N.W.2d 197 (1975) (same).

[30] See Levi v. City of Anniston, 155 Ala. 149, 46 So. 237 (1908); Levine v. Board of Adjustment, 125 Conn. 478, 7 A.2d 222 (1939); Shurman v. City of Atlanta, 148 Ga. 1, 95 S.E. 698 (1918); Grossman v. City of Indianapolis, 173 Ind. 157, 88 N.E. 945, reh. denied 173 Ind. 157, 89 N.E. 862 (1909); Knack v. Velick Scrap Iron & Machinery Co., 219 Mich. 573, 189 N.W. 54 (1922); Price v. Smith, 416 Pa. 560, 207 A.2d 887 (1965); Village of St. Johnsbury v. Aron, 103 Vt. 22, 151 A. 650 (1930); City of Milwaukee v. Ruplinger, 155 Wis. 391, 145 N.W. 42 (1914).

[31] See Shurman v. City of Atlanta, *supra* note 30 (bond requirement also imposed); City of St. Louis v. Baskowitz, 273 Mo. 543, 201 S.W. 870 (1918). Cf. Levi v. City of Anniston, *supra* note 30 (dealer must notify police of intent to purchase items, with description of the property and of person from whom to be bought).

[32] See Vermont Salvage Corp. v. Village of St. Johnsbury, *supra* note 28. Cf. Levine v. Board of Adjustment, *supra* note 30 (5-foot high fence).

[33] See Rotenberg v. City of Fort Pierce, 202 So.2d 782 (Fla.App.1967); State v. Buckley, 16 Ohio St.2d 128, 243 N.E.2d 66 (1968), appeal dism'd and cert. denied 395 U.S. 163, 89 S.Ct. 1647, 23 L.Ed.2d 174; Lenci v. City of Seattle, 63 Wash.2d 664, 388 P.2d 926 (1964), all sustaining—largely on aesthetic grounds—fencing requirements as to junkyards and salvage yards. As to exclusion of such uses from a city, see Oregon City v. Hartke, 240 Or. 35, 400 P.2d 255 (1965), sustaining a total ban on automobile wrecking yards in a city. See generally Comment, Municipal Regulation of Junk Yards, 12 Syracuse L.Rev. 79 (1960); Annot., Validity, Construction, and Application of Zoning Ordinance Relating to Operation of Junkyard or Scrap Metal Processing Plant, 50 A.L.R.3d 837 (1973). As to the application of zoning laws to junkyards and comparable land-uses, see also Section 18.4, note 52 *supra*, and accompanying text.

[34] Ex parte Le Protti, 68 Cal. 635, 10 P. 113 (1886); City of Newnan v. Atlanta Laundries, Inc., 174 Ga. 99, 162 S.E. 497 (1932); Ruban v. City of Chicago, 330 Ill. 97, 161 N.E. 133 (1928); State v. Dirnberger, 152 Minn. 44, 187 N.W. 972 (1922); Yee Bow v. City of Cleveland, 99 Ohio St. 269, 124 N.E. 132 (1919), error dism'd 255 U.S. 578, 41 S.Ct. 320, 65 L.Ed. 794 (upholding broad standards to be used by licensing authority). A reasonable license fee can be imposed. See Soon Hing v. Crowley, 113 U.S. 703, 5 S.Ct. 730, 28 L.Ed. 1145 (1885); Barbier v. Connolly, 113 U.S. 27, 5 S.Ct. 357, 28 L.Ed. 923 (1885). See generally 50 Am.Jur.2d Laundries, Dyers & Dry Cleaners §§ 5–6 (1970). See also Annot., Application of City Ordinance Requiring License for a Laundry to Supplier of Coin-Operated Laundry Machines Intended for Use in Apartment

required to meet certain standards for fire-protection and sanitation purposes.[35] Laundromats may be required to keep an attendant on the premises, particularly if the business remains open at night.[36] Similarly, a municipality may establish a system of licensing gasoline stations if, and only if, they meet designated safety standards.[37] Some authority has even upheld municipal prohibitions of self-service gasoline stations.[38]

Building, 65 A.L.R.3d 1296 (1975); Annots., Public Regulation of Dry Cleaning and Dyeing Establishments, 128 A.L.R. 678 (1940); 49 A.L.R. 110 (1927).

[35] See Ex parte Sing Lee, 96 Cal. 354, 31 P. 245 (1892); Ex parte Moynier, 65 Cal. 33, 2 P. 728 (1884); Yee Bow v. City of Cleveland, *supra* note 34 (upholding right of municipality to conduct inspections). Cf. Ex parte White, 67 Cal. 102, 7 P. 186 (1885) (upholding requirement that laundries be of brick and stone). While some types of regulation of laundries are less common today than in the past, a related type of restriction that has now appeared is regulation of the phosphate content of detergents that may be used in the locality, due to fear of "cultural eutrophication" of the waters, causing increased production of algae and aquatic plants. See Niehoff, Phosphates in Detergents: The Chicago-Type Ordinance and Other Remedies, 40 U.Cin.L.Rev. 548 (1971) (noting the Chicago ordinance, which provides a 2-stage phase-out of phosphates); Annot., Validity, Under Federal Constitution, of State Statute or Local Ordinance Regulating Phosphate Content of Detergents, 21 A.L.R.Fed. 365 (1974). See generally the discussion of water-pollution control Sec. 154 ns. 1–5 *infra*, and accompanying text. As to regulation of nail salons, see Note, Beyond the Polish: An Examination of Hazardous Conditions in Nail Salons and Potential Solutions for the Industry in New York City, 21 J. L. & Pol'y 243 (2012).

[36] See Gibbons v. City of Chicago, 34 Ill.2d 102, 214 N.E.2d 740 (1966), cert. denied 385 U.S. 829, 87 S.Ct. 63, 17 L.Ed.2d 65 (attendant required after 6 P.M., and laundromats required to close from 11:30 P.M. until 6:30 A.M.; upheld); Township of Little Falls v. Husni, 139 N.J.Super. 74, 352 A.2d 595 (1976); Schacht v. City of New York, 30 Misc.2d 77, 219 N.Y.S.2d 53 (1961), mod. 14 A.D.2d 526, 217 N.Y.S.2d 278 (upholding portion of ordinance requiring that attendant be present after 6 P.M. and that laundromats close between midnight and 6 A.M.). But cf. Heard v. Bolton, 107 Ga.App. 863, 131 S.E.2d 835 (1963) (ordinance requiring self-service laundry to close between 11 P.M. and 7 A.M. unless it had attendant on duty found unreasonable and void). See generally Annot., License, Regulation, and Taxation of Self-Service Laundries, 87 A.L.R.2d 1007 (1963).

In People v. Raub, 9 Mich.App. 114, 155 N.W.2d 878 (1967), the court upheld a requirement that *car* washes close between 10 P.M. and 7 A.M.

[37] See Appeal of Holley, 110 Conn. 80, 147 A. 300 (1929); City of Ottawa v. Brown, 372 Ill. 468, 24 N.E.2d 363 (1939); Scott v. City of Waterloo, 223 Iowa 1169, 274 N.W. 897 (1937); Fletcher Oil Co. v. Bay City, 247 Mich. 572, 226 N.W. 248 (1929); Hyma v. Seeger, 233 Mich. 659, 207 N.W. 834 (1926). The licensing standards can be fairly broad, not necessarily spelling out all requirements in detail. See City of Fordyce v. Dunn, 215 Ark. 276, 220 S.W.2d 430 (1949); Starkey v. City of Longmont, 91 Colo. 387, 15 P.2d 620 (1932) (gasoline station required to have attendant in charge; valid). But the standards cannot be so vague or general as to leave licensing authorities with nearly unbridled discretion. See D-X Sunray Oil Co. v. City of Stevens Point, 173 F.Supp. 431 (W.D.Wis.1959). See generally Phillips v. Town of Belleville, 135 N.J.L. 271, 52 A.2d 441 (1947) (ordinance concerning building of automobile service stations was invalid where it contained no norm for granting or refusing permits). A reasonable fee to cover costs of licensing and inspection may be levied. Fletcher Oil Co. v. Bay City, *supra*.

Closing-hour requirements as to gasoline stations have been upheld if found reasonable. See Bi-Lo Stations, Inc. v. Alsip, 22 Ill.App.3d 514, 318 N.E.2d 47 (1974).

[38] J & L Oil Co. v. City of Carrollton, 230 Ga. 817, 199 S.E.2d 190 (1973); Shell Oil Co. v. City of Revere, 383 Mass. 682, 421 N.E.2d 1181 (Mass. 1981); Town of North Hempstead v. Exxon Corp., 53 N.Y.2d 747, 439 N.Y.S.2d 342, 421 N.E.2d 834 (1981). Cf. Hawkins v. City of Red Cloud, 123 Neb. 487, 243 N.W. 431 (1932), appeal dism'd 289 U.S. 704, 53 S.Ct. 660, 77 L.Ed. 1461 (1933) (ordinance prohibiting coin-operated gasoline pumps upheld); Southern Wasco County Ambulance Serv., Inc. v. State, 156 Or.App. 543, 968 P.2d 848 (1998) (rational basis found for legislative classifications exempting certain consumers and sellers from general prohibition on self-service dispensing). But see Oil City Discount Center, Inc. v. City of Yonkers, 53 Misc.2d 191, 277 N.Y.S.2d 945 (1967) (ordinance prohibiting operation of self-service gasoline station void as not reasonably related to public health, safety, or welfare). Some ordinances allow self-service pumps only if an attendant is kept on duty. The "energy crunch" of recent times has resulted in discontinuance of operation of many gasoline stations—and conversion of many into other businesses. In Sun Oil Co. v. Goldstein, 453 F.Supp. 787 (D.Md.1978), aff'd without opinion 594 F.2d 859 (4th Cir.), the court upheld a Maryland statute declaring a two-year moratorium on conversion of full-service gas stations to lesser service facilities; the statute was passed due to concern about the availability of automotive repair facilities. Taxi companies and other providers of transportation have long been subject to government safety regulation; and such regulation,

§ 23.3 Restrictions on Hours and Days of Business Operation

Particularly controversial forms of municipal regulation of business are those that limit the hours of business operation. Courts tend to scrutinize such limitations closely to make sure there is some valid police-power purpose, such as protection of health, aid in lessening or detecting criminal activities, or prevention of noise that might be disturbing to neighboring residents. Ordinances reasonably aimed at some such purpose will normally be sustained, but not those that merely limit competition—and, in any case, not those that unreasonably discriminate against certain business. Thus, restrictions on restaurant hours have been upheld if reasonably necessary to noise-prevention;[39] limits on the business-hours of taverns have been sustained if necessary to enforcement of the liquor laws and/or to help curb violent and criminal activity;[40] closing hours for billiard halls may be justified if these places are reasonably regarded as breeding-grounds of crime;[41] and pawn-brokers and second-hand stores may be required

---

particularly at the municipal level, has sometimes now been extended to pedicabs. See Note, The Rise of the Pedicab: Municipal Regulation of an Emerging Industry, 53 Ariz. L. Rev. 255 (2011). Ride-sharing companies are also being regulated in some cities. See Rhodan, Hack Attacks—Cities Take Aim at Fast-growing Ride Services, Time magazine, March 31, 2014, at 18.

[39] State v. Grant, 107 N.H. 1, 216 A.2d 790 (1966); City of Burlington v. Jay Lee, Inc., 130 Vt. 212, 290 A.2d 23 (1972). But see City of Jackson v. Murray-Reed-Slone & Co., 297 Ky. 1, 178 S.W.2d 847 (1944). A closing-hour restriction on restaurants based on a desire to prevent sub rosa sale of intoxicating liquor was upheld in Churchill v. City of Albany, 65 Or. 442, 133 P. 632 (1913); but such a purpose was held an indirect and unreasonable means of dealing with the problem in Fincher v. City of Union, 186 S.C. 232, 196 S.E. 1 (1938). See Annot., Validity of Municipal Ordinance Regulating Time During Which Restaurant Business May be Conducted, 53 A.L.R.3d 942 (1973). See generally Reynolds, A Time to Open and a Time to Close—Municipal Regulation of Business Hours, 55 J. Urban & Contemp. L. 41 (1999); Annot., Validity of Statute or Ordinance Fixing Closing Hours for Certain Kinds of Business, 55 A.L.R. 242 (1928). See also Annot., What Constitutes a "Restaurant," 122 A.L.R. 1399 (1939); Annot., What Amounts to "Restaurant" or "Restaurant Business" Within Intoxicating Liquor Law, 105 A.L.R. 566 (1936). Many restrictions on restaurants are also imposed, of course, in order to insure that they serve healthful, uncontaminated food. See notes 22–24 *supra* and accompanying text. And zoning laws often forbid restaurants in many areas of a community. See Annot., Zoning Regulations as Forbidding or Restricting Restaurants, Diners, "Drive-ins," or the Like, 82 A.L.R.2d 989 (1962). Occasionally, restaurants are allowed in a certain zone only if they agree to restrictions on their hours of operation. See Annot. Imposing Restriction as to Hours or Days of Operation of Business as Condition of Allowance of Special Zoning Exception or Variance, 99 A.L.R.2d 227 (1965). Cf. City of Burlington v. Jay Lee, Inc., *supra* (ordinance prohibited restaurants in residential areas from being open during designated night-time hours; sustained). Compare New Hampshire Motor Transp. Ass'n v. Town of Plaistow, 67 F.3d 326 (1st Cir. 1995), upholding, as not pre-empted by federal laws, an ordinance limiting night-time access to a truck terminal in order to reduce noise, odors, dust, vibration, etc.; David E. Shelton Productions, Inc. v. City of Chicago, 167 Ill.App.3d 54, 117 Ill.Dec. 722, 520 N.E.2d 1073 (1988), upholding an ordinance barring "juice bars" from operating during early morning hours in order to curtail noise and prevent violations of curfew by youthful patrons.

[40] See The Other Place of Miami, Inc. v. City of Hialeah Gardens, 353 So.2d 861 (Fla.App.1977); State v. Calloway, 11 Idaho 719, 84 P. 27 (1906); City of Charleston v. Jenkins, 243 S.C. 205, 133 S.E.2d 242 (1963). The sale of liquor is often much regulated by the *state*; and state regulations will normally prevail over those of a municipality (even a home-rule municipality) in cases of *conflict*, though not if the local rule merely sets a higher standard. In some jurisdictions, the state is found to have totally pre-empted the field of liquor control; *then* its laws will prevail over local laws even in the absence of conflict. See Annot., Validity of Municipal Regulation More Restrictive Than State Regulation as to Time for Selling or Serving Intoxicating Liquor, 51 A.L.R.3d 1061 (1973). See also Annot., Validity, Construction, and Application of Statute or Ordinance Requiring Closing, During Certain Hours, of Places Where Intoxicating Liquor Is Sold, as Affected by Fact that Such Places Are Also Used for Other Business, 139 A.L.R. 756 (1942).

[41] Purvis v. City of Ocilla, 149 Ga. 771, 102 S.E. 241 (1920) (operation of pool or billiard room admits of strict regulation); City of Tarkio v. Cook, 120 Mo. 1, 25 S.W. 202 (1894); Ex parte Brewer, 68 Tex.Cr.R. 387, 152 S.W. 1068 (1913) (same reasoning that justified closing saloons between midnight and dawn justified closing billiard halls during those hours). Cf. State ex rel. Baylor v. City of Hinton, 109 W.Va. 653, 155 S.E. 912 (1930), upholding a total ban on pool halls on grounds of promoting morality. The hours of operation of

to close at night because of the use of these places to dispose of stolen property and the difficulty of apprehending such persons when they do this under cover of darkness.[42] But closing-hour legislation will often be invalidated as unreasonable if applied to such quiet, innocuous businesses as barbershops,[43] or to mercantile businesses in general.[44] And

---

massage parlors are also sometimes limited because such places are thought to be the scene of criminal or immoral activities. See City of Spokane v. Bostrom, 12 Wn.App. 116, 528 P.2d 500 (1974). But cf. Hart Health Studio v. Salt Lake County, 577 P.2d 116 (Utah 1978) (no reason to set different hours for masseurs who were sole practitioners; ordinance invalid). On massage parlors, see generally notes 127–129 *infra*, and accompanying text. In Star Satellite, Inc. v. City of Biloxi, 779 F.2d 1074 (5th Cir.1986), a zoning ordinance limiting an adult bookstore (as well as bars, nightclubs, massage parlors, and pool halls serving liquor) to certain days and hours of operation was held not to violate the operator's First and Fourteenth Amendment rights. Cf. Ben Rich Trading, Inc. v. City of Vineland, 126 F.3d 155 (3d Cir.1997), upholding against First Amendment attack ordinances limiting the operating hours of sexually oriented businesses.

[42] See Hyman v. Boldrick, 153 Ky. 77, 154 S.W. 369 (1913) (second-hand stores); Circle D Pawn No. 2, Inc. v. City of Norman, 956 P.2d 931 (Okl.Civ.App. 1998) (pawn shops); Solof v. City of Chattanooga, 180 Tenn. 296, 174 S.W.2d 471 (1943), reh. denied 180 Tenn. 296, 176 S.W.2d 816 (pawnbrokers). Cf. Davidson v. Phelps, 214 Ala. 236, 107 So. 86 (1926) (auctions); City of Butte v. Paltrovich, 30 Mont. 18, 75 P. 521 (1904) (pawnshops, loan offices, and second-hand stores); Biddles, Inc. v. Enright, 239 N.Y. 354, 146 N.E. 625 (1925) (auctions); City of Roanoke v. Fisher, 137 Va. 75, 119 S.E. 259 (1923) (jewelry auctions). It has been observed that there is a general tendency of the courts to be more willing to uphold "hours restrictions" on businesses if the social utility of those businesses is considered slight or doubtful. 1 Antieau, Municipal Corporation Law § 6.177, at 6–311 (1998).

[43] Ganley v. Claeys, 2 Cal.2d 266, 40 P.2d 817 (1935); City & County of Denver v. Schmid, 98 Colo. 32, 52 P.2d 388 (1935) (closing regulation as to barbershops but excepting beauty parlors; held arbitrary and unreasonable); City of Miami v. Shell's Super Store, 50 So.2d 883 (Fla.1951); Chaires v. City of Atlanta, 164 Ga. 755, 139 S.E. 559 (1927); City of Alexandria v. Hall, 171 La. 595, 131 So. 722 (1930) (unconstitutional to require barber shops to close at 6:30 p. m.); Eanes v. City of Detroit, 279 Mich. 531, 272 N.W. 896 (1937); Pavlik v. Johannes, 194 Minn. 10, 259 N.W. 537 (1935); Knight v. Johns, 161 Miss. 519, 137 So. 509 (1931); Ernesti v. City of Grand Island, 125 Neb. 688, 251 N.W. 899 (1933); Tomasi v. Township of Wayne, 126 N.J.Super. 169, 313 A.2d 229 (1973) (unconstitutional to require barber shops to close at 6:30 p.m. on weekdays); Oklahoma City v. Johnson, 183 Okl. 430, 82 P.2d 1057 (1938). An Ohio case once sustained an hours regulation as to barber shops on the ground that they may be lounging places for the idle and may serve as "fronts" for gambling and other illegal activities. Wilson v. City of Zanesville, 130 Ohio St. 286, 199 N.E. 187 (1935). But the court soon reversed its position and invalidated such a closing measure. City of Cincinnati v. Correll, 141 Ohio St. 535, 49 N.E.2d 412 (1943). See Fordham & Asher, Home Rule Powers in Theory and Practice, 9 Ohio St.L.J. 18, 64 (1948). See generally Annot., Validity of Statute or Ordinance Regulating Barbers, 98 A.L.R. 1088, 1093–96 (1935), noting that the majority of cases have invalidated closing-hour restrictions on barber shops.

[44] See Ex parte Harrell, 76 Fla. 4, 79 So. 166 (1918). Cf. Southland Corp. v. Township of Edison, 217 N.J.Super. 158, 524 A.2d 1336 (1986), judgment aff'd 220 N.J.Super. 294, 531 A.2d 1361 (1987) (township ordinance enacted to reduce late-night robberies by restricting the hours of many retail businesses invalidated as in violation of state constitutional guarantees of right to acquire, possess, and protect property and of the right to pursue lawful vocations); Fasino v. Mayor & Borough Council of Montvale, 122 N.J.Super. 304, 300 A.2d 195 (1973), aff'd 129 N.J.Super. 461, 324 A.2d 77 (ordinance requiring closing of all businesses for off-premises consumption from 11 p. m. to 6:30 a. m. unconstitutional); Crawford's Clothes, Inc. v. Board of Commissioners, 131 N.J.L. 97, 35 A.2d 38 (1944) (clothing stores); Cowan v. City of Buffalo, 247 App.Div. 591, 288 N.Y.S. 239 (1936) (markets); Dave Abrams, Inc. v. City of Buffalo, 276 N.Y. 494, 12 N.E.2d 174 (1937) (shoe stores); State v. Ray, 131 N.C. 814, 42 S.E. 960 (1902) (dry goods stores). Closing-hour regulations as to laundries are generally invalid. See Yee Gee v. City & County of San Francisco, 235 F. 757 (N.D.Cal.1916); Spann v. Gaither, 152 Md. 1, 136 A. 41 (1927) (laundry not obnoxious or unwholesome business). But as to self-service laundromats, they are often upheld. See Section 23.2, note 36 *supra* and cases cited therein. An ordinance forbidding soliciting between 6 p.m. and 9 a.m. was found to violate First Amendment free speech rights in Ohio Citizen Action v. City of Englewood, 671 F.3d 564 (6th Cir. 2012), because it was not narrowly tailored to protect privacy, prevent crime, or conserve public resources. On other restrictions on solicitors, see Section 23.6 *infra*.

Even if *some* restriction on hours might be justified as to a particular business, the closing-hour requirement specifically applied must be *reasonable*; and evidence of financial loss by a business is relevant to this question of reasonableness. See People ex rel. Pinello v. Leadbitter, 194 Misc. 481, 85 N.Y.S.2d 287 (1948). And if an ordinance is not uniformly applicable to all commercial enterprises but singles-out for regulation a First-Amendment-protected activity, the government must show that the regulation is narrowly and explicitly drawn and is necessary to further a legitimate government interest. See People v. Glaze, 27 Cal.3d 841, 166

such legislation will be invalidated as discriminatory if it exempts certain members of a particular trade,[45] or if it applies to some types of businesses, but not to other very similar types—such as an ordinance restricting the hours of clothing stores but not shoe stores.[46] Thus, closing-hour legislation must pass the twin tests of being (1) reasonably related to a valid police-power purpose, and (2) not unreasonably discriminatory as to certain businesses or classes of business.

Many of the same considerations enter the picture when local governments attempt to limit the *days* of operation of certain businesses (or the days on which certain commodities may be sold). The most common type of such restriction has been the "Sunday blue law." The U.S. Supreme Court has sustained such laws as not violative of the First Amendment of the U.S. Constitution;[47] and most courts have sustained such measures against arguments that they are not reasonably related to a police-power purpose, since some contribution to public health and general welfare can usually be found.[48] Occasional cases have failed to find sufficient purpose for a Sunday closing-

---

Cal.Rptr. 859, 614 P.2d 291 (1980) (hours regulation of "picture arcades" invalid; not justified as preventing masturbation).

[45] Heil v. Kauffman, 354 Mo. 271, 189 S.W.2d 276 (1945) (ordinance invalidated as not equally applicable to all gasoline stations in city).

[46] Crawford's Clothes, Inc. v. Board of Commissioners, *supra* note 44. Cf. McCulley v. City of Wichita, 151 Kan. 214, 98 P.2d 192 (1940) (ordinance applied to groceries and meat markets but exempted hotels, restaurants, etc.); Ernesti v. City of Grand Island, *supra* note 43 (ordinance applied to barber shops but not beauty parlors); Hart v. Teaneck Township, 135 N.J.L. 174, 50 A.2d 856 (1947) (ordinance applied to lunch wagons but not restaurants).

[47] Braunfeld v. Brown, 366 U.S. 599, 81 S.Ct. 1144, 6 L.Ed.2d 563 (1961), reh. denied 368 U.S. 869, 82 S.Ct. 22, 7 L.Ed.2d 70; Two Guys From Harrison-Allentown, Inc. v. McGinley, 366 U.S. 582, 81 S.Ct. 1135, 6 L.Ed.2d 551 (1961), reh. denied 368 U.S. 869, 82 S.Ct. 21, 7 L.Ed.2d 69; McGowan v. Maryland, 366 U.S. 420, 81 S.Ct. 1101, 6 L.Ed.2d 393 (1961). See Gallagher v. Crown Kosher Super Market, 366 U.S. 617, 81 S.Ct. 1122, 6 L.Ed.2d 536 (1961); Green Star Supermarket v. Stacy, 242 Ark. 54, 411 S.W.2d 871 (1967); City of Mount Vernon v. Julian, 369 Ill. 447, 17 N.E.2d 52 (1938) (good discussion of the arguments and cases).

[48] Opyt's Amoco, Inc. v. Village of South Holland, 209 Ill.App.3d 473, 154 Ill.Dec. 260, 568 N.E.2d 260 (1991) (upholding against a wide range of constitutional attacks an ordinance requiring the Sunday closing of most businesses); City of Harlan v. Scott, 290 Ky. 585, 162 S.W.2d 8 (1942); People v. Derose, 230 Mich. 180, 203 N.W. 95 (1925); GEM of St. Louis, Inc. v. City of Bloomington, 274 Minn. 471, 144 N.W.2d 552 (1966); Mack Paramus Co. v. Mayor & Council of Paramus, 103 N.J. 564, 511 A.2d 1179 (1986) (upholding a borough ordinance providing that no worldly employment, including computer use, could be practiced on Sunday; state blue law found to leave room for such local prohibitions); Masters-Jersey, Inc. v. Borough of Paramus, 32 N.J. 296, 160 A.2d 841 (1960); Town of West Orange v. Carr's Department Store, 53 N.J.Super. 237, 147 A.2d 97 (1958); Town of West Orange v. Jordan Corp., 52 N.J.Super. 533, 146 A.2d 134 (1958); Auto-Rite Supply Co. v. Mayor & Township Committeemen of Woodbridge, 25 N.J. 188, 135 A.2d 515 (1957) (municipalities may control and regulate Sunday activity, but particular ordinance void as conflicting with state law); S.S. Kresge Co. v. Tomlinson, 275 N.C. 1, 165 S.E.2d 236 (1969); State v. Solomon, 245 S.C. 550, 141 S.E.2d 818 (1965), appeal dism'd 382 U.S. 204, 86 S.Ct. 396, 15 L.Ed.2d 270; Bookout v. City of Chattanooga, 59 Tenn.App. 576, 442 S.W.2d 658 (1969). The valid purpose of such laws is usually said to be their assurance of a day of rest and quiet in the community. See Auto-Rite Supply Co. v. Mayor & Township Committeemen of Woodbridge, *supra*. Sometimes the laws are justified as preventing the harm that comes to persons from uninterrupted labor. See Hertz Washmobile System v. Village of South Orange, 41 N.J.Super. 110, 124 A.2d 68 (1956), aff'd 25 N.J. 207, 135 A.2d 524 (physical and moral debasement might otherwise occur—but particular ordinance found invalid as in conflict with state policy). Occasionally, courts mention that the laws may protect those who worship on Sunday from interruption of their services. See Pacesetter Homes, Inc. v. Village of South Holland, 18 Ill.2d 247, 163 N.E.2d 464 (1959), voiding a law as not contributing to this goal. See generally Annot., Validity, Construction, and Effect of "Sunday Closing" or "Blue" Laws—Modern Status, 10 A.L.R.4th 246 (1981) (noting that such laws have a long history in the United States but have been rare in the Far Western states); Annot., Constitutionality of Discrimination by Sunday Law or Ordinance as Between Different Kinds of Business, 119 A.L.R. 747 (1939). See also Annot., Validity, Under Establishment of Religion Clause of Federal or State Constitution, of Provision Making Day of Religious Observance a Legal Holiday, 90 A.L.R.3d 752 (1979); Annot., Establishment and Free Exercise of Religion Clauses of Federal Constitution's First Amendment as

law,[49] or have invalidated a municipal measure as in conflict with state law.[50] But if and when such laws are invalidated, it is usually on equal protection grounds; most of the laws contain classifications and exceptions, and the law will be invalidated if such categories serve no rational purpose. Exemptions of drug stores have generally been sustained,[51] as have exceptions for hotels and restaurants.[52] When the exception is expressed in terms of particular commodities, it may well be sustained if it covers such products as food, drugs, and gasoline.[53] But a law may be found violative of equal protection if it discriminates against larger businesses by allowing only small ones to remain open;[54] if it is so riddled with exceptions that it serves no general purpose;[55] or if it is so little, and so unevenly, enforced that it serves only to discriminate against isolated persons.[56] The history of such laws has been one of lax enforcement and considerable unpopularity,[57] and there are trends toward (1) providing additional exceptions in the

---

Applied to Governmental Regulations or Activities Allegedly Supporting Public Observance of Sabbath or of Religious Holiday, 106 L.Ed.2d 752 (1991).

49 See Pacesetter Homes, Inc. v. Village of South Holland, *supra* note 48 (saying that ordinary businesses don't disturb people in their worship or injure the peace of the community); Skag-Way Department Stores v. City of Omaha, 179 Neb. 707, 140 N.W.2d 28 (1966). Cf. S.E. Nichols Herkimer Corp. v. Village of Herkimer, 34 A.D.2d 371, 312 N.Y.S.2d 22 (1970), voiding an ordinance that required businesses to close on Memorial Day and Independence Day.

50 National Food Stores, Inc. v. Cefalu, 280 So.2d 903 (La.1973); Schacht v. City of New York, 30 Misc.2d 77, 219 N.Y.S.2d 53 (1961), mod. 14 A.D.2d 526, 217 N.Y.S.2d 278.

51 State v. Burbage, 172 N.C. 876, 89 S.E. 795 (1916) (against public policy of state for one to pursue his ordinary business on Sunday); Kirk v. Olgiati, 203 Tenn. 1, 308 S.W.2d 471 (1957).

52 Re Sumida, 177 Cal. 388, 170 P. 823 (1918) (hotels); State v. Towery, 239 N.C. 274, 79 S.E.2d 513 (1954), appeal dism'd 347 U.S. 925, 74 S.Ct. 532, 98 L.Ed. 1079. See generally Annot., What Is "Restaurant," "Cafe," or "Victualing House" Within Sunday Law, 9 A.L.R. 428 (1920).

53 See Humphrey Chevrolet v. City of Evanston, 7 Ill.2d 402, 131 N.E.2d 70 (1955), discussing the various kinds of Sunday-closing legislation; noting that in this instance certain commodities were forbidden to be sold, while the sale of others was allowed; and pointing out that all car dealers (the class to which plaintiff belonged) were treated alike under such a law. Cf. State v. Haase, 97 Ohio App. 377, 116 N.E.2d 224 (1953) (exception for "works of necessity" valid as not violating equal protection, but hardware business not a work of necessity). But see Skaggs Drug Centers, Inc. v. Ashley, 26 Utah 2d 38, 484 P.2d 723 (1971), striking down as void for vagueness a Sunday-closing law that contained exceptions for "goods or services necessary for maintenance of health, safety, or life."

54 See Piggly-Wiggly of Jacksonville, Inc. v. City of Jacksonville, 336 So.2d 1078 (Ala.1976) (statute exempted food stores in which not more than four persons regularly worked; held to create unreasonable classification). But some cases have upheld Sunday-closing laws that allow smaller businesses to remain open, since these businesses are thought not to disturb the peace and quiet of the "day of rest." City of Bismarck v. Materi, 177 N.W.2d 530 (N.D.1970) (grocery stores regularly employing no more than 3 persons could remain open). See City of Jackson v. Luckett, 336 So.2d 776 (Miss.1976). Cf. Caiola v. City of Birmingham, 288 Ala. 486, 262 So.2d 602 (1972) (upholding law permitting Sunday operation of grocery stores having on duty four or less employees), which was distinguished in the *Piggly-Wiggly* case *supra.*

55 Kroger Co. v. O'Hara Tp., 481 Pa. 101, 392 A.2d 266 (1978). See Millikan v. Jensen, 4 Ill.App.3d 580, 281 N.E.2d 401 (1972) (prohibition of public dances on Sunday void where no prohibition of other kinds of business); Spartan's Industries v. Oklahoma City, 498 P.2d 399 (Okl.1972), invalidating a Sunday-closing law as discriminating against some classes of merchants.

56 People v. Acme Markets, 37 N.Y.2d 326, 372 N.Y.S.2d 590, 334 N.E.2d 555 (1975), where the court noted a history of disuse and no policy of general enforcement, and held that under those circumstances, a prosecution at the instance of a group for its private purposes constituted a violation of equal protection.

57 See "Closing Up the Sunday Merchants," Bus. Week, Dec. 23, 1972, at 22, noting the non-enforcement of many "blue laws"; "Folks Blue Over Sunday Sales Law," Dallas Morning News, Jan. 31, 1977, at 1, noting a poll showing the unpopularity of such a law. With the repeal of North Dakota's "Sunday blue law" in 1991, no state remains in which Sunday shopping is totally prohibited. See "For North Dakota Shoppers, No More Minnesota Sundays," N.Y. Times, Feb. 12, 1991, at A12. For a discussion of the advantages of restrictions on Sunday activities, see Gibbs, And on the Seventh Day We Rested?, Time, Aug. 2, 2004, at 90.

existing laws, and (2) repealing, or invalidating (often because of the denial of equal protection created by the exceptions), the laws entirely. Where such laws remain, they often now provide an exception for persons wishing to observe—and close their business on—a day other than Sunday,[58] and the validity of such an exception has been sustained.[59]

§ 23.4 Local Regulation of Water and Air Pollution

Two problems of great modern importance are water pollution and air pollution. Regulation to reduce such pollution has been undertaken by the federal government; but there is generally still room, and often the need, for state and local regulation—some of which pre-dates the federal activity. While laws in this area can apply to all persons, businesses are particularly affected by many restrictions.

It has long been held that local governments can enact and enforce laws to reduce pollution of their water supply,[60] to protect waters within the locality in which people

---

Sunday blue laws, being penal in nature, are usually strictly construed and will not be enlarged by implication. See Denton v. Winner Communications, Inc., 726 P.2d 911 (Okl. App. 1986) (Sunday sale of stallion's stud services held not forbidden by Sabbath-breaking statute).

[58] See Berman's Petition, 344 Mich. 598, 75 N.W.2d 8 (1956), applying a Detroit ordinance with such an exception. Cf. Gibson Products Co. v. Texas, 545 S.W.2d 128 (Tex.1976), cert. denied 431 U.S. 955, 97 S.Ct. 2677, 53 L.Ed.2d 272, upholding the constitutionality of a law forbidding businesses to sell certain items on *both* Saturday and Sunday. See also 21 Okl. Stat.1981, § 909, allowing as a defense to the crime of "Sabbath-breaking" a person's honoring of another day-of-rest. But cf. Trans World Airlines, Inc. v. Hardison, 432 U.S. 63, 97 S.Ct. 2264, 53 L.Ed.2d 113 (1977), finding no violation of federal civil rights laws in an airline's refusal to allow clerks to work a four-day week if necessary in order to avoid working on their Sabbath.

[59] Marks Furs, Inc. v. City of Detroit, 365 Mich. 108, 112 N.W.2d 66 (1961). But cf. Thornton v. Caldor, Inc., 472 U.S. 703, 105 S.Ct. 2914, 86 L.Ed.2d 557 (1985), holding that a Connecticut statute which provided workers with an unqualified right not to work on their Sabbath violated the Establishment Clause, where it imposed on employers and employees an absolute duty to conform their business practices to the particular religious practices of the employee, provided no exception for special circumstances, and allowed no consideration of whether the employer had made reasonable accommodation proposals.

[60] See Shumaker v. Borough of Dalton, 51 F.2d 793 (M.D.Pa.1931) (interment of dead bodies near municipal water supply can be forbidden); State v. Finney, 65 Idaho 630, 150 P.2d 130 (1944) (ordinance forbidding the anchoring or maintaining of any craft, if used as a residence, on waters of lake); City of Shreveport v. Conrad, 212 La. 737, 33 So.2d 503 (1947) (vessels can be banned from municipal reservoir, and plane flights over it can be prohibited); City of New Rochelle ex rel. Conlon v. Burke, 288 N.Y. 406, 43 N.E.2d 463 (1942) (in interest of consumer's health and welfare, city has jurisdiction over water distribution system); Salt Lake City v. Young, 45 Utah 349, 145 P. 1047 (1915) (animals can be kept out of municipal water supply). Cf. City of West Frankfort v. Fullop, 6 Ill.2d 609, 129 N.E.2d 682 (1955) (city can prohibit drilling for oil and gas near source of water supply). But see Bino v. City of Hurley, 273 Wis. 10, 76 N.W.2d 571 (1956) (city could not ban swimming, etc. on lake which supplied city's water as would unconstitutionally deprive lake-front property owners of their property rights). On problems with some cities' drinking water, see "Troubled Water," Time, Aug. 31, 1970, at 40; "Warning: Your Drinking Water May Be Dangerous," U.S. News & World Rep., Jan. 16, 1984, at 51. See generally Hines, Nor any Drop to Drink: Public Regulation of Water Quality, 52 Iowa L.Rev. 186 (1966); Jacks, Local and Regional Water Pollution Control in Texas, 48 Tex.L.Rev. 1286 (1970); Robinson, Drinking Water Regulation, 10 Real Property, Probate & Trust J. 675 (1975). In Ayers v. Jackson Township, 106 N.J. 557, 525 A.2d 287 (1987), it was held that residents of a town whose water was contaminated by toxic pollutants had a claim against the township for infringement of their "quality of life" and for costs of medical surveillance. The claim was brought as a nuisance action under the New Jersey Tort Claims Act. See generally Owen, Urbanization, Water Quality, and the Regulated Landscape, 82 U. Colo. L. Rev. 431 (2011). See also Hoffer, The New York City Watershed Memorandum of Agreement: Forging a Partnership to Protect Water Quality, 18 U. Baltimore J. Envtl. L. 113 (2011). Some authorities recognize a human right to water. See Beail-Farkas, The Human Right to Water and Sanitation: Context, Contours, and Enforcement Prospects, 30 Wis. Int'l L. J. 761 (2013).

Municipalities, in operating the city water works, may *fluoridate* the city water supply. See Schuringa v. City of Chicago, 30 Ill.2d 504, 198 N.E.2d 326 (1964), cert. denied 379 U.S. 964, 85 S.Ct. 655, 13 L.Ed.2d 558 (with review of cases); Wilson v. City of Council Bluffs, 253 Iowa 162, 110 N.W.2d 569 (1961); Rogowski v. City

swim,[61] and to control discharge of waste and sewage into municipal sewers.[62] Those using a municipal sewer system may be required to pay reasonable charges to cover the cost of pollution control.[63] Local regulations designed to lessen or prevent water pollution must meet two tests in order to be upheld: (1) They must be authorized by state law, and (2) they must be reasonably designed to achieve the hoped-for goal.[64]

---

of Detroit, 374 Mich. 408, 132 N.W.2d 16 (1965); Kraus v. City of Cleveland, 163 Ohio St. 559, 127 N.E.2d 609 (1955), appeal dism'd, 351 U.S. 935, 76 S.Ct. 833, 100 L.Ed. 1463 (1956); Dowell v. City of Tulsa, 273 P.2d 859 (Okl.1954), cert. denied 348 U.S. 912, 75 S.Ct. 292, 99 L.Ed. 715, noted 8 Okl.L.Rev. 472 (1955); Hall v. Bates, 247 S.C. 511, 148 S.E.2d 345 (1966); Kaul v. City of Chehalis, 45 Wash.2d 616, 277 P.2d 352 (1954) (with review of authorities); Froncek v. City of Milwaukee, 269 Wis. 276, 69 N.W.2d 242 (1955). Cf. Attaya v. Town of Gonzales, 192 So.2d 188 (La.App.1966) (ordinance ordering fluoridation valid; invalidity of prior motion or resolution on the subject was immaterial). Even where the city's water is supplied by a privately operated utility, it is probable that the city may require that the water be fluoridated, unless there is conflicting state law or state pre-emption of the field. See Wilson v. City of Mountlake Terrace, 69 Wash.2d 148, 417 P.2d 632 (1966) (city purchased water district's water system within city limits and redelivered water received from district to district for distribution to users outside city limits; city could adopt water-fluoridation program). See generally Annot., Validity, Construction, and Effect of Statute, Ordinance, or Other Measure Involving Chemical Treatment of Public Water Supply, 43 A.L.R.2d 453 (1955). In some jurisdictions, regulation of *privately* owned water utilities is entirely occupied by state legislation. See New Haven Water Co. v. City of New Haven, 152 Conn. 563, 210 A.2d 449 (1965) (state commission has exclusive control). And in some jurisdictions, the state has pre-empted the *entire* field of water-pollution control. See Staiger v. Madill, 328 Mich. 99, 43 N.W.2d 77 (1950). On regulation of utilities, see generally Chapter 17 *supra*.

In recent years, the *federal* government has entered the field of regulating the quality of drinking-water supplies. The Safe Drinking Water Act of 1974, 42 U.S.C.A. § 300f, establishes a timetable for the setting of nationwide drinking-water standards. See Wheatley & Castaneda, Protection of Underground Drinking Water Supplies—The Gonzalez Amendment to the Safe Drinking Water Act, 8 St. Mary's L.J. 40 (1976) (summarizing entire Act and noting especially an amendment thereto applicable to communities which draw their drinking water from an aquifer). See generally Baroni, Whose Drop Is It, Anyway? Legal Issues Surrounding Our Nation's Water Resources (ABA Section of State & Local Government Law 2011). See also Renwick, The Effects of the Federal Safe Drinking Water Act on Oil, Gas, and Mining Operations: An Oil and Gas Lawyer's View, 23 Rocky Mt. Mineral L. Institute 975 (1977); Sanderson, The Effects of the Federal Safe Drinking Water Act on Oil, Gas, and Mining Operations: Bittersweet or Unpalatable?, 23 Rocky Mt. Mineral L. Institute 941 (1977).

[61] See State v. Finney, *supra* note 60 (houseboats can be banned from lakes where swimming occurs). Cf. City of Springfield v. Mecum, 320 S.W.2d 742 (Mo.App.1959) (use of certain types of outboard motors can be banned on lake where public swims).

[62] A. E. Staley Manufacturing Co. v. Environmental Protection Agency, 8 Ill.App.3d 1018, 290 N.E.2d 892 (1972); Village of Fox River Grove v. Aluminum Coil Anodizing Corp., 114 Ill.App.2d 226, 252 N.E.2d 225 (1969); Larsen Baking Co. v. New York City, 30 A.D.2d 400, 292 N.Y.S.2d 145 (1968) aff'd 24 N.Y.2d 1036, 303 N.Y.S.2d 80, 250 N.E.2d 356 (upholding code providing that certain pollutants could not be discharged into sewer system without permission of designated official and according to rules promulgated by him). The lead content of effluents deposited in the sewers by local industries can be limited by a municipality. See Rauland Division, Zenith Radio Corp. v. Metropolitan Sanitary District, 2 Ill.App.3d 35, 275 N.E.2d 756 (1971). On ordinances or regulations banning sale within a locality of detergents containing phosphorus, see Section 152, note 32 *supra*. On the problems that Cleveland, Ohio, once had with sewage discharge into the Cuyahoga River—and efforts to modernize the sewage system and clean up the river—, see "The Cities—The Price of Optimism," Time, Aug. 1, 1969, at 41. See also Wood, Ecological Drama Along the Cuyahoga; Students Fight Pollution in Cuyahoga River Watershed Region, Am.Educ., Jan., 1973, at 15.

[63] See Ivy Steel & Wire Co. v. City of Jacksonville, 401 F.Supp. 701 (M.D.Fla.1975). Cf. Larsen Baking Co. v. New York City, *supra* note 62 (surcharges can be levied for excess pollutants discharged into city sewers).

[64] See Westwood Forest Estates, Inc. v. Village of South Nyack, 23 N.Y.2d 424, 297 N.Y.S.2d 129, 244 N.E.2d 700 (1969) (municipal power to deal with problem of inadequate treatment of sewage); Larsen Baking Co. v. New York City, *supra* note 62. On federal, state, and local efforts to combat water pollution, see generally Fisher, New York's SEQR—Its Importance for Water Pollution Control, 50 N.Y.S.B.J. 572 (1978); Kuchenbecker & Long, Will Municipal Sewage Continue to Threaten Private Water-Control Recreation?: An Appraisal of the 1972 Water Pollution Control Act, 4 Rutgers Camden L.J. 260 (1973); Phillips, Developments in Water Quality and Land Use Planning: Problems in the Application of the Federal Water Pollution Control Act Amendments of 1972, 10 Urban L.Ann. 43 (1975).

The Federal Water Pollution Control Act of 1972, 33 U.S.C.A. §§ 1251–1376, provides a comprehensive program (including federal financial assistance—but not preempting the field; Askew v. American Waterways

Just as controls on water pollution promote public health and welfare, so do controls on polluted air. It has been held that the federal government has not pre-empted the

---

Operators, Inc., 411 U.S. 325, 93 S.Ct. 1590, 36 L.Ed.2d 280 (1973) reh. denied 412 U.S. 933, 93 S.Ct. 2746, 37 L.Ed.2d 162) for controlling and abating water pollution. See Train v. City of New York, 420 U.S. 35, 95 S.Ct. 839, 43 L.Ed.2d 1 (1975) (Administrator of Environmental Protection Agency could not allot to the states less than the entire amounts authorized to be appropriated under the Act). Cf. Environmental Protection Agency v. National Crushed Stone Association, 449 U.S. 64, 101 S.Ct. 295, 66 L.Ed.2d 268 (1980) (Environmental Protection Agency not required to include economic ability as factor in granting variances from 1977 effluent limitations). See generally Symposium, Water Quality Control: Federal Water Pollution Control Act Amendments of 1972, 7 Natural Resources Lawyer 225–56 (1974). See also Note, Clean Water Act of 1977: Great Expectations Unrealized, 47 U.Cin.L.Rev. 259 (1978). On the applicability of the federal water pollution legislation to nuclear facilities, see Miskovsky, Griffith, Bullerdick & Donnelly, Recent Developments in Urban Environment Law, 16 Urban Law. 821 (1984). On litigation over allocation of the cost of upgrading water and sewage treatment facilities to achieve compliance with federal laws, see Griffith, Fleming, Zeller & McCarthy, Recent Developments in Urban Environment Law, 19 Urban Law. 1093, 1101–03 (1987). See also United States v. City of Hoboken, 675 F.Supp. 189 (D.N.J.1987) (impossibility of compliance not a defense in enforcement action brought under Clean Water Act of 1977). As to the scope of federal authority under the Clean Water Act, see Note, Muddying the Waters: *United States v. Cundiff* Adds Confusion and Complexity to the Ongoing Debate Over the Scope of Federal Jurisdiction Under the Clean Water Act, 22 Vill. Envtl. L. J. 285 (2011), discussing United States v. Cundiff, 555 F.3d 200 (6th Cir. 2009). See generally Schempp, At the Confluence of the Clean Water Act and Prior Appropriation: The Challenge and Ways Forward, 43 Envtl. L. Rep. News & Analysis 10138 (2013); Comment, Did We Miss the Boat? The Clean Water Act and Sustainability, 47 U. Rich. L. Rev. 1267 (2013). A good overview of the federal law on water pollution is Evans (ed.), The Clean Water Handbook (American Bar Ass'n 1994). A good summary of developments concerning control of both water and air pollution (with emphasis on air pollution) is the Cato Symposium, 2 Cato J. 1–333 (Spring, 1982). A particularly thoughtful article, within that symposium, on water pollution is Milliman, Can Water Pollution Policy Be Efficient?, 2 Cato J. 165 (1982). As to regulation of water pollution from underground storage tanks, see Annot., State and Local Government Control of Pollution from Underground Storage Tanks, 11 A.L.R.5th 388 (1993). As to the effects of hydro fracking on *water* resources, see Rawlins, Planning for Fracking on the Barnett Shale: Soil and Water Contamination Concerns, and the Role of Local Government, 44 Envtl. L. 135 (2014); Comment, Hydraulic Fracturing in the United States and the European Union: Rethinking Regulation to Ensure the Protection of Water Resources, 30 Wis. Int'l L. J. 881 (2013).

field of air-pollution control;[65] but occasionally, state pre-emption may be found.[66] If there is no pre-emption, a local government may make reasonable and clear restrictions on activities likely to result in pollution of the air.[67] This power has been recognized for

---

[65] Houston Compressed Steel Corp. v. State, 456 S.W.2d 768 (Tex.Civ.App.1970). On local efforts to combat air pollution, see Note, Local Governments and Air Pollution, 33 Ohio St.L.J. 924 (1972); Recent Decision Note, Local Government—A Municipality Has the Power to Regulate by Local Ordinance the Emission of Air Pollutants, 22 Syracuse L.Rev. 1173 (1971). On special problems and efforts of some cities with particularly troublesome situations, see Chernow, Implementing the Clean Air Act in Los Angeles: The Duty to Achieve the Impossible, 4 Ecology L.Q. 537 (1975); Gartenberg, Air Pollution—The Landlords and New York City's New Air Code, 9 Colum.J.L. & Soc.Prob. 495 (1973); Walpole, Another Look at the Air Pollution Crisis in Birmingham, 3 Environmental Affairs 243 (1974). Air pollution has even invaded many areas of the Western U.S. See Gottschalk, Many Areas in West, Once Famed for the Air, Befouled by Pollution, Wall St. J., April 21, 1970, at 1. See also, on the air pollution problems of Beijing, China, and efforts to correct them, Ramzy, Airing Out Bejing, Time, Jan. 21, 2008, at Global 1.

Machinery for a unified federal-state battle against air pollution is set forth in the 1970 Clean Air Amendments to the Air Quality Act of 1967, 42 U.S.C.A. §§ 7401–7626. See Comment, Enforcement of the Clean Air Amendments of 1970, 10 Urban L.Ann. 297 (1975). The Act grants considerable rule-making power to the Administrator of the Environmental Protection Agency, and also permits the various states to submit plans for implementation and enforcement of emission standards. See Air Pollution Variance Board v. Western Alfalfa Corp., 416 U.S. 861, 94 S.Ct. 2114, 40 L.Ed.2d 607, on remand 35 Colo.App. 207, 534 P.2d 796, aff'd 191 Colo. 455, 553 P.2d 811 (1976) (state health inspector who entered outdoor premises, without knowledge or consent of owner, to observe smoke emission held not to have violated Fourth Amendment of U.S. Constitution); Annot., Air Pollution Control: Validity of Legislation Permitting Administrative Agency to Fix Permissible Standards of Pollutant Emission, 48 A.L.R.3d 326 (1973). See generally Currie, Air Pollution: Federal Law and Analysis (Callaghan & Co. 1981). Kramer, 1970 Clean Air Amendments: Federalism in Action or Inaction?, 6 Tex.Tech. L.Rev. 47 (1974); Luneberg, Federal-State Interaction Under the Clean Air Amendments of 1970, 14 Boston College Ind. & Comm.L.Rev. 637 (1973); Mandelker & Rothschild, Role of Land-Use Controls in Combating Air Pollution Under the Clean Air Act of 1970, 3 Ecology L.Q. 235 (1973); Strelow, Reviewing the Clean Air Act, 4 Ecology L.Q. 583 (1975); Comment, State Implementation Plans and Air Quality Enforcement, 4 Ecology L.Q. 595 (1975); "The Drive for Clean Air," U.S. News & World Rep., June 25, 1973, at 39; Annot., Orders or Penalties Against State or Its Officials for Failure to Comply with Regulations Directing State to Regulate Pollution-Creating Activities of Private Parties, Under § 113 of Clean Air Act, 31 A.L.R.Fed. 79 (1977). See also Annot., Validity and Construction of Statute or Ordinance Allowing Tax Exemption for Property Used in Pollution Control, 65 A.L.R.3d 434 (1975); Annot., Necessity of Showing Scienter, Knowledge, or Intent in Prosecution for Violation of Air Pollution or Smoke Control Statute or Ordinance, 46 A.L.R.3d 758 (1972) (intent or knowledge generally need *not* be shown). On municipal obligations and liabilities under federal law, see Smith & Grillo, Let's Clear the Air Once and For All: Municipal Liability for Failing to Comply with Section 110 of the Clean Air Act, 44 Catholic U.L. Rev. 1103 (1995). See generally Reitze, Air Pollution Control Law: Compliance & Enforcement (Environmental Law Institute 2001). See also Symposium, Clean Air, 43 Ariz. St. L. J. 665–949 (2011). On dealing with air pollution as a public nuisance, see Note, Tarheel Smokestack Blues: The Clean Air Act, Public Nuisance Law, and Abatement of Interstate Air Pollution, 30 Temple J. Sci. Tech. & Envtl. L. 311 (2011), noting North Carolina ex rel. Cooper v. Tennessee Valley Auth., 615 F.3d 291 (4th Cir. 2010).

There have at times been complaints of too many agencies, at too many levels of government, being involved in the fight against pollution, and of frequent changes in the standards. See MacGregor, Companies Complain That Pollution Laws Conflict, Change Often, Wall St. J., Dec. 23, 1970, at 1. As to air-pollution regulation in Indian Country, see Comment, Elusive Goal, Enduring Benefits: Regulation of Air Quality in Indian Country as a Tool to Promote Small Business Development, 8 Entrepreneurial Bus. L. J. 25 (2013).

As to federal pre-emption of air pollution regulation, see Pacific Merchant Shipping Ass'n v. Goldstene, 517 F.3d 1108 (9th Cir. 2008) (California state regulations limiting emissions from the auxiliary diesel engines of ocean-going vessels are pre-empted by federal Clean Air Act). On federal pre-emption, see generally Chapter 7 *supra*.

[66] See Village of Union v. Southern California Chemical Co., 59 Ill.App.3d 373, 16 Ill.Dec. 616, 375 N.E.2d 489 (1978) (state pre-emption). Cf. Borough of Verona v. Shalit, 92 N.J.Super. 65, 222 A.2d 145 (1966) aff'd 96 N.J.Super. 20, 232 A.2d 431 (conflict with state act, which allowed municipal regulations *not* in conflict with state law).

[67] Lees v. Bay Area Air Pollution Control District, 238 Cal.App.2d 850, 48 Cal.Rptr. 295 (Dist.Ct.1965); Marshall Field & Co. v. City of Chicago, 44 Ill.App. 410 (1892); City of New Orleans v. Lambert, 14 La.Ann. 247 (1859); People v. Lewis, 86 Mich. 273, 49 N.W. 140 (1891); Hudson Valley Light Weight Aggregate Corp. v. Schovel, 64 Misc.2d 814, 316 N.Y.S.2d 477 (1970); People v. Prince Jagendorf Greene, Inc., 7 N.Y.2d 42, 194

many decades,[68] and has been upheld by the U.S. Supreme Court even when exercised against vessels operating in interstate commerce under licenses from the United States.[69] While localities sometimes pass legislation specifically dealing with air pollution, it has been recognized that the power to terminate or curtail pollution-producing activities within the locality exists also under the general power to abate nuisances.[70] Comprehensive air-pollution-control ordinances have now been enacted by many municipalities; and they have been upheld as applied to businesses and to individuals; as with water-pollution restrictions, they must simply meet the tests of being authorized by the state, and being reasonable in nature.[71]

§ 23.5 Local Control of Trash and Garbage

A growing problem for many municipalities is the disposing of their residents' trash and garbage. As population grows, so does the amount of refuse that must be disposed of—in some manner that does not pose a threat to health or safety. Although a state may

---

N.Y.S.2d 498, 163 N.E.2d 325 (1959) (any accurate test could be used to determine volatile content of coal); City of Portland v. Lloyd A. Fry Roofing Co., 3 Or.App. 352, 472 P.2d 826 (1970) (with review of cases). See Oriental Boulevard Co. v. Heller, 58 Misc.2d 920, 297 N.Y.S.2d 431 (1969) aff'd 27 N.Y.2d 212, 316 N.Y.S.2d 226, 265 N.E.2d 72 (1970), appeal dism'd 401 U.S. 986, 91 S.Ct. 1234, 28 L.Ed.2d 527 (upholding ordinance regulating use of fuel burners and refuse incinerators). See generally Annot., Validity of State and local Air Pollution Administrative Rules, 74 A.L.R.4th 566 (1989). On the ways that local governments can deal with air pollution, see Elsom, Managing Urban Air Quality (Island Press 1996). On the 20-year anti-pollution plan adopted by a regional authority for the Los Angeles area in 1989, see "A Drastic Plan to Banish Smog," Time, March 27, 1989, at 65, noting that the plan was designed to curtail automobile use and to convert almost all vehicles to nonpolluting fuels by the year 2009. As to the possible effects of hydrofracking on *air* quality, see Rawlins, Planning for Fracking on the Barnett Shale: Urban Air Pollution, Improving Health-Based Regulation, and the Role of Local Governments, 31 Va. Envtl. L. J. 226 (2013).

[68] See City of Rochester v. Macauley-Fien Milling Co., 199 N.Y. 207, 92 N.E. 641 (1910) (ordinance could prescribe density of smoke allowed to issue from stacks within city limits); Department of Health v. Ebling Brewing Co., 78 N.Y.S. 11 (Mun.Ct.1902).

[69] Huron Portland Cement Co. v. City of Detroit, 362 U.S. 440, 80 S.Ct. 813, 4 L.Ed.2d 852 (1960). Cases have long upheld the general power of municipalities to regulate smoke emissions from vessels. Harmon v. City of Chicago, 110 Ill. 400 (1884). And from locomotives. See People ex rel. Greene v. Long Island Railroad, 31 N.Y.S.2d 537 (Ct.Spec.Sess.1941). Modern cases have upheld municipal controls on emissions from automobiles and other motor vehicles. See City of St. Louis v. Eskridge, 486 S.W.2d 648 (Mo.App.1972) (air pollution control ordinance, as applied to motor vehicles, upheld as not too indefinite).

[70] See Northwestern Laundry v. City of Des Moines, 239 U.S. 486, 36 S.Ct. 206, 60 L.Ed. 396 (1916). On the other hand, air pollution may be regulated by a locality even though the pollution is not yet bad enough to constitute a nuisance. Barber's Super Markets, Inc. v. City of Grants, 80 N.M. 533, 458 P.2d 785 (1969) (incinerator prohibited though not yet a nuisance). Cf. People v. Detroit Edison Co., 16 Mich.App. 423, 168 N.W.2d 320 (1969) (ordinance sustained making it unlawful for anyone to emit smoke greater than a designated density).

[71] See Hudson Valley Light Weight Aggregate Corp. v. Schovel, *supra* note 67; Oriental Boulevard Co. v. Heller, *supra* note 67; City of Portland v. Lloyd Fry Roofing Co., *supra* note 67.

Local governmental regulations are increasingly being enacted in other areas of environmental concern—for instance, biodiversity. See Tarlock, Local Government Protection of Biodiversity: What Is Its Niche?, 60 U. Chi. L. Rev. 555 (1993).

For discussion of regulation of greenhouse gases in order to lessen global warming, see Note, If Not Now, When? The California Global Warming Solutions Act of 2006: California's First Steps Toward Comprehensive Mandatory Greenhouse Gas Regulation, 13 Hastings W.–Nw. J. Envtl. L. & Pol'y 249 (2007). See generally Symposium, Reducing Greenhouse Gases: State Initiatives and Market-Based Solutions, 17 Fordham Envtl. L. Rev. 101–286 (2006); Symposium, Global Warming: Causes, Effects and Mitigation Strategies for States and Localities, 12 Penn St. Envtl. L. Rev. 1–217 (2004). See also Brower & Vespa, Thinking Globally, Acting Locally: The Role of Local Government in Minimizing Greenhouse Gas Emissions from New Development, 44 Idaho L. Rev. 589 (2008).

occasionally be found to have pre-empted the field,[72] most municipalities have express or implied authority to control the keeping, collection, and disposition of garbage.[73] Any regulations must be reasonable, as must any classifications or distinctions created thereby.[74] And there must be no undue burden on interstate commerce: The U.S. Supreme Court invalidated a New Jersey law that totally banned the sending into that state of waste that originated outside.[75] Many municipalities, of course, not only regulate

---

[72] See Town of Kearny v. Jersey City Incinerator Authority, 140 N.J.Super. 279, 356 A.2d 51 (1976); Ringlieb v. Township of Parsippany-Troy Hills, 59 N.J. 348, 283 A.2d 97 (1971). Compare Freiberg, (Don't) See More Butts: Preemption and Local Regulation of Cigarette Litter, 37 Hamline L. Rev. 205 (2014).

[73] See California Reduction Co. v. Sanitary Reduction Works, 199 U.S. 306, 26 S.Ct. 100, 50 L.Ed. 204 (1905) (private firms permitted to haul garbage can be regulated by municipality to insure sanitary conditions in city); City of Malden v. Flynn, 318 Mass. 276, 61 N.E.2d 107 (1945); Boulevard Apartments v. Borough of Lodi, 110 N.J.Super. 406, 265 A.2d 838 (1970). Again, as with air pollution (see Section 23.4 *supra*), regulation may come partly in the form of declaring the keeping of garbage a nuisance where it is not done under proper controls. See Board of Health v. Vink, 184 Mich. 688, 151 N.W. 672 (1915).

[74] See Campbell v. City of Frontenac, 527 S.W.2d 643 (Mo.App.1975), invalidating an ordinance that prohibited parking or storage of garbage trucks within the municipality. For a model ordinance, see Connolly, Small Town Trash: A Model Comprehensive Solid Waste Ordinance for Rural Areas of the United States, 53 Catholic U.L. Rev. 1 (2003).

[75] City of Philadelphia v. New Jersey, 437 U.S. 617, 98 S.Ct. 2531, 57 L.Ed.2d 475 (1978), noted 64 A.B.A.J. 1280 (1978); 92 Harv.L.Rev. (1978; part of summary of 1977 Supreme Court term); 18 Natural Resources J. 925 (1978). And some laws forbidding the bringing of garbage or trash into the community from outside its limits have been invalidated as outside the locality's power and/or as discriminatory. See Fort Gratiot Sanitary Landfill, Inc. v. Michigan Dep't of Natural Resources, 504 U.S. 353, 112 S.Ct. 2019, 119 L.Ed.2d 139 (1992), appeal after remand 71 F.3d 1197 (6th Cir.1995) (Michigan statute that generally prohibited private landfill operators from accepting solid waste that originated outside the county in which the landfill was located invalidated as violative of the commerce clause of U.S. Constitution); Boone Landfill, Inc. v. Boone County, 51 Ill.2d 538, 283 N.E.2d 890 (1972); Lutz v. Armour, 395 Pa. 576, 151 A.2d 108 (1959) (attempted distinction between local garbage and garbage from outside township is unrelated to township's health and general welfare). Cf. C & A Carbone, Inc. v. Town of Clarkstown, 511 U.S. 383, 114 S.Ct. 1677, 128 L.Ed.2d 399 (1994), on remand 208 A.D.2d 612, 617 N.Y.S.2d 482 (1994), invalidating as discriminating against interstate commerce a town ordinance that required all solid waste processed or handled within the town to be processed or handled at the town's transfer station; Oregon Waste Systems, Inc. v. Department of Environmental Quality, 511 U.S. 93, 114 S.Ct. 1345, 128 L.Ed.2d 13 (1994), on remand 319 Or. 251, 876 P.2d 749 (1994), finding that Oregon's imposition of a higher surcharge on disposal of out-of-state waste than was imposed on in-state waste was discriminatory on its face and thus violative of the commerce clause; Yaworski v. Canterbury, 21 Conn. Sup. 347, 154 A.2d 758 (1959), invalidating, as in conflict with state law, an ordinance prohibiting the transportation of garbage through a town. But see Wiggins v. Town of Somers, 4 N.Y.2d 215, 173 N.Y.S.2d 579, 149 N.E.2d 869 (1958), upholding a local prohibition on importation of garbage into the community. Compare State v. Wittenberg, 50 N.J.Super. 74, 141 A.2d 52 (1957), aff'd 26 N.J. 576, 141 A.2d 57 (1958), upholding a prohibition on importation of garbage into the community for the purpose of feeding pigs. See generally Gold, Solid Waste Management and the Constitution's Commerce Clause, 25 Urban Law. 21 (1993); Houpt, Roddewig & Sechen, The Commerce Clause and Waste Disposal Management Plans, 24 Urban Law. 907 (1992); Comment, State and Local Attempts to Restrict the Importation of Solid and Hazardous Waste: Overcoming the Dormant Commerce Clause, 40 U. Kan. L. Rev. 465 (1992).

After the *C & A Carbone* case, *supra*, it was widely believed that local governments had lost much of their power to control the movement of trash because it amounted to interference with the movement of an article of commerce. But in United Haulers Ass'n v. Oneida–Herkimer Solid Waste Management Auth., 261 F.3d 245 (2d Cir. 2001), cert. denied, 534 U.S. 1082, 122 S.Ct. 815, 151 L.Ed.2d 699 (2002), the Second Circuit held that local governments *can* permissibly direct the flow of waste to *public waste facilities* without running afoul of the U.S. Constitution's Commerce Clause. This helped revive flow control of solid waste by local governments. See Diederich, Municipalities Regain Control Over Trash, 35 Urban Law. 687 (2003).

On modern methods of, and problems with, garbage disposal, see generally Note, Garbage, the Police Power, and the Commerce Clause, 8 Capital U.L.Rev. 613 (1979); "The Garbage Can Crisis," Life, Nov. 7, 1969, at 32. See also Neal & Mealy, Recycling: Problems and Proposals, 2 Golden Gate L.Rev. 507 (1972). On provisions of the Refuse Act of 1899 prohibiting discharge of refuse into navigable waters except as permitted by the Army Corps of Engineers, see Note, The Refuse Act: Its Role Within the Scheme of Federal Water Quality Legislation, 46 N.Y.U.L.Rev. 304 (1971). On water pollution, see also Section 23.4 *supra*. *Air* pollution can also be a problem arising from garbage disposal, as where waste material is burned. See "Nashville's Trash

garbage accumulation and collection, but themselves engage in collecting and disposing of their inhabitants' garbage; power for a local government to do this is readily found in most states, even if the municipality exercises a monopoly on all garbage collection,[76] or grants an exclusive contract to a private company for such collection.[77] Where the

---

Crisis," Bus. Week, Feb. 23, 1976, at 52, discussing Nashville's efforts to run an incinerator-plant to burn garbage and, in the process, produce steam and chilled water for sale. Many cities are running out of landfill sites on which to bury garbage, and thus need to use incinerators—and modern incinerators *are* available that produce little pollution. See "Stamford Mines a Garbage Lode," Bus. Week, Sept. 25, 1971, at 142, on Stamford, Connecticut's, incinerator, using electrostatic precipitators and scrubbers. Sometimes, useful energy is even obtained from the destroying of garbage, either through incineration or through converting the garbage into liquid or gaseous fuel. See "Converting Garbage Into Energy," Bus. Week, March 30, 1974, at 44. On the effect of 1990 federal clean-air legislation on municipal waste incineration, see Kenderick-Hands, The Clean Air Act Amendments of 1990: New Standards for Municipal Solid Waste Incineration and Detroit's Resource Recovery Facility, 1991 Detroit C.L. Rev. 1. See generally Symposium, The Clean Air Act Amendments of 1990, 21 Environmental L. i–iii, 1549–2257 (1991). On problems with locating solid waste disposal facilities, see Houpt, Roddewig & Sechen, Report of the Subcommittee on Land Use and Solid Waste, 23 Urban Law. 753 (1991). See generally Comment, Taking Out the Trash—Where Will We Put All This Garbage?, 10 Pace Envtl. L. Rev. 925 (1993). On special regulation of hazardous waste, see Annot., Validity of Local Regulation of Hazardous Waste, 67 A.L.R.4th 822 (1989). See also Annot., Validity, Construction, and Application of State Hazardous Waste Regulations, 86 A.L.R.4th 401 (1991). A good overview of state and local regulation of waste disposal is O'Reilly, State & Local Government Solid Waste Management (Clark Boardman Callaghan 1994).

A possible alternative to traditional methods of disposing of solid waste is gasification: the conversion of solid waste into synthesis gas composed primarily of carbon monoxide and hydrogen via high temperatures. See Dudley & Collins, Gasification: Could It be an Answer to the Problem of Municipal Solid Waste Disposal?, 35 Urban Law. 693 (2003).

Another "waste control" problem is created by animals on city streets, etc. Some statutes (as in New York state—applicable to certain cities) and ordinances (as in Boston and Chicago) require owners of dogs to "clean up after them" if the canines defecate in any public area. See "Keeping New York Tidy," Time, Aug. 14, 1978, at 73.

[76] Cassidy v. City of Bowling Green, 368 S.W.2d 318 (Ky.1963); City of Hobbs v. Chesport, Limited, 76 N.M. 609, 417 P.2d 210 (1966). See Wheeler v. City of Boston, 233 Mass. 275, 123 N.E. 684 (1919) (farmers can be prohibited from transporting garbage through city streets to their farms); Pantlind v. City of Grand Rapids, 210 Mich. 18, 177 N.W. 302 (1920) (persons may be prohibited from transporting garbage from their own businesses). Cf. Laidlaw Waste Systems, Inc. v. City of Phoenix, 168 Ariz. 563, 815 P.2d 932 (App. 1991) (city garbage collection services in annexed area held lawful competition and not a "taking" of property of private trash haulers previously serving the area); Borough of Avalon v. Neithammer, 23 N.J.Super. 385, 93 A.2d 65 (1952) (homeowners can be forbidden to bury garbage on their premises, even if they do it for purpose of enriching the soil); City of Portsmouth v. McGraw, 21 Ohio St.3d 117, 488 N.E.2d 472 (1986) (city's requirement that every resident use, and pay a fee for, municipal garbage collection held a proper exercise of police power).

[77] See Gardner v. Michigan, 199 U.S. 325, 26 S.Ct. 106, 50 L.Ed. 212 (1905); California Reduction Co. v. Sanitary Reduction Works, 199 U.S. 306, 26 S.Ct. 100, 50 L.Ed. 204 (1905); Ponti v. Burastero, 112 Cal.App.2d 846, 247 P.2d 597 (Dist.Ct.1952); Ex parte Sozzi, 54 Cal.App.2d 304, 129 P.2d 40 (Dist.Ct.1942); Ex parte Zhizhuzza, 147 Cal. 328, 81 P. 955 (1905); State v. Orr, 68 Conn. 101, 35 A. 770 (1896); Strub v. Village of Deerfield, 19 Ill.2d 401, 167 N.E.2d 178 (1960); Schultz v. State, 112 Md. 211, 76 A. 592 (1910); City of Grand Rapids v. De Vries, 123 Mich. 570, 82 N.W. 269 (1900); State ex rel. City of Macon v. Belt, 561 S.W.2d 117 (Mo.1978); McKim v. Village of South Orange, 133 N.J.L. 470, 44 A.2d 784 (1945); Canton v. Van Voorhis, 61 Ohio App. 419, 22 N.E.2d 651 (1939); State ex rel. Moock v. City of Cincinnati, 120 Ohio St. 500, 166 N.E. 583 (1929); Dunn v. Gray, 238 Or. 71, 392 P.2d 1018 (1964); Wallis v. Fidelity & Deposit Co., 155 Wash. 618, 285 P. 656 (1930). Cf. Jansen Farms, Inc. v. City of Indianapolis, 202 Ind. 138, 171 N.E. 199 (1930) (food left from tables at restaurants, purchased for hog food, held not "garbage" under statute prohibiting collection of garbage except by department of sanitation); Troje v. City Council of Hastings, 310 Minn. 183, 245 N.W.2d 596 (1976) (city could properly refuse to grant more than one license for garbage collection); City of Spokane v. Carlson, 73 Wash.2d 76, 436 P.2d 454 (1968) (fact that garbage carted by defendant was harmless did not render unconstitutional, as to defendant, ordinance reserving to city the exclusive right to collect garbage in city). In Gomez v. City of Las Vegas, 61 N.M. 27, 293 P.2d 984 (1956), it was held that an exclusive contract for garbage collection could be entered into by a municipality despite a constitutional ban on exclusive privileges to any person or corporation. See Ventenbergs v. City of Seattle, 163 Wash.2d 92, 178 P.3d 960 (2008) (waste hauler did not have fundamental right to haul waste in city, and thus exclusive contracts granted to other haulers did not violate privileges and immunities clause of state constitution). But see Porter v. Suburban Sanitation Service, Inc., 283 N.C. 479, 196 S.E.2d 760 (1973).

municipality itself engages in collection of garbage and/or trash, it can charge a reasonable fee to those receiving the service.[78] Many of the same principles apply as with other utility-type services offered by local governments: Any classifications or differentials as to rates are constitutional only if rationally based on real differences;[79] the government cannot perform the service for *some* residents and arbitrarily deny it to others;[80] and reasonable controls (as on the type of garbage container used by residents) may be imposed in order to facilitate the local collection operation.[81]

§ 23.6 Local Regulation of Solicitors, Street Vendors, etc.

Another municipal problem—over which there has been a great amount of litigation—is the regulation of door-to-door salespersons, solicitors, canvassers, etc. Control of these persons' activities is often thought necessary to the health and well-being of the community. Some regulations distinguish among various categories of these persons, and thus a few definitions are helpful: *Peddlers* are usually said to be those who travel from place to place, selling and delivering their merchandise at the same time; *solicitors* or canvassers travel from place to place (or residence to residence) also, but don't carry goods with them—they merely take orders for future delivery; and *transient or itinerant merchants* occupy a temporary but fixed location (such as a stall or wagon)

---

[78] City of Naples v. Scatena, 240 So.2d 837 (Fla.App.1970); Mayor & Aldermen of Milledgeville v. Green, 221 Ga. 498, 145 S.E.2d 507 (1965), conf. to 112 Ga.App. 653, 145 S.E.2d 720; City of Lake Charles v. Wallace, 247 La. 285, 170 So.2d 654 (1964); Alexander v. City of Detroit, 392 Mich. 30, 219 N.W.2d 41 (1974). In City of Hobbs v. Chesport, Limited, *supra* note 76, it was held that such a fee could be imposed even on a resident who did not himself receive the municipality's garbage-collection service since he benefited from the service being performed for others. But in Montgomery v. City of Galva, 41 Ill.2d 562, 244 N.E.2d 193 (1969); it was held that a garbage-collection fee could not be added to the water bills of city residents since some who received water did not receive the garbage-collection service.

[79] See Pinellas Apartment Association, Inc. v. City of St. Petersburg, 294 So.2d 676 (Fla.App.1974); Alexander v. City of Detroit, 392 Mich. 30, 219 N.W.2d 41 (1974) (arbitrary classification is unconstitutional); Big Bear of North Carolina, Inc. v. City of High Point, 294 N.C. 262, 240 S.E.2d 422 (1978) (businesses, but not individual residents, had to pay fee for refuse collection; upheld). Cf. Minnesota v. Clover Leaf Creamery Co., 449 U.S. 456, 101 S.Ct. 715, 66 L.Ed.2d 659 (1981), reh. denied 450 U.S. 1027, 101 S.Ct. 1735, 68 L.Ed.2d 222 (1981) (to promote conservation and to ease waste disposal, state banned retail sale of milk in plastic, but not non-plastic containers if non-returnable and non-refillable; upheld). As to bans on plastic bags, see Comment, The Evolution of San Francisco's Plastic-bag Ban, 1 Golden Gate U. Envtl. L. J. 439 (2007). See generally Romer & Foley, A Wolf in Sheep's Clothing: The Plastic Industry's "Public Interest" Role in Legislation and Litigation of Plastic Bags in California, 5 Golden Gate U. Envtl. L. J. 377 (2012); Romer & Tamminen, Plastic Bag Reduction Ordinances: New York City's Proposed Charge on All Carryout Plastic Bags as a Model for U.S. Cities, 27 Tulane Envtl. L. J. 237 (2014). See also Note, San Francisco's Checkout Bag Fee Ordinance and the Problem of Proposition 26, 41 Hastings Const. L. Q. 151 (2013).

[80] Teagen Co. v. Borough of Bergenfield, 119 N.J.Super. 212, 290 A.2d 753 (1972); Boulevard Apartments v. Borough of Lodi, *supra* note 73 (garbage-collection service could not be denied residents of garden-type apartments). See generally Shean, The Politics of Trash, 16 Buffalo Envtl. L. J. 55 (2008–09).

[81] See Gardner v. Michigan, *supra* note 77 (recipients of service could be required to supply watertight container); Gardner v. City of Dallas, 81 F.2d 425 (5th Cir.1936), cert. denied 298 U.S. 668, 56 S.Ct. 834, 80 L.Ed. 1391; O'Neal v. Harrison, 96 Kan. 339, 150 P. 551 (1915); Pleasure Bay Apartments v. City of Long Branch, 66 N.J. 79, 328 A.2d 593 (1974) (garbage had to be left at curbside in approved containers; sustained); Sheek v. City of Newport News, 214 Va. 288, 199 S.E.2d 519 (1973) (businesses, including mobile home parks, had to put garbage in dumpmaster containers; sustained).

On the implementation of recycling programs by many local governments, see Copelan & Anderson, Government Recycling Objectives Frustrated by Lack of Demand, 15 Urban, State & Local L. Newsletter, No. 1, at 1 (Fall, 1991). See also O'Reilly, Recycling and Municipal Liability: Environmental Benefits and U.C.C. Risks, 23 Urban Law. 97 (1991).

from which they conduct business in a manner similar to that in which a permanent establishment would.[82]

One noted form of restriction on solicitors is the "Green River ordinance," which takes its name from one of its places of origin—Green River, Wyoming. Such an ordinance makes criminally punishable (often by declaring such action to be a nuisance) going in or upon private residential property without request or invitation of the owners. Such an ordinance has been sustained by the U.S. Supreme Court, and by some other courts, against constitutional objections;[83] but a majority of state courts have invalidated such measures—usually on the ground that they are unreasonably severe, amounting to practically total prohibitions.[84] Less extreme methods of regulation are usually upheld:

---

[82] See Rhyne, Burton, & Murphy, Municipal Regulation of Peddlers, Solicitors & Itinerant Merchants 79 (Nat'l Institute of Municipal Law Officers, Report No. 118) (1947); Montgomery, Municipal Regulation of the Itinerant Salesman, 10 Okl.L.Rev. 37 (1957). See generally Note, Streets of Wrath: The Constitutionality of the Town of Jupiter's Non-solicitation Ordinance, 37 Stetson L. Rev. 471 (2008).

[83] Breard v. Alexandria, 341 U.S. 622, 71 S.Ct. 920, 95 L.Ed. 1233, reh. denied 342 U.S. 843, 72 S.Ct. 21, 96 L.Ed. 637 (1951) (considering the community interest involved in promoting privacy in the home, this type of restriction is not a violation of due process and does not violate the Commerce Clause or infringe on free speech); Town of Green River v. Fuller Brush Co., 65 F.2d 112 (10th Cir. 1933) (upholding the Green River, Wyoming, ordinance); Larsen v. City of Colorado Springs, 142 F.Supp. 871 (D.C.Colo.1956); City of Shreveport v. Cunningham, 190 La. 481, 182 So. 649 (1938); Green v. Town of Gallup, 46 N.M. 71, 120 P.2d 619 (1941); People v. Bohnke, 287 N.Y. 154, 38 N.E.2d 478 (1941), cert. denied 316 U.S. 713, 62 S.Ct. 1306, 86 L.Ed. 1778; Village of West Jefferson v. Robinson, 1 Ohio St.2d 113, 205 N.E.2d 382 (1965); Ex parte Lewis, 141 Tex.Cr.R. 83, 147 S.W.2d 478 (1941); Town of Green River v. Bunger, 50 Wyo. 52, 58 P.2d 456 (1936), appeal dism'd 300 U.S. 638, 57 S.Ct. 510, 81 L.Ed. 854, reh. denied 300 U.S. 688, 57 S.Ct. 752, 81 L.Ed. 889 (upholding the Green River, Wyoming, ordinance). See McCormick v. City of Montrose, 105 Colo. 493, 99 P.2d 969 (1939). Such ordinances were particularly popular during the 1930's and 1940's; reportedly, over 400 municipalities adopted such ordinances from 1935 to 1939. McIntire & Rhyne, Municipal Legislative Barriers to a Free Market, 8 Law & Contemp. Prob. 359, 374 (1941).

As to the popularity of door-to-door soliciting, it has been reported to be on the increase again, due largely to the increased use of caller-ID and other devices that frustrate attempts at telephone solicitations. See Spencer, Ignore That Knocking: Door-to-Door Sales Make a Comeback, Wall St. J., April 30, 2003, at D.

In Watchtower Bible & Tract Soc'y of New York, Inc., v. Village of Stratton, 536 U.S. 150, 122 S.Ct. 2080, 153 L.Ed.2d 205 (2002), the Court, in an action brought by religious organizations, struck down as violative of the First Amendment an ordinance that required individuals to obtain a permit prior to engaging in door-to-door advocacy and required such solicitors to display the permit upon demand. See Comment, Constitutional Law—Freedom of Speech: Door-to-Door Permit Requirements for Noncommercial Canvassers, Domestic Threat or Freedom of Speech?, 79 N. Dak. L. Rev. 369 (2003); Note, U.S. Supreme Court Slams the Door on Small Town's Ordinance Requiring Solicitor Permits, 12 Widener L.J. 633 (2003). The *Watchtower* case, *supra*, was the latest in a line of cases that, for over 50 years, have invalidated restrictions on door-to-door canvassing and pamphleteering by Jehovah's Witnesses. See Murdock v. Pennsylvania, 319 U.S. 105, 63 S.Ct. 870, 87 L.Ed. 1292 (1943).

[84] Prior v. White, 132 Fla. 1, 180 So. 347 (1938); De Berry v. City of La Grange, 62 Ga.App. 74, 8 S.E.2d 146 (1940); City of Osceola v. Blair, 231 Iowa 770, 2 N.W.2d 83 (1942); City of Mount Sterling v. Donaldson Baking Co., 287 Ky. 781, 155 S.W.2d 237 (1941); Jewel Tea Co. v. City of Geneva, 137 Neb. 768, 291 N.W. 664 (1940); City of Washington v. Thompson, 160 N.E.2d 568 (Ohio Com.Pl.1949); City of Orangeburg v. Farmer, 181 S.C. 143, 186 S.E. 783 (1936) (ordinance declaring soliciting of sale of merchandise at private residences to be a nuisance held unreasonable); Ex parte Faulkner, 143 Tex.Cr.R. 272, 158 S.W.2d 525 (1942); White v. Town of Culpeper, 172 Va. 630, 1 S.E.2d 269 (1939). See New Jersey Good Humor, Inc. v. Board of Commissioners of Bradley Beach, 124 N.J.L. 162, 11 A.2d 113 (1940) (statute permitted municipality to *regulate* peddling; total *prohibition* by seashore community was not justified); Houston Credit Sales Co. v. City of Trinity, 269 S.W.2d 579 (Tex.Civ.App.1954) (city may regulate, but not prohibit, practice of solicitors going in and on private residences). Cf. City of McAlester v. Grand Union Tea Co., 186 Okl. 487, 98 P.2d 924 (1940) (house-to-house canvassing without permission of owners could not be *public* nuisance; at most was private nuisance as to individuals). The nuisance rationale was also partially relied on by the *Prior, Mount Sterling*, and *White* cases *supra*. See generally Note, Constitutional Law—Due Process—Freedom of Expression—Commerce Clause—"Green River" Ordinance as Applied to Door to Door Solicitation for Magazine Subscriptions, 50 Mich.L.Rev. 576 (1952); Note, Municipal Law—Ordinance Barring Uninvited Transient

Municipalities may require solicitors to register and give relevant information, including address and occupation.[85] Licenses can be required before a person is allowed to go door-to-door as a solicitor or canvasser,[86] but reasonably definite standards must be laid down so that those who wish to qualify may have a clear idea of the requirements.[87] A license

---

Vendors from City Residential Areas, 27 Miss.L.J. 148 (1956); Annot., Validity of Municipal Ordinance Prohibiting House-to-House Soliciting and Peddling Without Invitation, 35 A.L.R.2d 355 (1954); Annot. Validity of Municipal Regulation of Solicitation of Magazine Subscriptions, 9 A.L.R.2d 728 (1950). See also Comment, Political Speech in the Nonpublic Forum: Can Public Housing Facilities Limit Access to Political Canvassers?, 53 Case W. Reserve L. Rev. 569 (2002).

"Green River ordinances," because of the limitations they impose on free speech, may be invalidated if they are found not to be the least restrictive means of accomplishing a city's goals. See Project 80's, Inc. v. City of Pocatello, 857 F.2d 592 (9th Cir.1988), where a municipal ban on uninvited residential door-to-door solicitation was invalidated as not the least restrictive means available. The judgment was vacated and remanded, City of Idaho Falls v. Project 80's, Inc., 493 U.S. 1013, 110 S.Ct. 709, 107 L.Ed.2d 730 (1990), for further consideration in light of Board of Trustees of State University v. Fox, 492 U.S. 469, 109 S.Ct. 3028, 106 L.Ed.2d 388 (1989), on remand 764 F.Supp. 747 (N.D.N.Y.1991) (governmental restrictions on commercial speech need not be the absolutely least restrictive means to achieve a desired end). On remand, however, the Ninth Circuit again invalidated the ordinance as not sufficiently narrow. Project 80's, Inc. v. City of Pocatello, 942 F.2d 635 (9th Cir.1991). Such ordinances may also be given a strict construction. See MacLeod v. City of Los Altos, 182 Cal.App.2d 364, 6 Cal.Rptr. 326 (Dist. Ct.1960) (held inapplicable to members of a voluntary political group soliciting funds). And it has been argued that the burden should be on the property owner to post a "no-soliciting" notice, not on the solicitor to inquire whether such soliciting is wanted. See Reynolds, "Green River Ordinances": Where Does the Burden Belong?, 11 Fordham Urban L.J. 427 (1983).

[85] City of Washburn v. Ellquist, 242 Wis. 609, 9 N.W.2d 121 (1943), reh. denied 242 Wis. 609, 10 N.W.2d 292. Cf. The National Foundation v. City of Fort Worth, 307 F.Supp. 177 (N.D.Tex.1967), aff'd 415 F.2d 41, cert. denied 396 U.S. 1040, 90 S.Ct. 688, 24 L.Ed.2d 684 (solicitors for charities had to make accounting of funds; sustained); Acuff v. Mueller, 93 F.Supp. 146 (W.D.Mo.1950) (deposit of reasonable bond sustained); Mogolefsky v. Schoem, 50 N.J. 588, 236 A.2d 874 (1967) (requirement of supplying photograph, fingerprints, information on criminal record, etc. sustained); Moyant v. Borough of Paramus, 30 N.J. 528, 154 A.2d 9 (1959) (licensing requirement sustained, but fee and bond requirements held invalid; no statutory authority to raise revenue through such fees); Village of Mogadore v. Coe, 197 N.E.2d 570, 29 O.O.2d 44 (Ohio Com.Pl.1963) (solicitors can be required to reveal criminal record and obtain identification card, which they must carry when soliciting); Ex parte Killam, 144 Tex.Cr.R. 606, 162 S.W.2d 426 (1942), cert. denied sub nom. Killam v. Floresville, 317 U.S. 668, 63 S.Ct. 72, 87 L.Ed. 537, reh. denied 318 U.S. 801, 63 S.Ct. 826, 87 L.Ed. 1164 (regulations as to peddlers can be applied to minister of gospel selling books). But see Carolina Action v. Pickard, 420 F.Supp. 310 (W.D.N.C.1976) (solicitation license would be denied any charity whose cost of collection exceeded 25% of amount to be raised; unconstitutionally vague and overbroad); Pictorial Review Co. v. City of Alexandria, 46 F.2d 337 (W.D.La.1930) (bond of $100, and furnishing of such references as the mayor required; invalid); Robert v. City of Norfolk, 188 Va. 413, 49 S.E.2d 697 (1948) (regulation of solicitors found to violate freedom of press as applied to those soliciting magazine subscriptions). Cf. Ohio Citizen Action v. City of Englewood, 671 F.3d 564 (6th Cir. 2012), where a curfew on soliciting between 6 p.m. and 9 a.m. was invalidated as violating free-speech rights, though a requirement that solicitors carry a copy of the city's do-not-solicit list was upheld. Regulations may sometimes be upheld as to solicitation of or upon private residences but not as applied to business premises. See Day v. Klein, 225 Miss. 191, 82 So.2d 831 (1955) (ordinance upheld as applied to private residences—exception for sales of milk, dairy items, and certain other food products found reasonable).

[86] People v. Mobin, 237 Cal.App.2d 115, 46 Cal.Rptr. 605 (Dist.Ct.1965); Clifton v. Weber, 84 N.J.Super. 333, 202 A.2d 186 (1964) aff'd 44 N.J. 266, 208 A.2d 401 (permit required; was $3 fee); Slater v. Salt Lake City, 115 Utah 476, 206 P.2d 153 (1949). Cf. Re Hartmann, 25 Cal.App.2d 55, 76 P.2d 709 (Dist.Ct.1938) (magazine solicitors had to obtain permit if they had no established place of business in city; upheld). Sometimes ordinances imposing licensing, and related, requirements on solicitors are loosely termed "Green River ordinances"; but the term originally referred to regulations such as discussed in notes 83–84 *supra* and accompanying text.

[87] See Hynes v. Mayor & Council of Oradell, 425 U.S. 610, 96 S.Ct. 1755, 48 L.Ed.2d 243 (1976), invalidating an ordinance requiring solicitors and canvassers to give written notice to police; coverage was unclear, and ordinance did not specify what was necessary for compliance (what had to be included in notice, etc.); Staub v. City of Baxley, 355 U.S. 313, 78 S.Ct. 277, 2 L.Ed.2d 302 (1958), invalidating—as lacking definitive standards—an ordinance that allowed a mayor to decide whether or not to grant permits to solicit membership in organizations; the ordinance merely instructed the mayor to consider the applicant's character, the nature of the organization, and the effects on the general welfare of citizens. But some equally broad

fee may be charged if it is reasonable in amount;[88] but greater difficulty is presented by the question of charging such a fee to solicitors who operate in interstate commerce. Clearly if a fee or tax discriminates, or is likely to be applied so as to discriminate, against interstate commerce, it will be invalid.[89] But even where no discrimination is present, a license fee or bond requirement will be invalidated if it imposes a material burden on interstate commerce, and the U.S. Supreme Court found such a burden in a 1925 case involving an ordinance requiring a bond of $500 and license fees of $12.50 (for salespersons on foot) or $25 (for those using a vehicle).[90] The case seems to indicate that any fee on solicitors involved in interstate commerce would be unconstitutional; and several cases have found that an "undue burden" was imposed on such commerce by even fairly low fees.[91] Soliciting and canvassing for political support or charitable contributions may be regulated by municipalities in addition to their regulation of commercial solicitation; but courts will look with particular care at any restrictions on such activities, since important First Amendment rights are involved. Thus, the U.S. Supreme Court has invalidated a licensing requirement as applied to a candidate for public office and his supporters when the coverage of the ordinance, and the exact actions necessary for compliance, were unclear.[92] The same Court has invalidated as over-broad an ordinance prohibiting door-to-door or on-street solicitation by charities not using at least 75% of their receipts for charitable purposes.[93]

---

standards have sometimes been sustained, especially if First Amendment rights were not involved. See Moyant v. Borough of Paramus, *supra* note 85 (solicitor could be denied license if local official didn't find applicant "satisfactory").

[88] See Acuff v. Mueller, *supra* note 85 ($3 a day, $30 a month, or $75 a year reasonable). An unreasonable fee will be invalidated. Olan Mills, Inc. v. City of Nicholasville, 280 S.W.2d 522 (Ky.1955) (annual license fee of $50 found unreasonable); State v. Kromer, 34 N.J.Super. 465, 112 A.2d 804 (1955). A fee requirement may also be invalidated, on equal protection grounds, if it unreasonably discriminates against a particular class of sellers, but will be upheld if there is a reasonable basis for the different treatment. See Edwards v. City of Reno, 103 Nev. 347, 742 P.2d 486 (1987) (ordinance setting higher fees for peddlers than for solicitors upheld on basis of legitimate government purpose in preventing fraud by peddlers, whom the court regarded as a more transient class of sellers).

[89] Nippert v. City of Richmond, 327 U.S. 416, 66 S.Ct. 586, 90 L.Ed. 760 (1946) (license tax of $50 per year plus one-half of 1% of gross earnings (in excess of $1000) for preceding license year). Some jurisdictions have invalidated regulations as to solicitors that apply only to non-residents of the regulating locality. See Wilkins v. City of Harrison, 218 Ark. 316, 236 S.W.2d 82 (1951), noted 5 Ark.L.Rev. 429 (1951). Cf. Nafziger Baking Co. v. City of Salisbury, 329 Mo. 1014, 48 S.W.2d 563 (1932) (higher annual license fee for nonresident sellers than for residents; held void); Muhlenbrinck v. Long Branch Commissioners, 42 N.J.L. 364 (1880) (higher license fee charged some non-residents; found invalid). But some authority has sustained regulation of solicitors that exempts residents, or establishments having a permanent place of business in the locality. See Re Albrecht, 25 Cal.App.2d 750, 76 P.2d 713 (Dist.Ct.1938); People v. Bohnke, 287 N.Y. 154, 38 N.E.2d 478 (1941), cert. denied 316 U.S. 713, 62 S.Ct. 1306, 86 L.Ed. 1778. See also Goldberg v. Sweet, 488 U.S. 252, 109 S.Ct. 582, 102 L.Ed.2d 607 (1989) (Illinois tax on interstate telecommunications, which taxed only those calls originated or terminated in Illinois and charged to an Illinois service address, did not discriminate in favor of intrastate commerce at expense of interstate commerce).

[90] Real Silk Hosiery Mills v. City of Portland, 268 U.S. 325, 45 S.Ct. 525, 69 L.Ed. 982 (1925).

[91] *Id.* at 335–36. Cf. Village of Bel-Nor v. Barnett, 358 S.W.2d 832 (Mo.1962) (license cost $15 for 90 days; struck down as undue burden on interstate commerce); Moyant v. Paramus, *supra* note 85 ($25 for six months; were also requirements of a surety bond and certificate of freedom from disease; undue burden on interstate commerce found). See generally Jensen, Burdening Interstate Direct Selling Under Claims of State Police Power, 12 Rocky Mt.L.Rev. 257 (1940).

[92] Hynes v. Mayor & Council of Oradell, *supra* note 87.

[93] Village of Schaumburg v. Citizens for a Better Environment, 444 U.S. 620, 100 S.Ct. 826, 63 L.Ed.2d 73 (1980), reh. denied 445 U.S. 972, 100 S.Ct. 1668, 64 L.Ed.2d 250 noting that, while soliciting financial support is subject to reasonable regulation, any regulation must be undertaken with due regard for the informative and persuasive speeches, seeking support for particular causes or views, that often accompany the

solicitation. The Court held that even if the 75% requirement were valid as to some types of solicitation, it was unreasonable on its face as applied to advocacy-oriented organizations because it barred solicitation by them even where the funds would be used for reasonable salaries of those who gathered and disseminated information about the organization's purpose. See Secretary of State of Maryland v. Joseph H. Munson Co., 467 U.S. 947, 104 S.Ct. 2839, 81 L.Ed.2d 786 (1984), where the Court invalidated a Maryland statute which prohibited charitable organizations from paying expenses of more than 25% of the amount raised in connection with any fund-raising activity. The Court ruled that such a limitation was too imprecise a tool to achieve the legislative purpose of preventing mismanagement and that the statute was thus overbroad and created an unnecessary risk of chilling free speech because of its effect on the First Amendment rights of charities. Cf. Larson v. Valente, 456 U.S. 228, 102 S.Ct. 1673, 72 L.Ed.2d 33 (1982), reh. denied 457 U.S. 1111, 102 S.Ct. 2916, 73 L.Ed.2d 1323 (1982), invalidating a Minnesota statute that imposed certain registration and reporting requirements only on those religious organizations that solicit more than 50% of their funds from nonmembers; this was found to violate the Establishment Clause's clear command that one religious denomination not be officially preferred over another.

In Riley v. National Federation of the Blind of North Carolina, 487 U.S. 781, 108 S.Ct. 2667, 101 L.Ed.2d 669 (1988), a charitable solicitation statute's licensing requirement that professional fund raisers await a determination regarding their license application before engaging in solicitation, while volunteer fund raisers could solicit immediately upon submitting an application, was invalidated. A strict scrutiny standard was applied since restriction of free speech was involved, and the statute was thus found unconstitutional as permitting unlimited delay in issuing licenses to professional fund raisers. Cf. Green v. Village of Schaumburg, 676 F.Supp. 870 (N.D.Ill.1988) (ordinance making it unlawful for charitable organization to use a convicted felon as a solicitor held to violate First Amendment). See generally Strauss, First Amendment Protection of Charitable Solicitation, 13 Whittier L. Rev. 669 (1992).

Restrictions on the hours during which solicitation may occur have sometimes been invalidated as unnecessarily infringing on First Amendment rights considering the less restrictive alternatives available to achieve the goals of protecting privacy and preventing crime. City of Watseka v. Illinois Pub. Action Council, 796 F.2d 1547 (7th Cir.1986), aff'd without opinion 479 U.S. 1048, 107 S.Ct. 919, 93 L.Ed.2d 972 (1987) (three Justices dissenting); Wisconsin Action Coalition v. City of Kenosha, 767 F.2d 1248 (7th Cir.1985); Association of Community Organizations for Reform Now v. City of Frontenac, 714 F.2d 813 (8th Cir.1983). See, discussing the *Watseka* case *supra*, Kamen, High Court Restricts Curbs on Canvassing, Wash. Post, Jan. 21, 1987, at A8. Cf. New Jersey Citizen Action v. Edison Township, 797 F.2d 1250 (3d Cir.1986), cert. denied 479 U.S. 1103, 107 S.Ct. 1336, 94 L.Ed.2d 186 (1987), where an ordinance forbidding noncommercial door-to-door canvassing and solicitation during evening hours and requiring that canvassers be fingerprinted was held violative of the First Amendment.

As to restrictions on "panhandling" or begging, see Young v. New York City Transit Auth., 903 F.2d 146 (2d Cir.1990), cert. denied 498 U.S. 984, 111 S.Ct. 516, 112 L.Ed.2d 528 (1990), noted 57 Brooklyn L. Rev. 525 (1991), upholding restrictions imposed within the New York City Subway system. See generally Fleming, The New York Subway Cases: On or Off Track—*Young v. New York City Transit Authority*, 22 Urban Law. 919 (1990); Note, *Young v. New York City Transit Authority*: Silencing the Beggars in the Subways, 12 Pace L. Rev. 359 (1992). On enforcement of New York City's ordinance against begging within the subway system, see Henneberger, Subways Starting Panhandler Curb, N.Y. Times, Jan. 11, 1994, at A12. But in Loper v. New York City Police Dep't, 999 F.2d 699 (2d Cir. 1993), the same court that had upheld the general ban on begging in the subway system ruled that a statute criminalizing panhandling in the streets violated the First Amendment—a result that has been criticized as differing from the *Young* holding without offering any justification. See Nichols, The Panhandler's First Amendment Right: A Critique of *Loper v. New York City Police Department* and Related Academic Commentary, 48 S. Car. L. Rev. 267 (1997); Note, *Loper v. New York City Police Department* Begs the Question: Is Panhandling Protected by the First Amendment?, 60 Brooklyn L. Rev. 587 (1994). Note, Begging Underground? The Constitutionality of Regulations Banning Panhandling in the New York City Subway System, 27 Cardozo L. Rev. 1517 (2006); Comment, Examining a Beggar's First Amendment Right to Beg in an Era of Anti-begging Ordinances: The Presence and Persistence Test, 26 U. Dayton L. Rev. 155 (2000). See generally Ellickson, Controlling Chronic Misconduct in City Spaces: Of Panhandlers, Skid Rows, and Public Space Zoning, 105 Yale L.J. 1165 (1996); Annot., Laws Regulating Begging, Panhandling, or Similar Activity by Poor or Homeless Persons, 7 A.L.R.5th 455 (1992). Restrictions on soliciting money in a public forum may not survive the constitutional test, required as to any regulation based on content of speech, of having to be narrowly drawn to serve a compelling governmental interest. See State v. Boehler, 228 Ariz. 33, 262 P.3d 637 (App. 2011) (city's provision in anti-solicitation ordinance banning solicitors from orally asking passersby for cash after dark was not narrowly drawn to achieve its legitimate purpose of promoting safety in public areas after dark), discussed in Comment, Begging the (First Amendment) Question: The Constitutionality of Arizona's Prohibition of Begging in a Public Place, 45 Ariz. St. L. J. 1227 (2013). As to the "public forum" cases, see generally Section 23.9, note 153, para. 2, *infra*. See also Clatterbuck v. City of Charlottesville, 708 F.3d 549 (4th Cir. 2013), where the court dealt with an ordinance prohibiting

Where use of the public streets and ways is made for selling goods—as by transient merchants or hawkers—, some courts have said there can be no total ban, since such areas are by definition open to the public and there is no danger involved in such activities sufficient to justify a complete prohibition.[94] But what is probably the weight of authority supports the view that total prohibitions *can* be justified due to the traffic hazards otherwise presented, the need to keep pedestrian and vehicular traffic flowing smoothly, and—where sale of foodstuffs and certain other products is involved—the danger of contamination of the products being sold.[95] Most "prohibitions," however, are not really total, but only forbid selling in certain areas—such as ones particularly subject to traffic congestion. It is clear that many types of regulation less extreme than outright prohibition will be upheld: (1) Peddlers and hawkers can be prohibited from disrupting a neighborhood by too much noise, if the limitations are drawn with sufficient clarity.[96] (2) Parking on the street and attempting to sell goods from the parked vehicle, or other activities contributing to traffic congestion, can be forbidden.[97] (3) Licenses can be

---

solicitation of immediate donations of things of value within 50 feet of two streets that run through the downtown mall. The court found that the mall was a public forum and remanded the complaint, brought by homeless persons who wanted to beg at that location, for determination of whether the city enacted the ordinance with a censorial purpose in violation of the First Amendment.

[94] See City of Alexandria v. Jones, 216 La. 923, 45 So.2d 79 (1950); New Jersey Good Humor, Inc. v. Board of Commissioners, 124 N.J.L. 162, 11 A.2d 113 (1940); Good Humor Corp. v. City of New York, 290 N.Y. 312, 49 N.E.2d 153 (1943) (invalidating ordinance forbidding itinerant peddling on streets of city); Frecker v. City of Dayton, 88 Ohio App. 52, 85 N.E.2d 419 (1949), aff'd 153 Ohio St. 14, 90 N.E.2d 851. Cf. Higgins v. Krogman, 140 N.J.Eq. 518, 55 A.2d 175 (1947), aff'd 142 N.J.Eq. 691, 61 A.2d 444 (state law providing for issuance of hawkers' and peddlers' licenses to war veterans overrides local prohibition of peddling on beach and boardwalk); City of Eugene v. Miller, 318 Or. 480, 871 P.2d 454 (1994) (ordinance creating exception from general prohibition of sidewalk vending only for vendors selling "food, beverages, flowers, or balloons" violated free expression rights of vendor selling books on city sidewalks).

[95] See Shelton v. City of Mobile, 30 Ala. 540 (1857) (ban on peddling foodstuffs and meats on street); Kleiber v. City of Idaho Falls, 110 Idaho 501, 716 P.2d 1273 (1986) (issuance of business license to hot dog vendor did not confer on him any right to use public sidewalks for conduct of his business); Good Humor Corp. v. Village of Mundelein, 33 Ill.2d 252, 211 N.E.2d 269 (1965) (ban on peddling of ice cream on streets); State v. Perry, 151 N.C. 661, 65 S.E. 915 (1909) (ban on peddling fish); X-Cel Dairy v. City of Akron, 63 Ohio App. 147, 25 N.E.2d 700 (1939), appeal dism'd 136 Ohio St. 340, 25 N.E.2d 680 (ban on peddling of ice cream); Commonwealth v. Dunham, 191 Pa. 73, 43 A. 84 (1899); Dooley v. City of Cleveland, 175 Tenn. 439, 135 S.W.2d 649 (1940) (ban on selling food on streets); Ex parte Hogg, 70 Tex.Cr.R. 161, 156 S.W. 931 (1913) (general ban on selling merchandise on streets); Re Camp, 38 Wash. 393, 80 P. 547 (1905). Cf. John v. State, 577 S.W.2d 483 (Tex.Cr.App.1979) (ban on sale of tickets on city property). See generally Kettles, Regulating Vending in the Sidewalk Commons, 77 Temple L. Rev. 1 (2004). See also Meek, Street Vendors, Taxicabs, and Exclusion Zones: The Impact of Collateral Consequences of Criminal Convictions at the Local Level, 75 Ohio St. L. J. 1 (2014).

[96] See City of New Orleans v. Fargot, 116 La. 369, 40 So. 735 (1906) (peddlers prohibited from making loud outcries); Mister Softee v. Mayor and Council of Hoboken, 77 N.J.Super. 354, 186 A.2d 513 (1962) ("gong bells" and similar devices forbidden). But some courts may strike down, as not sufficiently definite and certain, ordinances prohibiting "loud" noises and not offering a clear definition of "loud." See Ex parte Westellison, 38 Okl.Cr. 207, 259 P. 873 (1927) (unlawful to announce contents of newspaper in a "loud voice"; ordinance held void).

[97] See City of Shreveport v. Dantes, 118 La. 113, 42 So. 716 (1907) (upholding prohibition of peddlers and hucksters stopping on streets and sidewalks unless making a sale); Borough of Harrington Park v. Hogenbirk, 52 N.J.Super. 223, 145 A.2d 161 (1958) (upholding ordinance providing that no one can park a vehicle on a public street and use it to sell goods to the occupants of other vehicles moving or standing on the road). Cf. Pittsford v. City of Los Angeles, 50 Cal.App.2d 25, 122 P.2d 535 (Dist.Ct.1942) (no vested right to do business in the public streets). See generally Comment, Location, Location, Location—The Food Truck's Battle for Common Ground, 44 Cumb. L. Rev. 283 (2013). In International Soc'y for Krishna Consciousness v. City of Baton Rouge, 668 F.Supp. 527 (M.D.La.1987), judgment aff'd 876 F.2d 494 (5th Cir.1989), a city's ordinance prohibiting solicitation of occupants of motor vehicles at traffic lights was upheld even as applied to religious solicitation, since the law was found to serve important public safety and traffic-flow concerns. Cf. United States v. Kokinda, 497 U.S. 720, 110 S.Ct. 3115, 111 L.Ed.2d 571 (1990), noted 25 Suffolk U.L. Rev. 772 (1991)

required of all peddlers or hawkers within a locality.[98] Classifications will be upheld if reasonable; and in general, peddlers and itinerant merchants have been unsuccessful when they have attacked legislation on the ground that it unreasonably discriminates against them and in favor of persons who operate businesses from permanent locations.[99]

It has been suggested that restrictions on street-peddlers and solicitors might provide a model for ordinances prohibiting "panic-peddling": the practice of real-estate brokers or others to induce the sale of real property by making the owners of such property fearful of an influx of minority or low-income persons into the area, and consequent lowering of property values.[100] A number of local ordinances do now make

---

(Postal Service Regulation prohibiting solicitation on postal premises, including postal sidewalk, upheld as applied to members of political advocacy group who were soliciting contributions, selling books, and distributing political literature); City of Seattle v. Webster, 115 Wash.2d 635, 802 P.2d 1333 (1990), cert. denied 500 U.S. 908, 111 S.Ct. 1690, 114 L.Ed.2d 85 (1991) (ordinance prohibiting intentional interference with pedestrian or vehicular traffic upheld; did not violate equal protection rights of homeless persons). But cf. Brown v. City of Newark, 113 N.J. 565, 552 A.2d 125 (1989) (court upheld most portions of an ordinance regulating street peddlers, but—contrary to the *Shreveport* case *supra*—invalidated, as not rationally related to the purpose of relieving sidewalk congestion, a portion that required venders to keep moving when not actually making sales). Special precautions may be required as to street-sales of goods attractive to children, since special dangers are then posed by the traffic hazards. See Trio Distributor Corp. v. City of Albany, 2 N.Y.2d 690, 163 N.Y.S.2d 585, 143 N.E.2d 329 (1957) (sustaining ordinance requiring street peddlers selling goods attractive to children to have along an attendant to guard the children from injury in the streets). Cf. Mister Softee v. Mayor and Council of Hoboken, *supra* note 96 (city can forbid sale of ice cream and similar products near schools during school hours). But unless some rational relationship to a police-power purpose is shown as to the distinction, an ordinance distinguishing vendors of goods likely to be appealing to children from vendors of other goods will be invalidated as discriminatory. See Frecker v. City of Dayton, *supra* note 94, criticized on the ground that such classification is reasonable in Note, Constitutional Law: Provisions in Ordinances Constituting Equal Protection of the Laws, 4 Okl.L.Rev. 494 (1951).

Restrictions on solicitation and/or peddling in certain limited areas of a city may well be found reasonable and thus upheld. See Slater v. Salt Lake City, 115 Utah 476, 206 P.2d 153 (1949) (business district). Cf. Re Mares, 75 Cal.App.2d 798, 171 P.2d 762 (Dist.Ct.1946) (ordinance prohibited solicitation for magazines or periodicals on any public street or sidewalk or any area abutting thereon; sustained). See also Annot., Peddlers: Right of Owner of Housing Development or Apartment Houses to Restrict Canvassing, Peddling, Solicitation of Contributions, etc., 3 A.L.R.2d 1431 (1949).

98 See Slater v. Salt Lake City, *supra* note 97. Reasonably definite standards must, as always, be provided those who are given power to grant or deny the licenses. Mister Softee v. Mayor and Council of Hoboken, *supra* note 96. A reasonable license fee may be charged. Jewel Tea Co. v. City of Troy, 80 F.2d 366 (7th Cir.1935); City of Joliet v. O'Sullivan, 303 Ill.App. 108, 24 N.E.2d 751 (1940). But if the fee is imposed under a municipality's *regulatory* power (as opposed to the separate power which may exist for tax for *revenue*), that fee must bear a reasonable relationship to the costs of policing; and in any case, a fee can be invalidated if it imposes an undue or material burden on interstate commerce. See ns. 7–10 *supra* and accompanying text.

99 See Jewel Tea Co. v. City of Troy, *supra* note 98. Cf. Hixon v. State, 523 S.W.2d 711 (Tex.Cr.App.1975) (ordinance prohibited sidewalk sales, but exempted vendors of flowers and ice cream; exemption held reasonable); Town of Sumner v. Ward, 126 Wash. 75, 217 P. 502 (1923) (courts will give great deference to municipal legislature in its classification as to peddlers). But cf. City of Eugene v. Miller, *supra* note 94 (ordinances under which sidewalk vending was generally prohibited but with exceptions for certain kinds of merchandise held invalid under state constitution as applied to sales of published matter).

100 Mandelker, Managing Our Urban Environment 852 (1st ed. 1966), noting an ordinance then proposed in Detroit making it unlawful to solicit by phone after the prospective customer has clearly requested the solicitor to cease. Mandelker notes that (1) the cited ordinance goes further than typical regulations of solicitors in that it applies to mail and phone solicitations, and the argument may be made that this is too restrictive, and (2) the panic-peddling problem might be solved by an ordinance applying only to real-estate agents, and a more sweeping regulation may be found unnecessarily broad—but an ordinance dealing only with realtors might be considered discriminatory. Cf. Mandelker, Managing Our Urban Environment 1030–32 (2d ed. 1971), noting similar *state* laws, and the origin of such measures in "Green River ordinances." Such a law was applied in Abel v. Lomenzo, 25 A.D.2d 104, 267 N.Y.S.2d 265 (1966), aff'd 18 N.Y.2d 619, 272 N.Y.S.2d 771, 219 N.E.2d 287. There is a federal anti-blockbusting law also. 42 U.S.C.A. §§ 3604(e), 3612. See

this activity unlawful, and such ordinances have been upheld.[101] But the U.S. Supreme Court invalidated, as unduly restrictive of the right of free speech, an ordinance banning "For Sale" and "Sold" signs from a township—the ordinance having been enacted to help stem a flight of home-owners from a racially integrating area.[102] There is an increasing movement toward state and local legislation limiting "junk phone calls"—unsolicited calls in which the caller seeks to sell goods or services—, as, for instance, by banning robot devices that place calls automatically.[103]

§ 23.7 Local Regulation of "Obscenity"

While free speech issues are raised in many of the cases involving local limitations on peddlers and solicitors,[104] even more difficult questions of this nature appear when a local government attempts to ban or censor publications. Since such attempted bans often occur because the publications are considered obscene or detrimental to morals, cases of this nature also raise the thorny issue of how far a government can go in legislating for the protection of "morality." Some moral basis is occasionally asserted for other restrictions on business activities—such as the restriction imposed by "Sunday blue laws"[105]—; but additional grounds for those restrictions can often be found. In the

---

generally Note, Blockbusting, 59 Geo.L.J. 170 (1970); Statute Note, An Anti-Blockbusting Ordinance, 7 Harv.J.Legis. 402 (1970).

[101] Chicago Real Estate Board v. City of Chicago, 36 Ill.2d 530, 224 N.E.2d 793 (1967); Summer v. Township of Teaneck, 53 N.J. 548, 251 A.2d 761 (1969) (no need for a single state-wide solution; may be useful to permit municipalities to act independently). See Brown v. State Realty Co., 304 F.Supp. 1236 (D.Ga.1969) (sustaining federal anti-blockbusting regulation); People v. C. Betts Realtors, Inc., 66 Ill.2d 144, 5 Ill.Dec. 258, 361 N.E.2d 581 (1977) (state anti-blockbusting statute sustained). Cf. Gladstone Realtors v. Village of Bellwood, 441 U.S. 91, 99 S.Ct. 1601, 60 L.Ed.2d 66 (1979) (complaint by area residents and village that real-estate brokers "steered" prospective home buyers to different residential areas according to race; village and residents held to have standing under federal Civil Rights Act); Organization for a Better Austin v. Keefe, 402 U.S. 415, 91 S.Ct. 1575, 29 L.Ed.2d 1 (1971) (real-estate broker denied injunction against distribution of literature alleging he was engaging in "block-busting" and "panic-peddling" activities). See generally Annot., Validity and Construction of Anti-Blockbusting Regulations Designed to Prevent Brokers from Inducing Sales of Realty Because of Actual or Rumored Entry by Racial Group into Neighborhood, 34 A.L.R.3d 1432 (1970).

[102] Linmark Associates, Inc. v. Township of Willingboro, 431 U.S. 85, 97 S.Ct. 1614, 52 L.Ed.2d 155 (1977). Cf. Campagna v. Shaffer, 73 N.Y.2d 237, 538 N.Y.S.2d 933, 536 N.E.2d 368 (1989) (order of New York Secretary of State prohibiting real estate brokers and salespersons from soliciting for sale residential realty in a particular area held to exceed authority granted that official by anti-blockbusting statute).

[103] See "A Revolt Against 'Junk Calls,'" Bus. Week, Feb. 20, 1978, at 26. On possible legal solutions to the problem of "junk calls," see Note, Unwanted Telephone Calls—A Legal Remedy?, 1967 Utah L.Rev. 379, noting (at 403 n. 137) a few municipal attempts to control telephone soliciting. But see Moser v. Frohnmayer, 315 Or. 372, 845 P.2d 1284 (1993) (statute prohibiting the use of automatic telemarketing devices for commercial solicitations invalidated as violative of free speech clause of Oregon Constitution). And one attempt by a law student to require the telephone company to indicate, by an asterisk beside his name in the telephone directory, that he did not want commercial or charitable calls soliciting his business or donation proved unsuccessful. McDaniel v. Pacific Tel. & Tel. Co., 60 P.U.R.3d 47 (Cal.Pub.Util.Comm'n 1965). See generally Seiler, Right of Privacy and Direct-Response Solicitation, 12 Forum 782 (1977). Federal legislation, the Fair Debt Collection Practices Act passed in 1978, forbids certain phone calls (as well as other conduct) engaged in by debt collectors. 15 U.S.C. § 1592.

[104] See Section 23.6, notes 83–87 & 92–98 *supra*, and accompanying text. On the special problems of restricting free speech, see Sunset Amusement Co. v. Board of Police Commissioners, 7 Cal.3d 64, 101 Cal.Rptr. 768, 496 P.2d 840 (1972), appeal dism'd 409 U.S. 1121, 93 S.Ct. 940, 35 L.Ed.2d 254, noting the difference between regulation involving exercise of First Amendment rights and regulation not concerning such rights, and upholding a licensing ordinance as to roller skating rinks, though a similar ordinance on motion-picture licensing had been invalidated for lack of sufficiently definite standards.

[105] See Section 23.3,notes 47–59 *supra*, and accompanying text.

cases of alleged obscenity, the morality-regulating, and the free-speech, issues are most clearly raised.

In 1957, in deciding the *Roth* case,[106] the U.S. Supreme Court ruled that local governments could forbid and prevent the sale of "obscene" materials if, and only if, the following test for obscenity was met: The material must be such that, to the average person, applying contemporary community standards, the dominant theme, taken as a whole, appeals to prurient interest. The Court emphasized that all ideas having even the slightest redeeming social importance are protected by the First Amendment so that their publication cannot be enjoined or published. In 1973, the Court, in the *Miller* case,[107] modified somewhat the definition of "obscenity" by laying down three requirements. Material was said to be obscene if (1) it describes or depicts sexual conduct in such a way that, taken as an entirety, it appeals to prurient interest in sex. (2) It describes or depicts the conduct in a patently offensive manner. And (3) it lacks, taken as an entirety, any serious literary, artistic, scientific, or political value. The proscribed conduct or publication must be specifically defined by the applicable state or local law,

---

[106] Roth v. United States, 354 U.S. 476, 77 S.Ct. 1304, 1 L.Ed.2d 1498 (1957) reh. denied 355 U.S. 852, 78 S.Ct. 8, 2 L.Ed.2d 60. See Butler v. Michigan, 352 U.S. 380, 77 S.Ct. 524, 1 L.Ed.2d 412 (1957), indicating a standard of the average adult rather than the unusually susceptible person. Cf. Manual Enterprises, Inc. v. Day, 370 U.S. 478, 82 S.Ct. 1432, 8 L.Ed.2d 639 (1962), holding that certain magazines designed to appeal to homosexuals could not be denied access to the mails. Among state cases applying *Roth,* good examples are Zeitlin v. Arnebergh, 59 Cal.2d 901, 31 Cal.Rptr. 800, 383 P.2d 152 (1963), cert. denied 375 U.S. 957, 84 S.Ct. 445, 11 L.Ed.2d 315; Attorney General v. Book Named "Tropic of Cancer", 345 Mass. 11, 184 N.E.2d 328 (1962); People v. Richmond County News, Inc., 9 N.Y.2d 578, 216 N.Y.S.2d 369, 175 N.E.2d 681 (1961); State v. Miller, 145 W.Va. 59, 112 S.E.2d 472 (1960). The "average person" of the *Roth* test was sometimes compared to the "reasonable person" of tort law. See State v. Nelson, 168 Neb. 394, 95 N.W.2d 678 (1959); State ex rel. Beil v. Mahoning Valley Distributing Agency, 84 O.L.A. 427, 169 N.E.2d 48 (Com.Pl.1960), aff'd 116 Ohio App. 57, 186 N.E.2d 631. See generally Comment, Obscenity—What Is the Test?, 5 Ariz.L.Rev. 265 (1964).

[107] Miller v. California, 413 U.S. 15, 93 S.Ct. 2607, 37 L.Ed.2d 419 (1973), reh. denied 414 U.S. 881, 94 S.Ct. 26, 38 L.Ed.2d 128, noted 6 Conn.L.Rev. 165 (1973); 23 Emory L.J. 551 (1974); 87 Harv.L.Rev. 160 (1973; part of summary of 1972 Supreme Court term); 51 J. Urban L. 314 (1973). See Jenkins v. Georgia, 418 U.S. 153, 94 S.Ct. 2750, 41 L.Ed.2d 642 (1974), holding the film *Carnal Knowledge* not obscene under the *Miller* test; City of Portland v. Jacobsky, 496 A.2d 646 (Me.1985) (city ordinance defining "obscenity" in line with elements listed in the *Miller* case and specifying use of contemporary community standards held not to infringe on freedom of expression as guaranteed by either federal or state constitution); Hildahl v. State, 536 P.2d 377 (Okl.Cr.App.1975), holding a state obscenity statute constitutional in light of the *Miller* decision. See generally Note, Community Standards, Class Actions, and Obscenity under *Miller v. California,* 88 Harv.L.Rev. 1838 (1975); Comment, Obscenity: Determined by Whose Standards?, 26 U.Fla. L.Rev. 324 (1974).

In Brockett v. Spokane Arcades, Inc., 472 U.S. 491, 105 S.Ct. 2794, 86 L.Ed.2d 394 (1985), the Supreme Court added to the *Miller* definitions by stating that material that only provokes normal, healthy sexual desires cannot be characterized as obscene but ruled that a statute which included any material inciting lust within its definition of "prurient" (thus making such material obscene) should not have been invalidated in its *entirety* where it contained a severability clause and could, without the offending provision on incitement of lust, be a valid and effective regulation. Cf. American Booksellers Ass'n v. Hudnut, 771 F.2d 323 (7th Cir.1985), aff'd without opinion 475 U.S. 1001, 106 S.Ct. 1172, 89 L.Ed.2d 291 (1986), reh. denied 475 U.S. 1132, 106 S.Ct. 1664, 90 L.Ed.2d 206 (1986), holding that an Indianapolis ordinance defining "pornography" as a practice that discriminates against women; declaring pornography to consist, under various designated circumstances, of the graphic, sexually explicit subordination of women in pictures or words; and not including in the definition any reference to prurient interests, offensiveness, or community standards violated the First Amendment; the court held that both offensiveness and an appeal to something other than normal sexual desires are essential to obscenity.

In Pope v. Illinois, 481 U.S. 497, 107 S.Ct. 1918, 95 L.Ed.2d 439 (1987), on remand 162 Ill.App.3d 299, 113 Ill.Dec. 547, 515 N.E.2d 356 (1987), appeal denied 118 Ill.2d 549, 117 Ill.Dec. 229, 520 N.E.2d 390 (1988), the Court ruled that the proper inquiry in deciding whether allegedly obscene matter has "literary, artistic, political, or scientific value" is not whether the ordinary member of any given community would find such value in the work but whether the *reasonable* person would find it in the material taken as a whole.

as written or authoritatively construed. The Court clearly allowed application by a community of *local* standards in determining whether the tests are met, and thus the decision was widely viewed as an invitation to local "crackdowns" on pornographic literature.[108] The manner in which a publication is advertised and sold can also be considered in determining if that publication is obscene.[109] Before the *Miller* case, the Court had specifically addressed the question of how the obscenity standard could be applied to a publication available to minors:[110] It could constitutionally be found obscene if (1) it has a predominant appeal to the prurient interests of minors; (2) it is patently offensive to the prevailing standards of the local adult community regarding what is suitable material for minors; and (3) it is without redeeming social importance for minors. Clearly, *Miller* modified the third requirement to provide that the material must lack serious literary, artistic, scientific, or political value for minors. And since *Miller,* the Supreme Court (in an opinion which, because of the time when the case arose, still applied the *Roth* test) ruled that children are not part of the relevant "community" for judging obscenity *if* children are not intended recipients of the material nor reasonably likely to receive the material.[111] It seems that it remains true, as held in a pre-*Miller*

---

[108] See "Hard-Nosed About Hard-Core," Time, July 2, 1973, at 42. See generally Weaver, Supreme Court Tightens Rule Governing Obscenity, Gives States New Power, N.Y. Times, June 22, 1973, at 1, col. 8, with continuation and related articles at 42. But local ordinances dealing with obscenity are still sometimes invalidated, of course; to be valid, they must now be in line with the *Miller* standards. See U. T. Inc. v. Brown, 457 F.Supp. 163 (W.D.N.C.1978). On the effects of *Miller*, see generally Project: An Empirical Inquiry into the Effects of *Miller v. California* on the Control of Obscenity, 52 N.Y.U.L.Rev. 810 (1977). On the standard of proof required in an obscenity case, see Cooper v. Mitchell Brothers' Santa Ana Theater, 454 U.S. 90, 102 S.Ct. 172, 70 L.Ed.2d 262 (1981), reh. denied 456 U.S. 920, 102 S.Ct. 1779, 72 L.Ed.2d 181 (1982) (federal Constitution does not require standard of proof beyond reasonable doubt; that choice is solely a matter of state law). On local efforts to curb pornography, see "Give-and-Take on Pornography," Time, March 10, 1986, at 67; "Porn Wars: Do's and Don'ts," U.S. News & World Rep., March 10, 1986, at 8.

[109] Splawn v. California, 431 U.S. 595, 97 S.Ct. 1987, 52 L.Ed.2d 606 (1977).

[110] Ginsberg v. New York, 390 U.S. 629, 88 S.Ct. 1274, 20 L.Ed.2d 195 (1968), reh. denied 391 U.S. 971, 88 S.Ct. 2029, 20 L.Ed.2d 887. Cf. Smith v. California, 361 U.S. 147, 80 S.Ct. 215, 4 L.Ed.2d 205 (1959), reh. denied 361 U.S. 950, 80 S.Ct. 399, 4 L.Ed.2d 383 (books cannot be kept from the adult reading public merely because they tend to corrupt the morals of youth); Katzev v. County of Los Angeles, 52 Cal.2d 360, 341 P.2d 310 (1959), noted 33 S.Cal.L.Rev. 325 (1960) (ordinance prohibiting sale and circulation of "crime comic books" to children under 18 ruled unconstitutional as overbroad, not justified by proof of clear and present danger to society, etc.).

[111] Pinkus v. United States, 436 U.S. 293, 98 S.Ct. 1808, 56 L.Ed.2d 293 (1978), on remand 579 F.2d 1174 (9th Cir.) cert. dism'd 439 U.S. 999, 99 S.Ct. 605, 58 L.Ed.2d 674, noting that in this case there was an affirmative representation that children were not involved; the Court also held that inclusion of "sensitive persons" as among the community to be considered was not error. Compare Upper Midwest Booksellers Ass'n v. City of Minneapolis, 780 F.2d 1389 (8th Cir.1985), where the court considered an ordinance making it unlawful to display for commercial purposes any material "harmful to minors" unless the material was in a sealed wrapper or otherwise segregated so that minors could not view it. The court held that, even though the law might be a content-based restriction impinging on the rights of adults, it was permissible as a reasonable means of controlling the merchandising to minors of sexually explicit material that was obscene as to them. For application of the *Miller* standards to a law attempting to protect minors from harmful material on the Internet, see Reno v. American Civil Liberties Union, 521 U.S. 844, 117 S.Ct. 2329, 138 L.Ed.2d 874 (1997) (challenged provisions found facially overbroad in violation of the First Amendment to extent those provisions prohibited transmission of speech that was indecent but not obscene). On laws giving special protection to minors, see also City of Dallas v. Stanglin, 490 U.S. 19, 109 S.Ct. 1591, 104 L.Ed.2d 18 (1989), upholding against equal protection attack a city ordinance restricting admission to certain dance halls to persons between the ages of 14 and 18. The Court found this rationally related to a legitimate effort to protect those in that age group from the possibly corrupting influence of older teenagers and young adults.

In Erznoznik v. City of Jacksonville, 422 U.S. 205, 95 S.Ct. 2268, 45 L.Ed.2d 125 (1975), the Court invalidated an ordinance prohibiting the showing of films containing nudity by a drive-in theatre with a screen visible from a public street or place. The Court stated that more stringent controls could be adopted as to materials accessible to minors, but that even as to minors, it could not be ruled that all nudity is obscene. See

case,[112] that conviction for the sale or transfer of obscene materials requires a showing of the seller's scienter—*i.e.*, knowledge of the obscene nature; and it would seem to remain true that possession of obscene materials in the privacy of one's home cannot be made criminal.[113] In 1982, the U.S. Supreme Court recognized that child pornography is, like obscenity, outside the scope of First Amendment protection and that its distribution or promotion may be banned and punished, provided the prohibited conduct is adequately defined by relevant state law. The Court limited "child pornography" to descriptions or depiction of sexual conduct involving live performance, or photographic or other visual reproduction of live performance, by children.[114]

---

generally, on regulation of drive-in movie theatres, notes 120–122 *infra*, and accompanying text. On regulation of adult businesses, see generally Gerard, Local Regulation of Adult Businesses (Clark Boardman Callaghan 1994).

As to the Child Online Protection Act, intended to protect children from harmful material on the Internet, see Ashcroft v. American Civil Liberties Union, 542 U.S. 656, 124 S.Ct. 2783, 159 L.Ed.2d 690 (2004) (Internet content providers and civil liberties groups were likely to prevail on claim that statute violated First Amendment; preliminary injunction upheld); Ashcroft v. American Civil Liberties Union, 535 U.S. 564, 122 S.Ct. 1700, 152 L.Ed.2d 771 (2002) (statute's reference to contemporary community standards in defining what was harmful to minors did not alone render statute unconstitutionally broad under First Amendment).

As to regulation of the sale or rental of video games to minors, see Entertainment Software Ass'n v. Blagojevich, 469 F.3d 641 (7th Cir. 2006) (Illinois law barring sale or rental of "sexually explicit" video games to minors held unconstitutional as not narrowly tailored to serve a compelling governmental interest under the strict scrutiny test). In Brown v. Entertainment Merchants Ass'n, 564 U.S. ___, 131 S.Ct. 2729, 180 L.Ed.2d 708 (2011), the Court, noting that the law restricted speech based on content, struck down a California statute prohibiting the sale or rental of "violent video games" to minors, finding that the law was not justified by a compelling government interest nor narrowly drawn to serve such an interest. See generally Note, *Video Software Dealers Association v. Schwarzenegger*: Defining the Constitutional Perimeter Around State Regulation of Violent Video Games, 13 S.M.U. Sci. & Tech. L. Rev. 219 (2010); Selected Material From 2010 International Summit on the Law and Business of Video Games, 13 S.M.U. Sci. & Tech. L. Rev. 139 (2010). See also Chemerinsky, Not a Free Speech Court, 53 Ariz. L. Rev. 723 (2011), citing the *Brown* case, *supra,* as one that was "protective of speech," but concluding that overall the current U.S. Supreme Court is "not a free speech Court." *Id.* at 734.

In United States v. Williams, 553 U.S. 285, 128 S.Ct. 1830, 170 L.Ed.2d 650 (2008), the Supreme Court upheld as not overbroad or impermissibly vague the Prosecutorial Remedies and Other Tools to End the Exploitation of Children Today (PROTECT) Act, criminalizing the pandering or solicitation of child pornography.

[112] Smith v. People of State of California, 361 U.S. 147, 80 S.Ct. 215, 4 L.Ed.2d 205 (1959), reh. denied 361 U.S. 950, 80 S.Ct. 399, 4 L.Ed.2d 383. Thus, in Pinkus v. United States, *supra* note 111, the Court applied a scienter requirement in dealing with the issue of availability to children of allegedly obscene materials: The defendant did not know or have reason to know that children were likely to receive the materials, and this fact was relied on in determining that children should not be included as part of the relevant community.

[113] See Stanley v. Georgia, 394 U.S. 557, 89 S.Ct. 1243, 22 L.Ed.2d 542 (1969) on remand 225 Ga. 273, 167 S.E.2d 756 (government may prohibit or regulate certain *public* actions respecting obscene material, but mere *private* possession of obscene matter cannot be made a crime). See generally Note, Obscenity in the Age of Direct Broadcast Satellite: A Final Burial for *Stanley v. Georgia*(?), A National Obscenity Standard, and Other Miscellany, 33 Wm. & M.L. Rev. 949 (1992). In New York v. P.J. Video, Inc., 475 U.S. 868, 106 S.Ct. 1610, 89 L.Ed.2d 871 (1986), on remand 68 N.Y.2d 296, 508 N.Y.S.2d 907, 501 N.E.2d 556 (1986), the Court held that an application for a warrant authorizing seizure of materials presumptively protected by the First Amendment (*i.e.*, protected unless found obscene or otherwise within one of the limited categories of speech not enjoying First Amendment protection) should be evaluated under the same standard of probable cause used to review warrant applications generally. No "higher" probable-cause standard is applied, but only the requirement that there be a "fair probability" that evidence of a crime will be found in the particular place to be searched.

[114] New York v. Ferber, 458 U.S. 747, 102 S.Ct. 3348, 73 L.Ed.2d 1113 (1982), on remand 57 N.Y.2d 256, 455 N.Y.S.2d 582, 441 N.E.2d 1100 (1982), noted 16 Creighton L. Rev. 509 (1983), 96 Harv. L. Rev. 141 (1982), 19 Wake Forest L. Rev. 95 (1983). See generally "The Court's Final Flurry," Time, July 12, 1982, at 52. In Osborne v. Ohio, 495 U.S. 103, 110 S.Ct. 1691, 109 L.Ed.2d 98 (1990), reh. denied 496 U.S. 913, 110 S.Ct. 2605, 110 L.Ed.2d 285 (1990), Ohio's prohibition against possessing and viewing child pornography was upheld as

Within those limits, local government may act to prevent the sale and dissemination of obscene materials and may provide for criminal punishment of those who engage in such sale or dissemination—unless, as has occurred in a few jurisdictions, the state is held to have pre-empted the field, leaving no room for local regulation.[115] The same basic rules apply to films as to written publications: A locality may prevent and/or punish the showing of obscene films or obscene parts of films,[116] but it cannot censor films, or punish

---

complying with the First Amendment. See generally United States v. X-Citement Video, Inc., 513 U.S. 64, 115 S.Ct. 464, 130 L.Ed.2d 372 (1994), on remand 77 F.3d 491 (9th Cir.1996), applying the federal criminal statute on sexual exploitation of children and holding that conviction thereunder requires a showing of defendant's knowledge of the elements of the crime, including minority of performers and sexually explicit nature of the material. In Ashcroft v. Free Speech Coalition, 535 U.S. 234, 122 S.Ct. 1389, 152 L.Ed.2d 403 (2002), the Child Pornography Prevention Act of 1996 was held, in its ban on virtual child pornography, to abridge the freedom to engage in a substantial amount of lawful speech and thus to be overbroad and unconstitutional under the First Amendment.

[115] Pierce v. City and County of Denver, 193 Colo. 347, 565 P.2d 1337 (1977); Chelsea Theater Corp. v. City of Burlington, 258 N.W.2d 372 (Iowa 1977); People v. Llewellyn, 401 Mich. 314, 257 N.W.2d 902 (1977), cert. denied 435 U.S. 1008, 98 S.Ct. 1879, 56 L.Ed.2d 390; Dover News Inc. v. City of Dover, 117 N.H. 1066, 381 A.2d 752 (1977) (state had not pre-empted *entire* field of regulating sexually explicit materials, but present city ordinance was invalid because it prohibited display of materials the state had not currently determined to be detrimental to children); City of Grafton v. Four G's, Inc., 252 N.W.2d 879 (N.D.1977) (state obscenity control statute pre-empted the field even as to regulation of obscene acts in places licensed by city for sale of alcoholic beverages). See City of Lynchburg v. Dominion Theatres, Inc., 175 Va. 35, 7 S.E.2d 157 (1940) (field of film censorship occupied by state). Cf. City of Spokane v. J-R Distributors, Inc., 90 Wash.2d 722, 585 P.2d 784 (1978) (some provisions of ordinance found in conflict with state statute; invalidated).

In addition to regulating or proscribing dissemination of obscene materials, states and localities may take steps against obscene speech or displays of obscene language. But the word "fuck" has been held not obscene because not erotic. Cohen v. California, 403 U.S. 15, 91 S.Ct. 1780, 29 L.Ed.2d 284 (1971), reh. denied 404 U.S. 876, 92 S.Ct. 26, 30 L.Ed.2d 124. See Hess v. Indiana, 414 U.S. 105, 94 S.Ct. 326, 38 L.Ed.2d 303 (1973), holding the words "We'll take the fucking street later (or again)" not obscene or otherwise punishable (as spoken to a crowd). Penalties may also be assessed for speaking or displaying language advocating use of force or of illegal action—but only if the advocacy is directed to inciting or producing imminent lawless action and is likely to incite or produce such conduct. See Hess v. Indiana, *supra*; Gooding v. Wilson, 405 U.S. 518, 92 S.Ct. 1103, 31 L.Ed.2d 408 (1972); Street v. New York, 394 U.S. 576, 89 S.Ct. 1354, 22 L.Ed.2d 572 (1969) on remand 24 N.Y.2d 1026, 302 N.Y.S.2d 848, 250 N.E.2d 250; Terminiello v. City of Chicago, 337 U.S. 1, 69 S.Ct. 894, 93 L.Ed. 1131 (1949), reh. denied 337 U.S. 934, 69 S.Ct. 1490, 93 L.Ed.2d 1740 (1949); Chaplinsky v. New Hampshire, 315 U.S. 568, 62 S.Ct. 766, 86 L.Ed. 1031 (1942); Annot., Supreme Court's View as to the Protection or Lack of Protection, Under the Federal Constitution, of the Utterance of "Fighting Words," 39 L.Ed.2d 925 (1975). See generally Rutzick, Offensive Language and the Evolution of First Amendment Protection, 9 Harv.Civ. Rights—Civ. Liberties L.Rev. 1 (1974); Note, "Offensive Speech" and the First Amendment, 53 Boston U.L.Rev. 834 (1973); Comment, Violence and Obscenity—*Chaplinsky* Revisited, 42 Fordham L.Rev. 141 (1973).

In City of Littleton, Colorado, v. Z.J. Gifts D–4, L.L.C., 541 U.S. 774, 124 S.Ct. 2219, 159 L.Ed.2d 84 (2004), it was held that where a city's "adult business" licensing procedure simply conditioned operation of adult business on compliance with neutral and nondiscretionary criteria and did not seek to censor content, the language in the ordinance providing for judicial review of adverse licensing decisions in accordance with the state's ordinary review procedures was sufficient to satisfy the First Amendment. Cf. Midvale City Corp. v. Haltom, 2003 Utah 26, 73 P.3d 334 (2003), cert. denied 540 U.S. 1049, 124 S.Ct. 826, 157 L.Ed.2d 698 (2003) (sale of sexual devices did not amount to expressive conduct protected by First Amendment; city's licensing system for a sexually oriented business was content-neutral time, place and manner restriction unrelated to expression).

[116] See Miller v. California, *supra* note 107; Motion Picture Appeal Board v. S. K. Films, 65 Ill.App.3d 217, 21 Ill.Dec. 809, 382 N.E.2d 103 (1978); Salt Lake City v. Piepenburg, 571 P.2d 1299 (Utah 1977) (city could punish showing of obscene film), noted 1978 Utah L.Rev. 375, defendant's conviction again aff'd, 602 P.2d 702 (Utah) (ordinance not unconstitutionally broad). Among the outstanding pre-*Miller* cases on films were Times Film Corp. v. City of Chicago, 365 U.S. 43, 81 S.Ct. 391, 5 L.Ed.2d 403 (1961), reh. denied 365 U.S. 856, 81 S.Ct. 798, 5 L.Ed.2d 820; City of Atlanta v. Columbia Pictures Corp., 218 Ga. 714, 130 S.E.2d 490 (1963) (films had to be submitted for censorship; upheld); Janus Films, Inc. v. City of Fort Worth, 354 S.W.2d 597 (Tex.Civ.App.1962) ref. n. r. e. 163 Tex. 616, 358 S.W.2d 589 (upholding power of municipal government to delete obscene portions from films). See generally Waples & White, Choice of Community Standards in

their showing, for reasons other than obscenity.[117] If a locality provides for screening and approval of films by some officer or agency before they may be shown in that locality, two requirements must be met: (1) The burden of proving that the film is obscene, and thus not protected by the First Amendment, rests with the censor. (2) The censor must—within a specified, brief period—either issue a license for the film to be shown or else go to court to restrain its showing; and there must be assurance of a prompt judicial decision if the censor takes the latter alternative.[118] Thus, although local administrators may temporarily delay the showing of a film, the film cannot be banned from the community until there is a final *judicial* determination. Stage and theatrical performances are, like films, forms of protected First Amendment expression, and may be banned and/or punished only if they meet the Supreme Court definition of "obscenity."[119] Of course,

---

Federal Obscenity Proceedings: The Role of the Constitution and the Common Law, 64 Va.L.Rev. 399 (1978). In Wall Distributors, Inc. v. City of Newport News, 782 F.2d 1165 (4th Cir.1986), an ordinance making it a criminal offense to exhibit films in enclosed booths was held a valid restriction on manner of speech that did not substantially impair the availability of constitutionally protected materials and that thus did not violate First Amendment rights. The court assumed the films in question were entitled to constitutional protection since, although erotic in nature, they had not been found obscene. Cf. Postscript Enterprises v. City of Bridgeton, 905 F.2d 223 (8th Cir. 1990), upholding an ordinance prohibiting doors or curtains on movie—arcade booths used by fewer than six persons; Berg v. Health & Hosp. Corp., 667 F.Supp. 639 (S.D.Ind.1987), judgment aff'd 865 F.2d 797 (7th Cir.1989), upholding a county ordinance—designed to decrease the spread of AIDS—that prohibited doors, curtains, or partitions on individual "entertainment booths."

[117] See Kingsley International Pictures Corp. v. Regents of University, 360 U.S. 684, 79 S.Ct. 1362, 3 L.Ed.2d 1512 (1959); Superior Films v. Department of Education, 346 U.S. 587, 74 S.Ct. 286, 98 L.Ed. 329 (1954); Gelling v. Texas, 343 U.S. 960, 72 S.Ct. 1002, 96 L.Ed. 1359 (1952); Joseph Burstyn, Inc. v. Wilson, 343 U.S. 495, 72 S.Ct. 777, 96 L.Ed. 1098 (1952).

[118] See Freedman v. Maryland, 380 U.S. 51, 85 S.Ct. 734, 13 L.Ed.2d 649 (1965). Thus, in Vance v. Universal Amusement Co., 445 U.S. 308, 100 S.Ct. 1156, 63 L.Ed.2d 413 (1980), reh. denied 446 U.S. 947, 100 S.Ct. 2177, 64 L.Ed.2d 804 (1980), a Texas nuisance statute was ruled unconstitutional because it authorized restraints of indefinite duration on the showing of motion pictures that had not been finally adjudicated as obscene.

Ordinances attempting to punish the showing of obscene films have also been invalidated if found not reasonably definite and certain. Rabe v. Washington, 405 U.S. 313, 92 S.Ct. 993, 31 L.Ed.2d 258 (1972), reh. denied 406 U.S. 911, 92 S.Ct. 1604, 31 L.Ed.2d 822; Interstate Circuit v. City of Dallas, 390 U.S. 676, 88 S.Ct. 1298, 20 L.Ed.2d 225 (1968).

[119] See Southeastern Promotions, Limited v. Conrad, 420 U.S. 546, 95 S.Ct. 1239, 43 L.Ed.2d 448 (1975) (denial of use of municipal facilities for production of the rock musical *Hair* amounted to unconstitutional prior restraint; same procedural safeguards must be accorded stage productions as films); State v. Walker, 568 P.2d 286 (Okl.Cr.App.1977) (statute pertaining to crime of outraging public decency did not mention sexual conduct, much less specifically define it; thus, under *Miller* guidelines, nude dancer could not constitutionally be charged with violation). But see, all upholding local government bans on indecent exposure in public, Yauch v. State, 109 Ariz. 576, 514 P.2d 709 (1973) (ordinance banning topless and bottomless performances); Davis v. State, 430 S.W.2d 217 (Tex.Cr.App.1968); City of Seattle v. Marshall, 83 Wash.2d 665, 521 P.2d 693 (1974), cert. denied 419 U.S. 1023, 95 S.Ct. 499, 42 L.Ed.2d 297 (conviction of stage performer under indecent exposure statute upheld; act of exposing her private parts to an all-male audience held obscene per se). Cf. New York State Liquor Authority v. Bellanca, 452 U.S. 714, 101 S.Ct. 2599, 69 L.Ed.2d 357 (1981) (New York statute prohibiting topless dancing in establishment licensed by state to serve liquor held constitutional); Crownover v. Musick, 9 Cal.3d 405, 107 Cal.Rptr. 681, 509 P.2d 497 (1973), cert. denied 415 U.S. 931, 94 S.Ct. 1443, 39 L.Ed.2d 489 (ordinance prohibited nudity by performers, waiters, and waitresses in places where food or beverages were served, but was exception for theatres; upheld); City of Seattle v. Buchanan, 90 Wash.2d 584, 584 P.2d 918 (1978) (ordinance punishing women who exposed themselves above the waist; upheld though didn't apply to men). In Barnes v. Glen Theatre, Inc., 501 U.S. 560, 111 S.Ct. 2456, 115 L.Ed.2d 504 (1991), on remand 941 F.2d 1212 (7th Cir.1991), the Court held that enforcement of a public indecency statute to require that dancers at adult entertainment establishments wear pasties and a G-string did not violate the First Amendment. The Court was, however, sharply divided, with the five Justices in the majority issuing three separate opinions; the four dissenters united in a single opinion. See Note, Nude Dancing and the First Amendment Question, 45 Vand. L. Rev. 237 (1992). Then in City of Erie v. Pap's A.M., 529 U.S. 277, 120 S.Ct. 1382, 146 L.Ed.2d 265 (2000), an ordinance forbidding nudity in public places was upheld as applied to nude erotic dancing; the ordinance was treated as a content-neutral regulation of symbolic speech. But see Triplett

theatres, like other businesses, may be required to obtain a license from the local government and to abide by certain health and safety standards—particularly in order to prevent fire dangers.[120]

Drive-in movie theatres pose special problems because they may constitute a danger if they distract those driving in traffic and because films therein exhibited may be viewed by minors even if those minors do not attend the theatre. Reasonable requirements that showings be screened from the view of drivers and pedestrians may be sustained.[121] But

---

Grille v. City of Akron, 40 F.3d 129 (6th Cir.1994) (ordinance prohibiting nude dancing invalidated as overbroad). The Court in *City of Erie* was again badly split. The opinion of Justice O'Connor was joined by Rehnquist, Kennedy, and Breyer, upholding the ordinance and finding that it was aimed at combating crime and other negative secondary effects of adult entertainment. Justices Scalia and Thomas concurred in the judgment but did so on the ground that the ordinance prohibited the act of going nude in public and thus was not subject to First Amendment scrutiny. Justice Souter concurred in part and dissented in part, finding the evidentiary record deficient as to the undesirable secondary effects. Justices Stevens and Ginsburg dissented. See generally Note, Constitutional Law—Freedom of Expression—Nude Dancing Conveying a Message of Eroticism and Sexuality Is Protected by the First Amendment But Can Be Limited Under State Police Powers Provided the Government Establishes a Content-Neutral Purpose, 23 St. Mary's L.J. 563 (1991). Compare Note, A Right to Bare All? Female Public Toplessness and Dealing With the Laws that Prohibit It, 8 Cardozo Pub. L. Pol'y & Ethics J. 453 (2010). See also Comment, Regulation of Nude Dancing in Bring Your Own Bottle Establishments in the Commonwealth of Pennsylvania: Are the Commonwealth's Municipalities Left to Fend for Themselves?, 99 Dickinson L. Rev. 169 (1994).

In American Bush v. City of South Salt Lake, 2006 Utah 40, 140 P.3d 1235 (2006), a city ordinance prohibiting nude dancing was held not to violate the free speech guarantees of the Utah Constitution. As to ordinances prohibiting physical contact between erotic dancers and patrons, compare City of Las Vegas v. Eighth Judicial Dist. of Nev., 122 Nev. 1041, 146 P.3d 240 (2006) (ordinance prohibiting certain physical contact between erotic dancers and patrons upheld as content-neutral and not unconstitutionally vague or overbroad), with City of Nyssa v. Dufloth, 339 Or. 330, 121 P.3d 639 (2005) (city ordinance that required nude dancers to remain at least four feet from audience violated free expression guarantees of Oregon Constitution; ordinance focused on restraining a particular variety of expression). See, focusing on the *City of Erie v. Pap's* case, *supra*, Note, *City of Erie v. Pap's A.M.*: Contorting Secondary Effects and Diluting Intermediate Scrutiny to Ban Nude Dancing, 30 Capital U.L. Rev. 823 (2002); Comment, The First Amendment Gone Awry: *City of Erie v. Pap's A.M.*, Ailing Analytical Structures, and the Suppression of Protected Expression, 150 U. Pa. L. Rev. 1021 (2002). For a discussion of the place of the *City of Erie v. Pap's* case in First Amendment law, see Mitchell, Comment: Nude Dancing and First Amendment Scrutiny, 34 Urban Law. 277 (2002). See generally Note, "Lewd and Immoral": Nude Dancing, Sexual Expression, and the First Amendment, 81 Chi.-Kent L. Rev. 1185 (2006).

Prior to the Supreme Court cases on obscenity in the 1960's and '70's convictions of stage performers were fairly common under statutes or ordinances (some of which might not pass constitutional muster today) prohibiting lewd, immoral, and/or indecent performances. See Brooks v. City of Birmingham, 32 F.2d 274 (N.D.Ala.1929); City of Grand Rapids v. Bateman, 93 Mich. 135, 53 N.W. 6 (1892); City of St. Louis v. Mikes, 372 S.W.2d 508 (Mo.App.1963); Bonserk Theatre Corp. v. Moss, 34 N.Y.S.2d 541 (Spec. Term 1942).

Any statute or ordinance punishing "obscene" stage performances must not only meet current Supreme Court standards on what can be declared "obscene," but must also be reasonably definite and certain as to exactly what acts are criminally punishable. See Birkenshaw v. Haley, 409 F.Supp. 13 (E.D.Mich.1974).

[120] See Hollywood Theatre Corp. v. City of Indianapolis, 218 Ind. 556, 34 N.E.2d 28 (1941) (inspection of theatres to reduce fire dangers upheld); Kalbfell v. City of St. Louis, 357 Mo. 986, 211 S.W.2d 911 (1948) (same); Ormsby v. Bell, 218 N.Y. 212, 112 N.E. 747 (1916) (theatre could be denied license because of proximity to fire hazard—dry cleaners storing benzine); William Fox Amusement Co. v. McClellan, 62 Misc. 100, 114 N.Y.S. 594 (1909). But cf. Re Walker, 84 Misc. 118, 146 N.Y.S. 519 (1914) (license cannot be denied arbitrarily); City of Seattle v. Bittner, 81 Wash.2d 747, 505 P.2d 126 (1973) (city could not deny motion-picture theatre licenses to all who had been convicted of certain crimes within past 5 years; ordinance did not purport to restrain only the showing of obscene movies, and it did not provide procedural safeguards necessary to prior restraints).

[121] Variety Theatres, Inc. v. Cleveland County, 282 N.C. 272, 192 S.E.2d 290 (1972), appeal dism'd 411 U.S. 911, 93 S.Ct. 1548, 36 L.Ed.2d 303. But see Olympic Drive-In Theatre v. City of Pagedale, 441 S.W.2d 5 (Mo.1969), voiding an ordinance requiring that the screen be so located that the picture could not be seen from public streets, where the protesting theatre showed it would cost them $252,000 to comply. As always, any penal or licensing ordinances as to drive-ins must be reasonably definite and certain. Thus, the *Olympic Drive-*

the U.S. Supreme Court invalidated an ordinance, as discriminatory on the basis of content, which prohibited the showing of films containing nudity by any drive-in theatre whose screen was visible from a public street or place.[122] The Court noted that more stringent controls on communicative materials available to youths may be justified than would be allowed as to materials for adults;[123] but it ruled that all nudity cannot be considered obscene even as to minors. Therefore, the ordinance was overbroad. Viewed as a traffic-safety measure, it was also overbroad in that sufficient justification was not offered for distinguishing movies containing nudity from all other movies.

§ 23.8 Local Regulation of Prostitution and Other "Immoral" Activities

Some attempts by local governments to regulate "morality" have (unlike the above-discussed regulations on reading materials and movie theatres) little or no connection with restrictions on "free speech." For instance, many localities have long prohibited prostitution and houses of prostitution, and have been held to have the power to enact such bans.[124] A prohibition on *solicitation* for prostitution will also generally be

---

In case, *supra*, also invalidated language that allowed revocation of theatre permits if a business was conducted so as to constitute a nuisance because of noise or immoral activity on the premises.

[122] Erznoznik v. City of Jacksonville, 422 U.S. 205, 95 S.Ct. 2268, 45 L.Ed.2d 125 (1975), ruling that all nudity cannot be considered obscene, even as to minors. Cf. State v. Jones, 177 Ariz. 94, 865 P.2d 138 (App. 1993) (ordinance requiring a special-use permit prior to operation of an establishment featuring "topless or bottomless dancers, strippers or similar entertainers" invalidated as unconstitutionally vague and overbroad); Wortham v. City of Tucson, 128 Ariz. 137, 624 P.2d 334 (App.1980) (nude or partially nude dancing subject to First Amendment protection); People v. Hardy, 77 Misc.2d 1092, 357 N.Y.S.2d 970 (1974) (per curiam) (mere proof of public nudity—sunbathing on public beach—held not to establish violation of anti-lewdness statute; no evidence defendant exposed herself in a lewd manner or committed a lewd act). But see Chapin v. Town of Southampton, 457 F.Supp. 1170 (E.D.N.Y.1978) (upholding ordinance prohibiting nudity on public beaches); Crownover v. Musick, *supra* note 119, upholding an ordinance that prohibited nudity by performers, waiters, and waitresses in places where food or beverages are served.

[123] Erznoznik v. City of Jacksonville, *supra* note 122, at 212–14. Cf. Interstate Circuit, Inc. v. City of Dallas, *supra* note 118 (ordinance attempting to control exhibition of films to minors voided as impermissibly vague and unclear). See generally, on controls as to materials available to minors, notes 110–111 *supra*, and accompanying text. See also Annot., Supreme Court's Views as to Validity of Laws Restricting or Prohibiting Sale or Distribution to Minors of Particular Types of Goods or Services Otherwise Available to Adults, 52 L.Ed.2d 892 (1978).

Many localities now leave the "rating" of motion pictures—as to whether or not children are allowed, allowed only with parents, or not allowed at all—to the Motion Picture Association of America (representing the largest motion picture distributors in the country), the International Film Importers & Distributors of America (representing many importers of foreign films), and the National Association of Theatre Owners, representing most theatre-owners in the nation. Together, these operate the Motion Picture Rating System. See Friedman, The Motion Picture Rating System of 1968: A Constitutional Analysis of Self-Regulation by the Film Industry, 73 Colum.L.Rev. 185 (1973), criticizing the system; Note, Private Ratings of Motion Pictures as a Basis for State Regulation, 59 Geo.L.J. 1205 (1971), also noting inadequacies of the system, and exploring legislative attempts to build or expand on its restrictions. See also Note, X-Rated Motion Pictures: From Restricted Theatres and Drive-Ins to the Television Screen, 8 Valparaiso U.L.Rev. 107 (1973). But a few cities retain their own reviewing boards. See Note, The Censorship of Violent Motion Pictures: A Constitutional Analysis, 53 Ind.L.J. 381 (1977–78), discussing a Chicago ordinance. Compare, as to the system in England, Note, Film Censorship—Something for Everyone, 40 Mod.L.Rev. 74 (1977). See generally Note, Constitutional Law—Procedural Guidelines Involved in Municipal Control of Motion Pictures, 41 Miss.L.J. 611 (1970). See also Alexander, Blue-Movie Blues, Newsweek Oct. 29, 1973, at 56; Stevenson, Aunt Julia's Movie Code, Am.Heritage, Dec., 1974, at 74; "Mysterious New Film Ratings" America, Jan. 15, 1972, at 33. On effects of and problems with the rating system over the years, see "Give the Rating System an X," Time, Aug. 27, 1990, at 56.

[124] See Yarbrough v. City of Birmingham, 353 So.2d 75 (Ala.Cr.App.1977); Rubey v. City of Fairbanks, 456 P.2d 470 (Alaska 1969); Atkinson v. Powledge, 123 Fla. 389, 167 So. 4 (1936); City of Evanston v. Hopkins,

upheld.[125] But occasionally, particular local ordinances aimed at prostitutes and their activities will be invalidated as void for vagueness—for instance, an ordinance stating that no prostitute or lewd woman should wander the streets at night.[126]

Reasonable regulations of the hours and/or methods of operation of massage parlors may be validly enacted by local governments, on the basis of protecting public health

---

330 Ill.App. 337, 71 N.E.2d 209 (1947); City of Chicago v. Clark, 359 Ill. 374, 194 N.E. 537 (1935); People v. Hanrahan, 75 Mich. 611, 42 N.W. 1124 (1889); State v. Poague, 245 Minn. 438, 72 N.W.2d 620 (1955); City of Farmington v. Phillips, 92 N.M. 304, 587 P.2d 451 (Ct.App.1978). Even where maintaining a house of prostitution is not *specifically* made a crime, it may be punishable as a kind of nuisance. See West v. State ex rel. Matthews, 233 Ala. 588, 173 So. 46 (1937); Griffith v. City of Hapeville, 182 Ga. 333, 185 S.E. 522 (1936). Certainly such establishments may be either public or private nuisances, or both. See generally Section 18.1 notes 1–5 *supra* and accompanying text.

But there has been some recent effort toward legalizing prostitution, and merely applying appropriate regulations to it; so far, such proposals have not resulted in much actual legislation. See "Prostitution Laws Under Attack in N.Y.C.," 66 A.B.A.J. 711 (1980) (noting argument that sex between consenting adults should be a private matter, not controlled by the government—but also noting that courts have rejected invasion-of-privacy arguments against prostitution laws); Essay, "Reflections on the Sad Profession," Time, Aug. 23, 1971, at 34 (noting that all states except Nevada have some laws against prostitution). Nevada actually permits prostitution, with restrictions, only in certain counties of the state. In other counties, prostitution is illegal, and even advertising of the brothels lawfully operating in other counties is not there allowed. See Princess Sea Indus., Inc. v. State, 97 Nev. 534, 635 P.2d 281 (1981), cert. denied 456 U.S. 926, 102 S.Ct. 1972, 72 L.Ed.2d 441 (1982), upholding the restriction on advertising within counties where prostitution is illegal.

[125] Junction City v. White, 2 Kan.App.2d 403, 580 P.2d 891 (1978). See Arcara v. Cloud Books, Inc., 478 U.S. 697, 106 S.Ct. 3172, 92 L.Ed.2d 568 (1986), on remand 68 N.Y.2d 553, 510 N.Y.S.2d 844, 503 N.E.2d 492 (1986) (Court upholds, against First Amendment attack, closing, pursuant to statute, of adult bookstore on premises on which it had been determined that solicitation of prostitution was taking place); City of Seattle v. Jones, 79 Wash.2d 626, 488 P.2d 750 (1971), upholding an ordinance against loitering for the purpose of soliciting prostitution. Cf. Salt Lake City v. Allred, 20 Utah 2d 298, 437 P.2d 434 (1968) (upholding ordinance punishing the directing of persons to a certain place to obtain sexual intercourse for hire); City of Seattle v. Slack, 113 Wash.2d 850, 784 P.2d 494 (1989) (city's prostitution loitering ordinance permitted police officer to consider whether suspect was "known prostitute" in order to infer suspect's intent; upheld). See also FW/PBS, Inc. v. City of Dallas, 493 U.S. 215, 110 S.Ct. 596, 107 L.Ed.2d 603 (1990), on remand 896 F.2d 864 (5th Cir.1990) (city could declare motels renting rooms for less than ten hours to be "sexually oriented businesses" and subject them to special regulation).

[126] City of St. Louis v. Burton, 478 S.W.2d 320 (Mo.1972). See Brown v. Municipality of Anchorage, 584 P.2d 35 (Alaska 1978); City of Detroit v. Bowden, 6 Mich.App. 514, 149 N.W.2d 771 (1967) (ordinance that known prostitutes or panderers could not stop motorists or pedestrians by making bodily gestures to them held void for vagueness). Restrictions on escort services have usually been upheld against constitutional attack. See IDK, Inc. v. County of Clark, 836 F.2d 1185 (9th Cir.1988) (county regulation of such services upheld, the court finding the services to be primarily commercial and therefore finding no impermissible burden on freedom of intimate association); Starlets International, Inc. v. Christensen, 106 Nev. 732, 801 P.2d 1343 (1990) (ordinance requiring person who provides outcall services to hotels and motels to satisfy licensing provisions, and requiring managers and entertainers to be similarly licensed, upheld as sufficiently clear and not violative of due process; said to facilitate legitimate governmental interest in controlling prostitution). But see Treants Enterprises, Inc. v. Onslow County, 83 N.C.App. 345, 350 S.E.2d 365 (1986), motion to dismiss appeal denied by 319 N.C. 411, 354 S.E.2d 730 (1987), aff'd by 320 N.C. 776, 360 S.E.2d 783 (1987) (city ordinance regulating businesses that offered male and/or female companions invalidated as vague, overbroad, and not rationally related to any legitimate governmental objective). See generally Annot., Laws Prohibiting or Regulating "Escort Services," "Outcall Entertainment," or Similar Services Used to Carry on Prostitution, 15 A.L.R.5th 900 (1993). On the requirement that all penal laws be reasonably definite and certain, see generally Chapter 10 *supra*.

Occasionally, a municipal ordinance on prostitution may be voided because the state is found to have pre-empted the field of such regulation. See Farmer v. Behmer, 9 Cal.App. 773, 100 P. 901 (Dist.Ct.1909); Pace v. City of Atlanta, 135 Ga.App. 399, 218 S.E.2d 128 (1975). On state pre-emption, see generally Chapter 6 *supra*. Certainly, this is an area where state law will prevail over all local laws (even those of home-rule cities) in cases of *conflict*; see Chapter 6 *supra*. See also Note, Revisiting the Prostitution Debate: Uniting Liberal and Radical Feminism in Pursuit of Policy Reform, 30 Law & Ineq. 19 (2010).

and morality.[127] Ordinances that prohibit the administration of massages, at public massage parlors or bath houses, by members of one sex to members of the other sex are fairly common and are obviously enacted largely in reliance on the "public morality" portion of the police power. Such ordinances are controversial and have been invalidated in a number of cases as violating equal protection through the use of invidious classifications.[128] But most authority, usually indicating that there is no "sex discrimination" involved and that a rational purpose (which generally can be found) will suffice to uphold these restrictions, supports the validity of such measures.[129]

The hours and manner of operation of pool and billiard halls can be regulated, largely on the basis of the possible detrimental effect of such establishments on

---

[127] See Pollard v. Cockrell, 578 F.2d 1002 (5th Cir.1978) (with review of cases); Rogers v. Miller, 401 F.Supp. 826 (E.D.Va.1975) (upholding regulation and annual license tax of $5000; tax not valid because it exceeded cost of regulation since local government also had power to tax); Wes Ward Enterprises, Limited v. Andrews, 42 Ill.App.3d 458, 355 N.E.2d 131 (1976); City of Indianapolis v. Wright, 267 Ind. 471, 371 N.E.2d 1298 (1978) appeal dism'd 439 U.S. 804, 99 S.Ct. 60, 58 L.Ed.2d 97; Caesar's Health Club v. St. Louis County, 565 S.W.2d 783 (Mo.App.1978), cert. denied 439 U.S. 955, 99 S.Ct. 353, 58 L.Ed.2d 346; Kisley v. City of Falls Church, 212 Va. 693, 187 S.E.2d 168 (1972), appeal dism'd 409 U.S. 907, 93 S.Ct. 237, 34 L.Ed.2d 169; City of Spokane v. Bostrom, 12 Wn.App. 116, 528 P.2d 500 (1974) (prohibition of massage parlors operating between 10 p. m. and 6 a. m.). Cf. Hollingsworth v. City of South Salt Lake, 624 P.2d 1149 (Utah 1981) (provision of city "massage parlor" ordinance making it unlawful for a masseur to touch or offer to touch the genitalia of customers was not void for vagueness). Ordinances regulating public bath houses, as to hours and methods of operation, have also been sustained. See Garaci v. City of Memphis, 379 F.Supp. 1393 (W.D.Tenn.1974); City of Spokane v. Bostrom, *supra*.

In Hart Health Studio v. Salt Lake County, 577 P.2d 116 (Utah 1978), the general power of state and local governments to regulate massage parlors was affirmed, but the court struck down ordinances setting different business-hours for masseurs who were sole practitioners and for those who were not, finding such a distinction arbitrary and unreasonable. Tattoo parlors may be regulated for purposes of health and safety, but total bans are likely to run afoul of the First Amendment. See Note, Preserving Access to Tattoos: First Amendment Trumps Municipal Ban in *Anderson v. City of Hermosa Beach*, 621 F.3d 1051 (9th Cir. 2010), noted 2011 B.Y.U. L. Rev. 131. See generally Hudson, You Gotta Fight for the Right to Tattoo, 98 A.B.A. J., Nov. 2012, at 12 (most state courts, but not Arizona's, have ruled that tattoos are not protected speech.

[128] Valley Health Systems, Inc. v. City of Racine, 369 F.Supp. 97 (E.D.Wis.1973); Joseph v. House, 353 F.Supp. 367 (E.D.Va.1973), aff'd 482 F.2d 575 (4th Cir. 1973). See Wheeler v. City of Rockford, 69 Ill.App.3d 220, 25 Ill.Dec. 702, 387 N.E.2d 358 (1979) (sex classifications in such ordinances should be voided unless a compelling interest is shown to support them). Cf. Bell v. Arlington County, Virginia, 673 F.Supp. 767 (E.D.Va.1987) (county ordinance prohibiting cross-sexual massages for pay held unconstitutionally vague); Cheek v. City of Charlotte, 273 N.C. 293, 160 S.E.2d 18 (1968) (unreasonable classifications found in particular ordinance—applied to massage parlors and health salons but not to beauty shops, barber shops, etc.); J.S.K. Enterprises v. City of Lacey, 6 Wn.App. 43, 492 P.2d 600 (1971), adhered to 6 Wn.App. 433, 493 P.2d 1015 (ordinance found unreasonable). In Cianciolo v. City of Knoxville, 376 F.Supp. 719 (E.D.Tenn.1974), an ordinance prohibiting members of one sex from massaging members of the opposite sex was held violative of the Federal Civil Rights Law.

[129] Tomlinson v. City of Savannah, 543 F.2d 570 (5th Cir.1976); Aldred v. Duling, 538 F.2d 637 (4th Cir.1976); Colorado Springs Amusements v. Rizzo, 524 F.2d 571 (3d Cir.1975), cert. denied 428 U.S. 913, 96 S.Ct. 3228, 49 L.Ed.2d 1222, noted 62 A.B.A.J. 233 (1976); Brown v. Haner, 410 F.Supp. 399 (W.D.Va.1976); Massage Parlors, Inc. v. City of Baltimore, 284 Md. 490, 398 A.2d 52 (1979); Smith v. Keator, 285 N.C. 530, 206 S.E.2d 203 (1974), appeal dism'd 419 U.S. 1043, 95 S.Ct. 613, 42 L.Ed.2d 636; Patterson v. City of Dallas, 355 S.W.2d 838 (Tex.Civ.App.1962) ref'd n. r. e. appeal dism'd 372 U.S. 251, 83 S.Ct. 873, 9 L.Ed.2d 732; Redwood Gym v. Salt Lake County Comm'n, 624 P.2d 1138 (Utah 1981); Kisley v. City of Falls Church, *supra* note 127. Cf. City of Chicago v. Geraci, 30 Ill.App.3d 699, 332 N.E.2d 487 (1975), ruling that "masturbatory massage parlors" may be enjoined as public nuisances. Cf. Techtow v. City Council of North Las Vegas, 105 Nev. 330, 775 P.2d 227 (1989) (court upheld ordinance regulating massage parlors' hours of operations, advertising, and other practices as not violative of First Amendment freedoms, and sustained a prohibition of massages by persons of the opposite sex, but invalidated as violative of freedom of association and rights of privacy the portions of the law which required windows on all doors and the keeping of records of the names of all patrons). See generally Annot., Validity and Construction of Statute or Ordinance Forbidding Treatment in Health Clubs or Massage Salons by Persons of the Opposite Sex, 51 A.L.R.3d 936 (1973).

morality.[130] The local restrictions can include requirements that operators of these establishments obtain licenses,[131] and limitations on those eligible for such licenses.[132] Even total bans on pool and billiard establishments in some communities have been upheld,[133] though regulation, rather than prohibition, seems more common in recent decades.

The suppression of gambling, or certain types of gambling activity, is occasionally pre-empted by a state government.[134] And, even in the absence of state pre-emption, state law will prevail over local regulations and prohibitions (even those of home-rule cities) in cases of *conflict*, since this is an area of state-wide concern.[135] But aside from those qualifications, local governments have power to enact legislation aimed at suppression of gambling, since this activity tends to corrupt public morals.[136] Thus, cities

---

130 Purvis v. City of Ocilla, 149 Ga. 771, 102 S.E. 241 (1920); State ex rel. Baer v. City of Milwaukee, 33 Wis.2d 624, 148 N.W.2d 21 (1967) (persons under 18 banned from premises, and no card-playing allowed on premises). Cf. B & B Vending Co. v. City of El Paso, 408 S.W.2d 545 (Tex.Civ.App.1966) (ordinance regulated ownership, location, and hours of operation of billiard halls and set standards for owners and employees upheld). But see Callaway v. City of Edmond, 791 P.2d 104 (Okl.Cr.App. 1990) (ordinance prohibited admission of minors to pool halls, snooker parlors, billiard parlors, or similar places of business; invalidated under Equal Protection as not rationally related to proper public purpose of inhibiting gambling since was no indication that the establishments in question were particularly prone to gambling activity by minors). On regulation of the playing of video games by minors, see Rothner v. City of Chicago, 725 F.Supp. 945 (N.D.Ill.1989), aff'd 929 F.2d 297 (7th Cir.1991), sustaining an ordinance making it unlawful for anyone under 17 to play any automatic amusement device during school hours at any location except airports. See generally Note, Is Violence Really Just Fun and Games?: A Proposal for a Violent Video Game Ordinance that Passes Constitutional Muster, 37 Valparaiso L. Rev. 429 (2002); Note, Insert Coins to Slay: Regulating Children's Access to Violent Arcade Games, 10 Villanova Sports & Entertainment L.J. 69 (2003).

131 See Wysong v. City of Lebanon, 163 Ind. 132, 71 N.E. 194 (1904) (reasonable license fee can also be charged); State ex rel. Reedhead v. City of Olympia, 122 Wash. 239, 210 P. 371 (1922) (proof of good moral character can be required of applicants for license). Cf. Purvis v. City of Ocilla, *supra* note 130 (license fee can be charged).

132 See Feinstein v. City of Whitehall, 198 N.E.2d 479 (Ohio Com.Pl.1964) (licenses denied those convicted of felony within the past 7 years); B & B Vending Co. v. City of El Paso, *supra* note 130 (requirement of good moral character held not too vague); State ex rel. Reedhead v. City of Olympia, *supra* note 131 (good moral character can be required of applicant). But a license cannot be denied arbitrarily or capriciously. Tillberg v. Kearney Township, 103 N.J.Super. 324, 247 A.2d 161 (1968). And if a license is so denied, mandamus will lie to compel issuance. State ex rel. Hardman v. Common Council of Glenville, 102 W.Va. 94, 134 S.E. 467 (1926); State ex rel. Hoffman v. Town of Clendenin, 93 W.Va. 618, 115 S.E. 583 (1923). Cf. Assaid v. City of Roanoke, 179 Va. 47, 18 S.E.2d 287 (1942) (opportunity for hearing must be given applicant).

133 State ex rel. Baylor v. City of Hinton, 109 W.Va. 653, 155 S.E. 912 (1930). Cf. Botes v. City of Franklin, 203 Ky. 357, 262 S.W. 282 (1924); Arms v. Vine Grove, 203 Ky. 213, 262 S.W. 11 (1924), both upholding license fees despite their being prohibitory in amount.

134 City of Piggott v. Eblen, 236 Ark. 390, 366 S.W.2d 192 (1963). See State v. Linn, 49 Okl. 526, 153 P. 826 (1915). Cf. In re Portnoy, 21 Cal.2d 237, 131 P.2d 1 (1942) (county anti-gambling ordinance conflicted with state penal code; invalid). See also Edmonds Shopping Center Associates v. City of Edmonds, 117 Wash.App. 344, 71 P.3d 233 (2003) (city ordinance prohibiting expansion of existing cardrooms beyond numbers authorized by gambling license was pre-empted by state law allowing cities to ban cardrooms but prohibiting them from changing scope of gambling license).

135 State ex rel. Sergi v. City of Youngstown, 68 Ohio App. 254, 40 N.E.2d 477 (1941) (where certain acts of gambling outlawed by state, locality cannot authorize them); City of Bartlett v. Hoover, 571 S.W.2d 291 (Tenn.1978) (where certain acts of gambling specifically allowed by state, locality cannot prohibit); Smith Amusement Co. v. City of Chattanooga, 205 Tenn. 712, 330 S.W.2d 320 (1959) (same).

136 On regulation of gambling as a nuisance, see People v. Lim, 18 Cal.2d 872, 118 P.2d 472 (1941); Approximately Fifty-Nine Gambling Devices v. People ex rel. Burke, 110 Colo. 82, 130 P.2d 920 (1942); Goose v. Commonwealth ex rel. Dummit, 305 Ky. 644, 205 S.W.2d 326 (1947); Garvey v. McNulty, 270 Mass. 260, 170 N.E. 58 (1930); People ex rel. Roberts v. Reille, 50 N.Y.S.2d 196 (City Ct. 1944). Cf. State ex rel. Dowling v. Tate, 306 Mich. 667, 11 N.W.2d 282 (1943) (upholding statute declaring any vehicle used for gambling purposes a public nuisance). A premises where gambling is conducted is often classified as a public nuisance even though there is no showing of excessive noise or boisterous conduct. See Ehrlick v. Commonwealth, 125

and towns have been upheld in banning particular gambling devices and games, so long as these were not sanctioned by state law;[137] and, on the other hand, local governments can authorize, regulate, and/or license particular forms of gambling that are not prohibited by state law.[138]

Much the same situation exists with local attempts at liquor controls as with local regulation of gambling: The state may occasionally be found to have pre-empted the field;[139] and despite a lack of state pre-emption, local regulations must yield to any

---

Ky. 742, 102 S.W. 289 (1907); Commonwealth v. Ciccone, 85 Pa.Super. 316 (1925). But cf. People v. Robbin, 53 Cal.App.2d 579, 128 P.2d 422 (Dist.Ct.1942) (premises must be frequented by disorderly or dissolute persons or be operated in a disorderly manner to be enjoinable as nuisance). See generally C.J.S. Nuisances § 48, at 800 (1950). See also Hunter v. Mayor & Council of Teaneck Township, 128 N.J.L. 164, 24 A.2d 553 (1942) (if no pre-emption by state, local government can prohibit gambling though state also has laws against such activity). On regulation and suppression of nuisances, see generally Chapter 18 *supra*. The power of municipalities to terminate gambling enterprises as nuisances may be considered comparable to the well-recognized power of such local units to destroy dangerous or harmful structures as nuisances. See McMahon v. City of Telluride, 79 Colo. 281, 244 P. 1017 (1926) (structural nuisance); Albert v. City of Mountain Home, 81 Idaho 74, 337 P.2d 377 (1959) (same); Sings v. City of Joliet, 237 Ill. 300, 86 N.E. 663 (1908) (buildings infected with disease); Rothenhoefer v. City of St. Louis, 410 S.W.2d 73 (Mo.1966) (burned-out building). But cf. Cole v. Kegler, 64 Iowa 59, 19 N.W. 843 (1884) (town and its authorities could be liable if destroyed structure was not actually a nuisance). See generally Section 115 *supra*. On the effect of recent legalization of gambling (discussed in Section 15.12 *supra*) on municipal power to regulate this activity, see Comment, The Promises and Perils of Legalized Gambling for Local Governments: Who Decides How to Stack the Deck?, 68 Temple L. Rev. 847 (1995).

[137] See Sharpe v. Johnson, 81 Cal.App.2d 939, 185 P.2d 340 (Dist.Ct.1947) (table games and marble games); Williams v. Mayor & Council of Athens, 122 Ga.App. 465, 177 S.E.2d 581 (1970) (pinball machines); Wallace v. City of Cartersville, 203 Ga. 63, 45 S.E.2d 63 (1947), cert. denied 333 U.S. 843, 68 S.Ct. 661, 92 L.Ed. 1126 (same); Kitt v. City of Chicago, 415 Ill. 246, 112 N.E.2d 607 (1953) (bagatelle); Coven Distributing Co. v. City of Chicago, 346 Ill.App. 448, 105 N.E.2d 137 (1952) (pinball machines); In re Albert Simon, Inc. v. Myerson, 36 N.Y.2d 300, 367 N.Y.S.2d 755, 327 N.E.2d 801 (1975), appeal dism'd 423 U.S. 908, 96 S.Ct. 209, 46 L.Ed.2d 137 (same); Benjamin v. City of Columbus, 167 Ohio St. 103, 146 N.E.2d 854 (1957), cert. denied 357 U.S. 904, 78 S.Ct. 1147, 2 L.Ed.2d 1155 (same); Westerhaus Co. v. City of Cincinnati, 165 Ohio St. 327, 135 N.E.2d 318 (1956) (bagatelle); Myers v. City of Cincinnati, 128 Ohio St. 235, 190 N.E. 569 (1934) (slot machines). Cf. People v. Mason, 261 Cal.App.2d 348, 68 Cal.Rptr. 17 (Dist. Ct.1968) (city could prohibit those pinball machines which are not predominantly games of skill; only those that are games of skill, not chance, were legalized by state statute); American Shuffleboard & Music Corp. v. City of Springfield, 40 Ill.App.3d 745, 353 N.E.2d 1 (1976) (coin-operated amusement devices can be licensed, with limit on the number); Columbus Legal Amusement Association v. City of Columbus, 50 O.L.A. 353, 79 N.E.2d 915 (1947) (mechanical amusement devices can be regulated; those readily convertible into gambling devices can be seized and destroyed); Dallmann v. Kluchesky, 229 Wis. 169, 282 N.W. 9 (1938) (ordinance prohibiting any device upon which money may be won or lost is valid—at least if construed to apply only to places in which numbers of people might gather). But cf. Curtis v. Hutchingson, 125 Fla. 435, 170 So. 134 (1936) (reasonable regulation of slot machines allowed, but prohibition of such machines more than 5 feet above or 3 feet below ground level of entrance of building held unreasonable). Even a gum-vending machine that also dispenses chances can be banned. State v. La Due, 198 Minn. 255, 269 N.W. 527 (1936). As can lotteries in general. See Glover v. City of Birmingham, 255 Ala. 596, 52 So.2d 521 (1951). Cf. Hagen v. City of Rock Island, 18 Ill.2d 174, 163 N.E.2d 495 (1959) (horse-racing machine can be prohibited); City of Wichita v. Stevens, 167 Kan. 408, 207 P.2d 386 (1949) ("punchboard" prohibited). On billiards, slot machines, etc., as "games of chance," see generally Annot., What Is Game of Chance, 60 A.L.R. 343 (1929). See also Fichtner, Carnival Games: Walking the Line Between Gambling and Amusement, 60 Drake L. Rev. 41 (2011).

[138] Sternall v. Strand, 76 Cal.App.2d 432, 172 P.2d 921 (1946); Ex parte Lawrence, 55 Cal.App.2d 491, 131 P.2d 27 (1942); Hallandale v. Broward County Kennel Club, 153 Fla. 302, 14 So.2d 397 (1943); Silfen v. City of Chicago, 299 Ill.App. 117, 19 N.E.2d 640 (1939); People v. Hess, 85 Mich. 128, 48 N.W. 181. (1891); Savoy Vending Co. v. Valentine, 178 Misc. 1, 33 N.Y.S.2d 324 (1942). See State ex rel. Grimes v. Board of Commissioners, 53 Nev. 364, 1 P.2d 570 (1931) (power to restrict number of gambling licenses inferred from statutory power to license and regulate gambling). See also Note, Unstacking the Deck: The Legalization of Online Poker, 50 Am. Crim. L. Rev. 519 (2013).

[139] See Los Angeles Brewing Co. v. City of Los Angeles, 8 Cal.App.2d 391, 48 P.2d 71 (Dist.Ct.1935) (under constitutional provision, state had exclusive right to license liquor dealers for revenue purposes; city could not impose license tax); 7-Eleven, Inc. v. McClain, 422 P.2d 455 (Okl.1967) (sale of alcoholic beverages

conflicting state laws,[140] since this is an area of state-wide, general concern—indeed, an area where uniform state legislation is often thought essential to adequate enforcement of the law. But within these limits, localities have unquestioned power to regulate the sale and distribution of liquor—not only for protection of morality, but for health and safety purposes.[141] Thus, taverns and liquor stores selling alcoholic beverages can be required to obtain licenses by local communities,[142] and can be banned from certain areas—as within a designated distance from a church, other places of worship, or school.[143] The powers of states and local governments to control liquor have been held so broad that entertainment in places serving alcoholic beverages can be regulated or

---

was a field "reserved" for *state* regulation; city zoning ordinance forbidding sale of beer in certain areas invalid). Cf. Mayor & Common Council of Prescott v. Randall, 67 Ariz. 369, 196 P.2d 477 (1948) (statute created state-wide control over traffic in liquor; city could license and tax any liquor-dealer licensed by the state, but could not refuse to issue license or limit number of licenses).

[140] See City of Canton v. Imperial Bowling Lanes, Inc., 7 Ohio Misc. 292, 220 N.E.2d 151 (Mun.Ct.1966); Town of Honea Path v. Flynn, 255 S.C. 32, 176 S.E.2d 564 (1970); City of Wichita Falls v. Abell, 566 S.W.2d 336 (Tex.Civ.App.1978), error dism'd ref'd n. r. e. Cf. Williams v. City of Jackson, 82 O.L.A. 177, 164 N.E.2d 195 (Com.Pl.1959) (city could not forbid sale of beer at hours when state allowed); Sparger v. Harris, 191 Okl. 583, 131 P.2d 1011 (1942) (city could not prohibit Sunday sale of beer, which was authorized by state statute).

[141] See Foster v. Police Commissioners, 102 Cal. 483, 37 P. 763 (1894); Nelson v. State ex rel. Gross, 157 Fla. 412, 26 So.2d 60 (1946); Cowan v. City of St. Petersburg, 149 Fla. 470, 6 So.2d 269 (1942); Mutchall v. City of Kalamazoo, 323 Mich. 215, 35 N.W.2d 245 (1948); State ex rel. Hewlett v. Womach, 355 Mo. 486, 196 S.W.2d 809 (1946); Greiner v. City of Hoboken, 68 N.J.L. 592, 53 A. 693 (1902); Driggs v. City of Denison, 420 S.W.2d 446 (Tex.Civ.App.1967). But local controls on liquor distribution will be invalidated if not reasonably definite and certain. See City of Canton v. Imperial Bowling Lanes, Inc., *supra* note 140. On various types of local controls over liquor, see generally Annot., Validity of Statute or Ordinance Making It an Offense to Consume or Have Alcoholic Beverages in Open Package in Motor Vehicle, 57 A.L.R.3d 1071 (1974); Annot., Validity of Municipal Regulation More Restrictive Than State Regulation as to Time for Selling or Serving Intoxicating Liquor, 51 A.L.R.3d 1061 (1973); Annot., Construction of Statute or Ordinance Making It an Offense to Possess or Have Alcoholic Beverages in Open Package in Motor Vehicle, 35 A.L.R.3d 1418 (1971). See also Annot., Degree or Nature of Intoxication for Purposes of Statute or Ordinance Making It a Criminal Offense to Operate Automobile While in That Condition, 142 A.L.R. 555 (1943).

[142] See Ex Parte Sikes, 102 Ala. 173, 15 So. 522 (1894) (license fee can be charged); Bumball v. Burnett, 115 N.J.L. 254, 179 A. 307 (1935) (local government need not issue maximum number of licenses authorized by ordinance); State ex rel. Boroo v. Town Board, 10 Wis.2d 153, 102 N.W.2d 238 (1960) (denial of license will be upheld if not arbitrary or capricious). See generally Note, The Power of Municipalities in Colorado to Levy an Occupational Tax on Liquor Dealers, 21 Rocky Mt.L.Rev. 209 (1948). Reasonably definite licensing standards must be provided or a license ordinance will be invalidated as denying due process. See Barnes v. Merritt, 428 F.2d 284 (5th Cir.1970). See generally Chapter 10 *supra*. See also Weeks, Issuing or Revoking Liquor Licenses: State and Local Authority under Recent Federal Decisions, 15 Urban Law. 379 (1983).

[143] Borough of Fanwood v. Rocco, 33 N.J. 404, 165 A.2d 183 (1960). See Barnes v. City of Dayton, 216 Tenn. 400, 392 S.W.2d 813 (1965) (license from Board of Commissioners, required for sale of beer, could be denied if would increase traffic congestion or be hazardous to public health; upheld); City of Clute v. Linscomb, 446 S.W.2d 377 (Tex. Civ.App.1969) (ordinance can restrict sale of beer to certain areas of city). Even the sale of beer may be banned near schools and churches, and within other designated districts of a municipality. See Harrison v. Buckhalt, 364 So.2d 283 (Ala.1978) (city can prohibit sale of beer within reasonable distance of school or church, but "grandfather clause" here found invalid as arbitrary; whole ordinance therefore ruled invalid). But see Larkin v. Grendel's Den, Inc., 459 U.S. 116, 103 S.Ct. 505, 74 L.Ed.2d 297 (1982), where it was held that a law vesting the governing bodies of churches and schools with the power to veto applications for liquor licenses amounted to a delegation of governmental power to private entities and violated the Establishment Clause of the First Amendment. Cf. Gas 'N Shop v. Nebraska Liquor Control Comm'n, 229 Neb. 530, 427 N.W.2d 784 (1988) (city ordinance prohibiting liquor sales on premises not separate from those on which other businesses are operated, but containing exceptions for certain establishments such as hotels and restaurants, held violative of equal protection); City of Clute v. Linscomb, *supra*. See generally Note, That's What I Like About Utah: *Larkin v. Grendel's Den* and the Alcoholic Beverage Control Act, 37 Columbia J.L. & Soc. Probs. 239 (2003).

Local restrictions on the hours of operation of taverns are quite common and are generally sustained. See South Daytona Restaurants v. City of South Daytona, 186 So.2d 78 (Fla.App.1966); State ex rel. Floyd v. Noel, 124 Fla. 852, 169 So. 549 (1936).

prohibited even though that entertainment does not qualify as "obscene" under U.S. Supreme Court definitions—there must simply be a reasonable relationship of the regulation or prohibition to some police-power purpose.[144]

Some municipalities regulate the sale of cigarettes and other smoking materials. The power of local governments to do this, as by requiring licenses of those who engage in such sales, has been upheld as based on legitimate police-power purposes.[145] Prohibitions on sale of cigarettes to minors have also been sustained when enacted at

---

[144] California v. LaRue, 409 U.S. 109, 93 S.Ct. 390, 34 L.Ed.2d 342 (1972), reh. denied 410 U.S. 948, 93 S.Ct. 1351, 35 L.Ed.2d 615. See City of Newport v. Iacobucci, 479 U.S. 92, 107 S.Ct. 383, 93 L.Ed.2d 334 (1986), reh. denied 479 U.S. 1047, 107 S.Ct. 913, 93 L.Ed.2d 862 (1987) (states' regulatory authority over intoxicating liquors includes power to ban nude dancing as part of its liquor license control program; state statutory delegation to city electorate of power to decide whether or not liquor could be served in local establishments did not prevent city legislative body from enacting a ban on nude dancing in local establishments licensed for sale of liquor for consumption on the premises); Geaneas v. Willetts, 911 F.2d 579 (11th Cir.1990), cert. denied 499 U.S. 955, 111 S.Ct. 1431, 113 L.Ed.2d 484 (1991) (city ordinance prohibiting exposure of certain body parts in establishments serving alcohol is valid exercise of police power under Twenty-First Amendment); Ranch House, Inc. v. City of Anniston, 678 So.2d 745 (Ala.1996) (city could prohibit nudity, partial nudity, or nude dancing in establishments where alcoholic beverages are sold or consumed); Crownover v. Musick, 9 Cal.3d 405, 107 Cal.Rptr. 681, 509 P.2d 497 (1973), cert. denied 415 U.S. 931, 94 S.Ct. 1443, 39 L.Ed.2d 489 (nudity banned in bars and taverns; upheld); City of Daytona Beach v. Del Percio, 476 So.2d 197 (Fla.1985) (ordinance applicable to establishments selling alcoholic beverages prohibited any female from exposing her breasts "below the top of the areola"; upheld); Olson v. City of West Fargo, 305 N.W.2d 821 (N.D.1981) (ordinance applicable to licensed liquor establishments prohibited any live performances that included dancing, removing of clothing, or performance or simulation of sexual acts; upheld); City of Portland v. Derrington, 253 Or. 289, 451 P.2d 111 (1969), cert. denied 396 U.S. 901, 90 S.Ct. 212, 24 L.Ed.2d 177 (topless dancing prohibited in establishment serving liquor; upheld); Wayside Restaurant, Inc. v. City of Virginia Beach, 215 Va. 231, 208 S.E.2d 51 (1974) (same); City of Milwaukee v. Piscuine, 18 Wis.2d 599, 119 N.W.2d 442 (1963) (female entertainers prohibited from sitting or standing at bar; upheld). Cf. Lanier v. City of Newton, Alabama, 842 F.2d 253 (11th Cir.1988) (town had authority under Twenty-First Amendment to ban nude dancing in liquor establishments and had not singled-out one bar owner for discriminatory treatment); Leverett v. City of Pinellas Park, 775 F.2d 1536 (11th Cir.1985) (court, while invalidating as overbroad an ordinance which prohibited nude or seminude entertainment in any commercial establishment, upheld ordinance which prohibited nude service of any food or drink). Even a ban on music in places where liquor is sold has been sustained; City of De Ridder v. Mangano, 186 La. 129, 171 So. 826 (1936). Cf. Mallach v. City of Mount Morris, 287 Mich. 666, 284 N.W. 600 (1939) (ban on dancing where alcohol sold; upheld); Zinn v. City of Steelville, 351 Mo. 413, 173 S.W.2d 398 (1943) (ban on juke boxes in places where liquor sold; upheld). But see Krueger v. City of Pensacola, 759 F.2d 851 (11th Cir.1985), where an ordinance banning topless dancing in establishments serving alcoholic beverages was invalidated for lack of evidence that any legitimate government interest motivated the city to impose such a restriction on communication; State of Arizona v. Western, 168 Ariz. 169, 812 P.2d 987 (1991), where an ordinance prohibiting striptease dancing in establishments serving food or alcohol was held unconstitutionally vague and overbroad. See also Annot., Validity, Construction, and Effect of Statutes, Ordinances, or Regulations Prohibiting or Regulating Advertising of Intoxicating Liquors, 20 A.L.R.4th 600 (1983), noting that under the states' regulatory powers, coupled with the broad grant of power vested in the states by the Twenty-First Amendment, state regulatory agencies have the power to restrict advertising, or forbid it entirely, when it concerns alcoholic beverages. But see Capital Cities Cable, Inc. v. Crisp, 467 U.S. 691, 104 S.Ct. 2694, 81 L.Ed.2d 580 (1984) (state regulation of retransmission by cable television stations pre-empted by federal regulations; state could not require cable television operators to delete all advertisements for alcoholic beverages). Cf. Rubin v. Coors Brewing Co., 514 U.S. 476, 115 S.Ct. 1585, 131 L.Ed.2d 532 (1995) (federal law prohibiting beer labels from displaying alcoholic content violated First Amendment's protection of commercial speech).

[145] See Gundling v. City of Chicago, 176 Ill. 340, 52 N.E. 44 (1898), aff'd 177 U.S. 183, 20 S.Ct. 633, 44 L.Ed. 725 (license required); Detroit Retail Druggists' Association v. City of Detroit, 267 Mich. 405, 255 N.W. 217 (1934) (same); Ex parte Nash, 55 Nev. 92, 26 P.2d 353 (1933). Cf. Lorillard Tobacco Co. v. Reilly, 533 U.S. 525, 121 S.Ct. 2404, 150 L.Ed.2d 532 (2001) (Massachusetts regulations requiring retailers to place tobacco products behind counters and requiring customers to have contact with salesperson before they are able to handle such products upheld against First Amendment attack, though some regulations governing advertising of tobacco products invalidated—see Section 23.9, note 151, *infra*). See also U.S. Smokeless Tobacco Mfg. Co. v. City of New York, 708 F.3d 428 (2d Cir. 2013) (city ordinance prohibiting the sale of flavored tobacco products held not pre-empted by federal statute).

the local level.[146] A number of states and municipalities have also now passed legislation prohibiting smoking throughout, or in certain portions of, designated public places, such as auditoriums and restaurants; while controversial, these ordinances are being enacted with increasing frequency and seem likely to be sustained by the courts.[147]

---

[146] State v. Crabtree Co., 218 Minn. 36, 15 N.W.2d 98 (1944) (saying need for regulation is presented partly because of dangers of marijuana cigarettes). Cf. Illinois Cigarette Service Co. v. City of Chicago, 89 F.2d 610 (7th Cir.1937), upholding a ban on cigarette-vending machines as a means of controlling sales to minors. See generally Annot., Supreme Court's Views as to Validity of Laws Restricting or Prohibiting Sale or Distribution to Minors of Particular Types of Goods or Services Otherwise Available to Adults, 52 L.Ed.2d 892 (1978).

[147] See Swanson v. City of Tulsa, 633 P.2d 1256 (Okl.Cr.App.1981) (ordinance not impermissibly vague); "Huffing Over All That Puffing," Time, April 24, 1978, at 59, observing that 30 states by then had legislation barring smoking in at least some public places. See generally Hostetler, Tobacco Pollution and the Nonsmoker's Rights, 4 Environmental Law 451 (1974); Comment, The Non-Smoker in Public: A Review and Analysis of Non-Smokers' Rights, 7 San Fernando U.L.Rev. 141 (1979). See also Garner, Cigarettes and Welfare Reform, 26 Emory L.J. 269 (1977); Note, Torts—Non-smokers' Rights—Duty of Employer to Furnish Safe Working Environment Will Support Injunction Against Smoking in the Work Area, 9 Texas Tech.L.Rev. 343 (1977–78). Some legislation requires that non-smoking areas be provided in certain public places, such as restaurants; but there is doubt as to the validity of such measures. See Alford v. City of Newport News, 220 Va. 584, 260 S.E.2d 241 (1979), discussed N.Y. Times, Nov. 24, 1979, at 10, col. 2, invalidating an anti-smoking ordinance as unreasonable; the ordinance required non-smoking areas in restaurants, and the court commented that smoke cannot be effectively segregated in an open room. And in the absence of legislation, non-smokers have been unsuccessful in attempts to force officials to ban smoking in public places. See Federal Employees for Non-Smokers' Rights v. United States, 446 F.Supp. 181 (D.D.C.1978), aff'd 598 F.2d 310 (D.C. Cir.) cert. denied 444 U.S. 926, 100 S.Ct. 265, 62 L.Ed.2d 182 (Federal Constitution does not require that smoking in federal buildings be confined to designated areas; plaintiffs alleged that their right to petition for redress of grievances was infringed by buildings' smoke-filled corridors); Gasper v. Louisiana Stadium & Exposition District, 418 F.Supp. 716 (E.D.La.1976) aff'd, 577 F.2d 897 (5th Cir.1978), cert. denied, 439 U.S. 1073, 99 S.Ct. 846, 59 L.Ed.2d 40 (1979) (nonsmokers stated no cause of action in attempt to enjoin Stadium District from allowing smoking in New Orleans Superdome). On possible judicial and legislative remedies for the nonsmoker bothered by tobacco smoke, see Reynolds, Extinguishing Brushfires: Legal Limits on the Smoking of Tobacco, 53 U. Cin. L. Rev. 435 (1984); Comment, Where There's Smoke There's Ire: The Search for Legal Paths to Tobacco-Free Air, 3 Colum. J. Envtl. L. 62 (1976); Comment, The Legal Conflict Between Smokers and Non-smokers: The Majestic Vice Versus the Right to Clean Air, 45 Mo. L. Rev. 444 (1980); Comment, The Resurgence and Validity of Antismoking Legislation, 7 U. Calif. Davis L. Rev. 167 (1974). See also Ranii, Tobacco's Legal Road, Nat'l L.J., April 9, 1984, at 1, col. 3. On the continuing trend toward restrictions on smoking, adopted both by legislative bodies and by private businesses, see "A Cloudy Forecast for Smokers," Time, April 7, 1986, at 45. By the late 1980's, some anti-smoking regulations were taking the form of *total* bans on smoking in restaurants and retail stores, such as the ban enacted in Beverly Hills, California. See "Hands Up and Butts Out," Time, April 27, 1987, at 78. A strict ban on smoking in many public places took effect in New York City in April, 1995. See "Marlboro Country It Ain't—Will an Anti-smoking Law Burn Big Apple Eateries?," Bus. Week, April 24, 1995, at 44. See generally "No Smoking Sweeps America," Bus. Week, July 27, 1987, at 40. On the validity and construction of such regulations, see Annot., Validity, Construction, and Application of Nonsmoking Regulations, 65 A.L.R.4th 1205 (1988). On the State of California's advertising campaign to discourage smoking, financed by a cigarette tax, see Mydans, California Opens All-Out War on Tobacco and Its Marketing, N.Y. Times, April 11, 1990, at A1. On municipal regulation of the sale, advertisement and use of tobacco products, see generally Hermer, Municipal Home Rule in New York: Tobacco Control at the Local Level, 65 Brooklyn L. Rev. 321 (1999).

Some municipalities have long restricted smoking in certain confined places and have been upheld in so doing. See State v. Heidenhain, 42 La.Ann. 483, 7 So. 621 (1890) (ordinance prohibiting smoking in streetcars, declaring it a nuisance, is valid). The same is true of restrictions on smoking where there is a high degree of fire danger, such as near large quantities of combustible material. See City of Zion v. Behrens, 262 Ill. 510, 104 N.E. 836 (1914) (but ordinance invalid where it prohibited carrying or using tobacco in streets or parks; such use could not reasonably offend others since streets wide and parks large). But older authority maintained that, except under such special circumstances, municipalities could not prohibit smoking in public places. See City of Zion v. Behrens, *supra*; Hershberg v. City of Barbourville, 142 Ky. 60, 133 S.W. 985 (1911) (ordinance prohibiting smoking of cigarettes within city limits void).

For discussion of particular state and local smoking bans, see Note, Smoked Out: Massachusetts Bans Smoking in Restaurants and Bars, 31 New England J. on Crim. & Civ. Confinement 401 (2005); Note, The Calabasas Smoking Ban: A Local Ordinance Points the Way for the Future of Environmental Tobacco Smoke

§ 23.9 Local Regulation of Advertising

What about local restraints on advertising—such as limitations on the distribution of handbills, on billboards, and on the use of sound trucks? Cases decided some decades ago by the U.S. Supreme Court indicated that prohibitions on distribution of religious or other noncommercial literature (or restrictions that entrusted the granting of permission to distribute such literature to the unbridled discretion of some official) would be invalidated,[148] but that commercial *advertising* would be treated on a different footing, and thus that the latter's distribution on public streets could be entirely forbidden.[149] But later, the Court clearly extended First Amendment protection to advertising.[150]

Regulation, 80 So. Cal. L. Rev. 393 (2007); Comment, Why Smoking Bans are a Butt to Texas: The Impact of Smoking Bans on Private Property Rights and Individual Freedom, 39 Tex. Tech L. Rev. 345 (2007). See generally Note, Examining the Underlying Purposes of Municipal and Statewide Smoking Bans, 80 Ind. L.J. 923 (2005). See also Comment, Indoor Air Quality: Options for Regulating Environmental Tobacco Smoke, 13 Mo. Envtl. L. & Pol'y Rev. 114 (2005–06). As to efforts to hold the tobacco industry liable for harm done by smoking, see Sokol, Smoking Abroad and Smokeless at Home: Holding the Tobacco Industry Accountable in a New Era, 13 N.Y.U. J. Legis. & Pub. Pol'y 175 (2010). As to possible nuisance liability of smokers, see Note, Smokers: Nuisances in Belmont City, California—In Their Homes, But Not in Public, 10 Minn. J. L. Sci. & Tech. 413 (2009).

Municipal smoking bans are sometimes attacked on grounds of violating state pre-emption or of being unconstitutionally vague, but these attacks are likely to fail. See Steffes v. City of Lawrence, 284 Kan. 380, 160 P.3d 843 (2007). Exceptions to smoking bans for particular businesses may, however, run afoul of equal protection or of prohibitions on special laws. See Comment, Atlantic City Special: Whether the Casino Exception to the New Jersey Smoke-Free Air Act Comports with the New Jersey Constitution's General Prohibition of Special Laws, 38 Seton Hall L. Rev. 359 (2008). As to whether state and/or local regulation of smoking is preferable to federal legislation, see Note, Anti-Smoking Legislation: Why Strong Local Legislation & Action Better Protect the Consumer Than Federal Legislation & Action, 23 Loyola Consumer L. Rev. 459 (2011).

[148] Lovell v. City of Griffin, 303 U.S. 444 58 S.Ct. 666, 82 L.Ed. 949 (1938), conf. to 57 Ga.App. 901, 197 S.E. 347 (dissemination of religious literature involved). Cf. Dulaney v. Municipal Court, 11 Cal.3d 77, 112 Cal.Rptr. 777, 520 P.2d 1 (1974) (ordinance declaring it unlawful to affix any notice or poster to utility pole without permission from person owning or controlling such pole invalidated as prior restraint on free speech; notice concerning an anti-war rally had sparked the case). But cf. Prince v. Massachusetts, 321 U.S. 158, 64 S.Ct. 438, 88 L.Ed. 645 (1944), reh. denied 321 U.S. 804, 64 S.Ct. 784, 88 L.Ed. 1090, upholding, even as applied to distribution of religious literature, a statute forbidding *children* under certain ages from selling in the streets and in public places, and making it unlawful for parents to allow their children to work in violation of the law.

[149] Valentine v. Chrestensen, 316 U.S. 52, 62 S.Ct. 920, 86 L.Ed. 1262 (1942) (prohibition on distribution of commercial advertising matter on streets upheld; Court said commercial handbills could be prohibited despite some inclusion—as in this case—of opinion on a civic matter therein). Cf. State ex rel. Department of Transportation v. Pile, 603 P.2d 337 (Okl.1979), cert. denied 453 U.S. 922, 101 S.Ct. 3158, 69 L.Ed.2d 1004 (1981) (statute prohibiting billboards on rural roads held inapplicable to those used for purposes of noncommercial speech; "pure speech" said to be protected in all public forums, though commercial speech is not).

[150] See Central Hudson Gas & Electric Corp. v. Public Service Commission, 447 U.S. 557, 100 S.Ct. 2343, 65 L.Ed.2d 341 (1980) (complete ban on promotional advertising by utility invalidated); Bates v. State Bar of Arizona, 433 U.S. 350, 97 S.Ct. 2691, 53 L.Ed.2d 810 (1977), reh. denied 434 U.S. 881, 98 S.Ct. 242, 54 L.Ed.2d 164 (commercial speech entitled to some First Amendment protection; total ban on lawyer advertising invalid); Carey v. Population Services International, 431 U.S. 678, 97 S.Ct. 2010, 52 L.Ed.2d 675 (1977) (prohibition of any advertisement or display of contraceptives held unconstitutional); Virginia State Board of Pharmacy v. Virginia Citizens Consumer Council, 425 U.S. 748, 96 S.Ct. 1817, 48 L.Ed.2d 346 (1976) (prohibition on pharmacists' advertising price of prescription drugs held unconstitutional). Cf. City of Cincinnati v. Discovery Network, Inc., 507 U.S. 410, 113 S.Ct. 1505, 123 L.Ed.2d 99 (1993) (ban on newsracks for commercial newspapers held not content-neutral and thus in violation of First Amendment); Shapero v. Kentucky Bar Ass'n, 486 U.S. 466, 108 S.Ct. 1916, 100 L.Ed.2d 475 (1988), on remand 763 S.W.2d 126 (Ky.1989) (state cannot absolutely prohibit lawyers from soliciting legal business for pecuniary gain by sending truthful, nondeceptive letters to potential clients known to have particular legal problems); Consolidated Edison Co. v. Public Service Commission, 447 U.S. 530, 100 S.Ct. 2326, 65 L.Ed.2d 319 (1980) (prohibition on inclusion by public utilities, in monthly bills, of inserts discussing controversial issues of public policy; held an invalid infringement on free

Finally, the Court has come to the position that (1) commercial speech *is* within the First Amendment; (2) but such speech has a special character, is less likely (because of its importance to business profits and because it is carefully calculated in advance) to be inhibited by reasonable regulations than are other types of communication, and is particularly in need of, and subject to, regulation to prevent deception; and (3) reasonable restrictions on time, place, and manner of expression may be permissible as to commercial speech even where impermissible as to non-commercial expression.[151]

---

speech); Bigelow v. Virginia, 421 U.S. 809, 95 S.Ct. 2222, 44 L.Ed.2d 600 (1975) (Virginia advertisements of New York organization engaged in arranging abortions were constitutionally protected); Griswold v. Connecticut, 381 U.S. 479, 85 S.Ct. 1678, 14 L.Ed.2d 510 (1965) (state law could not forbid use of contraceptives, or aiding or counseling therein); AIDS Action Committee v. Massachusetts Bay Transp. Auth., 42 F.3d 1 (1st Cir.1994) (transit authority's ban on condom advertisements enjoined as content-based discrimination); Anderson, Clayton & Co. v. Washington State Department of Agriculture, 402 F.Supp. 1253 (W.D.Wash.1975) (invalidating a statute prohibiting the use of any "dairy" words in the advertising of margarine). See generally Elman, The Constitutional Right to Advertise, 64 A.B.A.J. 206 (1978); Heller, The End of the "Commercial Speech" Exception—Good Riddance of More Headaches for the Courts, 67 Ky. L.J. 927 (1978–79); Stern, In Defense of the Imprecise Definition of Commercial Speech, 58 Md. L. Rev. 55 (1999); Comment, A Doctrine in Disarray—Why the First Amendment Demands the Abandonment of the *Central Hudson* Test for Commercial Speech, 27 Seton Hall L. Rev. 1626 (1997); Note, Commercial Speech in the Street: Regulation of Day Labor Solicitation, 9 S. Cal. Interdisc. L.J. 499 (2000). Annot., Applicability to Advertisements of First Amendment's Guaranty of Free Speech and Press—Federal Cases, 37 L.Ed.2d 1124 (1974). See also Annot., Statute or Ordinance Regulating or Prohibiting Advertising as Unconstitutional Burden on Interstate Commerce—Federal Cases, 10 L.Ed.2d 1386 (1964).

On the numerous legal clashes between advertisers and governments that refuse to allow certain ads on government property, see Ayers, What Rudy Hasn't Taken Credit For: First Amendment Limits on Regulation of Advertising on Government Property, 42 Ariz. L. Rev. 607 (2000), criticizing the public forum doctrine, and the commercial/noncommercial speech dichotomy with which it is often linked, as failing to uphold the First Amendment's prohibition of government censorship.

[151] See Board of Trustees of State University v. Fox, 492 U.S. 469, 109 S.Ct. 3028, 106 L.Ed.2d 388 (1989), on remand 764 F.Supp. 747 (N.D.N.Y. 1991) (governmental restrictions on commercial speech need not be the absolutely least restrictive means to achieve desired end); Bolger v. Youngs Drug Prods. Corp., 463 U.S. 60, 103 S.Ct. 2875, 77 L.Ed.2d 469 (1983) (federal statute prohibiting unsolicited mailing of contraceptive advertisements invalidated as overbroad, but Court noted that even content-based restrictions on commercial speech are sometimes permissible); Friedman v. Rogers, 440 U.S. 1, 99 S.Ct. 887, 59 L.Ed.2d 100 (1979), reh. denied 441 U.S. 917, 99 S.Ct. 2018, 60 L.Ed.2d 389, upholding a prohibition, by a Texas statute, of the practice of optometry under a trade name, since the prohibition was reasonably aimed at protecting the public from deceptive and misleading use of such names; Federal Election Comm'n v. Furgatch, 807 F.2d 857 (9th Cir.1987), cert. denied 484 U.S. 850, 108 S.Ct. 151, 98 L.Ed.2d 106 (1987) (newspaper advertisement advocating defeat of a political candidate is subject to reasonable regulation). Cf. Warner-Lambert Co. v. Federal Trade Commission, 562 F.2d 749 (D.C.Cir.1977), cert. denied 435 U.S. 950, 98 S.Ct. 1575, 55 L.Ed.2d 800 (corrective advertising order upheld); Robert L. Rieke Bldg. Co. v. City of Overland Park, 232 Kan. 634, 657 P.2d 1121 (1983) (court assumed that operation of searchlights for promotional purposes was a form of symbolic commercial speech, but municipal regulation of searchlights nonetheless upheld as protecting public interests); Oklahoma Alcoholic Beverage Control Board v. Burris, 626 P.2d 1316 (Okl.1980) (Alcoholic Beverage Control Board could predicate right to license on compliance with the rules governing advertisement, and this limitation does not violate First Amendment). Even the states' broad power to regulate liquor under the Twenty-First Amendment does not necessarily justify sweeping bans of advertising for liquor. 44 Liquormart, Inc. v. Rhode Island, 517 U.S. 484, 116 S.Ct. 1495, 134 L.Ed.2d 711 (1996) (state's complete statutory ban on price advertising for alcoholic beverages abridged First Amendment rights and was not saved by Twenty-First Amendment). See Comment, Strange Brew: The State of Commercial Speech Jurisprudence Before and After 44 *Liquormart, Inc. v. Rhode Island,* 47 Case Western Res. L. Rev. 681 (1997); Note, A First Amendment Look at the Statutory Ban on Tobacco Advertisements and the Self-regulation of Alcohol Advertisements, 65 Fed. Comm. L. J. 99 (2013). Cf. Rubin v. Coors Brewing Co., 514 U.S. 476, 115 S.Ct. 1585, 131 L.Ed.2d 532 (1995) (federal law prohibiting beer labels from displaying alcoholic content violated First Amendment's protection of commercial speech). See generally Note, Constitutional Law—Freedom of Speech—No Longer That Crazy Aunt in the Basement, Commercial Speech Joins the Family, 20 U. Ark. Little Rock L.J. 163 (1997); Note, The First Amendment, Commercial Speech, and the Future of Tobacco Advertising After *44 Liquormart, Inc. v. Rhode Island,* 43 Wayne L. Rev. 1505 (1997). States do, however, have wide powers to protect their residents against advertisements for activity that is illegal in the particular state or area. See

Courts have in recent years tended to invalidate prohibitions, or unduly restrictive licensing ordinances, applying to the distribution, on public property or throughout a locality, of commercial or non-commercial literature.[152] The U.S. Supreme Court has

---

United States v. Edge Broadcasting Co., 509 U.S. 418, 113 S.Ct. 2696, 125 L.Ed.2d 345 (1993), on remand 5 F.3d 63 (4th Cir.1993) (federal statutes prohibiting broadcast of lottery advertising to state not permitting lotteries, though allowing such broadcast to state that permits lotteries, upheld); Princess Sea Indus., Inc. v. State, 97 Nev. 534, 635 P.2d 281 (1981), cert. denied 456 U.S. 926, 102 S.Ct. 1972, 72 L.Ed.2d 441 (1982) (state could prohibit advertisements by legal brothels from appearing in those counties in which prostitution was illegal), discussed in Note, Chicken Ranch Cries Foul: Limitations on Commercial Expression—Why Can't Legal Prostitutes Advertise?, 4 Detroit C.L. Rev. 1613 (1983), with good review of cases concerning restrictions on commercial speech. Compare Greater New Orleans Broadcasting Ass'n v. United States, 527 U.S. 173, 119 S.Ct. 1923, 144 L.Ed.2d 161 (1999), noted 20 Loyola L.A. Ent. L. Rev. 605 (2000) (federal prohibition on broadcasting of lottery information could not be applied to advertisements of lawful private casino gambling that were broadcast by radio and television stations located in Louisiana, where such gambling was legal).

Some cases emphasize that not all bans or restrictions on commercial speech are unconstitutional. See, *e.g.*, City of Skagway v. Robertson, 143 P.3d 965 (Alaska 2006) (city ordinance that confined person-to-person solicitation activities within the historic district of city to enclosed structures or to areas containing at least 200 square feet of vending space applied only to commercial speech and was thus not unconstitutionally overbroad). But many restrictions on commercial advertising have nonetheless been ruled unconstitutional. See Lorillard Tobacco Co. v. Reilly, 533 U.S. 525, 121 S.Ct. 2404, 150 L.Ed.2d 532 (2001) (Massachusetts regulations prohibiting outdoor advertising of smokeless tobacco or cigars within 1000 feet of school or playground violated First Amendment); Thompson v. Western States Medical Center, 535 U.S. 357, 122 S.Ct. 1497, 152 L.Ed.2d 563 (2002) (provisions of federal Food and Drug Administration Modernization Act that exempted compounded drugs from Food and Drug Administration's drug approval requirements if providers of such drugs refrained from advertising, promoting, or soliciting prescriptions for particular compounded drugs were unconstitutional restrictions of commercial speech). In the *Lorillard* case, *supra*, many of the restrictions were also found pre-empted by the Federal Cigarette Labeling and Advertising Act. In any case, in a "Master Settlement Agreement" entered into by the tobacco industry in 1998, the participating tobacco manufacturers agreed to remove and discontinue most outdoor advertising, such as billboards. See Clisham, Commercial Speech, Federal Preemption, and Tobacco Signage: Obstacles to Eliminating Outdoor Tobacco Advertising, 36 Urban Law. 713 (2004), pointing out that there are exceptions to the "Master Agreement," as well as doubts as to its validity. *Id.* at 714–15. See generally Bonnie, The Impending Collision Between First Amendment Protection for Commercial Speech and the Public Health: The Case of Tobacco Control, 29 J. L. & Politics 599 (2014).

See generally Note, A First Amendment Look, *supra.* As to the federal legislation on tobacco warning labels, see Note, Smoke and Mirrors: Preventing Deception of Consumers in the Tobacco Market Through Graphic Warning Labels, 7 Albany Gov't L. Rev. 291 (2014); Note, Joe Camel v. Uncle Sam: The Constitutionality of Graphic Cigarette Warning Labels, 81 Fordham L. Rev. 2811 (2013); Comment, Enough Smoke and Mirrors!—Why the Graphic-warning Mandate Under the Family Smoking Prevention and Tobacco Control Act Is Speech Consumers Don't Want to Hear, 44 U. Toledo L. Rev. 659 (2013).

A Vermont statute restricting the sale, disclosure, and use of pharmacy records that reveal the prescribing practices of individual doctors was invalidated in Sorrell v. IMS Health, Inc., 564 U.S. ___, 131 S.Ct. 2653, 180 L.Ed.2d 544 (2011) (abrogating the 1st Circuit's opinion in IMS Health, Inc. v. Ayotte, 550 F.3d 42 (2008), cert, denied, 557 U.S. 939, 129 S.Ct. 2864, 174 L.Ed.2d 578 (2009), noted 25 Berkeley Tech. L. J. 649 (2010)). The Court applied heightened judicial scrutiny in finding violation of First Amendment protections because the statute was held to impose a specific content—and speaker—based restriction on protected expression. The Court observed that the government's legitimate interest in protecting consumers from commercial harm explains why commercial speech can be subject to greater governmental regulation than noncommercial speech, but here the state failed to show a "neutral justification" for its law. *Id.* at 2672.

[152] See In re Philipie, 82 Nev. 215, 414 P.2d 949 (1966) (ordinance banning distribution of noncommercial handbills invalid); City of Elizabeth v. Sullivan, 100 N.J.Super. 51, 241 A.2d 41 (1968) (ordinance requiring permit for distribution of literature held unconstitutional as applied to distribution of commercial handbills in community). Cf. Welton v. City of Los Angeles, 18 Cal.3d 497, 134 Cal.Rptr. 668, 556 P.2d 1119 (1976) (ordinance could not validly punish selling of maps showing location of movie stars' homes); Koffler v. Joint Bar Association, 51 N.Y.2d 140, 432 N.Y.S.2d 872, 412 N.E.2d 927 (1980) (direct mail solicitation of clients by lawyers is commercial speech, which may be regulated but not proscribed); Hillside Community Church, Inc. v. City of Tacoma, 76 Wash.2d 63, 455 P.2d 350 (1969) (city, which contracted to display advertising signs on exterior of city buses, could not refuse ads protesting the Vietnam War). But see Cardarella v. City of Overland Park, 228 Kan. 698, 620 P.2d 1122 (1980) (ordinance restricting sale or display of items identified with drug usage upheld; display of such items was not "commercial speech"). Cf. United

applied basically the same protection to distributors of such literature on the streets of a "company town"—and even some areas of a military base—as would apply to such distributors on the public property of any incorporated municipality.[153] For many years

---

States Postal Service v. Council of Greenburgh Civic Associations, 453 U.S. 114, 101 S.Ct. 2676, 69 L.Ed.2d 517 (1981), upholding a statute, applicable to both commercial and noncommercial materials, that prohibited the deposit of unstamped, mailable matter in a letter box.

In Krantz v. City of Fort Smith, 160 F.3d 1214 (8th Cir. 1998), cert. denied 527 U.S. 1037, 119 S.Ct. 2397, 144 L.Ed.2d 797 (1997), the court invalidated as overbroad an ordinance prohibiting anyone from putting leaflets on cars parked on city streets unless someone in the car gave permission. The case involved members of a church who were distributing religious information.

[153] On company towns, see Marsh v. Alabama, 326 U.S. 501, 66 S.Ct. 276, 90 L.Ed. 265 (1946) (Jehovah's Witness could not be criminally punished for distributing literature on street of unincorporated town). Cf. Tucker v. Texas, 326 U.S. 517, 66 S.Ct. 274, 90 L.Ed. 274 (1946) (federal defense housing village). As to a military base, see Flower v. United States, 407 U.S. 197, 92 S.Ct. 1842, 32 L.Ed.2d 653 (1972), conf. to 462 F.2d 1133 (5th Cir.) (street of military reservation was open to public; base commandant could not order defendant off the street for distributing leaflets). But see Greer v. Spock, 424 U.S. 828, 96 S.Ct. 1211, 47 L.Ed.2d 505 (1976), holding that there is no generalized constitutional right to make political speeches or distribute leaflets on a military reservation, and distinguishing the *Flower* case, *supra*, because military authorities had there abandoned any claim of special interest in who walked or talked on the street.

Public streets and sidewalks have sometimes been regarded as "public forums" in which free speech is entitled to special protection. See United States v. Grace, 461 U.S. 171, 103 S.Ct. 1702, 75 L.Ed.2d 736 (1983), on remand 717 F.2d 1480 (D.C.Cir.1983) (public sidewalks forming perimeter of U.S. Supreme Court grounds are public forums for First Amendment purposes); Lewis v. Colorado Rockies Baseball Club, Ltd., 941 P.2d 266 (Colo.1997) (sidewalks and walkways around baseball stadium were a traditional public forum for First Amendment purposes). See also Snyder v. Phelps, 562 U.S. 443, 131 S.Ct. 1207, 179 L.Ed.2d (2011) (public place adjacent to a public street treated as a public forum; *id.* at 1218). But apart from these special situations of streets and sidewalks surrounding certain properties, streets and sidewalks have often been ruled *not* public forums. See United States v. Kokinda, 497 U.S. 720, 110 S.Ct. 3115, 111 L.Ed.2d 571 (1990), noted 25 Suffolk U. L. Rev. 772 (1991) (sidewalk at a post office is not a public forum); Members of City Council v. Taxpayers for Vincent, 466 U.S. 789, 104 S.Ct. 2118, 80 L.Ed.2d 772 (1984), on remand 738 F.2d 353 (9th Cir.1984) (property covered by ordinance which prohibited posting of signs on any sidewalk, crosswalk, curb, street lamp-post, hydrant, etc. was not public forum subject to special First Amendment protection). Cf. Schenck v. Pro-Choice Network of Western New York, 519 U.S. 357, 117 S.Ct. 855, 137 L.Ed.2d 1 (1997) (governmental interests in ensuring public safety and order, prompting free flow of traffic on streets and sidewalks, protecting property rights, and protecting a woman's freedom to seek pregnancy-related services justified preliminary injunction appropriately tailored to assure unimpeded physical access to abortion clinics); Frisby v. Schultz, 487 U.S. 474, 108 S.Ct. 2495, 101 L.Ed.2d 420 (1988), on remand 857 F.2d 1175 (7th Cir.1988) (ordinance prohibiting picketing, even on public streets, before or about the dwelling of any individual upheld as narrowly tailored to serve significant government interest in protecting residential property). Compare Vittitow v. City of Upper Arlington, 43 F.3d 1100 (6th Cir.1995), cert. denied 515 U.S. 1121, 115 S.Ct. 2276, 132 L.Ed.2d 280 (1995) (ordinance against all residential picketing enjoined as overbroad). On the nature of public streets as forums for the expression of ideas, see generally Jamison v. Texas, 318 U.S. 413, 63 S.Ct. 669, 87 L.Ed. 869 (1943); Schneider v. State, 308 U.S. 147, 60 S.Ct. 146, 84 L.Ed. 155 (1939). A parking lot of a medical facility has been held not a public forum. Fardig v. Municipality of Anchorage, 785 P.2d 911 (Alaska App.1990), on reh. 803 P.2d 879 (1990) (trespassing ordinance could be enforced against anti-abortion protesters). Cf. Hill v. Colorado, 530 U.S. 703, 120 S.Ct. 2480, 147 L.Ed.2d 597 (2000) (upholding statute that prohibited any person from knowingly approaching within 8 feet of another person near health care facility without latter person's consent). And the U.S. Supreme Court has held an airport not to be a public forum. International Soc'y for Krishna Consciousness, Inc. v. Lee, 505 U.S. 672, 112 S.Ct. 2701, 120 L.Ed.2d 541 (1992) (prohibition on solicitation of contributions upheld). Cf. as to state fairgrounds Heffron v. International Soc'y for Krishna Consciousness, Inc., 452 U.S. 640, 101 S.Ct. 2559, 69 L.Ed.2d 298 (1981), on remand 311 N.W.2d 843 (Minn.1981), upholding a state fair rule prohibiting the sale or distribution of any merchandise, including printed or written material, except from fixed locations, in order to maintain orderly movement of crowds. A high-school newspaper has been held not a public forum. Hazelwood School Dist. v. Kuhlmeier, 484 U.S. 260, 108 S.Ct. 562, 98 L.Ed.2d 592 (1988), on remand 840 F.2d 596 (8th Cir.1988) (school officials could impose any restrictions that met test of reasonable relation to legitimate pedagogical concerns); Planned Parenthood of S. Nev., Inc. v. Clark County School Dist., 941 F.2d 817 (9th Cir.1991), criticized in Note, 38 Wayne L. Rev. 1897 (1992). But cf. Burch v. Barker, 861 F.2d 1149 (9th Cir.1988) (First Amendment prohibits school policies that require all student-written material to be submitted for school approval prior to distribution even if the distribution is not school-sponsored); Thompson v. Waynesboro Area School Dist., 673 F.Supp. 1379

now, public streets and traditional "downtowns" have, however, been rivaled or surpassed as public gathering-places by shopping centers—often located in largely residential or suburban areas and typically having a "mall" along which a great variety of retail establishments are located.[154] Thus, the question has also now arisen of the degree of protection afforded "free speech" within these malls. At one time, it seemed the Court would treat a shopping-center mall as equivalent to a public street of a municipality so far as rights of speech are concerned;[155] but the Court soon reconsidered

---

(M.D.Pa.1987) (school district violated students' freedom of speech by severely restricting distribution of religious literature). On problems of student rights and responsibilities that are raised by the *Hazelwood* and *Burch* cases *supra*, see generally Bittle, Bartlett & Hardt, Recent Developments in Public Education Law, 20 Urban Law. 1071, 1071–84 (1988). It has been held that the area surrounding a polling place *is* a public forum. Burson v. Freeman, 504 U.S. 191, 112 S.Ct. 1846, 119 L.Ed.2d 5 (1992) (Tennessee statute prohibiting solicitation of votes and displays or distributions of campaign materials within 100 feet of entrance to polling place was content-based regulation of political speech in a public forum and thus subject to strict scrutiny, but upheld as narrowly tailored to serve compelling interest). See generally Buchanan, The Case of the Vanishing Public Forum, 1991 U. Ill. L. Rev. 949, noting the changing nature of the public forum concept; Note, Closing the Door on the Public Forum, 26 Loyola L.A.L. Rev. 241 (1992). See also Bradburn v. North Central Regional Library Dist., 168 Wash. 2d 789, 231 P.3d 166 (2010) (Internet access in public libraries held neither a traditional nor a designated public forum). Where a public forum *is* found to exist, a content-based restriction on political speech can be upheld only if supported by a compelling governmental interest. See Burson v. Freeman, *supra* (statute restricting solicitation of votes or political advertising within 100 feet of polling place upheld); Boos v. Barry, 485 U.S. 312, 108 S.Ct. 1157, 99 L.Ed.2d 333 (1988) (District of Columbia law prohibiting signs or displays critical of foreign governments within 500 feet of embassies was not narrowly tailored to serve compelling government interest and was thus invalid).

[154] See "How Shopping Malls Are Changing Life in U.S.," U.S. News & World Rep., June 18, 1973, at 43, referring to shopping malls as a "new kind of civic center." Compare Comment, Shopping in the Marketplace of Ideas: Why *Fashion Valley Mall* Means Target and Trader Joe's Are the New Town Squares, 39 Golden Gate U. L. Rev. 261 (2009), discussing Fashion Valley Mall, LLC v. NLRB, 42 Cal. 4th 850, 69 Cal Rptr. 3d 288, 172 P.3d 742 (2007). On the different kinds of shopping centers, and trends apparent in the kinds that are now being built, see generally Trillin, U.S. Journal: New Orleans, The New Yorker, July 28, 1980, at 88, discussing "regionals," "specialty centers," and other kinds of shopping malls; "Malls: Now More Like Downtown," Bus. Week, July 14, 2003 at 14 (many large malls have failed, and some of them are being remade as outdoor shopping plazas, reminiscent of the town centers they replaced); "Call It Mall-mart," Bus. Week, July 14, 2003, at 40 (Wal–Mart and other discount stores are increasingly locating in malls); "The Discount Twist in Suburban Shopping Malls," Bus. Week, July 7, 1980, at 95, (an increasing number of malls consist largely or entirely of "discount" stores in various lines); "Shopping Centers of the Future: Smaller, More Fun," U.S. News and World Rep., Sept. 30, 1974, at 67 (there is some tendency toward building shopping centers in close-in locations, even the old downtowns); Queenan, All of America and Parking Too, N.Y. Times, Jan. 25, 2008, at D1 (shopping malls are becoming suitable travel destinations); "Melancholy Mall," Time, Oct. 20, 1980, at 77 (some slowdown in construction of suburban malls, but continued growth in shopping centers within old "downtown" areas). Shopping centers have generated some controversy, despite their popularity, since they pose a threat, if located in suburban areas, to traditional city-center shopping areas, and since some critics feel they contribute to traffic congestion and air pollution; see "A Pall Over the Suburban Mall," Time, Nov. 13, 1978, at 116.

Controversy has also developed over the tendency in some communities of street vendors simply to set up "business"—in a stall beside a public way or just on the sidewalk itself. See "'Free Enterprise' Stirs Storm on Sidewalks," U.S. News & World Rep., Jan. 10, 1977, at 59, noting opposition to such vendors because of the congestion they create and because they pay no rent, and often no sales or business taxes. Municipal regulations and prohibitions of the use of sidewalks and other public ways for vending have generally been upheld. See Annot., Authorization, Prohibition, or Regulation by Municipality of the Sale of Merchandise on Streets or Highways, or Their Use for Such Purpose, 14 A.L.R.3d 896 (1967). Cf. People v. Dmytro, 280 Mich. 82, 273 N.W. 400 (1937) (ordinance forbidding curb service upheld as reasonable in areas where congestion likely). It has been held that express statutory authority is necessary for a municipality to allow the use of a public way for commercial purposes, since such ways are ultimately under the control of the state. See Cowin v. City of Waterloo, 237 Iowa 202, 21 N.W.2d 705 (1946). On regulations applying to solicitors, peddlers, vendors, etc., see generally notes 82–99 *supra*, and accompanying text.

[155] Amalgamated Food Employees Union Local 590 v. Logan Valley Plaza, Inc., 391 U.S. 308, 88 S.Ct. 1601, 20 L.Ed.2d 603 (1968) (often called "the Logan Valley case"); the Court in this case affirmed the right of peaceful picketing within a shopping mall by members of a union who were protesting the non-union status of

this position and now treats shopping centers as basically private property, the owners of which may limit free speech without, at least, violating any *Federal* constitutional guarantees against governmental abridgment thereof.[156]

---

a store within the mall. The picketing took place in the immediate vicinity of the store involved in the controversy.

[156] See Hudgens v. National Labor Relations Board, 424 U.S. 507, 96 S.Ct. 1029, 47 L.Ed.2d 196 (1976), on remand 531 F.2d 1342 (peaceful picketing of retail store in shopping mall; held that rights and liability of parties were exclusively dependent on the National Labor Relations Act); Lloyd Corp. v. Tanner, 407 U.S. 551, 92 S.Ct. 2219, 33 L.Ed.2d 131 (1972), conf. to 463 F.2d 1095 (9th Cir.), noted 5 Urban Lawyer 598–604 (1973) (right of free speech in shopping center guaranteed only if expression's purpose is related to shopping center's business and no reasonable alternative forum is available). Cf. Steffel v. Thompson, 415 U.S. 452, 94 S.Ct. 1209, 39 L.Ed.2d 505 (1974), conf. to 494 F.2d 691 (5th Cir.) (petitioner, threatened with arrest for distributing literature in shopping center, brought suit for injunctive and declaratory relief, claiming his constitutional rights were being violated; case held to present an "actual controversy"). The *Hudgens* case, *supra*, stated that the rationale of *Logan Valley*, *supra* note 155, had not survived the *Lloyd* case, *supra*. And *Hudgens* indicated clear disapproval of *Lloyd* to the extent that the latter seemed to make the right of speech partly dependent on content of that speech. Thus, the *Logan Valley* case, *supra* note 155, seems effectively overruled, and *Lloyd*, *supra*, seems partly discredited; the law now is as stated in *Hudgens*: The shopping center is basically private property, and the rights of the parties are governed by relevant statutes. See Lechmere, Inc. v. National Labor Relations Bd., 502 U.S. 527, 112 S.Ct. 841, 117 L.Ed.2d 79 (1992) (barring union organizers from distributing handbills in employer's parking lots at shopping center did not constitute unfair labor practice); Cologne v. Westfarms Associates, 192 Conn. 48, 469 A.2d 1201 (1984) (rights of free speech and petition may not be exercised at regional shopping center contrary to wishes of its owners); SHAD Alliance v. Smith Haven Mall, 66 N.Y.2d 496, 498 N.Y.S.2d 99, 488 N.E.2d 1211 (1985) (under New York law, owner of a shopping mall was not required to permit distribution of anti-nuclear leaflets on its property but could enforce a blanket no-handbilling policy). Cf. State of Hawaii v. Viglielmo, 105 Hawai'i 197, 95 P.3d 952 (2004) (peaceful protesting activities in privately owned shopping center; Hawaii Constitution afforded no greater free speech protections than federal constitution and did not preclude prosecution). On the *Hudgens* case *supra*, see Schauer, *Hudgens v. N.L.R.B.* and the Problem of State Action in First Amendment Adjudication, 61 Minn. L. Rev. 433 (1977); Note, Shopping Center Picketing: The Impact of *Hudgens v. National Labor Relations Board*, 45 Geo. Wash. L. Rev. 812 (1977); Comment, Hudgens v. NLRB—A Final Definition of the Public Forum?, 13 Wake Forest L. Rev. 139 (1977).

But it has also been held that a *state* constitution *may* validly provide that individuals are entitled to exercise free-speech and -petition rights on the property of a privately owned shopping center to which the public is invited. PruneYard Shopping Center v. Robins, 447 U.S. 74, 100 S.Ct. 2035, 64 L.Ed.2d 741 (1980), noted 66 A.B.A.J. 1118 (1980) (California constitutional provision did not violate Federal Constitutional rights of owner of shopping center); Lloyd Corp., Ltd. v. Whiffen, 315 Or. 500, 849 P.2d 446 (1993), noted 30 Willamette L. Rev. 195 (1994) (implied right found under Oregon Constitution to gather signatures for initiative petitions in privately owned shopping centers). But cf. Woodland v. Michigan Citizens Lobby, 423 Mich. 188, 378 N.W.2d 337 (1985) (shopping mall could prohibit collection of signatures on its property for petition to put initiative question on ballot; state constitutional guarantee of free speech applies only to restrictions on speech by government, not by private landowners); Western Pennsylvania Socialist Workers 1982 Campaign v. Connecticut Gen. Life Ins. Co., 512 Pa. 23, 515 A.2d 1331 (1986) (under Pennsylvania Constitution, individuals do not have right to solicit signatures for a political candidate's nomination petition at a privately owned shopping mall without the mall owner's consent). See generally Berger, *PruneYard* Revisited: Political Activity on Private Lands, 66 N.Y.U.L. Rev. 633 (1991); Note (on state court opinion in *PruneYard* case), Federalism and State Protection of Free Speech, 10 Golden Gate U.L.Rev. 805 (1980); Comment, Constitutional Law—First Amendment—Distribution of Handbills in Mall of Private Shopping Center Is Not Constitutionally Protected When Purpose of Handbilling Is Unrelated to Shopping Center's Operation, 25 Ala.L.Rev. 76 (1972); Note, The Shopping Center as a Forum for the Exercise of First Amendment Rights, 37 Albany L.Rev. 556 (1973); Note, Lloyd Corp. v. Tanner: The Demise of Logan Valley and the Disguise of Marsh, 61 Geo.L.J. 1187 (1973); Note, Constitutional Law—First Amendment—Shopping Centers and the "Quasi-Public" Forum, 51 N.C.L.Rev. 123 (1972); Note, Constitutional Law—Free Speech Regulated in Shopping Centers, 8 Wake Forest L.Rev. 590 (1972); Comment, Speech Activists in Shopping Centers: Must Property Rights Give Way to Free Expression?, 64 Wash. L. Rev. 133 (1989); Comment, The Exercise of First Amendment Rights in Privately Owned Shopping Centers, 1973 Wash.U.L.Q. 427; Note, Constitutional Law—Free Speech on Premises of Privately Owned Shopping Center, 1973 Wis. L.Rev. 612.

In Sanders v. City of Seattle, 160 Wash.2d 198, 156 P.3d 874 (2007), a government easement through a privately owned shopping mall, created to provide access to a monorail, was held a nonpublic forum, and protestors using the easement to access the monorail were held validly subject to the shopping center's oral

Regulations on billboards and other advertising signs—and even complete prohibitions in certain areas—have been upheld if reasonably related to a police-power purpose. Increasingly, aesthetic factors are found sufficient to support such limitations;[157] but often, as in the case of regulations aimed at signs overhanging public streets or ways, other factors—such as safety—may be cited as also supporting the restrictions.[158]

---

policy requiring them not to display their signs in that area. The requirement was held reasonable and viewpoint-neutral and thus not violative of the protestors' freedom of expression. See generally Note, Finding a Forum in the Simulated City: Mega Malls, Gated Towns, and the Promise of *Pruneyard,* 13 Cornell J.L. & Pub. Pol'y 533 (2004). See also Fuchs, Free Exercise of Speech in Shopping Malls: Bases that Support an Independent Interpretation of Article 40 of the Maryland Declaration of Rights, 69 Albany L. Rev. 449 (2006); Peltz, Limited Powers in the Looking-glass: Otiose Textualism, and an Empirical Analysis of Other Approaches, When Activists in Private Shopping Centers Claim State Constitutional Liberties, 53 Clev. St. L. Rev. 399 (2005–06). Compare Sisk, Returning to the *PruneYard*: The Unconstitutionality of State-Sanctioned Trespass in the Name of Speech, 32 Harv. J. L. & Pub. Pol'y 389 (2009). In ACLU of Nevada v. City of Las Vegas, 466 F.3d 784 (9th Cir. 2006), it was held that a city could not prohibit all solicitation on a formerly public street that had been converted into a pedestrian shopping mall.

[157] See Members of City Council v. Taxpayers for Vincent, 466 U.S. 789, 104 S.Ct. 2118, 80 L.Ed.2d 772 (1984), on remand 738 F.2d 353 (9th Cir.1984) (ordinance banning the affixing of handbills or signs to utility poles, lamp-posts, trees, hydrants, sidewalks, curbs and other designated objects in public places upheld as reasonably necessary to aesthetic goal of avoiding visual clutter); United Advertising Corp. v. Borough of Metuchen, 42 N.J. 1, 198 A.2d 447 (1964) (total ban on advertising signs); Cromwell v. Ferrier, 19 N.Y.2d 263, 279 N.Y.S.2d 22, 225 N.E.2d 749 (1967) (upholding limits on location of billboards); Preferred Tires, Inc. v. Village of Hempstead, 173 Misc. 1017, 19 N.Y.S.2d 374 (1940) (upholding ordinance prohibiting signs extending over public ways). Cf. Metromedia, Inc. v. City of San Diego, 453 U.S. 490, 101 S.Ct. 2882, 69 L.Ed.2d 800 (1981), on remand 32 Cal.3d 180, 185 Cal.Rptr. 260, 649 P.2d 902 (1982) (seven Justices indicated that a prohibition on outdoor billboards would be upheld, though Court ruled that city could not limit the contents of billboards to commercial messages or permit some noncommercial messages but not others); Department of Transp. v. Shiflett, 251 Ga. 873, 310 S.E.2d 509 (1984) (statute prohibiting erection or maintenance of all outdoor advertising within 660 feet of right-of-way and visible from main travelled part of road held not to violate freedom of expression nor to constitute a taking without just compensation); Oscar P. Gustafson Co. v. City of Minneapolis, 231 Minn. 271, 42 N.W.2d 809 (1950) (noting that aesthetic factors may at least play an important and legitimate role in the prohibition of signs overhanging the street); Brayton v. City of New Brighton, 519 N.W.2d 243 (Minn.App.1994), cert. denied 514 U.S. 1036, 115 S.Ct. 1402, 131 L.Ed.2d 289 (1995) (content-neutral ordinance allowing a resident to post one noncommercial opinion sign on his or her property at any time and additional political signs at election season upheld). But see City of Ladue v. Gilleo, 512 U.S. 43, 114 S.Ct. 2038, 129 L.Ed.2d 36 (1994), invalidating an ordinance banning residential signs with only narrow exceptions; the ordinance was held to violate residents' right of free speech due to the sweeping nature of the prohibition. Cf. Metromedia, Inc. v. City of San Diego, 32 Cal.3d 180, 185 Cal.Rptr. 260, 649 P.2d 902 (1982) (on remand after U.S. Supreme Court opinion *supra*) (sign ordinance could not be fairly construed so as to preserve its constitutionality where limiting its scope to commercial signs would be inconsistent with ordinance's language and would invite constitutional difficulties with respect to distinguishing between commercial and noncommercial signs); City of Lakewood v. Colfax Unlimited Ass'n, 634 P.2d 52 (Colo.1981) (zoning ordinance confining permissible messages on "political" signs to information or advocacy concerning electoral issues and candidates was unconstitutional); State v. Calabria, Gillette Liquors, 301 N.J.Super. 96, 693 A.2d 949 (N.J.Super. Law Div. 1997) (ban on neon signs invalid where no showing that the ban served government interest in aesthetics); Miller v. City of Laramie, 880 P.2d 594 (Wyo.1994) (city may not ban distribution of all non-commercial speech which it views as litter). See generally Kramer, *Members of the City Council v. Taxpayers for Vincent*: A Step Backward for Political Campaigning, 17 Urban Law. 91 (1985).

As to regulation of the distribution of commercial handbills, which is often attempted in order to lessen litter, see Annot., Validity and Construction of Statutes or Ordinances Prohibiting or Restricting Distribution of Commercial Advertising to Private Residences—Modern Cases, 12 A.L.R. 4th 851 (1982), noting a split of authority on the validity of such regulation. See generally Note, Constitutional Law—Municipal Regulation of Commercial Handbilling, 9 Memphis St. U.L. Rev. 661 (1979). See also Comment, Windshield Leafleting Ordinances: A Permissible Use of Local Government Authority?, 79 U. Cinc. L. Rev. 749 (2010).

[158] See State v. Wightman, 78 Conn. 86, 61 A. 56 (1905); City of Nampa v. Swayne, 97 Idaho 530, 547 P.2d 1135 (1976); Ver Hoven Woodward Chevrolet, Inc. v. Dunkirk, 351 Mich. 190, 88 N.W.2d 408 (1958); Costopoulos v. Zoning Board of Adjustment, 23 Pa.Cmwlth. 159, 351 A.2d 318 (1976). See generally Annot., Validity and Construction of Provision Prohibiting or Regulating Advertising Sign Overhanging Street or

§ 23.10 Local Regulation of Noise

As noise has become an increasingly severe problem of modern times, many communities have enacted ordinances regulating the degree of noise allowed in the community and/or banning from the community certain particularly noisy activities. The authority of local governments to enact and enforce such measures has been upheld, so long as the measures are reasonable and are within the powers given those governments

---

Sidewalk, 80 A.L.R.3d 687 (1977); Annot., Validity and Construction of Zoning Ordinance Prohibiting Roof Signs, 76 A.L.R.3d 1162 (1977); Annot., Validity of Regulations Restricting Size of Freestanding Advertising Signs, 56 A.L.R.3d 1207 (1974); Annot., Power of Municipality as to Billboards and Outdoor Advertising, 72 A.L.R. 465 (1931), supplemented 58 A.L.R.2d 1314 (1958). See also Annot., Billboards and Other Outdoor Advertising Signs as Civil Nuisance, 38 A.L.R.3d 647 (1971).

by the state.[159] The restrictions have been upheld as applied to industrial noise.[160] And the U.S. Supreme Court, while invalidating a total ban on sound trucks,[161] has ruled

---

[159] See Ex parte Hall, 50 Cal.App. 786, 195 P. 975 (Dist.Ct.1920) (can be no question of city's authority to enact ordinances designed to prevent boisterous conduct and loud sounds); City of Tampa v. Islands Four, Inc., 364 So.2d 738 (Fla.App.1978); State v. Holland, 132 N.J.Super. 17, 331 A.2d 626 (1975) (upholding ordinance prohibiting unreasonably loud, disturbing, or unnecessary noise); Mister Softee v. Mayor & Council of Hoboken, 77 N.J.Super. 354, 186 A.2d 513 (1962) (citing cases); People v. Matherson, 64 Misc.2d 680, 315 N.Y.S.2d 596 (1970) (upholding ordinance providing that music played in any place of public assembly shall not be so loud as to be audible beyond the premises where the assembly is located); State v. Dorsett, 3 N.C.App. 331, 164 S.E.2d 607 (1968) (ordinance banning loud or unnecessary noise valid as applied to motorcycles); City of Portland v. Aziz, 47 Or.App. 937, 615 P.2d 1109 (1980) (ordinance applied to amplified sounds during specified night-time hours; upheld as reasonable). Cf. Einarsen v. City of Wheat Ridge, 43 Colo.App. 232, 604 P.2d 691 (Colo.App.1979) (noise abatement statute did not forbid residential development of property impacted by excessive noise and was not confiscatory). Noise ordinances have usually withstood constitutional attack. See Ward v. Rock Against Racism, 491 U.S. 781, 109 S.Ct. 2746, 105 L.Ed.2d 661 (1989), reh. denied 492 U.S. 937, 110 S.Ct. 23, 106 L.Ed.2d 636 (1989) (municipal noise regulation designed to ensure that music performances in city band-shell did not disturb surrounding residents held not violative of free speech rights of performers); Stokes v. City of Madison, 930 F.2d 1163 (7th Cir.1991) (requirement of a "street use permit" for amplified sound, except during stated hours, held a valid time, place, and manner restriction on expression). But cf. United States Labor Party v. Pomerleau, 557 F.2d 410 (4th Cir.1977) (anti-noise ordinance found too vague and overbroad). Sometimes, the power to control noise is treated as part of the power to enjoin nuisances. See State v. Dorsett, *supra*. Cf. Town of Davis v. Davis, 40 W.Va. 464, 21 S.E. 906 (1895) (town council could abate noisy merry-go-round as nuisance). On noise problems in modern cities, see generally "Crusader for Quiet," Time, Dec. 5, 1969, at 85.

Some aspects of noise control have been pre-empted by the Federal government. See City of Burbank v. Lockheed Air Terminal, Inc., 411 U.S. 624, 93 S.Ct. 1854, 36 L.Ed.2d 547 (1973) (noise made by aircraft in flight); Loma Portal Civic Club v. American Airlines, Inc., 61 Cal.2d 582, 39 Cal.Rptr. 708, 394 P.2d 548 (1964) (commercial flights conducted in strict compliance with federal regulations may not be enjoined as nuisances). But the city as operator or landlord of an airport may still take steps to lessen noise from aircraft, and may be held liable in tort by neighboring landowners for failure to do so. Greater Westchester Homeowners Association v. City of Los Angeles, 26 Cal.3d 86, 160 Cal.Rptr. 733, 603 P.2d 1329 (1979), cert. denied 449 U.S. 820, 101 S.Ct. 77, 66 L.Ed.2d 22 (observing that city, though to some extent relying on federal advice in operating airport, had not been compelled by federal government to choose particular location for airport or to expand the facility; also, city could install ground barriers to deflect noise, and could condemn an "aircraft noise easement"), noted 12 Urban Lawyer 617–20 (1980). See Comment, Federal Pre-Emption and Airport Noise Control, 8 Urban L.Ann. 229 (1974); "New Legal Squalls over Jet Noise," Bus.Week, Nov. 24, 1980, at 144. See generally Comment, Noise Pollution: Attempted Federal Control of Airplane Noise, 18 Natural Resources J. 621 (1978). The basic federal statute on noise control—the Noise Control Act of 1972, 42 U.S.C.A. §§ 4901–18—does not pre-empt the field but leaves room for state and local controls. See Note, Environmental Law: The Noise Control Act of 1972, 27 Okl.L.Rev. 55 (1974). On federal preemption see generally Section 7.4 *supra*.

A number of anti-noise ordinances have survived attacks based on vagueness and/or overbreadth. See Stevens v. Matanuska–Susitna Borough, 146 P.3d 3 (Alaska App. 2006) (did not unduly burden protected speech, and was not vague because it placed specific geographic and time limitations on forbidden noise); State of Idaho v. Medel, 139 Idaho 498, 80 P.3d 1099 (App. 2003) (not overbroad because was content-neutral in restricting all excessive sound levels). See generally Note, A Line in the Sand: Florida Municipalities Struggle to Determine the Line Between Valid Noise Ordinances and Unconstitutional Restrictions, 35 Stetson L. Rev. 461 (2006).

On particular problems of noise regulation at the local level, see Comment, Come On Feel the Noise: The Problem With Municipal Noise Regulation, 15 U. Miami Bus. L. Rev. 47 (2006). As to attempts to restrict noise in New Orleans, especially on Bourbon Street, see Robertson, In Rowdy New Orleans, a Noisy Fight Over Quiet, N. Y. Times, March 14, 2014, at 1 & 3 (International Ed.).

[160] See Singer v. Ben How Realty, 160 Fla. 53, 33 So.2d 409 (1948), reh. denied 160 Fla. 57, 34 So.2d 553 (industries using machinery that makes considerable noise can be restricted to operating in certain hours); Dube v. City of Chicago, 7 Ill.2d 313, 131 N.E.2d 9 (1955), cert. denied 350 U.S. 1013, 76 S.Ct. 658, 100 L.Ed. 873 (upholding ordinance prohibiting factory to be operated or maintained within 200 feet of a residence in such a way that loud and unusual noises were emitted, thus creating a nuisance). Cf. Southern Rock Products Co. v. Board of Zoning Adjustment, 282 Ala. 186, 210 So.2d 419 (1968) (applying ordinance prohibiting uses of property which cause noise, dust, or vibration affecting considerable portion of city). See also Gilbert v. Davidson Construction Co., 110 Kan. 298, 203 P. 1113 (1922) (rock crusher found nuisance—largely on basis of dust created). But cf. Reynolds v. Vulcan Materials Co., 279 Ala. 363, 185 So.2d 386 (1966) (rock-crushing

that reasonable regulations on the intensity, time, and place of operation of such trucks (and of other sound-amplifying equipment) are valid.[162]

---

plants could not be entirely prohibited, but could be regulated); In re Kelso, 147 Cal. 609, 82 P. 241 (1905) (rock quarries could not be forbidden in prescribed section of city).

[161] Saia v. New York, 334 U.S. 558, 68 S.Ct. 1148, 92 L.Ed. 1574 (1948). Cf. City of Eugene v. Powlowski, 116 Or.App. 186, 840 P.2d 1322 (1992) (city ordinance, adopting state statute, which restricted all hornhonking except as a warning invalidated as unconstitutionally overbroad).

[162] Kovacs v. Cooper, 336 U.S. 77, 69 S.Ct. 448, 93 L.Ed. 513 (1949), reh. denied 336 U.S. 921, 69 S.Ct. 638, 93 L.Ed. 1083, upholding use of words "loud and raucous" as sufficiently clear, without the need for reference to decibel levels. Cf. City of Farmington v. Wilkins, 106 N.M. 188, 740 P.2d 1172 (App. 1987), cert. denied 106 N.M. 174, 740 P.2d 1158 (1987) (conviction of operator of sound truck, broadcasting music, upheld under general noise control ordinances, which made no reference to decibel levels, even though sound was within the permissible decibels specified in another city ordinance). A number of limits on sound trucks and amplifiers—as to hours and places of operation, decibels of sound that may be emitted, etc.—have been upheld in state courts. See Brinkman v. City of Gainesville, 83 Ga.App. 508, 64 S.E.2d 344 (1951) (citing cases); State v. Smedberg, 31 N.C.App. 585, 229 S.E.2d 841 (1976), cert. allowed 291 N.C. 715, 232 S.E.2d 207. But cf. Wollam v. City of Palm Springs, 59 Cal.2d 276, 29 Cal.Rptr. 1, 379 P.2d 481 (1963) (ordinance prohibited use of sound trucks unless they were moving at speed of at least 10 miles per hour; void as unreasonable limit on free speech). See generally Annot., Public Regulation of Use of Sound Trucks in Streets or Highways—Federal Cases, 93 L.Ed. 532 (1950). See also Annot., Public Regulation and Prohibition of Sound Amplifiers or Loudspeaker Broadcasts in Streets or Other Public Places, 10 A.L.R.2d 627 (1950); Annot., Public Regulation of Advertising by Vehicles in Streets or High-ways—Federal Cases, 93 L.Ed. 543 (1949). On municipal noise-abatement enactments, see generally Hollister & Leigh, Authority of Municipal Corporations to Abate Unwanted Sounds, 10 Sw.U.L.Rev. 267 (1978); Comment, Toward the Comprehensive Abatement of Noise Pollution: Recent Federal and New York City Noise Control Legislation, 4 Ecology L.Q. 109 (1974); Comment, The New York City Noise Code: Not with a Bang, but a Whisper, 1 Fordham Urban L.J. 446 (1973); Comment, Noise Abatement at the Municipal Level, 7 U.San Francisco L.Rev. 478 (1973).

In City of Wichita v. Smith, 31 Kan.App.2d 837, 75 P.3d 1228 (2003), it was held that a music club's cabaret license did not exempt it from compliance with the city's noise ordinance. See also Laven, Turn Down the Volume: The Constitutionality of Ohio's Municipal Ordinances Regulating Sound from Car Stereo Systems, 51 Cleveland St. L. Rev. 1 (2004).

Another type of interference, particularly with astronomical activities, that some municipalities are now attempting to regulate is "light pollution." See Note, Light Pollution in the United States: An Overview of the Inadequacies of the Common Law and State and Local Regulation, 36 New England L. Rev. 985 (2002).

Chapter 24

LOCAL CONTROLS ON CRIMINAL ACTIVITY

Analysis

§ 24.1 The Problem of Urban Crime

The definition, prevention, detection, and punishment of criminal activity are all considered primarily functions of the *state,* rather than of local governments. Municipalities thus possess only such powers in this area as are clearly delegated by the state; and municipal police officers actually serve the whole state, not merely their own municipality.[1] State laws defining crimes and their punishment will, in cases of conflict, prevail over municipal laws to the contrary—even municipal laws of home-rule cities.[2] But much of the responsibility for keeping the peace within incorporated areas is commonly delegated to municipalities, and it has generally been held that an express delegation of the police power to a municipality carries with it the implied authority to put such power into effect by using proper means—including the imposition of reasonable penalties—to enforce municipal ordinances.[3]

---

[1] See City of Los Angeles v. Gurdane, 59 F.2d 161 (9th Cir.1932); Griffin v. City of Los Angeles, 134 Cal.App. 763, 26 P.2d 655 (Dist.Ct.1933). See generally 56 Am. Jur.2d Municipal Corporations § 131 (1971).

[2] See Mayor and Common Council of Prescott v. Randall, 67 Ariz. 369, 196 P.2d 477 (1948) (liquor control); Los Angeles Brewing Co. v. City of Los Angeles, 8 Cal.App.2d 391, 48 P.2d 71 (Dist.Ct.1935) (same); Farmer v. Behmer, 9 Cal.App. 773, 100 P. 901 (Dist.Ct.1909) (prostitution); State ex rel. Smith v. City of International Falls, 132 Minn. 298, 156 N.W. 249 (1916); State v. Linn, 49 Okl. 526, 153 P. 826 (1915) (gambling); Van Gilder v. City of Madison, 222 Wis. 58, 267 N.W. 25 (1936), reh. denied and adhered to 222 Wis. 58, 268 N.W. 108. In Colorado, the state has effectively pre-empted the field as to all acts made criminal by state law; cities (even home-rule cities) cannot provide punishment for such acts. See Gazotti v. City and County of Denver, 143 Colo. 311, 352 P.2d 963 (1960); Canon City v. Merris, 137 Colo. 169, 323 P.2d 614 (1958). On conflicts between state and municipal laws, and on state pre-emption of some fields, see generally Chapter 6 *supra.*

[3] See Ulrich v. City of St. Louis, 112 Mo. 138, 20 S.W. 466 (1892) (an ordinance without a penalty would be nugatory, and thus municipal corporations have implied power to provide for enforcement through fines); City of Detroit v. Fort Wayne & Belle Isle Railway, 95 Mich. 456, 54 N.W. 958 (1893); Ogden v. City of Madison, 111 Wis. 413, 87 N.W. 568 (1901). Cf. Denver City Railway v. City of Denver, 21 Colo. 350, 41 P. 826 (1895) (city has power to prescribe a penalty for failure to pay a lawful license tax); City of Tarkio v. Cook, 120 Mo. 1, 25 S.W. 202 (1894) (charter authorized fines of up to $100; ordinance imposing fine of not less than $25 and not more than $100 held reasonable). Clearly, a municipality in most jurisdictions may be given the power to imprison, for violation of its ordinances, by delegation from the state. In re Guerrero, 69 Cal. 88, 10 P. 261 (1886). But see State ex rel. Keefe v. Schmiege, 251 Wis. 79, 28 N.W.2d 345 (1947) (municipal and county authorities may be given power by state to impose fines, and to imprison in order to enforce fines, but no other power to imprison may be given). Some older authority refused to find *implied* power in a municipality to imprison ordinance-violators, where such power was not clearly spelled out by statute or home-rule charter.

The crowded conditions, racial unrest, and poverty of many urban areas have made enforcement of the criminal laws one of the most difficult tasks of local governments—especially the governments of our larger cities. "Violent crime in the United States," it has been observed, "is primarily a phenomenon of large cities."[4] Both rising crime statistics, and the constant *fear* of crime expressed by many city-dwellers, provide evidence that American cities have been far from entirely successful in "maintaining the peace."[5] Some observers have forecast that matters may become worse: the report of the National Commission on the Causes and Prevention of Violence, issued in 1969, forecast a city-of-the-future composed of high-rise, high-security apartment houses, surrounded by squalor, and ringed by suburbs in which nervous homeowners hid behind window

---

See State v. Bright, 38 La.Ann. 1 (1886) (infliction of punishment appertains exclusively to the sovereign). But the modern trend is toward inferring the power to imprison from broad grants of authority to do what is necessary for the general welfare of the municipality. See Dunn v. Mayor and Council of Wilmington, 59 Del. 287, 219 A.2d 153 (1966) (express authority was only to assess fines, but implied authority to imprison also found).

The U.S. Supreme Court has invalidated the "30 dollars or 30 days" type of penalty—once commonly provided for violators of municipal ordinances—under which a person is required to pay a fine, and must go to jail if, and only if, he is unable to pay. See Tate v. Short, 401 U.S. 395, 91 S.Ct. 668, 28 L.Ed.2d 130 (1971).

[4] "If Crime Goes Unchecked—What Big Cities Will Be Like," U.S. News & World Rep., Dec. 8, 1969, at 41, excerpting a statement (released Nov. 24, 1969) by Dr. Milton S. Eisenhower, who was then chair of the National Commission on the Causes and Prevention of Violence. See generally Krantz & Kramer, Urban Crisis and Crime, 50 Boston U.L.Rev. 343 (1970). On the possible connection between density of population in urban areas and the crime rate of those areas, see Lewyn, Are Spread Out Cities Really Safer (Or, Is Atlanta Safer than New York?), 41 Cleveland St. L. Rev. 279 (1993), concluding that while it has often been assumed that low-density urban areas are safer than high-density areas, this is not supported by crime-rate statistics. On the connection between fear of crime and strained relations between races, see Dowd, Fear of Crime Seems to Strain Race Relations, N.Y. Times, May 16, 1985, at B4, discussing a poll of New York City residents that indicated persons of all races believed crime was the city's most important problem. Due to their relatively low crime rate, rural areas sometimes lack legal staffing. See Note, The Problem of Low Crime: Constitutionally Inadequate Criminal Defense in Rural America, 22 Boston Univ. Pub. Interest L. J. 403 (2013).

On the laws—now in effect in all 50 states and the District of Columbia—by which sex offenders are required to register with local law enforcement upon their release from incarceration and whenever they change residence, see Locke & Chamberlin, Safe from Ex Offenders? Legislating Internet Publication of Sex Offender Registries, 39 Urban Law. 1 (2007), saying that little research has been done on the effects of online registries on recidivism rates. *Id.* at 18. Some municipalities have attempted to impose limits on where those who have been convicted of, or pled guilty to, sex-related crimes can live, but these are sometimes successfully attacked on constitutional grounds. See Note, Banished!—New Jersey Municipalities' Unconstitutional Trend of Banishing Sex Offenders, 31 Seton Hall Legis. J. 253 (2006). Some states and localities have attempted to ban convicted or admitted sex offenders from public libraries. In Doe v. City of Albuquerque, 667 F.3d 1111 (10th Cir. 2012), it was held that such a ban burdens fundamental First Amendment rights and can be sustained only if it is content-neutral and narrowly tailored to further a substantial governmental interest. See Note, Not in My Library: An Examination of State and Local Bans of Sex Offenders From Public Libraries, 44 Ind. L. Rev. 919 (2011). See generally on all these types of sex offender registration and restriction Carpenter & Beverlin, The Evolution of Unconstitutionality in Sex Offender Registration Laws, 63 Hastings L. J. 1071 (2012). As to satellite-based monitoring of recidivist sex offenders, see Grady v. North Carolina, ___ U.S. ___, 135 S.Ct. 1368 (2015) (such monitoring is a Fourth Amendment search, but Court declines to rule on its reasonableness in the first instance).

As to a statutory requirement that defendants charged with a felony be required to provide DNA samples, see State v. Johnson, 813 N.W. 2d 1 (Minn. 2012) (upheld against constitutional attack).

[5] See Rosenthal, The Cage of Fear in Cities Beset by Crime, Life, July 11, 1969, at 16–23. See generally "Patterns of Violence," 364 Annals I-157 (March, 1966) (series of articles); "The Curse of Violent Crime," Time, March 23, 1981, at 16.

grilles and kept guns ever handy.[6] Some writers even feared that downtowns would eventually have to be sealed-off at night by police.[7]

To meet current problems and to prevent worse situations later, a number of municipal efforts and proposals have been advanced: Pay raises for police officers have occurred in many major cities (though the pay is often still inadequate); these, and the use of higher standards for recruits, have helped improve the quality of many police forces.[8] Federal aid has at times in recent years been heavily concentrated on law-

---

[6] United States Nat'l Comm'n on the Causes and Prevention of Violence, To Establish Justice, To Ensure Domestic Tranquility; The Final Report (1970); "How to Heal a Violent Society," Time, Dec. 19, 1969, at 38 (summarizing the Report and noting that it found inaccurate the notion that most violent crime is committed by black offenders against white victims). See generally H. D. Graham & T. R. Gurr (eds.), The History of Violence in America: Historical & Contemporary Prospectives (Praeger 1969); Hofstadter & Wallace (eds.), American Violence; A Documentary History (Knopf 1970). See also United States President's Comm'n on Law Enforcement and Administration of Justice, The Challenge of Crime in a Free Society, A Report (Dutton 1969). A symposium on the latter report appeared in 43 Notre Dame Lawyer 811–907 (1968). See particularly Lumbard, State and Local Government Crime Control, *id.* at 889. See also Symposium on Riots, 43 Notre Dame Lawyer 908–1016 (1968).

[7] See "Future Cities—Armed Forts?", U.S. News & World Rep., Sept. 21, 1970, at 39, summarizing a staff-study prepared for the National Commission on the Causes and Prevention of Violence. See generally R. Harris, The Fear of Crime (Praeger 1969). See also J. H. Scheuer, To Walk the Streets Safely; The Role of Modern Science and Technology in our Criminal Justice System (1969). Some communities have installed surveillance cameras in areas where crimes are considered likely to occur. See Gregory, Cory Booker Is (Still) Optimistic that He Can Save Newark—Not Everyone Is, Time magazine, July 27, 2009, at 36, reporting (at 39) that more than 100 surveillance cameras had been installed throughout Newark, New Jersey, and noting that "The technology led to 109 arrests in its first 16 months of operation." But cf. Brannum v. Overton County School Bd., 516 F.3d 489 (6th Cir. 2008) (installation of video surveillance equipment by public officials in a middle-school locker room held a violation of students' Fourth Amendment rights; students had a constitutional right to privacy in locker room). See also Note, Seeing Red: The Legal Backlash Against Red-Light Cameras in Florida, 64 Fla. L. Rev. 1783 (2012); Comment, Satellites and Municipalities: One Town's Use of Google Earth for Residential Surveillance, 28 Touro L. Rev. 421 (2012).

[8] See "Police Under Attack But Standing Fast," U.S. News & World Rep., Sept. 21, 1970, at 38. See generally "Combating Crime," 374 Annals I-170 (Nov. 1967) (series of excellent articles). On the decrease in crime in the 1990's attributed to more effective police methods and use of technology, see Lacayo, Law and Order, Time, Jan. 15, 1996, at 48. Laws that allow police to "stop and frisk" persons they reasonably regard as suspicious are often considered to have contributed to the decrease in crime, but they remain controversial. See Ward, Stopping Stop and Frisk, 100 A.B.A. J. 38 (March 2014); Note, No to Bratton: A Rejection of Stop and Frisk, and a Call for Progressive Reform in Oakland, 11 Hastings Race & Poverty L. J. 223 (2014). Compare Bellin, The Inverse Relationship Between the Constitutionality and Effectiveness of New York City "Stop and Frisk," 94 Boston Univ. L. Rev. 1495 (2014).

Good discussions of the effect of terrorism, including the "9/11 attacks" on the United States, on police responsibilities and activities are found in Briffault, Facing the Urban Future After September 11, 2001, 34 Urban Law. 563 (2002); Local Policing in a Post-9/11 World, 32 Fordham Urb. L.J. 787 (2005); Ziegler, American Cities and Sustainable Development in the Age of Global Terrorism: Some Thoughts on Fortress America and the Potential for Defensive Dispersal II, 30 Wm. & Mary Envtl. L. & Pol'y Rev. 95 (2005). See generally Symposium, The New Normal: Grappling With Terrorism in Urban Spaces, 41 Fordham Urb. L. J. 1–176 (2013), especially Silber & Frey, Detect, Disrupt, and Detain: Local Law Enforcement's Critical Roles in Combating Homegrown Extremism and the Evolving Terrorist Threat, *id.* at 127.

On the allegations made in some communities that police-protection quality varies greatly according to the affluence or poverty of the neighborhood involved, see Note, Local Control vs. Poor Patrol: Can Discriminatory Police Protection Be Remedied Through the Education Finance Litigation Model?, 86 Boston U.L. Rev. 741 (2006).

Some communities have attempted to lessen displays of disrespect toward police officers by making it a criminal offense to curse or use obscene language toward an officer—but ordinances imposing penalties for such abusive language can seldom withstand constitutional attack. See Lewis v. City of New Orleans, 415 U.S. 130, 94 S.Ct. 970, 39 L.Ed.2d 214 (1974), invalidating an ordinance making it unlawful to curse or revile, or use obscene or opprobrious language toward or with reference to, any member of the city police in performance of his duties. See generally Gooding v. Wilson, 405 U.S. 518, 92 S.Ct. 1103, 31 L.Ed.2d 408 (1972). On the role that police officers play in our society, see Schultz ex rel. Schultz v. Pojoaque Tribal Police Dep't, 317 P.3d 866,

enforcement activities of local governments.[9] High-pressure sodium vapor street lighting has been employed in a growing number of municipalities; generating double the amount of illumination produced by the older mercury-vapor street lamps, these new lights owe their popularity largely to the belief of many people that they will help reduce criminal activity in the streets.[10] Again, the emphasis in supplying these aids has been on

---

871 (N. M. App. 2013) (police have a greater sense of duty to their employment than the average citizen). See also, as to the effects on crime when police presence on the streets is increased, Tierney, Prison Population Can Shrink When Police Crowd the Streets, N. Y. Times, Jan. 26, 2013, at A1 & A16. As to reforms in the use of force by police, see Note, Reforming Police Use-of-Force Practices: A Case Study of the Cincinnati Police Department, 46 Columbia J. L. & Soc. Probs. 539 (2013). As to the extent to which poor relations between city police and city citizens sometimes contributes to violence and riots (as in Baltimore in April, 2015), see Cobb, City Life, The New Yorker, May 11, 2015, at 19; Stolberg, Baltimore's "Broken Relationship" With Police, N.Y. Times, April 25, 2015, at A1; Van Drehle, The Roots of a Riot, Time magazine, May 11, 2015, at 34.

[9] The legislation creating the federal Law Enforcement Assistance Administration, and providing for federal grants through this agency to state and local units, is found at 42 U.S.C.A. §§ 3701–81. On the federal grants, see Clynch, Spending of Law Enforcement Assistance Administration Block Grants by the States: A Report, 2 Justice System J. 157 (1976). See generally Leonard, Bar and LEAA, 45 Wis.B.Bull. 37 (1972); Law Enforcement Assistance Administration: A Symposium on Its Operation and Impact, 5 Colum.Human Rights L.Rev. 1–214 (1973). See also McPheters & Stronge, Law Enforcement Expenditures and Urban Crime, 27 Nat. Tax J. 633 (1974). The first major emphasis on the need for federal assistance in local crime-control and crime-prevention programs was found in Title I of the Omnibus Crime Control and Safe Streets Act of 1968. See the up-dated authorization of expenditures in 42 U.S.C.A. § 3768, and Historical Note thereto. See also Note, Title II of the Omnibus Crime Control Act: A Study in Constitutional Conflict, 57 Geo.L.J. 438 (1968); Recent Statute Note, Title II of the Omnibus Crime Control and Safe Streets Act of 1968, 82 Harv.L.Rev. 1392 (1969), both discussing the portion of the Omnibus Act dealing with admissibility of evidence. But requirements for the federal aid were tightened when it appeared that most of the money was being spent on "hardware": guns, uniforms, equipment. See "Washington Limits Its Help to Police," Bus. Week, July 8, 1972, at 26, observing that over the preceding four years, the Law Enforcement Assistance Administration (LEAA) had turned over more than $1.5 billion in federal money to the states to aid crime-fighting efforts. This was called "the most ambitious venture yet in federal revenue-sharing." *Id.* The special federal aid given by LEAA was ended in 1980. It has been observed that its efforts and expenditures did not significantly reduce crime rates and that there is doubt the federal government can do much to reduce crime in various localities of the nation. See Pear, Experts Doubt Federal Role in Curbing Violent Crime, N. Y. Times, March 8, 1981, § 1, at 16. On the limits of federal power in fighting urban crime, see "Crackdown on Crime? Talk, But Little Action," U.S. News & World Rep., Sept. 27, 1982, at 65. See generally "What the Police Can—and Cannot—Do About Crime," Time, July 13, 1970, at 34.

[10] See "A Sodium-Vapor Attack on Street Crime," Bus. Week, May 12, 1973, at 172. Some people oppose such lighting, however, because they dislike the yellow-orange glow or because they fear potential hazards to health or because they think it will unduly interfere with the work of astronomers. Other technological developments aimed at crime detection and prevention include the use of better software. See Kedmey, Caught by the Cloud, Time magazine, May 25, 2015, at 18. And the wearing of body cameras by police. See Davis, Candid Cameras, A.B.A.J., June 2015, at 15. Cf. Williams, Police Cam Downside: Your Arrest Hits YouTube, N.Y. Times, April 27, 2015, at A1, reporting conflict over who is entitled to view the body camera recordings.

It has been suggested that cities should increasingly be planned and built with an eye to discouraging criminal activity. See Newman, Defensible Space: Crime Prevention Through Urban Design (1973); Schlomo, Discouraging Crime Through City Planning (1968). See generally Anderson et. al., Reducing Crime by Shaping the Built Environment With Zoning: An Empirical Study of Los Angeles, 161 U. Pa. L. Rev. 699 (2013); Katyal, Architecture as Crime Control, 111 Yale L.J. 1039 (2002); Ziegler, American Cities, Urban Planning, and Place-Based Crime Prevention, 39 Urban Law. 859 (2007), noting that the seminal work in this area is Newman's Defensible Space *supra,* and that since the publication of his book, a whole field of activity has developed known as Crime Prevention Through Environmental Design; *id.* at 859. See also Mitchell & Beckett, Securing the Global City: Crime, Consulting, Risk, and Ratings in the Production of Urban Space, 15 Ind. J. Global Legal Stud. 75 (2008).

Perhaps the ultimate in crime-prevention design was once suggested in the St. Louis suburb of Bellerive, Missouri: a 10-foot high chain-link fence to surround the entire 130-acre community. See "Fence Me In," Newsweek, March 4, 1974, at 78. See also "U.S. Gets Its First Walled City; Sugar Creek, Texas, Electronically Fortified," Bus. Week, March 6, 1971, at 28. Some neighborhoods in the Miami, Florida, area have erected street barricades as a crime-control device, complete in some cases with checkpoints and gates. Schmalz, Fearful and Angry Floridians Erect Street Barriers to Crime, N.Y. Times, Dec. 6, 1988, at A1, noting that most of the barricades were approved by the county commission and appeared to be legal. On the legality of a barrier

alleviating the problems of the big cities—in the central areas of which, it has been estimated, residents are a hundred times more likely to be victims of "crime in the street" than are suburban residents.[11]

§ 24.2 Nature of Ordinance-Violation Prosecutions; Right to Jury Trial

Overburdened by cases and fragmented into different regions and divisions, municipal law-enforcement systems are often in great need of overall supervision and co-ordination—thus, New York City in 1977 created the office of criminal-justice coordinator in order to provide a unified system for gathering and supplying information to, and unifying the efforts of, all the city's law-enforcement agencies.[12] Enforcement of

---

blocking off part of a community from the rest, see City of Memphis v. Greene, 451 U.S. 100, 101 S.Ct. 1584, 67 L.Ed.2d 769 (1981), reh. denied 452 U.S. 955, 101 S.Ct. 3100, 69 L.Ed.2d 965 (1981) (street closing did not violate Federal Civil Rights Act or Thirteenth Amendment). See generally Fleming, *City of Memphis v. N.T. Greene*: "Before I Built a Wall, I'd Ask to Know What I Was Walling in or Walling Out, And to Whom I Was Likely to Give Offense," 21 Urban Law. 961 (1989). On the growing popularity of gated communities, see Blakely & Snyder, Fortress America—Gated Communities in the United States (Brookings Institution Press 1997); Smith, Ross, Pritt, Woram, Witt & Welch, Gated Communities: Private Solution or Public Dilemma?, 29 Urban Law. 413 (1997); Stark, America, the Gated?, Wilson Quarterly, Winter, 1998, at 58. The effects on crime control remain unclear. See Perez, Walled Neighborhoods Spread, But Their Effects on Crime Are Unclear Trends: Although Residents Feel More Secure Behind Barricades, Some Say They Ruin Communities, L.A. Times, Nov. 24, 1996, at B3. See generally Schwartz, Public Gated Residential Communities: The Rosemont, Illinois, Approach and Its Constitutional Implications, 29 Urban Law. 123 (1997). See also Owens, Westec Story: Gated Communities and the Fourth Amendment, 34 Am. Crim. L. Rev. 1127 (1997); Note, Residential Associations as State Actors: Regulating the Impact of Gated Communities on Nonmembers, 105 Yale L.J. 761 (1995). See also Section 21.4, note 55 *supra*.

Some states have created funds for compensating the victims of certain crimes. See Lamborn, The Propriety of Governmental Compensation for Victims of Crime, 41 Geo. Wash.L.Rev. 446 (1973); Comment, Crime Victim Compensation: The New York Solution, 35 Albany L.Rev. 717 (1971); Comment, Compensation for Victims of Violent Crimes, 26 U.Kan.L.Rev. 227 (1978); Annot., Statutes Providing for Governmental Compensation for Victims of Crime, 20 A.L.R.4th 63 (1983). See generally "Easing the Pain for Crime Victims," U.S. News & World Rep., June 21, 1982, at 45. See also Hoelzel, A Survey of 27 Victim Compensation Programs, 63 Am. Judicature No. 10, at 485 (May, 1980).

[11] "Suburbs Hit by Only 1/100th as Much Crime as Ghetto," Stanford (University) Observer, Feb., 1970, at 6, summarizing views and findings in Packer, The Limits of the Criminal Sanction (Stanford University Press 1968). See generally Rainwater, Fear and the House-as-Haven in the Lower Class, 32 J.Am.Institute of Planners 23 (1966). It has sometimes been contended that city-center and minority neighborhoods receive less police protection than other areas. See Spiegel & Grau, Ghettoside: A True Story of Murder in America (2015), reviewed by Leovy, The Underpolicing of Black America, Wall St. J., Jan 24–25, 2015, at C-3. In some cities, residents themselves—often with the encouragement of police—have now formed "crime patrols" to detect and report criminal activity. See Henry, New Yorkers Patrolling Against Crime, N.Y. Times, May 4, 1981, at 15, col. 3; "The People's War Against Crime," U.S. News & World Rep., July 13, 1981, at 53.

On the "privatization" of police protection in some neighborhoods and communities, see generally Nelson, Private Neighborhoods and the Transformation of Local Government (2005), reviewed in Ammons, Private Governance for All: A Desirable Outcome or a Cause for Concern?, 9 N.Y.U.J. Legis. & Pub. Pol'y 503 (2005–2006). See generally Section 16.2, note 33, *supra*.

[12] See Wilkins, Crime in New York City: Specialists Are Looking to New Deputy Mayor for Solutions, N.Y. Times, Dec. 5, 1977, § C, at 67. On the history of the New York City police department, see generally Lardner & Reppetto, NYPD: A City and Its Police (Henry Holt 2000), reviewed Bus. Week, Sept. 4, 2000, at 22.

Though it has in the past been alleged that state and local courts are overwhelmed by the number of criminal cases coming before them, a study in 1982 indicated that court resources had actually increased more rapidly than the inflow of new cases, though case processing often lags and produces a backlog. See Jacob, Swank, Beecher & Rich, Keeping Pace: Court Resources and Crime in Ten U.S. Cities, 66 Am. Judicature No. 2, at 73 (Aug., 1982). On selection of local judges, see Atkins & Gertz, The Local Politics of Judicial Selection: Some Views of Law Enforcement Officials, 66 Am. Judicature No. 1, at 39 (June/July, 1982).

local criminal laws is still characterized not only by archaic structures, but also by quaint, often outdated doctrines—chief of which is the traditional rule that prosecutions for violations of municipal ordinances are civil, rather than criminal, proceedings. Several jurisdictions have now overthrown this doctrine and specifically recognized that such prosecutions are criminal proceedings,[13] or have adopted the position that violations of municipal ordinances amount to misdemeanors.[14] In these jurisdictions, an accused person normally enjoys all the usual rights of a criminal-case defendant, even though the prosecution is only for violation of a municipal, not a state or federal, law.[15] But many jurisdictions have clung to the rule that prosecutions of alleged violators of municipal ordinances are civil in nature[16]—a rule harking back to a day when municipalities enforced their ordinances by suits to recover a penalty that was considered in the nature of a "debt." Where the traditional rule is retained, defendants

---

[13] People v. Pacific Gas & Electric Co., 168 Cal. 496, 143 P. 727 (1914); City of Pueblo v. Clemmer, 150 Colo. 546, 375 P.2d 99 (1962); People v. Sarnoff, 302 Mich. 266, 4 N.W.2d 544 (1942); State ex rel. Salter v. McDonald, 121 Minn. 207, 141 N.W. 110 (1913); City of Deming v. Marquez, 74 N.M. 747, 398 P.2d 266 (1965); Salt Lake City v. Robinson, 39 Utah 260, 116 P. 442 (1911); City of Roanoke v. Donckers, 187 Va. 491, 47 S.E.2d 440 (1948). See Gibson City v. McClellan, 61 Ill.App.2d 218, 209 N.E.2d 363 (1965). Cf. City of St. Paul v. Whidby, 295 Minn. 129, 203 N.W.2d 823 (1972) (rules of criminal procedure apply if imprisonment may result); Diehl v. City of Shidler, 79 Okl.Cr. 355, 155 P.2d 269 (1945) (prosecutions are treated as criminal if possible punishment includes imprisonment, or fine over a certain limit).

[14] See State v. Walker, 265 N.C. 482, 144 S.E.2d 419 (1965) (ordinance required permit before person could repair own residence; held valid); City of Akron v. Sabol, 2 Ohio App.2d 109, 206 N.E.2d 575 (1965) (unlawfully disturbing the peace by intoxication); City of Sioux Falls v. Marshall, 48 S.D. 378, 204 N.W. 999 (1925) (possession of intoxicating liquor for sale).

In Alabama, Illinois, and Minnesota, ordinance-violation prosecutions are sometimes characterized as "quasi-criminal"; see Donahey v. City of Montgomery, 43 Ala.App. 20, 178 So.2d 832 (1965), cert. denied 278 Ala. 708, 178 So.2d 837; City of Danville v. Clark, 63 Ill.2d 408, 348 N.E.2d 844 (1976), cert. denied 429 U.S. 899, 97 S.Ct. 266, 50 L.Ed.2d 184; City of Chicago v. Berg, 48 Ill.App.2d 251, 199 N.E.2d 49 (1964); City of Chicago v. Williams, 45 Ill.App.2d 327, 195 N.E.2d 425 (1963); State v. Nelson, 157 Minn. 506, 196 N.W. 279 (1923).

A few cases, while not characterizing ordinance-violation cases as fully criminal in nature, have held that the procedural rules applicable to criminal prosecutions should apply in ordinance-prosecution situations. See City of Asbury Park v. Shure, 54 N.J.Super. 46, 148 A.2d 82 (1959); City of Minot v. Whitfield, 71 N.W.2d 766 (N.D.1955). Cf. City of Miami v. Gilbert, 102 So.2d 818 (Fla.App. 1958) (ordinance-violation proceedings partake of the nature of criminal proceedings). Missouri considers municipal ordinance violations to be only *quasi*-criminal: criminal to extent that the parties are bound by the criminal rules of procedure, the prosecution must establish guilt beyond a reasonable doubt, and the defendant may be incarcerated as punishment if convicted; but the case is otherwise considered primarily civil in nature. See City of Ferguson v. Nelson, 438 S.W. 2d 249, 255 (Mo. 1969); State of Kansas v. Lackey, 45 Kan. App. 2d 257, 246 P.3d 998 (2011) (applying Missouri law).

[15] See Thomas v. Yazoo City, 95 Miss. 395, 48 So. 821 (1909); State ex rel. Wallen v. Judges Noe, Towne, Johnson, etc., 78 Wn.2d 484, 475 P.2d 787 (1970). Cf. In re Wong Hane, 108 Cal. 680, 41 P. 693 (1895) (accused entitled to presumption of innocence and prosecution must prove case beyond a reasonable doubt); People v. Marcello, 25 N.Y.S.2d 533 (Mag.Ct.1941) (same); Cain v. State, 105 Tex.Cr. 204, 287 S.W. 262 (1926) (ordinance held unconstitutional as ex post facto in application to acts committed before its passage).

[16] See State v. Robitshek, 60 Minn. 123, 61 N.W. 1023 (1895); Kansas City v. Waller, 518 S.W.2d 202 (Mo.App.1974); City of St. Louis v. Flynn, 386 S.W.2d 44 (Mo.1965); City of St. Louis v. Fitch, 353 Mo. 706, 183 S.W.2d 828 (1944), transferred 238 Mo.App. 725, 187 S.W.2d 63; State v. Amick, 173 Neb. 770, 114 N.W.2d 893 (1962); Commonwealth v. Dortort, 205 Pa.Super. 211, 208 A.2d 797 (1965); O'Dell v. City of Knoxville, 54 Tenn.App. 59, 388 S.W.2d 150 (1964); Village of Bayside v. Bruner, 33 Wis.2d 533, 148 N.W.2d 5 (1967); City of Milwaukee v. Antczak, 24 Wis.2d 480, 129 N.W.2d 125 (1964). Cf. City of Highland Park v. Curtis, 83 Ill.App.2d 218, 226 N.E.2d 870 (1967) (enforcement of municipal ordinance not criminal; guilt need only be proven by preponderance of evidence, not beyond a reasonable doubt); Village of Riverside v. Kuhne, 335 Ill.App. 547, 82 N.E.2d 500 (1948), appeal transferred 397 Ill. 108, 73 N.E.2d 286 (suit to recover penalty for violation of ordinance is civil—no complaint necessary for prosecution). See also note 18 *infra* and cases cited therein (on lack of need for grand-jury indictment).

are not accorded the defenses and protections usually available, by state and federal constitution, to those charged with crimes.[17] Thus, a person accused of violating a municipal ordinance is not entitled to an indictment by a grand jury before being brought to trial,[18] and there is considerable authority that the Sixth Amendment's guarantee that an accused shall have the right in criminal prosecutions to be confronted with the witnesses against him does not apply to prosecutions for misdemeanor violations.[19] Also—although the U.S. Supreme Court has ruled that the "right-to-jury-trial" guarantee of the Federal Constitution applies to the states and is applicable wherever the accused faces a possible penalty of imprisonment in excess of six months[20]—persons

---

[17] City of Miami v. Gilbert, *supra* note 14; City of Webster Groves v. Quick, 319 S.W.2d 543 (Mo.1959), transferred to 323 S.W.2d 386. See Donahey v. City of Montgomery, *supra* note 14. Cf. Hunter v. State, 306 Or. 529, 761 P.2d 502 (1988) (persons convicted of violating municipal ordinances did not qualify as having been convicted under "laws of this state" and therefore were not entitled to use the provisions of state Post-Conviction Hearing Act).

[18] Burrow v. City of Hot Springs, 85 Ark. 396, 108 S.W. 823 (1908); Wright v. Worth, 83 Fla. 204, 91 So. 87 (1922); City of St. Louis v. Page, 259 S.W.2d 98 (Mo.App.1953) (report of police chief commences prosecution); Ex parte Lewis, 328 Mo. 843, 42 S.W.2d 21 (1931); Board of Health v. New York Central Railway, 10 N.J. 294, 90 A.2d 729 (1952) (indictment unnecessary *unless* offense constituted such a crime at common law as to make grand-jury indictment necessary); Brewer v. Watson, 191 Misc. 117, 77 N.Y.S.2d 97 (Sup.Ct.1947) (constitutional right to grand-jury indictment extends even to misdemeanors—but violation of this particular ordinance was not a misdemeanor); Finnical v. Village of Cadiz, 61 Ohio St. 494, 56 N.E. 200 (1900) (affidavit of mayor commences prosecution); Webster v. Knewel, 47 S.D. 142, 196 N.W. 549 (1924) (complaint can commence proceedings; no presentment of grand jury or information of public prosecutor needed). But cf. Ex parte Bochmann, 20 Okl.Cr. 78, 201 P. 537 (1921) (verified written complaint necessary under state constitution where punishment may be imprisonment or fine in excess of a certain amount; violation treated as criminal in nature—if prosecution is in court of record, must be upon presentment of grand jury, or indictment or information). See generally Crowe, Indictment and Information, 2 Okl.City U.L.Rev. 173 (1977) (part of symposium on Oklahoma law).

[19] State ex rel. Sellars v. Parker, 87 Fla. 181, 100 So. 260 (1924); City of Webster Groves v. Quick, *supra* note 17; Deitch v. City of Chattanooga, 195 Tenn. 245, 258 S.W.2d 776 (1953). But a state constitution *may* make the right to confront witnesses applicable in all proceedings, civil as well as criminal. See Ohio Const. Art. I, § 10.

The U.S. Supreme Court has held that the Sixth Amendment right (under the Federal Constitution) of an accused to confront witnesses against him in a criminal prosecution *does* apply to the states. Illinois v. Allen, 397 U.S. 337, 90 S.Ct. 1057, 25 L.Ed.2d 353 (1970), reh. denied 398 U.S. 915, 90 S.Ct. 1684, 26 L.Ed.2d 80. Thus, in those states in which ordinance-prosecution cases are considered criminal in nature, the right to confront witnesses will clearly now exist in such cases. Even before Illinois v. Allen *supra*, the state of Louisiana had recognized this right. City of Monroe v. Sharpe, 235 La. 1005, 106 So.2d 450 (1958). Cf. City of Detroit v. Morgan, 11 Mich.App. 656, 162 N.W.2d 104 (1968) (right of cross-examination applies to ordinance prosecutions).

Another unsettled question is whether a municipality has the right to appeal an unfavorable decision in an ordinance-violation case. See Annot., Right of Municipal Corporation to Review of Unfavorable Decision in Action or Prosecution for Violation of Ordinance—Modern Status, 11 A.L.R.4th 399 (1982), noting that the right of a municipality to obtain such judicial review is constantly changing in many jurisdictions and that many cases over the years have denied a municipality such right.

[20] Baldwin v. New York, 399 U.S. 66, 90 S.Ct. 1886, 26 L.Ed.2d 437 (1970); Duncan v. Louisiana, 391 U.S. 145, 88 S.Ct. 1444, 20 L.Ed.2d 491 (1968), reh. denied 392 U.S. 947, 88 S.Ct. 2270, 20 L.Ed.2d 1412, noted 35 Brooklyn L.Rev. 128 (1968); 82 Harv. L.Rev. 148 (1968) (portion of summary of term); 53 Minn.L.Rev. 414 (1968); 22 Sw. L.J. 875 (1968); 21 Vand.L.Rev. 1099 (1968). See generally Note, the Incorporation Doctrine: Sixth Amendment Trial by Jury, 15 Howard L.J. 164 (1968).

In the District of Columbia, a prosecution for violation of a local law has long required a jury trial if the offense with which the accused is charged is characterized as "grave" or "malum in se" or it was indictable under the common law, but not if the offense is considered petty. See District of Columbia v. Colts, 282 U.S. 63, 51 S.Ct. 52, 75 L.Ed. 177 (1930); Schick v. United States, 195 U.S. 65, 24 S.Ct. 826, 49 L.Ed. 99 (1904). Cf. District of Columbia v. Clawans, 300 U.S. 617, 57 S.Ct. 660, 81 L.Ed. 843 (1937) (prosecution for violation of Act of Congress involved; Court held that maximum imprisonment of 90 days did not prevent offense from being classified as "petty").

accused of violating a municipal ordinance are still held in most states not entitled, as a matter of constitutional right, to a jury trial.[21] It might be thought that even if constitutional guarantees of jury trial in *criminal* cases are considered here inapplicable, provisions for jury trials in *civil* cases would at least apply—but often, this has not been the reasoning of the courts. It has been ruled that provisions in state constitutions that the right of jury trial in civil cases shall remain inviolate apply only to cases triable by a jury at common law,[22] or at the time the state constitution was adopted.[23] It has often been noted, also, that there is a right of appeal in municipal-ordinance prosecutions to a state court of general jurisdiction, in which there *is* a right to a trial de novo with a jury.[24] This has generally been thought to satisfy any constitutional requirement of jury trial that might arguably be applicable, or at least relevant-by-analogy; but some jurists have argued to the contrary.[25] In a number of states, specific constitutional provisions *do* now guarantee a right to jury trial for ordinance-violations, at least in certain cases.[26]

---

[21] See Natal v. Louisiana, 139 U.S. 621, 11 S.Ct. 636, 35 L.Ed. 288 (1891); City of Birmingham v. Williams, 229 Ala. 101, 155 So. 877 (1934); State ex rel. Sellars v. Parker, *supra* note 19; Pearson v. Wimbish, 124 Ga. 701, 52 S.E. 751 (1906); City of Mount Sterling v. Holly, 108 Ky. 621, 57 S.W. 491 (1900); Norwood v. Wiseman, 141 Md. 696, 119 A. 688 (1922); Commonwealth v. Whitney, 108 Mass. 5 (1871); In re Cox, 129 Mich. 635, 89 N.W. 440 (1902); State v. Ketterer, 248 Minn. 173, 79 N.W.2d 136 (1956); State ex rel. Cole v. Nigro, 471 S.W.2d 933 (Mo.1971), appeal dism'd 404 U.S. 804, 92 S.Ct. 122, 30 L.Ed.2d 36 (1971), reh. denied 404 U.S. 960, 92 S.Ct. 309, 30 L.Ed.2d 278; Delaney v. Kansas City, 167 Mo. 667, 67 S.W. 589 (1902); Hudson v. City of Las Vegas, 81 Nev. 677, 409 P.2d 245 (1965); People v. Dobbertin, 202 Misc. 16, 114 N.Y.S.2d 147 (County Ct.1951); People v. Fenton, 144 Misc. 710, 259 N.Y.S. 913 (County Ct.1932); Ragsdale v. City of Danville, 116 Va. 484, 82 S.E. 77 (1914); City of Brookings v. Thomsen, 84 S.D. 651, 176 N.W.2d 46 (1970). Cf. Brewer v. Watson, *supra* note 18 (violation of village ordinance—punishment could not exceed fine of $50—no right to jury trial).

It has been held that the general rule, not requiring a jury trial, applies even though the offense would also be punishable under state law, and the accused would be entitled to a jury if tried under that law. See City of Gainesville v. Hilliard, 207 So.2d 520 (Fla.App.1968), aff'd 213 So.2d 689 (Fla.1968); State v. Parks, 199 Minn. 622, 273 N.W. 233 (1937); State v. Amick, *supra* note 16. Cf. City of Fort Scott v. Arbuckle, 165 Kan. 374, 196 P.2d 217 (1948) (immaterial that punishment possible under municipal ordinance greater than under state law). But see Canon City v. Merris, 137 Colo. 169, 323 P.2d 614 (1958) (where drunk driving was a crime under state law, the same act when punished under city ordinance must be prosecuted as a crime, not in a civil proceeding).

[22] State ex rel. Sellars v. Parker, *supra* note 19. See City of Mankato v. Arnold, 36 Minn. 62, 30 N.W. 305 (1886).

[23] See Hunt v. City of Jacksonville, 34 Fla. 504, 16 So. 398 (1894); City of Fort Scott v. Arbuckle, *supra* note 21; State ex rel. Curtis v. City of Topeka, 36 Kan. 76, 12 P. 310 (1886); Town of Montclair v. Stanoyevich, 6 N.J. 479, 79 A.2d 288 (1951) (date of adoption of original constitution, not present constitution, treated as determinative).

[24] See City of Des Moines v. Pugh, 231 Iowa 1283, 2 N.W.2d 754 (1942); City of Emporia v. Volmer, 12 Kan. 622 (Dassler 475) (1874) (opinion by Justice Brewer); Town of Moundsville v. Fountain, 27 W.Va. 182 (1885); City of Oshkosh v. Lloyd, 255 Wis. 601, 39 N.W.2d 772 (1949). Cf. Briggs v. Union City, 531 S.W.2d 106 (Tenn.1975) (cases involving violations of city ordinances are triable de novo on appeal in same manner as a tort action, with defendant then having right to jury trial).

[25] See Franks v. City of Muskogee, 14 Okl.Cr. 391, 171 P. 492 (1918) (availability of jury trial on appeal does not satisfy constitutional requirement). Cf. In re Jahn, 55 Kan. 694, 41 P. 956 (1895) (right to jury trial on appeal satisfies constitutional requirement only if no unreasonable restrictions on such right imposed). See generally Callan v. Wilson, 127 U.S. 540, 8 S.Ct. 1301, 32 L.Ed. 223 (1888) (police court of District of Columbia could not, without jury, convict defendant even though he could appeal to a higher court where jury available).

[26] See Village of New Miami v. White, 73 Ohio App. 12, 53 N.E.2d 664 (1943); City of Fremont v. Keating, 96 Ohio St. 468, 118 N.E. 114 (1917) (constitutional right of trial by jury where ordinance provides imprisonment as a direct punishment); Ex parte Johnson, 20 Okl.Cr. 66, 201 P. 533 (1921) (constitutional right to jury trial if imprisonment, or fine over a certain amount, is possible); Belatti v. Pierce, 8 S.D. 456, 66 N.W. 1088 (1896), aff'd 10 S.D. 63, 71 N.W. 755 (state constitution provides that right to trial by jury shall remain inviolate; this applies to all offenses triable by jury prior to adoption of constitution). Cf. Baker v. City of Fairbanks, 471 P.2d 386 (Alaska 1970) (right to jury trial wherever a direct penalty may be incarceration, and

§ 24.3 Rights of the Defendant in Ordinance-Violation Prosecutions

Aside from developments as to the right to jury trial (discussed in the preceding paragraph), those accused of violating municipal ordinances sometimes now enjoy many of the rights of other criminal-case defendants even where the municipal-ordinance prosecution is still treated as non-criminal in nature. This has come about in three ways: (1) Occasionally, court rules are adopted for municipal courts that guarantee ordinance-violation defendants appearing therein many of the rights of criminal-case defendants.[27] (2) Some rights have been held by the courts to be absolute, or very basic, and thus applicable to defendants in ordinance-violation cases despite the civil, or only quasi-criminal, nature of those matters. This is true of the right to bail before conviction, where that right is guaranteed by the state constitution;[28] the right to a speedy trial—meaning a trial initiated and conducted with reasonable promptness;[29] and the right to a public trial.[30] It is also true of the accused's right to know the nature and cause of the accusation against him—either because the state constitution guarantees that right in all cases, not just criminal;[31] or because the general constitutional guarantees of due process are held

---

also where penalty may be loss of a valuable license, and also wherever offense connotes "criminal conduct" in traditional sense of term); State v. Hoben, 256 Minn. 436, 98 N.W.2d 813 (1959) (right to jury trial where a violation of state traffic code charged, but not otherwise for ordinance prosecutions). But see City of Des Moines v. Pugh, *supra* note 24 (constitution guarantees jury trial in certain ordinance-prosecutions, but held satisfied by availability of jury on appeal). The Texas Constitution once guaranteed a jury trial in certain ordinance prosecutions. See Smith v. City of San Antonio, 17 Tex. 643 (1856) (ordinance empowering mayor to fine and imprison without jury trial was unconstitutional); Burns v. Town of La Grange, 17 Tex. 415 (1856). The present Constitution merely states in general terms that the right of jury trial shall remain inviolate. Vernon's Ann.Tex.Const. Art. 1, § 15. See generally Merrill, Sanctions and Fora for Enforcement of Municipal Ordinances in Oklahoma, 10 Okl.L.Rev. 1, 4–17 (1957), criticizing the Oklahoma rule guaranteeing a jury trial in many ordinance-prosecution cases.

[27] See City of Elvins v. DePriest, 398 S.W.2d 22 (Mo.App.1965), applying such a rule requiring that defendant be given a definite written statement of the alleged offense.

[28] See City of New Orleans v. Lacoste, 169 La. 717, 125 So. 865 (1930). Cf. City of Sioux Falls v. Marshall, 48 S.D. 378, 204 N.W. 999 (1925) (bail after conviction could be granted by trial judge *or* judge of Supreme Court, but application in first instance should be made to trial judge). In many states, there is no constitutional right to freedom on bail *after* conviction, pending appeal. See City of Sioux Falls v. Marshall, *supra* (absolute right inapplicable after conviction). But where there is such a right, it probably will apply to those convicted of violating municipal ordinances. See City of New Orleans v. Lacoste, *supra*. See generally Note, What the Right Hand Gives: Prohibitive Interpretations of the State Constitutional Right to Bail, 78 Fordham L. Rev. 267 (2009). See also Hegreness, America's Fundamental and Vanishing Right to Bail, 55 Ariz. L. Rev. 909 (2013), arguing that the Fifth and Fourteenth Amendments render invalid recent federal and state encroachments—as, for instance, for people deemed a "flight risk" or a "danger to the community"—on the right to bail.

[29] See City of Chicago v. Wisniewski, 54 Ill.2d 149, 295 N.E.2d 453 (1973); State ex rel. Wallen v. Judges Noe, Towne, Johnson, etc., 78 Wn.2d 484, 475 P.2d 787 (1970). As to what is "reasonable promptness," see City of Creston v. Nye, 74 Iowa 369, 37 N.W. 777 (1888) (trial at next jury term did not violate defendant's constitutional right).

[30] See People v. Crittenden, 93 Cal.App.2d 871, 209 P.2d 161 (Dist.Ct.1949); City of Creston v. Nye, *supra* note 29; Battenheiser v. City of Cincinnati, 41 Ohio App. 303, 180 N.E. 209 (1931). But see State ex rel. Sellars v. Parker, 87 Fla. 181, 100 So. 260 (1924), saying that constitutional right to a public trial would not apply to ordinance prosecutions because of their "civil" nature.

[31] Telheard v. City of Bay St. Louis, 87 Miss. 580, 40 So. 326 (1906); City of Akron v. Sabol, 2 Ohio App.2d 109, 206 N.E.2d 575 (1965); Village of Strongsville v. McPhee, 142 Ohio St. 534, 53 N.E.2d 522 (1944). See City of Seattle v. Cisel, 1 Wn.App. 236, 460 P.2d 287 (1969) review denied 77 Wash.2d 961 (1970) (charge is sufficient if it enables defendant to prepare defense and to plead any judgment as a bar to later prosecution for the same offense).

to require this.[32] It seems that ordinance-violation convictions, whether deemed criminal or civil, will also be reversed if the ordinance on which the conviction is based is not reasonably definite and certain in terminology.[33] And the privilege against self-incrimination is generally held available even in civil cases, and thus available in all ordinance-prosecution cases.[34] (3) The due process guaranteed by the Federal Constitution and by state constitutions applies to ordinance prosecutions; therefore, the defendant has the right to a reasonable opportunity to be heard,[35] and the right to be judged by an impartial tribunal.[36] On this basis also, it has been held that irrational

---

[32] See Donahey v. City of Montgomery, 43 Ala.App. 20, 178 So.2d 832 (1965), cert. denied 278 Ala. 708, 178 So.2d 837; Wright v. Worth, 83 Fla. 204, 91 So. 87 (1922); Telheard v. City of Bay St. Louis, *supra* note 31; City of Cleveland v. Gogola, 41 O.L.A. 452, 58 N.E.2d 101 (1944) (complaint must inform accused of exact nature of crime). Cf. Scott v. City and County of Denver, 125 Colo. 68, 241 P.2d 857 (1952) (complaint referred to offense only by numbers; insufficient); Town of Belleville v. Kiernan, 39 N.J.Super. 480, 121 A.2d 411 (1956) (complaint alleging violation of ordinance prohibiting funeral business in residential zone did not allege that residence where business conducted was *in* residential zone; defective). But sometimes—especially if the ordinance prosecution is considered civil in nature—the specificity required of indictments or informations is not here considered necessary. See City of Chicago v. Westphalen, 95 Ill.App.2d 331, 238 N.E.2d 225 (1968); City of New Orleans v. Adjmi, 249 La. 346, 186 So.2d 616 (1966); Kansas City v. Stricklin, 428 S.W.2d 721 (Mo.1968); People v. Kempner, 95 N.Y.S.2d 425 (Mag.Ct.1950).

[33] Beard, 246 Ala. 338, 20 So.2d 721 (1944); City of Shreveport v. Brewer, 225 La. 93, 72 So.2d 308 (1954). See Lambert v. California, 355 U.S. 225, 78 S.Ct. 240, 2 L.Ed.2d 228 (1957), modification and reh. denied 355 U.S. 937, 78 S.Ct. 410, 2 L.Ed.2d 419 (requirement of registration of convicted felons violates due process when applied to person with no knowledge of requirement). On the "reasonably definite and certain" requirement, see generally Chapter 10 *supra.*

[34] See City of Chicago v. Berg, 48 Ill.App.2d 251, 199 N.E.2d 49 (1964); City of Chicago v. Lord, 3 Ill.App.2d 410, 122 N.E.2d 439 (1954), aff'd 7 Ill.2d 379, 130 N.E.2d 504; City of Milwaukee v. Burns, 225 Wis. 296, 274 N.W. 273 (1937). Cf. State v. Beery, 198 Minn. 550, 270 N.W. 600 (1936) (trial judge has wide discretion in deciding whether witness has privilege of silence due to privilege against self-incrimination—here no such privilege); City of Seattle v. Hawley, 13 Wn.2d 357, 124 P.2d 961 (1942) (reference to failure of accused to testify in his own behalf violated his constitutional rights). Similarly, ordinances creating a presumption of an accused person's guilt, rebuttable *only* by that person's own testimony, have been invalidated, even where ordinance prosecutions are considered civil in nature. See People v. Hoogy, 277 Mich. 578, 269 N.W. 605 (1936). On presumptions, see also note 37 *infra* and accompanying text.

Constitutional bans on cruel and unusual punishment have also been held applicable to ordinance-prosecutions. See Edwards & Browne Coal Co. v. Sioux City, 213 Iowa 1027, 240 N.W. 711 (1932); Town of Montclair v. Stanoyevich, 6 N.J. 479, 79 A.2d 288 (1951); Mayor & Council of Hoboken v. Bauer, 26 N.J.Misc. 1, 55 A.2d 883 (1947), aff'd 137 N.J.L. 327, 59 A.2d 809 (1948).

The double jeopardy ban of the Fifth Amendment was applied to the states in Benton v. Maryland, 395 U.S. 784, 89 S.Ct. 2056, 23 L.Ed.2d 707 (1969), on remand 8 Md.App. 388, 260 A.2d 86. And in Waller v. Florida, 397 U.S. 387, 90 S.Ct. 1184, 25 L.Ed.2d 435 (1970), reh. denied 398 U.S. 914, 90 S.Ct. 1684, 26 L.Ed.2d 79, appeal after remand 270 So.2d 26, cert. denied 414 U.S. 945, 94 S.Ct. 256, 38 L.Ed.2d 168, it was held that a state and a municipality could not both prosecute a person for the same conduct, even though that conduct might constitute a violation of both state and local law. Clearly, this means that a person punished for particular conduct by a state, or acquitted by the state of charges based thereon, cannot subsequently be prosecuted by a municipality for that same conduct in a jurisdiction treating ordinance-violations as criminal in nature. And in such jurisdictions, the municipality could not appeal from a trial-court acquittal in situations where it is the municipality, rather than the state, that prosecutes for the conduct. It seems that, in light of the *Benton* and *Waller* cases *supra*, this same result should now occur even in jurisdictions treating ordinance-prosecutions as "civil" in nature. See Kansas City v. Bott, 509 S.W.2d 42 (Mo.1974) (double jeopardy clause applies to violations of municipal ordinances even if penalty does not exceed imprisonment for 6 months and there is no right to jury trial). On application of the rule against double jeopardy to state and local prosecutions, see generally Section 6.8, and Chapter 7, *supra.*

[35] See City of Portland v. City of Bangor, 65 Me. 120 (1876); Delaney v. Police Court, 167 Mo. 667, 67 S.W. 589 (1902).

[36] Thus, a judge should be disqualified if he has any pecuniary or proprietary interest that will be directly affected by the judgment to be rendered, or if he stands to gain from a particular judgment he might render—as where his salary is paid by fines assessed against those convicted. Tumey v. Ohio, 273 U.S. 510, 47 S.Ct. 437, 71 L.Ed. 749 (1927); Meyer v. City of San Diego, 121 Cal. 102, 53 P. 434 (1898). See Mayor of

presumptions cannot be used to convict a person of an ordinance violation;[37] and there is now authority that due process requires that an indigent defendant accused of an ordinance violation be furnished with legal counsel.[38]

§ 24.4 Local Controls on Breaches of the Peace, Drunkenness, and Firearms

Three types of municipal ordinance that have been of particular importance in attempts to "keep the peace" are breach-of-the peace ordinances, public drunkenness restrictions, and firearm controls.

Breach-of-the-peace ordinances have been held constitutional if their coverage is clearly delineated and if they are applied only to persons who have actually disturbed the peace or created a clear and present danger of such a disturbance.[39] Under general breach-of-the-peace ordinances or more specific ones, a municipality may punish those who disrupt a lawful meeting of the municipality's governing body.[40] Words which "by their very utterance inflict injury or tend to incite an immediate breach of the peace" are called "fighting words" and are beyond the scope of constitutional protection.[41] But an

---

Montezuma v. Minor, 73 Ga. 484 (1884). Cf. Ward v. Village of Monroeville, 409 U.S. 57, 93 S.Ct. 80, 34 L.Ed.2d 267 (1972) (mayor's court provided a large part of village's income, for which mayor held responsible; mayor held not an impartial judge). If the judge's salary is paid regardless of whether or not he convicts, or of how many persons he convicts, the basic system will usually be upheld. See Dugan v. Ohio, 277 U.S. 61, 48 S.Ct. 439, 72 L.Ed. 784 (1928).

[37] See City of St. Louis v. Cook, 359 Mo. 270, 221 S.W.2d 468 (1949); People v. Marcello, 25 N.Y.S.2d 533 (Mag.Ct.1941); City of Seattle v. Stone, 67 Wn.2d 886, 410 P.2d 583 (1966), appeal after remand 71 Wn.2d 905, 426 P.2d 604. The usual presumption of an accused person's innocence unless proven guilty beyond a reasonable doubt must here apply. See In re Wong Hane, 108 Cal. 680, 41 P. 693 (1895). Presumptions of a person's guilt that can be rebutted only by that person's testifying have been invalidated as in conflict with the rule against requiring self-incrimination. See note 34 *supra.*

[38] Application of Stevenson, 254 Or. 94, 458 P.2d 414 (1969) (calling right to counsel more essential to fair trial than right to jury). See Argersinger v. Hamlin, 407 U.S. 25, 92 S.Ct. 2006, 32 L.Ed.2d 530 (1972), noted 41 Fordham L.Rev. 722 (1973); 47 Tulane L.Rev. 446 (1973); 25 Vand.L.Rev. 1260 (1972), holding that due process requires that indigent defendant in misdemeanor cases, as well as felony prosecutions, must have counsel provided by the state where deprivation of liberty might result from a conviction; this clearly necessitates the supplying of counsel wherever an ordinance violation is deemed a misdemeanor *and* conviction may result in incarceration of any kind. The *Stevenson* case, *supra*, seems to go even beyond this, and requires appointment of such counsel wherever a person is deprived of his liberty. See generally Criminal Law, Constitutional Law—Right to Counsel for the Indigent Misdemeanant, 9 Washburn L.J. 469 (1970).

[39] City of Chicago v. Hunt, 374 Ill. 234, 29 N.E.2d 86 (1940); Town of Ponchatoula v. Bates, 173 La. 824, 138 So. 851 (1931); City of Cleveland Heights v. Christie, 128 Ohio St. 297, 190 N.E. 770 (1934), cert. denied 293 U.S. 574, 55 S.Ct. 86, 79 L.Ed. 672 (1934). Some ordinances are limited in application to punishing those who disturb the peace in or near educational institutions; these also have been sustained. Grayned v. City of Rockford, 408 U.S. 104, 92 S.Ct. 2294, 33 L.Ed.2d 222 (1972) (applicable to disturbances on public or private grounds adjacent to any building in which a school or class is in session); McAlpine v. Reese, 309 F.Supp. 136 (E.D.Mich.1970) (applicable to disturbances of the peace or good order of any school). But cf. Brown v. Louisiana, 383 U.S. 131, 86 S.Ct. 719, 15 L.Ed.2d 637 (1966) (protesting blacks who quietly "sat-in" a public library could not be convicted of breach of peace).

[40] State v. Guy, 196 Neb. 308, 242 N.W.2d 864 (1976) (ordinance sustained as not unduly vague).

[41] Chaplinsky v. New Hampshire, 315 U.S. 568, 62 S.Ct. 766, 86 L.Ed. 1031 (1942). See, invalidating particular breach-of-the-peace ordinances as vague and overly broad, Gooding v. Wilson, 405 U.S. 518, 92 S.Ct. 1103, 31 L.Ed.2d 408 (1972) ("opprobrious words or abusive language tending to cause a breach of the peace"); Cox v. Louisiana, 379 U.S. 536, 85 S.Ct. 453, 13 L.Ed.2d 471 (1965) (ordinance made it unlawful to "agitate, to arouse from a state of repose, to molest, to interrupt, to hinder, to disquiet"). Cf. Henry v. Rock Hill, 376 U.S. 776, 84 S.Ct. 1042, 12 L.Ed.2d 79 (1964) (speech cannot be punished merely because it stirs people to anger or brings about unrest). On cases invalidating ordinances for overbreadth and/or vagueness, see generally Chapter 10 *supra.*

ordinance that punishes constitutionally protected, as well as unprotected, speech will be struck down for over-breadth;[42] and a breach-of-peace ordinance that does not clearly define the prohibited conduct will be invalidated as in violation of due process—for instance, an ordinance prohibiting public display of any symbol, etc. that is likely to provoke a riot or breach of the peace.[43]

---

[42] Lewis v. New Orleans, 415 U.S. 130, 94 S.Ct. 970, 39 L.Ed.2d 214 (1974) (invalidating an ordinance making it a breach of the peace for anyone wantonly to curse, revile, or use obscene or opprobrious language toward or with reference to an on-duty city police officer). See note 41 *supra* and cases cited therein. Cf. Hill v. City of Houston, 764 F.2d 1156 (5th Cir.1985), on reh. 789 F.2d 1103 (5th Cir.1986) (ordinance that prohibited any interference with a police officer in the execution of his duty affected a substantial range of protected speech and was thus facially overbroad and unconstitutional). The Supreme Court affirmed the Fifth Circuit holding. City of Houston v. Hill, 482 U.S. 451, 107 S.Ct. 2502, 96 L.Ed.2d 398 (1987) (ordinance held substantially overbroad and thus invalid on its face under First Amendment). See also note 41 *supra*.

[43] People v. Young, 136 Cal.App. 699, 29 P.2d 440 (Dist.Ct.1934). See Cox v. Louisiana, *supra* note 41. Persons who create undue noise within a municipality are sometimes convicted of breaching the peace. See City of Louisiana v. Bottoms, 300 S.W. 316 (Mo.App.1927) (ordinance against shouting and disturbing the peace upheld). On municipal restrictions on noise, see generally Section 23.10 *supra*.

In an effort to preserve peace and order, some communities have imposed curfews prohibiting persons under a specified age from being on the streets after a designated hour. Such laws have usually been upheld if the restriction is reasonable in nature and for a legitimate municipal purpose. See In re Nancy C., 28 Cal.App.3d 747, 105 Cal.Rptr. 113 (Dist. Ct. 1972) (no unreasonable interference with personal rights); Chicago Park Dist. v. Altman, 127 Ill.App.2d 467, 262 N.E.2d 373 (1970) (reasonable exercise of park district's power); Thistlewood v. Trial Magistrate, 236 Md. 548, 204 A.2d 688 (1964) (ordinance forbidding minors from being on streets between midnight and 6 a.m. on Labor Day weekend was reasonable); City of Eastlake v. Ruggiero, 7 Ohio App.2d 212, 220 N.E.2d 126 (1966) (reasonable curfew as to minors). But see Alves v. Justice Court, 148 Cal.App.2d 419, 306 P.2d 601 (Dist. Ct. 1957) (curfew found an unreasonable invasion of personal liberty of citizens); Ex parte McCarver, 39 Tex. Cr. R. 448, 46 S.W. 936 (1898) (same). Cf. Johnson v. City of Opelousas, 658 F.2d 1065 (5th Cir.1981) (curfew infringed on rights of minors and parents). See generally Privor, Dusk 'til Dawn: Children's Rights and the Effectiveness of Juvenile Curfew Ordinances, 79 Boston U.L. Rev. 415 (1999); Note, Juvenile Curfews: Protection or Regulation?, 14 N.Y.L. Sch. J. Hum. Rts., 677 (1998); Note, Curfew Ordinances and the Control of Nocturnal Juvenile Crime, 107 U. Pa. L. Rev. 66 (1958). See also "Is Curfew the Cure?," Newsweek, Sept. 6, 1971, at 36. Curfews applicable to *all* persons, not just minors, will also usually be upheld if reasonable. See City of Portland v. Ledwidge, 50 Or.App. 355, 622 P.2d 1150 (1981) (upholding ordinance making it unlawful to be in a specified city park during certain hours). But many curfews have been aimed particularly at teenagers. See Note, Rethinking Judicial Attitudes Toward Freedom of Association Challenges to Teen Curfews: The First Amendment Exception Explored, 78 N.Y.U.L. Rev. 2278 (2003); Rawe, Bye-Bye Mall Rats, Time, July 9, 2007, at 41 (saying that a number of shopping malls now eject teenagers at 6 p.m. on Fridays and Saturdays unless they are with a parent or guardian). See generally Comment, The Government Is Establishing Your Child's Curfew, 21 St. John's J. Legal Comment 797 (2007). Curfews are one of the tools used by some communities in an effort to curtail gang violence. See Note, Achieving Peace in the Streets: How Legislative Efforts Fail in Combating Gang Violence in Comparison to Successful Local Community-based Initiatives, 35 New Eng. J. on Crim. & Civ. Confinement 243 (2009). In Ohio Citizen Action v. City of Englewood, 671 F.3d 564 (6th Cir 2012), a curfew on door-to-door soliciting between 6 p.m. and 9 a.m. was found an unconstitutional violation of free speech rights because it was not narrowly tailored to protect privacy, prevent crime, or conserve public resources.

An even more extreme step that, as a last resort, may be taken in order to preserve public order is the imposition of martial law and/or the calling-out of the National Guard by state or federal authorities. See Wiener, Martial Law Today, 49 Military L. Rev. 89 (1970) (especially note the discussion of the use of military forces in urban riots of 1967 and 1968, at 103); Note, Constitutional Law—Martial Law—Preserving Order in the State: A Traditional Reappraisal, 75 W. Va. L. Rev. 143 (1972). See generally Dennison, Martial Law: The Development of a Theory of Emergency Powers, 1776–1861, 18 Am. J. Leg. History 52 (1974); University of Colorado Law Revision Center, A Comprehensive Study of the Use of Military Troops in Civil Disorders with Proposals for Legislative Reform, 43 U. Colo. L. Rev. 399 (1972). See also Comment, Executive Military Power: A Path to American Dictatorship, 54 Neb. L. Rev. 111 (1975).

Localities can punish public drunkenness if (1) the state has not pre-empted the field,[44] and (2) the definition of the prohibited acts is reasonably definite and certain.[45] So far, statutes and ordinances punishing public drunkenness have withstood attacks alleging that, at least as applied to chronic alcoholics, such laws result in cruel and unusual punishment and/or deprivation of due process,[46] the theories being that such laws are necessary to the public welfare and that they punish behavior, not a status.

Historically, some gun-control ordinances of local governments have been sustained.[47] Ordinances have been upheld that generally forbid the discharge of firearms

---

[44] In re Koehne, 59 Cal.2d 646, 30 Cal.Rptr. 809, 381 P.2d 633 (1963) (ordinance making it a crime to be intoxicated in public place or place open to public view void due to state pre-emption). See People v. Lopez, 59 Cal.2d 653, 30 Cal.Rptr. 813, 381 P.2d 637 (1963) (since state had pre-empted field of regulation of criminal aspects of being intoxicated in public place, could be no prosecution under conflicting ordinance); In re Zorn, 59 Cal.2d 650, 30 Cal.Rptr. 811, 381 P.2d 635 (1963) (barber shop was "public place" within state statute preempting regulation of public intoxication). But see Ex parte Boza, 41 Cal.App.2d 25, 106 P.2d 29 (Dist.Ct.1940) (upholding ordinance making it unlawful to be intoxicated in public place or any place open to public view); Town of Bloomfield v. Trimble, 54 Iowa 399, 6 N.W. 586 (1880) (both state and city may have laws against drunkenness); People v. Johnson, 12 Mich.App. 139, 162 N.W.2d 667 (1968) (finding no conflict between ordinance and state law; so ordinance valid).

[45] See Quittner v. Thompson, 309 F.Supp. 684 (S.D.Fla.1970).

[46] See Powell v. Texas, 392 U.S. 514, 88 S.Ct. 2145, 20 L.Ed.2d 1254 (1968), reh. denied 393 U.S. 898, 89 S.Ct. 65, 21 L.Ed.2d 185 (1968) (but decision was 5 to 4, and Justice White, who cast the "swing" vote, indicated in his concurring opinion that punishment would be impermissible if defendant where shown to be a chronic alcoholic who could not resist drunkenness and subsequent appearance in public; *id.* at 548); City of Portland v. Juntunen, 6 Or.App. 632, 488 P.2d 806 (1971); City of Seattle v. Hill, 72 Wn.2d 786, 435 P.2d 692 (1967), cert. denied 393 U.S. 872, 89 S.Ct. 163, 21 L.Ed.2d 142 (with strong dissent). But cf. Easter v. District of Columbia, 361 F.2d 50 (D.C.Cir.1966) (chronic alcoholism is not itself a crime, and is a defense to charge of public intoxication; chronic alcoholic may be committed for treatment, but not punished for his alcoholism). See generally, predicting adoption of the "alcoholism defense," Nimmer, Court-Directed Reform of Vagrancy-Type Laws, 54 Am. Judicature 50, 53–54 (1970).

A notable controversy has concerned the validity, under the Fourth Amendment of the U.S. Constitution, of programs involving the stopping of motorists at checkpoints in order to detect intoxicated drivers. Most courts have upheld the validity of these operations. See, *e.g.*, State v. Pima County Superior Court, 143 Ariz. 45, 691 P.2d 1073 (1984); Ingersoll v. Palmer, 43 Cal.3d 1321, 241 Cal.Rptr. 42, 743 P.2d 1299 (1987); People v. Bartley, 109 Ill.2d 273, 93 Ill.Dec. 347, 486 N.E.2d 880 (1985), cert. denied 475 U.S. 1068, 106 S.Ct. 1384, 89 L.Ed.2d 608 (1986); Commonwealth v. Trumbull, 396 Mass. 81, 483 N.E.2d 1102 (1985); People v. Scott, 63 N.Y.2d 518, 483 N.Y.S.2d 649, 473 N.E.2d 1 (1984); State v. Alexander, 22 Ohio Misc.2d 34, 489 N.E.2d 1093 (1985); Lowe v. Commonwealth, 230 Va. 346, 337 S.E.2d 273 (1985), cert. denied 475 U.S. 1084, 106 S.Ct. 1464, 89 L.Ed.2d 720 (1986), Contra, State v. Muzik, 379 N.W.2d 599 (Minn. App. 1985); City of Seattle v. Mesiani, 110 Wash.2d 454, 755 P.2d 775 (1988) (city program). Cf. State v. Jones, 483 So.2d 433 (Fla.1986) (particular program invalidated, but court indicates possible approval of future programs meeting specified standards); Webb v. State, 695 S.W.2d 676 (Tex.App.1985), aff'd 739 S.W.2d 802 (Tex.Crim.App.1987) (stop at roadblock designed to detain all traffic in order to screen-out intoxicated drivers held unreasonable in absence of specific standards). The U.S. Supreme Court upheld the general constitutionality of highway sobriety check-point programs in Michigan Dep't of State Police v. Sitz, 496 U.S. 444, 110 S.Ct. 2481, 110 L.Ed.2d 412 (1990), on remand 193 Mich.App. 690, 485 N.W.2d 135 (1992), aff'd 443 Mich. 744, 506 N.W.2d 209 (1993). But cf. City of Indianapolis v. Edmond, 531 U.S. 32, 121 S.Ct. 447, 148 L.Ed.2d 333 (2000), where the court held that the city's drug interdiction checkpoint program was not justified by the lawful secondary purposes of keeping impaired motorists off the road and verifying licenses and registrations, if the primary purpose was narcotics detection. Violation of the Fourth Amendment was found.

[47] See Suter v. City of Lafayette, 57 Cal.App.4th 1109, 67 Cal.Rptr.2d 420 (Ct. App. 1997) (city had power to regulate sale, lease, or transfer of firearms); Township of Chester v. Panicucci, 62 N.J. 94, 299 A.2d 385 (1973) (ordinance banned possession of loaded gun within 300 feet of any dwelling or 400 feet of a school playground); People v. Judiz, 38 N.Y.2d 529, 381 N.Y.S.2d 467, 344 N.E.2d 399 (1976) (sale or possession of toy or imitation pistols covered; court says local ordinance entitled to same presumption of constitutionality as is a state law on the subject); City of Portland v. Bingham, 3 Or.App. 430, 474 P.2d 15 (1970) (unlawful to possess firearm unless ammunition removed and firing mechanism disassembled). It has been held that *reasonable* gun-control ordinances do not infringe on citizens' rights under the Second Amendment to the Federal Constitution. Brown v. City of Chicago, 42 Ill.2d 501, 250 N.E.2d 129 (1969); Photos v. City of Toledo,

throughout the city,[48] or that forbid such discharge in designated areas.[49] Prohibitions on possession of a firearm in a public place have been sustained,[50] as have registration

---

19 Ohio Misc. 147, 250 N.E.2d 916 (Ohio Ct.Pl.1969). See Comment, Constitutional Limitations on Firearms Regulation, 1969 Duke L.J. 775. Cf. City of Tucson v. Rineer, 193 Ariz. 160, 971 P.2d 207 (Ariz.App.1998) (city ordinance which prohibited use or possession of firearms within city parks held not to violate right to bear arms under state constitution). See generally Note; Firearms: Problems of Control, 80 Harv.L.Rev. 1328 (1967); Annot., Validity and Construction of Gun Control Laws, 28 A.L.R.3d 845 (1969). See also Annots., Constitutionality of Statutes Restricting Right of Aliens to Bear Arms, 34 A.L.R. 63 (1925); 24 A.L.R. 1119 (1923). For historical background, see Bellesiles, Gun Laws in Early America: The Regulation of Firearms Ownership, 1607–1794, 16 Law & Hist. Rev. 567 (1998). Most cases on the validity of firearms restrictions do turn on the question of violation of the Second Amendment. See Cramer, Johnson & Mocsary, "This Right Is Not Allowed by Governments That Are Afraid of the People": The Public Meaning of the Second Amendment When the Fourteenth Amendment Was Ratified, 17 Geo. Mason L. Rev. 823 (2010); Gulasekaram, "The People" of the Second Amendment: Citizenship and the Right to Bear Arms, 85 N.Y.U. L. Rev 1521 (2010). And see the U.S. Supreme Court's striking down of some state and local gun restrictions due to conflict with the Second Amendment; see note 52 *infra*, discussing the *Heller* and *McDonald* cases. Those cases have brought much scholarship regarding the Second Amendment. See Sturzenegger, The Second Amendment's Fixed Meaning and Multiple Purposes, 37 So. Ill. U. L. J. 337 (2013). Cf. Magarian, Speaking Truth to Firepower: How the First Amendment Destabilizes the Second, 91 Tex. L. Rev. 49 (2012). See generally Note, Loaded Question: A Suggested Constitutional Framework for the Right to Keep and Bear Arms, 96 Minn. L. Rev. 2182 (2012). On municipal lawsuits against gun manufacturers by which the municipalities attempt to recover some of their losses due to gun violence, see Vandall, O.K. Corral II: Policy Issues in Municipal Suits Against Gun Manufacturers, 44 Villanova L. Rev. 547 (1999) (a city's ability to recover often hinges on whether city can prove the gun manufacturers' conduct was a substantial cause of city's damages); Comment, Targeting the Gun Industry: Municipalities Aim to Hold Manufacturers Liable for Their Products and Actions, 24 S. Ill. U.L.J. 595 (2000); Note, Recovering the Costs of Public Nuisance Abatement: The Public and Private City Sue the Gun Industry, 113 Harv. L. Rev. 1521 (2000). See generally Comment, What in the Wide, Wide World of Torts Is Going On? First Tobacco, Now Guns: An Examination of Hamilton v. Accu-tek and the Cities' Lawsuits Against the Gun Industry, 69 Miss. L.J. 521 (1999), discussing municipal suits against gun manufacturers in light of the settlement of suits by 41 states against tobacco-product manufacturers, recovering some of those states' Medicaid expenditures. See also Landau, Recent Legislation—State Bans on City Gun Lawsuits, 37 Harv. J. Legis. 623 (2000).

On the use of public nuisance lawsuits against gun manufacturers, compare Note, A More Powerful Plaintiff: State Public Nuisance Lawsuits Against the Gun Industry, 70 Geo. Wash. L. Rev. 212 (2002), with Comment, Municipalities Versus Gun Manufacturers: Why Public Nuisance Claims Just Do Not Work, 31 U. Baltimore L. Rev. 273 (2002). On municipal lawsuits against gun manufacturers, see generally Bhowmik, Aiming for Accountability: How City Lawsuits Can Help Reform an Irresponsible Gun Industry, 11 J.L. & Pol'y 67 (2002); Note, The Right of the People to Keep and Bear Arms Shall Not Be Litigated Away: Constitutional Implications of Municipal Lawsuits Against the Gun Industry, 77 Ind. L.J. 873 (2002). As to legislation limiting gun manufacturers' civil liability, see Note, Tort Law—Civil Immunity—Congress Passes Prohibition of Qualified Civil Claims Against Gun Manufacturers and Distributors, 119 Harv. L. Rev. 1939 (2006) (noting Protection of Lawful Commerce in Arms Act, Pub. L. #109–92, 119 Stat. 2095, 15 U.S.C. §§ 7901–03 & 18 U.S.C. §§ 922, 924 (2005)); Note, Arming the Gun Industry: A Critique of Proposed Legislation Shielding the Gun Industry from Liability, 88 Minn. L. Rev. 1346 (2004). On the use of product liability law to hold gun manufacturers or sellers liable for violence committed with guns, see generally Symposium, Guns as a Consumer Product: New Public Health and Legal Strategies to Reduce Gun Violence, 4 J. Health Care L. & Pol'y 1–158 (2000).

[48] State v. Horn, 197 Neb. 755, 250 N.W.2d 912 (1977).

[49] Township of Chester v. Panicucci, *supra* note 47.

[50] City of St. Paul v. Kekedakis, 293 Minn. 334, 199 N.W.2d 151 (1972). See Annot., Offense of Carrying Weapon on Person as Affected by Place Where Defendant Was at the Time, 73 A.L.R. 839 (1931). See generally Annot., Offense of Carrying Concealed Weapon as Affected by Manner of Carrying or Place of Concealment, 43 A.L.R.2d 492 (1955). Many states and localities have laws against carrying a concealed weapon in schools. See Note, Missouri Concealed Carry and Schools, 73 U.M.L.C.L. Rev. 1165 (2005), noting that, while firearms cannot generally be carried onto school property in Missouri, the punishment imposed for violation of this restriction is only a small fine, which is criticized as inadequate. See also as to "right to carry" laws note 54 *infra* and accompanying text.

It is sometimes alleged that limits on the carrying of guns have been more vigorously enforced in minority neighborhoods. See Gardner, Separate and Unequal: Federal Tough-on-Guns Program Targets Minority Communities for Selective Enforcement, 12 Mich. J. Race & L. 305 (2007).

requirements.[51] But a sweeping gun ban in Washington, D.C., was invalidated by the U.S. Supreme Court.[52] There is extensive federal regulation of certain firearms, but the

---

[51] Galvan v. Superior Court, 70 Cal.2d 851, 76 Cal.Rptr. 642, 452 P.2d 930 (1969); Brown v. City of Chicago, 42 Ill.2d 501, 250 N.E.2d 129 (1969). Cf. City of Chicago v. Franklin, 126 Ill.App.2d 43, 261 N.E.2d 506 (1970) (ordinance required special registration if firearm purchased from anyone other than a licensed firearm dealer; upheld). See also Annot., Application of Statute or Regulation Dealing with Registration or Carrying of Weapons to Transient Non-Resident, 68 A.L.R.3d 1253 (1976). Some communities have in the past experimented with sweeping bans on possession of firearms. See "Out Front on Arms Control," Time, Feb. 1, 1982, at 19, discussing the Morton Grove, Illinois, ordinance. This Morton Grove ordinance, banning possession of all operable handguns (with limited exceptions), was upheld as a valid exercise of the police power, under the Illinois Constitution, in Kalodimos v. Village of Morton Grove, 103 Ill.2d 483, 83 Ill.Dec. 308, 470 N.E.2d 266 (1984). Emphasizing that the municipality had home-rule powers, the court found that the ordinance bears a rational relationship to legitimate governmental interests of reducing weapons-related injuries and accidents. Accord as to the same ordinance, Quilici v. Morton Grove, 695 F.2d 261 (7th Cir.1982), cert. denied 464 U.S. 863, 104 S.Ct. 194, 78 L.Ed.2d 170 (1983), rejecting challenges based on the Second and Ninth Amendments to the U.S. Constitution. On other anti-handgun ordinances, see Note, Handgun Prohibition: A Comparison of the San Francisco and the Morton Grove Ordinances, 6 Crim. Just. J. 21 (1982): "Shot Down," Time, July 12, 1982; at 17. See generally Anderson, An Extraordinary People, The New Yorker, Nov. 12, 1984, at 109.

[52] This ban had been one of the most sweeping firearm bans in the United States. See Lund, D.C's Handgun Ban and the Constitutional Right to Arms: One Hard Question?, 18 George Mason U. Civil Rights L.J. 229 (2008). This was invalidated in District of Columbia v. Heller, 554 U.S. 570, 128 S.Ct. 2783, 171 L.Ed.2d 637 (2008) (statutes banning handgun possession in the home violated Second Amendment). See generally Kates & Michel, Local Gun Bans in California: A Futile Exercise, 41 U. San Francisco L. Rev. 333 (2007); Symposium on Firearms, the Militia and Safe Cities: Merging History, Constitutional Law and Public Policy, 1 Albany Govt. Law Rev. 250–515 (2008). The District of Columbia's handgun ban was first declared invalid by the District of Columbia Circuit Court of Appeals in Parker v. District of Columbia, 478 F.3d 370 (D. C. Cir. 2007). See Note, *Parker v. District of Columbia*: Understanding the Broader Implications for the Future of Gun Control, 6 Geo. J. L. & Pub. Pol'y 643 (2008). Cf. Zimring, Handgun Control, the Second Amendment, and Judicial Legislation in the D. C. Circuit: A Note on *Parker v. District of Columbia*, 11 New Crim. L. Rev. 312 (2008). The Supreme Court granted certiorari; 128 S.Ct. 645, 169 L.Ed.2d 417 (2007). In a 5–4 decision, the Court affirmed the judgment of the Court of Appeals, striking down the Washington, D.C. handgun ban. District of Columbia v. Heller, 554 U.S. 570, 128 S.Ct. 2783, 171 L.Ed.2d 637 (2008).

The *Heller* case has been analyzed from many angles. See de Leeuw, Ready, Aim, Fire? *District of Columbia v. Heller* and Communities of Color, 25 Harv. Black Letter L. J. 133 (2009); Dery, Unintended Consequences: The Supreme Court's Interpretation of the Second Amendment in *District of Columbia v. Heller* Could Water-down Fourth Amendment Rights, 13 J. L. & Soc. Change 1 (2010); Greene, *Heller* High Water? The Future of Originalism, 3 Harv. L. & Pol'y Rev. 325 (2009); Kaufman, The Second Amendment: An Analysis of *District of Columbia v. Heller*, 25 Touro L. Rev. 703 (2009); Note, Come and Take It: The Status of Texas Handgun Legislation After *District of Columbia v. Heller*, 61 Baylor L. Rev. 215 (2009); Note, What the Hell(er)? The Fine Print Standard of Review Under *Heller*, 29 N. Ill. U. L. Rev. 605 (2009); Note, Gun-shy Originalism: The Second Amendment's Original Purpose in *District of Columbia v. Heller*, 44 Suffolk U. L. Rev. 505 (2011). Two Symposia also contain useful articles: Symposium, The Second Amendment After *Heller*, 60 Hastings, L. J. 1203–1505 (2009), particularly Little, *Heller* and Constitutional Interpretation: Originalism's Last Gasp, 60 Hastings L. J. 1415 (2009); Symposium, The Second Amendment After *District of Columbia v. Heller*, 13 Lewis & Clark L. Rev. 315–432 (2009). As to the effect of *Heller* on college campuses, see Langhauser, Gun Regulation on Campus: Understanding *Heller* and Preparing for Subsequent Litigation and Legislation, 36 J. College & University L. 63 (2009).

Because the *Heller* case, *supra*, invalidated a law of the District of Columbia, it left in doubt the validity of similar handgun bans passed by states. But in McDonald v. City of Chicago, 561 U.S. 742, 130 S.Ct. 3020, 177 L.Ed.2d 894 (2010), the Court held—again in a 5–4 decision—that the Second Amendment right to keep and bear arms is fully applicable to the states, and local governments within the states, by virtue of the Fourteenth Amendment. Handgun bans in two Illinois cities were thus invalidated. Some viewed the combination of this case and the *Heller* case as making a fundamental change in constitutional law. See Merkel, *Heller* as Hubris, and How *McDonald v. City of Chicago* May Well Change the Constitutional World as We Know It, 50 Santa Clara L. Rev. 1221 (2010); Note, The Changing Landscape of Firearm Legislation in the Wake of *McDonald v. City of Chicago*, 34 Harv. J. L. & Pub. Pol'y 1117 (2011). Some viewed *McDonald* as wrongly decided. See Note, Shooting Blanks: The Supreme Court's Flawed Analysis in *McDonald v. City of Chicago*, 66 U. Miami L. Rev. 197 (2011). Cf. Note, The Right Thing for the Wrong Reasons? The Incorporation of the Second Amendment in *McDonald v. City of Chicago*, 9 Ave Maria L. Rev. 335 (2011). And some view the *Heller* and *McDonald* cases as leaving the status of many firearm bans in a state of doubt. See Cohen, Jumping the Gun—As Second Amendment Advocates Celebrate a Court Decision, Its Impact Remains Hazy, Time magazine, July 12, 2010, at 23, noting that both cases "focused narrowly on people's right to use guns to protect themselves in their own homes." Cf. Comment, In Search of a Standard: Gun Regulation After *Heller* and *McDonald*, 70 Md. L. Rev. 1131 (2011). As to the *combined* effect of *Heller and* of *McDonald* on college campuses, see Wasserman, Gun Control on College and University Campuses in the Wake of *District of Columbia v. Heller* and *McDonald v. City of Chicago*, 19 Va. J. Soc. Pol'y & L. 1 (2011); Note, Guns on Campus: Continuing Controversy, 38 J. College & University L. 663 (2012).

As to the future of gun controls, see Sobel, The Tsunami of Legal Uncertainty: What's a Court to Do Post-*McDonald*?, 21 Cornell J. L. & Pub. Pol'y 489 (2012). Cf., applying *Heller*, United States v. Skoien, 614 F.3d 638 (7th Cir. 2010), noting that *Heller* indicates that some categorical prohibitions on possession of firearms will be allowed; the court thus upholds a statute disallowing an individual convicted of misdemeanor domestic violence from carrying a firearm. As to limits on the rights of mentally ill persons to carry firearms, see Record & Gostin, A Robust Individual Right to Bear Arms Versus the Public's Health: The Court's Reliance on Firearm Restrictions on the Mentally Ill, 6 Charleston L. Rev. 371 (2012); Vars & Young, Do the Mentally Ill Have a Right to Bear Arms?, 48 Wake Forest L. Rev. 1 (2013).

Many scholars have tried to predict the possible effects of *Heller* and/or *McDonald*. See Golimowski, Pulling the Trigger: Evaluating Criminal Gun Laws in a Post-*Heller* World, 49 Am. Crim. L. Rev. 1599 (2012). Some have looked to the history of our Constitution for help. See Miller, Text, History, and Tradition: What the Seventh Amendment Can Teach Us About the Second, 122 Yale L. J. 852 (2013). Cf. Note, History, *Heller*, and High-Capacity Magazines: What Is the Proper Standard of Review for Second Amendment Challenges?, 41 Fordham Urb. L. J. 1041 (2014). Some writers have concentrated on the effects on particular groups. See Comment, Keeping *Heller* Out of the Home: Homeowners Associations and the Right to Keep and Bear Arms, 15 U. Pa. J. Const. L. 1003 (2013). Or on the public health. See Dolce, To Keep and Bear Arms: Reconciling Firearms and the Public Health After *Heller* and *McDonald*, 15 Quinnipiac Health L. J. 155 (2011–12). Or on the law of self-defense. See Comment, In Defense of Self-Defense: *Heller*'s Second Amendment in Sensitive Places, 81 Miss. L. J. 1987 (2012). The treatment of the Supreme Court cases in lower courts has been studied. Symposium, A Second Amendment Quartet—*Heller* and *McDonald* in the Lower Courts, 71 Md. L. Rev. 1173–1230 (2012). As has the effect on laws allowing firearms to be openly carried in public, often called "open carry laws." See Frazer, Home, Sweet Home? The Second Amendment and the Right to Carry Firearms in Public, 4 Regent J. L. & Pub. Pol'y 1 (2012); Manley, Defining the Second Amendment Right to Carry: Objective Limits on a Fundamental Right, 14 Cooley J. Practical & Clinical L. 81 (2012). Cf. Comment, California's Unloaded Open Carry Bans: A Constitutional and Risky, But Perhaps Necessary, Gun Control Strategy, 61 UCLA L. Rev. 506 (2014). Even the effects of *Heller* on zoning officials have been analyzed. Boling & Denzin, When All *Heller* Breaks Loose: Gun Regulation Considerations for Zoning and Planning Officials Under the New Second Amendment, 44 Urban Law. 677 (2012), noting particularly the key exceptions listed in *Heller* (at 554 U.S. 626–27) for prohibitions on firearms for felons or the mentally ill, or near schools or government buildings.

federal statute specifically declares that it does not pre-empt the field.[53] Thus, there is possible room for local regulation—though occasionally, a *state* government may be found to have pre-empted the field in that jurisdiction.[54]

---

[53] 18 U.S.C.A. § 927. See Kreshesky v. Codd, 89 Misc.2d 439, 391 N.Y.S.2d 792 (1976). The basic federal firearms law is found at 18 U.S.C.A. §§ 921–28. See Zimring, Firearms and Federal Law: The Gun Control Act of 1968, 4 J.Legal Studies 133 (1975). A transfer tax on firearms is imposed by 26 U.S.C.A. §§ 5811–12. A tax on making firearms is imposed by 26 U.S.C.A. §§ 5821–22. A system for registering possession and transfers of certain firearms is established by 26 U.S.C.A. § 5841. The definitions of "firearms" and related terms are found in 26 U.S.C.A. § 5845. The registration provision of the federal law was sustained in United States v. Freed, 401 U.S. 601, 91 S.Ct. 1112, 28 L.Ed.2d 356 (1971), reh. denied 403 U.S. 912, 91 S.Ct. 2201, 29 L.Ed.2d 690, noted 57 A.B.A.J. 720 (1971). The provision authorizing the warrantless search of the premises of firearms dealers during business hours was sustained in United States v. Biswell, 406 U.S. 311, 92 S.Ct. 1593, 32 L.Ed.2d 87 (1972), noted 58 A.B.A.J. 746 (1972). The provision making it unlawful for a convicted felon to receive any firearm or ammunition which has been shipped in interstate or foreign commerce was applied in Barrett v. United States, 423 U.S. 212, 96 S.Ct. 498, 46 L.Ed.2d 450 (1976) (applied to felon's intrastate purchase of firearm that had previously been transported in interstate commerce from manufacturer to distributor and then from distributor to dealer). See generally, on this provision, Note, Prior Convictions and the Gun Control Act of 1968, 76 Colum.L.Rev. 326 (1976). See also Annot., Validity, Construction, and Application of Provision of Omnibus Crime Control and Safe Streets Act of 1968 Making It Federal Offense for Convicted Felon to Possess Firearm, 13 A.L.R.Fed. 103 (1972), noting a provision of the Omnibus Crime Control and Safe Streets Act of 1968—18 U.S.C.A.App. § 1202(a)(1)—which also deals with possession of firearms by felons.

On federal gun-control law, see generally Annot., Lawfulness of Sale or Other Disposition of Firearms or Ammunition Under 18 U.S.C. § 922(d), 34 A.L.R.Fed. 430 (1977); Annot., Validity, Construction, and Application of Provisions of Gun Control Act of 1968 and Implementing Regulations Relating to Firearms Registration and Recording Requirements Imposed Upon Federally Licensed Firearms Dealers, 33 A.L.R.Fed. 824 (1977). On enforcement of the federal law in municipalities, see Shannon, Have Gun? Will Travel, Time, Aug. 16, 1999, noting that in a number of cities those charged with certain crimes are being tried under federal statutes, which carry stiffer penalties than local laws usually do. For a comparison of U.S. laws with those in Canada, see Kopel, Canadian Gun Control: Should the United States Look North for a Solution to Its Firearms Problem?, 5 Temple Int'l & Comp. L.J. 1 (1991). As to Mexico's gun laws, see Kopel, Mexico's Gun-control Laws: A Model for the United States?, 18 Texas Rev. L. & Pol'y 27 (2013). See also Comment, Keep Off the Grass!: An Alternative Approach to the Gun Control Debate, 85 Ind. L. J. 1659 (2010).

In United States v. Lopez, 514 U.S. 549, 115 S.Ct. 1624, 131 L.Ed.2d 626 (1995), the federal Gun-Free School Zones Act was held invalid as in excess of Congress's power under the Commerce Clause. See generally Ching, Travelling Down the Unsteady Path: *United States v. Lopez, New York v. United States,* and the Tenth Amendment, 29 Loyola L.A.L. Rev. 99 (1995); Note, A *Lopez* Legacy?: The Federalism Debate Renewed, But Not Resolved, 17 N. Ill. U.L. Rev. 85 (1996). On the possible effects of the *Lopez* decision on jurisdiction over Indian tribes and Indian Country, see Garnett, Once More Into the Maze: *United States v. Lopez,* Tribal Self-Determination, and Federal Conspiracy Jurisdiction in Indian Country, 72 N.D.L. Rev. 433 (1996). In Printz v. United States, 521 U.S. 898, 117 S.Ct. 2365, 138 L.Ed.2d 914 (1997), the provisions of the federal Brady Handgun Violence Prevention Act of 1993 that required chief law enforcement officers in local jurisdictions to conduct background checks on prospective handgun purchasers were invalidated as imposing an unconstitutional obligation on state officers to execute federal laws. The Brady Law has been allowed to expire. For criticism of the current status of gun-control law in the United States, see Comment, Annie, Get Your Gun? An Analysis of Reactionary Gun Control Laws and Their Failure to Protect Americans From Violent Gun Crimes, 40 Southern Univ. L. Rev. 319 (2013). See also Note, Legal Judgment Day for the Rise of the Machines: A National Approach to Regulating Fully Autonomous Weapons, 56 Ariz. L. Rev. 1257 (2014), advocating Congressional passage of laws regulating such weapons.

[54] Schneck v. City of Philadelphia, 34 Pa.Cmwlth. 96, 383 A.2d 227 (1978). But see, finding no pre-emption, Galvan v. Superior Court, *supra* note 51; Junction City v. Lee, 216 Kan. 495, 532 P.2d 1292 (1975). On state gun-control legislation, see generally Annot., Validity of State Gun Control Legislation Under State Constitutional Provisions Securing the Right to Bear Arms, 86 A.L.R.4th 931 (1991). On what state and local controls on guns may still be allowed in light of the *Heller* and *McDonald* cases, *supra* note 52, see Blocher, Firearm Localism, 123 Yale L. J. 82 (2013). Cf. McCullough, Article 1 Section 13 of the Virginia Constitution: Of Militias and an Individual Right to Bear Arms, 48 U. Rich. L. Rev. 215 (2013); Note, State Legislatures Stand Up for Second Amendment Gun Rights While the U.S. Supreme Court Refuses to Order a Cease Fire on the Issue, 37 Seton Hall Legis. J. 411 (2013). An example of a gun-control law that has been upheld is found in Commonwealth of Massachusetts v. McGowan, 982 N. E. 2d 495 (Mass. 2013), where a state statute that required firearms to be rendered inoperable unless under the immediate control of the legal owner was ruled

not to violate the Second Amendment because it regulated conduct outside the amendment's scope and was rationally related to the state's interest in preventing unauthorized possession of firearms. Cf. Commonwealth of Massachusetts v. Reyes, 982 N. E. 2d 504 (Mass. 2013) (storage requirements as to firearms upheld). See also National Rifle Ass'n v. McCraw, 719 F.3d 338 (5th Cir. 2013) (state statutory scheme prohibiting 18–20 year olds from obtaining a license to carry handguns in public upheld); Peterson v. Martinez, 707 F.3d 1197 (10th Cir. 2013) (state statute banning non-residents from obtaining a concealed carry handgun license upheld).

With the prevalence of urban crime in recent times, many more city residents than previously have been arming themselves with guns, even when strict laws requiring permits are enacted. See "Record Number Ask Gun Permits in New York City," N.Y. Times, March 16, 1981, at 1, col. 5. See generally "The Duel over Gun Control," Time, March 23, 1981, at 33. See generally Kates, The Value of Civilian Handgun Possession as a Deterrent to Crime or a Defense Against Crime, 18 Am. J. Crim. L. 113 (1991). As to "right-to-carry" gun legislation, see generally Donohue, Guns, Crime, and the Impact of State Right-to-Carry Laws, 73 Fordham L. Rev. 623 (2004). See also note 50 *supra* and accompanying text.

Chapter 25

LOCAL CONTRACTUAL AND QUASI-CONTRACTUAL LIABILITY

Analysis

---

§ 25.1 Local Liability in Quasi-Contract

The contractual and the quasi-contractual liabilities of municipal corporations are overlapping topics, since whenever there is doubt as to the validity of a municipality's express, or implied-in-*fact*, contract, the question arises of the locality's possible liability in quasi-contract (an implied-in-*law* contract), or on some related theory. Thus, it is well to consider initially the basic principles governing a municipality's possible quasi-contractual liability, and related theories of liability. Then the requirements for, and limitations on, municipal contracts can be considered, and possible remedies where specific requirements have not been met can be discussed in more detail.

As with an individual or private corporation, a municipality can be held liable on an unjust enrichment theory for the reasonable value of goods provided or services performed, so long as the municipality has accepted the benefits of those goods or services. The law infers from the circumstances a promise to pay "quantum meruit"—the actual value.[1] Four requirements are usually applicable in such situations:[2] (1) Funds or materials must have been furnished, or services rendered, the municipality in order for it to become liable in quasi-contract. (2) These funds, materials, and/or services

---

[1] See City of Ingleside v. Stewart, 554 S.W.2d 939 (Tex.Civ.App.1977), ref. n.r.e. The distinction between an implied-in-law contract (or "quasi-contract") and an implied-in-fact contract is well discussed in Cameron, to Use of Cameron v. Eynon, 332 Pa. 529, 3 A.2d 423 (1939): Quasi-contract arises when the *law* imposes an obligation on a person, not because of any promise on his part, and perhaps even contrary to his intentions. It is a fictional creation. An implied-in-fact contract is a real agreement; the parties have agreed on the obligations they will incur, but their intention is not expressed in words, merely inferred from their acts.

[2] See the similar lists in City of Ingleside v. Stewart, *supra* note 1, at 943 (dividing the first requirement into two parts, and not listing the fourth—unjust enrichment—element); 1A Antieau, Municipal Corporation Law § 10.02, at 10–6 (1998), dividing the first requirement into two parts.

must have been accepted by the municipality. (3) This must have occurred under such circumstances as reasonably to inform the local government that the furnisher of the funds, goods, or services expected compensation in return from the locality. (4) The circumstances must be such that the local government would be unjustly enriched if it were not required to pay for what it has received. Quasi-contractual relief can be granted even though the parties have absolutely no contract-in-fact, and did not even attempt to enter into one.[3] But it *is* essential to quasi-contractual recovery that plaintiff show that defendant was actually enriched at plaintiff's expense; there can be no recovery, for instance, if whatever was furnished by plaintiff was worthless.[4] And the burden is on plaintiff to show with reasonable definiteness the *extent* to which defendant was actually enriched by the goods or services.[5]

Although the enrichment of defendant may thus be considered the key factor in these situations, it is not enough in itself to justify recovery. The "enriching" funds, goods, or services must have been accepted by some official authorized to do so. A hospital's offer of services in connection with treatment of a wounded city police officer, together with the rendering of such services, will not make the city liable to pay unless some authorized city agent has accepted the hospital's offer.[6] And even acceptance will not create liability where the locality reasonably believed there would be no obligation to pay for what was offered, as where city officials had reason to think that certain services were being rendered by other city officers or employees, not for extra compensation, but as part of their normal work.[7] Benefits voluntarily conferred on a locality will not result in quasi-contractual relief.[8] The public interest in not having public money put to unauthorized or improper uses must also be balanced here; and thus money paid under an unconstitutional or invalid statute or ordinance has been treated

---

[3] See City of New York v. Davis, 7 F.2d 566 (2d Cir.1925); Beardsley v. Town of Nashville, 64 Ark. 240, 41 S.W. 853 (1897); State ex rel. Beckstrom v. Glenn, 144 Kan. 461, 61 P.2d 1354 (1936); Jones v. City of Lake Charles, 295 So.2d 914 (La.App.1974); Sommers v. Putnam County Board of Education, 113 Ohio St. 177, 148 N.E. 682 (1925).

[4] Henningson, Durham & Richardson v. Prochnow, 13 Ariz.App. 411, 477 P.2d 285 (1970) (plans submitted by an engineering firm to an improvement district were worthless). Cf. Cline v. Red Bank Utility District, 194 Tenn. 255, 250 S.W.2d 362 (1952) (no profit to defendant from transaction; so could be no unjust enrichment).

[5] See Warren Brothers Co. v. Metropolitan Government, 540 S.W.2d 243 (Tenn.App.1976) (only the contract rate was shown, not the actual value of the goods furnished). Cf. Coats v. Garrett, 283 S.W.2d 289 (Tex.Civ.App.1955) (claimant for services rendered must show amount of work actually done, that fees charged were reasonable and services necessary, and that city accepted the services and derived benefit therefrom).

[6] Trinity Hospital Association v. City of Minot, 76 N.W.2d 916 (N.D.1956). See New Jersey Car-Spring & Rubber Co. v. Jersey City, 64 N.J.L. 544, 46 A. 649 (1900) (no quasi-contract liability unless local governing body had knowledge of receipt of the goods or services). Cf. Storrs v. City of Manchester, 88 N.H. 139, 184 A. 862 (1936) (no *ratification* because no showing of acceptance; quantum meruit also rejected).

[7] Nash v. City of Knoxville, 108 Tenn. 68, 64 S.W. 1062 (1901). See City of Chicago v. A. R. Beck Lumber Co., 93 Ill.App. 70 (1901) (sidewalk ordered to be built without authority, through mistake of employee; no quantum meruit); City of Jeffersonville v. Louisville & Jeffersonville Steam Ferry Co., 27 Ind. 100 (1866) (see later proceeding sub nom. City of Jeffersonville v. The John Shallcross, 35 Ind. 19 (1870)); Kerr v. King County, 42 Wn.2d 845, 259 P.2d 398 (1953) (overtime work with no expectation county would have to pay for it; no liability). Cf. Chandler v. Washington Toll Bridge Authority, 17 Wn.2d 591, 137 P.2d 97 (1943) (plaintiff expected to be paid by another party; couldn't recover in quasi-contract from defendant-local government; any benefit to that government was incidental).

[8] See Eastern Gentilly Civic Association v. New Orleans Sewerage & Water Board, 127 So.2d 788 (La.App.1961) (land-owners who made voluntary contributions to induce city to extend sewer lines, knowing city had policy of extending lines as soon as fixed percentage of total cost was contributed, could not recover their contributions, although city refunded contributions of landowners who had contributed *after* installation).

as "voluntarily" paid, and therefore not subject to recovery in quasi-contract,[9] unless it can be shown to have been paid under duress or compulsion.[10]

While, as noted, quasi-contractual recovery may be available even though no actual contract between the parties has been attempted, such relief is also often available today where the locality has endeavored to make a contract but has failed to comply with the applicable statutory (or home-rule charter) requirements. It has been said that the availability of such relief is necessitated by principles of honesty, justice, and fair dealing[11] and to prevent the locality's enriching itself at the expense of innocent persons.[12] It would seem that the great majority of U.S. jurisdictions now recognize the possibility of such relief against a local government, though a few jurisdictions may cling to long-held policies against such recovery;[13] and there continue to be occasional cases in which a court must deny such recovery because state law prescribes that there be no relief of any kind where certain requirements of municipal contracts are not met, such as public-bidding requirements[14] or a requirement that no payment of extra compensation be made after services have been rendered.[15] Some cases have indicated

---

[9] Jenad, Inc. v. Village of Scarsdale, 38 Misc.2d 658, 238 N.Y.S.2d 156 (1963) (money said to have been voluntarily paid under mistake of law).

[10] See Newport Building Corp. v. City of Santa Ana, 210 Cal.App.2d 771, 26 Cal.Rptr. 797 (Dist.Ct.1962); Five Boro Electric Contractors Association, Inc. v. New York City, 12 N.Y.2d 146, 237 N.Y.S.2d 315, 187 N.E.2d 774 (1962).

[11] See Hudson City Contracting Co. v. Jersey City Incinerator Authority, 17 N.J. 297, 111 A.2d 385 (1955); Luzerne Township v. Fayette County, 330 Pa. 247, 199 A. 327 (1938); Trull v. Lobelville, 554 S.W.2d 638 (Tenn.App.1976); Memphis Gaslight Co. v. City of Memphis, 93 Tenn. 612, 30 S.W. 25 (1894); County of Angelina v. O'Quinn, 429 S.W.2d 211 (Tex.Civ.App.1968) (plainest principles of justice said to require paying of reasonable value); Sluder v. City of San Antonio, 2 S.W.2d 841 (Tex.Comm'n App.1928), reh. denied 9 S.W.2d 1032 (common honesty and fair dealing require that compensation be paid).

[12] See Bethune v. City of Mountain Brook, 293 Ala. 89, 300 So.2d 350 (1974), appeal after remand 336 So.2d 148; Normandy Estates Metropolitan Recreation Dist. v. Normandy Estates, Limited, 191 Colo. 292, 553 P.2d 386 (1976); Loomis v. Fifth School Dist., 109 Conn. 700, 145 A. 571 (1929); Rieth-Riley Constr. Co. v. Town of Indian Village, 138 Ind.App. 341, 214 N.E.2d 208 (1966); Coleman v. Bossier City, 305 So.2d 444 (La.1974) (if arrangement not malum in se, citizen acting in good faith should recover from city); Jones v. City of Lake Charles, 295 So.2d 914 (La.App.1974); Grand Forks County v. City of Grand Forks, 123 N.W.2d 42 (N.D.1963) (unjust-enrichment basis of recovery emphasized). The malum in se v. malum prohibitum distinction applied in the *Coleman* case, *supra*, has been applied by some other cases. See Blum v. City of Hillsboro, 49 Wis.2d 667, 183 N.W.2d 47 (1971), with good discussion of the quasi-contract and estoppel bases of recovery.

[13] Louisville Extension Water Dist. v. Sloss, 314 Ky. 500, 236 S.W.2d 265 (Ky.1951) (no recovery in Kentucky against a municipal corporation on theory of implied contract); Gugenheim v. City of Marion, 242 Ky. 350, 46 S.W.2d 478 (1932) (same). Ohio took this view for a long time, and their Court of Appeals still adhered to it in 1952. Village of Eastlake v. Davis, 94 Ohio App. 71, 114 N.E.2d 627 (1952). But their Supreme Court has said that quasi-contract recovery may at least be allowed against a municipal corporation where it has received *money by mistake*. Village of Indian Hill v. Atkins, 153 Ohio St. 562, 93 N.E.2d 22 (1950).

[14] Bluthenthal v. Town of Headland, 132 Ala. 249, 31 So. 87 (1901); Reams v. Cooley, 171 Cal. 150, 152 P. 293 (1915); W. W. Cook & Son v. City of Cameron, 144 Mo.App. 137, 128 S.W. 269 (1910); J. A. Kreis & Co. v. City of Knoxville, 145 Tenn. 297, 237 S.W. 55 (1921); City of Bristol v. Dominion National Bank, 153 Va. 71, 149 S.E. 632 (1929). See generally Annot., Liability of Municipality on Quasi-Contract for Value of Property or Work Furnished Without Compliance With Bidding Requirements, 33 A.L.R.3d 1164 (1970).

[15] Stratton v. City of Detroit, 246 Mich. 139, 224 N.W. 649 (1929); Carpenter Construction Co. v. City of Detroit, 229 Mich. 285, 200 N.W. 955 (1924). Cf. Bauer v. City of Newark, 7 N.J. 426, 81 A.2d 727 (1951) (no quasi-contract where had been no prior appropriation). In some jurisdictions, a requirement that local government contracts be in writing may be considered of such importance that no recovery, even in quasi-contract, will be allowed where the requirement is not followed. See Missouri International Investigators, Inc. v. City of Pacific, 545 S.W.2d 684 (Mo.App.1976). But if a locality receives benefits under such a contract and does in fact pay for them, it will usually not be permitted to *recover* the payments. See Bride v. City of Slater, 263 S.W.2d 22 (Mo.1953). This is in accord with the general rule that cities retaining benefits under contracts, and having made payments thereon, will not be allowed to recover their payments. See Culver ex rel. Longyear

that quasi-contractual relief is possible when merely "directory" procedures as to municipal contracts are not followed, but that such relief is unavailable when "mandatory" requirements are disobeyed; but any such distinction has proven largely unworkable.[16]

The traditional measure of recovery in quasi-contract is the actual value of the benefits received by the defendant (here, the locality).[17] But two qualifications to this rule should be added: (1) Courts have often allowed the recovery to be measured by the amount of work done by plaintiff, not the benefit to defendant, where completion of such work was prevented by court order, act of God or other disaster, or something else beyond the plaintiff's control.[18] (2) There is now some authority that—especially where the defendant-municipality has been the party chiefly at fault in not following prescribed methods for entering into a contract—the reasonable value of improvements supplied is a fairer measure of relief than the actual value to the locality.[19]

§ 25.2 Local Liability Based on Ratification or Estoppel

Besides quasi-contract, there are two other theories on which relief may be granted a party who entered a contract with a municipality, only to learn later that the contract itself is invalid due to failure to abide by some legal requirements. *Ratification* is possible so long as the contract was not totally beyond the power of the municipality.[20] This requires that those steps or procedures that were not, in the first instance, followed, now be observed. Thus, if the original contract was void because the mayor voted thereon when he was not eligible to do so, another meeting of the proper municipal body should be called; another vote taken, with the mayor this time *not* voting; and the contract can then be treated as ratified.[21] Sometimes ratification is impossible because the disobeyed

---

v. Brown, 259 Mich. 294, 243 N.W. 10 (1932); Schell City v. L.M. Rumsey Manufacturing Co., 39 Mo.App. 264 (1890); City of Fremont v. Dodge County, 130 Neb. 856, 266 N.W. 771 (1936). But see Miller v. McKinnon, 20 Cal.2d 83, 124 P.2d 34 (1942) (action to recover money wrongly paid by county was properly brought by taxpayer after district attorney refused to bring such action); Miller v. City of Martinez, 28 Cal.App.2d 364, 82 P.2d 519 (Dist.Ct.1938) (taxpayer could sue to recover amount paid by city without need for city to return the goods received). Cf. City of Pasadena v. Estrin, 212 Cal. 231, 298 P. 14 (1931) (city could repudiate improperly made contract, recover value of what it had delivered thereunder, and not be liable for its repudiation).

[16] See Tooke, Quasi-Contractual Liability of Municipal Corporations, 47 Harv. L.Rev. 1143, 1162 (1934).

[17] See Luther v. Wheeler, 73 S.C. 83, 52 S.E. 874 (1905) (saying that if money was squandered, there can be no recovery; and if money was used for buildings or enterprises not reasonably necessary, there can be no recovery beyond actual benefit); Shulse v. City of Mayville, 223 Wis. 624, 271 N.W. 643 (1937), noted 36 Mich.L.Rev. 855 (1937). It is often indicated that the "actual" value claimed cannot exceed a "reasonable" amount. See City of Mesquite v. Scyene Investment Co., 295 S.W.2d 276 (Tex.Civ.App.1956), refused n.r.e.; City of Breckenridge v. Stoker, 264 S.W.2d 511 (Tex.Civ.App.1954), refused n.r.e.

[18] See Young v. City of Chicopee, 186 Mass. 518, 72 N.E. 63 (1904) (burning of bridge prevented completion of repairs); Armitage v. Essex Construction Co., 88 N.J.L. 640, 96 A. 889 (1916) (contract set aside by judicial action).

[19] See Edwards v. City of Renton, 67 Wn.2d 598, 409 P.2d 153 (1965).

[20] See Blount v. Baker, 177 Ark. 1162, 9 S.W.2d 802 (1928); City of Oakland v. Key System, 64 Cal.App.2d 427, 149 P.2d 195 (Dist.Ct.1944); Cohen v. City of Henderson, 182 Ky. 658, 207 S.W. 4 (1918); Ketterer v. Independent School District, 248 Minn. 212, 79 N.W.2d 428 (1956); In re Niland, 193 N.Y. 180, 85 N.E. 1012 (1908); Dullanty v. Vaughn, 77 Wis. 38, 45 N.W. 1128 (1890). Cf. Genesis Health Club, Inc. v. City of Wichita, 285 Kan. 1021, 181 P.3d 549 (2008) (no ratification can make lawful a municipal contract which is beyond the scope of the corporate powers).

[21] Day v. City of Beatrice, 169 Neb. 858, 101 N.W.2d 481 (1960). See Crane v. Bennington School-District, 61 Mich. 299, 28 N.W. 105 (1886); Edwards v. Mettler, 268 Minn. 472, 129 N.W.2d 805 (1964) (municipality can ratify or adopt what it could have done to begin with); Houman v. Borough of Pompton Lakes,

prerequisites can no longer be supplied—as where a contract has already been let without the necessary preliminary steps, such as the advertising for and obtaining of bids.[22] Then, the contract is simply void, and the whole process of entering into a contract must be repeated, but with all the proper procedures this time being observed. Ratification may occur where the original contract was void because not entered into by an authorized agent of the municipality. Ratification under these circumstances requires that (1) the contract itself satisfies all legal requirements;[23] (2) the contractual arrangement was originally attempted by a person who *purported* to act in behalf of the municipality;[24] and (3) the ratification is by the proper municipal officials—those who could have validly made the agreement in the first place.[25]

---

155 N.J.Super. 129, 382 A.2d 413 (1977); Landers v. Board of Education, 45 N.M. 446, 116 P.2d 690 (1941). The ratification must follow the form and procedures by which the contract could have initially been concluded. See Los Angeles Dredging Co. v. City of Long Beach, 210 Cal. 348, 291 P. 839 (1930); Goin v. Board of Education, 298 Ky. 645, 183 S.W.2d 819 (1944); Ballagh Realty Co. v. Borough of Dumont, 111 N.J.L. 32, 166 A. 491 (1933) (mayoral approval required for original contract; would be required for ratification); Paul v. City of Seattle, 40 Wash. 294, 82 P. 601 (1905) (where contract could only have been entered into by ordinance, ordinance necessary to ratify); Ellerbe & Co. v. City of Hudson, 1 Wis.2d 148, 83 N.W.2d 700 (1957), reh. Denied 1 Wis.2d 148, 85 N.W.2d 663 (funds must be provided before contract ratified). But cf. City of Kenai v. Filler, 566 P.2d 670 (Alaska 1977) (formalities necessary for the original contract need not be followed in ratifying).

[22] See Zottman v. City & County of San Francisco, 20 Cal. 96 (1862) (advertisement for bids, before contracting, was required, plus publication of proposed ordinance letting the contract; contract made in disregard of these requirements could not be ratified; a famous case in its day); Seim v. Independent District of Monroe, 70 S.D. 315, 17 N.W.2d 342 (1945).

[23] Ratajczak v. Board of Education of Perth Amboy, 114 N.J.L. 577, 177 A. 880 (1935), aff'd 116 N.J.L. 162, 183 A. 214 (ratification of hiring of school janitor). See Johnson v. Hospital Service Plan of New Jersey, 25 N.J. 134, 135 A.2d 483 (1957) ("implied ratification" when proper officials knew about contract, services were being performed for a long time, and officials made no attempt to repudiate; estoppel also found). Cf. State v. O'Connell, 83 Wn.2d 797, 523 P.2d 872 (1974), supplemented 84 Wn.2d 602, 528 P.2d 988 (acceptance of services creates implied promise to pay therefor where agent making contract acted with apparent authority).

[24] In re Settlement of Hanson, 206 Minn. 371, 288 N.W. 706 (1939). But "adoption" of an originally invalid agreement has also sometimes been allowed, and this need not satisfy all the requirements of ratification; the original actor need not then have been purporting to act for the adopting locality. Adoption is really the formation of a new, independent contract, though the contract is normally identical in content with the one earlier attempted. See Baker v. City of Palo Alto, 190 Cal.App.2d 744, 12 Cal.Rptr. 425 (Dist.Ct.1961) (voters in referendum approved purchase of property by city official *after* original contract of purchase; re-execution of same contract was then permissible).

[25] School Administrative Dist. No. 3 v. Maine School Dist. Commission, 158 Me. 420, 185 A.2d 744 (1962). Ratification need not be express. It may be implied in words or conduct. See Farmers' State Bank v. School District, 134 Kan. 47, 4 P.2d 404 (1931); Board of Education v. News Dispatch Printing & Audit Co., 117 Okl. 226, 245 P. 884 (1926) (receiving and retaining benefits of contract); City of East Orange v. Board of Water Commissioners, 73 N.J.Super. 440, 180 A.2d 185 (1962), aff'd 40 N.J. 334, 191 A.2d 747 (intent to ratify may be inferred from failure to repudiate); Frank v. Board of Education, 90 N.J.L. 273, 100 A. 211 (Ct. Err. & App.1917) (intent to ratify may be inferred from failure to repudiate). The retention of benefits may itself sometimes be found to constitute an implied ratification. See City of New Britain v. Hancock, 34 Conn.Sup. 14, 373 A.2d 859 (1976). Cf. City of Houston v. Howe & Wise, 323 S.W.2d 134 (Tex.Civ.App.1959), refused n.r.e. (knowingly accepting engineering services and benefiting thereby). It has been said that at the time of ratification, the local governmental officials attempting to ratify must know all material facts or else must be acting in willing disregard of such facts. Beckley-Cardy Co. v. West Point Special School District No. 3, 209 Ark. 792, 192 S.W.2d 540 (1946).

In Chemical Bank v. Washington Pub. Power Supply Sys., 102 Wash.2d 874, 691 P.2d 524 (1984), cert. denied 471 U.S. 1065, 105 S.Ct. 2140, 85 L.Ed.2d 497 (1985), & cert. denied 471 U.S. 1075, 105 S.Ct. 2154, 85 L.Ed.2d 510 (1985), it was held that the state legislature did not ratify agreements among municipalities, public utility districts, and the Washington Public Power Supply System to participate in the construction of nuclear power plants where the legislature had merely enacted legislation regulating any such agreements but not specifically acknowledging the particular agreements. Unjust enrichment against the municipalities which had participated in the projects was also denied the holders of bonds issued to finance those projects,

Local governments, like other parties, may generally be *estopped* from denying their contracts if (1) the other party had a right to rely, and did rely, on the locality's action, to the detriment of that other party,[26] and (2) the local government received benefits from the other party's performance of the contract.[27] Thus, if a person is employed by the city, and the city leads that person to believe that his contract of employment is valid and accepts the benefits of his services, the city will be estopped to deny that the official who hired the person had proper authority to make such a contract of employment.[28] But estoppel will generally not be applied by the courts if the purported contract was totally beyond the power of the municipality,[29] or is found to be against the public policy of the state.[30]

§ 25.3 Local Power to Contract and Limits Thereon

What limits exist on a local government's powers to contract? Or, to ask the question in a different way, under what circumstances will a municipality's contract be void, so that any recovery by the other party must be on one of the above-stated theories (quasi-contract, ratification, or estoppel)? A locality has basically the same scope of power in entering into contracts that it enjoys as to engaging in activities in general. Thus, it has been said that a city's power to contract may result from (1) the inherent power of the city to perform indispensable acts, (2) express provisions of a state statute or the city's own home-rule charter, *or* (3) implication, where the power is incidental to authority

---

since the municipalities were found totally lacking in statutory authority to enter into the participation agreements.

[26] Turney v. Town of Bridgeport, 55 Conn. 412, 12 A. 520 (1888). See Alford v. City of Gadsden, 349 So.2d 1132 (Ala.1977); Summer Cottagers' Association v. City of Cape May, 19 N.J. 493, 117 A.2d 585 (1955); Boiles v. City of Abilene, 276 S.W.2d 922 (Tex.Civ.App.1955), error refused. See City of Houston v. Finn, 149 S.W.2d 1000 (Tex.Civ.App.1941), rev'd 139 Tex. 111, 161 S.W.2d 776, noted 20 Tex.L.Rev. 109 (1941).

[27] Hitchcock v. Galveston, 96 U.S. 341, 24 L.Ed. 659 (1877). See L. C. Eddy, Inc. v. City of Arkadelphia, 303 F.2d 473 (8th Cir.1962); Chisholm Water Supply Co. v. City of Chisholm, 205 Minn. 245, 285 N.W. 895 (1939) (city had received water for several years under the "contract"; estopped from denying its validity even though bidding requirements had not been met); City of Corpus Christi v. Gregg, 155 Tex. 537, 289 S.W.2d 746 (1956) (estoppel despite insufficient public notice inviting bids; estoppel said available when city acting in its *proprietary* capacity). Cf. Board of County Comm'rs v. DeLozier, 917 P.2d 714 (Colo.1996) (promissory estoppel claim against county not barred by Governmental Immunity Act, which barred claims that lie in tort; court distinguished promissory estoppel, such as claim involved here that was based on alleged promise to hire a person in the future, from equitable estoppel, which applies to misstatements of fact). Riddlestorffer v. City of Rahway, 82 N.J.Super. 423, 197 A.2d 883 (1964) (estoppel applied though required salary ordinance had not been enacted). In estoppel (or ratification), recovery is permitted based on the contract price, rather than the (often lesser) value of the benefits received by the defendant, as under quasi-contract. See Blum v. City of Hillsboro, 49 Wis.2d 667, 183 N.W.2d 47 (1971), where recovery was allowed on an "unjust enrichment" theory but not on an estoppel basis.

[28] Edwards v. City of Kirkwood, 147 Mo.App. 599, 127 S.W. 378 (1910). Cf. Stahelin v. Board of Education, 87 Ill.App.2d 28, 230 N.E.2d 465 (1967) (school district had received new school under contract; estopped from denying validity of contract); 405 Monroe Co. v. City of Asbury Park, 40 N.J. 457, 193 A.2d 115 (1963) (private party had been led to spend large amount preparing building for anticipated use by city).

[29] Cleveland School Furniture Co. v. City of Greenville, 146 Ala. 559, 41 So. 862 (1906); Incorporated City of Humboldt v. Knight, 255 Iowa 22, 120 N.W.2d 457 (1963); Jenkins v. City of Henderson, 214 N.C. 244, 199 S.E. 37 (1938); City of Nederland v. Callihan, 299 S.W.2d 380 (Tex.Civ.App.1957), refused n.r.e. (dictum). See Genesis Health Club, Inc. v. City of Wichita, 285 Kan. 1021, 181 P.3d 549 (2008) (municipality cannot be made liable either on theory of estoppel or implied contract where it had no capacity to make the contract or where it was made in express violation of law).

[30] See Carter County v. City of Elizabethton, 39 Tenn.App. 685, 287 S.W.2d 934 (1955) (city had no power to enter into agreement with county whereby city would contribute its capital outlay funds toward repayment of county school bonds in return for right to participate in any future special levy by county or school bond issue; estoppel would not be applied since agreement contrary to public policy).

that is expressly given.[31] Local governments are usually accorded, by statute or home-rule charter, a general power of entering into contracts; and this authority has been interpreted to be as wide as necessary to accomplish any purposes that are not ultra vires.[32] But what if an agreement entered into by a locality *is* found to be ultra vires—completely beyond its scope of power? It is generally agreed that there can be no recovery on such a contract;[33] no specific performance will be granted;[34] no relief in quasi-contract will be granted;[35] and no ratification or estoppel is possible.[36] Three explanations have been given for this extreme result: (1) Courts are afraid that otherwise municipalities would attempt to expand their powers by contract, rather than recognizing that any such expansion must come through legislation. (2) There is also fear of extravagance on the part of local governments if their power to contract is extended beyond the scope of other powers given them by express provision or clear implication. (3) A person dealing with a local government is considered under a duty to determine the extent of the locality's authority to contract.[37] Thus, the power of a local government to contract—even where clearly stated in state laws or home-rule charters—has become a "dependent power"—

---

[31] Femmer v. City of Juneau, 97 F.2d 649 (9th Cir.1938), quoting 3 McQuillin, Municipal Corporations 806–07 (2d ed. 1928). See Long v. City of Neenah, 128 Wis. 40, 107 N.W. 10 (1906) (fair construction should be given). Cf. Roy v. Hampton, 108 N.H. 51, 226 A.2d 870 (1967) (reasonable, and not a rigid, construction).

[32] See Carruth v. City of Madera, 233 Cal.App.2d 688, 43 Cal.Rptr. 855 (Dist.Ct.1965) (city may contract in order to carry out its express or implied powers; agreement under which city promised to furnish water and sewer mains for housing development was valid); Collins v. City of Eldorado, 122 S.W.2d 690 (Tex.Civ.App.1938), error refused. Cf. Florida Power & Light Co. v. City of Miami, 98 F.2d 180 (5th Cir.1938), cert. denied 305 U.S. 644, 59 S.Ct. 147, 83 L.Ed. 415 (general power given municipalities to contract, coupled with power to provide water or lights, may authorize city to contract for water or lights at a stated price for a limited time).

[33] See Thomas v. City of Richmond, 79 U.S. (12 Wall.) 349, 20 L.Ed. 453 (1870); Kane v. City of Marion, 251 Iowa 1157, 104 N.W.2d 626 (1960) (no declaratory relief); State ex rel. Mitchell v. City of Coffeyville, 127 Kan. 663, 274 P. 258 (1929) (quo warranto proceeding; held that city could not sublease its airport); Barlum Realty Co. v. Heggblom, 273 Mich. 56, 262 N.W. 647 (1935) (no garnishment); Fitzgerald v. Town of Magnolia, 183 Miss. 334, 184 So. 59 (1938); Sinclair Refining Co. v. Bergen County, 103 N.J.Super. 426, 247 A.2d 484 (1968); Moody v. Transylvania County, 271 N.C. 384, 156 S.E.2d 716 (1967); Jenkins v. City of Henderson, 214 N.C. 244, 199 S.E. 37 (1938) (ultra vires contract is wholly void and cannot be ratified by either party); Crocker v. Town of Manchester, 178 Tenn. 67, 156 S.W.2d 383 (1941); Mineral County Court v. Town of Piedmont, 72 W.Va. 296, 78 S.E. 63 (1913); Waisman v. Wagner, 227 Wis. 193, 278 N.W. 418 (1938). Injunctive relief is sometimes available to prevent a local government's entering into or performing an ultra vires contract. See McKaig v. Mayor & City Council of Cumberland, 208 Md. 95, 116 A.2d 384 (1955) (court of equity will restrain municipality from performing illegal or ultra vires contract that might injuriously affect a taxpayer's rights—but relief here refused).

[34] Wheeler v. City of Sault Ste. Marie, 164 Mich. 338, 129 N.W. 685 (1911). Cf. People ex rel. Plugger v. Township Board, 11 Mich. 222 (1863) (no mandamus to compel performance). In Red Dog Saloon v. Sedgwick County Bd. of Comm'rs, 29 Kan.App.2d 928, 33 P.3d 869 (2001), it was held that a city lacks authority to contract away its police power and that such a contract is ultra vires and unenforceable.

[35] See Hovey v. Wyandotte County, 56 Kan. 577, 44 P. 17 (1896); Edwards House Co. v. City of Jackson, 138 Miss. 644, 103 So. 428 (1925) (contract to purchase land void under debt-limit statute); Wells v. Town of Salina, 119 N.Y. 280, 23 N.E. 870 (1890); Bloomsburg Land Improvement Co. v. Borough of Bloomsburg, 215 Pa. 452, 64 A. 602 (1906); Town of Worland v. Odell & Johnson, 79 Wyo. 1, 329 P.2d 797 (1958) (funds turned over to municipality under ultra vires contract). This is considered the *majority* view. But there are cases to the contrary; see note 39 *infra* and accompanying text.

[36] Cleveland School Furniture Co. v. City of Greenville, 146 Ala. 559, 41 So. 862 (1906) (no estoppel); Lamar Bath House Co. v. City of Hot Springs, 229 Ark. 214, 315 S.W.2d 884 (1958), appeal dism'd 359 U.S. 534, 79 S.Ct. 1137, 3 L.Ed.2d 1028 (same); City of Oakland v. Key System, 64 Cal.App.2d 427, 149 P.2d 195 (Dist.Ct.1944) (not subject to ratification); Williams v. City of Fargo, 63 N.D. 183, 247 N.W. 46 (1933) (no estoppel).

[37] See 1A Antieau, Municipal Corporation Law § 10.03[1] (1998). On the duty of persons contracting with the local government to inquire, at their peril, into the power of the government to make that contract, see Duncan Parking Meter Corp. v. City of Gurdon, 146 F.Supp. 280 (W.D.Ark.1956).

depending on, and limited by, other powers of the locality; the authority to contract really confers no separate or additional authority at all. Three objections to this result have been raised:[38] (1) If the locality attempts to exceed its powers, the proper remedy of the state is an action in quo warranto, and this should be adequate to protect the state's interests. (2) If the local officials become extravagant, the remedy of the citizens is through the electoral process. (3) The average person contracting with the local government cannot possibly be aware of the vast body of law interpreting the scope of municipal powers—and certainly cannot be expected to forecast how courts will rule on unsettled questions as to such powers; therefore, such a person should not be denied all relief when he performs a contract with the locality that is eventually ruled outside the locality's power. Though the denial of all recovery on such a contract remains the majority view, a number of courts have now allowed quasi-contractual relief where the attempted contract did not violate any specific prohibition of law and was not against the public policy of the state.[39]

Aside from the basic "ultra vires" rule—that a locality's power to contract is limited by its other statutory and charter powers—, a local government's contractual authority is circumscribed by four other types of limitation: (1) Some contracts are specifically prohibited by law. (2) Some are considered contrary to public policy. (3) Valid contracts can only be made by authorized agents of the locality. (4) Valid contracts must be made according to the procedures specified by law. By constitution, statute, or home-rule charter, certain contracts are often specifically forbidden. There is no recovery on a contract made in violation of such a prohibition;[40] even the return of goods delivered under such an agreement may be denied by some courts.[41] For instance, prohibitions often exist as to municipalities entering into contracts with their own officers; such

---

[38] See 1A Antieau, *supra* note 37, § 10.03. On the availability to the state government of quo warranto to prevent a locality's exceeding its powers, see State ex rel. Mitchell v. City of Coffeyville, *supra* note 33.

[39] See Allen v. Intendant and Councilmen of La Fayette, 89 Ala. 641, 8 So. 30 (1890) (action of implied assumpsit possible if contract simply unauthorized, as opposed to situation where contract specifically prohibited by law or offensive to public policy; in latter situations, no recovery possible); Butts County v. Jackson Banking Co., 129 Ga. 801, 60 S.E. 149 (1908) (obligation to account for money received rests on principle of common honesty); Schipper v. City of Aurora, 121 Ind. 154, 22 N.E. 878 (1889) (municipality liable to extent of value it has received); Thompson v. Town of Elton, 109 Wis. 589, 85 N.W. 425 (1901). Cf. Womack-Rayburn Co. v. Town of Worthington, 262 Ky. 710, 91 S.W.2d 13 (1936) (liability possible against municipality if payment is not made out of tax money), noted 25 Geo.L.J. 758 (1937); 50 Harv.L.Rev. 531 (1937). And a couple qualifications to the general rule against quasi-contractual recovery should be noted: (1) If a municipality appears to have power, based on legislation, to enter into a contract but the legislation is later declared unconstitutional, recovery against the city for the value of what it has received is likely to be allowed. See City of Henderson v. Redman, 185 Ky. 146, 214 S.W. 809 (1919) (bonds for street improvements invalid because ordinance passed pursuant to unconstitutional statute; city nonetheless liable). (2) If the local government itself has transferred funds or property under an ultra vires contract, it may recover the subject matter. School District No. 9 v. McLintock, 255 Mich. 197, 237 N.W. 539 (1931); Chaska v. Hedman, 53 Minn. 525, 55 N.W. 737 (1893). Cf. Village of Fort Edward v. Fish, 156 N.Y. 363, 50 N.E. 973 (1898) (statute prohibited contracts for sale of municipal obligations at less than par; no recovery by private party on contract; local government could recover its payments thereunder).

[40] Edison Electric Co. v. City of Pasadena, 178 F. 425 (9th Cir.1910) (no quasicontract); General Electric Co. v. Town of Fort Deposit, 174 Ala. 179, 56 So. 802 (1911); Ensley v. J. E. Hollingsworth & Co., 170 Ala. 396, 54 So. 95 (1909) (no quasicontract); Bluthenthal v. Town of Headland, 132 Ala. 249, 31 So. 87 (1901) (no quasi-contract or other relief where contract was in specific violation of statute prohibiting purchases on credit); Hope v. City of Alton, 214 Ill. 102, 73 N.E. 406 (1905) (no estoppel); Capital Bridge Co. v. Saunders County, 164 Neb. 304, 83 N.W.2d 18 (1957) (with review of cases); City of Bristol v. Dominion National Bank, 153 Va. 71, 149 S.E. 632 (1929), noted 16 Va.L.Rev. 628 (1930) (no quasi-contract).

[41] See General Electric Co. v. Town of Fort Deposit, *supra* note 40.

contracts are then treated as totally void.[42] The same is usually true of contracts made in excess of a municipal debt limitation,[43] though a few courts have allowed recovery of property delivered, or purchased with funds delivered, under such an agreement.[44]

Common examples of contracts made in violation of public policy are those made for an unreasonable length of time, those that promise particular governmental action or that promise not to exercise governmental powers, and those that attempt to convey the powers of government to others. In all these situations, recovery is uniformly denied on the contract itself; and even recovery under quasi-contract, or related theories, is usually denied. Thus, agreements whose duration exceeds that specified by statute or charter are void to the extent the limit is exceeded, and no relief is generally possible for such period to the person having made the agreement with a locality.[45] As discussed in an earlier chapter,[46] the time limitation as to municipal contracts in the absence of a specific statutory or charter provision is simply a limit of reasonableness.[47] If the contract is

---

[42] Bjelland v. City of Mankato, 112 Minn. 24, 127 N.W. 397 (1910); Neisius v. Henry, 142 Neb. 29, 5 N.W.2d 291 (1942) (distinguishing contract that is result of illegal exercise of authorized power, which might be ratified or sued on in quantum meruit, from contract that is illegal due to statutory disqualification, as to which no recovery possible).

[43] Litchfield v. Ballou, 114 U.S. 190, 5 S.Ct. 820, 29 L.Ed. 132 (1885); Turney v. Town of Bridgeport, 55 Conn. 412, 12 A. 520 (1888) (no estoppel); City of Joliet v. Alexander, 194 Ill. 457, 62 N.E. 861 (1902); Niles Water-Works v. City of Niles, 59 Mich. 311, 26 N.W. 525 (1886); Palmer v. City of Albuquerque, 19 N.M. 285, 142 P. 929 (1914); Miller v. Mayor of New York, 3 Hun. (10 N.Y.) 35 (Sup.Ct.1874) (no estoppel); J.B. Klein Iron & Foundry Co. v. Board of County Commissioners, 178 Okl. 72, 61 P.2d 1055 (1936); Fairbanks-Morse Co. v. Geary, 59 Okl. 22, 157 P. 720 (1916).

[44] Shaw v. Board of Education, 38 N.M. 298, 31 P.2d 993 (1934); Moe v. Millard County School District, 54 Utah 144, 179 P. 980 (1919). Cf. Bailey v. Miller County, 24 Ga.App. 746, 102 S.E. 178 (1920) (rental value of property used by local government awarded private party). But some courts have denied even this type of relief. See Klein v. Board of County Commissioners, *supra* note 43; Municipal Security Co. v. Baker County, 39 Or. 396, 65 P. 369 (1901).

[45] See City of Clay Center v. Clay Center Light & Power Co., 78 Kan. 390, 97 P. 377, 97 P. 800 (1908); Marble v. Town of Clinton, 298 Mass. 87, 9 N.E.2d 522 (1937) (but contract for one year with option in private party to renew for another year held not to violate statutory limit of one year); Hunt v. Fenlon, 313 Mich. 644, 21 N.W.2d 906 (1946). But some authority has allowed quasi-contractual relief. See City of Providence v. Providence Electric Light Co., 122 Ky. 237, 91 S.W. 664 (1906). And the agreement is usually treated as valid for the length of the statutory period. Cartersville Improvement, Gas & Water Co. v. Mayor of Cartersville, 89 Ga. 683, 16 S.E. 25 (1892); Columbus Water Co. v. City of Columbus, 48 Kan. 99, 28 P. 1097 (1892); Town of Highlands v. Weyant, 38 A.D.2d 256, 329 N.Y.S.2d 58 (1972), appeal dism'd 30 N.Y.2d 948, 335 N.Y.S.2d 699, 287 N.E.2d 389; State ex rel. Attorney General v. Ironton Gas Co., 37 Ohio St. 45 (1881). But see Manhattan Trust Co. v. City of Dayton, 59 F. 327 (6th Cir.1893); City of Wellston v. Morgan, 59 Ohio St. 147, 52 N.E. 127 (1898) (contract providing for street lighting for 99 years was totally void where statute set 10-year limit).

[46] See Chapter 8 *supra*, discussing limitations on the exercise of municipal powers.

[47] See Griffin v. Oklahoma Natural Gas Corp., 37 F.2d 545 (10th Cir. 1930); Bacon v. City of Detroit, 282 Mich. 150, 275 N.W. 800 (1937); Beverly Sewerage Authority v. Delanco Sewerage Authority, 65 N.J.Super. 86, 167 A.2d 46, aff'd 70 N.J.Super. 575, 176 A.2d 276 and 38 N.J. 354, 184 A.2d 864 (contract for sewage service for 40 years, with right of renewal in other party, upheld); Borough of West Caldwell v. Borough of Caldwell, 26 N.J. 9, 138 A.2d 402 (1958). Thus, in Wilmington Parking Authority v. Ranken, 34 Del.Ch. 439, 105 A.2d 614 (1954), a lease of space in parking facilities for 40 years, with an option in the tenant to renew for additional 10-year periods, was held unreasonable since the lessor-authority had a legal life of only 50 years and the city that would succeed to ownership of the property would be bound by a rental determined by the original construction cost. Cf. Hoskins v. City of Orlando, 51 F.2d 901 (5th Cir.1931) (lease of apartment for 99 years held unreasonable); Eastern Illinois State Normal School v. City of Charleston, 271 Ill. 602, 111 N.E. 573 (1916) (city had no power to bind itself, in consideration of location of state institution in or near city, to furnish for $5 all the water the institution would need for 50 years). But some contracts for very long periods have been sustained, especially where they provide for water being supplied the locality by a private company. See Vicksburg Waterworks Co. v. Vicksburg, 185 U.S. 65, 22 S.Ct. 585, 46 L.Ed. 808 (1902) (30 years); Walla Walla City v. Walla Walla Water Co., 172 U.S. 1, 19 S.Ct. 77, 43 L.Ed. 341 (1898) (25 years); New Orleans Water-works Co. v. Rivers, 115 U.S. 674, 6 S.Ct. 273, 29 L.Ed. 525 (1885) (50 years); State ex rel. Ferguson v.

considered "governmental" (or "legislative") in nature,[48] a rough rule-of-thumb employed by many courts is that contracts extending beyond the current term of the local governing body are unreasonably long.[49] But some jurisdictions avoid such a result by treating a local governing body as continuous in nature, regardless of changes in membership.[50] And it is usually agreed that this "beyond the term" rule is little more than a guideline, and that a contract for a longer time can be upheld if sufficient necessity is shown.[51] Furthermore, contracts of a "proprietary" (or business-like) nature

---

City of Wichita, 188 Kan. 1, 360 P.2d 186 (1961) (40-year contract for purchase of water from federal government). Cf. Beverly Sewerage Authority v. Delanco Sewerage Authority, *supra* (40-year contract for sewage disposal); Salt Lake City v. State, 22 Utah 2d 37, 448 P.2d 350 (1968) (contract by which state government received free water *from* Salt Lake City). And in Iowa, it seems that no limit of reasonableness applies to any contracts of a proprietary nature. See City of Des Moines v. City of West Des Moines, 239 Iowa 1, 30 N.W.2d 500 (1948), noted 34 Iowa L.Rev. 121 (1948) (contracts involving exercise of "legislative" powers distinguished).

[48] On what is "governmental" or "legislative" in nature, and what, on the other hand, is "proprietary," see Daly v. Stokell, 63 So.2d 644 (Fla.1953) (contract for removal of wrecks from city streets was proprietary; proprietary contracts redound to benefit of city or its people, while governmental have to do with some exercise of sovereignty); Plant Food Co. v. City of Charlotte, 214 N.C. 518, 199 S.E. 712 (1938) (giving numerous examples), noted approvingly 17 Tex.L.Rev. 501 (1939). Cf. New Castle County v. Mayor & Council of New Castle, 372 A.2d 188 (Del.1977) (agreement by county for sewer services to city held proprietary). See also the discussions of the terms "governmental" and "proprietary" in Chapter 1 *supra* and in the Tort Liability chapter.

[49] DeKalb County v. Georgia Paperstock Co., 226 Ga. 369, 174 S.E.2d 884 (1970) (contract by county to turn over to paper-company all waste corrugated boxes collected in county was not binding on succeeding boards of county commissioners); City of Douglas v. Cartrett, 109 Ga.App. 683, 137 S.E.2d 358 (1964); City of Warm Springs v. Bulloch, 212 Ga. 149, 91 S.E.2d 13 (1956) (fixing of water rates); City of Humboldt v. Knight, 255 Iowa 22, 120 N.W.2d 457 (1963) (contract to supply free water perpetually); Talty v. Board of Education, 10 N.J. 69, 89 A.2d 391 (1952); Harrison Central School District v. Nyquist, 59 A.D.2d 434, 400 N.Y.S.2d 218 (1977) (general rule is contract of employment cannot extend beyond governing board's term). Cf. Duggan v. City of Taunton, 360 Mass. 644, 277 N.E.2d 268 (1971), voiding a contract of employment (for legal services) running beyond the term of the appointing body but saying that not all such contracts are necessarily void.

[50] See Town of Graham v. Karpark Corp., 194 F.2d 616 (4th Cir.1952); In re Nicholson's Estate, 104 Colo. 561, 93 P.2d 880 (1939) (city council *could* bind future governing body by entering into contract with testator's heir whereby city was to renounce its right in the future to a charitable trust in consideration for payment, soon after contract was made, of a sum of money); City of Vincennes v. Citizens' Gaslight Co., 132 Ind. 114, 31 N.E. 573 (1892); City of North Newton v. Regier, 152 Kan. 434, 103 P.2d 873 (1940) (sewage contract proprietary; 15-year contract upheld); City of Biddeford v. Yates, 104 Me. 506, 72 A. 335 (1908); Davis v. Public Schools of Escanaba, 175 Mich. 105, 140 N.W. 1001 (1913); State ex rel. Great Falls Housing Authority v. City of Great Falls, 110 Mont. 318, 100 P.2d 915 (1940). In Daly v. Stokell, *supra* note 48, the court observed that the terms of the city commissioners were staggered and expired at different times. This was taken to establish that the commission was a continuing body, and thus that only a limit of reasonableness should apply to contracts made by it.

[51] See Board of Supervisors v. Udall, 38 Ariz. 497, 1 P.2d 343 (1931) (if necessity and public policy require, county supervisors can make contract extending beyond their term); Denio v. City of Huntington Beach, 22 Cal.2d 580, 140 P.2d 392 (1943) (contract made by municipal governing body may extend beyond term of office if appears fair and reasonable at time of execution and is prompted by necessities of situation or is advantageous to municipality—contract was for employment of attorneys as special counsel); Board of Commissioners v. Simmons, 159 Kan. 41, 151 P.2d 960 (1944); Town of Lovell v. Menhall, 386 P.2d 109 (Wyo.1963) (if contract is reasonable and not an improper delegation of power to private persons, can be upheld though extends beyond governing body's term—contract was for acquisition, installation, and operation of parking meters). But contracts made by a governing body near the end of its term will be carefully scrutinized by the courts and will be voided if bad faith is found. See Town of Tempe v. Corbell, 17 Ariz. 1, 147 P. 745 (1915) (contract for street-sprinkling made a few days before term ended, and executed after election of new council); Picket Publishing Co. v. Carbon County, 36 Mont. 188, 92 P. 524 (1907). The same is true of contracts that are not scheduled to begin until the term of a new governing body has begun. See Independent School District v. Pennington, 181 Iowa 933, 165 N.W. 209 (1917). But even these contracts are sometimes upheld. See King City Union High School District v. Waibel, 2 Cal.App.2d 65, 37 P.2d 861 (Dist.Ct.1934) (contract employing school superintendent valid though not to begin till after reorganization of school board which made it).

are not subject to any such rule, but only to the general standard of reasonableness as to time.[52]

Contracts to exercise governmental powers in particular ways are void as against public policy, and no relief may be obtained thereon.[53] This is, for instance, true of attempted agreements to enact a particular ordinance,[54] to zone land in a particular way,[55] or to open or close a street.[56] Similarly, a local government cannot validly promise a private party that governmental power will *not* be exercised in a particular way as to that party; such an agreement clearly curtails the legislative or administrative discretion that citizens are entitled to have from their government.[57] Thus, an agreement not to condemn a person's property is void,[58] as is an agreement not to zone a landowner's

---

Occasionally, a state statute or home-rule charter forbids contracts extending beyond the term of the present governing body. See Tanner Motor Tours, Limited v. Brown, 71 Nev. 73, 280 P.2d 291 (1955).

[52] See Perl-Mack Enterprises Co. v. City & County of Denver, 194 Colo. 4, 568 P.2d 468 (1977) (contract for sanitary services and fees); Southern Airways Co. v. DeKalb County, 102 Ga.App. 850, 118 S.E.2d 234 (1960) (lease of airport); City of Big Spring v. Board of Control, 404 S.W.2d 810 (Tex.1966) (fixing utility rates). Cf. City of Detroit v. Public Utilities Commission, 288 Mich. 267, 286 N.W. 368 (1938) (recognizing power of city to enter into franchise agreement revocable at will of city, though voiding particular arrangement as not such a franchise); Gillam v. City of Fort Worth, 287 S.W.2d 494 (Tex.Civ.App.1956), refused n.r.e. (ten-year contract for furnishing water made by council with 2-year term; no abuse of discretion); Tanner v. Town of Auburn, 37 Wash. 38, 79 P. 494 (1905) (contract for lighting streets and public places extended beyond term of officers making it; power to make such contract considered unquestionable).

[53] See San Francisco-Oakland Terminal Railways v. Alameda, 226 F. 889 (N.D.Cal.1914); City of Birmingham v. Holt, 239 Ala. 248, 194 So. 538 (1940); Williams v. Public Utility Protective League, 130 Fla. 603, 178 So. 286 (1938); City Council of Augusta v. Richmond County, 178 Ga. 400, 173 S.E. 140 (1934); City of New Albany v. New Albany Street Railroad, 172 Ind. 487, 87 N.E. 1084 (1909); Westminster Water Co. v. Mayor of Westminster, 98 Md. 551, 56 A. 990 (1904) (contract to levy taxes and pay proceeds to a water company, for water, for all time to come); New York, New Haven & Hartford Railroad v. Village of New Rochelle, 29 Misc. 195, 60 N.Y.S. 904 (1899); Born v. City of Pittsburgh, 266 Pa. 128, 109 A. 614 (1920). Cf. Leidigh v. Nebraska City, 138 Neb. 136, 292 N.W. 115 (1940) (pledge of credit beyond officers' term of office for purchase of real estate, with provision for forfeiture of land if ever was default on installments); City of Marshall v. Allen, 115 S.W. 849 (Tex.Civ.App.1909), error refused (agreement by city engineer that sidewalk would only be graded to a certain depth).

[54] Gardner v. City of Dallas, 81 F.2d 425 (5th Cir.1936), cert. denied 298 U.S. 668, 56 S.Ct. 834, 80 L.Ed. 1391 (1936) (promise to enact ordinance providing for collection of trash and garbage in separate containers).

[55] Beshore v. Town of Bel Air, 237 Md. 398, 206 A.2d 678 (1965); Pressman v. City of Baltimore, 222 Md. 330, 160 A.2d 379 (1960); Midtown Properties, Inc. v. Madison Township, 68 N.J.Super. 197, 172 A.2d 40 (1961), aff'd 78 N.J.Super. 471, 189 A.2d 226. See generally Trager, Contract Zoning, 23 Md.L.Rev. 121 (1963). See also, on zoning in general and contract zoning in particular, Chapter 18 *supra*.

[56] See Bessemer Improvement Co. v. City of Greensboro, 247 N.C. 549, 101 S.E.2d 336 (1958); Houston v. Town of West Greenville, 126 S.C. 484, 120 S.E. 236 (1922).

[57] See Moskovitz v. City of St. Paul, 218 Minn. 543, 16 N.W.2d 745 (1944); Seidel v. Seward, 178 Neb. 345, 133 N.W.2d 390 (1965); Cibolo Creek Municipal Authority v. Universal City, 568 S.W.2d 699 (Tex.Civ.App.1978). Cf. Lamar Bath House Co. v. City of Hot Springs, 229 Ark. 214, 315 S.W.2d 884 (1958) (municipality could not exempt United States government from sewer charges); American Oil Co. v. Marion County, 187 Miss. 148, 192 So. 296 (1939) (board of supervisors had no power to lease courthouse property).

[58] Contributors to Pennsylvania Hospital v. City of Philadelphia, 245 U.S. 20, 38 S.Ct. 35, 62 L.Ed. 124 (1917). Cf. Wheat Ridge Urban Renewal Auth. v. Cornerstone Group, 176 P.3d 737 (Colo. 2007) (contracts surrendering the power of eminent domain are void; court lacked power to order urban renewal authority to specifically perform contract with developer which required authority to exercise power of eminent domain.) But cf. Southern Indiana Gas & Electric Co. v. City of Boonville, 252 Ind. 385, 248 N.E.2d 343 (1969) (city utility may make contract which prevents it from thereafter taking property by eminent domain). Contracts between municipalities and utilities by which the government is absolutely bound to continue paying the same rate are likely to be held invalid. See Anchor Hocking Corp. v. Jacksonville Electric Authority, 419 F.Supp. 992 (M.D.Fla.1976).

property in a certain manner,[59] and (often at least) an agreement not to assess a landowner's property for local improvements.[60] It seems that the public policy against any such restrictions on municipal exercise of power is now so firmly established that everyone should be on guard against entering into these contracts and that all relief on these agreements will universally be denied.

It appears certain that contracts by which a local government conveyed to others its power to govern would be against public policy and hence void. But contracts in which this is found to have happened are seldom encountered. An agreement providing that disputes under a municipal contract will be submitted to arbitration is now generally agreed not to amount to an unlawful delegation of governing power,[61] unless there is legislation declaring that local authorities alone have power to decide the particular matter.[62] Similarly, contracts for the appraisal of property in the locality have been held not to delegate the discretionary or governmental power of the local government and thus not to be invalid.[63]

For a locality's contract to be valid, it must have been entered into by an agent with authority to make such an agreement; otherwise, there is no recovery on the contract itself.[64] It is often said in explanation and justification of this rule that persons dealing

---

[59] See Midtown Properties v. Madison Township, *supra* note 55. Cf. North Kansas City School District v. J. A. Peterson-Renner, Inc., 369 S.W.2d 159 (Mo.1963) (locality cannot surrender control of public sewers).

[60] Leggett v. City of Detroit, 137 Mich. 247, 100 N.W. 566 (1904); City of Cleveland v. Edwards, 109 Ohio St. 598, 143 N.E. 181 (1924). See State ex rel. Meyer v. Lancaster County, 173 Neb. 195, 113 N.W.2d 63 (1962); Little Falls Electric & Water Co. v. City of Little Falls, 74 Minn. 197, 77 N.W. 40 (1898) (promise to pay taxes on waterworks); Ehrlich v. City of Racine, 26 Wis.2d 352, 132 N.W.2d 489 (1965) (promise to pay tax rebate).

[61] Gary Excavating, Inc. v. Town of North Haven, 164 Conn. 119, 318 A.2d 84 (1972); Puget Sound Power & Light Co. v. Public Utility District, 17 Wn.App. 861, 565 P.2d 1221 (1977); City of Madison v. Frank Lloyd Wright Foundation, 20 Wis.2d 361, 122 N.W.2d 409 (1963). See Board of Education v. Philadelphia Federation of Teachers, 464 Pa. 92, 346 A.2d 35 (1975) (school boards may agree to arbitrate discharge of tenured teacher). Compulsory arbitration statutes applying to local governments have been held constitutional. Red Bank Bd. of Educ. v. Warrington, 138 N.J.Super. 564, 351 A.2d 778 (1976); Joint School Dist. v. Wisconsin Employment Relations Bd., 37 Wis.2d 483, 155 N.W.2d 78 (1967).

[62] Compare Dunellen Board of Education v. Dunellen Education Association, 64 N.J. 17, 311 A.2d 737 (1973) (decision to consolidate chairmanships of departments was not proper subject of arbitration or mandatory negotiation), with Milberry v. Board of Education, 467 Pa. 79, 354 A.2d 559 (1976) (board of education could submit to arbitration dispute over unsatisfactory rating of teacher).

[63] Hutchins v. Candler, 209 Ga. 415, 73 S.E.2d 191 (1952); Conroy v. City of Battle Creek, 314 Mich. 210, 22 N.W.2d 275 (1946); Stocklan v. Brackett, 95 N.H. 227, 61 A.2d 140 (1948).

An important development relating to municipal contracts has been the trend toward agreements by which municipalities turn over to private entities the operation of facilities or services that have traditionally been operated by local governments themselves. See Section 16.2 *infra*. See also Kmiec & Diamond, New Federalism Is Not Enough: The Privatization of Nonpublic Goods, 7 Harv. J. L. & Pub. Pol. 321 (1984), saying that privatization provides a mechanism for avoiding the monopoly-like power, thus inefficiency, of services provided by the government, even a local government.

[64] Brown v. City of St. Petersburg, 111 Fla. 718, 153 So. 141 (1933); Ingalls Iron Works Co. v. City of Forest Park, 99 Ga.App. 706, 109 S.E.2d 835 (1959); Folkers v. Butzer, 294 Ill.App. 1, 13 N.E.2d 624 (1938); Gontrum v. City of Baltimore, 182 Md. 370, 35 A.2d 128 (1943); Dos Santos v. Peabody, 327 Mass. 519, 99 N.E.2d 852 (1951) (contract by superintendent of municipal infirmary for collection of garbage); Skutt v. City of Grand Rapids, 275 Mich. 258, 266 N.W. 344 (1936); Doyle v. City of St. Paul, 204 Minn. 558, 284 N.W. 291 (1939); Henschel v. City of New York, 137 Misc. 310, 243 N.Y.S. 362 (1930); Newport Hospital v. Ward, 56 R.I. 45, 183 A. 571 (1936); American-LaFrance & Foamite Industries, Inc. v. Arlington County, 164 Va. 1, 178 S.E. 783 (1935). But cf. City of Grantsville v. Redevelopment Agency, 233 P.3d 461 (Utah 2010) (failure to comply with requirement that contracts with municipalities be countersigned by city recorder cannot be sole basis for defeating a contractual claim).

with the local government must, at their peril, know the extent of the authority of those officers or employees with whom they deal.[65] Where, by provision of statute or home-rule charter, the authorization of the local governing body is necessary to a contract, no agency—and hence no valid contract—exists without this.[66] But this is an area in which recovery apart from the contract is frequently allowed. Thus, a contract entered into by an unauthorized agent, but within the general powers of the locality, can be ratified by the locality.[67] And most authority has here recognized the possibility of estoppel if (1) the locality has clothed the supposed agent with apparent authority and the other party has acted reasonably and in good faith on such appearance,[68] *or* (2) the locality has taken advantage of the contract by accepting benefits thereunder.[69] Perhaps the strongest basis of all for recovery on a contract whose only defect is not having been entered into by an authorized agent is quasi-contract; the locality should be liable for the reasonable value of goods or services it has received, since the agreement was within its power—it was just not within the power of the individual who made it. Most authority *does* now allow quasi-contractual recovery in those situations.[70]

---

65 See City of Princeton v. Princeton Electric Light & Power Co., 166 Ky. 730, 179 S.W. 1074 (1915); School Administrative District No. 3 v. Maine School District Commission, 158 Me. 420, 185 A.2d 744 (1962); Inter-City Land Co. v. Baltimore County, 218 Md. 80, 145 A.2d 263 (1958); Rens v. City of Grand Rapids, 73 Mich. 237, 41 N.W. 263 (1889); Thatcher Chemical Co. v. Salt Lake City Corp., 21 Utah 2d 355, 445 P.2d 769 (1968) (person dealing with city is presumed to know municipal ordinances).

66 Satrom v. City of Grand Forks, 163 N.W.2d 522 (N.D.1968) (statute required authorization of governing body). See City of Jonesboro v. Shaw-Lightcap, Inc., 112 Ga.App. 890, 147 S.E.2d 65 (1966) (plaintiff not entitled to recover where his petition against city failed to show that contract sued on was entered into by mayor and council as a body, as required by city charter); Welch v. City of Lima, 89 Ohio App. 457, 102 N.E.2d 888 (1950) (governing body must act as a body, not through individual members).

67 See City of Pontiac v. Ducharme, 278 Mich. 474, 270 N.W. 754 (1936); DeMuro v. Martini, 1 N.J. 516, 64 A.2d 351 (1949); City Affairs Committee v. Board of Commissioners, 132 N.J.L. 552, 41 A.2d 798 (1945), aff'd 134 N.J.L. 180, 46 A.2d 425; New Jersey Car-Spring & Rubber Co. v. Jersey City, 64 N.J.L. 544, 46 A. 649 (1900); Lathrop Co. v. City of Toledo, 5 Ohio St.2d 165, 214 N.E.2d 408 (1966); Walthour v. McDowell, 109 Pa.Super. 118, 165 A. 746 (1933); Koch v. City of Milwaukee, 89 Wis. 220, 62 N.W. 918 (1895). Cf. M. & O. Disposal Co. v. Township of Middletown, 100 N.J.Super. 558, 242 A.2d 841 (1967), aff'd 52 N.J. 6, 242 A.2d 841 (1968) (ratification is based on knowledge and intention; where governing body not notified of plaintiffs' extra work, outside contract, till contract with them had terminated, could be no ratification by governing body of promise to pay for such work). The ratification must be by the group or authority that could have made the contract in the first place. See Yaeger v. Giguerre, 222 Minn. 41, 23 N.W.2d 22 (1946). Thus, where only the local governing body could have authorized the contract, it is the only body with authority to ratify. See B. F. Goodrich Rubber Co. v. Town of Collinsville, 101 S.W.2d 583 (Tex.Civ.App.1937).

68 George D. Barnard & Co. v. Sangamon County, 190 Ill. 116, 60 N.E. 109 (1901). See City of Chicago v. Sexton, 115 Ill. 230, 2 N.E. 263 (1885). Cf. Rason Asphalt, Inc. v. Town of Oyster Bay, 6 A.D.2d 810, 175 N.Y.S.2d 302 (1958) (advertising for sealed bids unnecessary where each contract was for less than amount for which such bids required, though total purchases exceeded that amount; town estopped from denying authority of superintendent of highways to procure materials). But cf. Giant Manufacturing Co. v. City of Wamego, 141 Kan. 329, 41 P.2d 744 (1935) (city not estopped from denying validity of park board's agreement to purchase flood lights—even though city had used the lights for a period of years).

69 See Norwalk Gaslight Co. v. Borough of Norwalk, 63 Conn. 495, 28 A. 32 (1894); Jones v. School District No. 3, 110 Mich. 363, 68 N.W. 222 (1896); Johnson v. Hospital Service Plan, 25 N.J. 134, 135 A.2d 483 (1957), noted 56 Mich.L.Rev. 1032 (1958); Goshorn's Executors v. County Court, 42 W.Va. 735, 26 S.E. 452 (1896). But see State ex rel. Workman v. Goldthait, 172 Ind. 210, 87 N.E. 133 (1909); Eureka Fire Hose Manufacturing Co. v. City of Portageville, 106 S.W.2d 513 (Mo.App.1937); American-LaFrance & Foamite Industries, Inc. v. Arlington County, *supra* note 64.

70 Condran v. City of New Orleans, 43 La.Ann. 1202, 9 So. 31 (1891); Central Bitulithic Paving Co. v. City of Mount Clemens, 143 Mich. 259, 106 N.W. 888 (1906); Miles v. Holt County, 86 Neb. 238, 125 N.W. 527 (1910); Kramrath v. City of Albany, 127 N.Y. 575, 28 N.E. 400 (1891); Abbott Realty v. City of Charlotte, 198 N.C. 564, 152 S.E. 686 (1930); Denison v. Foster, 28 S.W. 1052 (Tex.Civ.App.1894); Thompson v. Town of Elton, 109 Wis. 589, 85 N.W. 425 (1901). Cf. McCuistion v. City of Siloam Springs, 268 Ark. 148, 594 S.W.2d 233

Contracts may also be invalid if not entered into according to the procedures specified by state statute or home-rule charter. The traditional rule is that if the disobeyed specification is considered "mandatory," there is no recovery on the contract[71] or on any other basis.[72] But if a merely "directory" stipulation is not obeyed, there can generally be quasi-contractual relief,[73] and sometimes even relief on the contract itself.[74] However, attempts to distinguish "mandatory" and "directory" provisions have resulted in hair-splitting, in ignoring of underlying policies, and in contradictory decisions; it has been suggested that it is preferable for courts on each occasion to consider the purpose and importance of the violated law, the good or bad faith of the parties, the possibility of restoring the status quo, and whether, in general, it is feasible to grant some relief to the person who has contracted with the locality.[75]

(1980) (contract not formally authorized or approved by city council, but contractor could recover quantum meruit); Shulse v. City of Mayville, 223 Wis. 624, 271 N.W. 643 (1937), noted 36 Mich.L.Rev. 855 (1938) (plaintiff, not properly hired, performed work with acquiescence of city, and city accepted the work; cause of action stated for value of benefits city received). But some jurisdictions refuse quasi-contractual relief, reasoning that the party contracting with the government is obligated to know of an alleged agent's lack of authority and therefore deserves no relief. See Louisville Extension Water District v. Diehl Pump & Supply Co., 246 S.W.2d 585 (Ky.1952); City of Princeton v. Princeton Electric Light & Power Co., *supra* note 65; Bartlett v. City of Lowell, 201 Mass. 151, 87 N.E. 195 (1909); Groton Bridge & Manufacturing Co. v. Warren County, 80 Miss. 214, 31 So. 711 (1902); Hague v. City of Philadelphia, 48 Pa. 527 (1865). Cf. Seif v. City of Long Beach, 286 N.Y. 382, 36 N.E.2d 630 (1941), motion denied 287 N.Y. 836, 41 N.E.2d 164 (where legislation provides that valid city contracts may be made only by specified officers, is no implied contract to pay for services furnished under contract made by officer not so authorized; mayor not here authorized to hire special counsel).

[71] Utica State Savings Bank v. Village of Oak Park, 279 Mich. 568, 273 N.W. 271 (1937). See Note, Municipal Contracts—Debts and Contracts—Liability for Services Performed Under Void Contract, 34 Harv. L.Rev. 439 (1921); Note, Municipal Corporations—Ultra Vires—Liability in Quasi Contract for Benefits Received Under Ultra Vires Contract, 16 Va.L.Rev. 628 (1930).

[72] See Mullins v. Kansas City, 268 Mo. 444, 188 S.W. 193 (1916) (no estoppel); City of Plattsmouth v. Murphy, 74 Neb. 749, 105 N.W. 293 (1905) (no ratification); Scarborough Properties Corp. v. Village of Briarcliff Manor, 278 N.Y. 370, 16 N.E.2d 369 (1938), motion denied 253 A.D. 814, 1 N.Y.S.2d 1020 (no recovery in quasi-contract). But see, allowing recovery despite disregard of "mandatory" provisions, First National Bank v. Goodhue, 120 Minn. 362, 139 N.W. 599 (1913); First Wisconsin National Bank v. Town of Catawba, 183 Wis. 220, 197 N.W. 1013 (1924).

[73] See Webb v. Wakefield Township, 239 Mich. 521, 215 N.W. 43 (1927); Hines v. City of Bellefontaine, 74 Ohio App. 393, 57 N.E.2d 164 (1943). Cf. Alford v. City of Gadsden, 349 So.2d 1132 (Ala.1977) (estoppel will be applied to local government once it has accepted benefits); Hansen v. Town of Anthon, 187 Iowa 51, 173 N.W. 939 (1919) (ratification found). Compare Wilson v. Village of Forest View, 69 Ill.App.2d 400, 217 N.E.2d 398 (1966) (village's abandonment of special-assessment proceedings with regard to water-works improvement sewer system, after having entered into valid contract with engineer for plans, which engineer had then prepared, entitled engineer to recover the agreed compensation, not merely quantum meruit).

[74] Hatch v. Maple Valley Township Unit School, 310 Mich. 516, 17 N.W.2d 735 (1945); Saleno v. City of Neosho, 127 Mo. 627, 30 S.W. 190 (1895).

[75] See 1A Antieau, Municipal Corporation Law § 10.03[5], at 10–52, –53 (1998). Note that in the case of home-rule cities, city-charter provisions on the exact procedures for entering into contracts may prevail over state statutes. United States Elevator Corp. v. City of Tulsa, 610 P.2d 791 (Okl.1980) (specific procedures to be followed in advertising for and accepting competitive bids is a "municipal affair").

In 1979, the American Bar Association promulgated a Model Procurement Code for State and Local Governments, covering bidding requirements and other procedures and standards for public contracting. In 1982, a Model Procurement Ordinance for Local Governments, based on the Model Code and specially adapted to meet the needs of local jurisdictions, was approved by the Public Contract Law and the Urban, State, and Local Government Law sections of the American Bar. See Del Duca, Falvey & Adler, State and Local Government Procurement: Developments in Legislation and Litigation, 18 Urban Law. 301 (1986). See also Ethridge & Moul, Recent Developments in State and Local Procurement: Implementation of the Model Procurement Code Picks Up Pace, 17 Urban Law. 977 (1985).

§ 25.4 Competitive Bidding Requirements

One of the most frequently encountered requirements is one specifying that local contracts be let-out for bids and that the contract be awarded the lowest responsible bidder—*i.e.*, the reliable party who submits the bid that will cost the locality the least money. In the absence of constitutional, statutory, or charter provisions on the matter, there is no requirement that contracts be let-out for bids,[76] or that the contract be given the lowest bidder.[77] But legislation has made such requirements pervasive, though often they apply only to contracts above a specified amount. Where there is such a monetary limitation, the bidding requirement cannot be successfully evaded by breaking the contract into lesser amounts—the court will look to the gist of the matter and determine whether it truly involved several transactions, or just a single one.[78] Where bidding requirements are unmet, there can be no recovery on the contract;[79] and the traditional

---

[76] Davis v. City of Santa Ana, 108 Cal.App.2d 669, 239 P.2d 656 (Dist.Ct.1952); People ex rel. Adamowski v. Daley, 22 Ill.App.2d 87, 159 N.E.2d 18 (1959); Robinson v. City of Saginaw, 267 Mich. 557, 255 N.W. 396 (1934); George E. Gibson Co. v. New York City, 236 App.Div. 283, 258 N.Y.S. 320 (1932); Shaw Disposal, Inc. v. City of Auburn, 15 Wn.App. 65, 546 P.2d 1236 (1976) (not necessary in order to prevent corruption to impose competitive-bidding requirements as to long-term contracts); Akin v. Kewaskum Schools, 64 Wis.2d 154, 218 N.W.2d 494 (1974). Cf. Cullen v. Rock County, 244 Wis. 237, 12 N.W.2d 38 (1943) (if city not bound by bidding requirements it may, after deciding to invite bids, reject all bids and ask for new ones, or may contract on basis of reasonable business judgment, even with one who was not the lowest bidder). But cf. Eagle v. City of Corbin, 275 Ky. 808, 122 S.W.2d 798 (1938), imposing a competitive-bidding requirement on the sale of bonds though legislation did not specify this procedure.

While competitive-bidding requirements are usually found in statutes or home-rule charters, they are occasionally imposed by municipal ordinances. See Bunker v. City of Hutchinson, 74 Kan. 651, 87 P. 884 (1906); Cimarron Utilities Co. v. City of Guymon, 171 Okl. 344, 43 P.2d 143 (1935); Flinn v. City of Philadelphia, 258 Pa. 355, 102 A. 24 (1917).

[77] Case-Brothers Co., Inc. v. City of Ottawa, 226 Kan. 648, 602 P.2d 1316 (1979) (municipal officers have unlimited discretion in letting contract, so long as is no fraud); Deary v. Town of Dudley, 343 Mass. 192, 178 N.E.2d 83 (1961); Maribu v. Nohowec, 161 Misc. 944, 293 N.Y.S. 457 (1937).

[78] Menzl v. City of Milwaukee, 32 Wis.2d 266, 145 N.W.2d 198 (1966). Cf. Miller v. McKinnon, 20 Cal.2d 83, 124 P.2d 34 (1942) (cause of action found stated in taxpayer's suit to recover money paid contractor); State v. Kollarik, 22 N.J. 558, 126 A.2d 875 (1956) (criminal liability for conspiracy to split single contract into three separate ones, each within maximum amount); Signacon Controls, Inc. v. Mulroy, 32 N.Y.2d 410, 345 N.Y.S.2d 527, 298 N.E.2d 670 (1973) (bid requirement held applicable though nothing sold to county, but county agreed that supplier would charge override cost on each item sold to a non-county purchaser and county would assist in promoting the sales). But see Sanitary District v. George F. Blake Manufacturing Co., 179 Ill. 167, 53 N.E. 627 (1899) (competitive-bidding requirement applicable to contracts over $500; held inapplicable to contract for hiring pumps at $42.50 a day since contract was terminable at will, though total eventually paid did exceed $500). Cf. Hauger v. Earl, 275 App.Div. 437, 90 N.Y.S.2d 637 (1949) (purchase of parking meters to be paid for out of revenue from the meters was not within bidding requirement since was no "expenditure," but transfer of used meters as trade-ins was an "expenditure").

[79] Los Angeles Dredging Co. v. City of Long Beach, 210 Cal. 348, 291 P. 839 (1930); City of Owensboro v. Evansville & Ohio Valley Transit Co., 448 S.W.2d 375 (Ky.1969); Fluet v. Eberhardt, 294 Mass. 408, 2 N.E.2d 463 (1936); Salzer v. City of East Lansing, 263 Mich. 626, 249 N.W. 16 (1933); Bremerton Municipal League v. Bremer, 15 Wn.2d 231, 130 P.2d 367 (1942). On the reasons for requiring competitive bidding in order for a contract to be valid, see Village of Excelsior v. F. W. Pearce Corp., 303 Minn. 118, 226 N.W.2d 316 (1975) (such requirements intended to prevent fraud, collusion, favoritism, and improvidence, and to insure that locality receives high quality at reasonable prices); Land Constr. Co. v. Snohomish County, 40 Wash.App. 480, 698 P.2d 1120 (1985) (primary purpose of competitive bidding requirement is protection of general public, but another purpose is provision of a fair forum for those interested in undertaking a public project). Cf. Application of Borough of Saddle River, 71 N.J. 14, 362 A.2d 552 (1976) (strong public policy favors competitive bidding; statute requiring such bidding won't be found repealed by implication); Platt Electric Supply, Inc. v. City of Seattle, 16 Wn.App. 265, 555 P.2d 421 (1976), review denied 89 Wash.2d 1004 (1977) (when competitive bidding is required, must be substantial compliance with required procedure, and locality cannot negotiate privately with selected bidder or bidders in order to obtain a change in bids); Wagner v. City of Milwaukee, 196 Wis. 328, 220 N.W. 207 (1928) (where taxpayer sought to enjoin city from paying funds for public printing

policy of the law was to deny recovery even on quasi-contract[80] or related theories.[81] But the trend is now clearly to allow quasi-contractual recovery, and this seems the view of the majority of the more recent and/or better reasoned authority.[82] It is generally reasoned today that the municipality should have to pay for the reasonable value of what it has received despite the failure to minimize costs by taking bids and accepting the lowest. Since the measure of recovery does *not* include any profit to the private person with whom the contract was made, there is no real harm to the citizens of the community—and the lack of profit will presumably be sufficient deterrent to further violations, since it will put private parties on guard in future transactions with the

---

because contract had not been let to lowest bidder, attempt of city council to ratify acts of city officers and direct them to continue publication of proceedings without formal contract was nugatory). It has been held that statutes and regulations defining the rules of competitive bidding should be strictly construed against the government entity that solicits the bids. Planning & Design Solutions v. City of Santa Fe, 118 N.M. 707, 885 P.2d 628 (1994). But a competitive bidding requirement ordinarily applies only where the local government submits a project to private contractors or suppliers, not where the government performs all the work itself. See Montana Contractors' Ass'n v. Department of Highways, 220 Mont. 392, 715 P.2d 1056 (1986). It has been held that a contract obtained through competitive bidding is void if it materially differs from the invitation to bid. Orion Portfolio Services 2, LLC v. Clark County ex rel. University Medical Center of So. Nevada, 245 P.3d 527 (Nev. 2010).

[80] Zottman v. City & County of San Francisco, 20 Cal. 96 (1862) (the leading, and a famous, case); City & County of Denver v. Moorman, 95 Colo. 111, 33 P.2d 749 (1934), noted 7 Rocky Mt.L.Rev. 159 (1935); Pyrene Manufacturing Co. v. City of Atlanta, 27 Ga.App. 568, 110 S.E. 408 (1921), noted 31 Yale L.J. 779 (1922); Everds Brothers v. Gillespie, 256 Iowa 317, 126 N.W.2d 274 (1964); Frank v. Board of Education, 90 N.J.L. 273, 100 A. 211 (1917); La France Fire-Engine Co. v. City of Syracuse, 33 Misc. 516, 68 N.Y.S. 894 (1900); Probst v. City of Menasha, 245 Wis. 90, 13 N.W.2d 504 (1944), noted 29 Marq.L.Rev. 70 (1945).

[81] See, all denying relief on an estoppel theory, Folkers v. Butzer, 294 Ill.App. 1, 13 N.E.2d 624 (1938); Missoula Street Railway v. City of Missoula, 47 Mont. 85, 130 P. 771 (1913); Blum v. City of Hillsboro, 49 Wis.2d 667, 183 N.W.2d 47 (1971); Tobin v. Town Council of Sundance, 45 Wyo. 219, 17 P.2d 666 (1933). Some courts have even required a private party selling goods to a locality to return any payments already received thereon from that government if competitive-bidding requirements were not met—even if the goods can no longer be returned. Miller v. McKinnon, 20 Cal.2d 83, 124 P.2d 34 (1942); McNay v. Town of Lowell, 41 Ind.App. 627, 84 N.E. 778 (1908). See Wester v. Belote, 103 Fla. 976, 138 So. 721 (1931) (funds recoverable in taxpayers' suit). Cf. Gerzof v. Sweeney, 22 N.Y.2d 297, 292 N.Y.S.2d 640, 239 N.E.2d 521 (1968), supporting this rule but not requiring the seller to return the large amount—over three-quarters of a million dollars—he had received, but only to pay the city the difference between the improper bid and the actual low bid. But most authority will *not* require the return of funds received by a private party under a contract violative of competitive-bidding requirements, if the goods transferred in exchange for those funds can no longer be returned. Sacramento County v. Southern Pacific Co., 127 Cal. 217, 59 P. 568 (1899), reh. denied 127 Cal. 217, 59 P. 825 (1900); Grady v. City of Livingston, 115 Mont. 47, 141 P.2d 346 (1943); Scott Township School District Authority v. Branna Construction Corp., 409 Pa. 136, 185 A.2d 320 (1962); Ellefson v. Smith, 182 Wis. 398, 196 N.W. 834 (1924). See State for Use of Russell County v. Fourth National Bank, 270 Ala. 135, 117 So.2d 145 (1959); Burns v. City of Nashville, 142 Tenn. 541, 221 S.W. 828 (1919). Cf. City of St. Paul v. Dual Parking Meter Co., 229 Minn. 217, 39 N.W.2d 174 (1949), noted 63 Harv.L.Rev. 904 (1950) (city denied declaratory judgment awarding it receipts where contract violated competitive-bidding requirement; court leaves parties where it finds them).

[82] Lykes v. City of Texarkana, 223 Ark. 287, 265 S.W.2d 539 (1954); Corbello v. Jefferson Davis Parish Police Jury, 262 So.2d 151 (La.App.1972); Smith v. Town of Vinton, 216 La. 9, 43 So.2d 18 (1949), noted 24 Tul.L.Rev. 363 (1950); Hatch v. Maple Valley Township Unit School, 310 Mich. 516, 17 N.W.2d 735 (1945); Pillager v. Hewitt, 98 Minn. 265, 107 N.W. 815 (1906); O'Neill v. City of South Omaha, 102 Neb. 836, 170 N.W. 174 (1918); Poling v. Roman, 86 N.J.Super. 484, 207 A.2d 219 (1965); Home Owners Construction Co. v. Borough of Glen Rock, 34 N.J. 305, 169 A.2d 129 (1961); Abbott Realty Co. v. City of Charlotte, 198 N.C. 564, 152 S.E. 686 (1930); Merchants National Bank & Trust Co. v. City of Grand Forks, 130 N.W.2d 212 (N.D.1964); Womack v. Carson, 38 S.W.2d 184 (Tex.Civ.App.1931), aff'd 123 Tex. 260, 65 S.W.2d 485, reh. denied 123 Tex. 260, 70 S.W.2d 416; Edwards v. City of Renton, 67 Wn.2d 598, 409 P.2d 153 (1965). See Hudson City Contracting Co. v. Jersey City Incinerator Authority, 17 N.J. 297, 111 A.2d 385 (1955) (contractor could recover in quantum meruit for services performed in good faith under invalid contract with city incinerator authority); Blum v. City of Hillsboro, *supra* note 81. See generally Annot., Liability of Municipality on Quasi-Contract for Value of Property or Work Furnished Without Compliance with Bidding Requirements, 33 A.L.R.3d 1164 (1970).

locality. No quasi-contract or other relief will, of course, be granted if there has been collusion or bad faith by the party seeking recovery.[83]

Various exceptions to competitive-bidding requirements are usually specified in the relevant legislation; but certain exceptions have often been "read in" by the courts even if not specified: (1) Contracts for the renting of real property, or the hiring of a chattel of an unusual nature, are customarily excepted since the supply of suitable property is then likely to be quite limited.[84] (2) Contracts for the professional services of persons such as architects, engineers, and attorneys are not subject to such requirements since it is thought desirable that the locality have freedom to negotiate with those persons considered best qualified, rather than be bound to accept the lowest bid.[85] (3) Contracts for goods or services available only from a single source, such as utility services, are not usually considered subject to bidding requirements.[86] (4) Courts will generally create an exception where there is an emergency which necessitates quick action, without time for resorting to the bid process; despite failure to follow bidding requirements, relief will then be accorded, on the contract, a party contracting with a locality if that party did not

---

[83] See Jered Contracting Corp. v. New York City Transit Authority, 22 N.Y.2d 187, 292 N.Y.S.2d 98, 239 N.E.2d 197 (1968), with review of cases (collusive bidding makes contract voidable at option of local government). Cf. City of Oakland v. California Construction Co., 15 Cal.2d 573, 104 P.2d 30 (1940) (city as trustee for property owners had legal capacity to maintain action to recover proceeds of street-improvement contract allegedly void because of contractors' conspiracy to refrain from competitive bidding).

[84] See Angel v. Behnke, 166 Ind.App. 541, 337 N.E.2d 503 (1975) (lease of data processing equipment); Ambrozich v. City of Eveleth, 200 Minn. 473, 274 N.W. 635 (1937); Ex parte Houston, 93 Okl.Cr. 26, 224 P.2d 281 (1950); Wright v. Wagner, 405 Pa. 546, 175 A.2d 875 (1961), cert. denied 369 U.S. 849, 82 S.Ct. 933, 8 L.Ed.2d 9 (obtaining sites for dumping of debris). Cf. Hodgeman v. City of San Diego, 53 Cal.App.2d 610, 128 P.2d 412 (Dist.Ct.1942) (no reasonable basis of comparison among different parking meters; advertising for bids unnecessary); Hylton v. Mayor of Baltimore, 268 Md. 266, 300 A.2d 656 (1972) (bidding not necessary for building of unique solid-waste disposal facility).

[85] This has been applied to contracts for the services of attorneys. Commonwealth ex rel. Roberts v. Tice, 272 Pa. 447, 116 A. 316 (1922); Gibson v. Davis, 236 S.W. 202 (Tex.Civ.App.1921). And of engineers. Potts v. City of Utica, 86 F.2d 616 (2d Cir.1936); Rollins v. City of Salem, 251 Mass. 468, 146 N.E. 795 (1925); Hunter v. Whiteaker & Washington, 230 S.W. 1096 (Tex.Civ.App.1921), error refused (services of civil engineer to prepare plans for road work). And of architects. Miller v. Boyle, 43 Cal.App. 39, 184 P. 421 (Dist.Ct.1919); Foss v. Spitznagel, 77 S.D. 633, 97 N.W.2d 856 (1959); Tackett v. Middleton, 280 S.W. 563 (Tex.Com.App.1926) (employment of architect to draw plans for schoolhouse). And of actors and musicians. Adams v. Ziegler, 22 Cal.App.2d 135, 70 P.2d 537 (Dist.Ct.1937). And of various other professionals. In re Board of County Commissioners of Cook County (In re Myers), 146 Minn. 103, 177 N.W. 1013 (1920) (bond broker); Child v. Board of Commissioners of City of Newark, 8 N.J.Misc. 597, 151 A. 203 (1930) (real estate broker); Braaten v. Olson, 28 N.D. 235, 148 N.W. 829 (1914) (accountant); Hordin v. City of Cleveland, 77 Ohio App. 491, 62 N.E.2d 889 (1945) (car-advertising specialists); City of Cleveland v. Lausche, 71 Ohio App. 273, 49 N.E.2d 207 (1943) (services of museum in operation of zoo); Terry v. Commissioners of Cookeville, 184 Tenn. 347, 198 S.W.2d 1010 (1947) (financial agent). See Parker v. Panama City, 151 So.2d 469 (Fla.App.1963); City of Hazard v. Salyers, 311 Ky. 667, 224 S.W.2d 420 (1949) (financial and engineering firm); Transportation Displays, Inc. v. City of New Orleans, 346 So.2d 359 (La.App.1977); Mongiovi v. Doerner, 24 Or.App. 639, 546 P.2d 1110 (1976). But cf. O'Hare Express v. City of Chicago, 235 Ill.App.3d 202, 176 Ill.Dec. 148, 601 N.E.2d 846 (1992) (city's contract to provide bus service within area of airport held not for professional services and thus not within exception to competitive bidding requirement).

[86] Comley v. Board of Purchase & Supplies, 111 Conn. 147, 149 A. 410 (1930) (fire trucks; was only one seller); City of Hartford v. Hartford Electric Light Co., 65 Conn. 324, 32 A. 925 (1895); Hylton v. City of Baltimore, *supra* note 84; Mullen v. Town of Louisburg, 225 N.C. 53, 33 S.E.2d 484 (1945) (contract for supplying electricity); Washington Fruit & Produce Co. v. City of Yakima, 3 Wn.2d 152, 100 P.2d 8 (1940), aff'd en banc 3 Wn.2d 152, 103 P.2d 1106 (1940) (contract to purchase electric power for street lighting). But see Hunt v. Fenlon, 313 Mich. 644, 21 N.W.2d 906 (1946), requiring competitive bidding for electric service even though there was only one supplier, since the charter required such bidding in general terms.

have a part in creating the emergency.[87] A legislative declaration of an emergency, as by a city council, will be treated as prima facie evidence of the alleged state of affairs, but not as conclusive; thus there is judicial review of whether the emergency truly exists.[88] Most authority takes the view that the "emergency rule" also applies *after* a contract is let, and thus may be used to validate extra work ordered under a contract when the need for such work unexpectedly arises.[89] But, with that exception, there cannot ordinarily be substantial changes in a contract after it has been awarded pursuant to bidding requirements.[90]

Bidding requirements usually provide that there must be adequate notice to prospective bidders, and such notice normally takes the form of advertisements. The advertisement must contain such information as would be necessary in order for the reasonable bidder to prepare a proposal.[91] Ordinarily, the ad cannot limit the number of bidders or otherwise restrict competition.[92] Bids submitted are valid, and may be

---

[87] Los Angeles Dredging Co. v. City of Long Beach, 210 Cal. 348, 291 P. 839 (1930) (unforeseen conditions necessitated modifications in contract for dredging channel); Grimm v. City of Troy, 60 Misc.2d 579, 303 N.Y.S.2d 170 (1969); Sheehan v. City of New York, 37 Misc. 432, 75 N.Y.S. 802 (1902) (protecting greenhouse from frost); North River Electric Light & Power Co. v. City of New York, 48 App.Div. 14, 62 N.Y.S. 726 (1900) (temporary street lighting); Hoffman v. City of Mount Pleasant, 126 Tex. 632, 89 S.W.2d 193 (Com.App.1936) (sewage facilities); Tobin v. Town Council of Sundance, *supra* note 81 (garbage removal). But see Pyrene Manufacturing Co. v. City of Atlanta, *supra* note 80, refusing to recognize an exception for an emergency and denying even quasi-contractual relief.

[88] See Los Angeles Dredging Co. v. City of Long Beach, *supra* note 87; Reynolds Constr. Co. v. County of Twin Falls, 92 Idaho 61, 437 P.2d 14 (1968) (with review of cases); Continental Construction Co. v. City of Lawrence, 297 Mass. 513, 9 N.E.2d 550 (1937). Cf. West Virginia Coal Co. v. City of St. Louis, 324 Mo. 968, 25 S.W.2d 466 (1930) (under city charter, determination of emergency board of standardization was prerequisite to right to purchase large quantity of coal without advertising for bids).

[89] Los Angeles Dredging Co. v. City of Long Beach, *supra* note 87; Sekerez v. Lake County, 169 Ind.App. 52, 345 N.E.2d 865 (1976); Michigan City v. Witter, 218 Ind. 562, 34 N.E.2d 132 (1941); Jonathan Clark & Sons v. City of Pittsburg, 217 Pa. 46, 66 A. 154 (1907); Thomsen-Abbott Construction Co. v. City of Wausau, 9 Wis.2d 225, 100 N.W.2d 921 (1960) (additional work for lowering foundation footings due to discovery of unstable soil). See Todd Dry Dock Engineering & Repair Corp. v. New York City, 54 F.2d 490 (2d Cir.1931) (cost of extra work could be recovered in breach-of-contract suit). But see Zottman v. City & County of San Francisco, *supra* note 80.

[90] See Gjellefald v. Hunt, 202 Iowa 212, 210 N.W. 122 (1926), noted 15 Geo.L.J. 194 (1926); Hanna v. Board of Education, 200 Md. 49, 87 A.2d 846 (1952) (any changes in contract must be based on honest and reasonable business judgment and must not vary from the original plan to such an extent as to amount to a new undertaking); Robinson v. City of Saginaw, 267 Mich. 557, 255 N.W. 396 (1934); Ely v. City of Grand Rapids, 84 Mich. 336, 47 N.W. 447 (1890) (gutter work added to paving contract; found to be new undertaking necessitating new submission of bids); Diamond v. City of Mankato, 89 Minn. 48, 93 N.W. 911 (1903); Hibbs v. Arensberg, 276 Pa. 24, 119 A. 727 (1923). Cf. Warren v. Chandos, 115 Cal. 382, 47 P. 132 (1897) (contract for grading street ruled void where local officials changed grade-line of street after contract had been let). See generally McCormick, Contract Changes and Extras Clauses, Their Validity and Binding Effect, 10 Forum 5 (1974). See also Annot., Effect of Stipulation, in Public Building or Construction Contract, That Alterations or Extras Must Be Ordered in Writing, 1 A.L.R.3d 1273 (1965).

[91] See Parks v. City of Pocatello, 91 Idaho 241, 419 P.2d 683 (1966). Cf. Brewer Environmental Industries, Inc. v. A.A.T. Chem., Inc., 73 Haw. 344, 832 P.2d 276 (1992) (city's provision of supplemental information to one of two bidders held to have destroyed the requisite equal competitive footing of the bidders and thus to have invalidated the bidding process); City of Hartford v. King, 249 S.W.2d 13 (Ky.1952) (advertisement published the day before bids were due was not proper notice, especially where the ordinance authorizing the improvement for which bids sought hadn't even been passed yet; property owners could not be subjected to assessments to pay for improvement); Asbury Park Press v. City of Asbury Park, 23 N.J. 50, 127 A.2d 401 (1956) (notice of bids was published for minimum period required, but city offices were closed for substantial part of time between advertisement and receipt of bids, thus keeping prospective bidders from obtaining specifications).

[92] Rapp v. Salt Lake City, 527 P.2d 651 (Utah 1974); Mottner v. Town of Mercer Island, 75 Wn.2d 575, 452 P.2d 750 (1969). But a locality is usually allowed to specify a patented or trade-name article if such a

considered, only if in substantially the form provided by the relevant law; they must, for instance, be signed where that requirement is specified.[93] And they must be submitted within the specified time, though there is authority that a bid may be considered if it arrives just a few minutes late.[94]

The general rule is that a bid, once submitted, may not be revoked; it creates a vested contract right in the local government, and the government may not be deprived

---

specification is in the public interest. See Smith v. City of Seattle, 192 Wash. 64, 72 P.2d 588 (1937) (Mazda lamps specified). Cf. Tousey v. City of Indianapolis, 175 Ind. 295, 94 N.E. 225 (1911) (naming of patented article permissible if patentee has agreed to make the article available to the successful bidder). Before specifying a particular brand or a patented article, the locality must give careful attention to serviceability and cost of possible alternatives, if any. See Rewco, Inc. v. City of Cleveland, 183 N.E.2d 646 (Ohio Com.Pl.1961). Some authorities allow a brand name to be used if the words "or equal" are added following the specification of that name. See Shore Gas & Oil Co. v. Borough of Spring Lake, 27 N.J.Super. 33, 98 A.2d 689 (1953). But the addition of those words may not validate the specification if it is so drawn that only one brand can possibly qualify. See Hodge & Hammond, Inc. v. Burns, 23 Misc.2d 318, 202 N.Y.S.2d 133 (Sup.Ct.1960). But cf. Powercorp Alaska, LLC v. Alaska Industrial Development & Export Auth., 171 P.3d 159 (Alaska 2007) (requirement that a particular brand of programmable logic controller be used did not unduly restrict competition).

[93] Whitemarsh Township Authority v. Finelli Brothers, 408 Pa. 373, 184 A.2d 512 (1962). Contra, Eastside Disposal Co. v. City of Mercer Island, 9 Wn.App. 667, 513 P.2d 1047 (1973) (failure to sign bid was mere informality).

See, applying the rule of strict compliance, Nielsen v. City of St. Paul, 252 Minn. 12, 88 N.W.2d 853 (1958); L. Pucillo & Sons v. Borough of New Milford, 73 N.J. 349, 375 A.2d 602 (1977). Cf. Remsco Associates v. Raritan Township Municipal Utilities Authority, 115 N.J.Super. 326, 279 A.2d 860 (1971) (certified check for at least 10% of the amount bid had to be included with bid; failure to include it voided the bid). But cf. P. Michelotti & Sons v. Borough of Fair Lawn, 56 N.J.Super. 199, 152 A.2d 369 (1959), cert. granted 31 N.J. 75, 155 A.2d 173 (1959) (immaterial that uncertified check, later certified, was submitted).

It is often said that a minor irregularity in the form of the bid won't invalidate it if there is no fraud or bad faith. See Township of River Vale v. R.J. Longo Construction Co., 127 N.J.Super. 207, 316 A.2d 737 (1974) (township called for bids to be accompanied by security deposit in form of certified or cashier's check; could award contract to bidder whose deposit was in form of bid bond). In determining whether or not a departure from the required form is sufficiently material to invalidate a bid, the court will primarily consider whether the variation gave that bidder an advantage over others. See Duffy v. Village of Princeton, 240 Minn. 9, 60 N.W.2d 27 (1953); Marvec Allstate, Inc. v. Gray & Fear, Inc., 148 N.J.Super. 481, 372 A.2d 1156 (1977); Centric Corp. v. Barbarossa & Sons, Inc., 521 P.2d 874 (Wyo.1974). It is sometimes emphasized that there is a strong public policy favoring the government's acceptance of the lowest bid, and that if there is substantial compliance with requirements, this goal should not be defeated by strict adherence to technicalities. See Bryan Construction Co. v. Board of Trustees of Free Public Library, 31 N.J.Super. 200, 106 A.2d 303 (1954); Faist v. Mayor of Hoboken, 72 N.J.L. 361, 60 A. 1120 (1905) (bid bond attached instead of certified check; bid valid). If a deviation from bid requirements is major, it cannot be waived by local officials. Township of Hillside v. Sternin, 25 N.J. 317, 136 A.2d 265 (1957) (certified check for at least 10% of amount of bid had to accompany proposal; failure to include this could not be waived). But a minor irregularity can be waived. Murdock Contracting Co. v. Borough of Verona, 47 N.J.Super. 102, 135 A.2d 352 (1957) (bidder had failed to give proof that he could furnish a performance bond; held waivable); Consolidated Sheet Metal Works, Inc. v. Board of Education, 62 Misc.2d 445, 308 N.Y.S.2d 773 (1970) (bidder failed to file certificate of non-collusion; waivable). In JAL Constr., Inc. v. Friedman, 191 Or.App. 492, 83 P.3d 332 (2004), "substantial compliance" with bidding requirements was held to mean compliance in respect to essential matters necessary to assure every reasonable objective of the pertinent statutes. Here, the low bidder's timely delivery of the bid to the mailbox of the city purchasing manager in city hall, rather than to the city public works building, was held to constitute substantial compliance.

[94] Townsend v. McCall, 262 Ala. 554, 80 So.2d 262 (1955) (twenty minutes late); Critchfield v. Jersey City, 4 N.J.Misc. 299, 132 A. 321 (1926) (ten minutes late). Cf. Quinn Constr. Co., L.L.C. v. King County Fire Protection Dist., 111 Wash.App. 19, 44 P.3d 865 (2002) (bidder missed submission deadline by 5 to 10 seconds; considered a mere informality where no unfair advantage shown). See also Gostovich v. City of West Richland, 75 Wn.2d 583, 452 P.2d 737 (1969) (bid mailed 24 hours before appointed time for bid opening; city could validly accept).

of this without its consent.[95] This rule is strictly applied where the bidder's desire to withdraw a bid arises from discovery of a mistake by the bidder that resulted from his own negligence or other fault.[96] But over the years, the courts have recognized a qualification to the general rule; and they will usually now allow a bidder, if he has not ratified his bid or waived his right of withdrawal, to revoke a bid containing a mistake, and obtain return of any bond or deposit he has made, if 5 conditions are satisfied: (1) the mistake concerned a material aspect of the contract; (2) the mistake is serious enough that enforcement of such a contract would be unconscionable; (3) the mistake occurred without any violation of legal duty or failure of reasonable care; (4) the local government will not be seriously harmed by the withdrawal, except for losing the bargain; *and* (5) notice of the mistake was promptly given the local government.[97]

---

[95] See Carlin v. City of Newark, 36 N.J.Super. 74, 114 A.2d 761 (1955); City of Columbus v. Independent Towel Supply Co., 51 Ohio App.2d 250, 367 N.E.2d 915 (1977); Nelson, Inc. v. Sewerage Commission, 72 Wis.2d 400, 241 N.W.2d 390 (1976). Cf. Sinram-Marnis Oil Co. v. City of New York, 74 N.Y.2d 13, 544 N.Y.S.2d 119, 542 N.E.2d 337 (1989) (plaintiff was precluded from modifying its bid to include the right to charge tax as a separate line item and, not having withdrawn its original bid prior to being awarded the contract, it was bound by terms of original bid). The local government can enforce the bid through specific performance or sue on it for damages.

[96] Nelson, Inc. v. Sewerage Commission, *supra* note 95. But if the mistake is a merely clerical or mathematical one, as opposed to an error in judgment, and if the bid was made in good faith, there is now considerable authority allowing the contractor to rescind the bid prior to its acceptance if no harm results from the rescission. See Powder Horn Constructors, Inc. v. City of Florence, 754 P.2d 356 (Colo.1988) (good review of authorities). See generally Annot., Right of Bidder for State or Municipal Contract to Rescind Bid on Ground That Bid Was Based Upon His Own Mistake or That of His Employee, 2 A.L.R.4th 991 (1980).

[97] See Boise Junior College Dist. v. Mattefs Constr. Co., 92 Idaho 757, 450 P.2d 604 (1969); Santucci Construction Co. v. County of Cook, 21 Ill.App.3d 527, 315 N.E.2d 565 (1974); People ex rel. Department of Public Works & Buildings v. South East National Bank, 131 Ill.App.2d 238, 266 N.E.2d 778 (1971); Baltimore County v. John K. Ruff, Inc., 281 Md. 62, 375 A.2d 237 (1977); Conduit & Foundation Corp. v. Atlantic City, 2 N.J.Super. 433, 64 A.2d 382 (1949), noted 47 Mich.L.Rev. 1220 (1949); Jordan v. City of Beaumont, 337 S.W.2d 115 (Tex.Civ.App.1960), refused n.r.e. Cf. School District v. Olson Construction Co., 153 Neb. 451, 45 N.W.2d 164 (1950) (if mistake so fundamental that minds of parties haven't met, equity will act to prevent injustice by allowing withdrawal of bid). It has been held that a court can grant relief from a mistaken bid even if a statute or charter specifies that bids are irrevocable. City of Baltimore v. DeLuca-Davis Construction Co., 210 Md. 518, 124 A.2d 557 (1956).

Bidders have also been allowed to withdraw their bids where the locality with whom they have contracted attempts to impose on them substantial changes in the contract specifications. Cotter v. Casteel, 37 S.W. 791 (Tex.Civ.App.1896), error refused (bidder entitled to return of bid and deposit if substantial and material changes made by locality). But if the changes made by the locality are minor and don't substantially increase the private party's burden or lessen its prospective reward, the bidder cannot, on this ground, withdraw its bid. See City of Crockett v. Murdock, 440 S.W.2d 864 (Tex.Civ.App.1969), refused n.r.e. On mistakes in bids, changes in contract specifications, etc., see generally Survey of State and Local Government Contracts Law, 47 Geo.Wash.L.Rev. 1084 (1979).

A contract may certainly be avoided if the government has made substantial and material misrepresentations to the other party, or has breached a duty to disclose relevant information. In such cases, the government may (except as limited by governmental immunity) also be held civilly liable for fraud. See Sklute, Government Misrepresentation and Non-Disclosure of Superior Knowledge in Federal Procurement, 6 A.B.A.Pub. Contract L.J. 39 (1973–74); Annot., Public Contracts: Duty of Public Authority to Disclose to Contractor Information, Allegedly in Its Possession, Affecting Cost or Feasibility of Project, 86 A.L.R.3d 182 (1978). Cf. Los Angeles Unified School Dist. v. Great American Insurance Co., 49 Cal. 4th 739, 112 Cal. Rptr. 3d 230, 234 P.3d 490 (2010) (government misled contractor by giving him incorrect plans and specifications, causing contractor to submit a bid lower than he would otherwise have made; contractor could recover from government for extra work and expenses necessitated by conditions being other than as represented). See generally Leiblich, Failures of Communication in Government Contract Specifications, 6 A.B.A.Pub. Contract L.J. 1017 (1973–74). As to the notice required when the contractor sues the government for damages resulting from the government's conduct, see City of Gillette v. Hladky Constr., Inc., 196 P.3d 184 (Wyo. 2008) (contractor's notice of claim was sufficient where it was clear the contractor was seeking damages for city's

If a locality has not in some manner reserved the right to reject all bids, then it is usually considered obligated to accept the offer of the lowest responsible bidder.[98] But three important qualifications to this rule are recognized: (1) Statutes or charters may validly provide that a local government has the power to reject all bids; and such provisions are quite common. A locality's action in turning down all bidders will then be sustained unless there is a clear showing of fraud, other illegal conduct, or totally arbitrary action.[99] Occasionally, a statutory or charter provision states that the locality may reject all bids if "good cause" exists to do so. This somewhat broadens the scope of possible judicial review, and a low bidder may have the municipality's rejection of his bid overturned if no *reasonable* ground for the rejection exists.[100] (2) Statutes sometimes allow localities, if they find all bids unsatisfactory, to reject the initial bids and award a contract on the basis of further negotiations.[101] (3) Finally, it is generally agreed that any locality may reject all bids on a particular project if it has clearly reserved this right of rejection in its advertisement for the bids.[102]

A locality is by no means always obligated to accept *the lowest* bid it received on a contract; the basic requirement is that it accept the offer of the lowest *responsible* bidder. This gives it wide discretion, so long as it acts non-arbitrarily and in good faith, to determine the degree of responsibility of those who have bid on the job.[103] Courts will

---

changing the specifications for city hall expansion project and subsequent inaction in face of contractor's efforts to keep project on schedule).

[98] See Austin v. Housing Authority for Hartford, 143 Conn. 338, 122 A.2d 399 (1956); Otter Tail Power Co. v. Village of Elbow Lake, 234 Minn. 419, 49 N.W.2d 197 (1951); Kratz v. City of Allentown, 304 Pa. 51, 155 A. 116 (1931); Pearlman v. City of Pittsburgh, 304 Pa. 24, 155 A. 118 (1931). Cf. Poling v. Roman, 86 N.J.Super. 484, 207 A.2d 219 (1965) (council could refuse to award contract to lowest bidder if it determined after hearing that lowest bidder was not responsible, but must act with diligence as to hearing—lack of diligence could be considered lack of good faith). Cf. City of Golden v. Parker, 138 P.3d 285 (Colo. 2006) (developers had vested contract right to city council's exercise of its discretion in considering whether to make annual appropriations to developers under economic incentive agreements with city; there was no obligation that city make payments to the developers in any single year, the matter was left to the discretion of the city council, and the agreements were not contingent on the borrowing of funds, the extension of the city's credit, or any payments for which funds were not available).

[99] Bielec Wrecking & Lumber Co. v. McMorran, 21 A.D.2d 949, 251 N.Y.S.2d 331 (1964); Highway Express Lines v. Winter, 414 Pa. 340, 200 A.2d 300 (1964); A & A Construction Co. v. City of Corpus Christi, 527 S.W.2d 833 (Tex.Civ.App.1975). See Weber v. City of Philadelphia, 437 Pa. 179, 262 A.2d 297 (1970), mentioning fraud, collusion, bad faith, or arbitrary action.

[100] See Butler v. Federal Way School Dist., 17 Wn.App. 288, 562 P.2d 271 (1977), review denied 89 Wash.2d 1022 (1978), applying Washington statute.

[101] See Interstate Waste Removal Co., Inc. v. Board of Commissioners, 140 N.J.Super. 65, 355 A.2d 197 (1976), applying New Jersey statute.

[102] See Armitage v. City of Newark, 86 N.J.L. 5, 90 A. 1035 (1914); Straw v. City of Williamsport, 286 Pa. 41, 132 A. 804 (1926). Cf. Qonaar Corp. v. Metropolitan Atlanta Rapid Transit Authority, 441 F.Supp. 1168 (N.D.Ga.1977) (decision to reject all bids would be upheld unless arbitrary and capricious—applying specific statute on transit authority).

[103] Paul Goldman, Inc. v. Burns, 109 R.I. 236, 283 A.2d 673 (1971) (with review of cases). See Menke v. Board of Education, 211 N.W.2d 601 (Iowa 1973) (amount of bid is merely one factor to consider); Pioneer Co. v. Hutchinson, 159 W.Va. 276, 220 S.E.2d 894 (1975) (local governing body has broad discretion as long as it acts in good faith and honesty), overruled on other grounds, State ex rel. E.D.S. Federal Corp. v. Ginsberg, 163 W.Va. 647, 259 S.E.2d 618 (1979) (unsuccessful bidder had standing to bring action in mandamus or for injunction due to award of contract to another). Thus, the governing authorities may also consider the quality and suitability of the goods or services being offered. See West v. City of Oakland, 30 Cal.App. 556, 159 P. 202 (Dist.Ct.1916); Duffy v. Village of Princeton, 240 Minn. 9, 60 N.W.2d 27 (1953); Schulte v. Salt Lake City, 79 Utah 292, 10 P.2d 625 (1932). And the experience, skill, integrity, and financial situation of the various bidders. See Housing Authority v. Pittman Construction Co., 264 F.2d 695 (5th Cir.1959); Raymond v. Fresno School District, 123 Cal.App.2d 626, 267 P.2d 69 (Dist.Ct.1954); Jerry's Rides, Inc. v. City of Baltimore, 226 Md. 161,

not interfere with the decision unless bad faith or gross abuse of discretion is shown.[104] But it has been held that if a low bidder is to be "passed over" on the ground he is not sufficiently responsible, the locality must give that bidder notice of the situation and a reasonable opportunity to rebut the evidence against him and present his own case.[105]

---

172 A.2d 487 (1961) (concession to operate trackless trains at zoo; business experience and financial soundness could be considered); Commercial Cleaning Corp. v. Sullivan, 47 N.J. 539, 222 A.2d 4 (1966); Kandel v. Greene, 236 App.Div. 607, 260 N.Y.S. 502 (1932); Cal Wadsworth Constr. v. City of St. George, 898 P.2d 1372 (Utah 1995) (city may consider expertise, skill, ability, and honesty of bidders). Cf. Trap Rock Industries, Inc. v. Kohl, 59 N.J. 471, 284 A.2d 161 (1971) (contractor could be temporarily suspended from list of responsible bidders due to criminal charges filed against contractor's majority stockholder); Zara Contracting Co. v. Cohen, 45 Misc.2d 497, 257 N.Y.S.2d 479 (1964), aff'd 23 A.D.2d 718, 257 N.Y.S.2d 118 (1965) (contractor could be denied award, though was lowest bidder, due to its being under indictment for grand larceny in connection with another public contract); Kayfield Constructing Corp. v. Morris, 15 A.D.2d 373, 225 N.Y.S.2d 507 (1962) (low bidder had been guilty of making improper gifts to municipal employees); Pioneer Co. v. Hutchinson, *supra* (impending litigation against a bidder could be considered). And any other relevant factors. See Leskinen v. Pucelj, 262 Minn. 461, 115 N.W.2d 346 (1962). While statutes may set forth some requirements that bidders must meet, these do not preclude a contracting government from imposing additional requirements regarding experience, competence, and financial standing that must be met for a bidder to be considered "responsible." See Pflueger v. City & County of Honolulu, 5 Hawaii App. 13, 674 P.2d 1019 (1984) (bidder who failed to indicate his qualifications was estopped from asserting that he was denied an opportunity to be heard). Cf. Rollings Constr., Inc. v. Tulsa Metropolitan Water Auth., 745 P.2d 1176 (Okl.1987) (award of "Contractor's Prequalification Certificate" did not vest holder with absolute right to receive contract if it then submitted lowest bid; contracting authority still had discretion to choose lowest responsible bidder). See generally Grand Canyon Pipelines, Inc. v. City of Tempe, 168 Ariz. 590, 816 P.2d 247 (Ariz.App.1991) (low bidder on public construction project did not have protected property interest in being awarded contract; city could reject bid on ground bidder was not responsible). But see Hillside Landscape Contr., Inc. v. City of Lewiston, 151 Idaho 749, 264 P.3d 388 (2011) (city could not reject low bidder's bid on ground that low bidder, which possessed requisite license, did not possess necessary experience).

[104] See Hodgeman v. City of San Diego, 53 Cal.App.2d 610, 128 P.2d 412 (Dist.Ct.1942); Mayes Printing Co. v. Flowers, 154 So.2d 859 (Fla.App.1963); Culpepper v. Moore, 40 So.2d 366 (Fla.1949) (facts must reasonably support the decision); Koich v. Cvar, 111 Mont. 463, 110 P.2d 964 (1941); D. Stamato & Co., Inc. v. Township of Vernon, 131 N.J.Super. 151, 329 A.2d 65 (1974); Sellitto v. Cedar Grove Township, 133 N.J.L. 41, 42 A.2d 383 (1945) (lowest bid can be rejected if, and only if, would not be in best interest of locality to award contract to that bidder). Cf. Sandfort v. Atlantic City, 134 N.J.L. 311, 47 A.2d 553 (1946) (municipality could determine whether low bidders were so lacking in experience, financial ability, machinery, and facilities as to justify belief they would be unable to carry out garbage-collection contract). See generally Annot., Public Contracts: Low Bidder's Monetary Relief Against State or Local Agency for Nonaward of Contract, 65 A.L.R. 4th 93 (1988) (injunctive relief is most common remedy if lowest bidder is wrongfully denied contract, but some courts have now recognized a possible right to compensation). See also Mullins, Corruption in Municipal Procurement: Foreclosing Challenges of Disappointed Bidders—Augusta, Georgia, and the Need for Reform, 42 Pub. Contract L. J. 281 (2013); Annot., Standing of Disappointed Bidder on Public Contract to Seek Damages Under 42 U.S.C. § 1983 for Public Authorities' Alleged Violation of Bidding Procedures, 86 A.L.R. Fed. 904 (1988).

In Ritchie Paving, Inc., v. City of Deerfield, Kansas, 275 Kan. 631, 67 P.3d 843 (2003), it was held that an unsuccessful lowest responsible bidder on a city improvement project had a cause of action against the city on a theory of promissory estoppel, but the bidder's recovery was limited to costs incurred as a direct result of preparing and submitting a bid pursuant to the city's bidding documents. The city had awarded the contract based on factors that were not disclosed in the bidding documents, such as their preference for a commencement date for the project earlier than specified in those documents.

[105] See Inglewood-Los Angeles County Civic Center Authority v. Superior Court, 7 Cal.3d 861, 103 Cal.Rptr. 689, 500 P.2d 601 (1972); Seacoast Construction Corp. v. Lockport Urban Renewal Agency, 72 Misc.2d 372, 339 N.Y.S.2d 188 (1972).

In Metropolitan Express Servs., Inc. v. Kansas City, 23 F.3d 1367 (8th Cir.1994), appeal after remand 71 F.3d 273 (8th Cir.1995), the court allowed a company that had not submitted a bid for a city transportation contract to challenge the award of the contract where, prior to the award, the city's specifications were substantially altered so that if the challenging company had been aware of the new requirements it would have made a bid.

§ 25.5 Miscellaneous Procedural Requirements for Local Contracts

Electoral approval (*i.e.*, approval by the voters) of a local government's contract is unnecessary unless such a requirement is imposed by statute or charter.[106] This type requirement is, however, often thus imposed; and there can then be no recovery on a contract made in violation thereof.[107] But quasi-contractual relief in such situations has been afforded if good faith is shown.[108] Statutes or home-rule charters also frequently state that the making of a contract by a locality must be preceded by a budget item or general appropriation sufficient to cover the expenses which the locality will incur under such contract. Again, a contract entered into in violation of this rule will be void and there can be no recovery on the contract itself.[109] But the trend is to recognize the

---

[106] Baird v. Webster City, 256 Iowa 1097, 130 N.W.2d 432 (1964).

It is also true that, in the absence of a statutory or charter requirement, an ordinance is unnecessary in order to let a municipal contract. See Board of Public Works v. Sho-Me Power Corp., 362 Mo. 730, 244 S.W.2d 55 (1951). A resolution will suffice. State ex rel. Ferguson v. City of Wichita, 188 Kan. 1, 360 P.2d 186 (1961). But statutes and charters often *do* require an ordinance in order for a contract to be let; and if such a requirement is not obeyed, there can be no recovery on express contract. Division 26 v. City of Detroit, 330 Mich. 195, 47 N.W.2d 70 (1951); Homebuilders Association v. Kansas City, 431 S.W.2d 111 (Mo.1968); Ludwig Hommel & Co. v. Village of Woodsfield, 122 Ohio St. 148, 171 N.E. 23 (1930); Crocker v. Town of Manchester, 178 Tenn. 67, 156 S.W.2d 383 (1941). But quasi-contractual relief is usually possible. First National Bank v. City of Emmetsburg, 157 Iowa 555, 138 N.W. 451 (1912); Sluder v. City of San Antonio, 2 S.W.2d 841 (Tex.Com.App.1928), reh. denied 9 S.W.2d 1032; Brand v. City of San Antonio, 37 S.W. 340 (Tex.Civ.App.1896); Cade v. City of Belington, 82 W.Va. 613, 96 S.E. 1053 (1918). But see Lively v. Webb City, 106 S.W.2d 517 (Mo.App.1937); Paul v. City of Seattle, 40 Wash. 294, 82 P. 601 (1905). On the difference between ordinances and resolutions, see generally Section 11.2 *supra*.

[107] Iowa Electric Co. v. Incorporated Town of Winthrop, 198 Iowa 196, 198 N.W. 14 (1924); Utica State Savings Bank v. Village of Oak Park, 279 Mich. 568, 273 N.W. 271 (1937); Fairbanks-Morse Co. v. City of Geary, 59 Okl. 22, 157 P. 720 (1916); Bremerton Municipal League v. Bremer, 15 Wn.2d 231, 130 P.2d 367 (1942). Nor will the municipality be estopped from denying the validity of the contract where required electoral approval has not been obtained. See Wormstead v. City of Lynn, 184 Mass. 425, 68 N.E. 841 (1903); Hagerman v. Hagerman, 19 N.M. 118, 141 P. 613 (1914).

[108] City Council of Dawson v. Dawson Waterworks Co., 106 Ga. 696, 32 S.E. 907 (1899); Olsen v. Independent & Consolidated School District, 175 Minn. 201, 220 N.W. 606 (1928). See Hatch v. Maple Valley Township, 310 Mich. 516, 17 N.W.2d 735 (1945) (contractor's charges exceeded amount approved by electorate; could be quasi-contractual recovery). Cf. General Electric Co. v. Town of Fort Deposit, 174 Ala. 179, 56 So. 802 (1911) (contract void for lack of electoral approval, but seller could recover his property); American-La France & Foamite Industries, Inc. v. Arlington County, 169 Va. 1, 192 S.E. 758 (1937), noted 16 Tex.L.Rev. 267 (1937); 44 W.Va. L.Q. 160 (1937) (contractor could recover rent from county for use of property obtained under a contract that was void because not in compliance with constitutional requirements of electoral approval). But a few cases have denied even quasi-contractual relief when an electoral-approval requirement has not been met. Mountjoy & Frewen v. Cheyenne County High School Dist., 78 Colo. 162, 240 P. 464 (1925); Perry Water, Light & Ice Co. v. City of Perry, 29 Okl. 593, 120 P. 582 (1911).

[109] Empire Voting Machine Co. v. City of Chicago, 267 F. 162 (7th Cir.1920), cert. denied 254 U.S. 642, 41 S.Ct. 14, 65 L.Ed. 453, noted 34 Harv.L.Rev. 439 (1921); Guerine v. City of Northlake, 1 Ill.App.3d 603, 274 N.E.2d 625 (1971); May v. City of Chicago, 222 Ill. 595, 78 N.E. 912 (1906) (overtime pay denied employee); Hamer v. City of Huntington, 215 Ind. 594, 21 N.E.2d 407 (1939); Green v. City of Everett, 179 Mass. 147, 60 N.E. 490 (1901); Hurley v. City of Trenton, 66 N.J.L. 538, 49 A. 518 (1901), aff'd 51 A. 1109 (N.J. Err. & App. 1902); Roberts v. City of Fargo, 10 N.D. 230, 86 N.W. 726 (1901); Hinkle v. City of Philadelphia, 214 Pa. 126, 63 A. 590 (1906). See Miller v. City of Evansville, 244 Ind. 1, 189 N.E.2d 823 (1963) (taxpayer could be granted injunction against payment on contract entered into without required prior appropriation). Where there is a prior-appropriation requirement that has been unmet, a locality cannot ordinarily ratify the attempted contract by a later appropriation. See Burt v. Municipal Council of City of Taunton, 275 Mass. 535, 176 N.E. 511 (1931) (budget law designed to set rigid barriers against expenditures in excess of appropriations); Slurzberg v. City of Bayonne, 29 N.J. 106, 148 A.2d 171 (1959); Davis v. New York City, 50 Misc.2d 275, 270 N.Y.S.2d 265 (1966).

possibility of relief on a quasi-contractual or related theory.[110] A number of statutes and charters simply state that a local government must, before entering a contract, make *provision*, through taxation or other revenue, for payment of the obligations to be incurred. Violation of this kind of requirement will also mean there can be no recovery on the contract itself,[111] but the trend is to allow relief in quasi-contract.[112]

Requirements that contracts—or at least certain contracts—of localities be in writing are commonly encountered in statutes and home-rule documents, and such a requirement may occasionally be inferred.[113] Again, a violation will prevent any recovery on the agreement[114] but, by the trend view, will not prevent quasi-contractual

---

[110] Ohio Oil Co. v. Michigan City, 117 F.2d 391 (7th Cir.1941), noted 4 U.Det.L.J. 219 (1941); Omaha Road Equipment Co. v. Thurston County, 122 Neb. 35, 238 N.W. 919 (1931); Home Owners Construction Co. v. Borough of Glen Rock, 34 N.J. 305, 169 A.2d 129 (1961); Edwards v. City of Renton, 67 Wn.2d 598, 409 P.2d 153 (1965). Recovery has also sometimes been allowed on an estoppel theory. See Scott County v. Advance-Rumley Thresher Co., 288 F. 739 (8th Cir.1923); 405 Monroe Co. v. City of Asbury Park, 40 N.J. 457, 193 A.2d 115 (1963). But cf. Empire Voting Machine Co. v. City of Chicago, *supra* note 109 (acceptance of benefits does not necessarily estop municipality); Slurzberg v. City of Bayonne, *supra* note 109 (ratification, estoppel, and unjust enrichment should not be used to set at naught the laws requiring prior appropriations).

[111] See B.L. Nelson & Associates, Inc. v. City of Argyle, 535 S.W.2d 906 (Tex.Civ.App.1976) (violation of constitutional provision); First Wisconsin National Bank v. Town of Catawba, 183 Wis. 220, 197 N.W. 1013 (1924).

[112] See First Wisconsin National Bank v. Town of Catawba, *supra* note 111. Texas once refused to apply estoppel against a local government, and thus denied relief, where the locality had not provided for tax money to pay the contract, as required by the constitution. Noel v. City of San Antonio, 11 Tex.Civ.App. 580, 33 S.W. 263 (1895), error refused. But later authority in that jurisdiction at least allowed a private party, on a quasi-contractual or similar theory, to recover property received by a local government under a contract violative of requirements concerning provision for payment. See Fabric Fire Hose Co. v. City of Teague, 152 S.W. 506 (Tex.Civ.App.1912); Mineralized Rubber Co. v. City of Cleburne, 22 Tex.Civ.App. 621, 56 S.W. 220 (1900).

[113] See City of Hartford v. King, 249 S.W.2d 13 (Ky.1952), noting lack of certainty if contract not in writing. But cf. Wayman v. City of Cherokee, 204 Iowa 675, 215 N.W. 655 (1927) (contract with city to make street improvements need not be in writing).

In Sena School Bus Co. v. Board of Educ., 101 N.M. 26, 677 P.2d 639 (App. 1984), the court said that a statute granting governmental entities immunity from all contract actions but those based on a valid written contract did not deprive persons who allegedly had an oral contract with a governmental entity of their due process. But the court held it wasn't necessary to reach this constitutional issue anyhow, since any oral-contract action would have been barred by the statute of limitations.

[114] Cook v. Navy Point, Inc., 88 So.2d 532 (Fla.1956); Richard D. Kimball Co. v. City of Medford, 340 Mass. 727, 166 N.E.2d 708 (1960); Kearns v. City of Florissant, 393 S.W.2d 841 (Mo.App.1965); Bride v. Slater, 263 S.W.2d 22 (Mo.1953) (noting that requirement of a writing is a safeguard against fraud); Donovan v. Kansas City, 352 Mo. 430, 179 S.W.2d 108 (1944), appeal dism'd 322 U.S. 707, 64 S.Ct. 1049, 88 L.Ed. 1551 (1944); Angelotti v. Borough of Rankin, 341 Pa. 320, 19 A.2d 398 (1941). Ratification is also usually impossible. See Kansas City v. Rathford, 353 Mo. 1130, 186 S.W.2d 570 (1945); Arnott v. City of Spokane, 6 Wash. 442, 33 P. 1063 (1893). And estoppel has occasionally been denied. See Grauf v. City of Salem, 283 S.W.2d 14 (Mo. App.1955). But it is possible that estoppel will be applied if the case is strong enough. See Board of Public Works v. Sho-Me Power Corp., 362 Mo. 730, 244 S.W.2d 55 (1951) (estoppel may be applied with much caution against municipalities, in exceptional cases, but not here applied where contract made without required approval of common council). Cf. Lathrop Co. v. City of Toledo, 5 Ohio St.2d 165, 214 N.E.2d 408 (1966) (order for extra work not in writing, as required by city charter; city said to have obligation to issue a proper written order).

recovery.[115] The same rules apply to the situation in which a contract has not been signed by the proper local officer—*i.e.*, the one designated by statute or charter.[116]

§ 25.6 Breaches of Local Governmental Contracts

When a locality breaches its contract, the usual rules of contract law apply, and the usual remedies are available, including specific performance.[117] Debt limitations will ordinarily not be applied so as to restrict the money damages that may be awarded against breaching local governments.[118] Similarly, the general rules concerning third-

---

[115] See Webb v. Wakefield Township, 239 Mich. 521, 215 N.W. 43 (1927); Abbott Realty Co. v. City of Charlotte, 198 N.C. 564, 152 S.E. 686 (1930); Memphis Gaslight Co. v. City of Memphis, 93 Tenn. 612, 30 S.W. 25 (1894). But see McGovern v. City of Boston, 229 Mass. 394, 118 N.E. 667 (1918); W.W. Cook & Son v. City of Cameron, 144 Mo.App. 137, 128 S.W. 269 (1910) (city engineer could make incidental changes in carrying out contract for construction of city waterworks system, but where he ordered major changes, contractor could not recover without written contract).

[116] The contract is invalid if not properly signed, and there can be no recovery thereon. Lemery v. Twombly, 281 Mass. 93, 183 N.E. 171 (1932); Sharon Realty Co. v. Westlake, 172 Ohio St. 553, 179 N.E.2d 50 (1961); Press Pub. Co. v. City of Pittsburg, 207 Pa. 623, 57 A. 75 (1904); Lee v. City of Racine, 64 Wis. 231, 25 N.W. 33 (1885). Cf. Con P. Curran Printing Co. v. City of St. Louis, 213 Mo. 22, 111 S.W. 812 (1908) (not properly counter-signed). But there may be quasi-contractual relief. Charlotte Lumber & Manufacturing Co. v. City of Charlotte, 242 N.C. 189, 87 S.E.2d 204 (1955).

If a private party to a contract is required to post a bond or provide other security, these same general rules also apply: The private party will be denied relief on the contract if he did not comply with this requirement. City of Norwalk v. Daniele, 143 Conn. 85, 119 A.2d 732 (1955). But quasi-contractual recovery is generally allowed. Burt v. Road Improvement District, 159 Ark. 275, 253 S.W. 1 (1923); State ex rel. Morris v. Clark, 116 Minn. 500, 134 N.W. 129 (1912). Cf. Charlie Brown Constr. Co. v. Boulder City, 106 Nev. 497, 797 P.2d 946 (1990) (city which failed to follow its own mandatory ordinance requiring it to obtain payment bond from subdivider could be held liable to unpaid subcontractors for negligence). But see Mackey v. Columbus Township, 71 Mich. 227, 38 N.W. 899 (1888) (contractor built bridge without giving the security required by statute; bridge never accepted or used by township; contractor could not recover).

[117] See Interstate Materials Corp. v. City of Houston, 236 S.W.2d 653 (Tex.Civ.App.1951), refused n.r.e. Cf. City of Big Spring v. Board of Control, 389 S.W.2d 523 (Tex.Civ.App.1965), aff'd 404 S.W.2d 810 (Tex.) (in declaratory judgment action by city, contract by city to furnish water to state hospital as long as was maintained on present site held binding on city). See generally Denny Constr., Inc. v. City & County of Denver, 199 P.3d 742 (Colo. 2009) (political subdivision was not exempted by immunity legislation from breach of contract claim, and breach of contract action could include lost profits). There are some cases denying *specific performance* claims against the government on the ground of sovereign immunity. See Thompson Creek Townhomes, LLC v. Tabernash Meadows Water & Sanitation Dist., 240 P.3d 554 (Colo. App. 2010) (concept of sovereign immunity, based on maxim that "king can do no wrong," is broader than merely insulating government from tort liability). See also Tooele Associates Limited Partnership v. Tooele City, 251 P.3d 835 (Utah App. 2011) (for a court to order specific performance, the contract must be free from doubt, vagueness, or ambiguity; partnership not entitled to specific performance under development agreement with city in absence of provision that clearly imposed a continuing duty on city to maintain wastewater storage lakes). And while estoppel is seldom applied against governments, a local government *will* be estopped from denying its contractual obligations. See Sawyer v. City of San Diego, 138 Cal.App.2d 652, 292 P.2d 233 (Dist.Ct.1956). Cf. Boiles v. City of Abilene, 276 S.W.2d 922 (Tex.Civ.App.1955), error refused (municipal corporation estopped from denying validity of contract while exacting performance from other party and accepting benefits). But mandamus to compel a locality to perform its contract will rarely be granted. See Black v. City of Santa Monica, 13 Cal.App.2d 4, 56 P.2d 256 (Dist.Ct.1936) (mandamus won't issue unless is clear case to compel performance of act which law specifically requires as duty resulting from office, trust, or station); State ex rel. Cook v. Kelly, 142 S.W.2d 1091 (Mo.App.1940); City of Breckenridge v. Stoker, 264 S.W.2d 511 (Tex.Civ.App.1954), refused n.r.e.

A frequently encountered provision of government contracts is the "changed conditions' clause," allowing the party with whom the government contracts to recover additional costs added to the performance by physical conditions which materially differ from the specifications or from conditions ordinarily found in the type of work involved. For cases interpreting and applying such clauses, see Annot., Construction and Effect of "Changed Conditions" Clause in Public Works or Construction Contract with State or its Subdivision, 56 A.L.R.4th 1042 (1987).

[118] See DeKalb County v. Georgia Paperstock Co., 226 Ga. 369, 174 S.E.2d 884 (1970).

party beneficiaries govern the contracts of localities, and private persons qualifying as such beneficiaries will be allowed to sue on a municipality's contract.[119] For example, municipalities sometimes enter into contracts with public utilities under which the utilities contract to perform services for certain residents of the community; those residents may then be treated as third-party beneficiaries of the agreement.[120] The usual rules of contract law also apply to rescission and similar matters: Rescission may occur by mutual agreement,[121] as may changes in the contract.[122]

Of course, if the *other* party to a locality's contract breaches, the local government also has, under the law, all the usual remedies. Occasionally, a locality may try to recover sums paid on a contract on the ground that the contract was defectively executed by the locality itself. (Note that this is the reverse of the more common situation; instead of the other party seeking recovery on a defective agreement—in which case recovery on the agreement is usually denied, but often allowed in quasi-contract—, the locality is attempting to undo the matter and recover what it has paid.) Such relief is normally denied unless (1) unjust enrichment to the other party will otherwise result,[123] *or* (2) the contract is shown to have been totally outside the locality's power or made in violation of state statute or some strong public policy.[124]

§ 25.7 Legislation Limiting Those with Whom Locality May Contract

Some state statutes provide that preferences in the awarding of public contracts are to be given local products, suppliers, or laborers over those from other states or areas. Such provisions are valid[125] if (1) there is no violation of the Fourteenth Amendment, as

---

[119] Harlan Water Co. v. Carter, 220 Ky. 493, 295 S.W. 426 (1927); Williams v. City of North Las Vegas, 91 Nev. 622, 541 P.2d 652 (1975) (contract for benefit of general public under which city was obligated to inspect city's facilities; wrongful death action could be based on breach). See Ratzlaff v. Franz Foods, 250 Ark. 1003, 468 S.W.2d 239 (1971) (riparian owners could hold industrial plant to its contract with locality not to pollute stream). Cf. Dixon v. American Liberty Insurance Co., 332 So.2d 719 (Ala.1976) (by statute, citizen can sue against official bond of local officer where alleged breach of contract results in death of another and would give rise to wrongful-death action).

[120] See Woodbury v. Tampa Waterworks Co., 57 Fla. 243, 49 So. 556 (1909); Humphreys v. Central Kentucky Natural Gas Co., 109 Ky. 733, 229 S.W. 117 (1921); Morton v. Washington Light & Water Co., 168 N.C. 582, 84 S.E. 1019 (1915). Cf. Clear Lake Apartments, Inc. v. Clear Lake Utilities Co., 537 S.W.2d 48 (Tex.Civ.App.1976), modified 549 S.W.2d 385 (Tex.) (contract between privately owned utility and local authority could not be declared void where utility's customers, who would lose their utility service as a result of such declaration, were not made parties to action).

[121] See Minnesota Limited, Inc. v. Public Utilities Commission of Hibbing, 296 Minn. 316, 208 N.W.2d 284 (1973) (rescission by mutual consent found). Cf. Davis v. City of Bowling Green, 289 S.W.2d 506 (Ky.1955) (mutual abandonment); Carlin v. City of Newark, 36 N.J.Super. 74, 114 A.2d 761 (1955) (municipality can deal with its contract in same manner as natural person could).

[122] See Peters v. Ryan Constr. Corp., 125 Ind.App. 542, 127 N.E.2d 242 (1955). But cf. Ruck Construction Co. v. City of Tucson, 116 Ariz. 533, 570 P.2d 220 (App.1977) (city could not agree to change in subcontractors).

[123] City of St. Paul v. Dual Parking Meter Co., 229 Minn. 217, 39 N.W.2d 174 (1949), noted 63 Harv.L.Rev. 904 (1950). See City of New Britain v. Hancock, 34 Conn.Sup. 14, 373 A.2d 859 (1976); Scott Township School District Authority v. Branna Construction Corp., 419 Pa. 303, 214 A.2d 236 (1965).

[124] See School District No. 9 v. McLintock, 255 Mich. 197, 237 N.W. 539 (1931); Chaska v. Hedman, 53 Minn. 525, 55 N.W. 737 (1893). See generally, on when a locality may recover money paid under a contract, Vincennes Bridge Co. v. Board of County Commissioners, 248 F. 93 (8th Cir.1917).

[125] American Yearbook Co. v. Askew, 339 F.Supp. 719 (1972), aff'd without opinion 409 U.S. 904, 93 S.Ct. 230, 34 L.Ed.2d 168 (statute requiring all public printing of the state to be done within state). See City of Phoenix v. Superior Court, 109 Ariz. 533, 514 P.2d 454 (1973). Cf. Kloefkorn-Ballard Constr. & Dev., Inc. v. North Big Horn Hosp. Dist., 683 P.2d 656 (Wyo.1984) (corporation organized under Wyoming law and having

through unjust discrimination against aliens or other persons;[126] (2) there is no infringement on an area of exclusive federal control, such as immigration or foreign trade;[127] and (3) there is no unreasonable burden on interstate commerce.[128]

---

principal office and place of business in that state was resident Wyoming corporation for purposes of statute granting preference to resident corporation). But cf. Western Wyoming Constr. Co. v. Board of County Comm'rs of Sublette County, 301 P.3d 512 (Wyo. 2013) (resident contractor preference law does not pre-empt field of residential preferences in context of bidders who are both Wyoming residents; statute simply has no application in that context). It has been held that a local preference law does not violate the privileges and immunities clause of the U.S. Constitution. State v. Antonich, 694 P.2d 60 (Wyo.1985). But see United Bldg. & Constr. Trades Council of Camden v. Camden, 465 U.S. 208, 104 S.Ct. 1020, 79 L.Ed.2d 249 (1984) (ordinance requiring that at least 40% of workers on city construction projects be city residents may violate privileges and immunities clause). Cf. Owen of Georgia, Inc. v. Shelby County, 648 F.2d 1084 (6th Cir.1981) (county's preference for hiring local firms and county's consideration of a contractor's minority employment record did not constitute a "good cause" for awarding a construction bid to other than the lowest bidder). See generally Annot., Validity, Construction, and Effect of State and Local Laws Requiring Governmental Units to Give "Purchase Preference" to Goods Manufactured or Services Performed in State, 84 A.L.R.4th 419 (1991).

On state or local laws limiting governmental purchases from companies that do business in an allegedly repressive foreign state, see Crosby v. National Foreign Trade Council, 530 U.S. 363, 120 S.Ct. 2288, 147 L.Ed.2d 352 (2000) (Massachusetts statute which restricted ability of that state and its agencies to purchase goods or services from companies that do business with Burma (Myanmar) held invalid under Supremacy Clause). See generally Note, The Massachusetts Burma Law, 45 Villanova L. Rev. 137 (2000) (discussing the First Circuit's opinion, which had also invalidated the statute); "Can a State Have Its Own Foreign Policy?," Bus. Week., March 20, 2000, at 130, noting the controversy over the Massachusetts law. For the full history of the "Burma Law" dispute, see Note, The Winding Course of the Massachusetts Burma Law: Subfederal Sanctions in a Historical Context, 34 Geo. Wash. Int'l L. Rev. 435 (2002); Comment, Massachusetts, Myanmar, Market Participation, and the Federal Shutdown of Selective Purchasing Laws: Is the Power to Purchase Really the Power to Regulate?, 21 Nw. J. Int'l & Bus. L. 317 (2000).

[126] See Sugarman v. Dougall, 413 U.S. 634, 93 S.Ct. 2842, 37 L.Ed.2d 853 (1973) (statutory ban on employment of aliens in state civil service); People ex rel. Holland v. Bleigh Construction Co., 61 Ill.2d 258, 335 N.E.2d 469 (1975) (preferences against employment of resident aliens and against residents who had resided in state less than a year preceding employment held violative of equal protection; but preference for those who were residents at time of employment upheld). Cf. Construction & General Laborers Union Local 563 v. City of St. Paul, 270 Minn. 427, 134 N.W.2d 26 (1965) (ordinance required contractors doing work for city to hire only residents of that county; held an unreasonable classification and thus violative of equal protection and several other constitutional provisions). See generally Linde, Constitutional Rights in the Public Sector, 40 Wash.L.Rev. 10 (1965). See also Kasarda & Luther, Why Courts Must Subject Municipalities to Constitutional Tort Liability Under § 1983 When Unconstitutional Race- and Sex-Based Preference Statutes Deprive an Otherwise Lowest Qualified Bidder of a Public Contract, 19 George Mason U. Civ. Rts. L. J. 371 (2009); Mallory, Christy & Sears, An Evaluation of Local Laws Requiring Government Contractors to Adopt LGBT-related Workplace Policies, 5 Albany Gov't L. Rev. 478 (2012).

[127] Purdy & Fitzpatrick v. State, 71 Cal.2d 566, 79 Cal.Rptr. 77, 456 P.2d 645 (1969) (prohibition on employment of aliens held to infringe on Congress's exclusive control of immigration, as well as to violate equal protection); Bethlehem Steel Corp. v. Board of Commissioners, 276 Cal.App.2d 221, 80 Cal.Rptr. 800 (Dist.Ct.1969), noted 3 N.Y.U.J. Int'l L. & Pol. 164 (1970) (state's Buy America Act held to infringe on federal government's exclusive power over foreign trade). Cf. Baldwin-Lima-Hamilton Corp. v. Superior Court, 208 Cal.App.2d 803, 25 Cal.Rptr. 798 (Dist.Ct.1962) (specification for equipment manufactured in United States violated General Agreement on Tariffs and Trade). But see Mabey Bridge & Shore, Inc. v. Schoch, 666 F.3d 862 (3d Cir. 2012) (Pennsylvania statute restricting the use of foreign steel products for government-funded construction projects is not pre-empted by Federal Buy American Act and does not violate Commerce Clause). Cf. Antilles Cement Corp. v. Fortuno, 670 F.3d 310 (1st Cir. 2012) (federal Buy American Act does not pre-empt Puerto Rican law that restricts use of foreign cement on government-funded projects, though Puerto Rican labeling requirements differentiating local and foreign cement were discriminatory and unconstitutional).

[128] See Garden State Dairies of Vineland, Inc. v. Sills, 46 N.J. 349, 217 A.2d 126 (1966), noted 80 Harv.L.Rev. 1357 (1967), finding that a statute favoring the local milk industry in state contract could be invalid under the Commerce Clause and remanding the case for determination of whether there was an undue burden on interstate commerce. On remand, such a burden was found as to one of the requirements. 98 N.J.Super. 109, 236 A.2d 176 (1967), remanded for consideration of whether there was also an undue burden on interstate commerce in another part of the requirements, 53 N.J. 71, 248 A.2d 427 (1968).

Occasionally, legislation, instead of requiring a preference for certain contractors, may have the result of preventing a governmental agency from entering into an agreement with some contractors—as where civil rights legislation is interpreted as forbidding the state or its components from contracting with employers who discriminate, in their hiring, on the basis of race, creed, or color.[129]

---

[129] See Ethridge v. Rhodes, 14 Ohio Misc. 43, 268 F.Supp. 83 (S.D.Ohio.1967), noted 17 Am.U.L.Rev. 92 (1967); 81 Harv.L.Rev. 690 (1968); 46 N.Car.L.Rev. 149 (1967); 70 W.Va.L.Rev. 217 (1968); 1967 Wis.L.Rev. 1016 (injunction could issue against state officials to prevent contracts with contractors who used labor unions as source of their labor supply; alleged that unions discriminated against Negroes). A local government may provide by ordinance for setting aside contracts for bidding only among minority contractors and for designating a percentage of a contract's value to be subcontracted to minorities provided such affirmative action legislation is adopted on the basis of evidence of past discrimination, is narrowly tailored to the objective of remedying the past discrimination, and is constitutionally applied. See South Florida Chapter of Associated General Contractors of America, Inc. v. Metropolitan Dade County, 723 F.2d 846 (11th Cir.1984), later proceedings 729 F.2d 1468 (11th Cir.1984), cert. denied 469 U.S. 871, 105 S.Ct. 220, 83 L.Ed.2d 150 (1984). But cf. City of Richmond v. J. A. Croson Co., 488 U.S. 469, 109 S.Ct. 706, 102 L.Ed.2d 854 (1989), invalidating a city's plan requiring prime contractors awarded city construction contracts to subcontract at least 30% of the dollar amount of each contract to "Minority Business Enterprises." The Court found lacking the type of identified past discrimination against the minority enterprises that would establish the compelling government interest necessary to support such a plan. Cf. American Subcontractors Ass'n v. City of Atlanta, 259 Ga. 14, 376 S.E.2d 662 (1989), achieving the same result under the state constitution's equal protection clause. See generally Comment, Walking a Tightrope: Local Government Minority Business Enterprise Programs Since *City of Richmond v. J.A. Croson Co.*, 40 U.Kan.L.Rev.257 (1991). A good summary of affirmative-action developments after the *Richmond v. Croson* case is found in Symposium, Post-*Croson*, 26 Urban Law. 381–540 (1994). The power of the U.S. Congress to institute affirmative-action programs, including "set-aside" programs for minority contractors, has sometimes been found greater than the power of state and local governments in this regard. See Fullilove v. Klutznick, 448 U.S. 448, 100 S.Ct. 2758, 65 L.Ed.2d 902 (1980).

Statutes sometimes prohibit the award of government contracts to a person or business convicted of specified crimes, such as bribery. See Annot., Validity of State Statute Prohibiting Award of Government Contract to Person or Business Entity Previously Convicted of Bribery or Attempting to Bribe State Public Employee, 7 A.L.R.4th 1202 (1981).

Chapter 26

LOCAL GOVERNMENTAL LIABILITY IN TORT AND RELATED THEORIES

Analysis

§ 26.1 Historical Immunity of Municipalities for "Governmental" Functions

The immunity of governmental institutions from tort liability has long been recognized in the law of this nation and has been the subject of a considerable body of literature.[1] It has been traced to origins in the Roman law[2] and to the English doctrine that the King could do no wrong or, at least, that it was inconsistent with the King's sovereignty to allow him to be sued in his own courts.[3] Although the English rule began as a personal prerogative of the King, it came to be applied rather sweepingly to all levels of government, and, rather mystifyingly, became the basis of the American doctrine of immunity of the state and federal government.[4] The immunity was first applied to a local

---

[1] See Blachly & Oatman, Approaches to Governmental Liability in Tort: A Comparative Survey, 9 Law & Contemp. Prob. 181 (1942); Borchard, Governmental Responsibility in Tort, 28 Colum.L.Rev. 577, 734 (1928); Borchard, Government Liability in Tort, 34 Yale L.J. 1, 129, 221 (1924); Borchard, Government Responsibility in Tort, 36 Yale L.J. 1, 757, 1039 (1926); Davis, Tort Liability of Governmental Units, 40 Minn.L.Rev. 751 (1956); Harley & Wasinger, Governmental Immunity: Despotic Mantle or Creature of Necessity, 16 Washburn L.J. 12 (1976); James, Tort Liability of Government Units and Their Officers, 22 U.Chi.L.Rev. 610 (1955); Somerville, Governmental Tort Liability, 10 Urban Lawyer 376 (1976); Wangerin, Actions and Remedies Against Governmental Units and Public Officials for Nonfeasance, 11 Loyola (Chicago) U.L.J. 103 (1979); Note, Tort Claims Against the State of Illinois and Its Subdivisions, 47 Nw.U.L.Rev. 914 (1953); Note, Economic Analysis of Sovereign Immunity in Tort, 50 So.Cal. L.Rev. 515 (1977). The immunity applies only to tort liability—not liability on contractual or quasi-contractual theories. See Robinson v. Colorado State Lottery Division, 179 P.3d 998 (Colo. 2008) (lottery ticket buyer's breach of contract and unjust enrichment claims sounded in tort and were thus barred under state's Governmental Immunity Act). But see Section 25.6, note 117, as to possible immunity from specific performance. As to the possible injustices caused by sovereign immunity, see Phelan, A Synopsis of Texas and Federal Sovereign Immunity Principles: Are Recent Sovereign Immunity Decisions Protecting Wrongful Governmental Conduct?, 42 St. Mary's L. J. 725 (2011).

One type of immunity that is beyond the scope of this work is diplomatic immunity—the immunity of foreign diplomats in the United States from most civil or criminal proceedings and from many taxes. The law applicable in the United States is codified at 22 U.S.C.A. §§ 254a–58a and in the Vienna Convention on Diplomatic Relations, found at 55 Am.J.Int'l L. 1004 (1961). See generally Barnes, Diplomatic Immunity from Local Jurisdiction: Its Historical Development Under International Law and Application in United States Practice, 43 Dept. State Bull. 1735 (1960); Harris, Diplomatic Privilege and Immunities: A New Regime Is Soon to Be Adopted by the United States, 62 Am.J.Int'l L. 98 (1968). Local officials *do* occasionally encounter situations of diplomatic immunity, as in a celebrated incident in which two policemen arrested the Iranian minister to the United States for speeding, one of the officers allegedly saying "I've heard of Baptist ministers and Presbyterian ministers, but never of Iranian ministers." See Reeves, The Elkton Incident, 30 Am.J.Int'l L. 95 (1936).

[2] See Goodnow, Comparative Administrative Law 146, 169 (1893); Parker, The King Does No Wrong—Liability for Misadministration, 5 Vand.L.Rev. 167 (1952). See generally Watkins, The State as a Party Litigant 1–4 (1927).

[3] See Borchard, Governmental Responsibility in Tort, 36 Yale L.J. 1, 35 (1926); Holdsworth, The History of Remedies Against the Crown, 38 L.Q.Rev. 380 (1922); Jaffe, Suits Against Governments and Officers: Sovereign Immunity, 77 Harv.L.Rev. 1 (1963); Lawyer, Birth and Death of Governmental Immunity, 15 Clev.-Mar.L.Rev. 529 (1966). On the transfer of this immunity from the individual sovereign to the state, see Briggs v. Light-Boat Upper Cedar Point, 93 Mass. (11 Allen) 157, 162 (1865); Maier, Sovereign Immunity and Act of State: Correlative or Conflicting Policies, 35 U.Cin. L.Rev. 556 (1966). On sovereign immunity at the federal level, see generally Sisk, A Primer on the Doctrine of Federal Sovereign Immunity, 58 Okla. L. Rev. 439 (2005).

[4] Borchard, Government Liability in Tort, 34 Yale L.J. 1, 4 (1924). See Jaffe, Suits Against Governments and Officers: Damage Actions, 77 Harv.L.Rev. 209 (1963), suggesting that one reason for adoption of the immunity doctrine in the United States was that the courts had difficulty applying the usual principles of respondeat superior to governmental situations. It has been observed that there is irony in applications in this country of the maxim that "the King can do no wrong" since the country was founded due to the belief that the King had done wrong. Baer, Suing Uncle Sam in Tort, 26 N.C.L.Rev. 119 (1948). See Parker, The King Does No Wrong—Liability for Misadministration, *supra* note 2, concluding that the idea would be appropriate only where everything the chief-of-state does is law, as in an absolute monarchy. In an early case, the U.S. Supreme Court found sovereign immunity inconsistent with our system of popular sovereignty. Chisholm v. Georgia, 2 U.S. (2 Dall.) 419, 1 L.Ed. 440 (1793). Cf. Yick Wo v. Hopkins, 118 U.S. 356, 370, 6 S.Ct. 1064, 30 L.Ed. 220 (1886) (sovereignty is with the people). But before long, the Court adopted sovereign immunity of the government. Cohens v. Virginia, 19 U.S. (6 Wheat.) 264, 5 L.Ed. 257 (1821). See Reeside v. Walker, 52 U.S. (11 How.) 272, 13 L.Ed. 693 (1850). Until the Federal Tort Claims Act was passed in 1946, the United States was immune from tort liability except as the immunity was waived by a few limited

statutory provisions; usually the only possible relief was through special bills passed by Congress. See Gottlieb, Tort Claims Against the United States, 30 Geo. L.J. 462 (1942); Holtzoff, The Handling of Tort Claims Against the Federal Government, 9 Law & Contemp. Prob. 311 (1942). The Federal Tort Claims Act, 28 U.S.C.A. §§ 1346, 1402, 1504, 2110, 2401, 2402, 2411, 2412, 2671–80 contains a general waiver of the government's tort immunity, though a number of exceptions are still provided. See L. Jayson, Handling Federal Tort Claims (1974); W.B. Wright, The Federal Tort Claims Act (1957); Anderson, Recovery from the United States Under the Federal Tort Claims Act, 9 Law & Contemp. Prob. 311 (1942); Fisher, The Federal Tort Claims Act After Five Years, 3 Mercer L.Rev. 263 (1952); Gellhorn & Lauer, Federal Liability for Personal and Property Damage, 29 N.Y.U.L.Rev. 1325 (1954); Gellhorn & Schenk, Tort Actions Against the Federal Government, 47 Colum.L.Rev. 722 (1947); Gerwig, A Decade of Litigation Under the Federal Tort Claims Act, 24 Tenn. L.Rev. 301 (1953); Gottlieb, The Tort Claims Act Revisited, 49 Geo.L.J. 539 (1961); Gottlieb, The Federal Tort Claims Act—A Statutory Interpretation, 35 Geo. L.J. 1 (1946); Hulen, Suits on Tort Claims Against the United States, 7 F.R.D. 143 (1948); Johnson, Federal Tort Claims Act—A Substantive Survey, 6 U.Richmond L.Rev. 65 (1971). See generally Symposia, 26 Fed.B.J. 1–11 (1966); 24 Fed.B.J. 133–227 (1964) (with bibliography); Symposium, 7 Vand.L.Rev. 175–270 (1954). Of course, a private bill through Congress remains to this day a possible remedy where relief cannot be acquired under legislation. See Note, Private Bills, 79 Harv.L.Rev. 1684 (1966). It has been held that when an injured party sues the United States under the Federal Tort Claims Act, the United States waives sovereign immunity in circumstances where local law would make a private person liable in tort—not in circumstances where local law would make a state or municipal entity liable. United States v. Olson, 546 U.S. 43, 126 S.Ct. 510, 163 L.Ed.2d 306 (2005), noted 38 Urban Law. 359 (2006).

It has been stated that federal immunity was initially just a denial of the right to sue the federal government without its consent—basically a matter of procedure. See Kawananakoa v. Polyblank, 205 U.S. 349, 353, 27 S.Ct. 526, 51 L.Ed. 834 (1907) (Holmes opinion). But in time, a true substantive immunity was recognized. See Gibbons v. United States, 75 U.S. (8 Wall.) 269, 19 L.Ed. 453 (Ct.Cl.1868).

On the immunity doctrine as applied to *state* governments, see Anderson, Claims Against States, 7 Vand.L.Rev. 234 (1954); Leflar & Kantrowitz, Tort Liability of the States, 29 N.Y.U.L.Rev. 1363 (1954); Nutting, Legislative Practices Regarding Tort Claims Against the State, 4 Mo.L.Rev. 1 (1939); Shumate, Tort Claims Against State Governments, 9 Law & Contemp. Prob. 242 (1942). On the trend in recent decades to restrict or abolish such state immunity by either legislation or court decision, see Covey, New California Governmental Tort Liability Statutes, 1 Harv.J.Leg. 16 (1964); Olson, Governmental Immunity from Tort Liability—Two Decades of Decline, 31 Baylor L.Rev. 485 (1979); Van Alstyne, Governmental Tort Liability: A Decade of Change, 1966 U.Ill.L.F. 919. See generally Prosser & Keeton, Law of Torts 1043–51 (5th ed. 1984).

A case of considerable importance as to *state* tort liability was Nevada v. Hall, 440 U.S. 410, 99 S.Ct. 1182, 59 L.Ed.2d 416 (1979), reh. denied 441 U.S. 917, 99 S.Ct. 2018, 60 L.Ed.2d 389, noted 48 U.Cin. L.Rev. 1069 (1979), holding that a state may, despite the Eleventh Amendment, constitutionally provide a forum for its citizens to sue a sister state for a wrong committed in the forum state. See, discussing prior developments, Weick, Erosion of State Sovereign Immunity and the Eleventh Amendment by Federal Decisional Law, 10 Akron L.Rev. 583 (1977). But the case had less importance for municipalities, counties, and other political subdivisions of the state, since they have never shared the state's Eleventh Amendment immunity from suit in federal court. See, criticizing this distinction, Note, The Denial of Eleventh Amendment Immunity to Political Subdivisions of the States: An Unjustified Strain on Federalism, 1979 Duke L.J. 1042. On Eleventh Amendment problems, see generally Ripple, State Sovereignty—A Polished but Slippery Crown, 54 Notre Dame Lawyer 745 (1979). It has been held that a state's waiver of sovereign immunity as to tort liability does *not* impliedly waive the Eleventh Amendment's prohibitions of federal court actions against the state. Nichols v. Department of Corrections, 631 P.2d 746 (Okl.1981) (statute waived tort immunity, within limits of insurance or bond coverage, of state Department of Corrections).

government in the 1798 English case of Russell v. Men of Devon[5] and has, despite widespread criticism of such application,[6] been generally applied to municipalities in the United States. Fears of insolvency, and the belief that tax money raised for public use should not be diverted to compensate for the torts of government agents, have no doubt been considerably responsible for the doctrine's longevity.[7]

Except, however, in South Carolina, where local governments have *no* common-law tort liability,[8] the rule has not been one of complete immunity of municipalities in the United States, but has been qualified by the doctrine originated by an early New York decision that a municipality is immune only in the performance of its *governmental* functions, not its proprietary ones.[9] This qualified immunity doctrine has resulted in

---

[5] 2 Term Rep. 667, 100 Eng. Rep. 359 (1798) (county was only quasi-corporation and had no funds for satisfaction of judgment). It has been noted that at the time of this action, the local government was not yet clearly recognized as an entity separate from the population it governed; thus, the suit was in effect against the population of the county. Harno, Tort Immunity of Municipal Corporations, 4 Ill.L.Q. 28 (1921). See Barnett, The Foundations of the Distinction Between Public and Private Functions in Respect to the Common Law Tort Liability of Municipal Corporations, 16 Or. L.Rev. 250 (1937). It has been noted that Russell v. Men of Devon never mentioned the "King can do no wrong" doctrine, but relied on three other grounds for immunity: (1) fear that there would otherwise be an infinity of actions, (2) the lack of a fund out of which recovery could be made, and (3) the theory that it was better for an individual to suffer than for the public to suffer inconvenience. Ayala v. Philadelphia Board of Public Education, 453 Pa. 584, 305 A.2d 877 (1973) (abolishing governmental immunity in Pennsylvania; citing many cases).

[6] See Antieau, The Tort Liability of American Municipalities, 40 Ky.L.J. 131 (1952); David, Municipal Liability in Tort in California, 6 So.Cal.L.Rev. 269 (1933); 7 So.Cal.L.Rev. 48 (1933), 7 So.Cal.L.Rev. 214, 295, 372 (1934); Fuller & Casner, Municipal Tort Liability in Operation, 54 Harv. L.Rev. 437 (1941); Green, Municipal Liability for Torts, 38 Ill.L.Rev. 355 (1944); Harno, Tort Immunity of Municipal Corporations, 4 Ill.L.Q. 28 (1921); Repko, American Legal Commentary on the Doctrine of Municipal Tort Liability, 9 Law & Contemp. Prob. 214 (1942). See generally Smith, Municipal Tort Liability, 48 Mich.L.Rev. 41 (1949); Warp, The Law and Administration of Municipal Tort Liability, 28 Va.L.Rev. 630 (1942). Recent modifications and abrogations of municipal tort immunity are discussed *infra*. On early development of liability, see Tooke, The Extension of Municipal Liability in Tort, 19 Va.L.Rev. 97 (1932). See generally Comment, How to Sue the Government: An Open Courts Attack on Sovereign Immunity, 5 J.L. & Fam. Stud. 421 (2003).

[7] See Gossler v. City of Manchester, 107 N.H. 310, 221 A.2d 242 (1966), saying that abrogation of municipal immunity in tort would open the doors of the city treasury to unlimited claimants and would be financially disastrous to some communities. Cf. Riddle v. Proprietors of Merrimack River Locks & Canals, 7 Mass. 169, 187 (1810) (public corporations not liable, as they lack a corporate fund, but private corporations are liable). See also Coolidge v. Inhabitants of Brookline, 114 Mass. 592 (1874) (town cannot raise by taxation or pay from its treasury expenses incurred in opposing before the legislature annexation of part of its territory to another town). The prevalence of insurance would now seem to make this argument less persuasive. On the effects that insurance has had on immunity, see the discussion of the termination of immunity *infra*. See generally Gibbons, Liability Insurance and the Tort Immunity of State and Local Government, 1959 Duke L.J. 588; Comment, Municipal Corporations—Tort Liability—Purchase of Liability Insurance as Waiver of Immunity, 54 Mich.L.Rev. 404 (1956).

The case generally cited as the first United States application of tort immunity to a municipality is Mower v. Inhabitants of Leicester, 9 Mass. 247 (1812). It has been observed that since this case involved an incorporated town which could levy taxes to pay for damages, Russell v. Men of Devon, *supra* note 5, which was a suit against the *citizens* of a *county*, was incorrectly here relied on as precedent. Barnett, *supra* note 5, at 264, citing Borchard, Government Liability in Tort, 34 Yale L.J. 1, 41, 45 (1924).

[8] Pinkston v. Morrall, 236 S.C. 601, 115 S.E.2d 286 (1960); Furr v. City of Rock Hill, 235 S.C. 44, 109 S.E.2d 697 (1959); McKenzie v. City of Florence, 234 S.C. 428, 108 S.E.2d 825 (1959); Collins v. City of Greenville, 233 S.C. 506, 105 S.E.2d 704 (1958); Irvine v. Town of Greenwood, 89 S.C. 511, 72 S.E. 228 (1911). North Carolina has held that *state* sovereign immunity is absolute and unqualified except as expressly waived by statute. Guthrie v. North Carolina State Ports Auth., 307 N.C. 522, 299 S.E.2d 618 (1983) (North Carolina Ports Authority could not be sued in tort even if Authority's activities were proprietary in nature). But this rule of total immunity has only been applied to the state and its arms, not to municipalities, which are liable for their proprietary acts. See Aaser v. City of Charlotte, 265 N.C. 494, 144 S.E.2d 610 (1965).

[9] The distinction is usually traced to Bailey v. City of New York, 3 Hill 531 (1842), aff'd 1845 WL 4879 (1845). Until then, it had *usually* been assumed that municipalities would be liable for their torts just as

much "hair-splitting" and has, like the concept of governmental immunity itself, been much criticized.[10] But some generalizations can be drawn from the cases as to how the distinction works in practice: Governmental activities are normally undertaken for the good of the general public[11] and involve an exercise of the locality's sovereign powers, delegated from the state.[12] Activities undertaken for the financial profit of the municipality are, on the other hand, considered businesslike in nature, rather than connected with the locality's governing functions, and are thus proprietary.[13] Indeed, whenever a fee is charged by a municipality for the service rendered, that fee is strong evidence of the service's proprietary nature.[14] The reasoning (if it can be called that) behind the distinction seems to be that when a locality acts like a private business, or performs functions customarily performed by such businesses, it should be treated as on a par with private enterprises, and should be made to pay, just as they would, for harm

---

private corporations were. But there were some even-earlier indications of the governmental-proprietary distinction. See Barnett, *supra* note 5. See generally Doddridge, Distinction Between Governmental and Proprietary Functions of Municipal Corporations, 23 Mich.L.Rev. 325 (1925); Kraehe, "There's Something About Cities": Understanding Proprietary Functions of Texas Municipalities and Governmental Immunity, 32 Tex. Tech L. Rev. 1 (2000). Many of the cases applying this distinction have in effect been overruled by cases or statutes that abolish (though often with exceptions) municipal immunity in tort. On the governmental-proprietary distinction, see also Section 26.2 *infra*.

[10] See Weeks v. City of Newark, 62 N.J.Super. 166, 162 A.2d 314 (1960), aff'd 34 N.J. 250, 168 A.2d 11, saying the rules in this area are as logical as those governing French irregular verbs; Morris v. Mount Lebanon Township School District, 393 Pa. 633, 144 A.2d 737 (1958), saying there is no issue known to the law which is surrounded by more confusion than the question of whether a particular activity of a municipal corporation is governmental or proprietary; K.C. Davis, Administrative Law Treatise § 25.07, at 460 (1958), saying the distinction is one of the most unsatisfactory known to the law; Seasongood, Municipal Corporations: Objections to the Governmental or Proprietary Test, 22 Va.L.Rev. 910 (1936). See generally Fairweather, Test of Sovereign Immunity for Municipal Corporations, 13 Clev.-Mar.L.Rev. 151 (1964); Comment, Postscript: Tracing the Governmental-Proprietary Test, 53 U. Cinc. L. Rev. 561 (1984). Comment Note, Municipal Immunity from Liability for Torts, 60 A.L.R.2d 1198 (1958).

[11] Bolster v. City of Lawrence, 225 Mass. 387, 114 N.E. 722 (1917). See Felton v. City of Great Falls, 118 Mont. 586, 169 P.2d 229 (1946) (powers granted municipal corporation are (1) public or governmental, and (2) proprietary or quasi-private; operation of swimming pool held proprietary). Some authority limits governmental immunity to activities which can be effectively carried out *only* by the government. See Bokano v. Wayne-Westland Community Schools, 114 Mich.App. 79, 318 N.W.2d 613 (1982) (no immunity where school system acts as employment agency by placing students in jobs unrelated to their studies).

[12] See Grimes v. City of Henryetta, 208 Okl. 217, 254 P.2d 980 (1953) (city not liable for acts of its officers in attempting to enforce police regulations); Savage v. City of Tulsa, 174 Okl. 416, 50 P.2d 712 (1935) (city not liable for injuries to prisoner in city jail who was struck by car while doing street-maintenance work). Cf. City of Atlanta v. Mitcham, 296 Ga. 576, 769 S.E.2d 320 (2015) (care of jail inmates is governmental).

[13] See Dickinson v. City of Boston, 188 Mass. 595, 75 N.E. 68 (1905) (activity proprietary even if no profit actually realized); Glenn v. City of Raleigh, 248 N.C. 378, 103 S.E.2d 482 (1958). Cf. Britt v. City of Wilmington, 236 N.C. 446, 73 S.E.2d 289 (1952) ("commercial" activities are proprietary). Cf. Lane v. City of Seattle, 164 Wash. 2d 875, 194 P.3d 977 (2008) (providing fire hydrants held governmental; charge imposed on taxpayers to pay the cost of hydrants held an invalid tax). But some incidental financial advantage to a locality does not necessarily mean that the activity involved is proprietary if it was primarily undertaken for other reasons. See Day v. City of Berlin, 157 F.2d 323 (1st Cir.1946) (woman who fell on city-hall steps while on way to lavatory not entitled to recover from city merely because she intended to use pay toilet, not free toilet); Petty v. City of Atlanta, 40 Ga.App. 63, 148 S.E. 747 (1929).

[14] See Cornelisen v. City of Atlanta, 146 Ga. 416, 91 S.E. 415 (1917); Floyes v. City of Monroe, 194 So. 102 (La.App.1940); Sloper v. City of Quincy, 301 Mass. 20, 16 N.E.2d 14 (1938); Foss v. City of Lansing, 237 Mich. 633, 212 N.W. 952 (1927); Borwege v. City of Owatonna, 190 Minn. 394, 251 N.W. 915 (1933); Town of Douglas v. York, 445 P.2d 760 (Wyo.1968). But like most guidelines in this area, the "fee rule" is not absolute, and an activity may still be classified as governmental though a fee is charged. See Carr v. City & County of San Francisco, 170 Cal.App.2d 48, 338 P.2d 509 (Dist.Ct. 1959).

Some authority tends to equate proprietary activities with those of purely local concern to the community, and governmental activities with those of general or statewide concern. See Carter v. City of Greensboro, 249 N.C. 328, 106 S.E.2d 564 (1959).

done. A few courts, it should be noted, have substituted other distinctions for the governmental-proprietary test of determining the extent of municipal immunity. For instance, at times some tribunals have held that a local government is immune in the exercise of "mandatory" or "compulsory" powers—those that by law it and/or its agents *must* exercise—while no immunity exists as to activities voluntarily undertaken.[15] And some authority has found governmental immunity as to "discretionary" decisions and functions of local governmental agents, while finding no immunity as to "ministerial" undertakings—the thought being that free reign, without fear of creating governmental liability, should be given municipal officers and employees when they undertake planning or policy-making, but no such immunity should be accorded as to the day-to-day, routine carrying-out of laws and policies.[16] But neither of these two tests has gained strong support; and where municipal immunity is retained and is not modified by legislation, the governmental-proprietary distinction remains the test most often employed.

§ 26.2 Governmental v. Proprietary Distinction in Operation

In some areas of local activity, the *governmental* nature of the function is so evident that it is almost universally agreed, often with little discussion, that there is tort immunity. This is true, for instance, of a municipality's enactment of, or failure to enact,

---

[15] See Green v. City of Birmingham, 241 Ala. 684, 4 So.2d 394 (1941); Desmarais v. Wachusett Regional School District, 360 Mass. 591, 276 N.E.2d 691 (1971); Storti v. Town of Fayal, 194 Minn. 628, 261 N.W. 463 (1935); Byrnes v. City of Jackson, 140 Miss. 656, 105 So. 861 (1925) (city could be held liable for injuries inflicted by animal at city zoo, since was no mandatory obligation to keep a zoo); Eversole v. City of Columbus, 169 Ohio St. 205, 158 N.E.2d 515 (1959); Evans v. City of Sheboygan, 153 Wis. 287, 141 N.W. 265 (1913). But most authority has rejected this distinction. See Gillies v. City of Minneapolis, 66 F.Supp. 467 (D.Minn.1946); Martinson v. City of Alpena, 328 Mich. 595, 44 N.W.2d 148 (1950); Reynolds v. City of Nashua, 93 N.H. 28, 35 A.2d 194 (1943); Moulton v. City of Fargo, 39 N.D. 502, 167 N.W. 717 (1918).

[16] See Boucher v. Fuhlbruck, 26 Conn. Sup. 79, 213 A.2d 455 (1965) (saying "ministerial" acts are those that an official must perform without regard to his own judgment as to whether or not they should be done); Jones v. Sioux City, 185 Iowa 1178, 170 N.W. 445 (1919); Ely v. City of St. Louis, 181 Mo. 723, 81 S.W. 168 (1904); Fowler v. City of Cleveland, 100 Ohio St. 158, 126 N.E. 72 (1919); City of Tulsa v. Washington, 206 Okl. 61, 241 P.2d 194 (1952); Walters v. City of Carthage, 36 S.D. 11, 153 N.W. 881 (1915); Hoggard v. City of Richmond, 172 Va. 145, 200 S.E. 610 (1939), noted 24 Wash.U.L.Q. 425 (1939). Cf. Baker v. Washington, 448 F.2d 1200 (D.C.Cir.1971) (discretionary-ministerial distinction is measure of District of Columbia's common-law tort immunity as to both intentional and negligent torts). But the doctrine has been applied mainly in isolated cases and was never widely adopted as a permanent and general rule. It has been criticized on the ground there is no sound reason to immunize activities merely because there is some discretion involved in their exercise. See 1A Antieau, Municipal Corporation Law § 11.32, at 11–51 (1980). The Federal Tort Claims Act and a number of state laws contain exceptions under which the government remains immune as to the performance of, or failure to perform, discretionary functions; and these provisions have caused considerable difficulty in interpretation and application. See Cervone & Hardy, The Massachusetts Governmental Tort Liability Act and Its Discretionary Function Immunity: An Analysis and a Modest Proposal, 14 Suffolk U.L.Rev. 1251 (1980); James, The Federal Tort Claims Act and the "Discretionary Function" Exception, 10 U.Fla.L.Rev. 184 (1957); Peck, The Federal Tort Claims Act—A Proposed Construction of the Discretionary Function Exception, 31 Wash.L.Rev. 207 (1956); Reynolds, The Discretionary Function Exception of the Federal Tort Claims Act, 57 Geo.L.J. 81 (1968); Comment, Discretionary Function Exception to Federal Tort Liability, 2 Cumberland-Samford L.Rev. 383 (1970); Comment, Federal Tort Claims Act: Discretionary Function Exception Revisited, 31 U.Miami L.Rev. 161 (1976); Note, Torts—Federal Tort Claims Act—The Discretionary Function Exception to the Federal Tort Claims Act Is Limited Strictly to Policy Formulation, 45 U.Cin.L.Rev. 157 (1976). See also Heuser, Dalehite v. United States: A New Approach to the Federal Tort Claims Act, 7 Vand.L.Rev. 175 (1954), discussing an early, now largely discarded U.S. Supreme Court interpretation of the exception that gave the exception very wide scope.

Though usually rejected as to governmental liability, the discretionary-v.-ministerial test *is* much used in determining the *personal* liability of governmental officers and employees. See *infra* this chapter.

legislation[17]—even if an enacted measure proves to be unconstitutional or otherwise invalid.[18] Similarly, the enforcement of an ordinance is clearly a function of the local government *as* a governing power and therefore falls within the scope of immunity, even if the law enforced is declared invalid.[19] And the failure of a local government to enforce laws—statutes, ordinances, etc.—also involves an exercise of governmental, not corporate or business-like, power and cannot be made the basis of tort liability.[20] The instituting of legal proceedings, even if wrongfully done, is similarly classified, at least if the litigation is instituted for the benefit or protection of the municipality.[21]

Apart from these few generalizations, the categorization of activities as governmental or proprietary becomes quite difficult. If an attempt is made to base liability on the care and maintenance of a building (or lack thereof), the court must look to the use made of that particular structure by the locality. If, as is usually the case with a city hall, the building is used in connection with the city's governing activities, the immunity attaches to the building.[22] But the operation of a municipal garage is

---

[17] See Fidelity Laboratories v. Oklahoma City, 191 Okl. 473, 130 P.2d 834 (1942) (ordinance banning swine from city allegedly ruined plaintiff's hog cholera serum business); Mefford v. City of Dupontonia, 49 Tenn.App. 349, 354 S.W.2d 823 (1961). Cf. Young v. Jewish Welfare Federation, 371 S.W.2d 767 (Tex.Civ.App.1963), ref'd n.r.e. (amending of site plan for welfare center was exercise of governmental zoning power; no liability).

[18] City of Philadelphia ex rel. Warner Co. v. National Surety Corp., 48 F.Supp. 381 (E.D.Pa.1942), aff'd 140 F.2d 805; Elrod v. City of Daytona Beach, 132 Fla. 24, 180 So. 378 (1938); Curran v. Chicago Great Western Railway Co., 134 Minn. 392, 159 N.W. 955 (1916); Bean v. City of Moberly, 350 Mo. 975, 169 S.W.2d 393 (1943); Veling v. Borough of Ramsey, 94 N.J.Super. 459, 228 A.2d 873 (1967) (invalid amendment to zoning ordinance); Visidor Corp. v. Borough of Cliffside Park, 48 N.J. 214, 225 A.2d 105 (1966), cert. denied 386 U.S. 972, 87 S.Ct. 1166, 18 L.Ed.2d 132 (with review of cases); Whittaker v. Village of Franklinville, 265 N.Y. 11, 191 N.E. 716 (1934), affirming 239 App.Div. 881, 265 N.Y.S. 977, rearg. denied 266 N.Y. 505, 195 N.E. 174; Orange County v. Heath, 14 N.C.App. 44, 187 S.E.2d 345 (1972), cert. allowed 281 N.C. 514, 189 S.E.2d 34, aff'd 282 N.C. 292, 192 S.E.2d 308; Harrington v. Town of Greenville, 159 N.C. 632, 75 S.E. 849 (1912); Jones v. City of Williamsburg, 97 Va. 722, 34 S.E. 883 (1900); J.S.K. Enterprises, Inc. v. Lacey, 6 Wn.App. 433, 493 P.2d 1015 (1972), review denied 80 Wash.2d 1006 (1972); Wikstrom v. City of Laramie, 37 Wyo. 389, 262 P. 22 (1927). See Yellow Cab Co. v. City of Chicago, 186 F.2d 946 (7th Cir.1951); Bagni v. City of Bristol, 127 Conn. 38, 14 A.2d 716 (1940) (designation by city of places where coasting permitted on streets did not create liability for licensing a "public nuisance").

[19] See Mayhue v. City of Plantation, 375 F.2d 447 (5th Cir.1967).

[20] See Chambers v. Palaggi, 88 Ill.App.2d 221, 232 N.E.2d 69 (1967); Kretchmar v. City of Atchison, 133 Kan. 198, 299 P. 621 (1931) (municipality failed to enforce ordinances against fireworks; plaintiff lost eye as a result; no liability); Stranger v. New York State Electric & Gas Corp., 25 A.D.2d 169, 268 N.Y.S.2d 214 (1966) (failure to enforce fire regulations); Goggin v. City of Seattle, 48 Wn.2d 894, 297 P.2d 602 (1956) (no liability for failure to enforce laws against nuisances; court said no case imposing liability in such situation could be found). Cf. Roberson v. District of Columbia, 86 A.2d 536 (D.C.Mun.App.1952) (plaintiff struck by persons improperly allowed to loiter).

[21] Doyle v. City of Sandpoint, 18 Idaho 654, 112 P. 204 (1910). See Taulli v. Gregory, 223 La. 195, 65 So.2d 312 (1953) (no municipal liability for malicious prosecution); Creelman v. Svenning, 67 Wn.2d 882, 410 P.2d 606 (1966) (no state or county liability for malicious prosecution). The rule against liability for malicious prosecution is sometimes retained even where most municipal immunity has been abrogated. See Vivell v. City of Belmont, 274 Cal.App.2d 38, 78 Cal.Rptr. 841 (Dist.Ct. 1969). But see Watson v. New York City, 57 Misc.2d 542, 293 N.Y.S.2d 348 (1968) (city liable for malicious prosecution). Cf. Cone v. City of Lubbock, 431 S.W.2d 639 (Tex.Civ.App.1968), ref'd n.r.e. (city could be liable for wrongfully obtaining injunction involving proprietary function).

[22] Schwalk's Administrator v. City of Louisville, 135 Ky. 570, 122 S.W. 860 (1909); Snider v. City of St. Paul, 51 Minn. 466, 53 N.W. 763 (1892); Pleasants v. City of Greensboro, 192 N.C. 820, 135 S.E. 321 (1926); Huffman v. City of Columbus, 51 N.E.2d 410 (Ohio App.1943) (city not liable for negligence in manner of fastening iron bar to city-hall building). Cf. Griggs v. City of Goddard, 233 Kan. 915, 666 P.2d 695 (1983) (maintenance of courthouse grounds held governmental; county immune from liability to citizen who tripped over wire on courthouse lawn). But see Fox v. City of Philadelphia, 208 Pa. 127, 57 A. 356 (1904). Cf. Bucholz v. City of Sioux Falls, 77 S.D. 322, 91 N.W.2d 606 (1958) (city was liable to boy using police rifle range in

ordinarily classified as proprietary.[23] Occasional cases have held a locality liable if even *some* of the activities carried on in a building are proprietary in nature,[24] and a few courts have looked to the specific uses made of the portion of the building in which the injury was suffered.[25] The majority view would seem to be that municipal auditoriums, arenas, and convention halls are proprietary in nature.[26]

---

basement of city hall); Ring v. City of Mitchell, 64 S.D. 67, 263 N.W. 893 (1935) (city could be liable for defective condition of city-hall steps leading to public rest room).

[23] Bertiz v. City of Los Angeles, 74 Cal.App. 792, 241 P. 921 (Dist.Ct.1925). This is true though the garage is operated by, or for the benefit of, a "governmental" branch of city government, such as the police department. See City of Tulsa v. Hodge, 293 P.2d 344 (Okl.1956) (garage and repair shop for trucks that cleaned city streets); City of Tulsa v. Washington, 206 Okl. 61, 241 P.2d 194 (1952) (washing garbage trucks); Oklahoma City v. Haggard, 170 Okl. 473, 41 P.2d 109 (1935) (garage for police vehicles); Oklahoma City v. Foster, 118 Okl. 120, 247 P. 80 (1926) (same); City of Houston v. Shilling, 150 Tex. 387, 240 S.W.2d 1010 (1951), noted 30 Tex.L.Rev. 266 (1951) (garage for garbage trucks). Cf. Dallas v. City of St. Louis, 338 S.W.2d 39 (Mo.1960) (garage for garbage trucks and other city vehicles).

[24] See Carlisi v. City of Marysville, 373 Mich. 198, 128 N.W.2d 477 (1964); Bell v. City of Pittsburgh, 297 Pa. 185, 146 A. 567 (1929). Such cases illustrate the tendency long exhibited by some courts to keep municipal immunity within fairly narrow bounds. Thus, it has also usually been held that if a municipal government leases some or all of a building to another person or entity, the municipality loses its immunity as to the leased premises. See Little v. City of Holyoke, 177 Mass. 114, 58 N.E. 170 (1900); Munson v. Menominee County, 371 Mich. 504, 124 N.W.2d 246 (1963); Dean v. Board of Trustees, 65 Ohio App. 362, 29 N.E.2d 910 (1940). What if the locality is the tenant and another person is the landlord? In Davis v. County of Carbon, 495 P.2d 21 (Wyo.1972), a county was not liable for operation of a building it was leasing.

[25] See Tinsley v. City of Cincinnati, 146 N.E.2d 336, 4 O.O.2d 454 (Com.Pl. 1957) (window washer fell from portion of municipal building used for smoke-abatement program, a governmental activity). Cf. City & County of Denver v. Austria, 136 Colo. 454, 318 P.2d 1101 (1957) (plaintiff fell on left-over portion of Christmas decorations at municipal building; placing and removing of such decorations is not a governmental function; no immunity); Weiser v. Kansas City, 481 S.W.2d 568 (Mo.App.1972) (injury within city hall to employee of water department, which was housed there, held within proprietary area). But cf. Kelly v. City of Boston, 186 Mass. 165, 71 N.E. 299 (1904) (where plaintiff injured through negligence of city employees in throwing snow from city-hall roof, immaterial that city hall was occupied in part by city water department and city collector; no liability).

[26] See Sanders v. City of Long Beach, 54 Cal.App.2d 651, 129 P.2d 511 (Dist.Ct.1942) (auditorium); Chafor v. City of Long Beach, 174 Cal. 478, 163 P. 670 (1917) (auditorium); McGrury v. Kansas City, 397 S.W.2d 688 (Mo.App.1965) (auditorium); Leeds v. Atlantic City, 13 N.J.Misc. 868, 181 A. 892 (1935) (convention hall); Aaser v. City of Charlotte, 265 N.C. 494, 144 S.E.2d 610 (1965) (arena for exhibitions and athletic events); Bennett v. City of Portland, 124 Or. 691, 265 P. 433 (1928). Cf. City of Wichita Falls v. Lewis, 68 S.W.2d 388 (Tex.Civ.App.1933). But see Roberts v. City of Savannah, 54 Ga.App. 375, 188 S.E. 39 (1936) (auditorium treated as governmental); Ramirez v. Ogden City, 3 Utah 2d 102, 279 P.2d 463 (1955) (operation of community recreational center was governmental; city not liable when plaintiff's dress caught fire in ladies' powder room).

Fire-fighting, and fire-prevention and -control activities are generally agreed to be governmental,[27] as are law-enforcement activities of the police.[28] Thus, a municipality cannot, under the traditional governmental-proprietary distinction, be liable for tortious operation of a police vehicle,[29] or for the negligent installation of, or failure to install,

---

[27] See Thon v. City of Los Angeles, 203 Cal.App.2d 186, 21 Cal.Rptr. 398 (Dist.Ct.1962) (city failed to provide hose adequate to reach from nearest hydrant); Reynolds Boat Co. v. City of Haverhill, 357 Mass. 668, 260 N.E.2d 176 (1970) (municipality failed to provide enough water to fight fire); Howard v. City of Stillwater, 171 Minn. 391, 214 N.W. 656 (1927); Alexander v. City of Vicksburg, 68 Miss. 564, 10 So. 62 (1891); Motyka v. City of Amsterdam, 15 N.Y.2d 134, 256 N.Y.S.2d 595, 204 N.E.2d 635 (1965); Mabe v. City of Winston-Salem, 190 N.C. 486, 130 S.E. 169 (1925). Cf. Heieck & Moran v. City of Modesto, 64 Cal.2d 229, 49 Cal.Rptr. 377, 411 P.2d 105 (1966) (city employees closed water valve so that water was not available at hydrants near plaintiff's premises, and fire department failed to obtain other water, which would have been available from county); Canade, Inc. v. Town of Blue Grass, 195 N.W.2d 734 (Iowa 1972) (volunteer fire department of town went to blaze outside town, but withdrew when it found property-owner was not one of its subscribers); Steitz v. City of Beacon, 295 N.Y. 51, 64 N.E.2d 704 (1945), noted 39 Harv.L.Rev. 804 (1946) (city not liable for failure to create and maintain fire department or for failure to keep in repair water-pressure-and-flow-regulating valve); Valevais v. City of New Bern, 10 N.C.App. 215, 178 S.E.2d 109 (1970) (failure to respond to call outside city, though city had made valid contract to do so). The immunity often applies to operation of vehicles. See Annot., Liability for Personal Injury or Damage from Operation of Fire Department Vehicle, 82 A.L.R.2d 312 (1962). The immunity normally extends to failure to install or maintain fire hydrants properly. See Stang v. City of Mill Valley, 38 Cal.2d 486, 240 P.2d 980 (1952); Brink v. City of Grand Rapids, 144 Mich. 472, 108 N.W. 430 (1906). Cf. Bagwell v. City of Gainesville, 106 Ga.App. 367, 126 S.E.2d 906 (1962) (city deliberately turned off water). But when a locality provides fire service outside its borders in return for a fee, it may be held to be acting in a proprietary capacity. See City of Sand Springs v. Gray, 182 Okl. 248, 77 P.2d 56 (1938).

[28] See Wilford v. City of Jacksonville Beach, 79 So.2d 516 (Fla.1955); Allen v. City of Ogden, 210 Kan. 136, 499 P.2d 527 (1972); Gardner v. McDowell, 202 Kan. 705, 451 P.2d 501 (1969); Bale v. Ryder, 286 A.2d 344 (Me.1972); Tzatzken v. City of Detroit, 226 Mich. 603, 198 N.W. 214 (1924); Parks v. Town of Princeton, 217 N.C. 361, 8 S.E.2d 217 (1940); Blackman v. City of Cincinnati, 66 Ohio App. 495, 35 N.E.2d 164 (1941), 140 Ohio St. 25, 42 N.E.2d 158; Smeltz v. Copeland, 440 Pa. 224, 269 A.2d 466 (1970); Coffman v. City of Pulaski, 220 Tenn. 642, 422 S.W.2d 429 (1967) (police officer's shooting of suspect). Cf. Snell v. Murray, 117 N.J.Super. 268, 284 A.2d 381 (1971), aff'd 121 N.J.Super. 215, 296 A.2d 538 (city not liable for wounds inflicted by drunken police officer; no negligence in entrusting officer with pistol unless city had reason to know of officer's dangerous propensity). Compare Morales v. Oklahoma City, 230 P.3d 869 (Okla. 2010) (city was sued for injuries sustained by student during arrest by police officer following student's participation in fight; statutory immunity did not apply as officer was not providing protective services to student). If police officers engage in *unlawful* acts within the scope of their employment, any municipal immunity may be held inapplicable. See Dill v. Rader, 533 P.2d 650 (Okl.App. 1975) (in trying to prevent law suit against city, officials, including police chief, allegedly conspired to defame plaintiff; conspirators held to be acting for city in its proprietary capacity, and thus it did not enjoy immunity). Sometimes a local government's non-liability for failing to provide police protection or other such service has been based on the idea that any duty in this area is a public duty and does not run in favor of an individual. See Keane v. City of Chicago, 98 Ill.App.2d 460, 240 N.E.2d 321 (1968) (no greater duty owed school teacher on school premises than owed general public); Adamczyk v. Zambelli, 25 Ill.App.2d 121, 166 N.E.2d 93 (1960); Motyka v. City of Amsterdam, *supra* note 27 (dictum as to police). This public-duty limitation was applied in Massengill v. Yuma County, 104 Ariz. 518, 456 P.2d 376 (1969), but that case was overruled in Ryan v. State, 134 Ariz. 308, 656 P.2d 597 (1982), on remand 150 Ariz. 549, 724 P.2d 1218 (1986) (state can be liable for harm caused by escaped prisoner if state knew or should have known of likelihood of such harm). On limitations on governmental liability in Arizona, see generally Note, A Separation of Powers Analysis of the Absolute Immunity of Public Entities, 28 Ariz. L. Rev. 50 (1986), noting particularly that retention of the common law under the Arizona statute distinguishes that statute from the tort claims acts of many other states. And the common law of Arizona provides for governmental liability in tort in most situations, with immunity the exception. *Id.* at 52. On the duty concept, see also Section 26.3 *infra*.

[29] Poole v. City of Louisville, 107 Ga.App. 305, 130 S.E.2d 157 (1963); Taylor v. City of Berwyn, 372 Ill. 124, 22 N.E.2d 930 (1939) (police car was chasing murder suspect); Barnett v. City of Monroe, 124 So.2d 249 (La.App.1960); City of Hattiesburg v. Buckalew, 240 Miss. 323, 127 So.2d 428 (1961); Lewis v. Hunter, 212 N.C. 504, 193 S.E. 814 (1937) (mechanic driving police car while testing radio); Gabris v. Blake, 9 Ohio St.2d 71, 223 N.E.2d 597 (1967); Blackman v. City of Cincinnati, 66 Ohio App. 495, 35 N.E.2d 164 (1941), aff'd 140 Ohio St. 25, 42 N.E.2d 158 (police commandeered car to chase suspects); Johnson v. City of Jackson, 194 Tenn. 20, 250 S.W.2d 1 (1952) (policeman checking parking meters ran into plaintiff); Mayes v. City of Wichita Falls, 403 S.W.2d 852 (Tex.Civ.App.1966). See generally Annot., Liability Arising from Accidents Involving Police

traffic signals and other traffic-control devices.[30] Even negligent maintenance of traffic devices has generally been ruled within the area of immunity.[31] The bulk of authority traditionally took the view that health care was governmental,[32] and many cases have applied this rule even to the operation of hospitals.[33] But the trend is clearly toward classifying hospitals as proprietary operations for which a municipality can be liable in tort.[34] Similarly, the collection and disposal of garbage—an activity also related to the

---

Vehicles, 83 A.L.R.2d 383 (1962). See also Annot., Municipal Corporation's Safety Rules or Regulations as Admissible in Evidence in Action by Private Party Against Municipal Corporation or Its Officers or Employees for Negligent Operation of Vehicle, 82 A.L.R.3d 1285 (1978).

[30] See Urow v. District of Columbia, 316 F.2d 351 (D.C.Cir.1963), cert. denied 375 U.S. 826, 84 S.Ct. 69, 11 L.Ed.2d 59 (1963); Hoy v. Capelli, 48 N.J. 81, 222 A.2d 649 (1966) (removal of traffic-control light). Cf. Weiss v. Fote, 7 N.Y.2d 579, 200 N.Y.S.2d 409, 167 N.E.2d 63 (1960) (negligently designed traffic signals); Raisanen v. City of Milwaukee, 35 Wis.2d 504, 151 N.W.2d 129 (1967) (negligence in programming traffic signals). But see Abbett v. County of St. Louis, 424 N.W.2d 82 (Minn. App.1988) (county's decision not to erect a guardrail along a roadway held not discretionary and thus outside the area of immunity). See generally Annot., Liability of Highway Authorities Arising Out of Motor Vehicle Accident Allegedly Caused by Failure to Erect or Properly Maintain Traffic Control Device at Intersection, 34 A.L.R.3d 1008 (1970). See also Annot., Liability of Municipality for Failure to Erect Traffic Warnings Against Entering or Using Street Which Is Partially Barred or Obstructed by Construction or Improvement Work, 52 A.L.R.2d 689 (1957); Annot., Liability of Governmental Unit for Collision with Safety and Traffic-Control Devices in Traveled Way, 7 A.L.R.2d 226 (1949).

[31] Dorminey v. City of Montgomery, 232 Ala. 47, 166 So. 689 (1936), noted 21 Minn.L.Rev. 459 (1937); Hoel v. City of Los Angeles, 136 Cal.App.2d 295, 288 P.2d 989 (Dist.Ct.1955); Auslander v. City of St. Louis, 332 Mo. 145, 56 S.W.2d 778 (1933); Vickers v. City of Camden, 122 N.J.L. 14, 3 A.2d 613 (1939); Cleveland v. Town of Lancaster, 239 App.Div. 263, 267 N.Y.S. 673 (1933), aff'd 264 N.Y. 568, 191 N.E. 568 (1934); Glover v. City of South Houston, 424 S.W.2d 723 (Tex.Civ.App.1968); Parson v. Texas City, 259 S.W.2d 333 (Tex.Civ.App.1953) (signal showed green both ways). Cities have been held not liable for failure to fix traffic lights so that they will flash red in all directions when an emergency vehicle is going through the intersection. City of Ardmore v. Hendrix, 348 P.2d 497 (Okl.1960); Presley v. City of Odessa, 263 S.W.2d 293 (Tex.Civ.App.1952). But a few jurisdictions, even under the traditional governmental-proprietary test, have held municipalities liable for negligently failing to keep traffic signals in proper working order. See Johnston v. City of East Moline, 405 Ill. 460, 91 N.E.2d 401 (1950); Gorman v. Adams, 259 Iowa 75, 143 N.W.2d 648 (1966); McDaniel v. Welsh, 234 So.2d 833 (La.App.1970), writ refused 256 La. 616, 237 So.2d 397; Raisanen v. City of Milwaukee, 35 Wis.2d 504, 151 N.W.2d 129 (1967). Cf. Town of Ft. Oglethorpe v. Phillips, 224 Ga. 834, 165 S.E.2d 141 (1968) (defective traffic signal found a nuisance; liability); Fankhauser v. City of Mansfield, 19 Ohio St.2d 102, 249 N.E.2d 789 (1969) (malfunctioning traffic signal was nuisance; liability). The general liability of municipalities for nuisances, even where immunity otherwise still exists for governmental activities, is discussed in this section *infra*.

[32] See City of Brunswick v. Barrett, 58 Ga.App. 792, 199 S.E. 901 (1939); Evans v. City of Kankakee, 231 Ill. 223, 83 N.E. 223 (1907); Haley v. City of Boston, 191 Mass. 291, 77 N.E. 888 (1906); Martinson v. City of Alpena, 328 Mich. 595, 44 N.W.2d 148 (1950); Edwards v. City of Portsmouth, 237 Va. 167, 375 S.E.2d 747 (1989) (provision of emergency ambulance service by city held governmental); Hagerman v. City of Seattle, 189 Wash. 694, 66 P.2d 1152 (1937). Cf. Smyser v. City of Peoria, 215 Ariz. 428, 160 P.3d 1186 (App. 2007) (city's provision of emergency medical services was governmental); City of Memphis v. Bettis, 512 S.W.2d 270 (Tenn.1974) (operation of ambulance service governmental even though fee charged).

[33] See City & County of Denver v. Madison, 142 Colo. 1, 351 P.2d 826 (1960); Hall v. Hospital Authority, 93 Ga.App. 319, 91 S.E.2d 530 (1956); Butler v. Kansas City, 97 Kan. 239, 155 P. 12 (1916); Clark v. Ruidoso-Hondo Valley Hosp., 72 N.M. 9, 380 P.2d 168 (1963); Hyde v. City of Lakewood, 2 Ohio St.2d 155, 207 N.E.2d 547 (1965); McMahon v. Baroness Erlanger Hospital, 43 Tenn.App. 128, 306 S.W.2d 41 (1957) (negligence of nurse); Childs v. Greenville Hospital Authority, 479 S.W.2d 399 (Tex.Civ.App.1972) (nurse refused to admit woman). Cf. Tollefson v. City of Ottawa, 228 Ill. 134, 81 N.E. 823 (1907) (death caused by hospital employee); Frost v. City of Topeka, 103 Kan. 197, 173 P. 293 (1918) (injury caused by explosion of dynamite caps on hospital grounds); Gobel v. City of Houston, 455 S.W.2d 776 (Tex.Civ.App.1970) (employee delivering mail in vehicle for hospital). Some cases apply the immunity even to injuries suffered by paying patients. See Gillies v. City of Minneapolis, 66 F.Supp. 467 (D.Minn.1946); Schroeder v. City of St. Louis, 360 Mo. 293, 228 S.W.2d 677 (1950); Lloyd v. City of Toledo, 42 Ohio App. 36, 180 N.E. 716 (1931); Gartman v. City of McAllen, 130 Tex. 237, 107 S.W.2d 879 (1937) (negligence of nurse injured paying patient).

[34] See City of Miami v. Brooks, 70 So.2d 306 (Fla.1954) (patient burned when given X-ray treatments); Burton v. Somerset City Hospital, 388 S.W.2d 134 (Ky.1965); Swigerd v. City of Ortonville, 246 Minn. 339, 75

promotion of the community's health—was sometimes in the past held to be governmental in nature;[35] but the majority of more recent cases have recognized that it is basically a "business" type of activity, comparable to private enterprises, and have

---

N.W.2d 217 (1956) (negligent nurse). A number of cases have held that a local government's hospital will at least be liable to a *paying* patient. See Hernandez v. County of Yuma, 91 Ariz. 35, 369 P.2d 271 (1962) (patient burned when bedpan of boiling water placed under her); Suwannee County Hospital Corp. v. Golden, 56 So.2d 911 (Fla.1952) (patient injured through improper use of hot-water bottle); Henderson v. Twin Falls County, 56 Idaho 124, 50 P.2d 597 (1935) (administration of wrong injection); Carlson v. Marinette County, 264 Wis. 423, 59 N.W.2d 486 (1953). It has even been held that the state *cannot* immunize the county from liability to a *paying* patient. Suwannee County Hospital Corp. v. Golden, *supra*. But it is questionable whether a rule making hospitals potentially liable to paying patients but immune from liability to non-paying patients could withstand equal-protection attack today. On municipal liability for hospitals, see generally Note, Torts—Governmental Immunity—City Not Immune from Liability for Injuries Resulting from Malpractice in Municipal Hospital Because Operation of Hospital Is Not a Governmental Function, 57 U.Detroit J. Urban L. 165 (1979).

In Hershel v. University Hosp. Foundation, 610 P.2d 237 (Okl.1980), the operation of a state university hospital was, in an action brought for wrongful death of a patient, held a proprietary function. But in Neal v. Donahue, 611 P.2d 1125 (Okl.1980), a wrongful death action brought for a murder committed by a patient of defendant state hospital, it was held that the alleged improper supervision of the patient by the hospital fell within the governmental area since it involved protection of the public from those incarcerated. Subsequently, all functions of state mental health facilities were held governmental. Williams v. State, 678 P.2d 259 (Okl.1984). And the entire operation of a university hospital was, since it involves educational activity, then ruled governmental. McGaha v. Board of Regents, 691 P.2d 895 (Okl.1984).

Some cases finding a lack of immunity have relied on the particular hospital's nature as a profit-making or essentially business enterprise. See Holt v. City of Cincinnati, 2 Ohio St.2d 155, 207 N.E.2d 547 (1965); City of Shawnee v. Roush, 101 Okl. 60, 223 P. 354 (1924), noted 24 Colum.L.Rev. 679 (1924). Cf. Parker v. City of Highland Park, 404 Mich. 183, 273 N.W.2d 413 (1978) (municipal hospital not "governmental function" under statute granting immunity for such functions; court rejects common-law precedents on the governmental-proprietary distinction, but finds that a hospital is basically a business). See also Murray v. Beyer Memorial Hospital, 409 Mich. 217, 293 N.W.2d 341 (1980), holding the rule of the *Parker* case, *supra*, applicable to all cases pending on the date of that decision.

[35] See Manning v. City of Pasadena, 58 Cal.App. 666, 209 P. 253 (Dist.Ct.1922); Ethridge v. City of Lavonia, 101 Ga.App. 190, 112 S.E.2d 822 (1960) (fire spread from garbage dump to private property); Boone v. City of Columbus, 87 Ga.App. 701, 75 S.E.2d 338 (1953); Behrmann v. City of St. Louis, 273 Mo. 578, 201 S.W. 547 (1918); James v. City of Charlotte, 183 N.C. 630, 112 S.E. 423 (1922); Osborn v. City of Akron, 171 Ohio St. 361, 171 N.E.2d 492 (1960); Broughton v. City of Cleveland, 167 Ohio St. 29, 146 N.E.2d 301 (1957) (loaders of garbage truck threw a box and hit pedestrian); Scibilia v. City of Philadelphia, 279 Pa. 549, 124 A. 273 (1924) (collection of ashes); Boyd v. City of Knoxville, 171 Tenn. 401, 104 S.W.2d 419 (1937); Ashbury v. City of Norfolk, 152 Va. 278, 147 S.E. 223 (1929). Even in recent years, at least two states—Oklahoma and Texas—continued to hold garbage collection to be governmental. See Swart v. City of Vinita, 551 P.2d 1107 (Okl.1976); City of Purcell v. Hubbard, 401 P.2d 488 (Okl.1965); City of Houston v. George, 479 S.W.2d 257 (Tex.1972); C & C Construction Co. v. City of Plainview, 428 S.W.2d 108 (Tex.Civ.App.1968). But cf. City of Tulsa v. Washington, 206 Okl. 61, 241 P.2d 194 (1952) (washing garbage trucks was "ministerial" activity for which was no immunity); City of Houston v. Shilling, 150 Tex. 387, 240 S.W.2d 1010 (1951), noted 30 Tex.L.Rev. 266 (1951) (liability in connection with operation of garage for repair of garbage trucks).

accordingly held it proprietary.[36] Sewage disposal is also generally recognized as within the area of possible liability.[37]

Educational activities have usually been classified as governmental,[38] and the resulting immunity of municipalities as to the operation of schools has been applied even to the repair and maintenance of school buildings and grounds.[39] The immunity has also

---

[36] Beard v. City & County of San Francisco, 79 Cal.App.2d 753, 180 P.2d 744 (Dist.Ct.1947); City of Miami Beach v. Alexander, 61 So.2d 917 (Fla.1952); Schmidt v. City of Chicago, 284 Ill.App. 570, 1 N.E.2d 234 (1936); Missano v. Mayor of New York, 160 N.Y. 123, 54 N.E. 744 (1899); F. J. Kress Box Co. v. City of Pittsburgh, 333 Pa. 121, 4 A.2d 528 (1939), cert. denied 308 U.S. 562, 60 S.Ct. 73, 84 L.Ed. 472 (incinerator plant); Hutton v. Martin, 41 Wn.2d 780, 252 P.2d 581 (1953) (negligent driving of garbage truck); Adkins v. City of Hinton, 149 W.Va. 613, 142 S.E.2d 889 (1965) (negligent maintaining of garbage dump). Cf. McGuire v. City of Cedar Rapids, 189 N.W.2d 592 (Iowa 1971) (negligent operation of sewage disposal plant); Schweikert v. Kansas City, 358 S.W.2d 425 (Mo.App.1962) (garbage truck with defective brakes). Some courts have been influenced to find possible liability if the municipality makes a charge for its garbage service. See Foss v. City of Lansing, 237 Mich. 633, 212 N.W. 952 (1927); Koontz v. City of Winston-Salem, 280 N.C. 513, 186 S.E.2d 897 (1972) (sanitary landfill operation); Lasko v. City of Akron, 109 Ohio App. 409, 166 N.E.2d 771 (1958) (city disposed of garbage, for a fee, for other municipalities and private parties); Town of Douglas v. York, 445 P.2d 760 (Wyo.1968). And liability is found for some garbage-disposal operations on the ground they are nuisances—for which a municipality can be held liable even if the operation is considered governmental. See City of West Point v. Meadows, 236 Miss. 394, 110 So.2d 372 (1959); Milan v. City of Bethlehem, 372 Pa. 598, 94 A.2d 774 (1953). Cf. Burris v. City of New Orleans, 86 So.2d 549 (La.App.1956) (attractive nuisance). On liability for nuisances, see generally notes 57–60 *infra*, and accompanying text.

[37] McGuire v. City of Cedar Rapids, *supra* note 36; City of Altus v. Martin, 268 P.2d 228 (Okl.1954). See Accurate Die Casting Co. v. City of Cleveland, 2 Ohio App.3d 386, 442 N.E.2d 459 (1981) (when municipality superimposes sewer system on a natural watercourse, it must do so consistent with rights of riparian landowner or else be subject to tort liability for harm done land-owner); Peters v. City of Medford, 109 Or.App. 26, 818 P.2d 517 (1991) (homeowners suing city for flow of sewage into their home state negligence claim based on res ipsa loquitur); Thomas v. Clearfield City, 642 P.2d 737 (Utah 1982) (collection and disposal of sewage not essential to core of governmental activity and thus outside area of immunity). Cf. Chrislaw v. Village of Clinton, 29 Wis.2d 549, 139 N.W.2d 568 (1966) (discharge of outflow of sewer onto private property can be nuisance for which municipality is liable—but no nuisance created as to amount of effluent here involved); Kinnischtzke v. City of Glen Ullin, 79 N.D. 495, 57 N.W.2d 588 (1953) (sewage-disposal plant held a nuisance).

[38] Kinnare v. City of Chicago, 171 Ill. 332, 49 N.E. 536 (1898); Koehn v. Board of Education, 193 Kan. 263, 392 P.2d 949 (1964); Daszkiewicz v. Detroit Board of Education, 301 Mich. 212, 3 N.W.2d 71 (1942); Bank v. Brainerd School District, 49 Minn. 106, 51 N.W. 814 (1892); Finch v. Board of Education, 30 Ohio St. 37 (1876); Dahl v. Hughes, 347 P.2d 208 (Okl.1959); Iafrate v. Ramsden, 96 R.I. 216, 190 A.2d 473 (1963); Sarmiento v. City of Corpus Christi, 465 S.W.2d 813 (Tex.Civ.App.1971) (negligence of school crossing guard); Folk v. City of Milwaukee, 108 Wis. 359, 84 N.W. 420 (1900). See Cobb v. Fox, 113 Mich.App. 249, 317 N.W.2d 583 (1982), appeal denied 422 Mich. 892, 368 N.W.2d 235 (1985) (maintenance and operation of school bus system held governmental and within area of immunity).

[39] Lambert v. City of New Haven, 129 Conn. 647, 30 A.2d 923 (1943) (person fell on school steps); Molinari v. City of Boston, 333 Mass. 394, 130 N.E.2d 925 (1955) (steam radiator injured child); Wilson v. Gipson, 753 P.2d 1349 (Okl.1988) (maintenance of hot water heater in elementary school was governmental function); Husser v. School District, 425 Pa. 249, 228 A.2d 910 (1967) (students beaten on school grounds by known troublemakers); Dillon v. York City School District, 422 Pa. 103, 220 A.2d 896 (1966) (student fell on icy steps); Carlo v. Scranton School District, 319 Pa. 417, 179 A. 561 (1935) (school flagpole fell on boy). The immunity has generally extended to accidents occurring on school playgrounds and in athletic facilities. See Board of Education v. Bates, 114 Ga.App. 343, 151 S.E.2d 524 (1966); Hummer v. School City, 124 Ind.App. 30, 112 N.E.2d 891 (1953). But if the public is allowed to witness a school athletic event and admission is charged, liability may exist for negligence in maintenance of the facilities. See Briscoe v. School District No. 123, 32 Wn.2d 353, 201 P.2d 697 (1949). Cf. Sawaya v. Tucson High School District, 78 Ariz. 389, 281 P.2d 105 (1955) (high school rented stadium to another school). Even here, some cases have found the activity "governmental" and hence immune. Boyer v. Iowa High School Athletic Association, 256 Iowa 337, 127 N.W.2d 606 (1964) (with strong dissents); Watson v. Bay City School District, 324 Mich. 1, 36 N.W.2d 195 (1949).

extended to the operation of such educational institutions as libraries and museums.[40] But a sharp split of authority has long existed over how to categorize recreational facilities and functions. Many cases—chiefly older ones—classified recreational activities as, in general, governmental in nature.[41] But more recent cases have here, as in a number of other areas, recognized the analogy to private businesses and held that recreational endeavors are proprietary.[42] Many cases involving recreation have concerned the control and maintenance of public parks; and a number of cases ruled

[40] Parr v. City of Birmingham, 264 Ala. 224, 85 So.2d 888 (1955) (art museum); Seibold v. Kinston-Lenoir County Public Library, 264 N.C. 360, 141 S.E.2d 519 (1965), aff'd 268 N.C. 615, 151 S.E.2d 654. But see Johnston v. City of Chicago, 258 Ill. 494, 101 N.E. 960 (1913).

[41] Coste v. City of Superior, 231 F.Supp. 261 (W.D.Wis.1964) aff'd 343 F.2d 100 (7th Cir.) (toboggan slide); Chaffin v. City of Montgomery, 273 Ala. 492, 142 So.2d 267 (1962); Schmidt v. City of Vallejo, 122 Cal.App. 5, 10 P.2d 107 (Dist.Ct.1932); Kellar v. City of Los Angeles, 179 Cal. 605, 178 P. 505 (1919) (mountain camp); Williams v. City of Longmont, 109 Colo. 567, 129 P.2d 110 (1942); City of Louisville v. Pirtle, 297 Ky. 553, 180 S.W.2d 303 (1944); Mayor & Council of Baltimore v. State ex rel. Blueford, 173 Md. 267, 195 A. 571 (1937); Clark v. Waltham, 128 Mass. 567 (1880); Fahey v. Jersey City, 52 N.J. 103, 244 A.2d 97 (1968) (parks and play-grounds governmental); Bisbing v. Asbury Park, 80 N.J.L. 416, 78 A. 196 (1910); Blair v. Granger, 24 R.I. 17, 51 A. 1042 (1902). Cf. Herlihy Mid-Continent Co. v. Bay City, 293 F.2d 383 (6th Cir.1961) (city employees acted in governmental capacity when they turned off hydrant through which water was supplied to contractor for purpose of flooding a skating rink). But see Grappendorf v. Pleasant Grove City, 173 P.3d 166 (Utah 2007) (wrongful death action of parents whose son was killed when a gust of wind at city ballpark picked up a pitching mound and projected it through air; interpreting statute under which immunity was provided for natural conditions, but this was not a natural condition *on* the land; thus the city was not immune). Some courts have found no liability even where a fee was charged for the recreational activity that caused the harm. Warren v. City of Topeka, 125 Kan. 524, 265 P. 78 (1928); Vaughn v. Alcoa, 194 Tenn. 449, 251 S.W.2d 304 (1952).

[42] Jackson v. City of St. Louis, 422 S.W.2d 45 (Mo.1967) (steel post left in recreational area); Augustine v. Town of Brant, 249 N.Y. 198, 163 N.E. 732 (1928); City of Tulsa v. Goins, 437 P.2d 257 (Okl.1967); City of Lampasas v. Roberts, 398 S.W.2d 612 (Tex.Civ.App.1966) (liquid fertilizer left near picnic area; child killed); Dancer v. City of Houston, 384 S.W.2d 340 (Tex.1964). Cf. Beccue v. Rockford Park District, 94 Ill.App.2d 179, 236 N.E.2d 105 (1968) (jury question whether park district negligent, and thus liable, for maintaining area where tobogganer struck tree); Caldwell v. Village of Island Park, 304 N.Y. 268, 107 N.E.2d 441 (1952) (jury question of village negligence in failing to take measures to prevent injuries from fireworks where setting-off fireworks in park was customary on Fourth of July); Hill v. Allentown Housing Authority, 373 Pa. 92, 95 A.2d 519 (1953) (Housing Authority allowed use of its land as dump; could be liable for negligence in failing to guard dump against intrusion of immature children); Johnson v. Salt Lake City Corp., 629 P.2d 432 (Utah 1981) (child's sled collided with timber implanted in concrete in golf course during winter, when course used for sledding; prior authority partially overruled). Courts are particularly likely to hold recreational activities proprietary if a fee is charged for admission or use, or if revenue is obtained from the activity. See Glenn v. City of Raleigh, 248 N.C. 378, 103 S.E.2d 482 (1958) (operation of park brought in annual net revenue of $18,000; this was more than "incidental income," and thus governmental immunity should not be applied even to picnic-recreation area within park, though that particular area was open to public free of charge); Griffin v. Salt Lake City, 111 Utah 94, 176 P.2d 156 (1947).

these to be governmental.[43] But the *trend* has been clearly toward classifying them as proprietary.[44]

One of the best examples of a proprietary function of a municipality is the operation of a public utility, since the activity is obviously "business-like" in nature and involves the same type of activity as is performed by private companies. Thus, the operation of a

---

[43] Jones v. City of Birmingham, 284 Ala. 276, 224 So.2d 632 (1969) (poorly maintained walk); Carr v. City & County of San Francisco, 170 Cal.App.2d 48, 338 P.2d 509 (Dist.Ct.1959) (child tripped over merry-go-round attendant); Wysocki v. City of Derby, 140 Conn. 173, 98 A.2d 659 (1953) (child pushed through window of recreational center); Griffin v. City of Chicago, 317 Ill.App. 368, 45 N.E.2d 890 (1943) (monument in park fell); Baker v. City of Lexington, 310 S.W.2d 555 (Ky.1958) (wire across pathway in park caused plaintiff to fall); Penix v. City of St. Johns, 354 Mich. 259, 92 N.W.2d 332 (1958) (bleachers collapsed); Ballinger v. City of Dayton, 117 N.E.2d 469 (Ohio App.1952) (lawn mower in park injured employee); Rector v. City of Nashville, 23 Tenn.App. 495, 134 S.W.2d 892 (1939) (wire hanging in park electrocuted person); Davis v. Provo City Corp., 1 Utah 2d 244, 265 P.2d 415 (1953); Kilbourn v. City of Seattle, 43 Wn.2d 373, 261 P.2d 407 (1953) (dead limb fell on child). Cf. Davis v. Chicago Housing Auth., 136 Ill.2d 296, 144 Ill.Dec. 224, 555 N.E.2d 343 (1990) (providing of playground by Chicago Housing Authority is governmental function; immunity applies). In Dickey v. City of Flagstaff, 205 Ariz. 1, 66 P.3d 44 (2003), it was held that operation of a city park was a governmental function, and thus within a recreational use statute (see note 44 *infra*), where the city did not charge an admission fee or otherwise derive revenue from public's use of park, the city obtained land for the park from the federal government on stipulation that it be used as public park, and the park was open to everyone, not just city residents.

[44] See Woodford v. City of St. Petersburg, 84 So.2d 25 (Fla.1955); City of Jackson v. McFadden, 181 Miss. 1, 177 So. 755 (1938); Taylor v. Kansas City, 353 S.W.2d 814 (Mo.App.1961) transf. to 361 S.W.2d 797; State ex rel. Gerry v. Edwards, 42 Mont. 135, 111 P. 734 (1910); Coleman v. Township of Edison, 95 N.J.Super. 600, 232 A.2d 187 (1967); Spray v. City of Albuquerque, 94 N.M. 199, 608 P.2d 511 (N.M.1980) (golf course; upholding contract made by city); Murphy v. City of Carlsbad, 66 N.M. 376, 348 P.2d 492 (1960); Augustine v. Town of Brant, *supra* note 42; Rich v. City of Goldsboro, 15 N.C.App. 534, 190 S.E.2d 229 (1972) cert. allowed 281 N.C. 758, 191 S.E.2d 362, rev'd 282 N.C. 383, 192 S.E.2d 824; Dancer v. City of Houston, *supra* note 42. Cf. City of Kokomo v. Loy, 185 Ind. 18, 112 N.E. 994 (1916) (employee injured while loading cannon in park); Fetters v. City of Des Moines, 260 Iowa 490, 149 N.W.2d 815 (1967) (applying statute); City of Laurel v. Hutto, 220 Miss. 253, 70 So.2d 605 (1954) (hole in public park); Wallace v. State ex rel. Oklahoma Tourism & Recreation Dep't, 675 P.2d 436 (Okl.1983) (operation of park by state held proprietary). See generally Annot., Liability of Local Government Entity for Injury Resulting from Use of Outdoor Playground Equipment at Municipally Owned Park or Recreation Area, 73 A.L.R.4th 496 (1989). See also Kaczmarczyk v. City & County of Honolulu, 65 Hawaii 612, 656 P.2d 89 (1982) (city has duty to warn users of a beach park of extremely dangerous conditions in ocean along its beach frontage if such conditions were not known or obvious to persons of ordinary intelligence and were known or should reasonably have been known to city).–

In Whalen v. Mayor of Baltimore, 164 Md.App. 292, 883 A.2d 228 (2005), it was held that upkeep of public parks, including public ways adjacent to parks and areas contiguous thereto, was a proprietary, not governmental, function.

Some jurisdictions have "recreational use statutes," or provisions on recreational use within their governmental tort liability statutes, that provide immunity, often subject to exceptions for willful or wanton conduct, for governmental units maintaining and operating recreational facilities. Weinert v. City of Great Falls, 322 Mont. 38, 97 P.3d 1079 (2004) (Recreational Use Act provided immunity to city for injuries sustained by sledder who ran into safety net that city had installed at bottom of sledding hill in city park). As to what areas are covered by such statutes, see MacKinney v. City of Tucson, 299 P.3d 1282 (Ariz. App. 2013) (city golf course fit within common definition of a park and thus came under the recreational-use immunity statute). Cf. Daniel v. City of Colorado Springs, 327 P.3d 891 (Colo. 2014) (parking lot at golf course was part of recreation area for purposes of immunity waiver). But some jurisdictions hold that since "recreational use statutes" or provisions are intended to encourage landowners to open *private* lands to the public for recreation, such legislation does not apply to governmental landowners. Compare Sega v. State of New York, 60 N.Y.2d 183, 456 N.E.2d 1174, 469 N.Y.S.2d 51 (1983) (statute applies to local governments; public entities should be treated the same as private landowners), with Delta Farms Reclamation Dist. v. Superior Court of San Joaquin County, 33 Cal.3d 699, 660 P.2d 1168, 190 Cal.Rptr. 494 (1983), cert. denied 464 U.S. 915, 104 S.Ct. 277, 78 L.Ed.2d 257 (1983) (statute does not apply to local governments). See generally Annot., Effect of Statute Limiting Landowner's Liability for Personal Injury to Recreational User, 47 A.L.R. 4th 262 (1986); Dobbs, Law of Torts § 238, at 620–24 (2000).

municipal transit system has been ruled proprietary,[45] as has the operation of a city electric system,[46] gas works,[47] or water system.[48] What of the installation and maintenance of sewers and drains? Municipalities have usually been held under no obligation to provide sewers and drains, and therefore not liable for damage caused by a failure to do so.[49] But once the local government *does* undertake to provide such service,

---

45 Karsey v. City & County of San Francisco, 130 Cal.App. 655, 20 P.2d 751 (Dist.Ct.1933); Johnson v. City of Monroe, 164 So. 456 (La.App.1935); Staunton v. City of Detroit, 329 Mich. 516, 46 N.W.2d 569 (1951); Zangerle v. City of Cleveland, 145 Ohio St. 347, 61 N.E.2d 720 (1945); Tobin v. City of Seattle, 127 Wash. 664, 221 P. 583 (1923); Koch v. City of Seattle, 113 Wash. 583, 194 P. 572 (1921).

46 City of Troy v. McLendon, 279 Ala. 553, 188 So.2d 281 (1966); City of Decatur v. Parham, 268 Ala. 585, 109 So.2d 692 (1959); Welch v. City of Camilla, 86 Ga.App. 609, 72 S.E.2d 83 (1952); Eaton v. City of Weiser, 12 Idaho 544, 86 P. 541 (1906); Bathke v. Traverse City, 308 Mich. 1, 13 N.W.2d 184 (1944); Hamilton v. City of Rocky Mount, 199 N.C. 504, 154 S.E. 844 (1930); Pool v. Cushing, 184 Okl. 577, 89 P.2d 294 (1939); Saulman v. City of Nashville, 131 Tenn. 427, 175 S.W. 532 (1915). See Rice v. City of Lumberton, 235 N.C. 227, 69 S.E.2d 543 (1952) (municipal corporation, in supplying electricity for emolument, is regarded as a private corporation).

Most authority has found a municipality to be acting in a proprietary capacity even where it supplies electricity for lighting of streets. City of Madisonville v. Nisbet's Administrator, 270 Ky. 248, 109 S.W.2d 593 (1937); Roberts v. City of Lamar, 99 S.W.2d 498 (Mo.App.1936); Hamilton v. City of Rocky Mount, 199 N.C. 504, 154 S.E. 844 (1930); Ring v. Mitchell, 64 S.D. 67, 263 N.W. 893 (1935); Christian v. City of New London, 234 Wis. 123, 290 N.W. 621 (1940). But some cases have found the street-lighting function to be governmental. Schlicher v. New York City, 175 Misc. 696, 24 N.Y.S.2d 177 (1940); Steelman v. City of New Bern, 279 N.C. 589, 184 S.E.2d 239 (1971); Martin v. City of Canton, 41 Ohio App. 420, 180 N.E. 78 (1931); Irvine v. Town of Greenwood, 89 S.C. 511, 72 S.E. 228 (1911). See State ex rel. Fejes v. City of Akron, 5 Ohio St.2d 47, 213 N.E.2d 353 (1966).

47 City of Albany v. Burt, 88 Ga.App. 144, 76 S.E.2d 413 (1953); Brantman v. City of Canby, 119 Minn. 396, 138 N.W. 671 (1912); City of Richmond v. James, 170 Va. 553, 197 S.E. 416 (1938). Operation of a telephone system is also proprietary. Storti v. Town of Fayal, 194 Minn. 628, 261 N.W. 463 (1935).

48 City of Birmingham v. Lake, 243 Ala. 367, 10 So.2d 24 (1942); Richmond v. City of Norwich, 96 Conn. 582, 115 A. 11 (1921); City of Elberton v. J. C. Pool Realty Co., 111 Ga.App. 765, 143 S.E.2d 407 (1965); McGinley v. City of Cherryvale, 141 Kan. 155, 40 P.2d 377 (1935); Harvard Furniture Co. v. City of Cambridge, 320 Mass. 227, 68 N.E.2d 684 (1946); Carlisi v. City of Marysville, 373 Mich. 198, 128 N.W.2d 477 (1964); Henderson v. Kansas City, 177 Mo. 477, 76 S.W. 1045 (1903); Roberts Realty Corp. v. City of Great Falls, 160 Mont. 144, 500 P.2d 956 (1972); Faw v. Town of North Wilkesboro, 253 N.C. 406, 117 S.E.2d 14 (1960); Helz v. City of Pittsburgh, 387 Pa. 169, 127 A.2d 89 (1956); City of Waco v. Busby, 396 S.W.2d 469 (Tex.Civ.App.1965) refused n. r. e. See Hansen v. City of Pocatello, 145 Idaho 700, 184 P.3d 206 (2008) (city acts in proprietary capacity when it owns, maintains, and operates a water system, but no negligence found where pedestrian injured when lid of water meter flipped as she stepped on it); Iver Johnson Sporting Goods Co. v. City of Boston, 334 Mass. 401, 135 N.E.2d 658 (1956) (action for flooding of property owner's basement when city water main broke; question of fact whether city negligent); Oklahoma City v. Moore, 491 P.2d 273 (Okl.1971) (plaintiff fell into water-meter box installed and maintained by city; held proprietary function); Bennett v. Bow Valley Dev. Corp., 797 P.2d 419 (Utah 1990) (maintenance of water storage tank not a uniquely governmental function and thus not within area of immunity). Cf. Foust v. City of Durham, 239 N.C. 306, 79 S.E.2d 519 (1954) (water main burst, allegedly due to city's negligence; cause of action held stated). Most cases have found the city potentially liable even where the water is furnished for such usually "governmental" functions as fire-fighting and street-cleaning. See Cole Drug Co. v. City of Boston, 326 Mass. 199, 93 N.E.2d 556 (1950); Koch Brothers Bag Co. v. Kansas City, 315 S.W.2d 743 (Mo.1958); Bowling v. City of Oxford, 267 N.C. 552, 148 S.E.2d 624 (1966); Russell v. City of Grandview, 39 Wn.2d 551, 236 P.2d 1061 (1951). But see Cross v. Kansas City, 230 Kan. 545, 638 P.2d 933 (1982) (furnishing water for fire department is governmental function).

49 See Martinez v. Cook, 56 N.M. 343, 244 P.2d 134 (1952); McCutchen v. Village of Peekskill, 167 Misc. 460, 3 N.Y.S.2d 277 (1938); Boone v. City of Akron, 69 Ohio App. 95, 43 N.E.2d 315 (1942); Strauch v. City of Scranton, 353 Pa. 10, 44 A.2d 258 (1945). There is no liability where land floods simply because the locality has not provided drainage. See Daniels v. City of Denver, 2 Colo. 669 (1875); Beals v. Inhabitants of Brookline, 174 Mass. 1, 54 N.E. 339 (1899) (surface water flowed onto plaintiff's land); LaForm v. Bethelehem Township, 346 Pa.Super. 512, 499 A.2d 1373 (1985) (city not liable for death of motorist who drowned when her car became stalled in surface floodwaters in an adjacent township even though the city's developments had increased flow of surface waters); Patterson v. City of Bellevue, 37 Wash.App. 535, 681 P.2d 266 (1984), review denied 102 Wash.2d 1005 (1984) (city not liable for increasing rate of flow in drainway if it did not disturb natural drainage of area and no new water was collected or diverted into drainway). Nor does the local

it is usually reasoned that it must act reasonably. Thus, liability has been found for the negligent planning[50] or construction[51] of sewers and drains. And the great weight of authority supports the view that liability lies for negligence in the *maintenance* of sewers and drains.[52] Similarly, most authority supports liability as to the construction and

---

government have an obligation to provide drainage for water accumulating in its streets. Randle v. City of Rome, 23 Misc.2d 436, 195 N.Y.S.2d 373 (1960). But if the locality diverts water onto private property, it can be liable to the owner. See Dayley v. City of Burley, 96 Idaho 101, 524 P.2d 1073 (1974) (city enjoined from diverting storm waters into creek and ordered to remove water from landowners' property where city had accumulated water in storm drains and diverted it into creek that was not a natural water course); City of McComb v. Rodgers, 246 So.2d 913 (Miss.1971) (city changed drainage on street); Wilber Dev. Corp. v. Les Rowland Constr. Inc., 83 Wash.2d 871, 523 P.2d 186 (1974) (city not liable for damage occurring when it increases flow of surface water onto owner's property if damage arises wholly from changes produced by opening of streets, building of houses, and other such regular expansion of municipality, but is liable if, in course of authorized construction, it collects surface water by artificial channel or in large quantities and pours it in a body on land of private person to his injury). Compare Barney's Furniture Warehouse of Newark, Inc. v. City of Newark, 62 N.J. 456, 303 A.2d 76 (1973) (no city liability resulting from a gradually increasing functional incapacity of a sewer system due to increased urban development). See also note 62 *infra* and accompanying text.

[50] Bowman v. Town of Chenango, 227 N.Y. 459, 125 N.E. 809 (1920), noted 20 Colum.L.Rev. 619 (1920). See McCormick v. Town of Thermopolis, 478 P.2d 67 (Wyo.1970) (but municipality not liable for overflow of sewers caused by *extraordinary* rains or floods); Savage v. Town of Lander, 77 Wyo. 157, 309 P.2d 152 (1957) (municipality could be liable for negligence in planning or maintaining of gutter—but was insufficient evidence to show this caused plaintiff's injuries; said to be liability for negligent plan only if was so manifestly dangerous that its adoption was negligence as matter of law); But see Carlo v. City of Pittsfield, 339 Mass. 624, 161 N.E.2d 757 (1959) (no liability for an inadequacy in plan of sewers, but could be liability for negligent maintenance).

[51] Durante v. City of Oakland, 19 Cal.App.2d 543, 65 P.2d 1326 (Dist.Ct.1937); Galluzzi v. City of Beverly, 309 Mass. 135, 34 N.E.2d 492 (1941) (negligence in connecting property with sewer); Bean v. City of Moberly, 350 Mo. 975, 169 S.W.2d 393 (1943); Stoddard v. Village of Saratoga Springs, 127 N.Y. 261, 27 N.E. 1030 (1891); Accurate Die Casting Co. v. City of Cleveland, 68 O.L.A. 230, 113 N.E.2d 401 (1953); Rikansrud v. City of Canton, 79 S.D. 592, 116 N.W.2d 234 (1962); Hatten v. Mason Realty Co., 148 W.Va. 380, 135 S.E.2d 236 (1964). But a few cases have held the construction of sewers governmental. Register v. H. Burton Elliott, Inc., 229 A.2d 488 (Del.Super.1967), opinion supplemented by 1967 WL 90347 (Del.Super.1967); Elledge v. City of Des Moines, 259 Iowa 284, 144 N.W.2d 283 (1966). And Texas has treated construction of storm sewers as proprietary, but construction of sanitary sewers as governmental. See Chambers v. City of Dayton, 447 S.W.2d 425 (Tex.Civ. App.1969), ref'd n.r.e. See generally Annot., Municipality's Liability Arising from Negligence or Other Wrongful Act in Carrying Out Construction or Repair of Sewers and Drains, 61 A.L.R.2d 874 (1958).

[52] See Mulloy v. Sharp Park Sanitary District, 164 Cal.App.2d 438, 330 P.2d 441 (Dist.Ct.1958); Kellom v. City of Ecorse, 329 Mich. 303, 45 N.W.2d 293 (1951); Allen v. Town of Hampton, 107 N.H. 377, 222 A.2d 833 (1966); Ulibarri v. Village of Los Lunas, 79 N.M. 421, 444 P.2d 606 (1968); Barker v. City of Santa Fe, 47 N.M. 85, 136 P.2d 480 (1943); Pulliam v. City of Greensboro, 103 N.C.App. 748, 407 S.E.2d 567 (1991), review denied 330 N.C. 197, 412 S.E.2d 59 (1991) (maintenance, operation, and repair of sewer system held proprietary and thus subject to liability); Milner Hotels v. City of Raleigh, 268 N.C. 535, 151 S.E.2d 35 (1966), mod. on reh. 271 N.C. 224, 155 S.E.2d 543; Oklahoma City v. Romano, 433 P.2d 924 (Okl.1967); City of Watauga v. Taylor, 752 S.W.2d 199 (Tex.App.1988) (municipality immune from liability for negligent design or construction of drainage ditch but could be liable for negligent maintenance of ditch); Hayes v. City of Vancouver, 61 Wash. 536, 112 P. 498 (1911). Cf. The Lobster Pot v. City of Lowell, 333 Mass. 31, 127 N.E.2d 659 (1955) (city has duty of reasonable care to keep sewers free from obstructions—but insufficient evidence of negligence here); Dize Awning & Tent Co. v. City of Winston-Salem, 271 N.C. 715, 157 S.E.2d 577 (1967) (city was allegedly negligent in replacing pipes and culvert; court's dismissal of case was error); Ball v. Village of Reynoldsburg, 86 O.L.A. 293, 176 N.E.2d 739 (1960), aff'd 175 Ohio St. 128, 192 N.E.2d 51 (village allowed sewer line to be overloaded; jury question of negligence presented); Spencer v. City of Bristow, 165 P.3d 361 (Okla. Civ. App. 2007) (law requires municipalities to use reasonable diligence and care to see that sewer is not clogged; summary judgment for city on basis of immunity was precluded). It is sometimes emphasized that only reasonable care can be expected as to sewers and drains, and that municipalities furnishing such service are not insurers as to all damage caused thereby. See Kershner v. Town of Walden, 144 Colo. 67, 355 P.2d 77 (1960). See generally Annot., Municipality's Liability for Damage Resulting from Obstruction or Clogging of Drains or Sewers, 59 A.L.R.2d 281 (1958). See also Note, Down the Drain: How North Carolina Municipalities Lost Immunity for Storm Drains, 86 N.C. L. Rev. 2272 (2010), noting Jennings v. City of Fayetteville, 198 N.C App. 698, 680 S.E. 2d 757 (2009).

maintenance of public streets and ways.[53] Since dangers and defects in streets can occur frequently and suddenly, it is often emphasized that a municipality cannot be an insurer as to the condition of its streets and is not expected to keep them absolutely safe at all times, but is held only to the usual tort standard of reasonable care under the circumstances.[54] Not surprisingly, the same rule of possible liability that applies to streets has also been applied to construction and maintenance of municipal sidewalks.[55]

---

[53] City of Paducah v. Konkle, 236 Ky. 582, 33 S.W.2d 608 (1930); Shepherd v. City of Chattanooga, 168 Tenn. 153, 76 S.W.2d 322 (1934); City of Houston v. Glover, 355 S.W.2d 757 (Tex.Civ.App.1962), ref'd n.r.e.; Hewitt v. City of Seattle, 62 Wash. 377, 113 P. 1084 (1911). See Smith v. State, 93 Idaho 795, 473 P.2d 937 (1970) (construction and maintenance of highways is proprietary function of state; could be liability where flagman had left his post). Cf. Sherwin v. City of Aurora, 257 Ill. 458, 100 N.E. 938 (1913) (construction and maintenance of streets termed "ministerial"; possible liability); Latzoni v. City of Garfield, 22 N.J. 84, 123 A.2d 531 (1956) (active wrongdoing found; liability). A city's potential liability for failing to keep its streets in reasonably safe condition has been held to extend to failure to maintain a traffic turn signal, Schmeck v. City of Shawnee, 232 Kan. 11, 651 P.2d 585 (1982); Bowen v. Riverton City, 656 P.2d 434 (Utah 1982) (city said to have nondelegable duty to maintain streets, including traffic signals). A governmental entity's duty to maintain a road may also extend to the shoulder of that road, but this duty is sometimes held to apply only in favor of those using the shoulder in an emergency or under other special circumstances, not to those using it inadvertently. See Annot., Liability, in Motor Vehicle-Related Cases, of Governmental Entity for Injury, Death, or Property Damage Resulting from Defect or Obstruction in Shoulder of Street or Highway, 19 A.L.R.4th 532 (1983). But there have been cases, often now effectively overruled by a general termination of immunity, finding municipal activity throughout this area of street construction and maintenance to be governmental and thus immune. See Pluhowsky v. City of New Haven, 151 Conn. 337, 197 A.2d 645 (1964); Perry v. City of Wichita, 174 Kan. 264, 255 P.2d 667 (1953); State ex rel. Fejes v. City of Akron, 5 Ohio St.2d 47, 213 N.E.2d 353 (1966). Cf. Ruble v. Department of Transp., 660 P.2d 1049 (Okl.1983) (building and maintaining of state highways held a governmental function for which the state at the time enjoyed immunity); Bialk v. City of Hampton, 242 Va. 56, 405 S.E.2d 619 (1991) (municipal activities in connection with emergency cleaning of snow from streets held governmental, though ordinary street maintenance was classified as proprietary). Cf. DiFelici v. City of Lander, 312 P.3d 816 (Wyo. 2013) (pedestrian fell after stepping into hole in gutter of street; hole was result of street maintenance, which was statutorily excluded from waiver of immunity). See generally Sahm, Municipal Liability in Pennsylvania for Defective Streets, 45 Dickinson L.Rev. 113 (1941); Annot., Liability, in Motor-Vehicle-Related Cases, of Governmental Entity for Injury or Death Resulting from Failure to Repair Pothole in Surface of Highway or Street, 98 A.L.R.3d 101 (1980); Annot., Liability, in Motor-Vehicle-Related Cases, of Governmental Entity for Injury or Death Resulting from Ice or Snow on Surface of Highway or Street, 97 A.L.R.3d 11 (1980); Annot., Liability, in Motor-Vehicle-Related Cases, of Governmental Entity for Injury or Death Resulting from Defect or Obstruction on Roadside Parkway or Parking Strip, 98 A.L.R.3d 439 (1980). See also Munich v. Skagit Emergency Communication Center, 288 P.3d 328 (Wash. 2012) (county's express assurances promising action were not required to be false or inaccurate in order to create special relationship and thus possible negligence liability).

[54] See City of Grand Junction v. Lashmett, 126 Colo. 256, 247 P.2d 909 (1952) (no liability when child burned by torch near pit in street); Weiss v. City of Chicago, 23 Ill.App.2d 280, 162 N.E.2d 601 (1959); Pettinger v. Village of Winnebago, 239 Minn. 156, 58 N.W.2d 325 (1953); McCormick v. Kansas City, 250 S.W.2d 524 (Mo.1952); Rogers v. City of Asheville, 14 N.C.App. 514, 188 S.E.2d 656 (1972). Cf. Mosseller v. City of Asheville, 267 N.C. 104, 147 S.E.2d 558 (1966) (no liability for trivial defects in streets and sidewalks). But cf. Ames v. City of New York, 177 A.D.2d 528, 575 N.Y.S.2d 917 (1991) (municipality has absolute, nondelegable duty to keep highways in reasonably safe condition, and budget problems can't excuse failure).

[55] Turner v. City of Tacoma, 72 Wn.2d 1029, 435 P.2d 927 (1967). See Lane v. City of Tulsa, 402 P.2d 908 (Okl.1965) (maintenance of streets and sidewalks is proprietary); Koonce v. City of Mesquite, 343 S.W.2d 557 (Tex.Civ.App.1961) (liability if city negligently failed to maintain walkway in front of police and fire station). Cf. Colucci v. Town of Vail, 232 P.3d 218 (Colo. App. 2009) (pedestrian overpass perpendicular to interstate highway held a "sidewalk" within Colorado Governmental Immunity Act waiving immunity as to any sidewalk). But see Dugan v. City of Portland, 157 Me. 521, 174 A.2d 660 (1961); Gossler v. City of Manchester, 107 N.H. 310, 221 A.2d 242 (1966) (governmental immunity applied to suit based on fall on city sidewalk). Statutes sometimes specifically provide for municipal liability here. See Town of Antlers v. Benson, 247 F.2d 437 (10th Cir.1957); Wall v. City of Cincinnati, 150 Ohio St. 411, 83 N.E.2d 389 (1948). In Pennsylvania, the primary responsibility for keeping sidewalks in repair is with the abutting property owner; the locality has only a secondary duty. See Flynn v. City of Chester, 429 Pa. 170, 239 A.2d 322 (1968). Some cases involving sidewalks have adopted the "slight defect rule," whereby slight defects do not furnish a basis

There is one rule that has long been recognized as sweeping across the governmental-proprietary distinction as to municipal tort liability, even where that distinction is otherwise still applied: the rule that a municipality can be held liable, the same as any other property-owner, if it creates or maintains a nuisance.[56] This liability exists even though the nuisance resulted from the locality's performance of governmental acts.[57] On this basis, municipalities have, for instance, been held liable for garbage-disposal plants found to constitute nuisances,[58] and for the pollution of bodies of water.[59] By analogy, municipalities have been held liable for their creation of "*attractive* nuisances" that resulted in injury to children,[60] though this clearly involves confusion of the separate legal concepts of "nuisance" and "attractive nuisance." A tort

---

for negligence liability. See Ford v. City of Kinsley, 141 Kan. 877, 44 P.2d 255 (1935). But this has been held inapplicable to parking lots. Elstun v. Spangles, Inc., 289 Kan. 754, 217 P.3d 450 (2009).

56 Cleveland Wrecking Co. v. Struck Construction Co., 41 F.Supp. 70 (D.Ky.1941); Phillips v. City of Pasadena, 27 Cal.2d 104, 162 P.2d 625 (1945); Ambrosini v. Alisal Sanitary Dist., 154 Cal.App.2d 720, 317 P.2d 33 (Dist.Ct.1957); Cyr v. Town of Brookfield, 153 Conn. 261, 216 A.2d 198 (1965); Sparks v. City of Pella, 258 Iowa 187, 137 N.W.2d 909 (1965); Galleher v. City of Wichita, 179 Kan. 513, 296 P.2d 1062 (1956); Kurtigian v. City of Worcester, 348 Mass. 284, 203 N.E.2d 692 (1965); Alberts v. City of Muskegon, 146 Mich. 210, 109 N.W. 262 (1906); Windle v. City of Springfield, 320 Mo. 459, 8 S.W.2d 61 (1928); Herman v. City of Buffalo, 214 N.Y. 316, 108 N.E. 451 (1915); Oklahoma City v. Tytenicz, 171 Okl. 519, 43 P.2d 747 (1935); Adams v. City of Toledo, 163 Or. 185, 96 P.2d 1078 (1939), followed 163 Or. 193, 96 P.2d 1081; City of Paris v. Browning, 55 Tenn.App. 92, 396 S.W.2d 367 (1965). See Vickers v. City of Fitzgerald, 216 Ga. 476, 117 S.E.2d 316 (1960); Adams v. Arkansas City, 188 Kan. 391, 362 P.2d 829 (1961) (city's sewage-treatment plant was continuing nuisance; landowner could recover loss of market value); Schleissner v. Town of Provincetown, 27 Mass.App.Ct. 392, 538 N.E.2d 995 (1989) (municipality held liable in nuisance for maintaining a runoff collection facility which overflowed onto plaintiffs property; plaintiff could be awarded damages measured by loss of rental value plus a permanent injunction); Knight v. City of Missoula, 252 Mont. 232, 827 P.2d 1270 (1992) (creation of unlawful roadway could be nuisance); Kind v. Johnson City, 63 Tenn.App. 666, 478 S.W.2d 63 (1970); Taylor v. City of Charlottesville, 240 Va. 367, 397 S.E.2d 832 (1990) (city immune from negligence liability for street construction and failure to install lighting and safety devices, but not immune for creation of dangerous condition that constituted a public nuisance). But see Risk & Attridge, *Garitee v. Mayor and City Council of Baltimore*: A Gilded Age Debate on the Role and Limits of Local Government, 109 Md. Historical Mag. 453 (2014), discussing an 1880 Maryland public nuisance case in which the mayor and city council were dismissed as defendants, but it is unclear if sovereign immunity played a part in the dismissal. *Id.*, at 465. See generally Annot., Municipality's Liability Arising from Negligence or Other Wrongful Act in Carrying Out Construction or Repair of Sewers and Drains, 61 A.L.R.2d 874 (1958); Annot., Municipality's Liability for Damage Resulting from Obstruction or Clogging of Drains or Sewers, 59 A.L.R.2d 277, 310 (1958); Annot., Sewage Disposal Plant as Nuisance, 40 A.L.R.2d 1198 (1955). The governmental-proprietary distinction may also be treated as irrelevant in other (*i.e.*, non-nuisance) instances of invasions of private property—for instance, patent infringements. See Sommers, Municipal Liability for Patent Infringement, 24 A.B.A.J. 162 (1938).

57 See Thompson v. City of Eau Claire, 269 Wis. 76, 69 N.W.2d 239 (1955). See generally Annot., Rule of Municipal Immunity from Liability for Acts in Performance of Governmental Functions as Applicable to Injury or Death as Result of a Nuisance, 56 A.L.R.2d 1415 (1957).

58 Milan v. City of Bethlehem, 372 Pa. 598, 94 A.2d 774 (1953); Thompson v. City of Eau Claire, *supra* note 57. Cf. Edge v. City of Booneville, 226 Miss. 108, 83 So.2d 801 (1955) (odors from gas reduction station).

59 Newton v. Grundy Center, 246 Iowa 916, 70 N.W.2d 162 (1955). Cf. Thorson v. City of Minot, 153 N.W.2d 764 (N.D.1967) (landfill operation resulted in refuse being deposited on private property).

60 Stedwell v. City of Chicago, 297 Ill. 486, 130 N.E. 729 (1921); Hendren v. Kansas City, 172 Kan. 56, 238 P.2d 510 (1951) (deteriorated springhouse on unused part of city street); Davoren v. Kansas City, 308 Mo. 513, 273 S.W. 401 (1925); Latimer v. City of Clovis, 83 N.M. 610, 495 P.2d 788 (1972). Cf. Smith v. Iowa City, 213 Iowa 391, 239 N.W. 29 (1931) (court seems to assume city could be liable for attractive nuisance, but combined teeter-totter and merry-go-round not within doctrine since child not trespasser there). But several courts have refused to hold localities liable on an attractive-nuisance theory. See Conrad v. Takoma Park, 208 Md. 363, 118 A.2d 497 (1955) (warning flare); Lovin v. Town of Hamlet, 243 N.C. 399, 90 S.E.2d 760 (1956) (park); Ware v. City of Cincinnati, 93 Ohio App. 431, 111 N.E.2d 401 (1952); Clark v. City of Bremerton, 1 Wn.2d 689, 97 P.2d 112 (1939) (child burned himself on open flare near trench where city was excavating to install water main).

that truly *is* similar in nature to nuisance is trespass—both involve an interference with an owner's rights in his property, though trespass has traditionally required some tangible invasion while nuisance has not. It is thus appropriate that trespasses be here treated similarly to nuisances, and this has generally been done: A municipality has been held liable for its trespasses, regardless of whether they occur in connection with a governmental activity or a proprietary one.[61] On this basis, a municipality can be held liable for diverting waters from their natural course so as to cause flooding of a private person's land.[62]

§ 26.3 Alleviation and Abrogation of Governmental Immunity

Recent decades have witnessed a movement—gradual at first, now quite rapid—away from municipal immunity for governmental activities. The movement has occurred through (1) the obtaining of insurance by municipalities and subsequent holdings that immunity has been waived to the extent of the coverage, (2) statutes waiving immunity as to limited areas and specified functions, and (3) finally and most important, wholesale abrogation (though often with a few exceptions still) of the immunity by judicial and/or legislative action. Where a municipality has obtained insurance to cover possible liability for governmental activities, the courts have sometimes held such action ultra vires and of no effect.[63] This problem is now largely removed by statutes in most states specifically authorizing the purchasing of liability insurance to cover some or all governmental activities.[64] The argument can also be made that a local unit, even if it has power to

---

[61] City & County of Denver v. Talarico, 99 Colo. 178, 61 P.2d 1 (1936); Mayor & City Council of Havre de Grace v. Maxa, 177 Md. 168, 9 A.2d 235 (1939); Rix v. Town of Alamogordo, 42 N.M. 325, 77 P.2d 765 (1938); Persons v. Valley City, 26 N.D. 342, 144 N.W. 675 (1913); Hathaway v. Osborne, 25 R.I. 249, 55 A. 700 (1903) (trespassing on private land to lay out street). A trespass action can be used when a local government unlawfully destroys a building. See Michaud v. City of Bangor, 159 Me. 491, 196 A.2d 106 (1963), on appeal after remand, 160 Me. 285, 203 A.2d 687. The exception to governmental immunity for nuisances and trespasses has often been changed by statute. See Note, The Michigan Supreme Court Concludes that the Michigan Government Tort Liability Act Does Not Allow for the Common Law "Trespass-Nuisance" Exception to Governmental Immunity, as Applicable to Municipalities, 81 U. Detroit Mercy L. Rev. 91 (2003), commenting on Pohutski v. Allen Park, 465 Mich. 675, 641 N.W.2d 219 (2002) (overruling prior authority). Another possible theory which avoids the immunity problem and which can be used when property is damaged is "inverse (or reverse) condemnation"; see Chapter 19 *supra*.

[62] Corrington v. Kalicak, 319 S.W.2d 888 (Mo.App.1959). But cf. Williamson v. City of Hays, 275 Kan. 300, 64 P.3d 364 (2003) (as a general rule, a municipal corporation is not liable for damage caused by the increased or accelerated flow of surface waters which have not been diverted from their natural course, or by the incidental change or interruption in, the discharge of, or the increased or accelerated flow of, surface waters caused by the lawful improvement of its streets or the making of other public improvements). See generally Kinyon & McClure, Interferences with Surface Waters, 24 Minn.L.Rev. 891 (1940); Annot., Modern Status of Rules Governing Interference with Drainage of Surface Waters, 93 A.L.R.3d 1193 (1979). See also Annot., Liability of Government Entity for Issuance of Permit for Construction Which Caused Accelerated Flooding, 62 A.L.R.3d 514 (1975); Annot., Propriety of Injunctive Relief Against Diversion of Water by Municipal Corporation or Public Utility, 42 A.L.R.3d 426 (1972).

[63] See Looper v. City of Easley, 172 S.C. 11, 172 S.E. 705 (1934); Pohland v. City of Sheboygan, 251 Wis. 20, 27 N.W.2d 736 (1947) (statute authorized obtaining of liability insurance, but this held not to authorize such insurance for governmental operations). But if an insurance company has accepted payment of premiums by a municipality, then—even though the municipality was acting ultra vires—some authority supports the view that the company will be estopped from denying its liability on the policy. See McCaleb v. Continental Casualty Co., 132 Tex. 65, 116 S.W.2d 679 (1938).

[64] See Gibbons, Liability Insurance and the Tort Immunity of State and Local Government, 1959 Duke L.J. 588. It is possible, of course, that states retaining municipal immunity for governmental functions could hold such statutes unconstitutional, or interpret them as not covering governmental operations in order to avoid such invalidation. See Pohland v. City of Sheboygan, *supra* note 63.

purchase insurance, has no power to waive its governmental immunity; and this has sometimes been endorsed by the courts,[65] as has the argument that the mere purchase of liability insurance does not waive immunity.[66] But the trend has been toward upholding municipal power to waive immunity,[67] and toward finding that the purchase of liability insurance does, within the limits of the insurance, constitute such a waiver.[68] Some state statutes authorizing insurance speak to the question of a waiver of immunity: Some provide that the insurance is to have no effect on the areas of immunity and is to create no additional liability.[69] Some of the statutes declare that the insurance policies

---

Some state statutes provide that if liability insurance is maintained by an immune governmental unit, a person injured by that unit has a direct right of action against the insurance carrier. See Little Rock Port Auth. v. McCain, 296 Ark. 130, 752 S.W.2d 44 (1988), interpreting such a statute as authorizing a municipal authority to purchase liability insurance even if the authority was not subject to tort liability. As to the effects on local governments of recent changes in insurance regulation and of the trend toward a greater degree of "self-insurance," see Rynard, The Local Government as Insured or Insurer: Some New Risk Management Alternatives, 20 Urban Law. 103 (1988). See generally Wasserman & Phelus (eds.), Risk Management Today: A How-To Guide for Local Government (International City Management Ass'n 1985).

65 See Jones v. Scofield Brothers Inc., 73 F.Supp. 395 (D.C.Md.1947) (clause that insurer will not raise defense of governmental immunity treated as of no effect); Cushman v. Grafton County, 97 N.H. 32, 79 A.2d 630 (1951); Stephenson v. City of Raleigh, 232 N.C. 42, 59 S.E.2d 195 (1950) (insurance contract created rights only in the insured, not in third persons; and insured-city had no power to waive its immunity); Kesman v. School District, 345 Pa. 457, 29 A.2d 17 (1942); McKenzie v. City of Florence, 234 S.C. 428, 108 S.E.2d 825 (1959); Maffei v. Incorporated Town of Kemmerer, 80 Wyo. 33, 338 P.2d 808 (1959), reh. denied 80 Wyo. 33, 340 P.2d 759. Cf. Hale v. Smith, 254 Or. 300, 460 P.2d 351 (1969) (theory that plaintiff, suing city and police officer, was third-party beneficiary of insurance contract between city and insurer could not be raised where insurer was not party to action).

66 Barad v. Jefferson County, 178 N.W.2d 376 (Iowa 1970); Hughes v. County of Burlington, 99 N.J.Super. 405, 240 A.2d 177 (1968); Hale v. Smith, *supra* note 65. Cf. State ex rel. Cass Medical Center v. Mason, 796 S.W.2d 621 (Mo.1990) (en banc) (county hospital did not waive sovereign immunity by purchasing insurance to cover liabilities outside protection of such immunity).

67 The waiver is particularly likely to be found if the purchase of liability insurance is authorized by statute and the municipality then acts under such authorization. See Clark v. Scheld, 253 N.C. 732, 117 S.E.2d 838 (1961). But there is even authority that the purchase of the insurance by itself, though not authorized by statute, is a waiver of immunity to the extent of coverage. Thomas v. Broadlands Community Consolidated School District, 348 Ill.App. 567, 109 N.E.2d 636 (1952). Cf. Tracy v. Davis, 123 F.Supp. 160 (E.D.Ill.1954) (immunity of school district based on immunity of public funds, but non-public funds need not be available at time of entry of judgment; may be acquired afterwards); Beach v. City of Springfield, 32 Ill.App.2d 256, 177 N.E.2d 436 (1961) (municipality liable within coverage, though remained immune as to the deductible amount); Rogers v. Butler, 170 Tenn. 125, 92 S.W.2d 414 (1936) (in action against county, which had taken out liability insurance covering operation of school buses, court was authorized to render judgment against county but had to limit satisfaction to amount that could be obtained under liability policy).

68 Schoening v. United States Aviation Underwriters, Inc., 265 Minn. 119, 120 N.W.2d 859 (1963); My Sister's Place v. City of Burlington, 139 Vt. 602, 433 A.2d 275 (1981) (when city purchases policy of liability insurance, it waives its sovereign immunity and consents to being sued to extent of policy's coverage); Medlar v. Aetna Insurance Co., 127 Vt. 337, 248 A.2d 740 (1968); Marshall v. City of Green Bay, 18 Wis.2d 496, 118 N.W.2d 715 (1963). See Board of Educ. v. Kirby, 926 S.W.2d 455 (Ky.1996), noted 24 N. Ky. L. Rev. 319 (1997) (school district's purchase of liability insurance was implied waiver of immunity to extent of coverage); Lyles v. City of Charlotte, 344 N.C. 676, 477 S.E.2d 150 (1996), reh. denied 345 N.C. 355, 483 S.E.2d 170 (1997), noted 76 N.C.L. Rev. 269 (1997) (under North Carolina statute, city waives immunity by obtaining liability insurance or participating in risk pool, but no such waiver found here); Brown v. Egan Consolidated School Dist., 449 N.W.2d 259 (S.D.1989) (school district waived its immunity for injuries from bus accident to extent of its purchase of liability insurance coverage). But cf., distinguishing the *Marshall* case *supra*, Coste v. City of Superior, 231 F.Supp. 261 (W.D.Wis.1964), aff'd 343 F.2d 100 (7th Cir.) (no waiver found where insurer had merely agreed not to raise defense of immunity).

69 See Ga.Code Ann. § 20–2–1092 (1999) (covering negligent operation of school buses); Minn.Stat.Ann. § 466.06 (no effect on liability beyond coverage). Cf. City of Albuquerque v. Campbell, 68 N.M. 75, 358 P.2d 698 (1960) (provision of insurance for certain functions of sovereign does not affect sovereign's immunity).

must require the insurers not to raise the immunity defense.[70] But increasingly, most of the statutes simply provide that the municipality has, by acquiring liability insurance, waived its immunity, at least to the extent of the coverage.[71] This last-mentioned type of legislation removes most of the problems of interpretation and thus seems most desirable. Finally, however, some of the statutes authorizing municipalities to obtain liability insurance are silent on the question of whether the coverage effectuates a waiver. The trend in such situations is to find the waiver;[72] otherwise, public funds are being expended—wastefully, it would seem—to cover liability that doesn't exist. But it can be urged that common-law immunity should not be readily assumed to have been terminated, and thus that even the purchase of insurance under statutory authorization does not affect the waiver—and some courts have so held.[73] Again, the desirability of express provision in the statute for waiver (if that is intended) would seem clear.

For many years, statutes have existed in a number of states waiving municipal immunity for specified torts or, more commonly, for specified municipal activities. These statutes are often subjected to very narrow interpretation by the courts,[74] and thus the termination of immunity will occur only where this intent has been made extremely clear. Statutes abrogating immunity in limited areas fall into three principal categories: (1) Some are "safe place" statutes which impose liability for a failure to keep public

---

[70] See Ga.Code Ann. § 20–2–1092 (1999) (as to operation of school buses). Cf. Burns Ind. Stat. Ann. 34–13–3–20 (1998) (terms of policy govern rights and obligations of governmental entity and insurer). Sometimes such statutes are held to authorize a direct action by the injured party against the insurer. See Earl W. Baker & Co. v. Lagaly, 144 F.2d 344 (10th Cir.1944); Rome v. London & Lancashire Indem. Co., 169 So. 132 (La.App.1936). But see Shermoen v. Lindsay, 163 N.W.2d 738 (N.D.1968) (plaintiff who sued individual defendant and park district could not join park district's insurer as defendant in absence of specific "direct action" statute).

[71] See Minn.Stat.Ann. § 466.06, earlier version applied in Geislinger v. Village of Watkins, 269 Minn. 116, 130 N.W.2d 62 (1964); N.H.Rev.Stat.Ann. 412:3 (municipality or insurer cannot plead immunity). Cf. Ga. Code § 56–1013 (insurance to cover injuries by governmental motor vehicles). The waiver is only as to torts covered by the insurance policy. See Lively v. City of Blackfoot, 91 Idaho 80, 416 P.2d 27 (1966). Sometimes it is said that provisions of state law waiving governmental immunity are to be "read into" a policy purchased by the government. See Mott v. Mitchell, 209 Kan. 476, 496 P.2d 1297 (1972), applying statute now found at Kan.Stat.Ann. 74–4707 on purchase of insurance by state agencies. Cf. Allen v. City of Ogden, 210 Kan. 136, 499 P.2d 527 (1972), applying a former statute on municipal immunity.

[72] Taylor v. Knox County Board of Education, 292 Ky. 767, 167 S.W.2d 700 (1942); Vendrell v. School District No. 26C, 226 Or. 263, 360 P.2d 282 (1961); Collins v. Memorial Hospital, 521 P.2d 1339 (Wyo.1974). Cf. Rome v. London & Lancashire Co., *supra* note 69 (held that insurance company could not raise defense of immunity). Compare Surette v. Galiardo, 323 So.2d 53 (Fla.App.1975) (school board waived immunity for necessary functions by purchase of liability insurance), and Buffkin v. Board of County Commissioners, 320 So.2d 876 (Fla. App.1975) (mosquito control district waived immunity to extent of coverage of liability insurance), with Jolly v. Insurance Co., 331 So.2d 368 (Fla.App.1976) (cities and towns don't waive immunity by purchase of insurance). See generally Annot., Liability or Indemnity Insurance Carried by Governmental Unit as Affecting Immunity from Tort Liability, 68 A.L.R.2d 1437 (1959).

[73] Hummer v. School City of Hartford City, 124 Ind.App. 30, 112 N.E.2d 891 (1953); McGrath Building Co. v. City of Bettendorf, 248 Iowa 1386, 85 N.W.2d 616 (1957); Utz v. Board of Education, 126 W.Va. 823, 30 S.E.2d 342 (1944). Cf. Looper v. City of Easley, 172 S.C. 11, 172 S.E. 705 (1934) (city not estopped to assert immunity even though it had purchased insurance).

[74] See City of Bay Minette v. Quinley, 263 Ala. 188, 82 So.2d 192 (1955) (statute imposed liability for defects in buildings; court refused to apply to police building); Devers v. City of Scranton, 308 Pa. 13, 161 A. 540 (1932) (fire truck not within statute on motor vehicles); Abernathy v. City of Columbia, 213 S.C. 68, 48 S.E.2d 585 (1948) (treating as irrelevant a statutory provision on liability for defects or mismanagement of anything under municipal control); Sullivan v. School Dist., 179 Wis. 502, 191 N.W. 1020 (1923) (intent to change common law must be specifically stated or expressed in such manner as to leave no reasonable doubt).

buildings and/or other designated public places in reasonably safe condition.[75] (2) Some statutes impose liability for the negligent, or otherwise wrongful, driving of motor vehicles by employees of the locality within the scope of their employment.[76] (3) A number of these statutes pertain to the condition of streets and sidewalks and provide liability where injury results from a defect or unsafe condition in such a public way.[77] There are miscellaneous statutes providing municipal liability in particular situations, as where a change in the grade of a street or other public way causes damage to neighboring property,[78] or where specified municipal agents, such as medical practitioners at public institutions, negligently cause harm, or where riot damage occurs within a municipality.[79]

---

[75] *E.g.*, Ala.Code 1975, § 11–47–190; West's Ann.Cal.Gov.Code § 835 applied in Hibbs v. Los Angeles County Flood Control District, 252 Cal.App.2d 166, 60 Cal.Rptr. 364 (Dist.Ct.1967); Iowa Code Ann. § 364.12 (1976); Mich. Comp.Laws Ann. § 3.996 (106) (1977); Ohio Rev.Code Ann. § 723.01 (Page 1976), applied in Marshall v. City of Portsmouth, 11 Ohio Misc. 123, 229 N.E.2d 665 (1967) (parking lot held to be public ground under statute); Ware v. City of Cincinnati, 93 Ohio App. 431, 111 N.E.2d 401 (1952); Huffman v. City of Columbus, 51 N.E.2d 410 (Ohio App.1943). Cf. Wis. Stat.Ann. § 101.11 (1973) (safe place statute as to employers), discussed in Reuss, Thirty Years of the Safe Place Statute, 1940 Wis.L.Rev. 334; Note, Governmental Liability Under Safe Place Statute, 1959 Wis. L.Rev. 672.

[76] *E.g.*, West's Ann.Cal.Vehicle Code § 17001; Ill.Ann.Stat. § 1–4–4 (Smith-Hurd 1962) (negligent operation of motor vehicle by fireman); Mich. Compiled Laws Ann. § 3.996 (105); N.Y.Gen.Mun.Law § 50–a–c; Ohio Rev.Code § 701.02, applied in Rankin v. Sander, 96 Ohio App. 40, 121 N.E.2d 91 (1953); 11 Okl.Stat.Ann. § 23–101–08; Vernon's Ann.Tex.Civ.Stat. art. 6252–19, § 3. See generally Annot., What Is "Motor Vehicle" or the Like Within Statute Waiving Governmental Immunity as to Operation of Such Vehicles, 77 A.L.R.2d 945 (1961).

[77] *E.g.*, Ala.Code 1977, § 11–47–190; Conn.Gen.Stat.Ann. § 13–11 applied in Derfall v. Town of West Hartford, 25 Conn. Sup. 302, 203 A.2d 152 (1964); 23 Maine Rev.Stat.Ann. § 3655; Mass.Gen.Law Ann. c. 84, § 15; Mich.Comp.Laws Ann. § 3.996(101)–(104) (1977); Ohio Rev.Code § 723.01, applied in Griffin v. City of Cincinnati, 162 Ohio St. 232, 123 N.E.2d 11 (1954); McCave v. City of Canton, 140 Ohio St. 150, 42 N.E.2d 762 (1942); S.C.Code 1977, § 5–7–70, predecessor statute applied in Reeves v. City of Easley, 167 S.C. 231, 166 S.E. 120 (1932); Wis.Stat.Ann. 81.15, applied in McChain v. City of Fond Du Lac, 7 Wis.2d 286, 96 N.W.2d 607 (1959); Laffey v. City of Milwaukee, 4 Wis.2d 111, 89 N.W.2d 801 (1958) (sidewalk held within statute). Some cases under such statutes have also relied partly on a nuisance theory of liability. See Fankhauser v. City of Mansfield, 19 Ohio St.2d 102, 249 N.E.2d 789 (1969) (malfunctioning traffic signals). Cf. Dollar Savings & Trust Co. v. City of Youngstown, 19 Ohio App.2d 225, 250 N.E.2d 883 (1969) ("qualified nuisance" found where city eliminated crosswalk but allowed markings to remain on street). Streets and sidewalks, it should also be noted, are embraced within some of the statutes on "public property," discussed *supra* note 74, and accompanying text. See Duran v. Gibson, 180 Cal.App.2d 753, 4 Cal.Rptr. 803 (Dist.Ct. 1960) (street); Gentekos v. City & County of San Francisco, 163 Cal.App.2d 691, 329 P.2d 943 (Dist.Ct.1958) (sidewalk). But some of these statutes apply only to buildings. See Ball v. City of Madison, 1 Wis.2d 62, 82 N.W.2d 894 (1957), limiting the Wisconsin statute to structures having some of the characteristics of a building.

[78] *E.g.*, L.S.A.-Rev.Stat. 33:3742; Mo. V.A.M.S. § 88.080 (1971 Supp.1981); Mont. Code Ann. 7–14–4202; Neb.Rev. Stat. § 14–3,100,–3,101; N.D.Rev.Code § 40–39–03 (1968), applied in Kenner v. City of Minot, 98 N.W.2d 901 (N.D. 1959); 53 Pa.Stat. §§ 1674 & 1675 (1974); Tenn.Code Ann. § 7–31–112, applied in City of Knoxville v. Phillips, 162 Tenn. 328, 36 S.W.2d 434 (1931) (liberal construction to be given); Va. Code 1981, § 15.1–368 (damage from grading streets). Some of the statutes apply only to a certain group of municipalities. See Mich. Compiled Laws Ann. § 5.1812 (applicable in fourth class cities), applied in Speck v. Wayne County, 237 Mich. 202, 211 N.W. 626 (1927) (statute not to be extended by implication).

[79] An example of a statute on medical practitioners' negligence is N.Y.Gen.Mun. Law § 50d. Cf. Conn.Gen.Stat.Ann. § 7–308 (liability for torts of fire-fighters). Statutes occasionally provide relief to persons injured while attempting to aid a law-enforcement officer. See 24 Ill.Ann.Stat. § 1–4–6 (Smith-Hurd 1962 Supp. 1981), applied in Meador v. City of Salem, 51 Ill.2d 572, 284 N.E.2d 266 (1972) (absolute liability found). Cf. Sawyer v. Town of Southport, 6 A.D.2d 553, 179 N.Y.S.2d 897 (1958), applying a comparable New York law.

Mob violence statutes, often imposing strict liability, are discussed in Note, Municipal Liability for Riot Damage, 81 Harv. L. Rev. 653 (1968); Annot., Municipal Liability for Property Damage Under Mob Violence Statutes, 26 A.L.R. 3d 1198 (1969); Annot., Municipal Liability for Personal Injury or Death Under Mob Violence or Anti-Lynching Statutes, 26 A.L.R.3d 1142 (1969). See also Note, Regulating Flash Mobs: Seeking

The trend in recent years has been away from piece-meal waiver of municipal immunity for governmental actions, and toward full-scale liability. Florida took the lead in 1957, when it abolished municipal immunity in a case involving a prisoner who suffocated during a fire in the city jail.[80] This has been followed, in line with the general trend toward abolishing the old immunities, by an onslaught of cases, until it can be safely stated that municipal liability even as to governmental functions is possible in the great majority of states.[81] But six qualifications must be noted to the general rule of

---

a Middle Ground Approach That Preserves Free Expression and Maintains Public Order, 51 U. Louisville L. Rev. 375 (2013).

[80] Hargrove v. Town of Cocoa Beach, 96 So.2d 130 (Fla.1957), noted 7 Duke L.J. 142 (1958); 71 Harv.L.Rev. 744 (1958); 4 Howard L.J. 131 (1958); 56 Mich.L.Rev. 465 (1958); 11 U.Fla.L.Rev. 121 (1958); 16 U.Miami L.Rev. 572–74 (1962) (portion of Survey); 11 Vand.L.Rev. 263 (1957). On later developments in Florida's law on governmental tort liability, see Wetherington & Pollock, Tort Suits Against Governmental Entities in Florida, 44 Fla. L. Rev. 1 (1992). See generally Prosser & Keeton, Law of Torts 1052–56 (5th ed. 1984).

[81] See Scheele v. City of Anchorage, 385 P.2d 582 (Alaska 1963); City of Fairbanks v. Schaible, 375 P.2d 201 (Alaska 1962); Lorence v. Hospital Board, 294 Ala. 614, 320 So.2d 631 (1975); Jackson v. City of Florence, 294 Ala. 592, 320 So.2d 68 (1975) (with list of cases from other states); Veach v. City of Phoenix, 102 Ariz. 195, 427 P.2d 335 (1967); Town of Scottsdale v. State ex rel. Pickrell, 1 Ariz.App. 85, 399 P.2d 706 (1965); Stone v. Arizona Highway Commission, 93 Ariz. 384, 381 P.2d 107 (1963); Parish v. Pitts, 244 Ark. 1239, 429 S.W.2d 45 (1968); Muskopf v. Corning Hospital District, 55 Cal.2d 211, 11 Cal.Rptr. 89, 359 P.2d 457 (1961), modified sub nom. Corning Hospital District v. Superior Court, 57 Cal.2d 488, 20 Cal.Rptr. 621, 370 P.2d 325; Colorado Racing Commission v. Brush Racing Association, 136 Colo. 279, 316 P.2d 582 (1957); Murphy v. Ives, 151 Conn. 259, 196 A.2d 596 (1963); Hopper v. Idaho Board of Highway Directors, 93 Idaho 795, 473 P.2d 937 (1970); Molitor v. Kaneland Community Unit District, 18 Ill.2d 11, 163 N.E.2d 89 (1959), cert. denied 362 U.S. 968, 80 S.Ct. 955, 4 L.Ed.2d 900 (1960); Brinkman v. City of Indianapolis, 141 Ind.App. 662, 231 N.E.2d 169 (1967) (en banc); Gorrell v. City of Parsons, 223 Kan. 645, 576 P.2d 616 (1978); Burton v. Somerset City Hospital, 388 S.W.2d 134 (Ky.1965); Haney v. City of Lexington, 386 S.W.2d 738 (Ky. App.1964); Hamilton v. City of Shreveport, 247 La. 784, 174 So.2d 529 (1965), on remand 180 So.2d 30, writ denied 248 La. 700, 181 So.2d 399; Davies v. City of Bath, 364 A.2d 1269 (Me.1976); Williams v. City of Detroit, 364 Mich. 231, 111 N.W.2d 1 (1961); McCorkell v. City of Northfield, 266 Minn. 267, 123 N.W.2d 367 (1963); Spanel v. Mounds View School Dist., 264 Minn. 279, 118 N.W.2d 795 (1962); Tucker v. City of Okolona, 227 So.2d 475 (Miss.1969); Jones v. State Highway Comm'n, 557 S.W.2d 225 (Mo.1977), appeal after remand 593 S.W.2d 580 (saying 29 states and District of Columbia had already judicially abolished immunity); State v. District Court, 170 Mont. 15, 550 P.2d 382 (1976) (relying on statutes); Johnson v. Municipal University of Omaha, 184 Neb. 512, 169 N.W.2d 286 (1969), appeal after remand 187 Neb. 24, 187 N.W.2d 102; Brown v. City of Omaha, 183 Neb. 430, 160 N.W.2d 805 (1968); Rice v. Clark County, 79 Nev. 253, 382 P.2d 605 (1963); Bancroft v. Town of Canterbury, 118 N.H. 453, 388 A.2d 199 (1978); Merrill v. City of Manchester, 114 N.H. 722, 332 A.2d 378 (1974); Willis v. Department of Conservation, 55 N.J. 534, 264 A.2d 34 (1970); McAndrew v. Mularchuk, 33 N.J. 172, 162 A.2d 820 (1960); Hicks v. State, 88 N.M. 588, 544 P.2d 1153 (1975); Runkel v. New York City, 282 App. Div. 173, 123 N.Y.S.2d 485 (1953); Kitto v. Minot Park District, 224 N.W.2d 795 (N.D.1974); Ayala v. Philadelphia Board of Education, 453 Pa. 584, 305 A.2d 877 (1973); Laughlin v. City of Pittsburg, 226 Pa.Super. 431, 310 A.2d 289 (1973); Becker v. Beaudoin, 106 R.I. 562, 261 A.2d 896 (1970); Hosea v. City of Seattle, 64 Wn.2d 678, 393 P.2d 967 (1964); Kelso v. City of Tacoma, 63 Wn.2d 913, 390 P.2d 2 (1964); Long v. City of Weirton, 158 W.Va. 741, 214 S.E.2d 832 (1975); Holytz v. City of Milwaukee, 17 Wis.2d 26, 115 N.W.2d 618 (1962); Oroz v. Board of County Commissioners, 575 P.2d 1155 (Wyo.1978); Town of Douglas v. York, 445 P.2d 760 (Wyo.1968). Cf. Spencer v. General Hospital, 425 F.2d 479 (D.C.Cir.1969) (Washington, D.C.); Whitney v. City of Worcester, 373 Mass. 208, 366 N.E.2d 1210 (1977) (court will abolish municipal immunity if legislature does not act; legislature *did* subsequently pass statute, Mass. Gen.Laws Ann. c. 258, §§ 1–13; see generally Cervone & Hardy, The Massachusetts Governmental Tort Liability Act and Its Discretionary Function Immunity: An Analysis and a Modest Proposal, 14 Suffolk U.L.Rev. 1251 (1980)); Johnson v. Oman Construction Co., Inc., 519 S.W.2d 782 (Tenn.1975) (state has statute, but court does not regard it as dealing with subject in complete or comprehensive manner; court indicates it would be willing to abolish immunity more thoroughly, but not necessary in this case); City of Houston v. Bush, 566 S.W.2d 33 (Tex.Civ.App.1978), ref. n. r. e. (local government immune only if it meets burden of showing its activity was completely governmental; if activity partly governmental, and partly proprietary, is no immunity; even if function governmental, statute waives immunity to some extent). See generally K.C. Davis, Administrative Law of the Seventies ch. 25 (1976) & annual supps.; Vanlandingham, Local Governmental Immunity Re-Examined, 61 Nw. U.L.Rev. 237 (1967).

A variety of legislative and/or judicial approaches has been used in abolishing governmental immunity. Iowa has abolished municipal immunity by statute. Iowa Code § 613A.2. See Symmonds v. Chicago, Milwaukee & St. Paul R.R., 242 N.W.2d 262 (Iowa 1976), applying the statute to counties. On the gradual abolition of tort immunity by the court in Mississippi, see Case, From Pruett to Presley: The Long and Winding Road to Abrogation of Common Law Sovereign Immunity in Mississippi, 63 Miss. L. J. 537 (1994). In Oklahoma, the tort immunity of the state and local governments was prospectively abrogated, with limited exceptions, by the court in Vanderpool v. State, 672 P.2d 1153 (Okl.1983). This was followed by passage of a statute—the Governmental Tort Claims Act, 51 Okla. Stat. 1981, §§ 151–71—waiving sovereign immunity, subject to numerous exceptions. But in most states, statutes now deal with the subject of municipal tort liability, as well as (usually) state liability, and often contain designated exceptions—particularly for "discretionary" activities—to the general abrogation of immunity. See note 85 *infra*, and accompanying text. Pennsylvania statutes largely *retaining* local governmental immunity have been upheld. See Robson v. Penn Hills School Dist., 63 Pa.Cmwlth. 250, 437 A.2d 1273 (1981); Carroll v. County of York, 496 Pa. 363, 437 A.2d 394 (1981). On court interpretation of the Pennsylvania immunity statutes, see Doddo & Toth, The Emperor's New Clothes: A Survey of Significant Court Decisions Interpreting Pennsylvania's Sovereign Immunity Act and its Waivers, 32 Duquesne L. Rev. 1 (1993).

Some statutes waiving governmental immunity contain an exception as to injuries suffered by persons voluntarily using unimproved public property of the government and injured by natural conditions thereon. Such an exception, however, is likely to be held inapplicable to persons injured while using adjacent land. See Milligan v. City of Laguna Beach, 34 Cal.3d 829, 196 Cal.Rptr. 38, 670 P.2d 1121 (1983) (inapplicable when limbs from trees on government property injured adjacent property or persons thereon). Local governments also usually enjoy the same immunity from tort liability as enjoyed by other landowners under the widely adopted state "recreational use statutes." See Jackson v. Unified School Dist. 259, 268 Kan. 319, 995 P.2d 844 (2000) (school gymnasium could come within recreational use exception if used for recreational purposes). See generally Comment, The Connecticut Recreational Use Statute: Should a Municipality Be Immune from Tort Liability?, 15 Pace L. Rev. 963 (1995). See also Section 26.2, note 44, *supra*.

Statutory retention of immunity as to certain governmental units and certain activities has usually survived Equal Protection attack if supported by some rational basis. See Paulson v. County of Pierce, 99 Wash.2d 645, 664 P.2d 1202 (1983), appeal dism'd 464 U.S. 957, 104 S.Ct. 386, 78 L.Ed.2d 331 (1983) (county immune for noncontractual acts and omissions relating to flood protection; statute presumed constitutional unless challenging party shows it has no rational basis or that classification is contrary to purpose of legislation). On the rules of construction to be applied to statutes on governmental tort liability, compare Hoff v. Vacaville Unified School Dist., 19 Cal.4th 925, 80 Cal.Rptr.2d 811, 968 P.2d 522 (Cal. 1998) (public entity may be held liable only if statute so declares), and Vigil v. Ruettgers, 887 P.2d 521 (Wyo.1994) (under Wyoming statute, immunity is the rule and liability the exception; so liability is strictly construed), with Walton v. State, 968 P.2d 636 (Colo.1998) (immunity provisions should be construed strictly and waivers of immunity construed deferentially), and Bertrand v. Board of County Comm'rs, 872 P.2d 223 (Colo.1994) (governmental liability is now the common law of Colorado; statute creating immunity should be strictly construed). Cf. Tidwell v. City & County of Denver, 83 P.3d 75 (Colo. 2003) (Colorado Supreme Court construes broadly the provisions of Governmental Immunity Act that withhold immunity and construes the exceptions to these waivers strictly).

A good summary of the impacts, financial and otherwise, of municipal tort liability is Symposium, 44 Syracuse L. Rev. 829–966 (1993), particularly MacManus, The Impact of Litigation on Municipalities: Total Cost, Driving Factors, and Cost Containment Mechanisms, *id.* at 833. On particular statutes terminating municipal and other governmental immunity, see Comment, Wyoming's Governmental Claims Act: Sovereign Immunity with Exceptions—A Statutory Analysis, 15 Land & Water L.Rev. 619 (1980); Comment, Sovereign Immunity and the Tennessee Governmental Tort Liability Act, 41 Tenn.L.Rev. 885 (1974); Comment, Municipal Tort Liability Act, A Legislative Solution Balancing the Needs of Cities and Plaintiffs, 16 Urban L.Ann. 305 (1979); Note, Governmental Immunity: The Kansas Tort Claims Act (or The King *Can* Do Wrong), 19 Washburn L.J. 260 (1980). On the constitutionality of such statutes, see Note, Governmental Immunity—Kansas Supreme Court Upholds Governmental Immunity Statutes, 25 Kan. L.Rev. 140 (1976).

In Gladstone v. Bartlesville Independent School Dist., 66 P.3d 442 (Okla. 2003), Oklahoma's Governmental Tort Claims Act and its exceptions were upheld under equal protection and due process attacks based on both the United States and Oklahoma Constitutions. The constitutionality of limitations on the recoverable damages under Utah's Governmental Immunity Act was upheld in Tindley v. Salt Lake City School Dist., 2005 Utah 30, 116 P.3d 295 (2005). The purpose of government tort statutes was held to include the provision to the public entity of sufficient information to enable it to investigate claims and settle them, if appropriate, without the expense of litigation, in Stockett v. Association of Calif. Water Agencies Joint Powers Insurance Auth., 34 Cal.4th 441, 20 Cal.Rptr.3d 176, 99 P.3d 500 (2004). On notice and procedural requirements, see generally Note, Torts, Municipal Tort Liability, 6 Wm. Mitchell L.Rev. 490 (1980). See also Section 26.4 *infra*.

municipal liability: (1) The courts have often held that immunity remains as to legislative or judicial functions, since the need for a free exercise of judgment—without fear of possible liability—is considered especially great in these areas.[82] (2) A few courts have indicated that liability may be circumscribed by exceptions even wider than the above-mentioned legislative and judicial exception—for instance, a rule of continuing immunity as to "discretionary" actions by any agent of the local government,[83] or an exemption of liability as to even "quasi-judicial" or "quasi-legislative" tasks.[84] (3) The legislature has "gotten into the act" of abolishing governmental immunity in many states—usually *after* judicial action on the matter. A number of states now have statutes covering the liability of municipal corporations; and most of the statutes contain exceptions—specified torts or activities (such as "discretionary functions") for which the local governments remain immune.[85] (4) Many cases support the view that public policy

---

[82] See Middleton v. City of Fort Walton Beach, 113 So.2d 431 (Fla.App.1959); Gorrell v. City of Parsons, *supra* note 80 (Kansas); Haney v. City of Lexington, *supra* note 80 (Kentucky); Willis v. Department of Conservation, 55 N.J. 534, 264 A.2d 34 (1970); B. W. King, Inc. v. Town of West New York, 49 N.J. 318, 230 A.2d 133 (1967); Dusek v. Pierce County, 42 Wis.2d 498, 167 N.W.2d 246 (1969).

[83] See Parish v. Pitts, *supra* note 81 (Arkansas); City of Daytona Beach v. Palmer, 469 So.2d 121 (Fla.1985) (decisions on how to fight a particular fire were discretionary judgmental decisions); Everton v. Willard, 468 So.2d 936 (Fla.1985) (officer's decision not to make an arrest is discretionary and thus within area of immunity); Bergen v. Koppenal, 97 N.J.Super. 265, 235 A.2d 30 (1967), aff'd 52 N.J. 478, 246 A.2d 442; John v. City of Dresham, 214 Or.App. 305, 165 P.3d 1177 (2007) (genuine issue of material fact as to nature of city transportation engineer's decision to paint crosswalk precluded summary judgment based on discretionary immunity; case says such immunity does not apply to decisions not to decide). Cf. City of El Paso v. Higginbotham, 993 S.W.2d 819 (Tex.App.1999) (ambulance driver exercised governmental—as opposed to medical—discretion in deciding to un-strap patient, and thus immunity applied *if* discretion was exercised in good faith).

[84] See Steinhardt v. North Bay Village, 132 So.2d 764 (Fla.App.1961), cert. discharged 141 So.2d 737; Calbeck v. Town of South Pasadena, 128 So.2d 138 (Fla.App.1961); City of Miami v. Albro, 120 So.2d 23 (Fla.App.1960); City of Louisville v. Chapman, 413 S.W.2d 74 (Ky.1967); Haney v. City of Lexington, *supra* note 81 (Kentucky); Tarter v. State, 68 N.Y.2d 511, 510 N.Y.S.2d 528, 503 N.E.2d 84 (1986) (parole release decisions are quasi-judicial, and thus parole board is not liable for negligent paroling of dangerous prisoner). Cf. Pickle v. Board of County Comm'rs, 764 P.2d 262 (Wyo.1988) (enactment of statute waiving governmental immunity did not affect common-law doctrine of legislative and quasi-legislative immunity; but county's processing and reviewing of subdivision plan was not legislative or quasi-legislative since was purely an imperative administrative duty).

[85] See, *e.g.*, such exceptions found, in legislation generally waiving immunity, at West's Ann.Cal.Gov.Code §§ 810, 820.2, applied in McCorckle v. City of Los Angeles, 70 Cal.2d 252, 74 Cal.Rptr. 389, 449 P.2d 453 (1969) ("discretionary" exception said to apply where the activity involved personal deliberation, decision, and judgment); Ne Casek v. City of Los Angeles, 233 Cal.App.2d 131, 43 Cal.Rptr. 294 (Dist.Ct. 1965) (holding "discretion" present when police officer didn't adequately restrain arrested person, who thus escaped and injured plaintiff), and discussed (with special attention to the "discretionary" exception) in Note, The Discretionary Immunity Doctrine in California, 19 Hastings L.J. 561 (1968); Ill. Ann.Stat. §§ 85–2–103 to –109 (several exceptions, as for issuing or denying a permit, etc.); Iowa Code Ann. § 613A.4 (exceptions include collection or assessment of taxes and execution with due care of any statute or ordinance), liability applied in Strong v. Town of Lansing, 179 N.W.2d 365 (Iowa 1970) (no exception applicable); Mich. Compiled Laws Ann. § 9.2310 (1974), applied in Mullins v. Wayne County, 4 Mich.App. 359, 144 N.W.2d 829 (1966), aff'd 380 Mich. 151, 156 N.W.2d 546 (county not liable for failure to post warning sign where road ended, as decision was discretionary); Minn.Stat. Ann. § 466.03(6), discussed as to discretionary exception in Note, Discretionary Exception and Minnesota Tort Liability: A Reappraisal, 52 Minn.L.Rev. 1047 (1968); Nev. Rev.Stat. 41.032; 51 Okl.Stat. 1981, § 155 (exceptions for discretionary functions, legislative functions, judicial and quasi-judicial functions, etc.,); Or.Rev.Stat. 30.265, discussed in Henke, Oregon's Governmental Tort Liability Law from a National Perspective, 48 Or.L.Rev. 95 (1968) (with discussion of "discretionary exception" at 103–06). Cf. Wash.Rev.Code Ann. 4.96.010, applied in Haslund v. City of Seattle, 86 Wn.2d 607, 547 P.2d 1221 (1976) (saying discretionary exception is very limited).

On statutes restoring some degree of immunity following judicial termination, see generally Note, Governmental Immunity—The Doctrine of Immunity Judicially Abrogated and Legislatively Reinstated, 50 J.Urban L. 154 (1972).

Statutes have sometimes been invalidated if they attempt to limit the amount of recovery. See Treece v. Shawnee Community Unit School District, 39 Ill.2d 136, 233 N.E.2d 549 (1968). But the validity of a "cap" on monetary damages was upheld against attacks based on the state and federal constitutions in Smith v. City of Philadelphia, 512 Pa. 129, 516 A.2d 306 (1986), appeal dism'd 479 U.S. 1074, 107 S.Ct. 1265, 94 L.Ed.2d 127 (1987). Cf., interpreting such a limitation, Wood v. Milin, 134 Wis.2d 279, 397 N.W.2d 479 (1986) (joint-tenant property owners may recover separately up to statutory limit for harm to the jointly held property). Statutes may also be invalidated if they attempt to retain immunity for all governmental functions. See Maki v. East Tawas, 385 Mich. 151, 188 N.W.2d 593 (1971).

New York has long had a statute (the Court of Claims Act) waiving most immunity of the state. 29A (Part 2) New York Consol. Laws § 8. (McKinney 1963). And this has been held applicable to municipal corporations. Bernardine v. City of New York, 294 N.Y. 361, 62 N.E.2d 604 (1945). But the New York courts have been reluctant to impose liability under the statute for a *failure* to perform duties (as opposed to liability for tortious performance of duties). See Bass v. City of New York, 38 A.D.2d 407, 330 N.Y.S.2d 569 (1972), aff'd 32 N.Y.2d 894, 346 N.Y.S.2d 814, 300 N.E.2d 154. But see Schuster v. City of New York, 5 N.Y.2d 75, 180 N.Y.S.2d 265, 154 N.E.2d 534 (1958) (police had duty to provide protection to informer). Similarly, some cases have denied recovery on the ground that no duty was owed the particular plaintiff in the case. See King v. New York City, 3 Misc.2d 241, 152 N.Y.S.2d 110 (Sup.Ct.1956); Murrain v. Wilson Line, 270 App.Div. 372, 59 N.Y.S.2d 750 (1946), aff'd 296 N.Y. 845, 72 N.E.2d 29 (1947).

The "discretionary" exception found in many of the statutes is often modeled on that contained in the Federal Tort Claims Act, retaining the federal government's immunity as to performance, or failure to perform, discretionary functions; 28 U.S.C.A. § 2680(a). See Cervone & Hardy, The Massachusetts Governmental Tort Liability Act and Its Discretionary Function Immunity: An Analysis and a Modest Proposal, 14 Suffolk U.L.Rev. 1251 (1980). On the exception in the federal legislation, see Peck, The Federal Tort Claims Act—A Proposed Construction of the Discretionary Function Exception, 31 Wash.L.Rev. 207 (1956); Reynolds, The Discretionary Function Exception of the Federal Tort Claims Act, 57 Geo.L.J. 81 (1968); Comment, Federal Tort Claims Act: Discretionary Function Exception Revisited, 31 U. Miami L.Rev. 161 (1976).

Another test that has been proposed for deciding what are "discretionary functions" is that such functions must be the result of choice, involving the exercise of judgment; the choice must involve public policy, as opposed to routine day-to-day activities of public officials; and the public policy choice must be exercised by a person or body that has, either directly or by delegation, the responsibility or authority to make it. Sande v. City of Portland, 185 Or.App. 262, 59 P.3d 595 (2002). Compare Garrison v. Deschutes County, 334 Or. 264, 48 P.3d 807 (2002) (county officials protected by discretionary function exception in selecting final design for solid waste transfer station, even if decisions were negligently reached), with Sandberg v. Lehman, Jensen & Donahue, L.C., 2003 Utah App. 272, 76 P.3d 699 (2003) (decisions leading to omission of certain safety features at concrete pit at solid waste facility were not discretionary). Cf. Gilmore v. Board of Comm'rs of Logan County, 147 P.3d 296 (Okla. Civ. App. 2006) (county board of commissioners' decision to maintain a road as gravel rather than pave it was discretionary); Johnson v. Utah Dept. of Transp., 2006 Utah 15, 133 P.3d 402 (2006) (Department of Transportation's use of orange plastic barrels on highway construction project did not qualify for discretionary immunity).

On applying "discretionary" exceptions to state and municipal activities, see generally Spencer v. General Hospital, 425 F.2d 479 (D.C.Cir.1969) (no immunity for negligent treatment of paying patient); Johnson v. State, 69 Cal.2d 782, 73 Cal.Rptr. 240, 447 P.2d 352 (1968) (state not immune for parole officer's failure to warn plaintiff of danger of accepting paroled youth into her home); Martinez v. Maruszczak, 168 P.3d 720 (Nev. 2007) (physician's decisions with respect to diagnoses and treatment did not involve discretion); Merrill v. City of Manchester, 114 N.H. 722, 332 A.2d 378 (1974) (abrogation of municipal immunity did not extend to legislative, judicial, or policy-making functions). Cf. Antique Arts Corp. v. City of Torrance, 39 Cal.App.3d 588, 114 Cal.Rptr. 332 (Dist.Ct.1974) (city not liable to robbed store for value of items taken despite negligence of police radio dispatcher in alerting police; police function said to be immunized whether considered discretionary or ministerial); Jones v. State, 33 N.Y.2d 275, 352 N.Y.S.2d 169, 307 N.E.2d 236 (1973) (state not immune for intentional assault and battery). As to liability for water and sewer systems, compare Grabicki v. City of Lewiston, 302 P.3d 26 (Idaho 2013) (discretionary function exception does not apply to claim that city negligently designed storm-water drain system), with Jenkins v. Jordan Valley Water Conservancy Dist., 283 P.3d 1009 (Utah App. 2012) (district's decision on when to replace a water line section was discretionary function).

As a rule-of-thumb for determining what is within a "discretionary" exception, many cases have stated that, in general, planning-level or policy-formulating decisions are discretionary and thus immune, while operational-level activities are ministerial and outside the scope of immunity. See Lawton v. City of Pocatello, 126 Idaho 454, 886 P.2d 330 (1994) (routine matters will usually be deemed operational and thus subject to liability, while decisions involving consideration of financial, political, economic, and social effects will likely be classified as discretionary and thus immune); Czaplicki v. Gooding Joint School Dist., 116 Idaho 326, 775 P.2d 640 (1989) (discretionary function exception applies only to decisions entailing planning or policy (*i.e.*, the policy against penalizing innocent taxpayers and perhaps jeopardizing the financial stability of the government, from whose services all citizens are presumed to benefit) precludes the assessing of punitive (also called "exemplary") damages against a local government.[86] But while the majority view is clearly against the awarding of such

---

formulation and did not apply to school principal's operational actions of failing to call ambulance and render first aid to pupil); Jones v. City of St. Maries, 111 Idaho 733, 727 P.2d 1161 (1986) (allegation that city was negligent in inspecting and maintaining fire hydrants and water mains failed to establish whether city's conduct was planning or operational; thus city not entitled to dismissal on pleadings); Peavler v. Board of Comm'rs, 528 N.E.2d 40 (Ind.1988), appeal after remand 557 N.E.2d 1077 (Ind.App.1990) (counties not immune from liability in tort for failure to erect warning signs in absence of a showing that decision involved policy formulation); Bowers v. City of Chattanooga, 826 S.W.2d 427 (Tenn.1992), on remand 855 S.W.2d 583 (1992), noted 24 Memphis St. U.L. Rev. 168 (1993), 60 Tenn. L. Rev. 633 (1993) (adopting the planning-operational test, and abandoning the discretionary-ministerial text, and holding that bus driver's failure to make a scheduled stop did not involve planning and was thus not immune); Kerr v. City of Salt Lake, 322 P.3d 669 (Utah 2013) (city's decision not to remedy displaced sidewalk called a "classic operational determination," *id.* at 677; good review of cases); Nelson v. Salt Lake City, 919 P.2d 568 (Utah 1996) (immunity applies only to policy-making functions and thus did not apply to negligent failure to maintain fence between river and park); Chambers-Castanes v. King County, 100 Wash.2d 275, 669 P.2d 451 (1983) (endorsing planning-operational test and setting forth factors for courts to weigh in applying the distinction). Cf. Adams v. City of Tenakee Springs, 963 P.2d 1047 (Alaska 1998) (discretionary functions immune unless officials violate clearly established law, and planning decisions are considered discretionary, as with decisions on staffing of fire department); Dorsa Enterprises, Inc. v. City of Blackfoot, 144 Idaho 422, 163 P.3d 211 (2007) (greater rank or authority will often mean greater responsibility for planning or policy formation, but lower-ranking officials may occasionally make planning decisions that fall within the discretionary function immunity). See also Estate of Logusak v. City of Togiak, 185 P.3d 103 (Alaska 2008) (police officers have qualified immunity as to discretionary acts—no liability if they act within scope of authority, in good faith, and are not malicious or corrupt). Cases with particularly good discussion of the questions to be answered under the planning/operational test include Little v. Utah State Division of Family Services, 667 P.2d 49 (Utah 1983); Evangelical United Brethren Church of Adna v. State, 67 Wash. 2d 246, 407 P.2d 440 (1965).

Among the decisions that have been ruled "discretionary" within statutory exceptions from liability are the decision to install a particular type of traffic signal. Wainscott v. State, 642 P.2d 1355 (Alaska 1982) (flashing lights instead of sequential traffic signal). And the decision on whether or not to install traffic control devices. See Robinson v. City of Bartlesville Bd. of Educ., 700 P.2d 1013 (Okl.1985) (failure to install and maintain traffic control devices is discretionary, but construction and maintenance of high school parking lot were not). But cf. Walker v. City of Moore, 837 P.2d 876 (Okl.1992) (maintenance of existing paving markings on roadway is not discretionary). Failure to inspect and repair city sidewalks has been held discretionary. Sager v. City of Portland, 68 Or.App. 808, 684 P.2d 600 (1984), review denied 298 Or. 37, 688 P.2d 845 (1984). As have decisions regarding security at a high school. Randell v. Tulsa Independent School Dist. No. 1, 889 P.2d 1264 (Okl. App. 1994) (decisions on security immune, though could be liability for negligent performance of policy). And a decision with respect to making and enforcing disease-control regulations. Jasa v. Douglas County, 244 Neb. 944, 510 N.W.2d 281 (1994), noted 28 Creighton L. Rev. 247 (1994) (no liability for failing to warn of presence of bacterial meningitis at a day care center). But a decision to release a mental patient has been held not discretionary. Nguyen v. State, 788 P.2d 962 (Okl.1990). As has any violation of mandatory obligations. See Kansas State Bank & Trust Co. v. Specialized Transp. Services, Inc., 249 Kan. 348, 819 P.2d 587 (1991) (school district not entitled to immunity for employees' violation of mandatory reporting requirements). Or any violation of the law, since there is ordinarily no discretion to violate the law. See Gunn v. Consolidated Rural Water & Sewer Dist. No. 1, 839 P.2d 1345 (Okl.1992) (discharging employee contrary to statute is not exercise of discretionary function). In general, a "discretionary" function involves some element of judgment or choice. See United States v. Gaubert, 499 U.S. 315, 111 S.Ct. 1267, 113 L.Ed.2d 335 (1991), on remand 932 F.2d 376 (5th Cir.1991), interpreting the discretionary function exception of the Federal Tort Claims Act, on which many comparable provisions of state statutes are based. In Washington State, a statute precludes any municipal officer from being held liable for his actions while engaged in lawful performance of duties, and this has been held to immunize the municipality in such situations as well. Frost v. City of Walla Walla, 106 Wash.2d 669, 724 P.2d 1017 (1986). It has been held that a city's failure to raise the defense of discretionary function during the liability phase of the trial does not result in waiver of that defense and that it may be raised in the damages phase of the action. Boulder City v. Boulder Excavating, Inc., 124 Nev. 749, 191 P.3d 1175 (2008) (discretionary-act immunity is waived unless affirmatively pleaded, tried to consent, or otherwise litigated, but can be raised at any time before rendition of final judgment).

[86] Smith v. District of Columbia, 336 A.2d 831 (D.C.App.1975); Fisher v. City of Miami, 172 So.2d 455 (Fla.1965); Fulton County v. Baranan, 240 Ga. 837, 242 S.E.2d 617 (1978); Lane v. Yamamoto, 2 Haw.App.

damages, some cases have now held that these damages may be assessed against a municipality in circumstances where they would appropriately be levied against other defendants.[87] (5) The possible strict or "absolute" liability (*i.e.*, liability without fault) of a municipal corporation or other entity of local government remains in doubt in most jurisdictions. Unless such liability is specifically authorized by statute, courts are reluctant to impose it on governments.[88] Thus, a number of cases have declined to impose

---

176, 628 P.2d 634 (Haw. Intermediate Ct.App.1981) (even if city prosecutor acted with malice, city not liable for punitive damages); George v. Chicago Transit Authority, 58 Ill.App.3d 692, 15 Ill.Dec. 896, 374 N.E.2d 679 (1978); City of Gary v. Falcone, 169 Ind.App. 295, 348 N.E.2d 41 (1976); McHugh v. City of Wichita, 1 Kan.App.2d 180, 563 P.2d 497 (1977); Herilla v. City of Baltimore, 37 Md.App. 481, 378 A.2d 162 (1977); Desforge v. City of West St. Paul, 231 Minn. 205, 42 N.W.2d 633 (1950); Fisher v. Kansas City, 518 S.W.2d 138 (Mo.App.1974); Franchise Tax Bd. of California v. Hyatt, 335 P.3d 125 (Nev. 2014) (no punitive damages unless expressly authorized by statute); Ranells v. City of Cleveland, 41 Ohio St.2d 1, 321 N.E.2d 885 (1975); Moody v. City of Galveston, 524 S.W.2d 583 (Tex.Civ.App.1975), refused n.r.e. Cf. Foss v. Maine Turnpike Authority, 309 A.2d 339 (Me.1973) (abutting property owner suing for damages done by salting operations of turnpike authority would not be entitled to punitive damages). See generally Belli, Punitive Damages—An Historical Perspective, 13 Trial 40, 43 (Dec. 1977); Note, Municipal Corporations—Municipal Tort Liability for Punitive Damages, 7 U.Toledo L.Rev. 624 (1976). Some statutes waiving governmental immunity specifically provide that there can be no governmental liability for punitive damages—*e.g.*, Ill.Ann. Stat. § 85–2–102 (Smith-Hurd 1966); Ind. Code § 24–4–16.5–4; 51 Okl.Stat.1981, § 154. The Indiana statute was applied in State v. Denny, 177 Ind.App. 4, 377 N.E.2d 893 (1978), where the majority allowed damages in the nature of punitive against the state; the dissent (*Id.* at 895) noted the strong public policy against such an award and said the policy is based on Pogo's commentary that "I have met the enemy and he is us." *Id.* at 896. On appeal, the majority opinion was vacated and the dissent's view of the punitive-damage issue was adopted. 273 Ind. 556, 406 N.E.2d 240, aff'd on remand 409 N.E.2d 652 (Ind.App.1980). Cf. Hazen v. Municipality of Anchorage, 718 P.2d 456 (Alaska 1986) (in absence of statutory authorization, punitive damages are not available against a municipality regardless of nature of conduct involved); White v. State, 203 Mont. 363, 661 P.2d 1272 (1983) (rational basis exists for statutorily created immunity of state from punitive-damage liability, since deterrent effect of assessing such damages against the government would be very remote and innocent taxpayers would be punished); Vanderpool v. State, 672 P.2d 1153, 1157 n. 10 (Okl.1983) (in accord with the majority, Oklahoma adheres to rule that the government is not liable in exemplary damages).

Some authority also takes the view that, in the absence of specific legislative authorization, one governmental entity may not sue another for any form of damages. See District No. 55 v. Musselshell County, 245 Mont. 525, 802 P.2d 1252 (1990) (school district could not sue county for errors committed by county superintendent of schools and county board of commissioners regarding tax levy). On the confused situation in Pennsylvania on the punitive-damage problem, see Comment, Punitive Damage Liability of Municipal Corporations in Pennsylvania, 84 Dickinson L.Rev. 267 (1980). See also City of Newport v. Fact Concerts, Inc., 453 U.S. 247, 101 S.Ct. 2748, 69 L.Ed.2d 616 (1981) (punitive damages not recoverable against municipality under Federal Civil Rights Act—on Civil Rights Act actions in general, see Section 26.7 *infra*).

[87] See Hennigan v. Atlantic Refining Co., 282 F.Supp. 667 (E.D.Pa.1967), aff'd 400 F.2d 857 (3d Cir.), cert. denied 395 U.S. 904, 89 S.Ct. 1739, 23 L.Ed.2d 216 (applying Pennsylvania law); Young v. City of Des Moines, 262 N.W.2d 612 (Iowa 1978); Nixon v. Oklahoma City, 555 P.2d 1283 (Okl.1976) (municipality can be liable for punitive damages where has acted in a proprietary capacity and where taxpayers have condoned or approved conduct, but denied here). Cf. Providence Washington Ins. Co. v. City of Valdez, 684 P.2d 861 (Alaska 1984) (public policy of prohibiting liability insurance coverage for punitive damages would not prohibit a municipal corporation from insuring against punitive damage awards since the loss would otherwise fall on innocent taxpayers). See generally Comment, Sovereign Immunity: Negligent Performance of Proprietary Function by Oklahoma Municipality Results in Punitive Damages, 1 Okl. City U.L.Rev. 218 (1976) (noting that there has been some authority over the years that punitive damages may be awarded as to conduct of a municipality which was ratified by citizens as a whole, or where a statute specifically authorizes such damages); Annot., Recovery of Exemplary or Punitive Damages from Municipal Corporation, 1 A.L.R.4th 448 (1980).

[88] See Laird v. Nelms, 406 U.S. 797, 92 S.Ct. 1899, 32 L.Ed.2d 499 (1972), reh. denied 409 U.S. 902, 93 S.Ct. 95, 34 L.Ed.2d 165, noted 40 Tenn.L.Rev. 767 (1973); 59 Va.L.Rev. 1034 (1973) (federal government held not strictly liable under Federal Tort Claims Act); Kane v. Town of Estes Park, 786 P.2d 412 (Colo.1990) (town not strictly liable either at common law or under statute for damage caused by overflow of reservoir and dam maintained by it); McCurry v. City of Farmington, 97 N.M. 728, 643 P.2d 292 (App. 1982) (applying statute that waived immunity for negligence, court held city immune from strict liability for injuries allegedly caused by poisonous substances released into air during the burning of junked cars as part of firefighters' training);

strict liability on a municipality's operation of a zoo despite the common-law rule of strict liability for wild animals.[89] But over the years, there have been occasional cases imposing such liability on municipal zoos;[90] sometimes, there has been little apparent argument about the appropriateness of liability without fault, as in one case where a bear from the city zoo escaped from its den, was being led back by way of the adjacent municipal bathhouse, and bit plaintiff, a customer of the bathhouse, along the way.[91] (6) Though much of the authority supporting the rule is old, the rule may remain in effect that there is no municipal liability for "ultra vires" acts—that is, acts completely beyond the power of the municipality.[92] The increasing tendency of the courts, however, is to restrict this limitation and occasionally to ignore it.[93] It remains true, of course, that—applying

---

Richards v. City of Lawton, 629 P.2d 1260 (Okl.1981) (no common-law strict liability for damages to property from change in grade of abutting street). Cf. Guzman v. County of Monterey, 46 Cal. 4th 887, 95 Cal. Rptr. 3d 183, 209 P.3d 89 (2009) (state's Safe Drinking Water Act does not create a mandatory duty to deliver pure water, for purposes of tort liability). As to the *Laird* case, *supra*, see generally Peck, Laird v. Nelms: A Call for Review and Revision of the Federal Tort Claims Act, 48 Wash. L.Rev. 391 (1973); Reynolds, Strict Liability Under the Federal Tort Claims Act: Does "Wrongful" Cover a Few Sins, No Sins, or Non-Sins?, 23 Am.U.L.Rev. 813 (1974). See also Davis v. City of Tulsa, 87 P.3d 1106 (Okla. Civ. App. 2004) (in order for strict liability in tort to apply in a case of an abnormally dangerous activity, defendant must be the one who carries on such activity; port authority was thus not strictly liable for injury allegedly caused by release of arsine gas from chemical company that leased land from the authority, where the release happened on premises over which the company had exclusive control).

89 McKinney v. City & County of San Francisco, 109 Cal.App.2d 844, 241 P.2d 1060 (Dist.Ct.1952); City & County of Denver v. Kennedy, 29 Colo.App. 15, 476 P.2d 762 (1970), later appeal 31 Colo.App. 561, 506 P.2d 764; Guzzi v. New York Zoological Society, 192 App.Div. 263, 182 N.Y.S. 257 (1920), aff'd 233 N.Y. 511, 135 N.E. 897 (complaint properly dismissed since no allegation of negligence). Cf. Oklahoma City v. Hudson, 405 P.2d 178 (Okl.1965) (absolute liability inapplicable in case involving injury to zoo employee). See generally Annot., Governmental Liability from Operation of Zoo, 92 A.L.R.3d 832 (1979).

90 See Byrnes v. City of Jackson, 140 Miss. 656, 105 So. 861 (1925) (city has strict duty to keep wild animals safely confined, though negligence also found here); Willis v. Department of Conservation & Economic Development, 55 N.J. 534, 264 A.2d 34 (1970) (state tort immunity abolished; strict liability indicated possible); Moloney v. City of Columbus, 2 Ohio St.2d 213, 31 Ohio Op.2d 447, 208 N.E.2d 141 (1965). It is also possible for a zoo to be found a nuisance. See City of Fort Worth v. Wiggins, 5 S.W.2d 761 (Tex.Comm'n App.1928) (keeping bear could be nuisance). But see Grover v. City of Manhattan, 198 Kan. 307, 424 P.2d 256 (1967) (child bitten by coyote running loose in zoo; no nuisance since was temporary, isolated condition). See generally Annot., Zoo as Nuisance, 58 A.L.R.3d 1126 (1974).

Courts often have declined to impose strict liability against *any* defendant where there is specific statutory authorization to engage in the activity involved; this is called the defense of "privilege," and has been applied to prevent strict liability of zoo custodians. See Guzzi v. New York Zoological Society *supra* note 89. It is also one ground for denying strict liability of a *city* authorized to operate a zoo. See Hibbard v. City of Wichita, 98 Kan. 498, 159 P. 399 (1916). But this defense does not apply to a city operating a zoo without specific statutory or charter authorization. See Hyde v. City of Utica, 259 App.Div. 477, 20 N.Y.S.2d 335 (1940); Collentine v. City of New York, 279 N.Y. 119, 17 N.E.2d 792 (1938). And there is a tendency to keep the defense of privilege within narrow bounds, as by strictly construing authorizing statutes, finding that the manner of doing the work was not authorized, or applying the defense only when there is legal compulsion, not merely authorization. See generally Prosser & Keeton, Law of Torts 567 (5th ed. 1984).

91 City of Mangum v. Brownlee, 181 Okl. 515, 75 P.2d 174 (1938).

92 See Posey v. Town of North Birmingham, 154 Ala. 511, 45 So. 663 (1907); Town of Idaho Springs v. Filteau, 10 Colo. 105, 14 P. 48 (1887) (per curiam); Sturman v. City of Golden Beach, 355 So.2d 453 (Fla.App.1978); Town of Palm Beach v. Vlahos, 154 Fla. 159, 15 So.2d 848 (1944); Roughton v. City of Atlanta, 113 Ga. 948, 39 S.E. 316 (1901); Logan v. Mayor of Clarksdale, 240 Miss. 716, 128 So.2d 537 (1961); Wheeler v. Essex Public Road Bd., 39 N.J.L. 291 (1877); City of Radford v. Clark, 113 Va. 199, 73 S.E. 571 (1912). It has been held that a municipality is not estopped to plead immunity where it has acted ultra vires. Cunningham v. County Court, 148 W.Va. 303, 134 S.E.2d 725 (1964).

93 Krantz v. City of Hutchinson, 165 Kan. 449, 196 P.2d 227 (1948) (city had authority to control water for only 5 miles beyond city limits; but could not assert defense of ultra vires when it constructed a dike beyond the 5-mile limit); Whitacre v. City of Charlotte, 216 N.C. 687, 6 S.E.2d 558 (1940) (city had not properly maintained footbridge; not allowed to escape liability though had acted ultra vires in constructing bridge in

general principles of agency law—a municipality will not be held liable for torts of its personnel committed outside the scope of employment,[94] and will, subject to the generally recognized exceptions of agency law, not be liable for the torts of independent contractors.[95] There is also occasional difficulty in establishing municipal liability for intentional torts of officers and employees;[96] but often this is nothing more than the usual difficulty of showing that intentional misdeeds are within the scope of employment. Where it is established that an intentional tort was committed within the scope of municipal work, liability has now been allowed by most courts.[97]

---

that location). See Shinnick v. City of Marshalltown, 137 Iowa 72, 114 N.W. 542 (1908) (since city bound to keep its streets free from nuisances, ultra vires no defense to liability for injuries suffered by traveler who fell over rope stretched across street); Augustine v. Town of Brant, 249 N.Y. 198, 163 N.E. 732 (1928) (ultra vires no defense to town's liability for drowning at bathing beach in park though town had exceeded its powers in acquiring and equipping park lands), noted 14 Cornell L.Q. 351 (1929). See generally Note, Municipal Liability and Respondeat Superior: An Empirical Study and Analysis, 38 Suffolk U.L. Rev. 831 (2005).

[94] See Patterson v. City of Phoenix, 103 Ariz. 64, 436 P.2d 613 (1968); Brindamour v. Murray, 7 Cal.2d 73, 59 P.2d 1009 (1936); Newton v. Moultrie, 39 Ga.App. 702, 148 S.E. 299 (1929); Nelson v. Nuccio, 131 Ill.App.2d 261, 268 N.E.2d 543 (1971); Connelly v. City of Sedalia, 222 Mo.App. 109, 2 S.W.2d 632 (1928); Lazich v. City of Butte, 116 Mont. 386, 154 P.2d 260 (1944); Snell v. Murray, 121 N.J.Super. 215, 296 A.2d 538 (1972); Downing v. City of New York, 219 App.Div. 444, 220 N.Y.S. 76 (1927), aff'd 245 N.Y. 597, 157 N.E. 873; Boorse v. Springfield Township, 377 Pa. 109, 103 A.2d 708 (1954); Black v. Baker, 130 Tex. 454, 111 S.W.2d 706 (1938). If a municipal officer or employee acts outside the scope of authority, the municipality may nonetheless be liable if it ratifies the action. See City of Omaha v. Croft, 60 Neb. 57, 82 N.W. 120 (1900). A good statement of the vicarious liability of governmental entitles is found in Kisbey v. State, 36 Cal.3d 415, 204 Cal.Rptr. 428, 682 P.2d 1093 (1984) (public entity liable for act or omission of an employee committed within scope of employment if act or omission would give rise to cause of action against that employee). See generally Note, Municipal Liability and Respondeat Superior: An Empirical Study and Analysis, 38 Suffolk U.L. Rev. 831 (2005). See also Note, The State's Vicarious Liability for the Actions of the City, 124 Harv. L. Rev. 1036 (2011).

[95] See Walker v. City of Cedar Rapids, 251 Iowa 1032, 103 N.W.2d 727 (1960); State to Use of Reynolds v. City of Baltimore, 199 Md. 289, 86 A.2d 618 (1952); Weber v. Hurley, 13 Wis.2d 560, 109 N.W.2d 65 (1961). Two exceptions that are also recognized as to other employers of independent contractors have been applied in suits against municipalities: (1) The employer-municipality can be liable for the tort of an independent contractor where the contractor is hired to perform "inherently dangerous" work. Hazard Municipal Housing Commission v. Hinch, 411 S.W.2d 686 (Ky.1967) (blasting); Vannoy v. City of Warren, 15 Mich.App. 158, 166 N.W.2d 486 (1968), remanded by 382 Mich. 771, 387 N.W.2d 913 (1969). Cf. Behr v. Santa Cruz County, 172 Cal.App.2d 697, 342 P.2d 987 (Dist.Ct.1959) (county could be liable for spread of fire originating in refuse dump owned and operated by county, though the State Division of Forestry had by contract assumed fire-prevention work in the area—but no liability found here). (2) An employer-municipality is liable for the tort of an independent contractor if the contractor is carrying out a municipal obligation that is, by statute or common law, considered a "non-delegable duty." See Rogers v. City of Coffeyville, 95 Kan. 171, 147 P. 816 (1915); City of Laurel v. Upton, 253 Miss. 380, 175 So.2d 621 (1965) (duty to maintain streets and side-walks in safe condition); Bannister v. Farmers Alliance Mutual Insurance Co., 630 P.2d 1279 (Okl.1981) (same); Green v. Borough of Freeport, 218 Pa.Super. 334, 280 A.2d 412 (1971); Hendrix v. City of Maryville, 58 Tenn.App. 457, 431 S.W.2d 292 (1968) (also relying on fact that work done constituted a nuisance per se). On the non-liability of employers of independent contractors for torts of such contractors, and exceptions to the non-liability, see generally Prosser & Keeton Law of Torts 509–16 (5th ed. 1984). On the "non-delegable duty" rule, see in particular *Id.* 511–12.

[96] See McIntosh v. City & County of Denver, 98 Colo. 403, 55 P.2d 1337 (1936) (indicating no vicarious liability of municipality where malice essential to the tort; no such liability here for malicious prosecution); O'Connor v. Harms, 111 N.J.Super. 22, 266 A.2d 605 (1970); Schulman v. City of Cleveland, 30 Ohio St.2d 196, 283 N.E.2d 175 (1972) (intentional attack outside the scope of employment); Archer v. City of Cisco, 211 S.W.2d 955 (Tex.Civ.App.1948). Cf. Wiersma v. City of Long Beach, 41 Cal.App.2d 8, 106 P.2d 45 (Dist.Ct.1940) (wrestling matches held in city auditorium; city not liable for willful assault by wrestler on spectator). Cf. Mustain v. Grand River Dam Auth., 68 P.3d 991 (Okla. 2003) (Governmental Tort Claims Act barred claim based on alleged willful or malicious actions of governmental employee).

[97] Ruppe v. City of Los Angeles, 186 Cal. 400, 199 P. 496 (1921); Fisher v. City of Miami, 172 So.2d 455 (Fla.1965); City of Miami v. Simpson, 172 So.2d 435 (Fla.1965); Gilbert v. Bancroft, 80 Idaho 186, 327 P.2d 378 (1958) (water superintendent killed complaining customer); Prest v. Inhabitants of Farmington, 117 Me. 348,

Thus, islands of municipal immunity in tort still exist in many jurisdictions; and a few states still have broad municipal immunity. But the trend is clearly toward the abolition of immunity; and such abolition largely eliminates the distinction between governmental and proprietary activities, and all the difficulties attendant thereto. Many of the above-mentioned "piece-meal" statutes[98] on municipal liability have been repealed now, or else considerably reduced in importance since the general rule is now one of liability, not immunity. Of course, even where liability is possible, the question may arise in negligence actions of whether the municipality owed a duty to the particular plaintiff injured or whether, on the other hand, any duty owed was a "public duty," owed the general public but not an individual plaintiff. But here, as in most areas of negligence law, the concept of duty has been expanding in recent years. Thus, a municipality may be found to have breached its duty to provide police protection (1) where the municipality has, through its officers or employees, assured an individual or group that it will protect such person or persons, and it then negligently fails to do so;[99] *or* (2) where there is a

---

104 A. 521 (1918); Sherbutte v. Marine City, 374 Mich. 48, 130 N.W.2d 920 (1964); McAndrew v. Mularchuk, 33 N.J. 172, 162 A.2d 820 (1960); Osipoff v. City of New York, 286 N.Y. 422, 36 N.E.2d 646 (1941); Munick v. City of Durham, 181 N.C. 188, 106 S.E. 665 (1921). See Thomas v. Johnson, 295 F.Supp. 1025 (D.C.D.C.1968) (District of Columbia could be liable for "ministerial" act of its police officer in assaulting plaintiff). See generally Annot., Liability of Governmental Unit for Intentional Assault by Employee Other Than Police Officer, 17 A.L.R.4th 881 (1982). Some states still will not impose municipal liability for intentional torts, and this immunity has been criticized as leaving citizens at the mercy of municipal agents. See Note, Governmental Immunity—Pennsylvania Taxpayers No Longer Protected from Police Brutality, 68 Temple L. Rev. 977 (1995).

98 See notes 74–79 *supra* and accompanying text. On the general elimination of immunity in one jurisdiction, see Comment, Reining in Municipalities: How to Tame the Municipal Immunity Monster in Wisconsin, 2004 Wis. L. Rev. 1741.

99 See Morgan v. County of Yuba, 230 Cal.App.2d 938, 41 Cal.Rptr. 508 (Dist.Ct.1964); Bloom v. City of New York, 78 Misc.2d 1077, 357 N.Y.S.2d 979 (1974); Schuster v. City of New York, 5 N.Y.2d 75, 180 N.Y.S.2d 265, 154 N.E.2d 534 (1958). Cf. Sorichetti v. New York, 65 N.Y.2d 461, 492 N.Y.S.2d 591, 482 N.E.2d 70 (1985), where a police department was held to have a "special relationship," creating a duty, to a mother and child when the officers had knowledge of abusive behavior of the father toward the child and had led the mother to believe they would take action if the child was not returned to her by the father at the end of his court-ordered visitation period.

There is a split of authority as to whether a city's maintenance of a "911" emergency-number service creates a duty to help a potential crime victim from whom a call is received. Compare DeLong v. County of Erie, 60 N.Y.2d 296, 469 N.Y.S.2d 611, 457 N.E.2d 717 (1983) (acceptance of "911" call by city and county created special relationship and duty to victim, breach of which could result in liability for negligence when police were sent to wrong location), with Trezzi v. City of Detroit, 120 Mich.App. 506, 328 N.W.2d 70 (1982) (city's operation of "911" system is governmental function and immune from tort liability); Lovelace v. City of Shelby, 133 N.C.App. 408, 515 S.E.2d 722 (N.C.App.1999) (no special duty created when city dispatcher answered 911 call placed at request of homeowner whose house was on fire). Governmental liability in some "911" cases is denied on the basis that there were no express assurances of help made by the "911" operator. See Harvey v. County of Snohomish, 157 Wash.2d 33, 134 P.3d 216 (2006) (no express assurances to assault victim that created duty on part of county, sheriff, or other governmental entities); Cummins v. Lewis County, 156 Wash.2d 844, 133 P.3d 458 (2006) (evidence failed to show that "911" dispatcher provided decedent any express assurance that medical aid would be dispatched, upon which decedent could have justifiably relied).

The traditional view is that where public authorities fail to apprehend an intoxicated person, there can be no liability, due to lack of duty, to that person or others he may injure. See Marshall v. Ellison, 132 Ill.App.3d 732, 87 Ill.Dec. 704, 477 N.E.2d 830 (1985) (state statute authorizing police to transport intoxicated persons to detoxification centers did not create specific duty to intoxicated individual whom police failed to apprehend and who was subsequently injured on street, at least in absence of officer's having probable cause to believe individual was intoxicated); Mills v. City of Overland Park, 251 Kan. 434, 837 P.2d 370 (1992) (police officers owed no special duty to inebriated minor whom they questioned regarding disturbance he caused at bar; not liable when he subsequently fell asleep in field and froze to death); Phillips v. City of Billings, 233 Mont. 249, 758 P.2d 772 (1988) (police officer's general duty to protect does not give rise to liability for particular injury such as here suffered by victim of intoxicated motorist whom policy had failed to arrest); Gleason v. Peters, 568 N.W.2d 482 (S.D.1997), noted 43 S.D.L. Rev. 706 (1998) (no liability for police officers' failure to stop underage drinking party); Torres v. Salty Sea Days, Inc., 36 Wash.App. 668, 676 P.2d 512 (1984), review denied

foreseeable danger to a particular plaintiff or a group to which he belongs, and the municipality fails to offer adequate protection in light of this danger.[100]

---

101 Wash.2d 1008 (1984) (mere presence of police on evening cruise that was part of community festival did not create special relationship to minor who was on cruise, who was improperly served liquor, and who was later injured in automobile accident allegedly caused by her intoxication). See Coty v. Washoe County, 108 Nev. 757, 839 P.2d 97 (1992) (action of deputy sheriff in temporarily detaining but not arresting intoxicated teenage motorist held not to create governmental liability for death of motorist with whom the intoxicated driver collided). Cf. Parker v. Mineral County, 102 Nev. 593, 729 P.2d 491 (1986) (county officials were notified of ailing person lying alongside roadway, and they represented they would take care of situation; no duty found). But there is a trend in recent cases to find a duty in public authorities to protect an obviously intoxicated person from himself, and to protect others from him. See Olguin v. City of Burley, 119 Idaho 721, 810 P.2d 255 (1991) (person injured by drunk driver may assert claim for negligent entrustment against officer who failed to control motorist when officer had reason to believe driver was intoxicated); Fudge v. Kansas City, 239 Kan. 369, 720 P.2d 1093 (1986) (police owed duty to intoxicated person to take him into protective custody rather than let him drive away; could be liable for harm he subsequently caused third party with whom he collided); Irwin v. Town of Ware, 392 Mass. 745, 467 N.E.2d 1292 (1984) (negligent failure of police to remove from road a drunk driver, whom they had briefly detained. Cf. Leake v. Cain, 720 P.2d 152 (Colo.1986), rejecting altogether the "public duty" limitation on negligence liability in Colorado. Compare Coffel v. Clallam County, 58 Wash.App. 517, 794 P.2d 513 (1990), recognizing the public duty doctrine but stating that exceptions exist where a special relationship exists between a public agent and a particular individual and the individual relies on assurances by the public agent, and where the public agent has actual knowledge of a statutory violation and fails to enforce the law.

As to the duty of public officers toward persons injured while being apprehended by such officers, see City of Revere v. Massachusetts Gen. Hosp., 463 U.S. 239, 103 S.Ct. 2979, 77 L.Ed.2d 605 (1983), where the Court held that (1) Due Process requires the responsible government to provide medical assistance to persons injured while being apprehended by its peace officers, and (2) this Due Process obligation is fulfilled by seeing that the injured person is promptly taken to a hospital and that the needed medical care is provided. The U.S. Constitution does not, the Court said, dictate how the cost of the care should be allocated as between the governmental entity and the provider of the care, but leaves that matter to state law. Cf. Eklund v. Trost, 335 Mont. 112, 151 P.3d 870 (2006) (pedestrian injured when runaway from juvenile detention facility lost control of vehicle during a police chase was owed a special duty by law enforcement officers; applying statute that officers in such situations were not relieved from liability for driving in reckless disregard for the safety of others). On the ground that any duty owed is toward the general public and not particular individuals, there is often no municipal liability for failure to abate a nuisance. See Prosser v. Kennedy Enterprises, Inc., 342 Mont. 209, 179 P.3d 1178 (2008) (failure to take legal action against a casino); Ricketts v. Allegheny County, 409 Pa. 300, 186 A.2d 249 (1962) (permitting nuisance to exist within its jurisdiction).

[100] Some cases still show reluctance to find such a foreseeable danger. See Hayes v. State, 11 Cal.3d 469, 113 Cal.Rptr. 599, 521 P.2d 855 (1974) (no liability for failure to warn of possible criminal conduct); Simpson's Food Fair, Inc. v. City of Evansville, 149 Ind.App. 387, 272 N.E.2d 871 (1971) (where grocery went out of business due to crime wave in city, city not liable for failure to halt the criminal activity); Gatlin-Johnson v. Miles City, 291 P.3d 1129 (Mont. 2012) (public duty doctrine applies only if the public entity has a duty *only* to the public at large; inapplicable where child fell from a slide in city park); Bass v. City of New York, 38 A.D.2d 407, 330 N.Y.S.2d 569 (1972), aff'd 32 N.Y.2d 894, 346 N.Y.S.2d 814, 300 N.E.2d 154 (no liability of Housing Authority for failing to prevent rape and murder of tenant by another tenant of project); Riss v. City of New York, 22 N.Y.2d 579, 293 N.Y.S.2d 897, 240 N.E.2d 860 (1968) (city not liable to assault victim for failure to provide protection on request). Cf. Duran v. City of Tucson, 20 Ariz.App. 22, 509 P.2d 1059 (1973) (no liability for failure to enforce fire prevention code); Frye v. Clark County, 97 Nev. 632, 637 P.2d 1215 (1981) (no liability to citizen for fire department's failure to respond to call). See also Osborn v. Mason County, 157 Wash.2d 18, 134 P.3d 197 (2006) (parents of girl who was raped and murdered by convicted sex offender sued county for failure to warn them of offender's presence; because girl was not a foreseeable victim of offender, county had no special relationship and no duty to warn); Stiefel v. City of Kent, 132 Wash.App. 523, 132 P.3d 1111 (2006) (plaintiffs' claim against city and county for negligent failure to supply water for fire-fighting purposes or for negligent failure to enforce fire code provisions was barred by public duty doctrine).

The traditional, and still majority, view is that a city is not liable for negligent enforcement of its building code. See Trianon Park Condominium Ass'n, Inc. v. City of Hialeah, 468 So.2d 912 (Fla.1985) (city not liable to individual owners of condominiums who were allegedly injured by negligence of city building inspectors regarding enforcement of city building code); Ribeiro v. Town of Granby, 395 Mass. 608, 481 N.E.2d 466 (1985); Cracraft v. City of St. Louis Park, 279 N.W.2d 801 (Minn.1979); DeBry v. Noble, 889 P.2d 428 (Utah 1995) (city's issuance of temporary occupancy permit, alleged negligence in building inspections, and refusal to issue building permit were all within scope of governmental immunity). Cf. Siple v. City of Topeka, 235 Kan. 167,

679 P.2d 190 (1984) (no liability for city forester's inspection of tree). But see Wilson v. Nepstad, 282 N.W.2d 664 (Iowa 1979) (en banc), noted 29 Drake L. Rev. 207 (1979–80), 6 Wm. Mitchell L. Rev. 391 (1980) (negligent inspection as to fire safety of apartment building; municipality can be liable if breach of duty involves foreseeable risk to identifiable class to which plaintiff belongs). Cf. Hansen v. City of St. Paul, 298 Minn. 205, 214 N.W.2d 346 (1974) (city could be liable for failure to control vicious dogs on streets). At one time, Washington State held that a local government's building permit and inspection requirements did create a duty to one limited group: the builders. Thus, when a member of that class justifiably relied on the accuracy of the inspection and subsequently suffered economic loss due to inaccuracy of the government's agents, the government could be held liable. J. & B. Dev. Co. v. King County, 100 Wash.2d 299, 669 P.2d 468 (1983). Cf. Radach v. Gunderson, 39 Wash.App. 392, 695 P.2d 128 (1985), review denied 103 Wash.2d 1027 (1985) (city owed duty to builders of house who were issued building permit that violated zoning code; neighbors of illegally situated house were therefore entitled to equitable relief at expense of city). See generally Berth, Municipal Tort Liability for Erroneous Issuance of Building Permits: A National Survey, 58 Wash. L. Rev. 537 (1983). But that Washington Doctrine was overruled. Taylor v. Stevens County, 111 Wash.2d 159, 759 P.2d 447 (1988). Cf. Meaney v. Dodd, 111 Wash.2d 174, 759 P.2d 455 (1988) (county's issuance of special use permit for operation of sawmill did not create duty, and possible liability, of county to sawmill operator). This brings Washington's law on liability to builders into line with that of most jurisdictions. See Annot., Liability of Municipal Corporation for Negligent Performance of Building Inspector's Duties, 41 A.L.R.3d 567 (1972). And into line with Washington's law on governmental liability to persons *other* than builders. See Pierce v. Spokane County, 46 Wash.App. 171, 730 P.2d 82 (1986), review denied 108 Wash.2d 1012 (1987) (county could not be liable to purchasers of home on theory of county's negligence in inspecting house and underlying soil). Cf. Garibay v. State of Washington, 131 Wash.App. 454, 128 P.3d 617 (2006) (public duty doctrine held to shield the state Department of Labor and Industries from liability in a wrongful death action against the department by the surviving wife of a worker who died at a chemical production plant when a pipe burst, allegedly resulting from the department's negligent enforcement of safety regulations). See generally Carlisle, Coleman, Fontana, Moskowitz & Smith, Testing the Limits: A Report on the Uncertainties of Government Liability in 1982, 14 Urban Law. 687, 689–97 (1982); Markowitz, Municipal Liability for Negligent Inspection and Failure to Enforce Safety Codes, 15 Hamline J. Pub. L. & Pol'y 181 (1994); Comment, Municipal Liability for Negligent Building Inspections—Demise of the Public Duty Doctrine?, 65 Iowa L. Rev. 1416 (1980); Comment, The Public Duty Doctrine and Municipal Liability for Negligent Administration of Zoning Codes, 20 Seattle U.L. Rev. 803 (1997); Annot., Municipal Liability for Negligent Fire Inspection and Subsequent Enforcement, 69 A.L.R.4th 739 (1989). See also Barber v. Williams, 244 Kan. 318, 767 P.2d 1284 (1989) (city, by licensing fortune-tellers, did not assume duty to fortune-tellers' customers, in absence of physical harm to such customers).

Overall, there is a trend toward more often finding a foreseeable danger to a particular person or group, particularly in cases of possible municipal liability for failure to protect citizens against criminal acts of third persons. See City of Kotzebue v. McLean, 702 P.2d 1309 (Alaska 1985) (city owed duty to protect potential victims of caller who identified himself, gave his location, and informed police he was going to kill friend of his); Austin v. City of Scottsdale, 140 Ariz. 579, 684 P.2d 151 (1984) (city, having opted to provide policy protection, had duty to protect individual after being notified by anonymous caller that individual's life was in danger); Finken by Gutknecht v. Milwaukee County, 120 Wis.2d 69, 353 N.W.2d 827 (App. 1984) (city bus driver negligent in failing to protect passenger from assault by other passengers). Compare Gregoire v. City of Oak Harbor, 170 Wash. 2d 628, 244 P.3d 924 (2010) (jailer has special relationship with inmate due to custody of such person; can be liable for inmate's suicide). Cf. City of Pinellas Park v. Brown, 604 So.2d 1222 (Fla.1992), on remand 645 So.2d 1020 (Fla.App.1994) (municipality could be liable when its high-speed pursuit of traffic violator resulted in collision between violator's car and other vehicle; duty existed since a substantial part of the risk was created by the pursuing police). But cf. Davidson v. City of Westminster, 32 Cal.3d 197, 185 Cal.Rptr. 252, 649 P.2d 894 (1982) (mere fact that officers had recognized assault victim's assailant from a distance as a potential assailant because of his resemblance to a person suspected of committing a prior assault did not impose duty on officers to control assailant's conduct). See generally Forrell, Stopping the Violence: Mandatory Arrest and Police Tort Liability for Failing to Assist Battered Women, 6 Berkeley Women's L.J. 215 (1990–91); Shapo, Changing Frontiers in Torts: Vistas for the 70's, 22 Stan. L. Rev. 330 (1970); Note, Domestic Violence Victims v. Municipalities: Who Pays When the Police Will Not Respond?, 41 Case W. Res. L. Rev. 929 (1991); Annot., Governmental Tort Liability for Failure to Provide Police Protection to Specifically Threatened Crime Victim, 46 A.L.R.4th 948 (1986). A good summary of this area of the law—*i.e.*, the "public duty" doctrine and its exceptions—is found in Basil, A Primer on the Public Duty Doctrine as Applied to Police Protection, 37 Urban Law. 403 (2005). See also Dieringer & Grose, Judicial Deference or Bad Law: Why Massachusetts Courts Will Not Impose Municipal Liability for Failure to Enforce Restraining Orders, 38 Suffolk U.L. Rev. 557 (2005). For criticism of the "public duty" doctrine, see Note, Protecting the Greater Good: A Critique of the Public Duty Doctrine as Applied in Murray v. County of Person, 191 N. C. App. 575, 664 S.E. 2d 58 (2008), 88 N.C. L. Rev. 694 (2010).

§ 26.4 Notice Requirements

Does notice have to be given a local government before suit can be brought against it? At common law, no notice need be given.[101] But state statutes and home-rule charters commonly do require notice. Such a requirement has been said to serve the twin requirements of (1) giving the locality a chance to determine the circumstances surrounding the accident while the matter remains fresh in the minds of witnesses, and (2) informing the locality promptly so that it may correct the defect that caused the injury before further harm is caused by it.[102] Notice requirements will be upheld if reasonable;[103] but it has been held that even home-rule cities may not add further notice requirements to those imposed by state statute.[104] Notice requirements are mandatory, and failure to comply will preclude suit.[105] But it has repeatedly been held that

---

[101] Russell v. Mayor and Council of Wilmington, 35 Del. 193, 162 A. 71 (1932); Randolph v. City of Springfield, 302 Mo. 33, 257 S.W. 449 (1923); George v. City of Milwaukee, 41 Wis.2d 92, 163 N.W.2d 166 (1968). Cf. J.P. Asset Co. v. City of Wichita, 31 Kan.App.2d 650, 70 P.3d 711 (2003) (only tort victims are required to give written notice before filing suit against municipality; contract claims do not require written notice); Pellegrino v. State of Oklahoma, 63 P.3d 535 (Okla. 2003) (notice requirements do not apply to a tort claim against a governmental *employee* when the claim is based on acts outside the scope of employee's employment).

[102] See Erde v. City of Los Angeles, 116 Cal.App.2d 565, 254 P.2d 110 (Dist.Ct.1953); Lutsch v. City of Chicago, 318 Ill.App. 156, 47 N.E.2d 545 (1943); Cornett v. City of Neodesha, 187 Kan. 60, 353 P.2d 975 (1960); Winbush v. City of Mount Vernon, 306 N.Y. 327, 118 N.E.2d 459 (1954) (where administratrix of estate had, prior to her appointment, filed notice of claim against city, Supreme Court could, after her actual appointment, permit amendment of claim to show it was on her behalf as administratrix as well as individually). Cf. Allbritton v. City of Birmingham, 274 Ala. 550, 150 So.2d 717 (1963) (city given opportunity to investigate claim and decide on a defense or settlement); Duesterhaus v. City of Edmond, 634 P.2d 720 (Okl.1981) (purposes said to be the promoting of prompt investigation, providing an opportunity to repair any dangerous condition, providing for speedy and amicable settlement of meritorious claims, and allowing the city to prepare to meet fiscal liabilities). See generally Pigs Gun Club, Inc. v. Sanpete County, 2002 Utah 17, 42 P.3d 379 (2002) (purpose of notice provision is to provide the governmental entity an opportunity to correct the condition that caused the injury, evaluate the claim, and perhaps settle the matter without the expense of litigation). Compare Backus v. State, 220 Ariz. 101, 203 P.3d 499 (2009) (purposes of notice requirement are to allow the government to investigate and assess liability, to permit the possibility of settlement prior to litigation, and to assist the public entity in financial planning and budgeting).

[103] See Ragans v. City of Jacksonville, 106 So.2d 860 (Fla.App.1958); Waite v. Orgill, 203 Tenn. 146, 310 S.W.2d 179 (1958). But see Grubaugh v. City of St. Johns, 384 Mich. 165, 180 N.W.2d 778 (1970) (notice requirement violated due process as to person incapacitated by act of local government); Toler v. City of Huntington, 153 W.Va. 313, 168 S.E.2d 551 (1969) (home-rule city ordinance requiring 30-day written notice invalidated as in conflict with general state law).

[104] See Mikelsavage v. City of Detroit, 343 Mich. 566, 73 N.W.2d 266 (1955) (statute on notice to municipalities was intended to provide uniformity of procedure, prevailed over city ordinance delegating power to audit, and allow or reject, certain claims to corporation counsel).

[105] See Bituminous Casualty Corp. v. City of Evansville, 191 F.2d 572 (7th Cir.1951); Douglass v. City of Los Angeles, 5 Cal.2d 123, 53 P.2d 353 (1935); City of Miami Beach v. O'Hara, 166 So.2d 598 (Fla. App.1964); Allen v. City of Macon, 118 Ga.App. 88, 162 S.E.2d 783 (1968); Jones v. City of Augusta, 100 Ga.App. 268, 110 S.E.2d 691 (1959); McCarthy v. City of Chicago, 312 Ill.App. 268, 38 N.E.2d 519 (1941); City of Dawson Springs v. Reddish, 344 S.W.2d 826 (Ky.1961); Curtis v. City of Ellsworth, 292 A.2d 197 (Me.1972); MacLeod v. City of Takoma Park, 257 Md. 477, 263 A.2d 581 (1970); Hirth v. Village of Long Prairie, 274 Minn. 76, 143 N.W.2d 205 (1966); Millard v. Lewis, 17 Misc.2d 698, 185 N.Y.S.2d 708 (1959); Nevins v. City of Lexington, 212 N.C. 616, 194 S.E. 293 (1937); Pace v. Munday, 323 S.W.2d 609 (Tex.Civ.App.1959). Cf. Kowalczyk v. Bailey, 379 Mich. 568, 153 N.W.2d 660 (1967) (lack of notice barred suit; requirement not affected by judicial abrogation of old doctrine of municipal immunity); Wagstaff v. City of Groves, 419 S.W.2d 441 (Tex.Civ.App.1967) ref'd n.r.e. (suit against city barred by lack of notice though plaintiff had already recovered workmen's compensation benefits); Cooper v. City of Abilene, 416 S.W.2d 562 (Tex.Civ.App.1967) (notice requirement applicable where husband sought to recover for wife's injuries). The failure of plaintiff to give notice is sometimes treated as an affirmative defense that the municipality must plead. See Hunt v. Housing Authority of New Haven, 21 Conn. Supp. 65, 144 A.2d 539 (1958). See generally Deer Valley Unified School Dist. v. Houser, 214 Ariz. 293, 152

substantial compliance will suffice and that there need not be compliance with all the technical niceties required as to pleadings.[106] In one respect, courts are, however, quite strict in requiring compliance with notice requirements: the notice must be given within the *time* specified by the relevant legislation; filing even one day late will bar a claim.[107]

P.3d 490 (2007) (claim letter failed to comply with requirement of notice-of-claim statute that notice contain specific amount for which claim can be settled; this requirement is not satisfied by a reasonable estimate of value of claim); Cobbley v. City of Challis, 138 Idaho 154, 59 P.3d 959 (2002) (compliance with Idaho Tort Claims Act's notice requirement is mandatory condition of bringing suit no matter how legitimate the complaint; notice requirement is in addition to statute of limitations); Wooster v. Carbon County School Dist. No. 1, 2005 Wyo. 47, 109 P.3d 893 (2005) (two-year period for bringing a written claim against the government is not a mere procedural statute of limitations but is a jurisdictional non-claim statute, meaning that defective notice of claim cannot be cured via the relation-back doctrine by presentment of a non-defective notice of claim after the period has passed). See also Martinez, Hurry Up and Wait: Negative Statutes of Limitation in the Government Tort Liability Setting, 19 St. John's J. of Legal Commentary 259 (2005), arguing that "negative statutes of limitation," such as notice of claim requirements, should be viewed more as guidelines than actual rules.

As to what constitutes filing of notice by mail, see Lee v. State of Arizona, 218 Ariz. 235, 182 P.3d 1169 (2008) (proof of fact of mailing will, absent any contrary evidence, establish that delivery occurred; if addressee denies receipt, the presumption of delivery disappears, and it is for the factfinder to determine if the claim was in fact received prior to the statutory deadline).

[106] Tolbert v. City of Birmingham, 262 Ala. 674, 81 So.2d 336 (1955); Henry v. City of Los Angeles, 114 Cal.App.2d 603, 250 P.2d 643 (Dist.Ct.1952); City of Atlanta v. Frank, 120 Ga.App. 273, 170 S.E.2d 265 (1969). See Ray v. City of Birmingham, 275 Ala. 332, 154 So.2d 751 (1963); Bush v. City of Albany, 125 Ga.App. 558, 188 S.E.2d 245 (1972); City of Atlanta v. Fuller, 118 Ga.App. 563, 164 S.E.2d 364 (1968); Galbreath v. City of Indianapolis, 253 Ind. 472, 255 N.E.2d 225 (1970); Heck v. City of Knoxville, 249 Iowa 602, 88 N.W.2d 58 (1958); Paul v. City of Swartz Creek, 32 Mich.App. 472, 189 N.W.2d 66 (1971); Koontz v. City of St. Louis, 230 Mo.App. 128, 89 S.W.2d 586 (1936); Peacock v. City of Greensboro, 196 N.C. 412, 146 S.E. 3 (1928); Duschaine v. City of Everett, 5 Wn.2d 181, 105 P.2d 18 (1940). Cf. Weaver v. Village of Bancroft, 92 Idaho 189, 439 P.2d 697 (1968) (notice requirement met by letter to village referring to "this year's flood" and setting forth nature of injuries); Lucas v. Independent Pub. School Dist. No. 35, 674 P.2d 1131 (Okl.1983) (written statement given by injured party to the local government's insurance carrier held substantial compliance); Conway v. Ohio Cas. Ins. Co., 669 P.2d 766 (Okl.1983) (correspondence between attorney for child struck by school bus and school district's insurer held substantial compliance). But cf. Graves v. Rose, 663 P.2d 733 (Okl.1983) (accident report sent to appropriate state agency did not satisfy notice requirement). See also Myles v. Clark County, 170 Wash. App. 521, 289 P.3d 650 (2012) (statutory amendments require substantial, rather than strict, compliance, but can't be applied retroactively).

As to the nature of "substantial compliance," see Finnie v. Jefferson County School Dist. R–1, 79 P.3d 1253 (Colo. 2003) (timely notice provision requires substantial, not strict, compliance, and thus courts should evaluate compliance on a case-by-case basis, considering principles of agency and equity, the purposes of the notice statute, and concerns of preventing governmental entities from misleading plaintiffs); Sleeth v. Sedan City Hosp., 317 P.3d 782 (Kan. 2014) (substantial compliance means compliance in respect to the essential matters necessary to assure every reasonable objective of the statute requiring notice); Continental Western Ins. Co. v. Schultz, 304 P.3d 1239 (Kan. 2013) (notice must provide the municipality with what it needs for a full investigation and understanding of the merits of the claims advanced). Cf. Dicke v. Mabin, 101 P.3d 1126 (Colo. App. 2004), cert. denied 2004 WL 2659111 (Colo.2004) (whether one or more documents constitute a written notice of claim is a question of law subject to de novo review; only substantial compliance required to comply with statutory requirement that plaintiff's notice of claim contain a statement setting forth the amount of damages sought); Smith v. Mitton, 140 Idaho 893, 104 P.3d 367 (2004) (city employee suing for wrongful discharge was not required to plead compliance with notice requirements of Idaho Tort Claims Act). Compare Houghton v. Department of Health, 205 Utah 63, 125 P.3d 860 (2005) (although strict compliance with the notice of claim procedure is mandated, such notices are not required to meet the standards required to state a claim for relief; plaintiff need only include enough specificity to inform as to the nature of the claim so that defendant can appraise its potential liability). Actual notice and substantial compliance will not excuse a failure to file a claim within the statutory time limit. See Falcon ex rel. Sandoval v. Maricopa County, 213 Ariz. 525, 144 P.3d 1254 (2006).

[107] Gale v. Santa Barbara County, 118 Cal.App.2d 451, 257 P.2d 1000 (Dist.Ct.1953); Ray v. City of Wichita, 138 Kan. 686, 27 P.2d 288 (1933). See Shirk v. Vista Unified School Dist., 42 Cal.4th 201, 64 Cal.Rptr.3d 210, 164 P.3d 630 (2007) (timely presentation of a claim against a public entity is not merely a procedural requirement, but is a condition precedent to plaintiff's maintaining an action against defendant and is thus an element of plaintiff's cause of action); Olander v. Sperry & Hutchinson Co., 293 Minn. 162, 197

It has also been held that where a statute or charter requires personal service of the notice, this is mandatory, and a failure cannot be excused even though local officials had actual knowledge.[108] Notice requirements have often been held excused where plaintiff is a minor.[109] And the requirements have been held inapplicable to certain kinds of cases, as a suit in equity to enjoin a municipal tort.[110] Further, a number of courts have ruled that a municipality whose officials have actual knowledge of an occurrence will be *estopped* to claim lack of notice of such occurrence.[111] Statutes and charters also

---

N.W.2d 438 (1972) (substantial compliance suffices, but court will be stricter as to timeliness of notice and manner of service); Martin v. School Board, 301 N.Y. 233, 93 N.E.2d 655 (1950). Cf. Hoffman v. City of Palm Springs, 169 Cal.App.2d 645, 337 P.2d 521 (Dist.Ct.1959) (supplemental notice filed after statutory period has expired does not relate back to date of filing of original claim even though original was filed on time).

[108] Dicampli-Mintz v. Santa Clara County, 150 Cal. Rptr. 3d 111, 289 P.3d 884 (2012); Fannon v. City of Aurora, 106 Ill.App.2d 408, 245 N.E.2d 286 (1969). Cf. Dowers Farms, Inc. v. Lake County, 288 Or. 669, 607 P.2d 1361 (1980) (notice was not given county clerk, who was county's designated agent). See generally Annot., Actual Notice or Knowledge by Governmental Body or Officer of Injury or Incident Resulting in Injury as Constituting Required Claim or Notice of Claim for Injury—Modern Status, 7 A.L.R.4th 1063 (1981), saying that actual knowledge does not suffice for "substantial compliance" in most jurisdictions. But see note 111 *infra*, and accompanying text, on the possibility of estoppel.

[109] Wills v. Metz, 89 Ill.App.2d 334, 231 N.E.2d 628 (1967) (line of demarcation as to notice requirement is not based on physical or mental capacity but only on age); McDonald v. City of Spring Valley, 285 Ill. 52, 120 N.E. 476 (1918); Russo v. New York City, 258 N.Y. 344, 179 N.E. 762 (1932); Foster v. City of Charlotte, 206 N.C. 528, 174 S.E. 412 (1934); City of Tulsa v. Wells, 79 Okl. 39, 191 P. 186 (1920); McCrary v. City of Odessa, 482 S.W.2d 151 (Tex.1972); Simpson v. City of Abilene, 388 S.W.2d 760 (Tex.Civ.App.1965), ref'd n.r.e. But a few jurisdictions have held that even minority does not excuse non-compliance with notice requirements. Fox v. City of Overland Park, 210 Kan. 16, 499 P.2d 524 (1972); Dechant v. City of Hays, 112 Kan. 729, 212 P. 682 (1923); Ocampo v. City of Racine, 28 Wis.2d 506, 137 N.W.2d 477 (1965). Cf. McCrary v. Shows, 466 S.W.2d 803 (Tex.Civ.App.1971), judgment reversed in part 482 S.W.2d 151 (Tex.1972) (minority alone, without physical or mental incapacity, won't excuse); Wones v. City of Houston, 281 S.W.2d 133 (Tex.Civ.App.1955) (same).

[110] Floyd v. City of Butte, 147 Mont. 305, 412 P.2d 823 (1966) appeal after remand 151 Mont. 129, 439 P.2d 759. See Van v. Portneuf Medical Center, 147 Idaho 552, 212 P.3d 982 (2009) (wrongful termination claim under Whistleblower Act not subject to notice requirements of Idaho Tort Claims Act, nor were claims for breach of at-will employment contract, including breach of implied contract of good faith and fair dealing); Comcast of Oregon II, Inc. v. City of Eugene, 346 Or. 238, 209 P.3d 800 (2009) (declaratory judgment claim did not allege a tort and thus was not subject to notice requirement of Tort Claims Act). It is generally true that notice requirements apply only to tort suits and can be avoided by suing in quasi-contract. See Hunter v. City of Mobile, 244 Ala. 318, 13 So.2d 656 (1943); Holbrook v. City of Sarasota, 58 So.2d 862 (Fla.1952); Lux v. City of Topeka, 204 Kan. 179, 460 P.2d 541 (1969) (suit in quasi-contract for damages due to change in grade of street). And in at least some states, notice requirements are inapplicable to workmen's compensation suits. See City of Austin v. Powell, 321 S.W.2d 924 (Tex.Civ. App.1959), ref'd n.r.e. It has also been held that where other persons are joined as defendants with a municipality, those other defendants are not within the notice requirements. Alexander v. Gordon, 147 So.2d 595 (Fla.App.1962). See Walker v. City of Moore, 836 P.2d 1289 (Okl.1992) (spouse suing for loss of consortium and companionship did not have to file a separate written notice of the claim since it is derivative and was thus covered by the notice given of the primary claim). Cf. Belcastro v. Long Island Railroad, 55 Misc.2d 837, 286 N.Y.S.2d 945 (1968) (statutory provision on notice to railroad found too vague to be enforceable). See also Whaley v. Sharp, 343 P.3d 63 (Kan. 2014) (written 120-day notice requirement of Kansas statute did not apply to suit against municipal employees.

Note that where a municipality or other government entity is *plaintiff* in a tort case, most of the usual procedural and substantive requirements apply, and there is no special notice requirement. But statutes of limitation are often held not to apply to such a suit if the government is acting in its sovereign capacity to vindicate public rights. See Oklahoma City Municipal Improvement Auth. v. HTB, Inc., 769 P.2d 131 (Okl.1988).

[111] See City of Lubbock v. Green, 201 F.2d 146 (5th Cir.1953) (where father of injured child had discussed matter with city attorney and been led to believe he could wait till more certain about damages before filing claim, city estopped from asserting lack of notice); Farrell v. Placer County, 23 Cal.2d 624, 145 P.2d 570 (1944); Tillman v. City of Pompano Beach, 100 So.2d 53 (Fla.1957) (notice not filed within required time, but city officials had actual knowledge); City of Fairburn v. Clanton, 102 Ga.App. 556, 117 S.E.2d 197 (1960); City of Denison v. Fulce, 437 S.W.2d 277 (Tex.Civ.App.1969) (notice not given city manager, who was proper party under the law, because manager had told plaintiff to give notice to another); Smith v. City of Dallas, 404 S.W.2d

sometimes require that, before suit can be brought on a claim, the claim be presented to the municipality so that it has the opportunity to make payment or offer a compromise before being subjected to litigation.[112]

§ 26.5 Indemnity and Contribution

Where a municipality is held liable in tort, it may have an *indemnity* action over against another person; the same principles normally apply as in other indemnity actions. The action may be based on express[113] or implied-in-fact[114] contract. But it also may be grounded on restitutionary principles where the party against whom the indemnity is sought is found to have been more culpable than the municipality.[115] Thus, where a municipality is held vicariously liable for the tort of an officer or employee, the municipality has an action of indemnity over against this agent, just as any other

---

839 (Tex.Civ.App.1966), appeal after remand 425 S.W.2d 467; Harte v. City of Eagle River, 45 Wis.2d 513, 173 N.W.2d 683 (1970). Cf. Wilson v. City & County of Denver, 168 Colo. 43, 449 P.2d 822 (1969) (plaintiff gave no notice to clerk as required by statute, but did notify mayor as required by city charter); City of Atlanta v. Frank, 120 Ga.App. 273, 170 S.E.2d 265 (1969) (city estopped when city attorney had informed plaintiff that her claim had been investigated and no liability found). But some courts may be reluctant to find estoppel where time limits or personal-service requirements have not been met. See generally notes 107–108 *supra*, and accompanying text. And estoppel may be denied if the local official on whose conduct the alleged estoppel is based was acting beyond his authority. See Peek v. City of Albany, 101 Ga.App. 564, 114 S.E.2d 451 (1960).

[112] See Cochran v. City of Sumter, 242 S.C. 382, 131 S.E.2d 153 (1963). Cf. MacLeod v. Town of Milford, 25 Conn.Sup. 70, 196 A.2d 604 (1963) (claimant against municipality must, as separate and distinct requirements, give notice and present claim). Failure to file a claim may result in dismissal of the plaintiff's action. Dixon v. City of Mobile, 280 Ala. 419, 194 So.2d 825 (1967); Stambaugh v. City of Demorest, 221 Ga. 527, 145 S.E.2d 539 (1965); Foreway Express, Inc. v. City of Hilbert, 32 Wis.2d 371, 145 N.W.2d 668 (1966). But *contribution* may be obtained against a municipality despite failure to comply with a filing requirement. See Minneapolis, St. Paul & Sault Sainte Marie Railroad v. City of Fond du Lac, 297 F.2d 583 (7th Cir.1961). As usual with such requirements, the filing requirement is held satisfied by "substantial" compliance. See Holm v. City of San Diego, 35 Cal.2d 399, 217 P.2d 972 (1950) (compliance sufficient though addresses of claimants not included); Bush v. City of Albany, 125 Ga.App. 558, 188 S.E.2d 245 (1972); Spencer v. Salt Lake City, 17 Utah 2d 362, 412 P.2d 449 (1966).

[113] See De Vries v. City of Austin, 261 Minn. 52, 110 N.W.2d 529 (1961); Yearicks v. City of Wildwood, 23 N.J.Super. 379, 92 A.2d 873 (1952); Kurek v. Port Chester Housing Authority, 18 N.Y.2d 450, 276 N.Y.S.2d 612, 223 N.E.2d 25 (1966) (city was actively negligent itself also, but could nonetheless obtain indemnity from co-tortfeasor based on contract).

[114] See Washington Gaslight Co. v. District of Columbia, 161 U.S. 316, 16 S.Ct. 564, 40 L.Ed. 712 (1896) (city had action over against gas company for injuries due to gas box being out-of-order and unsafe); City of Fort Scott v. Pen Lubric Oil Co., 122 Kan. 369, 252 P. 268 (1927).

[115] See Miller v. DeWitt, 59 Ill.App.2d 38, 208 N.E.2d 249 (1965), aff'd in part, rev'd in part 37 Ill.2d 273, 226 N.E.2d 630 (municipality guilty of only passive, technical negligence may recover from actively negligent party); Inhabitants of Lowell v. Boston & Lowell Railroad, 40 Mass. (23 Pick.) 24 (1839) (if offense merely malum prohibitum and does not involve immoral conduct, court may inquire into relative fault of parties); City of Detroit v. Chaffee, 70 Mich. 80, 37 N.W. 882 (1888) (primary duty as to construction and repair of sidewalk is on adjacent owner); Weber v. City of New York, 18 Misc.2d 590, 186 N.Y.S.2d 769 (1959), aff'd 13 A.D.2d 823, 216 N.Y.S.2d 340, rearg. denied 13 A.D.2d 1024, 218 N.Y.S.2d 953 (indemnity possible if and only if party seeking it was passively negligent and other was actively negligent); Bonadonna v. City of Buffalo, 156 Misc. 225, 281 N.Y.S. 343 (1935) (indemnity possible if city only constructively negligent and other party was actually negligent); City of Spokane v. Crane Co., 98 Wash. 49, 167 P. 63 (1917) (person who actually created or maintained a dangerous condition can be liable for indemnity to city that was only passively negligent). Cf. Great Atlantic & Pacific Tea Co. v. Boyles, 102 F.2d 343 (3d Cir.1939) (in action against borough for injuries caused by defective sidewalk, evidence justified verdict against tenant of building abutting such sidewalk where tenant brought in as additional defendant); Hillyer v. City of East Cleveland, 155 Ohio St. 552, 99 N.E.2d 772 (1951) (since driveway on which plaintiff fell was constructed for property owner, such owner was primarily liable and city secondarily liable; but having settled claim with property owner, plaintiff barred from recovery from city). But see Ford v. City of Shreveport, 165 So.2d 325 (La.App.1964) (city had primary duty to keep sidewalks in repair, could not obtain indemnity from adjacent owner).

employer would have such an action.[116] Of course, indemnity can also work the other way, and a municipality may be held liable to another tortfeasor in such an action if (1) the municipality is the party primarily responsible or at fault, *and* if (2) the indemnity is not sought as to conduct for which the municipality enjoys immunity.[117] Outside their areas of immunity, municipalities may also be liable for *contribution* where private parties could be held so liable, either under common law allowing contribution[118] or under statutes providing for contribution.[119] And the municipality may similarly qualify to *obtain* contribution against others in appropriate cases.[120]

Where a statute or charter requires notice to a municipality before it can be sued in tort, does this requirement apply to a party seeking contribution or indemnity from the municipality? Ordinarily, the requirement does apply, but the party seeking the contribution or indemnity may obtain his rights by giving the proper notice even though the injured person failed to give the required notice.[121]

---

[116] See Village of Portland v. Citizens' Telephone Co., 206 Mich. 632, 173 N.W. 382 (1919). Common law indemnity has been said to arise from the equitable principle that one compelled to pay for damages caused by another should be able to seek recovery from the responsible party; but such recovery is usually denied someone who does not have "clean hands"—that is, someone whose own tortious conduct helped cause the injury. See State of Montana v. Butte–Silver Bow County, 353 Mont. 497, 220 P.3d 1115 (2009) (question of whether county owed indemnity to state presented issue of law for the court).

[117] Horrabin v. City of Des Moines, 198 Iowa 549, 199 N.W. 988 (1924) (contractor followed directions of city in beginning work on bridge on private property; when contractor held liable for trespass, he could obtain indemnity from city). But where a municipality continues to enjoy immunity as to certain activities, that extends to indemnity actions. See Town of Norwalk v. Warren County, 210 Iowa 1262, 232 N.W. 682 (1930) (county not liable for negligence in road improvements; could not be held liable in indemnity action); Devlin v. Philadelphia School District, 337 Pa. 209, 10 A.2d 408 (1940).

[118] See Bosin v. Minneapolis, St. Paul & Sault Saint Marie Railroad, 183 F.Supp. 820 (E.D.Wis.1960), aff'd sub nom. Minneapolis, St. Paul & Sault Saint Marie Railroad v. City of Fond Du Lac, 297 F.2d 583 (7th Cir.). As with indemnity, contribution—even though otherwise allowed by state law—will not be granted against a municipality as to its activities that are immune from tort liability. See Capital Transit Co. v. District of Columbia, 225 F.2d 38 (D.C.Cir.1955).

[119] See East Coast Freight Lines v. Mayor & City of Baltimore, 190 Md. 256, 58 A.2d 290 (1948); Titus v. Lindberg, 49 N.J. 66, 228 A.2d 65 (1967). Cf. Madsen v. Salt Lake City School Bd., 645 P.2d 658 (Utah 1982) (school board allowed to seek contribution against a city pursuant to a comparative negligence statute; governmental immunity statute held inapplicable since right to contribution is not the same as a "claim" covered by the immunity law). But cf. West v. City of New York, 276 N.Y. 524, 12 N.E.2d 458 (1937) (statute limited contribution to joint-tortfeasor situations; city found not to be joint tortfeasor even though it had joint duty with private contractor as to maintenance of sidewalk). As to the various meanings given the term "joint tortfeasors," see Prosser & Keeton, Law of Torts 322–30 (5th ed. 1984).

Contribution is now recognized by statute in most states; in a few states, the courts have recognized contribution without the aid of statute. See Prosser *supra*, at 336–41.

[120] See Fletcher v. County of Broome, 286 App.Div. 286, 143 N.Y.S.2d 76 (1955); Blauvelt v. Village of Nyack, 141 Misc. 730, 252 N.Y.S. 746 (1931) (contribution obtainable even against a defendant who had settled with injured person). But see Yearicks v. City of Wildwood, 23 N.J.Super. 379, 92 A.2d 873 (1952) (city could not obtain contribution as to tort judgment from injured party's employer, as employer's liability limited by workmen's compensation law). See generally 2 Antieau, Municipal Corporation Law §§ 13A.13–.14 (1980).

[121] See White v. Johnson, 272 Minn. 363, 137 N.W.2d 674 (1965). Cf. Royal Car Wash Co. v. City of Wilmington, 240 A.2d 144 (Del.Super.1968) (contribution claim against city not within statute requiring notice to city of claim within one year); Roehrig v. City of Louisville, 454 S.W.2d 703 (Ky.App.1970) (failure of defendant in personal injury case to give city statutory 90-day notice of claim did not bar defendant's action against city for contribution); Valstrey Service Corp. v. Board of Elections, 2 N.Y.2d 413, 161 N.Y.S.2d 52, 141 N.E.2d 565 (1957) (defendant's action against county for indemnity would not accrue until defendant had been cast in judgment by verdict in favor of injured plaintiff, and no filing of claim by defendant against county would be required); Geiger v. Calumet County, 18 Wis.2d 151, 118 N.W.2d 197 (1962) (where two counties jointly responsible for maintaining highway, failure to serve notice on one of the counties—where proper notice was given the other—did not prevent a finding of common liability which would support contribution).

§ 26.6 Tort Liability of the State and Its Arms

It has been observed that the courts have been somewhat more reluctant to abrogate the tort immunity of state governments than to terminate such immunity as to municipalities (whose immunity has, after all, never been total anyway).[122] But many courts have now terminated even the immunity of the state,[123] and legislation in many jurisdictions now achieves this result—though often with designated areas of continued immunity.[124] Since the "public quasi-corporations" discussed in Chapter 2 *supra*—such

---

On the effect that "notice-of-claim" requirements as to claims against municipalities (See Section 26.4 *supra*) may have on actions for contribution against municipalities, see generally Kutner, Contribution Among Tortfeasors: The Effects of Statutes of Limitations and Other Time Limitations, 33 Okl.L.Rev. 203, 255–63 (1980) (if notice of contribution claim is required, notice-period usually not deemed to commence at time of victim's injury, but only when contribution claim accrued). See also *Id.* at 241–43, discussing the possible effect on contribution actions against municipalities of "public authorities protection acts"—acts which place short statutes-of-limitations on actions done in pursuance or execution of a public duty (is split of authority, but contribution actions sometimes found outside scope of these laws since contribution is not an action in respect of the contribution-defendant's tortious act, or of the victim's injury, but in respect of the contribution-claimant's liability to the victim).

[122] See Prosser, Wade & Schwartz, Cases and Materials on Torts 622 n. 6 (9th ed. 1994), citing Henry v. Oklahoma Turnpike Auth., 478 P.2d 898 (Okl.1970). It has been held that state immunity is an affirmative defense which must be proven by the defendant, though the existence of the defense may appear within the complaint. See Van De Grift v. State of Utah, 299 P.3d 1043 (Utah 2013).

[123] See, *e.g.*, Stone v. Arizona Highway Commission, 93 Ariz. 384, 381 P.2d 107 (1963); Muskopf v. Corning Hospital District, 55 Cal.2d 211, 11 Cal.Rptr. 89, 359 P.2d 457 (1961), modified sub nom. Corning Hospital District v. Superior Court, 57 Cal.2d 488, 20 Cal.Rptr. 621, 370 P.2d 325; Smith v. State, 93 Idaho 795, 473 P.2d 937 (1970) (immunity terminated only as to "proprietary" functions); Molitor v. Kaneland Community Unit District, 18 Ill.2d 11, 163 N.E.2d 89 (1959), cert. denied 362 U.S. 968, 80 S.Ct. 955, 4 L.Ed.2d 900; Campbell v. State, 259 Ind. 55, 284 N.E.2d 733 (1972); Perkins v. State, 252 Ind. 549, 251 N.E.2d 30 (1969) (immunity terminated as to proprietary activities); Willis v. Department of Conservation & Economic Development, 55 N.J. 534, 264 A.2d 34 (1970); Hicks v. State, 88 N.M. 588, 544 P.2d 1153 (1975); Bulman v. Hulstrand Constr. Co., 521 N.W.2d 632 (N.D.1994) (common-law doctrine of state immunity from tort liability abrogated except as to discretionary acts; termination applied prospectively for claims arising 15 days after adjournment of state's next legislative session); Vanderpool v. State, 672 P.2d 1153 (Okl.1983) (immunity of state and its local governments terminated: termination applied retrospectively to plaintiff in this case, and prospectively to claims arising after 12:01 a.m. October 1, 1985); Ayala v. Philadelphia Board of Public Education, 453 Pa. 584, 305 A.2d 877 (1973) (abolishing all governmental immunity; list of many cases); Holytz v. City of Milwaukee, 17 Wis.2d 26, 115 N.W.2d 618 (1962). Cf. Board of Commissioners v. Splendour Shipping & Enterprises Co., 273 So.2d 19 (La.1973) (Board of Commissioners of Port of New Orleans and other such boards and agencies not immune in tort); Anderson v. City of Minneapolis, 296 N.W.2d 383 (Minn.1980) (state liable for obvious and palpably dangerous defect in plan for highway construction, for defect in original construction if state has reasonable notice of the danger, for negligence in construction if construction is under control and supervision of state, and for negligence in maintenance and repair of highways under state's control). On termination of state immunity, see Olson, Governmental Immunity from Tort Liability—Two Decades of Decline, 31 Baylor L.Rev. 485 (1979); Van Alstyne, Governmental Tort Liability: A Decade of Change, 1966 U.Ill.L.F. 919; Comment, Judicial Abrogation of Governmental and Sovereign Immunity: A National Trend with a Pennsylvania Perspective, 78 Dickinson L.Rev. 365 (1973).

[124] See, *e.g.*, Alaska Stat. 9.50.250 to .300, applied in State v. Abbott, 498 P.2d 712 (Alaska 1972) (with good discussion of history of immunity and of continued immunity for "discretionary" matters); West's Ann.Cal.Gov.Code §§ 810–996.6; Mass.Gen. Laws Ann. c. 258, §§ 1–13; N.J.Stat.Ann. 59:1–1 to 59:14–4; Okl. Stat. 1981, §§ 151–71 (declaring governmental immunity to be policy of state, then waiving that immunity subject to numerous specified exceptions; same waiver and exceptions apply to local governments as to state); Or.Rev.Stat. 30.260–30.400; Tenn. Code Ann. §§ 29–20–101 to –407; Vernon's Tex.Ann.Civ.Stat. § 6252–19; Utah Code Ann. 1978, 63–30–1 to 63–30–34; West's Wash.Rev.Code Ann. 4.92.010–4.96.030. See generally Anderson, Claims Against States, 7 Vand.L.Rev. 234 (1954); Cobey, New California Governmental Tort Liability Statutes, 1 Harv.J.Leg. 16 (1964); Note, The Discretionary Immunity Doctrine in California, 19 Hast.L.J. 560 (1967); Note, The Utah Governmental Immunity Act: An Analysis, 1967 Utah L.Rev. 120. Some statutes waive the immunity of municipalities and of most or all of the public quasi-corporations within a state, but not of the state itself—*e.g.*, 51 Okl. Stat.1981, §§ 151–70, ending immunity, with designated exceptions, of cities, towns, school districts and counties.

as counties, townships, and special function districts—are often technically regarded as arms of the state, their tort immunity might logically be governed by the same rules as apply to the state—and certainly the abolition of tort immunity as to the state will, if nothing to the contrary is provided, also terminate the immunity of these governments. But such governments are often, in reality, closer in nature to municipalities than to the state; and court decisions and statutes abrogating municipal immunity commonly cover such quasi-corporations as counties and school districts.[125]

Often, judicial termination of immunity has been followed by legislation partially restoring the immunity. See Note, Governmental Immunity—The Doctrine of Immunity Judicially Abrogated and Legislatively Reinstated, 50 J.Urban L. 154 (1972). See generally Cahn & Camper, The New Sovereign Immunity, 81 Harv.L.Rev. 919 (1968); Hamill, The Changing Concept of Sovereign Immunity, 13 Def.L.J. 653 (1964); Mann, New Developments in the Law of Sovereign Immunity, 36 Mod.L.Rev. 18 (1973); Schoenbrun, Sovereign Immunity, 44 Tex.L.Rev. 151 (1965); Note, Sovereign Immunity—Denial of Equal Protection, 52 Boston U.L.Rev. 202 (1972); Comment, Governmental Immunity: The End of "King's X," 34 La.L.Rev. 69 (1973); Note, An Insurance Program to Effectuate Waiver of Sovereign Tort Immunity, 26 U.Fla.L.Rev. 89 (1973). Some statutes merely authorize the state government to purchase liability insurance; these statutes are normally interpreted as allowing suit against the state only to the extent of the insurance coverage. See Schrom v. Oklahoma Industrial Development & Parks Department, 536 P.2d 904 (Okl.1975). As to the varying degrees of state liability that used to exist in different jurisdictions, see generally Blachly & Oatman, Approaches to Governmental Liability in Tort: A Comparative Survey, 9 Law & Contemp.Prob. 181 (1942).

The power of Congress under Section 5 of the Fourteenth Amendment to enforce the provisions of that amendment include the power to abrogate state sovereign immunity by authorizing private suits for damages against the states for violations of the amendment. United States v. Georgia, 546 U.S. 151, 126 S.Ct. 877, 163 L.Ed.2d 650 (2006) (Title II of the Americans With Disabilities Act validly abrogates state sovereign immunity insofar as it creates a private cause of action against the states for conduct that violates the Fourteenth Amendment). But Congress will be held to have abrogated state immunity only where it has made that intent unmistakably clear in a statute. See Coleman v. Court of Appeals of Maryland, 566 U.S.___, 132 S.Ct. 1327, 182 L.Ed.2d 296 (2012) (Congress did not validly abrogate states' sovereign immunity from suits for money damages in enacting self-care provision of Family and Medical Leave Act *despite* expressing a purpose to do so, as they did not identify a pattern of constitutional violations and tailor a remedy congruent and proportional to the documented violations); Sossamon v. Texas, 563 U.S. 277, 131 S.Ct. 1651, 179 L.Ed.2d 700 (2011) (provision of Religious Land Use and Institutionalized Persons Act creating private cause of action for violations of Act did not clearly and unequivocally notify states that by accepting federal funds, they were waiving their sovereign immunity to suits for money damages under the Act; so there was no waiver). As to recent U.S. Supreme Court rulings on sovereign immunity of the states, see generally Vladeck, State Sovereign Immunity and the Roberts Court, 5 Charleston L. Rev. 99 (2010).

It has been held that one state is not required to extend full faith and credit to statutes of another state that confer complete immunity on the latter state's agencies. Franchise Tax Bd. of Calif. v. Hyatt, 538 U.S. 488, 123 S.Ct. 1683, 155 L.Ed.2d 702 (2003) (Nevada court not required to extend full faith and credit to California statutes conferring complete immunity on California agencies).

[125] See Johnson v. City of Billings, 101 Mont. 462, 54 P.2d 579 (1936) (county not immune under general theory that sovereign cannot be sued without its consent); Terry v. Edgin, 598 P.2d 228 (Okl.1979) (county liable as to its proprietary activities under statute providing that counties can sue and be sued); Gooden v. County Comm'n of Webster County, 171 W.Va. 130, 298 S.E.2d 103 (1982) (immunity of county commissions found abolished; said to be no meaningful difference, in area of tort immunity, between municipal and county governments). Cf. Johnson v. Board of County Comm'rs of Pratt County, 259 Kan. 305, 913 P.2d 119 (1996) (county could be liable, as a private person would be, for flooding land of lower riparian landowner). See generally 4 Antieau, Local Government Law (County Law), ch. 38 (1998); Annots., Liability of County for Torts in Connection with Activities which Pertain, or Are Claimed to Pertain, to Private or Proprietary Function, 16 A.L.R.2d 1079 (1951); 101 A.L.R. 1166 (1936). See also Northern Insurance Co. of New York v. Chatham County, Georgia, 547 U.S. 189, 126 S.Ct. 1689, 164 L.Ed.2d 367 (2006) (county was not acting as arm of the state for Eleventh Amendment purposes when it was operating malfunctioning drawbridge; thus county was not entitled to sovereign immunity).

Where statutes or judicial decisions *retain* the state's tort immunity, public quasi-corporations will normally remain immune also. See Opinion of the Justices, 101 N.H. 546, 134 A.2d 279 (1957) (airport authority is agency of state, which enjoys broader immunity than does municipality). As to the liability of schools and school districts, see Annot., Modern Status of Doctrine of Sovereign Immunity as Applied to Public Schools and Institutions of Higher Learning, 33 A.L.R.3d 703 (1970). See generally 3A Antieau, Local

§ 26.7 Local Governmental Liability Under Federal Civil Rights Act

A new basis for municipal liability has emerged in recent decades: liability under Section 1983 of the Federal Civil Rights Act.[126] For many years, the U.S. Supreme Court narrowly limited recoveries under this Act by strictly construing the requirement that any liability be based on conduct occurring "under color of state law."[127] In 1961, the Court broadened its interpretation of this requirement and ruled that the Act was intended to give a remedy to anyone deprived of constitutional rights, privileges, or immunities by a public officer's abuse of position—but in the same decision, the Court ruled that municipalities were not subject to suit under the Act because they are not "persons."[128] Thus, the net effect of the 1961 decision was largely to open the door to suits against individual office-holders, but to keep the door firmly shut against civil-rights suits against municipalities. And the remedy against individual office-holders often proved worthless because of the difficulty of finding an identifiable, solvent officeholder

---

Government Law (Independent Local Government Entities), ch. 30(Q), part 14, at 30Q–417–47 (1998); L.O. Garber & N. Edwards, Tort and Contractual Liability of School Districts and School Boards (Interstate Pub.1963); Gardner, Changing Patterns in Illinois School Tort Immunity, 55 Chi.-Kent L.Rev. 605 (1979). See also, on liability of community and junior college districts, 3A Antieau, *supra*, ch. 30(C), § 30C.08, at 30C–15 (1998). As to liability for particular aspects of schools and school activities, see Annot., Tort Liability of Public Schools and Institutions of Higher Learning for Injuries Due to Condition of Grounds, Walks, and Playgrounds, 37 A.L.R.3d 738 (1971); Annot., Tort Liability of Public Schools and Institutions of Higher Learning for Accidents Occurring During Use of Premises and Equipment for Other Than School Purposes, 37 A.L.R.3d 712 (1971); Annot., Tort Liability of Public Schools and Institutions of Higher Learning for Injuries Caused by Acts of Fellow Students, 36 A.L.R.3d 330 (1971); Annot., Tort Liability of Public Schools and Institutions of Higher Learning for Accidents Associated with the Transportation of Students, 34 A.L.R.3d 1210 (1970); Annot., Tort Liability of Public Schools and Institutions of Higher Learning for Accidents Due to Condition of Buildings or Equipment, 34 A.L.R.3d 1166 (1970). *Some* public "quasi-corporations," such as *dependent* school districts and certain public authorities, are arms of a municipality, not of the state; these should certainly be governed by the same rules that apply to municipalities. See generally Chapter 2 *supra*.

It should be noted that the leading English case establishing tort immunity for local governments involved the citizens of a *county*. Russell v. Men of Devon, 2 Term Rep. 667, 100 Eng.Rep. 359 (1798).

[126] 42 U.S.C.A. § 1983. See Freilich, Rushing & Noland, 1978–79 Annual Review of Local Government Law: Undermining Municipal and State Initiative in an Era of Crisis and Uncertainty, 11 Urban Law. 547, 548–64 (1979). See generally Gelfand, Constitutional Litigation Under Section 1983 (2d ed. 1996), reviewed 30 Urban Law. 781 (1998).

On the great increase in lawsuits filed against municipalities due to the advent of municipal liability under the Federal Civil Rights Act, see "Dragging Cities into Court," Time, Sept. 13, 1982, at 101; "Yes, You Can Fight City Hall," U.S. News & World Rep., Dec. 20, 1982, at 59. On the resulting difficulties of municipalities in obtaining liability insurance at affordable rates, see Blodgett, Premium Hikes Stun Municipalities, 72 A.B.A.J. 48 (1986); "The Coverage Crisis at Town Hall," Bus. Week, Aug. 26, 1985, at 72. See generally "Cities Besieged," 71 A.B.A.J. 19 (1985). See also Carlisle, Harris, Skitol & Markides, Governmental Liability for Federal Statutory Torts: A Search for Precedent, 15 Urban Law. 817 (1983). A good summary of the development of municipal liability under the Federal Civil Rights Act is Pettit, The Evolution of Government Liability Under Section 1983, 24 St. Mary's L.J. 145 (1992). Another valuable source for material concerning municipal liability for constitutional violations is M.D. Gelfand, Suing and Defending Cities for Federal Constitutional Violations (3d ed. 2003), particularly Chapter 6 on "Bringing and Defending Constitutional Litigation Under Section 1983." See also Ross & Voss, Sword and Shield (American Bar Ass'n Section on State and Ross & Voss, Sword and Shield (American Bar Ass'n Section on State and Local Government Law 2006), tracing the history of Section 1983 of the Federal Civil Rights Act.

[127] See Developments in the Law—Section 1983 and Federalism, 90 Harv.L.Rev. 1133, 1191 (1977), with review of cases.

[128] Monroe v. Pape, 365 U.S. 167, 81 S.Ct. 473, 5 L.Ed.2d 492 (1961). The Court also held that (1) the federal statutory remedy is supplemental to any state remedy, and thus the state remedy need not be sought and refused before the federal one can be granted (*Id.* at 183), and (2) the cause of action under Section 1983 does not require that the alleged constitutional violation have been willful (*Id.* at 187).

whose conduct could be shown to have caused the plaintiff's harm.[129] But in 1978, the Supreme Court reversed its earlier view of the meaning of "persons," and held that municipalities and other local governments *are* "persons" within the meaning of Section 1983 of the Federal Civil Rights Act and can be sued under that Act for monetary, declaratory, and injunctive relief wherever allegedly unconstitutional action has been taken in the course of implementing official city policy.[130]

There are three main requirements for municipal liability under the Federal Civil Rights Act:[131] (1) The locality must, in taking the injury-producing action, have acted

---

[129] See Note, Damage Remedies Against Municipalities, 89 Harv.L.Rev. 922, 923 (1976). On the personal liability of officials of local governments under the Federal Civil Rights Act, and the "good faith" defense to such liability, see Section 26.9 *infra*.

[130] Monell v. Department of Social Services, 436 U.S. 658, 98 S.Ct. 2018, 56 L.Ed.2d 611 (1978), noted 14 Ga.L.Rev. 605 (1980). The Court also held that (1) official city policy can be shown by establishing custom, even if the custom has not received formal approval (*Id.* at 691), and (2) local governments may not be held liable for the actions of their agents on a mere respondeat superior basis, but there is no absolute immunity. See Kushnir, Impact of Section 1983 after Monell on Municipal Policy Formulation and Implementation, 12 Urban Law. 466 (1980); McCaffrey, Recent Developments in 42 U.S.C. Section 1983 Claims Against Municipalities and Their Police Departments, 15 Forum 747 (1980). See generally, on the *Monell* case and subsequent developments, Freilich, White-Wasson & Cofer, 1979–1980 Annual Review of Local Government Law: Municipal Liability and Other Certain Uncertainties, 12 Urban Law. 577, 578–93 (1980). See also Gelfand, Suing and Defending Cities for Federal Constitutional Violations: A Treatise for City Attorneys and Public Interest Litigators (Lexis Publ. 3d ed. 2001) (loose-leaf), reviewed by Salsich, 35 Urban Law. 379 (2003).

No punitive damages are awardable against a municipality in federal civil rights actions, unless taxpayers of the municipality can be shown directly responsible for an outrageous abuse of constitutional rights. City of Newport v. Fact Concerts, Inc., 453 U.S. 247, 101 S.Ct. 2748, 69 L.Ed.2d 616 (1981). See generally Annot., Punitive Damages in Actions for Violations of Federal Civil Rights Acts, 14 A.L.R.Fed. 608 (1973). On remedies available in actions brought under Section 1983, see generally Nahmod, Damages and Injunctive Relief under Section 1983, 16 Urban Law. 201 (1984). See also Stewart, The Supreme Court Rewrites a Law: Municipal Liability under Section 1983, 15 Urban Law. 503 (1983). For a strong endorsement of municipal liability for punitive damages, see Note, Paying the Price: It's Time to Hold Municipalities Liable for Punitive Damages Under 42 U.S.C. Section 1983, 10 J.L. & Pol'y 189 (2001).

On who is now considered a "person" under the Federal Civil Rights Act, see Will v. Michigan Dep't of State Police, 491 U.S. 58, 109 S.Ct. 2304, 105 L.Ed.2d 45 (1989) (neither a state nor its officials acting in their official capacities can qualify as "persons" under Federal Civil Rights Act). Cf. Ngiraingas v. Sanchez, 495 U.S. 182, 110 S.Ct. 1737, 109 L.Ed.2d 163 (1990) (neither Territory of Guam nor an officer of the Territory acting in an official capacity is a "person" under § 1983 of Federal Civil Rights Act). Compare Daddow v. Carlsbad Municipal School Dist., 120 N.M. 97, 898 P.2d 1235 (1995), cert. denied 516 U.S. 1067, 116 S.Ct. 753, 133 L.Ed.2d 700 (1996) (local school boards are "persons" under § 1983 unless they are state agencies or arms of the state). See generally Annot., Supreme Court's Views as to Who Is "Person" Under Civil Rights Statute (42 U.S.C. § 1983) Providing Private Rights of Action for Violation of Federal Rights, 105 L.Ed.2d 721 (1991). See also Annot., Supreme Court's Views as to Meaning of Term "Person," as Used in Statutory or Constitutional Provision, 56 L.Ed.2d 895 (1979).

In Lapides v. Board of Regents of the University Sys. of Ga., 535 U.S. 613, 122 S.Ct. 1640, 152 L.Ed.2d 806 (2002), it was reiterated that a state is not a "person" against whom a Section 1983 claim for money damages may be asserted—but it was here found that the state, when it voluntarily removed the case to federal court, had waived its Eleventh Amendment immunity from suit on state-law claims for money damages.

As to who are considered "persons" who may be sued under the Federal *Claims* Act, see Cook County, Illinois v. United States ex rel. Chandler, 538 U.S. 119, 123 S.Ct. 1239, 155 L.Ed.2d 247 (2003) (municipal corporations are "persons").

[131] Freilich, Rushing & Noland, *supra* note 126, at 550. See Mando v. Beame, 398 F.Supp. 569 (S.D.N.Y.1975) (municipal employee allowed to sue city for racial discrimination); Keyer v. Civil Service Commission, 397 F.Supp. 1362 (E.D.N.Y.1975) (civil service employee could sue under Section 1983 for wrongful dismissal). See generally Freilich & Carlisle (eds.), Section 1983: Sword and Shield (American Bar Ass'n 1983). See also, as to possible reconsideration of the scope of—and limitations on—municipal liability under the Federal Civil Rights Act, Symposium on Reconsidering *Monell's* Limitation Upon Municipal Liability for Civil Rights Violations, 31 Urban Law. 393–552 (1999).

under color of state law—usually meaning in furtherance of some official city policy.[132] This requirement may not be satisfied where, for instance, the action was an isolated

---

[132] See Rizzo v. Goode, 423 U.S. 362, 96 S.Ct. 598, 46 L.Ed.2d 561 (1976) (federal courts should not order relief against city officials accused of mistreatment of minority citizens since was no immediate case or controversy, since such interference in local affairs would upset principles of federalism, *and* since no *policy* of unconstitutional actions shown); Goss v. San Jacinto Junior College, 588 F.2d 96 (5th Cir.1979), mod. 595 F.2d 1119 (sufficient evidence that plaintiff discharged by college Board of Regents because of her First-Amendment-protected activities); Turpin v. Mailet, 579 F.2d 152 (2d Cir.1978), vac'd 439 U.S. 974, 99 S.Ct. 554, 58 L.Ed.2d 645, cert. denied 439 U.S. 988, 99 S.Ct. 586, 58 L.Ed.2d 662, on remand 591 F.2d 426, appeal after remand 619 F.2d 196, cert. denied 449 U.S. 1016, 101 S.Ct. 577, 66 L.Ed.2d 475 (official city policy found where police department failed to take disciplinary action against officer who acted unconstitutionally, but even rewarded him with a promotion); Molina v. Richardson, 578 F.2d 846 (9th Cir.1978), cert. denied 439 U.S. 1048, 99 S.Ct. 724, 58 L.Ed.2d 707 (where plaintiff did *not* argue that allegedly illegal conduct of police officers could be said to represent city policy, city immune from suit). The requirement that for plaintiff to recover against a municipality under Section 1983 of the Federal Civil Rights Act, an injury must have been caused by municipal policy, custom, usage or practice applies regardless of whether the remedy sought is money damages or prospective relief, such as an injunction or declaratory judgment. Los Angeles County v. Humphries, 562 U.S. 29, 131 S.Ct. 447, 178 L.Ed.2d 460 (2010). See generally as to the history of damages and other relief under the Act, Symposium, The Civil Rights Act at Fifty, 10 Stan. J. Civil Rights & Civil Liberties 159–250 (2014). Cf. District of Columbia v. Carter, 409 U.S. 418, 93 S.Ct. 602, 34 L.Ed.2d 613 (1973) reh. denied 410 U.S. 959, 93 S.Ct. 1411, 35 L.Ed.2d 694 (no action under Federal Civil Rights Act for conduct of District of Columbia officers, but might be action based on common law or constitution—but note that as of an amendment in 1979, the Civil Rights Act now applies to actions taken under color of laws of the District of Columbia; 42 U.S.C.A. § 1983); Green v. Dumke, 480 F.2d 624 (9th Cir.1973) (*state* college refused to award *federal* aid to student on ground he had been convicted of crime; college acting under color of state law and was not immune). As the *Green* case, *supra*, indicates, Section 1983 does not cover actions taken under color of *federal* law. See Soldevila v. Secretary of Agriculture, 512 F.2d 427 (1st Cir.1975); Junior Chamber of Commerce, Inc. v. United States Jaycees, 495 F.2d 883 (10th Cir.1974) cert. denied 419 U.S. 1026, 95 S.Ct. 505, 42 L.Ed.2d 301. See generally Winter, The Meaning of "Under Color of" Law, 91 Mich. L. Rev. 323 (1992); Note, When Off-Duty State Officials Act Under Color of State Law for the Purposes of Section 1983, 22 Memphis St. U.L. Rev. 725 (1992); Annot., Action of Private Organization Providing Legal Aid with Public Funds as State Action Within 42 U.S.C. § 1983, 49 A.L.R. Fed. 955 (1980).

On the changing views of what constitutes "official city policy," see Yuhas & Fluker, Recent Developments in Government Liability, 17 Urban Law. 765, 783–86 (1985). It has been held that a city's failure to discipline its officers or make changes in its procedures after an innocent bystander was shot in a bungled attempt to catch a suspect amounted to good evidence that the city had a "policy" of reckless disregard for human life. Grandstaff v. City of Borger, 767 F.2d 161 (5th Cir.1985), reh. denied 779 F.2d 1129 (5th Cir.1986). But it has been held that a single use of excessive force by policy officers does not justify an inference of inadequate training of those officers. Oklahoma City v. Tuttle, 471 U.S. 808, 105 S.Ct. 2427, 85 L.Ed.2d 791 (1985), reh. denied 473 U.S. 925, 106 S.Ct. 16, 87 L.Ed.2d 695 (1985). On when excessive force by state or local officers *is* actionable under Section 1983, see Gumz v. Morrissette, 772 F.2d 1395 (7th Cir.1985), cert. denied 475 U.S. 1123, 106 S.Ct. 1644, 90 L.Ed.2d 189 (1986) (force must cause severe injuries, be grossly disproportionate to the need, and must have been inspired by malice rather than mere carelessness). The U.S. Supreme Court has held that while inadequacy of police training may serve as a basis for Federal Civil Rights Act liability, this is true only if the failure to train is shown to amount to deliberate indifference to the rights of persons with whom the police come into contact. See City of Canton, Ohio v. Harris, 489 U.S. 378, 109 S.Ct. 1197, 103 L.Ed.2d 412 (1989). Cf. Davis v. Mason County, 927 F.2d 1473 (9th Cir.1991), cert. denied 502 U.S. 899, 112 S.Ct. 275, 116 L.Ed.2d 227 (1991) (county liable for sheriff's failure to train deputies concerning excessive force); Harris v. City of Pagedale, 821 F.2d 499 (8th Cir.1987), cert. denied 484 U.S. 1083, 108 S.Ct. 1066, 98 L.Ed.2d 1027 (1988) (deliberate indifference to police abuses establishes municipal custom sufficient to support Federal Civil Rights Act liability). But cf. Collins v. Harker Heights, Texas, 503 U.S. 115, 112 S.Ct. 1061, 117 L.Ed.2d 261 (1992) (city's alleged failure to train or warn its employees about known hazards in workplace did not violate due process); D.T. v. Independent School Dist., 894 F.2d 1176 (10th Cir.1990), cert. denied 498 U.S. 879, 111 S.Ct. 213, 112 L.Ed.2d 172 (1990) (no state action unless actor under a duty, or owes an obligation, to the state; school district not liable for teacher's acts of molestation). See generally Shoemaker, *D.T. v. Independent School District:* Limiting Liability Under 42 U.S.C. § 1983, 24 Urban Law. 393 (1992). Compare cases brought under Title IX of Education Amendments of 1992: Davis v. Monroe County Bd. of Educ., 526 U.S. 629, 119 S.Ct. 1661, 143 L.Ed.2d 839 (1999) (private damages action may lie against school board under Title IX in cases of student-on-student harassment but only where officials have acted with deliberate indifference and where harassment is so severe that it effectively bars victim's access to an educational opportunity or benefit); Gebser v. Lago Vista Independent School Dist., 524 U.S. 274, 118 S.Ct.

1989, 141 L.Ed.2d 277 (1998) (damages may not be recovered for teacher-student sexual harassment under Title IX unless a school district official who at a minimum has authority to institute corrective measures on district's behalf has actual notice of, and is deliberately indifferent to, teacher's misconduct).

The U.S. Supreme Court has made clear that municipal liability *may* be imposed under the Federal Civil Rights Act for even a *single decision* of municipal policymakers; what is required is some showing that the act was officially sanctioned or ordered. See Pembaur v. City of Cincinnati, 475 U.S. 469, 106 S.Ct. 1292, 89 L.Ed.2d 452 (1986), on remand 792 F.2d 57 (6th Cir.1986), where a county prosecutor ordered deputy sheriffs to enter a physician's clinic to serve capiases on third parties in connection with an investigation of alleged welfare fraud. Since the prosecutor was acting as final decisionmaker for the county, the Court held that the county could be liable under Section 1983 for a violation of the physician's Fourth Amendment rights. Compare Board of County Comm'rs of Bryan County v. Brown, 520 U.S. 397, 117 S.Ct. 1382, 137 L.Ed.2d 626 (1997), reh. denied 520 U.S. 1283, 117 S.Ct. 2472, 138 L.Ed.2d 227 (1997) (evidence failed to establish that sheriff's isolated failure to perform adequate screening reflected deliberate indifference to high risk that deputy could use excessive force). Cf. McMillan v. Monroe County, Alabama, 520 U.S. 781, 117 S.Ct. 1734, 138 L.Ed.2d 1 (1997) (sheriff was policymaker for State of Alabama, not a final policy-making authority for county; therefore county not liable for his conduct in a Section 1983 action); City of St. Louis v. Praprotnik, 485 U.S. 112, 108 S.Ct. 915, 99 L.Ed.2d 107 (1988), on remand 879 F.2d 1573 (8th Cir.1989) (only municipal officers who have final policy-making authority may subject government to Section 1983 liability, and whether particular official has such authority is question of state law). See generally Brown-Graham & Williams, *Board of the County Commissioners v. Brown*: Virtual Reality in Single-Incident Municipal Liability Cases?, 29 Urban Law. 749 (1997); Cushman, Municipal Liability Under § 1983: Toward a New Definition of Municipal Policymaker, 34 Boston C. L. Rev. 693 (1993); Note, Constitutional Law—Single-Hiring Decisions and Municipalities: The United States Supreme Court's Latest Safeguard Against Municipal Liability Under 42 U.S.C. § 1983, 20 U. Ark. Little Rock L.J. 327 (1998).

Liability under Section 1983 also requires that the agents of the city who allegedly deprived plaintiff of his rights were acting in their official capacity at the time. See Brandon v. Holt, 469 U.S. 464, 105 S.Ct. 873, 83 L.Ed.2d 878 (1985), on remand 645 F.Supp. 1261 (W.D.Tenn.1986) (judgment against public servant in his official capacity imposes liability on the governmental entity). Cf. City of Los Angeles v. Heller, 475 U.S. 796, 106 S.Ct. 1571, 89 L.Ed.2d 806 (1986) (jury verdict *for* city police officer and against civil rights plaintiff who claimed he had been victim of excessive force by officer removed any basis for liability of city and members of its police commission). But the requisite "state action" may be found even if the conduct was that of a private citizen, or an off-duty police officer, so long as significant aid was obtained from a state official or agency or the authority of public officials put the weight of the state behind the private party's acts. See Lugar v. Edmondson Oil Co., 457 U.S. 922, 102 S.Ct. 2744, 73 L.Ed.2d 482 (1982); Motes v. Myers, 810 F.2d 1055 (11th Cir.1987), reh. denied 837 F.2d 1095 (11th Cir.1988); Greco v. Guss, 775 F.2d 161 (7th Cir.1985) (deputy sheriff conspired with private persons in wrongfully serving distress-for-rent warrant on restaurant owner). But mere use of state forms or directives does not suffice to make a party's action that of the state. See Jerry's Sport Center, Inc. v. Novick, 122 N.H. 636, 448 A.2d 404 (1982) (recording of a notice of *lis pendens* not state action). And it has been held that a state's failure to protect an individual against private violence—such as failing to protect a child from his father—does not constitute a violation of due process so as to give rise to Federal Civil Rights Act liability. DeShaney v. Winnebago County Dep't of Social Services, 489 U.S. 189, 109 S.Ct. 998, 103 L.Ed.2d 249 (1989), noted 87 St. John's L. Rev. 1071 (2013). On private persons' conduct as establishing a violation of the Federal Civil Rights Act, see generally Chen, Liability of Private Firms Performing Public Functions, 35 Trial, No. 10, at 60 (Oct. 1999); Annot., Action of Private Organization Providing Legal Aid with Public Funds as State Action Within 42 U.S.C. § 1983, 49 A.L.R. Fed. 955 (1980). It has been held that state regulation and state funding, as of nursing homes, do not by themselves transform the conduct of the object of the regulation and funding into "state action." See Daigle v. Opelousas Health Care, Inc., 774 F.2d 1344 (5th Cir.1985) (woman was allegedly beaten to death in nursing home; general state involvement with the business held insufficient basis for Section 1983 claim).

As to vicarious liability of a city under Section 1983, see Jett v. Dallas Independent School Dist., 491 U.S. 701, 109 S.Ct. 2702, 105 L.Ed.2d 598 (1989), on remand 7 F.3d 1241 (5th Cir.1993) (municipality may not be held liable under *respondeat superior* for its employees' violations of Section 1981 of Federal Civil Rights Act; Section 1983 provides exclusive federal damages remedy for violations of Section 1981 when alleged violation is by a state actor); City of Phoenix v. Yarnell, 184 Ariz. 310, 909 P.2d 377 (Ariz.1995) (municipal liability under Section 1983 cannot be imposed on basis of *respondeat superior*). The Supreme Court's exclusion of Section 1983 *respondeat superior* municipal liability has been criticized. See Note, Who's Afraid of Municipal Liability? The Supreme Court's Strange Exclusion of § 1983 Respondeat Superior Municipal Liability, 38 Ohio No. U. L. Rev. 461 (2011). Compare Faragher v. City of Boca Raton, 524 U.S. 775, 118 S.Ct. 2275, 141 L.Ed.2d 662 (1998) (former city employees sued city under Title VII of Federal Civil Rights Act for sexual harassment based on conduct of city supervisors; city held vicariously liable in view of its failure to exercise reasonable care to prevent harassing behavior). See generally Achtenberg, Taking History Seriously: Municipal Liability

incident, or was taken by city employees without knowledge of higher officials.[133] (2) The action must have deprived plaintiff of some right or rights protected under Section 1983; those rights are the ones protected by the Bill of Rights and made applicable to the state under the 14th Amendment, and those provided for by federal statute.[134] (3) The

---

Under 42 U.S.C. Section 1983 and the Debate Over *Respondeat Superior*, 73 Fordham L. Rev. 2183 (2005); Blum, Municipal Liability Under Section 1983 Independent of Employee Liability, 17 Touro L. Rev. 551 (2001). As to the problems of showing improper motive when the actor is a multi-member municipal board, see Note, Municipal Liability Under § 1983: The Difficulty of Determining Improper Motives of a Multi-member Municipal Board, 42 N. Eng. L. Rev. 865 (2008).

[133] See Reimer v. Short, 578 F.2d 621 (5th Cir.1978) cert. denied 440 U.S. 947, 99 S.Ct. 1425, 59 L.Ed.2d 635. Cf. Rizzo v. Goode, *supra* note 132 (no Federal Civil Rights Act remedy where no immediate injury threatened and local authorities were not shown to have played any affirmative part in alleged misconduct); Jones v. City of Memphis, 586 F.2d 622 (6th Cir.1978), cert. denied 440 U.S. 914, 99 S.Ct. 1230, 59 L.Ed.2d 464 (where arrestee's cause of action was based solely on fact that officers who mistreated him were employed by city, city not liable under Fourteenth Amendment and general federal question statute); Leite v. City of Providence, 463 F.Supp. 585 (D.R.I.1978) (mere negligence of municipality in hiring, training, and supervising police officers does not suffice); Kohler v. Hirst, 460 F.Supp. 412 (E.D.Va.1978) (mere failure to act does not suffice). See generally Note, Municipal Liability Under 42 U.S.C. § 1983 for Failing to Equip Police With Tasers, 28 Quinnipiac L. Rev. 225 (2009). See also Bosteder v. City of Renton, 155 Wash.2d 18, 117 P.3d 316 (2005) (municipality not liable under Section 1983 solely because it employs a tortfeasor; rather, plaintiff wishing to establish Section 1983 liability of a municipality must show that an official policy or pervasive custom of the city caused plaintiff's injury).

[134] See Maine v. Thiboutot, 448 U.S. 1, 100 S.Ct. 2502, 65 L.Ed.2d 555 (1980), indicating that a violation of any federal law may be actionable under the Federal Civil Rights Act. See generally Freilich, Rushing & Noland, *supra* note 126, at 551, noting that, in addition, some civil rights have been found *implied* by the courts—notably the right to privacy (citing Shuman v. City of Philadelphia, 470 F.Supp. 449 (E.D.Pa.1979)). On invasion of privacy as a violation of federal civil rights, see generally Annot., State or Municipal Liability for Invasion of Privacy, 87 A.L.R.3d 145 (1978). See also Rehnquist, Is an Expanded Right of Privacy Consistent with Fair and Effective Law Enforcement?, 23 Kan.L.Rev. 1 (1974). It has been held that an official's merely negligent act, even though causing injury, does not constitute a deprivation of due process such as will result in a claim under Section 1983. County of Sacramento v. Lewis, 523 U.S. 833, 118 S.Ct. 1708, 140 L.Ed.2d 1043 (1998) (liability for negligently inflicted harm is categorically beneath threshold of constitutional due process; therefore, high-speed police chase with no intent to harm suspects physically or to worsen their legal plight did not give rise to redressable action under Section 1983). See Davidson v. Cannon, 474 U.S. 344, 106 S.Ct. 668, 88 L.Ed.2d 677 (1986); Daniels v. Williams, 474 U.S. 327, 106 S.Ct. 662, 88 L.Ed.2d 662 (1986), both involving suits by prisoners based on alleged negligence of state prison officials. These cases overruled in part Parratt v. Taylor, 451 U.S. 527, 101 S.Ct. 1908, 68 L.Ed.2d 420 (1981) (prison officials' misconduct in giving cell keys to some inmates did not result in a Section 1983 claim since it was not done pursuant to a state policy). On the ruling in *Parratt v. Taylor*, *supra*, that a Section 1983 claim *could* be based on merely negligent conduct, see Blum, The Implications of *Parratt v. Taylor* for Section 1983 Litigation, 16 Urban Law. 363 (1984). Compare McLin v. Trimble, 795 P.2d 1035 (Okl.1990) (mere allegations of negligent treatment of prison inmate insufficient to state claim for deprivation of inmate's due process), with Rushing v. Wayne County, 436 Mich. 247, 462 N.W.2d 23 (1990), cert. denied 499 U.S. 920, 111 S.Ct. 1310, 113 L.Ed.2d 245 (1991), noted 1991 Thomas M. Cooley L. Rev. 703 (1991) (*deliberate* indifference to deprivation of rights of detainee would state claim under Section 1983). See generally Kritchevsky, Making Sense of State of Mind: Determining Responsibility in Section 1983 Municipal Liability Litigation, 60 Geo. Wash. L. Rev. 417 (1992).

It has also been held that a mere breach of state law does not constitute a violation of the federal Constitution and is therefore not actionable under Section 1983. Archie v. City of Racine, 847 F.2d 1211 (7th Cir.1988), cert. denied 489 U.S. 1065, 109 S.Ct. 1338, 103 L.Ed.2d 809 (1989) (action for deprivation of civil rights did not lie against a city or its dispatcher-employee for dispatcher's failure to send an ambulance to ill woman). See Chesterfield Dev. Corp. v. City of Chesterfield, 963 F.2d 1102 (8th Cir.1992) (mere violation of state law, as by enforcement of invalid zoning ordinance, is not the kind of "truly irrational" government action that gives rise to claim for violation of substantive due process).

Thus, what is needed for Section 1983 liability is either (1) a deliberate action, not mere negligence, *or* (2) a truly irrational violation of state law, not merely an inadvertent violation.

In City of Rancho Palos Verdes, Calif., v. Abrams, 544 U.S. 113, 125 S.Ct. 1453, 161 L.Ed.2d 316 (2005), it was held that an individual may not enforce, through a Section 1983 action, the limitations placed by the Telecommunications Act of 1996 on regulation by local zoning authorities of facilities for wireless communications. A judicial remedy is expressly authorized by the Telecommunications Act, and Congress did

deprivation of plaintiff's constitutional or statutory right(s) must have resulted in injury to him. This requirement is met where, for example, plaintiff shows that he was deprived of his property without due process,[135] as where plaintiff has wrongfully been fired from his job.[136] This third requirement may be satisfied by showing that plaintiff was deprived of property without just compensation, as where an uncompensated "taking" of property rights has occurred.[137] This last-mentioned theory for recovery opens the door for possible suits under Section 1983 for so-called "inverse condemnation" actions—actions by property-owners who allege that their property has in effect been taken without the payment requirements for eminent domain having been met.[138] The provisions of the Federal Civil Rights Act must, of course, be read in conjunction with other relevant laws; it has, for instance, been held that the doctrine of collateral estoppel will be applied in

---

not mean this to coexist with a Section 1983 action, which would distort the scheme of judicial review and the limited remedies created by the Telecommunications Act.

[135] Lynch v. Household Finance Corp., 405 U.S. 538, 92 S.Ct. 1113, 31 L.Ed.2d 424 (1972), reh. denied 406 U.S. 911, 92 S.Ct. 1611, 31 L.Ed.2d 822, on remand 360 F.Supp. 720 (D.C.Conn.). Cf. Scott v. Harris, 550 U.S. 372, 127 S.Ct. 1769, 167 L.Ed.2d 686 (2007) (motorist brought Section 1983 action against county deputy and others, alleging excessive use of force during high-speed chase; held that deputy acted reasonably when he terminated car chase and thus did not violate motorist's Fourth Amendment right against unreasonable seizure); Kruzhkov v. State, 144 P.3d 186 (Okla. Civ. App. 2006) (substantive due process only imposes upon a state the duty to protect those persons who are in actual custody; thus, motorist who was not in custody could not maintain civil rights claim against state trooper and the state itself). The damage requirement is not satisfied by showing loss of the merely abstract value of constitutional rights, and such loss is not a permissible element of compensable damages in a Section 1983 action. Memphis Community School Dist. v. Stachura, 477 U.S. 299, 106 S.Ct. 2537, 91 L.Ed.2d 249 (1986), on remand 803 F.2d 721 (6th Cir. 1986). But cf. Griffith v. Butte School Dist. No. 1, 358 Mont. 193, 244 P.3d 321 (2010) (delivering a valedictory speech at high-school graduation was an important benefit, and student who was denied right to speak because her proposed speech contained religious references stated a § 1983 claim for damages).

[136] Perry v. Sindermann, 408 U.S. 593, 92 S.Ct. 2694, 33 L.Ed.2d 570 (1972); Board of Regents v. Roth, 408 U.S. 564, 92 S.Ct. 2701, 33 L.Ed.2d 548 (1972). Cf. Fulton Market Cold Storage Co. v. Cullerton, 582 F.2d 1071 (7th Cir.1978), cert. denied 439 U.S. 1121, 99 S.Ct. 1033, 59 L.Ed.2d 82 (systematic and fraudulent over-assessment of taxes); Roberson v. Wood, 464 F.Supp. 983 (E.D.Ill.1979) (protecting right of nursing home residents, on Medicaid, to continued residence in facility of their choice).

[137] Lake Country Estates, Inc. v. Tahoe Regional Planning Agency, 440 U.S. 391, 99 S.Ct. 1171, 59 L.Ed.2d 401 (1979), on remand 474 F.Supp. 901 (D.C.Nev.) (land-use ordinance alleged to have destroyed value of property).

[138] See Freilich, Rushing & Noland, *supra* note 126, at 552–53; Freilich, White-Wasson & Cofer, *supra* note 130, at 608–12. See generally Kanner, The Consequences of Taking Property by Regulation, 24 Prac. Lawyer 75 (1978); Searles, An Overview of Inverse Condemnation, 33 The Record 20 (1978). On inverse condemnation, see generally Section 19.2 *supra*.

Exhaustion of state administrative remedies is not a prerequisite to an action under the Federal Civil Rights Act. Patsy v. Board of Regents of Fla., 457 U.S. 496, 102 S.Ct. 2557, 73 L.Ed.2d 172 (1982), on remand 693 F.2d 558 (5th Cir.1982). And a state statutory limit on damage awards has been held inapplicable to an award under 42 U.S.C.A. § 1983. Thompson v. Village of Hales Corners, 115 Wis.2d 289, 340 N.W.2d 704 (1983), noted 53 U. Cinc. L. Rev. 667 (1984). It has been held, however, that a person claiming that his property has been taken for public use without just compensation may not pursue redress under Section 1983 in federal court where the state courts provide adequate means for compensating property owners whose property is taken for public use. Collier v. City of Springdale, 733 F.2d 1311 (8th Cir.1984), cert. denied 469 U.S. 857, 105 S.Ct. 186, 83 L.Ed.2d 120 (1984) (plaintiff's trout farm flooded by city sewage facility). See Wilhelm v. Gray, 766 P.2d 1357 (Okl.1988), cert. denied 490 U.S. 1092, 109 S.Ct. 2436, 104 L.Ed.2d 992 (1989) (adequate state remedy to redress property damage inflicted by state officers avoids conclusion that there has been deprivation of property without due process). Cf. Punton v. City of Seattle, 805 F.2d 1378 (9th Cir.1986), cert. denied 481 U.S. 1029, 107 S.Ct. 1954, 95 L.Ed.2d 527 (1987) (wrongfully dismissed police officer who had won reinstatement with back pay from state court had received adequate state remedy and thus had no claim under Federal Civil Rights Act for emotional distress and attorney fees); Sintra, Inc. v. City of Seattle, 119 Wash.2d 1, 829 P.2d 765 (1992), cert. denied 506 U.S. 1028, 113 S.Ct. 676, 121 L.Ed., 2d 598 (1992) (housing preservation ordinance could give rise to Section 1983 claim for taking, but no such claim available here because no decision had been obtained under state inverse condemnation law).

an action under the Act where a state court has given the parties a full and fair opportunity to litigate federal claims.[139] But the result of Supreme Court cases in this area has been to create a broad new field of municipal liability,[140] and it has been held—in a case in which plaintiff had been deprived of procedural due process by not being provided with a name-clearing hearing in the course of his termination from employment—that the presence of "good faith" on the part of the locality and its agent does not provide the locality with any immunity.[141]

§ 26.8 Local Governmental Liability Under Anti-Trust Laws

Another developing category of lawsuits against municipalities is anti-trust litigation. For years, anti-trust liability was considered generally impossible on the part of local governments because immunity, under anti-trust laws, was accorded "state action" by the U.S. Supreme Court decision in Parker v. Brown.[142] But in a 1978 decision,

---

[139] Allen v. McCurry, 449 U.S. 90, 101 S.Ct. 411, 66 L.Ed.2d 308 (1980), noting that the main goal of the federal Civil Rights Act of 1871 was to override the corrupting influence of the Ku Klux Klan and its sympathizers on the governments of southern states, and a strong motive behind enactment of the law was concern that state courts had been deficient in protecting federal rights. See Koch v. City of Hutchinson, 814 F.2d 1489 (10th Cir.1987), reh. granted 847 F.2d 1435, cert. denied 488 U.S. 909, 109 S.Ct. 262, 102 L.Ed.2d 250 (1988) (plaintiff—a fire marshall who had been demoted—was collaterally estopped from asserting due process claim in federal civil rights action as he had been afforded full and fair opportunity to litigate this claim at state level). Cf. Keller v. Prince George's County, 827 F.2d 952 (4th Cir.1987), appeal after remand 923 F.2d 30 (4th Cir.1991) (Congress did not intend that Federal Civil Rights Act pre-empt other remedies against state as employer). On the relevant state statute of limitations for Section 1983 actions, see Owens v. Okure, 488 U.S. 235, 109 S.Ct. 573, 102 L.Ed.2d 594 (1989) (where state has multiple statutes of limitations for personal injury actions, Section 1983 cases are governed by state's general or residual personal injury statute of limitations).

[140] See Nahmood, Government Liability Under Section 1983: The Present Is Prologue, 21 Urban Law. 1 (1989), discussing the future of government liability under the Federal Civil Rights Act. Many *states* now have Civil Rights Acts also, giving rise to possible criminal and civil actions. See Note, Municipal Law—How Broad a Remedy? Municipal Liability and the Massachusetts Civil Rights Act, 20 W. New England L. Rev. 841 (2007).

[141] Owen v. City of Independence, 421 F.Supp. 1110 (W.D.Mo.1976), aff'd in part rev'd in part 560 F.2d 925 (8th Cir.) vac'd and remanded for reconsideration, 438 U.S. 902, 98 S.Ct. 3118, 57 L.Ed.2d 1145, mod. on remand, 589 F.2d 335 (8th Cir.), rev'd and remanded 445 U.S. 622, 100 S.Ct. 1398, 63 L.Ed.2d 673, on remand 623 F.2d 550 (8th Cir.) reh. denied 446 U.S. 993, 100 S.Ct. 2979, 64 L.Ed.2d 850. See Carlisle, The Evolution of Section 1983—Verdict In on Liability but Jury Out on Remedy, 12 Urban Law. 727 (1980); Peters, Municipal Liability After Owen v. City of Independence and Maine v. Thiboutot, 13 Urban Law. 407 (1981). Cf. Jefferson v. Ysleta Independent School Dist., 817 F.2d 303 (5th Cir.1987) (no defense of qualified immunity for a school district where a school official violated what a reasonable person would know to be an established statutory or constitutional right). See also Carlisle. *Owen v. City of Independence:* Toward Constructing a Model for Municipal Liability After Monnell, 12 Urban Law. 292 (1980), written prior to the Supreme Court's final decision in the *Owen* case, *supra*, and urging that the government be accorded all the tort defenses traditionally accorded individual government employees when they are personally sued.

Immunity, under state law, from tort liability does not prevent liability under Section 1983 of the Federal Civil Rights Act; otherwise, the *Monnell* decision, *supra* note 130, would be meaningless. See Monnell v. New York City Department of Social Services, *supra* note 130, at 701. See also Ex parte Young, 209 U.S. 123, 28 S.Ct. 441, 52 L.Ed. 714 (1908) (federal court may enjoin individual or state officer from enforcing state statute because of its unconstitutionality, though may not restrain state court from acting in any case brought before it).

A covenant not to sue under Section 1983 may be valid if its execution is voluntary, deliberate, and informed. See Town of Newton v. Rumery, 480 U.S. 386, 107 S.Ct. 1187, 94 L.Ed.2d 405 (1987) (agreement enforceable where defendant entered into it voluntarily and prosecutor had legitimate reason to make it in connection with his prosecutorial responsibilities).

[142] 317 U.S. 341, 63 S.Ct. 307, 87 L.Ed. 315 (1943), upholding a California program that limited the marketing of raisins in order to maintain prices, since the Sherman Anti-Trust Act, 15 U.S.C.A. §§ 1–7, did not prohibit state-imposed restraints on trade. Though the *Parker* case involved only the Sherman Act, it was generally assumed that its holding encompassed other anti-trust laws as well. See Note, Parker v. Brown

the Court terminated the absolute immunity and held that the "*Parker* doctrine" exempts, from the anti-trust laws, only state or local anti-competitive conduct that (1) is authorized or directed by the state, *and* (2) is so authorized or directed in order to fulfill a state policy of substituting regulation, or governmental monopoly service, for competition.[143] Following this, a number of decisions recognized possible anti-trust

---

Revisited: The State Action Doctrine After Goldfarb, Cantor, and Bates, 77 Colum.L.Rev. 898 (1977). It was urged by some that the *Parker* decision, *supra*, should not bar suits under Section 5 of the Federal Trade Commission Act, 15 U.S.C.A. § 45 (a)(1). See Note, The State Action Exemption and Antitrust Enforcement Under the Federal Trade Commission Act, 89 Harv.L.Rev. 715 (1976). See generally Teply, Antitrust Immunity of State and Local Government Action, 48 Tulane L.Rev. 272 (1974); Note, The Antitrust Liability of Municipalities Under the Parker Doctrine, 57 Boston U.L.Rev. 368 (1977).

Prior to *Parker*, antitrust challenges to state actions had been unsuccessful, but the courts had not expressly held that the Sherman Act did not apply to state action. See Olsen v. Smith, 195 U.S. 332, 25 S.Ct. 52, 49 L.Ed. 224 (1904) (state licensing of harbor pilots was not an unreasonable restraint of trade); Lowenstein v. Evans, 69 F. 908 (C.C.S.C.1895) (state monopoly on liquor sales upheld).

On the extent to which the "state action" doctrine may protect private persons from antitrust liability, see Patrick v. Burget, 486 U.S. 94, 108 S.Ct. 1658, 100 L.Ed.2d 83 (1988), reh. denied 487 U.S. 1243, 108 S.Ct. 2921, 101 L.Ed.2d 952 (1988) (to qualify as "state action" exempt from antitrust laws, conduct of private parties must be clearly articulated and affirmatively expressed as state policy, and actively supervised by the state itself; doctrine did not protect Oregon physicians from federal antitrust liability for initiating and participating in hospital peer-review committee proceedings to terminate a surgeon's privileges at city hospital).

[143] City of Lafayette v. Louisiana Power & Light Co., 435 U.S. 389, 98 S.Ct. 1123, 55 L.Ed.2d 364 (1978), noted 45 Brooklyn L.Rev. 165 (1978); 11 Conn.L.Rev. 126 (1978); 28 Drake L.Rev. 513 (1978–79); 92 Harv.L.Rev. 277 (1978); 15 Wake Forest L.Rev. 89 (1979). A later, even more sweeping decision is Community Communications, Inc. v. City of Boulder, 455 U.S. 40, 102 S.Ct. 835, 70 L.Ed.2d 810 (1982) (home-rule city's three-month moratorium on expansion of cable television business not immune from anti-trust laws). See Melton, The State Action Antitrust Defense for Local Governments: A State Authorization Approach, 12 Urban Lawyer 315 (1980). Cf. Cantor v. Detroit Edison Co., 428 U.S. 579, 96 S.Ct. 3110, 49 L.Ed.2d 1141 (1976) (where state policy was "neutral," a state-regulated utility was not immune from antitrust liability for distributing free light bulbs to its electricity customers). The *City of Lafayette* case, *supra*, and its effects are well discussed in Curtin, Antitrust Comes to the Cities—Analysis of City of Lafayette v. Louisiana Power & Light Co. and Its Effect on Municipal Antitrust Liability, 5 U. Dayton L.Rev. 7 (1980); Rose, Municipal Activities and the Antitrust Laws After City of Lafayette, 57 U.Detroit J. Urban L. 483 (1980); Sims, Antitrust Comes to City Hall, Regulation, July/Aug., 1979, at 35; Thomas, City of Lafayette's State Action Test Reformulated: A Meaningful Standard of Antitrust Immunity for Cities, 2 Ariz. St.L.J. 345 (1980). The *City of Boulder* case *supra* was attacked as undermining the viability of home rule in America. Editor's Comment, The *Community Communications* Case: A Return to the Dark Ages before Home Rule, 14 Urban Law. No. 2, at v (Spring, 1982). And it was called potentially devastating to local governmental finances. See Moore, Antitrust Lawsuits Threaten Local Governments' Budgets, Wash. Post, Sept. 29, 1984, at A-1. On the significance of the *City of Boulder* case to cable television franchising, see Ryerson, Cable Television Franchising Without Antitrust Immunity, 16 Urban Law. 387 (1984). On the significance to airport regulation, see Dolley & Barker, Airport Antitrust Regulation, 14 Urban Law. 673 (1982). A good summary of many of the cases on municipal antitrust liability is found in Yuhas & Temple, Recent Developments in Government Liability, 16 Urban Law. 655 (1984). See generally Siena, Antitrust & Local Government (Nat'l League of Cities 1982); Carlisle, Coleman, Fontana, Moskowitz & Smith, Testing the Limits: A Report on the Uncertainties of Government Liability in 1982, 14 Urban Law. 687, 698–723 (1982); Freilich, Donovan & Ralls, Antitrust Liability and Preemption of Authority: Trends and Developments in Urban, State and Local Government Law, 15 Urban Law. 705, 707–37 (1983); Roberts, Municipal Antitrust Immunity and the State-Action Exemption: Developments in the Law, 58 State Gov't 164 (1986). On the concern created for municipal officials in the early 1980's by the prospect of municipal antitrust liability, see Spiegel, Local Governments and the Terror of Antitrust, 69 A.B.A.J. 163 (1983).

A couple U.S. Supreme Court cases in 1985, however, widened possible immunity from antitrust liability. In Southern Motor Carriers Rate Conference, Inc. v. United States, 471 U.S. 48, 105 S.Ct. 1721, 85 L.Ed.2d 36 (1985), on remand 764 F.2d 748 (11th Cir.1985), it was held that private anticompetitive behavior conducted pursuant to a clearly articulated state policy to permit such conduct may be immune from federal antitrust liability if the state actively supervises the conduct of the private parties. Thus, antitrust immunity was found in situations where states permitted motor carriers to submit collective rate proposals to public service commissions which could accept, modify, or reject those rate schedules. See Patrick v. Burget, *supra* note 142. In the other 1985 case, it was held that a municipality's anticompetitive activities are immune from antitrust liability if they are merely *authorized*, not necessarily compelled, by the state, and may be immune though the

liability of local governments in a variety of areas,[144] and it has been noted that many activities of such governments have potential anti-trust consequences.[145] It has been observed that municipal anti-trust violations should certainly not be found in any situations in which private parties could lawfully engage in the same conduct.[146] There remained doubt as to the scope of the Supreme Court's termination of the former immunity, and it was suggested that the Court should act to clarify this area of liability.[147] Before the Court had fully clarified the law, however, Congress acted by

---

state does not actively supervise the anticompetitive conduct. Town of Hallie v. City of Eau Claire, 471 U.S. 34, 105 S.Ct. 1713, 85 L.Ed.2d 24 (1985) (Wisconsin statutes authorizing city to provide sewage services and to determine areas to be served constituted a clear articulation of state policy to displace competition with regulation, thus giving antitrust immunity). A number of cases following the *Town of Hallie* case *supra* found municipal activity immune from antitrust liability due to state authorization. See McCallum v. City of Athens, 976 F.2d 649 (11th Cir.1992) (state statutes set forth policy of displacing competition in field of municipal water distribution; thus, operation of municipality's water system was exempt from Sherman Act scrutiny); LaSalle Nat'l Bank of Chicago v. County of DuPage, 777 F.2d 377 (7th Cir.1985), cert. denied 476 U.S. 1170, 106 S.Ct. 2892, 90 L.Ed.2d 979 (1986) (agreement between villages to divide unincorporated land between them so that each had the exclusive right to annex, and to provide water service to, a designated area held authorized by state law and thus exempt from antitrust liability). Cf. Allright Colorado, Inc. v. City & County of Denver, 937 F.2d 1502 (10th Cir.1991), cert. denied 502 U.S. 983, 112 S.Ct. 994, 117 L.Ed.2d 155 (1992) (municipality's activities regulating shuttle bus services to and from airport parking held immune from antitrust laws); Oberndorf v. City & County of Denver, 696 F.Supp. 552 (D.Colo.1988), aff'd 900 F.2d 1434 (10th Cir.1990), cert. denied 498 U.S. 845, 111 S.Ct. 129, 112 L.Ed.2d 97 (1990) (adoption and implementation of urban renewal plan and accompanying project were not violative of antitrust laws and, in any event, the city and other parties involved were immune).

Finally, in City of Columbia v. Omni Outdoor Advertising, Inc., 499 U.S. 365, 111 S.Ct. 1344, 113 L.Ed.2d 382 (1991), on remand 974 F.2d 502 (4th Cir.1992), it was held that a city was not deprived of immunity from antitrust liability on the ground that its action was not taken to promote police-power purposes (health, safety, morality, or general welfare) and thus was not even authorized by state law. On the expansion of immunity brought about by this case, see Note, *City of Columbia v. Omni Outdoor Advertising, Inc.*: The Expansion of State Action Immunity to Municipal Regulation, 18 J. Contemp. L. 309 (1992); Note, Municipal Antitrust Immunity After *City of Columbia v. Omni Outdoor Advertising, Inc.*, 67 Wash. L. Rev. 479 (1992). But it has been held that a *nonsovereign* actor enjoys *Parker* immunity only if the challenged restraint is clearly articulated and affirmatively expressed as state policy that is actively supervised by the state. North Caroliina State Bd. of Dental Examiners v. Federal Trade Comm'n, ___ U.S. ___, 135 S.Ct. 1101 (2015).

[144] See Woolen v. Surtran Taxicabs, Inc., 461 F.Supp. 1025 (N.D.Tex.1978) (exclusive permit for soliciting taxicab passengers at airport); Star Lines, Limited v. Puerto Rico Maritime Shipping Authority, 451 F.Supp. 157 (S.D.N.Y.1978) (control over commercial freight between Puerto Rico and the East and Gulf Coast of the U.S. mainland). In all three circuit court cases vacated and remanded by the U.S. Supreme Court following the *Lafayette* decision, *supra* note 143, the courts subsequently reinstated their pre-*Lafayette* denials of "state action" motions to dismiss, or motions for summary judgment, made by local governments. See generally Taurman, Reflections on *City of Lafayette:* Applying the Antitrust "State Action" Exemption to Local Governments, 13 Urban Law. 159 (1981).

[145] See Melton, *supra* note 143, at 318–19 & note 14, listing ten categories of municipal activities having antitrust implications—including zoning, occupational licensing, housing and urban development, transportation, operation of airports, and operation of utilities. As to hospitals and health care, see Federal Trade Comm'n v. Phoebe Putney Health System, Inc., ___ U.S. ___, 133 S.Ct. 1003 (2013) (in order to receive state-action antitrust immunity, a state must clearly articulate and affirmatively express that a political subdivision that provides health care services has the ability to make acquisitions even where they substantially reduce competition; authority that operated hospital attempted to acquire other local hospital; immunity applies only if the anticompetitive effect was a foreseeable result of state legislature's authorization, and there was no evidence of such foreseeability here). See generally "Municipalities and Antitrust Litigation," The Municipal Attorney 384 (Dec., 1978). As to the liability of special function districts, see generally Comment, Special Districts, Antitrust Law and the Infrastructure Crisis, 43 Gonzaga L. Rev. 671 (2007–08). See also, discussing possible antitrust problems in public housing, Strauss & Stegman, Moderate-Cost Housing After *La Fayette:* A Proposal, 11 Urban Lawyer 209 (1979).

[146] Survey, The Supreme Court, 1977 Term, 92 Harv.L.Rev. 1, 277, 284–85 (1978). See generally 1 P. Areeda & D. Turner, Antitrust Law § 217a2 (1978).

[147] Melton, *supra* note 143, at 321. It has been agreed by most commentators that the legislative history of the Sherman Act does not indicate that Congress seriously considered the "state action" problem when

passing the Local Government Antitrust Act of 1984, which bars anti-trust damage recovery against local governments and officials, though leaving the possibility of injunctive relief against local governmental activity that falls outside judicially developed immunity for state action.[148]

§ 26.9 Local Governmental Liability for Restitution

Another possible kind of relief against local governments, which has been partially considered in the discussion of municipal contracts,[149] is restitution. This relief has, for instance, been granted when a municipal corporation holds a deposit or bond that in justice belongs to another—as where a bidder on a municipal contract has made an honest mistake in his bid and gives notice to the municipality before it has opened the bids submitted.[150] Similarly, property owners who have paid assessments to a local government can recover them in a restitution action if the levies turn out to have been invalid;[151] and a subdivider has been allowed to recover fees or properties illegally

---

passing the Act. See Slater, Antitrust and Government Action: A Formula for Narrowing Parker v. Brown, 69 Nw.U.L.Rev. 71, 81–86 (1974); White, Participant Governmental Action Immunity from the Antitrust Laws: Fact or Fiction?, 50 Tex.L.Rev. 474, 498 (1972). See generally Tepley, Antitrust Immunity of State and Local Government Action, 48 Tul.L.Rev. 272 (1974).

[148] 15 U.S.C.A. §§ 34–36. In passing the law, Congress rejected proposals that all types of antitrust actions based on governmental activities of local governments be precluded. See Yuhas & Fluker, Recent Developments in Government Liability, 17 Urban Law. 765, 767–75 (1985). Regarding the importance of this change in the law as to the land-use area, see Duerksen & Bean, Land and the Law 1985: A Run on the Bank, 17 Urban Law. 827, 833–38 (1985). See generally Harris, Local Government Antitrust Act of 1984, 8 Urban, State & Local L. Newsletter, No. 3, at 1 (Winter, 1985).

In City Communications, Inc. v. City of Detroit, 660 F.Supp. 932 (E.D.Mich.1987), the court found that genuine issues of material fact precluded summary judgment as to whether the state action immunity doctrine and the Local Government Antitrust Act protected a successful bidder for a cable television franchise from suit under the Sherman Act. Cf. Fine Airport Parking, Inc. v. City of Tulsa, 71 P.3d 5 (Okla. 2003) (an anti-competitive municipal regulation is "supervised" by the state, as required for the state-action immunity doctrine to protect a municipality's anti-competitive conduct from federal antitrust liability, if the municipality *actively* supervises the regulation). Compare First American Title Co. v. Devaugh, 480 F.3d 438 (6th Cir. 2007) (county's practice of conditioning the provision of nonpaper reproductions or bulk discounts for paper reproductions of real-estate title records on the purchaser's agreement not to resell copies or the information contained therein does *not* qualify for state-action immunity because the anti-competitive practices were neither clearly articulated and affirmatively expressed by the legislature as intended policy, nor were they the logical and foreseeable result of the legislature's expressed policy).

On local governments' exemption from *state* anti-trust laws, see County of Milwaukee v. Williams, 295 Wis.2d 389, 720 N.W.2d 177 (2006), noted 2007 Wis. L. Rev. 1355.

[149] See Chapter 25 on contract liability, *supra*.

[150] City of Hattiesburg v. Cobb Brothers Construction Co., 183 Miss. 482, 184 So. 630 (1938); Gavahan v. Village of Shorewood, 200 Wis. 429, 228 N.W. 497 (1930). But see Mayor & City Council of Baltimore v. J. L. Robinson Construction Co., 123 Md. 660, 91 A. 682 (1914) (bidder had tried to withdraw his bid, and then upon contract being awarded him, refused to sign it; not allowed to recover amount of check that accompanied bid). Some authority denies restitutionary relief to a bidder who was negligent. See A.J. Colella, Inc. v. County of Allegheny, 391 Pa. 103, 137 A.2d 265 (1958). Cf. Jordan v. City of Beaumont, 337 S.W.2d 115 (Tex.Civ.App.1960) ref'd n.r.e. (bidder had made honest mistake and was *not* negligent; entitled to return of bid deposit unless he had ratified bid or waived right to withdraw it). And other authority denies relief to a *grossly* negligent bidder. See Union & Peoples National Bank v. Anderson-Campbell Co., 256 Mich. 674, 240 N.W. 19 (1932).

[151] See Carolina & North Western Railway v. Town of Clover, 46 F.2d 395 (4th Cir.1931); Smith v. City of Boston, 194 Mass. 31, 79 N.E. 786 (1907); Blanchard v. City of Detroit, 253 Mich. 491, 235 N.W. 230 (1931). But to be recoverable, the payment must have been made under duress, as well as having been illegal; "voluntary" payments generally cannot be recovered. See Garibaldi v. Daly City, 61 Cal.App.2d 514, 143 P.2d 397 (Dist.Ct.1943); Kirchner v. City of Pittsfield, 312 Mass. 342, 44 N.E.2d 634 (1942); Corby v. City of Detroit, 180 Mich. 208, 146 N.W. 670 (1914); Horn v. City of Minneapolis, 182 Minn. 172, 234 N.W. 289 (1930). The required "duress" means pressure compelling an exaction or payment in order to release property from some

required by a municipality as a condition for subdivision approval.[152] A person who is not a volunteer and who has performed a duty which the law imposes on another person, who has failed to perform that duty, is, under general legal principles, accorded an action for restitution against that other if (1) prompt performance of the duty is of grave concern to the public, (2) the person on whom the duty rests failed or refused to act with knowledge of the facts, or found it impossible to perform the duty, and (3) the person who intervened was not a mere intermeddler but a proper person to carry out the task.[153] Applying these principles to a situation in which a local government has failed to perform a duty, courts have allowed restitution to an individual or institution that has provided care for poor persons where the government had the duty to render such care.[154] Restitution can also be utilized when one governmental unit receives funds that rightfully belong to another, as where taxes are by mistake paid the wrong governmental unit.[155]

§ 26.10 Liability to, and Personal Liability of, Local Governmental Officers and Employees

What rules govern the possible liability of municipalities *to* their own officers and employees? It has been held that common-law and statutory obligations of the employer-locality to provide a reasonably *safe place to work* apply regardless of whether the municipal worker was engaged in a "governmental" or a "proprietary" function.[156]

---

hold or lien on it. See Adrico Realty Corp. v. City of New York, 250 N.Y. 29, 164 N.E. 732 (1928). Cf. Newberry v. City of Detroit, 184 Mich. 188, 150 N.W. 838 (1915) (payment to remove lien was involuntary). A payment made under protest is generally held involuntary. See Peterson v. City of Missoula, 135 Mont. 96, 337 P.2d 367 (1959). But if the involuntariness of the payment is otherwise shown, there is no need to show that a protest was made at the time of the payment. Newberry v. City of Detroit, *supra*.

Payment of taxes has often been held non-reimbursable under restitutionary principles if the payment is characterized as voluntary. See Carr v. City of Memphis, 22 F.2d 678 (6th Cir.1927); Pitt v. Town of Stamford, 117 Conn. 388, 167 A. 919 (1933); People ex rel. Eitel v. Lindheimer, 371 Ill. 367, 21 N.E.2d 318 (1939), appeal dism'd 308 U.S. 505, 60 S.Ct. 111, 84 L.Ed. 432, reh. denied 308 U.S. 636, 60 S.Ct. 137, 84 L.Ed. 529; Dupre v. City of Opelousas, 161 La. 272, 108 So. 479 (1926) (taxes not recoverable if taxpayer not coerced into payment); Mercury Machine Importing Co. v. City of New York, 3 N.Y.2d 418, 165 N.Y.S.2d 517, 144 N.E.2d 400 (1957); Wilson v. School District of Philadelphia, 328 Pa. 225, 195 A. 90 (1937). Similarly, illegally collected license fees cannot be recovered if voluntarily paid. See Manufacturer's Casualty Insurance Co. v. Kansas City, 330 S.W.2d 263 (Mo.1959); Simpson v. City of New Orleans, 133 La. 384, 63 So. 57 (1913); City of Charlottesville v. Marks' Shows, Inc., 179 Va. 321, 18 S.E.2d 890 (1942).

[152] Ridgemont Development Co. v. City of East Detroit, 358 Mich. 387, 100 N.W.2d 301 (1960). Cf. Kelber v. City of Upland, 155 Cal.App.2d 631, 318 P.2d 561 (Dist.Ct.1957) (ordinances required subdivider, as condition of approval of subdivision map, to pay $30 per lot into fund for parks and schools and $99.07 per acre into drainage fund; fees held not authorized by statute).

[153] 3 Antieau, Municipal Corporation Law § 30.06, at 30–19 (1998).

[154] William W. Backus Hospital, Inc. v. City of Norwich, 146 Conn. 686, 155 A.2d 916 (1959); City of Worcester v. Town of Charlton, 336 Mass. 525, 146 N.E.2d 675 (1957); Mary Lanning Memorial Hospital v. Clay County, 170 Neb. 61, 101 N.W.2d 510 (1960); De Goesbriand Memorial Hospital v. Town of Alburg, 122 Vt. 275, 169 A.2d 360 (1961). See Patrick v. Town of Baldwin, 109 Wis. 342, 85 N.W. 274 (1901). The duty to care for indigents is generally held not to exist at common law, and therefore any such duty must be based on statute. See Robbins v. Town of Homer, 95 Minn. 201, 103 N.W. 1023 (1905).

[155] Colusa County v. Glenn County, 117 Cal. 434, 49 P. 457 (1897); Town of Balkan v. Village of Buhl, 158 Minn. 271, 197 N.W. 266 (1924); Strough v. Board of Supervisors, 119 N.Y. 212, 23 N.E. 552 (1890); Village of Indian Hill v. Atkins, 153 Ohio St. 562, 93 N.E.2d 22 (1950); City of Norfolk v. Norfolk County, 120 Va. 356, 91 S.E. 820 (1917). Cf. First National Bank v. Town of York, 212 Wis. 270, 249 N.W. 515 (1933) (school district could recover from town the moneys collected for it by town, acting as its agent). Here, it is irrelevant that the payment may have been voluntarily made. See Town of Balkan v. Village of Buhl, *supra*.

[156] See Roberts v. City of St. Marys, 86 Kan. 403, 121 P. 367 (1912); Bowden v. Kansas City, 69 Kan. 587, 77 P. 573 (1904) (fireman). Cf. Spear v. City of Wichita, 113 Kan. 686, 216 P. 305 (1923) (worker in city

Otherwise, the same rules apply to tort actions against a local government by one of the government's workers as would apply to other tort suits against such locality. Where immunity has been generally applied to the governmental activities of municipalities, this has been applied in actions by a municipality's officers and employees, who have then been denied recovery against the municipality if the injury was suffered while the worker was engaged in "governmental" activities.[157] But recovery has been allowed if the injury occurred while the worker was engaged in "corporate" or "proprietary" functions.[158] Liability has sometimes been denied if the activity in which the worker was engaged was found ultra vires the local government.[159] But gradually, the areas of non-liability are disappearing. Increasingly, local government workers are covered, as to injuries suffered on the job, by state workmen's compensation statutes.[160] And increasingly, as in other areas of possible tort liability of municipalities, the old distinctions—in particular, the distinction between "governmental" and "proprietary" functions—are being swept aside, and liability is being recognized as possible, with limited exceptions, regardless of how the area of activity involved is characterized.

Similarly, the distinctions often applied in the past as to municipal tort liability have usually been held irrelevant as to the *personal* tort liability of municipal officers

---

park); Schmitt v. New York City, 55 N.Y.S.2d 865 (Sup.Ct.1945) (fireman who was inexperienced as a tillerman on a hook-and-ladder truck but was ordered by supervisor to occupy that post, leading to his death).

[157] Hillis v. City of Huntsville, 274 Ala. 663, 151 So.2d 240 (1963) (employee cutting weeds along city streets); Brannan v. City of Brunswick, 49 Ga.App. 62, 174 S.E. 186 (1934) (policeman); Watrous v. City of St. Louis, 281 S.W.2d 594 (Mo.App.1955); Reynolds v. City of Nashua, 93 N.H. 28, 35 A.2d 194 (1943) (street-construction worker); White v. City of Lawton, 373 P.2d 25 (Okl.1961) (police department employee repainting traffic-meter spaces); Ashburn v. Oklahoma City, 192 Okl. 46, 134 P.2d 365 (1943) (garbage collector); Howard v. City of Chattanooga, 170 Tenn. 663, 98 S.W.2d 510 (1936) (prisoner at rock quarry); Bean v. City of Monahans, 403 S.W.2d 155 (Tex. Civ.App.1966), ref'd n.r.e. (garbage truck driver); City of Wichita Falls v. Robison, 121 Tex. 133, 46 S.W.2d 965 (1932) (employee in sanitation department); Haney v. Town of Rainelle, 125 W.Va. 397, 25 S.E.2d 207 (1943) (jailer). Some of these cases would no longer be decided the same way since many jurisdictions have, by statute or judicial action, overturned or limited the effect of the old "governmental-v.-proprietary" distinction.

[158] City of Troy v. McLendon, 279 Ala. 553, 188 So.2d 281 (1966) (electric-utility worker); Sumid v. City of Prescott, 27 Ariz. 111, 230 P. 1103 (1924) (waterworks employee); Ballard v. City of Tampa, 124 Fla. 457, 168 So. 654 (1936) (keeper of prisoners, working-out their sentences on city streets, was negligent, causing a prisoner's death); Rivers v. City of Gainesville, 106 Fla. 267, 143 So. 235 (1932), adhered to 106 Fla. 267, 107 Fla. 774, 144 So. 481 (boiler worker); King v. City of St. Louis, 155 S.W.2d 557 (Mo.App.1941) (auditorium worker); Josupeet v. City of Niagara Falls, 70 Misc. 638, 127 N.Y.S. 527 (Sup.Ct.1910), aff'd 147 A.D. 919, 131 N.Y.S. 1122, appeal denied 148 A.D. 935, 133 N.Y.S. 1127 (city liable for negligence of foreman of street-gang in directing employees to work under overhanging bank); George v. City of Youngstown, 139 Ohio St. 591, 41 N.E.2d 567 (1942) (municipal blacksmith shop); Oklahoma City v. Dobbs, 193 Okl. 183, 142 P.2d 369 (1943) (worker on power shovel); City of Panhandle v. Byrd, 130 Tex. 96, 106 S.W.2d 660 (1937) (city employee operating street grader); Williams v. City of Spokane, 73 Wash. 237, 131 P. 833 (1913) (bridge-construction worker); Parr v. City of Spokane, 67 Wash. 164, 121 P. 453 (1912) (same).

[159] See Foxen v. City of Santa Barbara, 166 Cal. 77, 134 P. 1142 (1913); Roush v. Town of Esmond, 73 S.D. 406, 43 N.W.2d 547 (1950).

[160] See City of St. Petersburg v. Cashman, 71 So.2d 733 (Fla.1954); Crowe v. De Soto Consolidated School District, 246 Iowa 402, 68 N.W.2d 63 (1955); Howard v. City of Detroit, 377 Mich. 102, 139 N.W.2d 677 (1966); Koktavy v. City of New Prague, 246 Minn. 550, 75 N.W.2d 774 (1956) (volunteer fireman covered); Fiore v. New York City, 256 App.Div. 293, 10 N.Y.S.2d 195 (1939) (workmen's compensation remedy is exclusive); Brinker v. City of Greensburg, 409 Pa. 110, 185 A.2d 593 (1962). But some state workmen's compensation laws do *not* cover local government employees. See Bartram v. City of Atlanta, 71 Ga.App. 313, 30 S.E.2d 780 (1944). And some apply only to employees in "proprietary" activities. See Bellevue v. Hall, 295 Ky. 57, 174 S.W.2d 24 (1943). Some do not cover "volunteers" who aid in emergencies. See Seward v. Wisdom, 413 P.2d 931 (Alaska 1966). And some are applicable to local government employees only at the option of the local government. See City of Wichita v. Wyman, 158 Kan. 709, 150 P.2d 154 (1944).

and employees. Municipal workers have been held potentially liable for their on-the-job torts even when engaged in "governmental" functions.[161] And they can be held personally liable even if acting beyond the scope of their authority.[162] But personal immunity *does* apply to certain municipal workers in certain of their undertakings. The immunity is perhaps at its broadest as to judges of local courts; they are immune as to their judicial actions so long as acting with color of jurisdiction.[163] Even *they* are, however, potentially liable if they act completely outside their jurisdiction,[164] though their immunity is not necessarily destroyed merely because they act maliciously.[165] Members of local legislative bodies also enjoy broad immunity, and cannot be held liable for their enactment or non-enactment of legislation.[166] As to executive and administrative

---

[161] See Jabs v. Town of Burlington, 23 Conn.Sup. 158, 178 A.2d 280 (1962); City of Memphis v. Bettis, 512 S.W.2d 270 (Tenn.1974). Compare, as to personal liability of federal officers and employees, Osborn v. Haley, 549 U.S. 225, 127 S.Ct. 881, 166 L.Ed.2d 819 (2007) (federal statute commonly known as the Westfall Act accords federal employees absolute immunity from tort claims arising out of acts undertaken in their official duties; United States will be substituted as defendant in place of a sued employee or officer, and the action is thereafter governed by the Federal Tort Claims Act).

[162] Shellburne v. Roberts, 43 Del.Ch. 485, 238 A.2d 331 (1967); Odinetz v. Budds, 315 Mich. 512, 24 N.W.2d 193 (1946); Connelly v. City of Sedalia, 222 Mo.App. 109, 2 S.W.2d 632 (1928). Both statutes and common law rules grant immunity to officers and employees only if acting within their duties. See Henning v. Rounds, 142 N.M. 803, 171 P.3d 317 (App. 2007) (state statute grants immunity only to public employees for actions performed while in scope of their duties; whether or not employee is within scope of duties is question of fact). But it is sometimes presumed that officers and employees are acting within their authority. See Holgerson v. City of Devils Lake, 63 N.D. 155, 246 N.W. 641 (1933).

[163] Calhoun v. Little, 106 Ga. 336, 32 S.E. 86 (1898); Stewart v. Case, 53 Minn. 62, 54 N.W. 938 (1893). See Cashen v. Spann, 125 N.J.Super. 386, 311 A.2d 192 (1973) mod. 66 N.J. 541, 334 A.2d 8, cert. denied 423 U.S. 829, 96 S.Ct. 48, 46 L.Ed.2d 46, on remand 143 N.J.Super. 560, 364 A.2d 21, aff'd 150 N.J.Super. 500, 376 A.2d 186, rev'd 77 N.J. 138, 389 A.2d 969. Cf. Going v. Dinwiddie, 86 Cal. 633, 25 P. 129 (1890) (justice of the peace). See generally Rubinstein, Liability in Tort of Judicial Officers, 15 U. Toronto L.Rev. 317 (1964); Thompson, Judicial Immunity and the Protection of Justices, 21 Mod. L.Rev. 517 (1958); Note, Torts—Judicial Immunity, 11 Ind.L.Rev. 489 (1978). In recent years, the nearly total immunity of judges has been criticized, and a number of the critics have suggested the substitution of a *qualified* immunity—allowing, for instance, possible liability for judicial malice or for at least the more extreme forms of judicial negligence. See Katz, The Quest for Qualified Judicial Immunity, 36 J.Mo.Bar 376 (1980); Way, A Call for Limits to Judicial Immunity: Must Judges Be Kings in Their Courts?, 64 Judicature 390 (1981); Note, Immunity of Federal and State Judges from Civil Suit—Time for a Qualified Immunity?, 27 Case W. Res.L.Rev. 727 (1977). On judicial immunity under the Federal Civil Rights Act, see note 182 *infra* and accompanying text.

[164] See Nelson v. Kellogg, 162 Cal. 621, 123 P. 1115 (1912) (judge liable when exceeds jurisdiction); Osbekoff v. Mallory, 188 N.W.2d 294 (Iowa 1971); Hoppe v. Klapperich, 224 Minn. 224, 28 N.W.2d 780 (1947); Vickrey v. Dunivan, 59 N.M. 90, 279 P.2d 853 (1955).

[165] The immunity of judges has usually been held not to be overcome by a showing that a judge acted maliciously or corruptly. See Cuiksa v. City of Mansfield, 250 F.2d 700 (6th Cir.1957), cert. denied 356 U.S. 937, 78 S.Ct. 779, 2 L.Ed.2d 813; Curnow v. Kessler, 110 Mich. 10, 67 N.W. 982 (1896). On the reasons for this nearly total immunity of judges, see Jennings, Tort Liability of Administrative Officers, 21 Minn.L.Rev. 263, 271–72 (1937). But *some* authority has found the judicial immunity terminated where the judge acts with malice. Stewart v. Cooley, 23 Minn. 347 (1877). See Osbekoff v. Mallory, *supra* note 164 (when minor magistrate acts wholly without jurisdiction, civil liability attaches for malicious abuse of process, or oppression); Dean v. Kochendorfer, 237 N.Y. 384, 143 N.E. 229 (1924) (if magistrate instigates prosecution before himself without probable cause and deliberately uses process to gratify his personal feelings of importance, this can be illegal abuse of process). See also note 163 *supra* on proposals for limiting judicial immunity.

Public prosecutors often enjoy immunity comparable to that of judges. See Rosenthal v. County of Madison, 339 Mont. 419, 170 P.3d 493 (2007) (prosecutors are entitled to absolute immunity as quasi-judicial officers when their judgment and conduct are functionally comparable to those implemented by judges, as in filing and maintaining criminal charges).

[166] Hough v. Amato, 260 So.2d 537 (Fla.App.1972); Allen v. Secor, 195 So.2d 586 (Fla.App.1967) (zoning ordinance); Bricker v. Sims, 195 Tenn. 361, 259 S.W.2d 661 (1953) (rule applies even if members of legislative body exceeded authority and passed an invalid act). See Pawlowski v. Jenks, 115 Mich. 275, 73 N.W. 238

officers, two distinctions have been of importance: (1) Some courts, even where willing to impose liability for misfeasance (affirmative misconduct), have been reluctant to apply liability to mere nonfeasance—passive inaction or failure to act.[167] (2) As to misfeasance, municipal workers are immune from liability as to their "*discretionary*" acts, but are potentially liable for their "*ministerial*" activities.[168] "Discretionary" acts are those as to which the worker is free to exercise judgment in determining the manner in which the work is performed[169]—for instance, the decision of members of a local housing authority

---

(1897); Incorporated Village of Hicksville v. Blakeslee, 103 Ohio St. 508, 134 N.E. 445 (1921). The immunity of members of the local legislative body as to defamation is generally regarded as qualified; it applies if the statements were made (1) at a duly called meeting, or in the necessary exercise of the member's duties, and (2) concerning a legitimate municipal matter that was being considered or handled at the time, and (3) without malice. See Mills v. Denny, 245 Iowa 584, 63 N.W.2d 222 (1954). Cf. Clark v. McGee, 49 N.Y.2d 613, 427 N.Y.S.2d 740, 404 N.E.2d 1283 (1980), noted 66 A.B.A.J. 1293 (1980) (town supervisor not absolutely immune for remarks made on local radio show). Otherwise, there can be liability. Stanley v. Prince, 118 Me. 360, 108 A. 328 (1919). On the possible liability of municipal legislators when they are engaged in administering the government, rather than legislating, see note 170 *infra*.

[167] See Montanick v. McMillin, 225 Iowa 442, 280 N.W. 608 (1938); Desmarais v. Wachusett Regional School District, 360 Mass. 591, 276 N.E.2d 691 (1971); Trum v. Town of Paxton, 329 Mass. 434, 109 N.E.2d 116 (1952); Fulgoni v. Johnston, 302 Mass. 421, 19 N.E.2d 542 (1939). But many courts have ignored the nonfeasance-misfeasance dichotomy; and courts have been particularly willing to impose liability even for nonfeasance where the inaction involved a failure to perform an absolute obligation imposed by the law. See note 175 *infra*, and accompanying text. On the nonfeasance-misfeasance distinction as generally applied in the tort law of negligence, see Prosser & Keeton, Law of Torts 373–82 (5th ed. 1984).

[168] Elder v. Anderson, 205 Cal.App.2d 326, 23 Cal.Rptr. 48 (Dist.Ct.1962); Lusietto v. Kingan, 107 Ill.App.2d 239, 246 N.E.2d 24 (1969); Weast v. Budd, 186 Kan. 249, 349 P.2d 912 (1960); Gildea v. Ellershaw, 363 Mass. 800, 298 N.E.2d 847 (1973); Weaver v. Lane County, 10 Or.App. 281, 499 P.2d 1351 (1972); Blalock v. Johnston, 180 S.C. 40, 185 S.E. 51 (1936). Cf. City of Homestead v. International Association of Firefighters, 291 So.2d 38 (Fla.App.1974) (applying immunity to "discretionary and legislative" acts); Clark v. Ferling, 220 Md. 109, 151 A.2d 137 (1959) (immunity applied to discretionary, nonmalicious acts of *officials*). See generally Note, Public Officers—Federal Officer's Liability for Damages Done to Property Pursuant to Statutory Authorization, 38 Mich.L.Rev. 1344 (1940); Symposium on civil liability of government officials, 42 Law & Contemp. Prob. 1–114 (Winter, 1978); Prosser, Law of Torts 987–92 (4th ed. 1971). Some commentators have urged abandonment of the "discretionary-v.-ministerial" test in favor of possible liability wherever an officer or employee acts with improper motive or without due care. See Gray, Private Wrongs of Public Servants, 47 Calif.L.Rev. 303 (1959); Jennings, Tort Liability of Administrative Officers, 21 Minn.L.Rev. 263 (1937); Mathes & Jones, Toward a "Scope of Official Duty" Immunity for Police Officers in Damage Actions, 53 Geo.L.J. 889 (1965). Compare, urging total immunity of public officers within the scope of their offices, Davis, Administrative Officers' Tort Liability, 55 Mich.L.Rev. 201 (1956) (government should be made liable for all torts of officers, but should be no personal liability of the officers). See generally Mashaw, Discussion of Civil Liability of Government Officials, 42 Law & Contemp.Prob. 80 (1978).

Some high-level executive officers, at least at the federal and state level, may be immune as to all their official acts, either because all such acts are considered to involve discretion, or simply because such immunity is considered necessary to the desired independence of their conduct. See Nixon v. Fitzgerald, 457 U.S. 731, 102 S.Ct. 2690, 73 L.Ed.2d 349 (1982) (due to special nature of office and functions of President of the U.S., absolute immunity exists as to President's official acts and even for acts within "outer perimeter" of official responsibility). Cf. Bush v. Lucas, 462 U.S. 367, 103 S.Ct. 2404, 76 L.Ed.2d 648 (1983) (aerospace engineer denied judicial remedy against director of federal space flight center for alleged retaliatory demotion); Chappell v. Wallace, 462 U.S. 296, 103 S.Ct. 2362, 76 L.Ed.2d 586 (1983) (Navy enlisted men denied judicial action against superior officers for alleged racial discrimination). Compare Harlow v. Fitzgerald, 457 U.S. 800, 102 S.Ct. 2727, 73 L.Ed.2d 396 (1982) (Presidential aides enjoy only qualified immunity; immune as to their discretionary functions so long as they don't violate clearly established constitutional or statutory rights of which a reasonable person would have known). See generally Oren, Immunity and Accountability in Civil Rights Litigation: Who Should Pay?, 50 U. Pitt. L. Rev. 935 (1989) (particularly discussing the *Harlow* case *supra* and its impact); "Shielding the President," Time, July 5, 1982, at 48. See also Westfall v. Erwin, 484 U.S. 292, 108 S.Ct. 580, 98 L.Ed.2d 619 (1988) (conduct by federal officials must be discretionary in nature, as well as within scope of their employment, before conduct is absolutely immune from state-law tort liability).

[169] Blalock v. Johnston, *supra* note 168. See Churchill v. McKay, 17 Alaska 633, 163 F.Supp. 339 (1958) (municipal clerk charged with statutory duty of keeping records of city owed no duty to taxicab owner to make correct copy of taxicab ordinance as passed and distribute correct copies to cab owners and operators). The

to order the taking and destruction of private property,[170] and a city engineer's acceptance of sewers from a developer.[171] When little or nothing is left to the individual's judgment as to the manner in which to perform a duty, the performance of such duty is "ministerial"[172]—as a peace officer's making an improper arrest[173] or using unnecessary force to effectuate an arrest.[174] Despite the nonfeasance-v.-misfeasance distinction

---

Churchill case *supra* illustrates that the "duty limitation" can also help preclude liability of a government officer or employee, just as that limitation sometimes prevents liability of governmental entities; see section on Alleviation and Abrogation of Governmental Immunity *supra*. Thus, it has been held that a state highway patrol officer ordinarily has a right but no duty to investigate accidents or come to the aid of stranded motorists; but once such an officer undertakes, even voluntarily, to render aid to, or protect, certain members of the public, that officer must perform the undertaking as the reasonably prudent person would. Williams v. State, 34 Cal.3d 18, 192 Cal.Rptr. 233, 664 P.2d 137 (1983). Cf. Dauffenbach v. City of Wichita, 233 Kan. 1028, 667 P.2d 380 (1983) (police officer not liable on claim arising from general duty to prevent crime and enforce laws, but only when there has been breach of specific duty owed an individual); Hendrix v. City of Topeka, 231 Kan. 113, 643 P.2d 129 (1982) (same).

[170] Bridges v. Alaska Housing Authority, 375 P.2d 696 (Alaska 962). Cf. Johnson v. Fossum, 280 Minn. 386, 159 N.W.2d 791 (1968) (municipal fire chief not liable for destruction of property); Buckhannon v. Reppert, 118 W.Va. 10, 188 S.E. 870 (1936) (officer who shot plaintiff's dog not liable for plaintiff's miscarriage, which allegedly resulted from the shooting).

When the local legislative body acts administratively in conducting governmental affairs, the rules generally applied to administrators—including the "discretionary-v.-ministerial" distinction—are applied. Compare Martelli v. Pollock, 162 Cal.App.2d 655, 328 P.2d 795 (Dist.Ct.1958) (fixing terms of contract and rejecting a particular bid held discretionary), and Lacy v. City of Des Moines, 253 Iowa 621, 113 N.W.2d 279 (1962) (authorizing destruction of property was discretionary), with Lemmon v. Clayton, 128 F.Supp. 771 (D.C.Idaho 1955) (duty to maintain public streets is ministerial). Cf. Wille Wittbold & Co. v. Gregory, 41 Mich.App. 511, 200 N.W.2d 351 (1972) (illegally ordering destruction of property held ministerial).

[171] Panepinto v. Edmart, 129 N.J.Super. 319, 323 A.2d 533 (1974).

[172] Pluhowsky v. City of New Haven, 151 Conn. 337, 197 A.2d 645 (1964); State ex rel. Hammond v. Wimberly, 184 Tenn. 132, 196 S.W.2d 561 (1946); Clausen v. Eckstein, 7 Wis.2d 409, 97 N.W.2d 201 (1959); Meyer v. Carman, 271 Wis. 329, 73 N.W.2d 514 (1955). See State v. Stanley, 506 P.2d 1284 (Alaska 1973), reh. denied 509 P.2d 279 (alleged failures of state employees causing sinking of plaintiff's vessel, which had been seized by them, were at operational, not planning, level, and thus not immune); Poch v. Town of East Hartford, 27 Conn.Sup. 463, 243 A.2d 84 (1968) (complaint against municipal sidewalk inspector and building superintendent not subject to demurrer on ground duties discretionary rather than ministerial where complaint did not disclose whether duties discretionary or ministerial). Cf. Gardels v. Murphy, 377 F.Supp. 1389 (N.D.Ill.1974) (Director of White House Advance Office enjoyed immunity, but volunteer "advanceman" whose duties were considered menial did not have immunity).

[173] See McIver v. Russell, 264 F.Supp. 22 (D.Md.1967); Collins v. Los Angeles County, 241 Cal.App.2d 451, 50 Cal.Rptr. 586 (Dist.Ct.1966); Miller v. Fano, 134 Cal. 103, 66 P. 183 (1901) (arrest of innocent person); Wrains v. Rose, 175 So.2d 75 (Fla. App.1965). Cf. Collins v. Jones, 131 Cal.App. 747, 22 P.2d 39 (Dist.Ct.1933) (police captain had woman improperly confined for psychopathic observation); Stine v. Shuttle, 134 Ind.App. 67, 186 N.E.2d 168 (1962) (clerk of court can be liable for issuing warrant for unlawful arrest).

[174] McIver v. Russell, *supra* note 173; Gardner v. McDowell, 202 Kan. 705, 451 P.2d 501 (1969) (liability for needless and wanton injury); Stephens v. City of St. Helens, 231 Or. 1, 371 P.2d 686 (1962). See Sheldon v. City of Ambler, 178 P.3d 459 (Alaska 2008) (police officer who used a bear hug and a "take down" on an intoxicated arrestee, resulting in arrestee's death, could have reasonably believed that his use of force was lawful and not excessive, and thus officer was entitled to qualified immunity from claim of excessive force); Benally v. Robinson, 14 Utah 2d 6, 376 P.2d 388 (1962) (arresting officers owe person arrested a duty of reasonable care). But see Mecham v. Frazier, 193 P.3d 630 (Utah 2008) (state troopers sued for alleged use of excessive force during roadside arrest; Utah Governmental Immunity Act held to confer immunity from *suit*, not just from liability, as to troopers). It is generally agreed that police officers are liable for their negligence in the operation of vehicles. See Wood v. Morris, 109 Ga.App. 148, 135 S.E.2d 484 (1964) (accident while driving child to hospital in police car); Both v. Collins, 339 Ill.App. 437, 90 N.E.2d 285 (1950) (collision with another vehicle); Manwaring v. Geisler, 191 Ky. 532, 230 S.W. 918 (1921) (officer on motorcycle struck and injured child). Cf. Moore v. Cook, 22 Ill.App.2d 48, 159 N.E.2d 496 (1959) (police officer chasing traffic violator struck and injured innocent person; court finds liability, noting that statute requires municipality to indemnify officer held liable under such circumstances).

There is authority that a police officer who wrongfully or negligently shoots a person while the officer is trying to apprehend or arrest a suspect can be held liable. Askay v. Maloney, 85 Or. 333, 166 P. 29 (1917), reh.

mentioned *supra*, liability is often imposed even for failure to act where the failure occurs as to "ministerial" tasks. Thus, it has been held that if a local government officer negligently fails to perform a ministerial duty that is absolutely imposed on him by law, he can be personally liable for his non-performance.[175] And one other principle sweeps across the nonfeasance-misfeasance distinction and various rules on immunity: executive and administrative workers are usually held liable if they act with malice or bad faith, even though acting within an area where they would otherwise enjoy immunity.[176]

The usual rules of vicarious liability don't apply to municipal officials. Such officials are liable for the torts of subordinates only if (1) they order, direct, or participate in the tort, *or* (2) they know or have reason to know that unlawful acts are being committed or have been committed and do nothing to rectify the situation, *or* (3) they ratify or countenance a tort.[177] Thus, a chief of police or sheriff is not ordinarily liable for a false

---

denied 92 Or. 566, 179 P. 899 (jury question whether city detectives were negligent in shooting, on street, at thief who escaped from their custody). But cf. Berry v. Hamman, 203 Va. 596, 125 S.E.2d 851 (1962) (defendant officer not negligent in accidental shooting of another officer while shooting at escaping felon, *and* other officer assumed risk of injury by moving into the open).

Liability in such cases can be based either on intent—but it must then be considered whether the officer was acting within the scope of some privilege such as the privilege of arrest—or on negligence—but the officer's conduct must then be judged under the circumstances, which may have involved an emergency.

[175] See Ellis v. City Council of Burlingame, 222 Cal.App.2d 490, 35 Cal.Rptr. 317 (Dist.Ct.1963) (failure to issue permit to one who qualified); Mock v. City of Santa Rosa, 126 Cal. 330, 58 P. 826 (1899); Upchurch v. Clinton County, 330 S.W.2d 428 (Ky.1959); Ottmann v. Village of Rockville Centre, 275 N.Y. 270, 9 N.E.2d 862 (1937); Meyer v. Carman, 271 Wis. 329, 73 N.W.2d 514 (1955). Cf. Kitchen v. CSX Transp., Inc., 6 F.3d 727 (11th Cir.1993), appeal after remand 19 F.3d 601 (11th Cir.1994) (county commissioner had duty to erect barricades and signs required by state regulation; could be held liable for failure). But in some states, statutes require gross negligence or other extreme misconduct for personal liability of government workers. See Note, Michigan Sovereign Immunity—Michigan Governmental Immunity Statute—Government Employee Tort Liability Is Limited to Those Situations in Which the Conduct at Issue Is Substantially More Than Negligent, 72 U. Detroit Mercy L. Rev. 685 (1995).

It has been held that the doctrine of state sovereignty, as embodied in the Eleventh Amendment to the U.S. Constitution, bars federal courts from ordering state officials to obey state law. Pennhurst State School & Hosp. v. Halderman, 465 U.S. 89, 104 S.Ct. 900, 79 L.Ed.2d 67 (1984) (sometimes called "Pennhurst II"). See generally Freilich, Acconcia & Martin, Judicial Federalism and State Sovereignty, 16 Urban Law. 539 (1984).

[176] See Trimble v. City & County of Denver, 697 P.2d 716 (Colo.1985) (city official's immunity for discretionary acts applies only insofar as conduct is not willful, malicious, or intentionally harmful; could be liability for intentional interference with contract); Shellburne v. Roberts, 43 Del.Ch. 485, 238 A.2d 331 (1967); Runnels v. Okamoto, 56 Hawaii 1, 525 P.2d 1125 (1974); Medeiros v. Kondo, 55 Hawaii 499, 522 P.2d 1269 (1974). Cf. Pluhowsky v. City of New Haven, 151 Conn. 337, 197 A.2d 645 (1964) (local government official not personally liable if acts in good faith and not maliciously); Russell v. Bell, 224 Ky. 298, 6 S.W.2d 236 (1928) (immunity exists if malice or bad faith is not proved); Bahrle v. Mirabelli, 107 N.J.Super. 361, 258 A.2d 383 (1969) (no liability of town clerk or township where clerk made mistake out of ignorance, not due to malice or bad faith); Utah State Univ. v. Sutro & Co., 646 P.2d 715 (Utah 1982) (college officials not liable for mere errors in judgment in investing state funds in common stocks). In one area in particular—liability for refusing to register a prospective voter, or refusing to allow someone to vote—, liability has often been held to depend on improper motive; good faith is a sound defense. See Annot., Personal Liability of Public Officer for Breach of Duty in Respect of Election or Primary Election Laws, 153 A.L.R. 109 (1944).

[177] See Carter v. City of Gadsden, 264 Ala. 544, 88 So.2d 689 (1955); Kangieser v. Zink, 134 Cal.App.2d 559, 285 P.2d 950 (Dist.Ct.1955); Abrahamson v. Ceres, 90 Cal.App.2d 523, 203 P.2d 98 (Dist.Ct.1949); Carter v. Allan, 94 Idaho 190, 484 P.2d 739 (1971) (suit against mayor and city councilman for negligently constructed sidewalk); Taylor v. City of Alexandria, 261 So.2d 92 (La.App.1972); Brown v. City of Shreveport, 129 So.2d 540 (La.App.1961); Hirych v. State, 376 Mich. 384, 136 N.W.2d 910 (1965); Webber v. Andersen, 187 Neb. 9, 187 N.W.2d 290 (1971); Antonelli v. City of Mt. Vernon, 234 N.Y.S.2d 550 (Sup.Ct.1962); Antin v. Union High School District, 130 Or. 461, 280 P. 664 (1929); Commonwealth v. Roberts, 392 Pa. 572, 141 A.2d 393 (1958). Cf. Klam v. Boehm, 72 Idaho 259, 240 P.2d 484 (1952) (chief of police not liable for violent acts committed on

arrest or other tort committed by his subordinate,[178] but can be held liable for his own negligence in failing to discharge a subordinate he knew or should reasonably have known was incompetent.[179]

Besides having possible common-law tort liability, local government officers and employees are also potentially liable—civilly as well as criminally—under the Federal Civil Rights Act.[180] There is usually no immunity under Section 1983 if an officer or

---

prisoner by police officers where chief did not know or have reason to know of acts). But see Bosh v. Cherokee County Building Auth., 305 P.3d 994 (Okla. 2013) (common law doctrine of *respondeat superior* applies to municipal corporations in tort actions). See generally Blum & others, Municipal Liability and Liability of Superiors: Litigation Significance of Recent Trends and Developments, 29 Touro L. Rev. 93 (2012).

[178] Giroux v. Murphy, 88 R.I. 280, 147 A.2d 465 (1959). See Jordan v. Kelly, 223 F.Supp. 731 (W.D.Mo.1963) (with review of cases); Marshall v. County of Los Angeles, 131 Cal.App.2d 812, 281 P.2d 544 (Dist.Ct.1955). Cf. Baisley v. Henry, 55 Cal.App. 760, 204 P. 399 (Dist.Ct.1921) (city trustees not liable for negligence of police chief). Similarly, it has been held that a park commissioner is not liable for the negligence of park employees. Shannon v. Fleischhacker, 116 Cal.App. 258, 2 P.2d 835 (Dist.Ct.1931).

Some cases—mostly older ones—denying a police chief's liability for the torts of his officers based the non-liability on the rule that any misconduct of the chief was mere "nonfeasance," and/or on the rule that if the chief was not shown to have acted maliciously, he could not be liable. See Pearson v. Zehr, 138 Ill. 48, 29 N.E. 854 (1891); Miller v. Horton, 152 Mass. 540, 26 N.E. 100 (1891).

[179] Robinson v. Smith, 211 Cal.App.2d 473, 27 Cal.Rptr. 536 (Dist.Ct.1962); Still v. San Francisco Railroad, 154 Cal. 559, 98 P. 672 (1908); Shirley v. Winnfield, 41 So.2d 136 (La.App.1949). See Beverly v. Morris, 470 F.2d 1356 (5th Cir.1972) (supervisory personnel can be held liable for own negligence in failing to train and supervise subordinates). A police chief or other law-enforcement officer may also be held vicariously liable for the tort of a personally appointed, personally supervised deputy. See Bostatter v. Hinchman, 243 Mich. 589, 220 N.W. 775 (1928).

[180] 42 U.S.C.A. § 1983. See Monroe v. Pape, 365 U.S. 167, 81 S.Ct. 473, 5 L.Ed.2d 492 (1961); Dean v. Gladney, 621 F.2d 1331 (5th Cir.1980), cert. denied 450 U.S. 983, 101 S.Ct. 1521, 67 L.Ed.2d 819 (law enforcement officers liable under Section 1983, but municipality not liable thereunder on a mere *respondeat superior* basis); O'Neal v. Gresham, 519 F.2d 803 (4th Cir.1975) (employee dismissed because she wouldn't disclose how she voted in recent election); Pierson v. Ray, 352 F.2d 213 (5th Cir.1965); mod. 386 U.S. 547, 87 S.Ct. 1213, 18 L.Ed.2d 288 (1967); Hornsby v. Allen, 326 F.2d 605 (5th Cir.1964), reh. denied 330 F.2d 55 (wrongful refusal of liquor license); Jordan v. Kelly, 223 F.Supp. 731 (W.D.Mo.1963) reh. denied 425 U.S. 985, 96 S.Ct. 2194, 48 L.Ed.2d 811. Compare Paul v. Davis, 424 U.S. 693, 96 S.Ct. 1155, 47 L.Ed.2d 405 (1976), reh. denied 425 U.S. 985, 96 S.Ct. 2194, 48 L.Ed.2d 811 (1976), (plaintiff charged that police chiefs had deprived him of constitutional right to privacy by distributing defamatory flyer; held that no civil-rights claim stated). See generally C. Antieau, Federal Civil Rights Acts—Civil Practice (1971); Hardy & Weeks, Personal Liability of Public Officials Under Federal Law (Institute of Government, Univ. of Ga.1980), reviewed 13 Urban Law. 528 (1981); Jaron, The Threat of Personal Liability Under the Federal Civil Rights Act: Does It Interfere with the Performance of State and Local Government?, 13 Urban Law. 1 (1981); Note, Civil Rights Suits Against State and Local Governmental Entities and Officials: Rights of Action, Immunities, and Federalism, 53 S. Cal. L. Rev. 945 (1980) (good review of liability of both local governments and their agents); Annot., Actionability, Under 42 U.S.C. § 1983, of Claims Against Persons Other Than Police Officers for False Arrest or False Imprisonment, 44 A.L.R.Fed. 225 (1979); Annot., Police Action in Connection with Arrest as Violation of Civil Rights Act, 1 A.L.R.Fed. 519 (1969). See also Newman, Suing the Lawbreakers: Proposals to Strengthen the Section 1983 Damage Remedy for Law Enforcers' Misconduct, 87 Yale L.J. 447 (1978).

On *vicarious* personal liability under the Federal Civil Rights Act, see Annot., Vicarious Liability of Superior Under 42 U.S.C. § 1983 for Subordinate's Acts in Deprivation of Civil Rights, 51 A.L.R.Fed. 285 (1981). As to the standard for liability, see Vance v. Ball State University, ___ U.S. ___, 133 S.Ct. 2434 (2013) (employee is a "supervisor" for purposes of Title VII of Federal Civil Rights Act only if he or she is empowered by the employer to take tangible employment actions against the victim, and thus the employer may be vicariously liable under Title VII only if the tortfeasor meets that definition). There is considerable confusion over whether a government supervisor can be held vicariously liable under Section 1983. There is dictum in Ashcroft v. Iqbal, 556 U.S. 662, 129 S.Ct. 1937 (2009), indicating there is no such supervisory vicarious liability. But Connick v. Thompson, 563 U.S. 51, 131 S.Ct. 1350, 179 L.Ed.2d 417 (2011), seems to the contrary, though applying a stringent standard that requires deliberate indifference and finding the standard not met here. See Comment, Supervisory Liability Under 42 U.S.C. § 1983 in the Wake of *Iqbal* and *Connick*: It May Be Misconceived, But It's Not a Misnomer, 56 Ariz. L. Rev. 602 (2014). See generally Note, Municipal Liability? Not So Fast: What *Connick v. Thompson* Means for Future Prosecutorial Misconduct, 63 Mercer L. Rev. 1113

employee knew or should reasonably have known that some action he took would violate a person's constitutional rights, or if the action was taken with the malicious intention of depriving a person of some such right.[181] But judicial officers are nonetheless treated

---

(2012). See also Gelfand, Suing and Defending Cities for Federal Constitutional Violations (Lexis 3d ed. 2003) (dealing with Section 1983 claims in §§ 6.01–.05). While Monroe v. Pape, *supra*, denied any liability of a *municipality* under Section 1983 of the Federal Civil Rights Act, this rule was changed by Monell v. Department of Social Services, 436 U.S. 658, 98 S.Ct. 2018, 56 L.E.2d 611 (1978).

It has been held that Federal Civil Rights Act suits against local governments and/or their agents should be characterized as personal injury actions for statute-of-limitations purposes. Wilson v. Garcia, 471 U.S. 261, 105 S.Ct. 1938, 85 L.Ed.2d 254 (1985) (action against police officer and chief of police; New Mexico three-year limitations statute governing actions for injury to person held to govern Section 1983 suit). Cf. Wallace v. Kato, 549 U.S. 384, 127 S.Ct. 1091, 166 L.Ed.2d 973 (2007), reh. denied 549 U.S. 1362, 127 S.Ct. 2090, 167 L.Ed.2d 807 (2007) (state statute of limitations for personal-injury torts applies in a Section 1983 action, but accrual date is question of federal law).

Some cases have also recognized that there may be a cause of action directly under the federal Constitution for violation of a person's constitutional rights. See Bivens v. Six Unknown Named Agents of Federal Bureau of Narcotics, 403 U.S. 388, 91 S.Ct. 1999, 29 L.Ed.2d 619 (1971) (cause of action under Fourth Amendment). Cf. District of Columbia v. Carter, 409 U.S. 418, 432–433, 93 S.Ct. 602, 610, 34 L.Ed.2d 613 (1973), reh. denied 410 U.S. 959, 93 S.Ct. 1411, 35 L.Ed.2d 694 (District of Columbia and its officers not liable under Federal Civil Rights Act—prior to 1979 amendment—, but Court says could be liability of officer for deprivation of constitutional rights). But only personal liability—not vicarious liability under *respondeat superior*—can be based on such violation of constitutional rights. See Dean v. Gladney, *supra* (liability could not be imposed on county or municipalities for unlawful arrests made by their employees). See generally Dellinger, Of Rights and Remedies: The Constitution as a Sword, 85 Harv.L.Rev. 1532 (1972); Lehmann, *Bivens* and its Progeny: The Scope of a Constitutional Cause of Action for Torts Committed by Government Officials, 4 Hastings Con. L.Q. 531 (1977); Annot., Implication of Private Right of Action from Provision of United States Constitution—Federal Cases, 64 L.Ed.2d 872 (1981) (noting that the *Monell* case, *supra*, usually renders unnecessary the implication of a cause of action under the Fourteenth Amendment in order to redress a violation of constitutional rights). See also Comment, *Bivens* Actions for Equal Protection Violations: *Davis v. Passman*, 92 Harv.L.Rev. 745 (1979). In Wilkie v. Robbins, 551 U.S. 537, 127 S.Ct. 2588, 168 L.Ed.2d 389 (2007), the Court held that a landowner did not have a private action under *Bivens* against Bureau of Land Management employees where their alleged activities of trying to induce the landowner to grant an easement for public use were perfectly legitimate and where the government, as a landowner, had a valid interest in gaining access to neighboring lands. As to property cases under the *Bivens* doctrine, see generally Note, An End-run Around the Takings Clause? The Law and Economics of *Bivens* Actions for Property Rights Violations, 50 Wm. & Mary L. Rev. 1739 (2009).

The U.S. Supreme Court has said that the factors necessary to establish a *Bivens* violation of the U.S. Constitution vary according to the constitutional provision at issue and that if the claim is for invidious discrimination in contravention of the First and Fifth Amendments, plaintiff must plead and prove that the defendant acted with discriminatory purpose. Ashcroft v. Iqbal, *supra* (Muslim Pakistani detainee alleged that government officials took series of unconstitutional actions against him in connection with his confinement; complaint failed to plead sufficient facts to state a claim for purposeful and unlawful discrimination). See Blum, Supervisory Liability After *Iqbal*: Misunderstood But Not Misnamed, 43 Urban Law. 541 (2011) (where plaintiff alleges a claim that requires a showing of discriminatory purpose, plaintiff must allege and prove that a supervisor himself had the impermissible purpose in order to establish supervisor's liability; mere knowledge of a subordinate's discriminatory purpose is not enough; *id.* at 542).

As to possible tort liability for constitutional violations apart from the *Bivens* doctrine, see M. Haskel & W. Haskel, Truth, Justice and a Healthy Fear of Deceiving the Public: An Argument for Imposing Constitutional Tort Liability for Fraudulent Misrepresentations by Executive Branch Officers, 28 Quinnipiac L. Rev. 491 (2010). In some cases, a plaintiff asserts a claim under Section 1983 of the Federal Civil Rights Act and alternatively under the *Bivens* Doctrine. See Reichle v. Howards, 566 U.S. ___, 132 S.Ct. 2088, 182 L.Ed.2d 985 (2012) (Secret Service agents enjoyed qualified immunity under both theories; this immunity shields government officials from civil damages liability for violating a constitutional right unless the right was clearly established at the time of the challenged conduct).

[181] Wood v. Strickland, 420 U.S. 308, 95 S.Ct. 992, 43 L.Ed.2d 214 (1975), reh. denied 421 U.S. 921, 95 S.Ct. 1589, 43 L.Ed.2d 790 (school officials enjoy "qualified" good faith immunity but not immune if they acted with malice or if they knew or should have known their actions would violate students' constitutional rights); McGhee v. Draper, 564 F.2d 902 (10th Cir.1977). Immunity may thus be said to require "good faith." See Gomez v. Toledo, 446 U.S. 635, 100 S.Ct. 1920, 64 L.Ed.2d 572 (1980) (plaintiff need not allege that defendant-official acted in bad faith; burden is on defendant to plead good faith as an affirmative defense); O'Connor v.

as having nearly complete immunity. Thus, a judge is immune under the Federal Civil Rights Act unless acting in the clear absence of all jurisdiction,[182] and a prosecuting

---

Donaldson, 422 U.S. 563, 95 S.Ct. 2486, 45 L.Ed.2d 396 (1975), on remand 519 F.2d 59 (5th Cir.) (superintendent of state hospital could be liable if he kept patient confined maliciously or if superintendent knew or should reasonably have known his action violated patient's constitutional rights). Compare Owen v. City of Independence, 445 U.S. 622, 100 S.Ct. 1398, 63 L.Ed.2d 673 (1980), on remand 623 F.2d 550 (8th Cir.) (*municipality* may not assert good faith of its officers as defense to *municipal* liability under Section 1983). "Good faith" is thus a valid defense in a Section 1983 action against an individual government agent, but is not a valid defense as to the government itself. See Annot., Defense of Good Faith in Action for Damages Against Law Enforcement Official Under 42 U.S.C. § 1983, Providing for Liability of Person Who, Under Color of Law, Subjects Another to Deprivation of Rights, 61 A.L.R. Fed. 7 (1983). On personal liability of municipal officials under Section 1983, see generally Weeks, Personal Liability Under Federal Law: Major Developments Since *Monell*, 12 Urban Lawyer 263 (1980). On criminal liability of state and local officials, see United States v. Gillock, 445 U.S. 360, 100 S.Ct. 1185, 63 L.Ed.2d 454 (1980) (in federal criminal prosecution against state legislator, there is no privilege barring introduction of evidence of the legislator's legislative acts).

There is clearly no liability under the Federal Civil Rights Act unless plaintiff meets the threshold requirement of showing that he was deprived of a right secured by the Constitution and laws. See Baker v. McCollan, 443 U.S. 137, 99 S.Ct. 2689, 61 L.Ed.2d 433 (1979), on remand 601 F.2d 903 (5th Cir.) (due to mistaken identity, plaintiff had been arrested and jailed for crime he did not commit; but was no deprivation of rights since Constitution does not guarantee that only the guilty will be arrested). It has been held that the Attorney General of the United States enjoys only qualified immunity under the Federal Civil Rights Act—*i.e.*, immunity so long as his actions do not violate clearly established statutory or constitutional rights of which a reasonable person would have known. Mitchell v. Forsyth, 472 U.S. 511, 105 S.Ct. 2806, 86 L.Ed.2d 411 (1985), on remand 772 F.2d 894 (3d Cir.1985). Cf. Davis v. Scherer, 468 U.S. 183, 104 S.Ct. 3012, 82 L.Ed.2d 139 (1984), reh. denied 468 U.S. 1226, 105 S.Ct. 26, 82 L.Ed.2d 919 (1984) (officials not liable for discharge of highway patrol employee where there was no clearly established Due Process right that was violated when the employee, who was in the civil service, was discharged without a pretermination hearing). Compare Malley v. Briggs, 475 U.S. 335, 106 S.Ct. 1092, 89 L.Ed.2d 271 (1986) (possible liability of police officer who caused plaintiffs to be unconstitutionally arrested by presenting judge with a complaint and affidavit which failed to establish probable cause). Cf. West v. Atkins, 487 U.S. 42, 108 S.Ct. 2250, 101 L.Ed.2d 40 (1988) (physician who was under contract with the state to provide medical services to inmates at state prison hospital was potentially liable under Federal Civil Rights Act for his conduct).

While an officer sued in an official capacity enjoys only those immunities possessed by the governmental entity for whom he works, an officer sued in his personal capacity may assert such personal immunity defenses as reasonable reliance on existing law. Hafer v. Melo, 502 U.S. 21, 112 S.Ct. 358, 116 L.Ed.2d 301 (1991). See generally Lee, Qualified Immunity Under 42 U.S.C. § 1983 for Public Officials, 25 Urban Law. 97 (1993); Micas, The Doctrinal Bases for Absolute and Qualified Public Official Immunities, 29 Urban Law. 47 (1997). On what constitutes the "qualified immunity" often granted public officials, see Pearson v. California, 555 U.S. 223, 129 S.Ct. 808, 172 L.Ed.2d 565 (2009) (qualified immunity protects government officials from liability for civil damages insofar as their conduct does not violate clearly established statutory or constitutional rights of which a reasonable person would have known). On the disagreement as to the *extent of supervisory* liability under Section 1983, see Kinports, The Buck Does Not Stop Here: Supervisory Liability in Section 1983 Cases, 1997 U. Ill. L. Rev. 147 (courts have rejected negligence or vicarious liability in favor of a higher culpability requirement). Cf. Prentzel v. State of Alaska, 53 P.3d 587 (Alaska 2002) (a supervisor may be liable under Section 1983 only if there exists either his or her personal involvement in the constitutional deprivation *or* there is a sufficient causal connection between the supervisor's wrongful conduct and the constitutional violation). Cf. note 180, para. 2, *supra*.

[182] Stump v. Sparkman, 435 U.S. 349, 98 S.Ct. 1099, 55 L.Ed.2d 331 (1978), reh. denied 436 U.S. 951, 98 S.Ct. 2862, 56 L.Ed.2d 795, on remand 601 F.2d 261 (7th Cir.). Cf. Butz v. Economou, 438 U.S. 478, 98 S.Ct. 2894, 57 L.Ed.2d 895 (1978), on remand 466 F.Supp. 1351 (D.C.N.Y.), aff'd 633 F.2d 203 (2d Cir.) (persons performing adjudicatory functions within federal agencies are also entitled to absolute immunity from civil liability for their judicial acts). Compare Dennis v. Sparks, 449 U.S. 24, 101 S.Ct. 183, 66 L.Ed.2d 185 (1980) (fact that state court judge had been dismissed from action on grounds of immunity did not preclude action against private parties alleged to have conspired with him; noted that even the judge, though immune from civil liability, could be found *criminally* liable for the violation of civil rights under 18 U.S.C.A. § 242). See generally Rosenberg, *Stump v. Sparkman*: The Doctrine of Judicial Immunity, 64 Va.L.Rev. 833 (1978); Note, Liability of Judicial Officers Under Section 1983, 79 Yale L.J. 322 (1969); Annot., Supreme Court's Views as to Civil Liability of Judges, 55 L.Ed.2d 850 (1979). See also Annot., Rights to Relief Under Federal Civil Rights Act of 1871 for Alleged Wrongful Commitment to or Confinement in Mental Hospital, 16 A.L.R.Fed. 440 (1973), noting the roadblocks to recovery—including judicial immunity—in wrongful commitment cases. The absolute immunity of judges from Section 1983 liability is, however, limited to the judges' adjudicatory functions, as

attorney acting within the scope of his duties is totally immune.[183] Where a state or municipal officer or employee is held liable under the Federal Civil Rights Act, the liability *can* include punitive damages if the defendant's conduct was motivated by evil intent or involved callous indifference to federally protected rights.[184]

---

opposed to administrative functions. Forrester v. White, 484 U.S. 219, 108 S.Ct. 538, 98 L.Ed.2d 555 (1988), on remand 846 F.2d 29 (7th Cir.1988) (immunity did not extend to a state judge's allegedly wrongful demotion and dismissal of a probation officer). See generally Mireles v. Waco, 502 U.S. 9, 112 S.Ct. 286, 116 L.Ed.2d 9 (1991), on remand 962 F.2d 865 (9th Cir.1992) (judge's immunity is overcome in only two sets of circumstances: where actions are not taken by judge in judicial capacity, and where actions, though judicial, are taken in complete absence of all jurisdiction).

[183] Imbler v. Pachtman, 424 U.S. 409, 96 S.Ct. 984, 47 L.Ed.2d 128 (1976). See Burns v. Reed, 500 U.S. 478, 111 S.Ct. 1934, 114 L.Ed.2d 547 (1991), on remand 958 F.2d 374 (7th Cir.1992) (state prosecutor's appearance in court in support of application for search warrant and presentation of evidence at hearing were protected by absolute immunity). But see Barbera v. Smith, 836 F.2d 96 (2d Cir.1987), cert. denied 489 U.S. 1065, 109 S.Ct. 1338, 103 L.Ed.2d 808 (1989) (prosecutors sued on constitutional tort theory are entitled to qualified, not absolute, immunity in performance of investigatory duties so long as is no clear violation of constitutional or statutory rights). Compare Van de Kamp v. Goldstein, 555 U.S. 335, 129 S.Ct. 855, 172 L.Ed.2d 706 (2009) (district attorney and chief deputy district attorney were entitled to *absolute* prosecutorial immunity in Section 1983 due process action), with Filarsky v. Delia, 566 U.S. ___, 132 S.Ct. 1657, 182 L.Ed.2d 662 (2012) (attorney who was retained by city to assist in conducting official investigation into firefighter's potential wrongdoing was entitled to seek *qualified* immunity in Section 1983 suit alleging violation of Fourth Amendment rights). Cf. Whitlock v. Brueggemann, 682 F.3d 567 (7th Cir. 2012) (prosecutors have absolute immunity only in the prosecutorial stage and are not protected by even qualified immunity where they have participated in falsifying evidence in the investigative phase of a criminal investigation). See generally Annot., Immunity of Prosecuting Attorney or Similar Officer from Action for False Arrest or Imprisonment, 79 A.L.R.3d 882 (1977). A public defender cannot be held liable under the Federal Civil Rights Act for conduct in connection with representing an indigent, since the attorney-client relationship is essentially a private, nongovernmental one. Polk County v. Dodson, 454 U.S. 312, 102 S.Ct. 445, 70 L.Ed.2d 509 (1981). See Black v. Bayer, 672 F.2d 309 (3d Cir.1982), cert. denied sub nom. Stoica v. Stewart, 459 U.S. 916, 103 S.Ct. 230, 74 L.Ed.2d 182 (1982) (absolute immunity accorded both public and privately retained counsel paid by the state, and absolute immunity is granted a public defender and an investigator against charges of conspiring with the prosecuting attorney). But see Tower v. Glover, 467 U.S. 914, 104 S.Ct. 2820, 81 L.Ed.2d 758 (1984) (public defender is not immune from Section 1983 liability for conspiring with other officials to deprive his client of constitutional rights). Cf. on conspiracy liability Dennis v. Sparks, *supra* note 182 (even the absolute immunity of one person does not provide immunity to a person who conspired with him, or acted in concert with him). As to the possible immunity of witnesses from Section 1983 liability, see Briscoe v. LaHue, 460 U.S. 325, 103 S.Ct. 1108, 75 L.Ed.2d 96 (1983) (action against a private or governmental witness—in this case, a police officer—for allegedly perjured testimony cannot be brought under Section 1983; Federal Civil Rights Act held not to have abrogated the common-law immunity of witnesses, though the possibility of criminal liability remains).

Absolute immunity has been accorded officials acting in a legislative capacity. Bogan v. Scott-Harris, 523 U.S. 44, 118 S.Ct. 966, 140 L.Ed.2d 79 (1998) (local legislators are absolutely immune from Section 1983 liability for their legislative activities, such as passage of ordinance); Lake Country Estates v. Tahoe Regional Planning Agency, 440 U.S. 391, 99 S.Ct. 1171, 59 L.Ed.2d 401 (1979), on remand 474 F.Supp. 901 (D.C. Nev.); Hernandez v. City of Lafayette, 643 F.2d 1188 (5th Cir.1981), reh. denied 649 F.2d 336. See Latino Political Action Committee, Inc. v. City of Boston, 581 F.Supp. 478 (D.Mass.1984) (members of city council absolutely immune under Section 1983 for acts within sphere of legitimate activity, such as adoption of election district plan, but mayor found not immune from suit on ground that he had failed to show that complaint ran against him only in his legislative capacity); Searingtown Corp. v. Incorporated Village of North Hills, 575 F.Supp. 1295 (E.D.N.Y.1981) (zoning board absolutely immune from suit for damages and equitable relief regarding its legislative activities).

[184] Smith v. Wade, 461 U.S. 30, 103 S.Ct. 1625, 75 L.Ed.2d 632 (1983) (reformatory guard could be liable in punitive damages on a finding of reckless or careless disregard or indifference to inmate's rights or safety; same threshold for punitive damages applies even where, as here, the underlying standard for compensatory—damage liability is also one of recklessness). See Yeager v. Hurt, 433 So.2d 1176 (Ala.1983) (punitive damages upheld against police officer, sued under Section 1983, where officer had legitimately seized plaintiff's motorcycle pursuant to search warrant but then failed to return the cycle for over two years). See also Kolstad v. American Dental Ass'n, 527 U.S. 526, 119 S.Ct. 2118, 144 L.Ed.2d 494 (1999) (in action for gender-based discrimination brought under Title VII of Federal Civil Rights Act, employer could be held liable for punitive damages if the employer discriminated in face of perceived risk that its actions would violate federal law). Compare City of Newport v. Fact Concerts, Inc., 453 U.S. 247, 101 S.Ct. 2748, 69 L.Ed.2d 616 (1981)

It should be noted that statutes in a number of states require local governments to indemnify their officers or employees who are held liable for torts committed in the good faith performance of their duties; such statutes have been upheld.[185] Some statutes merely *authorize* local governments to indemnify their workers for tort liability incurred, without malice or bad faith, in the course of local government employment; these, too, have been sustained by the courts,[186] as have statutes either authorizing or requiring local governmental units to obtain liability insurance covering their officers or employees for liability arising from their employment.[187]

A developing area of liability of municipal officers and employees consists of what are often called the "implication cases." These are cases in which damage and/or injunctive suits are brought by individuals claiming that state or local officials (or the officials of non-profit organizations) have violated the standards of federal grants, made to such governments or organizations, to the prejudice of the suing individuals. It has long been recognized that private causes of action could be based on the violation of federal regulatory statutes; but such statutes, and thus such actions, have been confined to rather limited areas.[188] The prevalence in recent times of federal grants, together with the developing judicial rule that a private cause of action may be maintained by a person harmed by violation of a grant's standards if a legislative intent to allow such a remedy can be found, has opened up a potentially broad new road to tort recoveries against local officials.[189]

(municipality not liable for punitive damages under Section 1983 unless taxpayers of the municipality can be shown directly responsible for an outrageous abuse of constitutional rights). Cf. Barnes v. Gorman, 536 U.S. 181, 122 S.Ct. 2097, 153 L.Ed.2d 230 (2002), holding that punitive damages may not be awarded in private suits brought under the Americans with Disabilities Act and the Rehabilitation Act.

[185] Titus v. Lindberg, 49 N.J. 66, 228 A.2d 65 (1967); City of Chattanooga v. Harris, 223 Tenn. 51, 442 S.W.2d 602 (1969). Most of the statutes contain exceptions—often providing that there is no duty to indemnify for punitive damages, or for *any* damages paid due to willful wrongdoing. Some statutes apply only to the torts (with the usual exceptions) of police officers and firefighters. See Arnolt v. City of Highland Park, 52 Ill.2d 27, 282 N.E.2d 144 (1972) (police); Hansen v. Raleigh, 391 Ill. 536, 63 N.E.2d 851 (1945) (firemen). See generally Annot., Validity and Construction of Statute Authorizing or Requiring Governmental Unit to Indemnify Public Officer or Employee for Liability Arising out of Performance of Public Duties, 71 A.L.R.3d 90 (1976).

[186] See Douglas v. City of Minneapolis, 304 Minn. 259, 230 N.W.2d 577 (1975). Cf. City of Kingsport v. Quillen, 512 S.W.2d 569 (Tenn.1974) (city "authorized and required" by charter to provide indemnity unless judgment arose from willful wrong-doing). See generally Annot., *supra* note 185.

[187] Marshall-Putnam Farm Bureau, Inc. v. Shaver, 12 Ill.App.3d 402, 299 N.E.2d 10 (1973); Sullivan v. Midlothian Park District, 51 Ill.2d 274, 281 N.E.2d 659 (1972); City of Albuquerque v. Campbell, 68 N.M. 75, 358 P.2d 698 (1960). See generally Annot., Validity and Construction of Statute Authorizing or Requiring Governmental Unit to Procure Liability Insurance Covering Public Officers or Employees for Liability Arising out of Performance of Public Duties, 71 A.L.R.3d 6 (1976). On the implied power of municipal corporations to carry insurance, see 56 Am. Jur.2d Municipal Corporations, Counties, and Other Political Subdivisions § 548 (1971). On implied powers, see generally Chapter 8 *supra*.

[188] See Pillai, Negative Implication: The Demise of Private Rights of Action in Federal Courts, 47 U.Cin.L.Rev. 1 (1978).

[189] See Cappalli, Federal Grants and the New Statutory Tort: State and Local Officials Beware!, 12 Urban Lawyer 445 (1980). See generally R. Cappalli, Rights and Remedies Under Federal Grants 115–15, 137–42, 343–44 (Bureau of Nat'l Affairs 1979). On the number and importance of federal grants in recent years, see Cappalli, Federal Grants Disputes: The Lawyer's Next Domain, 11 Urban Law. 377, 392–93 (1979). The "implication" doctrine received its major impetus in Cort v. Ash, 422 U.S. 66, 95 S.Ct. 2080, 45 L.Ed.2d 26 (1975), in which the Court (in an opinion by Justice Brennan) *denied* a private claim in behalf of stockholders based on corporate expenditures alleged to have violated criminal laws but in which the Court also laid down the principles to be considered in an "implication" case. A notable use of the "implication" doctrine occurred in Naughton v. Bevilacqua, 458 F.Supp. 610 (D.R.I.1978), aff'd 605 F.2d 586 (1st Cir.), where the court inferred a private tort claim from grant-in-aid standards applicable to a federal grant to a doctor, who had injured

plaintiff-patient, at a state mental institution. Compare Pennhurst State School Hospital v. Halderman, 451 U.S. 1, 101 S.Ct. 1531, 67 L.Ed.2d 694 (1981) (Developmentally Disabled Assistance and Bill of Rights Act did not create substantive rights to appropriate treatment in individual mental-health patients).

Chapter 27

EXTRAORDINARY ACTIONS AND REMEDIES AS TO LOCAL GOVERNMENTS

Analysis

§ 27.1 Kinds of Extraordinary Remedies

Apart from the regular legislative and judicial processes, certain exceptional remedies are sometimes available to citizens of a municipality. Some—such as initiative and referendum—are employed to enact legislation, amend existing legislation, or reject proposed legislative measures. Recall is a "popular" method that can be used to oust a public officer. Injunctions and mandamus are among the exceptional *judicial* remedies that may occasionally be used to compel or to prevent particular action by municipal agents.

§ 27.2 The Initiative

In many jurisdictions, the state constitution or a state statute provides that local governments may enact legislation through the process of initiative—*i.e.*, a process by which the electorate petitions for and votes on a proposed law.[1] The power of initiative

---

[1] See Crouch, The Initiative and Referendum in Cities, 37 Am.Pol.Sci.Rev. 491 (1943); Sirico, Constitutionality of the Initiative and Referendum, 65 Iowa L.Rev. 637 (1980); Stewart, Law of Initiative Referendum in Massachusetts, 12 New England L.Rev. 455 (1977); Note, Initiative and Referendum—Do They Encourage or Impair Better State Government?, 5 Fla.St. U.L.Rev. 925 (1977); Note, Constitutional Constraints on Initiative and Referendum, 32 Vand.L.Rev. 1143 (1979); Note, Constitutionality of the Referendum, 41 Yale L.J. 132 (1931). For a critical view of the initiative and referendum, see Warner, Direct Democracy: The Right of the People to Make Fools of Themselves; The Use and Abuse of Initiative and Referendum, A Local Government Perspective, 19 Seattle U.L. Rev. 47 (1995). For good discussions of experiences with the initiative and referendum in particular states, see Bradley & Williams, "Be It Enacted by the People of the State of Alaska . . ."—A Practitioner's Guide to Alaska's Initiative Law, 9 Alaska L. Rev. 279 (1992); Gray & Kiley, The Initiative and Referendum in Massachusetts, 26 New England L. Rev. 27 (1991); Comment, Executive, Legislative, and Judicial Power over Direct Legislation in Arizona, 23 Ariz. St. L.J. 1111 (1991); Comment, The Current Use of the Initiative and Referendum in Ohio and Other States, 53 U. Cinc. L. Rev. 541 (1984). See generally Dubois & Feeney, Lawmaking by Initiative: Issues, Options, and Comparisons (Agathon Press 1998); Schrag, Paradise Lost: California's Experience, America's Future (The New Press 1998), both reviewed in Clark, Direct Democracy in America, 97 Mich. L. Rev. 1560 (1999). On proposals for a *national* initiative, see Allen, National Initiative Proposal: A Preliminary Analysis, 58 Neb.L.Rev. 965 (1979); Black,

can never be broader than the general powers of the local government; and an initiative measure must, just like any other law of the local unit, be within those powers expressly or impliedly given that unit by state statute or home-rule charter.[2] And a law passed by initiative even in a home-rule city must yield to any conflicting state law as to all matters of state-wide, or general, concern.[3]

There are three steps that are customarily required for the passage of an ordinance by the initiative process, and there must be substantial compliance with all requirements.[4] (1) It is often required that there be some form of published notice of the

---

National Lawmaking by Initiative? Let's Think Twice, 8 Human Rights 28 (1979). For adverse criticisms of use of the initiative, see Abrams, The Majority Will: A Case Study of Misinformation, Manipulation, and the Oregon Initiative Process, 87 Or. L. Rev. 1025 (2008); Vitiello, Why the Initiative Process Is the Wrong Way to Go: Lessons We Should Have Learned From Proposition 215, 43 McGeorge L. Rev. 63 (2012). See also Ngo, The Elephant in the Room: A Critique of California's Constitutional Amendment Process that Gave Birth to the Baby Elephant (Proposition 8) and a Call for Its Reform, 33 T. Jefferson L. Rev. 235 (2011).

2 See Municipality of Anchorage v. Frohne, 568 P.2d 3 (Alaska 1977); Mitchell v. Walker, 140 Cal.App.2d 239, 295 P.2d 90 (Dist.Ct.1956); Baum v. City of St. Louis, 343 Mo. 738, 123 S.W.2d 48 (1938); State ex rel. Andersen v. Leahy, 189 Neb. 92, 199 N.W.2d 713 (1972); Custer v. City of Robinson, 79 S.D. 91, 108 N.W.2d 211 (1961). Cf. Bagley v. City of Manhattan Beach, 18 Cal.3d 22, 132 Cal.Rptr. 668, 553 P.2d 1140 (1976) (local government had no power to set compensation of public employees by administrative order or arbitrator's award; such power could not be created by an initiative). But cf. City of Youngstown v. Craver, 127 Ohio St. 195, 187 N.E. 715 (1933) (home-rule charter city could abolish its charter under initiative and referendum provisions of general state law). Of course, initiated measures are subject to constitutional limitations, just as other ordinances are. See City & County of San Francisco v. Market Street Railway, 98 F.2d 628 (9th Cir.1938), cert. denied 305 U.S. 657, 59 S.Ct. 357, 83 L.Ed. 426 (1939), reh. denied 306 U.S. 667, 59 S.Ct. 460, 83 L.Ed. 1062 (ordinance cannot be unreasonable or discriminatory); Snowden v. Smith, 328 S.W.2d 528 (Ky.1959) (ordinance cannot violate Contract Clause); In re Initiative Petition No. 332, 776 P.2d 556 (Okl.1989) (proposed state law gave commission unlimited authority to disburse public funds, thus unconstitutionally delegating legislative power).

Within the above-stated limitations, the power of initiative—it is often observed—should be liberally construed. See Barnes v. City of Miami, 47 So.2d 3 (Fla.1950); State ex rel. Sharpe v. Hitt, 155 Ohio St. 529, 99 N.E.2d 659 (1951); Glass v. Smith, 150 Tex. 632, 244 S.W.2d 645 (1951). Cf. D'Ascensio v. Benjamin, 137 N.J.Super. 155, 348 A.2d 219 (1975), aff'd 142 N.J.Super. 52, 359 A.2d 885 (provisions for initiative and referendum are to be liberally construed; petition not outdated though it took 18 months to collect signatures). And courts are often reluctant to rule on the validity of laws proposed by initiative prior to those laws being actually enacted. See In re Initiative Petition No. 360, 879 P.2d 810 (Okl.1994) (whether initiative measure violated qualification clauses of U.S. Constitution or free speech and associational rights under First Amendment could not be considered during pre-election stage of initiative proceedings); Boytano v. Fritz, 131 Or.App. 466, 886 P.2d 31 (1994), aff'd 321 Or. 498, 901 P.2d 835 (1995) (statute prohibiting enactment of measures singling-out citizens on account of sexual orientation does not prohibit submitting such measures to vote under initiative power). Cf. Winkle v. City of Tucson, 190 Ariz. 413, 949 P.2d 502 (Ariz. 1997) (question of state pre-emption was not ripe for judicial review before enactment of initiative by voters); City of Rocky Ford v. Brown, 133 Colo. 262, 293 P.2d 974 (1956) (ordinance proposed pursuant to initiative and referendum laws was presumed valid in first instance when challenged in mandamus proceedings before enactment). See generally Annot., Injunctive Relief Against Submission of Constitutional Amendment, Statute, Municipal Charter, or Municipal Ordinance, on Ground That Proposed Action Would Be Unconstitutional, 19 A.L.R.2d 519 (1951); Annot., Capacity of Taxpayers to Maintain Suit to Enjoin Submission of Initiative, Referendum, or Recall Measure to Voters, 6 A.L.R.2d 557 (1949). See also notes 7–8 *infra* and accompanying text.

3 See Alexander v. Mitchell, 119 Cal.App.2d 816, 260 P.2d 261 (Dist.Ct.1953).

4 See Fox Bakersfield Theatre Corp. v. City of Bakersfield, 36 Cal.2d 136, 222 P.2d 879 (1950); Baum v. City of St. Louis, 343 Mo. 738, 123 S.W.2d 48 (1938); State ex rel. Kurtz v. Shaffer, 155 Ohio St. 491, 99 N.E.2d 479 (1951); In re Initiative Petition No. 1, Drumright, 298 P.2d 409 (Okl.1956); In re Initiative Petition No. 9 of Oklahoma City, 185 Okl. 165, 90 P.2d 665 (1939); Whitson v. City of Kingfisher, 176 Okl. 145, 54 P.2d 616 (1936). Cf. City of Dayton v. City Railway, 16 F.2d 401 (6th Cir.1926) (method of testing sufficiency of referendum petitions governed by city's home-rule charter, not by state law); In re Initiative Petition No. 4, 176 Okl. 20, 54 P.2d 347 (1936) (where protestants to sufficiency of initiative petition file court proceedings and submit brief reasonably supporting their allegations, and proponents of measure make no response, court can sustain protest). Minor deviations in procedure will not invalidate the process. See Johnson v. Munger, 260 Ark. 613, 542 S.W.2d 753 (1976) (minor deviations as to publication requirement). See generally Feldmeier

proposed ordinance and of the time and place of the proposed election thereon.[5] (2) There is almost always a requirement of a petition supporting the election on the proposed law and signed by a specified number of qualified voters of the locality. Usually the circulators of the petition must swear that they believe the signers signed with knowledge of the petition's contents.[6] The petition, with the requisite number of signatures, must be presented to a designated municipal official or board for determination of the sufficiency of the signatures. That official's (or board's) conclusion will be judicially reversed only if there is a showing of fraud or palpable error.[7] But if

---

v. Watson, 211 Ariz. 444, 123 P.3d 180 (2005) (in the context of formal requirements for initiatives, "substantial compliance" means that the petition as circulated fulfills the purpose of the relevant statutory or constitutional requirements, despite a lack of strict or technical compliance). See generally Comment, We the People: A Needed Reform of State Initiative and Referendum Procedures, 78 Mo. L. Rev. 1401 (2013). California has the rule that, while statewide initiatives may be placed directly on the ballot, city and county initiatives can only be submitted to voters if the initiatives have been first presented to, but not enacted by, the local legislative body. Tuolumne Jobs & Small Business Alliance v. Superior Court, 175 Cal. Rptr. 3d 601, 330 P.3d 912 (2014).

As to requirements for the title of ballot initiatives, see Caruthers v. Myers, 343 Or. 162, 166 P.3d 514 (2007) (state statute required a title that included result that would occur if the initiative was approved; proposed property tax exemption for senior citizen's primary residence was required to include in the title a discussion of the fiscal impact of the measure on local tax revenues). On titles of ordinances, see generally Section 11.1 *supra*.

5 See Wood v. City of St. Joseph, 238 Mo.App. 1212, 186 S.W.2d 212 (1945) (failure to publish initiative proposal or to mention proposal in proclamation giving public notice of election invalidated vote on initiative measure, even though it received majority approval).

6 See Kerley v. Wetherell, 61 Idaho 31, 96 P.2d 503 (1939); State ex rel. Abrams v. Bachrach, 175 Ohio St. 257, 193 N.E.2d 517 (1963) (requirement that each initiative petition contain affidavit of person soliciting signatures that he believes signers signed with knowledge of contents is mandatory). Cf. In re Initiative Petition in Tulsa, 597 P.2d 1208 (Okl.1979) (petition void when not properly verified that circulator of petition was qualified elector of state, as required by statute). The language of the proposed law must, of course, be sufficiently clear that petition-signers and voters will understand what it will do if enacted. See Morehead v. Dyer, 518 P.2d 1105 (Okl.1973).

Restrictions on petition-circulators will be invalidated as infringing on First Amendment rights if those restrictions unduly hinder political conversations and exchange of ideas. See Buckley v. American Constitutional Law Foundation, Inc., 525 U.S. 182, 119 S.Ct. 636, 142 L.Ed.2d 599 (1999), invalidating Colorado statutory requirements that circulators be registered voters, that circulators wear identification badges, and that the names and addresses of all paid circulators, and the amount paid each circulator, be reported; Meyer v. Grant, 486 U.S. 414, 108 S.Ct. 1886, 100 L.Ed.2d 425 (1988), invalidating as an unnecessary infringement on free speech a state prohibition on paying the circulators of initiative and referendum petitions. Cf. Yes on Term Limits, Inc. v. Savage, 550 F.3d 1023 (10th Cir. 2008) (Oklahoma's ban on non-resident petition circulators violates First and Fourteenth Amendments to U.S. Constitution because it is not sufficiently tailored to protect the integrity and reliability of the initiative process).

As to the invalidation of signatures on an initiative petition, see generally Montanans for Justice v. State of Montana ex rel. McGrath, 334 Mont. 237, 146 P.3d 759 (2006) (evidence established that out-of-state signature gatherers falsely attested that they personally gathered or assisted in gathering signatures, that such signature gatherers gave false or fictitious addresses in their certification affidavits, and that a large percentage of such signature gatherers used a bait-and-switch tactic to obtain signatures; signatures obtained by out-of-state gatherers were thus invalidated).

7 See State ex rel. Griffith v. City of Walnut, 166 Kan. 296, 201 P.2d 635 (1949); State ex rel. Malone v. Jacobs, 135 Kan. 513, 11 P.2d 739 (1932). But if an initiative measure is, on its face, clearly unconstitutional or otherwise illegal, a court may order that it not appear on (or that it be removed from) the ballot. See Whitson v. Anchorage, 608 P.2d 759 (Alaska 1980) (proposed amendment to municipal charter contradicted state statutes); In re Initiative Petition No. 366, 46 P.3d 123 (Okla. 2002) (pre-election judicial review of an initiative petition for an "English-only law" was appropriate to prevent an election to enact an unconstitutional law where the law would clearly violate state constitutional rights to freedom of speech and petition for redress of grievances, would be void for vagueness under the state due process clause, and would delegate legislative authority to agencies in violation of the non-delegation doctrine). Cf. Carmony v. McKechnie, 217 P.3d 818 (Alaska 2009) (courts are empowered to conduct pre-election review of initiative where it is challenged on the basis it does not comply with state constitutional and statutory provisions regulating initiatives or where the initiative is clearly unconstitutional or unlawful; borough clerk's rejection of application upheld). See generally

there are sufficient valid signatures, it is incumbent on the official or board to submit the proposal to a public vote, and the submission can be compelled by mandamus.[8] (3) An election must then be held on the question, with the ballot clearly and fully stating the proposed measure.[9]

It has frequently been ruled by the courts that the initiative power extends only to "legislative" ordinances, not those dealing with merely administrative matters. A measure is considered legislative if it establishes a new law or policy, but is looked upon as administrative if it only provides for the enforcement of existing law or policy.[10] Thus,

---

Harnett, State and Local Anti-Immigrant Initiatives: Can They Withstand Legal Scrutiny?, 17 Widener L.J. 365 (2008). See also note 2 *supra*.

On the scope of judicial review in one particular state, see Norway, Judicial Review of Initiative Petitions in Florida, 5 Fla. Coastal L. Rev. 15 (2004).

It has been held that a proposed initiative is beyond the scope of the initiative power if it involves powers granted by the legislature to the governing body of a city, rather than to the city itself. City of Sequim v. Malkasian, 157 Wash.2d 251, 138 P.3d 943 (2006). See City of Seattle v. Yes for Seattle, 122 Wash.App. 382, 93 P.3d 176 (2004) (initiative process is not available when the legislature delegates power exclusively to the legislative authority of a city, as opposed to the city as a corporate entity). Cf. City of Longview v. Wallin, 301 P.3d 45 (Wash. App. 2013) (grant of power to city's legislative authority or legislative body means exclusively the mayor and city council, not the electorate); Mukilteo Citizens for Simple Government v. City of Mukilteo, 174 Wash. 2d 41, 272 P.3d 227 (2012) (same).

[8] City of Rocky Ford v. Brown, *supra* note 7; Plageman v. Board of Commissioners, 569 S.W.2d 191 (Ky.App.1978); Powelsland v. City of Toledo, 15 Ohio App. 198 (1921); Black v. Wood, 207 Okl. 368, 249 P.2d 699 (1952); State ex rel. Schreyer v. City of Wheeling, 146 W.Va. 467, 120 S.E.2d 389 (1961); State ex rel. Althouse v. City of Madison, 79 Wis.2d 97, 255 N.W.2d 449 (1977). See generally Annot., Time Within Which Officer Must Perform Duty to Pass Upon Sufficiency of Initiative, Referendum, or Recall Petition, 102 A.L.R. 51 (1936). In some jurisdictions, criminal penalties are provided for officials who refuse to submit a properly presented initiative measure to the voters. See City of Rocky Ford v. Brown, *supra*.

It is ordinarily for the *courts*, not other municipal officers or boards, to rule on the alleged unconstitutionality of a proposed measure; thus, the official or board to whom the initiative petition is presented cannot ordinarily refuse to place a measure on the ballot on the ground of its alleged unconstitutionality. See Johnson v. City of Astoria, 227 Or. 585, 363 P.2d 571 (1961). But cf. Citizens for Responsible Behavior v. Superior Court, 1 Cal.App.4th 1013, 2 Cal.Rptr.2d 648 (1991) (city acted properly in refusing to place measure on ballot where it violated equal protection, patently fostered unlawful private discrimination, and was an illegal disguised attempt to amend the city charter). Compare Kodiak Island Borough v. Mahoney, 71 P.3d 896 (Alaska 2003) (voter initiative that erroneously proposed a ballot measure, rather than an ordinance, to establish mayoral term limits was not subject to rejection by the municipal clerk, where parties agreed that the best way to handle the technically flawed initiative was for the clerk to point out the deficiency, inform the proposing citizen what was necessary to correct it, and permit the citizen to resubmit the initiative).

[9] See City of Covington v. Reagan, 284 S.W.2d 323 (Ky.1955); Morehead v. Dyer, *supra* note 6.

[10] Lewis v. City of South Hutchinson, 162 Kan. 104, 174 P.2d 51 (1946); City of Newport v. Gugel, 342 S.W.2d 517 (Ky. 1960); Whitbeck v. Funk, 140 Or. 70, 12 P.2d 1019 (1932); Bachmann v. Goodwin, 121 W.Va. 303, 3 S.E.2d 532 (1939). Often an ordinance is classified as "legislative" but the power of initiative is nonetheless denied if some board or commission is required by a state statute or home-rule charter to hold hearings before such ordinance can be enacted. Baum v. City of St. Louis, *supra* note 4. Or if *public* hearings are thus required. See Southwestern Telegraph & Telephone Co. v. City of Dallas, 104 Tex. 114, 134 S.W. 321 (1911) (ordinance regulating telephone rates could not be passed by initiative). On the basic limitation of the initiative process to "legislative" matters, see Collins v. City & County of San Francisco, 112 Cal.App.2d 719, 247 P.2d 362 (Dist.Ct.1952); Bean v. City of Knoxville, 180 Tenn. 448, 175 S.W.2d 954 (1943); State ex rel. Payne v. City of Spokane, 17 Wn.2d 22, 134 P.2d 950 (1943). Cf. Seaton v. Lackey, 298 Ky. 188, 182 S.W.2d 336 (1944) (adoption of ordinance for sale of franchise found "administrative," not legislative). See generally 42 Am.Jur.2d Initiative and Referendum §§ 7–8 (2000). By some authority, the initiative process is limited to the proposing of legislation of a *permanent* nature. See State v. City of St. Petersburg, 61 So.2d 416 (Fla.1952). See generally Annot., Character or Subject Matter of Ordinance Within Operation of Initiative and Referendum Provisions, 122 A.L.R. 769 (1939). Some authority treats traffic regulations as an inappropriate subject-matter for initiative. See In re Certain Petitions, 154 N.J.Super. 482, 381 A.2d 1217 (1977).

proposed laws establishing the salaries of local officers or employees have been ruled administrative and not subject to the initiative,[11] as have laws setting rates for utility services.[12]

Traditionally, zoning laws could not be enacted by the initiative method since detailed provisions, often involving the holding of hearings and the obtaining of planning-commission recommendations, usually apply to their enactment. See Korash v. City of Livonia, 388 Mich. 737, 202 N.W.2d 803 (1972); State ex rel. Powers v. Donohue, 368 S.W.2d 432 (Mo.1963); Dewey v. Doxey-Layton Realty Co., 3 Utah 2d 1, 277 P.2d 805 (1954). Cf. Vara v. City of Houston, 583 S.W.2d 935 (Tex.Civ.App.1979), refused n.r.e., appeal dism'd 449 U.S. 807, 101 S.Ct. 54, 66 L.Ed.2d 11 (initiative could not be used to *disannex* property from city). But some authority now supports the use of the initiative as to zoning laws. See Associated Home Builders v. Livermore, 18 Cal.3d 582, 135 Cal.Rptr. 41, 557 P.2d 473 (1976); Builders Association v. Superior Court, 13 Cal.3d 225, 118 Cal.Rptr. 158, 529 P.2d 582 (1974), appeal dism'd 427 U.S. 901, 96 S.Ct. 3184, 49 L.Ed.2d 1195; San Diego Building Contractors Association v. City Council of San Diego, 13 Cal.3d 205, 118 Cal.Rptr. 146, 529 P.2d 570 (1974), appeal dism'd 427 U.S. 901, 96 S.Ct. 3184, 49 L.Ed.2d 1195; Allison v. Washington County, 24 Or.App. 571, 548 P.2d 188 (1976). In Sevier Power Co., LLC v. Board of Sevier County Comm'rs, 196 P.3d 583 (Utah 2008), the court held that a state statute providing that voters may not initiate a land-use ordinance or a budget violated the State Constitution's guarantee to the people of the right to initiate any desired legislation and submit it to the voters for approval or rejection.

The initiative process is particularly likely to be allowed if the proposed measure is of a general, policy-making nature, rather than involving the zoning of specific property, since the measure can then be more readily categorized as "legislative." See Annot., Adoption of Zoning Ordinance or Amendment Thereto Through Initiative Process, 72 A.L.R.3d 991 (1976). Cf. DeVita v. County of Napa, 9 Cal.4th 763, 38 Cal.Rptr.2d 699, 889 P.2d 1019 (1995) (initiative could validly be used to amend county's general plan so that any redesignation of existing agricultural land or open space would for the next thirty years require majority voter approval). But cf. Vagneur v. City of Aspen, 295 P.3d 493 (Colo. 2013) (citizen-initiated proposed ordinances regarding design and construction of a state highway entrance to city were administrative in character); City of Wichita v. Kansas Taxpayers Network, Inc., 255 Kan. 534, 874 P.2d 667 (1994) (ordinance establishing storm water utility system was administrative and thus outside scope of initiative and referendum powers); Terry v. Bishop, 158 P.3d 1067 (Okla. 2007) (initiative petition was legally insufficient because it sought to bind city unconstitutionally by limiting its power to rezone specific property for ten years); Foster v. Clark, 309 Or. 464, 790 P.2d 1 (1990) (renaming of city street was administrative matter and thus not subject to initiative process, regardless of whether initial renaming of street, which the initiative sought to undo, was legislative action). See also, on the use of the initiative to enact zoning and related laws, Section 120 *supra*. On other land-use matters, compare Eller Media Co. v. City of Reno, 118 Nev. 767, 59 P.3d 437 (2002) (proposal to prohibit city from issuing permits for construction of new off-premises advertising billboards was legislative in character and thus a proper subject for initiative), with Citizens for a Public Train Trench Vote v. City of Reno, 118 Nev. 574, 53 P.3d 387 (2002) (initiative which proposed prohibition of railroad trench within existing railroad right of way was administrative), and Glover v. Concerned Citizens for Fuji Park, 118 Nev. 488, 50 P.3d 546 (2002) (proposed initiative to preserve park in perpetuity was an administrative act and thus not within the constitutional initiative power of the people). Cf. Horne v. City of Mesquite, 120 Nev. 700, 100 P.3d 168 (2004) (initiative ordinance that required city to conduct all land sales by public auction or public sealed-bid process was repugnant to state statute and thus invalid). See also McAlister v. City of Fairway, 289 Kan. 391, 212 P.3d 184 (2009) (proposed ordinance that would prohibit city from allowing rezoning, eminent domain, or condemnation of certain properties and would restrict commercial development was principally administrative).

[11] City of Lawrence v. McArdle, 214 Kan. 862, 522 P.2d 420 (1974) (proposed measure would have equalized firemen's salaries with those of police officers). Cf. Fite v. Lacey, 691 P.2d 901 (Okl.1984) (proposed amendment to city charter providing for collective bargaining and arbitration for firefighters and police officers was administrative in nature and thus not a proper subject of initiative petition); In re Initiative Petition in Tulsa, 597 P.2d 1208 (Okl.1979) (initiative could not be used to establish minimum number of policemen in city). But see Parrack v. City of Phoenix, 84 Ariz. 382, 329 P.2d 1103 (1958) (initiative could be used to fix salaries of fire department employees). See generally In re Initiative Petition No. 27 of Oklahoma City, 82 P.3d 90 (Okla. 2003) (subject matter of initiative petition that dealt with wages, hours, and other conditions of city employment was administrative, not legislative, and thus violative of state constitution).

[12] McKinley v. City of Fraser, 366 Mich. 104, 114 N.W.2d 341 (1962); In re Supreme Court Adjudication of Initiative Petitions in Norman, 534 P.2d 3 (Okl.1975) (but initiative method *could* be used to amend city charter to require that voters henceforth would have to approve any increase in utility rates before such increase could be passed by local legislative body).

Financial matters are often held "administrative" and thus outside the scope of the initiative power. See Chicago Bar Ass'n v. State Bd. of Elections, 137 Ill.2d 394, 148 Ill.Dec. 744, 561 N.E.2d 50 (1990), noted 22

Often it is provided by state law that when an initiative petition is presented to local officials, the local governing body has a specified period of time within which it may enact the suggested measure, eliminating the need for an election thereon.[13] It is also frequently provided in state law that once a measure is passed by the initiative process, it may not be repealed or amended—or at least may not be repealed or amended within a specified length of time—by the legislative body.[14] In the absence of any such limitation, courts will usually uphold the power of the legislative body to repeal initiated ordinances in the same manner as other ordinances.[15]

Loyola (Chicago) U.L.J. 1119 (1991) (initiative could not be used to amend state constitution so as to change legislative revenue-raising process); Rauh v. City of Hutchinson, 223 Kan. 514, 575 P.2d 517 (1978) (issuance of revenue bonds to aid industry); Dieruf v. City of Bozeman, 173 Mont. 447, 568 P.2d 127 (1977) (creation of local improvement district to be financed by special assessments). Cf. City of Idaho Springs v. Blackwell, 731 P.2d 1250 (Colo.1987) (petitions for initiated ordinances relating to purchase of site for city hall related to administrative matters and could not validly be made subject of initiative vote); Bidwell v. City of Bellevue, 65 Wash.App. 43, 827 P.2d 339 (1992), review denied 119 Wash.2d 1023, 838 P.2d 690 (1992) (proposed initiative that would require convention center authority to obtain voter approval prior to issuing revenue bonds would impair authority's contracts in violation of state and federal constitutions). See also State ex rel. Card v. Kaufman, 517 S.W.2d 78 (Mo.1974); State ex rel. Sessions v. Bartle, 359 S.W.2d 716 (Mo.1962), both applying constitutional provision that initiative not be used for appropriation of money, except of new revenues created and provided for by the appropriating law. But see City of Fairbanks v. Fairbanks Convention & Visitors Bureau, 818 P.2d 1153 (Alaska 1991) (voter initiative which would set aside hotel bed tax revenues for deposit in city council discretionary fund would not restrict power of city council in distributing revenues and could thus validly be made subject of initiative); Rossi v. Brown, 9 Cal.4th 688, 38 Cal.Rptr.2d 363, 889 P.2d 557 (1995) (city charter prohibiting referenda on tax ordinances did not prevent voters from using initiative power prospectively to repeal a tax ordinance and to prevent adoption of any future ordinance imposing a similar tax); State ex rel. Boyer v. Grady, 201 Neb. 360, 269 N.W.2d 73 (1978) (enactment of sales tax could be repealed by initiative); In re Initiative Petition No. 348, 820 P.2d 772 (Okl. 1991) (initiative petition to amend state constitution to require approval of revenue-raising bills by people at next general election held valid).

State statutes or constitutional provisions sometimes specifically prohibit the use of the initiative power as to "appropriations." See Alaska Action Center, Inc. v. Municipality of Anchorage, 84 P.3d 989 (Alaska 2004) (under such provisions, "appropriation" is often understood to refer to money, but an initiative setting aside land or other governmental property may also be an appropriation; here, a proposed municipal initiative to designate a specific parcel of land as parkland was an "appropriation" and therefore barred by state constitution and statute). Cf. Staudenmaier v. Municipality of Anchorage, 139 P.3d 1259 (Alaska 2006) (initiatives requiring municipality to sell two city-owned utilities violated constitutional provision prohibiting the making of appropriations by voter initiative). See also City of Colorado Springs v. Bull, 143 P.3d 1127 (Colo. App. 2006) (provisions in revenue initiative relating to street light charges were administrative in nature and thus not proper subject for an initiative).

[13] See Rea v. City of Reno, 76 Nev. 483, 357 P.2d 585 (1960), where a statute *compelling* the local legislative body to adopt an initiated proposal was declared unconstitutional, since the basic purpose of initiative is merely to give the voters a *chance* to enact (and a chance to reject) the proposed legislation. A few states have laws allowing initiatives that are merely advisory in nature. But it has been held that there is no federal constitutional prohibition of laws that forbid such initiatives, and that is the usual rule. See Proulx v. Salt Lake City Recorder, 297 P.3d 573 (Utah 2013) (state constitutional prohibition of advisory initiatives does not violate right of free speech in U.S. Constitution).

[14] See, applying such limiting statutes, State ex rel. Harley v. City of Wichita, 151 Kan. 390, 99 P.2d 812 (1940); City of Shreveport v. Gregory, 186 La. 407, 172 So. 435 (1937); State ex rel. Ausburn v. City of Seattle, 190 Wash. 222, 67 P.2d 913 (1937). Cf. People v. Kelly, 47 Cal. 4th 1008, 103 Cal. Rptr. 3d 733, 222 P.3d 186 (2010) (state constitution prohibits legislature from amending an initiative statute unless authorized by the measure itself, though legislature remains free to address a related but distinct area or a matter that an initiative measure does not specifically authorize or prohibit).

[15] See Jackson v. Denver Producing & Refining Co., 96 F.2d 457 (10th Cir. 1938); La Fleur ex rel. Anderson v. Frost, 146 Me. 270, 80 A.2d 407 (1951); State ex rel. Singer v. Cartledge, 129 Ohio St. 279, 195 N.E. 237 (1935). Cf. Granger v. City of Tulsa, 174 Okl. 565, 51 P.2d 567 (1935) (city legislative body could repeal initiative measure, thereby diminishing salaries of members of fire department). In Gibbons v. Cenarrusa, 140 Idaho 316, 92 P.3d 1063 (2002), it was held that the legislature could immediately enact the repeal of a voter-enacted term-limits initiative by declaring an emergency; statutes created by initiative could be repealed like ones enacted by the legislature, and the discretion to declare an emergency lay entirely with

§ 27.3 The Referendum

Similar in nature to the initiative is the referendum. This refers to the process by which legislation passed by the governing body is submitted to the electorate for its approval or disapproval. There is no inherent right of referendum in the electorate, and thus the process is not available at common law.[16] But statutes and home-rule charters often provide for it, sometimes specifying that where the process is used, the governing body is given a designated time within which to repeal the ordinance in question, which will then be submitted to the voters if such repeal does not occur.[17] There are many similarities here to the rules on initiative. Once again, even a home-rule city cannot use this method of "popular legislation" to defeat the superiority of state law over local law as to matters of state-wide, or general, concern.[18] And again, the method applies only to "legislative" ordinances, not to those that are administrative or executive in nature.[19] An ordinance is administrative if it is designed merely to enforce or carry into effect a basic policy that has been already established.[20] It is also often observed that an ordinance is

---

the legislature. See generally Annot., Power of Legislative Body to Amend, Repeal, or Abrogate Initiative or Referendum Measure, or to Enact Measure Defeated on Referendum, 33 A.L.R.2d 1118 (1954).

[16] See City of Mt. Olive v. Braje, 366 Ill. 132, 7 N.E.2d 851 (1937); Wright v. Village of South Orange, 79 N.J.Super. 96, 190 A.2d 675 (1963). See generally Shapiro, The Referendum Process in Maryland: Balancing Respect for Representative Government With the Right to Direct Democracy, 44 U. Baltimore L. J. 1 (2013).

[17] See State ex rel. Dawson v. Board of Commissioners of Pratt, 92 Kan. 247, 139 P. 1191 (1914); Gorman v. Peabody, 312 Mass. 560, 45 N.E.2d 939 (1942); State ex rel. Middletown v. City Commission of Middletown, 140 Ohio St. 368, 44 N.E.2d 459 (1942). Cf. Washington's Army v. City of Seward, 181 P.3d 1102 (Alaska 2008) (where city council had not passed any ordinance or resolution regarding vacation of street, referendum on the vacation could not be held; council had voted twice on the proposal, but fewer than the required four votes were cast for either possible result). It is often said that the power of referendum is to be liberally construed. Whittemore v. Seydel, 74 Cal.App.2d 109, 168 P.2d 212 (Dist.Ct.1946); Burks v. City of Lafayette, 142 Colo. 61, 349 P.2d 692 (1960) (ordinance providing for improvement district to carry out street-paving program was subject to referendum); State ex rel. Sutton v. Caldwell, 195 La. 507, 197 So. 214 (1940).

[18] State ex rel. Guthrie v. City of Richland, 80 Wn.2d 382, 494 P.2d 990 (1972).

[19] Greenlee v. Munn, 262 Ark. 663, 559 S.W.2d 928 (1978); Reagan v. City of Sausalito, 210 Cal.App.2d 618, 26 Cal.Rptr. 775 (Dist.Ct.1962); Housing Authority v. Superior Court, 35 Cal.2d 550, 219 P.2d 457 (1950); People ex rel. Holvey v. Kapp, 355 Ill. 596, 189 N.E. 920 (1934); State ex rel. Hall v. Morton, 128 Kan. 125, 276 P. 62 (1929); Katter, Inc. v. Brockman, 349 S.W.2d 838 (Ky.1961); Read v. City of Scottsbluff, 139 Neb. 418, 297 N.W. 669 (1941); State ex rel. Barberis v. City of Bay Village, 31 Ohio Misc. 203, 281 N.E.2d 209, 59 O.O.2d 366 (Com.Pl.1971); Tillamook District v. Coates, 174 Or. 476, 149 P.2d 558 (1944) (ordinance specifying denomination and form of bonds—previously approved by voters—, rate of interest on them, maturity dates, etc. was "administrative"); Denman v. Quin, 116 S.W.2d 783 (Tex.Civ.App.1938), error refused; Keigley v. Bench, 97 Utah 69, 89 P.2d 480 (1939); Neils v. City of Seattle, 185 Wash. 269, 53 P.2d 848 (1936). See Carson v. Oxenhandler, 334 S.W.2d 394 (Mo.App.1960). The rationale for the distinction is discussed in Wennerstrom v. City of Mesa, 169 Ariz. 485, 821 P.2d 146 (1991) (rationale for limiting referendum to legislative action is that to permit referenda on executive and administrative actions would hamper administration of local governments; approval of city street improvement project held not legislative and thus not subject to referendum). Accord as to the rationale, but saying the efficiency rationale must be balanced against the obligation of broadly construing initiative and referendum powers to maintain maximum power in the people, Phillips v. City of Whitefish, 330 P.3d 442 (Mont. 2014) (city council resolution as to zoning power over extraterritorial area held principally administrative). Compare, both applying the administrative-legislative distinction, Friends of Maple Mountain, Inc. v. Mapleton City, 228 P.3d 1238 (Utah 2010) (city council's adoption of new zoning classification is per se legislative action), with Citizens for Responsible Transportation v. Draper City, 190 P.3d 1245 (Utah 2008) (city council resolution endorsing proposed commuter rail corridor was administrative action without the force of law and therefore not subject to referendum). The difficulty of applying the legislative-v.-administrative distinction has, however, been noted. See Whitehead v. H & C Development Corp., 204 Va. 144, 129 S.E.2d 691 (1963).

[20] See Scroggins v. Kerr, 217 Ark. 137, 228 S.W.2d 995 (1950); Kleiber v. City & County of San Francisco, 18 Cal.2d 718, 117 P.2d 657 (1941); Seaton v. Lackey, 298 Ky. 188, 182 S.W.2d 336 (1994); Kelley v. John, 162 Neb. 319, 75 N.W.2d 713 (1956); Read v. City of Scottsbluff, *supra* note 20; State ex rel. Didelius

administrative if it deals with a temporary situation or with matters of routine or detail, but legislative if it is permanent and general in nature.[21] Ordinances establishing utility

---

v. City Commission of City of Sandusky, 131 Ohio St. 356, 2 N.E.2d 862 (1936). Cf. Moore v. School Committee of Newton, 375 Mass. 443, 378 N.E.2d 47 (1978) (matter is "legislative" if it involves a sweeping determination of municipal policy). As in the case of the initiative—see preceding section—, there has been some difficulty over whether the referendum can apply to zoning and other land-use laws, and some cases have denied such application. Minneapolis-Honeywell Regulator Co. v. Nadasdy, 247 Minn. 159, 76 N.W.2d 670 (1956); Kelley v. John, *supra*; Snohomish County v. Anderson, 123 Wash.2d 151, 868 P.2d 116 (1994) (ordinance mandating development and implementation of countywide planning policies was not subject to referendum as power had been statutorily delegated to legislative authority). Cf. Witcher v. Canon City, 716 P.2d 445 (Colo.1986) (amendment to lease was administrative act, not subject to referendum); City of Shelby v. Sandholm, 208 Mont. 77, 676 P.2d 178 (1984) (resolution creating special improvement district encompassing less than entire area of city was administrative act, not subject to referendum); Heider v. City of Seattle, 100 Wash.2d 874, 675 P.2d 597 (1984) (change in street name is administrative and immune from referendum). But the tendency is to allow the referendum process here. See Yost v. Thomas, 36 Cal.3d 561, 205 Cal.Rptr. 801, 685 P.2d 1152 (1984) (adoption of specific land-use plan for coastal zone was a legislative act subject to referendum); City of Fort Collins v. Dooney, 178 Colo. 25, 496 P.2d 316 (1972); City of Coral Gables v. Carmichael, 256 So.2d 404 (Fla.App.1972), cert. dism'd 268 So.2d 1 (Fla.); Reva v. Township of Portage, 356 Mich. 381, 96 N.W.2d 778 (1959); Stadle v. Township of Battle Creek, 346 Mich. 64, 77 N.W.2d 329 (1956); Denney v. City of Duluth, 295 Minn. 22, 202 N.W.2d 892 (1972); Greens at Fort Missoula v. City of Missoula, 271 Mont. 398, 897 P.2d 1078 (1995) (zoning and rezoning ordinances are legislative and are subject to referendum power of public). Some authority would allow comprehensive zoning ordinances, laying down a general plan, to be subjected to referendum, but not ordinances merely zoning or rezoning particular land or amending a comprehensive ordinance. Compare West v. City of Portage, 392 Mich. 458, 221 N.W.2d 303 (1974) (amendment affecting single tract not subject to referendum), and State ex rel. Srovnal v. Linton, 46 Ohio St.2d 207, 346 N.E.2d 764 (1976) (grant of use exception was "administrative," not subject to referendum), with Anne Arundel County v. McDonough, 277 Md. 271, 354 A.2d 788 (1976) (comprehensive zoning ordinance was subject to referendum), and Hilltop Realty, Inc. v. City of South Euclid, 110 Ohio App. 535, 164 N.E.2d 180 (1960), appeal dism'd 170 Ohio St. 585, 166 N.E.2d 924 (amendment to comprehensive zoning ordinance subject to referendum). See generally Annot., Adoption of Zoning Ordinance or Amendment Thereto as Subject to Referendum, 72 A.L.R.3d 1030 (1976). See also, as to the use of referendum in zoning matters, Section 18.6 *supra*. In City of Eastlake v. Forest City Enterprises, Inc., 426 U.S. 668, 96 S.Ct. 2358, 49 L.Ed.2d 132 (1976), it was held that the referendum process does not in itself violate federal due process when applied to a rezoning ordinance.

On the use of a referendum as to location of a housing project in a community, see James v. Valtierra, 402 U.S. 137, 91 S.Ct. 1331, 28 L.Ed.2d 678 (1971) (referendum permissible), noted 13 Boston College Ind. & Comm.Rev. 603 (1972); Hunter v. Erickson, 393 U.S. 385, 89 S.Ct. 557, 21 L.Ed.2d 616 (1969) (referendum requirement not permissible where applied *only* to discrimination-in-housing laws). In City of Cuyahoga Falls, Ohio v. Buckeye Community Hope Foundation, 538 U.S. 188, 123 S.Ct. 1389, 155 L.Ed.2d 349 (2003), a city had submitted to voters a facially neutral referendum petition calling for repeal of a municipal housing ordinance authorizing construction of a low-income housing complex and had refused to issue building permits while the petition was pending. The Court held the city's subjection of the site-plan ordinance to the referendum process did not constitute arbitrary government conduct in violation of substantive due process. See generally Note, The Use of Zoning Laws to Prevent Poor People from Moving into Suburbia, 16 Howard L.J. 351 (1971); Annot., Referendum Relating to Low- or Moderate-Income Housing Projects as Constituting Racial Discrimination in Violation of Federal Constitution, 15 A.L.R.Fed. 613 (1973). See also Chapter 20 *supra*.

[21] See People ex rel. Austin v. Graham, 70 Colo. 509, 203 P. 277 (1921); Long v. City of Portland, 53 Or. 92, 98 P. 1111 (1909); Whitehead v. H. & C. Development Corp., *supra* note 19. Cf. State ex rel. Malone v. Jacobs, 135 Kan. 513, 11 P.2d 739 (1932) (ordinance providing for condemnation to widen a street is subject to referendum since gist of the legislation—the widening of the street—is "legislative" in nature). If a matter is considered of general or community-wide concern, an ordinance dealing therewith is often treated as subject to referendum. See State ex rel. Mitchell v. Council of Milan, 133 Ohio St. 499, 14 N.E.2d 772 (1938) (contract to purchase electricity); State ex rel. Lindstrom v. Goetz, 73 S.D. 633, 47 N.W.2d 566 (1951). This is true even as to some subject-matters (See notes 10–12 *supra*) that are often held not within the *initiative* process, such as municipal salaries. See Collins v. City & County of San Francisco, 112 Cal.App.2d 719, 247 P.2d 362 (Dist.Ct.1952); Morra v. City Clerk of New Bedford, 340 Mass. 240, 163 N.E.2d 268 (1960) (wage increase for police officers and firefighters). And utility rates. Walker Bros. Catering Co. v. Detroit City Gas Co., 230 Mich. 564, 203 N.W. 492 (1925). And some financial matters affecting the municipality. See Keigley v. Bench, *supra* note 19 (bond election for municipal electric system). (But see note 23 *infra* and accompanying text.) It is, however, also sometimes noted that the referendum should *not* be allowed as to matters on which city governing authorities may be considered to have special expertise or information. See State ex rel. Conine v.

rates have normally been held administrative and non-referable.[22] Besides the general exception for administrative matters, three other exceptions are generally either specified by legislation or are "read into" the authorizing legislation by the courts: (1) Ordinances approving or otherwise dealing with the budget, plus general appropriation ordinances, are held non-referable.[23] (2) Emergency ordinances are normally not subject

---

Hunter, 97 Conn. 579, 117 A. 548 (1922) (hiring manager). Or as to nonpermanent regulations. See In re Village of Ridgefield Park, 149 N.J.Super. 530, 374 A.2d 83 (1977), aff'd 154 N.J.Super. 482, 381 A.2d 1217 (traffic regulations). As to the administrative v. legislative distinction in the context of referendums, see generally Redelsperger v. City of Avondale, 207 Ariz. 430, 87 P.3d 843 (App. 2004) (court must consider whether the action is (1) permanent or temporary, (2) of general or of specific, limited application, and (3) a matter of policy creation or a form of policy implementation).

[22] City of Aurora v. Zwerdlinger, 194 Colo. 192, 571 P.2d 1074 (1977); Hoover v. Carpenter, 188 Neb. 405, 197 N.W.2d 11 (1972) (electric rates); Johnson v. City of Alamogordo, 121 N.M. 232, 910 P.2d 308 (1996) (city ordinance increasing rates for water and sewer service by city-owned utility not subject to review by referendum); Hatten v. City of Houston, 373 S.W.2d 525 (Tex.Civ.App.1963), ref'd n. r. e. (water rates). Cf. Town of Whitehall v. Preece, 288 Mont. 55, 956 P.2d 743 (1998) (town's water metering ordinance was administrative and thus not subject to referendum). But see City of North Little Rock v. Gorman, 264 Ark. 150, 568 S.W.2d 481 (1978) (rate-making for municipal utility held "legislative"); Walker Brothers v. Detroit City Gas Co., *supra* note 21 (ordinance setting rates for gas utility was subject to referendum). Cf. State ex rel. Whittington v. Strahm, 374 S.W.2d 127 (Mo.1963) (ordinance providing for fluoridation of municipal water supply was "legislative" and thus subject to referendum).

In Stop Exploiting Taxpayers v. Jones, 211 Ariz. 576, 125 P.3d 396 (App. 2005), the court ruled that municipal ordinances setting rates for city-owned utility services were administrative, not legislative, and thus not subject to referendum where the ordinances listed specific utility services that the city provided and contained schedules modifying the rates charged for those services, the ordinances did not affect the underlying statutes and ordinances through which the city owned and operated its utilities, and the rate changes were considered annually as part of the city's budget process. Cf. Low v. City of Monticello, 2002 Utah 90, 54 P.3d 1153 (2002) (city's decision to exercise option to repurchase electrical power distribution system was an administrative decision not subject to referendum).

[23] Hawkins v. City of Birmingham, 239 Ala. 185, 194 So. 533 (1940); State ex rel. Keefe v. City of St. Petersburg, 106 Fla. 742, 145 So. 175 (1933); Sparta Township v. Spillane, 125 N.J.Super. 519, 312 A.2d 154 (1973), cert. denied 64 N.J. 493, 317 A.2d 706; Vansuch v. State ex rel. Fetch, 112 Ohio St. 688, 148 N.E. 232 (1925); In re Referendum Petition, 182 Okl. 419, 77 P.2d 1152 (1938). See City of Woodlake v. Logan, 230 Cal.App.3d 1058, 282 Cal.Rptr. 27 (1991) (statewide initiative proposition that prohibited local government from imposing any general tax unless first submitted for voter approval held to place an unconstitutional referendum requirement on taxing powers). Cf. Voters for Responsible Retirement v. Board of Supervisors, 8 Cal.4th 765, 35 Cal.Rptr.2d 814, 884 P.2d 645 (1994) (county's determination to enter into arrangement whereby its employees were to join state's public employee retirement system not subject to referendum); City of Fort Collins v. Dooney, *supra* note 20 (charter provided that all ordinances subject to referendum except those making tax levy or appropriation or ordering improvements initiated by petition; so zoning map amendment *was* thus subject); State ex rel. City of Fostoria v. King, 154 Ohio St. 213, 94 N.E.2d 697 (1950) (ordinance adopting sewer charges not subject to referendum—ordinance was also adopted as emergency measure). Compare Municipality of Anchorage v. Holleman, 321 P.3d 378 (Alaska 2014) (referendum allowing a popular vote to amend employment relations chapter of municipal code did not violate state constitution's prohibition of referendum on revenue or appropriations, or city charter's prohibition as to budgets or appropriating funds). But see Citizens for Financially Responsible Gov't v. City of Spokane, 99 Wash.2d 339, 662 P.2d 845 (1983) (ordinance imposing a general business and occupations tax was a legislative act and subject to referendum). Sometimes, the power of granting street franchises is also considered non-referable. See Washington Water Power Co. v. Rooney, 3 Wn.2d 642, 101 P.2d 580 (1940). On street franchises, see generally Chapter 17 *supra*. See also Annot., Inclusion of Different Franchise Rights or Purposes in Same Ordinance, 127 A.L.R. 1049 (1940).

to the referendum process.[24] (3) The referendum procedure also does not apply to actions of the governing body that are considered judicial, or quasi-judicial, in nature.[25]

A referendum election is called by much the same method as that for calling a vote on an initiated measure: The key element is the filing of a petition signed by a designated number of electors within the locality. State statute or home-rule charter usually specifies that the petition must be filed within a certain number of days from passage or publication of the ordinance in question, and compliance with this time-limit is mandatory.[26] The petition must be presented to a designated officer or board, which

---

[24] See Hawkins v. City of Birmingham, *supra* note 23; Shryock v. City of Zanesville, 92 Ohio St. 375, 110 N.E. 937 (1915). In most jurisdictions, the courts will, however, look behind the legislative declaration of an emergency and determine for themselves whether an emergency actually existed. See Klassen v. Burton, 110 Cal.App.2d 539, 243 P.2d 28 (Dist.Ct.1952); Continental Constr. Co. v. City of Lawrence, 297 Mass. 513, 9 N.E.2d 550 (1937); State ex rel. Asotsky v. Regan, 317 Mo. 1216, 298 S.W. 747 (1927); Swartout v. City of Spokane, 21 Wn.App. 665, 586 P.2d 135 (1978), review denied 91 Wash.2d 1023 (1979); State ex rel. Gray v. Martin, 29 Wn.2d 799, 189 P.2d 637 (1948). But a minority view treats the legislative declaration as binding. See State ex rel. Schorr v. Kennedy, 132 Ohio St. 510, 9 N.E.2d 278 (1937); Greenberg v. Lee, 196 Or. 157, 248 P.2d 324 (1952). On the effect that such a "conclusive" rule can have, compare Tamele v. Brinkman, 30 Ohio Misc. 49, 284 N.E.2d 210 (1972) (statute providing for effective date of annexation recognized right of electors to require referendum on annexation and thus modified the statute on enactment of emergency ordinances), with State ex rel. Tester v. Board of Elections, 174 Ohio St. 15, 185 N.E.2d 762 (1962) (council could prevent electorate from voting on ordinance, which had not been passed as emergency measure and on which valid referendum petition had been filed, by repealing the ordinance originally passed and then re-enacting same ordinances as emergency measure). But, although Ohio applies this "conclusive" rule, it has been held in that state that home-rule cities can by charter provide for possible referendums even on emergency measures. State ex rel. Bramblette v. Yordy, 24 Ohio St.2d 147, 265 N.E.2d 273 (1970). See generally Page, State of Emergency: Washington's Use of Emergency Clauses and the People's Right to Referendum, 44 Gonzaga L. Rev. 219 (2008/09).

In McKee v. City of Louisville, 200 Colo. 525, 616 P.2d 969 (1980), voters filed referendum petitions before and immediately after the adoption of an annexation ordinance, but these were rejected because of the emergency clause in the annexation ordinance. The court held, however, that when the voters, immediately after adoption of the ordinance, filed *initiative* petitions for repeal of the annexation ordinance, the voters had a constitutional right to have the question submitted to the electorate.

[25] See Scroggins v. Kerr, 217 Ark. 137, 228 S.W.2d 995 (1950) (city ordinance authorizing execution of public housing cooperation agreement between city and federal agency held subject to referendum).

[26] Railey v. City of Magnolia, 197 Ark. 1047, 126 S.W.2d 273 (1939); Borough of Eatontown v. Danskin, 121 N.J.Super. 68, 296 A.2d 81 (1972) (with review of cases). See Kochen v. Young, 252 Iowa 389, 107 N.W.2d 81 (1961) (insufficient petition cannot be amended so as to make it sufficient after time for filing has expired). There must be substantial compliance with all requirements concerning circulation, filing, and verification of referendum petitions. See Western Devcor, Inc. v. Massie, 168 Ariz. 426, 814 P.2d 767 (1991) (referendum petitions stated that circulators believed signers were qualified electors of state; held not to comply strictly with requirement that circulators believe each signer is a qualified *city* elector; thus petitions invalid); Clark v. City of Aurora, 782 P.2d 771 (Colo.1989) (city ordinance upheld imposing requirements regarding signatures on referendum petitions: elector must print name after signature, ditto marks could not be used for any required information, etc.); Corbly v. City of Colton, 278 N.W.2d 459 (S.D.1979); Compare Riverton Citizens for Constitutional Government v. Beckstead, 631 P.2d 885 (Utah 1981) (city recorder's checking and certification of signatures on referendum petition was not substantial compliance with statutory requirement that petitions be checked and certified with county clerk and filed with city recorder). It is often emphasized that referendum laws are to be liberally construed in favor of the petitioners. See Johnson v. Maehling, 123 Ariz. 15, 597 P.2d 1 (1979); Ley v. Dominguez, 212 Cal. 587, 299 P. 713 (1931); State ex rel. Sutton v. Caldwell, 195 La. 507, 197 So. 214 (1940); In re Neuendorffer, 256 App.Div. 941, 9 N.Y.S.2d 950 (1939). But see Gittings v. Board of Supervisors of Elections, 38 Md.App. 674, 382 A.2d 349 (1978) (must be *strict* compliance with referendum law). If there is *not* the required degree of compliance with procedures, the referendum election can be enjoined.

Where the deadline for filing the petition is established as a certain number of days after the legislation's "passage," this period commences when the council votes approval, not the day when the ordinance is posted. Bissland v. Bankhead, 171 P.3d 430 (Utah 2007) ("passage" means "the event at which a legislative body conducts a vote favorable to a piece of proposed legislation"; *id.* at 433).

passes on its sufficiency. The decision of the officer or board as to the petition's adequacy will not be judicially overturned unless there is a showing of fraud, bad faith, or clear error.[27] If all the required steps for calling a referendum have been met by the petitioners, mandamus will lie to compel the appropriate officer to order the necessary election.[28] The will of the voters will then determine what happens to the measure in question—but an election can subsequently be invalidated if it is found the ballot did not contain a sufficiently clear statement of the issue.[29]

An ordinance is not nullified by the filing of a referendum petition,[30] but the law involved in the referendum is suspended and held in abeyance unless and until it is approved by the voters.[31] Usually the local legislative body has no power, during the time between filing of the petition and the holding of the election, to repeal or re-enact the law, or to legislate at all on that specific subject-matter,[32] except as some statutory or charter provisions specifically allow the legislature a certain time after the filing of the petition within which to repeal the law, thus eliminating the need for an election.[33]

Statutes or constitutional provisions generally require that only qualified, registered voters can sign the referendum petition. But it has been held that an opponent of such petition bears the burden of producing sufficient competent evidence to overcome the presumption that the signers are thus qualified. In re Referendum Petition No. 0203–1, City of Norman, 92 P.3d 715 (Okla. Civ. App. 2004). Where the law specifies that the signatures on a municipal referendum petition must equal a certain percentage of the total votes cast at "the next preceding election," that has been held to refer to the most recent general municipal election. Neidy v. City of Chickasha, 188 P.3d 128 (Okla. 2008) (reference was to general municipal election to elect three city council members, not a subsequent special election to determine increase in sales tax).

In Doe #1 v. Reed, 561 U.S. 186, 130 S.Ct. 2811, 177 L.Ed.2d 493 (2010), the Court held that a referendum petition, containing the names and addresses of signers, was subject to the disclosure provisions of the Washington State Public Record Act. The disclosure requirements as here applied were upheld as sufficiently related to the state's interest in protecting the integrity of the electoral process.

[27] See State ex rel. Griffith v. City of Walnut, 166 Kan. 296, 201 P.2d 635 (1949). It has even been held that courts will not restrain a referendum election on the basis of alleged unconstitutionality or other invalidity of the proposed law. See Queen Creek Land & Cattle Corp. v. Yavapai County, 108 Ariz. 449, 501 P.2d 391 (1972).

[28] State ex rel. Ford v. Brawley, 514 S.W.2d 97 (Mo.App.1974); State ex rel. City of Middletown v. City Commission of Middletown, 140 Ohio St. 368, 44 N.E.2d 459 (1942); State ex rel. Mitchell v. Council of Milan, 133 Ohio St. 499, 14 N.E.2d 772 (1938); State ex rel. Plymale v. Garner, 147 W.Va. 293, 128 S.E.2d 185 (1962).

[29] Anne Arundel County v. McDonough, *supra* note 20; Troland v. City of Malden, 332 Mass. 351, 125 N.E.2d 134 (1955). Cf. Portmann v. Board of Elections, 60 Ohio App. 54, 19 N.E.2d 531 (1938) (voters entitled to clear statement of issues at the election). A law limiting campaign contributions in referendum elections was struck down as a direct restraint on freedom of expression in Citizens Against Rent Control/Coalition for Fair Housing v. City of Berkeley, 454 U.S. 290, 102 S.Ct. 434, 70 L.Ed.2d 492 (1981). See Barbash, Court Strikes Down Contribution Limits in Referendum Campaigns, Wash. Post, Dec. 15, 1981, at A 8.

[30] Utah Power & Light Co. v. Ogden City, 95 Utah 161, 79 P.2d 61 (1938) (filing of referendum petition against ordinance, without further action, merely suspended ordinance).

[31] Jackson v. Denver Producing & Refining Co., 96 F.2d 457 (10th Cir. 1938) (emergency clause could not be attached to ordinance after referendum petition as to that ordinance had been filed); Kerley v. Wetherell, 61 Idaho 31, 96 P.2d 503 (1939). The suspension is sometimes specifically provided by state statute or home-rule charter. See Burks v. City of Lafayette, 142 Colo. 61, 349 P.2d 692 (1960) (charter provided that operation of ordinance would be suspended pending repeal by council or final determination by electors). This suspension of the law has been mentioned as a reason for requiring strict compliance with constitutional and statutory provisions where exercises of the referendum power are concerned. Sklar v. Town of Fountain Hills, 220 Ariz. 449, 207 P.3d 702 (App. 2008) (referendum power allows a minority to hold up the effective date of legislation which may well represent the wishes of the majority).

[32] See Jackson v. Denver Producing & Refining Co., *supra* note 31; In re Opinion of the Justices, 132 Me. 512, 174 A. 853 (1933); State ex rel. Drain v. Becker, 240 S.W. 229 (Mo.1922); In re Referendum Petition, Sand Springs, 203 Okl. 298, 220 P.2d 454 (1950).

[33] See Gilbert v. Ashley, 93 Cal.App.2d 414, 209 P.2d 50 (Dist.Ct.1949); Keigley v. Bench, 90 Utah 569, 63 P.2d 262 (1936). See generally note 17 *supra*, and accompanying text.

Unless limited by statute or charter, the legislature has the power, once a measure is approved in a referendum, subsequently to amend or repeal that measure.[34] More difficulty arises over the question of whether, if the electorate has rejected a proposed law, the legislative body may subsequently enact it. Most authority takes the view that the legislature may subsequently legislate on the same subject matter so long as any law it passes differs in some essential feature or features from the defeated measure.[35] Many statutory and charter provisions now clarify this situation by declaring that the governing body cannot legislate on the subject-matter for a designated period of time after the electoral rejection.[36]

§ 27.4 Withdrawal of Signatures from Initiative and Referendum Petitions

One recurring problem that arises both in referendum and initiative situations is that of the petition-signer who changes his mind—what if a voter has signed the petition but later wants to withdraw the signature? Statutes or charters occasionally provide a solution by setting a deadline after which signatures may not be withdrawn. If no such solution is provided, the majority view is that a signature may be withdrawn up until the time that final action is taken thereon (*i.e.*, either an election is called on the basis

---

[34] Jackson v. Denver Producing & Refining Co., *supra* note 31; State v. Cartledge, 129 Ohio St. 279, 195 N.E. 237 (1935); Granger v. City of Tulsa, 174 Okl. 565, 51 P.2d 567 (1935). But see State ex rel. Knez v. City of Seattle, 176 Wash. 283, 28 P.2d 1020 (1934), adhered to on reh. 176 Wash. 283, 33 P.2d 905. See generally Note, Municipal Corporations—Power of Council of Non-Charter City to Amend or Repeal Initiated Ordinances, 2 Ohio St.L.J. 56 (1935). Sometimes, initiated ordinances themselves provide that the ordinance shall not be repealed or modified except by another vote of the electorate. See City & County of San Francisco v. Market Street Railway, 98 F.2d 628, 635–36 (9th Cir.1938), cert. denied 305 U.S. 657, 59 S.Ct. 357, 83 L.Ed. 426, reh. denied 306 U.S. 667, 59 S.Ct. 460, 83 L.Ed. 1062 (regulation concerning street railway operation). And occasionally, state constitutions or statutes, or home-rule charters, provide that an ordinance approved at a referendum cannot be repealed or amended by the legislative body.

[35] See Martin v. Smith, 176 Cal.App.2d 115, 1 Cal.Rptr. 307 (Dist.Ct.1959); In re Statham, 45 Cal.App. 436, 187 P. 986 (Dist. Ct.1920); Trumbull v. Ehrsam, 148 Conn. 47, 166 A.2d 844 (1961) (legislation valid if legislative body acts in good faith and if the legislation differs essentially from the measure rejected by the voters); City of Mattoon v. Henne, 372 Ill. 89, 22 N.E.2d 940 (1939); Eagle v. City of Corbin, 275 Ky. 808, 122 S.W.2d 798 (1938); State ex rel. Megnella v. Meining, 133 Minn. 98, 157 N.W. 991 (1916); McKann v. Town of Irvington, 133 N.J.L. 63, 42 A.2d 391 (1945), aff'd 133 N.J.L. 575, 45 A.2d 494. Cf. Selle v. City of Henderson, 309 Ky. 599, 218 S.W.2d 645 (1949) (referendum election which defeated bond issue did not preclude subsequent adoption of initiative also providing for bond issue, but with alterations over the referendum measure).

[36] See Martin v. Smith, *supra* note 35, applying California statute specifying that defeated measure cannot be enacted by municipal legislative body for a year after the rejection. Cf. Columbus Gas & Fuel Co. v. City of Columbus, 42 F.Supp. 762 (S.D.Ohio 1941) (charter provided that ordinance rejected by referendum could not be subsequently enacted except by electoral vote—but inapplicable to a second measure not substantially similar to the first); Stetson v. City of Seattle, 74 Wash. 606, 134 P. 494 (1913) (under charter, ordinance adopted by referendum can only be repealed, altered or amended by vote of electors). It has been held that where an ordinance is rejected in a referendum, the same or a similar law may subsequently be enacted by initiative. Hall v. City of Denver, 115 Colo. 538, 177 P.2d 234 (1946); City of Shreveport v. Gregory, 186 La. 407, 172 So. 435 (1937). Cf. Selle v. City of Henderson, *supra* note 35 (were changes from the defeated referendum measure).

In some jurisdictions, state constitutional or statutory provisions declare that measures rejected in an initiative or referendum election cannot be resubmitted to the electorate for a certain length of time. See In re Initiative Petition No. 314, 625 P.2d 595 (Okl.1980), applying an Oklahoma constitutional limitation of three years unless a higher-than-usual percentage of voters sign the petition. Cf. Pelkey v. City of Fargo, 453 N.W.2d 801 (N.D.1990), where the court upheld a statute which prohibited submitting any proposal to amend or repeal a home-rule charter more often than biennially. But see Bishel v. City of Middletown, 21 Conn.Sup. 212, 151 A.2d 893 (1959) (where is no statutory or charter restriction, measure defeated at referendum election could be resubmitted to people at the will of local legislative body).

of the petition, or the petition is found insufficient) by the appropriate officials.[37] But some authority holds that names may not be withdrawn once the petition is *filed* with the proper authorities.[38]

§ 27.5 Recall of Officers

Just as initiative and referendum provisions give voters a way to express themselves on proposed legislation, so the device known as "recall" provides voters with a means, during an elected officer's term, to vote on removing or retaining that officer. Recall provisions are found in some state constitutions and in many state statutes and home-rule charters; they have been upheld against constitutional attacks.[39] Again, as with referendum and initiative procedures, the recall process is generally commenced by a petition containing the signatures of a specified number of eligible voters. There are often additional requirements as to the petition: In some jurisdictions, each petition must be limited to the proposed recall of a single officer,[40] and in some states the alleged cause for the recall must be stated in the petition.[41] The grounds for removal by recall are limited in some jurisdictions to specified (though usually rather broad) kinds of conduct, such as abuse of office.[42] In such cases, the courts will prevent recall procedures

---

[37] Birmingham Gas Co. v. City of Bessemer, 250 Ala. 137, 33 So.2d 475 (1947); Littell v. Board of Supervisors, 198 Ill. 205, 65 N.E. 78 (1902); Weltmer v. Montrose Rural High School District, 169 Kan. 653, 219 P.2d 1071 (1950); State ex rel. Wehr v. Council of Bellevue, 138 Ohio St. 93, 32 N.E.2d 839 (1941); State ex rel. Mohr v. City of Seattle, 59 Wash. 68, 109 P. 309 (1910). Cf. Territory ex rel. Stockard v. Mayor & Council of Roswell, 16 N.M. 340, 117 P. 846 (1911) (withdrawal of signatures during period in which validity of all signatures on petition was being investigated; withdrawals held effective); Stevens v. Board of Elections, 108 Ohio App. 37, 160 N.E.2d 366 (1957) (voter who withdrew name from petition before any action was taken thereon could have name restored to petition before action taken). See generally Note, Petitions—Rights of Signers to Withdraw from Petition, 32 Neb.L.Rev. 112 (1952).

[38] Knowlton v. Hezmalhalch, 32 Cal.App.2d 419, 89 P.2d 1109 (Dist.Ct.1939); Fischer v. Washtenaw County, 156 Mich. 1, 120 N.W. 13 (1909).

[39] Lanahan v. City of Los Angeles, 14 Cal.2d 128, 92 P.2d 1014 (1939); Campbell v. Johnson, 182 So.2d 244 (Fla.1966); Karwick v. Grazewski, 253 Mich. 110, 234 N.W. 168 (1931); Stone v. Wyckoff, 102 N.J.Super. 26, 245 A.2d 215 (1968) (recall held not "cruel and unusual punishment" to officeholder); Leers v. Diehl, 11 N.J.Misc. 525, 167 A. 216 (1933); Chesney v. Jones, 31 Okl. 363, 126 P. 715 (1912). It has often been said that recall provisions should be liberally construed in favor of the electorate. See Westpy v. Burnett, 82 N.J.Super. 239, 197 A.2d 400 (1964); In re Recall of Certain Officials of Delafield, 63 Wis.2d 362, 217 N.W.2d 277 (1974). But cf. Simons v. Canty, 195 Conn. 524, 488 A.2d 1267 (1985) (statute authorizing municipal governing body to fix terms of office does not empower that body to provide for officers' recall).

[40] See, applying such provisions, Bricker v. Banks, 98 Cal.App. 87, 276 P. 399 (Dist. Ct.1929); State ex rel. Brown v. Howell, 134 Tenn. 93, 183 S.W. 517 (1916); McCush v. Pratt, 113 Wash. 7, 192 P. 964 (1920).

[41] See People v. O'Hara, 246 Mich. 312, 224 N.W. 384 (1929). Cf. Batchelor v. Eighth Judicial District Court, 81 Nev. 629, 408 P.2d 239 (1965) (under state constitution, the reason for recall must be stated in petition, but merit of reason is for electorate to determine, not for court to judge).

In the case of all procedures required for recall, substantial compliance is usually demanded. See Bab v. Hoyt, 79 N.J.Super. 531, 192 A.2d 190 (1963). On procedures, see generally 2A Antieau, Municipal Corporation Law § 22.199 (1998); 4 McQuillin, Municipal Corporations §§ 12.251–.251.40 (3d rev. ed. 1992). As to the specificity with which grounds for recall must be stated, see State ex rel. Lottman v. Board of Education, 201 Neb. 486, 268 N.W.2d 435 (1978) (greater specificity than found in statute usually not required for petition). See also note 45 *infra*, and accompanying text.

[42] See Sproat v. Arnau, 213 So.2d 692 (Fla.1968) (applying city-charter provisions); Jacobsen v. Nagel, 255 Minn. 300, 96 N.W.2d 569 (1959) (interpreting constitutional provision requiring malfeasance or nonfeasance in office); Westpy v. Burnett, *supra* note 39 (applying state statute requiring a cause connected with office). Cf. Taines v. Galvin, 279 So.2d 9 (Fla.1973), saying that city charters may create less onerous requirements for recall petitions as to local offices than the requirements found in state laws. It has been stated that where state constitutions and statutes, and the home-rule charter if one is applicable, do not specify the grounds for recall, there need be no allegation of misfeasance, nonfeasance, etc. See In re Bower, 91 Ill.App.2d 63, 233 N.E.2d 225 (1967), aff'd 41 Ill.2d 277, 242 N.E.2d 252; Wallace v. Tripp, 358 Mich. 668, 101 N.W.2d

from continuing if the specified grounds are not alleged.[43] But aside from that, recall is considered a political process, and the courts will not interfere with it on the basis of

---

312 (1960). But cf. Taines v. Galvin, *supra*, indicating that wherever a statement of grounds must be made, such statement must allege specific misdeeds having some relationship to the officeholder's job.

Often the relevant state statutes *do* require a showing of misfeasance, malfeasance, or violation of the official's oath of office. See, applying such a provision, In re Recall of Ward, 282 P.3d 1093 (Wash. 2012) (commissioners of county fire protection district alleged to have falsified minutes of meeting; statutory requirement satisfied). "Misfeasance" and "malfeasance," where thus specified, have been held to mean any wrongful conduct that affects, interrupts, or interferes with the performance of official duty. In re Recall of Robinson, 156 Wash.2d 704, 132 P.3d 124 (2006). Compare In re Recall of Davis, 164 Wash. 2d 361, 193 P.3d 98 (2008) (charges that commissioner committed malfeasance by voting in an executive session in violation of Open Public Meetings Act were not legally and factually sufficient to justify recall, but charges that commissioner entered into unauthorized agreement with outgoing port employee for payment of moneys outside his employment with intent to commit malfeasance were sufficient). It has been stated that even if a governing statute provides that a petition for recall must allege malfeasance or misfeasance while in office or violation of the oath of office, the petition does not have to contain the specific terms "misfeasance," "malfeasance," or "violation of the oath of office." In re Heiberg, 171 Wash. 2d 771, 257 P.3d 565 (2011) (but here the charges—that the mayor violated the law by purchasing a pickup truck and by authorizing the destruction of a resolution calling for a vote of no confidence—were found insufficient). An elected official cannot be recalled for appropriately exercising the discretion granted him or her by law. In re Recall of Reed, 156 Wash.2d 53, 124 P.3d 279 (2005). Charges in a recall petition that an elected mayor offered the assistance of his office in obtaining an internship in order to promote a potential sexual relationship have been held sufficient to raise an inference of wrongful conduct. In re Recall of West, 155 Wash.2d 659, 121 P.3d 1190 (2005). As have charges that school board members knowingly broke a collective bargaining agreement and unnecessarily caused financial harm. In re Recall of Young, 152 Wash.2d 848, 100 P.3d 307 (2004). There is no requirement that the petitioner attempting to recall an elected official have *firsthand* knowledge of the official's improper acts, but he or she must have *some* knowledge of the facts underlying the charges. See In re Recall of Wasson, 149 Wash.2d 787, 72 P.3d 170 (2003).

[43] Bent v. Ballantyne, 368 So.2d 351 (Fla.1979); Tolar v. Johns, 147 So.2d 196 (Fla.App.1962); Amberg v. Welsh, 325 Mich. 285, 38 N.W.2d 304 (1949); Foster v. Kovich, 207 Mont. 139, 673 P.2d 1239 (1983) (allegations that mayor "misconducted" himself by removing a police officer from that position, violating his oath by failing to follow the prescribed order of business, and demonstrated his incompetence by failing to conduct an orderly council meeting and by using vulgar language at the meeting held not to state with sufficient specificity the mayor's misconduct and lack of qualifications); In re Anderson, 131 Wash.2d 92, 929 P.2d 410 (1997) (petitions which alleged that mayor and council members violated Open Public Meetings Act but did not allege that they intended to violate the Act held insufficient); In re Shipman, 125 Wash.2d 683, 886 P.2d 1127 (1995) (charges that county public utility district commissioners committed acts of misfeasance by arbitrarily and unreasonably approving 300% water rate increase without adequate accounting data and contrary to recommendation of experts did not establish prima facie case of manifest abuse of discretion and was legally insufficient); In re Recall of Wade, 115 Wash.2d 544, 799 P.2d 1179 (1990) (petition which alleged discrimination on basis of sex by school board in hiring of principal but which did not set forth prima facie showing of that discrimination held insufficient); In re Zufelt, 112 Wash.2d 906, 774 P.2d 1223 (1989) (petition which did not allege how acts of mayor therein described constituted misfeasance, malfeasance, or violation of oath of office held insufficient); Chandler v. Otto, 103 Wash.2d 268, 693 P.2d 71 (1984) (allegations council members abused discretion and contravened the public interest by voting to award contract to a particular bidder held insufficient where was no allegation of fraud, arbitrary conduct, or other misfeasance or violation of oath); Cudihee v. Phelps, 76 Wash. 314, 136 P. 367 (1913). It has been said that under recall statutes, the courts serve as gatekeepers to ensure that public officials are not subject to frivolous or unsubstantiated charges. In re Recall of Lindquist, 172 Wash. 2d 120, 258 P.3d 9 (2011) (recall petition found intentionally frivolous). In general, officials may not be recalled for discretionary acts unless the official exercised discretion in a manifestly unreasonable manner. See In re Recall of Bolt, 298 P.3d 710 (Wash. 2013) (allegations of bullying, using town vehicle for personal purposes, etc. all found insufficient). Cf. Piver v. Stallman, 198 So.2d 859 (Fla. App.1967) (order of mandamus to call recall election reversed where no legally sufficient grounds for the recall were alleged). Mandamus will not lie to force a recall election if there has been no such specification of grounds as is required by state law or local charter. Joyner v. Shuman, 116 So.2d 470 (Fla.App.1959). If such grounds as misfeasance or nonfeasance in office are required, a petition indicating only that the voters disagree with the officeholder on matters of policy will not suffice. See Richard v. Tomlinson, 49 So.2d 798 (Fla.1951) (not enough to allege conduct inimical to best interests of the citizens); State ex rel. Citizens Against Mandatory Bussing v. Brooks, 80 Wn.2d 121, 492 P.2d 536 (1972), noted 48 Wash.L.Rev. 503 (1973). Cf. Collins v. City of Opa-Locka, 251 So.2d 709 (Fla.App.1971) (affidavits insufficient as allegations lacked foundation or relation to performance of office, and were in part ambiguous). Nor will allegation of mere errors in judgment suffice.

allegations that the charges against the officer are insufficient or untrue.[44] Wherever the recall petition must allege grounds, the statement of those grounds has to be made with sufficient clarity to enable the officer to know the charges against which he will have to defend himself.[45]

A recall petition must usually be presented to a designated officer or board, whose duty it is—if the petition is sufficient—to call an election. Mandamus will lie to compel the calling of the election if the petition is adequate and the proper official does not promptly act thereon.[46] At the election, the eligible voters will determine whether to remove the officer or retain him. If he is removed, the statutory and charter provisions on filling vacancies in office must be consulted. Normally, the removed officer is not eligible to succeed himself for the balance of his unexpired term.[47] In a few jurisdictions,

---

Taines v. Galvin, *supra* note 42. Cf. Matter of Recall of Call, 109 Wash.2d 954, 749 P.2d 674 (1988) (charge that a city council member proposed an improper resolution was legally insufficient to support a recall petition). But if even *one* valid ground for recall is stated, that will suffice. People v. O'Hara, *supra* note 41; Danielson v. Faymonville, 72 Wn.2d 854, 435 P.2d 963 (1967); Morton v. McDonald, 41 Wn.2d 889, 252 P.2d 577 (1953).

[44] See Abbey v. Green, 28 Ariz. 53, 235 P. 150 (1925); Bernzen v. City of Boulder, 186 Colo. 81, 525 P.2d 416 (1974); State ex rel. Landis v. Tedder, 106 Fla. 140, 143 So. 148 (1932); Wallace v. Tripp, 358 Mich. 668, 101 N.W.2d 312 (1960); State ex rel. Topping v. Houston, 94 Neb. 445, 143 N.W. 796 (1913); State ex rel. Hackley v. Edmonds, 150 Ohio St. 203, 80 N.E.2d 769 (1948); Dunham v. Ardery, 43 Okl. 619, 143 P. 331 (1914); In re Cy Sun, 299 P.3d 651 (Wash. 2013) (court does not evaluate the truthfulness of the allegations); Pederson v. Moser, 99 Wash.2d 456, 662 P.2d 866 (1983) (court will not inquire into truth of recall charges but will consider only their legal sufficiency); Bocek v. Bayley, 81 Wn.2d 831, 505 P.2d 814 (1973) (court must assume truth of charges in determining whether legally sufficient grounds are stated). The view has sometimes been expressed that stricter standards are needed to protect public officials from groundless recall efforts. See Comment, Electoral Recall in Washington State and California: California Needs Stricter Standards to Protect Elected Officials from Harassment, 28 Seattle U.L. Rev. 145 (2004).

[45] Gilbert v. Morrow, 277 So.2d 812 (Fla.App.1973); State ex rel. LaMon v. Town of Westport, 73 Wn.2d 255, 438 P.2d 200 (1968); In re Recall of Certain Officials of Delafield, *supra* note 39. See Matter of Recall of Lee, 122 Wash.2d 613, 859 P.2d 1244 (1993) (charges in recall petition must be made with sufficient precision and detail to enable both the electorate and the challenged official to make informed decisions in the recall process; sufficient facts must be alleged to make out a prima facie case of misfeasance, malfeasance, or violation of oath of office). But the charges are never required to be so definite as would be necessary in a criminal information or indictment. See Danielson v. Faymonville, *supra* note 43. See also note 41, *supra*, and accompanying text. In Gordon v. Leatherman, 325 F.Supp. 494 (S.D.Fla.1971), the district court held that due process requires notice to the officer of the grounds for his attempted recall. But the Court of Appeals reversed—450 F.2d 562 (5th Cir.)—and said that the Florida cases on which the lower court had relied merely indicated that where constitution, statute, or home-rule charter expressly requires a statement of reasons, this means a clear statement of grounds having some relation to the officeholder's performance in office.

[46] Blue v. Stockton, 355 P.2d 395 (Alaska 1960); Struhm v. City of Berkeley, 229 Cal.App.2d 278, 40 Cal.Rptr. 230 (Dist.Ct.1964); Miller v. State ex rel. Meyers, 53 S.W.2d 838 (Tex.Civ.App.1932) (mandamus can be employed against officials who have duty to act on petition where it is those officials themselves whose recall is sought). But cf. State ex rel. Goodhope v. Leyse, 60 S.D. 384, 244 N.W. 529 (1932) (action of person with whom petition is filed is final unless that person has acted fraudulently or arbitrarily, in which case the action may be reviewed by mandamus).

Recall statutes and constitutional provisions often provide that the number of signatures required for a valid recall petition be equivalent to a certain percentage of the votes cast in the "last general election." In a situation involving a locally elected official, this has been held to mean the designated percentage of those who voted in the last general election for the office of the local officer sought to be recalled. Richards v. Schmidt, 274 Kan. 753, 56 P.3d 274 (2002).

[47] Bernzen v. City of Boulder, *supra* note 44; In re Recall Election of Hackensack, 57 N.J.Super. 257, 154 A.2d 639 (1959), aff'd 31 N.J. 592, 158 A.2d 505; Recall Bennett Committee v. Bennett, 196 Or. 299, 249 P.2d 479 (1952) (officer's resignation on day after his recall, but before vote was officially canvassed, was immaterial in determining his right to run for remainder of term). But see Hurt v. Naples, 299 So.2d 17 (Fla.1974), conformed to 301 So.2d 31 (recalled officer can run for remainder of term if no statutory or charter provision to contrary). Cf. Anchor Bay Concerned Citizens v. People ex rel. Kelley, 55 Mich.App. 428, 223 N.W.2d 3 (1974), appeal denied 394 Mich. 779, 229 N.W.2d 338 (recall petition rendered void when its filing

the choosing of a successor (in case the recall succeeds) may be combined in the same election with the decision on the recall itself.[48]

§ 27.6 Exceptional Judicial Remedies: Mandamus and Injunctions

Certain exceptional judicial remedies are sometimes available to persons with a claim or complaint against a municipality. Chief among these are writs of mandamus and injunctions. The latter may be either mandatory or prohibitory. The writ of mandamus will lie to compel performance of a public duty. There are three principal requirements:[49] (1) Since this is an exceptional remedy, there must be no other adequate relief. (2) The writ must be sought to enforce a duty imposed by law, not merely by contract.[50] (3) The duty sought to be enforced must be a mandatory one.[51] It is also true

---

was followed by election at which named officers were re-elected). In Matsumoto v. Pua, 775 F.2d 1393 (9th Cir.1985), the court considered the validity of a city charter provision disqualifying recalled city officials from running for city office for two years. Finding that the provision would likely be ruled unconstitutional, the court granted a preliminary injunction prohibiting the city clerk from enforcing the provision against recalled council members who sought to run in a special election to fill the vacancies created by their recall. The court expressed no view on the constitutionality of a *limited* ban on recalled officials seeking to fill the vacancies created by their recall, but noted that this was a general ban making no distinction between that type of election and other elections.

Under some constitutions, statutes, or charters, an officer cannot be recalled until he has held office for a certain length of time. See Poole v. Lawrence, 86 N.J.L. 90, 90 A. 668 (1914) (one year in office required; resignation and immediate reappointment of officer did not vest him with new term).

[48] See Martin v. Board of Trustees, 96 Cal.App. 705, 274 P. 1015 (Dist.Ct.1929). In re Hickenlooper, 312 P.3d 153 (Colo. 2013), held unconstitutional, under the First and Fourteenth Amendments of the U.S. Constitution, a state constitutional provision requiring an elector who wished to vote for a successor in a recall election also to cast a vote on the recall issue.

[49] See Fordham, Local Government Law 635–36 (2d rev. ed. 1986). See generally Ferris & Ferris, The Law of Extraordinary Legal Remedies (Thomas Law Book Co. 1926); Note, Mandamus of Unexecuted Executive Discretionary Powers, 33 Ark.L.Rev. 765 (1980); Note, Mandamus Proceedings Against Public Officials, 9 N.M.L.Rev. 195 (1978–79). See also Freeman v. Gregoire, 171 Wash. 2d 316, 256 P.3d 264 (2011) (to compel an action in mandamus, a duty must be mandatory and ministerial). On the use of mandamus in one particular jurisdiction, see Koehler & Williams, Mandamus Decisions of the Texas Supreme Court, 64 S.M.U. L. Rev. 393 (2011).

[50] But municipal obligations are sometimes rather easily found to be based on a law. See Commercial National Bank v. Robinson, 66 Okl. 235, 168 P. 810 (1917) (pursuant to statute, municipal officers entered into contract for street improvements to be paid for by delivery of bonds; delivery of the bonds may be compelled by mandamus). And some revenue-bond enabling acts specifically authorize the enforcement of bond-holders rights through mandamus.

[51] See Fordham, Methods of Enforcing Satisfaction of the Obligations of Public Corporations, 33 Colum.L.Rev. 28, 32–53 (1933). Cf. Detroit Fire Fighters Ass'n v. City of Detroit, 199 Mich.App. 129, 501 N.W.2d 202 (1993) (fire fighters' union and union officers lacked standing to seek writ of mandamus to compel city officials to spend money which had been appropriated for new fire department squad; city not required to spend appropriated funds); State Bd. of Educ. v. Houghton Lake Community Schools, 430 Mich. 658, 425 N.W.2d 80 (1988) (mandamus will lie to compel exercise of discretion by one duty-bound to do so but does not lie to compel exercise in a particular manner); Morton v. Adair County Excise Bd., 780 P.2d 707 (Okl.1989) (county excise board should not have withdrawn funding for statutorily mandated position, but since fiscal year had passed, the question was moot); TIB Corp. v. Edmondson, 630 P.2d 1296 (Okl.1981) (mandamus will lie to compel an executive officer—here, at the state level—to perform an act required by law where officer is not required to exercise discretion); Cordill v. City of Estacada, 67 Or.App. 481, 678 P.2d 1257 (1984) (mandamus would not issue to control city's exercise of a legislative function—specifically, to preclude the city from amending a zoning ordinance to permit carwash operations in a particular area). It has been held that a writ of mandamus may be used in a prohibitory manner to prevent unconstitutional official action. American Federation of State, County & Municipal Employees v. Martinez, 159 N.M. 132, 257 P.3d 952 (2011). See generally McCarthy & Laurie Reynolds, Local Government Law in a Nutshell 467–468 (5th ed. 2003), noting that a citizen or taxpayer can often enforce performance of non-discretionary duties through mandamus.

that there must ordinarily have already been a default in the obligation to be enforced, though courts have occasionally allowed this remedy where a default seems imminent and practically inevitable.[52]

Where the legal remedy of mandamus exists, there is usually no need for a mandatory injunction—*i.e.*, a court order specifying action that must be taken—against a municipality or its officers; and since mandamus provides an adequate remedy at law, such an injunction is likely then to be denied.[53] But the mandatory injunction is not limited by any requirement that the underlying duty being enforced must be based on law, not contract. Therefore, this form of relief may be available and particularly appropriate for those who *do* base their claim on some contractual undertaking, such as bonds issued by the municipality.[54] *Prohibitory* injunctions are also often an appropriate form of relief for bond-holders if no adequate remedy at law is available. For instance, a general-obligation creditor may attempt to restrain diversion of funds that had been dedicated or appropriated for payment of claims of his general class.[55] Revenue-bond holders may attempt to prevent action by the municipality which would harm the revenue-producing facility in which they have invested, or would interfere with the flow of revenue therefrom.[56]

The general rule is that a prohibitory injunction will not issue to restrain the passage or enactment of an ordinance or other municipal law.[57] Injunctive or other relief

---

[52] See State ex rel. Harrington v. City of Daytona Beach, 118 Fla. 773, 160 So. 501 (1935) (city already in default on some bonds and had prepared budget making no provision for debt-service taxes). See generally Note, Creditors' Remedies in Municipal Default, 1976 Duke L.J. 1363, 1375. An action already done cannot be undone by mandamus, however erroneous the action may have been. See Beasley v. Flathead County Bd. of Adjustments, 350 Mont. 171, 205 P.3d 812 (2009).

[53] George v. City of Asheville, 80 F.2d 50 (4th Cir.1935) (in bondholders' suit for injunction to restrain diversion of revenues, court could not order officers to levy, assess, or collect taxes or fix water rates since that would be equivalent to legal remedy of mandamus); Tyler County v. Town, 23 F.2d 371 (5th Cir.1928), cert. denied 278 U.S. 601, 49 S.Ct. 9, 73 L.Ed. 530 (mandamus is extraordinary *legal* remedy); McClintock, Principles of Equity 452 (2d ed.1948), noting that if a person seeks to enforce the duties of officers as to the conduct of elections, relief is generally refused on the ground that mandamus furnishes an adequate remedy. But cf. Board of Education v. James, 49 F.2d 91 (10th Cir. 1931) (purchaser of school bonds *could* sue for injunction against diversion of funds set aside for payment of bonds).

[54] See Fordham, Revenue Bond Sanctions, 42 Colum.L.Rev. 395, 425 (1942). The mandatory injunction may be coupled with another remedy such as an accounting or even a receivership. *Id.* On accounting, see generally *id.* 414–19; on receiverships and trusteeships, see *id.* 428–33.

[55] See Tyler County v. Town, *supra* note 53.

[56] See Fordham, Local Government Law 636–37 (2d rev. ed. 1986), saying an injunction is the obvious remedy to prevent violation of negative covenants supporting revenue bonds. Cf. George v. City of Asheville, *supra* note 53 (under statute requiring net revenues of municipal enterprise to be applied to payment of bonds—if net revenues were in danger of being diverted, bondholders entitled to injunctive relief). Prohibitory injunctions are also available to halt the maintaining by municipalities of conditions that amount to nuisances. See City of Rome v. Turk, 235 Ga. 223, 219 S.E.2d 97 (1975) (construction and maintenance of sewer and drainage system can be abated when it becomes a nuisance even though it involves "governmental" function); Malhame v. Borough of Demarest, 162 N.J.Super. 248, 392 A.2d 652 (1978) (noise from fire-alarm system could be abated by injunction). Cf. Duffield v. DeKalb County, 242 Ga. 432, 249 S.E.2d 235 (1978) (continuing nuisance by county subject to injunction). But cf. City of Newport News v. Hertzler, 216 Va. 587, 221 S.E.2d 146 (1976) (operation of park would not be enjoined merely because of occasional annoyance to neighbors). On municipal liability for nuisances, see generally Chapter 26 *supra*.

[57] See New Orleans Water Works Co. v. New Orleans, 164 U.S. 471, 17 S.Ct. 161, 41 L.Ed. 518 (1896); City & County of Denver v. Board of County Commissioners, 141 Colo. 102, 347 P.2d 132 (1959) (passage of annexation ordinance not enjoined); Zaring v. Adams, 188 Ga. 97, 3 S.E.2d 635 (1939); Randall v. Township Board, 342 Mich. 605, 70 N.W.2d 728 (1955); City of Detroit v. Hosmer, 79 Mich. 384, 44 N.W. 622 (1890); Smith v. Brock, 83 R.I. 432, 118 A.2d 336 (1955); Rose Manor Realty Co. v. City of Milwaukee, 272 Wis. 339, 75 N.W.2d 274 (1956). Cf. Hackney v. City of Guthrie, 171 Okl. 320, 41 P.2d 705 (1935) (enactment of ordinance

is available only after the law is actually passed, not while it remains a hypothetical possibility. At times, various courts have recognized at least three possible exceptions (though none of these is as yet supported by any large amount of authority): (1) If it is clear that the contemplated legislation would be beyond the scope of any possible municipal power, an injunction may be granted.[58] (2) It is possible that a court may restrain enactment of a law if the challenging party can demonstrate that the law will be invalid and that extreme hardship will result if it cannot be challenged prior to passage.[59] (3) If a multiplicity of suits can thereby be avoided, a court may enjoin passage of an invalid law.[60] With those possible exceptions, courts are hesitant to interfere with the legislative process or to judge in advance the validity of a proposed piece of legislation.

§ 27.7 The Ombudsperson

Apart from legislative and judicial remedies, a citizen with a complaint against a local government may also be able to avail himself of the services of an "ombudsman" or "ombudsperson." This may be defined as an officer or agency, detached from politics and independent of other branches of the government, that supplies information about the government, and receives and investigates complaints. The origin of this institution is usually traced to Sweden in 1809; in recent times, it has become a highly popular concept throughout much of the world and has been employed at levels of government ranging from local to national.[61] The institution may be called by a great variety of names,

---

won't be enjoined *unless* city legislative body is acting outside its power; or threatening thus to act, thereby invading complainant's property rights; or where a threatened act is ministerial, not legislative).

[58] See City of Norman v. Allen, 47 Okl. 74, 147 P. 1002 (1915); Smith v. Brock, *supra* note 57. But cf. Durrett Hardware & Furniture Co. v. City of Monroe, 199 La. 329, 5 So.2d 911 (1942), noted 16 Tul. L.Rev. 632 (1942) (equity will not interfere on mere complaint that legislative body is acting outside its powers if it does not appear to be acting in direct violation of prohibitory law).

[59] See International Trading-Stamp Co. v. City of Memphis, 101 Tenn. 181, 47 S.W. 136 (1898) (injunction would issue to restrain city from passing ultra vires ordinance imposing tax on many persons).

[60] See State ex rel. Abel v. Gates, 190 Mo. 540, 89 S.W. 881 (1905); People ex rel. Davis v. Sturtevant, 9 N.Y. 263 (1853). Cf. Spring Valley Water-Works v. Bartlett, 16 F. 615 (D.Cal.1883) (court can enjoin passage of ordinance void on its face—but will do so only if some irreparable injury would result from passage).

[61] See Philadelphia Mayor's Ad Hoc Committee on Improvement in Municipal Standards and Practices, Final Report (1962), relevant part reproduced in Fordham, Local Government Law 294–97 (2d rev. ed. 1986). Compare, describing a unique program in Utah to resolve property rights disputes, Call, Resolving Land Use and Impact Fee Disputes: Utah's Innovative Ombudsman Program, 42/43 Urban Law. 375 (2010–11). See generally on ombudsmen S.V. Anderson, Ombudsman Papers: American Experience and Proposals (Institute of Governmental Studies, University of Calif.1969); R.V. Peel (ed.), The Ombudsman or Citizen's Defender; A Modern Institution (American Academy of Political & Social Science 1968); Moore, Ombudsman and the Ghetto, 1 Conn.L.Rev. 244 (1968); Tibbles, Ombudsman: Who Needs Him?, 47 J.Urban L. 1 (1969); Toxey, Ombudsman in the Common Law System—Administrative Justice, 11 Wm. & M.L.Rev. 138 (1969). See also Hill, Institutionalization, the Ombudsman, and Bureaucracy, 68 Am.Pol.Sci.Rev.1075 (1974). An ombudsman system has been instituted at the *state* level in Hawaii, while notable experiments at the municipal level have occurred in Buffalo, New York, and New York City. See S.V. Anderson (ed.), Ombudsman for American Government? (Prentice-Hall 1968), reviewed 22 Okl.L.Rev. 122 (1969); Green & Eisner, The Public Advocate for New York City: An Analysis of the Country's Only Elected Ombudsman, 42 N.Y.L. School L. Rev. 1093 (1998). Cf. Haemmel, The Ombudsman, or Citizens Defender—The North Carolina Experience, 10 N.C.Central L.J. 227 (1979) (good discussion of history of concept). See generally on state and local ombudsman programs S.V. Anderson & J.E. Moore (eds.), Ombudsman Workshop, Honolulu—Establishing Ombudsman Offices: Recent Experience in the United States (Institute of Governmental Studies, University of Calif. 1972). On the use of ombudsmen in federal agencies in the United States, see Krent, Federal Agency Ombuds: The Costs, Benefits, and Countenance of Confidentiality, 52 Admin. L. Rev. 17 (2000) (using the terms "ombud" and "ombudsman" interchangeably, since the Alternative Dispute Resolution Act of 1996, 5 U.S.C. § 573 (e)(3) (Supp. III 1997) uses the term "ombud"). An excellent summary of the qualifications and responsibilities of

including titles such as "Bureau of Information and Complaints." But at its best, it is more than a complaint bureau and has broad powers of investigation, acting either on its own motion *or* upon the request of a citizen. It is hoped that the increased use of this and similar devices may improve governmental responsiveness to citizen complaints and may aid local governments in fulfilling their long-standing purpose: serving the needs of their citizens.

---

ombudspersons is found in Special Feature, Ombuds Standards, 54 Admin. L. Rev. 535 (2002). On the need for some person or agency to make known to the governments the necessity that local communities achieve sustainability, see Salkin, Can You Hear Me Up There? Giving Voice to Local Communities Imperative for Achieving Sustainability, 4 Envtl. & Energy L. & Pol'y J. 256 (2009).

Outstanding works on ombudsman programs in other countries include W. Gellhorn, Ombudsmen and Others: Citizens' Protectors in Nine Countries (Harvard University Press 1966); Hill, The New Zealand Ombudsman's Authority System, in Readings in New Zealand Government 163–69 (L. Cleveland & A.D. Robinson, eds. Reed Publ. 1972); K.M. Weeks, Ombudsmen Around the World (Institute of Governmental Studies, University of California 1978).

Table of Cases

Index

References are to Pages